ROYAL HISTORICAL SOCIETY

GUIDES AND HANDBOOKS

No. 17

GUIDE TO THE

LOCAL ADMINISTRATIVE UNITS OF ENGLAND

ROYAL HISTORICAL SOCIETY

GUIDES AND HANDBOOKS

ISSN 0080-4398

MAIN SERIES

1. *Guide to English commercial statistics, 1696–1782.* By G. N. Clark and Barbara M. Franks. 1938.
2. *Handbook of British chronology.* Edited by F. M. Powicke, Charles Johnson and W. J. Harte. 1939. 2nd edition, edited by F. M. Powicke and E. B. Fryde, 1961. 3rd edition, edited by E. B. Fryde, D. E. Greenway, S. Porter and I. Roy, 1986.
3. *Medieval libraries of Great Britain. A list of surviving books.* Edited by N. R. Ker. 1941. 2nd edition, 1964.
4. *Handbook of dates for students of English history.* Edited by C. R. Cheney. 1945. Reprinted, 1991.
5. *Guide to the national and provincial directories of England and Wales, excluding London, published before 1856.* By Jane E. Norton, 1950.
6. *Handbook of oriental history.* Edited by C. H. Philips. 1951.
7. *Texts and Calendars. An analytical guide to serial publications.* By E. L. C. Mullins. 1958. Reprinted (with corrections), 1978.
8. *Anglo-Saxon Charters. An annotated list and bibliography.* By P. H. Sawyer. 1968.
9. *A Centenary Guide to the publications of the Royal Historical Society 1868–1968 and of the former Camden Society 1838–1897.* By Alexander Taylor Milne. 1968.
10. *Guide to the local administrative units of England.* Volume I. *Southern England.* By Frederic A. Youngs, Jr. 1980. Reprinted, 1981.
11. *Guide to bishops' registers of England and Wales. A survey from the middle ages to the abolition of episcopacy in 1646.* By David M. Smith. 1981.
12. *Texts and Calendars II. An analytical guide to serial publications 1957–1982.* By E. L. C. Mullins. 1983.
13. *Handbook of Medieval Exchange.* By Peter Spufford, with the assistance of Wendy Wilkinson and Sarah Tolley. 1986.
14. *Scottish Texts and Calendars. An analytical guide to serial publications.* By David and Wendy Stevenson. 1987.
15. *Medieval libraries of Great Britain.* Edited by N. R. Ker. *Supplement to the second edition.* Edited by Andrew G. Watson. 1987.
16. *A Handlist of British diplomatic representatives 1509–1688.* By Gary M. Bell. 1990.

SUPPLEMENTARY SERIES

1. *A Guide to the papers of British Cabinet Ministers, 1900–1951.* Compiled by Cameron Hazlehurst and Christine Woodland. 1974.
2. *A Guide to the reports of the U.S. Strategic Bombing Survey.* I *Europe.* II *The Pacific.* Edited by Gordon Daniels. 1981.

Guide to the Local Administrative Units of England

VOLUME II: Northern England

BY
FREDERIC A. YOUNGS, JR.

LONDON
OFFICES OF THE ROYAL HISTORICAL SOCIETY
UNIVERSITY COLLEGE LONDON, GOWER STREET
LONDON WC1E 6BT
1991

FOR
CHARLES AND GEOFF

© Royal Historical Society 1991

First published 1991

Distributed for the Royal Historical Society
by Boydell & Brewer Ltd
PO Box 9 Woodbridge Suffolk IP12 3DF
and Boydell & Brewer Inc.
PO Box 41026 Rochester NY 14604 USA

ISBN 0 86193 127 0

British Library Cataloguing-in-Publication Data
Guide to the local administrative units of England: Vol 2. Northern
England. — (Royal Historical Society guides and handbooks)
  I. Youngs, Frederic A. II. Series
  352.0427
  ISBN 0-86193-127-0

This publication is printed on acid-free paper

Printed and bound in Great Britain by
Woolnough Bookbinding Ltd, Irthlingborough, Northants.

CONTENTS

PREFACE   vi

HOW TO USE THE GUIDE   vii

PART I: THE PARISHES OF ENGLAND   1

PART II: LOCAL GOVERNMENT UNITS   635

PART III: PARLIAMENTARY CONSTITUENCIES   799

PART IV: THE DIOCESES OF ENGLAND   859

NOTES FOR ENTRIES   875

CORRIGENDA FOR VOLUME I   913

PREFACE

It is a pleasure to thank those whose assistance has been so important in the preparation of Volume II of the *Guide*. Several members of the Royal Historical Society have assisted in their official capacities, especially those who served as literary directors, Dr. Ian Roy, Dr. H. C. G. Matthew, and Dr. John Ramsden.

I am grateful to the National Endowment for the Humanities for a grant from the Research Tools fund which financed a great part of the research for this Volume. Ronald H. Fritze served as Research Associate. Sara Murphy, Anna Oivanki, and Sue Roider were on the staff. William B. Robison provided valuable research assistance.

My greatest appreciation goes to Mr. David Armstrong, Records Officer for the Church Commissioners, and to Mr. Christopher Elrington, Editor of the Victoria History of the Counties of England. They have helped at every stage, both professionally and personally. My colleagues at Louisiana State University, Baton Rouge—where I was on the faculty from 1973 to 1988—were very supportive, especially Dean Henry Snyder of the College of Arts and Sciences and Professor John L. Loos, Chairman of the Department of History.

Mr. John Gilbert of the British Library, at his own initiative, undertook to reread in its entirety Volume I of the *Guide*. I am most grateful for his work, which forms the major part of the Corrigenda presented at the end of this Volume.

This volume is lovingly dedicated to my two sons, Charles and Geoff Youngs.

Frederic A. Youngs, Jr.

ACKNOWLEDGEMENTS

Borthwick Institute of Historical Research, University of York: Mr. D. M. Smith, Mr. W. Shields, Mr. Christopher Webb, Mr. Oliver. Cheshire Record Office: Mr. Brian C. Redwood, Mr. F. I. Dunn. Cumbria County Record Ofrice: Mr. B. C. Jones (Carlisle), Mr. J. P. Godwin (Carlisle), Miss S. J. MacPherson (Kendal). Derbyshire Record Office: Miss Joan Sinar. Durham County Record Office: Mr. D. Butler, Mrs. A. Mitchell. Hereford and Worcester Record Office: Mr. A. M. Wherry (Hereford), Mr. E. H. Sargeant (Worcester), Mrs. Meller (Worcester). Humberside County Record Office: Mr. K. D. Holt. Lancashire Record Office: Mr. K. Hall. Leeds Archives Department: Mr. J. M. Collinson. Leicestershire Record Office: Miss K. M. Thompson, Mr. L. A. Parker. Lincolnshire Record Office: Mr. C. M. Lloyd, Mr. C. P. C. Johnson. Liverpool Diocesan Registry: Mr. Christopher H. Tyne. Manchester Diocesan Registry: Mr. M. C. Darlington. North Yorkshire County Record Office: Mr. M. Y. Ashcroft. Northamptonshire Record Office: Mr. P. I. King, Mr. C. Tonge. Northumberland County Record Office: Mr. R. M. Gard. Nottinghamshire Archives Office: Mr. Adrian Henstock. Salop Record Office: Mrs. M. T. Halford. Staffordshire Record Office: Mr. D. V. Fowkes, Mr. F. B. Stitt. Warwickshire County Record Office: Mr. M. W. Farr, Miss Monica Ory. West Yorkshire Record Office: Mrs. E. K. Berry.

HOW TO USE THE GUIDE

THE SCOPE AND USE OF THE GUIDE

This volume (*Northern England*) is the second of a two volume set, and includes the eighteen ancient counties north of a line drawn roughly from the Severn to the Wash. The first volume (*Southern England*, 1980, *Guides and Handbooks* 10) included the twenty-one southern counties and the City of London. This introductory section differs from that in Volume I only in the addition and deletion of terms and abbreviations particular to the relevant counties (e.g., the inclusion of 'Wapentakes' for some northern counties, the deletion of 'Lathes' appropriate only to entries for Sussex) and in a clarifying addition on the following page about the distinction between the legal creation of an ecclesiastical parish and the date of its first registers.

The basis of the *Guide* is the parish, a unit of medieval origins which at first had solely ecclesiastical rights and obligations. From the late sixteenth century civil responsibilities were imposed upon it, and when parliamentary constituencies were restructured in the nineteenth and twentieth centuries, they were defined in terms of governmental units comprised of parishes. Thus in time the parish became a fundamental unit in the civil, parliamentary and ecclesiastical organisation of England, important both for royal and local government.

These introductory pages provide the information and procedures necessary to use the *Guide*. First there is a section on ORGANISATION AND FORMAT which explains the plan of the entire *Guide* and of the many types of entries within it. It will be noted here and also in the third section, ABBREVIATIONS, that numerous devices have been employed to express information as succinctly as possible—a necessity considering that over 10,000 parishes are included, each with a multiplicity of detail. The second section, DEFINITIONS OF TERMS, supplies a basic understanding not only of the nature of the units but also of the sources used in gathering information about each of them. The final section, DATES, is necessary because, unlike a gazetteer which deals with areas at one fixed moment in time, the *Guide* presents information which on the ecclesiastical and parliamentary side dates from the middle ages, and on the civil side from the late sixteenth century—all in a continuous presentation up to 1 April 1974.

It is important to note what the *Guide* is not intended to do. On the ecclesiastical side, it is not concerned with the medieval origin of the parish. There has been no original research to date the inception of a parish, but of course where the research of others had made this clear, the information is provided. For the period after the Reformation, the *Guide* deals only with the established Church of England, so that there is no information about the organisation of disseneters, Catholics or non-Christian groups.

On the civil side, the *Guide* is concerned with administrative and not judicial organisation. It makes no attempt to date the medieval origin of boroughs but does indicate the first date at which a borough was represented in the House of Commons. The *Guide* deals only with local governmental units which either had an exceptional importance over a long period of time (the hundreds, for example) or which are important links in the historical evolution of major administrative units (the poor law unions became the basis for the structure of the sanitary districts, which in turn became the basis of administrative county districts from 1894). Thus many important units such as highway districts or town improvement commissions are not included. It will be appreciated that it was necessary to exclude a number of areas in order to keep the size of the *Guide* manageable.

Several comments about completeness of details and accuracy are needed. Any historian's work reductively depends on the completeness of sources; in a work which intends to deal with the totality of the parishes the problem becomes particularly acute. It will be clear from the description of sources used that an effort was made to use as wide a range of sources as possible, and to use them as checks on each other. It must be realised that in spite of this there are many instances in which information cannot be found, and that there is a limit on reconstruction, so that exact answers are beyond the possibility of historical certainty. It should also be noted that a goal of the *Guide* is to furnish not only the dates of changes but also the exact authority for the change. In many cases dates are generally understood but formal orders lacking, so that the date is noted but the footnote will indicate 'authority not found'.

Finally, every attempt has been made to be accurate. Citations and information have been compared and checked. The compiler has visited every county record office at least once and sent a copy of the result to the county for the archivist's review. Naturally any errors which remain are the sole responsibility of the compiler. Corrigenda arising from the first printing of Volume I are reproduced at the end of this volume.

ORGANISATION AND FORMAT

PART I: THE PARISHES OF ENGLAND

This part is arranged alphabetically by ancient counties, and within each by its constituent parishes in alphabetical order. To the extent allowed by the nature of each parish, a variety of information in presented.

Information
Creation, Abolition.

For each civil parish (CP) and ecclesiastical parish (EP), the date of creation, the names of other parishes from which it was formed and a footnote reference to the authority for the creation. For each ancient parish (AP), CP and EP, the date of the abolition (if any), the names of the parishes into which its territory was dispersed and a footnote reference to the authority for the abolition. It is possible for a parish to be abolished for one purpose and to continue to exist for the others, e.g., an AP which loses its civil identity to an expanding nearby town while remaining ecclesiastically separate.

Parish Registers and the Creation of Parishes.

Of particular interest to genealogists is the earliest date for which registers are available, whether of births, marriages, or deaths. It should be noted that very rarely do such dates coincide with the date a parish became separate. Please see the entries for PARISH in the section which follows, DEFINITION OF TERMS, for norms as to when parishes become independent.

Registers have importance only in regard to the ecclesiastical functions of parishes, and thus no relation to CPs. Because registers are kept regularly for all practical purposes only from the 1530s upon the order of Henry VIII, they are almost never important in dating the origins of APs. In regard to EPs, it is possible that the date of the earliest registers coincides with the separate status gained by a chapelry, and such a date is used rarely in the *Guide* when no other source can be found. Usually, however, the dates will not coincide for one of the following reasons: the chapelry existed and had registers because baptisms could be performed there, but never became separate from the mother parish; the registers record baptisms yet independence came later, either when the chapelry was augmented as a perpetual curacy or explicitly constituted an EP; the registers may be lost for an earlier period, and thus do not accurately reflect the earliest date baptisms were performed.

Alterations of Boundaries.

For all parishes, the dates when boundaries were altered, for any purpose, with a footnote reference to the authority for the change. The names of other parishes are not generally cited for economy of space, except when the change resulted in the creation of a new parish, when another parish was gained in its entirety, when the boundary of a county was altered (changes in APs, CPs) or when the boundary of a diocese was affected (APs, EPs).

Civil Organisation.

For APs and CPs, to the extent that the parish was in existence at any time, inclusion in hundreds (late 16th cent—1889), boroughs (at any time), poor law unions (1830s—1930), sanitary districts (1875—94) and administrative county units (1894—1974).

Parliamentary Organisation.

For APs and CPs, to the extent that the parish was in existence at any time, inclusion in parliamentary boroughs (at any time) and divisions or county constituencies (after 1832).

Ecclesiastical Organisation.

For APs and EPs, the rural deaneries in which the parish was organised. A reference to the entries at the beginning of the county's section will indicate how the rural deaneries were organised in dioceses and archdeaconries.

Sample Entries

For the instances below and for all entries, references must be made both to the General Abbreviations (below in this section), applicable throughout the *Guide*, and to the abbreviations particular to each individual county.

EXAMPLE A: NAUNTON BEAUCHAMP
  Worcs   AP *LG* Seq 17. *Parl* Seq 3. *Eccl* Seq 7.

EXAMPLE B: MOBBERLEY
  Ches   AP *LG* Seq 8. Civ bdry: 1936.[7] *Parl* Seq 2. *Eccl* Maccl.
                   RDn (until 1873), Maccl. North RDn (1873—80),
                   Bowdon RDn (1880—1953), Knutsf. RDn (1953—
                   *). Eccl bdry: 1881 (help cr Ashley EP).[41]

EXAMPLE C: OLLERTON
  Notts   Chap in Edwinstowe AP (eccl 'Edwinstowe with
                   Carburton'), sep CP 1866,[2] sep EP 1888.[91] *LG* Seq
                   3. Civ bdry: 1957.[93] *Parl* Seq 2. *Eccl* Worksop
                   RDn. Eccl bdry: 1931.[48]

EXAMPLE D: MATLOCK BATH
  Derbys   EP Cr 1842 from Matlock AP.[9] Ashov. RDn (1842—
                   87), Bakew. RDn (1887—*).

EXAMPLE E: ASHBY WOULDS
  Leics   CP Cr 1894 from the pt of Ashby de la Zouch AP in
                   Ashb. Would UD.[22] *LG* Ashb. de la Z. PLU, Ashb.
                   Woulds UD. Bdry: 1897 (help cr Woodville CP, to
                   be in Derbys),[32] 1936,[23] 1956.[24] *Parl* Loughb. Dv/
                   CC (1918—*).

Creation, Abolition.

        Ashby Woulds (E) is a civil parish only and its formation from Ashby de la Zouch AP, while reducing the latter for civil purposes, in no way affected it for ecclesiastical purposes. Matlock Bath (D) is an ecclesiastical parish only, and its formation did not affect Matlock AP for civl purposes. Ollerton (C) was a subordinate part of Edwinstowe AP (as it was called for civil purposes, while called 'Edwinstowe with Carburton' ecclesiastically), gaining separate separate civil status as a parish (CP) in 1866 and separate ecclesiastical status as a parish (EP) in 1888. Naunton Beauchamp (A) and Mobberley (B) are ancient parishes and the *Guide* does not attempt to date their medieval origins.

Alteration of Boundaries.

        Naunton Beauchamp (A) underwent no boundary changes whatsoever. Ashby Woulds (E) as a CP was capable only of civil boundary alteration; Matlock Bath (D), only of ecclesiastical. The changes for Mobberley (B) in 1936 and for Ollerton (C) in 1957 are labelled 'civ bdry' because the parishes boundaries were altered only for civil purposes in those instances. The changes in Mobberley (B) in 1881 and Ollerton (C) in 1931 are labelled 'eccl bdry' because the alterations were exclusively ecclesiastical. The change in the latter is cited by year only because no new parishes were created or existing ones gained, but there is an elaboration in the former instance because the change resulted in the creation of a new parish. The civil change in Ashby Woulds in 1897 is detailed since it involved a reduction in the area of Leicestershire to help create a new parish in Derbyshire.

Civil Organisation.

        The arrangement of the parish within the civil structure of its county is marked off in examples A, B, C and E by *LG* for *Local Government*; Matlock Bath (D) has no civil status. For Naunton Beauchamp (A), Mobberley (B) and Ollerton (C) an abbreviated entry prefixed by 'Seq' is used to shorten the entry. By reference to the initial page of the entry for Worcs under 'Local Government Sequences' it will be found that Naunton Beauchamp and other parishes with Sequence 17 were in Pershore Hd, Pershore PLU and RSD, and in Pershore RD. The organisation is presented in full for Ashby Woulds (E) because it was in an urban district and because its organisation in Ashby de la Zouch PLU was only for the years 1894—1930 instead of the fullest possible extent from the creation in the 1830s until 1930.

Parliamentary Organisation.

        The abbreviation *Parl* sets off the arrangement of A, B, C and E for parliamentary constituencies. The inclusive years within particular constituencies were shown because the arrangement would apply not only to general but also to bye elections. The abbreviated sequence is used for A, B and C because they shared a similar arrangement with other parishes in their respective counties. Ashby Woulds (E) has the constituencies named explicitly because the parish existed only for part of the period covered by the sequence and thus the sequence would not be applicable.

Ecclesiastical Organisation.

The appropriate entries for A, B and C are set off with *Eccl.* There is no such heading for D because, as an EP, it could have no organisation other than ecclesiastical, and it is thus understood. A sequence is used for Naunton Beauchamp. There is no sequence for B or C and instead the rural deaneries are named explicitly because each's arrangement in rural deaneries was unique to that parish, not shared by any other parish in the respective counties. An explicit citation of rural deaneries is given for D because the EP existed only from 1842, and thus the citation by sequence would be inappropriate.

Sample Entry for Major Urban Area.

The entries for 'Warwick' (Warws) are presented in order to illustrate a special form of abbreviated entry.

> WARWICK
> The following have 'Warwick' in their names. Insofar as any existed at a given time: *LG* Knight. Hd, Warw. Bor/MB, PLU, USD. *Parl* Warw. Parl Bor (1295—1918), Warw. & Leam. Dv/CC (1918—*). *Eccl* Warw. RDn.
> CP1—WARWICK—Cr 1921 by union AP1, AP2.[338] Bdry: 1931.[74]
> —WARWICK ALL SAINTS—Name used now for EP cr 1867 as 'Emscote' qv.
> AP1—WARWICK ST MARY—Abol civ 1921 to help cr CP1.[338] Eccl bdry: 1844 (cr EP1).[339]
> AP2—WARWICK ST NICHOLAS—Abol civ 1921 to help cr CP1.[338] Eccl bdry: 1861 (cr Emscote EP, now called 'Warwick All Saints'),[101] 1957.[275]
> EP1—WARWICK ST PAUL—Cr 1844 from AP1.[339]

Many of the details of the entries follow the norms expressed above: civil and ecclesiastical boundary alterations are clearly separated (Warwick St Mary), some units have only civil status (Warwick) so that the boundary alteration is of necessity only civil, and so forth. The principal change is the indication of a parish's name by a special entry (CP1, EP1, AP1) so that the name need not be repeated each time in which it was involved with changes with other parishes in Warwick (to which alone the arrangement is restricted). The saving in space is substantial, particularly when applied to all the parishes in Manchester, York or Lincoln, for example. The other change is that the organisation for civil, parliamentary and ecclesiastical purposes is expressed once only, in the headnote. Unless stated otherwise in the entry for particular purposes, it is assumed that each ancient and civil parish was in the borough, poor law union, and so on, to the extent possible given the nature of each unit (only the arrangement in Warwick RDn will apply to APs and the EP, for example, because only they had ecclesiastical status).

PART II: LOCAL GOVERNMENT UNITS

The entries in this Part summarise from a different aspect information provided in Part I. Here the perspective is the composition in their totality of local government units rather than the place of the individual parish.

Arrangement by Counties.

The basic arrangement is alphabetical by ancient county, but because these were followed by administrative and then metropolitan and non-metropolitan counties, a partial rearrangement has been necessary. As regards *administrative counties*, the three administrative counties of the Parts of Lincolnshire (Parts of Holland, Parts of Kesteven, Parts of Lindsey) are presented with Lincolnshire, those parishes constituting the Soke of Peterborough are listed separately (although in Part I the parishes are included among the entries for Northamptonshire), and the three administrative counties of the Ridings of Yorkshire (Yorkshire East Riding, Yorkshire North Riding, Yorkshire West Riding) are presented with Yorkshire. As regards *metropolitan* and *non-metropolitan counties*, these are interspersed alphabetically among the other county entries, by first letter of the first name (e.g., Greater Manchester under 'G', West Midlands under 'W').

Alterations in County Boundaries.

For each of the ancient and administrative counties there is a summary of the changes in county boundaries, arranged by the years in which the alterations took place. It will then be necessary to note the parishes affected and then to refer to Part I to determine the nature of the change each underwent. For the metropolitan and non-metropolitan counties, the constitution as of 1 Apr 1974 is given in terms of administrative counties as of 31 Mar 1974.

Organisation within Local Government Units.

The major portion of Part II consists of summary lists of constituent parishes for the hundreds, boroughs, poor law unions, sanitary districts and administrative county districts within the county.

EXAMPLE — HUNDREDS
>ALSTOW HD
>>Ashwell, Barrow (from 1866), Burley, Cottesmore, Exton, Greetham, Horn, Market Overton, Stretton, Teigh, Thistleton, Whissendine, Whitwell

In this example from Rutland, it will be noted that parishes may be assumed to be within the hundred throughout their entire history unless their place in it is limited by dates of inclusion. Barrow, for example, became recognised as a civil parish in 1866, having previously been considered a chapelry within Cottesmore (as can be ascertained from Part I of the *Guide*). The principles stated here apply to the other entries in Part II. It will be noted that Poor Law Unions were entirely within the county unless noted otherwise; in the latter instance, it will be necessary to look under each county indicated to ascertain the complete parochial composition of the union.

PART III: PARLIAMENTARY CONSTITUENCIES

The entries in theis Part are similar to those in Part II in that there are summary lists of the composition of each parliamentary constituency. It is possible to shorten the entries substantially because the practice from 1832—85 was to express divisions in terms of hundreds and liberties, and from 1918 onward in terms of administrative county units. As will be noted below, the dates at which boroughs first sent representatives to parliament are based on the lists of MPs in *Parliamentary Papers* and not on original research, and that it has been necessary to provide a complete survey of the parochial composition of county divisions for 1885—1918 because the latter were expressed in terms of petty sessional divisions.

PART IV: THE DIOCESES OF ENGLAND

Part IV is similar to Parts II and III in that it is a summary of information provided in Part I, but differs in that there are no summary lists of the parochial composition because of limitations of space. Instead the summary lists are of rural deaneries within the respective dioceses and archdeaconries. The dates and authorities for changes in these units are also summarised.

DEFINITIONS OF TERMS

PRELIMINARY NOTE:
>The *definitions* below are for the purposes of the *Guide* only. A full definition would include the powers assigned to each unit and thus would introduce matters outside the *Guide's* scope which is limited to the areas in which those powers were used.
>*Sources* used for particular districts are specified. In addition there was an extensive use of *The Victoria History of the Counties of England*, directories, gazeteers such as Samuel Lewis, *A Topographical Dictionary of England*, internal memoranda and manuscipt sources in county records offices. Many of these are cited in the footnotes.

ADMINISTRATIVE COUNTY—see COUNTY
ANCIENT COUNTY—see COUNTY
ANCIENT PARISH—see PARISH
ARCHDEACONRY—see DIOCESE
BOROUGH
>*Borough ('Bor')*.
>>There is agreement neither on what constitutes a borough in the early period, nor on how many there were. Some towns had ancient charters, others claimed the right by prescription, some were incorporated and some had several claims to the title. Among distinguishing marks were the borough's own officers and institutions which included some degree of exemption from the county's jurisdiction, special schemes of taxation, the right to hold fairs and markets and the right to representation in parliament. Since the *Guide* is not concerned with the medieval origins of units, the inclusion of a unit as a borough is based on the research of others (see *Sources* below). Because many boroughs disappeared early or because the extent of the borough gradually increased or was even in dispute, the inclusion of a parish as a constituent part of a particular

borough must be provisional, and it cannot be assumed that the parish's area was entirely subject to the borough's jurisdiction. Some boroughs were of such importance that they gained the status of 'counties of themselves' (see COUNTY).

Municipal Borough ('MB').

These were established by authority of the Municipal Corporations Act, 1835 (5 & 6 Wm IV, *c* 76), either by inclusion in the schedule to the act of 1835 or by later charter. A number of earlier boroughs were not made municipal boroughs, and those which did not gain the status by the mid-1880s were disfranchised. The scheme of municipal boroughs was ended in 1974, so that if inclusive dates are not expressed in Part II of the *Guide* after a borough's name, it is to be understood that it was in existence from 1835 to 1974.

County Borough ('CB').

Towns of exceptional importance were made county boroughs, either by inclusion in the original schedule in the Local Government Act, 1888 (51 & 52 Vict, *c* 41, effective 1889) or by later charter. This status carried complete exemption from the jurisdiction of the surrounding or adjacent administrative county (see COUNTY), but it was common to include returns of the area in census and other reports along with the county with which they were 'associated', usually the area from which they first won independence. This procedure is followed in the *Guide*; a table later in this section lists county boroughs alphabetically and the names of the 'associated' counties. This scheme was also terminated in 1974, so that a lack of dates by a name in Part II of the *Guide* indicates the county borough's existence from 1889 to 1974.

Wards.

Boroughs, municipal boroughs and county boroughs of any size were divided into wards, the composition of which varied over the years. Because the wards only rarely coincided with parishes, the basic unit of the *Guide*, schemes of wards are generally ignored. The only exception is with the constitution of parliamentary constituencies when stated in terms of wards. These are then presented in Part III under the respective counties when needed. (Wards also existed in the northernmost counties as equivalents to 'hundreds' in the south; see ANCIENT COUNTY).

Sources and Boundaries.

The inclusion of a borough of medieval origin rests primarily upon M. W. Beresford and H. P. R. Finberg, *English Medieval Boroughs: A Hand-List* (1973), on other secondary sources and on consultation with the archivists of the various counties, but not on original research. Schedules of municipal and county boroughs appear in the original acts and later incorporations are summarised in the census returns. At the time the act of 1835 was contemplated, a survey was made of the then existing boroughs, with results published in *Parliamentary Papers*. The returns were voluntary and thus incomplete, but valuable particulars of changes in boundaries in the early periods are often included. For the period 1875—94 when municipal boroughs were also urban sanitary disticts (see SANITARY DISTRICTS), changes in the boundaries of one did not automatically alter the other, and differences are noted in Part II of the *Guide* under each county. Thereafter alterations in the boundaries of constituent parishes also altered the boundaries of the municipal or county borough.

BOROUGH CONSTITUENCY—see PARLIAMENTARY CONSTITUENCIES
BOUNDARY ALTERATIONS—see each major unit where boundary alterations particular to it are noted
CHAPELRY—see PARISH
CIVIL PARISH—see PARISH
COUNTY

Ancient County ('Anc Co').

Counties are geographic entities whose origins reach back into the pre-Conquest period. They were derived either from Anglo-Saxon kingdoms whose size made them suitable administrative units when England was unified in the tenth century, or as artificial creations formed from larger kingdoms. The number of 'shires' (the Anglo-Saxon term) or 'counties' (Norman term) varied in the medieval period, particularly in the north of England—Westmorland became a county, for example, only in the sixteenth century.

Ancient counties were divided into smaller geographic districts called by a variety of names, according to local custom. In southern England and in the southmost of those counties included in this volume, the units were *Hundreds ('Hd')*, the origins and roles of which are debated by historians. In the areas included within the Danelaw in the pre-Conquest centuries, the term *Wapentake ('Wap')* is more commonly used. In the far north, the subdivisions are usually called *Wards ('Wd')*. Hundreds or their equivalents were comprised of vills in the medieval period, and of parishes only by the late sixteenth century, thus providing the starting point for the *Guide*. The vast restructuring of hundreds in the middle ages thus falls outside the scope of the *Guide*. By the later nineteenth century hundreds had lost administrative importance. They are thus ignored in the *Guide* after 1889, at which time ancient counties were supplanted by administrative counties.

Administrative County ('Adm Co').

A new scheme of administrative counties was created in 1889 by the Local Government Act, 1888 (51 & 52 Vict, *c* 41, effective 1889). The new counties consisted of Municipal Boroughs (see BOROUGHS) and, from 1894, Urban and Rural Districts (as established by the Local Government Act, 1894, 57 & 58 Vict, *c* 58). *Urban Districts ('UD')* and *Rural Districts ('RD')* were either successors to previously existing urban or rural sanitary districts (see SANITARY DISTRICTS) or were created by later order. The scheme of administrative counties and constituent units was abolished in 1974.

County Boroughs ('CB').

The Local Government Act, 1888, also conferred on a number of important boroughs the status of county borough which entailed complete independence from the surrounding or adjacent county upon which it had once been dependent. For details, see BOROUGHS.

Metropolitan and Non-Metropolitan Counties.

The Local Government Act, 1972 (20 & 21 Eliz II, *c* 70, effective 1974) supplanted administrative counties and county boroughs with a new scheme of six metropolitan and thirty-nine non-metropolitan counties (excluding Greater London as constituted in 1965; see LONDON in the introduction to Volume I of the *Guide*). The new counties were divided respectively into metropolitan districts and districts; all of the metropolitan counties are in the north of England and fall within the scope of this Volume of the *Guide*. This new arrangement provided a logical terminus for the *Guide*, which does, however, state in Part II the constitution of each metropolitan and non-metropolitan county in northern England as of its erection on 1 April 1974.

County of Itself.

Certain important towns enjoyed the right to name their own sheriffs and were known as 'counties of themselves', 'counties of cities' or 'counties of towns'. These are included by special notation within the counties in which their area was located: Berwick upon Tweed (1835) in Northumberland, Chester (*ca* 1121/ 1129 and more continuously from 1238/39) in Cheshire, Coventry (1452) in Warwickshire, Kingston upon Hull (1440) in Yorkshire, Lichfield (1556) in Staffordshire, Lincoln (1410) in Lincolnshire, Newcastle upon Tyne (1400) in Northumberland, and Nottingham (1448) in Nottinghamshire.

Poor Law Counties (or Registration Counties).

When the Poor Law Commissioners organised poor law unions after 1834 (see POOR LAW), the unions of parishes often included parishes in two or more ancient counties. The census returns from 1851 created an artificial 'poor law' or 'registration' county, grouping under one county those unions predominantly comprised of parishes within that ancient county. The arrangement is ignored in Part I of the *Guide* but is reflected in Part II where poor law unions are identified as belonging to one or the other poor law county. Where a union included parishes from several counties, it will be necessary to refer to each county involved to ascertain the complete composition of the union.

Sources and Boundaries.

The schedules to the acts of 1888 and 1972 are the initial source, modified by later governmental orders (see PARISHES, *Sources and Boundaries* where the agencies are stated). In Part I of the *Guide* any changes which affected the boundary of a county are indicated under the name of the border parishes affected, with the names of parishes affected in the adjacent county or county borough as well. In Part II all changes which affected county boroughs are summarised by year in the entry 'Associated County Borough(s)'.

COUNTY BOROUGH—see BOROUGH and COUNTY
COUNTY CONSTITUENCY—see PARLIAMENTARY CONSTITUENCIES
COUNTY OF ITSELF—see COUNTY
DIOCESE

Diocese ('Dioc').

The diocese was the basic geographic division of the church from the earliest times. There was a continual rearrangement of dioceses before the Normans, but the system established by them in the eleventh century remained until the nineteenth centruy, altered only slightly in the sixteenth century. The *Guide* includes all dioceses of the established church from the Norman period until 1974, the terminal date for all entries, even though the ecclesiastical structure remains after that date with no loss in continuity. Dioceses are directed by a *bishop ('bp')* with ordinary jurisdiction, and the town in which his cathedral is located is properly called a *city*. On occasion the term 'city' has been granted to other towns by royal letters patent.

Archdeaconries ('AD') and Rural Deaneries ('RDn').

From the twelfth and thirteenth centuries dioceses were divided into geographic areas with special administrative and judicial roles under the direction of an archdeacon. These is turn were divided into rural deaneries, 'rural' used to distinguish them from the dean and chapter of the cathedral of the diocese. The system of rural deaneries was in abeyance from the sixteenth to the early nineteenth century when it was revived.

Rearrangements of dioceses, archdeaconries and rural deaneries were frequent from the early nineteenth century. To note all three jurisdictions in each of the parochial entries would expand the *Guide* to unmanageable size, so only the rural deaneries in which a parish were organised are noted. At the beginning of the entries for each county in Part I, the arrangement of rural deaneries in which that county's parishes were organised is specified, with details of the organisation of rural deaneries within dioceses and archdeaconries. Part IV of the *Guide* lists the complete composition of the dioceses, regardless of the counties in which constituent parishes were located.

Peculiars.

A number of parishes were geographically within the area of a diocese yet exempt in part or entirely from the jurisdiction of the bishop, archdeacon, other official or ecclesiastical courts. These *pecular jurisdictions ('pec jurisd')* are specified in Part I of the *Guide* only. Most peculiar jurisdictions were abolished in the late 1840s but some persist; the terminal date of inclusion within the peculiar is noted.

Sources and Boundaries.

Changes in dioceses in Henry VIII's reign were made by letters patent, printed in Rymer's *Foedera*. Since the nineteenth century the new dioceses have been created by statutory authority, brought into effect by orders in council published in the *London Gazette*. The effective date of the change was usually the date gazetted, but sometimes at a later specified date or upon the vacancy of an incumbent.

Arrangements of parishes within the diocesan framework are noted for 1291 in *Taxatio Ecclesiastica Angliae et Walliae Auctoritate P. Nicholai IV* (1802), and for the 1530s in *Valor Ecclesiasticus Temp. Henr. VIII. Auctoritate Regia Institutus* (1817), and for later times in John Bacon, *Liber Regis vel Thesaurus Rerum Ecclesiasticarum* (1786 edition used). Rearrangements since the nineteenth century were made by gazetted orders in council; changes before 1875 were often on the bishop's authority and not published. In these cases the date cited in the *Guide* is the date in which the changes first appeared in the *Clergy List*.

There were other ways for the composition of a rural deanery to be changed in addition to an explicit order: constituent parishes could be abolished or new ones created; alterations of boundaries involving parishes in different dioceses, archdeaconries or rural deaneries could occur; or parishes could become organised in unions of benefices with parishes in adjacent jurisdictions, and thereby be drawn into the ecclesiastical organisation of the neighbouring parish.

DISTRICT—see *Metropolitan District* and *District* under COUNTY, *Urban District* and *Rural District* under COUNTY, *Urban Sanitary District* and *Rural Sanitary District* under SANITARY DISTRICTS
DIVISION—see PARLIAMENTARY CONSTITUENCIES
ECCLESIASTICAL PARISH—see PARISH
EXTRA-PAROCHIAL

Certain geographic areas were not organised as parishes and hence were called *extra-parochial ('ex-par')*. There were a variety of reasons, including association with the crown, with a religious house before the Dissolution or with a cathedral chapter, or with other corporate bodies. An attempt was made to extinguish these for civil purposes in the late 1850s, notably in the statute 20 Vict, *c* 19, effective 1 Jan 1858, which stipulated that these places should either become separate civil parishes or be incorporated into an adjacent civil parish. Although this established the principle, a series of supplementary orders was often required to make the plan uniform (see PARISHES, *Sources and Boundaries*). These civil changes had no effect whatsoever on the ecclesiastical status of the extra-parochial places and a good many remain in that status. Over the years many have been altered, made parishes or amalgamated with other units, and these are indicated in the *Guide*.

GILBERT UNION—see POOR LAW
HAMLET—see PARISH
HUNDRED—see COUNTY
INCORPORATION—see BOROUGH, POOR LAW
LIBERTY—see PARISH
LORDSHIP—see PARISH
METROPOLITAN COUNTY—see COUNTY
MUNICIPAL BOROUGH—see BOROUGH
NON-METROPOLITAN COUNTY—see COUNTY

There can be no single definition of 'parish'—indeed, the parish in origin was more a conglomeration of rights rather than a specific geographic area. Because the *Guide* deals with the areas in which these rights were exercised, the definition must be subdivided into ancient, civil and ecclesiastical parishes.

Ancient Parish ('AP').

As used for the purposes of the *Guide*, an ancient parish is one which existed at first for ecclesiastical purposes, as an area under the jurisdiction of a clergyman with cure of souls, but which gained secular functions in later periods. The first secular function was the relief of the poor, under successive statutory authorities beginning with the Elizabethan poor law of 1597. Therefore 'ancient parish' is used for a parish which existed before 1597 and which thereafter served both secular and ecclesiastical roles.

Civil Parish ('CP').

These units served only civil roles. It was common to define parishes in this sense as areas 'for which a separate poor rate is or can be assessed', a definition of no use after 1930. The existence, alteration or abolition of these units made no effect on the ecclesiastical arrangements of the identical geographic area.

Many civil parishes were in effect areas at first subordinate to a mother parish, which came in time to enjoy independence. These units were variously called *hamlets* ('hmlt') (small settlements), *tithings* ('tg'), or *townships* ('tp') (generally subdivisions for poor law purposes), *chapelries* ('chap', areas with a clergyman dependent upon the incumbent of the mother parish), *liberties* ('lbty'), or *lordships* (areas with an early dependence upon a secular or ecclesiastical lord), or were called by a variety of other names with local importance. If a separate poor law rate was levied in the subordinate unit, it was then called by its own 'rank' such as 'township' and/or as 'parish'. To avoid this confusion the Poor Law Amendment Act, 1866 (29 & 30 Vict, *c* 113) stipulated that these areas should thereafter be called 'parishes'. It has been noted elsewhere (see EXTRA-PAROCHIAL) that many areas not within the parochial framework also became civil parishes, particularly in 1858.

Ecclesiastical Parishes ('EP').

These units came into existence after 1597 to serve only ecclesiastical roles. The number of these was much greater than for civil parishes, particularly as efforts were made to build new churches in increasingly populated urban areas. Many ecclesiastically subordinate areas within parishes such as chapelries were raised to parochial rank, and many formed with no earlier status. The Commissioners of Queen Anne's Bounty provided financial assistance to clergymen of cures with inadequate financial resources, after which the benefice was styled a 'perpetual curacy'. This had no effect on the independence of previously separate parishes, but 'augmentation' of revenues for hitherto subordinate units gave them new independent status (1 Geo I, *c* 10), and many ecclesiastical parishes therefore date from that augmentation. In the nineteenth and twentieth centuries a number of statutory provisions allowed the creation of many different types of ecclesiastical parishes, alike only in the newly independent status. It was thus not unusual for a parish to be 'refounded' to gain privileges and rights according to newer statutes which it had not earlier enjoyed as a perpetual curacy. The various types of ecclesiastical parishes are ignored because the reference to the original order will make the status clear; an exception is made for *particular districts* ('part dist') which are mentioned in the footnotes because their creation often rested on the authority of the particular bishop or other agency and because these orders were not generally published in the *London Gazette*.

Sources and Boundaries.

Civil parishes have been created and abolished, and their boundaries altered, by parliamentary statutes and by orders of a succession of governmental agencies (the Local Government Board, the Ministry of Health, the Ministry of Housing and Local Government, and the Department of the Environment). The census has been the main source for these changes because the orders published in the intercensal periods are recapitulated in every new census.

The archives of the Church Commissioners (originally Ecclesiastical Commissioners) have been used to trace the ecclesiastical changes. For the period to 1939 the orders in council making the changes were published as an appendix to the Commissioners' report to parliament, so that one need not work through the bulky *London Gazette*, nor sort through the files or copies of the records in the diocesan record offices. Since 1939 the *London Gazette* is the principal source, although lately the orders have been published by name only, so that one must consult the originals.

Full details of all parishes affected by creations and abolitions of civil and ecclesiastical parishes are provided, with a footnote reference to the authority. Boundary alterations are cited by date with footnote reference to the authority, without further details, except when the alteration affected the boundaries of the county (civil parish) or diocese (ecclesiastical parish), in which case full particulars are included.

A particularly complicating element arises because many parishes consisted of two or more geographically separate portions. The elements of a parish existing apart were called 'detached parts', and conversely elements of other parishes included within a parish were called 'foreign parts'. A determined effort was made in the 1880s to eliminate these for civil purposes, notably in the statute 45 & 46 Vict, c 58 (effective 1883) which ordered that detached parts be incorporated into the parish which surrounded them or with which they enjoyed the longest common boundary. A series of orders was needed, however, to implement the principle fully; orders in the 1880s changing civil boundaries are nearly all of this type. These changes had no effect whatsoever on the ecclesiastical constitution of the parish, unless separate orders in council to that purpose were issued later.

PARLIAMENTARY BOROUGH—see PARLIAMENTARY CONSTITUENCIES
PARLIAMENTARY CONSTITUENCIES

Rearrangement of Constituencies.

Representatives of the counties of England in the House of Commons were called knights of the shire, with two representing each county. From 1832 onwards a number of statutes divided counties for parliamentary purposes: from 1832 to 1948 these were called *divisions ('Dv')* of the county, and since 1948 *county constituencies ('CC')*. A large number of boroughs were also represented in the House of Commons, called *parliamentary boroughs ('Parl Bor')* until 1948, *borough constituencies ('BC')* thereafter. Other interests such as the universities were also represented at different times.

In 1832 and 1867, with a few exceptions, county divisions were expressed in terms of constituent hundreds and liberties. In 1885 the definition was in terms of *Petty Sessional Divisions ('PSD')*, judicial units with which the *Guide* is not otherwise concerned. It has been necessary, therefore, to provide the parochial composition of the constituencies in the period 1885—1918 in Part III of the *Guide*. From 1918 onward the elements were stated in constitutive administrative county units.

Sources and Boundaries.

Dates of medieval representation of boroughs in parliament have been taken from the list of MPs in *Parliamentary Papers*, with no additional research other than secondary sources. Dates are shown as inclusive between alterations rather than by date of general elections (e.g., 1832—67) since bye elections would be based on the earlier arrangement. Changes from 1832—1918 and for 1948 are based on schedules in the following acts: 1832 (2 & 3 Wm IV, c 45); 1867 (30 & 31 Vict, c 102); 1885 (48 & 49 Vict, c 3, 23); 1918 (7 & 8 Geo V, c 64); 1948 (11 & 12 Geo VI, c 65). Changes in 1945 and 1970 rest on schedules published as statutory instruments (1945/701, 1970/1674). From 1951 onward a number of changes are made on specific individual cases without awaiting a general rearrangement; these are published as statutory instruments. Many of the latter also change boundaries for parliamentary purposes, usually to bring the boundaries of borough constituencies into line with previously altered boundaries of municipal and county boroughs.

PARTICULAR DISTRICTS—see PARISH
PECULIARS—see DIOCESE
PETTY SESSIONAL DIVISION—see PARLIAMENTARY CONSTITUENCIES
POOR LAW

The Elizabethan Poor Law.

The poor law acts of 1597 and 1601 assigned to the parishes the responsibility for administering the relief of the poor. These and numerous acts thereafter also allowed units within the parishes but without parochial status (chapelries, hamlets and the like) to be distinct and separate poor law units. It is impossible to date when most of these units assumed those responsibilities, but at the time they did so they became civil parishes (see PARISHES). This assumption of status is indicated in the *Guide* by the entry 'separate civil identity early'.

Incorporations and Gilbert Unions.

From the eighteenth century there was a growing awareness that a regional and/or particular rather than a parochial approach was needed in poor law matters. A number of parishes and groups of parishes sought special provisions through acts in parliament and are thus called *incorporations ('incorp')* for poor law purposes. The necessity for seeking special privileges through legislation was obviated by the permissive 'Gilbert's Act' of 1783 (22 Geo III, c 83) which allowed voluntary associations of parishes for poor law purposes as *Gilbert's Unions ('GilbU')*.

Poor Law Unions ('PLU').

The next step in forming unions of parishes was compulsory: the Poor Law Amendment Act, 1834 (4 & 5 Wm IV, c 76) authorised Poor Law Commissioners to create poor law unions throughout the realm. Many of the parishes and groups of parishes already under incorporations or Gilbert Unions were subsumed into the new poor law unions, but others remained separate for varying periods of time. For the purposes of the *Guide*, incorporations and Gilbert unions are not included unless they maintained their independence after the scheme of poor law unions. The Local Government Act, 1929 (19 & 20 Geo V, *c* 17, effective 1930) abolished poor law unions and transferred those functions to the county councils of the administrative counties.

Sources and Boundaries.

The Poor Law Commissioners made annual reports to parliament in which the establishment of and changes in poor law unions can be found, particularly in 1835 and 1836 (published in *Parliamentary Papers*). Many changes of parishes from one union to another are recorded only in the minute books of the unions, usually held now in county record offices; since many of these are lost, it is sometimes possisble to date changes only by reference to county directories, looking for the first appearance of a parish in a new union.

See also: Poor Law County under COUNTY

POOR LAW COUNTY—see COUNTY
POOR LAW UNION—see POOR LAW
RURAL DEANERY—see DIOCESE
RURAL DISTRICT—see COUNTY
RURAL SANITARY DISTRICT—see SANITARY DISTRICTS
SANITARY DISTRICTS
Urban Sanitary Districts ('USD') and Rural Sanitary Districts ('RSD')

The Public Health Acts of 1873 and 1875 (35 & 36 Vict, *c* 79, effective 1875, and 38 & 39 Vict, *c* 55) created new authorities with responsibilities in public health. Urban areas, already included in municipal boroughs or in other bodies such as towns with improvement commissioners, were to form urban sanitary districts, the number of which was gradually enlarged in succeeding years. The remainder of the realm was to be divided into rural sanitary districts to be co-terminous with poor law unions less the areas in urban sanitary districts. The system was abolished by the Local Government Act, 1894 (57 & 58 Vict, *c* 58) which transformed existing urban and rural sanitary districts into general-purpose *urban districts ('UD')* and *rural districts ('RD')* respectively, in the new scheme of administrative counties (see COUNTY).

Sources and Boundaries.

Creations, abolitions and changes in these units are summarised in the census reports. The incorporation of a town as a municipal borough (see BOROUGHS) also made it an urban sanitary district. Changes in the boundaries of one did not always affect the other; changes are specified in Part II of the *Guide* under sanitary districts.

TITHING—see PARISH
TOWNSHIP—see PARISH
URBAN DISTRICT—see COUNTY
URBAN SANITARY DISTRICT—see SANITARY DISTRICTS
WARDS—see COUNTY and PARLIAMENTARY CONSTITUENCIES

GENERAL ABBREVIATIONS

MONARCHS, MONTHS

The usual abbreviations are used for names of monarchs and months of the year.

ABBREVIATIONS PARTICULAR TO COUNTIES

These are the initial entries for each county in Part I of the *Guide*.

COUNTIES

Bucks	Buckinghamshire	Cumb	Cumberland
Cambs	Cambridgeshire	Derbys	Derbyshire
Ches	Cheshire	Flints	Flintshire
Clev	Cleveland	Glos	Gloucestershire

Heref	Herefordshire	Northants	Northamptonshire
Holl	Holland	Northumb	Northumberland
Humb	Humberside	Notts	Nottinghamshire
Hunts	Huntingdonshire	Oxon	Oxfordshire
IoE	Isle of Ely	Peterb	Peterborough
Kestev	Kesteven	Rutl	Rutland
Lancs	Lancashire	Salop	Shropshire
Leics	Leicestershire	Staffs	Staffordshire
Lincs	Lincolnshire	Warws	Warwickshire
Lind	Lindsey	Westm	Westmorland
Monm	Monmouth	Worcs	Worcestershire
Montg	Montgomeryshire	Yorks	Yorkshire

DIOCESES

Birm	Birmingham	Linc	Lincoln
Blackb	Blackburn	Manch	Manchester
Bradf	Bradford	Newc	Newcastle
Cov	Coventry	Sheff	Sheffield
Heref	Hereford	S'well	Southwell
Leic	Leicester	Wakef	Wakefield
Lichf	Lichfield	Worc	Worcester

TERMS

abol	abolished	ent	entire(ly)
AD	Archdeaconry	Envirn	Environment
addtl	additional	EP	Ecclesiastical Parish
Adm	Administrative	ex-par	extra-parochial
alt	alteration	Gt	Great
Anc	Ancient	Gtr	Greater
AP	Ancient Parish	Hd	Hundred
apptd	appointed	hmlt	hamlet
Archbp	Archbishop	incl	included
BC	Borough Constituency	incorp	incorporated
Bd	Board	Instr	Instrument
bdry	boundary	jurisd	jurisdiction
Bor	Borough	lbty	liberty
Bp	Bishop	LG	Local Government
c	chapter (statute)	LGB	Local Government Board
ca	*circa*	LGBO	Local Government Board Order
Cath	Cathedral	lic min	effective when minister
CB	County Borough		licensed to the cure
CBC	Church Building Commissioners	*Lond Gaz*	*London Gazette*
CC	County Constituency	MB	Municipal Borough
chap	chapel(ry)	mediev	medieval
civ	civil(ly)	Metrop	Metropolitan
Co	County	mbr(s)	member(s)
conf	confirmed	MHealthO	Ministry of Health Order
consecr	consecrated	MHousLGO	Ministry of Housing and
Const	Constituency		Local Government Order
CP	Civil Parish	N (N'rn)	North (Northern)
cr	created	No	Number
d	dorse	Non-Metrop	Non-Metropolitan
Decl	Declaration	O	Order
Dept	Department	OC	Order in Council
dioc	diocese	orig	original(ly)
Dist	District	o'wise	otherwise
Dv	Division	par(s)	parish(es)
E (E'rn)	East (Eastern)	Parl	Parliamentary
eccl	ecclesiastical	Part Dist	Particular District

PC	Perpetual Curacy	RSD	Rural Sanitary District
pec	peculiar	S (S'rn)	South (Southern)
PLU	Poor Law Union	sep	separate
prev	previous(ly)	Seq	Sequence
prob	probably	SI	Statutory Instrument
ProvO	Provisional Order	St	Saint
PSD	Petty Sessional Division	supp	supplemental
pt	part(ly)	*temp*	*tempore*
Pts	Parts [Lincolnshire]	tg	tithing
QAB	augmented by Commissioners	tp	township
	of Queen Anne's Bounty	transf	transferred
qv	for which see separate entry	UD	Urban District
RD	Rural District	USD	Urban Sanitary District
RDn	Rural Deanery	vac	effective upon vacancy
RO	Record Office	W (W'rn)	West (Western)

FREQUENTLY CITED SOURCES

Beresford & Finberg	M. W. Beresford and H. P. R. Finberg, *English Medieval Boroughs: A Hand-List*
Liber Regis	John Bacon, *Liber Regis* (1786)
Lond Gaz	*London Gazette*
VCH	*Victoria History of the Counties of England*
Valor	*Valor Ecclesiasticus* (1535)

DATES

The terminal date of the *Guide* is 1 April 1974 at which time the Local Government Act, 1972, became effective. Since that act did not affect ecclesiastical or parliamentary units, the character * is used to indicate that the ecclesiastical or parliamentary units continued to exist after 1 April 1974.

'ASSOCIATED' COUNTY BOROUGHS AND COUNTIES OF THEMSELVES

The entries in italics were counties of themselves only. Those marked with + were counties of themselves and later county boroughs as well. The entry is paired with the name of the 'associated' county with which its entries are found in the *Guide*.

Barnsley	Yorks W Riding	Gateshead	Durham
Barrow in Furness	Lancs	Grimsby	Lincs Pts Lind
Berwick upon Tweed	Northumb	Halifax	Yorks W Riding
Birkenhead	Ches	Hanley	Staffs
Birmingham	Warws	Hartlepool	Durham
Blackburn	Lancs	Huddersfield	Yorks W Riding
Blackpool	Lancs	Kingston upon Hull +	Yorks E Riding
Bolton	Lancs	Leeds	Yorks W Riding
Bootle	Lancs	Leicester	Leics
Bradford	Yorks W Riding	*Lichfield*	Staffs
Burnley	Lancs	Lincoln +	Lincs Pts Lind
Burton upon Trent	Staffs	Liverpool	Lancs
Bury	Lancs	Manchester	Lancs
Carlisle	Cumb	Middlesbrough	Yorks N Riding
Chester +	Ches	Newcastle upon Tyne +	Northumb
Coventry +	Warws	Northampton	Northants
Darlington	Durham	Nottingham +	Notts
Derby	Derbys	Oldham	Lancs
Dewsbury	Yorks W Riding	Preston	Lancs
Doncaster	Yorks W Riding	Rochdale	Lancs
Dudley Worcs	(1889—1966); Staffs (1966—74)	Rotherham	Yorks W Riding
		Salford	Lancs

Sheffield	Yorks W Riding	Wakefield	Yorks W Riding
Smethwick	Staffs	Wallasey	Ches
Solihull	Warws	Walsall	Staffs
South Shields	Durham	Warley	Worcs
Southport	Lancs	Warrington	Lancs
St Helen's	Lancs	West Bromwich	Staffs
Stockport	Ches	West Hartlepool	Durham
Stoke on Trent	Staffs	Wigan	Lancs
Sunderland	Durham	Wolverhampton	Staffs
Teesside	Yorks N Riding	Worcester	Worcs
Tynemouth	Northumb	York	Yorks (not assoc with a Riding)

EARLIER COUNTIES ABSORBED INTO OTHERS

Hexhamshire	Northumb	Islandshire	Northumb
Howdenshire	Yorks N Riding	Norhamshire	Northumb

Part I: The Parishes of England

CHESHIRE

ABBREVIATIONS

Abbreviations particular to Ches follow. Those general abbreviations in use throughout the *Guide* are found on pages xvii—xix.

Altr.	Altrincham
Beb.	Bebington
Birk.	Birkenhead
Bough.	Boughton
Brox.	Broxton
Buckl.	Bucklow
Budw.	Budworth
Congl.	Congleton
Edd.	Eddisbury
Ellesm.	Ellesmere
Frod.	Frodsham
Gt Bough.	Great Boughton
Haward.	Hawarden
Knutsf.	Knutsford
Maccl.	Macclesfield
Middlew.	Middlewich
Mkt. Dray.	Market Drayton
Mott.	Mottram
Nantw.	Nantwich
Northw.	Northwich
Runc.	Runcorn
Stalybr.	Stalybridge
Stockpt.	Stockport
Tarv.	Tarvin
Tintw.	Tintwistle
Wall.	Wallasey
Warr.	Warrington
Whitch.	Whitchurch
Wrex.	Wrexham

SEQUENCES

An abbreviated entry prefixed by 'Seq' is used in the parochial entries to avoid repeating often the names of superior units of administration. The content of each sequence is shown below.

Local Government Sequences ('LG')

SEQ 1 Brox. Hd, Gt Bough. PLU (1837—71), Chester PLU (1871—1930), RSD, RD

SEQ 2 Brox. Hd, Gt Bough. PLU (1837—53), Haward. PLU (1853—71), Chester PLU (1871—1930), RSD, RD

SEQ 3 Brox. Hd, Gt Bough. PLU (1837—71), Tarv. PLU (1871—1930), RSD, RD

SEQ 4 Brox. Hd, Gt Bough. PLU (1837—71), Tarv. PLU (1871—1930), RSD, RD (1894—1936), Chester RD (1936—74)

SEQ 5 Brox. Hd, Nantw. PLU, RSD, RD

SEQ 6 Brox. Hd, Nantw. PLU (1837—53), Whitch. PLU (1853—1930), RSD, Malpas RD (1894—1936), Tarv. RD (1936—74)

SEQ 7 Brox. Hd, Wrex. PLU (1837—53), Whitch. PLU (1853—1930), RSD, Malpas RD (1894—1936), Tarv. RD (1936—74)

SEQ 8 Buckl. Hd, Altr. PLU (1836—95), RSD, RD (1894—95), Buckl. PLU (1895—1930), RD (1895—1974)

SEQ 9 Buckl. Hd, Northw. PLU, RSD, RD

SEQ 10 Buckl. Hd, Runc. PLU, RSD, RD

SEQ 11 Edd. Hd, Gt Bough. PLU (1837—71), Chester PLU (1871—1930), RSD, RD

SEQ 12 Edd. Hd, Gt Bough. PLU (1837—71), Tarv. PLU (1871—1930), RSD, RD

SEQ 13 Edd. Hd, Nantw. PLU, RSD, RD

SEQ 14 Edd. Hd, Nantw. PLU (1837—92), RSD (1875—92), Tarv. PLU (1892—1930), RSD (1892—94), RD

SEQ 15 Edd. Hd, Northw. PLU, RSD, RD
SEQ 16 Edd. Hd, Runc. PLU, RSD, RD
SEQ 17 Maccl. Hd, PLU, RSD, RD
SEQ 18 Nantw. Hd, PLU, RSD, RD
SEQ 19 Nantw. Hd, PLU (1837—53), Whitch. PLU (1853—1930), Malpas RD (1894—1936), Nantw. RD (1936—74)
SEQ 20 Nantw. Hd, Congl. PLU, RSD, RD
SEQ 21 Northw. Hd, PLU, RSD, RD
SEQ 22 Northw. Hd, Congl. PLU, RSD, RD
SEQ 23 Northw. Hd, Nantw. PLU, RSD, RD
SEQ 24 Wirral Hd, PLU, RSD, RD (1894—1933), Chester RD (1933—74)
SEQ 25 Wirral Hd, Gt Bough. PLU (1837—71), Chester PLU (1871—1930), RSD, RD
SEQ 26 Wirral Hd, Gt Bough. PLU (1871—53), Haward. PLU (1853—71), Chester PLU (1871—1930), RSD, RD

Parliamentary Sequences ('Parl')

SEQ 1   N'rn Dv (1832—67), Mid Dv (1867—85), Altr. Dv (1885—1945), Buckl. Dv (1945—48), Knutsf. CC (1948—*)
SEQ 2   N'rn Dv (1832—67), Mid Dv (1867—85), Knutsf. Dv/CC (1885—*)
SEQ 3   N'rn Dv (1832—67), Mid Dv (1867—85), Knutsf. Dv (1885—1948), Runc. CC (1948—*)
SEQ 4   N'rn Dv (1832—67), Mid Dv (1867—85), Northw. Dv/CC (1885—*)
SEQ 5   N'rn Dv (1832—67), Mid Dv (1867—85), Northw. Dv (1885—1948), Runc. CC (1948—*)
SEQ 6   N'rn Dv (1832—67), North Dv (1867—85), Knutsf. Dv (1885—1918), Maccl. Dv/CC (1918—*)
SEQ 7   N'rn Dv (1832—67), North Dv (1867—85), Knutsf. Dv (1885—1948), Maccl. CC (1948—*)
SEQ 8   N'rn Dv (1832—67), North Dv (1867—85), Maccl. Dv/CC (1885—*)
SEQ 9   S'rn Dv (1832—67), Mid Dv (1867—85), Crewe Dv (1885—1948), Knutsf. CC (1948—*)
SEQ 10 S'rn Dv (1832—67), Mid Dv (1867—85), Edd. Dv (1885—1948), Crewe CC (1948—55), Nantw. CC (1955—*)
SEQ 11 S'rn Dv (1832—67), Mid Dv (1867—85), Edd. Dv (1885—1918), Northw. Dv (1918—48), Knutsf. CC (1948—*)
SEQ 12 S'rn Dv (1832—67), Mid Dv (1867—85), Knutsf. Dv/CC (1885—*)
SEQ 13 S'rn Dv (1832—67), Mid Dv (1867—85), Knutsf. Dv (1885—1948), Northw. CC (1948—*)
SEQ 14 S'rn Dv (1832—67), Mid Dv (1867—85), Maccl.Dv (1885—1948), Knutsf. CC (1948—*)

SEQ 15 S'rn Dv (1832—67), Mid Dv (1867—85), Northw. Dv/CC (1885—*)
SEQ 16 S'rn Dv (1832—67), South Dv (1867—85), Crewe Dv/CC (1885—*)
SEQ 17 S'rn Dv (1832—67), South Dv (1867—85), Crewe Dv (1885—1948), Knutsf. CC (1948—*)
SEQ 18 S'rn Dv (1832—67), South Dv (1867—85), Crewe Dv/CC (1885—1955), Nantw. CC (1955—*)
SEQ 19 S'rn Dv (1832—67), South Dv (1867—85), Edd. Dv (1885—1918), City of Chester Dv/CC (1918—*)
SEQ 20 S'rn Dv (1832—67), South Dv (1867—85), Edd. Dv (1885—1948), City of Chester CC (1948—*)
SEQ 21 S'rn Dv (1832—67), South Dv (1867—85), Edd. Dv (1885—1948), Crewe CC (1948—55), Nantw. CC (1955—*)
SEQ 22 S'rn Dv (1832—67), South Dv (1867—85), Edd. Dv (1885—1948), Northw. CC (1948—*)
SEQ 23 S'rn Dv (1832—67), South Dv (1867—85), Edd. Dv (1885—1948), Northw. CC (1948—55), Nantw. CC (1955—*)
SEQ 24 S'rn Dv (1832—67), South Dv (1867—85), Edd. Dv (1885—1948), Runc. CC (1948—*)
SEQ 25 S'rn Dv (1832—67), South Dv (1867—85), Northw. Dv/CC (1885—*)
SEQ 26 S'rn Dv (1832—67), South Dv (1867—85), Wirral Dv/CC (1885—*)
SEQ 27 S'rn Dv (1832—67), South Dv (1867—85), Wirral Dv (1885—1948), City of Chester CC (1948—*)
SEQ 28 S'rn Dv (1832—67), South Dv (1867—85), Wirral Dv (1885—1948), Beb. BC (1948—70), Beb. & Ellesm. Port BC (1970—*)

Ecclesiastical Sequences ('Eccl')

SEQ 1   Brox. RDn (until after 1382), Malpas RDn (after 1382—*)
SEQ 2   Chester RDn
SEQ 3   Chester RDn (until 1935), Frod. RDn (1935—*)
SEQ 4   Frod. RDn (until 1869), Frod. East RDn (1869—80), Bowdon RDn (1880—*)
SEQ 5   Frod. RDn (until 1869), Frod. West RDn (1869—80), Frod. RDn (1880—*)
SEQ 6   Maccl. RDn (until 1873), Maccl. South RDn (1873—80), Maccl. RDn (1880—*)
SEQ 7   Middlew. RDn
SEQ 8   Middlew. RDn (until 1880), Congl. RDn (1880—*)
SEQ 9   Nantw. RDn
SEQ 10 Wirral RDn (until 1935), Wirral North RDn (1935—*)
SEQ 11 Wirral RDn (until 1935), Wirral South RDn (1935—*)

DIOCESES AND ARCHDEACONRIES

Ches pars were arranged in Archdeaconries and
Rural Deaneries as follows:

CHESTER DIOC (1541—*)
Chester AD: Bangor RDn (1541—1847), Birk. RDn (1888—*), Gt Budw. RDn (1935—*), Chester RDn, Frod. RDn (1541—1869), Frod. RDn (1880—*), Frod. East RDn (1869—80), Frod. West RDn (1869—80), Maccl. RDn (1541—1873), Maccl. North RDn (1873—80), Maccl. South RDn (1873—80), Malpas RDn, Middlew. RDn, Nantw. RDn (1541—1966), Wall. RDn (1907—*), Wirral RDn (1541—1847), Wirral RDn (1880—1935), Wirral North RDn (1935—*), Wirral South RDn (1935—*)
Liverpool AD (1847—80): Wirral RDn
Maccl. AD (1880—*): Bowdon RDn, Congl. RDn, Knutsf. RDn (1935—*), Maccl. RDn, Mott. RDn (1888—*), Nantw. RDn (1966—*), Stockpt. RDn

COVENTRY AND LICHFIELD DIOC (until 1541) [before 1837 variously styled 'Lichfield' (until 1075), 'Chester' (1075—1102), 'Coventry' (1102—1228), 'Coventry and Lichfield' (1228—Reformation), 'Lichfield and Coventry' (Reformation—1837)]
Chester AD: Brox. RDn (until after 1382), Chester RDn, Frod. RDn, Maccl. RDn, Malpas RDn (after 1382—1541), Middlew. RDn, Nantw. RDn, Wirral RDn

MANCHESTER DIOC (1847—*)
Manchester AD: Heaton RDn (1934—65), Withington RDn (1965—*)

THE PARISHES OF CHESHIRE

ACTON
AP Incl chap Church Minshull (sep par at Dissolution, 1st rector 1541[1]), chap Nantwich (1st independent status 1677 but sep status early debated[2]), chap Wrenbury cum Frith (sep civ identity early [qv for its tps], sep EP 1730 as 'Wrenbury'[3]); incl tps Worleston, Ashton juxta Mondrum, Cholmondeston, Poole (each of the 4 a sep CP 1866,[4] the 4 eccl united 1873 as 'Worleston' EP[5]); incl tps Austerson, Baddington, Brindley, Burland, Coole Pilate, Edleston, Faddiley, Henhull, Hurleston, Stoke (each a sep CP 1866[4]), tp Sound (orig in this par; after chap Wrenbury cum Frith gains sep civ identity, tp Sound pt in this par and pt in the latter, sep CP 1866[4]). LG Pt Nantw. Bor (until Nantwich gains sep civ identity), Seq 18. Addtl civ bdry alt: 1888,[6] 1936.[7] Parl S'rn Dv (1832—67), South Dv (1867—85), Northw. Dv (1885—1945), Edd. Dv (1945—48), Crewe CC (1948—55), Nantw. CC (1955—*). Eccl Seq 9. Addtl eccl bdry alt: 1930.[8]

ACTON
Tp in Weaverham cum Milton AP (eccl, 'Weaverham'), sep CP 1866.[4] LG Edd. Hd, Northw. PLU, RSD, RD. Bdry: 1936.[7] Renamed 1967 'Acton Bridge'.[9] Parl S'rn Dv (1832—67), South Dv (1867—85), Northw. Dv/CC (1885—1970).

ACTON BRIDGE
CP Renaming 1967 of Acton CP.[9] LG Northw. RD. Parl Northw. CC (1970—*).

ACTON GRANGE
Tp in Runcorn AP, before sep civ gains 1858 the area of prev ex-par Middleton Grange,[10] 'Acton Grange' thus enlarged a sep CP 1866,[4] eccl in chap Daresbury (sep EP 1738 from Runcorn AP [qv for other constituent areas incl ex-par Middleton Grange],[3] pt of Daresbury EP eccl severed [incl pt of this tp] 1879 to help cr Walton EP,[11] the remainder refounded 1880 as 'Daresbury' EP[12]). LG Buckl. Hd, Runc. PLU, RSD, RD. Bdry: 1933 (loses pt to Penketh CP, Lancs).[13] Abol 1936 to help cr Walton CP.[7] Parl N'rn Dv (1832—67), Mid Dv (1867—85), Knutsf. Dv (1885—1948).

ADLINGTON
Chap in Prestbury AP, sep CP 1866.[4] LG Seq 17. Bdry: 1936.[7] Parl Seq 7.

AGDEN
Tp pt in Bowdon AP, pt in Rostherne AP, sep CP 1866 from both pars,[4] the pts in both pars eccl severed 1869 to help cr Bollington [Holy Trinity] EP.[14] LG Seq 8. Bdry: 1936.[7] Parl Seq 1.

AGDEN
Tp in Malpas AP, sep CP 1866,[4] eccl severed 1824 to help cr Malpas St Chad EP,[3] the latter refounded 1860.[15] LG Seq 7. Parl Seq 23.

ALDERLEY
AP Incl tps Nether Alderley, Over Alderley, Great Warford (each a sep CP 1866[4]) so that 'Alderley' has no sep civ identity after 1866. LG Maccl. Hd. Parl N'rn Dv (1832—67). Eccl Maccl. RDn (until 1873), Maccl. South RDn (1873—80), Maccl. RDn (1880—1935), Knutsf. RDn (1935—*). Eccl bdry: 1890 (help cr Birtles EP).[16]

NETHER ALDERLEY
Tp in Alderley AP, sep CP 1866.[4] LG Seq 17. Bdry: 1910.[17] Parl Seq 7.

OVER ALDERLEY
Tp in Alderley AP, sep CP 1866.[4] LG Seq 17. Bdry: 1936.[7] Parl Seq 7.

ALDERLEY EDGE
CP Cr 1894 from the pt of Chorley CP in Chorley USD (renamed effective 5 Sept 1894 'Alderley Edge' UD[18]).[19] LG Maccl. PLU, Alderley Edge UD.

Bdry: 1895,[20] 1910,[17] 1936,[7] 1954.[21] *Parl* Knutsf. Dv/CC (1918—70), Maccl. CC (1970—*).

ALDERSEY
    Tp in Coddington AP, sep CP 1866.[4] *LG* Seq 3. *Parl* Seq 23.

ALDFORD
    AP Incl tps Buerton, Churton by Aldford, Edgerley (each a sep CP 1866[4]). *LG* Seq 4. Addtl civ bdry alt: 1936.[7] *Parl* Seq 20. *Eccl* Malpas RDn (until 1967), Chester RDn (1967—72), Malpas RDn (1972—*).

ALLOSTOCK
    Tp in Great Budworth AP, sep CP 1866,[4] eccl severed 1814 to help cr Lower Peover EP.[3] *LG* Seq 21. *Parl* Seq 13.

ALPRAHAM
    Tp in Bunbury AP, sep CP 1866,[4] eccl severed and transf 1901 to Tilstone Fearnall EP.[22] *LG* Seq 13. *Parl* Seq 21.

ALSAGER
    Tp in Bartholmey AP (Ches, Staffs until 1866, ent Ches thereafter), sep CP 1866 in Ches,[4] sep EP 1898.[23] *LG* Nantw. Hd, Congl. PLU, RSD (1875—Jan 1894), Alsager USD (Jan—Apptd Day 1894), UD. *Parl* S'rn Dv (1832—67), South Dv (1867—85), Crewe Dv (1885—1948), Knutsf. CC (1948—55), Crewe CC (1955—*). *Eccl* Congl. RDn (1898—1972), Malpas RDn (1972—*). Eccl bdry: 1946 (cr Alsager Christ Church EP).[24]

ALSAGER CHRIST CHURCH
    EP Cr 1946 from Alsager EP.[24] Congl. RDn. Bdry: 1952.[25]

ALTRINCHAM
    Chap (built 1799) and bor in Bowdon AP, sep CP 1866,[4] sep EP 1812 [St George],[3] eccl refounded 1860.[26] *LG* Buckl. Hd, Altr. Bor, PLU (1836—95), USD, UD (1894—1937), MB (1937—74), Buckl. PLU (1895—1930). Civ bdry: 1920,[27] 1936.[7]. Transf 1974 to Gtr Manch.[28] *Parl* N'rn Dv (1832—67), Mid Dv (1867—85), Altr. Dv (1885—1945), Altr. & Sale Parl Bor/BC (1945—*). *Eccl* Frod. RDn (1812—69), Frod. East RDn (1869—80), Bowdon RDn (1880—*). Eccl bdry: 1911 (cr Broadheath EP).[29]

ALTRINCHAM ST JOHN THE EVANGELIST
    EP Cr 1867 from Bowdon AP, Dunham Massey EP, Timperley EP.[30] Frod. RDn (1867—69), Frod. East RDn (1869—80), Bowdon RDn (1880—*). Bdry: 1906 (help cr Hale EP).[31]

ALVANLEY
    Chap in Frodsham AP, sep CP 1866,[4] sep EP 1741,[3] eccl refounded 1861.[32] *LG* Seq 16. Civ bdry: 1936.[7] *Parl* Seq 24. *Eccl* Frod. RDn (1741—1869), Frod. West RDn (1869—80), Frod. RDn (1880—*). Eccl bdry: 1930.[33]

ALVASTON
    Tp in Nantwich AP, sep CP 1866.[4] *LG* Nantw. Hd, PLU, RSD, RD. Abol 1899 ent to Worleston CP.[34] *Parl* S'rn Dv (1832—67), South Dv (1867—85), Crewe Dv (1885—1918).

ANDERTON
    Tp in Great Budworth AP, sep CP 1866.[4] *LG* Seq 9. *Parl* Seq 4.

ANTROBUS
    Tp in Great Budworth AP, sep CP 1866,[4] sep EP 1848.[3] *LG* Seq 10. Civ bdry: 1881,[35] 1881,[36] 1936 (gains Crowley CP, Seven Oaks CP).[7] *Parl* Seq 3. *Eccl* Frod. RDn (1848—69), Frod. West RDn (1869—80), Frod. RDn (1880—1935), Gt Budw. RDn (1935—*).

APPLETON
    Tp in Great Budworth AP (sometimes early 'Hull and Appleton'), sep CP 1866.[4] *LG* Seq 10. Bdry: 1896 (loses pt to Warr. CB [assoc with Lancs] and to Latchford CP),[37] 1897 (cr Stockton Heath CP).[38] *Parl* Seq 3.

APPLETON THORN
    EP Cr 1887 from Stretton EP.[39] Frod. RDn (1887—1935), Gt Budw. RDn (1935—*).

ARCLID
    Tp in Sandbach AP, sep CP 1866.[4] *LG* Seq 22. *Parl* Seq 9.

ARROWE
    Tp in Woodchurch AP, sep CP 1866.[4] *LG* Wirral Hd, PLU, RSD, RD. Abol 1933 pt to Birk. CB (assoc with Ches) & AP, pt to Irby CP to help cr Wirral UD.[40] *Parl* S'rn Dv (1832—67), South Dv (1867—85), Wirral Dv (1885—1948).

ASHLEY
    Tp in Bowdon AP, sep CP 1866,[4] sep EP 1881 (sometimes 'Ashley Hayes') from Bowdon AP (most of tp Ashley), Mobberley AP, Rostherne AP.[41] *LG* Seq 8. Civ bdry: 1936.[7] *Parl* Seq 1. *Eccl* Bowdon RDn.

ASHTON
    Tp in Tarvin AP, sep CP 1866.[4] *LG* Seq 12. *Parl* Seq 22.

ASHTON UNDER LYME
    AP Lancs par (Salford Hd), civ organisation primarily in Lancs, pt Stalybr. MB ([Ches, Lancs] 1857—94 [enlarged pt 1881—94]), pt Stalybr. USD (Ches, Lancs). This pt becomes 1889 pt of Ches, abol 1894 to help cr Stalybridge CP.[42] For remainder of civ organisation, for parl organisation (incl pt in Stalybr. Parl Bor [Ches, Lancs] 1867—1918), and for eccl organisation, see main entry in Lancs.

ASHTON UPON MERSEY
    AP Incl tp Sale (sep CP 1866,[4] sep EP 1856[43]). *LG* Buckl. Hd, Altr. PLU (1836—95), RSD, Buckl. PLU (1895—1930), RD (1894—95), Ashton upon Mersey UD (1895—1930), Sale UD (1930—35), MB (1935—36). Addtl civ bdry alt: 1908.[44] Abol civ 1936 ent to Sale CP.[7] *Parl* N'rn Dv (1832—67), Mid Dv (1867—85), Altr. Dv (1885—1945), Altr. & Sale Parl Bor (1945—48). *Eccl* Seq 4. Addtl eccl bdry alt: 1887,[45] 1894 (cr Ashton upon Mersey St Mary Magdalene EP).[46]

ASHTON UPON MERSEY ST MARY MAGDALENE
    EP Cr 1894 from Ashton upon Mersey AP.[46] Bowdon RDn.

ASTBURY
    AP Incl in Northw. Hd tp Buglawton (sep CP 1866,[4] sep EP 1841 [incl pt tp Eaton][47]), chap and bor Congleton (sep CP 1866,[4] sep EP 1720[3] [qv for cr of other EPs before remainder refounded 1867 as

'Congleton' EP[48]]), tp Davenport (sep CP 1866,[4] eccl severed 1880 and transf to Swettenham AP[49]), tp Eaton (sep CP 1866,[4] pt eccl severed 1841 to help cr Buglawton EP,[47] the remainder cr 1858 'Eaton' EP[50]), tp Hulme Walfield, tp Radnor (each a sep CP 1866,[4] the 2 united 1878 with tp Somerford Booths in Maccl. Hd to cr 'Hulme Walfield' EP 1878[39]), tp Moreton cum Alcumlow (sep CP 1866[4]), tp Newbold Astbury (sep CP 1866[4]), tp Odd Rode (sep CP 1866,[4] sep EP 1860[51]), tp Smallwood (sep CP 1866,[4] sep EP 1848[3]), tp Somerford (sep CP 1866[4]); incl in Maccl. Hd tp Somerford Booths (sep CP 1866,[4] eccl severed 1878 to help cr Hulme Walfield EP, as noted above) so that 'Astbury' has no sep civ identity after 1866. Parl Pt N'rn Dv, pt S'rn Dv (1832—67). Eccl Seq 8. Addtl eccl bdry alt: 1858 (cr Mossley EP).[3]

ASTON
CP Cr 1936 by union Aston by Sutton CP, Aston Grange CP.[7] LG Runc. RD. Bdry: 1967.[52] Parl Runc. CC (1948—*).

ASTON
Chap in Runcorn AP, sep EP 1861 from Runcorn AP (tps Sutton, Aston by Sutton, Aston Grange, and the pt of tp Dutton [o'wise in Great Budworth AP] eccl in this par), area of eccl ex-par Middleton Grange,[53] the area in Runcorn AP a sep CP 1866 as 'Aston by Sutton',[4] qv. Eccl Frod. RDn (1867—85), Frod. West RDn (1869—80), Frod. RDn (1880—*).

ASTON BY BUDWORTH
Tp in Great Budworth AP, sep CP 1866.[4] LG Seq 8. Parl Seq 2.

ASTON BY SUTTON
Chap in Runcorn AP, sep CP 1866,[4] sep EP 1861 as 'Aston' from Runcorn AP (tps Sutton, Aston by Sutton, Aston Grange, and the pt of tp Dutton [o'wise in Great Budworth AP] in this par), area of eccl ex-par Middleton Grange,[53] qv. LG Buckl. Hd, Runc. PLU, RSD, RD. Abol civ 1936 to help cr Aston CP.[7] Parl N'rn Dv (1832—67), Mid Dv (1867—85), Northw. Dv (1885—1948). Eccl Frod. RDn (1861—69), Frod. West RDn (1869—80), Frod. RDn (1880—*).

ASTON GRANGE
Tp in Runcorn AP, sep CP 1866,[4] eccl severed 1861 to help cr Aston EP.[53] LG Buckl. Hd, Runc. PLU, RSD, RD. Abol 1936 to help cr Aston CP.[7] Parl N'rn Dv (1832—67), Mid Dv (1867—85), Northw. Dv (1885—1948).

ASTON JUXTA MONDRUM
Tp in Acton AP, sep CP 1866,[4] eccl severed 1873 to help cr Worleston EP.[5] LG Seq 18. Parl Seq 21.

AUDENSHAW ST HILDA
EP Cr 1923 from Audenshaw EP, Denton EP (both Lancs, dioc Manch), Haughton St Anne EP (Lancs, Ches, dioc Manch) to be in dioc Manch.[54] See main entry in Lancs.

AUDLEM
AP Incl tps Buerton, Hankelow, Tittenley (each a sep CP 1866[4]), tp Newhall (reported in 1871 census as pt in this par, pt in Wrenbury AP, o'wise and generally considered ent in this par, sep CP 1866[4]),

pt tp Dodcott cum Wilkesley (sep CP 1866[4]). LG Seq 18. Addtl civ bdry alt: 1888.[6] Parl Seq 21. Eccl Seq 9. Eccl bdry: 1869 (help refound Burleydam EP).[55]

AUSTERSON
Tp in Acton AP, sep CP 1866.[4] LG Seq 18. Bdry: 1936.[7] Parl Seq 21.

BACHE
Tp in Chester St Oswald AP, sep CP 1866.[4] LG Seq 1. Parl Seq 19.

BACKFORD
AP Tp 'Backford' in Wirral Hd as were tps Chorlton by Backford, Lea by Backford, Mollington Tarrant (sometimes 'Great Mollington') (each of the 3 a sep CP 1866[4]); incl in Brox. Hd tp Caughall (sep CP 1866[4]). LG Gt Bough. PLU (1837—71), Chester PLU (1871—1930), RSD, RD. Parl Seq 19. Eccl Wirral RDn (until 1880), Chester RDn (1880—1935), Wirral South RDn (1935—*).

BADDILEY
AP LG Seq 18. Civ bdry: 1883,[56] 1888.[6] Parl Seq 21. Eccl Seq 9. Eccl bdry: 1930.[8]

BADDINGTON
Tp in Acton AP, sep CP 1866.[4] LG Seq 18. Bdry: 1936.[7] Parl Seq 21.

BAGULEY
Tp in Bowdon AP (reported in 1871 census as pt in Bowdon AP, pt in Northenden AP, o'wise and generally considered ent in Bowdon), sep CP 1866,[4] sep EP 1848,[3] eccl refounded 1868 from Timperley EP, Sale EP.[57] LG Buckl. Hd, Altr. PLU (1836—95), RSD, RD (1894—95), Buckl. PLU (1895—1930), RD (1895—1931). Abol civ 1931 ent to Manch CB (assoc with Lancs) & AP.[58] Parl N'rn Dv (1832—67), Mid Dv (1867—85), Altr. Dv (1885—1945), Buckl. Dv (1945—48). Eccl Frod. RDn (1848—69), Frod. East RDn (1869—80), Bowdon RDn (1880—*). Eccl bdry: 1886,[59] 1937 (help cr Lawton Moor EP),[60] 1960 (incl help cr Wythenshawe EP).[61]

BARNSTON
Tp in Woodchurch AP, sep CP 1866,[4] sep EP 1870.[62] LG Wirral Hd, PLU, RSD, RD (1894—1933), Wirral UD (1933—74). Bdry: 1933.[40] Transf 1974 to Merseyside.[28] Parl Seq 26. Eccl Wirral RDn (1870—1935), Wirral North RDn (1935—*). Eccl bdry: 1880 (gains tp Pensby from from Woodchurch AP),[12] 1959.[63]

BARNTON
Tp in Great Budworth AP, sep CP 1866,[4] sep EP 1843 (tp Barnton and a further pt of Great Budworth AP).[64] LG Seq 9. Civ bdry: 1936.[7] Parl Seq 4. Eccl Frod. RDn (1843—69), Frod. West RDn (1869—80), Frod. RDn (1880—1935), Gt Budw. RDn (1935—*).

BARROW
AP Incl areas Great Barrow, Little Barrow (each orig sep rated in Gt Bough. PLU but sep staus as pars not gained and thereafter 'Barrow' alone has civ identity). LG Edd. Hd, Gt Bough. PLU (soon after 1837[65]—71), Tarv. PLU (1871—1930), RSD, RD (1894—1936), Chester RD (1936—74). Civ bdry: 1967.[66] Parl Seq 20. Eccl Seq 2.

GREAT BARROW, LITTLE BARROW—see prev entry

BARTHOMLEY

AP Tp 'Barthomley' in Ches (Nantw. Hd) as were chap Alsager (sep CP 1866,[4] sep EP 1852[59]), tp Crewe (sep CP 1866,[4] sep EP 1857[67]), chap Haslington (sep CP 1866,[4] sep EP 1766,[3] eccl refounded 1860[68]); incl in Staffs (N Pirehill Hd) tp Balterley (sep CP 1866 in Staffs[4] so that this par ent Ches thereafter). LG Ches pt, Seq 18. Parl Ches pt, Seq 16. Eccl Nantw. RDn (until 1880), Congl. RDn (1880—*). Addtl eccl bdry alt: 1898 (cr Alsager St Mary Magdalene EP).[23]

BARTINGTON

Tp in Great Budworth AP, sep CP 1866.[4] LG Buckl. Hd, Runc. PLU, RSD, RD. Abol 1936 ent to Dutton CP.[7] Bdry: 1898.[69] Parl N'rn Dv (1832—67), Mid Dv (1867—85), Northw. Dv (1885—1948).

BARTON

Tp in Farndon AP, sep CP 1866.[4] LG Seq 3. Parl Seq 23.

BASFORD

Tp in Wybunbury AP, sep CP 1866.[4] LG Seq 18. Parl Seq 18.

BATHERTON

Tp in Wybunbury AP, sep CP 1866.[4] LG Seq 18. Parl Seq 21.

BEBINGTON

AP Usual civ spelling; for eccl see 'Nether Bebington'. Incl tp Higher Bebington (sep CP 1866,[4] sep EP 1844 as 'Rock Ferry',[70] sometimes 'Higher Bebington St Peter'), tp Lower Bebington (sep CP 1866[4]; incl area church St Andrew, qv below under 'Nether Bebington'), tp Poulton cum Spital, tp Storeton (each a sep CP 1866[4]), tp Tranmere (sep CP 1866,[4] sep EP 1842[71]) so that 'Bebington' has no sep civ identity after 1866. LG Wirral Hd. Parl S'rn Dv (1832—67).

HIGHER BEBINGTON

Tp in Bebington AP, sep CP 1866,[4] sep EP 1844 as 'Rock Ferry' EP,[70] qv sometimes eccl called 'Higher Bebington St Peter'. LG Wirral Hd, PLU, pt Higher Beb. USD, pt Birk. MB (1877—89), pt Birk. CB (1889—94), pt Birk. USD (1877—94), pt Wirral RD (1875—77), Higher Beb. UD. Bdry: 1894 (loses the pt in Birk. CB [assoc with Ches] to cr Rock Ferry CP).[19] Abol 1922 to help cr Beb. & Bromborough UD & CP.[72] Parl S'rn Dv (ent 1832—59, pt 1859—67), pt Birk. Parl Bor (1859—1918), pt South Dv (1867—85), Wirral Dv (pt 1885—1918, ent 1918—48).

HIGHER BEBINGTON CHRIST CHURCH

EP Cr 1877 from Rock Ferry EP (sometimes 'Higher Bebington St Peter').[73] Wirral RDn (1877—1935), Wirral North RDn (1935—*).

HIGHER BEBINGTON ST PETER—see ROCK FERRY

LOWER BEBINGTON

Tp (incl area church St Andrew; for eccl see 'Nether Bebington') in Bebington AP, sep CP 1866.[4] LG Wirral Hd, PLU, Lower Beb. USD, UD. Bdry: 1898 (loses pt to Birk. CB [assoc with Ches] & CP),[74] 1911.[75] Abol 1922 to help cr Beb. & Bromborough UD & CP.[72] Parl S'rn Dv (1832—

67), South Dv (1867—85), Wirral Dv (1885—1948).

NETHER BEBINGTON

AP Usual eccl spelling (sometimes 'Lower Bebington'); for civ and civ and eccl sep tps, see 'Bebington'. Eccl Seq 10. Addtl eccl bdry alt: 1888 (cr New Ferry EP).[76]

BEBINGTON AND BROMBOROUGH

CP Cr 1922 by union Higher Beb. UD & CP, Lower Beb. UD & CP, Bromborough UD & AP.[72] LG Wirral PLU, Beb. & Bromborough UD (1922—33), Beb. UD (1933—37), MB (1937—74). Transf 1974 to Merseyside.[28] Parl Beb. BC (1948—70), Beb. & Ellesm. Port BC (1970—*).

BEESTON

Tp in Bunbury AP, sep CP 1866.[4] LG Seq 14. Parl Seq 23.

BENCHILL

EP Cr 1936 from Northenden AP (Ches AP, civ in Manch CB [assoc with Lancs] from 1931).[77] Heaton RDn (1936—65), Withington RDn (1965—*). Bdry: 1963,[78] 1963 (help cr Wythenshawe The William Temple Church),[79] 1964,[80] 1971 (cr Wythenshawe St Richard of Chichester EP).[81]

BETCHTON

Tp in Sandbach AP, sep CP 1866.[4] LG Seq 20. Parl Seq 17.

BEXTON

Tp in Knutsford CP (orig chap in Rostherne AP, sep par 1741[82]), 'Bexton' a sep CP 1866.[4] LG Seq 8. Bdry: 1936.[7] Parl Seq 2.

BICKERTON

Tp in Malpas AP, sep CP 1866,[4] sep EP 1840 (presumed[83] incl tps Broxton, Bulkeley, Duckington, Egerton, Larkton),[3] eccl refounded 1843.[84] LG Seq 5. Parl Seq 21.

BICKLEY

Tp in Malpas AP, sep CP 1866,[4] pt eccl severed 1842 to help cr Malpas St Chad EP,[15] the latter refounded 1860,[15] 'Bickley' a sep EP 1893 from Malpas AP, Marbury EP, Wrenbury AP.[85] LG Seq 6. Parl Seq 23. Eccl Malpas RDn.

BIDSTON

AP Usual eccl spelling; for civ and civ and eccl sep tps, see following entry. Eccl Wirral RDn (until 1888), Birk. RDn (1888—*). Addtl eccl bdry alt: 1876 (help cr Claughton cum Grange EP),[86] 1905,[87] 1911 (help cr Birkenhead St Bede EP),[29] 1957 (help cr Leasowe EP).[88]

BIDSTON CUM FORD

AP Usual civ spelling; for eccl and cr EP not an orig tp, see prev entry. Incl chap Birkenhead (sep CP 1866,[4] sep EP [St Mary] 1738[3]), tp Claughton with Grange (reported in 1871 census to be pt in this par, pt in Woodchurch AP, o'wise and generally considered ent in this par, sep CP 1866[4]), tp Moreton [sometimes 'Moreton cum Lingham'], tp Saughall Massie (each a sep CP 1866,[4] the 2 tps eccl united 1864 as 'Moreton' EP[89]). LG Wirral Hd, PLU (1836—91), RSD (1875—91), Birk. PLU (1891—1930), RSD (1891—94), Wirral RD. Addtl civ bdry alt: 1928 (loses pt to Birk. CB [assoc with Ches] & AP),[90] 1928 (loses pt to Wall. CB [assoc with Ches] & CP).[91] Abol civ 1933 pt to Birk. CB & AP, pt to Wall. CB & CP (both CBs assoc with Ches).[40] *Parl* S'rn Dv (1832—67), South Dv (1867—85), Wirral Dv (1885—1948).

BIRCHES

Tp in Great Budworth AP, sep CP 1866,[4] eccl in chap Witton (sep EP 1723 from Great Budworth [see Witton for other constituent pts and EPs cr later reducing the area],[3] the reduced area refounded 1900 as 'Witton (otherwise Northwich St Helen)' EP,[14] qv). *LG* Northw. Hd, PLU, RSD. Abol 1892 ent to Lach Dennis CP.[92] *Parl* S'rn Dv (1832—67), Mid Dv (1867—85), Knutsf. Dv (1885—1918).

BIRKENHEAD

The following have 'Birkenhead' in their names. Insofar as any existed at a given time: *LG* Wirral Hd, PLU (1836—91), RSD (1875—77), Birk. PLU (1891—1930), MB (1877—89), USD (1877—94), CB (1889—1974). *Parl* S'rn Dv (1832—57), Birk. Parl Bor (1859—1918); pt Birk. East Parl Bor, pt Birk. West Parl Bor (1918—48); pt Beb. BC, pt Birk. BC (1948—70); pt Birk. BC, pt Wirral CC (1970—*) [see Part III of the *Guide* for compositions of Parl Bor/BC/CC constituencies by wards of the CB]. *Eccl* Wirral RDn (1738—1888), Birk. RDn (1888—*).

CP1/EP1—BIRKENHEAD [ST MARY]—Chap in Bidston cum Ford AP (eccl, 'Bidston'), sep CP 1866,[4] sep EP 1738.[3] Civ bdry: 1898 (gains the following in Birk. CB: Claughton with Grange CP, Oxton CP, Rock Ferry CP, Tranmere CP, and gains pt Lower Bebington UD & CP),[74] 1928 (gains pt Bidston cum Ford CP),[91] 1933 (incl gains Landican CP, Noctorum CP, Prenton CP, Thingwall CP, Woodchurch AP).[40] Transf 1974 to Merseyside.[28] Eccl bdry: 1841 (cr EP2),[93] 1859 (cr EP7,[3] refounded same year[94]), 1862 (cr EP11,[3] refounded 1864[95]), 1869 (cr EP5),[96] 1881.[97] Abol eccl 1948 to help cr EP9.[98]

EP2—BIRKENHEAD HOLY TRINITY—Cr 1841 from EP1.[93] Bdry: 1861 (cr EP3),[99] 1868 (cr EP12),[100] 1914 (cr EP10).[101]

EP3—BIRKENHEAD ST ANNE—Cr 1861 from EP2.[99] Bdry: 1905.[87]

EP4—BIRKENHEAD ST BEDE—Cr 1911 from Oxton EP, Bidston AP.[29] Abol 1972 to help cr EP6.[102]

EP5—BIRKENHEAD ST JAMES—Cr 1869 from EP1.[96] Bdry: 1876 (help cr Claughton cum Grange EP).[86] Abol 1972 to help cr EP6.[102]

EP6—BIRKENHEAD ST JAMES WITH ST BEDE—Cr 1972 by union EP5, EP4.[102]

EP7—BIRKENHEAD ST JOHN—Cr 1859 from EP1,[3] refounded same year.[94] Bdry: 1881,[97] 1905,[87] 1922 (cr EP8).[103]

EP8—BIRKENHEAD ST MARK—Cr 1922 from EP7.[103]

EP9—BIRKENHEAD ST MARY AND ST PAUL—Cr 1948 by union EP1, EP11.[98]

EP10—BIRKENHEAD ST MATTHEW—Cr 1914 from EP2.[101] Abol 1969 to help cr EP13.[104]

EP11—BIRKENHEAD ST PAUL—Cr 1862 from EP1,[3] refounded 1864.[95] Bdry: 1881.[97] Abol 1948 to help cr EP9.[98]

EP12—BIRKENHEAD ST PETER—Cr 1868 from EP2.[100] Abol 1969 to help cr EP13.[104]

EP13—BIRKENHEAD ST PETER WITH ST MATTHEW—Cr 1969 by union EP12, EP10.[104]

BIRTLES

Chap (erected 1840[105]) and tp in Prestbury AP, sep CP 1866,[4] sep EP 1890 from Alderley AP, Prestbury AP.[16] *LG* Maccl. Hd, PLU, RSD, RD. Abol civ 1936 pt to help cr Henbury CP, pt to Over Alderley CP.[106] *Parl* N'rn Dv (1832—67), North Dv (1867—85), Maccl. Dv (1885—1948). *Eccl* Maccl. RDn.

BLACKDEN

Tp in Sandbach AP, sep CP 1866[4]; eccl in chap Goostrey (sep EP 1724 from Sandbach,[3] qv). *LG* Northw. Hd, Congl. PLU, RSD, RD. Abol 1936 to help cr Goostrey CP.[106] *Parl* S'rn Dv (1832—67), Mid Dv (1867—85), Knutsf. Dv (1885—1948).

BLACON CUM CRABWALL

Tp in Chester Holy Trinity AP, sep CP 1866,[4] pt of the area considered eccl in Chester St Oswald AP, that pt eccl severed 1882 to help refound Upton EP.[107] *LG* Wirral Hd, Gt Bough. PLU (1837—71), Chester PLU (1871—1930), RSD, RD. Bdry: 1899 (gains pt Chester CB [assoc with Ches] & CP).[108] Abol 1936 pt to Chester CB (assoc with Ches) & CP, pt to Mollington CP.[7] *Parl* S'rn Dv (1832—67), South Dv (1867—85), Edd. Dv (1885—1918), City of Chester Dv (1918—48).

BLAKENHALL

Tp in Wybunbury AP, sep CP 1866.[4] *LG* Seq 18. Bdry: 1888,[6] 1965 (loses pt to Betley CP, Staffs).[109] *Parl* Seq 21.

BOLLINFEE

Tp in Wilmslow AP, sep CP 1866.[4] *LG* Maccl. Hd, Altr. PLU (1836—95), Buckl. PLU (1895—1930), Chorley USD (ent 1875—89, pt 1889—94 [the USD renamed 5 Sept 1894 'Alderley Edge'[18]]), pt Wilmslow USD (1888—94), Alderley Edge UD. Bdry: 1883,[56] 1888 (gains detached pt Pownall Fee CP and thus becomes pt Wilmslow USD),[110] 1894 (loses the pt in Wilmslow USD to help cr Wilmslow CP),[111] 1894 (gains the pt of Fulshaw CP in Alderley Edge UD).[112] Abol 1936 pt to Alderley Edge CP, pt to Wilmslow UD & CP.[7] *Parl* N'rn Dv (1832—67), North Dv (1867—85), Knutsf. Dv (1885—1948).

BOLLINGTON

Tp pt in Bowdon AP, pt in Rostherne AP, sep CP 1866 from both pars,[4] sep EP [Holy Trinity] 1869 (from both pars, incl tp Agden with pt in both pars).[14] *LG* Seq 8. Civ bdry: 1883 (loses pt to Bowdon AP which did not however become pt Bowdon USD,[56] this pt becoming 1894 'Unnamed' CP, qv). *Parl* Seq 1. *Eccl* Frod. East RDn (1869—80), Bowdon RDn (1880—1973). Abol eccl 1973 to help cr Rostherne with Bollington EP.[113]

BOLLINGTON

Tp in Prestbury AP, sep CP 1866,[4] sep EP [St John the Baptist] 1842.[114] *LG* Maccl. Hd, PLU, pt Bollington USD, pt Maccl. RSD, Bollington UD. Civ bdry: 1894 (the pt not in the UD cr Kerridge

CP),[19] 1900 (gains Kerridge CP),[115] 1936.[7] *Parl* Seq 7. *Eccl* Maccl. RDn (1842—73), Maccl. South RDn (1873—80), Maccl. RDn (1880—*). Eccl bdry: 1968.[116]

BOSDEN
Pt of tp Handforth cum Bosden (sep CP 1866 from Cheadle AP),[4] the latter divided 1877 into 2 CPs of Handforth, Bosden,[117] the area of Bosden eccl severed 1878 from Cheadle AP and transf to Norbury EP.[118] *LG* Maccl. Hd, Stockpt. PLU, RSD, RD. Abol 1900 ent to help cr Hazel Grove & Bramhall UD & CP.[119] *Parl* Hyde Dv (1885—1918).

BOSLEY
Chap in Prestbury AP, sep CP 1866,[4] sep EP 1883.[55] *LG* Seq 17. Civ bdry: 1933.[7] *Parl* Seq 8. *Eccl* Maccl. RDn.

BOSTOCK
Tp in Davenham AP, sep CP 1866,[4] eccl severed 1877 to help cr Moulton EP.[106] *LG* Seq 21. Bdry: 1883,[56] 1936 (incl loses the pt transf to Winsford UD to help cr Winsford CP).[7] *Parl* Seq 15.

GREAT BOUGHTON
Tp in Chester St Oswald AP, sep CP 1866.[4] *LG* Brox. Hd, Gt Bough. PLU (1837—71), Chester PLU (1871—1930), pt Chester MB (1835—84), Chester RSD (pt 1875—84, ent 1884—94), Chester RD. Bdry: 1936 (incl exchanges pts with Chester CB [assoc with Ches] & CP).[7] *Parl* Chester Parl Bor (pt 1832—67, ent 1867—1918), Chester Dv/CC (1918—*).

BOWDON
AP Incl chap (built 1779) and bor Altrincham (sep CP 1866,[4] sep EP 1812,[3] eccl refounded 1860[26]), chap Carrington (sep CP 1866,[4] chap built and sep EP 1759 [sometimes early 'Bowdon St George', incl tp Partington in same par],[3] 'Partington' a sep EP 1885 from Carrington,[120] the remainder eccl refounded 1887 as 'Carrington' EP[39]), tp Ashley (sep CP 1866,[4] sep EP 1881 from Bowdon AP [most of tp Ashley], Mobberley AP, Rostherne AP[41]), tp Baguley ([reported in 1871 census as pt in Bowdon AP, pt in Northenden AP, o'wise and generally considered ent in this par] sep CP 1866,[4] sep EP 1848,[3] eccl refounded 1868 from Timperley EP, Sale EP[57]), tp Dunham Massey (sep CP 1866,[4] sep EP 1855[121]), tp Hale (sep CP 1866,[4] sep EP 1906 from Bowdon AP, Altrincham St John the Evangelist EP[31]), tp Partington (sep CP 1866,[4] eccl severed 1759 to help cr Carrington EP as noted above, 'Partington' a sep EP 1885 from Carrington EP[120]), tp Timperley (sep CP 1866,[4] sep EP 1852[122]); incl pt tp Agden, pt tp Bollington (each a sep CP from Bowdon AP, Rostherne AP,[4] the pts in of both tps in both pars united eccl 1869 to cr 'Bollington' [Holy Trinity] EP[14]). *LG* Pt Altr. Bor (until 1866), Buckl. Hd, Altr. PLU (1836—95), Buckl. PLU (1895—1930), Bowdon USD (ent 1875—83, pt 1883—94), pt Altr. RSD (1883—94). Addtl civ bdry alt: 1883,[56] 1894 (the former detached pt of Bollington CP gained in 1883, never made a pt of Bowdon USD, cr Unnamed CP),[123] 1936 (incl gains Unnamed CP).[7] Transf 1974 to Gtr

Manch.[28] *Parl* Seq 1. *Eccl* Seq 4. Addtl eccl bdry alt: 1722 (cr Ringway EP,[3] refounded 1863[124]), 1866 (cr Dunham Massey St Mark EP,[3] sometimes 'Dunham Town', refounded 1873[5]), 1867 (help cr Altrincham St John the Evangelist EP),[30] 1893.[45]

BRADLEY
Tp in Malpas AP, sep CP 1866,[4] pt eccl severed 1824 to help cr Malpas St Chad EP,[3] the latter eccl refounded 1860.[15] *LG* Seq 7. *Parl* Seq 23.

BRADWALL
Tp in Sandbach AP, sep CP 1866.[4] *LG* Seq 22. Bdry: 1883,[56] 1936.[7] *Parl* Seq 11.

BRAMHALL
Tp in Stockport AP, sep CP 1866,[4] eccl severed 1827 to help cr Stockport St Thomas EP,[3] the latter refounded 1839,[125] 'Bramhall' a sep EP 1911 from Stockport St Thomas EP.[29] *LG* Maccl. Hd, Stockpt. PLU, RSD, RD. Civ bdry: 1883.[56] Abol civ 1900 to help cr Hazel Grove & Bramhall UD & CP.[119] *Parl* N'rn Dv (1832—67), North Dv (1867—85), Altr. Dv (1885—1918). *Eccl* Stockpt. RDn.

BREDBURY
Tp in Stockport AP, sep CP 1866,[4] sep EP 1846.[67] *LG* Maccl. Hd, Stockpt. PLU, Bredbury & Romiley USD, UD. Civ bdry: 1901 (loses pt to Stockpt. CB [assoc with Ches] & AP),[126] 1902 (gains Brinnington CP).[127] Abol civ 1936 to help cr Bredbury and Romiley CP, pt to Stockpt. CB (assoc with Ches) & AP, pt to Marple UD & CP.[7] *Parl* N'rn Dv (1832—67), North Dv (1867—85), Hyde Dv (1885—1918), Maccl. Dv (1918—48). *Eccl* Maccl. RDn (1848—73), Maccl. North RDn (1873—80), Stockpt. RDn (1880—*). Eccl bdry: 1893 (help cr Stockport Hall Street EP),[101] 1963 (help cr Brinnington EP).[128]

BREDBURY AND ROMILEY
CP Cr 1936 by union pts Bredbury CP, Compstall CP, Hyde CP, Marple CP, Romiley CP.[7] *LG* Bredbury & Romiley UD. Bdry: 1952 (loses pt to Stockpt. CB [assoc with Ches] & AP).[129] Transf 1974 to Gtr Manch.[28] *Parl* Cheadle CC (1948—70), Hazel Grove BC (1970—*). Parl bdry: 1953.[130]

BRERETON
CP Cr 1936 by union Brereton cum Smethwick AP, Davenport CP.[7] *LG* Congl. RD. *Parl* Knutsf. CC (1948—*).

BRERETON CUM SMETHWICK
AP *LG* Northw. Hd, Congl. PLU, RSD, RD. Abol civ 1936 to help cr Brereton CP.[7] *Parl* S'rn Dv (1832—67), Mid Dv (1867—85), Knutsf. Dv (1885—1948). *Eccl* Middlew. RDn (until 1880), Congl. RDn (1880—1971). Abol eccl 1971 to help cr Brereton with Swettenham EP.[131]

BRERETON WITH SWETTENHAM
EP Cr 1971 by union Brereton cum Smethwick AP, Swettenham AP.[131] Congl. RDn.

BRIDGEMERE
Tp in Wybunbury AP, sep CP 1866.[4] *LG* Seq 18. *Parl* Seq 21.

NEW BRIGHTON ALL SAINTS
EP Cr 1929 from New Brighton St James EP, Wallasey AP.[132] Wall. RDn.

NEW BRIGHTON EMMANUEL
EP Cr 1909 from New Brighton St James EP.[133] Wall. RDn.

NEW BRIGHTON ST JAMES
EP Cr 1861 from Wallasey AP.[134] Wirral RDn (1861—88), Birk. RDn (1888—1907), Wall. RDn (1907—*). Bdry: 1907,[135] 1909 (cr New Brighton Emmanuel EP),[133] 1929 (help cr New Brighton All Saints EP).[132]

BRIMSTAGE
Tp in Bromborough AP, sep CP 1866,[4] eccl severed 1869 to help cr Thornton Hough EP.[136] LG Wirral Hd, PLU, RD (1894—1933), Beb. UD (1933—37), MB (1937—74). Bdry: 1933 (pt transf to Barnston CP to help cr Wirral UD).[40] Transf 1974 to Merseyside.[28] Parl Seq 28.

BRINDLEY
Tp in Acton AP, sep CP 1866.[4] LG Seq 18. Bdry: 1883,[56] 1888.[6] Parl Seq 21.

BRINKSWAY
EP Cr 1893 from Cheadle AP, Stockport St Matthew EP, Stockport St Peter EP.[116] Stockpt. RDn.

BRINNINGTON
Tp in Stockport AP, sep CP 1866,[4] pt eccl severed 1844 to cr Portwood EP,[137] 'Brinnington' a sep EP 1963 from Portwood EP, Bredbury EP.[128] LG Maccl. Hd, Stockpt. PLU, pt Stockpt.Bor/MB (until 1889), pt Stockp. CB (1889—94), pt Stockpt. USD, pt Stockpt. RSD, Stockpt. RD. Civ bdry: 1894 (loses the pt in the CB to Stockport AP),[138] 1901 (loses pt to Stockpt. CB [assoc with Ches] & AP).[126] Abol civ 1902 ent to Bredbury & Romiley UD and to Bredbury CP.[127] Parl Pt Stockpt. Parl Bor (1832—1918), pt N'rn Dv (1832—67), pt North Dv (1867—85), pt Hyde Dv (1885—1918). Eccl Stockpt. RDn. Abol eccl 1971 to help cr Brinnington with Portwood EP.[139]

BRINNINGTON WITH PORTWOOD
EP Cr 1971 by union Brinnington EP, Portwood EP.[139] Stockpt. RDn.

BROADHEATH
EP Cr 1911 from Altrincham EP.[29] Bowdon RDn.

BROMBOROUGH
AP Incl chap Eastham (the 2 areas of Bromborough and Eastham a single vill but Eastham eccl dependent until the Dissolution when the 2 become sep pars[140] [see Eastham for its dependent tps]), tp Brimstage (sep CP 1866[4]). LG Wirral Hd, PLU, Bromborough USD, UD. Addtl civ bdry alt: 1895,[141] 1911.[75] Abol 1922 to help cr Beb. & Bromborough UD & CP.[72] Parl S'rn Dv (1832—67), South Dv (1867—85), Wirral Dv (1885—1948). Eccl Seq 11. Eccl bdry: 1869 (help cr Thornton Hough EP),[136] 1968.[142]

BROMHALL
Tp in Wrenbury cum Frith AP (eccl, 'Wrenbury'), sep CP 1866.[4] LG Seq 18. Parl Seq 21.

BROXTON
Tp in Malpas AP, sep CP 1866,[4] presumed[83] eccl severed 1840 to help cr Bickerton EP,[3] the latter eccl refounded 1843.[84] LG Seq 3. Parl Seq 23.

BRUERA
Tp in Chester St Oswald AP, sep EP 1868 as 'Bruera',[143] sep CP 1866 as 'Churton Heath',[4] qv. Eccl Chester RDn (1868—1935), Malpas RDn (1935—*).

GREAT BUDWORTH
AP Tp 'Great Budworth' in Buckl. Hd as were chap Aston by Budworth (sep CP 1866[4]), chap Little Leigh (sep CP 1866,[4] sep EP 1728,[3] eccl refounded 1834[144]), chap Stretton (sep CP 1866,[4] sep EP 1830,[3] eccl refounded 1834[145]), tp Anderton (sep CP 1866[4]), tp Antrobus (sep CP 1866,[4] sep EP 1848[3]), tp Appleton (sometimes early 'Hull and Appleton', sep CP 1866[4]), tp Barnton (sep CP 1866,[4] sep EP 1843 [tp Barnton and further pt Great Budworth][64]), tps Bartington, Cogshall, Comberbach, Crowley (each of the 4 a sep CP 1866[4]), tp Dutton (sep CP 1866,[4] pt of the tp eccl in Runcorn AP, that pt eccl severed 1861 to help cr Aston EP[53]), tp Marbury (sep CP 1866[4]), tp Marston (sep CP 1866,[4] sep EP 1875 from Great Budworth AP, Lostock Gralam EP[146]), tp Peover Inferior (sep CP 1866,[4] sep EP 1814 [incl tp Allostock in Northw. Hd] as 'Lower Peover'[3]), tps Pickmere, Plumley, Seven Oaks, Tabley Inferior (each of the 4 a sep CP 1866[4]), tp Higher Whitley (sometimes 'Over Whitley', sep CP 1866[4]), tp Lower Whitley (sep CP 1866,[4] sep EP 1824,[3] eccl refounded 1834[144]), tp Wincham (sep CP 1866[4]); incl in Edd. Hd pt chap Hartford, tps Castle Northwich, Winnington (each a sep CP 1866,[4] each eccl pt of chap Witton [sep EP 1723[3]], pt of the EP [orig areas Hartford, pt Castle Northwich] severed 1825 to cr Hartford EP[3] [qv for later refounding], pt of the EP severed 1846 to help cr Dane Bridge EP,[147] 'Witton' EP refounded 1900 as 'Witton (otherwise Northwich St Helen)' EP,[14] orig area of Castle Northwich severed 1929 from Hartford EP, Witton (otherwise Northwich St Helen) EP to cr Northwich Holy Trinity EP,[132] 'Winnington' a sep EP 1931 from Witton (otherwise Northwich St Helen) EP[148]); incl in Northw. Hd chap Nether Peover (sep CP 1866[4]), tp Allostock (sep CP 1866,[4] eccl severed 1814 to help cr Lower Peover EP[3]), tps Birches, Hulse, Lach Dennis, Northwich, Witton cum Twambrooks (each a sep CP 1866,[4] all pt of chap/EP Witton and its later refounding as noted above), tp Lostock Gralam (sep CP 1866,[4] eccl in chap/EP Witton, 'Lostock Gralam' a sep EP 1842 from Great Budworth AP, Witton EP[149]), tp Rudheath (reported in 1871 census as pt in this AP, pt in Davenham AP, pt in Sandbach AP, o'wise and generally considered pt in Davenham, pt in Sandbach only, sep CP 1866,[4] eccl in chap/EP Witton and its later refounding). LG Pt Northw. Bor, Runc. PLU, RSD, RD. Parl Seq 5. Eccl Frod. RDn (until 1869), Frod. West RDn (1869—80), Frod. RDn (1880—1935), Gt Budw. RDn (1935—*). Addtl eccl bdry alt: 1838 (help cr Stockton Heath EP [Ches, Lancs]),[150] 1965 (gains Marston EP),[98] 1968,[116] 1973.[113]

LITTLE BUDWORTH
AP Appropriated to nunnery of Chester St Mary, called free chap in Over AP, sep par from Dissolution.[151] LG Seq 15. Civ bdry: 1892 (gains Low Oulton CP),[92] 1936.[7] Parl Seq 22. Eccl Middlew. RDn.

Abol eccl 1971 to help cr Whitegate with Little Budworth EP.[152]

BUERTON

Tp in Aldford AP, sep CP 1866,[4] *LG* Seq 4. *Parl* Seq 20.

BUERTON

Tp in Audlem AP, sep CP 1866.[4] *LG* Seq 18. *Parl* Seq 21.

BUGLAWTON

Chap in Astbury AP, sep CP 1866,[4] sep EP 1841 (incl pt tp Eaton in same par).[47] *LG* Northw. Hd, Congl. PLU, Buglawton USD, UD. Abol civ 1936 pt to Congl. MB & CP, pt to Eaton CP, pt to North Rode CP.[7] *Parl* S'rn Dv (1832—67), Mid Dv (1867—85), Maccl. Dv (1885—1948). *Eccl* Middlew. RDn (1841—80), Congl. RDn (1880—*).

BULKELEY

Tp in Malpas AP, sep CP 1866,[4] presumed[83] eccl severed 1840 to help cr Bickerton EP,[3] the latter eccl refounded 1843[84]). *LG* Seq 5. *Parl* Seq 21.

BUNBURY

AP Tp 'Bunbury' in Edd. Hd as were chap Tilstone Fearnall (sep CP 1866,[4] sep EP 1837[22]), tps Beeston, Calveley, Haughton, Peckforton, Ridley, Spurstow, Wardle (each a sep CP 1866[4]), tps Alpraham, Tiverton (each a sep CP 1866,[4] each eccl severed 1901 and transf to Tilstone Fearnall EP[22]); incl in Brox. Hd chap Burwardsley (sep CP 1866,[4] chap built 1735, sep EP 1767[3]). *LG* Nantw. PLU, RSD, RD. Addtl civ bdry alt: 1936.[7] *Parl* Seq 21. *Eccl* Nantw. RDn (until 1888), Malpas RDn (1888—*).

BURLAND

Tp in Acton AP, sep CP 1866.[4] *LG* Seq 18. *Parl* Seq 21.

BURLEYDAM

EP Cr 1738 from Wrenbury EP,[3] refounded 1869 from Wrenbury EP, Audlem AP.[55] Nantw. RDn.

BURTON

AP Incl tp Puddington (sep CP 1866[4]). *LG* Wirral Hd, PLU, RSD, RD (1894—1933), Neston UD (1933—74). Addtl civ bdrty alt: 1933.[40] *Parl* Seq 26. *Eccl* Wirral RDn (until 1880), Chester RDn (1880—88), Wirral RDn (1888—1935), Wirral South RDn (1935—*).

BURTON BY TARVIN

Tp in Tarvin AP, sep CP 1866.[4] *LG* Seq 12. *Parl* Seq 22.

BURTONWOOD

CP Lancs par transf 1974 to Ches.[28]

BURWARDSLEY

Tp (Brox. Hd) in Bunbury AP (o'wise Edd. Hd), sep CP 1866,[4] chap built 1735, sep EP 1767.[3] *LG* Brox. Hd, Nantw. PLU (1837—92), RSD (1875—92), Tarv. PLU (1892—1930), RSD (1892—94), Tarv. RD. *Parl* Seq 23. *Eccl* Nantw. RDn (1767—1888), Malpas RDn (1888—*).

BUTLEY

Tp in Prestbury AP, sep CP 1866.[4] *LG* Maccl. Hd, PLU, RSD, RD. Abol 1936 pt to Bollington UD & CP, pt to Prestbury AP.[7] *Parl* N'rn Dv (1832—67), North Dv (1867—85), Knutsf. Dv (1885—1948).

BYLEY

Tp (sometimes early civ 'Byley cum Yatehouse') in Middlewich AP, sep CP 1866,[4] sep EP 1848.[153] *LG* Northw. Hd, PLU, pt Middlew. USD (1893—94), Northw. RSD (ent 1875—93, pt 1893—94), Northw. RD. Civ bdry: 1892 (gains Croxton CP, Ravenscroft CP),[92] 1894 (the pt in the UD transf to Middlewich AP),[154] 1936.[7] *Parl* Seq 13. *Eccl* Middlew. RDn. Eccl bdry: 1909.[155]

CADISHEAD

EP Cr 1925 from Irlam EP, Flixton EP (both Lancs, dioc Manch), Partington EP, Carrington EP (both Ches, dioc Chester), to be dioc Manch.[156] For organisation in RDns, see main entry in Lancs.

CALDECOTT

Tp in Shocklach AP, sep CP 1866.[4] *LG* Seq 3. Bdry: 1888.[157] *Parl* Seq 23.

CALDY

Tp in West Kirby AP, sep CP 1866.[4] *LG* Wirral Hd, PLU, RSD, RD (1894—1933), Hoylake UD (1933—74). Transf 1974 to Merseyside.[28] *Parl* Seq 26.

CALVELEY

Tp in Bunbury AP, sep CP 1866.[4] *LG* Seq 13. *Parl* Seq 21.

CAPENHURST

Tp in Shotwick AP, sep CP 1866,[4] sep EP 1859 from Shotwick AP (tp Capenhurst), Neston AP (tp Ledsham).[158] *LG* Seq 25. *Parl* Seq 19. *Eccl* Wirral RDn (1859—80), Chester RDn (1880—88), Wirral RDn (1888—1935), Wirral South RDn (1935—*).

CAPESTHORNE

Tp and chap (built 1722) in Prestbury AP, sep CP 1866,[4] sep EP 1722.[3] *LG* Maccl. Hd, PLU, RSD, RD. Abol civ 1936 ent to Siddington CP.[7] *Parl* N'rn Dv (1832—67), North Dv (1867—85), Knutsf. Dv (1885—1948). *Eccl* Maccl. RDn. Abol eccl 1846 to help cr Capesthorne with Siddington EP.[159]

CAPESTHORNE WITH SIDDINGTON

EP Cr 1846 by union Capesthorne EP, Siddington EP.[159] Maccl. RDn (1846—73), Maccl. South RDn (1873—80), Maccl. RDn (1880—*).

CARDEN

Tp in Tilston AP, sep CP 1866.[4] *LG* Seq 3. *Parl* Seq 23.

CARRINGTON

Chap in Bowdon AP, sep CP 1866,[4] chap built and sep EP 1759 (incl tp Partington in same par),[3] sometimes early called 'Bowdon St George', the orig area of Partington eccl severed 1885 to cr Partington EP,[120] the remainder eccl refounded 1887 as 'Carrington' EP.[39] *LG* Seq 8. Civ bdry: 1920 (exchanges pts with Irlam CP, Flixton AP, both Lancs),[160] 1920.[27] Transf 1974 to Gtr Manch.[28] *Parl* Seq 1. Parl bdry: 1945.[161] *Eccl* Frod. RDn (1759—1869), Frod. East RDn (1869—80), Bowdon RDn (1880—*). Eccl bdry: 1925 (help cr Cadishead EP [Lancs, Ches, to be dioc Manch]).[156]

CASTLE HALL

EP Cr 1846 from Stockport AP (the pt of tp Dukinfield not prev cr Dukinfield EP).[162] Maccl. RDn (1846—73), Maccl. North RDn (1873—80), Stockpt. RDn

(1880—88), Mott. RDn (1888—*). Bdry: 1959.[163]

CAUGHALL

Tp (Brox. Hd) in Backford AP (o'wise Wirral Hd), sep CP 1866.[4] *LG* Seq 1. *Parl* Seq 19.

CHADKIRK

EP Cr 1745 from Stockport AP (pt chap Romiley),[3] refounded 1876.[164] Maccl. RDn (1745—1873), Maccl. North RDn (1873—80), Stockpt. RDn (1880—*).

CHEADLE

AP Incl tps Cheadle Bulkeley, Cheadle Moseley (each a sep CP 1866[4]), tp Handforth cum Bosden (sep CP 1866,[4] the CP divided 1877 into 2 CPs of Handforth, Bosden,[117] the area of Handforth eccl severed 1877 [incl an additional pt of Cheadle AP] to cr 'Handforth' EP,[106] the area of Bosden eccl severed 1878 and transf to Norbury EP[118]) so that 'Cheadle' has no sep civ identity 1866—79 (see following entry). *LG* Maccl. Hd, pt Stockpt. Bor/MB. *Parl* Pt Stockpt. Parl Bor, pt N'rn Dv (1832—67). *Eccl* Maccl. RDn (until 1873), Maccl. North RDn (1873—80), Stockpt. RDn (1880—*). Eccl bdry: 1868 (help cr Cheadle Hulme All Saints EP),[100] 1893 (help cr Brinksway EP),[116] 1907,[165] 1937,[166] 1959 (cr Cheadle Hulme St Andrew EP).[167]

CP Cr 1879 by union Cheadle Bulkeley CP, Cheadle Moseley CP.[168] *LG* Maccl. Hd, Stockpt. PLU (1879—1930), pt Stockpt. MB (1879—89), pt Stockpt. USD (1879—94), pt Stockpt. CB (1889—94), pt Cheadle & Gatley USD (1886—94), pt Maccl. RSD (1879—86), Cheadle & Gatley UD. Bdry: 1883,[56] 1894 (loses the pt in the CB to Stockport AP),[138] 1901 (loses pt to Stockpt. CB [assoc with Ches] & AP).[126] Abol 1930 to help cr Cheadle and Gatley CP.[169] *Parl* Pt Stockpt. Parl Bor (1885—1918), Altr. Dv (pt 1885—1918, ent 1918—45).

CHEADLE AND GATLEY

CP Cr 1930 by union Cheadle CP, Stockport Etchells CP.[169] *LG* Cheadle & Gatley UD. Bdry: 1936 (incl loses pt to Wilmslow UD & CP).[7] Transf 1974 to Gtr Manch.[28] *Parl* Buckl. Dv (1945—48), Cheadle CC (1948—70), Cheadle BC (1970—*). Parl bdry: 1945.[161]

CHEADLE BULKELEY

Tp in Cheadle AP, sep CP 1866.[4] *LG* Maccl. Hd, Stockpt. PLU, pt Stockpt. MB, pt Maccl. RSD. Abol 1879 to help cr Cheadle CP.[168] *Parl* Pt Stockpt. Parl Bor (1832—85), pt N'rn Dv (1832—67), pt North Dv (1867—85).

CHEADLE HULME ALL SAINTS

EP Cr 1868 from Cheadle AP, Gatley EP.[100] Maccl. RDn (1868—73), Maccl. North RDn (1873—80), Stockpt. RDn (1880—*). Bdry: 1958.[170]

CHEADLE HULME ST ANDREW

EP Cr 1959 from Cheadle AP, Gateley EP.[167] Stockpt. RDn.

CHEADLE MOSELEY

Tp in Cheadle AP, sep CP 1866.[4] Organisation as for Cheadle Bulkeley.

CHECKLEY CUM WRINEHILL

Tp in Wybunbury AP, sep CP 1866.[4] *LG* Seq 18.

Bdry: 1883,[56] 1965 (loses pt to Betley CP, Staffs).[109] *Parl* Seq 21.

CHELFORD

Chap in Prestbury AP, sep CP 1866,[4] sep EP 1720,[3] eccl refounded 1880 as 'Chelford with Old Withington',[171] qv. *LG* Seq 17. *Parl* Seq 7. *Eccl* Maccl. RDn (1720—1873), Maccl. South RDn (1873—80).

CHELFORD WITH OLD WITHINGTON

EP Refounding 1880 of Chelford EP (qv in prev entry for cr 1720 from Prestbury AP) from Prestbury AP, Over Peover EP.[171] Maccl. RDn (1880—1935), Knutsf. RDn (1935—*). Bdry: 1915.[172]

CHESTER

The following have 'Chester' in their names. Insofar as any existed at a given time: *LG* Chester Co of Itself (from 1121/1129, more continuously from 1238/1239), Chester Incorp for poor (1762—1869), PLU (1869—1930), Bor/MB/CB, USD sep noted. *Parl* Sep noted. *Eccl* Chester RDn.

CP1—CHESTER—Cr 1884 by union pars in Chester CB: CP2, AP1, AP2, AP3, AP4, AP5, AP6, AP7, AP8, AP9, Spital Boughton CP.[173] Chester MB/CB, USD. Bdry: 1899 (exchanges pts with CP3, loses pt to Blacon cum Crabwall CP),[108] 1936 (incl exchanges pts with Great Boughton CP),[7] 1954.[174] Transf 1974 to Ches.[28] *Parl* Chester Parl Bor (1885—1918), City of Chester Dv/CC (1918—*).

EP1—CHESTER—Cr 1973 by union AP3, EP6, EP2, EP4, AP9, EP5.[175]

CP2—CHESTER ABBEY PRECINCTS—Ex-par place (eccl, 'Chester Cathedral Church Precinct'), sep CP 1858.[10] *LG* Chester Bor/MB, USD. Abol 1884 to help cr CP1.[173] *Parl* Chester Parl Bor (1553—1885).

CP3—CHESTER CASTLE—Ex-par place, sep CP 1858.[10] *LG* Chester PLU (1869—1930), not in a USD or RSD, put 1889 into Chester RD. Bdry: 1899 (exchanges pts with Chester CB [assoc with Ches] & CP1).[108] *Parl* S'rn Dv (1832—67), South Dv (1867—85), Edd. Dv (1885—1918), City of Chester Dv/CC (1918—*).

—CHESTER CATHEDRAL CHURCH PRECINCT—see CP2

EP2—CHESTER CHRIST CHURCH—Cr 1843 from AP8 and from tp Hoole (pt in Plemstall AP, AP3).[176] Bdry: 1872 (cr Hoole EP).[177] Abol 1973 to help cr EP1.[175]

AP1—CHESTER HOLY TRINITY—Tp 'Chester Holy Trinity' in Chester Bor/MB/CB, USD; incl in Wirral Hd tp Blacon cum Crabwall (sep CP 1866,[4] pt considered eccl in AP8, that pt eccl severed 1882 to help refound Upton EP[107]). Abol civ 1884 to help cr CP1.[173] *Parl* Chester Parl Bor (pt 1553—1867, ent 1867—85), pt S'rn Dv (1832—67), pt South Dv (1867—85). Eccl bdry: 1882,[178] 1887.[179] Abol eccl 1960, pt to AP9, the remainder (with area of new church), after exchanging pts with AP8, reconstituted as EP3.[180]

EP3—CHESTER HOLY TRINITY WITHOUT THE WALLS—Reconstitution 1960 of AP1 after the latter loses pt (incl the old church) to AP9, and main area (incl the new church) exchanges pts with AP8.[180]

—CHESTER LITTLE ST JOHN—Ex-par place situated ent within AP8, not sep civ but a sep eccl benefice, abol eccl 1967 to help cr EP6.[181]

AP2—CHESTER ST BRIDGET—*LG* Chester Bor/MB, USD. Abol civ 1884 to help cr CP1.[173] *Parl* Chester Parl Bor (1553—1885). *Eccl* Abol eccl 1842 to help cr EP4.[182]

EP4—CHESTER ST BRIDGET AND ST MARTIN—Cr 1842 by union AP2, AP4.[182] Bdry: 1882,[178] 1887.[179] Abol 1973 to help cr EP1.[175]

AP3—CHESTER ST JOHN THE BAPTIST—Collegiate, parochial at the Dissolution.[183] Tp 'Chester St John the Baptist' in Chester Bor/MB/CB, USD; incl in Brox. Hd pt tp Hoole (sep CP 1866,[4] the ent tp [incl pt in Plemstall AP] eccl severed 1843 to help cr EP2[176]). Abol civ 1884 to help cr CP1.[173] *Parl* Organisation as for AP1. Eccl bdry: 1846 (help cr EP7),[184] 1879.[185] Abol eccl 1973 to help cr EP1.[175]

AP4—CHESTER ST MARTIN—*LG* Chester Bor/MB, USD. Abol civ 1884 to help cr CP1.[173] *Parl* Organisation as for AP2. *Eccl* Abol eccl 1842 to help cr EP4.[182]

AP5—CHESTER ST MARY ON THE HILL—Sometimes 'Chester St Mary Without the Walls'. Gains after Dissolution Overchurch AP (Brox. Hd, Middlew. RDn, earlier appropriated to Dean and Chapter of Chester, in ruins by Dissolution and thereafter considered chap or tp civ ent in this par, civ called 'Upton by Chester' and as such sep CP 1866,[4] eccl considered pt in this AP, pt in AP8, eccl called 'Upton', the pt considerd eccl in this par severed 1743 to help cr 'Upton' EP [incl also tp Moston, tp Mollington Banastre (sometimes 'Little Mollington')],[3] eccl refounded as 'Upton' 1882 from AP5, AP8 [the remainder of tp Upton considered eccl in that AP and the pt of tp Blacon cum Crabwall also considered eccl in that par[107]]); incl also in Brox. Hd tp Marlston cum Lache (sep CP 1866[4]), tp Moston (sep CP 1866,[4] eccl severed 1743 to help cr Upton EP,[3] qv above for later refounding); incl in Wirral Hd tp Mollington Banastre (sometimes 'Little Mollington', sep CP 1866,[4] eccl severed 1743 to help cr Upton EP,[3] qv above for later refounding). *LG* Chester Bor/MB (pt until 1866, ent 1866—84), Chester USD. Abol civ 1884 to help cr CP1.[173] *Parl* Organisation as for AP1. *Eccl* Addtl eccl bdry alt: 1855 (help cr Lache cum Saltney EP [Ches, Flints]),[186] 1887,[179] 1923.[187]

AP6—CHESTER ST MICHAEL—*LG* Chester Bor/MB, USD. Abol civ 1884 to help cr CP1.[173] *Parl* Organisation as for AP2. *Eccl* Abol eccl 1839 to help cr EP5.[188]

EP5—CHESTER ST MICHAEL WITH ST OLAVE—Cr 1839 by union AP6, AP7.[188] Bdry: 1887.[179] Abol 1973 to help cr EP1.[175]

AP7—CHESTER ST OLAVE—Organisation as for AP6.

AP8—CHESTER ST OSWALD—Incl in Edd. Hd tp Iddinshall (sep CP 1866[4]); incl in Brox. Hd chap Churton Heath (sep CP 1866,[4] sep EP 1868 as

'Bruera'[143]), tps Bache, Great Boughton, Huntington, Lea Newbold, Newton by Chester, Saighton, Wervin (each a sep CP 1866[4]); incl in Wirral Hd tp Croughton (sep CP 1866[4]); considered to incl eccl pt tp Upton (qv for orig status as Overchurch AP), pt tp Blacon cum Crabwall (civ considered ent in AP5, AP1 respectively, qv in each instance for the sep civ identities of the areas 1866, the areas eccl in this par of both eccl severed 1882 to help refound Upton EP[107]). *LG* Chester Bor/MB (pt until 1866, ent 1866—84), Chester USD. Abol civ 1884 to help cr CP1.[173] *Parl* Organisation as for AP1. *Eccl* Addtl eccl bdry alt: 1846 (help cr EP7),[184] 1882,[178] 1960 (exchanges pts with AP1 as latter with other alterations reconstituted as EP3).[180] Gains 1967 ex-par (but sep benefice) Chester Little St John (situated ent within this par) to cr EP6.[181]

EP6—CHESTER ST OSWALD WITH LITTLE ST JOHN—Cr 1967 when AP8 gains ex-par (but sep benefice) Chester Little St John (situated ent within AP8).[181] Abol 1973 to help cr EP1.[175]

EP7—CHESTER ST PAUL—Cr 1846 from AP3, AP8.[184] Bdry: 1879,[185] 1934.[189]

AP9—CHESTER ST PETER—*LG* Chester Bor/MB, USD. Abol civ 1884 to help cr CP1.[173] *Parl* Organisation as for AP2. *Eccl* Eccl bdry: 1882,[178] 1960.[180] Abol eccl 1973 to help cr EP1.[175]

CHIDLOW
Tp in Malpas AP, sep CP 1866,[4] eccl severed 1824 to help cr Malpas St Chad EP,[3] eccl refounded 1860.[15] *LG* Seq 7. *Parl* Seq 23.

CHOLMONDELEY
Tp in Malpas AP, sep CP 1866.[4] *LG* Seq 5. *Parl* Seq 21.

CHOLMONDESTON
Tp in Acton AP, sep CP 1866,[4] eccl severed 1873 to help cr Worleston EP.[5] *LG* Seq 18. *Parl* Seq 21.

CHORLEY
Tp in Wilmslow AP, sep CP 1866,[4] sep EP 1855,[3] eccl refounded 1866.[190] *LG* Maccl. Hd, PLU, pt Chorley USD (renamed effective 5 Sept 1894 'Alderley Edge'[18]), pt Maccl. RSD, Maccl. RD. Civ bdry: 1894 (the pt in the USD cr Alderley Edge CP),[19] 1895,[20] 1936.[7] *Parl* Seq 7. *Eccl* Maccl. RDn (1855—73), Maccl. North RDn (1873—80), Maccl. RDn (1880—1935), Knutsf. RDn (1935—*). Eccl bdry: 1877 (cr Lindow EP).[106]

CHORLEY
Tp in Wrenbury cum Frith (chap in Acton AP, sep civ identity early, sep EP 1730 as 'Wrenbury'[3]), sep CP 1866.[4] *LG* Seq 18. *Parl* Seq 21.

CHORLTON
Tp in Malpas AP, sep CP 1866.[4] *LG* Seq 7. *Parl* Seq 23.

CHORLTON
Tp in Wybunbury AP, sep CP 1866.[4] *LG* Seq 18. Civ bdry: 1965 (gains pt Balterley CP, Staffs).[109] *Parl* Seq 18.

CHORLTON BY BACKFORD
Tp in Backford AP, sep CP 1866.[4] *LG* Seq 25. *Parl* Seq 19.

CHOWLEY
Tp in Coddington AP, sep CP 1866.[4] *LG* Seq 3. *Parl* Seq 23.

CHRISTLETON
AP Incl tps Cotton Abbotts, Cotton Edmunds, Littleton, Rowton (each a sep CP 1866[4]). *LG* Seq 1. Addtl civ bdry alt: 1888,[157] 1963.[66] *Parl* Seq 19. *Eccl* Seq 2.

CHURTON BY ALDFORD
Tp in Aldford AP, sep CP 1866.[4] *LG* Seq 3. Bdry: 1936.[7] *Parl* Seq 23.

CHURTON BY FARNDON
Tp in Farndon AP, sep CP 1866.[4] *LG* Seq 3. *Parl* Seq 23.

CHURTON HEATH
Tp in Chester St Oswald AP, sep CP 1866,[4] sep EP 1868 as 'Bruera',[143] qv. *LG* Seq 4. *Parl* Seq 20.

CLAUGHTON CUM GRANGE
EP Cr 1958 by union Claughton cum Grange Christ Church EP, Claughton St Michael and All Angels EP.[191] Birk. RDn. Renamed 1960 'Claughton cum Grange Christ Church and St Michael' EP.[192]

CLAUGHTON CUM GRANGE CHRIST CHURCH
EP Cr 1876 from Bidston AP, Birkenhead St James EP, Oxton EP.[86] Wirral RDn (1876—88), Birk. RDn (1888—1958). Bdry: 1912 (help cr Claughton St Michael and All Angels EP).[193] Abol 1958 to help cr Claughton cum Grange EP.[191]

CLAUGHTON CUM GRANGE CHRIST CHURCH AND ST MICHAEL
EP Renaming 1960 of Claughton cum Grange EP.[192] Birk. RDn.

CLAUGHTON ST MICHAEL AND ALL ANGELS
EP Cr 1912 from Claughton cum Grange Christ Church EP, Tranmere EP.[193] Wirral RDn (1912—35), Birk. RDn (1935—58). Abol 1958 to help cr Claughton cum Grange EP.[191]

CLAUGHTON WITH GRANGE
Tp in Bidston cum Ford (eccl, 'Bidston') AP (reported in 1871 census as pt in this par, pt in Woodchurch AP, o'wise and generally considered ent in Bidston cum Ford), sep CP 1866.[4] *LG* Wirral Hd, PLU (1836—91), RSD (1875—77), Birk. PLU (1891—98), MB (1877—89), CB (1889—98), USD (1877—94). Abol 1898 ent to Birkenhead CP.[74] *Parl* S'rn Dv (1832—59), Birk. Parl Bor (1859—1918).

CLAVERTON
Ex-par place, sep CP 1858.[10] *LG* Brox. Hd, Haward. PLU (1853—71), Chester PLU (1871—1930), RSD, RD. Bdry: 1936 (loses pt to Chester CB & CP).[7] *Parl* Edd. Dv (1885—1918), City of Chester Dv/CC (1918—*).

CLIFTON
Tp in Runcorn AP, sep CP 1866.[4] *LG* Buckl. Hd, Runc. PLU, RSD, RD. Abol 1936 pt to Runc. UD & AP, pt to Sutton CP.[7] *Parl* N'rn Dv (1832—67), Mid Dv (1867—85), Northw. Dv (1885—1948).

CLIVE
Tp in Middlewich AP, sep CP 1866.[4] *LG* Northw. Hd, PLU, RSD, RD. Abol 1936 pt to Winsford UD to help cr Winsford CP, pt to Stanthorne CP.[7] *Parl* S'rn Dv (1832—67), Mid Dv (1867—85), Northw. Dv (1885—1948).

CLOTTON HOOFIELD
Tp in Tarvin AP, sep CP 1866.[4] *LG* Seq 12. *Parl* Seq 22.

CLUTTON
Tp in Farndon AP, sep CP 1866.[4] *LG* Seq 3. *Parl* Seq 23.

CODDINGTON
AP Incl tps Aldersey, Chowley (each a sep CP 1866[4]). *LG* Seq 3. *Parl* Seq 23. *Eccl* Bangor RDn (until 1847), Malpas RDn (1847—*). Eccl bdry: 1963.[62]

COGSHALL
Tp in Great Budworth AP, sep CP 1866.[4] *LG* Buckl. Hd, Northw. PLU, RSD, RD. Abol 1936 ent to Comberbach CP.[7] *Parl* N'rn Dv (1832—67), Mid Dv (1867—85), Northw. Dv (1885—1948).

COMBERBACH
Tp in Great Budworth AP, sep CP 1866.[4] *LG* Seq 9. Bdry: 1936 (gains Cogshall CP).[7] *Parl* Seq 4.

COMPSTALL
CP Renaming 1897 of Werneth CP.[194] *LG* Stockpt. PLU, RD (1897—1902), Compstall UD (1902—36). Abol 1936 pt to Bredbury & Romiley UD to help cr Bredbury and Romiley CP, pt to Hyde MB & CP.[7] *Parl* Maccl. Dv (1918—48).

CONGLETON
Chap and bor in Astbury AP, sep CP 1866,[4] sep EP [St Peter] 1720,[3] pt eccl severed 1844 to cr Congleton St James EP,[195] a further pt eccl severed 1845 to cr Congleton St Stephen EP,[191] the remainder refounded 1867 as 'Congleton' EP.[50] *LG* Northw. Hd, Congl. PLU, Bor/MB, USD. Civ bdry: 1936.[7] *Parl* S'rn Dv (1832—67), Mid Dv (1867—85), Maccl. Dv/CC (1885—*). *Eccl* Middlew. RDn (1720—1880), Congl. RDn (1880—*).

CONGLETON ST JAMES
EP Cr 1844 from Congleton EP.[195] Middlew. RDn (1844—80), Congl. RDn (1880—*).

CONGLETON ST STEPHEN
EP Cr 1845 from Congleton EP.[191] Middlew. RDn (1845—80), Congl. RDn (1880—*).

COOLE PILATE
Tp in Acton AP, sep CP 1866.[4] *LG* Seq 18. *Parl* Seq 21.

COPPENHALL
AP Incl tp Church Coppenhall (sep CP 1866,[4] incl area of par church), tp Monks Coppenhall (sep CP 1866,[4] pt a sep EP 1855 as 'Crewe Christ Church',[196] the remainder cr 1869 Coppenhall St Paul EP[197]) so that 'Coppenhall' has no sep civ identity after 1866. *LG* Nantw. Hd. *Parl* S'rn Dv (1832—67). *Eccl* Seq 9. Addtl eccl bdry alt: 1931 (help cr Crewe St Peter EP),[198] 1961.[116]

CHURCH COPPENHALL
Tp in Coppenhall AP, sep CP 1866[4]; incl area of par church, thus see prev entry for eccl organisation. *LG* Nantw. Hd, PLU, pt Crewe MB & USD (1892—94), Nantw. RSD (ent 1875—92, pt 1892—94), Nantw. RD. Bdry: 1894 (loses the pt in the MB to Monks Coppenhall CP).[199] Abol civ 1936 ent to Monks Coppenhall CP.[7] *Parl* S'rn Dv (1832—67), South Dv (1867—85), Crewe Dv (1885—1948).

MONKS COPPENHALL
Tp in Coppenhall AP, sep CP 1866,[4] pt eccl severed

1855 to cr Crewe Christ Church EP,[196] the remainder cr 1869 Coppenhall St Paul EP.[197] *LG* Nantw. Hd, PLU, RSD (1875—77), Crewe MB (1877—1974), USD (1877—94). Bdry: 1894 (gains the pt in Crewe MB of Church Coppenhall CP, Shavington cum Gresty CP, Wistaston CP),[199] 1936 (incl gains Church Coppenhall CP).[7] *Parl* S'rn Dv (1832—67), South Dv (1867—85), Edd. Dv (1885—1918), Crewe Dv/CC (1918—*).

COPPENHALL ST PAUL
EP Cr 1869 from Coppenhall AP (the remainder of tp Monks Coppenhall not cr 1855 'Crewe Christ Church' EP[196]).[197] Nantw. RDn. Bdry: 1886 (cr Crewe St Barnabas EP),[200] 1914 (help cr Crewe St John Baptist EP),[201] 1923,[15] 1931 (help cr Crewe St Peter EP),[198] 1961.[116]

COTTON
Tp in Sandbach AP, sep CP 1866.[4] *LG* Northw. Hd, Congl. PLU, RSD, RD. Abol 1936 ent to Cranage CP.[7] *Parl* S'rn Dv (1832—67), Mid Dv (1867—85), Knutsf. Dv (1885—1948).

COTTON ABBOTTS
Tp in Christleton AP, sep CP 1866.[4] *LG* Seq 3. Bdry: 1888.[202] *Parl* Seq 22.

COTTON EDMUNDS
Tp in Christleton AP, sep CP 1866.[4] Organisation as for Cotton Abbotts, with addtl bdry alt 1963.[66]

CRANAGE
Tp in Sandbach AP, sep CP 1866,[4] eccl in chap Church Hulme (sep EP 1733 from Sandbach[3]). *LG* Seq 22. Bdry: 1889,[203] 1936 (incl gains Cotton CP).[7] *Parl* Seq 12.

CREWE
Tp in Barthomley AP (Ches, Staffs until 1866, ent Ches thereafter), sep CP 1866 in Ches,[4] sep EP [St Michael] 1857,[67] later called 'Crewe Green'. *LG* Seq 18. Civ bdry: 1936.[7] *Parl* Seq 16. *Eccl* Nantw. RDn (1857—80), Congl. RDn (1880—*).

CREWE
Tp in Farndon AP, sep CP 1866.[4] *LG* Seq 3. *Parl* Seq 23.

CREWE CHRIST CHURCH
EP Cr 1855 from Coppenhall AP (pt tp Monks Coppenhall).[196] Nantw. RDn. Bdry: 1914 (help cr Crewe St John Baptist EP),[201] 1926 (help cr Crewe St Andrew EP),[177] 1961.[116]

CREWE ST ANDREW
EP Cr 1926 from Crewe Christ Church EP, Wistaston AP, Wybunbury AP.[177] Nantw. RDn.

CREWE ST BARNABAS
EP Cr 1886 from Coppenhall St Paul EP.[200] Nantw. RDn. Bdry: 1951,[14] 1961.[116]

CREWE ST JOHN BAPTIST
EP Cr 1914 from Crewe Christ Church EP, Coppenhall St Paul EP.[201] Nantw. RDn. Bdry: 1923,[15] 1961.[116]

CREWE ST PETER
EP Cr 1931 from Coppenhall St Peter EP, Coppenhall AP.[198] Nantw. RDn.

CREWE GREEN—see 1st CREWE above

CROFT
CP Lancs par transf 1974 to Ches.[28]

CROSS TOWN—see KNUTSFORD ST CROSS

CROUGHTON
Tp in Chester St Oswald AP, sep CP 1866.[4] *LG* Seq 25. *Parl* Seq 19.

CROWLEY
Tp in Great Budworth AP, sep CP 1866.[4] *LG* Buckl. Hd, Runc. PLU, RSD, RD. Abol 1936 ent to Antrobus CP.[7] *Parl* N'rn Dv (1832—67), Mid Dv (1867—85), Knutsf. Dv (1885—1948).

CROWTON
Tp in Weaverham cum Milton AP (eccl, 'Weaverham'), sep CP 1866,[4] sep EP 1872 from Weaverham AP, Norley EP.[204] *LG* Seq 15. Civ bdry: 1881,[205] 1883,[56] 1892 (gains Onston CP).[92] *Parl* Seq 22. *Eccl* Frod. West RDn (1872—80), Frod. RDn (1880—88), Middlew. RDn (1888—*).

CROXTON
Tp in Middlewich AP, sep CP 1866.[4] *LG* Northw. Hd, PLU, RSD, RD. Abol 1892 ent to Byley CP.[92] *Parl* S'rn Dv (1832—67), Mid Dv (1867—85), Northw. Dv (1885—1918).

CUDDINGTON
Tp in Malpas AP, sep CP 1866.[4] *LG* Seq 7. *Parl* Seq 23.

CUDDINGTON
Tp in Weaverham cum Milton AP (eccl, 'Weaverham'), sep CP 1866.[4] *LG* Seq 15. Bdry: 1936.[7] *Parl* Seq 22.

CUERDLEY
CP Lancs par transf 1974 to Ches.[28]

DANE BRIDGE
EP Cr 1846 from Davenham AP, Witton EP.[147] Middlew. RDn. Abol 1930 pt to Davenham AP, pt to Witton (otherwise Northwich St Helen) EP.[206]

DARESBURY
Chap in Runcorn AP, sep CP 1866,[4] eccl incl tps Acton Grange, Hatton, Keckwick, Moore, Newton by Daresbury, Preston on the Hill (all in same par), the ent area and ex-par Middleton Grange cr 1738 'Daresbury' EP,[3] pt of the latter eccl severed 1879 (pt tp Acton Grange, pt tp Moore) to help cr Walton EP,[11] the remainder refounded 1880 as 'Daresbury' EP.[12] *LG* Seq 10. Civ bdry: 1936 (gains Keckwick CP, Newton by Daresbury CP),[7] 1967.[52] *Parl* Seq 3. *Eccl* Frod. RDn (1738—1869), Frod. West RDn (1869—80), Frod. RDn (1880—1935), Gt Budw. RDn (1935—*).

DARNHALL
Tp in Whitegate AP, sep CP 1866,[4] eccl severed 1876 and transf to Over AP.[207] *LG* Seq 15. Civ bdry: 1892 (gains Weaver CP),[92] 1936 (incl loses pt to Winsford CP to help cr Winsford UD).[7] *Parl* Seq 23.

DAVENHAM
AP Incl tps Bostock, Moulton (each a sep CP 1866,[4] the 2 eccl severed 1877 to cr 'Moulton' EP[106]), tps Eaton, Leftwich, Newhall, Shipbrook, Shurlach, Stanthorne (each a sep CP 1866[4]), tp Wharton (sep CP 1866,[4] sep EP 1860[147]), tp Whatcroft, pt tp Rudheath (each a sep CP 1866[4]). *LG* Seq 21. Addtl civ bdry alt: 1936,[7] 1955.[208] *Parl* Seq 15. *Eccl* Seq 7. Addtl eccl bdry alt: 1846 (help cr Dane Bridge EP),[147] 1930.[206]

DAVENPORT
Tp in Astbury AP, sep CP 1866,[4] eccl severed 1880 and transf to Swettenham AP.[49] *LG* Northw. Hd, Congl. PLU, RSD, RD. Abol 1936 to help cr Brereton CP.[7] *Parl* S'rn Dv (1832—67), Mid Dv (1867—85), Knutsf. Dv (1885—1948).

DELAMERE
Ex-par place, pt of Delamere Forest, made a sep par 1812 by union this area, tps Eddisbury, Kingswood Oakmere[209] (each of the 3 tps a sep CP 1866 from Delamere[4]). *LG* Seq 15. Addtl civ bdry alt: 1936 (incl gains Eddisbury CP).[7] *Parl* Seq 22. *Eccl* Chester RDn (1812—80), Frod. RDn (1880—88), Middlew. RDn (1888—*). Eccl bdry: 1935 (help cr Sandiway EP),[165] 1956 (help cr Kelsall EP).[210]

DISLEY
Chap in Stockport AP, sep CP 1866 in Ches,[4] pt in New Mills USD (o'wise ent Derbys), that pt becomes 1889 pt Derbys and cr 1894 Newton CP in that co,[211] and Disley ent Ches thereafter, Disley a sep EP 1741,[3] eccl refounded 1913.[212] *LG* Maccl. Hd, Hayfield PLU, pt New Mills USD, pt Hayfield RSD, Disley RD. Addtl civ bdry alt: 1936 (incl exchanges pts with New Mills CP, Derbys, and loses pt to help cr Whaley Bridge UD & CP, to be in Derbys).[213] *Parl* Seq 6. *Eccl* Maccl. RDn (1741—1873), Maccl. North RDn (1873—80), Stockpt. RDn (1880—*). Eccl bdry: 1923.[214]

DODCOTT CUM WILKESLEY
Tp pt in Audlem AP, pt in Wrenbury cum Frith CP (chap in Acton AP, sep civ identity early, sep EP 1730 as 'Wrenbury'[3]), sep CP 1866.[4] *LG* Seq 18. Bdry: 1888.[6] *Parl* Seq 21.

DODDINGTON
Tp in Wybunbury AP, sep CP 1866,[4] sep EP 1841.[3] *LG* Seq 18. *Parl* Seq 21. *Eccl* Nantw. RDn.

DODLESTON
AP Tp 'Dodleston' in Ches (Brox. Hd) as was tp Lower Kinnerton (sep CP 1866[4]); incl in Flints (Maylor Hd) tp Higher Kinnerton (sep CP 1866 in that co[4]) so that Dodleston ent Ches thereafter. *LG* Gt Bough. PLU (1837—53), Haward. PLU (1853—71), Chester PLU (1871—1930), RSD, RD. *Parl* Seq 19. *Eccl* Seq 2.

DOWNES—see POTT SHRIGLEY

DUCKINGTON
Tp in Malpas AP, sep CP 1866,[4] presumed[83] eccl severed 1840 to help cr Bickerton EP,[3] the latter eccl refounded 1843.[84] *LG* Brox. Hd, Gt Bough. PLU (1837—53), Whitch. PLU (1853—1930), RSD, Malpas RD (1894—1936), Tarv. RD (1936—74). *Parl* Seq 23.

DUDDON
Tp in Tarvin AP, sep CP 1866.[4] *LG* Seq 12. *Parl* Seq 22.

DUKINFIELD
The following have 'Dukinfield' in their names. Insofar as any existed at a given time: *LG* Maccl. Hd, Ashton under Lyne PLU, pt Stalybr. MB ([Ches, Lancs] 1857—94), pt Stalybr. USD (Ches, Lancs), Dukinfield UD (pt 1894—98, ent 1898—99), MB (1899—1974). *Parl* N'rn Dv (1832—67), pt Ashton under Lyme Parl Bor ([Lancs, Ches]

1867—1918), pt Stalybr. Parl Bor ([Lancs, Ches, Yorks W Riding] 1867—1918), Stalybr. & Hyde Dv/CC (1918—*). *Eccl* Maccl. RDn (1846—73), Maccl. North RDn (1873—80), Stockpt. RDn (1880—88), Mott. RDn (1888—*).

CP1/EP1—DUKINFIELD [ST MARK]—Chap in Stockport AP, sep CP 1866,[4] pt cr 1846 'Dukinfield' EP,[196] the remainder cr 1846 'Castle Hall' EP.[162] Civ bdry: 1894 (loses the pt in Stalybr. MB to help cr Stalybridge CP),[42] 1898 (loses pt to Ashton under Lyne AP, Lancs),[215] 1915 (bdry with Newton CP defined),[216] 1936.[7] Transf 1974 to Gtr Manch.[28] Eccl bdry: 1906 (help cr EP4),[133] 1906.[217]

EP2—DUKINFIELD CHRIST CHURCH—Cr 1880 from EP3 (Ches), Ashton under Lyne AP, New Stalybridge St George EP (both Lancs).[12]

EP3—DUKINFIELD ST JOHN THE EVANGELIST—Cr 1843 from Stockport AP.[218] Bdry: 1880 (help cr EP2 [Ches, Lancs]),[12] 1906 (help cr EP4),[133] 1906.[217]

EP4—DUKINFIELD ST LUKE—Cr 1906 from EP3, EP1.[133]

DUNHAM MASSEY
Tp in Bowdon AP, sep CP 1866,[4] sep EP 1855.[121] *LG* Seq 8. Civ bdry: 1920,[27] 1936.[7] Transf 1974 to Gtr Manch.[28] *Parl* Seq 1. *Eccl* Frod. RDn (1855—69), Frod. East RDn (1869—80), Bowdon RDn (1880—*). Eccl bdry: 1867 (help cr Altrincham St John the Evangelist EP).[30]

DUNHAM MASSEY ST MARK
EP Cr 1866 from Bowdon AP,[3] refounded 1873.[5] Frod. RDn (1866—69), Frod. East RDn (1869—80), Bowdon RDn (1880—*). Sometimes called 'Dunham Town'.

DUNHAM ON THE HILL
Tp in Thornton le Moors AP, sep CP 1866,[4] sep EP 1888 (tps Dunham on the Hill, Hapsford, both in Thornton le Moors).[219] *LG* Seq 11. *Parl* Seq 19. *Eccl* Chester RDn (1888—1935), Frod. RDn (1935—*).

DUTTON
Tp in Great Budworth AP, sep CP 1866,[4] pt eccl in Runcorn AP, the latter severed 1861 to help cr Aston EP.[53] *LG* Seq 10. Bdry: 1898,[69] 1936 (incl gains Bartington CP),[7] 1967.[52] *Parl* Seq 5.

EASTHAM
AP Formed with Bromborough AP a single vill but Eastahm eccl dependent until Dissolution when the 2 became sep pars.[140] Incl tps Hootton, Little Sutton, Childer Thornton (each a sep CP 1866,[4] the 3 united eccl 1862 as 'Hootton' EP[220]); incl tp Netherpool, tp Overpool, pt tp Whitby (each a sep CP 1866[4], the 2 tps and the pt in this par of the 3rd united 1871 as 'Ellesmere Port' EP[221]); incl tp Great Sutton (sep CP 1866,[4] sep EP 1880[222]). *LG* Wirral Hd, PLU, RSD, RD (1894—1933), Beb. UD (1933—37), MB (1937—74). Addtl civ bdry alt: 1933 (loses pt to Childer Thornton CP to help cr Ellesm. Port UD, gains pt Childer Thornton CP and pt Hooton CP to help cr Beb. UD).[40] Transf 1974 to Merseyside.[28] *Parl* Seq 28. *Eccl* Seq 11. Addtl eccl bdry alt: 1968.[142]

EATON

Tp in Astbury AP, sep CP 1866,[4] pt eccl severed 1841 to help cr Buglawton EP,[47] the remainder cr 1858 'Eaton' EP.[50] *LG* Northw. Hd, Maccl. PLU, RSD, RD. Civ bdry: 1936.[7] *Parl* S'rn Dv (1832—67), Mid Dv (1867—85), Maccl. Dv/CC (1885—*). *Eccl* Middlew. RDn (1858—80), Congl. RDn (1880—*).

EATON

Tp in Davenham AP, sep CP 1866.[4] *LG* Northw. Hd, PLU, RSD, RD. Abol 1936 pt transf to Winsford UD to help cr Winsford CP, pt to Davenham AP, pt to Hartford CP.[7] *Parl* S'rn Dv (1832—67), Mid Dv (1867—85), Northw. Dv (1885—1948).

EATON

Tp in Eccleston AP, sep CP 1866.[4] *LG* Seq 2. *Parl* Seq 19.

EATON

Tp in Tarporley AP, sep CP 1866.[4] *LG* Edd. Hd, Nantw. PLU (1837—94), Tarv. PLU (1894—1930), Tarporley USD, UD. Abol 1936 pt to Tarporley AP, pt to Rushton CP, pt to Utkinton CP.[7] *Parl* S'rn Dv (1832—67), South Dv (1867—85), Edd. Dv (1885—1948).

ECCLESTON

AP Incl tp Eaton (sep CP 1866[4]). *LG* Seq 2. *Parl* Seq 19. *Eccl* Chester RDn. Abol eccl 1973 to help cr Eccleston and Pulford EP.[223]

ECCLESTON AND PULFORD

EP Cr 1973 by union Eccleston AP, Pulford AP.[223] Chester RDn.

EDDISBURY

Tp in Delamere CP (orig ex-par place, pt of Delamere Forest, made a sep par 1812 by union Delamere, tp Eddisbury, and 2 other tps [see Delamere][209]), 'Eddisbury' a sep CP 1866.[4] *LG* Edd. Hd, Northw. PLU, RSD, RD. Abol 1936 ent to Delamere CP.[7] *Parl* S'rn Dv (1832—67), South Dv (1867—85), Edd. Dv (1885—1948).

EDGE

Tp in Malpas AP, sep CP 1866.[4] *LG* Brox. Hd, Gt Bough. PLU (1837—53), Whitch. PLU (1853—1930), Malpas RD (1894—1936), Tarv. RD (1936—74). *Parl* Seq 23.

EDGERLEY

Tp in Aldford AP, sep CP 1866.[4] *LG* Seq 3. *Parl* Seq 23.

EDLESTON

Tp in Acton AP, sep CP 1866.[4] *LG* Seq 18. *Parl* Seq 21.

EGERTON

Tp in Malpas AP, sep CP 1866,[4] presumed[83] eccl severed 1840 to help cr Bickerton EP,[3] the latter refounded 1843.[84] *LG* Seq 5. *Parl* Seq 21.

EGREMONT (OTHERWISE LISCARD)

EP Cr 1884 from Wallasey AP, Seacombe EP.[224] Wirral RDn (1884—88), Birk. RDn (1888—1907), Wall. RDn (1907—*). Bdry: 1922 (cr Egremont St Columba EP).[225]

EGREMONT ST COLUMBA

EP Cr 1922 from Egremont (otherwise Liscard) EP.[225] Wall. RDn. Abol 1971 to help cr Liscard St Mary with St Columba EP.[226]

ELLESMERE PORT

EP Cr 1871 from Eastham AP (tp Netherpool, tp Overpool, the pt of tp Whitby in Eastham AP).[221] Chester RDn (1871—88), Wirral RDn (1888—1935), Wirral South RDn (1935—*). Bdry: 1964 (gains ex-par Great Stanney),[227] 1967,[228] 1971 (gains Stoak AP, Thornton le Moors AP).[229]

CP Cr 1911 by union Netherpool CP, Overpool CP, Whitby CP.[230] *LG* Wirral PLU, Ellesm. Port & Whitby UD (1911—33), Ellesm. Port UD (1933—55), MB (1955—74). Bdry: 1950 (gains the other pars in the UD: Hooton CP, Ince AP, Great Stanney CP, Great Sutton CP, Little Sutton CP, Childer Thornton CP),[231] 1963,[232] 1967.[233] *Parl* Wirral Dv/CC (1918—70), Beb. & Ellesm. Port BC (1970—*).

ELTON

Tp in Thornton le Moors AP, sep CP 1866.[4] *LG* Seq 11. *Parl* Seq 19.

ELTON

Tp in Warmingham AP, sep CP 1866.[4] *LG* Northw. Hd, Congl. PLU, RSD, RD. Bdry: 1936.[7] Abol 1970 to help cr Moston CP.[234] *Parl* S'rn Dv (1832—67), Mid Dv (1867—85), Crewe Dv (1885—1918), Northw. Dv (1918—48), Knutsf. CC (1948—*).

ELWORTH

EP Cr 1847 from Sandbach AP, Warmingham AP.[235] Middlew. RDn (1847—80), Congl. RDn (1880—*).

NORTHERN ETCHELLS

Tp in Northenden AP, sep CP 1866.[4] *LG* Maccl. Hd, Altr. PLU (1836—95), RSD, RD (1894—95), Buckl. PLU (1895—1930), RD (1895—1931). Abol 1931 ent to Manch CB (assoc with Lancs) & AP.[58] *Parl* N'rn Dv (1832—67), North Dv (1867—85), Altr. Dv (1885—1945), Buckl. Dv (1945—48).

STOCKPORT ETCHELLS

Tp in Stockport AP, sep CP 1866,[4] eccl severed 1827 to help cr Stockport St Thomas EP,[3] the latter refounded 1839,[125] the area of the orig tp severed 1882 from Stockport St Thomas EP to cr 'Gatley' EP.[236] *LG* Maccl. Hd, Stockpt. PLU, RSD (1875—86), Cheadle & Gatley USD (1886—94), UD. Abol 1930 to help cr Cheadle and Gatley CP.[169] *Parl* N'rn Dv (1832—67), North Dv (1867—85), Altr. Dv (1885—1945).

FADDILEY

Tp in Acton AP, sep CP 1866.[4] *LG* Seq 18. Bdry: 1883,[56] 1888.[6] *Parl* Seq 21.

FALLIBROOME

Tp in Prestbury AP, sep CP 1866.[4] *LG* Maccl. Hd, PLU, RSD, RD. Abol 1936 pt to Maccl. MB & CP, pt to Prestbury AP.[7] *Parl* N'rn Dv (1832—67), North Dv (1867—85), Knutsf. Dv (1885—1948).

FARNDON

AP Incl tps Barton, Churton by Farndon, Clutton, Crewe (each a sep CP 1866[4]). *LG* Seq 3. *Parl* Seq 23. *Eccl* Chester RDn (until 1880), Malpas RDn (1880—*). Eccl bdry: 1963.[62]

FRANKBY

Tp in West Kirby AP, sep CP 1866,[4] sep EP 1861 from West Kirby AP (tp Frankby, pt tp Greasby, pt tp Grange, pt tp Newton with Larton), Thurstaston AP (the remainder of tp Greasby).[237] *LG* Wirral Hd, PLU, RSD, RD (1894—1933), Hoylake UD (1933—74). Transf 1974 to Meryseyside.[28] *Parl* Seq 26. *Eccl* Wirral RDn (1861—1935), Wirral North RDn (1935—*). Eccl bdry: 1937 (help cr Great Meols EP).[238]

FRIEZLAND

EP Cr 1848 from Saddleworth EP, Lydgate EP (both Yorks W Riding), Stalybridge St Paul EP (Ches) to be dioc Manch.[239] Bdry: 1869 (the pt in Yorks severed to help cr Roughtown EP).[240] For RDns and for cr of Greenfield EP 1876 from area ent in Yorks W Riding, see main entry in Yorks.

FRODSHAM

AP Incl chap Alvanley (sep CP 1866,[4] sep EP 1741,[3] eccl refounded 1861[32]), chap Norley (sep CP 1866,[4] sep EP 1861[241]), tp Frodsham Lordship (sep CP 1866[4]), tp Helsby (sep CP 1866,[4] sep EP 1875[242]), tp Kingsley (sep CP 1866,[4] sep EP 1853[3]), tps Manley, Newton by Frodsham (each a sep CP 1866[4]); incl from 1866 undivided pt Lands Common to Frodsham and Frodsham Lordship, abol 1936 as below. *LG* Frod. Bor, Seq 16. Addtl civ bdry alt: 1881,[205] 1883,[56] 1936 (gains Frodsham Lordship CP, Lands Common to Frodsham and Frodsham Lordship).[7] *Parl* Seq 24. *Eccl* Seq 5. Addtl eccl bdry alt: 1930.[33]

FRODSHAM LORDSHIP

Tp in Frodsham AP, sep CP 1866.[4] Incl undivided pt Lands Common to Frodsham and Frodsham Lordship. *LG* Edd. Hd, Runc. PLU, RSD, RD. Bdry: 1883.[56] Abol 1936 ent to Frodsham AP (abol at same time, also to Frodsham AP, Lands Common to Frodsham and Frodsham Lordship).[7] *Parl* S'rn Dv (1832—67), South Dv (1867—85), Edd. Dv (1885—1948).

FULSHAW

Tp in Wilmslow AP, sep CP 1866.[4] *LG* Maccl. Hd, Altr. PLU (1836—95), pt Chorley UD (renamed effective 5 Sept 1894 'Alderley Edge'[18]), pt Wilmslow USD. Bdry: 1883,[56] 1888.[110] Abol 1894 the pt in Alderley Edge UD transf to Bollinfee CP,[112] the pt in Wilmslow UD to help cr Wilmslow CP.[111] *Parl* N'rn Dv (1832—67), North Dv (1867—85), Knutsf. Dv (1885—1918).

GATLEY

EP Cr 1882 from Stockport St Thomas EP (area of tp Stockport Etchells orig in Stockport AP).[236] Stockpt. RDn. Bdry: 1868 (incl help cr Cheadle Hulme All Saints EP),[100] 1958 (help cr Heald Green EP),[170] 1964 (exchanges pts with Benchill EP, gains pt Didsbury EP, both Lancs and dioc Manch).[243]

GAWSWORTH

AP *LG* Seq 17. Civ bdry: 1936,[7] 1955.[244] *Parl* Seq 8. *Eccl* Seq 6. Eccl bdry: 1962.[245]

GAYTON

Tp in Heswall cum Oldfield AP (eccl, 'Heswall'), sep CP 1866.[4] *LG* Wirral Hd, PLU, RSD, RD (1894—1933), Wirral UD (1933—74). Bdry: 1933.[40] Transf 1974 to Merseyside.[28] *Parl* Seq 26.

GEE CROSS

EP Cr 1880 from Werneth EP, Hyde St George EP,

Hyde EP.[12] Stockpt. RDn (1880—88), Mott. RDn (1888—*).

GODLEY

Tp in Mottram AP, sep CP 1866,[4] eccl severed 1847 to help cr Godley cum Newton Green EP.[246] *LG* Maccl. Hd, Ashton under Lyne PLU, Hyde USD, MB (1881—1923). Abol 1923 ent to Hyde CP.[247] *Parl* N'rn Dv (1832—67), North Dv (1867—85), Hyde Dv (1885—1918), Stalybr. & Hyde Dv (1918—48).

GODLEY CUM NEWTON GREEN

EP Cr 1847 from Mottram AP (tp Godley), Newton in Mottram EP.[246] Maccl. RDn (1847—73), Maccl. North RDn (1873—80), Stockpt. RDn (1880—88), Mott. RDn (1888—*). Bdry: 1966 (incl help cr Hattersley EP).[248]

GOLBORNE

CP Lancs par (comprising Golborne UD) transf 1974 pt to Ches [wards of Culcheth, Newchurch (area ceases to be in a par)], pt [the remainder] to Gtr Manch.[28]

GOLBORNE BELLOW

Tp in Tattenhall AP, sep CP 1866.[4] *LG* Seq 3. *Parl* Seq 23.

GOLBORNE DAVID

Tp in Handley AP, sep CP 1866.[4] *LG* Seq 3. *Parl* Seq 23.

GOOSTREY

Tp in Sandbach AP, sep EP 1724 as 'Goostrey' (incl tp Blackden in same par),[3] sep CP 1866 as 'Goostrey cum Barnshaw',[4] qv. Middlew. RDn (1724—1880), Congl. RDn (1880—*).

CP Cr 1936 by union Blackden CP, Goostrey cum Barnshaw CP.[7] *LG* Congl. RD. *Parl* Knutsf. CC (1948—*).

GOOSTREY CUM BARNSHAW

Chap in Sandbach AP, sep CP 1866,[4] sep EP 1724 as 'Goostrey',[3] qv. *LG* Northw. Hd, Congl. PLU, RSD, RD. Abol 1936 to help cr Goostrey CP.[7] *Parl* S'rn Dv (1832—67), Mid Dv (1867—85), Knutsf. Dv (1885—1948).

GRAFTON

Tp in Tilston AP, sep CP 1866.[4] *LG* Seq 3. *Parl* Seq 23.

GRANGE

Tp in West Kirby AP, sep CP 1866,[4] pt eccl severed 1861 to help cr Frankby EP.[237] *LG* Wirral Hd, PLU, pt West Kirby & Hoylake USD (1891—94), Wirral RSD (ent 1875—91, pt 1891—94), Wirral RD (1894—1933), Hoylake UD (1933—74). Civ bdry: 1889 (gains Newton with Larton CP),[249] 1894 (loses the pt in West Kirby & Hoylake UD to help cr Hoylake cum West Kirby CP),[250] 1915,[251] 1933.[40] Transf 1974 to Merseyside.[28] *Parl* Seq 26.

GRAPPENHALL

AP Incl chap Latchford (deemed civ ent Ches [Buckl. Hd], the pt eccl deemed in Lancs a sep EP 1796 as 'Latchford St James',[3] refounded 1866 from Grappenhall AP, Thelwall EP [both Ches], Warrington AP [Lancs],[252] the pt eccl deemed in Ches cr 1866 'Latchford Christ Church' EP[253]). *LG* Buckl. Hd, Runc. PLU (1836—45), Warr. PLU (1845—1930), RSD, RD. Addtl civ bdry alt: 1933 (exchanges pts with Warr. CB [assoc with Lancs] & AP),[254] 1933 (exchanges pts with Woolston with Martinscroft CP, Lancs),[13] 1936 (gains Thelwall CP),[7] 1953.[255] *Parl* Seq 3. Parl bdry: 1945.[161] *Eccl* Frod. RDn (until 1869), Frod. West RDn (1869—80), Frod. RDn (1880—1935), Gt Budw. RDn (1935—*). Addtl eccl bdry alt: 1968.[190]

GREASBY

Tp pt in Thurstaston AP, pt in West Kirby AP, sep CP 1866,[4] eccl severed 1861 to help cr Frankby EP.[237] *LG* Wirral Hd, PLU, RSD, RD (1894—1933), Hoylake UD (1933—74). Transf 1974 to Merseyside.[28] *Parl* Seq 26.

HALE

Tp in Bowdon AP, sep CP 1866,[4] sep EP 1906 from Bowdon AP, Altrincham St John the Evangelist EP.[31] *LG* Buckl. Hd, Altr. PLU (1836—95), RSD, RD (1894—95), Buckl. PLU (1895—1930), RD (1895—1900), Hale UD (1900—74). Bdry: 1900 (the pt not constituted Hale UD cr Ringway CP),[256] 1936.[7] Transf 1974 to Gtr Manch.[28] *Parl* Seq 1. *Eccl* Bowdon RD.

HALE

CP Lancs par transf 1974 to Ches.[28]

HALTON

Chap in Runcorn AP, sep CP 1866,[4] sep EP 1718,[3] eccl refounded 1860 from Runcorn AP, Runcorn Holy Trinity EP.[198] *LG* Buckl. Hd, Runc. PLU, pt Runc. USD (1875—83), Runc. RSD (pt 1875—83, ent 1883—94), RD. Civ bdry: 1883,[56] 1884,[257] 1936,[7] 1955.[258] Abol civ 1967 ent to Runc. UD & AP.[52] *Parl* N'rn Dv (1832—67), Mid Dv (1867—85), Northw. Dv (1885—1948), Runc. CC (1948—70). *Eccl* Frod. RDn (1718—69), Frod. West RDn (1869—80), Frod. RDn (1880—1973). Eccl bdry: 1960,[259] 1963 (cr Runcorn Grange EP).[260] Abol eccl 1973 to help cr East Runcorn with Halton EP.[261]

HAMPTON

Tp in Malpas AP, sep CP 1866,[4] pt eccl severed 1842 to help cr Malpas St Chad EP,[3] refounded 1860.[15] *LG* Seq 6. *Parl* Seq 23.

HANDFORTH

CP Cr 1877 when Handforth cum Bosden CP divided into 2 CPs of 'Handforth', 'Bosden'.[117] *LG* Maccl. Hd, Stockpt. PLU, RSD, RD (1894—1904), Handforth UD (1904—36). Abol 1936 pt to Cheadle & Gatley UD & CP, pt to Wilmslow UD & CP.[7] *Parl* Altr. Dv (1885—1945).

EP Tp in Cheadle AP, sep EP 1877 (the tp and a further pt of Cheadle AP),[106] sep CP 1866 as 'Handforth cum Bosden',[4] qv. Maccl. North RDn (1877—80), Stockpt. RDn (1880—1935), Knutsf. RDn (1935—54), Stockpt. RDn (1954—*). Eccl bdry: 1958 (help cr Heald Green EP).[170]

HANDFORTH CUM BOSDEN

Tp in Cheadle AP, sep CP 1866,[4] sep EP 1877 as 'Handforth' (the tp and a further pt of Cheadle AP),[106] qv. *LG* Maccl. Hd, Stockpt. PLU, RSD. *Parl* N'rn Dv (1832—67), North Dv (1867—85).

HANDLEY

AP Incl tp Golborne David (sep CP 1866[4]). *LG* Seq 3. *Parl* Seq 23. *Eccl* Seq 1.

HANKELOW

Tp in Audlem AP, sep CP 1866.[4] *LG* Seq 18. Bdry: 1888.[6] *Parl* Seq 21.

HAPSFORD

Tp in Thornton le Moors AP, sep CP 1866,[4] eccl severed 1888 to help cr Dunham on the Hill EP.[219] *LG* Seq 11. *Parl* Seq 19.

HARGRAVE

EP Cr 1878 from Tarvin (tp Foulk Stapleford), Waverton AP (tp Huxley).[50] Chester RDn (1878—1935), Malpas RDn (1935—*). Sometimes 'Foulk Stapleford'.

HARTFORD

Chap pt in Great Budworth AP, pt in Weaverham cum Milton (eccl, 'Weaverham') AP, sep CP 1866,[4] eccl in chap Witton (sep EP 1723 from Great Budworth [qv for other constituent pts]3), 'Hartford' a sep EP 1825 from Witton EP (incl pt orig area tp Castle Northwich),[3] refounded 1863.[124] *LG* Edd. Hd, Northw. PLU, pt Northw. USD, pt Northw. RSD, Northw. RD. Civ bdry: 1894 (loses the pt in the UD to Northwich CP),[262] 1936,[7] 1955.[208] *Parl* Seq 25. *Eccl* Frod. RDn (1825—88), Middlew. RDn (1888—*). Eccl bdry: 1929 (the pt of orig tp Castle Northwich severed to help cr Northwich Holy Trinity EP).[132]

HARTHILL

AP *LG* Seq 3. *Parl* Seq 23. *Eccl* Seq 1.

HASLINGTON

Chap in Barthomley AP (Ches, Staffs until 1866, ent Ches thereafter), sep CP 1866 in Ches,[4] sep EP 1766,[3] eccl refounded 1860.[68] *LG* Seq 18. Civ bdry: 1936.[7] *Parl* Seq 16. *Eccl* Nantw. RDn (1766—1880), Congl. RDn (1880—*). Eccl bdry: 1952.[25]

HASSALL

Tp in Sandbach AP, sep CP 1866.[4] *LG* Seq 20. *Parl* Seq 17.

HATHERTON

Tp in Wybunbury AP, sep CP 1866.[4] *LG* Seq 18. *Parl* Seq 21.

HATTERSLEY

Tp in Mottram (eccl 'Mottram in Longendale') AP, sep CP 1866,[4] eccl severed and united 1966 with pt Mottram in Longendale AP, pt Godby cum Newton Green EP to cr 'Hattersley' EP.[248] *LG* Maccl. Hd, Asht. under Lyne PLU, RSD, Tintw. RD. Abol civ 1936 pt to Hyde MB & CP, pt to help cr Longendale UD & CP.[7] *Parl* N'rn Dv (1832—67), North Dv (1867—85), Hyde Dv (1885—1918), Stalybr. & Hyde Dv (1918—48). *Eccl* Mott. RDn.

HATTON

Tp in Runcorn AP, sep CP 1866,[4] eccl in chap Daresbury (sep EP 1738 from Runcorn AP,[3] qv for later refounding). *LG* Seq 10. *Parl* Seq 3.

HATTON

Tp in Waverton AP, sep CP 1866.[4] *LG* Seq 3. *Parl* Seq 22.

HAUGHTON

Tp in Bunbury AP, sep CP 1866.[4] *LG* Seq 13. Bdry: 1888.[6] *Parl* Seq 21.

HAUGHTON ST ANNE

EP Cr 1881 from Denton Christ Church EP (Lancs),

Stockport AP (Ches).[263] Asht. under Lyne RDn (1881—1910), Ardw. RDn (1910—*). Bdry: 1923 (help cr Audenshaw St Hilda EP [Lancs, Ches] to be in dioc Manch).[54]

HAZEL GROVE AND BRAMHALL

CP Cr 1900 by union Bosden CP, Bramhall CP, Norbury CP, Offerton CP, Torkington CP.[119] LG Stockpt. PLU, Hazel Grove & Bramhall UD. Bdry: 1901 (loses pt to Stockpt. CB [assoc with Ches] & AP),[126] 1935 (loses pt to Stockpt. CB [assoc with Ches] & AP),[264] 1936 (incl loses pt to Stockpt. CB [assoc with Ches] & AP),[7] 1939 (gains Woodford CP).[265] Transf 1974 to Gtr Manch.[28] Parl Knutsf. Dv (1918—48), Cheadle CC (1948—70), Hazel Grove BC (1970—*).

HEALD GREEN

EP Cr 1958 from Gatley EP, Handforth EP.[170] Stockpt. RDn.

HELSBY

Tp in Frodsham AP, sep CP 1866,[4] sep EP 1875.[242] LG Seq 16. Bdry: 1936.[7] Parl Seq 24. Eccl Frod. West RDn (1869—80), Frod. RDn (1880—*).

HENBURY

Tp in Prestbury AP, sep EP 1851,[51] sep CP 1866 as 'Henbury cum Pexall',[4] qv. Maccl. RDn (1851—73), Maccl. North RDn (1873—80), Maccl. RDn (1880—*). Bdry: 1962.[245]

CP Cr 1936 by union ent Henbury cum Pexall CP, pt Birtles CP, pt Macclesfield CP.[7] LG Maccl. RD. Parl Maccl. CC (1948—*).

HENBURY CUM PEXALL

Tp in Prestbury AP, sep CP 1866,[4] sep EP 1851 as 'Henbury',[51] qv. LG Maccl. Hd, PLU, RSD, RD. Abol 1936 to help cr Henbury CP.[7] Parl N'rn Dv (1832—67), North Dv (1867—85), Maccl. Dv (1885—1948).

HENHULL

Tp in Acton AP, sep CP 1866.[4] LG Seq 18. Bdry: 1936.[7] Parl Seq 21.

HESWALL

AP Usual eccl spelling; for civ and civ sep tp, see following entry. Eccl Seq 10.

HESWALL CUM OLDFIELD

AP Usual civ spelling; for eccl see prev entry. Incl tp Gayton (sep CP 1866[4]). LG Wirral Hd, PLU, RSD (1894—1933), UD (1933—74). Transf 1974 to Merseyside.[28] Parl Seq 26.

HIGH LANE

EP Cr 1860 from Poynton with Worth EP, Marple EP, Stockport AP (pt tp Torkington), Norbury EP.[51] Maccl. RDn (1860—73), Maccl. North RDn (1873—80), Stockpt. RDn (1880—*). Bdry: 1871 (loses pt to help refound Poynton with Worth EP as 'Poynton' EP),[185] 1934.[266]

HOCKENHULL

Tp in Tarvin AP, sep CP 1866.[4] LG Seq 12. Bdry: 1963.[66] Parl Seq 22.

HOLLINGWORTH

Tp in Mottram AP (eccl, 'Mottram in Longendale'), sep CP 1866,[4] eccl severed 1840 to help cr Tintwistle EP,[3] 'Hollingworth' a sep EP 1922 from Tintwistle EP.[267] LG Maccl. Hd, Ashton under Lyne PLU, Hollingworth USD, UD. Abol 1936 to

help cr Longendale UD & CP.[7] Parl N'rn Dv (1832—67), North Dv (1867—85), Hyde Dv (1885—1918), Stalybr. & Hyde Dv (1918—48).

HOOLE

Tp pt in Plemstall AP, pt in Chester St John the Baptist AP, sep CP 1866,[4] eccl severed 1843 to help cr Chester Christ Church EP,[176] 'Hoole' a sep EP 1872 from Chester Christ Church EP.[177] LG Brox. Hd, Gt Bough. PLU (1837—71), Chester PLU (1871—1930), pt Hoole USD, pt Chester RSD, Hoole UD. Civ bdry: 1894 (the pt not in Hoole UD cr Hoole Village CP),[19] 1936 (incl loses pt to Chester CB [assoc with Ches] & CP).[7] Abol civ 1954 pt to Chester CB (assoc with Ches) & CP, pt to Guilden Sutton AP, pt to Hoole Village CP.[174] Parl S'rn Dv (1832—67), pt Chester Parl Bor (1867—1918), pt South Dv (1867—85), pt Knutsf. Dv (1885—1918), City of Chester Dv/CC (1918—70). Eccl Chester RDn. Eccl bdry: 1934,[189] 1959.[268]

HOOLE VILLAGE

CP Cr 1894 from the pt of Hoole CP not in Hoole UD.[19] LG Chester PLU, RD. Bdry: 1936,[7] 1954.[174] Parl City of Chester Dv/CC (1918—*).

HOOSE

Tp in West Kirby AP, sep CP 1866,[4] sep EP 1839,[3] refounded 1860 as 'Holy Trinity in Hoose otherwise the Holy Trinity Hoylake',[269] soon and thereafter called 'Hoylake', qv. LG Wirral Hd, PLU, RSD (1875—91), Hoylake USD (1891—94). Abol 1894 to help cr Hoylake cum West Kirby CP.[250] Parl S'rn Dv (1832—67), South Dv (1867—85), Wirral Dv (1885—1918).

HOOTON

Tp in Eastham AP, sep CP 1866,[4] sep EP 1862 (tps Hooton, Little Sutton, Childer Thornton, all in Eastham AP).[220] LG Wirral Hd, PLU, RSD, RD (1894—1933), Ellesm. Port UD (1933—50). Civ bdry: 1933 (incl pt transf to Eastham AP to help cr Beb. UD).[69] Abol civ 1950 ent to Ellesmere Port CP.[231] Parl S'rn Dv (1832—67), South Dv (1867—85), Wirral Dv/CC (1885—1970). Eccl Wirral RDn (1862—1935), Wirral South RDn (1935—*).

HORTON

Tp in Tilston AP, sep CP 1866.[4] LG Seq 3. Parl Seq 23.

HORTON CUM PEEL

Tp (sometimes 'Little Mouldsworth') in Tarvin AP, sep CP 1866.[4] LG Seq 12. Parl Seq 22.

HOUGH

Tp in Wybunbury AP, sep CP 1866.[4] LG Seq 18. Parl Seq 18.

HOYLAKE

EP Cr 1839 from West Kirby AP as 'Hoose',[3] refounded 1860 as 'Holy Trinity in Hoose otherwise the Holy Trinity Hoylake',[269] soon and thereafter called 'Hoylake'. Wirral RDn (1839—1935), Wirral North RDn (1935—*). Bdry: 1889,[270] 1937 (help cr Great Meols EP).[238]

HOYLAKE CUM WEST KIRBY

CP Cr 1894 by union pars in W Kirby & Hoylake UD: Hoose CP, West Kirby AP, Great Meolse CP, Little Meolse CP, pt Grange CP.[250] LG Wirral PLU, W Kirby & Hoylake UD (1894—97), Hoylake & W

Kirby UD (1897—1933), Hoylake UD (1933—74). Bdry: 1915.[251] Transf 1974 to Merseyside.[28] *Parl* Wirral Dv/CC (1918—*).

HULL AND APPLETON—see APPLETON

CHURCH HULME
Chap in Sandbach AP, sep CP 1866,[4] sep EP 1733 (incl tp Cranage in same par).[3] *LG* Seq 22. *Parl* Seq 12. *Eccl* Middlew. RDn (1733—1880), Congl. RDn (1880—*).

HULME WALFIELD
Tp in Astbury AP, sep CP 1866,[4] sep EP 1878 (tps Hulme Walfield, Radnor, Somerforrd Booths, all in Astbury AP).[39] *LG* Seq 22. Civ bdry: 1933.[7] *Parl* Seq 14. *Eccl* Middlew. RDn (1878—80), Congl. RDn (1880—*).

HULSE
Tp in Great Budworth AP, sep CP 1866,[4] eccl in chap Witton (sep CP 1723 from Great Budworth [qv for other constituent pts],[3] eccl refounded after severing of other pts [see Witton] as 'Witton (otherwise Northwich St Helen)' EP[14]). *LG* Northw. Hd, PLU, RSD. Bdry: 1889.[271] Abol 1892 ent to Lach Dennis CP.[92] *Parl* S'rn Dv (1832—67), Mid Dv (1867—85), Northw. Dv (1885—1918).

HUNSTERSON
Tp in Wybunbury AP, sep CP 1866.[4] *LG* Seq 18. *Parl* Seq 21.

HUNTINGTON
Tp in Chester St Oswald AP, sep CP 1866.[4] *LG* Seq 4. *Parl* Seq 20.

HURDSFIELD
Tp in Prestbury AP, sep CP 1866,[4] eccl in chap Macclesfield (sep EP [St Paul] 1813,[3] refounded 1844,[195] 'Hurdsfield' a sep EP 1840 from Macclesfield EP.[272] *LG* Maccl. Hd, PLU, pt Maccl. MB (1835—94), pt Maccl. USD, pt Maccl. RSD, Maccl. RD. Civ bdry: 1894 (loses the pt in the MB to Macclesfield CP),[273] 1936.[7] *Parl* Pt Maccl. Parl Bor (1832—85), pt N'rn Dv (1832—67), pt North Dv (1867—85), Maccl. Dv/CC (1885—*). *Eccl* Maccl. RDn (1853—73), Maccl. South RDn (1873—80), Maccl. RDn (1880—*). Eccl bdry: 1886,[274] 1968.[116]

HURLESTON
Tp in Acton AP, sep CP 1866.[4] *LG* Seq 18. *Parl* Seq 21.

HUXLEY
Tp in Waverton AP, sep CP 1866,[4] eccl severed 1878 to help cr Hargrave EP.[50] *LG* Seq 3. Bdry: 1963.[66] *Parl* Seq 22.

HYDE
Chap in Stockport AP, sep CP 1866,[4] pt a sep EP 1846.[67] *LG* Maccl. Hd, Stockpt. PLU, Hyde USD, MB (1881—1974). Civ bdry: 1894 (gains the pt in Hyde MB of Werneth CP),[274a] 1923 (gains the other pars in Hyde MB: Godley CP, Newton CP),[247] 1936 (incl help cr Bredbury and Romiley CP).[7] Transf 1974 to Gtr Manch.[28] *Parl* N'rn Dv (1832—67), North Dv (1867—85), Hyde Dv (1885—1918), Stalybr. & Hyde Dv/CC (1918—*). *Eccl* Maccl. RDn (1846—73), Maccl. North RDn (1873—80), Stockpt. RDn (1880—88), Mott. RDn (1888—*). Eccl bdry: 1880 (help cr Gee Cross EP).[12]

HYDE ST GEORGE
EP Cr 1843 from Stockport AP.[218] Maccl. RDn (1843—73), Maccl. North RDn (1873—80), Stockpt. RDn (1880—88), Mott. RDn (1888—*). Bdry: 1880 (help cr Gee Cross EP),[12] 1881 (help refound Denton Christ Church EP [Lancs]),[275] 1891 (help cr Newton Flowery Field EP).[276]

IDDINSHALL
Tp in Chester St Oswald AP, sep CP 1866.[4] *LG* Seq 12. *Parl* Seq 22.

INCE
AP *LG* Edd. Hd, Gt Bough. PLU (1837—71), Chester PLU (1871—1930), RSD, RD (1894—1933), Ellesm. Port UD (1933—50). Civ bdry: 1933.[40] Abol civ 1950 ent to Ellesmere Port CP.[231] *Parl* S'rn Dv (1832—67), South Dv (1867—85), Edd. Dv (1885—1918), City of Chester Dv (1918—48), Wirral CC (1948—70). *Eccl* Seq 3.

IRBY
Tp pt in Thurstaston AP, pt in Woodchurch AP, sep CP 1866.[4] *LG* Wirral Hd, PLU, RSD, RD (1894—1933), Wirral UD (1933—74). Bdry: 1933.[40] Transf 1974 to Merseyside.[28] *Parl* Seq 26.

KECKWICK
Tp in Runcorn AP, sep CP 1866,[4] eccl severed 1738 to help cr Daresbury EP,[3] qv for later refounding. *LG* Buckl. Hd, Runc. PLU, RSD, RD. Abol 1936 ent to Daresbury CP.[7] *Parl* N'rn Dv (1832—67), Mid Dv (1867—85), Knutsf. Dv (1885—1948).

KELSALL
Tp in Tarvin AP, sep CP 1866,[4] sep EP 1956 incl pt Delamere EP.[210] *LG* Seq 12. *Parl* Seq 22. *Eccl* Chester RDn. Eccl bdry: 1965 (gains eccl ex-par Willington).[142]

KERMINCHAM
Tp in Swettenham AP, sep CP 1866.[4] *LG* Northw. Hd, Congl. PLU, RSD, RD. Abol 1936 ent to Swettenham AP.[7] *Parl* S'rn Dv (1832—67), Mid Dv (1867—85), Knutsf. Dv (1885—1948).

KERRIDGE
CP Cr 1894 from the pt of Bollington CP not in Bollington UD.[19] *LG* Maccl. PLU, RD. Abol 1900 ent to Bollington CP.[115]

KETTLESHULME
Tp in Prestbury AP, sep CP 1866,[4] eccl in chap Macclesfield (sep EP 1813 from Prestbury AP,[3] eccl refounded 1835[277]), the area of Kettleshulme eccl severed 1864 from Macclesfield EP to help cr Salterford cum Kettleshulme EP.[41] *LG* Seq 17. Bdry: 1936 (loses pt to help cr Whaley Bridge UD & CP, Derbys).[213] *Parl* Seq 6.

KINDERTON
CP Cr 1894 from the pts not in Middlew. UD of Kinderton cum Hulme CP, Newton CP.[278] *LG* Northw. PLU, RD. Abol 1936 pt to Northw. UD & CP, pt to Bradwall CP, pt to Tetton CP, pt to Byley CP, pt to Sproston CP, pt to Stanthorne CP, pt to Wimboldsley CP.[7] *Parl* Northw. Dv (1918—48).

KINDERTON CUM HULME
Tp in Middlewich AP, sep CP 1866.[4] *LG* Northw. Hd, PLU, pt Middlew. USD (enlarged pt 1893—94), pt Northw. RSD (reduced pt 1893—94). Bdry: 1883.[56] Abol 1894 the pt in the UD transf to

Middlewich AP, the remainder to help cr Kinderton CP.[278] *Parl* S'rn Dv (1832—67), Mid Dv (1867—85), Northw. Dv (1885—1948).

KINGS MARSH

Ex-par place, sep CP 1858,[10] eccl abol 1963 pt to Farndon AP, pt to Shocklach AP.[62] *LG* Seq 3. Civ bdry: 1888.[157] *Parl* Seq 23.

KINGSLEY

Tp in Frodsham AP, sep CP 1866,[4] sep EP 1853.[3] *LG* Seq 16. Civ bdry: 1881,[279] 1936 (incl gains Newton by Frodsham CP).[7] *Parl* Seq 24. *Eccl* Frod. RDn (1853—69), Frod. North RDn (1869—80), Frod. RDn (1880—*).

KINGSWOOD

Tp in Delamere CP (orig ex-par place, pt of Delamere Forest, made a sep par 1812 by union Delamere, tp Kingswood, and 2 other tps [see Delamere][209]), 'Kingswood' a sep CP 1866.[4] *LG* Edd. Hd, Runc. PLU, RSD, RD. Abol 1936 pt to Kingsley CP, pt to Manley CP, pt to Norley CP.[7] *Parl* S'rn Dv (1832—67), South Dv (1867—85), Edd. Dv (1885—1948).

LOWER KINNERTON

Tp in Dodleston AP (Ches, Flints until 1866, ent Ches from 1866), sep CP 1866 in Ches.[4] *LG* Seq 2. *Parl* Seq 19.

WEST KIRBY

AP Incl tps Caldy, Great Meolse, Little Meolse (each a sep CP 1866[4]); tp Hoose (sep CP 1866,[4] sep EP 1839,[3] refounded 1860 as 'Holy Trinity in Hoose otherwise the Holy Trinity Hoylake' EP,[269] soon and thereafter called 'Hoylake'); tp Frankby, tp Grange, tp Newton with Larton, pt tp Greasby (each a sep CP 1866,[4] the ent tps of Frankby, Greasby [incl the pt of tp Greasby in Thurstaston AP] and pt tps Grange, Newton with Larton eccl severed 1861 to cr Frankby EP[237]). *LG* Wirral Hd, PLU, RSD (1875—91), W Kirby & Hoylake USD (1891—94). Abol civ 1894 to help cr Hoylake cum West Kirby CP.[250] *Parl* S'rn Dv (1832—67), South Dv (1867—85), Wirral Dv (1885—1918). *Eccl* Seq 10. Addtl eccl bdry alt: 1874,[280] 1889,[270] 1920 (cr West Kirby St Andrew EP).[177]

WEST KIRBY ST ANDREW

EP Cr 1920 from West Kirby AP.[177] Wirral North RDn. Bdry: 1937 (help cr Great Meols EP).[238]

KNUTSFORD

Chap in Rostherne AP, sep par 1741.[82] Incl tps Bexton, Knutsford Nether, Ollerton (each a sep CP 1866[4]), tp Knutsford Over (sep CP 1866,[4] sep EP 1858 as 'Knutsford St Cross',[3] [sometimes 'Cross Town' or 'Cross Town St Cross'], refounded 1860[51]), tp Toft (sep CP 1866,[4] sep EP 1854,[3] eccl refounded 1855[281]) so that 'Knutsford' has no sep civ identity 1866—95 (see following entry). *LG* Buckl. Hd, pt Knutsf. Bor. *Parl* N'rn Dv (1832—67). *Eccl* Frod. RDn (1741—1869), Frod. East RDn (1869—80), Bowdon RDn (1880—1935), Knutsf. RDn (1935—*). Addtl eccl bdry alt: 1840 (help cr Marthall EP),[282] 1968.[116]

CP Cr 1895 by union Knutsford Nether CP, Knutsford Over CP.[283] *LG* Buckl. PLU, Knutsf. UD. Bdry: 1936.[7] *Parl* Knutsf. Dv/CC (1918—*).

KNUTSFORD NETHER

Tp in Knutsford AP, sep CP 1866.[4] *LG* Buckl. Hd, Altr. PLU, RSD, RD. Abol 1895 to help cr Knutsford CP.[283] *Parl* N'rn Dv (1832—67), Mid Dv (1867—85), Knutsf. Dv (1885—1918).

KNUTSFORD OVER

Tp in Knutsford AP, sep CP 1866,[4] eccl cr 1858 as 'Knutsford St Cross' EP[3] [sometimes 'Cross Town' or 'Cross Town St Cross'], refounded 1860,[51] qv. *LG* Buckl. Hd, Altr. PLU, RSD, RD. Abol civ 1895 to help cr Knutsford CP.[283] *Parl* N'rn Dv (1832—67), Mid Dv (1867—85), Knutsf. Dv (1885—1918).

KNUTSFORD ST CROSS

EP Cr 1858 (sometimes 'Cross Town' or 'Cross Town St Cross') from Knutsford AP (for civ see prev entry),[3] refounded 1860.[51] Bowdon RDn (1858—1935), Knutsf. RDn (1935—*).

LACH DENNIS

Tp in Great Budworth AP, sep CP 1866,[4] eccl in chap Witton (sep EP 1723 from Great Budworth AP,[3] eccl refounded 1900 [after other areas severed from it, qv] as 'Witton (otherwise Northwich St Helen)' EP[14]). *LG* Seq 21. Bdry: 1892 (gains Hulse CP, Birches CP, Stublach CP, Newhall CP),[92] 1936.[7] *Parl* Seq 13.

LACHE CUM SALTNEY

EP Cr 1855 from Chester St Mary on the Hill AP (Ches, dioc Chester), Hawarden AP (Flints, dioc St Asaph) to be in dioc Chester.[186] Chester RDn. Bdry: 1904 (gains pt Hawarden AP, Flints, dioc St Asaph),[284] 1923.[187]

LANDS COMMON TO FRODSHAM AND FRODSHAM LORDSHIP

Exists from 1866 when Frodsham Lordship a sep CP from Frodsham AP.[4] *LG* Runc. RD. Abol 1936 ent to Frodsham AP.[7] *Parl* Edd. Dv (1918—48).

LANDICAN

Tp in Woodchurch AP, sep CP 1866.[4] *LG* Wirral Hd, PLU, RSD, RD (1894—1928), Birk. CB (1928—33). Abol 1933 ent to Birkenhead CP.[40] *Parl* S'rn Dv (1832—67), South Dv (1867—85), Wirral Dv (1885—1948).

LARKTON

Tp in Malpas AP, sep CP 1866,[4] presumed[83] eccl severed 1840 to help cr Bickerton EP,[3] eccl refounded 1843.[84] *LG* Seq 6. *Parl* Seq 23.

LATCHFORD

Chap in Grappenhall AP, deemed civ ent in Ches, sep CP 1866,[4] deemed eccl pt in Lancs, that pt a sep EP 1796 as 'Latchford St James',[3] eccl refounded 1866 from Grappenhall AP, Thelwall EP (both Ches) and from Warrington AP (Lancs),[252] the pt deemed eccl in Ches a sep EP 1866 from Grappenhall AP as 'Latchford Christ Church'.[253] *LG* Buckl. Hd, Runc. PLU (1836—45), Warr. PLU (1845—1930), pt Warr. MB ([Lancs, Ches] 1847—94, ent [Lancs] 1894—98), pt Warr. USD, pt Runc. RSD. Civ bdry: 1884,[285] 1884 (gains pt Warrington AP, Lancs, and gains the pt in Warr. MB of Thelwall CP),[286] 1894 (the pt in Ches, not in Warr. MB, cr Latchford Without CP),[287] 1896 (when in Warr. MB, gains pts from Ches pars of Appleton CP, Latchford Without CP, Walton Inferior CP).[37]

Abol 1898 ent to Warrington AP.[211] *Parl* Warr.
Parl Bor ([Lancs, Ches] 1832—1918).

LATCHFORD CHRIST CHURCH
EP Cr 1866 from Grappenhall AP (the pt of chap
Latchford [Ches, Lancs] in Ches).[253] RDns as for
Latchford St James, from 1866. Bdry: 1968.[190]

LATCHFORD ST JAMES
EP Cr 1796 from the Lancs pt of chap Latchford (Ches,
Lancs) in Grappenhall AP,[3] refounded 1866 from
Grappenhall AP, Thelwall EP (both Ches), Warr-
ington AP (Lancs).[252] Frod. RDn (until 1869),
Frod. West RDn (1869—80), Frod. RDn (1880—
1935), Gt Budw. RDn (1935—*).

LATCHFORD WITHOUT
CP Cr 1894 from the pt of Latchford CP in Ches (the pt
not in Warr. MB [Lancs]).[287] *LG* Runc. PLU, RD.
Bdry: 1896 (loses pt to Warr. MB [Lancs] and to
Latchford CP),[37] 1933 (loses pt to Warr. CB [assoc
with Lancs] & AP).[254] Abol 1936 ent to Stockton
Heath CP.[7] *Parl* Knutsf. Dv (1918—48).

LAWTON OR CHURCH LAWTON—see following
entry

CHURCH LAWTON
AP *LG* Seq 22. Civ bdry: 1965 (exchanges pts with
Kidsgrove UD & CP, Staffs).[109] *Parl* Seq 9. *Eccl*
As 'Lawton or Church Lawton'. Seq 8.

LAWTON MOOR
EP Cr 1937 from Northenden AP (Ches par, since 1931
in Manch CB [assoc with Lancs]), Baguley EP, to
be in dioc Manch.[60] Heaton RDn (1937—65),
Withington RDn (1965—*).

LEA
Tp in Wybunbury AP, sep CP 1866.[4] *LG* Seq 18.
Parl Seq 21.

LEA BY BACKFORD
Tp in Backford AP, sep CP 1866.[4] *LG* Seq 25. *Parl*
Seq 19.

LEA NEWBOLD
Tp in Chester St Oswald AP, sep CP 1866.[4] *LG* Seq
4. *Parl* Seq 20.

LEASOWE
EP Cr 1957 from Moreton EP, Great Meols EP,
Bidston AP, Wallasey AP, Wallasey St Nicholas
EP.[88] Wall. RDn.

LEDSHAM
Tp in Neston AP, sep CP 1866,[4] eccl severed 1859
to help cr Capenhurst EP.[158] *LG* Seq 24. Bdry:
1933.[40] *Parl* Seq 27.

LEESE
Tp in Sandbach AP (described in 1871 census as pt
Sandbach, pt Middlewich AP, o'wise considered
ent in Sandbach), sep CP 1866.[4] *LG* Northw. Hd,
Congl. PLU, RSD, RD. Abol 1936 pt to Cranage
CP, pt to Byley CP, pt to Lach Dennis CP.[7] *Parl*
S'rn Dv (1832—67), Mid Dv (1867—85), Knutsf.
Dv (1885—1948).

LEFTWICH
Tp in Davenham AP, sep CP 1866.[4] *LG* Northw.
Hd, PLU, pt Northw. USD, pt Northw. RSD,
Northw. RD. Bdry: 1883,[56] 1894 (loses the pt in the
UD to Northwich CP).[262] Abol 1936 pt to Northw.
UD & CP, pt to Davenham AP, pt to Hartford CP.[7]
Parl S'rn Dv (1832—67), Mid Dv (1867—85),

Northw. Dv (1885—1948).

HIGH LEGH
Chap in Rostherne AP, sep CP 1866,[4] sep EP
1817,[3] sep eccl status not sustained, re-cr 1973.[288]
LG Seq 8. *Parl* Seq 1. *Eccl* Frod. RDn (orig cr),
Knutsf. RDn (1973—*).

LITTLE LEIGH
Chap in Great Budworth AP, sep CP 1866,[4] sep EP
1728,[3] eccl refounded 1834.[144] *LG* Seq 9. *Parl* Seq
4. *Eccl* Frod. RDn (1728—1869), Frod. West RDn
(1869—80), Frod. RDn (1880—1935), Gt Budw.
RDn (1935—*).

LEIGHTON
Tp in Nantwich AP, sep CP 1866,[4] eccl severed
1850 to help cr Leighton with Minshull EP
(sometimes 'Leighton cum Minshull Vernon').[3] *LG*
Seq 18. Bdry: 1936.[7] *Parl* Seq 21.

LEIGHTON
Tp in Neston AP, sep CP 1866.[4] *LG* Wirral Hd,
PLU, Neston & Parkgate USD. Abol 1894 to help
cr Neston cum Parkgate CP.[289] *Parl* S'rn Dv
(1832—67), South Dv (1867—85), Wirral Dv
(1885—1948).

LEIGHTON CUM MINSHULL VERNON—see following entry

LEIGHTON WITH MINSHULL
EP Cr 1850 by union tp Leighton in Nantwich AP, tp
Minshull Vernon in Middlewich AP.[3] Nantw. RDn
(1850—80), Middlew. RDn (1880—1935), Nantw.
RDn (1935—*). Bdry: 1951.[14] Sometimes
'Leighton cum Minshull Vernon'.

LINDOW
EP Cr 1877 from Chorley EP.[106] Maccl. North RDn
(1877—80), Bowdon RDn (1880—88), Maccl. RDn
(1888—1935), Knutsf. RDn (1935—*).

LISCARD
Tp in Wallasey AP, sep CP 1866,[4] pt a sep EP
1878.[290] *LG* Wirral Hd, PLU (1836—91), Birk.
PLU (1891—1912), Wall. USD, UD (1894—1910),
MB (1910—12). Abol civ 1912 ent to Wallasey
AP.[291] *Parl* S'rn Dv (1832—67), South Dv (1867—
85), Wirral Dv (1885—1918), Wall. Parl Bor
(1918—48). *Eccl* Wirral RDn (1878—88), Birk.
RDn (1888—1907), Wall. RDn (1907—*). Eccl
bdry: 1907,[135] 1925 (cr Liscard St Thomas EP).[148]
Abol eccl 1971 to help cr Liscard St Mary with St
Columba EP.[226]

LISCARD ST MARY WITH ST COLUMBA
EP Cr 1971 by union Liscard EP, Egremont St
Columba EP.[226] Wall. RDn.

LISCARD ST THOMAS
EP Cr 1925 from Liscard EP.[148] Wall. RDn.

LITTLETON
Tp in Christleton AP, sep CP 1866.[4] *LG* Seq 1. *Parl*
Seq 19.

LONGENDALE
CP Cr 1936 by union ent Mott. in Longendale UD &
Mottram CP, ent Hollingworth UD & CP, pt
Hattersley CP, pt Matley CP.[7] *LG* Longendale UD.
Transf 1974 to Gtr Manch.[28] *Parl* Stalybr. & Hyde
CC (1948—*).

LOSTOCK GRALAM
Tp in Great Budworth AP, sep CP 1866,[4] eccl in

chap Witton (sep EP 1723 from Great Budworth AP[3]), 'Lostock Gralam' a sep 1842 from Great Budworth EP, Witton EP.[149] *LG* Seq 21. Civ bdry: 1936.[7] *Parl* Seq 13. *Eccl* Frod. RDn (1842—69), Frod. West RDn (1869—80), Frod. RDn (1880—1935), Gt Budw. RDn (1935—54), Middlew. RDn (1954—*). Eccl bdry: 1875 (help cr Marston EP).[146]

LYME HANDLEY
Tp in Prestbury AP, sep CP 1866.[4] *LG* Seq 17. *Parl* Seq 6.

LYMM
AP *LG* Buckl. Hd, Altr. PLU (1836—95), Buckl. PLU (1895—1930), Lymm USD, UD. Civ bdry: 1933 (incl exchanges pts with Rixton with Glazebrook CP, and loses pt to Woolston with Martinscroft EP, both Lancs),[13] 1936.[7] *Parl* N'rn Dv (1832—67), Mid Dv (1867—85), Altr. Dv (1885—1945), Buckl. Dv (1945—48), Runc. CC (1948—*). *Eccl* After Dissolution free chap of Warburton (orig a sep AP, sep civ identity retained) presented with Lymm AP (Warburton ent sep eccl 1869[292]), Seq 4. Addtl eccl bdry alt: 1881 (cr Oughtrington EP [proposed 1874, confirmed 1881]).[293]

MACCLESFIELD
The following have 'Macclesfield' in their names. Insofar as any existed at a given time: *LG* Maccl. Hd, PLU, Bor/MB, USD. *Parl* Maccl. Parl Bor (1832—85), Dv/CC (1885—*). *Eccl* Maccl. RDn (cr—1873), Maccl. South RDn (1873—80), Maccl. RDn (1880—*).

CP1/EP1—MACCLESFIELD [ST MICHAEL]—Tp in Prestbury AP, sep CP 1866,[4] sep EP 1813 incl tp Hurdsfield, tp Kettleshulme in same par,[3] eccl refounded 1835.[277] Civ bdry: 1894 (gains the pts in the MB of Hurdsfield CP, Sutton CP),[273] 1936 (incl help cr Henbury CP),[7] 1955.[244] Addtl eccl bdry alt: 1837 (cr EP1,[3] refounded 1888[294]), 1840 (cr Hurdsfield EP),[272] 1844 (cr EP3),[195] 1844 (cr EP4),[30] 1864 (tp Kettleshulme severed to help cr Salterford cum Kettleshulme EP),[41] 1888 (cr EP2),[295] 1888 (refound EP1),[294] 1962,[245] 1963,[296] 1968.[116]

EP1—MACCLESFIELD CHRIST CHURCH—Cr 1837 from EP1,[3] refounded 1888.[294]

EP2—MACCLESFIELD ST JOHN THE EVANGELIST—Cr 1888 from EP1.[295] Bdry: 1962,[245] 1963.[296]

EP3—MACCLESFIELD ST PAUL—Cr 1844 from EP1.[195] Bdry: 1886.[274]

EP4—MACCLESFIELD ST PETER—Cr 1844 from EP1.[30]

MACCLESFIELD FOREST
Tp in Prestbury AP, sep CP 1866,[4] sep EP 1737 (incl tp Wildboarclough in same par) as 'Macclesfield Forest with Wildboarclough',[3] eccl refounded 1906,[297] qv. *LG* Seq 17. *Parl* Seq 6.

MACCLEFIELD FOREST WITH WILDBOARCLOUGH
EP Cr 1737 when tps Macclesfield Forest, Wildboarclough eccl severed from Prestbury AP,[3] refounded 1906.[297] Maccl. RDn (1737—1873), Maccl. South RDn (1873—80), Maccl. RDn (1880—1973). Abol

1973 the area of Wildboarclough CP to help cr Wincle and Wildboarclough EP, the remainder to help cr Rainow with Salterford and Forest EP.[298]

MACEFEN
Tp in Malpas AP, sep CP 1866,[4] eccl severed 1824 to help cr Malpas St Chad EP,[3] the latter refounded 1860.[15] *LG* Seq 6. *Parl* Seq 23.

MALPAS
AP Tp 'Malpas' in Ches (Brox. Hd) as were tps Agden, Bradley, Chidlow, Macefen, Tushingham cum Grindley (sometimes 'Tushingham' or 'Tushingham with Grindley') (each of the 5 a sep CP 1866,[4] the 5 eccl united 1824 incl pt tps Bickley, Hampton, main tp of Malpas as 'Malpas St Chad' EP,[3] refounded 1860[196]); incl tps Bickerton, Broxton, Bulkeley, Duckington, Egerton, Larkton (each of the 6 a sep CP 1866,[4] all presumed[83] eccl united 1840 as 'Bickerton' EP,[3] the latter eccl refounded 1843[84]), tp Bickley (sep CP 1866,[4] pt eccl severed 1824 to help cr Malpas St Chad EP,[3] qv for refounding, 'Bickley' a sep EP 1893 from Malpas AP, Marbury EP, Wrenbury AP[85]), tps Cholmondeley, Chorlton, Cuddington, Edge (each of the 4 a sep CP 1866[4]), tp Hampton (sep CP 1866,[4] pt eccl severed 1824 to help cr Malpas St Chad EP,[3] qv for refounding), tps Newton by Malpas, Oldcastle, Overton, Stockton, Wigland, Wychough (each of the 6 a sep CP 1866[4]); incl in Flints (Maylor Hd) chap Iscoyd (sep CP 1866 in Flints[4] so that 'Malpas' ent Ches thereafter, Iscoyd a sep EP 1880 in Flints as 'Whitewell'[299]). *LG* Ches pt, pt Malpas Bor, Seq 7. *Parl* Ches pt, Seq 23. *Eccl* Seq 1. Eccl bdry: 1880 (the tps and pts of tps not cited above as eccl severed refounded as 'Malpas').[299]

MALPAS ST CHAD
EP Cr 1824 from Malpas AP (tps Agden, Bradley, Chidlow, Macefen, Tushingham cum Grindley, pt tps Bickley, Hampton, main tp of Malpas),[3] refounded 1860.[15] Malpas RDn. Sometimes 'Tushingham'.

MANLEY
Tp in Frodsham AP, sep CP 1866.[4] *LG* Seq 16. Bdry: 1936.[7] *Parl* Seq 24.

MARBURY
Tp in Great Budworth AP, sep CP 1866.[4] *LG* Seq 9. *Parl* Seq 4.

MARBURY
Chap (Ches, Nantw. Hd) in Whitchurch AP [Salop [N Bradford Hd], Ches until 1866, ent Salop thereafter) comprised of tps Marbury with Quoisley, Norbury, the ent area a sep EP 1870 as 'Marbury',[300] each of the tps CP 1866 in Ches,[4] qv. Maccl. RDn (1870—80), Nantw. RDn (1880—1935), Malpas RDn (1935—*). Eccl bdry: 1893 (help cr Bickley EP).[85]

MARBURY CUM QUOISLEY—see following entry
MARBURY WITH QUOISLEY
Chap (Ches, Nantw. Hd) in Whitchurch AP [Salop [N Bradford Hd], Ches until 1866, ent Salop from 1866), comprised of tps Marbury with Quoisley, Norbury (each a sep CP 1866 in Ches[4]), the ent area a sep EP 1870 as 'Marbury',[300] qv. *LG* Seq 19. By 1971 census, called 'Marbury cum Quoisley'. Bdry:

1965 (gains pt Whitchurch UD & Whitchurch Urban CP, Salop).[109] *Parl* Seq 21.

MARLSTON CUM LACHE

Tp in Chester St Mary on the Hill AP, sep CP 1866.[4] *LG* Seq 2. Bdry: 1936 (loses pt to Chester CB [assoc with Ches] & CP).[7] *Parl* Seq 19.

MARPLE

Chap in Stockport AP, sep CP 1866,[4] sep EP 1738,[3] pt eccl severed 1860 to help cr High Lane EP,[51] pt eccl severed 1870 to cr Marple Low EP,[301] the remainder eccl refounded 1876 as 'Marple'.[73] *LG* Maccl. Hd, Stockpt. PLU, Marple USD, UD. Civ bdry: 1936 (incl help cr Bredbury and Romiley CP),[7] 1936 (gains Ludworth CP, Mellor CP, both Derbys),[213] 1936 (gains pt Stockpt. CB [assoc with Ches] & AP).[7] Transf 1974 to Gtr Manch.[28] *Parl* N'rn Dv (1832—67), North Dv (1867—85), Hyde Dv (1885—1918), Maccl. Dv (1918—48), Cheadle CC (1948—70), Hazel Grove BC (1970—*). *Eccl* Maccl. RDn (1738—1873), Maccl. North RDn (1873—80), Stockpt. RDn (1880—*). Eccl bdry: 1934.[266]

MARPLE LOW

EP Cr 1870 from Marple EP.[301] Maccl. RDn (1870—73), Maccl. North RDn (1873—80), Stockpt. RDn (1880—88), Mott. RDn (1888—1935), Stockpt. RDn (1935—*).

MARSTON

Tp in Great Budworth AP, sep CP 1866,[4] sep EP 1875 from Great Budworth AP, Lostock Gralam EP.[146] *LG* Seq 9. Civ bdry: 1883,[56] 1889.[271] *Parl* Seq 4. *Eccl* Frod. West RDn (1875—80), Frod. RDn (1880—1935), Gt Budw. RDn (1935—65). Abol eccl 1965 ent to Great Budworth AP.[98]

MARTHALL

Tp in Rostherne AP, sep CP 1866 as 'Marthall cum Warford',[4] qv, sep EP 1840 as 'Marthall' from Rosthorne AP, Knutsford AP.[282] Frod. RDn (1840—69), Frod. East RDn (1869—80), Bowdon RDn (1880—1935), Knutsf. RDn (1935—*).
CP Cr 1951 when Marthall cum Warford CP divided into 2 CPs of 'Marthall', 'Little Warford'.[302] *LG* Buckl. RD. *Parl* Knutsf. CC (1955—*).

MARTHALL CUM WARFORD

Tp in Rostherne AP, sep CP 1866[4]; for eccl see 'Marthall'. *LG* Buckl. Hd, Altr. PLU (1836—95), RSD, RD (1894—95), Buckl. PLU (1895—1930), RD (1895—1951). Abol 1951 divided into 2 CPs of 'Marthall', 'Little Warford'.[302] *Parl* N'rn Dv (1832—67), Mid Dv (1867—85), Knutsf. Dv (1885—1948).

MARTON

Chap in Prestbury AP, sep CP 1866,[4] sep EP 1728.[3] *LG* Seq 17. *Parl* Seq 7. *Eccl* Maccl. RDn (1728—1873), Maccl. South RDn (1873—80), Maccl. RDn (1880—*).

MARTON

Tp in Whitegate AP, sep CP 1866.[4] *LG* Seq 15. Bdry: 1883 (loses detached pt to Over AP which was not part of Winsford USD and thus in 1894 became 'Unnamed' CP, qv),[56] 1927,[303] 1936 (incl loses pt to Winsford UD to help cr Winsford CP).[7] *Parl* Seq 22.

MATLEY

Tp in Mottram AP (eccl, 'Mottram in Longendale'), sep CP 1866.[4] *LG* Maccl. Hd, Ashton under Lyne PLU, RSD, Tintw. RD. Abol 1936 pt to Dukinfield MB & CP, pt to Hyde MB & CP, pt to help cr Longendale UD & CP, pt to Stalybr. MB & CP.[7] *Parl* N'rn Dv (1832—67), North Dv (1867—85), Hyde Dv (1885—1918), Stalybr. & Hyde Dv (1918—48).

GREAT MEOLS

EP Cr 1937 from Hoylake EP, Moreton EP, West Kirby St Andrew EP, Frankby EP.[238] Wirral North RDn. Bdry: 1957 (help cr Leasowe EP),[88] 1959.[268]

GREAT MEOLSE

Tp in West Kirby AP, sep CP 1866.[4] *LG* Wirral Hd, PLU, RSD (1875—91), W Kirby & Hoylake USD (1891—94). Abol 1894 to help cr Hoylake cum West Kirby CP.[250] *Parl* S'rn Dv (1832—67), South Dv (1867—85), Wirral Dv (1885—1918).

LITTLE MEOLSE

Tp in West Kirby AP, sep CP 1866.[4] Organisation as for Great Meolse.

MERE

Tp in Rostherne AP, sep CP 1866.[4] *LG* Seq 8. *Parl* Seq 2.

MICKLEHURST

EP Cr 1962 from Millbrook EP (Ches, dioc Chester), Mossley EP (Lancs, dioc Manch) to be in Manch dioc.[172] Mottram RDn.

MIDDLETON GRANGE

Ex-par place (Buckl. Hd), united civ 1858 with tp Acton Grange in Runcorn AP,[10] abol eccl 1861 to help cr Aston EP.[53]

MIDDLEWICH

AP Tp 'Middlewich' in Northw. Hd as were tp Byley ([sometimes civ early called 'Byley cum Yatehouse], sep CP 1866 as 'Byley',[4] sep EP 1848 as 'Byley'[153]), tps Clive, Croxton, Kinderton cum Hulme (each a sep CP 1866[4]), tp Minshull Vernon (sep CP 1866,[4] eccl severed 1850 to help cr Leighton with Minshull EP [sometimes 'Leighton cum Minshull Vernon']3), tps Mooresbarow cum Parme, Newton, Occlestone, Ravenscroft, Sproston, Stublach, Sutton, Wimboldsley (each a sep CP 1866[4]), reported in 1871 census that this par incl pt tp Leese (o'wise generally considered ent in Sandbach AP, qv for sep identity of the tp 1866[4]); incl in Edd. Hd tp Weaver (sep CP 1866[4]). *LG* Northw. PLU, Middlew. USD, UD. Addtl civ bdry alt: 1894 (gains the pts in Middlew. UD of Kinderton cum Hulme CP, Newton CP, Byley CP),[154] 1936.[7] *Parl* S'rn Dv (1832—67), Mid Dv (1867—85), Northw. Dv/CC (1918—55), Nantw. CC (1955—*). *Eccl* Seq 7.

MILLBROOK

EP Cr 1863 from Stalybridge St Paul EP.[124] Maccl. RDn (1863—73), Maccl. North RDn (1873—80), Stockpt. RDn (1880—88), Mott. RDn (1888—*). Bdry: 1962 (help cr Micklehurst EP [Ches, Lancs] to be in dioc Chester, and loses pt to Mossley EP [Lancs, dioc Manch]).[172]

MILLINGTON

Tp in Rostherne AP, sep CP 1866.[4] *LG* Seq 8. *Parl*

Seq 1.

CHURCH MINSHULL

AP Chap in Acton AP, sep par at Dissolution, 1st rector 1541.[1] *LG* Seq 18. *Parl* Seq 21. *Eccl* Nantw. RDn (until 1880), Middlew. RDn (1880—1935), Nantw. RDn (1935—*). Eccl bdry: 1951.[14]

MINSHULL VERNON

Tp in Middlewich AP, sep CP 1866,[4] eccl severed 1850 to help cr Leighton with Minshull EP (sometimes 'Leighton cum Minshull Vernon').[3] *LG* Seq 23. *Parl* Seq 10.

MOBBERLEY

AP *LG* Seq 8. Civ bdry: 1936.[7] *Parl* Seq 2. *Eccl* Maccl. RDn (until 1873), Maccl. North RDn (1873—80), Bowdon RDn (1880—1935), Knutsf. RDn (1935—*). Eccl bdry: 1881 (help cr Ashley EP).[41]

MOLLINGTON

CP Cr 1901 by union Mollington Banastre CP, Mollington Tarrant CP.[198] *LG* Chester PLU, RD. Bdry: 1936.[7] *Parl* City of Chester Dv/CC (1918—*).

MOLLINGTON BANASTRE

Tp (sometimes 'Little Mollington') in Chester St Mary on the Hill AP, sep CP 1866,[4] eccl severed 1743 to help cr Upton EP,[3] the latter refounded 1882.[107] *LG* Wirral Hd, Gt Bough. PLU (1837—71), Chester PLU (1871—1901), RSD, RD. Abol 1901 to help cr Mollington CP.[304] *Parl* S'rn Dv (1832—67), South Dv (1867—85), Edd. Dv (1885—1918).

MOLLINGTON TARRANT

Tp (sometimes 'Great Mollington') in Backford AP, sep CP 1866.[4] Organisation as for Mollington Banastre.

MOORE

Tp in Runcorn AP, sep CP 1866,[4] eccl severed 1738 to help cr Daresbury EP,[3] pt of orig area of tp Moore severed 1879 from the latter to help cr Walton EP,[11] the remainder of Daresbury EP refounded 1880 as such.[12] *LG* Seq 10. Bdry: 1933 (loses pt to Penketh CP, Lancs),[13] 1967.[52] *Parl* Seq 3.

MOORESBARROW CUM PARME

Tp in Middlewich AP, sep CP 1866.[4] *LG* Northw. Hd, PLU, RSD. Abol 1892 ent to Sproston CP.[92] *Parl* S'rn Dv (1832—67), Mid Dv (1867—85), Knutsf. Dv (1885—1918).

MORETON

Tp (sometimes called 'Moreton cum Lingham') in Bidston cum Ford AP (eccl, 'Bidston'), sep CP 1866 as 'Moreton',[4] sep EP 1864 (incl tp Saughall Massie in the same par).[89] *LG* Wirral Hd, PLU, RSD, RD. Civ bdry: 1915.[251] Abol civ 1928 ent to Wall. CB (assoc with Ches) & AP.[90] *Parl* S'rn Dv (1832—67), South Dv (1867—85), Wirral Dv (1885—1918). *Eccl* Wirral RDn (1864—1935), Wirral North RDn (1935—*). Eccl bdry: 1937 (help cr Great Meols EP),[238] 1957 (help cr Leasowe EP),[88] 1959.[268]

MORETON CUM ALCUMLOW

Tp in Astbury AP, sep CP 1866.[4] *LG* Seq 22. *Parl* Seq 9.

MOSSLEY

EP Cr 1858 from Astbury AP.[3] Middlew. RDn (1858—80), Congl. RDn (1880—*).

MOSTON

Tp in Chester St Mary on the Hill AP, sep CP 1866,[4] eccl severed 1743 to help cr Upton EP,[3] the latter refounded 1882.[107] *LG* Seq 1. *Parl* Seq 19.

MOSTON

Tp in Warmingham AP, sep CP 1866.[4] *LG* Northw. Hd, Congl. PLU, RSD, RD. Abol 1936 ent to Tetton CP.[7] *Parl* S'rn Dv (1832—67), Mid Dv (1867—85), Edd. Dv (1885—1918), Northw. Dv (1918—48).

MOSTON

CP Cr 1970 by union Elton CP, Tetton CP.[234] *LG* Congl. RD.

MOTTRAM

AP Usual civ spelling; for eccl see following entry. Incl tp Godley (sep CP 1866,[4] eccl severed 1847 to help cr Godley cum Newton Green EP[246]), tp Hattersley (sep CP 1866,[4] eccl severed 1966 and united with pt Godley cum Newton Green EP to help cr Hattersley EP[248]), tp Hollingworth (sep CP 1866,[4] eccl severed 1840 to help cr Tintwistle EP,[3] 'Hollingworth' a sep EP 1922 from Tintwistle EP[267]), tp Matley (sep CP 1866[4]), tp Newton (sep CP 1866,[4] sep EP 1840 as 'Newton in Mottram',[3] eccl refounded 1841,[76] the EP sometimes called 'Newton Moor'), tp Stayley (sep CP 1866,[4] sep EP 1840 as 'Staleybridge St Paul'[305]), tp Tintwistle (sep CP 1866,[4] sep EP 1840 [incl tp Hollingworth in same par][3]). *LG* Maccl. Hd, Ashton under Lyne PLU, Mott. in Longendale USD, UD. Abol civ 1936 to help cr Longendale UD & CP.[7] *Parl* N'rn Dv (1832—67), North Dv (1867—85), Hyde Dv (1885—1918), Stalybr. & Hyde Dv (1918—48).

MOTTRAM IN LONGENDALE

AP Usual eccl spelling; for civ and civ and eccl sep tps, see prev entry. *Eccl* Maccl. RDn (until 1873), Maccl. North RDn (1873—80), Stockpt. RDn (1880—88), Mott. RDn (1888—*). Addtl eccl bdry alt: 1724 (cr Woodhead EP).[3]

MOTTRAM ST ANDREW

Tp in Prestbury AP, sep CP 1866.[4] *LG* Seq 17. Bdry: 1936 (incl gains Newton CP).[7] *Parl* Seq 7.

MOULDSWORTH

Tp in Tarvin AP, sep CP 1866.[4] *LG* Seq 12. *Parl* Seq 22.

LITTLE MOULDSWORTH—see HORTON CUM PEEL

MOULTON

Tp in Davenham AP, sep CP 1866,[4] sep EP 1877 (incl tp Bostock in same par).[106] *LG* Seq 21. Civ bdry: 1883,[56] 1936 (loses pt to Winsford UD to help cr Winsford CP).[7] *Parl* Seq 15.

NANTWICH

Chap in Acton AP, 1st independent status 1677 but sep status early debated.[2] Incl tps Alvaston, Woolstanwood, pt tp Willaston (each a sep CP 1866[4]), tp Leighton (sep CP 1866,[4] eccl severed 1850 to help cr Leighton with Minshull EP [sometimes 'Leighton cum Minshull Vernon']3). *LG* Pt Nantw. Bor, Nantw. Hd, PLU, USD, UD. Addtl civ bdry alt: 1936.[7] *Parl* Seq 18. *Eccl* Nantw. RDn. Addtl eccl bdry alt: 1927,[290] 1930,[8] 1951.[14]

NESS

Tp in Neston AP, sep CP 1866.[4] *LG* Wirral Hd, PLU, RSD, RD (1894—1933), Neston UD (1933—74). *Parl* Seq 26.

NESTON

AP Incl tp Ledsham (sep CP 1866,[4] eccl severed 1859 to help cr Capenhurst EP[158]), tps Leighton, Ness, Great Neston, Little Neston (each of the 4 a sep CP 1866[4]), tps Raby, Thornton Hough, Willaston (each of the 3 a sep CP 1866,[4] ent tp Thornton Hough and pt tps Raby, Willaston eccl severed 1865 and united with an addtl pt of Neston AP to cr 'Willaston' EP,[146] the orig areas of ent tp Thornton Hough, pt tp Raby, pt Neston AP severed 1869 from Willaston EP to cr 'Thornton Hough' EP[136]), so that 'Neston' has no sep civ identity after 1866. *LG* Wirral Hd. *Parl* S'rn Dv (1832—67). *Eccl* Seq 11.

GREAT NESTON

Tp in Neston AP, sep CP 1866.[4] *LG* Wirral Hd, PLU, Neston & Parkgate USD. Abol 1894 to help cr Neston cum Parkgate CP.[289] *Parl* S'rn Dv (1832—67), South Dv (1867—85), Wirral Dv (1885—1918).

LITTLE NESTON

Tp in Neston AP, sep CP 1866.[4] Organisation as for Great Neston, with bdry alt 1883,[56] 1889.[306]

NESTON CUM PARKGATE

CP Cr 1894 by union pars in Neston and Parkgate UD: Leighton CP, Great Neston CP, Little Neston CP.[289] *LG* Wirral PLU, Neston and Parkgate UD (1894—1933), Neston UD (1933—74). Bdry: 1933 (incl gains pt Raby CP and pt Thornton Hough CP to help cr Neston UD, and loses pt to Raby CP to help cr Beb. UD).[69] *Parl* Wirral Dv/CC (1918—*).

NETHERPOOL

Tp in Eastham AP, sep CP 1866,[4] eccl severed 1871 to help cr Ellesmere Port EP.[221] *LG* Wirral Hd, PLU, RSD, RD (1894—1910), Ellesm. Port & Whitby UD (1901—11). Abol 1911 to help cr Ellesmere Port CP.[230] *Parl* S'rn Dv (1832—67), South Dv (1867—85), Wirral Dv (1885—1918).

NEW FERRY

EP Cr 1888 from Nether Bebington AP (civ, 'Bebington').[76] Wirral RDn (1888—1935), Wirral North RDn (1935—*).

NEWALL GREEN

EP Cr 1960 from Northenden AP (Ches par, civ in Manch CB from 1931).[214] Heaton RDn (1960—65), Withington RDn (1965—*).

NEWBOLD ASTBURY

Tp in Astbury AP, sep CP 1866.[4] *LG* Seq 22. Bdry: 1936.[7] *Parl* Seq 14.

NEWHALL

Tp in Audlem AP (reported in 1871 census as pt in Audlem AP, pt in Wrenbury cum Frith AP, o'wise and generally considered ent in Audlem), sep CP 1866.[4] *LG* Seq 18. *Parl* Seq 21.

NEWHALL

Tp in Davenham AP, sep CP 1866.[4] *LG* Northw. Hd, PLU, RSD. Abol 1892 ent to Lach Dennis CP.[92] *Parl* S'rn Dv (1832—67), Mid Dv (1867—85), Knutsf. Dv (1885—1918).

NEWTON

Tp in Middlewich AP, sep CP 1866.[4] *LG* Northw. Hd, PLU, pt Middlew. USD (enlarged pt 1893—94), pt Northw. RSD (reduced pt 1893—94). Bdry: 1892 (gains Sutton CP).[92] Abol 1894 the pt in the UD transf to Middlewich AP, the remainder to help cr Kinderton CP.[278] *Parl* S'rn Dv (1832—67), Mid Dv (1867—85), Northw. Dv (1885—1918).

NEWTON

Tp in Mottram (eccl, 'Mottram in Longendale') AP, sep CP 1866,[4] sep EP 1840 as 'Newton in Mottram',[3] refounded 1841,[76] qv, sometimes called 'Newton Moor'. *LG* Maccl. Hd, Ashton under Lyne PLU, Hyde USD, MB (1881—1923). Bdry: 1915 (bdry with Dukinfield CP defined).[216] Abol civ 1923 ent to Hyde CP.[247] *Parl* N'rn Dv (1832—67), North Dv (1867—85), Hyde Dv (1885—1918), Stalybr. & Hyde Dv (1918—48).

NEWTON

Tp in Prestbury AP, sep CP 1866.[4] *LG* Maccl. Hd, PLU, RSD, RD. Abol 1936 ent to Mottram St Andrew CP.[7] *Parl* N'rn Dv (1832—67), North Dv (1867—85), Knutsf. Dv (1885—1948).

NEWTON BY CHESTER

Tp in Chester St Oswald AP, sep CP 1866.[4] *LG* Brox. Hd, Gt Bough. PLU (1837—71), Chester PLU (1871—1930), RSD, RD. Abol 1936 pt to Chester CB & CP, pt to Hoole UD & CP.[7] *Parl* S'rn Dv (1832—67), pt Chester Parl Bor (1867—1918), pt South Dv (1867—85), pt Edd. Dv (1885—1918), City of Chester Dv (1918—48).

NEWTON BY DARESBURY

Tp in Runcorn AP, sep CP 1866,[4] eccl severed 1783 to help cr Daresbury EP,[3] qv for later refounding. *LG* Buckl. Hd, Runc. PLU, RSD, RD. Abol 1936 ent to Daresbury CP.[7] *Parl* N'rn Dv (1832—67), Mid Dv (1867—85), Knutsf. Dv (1885—1948).

NEWTON BY FRODSHAM

Tp in Frodsham AP, sep CP 1866.[4] *LG* Edd. Hd, Runc. PLU, RSD, RD. Abol 1936 ent to Kingsley CP.[7] *Parl* S'rn Dv (1832—67), Edd. Dv (1885—1948).

NEWTON BY MALPAS

Tp in Malpas AP, sep CP 1866.[4] *LG* Seq 7. *Parl* Seq 23.

NEWTON BY TATTENHALL

Tp in Tattenhall AP, sep CP 1866.[4] *LG* Seq 3. *Parl* Seq 23.

NEWTON FLOWERY FIELD

EP Cr 1891 from Newton in Mottram EP, Hyde St George EP.[276] Mott. RDn.

NEWTON IN MOTTRAM

Tp in Mottram (eccl, 'Mottram in Longendale') AP, sep EP 1840,[3] eccl refounded 1841,[76] sometimes called 'Newton Moor', sep CP 1866 as 'Newton',[4] qv (2nd Newton above). *Eccl* Maccl. RDn (1840—73), Maccl. North RDn (1873—80), Stockpt. RDn (1880—88), Mott. RDn (1888—*). Bdry: 1847 (help cr Godley cum Newton Green EP),[246] 1891 (help cr Newton Flowery Field EP).[276]

NEWTON WITH LARTON

Tp in West Kirby AP, sep CP 1866,[4] pt eccl severed 1861 to help cr Frankby EP.[237] *LG* Wirral Hd,

PLU, RSD. Abol 1889 ent to Grange CP.[249] *Parl* S'rn Dv (1832—67), South Dv (1867—85), Wirral Dv (1885—1918).

NOCTORUM

Tp in Woodchurch AP, sep CP 1866.[4] *LG* Wirral Hd, PLU (1836—91), RSD (1875—91), Birk. PLU (1891—1930), RSD (1891—94), Wirral RD. Abol 1933 ent to Birk. CB (assoc with Ches) & CP.[40] *Parl* S'rn Dv (1832—67), South Dv (1867—85), Wirral Dv (1885—1948).

NORBURY

Tp in chap Marbury (Ches, Nantw. Hd, comprised of tps Marbury with Quoisley, Norbury) in Whitchurch AP (Salop [N Bradford Hd], Ches until 1866, ent Salop thereafter), the 2 tps each a sep CP 1866 in Ches,[4] 'Marbury' a sep EP 1870 (ent chap comprised of both tps).[300] *LG* Seq 19. *Parl* Seq 21.

NORBURY

Chap in Stockport AP, sep CP 1866,[4] sep EP 1737,[3] eccl refounded 1843.[218] *LG* Maccl. Hd, Stockpt. PLU, RSD, RD. Abol civ 1900 to help cr Hazel Grove and Bramhall UD & CP.[119] *Parl* N'rn Dv (1832—67), North Dv (1867—85), Altr. Dv (1885—1918). *Eccl* Maccl. RDn (1737—1873), Maccl. North RDn (1873—80), Stockpt. RDn (1880—*). Bdry: 1860 (help cr High Lane EP),[51] 1878 (gains area tp Bosden from Cheadle AP, gains remainder of area tp Torkington [the pt not severed 1860 to help cr High Lane EP[51]] from Stockport AP).[118]

NORLEY

Chap in Frodsham AP, sep CP 1866,[4] sep EP 1861.[241] *LG* Seq 16. Bdry: 1881,[279] 1881,[205] 1883,[56] 1936.[7] *Parl* Seq 24. *Eccl* Frod. RDn (1861—69), Frod. West RDn (1869—80), Frod. RDn (1880—*). Eccl bdry: 1872 (help cr Crowton EP).[204]

NORTHENDEN

AP Incl tp Northern Etchells (sep CP 1866[4]), reported in 1871 census to incl pt tp Baguley (o'wise and generally considered ent in Bowdon AP, qv for sep civ and eccl status of Baguley). *LG* Maccl. Hd, Altr. PLU (1836—95), RSD, RD (1894—95), Buckl. PLU (1895—1930), RD (1895—1931). Abol civ 1931 ent to Manch CB (assoc with Lancs) & AP.[58] *Parl* N'rn Dv (1832—67), North Dv (1867—85), Altr. Dv (1885—1945). *Eccl* Maccl. RDn (until 1873), Maccl. North RDn (1873—80), Bowdon RDn (1880—1934), Heaton RDn (dioc Manch, 1934—65), Withington RDn (dioc Manch, 1965—*). Eccl bdry: 1936 (cr Benchill EP),[77] 1937 (help cr Lawton Moor EP [Ches, Lancs]),[60] 1960 (cr Newall Green EP),[214] 1963 (incl help cr Wythenshawe The William Temple Church EP).[79]

NORTHWICH

Tp in Great Budworth AP, sep CP 1866,[4] eccl in chap Witton (sep EP 1723 from Great Budworth,[3] after severing of area to cr several EPs [see Witton] eccl refounded 1900 as 'Witton (otherwise Northwich St Helen)' EP[14]). *LG* Northw. Hd, PLU, Northw. USD, UD. Civ bdry: 1894 (gains the following par and pts of pars in Northw. UD: ent Castle Northwich CP and pts Hartford CP, Leftwich

CP, Winnington CP),[262] 1936,[7] 1955.[208] *Parl* Seq 15.

CASTLE NORTHWICH

Tp in Great Budworth AP, sep CP 1866,[4] eccl in chap Witton (sep EP 1723 from Great Budworth,[3] pt of area of orig tp Castle Northwich eccl severed 1825 from Witton EP to help cr Hartford EP [qv for later refounding],[3] the remainder of the area of the tp remains in Witton EP, the latter refounded 1900 as 'Witton (otherwise Northwich St Helen)' EP,[14] the area of Castle Northwich severed 1929 from Witton (otherwise Northwich St Helen) EP, Hartford EP to cr 'Northwich Holy Trinity' EP.[132] *LG* Edd. Hd, Northw. PLU, USD. Abol 1894 ent to Northwich CP.[262] *Parl* S'rn Dv (1832—67), South Dv (1867—85), Northw. Dv (1885—1918).

NORTHWICH HOLY TRINITY

EP Cr 1929 from the area of orig tp Castle Northwich (qv in prev entry for civ and eccl status before 1929) in Witton (otherwise Northwich St Helen) EP, Hartford EP.[132] Middlew. RDn.

NORTHWICH ST HELEN—see WITTON (OTHERWISE NORTHWICH ST HELEN)

NORTON

Tp in Runcorn AP, sep CP 1866.[4] *LG* Buckl. Hd, Runc. PLU, RSD, RD. Bdry: 1936 (incl gains Stockham CP [Ches], loses pt to Cuerdley CP [Lancs], loses pt to help cr Preston Brook CP [Ches]).[7] Abol 1967 pt to Runc. UD & AP, pt to Daresbury CP.[52] *Parl* N'rn Dv (1832—67), Mid Dv (1867—85), Northw. Dv (1885—1948), Runc. CC (1948—70).

OAKMERE

Tp in Delamere CP (orig ex-par place, pt of Delamere Forest, made a sep par 1812 by union Delamere, tp Oakmere, and 2 other tps [see Delamere][209]), 'Oakmere' a sep CP 1866.[4] *LG* Seq 15. Bdry: 1936.[7] *Parl* Seq 22.

OCCLESTONE

Tp in Middlewich AP, sep CP 1866.[4] *LG* Northw. Hd, PLU, RSD. Abol 1892 ent to Wimboldsley CP.[92] *Parl* S'rn Dv (1832—67), Mid Dv (1867—85), Edd. Dv (1885—1918).

ODD RODE

Tp in Astbury AP, sep CP 1866,[4] sep EP 1860.[51] *LG* Seq 22. Civ bdry: 1965 (exchanges pts with Kidsgrove UD & CP, Staffs).[109] *Parl* Seq 9. *Eccl* Middlew. RDn (1860—80), Congl. RDn (1880—*).

OFFERTON

Tp in Stockport AP, sep CP 1866.[4] *LG* Maccl. Hd, Stockpt. PLU, RSD, RD. Abol 1900 to help cr Hazel Grove and Bramhall UD & CP.[119] *Parl* N'rn Dv (1832—67), North Dv (1867—85), Hyde Dv (1885—1918).

OLDCASTLE

Tp in Malpas AP, sep CP 1866.[4] *LG* Seq 7. *Parl* Seq 23.

OLLERTON

Tp in Knutsford AP, sep CP 1866.[4] *LG* Seq 8. *Parl* Seq 2.

ONSTON

Tp in Weaverham cum Milton AP (eccl, 'Weaverham'), sep CP 1866.[4] *LG* Edd. Hd,

Northw. PLU, RSD. Abol 1892 ent to Crowton CP.[92] *Parl* S'rn Dv (1832—67), South Dv (1867—85), Edd. Dv (1885—1918).

OUGHTRINGTON

EP Cr 1881 (as proposed 1874, confirmed 1881) from Lymm AP.[293] Bowdon RDn.

LOW OULTON

Tp in Over AP, sep CP 1866.[4] *LG* Edd. Hd, Northw. PLU, RSD. Abol 1892 ent to Little Budworth AP.[92] *Parl* S'rn Dv (1832—67), South Dv (1867—85), Edd. Dv (1885—1918).

OVER

AP Incl chap Little Budworth (appropriated to nunnery of Chester St Mary, called free chap in Over AP, sep par from Dissolution[151]), chap Whitegate (sep par 1542[307]), tp Low Oulton (sep CP 1866[4]), chap Wettenhall (sep CP 1866,[4] sep EP 1720[3]); tp Over reported in 1871 census as pt in Over AP, pt in Whitegate AP, o'wise and generally considered ent in Over AP. *LG* Pt Over Bor, Edd. Hd, Northw. PLU, Winsford USD (ent 1875—83, pt 1883—94), pt Northw. RSD (1883—94), Winsford UD. Addtl civ bdry alt: 1883 (gains the detached pt of Marton CP but the area not made pt of the USD and hence became 1894 'Unnamed' CP, qv),[123] 1927.[303] Abol civ 1936 pt to Winsford UD to help cr Winsford CP, pt to Darnhall CP, pt to Davenham AP, pt to Marton CP.[7] *Parl* S'rn Dv (1832—67), South Dv (1867—85), Northw. Dv (1885—1948). *Eccl* Seq 7. Addtl eccl bdry alt: 1863 (help cr Over St John the Evangelist EP),[308] 1876 (gains tp Darnhall from Whitegate AP).[207]

OVER ST JOHN THE EVANGELIST

EP Cr 1863 from Over AP, Whitegate AP.[308] Middlew. RDn.

OVERCHURCH

AP Rectory (Brox. Hd, Middlew. RDn) appropriated to Dean and Chapter of Chester, in ruins after the Dissoluton, thereafter considered chap or tp in Chester St Mary on the Hill AP, civ called 'Upton by Chester' and as such sep CP 1866,[4] eccl called 'Upton', sep EP 1743 (greater pt tp Upton, ent tp Moston, ent tp Mollington Banastre, all in Chester St Mary on the Hill),[3] eccl refounded 1882 from Chester St Mary on the Hill AP, Chester St Oswald AP (remainder of tp Upton, pt tp Blacon cum Crabwall).[107]

OVERPOOL

Tp in Eastham AP, sep CP 1866,[4] eccl severed 1871 to help cr Ellesmere Port EP.[221] *LG* Wirral Hd, PLU, RSD, RD (1894—1910), Ellesm. Port & Whitby UD (1910—11). Bdry: 1889.[309] Abol 1911 to help cr Ellesmere Port CP.[230] *Parl* S'rn Dv (1832—67), South Dv (1885—85), Wirral Dv (1885—1918).

OVERTON

Tp in Malpas AP, sep CP 1866.[4] *LG* Seq 7. *Parl* Seq 23.

OXTON

Tp in Woodchurch AP, sep CP 1866,[4] sep EP 1865.[310] *LG* Wirral Hd, PLU (1836—91), RSD (1875—77), Birk. PLU (1891—98), Birk. MB (1877—89), CB (1889—98), USD (1877—94).

Abol civ 1898 ent to Birkenhead CP.[74] *Parl* S'rn Dv (1832—59), Birk. Parl Bor (1859—1918). *Eccl* Wirral RDn (1865—88), Birk. RDn (1888—*). Eccl bdry: 1876 (help cr Claughton cum Grange EP),[86] 1902 (help cr Prenton EP),[311] 1911 (help cr Birkenhead St Bede EP),[29] 1948.[12]

PARTINGTON

Tp in Bowdon AP, sep CP 1866,[4] eccl in chap Carrington (sep EP 1759 from Bowdon AP[3]), 'Partington' a sep EP 1885 from Carrington EP.[120] *LG* Seq 8. Civ bdry: 1920 (exchanges pts with Irlam CP, loses pt to Rixton with Glazebrook CP, both Lancs).[160] Transf 1974 to Gtr Manch.[28] *Parl* Seq 1. Parl bdry: 1945.[161] *Eccl* Bowdon RDn. Eccl bdry: 1925 (help cr Cadishead EP [Ches, Lancs], to be in dioc Manch).[156]

PECKFORTON

Tp in Bunbury AP, sep CP 1866.[4] *LG* Seq 13. *Parl* Seq 21.

PENKETH

EP Lancs par transf 1974 to Ches.[28]

PENSBY

Tp in Woodchurch AP, sep CP 1866,[4] eccl severed 1880 and transf to Barnston EP.[12] *LG* Wirral Hd, PLU, RSD, RD (1894—1933), Wirral UD (1933—74). Transf 1974 to Merseyside.[28] *Parl* Seq 26.

LOWER PEOVER

Tp in Great Budworth AP, sep EP 1814 (incl tp Allostock in same par),[3] sep CP 1866 as 'Peover Inferior',[4] qv. Frod. RDn (1814—69), Frod. West RDn (1869—80), Frod. RDn (1880—1907), Bowdon RDn (1907—35), Knutsf. RDn (1935—*). Bdry: 1909.[155]

NETHER PEOVER

Chap in Great Budworth AP, sep CP 1866.[4] *LG* Seq 21. *Parl* Seq 13.

OVER PEOVER

Tp in Rostherne AP, sep EP 1827,[3] sep CP 1866 as 'Peover Superior',[4] qv. Frod. RDn (1827—69), Frod. East RDn (1869—80), Bowdon RDn (1880—1935), Knutsf. RDn (1935—*). Bdry: 1880 (help refound Chilford EP as 'Chilford with Old Withington' EP).[171]

PEOVER INFERIOR

Tp in Great Budworth AP, sep CP 1866,[4] sep EP 1814 as 'Lower Peover' (incl tp Allostock in same par),[3] qv. *LG* Seq 8. *Parl* Seq 2.

PEOVER SUPERIOR

Chap in Rostherne AP, sep CP 1866,[4] sep EP 1827 as 'Over Peover',[3] qv. *LG* Seq 8. *Parl* Seq 2.

PICKMERE

Tp in Great Budworth AP, sep CP 1866.[4] *LG* Seq 8. Bdry: 1936.[7] *Parl* Seq 2.

PICTON

Tp in Plemstall AP, sep CP 1866.[4] *LG* Seq 1. Bdry: 1963.[66] *Parl* Seq 19.

PLEMSTALL

AP Incl in Brox. Hd tps Picton, Mickle Trafford, pt tp Hoole (each a sep CP 1866[4]); incl in Edd. Hd tp Bridge Trafford (sep CP 1866[4]) so that 'Plemstall' has no sep civ identity after 1866. *Parl* N'rn Dv (1832—67). *Eccl* Seq 2. Eccl bdry: 1934,[189] 1959.[268]

PLUMLEY
Tp in Great Budworth AP, sep CP 1866.[4] *LG* Seq 8. *Parl* Seq 2.

POOLE
Tp in Acton AP, sep CP 1866,[4] eccl severed 1873 to help cr Worleston EP.[5] *LG* Seq 18. *Parl* Seq 21.

POOLTON—see POULTON

PORTWOOD
EP Cr 1844 from pt of tp Brinnington in Stockport AP.[137] Sometimes called 'Stockport St Matthew'. Maccl. RDn (1844—73), Maccl. North RDn (1873—80), Stockpt. RDn (1880—1971). Bdry: 1852,[312] 1876,[164] 1963 (help cr Brinnington EP).[128] Abol 1971 to help cr Brinnington with Portwood EP.[139]

POTT SHRIGLEY
Chap (sometimes 'Downes') in Prestbury AP, sep CP 1866,[4] sep EP 1719,[3] eccl refounded 1880.[313] *LG* Seq 17. *Parl* Seq 6. *Eccl* Maccl. RDn (1719—1873), Maccl. South RDn (1873—80), Maccl. RDn (1880—*).

POULTON
Tp in Pulford AP, sep CP 1866.[4] *LG* Seq 2. *Parl* Seq 19.

POULTON
EP Cr 1907 (orig 'Poolton') from Wallasey AP,[314] sep CP 1866 as 'Poulton cum Seacombe',[4] qv. Birk. RDn (1907), Wall. RDn (1907—*).

POULTON CUM SEACOMBE
Tp in Wallasey AP, sep CP 1866,[4] sep EP 1907 as 'Poulton' (orig, 'Poolton'),[314] qv. *LG* Wirral Hd, PLU (1836—91), Birk. PLU (1891—1912), Wall. USD, UD (1894—1910), MB (1910—12). Abol 1912 ent to Wallasey CP.[291] *Parl* S'rn Dv (1832—67), South Dv (1867—85), Wirral Dv (1885—1918).

POULTON CUM SPITAL
Tp in Bebington AP, sep CP 1866.[4] *LG* Wirral Hd, PLU, RSD, RD (1894—1933), Beb. UD (1933—37), MB (1937—74). Bdry: 1895.[141] Transf 1974 to Merseyside.[28] *Parl* Seq 28.

POULTON WITH FEARNHEAD
CP Lancs par transf 1974 to Ches.[28]

POWNALL FEE
Tp in Wilmslow AP, sep CP 1866.[4] *LG* Maccl. Hd, Altr. PLU, pt Chorley USD (1875—88), pt Wilmslow USD (1888—94), pt Altr. RSD. Bdry: 1883,[56] 1888.[110] Abol 1894 the pt in Wilmslow UD to help cr Wilmslow CP,[111] the remainder cr Styal CP.[19] *Parl* N'rn Dv (1832—67), North Dv (1867—85), Knutsf. Dv (1885—1918).

POYNTON
Chap in Prestbury AP, sep CP 1866,[4] eccl united 1745 with tp Worth in same par to cr Poynton with Worth EP,[3] eccl refounded 1871 as 'Poynton' from Prestbury AP, High Lane EP (the area of the orig chap and tp).[185] *LG* Maccl. Hd, PLU, RSD. Abol civ 1880 to help cr Poynton with Worth CP.[315] *Parl* N'rn Dv (1832—67), North Dv (1867—85). *Eccl* Maccl. RDn (1871—73), Maccl. South RDn (1873—80), Maccl. RDn (1880—1935), Stockpt. RDn (1935—*).

POYNTON WITH WORTH
EP Cr 1745 by union chap Poynton, tp Worth, both in Prestbury AP,[3] refounded 1871 as 'Poynton' from Prestbury AP, High Lane EP (the area of the orig chap and tp).[185] Maccl. RDn. Bdry: 1860 (help cr High Lane EP).[51]
CP Cr 1880 by union Poynton CP, Worth CP.[315] *LG* Maccl. Hd, PLU, RSD, RD. *Parl* Knutsf. Dv (1885—1948), Maccl. CC (1948—*).

PRENTON
Tp in Woodchurch AP, sep CP 1866,[4] sep EP 1902 from Woodchurch AP, Tranmere St Paul EP, Oxton EP.[311] *LG* Wirral Hd, PLU, RSD, RD (1894—1928), Birk. CB (1928—33). Abol civ 1933 ent to Birk. CB (assoc with Ches) & CP.[40] *Parl* S'rn Dv (1832—67), South Dv (1867—85), Wirral Dv (1885—1948). *Eccl* Birk. RDn. Eccl bdry: 1948.[12]

PRESTBURY
AP Incl chap Adlington (sep CP 1866[4]), chap Bollington (sep CP 1866,[4] sep EP [St John the Baptist] 1842[114]), chap Bosley (sep CP 1866,[4] sep EP 1883[55]), chap Chelford (sep CP 1866,[4] sep EP 1720,[3] eccl refounded 1880 as 'Chelford with Old Withington' EP from Prestbury AP, Over Peover EP[171]), chap and bor Macclesfield (sep CP 1866[4] sep EP 1813 [incl tp Hurdsfield, tp Kettleshulme, both in Prestbury],[3] eccl refounded 1835[277]), chap Macclesfield Forest (sep CP 1866,[4] eccl severed 1737 to help cr Macclesfield Forest with Wildboarclough EP,[3] eccl refounded 1906[297]), chap Marton (sep CP 1866,[4] sep EP 1728[3]), chap Newton (sep CP 1866[4]), chap Pott Shrigley ([sometimes 'Downes'] sep CP 1866 as 'Pott Shrigley',[4] sep EP 1719,[3] eccl refounded 1880[313]), chap Poynton, tp Worth (each a sep CP 1866,[4] the 2 eccl united 1745 as 'Poynton with Worth' EP,[3] the orig areas of the chap and tp eccl refounded 1871 as 'Poynton' from Prestbury AP, High Lane EP[185]), chap Rainow (sep CP 1866,[4] sep EP 1785,[3] eccl refounded 1863[316]), chap Siddington (sep CP 1866,[4] sep EP 1728[3]), chap Sutton (sep CP 1866,[4] pt severed 1835 to cr Sutton St George EP,[276] the remainder cr 1859 Sutton St James EP[3]), chap Wincle (sep CP 1866,[4] sep EP 1725,[3] eccl refounded 1869[14]), tp and chap (erected 1840[105]) Birtles (sep CP 1866,[4] sep EP 1890 from Alderley AP, Prestbury AP[16]), tp Butley (sep CP 1866[4]), tp and chap (built 1722) Capesthorne (sep CP 1866,[4] sep EP 1722[3]), tp Fallibroome (sep CP 1866[4]), tp Henbury cum Pexall (sep CP 1866,[4] sep EP 1851 as 'Henbury'[51]), tp Hurdsfield (sep CP 1866,[4] eccl in chap/EP Macclesfield [qv above], 'Hurdsfield' a sep EP 1840 from the latter[272]), tp Kettleshulme (sep CP 1866,[4] eccl in chap/EP Macclesfield [qv above], area of Kettleshulme eccl severed 1864 from the latter to help cr Salterford cum Kettleshulme EP[41]), tp Lyme Handley (sep CP 1866[4]), tp Mottram St Andrew (sep CP 1866[4]), tp North Rode (sep CP 1866,[4] sep EP 1846[317]), tp Tytherington (sep CP 1866[4]), tp Upton (sep CP 1866[4]), tp Wildboarclough (sep CP 1866,[4] eccl severed 1737 to help cr Macclesfield Forest with Wildboarclough EP,[3] eccl refounded 1906[297]), tp Lower Withington, tp Old Withington

(each a sep CP 1866[4]), tp Woodford (sep CP 1866,[4] sep EP 1873[5]). *LG* Seq 17. Addtl civ bdry alt: 1936.[7] *Parl* Pt Maccl. Parl Bor (1832—67), remainder and later, Seq 7. *Eccl* Seq 6. Addtl eccl bdry alt: 1780 (cr Salterford EP,[3] refounded 1864 as 'Salterford cum Kettleshulme'[41]), 1886,[274] 1915,[172] 1968.[116]

PRESTON BROOK
CP Cr 1936 by union ent Preston on the Hill CP, pt Norton CP.[7] *LG* Runc. RD. Bdry: 1967.[52] *Parl* Runc. CC (1948—*).

PRESTON ON THE HILL
Tp in Runcorn AP, sep CP 1866,[4] eccl severed 1738 to help cr Daresbury EP,[3] qv for later refounding. *LG* Buckl. Hd, Runc. PLU, RSD, RD. Abol 1936 to help cr Preston Brook CP.[7] *Parl* N'rn Dv (1832—67), Mid Dv (1867—85), Knutsf. Dv (1885—1948).

PRIOR'S HEYS
Ex-par place, sep CP 1858,[10] abol eccl 1964 ent to Tarvin AP.[227] *LG* Edd. Hd, Gt Bough. PLU (1858—71), Trav. PLU (1871—1930), RSD, RD. *Parl* Seq 22.

PUDDINGTON
Tp in Burton AP, sep CP 1866.[4] *LG* Seq 24. Bdry: 1936.[7] *Parl* Seq 27.

PULFORD
AP Incl tp Poulton (sep CP 1866[4]). *LG* Seq 2. *Parl* Seq 19. *Eccl* Chester RDn. Abol eccl 1973 to help cr Eccleston and Pulford EP.[223]

RABY
Tp in Neston AP, sep CP 1866,[4] pt eccl severed 1865 to help cr Willaston EP,[146] that same area severed 1869 from Willaston EP to help cr Thornton Hough EP.[136] *LG* Wirral Hd, PLU, RSD, RD (1894—1933), Beb. UD (1933—37), MB (1937—74). Bdry: 1883,[56] 1889,[306] 1933 (gains pt Neston cum Parkgate CP, pt Willaston CP to cr Beb. UD, loses pt to Neston cum Parkgate CP to help cr Neston UD).[69] Transf 1974 to Merseyside.[28] *Parl* Seq 28.

RADNOR
Tp in Astbury AP, sep CP 1866,[4] eccl severed 1878 to help cr Hulme Walfield EP.[39] *LG* Northw. Hd, Congl. PLU, RSD, RD. Abol 1895 ent to Somerford CP.[318] *Parl* S'rn Dv (1832—67), Mid Dv (1867—85), Maccl. Dv (1885—1918).

RAINOW
Chap in Prestbury AP, sep CP 1866,[4] sep EP 1785,[3] eccl refounded 1863.[316] *LG* Seq 17. *Parl* Seq 6. *Eccl* Maccl. RDn (1785—1873), Maccl. South RDn (1873—80), Maccl. RDn (1880—1921). Abol eccl 1921 to help cr Rainow with Salterford EP.[319]

RAINOW WITH SALTERFORD
EP Cr 1921 by union Rainow EP, area Salterford in Salterford cum Kettleshulme EP.[319] Maccl. RDn. Abol 1973 to help cr Rainow with Salterford and Forest EP.[298]

RAINOW WITH SALTERFORD AND FOREST
EP Cr 1973 by union ent Rainow with Salterford EP, pt Macclesfield Forest with Wildboarclough EP.[298] Maccl. RDn.

RAVENSCROFT
Tp in Middlewich AP, sep CP 1866.[4] *LG* Northw.

Hd, PLU, RSD. Abol 1892 ent to Byley CP.[92] *Parl* S'rn Dv (1832—67), Mid Dv (1867—85), Northw. Dv (1885—1918).

RIDLEY
Tp in Bunbury AP, sep CP 1866.[4] *LG* Seq 13. *Parl* Seq 21.

RINGWAY
EP Cr 1722 from Bowdon AP,[3] refounded 1863.[124] Frod. RDn (1722—1869), Frod. East RDn (1869—80), Bowdon RDn (1880—*).
CP Cr 1900 from the pt of Hale CP not constituted Hale UD.[256] *LG* Buckl. PLU, RD. Bdry: 1936.[7] Transf 1974 to Gtr Manch.[28] *Parl* Altr. Dv (1918—45), Buckl. Dv (1945—48), Knutsf. CC (1948—*).

RIXTON WITH GLAZEBROOK
CP Lancs par transf 1974 to Ches.[28]

ROCK FERRY
CP Cr 1894 from the pt of Higher Bebington CP in Birk. CB (assoc with Ches).[19] *LG* Wirral PLU, Birk. CB. Abol 1898 ent to Birkenhead CP.[74]
EP Cr 1844 from area tp Higher Bebington (qv for sep civ identity 1866) in Bebington AP.[70] Wirral RDn (1844—88), Birk. RDn (1888—*). Sometimes 'Higher Bebington St Peter'. Bdry: 1877 (cr Higher Bebington Christ Church EP),[73] 1900.[14]

NORTH RODE
Tp in Prestbury AP, sep CP 1866,[4] sep EP 1846.[317] *LG* Seq 17. Civ bdry: 1936.[7] *Parl* Seq 8. *Eccl* Maccl. RDn (1846—73), Maccl. South RDn (1873—80), Maccl. RDn (1880—*).

ROMILEY
Chap in Stockport AP, sep CP 1866,[4] pt cr 1745 'Chadkirk',[3] as such eccl refounded 1876,[164] the remainder of the orig chap transf 1877 to Werneth EP.[320] *LG* Maccl. Hd, Stockpt. PLU, Bredbury & Romiley USD, UD. Abol 1936 pt to help cr Bredbury and Romiley CP, pt to Marple UD & CP.[7] *Parl* N'rn Dv (1832—67), North Dv (1867—85), Hyde Dv (1885—1918), Maccl. Dv (1918—48).

ROPE
Tp in Wybunbury AP, sep CP 1866.[4] *LG* Seq 18. *Parl* Seq 18.

ROSTHERNE
AP Tp 'Rostherne' in Buckl. Hd as were chap & bor Knutsford (sep par 1741[82] [qv for its tps and their sep civ and eccl identity]), chap Peover Superior (sep CP 1866,[4] sep EP 1827 as 'Over Peover'[3]), tp High Legh (sep CP 1866,[4] sep EP 1817,[3] sep eccl status not sustained, re-cr 1973[288]), tp Marthall cum Warford (sep CP 1866,[4] 'Marthall' a sep EP 1840 from Rostherne AP, Knutsford AP[282]), tps Mere, Millington (each a sep CP 1866[4]), tp Tabley Superior (sep CP 1866,[4] sep EP 1855 as 'Over Tabley'[321]), tp Tatton (sep CP 1866[4]), pt tp Agden (sep CP 1866[4]), pt tp Bollington (sep CP 1866,[4] the ent tp [incl the pt in Bowdon AP] a sep EP 1869 as 'Bollington [Holy Trinity]' EP[14]); incl in Maccl. Hd tp Snelson (sep CP 1866[4]). *LG* Altr. PLU (1836—95), RSD, RD (1894—95), Buckl. PLU (1895—1930), RD (1895—1974). *Parl* Seq 1. *Eccl* Frod. RDn (until 1869), Frod. East RDn (1869—80), Bowdon RDn (1880—1935), Knutsf. RDn (1935—73). Addtl eccl bdry alt: 1881 (help cr

Ashley EP).[41] Abol eccl 1973 to help cr Rostherne with Bollington EP.[113]

ROSTHERNE WITH BOLLINGTON

EP Cr 1973 by union Rostherne AP, Bollington [Holy Trinity] EP.[113] Knutsf. RDn.

ROWTON

Tp in Christleton AP, sep CP 1866.[4] *LG* Seq 4. *Parl* Seq 20.

RUDHEATH

Tp pt in Davenham AP, pt in Sandbach AP (in 1871 census reported also as pt in Great Budworth AP, o'wise and generally considered only in the 2 stated APs), sep CP 1866,[4] eccl in chap Witton (sep EP 1723 from Great Budworth AP,[3] eccl refounded 1900 [after bdry alts, qv under Witton] as 'Witton (otherwise Northwich St Helen)' EP[14]). *LG* Seq 21. Bdry: 1883,[56] 1889,[271] 1889,[203] 1892 (gains Shurlach CP),[92] 1936,[7] 1955.[208] *Parl* Seq 13.

RUNCORN

AP Incl chap Aston by Sutton, tp Aston Grange, tp Sutton (each a sep CP 1866,[4] the 3 eccl united 1861, adding the pt of tp Dutton in Runcorn AP and the prev ex-par area of Middleton Grange as 'Aston' EP[53]), chap Daresbury (sep CP 1866,[4] sep EP 1738 [incl tps Acton Grange, Hatton, Keckwick, Moore, Newton by Daresbury, Preston on the Hill, all in the same par],[3] eccl refounded 1880[12]), chap Halton (sep CP 1866,[4] sep EP 1718,[3] eccl refounded 1860 from Runcorn AP, Runcorn Holy Trinity EP[198]), chap Thelwall (sep CP 1866,[4] sep EP 1737,[3] pt of the latter eccl severed 1866 to help cr Latchford St James EP [Ches, Lancs],[252] the remainder refounded 1870 as 'Thelwall'[322]), tp Acton Grange ([gains civ 1858 area of prev ex-par Middleton Grange[10], sep CP 1866,[4] eccl in chap/EP Daresbury, qv above), tp Clifton (sep CP 1866[4]), tps Hatton, Keckwick, Moore, Newton by Daresbury (each of the 4 a sep CP 1866,[4] each eccl in chap/EP Daresbury, qv above), tp Norton (sep CP 1866[4]), tp Preston on the Hill (sep CP 1866,[4] eccl in chap/EP Daresbury, qv above), tp Stockham (sep CP 1866[4]), tps Walton Inferior, Walton Superior (each a sep CP 1866[4]). *LG* Pt Halton Bor, Buckl. Hd, Runc. PLU, USD, UD. Addtl civ bdry alt: 1883,[56] 1884,[257] 1936 (incl gains Weston CP),[7] 1955,[258] 1967 (incl gains Halton CP).[52] *Parl* Seq 5. *Eccl* Seq 5. Addtl eccl bdry alt: 1838 (help cr Stockton Heath [Ches, Lancs] EP),[150] 1840 (cr Runcorn Holy Trinity EP),[323] 1842 (cr Runcorn Weston St John EP),[324] 1930 (cr Runcorn Weston St John EP),[68] 1931 (cr Runcorn St Michael and All Angels EP),[325] 1960.[259]

EAST RUNCORN WITH HALTON

EP Cr 1973 by union Halton EP, Runcorn Grange EP, Runcorn Holy Trinity EP.[261] Frod. RDn.

RUNCORN HOLY TRINITY

EP Cr 1840 from Runcorn AP.[323] Frod. RDn (1840—69), Frod. West RDn (1869—80), Frod. RDn (1880—1973). Bdry: 1860 (help refound Halton EP),[198] 1960.[259] Abol 1973 to help cr East Runcorn with Halton EP.[261]

RUNCORN ST MICHAEL AND ALL ANGELS

EP Cr 1931 from Runcorn AP.[325] Frod. RDn. Bdry: 1960.[259]

RUNCORN GRANGE

EP Cr 1963 from Halton EP.[260] Frod. RDn. Abol 1973 to help cr East Runcorn with Halton EP.[261]

RUNCORN WESTON ST JOHN

EP Cr 1842 from Runcorn AP.[324] Frod. RDn (1842—69), Frod. West RDn (1869—80), Frod. RDn (1880—*). Bdry: 1960.[324] Sometimes 'Weston Point'.

RUSHTON

Tp in Tarporley AP, sep CP 1866.[4] *LG* Edd. Hd, Nantw. PLU (1837—94), Tarv. PLU (1894—1930), Tarporley USD, UD (1894—1936), Northw. RD (1936—74). Bdry: 1936.[7] *Parl* Seq 22.

SAIGHTON

Tp in Chester St Oswald AP, sep CP 1866.[4] *LG* Seq 4. *Parl* Seq 20.

SALE

Tp in Ashton upon Mersey AP, sep CP 1866,[4] sep EP 1856.[43] *LG* Buckl. Hd, Altr. PLU (1836—95), Buckl. PLU (1895—1930), Sale USD, UD (1894—1936), MB (1936—74). Civ bdry: 1908,[44] 1936 (incl gains Ashton upon Mersey AP).[7] Transf 1974 to Gtr Manch.[28] *Parl* N'rn Dv (1832—67), Mid Dv (1867—85), Altr. Dv (1885—1945), Altr. & Sale Parl Bor/BC (1945—*). *Eccl* Frod. RDn (1856—69), Frod. East RDn (1869—80), Bowdon RDn (1880—*). Eccl bdry: 1868 (help refound Baguley EP),[57] 1884 (cr Sale St Paul EP),[326] 1886.[59]

SALE ST PAUL

EP Cr 1884 from Sale EP.[326] Bowdon RDn.

SALTERFORD

EP Cr 1780 from Prestbury AP.[3] Maccl. RDn. Refounded 1864 as 'Salterford cum Kettleshulme', qv, when gains tp Kettleshulme (orig in Prestbury AP, eccl severed 1843 to help cr Macclesfield EP, qv) from Macclesfield EP.[41]

SALTERFORD CUM KETTLESHULME

EP Cr 1864 by union Salterford EP, area of Kettleshulme in Macclesfield EP (Salterford a sep EP 1780 from Prestbury AP, Kettleshulme eccl severed 1843 from Prestbury AP to help cr Macclesfield EP, qv).[41] Maccl. RDn (1864—73), Maccl. South RDn (1873—80), Maccl. RDn (1880—1921). Abol 1921 pt to help cr Rainow with Salterford EP, pt to help cr Taxal with Kettleshulme EP.[319]

SANDBACH

AP Tp 'Sandbach' in Northw. Hd as were chap Church Hulme (sep CP 1866,[4] sep EP 1733 incl tp Cranage[3]), chap Goostrey cum Barnshaw (sep CP 1866,[4] sep EP 1724 as 'Goostrey' [incl tp Blackden][3]), tp Arclid (sep CP 1866[4]), tp Blackden (sep CP 1866,[4] eccl in chap/EP Goostrey as above), tp Bradwall (sep CP 1866[4]), tp Cotton (sep CP 1866[4]), tp Cranage (sep CP 1866,[4] eccl in chap/EP Church Hulme as above), tp Leese (reported in 1871 census as pt in Sandbach AP, pt in Middlewich AP, o'wise and generally considered ent in this par, sep CP 1866[4]), tp Twemlow (sep CP 1866[4]), tp Wheelock (sep CP 1866,[4] sep EP 1840[327]), pt tp Rudheath (in 1871 census reported as pt in Sandbach AP, pt in Great Budworth AP, o'wise and generally considered pt Sandbach, pt Davenham AP, sep CP 1866[4]); incl in Nantw. Hd tps Betchton, Hassall (each a sep CP 1866[4]). *LG* Congl. PLU, Sandbach USD, UD. Addtl civ bdry alt: 1936.[7] *Parl* S'rn Dv (1832—67), Mid Dv (1867—85), Crewe Dv (1885—1948), Knutsf. CC (1948—55), Crewe CC (1955—*). *Eccl* Seq 8. Addtl eccl bdry alt: 1847 (help cr Elworth EP),[235] 1861 (cr Sandbach Heath EP).[328]

SANDBACH HEATH
EP Cr 1861 from Sandbach AP.[328] Middlew. RDn (1861—80), Congl. RDn (1880—*).

SANDIWAY
EP Cr 1935 from Whitegate AP, Delamere EP, Weaverham cum Milton AP.[165] Middlew. RDn.

GREAT SANKEY
CP Lancs par transf 1974 to Ches.[28]

SAUGHALL
CP Cr 1948 by union Great Saughall CP, Little Saughall CP.[329] *LG* Chester RD. *Parl* City of Chester CC (1970—*).

GREAT SAUGHALL
Tp in Shotwick AP, sep CP 1866,[4] sep EP 1921 from Shotwick AP, ent eccl ex-par Shotwick Park.[330] *LG* Wirral Hd, Gt Bough. PLU (1837—53), Haward. PLU (1853—71), Chester PLU (1871—1930), RSD, RD. Civ bdry: 1888.[331] Abol civ 1948 to help cr Saughall CP.[329] *Parl* S'rn Dv (1832—67), South Dv (1867—85), Edd. Dv (1885—1918), City of Chester Dv/CC (1918—70). *Eccl* Wirral RDn (1921—35), Wirral South RDn (1935—*).

LITTLE SAUGHALL
Tp in Shotwick AP, sep CP 1866.[4] Civ, parl organisation as for Great Saughall, with addtl civ bdry alt 1936 (loses pt to Chester CB [assoc with Ches] & CP).[7]

SAUGHALL MASSIE
Tp in Bidston cum Ford AP (eccl, 'Bidston'), sep CP 1866,[4] eccl severed 1864 to help cr Moreton EP.[89] *LG* Wirral Hd, PLU, RSD, RD. Bdry: 1915.[251] Abol 1933 pt to Wall. CB (assoc with Ches) & AP, pt to Grange CP to help cr Hoylake UD.[40] *Parl* S'rn Dv (1832—67), South Dv (1867—85), Wirral Dv (1885—1948).

SEACOMBE
EP Cr 1847 from Wallasey AP.[332] Wirral RDn (1847—88), Birk. RDn (1888—1907), Wall. RDn (1907—*). Bdry: 1884 (help cr Egremont (otherwise Liscard) EP).[224]

SEVEN OAKS
Tp in Great Budworth AP, sep CP 1866.[4] *LG* Buckl. Hd, Runc. PLU, RSD, RD. Bdry: 1881,[35] 1881.[36] Abol 1936 ent to Antrobus CP.[7] *Parl* N'rn Dv (1832—67), Mid Dv (1867—85), Knutsf. Dv (1885—1948).

SHAVINGTON CUM GRESTY
Tp in Wybunbury AP, sep CP 1866.[4] *LG* Nantw. Hd, PLU, pt Crewe MB & USD (1892—94), Nantw. RSD (ent 1875—92, pt 1892—94), Nantw. RD. Bdry: 1894 (loses the pt in the MB to Monks Coppenhall CP),[199] 1936.[7] *Parl* Seq 18.

SHIPBROOK
Tp in Davenham AP, sep CP 1866.[4] *LG* Northw. Hd, PLU, RSD. Abol 1892 ent to Whatcroft CP.[92] *Parl* S'rn Dv (1832—67), Mid Dv (1867—85), Knutsf. Dv (1885—1918).

SHOCKLACH
AP Incl tps Caldecott, Church Shocklach, Shocklach Oviatt (each a sep CP 1866[4]) so that 'Shocklach' has no sep civ identity after 1866. *LG* Brox. Hd. *Parl* S'rn Dv (1832—67). *Eccl* Bangor RDn (until 1847), Malpas RDn (1847—*). Eccl bdry: 1963.[62]

CHURCH SHOCKLACH
Tp in Shocklach AP, sep CP 1866.[4] *LG* Brox. Hd, Wrex. PLU (1837—94), RSD, Tarv. PLU (1894—1930), RSD, RD. *Parl* Seq 23.

SHOCKLACH OVIATT
Tp in Shocklach AP, sep CP 1866.[4] Organisation as for Church Shocklach.

SHOTWICK
AP Incl tp Capenhurst (sep CP 1866,[4] sep EP 1859 from Shotwick AP [tp Capenhurst], Neston AP [tp Ledsham])[158]), tp Great Saughall (sep CP 1866,[4] eccl severed 1921 and united with eccl ex-par Shotwick Park as 'Great Saughall' EP[330]), tps Little Saughall, Woodbank (each a sep CP 1866[4]). *LG* Seq 26. *Parl* Seq 19. *Eccl* Wirral RDn (until 1880), Chester RDn (1880—88), Wirral RDn (1888—1935), Wirral South RDn (1935—*).

SHOTWICK PARK
Ex-par place, sep CP 1858,[10] eccl abol 1921 to help cr Great Saughall EP.[332] *LG* Seq 26. *Parl* Seq 19.

SHURLACH
Tp in Davenham AP, sep CP 1866.[4] *LG* Northw. Hd, PLU, RSD. Bdry: 1883.[56] Abol 1892 ent to Rudheath CP.[92] *Parl* S'rn Dv (1832—67), Mid Dv (1867—85), Knutsf. Dv (1885—1918).

SIDDINGTON
Tp in Prestbury AP, sep CP 1866,[4] sep EP 1728.[3] *LG* Seq 17. Civ bdry: 1936 (gains Capesthorne CP).[7] *Parl* Seq 7. *Eccl* Maccl. RDn. Abol 1846 to help cr Capesthorne with Siddington EP.[159]

SMALLWOOD
Tp in Astbury AP, sep CP 1866,[4] sep EP 1848.[3] *LG* Seq 22. *Parl* Seq 9. *Eccl* Middlew. RDn (1848—80), Congl. RDn (1880—*).

SNELSON
Tp (Maccl. Hd) in Rostherne AP (o'wise Buckl. Hd), sep CP 1866.[4] *LG* Seq 17. *Parl* Seq 7.

SOMERFORD
Tp in Astbury AP, sep CP 1866.[4] *LG* Seq 22. Bdry: 1895 (gains Radnor CP).[318] *Parl* Seq 12.

SOMERFORD BOOTHS
Tp in Astbury AP, sep CP 1866,[4] eccl severed 1878 to help cr Hulme Walfield EP.[39] *LG* Maccl. Hd, Congl. PLU, RSD, RD. *Parl* N'rn Dv (1832—67), North Dv (1867—85), Knutsf. Dv/CC (1885—*).

SOUND
Tp orig in Acton AP, then pt in Acton AP, pt in Wrenbury cum Frith CP (after latter gains sep civ identity from Acton; the area eccl, 'Wrenbury'), 'Sound' a sep CP 1866.[4] *LG* Seq 18. *Parl* Seq 21.

SPITAL BOUGHTON
Ex-par place, sep CP 1858.[10] *LG* Chester Bor/MB,

Chester PLU (1869—84), USD. Abol civ 1884 to help cr Chester CP.[173] *Parl* Chester Parl Bor (1553—85).

SPROSTON

Tp in Middlewich AP, sep CP 1866.[4] *LG* Seq 21. Bdry: 1892 (gains Mooresbarrow with Parme CP),[92] 1936.[7] *Parl* Seq 13.

SPURSTOW

Tp in Bunbury AP, sep CP 1866.[4] *LG* Seq 13. Bdry: 1888.[6] *Parl* Seq 21.

STALYBRIDGE

CP Cr 1894 by union of the following in Stalybr. MB: ent Stayley CP, pt Dukinfield CP, pt (prev to 1889 in Lancs) Ashton under Lyne AP.[42] *LG* Ashton under Lyne PLU, Stalybr. MB. Bdry: 1936.[7] Transf 1974 to Gtr Manch.[28] *Parl* Stalybr. & Hyde Dv/CC (1918—*).

STALYBRIDGE ST PAUL

Tp 'Stayley' in Mottram AP (eccl, 'Mottram in Longendale') a sep CP 1866,[4] sep EP 1840 as 'Stalybridge St Paul'.[305] Maccl. RDn (1840—73), Maccl. North RDn (1873—80), Stockpt. RDn (1880—88), Mott. RDn (1888—*). Bdry: 1848 (help cr Friezeland EP to be in dioc Manch),[239] 1863 (cr Millbrook EP),[124] 1959.[163]

STANLOW

Ex-par place, sep CP 1858.[10] *LG* Wirral Hd, Gt Bough. PLU (1837—71), Chester PLU (1871—1911), RSD, RD (1894—1910), Ellesm. Port & Whitby UD (1910—11). Civ bdry: 1888.[331] Abol civ 1911 ent to Great Stanney CP.[230] *Parl* S'rn Dv (1832—67), South Dv (1867—85), Edd. Dv (1885—1918).

GREAT STANNEY

Ex-par place, sep CP 1858,[10] abol eccl 1964 ent to Ellesmere Port EP.[227] *LG* Edd. Hd, Gt Bough. PLU (1837—71), Chester PLU (1871—1930), RSD, RD (1894—1910), Ellesm. Port & Whitby UD (1910—33), Ellesm. Port UD (1933—50). Civ bdry: 1888,[331] 1911 (gains Stanlow CP).[230] Abol civ 1950 ent to Ellesmere Port CP.[231] *Parl* S'rn Dv (1832—67), South Dv (1867—85), Edd. Dv (1885—1918), Wirral Dv/CC (1918—70).

LITTLE STANNEY

Tp in Stoke AP, sep CP 1866.[4] *LG* Seq 25. Bdry: 1963,[232] 1967.[233] *Parl* Seq 19.

STANTHORNE

Tp in Davenham AP, sep CP 1866.[4] *LG* Seq 21. Bdry: 1936 (incl loses pt to Winsford UD to help cr Winsford CP).[7] *Parl* S'rn Dv (1832—67), Mid Dv (1867—85), Northw. Dv/CC (1885—1955), Nantw. CC (1955—*).

STAPELEY

Tp in Wybunbury AP, sep CP 1866.[4] *LG* Seq 18. Bdry: 1936,[7] 1938.[42] *Parl* Seq 18.

BRUEN STAPLEFORD

Tp in Tarvin AP, sep CP 1866.[4] *LG* Seq 12. Bdry: 1963.[66] *Parl* Seq 22.

FOULK STAPLEFORD

Tp (Brox. Hd) in Tarvin AP (o'wise Edd. Hd), sep CP 1866,[4] eccl severed 1878 to help cr Hargrave EP.[48] *LG* Seq 3. Bdry: 1963.[66] *Parl* Seq 22.

STAYLEY

Tp in Mottram AP (eccl, 'Mottram in Longendale'), sep CP 1866,[4] sep EP 1840 as 'Stalybridge St Paul',[305] qv. *LG* Maccl. Hd, Ashton under Lyne PLU, pt Stalybr. MB & USD ([Lancs, Ches] 1857—94 [enlarged pt 1881—94]), pt Stayley USD (1875—81), pt Stalybr. USD (enlarged pt 1881—94), pt Mossley USD (Lancs, Ches 1875—85; Lancs, Ches, Yorks W Riding 1885—94), pt Mossley MB (Lancs, Ches, Yorks W Riding 1885—89, ent Lancs 1889—94). The pt in Mossley MB becomes 1889 pt of Lancs (that pt abol 1894 to help cr Mossley CP in Lancs[211]) and Stayley ent Ches 1889—94. Abol 1894 to help Stalybridge CP.[42] *Parl* N'rn Dv (1832—67), pt Stalybr. Parl Bor ([Lancs, Ches, Yorks W Riding] 1867—1918), pt North Dv (1867—85), pt Hyde Dv (1885—1918).

STOAK

AP Usual eccl spelling; for civ and civ sep tps, see 'Stoke'. *Eccl* Wirral RDn (until 1880), Chester RDn (1880—1935), Wirral South RDn (1935—71). Eccl bdry: 1967.[228] Abol eccl 1971 ent to Ellesmere Port EP.[229]

STOCKHAM

Tp in Runcorn AP, sep CP 1866.[4] *LG* Buckl. Hd, Runc. PLU, RSD, RD. Abol 1936 ent to Norton CP.[7] *Parl* N'rn Dv (1832—67), Mid Dv (1867—85), Northw. Dv (1885—1948).

STOCKPORT

The following have 'Stockport' in their names. Insofar as any existed at a given time: *LG* Maccl. Hd, Stockpt. PLU, Bor/MB,CB, USD. *Parl* Stockpt. Parl Bor (1832—1948), pt Stockpt. North BC, pt Stockpt. South BC (1948—*) (see Part III of the *Guide* for composition of BCs by wards of the CB). *Eccl* Maccl. RDn (until 1873), Maccl. North RDn (1873—80), Stockpt. RDn (1880—*).

AP1—STOCKPORT [ST MARY]—Incl chap Disley (sep CP 1866,[4] sep EP 1741 [incl tp Newtown, not sep civ],[3] eccl refounded 1913[212]), chap Dukinfield (sep CP 1866,[4] pt a sep EP 1846 as 'Dukinfield',[196] the remainder cr 1846 'Castle Hall' EP[162]), chap Hyde (sep CP 1866,[4] pt cr 1846 'Hyde' EP[67]), chap Marple (sep CP 1866,[4] sep EP 1738,[3] pts of the latter severed 1860, 1870 [qv], the remainder eccl refounded 1876 as 'Marple'[73]), chap Norbury (sep CP 1866,[4] sep EP 1737,[3] eccl refounded 1843[218]), chap Romiley (sep CP 1866,[4] pt cr 1745 'Chadkirk' EP,[3] as such eccl refounded 1876,[164] the remainder of orig area chap Romiley transf 1877 to Werneth EP[320]), tp Bramhall (sep CP 1866,[4] eccl severed 1827 to help cr EP7,[3] the latter refounded 1839,[125] 'Bramhall' a sep EP 1911 from EP7[29]), tp Bredbury (sep CP 1866,[4] sep EP 1846[67]), tp Brinnington (sep CP 1866,[4] pt eccl severed 1844 to cr Portwood EP,[137] 'Brinnington' a sep EP 1963 from Portwood EP, Bredbury EP[128]), tp Stockport Etchells (sep CP 1866,[4] eccl severed 1827 to help cr EP7,[3] the latter refounded 1839,[125] the area of the orig tp severed 1882 from EP7 as 'Gatley' EP[236]), tp Offerton (sep CP 1866[4]), tp Torkington (sep CP 1866,[4] pt eccl severed 1860 to help cr High Lane EP,[51] the remainder eccl severed 1878 and transf to Norbury EP[118]), tp Werneth (sep CP 1866,[4] sep EP 1841[333]). Addtl civ bdry alt: 1894 (gains the pts in the CB of Brinnington CP, Cheadle CP [both orig Ches], Heaton Norris CP [orig Lancs]),[138] 1901 (gains pts Bredbury CP, Brinnington CP, Cheadle CP, Hazel Grove and Bramhall CP [all Ches], Heaton Norris CP [Lancs]),[126] 1913 (gains Heaton Norris UD & CP, Lancs, to be a constituent par in Stockpt. CB),[334] 1935 (incl gains Heaton Norris CP, Reddish CP [orig Lancs, in Stockpt. CB 1901—35]),[264] 1936 (incl loses pt to Marple UD & CP),[7] 1937 (exchanges pts with Denton UD & CP, Lancs),[335] 1952 (gains pt Bredbury & Romiley UD & CP, Ches).[129] Transf 1974 to Gtr Manch.[28] Parl bdry: 1953.[130] Addtl eccl bdry alt: 1765 (cr EP5,[3] refounded 1839[125]), 1827 (cr EP7,[3] refounded 1839[125]), 1843 (cr Hyde St George EP, cr Dukinfield St John the Evangelist EP),[218] 1852,[312] 1876,[164] 1881 (help cr Haughton St Anne EP [Lancs, Ches]),[263] 1893 (help cr EP1),[101] 1963 (help cr Wythenshawe The William Temple Church EP, to be dioc Manch).[79]

EP1—STOCKPORT HALL STREET—Cr 1893 from AP1, Bredbury EP.[101] Bdry: 1895,[336] 1934 (help cr EP6).[337]

EP2—STOCKPORT ST GEORGE—Cr 1897 from EP7.[98] Bdry: 1934 (help cr EP6),[337] 1937.[166]

EP3—STOCKPORT ST MARK—Cr 1911 from EP4.[338]

EP4—STOCKPORT ST MATTHEW—Cr 1844 from EP7.[137] Bdry: 1852,[312] 1893 (help cr Brinksway EP),[116] 1907,[165] 1911 (cr EP3).[338]

EP5—STOCKPORT ST PETER—Cr 1765 from AP1,[3] refounded 1839.[125] Bdry: 1893 (help cr Brinksway EP).[116]

EP6—STOCKPORT ST SAVIOUR—Cr 1934 from EP2, EP1.[337]

EP7—STOCKPORT ST THOMAS—Cr 1827 from AP1 (incl tp Bramhall and tp Stockport Etchells in the same par),[3] refounded 1839.[125] Bdry: 1844 (cr EP4),[137] 1878,[118] 1882 (area of orig tp Stockport Etchells severed to cr Gatley EP),[236] 1897 (cr EP2),[98] 1911 (area of orig tp Bramhall severed to cr Bramhall EP).[29]

STOCKTON
    Tp in Malpas AP, sep CP 1866.[4] LG Seq 7. Parl Seq 23.

STOCKTON HEATH
    EP Cr 1838 from Great Budworth AP, Runcorn AP (both Ches), Warrington AP (Lancs).[150] Frod. RDn (1838—69), Frod. West RDn (1869—80), Frod. RDn (1880—1935), Gt Budw. RDn (1935—*). Bdry: 1879 (help cr Walton EP),[11] 1963,[339] 1968.[190]
    CP Cr 1897 from Appleton EP.[38] LG Runc. PLU, RD. Bdry: 1933 (loses pt to Warr. CB [assoc with Lancs] & AP),[254] 1936 (gains Latchford Without CP),[7] 1953.[255] Parl Knutsf. Dv (1918—48), Runc. CC (1948—*).

STOKE
    AP Usual civ spelling; for eccl, see 'Stoak'. Incl tp Little Stanney, pt tp Whitby (each a sep CP 1866[4]). LG Seq 25. Addtl civ bdry alt: 1963.[66] Parl Seq 19.

STOKE
    Tp in Acton AP, sep CP 1866.[4] LG Seq 18. Parl Seq 21.

STORETON
    Tp in Bebington AP, sep CP 1866.[4] LG Wirral Hd, PLU, RSD, RD (1894—1933), Beb. UD (1933—37), MB (1937—74). Transf 1974 to Merseyside.[28] Parl Seq 28.

STRETTON
    Chap in Great Budworth AP, sep CP 1866,[4] sep EP 1830,[3] eccl refounded 1834.[145] LG Seq 10. Parl Seq 3. Eccl Frod. RDn (1830—69), Frod. West RDn (1869—80), Frod. RDn (1880—1935), Gt Budw. RDn (1935—*). Eccl bdry: 1887 (cr Appleton Thorn EP).[39]

STRETTON
    Tp in Tilston AP, sep CP 1866.[4] LG Seq 3. Parl Seq 23.

STUBLACH
    Tp in Middlewich AP, sep CP 1866.[4] LG Northw. Hd, PLU, RSD. Bdry: 1889.[271] Abol 1892 ent to Lach Dennis CP.[92] Parl S'rn Dv (1832—67), Mid Dv (1867—85), Knutsf. Dv (1885—1918).

STYAL
    CP Cr 1894 from the pt of Pownall Fee CP not in Wilmslow UD.[19] LG Altr. PLU (1894—95), RD (1894—95), Buckl. PLU (1895—1930), RD (1895—1936). Abol 1936 pt to Wilmslow UD & CP, pt to Mobberley AP.[7] Parl Knutsf. Dv (1918—48).

SUTTON
    Tp in Middlewich AP, sep CP 1866.[4] LG Northw. Hd, PLU, RSD. Abol 1892 ent to Newton CP.[92] Parl S'rn Dv (1832—67), Mid Dv (1867—85), Edd. Dv (1885—1918).

SUTTON
    Chap in Prestbury AP, sep CP 1866,[4] pt cr 1835 Sutton St George EP,[276] the remainder cr 1859 Sutton St James EP,[3] both qv. LG Maccl. Hd, PLU, pt Maccl. MB (1835—94), pt Maccl. USD, pt Maccl. RSD, Maccl. RD. Bdry: 1894 (loses the pt in the UD to Macclesfield CP),[273] 1936.[7] Parl Pt Maccl. Parl Bor (1832—85), pt N'rn Dv (1832—67), pt North Dv (1867—85), Maccl. Dv/CC (1885—*).

SUTTON
    Tp in Runcorn AP, sep CP 1866,[4] eccl severed 1861 to help cr Aston EP.[53] LG Seq 10. Bdry: 1936,[7] 1955,[258] 1967.[52] Parl Seq 5.

GREAT SUTTON
    Tp in Eastham AP, sep CP 1866,[4] sep EP 1880.[222] LG Wirral Hd, PLU, RSD, RD (1894—1933), Ellesm. Port UD (1933—50). Civ bdry: 1889.[309] Abol civ 1950 ent to Ellesmere Port CP.[231] Parl S'rn Dv (1832—67), South Dv (1867—85), Wirral Dv/CC (1885—1970). Eccl Chester RDn (1880—88), Wirral RDn (1888—1935), Wirral South RDn (1935—*).

GUILDEN SUTTON

AP *LG* Seq 4. Civ bdry: 1936,[7] 1954,[174] 1963.[66] *Parl* Seq 20. *Eccl* Seq 2.

LITTLE SUTTON

Tp in Eastham AP, sep CP 1866,[4] eccl severed 1862 to help cr Hooton EP.[220] *LG* Wirral Hd, PLU, RSD, RD (1894—1933), Ellesm. Port UD (1933—50). Bdry: 1933.[69] Abol 1950 ent to Ellesmere Port CP.[231] *Parl* S'rn Dv (1832—67), South Dv (1867—85), Wirral Dv/CC (1885—1970).

SUTTON ST GEORGE

EP Cr 1835 from pt chap Sutton in Prestbury AP.[276] Maccl. RDn (1835—73), Maccl. South RDn (1873—80), Maccl. RDn (1880—*). Bdry: 1962.[245]

SUTTON ST JAMES

EP Cr 1859 from the pt of chap Sutton in Prestbury AP not cr 1835 Sutton St George.[3] RDns as for Sutton St George, from 1859.

SWETTENHAM

AP Incl tp Kermincham (sep CP 1866[4]). *LG* Seq 22. Addtl civ bdry alt: 1936 (gains Kermincham CP).[7] *Parl* Seq 12. *Eccl* Middlew. RDn (until 1880), Congl. RDn (1880—1971). Eccl bdry: 1880 (gains tp Davenport from Astbury AP).[49] Abol eccl 1971 to help cr Brereton with Swettenham EP.[131]

OVER TABLEY

Tp in Rostherne AP, sep EP 1855,[321] sep CP 1866 as 'Tabley Superior',[4] qv. *Eccl* Frod. RDn (1855—69), Frod. East RDn (1869—80), Bowdon RDn (1880—1935), Knutsf. RDn (1935—*). Eccl bdry: 1968,[116] 1973.[113]

TABLEY INFERIOR

Tp in Great Budworth AP, sep CP 1866.[4] *LG* Seq 8. Bdry: 1936.[7] *Parl* Seq 2.

TABLEY SUPERIOR

Tp in Rostherne AP, sep CP 1866.[4] sep EP 1855 as 'Over Tabley',[321] qv. *LG* Seq 8. Civ bdry: 1936.[7] *Parl* Seq 2.

TARPORLEY

AP Incl tps Eaton, Rushton, Utkinton (each a sep CP 1866[4]). *LG* Edd. Hd, Tarporley Bor, Nantw. PLU (1837—94), Tarv. PLU (1894—1930), Tarporley USD, UD (1894—1936), Northw. RD (1936—74). Addtl civ bdry alt: 1936.[7] *Parl* Seq 22. *Eccl* Chester RDn (until 1880), Middlew. RDn (1880—1954), Malpas RDn (1954—*).

TARVIN

AP Tp 'Tarvin' in Edd. Hd (sometimes early 'Tarvin with Oscroft') as were tps Ashton, Burton by Tarvin, Clotton Hoofield, Duddon, Hockenhull, Horton cum Peel (sometimes 'Little Mouldsworth'), Mouldsworth, Bruen Stapleford (each a sep CP 1866[4]), tp Kelsall (sep EP 1866,[4] eccl severed 1956 and united with pt Delamere EP to cr 'Kelsall' EP[210]); incl in Brox. Hd tp Foulk Stapleford (sep CP 1866,[4] eccl severed 1878 to help cr Hargrave EP[48]). *LG* Gt Bough. PLU (1837—71), Tarv. PLU (1871—1930), RSD, RD. Addtl civ bdry alt: 1963.[66] *Parl* Seq 22. *Eccl* Seq 2. Addtl eccl bdry alt: 1964 (gains ex-par Prior's Heys).[227]

TATTENHALL

AP Incl tps Golborne Bellow, Newton by Tattenhall (each a sep CP 1866[4]). *LG* Seq 3. *Parl* Seq 23. *Eccl*

Seq 1.

TATTON

Tp in Rostherne AP, sep CP 1866.[4] *LG* Seq 8. *Parl* Seq 2.

TAXAL

AP Incl tp Yeardsley cum Whaley (sep CP 1866[4]). *LG* Maccl. Hd, PLU, RSD, RD. Abol civ 1936 (by which time called 'Taxall') pt to Wildboarclough CP, Ches, pt to help cr Whaley Bridge UD & CP to be in Derbys, pt to Hartington Upper Quarter CP, Derbys.[213] *Parl* N'rn Dv (1832—67), North Dv (1867—85), Knutsf. Dv (1885—1918), Maccl. Dv (1918—48). *Eccl* Maccl. RDn (until 1873), Maccl. North RDn (1873—80), Stockpt. RDn (1880—1921). Abol eccl 1921 to help cr Taxal with Kettleshulme EP.[319]

TAXAL WITH KETTLESHULME

EP Cr 1921 by union Taxal AP, area Kettleshulme in Salterford cum Kettleshulme EP.[319] Stockpt. RDn. Bdry: 1923.[214]

TAXALL—see TAXAL

TETTON

Tp in Warmingham AP, sep CP 1866.[4] *LG* Northw. Hd, Congl. PLU, RSD, RD. Bdry: 1936 (incl gains Moston CP).[7] Abol 1970 to help cr Moston CP.[234] *Parl* Seq 11.

THELWALL

Chap in Runcorn AP, sep CP 1866,[4] sep EP 1737,[3] pt of the latter severed 1866 to help refound Latchford St James EP (Ches, Lancs),[252] the remainder refounded 1870 as 'Thelwall' EP.[322] *LG* Buckl. Hd, Runc. PLU (1836—45), Warr. PLU (1845—1930), pt Warr. MB ([Lancs, Ches] 1847—84), Warr. USD ([Lancs, Ches] 1875—84), Runc. RSD (1884—94), Runc. RD. Civ bdry: 1884 (loses the pt in Warr. MB & USD to Latchford CP),[286] 1885 (loses pt to Woolston with Martinscroft CP, Lancs),[340] 1933 (exchanges pts with Woolston with Martinscroft CP, Lancs).[13] Abol 1936 ent to Grappenhall AP.[7] *Parl* Warr. Parl Bor ([Lancs, Ches] 1832—85), Altr. Dv (1885—1918), Knutsf. Dv (1918—45). *Eccl* Frod. RDn (1737—1869), Frod. West RDn (1869—80), Frod. RDn (1880—1935), Gt Budw. RDn (1935—*).

THINGWALL

Tp in Woodchurch AP, sep CP 1866.[4] *LG* Wirral Hd, PLU, RSD, RD (1894—1928), Birk. CB (1928—33). Abol 1933 ent to Birkenhead CP.[40] *Parl* S'rn Dv (1832—67), South Dv (1867—85), Wirral Dv (1885—1948).

CHILDER THORNTON

Tp in Eastham AP, sep CP 1866,[4] eccl severed 1862 to help cr Hooton EP.[220] *LG* Wirral Hd, PLU, RSD, RD (1894—1933), Ellesm. Port UD (1933—50). Bdry: 1933 (incl gains pt Eastham AP, pt Willaston CP as enlarged area constituted Ellesm. Port UD, loses pt to Eastham AP to help cr Beb. UD).[40] Abol 1950 ent to Ellesmere Port CP.[231] *Parl* S'rn Dv (1832—67), South Dv (1867—85), Wirral Dv/CC (1885—1970).

THORNTON HOUGH

Tp in Neston AP, sep 1866,[4] eccl severed 1865 to help cr Willaston EP,[146] the orig area severed 1869 from Willaston EP and united with pt Neston AP (pt tp Raby and addtl pt of the AP), pt Bromborough AP (tp Brimstage) to cr 'Thornton Hough' EP.[136] *LG* Wirral Hd, PLU, RSD, RD (1894—1933), Beb. UD (1933—37), MB (1937—74). Civ bdry: 1933 (incl loses pt Neston cum Parkgate CP to help cr Neston UD).[69] Transf 1974 to Merseyside.[28] *Parl* Seq 28. *Eccl* Wirral RDn (1869—1935), Wirral South RDn (1935—*). Eccl bdry: 1905.[341]

THORNTON LE MOORS

AP Incl tp Dunham on the Hill, tp Hapsford (each a sep CP 1866,[4] the 2 eccl united 1888 to cr 'Dunham on the Hill EP'[219]), tps Elton, Wimbolds Trafford (each a sep CP 1866[4]). *LG* Seq 11. Addtl civ bdry alt: 1933,[40] 1963.[66] *Parl* Seq 19. *Eccl* Chester RDn (until 1935), Frod. RDn (1935—71). Abol eccl 1971 ent to Ellesmere Port EP.[229]

THREAPWOOD

Ex-par place, pt Flints (Maylor Hd), pt Ches (Brox. Hd), made 1896 ent Ches,[342] although eccl ex-par considered a sep benefice, eccl refounded as sep par 1968.[343] *LG* Wrex. PLU (1837—94), RSD, Whitch. PLU (1894—1930), Malpas RD (pt 1894—96, ent 1896—1936), pt sep RD in Flints (1894—96), Tarv. RD (1936—74). *Parl* Seq 23. *Eccl* Malpas RDn (1968—*).

THURSTASTON

AP Incl pt tp Greasby (sep CP 1866,[4] eccl severed 1861 to help cr Frankby EP[237]), pt tp Irby (sep CP 1866[4]). *LG* Wirral Hd, PLU, RSD, RD (1894—1933), UD (1933—74). Transf 1974 to Merseyside.[28] *Parl* Seq 26. *Eccl* Seq 10. Addtl eccl bdry alt: 1874,[280] 1959.[63]

TILSTON

AP Incl tps Carden, Grafton, Horton, Stretton (each a sep CP 1866[4]). *LG* Seq 3. *Parl* Seq 23. *Eccl* Seq 1.

TILSTONE FEARNALL

Chap in Bunbury AP, sep CP 1866,[4] sep EP 1837.[22] *LG* Seq 14. Civ bdry: 1936.[7] *Parl* Seq 22. *Eccl* Nantw. RDn (1837—88), Malpas RDn (1888—*). Eccl bdry: 1901 (gains tps Alpraham, Tiverton from Bunbury AP).[22]

TIMPERLEY

Tp in Bowdon AP, sep CP 1866,[4] sep EP 1852.[122] *LG* Buckl. Hd, Altr. PLU (1836—95), RSD, RD (1894—95), Buckl. PLU (1895—1930), RD (1895—1936). Abol 1936 pt to Altr. UD & CP, pt to Hale UD & CP, pt to Sale MB & CP.[7] *Parl* N'rn Dv (1832—67), Mid Dv (1867—85), Altr. Dv (1885—1945), Buckl. Dv (1945—48). *Eccl* Frod. RDn (1852—69), Frod. East RDn (1869—80), Bowdon RDn (1880—*). Eccl bdry: 1867 (help cr Altrincham St John the Evangelist EP).[30] 1868 (help refound Baguley EP).[57]

TINTWISTLE

Tp in Mottram (eccl, 'Mottram in Longendale') AP, sep CP 1866,[4] sep EP 1840 (incl tp Hollingworth in same par).[3] *LG* Maccl. Hd, Ashton under Lyne PLU, pt Mossley MB ([Lancs, Ches] 1885—94), pt Mossley USD (Lancs, Ches 1875—85; Lancs, Ches, Yorks W Riding 1885—89, ent Lancs 1889—94), pt Ashton under Lyne RSD, Tintw. RD. The pt in Mossley MB becomes 1889 pt of Lancs (that pt

abol 1894 to help cr Mossley CP in Lancs[211]) and Tintwistle ent Ches thereafter. Transf 1974 to Derbys.[28] *Parl* N'rn Dv (1832—67), North Dv (1867—85), Hyde Dv (1885—1918), Stalybr. & Hyde Dv/CC (1918—*). *Eccl* Maccl. RDn (1840—73), Maccl. North RDn (1873—80), Stockpt. RDn (1880—88), Mott. RDn (1888—*). Eccl bdry: 1922 (orig area tp Hollingworth severed to cr Hollingworth EP).[267]

TITTENLEY

Tp in Audlem AP, sep CP 1866.[4] *LG* Nantw. Hd, Mkt. Dray. PLU, RSD, sep RD in Ches (1894—95). Transf 1895 to Salop.[344] *Parl* S'rn Dv (1832—67), South Dv (1867—85), Edd. Dv (1885—1918).

TIVERTON

Tp in Bunbury AP, sep CP 1866,[4] eccl transf 1901 to Tilstone Fearnall EP.[22] *LG* Seq 14. *Parl* Seq 22.

TOFT

Tp in Knutsford AP, sep CP 1866,[4] sep EP 1854,[3] eccl refounded 1855.[281] *LG* Seq 8. Civ bdry: 1936.[7] *Parl* Seq 2. *Eccl* Frod. RDn (1854—69), Frod. East RDn (1869—80), Bowdon RDn (1880—1935), Knutsf. RDn (1935—*). Eccl bdry: 1968.[116]

TORKINGTON

Tp in Stockport AP, sep CP 1866,[4] pt eccl severed 1860 to help cr High Lane EP,[51] the remainder transf 1878 to Norbury EP.[118] *LG* Maccl. Hd, Stockpt. PLU, RSD, RD. Abol civ 1900 to help cr Hazel Grove and Bramhall UD & CP.[119] *Parl* N'rn Dv (1832—67), North Dv (1867—85), Hyde Dv (1885—1918).

BRIDGE TRAFFORD

Tp (Edd. Hd) in Plemstall AP (o'wise Brox. Hd), sep CP 1866.[4] *LG* Seq 11. Bdry: 1888,[331] 1963.[66] *Parl* Seq 19.

MICKLE TRAFFORD

Tp in Plemstall AP, sep CP 1866.[4] *LG* Seq 1. Bdry: 1963.[66] *Parl* Seq 19.

WIMBOLDS TRAFFORD

Tp in Thornton le Moors AP, sep CP 1866.[4] *LG* Seq 11. Bdry: 1888,[331] 1963.[66] *Parl* Seq 19.

TRANMERE

Chap in Bebington AP (eccl, 'Nether Bebington'), sep CP 1866,[4] sep EP 1842.[71] *LG* Wirral Hd, PLU (1836—91), RSD (1875—77), Birk. PLU (1891—98), MB (1877—89), CB (1889—98), USD (1877—94). Abol civ 1898 ent to Birkenhead CP.[74] *Parl* S'rn Dv (1832—59), Birk. Parl Bor (1859—1918). *Eccl* Wirral RDn (1842—88), Birk. RDn (1888—*). Eccl bdry: 1858 (cr Tranmere St Paul EP),[345] 1881,[97] 1883 (help cr Lower Tranmere EP),[346] 1902 (help cr Prenton EP),[311] 1912 (help cr Claughton St Michael and All Angels EP).[193]

LOWER TRANMERE

EP Cr 1883 from Tranmere EP, Tranmere St Paul EP.[346] Wirral RDn (1883—88), Birk. RDn (1888—1971). Abol 1971 to help cr Tranmere St Paul with St Luke EP.[347]

TRANMERE ST PAUL

EP Cr 1858 from Tranmere EP.[345] Wirral RDn (1858—88), Birk. RDn (1888—1971). Bdry: 1883 (help cr Lower Tranmere EP).[346] Bdry: 1900,[14] 1902 (help cr Prenton EP).[311] Abol 1971 to help cr

Tranmere St Paul with St Luke EP).[347]

TRANMERE ST PAUL WITH ST LUKE
EP Cr 1971 by union Tranmere St Paul EP, Lower Tranmere EP.[347] Birk. RDn.

TUSHINGHAM CUM GRINDLEY
Tp in Malpas AP (sometimes 'Tushingham' or 'Tushingham with Grindley'), sep CP 1866,[4] sep EP 1824 as 'Malpas St Chad', qv, by union of this tp and 4 others in Malpas: Agden, Bradley, Chidlow, Macefen,[3] as such eccl refounded 1860.[15] *LG* Seq 6. *Parl* N'rn Dv (1832—67), North Dv (1867—85), Edd. Dv (1885—1948), Northw. CC (1948—55), Nantw. CC (1955—*).

TWEMLOW
Tp in Sandbach AP, sep CP 1866.[4] *LG* Seq 22. Bdry: 1889.[203] *Parl* Seq 12.

TYTHERINGTON
Tp in Prestbury AP, sep CP 1866.[4] *LG* Maccl. Hd, PLU, RSD, RD. Abol 1936 pt to Maccl. MB & CP, pt to Bollington CP.[7] *Parl* N'rn Dv (1832—67), pt Maccl. Parl Bor (1867—85), pt North Dv (1867—85), Knutsf. Dv (1885—1948).

UNNAMED
CP Cr 1894 from the pt of Bowdon AP gained 1883 from Bollington CP (a former detached pt of latter) but not made pt of Bowdon USD.[123] *LG* Altr. PLU (1894—95), RD (1894—95), Buckl. PLU (1895—1930), RD (1895—1936). Abol 1936 ent to Bowdon UD & AP.[7] *Parl* Altr. Dv (1918—45), Buckl. Dv (1945—48).

UNNAMED
CP Cr 1894 from pt of the pt of Marton CP gained 1883 from Over AP (a former detached pt of latter) which became pt of Winsford USD.[123] *LG* Northw. PLU, Winsford UD. Abol 1936 to help cr Winsford CP.[7] *Parl* Northw. Dv (1918—48).

UNNAMED
CP Cr 1894 from pt of the pt of Marton CP gained 1883 from Over AP (a former detached pt of latter) but not made pt of Winsford USD.[123] *LG* Northw. PLU, RD. Abol 1936 to help cr Winsford CP.[7] *Parl* Northw. Dv (1918—48).

UPTON—see UPTON BY CHESTER

UPTON
Tp in Prestbury AP, sep CP 1866.[4] *LG* Maccl. Hd, PLU, RSD, RD. Abol 1936 pt to Maccl. MB & CP, pt to Prestbury AP.[7] *Parl* N'rn Dv (1832—67), North Dv (1867—85), Knutsf. Dv (1885—1948).

UPTON BY BIRKENHEAD
AP *LG* Wirral Hd, PLU, RSD, RD. Abol civ 1933 pt to Birk. CB (assoc with Ches) & CP, pt to Wall. CB (assoc with Ches) & AP.[40] *Parl* S'rn Dv (1832—67), South Dv (1867—85), Wirral Dv (1885—1948). *Eccl* Seq 10. Eccl bdry: 1969.[103]

UPTON BY CHESTER
Chap or tp in Chester St Mary on the Hill AP, orig a sep rectory as 'Overchurch' (Brox. Hd, Middlew. RDn) appropriated to Dean and Chapter of Chester, after Dissolution considered in Chester St Mary on the Hill, sep CP 1866 as 'Upton',[4] sep EP 1743 as 'Upton' (tp Moston, tp Mollington Banastre [sometimes Little Mollington], gtr pt of tp Upton),[3] as such refounded 1882 from Chester St Mary on the

Hill AP, Chester St Oswald AP (remainder of tp Upton, pt tp Blacon with Crabwall).[107] *LG* Seq 1. Civ bdry: 1954 (loses pt to Chester CB [assoc with Ches] & CP).[174] *Parl* Seq 19. *Eccl* Wirral RDn (1743—1935), Wirral North RDn (1935—*).

UTKINTON
Tp in Tarporley AP, sep CP 1866.[4] *LG* Edd. Hd, Nantw. PLU (1837—94), Tarv. PLU (1894—1930), Tarporley USD, UD (1894—1936), Northw. RD (1936—74). Bdry: 1936.[7] *Parl* Seq 22.

WALGHERTON
Tp in Wybunbury AP, sep CP 1866.[4] *LG* Seq 18. *Parl* Seq 21.

WALLASEY
AP Incl tp Liscard (sep CP 1866,[4] pt a sep EP 1878[290]), tp Poulton cum Seacombe (sep CP 1866,[4] sep EP [orig as 'Poolton'] 1907 as 'Poulton'[314]). *LG* Wirral Hd, PLU (1836—91), Birk. PLU (1891—1930), Wall. USD, UD (1894—1910), MB (1910—13), CB (1913—74). Addtl civ bdry alt: 1912 (gains Liscard CP, Poulton cum Seacombe CP),[291] 1928 (gains pt Bidston cum Ford AP, ent Moreton CP),[90] 1933.[40] Transf 1974 to Merseyside.[28] *Parl* S'rn Dv (1832—67), South Dv (1867—85), Wirral Dv (1885—1918), Wall. Parl Bor/BC (1918—*). *Eccl* Wirral RDn (until 1888), Birk. RDn (1888—1907), Wall. RDn (1907—*). Addtl eccl bdry alt: 1847 (cr Seacombe EP),[332] 1861 (cr New Brighton St James EP),[134] 1884 (help cr Egremont (otherwise Liscard) EP),[224] 1907,[135] 1912 (cr Wallasey St Nicholas EP),[268] 1929 (help cr New Brighton All Saints EP),[132] 1957 (help cr Leasowe EP).[88]

WALLASEY ST NICHOLAS
EP Cr 1912 from Wallasey AP.[268] Wall. RDn. Bdry: 1957 (help cr Leasowe EP).[88]

WALLERSCOAT
Tp in Weaverham cum Milton (eccl, 'Weaverham') AP, sep CP 1866.[4] *LG* Edd. Hd, Northw. PLU, RSD. Abol 1892 ent to Winnington CP.[92] *Parl* S'rn Dv (1832—67), South Dv (1867—85), Northw. Dv (1885—1918).

WALTON
CP Cr 1936 by union Walton Superior CP, Acton Grange CP, Walton Inferior CP.[7] *LG* Runc. RD. *Parl* Runc. CC (1948—*).
EP Cr 1879 from Daresbury EP (incl pt orig tp Acton Grange, pt orig tp Moore), Stockton Heath EP (Ches, Lancs).[11] Frod. West RDn (1879—80), Frod. RDn (1880—1935), Gt Budw. RDn (1935—*). Bdry: 1963.[339]

WALTON INFERIOR
Tp in Runcorn AP, sep CP 1866.[4] *LG* Buckl. Hd, Runc. PLU, RSD, RD. Bdry: 1896 (loses pt to Warr. CB [assoc with Lancs] and to Latchford CP),[37] 1933 (loses pt to Warr. CB [assoc with Lancs] & AP).[254] Abol 1936 to help cr Walton CP.[7] *Parl* N'rn Dv (1832—67), Mid Dv (1867—85), Knutsf. Dv (1885—1948).

WALTON SUPERIOR
Tp in Runcorn AP, sep CP 1866.[4] *LG* Buckl. Hd, Runc. PLU, RSD, RD. Abol 1936 to help cr Walton CP.[7] *Parl* As for Walton Inferior.

WARBURTON

AP Orig sep AP, after Dissolution free chap of Warburton presented with Lymm AP, sep civ identity retained, ent sep eccl 1869.[292] *LG* Seq 8. Civ bdry: 1920 (loses pt to Rixton with Glazebrook CP, Lancs),[160] 1933 (incl exchanges pts with Rixton with Glazebrook CP, Lancs).[13] Transf 1974 to Gtr Manch.[28] *Parl* Seq 1. Parl bdry: 1945.[161] *Eccl* Ford. RDn (when AP), Frod. East RDn (1869—80), Bowdon RDn (1880—*).

WARDLE

Tp in Bunbury AP, sep CP 1866.[4] *LG* Seq 13. *Parl* Seq 21.

GREAT WARFORD

Tp in Alderley AP, sep CP 1866.[4] *LG* Seq 17. Bdry: 1936.[7] *Parl* Seq 7.

LITTLE WARFORD

CP Cr 1951 when Marthall cum Warford CP divided into 2 CPs of 'Marthall', 'Little Warford'.[302] *LG* Buckl. RD. *Parl* Knutsf. CC (1955—*).

WARMINGHAM

AP Incl tps Elton, Moston, Tetton (each a sep CP 1866[4]). *LG* Seq 23. Addtl civ bdry alt: 1936.[7] *Parl* Seq 10. *Eccl* Seq 8. Eccl bdry: 1847 (help cr Elworth EP).[235]

WAVERTON

AP Incl tp Hatton (sep CP 1866[4]), tp Huxley (sep CP 1866,[4] eccl severed 1878 to help cr Hargrave EP[48]). *LG* Seq 3. Addtl civ bdry alt: 1888.[157] *Parl* Seq 22. *Eccl* Chester RDn (until 1935), Malpas RDn (1935—*).

WEAVER

Tp (Edd. Hd) in Middlewich AP (o'wise Northw. Hd), sep CP 1866.[4] *LG* Edd. Hd, Northw. PLU, RSD. Abol 1892 ent to Darnhall CP.[92] *Parl* S'rn Dv (1832—67), South Dv (1867—85), Edd. Dv (1885—1918).

WEAVERHAM

AP Usual eccl spelling; for civ and sep chap and tps, see following entry. *Eccl* Frod. RDn (until 1869), Frod. West RDn (1869—88), Middlew. RDn (1888—*). Addtl eccl bdry alt: 1935 (help cr Sandiway EP).[165]

WEAVERHAM CUM MILTON

AP Usual civ spelling; for eccl see prev entry. Incl pt chap Hartford ([remainder in Great Budworth AP] sep CP 1866,[4] eccl in chap Witton [sep EP 1723 from Great Budworth AP (qv for other constituent pts)], 'Hartford' a sep EP 1825 from Witton EP,[3] refounded 1863[124]), tp Crowton (sep CP 1866,[4] sep EP 1872 from Weaverham AP, Norley EP[204]), tps Acton, Cuddington, Onston, Wallerscoat (each a sep CP 1866[4]). In 1871 census tp Weaverham reported to be pt in this AP, pt in Whitegate AP, o'wise and generally considered ent in this AP. *LG* Seq 15. Addtl civ bdry alt: 1936.[7] *Parl* Seq 25.

WERNETH

Tp in Stockport AP, sep CP 1866,[4] sep EP 1841.[333] *LG* Maccl. Hd, Stockpt. PLU, pt Hyde MB (1881—94), pt Hyde USD, pt Stockpt. RSD, Stockpt. RD. Civ bdry: 1894 (loses the pt in the MB to Hyde CP).[274a] Renamed 1897 'Compstall' CP.[194] *Parl* N'rn Dv (1832—67), North Dv (1867—85), Hyde Dv (1885—1918). *Eccl* Maccl. RDn (1851—73),

Maccl. North RDn (1873—80), Stockpt. RDn (1880—88), Mott. RDn (1888—1935), Stockpt. RDn (1935—*). Eccl bdry: 1877,[320] 1880 (help cr Gee Cross EP).[12]

WERVIN

Tp in Chester St Oswald AP, sep CP 1866.[4] *LG* Seq 1. Bdry: 1963.[66] *Parl* Seq 19.

WESTON

Tp in Runcorn AP, sep CP 1866.[4] *LG* Buckl. Hd, Runc. PLU, RSD, RD. Abol 1936 ent to Runcorn AP.[7] *Parl* N'rn Dv (1832—67), Mid Dv (1867—85), Crewe Dv (1885—1918), Northw. Dv (1918—48).

WESTON

Tp in Wybunbury AP, sep CP 1866,[4] sep EP 1841.[3] *LG* Seq 18. Civ bdry: 1965 (exchanges pts with Balterley CP, Staffs).[109] *Parl* S'rn Dv (1832—67), South Dv (1867—85), Northw. Dv (1885—1918), Crewe Dv/CC (1918—*). *Eccl* Nantw. RDn.

WETTENHALL

Chap in Over AP, sep CP 1866,[4] sep EP 1720.[3] *LG* Seq 13. *Parl* Seq 21. *Eccl* Middlew. RDn (1720—1969), Malpas RDn (1969—*).

WHARTON

Tp in Davenham AP, sep CP 1866,[4] sep EP 1860.[147] *LG* Northw. Hd, PLU, Winsford USD, UD. Abol civ 1936 pt to help cr Winsford CP, pt to Bostock CP.[7] *Parl* S'rn Dv (1832—67), Mid Dv (1867—85), Northw. Dv (1885—1948). *Eccl* Middlew. RDn.

WHATCROFT

Tp in Davenham AP, sep CP 1866.[4] *LG* Seq 21. Bdry: 1892 (gains Shipbrook CP),[92] 1955.[208] *Parl* S'rn Dv (1832—67), Mid Dv (1867—85), Northw. Dv (1885—1918), Knutsf. Dv (1918—48), Northw. CC (1948—*).

WHEELOCK

Tp in Sandbach AP, sep CP 1866,[4] sep EP 1840.[327] *LG* Northw. Hd, Congl. PLU, RSD, RD. Abol civ 1936 pt to Sandbach UD & AP, pt to Haslington CP.[7] *Parl* S'rn Dv (1832—67), Mid Dv (1867—85), Crewe Dv (1885—1948). *Eccl* Middlew. RDn (1840—80), Congl. RDn (1880—*).

WHITBY

Tp pt in Eastham AP, pt in Stoke AP, sep CP 1866,[4] the pt in Eastham AP eccl severed 1871 to help cr Ellesmere Port EP.[221] *LG* Wirral Hd, PLU, RSD, RD (1894—1902), Ellesm. Port UD (1902—11). Abol 1911 to help cr Ellesmere Port CP.[230] *Parl* S'rn Dv (1832—67), South Dv (1867—85), Edd. Dv (1885—1918).

WHITCHURCH

AP Mostly Salop (N Bradford Hd), incl in Ches (Nantw. Hd) chap Marbury (sep EP 1870,[3] comprised of tps Marbury with Quoisley, Norbury, each a sep CP 1866 in Ches[4]), tp Wirswall (sep CP 1866 in Ches[4]), so that 'Whitchurch' ent Salop from 1866. *Parl* Ches pt, S'rn Dv (1832—67). *Eccl* See main entry in Salop.

WHITEGATE

AP Orig chap in Over AP, sep par 1542.[307] Incl tp Darnhall (sep CP 1866,[4] eccl severed 1876 and transf to Over AP[207]), tp Marton (each a sep CP 1866[4]) so that 'Whitegate' has no sep civ identity after 1866. The 1871 census described tp Over and tp Weaverham as each pt in this AP, each o'wise and generally considered ent in its respective AP. *LG* Edd. Hd. *Parl* S'rn Dv (1832—67). *Eccl* Middlew. RDn. Eccl bdry: 1863 (help cr Over St John the Evangelist EP),[308] 1935 (help cr Sandiway EP).[165] Abol eccl 1971 to help cr Whitegate with Little Budworth EP.[152]

WHITEGATE WITH LITTLE BUDWORTH
EP Cr 1971 by union Whitegate AP, Little Budworth AP.[152] Middlew. RDn.

WHITLEY
CP Cr 1936 by union Higher Whitley CP, Lower Whitley CP.[7] *LG* Runc. RD. *Parl* Runc. CC (1948—*).

HIGHER WHITLEY
Tp (sometimes 'Over Whitley') in Great Budworth AP, sep CP 1866.[4] *LG* Buckl. Hd, Runc. PLU, RSD, RD. Abol 1936 to help cr Whitley CP.[7] *Parl* N'rn Dv (1832—67), Mid Dv (1867—85), Knutsf. Dv (1885—1948).

LOWER WHITLEY
Tp in Great Budworth AP, sep CP 1866,[4] sep EP 1824,[3] eccl refounded 1834.[144] Civ and parl organisation as for Higher Whitley. *Eccl* Frod. RDn (1824—69), Frod. West RDn (1869—80), Frod. RDn (1880—1935). Gt Budw. RDn (1935—*).

WIDNES
CP Lancs par transf 1974 to Ches.[4]

WIGLAND
Tp in Malpas AP, sep CP 1866.[4] *LG* Seq 7. *Parl* Seq 23.

WILDBOARCLOUGH
Tp in Prestbury AP, sep CP 1866,[4] eccl severed 1737 to help cr Macclesfield Forest with Wildboarclough EP,[3] the latter refounded 1906,[297] qv for division on abol 1973 incl orig area Wildboarclough. *LG* Seq 17. Bdry: 1888,[348] 1936.[213] *Parl* Seq 8.

WILLASTON
Tp in Neston AP, sep CP 1866,[4] sep EP 1865 (pt tp Willaston, tp Thornton Hough, pt tp Raby, addtl pt of Neston AP).[146] *LG* Wirral Hd, PLU, RSD, RD (1894—1933), Neston UD (1933—74). Civ bdry: 1933 (incl pt transf to Raby CP to help cr Beb. UD, pt to Childer Thornton CP to help cr Ellesm. Port UD, pt to Little Sutton CP),[7] 1936.[7] *Parl* Seq 26. *Eccl* Wirral RDn (1865—1935), Wirral South RDn (1935—*). Eccl bdry: 1869 (orig area of tp Thornton Hough, pt tp Raby, addtl pt of Neston AP severed to help cr Thornton Hough EP),[136] 1905.[341]

WILLASTON
Tp pt in Wybunbury AP, pt in Nantwich AP, sep CP 1866.[4] *LG* Seq 18. Bdry: 1936,[7] 1938.[42] *Parl* Seq 18.

WILLINGTON
Ex-par place, sep CP 1858,[10] eccl abol 1968 ent to Kelsall EP.[142] *LG* Seq 12. *Parl* Seq 22.

WILMSLOW
AP Incl tp Bollinfee (sep CP 1866[4]), tp Chorley (sep CP 1866,[4] sep EP 1855,[3] eccl refounded 1866[190]), tp Fulshaw, tp Pownall Fee (each a sep CP 1866[4]) so that 'Wilmslow' has no sep civ identity 1866—94 (see following entry). *LG* Maccl. Hd. *Parl* N'rn Dv (1832—67). *Eccl* Maccl. RDn (until 1873), Maccl. North RDn (1873—80), Stockpt. RDn (1880—1935), Knutsf. RDn (1935—*).

CP Cr 1894 by union of the pts in Wilmslow UD of Bollinfee CP, Fulshaw CP, Pownall Fee CP.[111] *LG* Altr. PLU (1894—95), Buckl. PLU (1895—1930), Wilmslow UD. Bdry: 1936,[7] 1954.[21] *Parl* Knutsf. Dv/CC (1918—*). Parl bdry: 1945.[161]

WIMBOLDSLEY
Tp in Middlewich AP, sep CP 1866.[4] *LG* Seq 21. Bdry: 1892 (gains Occleston CP),[92] 1936.[7] *Parl* S'rn Dv (1832—67), Mid Dv (1867—85), Edd. Dv (1885—1948), Northw. CC (1948—55), Nantw. CC (1955—*).

WINCHAM
Tp in Great Budworth AP, sep CP 1866.[4] *LG* Seq 9. Bdry: 1899,[271] 1936.[7] *Parl* Seq 4.

WINCLE
Chap in Prestbury AP, sep CP 1866,[4] sep EP 1725,[3] eccl refounded 1869.[14] *LG* Seq 17. Civ bdry: 1888.[348] *Parl* Seq 8. *Eccl* Maccl. RDn (1725—1873), Maccl. South RDn (1873—80), Maccl. RDn (1880—1973). Abol eccl 1973 to help cr Wincle and Wildboarclough EP.[298]

WINCLE AND WILDBOARCLOUGH
EP Cr 1973 by union Wincle EP, area Wildboarclough in Macclesfield Forest with Wildboarclough EP.[298] Maccl. RDn.

WINNINGTON
Tp in Great Budworth AP, sep CP 1866,[4] eccl in chap Witton (sep EP 1723 from Great Budworth AP,[3] qv for areas eccl severed before Witton EP refounded 1900 as 'Witton (otherwise Northwich St Helen)' EP,[14] 'Winnington' a sep EP 1931 from the latter.[148] *LG* Edd. Hd, Northw. PLU, pt Northw. USD, pt Northw. RSD, Northw. RD. Civ bdry: 1892 (gains Wallerscoat EP),[92] 1894 (loses the pt in the UD to Northwich CP).[262] Abol civ 1936 pt to Maccl. MB & CP, pt to Hartford CP, pt to Weaverham cum Milton AP.[7] *Parl* S'rn Dv (1832—67), South Dv (1867—85), Northw. Dv (1885—1948). *Eccl* Middlew. RDn.

WINSFORD
CP Cr 1936 by union Unnamed CP (in Winsford UD), Unnamed CP (in Northw. RD) and pts Bostock CP, Clive CP, Darnhall CP, Eaton CP, Marton CP, Moulton CP, Over AP, Stanthorne CP, Wharton CP.[7] *LG* Winsford RD. *Parl* Northw. CC (1948—55), Nantw. CC (1955—*).

WINWICK
AP Lancs par transf 1974 to Ches.[28]

WIRSWALL
Tp in Whitchurch AP (Salop, Ches until 1866, ent Salop thereafter), sep CP 1866 in Ches.[4] *LG* Seq 19. *Parl* Seq 21.

WISTASTON
AP *LG* Nantw. Hd, PLU, pt Crewe MB & USD (1892—94), Nantw. RSD (ent 1875—92, pt 1892—94), Nantw. RD. Civ bdry: 1894 (loses the pt in Crewe MB to Monks Coppenhall CP),[199] 1936.[7]

Parl Seq 18. *Eccl* Seq 9. Eccl bdry: 1926 (help cr Crewe St Andrew EP),[177] 1961.[116]

WITHINGTON
CP Cr 1936 by union Lower Withington CP, Old Withington CP.[7] *LG* Maccl. RD. *Parl* Maccl. CC (1948—*).

LOWER WITHINGTON
Tp in Prestbury AP, sep CP 1866.[4] *LG* Maccl. Hd, PLU, RSD, RD. Abol 1936 to help cr Witton CP.[7] *Parl* N'rn Dv (1832—67), North Dv (1867—85), Knutsf. Dv (1885—1948).

OLD WITHINGTON
Tp in Prestbury AP, sep CP 1866.[4] Organisation as for Lower Withington.

WITTON
Chap in Great Budworth AP, sep EP 1723 (incl chap Hartford, tps Birches, Hulse, Lach Dennis, Lostock Gralam, Northwich, Castle Northwich, Rudheath, Winnington, Witton cum Twanbrooks [see each for sep civ identity]).[3] Frod. RDn (1723—1869), Frod. West RDn (1869—80), Frod. RDn (1880—88), Middlew. RDn (1888—1900). Bdry: 1825 (orig areas Hartford, pt Castle Northwich severed to cr Hartford EP[3] [qv for refounding 1863]), 1842 (pt severed to help cr Lostock Gralam EP),[149] 1846 (help cr Dane Bridge EP).[147] The remainder refounded 1900 as 'Witton (otherwise Northwich St Helen' EP.[14]

WITTON (OTHERWISE NORTHWICH ST HELEN)
EP Refounding 1900 of Witton EP (qv in prev entry for cr 1723, and for its reduction by cr of pars from it in 1825, 1842, 1846).[14] Middlew. RDn (1900—*). Bdry: 1929 (orig area of Castle Northwich severed 1929 to help cr Northwich Holy Trinity EP),[132] 1930,[206] 1931 (cr Winnington EP).[148]

WOODBANK
Tp in Shotwick AP, sep CP 1866.[4] *LG* Seq 26. Bdry: 1888.[331] *Parl* Seq 19.

WOODCHURCH
AP Incl tp Arrowe (sep CP 1866[4]), tp Barnston (sep CP 1866,[4] sep EP 1870[62]), tps Landican, Noctorum (each a sep CP 1866[4]), tp Oxton (sep CP 1866,[4] sep EP 1865[312]), tp Pensby (sep CP 1866,[4] eccl severed 1880 and transf to Barnston EP[12]), tp Thingwall (sep CP 1866[4]), pt tp Irby (sep CP 1866[4]), tp Prenton (sep CP 1866,[4] sep EP 1902 from Woodchurch AP, Tranmere EP, Tranmere St Paul EP, Oxton EP[311]). In 1871 census Woodchurch described as incl pt tp Claughton with Grange, o'wise and generally considered ent in Bidston cum Ford AP. *LG* Wirral Hd, PLU, RSD, RD. Abol civ 1933 ent to Birk. CB (assoc with Ches) & CP.[40] *Parl* S'rn Dv (1832—67), South Dv (1867—85), Wirral Dv (1885—1948). *Eccl* Wirral RDn (until 1935), Wirral North RDn (1935—70), Birk. RDn (1970—*). Addtl eccl bdry alt: 1948,[12] 1959,[63] 1969.[103]

WOODCOTT
Tp in Wrenbury cum Frith AP (eccl, 'Wrenbury'), sep CP 1866.[4] *LG* Seq 18. *Parl* Seq 21.

WOODFORD
Tp in Prestbury AP, sep CP 1866,[4] sep EP 1873.[5] *LG* Maccl. Hd, PLU, RSD, RD. Civ bdry: 1963.[7] Abol civ 1939 ent to Hazel Grove & Bramhall UD

& CP.[265] *Parl* N'rn Dv (1832—67), North Dv (1867—85), Knutsf. Dv (1885—1948). *Eccl* Maccl. North RDn (1873—80), Stockpt. RDn (1880—1935), Knutsf. RDn (1935—*).

WOODHEAD
EP Cr 1724 from Mottram in Longendale AP (civ, 'Mottram').[3] Maccl. RDn (1724—1873), Maccl. North RDn (1873—80), Stockpt. RDn (1880—88), Mott. RDn (1888—*).

WOOLSTANWOOD
Tp in Nantwich AP, sep CP 1866.[4] *LG* Seq 18. Bdry: 1933.[7] *Parl* S'rn Dv (1832—67), South Dv (1867—85), Crewe Dv (1885—1918), Edd. Dv (1918—48), Crewe CC (1948—55), Nantw. CC (1955—*).

WOOLSTON
CP Lancs par transf 1974 to Ches.[28]

WORLESTON
Tp in Acton AP, sep CP 1866,[4] sep EP 1873 (tps Worleston, Aston juxta Mondrem, Cholmondeston, Poole, all in Acton AP).[5] *LG* Seq 18. Civ bdry: 1899 (gains Alvaston CP),[34] 1936.[7] *Parl* Seq 21. *Eccl* Nantw. RDn.

WORTH
Tp in Prestbury AP, sep CP 1866,[4] eccl united 1745 with chap Poynton in same par to cr Poynton with Worth EP,[3] refounded 1871 as 'Poynton' from Prestbury AP, High Lane EP.[185] *LG* Maccl. Hd, PLU, RSD. Abol civ 1880 to help cr Poynton with Worth with Worth CP.[315] *Parl* N'rn Dv (1832—67), North Dv (1867—85).

WRENBURY
Chap in Acton AP, sep EP 1730,[3] sep civ identity early as 'Wrenbury cum Frith', qv (incl sep civ identities of tps). *Eccl* Nantw. RDn. Eccl bdry: 1738 (cr Burleydam EP,[3] refounded 1869 from Wrenbury EP, Audlem AP[55]), 1893 (help cr Bickley EP),[85] 1930.[8]

WRENBURY CUM FRITH
Chap in Acton AP, sep civ identity early, sep EP 1730 as 'Wrenbury',[3] qv in prev entry. Incl tps Bromhall, Chorley, Woodcott (each a sep CP 1866[4]), incl pt tp Dodcott cum Wilkesley (sep CP 1866[4]), pt tp Sound (orig ent in Acton AP, then pt in Acton, pt in Wrenbury cum Frith when latter gains sep civ identity early from Acton), 'Sound' a sep CP 1866[4]. In 1871 census tp Newhall reported as pt in this par, pt in Audlem AP, o'wise and generally considered ent in Audlem AP. *LG* Seq 18. *Parl* Seq 21.

WYBUNBURY
AP Incl tps Basford, Batherton, Blakenhall, Bridgemere, Checkley cum Wrinehill, Chorlton, Hatherton, Hough, Hunsterson, Lea, Rope, Shavington cum Gresty, Stapeley, Walgherton (each a sep CP 1866[4]), tp Doddington (sep CP 1866,[4] sep EP 1841[3]), tp Weston (sep CP 1866,[4] sep EP 1841[3]), pt tp Willaston (sep CP 1866[4]). *LG* Seq 18. *Parl* Seq 18. *Eccl* Seq 9. Addtl eccl bdry alt: 1926 (help cr Crewe St Andrew EP),[177] 1927.[290]

WYCHOUGH
Tp in Malpas AP, sep CP 1866.[4] *LG* Seq 7. *Parl* Seq 23.

WYTHENSHAWE ST RICHARD OF CHICHESTER
EP Cr 1971 from Benchill EP.[81] Withington RDn.
WYTHENSHAWE THE WILLIAM TEMPLE CHURCH
EP Cr 1963 from Benchill EP (Ches, dioc Manch), Northenden AP (Ches until 1931, area within Manch CB thereafter, dioc Manch), Stockport AP (Ches, dioc Chester).[79] Heaton RDn (1963—65),

Withington RDn (1965—74).
YEARDSLEY CUM WHALLEY
Tp in Taxal AP, sep CP 1866.[4] *LG* Maccl. Hd, PLU, Yeardsley cum Whalley USD, UD. Abol 1936 pt to Disley CP, pt to help cr Whaley Bridge UD & CP to be in Derbys.[213] *Parl* N'rn Dv (1832—67), North Dv (1867—85), Knutsf. Dv (1885—1918), Maccl. Dv (1918—48).

CUMBERLAND

ABBREVIATIONS

Abbreviations particular to Cumb follow. Those general abbreviations in use throughout the *Guide* are found on pages xvii—xix.

Allerd.	Allerdale
Bramp.	Brampton
Cockerm.	Cockermouth
Copel.	Copeland
Derw.	Derwent
Egrem.	Egremont
Ennerd.	Ennerdale
Esk.	Eskdale
Gosf.	Gosforth
Greyst.	Greystoke
Kesw.	Keswick
Kirkosw.	Kirkoswald
Maryp.	Maryport
Longt.	Longtown
Penr.	Penrith
Ulv.	Ulverston
Whiteh.	Whitehaven
Wigt.	Wigton
Work.	Workington

SEQUENCES

An abbreviated entry prefixed by 'Seq' is used in the parochial entries to avoid repeating often the names of superior units of administration. The content of each sequence is shown below.

Local Government Sequences ('LG')

SEQ 1 Allerd. above Derw Wd, Bootle PLU, RSD, RD (1894—1934), Millom RD (1934—74)

SEQ 2 Allerd. above Derw. Wd, Cockerm. PLU, RSD, RD

SEQ 3 Allerd. above Derw. Wd, Whiteh. PLU, RSD, RD (1894—1934), Ennerd. RD (1934—74)

SEQ 4 Allerd. below Derw. Wd, Cockerm. PLU, RSD, RD

SEQ 5 Allerd. below Derw. Wd, Wigt. PLU, RSD, RD

SEQ 6 Cumb Wd, Carl PLU, RSD, RD (1894—1934), Border RD (1934—74)

SEQ 7 Cumb Wd, Wigt. PLU, RSD, RD

SEQ 8 Esk. Wd, Bramp. PLU, RSD, RD (1894—1934), Border RD (1934—74)

SEQ 9 Esk. Wd, Longt. PLU, RSD, RD (1894—1934), Border RD (1934—74)

SEQ 10 Leath Wd, Penr. PLU, RSD, RD

Parliamentary Sequences ('Parl')

SEQ 1 E'rn Dv (1832—85), Esk. Dv (1885—1918), N'rn Dv (1918—48), Penr. & the Border CC (1948—*)

SEQ 2 E'rn Dv (1832—85), Penr. Dv (1885—1918), N'rn Dv (1918—48), Penr. & the Border CC (1948—*)

SEQ 3 E'rn Dv (1832—85), Penr. Dv (1885—1918), Penr. & Cockerm. Dv (1918—48), Penr. & the Border CC (1948—*)

SEQ 4 W'rn Dv (1832—85), Cockerm. Dv (1885—1918), Work. Dv/CC (1918—*)

SEQ 5 W'rn Dv (1832—85), Egrem. Dv (1885—1918), Whiteh. Dv/CC (1918—*)

SEQ 6 W'rn Dv (1832—85), Egrem. Dv (1885—1918), Work. Dv (1918—48), Whiteh. CC (1948—*)

SEQ 7 W'rn Dv (1832—85), Esk. Dv (1885—1918), N'rn Dv (1918—48), Penr. & the Border CC (1948—*)

SEQ 8 W'rn Dv (1832—85), Penr. Dv (1885—1918), N'rn Dv (1918—48), Penr. & the Border CC (1948—*)

SEQ 9 W'rn Dv (1832—85), Penr. Dv (1885—1918), Penr. & Cockerm. Dv (1918—48), Work. CC (1948—*)

Ecclesiastical Sequences ('Eccl')

Orig in Carlisle dioc

SEQ 1   Allerd. RDn (until 1859), Cockerm. RDn (1859—71), Maryp. RDn (1871—1970), Solway RDn (1970—*)

SEQ 2   Allerd. RDn (until 1857), Cumb RDn (1857—59), Greyst. RDn (1859—82), Penr. West RDn (1882—1926), Penr. RDn (1926—*)

SEQ 3   Allerd. RDn (until 1857), Cumb RDn (1857—59), Penr. RDn (1859—82), Penr. East RDn (1882—1926), Kirkosw. RDn (1926—70), Penr. RDn (1970—*)

SEQ 4   Allerd. RDn (until 1859), Kesw. RDn (1859—1970), Derw. RDn (1970—*)

SEQ 5   Allerd. RDn (until 1859), Wigt. RDn (1859—1970), Carl RDn (1970—*)

SEQ 6   Allerd. RDn (until 1859), Wigt. RDn (1859—1970), Derw. RDn (1970—*)

SEQ 7   Carl RDn (until 1859), Bramp. RDn (1859—*)

SEQ 8   Carl RDn (until 1871), Carl North RDn (1871—1926), Bramp. RDn (1926—*)

SEQ 9   Carl RDn (until 1871), Carl North RDn (1871—1926), Carl RDn (1926—*)

SEQ 10   Carl RDn (until 1871), Carl North RDn (1871—1926), Carl RDn (1926—70), Bramp. RDn (1970—*)

SEQ 11   Carl RDn (until 1871), Carl South RDn (1871—1926), Carl RDn (1926—*)

SEQ 12   Carl RDn (until 1871), Carl South RDn (1871—1926), Carl RDn (1926—70), Bramp. RDn (1970—*)

SEQ 13   Carl RDn (until 1871), Carl South RDn (1871—82), Carl North RDn (1882—1926), Carl RDn (1926—*)

SEQ 14   Carl RDn (until 1859), Wigt. RDn (1859—1970), Carl RDn (1970—*)

Orig in York dioc

SEQ 15   Copel. RDn (until 1859), Gosf. RDn (1859—1970), Calder RDn (1970—*)

SEQ 16   Copel. RDn (until 1859), Whiteh. RDn (1859—1970), Calder RDn (1970—*)

DIOCESES AND ARCHDEACONRIES

Cumb pars are primarily in Carlisle Dioc and were organised in Archdeaconries and Rural Deaneries as follows:

CARLISLE AD

Allerd. RDn (until 1859), Bramp. RDn (1859—*), Carl RDn (until 1871), Carl RDn (1926—*), Carl North RDn (1871—1926), Carl South RDn (1871—1926), Cumb RDn (1857—59), Greyst. RDn (1859—82), Kesw. RDn (1859—84), Kirkosw. RDn (1926—70), Maryp. RDn (1871—1959), Penr. RDn (1859—82), Penr. RDn (1926—*), Penr. East RDn (1882—1926), Penr. West RDn (1882—1926), Wigt. RDn (1859—1970)

WEST CUMBERLAND AD (1959—*)

Calder RDn (1970—*), Cockerm. & Work. RDn (1959—70), Derw. RDn (1970—*), Gosf. RDn (1959—70), Kesw. RDn (1959—70), Maryp. RDn (1959—70), Solway RDn (1970—*), Whiteh. RDn (1959—70)

FURNESS AD (1884—1959)

Gosf. RDn, Ulv. RDn

WESTMORLAND AD (1856—1959)

Cockerm. RDn (1859—82), Cockerm. & Work. RDn (1882—1959), Copel. RDn (1856—59), Gosf. RDn (1859—84), Kesw. RDn (1884—1959), Ulv. RDn (1859—84), Whiteh. RDn (1859—1959)

WESTMORLAND AND FURNESS AD (1959—*)

Furness RDn (1970—*), Kendal RDn, Ulv. RDn (1959—70)

THE PARISHES OF CUMBERLAND

Cumb pars were transf 1974 to help cr Cumbria Non-Metrop Co.

ABBEYTOWN—see HOLME ABBEY

ABOVE DERWENT

Tp in Crosthwaite AP, sep CP 1866.[1] *LG* Allerd. above Derw. Wd, Cockerm. PLU (soon after 1838[2]—1930), RSD, RD. Civ bdry: 1946.[3] *Parl* Seq 9.

ADDINGHAM

AP Incl tps Gamblesby, Glassonby, Hunsonby and Winskill (each a sep CP 1866[1]), tp (orig chap) Little Salkeld (sep CP 1866[1]) so that 'Addingham' has no sep civ identity after 1866. *LG* Leath Wd. *Parl* E'rn Dv (1832—67). *Eccl* Seq 3.

AIKTON

AP *LG* Seq 7. *Parl* Seq 1. *Eccl* Seq 14.

AINSTABLE

AP *LG* Seq 10. Civ bdry: 1934.[4] *Parl* Seq 3. *Eccl* Seq 3. Eccl bdry: 1973 (cr Armathwaite EP [qv for earlier eccl status and uncertainties]).[5]

ALLHALLOWS

Chap in Aspatria AP, sep civ identity early, sep EP 1746.[6] *LG* Seq 5. *Parl* Seq 8. *Eccl* Allerd. RDn (1746—1859), Cockerm. RDn (1859—71), Maryp. RDn (1871—82), Wigt. RDn (1882—1970), Solway RDn (1970—*).

ALLONBY

Chap (founded 1744) in Bromfield AP, sep EP 1746,[6] eccl refounded 1906,[7] civ united with tp West Newton in same par as 'West Newton and Allonby', as such a sep CP 1866,[1] 'Allonby' a sep CP 1894 from West Newton and Allonby CP.[8] *LG* Wigt. PLU, RD. *Parl* Work. Dv (1918—48), Penr. & the Border CC (1948—*). *Eccl* Allerd. RDn (1746—1859), Wigt. RDn (1859—71), Maryp. RDn (1871—1970), Solway RDn (1970—*).

ALSTON WITH GARRIGILL

AP *LG* Leath Wd, Alston with Garrigill PLU, RSD, RD. *Parl* Seq 3. *Eccl* Corbr. RDn (until 1845), Hexham RDn (1845—*) (dioc Durham until 1884, dioc Newc thereafter). Eccl bdry: 1846 (cr Nenthead EP).[9]

ARLECDON

AP Allerd. above Derw. Wd, Whiteh. PLU, pt Arlecdon & Frizington USD (1882—94), Whiteh. RSD (ent 1875—82, pt 1882—94), Arlecdon & Frizington UD (1894—1934). Renamed civ 1934 'Arlecdon and Frizington'.[3] *Parl* W'rn Dv (1832—85), Egrem. Dv (1885—1918), Work. Dv (1918—48). *Eccl* Seq 16. Eccl bdry: 1910 (cr Frizington EP).[10]

ARLECDON AND FRIZINGTON

CP Renaming 1934 of Arlecdon AP.[3] *LG* Ennerd. RD. *Parl* Whiteh. CC (1948—*).

ARMATHWAITE

EP Cr 1745 from Hesket in the Forest (qv for early status),[6] eccl refounded 1973 at which time declared never before to have been legally constituted.[5] Penr. RDn (1973—*).

ARTHURET

AP *LG* Seq 9. Civ bdry: 1883.[11] *Parl* Seq 1. *Eccl* Seq 10.

ASKERTON

Tp in Lanercost AP, sep CP 1866.[1] *LG* Seq 8. *Parl* Seq 1.

ASPATRIA

AP Incl tps Aspatria and Brayton, Oughterside and Allerby (each a sep CP 1866[1]), chap Hayton (sep EP 1741,[6] eccl refounded 1868,[9] civ united with Mealo as 'Hayton and Mealo' and as such sep CP 1866[1]), chap Allhallows (sep civ identity early, sep EP 1746[6]), so that 'Aspatria' has no sep civ identity 1866—1934 (see following entry). *LG* Allerd. below Derw. Wd. *Parl* W'rn Dv (1832—67). *Eccl* Seq 1.

CP Cr 1934 from Aspatria and Brayton CP, Oughterside and Allerby CP.[3] *LG* Wigt. RD. *Parl* Penr. & the Border CC (1948—*).

ASPATRIA AND BRAYTON

Tp in Aspatria AP, sep CP 1866.[1] *LG* Allerd. below Derw. Wd, Wigt. PLU, RSD (1875—92), Aspatria USD (1892—94), UD. Abol 1934 pt to help cr Aspatria CP, pt to Hayton and Mealo CP, pt to Oughterside and Allerby CP.[3] *Parl* W'rn Dv (1867—85), Esk. Dv (1885—1918), Work. Dv (1918—48).

BASSENTHWAITE

AP *LG* Seq 4. *Parl* Seq 9. *Eccl* Seq 4. Eccl bdry: 1955.[12]

BEAUMONT

AP *LG* Seq 6. Civ bdry: 1887,[13] 1934 (gains Grinsdale AP, Kirkandrews upon Eden AP),[3] 1951 (loses pt to Carl CB [assoc with Cumb] & CP).[14] *Parl* Seq 1. Parl bdry: 1951.[15] *Eccl* Carl RDn. Abol eccl 1692 to help cr Kirkandrews on Eden with Beaumont EP.[16]

BECKERMET ST BRIDGET

AP Sometimes 'St Bride's'. Incl area Calderbridge (not sep). *LG* Seq 3. Civ bdry: 1881,[17] 1935.[18] *Parl* Seq 5. *Eccl* Copel. RDn (until 1859), Whiteh. RDn (1859—1957). Abol eccl 1957 to help cr Beckermet St Bridget with Ponsonby EP.[19]

BECKERMET ST BRIDGET WITH PONSONBY

EP Cr 1957 by union Beckermet St Bridget AP, Ponsonby AP.[19] Whiteh. RDn (1957—70), Calder RDn (1970—*). Bdry: 1963.[20]

BECKERMET ST JOHN

AP *LG* Allerd. above Derw. Wd, Whiteh. PLU, pt Egrem. USD (1890—94), Whiteh. RSD (ent 1875—90, pt 1890—94), Whiteh. RD (1894—1934), Ennerd. RD (1934—74). Civ bdry: 1894,[21] 1935.[18] *Parl* Seq 5. *Eccl* Copel. RDn (until 1859), Whiteh. RDn (1859—71), Gosf. RDn (1871—1970), Calder RDn (1970—*). Eccl bdry: 1963.[20]

BELLBANK

Tp in Stapleton AP, sep CP 1866.[1] *LG* Esk. Wd, Longt. PLU, RSD, RD. Abol 1934 ent to Stapleton AP.[3] *Parl* E'rn Dv (1867—85), Esk. Dv (1885—1918), N'rn Dv (1918—48).

BELLE VUE

CP Cr 1894 from the pt of Caldewgate CP not in Carl MB.[22] *LG* Carl PLU, RD. Abol 1912 pt to Carl MB & CP, pt to Grinsdale AP.[23]

BERRIER AND MURRAH

Tp in Greystoke AP, sep CP 1866,[1] pt eccl severed 1926 to help refound Mungrisdale EP.[24] *LG* Leath Wd, Penr. PLU, RSD, RD. Abol 1934 ent to Mungrisdale CP.[3] *Parl* E'rn Dv (1867—85), Penr. Dv (1885—1918), Penr. & Cockerm. Dv (1918—48).

BEWALDETH AND SNITTLEGARTH

Tp in Torpenhow AP, sep CP 1866.[1] *LG* Seq 4. Civ bdry: 1934.[4] *Parl* Seq 4.

BEWCASTLE

AP *LG* Seq 9. *Parl* Seq 2. *Eccl* Seq 7.

BIRKER AND AUSTHWAITE

Tp in Millom AP, sep CP 1866.[1] *LG* Allerd. above Derw. Wd, Bootle PLU, RSD, RD. Abol 1934 to help cr Eskdale CP.[3] *Parl* W'rn Dv (1867—85), Egrem. Dv (1885—1918), Whiteh. Dv (1918—48).

BLACKFORD

EP Cr 1871 by union tp Westlinton in Kirklinton AP, pt Rockcliffe AP.[25] Carl RDn (1871), Carl North RDn (1871—1926), Carl RDn (1926—61), Bramp. RDn (1961—*).

BLENCOGO

Tp in Bromfield AP, sep CP 1866.[1] *LG* Cumb Wd, Wigt. PLU, RSD, RD. Abol 1934 ent to Bromfield AP.[3] *Parl* E'rn Dv (1867—85), Penr. Dv (1885—1918), N'rn Dv (1918—48).

BLENNERHASSET AND KIRKLAND

Tp in Torpenhow AP, sep CP 1866.[1] *LG* Allerd.

below Derw. Wd, Wigt. PLU, RSD, RD. Abol 1934 to help cr Blennerhasset and Torpenhow CP.[3] *Parl* W'rn Dv (1867—85), Penr. Dv (1885—1918), N'rn Dv (1918—48).

BLENNERHASSET AND TORPENHOW
CP Cr 1934 by union Blennerhasset and Kirkland CP, pt Torpenhow and Whitrigg CP.[3] *LG* Wigt. RD. *Parl* Penr. & the Border CC (1948—*).

BLINDBOTHEL
Tp in Brigham AP, sep CP 1866.[1] *LG* Seq 2. Bdry: 1934 (gains Mosser CP, Whinfell CP).[3] *Parl* Seq 4.

BLINDCRAKE
CP Cr 1934 by union Blindcrake Isel and Redmaine CP, Isel Old Park CP, Sunderland CP.[3] *LG* Cockerm. RD. *Parl* Work. CC (1948—*).

BLINDCRAKE ISEL AND REDMAINE
Tp in Isel AP, sep CP 1866.[1] *LG* Allerd. below Derw. Wd, Cockerm. PLU, RSD, RD. Abol 1934 to help cr Blindcrake CP.[3] *Parl* W'rn Dv (1867—85), Cockerm. Dv (1885—1918), Penr. & Cockerm. Dv (1918—48).

BOLTON
AP Incl tps Bolton High, Bolton Low (each a sep CP 1866[1]) so that 'Bolton' has no sep civ identity after 1866. *LG* Allerd. below Derw. Wd. *Parl* W'rn Dv (1832—67). *Eccl* Seq 6.

BOLTON HIGH
Tp in Bolton AP, sep CP 1866.[1] *LG* Allerd. below Derw. Wd, Wigt. PLU, RSD, RD. Abol 1887 to help cr Boltons CP.[26] *Parl* W'rn Dv (1867—85), Penr. Dv (1885—1918).

BOLTON LOW
Organisation as for Bolton High.

BOLTONS
CP Cr 1887 by union Bolton High CP, Bolton Low CP.[26] *LG* Allerd. below Derw. Wd, Wigt. PLU, RSD, RD. *Parl* N'rn Dv (1918—48), Penr. & the Border CC (1948—*).

BOOTLE
AP *LG* Seq 1. *Parl* Seq 5. *Eccl* Seq 15.

BORROWDALE
Chap in Crosthwaite AP, sep CP 1866,[1] sep EP 1743,[6] pt severed 1859 to help refound Keswick EP,[27] the remainder cr 1865 'Borrowdale' EP.[28] *LG* Seq 2. *Parl* Seq 9. *Eccl* Allerd. RDn (1743—1859), Kesw. RDn (1859—1970), Derw. RDn (1970—*).

BOTCHERGATE
Tp in Carlisle St Cuthbert AP, sep CP 1894 from the pt of St Cuthbert Without CP in Carl MB,[22] sep EP 1832,[6] eccl refounded 1854,[29] the usual eccl name 'Carlisle Christ Church', qv. *LG* Carl PLU, MB. Abol 1904 to help cr Carlisle CP.[30]

BOTHEL AND THREAPLAND
Tp in Torpenhow AP, sep CP 1866.[1] *LG* Seq 4. *Parl* Seq 4.

BOWNESS
AP *LG* Cumb Wd, Wigt. PLU (soon after 1837[31]—1930), RSD, RD. *Parl* Seq 1. *Eccl* Carl RDn (until 1859), Wigt. RDn (1859—82), Carl North RDn (1882—1926), Wigt. RDn (1926—70), Carl RDn (1970—*).

BOWSCALE
Tp in Greystoke AP, sep CP 1866,[1] eccl severed

1926 to help refound Mungrisdale EP.[24] *LG* Leath Wd, Penr. PLU, RSD, RD. Abol 1934 ent to Mungrisdale CP.[3] *Parl* E'rn Dv (1867—85), Penr. Dv (1885—1918), Penr. & Cockerm. Dv (1918—48).

BRACKENTHWAITE
Tp mostly in chap Lorton (sep civ identity early from Brigham AP, sep EP 1744,[6] eccl refounded 1883, qv for constituent pars then[32]), sep CP 1866,[1] pt eccl severed 1884 to help refound Buttermere EP,[33] the remainder severed 1886 to help refound Loweswater EP.[34] *LG* Allerd. above Derw. Wd, Cockerm. PLU, RSD, RD. Bdry: 1883,[12] 1887.[35] Abol 1934 ent to Buttermere CP.[3] *Parl* W'rn Dv (1867—85), Cockerm. Dv (1885—1918), Penr. & Cockerm. Dv (1918—48).

BRAMPTON
AP *LG* Seq 8. Civ bdry: 1883,[36] 1934.[4] *Parl* Seq 1. *Eccl* Seq 7. Eccl bdry: 1937.[24]

BRIDEKIRK
AP Incl tps Dovenby, Papcastle, Tallentire (each a sep CP 1866[1]), tps Great Broughton, Little Broughton, Ribton (each a sep CP 1866,[1] eccl united 1863 to cr Great Broughton EP[37]). *LG* Seq 4. Addtl civ bdry alt: 1887,[35] 1934 (gains Dovenby CP, Tallentire CP).[3] *Parl* Cockerm. Bor (1832—85), Esk. Dv (1885—1918), Penr. & Cockerm. Dv (1918—48), Work. CC (1948—*). *Eccl* Allerd. RDn (until 1859), Cockerm. RDn (1859—71), Maryp. RDn (1871—1970), Derw. RDn (1970—*).

BRIERY COTTAGES
Ex-par place, sep CP 1858,[38] eccl severed 1839 to help refound Keswick EP.[39] *LG* Allerd. below Derw. Wd, Cockerm. PLU (1858—94), RSD. Abol 1894 ent to Keswick CP.[40] *Parl* W'rn Dv (1867—85), Penr. Dv (1885—1918).

BRIGHAM
AP Incl chap chap Buttermere (sep CP 1866,[1] sep EP 1748,[6] eccl refounded 1884 by union pt orig area [remainder to help refound Lorton EP, qv], the pt of Lorton EP not used 1883 to help refound that par, the pt of tp Brackenthwaite not in Lorton EP,[33] the pt of tp Whinfell not eccl incl 1883 in Mosser EP[32]), chap Cockermouth (sep CP 1866,[1] sep EP 1806[6]), chap Embleton (sep CP 1866,[1] sep EP 1747[6]), chap Lorton (sep civ identity early, sep EP 1744 [incl eccl chap Wythop, most of tp Brackenthwaite],[6] refounded 1883 [remainder after areas severed 1738 to cr Wythrop EP, and severed 1883 to help refound Buttermere EP][33]), chap & tp Mosser (sep CP 1866,[1] sep EP 1774,[6] eccl refounded 1883 by union orig area, tp Eaglesfield, tp Blindbothel, pt tp Whinfell[41]), chap Setmurthy (sep CP 1866,[1] sep EP 1748[6]), chap Wythop (sep CP 1866, orig incl in area chap/EP Lorton [qv above], 'Wythop' a sep EP 1738 from Lorton EP[6]), tp Brackenthwaite (sep CP 1866,[1] eccl mostly incl in chap/EP [qv above], pt orig area tp severed 1884 to help refound Buttermere EP,[33] the remainder severed 1886 to help refound Loweswater EP[34]), tp Blindbothel (sep CP 1866,[1] eccl severed 1883 to help refound Mosser EP[41]), tp Eaglesfield (sep CP 1866,[1] eccl

severed 1883 to help refound Mosser EP[41]), tp Greysouthen (sep CP 1866[1]), tp Whinfell (sep CP 1866,[1] pt eccl severed 1883 to help refound Mosser EP[41]). *LG* Allerd. above Derw. Wd, pt (area of Cockermouth) Cockerm. Bor (status not sustained), Cockerm. PLU, RSD, RD. *Parl* Cockerm. Parl Bor (pt [Cockermouth] 1295, 1640—1835, ent par 1835—85), Cockerm. Dv (1885—1918), Penr. & Cockerm. Dv (1918—48), Work. CC (1948—*). *Eccl* Copel. RDn (until 1859), Cockerm. RDn (1859—82), Cockerm. & Work. RDn (1859—1970), Derw. RDn (1970—*).

BROCKLEYMOOR—see PLUMPTON WALL

BROMFIELD

AP Tp 'Bromfield' in Allerd. below Derw. Wd as were tp Landrigg and Mealrigg (sep CP 1866[1], pt eccl severed 1863 to help cr Westnewton EP[42]), tp West Newton and Allonby (sep CP 1866 comprised of chap Allonby [sep EP 1746,[6] eccl refounded 1906[6]], area West Newton [sep EP 1863 as 'Westnewton' by union tp West Newton, pt tp Langrigg and Mealrigg[42]]); incl in Cumb Wd tp Blencogo (sep CP 1866[1]), tp Dundraw (sep CP 1866,[1] eccl severed 1902 to help cr Waverton EP[43]). *LG* Wigt. PLU, RSD, RD. Addtl civ bdry alt: 1934 (gains Blencogo CP, Langrigg and Mealrigg CP).[3] *Parl* Seq 7. *Eccl* Seq 5.

BROUGHTON

CP Cr 1898 by union pt Great Broughton CP, pt Little Broughton CP.[44] *LG* Cockerm. PLU, RD. *Parl* Work. Dv/CC (1918—*).

GREAT BROUGHTON

Tp in Bridekirk AP, sep CP 1866,[1] eccl united 1863 with tps Little Broughton, Ribton in same par as 'Great Broughton' EP.[37] *LG* Allerd. below Derw. Wd, Cockerm. PLU, RSD, RD. Bdry: 1887.[35] Abol 1898 pt to help cr Broughton CP, pt to help cr Broughton Moor CP.[44] *Parl* W'rn Dv (1867—85), Cockerm. Dv (1885—1918). *Eccl* Maryp. RDn (1863—1970), Solway RDn (1970—*).

LITTLE BROUGHTON

Tp in Bridekirk AP, sep CP 1866,[1] eccl severed 1863 to help cr Great Broughton EP.[37] Organisation as for Great Broughton.

BROUGHTON MOOR

CP Cr 1898 by union pt Great Broughton CP, pt Little Broughton CP.[44] *LG* Cockerm. PLU, RD. *Parl* Work. Dv/CC (1918—*).

BURGH BY SANDS

AP *LG* Seq 6. *Parl* Seq 1. *Eccl* Seq 13.

BURTHOLME

Tp in Lanercost AP, sep CP 1866.[1] *LG* Seq 8. Bdry: 1883,[45] 1934.[4] *Parl* Seq 1.

BUTTERMERE

Chap in chap Lorton (sep civ identity early from Brigham AP, sep EP 1744,[6] eccl refounded 1883, qv for constituent pars then[32]), sep CP 1866,[1] sep EP 1748,[6] eccl refounded 1884 by union pt orig area (remainder eccl severed 1883 to help refound Lorton EP[34]), pt tp Brackenthwaite.[33] *LG* Seq 2. Civ bdry: 1887,[35] 1934 (gains Brackenthwaite CP),[3] 1946.[46] *Parl* Seq 4. *Eccl* Copel. RDn (1748—1859), Kesw. RDn (1859—71), Cockerm. RDn

(1871—82), Cockerm. & Work. RDn (1882—1970), Derw. RDn (1970—*).

CALDBECK

AP Incl tp Mosedale (sep CP 1866,[1] eccl severed 1926 to help refound Mungrisdale EP[24]). *LG* Seq 5. Addtl civ bdry alt: 1971.[47] *Parl* Seq 8. *Eccl* Seq 5. Addtl eccl bdry alt: 1958.[48]

CALDERBRIDGE—see BECKERMET ST BRIDGET

CALDEWGATE

Tp in Carlisle St Mary AP, sep CP 1866,[1] sep EP 1832,[6] eccl refounded 1834,[49] eccl usually as 'Carlisle Holy Trinity', qv. *LG* Cumb Wd, Carl PLU, MB (pt 1835—94, ent 1894—1904), pt Carl USD, pt Carl RSD. Civ bdry: 1894 (the pt not in Carl MB cr Belle Vue CP,[22] and gains the pt of Cummersdale CP in the MB[50]). Abol civ 1904 to help cr Carlisle CP.[30] *Parl* Carl Parl Bor (1832—1918).

CALTHWAITE—see HESKET IN THE FOREST

CAMERTON

AP Incl tp Seaton (sep CP 1866[1]), chap Flimby (sep civ identity early, sometimes deemed ex-par,[51] sep EP 1744[6]). *LG* Seq 4. Addtl civ bdry alt: 1934 (gains Ribton CP).[3] *Parl* Seq 4. *Eccl* Seq 1. Addtl eccl bdry alt: 1893 (cr West Seaton EP).[52]

CARLATTON

AP Orig AP, appropriated to Lanercost Priory, no presentation after 15th cent and considered ex-par from Dissolution,[53] sep CP 1858,[38] eccl abol 1971 pt to Cumrew AP, pt to Cumwhitton AP.[54] *LG* Esk. Wd, own overseers for poor (until 1861), Bramp. PLU (1861—1930), RSD, RD (1894—1934), Border RD (1934—74). *Parl* Seq 1.

CARLETON—see CARLISLE ST CUTHBERT

CARLISLE

The following have 'Carlisle' in their names. Insofar as any existed at a given time: *LG* Carl PLU; Bor/MB, USD, CB sep noted. *Parl* Sep noted. *Eccl* Unless o'wise noted, Carl RDn (until 1871) and Carl RDn (1926—*); sep noted (1871—1926).

CP1—CARLISLE—Cr 1904 by union pars in Carl MB: Botchergate CP, Caldewgate CP, Eaglesfield Abbey CP, Rickergate CP, St Cuthbert Within CP, St Mary Within CP.[30] *LG* Carl MB (1904—14), CB (1914—74). Civ bdry: 1912,[23] 1951.[14] *Parl* Carl Parl Bor (1918—*). Parl bdry: 1951.[15]

EP1—CARLISLE CHRIST CHURCH—Cr 1832 from AP1,[6] refounded 1854[29]; for civ see 'Botchergate'. Carl South RDn (1871—1926). Bdry: 1865 (help cr EP11),[55] 1867 (help cr EP8).[56] Abol 1932 to help cr EP4.[57]

EP2—CARLISLE HOLY TRINITY—Cr 1832 from AP2,[6] refounded 1834.[49]; for civ see 'Caldewgate'. Carl North RDn (1871—1926). Bdry: 1934 (cr EP5),[6] 1968 (cr EP9).[58]

EP3—CARLISLE ST AIDAN—Cr 1902 from EP10, EP8.[59] Carl North RDn (1902—26). Abol 1932 to help cr EP4.[57]

EP4—CARLISLE ST AIDAN WITH CHRIST CHURCH—Cr 1932 by union EP3, EP1.[57]

EP5—CARLISLE ST BARNABAS—Cr 1934 from EP2.[6]

AP1—CARLISLE ST CUTHBERT—Incl tp Botcher-gate (sep EP 1832,[6] eccl refounded 1854,[29] eccl name as EP1, qv; civ not orig in Carl Bor, incl within area of MB from 1835 but the tp was civ within St Cuthbert [1866—94], 'Botchergate' a sep CP 1894 from the pt of St Cuthbert Without in the MB[22]), tp Carleton (not sep). The pts of AP1 within and without the MB sep rated for poor law purposes and each a sep CP 1866, as 'St Cuthbert Within' CP, 'St Cuthbert Without' CP,[1] so that AP1 has no sep civ identity after 1866. *Parl* Pt Carl Parl Bor (1295—1832 [enlarged pt 1832—67]), pt E'rn Dv (1832—67). Carl North RDn (1871—1926), Bramp. RDn (1970—*). Eccl bdry: 1771 (cr Upperby EP,[6] refounded 1860[60]), 1865 (help cr EP11).[55]

EP6—CARLISLE ST ELISABETH, HARRABY—Cr 1960 from Upperby EP, Scotby EP.[61] Bdry: 1969.[62]

EP7—CARLISLE ST HERBERT WITH ST STE-PHEN—Cr 1962 by union Currock EP, pt EP11.[63]

—CARLISLE ST JAMES—Name commonly used for EP cr 1863 as 'Denton Holme', qv.

EP8—CARLISLE ST JOHN THE EVANGELIST—Cr 1867 from EP1, Upperby EP.[56] Carl North RDn (1871—73), Carl South RDn (1873—1926). Bdry: 1902 (help cr EP3),[59] 1969.[62]

EP9—CARLISLE ST LUKE, MORTON—Cr 1968 from EP2.[58]

AP2—CARLISLE ST MARY—Mainly in Bor/MB; incl in Cumb Wd tp Caldewgate (sep CP 1866,[1] sep EP 1832,[6] eccl refounded 1834,[49] eccl name as EP2, qv), tp Rickergate (sep CP 1866,[1] eccl severed 1868 to help cr EP10[31]), tp Cummersdale (sep CP 1866[1]); incl in Leath Wd tp Middlesceugh and Braithwaite (sep CP 1866[1]). The pts of AP2 within and without the MB sep rated for poor law purposes and each a sep CP 1866, as 'St Mary Within' CP, 'St Mary Without' CP,[1] so that AP2 has no sep civ identity after 1866. *Parl* As for AP1, except no enlarged pt 1832—67. Carl North RDn (1871—1926). Eccl bdry: 1863 (cr Denton Holme EP, later called 'Carlisle St James'),[37] 1867 (help refound Ivegill EP),[64] 1868 (cr EP10 [incl area tp Rickergate]),[31] 1932 (gains EP10).[65]

EP10—CARLISLE ST MARY WITHOUT—Cr 1868 from AP2 (incl area tp Rickergate).[31] After cr 1875 of church St Paul, commonly called 'Carlisle St Paul'. Carl North RDn (1871—1926). Bdry: 1902 (help cr EP3).[59] Abol 1932 ent to AP2.[65]

—CARLISLE ST PAUL—See EP10

EP11—CARLISLE ST STEPHEN—Cr 1865 from AP1, Upperby EP, EP1.[55] Carl South RDn (1871—1926). Bdry: 1893,[29] 1897,[66] 1937 (help cr Currock EP),[67] 1962 (help cr EP7).[63]

CASTLE CARROCK
AP *LG* Seq 8. *Parl* Seq 1. *Eccl* Seq 7. Eccl bdry: 1971 (gains eccl ex-par Geltsdale).[54]

CASTLE SOWERBY
AP *LG* Seq 10. Civ bdry: 1886,[68] 1934,[4] 1935.[19] *Parl* Seq 3. *Eccl* Allerd. RDn (until 1857), Cumb RDn (1857—59), Greyst. RDn (1859—82), Penr. West

RDn (1882—1926), Penr. RDn (1926—58), Carl RDn (1958—*). Eccl bdry: 1737 (cr Raughton Head with Gatesgill EP,[6] refounded 1868 [incl pt Dalston AP[25]), 1958.[48]

CASTLERIGG ST JOHN'S AND WYTHBURN
Tp Castlerigg St John's, chap Wythburn (for eccl, qv) each in Crosthwaite AP, civ one unit and as such CP 1866.[1] *LG* Allerd. below Derw. Wd, Cockerm. PLU (soon after 1838[2]—1930), pt Kesw. USD, pt Cockerm. RSD, Cockerm. RD. Bdry: 1883,[12] 1894 (the pt in the USD transf to Keswick CP),[19] 1935.[19] *Parl* Seq 9.

CATTERLEN
Tp in Newton Reigny AP, sep CP 1866.[1] *LG* Seq 10. Bdry: 1934 (gains Newton Reigny AP).[3] *Parl* Seq 3.

CLEATOR
AP *LG* Allerd. above Derw. Wd, Whiteh. PLU, Cleator Moor USD, UD. Renamed civ 1934 'Cleator Moor'.[3] *Parl* W'rn Dv (1832—85), Egrem. Dv (1885—1918), Whiteh. Dv (1918—48). *Eccl* Seq 16. Eccl bdry: 1869 (cr Cleator Moor EP).[69]

CLEATOR MOOR
EP Cr 1869 from Cleator AP.[69] Whiteh. RDn (1869—1970), Calder RDn (1970—*).
CP Renaming civ 1934 of Cleator AP.[3] *LG* Ennerd. RD. *Parl* Whiteh. CC (1948—*).

CLIFTON
Chap in Workington AP, sep EP 1733[6]; for civ see constituent tps of Great Clifton, Little Clifton. Copel. RDn (1733—1859), Cockerm. RDn (1859—82), Cockerm. & Work. RDn (1882—1970), Solway RDn (1970—*).

GREAT CLIFTON
Tp in Workington AP, sep CP 1866[1]; pt of chap Clifton (sep EP 1733[6], qv). *LG* Seq 2. Bdry: 1887.[35] *Parl* Seq 4.

LITTLE CLIFTON
Organisation as for Great Clifton.

CLOFFOCKS
Ex-par place, sep CP 1858.[38] *LG* Allerd. above Derw. Wd, Cockerm. PLU, RSD (1875—83), Work. MB (1883—1934), USD (1882—94). Abol 1934 ent to Workington AP.[3] *Parl* N'rn Dv (1867—85), Penr. Dv (1885—1918), Work. Dv (1918—48).

COCKERMOUTH
Chap in Brigham AP, sep EP 1806,[6] sep CP 1866.[1] *LG* Allerd. above Derw. Wd, Cockerm. PLU, USD, UD. Civ bdry: 1935.[19] *Parl* Cockerm. Parl Bor (orig as pt Brigham, then with sep civ identity: 1295, 1640—1885), Cockerm. Dv (1885—1918), Penr. & Cockerm. Dv (1918—48), Work. CC (1948—*). *Eccl* Copel. RDn (1806—59), Cockerm. RDn (1859—82), Cockerm. & Work. RDn (1882—1970), Derw. RDn (1970—*). Eccl bdry: 1865 (cr Cockermouth Christ Church EP).[55]

COCKERMOUTH CHRIST CHURCH
EP Cr 1865 from Cockermouth EP.[55] RDns as for Cockermouth, from 1865.

CORNEY
AP *LG* Allerd. above Derw. Wd, Bootle PLU, RSD,

RD. Civ bdry: 1886.[70] Abol civ 1934 ent to Waberthwaite AP.[3] *Parl* W'rn Dv (1832—85), Egrem. Dv (1885—1918), Whiteh. Dv (1918—48). *Eccl* Seq 15. Eccl bdry: 1956.[71]

COTEHILL AND CUMWHITTON
EP Cr 1868 from Wetheral AP.[72] Carl RDn (1868—71), Carl South RDn (1871—1926), Carl RDn (1926—70), Bramp. RDn (1970—*).

CROGLIN
AP *LG* Leath Wd, Penr. PLU, RSD, RD. Abol civ 1934 pt to Ainstable AP, pt to Cumrew AP.[3] *Parl* E'rn Dv (1832—85), Penr. Dv (1885—1918), Penr. & Cockerm. Dv (1918—48). *Eccl* Allerd. RDn (until 1857), Cumb RDn (1857—59), Penr. RDn (1859—82), Penr. East RDn (1882—1926), Kirkosw. RDn (1926—54), Bramp. RDn (1954—*).

CROSBY ON EDEN
AP Usual eccl spelling; for civ see following entry. *Eccl* Seq 10.

CROSBY UPON EDEN
AP Usual civ spelling; for eccl see prev entry. *LG* Esk. Wd, Carl PLU, RSD, RD. Abol civ 1934 pt to Stanwix AP, pt to Wetheral AP.[3] *Parl* E'rn Dv (1832—85), Esk. Dv (1885—1918), N'rn Dv (1918—48).

CROSSCANONBY
AP Incl area Maryport (sep EP 1763,[6] refounded 1863 [tps Netherall, Dearham, neither with sep civ identity],[73] sep CP 1928 by union pars in Maryp. UD, qv). *LG* Allerd. below Derw. Wd, Cockerm. PLU (soon after 1838[2]—1930), pt Maryp. USD, pt Cockerm. RSD, Cockerm. RD. Civ bdry: 1894 (the pt in the USD cr Netherhall CP).[22] *Parl* Seq 4. *Eccl* Seq 1.

CROSTHWAITE
AP Incl in Allerd. above Derw. Wd chap Borrowdale (sep CP 1866,[1] sep EP 1743,[6] pt of the EP severed 1859 to help refound Keswick EP,[27] the remainder refounded 1865 as Borrowdale EP[28]), chap Newlands (sep EP 1748,[6] eccl refounded 1868,[29] not sep civ), chap St John's in the Vale (pt severed 1859 to help refound Keswick EP,[27] the remainder cr 1863 'St John's in the Vale' EP[74]), tp Above Derwent (sep CP 1866[1]); incl in Allerd. below Derw. Wd chap Wythburn (sep EP 1745,[6] eccl refounded 1867[75]), tp Castlerigg St John's (civ united with Wythburn as 'Castlerigg St John's and Wythburn' and as such sep CP 1866[1]), tp Underskiddaw (sep CP 1866[1]), chap and bor Keswick (bor status not sustained, sep CP 1866,[1] sep EP 1717,[6] eccl refounded 1839, 1859, qv for constituent pars) so that after 1866, 'Crosthwaite' has no sep civ identity. *Parl* W'rn Dv (1832—67). *Eccl* Seq 4. Addtl eccl bdry alt: 1717 (cr Thornthwaite EP,[6] eccl refounded 1841[64]), 1926.[60]

CULGAITH
Chap in Kirkland AP, sep CP 1866,[1] sep EP 1739,[6] eccl refounded 1879.[76] *LG* Seq 10. Civ bdry: 1934 (gains Kirkland and Blencarn CP, Skirwith CP).[3] *Parl* Seq 3. *Eccl* Allerd. RDn (1739—1857), Cumb RDn (1857—59), Penr. RDn (1859—82), Penr. East RDn (1882—1926), Kirkosw. RDn (1926—

70), Penr. RDn (1970—*).

CUMMERSDALE
Tp in Carlisle St Mary AP, sep CP 1866.[1] *LG* Cumb Wd, Carl PLU, pt Carl MB & USD (1887—94), Carl RSD (ent 1875—87, pt 1887—94), Carl RD (1894—1934), Border RD (1934—74). Bdry: 1894 (loses the pt in the MB to Caldewgate CP),[50] 1912,[68] 1951 (loses pt to Carl CB [assoc with Cumb] & CP).[14] *Parl* E'rn Dv (1867—85), Esk. Dv (1885—1918), N'rn Dv (1918—48), Penr. & the Border CC (1948—*). *Parl* bdry: 1951.[15]

CUMREW
AP *LG* Seq 8. Civ bdry: 1934.[4] *Parl* Seq 1. *Eccl* Seq 7. Eccl bdry: 1971.[54]

CUMWHITTON
AP Orig sep AP, appropriated to Carl Priory, after Dissolution deemed chap in Wetheral AP,[77] sep civ identity early, sep EP 1740.[6] *LG* Seq 8. Civ bdry: 1934.[4] *Parl* Seq 1. *Eccl* Seq 7. Eccl bdry: 1955,[78] 1971.[54]

CURROCK
EP Cr 1937 from Upperby EP, Carlisle St Stephen EP.[67] Carl RDn. Abol 1962 to help cr Carlisle St Herbert with St Stephen EP.[63]

DACRE
AP *LG* Seq 10. *Parl* Seq 3. *Eccl* Seq 2.

DALSTON
AP *LG* Seq 6. Civ bdry: 1886,[68] 1934.[4] *Parl* Seq 1. *Eccl* Carl RDn (until 1859), Wigt. RDn (1859—1926), Carl RDn (1926—*). Eccl bdry: 1771 (cr Ivegill [sometimes 'Highhead'] EP,[6] refounded 1867, qv for other constituent pars[64]), 1868 (help refound Raughton Head with Gatesgill EP),[25] 1971.[37]

DEAN
AP *LG* Seq 2. Civ bdry: 1934 (gains Eaglesfield CP).[3] *Parl* Seq 4. *Eccl* Copel. RDn (until 1859), Whiteh. RDn (1859—82), Cockerm. & Work. RDn (1882—1970), Derw. RDn (1970—*).

DEARHAM
AP Incl tp Ellenborough and Ewanrigg (sep CP 1866[1]). *LG* Seq 4. *Parl* Seq 4. *Eccl* Seq 1. Eccl bdry: 1911 (cr Netherton EP),[79] 1914.[29]

NETHER DENTON
AP *LG* Seq 8. Civ bdry: 1883.[80] *Parl* Seq 1. *Eccl* Seq 7. Eccl bdry: 1937.[24]

OVER DENTON
AP Usual eccl spelling; for civ see following entry. *Eccl* Carl RDn (until 1859), Bramp. RDn (1859—1970). Abol eccl 1970 ent to Gilsland EP.[81]

UPPER DENTON
AP Usual civ spelling; for eccl see prev entry. *LG* Seq 8. *Parl* Seq 1.

DENTON HOLME
EP Cr 1863 from Carlisle St Mary AP.[37] Carl RDn (1863—71), Carl South RDn (1871—1926), Carl RDn (1926—*). Now usually called 'Carlisle St James'.

DISTINGTON
AP *LG* Seq 3. *Parl* Seq 6. *Eccl* Copel. RDn (until 1859), Whiteh. RDn (1859—1970), Solway RDn (1970—*). Eccl bdry: 1954.[82]

DOVENBY

Tp in Bridekirk AP, sep CP 1866.[1] *LG* Allerd. below Derw. Wd, Cockerm. PLU, RSD, RD. Bdry: 1887.[35] Abol 1934 ent to Bridekirk AP.[3] *Parl* Pt Cockerm. Parl Bor, pt W'rn Dv (1832—85), Cockerm. Dv (1885—1918), Penr. & Cockerm. Dv (1918—48).

DRIGG

AP Usual eccl spelling; for civ see following entry. *Eccl* Seq 15. Eccl bdry: 1904 (help cr Seascale EP).[83]

DRIGG AND CARLETON

AP Usual civ spelling; for eccl see prev entry. *LG* Seq 1. Civ bdry: 1901.[84] *Parl* Seq 5.

DUNDRAW

Tp in Bromfield AP, sep CP 1866,[1] eccl severed 1902 to help cr Waverton EP.[43] *LG* Seq 7. Bdry: 1946.[85] *Parl* Seq 2.

EAGLESFIELD

Tp in Brigham AP, sep CP 1866.[1] *LG* Allerd. above Derw. Wd, Cockerm. PLU, RSD, RD. Abol 1934 ent to Dean AP.[3] *Parl* Cockerm. Parl Bor (1832—85), Cockerm. Dv (1885—1918), Penr. & Cockerm. Dv (1918—48).

EAGLESFIELD ABBEY

Ex-par place, sep CP 1858.[38] *LG* Carl Bor/MB, PLU (1862—1904), USD. Abol 1904 to help cr Carlisle CP.[30] *Parl* Carl Parl Bor (until 1918).

EASTON

AP Orig sep AP, Carl RDn, lost by late 14th cent and incl in Kirkandrews upon Esk AP (eccl, 'Kirkandrews on Esk').[86]

EDENHALL

AP Usual civ spelling; incl eccl Langwathby (seemingly orig AP and later styled 'vicarage', but sep eccl status not sustained,[87] hence this par usually eccl 'Edenhall with Langwathby', qv). *LG* Leath Wd, Penr. PLU, RSD, RD. Abol 1934 ent to Langwathby CP.[3] *Parl* E'rn Dv (1832—85), Penr. Dv (1885—1918), Penr. & Cockerm. Dv (1918—48).

EDENHALL WITH LANGWATHBY

AP Usual eccl spelling; for civ and for eccl inclusion of Langwathby, see prev entry. *Eccl* Seq 3.

EGREMONT

AP *LG* Allerd. above Derw. Wd, Egrem. Bor (status not sustained), Whiteh. PLU, Egrem. USD, UD (1894—1934), Ennerd. RD (1934—74). Civ bdry: 1881,[88] 1894.[21] *Parl* Egrem. Parl Bor (1295 only), Seq 5. *Eccl* Seq 16. Eccl bdry: 1963.[20]

ELLENBOROUGH AND EWANRIGG

Tp in Dearham AP, sep CP 1866,[1] eccl severed 1911 to help cr Netherton EP.[79] *LG* Allerd. below Derw. Wd, Cockerm. PLU, pt Maryp. USD, pt Cockerm. RSD, Maryp. UD. Abol 1928 to help cr Maryport.[89] *Parl* W'rn Dv (1867—85), Cockerm. Dv (1885—1918), Work. Dv (1918—48).

EMBLETON

Chap in Brigham AP, sep CP 1866,[1] sep EP 1747.[6] *LG* Seq 2. Civ bdry: 1887.[90] *Parl* Seq 4. *Eccl* Copel. RDn (1747—1859), Cockerm. RDn (1859—82), Cockerm. & Work. RDn (1882—1970), Derw. RDn (1970—*). Eccl bdry: 1971.[91]

ENNERDALE

Chap in St Bees AP, sep EP 1743,[6] incl tp Kinniside and as 'Ennerdale and Kinniside' sep CP 1866,[1] qv. *Eccl* Copel. RDn (1743—1859), Whiteh. RDn (1859—1970), Calder RDn (1970—*).

ENNERDALE AND KINNISIDE

Civ name for CP cr 1866 from chap Ennerdale (sep EP 1743,[6] qv) which incl area Kinniside.[1] *LG* Seq 3. *Parl* Seq 5.

ESKDALE

Chap in St Bees AP, sep EP 1747,[6] civ united with chap Wasdale Head in same par as 'Eskdale and Wasdale', as such sep CP 1866,[1] qv. *Eccl* Copel. RDn (1747—1859), Gosf. RDn (1859—1970), Calder RDn (1970—*).

CP Cr 1934 by union Birker and Austhwaite CP, pt Eskdale and Wasdale CP.[3] *LG* Millom RD. *Parl* Whiteh. CC (1948—*).

ESKDALE AND WASDALE

Civ union of chaps Eskdale, Wasdale Head, each in St Bees AP (for eccl independence and organisation, see the 2 chaps), sep CP 1866.[1] *LG* Allerd. above Derw. Wd, Bootle PLU, RSD, RD. Abol 1934 pt to help cr Eskdale CP, pt to Nether Wasdale CP.[3] *Parl* W'rn Dv (1867—85), Egrem. Dv (1885—1918), Whiteh. Dv (1918—48).

ESKETT—see SALTER AND ESKETT

FARLAM

AP *LG* Seq 8. Civ bdry: 1883,[92] 1934.[4] *Parl* Seq 1. *Eccl* Carl RDn (1740—1859), Bramp. RDn (1859—*). Eccl bdry: 1937.[24]

FLIMBY

Chap in Camerton AP, sep civ identity early, sometimes deemed ex-par,[51] sep EP 1744.[6] *LG* Allerd. below Derw. Wd, Cockerm. PLU, RSD, RD (1894—1934), Maryp. UD (1934—74). *Parl* Seq 4. *Eccl* Allerd. RDn (1744—1859), Cockerm. RDn (1859—71), Maryp. RDn (1871—1970), Solway RDn (1970—*).

FRIZINGTON

EP Cr 1910 from Arlecdon AP.[10] Whiteh. RDn (1910—70), Calder RDn (1970—*).

GAMBLESBY

Tp in Addingham AP, sep CP 1866.[1] *LG* Leath Wd, Penr. PLU, RSD, RD. Bdry: 1886.[93] Abol 1934 ent to Glassonby CP.[3] *Parl* E'rn Dv (1867—85), Penr. Dv (1885—1918), Penr. & Cockerm. Dv (1918—48).

GELTSDALE

Ex-par place, sep CP 1858,[38] eccl abol 1971 ent to Castle Carrock AP.[54] *LG* Esk. Wd, own overseers for poor (until 1861), Bramp. RDn (1861—1930), RSD, RD (1894—1934), Border RD (1934—74). *Parl* Seq 1.

GILCRUX

AP *LG* Seq 4. *Parl* Seq 4. *Eccl* Seq 1.

GILSLAND

EP Cr 1854 from Lanercost AP,[94] refounded 1855.[95] Carl RDn (1854—59), Bramp. RDn (1859—*). Bdry: 1970 (gains Over Denton AP).[81]

GLASSONBY

Tp in Addingham AP, sep CP 1866.[1] *LG* Seq 10. Bdry: 1886,[93] 1934 (gains Gamblesby CP).[3] *Parl*

Seq 3.

GOSFORTH

AP *LG* Seq 3. Civ bdry: 1881,[17] 1897 (cr Seascale CP).[96] *Parl* Seq 5. *Eccl* Seq 15. Eccl bdry: 1904 (help cr Seascale EP).[83]

GREYSOUTHEN

Tp in Brigham AP, sep CP 1866.[1] *LG* Seq 2. *Parl* Seq 4.

GREYSTOKE

AP Incl tps Berrier and Murrah, Hutton Roof (each a sep CP 1866,[1] pt of each eccl severed 1926 to help refound Mungrisdale EP[24]), tp Bowscale (sep CP 1866,[1] eccl severed 1926 to help refound Mungrisdale EP[24]), tps Hutton Soil, Hutton John (each a sep CP 1866[1]), chap Matterdale (sep CP 1866,[1] sep EP 1742,[6] eccl refounded 1865[29]), chap Mungrisdale (sep CP 1866,[1] sep EP 1740,[6] eccl refounded 1929 by union Mungrisdale EP, tp Bowscale, pt tps Berrier and Murrah, Hutton Roof [all orig in Greystoke AP], pt tp Mosedale in Caldbeck AP, pt Matterdale EP[24]), chap Threkeld (sep CP 1866,[1] sep EP 1747[6]), chap Watermillock (sep CP 1866,[1] sep EP 1742[6]). *LG* Pt Greystoke Bor (status not sustained), Seq 10. *Parl* Seq 3. *Eccl* Seq 2.

GRINSDALE

AP *LG* Cumb Wd, Carl PLU, RSD, RD. Civ bdry: 1912.[23] Abol 1934 ent to Beaumont AP.[3] *Parl* E'rn Dv (1832—85), Esk. Dv (1885—1918), N'rn Dv (1918—48). *Eccl* Seq 13.

HAILE

AP *LG* Seq 3. Civ bdry: 1935.[19] *Parl* Seq 5. *Eccl* Copel. RDn (until 1859), Whiteh. RDn (1859—71), Gosf. RDn (1871—1970), Calder RDn (1970—*). Eccl bdry: 1963.[20]

HARRINGTON

AP *LG* Allerd. above Derw. Wd, Whiteh. PLU, RSD (1875—91), Harrington USD (1891—94), UD (1894—1934), Work. MB (1934—74). Civ bdry: 1934 (the pt not transf to Work. MB cr Lowca CP).[3] *Parl* W'rn Dv (1832—85), Egrem. Dv (1885—1918), Work. Dv/CC (1918—*). *Eccl* Copel. RDn (until 1859), Whiteh. RDn (1859—1954), Cockerm. & Work. RDn (1954—70), Solway RDn (1970—*). Eccl bdry: 1954.[82]

HAYTON

AP *LG* Seq 8. *Parl* Seq 1. *Eccl* Seq 7. Eccl bdry: 1843 (help cr Holme Eden EP),[97] 1955.[78]

HAYTON

Chap in Aspatria AP, sep EP 1741,[6] eccl refounded 1868,[9] civ united with Mealo as 'Hayton and Mealo' and as such sep CP 1866,[1] qv. *Eccl* Allerd. RDn (1741—1859), Cockerm. RDn (1859—71), Maryp. RDn (1871—1970), Solway RDn (1970—*).

HAYTON AND MEALO

Civ name for tp in Aspatria AP (for eccl and EP cr therefrom, see prev entry), sep CP 1866.[1] *LG* Seq 5. Bdry: 1934.[4] *Parl* W'rn Dv (1867—85), Esk. Dv (1885—1918), Work. Dv (1918—48), Penr. & the Border CC (1948—*).

HENSINGHAM

Chap in St Bees AP, sep CP 1866,[1] sep EP 1867.[75]

LG Allerd. above Derw. Wd, Whiteh. PLU, RSD, RD. Civ bdry: 1881 (incl gains Low Keekle CP).[98] Abol 1934 pt to Weddicar CP, pt to Whitehaven CP, pt to St Bees AP.[3] *Parl* W'rn Dv (1867—85), Egrem. Dv (1885—1918), Whiteh. Dv (1918—48). *Eccl* Whiteh. RDn (1867—1970), Calder RDn (1970—*). Eccl bdry: 1934,[99] 1961 (help cr Mirehouse EP).[100]

HESKET

CP Cr 1934 by union Hesket in the Forest AP, Plumpton Wall CP.[3] *LG* Penr. RD. *Parl* Penr. & the Border CC (1948—*).

HESKET IN THE FOREST

AP Orig chap in Carlisle St Mary AP, date of sep status uncertain, perhaps as early as 14th cent, perhaps 16th cent after erection of chapel 1530.[101] Incl tps Calthwaite, Plumpton Street (neither sep). *LG* Leath Wd, Penr. PLU, RSD, RD. Abol civ 1934 to help cr Hesket CP.[3] *Parl* E'rn Dv (1832—85), Penr. Dv (1885—1918), Penr. & Cockerm. Dv (1918—48). *Eccl* Carl RDn (cr—1871), Carl North RDn (1871—82), Carl South RDn (1882—1926), Penr. RDn (1926—*). Eccl bdry: 1867 (help refound Ivegill EP),[64] 1869 (help refound Wreay EP),[102] 1873 (help refound Plumpton Wall EP),[103] 1973.[4]

HETHERSGILL

Tp in Kirklinton AP, sep CP 1866.[1] *LG* Seq 9. Bdry: 1883.[12] *Parl* Seq 1.

HIGHHEAD—See IVEGILL

HOLM CULTRAM

AP Incl tps Holme Abbey, Holme East Waver, Holme St Cuthbert (each a sep CP 1866[1]), tp Holme Low (sep CP 1866,[1] sep EP 1851[6]) so that 'Holm Cultram' has no sep civ identity after 1866. Incl Skinburness Marsh (after 1866 common to Holme Abbey CP, Holme Low CP, Holme St Cuthbert CP). Other bdry alt: ca 1305 (cr Skinburness AP, soon removed to Newton Arlosh, later only a chap in this par until 1849).[104] *LG* Pt Wavermouth Bor (1300—01), replaced by Skinburness Bor (1301—05), replaced by Newton Arlosh Bor (sometimes 'Kirkby Johnannis', status not sustained), Allerd. below Derw. Wd. *Parl* W'rn Dv (1832—67). *Eccl* Allerd. RDn (until 1859), Wigt. RDn (1859—after 1940), Maryp. RDn (after 1940—70), Solway RDn (1970—*). Addtl eccl bdry alt: 1849 (cr Newton Arlosh EP, Silloth Christ Church EP, Silloth St Paul EP).[105]

HOLME ABBEY

Tp (sometimes 'Abbeytown') in Holm Cultram AP, sep CP 1866.[1] *LG* Allerd. below Derw. Wd, Wigt. PLU, Holme Cultram USD, UD (1894—1934), Wigt. RD (1934—74). Bdry: 1883,[12] 1887,[106] 1934.[4] *Parl* Seq 7.

HOLME EAST WAVER

Tp in Holm Cultram AP, sep CP 1866.[1] Organisation as for Holme Abbey.

HOLME EDEN

EP Cr 1843 from Wetheral AP, Hayton EP.[97] Carl RDn (1843—59), Bramp. RDn (1859—71), Carl South RDn (1871—1926), Carl RDn (1926—70), Bramp. RDn (1970—*). Bdry: 1955.[78]

HOLME LOW

Tp (sometimes 'Holme St Paul') in Holm Cultram AP, sep CP 1866,[1] sep EP 1851.[6] *LG* Allerd. below Derw. Wd, Wigt. PLU, Holme Cultram USD, UD. Bdry: 1883,[12] 1887,[106] 1934 (incl help cr Silloth CP).[3] *Parl* Seq 7. *Eccl* Allerd. RDn (1851—59), Bramp. RDn (1859—71), Carl North RDn (1871—1926), Carl RDn (1926—*).

HOLME ST CUTHBERT

Tp in Holm Cultram AP, sep CP 1866.[1] Organisation as for Holme Abbey.

HOLME ST PAUL—see HOLME LOW

HOUGHTON ST JOHN

EP Cr 1841 from Stanwix AP, ent ex-par Kingmoor.[107] Carl RDn (1841—59), Bramp. RDn (1859—71), Carl North RDn (1871—1926), Carl RDn (1926—*). Sometimes 'Houghton St John with Kingmoor'.

HUNSONBY

CP Cr 1934 by union Hesket in the Forest AP, Hunsonby and Winskill CP.[3] *LG* Penr. RD. *Parl* Penr. & the Border CC (1948—*).

HUNSONBY AND WINSKILL

Tp in Addingham AP, sep CP 1866.[1] *LG* Leath Wd, Penr. PLU, RSD, RD. Abol 1934 to help cr Hunsonby CP.[3] *Parl* E'rn Dv (1867—85), Penr. Dv (1885—1918), Penr. & Cockerm. Dv (1918—48).

HUTTON

CP Cr 1934 by union Hutton John CP, Hutton Soil CP.[3] *LG* Penr. RD. *Parl* Penr. & the Border CC (1948—*).

HUTTON IN THE FOREST

AP *LG* Leath Wd, Penr. PLU, RSD, RD. Abol civ 1934 ent to Skelton AP.[3] *Parl* E'rn Dv (1832—85), Penr. Dv (1885—1918), Penr. & Cockerm. Dv (1918—48). *Eccl* Seq 2.

HUTTON JOHN

Tp in Greystoke AP, sep CP 1866.[1] *LG* Leath Wd, Penr. PLU, RSD, RD. Bdry: 1883.[12] Abol 1934 to help cr Hutton CP.[3] *Parl* E'rn Dv (1867—85), Penr. Dv (1885—1918), Penr. & Cockerm. Dv (1918—48).

HUTTON ROOF

Tp in Greystoke AP, sep CP 1866,[1] pt eccl severed 1926 to help refound Mungrisdale EP.[24] *LG* Leath Wd, Penr. PLU, RSD, RD. Abol 1934 ent to Mungrisdale CP.[3] *Parl* As for Hutton John.

HUTTON SOIL

Tp in Greystoke AP, sep CP 1866.[1] Organisation as for Hutton John.

IREBY

AP Incl tps High Ireby, Low Ireby (each a sep CP 1866[1]) so that 'Ireby' has no sep civ identity 1866—1934 (see following entry). *LG* Allerd. below Derw. Wd. *Parl* W'rn Dv (1832—67). *Eccl* Seq 6.

CP Cr 1934 by union High Ireby CP, Low Ireby CP, Uldale AP.[3] *LG* Wigt. RD. *Parl* Penr. & the Border CC (1948—*).

HIGH IREBY

Tp in Ireby AP, sep CP 1866.[1] *LG* Allerd. below Derw. Wd, Wigt. PLU, RSD, RD. Abol 1934 to help cr Ireby CP.[3] *Parl* W'rn Dv (1867—85), Penr. Dv (1885—1918), N'rn Dv (1918—48).

LOW IREBY

Organisation as for High Ireby.

IRTHINGTON

AP *LG* Seq 8. *Parl* Seq 1. *Eccl* Seq 7.

IRTON

AP Pt of single tp 'Irton, Santon and Melthwaite' orig in St Bees AP, as such a sep CP 1866,[1] later called 'Irton'. *LG* Seq 1. Civ bdry: 1934.[4] *Parl* Seq 5. *Eccl* Seq 15.

IRTON, SANTON AND MELTHWAITE—see prev entry

ISEL

AP Incl tps Blindcrake Isel and Redmaine, Isel Old Park, Sunderland (each a sep CP 1866[1]) so that 'Isel' has no sep civ identity after 1866. *LG* Allerd. below Derw. Wd. *Parl* W'rn Dv (1832—67). *Eccl* Allerd. RDn (until 1859), Cockerm. RDn (1859—71), Maryp. RDn (1871—1961), Kesw. RDn (1961—70), Derw. RDn (1970—*).

ISEL OLD PARK

Tp in Isel AP, sep CP 1866.[1] *LG* Allerd. below Derw. Wd, Cockerm. PLU, RSD, RD. Abol 1934 to help cr Blindcrake CP.[3] *Parl* W'rn Dv (1867—85), Cockerm. Dv (1885—1918), Penr. & Cockerm. Dv (1918—48).

IVEGILL

Chap (sometimes 'Highhead') in Dalston AP, sep EP 1771,[6] eccl refounded 1867 from Dalston AP, Hesket in the Forest AP, Carlisle St Mary AP.[64] Wigt. RDn (1771—1871), Carl South RDn (1871—1926), Penr. RDn (1926—*). Bdry: 1971.[37]

LOW KEEKLE

Ex-par place, sep CP ca 1871.[108] *LG* Allerd. above Derw. Wd, Whiteh. PLU (1873—81), RSD. Abol 1881 ent to Hensingham CP.[109] *Parl* W'rn Dv (1867—85).

KELLS

EP Cr 1935 from Whitehaven Holy Trinity with Christ Church EP.[110] Whiteh. RDn (1935—70), Calder RDn (1970—*).

KESWICK

Chap in Crosthwaite AP, sep CP 1866,[1] sep EP 1717,[6] eccl refounded 1839 (incl ex-par Briery Cottages),[39] eccl refounded 1859 (incl pts chaps St John's in the Vale, Borrowdale, each in Crosthwaite AP).[27] *LG* As chap: Kesw. Bor (status not sustained); then and as par, Allerd. below Derw. Wd, Cockerm. PLU, Kesw. USD, UD. Civ bdry: 1883,[12] 1894 (gains the following in Kesw. USD: Briery Cottages CP and pts of Castlerigg St John's and Wythburn CP, Underskiddaw CP), 1935.[19] *Parl* Seq 9. *Eccl* Allerd. RDn (1717—1859), Kesw. RDn (1859—1970), Derw. RDn (1970—*). Eccl bdry: 1970.[111]

KINGMOOR

Ex-par place (incl area hmlt Kingstown, not sep), sep CP 1858,[38] eccl abol 1841 to help cr Houghton St John EP.[107] *LG* Esk. Wd, Carl PLU, RSD, RD (1894—1934), Border RD (1934—74). Civ bdry: 1912,[23] 1951 (loses pt to Carl CB [assoc with Cumb] & CP).[14] *Parl* Seq 1. *Parl* bdry: 1951.[15]

KINGSTOWN—see prev entry

KINGWATER

Tp in Lanercost AP, sep CP 1866.[1] *LG* Seq 8. *Parl* Seq 1.

KIRKANDREWS

CP Cr 1934 by union Kirkandrews Middle CP, Kirkandrews Moat CP, Kirkandrews Nether CP.[3] *LG* Border RD. *Parl* Penr. & the Border CC (1948—*).

KIRKANDREWS MIDDLE

Tp in Kirkandrews upon Esk AP, sep CP 1866.[1] *LG* Esk. Wd, Longt. PLU, RSD, RD. Abol 1934 to help cr Kirkandrews CP.[3] *Parl* E'rn Dv (1867—85), Esk. Dv (1885—1918), N'rn Dv (1918—48).

KIRKANDREWS MOAT

Organisation as for Kirkandrews Middle.

KIRKANDREWS NETHER

Organisation as for Kirkandrews Middle.

KIRKANDREWS ON EDEN

AP Usual eccl spelling; for civ see 'Kirkandrews upon Eden'. *Eccl* Carl RDn. Gains eccl 1692 Beaumont AP, thereafter 'Kirkandrews on Eden with Beaumont' EP,[16] qv.

KIRKANDREWS ON EDEN WITH BEAUMONT

EP Cr 1692 by union Kirkandrews on Eden AP, Beaumont AP.[16] *Eccl* Seq 13.

KIRKANDREWS ON ESK

AP Usual eccl spelling; for civ and early reestablishment of this par, see 'Kirkandrews upon Esk'. *Eccl* Seq 10.

KIRKANDREWS UPON EDEN

AP Usual civ spelling; for eccl and eccl gain of Beaumont AP, see 'Kirkandrews on Eden'. *LG* Cumb Wd, Carl PLU, RSD, RD. Abol civ 1934 ent to Beaumont AP.[3] *Parl* E'rn Dv (1832—85), Esk. Dv (1885—1918), N'rn Dv (1918—48).

KIRKANDREWS UPON ESK

AP Usual civ spelling; for eccl see 'Kirkandrews on Esk'. Gains late 14th cent Easton AP[86]. This par later in ruins, reestablished 1632 (incl Nichol Forest as its chap) (sep CP 1866,[1] sep EP 1744,[6] eccl usually 'Nicholforest'); also incl tps Kirkandrews Middle, Kirkandrews Moat, Kirkandrews Nether (each a sep CP 1866[1]) so that 'Kirkandrews upon Esk' has no sep civ identity after 1866. *LG* Esk. Wd. *Parl* E'rn Dv (1832—67).

KIRKBAMPTON

AP *LG* Cumb Wd, Wigt. PLU (soon after 1837[2]—1930), RSD, RD. *Parl* Seq 1. *Eccl* Seq 10.

KIRKBRIDE

AP *LG* Seq 7. *Parl* E'rn Dv (1832—85), Cockerm. Dv (1885—1918), N'rn Dv (1918—48), Penr. & the Border CC (1948—*). *Eccl* Seq 5.

KIRKCAMBECK

AP Orig sep AP, Carl RDn, not mentioned after 14th cent and incl in Lanercost AP (hence thereafter eccl 'Lanercost with Kirkcambeck').[112]

KIRKLAND

AP Incl chap Culgaith (sep CP 1866,[1] sep EP 1739,[6] eccl refounded 1879[76]), tp Skirwith (sep CP 1866,[1] sep EP 1867[113]), tp Kirkland and Blencarn (sep CP 1866[1]) so that 'Kirkland' has no sep civ identity after 1866. *LG* Leath Wd. *Parl* E'rn Dv (1832—67). *Eccl* Seq 3.

KIRKLAND AND BLENCARN

Tp in Kirkland AP, sep CP 1866.[1] *LG* Leath Wd, Penr. PLU, RSD, RD. Abol 1934 ent to Culgaith CP.[3] *Parl* E'rn Dv (1867—85), Penr. Dv (1885—1918), Penr. & Cockerm. Dv (1918—48).

KIRKLINTON

AP Incl tps Hethersgill, Kirklinton Middle (each a sep CP 1866[1]), tp Westlinton (sep CP 1866,[1] eccl severed 1871 to help cr Blackford EP[25]) so that 'Kirklinton' has no sep civ identity after 1866. *LG* Esk. Wd. *Parl* E'rn Dv (1832—67). *Eccl* Seq 8.

KIRKLINTON MIDDLE

Tp in Kirklinton AP, sep CP 1866.[1] *LG* Seq 9. *Parl* Seq 1.

KIRKOSWALD

AP Incl tp Staffield (sep CP 1866[1]). *LG* Seq 10. Addtl civ bdry alt: 1934 (gains Renwick AP, Staffield CP).[3] *Parl* Seq 3. *Eccl* Seq 3.

LAMPLUGH

AP *LG* Seq 3. Civ bdry: 1934 (gains Salter and Eskett CP).[3] *Parl* Seq 5. *Eccl* Seq 16.

LANERCOST

AP Gains after 14th cent Kirkcambeck AP,[112] thereafter eccl 'Lanercost with Kirkcambeck', qv. Incl tps Askerton, Burtholme, Kingwater, Waterhead (each a sep CP 1866[1]) so that 'Lanercost' has no sep civ identity after 1866. *LG* Esk. Wd. *Parl* E'rn Dv (1832—67).

LANERCOST WITH KIRKCAMBECK

AP Eccl name for union after late 14th cent of Lanercost AP, Kirkcambeck AP,[112] the name 'Lanercost' used civ, qv for civ and for civ sep tps. *Eccl* Seq 7. Eccl bdry: 1854 (cr Gilsland EP,[94] refounded 1855[95]), 1937.[24]

LANGRIGG AND MEALRIGG

Tp in Bromfield AP, sep CP 1866,[1] pt eccl severed 1863 to help cr Westnewton EP.[42] *LG* Allerd. below Derw. Wd, Wigt. PLU, RSD, RD. Abol 1934 ent to Bromfield AP.[3] *Parl* W'rn Dv (1867—85), Esk. Dv (1885—1918), N'rn Dv (1918—48).

LANGWATHBY

AP Seemingly orig AP and later styled 'vicarage', sep eccl status seemingly not sustained and incl in Edenhall AP,[87] hence usually eccl 'Edenhall with Langwathby', sep civ identity maintained. *LG* Seq 10. Civ bdry: 1886,[93] 1934 (gains Edenhall AP).[3] *Parl* Seq 3.

LAZONBY

AP Incl chap Plumpton Wall (sep CP 1866,[1] sep EP 1769,[6] eccl refounded 1873 [qv for constituent pars then][103]). *LG* Seq 10. *Parl* Seq 3. *Eccl* Seq 3. Addtl eccl bdry alt: 1973.[4]

LONGNEWTON—see NEWTON ARLOSH

LORTON

Chap in Brigham AP, sep civ identity early, sep EP 1744,[6] eccl refounded 1883 by union Lorton EP, pt Buttermere EP, pt tp Whinfell (the pt not incl 1883 in refounded Mosser EP).[34] Incl chap & tp Wythop (sep CP 1866,[1] sep EP 1738[6]), tp Brackenthwaite (sep CP 1866,[1] most eccl in Lorton, pt eccl severed 1884 to help refound Buttermere EP,[33] the remainder severed 1886 to help refound Loweswater EP[34]). *LG* Seq 2. Addtl civ bdry alt: 1883,[12]

1887.[35] *Parl* Seq 4. *Eccl* Copel. RDn (1744—1859), Kesw. RDn (1859—71), Cockerm. RDn (1871—82), Cockerm. & Work. RDn (1882—1970), Derw. RDn (1970—*). Addtl eccl bdry alt: 1884 (help refound Buttermere EP).[33]

LOWCA
CP Cr 1934 from the pt of Harrington AP not transf to Work. MB.[3] *LG* Ennerd. RD. *Parl* Whiteh. CC (1948—*).

LOWESWATER
Chap in St Bees AP, sep civ identity early, sep EP 1723,[6] eccl refounded 1886 by union Loweswater, the pt of tp Brackenthwaite (in Brigham AP) in neither Lorton EP nor Buttermere EP.[34] *LG* Seq 2. Civ bdry: 1946.[46] *Parl* Seq 4. *Eccl* Copel. RDn (1723—1859), Whiteh. RDn (1859—71), Cockerm. RDn (1871—82), Cockerm. & Work. RDn (1882—*).

LOWSIDE QUARTER
Tp in St Bees AP, sep CP 1866.[1] *LG* Seq 3. Bdry: 1894,[21] 1935.[19] *Parl* Seq 5.

MARYPORT
Area in Crosscanonby AP, sep EP 1763,[6] eccl refounded 1893 by union tps Netherall, Dearham (neither with sep civ identity) in Crosscanonby AP,[73] sep CP 1928 by union pars in Maryp. UD: Ellenborough and Ewanrigg CP, Netherall CP.[89] *LG* Cockerm. PLU, Maryp. UD. *Parl* Work. CC (1948—*). *Eccl* Allerd. RDn (1763—1859), Cockerm. RDn (1859—71), Maryp. RDn (1871—1970), Solway RDn (1970—*).

MATTERDALE
Chap and tp (area of tp smaller than chap) in Greystoke AP, sep EP 1742,[6] eccl refounded 1865,[28] the smaller tp a sep CP 1866.[1] *LG* Seq 10. Civ bdry: 1886,[114] 1934 (gains Watermillock CP).[4] *Parl* Seq 3. *Eccl* Allerd. RDn (1742—1857), Cumb. RDn (1857—59), Greyst. RDn (1859—82), Penr. West RDn (1882—1926), Penr. RDn (1926—*). Eccl bdry: 1926 (help refound Mungrisdale EP).[24]

MELMERBY
AP *LG* Leath Wd, Penr. PLU, RSD, RD. Abol civ 1934 ent to Ousby AP.[4] *Parl* E'rn Dv (1832—85), Penr. Dv (1885—1918), Penr. & Cockerm. Dv (1918—48). *Eccl* Seq 3.

MIDDLESCEUGH AND BRAITHWAITE
Hmlt in Carlisle St Mary AP, sep CP 1866.[1] *LG* Leath Wd, Penr. PLU, RSD, RD. Abol 1934 ent to Skelton AP.[4] *Parl* E'rn Dv (1832—85), Penr. Dv (1885—1918), Penr. & Cockerm. Dv (1918—48).

MIDGEHOLME
Ex-par place, sep CP 1858.[38] *LG* Esk. Wd, own overseers for poor until 1861, Bramp. PLU (1861—1930), RSD, RD (1894—1934), Border RD (1934—74). Bdry: 1883.[11] *Parl* Seq 1.

MILLOM
AP Incl chap Ulpha (sep CP 1866,[1] sep EP 1747[6]), chap Thwaites (sep EP 1717,[6] refounded 1925[115]), tp Birker and Austhwaite (sep CP 1866[1]). *LG* Allerd. above Derw. Wd, Bootle PLU, pt Millom USD, pt Bootle RSD, Millom UD (1894—1934), Millom RD (1934—74). Addtl civ bdry alt: 1886,[70] 1894 (the pt not in the USD cr Millom Rural CP).[22] *Parl*

Seq 5. *Eccl* Copel. RDn (until 1859), Gosf. RDn (1859—1970), Furness RDn (1970—*). Addtl eccl bdry alt: 1879 (cr Millom St George EP),[103] 1970.[116]

MILLOM RURAL
CP Cr 1894 from the pt of Millom AP not in Millom USD.[22] *LG* Bootle PLU, RD. Renamed 1934 'Millom Without' CP.[4] *Parl* Whiteh. Dv (1918—48).

MILLOM ST GEORGE
EP Cr 1879 from Millom AP.[103] Gosf. RDn (1879—1970), Furness RDn (1970—*).

MILLOM WITHOUT
CP Renaming 1934 of Millom Rural CP.[4] *LG* Millom RD. Bdry: 1935 (loses pt to Broughton West CP, Lancs).[117] *Parl* Whiteh. CC (1948—*).

MIREHOUSE
EP Cr 1961 from Hensingham EP, Whitehaven Holy Trinity with Christ Church EP.[100] Whiteh. RDn (1961—70), Calder RDn (1970—*).

MORESBY
AP Incl tp Parton (sep CP 1866[1]). *LG* Seq 3. Addtl civ bdry alt: 1900,[118] 1934.[4] *Parl* Seq 6. *Eccl* Seq 16. Eccl bdry: 1934.[99]

MOSEDALE
Tp in Caldbeck AP, sep CP 1866,[1] eccl severed 1926 to help refound Mungrisdale EP.[24] *LG* Allerd. below Derw. Wd, Penr. PLU, RSD, RD. Abol 1934 ent to Mungrisdale CP.[4] *Parl* W'rn Dv (1867—85), Penr. Dv (1885—1918), Penr. & Cockerm. Dv (1918—48).

MOSSER
Chap in Brigham AP, sep CP 1866,[1] sep EP 1774,[6] eccl refounded 1883 by union Mosser, tp Eaglesfield, pt tp Whinfell, all in Brigham AP.[41] *LG* Allerd. above Derw. Wd, Cockerm. PLU, RSD, RD. Abol 1934 ent to Blindbothel CP.[4] *Parl* W'rn Dv (1867—85), Cockerm. Dv (1885—1918), Penr. & Cockerm. Dv (1918—48). *Eccl* Copel. RDn (1774—1859), Cockerm. RDn (1859—82), Cockerm. & Work. RDn (1882—1970), Derw. RDn (1970—*).

MOUNT PLEASANT
EP Cr 1845 from St Bees AP (pt tp Preston Quarter).[99] Later called 'Whitehaven Christ Church'. Copel. RDn (1845—59), Whiteh. RDn (1859—1935). Abol 1935 to help cr Whitehaven Holy Trinity with Christ Church EP.[119]

MUNCASTER
AP *LG* Seq 1. Civ bdry: 1886.[70] *Parl* Seq 5. *Eccl* Seq 15.

MUNGRISDALE
Chap in Greystoke AP, sep CP 1866,[1] sep EP 1740,[6] eccl refounded 1926 by union pt Greystoke AP (tps Mungrisdale, Bowscale, pt tps Berrier and Murrah, Hutton Roof), pt Caldbeck AP (tp Mosedale), pt Matterdale EP.[24] *LG* Seq 10. Civ bdry: 1934 (gains Berrier and Murrah CP, Bowscale CP, Hutton Roof CP, Mosedale CP).[4] *Parl* Seq 3. *Eccl* Allerd. RDn (1740—1857), Cumb. Wd (1857—59), Greyst. RDn (1859—82), Kesw. RDn (1882—1970), Carl RDn (1970—*).

NENTHEAD

EP Cr 1846 from Alston with Garrigill AP.[9] Hexham RDn (dioc Durham until 1884, dioc Newc thereafter).

NETHERHALL

CP Cr 1894 from the pt of Crosscanonby AP in Maryp. USD[22]; for eccl severing 1893 see Maryport EP. *LG* Cockerm. PLU, Maryp. UD. Abol 1928 to help cr Maryport CP.[89] *Parl* Work. Dv (1918—48).

NETHERTON

EP Cr 1911 from Dearham AP.[79] Maryp. RDn (1911—70), Solway RDn (1970—*). Bdry: 1914.[19]

NEWLANDS

EP Cr 1748 from Crosthwaite AP,[6] refounded 1868.[29] Allerd. RDn (1748—1859), Kesw. RDn (1859—1970), Derw. RDn (1970—*). Bdry: 1926.[60]

WEST NEWTON AND ALLONBY—see below in entries for 'W'

NEWTON ARLOSH

AP Cr *ca* 1305 from Holme Cultram AP at Skinburness, soon transf to Newton Arlosh, later considered only chap in Holme Cultram,[104] eccl refounded 1849.[105] Allerd. RDn (orig, 1849—59), Wigt.RDn (1859—1970), Carl RDn (1970—*).

NEWTON REIGNY

AP Often called 'chap' because early appropriated to Bp Carl, but a sep AP (though often held with Penrith AP).[120] Incl tp Catterlen (sep CP 1866[1]). *LG* Leath Wd, Penr. PLU, RSD, RD. Abol civ 1934 ent to Catterlen CP.[4] *Parl* E'rn Dv (1832—85), Penr. Dv (1885—1918), Penr. & Cockerm. Dv (1918—48). *Eccl* Allerd. RDn (until 1857), Cumb RDn (1857—59), Penr. RDn (1859—82), Penr. West RDn (1882—1926), Penr. RDn (1926—*).

NICHOL FOREST

Orig sep area, incl 1632 in Kirkandrews upon Esk AP, sep EP 1744 as 'Nicholforest',[6] qv, sep CP 1866.[1] *LG* Seq 9. *Parl* Seq 1.

NICHOLFOREST

Orig sep area, incl 1632 in Kirkandrews upon Esk AP, sep EP 1744,[6] sep CP 1866 as 'Nichol Forest',[1] qv. *Eccl* Allerd. RDn (1744—1859), Bramp. RDn (1859—71), Carl North RDn (1871—1926), Carl RDn (1926—70), Bramp. RDn (1970—*).

ORTON

AP Usual civ spelling; for eccl see following entry. *LG* Seq 6. *Parl* Seq 1.

GREAT ORTON

AP Usual eccl spelling; for civ see prev entry. *Eccl* Carl RDn (until 1871), Carl North RDn (1871—82), Carl South RDn (1882—1926), Carl RDn (1926—*).

OUGHTERSIDE AND ALLERBY

Tp in Aspatria AP, sep CP 1866.[1] *LG* Seq 4. Bdry: 1934 (incl help cr Aspatria CP).[4] *Parl* Seq 4.

OULTON

Tp in Wigton AP, sep CP 1866.[1] *LG* Cumb. Wd, Wigt. PLU, RSD, RD. Abol 1934 ent to Woodside CP.[4] *Parl* E'rn Dv (1867—85), Esk. Dv (1885—1918), N'rn Dv (1918—48).

OUSBY

AP *LG* Seq 10. Civ bdry: 1934 (gains Melmerby AP).[4] *Parl* Seq 3. *Eccl* Seq 3.

PAPCASTLE

Tp in Bridekirk AP, sep CP 1866.[1] *LG* Seq 4. Bdry: 1935.[18] *Parl* Cockerm. Parl Bor (1832—85), Cockerm. Dv (1885—1918), Penr. & Cockerm. Dv (1885—1918), Work. CC (1948—*).

PARTON

Tp in Moresby AP, sep CP 1866.[1] *LG* Seq 3. *Parl* Seq 5.

PENRITH

AP *LG* Leath Wd, Penr. Bor, PLU, USD, UD. *Parl* Seq 3. *Eccl* Allerd. RDn (until 1857), Cumb. RDn (1857—59), Penr. RDn (1859—82), Penr. West RDn (1882—1926), Penr. RDn (1926—*). Eccl bdry: 1862 (cr Penrith Christ Church EP),[12] 1873 (help refound Plumpton Wall EP),[103] 1968 (gains Penrith Christ Church EP).[121]

PENRITH CHRIST CHURCH

EP Cr 1862 from Penrith AP.[12] Penr. RDn (1862—82), Penr. West RDn (1882—1926), Penr. RDn (1926—*). Bdry: 1873 (help refound Plumpton Wall EP).[103] Abol 1968 ent to Pentrith AP.[121]

PLUMBLAND

AP *LG* Seq 4. *Parl* Seq 4. *Eccl* Seq 1.

PLUMPTON—see PLUMPTON WALL

PLUMPTON STREET—see HESKET IN THE FOREST

PLUMPTON WALL

Chap (usually colloquially 'Plumpton') in Lazonby AP, sep CP 1866,[1] sep EP 1769,[6] eccl refounded 1873 from Lazonby AP, Hesket in the Forest AP, Penrith AP, Penrith Christ Church EP.[103] *LG* Leath Wd, Penr. PLU, RSD, RD. Abol civ 1934 to help cr Hesket CP.[4] *Parl* E'rn Dv (1867—85), Penr. Dv (1885—1918), Penr. & Cockerm. Dv (1918—48). *Eccl* Sometimes as 'Salkeld Gate(s) and Brockleymoor', Allerd. RDn (1769—1857), Cumb. RDn (1857—59), Penr. RDn (1859—82), Penr. East RDn (1882—1926), Penr. RDn (1926—*). Eccl bdry: 1973.[5]

PONSONBY

AP *LG* Seq 3. *Parl* Seq 5. *Eccl* Copel. RDn (until 1859), Gosf. RDn (1859—1957). Abol eccl 1957 to help cr Beckermet St Bridget with Ponsonby EP.[19]

PRESTON QUARTER

Tp in St Bees AP, sep CP 1866,[1] pt eccl severed 1845 to cr Mount Pleasant EP (later called 'Whitehaven Christ Church').[99] *LG* Allerd. above Derw. Wd, Whiteh. PLU, MB (1894—96), pt Whiteh. USD, pt Whiteh. RSD. Bdry: 1881,[122] 1894 (the pt not incl in Whiteh. MB cr Preston Quarter Rural CP).[22] Abol 1896 ent to Whitehaven CP.[123] *Parl* Pt Whiteh. Parl Bor, pt W'rn Dv (1832—85), Egrem. Dv (1885—1918).

CP Renaming 1896 of the pt of Preston Quarter Rural CP not transf to Whitehaven CP.[123] *LG* Whiteh. PLU, RD. Bdry: 1896,[124] 1900.[118] Abol 1934 pt to Rottington CP, pt to Whitehaven CP.[4] *Parl* Whiteh. Dv (1918—48).

PRESTON QUARTER RURAL

CP Cr 1894 from the pt of Preston Quarter CP not incl in Whiteh. MB.[22] *LG* Whiteh. PLU, RD. Abol 1896 pt transf to Whitehaven CP, the remainder renamed 'Preston Quarter' CP.[123]

RAUGHTON HEAD—See following entry

RAUGHTON HEAD WITH GATESGILL

EP Cr 1737 as 'Raughton Head' (sometimes 'Raughtonhead') from Castle Sowerby AP,[6] refounded 1868 as 'Raughton Head with Gatesgill' from Castle Sowerby AP, Dalston AP.[25] Allerd. RDn (1737—1857), Cumb. RDn (1857—59), Greyst. RDn (1859—82), Carl South RDn (1882—1926), Carl RDn (1926—*). Bdry: 1958,[48] 1971.[37]

RENWICK

AP LG Leath Wd, Penr. PLU, RSD, RD. Abol civ 1934 ent to Kirkoswald AP.[4] Parl E'rn Dv (1832—85), Penr. Dv (1885—1918), Penr. & Cockerm. Dv (1918—48). Eccl Seq 3.

RIBTON

Tp in Bridekirk AP, sep CP 1866,[1] eccl severed 1863 to help cr Great Broughton EP.[37] LG Allerd. below Derw. Wd, Cockerm. PLU, RSD, RD. Abol 1934 ent to Camerton AP.[4] Parl W'rn Dv (1867—85), Cockerm. Dv (1885—1918), Work. Dv (1918—48).

RICKERGATE

Tp in Carlisle St Mary AP, sep CP 1866,[1] eccl severed 1868 to help cr Carlisle St Mary Without EP.[29] LG Cumb. Wd, Carl PLU, MB (1835—1904), USD. Bdry: 1894 (gains the pt of Stanwix AP in Carl MB).[50] Abol 1904 to help cr Carlisle CP.[30] Parl Carl Parl Bor (1832—1918).

ROCKCLIFFE

AP LG Seq 6. Parl Seq 1. Eccl Seq 9. Eccl bdry: 1871 (help cr Blackford EP).[25]

ROSLEY WITH WOODSIDE

EP Cr 1868 from Westward AP.[29] Wigt. RDn (1868—1970), Carl RDn (1970—*).

ROTTINGTON

Tp in St Bees AP, sep CP 1866.[1] LG Seq 3. Bdry: 1934.[4] Parl Seq 5.

ST BEES

AP Incl chap Ennerdale (sep EP 1743 [incl tp Kinniside],[6] the area civ 'Ennerdale and Kinniside', as such a sep CP 1866[1]), chap Eskdale (sep EP 1747,[7] the area civ a pt of 'Eskdale and Wasdle', qv below), chap Hensingham (sep CP 1866,[1] sep EP 1867[75]), chap Loweswater (sep civ identity early, sep EP 1723,[6] eccl refounded 1886 by union Loweswater and the pt of tp Brackenthwaite in Brigham AP neither in Lorton EP nor Buttermere EP[34]), chap Nether Wasdale (sep CP 1866,[1] sep EP 1715[6]), chap Wasdale Head ([sometimes 'Upper Wasdale'], sep EP 1719,[6] civ a pt of 'Eskdale and Wasdale', as such a sep CP 1866[1]), chap Whitehaven (sep CP 1866,[1] sep EP 1736 as 'Whitehaven St Nicholas',[6] eccl refounded 1835[125]); tp Irton, Santon and Melthwaite (sep CP 1866,[1] later called 'Irton'); tps Lowside Quarter, Rottington, Sandwith, Weddicar (each a sep CP 1866[1]), tp Preston Quarter (sep CP 1866,[1] pt eccl severed 1845 to cr Mount Pleasant EP,[99] later called 'Whitehaven Christ Church'). LG Seq 3. Parl Seq 5. Eccl Seq 16. Addtl eccl bdry alt: 1812 (cr Whitehaven St James EP,[6] refounded 1835[125]), 1835 (cr Whitehaven Holy Trinity EP),[125] 1963.[20]

ST CUTHBERT WITHIN

CP Cr 1866 from pt of the pt of Carlisle St Cuthbert AP in Carl MB.[1] LG Carl PLU, MB, USD. Abol 1904 to help cr Carlisle CP.[30] Parl Carl Parl Bor (1867—1918).

ST CUTHBERT WITHOUT

CP Cr 1866 from the pt of Carlisle St Cuthbert AP not in Carl MB and from another pt (chap Botchergate, not yet sep civ) in Carl MB.[1] LG Pt Cumb. Wd, Carl PLU, pt Carl MB (1866—94), pt Carl USD, pt Carl RSD, Carl RD (1894—1934), Border RD (1934—74). Bdry: 1883,[11] 1887,[13] 1894 (the pt in Carl MB cr Botchergate CP),[22] 1912,[23] 1934 (gains Wreay CP),[4] 1951 (loses pt to Carl CB [assoc with Cumb] & CP).[14] Parl Pt Carl Parl Bor (1867—1918), pt E'rn Dv (1867—85), pt Esk. Dv (1885—1918), N'rn Dv (1918—48), Penr. & the Border CC (1948—*). Parl bdry: 1951.[15]

ST JOHN'S IN THE VALE

Chap in Crosthwaite AP, pt severed 1859 to help refound Keswick EP,[27] the remainder constituted 1863 'St John's in the Vale' EP.[74] Kesw. RDn (1863—1970), Derw. RDn (1970—*).

ST MARY WITHIN

CP Cr 1866 from the pt of Carlisle St Mary AP in Carl MB.[1] LG Carl PLU, MB, USD. Bdry: 1883.[11] Abol 1904 to help cr Carlisle CP.[30] Parl Carl Parl Bor (1867—1918).

GREAT SALKELD

AP LG Seq 10. Civ bdry: 1886.[93] Parl Seq 3. Eccl Seq 3.

LITTLE SALKELD

Tp (orig chap) in Addingham AP, sep CP 1866.[1] LG Leath Wd, Penr. PLU, RSD, RD. Bdry: 1886.[93] Abol 1934 to help cr Hunsonby CP.[4] Parl E'rn Dv (1867—85), Penr. Dv (1885—1918), Penr. & Cockerm. Dv (1918—48).

SALKELD GATE(S) AND BROCKLEYMOOR—See PLUMPTON WALL

SALTER AND ESKETT

Ex-par place, sep CP 1858.[38] LG Allerd. above Derw. Wd, own overseers for poor (until 1861), Whiteh. PLU (1861—1930), RSD, RD. Abol 1934 ent to Nether Wasdale CP.[4] Parl W'rn Dv (1867—85), Egrem. Dv (1885—1918), Whiteh. Dv (1918—48).

SANDWITH

Tp in St Bees AP, sep CP 1866.[1] LG Allerd. above Derw. Wd, Whiteh. PLU, RSD, RD. Bdry: 1881.[126] Abol 1934 pt to Whitehaven CP, pt to Rottington CP.[4] Parl W'rn Dv (1867—85), Egrem. Dv (1885—1918), Whiteh. Dv (1918—48).

SCALEBY

AP LG Seq 9. Civ bdry: 1883.[11] Parl Seq 1. Eccl Seq 8.

SCOTBY

EP Cr 1862 from Wetheral AP.[127] Bramp. RDn (1862—71), Carl South RDn (1871—1926), Carl RDn (1926—70), Bramp. RDn (1970—*). Bdry: 1960 (help cr Carlisle St Elisabeth, Harraby EP),[61] 1969.[62]

SEASCALE

CP Cr 1897 from Gosforth AP.[96] LG Whiteh. PLU (1897—1901), RD (1897—1901), Bootle PLU (1901—30), RD (1901—34), Millom RD (1934—74). Bdry: 1901.[84] Parl Whiteh. Dv/CC (1918—*).

EP Cr 1904 from Gosforth AP, Drigg AP.[83] Gosf. RDn (1904—70), Calder RDn (1970—*).

SEATON
Tp in Camerton AP, sep CP 1866.[1] *LG* Seq 4. Bdry: 1899.[128] *Parl* Seq 4.

WEST SEATON
EP Cr 1893 from Camerton AP.[52] Maryp. RDn (1893—1970), Solway RDn (1970—*). Sometimes 'North Side', sometimes 'Workington North Side'.

SEBERGHAM
AP *LG* Seq 7. Civ bdry: 1934,[4] 1935,[18] 1971.[47] *Parl* Seq 2. *Eccl* Allerd. RDn (until 1859), Greyst. RDn (1859—82), Carl South RDn (1882—1926), Wigt. RDn (1926—70), Carl RDn (1970—*). Eccl bdry: 1958,[48] 1971.[37]

SETMURTHY
Chap in Brigham AP, sep CP 1866,[1] sep EP 1748.[6] *LG* Seq 2. Civ bdry: 1887,[90] 1935.[18] *Parl* Seq 4. *Eccl* Copel. RDn (1748—1859), Cockerm. RDn (1859—82), Cockerm. & Work. RDn (1882—1970), Derw. RDn (1970—*). Eccl bdry: 1971.[91]

SILLOTH
CP Cr 1934 from Holme Low CP, Skinburness Marsh (land common to Holme Abbey CP, Holme Low CP, Holme St Cuthbert CP).[4] *LG* Wigt. RD. *Parl* Penr. & the Border CC (1948—*).

SILLOTH CHRIST CHURCH
EP Cr 1849 from Holme Cultram AP.[105] Allerd. RDn (1849—59), Wigt. RDn (1859—1948). Abol 1948 to help cr Silloth Christ Church with St Paul EP.[58]

SILLOTH CHRIST CHURCH WITH ST PAUL
EP Cr 1948 by union Silloth Christ Church EP, Silloth St Paul EP.[58] Wigt. RDn (1948—70), Solway RDn (1970—*).

SILLOTH ST PAUL
EP Organisation as for Silloth Christ Church.

SKELTON
AP *LG* Seq 10. Civ bdry: 1934 (incl gains Hutton in the Forest AP, Middlesceugh and Braithwaite CP).[4] *Parl* Seq 3. *Eccl* Seq 2.

SKIDDAW
Ex-par place (mountain, sometimes 'Skiddaw Forest'), sep CP 1858.[38] *LG* Allerd. below Derw. Wd, Cockerm. PLU (1862—1930), RSD, RD. Abol 1934 ent to Underskiddaw CP.[4] *Parl* W'rn Dv (1867—85), Penr. Dv (1885—1918), Penr. & Cockerm. Dv (1918—48).

SKINBURNESS—See NEWTON ARLOSH
SKINBURNESS MARSH
Orig in Holme Cultram AP, after 1866 common to Holme Abbey CP, Holme Low CP, Holme St Cuthbert CP. *LG* Wigt. PLU, Holme Cultram USD, UD (1894—1934), Wigt. RD (1934—74). Bdry: 1894 (help cr Silloth CP).[4] *Parl* N'rn Dv (1918—48), Penr. & the Border CC (1948—*).

SKIRWITH
Area in Kirkland AP, sep CP 1866,[1] sep EP 1867.[113] *LG* Leath Wd, Penr. PLU, RSD, RD. Abol 1934 ent to Culgaith CP.[4] *Parl* E'rn Dv (1867—85), Penr. Dv (1885—1918), Penr. & Cockerm. Dv (1918—48). *Eccl* Penr. RDn (1867—82), Penr. East RDn (1882—1926), Kirkosw. RDn (1926—70), Penr. RDn (1970—*).

SOLPORT
Tp in Stapleton AP, sep CP 1866.[1] *LG* Seq 9. Bdry: 1934 (gains Trough CP).[4] *Parl* Seq 1.

STAFFIELD
Tp in Kirkoswald AP, sep CP 1866.[1] *LG* Leath Wd, Penr. PLU, RSD, RD. Abol 1934 ent to Kirkoswald AP.[4] *Parl* E'rn Dv (1867—85), Penr. Dv (1885—1918), Penr. & Cockerm. Dv (1918—48).

STAINBURN
Tp in Workington AP, sep CP 1866.[1] *LG* Allerd. above Derw. Wd, Cockerm. PLU, RSD, RD. Abol 1934 pt to Workington AP, pt to Winscales CP.[4] *Parl* W'rn Dv (1867—85), Cockerm. Dv (1885—1918), Work. Dv (1918—48).

STANWIX
AP *LG* Pt Esk. Wd, pt Cumb. Wd, Carl PLU, pt Carl MB & USD (1887—94), Carl RSD (ent 1875—87, pt 1887—94), Carl RD (1894—1934), Border RD (1934—66). Civ bdry: 1883,[11] 1894 (the pt in Carl MB transf to Rickergate CP),[50] 1912,[23] 1934,[4] 1951 (loses pt to Carl CB [assoc with Cumb] & CP).[14] Renamed 1966 'Stanwix Rural' CP.[129] *Parl* E'rn Dv (1832—85), Esk. Dv (1885—1918), N'rn Dv (1918—48), Penr. & the Border CC (1948—70). Parl bdry: 1951.[15] *Eccl* Seq 9. Eccl bdry: 1841 (help cr Houghton St John EP).[107]

STANWIX RURAL
CP Renaming 1966 of Stanwix AP.[129] *LG* Border RD. *Parl* Penr. & the Border CC (1970—*).

STAPLETON
AP Incl tps Bellbank, Solport, Trough (each a sep CP 1866[1]). *LG* Seq 9. Addtl civ bdry alt: 1934 (gains Bellbank CP).[4] *Parl* Seq 1. *Eccl* Seq 7.

SUNDERLAND
Tp in Isel AP, sep CP 1866.[1] *LG* Allerd. below Derw. Wd, Cockerm. PLU, RSD, RD. Abol 1934 to help cr Blindcrake CP.[4] *Parl* W'rn Dv (1867—85), Cockerm. Dv (1885—1918), Penr. & Cockerm. Dv (1918—48).

TALLENTIRE
Tp in Bridekirk AP, sep CP 1866.[1] *LG* Allerd. below Derw. Wd, Cockerm. PLU, RSD, RD. Abol 1934 ent to Birdekirk AP.[4] *Parl* W'rn Dv (1867—85), Cockerm. Dv (1885—1918), Penr. & Cockerm. Dv (1918—48).

THORNTHWAITE
EP Cr 1717 from Crosthwaite AP,[6] refounded 1841.[64] Allerd. RDn (1717—1859), Kesw. RDn (1859—1970), Derw. RDn (1970—*). Bdry: 1926.[60]

THRELKELD
Chap in Greystoke AP, sep EP 1747,[6] sep CP 1866.[1] *LG* Seq 10. *Parl* Seq 3. *Eccl* Allerd. RDn (1747—1857), Cumb. RDn (1857—59), Kesw. RDn (1859—1970), Derw. RDn (1970—*).

THURSBY
AP *LG* Seq 7. *Parl* Seq 2. *Eccl* Seq 14.

THWAITES
EP Chap in Millom AP, sep EP 1717,[6] refounded 1925.[115] Copel. RDn (1717—1859), Gosf. RDn (1859—1970), Furness RDn (1970—*).

TORPENHOW
AP Incl tps Bewaldeth and Snittlegarth, Blennerhasset and Kirkland, Bothel and Threapland, Torpenhow

and Whitrigg (each a sep CP 1866[1]) so that 'Torpenhow' has no sep civ identity after 1866. *LG* Allerd. below Derw. Wd. *Parl* W'rn Dv (1832—67). *Eccl* Seq 1. Eccl bdry: 1955.[12]

TORPENHOW AND WHITRIGG

Tp in Torpenhow AP, sep CP 1866.[1] *LG* Allerd. below Derw. Wd, Wigt. PLU, RSD, RD. Abol 1934 pt to help cr Blennerhasset and Torpenhow CP, pt to Bewaldeth and Snittlegarth CP.[4] *Parl* W'rn Dv (1867—85), Penr. Dv (1885—1918), N'rn Dv (1918—48).

TROUGH

Tp in Skelton AP, sep CP 1866.[1] *LG* Esk. Wd, Longt. PLU, RSD, RD. Abol 1934 ent to Solport CP.[4] *Parl* E'rn Dv (1867—85), Esk. Dv (1885—1918), N'rn Dv (1918—48).

ULDALE

AP *LG* Allerd. below Derw. Wd, Wigt. PLU, RSD, RD. Abol civ 1934 to help cr Ireby CP.[4] *Parl* W'rn Dv (1832—85), Penr. Dv (1885—1918), N'rn Dv (1918—48).

ULPHA

Chap in Millom AP, sep CP 1866,[1] EP 1747.[6] *LG* Seq 1. Civ bdry: 1935 (gains pt Dunnerdale with Seathwaite CP, Lancs).[130] *Parl* Seq 5. *Eccl* Copel. RDn (1747—1859), Ulv. RDn (1859—82), Gosf. RDn (1882—1970), Furness RDn (1970—*).

UNDERSKIDDAW

Tp in Crosthwaite AP, sep CP 1866.[1] *LG* Seq 4. Civ bdry: 1894,[40] 1934 (gains Skiddaw CP),[4] 1946.[3] *Parl* Seq 9.

UPPERBY

EP Cr 1771 from Carlisle St Cuthbert AP,[6] refounded 1860.[60] Carl RDn (1771—1871), Carl South RDn (1871—1926), Carl RDn (1926—*). Bdry: 1865 (help cr Carlisle St Stephen EP),[55] 1867 (help cr Carlisle St John the Evangelist EP),[56] 1869 (help refound Wreay EP),[102] 1893,[28] 1897,[66] 1937 (help cr Currock EP),[67] 1960 (help cr Carlisle St Elisabeth, Harraby EP),[61] 1969.[62]

WABERTHWAITE

AP *LG* Seq 1. Civ bdry: 1886,[70] 1934 (gains Corney AP).[4] *Parl* Seq 5. *Eccl* Seq 15. Eccl bdry: 1956.[71]

WALTON

AP *LG* Seq 8. *Parl* Seq 1. *Eccl* Seq 7.

WARWICK

Chap in Wetheral AP, sep civ identity early, presented jointly with Wetheral and augmented 1815 as 'Wetheral and Warwick',[131] qv for eccl organisation. *LG* Pt Cumb. Wd, pt Esk. Wd, Carl PLU, RSD, RD. Abol 1934 ent to Wetheral AP.[4] *Parl* E'rn Dv (1832—85), Esk. Dv (1885—1918), N'rn Dv (1918—48).

NETHER WASDALE

Chap in St Bees AP, sep CP 1866,[1] sep EP 1715.[6] *LG* Seq 3. Civ bdry: 1934.[4] *Parl* Seq 5. *Eccl* Copel. RDn (1725—1859), Gosf. RDn (1859—1970), Calder RDn (1970—*).

WASDALE HEAD

Chap in St Bees AP, sometimes 'Upper Wasdale', sep EP 1719,[6] civ united with chap Eskdale as 'Eskdale and Wasdale' and as such sep CP 1866,[1] qv. Copel. RDn (1719—1859), Gosf. RDn (1859—

1970), Calder RDn (1970—*).

WATERHEAD

Tp in Lanercost AP, sep CP 1866.[1] *LG* Seq 8. Bdry: 1883,[45] 1934.[4] *Parl* Seq 1.

WATERMILLOCK

Tp in Greystoke AP, sep CP 1866,[1] sep EP 1742.[6] *LG* Leath Wd, Penr. PLU, RSD, RD. Civ bdry: 1886.[114] Abol 1934 ent to Matterdale CP.[4] *Parl* E'rn Dv (1867—85), Penr. Dv (1885—1918), Penr. & Cockerm. Dv (1918—48). *Eccl* Allerd. RDn (1742—1857), Cumb. RDn (1857—59), Greyst. RDn (1859—82), Penr. West RDn (1882—1926), Penr. RDn (1926—*).

WAVERTON

Tp in Wigton AP, sep CP 1866,[1] sep EP 1902 by union Waverton, pt tp Dundraw in Bromfield AP.[43] *LG* Seq 7. Civ bdry: 1883,[11] 1887 (help cr Wigton cum Woodside CP),[132] 1946.[85] *Parl* Seq 2. *Eccl* Wigt. RDn (1902—70), Carl RDn (1970—*).

WEDDICAR

Tp in St Bees AP, sep CP 1866.[1] *LG* Seq 3. Bdry: 1934.[4] *Parl* Seq 6.

WESTFIELD

EP Cr 1958 from Workington AP, Workington St John EP.[133] Cockerm. & Work. RDn (1958—70), Solway RDn (1970—*).

WESTLINTON

Tp in Kirklington AP, sep CP 1866,[1] eccl severed 1871 to help cr Blackford EP.[25] *LG* Seq 9. Bdry: 1883.[11] *Parl* Seq 1.

WEST NEWTON AND ALLONBY

Civ union of tp West Newton, chap Allonby, each in Bromfield AP, sep CP 1866[1]; for eccl independence of each, see entries for 'Westnewton', 'Allonby'. *LG* Allerd. below Derw. Wd, Wigt. PLU, RSD. Abol 1894 to cr 2 CPs, Allonby, West Newton, the latter later called 'Westnewton'.[8] *Parl* W'rn Dv (1867—85), Esk. Dv (1885—1918).

WESTNEWTON

EP Tp in Bromfield AP, sep EP 1863 (tps West Newton, pt Langrigg and Mealrigg)[42]; for civ see 'West Newton and Allonby'. Wigt. RDn (1863—82), Maryp. RDn (1882—1970), Solway RDn (1970—*).

CP Cr 1894 from West Newton and Allonby CP, orig as 'West Newton', later 'Westnewton'. *LG* Wigt. PLU, RD. *Parl* Work. Dv (1918—48), Penr. & the Border CC (1948—*).

WESTWARD

AP *LG* Seq 5. *Parl* Seq 8. *Eccl* Seq 5. Eccl bdry: 1868 (cr Rosley with Woodside EP).[29]

WETHERAL

AP Gains after Dissolution Cumwhitton AP (thereafter deemed chap in this par[77] until sep civ identity regained early, sep EP 1740[6]). Incl chap Warwick (sep civ identity early, jointly presented and augmented 1815 as 'Wetheral and Warwick',[6] qv for eccl organisation). *LG* Pt Esk. Wd, pt Cumb. Wd, Carl PLU, RSD, RD (1894—1934), Border RD (1934—74). Addtl civ bdry alt: 1912,[23] 1934 (gains Warwick CP),[4] 1951 (loses pt to Carl CB [assoc with Cumb] & CP).[14] *Parl* Seq 1. Parl bdry: 1951.[15]

WETHERAL WITH WARWICK
AP Name used ecl for joint presentation of Wetheral, chap Warwick (qv for civ) from time of joint augmentation 1815.[6] *Eccl* Seq 12. Eccl bdry: 1843 (help cr Holme Eden EP),[97] 1862 (cr Scotby EP),[127] 1868 (cr Cotchill and Cumwhitton EP),[72] 1955.[78]

WHICHAM
AP *LG* Seq 1. Civ bdry: 1934 (gains Whitbeck AP).[4] *Parl* Seq 5. *Eccl* Seq 15. Eccl bdry: 1970.[116]

WHINFELL
Tp in Brigham AP, sep CP 1866.[1] *LG* Allerd. above Derw. Wd, Cockerm. PLU, RSD, RD. Abol 1934 ent to Blindbothel CP.[4] *Parl* W'rn Dv (1867—85), Cockerm. Dv (1885—1918), Penr. & Cockerm. Dv (1918—48).

WHITBECK
AP *LG* Allerd. above Derw. Wd, Bootle PLU, RSD, RD. Abol civ 1934 ent to Whicham AP.[4] *Parl* W'rn Dv (1832—85), Egrem. Dv (1885—1918), Whiteh. Dv (1918—48). *Eccl* Seq 15.

WHITEHAVEN
The following have 'Whitehaven' in their names. Insofar as any existed at a given time: *LG* Allerd. above Derw. Wd, Whiteh. PLU, USD, MB (1894—1974). *Parl* Whiteh. Parl Bor (1832—85), Egrem. Dv (1885—1918), Whiteh. Dv/CC (1918—*). *Eccl* Copel. RDn (cr—1859), Whiteh. RDn (1859—1970), Calder RDn (1970—*).

CP1/EP1—WHITEHAVEN [ST NICHOLAS]—Chap in St Bees AP, sep CP 1866,[1] sep EP 1736,[6] eccl refounded 1835,[125] eccl usually 'Whitehaven St Nicholas'. Civ bdry: 1896 (gains Preston Quarter CP, pt Preston Quarter Rural CP [the remainder of the latter then renamed 'Preston Quarter' CP]),[123] 1900,[118] 1934.[4] Eccl bdry: 1888,[134] 1934.[99]

—WHITEHAVEN CHRIST CHURCH—Name commonly used for EP cr 1845 as 'Mount Pleasant', qv.

EP2—WHITEHAVEN HOLY TRINITY—Cr 1835 from St Bees AP.[125] Abol eccl 1935 to help cr EP3.[119]

EP3—WHITEHAVEN HOLY TRINITY WITH CHRIST CHURCH—Cr 1935 by union EP2, Mount Pleasant EP (commonly called 'Whitehaven Christ Church').[119] Bdry: 1935 (cr Kells EP),[110] 1961 (help cr Mirehouse EP).[100]

EP4—WHITEHAVEN ST JAMES—Cr 1812 from St Bees AP,[6] refounded 1835.[125] Bdry: 1934.[99]

—WHITEHAVEN ST NICHOLAS—See CP1/EP1

WIGTON
AP Incl tps Oulton, Waverton, Woodside Quarter (each a sep CP 1866[1]). *LG* Cumb. Wd, Wigt. PLU, USD. Abol civ 1887 to help cr Wigton cum Woodside CP.[132] *Parl* E'rn Dv (1832—85), Penr. Dv (1885—1918). *Eccl* Seq 5.

CP Cr 1894 from Wigton cum Woodside CP.[22] *LG* Wigt. PLU, UD (1894—1934), RD (1934—74). *Parl* N'rn Dv (1918—48), Penr. & the Border CC (1948—*).

WIGTON CUM WOODSIDE
CP Cr 1887 by union Wigton AP, Woodside Quarter CP, pt Waverton CP.[132] *LG* Cumb. Wd, Wigt. PLU, RSD. Abol 1894 to cr the 2 CPs of Wigton, Woodside.[22]

WINSCALES
Tp in Workington AP, sep CP 1866.[1] *LG* Seq 2. Bdry: 1934.[4] *Parl* Seq 4.

WOODSIDE
CP Cr 1894 from Wigton cum Woodside CP.[22] *LG* Wigt. PLU, RD. Bdry: 1934 (gains Oulton CP).[4] *Parl* N'rn Dv (1918—48), Penr. & the Border CC (1948—*).

WOODSIDE QUARTER
Tp in Wigton AP, sep CP 1866.[1] *LG* Cumb. Wd, Wigt. PLU, RSD. Abol 1887 to help cr Wigton cum Woodside CP.[132] *Parl* E'rn Dv (1867—85), Penr. Dv (1885—1918).

WORKINGTON
AP Incl chap Clifton (sep EP 1733,[6] civ comprised of tps Great Clifton, Little Clifton [each a sep CP 1866[1]]), tps Stainburn, Winscales (each a sep CP 1866[1]). *LG* Allerd. above Derw. Wd, Cockerm. PLU, Work. MB (pt 1883—94, ent 1894—1974), pt Work. USD (1883—94), Work. RSD (ent 1875—83, pt 1883—94). Addtl civ bdry alt: 1894 (the pt not in Work. MB cr Workington Rural CP),[22] 1899,[128] 1934 (incl gains Cloffocks CP).[4] *Parl* Seq 4. *Eccl* Copel. RDn (until 1859), Whiteh. RDn (1859—82), Cockerm. & Work. RDn (1882—1970), Solway RDn (1970—*). Addtl eccl bdry alt: 1835 (cr Workington St John EP),[135] 1954,[82] 1958 (help cr Westfield EP).[133]

WORKINGTON RURAL
CP Cr 1894 from the pt of Workington AP not in Work. MB.[22] *LG* Cockerm. PLU, RD. Abol 1934 pt to Workington AP, pt to Winscales CP.[4] *Parl* Work. Dv (1918—48).

WORKINGTON ST JOHN
EP Cr 1835 from Workington AP.[135] Copel. RDn (1835—59), Whiteh. RDn (1859—1970), Solway RDn (1970—*). Bdry: 1954,[82] 1958 (help cr Westfield EP).[133]

WREAY
Chap in Carlisle St Mary AP, sep CP 1866,[1] sep EP 1738,[6] eccl refounded 1869 from Carlisle St Mary AP, Hesket in the Forest AP, Upperby EP.[102] *LG* Cumb. Wd, Carl PLU, RSD, RD. Civ bdry: 1883.[11] Abol civ 1934 ent to St Cuthbert Without CP.[4] *Parl* E'rn Dv (1867—85), Esk. Dv (1885—1918), N'rn Dv (1918—48). *Eccl* Carl RDn (1738—1871), Carl South RDn (1871—1926), Carl RDn (1926—*).

WYTHOP
Tp in chap Lorton (sep civ identity early from Brigham AP, sep EP 1744,[6] eccl refounded 1883, qv for constituent pars then), 'Wythop' a sep CP 1866,[1] sep EP 1738.[6] *LG* Seq 2. *Parl* Seq 4. *Eccl* Copel. RDn (1738—1859), Kesw. RDn (1859—71), Cockerm. RDn (1871—82), Cockerm. & Work. RDn (1882—1970), Derw. RDn (1970—*).

WYTHBURN
Chap in Crosthwaite AP, sep EP 1745,[6] eccl refounded 1867,[75] civ united with tp Castlerigg St John's in same par and as 'Castlerigg St John's and Wythburn' sep CP 1866.[1] Allerd. RDn (1745—1859), Kesw. RDn (1859—1970), Derw. RDn (1970—*).

DERBYSHIRE

ABBREVIATIONS

Abbreviations particular to Derbys follow. Those general abbreviations in use throughout the *Guide* are found on pages xvii—xix.

Alf.	Alfreton
Appl.	Appletree
Ashb.	Ashbourne
Ashov.	Ashover
Bakew.	Bakewell
Basf.	Basford
Blackw.	Blackwell
Bols.	Bolsover
Bramp.	Brampton
Burt. upon Tr.	Burton upon Trent
Castil.	Castilar
Castlet.	Castleton
Chap. en le Fr.	Chapel en le Frith
Chestf.	Chesterfield
Dronf.	Dronfield
Duff.	Duffield
Eccl.-Bierl.	Ecclesall-Bierlow
Gloss.	Glossop
Gres.	Gresley
Hartsh.	Hartshorn
Hayf.	Hayfield
High Pk.	High Peak
Ilk.	Ilkeston
Longf.	Longford
Lull.	Lullington
Mansf.	Mansfield
Melb.	Melbourne
Morl. & Lit.	Morleston and Litchurch
Ockb.	Ockbrook
Radb.	Radbourne
Roth.	Rotherham
Scar.	Scarsdale
Shard.	Shardlow
Stant. by Br.	Stanton by Bridge
Stav.	Staveley
Sudb.	Sudbury
Tamw.	Tamworth
Uttox.	Uttoxeter
Will.	Willington
Wirksw.	Wirksworth
Youlg.	Youlgreave

SEQUENCES

An abbreviated entry prefixed by 'Seq' is used in the parochial entries to avoid repeating often the names of superior units of administration. The content of each sequence is shown below.

Local Government Sequences ('LG')

SEQ 1 Appl. Hd, Ashb. PLU, RSD, RD

SEQ 2 Appl. Hd, Belper PLU, RSD, RD

SEQ 3 Appl. Hd, Burt. upon Tr. PLU, RSD, Repton RD

SEQ 4 Appl. Hd, Shard. PLU, RSD, RD (1894—1959), S E Derbys RD (1959—74)

SEQ 5 Appl. Hd, Uttox. PLU, RSD, Sudb. RD (1894—1934), Ashb. RD (1934—74)

SEQ 6 High Pk. Hd, Bakew. PLU, RSD, RD

SEQ 7 High Pk. Hd, Chap. en le Fr. PLU, RSD, RD

SEQ 8 High Pk. Hd, Hayf. PLU, RSD, RD (1894—1934), Chap. en le Fr. RD (1934—74)

SEQ 9 Morl. & Lit. Hd, Belper PLU, RSD, RD

SEQ 10 Morl. & Lit. Hd, Burt. upon Tr. PLU, RSD, Repton RD

SEQ 11 Morl. & Lit. Hd, Shard. PLU, RSD, RD (1894—1959), S E Derbys RD (1959—74)

SEQ 12 Repton & Gres. Hd, Ashby de la Zouch PLU, Hartsh. & Seals RD (1894—1934), Repton RD (1934—74)

SEQ 13 Repton & Gres. Hd, Burt. upon Tr. PLU, RSD, Repton RD

SEQ 14 Repton & Gres. Hd, Shard. PLU, RSD, RD (1894—1959), S E Derbys RD (1959—74)

SEQ 15 Scar. Hd, Chestf. PLU, RSD, RD

SEQ 16 Scar. Hd, Mansf. PLU, RSD, Blackw. RD

SEQ 17 Scar. Hd, Worksop PLU, RSD, Clowne RD

SEQ 18 Wirksw. Hd, Ashb. PLU, RSD, RD

SEQ 19 Wirksw. Hd, Bakew. PLU, RSD, RD

Parliamentary Sequences ('Parl')

SEQ 1 N'rn Dv (1832—67), East Dv (1867—85), Chestf. Dv (1885—1948), N E Derbys CC (1948—*)

SEQ 2 N'rn Dv (1832—67), East Dv (1867—85), Chestf. Dv (1885—1918), Clay Cross Dv (1918—48), Bols. CC (1948—*)

SEQ 3 N'rn Dv (1832—67), East Dv (1867—85), Chestf. Dv (1885—1918), Clay Cross Dv (1918—48), N E Derbys CC (1948—*)

SEQ 4 N'rn Dv (1832—67), East Dv (1867—85), Mid Dv (1885—1918), Clay Cross Dv (1918—48), Bols. CC (1948—*)

SEQ 5 N'rn Dv (1832—67), East Dv (1867—85), Mid Dv (1885—1918), Clay Cross Dv (1918—48), N E Derbys CC (1948—*)

SEQ 6 N'rn Dv (1832—67), East Dv (1867—85), N-E'rn Dv (1885—1948), Bols. CC (1948—*)

SEQ 7 N'rn Dv (1832—67), East Dv (1867—85), N-E'rn Dv (1885—1948), N E Derbys CC (1948—*)

SEQ 8 N'rn Dv (1832—67), North Dv (1867—85), High Pk. Dv/CC (1885—*)

SEQ 9 N'rn Dv (1832—67), North Dv (1867—85), W'rn Dv (1885—1948), W Derbys CC (1948—*)

SEQ 10 S'rn Dv (1832—67), North Dv (1867—85), W'rn Dv (1885—1948), W Derbys CC (1948—*)

SEQ 11 S'rn Dv (1832—67), South Dv (1867—85), Ilk. Dv/CC (1885—*)

SEQ 12 S'rn Dv (1832—67), South Dv (1867—85), Ilk. Dv (1885—1918), Belper Dv/CC (1918—*)

SEQ 13 S'rn Dv (1832—67), South Dv (1867—85), Ilk. Dv (1885—1918), S'rn Dv (1918—48), S E Derbys CC (1948—*)

SEQ 14 S'rn Dv (1832—67), South Dv (1867—85), Mid Dv (1885—1918), Belper Dv/CC (1918—*)

SEQ 15 S'rn Dv (1832—67), South Dv (1867—85), S'rn Dv (1885—1918), Belper Dv/CC (1918—*)

SEQ 16 S'rn Dv (1832—67), South Dv (1867—85), S'rn Dv (1885—1948), Belper CC (1948—*)

SEQ 17 S'rn Dv (1832—67), South Dv (1867—85), S'rn Dv (1885—1948), S E Derbys CC (1948—*)

SEQ 18 S'rn Dv (1832—67), South Dv (1867—85), S'rn Dv (1885—1918), W'rn Dv (1918—48), W Derbys CC (1948—*)

SEQ 19 S'rn Dv (1832—67), South Dv (1867—85), W'rn Dv (1885—1948), Belper CC (1948—*)

SEQ 20 S'rn Dv (1832—67), South Dv (1867—85), W'rn Dv (1885—1948), W Derbys CC (1948—*)

Ecclesiastical Sequences ('Eccl')

SEQ 1 Ashb. RDn

SEQ 2 Ashb. RDn (until 1846), Wirksw. RDn (1846—*)

SEQ 3 Castil. RDn (until 1846), Cubley RDn (1846—87), Ashb. RDn (1887—*)

SEQ 4 Castil. RDn (until 1846), Cubley RDn (1846—87), Longf. RDn (1887—*)

SEQ 5 Castil. RDn (until 1846), Radb. RDn (1846—87), Longf. RDn (1887—*)

SEQ 6 Castil. RDn (until 1846), Will. RDn (1846—51), Radb. RDn (1851—87), Longf. RDn (1887—*)

SEQ 7 Chestf. RDn (until 1846), Alf. RDn (1846—*)

SEQ 8 Derby RDn (until 1846), Duff. RDn (1846—*)

SEQ 9 Derby RDn (until 1846), Duff. RDn (1846—87), Ilk. RDn (1887—*)

SEQ 10 Derby RDn (until 1846), Ockb. RDn (1846—87), Ilk. RDn (1887—*)

SEQ 11 Derby RDn (until 1846), Radb. RDn (1846—87), Duff. RDn (1887—*)

SEQ 12 Derby RDn (until 1846), Stant. by Br. RDn (1846—87), Melb. RDn (1887—*)

SEQ 13 High Pk. RDn (until 1846), Eyam RDn (1846—*)

SEQ 14 High Pk. RDn (until 1846), Youlg. RDn (1846—47), Bakew. RDn (1847—*)

SEQ 15 Repton RDn (until 1846), Hartsh. RDn (1846—55), Lull. RDn (1855—66), Hartsh. RDn (1866—87), Repton RDn (1887—1927), W Akeley RDn (dioc Leic, 1927—*)

SEQ 16 Repton RDn (until 1846), Hartsh. RDn (1846—87), Repton RDn (1887—*)

SEQ 17 Repton RDn (until 1846), Hartsh. RDn (1846—55), Lull. RDn (1855—87), Repton RDn (1887—*)

SEQ 18 Repton RDn (until 1846), Stant. by Br. RDn (1846—87), Melb. RDn (1887—*)

DIOCESES AND ARCHDEACONRIES

Derbys pars were organised in Archdeaconries and Rural Deaneries as follows:

CHESTER DIOC (1966—*)
Macclesfield AD: Fernilee RDn (1966—*), Stockport RDn (1966—*)

DERBY DIOC (1927—*)
Chestf. AD: Alf. RDn, Bakew. RDn (1971—*), Bols. RDn, Buxton RDn (1971—*), Chestf. RDn, Eyam RDn, Gloss. RDn, Heanor RDn, Stav. RDn
Derby AD: Ashb. RDn, Bakew. RDn (1927—71), Buxton RDn (1927—71), Derby RDn, Duff. RDn, Ilk. RDn, Longf. RDn, Melb. RDn, Repton RDn, Wirksw. RDn

LEICESTER DIOC (1927—*)
Loughborough AD: W Akeley RDn

LICHFIELD DIOC (1837—84)
Derby AD: Alf. RDn (1846—84), Ashb. RDn, Ashov. RDn (1846—84), Bakew. RDn (1847—84), Bols. RDn (1875—84), Bramp. RDn (1846—84), Buxton RDn (1847—84), Castil. RDn (1837—46), Castlet. RDn (1846—84), Chestf. RDn, Cubley RDn (1846—84), Derby RDn, Duff. RDn (1846—84), Eyam RDn (1846—84), Hartsh. RDn (1846—84), High Pk. RDn (1837—46), Lull. RDn (1855—84), Ockb. RDn (1846—84), Radb. RDn (1846—84), Repton RDn (1837—46), Stant. by Br. RDn (1846—84), Stav. RDn (1846—84), Will. RDn (1846—47), Wirksw. RDn (1846—84), Youlg. RDn (1846—47)

LICHFIELD AND COVENTRY DIOC (until 1837)
[before 1837 variously styled 'Lichfield' (until 1075), 'Chester' (1075—1102), 'Coventry' (1102—1228), 'Coventry and Lichfield' (1228—Reformation), 'Lichfield and Coventry' (Reformation—1837)]
Derby AD: Ashb. RDn, Castil. RDn, Chestf. RDn, Derby RDn, High Pk. RDn, Repton RDn

SHEFFIELD DIOC (1914—*)
Sheff AD: Attercliffe RDn (1974—*), Ecclesall RDn (1942—*), Sheffield RDn (1914—42)

SOUTHWELL DIOC (1884—1927)
Derby AD: Alf. RDn (1884—1910), Ashb. RDn, Ashov. RDn (1884—87), Bakew. RDn, Bols. RDn (1884—87), Bramp. RDn (1884—87), Buxton RDn, Castlet. RDn (1884—87), Chestf. RDn (1884—1910), Cubley RDn (1884—87), Derby RDn, Dronf. RDn (1887—1910), Duff. RDn, Eyam RDn (1884—1910), Gloss. RDn (1887—1910), Hartsh. RDn (1884—87), Ilk. RDn (1887—1927), Longf. RDn (1887—1927), Lull. RDn (1884—87), Melb. RDn (1887—1927), Repton RDn (1887—1927), Ockb. RDn (1884—87), Radb. RDn (1884—87), Stant. by Br. RDn (1884—87), Stav. RDn (1887—1910), Wirksw. RDn

THE PARISHES OF DERBYSHIRE

ABBEY DALE
EP Cr 1878 from Dore EP, Norton AP.[1] Bramp. RDn (1878—87), Dronf. RDn (1887—1910), Eyam RDn (1910—74), Ecclesall RDn (dioc Sheff, 1974—*). Bdry: 1922 (help cr Totley EP).[2]

ABNEY AND ABNEY GRANGE
Hmlt in Hope AP, sep CP 1866,[3] eccl severed 1875 to help cr Bradwell EP.[4] LG Seq 6. Parl Seq 9.

ALDERWASLEY
Chap in Wirksworth AP, sep CP 1866.[3] LG Seq 2. Bdry: 1886.[5] Parl Seq 14.

ALDWARK
Tp in Bradbourne AP, sep CP 1866.[3] LG Seq 19. Parl Seq 10.

ALFRETON
AP LG Scar. Hd, Belper PLU (soon after 1837[6]—1930), Alf. USD (pt 1875—88, ent 1888—94), pt Belper RSD (1875—88), Alf. UD. Civ bdry: 1934.[7] Parl N'rn Dv (1832—67), East Dv (1867—85), Mid Dv (1885—1918), Belper Dv (1918—48), Ilk. CC (1948—*). Eccl Seq 7. Eccl bdry: 1835 (cr Riddings EP),[8] 1854 (help cr Somercotes EP,[9] refounded 1898[10]), 1861 (help cr Swanwick EP).[11]

ALKMONTON
Chap and tp in Longford AP, sep CP 1866,[3] sep EP 1848 (incl lbty Hungy Bentley [qv for sep civ status from 1866],[9] eccl refounded 1849[12]). LG Seq 1. Civ bdry: 1887.[13] Parl Seq 20. Eccl Cubley RDn (1848—87), Longf. RDn 1887—*).

ALLENTON AND SHELTON LOCK
EP Cr 1948 from Alvaston EP, Boulton EP, Derby St Bartholomew EP, pt ex-par Sinfin Moor.[14] Melb. RDn. Bdry: 1963.[15]

ALLESTREE
Chap in Mackworth AP, sep civ identity early, sep EP 1849.[16] LG Morl. & Lit. Hd, Belper PLU, RSD, RD. Civ bdry: 1934.[7] Abol civ 1968 pt to Derby CB (assoc with Derbys) & CP, pt to Quarndon CP, pt to Little Eaton CP.[17] Parl S'rn Dv (1832—67), South Dv (1867—85), S'rn Dv (1885—1918), Belper Dv/CC (1918—70). Eccl Duff. RDn. Eccl bdry: 1958,[18] 1965 (incl help cr Allestree St Nicholas EP).[19]

ALLESTREE ST NICHOLAS
EP Cr 1965 from Allestree EP, Mackworth AP, Quarndon EP.[19] Duff. RDn.

ALSOP EN LE DALE
Chap in Ashbourne AP, sep EP 1737 (incl area Eaton),[9] sep civ identity early as 'Eaton and Alsop', qv. *Eccl* Ashb. RDn.

ALVASTON
Chap (Morl. & Lit. Hd) in Derby St Michael AP (o'wise Derby Bor), sep civ identity early, sep EP 1772.[9] *LG* Shard. PLU, Alvaston & Boulton USD. Abol civ 1884 pt to help cr Alvaston and Boulton CP, pt to Elvaston AP.[20] *Parl* S'rn Dv (1832—67), South Dv (1867—85). *Eccl* Derby RDn (1772—1846), Stant. by Br. RDn (1846—87), Melb. RDn (1887—*). Eccl bdry: 1948 (help cr Allenton and Shelton Lock EP),[13] 1962.[21]

ALVASTON AND BOULTON
CP Cr 1884 by union Boulton CP, pt Alvaston CP.[20] *LG* Morl. & Lit. Hd, Shard. PLU, Alvaston & Boulton USD, UD (1894—1934), Shard. RD (1934—59), S E Derbys RD (1959—68). Bdry: 1901 (loses pt to Derby CB [assoc with Derbys] & CP),[22] 1928 (loses pt to Derby CB [assoc with Derbys] & CP.[23] Abol 1968 pt to Derby CB (assoc with Derbys) & CP, pt to Elvaston AP.[17] *Parl* S'rn Dv (1885—1948), S E Derbys CC (1948—*).

AMBERGATE
EP Cr 1899 from Heage EP.[24] Duff. RDn. Bdry: 1901.[25]

APPLEBY
AP Mostly Leics (Sparkenhoe Hd), pt Derbys (Repton & Gres. Hd). *LG* Ashby de la Zouch PLU, RSD. Abol civ 1889 to cr 2 CPs, one in each co, each 'Appleby'.[26] *Parl* Derbys pt, S'rn Dv (1832—67), South Dv (1867—85), S'rn Dv (1885—1918). *Eccl* For RDns see entry in Leics.
CP Cr 1889 from the Derbys pt of Appleby AP (Leics, Derbys).[26] *LG* Ashby de la Zouch PLU, sep RD in Derbys. Transf 1897 to Leics and renamed 'Appleby Magna North'.[27]

ASH
Hmlt (eccl ex-par) in Sutton on the Hill AP, sep CP 1866.[3] *LG* Appl. Hd, Burt. upon Tr. PLU (soon after 1837[6]—1930, RSD, Repton RD. *Parl* Seq 15.

ASHBOURNE
AP Tp 'Ashbourne' in Wirksw. Hd as was chap Eaton and Alsop (sep civ identity early, sep EP 1737 as 'Alsop en le Dale' [incl area Eaton][9]), chap Hognaston (sep par early but independence disputed 17th cent[28]), chap Kniveton (sep par 1290[29]), chap Parwich (sep civ identity early, sep EP 1791[9]), lbty Offcote and Underwood, hmlt Newton Grange (each a sep CP 1866[3]); incl in Appl. Hd tps Hulland, Hulland Ward (each a sep CP 1866,[3] eccl united 1853 as 'Hulland' EP[9]), tps Hulland Ward Intakes, Sturston, Yeldersley (each a sep CP 1866[3]); incl in Morl. & Lit. Hd chap Clifton and Compton (sep CP 1866,[3] sep EP 1846 as 'Clifton'[30]). *LG* Ashb. PLU, USD, UD. Addtl civ bdry alt: 1894 (gains the pts in Ashb. UD of Clifton and Compton CP, Offcote and Underwood CP, Sturston CP),[31] 1924,[32] 1934.[7] *Parl* Seq 10. *Eccl* Ashb. RDn. Gains early eccl Mapleton AP to cr Ashbourne with Mapleton EP,[33] qv.

ASHBOURNE WITH MAPLETON
EP Cr early by union Ashbourne AP, Mapleton AP.[33] Ashb. RDn.

ASHFORD
Chap in Bakewell AP, sep CP 1866,[3] sep EP 1731 (incl tp Brushfield in same par),[9] eccl refounded 1871,[34] eccl abol 1872 to help cr Ashford with Sheldon EP.[35] *LG* High Pk. Hd, Bakew. PLU, RSD, RD. Renamed civ 1953 'Ashford in the Water'.[36] *Parl* N'rn Dv (1832—67), North Dv (1867—85), W'rn Dv (1885—1948), W Derbys CC (1948—70). *Eccl* Pec jurisd Bakew. (until 1846), Bakew. RDn (1846—72).

ASHFORD IN THE WATER
CP Renaming 1953 of Ashford CP.[36] *LG* Bakew. RD. *Parl* W Derbys CC (1970—*).

ASHFORD WITH SHELDON
EP Cr 1872 by union Ashford EP, Sheldon EP.[35] Bakew. RDn.

ASHLEYHAY
Tp in Wirksworth AP, sep CP 1866.[3] *LG* Seq 2. Bdry: 1886.[5] *Parl* Seq 14.

ASHOVER
AP Tp 'Ashover' in Scar. Hd; incl in Wirksw. Hd tp (orig chap, long destroyed) Dethick and Lea (sep CP 1866,[3] sep EP 1741 as 'Dethick Lea and Holloway',[9] as such eccl refounded 1899[37]). *LG* Scar. Hd (pt until 1866, ent from 1866), pt Wirksw. Hd (until 1866), Chestf. PLU, RSD, RD, *Parl* Area Dethick and Lea in S'rn Dv (1832—67); remainder and later, Seq 3. *Eccl* Chestf. RDn (until 1846), Ashov. RDn (1846—87), Chestf. RDn (1887—*).

ASTON
Tp in Hope AP, sep CP 1866.[3] *LG* Seq 7. *Parl* Seq 8.

ASTON ON TRENT
AP Usual eccl spelling; for civ and civ sep tp, see following entry. *Eccl* Seq 12.

ASTON UPON TRENT
AP Usual civ spelling; for eccl see prev entry. Incl tp Shardlow and Great Wilne (see CP 1866,[3] sep EP 1839 as 'Shardlow'[11]). *LG* Seq 11. Addtl civ bdry alt: 1968 (incl loses pt to Derby CB [assoc with Derbys] & CP).[17] *Parl* Seq 17.

ATLOW
Chap (Appl. Hd) in Bradbourne AP (o'wise Wirksw. Hd), sep CP 1866,[3] sep EP 1716.[9] *LG* Seq 1. *Parl* Seq 20. *Eccl* Ashb. RDn (1716—1846), Wirksw. RDn (1846—84), Ashb. RDn (1884—*).

AULT HUCKNALL
AP *LG* Seq 16. *Parl* Seq 2. *Eccl* Chestf. RDn (until 1846), Stav. RDn (1846—51), Chestf. RDn (1851—75), Bols. RDn (1875—87), Chestf. RDn (1887—1955), Bols. RDn (1955—*). Eccl bdry: 1954.[38]

BAKEWELL
AP Incl chap Ashford (sep CP 1866,[3] sep EP 1731 incl tp Brushfield [the latter a sep CP from Bakewell],[9] 'Ashford' eccl refounded 1871[34]), chap Sheldon (sep CP 1866,[3] sep EP 1741,[9] eccl refounded 1871[34]) (Ashford EP, Sheldon EP united 1872 as 'Ashford with Sheldon'[35]); incl chap Baslow (sep EP 1770 [comprised of 5 tps of Baslow and Bubnell, Calver, Curbar, Froggatt, Rowland, each a sep CP

1866 from Bakewell],[9] the ent orig areas of Calver, Frogatt and pt of orig areas of Curbar, Baslow and Bubnell [pt area Bubnell] eccl severed from Baslow EP to cr Curbar EP[39]); incl chap Beeley (sep CP 1866,[3] sep EP 1766[9]), chap Buxton (sep EP 1866,[3] sep EP 1728 incl pt Hope AP [tp Fernilee, chap (donative) Fairfield (Fernilee a sep EP 1905 from Buxton EP[40]] and pt Bakewell AP [area King Sterndale,[9] 'King Sterndale' a sep EP 1850 from Buxton EP,[9] refounded 1851 from Buxton EP, Hope AP, Hartington AP[40]], 'Buxton' eccl refounded 1898[10]; incl chap Chelmorton (sep CP 1866,[3] sep EP 1743 incl tp Flagg [the latter a sep CP 1866 from Bakewell AP[3]]), chap Longstone (sep EP 1830 comprised of tps Great Longstone, Little Longstone, and the pt of tp Wardlow in this par [the first 2 each a sep CP 1866 from Bakewell AP, the last a sep CP 1866 from Bakewell AP, Hope AP[3]][9]), chap Monyash (sep CP 1866,[3] sep EP 1744[9]), chap Taddington (sep CP 1866,[3] sep EP 1748 incl tp Blackwell [the latter a sep CP 1866 from Bakewell[3]][9]); also incl tps Nether Haddon, Over Haddon (each a sep CP 1866[3]; these 2 tps comprised chap Haddon, not sep eccl), tps Harthill, Hassop (each a sep CP 1866[3]), tp Great Rowsley (sep CP 1866,[3] although later civ called 'Rowsley', sep EP 1859 as 'Rowsley',[9] as such eccl refounded 1860[43]). LG High Pk. Hd, Bakew. Bor, PLU, USD, UD. Addtl civ bdry alt: 1894,[41] 1903.[42] Parl Seq 9. Eccl Pec jurisd Bakew. (until 1846), Bakew. RDn (1846—*).

BALLIDON

Tp in Bradbourne AP, sep CP 1866.[3] LG Seq 18. Parl Seq. 10.

BAMFORD

Hmlt in Hathersage AP, sep CP 1866,[3] sep EP 1860,[9] eccl refounded 1861.[44] LG Seq 7. Parl Seq 8. Eccl Eyam RDn. Eccl bdry: 1943 (gains Derwent Woodlands EP).[45]

BARLBOROUGH

AP LG Seq 17. Civ bdry: 1935.[46] Parl Seq 6. Eccl Chestf. RDn (until 1851), Stav. RDn (1851—1920), Bols. RDn (1920—*).

BARLOW

EP Cr 1724 from Staveley AP.[9] Chestf. RDn (1724—1846), Bramp. RDn (1846—87), Dronf. RDn (1887—1910), Chestf. RDn (1910—*).

CP Cr 1871 by union Great Barlow CP, Little Barlow CP.[47] LG Scar. Hd, Chestf. PLU, RSD, RD. Parl Chestf. Dv (1885—1948), N E Derbys CC (1948—*).

GREAT BARLOW

Chap in Staveley, AP, sep CP 1866.[3] LG Scar. Hd, Chestf. PLU, RSD. Abol 1871 to help cr Barlow CP.[47] Parl N'rn Dv (1832—67), East Dv (1867—85).

LITTLE BARLOW

Hmlt in Dronfield AP, sep CP 1866.[3] Organisation o'wise as for Great Barlow.

BARROW HILL

EP Cr 1928 from Staveley AP.[48] Stav. RDn. Abol 1973 to help cr Staveley and Barrowhill EP.[49]

BARROW UPON TRENT

AP Usual civ spelling; for eccl see following entry. Tp 'Barrow upon Trent' in Morl. & Lit. Hd; incl in Appl. Hd chap Twyford and Stenson, lbty Sinfin and Arleston (each a sep CP 1866[3]). LG Shard. PLU, RDS, RD (1894—1959), S E Derbys RD (1959—74). Addtl civ bdry alt: 1968.[17] Parl Seq 17.

BARROW WITH TWYFORD

AP Usual eccl spelling; for civ and civ sep chap and lbty, see prev entry. Eccl Seq 12.

BARTON BLOUNT

AP LG Appl. Hd, Burt. upon Tr. PLU (soon after 1837[6]—1930, RSD, Repton RD. Civ bdry: 1886 (loses pt to Tatenhill AP, Staffs).[50] Parl Seq 19. Eccl Castil. RDn (until 1846), Cubley RDn (1846—87), Longf. RDn (1887—1924). Abol eccl 1924 to help cr Church Broughton with Barton Blount EP.[51])

BASLOW

Chap in Bakewell AP comprised of tps Baslow and Bubnell, Calver, Curbar, Froggatt, Rowland (each a sep CP 1866 from Bakewell AP[3]), 'Baslow' a sep EP 1770,[9] the orig area of the last 2 tps eccl severed 1869 and united with pts orig areas of Curbar, Baslow and Bubnell (pt area Bubnell) to cr 'Curbar EP' and the remainder then refounded as 'Baslow' EP.[39] Pec jurisd Bakew. (until 1846), Eyam RDn (1846—*).

BASLOW AND BUBNELL

Tp in Bakewell AP, sep CP 1866[3]; for eccl organisation in Baslow chap/EP and 1869 re-arrangement in Baslow EP and Curbar EP, see prev entry. LG High Pk. Hd, Bakew. PLU, Baslow & Bubnell USD, UD (1894—1934), Bakew. RD (1934—74). Bdry: 1934.[7] Parl Seq 9.

BEARD—see following entry

BEARD, THORNSETT, OLLERSETT AND WHITTLE

Hmlt in Glossop AP, pt situated on Ches side of River Goyt (uncertain as to which co belonged, the tp declared to be ent Derbys 1832 for parl purposes, 1844 for civ purposes[52]), the ent area a sep CP 1866,[3] sep EP 1844 as 'Beard',[53] later eccl called 'New Mills', qv. LG High Pk. Hd, Hayf. PLU, New Mills USD. Renamed civ 1885 'New Mills'.[54] Parl N'rn Dv (1832—67), North Dv (1867—85), High Pk. Dv (1885—1918).

BEARWARDCOTE

Tp in Etwall AP, sep CP 1866.[3] LG App. Hd, Burt. upon Tr. PLU (soon after 1837[6]—1930), RSD, Repton RD. Bdry: 1886.[55] Parl Seq 15.

BEAUCHIEF

Ex-par place, sep CP 1858,[56] eccl 'Beauchief Abbey', pt eccl severed 1912 to help cr Norton Woodseats St Chad EP,[57] the remainder transf 1973 from dioc Derby (situated then in Stav. RDn) to dioc Sheff, Ecclesall RDn.[58] LG Scar. Hd, Eccl.-Bierl. PLU, RSD, Norton RD. Civ bdry: 1901 (pt transf to Sheff CB [assoc with Yorks W Riding] to help cr Norton Within CP).[59] Abol civ 1934 ent to Sheff CB (assoc with Yorks W Riding) & AP.[60] Parl N'rn Dv (1832—67), East Dv (1867—85), N-E'rn Dv (1885—1948).

BEAUCHIEF ABBEY—see prev entry

BEELEY

Chap in Bakewell AP, sep CP 1866,[3] sep EP 1766.[9]

LG Seq 6. *Parl* Seq 9. *Eccl* Pec jurisd Bakew. (until 1846), Eyam RDn (1846—84), Bakew. RDn (1884—*).

BEIGHTON

AP *LG* Scar. Hd, Rotherham PLU, RSD, Chestf. RD. Abol civ 1967 pt to Sheff CB (assoc with Yorks W Riding) & AP, pt to Wales CP, pt to Aston cum Aughton CP (the last 2 in Yorks W Riding), pt to Eckington AP, pt to Killamarsh CP (both Derbys).[61] *Parl* N'rn Dv (1832—67), East Dv (1867—85), N-E'rn Dv (1885—1948), N E Derbys CC (1948—70). *Eccl* Chestf. RDn (until 1846), Bramp. RDn (1846—55), Stav. RDn (1855—1974), Attercliffe RDn (dioc Sheff. 1974—*). Eccl bdry: 1943 (cr Frecheville EP),[45] 1957 (cr Hackenthorpe EP).[62]

BELPER

Chap in Duffield AP, sep CP 1866,[3] sep EP 1843.[9] *LG* Appl. Hd, Belper PLU, USD, UD. *Parl* Seq 14. *Eccl* Derby RDn (until 1846), Duff. RDn (1846—55), Alf. RDn (1855—66), Duff. RDn (1866—*). Eccl bdry: 1845 (cr Bridge Hill EP,[63] later sometimes called 'Belper Christ Church'), 1846 (help cr Milford EP).[64]

BELPER CHRIST CHURCH

EP Name sometimes used now for EP cr 1845 as 'Bridge Hill', qv.

FENNY BENTLEY

AP *LG* Seq 18. *Parl* Seq 10. *Eccl* Seq 1.

HUNGRY BENTLEY

Lbty in Longford AP, sep CP 1866,[3] eccl in chap Alkmonton (sep EP 1848 from Longford AP,[9] eccl refounded 1849[12]). *LG* Seq 1. *Parl* S'rn Dv (1832—67), South Dv (1867—85), W'rn Dv (1885—1948), W Derbys CC (1948—*).

BIGGIN

EP Cr 1848 from Hartington AP (while in the AP, pec jurisd Bakew., until 1846).[65] Buxton RDn.

BIGGIN

Tp in Wirksworth AP, sep CP 1866.[3] *LG* Seq 1. Bdry: 1887.[13] *Parl* Seq 20.

BIRCHOVER

Chap in Youlgreave AP, sep CP 1866,[3] pt eccl severed 1876 to help cr Stanton in Peak EP,[66] later called 'Stanton in Peak with Birchover or Rowston'. *LG* Seq 6. Bdry: 1883,[67] 1934.[7] *Parl* Seq 9.

BLACKWELL

AP *LG* Seq 16. *Parl* Seq 4. *Eccl* Seq 7.

BLACKWELL

Tp in Bakewell AP, sep CP 1866,[3] eccl in chap Taddington (sep EP 1748 from Bakewell AP[9]). *LG* High Pk. Hd, Bakew. PLU (soon after 1838[6]—1930), RSD, RD. *Parl* N'rn Dv (1832—67), North Dv (1867—85), Mid Dv (1885—1918), W'rn Dv (1918—48), W Derbys CC (1948—*).

BOLSOVER

AP Incl hmlt Glapwell (sep CP 1866[3]). *LG* Scar. Hd, Chestf. PLU, RSD (1875—93), Bols. USD (1893—94), UD. Addtl civ bdry alt: 1885,[68] 1935.[46] *Parl* Seq 6. *Eccl* Chestf. RDn (until 1875), Bols. RDn (1875—87), Chestf. RDn (1887—1910), Stav. RDn (1910—20), Bols. RDn (1920—*). Eccl bdry: 1924 (help cr Whaley Thorns EP [Derbys, Notts]).[66]

1954.[38]

BONSALL

AP *LG* Wirksw. Hd, Ashb. PLU, Bonsall USD, UD (1894—1934), Matlock UD (1934—74). *Parl* Seq 10. *Eccl* Ashb. RDn (until 1846), Ashov. RDn (1846—87), Wirksw. RDn (1877—*).

BOULTON

Chap (Morl. & Lit. Hd) in Derby St Peter AP (mostly Derby Bor, qv below), sep civ identity early, sep EP 1733.[9] *LG* Shard. PLU, Alvaston & Boulton USD. Abol civ 1884 to help cr Alvaston and Boulton CP.[20] *Parl* S'rn Dv (1832—67), South Dv (1867—85). *Eccl* Derby RDn (1733—1846), Stant. by Br. RDn (1846—87), Melb. RDn (1887—*). Eccl bdry: 1948 (help cr Allenton and Shelton Lock EP),[14] 1962,[21] 1963.[15]

THE BOUNDARY

Ex-par place, sep CP 1858.[56] *LG* Repton & Gres. Hd, Ashby de la Zouch PLU (1858—1930), RSD, Hartsh. & Seals RD. Abol civ 1934 ent to Smisby AP.[7] *Parl* S'rn Dv (1832—67), South Dv (1867—85), S'rn Dv (1885—1948).

BOYLESTON

AP *LG* Seq 5. *Parl* Seq 20. *Eccl* Seq 4.

BRACKENFIELD

Tp in Morton AP, see CP 1866,[3] sep EP 1758,[9] eccl refounded 1844.[69] *LG* 15. *Parl* Seq 5. *Eccl* Chestf. RDn (1758—1846), Ashov. RDn (1846—87), Alf. RDn (1887—*).

BRADBOURNE

AP Usual civ spelling; for eccl see following entry. Tp 'Bradbourne' in Wirksw. Hd as was chap Brassington (sep CP 1866.[3]), chap Tissington (sep civ identity early, sep EP 1819 (tps Aldwark, Ballidon, hmlt Lea Hall (each of the 3 a sep CP 1866[3]); incl in Appl. Hd chap Atlow (sep CP 1866,[3] sep EP 1716[9]). *LG* Ashb. PLU, RSD, RD. *Parl* Seq 10.

BRADBOURNE WITH BALLIDON

AP Usual eccl spelling; for civ and civ sep chaps, tps and hmlt, see prev entry. *Eccl* Ashb. RDn (until 1958), Wirksw. RDn (1958—*).

BRADLEY

AP *LG* Seq 1. Civ bdry: 1934.[7] *Parl* Seq 20. *Eccl* Seq 1.

BRADWELL

Tp in Hope AP, sep CP 1866,[3] sep EP 1875 (tps Bradwell, Grindlow; hmlts Abney and Abney Grange, Great Hucklow, Little Hucklow; lordship Hazlebadge; and the pt of tp Wardlow in Hope AP).[4] *LG* High Pk Hd, Bakew. PLU (soon after 1838[6]—1930), RSD, RD. *Parl* N'rn Dv (1832—67), North Dv (1867—85), High Pk. Dv (1885—1948), W Derbys CC (1948—*). *Eccl* Castleford RDn (1875—87), Eyam RDn (1887—*).

BRAILSFORD

AP Incl chap Osmaston (sep civ identity early, sep EP 1849 as 'Osmaston by Ashbourne'[70]). *LG* Seq 1. Addtl civ bdry alt: 1883.[67] *Parl* Seq 18. *Eccl* Castil. RDn (until 1846), Radb. RDn (1846—87), Ashb. RDn (1887—*). Eccl bdry: 1860 (help cr Long Lane EP),[43]

BRAMPTON

AP Usual civ spelling, eccl sometimes 'Old Brampton'. *LG* Scar. Hd, Chestf. PLU, Bramp. & Walton USD (ent 1875—92, pt 1892—26 Mar 1894, ent 26 Mar—apptd day 1894), pt Chestf. MB & USD (1892—26 Mar 1894), Bramp. & Walton UD (1894—1935), Chestf. RD (1935—74). Civ bdry: 1894 (26 Mar, loses the pt in Chestf. MB to Chestfield AP),[71] 1910,[72] 1920,[73] 1935.[46] *Parl* Seq 1. *Eccl* Derby RDn (until 1846), Bramp. RDn (1846—87), Chestf. RDn (1887—*). Eccl bdry: 1834 (help cr Brampton St Thomas EP),[74] 1962 (cr Brampton St Mark EP).[75]

OLD BRAMPTON—see prev entry

BRAMPTON ST MARK

EP Cr 1962 from Brampton AP.[75] Chestf. RDn.

BRAMPTON ST THOMAS

EP Cr 1834 from Brampton AP, Chesterfield AP.[74] RDns as for Brampton, from 1834. Bdry: 1861 (help cr Newbold with Dunston EP),[76] 1908,[77] 1926 (help cr Chesterfield St Augustine EP).[38]

BRASSINGTON

Chap in Bradbourne AP, sep CP 1866,[3] sep EP 1743.[9] *LG* Seq 18. *Parl* Seq 10. *Eccl* Ashb. RDn (1743—1846), Wirksw. RDn (1846—*).

BREADSALL

AP *LG* Seq 4. Civ bdry: 1934,[7] 1968 (loses pt to Derby CB [assoc with Derbys] & CP).[17] *Parl* Seq 17. *Eccl* Seq 9. Eccl Bdry: 1955 (help cr Chaddesdon St Philip EP).[78]

BREASTON

Chap in chap Wilne (sep civ identity early from Sawley AP), 'Breaston' a sep EP 1719 from Sawley AP,[9] sep CP 1866 from Wilne CP.[3] *LG* Seq 11. Civ bdry: 1934,[7] 1965 (gains pt Lockington-Hemington CP, Leics).[79] *Parl* Seq 13. *Eccl* Pec jurisd Prebend Sawley (until 1846), Ockb. RDn (1846—87), Ilk. RDn (1887—*).

BRETBY

Chap (donative) in Repton AP, sep CP 1866,[3] sep EP 1922.[40] *LG* Seq 13. Civ bdry: 1885,[80] 1886,[55] 1894 (gains pt of the pt of Stapenhill AP not in Burt. upon Tr. CB [assoc with Staffs]),[81] 1934 (incl loses pt to Burt. upon Tr. CB [assoc with Staffs] & AP).[7] *Parl* Seq 15. *Eccl* Repton RDn.

BRIDGE HILL

EP Cr 1845 from Belper EP.[63] Duff. RDn (1846—55), Alf. RDn (1855—66), Duff. RDn (1866—*). Now sometimes called 'Belper Christ Church'.

BRIMINGTON

Chap in Chesterfield AP, sep CP 1866,[3] sep EP 1737,[9] eccl refounded 1844.[82] *LG* Seq 15. Civ bdry: 1883,[67] 1883,[83] 1920.[73] *Parl* N'rn Dv (1832—67), East Dv (1867—85), Chestf. Dv (1885—1948), Chestf. BC (1948—*). *Eccl* Chestf. RDn (1737—1955), Stav. RDn (1955—*).

BROUGH AND SHATTON

Tp in Hope AP, sep CP 1866.[3] *LG* Seq 7. *Parl* Seq 8.

CHURCH BROUGHTON

AP *LG* Seq 3. Civ bdry: 1883,[67] 1885,[84] 1934.[7] *Parl* Seq 19. *Eccl* Castil. RDn (until 1846), Cubley RDn (1846—87), Longf. RDn (1887—1924). Abol eccl 1924 to help cr Church Broughton with Barton Blount EP.[51]

CHURCH BROUGHTON WITH BARTON BLOUNT

EP Cr 1924 by union Church Broughton AP, Barton Blount AP.[51] Longf. RDn.

BRUSHFIELD

TP in Bakewell AP, sep CP 1866;[3] eccl in chap Ashford (sep EP 1731 from Bakewell AP,[9] eccl refounded 1871[34]; see Ashford for later union). *LG* Seq 6. Bdry: 1934.[7] *Parl* Seq 9.

BURBAGE

EP Cr 1869 from Hartington AP (area in pec jurisd Bakew. even before sep, until 1846).[85] Buxton RDn.

CP Cr 1894 from the pt of Hartington Upper Quarter CP in Buxton UD.[86] *LG* Chap en le Fr. PLU, Buxton UD (1894—1917), MB (1917—74). Bdry: 1934.[7] *Parl* High Pk. Dv/CC (1918—*).

BURNASTON

Tp in Etwall AP, sep CP 1866.[3] *LG* Seq 3. Bdry: 1968.[17] *Parl* Seq 15.

BURTON UPON TRENT

AP Staffs par (N Offlow Hd) incl in Derbys chap and tp Chilcote (Repton & Gres. Hd, sep CP 1866 in Derbys,[3] eccl severed early and united with Clifton Campville AP [Staffs][87]), tp Winshill (Repton & Gresley Hd, sep CP 1866 in Derbys,[3] eccl severed 1825 to help cr Burton upon Trent Holy Trinity EP,[9] the latter eccl refounded 1842,[88] 'Winshill' a sep EP 1867 from Burton upon Trent Holy Trinity EP[89]) so that 'Burton upon Trent' ent Staffs after 1866, qv in that co.

BURTON UPON TRENT HOLY TRINITY

EP Cr 1825 from Burton upon Trent AP (incl Staffs tps Horninglow, Stretton, Derbys tp Winshill),[9] eccl refounded 1842.[88] Tamw. & Tutb. RDn (1825—51), Tutb. RDn (1851—*) (dioc Lichf). Bdry: affecting Staffs areas only in 1844, 1867, 1873 (qv in entries in Staffs, incl abol 1969); affecting Derbys, 1867 (area of Winshill severed to cr Winshill EP).[89]

BUXTON

Chap (pec jurisd. Bakew.) in Bakewell AP, sep CP 1866,[3] sep EP 1728 from Bakewell AP (incl area King Sterndale, sep EP as below), Hope AP (tp Fernilee, chap Fairfield [see Fernilee for later eccl identity]9), 'Buxton' eccl refounded 1898.[10] *LG* High Pk. Hd, Chap en le Fr. PLU, pt Buxton USD, pt Chap. en le Fr. RSD, Buxton UD (1894—1917), MB (1917—74). Civ bdry: 1894 (pt of the pt not in Buxton UD cr King Sterndale CP, later called 'Kingsterndale',[86] the remainder not in the UD made pt of the UD[90]), 1894 (gains the pt of Fernilee CP in Buxton UD).[91] *Parl* N'rn Dv (1832—67), North Dv (1867—85), High Pk. Dv/CC (1885—*). *Eccl* Pec jurisd Bakew. (until 1846), Buxton RDn (1846—*). Eccl bdry: 1850 (cr King Sterndale EP,[9] refounded 1851 from Buxton EP, Hope AP, Hartington AP[40]), 1905 (cr Fernilee EP).[41]

BUXWORTH WITH CHINLEY— see CHINLEY WITH BUGSWORTH

CALDWELL

Hmlt in Stapenhill AP, sep CP 1866.[3] *LG* Seq 13.

Parl Seq 16. Sometimes later called 'Cauldwell'.

CALKE

AP *LG* Seq 12. *Parl* Seq 16. *Eccl* Repton RDn; early loses sep eccl status and incl in Ticknall AP.[92]

CALLOW

Hmlt in Wirksworth AP, sep CP 1866.[3] *LG* Seq 18. Bdry: 1883.[67] *Parl* Seq 10.

CALOW

Tp in Chesterfield AP, sep CP 1866,[3] sep EP 1900 (main pt exclusive of 2 detached pts).[4] *LG* Seq 15. Civ bdry: 1901.[72] *Parl* Seq 1. *Eccl* Chestf. RDn.

CALVER

Tp in Bakewell AP, sep CP 1866,[3] eccl in chap Baslow (sep EP 1770 from Bakewell AP [qv for other constituent tps in Bakewell AP],[9] the orig area of Calver eccl severed 1869 from Baslow EP to help cr Curbar EP[39]). *LG* Seq 9. *Parl* Seq 9.

CARSINGTON

AP *LG* Seq 18. *Parl* Seq 10. *Eccl* Seq 2.

CASTLETON

AP Incl tp Edale (sep CP 1866,[3] sep EP 1722,[9] eccl refounded 1863[93]). *LG* Castlet. Bor, Seq 7. *Parl* Seq 8. *Eccl* High Pk. RDn (1722—1846), Castlet. RDn (1846—87), Eyam RDn (1887—*).

CATTON

Tp (Derbys. Repton & Gres. Hd) in Croxall AP (Derbys, Staffs [N Offlow Hd]), sep CP 1866 in Derbys.[3] *LG* Burt. upon Tr. PLU (soon after 1837[6]—1930), RSD, Repton RD. *Parl* Seq 16.

CAULDWELL— see CALDWELL

CHADDESDEN

Chap in Spondon AP, sep civ identity early, sep EP 1829,[9] eccl refounded 1851.[94] *LG* Appl. Hd, Shard. PLU, RSD, RD (1894—1959), S E Derbys RD (1959—68). Civ bdry: 1901 (loses pt to Derby CB [assoc with Derbys] & CP),[22] 1928 (loses pt to Derby CB [assoc with Derbys] & CP),[23] 1934 loses pt to Derby CB [assoc with Derbys] & CP).[7] Abol civ 1968 pt to Derby CB (assoc with Derbys) & CP, pt to Morley AP.[17] *Parl* S'rn Dv (1832—67), South Dv (1867—85), S'rn Dv (1885—1948), S E Derbys CC (1948—55), Derby North BC (1955—70). *Eccl* [St Mary] Derby RDn (1829—46), Ockb. RDn (1846—87), Ilk. RDn (1887—1955), Derby RDn (1955—*). Eccl bdry: 1955 (incl help cr Chaddesden St Philip EP).[78]

CHADDESDEN ST PHILIP

EP Cr 1955 from Chaddesden EP, Breadsall AP.[78] Derby RDn.

CHAPEL EN LE FRITH

AP *LG* Seq 7. Civ bdry: 1934,[76] 1936 (help cr Whaley Bridge UD & CP [qv for other constituent pars in Derbys, Ches]).[95] *Parl* Seq 8. *Eccl* Pec jurisd Bakew. (until 1846), Castlet. RDn (1846—87), Buxton RDn (1887—*). Eccl bdry: 1960,[96] 1966 (help cr Taxal and Fernilee EP [Ches, Derbys] to be in dioc Chester).[97]

CHARLESWORTH

Chap in Glossop AP, incl for poor law purposes the following areas: Chunal, Dinting, Hadfield, Padfield, Whitfield (none sep civ, the first 3 and pt of last 2 united 1845 as Whitfield EP,[98] the orig area of Hadfield and pt Padfield severed 1875 from Whitfield EP and united with remainder of Padfield [in Glossop AP] to cr Hadfield EP[99]), areas Glossop Dale, Simmondley (neither sep civ, the 2 united eccl 1845 with main area Charlesworth and area Chisworth [in tp Ludworth and Chisworth] from Mellow EP to cr 'Charlesworth' EP[98], 'Charlesworth' a sep CP 1894 from the pt of Glossop AP not in Gloss. MB.[99] *LG* Gloss. PLU, Gloss. Dale RD (1894—1934), Chap. en le Fr. RDn (1934—74). *Parl* High Pk. Dv/CC (1918—*). *Eccl* High Pk. RDn (1845—46), Castlet. RDn (1846—87), Gloss. RDn (1887—*).

CHATSWORTH

Ex-par lbty, sometimes incorrectly deemed tp in Edensor AP,[100] sep CP 1858.[56] *LG* High Pk. Hd, Bakew. PLU (1861—1930), RSD, RD. *Parl* Seq 9.

CHELLASTON

AP *LG* Repton & Gres. Hd, Shard. PLU, RSD, RD (1894—1959), S E Derbys RD (1959—68). Abol civ 1968 pt to Derby CB (assoc with Derbys) & CP, pt to Elvaston AP, pt to Aston upon Trent AP, pt to Swarkestone AP.[17] *Parl* S'rn Dv (1832—67), South Dv (1867—85), S'rn Dv (1885—1948), S E Derbys CC (1948—70). *Eccl* Castil. RDn (until 1846), Stant. by Br. RDn (1846—87), Melb. RDn (1887—*).

CHELMORTON

Chap in Bakewell AP, sep CP 1866,[3] sep EP 1743 (incl tp Flagg in same par).[9] *LG* Seq 6. *Parl* Seq 9. *Eccl* Pec jurisd Bakew. (until 1846), Buxton RDn (1846—*).

LITTLE CHESTER

Tp (Morl. & Lit. Hd) in Derby St Alkmund AP (mostly Derby Bor, qv below), sep CP 1866.[3] *LG* Derby PLU, USD, MB (1877—89), CB (1889—98). Abol 1898 to help cr Derby CP.[101] *Parl* S'rn Dv (1832—67), Derby Parl Bor (1867—1918).

CHESTERFIELD

The following have 'Chesterfield ' in their names. Insofar as any existed at a given time: *LG* Scar. Hd, Chestf. PLU, Chestf. Bor/MB, USD. *Parl* N'rn Dv (1832—67), East Dv (1867—85), Chestf. Dv (1885—1948), Chestf. BC (1948—*). *Eccl* Chestf. RDn.

AP1—CHESTERFIELD [ST MARY AND ALL SAINTS]—Incl chap Brimington (see CP 1866,[3] sep EP 1737,[9] eccl refounded 1844[84]), chap Walton (sep CP 1866[3]), chap Wingerworth (sep civ identity early, sep EP 1728[9]), tp Calow (sep CP 1866,[3] sep EP 1900 [main pt exclusive of 2 detached pts[4]]), tp Hasland (sep CP 1866,[3] sep EP 1851[102]), tp Newbold and Dunston (sep CP 1866,[3] sep EP 1861 as 'Newbold with Dunston' from Brampton St Thomas EP, EP2, Whittington AP[76]), tp Temple Normanton (sep CP 1866,[3] sep EP 1793[9]), tp Tapton (sep CP 1866[3]). Addtl civ bdry alt: 1894 (gains the pts in Chestf. MB of Brampton AP, Hasland CP, Newbold and Dunston CP, Walton CP),[71] 1901,[72] 1920 (incl gains Whittington AP, Tapton CP).[73] *Eccl* Addtl eccl bdry alt: 1834 (help cr Brampton St Thomas EP),[74] 1841 (cr EP2),[103] 1908,[77] 1926 (help cr EP3).[38]

EP1—CHESTERFIELD CHRIST CHURCH—Cr 1914 from EP2, Newbold with Dunston EP.[104]

EP2—CHESTERFIELD HOLY TRINITY—Cr 1841 from AP1.[103] Bdry: 1861 (help cr Newbold with Dunston EP),[76] 1908,[77] 1914 (help cr EP1).[104]

EP3—CHESTERFIELD ST AUGUSTINE—Cr 1926 from AP1, Brampton St Thomas EP.[38]

CHILCOTE

Chap and tp (Derbys, Repton & Gres. Hd) in Burton upon Trent AP (mostly Staffs, N Offlow Hd), sep CP 1866 in Derbys,[3] eccl severed and united early to Clifton Campville AP (Staffs).[87] LG Tamw. PLU, RSD, sep RD in Derbys (1894—97). Transf 1897 to Leics.[105] Parl S'rn Dv (1832—67), South Dv (1867—85), S'rn Dv (1885—1918); see entry in Leics for parl organisation thereafter.

CHINLEY, BUGSWORTH AND BROWNSIDE

Chap in Glossop AP, sep CP 1866,[3] sep EP 1915 as 'Chinley with Bugsworth' EP,[106] qv, sometimes later called 'Buxworth with Chinley'. LG Seq 7. Parl Seq 8.

CHINLEY WITH BUGSWORTH

Chap in Glossop AP, sep EP 1915,[106] sep CP 1866 as 'Chinley, Bugsworthy and Brownside',[3] qv. Gloss. RDn. Bdry: 1960.[96] Sometimes 'Buxworth with Chinley'.

CHISWORTH

Area in tp Ludworth and Chisworth (sep CP 1866 from Glossop AP[3]), 'Chisworth' a sep CP 1896 from Ludworth and Chisworth CP,[107] the orig area eccl severed 1737 to help cr Mellor EP,[9] orig area severed 1845 from Mellor EP to help cr Charlesworth EP.[98] LG Gloss. PLU, Gloss. Dale RD (1896—1934), Chap. en le Fr. RD (1934—74). Parl High Pk. Dv/CC (1918—*).

CLAY CROSS

EP Cr 1852 from North Wingfield AP (tps Clay Lane, Stretton, Woodthorpe, and area Handley [not sep civ]).[108] Ashov. RDn (1852—87), Chestf. RDn (1887—*).

CP Cr 1935 by union Clay Lane CP, Egstow CP, and pts Pilsley CP, Stretton CP, Tupton CP, Woodthorpe CP.[46] LG Clay Cross UD. Parl N E Derbys CC (1948—*).

CLAY LANE

Tp in North Wingfield AP, sep CP 1866,[3] eccl severed 1852 to help cr Clay Cross EP.[108] LG Scar. Hd, Chestf. PLU, Clay Lane USD (1875—93), Clay Cross USD (1893—94), UD. Bdry: 1883.[83] Abol 1935 to help cr Clay Cross CP.[46] Parl N'rn Dv (1832—67), East Dv (1867—85), Chestf. Dv (1885—1918), Clay Cross Dv (1918—48).

CLIFTON

Chap in Ashbourne AP, sep EP 1846,[109] sep CP 1866 as 'Clifton and Compton',[3] qv. Ashb. RDn.

CLIFTON AND COMPTON

Chap in Ashbourne AP, sep CP 1866,[3] sep EP 1846 as 'Clifton',[109] qv. LG Morl. & Lit. Hd, Ashb. PLU, pt Ashb. USD, pt Ashb. RSD, Ashb. RD. Bdry: 1887 (incl gains pt Mayfield AP, Staffs),[13] 1894 (loses the pt in the UD to Ashbourne AP),[31] 1934.[7] Parl Seq 18.

CLIFTON CAMPVILLE

AP Staffs par (N Offlow Hd), gains eccl early chap and tp Chilcote (Derbys, qv for sep civ identity 1866 in Derbys) from Burton upon Trent AP (o'wise Staffs).[87] See main entry in Staffs.

CLOWNE

AP LG Seq 17. Civ bdry: 1885,[68] 1935.[46] Parl Seq 6. Eccl Chestf. RDn (until 1851), Stav. RDn (1851—1920), Bols. RDn (1920—*).

COAL ASTON

Tp in Dronfield AP, sep CP 1866.[3] LG Scar. Hd, Chestf. PLU, RSD, RD. Bdry: 1883,[83] 1934.[60] Abol 1935 pt to Dronf. UD & AP, pt to Eckington AP.[46] Parl N'rn Dv (1832—67), East Dv (1867—85), N-E'rn Dv (1885—1948).

CODNOR

EP Cr 1927 when Codnor and Loscoe EP divided into 2 EPS of Codnor, Loscoe.[110] Heanor RDn.

CODNOR AND LOSCOE

Hmlt in Heanor AP, sep CP 1866,[3] sep EP 1844 from Heanor AP, Pentrich AP, Denby AP, pt ex-par Codnor Park.[111] LG Morl. & Lit. Hd, Basf. PLU, RSD, Unnamed RD (1894—99), Heanor UD (1899—1974). Civ bdry: 1934.[7] Parl Seq 11. Eccl Alf. RDn (1844—1920), Heanor RDn (1920—27). Eccl bdry: 1850 (help cr Ironville EP [Derbys, Notts]).[112] Abol eccl 1927 pt to cr Codnor EP, pt to help cr Loscoe.[110]

CODNOR PARK

Ex-par place, sep CP 1858,[56] pt eccl severed 1844 to help cr Codnor and Loscoe EP,[111] the remainder abol 1850 to help cr Ironville EP (Derbys, Notts).[112] LG Morl. & Lt. Hd, Basf. PLU, RSD, Unnamed RD (in Derbys, administered by Basford Co Council, Notts, 1894—1934). Abol civ 1934 pt to Alf. UD & AP, pt to Heanor UD and to Codnor and Loscoe CP.[7] Parl S'rn Dv (1832—67), South Dv (1867—85), Ilk. Dv (1885—1948).

COTMANHAY

EP Cr 1845 from Heanor AP (pt lbty and tp Shipley), Ilkeston AP.[113] Derby RDn (1845—46), Ockb. RDn (1846—87), Ilk. RDn (1887—*). Bdry: 1888 (help cr Ilkeston Holy Trinity EP),[48] 1962 (help cr Marlpool EP).[114]

COTON IN THE ELMS

Tp in Lullington AP, sep CP 1866,[3] sep EP 1859,[9] eccl refounded 1865.[115] LG Seq 13. Parl Seq 16. Eccl Lull. RDn (1859—87), Repton RDn (1887—*).

CRICH

AP Tp 'Crich' in Morl. & Lit. Hd; incl in Scar. Hd tp Wessington (sep CP 1866,[3] see EP 1859[116]); incl in Wirksw. Hd tp Tansley (sep CP 1866,[3] sep EP 1840,[9] eccl refounded 1844[53]). LG Morl. & Lit. Hd (pt until 1866, ent from 1866), pt Scar. Hd (until 1866), pt Wirksw. Hd (until 1866), Belper PLU, RSD, RD. Addtl civ bdry alt: 1897 (help cr Dethick and Holloway CP),[117] 1934.[7] Parl Seq 14. Eccl Derby RDn (until 1846), Alf. RDn (1846—55), Ashov. RDn (1855—87), Alf. RDn (1887—*). Addtl eccl bdry alt: 1901.[25]

CROMFORD

Chap in Wirksworth AP, sep CP 1866,[3] sep EP

1798,[9] eccl refounded 1869 from Wirksworth AP, Middleton by Wirksworth EP,[85] *LG* Wirksw. Hd, Bakew. PLU, RSD, RD (1894—1924), The Matlocks UD (1924—34), Matlock UD (1934—74). Civ bdry: 1934.[7] *Parl* Seq 10. *Eccl* Ashb. RDn (1798—1846), Ashov. RDn (1846—87), Wirksw. RDn (1887—*).

CROSS GREEN—see SOUTH DARLEY

CROXALL
AP Tp 'Croxall' in Derbys (Repton & Gres. Hd), pt in Staffs (N Offlow Hd); incl in Derbys (Repton & Gres. Hd) tp Catton (sep CP 1866 in Derbys[3]), the par made 1895 ent Staffs.[118] *LG* Tamw. PLU, RSD, pt sep RD in Derbys (1894—95). *Parl* Derbys pt, S'rn Dv (1832—67), South Dv (1867—85), S'rn Dv (1885—1918); see Staffs for remainder and later. *Eccl* Repton RDn (until 1846), Hartsh. RDn (1846—55), Lull. RDn (1855—87), Repton RDn (1887—*).

CUBLEY
AP *LG* Appl. Hd, Uttox. PLU (soon after 1837[6]—1930), RSD, Sudb. RD (1894—1934), Ashb. RD (1934—74). *Parl* Seq 20. *Eccl* Seq 3.

CURBAR
Tp in Bakewell AP, sep CP 1866,[3] eccl in chap Baslow (sep EP 1770 from Bakewell AP [qv for other constituent tps in Bakewell AP][9]), 'Curbar' a sep EP 1869 from Baslow EP (pt orig area Curbar [the rest remains in Baslow EP], area of orig tps Calver, Froggatt, and pt orig area tp Baslow and Bubnell [pt area Bubnell]).[39] *LG* Seq 6. Civ bdry: 1934.[7] *Parl* Seq 9. *Eccl* Eyam RDn.

DALBURY
AP Usual eccl spelling; for civ see following entry. *Eccl* Seq 5.

DALBURY LEES
AP Usual civ spelling; for eccl see prev entry. *LG* Seq 3. *Parl* Seq 15.

DALE ABBEY
AP Orig private pec owned by Stanhope family, sometimes eccl considered chap in Stanton by Dale AP, sometimes considered a sep EP,[119] no longer considered sep by 1893 and eccl incl thereafter in Stanton by Dale (qv for RDns). *LG* Seq 11. Civ bdry: 1884,[120] 1934,[7] 1968.[17] *Parl* Seq 13.

DARLEY
AP Tp 'Darley' in High Pk. Hd; incl in Wirksw. Hd tp Wensley and Snitterton (sep CP 1866,[3] eccl severed 1845 to cr South Darley EP[121]). *LG* High Pk. Hd (pt until 1866, ent from 1866), pt Wirksw. Hd (until 1866), Bakew. PLU, N Darley USD, UD (1894—1934), Matlock UD (1934—74). *Parl* Seq 9. *Eccl* Seq 14.

SOUTH DARLEY
EP Cr 1845 from Darley AP (tp Wensley and Snitterton, qv for sep civ identity 1866).[121] Sometimes early 'Cross Green' or 'Darley Dale'. Bakew. RDn.

DARLEY ABBEY
Area in Derby St Alkmund AP, sep EP 1847,[122] sep CP 1894 from the pt of Derby St Alkmund not in Derby CB.[99] *LG* Derby PLU, Belper RD. Civ bdry: 1928 (loses pt to Derby CB [assoc with Derbys] & CP),[23] 1934.[7] Abol civ 1968 ent to Derby CB (assoc with Derbys) & CP.[17] *Parl* Belper Dv/CC (1918—70). *Eccl* Derby RDn (1847—87), Duff. RDn (1887—1955), Derby RDn (1955—*). Eccl bdry: 1958.[18]

DENBY
AP *LG* Seq 9. Civ bdry: 1886.[5] *Parl* Seq 12. *Eccl* Castil. RDn (until 1846), Alf. RDn (1846—47), Duff. RDn (1847—*). Eccl bdry: 1844 (help cr Codnor and Loscoe EP).[111]

DERBY
The following have 'Derby' in their names (entry for Derby Hills follows this listing). Insofar as any existed at a given time: *LG* Derby PLU; Bor, MB, CB, USD, RSD sep noted. *Parl* Derby Parl Bor (1295—1918); sep listed thereafter. *Eccl* Derby RDn.

CP1—DERBY—Cr 1898 by union pars in Derby CB: Little Chester CP, AP1, AP2, AP3, AP4, AP5, Litchurch CP, New Normanton CP, Rowditch CP.[101] *LG* Derby CB. Bdry: 1901,[22] 1928,[23] 1934,[7] 1968 (incl gains Darley Abbey CP and exchanges pts with Mackworth AP).[17] *Parl* Derby Parl Bor/BC (1918—48); pt Derby North BC, pt Derby South BC (1848—*; see Part II of the *Guide* for composition of the 2 BCs by wards of the CB).

AP1—DERBY ALL SAINTS—*LG* Derby Bor/MB/CB, USD. Abol civ 1898 to help cr CP1.[101] *Parl* Derby Parl Bor (1295—1918). Cathedral church from 1927. Eccl bdry: 1847 (help cr EP13),[123] 1946,[124] 1958 (gains AP3).[125]

EP1—DERBY CHRIST CHURCH—Cr 1867 from AP4.[9] Bdry: 1882 (help cr EP11).[126] Abol 1972 to help cr EP2.[66]

EP2—DERBY CHRIST CHURCH AND HOLY TRINITY—Cr 1972 by union EP1, EP3.[66]

EP3—DERBY HOLY TRINITY—Cr 1855 from AP4.[9] Abol 1972 to help cr EP2.[66]

AP2—DERBY ST ALKMUND—Tp 'Derby St Alkmund' pt in Derby Bor, pt Morl. & Lit. Hd; incl in Morl. & Lit. Hd chap Little Eaton (sep CP 1866,[3] sep EP 1792,[9] eccl refounded 1862[127]), tp Little Chester (sep CP 1866[3]), chap Quorndon (sep civ identity early, sep EP 1732[9]). *LG* Derby Bor/MB/CB (pt until 1894 [enlarged pt 1866—94], ent 1894—98), pt Derby USD, pt Derby RSD. Addtl civ bdry alt: 1894 (the pt not in the CB cr Darley Abbey CP).[99] Abol civ 1898 to help cr CP1.[101] *Parl* Pt Derby Parl Bor (1295—1918 [enlarged pt 1867—1918]), pt S'rn Dv (1832—67), pt South Dv (1867—85), pt S'rn Dv (1885—1918). Addtl eccl bdry alt: 1844 (cr EP16),[128] 1847 (cr Darley Abbey EP),[122] 1847 (help cr EP13),[123] 1867 (help cr EP6),[129] 1946,[124] 1965.[19]

EP4—DERBY ST ANDREW—Cr 1867 from AP4.[130] Abol 1969 to help cr EP5.[131]

EP5—DERBY ST ANDREW WITH ST OSMUND—Cr 1969 by union EP4, pt Osmaston by Derby EP.[131]

EP6—DERBY ST ANNE—Cr 1873 from AP2, EP13.[129] Abol 1972 to help cr EP7.[132]

EP7—DERBY ST ANNE AND ST JOHN—Cr 1972 by union EP6, EP13.[132]

EP8—DERBY ST AUGUSTINE—Cr 1908 from EP11.[133]

EP9—DERBY ST BARNABAS—Cr 1886 from EP13.[134] Bdry: 1961.[135]

EP10—DERBY ST BARTHOLOMEW—Cr 1928 from Osmaston by Derby EP, EP12, Normanton EP.[136] Bdry: 1948 (help cr Allenton and Shelton Lock EP),[14] 1969.[131]

EP11—DERBY ST CHAD MILL HILL—Cr 1882 from EP1, EP12, Normanton EP.[126] Bdry: 1908 (cr EP8).[133]

EP12—DERBY ST JAMES THE GREATER—Cr 1856 from AP4.[137] Bdry: 1882 (help cr EP11),[126] 1883 (cr EP17),[138] 1928 (help cr EP10).[136]

EP13—DERBY ST JOHN—Cr 1847 from AP5, AP2, AP1.[123] Bdry: 1873 (help cr EP6),[129] 1886 (cr EP9).[134] Abol 1972 to help cr EP7.[132]

EP14—DERBY ST LUKE—Cr 1872 from AP5.[139]

EP15—DERBY ST MARK—Cr 1937 from EP16.[45] Bdry: 1955.[78]

AP3—DERBY ST MICHAEL—Tp 'Derby St Michael' in Derby Bor; incl in Morl. & Lit. Hd chap Alvaston (sep civ identity early, sep EP 1772[9]). *LG* Pt Morl. & Lit. Hd (until 1877 [reduced pt when Alvaston gains sep civ identity]), pt Derby Bor (enlarged pt when Alvaston gains sep civ identity), Derby MB (pt 1835—77, ent 1877—89), Derby USD, CB (1889—98). Abol civ 1898 to help cr CP1.[101] *Parl* Derby Parl Bor (pt 1295—1885, ent 1885—1918), pt S'rn Dv (1832—67), pt South Dv (1867—85). Abol eccl 1958 ent to AP1.[125]

EP16—DERBY ST PAUL—Cr 1844 from AP2.[128] Bdry: 1937 (cr EP15).[45]

AP4—DERBY ST PETER—Incl in Repton & Gres. Hd chap Normanton (sep civ identity early, sep EP 1877[140]); incl in Morl. & Lit. Hd chap Boulton (sep civ identity early, sep EP 1733[9]), tp Litchurch (sep CP 1866[3]). *LG* Pt Repton & Gres. Hd (until Normanton gains sep civ identity), pt Morl. & Lit. Hd (until 1866 [reduced pt after Boulton gains sep civ identity]), pt Derby Bor, Derby MB (pt 1835—77, ent 1877—89), Derby USD, CB (1889—98). Abol civ 1898 to help cr CP1.[101] *Parl* Derby Parl Bor (pt 1295—1885, ent 1885—1918), pt S'rn Dv (1832—67), pt South Dv (1867—85). Addtl eccl bdry alt: 1855 (cr EP2),[9] 1856 (cr EP12),[137] 1867 (cr EP1),[9] 1867 (cr EP4).[130]

EP17—DERBY ST THOMAS—Cr 1883 from EP12.[138]

AP5—DERBY ST WERBURGH—Incl in Repton & Gres. Hd chap Osmaston (sep civ identity early, sep EP 1733 as 'Osmaston by Derby'[9].) *LG* Derby Bor (pt until Osmaston gains sep civ identity, ent thereafter), pt Morl. & Lit. Hd (until Osmaston gains sep civ identity), Derby MB/CB, USD. Addtl civ bdry alt: 1890 (gains the pt in Derby USD of Littleover CP).[141] Abol civ 1898 to help cr CP1.[101] *Parl* Derby Parl Bor (pt 1295—1885 [enlarged pt when Osmaston gains sep civ identity], ent 1885—1918). Addtl eccl bdry alt: 1847 (help cr EP13),[123] 1872 (cr EP14).[139]

DERBY HILLS
Ex-par lbty, sep CP 1858.[56] *LG* Seq 14. *Parl* Seq 17.

DERWENT
Chap in Hathersage AP, sep CP 1866,[3] sep EP 1722,[9] eccl refounded 1871 as 'Derwent Woodlands' when united with pt Hope AP.[142] *LG* Seq 7. Civ bdry: 1929 (loses pt to Sheff CB [assoc with Yorks W Riding] and to Ecclesall CP),[143] 1934.[7] *Parl* N'rn Dv (1832—67), North Dv (1867—85), High Pk Dv (ent 1885—1918, pt 1918—48), pt W'rn Dv (1918—48), High Pk. CC (1948—*). *Eccl* Derby RDn (1722—1846), Eyam RDn (1846—51), Castlet. RDn (1851—66), Eyam RDn (1866—71).

DERWENT WOODLANDS
EP Refounding 1871 of Derwent EP when the latter united with pt Hope AP.[142] Eyam RDn. Abol 1943 ent to Bamford EP.[45]

DETHICK AND HOLLOWAY
CP Cr 1897 by union Dethick and Lea CP, pt Crich AP.[117] *LG* Belper PLU, RD. *Parl* Belper Dv/CC (1918—*).

DETHICK AND LEA
Tp (orig a chap in Wirksw. Hd, long destroyed) in Ashover AP (o'wise Scar. Hd), sep CP 1866,[3] sep EP 1741 as 'Dethick Lea and Holloway',[9] as such eccl refounded 1899.[37] *LG* Belper PLU, RSD, RD. Abol 1897 to help cr Dethick and Holloway CP.[117] *Parl* S'rn Dv (1832—67), East Dv (1867—85), W'rn Dv (1885—1918).

DETHICK LEA AND HOLLOWAY
EP Tp (orig a chap, long destroyed) in Ashover AP, sep EP 1741,[9] eccl refounded 1899,[37] sep CP 1866 as 'Dethick and Lea',[3] qv. *Eccl* Chestf. RDn (1741—1846), Ashov. RDn (1846—87), Alf. RDn (1887—*). Bdry: 1901.[25]

DINTING VALE
EP Cr 1879 from Whitfield EP.[144] Castlet. RDn (1879—87), Gloss. RDn (1887—*).

DISLEY
CP Ches Par (Hayf. PLU), pt in New Mills USD (o'wise ent Derbys), the pt in the USD becomes 1889 pt Derbys, that pt cr 1894 Newtown CP in Derbys,[145] so that 'Disley' ent Ches thereafter.

DONISTHORPE
Hmlt in Church Gresley AP, Measham AP (both Derbys, dioc Lichf), Seal AP, Ashby de la Zouch AP (both Leics, dioc Peterb), civ united with hmlt Oakthorpe (ent Derbys, in Church Gresley AP, Stretton en le Field AP, Measham AP) as 'Oakthorpe and Donisthorpe', qv for sep civ identity 1866 in both cos,[3] the combined area a sep EP 1869 as 'Donisthorpe'.[146] Hartsh. RDn (1869—87), Repton RDn (1887—1937), W Akeley RDn (dioc Leic, 1927—*). Now eccl called 'Donisthorpe and Moira'.

DONISTHORPE AND MOIRA—see prev entry

DORE
Chap in Dronfield AP, sep CP 1866,[3] sep EP 1720 (incl tp Totley in same par),[9] eccl refounded 1844.[147] *LG* Scar. Hd, Eccl.-Bierl. PLU, RSD, Norton RD. Civ bdry: 1929 (loses pt to Sheff CB [assoc with Yorks W Riding] and to Ecclesall

CP).[143] Abol civ 1934 ent to Sheff CB (assoc with Yorks W Riding) and AP.[60] *Parl* N'rn Dv (1832—67), East Dv (1867—85), N-E'rn Dv (1885—1948). *Eccl* Chestf. RDn (1720—1846), Bramp. RDn (1846—87), Dronf. RDn (1887—1910), Eyam RDn (1910—74), Ecclesall RDn (dioc Sheff, 1974—*). Eccl bdry: 1878 (help cr Abbey Dale EP),[1] 1922 (help cr Totley EP),[2] 1974.[148]

DOVERIDGE

AP *LG* Seq 5. Civ bdry: 1883 (gains pt Croxden AP, Staffs),[67] 1934.[7] *Parl* Seq 20. *Eccl* Seq 4.

DRAKELOW

Tp in Church Gresley AP, sep CP 1866.[3] *LG* Seq 13. Civ bdry: 1894 (gains pt of the pt of Stapenhill AP not in Burt. upon Tr. CB [assoc with Staffs]).[81] *Parl* Seq 16.

DRAYCOTT AND CHURCH WILNE

Lbty in chap (pec jurisd Prebend Sawley) Wilne (sep civ identity early from Sawley AP), 'Draycott and Church Wilne' a sep CP 1866 from Wilne CP,[3] the area eccl severed 1822 from Sawley AP to help cr 'Wilne with Draycott' EP,[9] as such eccl refounded 1857.[149] *LG* Seq 11. *Parl* Seq 13.

DRONFIELD

AP Incl chap Dore (sep CP 1866,[3] sep EP 1720 incl tp Totley [qv for later eccl status],[9] eccl refounded 1844[147]), chap Holmesfield (sep CP 1866,[3] sep EP 1720,[9] eccl refounded 1857[150]), tp Totley (sep CP 1866,[3] eccl in chap/EP Dore as noted above, 'Totley' a sep EP 1922 from Dore EP, Abbey Dale EP[2]), hmlt Little Barlow, tp Coal Aston, tp Unstone (each of the 3 a sep CP 1866[3]). *LG* Scar. Hd, Chestf. PLU, pt Dronf. USD, pt Chestf. RSD, Dronf. UD. Addtl civ bdry alt: 1894 (the pt not in the UD cr Dronfield Woodhouse CP),[151] 1935,[46] 1967 (exchanges pts with Sheff CB [assoc with Yorks W Riding] & AP).[61] *Parl* Seq 7. *Eccl* Chestf. RDn (until 1846), Bramp. RDn (1846—87), Dronf. RDn (1887—1910), Chestf. RDn (1910—*). Addtl eccl bdry alt: 1974.[148]

DRONFIELD WOODHOUSE

CP Cr 1894 from the pt of Dronfield AP not in Dronf. UD.[151] *LG* Chestf. PLU, RD. Abol 1935 pt to Dronf. UD & AP, pt to Holmesfield CP.[46] *Parl* N-E'rn Dv (1918—48).

DUFFIELD

AP Incl chap Belper (sep CP 1866,[3] sep EP 1743[9]), chap Heage (sep CP 1866,[3] sep EP 1784[9]), chap Hobrook (sep CP 1866,[3] sep EP 1811,[9] eccl refounded 1863[152]), chap Turnditch (sep CP 1866,[3] sep EP 1737[9]), tps Hazlewood, Shottle and Postern (each a sep CP 1866,[3] eccl united 1846 as 'Hazlewood' EP[153]), tp Windley (sep CP 1866[3]). *LG* Seq 2. Addtl civ bdry alt: 1886,[5] 1897 (cr Milford CP),[154] 1968 (loses pt to Derby CB [assoc with Derbys] & CP).[17] *Parl* Seq 14. *Eccl* Seq 8. Addtl eccl bdry alt: 1846 (tps Milford, Makeney [neither sep civ] severed to help cr Milford EP),[64] 1856 (help cr Idridgehay EP),[155] 1962,[114] 1967.[156]

EARLSTERNDALE—see EARL STERNDALE

LITTLE EATON

Chap in Derby St Alkmund AP, sep CP 1866,[3] sep EP 1792,[9] eccl refounded 1862.[127] *LG* Seq 11. Civ

bdry: 1934,[7] 1968.[17] *Parl* Seq 17. *Eccl* Derby RDn (1792—1847), Duff. RDn (1847—*).

LONG EATON

Tp (pec jurisd Prebend Sawley, until 1846) in Sawley AP, sep CP 1866,[3] sep EP 1864.[157] *LG* Morl. & Lit. Hd, Shard. PLU, Long Eaton USD, UD. Civ bdry: 1921,[158] 1934.[7] *Parl* Seq 13. *Eccl* Ockb. RDn (1864—87), Ilk. RDn (1887—*). Eccl bdry: 1922 (cr Long Eaton St John EP).[37]

LONG EATON ST JOHN

EP Cr 1922 from Long Eaton AP.[37] Ilk. RDn. Bdry: 1929.[116]

EATON AND ALSOP

Chap in Ashbourne AP, sep civ identity early, sep EP 1737 as 'Alsop en le Dale' (incl area Eaton),[9] qv. *LG* Seq 18. *Parl* Seq 10.

ECKINGTON

AP Incl chap Killamarsh (see civ identity early, sep EP 1843[159]). *LG* Seq 15. Addtl civ bdry alt: 1935,[46] 1967 (incl loses pt to Sheff CB [assoc with Yorks W Riding] & AP).[61] *Parl* Seq 7. *Eccl* Chestf. RDn (1843—51), Stav. RDn (1851—*). Addtl eccl bdry alt: 1842 (cr Ridgeway EP,[160] refounded 1843[161]), 1929 (cr Mosbrough EP),[162] 1957.[163]

EDALE

Chap in Castleton AP, sep CP 1866,[3] sep EP 1722,[9] eccl refounded 1863.[93] *LG* Seq 7. *Parl* Seq 8. *Eccl* High Pk RDn (1722—1846), Castlet. RDn (1846—87), Eyam RDn (1887—*).

EDENSOR

AP Incl tp Pilsley (sep CP 1866[3]); the ex-par place of Chatsworth sometimes incorrectly deemed a tp in this par.[100] *LG* Seq 6. *Parl* Seq 9. *Eccl* High Pk. RDn (until 1846), Youlg. RDn (1846—47), Eyam RDn (1847—84), Bakew. RDn (1884—*).

EDLASTON

AP Usual eccl spelling; for civ see following entry. *Eccl* Seq 1.

EDLASTON AND WYASTON

AP Usual civ spelling; for eccl see prev entry. *LG* Seq 1. *Parl* Seq 20.

EGGINTON

AP *LG* Seq 10. *Parl* Seq 15. *Eccl* Seq 6.

EGSTOW

CP Cr 1894 by union of the pts in Clay Cross UD of Pilsley CP, Woodthorpe CP.[151] *LG* Chestf. PLU, Clay Cross UD. Bdry: 1898.[164] Abol 1935 to help cr Clay Cross CP.[46] *Parl* Clay Cross Dv (1918—48).

ELMTON

AP Usual civ spelling; for eccl see following entry. *LG* Seq 17. Bdry: 1935.[46] *Parl* Seq 6.

ELMTON WITH CRESSWELL

AP Usual eccl spelling; for civ see prev entry. *Eccl* Chestf. RDn (until 1846), Stav. RDn (1846—1920), Bols. RDn (1920—*).

ELTON

Chap (Wirksw. Hd) in Youlgreave AP (o'wise High Pk. Hd), sep civ identity early, sep EP 1728.[9] *LG* Wirksw. Hd, Bakew. PLU (soon after 1838[6]—1930), RSD, RD. *Parl* Seq 10. *Eccl* High Pk. RDn (1728—1846), Youlg. RDn (1846—47), Bakew. RDn (1847—*).

ELVASTON

AP Usual civ spelling; for eccl see following entry. *LG* Morl. & Lit. Hd, Shard. PLU, pt Alvaston & Boulton USD (1884—94), Shard RSD (ent 1875—84, pt 1884—94), Shard. RD (1894—1959), S E Derbys RD (1959—74). Civ bdry: 1884 (gains pt of Alvaston CP in the USD),[120] 1894 (the pt of this par in the UD becomes a new and sep par, 'Unnamed'),[165] 1897 (gains Unnamed CP),[166] 1968 (incl loses pt to Derby CB [assoc with Derbys] & CP).[17] *Parl* Seq 17.

ELVASTON CUM THURLSTON AND AMBASTON

AP Usual eccl spelling; for civ see prev entry. *Eccl* Seq 12.

ETWALL

AP Incl tps Bearwardcote, Burnaston (each a sep CP 1866[3]). *LG* Seq 3. Addtl civ bdry alt: 1886.[55] *Parl* Seq 15. *Eccl* Seq 6.

EYAM

AP Incl tp Eyam Woodlands, hmlt Foolow (each a sep CP 1866[3]). *LG* Seq 6. Addtl civ bdry alt: 1883,[67] 1934.[7] *Parl* Seq 9. *Eccl* Seq 13. Eccl bdry: 1936.[167]

EYAM WOODLANDS

Tp in Eyam AP, sep CP 1866.[3] *LG* Seq 6. Bdry: 1883,[67] 1934.[7] *Parl* Seq 9.

FAIRFIELD

Chap (donative) in Hope AP, sep CP 1866,[3] eccl severed 1728 to help cr Buxton EP,[9] the latter eccl refounded 1898.[10] *LG* High Pk. Hd, Chap. en le Fr. PLU, pt Fairfield USD, pt Buxton USD, pt Fairfield UD (1894—1917), pt Buxton UD (1894—1917), Buxton MB (1917—74). Civ bdry: 1917 (the pt not in Buxton UD [being constituted Buxton MB] cr Green Fairfield CP),[168] 1934.[7] *Parl* Seq 8. *Eccl* Pec jurisd Bakew. (until 1846), Buxton RDn (1846—*). Eccl bdry: 1960.[96]

GREEN FAIRFIELD

CP Cr 1917 from the pt of Fairfield CP not in Buxton UD (as the latter enlarged to constitute Buxton MB).[168] *LG* Chap. en le Fr. PLU, RD. Bdry: 1934.[7] *Parl* High Pk. Dv/CC (1918—*).

FERNILEE

Tp in Hope AP, sep CP 1866,[3] eccl severed 1728 to help cr Buxton EP,[9] the latter refounded 1898,[10] 'Fernilee' a sep EP 1905 from Buxton EP.[40] *LG* High Pk. Hd, Chap. en le Fr. PLU, pt Buxton USD, pt Chap. en le Fr. RSD, Chap. en le Fr. RD. Civ bdry: 1894 (loses the pt in the UD to Buxton CP),[91] 1934,[7] 1936 (help cr Whaley Bridge UD & CP [qv for other constituent pars in Derbys, Ches]).[95] *Parl* N'rn Dv (1832—67), North Dv (1867—85), High Pk. Dv (1885—1948). *Eccl* Buxton RDn. Abol eccl 1966 to help cr Taxal and Fernilee EP to be in dioc Chester, Stockport RDn.[169]

FINDERN

Chap in Mickleover AP, sep CP 1866,[3] sep EP 1866.[170] *LG* Seq 10. Civ bdry: 1968 (incl loses pt to Derby CB [assoc with Derbys] & CP).[17] *Parl* Seq 15. *Eccl* Radb. RDn (1866—87), Melb. RDn (1887—1955), Repton RDn (1955—*).

FLAGG

Tp in Bakewell AP, sep CP 1866,[3] eccl in chap Chelmorton (sep EP 1743 from Bakewell AP[9]). *LG*

Seq 6. Bdry: 1934.[7] *Parl* Seq 9.

FOOLOW

Hmlt in Eyam AP, sep CP 1866.[3] *LG* Seq 6. Bdry: 1883,[67] 1934.[7] *Parl* Seq 9.

FOREMARK

AP Incl tp Ingleby (sep CP 1866[3]). *LG* Seq 13. *Parl* Seq 15. *Eccl* Repton RDn (until 1846), Will. RDn (1846—51), Stant. by Br. RDn (1851—87), Melb. RDn (1887—1955), Repton RDn (1955—*).

FOSTON AND SCROPTON

Tp in Scropton AP (area Foston ent Derbys [Appl. Hd], area Scropton pt Derbys [Appl. Hd], pt Staffs [N Offlow Hd], pt but not all of the area in Derbys transf to Staffs 1832 for parl purposes, 1844 for civ purposes[52], the tp a sep CP 1866 with pt in each co.[3] *LG* Burt. upon Tr. PLU, RSD, Repton RD. Bdry: 1885,[84] 1890 (loses the pt in Staffs to Staffs pars of Tutbury AP, Tatenhill AP, Yoxall AP, so that 'Foston and Scropton' ent Derbys thereafter).[171] *Parl* Derbys pt, Seq 19.

FRECHEVILLE

EP Cr 1943 from Beighton AP.[45] Stav. RDn. Abol 1972 to help cr Frecheville and Hackenthorpe EP.[172]

FRECHEVILLE AND HACKENTHORPE

EP Cr 1972 by union Frecheville EP, Hackenthorpe EP.[172] Stav. RDn (1972—74), Attercliffe RDn (dioc Sheff, 1974—*). Bdry: 1974,[148] 1974.[162]

FROGGATT

Tp in Bakewell AP, sep CP 1866,[3] eccl in chap Baslow (sep EP 1770 from Bakewell AP [qv for other constituent tps in Bakewell AP][9]), the orig area of Froggatt eccl severed 1869 from Baslow EP to help cr Curbar EP.[39] *LG* Seq 6. *Parl* Seq 9.

GLAPWELL

Hmlt in Bolsover AP, sep CP 1866.[3] *LG* Scar. Hd, Mansf. PLU (soon after 1836[6]—1930), RSD, RD. *Parl* Seq 2.

GLEADLESS VALLEY

EP Cr 1974 from Norton AP (Derbys), Heeley EP, Gleadless EP (both Yorks W Riding) to be dioc Sheff.[148] Attercliffe RDn (dioc Sheff, 1974—*).

GLOSSOP

AP Incl chap Charlesworth (incl for poor law purposes areas Chunal, Dinting, Hadfield, Padfield, Whitfield [none sep civ], the first 3 and pt of last 2 united 1845 as Whitfield EP,[98] the pt of the orig area of Padfield and ent Hadfield severed 1875 from Whitfield EP and united with remainder of Padfield to cr Hadfield EP[97]; also incl for poor law purposes Glossop Dale, Simmondley (neither sep civ), the 2 united 1845 with main area Charlesworth and area of Chisworth from Mellor EP to cr 'Charlesworth' EP,[98] 'Charlesworth' a sep CP 1894 from the pt of Glossop AP not in Gloss. MB[99]), chap Chinley, Bugsworth and Brownside (sep CP 1866,[3] sep EP 1915 as 'Chinley with Bugsworth',[106] the latter sometimes called 'Buxworth with Chinley'), chap Hayfield (sep CP 1866,[3] sep EP 1733[9]), chap Mellor (sep CP 1866,[3] sep EP 1737 [incl tp Ludworth and Chisworth],[9] the area of Chisworth eccl severed 1845 from Mellor EP to help cr Charlesworth EP[98]); also incl tp Beard, Thornsett,

Ollersett and Whittle ([pt situated on Ches side of River Goyt, uncertain as to which co belonged, the tp declared to be ent Derbys 1832 for parl purposes, 1844 for civ purposes[52]] 'Beard, Thornsett, Ollersett and Whittle' a sep CP 1866,[3] sep EP 1844 as 'Beard',[53] later called 'New Mills'). LG High Pk. Hd, Gloss. PLU, pt Gloss. USD, pt Gloss. RSD, Gloss. MB (pt 1866—94, ent 1894—1974). Addtl civ bdry alt: 1934.[7] Parl Seq 8. Eccl High Pk. RDn (until 1846), Castlet. RDn (1846—87), Gloss. RDn (1887—*).

GRATTON
Hmlt in Youlgreave AP, sep CP 1866.[3] LG Seq 6. Parl Seq 9.

GREENHILL
EP Cr 1959 from Norton AP.[173] Stav. RDn (1959—74), Ecclesall RDn (dioc Sheff, 1974—*).

CASTLE GRESLEY
Hmlt in Church Gresley AP, sep CP 1866.[3] LG Seq 13. Bdry: 1883,[67] 1886,[55] 1934.[7] Parl Seq 16.

CHURCH GRESLEY
AP Incl hmlt Castle Gresley, tps Drakelow, Linton (each a sep CP 1866[3]), tp Swadlincote (sep CP 1866,[3] sep EP 1849[174]), pt hmlt Donisthorpe (Derbys, Leics), pt hmlt Oakthorpe (ent Derbys) (the 2 hmlts civ united and sep CP 1866 as 'Oakthorpe and Donisthorpe'[3] with pt in each co [qv for pt other constituent areas in the CP], the ent combined area a sep EP 1869 as 'Donisthorpe'[146]). LG Repton & Gres. Hd, Burt. upon Tr. PLU, Swadlincote Dist USD, UD (1894—1951), Swadlincote UD (1951—74). Addtl civ bdry alt: 1883,[67] 1886,[55] 1934.[7] Parl Seq 16. Eccl Seq 16.

GRIFFE GRANGE
Ex-par place, united civ 1858 with tp Hopton in Wirksworth AP to cr tp Hopton and Griffe Grange,[175] as such sep CP 1866,[3] qv.

GRINDLOW
Tp in Hope AP, sep CP 1866,[3] eccl severed 1875 to help cr Bradwell EP.[4] LG Seq 6. Parl Seq 9.

HACKENTHORPE
EP Cr 1957 from Beighton AP.[62] Stav. RDn. Abol 1972 to help cr Frecheville and Hackenthorpe EP.[172]

HADDON—see following 2 entries

NETHER HADDON
Tp in Bakewell AP (in chap Haddon, not sep eccl), sep CP 1866.[3] LG High Pk. Hd, Bakew. PLU (1861—1930), RSD, RD. Parl Seq 9.

OVER HADDON
Tp in Bakewell AP (in chap Haddon, not sep eccl), sep CP 1866.[3] LG Seq 6. Bdry: 1894.[41] Parl Seq 9.

HADFIELD
EP Cr 1875 from Whitfield EP (areas of orig tp Hadfield, pt tp Padfield), Glossop AP (remainder of area tp Padfield).[97] Castlet. RDn (1875—87), Gloss. RDn (1887—*).

KIRK HALLAM
AP Tp 'Kirk Hallam' in Morl. & Lit. Hd; incl in Appl. Hd tp Mapperley (sep CP 1866,[3] sep EP 1870[176]). LG Shard. PLU, RSD, RD. Addtl civ bdry alt: 1884.[120] Abol civ 1934 pt to Ilk. MB & AP, pt to Dale Abbey CP.[7] Parl S'rn Dv (1832—67), South

Dv (1867—85), Ilk. Dv (1885—1918), S'rn Dv (1918—48). Eccl Seq 10.

WEST HALLAM
AP LG Seq 11. Civ bdry: 1884.[120] Parl Seq 13. Eccl Seq 10.

HARGATE MANOR
Ex-par place, sep CP 1858.[56] LG Appl. Hd, Burt. upon Tr. PLU (1862—85), RSD. Abol civ 1885 ent to Hilton CP.[177] Parl S'rn Dv (1832—85), W'rn Dv (1885—1918).

HARTHILL
Tp in Bakewell AP, sep CP 1866.[3] LG Seq 6. Parl Seq 9.

HARTINGTON
AP Incl chap Earl Sterndale (sep EP 1763[9]); ent par civ divided into tps Hartington Middle Quarter, Hartington Nether Quarter, Hartington Town Quarter, Hartington Upper Quarter (each a sep CP 1866[3]) so that 'Hartington' has no sep civ identity after 1866. LG Wirksw. Hd. Parl N'rn Dv (Middle and Town Quarters), pt S'rn Dv (Nether and Upper Quarters) (1832—67). Eccl Pec jurisd Bakew. (until 1846), Bakew. RDn (1846—*). Addtl eccl bdry alt: 1848 (cr Biggin EP),[65] 1851 (help refound King Sterndale EP),[40] 1868 (cr Burbage EP).[85]

HARTINGTON MIDDLE QUARTER
Tp in Hartington AP, sep CP 1866.[3] LG Seq 19. Parl Seq 9.

HARTINGTON NETHER QUARTER
Tp in Hartington AP, sep CP 1866.[3] LG Seq 18. Parl S'rn Dv (1832—67), North Dv (1867—85), W'rn Dv (1885—1918), N-E'rn Dv (1918—48), Bols. CC (1948—*).

HARTINGTON TOWN QUARTER
Tp in Hartington AP, sep CP 1866.[3] LG Seq 18. Parl Seq 10.

HARTINGTON UPPER QUARTER
Tp in Hartington AP, sep CP 1866.[3] LG Wirksw. Hd, Chap. en le Fr. PLU, pt Buxton USD, pt Chap. en le Fr. RSD, Chap. en le Fr. RD. Civ bdry: 1894 (the pt in the UD cr Burbage CP),[86] 1934,[7] 1936 (incl gains pt Taxal AP [by 1936 called 'Taxall'], Ches).[95] Parl Seq 8.

HARTSHORNE
AP LG Seq 12. Civ bdry: 1883,[67] 1897 (help cr Woodville CP to be ent Derbys [qv for other constituent pt from Leics]),[105] 1934.[7] Parl Seq 16. Eccl Seq 16. Eccl bdry: 1847 (help cr Woodville EP [qv for other constituent pt from Leics]).[178]

HASLAND
Tp in Chesterfield AP, sep CP 1866,[3] sep EP 1851.[105] LG Scar. Hd, Chestf. PLU, pt Chestf. MB & USD (1892—26 Mar 1894), Chestf. RSD (ent 1875—92, pt 1892—26 Mar 1894, ent 26 Mar—apptd day 1894), Chestf. RD. Civ bdry: 1883,[67] 1894 (26 Mar, loses the pt in the MB to Chesterfield AP),[71] 1901,[72] 1920.[73] Parl Seq 1. Eccl Chestf. RDn.

HASSOP
Tp in Bakewell AP, sep CP 1866.[3] LG Seq 6. Bdry: 1934.[7] Parl Seq 9.

HATHERSAGE
AP Incl hmlt Bamford (sep CP 1866,[3] sep EP 1860,[9]

eccl refounded 1861[44]), chap Derwent (sep CP 1866,[3] sep EP 1722,[9] eccl refounded 1871 as 'Derwent Woodlands' when gains pt Hope AP[142]), chap Stony Middleton (sep CP 1866,[3] sep EP 1743[9]), hmlt Outseats (sep CP 1866[3]). *LG* Seq 6. Addtl civ bdry alt: 1883,[67] 1929 (loses pt to Sheff CB [assoc with Yorks W Riding] and to Ecclesall CP),[143] 1934.[7] *Parl* Seq 9. *Eccl* Seq 13. Addtl eccl bdry alt: 1974.[148]

HATTON
Tp in Marston on Dove AP, sep CP 1866.[3] *LG* Seq 3. Bdry: 1883,[67] 1885,[84] 1934.[7] *Parl* Seq 19.

HAYFIELD
Chap in Glossop AP, sep CP 1866,[3] sep EP 1733.[9] *LG* Seq 8. *Parl* Seq 8. *Eccl* High Pk. RDn (1733—1846), Castlet. RDn (1846—87), Gloss. RDn (1887—*).

HAZLEBADGE
Lordship in Hope AP, sep CP 1866,[3] eccl severed 1875 to help cr Bradwell CP.[4] *LG* Seq 6. *Parl* Seq 9.

HAZLEWOOD
Tp in Duffield AP, sep CP 1866,[3] sep EP 1846 (incl tp Shottle and Postern in same par).[153] *LG* Seq 2. Bdry: 1886.[5] *Parl* Seq 14. *Eccl* Duff. RDn. Eccl bdry: 1967.[156]

HEAGE
Chap in Duffield AP, sep CP 1866,[3] sep EP 1784.[9] *LG* Appl. Hd, Belper PLU, Heage USD, UD (1894—1934), Ripley UD (1934—74). Civ bdry: 1934.[7] *Parl* S'rn Dv (1832—67), South Dv (1867—85), Mid Dv (1885—1918), Belper Dv (1918—48), Ilk. CC (1948—*). *Eccl* Derby RDn (1784—1846), Duff. RDn (1846—*). Eccl bdry: 1899 (cr Ambergate EP).[24]

HEANOR
AP Incl hmlt Codnor and Loscoe (sep CP 1866,[3] sep EP 1844 from Heanor AP, Pentrich AP, Denby AP, pt ex-par Codnor Park[111]), lbty and tp Shipley (sep CP 1866,[3] pt eccl severed 1845 to help cr Cotmanhay EP[113]). *LG* Morl. & Lit. Hd, Basf. PLU, Heanor USD, UD. *Parl* Seq 11. *Eccl* Derby RDn (until 1846), Alf. RDn (1846—1920), Heanor RDn (1920—*). Addtl eccl bdry alt: 1913 (cr Langley Mill EP),[179] 1927 (help cr Loscoe EP),[110] 1962 (help cr Marlpool EP).[114]

HEATH
AP Sometimes 'Lowne'. *LG* Seq 15. *Parl* Seq 3. *Eccl* Castil. RDn (until 1846), Stav. RDn (1846—51), Chestf. RDn (1851—75), Bols. RDn (1875—*). Eccl bdry: 1954.[180]

HIGHLOW
Lordship in Hope AP, sep CP 1866.[3] *LG* Seq 6. *Parl* Seq 9.

HILTON
Tp in Marston on Dove AP, sep CP 1866.[3] *LG* Seq 3. Bdry: 1885 (gains Hargate Manor CP).[177] *Parl* Seq 19.

HOGNASTON
AP Chap in Ashbourne AP, sep par early but independence disputed 17th cent.[28] *LG* Seq 18. *Parl* Seq 10. *Eccl* Seq 2.

HOLBROOK
Chap in Duffield AP, sep CP 1866,[3] sep EP 1811,[9] eccl refounded 1863.[152] *LG* Seq 2. *Parl* Seq 14. *Eccl* Derby RDn (1811—46), Duff. RDn (1846—*).

HOLLINGTON
Tp in Longford AP, sep CP 1866.[3] *LG* Seq 1. Bdry: 1883,[67] 1887.[13] *Parl* Seq 20.

HOLMESFIELD
Chap in Dronfield AP, sep CP 1866,[3] sep EP 1720,[9] eccl refounded 1857.[150] *LG* Seq 15. Civ bdry: 1934,[60] 1935,[46] 1967 (exchanges pts with Sheff CB [assoc with Yorks W Riding] & AP).[61] *Parl* Seq 7. *Eccl* Chestf. RDn (1720—1846), Bramp. RDn (1846—87), Dronf. RDn (1887—1910), Chestf. RDn (1910—*). Eccl bdry: 1974.[148]

HOON
Tp in Marston on Dove AP, sep CP 1866.[3] *LG* Seq 3. *Parl* Seq 19.

HOPE
AP Incl chap Fairfield, tp Fernilee (each a sep CP 1866,[3] both eccl severed 1728 to help cr Buxton EP,[9] the latter eccl refounded 1898,[10] 'Fernilee' a sep EP 1905 from Buxton EP[40]), hmlt Abney and Abney Grange, tp Bradwell, tp Grindlow, lordship Hazlebadge, hmlt Great Hucklow, hmlt Little Hucklow, the pt of tp Wardlow in Hope AP (each of the 7 a sep CP 1866,[3] all 7 eccl united 1875 (along with the pt of tp Wardlow in Hope AP [sep CP 1866 from Hope AP, Bakewell AP[3]] as 'Bradwell' EP[4]), tp Aston, tp Brough and Shatton, lordship Highlow, hmlt Hope Woodlands, hmlt Offerton, hmlt Nether Padley, tp Stoke, tp Thornhill (each of the 8 a sep CP 1866[3]). *LG* Seq 7. Addtl civ bdry alt: 1934.[7] *Parl* Seq 8. *Eccl* Pec jurisd Bakew. (until 1846), Castlet. RDn (1846—84), Eyam RDn (1884—*). Addtl eccl bdry alt: 1851 (help refound King Sterndale EP),[40] 1871 (help refound Derwent EP as 'Derwent Woodlands' EP).[142]

HOPE WOODLANDS
Hmlt in Hope AP, sep CP 1866.[3] *LG* Seq 7. Bdry: 1934.[7] *Parl* Seq 8.

HOPTON—see following entry

HOPTON AND GRIFFE GRANGE
Tp cr 1858 by union tp Hopton in Wirksworth AP, ex-par area Griffe Grange,[175] the whole a sep CP 1866.[3] *LG* Seq 18. *Parl* Seq 10.

HOPWELL
Hmlt in chap Wilne (sep civ identity early from Sawley AP), 'Hopwell' a sep CP 1866 from Wilne CP.[3] *LG* Seq 11. *Parl* Seq 13.

HORSLEY
AP Incl tp Horsley Woodhouse (sep CP 1866,[3] pt eccl severed 1877 to help cr Smalley EP,[181] the remainder cr 1878 'Horsley Woodhouse' EP[182]), tp Kilburn (sep CP 1866[3]). *LG* Seq 9. *Parl* Seq 12. *Eccl* Seq 8.

HORSLEY WOODHOUSE
Tp in Horsley AP, sep CP 1866,[3] pt eccl severed 1877 to help cr Smalley EP,[181] the remainder cr 1878 'Horsley Woodhouse' EP.[182] *LG* Seq 9. *Parl* Seq 12. *Eccl* Duff. RDn.

GREAT HUCKLOW
Hmlt in Hope AP, sep CP 1866,[3] eccl severed 1875

to help cr Bradwell EP.[4] *LG* Seq 6. Bdry: 1883,[67] 1934.[7] *Parl* Seq 9.

LITTLE HUCKLOW

Organisation and bdry alts as for Great Hucklow.

HULLAND

Tp in Ashbourne AP, sep CP 1866,[3] eccl united 1853 with tp Hulland Ward in same par to cr 'Hulland' EP.[9] *LG* Seq 1. Civ bdry: 1886,[183] 1887.[13] *Parl* Seq 20. *Eccl* Ashb. RDn.

HULLAND WARD

Tp in Ashbourne AP, sep CP 1866,[3] eccl united 1853 with tp Hulland in same par to cr 'Hulland' EP.[9] *LG* Seq 1. Bdry: 1886,[183] 1886,[184] 1934 (gains Hulland Ward Intakes CP).[7] *Parl* Seq 22.

HULLAND WARD INTAKES

Tp in Ashbourne AP, sep CP 1866.[3] *LG* Appl. Hd, Ashb. PLU, RSD, RD. Abol 1934 ent to Hulland Ward CP.[7] *Parl* S'rn Dv (1832—67), South Dv (1867—85), W'rn Dv (1885—1948).

IBLE

Tp in Wirksworth AP, sep CP 1866,[3] eccl severed 1841 to help cr Middleton by Wirksworth EP,[9] the latter eccl refounded 1847.[185] *LG* Seq 18. *Parl* Seq 11.

IDRIDGEHAY

EP Cr 1856 from Wirksworth AP (tp Idridgehay and Alton), Kirk Ireton AP (tp Ireton Wood), Duffield AP.[155] Wirksw. RDn.

IDRIDGEHAY AND ALTON

Tp in Wirksworth AP, sep CP 1866,[3] eccl severed 1856 to help cr Idridgehay EP,[155] qv. *LG* Seq 2. Bdry: 1886,[5] 1889.[186] *Parl* S'rn Dv (1832—67), South Dv (1867—85), W'rn Dv (1885—1918), Belper Dv/CC (1918—*).

ILKESTON

AP *LG* Morl. & Lit. Hd, Basf. PLU, Ilk. USD, MB (1887—1974). Civ bdry: 1934.[7] *Parl* Seq 11. *Eccl* Seq 10. Eccl bdry: 1845 (help cr Cotmanhay EP),[113] 1888 (help cr Ilkeston Holy Trinity EP),[48] 1912 (cr Ilkeston St John EP),[187] 1954.[188]

ILKESTON HOLY TRINITY

EP Cr 1888 from Ilkeston AP, Cotmanhay EP.[48] Ilk. RDn. Bdry: 1954.[188]

ILKESTON ST JOHN

EP Cr 1912 from Ilkeston AP.[187] Ilk. RDn.

INGLEBY

Tp in Foremark AP, sep CP 1866.[3] *LG* Seq 13. *Parl* Seq 15.

KIRK IRETON

AP Incl tp Ireton Wood (sep CP 1866,[3] eccl severed 1856 to help cr Idridgehay EP[155]). *LG* Seq 18. Addtl civ bdry alt: 1889.[186] *Parl* Seq 10. *Eccl* Seq 2.

IRETON WOOD

Tp in Kirk Ireton AP, sep CP 1866,[3] eccl severed 1856 to help cr Idridgehay EP.[155] *LG* Wirksw. Hd, Belper PLU, RSD. Abol 1889 pt to Idridgehay and Alton CP, pt to Kirk Ireton AP.[186] *Parl* S'rn Dv (1832—67), North Dv (1867—85), W'rn Dv (1885—1918).

IRONVILLE

EP Cr 1850 from Notts par of Selston with Underwood and Westwood AP (civ, 'Selston') and from 4 Derbys areas of Codnor and Loscoe EP, Pentrich

AP, Riddings EP, ent ex-par Codnor Park (the area not eccl severed 1844 to help cr Codnor and Loscoe EP).[112] Alf. RDn (1850—1920), Heanor RDn (1920—*).

IVONBROOK GRANGE

Hmlt in Wirksworth AP, sep CP 1866,[3] eccl severed 1841 to help cr Middleton by Wirksworth EP,[9] the latter eccl refounded 1847.[185] *LG* Seq 6. *Parl* Seq 9.

KEDLESTON

AP *LG* Seq 2. *Parl* Seq 15. *Eccl* Seq 11.

KILBURN

Tp in Horsley AP, sep CP 1866.[3] *LG* Seq 9. Bdry: 1886.[5] *Parl* Seq 14.

KILLAMARSH

Chap in Eckington AP, sep civ identity early, sep EP 1843.[159] *LG* Seq 15. Civ bdry: 1967 (incl loses pt to Sheff CB [assoc with Yorks W Riding] & AP).[61] *Parl* Seq 7. *Eccl* Chestf. RDn (1843—51), Stav. RDn (1851—*).

KINGSTERNDALE—see KING STERNDALE

KNIVETON

AP Chap in Ashbourne AP, sep par 1290.[29] *LG* Seq 18. *Parl* Seq 10. *Eccl* Pec jurisd Kniveton (until 1846), Ashb. RDn (1846—*).

KIRK LANGLEY

AP *LG* Seq 9. *Parl* Seq 15. *Eccl* Seq 11.

LANGLEY MILL

EP Cr 1913 from Heanor AP.[179] Alf. RDn (1913—20), Heanor RDn (1920—*).

UPPER LANGWITH

AP *LG* Scar. Hd, Mansf. PLU, RSD, Blackw. RD. Civ bdry: 1884.[189] Abol civ 1935 pt to Scarcliffe AP, pt to Shirebrook CP.[46] *Parl* N'rn Dv (1832—67), East Dv (1867—85), Chestf. Dv (1885—1918), Clay Cross Dv (1918—48), *Eccl* Chestf. RDn (until 1846), Stav. RDn (1846—51), Chestf. RDn (1851—75), Bols. RDn (1875—87), Stav. RDn (1887—1920), Bols. RDn (1920—*). Eccl bdry: 1924 (help cr Whaley Thorns EP [Derbys, Notts]).[66]

LEA HALL

Hmlt in Bradbourne AP, sep CP 1866.[3] *LG* Seq 18. *Parl* Seq 10.

LINTON

Tp in Church Gresley AP, sep CP 1866.[3] *LG* Seq 13. *Parl* Seq 16.

LITCHURCH

Tp in Derby St Peter AP, sep CP 1866.[3] *LG* Morl. & Lit. Hd, Derby PLU, USD, MB (1877—89), CB (1889—98). Abol 1898 to help cr Derby CP.[101] *Parl* S'rn Dv (1832—67), Derby Parl Bor (1867—1918).

LITTLEOVER

Chap in Mickleover AP, sep CP 1866,[3] sep EP 1866.[190] *LG* Morl. & Lit. Hd, Shard. PLU, pt Derby USD (1875—90), Shard. RSD (pt 1875—90, ent 1890—94), Shard. RD (1894—1959), S E Derbys RD (1959—68). Civ bdry: 1890 (loses the pt in the USD to Derby St Werburgh AP),[141] 1928 (incl loses pt to Derby CB [assoc with Derbys] & CP).[23] Abol civ 1968 pt to Derby CB (assoc with Derbys) & CP, pt to Findern CP.[17] *Parl* S'rn Dv (1832—67), South Dv (1867—85), S'rn Dv (1885—

1948), S E Derbys CC (1948—55), Derby South BC (1955—70). *Eccl* Radb. RDn (1866—87), Derby RDn (1887—*). Eccl bdry: 1962 (incl help cr Mickleover St John EP).[135]

LITTON

Hmlt in Tideswell AP, sep CP 1866.[3] *LG* Seq 6. *Parl* Seq 9.

LONG LANE

EP Cr 1860 from Brailsford AP, Trusley AP, Sutton on the Hill AP (tp Orleston and Thurvaston).[43] Radb. RDn (1860—87), Longf. RDn (1887—*).

LONGFORD

AP Incl chap and tp Alkmonton (sep CP 1866,[3] sep EP 1843 [incl lbty Hungry Bentley],[9] eccl refounded 1849[12]), tp Hollington, hmlt Rodsley (each a sep CP 1866[3]), lbty Hungry Bentley (sep CP 1866,[3] eccl in chap/EP Alkmonton as noted above). *LG* Seq 1. Addtl civ bdry alt: 1883,[67] 1887.[13] *Parl* Seq 20. *Eccl* Seq 4.

LONGSTONE

Chap in Bakewell AP comprised of tps Great Longstone, Little Longstone, and the pt of tp Wardlow in Bakewell AP (see the sep tps for their sep civ identities), the chap a sep EP 1830.[9] Pec jurisd Bakew. (until 1846), Bakew. RDn (1846—*).

GREAT LONGSTONE

Tp in Bakewell AP, sep CP 1866,[3] eccl in chap Longstone (sep EP 1830,[9] qv for other constituent areas). *LG* Seq 6. Bdry: 1883,[67] 1894,[41] 1903,[42] 1934.[7] *Parl* Seq 9.

LITTLE LONGSTONE

Tp in Bakewell AP, sep CP 1866,[3] eccl in chap Longstone (sep EP 1830,[9] qv for other constituent areas). *LG* Seq 6. Bdry: 1934.[7] *Parl* Seq 9.

LOSCOE

EP Cr 1927 from Codnor and Loscoe EP, Heanor AP.[110] Heanor RDn.

LUDWORTH

CP Cr 1896 from Ludworth and Chisworth CP.[107] *LG* Gloss. PLU, Gloss. Dale RD (1896—1934), Chap. en le Fr. RD (1934—36). Transf 1936 to Ches.[95] *Parl* High Pk. Dv (1918—48).

LUDWORTH AND CHISWORTH

Tp in Glossop AP, sep CP 1866,[3] eccl in chap Mellor (sep EP 1737 from Glossop AP[9]), the area of Chisworth eccl severed 1843 from Mellor EP to help cr Charlesworth EP.[98] *LG* High Pk. Hd, Gloss. PLU, RSD, Gloss. Dale RD. Abol 1896 to cr 2 CPs of Ludworth, Chisworth.[107] *Parl* N'rn Dv (1832—67), North Dv (1867—85), High Pk. Dv (1885—1918).

LULLINGTON

AP Incl tp Coton in the Elms (sep CP 1866,[3] sep EP 1859,[9] eccl refounded 1865[115]). *LG* Seq 13. *Parl* Seq 16. *Eccl* Seq 17.

MACKWORTH

AP Incl chap Allestree (sep civ identity early, sep EP 1849[16]), tp Markeaton (sep CP 1866[3]). *LG* Seq 9. Addtl civ bdry alt: 1886,[5] 1934 (incl loses pt to Derby CB [assoc with Derbys] & CP),[7] 1968 (incl exchanges pts with Derby CB [assoc with Derbys] & CP).[17] *Parl* Seq 15. *Eccl* Seq 11. Addtl eccl bdry alt: 1954 (cr Mackworth St Francis EP),[191] 1958,[18]

1965 (incl help cr Allestree St Nicholas EP).[19]

MACKWORTH ST FRANCIS

EP Cr 1954 from Mackworth AP.[191] Derby RDn. Bdry: 1961,[135] 1962 (help cr Mickleover St John EP).[135]

MAPLETON

AP *LG* Seq 18. Civ bdry: 1887 (incl exchanges pts with Mayfield AP and exchanges pts with Okeover CP [early status as AP uncertain; see entry in Staffs], both Staffs).[13] *Parl* Seq 10. *Eccl* Ashb. RDn. Abol eccl early to help cr Ashbourne with Mapleton EP.[33]

MAPPERLEY

Tp (Appl. Hd) in Kirk Hallam AP (o'wise Morl. & Lit. Hd), sep CP 1866,[3] sep EP 1870.[176] *LG* Seq 2. *Parl* Seq 12. *Eccl* Ockb. RDn (1870—87), Ilk. RDn (1887—*).

MARKEATON

Tp in Mackworth AP, sep CP 1866.[3] *LG* Morl. & Lit. Hd, Belper PLU, pt Derby USD (1875—90), Belper RSD (pt 1875—90, ent 1890—94), Belper RD. Bdry: 1886,[5] 1890 (the pt in Derby USD [brought at this time into Derby CB] cr Rowditch CP to be a constituent par in the CB),[141] 1928 (loses pt to Derby CB [assoc with Derbys] & CP).[23] Abol 1934 pt to Derby CB (assoc with Derbys) & CP, pt to Allestree CP, pt to Darley Abbey CP, pt to Mackworth AP.[7] *Parl* S'rn Dv (1832—67), South Dv (1867—85), S'rn Dv (1885—1918), Belper Dv (1918—48).

MARLPOOL

EP Cr 1962 from Cotmanhay EP, Heanor AP.[114] Heanor RDn.

MARSTON MONTGOMERY

AP *LG* Appl. Hd, Uttox. PLU (soon after 1837[6]—1930), RSD, Sudb. RD (1894—1934), Ashb. RD (1934—74). *Parl* Seq 20. *Eccl* Castil. RDn (until 1846), Cubley RDn (1846—87), Ashb. RDn (1887—*).

MARSTON ON DOVE

AP Usual civ spelling; for eccl until 1974 see 'Marston upon Dove'. Incl tps Hatton, Hilton, Hoon (each a sep CP 1866[3]). *LG* Seq 3. Addtl civ bdry alt: 1903 (gains the pt of Rolleston AP in Derbys [Rolleston considered in 19th cent and earlier to be ent Staffs, a small pt without population deemed later to be in Derbys]).[192] *Parl* Seq 19.

MARSTON ON DOVE WITH SCROPTON

EP Cr 1974 by union Marston upon Dove AP (Derbys), Scropton AP (Staffs, Derbys until 1866 [reduced area in Derbys from 1844], ent Staffs thereafter).[193] Longf. RDn.

MARSTON UPON DOVE

AP Usual eccl spelling until 1974; for civ and civ sep tps, see 'Marston on Dove'. *Eccl* Castil. RDn (until 1846), Cubley RDn (1846—47), Will. RDn (1847—51), Radb. RDn (1851—87), Longf. RDn (1887—1974). Abol eccl 1974 to help cr Marston on Dove with Scropton EP.[193]

MATLOCK

AP *LG* Wirksw. Hd, Bakew. PLU, pt Matlock USD, pt Matlock Bath and Scarthin Nick USD, Matlock UD (1894—1924), The Matlocks UD (1924—34),

Matlock UD (1934—74). Civ bdry: 1894 (the pt in Matlock Bath and Scarthin Nick UD cr Matlock Bath CP).[99] *Parl* Seq 10. *Eccl* Ashb. RDn (until 1846), Ashov. RDn (1846—87), Bakew. RDn (1887—*). Eccl bdry: 1842 (cr Matlock Bath EP),[9] 1865,[194] 1886 (cr Matlock Bank EP).[195]

MATLOCK BANK
EP Cr 1886 from Matlock AP.[195] Ashov. RDn (1886—87), Bakew. RDn (1887—*).

MATLOCK BATH
EP Cr 1842 from Matlock AP.[9] Ashov. RDn (1842—87), Bakew. RDn (1887—*).
CP Cr 1894 from the pt of Matlock AP in Matlock Bath and Scarthin Nick UD.[99] *LG* Bakew. PLU, Matlock Bath and Scarthin Nick UD (1894—1924), The Matlocks UD (1924—34), Matlock UD (1934—74). *Parl* W'rn Dv (1918—48), W Derbys CC (1948—*).

MEASHAM
AP Incl pt hmlt Oakthorpe (ent Derbys), pt (in Derbys) of hmlt Donisthorpe (Derbys, Leics) (the 2 hmlts united as single tp 'Oakthorpe and Donisthorpe', as such sep CP 1866 with pt in each co,[3] the area a sep EP 1869 as 'Donisthorpe',[146] qv for other constituent areas). *LG* Repton & Gres. Hd, Ashby de la Zouch PLU, RSD, sep RD in Derbys (1894—97). Addtl civ bdry alt: 1884,[196] 1885.[80] Transf 1897 to Leics.[105] *Parl* S'rn Dv (1832—67), South Dv (1867—85), S'rn Dv (1885—1918); see Leics for later civ and parl organisation. *Eccl* Repton RDn (until 1846), Hartsh. RDn (1846—55), Lullington RDn (1855—66), Hartsh. RDn (1866—87), Repton RDn (1887—1927), S Akeley RDn (dioc Leic, 1927—*).

MELBOURNE
AP *LG* Seq 14. Civ bdry: 1965 (loses pt to Breedon on the Hill AP, exchanges pts with Donington AP, both Leics).[79] *Parl* Seq 17. *Eccl* Seq 18.

MELLOR
Chap in Glossop AP, sep CP 1866,[3] sep EP 1737 incl tp Ludworth and Chisworth,[9] the area of Chisworth eccl severed 1843 from Mellor EP to help cr Charlesworth EP.[98] *LG* High Pk. Hd, Hayf. PLU, RSD, RD (1894—1934), Chap. en le Fr. RD (1934—36). Transf 1936 to Ches.[95] *Parl* N'rn Dv (1832—67), North Dv (1867—85), High Pk. Dv (1885—1948). *Eccl* High Pk. RDn (1737—1846), Castlet. RDn (1846—87), Gloss. RDn (1887—*).

MERCASTON
Tp in Mugginton AP, sep CP 1866.[3] *LG* Seq 1. *Parl* Seq 18.

MICKLEOVER
AP Incl chap Findern (sep CP 1866,[3] sep EP 1866[170]), chap Littleover (sep CP 1866,[3] sep EP 1866[190]). *LG* Morl. & Lit. Hd, Burt. upon Tr. PLU, RSD, Repton RD. Addtl civ bdry alt: 1928 (loses pt to Derby CB [assoc with Derbys] & CP).[23] Abol civ 1968 pt to Derby CB (assoc with Derbys) & CP, pt to Burnaston CP, pt to Findern CP, pt to Radbourne AP.[17] *Parl* S'rn Dv (1832—67), South Dv (1867—85), S'rn Dv (1885—1918), Belper Dv/CC (1918—70). *Eccl* Derby RDn (until 1846), Will. RDn (1846—51), Radb. RDn (1851—87), Longf. RDn

(1887—*). Addtl eccl bdry alt: 1962 (incl help cr Mickleover St John EP).[135]

MICKLEOVER ST JOHN
EP Cr 1962 from Mickleover AP, Littleover EP, Mackworth St Francis EP.[135] Derby RDn.

MIDDLETON AND SMERRILL
Chap in Youlgreave AP, sep CP 1866.[3] *LG* Seq 17. *Parl* Seq 9.

MIDDLETON BY WIRKSWORTH
Hmlt in Wirksworth AP, sep CP 1866,[3] sep EP 1841 incl tp Ible, hmlt Ivonbrook Grange, both in same par,[9] eccl refounded 1847.[185] *LG* Wirksw. Hd, Ashb. PLU, RSD, RD. Abol civ 1934 ent to Wirksw. UD & AP.[7] *Parl* S'rn Dv (1832—67), North Dv (1867—85), W'rn Dv (1885—1948). *Eccl* Ashb. RDn (1841—46), Wirksw. RDn (1846—*). Eccl bdry: 1869 (help refound Cromford EP).[85]

MILFORD
EP Cr 1846 from Belper EP, Duffield AP (tps Milford, Makeney [neither sep civ]).[64] Duff. RDn.
CP Cr 1897 from Duffield AP.[154] *LG* Belper PLU, RD (1894—1934), UD (1934—74). *Parl* Belper Dv/CC (1918—*).

MONYASH
Chap in Bakewell AP, sep CP 1866,[3] sep EP 1744.[9] *LG* Seq 6. *Parl* Seq 9. *Eccl* Pec jurisd Bakew. (until 1846), Bakew. RDn (1846—84), Buxton RDn (1884—*).

MORLEY
AP Incl chap Smalley (sep CP 1866,[3] sep EP 1877 incl pt Horsley AP [pt tp Horsley Woodhouse][181]).Bartholomew EP).[136] *LG* Morl. & Lit. Hd, Belper PLU, RSD, RD (1894—1934), Shard. RD (1934—59), S E Derbys RD (1959—74). Addtl civ bdry alt: 1968.[17] *Parl* S'rn Dv (1832—67), South Dv (1867—85), Ilk. Dv (1885—1918), Belper Dv (1918—48), S E Derbys CC (1948—*). *Eccl* Seq 9.

MORTON
AP Incl tp Brackenfield (sep CP 1866,[3] sep EP 1758,[9] eccl refounded 1844[69]). *LG* Scar. Hd, Chestf. PLU, pt Clay Lane USD (1875—83), Chestf. RSD (pt 1875—83, ent 1883—94), Chestf. RD. Addtl civ bdry alt: 1883.[83] *Parl* Seq 5. *Eccl* Chestf. RDn (until 1846), Alf. RDn (1846—66), Ashov. RDn (1866—84), Alf. RDn (1884—*).

MOSBROUGH
EP Cr 1929 from Eckington AP.[162] Stav. RDn (1929—74), Attercliffe RDn (dioc Sheff, 1974—*). Bdry: 1974,[148] 1974.[162]

MUGGINGTON
AP Tp 'Muggington' in Appl. Hd as was tp Mercaston, hmlt Ravensdale Park (each a sep CP 1866[3]); incl in Morl. & Lit. Hd tp Weston Underwood (sep CP 1866[3]). *LG* Belper PLU, RSD. Abol civ 1886 pt to Hulland Ward CP, pt to Weston Underwood CP.[184] *Parl* S'rn Dv (1832—67), South Dv (1867—85), S'rn Dv (1885—1918). *Eccl* Derby RDn (until 1846), Radb. RDn (1846—87), Duff. RDn (1887—*).

NETHERSEAL
CP Leics par ('Nether Seal') transf 1897 to Derbys where soon called 'Netherseal.'[105] *LG* Ashby de la

Zouch PLU, Hartsh. & Seals RD (1897—1934), Repton RD (1934—74). *Parl* S'rn Dv (1918—48), Belper CC (1948—*).

NEW MILLS

EP Cr 1844 from Glossop AP as 'Beard' EP (for civ see following entry),[53] later called 'New Mills'. High Pk. RDn (1844—46), Castlet. RDn (1846—87), Gloss. RDn (1887—*).

CP Renaming 1885 of Beard, Thornsett, Ottersett and Whittle CP (orig tp in Glossop AP; for eccl see prev entry).[54] *LG* High Pk. Hd, Hayf. PLU, New Mills USD, UD. Bdry: 1934 (gains Newtown CP),[7] 1936 (exchanges pts with Disley CP, Ches).[95] *Parl* High Pk. Dv/CC (1918—*).

NEWBOLD AND DUNSTON

Tp in Chesterfield AP, sep CP 1866.[3] *LG* Scar. Hd, Chestf. PLU, Newbold & Dunston USD (ent 1875—92, pt 1892—26 Mar 1894, ent 26 Mar—apptd day 1894), pt Chestf. MB & USD (1882—26 Mar 1894), Newbold & Dunston UD (1894—1911), Whittington & Newbold UD (1911—20). Bdry: 1894 (26 Mar, loses the pt in the MB to Chesterfield AP),[71] 1901.[72] Abol 1920 pt to Chestf. MB & AP, pt to Brampton AP.[73] *Parl* N'rn Dv (1832—67), East Dv (1867—85), Chestf. Dv (1885—1948).

NEWBOLD WITH DUNSTON

EP Cr 1861 from Brampton St Thomas EP, Chesterfield Holy Trinity EP, Whittington AP.[76] Chestf. (1861—84), Bramp. RDn (1884—87), Dronf. RDn (1887—1910), Chestf. RDn (1910—*). Bdry: 1908,[77] 1914 (help cr Chesterfield Christ Church EP).[104]

NEWHALL

EP Cr 1835 from Stapenhill AP.[9] Hartsh. RDn (1835—66), Lull. RDn (1866—87), Repton RDn (1887—*).

NEWTON GRANGE

Hmlt in Ashbourne AP, sep CP 1866.[3] *LG* Seq 18. Bdry: 1887.[13] *Parl* Seq 10.

NEWTON SOLNEY

AP *LG* Seq 13. Civ bdry: 1885,[80] 1886,[55] 1894 (gains the pt of Winshill CP not in Burton upon Tr. CB [assoc with Staffs] so that Winshill CP thereafter ent in the CB).[81] *Parl* Seq 15. *Eccl* Repton RDn (until 1846), Will. RDn (1846—51), Hartsh. RDn (1851—66), Lull. RDn (1866—87), Repton RDn (1887—*).

NEWTOWN

CP Cr 1894 from the pt of Disley CP (o'wise Ches) in Derbys.[145] *LG* Hayf. PLU, New Mills UD. Abol 1934 ent to New Mills CP.[7] *Parl* High Pk. Dv (1918—48).

NO MAN'S HEATH

Ex-par area, uncertain if within or near junction of any of 3 cos of Derbys, Leics, Warws, or whether in diocs of Worc, Lichf, or Peterb, the area civ abol 1888 ent to Newton Regis AP, Warws,[197] 'No Man's Heath' a sep EP 1873 from ent ex-par area and pt Newton Regis AP, Warws, to be in dioc Lichf (Tamworth RDn, 1873—*).[113]

NORBURY

AP Usual eccl spelling; for civ and civ and eccl sep chap, see following entry. *Eccl* Seq 1.

NORBURY AND ROSTON

AP Usual civ spelling; for eccl see prev entry. Incl chap Snelston (sep civ identity early, sep EP 1871[198]). *LG* Appl. Hd, Uttox. PLU (soon after 1837[6]—1930), RSD, Sudb. RD (1894—1934), Ashb. RD (1934—74). *Parl* Seq 20.

NORMANTON

Chap in Derby St Peter AP, sep civ identity early, sep EP 1877.[140] *LG* Repton & Gres. Hd, Shard. PLU, RSD, RD. Civ bdry: 1890 (the pt in Derby USD [brought at this time into Derby CB] cr New Normanton CP to be in the CB),[141] 1901 (loses pt to Derby CB [assoc with Derbys] & CP).[22] Abol civ 1928 pt to Derby CB (assoc with Derbys) & CP, pt to Littleover CP, pt to Sinfin Moor CP.[23] *Parl* S'rn Dv (1832—67), South Dv (1867—85), S'rn Dv (1885—1948). *Eccl* Derby RDn. Eccl bdry: 1882 (help cr Derby St Chad Mill Hill EP),[126] 1928 (help cr Derby St Bartholomew EP).[136]

NEW NORMANTON

CP Cr 1890 from the pt of Normanton CP (prev in Derby USD) now brought into Derby CB.[141] *LG* Shard. PLU, Derby CB. Abol 1898 to help cr Derby CP.[101]

SOUTH NORMANTON

AP *LG* Seq 16. *Parl* Seq 4. *Eccl* Seq 7.

TEMPLE NORMANTON

Tp in Chesterfield AP, sep CP 1866,[3] sep EP 1793.[9] *LG* Seq 15. *Parl* Seq 1. *Eccl* Chestf. RDn (1793—1846), Ashov. RDn (1846—66), Chestf. RDn (1866—*).

NORTON

AP *LG* Scar. Hd, Eccl.-Bierl. PLU, RSD, Norton RD. Civ bdry: 1901 (pt transf to Sheff CB [assoc with Yorks W Riding] to help cr Norton Within CP in that CB).[59] Abol civ 1934 pt to Sheff CB (assoc with Yorks W Riding) & AP, pt to Coal Aston CP.[60] *Parl* N'rn Dv (1832—67), East Dv (1867—85), N-E'rn Dv (1885—1948). *Eccl* Chestf. RDn (until 1846), Bramp. RDn (1846—87), Dronf. RDn (1887—1910), Stav. RDn (1910—74), Ecclesall RDn (dioc Sheff, 1974—*). Eccl bdry: 1874 (cr Norton Woodseats EP),[136] 1878 (help cr Abbey Dale EP),[1] 1912 (help cr Norton Woodseats St Chad EP),[57] 1959 (cr Greenhill EP),[173] 1974 (incl help cr Gleadless Valley EP [Derbys, Yorks W Riding[148]).

NORTON WOODSEATS

EP Cr 1874 from Norton AP.[136] Bramp. RDn (1874—87), Dronf. RDn (1887—1910), Eyam RDn (1910—14), Sheffield RDn (dioc Sheff, 1914—42), Ecclesall RDn (dioc Sheff, 1942—*). Bdry: 1912 (help cr Norton Woodseats St Chad EP).[57] Now sometimes called 'Norton Lees'.

NORTON WOODSEATS ST CHAD

EP Cr 1912 from Norton Woodseats EP, Norton AP, pt ex-par Beauchief Abbey.[57] Eyam RDn (1912—14), Sheffield RDn (dioc Sheff, 1914—42), Ecclesall RDn (dioc Sheff, 1942—*).

OAKTHORPE AND DONISTHORPE

Tp comprised of hmlt Oakthorpe (ent Derbys: in Stretton en le Field AP, Church Gresley AP, Measham AP), hmlt Donisthorpe (pt Derbys: in Church Gresley AP, Measham AP; pt Leics: W

Goscote Hd, in Seal AP), sep CP 1866 with pt in each co,[3] eccl severed 1869 to help cr 'Donisthorpe' EP.[146] *LG* Derbys pt, Repton & Gres. Hd, Ashby de la Zouch PLU, RSD, sep RD in Derbys (1894—97), the par made 1897 ent Leics.[105] Bdry: 1884,[196] 1884,[80] 1884 (gains pt Over and Nether Seal CP, Leics),[199] 1884.[200] *Parl* Derbys pt, S'rn Dv (1832—67), South Dv (1867—85), S'rn Dv (1885—1918). For later civ and parl organisation, see entry in Leics.

OCKBROOK
AP *LG* Seq 11. Civ bdry: 1954,[201] 1968.[17] *Parl* Seq 13. *Eccl* Seq 10. Eccl bdry: 1964.[202]

OFFCOTE AND UNDERWOOD
Lbty in Ashbourne AP, sep CP 1866.[3] *LG* Wirksw. Hd, Ashb. PLU, pt Ashb. USD, pt Ashb. RSD, Ashb. RD. Civ bdry: 1887,[13] 1894 (loses the pt in the UD to Ashbourne AP),[31] 1924,[32] 1934.[7] *Parl* Seq 10.

OFFERTON
Hmlt in Hope AP, sep CP 1866.[3] *LG* High Pk. Hd, Bakew. PLU (soon after 1838[6]—1930), RSD, RD. Bdry: 1883.[67] *Parl* Seq 9.

OSLETON AND THURVASTON
Tp in Sutton on the Hill AP, sep CP 1866,[3] eccl severed 1860 to help cr Long Lane EP.[43] *LG* Appl. Hd, Burt. upon Tr. PLU (soon after 1837[6]—1930), RSD, Repton RD. Bdry: 1883.[67] *Parl* Seq 19.

OSMASTON
Chap in Brailsford AP, sep civ identity early, sep EP 1849 as 'Osmaston by Ashbourne',[70] qv. *LG* Seq 1. *Parl* Seq 20.

OSMASTON
Chap in Derby St Werburgh AP, sep civ identity early, sep EP 1733 as 'Osmaston by Derby',[9] qv. *LG* Repton & Gres. Hd, Shard. PLU, RSD, RD. Civ bdry: 1884,[120] 1901 (loses pt to Derby CB [assoc with Derbys] & CP).[22] Abol civ 1902 ent to Sinfin Moor CP.[203] *Parl* S'rn Dv (1832—67), South Dv (1867—85), S'rn Dv (1885—1918), Belper Dv (1918—48).

OSMASTON BY ASHBOURNE
Chap in Brailsford AP, sep EP 1849,[70] sep civ identity early as 'Osmaston', qv above (1st 'Osmaston'). *Eccl* Radb. RDn (1849—55), Ashb. RDn (1855—*).

OSMASTON BY DERBY
Chap in Derby St Werburgh AP, sep EP 1733,[9] sep civ identity early as 'Osmaston', qv above (2nd 'Osmaston'). *Eccl* Derby RDn. Eccl bdry: 1928 (help cr Derby St Bartholomew EP).[136] Abol eccl 1969 pt to help cr Derby St Andrew with St Osmund EP, pt to Derby St Bartholomew EP.[131]

OUTSEATS
Hmlt in Hathersage AP, sep CP 1866.[3] *LG* High Pk. Hd, Bakew. PLU (soon after 1838[6]—1930), RSD. RD. Bdry: 1883,[67] 1929 (loses pt to Sheff CB [assoc with Yorks W Riding] and to Ecclesall CP),[143] 1934.[7] *Parl* N'rn Dv (1832—67), North Dv (1867—85), W'rn Dv (ent 1885—1918, pt 1918—48), pt High Pk. Dv (1918—48), W Derbys CC (1948—*).

OVERSEAL
CP Leics par ('Over Seal') transf 1897 to Derbys where soon called 'Overseal'.[105] *LG* Ashby de la Zouch PLU, Hartsh. & Seals RD (1897—1934), Repton RD (1934—74). *Parl* S'rn Dv (1918—48), Belper CC (1948—*).

PACKINGTON
AP Tp 'Packington' mostly Leics (W Goscote Hd), pt Derbys (Repton & Gres. Hd) as was chap Snibston [not sep civ]. *LG* Ashby de la Zouch PLU, RSD. Reconstituted 1884, the 3 Derbys pts of this par (incl chap Snibston) severed to help cr Ravenstone and Snibston CP to be ent Leics[204] so that 'Packington' ent Leics thereafter, 'Snibston' a sep EP 1910.[205] See entry in Leics.

NETHER PADLEY
Hmlt in Hope AP, sep CP 1866.[3] *LG* Seq 6. Bdry: 1934.[7] *Parl* Seq 9.

PARWICH
Chap in Ashbourne AP, sep civ identity early, sep EP 1791.[9] *LG* Seq 18. *Parl* Seq 10. *Eccl* Ashb. RDn (1791—1846), Wirksw. RDn (1846—55), Ashb. RDn (1855—*).

PEAK FOREST
Ex-par chap & lbty in King's Forest, sep CP 1858,[56] donative with sep eccl independence maintained. *LG* Seq 7. *Parl* Seq 8. *Eccl* Pec jurisd Bakew. (until 1846), Eyam RDn (1846—87), Buxton RDn (1887—*).

PENTRICH
AP Sometimes early 'Pentridge'. Incl chap Ripley (sep CP 1866,[3] sep EP 1822,[9] eccl refounded 1855[206]). *LG* Seq 9. Addtl civ bdry alt: 1886.[5] *Parl* Seq 12. *Eccl* Derby RDn (until 1846), Alf. RDn (1846—1920), Heanor RDn (1920—56), Alf. RDn (1956—*). Addtl eccl bdry alt: 1844 (help cr Codnor and Loscoe EP),[111] 1850 (help cr Ironville EP [Derbys, Notts]).[112]

PILSLEY
Tp in Edensor AP, sep CP 1866.[3] *LG* Seq 6. Bdry: 1883.[83] *Parl* Seq 9.

PILSLEY
Hmlt in North Wingfield AP, sep CP 1866,[3] sep EP 1874.[207] *LG* Scar. Hd, Chestf. PLU, pt Clay Lane USD (1875—83), pt Clay Cross USD (1893—94), pt Chestf. RSD, Chestf. RD. Civ bdry: 1894 (loses the pt in the UD to help cr Egstow CP),[151] 1935 (help cr Clay Cross CP).[46] *Parl* Seq 5. *Eccl* Chestf. RDn. Abol eccl 1973 to help cr North Wingfield, Pilsley and Tupton EP.[208]

PINXTON
AP Derbys par considered most of 19th cent and earlier to be ent Derbys, by 1891 census a small pt deemed in Notts. *LG* Seq 16. Civ bdry: 1895 (exchanges pts wth Kirkby in Ashfield AP, Notts and Pinxton ent Derbys thereafter).[209] *Parl* Seq 4. *Eccl* Seq 7. Eccl bdry: 1873 (gains pt Kirkby in Ashfield AP, dioc S'well).[43]

PLEASLEY
AP Incl chap Shirebrook (sep EP 1849,[210] sep CP 1904[211]). *LG* Seq 16. Addtl civ bdry alt: 1884.[189] *Parl* Seq 2. *Eccl* Chestf. RDn (until 1846), Stav. RDn (1846—51), Chestf. RDn (1851—75), Bols.

RDn (1875—87), Alf. RDn (1887—1910), Stav. RDn (1910—20), Bols. RDn (1920—*).

QUARNDON
Chap in Derby St Alkmund AP, sep civ identity early, sep EP 1732.[9] *LG* Seq 9. Civ bdry: 1968 (incl loses pt to Derby CB [assoc with Derbys] & CP).[17] *Parl* Seq 15. *Eccl* Derby RDn (1732—1846), Duff. RDn (1846—*). Eccl bdry: 1958,[18] 1962,[114] 1965 (incl help cr Allestree St Nicholas EP).[19]

RADBOURNE
AP *LG* Seq 3. Civ bdry: 1968 (incl loses pt to Derby CB [assoc with Derbys] & CP).[17] *Parl* Seq 15. *Eccl* Derby RDn (until 1846), Radb. RDn (1846—87), Longf. RDn (1887—*). Eccl bdry: 1961.[135]

RAVENSDALE PARK
Hmlt in Muggington AP, sep CP 1866.[3] *LG* Appl. Hd, Belper PLU (soon after 1837[6]—1930), RSD, RD. *Parl* Seq 15.

RAVENSTONE
AP Mostly Leics (W Goscote Hd), pt Derbys (Repton & Gres. Hd). *LG* Ashby de la Zouch PLU, RSD. Reconstituted 1884 as 'Ravenstone with Snibston' CP to be ent Leics when gains pt Ashby de la Zouch AP (Leics), the 3 pts (incl chap Snibston [not sep civ, sep EP 1910[205]] in Derbys of Packington AP (prev Leics, Derbys, thereafter ent Leics).[204] *Parl* Derbys pt, S'rn Dv (1832—67), South Dv (1867—85). *Eccl* Repton RDn (until 1846), Hartsh. RDn (1846—87), Repton RDn (1887—1927), S Akeley RDn (dioc Leic, 1927—*).

REPTON
AP Incl chap Bretby (sep CP 1866,[3] donative, sep EP 1922[40]). *LG* Seq 13. Addtl civ bdry alt: 1880,[212] 1880.[213] *Parl* Seq 15. *Eccl* Repton RDn (until 1846), Will. RDn (1846—51), Hartsh. RDn (1851—87), Repton RDn (1887—*).

RIDDINGS
EP Cr 1835 from Alfreton AP.[8] Chestf. RDn (1835—46), Alf. RDn (1846—*). Bdry: 1850 (help cr Ironville EP [Derbys, Notts],[112] 1854 (help cr Somercotes EP,[9] refounded 1898[10]), 1861 (help cr Swanwick EP),[11] 1962.[114]

RIDGEWAY
EP Cr 1842 from Eckington AP,[160] refounded 1843.[161] Chestf. RDn (1842—51), Stav. RDn (1851—*). Bdry: 1974.[148]

RIPLEY
Chap in Pentrich AP, sep CP 1866,[3] sep EP 1822,[9] eccl refounded 1855.[206] *LG* Morl. & Lit. Hd, Belper PLU, pt Ripley USD, pt Belper RSD, Ripley UD. Civ bdry: 1886,[5] 1894 (bdry unaltered but par made ent in the UD).[214] *Parl* Seq 11. *Eccl* Derby RDn (1822—46), Alf. RDn (1846—1920), Heanor RDn (1920—*).

RISLEY
Chap (pec jurisd Prebend Sawley) in chap Wilne (sep civ identity early from Sawley AP), 'Risley' a sep EP 1719 from Sawley AP,[9] sep CP 1866 from Wilne CP.[3] *LG* Seq 11. *Parl* Seq 13. Pec jurisd Prebend Sawley (until 1846), Ockb. RDn (1846—87), Ilk. RDn (1887—*).

RODSLEY
Hmlt in Longford AP, sep CP 1866.[3] *LG* Seq 1.

Parl Seq 20.

ROLLESTON
AP Staffs par considered in 19th cent and earlier to be ent Staffs, a small pt without population deemed later to be in Derbys, the latter transf 1903 to Marston on Dove AP (Derbys) and Rolleston ent Staffs thereafter.[192] See main entry in Staffs.

ROSLISTON
Chap in Walton upon Trent AP (eccl, 'Walton on Trent'), sep civ identity early, sep EP 1856.[215] *LG* Seq 13. *Parl* Seq 17. *Eccl* Lull. RDn (1856—66), Hartsh. RDn (1866—87), Repton RDn (1887—*).

ROWDITCH
CP Cr 1890 from the pt of Markeaton CP prev in Derby USD, now brought into Derby CB.[141] *LG* Belper PLU, Derby CB. Abol 1898 to help cr Derby CP.[101]

ROWLAND
Tp in Bakewell AP, sep CP 1866,[3] eccl in chap Baslow (sep EP 1770 from Bakewell AP [qv for other constituent tps in Bakewell AP]).[9] *LG* High Pk. Hd, Bakew. PLU (soon after 1838[6]—1930), RSD, RD. *Parl* Seq 9.

ROWSLEY
Tp in Bakewell AP, sep EP 1859,[9] eccl refounded 1860,[43] sep CP 1866 as 'Great Rowsley',[3] qv although by mid 20th cent civ called 'Rowsley'. *Eccl* Bakew. RDn. Eccl bdry: 1876 (help cr Stanton in Peake EP).[66]

GREAT ROWSLEY
Tp in Bakewell AP, sep CP 1866,[3] by mid 20th cent civ called 'Rowsley', sep EP 1859 as 'Rowsley',[9] as such eccl refounded 1860,[43] qv. *LG* Seq 6. Civ bdry: 1934.[7] *Parl* Seq 9.

SANDIACRE
AP *LG* Seq 11. Civ bdry: 1884,[120] 1921.[158] *Parl* Seq 13. *Eccl* Pec jurisd Prebend Sandiacre (until 1846), Seq 10 thereafter. Eccl bdry: 1929.[116]

SAWLEY
AP Incl chap Wilne (sep civ identity early, civ comprised of chap Breaston, chap Risley [each a sep EP 1719 from Sawley AP,[9] each a sep CP 1866 from Wilne CP[3], tp Draycott and Church Wilne [sep CP 1866 from Wilne CP,[3] sep EP 1822 as 'Wilne with Draycott' from Sawley AP,[9] as such eccl refounded 1857[149]], hmlt Hopwell [sep CP 1866 from Wilne CP[3]]), tp Long Eaton (sep CP 1866,[3] sep EP 1864[157]), tp Sawley and Wilsthorpe (sep CP 1866[3]) so that 'Sawley' has no sep civ identity after 1866. *LG* Morl. & Lit. Hd. *Parl* S'rn Dv (1832—67). *Eccl* Pec jurisd Prebend Sawley (incl chaps, until 1846), Seq 10 thereafter.

SAWLEY AND WILSTHORPE
Tp in Sawley AP, sep CP 1866.[3] *LG* Morl. & Lit. Hd, Shard. PLU, RSD, RD. Bdry: 1884 (loses pt to Lockington AP, Leics),[216] 1921.[158] Abol 1934 pt to Long Eaton UD & CP, pt to Breaston CP.[7] *Parl* S'rn Dv (1832—67), South Dv (1867—85), Ilk. Dv (1885—1918), S'rn Dv (1918—48).

SCARCLIFFE
AP *LG* Seq 16. Civ bdry: 1935.[46] *Parl* Seq 2. *Eccl* Chestf. RDn (until 1875), Bols. RDn (1875—87), Stav. RDn (1887—1920), Bols. RDn (1920—*).

Eccl bdry: 1924 (help cr Whaley Thorns EP [Derbys, Notts]).[66]

SCROPTON

AP Incl tp Foston and Scropton (area Foston ent Derbys [Appl. Hd], area Scropton pt Derbys [Appl. Hd], pt Staffs [N Offlow Hd], pt but not all of the area in Derbys transf to Staffs 1832 for parl purposes, 1844 for civ purposes,[52] the tp a sep CP 1866 with pt in each co[3]) so that Scropton AP pt Derbys, mostly Staffs until 1844, ent Staffs thereafter. See main entry in Staffs for civ and parl organisation thereafter. *Eccl* Donative, Derby RDn (until 1846), Will. RDn (1846—47), Cubley RDn (1847—87), Longf. RDn (1887—1974). Abol eccl 1974 to help cr Marston on Dove with Scropton EP.[193] Eccl bdry alt but ent from Staffs pts: 1884 (help cr Rangemore EP),[217] 1895 (help cr Needwood EP).[218]

SHARDLOW

Tp in Aston upon Trent AP, sep EP 1839,[11] sep CP 1866 as 'Shardlow and Great Wilne',[3] qv. *Eccl* Derby RDn (1839—46), Stant. by Br. RDn (1846—87), Melb. RDn (1887—*).

SHARDLOW AND GREAT WILNE

Tp in Aston upon Trent AP, sep CP 1866,[3] sep EP 1839 as 'Shardlow'.[11] *LG* Seq 11. Civ bdry: 1965 (loses pt to Lockington-Hemington CP, exchanges pts with Castle Donington AP, both Leics).[79] *Parl* Seq 17.

SHELDON

Chap in Bakewell AP, sep CP 1866,[3] sep EP 1741,[9] eccl refounded 1871.[34] *LG* Seq 6. *Parl* Seq 9. *Eccl* Pec jurisd Bakew. (until 1846), Bakew. RDn (1846—72). Abol eccl 1872 to help cr Ashford with Sheldon EP.[35]

SHIPLEY

Lbty and tp in Heanor AP, sep CP 1866,[3] pt eccl severed 1845 to help cr Cotmanhay EP.[113] *LG* Morl. & Lit. Hd, Basf. PLU, RSD, Unnamed RD (administered by Basf. RD Council, Notts, 1894—1934), Belper RD (1934—74). Bdry: 1934.[7] *Parl* Seq 11.

SHIREBROOK

Chap in Pleasley AP, sep EP 1849,[210] sep CP 1904.[211] *LG* Mansf. PLU, Blackw. RD. Civ bdry: 1935.[46] *Parl* Clay Cross Dv (1918—48), Bols. CC (1948—*). *Eccl* Chestf. RDn (1849—75), Bols. RDn (1875—87), Alf. RDn (1887—1910), Stav. RDn (1910—20), Bols. RDn (1920—*).

SHIRLAND

AP Usual eccl spelling; for civ see following entry. *Eccl* Seq 7. Eccl bdry: 1910 (help cr Stonebroom EP).[219]

SHIRLAND AND HIGHAM

AP Usual civ spelling; for eccl see prev entry. *LG* Seq 15. *Parl* Seq 5.

SHIRLEY

AP Incl tp Stydd (sep CP 1866[3]), tp Yeavesley (sep CP 1866,[3] sep EP 1844[220]). *LG* Seq 1. Addtl civ bdry alt: 1887.[13] *Parl* Seq 20. *Eccl* Seq 3.

SHOTTLE AND POSTERN

Tp in Duffield AP, sep CP 1866,[3] eccl severed 1846 to help cr Hazlewood EP.[153] *LG* Seq 2. Bdry: 1886.[5] *Parl* Seq 14.

SINFIN AND ARLESTON

Lbty in Barrow upon Trent AP, sep CP 1866.[3] *LG* Appl. Hd, Shard. PLU (soon after 1837[6]—1930), RSD, RD (1894—1959), S E Derbys RD (1959—68). Abol 1968 pt to to Derby CB (assoc with Derbys) & CP, pt to Barrow upon Trent AP.[17] *Parl* S'rn Dv (1832—67), South Dv (1867—85), S'rn Dv (1885—1948), S E Derbys CC (1948—70).

SINFIN MOOR

Ex-par lbty, sep CP 1858,[56] pt eccl severed 1948 to help cr Allenton and Shelton Lock EP.[14] *LG* Morl. & Lit. Hd, Shard. PLU (1861—1930), RSD, RD (1894—1959), S E Derbys RD (1959—68). Bdry: 1902 (gains Osmaston CP [the remainder of that par, the pt not transf 1901 to Derby CB & CP]),[203] 1928 (incl loses pt to Derby CB [assoc with Derbys] & CP.[23] Abol civ 1968 pt to Derby CB (assoc with Derbys) & CP, pt to Barrow upon Trent AP, pt to Swarkestone AP.[17] *Parl* S'rn Dv (1832—67), South Dv (1867—85), S'rn Dv (1885—1948), S E Derbys CC (1948—70).

SMALLEY

Chap in Morley AP, sep CP 1866,[3] sep EP 1877 from Morley AP, Horsley AP (pt tp Horsley Woodhouse).[181] *LG* Seq 9. Civ bdry: 1934.[7] *Parl* Seq 12. *Eccl* Duff. RDn (1877—87), Ilk. RDn (1887—1905), Heanor RDn (1955—*). Eccl bdry: 1965.[45]

SMISBY

AP *LG* Seq 12. Civ bdry: 1880,[212] 1883,[67] 1934 (gains The Boundry CP).[7] *Parl* Seq 16. *Eccl* Derby RDn (until 1846), Hartsh. RDn (1846—87), Repton RDn (1887—*).

SNELSTON

Chap in Norbury and Roston AP (eccl, 'Norbury'), sep civ identity early, sep EP 1871.[198] *LG* Seq 1. Civ bdry: 1886,[221] 1887 (incl loses pt to Calwich AP, exchanges pts with Mayfield AP, both Staffs).[13] *Parl* Seq 20. *Eccl* Ashb. RDn.

SOMERCOTES

EP Cr 1854 from Alfreton AP, Riddings EP,[9] refounded 1898.[10] Alf. RDn. Bdry: 1962.[114]

SOMERSAL HERBERT

AP *LG* Seq 5. Civ bdry: 1934.[7] *Parl* Seq 20. *Eccl* Seq 4.

SPONDON

AP Incl chap Chaddesden (sep civ identity early, sep EP 1829,[9] eccl refounded 1851[94]), chap Stanley (sep CP 1866,[3] sep EP 1828,[9] eccl refounded 1851[94]). *LG* Appl. Hd, Shard. PLU, RSD, RD (1894—1959), S E Derbys RD (1959—68). Addtl civ bdry alt: 1884,[120] 1901 (loses pt to Derby CB [assoc with Derbys] & CP),[22] 1928 (loses pt to Derby CB [assoc with Derbys] & CP),[23] 1934 (loses pt to Derby CB [assoc with Derbys] & CP),[7] 1954.[201] Abol civ 1968 pt to Derby CB (assoc with Derbys) & CP, pt to Dale Abbey AP, pt to Ockbrook AP.[17] *Parl* S'rn Dv (1832—67), South Dv (1867—85), S'rn Dv (1885—1948), S E Derbys CC (1948—70). *Eccl* Derby RDn (until 1846), Ockb. RDn (1846—47), Ilk. RDn (1887—*). Addtl eccl bdry alt: 1955,[78] 1964.[202]

STANLEY

Chap in Spondon AP, sep CP 1866,[3] sep EP 1828,[9] eccl refounded 1851.[94] *LG* Seq 4. Civ bdry: 1884,[120] 1934.[7] *Parl* Seq 13. *Eccl* Derby RDn (1828—46), Ockb. RDn (1846—87), Ilk. RDn (1887—*). Eccl bdry: 1965.[45]

STANTON

Chap in Youlgreave AP, sep CP 1866,[3] pt eccl severed 1876 to help cr Stanton in Peake EP.[66] *LG* Seq 6. Bdry: 1883,[67] 1934.[7] *Parl* Seq 9.

STANTON AND NEWHALL

Tp in Stapenhill AP, sep CP 1866.[3] *LG* Repton & Gres. Hd, Burt. upon Tr. PLU, Swadlincote Dist USD, UD (1894—1951), Swadlincote UD (1951—74). Bdry: 1934.[7] *Parl* Seq 16.

STANTON BY BRIDGE

AP *LG* Seq 14. Civ bdry: 1884.[200] *Parl* Seq 17. *Eccl* Seq 18.

STANTON BY DALE

AP *LG* Seq 11. Civ bdry: 1884.[120] *Parl* Seq 13. *Eccl* Repton RDn (until 1846), Ockb. RDn (1846—87), Ilk. RDn (1887—*). Area of Dale Abbey AP (orig private pec owned by Stanhope family) sometimes eccl considered chap in this par, sometimes considered a sep EP,[119] no longer considered sep by 1893 and eccl incl thereafter in this par.

STANTON IN PEAK

EP Cr 1876 from Youlgreave AP (pt tps Stanton, Birchover), Rowsley EP.[66] Bakew. RDn. Later called 'Stanton in Peak with Birchover or Rowston'.

STANTON IN PEAK WITH BIRCHOVER AND ROWSTON—see prev entry

STAPENHILL

AP Usual civ spelling; for eccl see following entry. Incl hmlt Caldwell (sep CP 1866[3]), tp Stanton and Newhall (sep CP 1866[3]). *LG* Repton & Gres. Hd, Burt. upon Tr. PLU, pt Burt. upon Tr. MB (1878—89), Burt. upon Tr. CB [assoc with Staffs] (pt 1889—94, ent 1894—1904), pt Burt. upon Tr. USD (1878—94), Burt. upon Tr. RSD (ent 1875—78, pt 1878—94). Civ bdry: 1894 (the pts not in the CB transf 1894 to Bretby CP, Drakelow CP [both Derbys] so that Stapenhill ent Burt. upon Tr. CB thereafter).[81] Abol civ 1904 ent to Burton upon Trent AP.[222] *Parl* S'rn Dv (1832—67), South Dv (1867—85), S'rn Dv (1885—1918). *Eccl* Pec jurisd Bakew. (until 1846), Hartsh. RDn (1846—66), Lull. RDn (1866—87), Repton RDn (1887—*). Eccl bdry: 1835 (cr Newhall EP).[9]

STAVELEY

AP Incl tp Great Barlow (sep CP 1866[3]). *LG* Scar. Hd, Chestf. PLU, RSD, RD (1894—1935), Stav. UD (1935—74). Addtl civ bdry alt: 1935.[46] *Parl* N'rn Dv (1832—67), East Dv (1867—85), N-E'rn Dv (1885—1948), Chestf. BC (1948—*). *Eccl* Chestf. RDn (until 1846), Stav. RDn (1846—1973). Eccl bdry: 1724 (cr Barlow EP),[93] 1928 (cr Barrow Hill EP),[48] 1957.[163] Abol eccl 1973 to help cr Staveley and Barrowhill EP.[49]

STAVELEY AND BARROWHILL

EP Cr 1973 by union Staveley AP, Barrow Hill EP.[49] Stav. RDn.

EARL STERNDALE

EP Chap in Hartington AP, sep EP 1763.[9] Pec jurisd Bakew. (until 1846), Ashb. RDn (1846—47), Buxton RDn (1847—*). Sometimes 'Earlsterndale'.

KING STERNDALE

EP Cr 1850 from Buxton EP,[9] refounded 1851 from Buxton EP, Hope AP, Hartington AP.[40] Buxton RDn.

CP Cr 1894 as 'King Sterndale' from pt of the pt of Buxton CP not in Buxton UD,[86] later called 'Kingsterndale'. *LG* Chap. en le Fr. PLU, RD. Bdry: 1934.[7] *Parl* High Pk.Dv/CC (1918—*).

STOKE

Tp in Hope AP, sep CP 1866.[3] *LG* Seq 6. *Parl* Seq 9.

STONEBROOM

EP Cr 1910 from Shirland AP, Tibshelf AP.[219] Alf. RDn.

STONY MIDDLETON

Chap in Hathersage AP, sep CP 1866,[3] sep EP 1743.[9] *LG* Seq 6. Civ bdry: 1934.[7] *Parl* Seq 9. *Eccl* High Pk. RDn (1843—1846), Eyam RDn (1846—*). Eccl bdry: 1936.[167]

STRETTON

Tp in North Wingfield AP, sep CP 1866,[3] eccl severed 1852 to help cr Clay Cross EP.[118] *LG* Seq 15. Bdry: 1935 (help cr Clay Cross CP).[46] *Parl* Seq 3.

STRETTON EN LE FIELD

AP Incl pt hmlt Oakthorpe (ent Derbys), in tp Oakthorpe with Donisthorpe (the latter a sep CP 1866[3] with pts in Derbys, Leics, qv for other areas, the pt of the hmlt Oakthorpe in this par eccl severed 1869 to help cr Donisthorpe EP[146]). *LG* Repton & Gres. Hd, Ashby de la Zouch PLU, RSD, sep RD in Derbys (1894—97). Addtl civ bdry alt: 1884,[200] 1884.[223] Transf 1897 to Leics.[105] *Parl* S'rn Dv (1832—67), South Dv (1867—85), S'rn Dv (1885—1918), Leics thereafter. *Eccl* Repton RDn (until 1846), Hartsh. RDn (1846—55), Lull. RDn (1855—66), Hartsh. RDn (1866—87), Repton RDn (1887—1927), W Akeley RDn (dioc Leic, 1927—*).

STURSTON

Tp in Ashbourne AP, sep CP 1866.[3] *LG* Appl. Hd, Ashb. PLU, pt Ashb. USD, pt Ashb. RSD, Ashb. RD. Bdry: 1894 (loses the pt in the UD to Ashbourne AP),[31] 1924.[32] Abol 1934 pt to Ashb. UD & AP, pt to Bradley AP, pt to Offcote and Underwood CP.[7] *Parl* S'rn Dv (1832—67), South Dv (1867—85), W'rn Dv (1885—1948).

STYDD

Tp in Shirley AP, sep CP 1866.[3] *LG* Appl. Hd, Ashb. PLU, RSD. Abol 1886 pt to Yeavesley CP, pt to Snelston CP.[221] *Parl* S'rn Dv (1832—67), South Dv (1867—85), W'rn Dv (1885—1948).

SUDBURY

AP *LG* Seq 5. Civ bdry: 1934.[7] *Parl* Seq 20. *Eccl* Seq 4.

SUTTON CUM DUCKMANTON

AP Sometimes early 'Sutton in the Dale'. *LG* Seq 15. Civ bdry: 1935.[46] *Parl* Seq 1. *Eccl* Chestf. RDn (until 1910), Stav. RDn (1910—55), Bols. RDn (1955—*).

SUTTON IN THE DALE—see prev entry

SUTTON ON THE HILL
AP Incl hmlt Ash (sep CP 1866[3]), tp Orleston and Thurvaston (sep CP 1866,[3] eccl severed 1860 to help cr Long Lane EP[43]). *LG* Seq 3. Addtl civ bdry alt: 1883.[67] *Parl* Seq 21. *Eccl* Seq 5.

SWADLINCOTE
Tp in Church Gresley AP, sep CP 1866,[3] sep EP 1849.[174] *LG* Repton & Gres. Hd, Burt. upon Tr. PLU, Swadlincote Dist USD, UD (1894—1951), Swadlincote UD (1951—74). Civ bdry: 1934.[7] *Parl* Seq 16. *Eccl* Hartsh. RDn (1849—66), Lull. RDn (1866—87), Repton RDn (1887—*).

SWANWICK
EP Cr 1861 from Alfreton AP, Riddings EP.[11] Alf. RDn.

SWARKESTONE
AP *LG* Seq 14. Civ bdry: 1968 (incl loses pt to Derby CB [assoc with Derbys] & CP).[17] *Parl* Seq 17. *Eccl* Derby RDn (until 1846), Stant. by Br. RDn (1846—87), Melb. RDn (1887—*).

TADDINGTON
Chap in Bakewell AP, sep CP 1866,[3] sep EP 1748 (incl tp Blackwell in same par).[9] *LG* High Pk. Hd, Bakew. PLU (soon after 1838[6]—1930), RSD, RD. *Parl* Seq 9. *Eccl* Pec jurisd Bakew. (until 1846), Bakew. RDn (1846—*).

TANSLEY
Tp in Crich AP, sep CP 1866,[3] sep EP 1840,[9] eccl refounded 1844.[53] *LG* Wirksw. Hd, Bakew. PLU (soon after 1838[6]—1930), RSD, RD (1894—1924), The Matlocks UD (1924—34), Matlock UD (1934—74). *Parl* Seq 10. *Eccl* Derby RDn (1840—47), Ashov. RDn (1847—87), Bakew. RDn (1887—*). Eccl bdry: 1865.[194]

TAPTON
Tp in Chesterfield AP, sep CP 1866.[3] *LG* Scar. Hd, Chestf. PLU, RSD, RD. Civ bdry: 1883,[67] 1883.[83] Abol 1920 ent to Chestf. MB & AP.[73] *Parl* N'rn Dv (1832—67), East Dv (1867—85), Chestf. Dv (1885—1948).

TAXAL AND FERNILEE
EP Cr 1966 by union Taxal with Kettleshulme EP (Ches), ent Fernilee EP, pt Chapel en le Frith AP (both Derbys), to be dioc Chester, Stockport RDn.[97]

THORNHILL
Tp in Hope AP, sep CP 1866.[3] *LG* Seq 7. *Parl* Seq 8.

THORPE
AP *LG* Seq 18. Civ bdry: 1887 (incl gains pt Okeover CP [early status as AP uncertain; see entry in Staffs], Staffs).[13] *Parl* Seq 10. *Eccl* Seq 1.

TIBSHELF
AP *LG* Seq 16. *Parl* Seq 4. *Eccl* Chestf. RDn (until 1846), Ashov. RDn (1846—66), Chestf. RDn (1866—75), Bols. RDn (1875—87), Alf. RDn (1887—*). Eccl bdry: 1910 (help cr Stonebroom EP).[219]

TICKNALL
AP *LG* Seq 12. Civ bdry: 1884,[200] 1884.[213] *Parl* Seq 16. *Eccl* Seq 12. Eccl gains early Calke AP (sep civ identity retained, sep eccl status lost).[92]

TIDESWELL
AP Incl chap Wormhill (sep CP 1866,[3] sep EP 1748,[9] eccl refounded 1859[30]), tps Litton, Wheston (each a sep CP 1866[3]). *LG* Seq 6. Addtl civ bdry alt: 1883,[67] 1913 (bdry with Wheston CP defined),[224] 1934.[7] *Parl* Seq 9. *Eccl* Pec jurisd Bakew. (until 1846), Eyam RDn (1846—87), Buxton RDn (1887—*).

TINTWISTLE
CP Ches par, transf 1974 to Derbys.[225]

TISSINGTON
Chap in Bradbourne AP, sep civ identity early, sep EP 1819.[9] *LG* Seq 18. *Parl* Seq 10. *Eccl* Ashb. RDn.

TOTLEY
Tp in Dronfield AP, sep CP 1866,[3] eccl in chap Dore (sep EP 1720 from Dronfield,[9] eccl refounded 1844[147]), 'Totley' a sep EP 1922 from Dore EP, Abbey Dale EP (together the same area as Totley CP).[2] *LG* Scar. Hd, Eccl.-Bierl. PLU, RSD, Norton RD. Civ bdry: 1929 (loses pt to Sheff CB [assoc with Yorks W Riding] and to Ecclesall CP).[143] Abol civ 1934 pt to Sheff CB (assoc with Yorks W Riding) & AP, pt to Holmesfield CP.[60] *Parl* N'rn Dv (1832—67), East Dv (1867—85), N-E'rn Dv (1885—1948). *Eccl* Eyam RDn (1922—74), Ecclesall RDn (Sheffield dioc, 1974—*). Eccl bdry: 1974.[148]

TRUSLEY
AP *LG* Seq 3. *Parl* Seq 15. *Eccl* Seq 5. Eccl bdry: 1860 (help cr Long Lane EP).[43]

TUPTON
Tp in North Wingfield AP, sep CP 1866.[3] *LG* Seq 15. Bdry: 1935 (incl help cr Clay Cross CP).[46] *Parl* Seq 3.

TURNDITCH
Chap in Duffield AP, sep CP 1866,[3] sep EP 1737.[9] *LG* Seq 2. Civ bdry: 1886.[183] *Parl* Seq 14. *Eccl* Derby RDn (1737—1846), Duff. RDn (1846—87), Wirksw. RDn (1887—*).

TWYFORD AND STENSON
Chap in Barrow upon Trent AP, sep CP 1866.[3] *LG* Seq 3. Bdry: 1968 (loses pt to Derby CB [assoc with Derbys] & CP).[17] *Parl* Seq 15.

UNNAMED
CP Pt of Elvaston AP in Alvaston and Bulton UD, sep CP 1894.[165] *LG* Shard. PLU, Alvaston and Boulton UD. Abol 1897 ent to Elvaston AP, to be ent Shardlow RD.[166]

UNSTONE
Tp in Dronfield AP, sep CP 1866.[3] *LG* Seq 15. Bdry: 1883,[83] 1935.[46] *Parl* Seq 7.

WALTON
Tp in Chesterfield AP, sep CP 1866.[3] *LG* Scar. Hd, Chestf. PLU, Bramp. & Walton USD (ent 1875—92, pt 1892—26 Mar 1894, ent 26 Mar—apptd day 1894), pt Chestf. MB & USD (1892—26 Mar 1894), Bramp. & Walton UD (1894—1935), Chestf. RD (1935—74). Bdry: 1894 (26 Mar, loses the pt in the MB to Chesterfield AP),[71] 1901,[72] 1920,[73] 1935.[46]

WALTON ON TRENT
AP Usual eccl spelling; for civ and civ and eccl sep

chap, see following entry. *Eccl* Seq 17.

WALTON UPON TRENT

AP Usual civ spelling; for eccl see prev entry. Incl chap Rosliston (sep civ identity early, sep EP 1856[215]). *LG* Seq 13. *Parl* Seq 16.

WARDLOW

Tp pt in Bakewell AP (this pt in chap Longstone in same par, 'Longstone' a sep EP 1830[9] [qv for other constituent pars]), pt in Hope AP (this pt eccl severed 1875 to help cr Bradwell EP[4]), 'Wardlow' a sep CP 1866.[3] *LG* Seq 6. Bdry: 1883.[67] *Parl* Seq 9.

WENSLEY AND SNITTERTON

Tp (Wirksw. Hd) in Darley AP (o'wise High Pk. Hd), sep CP 1866,[3] eccl severed 1845 to cr South Darley EP.[121] *LG* Wirksw. Hd, Bakew. PLU, S Darley USD, UD (1894—1934), Matlock UD (1934—74). *Parl* Seq 9.

WESSINGTON

Tp in Crich AP, sep CP 1866,[3] sep EP 1859.[116] *LG* Seq 15. *Parl* Seq 5. *Eccl* Ashov. RDn (1859—87), Alf. RDn (1887—*).

WESTON UNDERWOOD

Tp (Morl. & Lit. Hd) in Muggington AP (o'wise Appl. Hd), sep CP 1866.[3] *LG* Seq 9. Bdry: 1886.[184] *Parl* Seq 15.

WESTON ON TRENT

AP Usual eccl spelling; for civ see following entry. *Eccl* Seq 12.

WESTON UPON TRENT

AP Usual civ spelling; for eccl see prev entry. *LG* Seq 11. Civ bdry: 1965 (loses pt to Castle Donington AP, Leics).[79] *Parl* Seq 17.

WHALEY BRIDGE

CP Cr 1936 by union pts 4 pars in Ches (Yeardsley and Whaley UD & CP, Disley CP, Kettleshulme CP, Taxall AP [orig 'Taxal', later 'Taxall']) and pts 2 pars in Derbys (Fernilee CP, Chapel en le Frith AP).[95] *LG* Whaley Bridge UD. *Parl* High Pk. CC (1948—*).

WHALEY THORNS

EP Cr 1924 from Bolsover AP, Scarcliffe AP, Upper Langwith AP (all Derbys), Norton Cuckney AP (Notts).[66] Bols. RDn.

WHESTON

Hmlt in Tideswell AP, sep CP 1866.[3] *LG* Seq 6. Bdry: 1883,[67] 1913 (bdry with Tideswell defined),[224] 1934.[7] *Parl* Seq 9.

WHITFIELD

Area for poor law purposes in chap Charlesworth (the latter a sep CP 1866 from Glossop AP[3]), 'Whitfield' a sep EP 1845 by union pts areas Padfield, Whitfield and ent areas Chunall, Dinting, Hadfield (each also in hmlt/CP Charlesworth).[98] High Pk. RDn (1845—46), Castlet. RDn (1846—87), Gloss. RDn (1887—*). Bdry: 1875 (orig area Hafield and the pt of Padfield in the par severed to help cr Hadfield EP),[97] 1879 (cr Dinting Vale EP).[144]

WHITTINGTON

AP *LG* Scar. Hd, Chestf. PLU, Whittington USD, UD (1894—1911), Whittington & Newbold UD (1911—20). Abol civ 1920 ent to Chestf. MB & AP.[73] *Parl* N'rn Dv (1832—67), East Dv (1867—85), N-E'rn

Dv (1885—1918), Chestf. Dv (1918—48). *Eccl* Chestf. RDn (until 1846), Bramp. RDn (1846—87), Dronf. RDn (1887—1910), Stav. RDn (1910—55), Chestf. RDn (1955—*). Eccl bdry: 1861 (help cr Newbold with Dunston EP),[76] 1927 (cr New Whittington EP).[226]

NEW WHITTINGTON

EP Cr 1927 from Whittington AP.[226] Stav. RDn (1927—55), Chestf. RDn (1955—*).

WHITWELL

AP *LG* Seq 17. Civ bdry: 1934.[46] *Parl* Seq 6. *Eccl* Chestf. RDn (until 1846), Stav. RDn (1846—1920), Bols. RDn (1920—*).

WILLESLEY

AP *LG* Repton & Gres. Hd, Ashby de la Zouch PLU, RSD, sep RD in Derbys (1894—97). Transf 1897 to Leics.[105] *Parl* S'rn Dv (1832—67), South Dv (1867—85), S'rn Dv (1885—1918), Leics thereafter. *Eccl* Seq 15.

WILLINGTON

AP *LG* Seq 10. *Parl* Seq 15. *Eccl* Derby RDn (until 1846), Will. RDn (1846—51), Hartsh. RDn (1851—66), Lull. RDn (1866—87), Repton RDn (1887—*).

WILNE

Chap (pec jurisd Prebend Sawley) in Sawley AP (comprised of chap Breaston, chap Risley [each a sep EP 1719 from Sawley AP,[9] each a sep CP 1866 from Wilne CP[3]], tp Draycott and Church Wilne [sep CP 1866 from Wilne CP,[3] sep EP 1822 as 'Wilne with Draycott' from Sawley AP[9]], hmlt Hopwell [sep CP 1866 from Wilne CP[3]]), 'Wilne' with sep civ identity early from Sawley AP but with no sep civ identity from 1866 after civ sep of the 4 subordinate units. *LG* Morl. & Lit. Hd. *Parl* South Dv (1832—67).

WILNE WITH DRAYCOTT

EP Cr 1822 from Sawley AP (reduced area of chap Wilne [qv in prev entry for units civ contained, the area of the EP the orig chap less chaps Breaston, Risley which had each become sep EPs in 1719],[9] eccl refounded 1857.[149] Pec jurisd Prebend Sawley (until 1846), Stant. by Br. RDn (1846—55), Ockb. RDn (1855—87), Ilk. RDn (1887—*).

WINDLEY

Tp in Duffield AP, sep CP 1866.[3] *LG* Seq 2. *Parl* Seq 14.

WINGERWORTH

Chap in Chesterfield AP, sep civ identity early, sep EP 1728.[9] *LG* Seq 15. Civ bdry: 1935.[46] *Parl* Seq 1. *Eccl* Chestf. RDn (until 1846), Bramp. RDn (1846—84), Chestf. RDn (1884—*).

NORTH WINGFIELD

AP Incl tps Clay Lane, Stretton, Woodthorpe (each a sep CP 1866,[3] eccl united 1852 (incl area Handley [not sep civ]) as 'Clay Cross' EP[118]), hmlt Pilsley (sep CP 1866,[3] sep EP 1874[207]), tp Tupton (sep CP 1866[3]). *LG* Scar. Hd, Chestf. PLU, pt Clay Lane USD (1875—83), Chestf. RSD (pt 1875—83, ent 1883—94), Chestf. RD. Addtl civ bdry alt: 1883,[67] 1898.[164] *Parl* Seq 3. *Eccl* Chestf. RDn (until 1846), Ashov. RDn (1846—87), Chestf. RDn (1887—1973). Addtl eccl bdry alt: 1954.[180] Abol eccl 1973 to help cr North Wingfield, Pilsley and Tupton EP.[208]

NORTH WINGFIELD, PILSLEY AND TUPTON

EP Cr 1973 by union North Wingfield AP, Pilsley EP.[208] Chestf. RDn.

SOUTH WINGFIELD

AP *LG* Scar. Hd, Belper PLU, RSD, RD. *Parl* N'rn Dv (1832—67), East Dv (1867—85), Mid Dv (1885—1918), Belper Dv/CC (1918—*). *Eccl* Seq 7.

WINSHILL

Tp in Derbys (Repton & Gres. Hd) in Burton upon Trent AP (mostly Staffs, N Offlow Hd), sep CP 1866 in Derbys,[3] eccl severed 1825 to help cr Burton upon Trent Holy Trinity EP,[9] the latter refounded 1842,[88] 'Winshill' a sep EP 1867 from Burton upon Trent Holy Trinity EP.[89] *LG* Burt. upon Tr. PLU, pt Burt. upon Tr. MB (1878—89), Burt. upon Tr. CB [assoc with Staffs] (pt 1889—94, ent 1894—1909), pt Burt. upon Tr. USD (1878—94), Burt. upon Tr. RSD (ent 1875—78, pt 1878—94). Civ bdry: 1894 (loses the pt not in the CB to Newton Solney AP and the par thereafter ent in Burt. upon Tr. CB [assoc with Staffs]).[81] Abol civ 1904 ent to Burton upon Trent AP.[222] *Parl* S'rn Dv (1832—67), South Dv (1867—85), S'rn Dv (1885—1918). *Eccl* Lull. RDn (1867—87), Repton RDn (1887—*).

WINSTER

Chap in Youlgreave AP, sep civ identity early, sep EP 1727.[9] *LG* Seq 6. *Parl* Seq 9. *Eccl* Pec jurisd Bakew. (until 1846), Youlg. RDn (1846—47), Bakew. RDn (1847—*).

WIRKSWORTH

AP Tp 'Wirksworth' in Wirksw. Hd as was tp Ible, hmlt Middleton by Wirksworth (each a sep CP 1866,[3] the 2 eccl united 1841 with hmlt Ivonbrook Grange [for civ, see below] as 'Middleton by Wirksworth' EP,[9] as such eccl refounded 1847[185]), hmlt Callow (sep CP 1866[3]), chap Cromford (sep CP 1866,[3] sep EP 1798,[9] eccl refounded 1869 from Wirksworth AP, Middleton by Wirksworth EP[85]), tp Hopton and Griffe Grange (tp cr 1858 by union of tp Hopton in this par, ex-par area Griffe Grange,[175] the whole a sep CP 1866[3]); incl in High Pk. Hd hmlt Ivonbrook Grange (sep CP 1866,[3] eccl severed 1841 to help cr Middleton by Wirksworth EP,[9] the latter eccl refounded 1847[185]); incl in Appl. Hd chap Alderwasley, tps Ashleyhay, Biggin (each a sep CP 1866[3]), tp Idridgehay and Alton (sep CP 1866,[3] eccl severed 1856 to help cr Idridgehay EP,[155] qv for other constituent pars). *LG* Wirksw. Hd (pt until 1866, ent from 1866), pt High. Pk Hd (until 1866), pt Appl. Hd (until 1866), Belper PLU,

Wirksw. USD, UD. Addtl civ bdry alt: 1934 (incl gains Middleton by Wirksworth CP and loses pt to Cromford CP to help cr Matlock UD).[7] *Parl* Seq 10. *Eccl* Seq 2.

WOODTHORPE

Tp in North Wingfield AP, sep CP 1866,[3] eccl severed 1852 to help cr Clay Cross EP.[118] *LG* Scar. Hd, Chestf. PLU, pt Clay Lane USD (1875—93), pt Clay Cross USD (1893—94), Chestf. RD. Bdry: 1883,[83] 1894 (loses the pt in Clay Cross UD to help cr Egstow CP).[151] Abol civ 1935 pt to Clay Cross UD to help cr Clay Cross CP, pt to Tupton CP, pt to Wingerworth CP.[46] *Parl* N'rn Dv (1832—67), East Dv (1867—85), Chestf. Dv (1885—1918), Clay Cross Dv (1918—48).

WOODVILLE

EP Cr 1847 from Ashby de la Zouch AP (Leics), Hartshorne AP (Derbys).[178] Repton RDn.

CP Cr 1897 by union pt Hartshorn AP (Derbys), pt Ashby Woulds CP, pt Blackfordby CP (both Leics).[105] *LG* Ashby de la Zouch PLU, Hartsh. & Seals RD (1897—1934), Repton RD (1934—74). Bdry: 1934.[105] *Parl* S'rn Dv (1918—48), Belper CC (1948—*).

WORMHILL

Chap in Tideswell AP, sep CP 1866,[3] sep EP 1748,[9] eccl refounded 1859.[30] *LG* High Pk. Hd, Chap. en le Fr. PLU (soon after 1837[6]—1930), pt Fairfield USD, pt Chap. en le Fr. RSD, Chap. en le Fr. RD. Civ bdry: 1934.[7] *Parl* Seq 8. *Eccl* Pec jurisd Bakew. (until 1847), Buxton RDn (1847—*).

YEAVELEY

Tp in Shirley AP, sep CP 1866,[3] sep EP 1844.[220] *LG* Seq 1. Civ bdry: 1886.[221] *Parl* Seq 20. *Eccl* Castil. RDn (1844—46), Cubley RDn (1846—87), Ashb. RDn (1887—1923), Longf. RDn (1923—*).

YELDERSLEY

Tp in Ashbourne AP, sep CP 1866.[3] *LG* Seq 1. *Parl* Seq 20.

YOULGREAVE

AP Usual civ spelling; for eccl see following entry. Tp 'Youlgreave' in High Pk. Hd as was chap Birchover, chap Stanton (each a sep CP 1866,[3] pt of each eccl severed 1876 to help cr Stanton in Peak EP[66]), chap Winster (sep civ identity early, sep EP 1727[9]), hmlt Gratton (sep CP 1866[3]); incl in Wirksw. Hd chap Middleton and Smerrill (sep CP 1866[3]), tp Elton (sep CP 1866[3]). *LG* Bakew. PLU (soon after 1838[6]—1930), RSD, RD. Addtl civ bdry alt: 1934.[7] *Parl* Seq 9.

YOULGREAVE WITH MIDDLETON

AP Usual eccl spelling; for civ and civ and eccl sep units, see prev entry. *Eccl* Seq 14.

COUNTY DURHAM

ABBREVIATIONS

Abbreviations particular to Durham follow. Those general abbreviations in use throughout the *Guide* are found on pages xvii—xix.

(Bp) Auckl.	(Bishop) Auckland
Barn. Cast.	Barnard Castle
Blayd.	Blaydon
Chest. (le Str.)	Chester (le Street)
Darl.	Darlington
Eas.	Easington
Gatesh.	Gateshead
Hartl.	Hartlepool
Hough. le Spr.	Houghton le Spring
Lanch.	Lanchester
Sedg.	Sedgefield
Spennym.	Spennymoor
Stanh.	Stanhope
Stock.	Stockton
Sund.	Sunderland
Teesd.	Teesdale
Wash.	Washington
Weard.	Weardale
Wearm.	Wearmouth

SEQUENCES

An abbreviated entry prefixed by 'Seq' is used in the parochial entries to avoid repeating often the names of superior units of administration. The content of each sequence is shown below.

Local Government Sequences ('LG')

SEQ 1 Chest. Wd, Chest. le Str. PLU, RSD, RD
SEQ 2 Chest. Wd, Lanch. PLU, RSD, RD
SEQ 3 Chest. Wd, Weard. PLU, RSD, RD
SEQ 4 Darl. Wd, PLU, RSD, RD
SEQ 5 Darl. Wd, Auckl. PLU, RSD, RD (1894—1937), Barn. Cast. RD (1937—74)
SEQ 6 Darl. Wd, Sedg. PLU, RSD, RD
SEQ 7 Darl. Wd, Teesd. PLU, RSD, RD, Barn. Cast. RD
SEQ 8 Darl. Wd (until 1829), Durham Wd (from 1829), Durham PLU, RSD, RD
SEQ 9 Eas. Wd, PLU, RSD, RD
SEQ 10 Eas. Wd, Chest. le Str. PLU, RSD, RD
SEQ 11 Eas. Wd (until 1829), Durham Wd (from 1829), Durham PLU, RSD, RD
SEQ 12 Stock. Wd, PLU, RSD, RD
SEQ 13 Stock. Wd, PLU (1837—59), Hartl. PLU (1859—1930), RSD, RD (1894—1936), Stock. RD (1936—74)
SEQ 14 Stock. Wd, Sedg. PLU, RSD, RD
SEQ 15 Stock. Wd, Sedg. PLU, RSD, RD (1894—1937), Darl. RD (1937—74)
SEQ 16 Stock. Wd (until 1829), Darl. Wd (from 1829), Darl. PLU, RSD, RD
SEQ 17 Stock. Wd (until 1829), Durham Wd (from 1829), Sedg. PLU, RSD, RD

Parliamentary Sequences ('Parl')

SEQ 1 N'rn Dv (1832—85), Chest. le Spr. Dv/CC (1885—*)
SEQ 2 N'rn Dv (1832—85), Hough. le Spr. Dv (1885—1918), Chest. le Str. Dv/CC (1918—*)
SEQ 3 N'rn Dv (1832—85), Hough. le Spr. Dv (1885—1918), Seaham Dv (1918—48), Eas. CC (1948—70), Hough. le Spr. CC (1970—*)
SEQ 4 N'rn Dv (1832—85), Mid Dv (1885—1918), Durham Dv/CC (1918—*)
SEQ 5 N'rn Dv (1832—85), N-W'rn Dv (1885—1918), Barn. Cast. Dv (1918—48), N W Durham CC (1948—*)
SEQ 6 N'rn Dv (1832—85), S-E'rn Dv (1885—1918), Seaham Dv (1918—48), Eas. CC (1948—*)
SEQ 7 S'rn Dv (1832—85), Barn. Cast. Dv (1885—1918), Bp Auckl. Dv/CC (1918—*)
SEQ 8 S'rn Dv (1832—85), Barn. Cast. Dv (1885—1948), Bp Auckl. CC (1948—*)
SEQ 9 S'rn Dv (1832—85), Barn. Cast. Dv (1885—1948), N W Durham CC (1948—*)

SEQ 10 S'rn Dv (1832—85), Mid Dv (1885—1918), Durham Dv/CC (1918—*)

SEQ 11 S'rn Dv (1832—85), Mid Dv (1885—1918), Sedg. Dv/CC (1918—70), Durham CC (1970—*)

SEQ 12 S'rn Dv (1832—85), S-E'rn Dv (1885—1918), Sedg. Dv/CC (1918—70), Bp Auckl. CC (1970—*)

SEQ 13 S'rn Dv (1832—85), S-E'rn Dv (1885—1918), Sedg. Dv/CC (1918—70), Durham CC (1970—*)

SEQ 14 S'rn Dv (1832—85), S-E'rn Dv (1885—1918), Sedg. Dv/CC (1918—70), Eas. CC (1970—*)

Ecclesiastical Sequences ('Eccl')

SEQ 1 Darl. RDn (before 1291—early 19th cent), Durham RDn (early 19th cent—1842), Darl. RDn (1842—74), Darl. RDn (S'rn Dv) (1874—80), Darl. RDn (1880—*)

SEQ 2 Darl. RDn (before 1291—early 19th cent), Durham RDn (early 19th cent—1842), Darl. RDn (1842—74), Darl. RDn (S'rn Dv) (1874—80), Darl. RDn (1880—*)

SEQ 3 Darl. RDn (before 1291—early 19th cent), Durham RDn (early 19th cent—1842), Darl. RDn (1842—74), Darl. RDn (S'rn Dv) (1874—80), Darl. RDn (1880—1924), Barn. Cast. RDn (1924—*)

SEQ 4 Darl. RDn (before 1291—early 19th cent), Durham RDn (early 19th cent—1842), Stock. RDn (1842—*)

SEQ 5 Darl. RDn (before 1291—early 19th cent), Durham RDn (early 19th cent—1842), Stock. RDn (1842—80), Darl. RDn (1880—*)

SEQ 6 Durham RDn (before 1291—before 1535), Chest. le Str. RDn (before 1535—early 19th cent), Durham RDn (early 19th cent—1842), Chest. le Str. RDn (1842—74), Chest. RDn (W'rn Dv) (1874—80), Ryton RDn (1880—91), Chest. le Str. RDn (1891—*)

SEQ 7 Durham RDn (before 1291—before 1535), Chest. le Str. RDn (before 1535—early 19th cent), Durham RDn (early 19th cent—1842), Darl. RDn (1842—74), Darl. RDn (N'rn Dv) (1874—80), Stanh. RDn (1880—*)

DIOCESE AND ARCHDEACONRIES

Durham pars are primarily in Durham Dioc and were organised in Archdeaconries and Rural Deaneries as follows:

AUCKLAND AD (1882—*)
Auckl. RDn, Barn. Cast. RDn (1924—*), Darl. RDn, Hartl. RDn (1888—*), Stanh. RDn, Stock. RDn

DURHAM AD
Auckl. RDn (until early 19th cent), Auckl. RDn (1880—82), Chest. RDn (E'rn Dv) (1874—80), Chest. RDn (W'rn Dv) (1874—80), Chest. le Str. RDn (before 1535—early 19th cent), Chest. le Str. RDn (1842—74), Chest. le Str. RDn (1880—*), Darl. RDn (before 1291—early 19th cent), Darl. RDn (1842—74), Darl. RDn (1880—82), Darl. RDn (N'rn Dv) (1874—80), Darl. RDn (S'rn Dv) (1874—80), Durham RDn (until 1842), Durham RDn (1880—*), Eas. RDn (1842—74), Eas. RDn (1880—*), Eas. RDn (N'rn Dv) (1874—80), Eas. RDn (S'rn Dv) (1874—80), Gatesh. RDn (1891—*), Hough. le Spr. RDn (1880—*), Jarrow RDn (1880—*), Lanch. RDn (until early 19th cent), Lanch. RDn (1891—*), Ryton RDn (1880—91), Stanh. RDn (1880—82), Stock. RDn (1842—82), Wearm. RDn (1880—*)

THE PARISHES OF COUNTY DURHAM

AISLABY
Tp in Egglescliffe AP, sep CP 1866.[1] *LG* Seq 12. Transf 1974 to Clev.[2] *Parl* Seq 14.

ALBERT HILL—see DARLINGTON ST JAMES, ALBERT HILL

ANCROFT
Chap in Holy Island AP, sep civ identity early, sep EP 1733.[3] *LG* Islandshire, Berw. PLU, transf to Northumb 1832 for parl purposes, 1844 for civ purposes.[4] *Parl* In Durham until 1832, Northumb thereafter. See main entry in Northumb for later civ, parl organisation and for all eccl organisation, incl cr 1844 of Scremerston EP.

ANFIELD PLAIN
EP Cr 1914 from Collierley EP, Lanchester AP, Holmside EP.[5] Lanch. RDn. Bdry: 1899,[6] 1929.[7]

ARCHDEANON NEWTON
Tp in Darlington AP, sep CP 1866,[1] eccl severed 1843 to help cr Darlington Holy Trinity EP.[8] *LG* Seq 4. Bdry: 1915,[9] 1930 (loses pt to Darl. CB [assoc with Durham] & AP).[10] *Parl* Seq 12.

BISHOP AUCKLAND
Tp and bor in chap Escomb (sep civ identity early from Auckland St Andrew AP, sep EP 1743,[3] eccl refounded 1893 [qv for constituent pars then][11]), 'Bishop Auckland' a sep CP 1866.[1] *LG* Darl. Wd, Auckl. PLU, Bp Auckl. USD. Bdry: 1883.[12] Abol 1886 to help cr Bishop Auckland and Pollard's Lands CP.[13] *Parl* S'rn Dv (1832—85), Bp Auckl. Dv (1885—1918).

CP Cr 1894 from the pt of Bishop Auckland and Pollard's Lands CP in Bp Auckl. UD.[14] *LG* Auckl. PLU, Bp Auckl. UD. Bdry: 1937 (incl gains Binchester CP, Coundon CP, Coundon Grange CP).[15] *Parl* Bp Auckl. Dv/CC (1918—*).

BISHOP AUCKLAND AND POLLARD'S LANDS

CP Cr 1886 by union Bishop Auckland CP, Pollard's Lands CP.[13] *LG* Darl. Wd, Auckl. PLU, pt Bp Auckl. USD, pt Auckl. RSD. Abol 1894 the pt in the USD to cr Bishop Auckland CP, the remainder to cr Pollard's Lands CP.[14]

WEST AUCKLAND

Tp in chap Auckland St Helen (sep civ identity early from Auckland St Andrew AP, sep EP 1724[3]), 'West Auckland' a sep CP 1866,[1] the detached pt eccl severed 1863 to help cr Evenwood EP.[13] Incl undivided pt Land Common to Evenwood and Barony and West Auckland (abol 1937 pt to this par, pt to Bp Auckl. UD & CP[15]). *LG* Darl. Wd, Auckl. PLU, RSD, RD (1894—1937), Barn. Cast. RD (1937—39). Addtl civ bdry alt: 1883,[12] 1937.[15] Renamed 1939 'Etherley' CP.[16] *Parl* S'rn Dv (1832—85), Barn. Cast. Dv (1885—1918), Bp Auckl. Dv/CC (1918—53).

AUCKLAND ST ANDREW

AP At one time Collegiate. Incl chap Auckland St Helen (sep civ identity early, sep EP 1724 [incl main pt tp West Auckland, tp Evenwood and Barony,[3] pt of the latter eccl severed 1834 to help cr Etherley EP,[17] the remainder united eccl 1863 with detached pt tp West Auckland to cr Evenwood EP][18]), pt chap and tp Byers Green (sep CP 1866,[1] sep EP 1845 [incl pt tp Binchester][19]), chap and tp Coundon (sep CP 1866,[1] pt a sep EP 1842 [incl tps Westerton, Windlestone][20]), chap Escomb (sep civ identity early, sep EP 1869 as 'Witton Park',[21] eccl refounded 1893 as 'Escomb' by union of the pt of tp Escomb neither in Etherley EP nor in Hunwick EP, pt tps Bishop Auckland, Pollard's Lands[11]), chap Hamsterley (sep civ identity early, sep EP 1724[3]), chap Shildon (sep CP 1866,[1] sep EP 1837 [tps Eldon, Middridge, Shildon, East Thicklerley][22]), chap Witton le Wear (sep civ identity early, sep EP 1724 [incl tp North Bedburn][3]), tp and bor Bishop Auckland (sep CP 1866,[1] pt eccl severed 1872 to cr Auckland St Peter EP[23]), tp West Auckland (sep CP 1866,[1] main pt eccl severed 1724 to help cr Auckland St Helen EP,[3] the detached pt eccl severed 1863 to help cr Evenwood EP[18]), tp North Bedburn (sep CP 1866,[1] eccl severed 1724 to help cr Witton le Wear EP[3]), tps South Bedburn, Lynesack and Softley (each a sep CP 1866,[1] pts of each eccl severed 1850 and united with pt tp Hamsterley in Hamsterley EP to cr Lynesack EP[22]), tp Binchester (sep CP 1866,[1] pt eccl severed 1845 to help cr Byers Green EP[19]), tp Coundon Grange (sep CP 1866[1]), tp Eldon (sep CP 1866,[1] eccl severed 1837 to help cr Shildon EP[22]), tp Evenwood and Barony (sep CP 1866,[1] eccl severed 1724 to help cr Auckland St Helen AP,[3] pt of the latter eccl severed 1834 to help cr Etherley EP,[17] the remainder united eccl 1863 with detached pt tp West Auckland to cr Evenwood EP[18]), tp Hunwick and Helmington (sep CP 1866,[1] eccl severed 1845 to help cr Hunwick EP[19]), tp Middridge (sep CP 1866,[1] eccl severed 1837 to help cr Shildon EP[22]), tp Middlestone (sep CP 1866,[1] eccl severed 1845 and transf to Merrington AP[24]), tp Newfield (sep CP 1866[1]), tp Old Park (sep CP 1866[1]), tp Newton Cap (sep CP 1866,[1] pt eccl severed 1845 to help cr Hunwick EP[19]), tp Pollard's Lands (sep CP 1866,[1] pt eccl severed 1893 to help refound Escomb EP[15]), tp East Thickerley (sep CP 1866,[1] eccl severed 1837 to help cr Shildon EP[22]), tps Westerton, Windlestone (each a sep CP 1866,[1] both eccl severed 1842 to help cr Coundon EP[20]); also incl land which, after cr 1866 of CPs, becomes Land Common to Evenwood and Barony and West Auckland (qv under respective CPs). *LG* Darl. Wd, pt Bp Auckl. Bor, Auckl. PLU, RSD, RD. Abol civ 1937 pt to Bp Auckl. UD & CP, pt to Shildon UD & CP.[15] *Parl* S'rn Dv (1832—85), Bp Auckl. Dv (1885—1948). *Eccl* Auckl. RDn (before 1291—early 19th cent), Durham RDn (early 19th cent—1842), Darl. RDn (1842—74), Darl. RDn (N'rn Dv) (1874—80), Auckl. RDn (1880—*). Addtl eccl bdry alt: 1782 (cr Auckland St Anne EP),[3] 1869 (help cr New Shildon EP),[25] 1877 (help cr Eldon EP),[26] 1894,[27] 1961 (incl help cr Newton Aycliffe EP).[28]

AUCKLAND ST ANNE

EP Cr 1782 from Auckland St Andrew AP.[3] RDns as for Auckland St Andrew, from 1782.

AUCKLAND ST HELEN

Chap in Auckland St Andrew AP, sep civ identity early, sep EP 1724[3]; comprised of tps West Auckland, Evenwood and Barony (each a sep CP 1866,[1] pt of the latter eccl severed 1834 to help cr Etherley EP,[17] the remainder united 1863 with detached pt tp West Auckland to cr Evenwood EP[18]). *LG* Darl. Wd, Auckl. PLU, RSD, RD. Abol civ 1937 pt to Bp Auckl. UD & CP, pt to West Auckland CP.[15] *Parl* S'rn Dv (1832—85), Barn. Cast. Dv (1885—1918), Bp Auckl. Dv (1918—48). *Eccl* RDns as for Auckland St Andrew, from 1724.

AUCKLAND ST PETER

EP Cr 1872 from Escomb EP (pt orig tp Bishop Auckland).[23] RDns as for Auckland St Andrew, from 1872. Bdry: 1894.[22]

AYCLIFFE

AP Incl tps Great Aycliffe, Brafferton, Preston le Skerne, Woodham (each a sep CP 1866[1]) so that 'Aycliffe' has no sep civ identity after 1866. *LG* Darl. Wd. *Parl* S'rn Dv (1832—67). *Eccl* Seq 1. Eccl bdry: 1925 (help cr Chilton EP),[29] 1961 (incl help cr Newton Aycliffe EP).[28]

GREAT AYCLIFFE

Tp in Aycliffe AP, sep CP 1866.[1] *LG* Seq 4. Civ bdry: 1884,[30] 1952,[31] 1969,[32] 1974 (gains the pt of Heighington AP transf to Sedg. Dist [the remainder of the latter to be in Darl. Dist]).[2]

NEWTON AYCLIFFE

EP Cr 1961 from Shildon EP, Heighington AP, Aycliffe AP, Auckland St Andrew AP.[28] Darl. RDn.

SCHOOL AYCLIFFE

Tp in Heighington AP, sep CP 1866.[1] *LG* Darl. Wd, PLU, RSD, RD. Bdry: 1885.[33] Abol 1946 ent to Heighington AP.[34] *Parl* S'rn Dv (1832—85), S-E'rn Dv (1885—1918), Sedg. Dv/CC (1918—52).

AYRES QUAY

EP Cr 1878 from Deptford St Andrew EP, Bishopwear-mouth AP.[35] Wearm. RDn. Sometimes called 'Bishopwearmouth St Stephen'. Abol 1950 ent to Millfield St Mark EP.[36]

NORTH BAILEY—see DURHAM ST MARY LE BOW

SOUTH BAILEY—see DURHAM ST MARY THE LESS

BAMBURGH

AP Northumb par incl chap Belford (mostly in North-umb, pt in Durham); see entry under Belford for its sep organisation, and for tps incl and their cos before and after 1844.

BARMPTON

Tp in Haughton le Skerne AP, sep CP 1866.[1] *LG* Seq 4. Bdry: 1930.[10] *Parl* Seq 12.

BARMSTON

Tp in Washington AP, sep CP 1866.[1] *LG* Chest. Wd, Chest. le Str. PLU, RSD, RD (1894—1922), Wash. UD (1922—37). Abol 1937 ent to Wash-ington AP.[15] *Parl* N'rn Dv (1832—85), Chest. le Str. Dv (1885—1948).

BARNARD CASTLE

Chap in Gainford AP, sep CP 1866,[1] sep EP 1723,[3] eccl refounded 1850.[37] *LG* Darl. Wd, Teesd. PLU, Barn. Cast. USD (ent 1875—84, pt 1884—94), pt Teesd. RSD (1884—94), Barn. Cast. UD. Civ bdry: 1883,[12] 1884 (incl gains Marwood CP, a pt not in the USD),[38] 1894 (the pt not in Barn. Cast. UD cr Marwood CP).[39] *Parl* Seq 8. *Eccl* Darl. RDn (1723—early 19th cent), Durham RDn (early 19th cent—1842), Darl. RDn (1842—74), Darl. RDn (S'rn Dv) (1874—80), Darl. RDn (1880—1924), Barn. Cast. RDn (1924—*).

BEAMISH

EP Cr 1873 from Tanfield EP, Collierley EP, Lanches-ter AP.[40] Chest. le Str. RDn (1873—74), Chest. RDn (E'rn Dv) (1874—80), Ryton RDn (1880—91), Chest. le Str. RDn (1891—1970), Lanch. RDn (1970—*). Bdry: 1897,[41] 1912 (help cr South Moor EP),[42] 1912,[43] 1929.[44]

BEARPARK

EP Cr 1879 from Durham St Oswald AP.[45] Durham RDn. Eccl bdry: 1914 (help cr Ushaw Moor EP),[46] 1962.[41]

CP Cr 1894 from the pt of Elvet CP not in Durham MB.[47] *LG* Durham PLU, RD. Civ bdry: 1895 (cr St Oswald's CP),[48] 1935,[49] 1946.[50] *Parl* Durham Dv/CC (1918—*).

NORTH BEDBURN

Tp in chap Witton le Wear (sep civ identity early from Auckland St Andrew AP, sep EP 1724[3]), 'North Bedburn' a sep CP 1866,[1] eccl severed 1862 from Witton le Wear EP to help cr Fir Tree EP.[51] *LG* Darl. Wd, Auckl. PLU, RSD, RD. Bdry: 1883.[12] Abol civ 1937 to help cr Crook & Willington UD & CP, pt to South Bedburn CP, pt to Wolsingham AP.[15] *Parl* S'rn Dv (1832—85), Barn. Cast. Dv (1885—1918), Spennym. Dv (1918—48).

SOUTH BEDBURN

Tp in chap Hamsterley (sep civ identity early from Auckland St Andrew AP, sep EP 1724[3]), 'South Bedburn' a sep CP 1866,[1] pt orig area tp eccl severed 1850 from Hamsterley EP to help cr Lynesack EP.[22] Incl undivided pt Undivided Moor Common to Lynesack and Softley, Hamsterley and South Bedburn. *LG* Seq 5. Bdry: 1883,[12] 1885,[52] 1937.[15] *Parl* Seq 8.

BEDLINGTON

AP *LG* Bedlingtonshire (orig sep jurisd, later in co Durham), Morpeth PLU, transf to Northumb 1832 for parl purposes, 1844 for civ purposes.[4] For later civ and parl organisation (incl in Morpeth Parl Bor [o'wise ent Northumb] from 1832, qv), and for all eccl organisation incl cr of 1863 of Cambois EP and of Choppington EP, cr 1906 of Sleekburn EP, see entry in 1878 (cr Ayres Quay EP, later called 'Bishopwearmouth St Northumb.

BELFORD

Chap (pt Durham [Islandshire], pt Northumb [Bamburgh Wd]) in Bamburgh AP (o'wise North-umb [Bamburgh Wd]), 'Belford' with sep civ identity early, sep EP 1735.[3] Tp 'Belford' in Northumb (Bamb. Wd) as were tps Detchant, Easington, Easington Grange, Middleton (the 4 each a sep CP 1866[1]); incl in Durham (Islandshire) tp Ross); incl (pt Durham, pt Northumb) tp Elwick, the tps of Ross, Elwick each transf ent to Northumb 1832 for parl purposes, 1844 for civ purposes,[4] each a sep CP 1866 in Northumb.[1] For later civ and parl organisation, and for ent eccl organisation, see entry in Northumb.

BELMONT

Chap in Durham St Giles AP, sep EP 1852,[53] sep CP 1894 from the pt of Durham St Giles not in Durham MB.[47] *LG* Durham PLU, RD. Civ bdry: 1896,[54] 1935,[49] 1958.[55] *Parl* Durham Dv/CC (1918—*). *Eccl* Eas. RDn (1852—74), Eas. RDn (S'rn Dv) (1874—80), Durham RDn (1880—*). Eccl bdry: 1920,[56] 1940,[57] 1946.[58]

BENFIELDSIDE

Tp in chap Medomsley (sep CP 1866 from Lanches-ter AP,[1] sep EP 1765[3]), 'Benfieldside' a sep CP 1866,[1] pt eccl severed 1847 from Medomsley EP and united with pt tp Conside and Knitsley in Medomsley EP, pt Ebchester EP to cr 'Benfieldside' EP.[59] *LG* Chest. Wd, Lanch. PLU, pt Benfieldside USD, pt Lanch. RSD, Benfieldside UD (1894—1937). Civ bdry: 1883,[12] 1887,[60] 1887,[61] 1894 (loses the pt not in the UD to Healeyfield CP).[62] Abol civ 1937 ent to Consett UD & CP.[15] *Parl* N'rn Dv (1832—85), N-W'rn Dv (1885—1918), Consett Dv (1918—48). *Eccl* Chest. le Str. RDn (1847—74), Chest. RDn (W'rn Dv) (1874—80), Ryton RDn (1880—91), Lanch. RDn (1891—*). Eccl bdry: 1862 (cr Consett EP),[51] 1884 (help cr Blackhill EP).[63]

BENSHAM—see GATESHEAD ST CHAD, BENSHAM AND GATESHEAD ST CUTHBERT, BEN-SHAM

COWPEN BEWLEY

Tp in Billingham AP, sep CP 1866.[1] *LG* Stock. Wd, PLU, RSD, RD. Abol 1937 pt to Billingham UD & AP, pt to Newton Bewley CP.[15] *Parl* S'rn Dv (1832—85), S-E'rn Dv (1885—1918), Sedg. RDn (1918—48).

NEWTON BEWLEY

Tp in Billingham AP, sep CP 1866,[1] eccl in chap Wolviston (sep EP 1738 from Billingham AP,[3] eccl refounded 1859[64]). *LG* Seq 12. Bdry: 1937,[15] 1968.[65] Transf 1974 to Clev.[2] *Parl* Seq 14.

SOUTH BIDDICK

Tp in chap Penshaw (sep CP 1866 from Houghton le Spring AP,[1] sep EP 1752,[3] eccl refounded 1838[27]), 'South Biddick' a sep CP 1866,[1] eccl severed 1866 from Penshaw EP to help cr Burnmoor EP.[66] *LG* Seq 12. Civ bdry: 1937,[15] 1974 (main pt remains in Durham as 'South Biddick', the pt [in Wash. New Town] transf to Tyne & Wear not to be in a par).[2] *Parl* Seq 2.

BILLINGHAM

AP Incl chap Wolviston (sep CP 1866,[1] sep EP 1738 [incl tp Newton Bewley],[3] eccl refounded 1859[64]), tp Newton Bewley (sep CP 1866,[1] eccl in chap/EP Wolviston as noted), tp Cowpen Bewley (sep CP 1866[1]). *LG* Stock. Wd, PLU, RSD, RD (1894—1923), Billingham UD (1923—67). Addtl civ bdry alt: 1937.[15] Abol civ 1968 pt to Newton Bewley CP, pt to Brindon AP, pt to cr Wolviston CP, pt to help cr Teeside CB (assoc with Yorks N Riding) & CP.[65] *Parl* S'rn Dv (1832—85), S-E'rn Dv (1885—1918), Sedg. Dv/CC (1918—70). *Eccl* Durham RDn (before 1291—before 1535), Darl. RDn (before 1535—early 19th cent), Durham RDn (early 19th cent—1842), Stock. RDn (1842—88), Hartl. RDn (1888—1924), Stock. RDn (1924—*). Addtl eccl bdry alt: 1862 (cr Haverton Hill EP),[51] 1937,[67] 1957,[68] 1959 (cr Billingham St Aidan EP).[69]

BILLINGHAM ST AIDAN

EP Cr 1959 from Billingham AP.[69] Stock. RDn. Bdry: 1969.[61]

BILLINGSIDE

Tp in Lanchester AP, sep CP 1866,[1] eccl severed 1843 to help cr Collierley EP.[71] *LG* Chest. Wd, Lanch. PLU, RSD, RD. Abol 1887 pt to Medomsley CP, pt to Lanchester AP.[60] *Parl* N'rn Dv (1832—85), N-W'rn Dv (1885—1918).

BINCHESTER

Tp in Auckland St Andrew AP, sep CP 1866,[1] pt eccl severed 1845 to help cr Byers Green EP.[19] *LG* Darl. Wd, Auckl. PLU, RSD, RD. Bdry: 1885.[72] Abol 1937 ent to Bp Auckl. UD & CP.[60] *Parl* S'rn Dv (1832—85), Bp Auckl. Dv (1885—1918).

BIRTLEY

Chap in Chester le Street AP, sep CP 1866,[1] sep EP 1850 (incl tp Harraton in same par).[52] *LG* Seq 1. Transf 1974 to Tyne & Wear (the pt in Gatesh. Metrop Dist to be 'Birtley' par, the pt in Sund. Metrop Dist not to be in a par).[2] *Parl* Seq 1. *Eccl* Chest. le Str. RDn (1850—74), Chest. RDn (E'rn Dv) (1874—80), Chest. le Str. RDn (1880—*). Eccl bdry: 1875,[73] 1875 (help cr Fatfield EP),[74] 1963.[75]

BISHOP MIDDLEHAM

AP Incl tp Cornforth (sep CP 1866,[1] eccl severed 1865, pt to help cr Cassop cum Quarrington EP, pt to help cr Coxhoe EP, the remainder to be 'Cornforth' EP[76]), tps Garmondsway Moor, Mainsforth, Thrislington (each a sep CP 1866[1]). *LG* Seq 17. *Parl* Seq 11. *Eccl* Durham RDn (before 1291—before 1535), Darl. RDn (before 1535—early 19th cent), Durham RDn (early 19th cent—1842), Stock. RDn (1842—*).

BISHOPTON

AP Incl tps East and West Newbiggin, Little Stainton (each a sep CP 1866[1]). *LG* Seq 15. *Parl* Seq 12. *Eccl* Darl. RDn (before 1291—early 19th cent), Durham RDn (early 19th cent—1842), Stock. RDn (1842—*).

BISHOPWEARMOUTH

The following have 'Bishopwearmouth' in their names. Insofar as any existed at a given time: *LG* Eas. Wd, Sund. PLU; Bor/MB, USD, RSD, RD sep noted. *Parl* Sep noted. *Eccl* Durham RDn (before 1291—before 1535), Chest. le Str. RDn (before 1535—early 19th cent), Durham RDn (early 19th cent—1842), Eas. RDn (1842—74), Eas. RDn (N'rn Dv) (1874—80), Wearm. RDn (1880—*).

AP1—BISHOPWEARMOUTH [ST MICHAEL AND ALL ANGELS]—Incl chap Ryhope (sep CP 1866,[1] sep EP 1829 [incl tps Burdon, Tunstall],[3] eccl refounded 1854[77]), area and bor Sunderland (sep par 1719[78]), tp Bishopwearmouth Panns (sep CP 1866[1]), tps Burdon, Tunstall (each a sep CP 1866,[1] each in chap/EP Ryhope as noted above), tp Ford (sep CP 1866,[1] sep EP 1854 as 'South Hylton (Ford)'[77]), tp Silksworth (sep CP 1866,[1] sep EP 1868[79]). Pt Sund. Bor (until 1719), pt Sund. MB (1835—89), Sund. CB (pt 1889—94, ent 1894—97), Sund. USD, pt Sund. RSD. Addtl civ bdry alt: 1894 (the pt not in the CB cr CP2),[47] 1895 (gains pt CP2).[80] Abol civ 1897 ent to Sunderland CP.[81] *Parl* Sund. Parl Bor (pt 1832—67, ent 1867—1918), pt N'rn Dv (1832—67). Addtl eccl bdry alt: 1844 (cr EP7, cr Deptford St Andrew EP),[82] 1854 (cr Hendon EP),[83] 1868 (cr Millfield St Mark EP, cr EP6),[79] 1875 (cr EP1),[84] 1878 (cr Ayres Quay EP, later called 'Bishopwearmouth St Stephen'),[35] 1904 (cr EP3),[86] 1929,[43] 1936 (cr EP5),[87] 1948 (gains EP6),[88] 1951.[73] Abol eccl 1970 to help cr EP4.[89]

EP1—BISHOPWEARMOUTH CHRIST CHURCH—Cr 1875 from AP1.[90] Bdry: 1929,[43] 1950,[76] 1953,[90] 1970.[91]

EP2—BISHOPWEARMOUTH GOOD SHEPHERD—Cr 1951 from South Hylton (Ford) EP.[92]

CP1—BISHOPWEARMOUTH PANNS—Tp in AP1, sep CP 1866.[1] *LG* Sund. MB/CB, USD. Abol 1897 ent to Sunderland CP.[81] *Parl* Sund. Parl Bor (1832—1918).

EP3—BISHOPWEARMOUTH ST GABRIEL—Cr 1904 from AP1.[86] Bdry: 1929,[43] 1950,[76] 1951.[73]

EP4—BISHOPWEARMOUTH ST MICHAEL WITH ST HILDA—Cr 1970 by union AP1, Millfield St Hilda EP.[89]

EP5—BISHOPWEARMOUTH ST NICHOLAS—Cr 1936 from AP1.[87] Bdry: 1950.[76]

EP6—BISHOPWEARMOUTH ST PETER—Cr 1868 from AP1.[79] Abol 1948 ent to AP1.[88]

—BISHOPWEARMOUTH ST STEPHEN—see AYRES QUAY

EP7—BISHOPWEARMOUTH ST THOMAS—Cr 1844 from AP1.[82] Sometimes 'Deptford St

Thomas'. Abol 1898 ent to Sunderland EP.[88]

CP2—BISHOPWEARMOUTH WITHOUT—Cr 1894 from the pt of AP1 not in Sund. CB.[47] *LG* Sund. PLU, RD. Bdry: 1895 (loses pt to Sund. CB [assoc with Durham] & to AP1).[80] Abol 1928 ent tp Sund. CB (assoc with Durham) & CP.[93] *Parl* Hough. le Spr. Dv (1918—48).

BLACKHALL

EP Cr 1925 from Monk Hesleden St John with St Mary EP.[94] Hartl. RDn.

BLACKHILL

EP Cr 1884 from Benfieldside EP, Consett EP.[63] Ryton RDn (1884—91), Lanch. RDn (1891—*). Bdry: 1963.[75]

BLACKWELL

Tp in Darlington AP, sep CP 1866,[1] pt eccl severed 1845 to help cr Darlington St John EP.[95] *LG* Darl. Wd, PLU, RSD, RD. Bdry: 1915 (gains pt Darl. MB & AP as remainder of the latter [augmented by gains pts other pars, qv] constituted Darl. CB),[9] 1930 (loses pt to Darl. CB [assoc with Durham] & AP).[10] Abol 1967 pt to Cleasby CP (Yorks N Riding), pt to Darl. CB (assoc with Durham) & AP, pt to Hurworth AP (Durham).[96] *Parl* S'rn Dv (1832—85), S-E'rn Dv (1885—1918), Sedg. Dv/ CC (1918—70).

BLAYDON

CP Cr 1937 by union pars in Blaydon UD: Chopwell CP, Stella CP.[97] *LG* Blayd. UD. Bdry: 1896,[98] 1937.[15] Transf 1974 to Tyne & Wear.[2] *Parl* Blayd. CC (1948—70), Blayd. BC (1970—*).

BOLAM

Tp in Gainford AP, sep CP 1866,[1] sep EP 1867 (incl tp Morton Tinmouth in same par).[99] *LG* Seq 5. *Parl* Seq 7. *Eccl* Darl. RDn (1867—74), Darl. RDn (S'rn Dv) (1874—80), Darl. RDn (1880—1945). Abol eccl 1945, the pt in Morton Tinmouth CP to Ingleton EP, the pt in Bolam CP to Heighington AP.[100]

BOLDON

AP *LG* Chest. Wd, S Shields PLU, RSD, RD (1894—1936), Boldon UD (1936—74). Civ bdry: 1883,[12] 1895 (cr Boldon Colliery CP),[101] 1901,[102] 1921 (loses pt to S Shields CB [assoc with Durham & CP),[103] 1936 (loses pt to S Shields CB [assoc with Durham] & CP),[97] 1951 (loses pt to S Shields CB [assoc with Durham] & CP),[104] 1967 (loses pt to Sund. CB [assoc with Durham] & CP, loses pt to Jarrow MB & CP).[105] Transf 1974 to Tyne & Wear.[2] *Parl* N'rn Dv (1832—85), Jarrow Dv (1885—1918), Hough. le Spr. Dv (1918—48), Jarrow CC (1948—51), Jarrow BC (1951—*). *Eccl* Durham RDn (before 1291—before 1535), Chest. le Str. RDn (before 1535—early 19th cent), Durham RDn (early 19th cent—1842), Chest. le Str. RDn (1842—74), Chest. RDn (E'rn Dv) (1874—80), Jarrow RDn (1880—*). Eccl bdry: 1848 (help cr Hedworth EP),[106] 1930 (help cr East Boldon EP),[51] 1930.[107]

EAST BOLDON

EP Cr 1930 from Boldon AP, Hedworth EP, Cleadon EP.[51] Jarrow RDn. Bdry: 1961.[108]

BOLDON COLLIERY

CP Cr 1895 from Boldon AP.[101] *LG* S Shields PLU, RD. Abol 1936 pt to help cr Boldon UD and transf to Boldon AP, pt to Felling UD and transf to Heworth CP, pt to Jarrow MB & CP.[97] *Parl* Hough. le Spr. Dv (1918—48).

BOURNMOOR—see BURNMOOR

BRADBURY

Tp in Sedgeield AP, sep CP 1866.[1] Sometimes called 'Bradbury and the Isle'. *LG* Seq 14. *Parl* Seq 13.

BRAFFERTON

Tp in Aycliffe AP, sep CP 1866.[1] *LG* Seq 4. *Parl* Seq 12.

BRANCEPETH

AP Incl chap Crook (sep EP 1845 [incl pt tp Willington],[109] the tp called 'Crook and Billy Row' and as such a sep CP 1866[1]), tp Brandon and Byshottles (sep CP 1866,[1] sep EP 1877 as 'Brandon'[110]), tp Hedleyhope (sep CP 1866,[1] pt eccl severed 1735 to help cr Satley EP[3]), tp Helmington Row (sep CP 1866[1]), tp Stockley (sep CP 1866,[1] pt eccl severed 1858 to help cr Willington EP[111]), tp Willington (sep CP 1866,[1] pt eccl severed 1845 to help cr Crook EP,[109] the remainder eccl united 1888 with pt tp Brancepeth, pt tp Stockley to cr 'Willington' EP[111]). *LG* Seq 8. Addtl civ bdry alt: 1881.[112] *Parl* S'rn Dv (1832—85), Mid Dv (1885—1918), Spennym. Dv (1918—48), Durham CC (1948—70), N W Durham CC (1970—*). *Eccl* Durham RDn (before 1291—before 1535), Chest. le Str. RDn (before 1535—early 19th cent), Durham RDn (early 19th cent—1842), Darl. RDn (1842—74), Darl. RDn (N'rn Dv) (1874—80), Durham RDn (1880—*). Addtl eccl bdry alt: 1865 (help cr Tudhoe EP),[113] 1879 (cr Waterhouses EP).[114]

BRANDON

EP Cr 1877 from Brancepeth AP[110]; for civ see following entry. Darl. RDn (N'rn Dv) (1877—80), Durham RDn (1880—*). Bdry: 1947,[115] 1962.[41]

BRANDON AND BYSHOTTLES

Tp in Brancepeth AP, sep CP 1866[1]; for eccl see prev entry. *LG* Darl. Wd, Durham PLU, Brandon & Byshottles USD, UD. Bdry: 1881,[116] 1935,[49] 1937 (incl help cr Spennymoor CP in Spennym. UD).[15] *Parl* S'rn Dv (1832—85), Mid Dv (1885—1918), Spennym. Dv (1918—48), N W Durham CC (1948—*).

BRIERTON

Tp in Stranton AP, sep CP 1866.[1] *LG* Seq 13. Bdry: 1967 (loses pt to Hartlepool CP to help constitute Hartl. CB).[117] Transf 1974 to Clev.[2] *Parl* Seq 14.

BROOM

Tp in St Oswald AP, sep CP 1866.[1] *LG* Chest. Wd (until 1829), Durham Wd (from 1829), Durham PLU, RSD, RD. Abol 1937 pt to Brandon & Byshottles UD & CP, pt to Bearpark CP.[15] *Parl* N'rn Dv (1832—85), Mid Dv (1885—1918), Durham Dv (1918—48).

BURDON

Tp in chap Ryhope (sep CP 1866 from Bishopwearmouth AP,[1] sep EP 1829,[3] eccl refounded 1854[77]), 'Burdon' a sep CP 1866.[1] *LG*

Seq 9. Bdry: 1937,[15] 1967 (loses pt to Sund. CB [assoc with Durham] & AP).[118] Transf 1974 to Tyne & Wear.[2] *Parl* Seq 3.

GREAT BURDON
Tp in Haughton le Skerne AP, sep CP 1866.[1] *LG* Seq 4. Bdry: 1967 (exchanges pts with Darl. CB [assoc with Durham] & AP).[96] *Parl* Seq 12.

BURNMOOR
Tp in chap Penshaw (sep CP 1866 from Houghton le Spring AP,[1] sep EP 1752,[3] eccl refounded 1838[27]), 'Burnmoor' [sometimes 'Bournmoor'] a sep CP 1866,[1] eccl severed 1866 and united with orig area tp South Biddick, also in Penshaw EP, to cr 'Burnmoor' EP.[66] *LG* Seq 12. *Parl* Seq 2. *Eccl* Durham RDn (1752—1842), Eas. RDn (1842—74), Eas. RDn (N'rn Dv) (1874—80), Hough. le Spr. RDn (1880—*). Eccl bdry: 1867,[119] 1875.[73]

BURNOPFIELD
EP Cr 1871 from Tanfield EP, Lanchester AP, Medomsley EP, Whickham AP, Collierley EP.[120] Chest. le Str. RDn (1871—74), Chest. RDn (W'rn Dv) (1874—80), Ryton RDn (1880—91), Chest. le Str. RDn (1891—*). Bdry: 1953.[121]

BUTTERWICK AND OLDACRES
Tp in Sedgefield AP, sep CP 1866.[1] *LG* Seq 14. *Parl* Seq 13.

BYERS GREEN
Chap and tp pt in Auckland St Andrew AP, pt in Whitworth AP, sep CP 1866,[1] sep EP 1845 from Auckland St Andrew AP (incl pt tp Binchester).[19] *LG* Darl. Wd, Auckl. PLU, RSD, RD. Civ bdry: 1885,[72] 1912.[122] Abol civ 1937 pt to Bp Auckl. UD & CP, pt to help cr Crook & Willington UD & CP, pt to Spennym. UD & to help cr Spennymoor CP.[15] *Parl* S'rn Dv (1832—85), Bp Auckl. Dv (1885—1948). *Eccl* Darl. RDn (1845—74), Darl. RDn (N'rn Dv) (1874—80), Auckl. RDn (1880—*). Eccl bdry: 1940.[123]

CARLTON
Chap in Redmarshall AP, sep CP 1866.[1] *LG* Seq 12. Bdry: 1968 (incl loses pt to help cr Teeside CB [assoc with Yorks N Riding] & CP).[65] Transf 1974 to Clev.[2] *Parl* Seq 14.

CASSOP
Tp in Kelloe AP, sep CP 1866,[1] pt eccl united 1865 with other areas (see following entry) to help cr Cassop cum Quarrington EP.[76] *LG* Eas. Wd (until 1829), Durham Wd (from 1829), Durham PLU, RSD. Abol civ 1887 to help cr Cassop cum Quarrington CP.[124] *Parl* N'rn Dv (1832—85), Mid Dv (1885—1918).

CASSOP CUM QUARRINGTON
EP Cr 1865 from Kelloe AP (pt tp Cassop, pt tp Quarrington), Bishop Middleham AP (pt tp Cornforth).[76] Eas. RDn (1865—74), Eas. RDn (S'rn Dv) (1874—80), Eas. RDn (1880—*). Eccl bdry: 1937,[125] 1960.[126]
CP Cr 1887 by union Cassop CP, Quarrington CP.[124] *LG* Durham Wd, PLU, RSD, RD. Civ bdry: 1946,[50] 1953.[127] *Parl* Durham Dv/CC (1918—*).

CASTLE EDEN
AP Orig chap appropriated to Guisborough Priory, sep par at Reformation. *LG* Seq 9. Civ bdry: 1946,[128] 1956.[129] *Parl* Seq 6. *Eccl* Durham RDn (until 1842), Eas. RDn (1842—74), Eas. RDn (S'rn Dv) (1874—80), Eas. RDn (1880—1924), Hartl. RDn (1924—*). Eccl bdry: 1842 (help cr Wingate Grange EP),[99] 1925,[130] 1963.[131]

CASTLESIDE
EP Cr 1863 from Lanchester AP, Ebchester EP, Medomsley EP, Satley EP, Muggleswick EP.[94] Chest. le Str. RDn (1863—74), Chest. RDn (W'rn Dv) (1874—80), Ryton RDn (1880—91), Lanch. RDn (1891—*). Bdry: 1966.[132]

CASTLETOWN—see NORTH HYLTON ST MARGARET, CASTLETOWN

CHESTER LE STREET
AP Tp 'Chester le Street' in Chest. Wd as were chap Birtley (sep CP 1866,[1] sep EP 1819[3]), chap Lamsley (sep CP 1866,[1] sep EP 1819[3]), chap Tanfield (sep CP 1866,[1] sep EP 1768[3]), tp Edmondsley (sep CP 1866,[1] pt eccl severed 1843 to help cr Pelton EP[133]), tp Harraton (sep CP 1866[1]), tp Ouston (sep CP 1866,[1] eccl severed 1843 to help cr Pelton EP[133]), tp Pelton (sep CP 1866,[1] sep EP 1843 [incl tp Ouston, pt tps Edmondsley, Urpeth][133]), tp Plawsworth (the only pt of the par transf 1829 to Durham Wd, sep CP 1866[1]), tp Urpeth (sep CP 1866,[1] eccl severed 1843 to help cr Pelton EP[133]), tp Waldridge (sep CP 1866[1]); incl in Eas. Wd tps Lambton, Great Lumley, Little Lumley (each a sep CP 1866,[1] the 3 tps eccl united 1862 to cr Lumley EP[134]). *LG* Chest. le Str. PLU, RSD, RD (1894—1909), Chest. le Str. UD (1909—74). Addtl civ bdry alt: 1881,[135] 1883,[12] 1885,[136] 1912,[137] 1921,[138] 1935.[15] *Parl* Seq 1. *Eccl* Chest. le Str. RDn (until early 19th cent), Durham RDn (early 19th cent—1842), Chest. le Str. RDn (1842—74), Chest. RDn (E'rn Dv) (1874—80), Chest. le Str. RDn (1880—*). Addtl eccl bdry alt: 1863 (help cr Sacriston EP),[139] 1865 (help cr Holmside EP),[140] 1876 (help cr West Pelton EP),[141] 1923 (help cr Kimblesworth EP),[142] 1963.[75]

CHILTON
Tp in Merrington AP, sep CP 1866,[1] eccl severed 1843 to help cr Ferryhill EP.[143] *LG* Seq 6. Bdry: 1946.[144] *Parl* S'rn Dv (1832—85), Bp Auckl. Dv (1885—1918), Sedg. Dv/CC (1918—70), Durham RDn (1970—*).

CHILTON
EP Cr 1925 from Ferryhill EP, Aycliffe AP, Coundon EP.[29] Eas. RDn.

CHILTON MOOR
EP Cr 1872 from Houghton le Spring AP, Rainton EP, East Rainton EP, Newbottle EP.[145] Eas. RDn (1872—74), Eas. RDn (S'rn Dv) (1874—80), Hough. le Spr. RDn (1880—*).

CHOPWELL
Tp in chap Winlaton (sep civ identity early from Ryton AP, sep EP 1832[146]), 'Chopwell' a sep CP 1866,[1] eccl severed 1916 from Winlaton EP as 'Chopwell' EP.[147] *LG* Chest. Wd, Gatesh. PLU, Blayd. USD, UD. Civ bdry: 1901.[148] Abol civ 1936 to help cr Blaydon CP.[97] *Parl* N'rn Dv (1832—85), Chest. le Str. Dv (1885—1918), Blayd. Dv (1918—48). *Eccl* Chest. le Str. RDn.

CLAXTON

Orig chap in Billingham AP, transf to Greatham by 16th cent,[149] sep CP 1866.[1] *LG* Seq 13. Transf 1974 to Clev.[2] *Parl* Seq 14.

CLEADON

EP Cr 1911 from Whitburn AP (tp Cleadon, pt tp Whitburn).[150] Wearm. RDn. Bdry: 1930 (help cr East Boldon EP),[51] 1930,[107] 1951,[151] 1952 (incl help cr Cleadon Park EP, help cr Horton EP).[152]

CLEADON PARK ST CUTHBERT

EP Cr 1952 from Cleadon EP, Harton EP.[152] Jarrow RDn. Bdry: 1958.[153] Renamed 1961 'Cleadon Park St Mark and St Cuthbert'.[154]

CLEADON PARK ST MARK AND ST CUTHBERT

EP Renaming 1961 of Cleadon Park St Cuthbert EP.[154] Jarrow RDn. Bdry: 1967.[155]

CLEATLAM

Tp pt in Gainford AP, pt in Staindrop AP, pt in Winston AP, sep CP 1866.[1] *LG* Seq 7. *Parl* Seq 8.

COATHAM MUNDEVILLE

Orig in co Sadberge (Northumb until 1189, Durham thereafter, considered a sep co until mid 15th cent, then in other Wards). Tp in Haughton le Skerne AP, sep CP 1866.[1] *LG* Seq 16. Bdry: 1884.[30] *Parl* Seq 12.

COATSAY MOOR

Tp in Heighington AP, sep CP 1866.[1] *LG* Darl. Wd, PLU, RSD. Abol 1884 ent to Heighington AP.[156] *Parl* S'rn Dv (1832—85).

COCKEN

Tp in chap West Rainton (sep CP 1866 from Houghton le Spring AP,[1] sep EP 1836 as 'Rainton'[27] [qv for constituent areas]), 'Cocken' a sep CP 1866.[1] *LG* Eas. Wd, Chest. le Str. PLU, RSD, RD. Abol 1937 pt to Framwellgate Moor CP, pt to West Rainton CP.[15] *Parl* N'rn Dv (1832—85), Hough. le Spr. Dv (1885—1918), Chest. le Str. Dv (1918—48).

COCKERTON

Tp in Darlington AP, sep CP 1866,[1] eccl severed 1843 to help cr Darlington Holy Trinity EP,[8] orig area tp Cockerton severed 1925 from the latter as 'Cockerton' EP.[157] *LG* Darl. Wd, PLU, pt Darl. MB (1872—94), pt Darl. USD, pt Darl. RSD, Darl. RD. Civ bdry: 1894 (loses the pt in Darl. MB to help cr Harrowgate Hill CP).[158] Abol civ 1915 pt to Archdeacon Newton CP, pt to Darlington AP as Darl. MB constituted a CB.[9] *Parl* S'rn Dv (1832—85), pt Darl. Parl Bor, pt S-E'rn Dv (1885—1918). *Eccl* Darl. RDn. Eccl bdry: 1966.[18]

COCKFIELD

AP Incl tp Woodland (sep CP 1866[1]). *LG* Seq 7. Addtl civ bdry alt: 1884.[159] *Parl* Seq 8. *Eccl* Seq 3. Eccl bdry: 1969.[160]

COLD HESLEDON

Tp in Dalton le Dale AP, sep CP 1866.[1] *LG* Seq 9. Bdry: 1954.[161] *Parl* N'rn Dv (1832—85), S-E'rn Dv (1885—1918), Seaham Dv (1918—48), Eas. CC (1948—70), Hough. le Spr. CC (1970—*).

COLLIERLEY

Chap and tp in Lanchester AP, sep CP 1866,[1] sep EP 1843 (incl tps Kyo, Billingside, pt tp Greencroft).[71] *LG* Chest. Wd, Lanch. PLU, RSD, RD

(1894—96), Annfield Plain UD (1896—1937). Civ bdry: 1886,[162] 1887.[60] Sometimes civ 'Collierley and Pontop'. Abol civ 1937 pt to Consett UD & CP, pt to Stanley UD & CP.[15] *Parl* N'rn Dv (1832—85), N-W'rn Dv (1885—1918), Consett Dv (1918—48). *Eccl* Chest. le Str. RDn (1842—74), Chest. RDn (W'rn Dv) (1874—80), Ryton RDn (1880—91), Lanch. RDn (1891—*). Eccl bdry: 1871 (help cr Burnopfield EP),[120] 1873 (help cr Beamish EP),[40] 1883 (help cr Dipton EP),[163] 1914 (help cr Annfield Plain EP),[5] 1953.[121]

CONISCLIFFE

AP Orig in co Sadberge (Northumb until 1189, Durham thereafter, considered a sep co until mid 15th cent, then in other Wards). Incl tps High Coniscliffe, Low Coniscliffe (each a sep CP 1866[1]) so that 'Coniscliffe' has no sep civ identity after 1866. *LG* Darl. Wd. *Parl* S'rn Dv (1832—85). *Eccl* Seq 2.

HIGH CONISCLIFFE

Tp in Coniscliffe AP, sep CP 1866.[1] *LG* Seq 4. Bdry: 1884.[30] *Parl* Seq 12.

LOW CONISCLIFFE

Tp in Coniscliffe AP, sep CP 1866.[1] Organisation as for High Coniscliffe, with addtl civ bdry alt 1967 (exchanges pts with Darl. CB [assoc with Durham] & AP).[96]

CONSETT

EP Cr 1862 from Benfieldside EP.[51] Chest. le Str. RDn (1862—74), Chest. RDn (W'rn Dv) (1874—80), Ryton RDn (1880—91), Lanch. RDn (1891—*). Eccl bdry: 1884 (help cr Blackhill EP),[63] 1963,[75] 1966.[132]

CP Cr 1894 from the pt of Conside and Knitsley CP in Consett UD.[62] *LG* Lanch. PLU, Consett UD. Civ bdry: 1920,[164] 1937 (incl gains Benfieldside CP, Ebchester CP).[15] *Parl* Consett Dv/CC (1918—*).

CONSIDE AND KNITSLEY

Tp in chap Medomsley (sep CP 1866 from Lanchester AP,[1] sep EP 1765[3]), 'Conside and Knitsley' a sep CP 1866,[1] pt eccl severed 1847 from Medomsley EP to help cr Benfieldside EP.[59] *LG* Chest. Wd, Lanch. PLU, pt Consett USD, pt Lanch. RSD. Bdry: 1883,[12] 1887,[60] 1887.[61] Abol 1894 the pt in Consett UD to help cr Consett CP, the remainder to cr Knitsley CP.[62] *Parl* N'rn Dv (1832—85), N-W'rn Dv (1885—1918).

CONFORTH

Tp in Bishop Middleham AP, sep CP 1866,[1] pt eccl severed 1865 to help cr Cassop cum Quarrington EP, pt to help cr Coxhoe EP, the remainder eccl united with pt tp Bishop Middleham to cr 'Conforth' EP.[76] *LG* Seq 17. Civ bdry: 1937,[15] 1946.[144] *Parl* Seq 11. *Eccl* Stock. RDn (1865—80), Eas. RDn (1880—*). Eccl bdry: 1937.[125]

CORNHILL ON TWEED

Chap in Norham AP, sep CP 1866,[1] sep EP 1730.[3] *LG* Norhamshire, Berwick PLU, transf to Northumb 1832 for parl purposes, 1844 for civ purposes.[4] *Parl* In Durham until 1832, Northumb thereafter. For later civ and parl organisation, and for ent eccl organisation, see entry in Northumb.

CORNSAY

Tp in Lanchester AP, sep CP 1866.[1] *LG* Darl. Wd,

Lanch. PLU, pt Tow Law USD, pt Lanch. RSD, Lanch. RD. Bdry: 1883,[12] 1894 (loses the pt in Tow Law UD to help cr South Cornsay CP),[62] 1946,[165] 1956.[166] *Parl* S'rn Dv (1832—85), N-W'rn Dv (1885—1918), Barn. Cast. Dv (1918—48), N W Durham CC (1948—*).

SOUTH CORNSAY
CP Cr 1894 from the pts in Tow Law UD of Cornsay CP, Hedleyhope CP.[62] *LG* Lanch. PLU, Tow Law UD. *Parl* Spennym. Dv (1918—48), N W Durham CC (1948—*).

COUNDON
Chap and tp in Auckland St Andrew AP, sep CP 1866,[1] sep EP 1842 (tps Westerton, Windlestone, pt tp Coundon).[20] *LG* Darl. Wd, Auckl. PLU, RSD, RD. Civ bdry: 1886.[13] Abol civ 1937 ent to Bp Auckl. UD & CP.[15] *Parl* S'rn Dv (1832—85), Bp Auckl. Dv (1885—1948). *Eccl* Darl. RDn (1842—74), Darl. RDn (N'rn Dv) (1874—80), Auckl. RDn (1880—*). Eccl bdry: 1925 (help cr Chilton EP).[29]

COUNDON GRANGE
Tp in Auckland St Andrew AP, sep CP 1866.[1] *LG* Darl. Wd, Auckl. PLU, RSD, RD. Bdry: 1886.[13] Abol 1937 ent to Bp Auckl. UD & CP.[15] *Parl* S'rn Dv (1832—85), Bp Auckl. Dv (1885—1948).

COXHOE
Tp in Kelloe AP, sep CP 1866,[1] pt eccl severed 1865 and united with pt tp Cornforth in Bishop Middleham AP to cr 'Coxhoe' EP.[76] *LG* Seq 11. Addtl civ bdry alt: 1937,[15] 1946.[50] *Parl* Seq 4. *Eccl* Eas. RDn (1865—74), Eas. RDn (S'rn Dv) (1874—80), Eas. RDn (1880—*). Eccl bdry: 1936.[125]

CRAGHEAD
CP Cr 1896 from Lanchester AP, Edmonsley CP.[167] *LG* Lanch. PLU, RD. Abol 1937 pt to Stanley UD & CP, pt to Lanchester AP.[15] *Parl* Consett Dv (1918—48).

EP Cr 1912 from Holmside EP.[168] Lanch. RDn.

CRAWBROOK
Tp in Ryton AP, sep CP 1866.[1] *LG* Chest. Wd, Gatesh. PLU, Ryton USD, UD. Bdry: 1883.[12] Abol 1914 ent to Ryton AP.[169] *Parl* N'rn Dv (1832—85), Chest. le Str. Dv (1885—1918), Blayd. Dv (1918—48).

CRAYKE
AP Durham par (Stock. Wd), transf to Yorks N Riding (Bulmer Wap) 1832 for parl purposes, 1844 for civ purposes.[4] For later civ and parl organisation, and for all eccl organisation (incl orig in pec jurisd Dean & Chapter of Durham), see entry in Yorks.

CROOK
Chap in Brancepeth AP, sep EP 1845 by union tp tp Crook and Billy Row, pt tp Willington[109]; for civ see following entry. *Eccl* Darl. RDn (1845—74), Darl. RDn (N'rn Dv) (1874—80), Auckl. RDn (1880—91), Stanh. RDn (1891—*). Bdry: 1872 (cr Stanley EP),[170] 1899 (help cr Sunnybrow EP),[171] 1903.[5]

CROOK AND BILLY ROW
Tp in Brancepeth AP, sep CP 1866[1]; for eccl see prev entry. *LG* Darl. Wd (until 1829), Durham Wd (from 1829), Auckl. PLU, RSD, RD (1894—98), Crook UD (1898—1937). Abol civ 1937 to help cr Crook and Willington UD & CP.[15] *Parl* S'rn Dv (1832—85), Barn Cast. Dv (1885—1918), Spennym. Dv (1918—48).

CROOK AND WILLINGTON
CP Cr 1937 by union Crook UD (Crook and Billy Row CP), Helmington Row CP, Hunwick and Helmington CP, Stockley CP, and pts Byers Green CP, Escomb CP, Newton Cap CP, North Bedburn CP, Willington CP, Witton le Wear CP, Lands Common to Witton le Wear and North Bedburn.[15] *LG* Crook & Willington UD. *Parl* N W Durham CC (1948—*).

CROSSGATE
Tp in chap Durham St Margaret (sep EP 1748 from Durham St Oswald EP[3]), 'Crossgate' a sep CP 1866.[1] *LG* Chest. Wd (until 1829), Durham Wd (from 1829), Durham PLU, MB (pt 1835—94, ent 1894—1916), pt Durham USD, pt Durham RSD. Bdry: 1894 (the pt not in Durham MB cr Neville Cross CP),[39] 1905.[172] Abol 1916 to help cr Durham CP.[173] *Parl* Pt Durham Parl Bor (1832—1918), pt N'rn Dv (1832—85), pt Mid Dv (1885—1918), Durham Dv (1918—48).

CROXDALE
Chap in Durham St Oswald AP, sep EP 1738,[3] eccl refounded 1843 by union tp Sunderland Bridge, pt tp Elvet (both in Durham St Oswald EP), tp Hett, pt tp Ferryhill (both in Merrington AP).[174] Durham RDn (1738—1842), Eas. RDn (1842—74), Eas. RDn (S'rn Dv) (1874—80), Durham RDn (1880—*).

DALTON LE DALE
AP Incl tps Cold Hesledon, Dawdon, East Morton (each a sep CP 1866[1]). *LG* Seq 9. Addtl civ bdry alt: 1954.[161] *Parl* Seq 3. *Eccl* Durham RDn (before 1291—before 1535), Darl. RDn (before 1535— early 19th cent), Durham RDn (early 19th cent— 1842), Eas. RDn (1842—74), Eas. RDn (N'rn Dv) (1874—80), Hough. le Spr. RDn (1880—*). Eccl bdry: 1843 (cr Seaham Harbour EP),[175] 1962.[176]

DALTON PIERCY
Tp in Hart AP, sep CP 1866.[1] *LG* Seq 13. Bdry: 1932,[177] 1953 (loses pt to W Hartl. CB [assoc with Durham] & CP),[178] 1967 (incl loses pt to Hartlepool CP to help constitute Hartl. CB [assoc with Durham]).[117] Transf 1974 to Clev.[2] *Parl* Seq 14. Parl bdry: 1953.[179]

DARLINGTON
The following have 'Darlington' in their names. Insofar as any existed at a given time: *LG* Darl. Wd, PLU, MB (1867—1915), USD, CB (1915—74). *Parl* S'rn Dv (1832—67), Darl. Parl Bor (1867—*). *Eccl* Darl. RDn (before 1291—early 19th cent), Durham RDn (early 19th cent—1842), Darl. RDn (1842—74), Darl. RDn (S'rn Dv) (1874—80), Darl. RDn (1880—*).

AP1—DARLINGTON [ST CUTHBERT]—At one time Collegiate. Incl tp Archdeacon Newton (sep CP 1866,[1] eccl severed 1840 to help cr EP1,[3] the latter eccl refounded 1843[8]), tp Blackwell (sep CP 1866,[1] pt eccl severed 1845 to help cr EP3[95]), tp Cockerton (sep CP 1866,[1] eccl severed 1840 to help cr EP1,[3] the latter refounded 1843,[8] 'Cockerton' a sep EP 1925 from EP1[157]). Addtl civ bdry alt: 1915 (loses pt to Blackwell CP, gains pts Cockerton CP, Haughton le Skerne AP as the reconstituted par constituted Darl. CB),[9] 1930,[10] 1967 (incl exchanges pts with Great Burdon CP, Hurworth AP, Low Coniscliffe CP).[96] Addtl eccl bdry alt: 1840 (pt of tp Darlington severed to help cr EP1,[3] refounded 1843[8]), 1845 (help cr EP3),[95] 1868 (cr EP9),[18] 1884 (help cr EP5),[111] 1962.[180]

EP1—DARLINGTON HOLY TRINITY—Cr 1843 from AP1 (tps Archdeacon Newton, Cockerton, pt main area AP1),[3] refounded 1843.[8] Bdry: 1884 (help cr EP5),[111] 1925 (help cr EP8),[53] 1925 (cr Cockerton EP),[157] 1966.[18]

EP2—DARLINGTON ST JAMES—Cr 1872 from EP3.[145] Bdry: 1962.[180]

EP3—DARLINGTON ST JOHN—Cr 1845 from AP1 (pt main tp AP1, pt tp Blackwell).[95] Bdry: 1872 (cr EP2),[145] 1889 (cr EP4).[181]

EP4—DARLINGTON ST HILDA—Cr 1889 from EP3.[181] Bdry: 1962.[18]

EP5—DARLINGTON ST LUKE—Cr 1884 from EP9, EP1, AP1.[111] Bdry: 1925 (help cr EP8).[53]

EP6—DARLINGTON ST MARK—Cr 1929 from EP9, Haughton le Skerne AP.[43] Abol 1973 to help cr EP7.[182]

EP7—DARLINGTON ST MARK WITH ST PAUL—Cr 1973 by union EP6, EP9.[182]

EP8—DARLINGTON ST PAUL—Cr 1868 from AP1.[18] Bdry: 1884 (help cr EP5),[111] 1929 (help cr EP6).[43] Abol 1973 to help cr EP7.[182]

DAWDON
Tp in Dalton le Dale AP, sep CP 1866,[1] sep EP 1843 as 'Seaham Harbour',[175] 'Dawdon' a sep EP 1912 from Seaham Harbour EP.[183] LG Eas. Wd, PLU, Seaham Harbour USD, UD. Abol civ 1937 ent to Seaham AP to help constitute Seaham UD.[15] Parl N'rn Dv (1832—85), S-E'rn Dv (1885—1918), Seaham Dv (1918—48). Eccl Hough. le Spr. RDn. Eccl bdry: 1940.[184]

DEAF HILL CUM LANGDALE
EP Cr 1874 from Trimdon AP, Wingate Grange EP.[185] Bdry: 1889,[186] 1963.[131]

DENTON
Chap in Gainford AP, sep CP 1866,[1] sep EP 1837.[3] LG Seq 4. Parl Seq 12. Eccl Durham RDn (1837—42), Darl. RDn (1842—74), Darl. RDn (S'rn Dv) (1874—80), Darl. RDn (1880—*). Eccl bdry: 1932 (gains area of Summerhouse CP from Gainford AP).[187]

DEPTFORD ST ANDREW
EP Cr 1844 from Bishopwearmouth AP.[82] Eas. RDn (1844—74), Eas. RDn (N'rn Dv) (1874—80), Wearm. RDn (1880—1950). Bdry: 1868 (cr Pallion EP),[71] 1873,[188] 1878 (help cr Ayres Quay EP).[35] Abol 1950 pt to Millfield St Mark EP, pt to Millfield St Mary Magdalene EP, pt to Pallion EP.[36]

DEPTFORD ST THOMAS—see BISHOPWEAR-MOUTH ST THOMAS

DINSDALE
AP Usual eccl spelling; for civ see following entry. Eccl Seq 5. Eccl bdry: 1945.[189]

LOW DINSDALE
AP Orig in co Sadberge (Northumb until 1189, Durham thereafter, considered a sep co until mid 15th cent, then in other Wards). Usual civ spelling (as opposed to Over Dinsale in Yorks N Riding); for eccl see prev entry. LG Seq 16. Parl Seq 12.

DIPTON
EP Cr 1883 from Collierley EP, Tanfield EP.[163] Ryton RDn (1883—91), Lanch. RDn (1891—*). Bdry: 1953.[121]

DUDDO
Tp in Norham AP, sep CP 1866,[1] sep EP 1865.[190] LG Norhamshire, Berwick PLU, transf to Northumb 1832 for parl purposes, 1844 for civ purposes.[4] Parl In Durham until 1832, Northumb thereafter. For later civ and parl organisation, and for ent eccl organisation, see entry in Northumb.

DUNSTON CHRIST CHURCH
EP Cr 1872 from Whickham AP.[7] Chest. le Str. RDn (1872—74), Chest. RDn (W'rn Dv) (1874—80), Chest. le Str. RDn (1880—91), Gatesh. RDn (1891—*). Bdry: 1936 (help cr Dunston St Nicholas EP).[191]

DUNSTON ST NICHOLAS
EP Cr 1936 from Dunston Christ Church EP, Whickham AP.[191] Gatesh. RDn. Bdry: 1949 (cr Lobley Hill EP).[192]

DURHAM
The following have 'Durham' in their names. Insofar as any existed at a given time: LG Eas. Wd (until 1829), Durham Wd (from 1829), Durham PLU; Bor/MB, USD, RSD sep noted. Parl Sep noted. Eccl Sep noted before 1880, Durham RDn (1880—*).

CP1—DURHAM—Cr 1916 by union pars in Durham MB: Crossgate CP, CP2, CP3, CP4, AP2, AP3, AP4, Elvet CP, Framwellgate CP, St Giles AP.[173] Bdry: 1935,[49] 1955.[193] Parl Durham Dv/CC (1918—*).

—DURHAM NORTH BAILEY—see AP2

—DURHAM SOUTH BAILEY—see AP3

CP2—DURHAM CASTLE AND PRECINCTS—Ex-par place, sep CP 1858.[194] LG Not in Bor, Durham MB (1835—1916), USD. Abol civ 1916 to help cr CP1.[173] Parl Durham Parl Bor (1832—1918).

EP3—DURHAM COLLEGE—Ex-par place, sep CP 1858.[194] LG, civ abol, Parl as for CP2.

CP4—DURHAM MAGDALEN PLACE—The chap at the Hospital of St Mary early considered a parochial church, early in ruins and no presentations from late 17th cent,[195] thereafter considered ex-par, sep CP 1858.[194] LG, civ abol, Parl as for CP2.

EP1—DURHAM ST CUTHBERT—Cr 1858 from AP5 (civ, 'St Oswald') (pt of area chap Durham St Margaret in that par).[196] Chest. RDn (1858—74), Chest. RDn (W'rn Dv) (1874—80). Bdry: 1923 (help cr Kimblesworth EP).[142]

AP1—DURHAM ST GILES—Usual eccl name; for civ and bor, see 'St Giles'. Incl chap St Oswald (sep par 12th cent as AP5 [qv for areas incl][197]). Eccl Durham RDn (until 1842), Eas. RDn (1842—74),

Eas. RDn (S'rn Dv) (1874—80). Eccl bdry: 1852 (cr Belmont EP),[53] 1940,[57] 1946.[58]

EP3—DURHAM ST MARGARET—Chap in AP5, sep EP 1748[3]; civ comprised of tps Crossgate, Framwellgate (each a sep CP 1866[1]). Durham RDn (1748—early 19th cent), Chest. le Str. RDn (early 19th cent—1874), Chest. le Str. RDn (W'rn Dv) (1874—80). Bdry: 1962.[198]

AP2—DURHAM ST MARY LE BOW—Sometimes 'North Bailey' or 'Durham North Bailey'. *LG* Castle jurisd (seat of Palatinate) (until 1835), Durham MB (1835—1916), USD. Abol civ 1916 to help cr CP1.[173] *Parl* Durham Parl Bor (1832—1918). *Eccl* Chest. le Str. RDn. Incl from late 17th cent AP3 (presentations not made in latter after 1578[199]), the union called as EP2, qv.

EP2—DURHAM ST MARY LE BOW WITH ST MARY THE LESS—Name used from late 17th cent when AP2 gains area AP3 (no presentations to latter after 1578[199]). Chest. le Str. RDn (cr—early 19th cent), Durham RDn (early 19th cent—1842), Eas. RDn (1842—74), Eas. RDn (S'rn Dv) (1874—80). Abol 1967 ent to AP5.[200]

AP3—DURHAM ST MARY THE LESS—Sometimes 'South Bailey' or 'Durham South Bailey'. *LG*, civ abol, *Parl* as for AP2. *Eccl* Chest. le Str. RDn. Abol civ late 17th cent (no presentations to this par after 1578[199]), thereafter incl within area AP2, name as EP2.

AP4—DURHAM ST NICHOLAS—*LG* Durham Bor (sometimes 'Bishop's Bor' or 'Old Borough' of 'Crossgate', until 1565), Durham and Framwellgate Bor (1565—1835), Durham MB (1835—1916), USD. Abol civ 1916 to help cr CP1.[173] *Parl* Durham and Framwellgate Parl Bor (1678—1832), Durham Parl Bor (1832—1918). *Eccl* Durham RDn (until 1842), Eas. RDn (1842—74), Eas. RDn (S'rn Dv) (1874—80).

AP5—DURHAM ST OSWALD—Usual eccl name; for civ and bor, see 'St Oswald'. Orig chap in AP1, sep par in 12th cent.[197] Incl chap St Margaret (sep EP 1748[3]; civ comprised of tps Crossgate, Framwellgate [each a sep CP 1866[1]], the latter in Framwellgate Bor until 1535, pt in Durham Bor 1565—1835, qv for later), tp Elvet (sep CP 1866[1] [Barony and Bor of Elvet until 1835, qv for later]), tp Shincliffe (sep CP 1866[1], sep EP 1827[3]), chap Croxdale (sep EP 1738,[3] eccl refounded 1843 from AP5, Merrington AP[174]), chap Witton Gilbert (sep par 1423,[201] incl from 1593 Kimblesworth AP [orig sep AP, in ruins by 16th cent[202]], the union eccl 'Witton Gilbert and Kimblesworth', pt eccl severed 1863 to help cr Sacriston EP,[139] 'Kimblesworth' deemed civ ex-par, sep CP 1858[194]). *Eccl* Durham RDn (until 1842), Chest. le Str. RDn (1842—74), Chest. RDn (W'rn Dv) (1874—80). Addtl eccl bdry alt: 1858 (cr EP1),[196] 1879 (cr Bearpark EP),[45] 1962,[200] 1967 (gains EP2).[200]

EASINGTON

AP Incl tps Haswell, Shotton (each a sep CP 1866[1], pt of each united eccl 1863 with pt tp Easington to cr 'Shotton with Haswell' EP,[203] the latter divided 1870 into 2 EPS of 'Haswell', 'Shotton'[204]), tp Hawthorn (sep CP 1866,[1] pt eccl severed 1863 to help cr South Hetton EP,[203] the remainder united eccl 1863 with pt tp Haswell [the pt not prev severed to help cr Shotton with Haswell EP, qv above] to cr 'Hawthorn' EP[203]). *LG* Seq 9. Addtl civ bdry alt: 1915,[205] 1946,[128] 1956 (help cr Peterlee CP).[206] *Parl* Seq 6. *Eccl* Appropriated to Archdeacon of Durham, in Durham RDn (until 1842), Eas. RDn (1842—74), Eas. RDn (S'rn Dv) (1874—80), Eas. RDn (1880—*). Addtl eccl bdry alt: 1863 (cr South Hetton EP [pt orig tp Haswell, pt tp Hawthorn]),[203] 1913 (cr Horden EP),[207] 1924 (cr Easington Colliery EP),[111] 1956,[163] 1957 (help cr Peterlee EP).[208]

EASINGTON COLLIERY

EP Cr 1924 from Easington AP.[111] Eas. RDn. Bdry: 1956,[163] 1957 (help cr Peterlee EP).[208]

EASINGTON LANE—see LYONS

EASTGATE

EP Cr 1885 from Stanhope AP.[209] Sometimes 'Stanhope All Saints, Eastgate'. Stanh. RDn.

EBCHESTER

Chap in Lanchester AP, sep civ identity early, sep EP 1743.[3] *LG* Chest. Wd, Lanch. PLU, pt Consett USD (1875—83), pt Benfieldside USD (1875—83), Lanch. RSD (pt 1875—83, ent 1883—94), Lanch. RD. Civ bdry: 1883,[12] 1887,[60] 1887.[61] Abol civ 1937 ent to Consett UD & CP.[15] *Parl* N'rn Dv (1832—85), N-W'rn Dv (1885—1918), Consett Dv (1918—48). *Eccl* Durham RDn (1743—1842), Chest. le Str. RDn (1842—74), Chest. RDn (W'rn Dv) (1874—80), Ryton RDn (1880—91), Lanch. RDn (1891—*). Eccl bdry: 1847 (help cr Benfieldside EP),[59] 1863 (help cr Castleside EP).[94]

EDMONDBYERS

AP Incl chap Hunstanworth (sep CP 1866,[1] sep EP 1727[3]). *LG* Seq 3. Addtl civ bdry alt: 1883.[12] *Parl* Seq 5. *Eccl* Durham RDn (before 1291—before 1535), Chest. le Str. RDn (before 1535—early 19th cent), Durham RDn (early 19th cent—1842), Chest. le Str. RDn (1842—74), Chest. RDn (W'rn Dv) (1874—80), Stanh. RDn (1880—*). Addtl eccl bdry alt: 1959.[210]

EDMONDSLEY

Tp in Chester le Street AP, sep CP 1866,[1] pt eccl severed 1843 to help cr Pelton EP.[133] *LG* Seq 1. Bdry: 1883,[12] 1885,[136] 1886,[211] 1887,[60] 1896 (help cr Craghead CP),[167] 1896,[212] 1946.[213] *Parl* Seq 1.

EGGLESCLIFFE

AP Orig in co Sadberge (Northumb until 1189, Durham thereafter, considered a sep co until mid 15th cent, then in other Wds). Incl tps Aislaby, Newsham (each a sep CP 1866[1]). *LG* Seq 12. Transf 1974 to Clev.[2] *Parl* Seq 14. *Eccl* Seq 4. Eccl bdry: 1924 (help cr Preston upon Tees EP).[214]

EGGLESTON

Chap in Middleton in Teesdale AP, sep CP 1866,[1] sep EP 1744,[3] eccl refounded 1859.[215] *LG* Seq 7. Civ bdry: 1883,[12] 1884.[38] *Parl* Seq 8. *Eccl* Darl. RDn (1744—1874), Darl. RDn (1842—74), Darl. RDn (S'rn Dv) (1874—80), Darl. RDn (1880—1924), Barn. Cast. RDn (1924—*).

EIGHTON BANKS

EP Cr 1863 from Lamesley EP, Gateshead Fell EP.[216] Chest. le Str. RDn (1863—74), Chest. RDn (E'rn Dv) (1874—80), Chest. le Str. RDn (1880—1924), Gatesh. RDn (1924—*). Bdry: 1955,[217] 1964.[218]

ELDON

Tp in chap Shildon (sep CP 1866 from Auckland St Andrew AP,[1] sep EP 1837[22]), 'Eldon' a sep CP 1866,[1] sep EP 1877 from Auckland St Andrew AP, Shildon EP.[26] LG Darl. Wd, Auckl. PLU, RSD, RD. Abol civ 1937 pt to Shildon UD & CP, pt to Windlestone CP.[15] Parl S'rn Dv (1832—85), Bp Auckl. Dv (1885—1948). Eccl Darl. RDn (S'rn Dv) (1877—80), Auckl. RDn (1880—*).

ELSTOB

Tp in Great Stainton AP, sep CP 1866.[1] LG Seq 14. Parl Seq 13.

ELTON

AP Orig in co Sadberge (Northumb until 1189, Durham thereafter), considered a sep co until mid 15th cent, then in other Wds). Perhaps orig a chap in Norton AP, sep par by 1291.[219] LG Seq 12. Civ bdry: 1913,[220] 1951,[221] 1968 (loses pt to help cr Teeside CB [assoc with Yorks N Riding] & CP).[65] Transf 1974 to Clev.[2] Parl Seq 14. Parl bdry: 1952.[137] Eccl Seq 4.

ELVET

Tp in St Oswald AP (eccl, 'Durham St Oswald'), sep CP 1866.[1] LG Chest. Wd (until 1829), Durham Wd (from 1829), Elvet Barony & Bor (until 1835), Durham PLU, MB (pt 1835—94, ent 1894—1916), pt Durham USD, pt Durham RSD. Bdry: 1886,[222] 1894 (the pt not in Durham MB cr Bearpark CP).[47] Abol 1916 to help cr Durham CP.[173] Parl Pt Durham Parl Bor (1835—1918), pt N'rn Dv (1832—85), pt Mid Dv (1885—1918).

ELWICK

Pt in Durham (Islandshire), pt in Northumb (Bamburgh Wd), made ent Northumb 1832 for parl purposes, 1844 for civ purposes.[4] Tp in Norham AP, sep CP 1866.[1] LG Belford PLU. Parl Pt in Durham, pt in Northumb (until 1832), ent Northumb thereafter. For later civ and parl organisation, see entry in Northumb.

ELWICK

Tp in Hart AP, sep CP 1866.[1] LG Seq 13. Bdry: 1932,[177] 1967 (incl loses pt to Hartlepool CP to help constitute Hartl. CB [assoc with Durham]).[117] Transf 1974 to Clev.[2] Parl Seq 14.

ELWICK HALL

AP Orig in co Sadberge (Northumb until 1189, Durham thereafter, considered a sep co until mid 15th cent, then in other Wds). LG Seq 13. Transf 1974 to Clev.[2] Parl Seq 14. Eccl Durham RDn (until before 1535), Darl. RDn (before 1535—early 19th cent), Durham RDn (early 19th cent—1842), Stock. RDn (1842—80), Eas. RDn (1880—88), Hartl. RDn (1888—*).

EMBLETON

Chap in Sedgefield AP, sep CP 1866.[1] LG Seq 14. Parl Seq 13.

EPPLETON

Area in chap Hetton le Hole (sep CP 1866 from Houghton le Spring AP,[1] sep EP 1838 [tps Hetton le Hole, Great Eppleton, Little Eppleton][27]), 'Eppleton' a sep EP 1883 [tps Great Eppleton, Little Eppleton) from Hetton le Hole EP.[130] Hough. le Spr. RDn.

GREAT EPPLETON

Tp in chap Hetton le Hole (sep CP 1866 from Houghton le Spring AP,[1] sep EP 1838 [tps Hetton le Hole, Great Eppleton, Little Eppleton][27]), 'Eppleton' a sep CP 1866 from Houghton le Spring AP,[1] eccl severed 1883 from Hetton le Hole EP to help cr 'Eppleton' EP.[130] LG Eas. Wd, Hough. le Spr. PLU, RSD, RD. Abol civ 1937 to help cr Hetton CP in Hetton UD.[15] Parl N'rn Dv (1832—85), Hough. le Spr. Dv (1885—1918), Durham Dv (1918—48).

LITTLE EPPLETON

Orig status as tp, sep civ and eccl status (sequentially), civ and parl organisation as for Great Eppleton.

ESCOMB

Chap in Auckland St Andrew AP, sep civ identity early, sep EP 1743 (incl tps Bishop Auckland, Witton Park [the latter with no sep civ identity]),[3] eccl refounded 1893 by union Escomb EP (after reductions in 1834, 1845, 1869, 1872 as noted below), pt tp Pollard's Lands in Auckland St Andrew AP.[11] LG Darl. Wd, Auckl. PLU, RSD, RD. Civ bdry: 1883,[12] 1886.[13] Abol civ 1937 pt to Bp Auckl. UD & CP, pt to West Auckland CP, pt to help cr Crook & Willington UD & CP.[15] Parl S'rn Dv (1832—85), Bp Auckl. Dv (1885—1948). Eccl Auckl. RDn (1743—early 19th cent), Durham RDn (early 19th cent—1842), Darl. RDn (1842—74), Darl. RDn (N'rn Dv) (1874—80), Auckl. RDn (1880—*). Eccl bdry: 1834 (help cr Etherley EP),[17] 1845 (help cr Hunwick EP),[19] 1869 (cr Witton Park EP),[21] 1872 (cr Auckland St Peter EP).[170]

ESH

Chap in Lanchester AP, sep CP 1866,[1] sep EP 1733.[3] LG Chest. Wd (until 1829), Durham Wd (from 1829), Lanch. PLU, RSD, RD. Civ bdry: 1883,[12] 1887,[60] 1937,[15] 1946,[165] 1956.[166] Parl Seq 5. Eccl Lanch. RDn (until early 19th cent), Durham RDn (early 19th cent—1842), Chest. le Str. RDn (1842—74), Chest. RDn (W'rn Dv) (1874—80), Durham RDn (1880—91), Lanch. RDn (1891—*). Eccl bdry: 1873 (cr Hamsteels EP),[223] 1914 (help cr Ushaw Moor EP),[46] 1962.[41]

ETHERLEY

EP Cr 1834 from Escomb EP, Auckland St Helen EP (pt orig area tps Evenwood and Barony, Hunwick and Helmington).[17] Durham RDn (1834—42), Darl. RDn (1842—74), Darl. RDn (N'rn Dv) (1874—80), Auckl. RDn (1880—*).

CP Renaming 1939 of West Auckland CP.[16] LG Barn. Cast. RD. Bdry: 1946.[224] Parl Bp Auckl. CC (1948—*).

EVENWOOD

EP Cr 1863 by union areas orig tp Evenwood and Barony (after pt eccl severed 1834 to help cr Etherley EP[17]), detached pt tp West Auckland, each in Auckland St Helen EP.[18] Darl. RDn (1863—74),

Darl. RDn (N'rn Dv) (1874—80), Auckl. RDn (1880—1924), Barn. Cast. RDn (1924—*).

EVENWOOD AND BARONY
Tp in chap Auckland St Helen (sep civ identity early from Auckland St Andrew AP, sep EP 1724[3]), 'Evenwood and Barony' a sep CP 1866,[1] pt eccl severed 1834 to help cr Escomb EP,[17] the remainder eccl severed 1863 to help cr Evenwood EP.[18] Incl undivided pt Land Common to Evenwood and Barony and West Auckland (abol 1937 pt to Bp Auckl. UD & CP, pt to West Auckland CP[15]). LG Seq 5. Addtl civ bdry alt: 1883,[12] 1937,[15] 1946.[224] Parl Seq 7.

FARNE ISLANDS
Ex-par islands in Durham, transf to Northumb 1832 for parl purposes, 1844 for civ purposes.[4] LG Not in a Wd, Belford PLU. Parl In Durham until 1832, Northumb thereafter. For later civ and parl organisation, see entry in Northumb.

FATFIELD
EP Cr 1875 from Birtley EP, Usworth EP.[74] Chest. RDn (E'rn Dv) (1875—80), Chest. le Str. RDn (1880—*). Bdry: 1957,[139] 1963.[75]

FELKINGTON
Tp in Norham AP, sep CP 1866.[1] LG Norhamshire, Berwick PLU, transf to Northumb 1832 for parl purposes, 1844 for civ purposes.[4] Parl In Durham until 1832, Northumb thereafter. For later civ and parl organisation, see entry in Northumb.

FELLING
EP Cr 1866 from Heworth EP.[225] Chest. le Str. RDn (1866—74), Chest. RDn (E'rn Dv) (1874—80), Chest. le Str. RDn (1880—91), Gatesh. RDn (1891—*).

FERRYHILL
Tp in Merrington AP, sep CP 1866,[1] sep EP (incl tp Chilton in Merrington AP, tp Tudhoe in Whitworth AP).[143] LG Darl. Wd (until 1829), Durham Wd (from 1829), Sedg. PLU, RSD, RD. Civ bdry: 1886,[226] 1894 (the pt transf to Spennym. UD cr Low Spennymoor CP,[227] an addtl pt of this par also transf to Low Spennymoor CP[228]), 1946.[144] Parl Seq 11. Eccl Darl. RDn (1843—74), Darl. RDn (N'rn Dv) (1874—80), Eas. RDn (1880—*). Eccl bdry: 1865 (orig area of tp Tudhoe severed to help cr Tudhoe EP,[229] 1925 (help cr Chilton EP).[29]

FIRTREE
EP Cr 1862 from Witton le Wear EP (tp North Bedburn, pt main area Witton le Wear EP).[51] Darl. RDn (1862—74), Darl. RDn (N'rn Dv) (1874—80), Auckl. RDn (1880—*).

FISHBURN
Tp in Sedgefield AP, sep CP 1866.[1] LG Seq 14. Bdry: 1937.[15] Parl Seq 13.

FORD
Tp in Bishopwearmouth AP, sep CP 1866,[1] sep EP 1854 as 'South Hylton (Ford)',[77] qv. LG Eas. Wd, Sund. PLU, RSD, RD. Civ bdry: 1928 (loses pt to Sund. CB [assoc with Durham] & CP),[93] 1936 (loses pt to Sund. CB [assoc with Durham] & CP),[230] 1951 (loses pt to Sund. CB [assoc with Durham] & CP).[81] Abol civ 1967 pt to Sund. CB (assoc with Durham) & CP, pt to Hough. le Spr.

UD & AP.[231] Parl N'rn Dv (1832—85), Hough. le Spr. Dv/CC (1885—1970). Parl bdry: 1952.[232]

FOREST AND FRITH
Tp in Middleton in Teesdale AP, sep CP 1866,[1] sep EP 1875.[233] LG Seq 7. Parl Seq 8. Eccl Darl. RDn (S'rn Dv) (1875—80), Darl. RDn (1880—1924), Barn. Cast. RDn (1924—*).

FOXTON AND SHOTTON
Tp in Sedgefield AP, sep CP 1866,[1] eccl severed 1886 and transf to Stillington EP.[234] LG Seq 14. Parl Seq 13.

FRAMWELLGATE
Tp in chap Durham St Margaret (sep EP 1748 from Durham St Oswald AP[3]), 'Framwellgate' a sep CP 1866.[1] LG Chest. Wd (until 1829), Durham Wd (from 1829), Durham PLU, Framwellgate Bor (until 1565), Durham & Framwellgate Bor (1565—1835), Durham MB (pt 1835—94, ent 1894—1916), pt Durham USD, pt Durham RSD. Bdry: 1883,[12] 1886,[222] 1894 (the pt not in Durham MB cr Framwellgate Moor CP),[39] 1905.[172] Abol 1916 to help cr Durham CP.[173] Parl While tp and when CP: pt Durham & Framwellgate Parl Bor (1678—1832), Durham Parl Bor (pt 1832—67, ent 1867—1918), pt N'rn Dv (1832—67).

FRAMWELLGATE MOOR
CP Cr 1894 from the pt of Framwellgate CP not in Durham MB.[39] LG Durham PLU, RD. Bdry: 1905,[172] 1935,[49] 1937,[15] 1955.[193] Parl Durham Dv/CC (1918—*).

FROSTERLEY
EP Cr 1866 from Stanhope AP, Wolsingham AP.[235] Darl. RDn (1866—74), Darl. RDn (N'rn Dv) (1874—80), Stanh. RDn (1880—*).

FULWELL
Tp in Monkwearmouth AP, sep CP 1866,[1] eccl severed 1844 to help cr Monkwearmouth All Saints EP.[225] LG Chest. Wd (until 1829), Eas. Wd (from 1829), Sund. PLU, RSD, RD. Bdry: 1887.[236] Abol 1928 ent to Sund. CB (assoc with Durham) & CP.[93] Parl N'rn Dv (1832—85), Hough. le Spr. Dv (1885—1948).

GAINFORD
AP Orig in co Sadberge (Northumb until 1189, Durham thereafter, considered a sep co until mid 15th cent, then in other Wds). Incl chap Barnard Castle (sep CP 1866,[1] sep EP 1723,[3] eccl refounded 1850[37]), chap Denton (sep CP 1866,[1] sep EP 1837[3]), chap Whorlton (sep CP 1866,[1] sep EP 1767[3]), tp Bolam (sep CP 1866,[1] sep EP 1837 [incl tp Morton Tinmouth][99]), tp Morton Tinmouth (sep CP 1866,[1] eccl severed 1837 to help cr Bolam EP[99]), tp Summerhouse (sep CP 1866,[1] eccl severed 1932 and transf to Denton EP[187]), tps Headlam, Houghton le Side, Langton, Marwood, Piercebridge, Streatham and Stainton, Westham, pt tp Cleatlam (each a sep CP 1866[1]). LG Seq 7. Parl Seq 8. Eccl Seq 3. Addtl eccl bdry alt: 1932.[187]

GARMONDSWAY MOOR
Tp in Bishop Middleham AP, sep CP 1866,[1] later regarded as eccl ex-par.[237] LG Stock. Wd (until 1829), Durham Wd (from 1829), Sedg. PLU, RSD, RD. Abol 1937 pt to Fishburn CP, pt to Kelloe

AP.[15] *Parl* S'rn Dv (1832—85), S-E'rn Dv (1885—1918), Sedg. Dv (1918—48).

GATESHEAD

The following have 'Gateshead' in their names. Insofar as any existed at a given time: *LG* Chest. Wd, Gatesh. PLU, MB/CB, USD. *Parl* Gatesh. Parl Bor (1832—1948), pt Gatesh. East BC, pt Gatesh. West BC (1948—*). *Eccl* Durham RDn (before 1291—before 1535), Chest. le Str. RDn (before 1535—early 19th cent), Durham RDn (early 19th cent—1842), Chest. le Str. RDn (1842—74), Chest. RDn (E'rn Dv) (1874—80), Chest. le Str. RDn (1880—91), Gatesh. RDn (1891—*).

AP1—GATESHEAD [ST MARY]—Civ bdry: 1907 (gains Heworth Within CP),[238] 1933,[239] 1936,[97] 1954.[240] Transf 1974 to Tyne & Wear.[2] Eccl bdry: 1809 (cr EP11),[241] 1864 (cr EP2),[58] 1864 (cr EP9),[242] 1865 (cr EP5),[243] 1865 (cr EP6),[244] 1865,[140] 1874 (cr EP1),[245] 1876 (help cr EP8),[94] 1966 (gains EP2),[246] 1973 (gains EP6, EP10).[247]

EP1—GATESHEAD CHRIST CHURCH—Cr 1874 from AP1.[245] Bdry: 1904 (help cr EP7).[248]

EP2—GATESHEAD HOLY TRINITY—Cr 1864 from AP1.[58] Abol 1966 ent to AP1.[246]

EP3—GATESHEAD ST AIDAN—Cr 1889 from Low Team EP, EP5.[99]

EP4—GATESHEAD ST CHAD, BENSHAM—Cr 1909 from EP5.[249]

EP5—GATESHEAD ST CUTHBERT—Cr 1865 from AP1.[76] Commonly called 'Gateshead St Cuthbert, Bensham'. Bdry: 1871 (cr Low Team EP),[95] 1876 (help cr EP8),[94] 1889 (help cr EP3),[99] 1900 (cr EP4).[249]

EP6—GATESHEAD ST EDMUND—Cr 1865 from AP1, Heworth EP, EP11.[244] Bdry: 1885 (help cr EP10).[250] Abol 1973 ent to AP1.[247]

EP7—GATESHEAD ST GEORGE—Cr 1904 from EP1, EP11, Heworth EP.[248]

EP8—GATESHEAD ST HELEN—Cr 1876 from EP11, AP1, EP5.[94]

EP9—GATESHEAD ST JAMES—Cr 1864 from AP1.[242] Bdry: 1885 (help cr EP10).[250]

—GATESHEAD ST PAUL—see LOW TEAM

EP10—GATESHEAD THE VENERABLE BEDE—Cr 1885 from EP6, EP9.[250] Abol 1973 ent to AP1.[247]

EP11—GATESHEAD FELL [ST JOHN]—Cr 1809 from AP1.[241] Bdry: 1863 (cr Eighton Banks EP),[216] 1865 (help cr EP6),[244] 1876 (help cr EP8),[94] 1904 (help cr EP7),[248] 1964.[218]

GILLIGATE—see DURHAM ST GILES (eccl), ST GILES (civ)

GRANGETOWN

EP Cr 1911 from Ryhope EP.[120] Bdry: 1952,[90] 1970.[91]

GREATHAM

AP Orig (except for area Claxton) in co Sadberge (Northumb until 1189, Durham thereafter, considered a sep co until mid 15th cent, then in other Wds). By 16th cent gains chap Claxton (orig chap in Billingham, transf to Greatham by 16th cent,[149] 'Claxton' a sep CP 1866[1]). *LG* Seq 13. Addtl civ bdry alt: 1946,[251] 1953 (loses pt to W Hartl. CB [assoc with Durham] & CP),[178] 1967 (loses pt to Hartlepool CP to help constitute Hartl. CB [assoc

with Durham]).[117] Transf 1974 to Clev.[2] *Parl* Seq 14. Parl bdry: 1953.[179] *Eccl* Durham RDn (before 1291—before 1535), Darl. RDn (before 1535—early 19th cent), Durham RDn (early 19th cent—1842), Stock. RDn (1842—88), Hartl. RDn (1888—*).

GREENCROFT

Tp in Lanchester AP, sep CP 1866,[1] pt eccl severed 1843 to help cr Collierley EP.[71] *LG* Seq 2. Bdry: 1883,[12] 1887,[60] 1896 (loses pt to help cr Annfield Plain UD as 'Greencroft Within' CP).[252] *Parl* Seq 5.

GREENCROFT WITHIN

CP in 1896 from the pt of Greencroft CP to help constitute Annfield Plain UD.[252] *LG* Lanch. PLU, Annfield Plain UD. Abol 1937 ent to Stanley UD & CP.[15] *Parl* Consett Dv (1918—48).

GREENSIDE

EP Cr 1886 from Ryton AP.[235] Ryton RDn (1886—91), Chest. le Str. RDn (1891—*).

GRINDON

AP Incl tp Whitton (sep CP 1866,[1] eccl severed 1872 to help cr Stillington EP[243]). *LG* Seq 12. Addtl civ bdry alt: 1937,[15] 1968 (loses pt to help cr Teeside CB [assoc with Yorks N Riding] & CP).[65] Transf 1974 to Clev.[2] *Parl* Seq 14. *Eccl* Darl. RDn (before 1291—early 19th cent), Durham RDn (early 19th cent—1842), Stock. RDn (1842—*).

GRINDON

Tp in Norham AP, sep CP 1866.[1] *LG* Norhamshire, Berwick PLU, transf to Northumb 1832 for parl purposes, 1844 for civ purposes.[4] *Parl* In Durham until 1832, Northumb thereafter. For later civ and parl organisation, see entry in Northumb.

HAMSTEELS

EP Cr 1873 from Esh EP.[223] Chest. le Str. RDn (1873—74), Chest. RDn (W'rn Dv) (1874—80), Durham RDn (1880—91), Lanch. RDn (1891—*).

HAMSTERLEY

Chap in Auckland St Andrew AP, sep civ identity early, sep EP 1724.[3] Incl tp South Bedburn (sep CP 1866,[1] pt eccl severed 1850 to help cr Lynesack EP[22]), tp Lynesack and Softley (sep CP 1866,[1] pt eccl severed 1850 to help cr Lynesack EP[22]); after 1866 incl undivided pt Undivided Moor Common to Lynesack and Softley, Hamsterley and South Bedburn. *LG* Seq 5. Addtl civ bdry alt: 1883,[12] 1885.[72] *Parl* Seq 8. *Eccl* Auckl. RDn (1724—early 19th cent), Durham RDn (early 19th cent—1842), Darl. RDn (1842—74), Darl. RDn (N'rn Dv) (1874—80), Auckl. RDn (1880—*).

HARRATON

Tp in Chester le Street AP, sep CP 1866,[1] eccl severed 1850 to help cr Birtley EP.[52] *LG* Seq 1. Bdry: 1883,[253] 1937.[15] Abol 1937, the pt remaining in Durham cr North Lodge CP, the pt transf to Tyne and Wear (incl the pt in Wash. New Town) not to be in a par.[2] *Parl* Seq 1.

HARROWGATE HILL

CP Cr 1894 from the pts in Darl. MB of Cockerton CP, Haughton le Skerne AP.[158] *LG* Darl. PLU, MB. Abol 1907 ent to Darlington AP.[254]

HART

AP Orig in co Sadberge (Northumb until 1189, Durham thereafter, considered a sep co until mid 15th cent, then in other Wds). Tp 'Hart' in Stock. Wd as were area Hartlepool (sep civ identity early, sep EP 1724[3]), tps Dalton Piercy, Elwick, Throston (each a sep CP 1866[1]); incl in Eas. Wd tps Nesbitt, Thorpe Bulmer (each a sep CP 1866[1]). *LG* Hartl. PLU, RSD, RD (1894—1936), Stock. RD (1936—74). Addtl civ bdry alt: 1897,[25] 1936,[97] 1967 (loses pt to Hartlepool CP to help constitute Hartl. CB [assoc with Durham]).[117] Transf 1974 to Clev.[2] *Parl* Seq 14. *Eccl* Durham RDn (before 1291—before 1535), Darl. RDn (before 1535—early 19th cent), Stock. RDn (early 19th cent—1842), Stock. RDn (1842—80), Eas. RDn (1880—88), Hartl. RDn (1888—*). Eccl bdry: 1853 (cr Hartlepool Holy Trinity EP),[256] 1926 (help cr West Hartlepool St Luke EP),[257] 1954,[258] 1957,[259] 1974.[82]

EAST HARTBURN

Tp in chap Stockton on Tees (sep par 1713 from Norton AP[260]), 'East Hartburn' a sep CP 1866.[1] Stock. Wd, PLU, RSD, RD. Abol 1913 pt to Stock. on Tees MB & CP, pt to Elton AP.[220] *Parl* S'rn Dv (1832—85), S-E'rn Dv (1885—1918).

HARTLEPOOL

The following have 'Hartlepool' in their names. Insofar as any existed at a given time: *LG* Orig in co Sadberge (Northumb until 1189, Durham thereafter, considered a sep co until mid 15th cent, then in other Wds). *LG* Stock. Wd, Hartl. PLU; MB, CB, USD sep noted. *Parl* S'rn Dv (1832—67), The Hartlepools Parl Bor (1867—*). *Eccl* Darl. RDn (cr—early 19th cent), Durham RDn (early 19th cent—1842), Stock. RDn (1842—88), Hartl. RDn (1888—*).

EP1/EP1—HARTLEPOOL [ST HILDA]—Area in Hart AP, sep civ identity early, sep EP 1724.[3] Hartl. MB (1850—1967), USD, CB (1967—74). Civ bdry: 1932,[177] 1936,[97] 1967 (incl gains W Hartl. CB [assoc with Durham] & CP, gains Seaton CP).[117] Transf 1974 to Clev.[2] Eccl bdry: 1954.[258]

EP2—HARTLEPOOL ALL SAINTS, STRANTON—Renaming 1968 of Stranton AP.[76] Abol 1973 pt to help cr Stranton All Saints EP, pt to EP5, pt to EP8.[261]

EP3—HARTLEPOOL CHRIST CHURCH—Renaming 1968 of EP9.[76] Bdry: 1957.[75] Abol 1973, pt to help cr Stranton All Saints EP, pt to EP7, pt to EP8.[261]

EP4—HARTLEPOOL HOLY TRINITY—Cr 1853 from Hart AP.[256] Bdry: 1954,[258] 1974.[262]

EP5—HARTLEPOOL ST AIDAN—Renaming 1968 of EP10.[76] Bdry: 1973.[261]

EP6-HARTLEPOOL ST LUKE—Renaming 1968 of EP12.[76] Bdry: 1974.[262]

EP7—HARTLEPOOL ST OSWALD—Renaming 1968 of EP13.[76] Bdry: 1973.[261]

EP8—HARTLEPOOL ST PAUL—Renaming 1968 of EP14.[76] Bdry: 1973.[261]

CP2—WEST HARTLEPOOL—Cr 1894 from the pt of Stranton AP in W Hartl. MB.[47] W Hartl. MB

(1894—1902), CB (1902—67). Bdry: 1897,[263] 1921 (gains Seaton Carew CP),[264] 1932.[177] Abol 1967 to help cr Hartl. CB (assoc with Durham) & CP.[117] Parl bdry: 1953.[179]

EP9—WEST HARTLEPOOL CHRIST CHURCH—Cr 1855 from Stranton AP,[3] refounded 1859.[265] Bdry: 1870 (cr EP11),[181] 1901,[266] 1904 (cr EP13),[267] 1957.[75] Renamed 1968 as EP3.[76]

EP10—WEST HARTLEPOOL ST AIDAN—Cr 1891 from Stranton AP, Seaton Carew EP.[268] Bdry: 1932,[125] 1957.[259] Renamed 1968 as EP5.[76]

EP11—WEST HARTLEPOOL ST JAMES—Cr 1870 from EP9.[181] Bdry: 1898.[204] Abol 1957, pt to EP9, pt to Stranton AP.[75]

EP12—WEST HARTLEPOOL ST LUKE—Cr 1926 from EP14, Hart AP.[257] Bdry: 1957.[259] Renamed 1968 as EP6.[76]

EP13—WEST HARTLEPOOL ST OSWALD—Cr 1904 from EP9.[267] Renamed 1968 as EP7.[76]

EP14—WEST HARTLEPOOL ST PAUL—Cr 1886 from Stranton AP.[269] Bdry: 1901,[266] 1926 (help cr EP12).[257] Renamed 1968 as EP8.[76]

HARTON

Tp in Jarrow AP, sep CP 1866,[1] eccl severed 1845 to help cr South Shields [St Hilda] EP,[270] pt of orig area tp severed 1848 from the latter to help cr South Shields Holy Trinity EP,[271] 'Harton' a sep EP 1864 from South Shields EP, South Shields Holy Trinity EP.[272] *LG* Chest. Wd, S Shields PLU, pt Southwick on Wear USD (1887), S Shields RSD (ent 1875—87, pt 1887, ent 1887—94), S Shields RD (1894—1921). Civ bdry: 1883,[12] 1887,[236] 1901 (loses pt to S Shields CB [assoc with Durham] & CP).[102] Abol civ 1921 pt to S Shields CB (assoc with Durham) & CP, pt to Whitburn AP.[103] *Parl* N'rn Dv (1832—85), Jarrow Dv (1885—1948). *Eccl* Chest. le Str. RDn (1864—74), Chest. RDn (E'rn Dv) (1874—80), Jarrow RDn (1880—*). Eccl bdry: 1890 (help cr Harton Colliery EP),[274] 1951,[151] 1952 (help cr Cleadon Park St Cuthbert EP),[152] 1967.[155]

WEST HARTON—see following entry

HARTON COLLIERY

EP Cr 1890 from Harton EP, South Shields St Simon EP.[274] Jarrow RDn. Bdry: 1903 (help cr South Shields St Oswin EP),[275] 1930,[107] 1954,[259] 1961,[108] 1967.[155] Sometimes 'West Harton'.

HASWELL

Tp in Easington AP, sep CP 1866,[1] pts eccl severed 1863 to help cr 2 EPs of Shotton with Haswell, South Hetton,[203] 'Haswell' a sep EP 1870 from Shotton with Haswell EP.[204] *LG* Seq 9. Civ bdry: 1914,[276] 1921,[274] 1946,[128] 1954.[161] *Parl* Seq 6. *Eccl* Eas. RDn (1870—74), Eas. RDn (S'rn Dv) (1874—80), Eas. RDn (1880—*).

HAUGHTON LE SKERNE

AP Pt (areas of Coatham Mundeville, Sadberge) in co Sadberge (Northumb until 1189, Durham thereafter, considered a sep co until mid 15th cent, then in other Wds). Tp 'Haughton le Skerne' in Darl. Wd as were tps Barmpton, Great Burdon (each a sep CP 1866[1]); incl in Stock. Wd (until 1829), Darl. Wd (from 1829) chap Sadberge (sep CP 1866,[1] sep EP 1856[278]), *LG* Darl. PLU, pt Darl. MB (1872—

94), pt Darl. USD, pt Darl. RSD, Darl. RD. Addtl civ bdry alt: 1894 (loses the pt in the MB to help cr Harrowgate Hill CP),[158] 1915 (loses pt to Darlington AP as the enlarged Darl. MB constituted Darl. CB [assoc with Durham]).[9] Abol civ 1930 pt to Darl. CB (assoc with Durham) & AP, pt to Barmpton CP.[10] *Parl* S'rn Dv (1832—67), Darl. Parl Bor (1867—1918), Sedg. Dv (1918—48). *Eccl* Seq 2. Addtl eccl bdry alt: 1929 (help cr Darlington St Mark EP),[43] 1965.[56]

HAVERTON HILL
EP Cr 1862 from Billingham AP.[51] Stock. RDn (1862—88), Hartl. RDn (1888—1924), Stock. RDn (1924—*). Bdry: 1937.[67]

HAWTHORN
Tp in Easington AP, sep CP 1866,[1] pt eccl severed 1863 to help cr South Hetton EP,[203] the remainder cr 1864 'Hawthorn' EP.[23] *LG* Seq 9. Civ bdry: 1914,[276] 1921,[271] 1946,[128] 1956.[161] *Parl* Seq 6. *Eccl* Eas. RDn (1864—74), Eas. RDn (S'rn Dv) (1874—80), Eas. RDn (1880—*). Eccl bdry: 1962.[176]

HEADLAM
Tp in Gainford AP, sep CP 1866.[1] *LG* Seq 7. *Parl* Seq 8.

HEALEYFIELD
Tp in Lanchester AP, sep CP 1866.[1] *LG* Seq 2. Bdry: 1883,[12] 1887,[60] 1887,[61] 1894,[62] 1920,[164] 1937.[15] *Parl* N'rn Dv (1832—85), N-W'rn Dv (1885—1918), Consett Dv (1918—48), N W Durham CC (1948—*).

HEATHERYCLEUGH
EP Cr 1827 from Stanhope AP,[3] refounded 1866.[273] Durham RDn (1827—42), Darl. RDn (1842—74), Darl. RDn (N'rn Dv) (1874—80), Stanh. RDn (1880—*).

HEBBURN
CP Cr 1894 from the pt of Hedworth, Monkton and Jarrow CP in Hebburn UD.[47] *LG* S Shields PLU, Hebburn UD. Bdry: 1936.[97] Transf 1974 to Tyne & Wear.[2] *Parl* Jarrow Dv/CC (1918—70), Jarrow BC (1970—*).

HEBBURN ST CUTHBERT
EP Cr 1875 from Jarrow AP.[274] Chest. RDn (E'rn Dv) (1875—80), Jarrow RDn (1880—*). Bdry: 1881 (cr Hebburn St Oswald EP),[275] 1885 (cr Hebburn St John EP),[279] 1901.[274]

HEBBURN ST JOHN
EP Cr 1885 from Hebburn St Cuthbert EP.[279] Jarrow RDn. Bdry: 1901.[274]

HEBBURN ST OSWALD
EP Cr 1881 from Hebburn St Cuthbert EP.[275] Jarrow RDn.

HEDGEFIELD
EP Cr 1914 from Ryton AP.[277] Chest. le Str. RDn.

HEDLEY—see LAMESLEY

HEDLEYHOPE
Tp in Brancepeth AP, sep CP 1866,[1] pt eccl severed 1735 to help cr Satley EP.[3] *LG* Darl. Wd, Lanch. PLU, pt Tow Law USD, pt Lanch. RSD, Lanch. RD. Bdry: 1894 (loses the pt in Tow Law UD to help cr South Cornsay CP),[62] 1956.[166] *Parl* S'rn Dv (1832—85), N-W'rn Dv (1885—1918), Spennym.

Dv (1918—48), N W Durham CC (1948—*).

HEDWORTH
EP Cr 1878 from Harrow AP, Boldon AP, Monkwearmouth AP, Whitburn AP[106]; for civ see following entry. Chest. RDn (E'rn Dv) (1878—80), Jarrow RDn (1880—*). Bdry: 1920 (help cr East Boldon EP),[51] 1954,[259] 1969.[160]

HEDWORTH, MONKTON AND JARROW
Tp in Jarrow AP, sep CP 1866[1]; for eccl see prev entry. *LG* Chest. Wd, S Shields PLU, pt Jarrow MB & USD (1875—94), pt Hebburn USD, pt S Shields RSD. Bdry: 1887.[236] Abol 1894 the pt in Jarrow MB cr Jarrow CP, the pt in Hebburn UD cr Hebburn CP, the remainder cr Monkton CP.[39] *Parl* N'rn Dv (1832—85), Jarrow Dv (1885—1918).

HEIGHINGTON
AP Incl tps School Aycliffe, Coatsay Moor, Redworth, Walworth, pt tp Middridge Grange (each a sep CP 1866[1]), tp Killerby (sep CP 1866,[1] eccl severed 1850 and transf to Ingleton AP).[278] *LG* Seq 4. Addtl civ bdry alt: 1883,[12] 1884,[280] 1884 (gains Coatsay Moor CP),[156] 1885,[33] 1885,[72] 1937,[15] 1946 (gains School Aycliffe CP),[34] 1952,[128] 1969,[32] 1974 (loses the pt in Sedg. Dist to Great Aycliffe CP, the remainder to be in Darl. Dist).[2] *Parl* Seq 12. Parl bdry: 1953.[179] *Eccl* Seq 1. Eccl bdry: 1961 (incl help cr Newton Aycliffe EP),[28] 1945.[100]

HELMINGTON ROW
Tp in Brancepeth AP, sep CP 1866.[1] *LG* Darl. Wd, Auckl. PLU, RSD, RD. Bdry: 1881.[281] Abol 1937 to help cr Crook & Willington UD & CP.[15] *Parl* S'rn Dv (1832—85), Bp Auckl. Dv (1885—1918), Spennym. Dv (1918—48).

HENDON [ST PAUL]
EP Cr 1854 from Bishopwearmouth AP.[77] Eas. RDn (1854—74), Eas. RDn (N'rn Dv) (1874—80), Wearm. RDn (1880—*). Bdry: 1876 (cr Middle Hendon EP),[157] 1889 (cr Hendon St Ignatius EP),[99] 1970 (incl gains Hendon St Ignatius EP).[91]

HENDON ST IGNATIUS
EP Cr 1889 from Hendon EP.[99] Wearm. RDn. Abol 1970 ent to Hendon EP.[91]

MIDDLE HENDON
EP Cr 1876 from Hendon EP.[157] Eas. RDn (N'rn Dv) (1876—80), Wearm. RDn (1880—9170). Bdry: 1906,[185] 1950.[276] Abol 1970 pt to Hendon EP, pt to Bishopwearmouth Christ Church EP, pt to Grangetown EP.[91]

HERRINGTON
EP Cr 1884 from Newbottle EP.[111] Hough. le Spr. RDn. Bdry: 1913 (help cr Shiney Row EP),[282] 1950,[76] 1962 (cr East Herrington EP).[283]
CP Cr 1946 by union pts East and Middle Herrington CP, West Herrington CP, Silksworth CP.[284] *LG* Sund. RD. Civ bdry: 1951 (loses pt to Sund. CB [assoc with Durham] & CP).[285] Abol 1967 pt to Sund. CB (assoc with Durham) & CP, pt to Hough. le Spr. UD & AP.[231] *Parl* Hough. le Spr. CC (1948—70). Parl bdry: 1952.[232]

EAST HERRINGTON
EP Cr 1962 from Herrington EP.[283] Wearm. RDn.

EAST AND MIDDLE HERRINGTON
Tp in Houghton le Spring AP, sep CP 1866.[1] *LG*

Eas. Wd, Hough. le Spr. PLU, RSD, RD (1894—1937), Sund. RD (1937—46). Bdry: 1886,[286] 1937.[15] Abol 1946 pt to help cr Herrington CP, pt to Offerton CP.[284] *Parl* N'rn Dv (1832—85), Hough. le Spr. Dv (1885—1948).

WEST HERRINGTON
Tp in Houghton le Spring AP, sep CP 1866.[1] *LG*, civ bdry alt, civ abol, *Parl* as for East and Middle Herrington.

HETT
Tp in Merrington AP, sep CP 1866.[1] *LG* Seq 8. Bdry: 1937 (help cr Spennymoor CP in Spennym. UD).[15] *Parl* Seq 10.

HETTON
CP Cr 1937 by union Great Eppleton CP, Little Eppleton CP, Hetton le Hole CP, Moorsley CP and pts Pittington AP, East Rainton CP.[15] *LG* Hetton UD. Transf 1974 to Tyne & Wear.[2] *Parl* Durham CC (1948—70), Hough. le Spr. CC (1970—*).

SOUTH HETTON
EP Cr 1863 from Easington AP (pt tps Haswell, Hawthorn).[203] Eas. RDn (1863—74), Eas. RDn (S'rn Dv) (1874—80), Eas. RDn (1880—*). Bdry: 1962.[176]

HETTON LE HOLE
Chap in Houghton le Spring AP, sep CP 1866,[1] sep EP 1838 (incl tps Great Eppleton, Little Eppleton).[27] *LG* Eas. Wd, Hough. le Spr. PLU, RSD, RD (1894—95), Hetton UD (1895—1937). Abol civ 1937 to help cr Hetton CP.[15] *Parl* N'rn Dv (1832—85), Hough. le Spr. Dv (1885—1918), Durham Dv (1918—48). *Eccl* Durham RDn (1838—42), Eas. RDn (1842—74), Eas. RDn (N'rn Dv) (1874—80), Hough. le Spr. RDn (1880—*). Eccl bdry: 1869 (help cr Lyons EP),[142] 1883 (cr Eppleton EP),[130] 1956,[287] 1974.[288]

HEWORTH [ST MARY]
Chap in Jarrow AP, sep CP 1866,[1] sep EP 1815.[3] *LG* Chest. Wd, Gatesh. PLU, pt Gatesh. MB (1835—89), pt Gatesh. CB (1889—94), pt Felling USD, Felling UD. Civ bdry: 1894 (the pt in Gatesh. CB cr Heworth Within CP),[39] 1936,[97] 1954 (loses pt to Gatesh. CB [assoc with Durham] & AP).[240] Transf 1974 to Tyne & Wear.[2] *Parl* Pt Gatesh. Parl Bor (1832—1918), pt N'rn Dv (1832—85), Jarrow Dv (pt 1885—1918, ent 1918—51), Jarrow BC (1951—55), Gatesh. East BC (1955—*). *Eccl* Durham RDn (1815—42), Chest. RDn (1842—74), Chest. RDn (E'rn Dv) (1874—80), Jarrow RDn (1880—1924), Gatesh. RDn (1924—*). Eccl bdry: 1843 (cr Heworth St Alban EP),[289] 1865 (help cr Gateshead St Edmund EP),[244] 1865,[140] 1866 (cr Felling EP),[225] 1904 (help cr Gateshead St George EP),[248] 1955.[217] Sometimes eccl called 'Windynook'.

HEWORTH ST ALBAN
EP Cr 1843 from Heworth CP.[289] RDns as for Heworth, from 1843.

HEWORTH WITHIN
CP Cr 1894 from the pt of Heworth CP in Gatesh. CB.[39] *LG* Gatesh. PLU, CB. Abol 1907 ent to Gateshead AP.[238]

HILTON
Tp in tp (chap built 1843) Ingleton (sep CP 1866 from Staindrop AP,[1] sep EP 1845 (incl tps Hilton, Wackerfield[109]), 'Hilton' a sep CP 1866.[1] *LG* Seq 7. *Parl* Seq 8.

HOLMSIDE
EP Cr 1865 from Lanchester AP, Chester le Street AP, Witton Gilbert with Kimblesworth EP, Tanfield EP.[140] Chest. le Str. RDn (1865—74), Chest. RDn (W'rn Dv) (1874—80), Durham RDn (1880—91), Lanch. RDn (1891—*). Bdry: 1897,[41] 1912 (help cr South Moor EP),[42] 1912 (cr Craghead EP),[168] 1912,[43] 1914 (help cr Annfield Plain EP).[5]

HOLY ISLAND
AP Tp 'Holy Island' in Durham (Islandshire) as were chap Ancroft (sep civ identity early, sep EP 1733[3]), chap Kyloe (sep civ identity early, sep EP 1738[3]), chap Tweedmouth (sep civ identity early, sep EP 1737[3]), all these transf to Northumb 1832 for parl purposes, 1844 for civ purposes[4]; incl in Northumb (Glendale Wd) chap Lowick (sep civ identity early, sep EP 1732[3]). *LG* Holy Island Bor (status not sustained), Berwick PLU. *Parl* In Durham until 1832, Northumb thereafter. For later civ and parl organisation, and for ent eccl organisation, see entry in Northumb.

HORDEN
Area in Easington AP, sep EP 1913,[207] sep CP 1947 from Shotton CP (orig in Easington, qv).[290] *LG* Eas. RD. Civ bdry: 1956 (help cr Peterlee CP).[206] *Parl* Eas. CC (1948—*). *Eccl* Eas. RDn (1913—24), Hartl. RDn (1924—*). Eccl bdry: 1956,[69] 1957 (help cr Peterlee EP).[208]

HORNCLIFFE
Tp in Norham AP, transf with the latter to Northumb 1832 for parl purposes, 1844 for civ purposes,[4] 'Horncliffe' a sep CP 1866 in Northumb.[1] *LG* Norhamshire, Berwick PLU. *Parl* In Durham until 1832, Northumb thereafter. For later civ and parl organisation, see entry in Northumb.

HOUGHTON LE SIDE
Tp in chap Denton (sep CP 1866 from Gainford,[1] sep EP 1837[3]). *LG* Seq 4. *Parl* Seq 12.

HOUGHTON LE SPRING
AP Incl chap Hetton le Hole (sep CP 1866,[1] sep EP 1838 [incl tps Great Eppleton, Little Eppleton][27]), chap Penshaw (sep CP 1866,[1] sep EP 1752 [incl tps South Biddick, Burnmoor],[3] eccl refounded 1838,[27] orig area tps South Biddick, Burmoor eccl severed 1866 to cr Burnmoor EP[66]), chap West Rainton (sep CP 1866,[1] 'Rainton' a sep EP 1836 [tps East Rainton, West Rainton, Cocken, Moor House, Moorsley[27]], tps South Biddick, Burnmoor (each a sep CP 1866,[1] each eccl severed 1752 to help cr Penshaw EP,[3] each eccl severed 1866 from the latter to help cr Burnmoor EP[66]), tps Cocken, Moor House, Moorsley, East Rainton, West Rainton (each a sep CP 1866, together constituted 1752 'Rainton' EP[27]), tp Great Eppleton, Little Eppleton (each a sep CP 1866,[1] each eccl severed 1838 to help cr Hetton le Hole EP[27]), tp Newbottle (sep CP 1866,[1] pt eccl severed 1752 to help cr Penshaw EP,[3] qv for refounding 1838, the remainder cr 1865

'Newbottle' EP[291]), tps East and Middle Herrington, West Herrington, Morton Grange, Offerton, Warden Law (each a sep CP 1866[1]). *LG* Eas. Wd (ent until 1829, pt 1829—66 [all except pts transf 1829 to Durham Wd], ent from 1866), pt Durham Wd (1829—66: Moor House, Moorsley), Hough. le Spr. PLU, USD, UD. Addtl civ bdry alt: 1967 (incl gains pt Sund. CB [assoc with Durham] & AP).[118] Transf 1974 to Tyne & Wear.[2] *Parl* N'rn Dv (1832—85), Hough. le Spr. Dv/CC (1885—*). *Eccl* Durham RDn (before 1291—before 1535), Darl. RDn (before 1535—early 19th cent), Eas. RDn (1842—74), Eas. RDn (N'rn Dv) (1874—80), Hough. le Spr. RDn (1880—*). Addtl eccl bdry alt: 1872 (help cr Chilton Moor EP).[145]

HUNSTANWORTH
Chap in Edmondbyers AP, sep CP 1866,[1] sep EP 1747.[3] *LG* Seq 3. *Parl* Seq 5. *Eccl* Chest. le Str. RDn (1727—early 19th cent), Durham RDn (early 19th cent—1842), Chest. le Str. RDn (1842—74), Chest. RDn (W'rn Dv) (1874—80), Stanh. RDn (1880—1930), Corbridge RDn (dioc Newc, 1930—*).

HUNWICK
EP Cr 1845 from Auckland St Andrew AP (tp Hunwick and Helmington [for civ, see following entry], pt tp Newton Cap), Escomb EP.[19] Darl. RDn (1845—74), Darl. RDn (N'rn Dv) (1874—80), Auckl. RDn (1880—*).

HUNWICK AND HELMINGTON
Tp in Auckland St Andrew AP, sep CP 1866,[1] eccl severed 1845 to help cr Hunwick EP.[19] *LG* Darl. Wd, Auckl. PLU, RSD, RD. Bdry: 1883,[3] 1885.[72] Abol civ 1937 to help cr Crook & Willington UD & CP.[15] *Parl* S'rn Dv (1832—85), Bp Auckl. Dv (1885—1918), Spennym. Dv (1918—48).

HURWORTH
AP Orig in co Sadberge (Northumb until 1189, Durham thereafter, considered a sep co until mid 15th cent, then in other Wds). Incl tp Neasham (sep CP 1866[1]). *LG* Seq 16. Addtl civ bdry alt: 1967 (incl exchanges pts with Darl. CB [assoc with Durham] & AP).[96] *Parl* Seq 12. *Eccl* Seq 5.

HUTTON HENRY
Tp in Monk Hesleden AP, sep CP 1866.[1] *LG* Seq 9. Bdry: 1956.[129] *Parl* Seq 6.

HYLTON
Tp in Monkwearmouth AP, sep CP 1866,[1] eccl severed 1847 to help cr Southwick EP (area of tps North Hylton, South Hylton, neither sep civ [for former eccl, see following entry])[292]). *LG* Chest. Wd (until 1829), Eas. Wd (from 1829), Sund. PLU, RSD, RD. Civ bdry: 1937,[15] 1951 (loses pt to Sund. CB [assoc with Durham] & CP).[285] Abol civ 1967 pt to Sund. CB (assoc with Durham) & CP, pt to Wash. UD & AP.[118] *Parl* N'rn Dv (1832—85), Hough. le Spr. Dv/CC (1885—1970). Parl bdry: 1952.[232]

NORTH HYLTON
EP Cr 1874 from Southwick EP (tp North Hylton, not sep civ [for 'Hylton', see prev entry]).[277] Chest. RDn (E'rn Dv) (1874—80), Wearm. RDn (1880—*). Bdry: 1951,[73] 1958.[293] Sometimes called 'North

Hylton St Margaret, Castletown' or 'Castletown'.

SOUTH HYLTON (FORD)
Tp in Bishopwearmouth AP, sep EP 1854,[3] sep CP 1866 as 'Ford',[1] qv. Eas. RDn (1854—74), Eas. RDn (N'rn Dv) (1874—80), Wearm. RDn (1880—*). Bdry: 1950,[76] 1951,[294] 1951,[73] 1951 (cr Bishopwearmouth Good Shepherd EP).[92]

INGLETON
Tp (chap built 1843) in Staindrop AP, sep CP 1866,[1] sep EP 1845 (incl tps Hilton, Wackerfield).[109] *LG* Seq 7. *Parl* Seq 8. *Eccl* Darl. RDn (1845—74), Darl. RDn (S'rn Dv) (1874—80), Darl. RDn (1880—*). Eccl bdry: 1850 (gains tp Killerby from Heighington AP),[278] 1932,[187] 1945 (gains area Morton Tinmouth CP in Bolam AP).[100]

IVESTON
Tp in Lanchester AP, sep CP 1866.[1] *LG* Chest. Wd, Lanch. PLU, pt Leadgate USD (enlarged pt 1884—94), pt Consett USD, Leadgate UD. Bdry: 1883,[12] 1887,[60] 1888 (the detached pt [gained 1883 from Greencroft CP] incl in Leadgate USD), 1894 (gains the pt of Medomsley CP in Leadgate USD, loses the pt in Consett UD to help cr Consett CP).[62] Abol 1937 pt to Consett UD & CP, pt to Stanley UD & CP.[15] *Parl* N'rn Dv (1832—85), N-W'rn Dv (1885—1918), Consett Dv (1918—48).

JARROW
AP Incl chap Heworth (sep CP 1866,[1] sep EP 1815[3]), chap Westoe (sep CP 1866,[1] sep EP 1821,[3] eccl refounded 1864 [qv for constituent pars then][295]), tps Harton; Hedworth, Monkton and Jarrow (each a sep CP 1866[1]), tp South Shields (sep CP 1866,[1] sep EP [St Hilda] 1845[270]) so that 'Jarrow' has no sep civ identity 1866—94 (see following entry). *LG* Chest. Wd. *Parl* N'rn Dv (1832—67). *Eccl* Durham RDn (until 1842), Chest. le Str. RDn (1842—74), Chest. RDn (E'rn Dv) (1874—80), Jarrow RDn (1880—*). Addtl eccl bdry alt: 1868 (cr Jarrow Grange EP),[296] 1875 (cr Hebburn St Cuthbert EP),[274] 1878 (cr Hedworth EP),[106] 1881 (cr Jarrow St Peter EP),[40] 1906 (cr Jarrow St Mark EP),[297] 1969,[140] 1969 (gains Jarrow St Peter EP).[298]

CP Cr 1894 from the pt of Hedworth, Monkton and Jarrow CP in Jarrow MB.[47] *LG* S Shields PLU, Jarrow MB. Bdry: 1936 (incl gains pt S Shields CB [assoc with Durham] & CP),[97] 1967.[105] Transf 1974 to Tyne & Wear.[2] *Parl* Jarrow Dv/CC (1918—51), Jarrow BC (1951—*).

JARROW ST MARY
EP Cr 1906 from Jarrow AP.[297] Jarrow RDn.

JARROW ST PETER
EP Cr 1881 from Jarrow AP.[40] Jarrow RDn. Abol 1969 ent to Jarrow AP.[298]

JARROW ST STEPHEN—see SOUTH SHIELDS ST STEPHEN

JARROW DOCKS
EP Cr 1864 from South Shields EP, South Shields Holy Trinity EP.[299] RDns as for Jarrow, from 1864. Sometimes 'Tyne Docks' or 'South Shields St Mary'. Bdry: 1875 (cr South Shields St Simon EP),[74] 1910 (help cr South Shields St Francis EP).[300]

JARROW GRANGE

EP Cr 1868 from Jarrow AP.[296] RDns as for Jarrow, from 1868.

KELLOE

AP Incl chap Thornley (sep CP 1866,[1] sep EP 1844 [incl tp Wingate][44]), chap Trimdon (sep civ identity early, sep EP 1755[3]), tp Coxhoe (sep CP 1866,[1] eccl severed 1865 to help cr Coxhoe EP [qv for other constituent areas][76]), tps Cassop, Quarrington (each a sep CP 1866,[1] pt of each eccl severed 1865 to help cr Cassop cum Quarrington EP [qv for other constituent areas][76]), tp Wingate (sep CP 1866,[1] eccl in chap/EP Thornley, qv above, orig area of the tp eccl severed 1914 from Thornley EP to help cr Wheatley Hill EP[46]). *LG* Eas. Wd (ent until 1829, pt [tp 'Kelloe', tps Thornley, Wingate] 1829—66), pt Durham Wd (1829—66: Cassop, Coxhoe, Quarrington), Eas. PLU. RSD, RD (1894—1937), Durham RD (1937—74). Addtl civ bdry alt: 1937.[15] *Parl* N'rn Dv (1832—85), S-E'rn Dv (1885—1918), Seaham Dv (1918—48), Durham CC (1948—*). *Eccl* Durham RDn (before 1291—before 1535), Darl. RDn (before 1535—1842), Eas. RDn (1842—74), Eas. RDn (S'rn Dv) (1874—80), Eas. RDn (1880—*). Addtl eccl bdry alt: 1842 (help cr Wingate Grange EP),[99] 1865 (help cr Cornforth EP),[76] 1889,[8] 1896 (gains area Trimdon Grange from Trimdon AP),[301] 1920 (cr Trimdon Grange EP),[84] 1937.[125]

KIBBLESWORTH—see LAMESLEY

KILLERBY

Tp in Heighington AP, sep CP 1866,[1] eccl severed 1850 and transf to Ingleton EP.[278] *LG* Seq 4. *Parl* Seq 12.

KIMBLESWORTH

AP Orig AP and pec of Durham Abbey, annexed 1593 to Witton Gilbert AP for eccl purposes as 'Witton Gilbert with Kimblesworth' EP,[202] pt eccl severed 1863 to help cr Sacriston EP,[139] 'Kimblesworth' considered civ ex-par, sep CP 1858.[194] *LG* Chest. Wd (until 1829), Durham Wd (from 1829), Durham PLU, RSD, RD. Civ bdry: 1881,[135] 1885,[156] 1937.[15] *Parl* Seq 4.

EP Cr 1923 from Witton Gilbert with Kimblesworth EP, Chester le Street AP, Durham St Cuthbert EP, Sacriston EP.[142] Durham RDn.

KNITSLEY

CP Cr 1894 from the pt of Conside and Knitsley CP not in Consett UD.[62] *LG* Lanch. PLU, RD. Bdry: 1920.[164] Abol 1937 pt to Consett UD & CP, pt to Healeyfield CP.[15] *Parl* Consett Dv (1918—48).

KYLOE

Chap in Holy Island AP, sep civ identity early, sep EP 1738.[3] *LG* Islandshire, Berwick PLU, transf to Northumb 1832 for parl purposes, 1844 for civ purposes.[4] For later civ and parl organisation and for ent eccl organisation, see entry in Northumb.

KYO

Tp in Lanchester AP, sep CP 1866,[1] eccl severed 1843 to help cr Collierly EP.[71] *LG* Chest. Wd, Lanch. PLU, pt Stanley USD (1892—94), Lanch. RSD (ent 1875—92, pt 1892—94), Lanch. RD (1894—96), Annfield Plain UD (1896—1937).

Bdry: 1883,[12] 1886,[162] 1887,[60] 1894 (loses the pt in Stanley UD to cr Oxhill CP),[62] 1895,[302] 1899.[303] Abol 1937 ent to Stanley UD & CP.[15] *Parl* N'rn Dv (1832—85), N-W'rn Dv (1885—1918), Consett Dv (1918—48).

LAMBTON

Tp in Chester le Street AP, sep CP 1866,[1] eccl severed 1862 to help cr Lumley EP.[134] *LG* Seq 12. *Parl* Seq 2.

LAMESLEY

Chap in Chester le Street AP, sep CP 1866,[1] sep EP 1812 (incl tps Ravensworth, Kibblesworth, Hedley [none sep civ]).[3] *LG* Seq 1. Civ bdry: 1883,[12] 1933 (loses pt to Gatesh. CB [assoc with Durham] & AP),[239] 1936 (loses pt to Gatesh. CB [assoc with Durham] & AP),[97] 1937.[15] Transf 1974 to Tyne & Wear.[2] *Parl* Seq 1. *Eccl* Durham RDn (1812—42), Chest. le Str. RDn (1842—74), Chest. RDn (E'rn Dv) (1874—80), Chest. le Str. RDn (1880—1924), Gatesh. RDn (1924—*). Eccl bdry: 1843 (help cr Pelton EP),[133] 1863 (help cr Eighton Banks EP),[216] 1874 (help cr Marley Hill EP).[304]

LANCHESTER

AP Orig Collegiate. Tp 'Lanchester' in Chest. Wd as were chap and tp Benfieldside (sep CP 1866,[1] eccl in chap/EP Medomsley, qv below, eccl severed 1847 from Medomsley EP and united with pt tp of Conside and Knitsley to cr 'Benfieldside' EP[59]), chap Collierley (sep CP 1866,[1] sep EP 1843 [incl tps Billingside, Kyo, pt tp Greencroft][71]), chap Ebchester (sep civ identity early, sep EP 1743[3]), chap Medomsley (sep CP 1866,[1] sep EP 1765 [incl chap & tp Benfieldside, tp Consett and Knitsley][3]), chap Satley (sep CP 1866,[1] sep EP 1735 [incl pt tp Hedleyhope][3]), pt Billingside (sep CP 1866,[1] eccl severed 1842 to help cr Collierley EP[71]), pt Conside and Knitsley (sep CP 1866,[1] eccl in chap/EP Medomsley, qv above, pt of orig tp eccl severed 1847 from Medomsley EP to help cr Benfieldside EP[59]), tp Greencroft (sep CP 1866,[1] pt eccl severed 1842 to help cr Collierley EP[71]), tp Kyo (sep CP 1866,[1] eccl severed 1842 to help cr Collierley EP[71]), tps Healeyfield, Iveston, Langley (each a sep CP 1866[1]); incl in Darl. Wd tp Cornsay (sep CP 1866[1]); incl in Durham Wd chap Esh (sep CP 1866,[1] sep EP 1733[3]). *LG* Lanch. PLU, pt Stanley USD (1892—94), Lanch. RSD (ent 1875—92, pt 1892—94), Lanch. RD. Addtl civ bdry alt: 1886,[211] 1895.[302] *Parl* N'rn Dv (pt 1832—67, ent 1867—85), pt S'rn Dv (1832—67), N-W'rn Dv (1885—1918), Barn. Cast. Dv (1918—48), N W Durham CC (1948—*). *Eccl* Lanch. RDn (until early 19th cent), Durham RDn (early 19th cent—1842), Chest. le Str. RDn (1842—74), Chest. RDn (W'rn Dv) (1874—80), Durham RDn (1880—91), Lanch. RDn (1891—*). Addtl eccl bdry alt: 1863 (help cr Leadgate EP, help cr Castleside EP),[94] 1865 (help cr Holmside EP),[140] 1871 (help cr Burnopfield EP),[120] 1873 (help cr Beamish EP),[40] 1914 (help cr Annfield Plain EP).[5]

LAND COMMON TO EVENWOOD AND BARONY AND WEST AUCKLAND

LG Auckl. RD. Abol 1937 pt to Bp Auckl. UD &

CP, pt to West Auckland CP.[15] *Parl* Bp Auckl. Dv (1918—48).

LANGDALE—see DEAF HILL CUM LANGDALE

LANGLEY

Tp in Lanchester AP, sep CP 1866.[1] *LG* Seq 2. Bdry: 1883,[12] 1887.[60] *Parl* Seq 5.

LANGLEYDALE AND SHOTTON

Tp in Staindrop AP, sep CP 1866.[1] *LG* Seq 7. Bdry: 1884.[38] *Parl* Seq 8.

LANGTON

Tp in Gainford AP, sep CP 1866.[1] *LG* Seq 7. *Parl* Seq 8.

LEADGATE

EP Cr 1863 from Lanchester AP, Medomsley EP.[94] Chest. le Str. RDn (1863—74), Chest. RDn (W'rn Dv) (1874—80), Ryton RDn (1880—91), Lanch. RDn (1891—*). Bdry: 1963.[75]

LOAN END

Tp in Norham AP, sep CP 1866.[1] *LG* Norhamshire, Berwick PLU, transf to Northumb 1832 for parl purposes, 1844 for civ purposes.[4] *Parl* In Durham until 1832, Northumb thereafter. For later civ and parl organisation, see entry in Northumb.

LOBLEY HILL

EP Cr 1949 from Dunston St Nicholas EP.[192] Gatesh. RDn.

NORTH LODGE

CP Cr 1974 from the pt of Harraton CP remaining in Durham (the remainder, transf to Tyne & Wear [in Wash. New Town] not to be in a par).[2]

LONGRIDGE

Tp in Norham AP, sep CP 1866.[1] *LG* Norhamshire, Berwick PLU, transf to Northumb 1832 for parl purposes, 1844 for civ purposes.[4] *Parl* In Durham until 1832, Northumb thereafter. For later civ and parl organisation, see entry in Northumb.

LOW TEAM

EP Cr 1871 from Gateshead St Cuthbert EP.[95] Chest. le Str. RDn (1871—74), Chest. RDn (E'rn Dv) (1874—80), Chest. le Str. RDn (1880—91), Gatesh. RDn (1891—*). Bdry: 1889 (help cr Gateshead St Aidan EP).[99] Sometimes 'Gateshead St Paul'.

LUMLEY

EP Cr 1862 from Chester le Street AP (tps Great Lumley, Little Lumley, Lambton).[134] Chest. le Str. RDn (1862—74), Chest. RDn (E'rn Dv) (1874—80), Chest. le Str. RDn (1880—*). Bdry: 1867.[119]

GREAT LUMLEY

Tp in Chester le Street AP, sep CP 1866,[1] eccl severed 1862 to help cr Lumley EP.[134] *LG* Seq 12. *Parl* Seq 2.

LITTLE LUMLEY

Tp in Chester le Street AP, sep CP 1866,[1] eccl severed 1862 to help cr Lumley EP.[134] Organisation as for Great Lumley, incl also civ bdry alt 1912.[305]

LYNESACK

EP Cr 1850 by union of pts of the following tps in Hamsterley EP (orig in Auckland St Andrew AP): Hamsterley, Lynesack and Softley, South Bedburn.[22] Darl. RDn (1850—74), Darl. RDn (S'rn Dv) (1874—80), Auckl. RDn (1880—1924), Barn. Cast. RDn (1924—*). Bdry: 1967.[160]

LYNESACK AND SOFTLEY

Chap and tp in chap Hamsterley (sep civ identity early from Auckland St Andrew AP, sep EP 1724[3]), 'Lynesack and Softley' a sep CP 1866,[1] pt eccl severed 1850 to help cr Lynesack EP.[22] Incl undivided pt Undivided Moor Common to Lynesack and Softley, Hamsterley and South Bedburn. *LG* Seq 5. Bdry: 1885.[72] *Parl* S'rn Dv (1832—85), Barn. Cast. Dv (1885—1918), Bp Auckl. Dv/CC (1918—*).

LYONS

EP Cr 1869 from Hetton le Hole EP, Pittington AP.[142] Eas. RDn (1869—74), Eas. RDn (N'rn Dv) (1874—80), Hough. le Spr. RDn (1880—*). Sometimes 'Easington Lane'.

MAINSFORTH

Tp in Bishop Middleham AP, sep CP 1866.[1] *LG* Seq 17. Bdry: 1946.[144] *Parl* Seq 11.

MARLEY HILL

EP Cr 1874 from Whickham AP, Lamesley EP, Tanfield EP.[304] Chest. RDn (E'rn Dv) (1874—80), Ryton RDn (1880—91), Chest. le Str. RDn (1880—*). Bdry: 1953.[121]

MARWOOD

Tp in Gainford AP, sep CP 1866.[1] *LG* Darl. Wd, Teesd. PLU, tp Barn. Cast. USD, pt Teesd. RSD. Abol 1884 ent to Barnard Castle CP.[38] *Parl* S'rn Dv (1832—85).

CP Cr 1894 from the pt of Barnard Castle CP not in Barn. Cast. UD.[39] *LG* Teesd. PLU, Barn. Cast. RD. *Parl* Barn. Cast. Dv (1918—48), Bp Auckl. CC (1948—*).

MEDOMSLEY

Chap in Lanchester AP, sep CP 1866,[1] sep EP 1765 (incl chap and tp Benfieldside, tp Consett and Knitsley).[3] *LG* Chest. Wd, Lanch. PLU, pt Leadgate USD, pt Lanch. RSD, Lanch. RD. Civ bdry: 1883,[12] 1887 (gains pt Hedley Woodside CP, Northumb),[60] 1894 (the pt in Leadgate UD transf to Iveston CP),[62] 1901.[148] Abol civ 1937 pt to Consett UD & CP, pt to Stanley UD & CP.[15] *Parl* N'rn Dv (1832—85), N-W'rn Dv (1885—1918), Consett Dv (1918—48). *Eccl* Lanch. RDn (1765—early 19th cent), Chest. le Str. RDn (early 19th cent—1874), Chest. RDn (W'rn Dv) (1874—80), Ryton RDn (1880—91), Lanch. RDn (1891—*). Eccl bdry: 1847 (orig area of chap and tp Benfieldside, pt tp Consett and Knitsley eccl severed and united with pt Ebchester EP to cr Benfieldside EP),[59] 1863 (help cr Castleside EP, help cr Leadgate EP),[94] 1871 (help cr Burnopfield EP),[120] 1953,[121] 1963.[75]

MERRINGTON

AP Incl tp Ferryhill (sep CP 1866,[1] sep EP 1843[143]), tps Chilton, Hett (each a sep CP 1866[1]). *LG* Darl. Wd (ent until 1829, pt 1829—66, ent from 1866), pt Durham Wd 1829—66 [Ferryhill, Hett]), Auckl. PLU, RSD. Addtl civ bdry alt: 1894 (the pt transf to Spennym. UD[306] and an addtl pt of Merrington AP[228] cr Merrington Lane CP). Abol civ 1937 pt to Bp Auckl. UD & CP, pt to Spennym. UD to help cr Spennymoor CP.[15] *Parl* S'rn Dv (1832—85), Bp Auckl. Dv (1885—1948). *Eccl* Durham RDn (before 1291—before 1535), Darl.

RDn (before 1535—early 19th cent), Durham RDn (early 19th cent—1842), Darl. RDn (1842—74), Darl. RDn (N'rn Dv) (1874—80), Auckl. RDn (1880—*). Eccl bdry: 1845 (gains eccl tp Middlestone from Auckland St Andrew AP), 1865 (help cr Tudhoe EP).[229]

MERRINGTON LANE
CP Cr 1894 from the pt of Merrington AP transf to Spennym. UD[306] and an addtl pt of Merrington AP.[228] *LG* Auckl. PLU, Spennym. UD. Abol 1937 to help cr Spennymoor CP.[15] *Parl* Spennym. Dv (1918—48).

MIDDLESTONE
Tp in Auckland St Andrew AP, sep CP 1866,[1] eccl severed 1845 and transf to Merrington AP.[24] *LG* Darl. Wd, Auckl. PLU, RSD, RD. Abol 1937 pt to Bp Auckl. UD & CP, pt to Spennym. UD to help cr Spennymoor CP.[15] *Parl* S'rn Dv (1832—85), Bp Auckl. Dv (1885—1948).

MIDDLETON
CP Cr 1894 from the pt of Stranton AP in Hartl. MB.[39] *LG* Hartl. PLU, MB. Abol 1936 ent to Hartl. MB & CP.[47] *Parl* The Hartlepools Parl Bor (1918—48).

MIDDLETON IN TEESDALE
AP Incl chap Eggleston (sep CP 1866,[1] sep EP 1741,[3] eccl refounded 1859[215]), tp Forest and Frith (sep CP 1866,[1] sep EP 1875[233]), tp Newbiggin (sep CP 1866[1]). *LG* Seq 7. Addtl civ bdry alt: 1883,[12] 1884 (loses pt to Holwick CP, Yorks N Riding).[159] *Parl* Seq 8. *Eccl* Darl. RDn (before 1291—early 19th cent), Durham RDn (early 19th cent—1842), Darl. RDn (1842—74), Darl. RDn (S'rn Dv) (1874—80), Darl. RDn (1880—1924), Barn. Cast. RDn (1924—*).

MIDDLETON ST GEORGE
AP Orig in co Sadberge (Northumb until 1189, Durham thereafter, considered a sep co until mid 15th cent, then in other Wds). Pt of tp Middleton St George in Long Newton AP. *LG* Stock. Wd, Darl. PLU, RSD, RD. *Parl* Seq 12. *Eccl* Seq 5. Eccl bdry: 1945.[189]

MIDDRIDGE
Tp in chap Shildon (sep CP 1866 from Auckland St Andrew AP,[1] sep EP 1837[22]), 'Middridge' a sep CP 1866.[1] *LG* Darl. Wd, Auckl. PLU, RSD, RD. Bdry: 1883,[12] 1885.[72] Abol 1937 ent to Shildon UD & CP.[15] *Parl* S'rn Dv (1832—85), Bp Auckl. Dv (1885—1948).

MIDDRIDGE GRANGE
Tp pt in Auckland St Andrew AP, pt in Heighington AP, sep CP 1866.[1] *LG* Darl. Wd, Auckl. PLU, RSD, RD. Bdry: 1883,[12] 1885.[72] Abol 1937 pt to Shildon UD & CP, pt to Heighington AP.[15] *Parl* S'rn Dv (1832—85), Bp Auckl. Dv (1885—1948).

MILLFIELD ST HILDA
EP Cr 1894 from Millfield St Mark EP, Bishopwearmouth AP.[85] Wearm. RDn. Abol 1970 to help cr Bishopwearmouth St Michael with St Hilda EP.[89]

MILLFIELD ST MARK
EP Cr 1868 from Bishopwearmouth AP.[79] Eas. RDn (1868—74), Eas. RDn (N'rn Dv) (1874—80), Wearm. RDn (1880—*). Bdry: 1873,[188] 1894 (help cr Millfield St Hilda EP),[85] 1899,[70] 1950 (incl gains Ayres Quay EP).[36]

MILLFIELD ST MARY MAGDALENE
EP Cr 1907 from Pallion EP.[307] Wearm. RDn. Bdry: 1950.[36]

MONK HESLEDEN
AP Incl tps Hutton Henry, Sheraton with Hulam (each a sep CP 1866[1]). *LG* Seq 9. Addtl civ bdry alt: 1936,[97] 1946.[128] *Parl* Seq 6. *Eccl* Durham RDn (before 1291—before 1535), Darl. RDn (before 1535—early 19th cent), Durham RDn (early 19th cent—1842), Eas. RDn (1842—74), Eas. RDn (S'rn Dv) (1874—80), Eas. RDn (1880—1924), Hartl. RDn (1924—25). Eccl bdry: 1882 (cr Monk Hesleden St John EP),[308] 1885.[309] Abol eccl 1925 to help cr Monk Hesleden St John with St Mary EP.[130]

MONK HESLEDEN ST JOHN
EP Cr 1882 from Monk Hesleden AP.[308] Eas. RDn (1882—1924), Hartl. RDn (1924—25). Abol 1925 to help cr Monk Hesleden St John with St Mary EP.[130]

MONK HESLEDEN ST JOHN WITH ST MARY
EP Cr 1925 by union Monk Hesleden AP, Monk Hesleden St John EP.[130] Hartl. RDn. Bdry: 1925 (cr Blackhall EP),[94] 1963.[131]

MONKS HOUSE
Ex-par place, Islandshire, Belford PLU, transf to Northumb 1832 for parl purposes, 1844 for civ purposes,[4] sep CP 1858 in Northumb.[194] *Parl* In Durham until 1832, Northumb thereafter. For later civ and parl organisation, see entry in Northumb.

MONKTON
CP Cr 1894 from the pt of Hedworth, Monkton and Jarrow CP neither in Jarrow MB nor Hebburn UD.[39] *LG* S Shields PLU, RD. Bdry: 1901.[102] Abol 1936 pt to S Shields CB (assoc with Durham) & CP, pt to help cr Boldon UD & CP, pt to Felling UD & to Heworth CP, pt to Hebburn UD & CP, pt to Jarrow MB & AP.[97] *Parl* Hough. le Spr. Dv (1918—48).

MONKWEARMOUTH
The following have 'Monkwearmouth' in their names. Insofar as any existed at a given time: *LG* Chest. Wd (until 1829), Eas. Wd (from 1829), Sund. PLU; remainder sep noted. *Parl* Sep noted. *Eccl* Durham RDn (cr—1842), Chest. le Str. RDn (1842—74), Chest. RDn (E'rn Dv) (1874—80), Wearm. RDn (1880—*).

AP1—MONKWEARMOUTH [ST PETER]—Incl tp Fulwell (sep CP 1866,[1] eccl severed 1844 and united with tp 'Monkwearmouth' to cr EP2[225]), tp Hylton (sep CP 1866,[1] eccl severed 1847 to help cr Southwick EP [area of tps North Hylton, South Hylton, neither sep civ][114]), tp Monkwearmouth Shore (sep CP 1866,[1] only pt eccl remaining as 'St Peter' after main tp severed 1844 as noted above), tp Southwick (sep CP 1866,[1] sep EP 1847 [incl area tps North Hylton, South Hylton, neither sep civ][114]). *LG* Sund. MB (ent 1835—87, pt 1887—89), Sund. CB (pt 1889—94, ent 1894—97), Sund. USD (ent 1875—87, pt 1887—94), pt Sund. RSD (1887—94). Addtl civ bdry alt: 1883,[12] 1887,[236] 1894 (the pt not in Sund. CB cr CP2),[39]

1895 (gains CP1).[310] Abol 1897 ent to Sunderland CP.[81] *Parl* Sund. Parl Bor (1832—1918). Addtl eccl bdry alt: 1871 (help cr EP6),[311] 1878 (help cr Hedworth EP),[106] 1880 (cr EP4).[312] Abol eccl 1935 to help cr EP5.[183]

EP1—MONKWEARMOUTH—Cr 1962 by union EP5, EP6.[176]

EP2—MONKWEARMOUTH ALL SAINTS—Cr 1844 from AP1 (union tp Fulwell, tp 'Monkwearmouth').[225] Bdry: 1871 (help cr EP6),[311] 1884 (help cr Southwick St Columba EP),[313] 1886,[139] 1907 (cr EP3),[42] 1919,[314] 1931,[315] 1962.[176]

EP3—MONKWEARMOUTH ST ANDREW—Cr 1907 from EP2.[42] Bdry: 1919,[314] 1931,[315] 1962.[176]

EP4—MONKWEARMOUTH ST CUTHBERT—Cr 1880 from AP1.[312] Abol 1935 to help cr EP5.[183]

EP5—MONKWEARMOUTH ST PETER WITH ST CUTHBERT—Cr 1935 by union AP1, EP4.[183] Abol 1962 to help cr EP1.[176]

EP6—MONKWEARMOUTH THE VENERABLE BEDE—Cr 1871 from AP1, EP2.[311] Bdry: 1886.[139] Abol 1962 pt to help cr EP1, pt to EP2, pt to EP3, pt to Southwick St Columba EP.[176]

CP1—MONKWEARMOUTH SHORE—Tp in AP1, sep CP 1866,[1] the sole tp constituting AP1 after tp 'Monkwearmouth' eccl severed 1844, qv above. *LG* Sund. MB (1835—89), CB (1889—97), USD. Bdry: 1883.[12] Abol 1897 ent to Sunderland CP.[81] *Parl* Sund. Parl Bor (1832—1918).

CP2—MONKWEARMOUTH WITHOUT—Cr 1894 from the pt of AP1 not in Sund. CB.[39] *LG* Sund. PLU, RD. Abol 1895 ent to AP1.[310]

SOUTH MOOR
CP Cr 1894 from the pt of Lanchester AP in Stanley UD.[62] *LG* Lanch. PLU, Stanley UD. Bdry: 1895.[316] Abol 1916 ent to Stanley CP.[317]
EP Cr 1912 from Holmside EP, Beamish EP.[42] Lanch. RDn. Bdry: 1929.[7]

MOOR HOUSE
Tp in Houghton le Spring AP, sep CP 1866,[1] eccl severed 1836 to help cr Rainton EP.[27] *LG* Eas. Wd (until 1829), Durham Wd (from 1829), Hough. le Spr. PLU, RSD, RD (1894—1937), Durham RD (1937—46). Abol 1946 ent to West Rainton CP.[318] *Parl* N'rn Dv (1832—85), Hough. le Spr. Dv (1885—1918), Durham Dv (1918—48).

MOORSLEY
Tp in Houghton le Spring AP, sep CP 1866,[1] eccl severed 1836 to help cr Rainton EP.[27] *LG* Eas. Wd (until 1829), Durham Wd (from 1829), Hough. le Spr. PLU, RSD, RD. Abol 1937 to help cr Hetton CP in Hetton UD.[15] *Parl* N'rn Dv (1832—85), Hough. le Spr. Dv (1885—1918), Durham Dv (1918—48).

MORDON
Tp in Sedgefield AP, sep CP 1866.[1] *LG* Seq 14. *Parl* Seq 13.

MORTON GRANGE
Tp in Houghton le Spring AP, sep CP 1866.[1] *LG* Eas. Wd, Hough. le Spr. PLU, RSD, RD. Abol 1937 pt to Hough. le Spr. UD & AP, pt to West Rainton CP.[15] *Parl* N'rn Dv (1832—85), Hough. le Spr. Dv (1885—1948).

MORTON PALMS
Tp in Haughton le Skerne AP, sep CP 1866.[1] *LG* Seq 16. *Parl* Seq 12.

MORTON TINMOUTH
Tp in Gainford AP, sep CP 1866,[1] eccl severed 1867 to help cr Bolam EP,[99] on abol of latter 1945 transf to Ingleton EP.[100] *LG* Seq 7. *Parl* Seq 8.

MUGGLESWICK
AP *LG* Seq 2. Civ bdry: 1883,[12] 1887.[60] *Parl* Seq 5. *Eccl* Durham RDn (until 1842), Chest. le Str. RDn (1842—74), Chest. RDn (W'rn Dv) (1874—80), Stanh. RDn (1880—*). Eccl bdry: 1863 (help cr Castleside EP),[94] 1959.[210]

EAST MURTON
Tp in Dalton le Dale AP, sep CP 1866.[1] *LG* Seq 9. Bdry: 1914.[276] *Parl* Seq 3.

NEASHAM
Tp in Hurworth AP, sep CP 1866.[1] *LG* Seq 16. *Parl* Seq 12.

NESBITT
Tp in Hart AP, sep CP 1866.[1] *LG* Seq 9. *Parl* Seq 6.

NEVILLE'S CROSS
CP Cr 1894 from the pt of Crossgate CP not in Durham MB.[39] *LG* Durham PLU, RD. Bdry: 1905.[172] Abol 1935 ent to Durham MB & CP.[49] *Parl* Durham Dv (1918—48).

NEWBIGGIN
Tp in Middleton in Teesdale AP, sep CP 1866.[1] *LG* Seq 7. Bdry: 1883,[12] 1884 (incl loses pt to Holwick CP, Yorks N Riding).[319] *Parl* Seq 8.

EAST AND WEST NEWBIGGIN
Tp in Bishopton AP, sep CP 1866.[1] *LG* Seq 15. *Parl* Seq 12.

NEWBOTTLE
Tp in Houghton le Spring AP, sep CP 1866,[1] pt eccl severed 1752 to help cr Penshaw EP,[3] qv for refounding 1838, the remainder constituted 1865 'Newbottle' EP.[291] *LG* Eas. Wd, Hough. le Spr. PLU, RSD, RD. Abol civ 1937 pt to Hough. le Spr. UD & AP, pt to East and Middle Herrington CP.[15] *Parl* N'rn Dv (1832—85), Hough. le Spr. Dv (1885—1948). *Eccl* Eas. RDn (1865—74), Eas. RDn (N'rn Dv) (1874—80), Hough. le Spr. RDn (1880—*). Eccl bdry: 1872 (help cr Chilton Moor EP),[145] 1884 (cr Herrington EP),[111] 1913 (help cr Shiney Row EP).[282]

NEWFIELD
Tp in Auckland St Andrew AP, sep CP 1866,[1] eccl severed 1845 to help cr Byers Green EP.[19] *LG* Darl. Wd, Auckl. PLU, RSD, RD. Bdry: 1912.[122] Abol 1937 pt to Bp Auckl. UD & CP, pt to Spennym. UD to help cr Spennymoor CP.[15] *Parl* S'rn Dv (1832—85), Bp Auckl. Dv (1885—1948).

NEWSHAM
Tp in Egglescliffe AP, sep CP 1866.[1] *LG* Seq 12. Bdry: 1887.[320] Transf 1974 to Clev.[2] *Parl* Seq 14.

LONG NEWTON
AP Orig in co Sadberge (Northumb until 1189, Durham thereafter, considered a sep co until mid 15th cent, then in other Wds). Incl pt tp Middleton St George (o'wise in that AP). *LG* Seq 12. Transf 1974 to

Clev.[2] *Parl* Seq 14. *Eccl* Darl. RDn (before 1291—
before 1535), Durham RDn (before 1535—1842),
Stock. RDn (1842—*).

NEWTON CAP
Tp in Auckland St Andrew AP, sep CP 1866,[1] pt
eccl severed 1845 to help cr Hunwick EP.[19] *LG*
Darl. Wd, Auckl. PLU, RSD, RD. Bdry: 1883.[12]
Abol 1937 pt to Bp Auckl. UD & CP, pt to help cr
Crook & Willington UD & CP.[15] *Parl* S'rn Dv
(1832—85), Bp Auckl. Dv (1885—1948).

NORHAM
AP *LG* Norhamshire, Berwick PLU, transf to Northumb 1832 for parl purposes, 1844 for civ purposes.[4]
Incl chap Cornhill on Tweed (also transf to
Northumb, sep CP 1866 in Northumb,[1] sep EP
1732[3]), tps Duddo, Felkington, Grindon, Horncliffe, Loanend, Longridge, Norham Mains, Shoreswood, Thornton, Twizell (each also transf to
Northumb, each a sep CP 1866 in Northumb[1]). *Parl*
In Durham until 1832, Northumb thereafter. For
later civ and parl organisation, and for ent eccl
organisation, see entry in Northumb.

NORHAM MAINS
Tp in Norham AP, sep CP 1866.[1] *LG* Norhamshire,
Berwick PLU, transf to Northumb 1832 for parl
purposes, 1844 for civ purposes.[4] *Parl* In Durham
until 1832, Northumb thereafter. For later civ and
parl organisation, see entry in Northumb.

NORTON
AP Incl chap Stockton on Tees (sep par 1713,[260] eccl
'Stockton upton Tees'), perhaps incl chap Elton (sep
par by 1291[219]). *LG* Stock. Wd, PLU, RSD, RD.
Civ bdry: 1887,[321] 1913,[220] 1951.[221] Abol 1968 pt
to Carlton CP, pt to Grindon AP, pt to Redmarshall
AP, pt to help cr Teeside CB (assoc with Yorks N
Riding) & CP.[65] *Parl* S'rn Dv (ent 1832—67, pt
1867—85), pt Stock. on Tees Parl Bor (1867—
1918), pt S-E'rn Dv (1885—1918), Sedg. Dv/CC
(1918—70). Parl bdry: 1952.[137] *Eccl* Seq 4. Eccl
bdry: 1918 (help cr Norton St Michael and All
Angels EP),[322] 1928,[323] 1959,[198] 1959 (cr Stockton
on Tees St Chad EP).[324]

NORTON ST MICHAEL AND ALL ANGELS
EP Cr 1918 from Norton AP, Stockton upon Tees AP,
Stockton upon Tees St John the Baptist EP.[322]
Stock. RDn. Bdry: 1959.[198]

OFFERTON
Tp in chap Penshaw (sep CP 1866 from Houghton le
Spring AP, sep EP 1752 [qv for constituent tps and
later eccl refounding][3]), 'Offerton' a sep CP 1866.[1]
LG Eas. Wd, Hough. le Spr. PLU, RSD, RD
(1894—1937), Sund. RDn (1937—67). Bdry:
1886,[286] 1937,[15] 1946.[284] Abol 1967 pt to Sund CB
(assoc with Durham) & CP, pt to Hough. le Spr.
UD & AP.[118] *Parl* N'rn Dv (1832—85), Hough. le
Spr. Dv/CC (1885—1970).

OLD PARK
Tp in Auckland St Andrew AP, sep CP 1866.[1] *LG*
Darl. Wd, Auckl. PLU, RSD, RD. Abol 1937 pt to
Bp Auckl. UD & CP, pt to Spennym. UD and to
help cr Spennymoor CP.[15] *Parl* S'rn Dv (1832—
85), Bp Auckl. Dv (1885—1948).

OUSTON
Tp in Chester le Street AP, sep CP 1866,[1] eccl
severed 1843 to help cr Pelton EP.[133] *LG* Seq 1.
Parl Seq 1.

OXHILL
CP Cr 1894 from the pt of Kyo CP in Stanley UD.[62] *LG*
Lanch. PLU, Stanley UD. Bdry: 1895.[302] Abol
1916 ent to Stanley CP.[317]

PALLION
EP Cr 1868 from Deptford St Andrew EP.[79] Eas. RDn
(1868—74), Eas. RDn (N'rn Dv) (1874—80),
Wearm. RDn (1880—*). Bdry: 1907 (cr Millfield
St Mary Magdalene EP),[307] 1950,[36] 1951.[294]

PELTON
Tp in Chester le Street AP, sep CP 1866,[1] sep EP
1843 (incl tp Ouston, pt tps Edmondsley, Urpeth, pt
tp 'Chester le Street', and also pt Lamesley EP[319]).
LG Seq 1. Civ bdry: 1883,[12] 1885,[325] 1921.[138] *Parl*
Seq 1. *Eccl* Chest. le Str. RDn (1843—74), Chest.
RDn (E'rn Dv) (1874—80), Chest. le Str. RDn
(1880—*). Eccl bdry: 1876 (help cr West Pelton
EP),[141] 1963.[75]

WEST PELTON
EP Cr 1876 from Pelton EP, Chester le Street AP,
Tanfield EP.[141] Chest. RDn (E'rn Dv) (1876—80),
Chest. le Str. RDn (1880—*).

PENSHAW
Chap in Houghton le Spring AP, sep CP 1866,[1] sep
EP 1752 (incl tps South Biddick, Burnmoor,
Offerton, pt tp Newbottle),[3] eccl refounded 1838,[27]
the orig area of tps South Biddick, Burnmoor eccl
severed 1866 and united to cr Burnmoor EP.[66] *LG*
Eas. Wd, Hough. le Spr. PLU, RSD, RD. Abol civ
1937 to Hough. le Spr. UD & AP, pt to Offerton
CP.[15] *Parl* N'rn Dv (1832—85), Hough. le Spr. Dv
(1885—1948). *Eccl* Darl. RDn (1752—early 19th
cent), Durham RDn (early 19th cent—1842), Eas.
RDn (1842—74), Eas. RDn (N'rn Dv) (1874—80),
Hough. le Spr. RDn (1880—*). Addtl eccl bdry alt:
1913 (help cr Shiney Row EP).[282]

PETERLEE
CP Cr 1956 from Easington AP, Horden CP, Shotton
CP.[206] *LG* Eas. RD. *Parl* Eas. CC (1970—*).
EP Cr 1957 from Horden EP, Easington AP, Easington
Colliery EP.[208] Eas. RDn.

PIERCEBRIDGE
Tp in Gainford AP, sep CP 1866.[1] *LG* Seq 4. *Parl*
Seq 12.

PITTINGTON
AP Incl tp Shadforth (sep CP 1866,[1] sep EP 1841[186]),
tp Sherburn (sep CP 1866,[1] sep EP 1855[326]). *LG*
Seq 11. Addtl civ bdry alt: 1881,[327] 1896,[54] 1937
(help cr Hetton CP in Hetton UD).[15] *Parl* Seq 4.
Eccl Durham RDn (before 1291—before 1535),
Darl. RDn (before 1535—early 19th cent), Durham
RDn (early 19th cent—1842), Eas. RDn (1842—
74), Eas. RDn (S'rn Dv) (1874—80), Eas. RDn
(1880—1970), Durham RDn (1970—*). Eccl bdry:
1869 (help cr Lyons EP),[142] 1920.[56]

PLAWSWORTH
Tp in Chester le Street AP, sep CP 1866.[1] *LG*
Chest. Wd (until 1829), Durham Wd (from 1829),
Chest. le Str. PLU, RSD. Bdry: 1883,[12] 1885,[328]

1885,[329] 1937.[15] *Parl* Seq 1.

POLLARD'S LAND

Tp in Auckland St Andrew AP, sep CP 1866,[1] pt eccl severed 1893 to help refound Escomb EP.[11] *LG* Darl. Wd, Auckl. PLU, RSD. Abol 1886 to help cr Bishop Auckland and Pollard's Lands CP.[13] *Parl* S'rn Dv (1832—85), Bp Auckl. Dv (1885—1918).

CP Cr 1894 from the pt of Bishop Auckland and Pollard's Lands CP not in Bp Auckl. UD.[14] *LG* Auckl. PLU, RD. Abol 1937 pt to Bp Auckl. UD & CP, pt to West Auckland CP.[15] *Parl* Bp Auckl. Dv (1918—48).

PRESTON LE SKERNE

Tp in Aycliffe AP, sep CP 1866.[1] *LG* Seq 6. Bdry: 1937.[15] *Parl* Seq 13.

PRESTON ON TEES

Tp in area Stockton on Tees (eccl, 'Stockton upon Tees', sep par 1713 from Norton AP[260]), 'Preston on Tees' a sep CP 1866,[1] sep EP 1924 from Stockton upon Tees Holy Trinity EP, Egglescliffe EP.[214] *LG* Seq 12. Civ bdry: 1951,[221] 1968 (loses pt to Teeside CB [assoc with Yorks N Riding] & CP).[65] Transf 1974 to Clev.[2] *Parl* Seq 14. Parl bdry: 1952.[137] *Eccl* Stock. RDn.

QUARRINGTON

Tp in Kelloe AP, sep CP 1866,[1] pt eccl severed 1865 to help cr Cassop cum Quarrington EP.[76] *LG* Eas. Wd (until 1829), Durham Wd (from 1829), Durham PLU, RSD. Abol 1887 to help cr Cassop cum Quarrington CP.[124] *Parl* N'rn Dv (1832—85), Mid Dv (1885—1918).

RABY WITH KEVERSTONE

Tp in Staindrop AP, sep CP 1866.[1] *LG* Seq 7. *Parl* Seq 8.

RAINTON

EP Cr 1836 by union of following tps in Houghton le Spring AP: East Rainton, West Rainton, Moorsley, Moor House, Cocken.[27] Durham RDn (1836—42), Eas. RDn (1842—74), Eas. RDn (N'rn Dv) (1874—80), Hough. le Spr. RDn (1880—*). Bdry: 1866 (area of orig tp East Rainton, pt tp Moorsley eccl severed to cr East Rainton EP),[326] 1872 (help cr Chilton Moor EP).[145]

EAST RAINTON

Tp in Houghton le Spring AP, sep CP 1866,[1] eccl severed 1836 to help cr Rainton EP,[27] the orig area of East Rainton eccl severed 1866 from the latter and united with pt area tp Moorsley in same EP to cr 'East Rainton' EP.[326] *LG* Eas. Wd, Hough. le Spr. PLU, RSD. Abol civ 1937 pt to help cr Hetton CP in Hetton UD, pt to Hough. le Spr. UD & AP.[15] *Parl* N'rn Dv (1832—85), Hough. le Spr. Dv (1885—1918), Durham Dv (1918—48). *Eccl* Eas. RDn (1866—74), Eas. RDn (W'rn Dv) (1874—80), Hough. le Spr. RDn (1880—*). Eccl bdry: 1872 (help cr Chilton Moor EP),[145] 1956,[287] 1974.[288]

WEST RAINTON

Tp in Houghton le Spring AP, sep CP 1866,[1] eccl severed 1836 to help cr Rainton EP.[27] *LG* Eas. Wd, Hough. le Spr. PLU, RSD, RD (1894—1937), Durham Dv (1937—74). Bdry: 1881,[327] 1937,[15] 1946 (gains Moor House CP).[318] *Parl* N'rn Dv (1832—85), Hough. le Spr. Dv (1885—1918),

Durham Dv/CC (1918—*).

RAVENSWORTH—see LAMESLEY

REDMARSHALL

AP Incl chap Carlton (sep CP 1866[1]), chap Stillington (sep CP 1866,[1] sep EP 1872 by union this chap, tp Whitton in Grindon AP[243]). *LG* Seq 12. Addtl civ bdry alt: 1968.[65] Transf 1974 to Clev.[2] *Parl* Seq 14. *Eccl* Seq 4.

REDWORTH

Tp in Heighington AP, sep CP 1866.[1] *LG* Darl. Wd, PLU, RSD, RD. Abol 1937 pt to Shildon UD & CP, pt to Heighington AP.[15] *Parl* S'rn Dv (1832—85), S-E'rn Dv (1885—1918), Sedg. Dv (1918—48).

ROOKHOPE

EP Cr 1866 from Stanhope AP.[272] Darl. RDn (1866—74), Darl. RDn (N'rn Dv) (1874—80), Stanh. RDn (1880—*). Sometimes called 'Stotfield Burn'.

RYHOPE

Chap in Bishopwearmouth AP, sep CP 1866,[1] sep EP 1829 (incl tps Burdon, Tunstall),[3] eccl refounded 1854.[77] *LG* Eas. Wd, Sund. PLU, pt Sund. MB (1867—89), Sund. CB (pt 1889—94, ent 1894—1967), pt Sund. USD, pt Sund. RSD. Civ bdry: 1894 (the pt in the CB cr Ryhope Within CP),[39] 1928 (loses pt to Sund. CB [assoc with Durham] & CP).[93] Abol civ 1967 pt to Sund. CB (assoc with Durham) & CP, pt to Seaham UD & AP.[118] *Parl* N'rn Dv (ent 1832—67, pt 1867—85), pt Sund. Parl Bor (1867—1918), Hough. le Spr. Dv/CC (pt 1885—1918, ent 1918—70). *Eccl* Durham RDn (1829—42), Eas. RDn (1842—74), Eas. RDn (N'rn Dv) (1874—80), Wearm. RDn (1880—*). Eccl bdry: 1906,[185] 1911 (help cr Grangetown EP),[120] 1952.[90]

RYHOPE WITHIN

CP Cr 1894 from the pt of Ryhope CP in Sund. CB.[39] *LG* Sund. PLU, CB. Abol 1897 ent to Sunderland CP.[81]

RYTON

AP Incl area Winlaton (sep civ identity early [incl tp Chopwell], sep EP 1834 [incl tp Chopwell],[146] Chopwell a sep CP 1866,[1] sep EP 1916[147]), tp Stella (sep CP 1866,[1] sep EP 1845 [incl pt Winlaton EP][330]), tps Crawcrook, Ryton Woodside (each a sep CP 1866[1]). *LG* Chest. Wd, Gatesh. PLU, Ryton USD, UD. Addtl civ bdry alt: 1914 (gains Crawcrook CP, Ryton Woodside CP).[169] Transf 1974 to Tyne & Wear.[2] *Parl* N'rn Dv (1832—85), Chest. le Str. Dv (1885—1918), Blayd. Dv/CC (1918—70), Blayd. BC (1970—*). *Eccl* Seq 6. Addtl eccl bdry alt: 1886 (cr Greenside EP),[235] 1914 (cr Hedgefield EP).[277]

RYTON WOODSIDE

Tp in Ryton AP, sep CP 1866.[1] *LG* Chest. Wd, Gatesh. PLU, Ryton USD, UD. Bdry: 1883.[12] Abol 1914 ent to Ryton AP.[169] *Parl* N'rn Dv (1832—85), Chest. le Str. Dv (1885—1918).

SACRISTON

EP Cr 1863 from Witton Gilbert with Kimblesworth EP, Chester le Street AP.[139] Chest. le Str. RDn (1863—74), Chest. RDn (W'rn Dv) (1874—80), Durham RDn (1880—*).

CP Cr 1937 from Witton Gilbert AP.[15] *LG* Chest. le Str. RD. Bdry: 1946.[212] *Parl* Chest. le Str. CC (1948—*).

SADBERGE

Orig in co Sadberge (Northumb until 1189, Durham thereafter, considered a sep co until mid 15th cent, then in other Wds). Tp in Haughton le Skerne AP, sep CP 1866,[1] sep EP 1856.[331] *LG* Seq 16. *Parl* Seq 12. *Eccl* Darl. RDn (1856—74), Darl. RDn (S'rn Dv) (1874—80), Darl. RDn (1880—*).

ST GILES

AP Usual civ spelling (sometimes 'Gilligate'); for eccl and for inclusion of chap Durham St Oswald (civ, 'St Oswald'), see 'Durham St Giles'. *LG* Eas. Wd (until 1829), Durham Wd (from 1829), St Giles Bor, Durham PLU, Durham MB (pt 1835—94, ent 1894—1916), pt Durham USD, pt Durham RSD. Civ bdry: 1894 (the pt not in the MB cr Belmont CP).[47] Abol civ 1916 to help cr Durham CP.[173] *Parl* Pt Durham Parl Bor (1832—1918), pt N'rn Dv (1832—85), pt Mid Dv (1885—1918).

ST JOHN IN WEARDALE—see WEARDALE

ST OSWALD

AP Orig chap in Durham St Giles AP (civ, 'St Oswald'), sep par in 12th cent[197]; for chap and tps (each sep rated for poor law purposes, qv), see 'Durham St Oswald'; after last is sep in 1866, 'St Oswald' has no sep civ identity. *LG* Pt Darl. Wd, pt Eas. Wd (until 1829), Durham Wd (from 1829), pt Durham Old Borough (or Crossgate) (until 1565), pt Durham Bishop's Borough ([pt Framwellgate] until 1565), pt Framwellgate Bor (until 1565), pt Durham and Framwellgate Bor ([Framwellgate] 1565—1835), pt Elvet Barony and Bor ([Elvet] until 1835), pt Durham MB (1835—66). *Parl* Pt Durham and Framwellgate Parl Bor (1678—1832), pt Durham Parl Bor (1832—67), pt N'rn Dv (1832—67).

ST OSWALD'S

CP Cr 1895 from Bearpark CP.[48] *LG* Durham PLU, RD. Abol 1935 pt to Durham MB & CP, pt to Shincliffe CP, pt to Sunderland Bridge CP.[49] *Parl* Durham Dv (1918—48).

SATLEY

Chap in Lanchester AP, sep CP 1866,[1] sep EP 1735 (incl pt tp Hedleyhope in Brancepeth AP[3]). *LG* Seq 2. Civ bdry: 1883,[12] 1887.[98] *Parl* Seq 5. *Eccl* Lanch. RDn (1735—early 19th cent), Durham RDn (early 19th cent—1842), Chest. le Str. RDn (1842—74), Chest. RDn (W'rn Dv) (1874—80), Auckl. RDn (1880—91), Stanh. RDn (1891—*). Eccl bdry: 1863 (help cr Castleside EP),[94] 1878 (help cr Towlaw EP),[183] 1921.[332]

SEAHAM

AP Incl tp Seaton with Slingley (sep CP 1866[1]). *LG* Eas. Wd, PLU, RSD, RD (1894—1937), Seaham UD (1937—74). Addtl civ bdry alt: 1937 (loses pt to Burdon CP, gains Dawdon CP, the altered par then constituted Seaham UD),[15] 1967 (incl loses pt to Sund. CB [assoc with Durham] & CP).[118] *Parl* N'rn Dv (1832—85), Hough. le Spr. Dv (1885—1918), Seaham Dv (1918—48), Hough. le Spr. CC (1948—*). *Eccl* Durham RDn (before 1291—before 1535), Darl. RDn (before 1535—early 19th cent), Durham RDn (early 19th cent—1842), Eas. RDn (1842—74), Eas. RDn (N'rn Dv) (1874—80), Hough. le Spr. RDn (1880—*). Eccl bdry: 1861 (cr New Seaham EP).[87]

NEW SEAHAM

EP Cr 1861 from Seaham AP.[87] RDns as for Seaham, from 1861. Bdry: 1940.[184]

SEAHAM HARBOUR

EP Cr 1843 from Dalton le Dale AP (tp Dawdon, qv for sep civ identity).[175] RDns as for Seaham, from 1843. Bdry: 1912 (cr Dawdon EP),[183] 1940.[184]

SEATON

CP Cr 1894 from the pt of Seaton Carew CP not in W Hartl. CB.[39] *LG* Hartl. PLU, RD (1894—1936), Stock. RD (1936—67). Bdry: 1932 (loses pt to W Hartl. CB [assoc with Durham] & CP),[177] 1946,[251] 1953 (loses pt to W Hartl. CB [assoc with Durham] & CP).[178] Abol 1967 to help cr Hartl. CB (assoc with Durham) and to Hartlepool CP.[117] *Parl* Sedg. Dv (1918—48). Parl bdry: 1953.[179]

SEATON CAREW

Tp in Stranton AP, sep CP 1866,[1] sep EP 1833,[3] eccl refounded 1843.[333] *LG* Stock. Wd, Hartl. PLU, pt Seaton Carew USD (1875—83), W Hartl. MB (pt 1883—94, ent 1894—1902), pt W Hartl. USD (1883—94), pt Hartl. RSD, W Hartl. CB (1902—21). Civ bdry: 1894 (the pt not in W Hartl. CB cr Seaton CP).[47] Abol 1921 ent to West Hartlepool CP.[264] *Parl* S'rn Dv (1832—67), The Hartlepools Parl Bor (1867—1948). *Eccl* Durham RDn (1833—42), Stock. RDn (1842—88), Hartl. RDn (1888—*). Eccl bdry: 1891 (help cr West Hartlepool St Aidan EP).[268]

SEATON WITH SLINGLEY

Tp in Seaham AP, sep CP 1866.[1] *LG* Seq 9. *Parl* Seq 3.

SEDGEFIELD

AP Incl chap Embleton, tps Bradbury, Butterwick and Old Acres, Fishburn, Mordon (each a sep CP 1866[1]), tp Foxton and Shotton (sep CP 1866,[1] eccl severed 1886 and transf to Stillington EP[234]). *LG* Seq 14. *Parl* Seq 13. *Eccl* Durham RDn (before 1291—before 1535), Darl. RDn (before 1535—early 19th cent), Durham RDn (early 19th cent—1842), Stock. RDn (1842—*).

SHADFORTH

Tp in Pittington AP, sep CP 1866,[1] sep EP 1841 (incl pt tp Sherburn in same par).[186] *LG* Seq 11. *Parl* Seq 4. *Eccl* Durham RDn (1841—42), Eas. RDn (1842—74), Eas. RDn (S'rn Dv) (1874—80), Eas. RDn (1880—1970), Durham RDn (1970—*). Eccl bdry: 1914 (help cr Wheatley Hill EP).[46]

SHERATON WITH HULAM

Tp in Monk Hesleden AP, sep CP 1866.[1] *LG* Seq 9. *Parl* Seq 6.

SHERBURN

Tp in Pittington AP, sep CP 1866,[1] pt eccl severed 1841 to help cr Shadforth EP,[186] the remainder cr 1866 'Sherburn' EP.[326] *LG* Seq 11. Civ bdry: 1958.[55] *Parl* Seq 4. *Eccl* Eas. RDn (1866—74), Eas. RDn (S'rn Dv) (1874—80), Eas. RDn (1880—1970), Durham RDn (1970—*).

SHERBURN HOUSE

Ex-par place, sep CP 1858.[194] *LG* Seq 11. Bdry: 1946.[50] *Parl* Seq 4.

SOUTH SHIELDS

The following have 'South Shields' in their names. Insofar as any existed at a given time: *LG* Chest. Wd, S Shields PLU, MB (1850—89), CB, USD. *Parl* S Shields Parl Bor/BC (1832—*). *Eccl* Durham RDn (cr—1842), Chest. le Str. RDn (1842—74), Chest. RDn (E'rn Dv) (1874—80), Jarrow RDn (1880—*).

CP1/EP1—SOUTH SHIELDS [ST HILDA]—Tp in Jarrow AP, sep CP 1866,[1] sep EP 1845 (incl tp Harton in same par).[270] Civ bdry: 1897 (gains Westoe CP),[334] 1901,[102] 1921 (gains Harton CP),[103] 1936 (loses pt to Jarrow MB),[97] 1951.[104] Transf 1974 to Tyne & Wear.[2] Parl bdry: 1951.[335] Eccl bdry: 1848 (cr EP2),[271] 1848 (cr EP10),[336] 1864 (help cr Jarrow Docks EP),[229] 1864 (help cr Harton EP),[272] 1864 (help cr Westoe EP),[295] 1878 (cr South Westoe EP),[6] 1885 (help cr EP3).[85] Abol 1963 to help cr EP5.[337]

EP2—SOUTH SHIELDS HOLY TRINITY—Cr 1848 from EP1.[271] Bdry: 1864 (help cr Jarrow Docks EP),[229] 1864 (help cr Harton EP),[272] 1864 (help cr Westoe EP),[295] 1873 (cr EP7),[338] 1883 (cr EP6),[339] 1886,[340] 1961.[341]

EP3—SOUTH SHIELDS ST AIDAN—Cr 1885 from EP10, EP1.[85]

EP4—SOUTH SHIELDS ST FRANCIS—Cr 1910 from Jarrow Docks EP, EP6.[300]

EP5—SOUTH SHIELDS ST HILDA WITH ST THOMAS—Cr 1963 by union EP1, Westoe EP.[337]

EP6—SOUTH SHIELDS ST JUDE—Cr 1883 from EP2.[339] Bdry: 1886,[340] 1910 (help cr EP4),[300] 1959,[342] 1961.[341]

EP7—SOUTH SHIELDS ST MARK—Cr 1873 from EP2.[338] Abol 1961 pt to EP6, pt to EP2.[341]

—SOUTH SHIELDS ST MARY—see JARROW DOCKS

EP8—SOUTH SHIELDS ST OSWIN—Cr 1910 from South Westoe EP, Harton Colliery EP.[275] Bdry: 1959,[342] 1967.[155]

EP9—SOUTH SHIELDS ST SIMON—Cr 1875 from Jarrow Docks EP.[74] Bdry: 1890 (help cr Harton Colliery EP),[274] 1954,[259] 1969.[140]

EP10—SOUTH SHIELDS ST STEPHEN—Cr 1848 from EP1.[336] Bdry: 1885 (help cr EP3).[308]

SHILDON

Chap in Auckland St Andrew AP, sep CP 1866,[1] sep EP 1837 (incl tps Eldon, Middridge, East Thickley).[22] *LG* Darl. Wd, Auckl. PLU, Shildon & E Thickley USD, UD (1894—1907), Shildon UD (1907—74). Civ bdry: 1937 (incl gains East Thickley CP, Middridge CP),[15] 1952,[31] 1969.[32] *Parl* S'rn Dv (1832—85), Bp Auckl. Dv/CC (1885—*). *Eccl* Durham RDn (1837—42), Darl. RDn (1842—74), Darl. RDn (S'rn Dv) (1874—80), Auckl. RDn (1880—*). Eccl bdry: 1869 (help cr New Shildon EP),[25] 1877 (help cr Eldon EP),[26] 1961 (incl help cr Newton Aycliffe EP).[28]

NEW SHILDON

EP Cr 1869 from Auckland St Andrew AP, Shildon EP.[25] RDns as for Shildon, from 1869.

SHINCLIFFE

Tp in St Oswald AP (eccl, 'Durham St Oswald'), sep CP 1866,[1] sep EP 1827,[3] eccl refounded 1831.[132] *LG* Seq 11. Civ bdry: 1935,[15] 1946,[50] 1953.[127] *Parl* Seq 4. *Eccl* Durham RDn (1827—42), Eas. RDn (1842—74), Eas. RDn (S'rn Dv) (1874—80), Durham RDn (1880—*). Eccl bdry: 1940,[57] 1960.[126]

SHINEY ROW

EP Cr 1913 from Penshaw EP, Newbottle EP, Herrington EP.[282] Hough. le Spr. RDn.

SHORESWOOD

Tp in Norham AP, sep CP 1866.[1] *LG* Norhamshire, Berwick PLU, transf to Northumb 1832 for parl purposes, 1844 for civ purposes.[4] For later civ and parl organisation, see entry in Northumb.

SHOTTON

Tp in Easington AP, sep CP 1866,[1] pt eccl severed 1863 and united with pt tp Haswell in same par, pt tp Easington to cr Shotton with Haswell EP,[203] the latter divided 1870 into the 2 EPs of Shotton, Haswell.[204] *LG* Seq 9. Civ bdry: 1915,[205] 1946,[128] 1947 (cr Horden EP),[290] 1956 (help cr Peterlee CP).[206] *Parl* Seq 6.

EP Cr 1870 when Shotton with Haswell EP divided into 2 EPs of Shotton, Haswell.[204] Eas. RDn (1870—74), Eas. RDn (S'rn Dv) (1874—80), Eas. RDn (1880—*). Bdry: 1956,[163] 1957,[208] 1963.[131]

SHOTTON WITH HASWELL

EP Cr 1863 from Easington AP (pt tps Shotton, Haswell, pt tp Easington).[203] Eas. RDn. Divided 1870 into 2 EPs of Shotton, Haswell EP.[204]

SILKSWORTH

Tp in Bishopwearmouth AP, sep CP 1866,[1] sep EP 1868.[79] *LG* Eas. Wd, Hough. le Spr. PLU, RSD, RD (1894—1937), Sund. RD (1937—67). Civ bdry: 1928 (loses pt to Sund. CB [assoc with Durham] & CP),[93] 1936 (loses pt to Sund. CB [assoc with Durham] & CP),[230] 1946 (help cr Herrington EP).[284] Abol civ 1967 pt to Sund. CB (assoc with Durham) & CP, pt to Houghton le Spring UD & AP.[118] *Parl* N'rn Dv (1832—85), Hough. le Spr. Dv/CC (1885—1970). Parl bdry: 1952.[232] *Eccl* Eas. RDn (1868—74), Eas. RDn (N'rn Dv) (1874—80), Wearm. RDn (1880—*). Eccl bdry: 1950,[76] 1952.[90]

SOCKBURN

AP Tp 'Sockburn' in Durham (Stock. Wd [until 1829], Darl. Wd [from 1829]); incl in Yorks N Riding (Allerton Wap) tps Girsby, Over Dinsdale (each a sep CP 1866 in Yorks[1]) so that Sockburn ent Durham thereafter. *LG* Darl. PLU, RSD, RD. *Parl* Durham pt, Seq 12. *Eccl* Seq 5.

SOUTHWICK

Tp in Monkwearmouth AP, sep CP 1866,[1] sep EP 1847 by union tp Southwick, tps North Hylton, South Hylton (neither sep civ; for civ, see 'Hylton').[113] *LG* Chest. Wd (until 1829), Eas. Wd (from 1829), Sund. PLU, Southwick on Wear USD (ent 1875—87, pt 1887, ent 1887—94), pt Sund. RSD (1887), Southwick on Wear UD (1894—1928). Civ bdry: 1887.[236] Abol civ 1928 ent to

Sund. CB (assoc with Durham) & CP.[93] *Parl* Sund. Parl Bor (1832—1948). *Eccl* Chest. le Str. RDn (1847—74), Chest. RDn (E'rn Dv) (1874—80), Wearm. RDn (1880—*). Eccl bdry: 1874 (cr North Hylton EP),[277] 1884 (cr Southwick St Columba EP),[313] 1951,[73] 1958.[293]

SOUTHWICK ST COLUMBA
EP Cr 1884 from Monkwearmouth All Saints EP, Southwick EP.[313] Wearm. RDn. Bdry: 1962.[176]

SPENNYMOOR
EP Cr 1875 from Whitworth EP.[74] Darl. RDn (N'rn Dv) (1875—80), Auckl. RDn (1880—1940). Bdry: 1884 (help cr Tudhoe Grange EP).[204] Abol 1940 to help cr Whitworth with Spennymoor EP.[123]

CP Cr 1937 by union Low Spennymoor CP, Merrington Lane CP, Tudhoe CP, Whitworth AP, Whitworth Without CP, and pts Brandon and Byshottles CP, Byers Green CP, Hett CP, Merrington AP, Middlestone CP, Newfield CP, Old Park CP, Westerton CP.[15] *LG* Spennym. UD. *Parl* Durham CC (1948—70), N W Durham CC (1970—*).

LOW SPENNYMOOR
CP Cr 1894 from the pt of Ferryhill CP transf to Spennym. UD,[227] and from addtl pts of Ferryhill CP, Whitworth AP, Tudhoe CP.[228] *LG* Sedg. PLU, Spennym. UD. Abol 1937 to help cr Spennymoor CP.[15] *Parl* Spennym. Dv (1918—48).

STAINDROP
AP Incl tp Ingleton (sep CP 1866,[1] sep EP 1845[109]), tps Hilton, Langleydale and Shotton, Raby with Keverstone, Wackerfield, pt tp Cleatham (each a sep CP 1866[1]). *LG* Seq 7. *Parl* Seq 8. *Eccl* Seq 3.

GREAT STAINTON
AP Orig in co Sedberge (Northumb until 1189, Durham thereafter, considered a sep co until mid 15th cent, thereafter in other wards). Sometimes called 'Stainton le Street'. Incl tp Elstob (sep CP 1866[1]). *LG* Seq 15. *Parl* Seq 12. *Eccl* Darl. RDn (before 1291—early 19th cent), Durham RDn (early 19th cent—1842), Stock. RDn (1842—80), Darl. RDn (1880—1927), Stock. RDn (1927—*).

LITTLE STAINTON
Tp in Bishopton AP, sep CP 1866.[1] *LG* Seq 15. *Parl* Seq 12.

STAINTON LE STREET—see GREAT STAINTON
STANHOPE
AP *LG* Darl. Wd, Weard. PLU, pt Stanh. USD, pt Weard. RSD, Weard. RD. Civ bdry: 1883,[12] 1894 (the pt in Stanh. UD cr Stanhope Urban CP),[39] 1937 (gains Stanhope Urban CP),[15] 1946.[343] *Parl* Seq 9. *Eccl* Seq 7. Eccl bdry: 1817 (cr Weardale St John EP,[3] refounded 1866[272]), 1827 (cr Heatherycleugh EP,[3] refounded 1866[272]), 1866 (cr Rookhope EP),[272] 1866 (help cr Frosterley EP),[94] 1885 (cr Eastgate [sometimes 'Stanhope All Saints, Eastgate'] EP).[209]

STANHOPE ALL SAINTS, EASTGATE—see EASTGATE
STANHOPE URBAN
CP Cr 1894 from the pt of Stanhope AP in Stanh. UD.[39] *LG* Weard. PLU, Stanh. UD. Abol 1937 ent to Stanhope AP.[15] *Parl* Barn. Cast. Dv (1918—48).

STANLEY
EP Cr 1872 from Crook EP.[170] Darl. RDn (1872—74), Darl. RDn (N'rn Dv) (1874—80), Auckl. RDn (1880—91), Stanh. RDn (1891—*).
CP Cr 1894 from the pt of Tanfield CP in Stanley UD.[62] *LG* Lanch. PLU, Stanley UD. Bdry: 1895,[295] 1916,[317] 1937 (incl gains Greencroft Within CP, Kyo CP).[15] *Parl* Consett Dv/CC (1918—*).

STELLA
Tp in Ryton AP, sep CP 1866,[1] sep EP 1845 (incl pt Winlaton EP).[330] *LG* Chest. Wd, Gatesh. PLU, Blaydon USD, UD. Abol 1937 to help cr Blaydon CP.[15] *Parl* N'rn Dv (1832—85), Chest. le Str. Dv (1885—1918), Blayd. Dv (1918—48). *Eccl* Chest. le Str. RDn (1845—74), Chest. RDn (W'rn Dv) (1874—80), Ryton RDn (1880—91), Chest. le Str. RDn (1891—*). Eccl bdry: 1905 (help cr Swalwell EP).[245]

STILLINGTON
Chap in Redmarshall AP, sep CP 1866,[1] sep EP 1872 by union chap Stillington, tp Whitton in Grindon AP.[243] *LG* Seq 14. *Parl* Seq 13. *Eccl* Stock. RDn. Eccl bdry: 1886 (gains tp Foxton and Shotton from Sedgefield AP).[234]

STOCKLEY
Tp in Brancepeth AP, sep CP 1866,[1] pt eccl severed 1858 to help cr Willington EP.[111] *LG* Darl. Wd (until 1829), Durham Wd (from 1829), Durham PLU, RSD, RD (1875—81), Willington USD (1881—94), UD (1894—1937). Bdry: 1881.[343] Abol 1937 to help cr Crook & Willington UD & CP.[15] *Parl* S'rn Dv (1832—85), Mid Dv (1885—1918), Spennym. Dv (1918—48).

STOCKTON ON TEES
The following have 'Stockton on Tees' (civ) or 'Stockton upon Tees' (eccl) in their names. Insofar as any existed at a given time: *LG* Stock. Wd, PLU, Stock. on Tees MB (pt 1835—89, ent 1889—1967), Stock. USD (pt 1875—89, ent 1889—94), pt Stock. RSD (1875—89). *Parl* S'rn Dv (1832—67), Stock. on Tees Parl Bor/BC (1867—1970). *Eccl* Darl. RDn (cr—early 19th cent), Durham RDn (early 19th cent—1842), Stock. RDn (1842—*).

CP1/EP1—STOCKTON ON [eccl, UPON] TEES [ST THOMAS]—Chap in Norton AP, sep par 1713.[260] Incl tp Preston on Tees (sep CP 1866,[1] sep EP 1924 from EP2, Egglescliffe EP[214]), tp East Hartburn (sep CP 1866[1]). Addtl civ bdry alt: 1887,[321] 1887 (loses pt to Thornaby AP, Yorks N Riding),[344] 1895 (gains pt Linthorpe CP, Yorks N Riding),[345] 1913,[220] 1951.[221] Abol 1968 ent to help cr Teeside CB (assoc with Yorks N Riding) & CP.[65] Parl bdry: 1952.[137] Addtl eccl bdry alt: 1837 (cr EP2),[346] 1864 (cr EP4),[242] 1871 (cr EP5),[341] 1875 (help cr EP6, help cr EP7),[74] 1918 (help cr Norton St Michael and All Angels EP),[322] 1928.[323]

EP2—STOCKTON UPON TEES HOLY TRINITY—Cr 1837 from EP1.[346] Bdry: 1875 (help cr EP6, help cr EP7),[74] 1924 (help cr Preston on Tees EP),[214] 1928.[323]

EP3—STOCKTON UPON TEES ST CHAD—Cr 1959

from Norton AP.[324]

EP4—STOCKTON UPON TEES ST JAMES—Cr 1864 from EP1.[242] Bdry: 1928.[323]

EP5—STOCKTON UPON TEES ST JOHN THE BAPTIST—Cr 1871 from EP1.[341] Bdry: 1918 (help cr Norton St Michael and All Angels EP),[322] 1928.[323]

EP6—STOCKTON UPON TEES ST PAUL—Cr 1875 from EP1, EP2.[74] Bdry: 1928.[323]

EP7—STOCKTON UPON TEES ST PETER—Cr 1875 from EP1, EP2.[74] Bdry: 1928.[323]

STOTFIELD BURN—see ROOKHOPE

STRANTON

AP Orig in co Sadberge (Northumb until 1189, Durham thereafter, considered a sep co until mid 15th cent, then in other Wds). Incl tp Brierton (sep CP 1866[1]), tp Seaton Carew (sep CP 1866,[1] sep EP 1843[333]). *LG* Stock. Wd, Hartl. PLU, pt Middleton in Stranton USD (1875—83), pt Hartl. MB & USD (1883—94), pt W Hartl. MB & USD (1887—94), Hartl. RD. Addtl civ bdry alt: 1894 (the pt in Hartl. MB cr Middleton CP, the pt in W Hartl. MB cr West Hartlepool CP).[39] Abol civ 1932 pt to W Hartl. CB (assoc with Durham) & CP, pt to Dalton Piercy CP.[177] *Parl* S'rn Dv (1832—67), The Hartlepools Parl Bor (1867—1918), Sedg. Dv (1918—48). *Eccl* Durham RDn (before 1291—before 1535), Darl. RDn (before 1535—early 19th cent), Durham RDn (early 19th cent—1842), Stock. RDn (1842—88), Hartl. RDn (1888—1968). Addtl eccl bdry alt: 1885 (cr West Hartlepool EP,[1] refounded 1859[265]), 1886 (cr West Hartlepool St Paul EP),[269] 1891 (help cr West Hartlepool St Aidan EP),[268] 1898,[204] 1932,[259] 1957,[75] 1957.[259] Renamed eccl 1968 'Hartlepool All Saints, Stranton' EP.[76]

STRANTON ALL SAINTS

EP Cr 1973 by union pt Hartlepool Christ Church EP, pt Hartlepool All Saints, Stranton EP.[261] Hartl. RDn.

STREATLAM AND STAINTON

Tp in Gainford AP, sep CP 1866.[1] *LG* Seq 7. Bdry: 1883,[12] 1884.[38] *Parl* Seq 8.

SUMMERHOUSE

Tp in Gainford AP, sep CP 1866,[1] pt eccl severed 1932 and transf to Denton EP.[187] *LG* Seq 4. *Parl* Seq 12.

SUNDERLAND

Area in Bishopwearmouth AP, sep par 1719.[78] *LG* Eas. Wd, Sund. PLU, MB/CB, USD. Civ bdry: 1897 (gains the other pars in Sund. CB: Bishopwearmouth AP, Bishopwearmouth Panns CP, Monkwearmouth AP, Monkwearmouth Shores CP, Ryhope Within CP),[81] 1928 (incl gains Southwick on Wear UD & Southwick CP, gains Bishopwearmouth Without CP, Fulwell CP),[93] 1936,[230] 1967 (incl gains Tunstall CP and loses pt to Hough. le Spr. UD & AP).[231] Transf 1974 to Tyne & Wear.[2] *Parl* Sund. Parl Bor (1832—1948), pt Sund. North BC, pt Sund. South BC (1948—*). Parl bdry: 1952.[232] *Eccl* Chest. le Str. RDn (1769—1842), Eas. RDn (1842—74), Eas. RDn (N'rn Dv) (1874—80), Wearm. RDn (1880—*). Eccl bdry:

1769 (cr Sunderland St John EP,[1] refounded 1875[347]), 1948 (gains Bishopwearmouth St Thomas EP, Sunderland St John EP).[88]

SUNDERLAND ST JOHN

EP Cr 1769 from Sunderland EP,[3] refounded 1875.[347] Chest. le Str. RDn (1769—1842), Eas. RDn (1842—74), Eas. RDn (N'rn Dv) (1874—80), Wearm. RDn (1880—1948). Abol 1948 ent to Sunderland EP.[88]

SUNDERLAND BRIDGE

Tp in St Oswald AP (eccl, 'Durham St Oswald'), sep CP 1866.[1] *LG* Seq 8. Bdry: 1935,[49] 1937.[15] *Parl* Seq 10.

SUNNYBROW

EP Cr 1899 from Crook EP, Willington EP.[171] Auckl. RDn. Bdry: 1903.[5]

SWALWELL

EP Cr 1905 from Whickham AP, Winlaton EP, Stella EP.[245] Chest. le Str. RDn.

TANFIELD

Chap in Chester le Street AP, sep CP 1866,[1] sep EP 1768.[3] *LG* Chest. Wd, Lanch. PLU, pt Stanley USD (1892—94), pt Whickham USD (1883—94), Lanch. RSD (ent 1875—83, pt 1883—94 [reduced pt 1892—94]), Lanch. RD (1894—95), Tanfield UD (1895—1937). Civ bdry: 1883,[1] 1886,[162] 1887,[60] 1894 (the pt in Whickham USD transf to Whickham AP),[348] 1895,[305] 1896,[98] 1899.[303] Abol civ 1937 pt to Consett UD & CP, pt to Stanley UD & CP, pt to Lamesley CP.[15] *Parl* N'rn Dv (1832—85), N-W'rn Dv (1885—1918), Blayd. Dv (1918—48). *Eccl* Chest. le Str. RDn (1768—early 19th cent), Durham RDn (early 19th cent—1842), Chest. le Str. RDn (1842—74), Chest. RDn (W'rn Dv) (1874—80), Ryton RDn (1880—91), Chest. le Str. RDn (1891—*). Eccl bdry: 1865 (help cr Holmside EP),[242] 1871 (help cr Burnopfield EP),[120] 1873 (help cr Beamish EP),[40] 1874 (help cr Marley Hill EP),[304] 1876 (help cr West Pelton EP),[141] 1883 (help cr Dipton EP),[163] 1953.[121]

EAST THICKLEY

Tp in Auckland St Andrew AP, sep CP 1866,[1] eccl severed 1837 to help cr Shildon EP.[22] *LG* Darl. Wd, Auckl. PLU, Shildon & E Thickley USD, UD (1894—1907), Shildon UD (1907—37). Abol 1937 ent to Shldon CP.[15] *Parl* S'rn Dv (1832—85), Bp Auckl. Dv (1885—1948).

THORNLEY

Tp in Kelloe AP, sep CP 1866,[1] sep EP 1844 (incl tp Wingate in same par).[46] *LG* Seq 9. *Parl* Seq 6. *Eccl* Eas. RDn (1844—74), Eas. RDn (S'rn Dv) (1874—80), Eas. RDn (1880—*). Eccl bdry: 1885,[309] 1914 (the orig area of tp Wingate severed to help cr Wheatley Hill EP),[46] 1965.[24]

THORNLEY ST BARTHOLOMEW

Chap in Wolsingham AP (incl area Tow Law, no sep civ identity until 1894, qv), sep EP 1848.[349] Darl. RDn (1848—74), Darl. RDn (N'rn Dv) (1874—80), Auckl. RDn (1880—91), Stanh. RDn (1891—*). Bdry: 1878 (orig area of Tow Law severed to help cr Towlaw EP).[183]

THORNTON

Tp in Norham AP, sep CP 1866.[1] *LG* Norhamshire,

Berwick PLU, transf to Northumb 1832 for parl purposes, 1844 for civ purposes.[4] *Parl* In Durham until 1832, Northumb thereafter. For later civ and parl organisation, see entry in Northumb.

THORPE BULMER

Tp in Hart AP, sep CP 1866.[1] *LG* Eas. Wd, Hartl. PLU, RSD, RD. Abol 1936 pt to Hartl. MB & CP, pt to Monk Hesleden AP, pt to Hart AP.[97] *Parl* N'rn Dv (1832—85), S-E'rn Dv (1885—1918), Sedg. Dv (1918—48).

THRISLINGTON

Tp in Bishop Middleham AP, sep CP 1866.[1] *LG* Stock. Wd (until 1829), Durham Wd (from 1829), Sedg. PLU, RSD, RD. Abol 1946 pt to Cornforth CP, pt to Ferryhill CP.[144] *Parl* S'rn Dv (1832—85), Mid Dv (1885—1918), Sedg. Dv (1918—52).

THROSTON

Tp in Hart AP, sep CP 1866.[1] *LG* Stock. Wd, Hartl. PLU, pt Throston USD (1875—83), Hartl. MB (pt 1883—94, ent 1894—1936), pt Hartl. USD (1883—94), pt Hartl. RSD. Bdry: 1894 (the pt not in Hartl. MB cr Throston Rural EP),[47] 1897.[255] Abol 1936 ent to Hartlepool CP.[97] *Parl* S'rn Dv (1832—85), The Hartlepools Parl Bor (1867—1948).

THROPSTON RURAL

CP Cr 1894 from the pt of Throston CP not in Hartl. MB.[47] *LG* Hartl. PLU, RD. Bdry: 1897,[255] 1897.[263] Abol 1932 pt to W Hartl. CB (assoc with Durham) & CP, pt to Hartl. MB & CP, pt to Elwick CP.[177] *Parl* Sedg. Dv (1918—48).

TOW LAW

Area in chap Thornley (sep EP 1848 from Wolsingham AP[329]), 'Towlaw' a sep EP 1878 from Thorney EP, Satley EP,[183] qv in following entry, 'Tow Law' a sep CP 1894 from the pt of Wolsingham AP in Tow Law UD.[39] *LG* Weard. PLU, Tow Law UD. *Parl* Spennym. Dv (1918—48), N W Durham CC (1948—*).

TOWLAW

Area in chap Thornely (sep EP 1848 from Wolsingham AP[329]), 'Towlaw' a sep EP 1878 from Thornley EP, Satley EP,[183] 'Tow Law' a sep CP 1894 from the pt of Wolsingham AP in Tow Law UD,[39] qv in prev entry. *Eccl* Darl. RDn (N'rn Dv) (1878—80), Auckl. RDn (1880—91), Stanh. RDn (1891—*). Eccl bdry: 1921,[332] 1965.[24]

TRIMDON

Chap in Kelloe AP, sep civ identity early, sep EP 1755.[3] *LG* Eas. Wd, Sedg. PLU, RSD, RD. Civ bdry: 1937.[15] *Parl* N'rn Dv (1832—85), S-E'rn Dv (1885—1918), Sedg. Dv/CC (1918—70), Durham CC (1970—*). *Eccl* Darl. RDn (1755—1842), Eas. RDn (1842—74), Eas. RDn (S'rn Dv) (1874—80), Eas. RDn (1880—*). Eccl bdry: 1874 (help cr Deaf Hill cum Langdale EP),[185] 1896 (area of Trimdon Grange severed and transf to Kelloe EP [qv for cr 1920 as 'Trimdon Grange' EP]).[301]

TRIMDON GRANGE

EP Cr 1920 from Kelloe AP (for prev status in Trimdon AP, see prev entry).[84] Eas. RDn.

TUDHOE

Tp in Whitworth AP, sep CP 1866,[1] eccl severed 1843 to help cr Ferryhill EP,[143] eccl severed 1865

from latter and gains pt Brancepeth AP, Merrington AP, to cr 'Tudhoe' EP.[229] *LG* Darl. Wd, Durham PLU, RSD, Spennym. UD (1894—1937). Civ bdry: 1886,[226] 1894.[228] Abol civ 1937 to help cr Spennymoor CP.[15] *Parl* S'rn Dv (1832—85), Mid Dv (1885—1918), Spennym. Dv (1918—48). *Eccl* Darl. RDn (1865—74), Darl. RDn (N'rn Dv) (1874—80), Auckl. RDn (1880—*). Eccl bdry: 1884 (help cr Tudhoe Grange EP).[204]

TUDHOE GRANGE

EP Cr 1884 from Tudhoe EP, Spennymoor EP.[204] Auckl. RDn.

TUNSTALL

Tp in Bishopwearmouth AP, sep CP 1866,[1] eccl severed 1829 to help cr Ryhope EP,[3] the latter eccl refounded 1854.[77] *LG* Eas. Wd, Sund. PLU, RSD, RD. Civ bdry: 1928 (loses pt to Sund. CB [assoc with Durham] & CP),[93] 1946.[284] Abol 1967 ent to Sund. CB (assoc with Durham) & CP.[231] *Parl* N'rn Dv (1832—85), Hough. le Spr. Dv/CC (1885—1970).

TWEEDMOUTH

Chap in Holy Island AP, sep civ identity early, sep EP 1737.[3] *LG* Islandshire, Berwick PLU, pt Berwick upon Tweed MB (from 1835), transf to Northumb 1832 for parl purposes, 1844 for civ purposes.[4] *Parl* In Durham until 1832, Northumb thereafter. For later civ and parl organisation, and for ent eccl organisation (incl cr 1844 of Scremerston EP), see entry in Northumb.

TWIZELL

Tp in Norham AP, sep CP 1866.[1] *LG* Norhamshire, Berwick PLU, transf to Northumb 1832 for parl purposes, 1844 for civ purposes.[4] *Parl* In Durham until 1832, Northumb thereafter. For later civ and parl organisation, see entry in Northumb.

TYNE DOCKS—see JARROW DOCKS

UNDIVIDED MOOR COMMON TO LYNESACK AND SOFTLEY, HAMSTERLEY AND SOUTH BEDBURN

LG Auckl. RD (1894—1937), Barn. Cast. RD (1937—74). *Parl* Bp Auckl. Dv/CC (1918—*).

URPETH

Tp in Chester le Street AP, sep CP 1866,[1] eccl severed 1843 to help cr Pelton EP.[133] *LG* Seq 1. Bdry: 1883,[12] 1886,[162] 1937.[15] *Parl* Seq 1.

USHAW MOOR

EP Cr 1914 from Esh EP, Bearpark EP.[46] Lanch. RDn (1914—24), Durham RDn (1924—*). Bdry: 1947,[115] 1962.[41]

USWORTH

Chap in Washington AP, sep CP [sometimes 'Great and Little Usworth'] 1866,[1] sep EP 1837.[3] *LG* Chest. Wd, Chest. le Str. PLU, RSD, RD (1894—1922), Wash. UD (1922—37). Civ bdry: 1881.[253] Abol civ 1937 ent to Washington AP.[15] *Parl* N'rn Dv (1832—85), Chest. le Str. Dv (1885—1948). *Eccl* Durham RDn (1837—42), Chest. le Str. RDn (1842—74), Chest. RDn (W'rn Dv) (1874—80), Chest. le Str. RDn (1880—1924), Gatesh. RDn (1924—65), Chest. le Str. RDn (1965—*). Eccl bdry: 1875 (help cr Fatfield EP).[74]

WACKERFIELD

Tp in Staindrop AP, sep CP 1866,[1] eccl severed 1845 to help cr Ingleton EP.[109] *LG* Seq 7. *Parl* Seq 8.

WALDRIDGE

Tp in Chester le Street AP, sep CP 1866.[1] *LG* Seq 1. Bdry: 1896,[212] 1937.[15] *Parl* Seq 1.

WALWORTH

Tp in Heighington AP, sep CP 1866.[1] *LG* Seq 4. *Parl* Seq 12.

WARDEN LAW

Tp in Houghton le Spring AP, sep CP 1866.[1] *LG* Eas. Wd, Hough. le Spr. PLU, RSD, RD (1894—1937), Eas. RD (1937—74). Transf 1974 to Tyne & Wear.[2] *Parl* N'rn Dv (1832—85), Hough. le Spr. Dv (1885—1948), Eas. CC (1948—70), Hough. le Spr. CC (1970—*).

WASHINGTON

AP Incl tps Barmston, Usworth (each a sep CP 1866[1]). *LG* Chest. Wd, Chest. le Str. PLU, RSD, RD (1894—1922), Wash. UD (1922—74). Addtl civ bdry alt: 1937 (incl gains Bramston CP, Usworth CP),[15] 1967.[118] Transf 1974 to Tyne & Wear.[2] *Parl* Seq 1. *Eccl* Durham RDn (before 1291—before 1535), Chest. le Str. RDn (before 1535—early 19th cent), Chest. le Str. RDn (1842—74), Chest. RDn (W'rn Dv) (1874—80), Chest. le Str. RDn (1880—*). Eccl bdry: 1875 (help cr Fatfield EP),[74] 1957.[139]

WATERHOUSES

EP Cr 1879 from Brancepeth AP (incl area hmlt Waterhouses).[113] Darl. RDn (N'rn Dv) (1879—80), Durham RDn (1880—*). Bdry: 1921.[332]

WEARDALE ST JOHN

EP Cr 1817 from Stanhope AP,[3] refounded 1866.[272] Durham RDn (1817—42), Darl. RDn (1842—74), Darl. RDn (N'rn Dv) (1874—80), Stanh. RDn (1880—*). Bdry: 1867 (cr Westgate EP).[350] Usually called 'St John in Weardale'.

WESTERTON

Tp in Auckland St Andrew AP, sep CP 1866,[1] eccl severed 1842 to help cr Coundon EP.[20] *LG* Darl. Wd, Auckl. PLU, RSD, RD. Abol 1937 pt to Bp Auckl. UD & CP, pt tp Spennym. UD to help cr Spennymoor CP.[15] *Parl* S'rn Dv (1832—85), Bp Auckl. Dv (1885—1948).

WESTGATE

EP Cr 1867 from Weardale St John EP.[350] Darl. RDn (1867—74), Darl. RDn (N'rn Dv) (1874—80), Stanh. RDn (1880—*).

WESTOE

Tp in chap South Shields (sep CP 1866 from Jarrow AP,[1] sep EP 1845[270]), 'Westoe' a sep CP 1866,[1] sep EP 1821,[3] eccl refounded 1864 from South Shields EP, South Shields Holy Trinity EP.[295] *LG* Chest. Wd, S Shields PLU, MB (1850—89), USD, CB (1889—97). Abol civ 1897 ent to South Shields CP.[334] *Parl* S Shields Parl Bor (1832—1918). *Eccl* Durham RDn (1821—42), Chest. le Str. RDn (1842—74), Chest. RDn (E'rn Dv) (1874—80), Jarrow RDn (1880—1963). Eccl bdry: 1885 (help cr South Shields St Aidan EP).[85] Abol eccl 1963 to help cr South Shields St Hilda with St Thomas

EP.[337]

SOUTH WESTOE

EP Cr 1878 from South Shields EP.[6] Chest. RDn (E'rn Dv) (1878—80), Jarrow RDn (1880—*). Bdry: 1903 (help cr South Shields St Oswin EP),[275] 1967.[155]

WESTWICK

Tp in Gainford AP, sep CP 1866.[1] *LG* Seq 7. *Parl* Seq 8.

WHEATLEY HILL

EP Cr 1914 from Thornley EP (area of Wingate CP), Shadforth EP.[46] Eas. RDn. Bdry: 1963.[131]

WHESSOE

Tp in Haughton le Skerne AP, sep CP 1866.[1] *LG* Seq 4. Bdry: 1930 (loses pt to Darl. CB [assoc with Durham] & AP).[10] *Parl* S'rn Dv (1832—85), S-E'rn Dv (1885—1918), Sedg. Dv/CC (1918—70), Bp Auckl. CC (1970—*).

WHICKHAM

AP *LG* Chest. Wd, Gatesh. PLU, Whickham USD (ent 1875—83, pt 1883—94), pt Gatesh. RSD (1883—94), Whickham UD. Civ bdry: 1883,[12] 1894 (the par made ent in the UD),[348] 1896,[98] 1899,[303] 1936 (loses pt to Gatesh. CB [assoc with Durham] & AP),[97] 1937.[15] Transf 1974 to Tyne & Wear.[2] *Parl* N'rn Dv (1832—85), Chest. le Str. Dv (1885—1918), Blayd. Dv/CC (1918—70), Blayd. BC (1970—*). *Eccl* Seq 6. Eccl bdry: 1871 (help cr Burnopfield EP),[120] 1872 (help cr Dunston Christ Church EP),[7] 1874 (help cr Marley Hill EP),[304] 1905 (help cr Dunston St Nicholas EP),[191] 1905 (help cr Swalwell EP),[245] 1936 (help cr Dunston St Nicholas EP),[191] 1953.[121]

WHITBURN

AP *LG* Chest. Wd, S Shields PLU, RSD, RD. Civ bdry: 1883,[12] 1887,[236] 1921 (loses pt to S Shields CB [assoc with Durham] & CP),[103] 1928 (loses pt to Sund. CB [assoc with Durham] & CP).[93] Abol civ 1936 pt to S Shields CB (assoc with Durham) & CP, pt to Boldon UD & AP.[97] *Parl* N'rn Dv (1832—85), Jarrow Dv (1885—1918), Hough. le Spr. Dv (1918—48). *Eccl* Durham RDn (before 1291—before 1535), Chest. le Str. RDn (before 1535—early 19th cent), Durham RDn (early 18th cent—1842), Chest. le Str. RDn (1842—74), Chest. RDn (E'rn Dv) (1874—80), Wearm. RDn (1880—*). Eccl bdry: 1878 (help cr Hedworth EP),[106] 1911 (cr Cleadon EP),[150] 1958.[153]

WHITTON

Tp in Grindon AP, sep CP 1866,[1] eccl severed 1872 to help cr Stillington EP.[243] *LG* Seq 12. Transf 1974 to Clev.[2] *Parl* Seq 14.

WHITWELL HOUSE

Ex-par place, sep CP 1858,[194] eccl reduced in area 1960 when pt transf to Cassop cum Quarrington EP.[126] *LG* Seq 11. Civ bdry: 1953.[127] *Parl* Seq 4.

WHITWORTH

AP Incl tp Tudoe, pt tp Byers Green (each a sep CP 1866[1]). *LG* Darl. Wd, Auckl. PLU, pt Spennym. USD, pt Auckl. RSD, Spennym. UD. Civ bdry: 1894 (the pt not in the UD transf to Low Spennymoor CP,[14] gains pts other pars,[228] the remainder cr Whitworth Without CP[14]). Abol civ

1937 to help cr Spennymoor CP.[15] *Parl* S'rn Dv (1832—85), Bp Auckl. Dv (1885—1918), Spennym. Dv (1918—48). *Eccl* Durham RDn (until 1842), Darl. RDn (1842—74), Darl. RDn (N'rn Dv) (1874—80), Auckl. RDn (1880—1940). Eccl bdry: 1875 (cr Spennymoor EP).[74] Abol eccl 1940 pt to Byers Green EP, pt to help cr Whitworth with Spennymoor EP).[123]

WHITWORTH WITH SPENNYMOOR

EP Cr 1940 by union Spennymoor EP, pt Whitworth EP.[123] Auckl. RDn.

WHITWORTH WITHOUT

CP Cr 1894 from the pt of Whitworth AP not in Spennym. UD.[14] *LG* Auckl. PLU, RD. Abol 1937 ent to Spennym. UD to help cr Spennymoor CP.[15] *Parl* Bp Auckl. Dv (1918—48).

WHORLTON

Chap in Gainford AP, sep CP 1866,[1] sep EP 1767.[3] *LG* Seq 7. *Parl* Seq 8. *Eccl* Darl. RDn (1767—early 19th cent), Durham RDn (early 19th cent—1842), Darl. RDn (1842—74), Darl. RDn (S'rn Dv) (1874—80), Darl. RDn (1880—1924), Barn. Cast. RDn (1924—*).

WILLINGTON

Tp in Brancepeth AP, sep CP 1866,[1] pt eccl severed 1845 to help cr Crook EP,[109] the remainder united 1858 with pt tp Brancepeth, pt tp Stockley in the same par to cr 'Willington' EP.[111] *LG* Darl. Wd, Durham PLU, RSD (1875—81), Willington USD (1881—94), UD. Civ bdry: 1881,[351] 1881.[281] Abol 1937 pt to Bp Auckl. UD & CP, pt to help cr Crook and Willington UD & CP.[15] *Parl* S'rn Dv (1832—85), Mid Dv (1885—1918), Spennym. Dv (1918—48). *Eccl* Darl. RDn (1858—74), Darl. RDn (N'rn Dv) (1874—80), Durham RDn (1880—1924), Auckl. RDn (1924—*). Eccl bdry: 1889 (help cr Sunnybrow EP).[171]

WINDLESTONE

Tp in Auckland St Andrew AP, sep CP 1866,[1] eccl severed 1842 to help cr Coundon EP.[20] *LG* Darl. Wd, Auckl. PLU, RSD, RD (1894—1937), Sedg. RD (1937—74). Bdry: 1937.[15] *Parl* S'rn Dv (1832—85), Bp Auckl. Dv (1885—1948), Sedg. CC (1948—70), Durham CC (1970—*).

WINDYNOOK—see HEWORTH ST ALBAN

WINGATE

Tp in Kelloe AP, sep CP 1866,[1] eccl in chap Thornley (sep EP 1844 from Kelloe[44]), orig area Kelloe eccl severed 1914 from Thornley EP to help cr Wheatley Hill EP.[46] *LG* Seq 9. Bdry: 1946.[128] *Parl* Seq 6.

WINGATE GRANGE

EP Cr 1842 from Castle Eden AP, Kelloe AP.[99] Eas. RDn (1842—74), Eas. RDn (S'rn Dv) (1874—80), Eas. RDn (1880—*). Bdry: 1874 (help cr Deaf Hill cum Langdale EP),[185] 1925,[130] 1963.[131]

WINLATON

Tp (private chap built later) in Ryton AP, sep civ identity early (incl tp Chopwell, a sep CP 1866[1]), the tps of Winlaton, Chopwell eccl united 1832 as 'Winlaton' EP,[146] orig area of Chopwell eccl severed 1916 from the later to cr 'Chopwell' EP.[147] *LG* Chest. Wd, Gatesh. PLU, Blaydon USD, UD.

Addtl civ bdry alt: 1896.[98] Abol civ 1937 pt to Blaydon CP, pt to Stanley UD & CP, pt to Whickham UD & AP.[15] *Parl* N'rn Dv (1832—85), Chest. le Str. Dv (1885—1918), Blayd. Dv (1918—48). *Eccl* Durham RDn (1834—42), Chest. le Str. RDn (1842—74), Chest. RDn (W'rn Dv) (1874—80), Ryton RDn (1880—91), Chest. le Str. RDn (1891—*). Addtl eccl bdry alt: 1845 (help cr Stella EP),[330] 1905 (help cr Swalwell EP).[245]

WINSTON

AP Incl pt tp Cleatlam (sep CP 1866[1]). *LG* Seq 7. *Parl* S'rn Dv (1832—85), Chest. le Str. Dv (1885—1918), Barn. Cast. Dv (1918—48), Bp Auckl. CC (1948—*). *Eccl* Seq 3.

WITTON GILBERT

AP Orig chap in St Oswald AP (eccl, 'Durham St Oswald'), sep par 1423.[201] Gains eccl 1593 Kimblesworth AP, the union eccl 'Witton Gilbert with Kimblesworth',[202] qv below (Kimblesworth retains sep civ identity as ex-par place, sep CP 1858[194]). *LG* Chest. Wd (until 1829), Durham Wd (from 1829), Chest. le Str. PLU, RSD, RD (1894—1937), Durham RD (1937—74). Civ bdry: 1883,[12] 1885,[60] 1887,[325] 1937 (cr Sacriston CP),[15] 1946.[50] *Parl* N'rn Dv (1832—85), Mid Dv (1885—1918), Chest. le Str. Dv (1918—48), Durham CC (1948—*). *Eccl* Chest. le Str. RDn.

EP Name used from 1923 for remainder of Witton Gilbert with Kimblesworth EP after Kimblesworth (incl other areas, qv) cr a sep EP.[142] Durham RDn. Bdry: 1962.[41]

WITTON GILBERT WITH KIMBLESWORTH

EP Cr 1593 by union Witton Gilbert AP, Kimblesworth AP (sep civ identity of each retained, qv, the latter as civ ex-par).[202] Chest. le Str. RDn (1593—early 19th cent), Durham RDn (early 19th cent—1842), Chest. le Str. RDn (1842—74), Chest. RDn (W'rn Dv) (1874—80), Durham RDn (1880—1923). Bdry: 1863 (help cr Sacriston EP),[139] 1865 (help cr Holmside EP).[140] Abol 1923, pt to help cr Kimblesworth EP, the remainder to be 'Witton Gilbert'.[142]

WITTON LE WEAR

Chap in Auckland St Andrew AP, sep civ identity early, sep EP 1724.[3] Incl tp North Bedburn (sep CP 1866,[1] eccl remains in chap Witton le Wear until eccl severed 1862 and united with another pt Witton le Wear EP to cr Firtree EP[51]). *LG* Darl. Wd, Auckl. PLU, RSD, RD. Addtl civ bdry alt: 1883.[12] Abol 1937 pt to Bp Auckl. UD & CP, pt to help cr Crook & Willington UD & CP, pt to Evenwood and Barony CP, pt to Wolsingham AP.[15] *Parl* S'rn Dv (1832—85), Barn. Cast. Dv (1885—1918), Bp Auckl. Dv (1918—48). *Eccl* Auckl. le Str. RDn (1724—early 19th cent), Durham RDn (early 19th cent—1842), Darl. RDn (1842—74), Darl. RDn (N'rn Dv) (1874—80), Auckl. RDn (1880—*).

WITTON PARK

Tp (not sep civ) in chap Escomb (sep civ identity early from Auckland St Andrew AP, sep EP 1743[3]), the orig area of the tp eccl severed 1869 from Escomb EP as 'Witton Park' EP.[21] Darl. RDn (1869—74), Darl. RDn (N'rn Dv) (1874—80),

Auckl. RDn (1880—*).

WOLSINGHAM

AP *LG* Darl. Wd, Weard. PLU, pt Tow Law USD, pt Weard. RSD, Weard. RD. Civ bdry: 1883,[12] 1894 (the pt in Tow Law UD cr Tow Law CP),[39] 1937,[15] 1946.[352] *Parl* Seq 9. *Eccl* Seq 7. Eccl bdry: 1848 (cr Thornley EP),[349] 1866 (help cr Frosterley EP).[235]

WOLVISTON

Chap in Billimgham AP, sep CP 1866,[1] sep EP 1738 (incl tp Newton Bewley),[3] eccl refounded 1859.[64] *LG* Stock. Wd, PLU, RSD, RD. Abol civ 1937 pt to Billingham UD & AP, pt to Grindon AP.[15] *Parl* S'rn Dv (1832—85), S-E'rn Dv (1885—1918), Sedg. Dv (1918—48). *Eccl* Darl. RDn (1738—early 19th cent), Durham RDn (early 19th cent—1842), Stock. RDn (1842—88), Hartl. RDn (1888—1924), Stock. RDn (1924—*). Eccl bdry: 1957,[68] 1969.[70]

CP Cr 1968 from Billingham UD & AP.[65] *LG* Stock. RD. Transf 1974 to Clev.[2] *Parl* Eas. CC (1970—*).

WOODHAM

Tp in Aycliffe AP, sep CP 1866.[1] *LG* Seq 6. Civ bdry: 1884,[280] 1937,[15] 1952.[31] *Parl* Seq 13.

WOODLAND

Tp in Cockfield AP, sep CP 1866.[1] *LG* Seq 7. Bdry: *Parl* Seq 8.

HEREFORDSHIRE

ABBREVIATIONS

Abbreviations particular to Heref follow. Those general abbreviations in use throughout the *Guide* are found on pages xvii—xix.

Abbeyd.	Abbeydore
Archenf.	Archenfield
Bredw.	Bredwardine
Bromyd.	Bromyard
Brox.	Broxash
Ewy. Lacy	Ewyas Lacy
Greyt.	Greytree
Grimsw.	Grimsworth
Hunt.	Huntington
Kingsl.	Kingsland
Kingt.	Kington
Knight.	Knighton
Ledb.	Ledbury
Leom.	Leominster
Ludl.	Ludlow
Prest.	Presteigne
Radl.	Radlow
Stretf.	Stretford
Tenb.	Tenbury
Webt.	Webtree
Weob.	Weobley
Whitch.	Whitchurch
Wigm.	Wigmore
Wolp.	Wolphy
Worm.	Wormelow

SEQUENCES

An abbreviated entry prefixed by 'Seq' is used in the parochial entries to avoid repeating often the names of superior units of administration. The content of each sequence is shown below.

Local Government Sequences ('LG')

SEQ 1   Brox. Hd, Bromyd. PLU, RSD, RD

SEQ 2   Brox. Hd, Heref PLU, RSD, RD

SEQ 3   Ewy. Lacy Hd, Dore PLU, RSD, RD (1894—1934), Dore & Bredw. RD (1934—74)

SEQ 4   Greyt. Hd, Heref PLU, RSD, RD

SEQ 5   Greyt. Hd, Ledb. PLU, RSD, RD

SEQ 6   Greyt. Hd, Newent PLU (1835—36), Ross PLU (1836—1930), RSD, RD (1894—1931), Ross & Whitch. RD (1931—74)

SEQ 7   Greyt. Hd, Ross PLU, RSD, RD (1894—1931), Ross & Whitch. RD (1931—74)

SEQ 8   Grimsw. Hd, Heref PLU, RSD, RD

SEQ 9   Grimsw. Hd, Weob. PLU, RSD, RD

SEQ 10   Hunt. Hd, Kingt. PLU, RSD, RD

SEQ 11   Radl. Hd, Bromyd. PLU, RSD, RD

SEQ 12   Radl. Hd, Heref PLU, RSD, RD

SEQ 13   Radl. Hd, Ledb. PLU, RSD, RD

SEQ 14   Stretf. Hd, Kingt. PLU, RSD, RD

SEQ 15   Stretf. Hd, Leom. PLU, RSD, RD (1894—1930), Leom. & Wigm. RD (1930—74)

SEQ 16   Stretf. Hd, Weob. PLU, RSD, RD

SEQ 17   Webt. Hd, Dore PLU, RSD, RD (1894—1934), Dore & Bredw. RD (1934—74)

SEQ 18   Webt. Hd, Hay PLU, RSD, Bredw. RD (1894—1934), Dore & Bredw. RD (1934—74)

SEQ 19   Webt. Hd, Heref PLU, RSD, RD

SEQ 20   Webt. Hd, Weob. PLU, RSD, RD

SEQ 21   Wigm. Hd, Knight. PLU, RSD, Wigm. RD (1894—1930), Leom. & Wigm. RD (1930—74)

SEQ 22   Wigm. Hd, Ludl. PLU, RSD, Wigm. RD (1894—1930), Leom. & Wigm. RD (1930—74)

SEQ 23   Wigm. Hd, Prest. PLU (1836), Kingt. PLU (1836—1930), RSD, RD

SEQ 24   Wolp. Hd, Leom. PLU, RSD, RD (1894—1930), Leom. & Wigm. RD (1930—74)

SEQ 25 Wolp. Hd, Tenb. PLU, RSD, Leom. RD (1894—1930), Leom. & Wigm. RD (1930—74)

SEQ 26 Worm. Hd, Dore PLU, RSD, RD (1894—1934), Dore & Bredw. RD (1934—74)

SEQ 27 Worm. Hd, Heref PLU, RSD, RD

SEQ 28 Worm. Hd, Monm PLU, RSD, Whitch. RD (1894—1931), Ross & Whitch. RD (1931—74)

SEQ 29 Worm. Hd, Ross PLU, RSD, RD (1894—1931), Ross & Whitch. RD (1931—74)

Parliamentary Sequences ('Parl')

Heref was undivided for parl purposes until 1885.

SEQ 1 Leom. Dv/CC (1885—*)

SEQ 2 Leom. Dv (1885—1948), Heref CC (1948—*)

SEQ 3 Ross Dv (1885—1918), Heref Dv/CC (1918—*)

SEQ 4 Ross Dv (1885—1918), Heref Dv (1918—48), Leom. CC (1948—*)

SEQ 5 Ross Dv (1885—1918), Leom. Dv/CC (1918—*)

Ecclesiastical Sequences ('Eccl')

Orig in Heref dioc:

SEQ 1 Archenf. RDn (until 1898), Abbey Dore RDn (1898—1972), Abbeyd. RDn (1972—*)

SEQ 2 Archenf. RDn (until 1898), Heref RDn (1898—1923), Abbey Dore RDn (1923—72), Abbeyd. RDn (1972—*)

SEQ 3 Archenf. RDn (until 1923), Heref (S) RDn (1923—72), Heref Rural RDn (1972—*)

SEQ 4 Archenf. RDn (until 1898), Ross RDn (1898—1923), Ross & Archenf. RDn (1923—*)

SEQ 5 Archenf. RDn (until 1923), Ross & Archenf. RDn (1923—*)

SEQ 6 Frome RDn (until 1878), N Frome RDn (1878—98), Bromyd. RDn (1898—*)

SEQ 7 Frome RDn (until 1878), N Frome RDn (1878—98), Weston RDn (1898—1972), Heref Rural RDn (1972—*)

SEQ 8 Frome RDn (until 1878), S Frome RDn (1878—98), Ledb. RDn (1898—*)

SEQ 9 Heref RDn (until 1923), Heref (City) RDn (1923—72), Heref City RDn (1972—*)

SEQ 10 Heref RDn (until 1923), Heref (S) RDn (1823—72), Abbeyd. RDn (1972—*)

SEQ 11 Heref RDn (until 1923), Heref (S) RDn (1923—72), Heref Rural RDn (1972—*)

SEQ 12 Heref RDn (until 1898), Weob. RDn (1898—1972), Abbeyd. RDn (1972—*)

SEQ 13 Heref RDn (until 1898), Weston RDn (1898—1972), Heref RDn (1972—*)

SEQ 14 Leom. RDn (until 1878), Leom. 1 RDn (1878—98), Kingsl. RDn (1898—1923), Kingt. RDn (1923—72), Kingt. & Weob. RDn (1972—*)

SEQ 15 Leom. RDn (until 1878), Leom. 1 RDn (1878—98), Kingsl. RDn (1898—1923), Leom. RDn (1923—*)

SEQ 16 Leom. RDn (until 1878), Leom. 1 RDn (1878—98), Kingsl. RDn (1898—1923), Wigm. RDn (1923—58), Leom. RDn (1958—*)

SEQ 17 Leom. RDn (until 1878), Leom. 2 RDn (1878—98), Leom. RDn (1898—*)

SEQ 18 Ross RDn (until 1898), Heref RDn (1898—1923), Heref (S) RDn (1923—72), Heref Rural RDn (1972—*)

SEQ 19 Ross RDn (until 1923), Ross & Archenf. RDn (1923—*)

SEQ 20 Weob. RDn (until 1878), Weob. 1 RDn (1878—98), Abbey Dore RDn (1898—1972), Abbeyd. RDn (1972—*)

SEQ 21 Weob. RDn (until 1878), Weob. 1 RDn (1878—98), Weob. RDn (1898—1972), Heref Rural RDn (1972—*)

SEQ 22 Weob. RDn (until 1878), Weob. 1 RDn (1878—98), Weob. RDn (1878—1972), Kingt. & Weob. RDn (1972—*)

SEQ 23 Weob. RDn (until 1878), Weob. 2 RDn (1878—98), Abbey Dore RDn (1898—1972), Abbeyd. RDn (1972—*)

SEQ 24 Weob. RDn (until 1878), Weob. 3 RDn (1878—98), Kingt. RDn (1898—1972), Kingt. & Weob. RDn (1972—*)

SEQ 25 Weob. RDn (until 1878), Weston RDn (1878—1972), Heref Rural RDn (1972—*)

SEQ 26 Weston RDn (until 1972), Heref Rural RDn (1972—*)

Orig in St David's dioc:

SEQ 27 Brecknock RDn (until mid 19th cent), Brecknock 3 RDn (mid 19th cent—later 19th cent), Weob. RDn (later 19th cent—1878), Weob. 2 RDn (1878—98), Abbey Dore RDn (1898—1972), Abbeyd. RDn (1972—*)

DIOCESES AND ARCHDEACONRIES

Heref pars were organised in Archdeaconries and Rural Deaneries as follows:

HEREFORD DIOC

Heref AD: Abbey Dore RDn (1898—1972), Abbeyd. RDn (1972—*), Archenf. RDn (until 1923), Bromyd. RDn (1898—*), Frome RDn (until 1878), N Frome RDn (1878—98), S Frome RDn (1878—98), Heref RDn (until 1923), Heref (City) RDn (1923—72), Heref City RDn (1972—*), Heref Rural RDn (1972—*), Heref (S) RDn (1923—72), Kingsl. RDn (1898—1923), Kingt. RDn (1898—1972), Kingt. & Weob. RDn (1972—*), Ledb. RDn (1898—*), Leom. RDn (until 1878), Leom. RDn (1898—*), Leom. 1 RDn (1878—98), Leom. 2 RDn (1878—98), Ross RDn (until 1923), Ross & Archenf. RDn (1923—*), Weob. RDn (until 1878),

Weob. RDn (1898—1972), Weob. 1 RDn (1878—98), Weob. 2 RDn (1878—98), Weob. 3 RDn (1878—98), Weston RDn (until 1972), Wigm. RDn (1923—58)

ST DAVID'S DIOC (until later 19th cent)
Brecon AD: Brecknock RDn (until mid 19th cent), Brecknock 3 RDn (mid 19th cent—later 19th cent)

THE PARISHES OF HEREFORDSHIRE

Heref pars were transf 1974 to help cr Hereford & Worcester Non-Metrop Co.

ABBEY DORE
AP Orig pt of Dore Abbey, sep par from Dissolution. *LG* Seq 17. *Parl* Seq 2. *Eccl* Seq 23.
ACONBURY
AP *LG* Seq 27. *Parl* Seq 3. *Eccl* Archenf. RDn (until 1923), Heref (S) RDn (1923—72), Heref RDn (1972—74). Abol eccl 1974 to help cr Little Dewchurch with Aconbury EP.[1]
ACTON BEAUCHAMP
AP Worcs par transf 1897 to Heref.[2] *LG* Bromyd. PLU, RD. *Parl* Leom. Dv/CC (1918—*). *Eccl* Powyke RDn (dioc Worc, until 1919), Bromyd. RDn (1919—*).
ADFORTON
Tp in Lentwardine AP, sep CP 1866.[3] *LG* Seq 21. *Parl* Seq 1.
ALLENSMORE
AP *LG* Webt. Hd, Heref PLU (soon after 1836[4]—1930), RSD, RD. *Parl* Seq 3. *Eccl* Seq 10.
ALMELEY
AP *LG* Seq 16. *Parl* Seq 1. *Eccl* Seq 22.
AMBERLEY
Chap in Marden AP, sep CP 1866.[3] *LG* Brox. Hd, Heref PLU, RSD. Bdry: 1883.[5] Abol 1887 pt to Sutton CP, pt to Bodenham AP.[6] *Parl* Ross Dv (1885—1918).
ASHFORD CARBONNELL
EP Cr 1880 from Little Hereford AP.[7] Ludl. RDn.
ASHPERTON
Chap in Stretton Grandison AP, sep civ identity early. *LG* Seq 13. Bdry: 1884,[8] 1885,[9] 1885.[10] *Parl* Seq 5.
ASTON
AP *LG* Seq 22. By late 20th cent, called civ 'Pipe Aston'. *Parl* Seq 1. *Eccl* Clun RDn (Salop AD, until 1878), Ludl. RDn (1878—98), Kingsl. RDn (1898—1923), Wigm. RDn (1923—1958), Ludl. RDn (1958—*).
PIPE ASTON—see prev entry
ASTON INGHAM
AP *LG* Seq 6. Civ bdry: 1965 (loses pt to Newent AP, Glos).[11] *Parl* Seq 3. *Eccl* Seq 19.
AVENBURY
AP *LG* Seq 1. Civ bdry: 1884,[12] 1884.[13] *Parl* Seq 1. *Eccl* Frome RDn (until 1878), N Frome RDn (1878—98), Bromyd. RDn (1898—1931). Eccl bdry: 1882,[14] 1928.[15] Abol eccl 1931 pt to Bromyard AP, pt to Stoke Lacy AP.[16]
AYLTON
AP Orig chap in Ledbury AP, prob sep at Reformation, sep status noted 1587.[17] *LG* Seq 13. *Parl* Seq 4. *Eccl* Seq 8.

AYMESTREY
AP Incl chap Leinthall Earles (sep EP 1756[18]), chap Leinthall Starkes (sep civ identity early, sep EP 1783[18]). *LG* Pt Stretf. Hd, pt Wigm. Hd, Leom. PLU, RSD, RD (1894—1930), Leom. & Wigm. RD (1930—74). *Parl* Seq 1. *Eccl* Leom. RDn (until 1878), Leom. 1 RDn (1878—98), Kingsl. RDn (1898—1923), Wigm. RDn (1923—37). Abol eccl 1937 to help cr Aymestry with Leinthall Earles EP.[19]
AYMESTRY WITH LEINTHALL EARLES
EP Cr 1937 by union Aymestry AP, Leinthall Earles EP.[19] Wigm. RDn (1937—58), Leom. RDn (1958—*).
BACTON
AP *LG* Seq 17. *Parl* Seq 3. *Eccl* Seq 23.
BALLINGHAM
AP Chap in Holme Lacy AP, prob sep par at Reformation and so thereafter for civ purposes, eccl united then with chap Bolstone in same par as 'Ballingham and Bolstone',[20] qv. *LG* Seq 29. Bdry: 1884.[21] *Parl* Seq 3.
BALLINGHAM AND BOLSTONE
AP Union for eccl purposes prob at Reformation of chaps Ballingham, Bolstone, both in Holme Lacy AP[20] (for sep civ status of each from that time, see the respective pars). *Eccl* Archenf. RDn (cr—1923), Ross & Archenf. RDn (1923—46), Heref (S) RDn (1946—72), Heref Rural RDn (1972—*).
BARTESTREE
Chap in Dormington AP, sep CP 1866,[3] sep EP 1729,[18] sep eccl status not sustained and remains in Dormington until eccl severed 1928 to help cr Lugwardine with Bartestree EP.[22] *LG* Seq 4. *Parl* Seq 5. *Eccl* Weston RDn.
LITTLE BIRCH
AP *LG* Seq 27. *Parl* Seq 3. *Eccl* Seq 3.
MUCH BIRCH
Prob chap in Much Dewchurch AP, sep par by 1621.[23] *LG* Seq 27. *Parl* Seq 3. *Eccl* Seq 3.
BIRLEY
AP *LG* Seq 16. Civ bdry: 1884.[24] *Parl* Seq 1. *Eccl* Weston RDn (until 1878), Leom. 1 RDn (1878—98), Weob. RDn (1898—1972), Leom. RDn (1972—*). Eccl bdry: 1956.[25]
BISHOPSTONE
AP *LG* Seq 9. Civ bdry: 1884.[24] *Parl* Seq 1. *Eccl* Weob. RDn (until 1878), Weob. 1 RDn (1878—98), Weob. RDn (1898—1923), Weston RDn (1923—72), Heref Rural RDn (1972—*).
BISHOP'S WOOD
EP Cr 1845 from Walford AP (Heref), Ruardean EP (Glos).[26] Ross RDn (1845—1923), Ross &

Archenf. RDn (1923—*).

BLAKEMERE

AP *LG* Webt. Hd, Weob. PLU (soon after 1836[4]—1930), RSD, RD. *Parl* Seq 1. *Eccl* Seq 12.

BOCKLETON

AP Mostly Worcs (Doddingtree Hd), incl hmlt Hampton Charles in Heref (Brox. Hd), the latter a sep CP 1866 in Heref[3] and Bockleton ent Worcs thereafter, qv for all organisation.

BODENHAM

AP *LG* Brox. Hd, Leom. PLU, RSD, RD (1894—1930), Leom. & Wigm. RD (1930—74). Civ bdry: 1883,[5] 1884,[27] 1887.[6] *Parl* Seq 1. *Eccl* Seq 26.

BOLSTONE

AP Chap in Holme Lacy AP, prob sep par at Reformation and so thereafter for civ purposes, eccl united then with Ballingham in same par as 'Ballingham and Bolstone',[20] qv. *LG* Seq 27. Bdry: 1884.[21] *Parl* Seq 3.

BOSBURY

AP *LG* Seq 13. *Parl* Seq 5. *Eccl* Seq 8.

BRAMPTON ABBOTTS

Chap in Ross AP, sep par 1671.[28] *LG* Seq 7. Civ bdry: 1884.[29] *Parl* Seq 3. *Eccl* Seq 19. Eccl bdry: 1960.[30]

BRAMPTON BRYAN

AP Main tp in Heref (Wigm. Hd), incl in Radnor (Knight. Hd) lordship Stanage (sep CP 1866 in Radnor[3]) and this par ent Heref thereafter. *LG* Wigm. Hd (ent from 1866), Knight. PLU, RSD, Wigm. RD (1894—1930), Leom. & Wigm. RD (1930—74). Addtl civ bdry alt: 1894 (gains the pt in Heref of Bucknell AP [o'wise ent Salop, ent Salop thereafter]).[31] *Parl* Heref pt, Seq 1. *Eccl* Clun RDn (Salop AD, until 1923), Wigm. RDn (1923—58), Kingt. RDn (1958—72), Kingt. & Weob. RDn (1972—*).

BREDENBURY

AP *LG* Seq 1. Civ bdry: 1884.[12] *Parl* Seq 1. *Eccl* Frome RDn. Abol eccl 1875 to help cr Brednebury with Wacton EP.[32]

BREDENBURY WITH GRENDON BISHOP AND WACTON

EP Cr 1948 by union pt Bredenbury with Wacton EP, Grendon Bishop EP.[33] Bromyd. RDn.

BREDENBURY WITH WACTON

EP Cr 1875 by union Bredenbury AP, Wacton EP.[32] Frome RDn (1875—78), N Frome RDn (1878—98), Bromyd. RDn (1898—1948). Bdry: 1882.[14] Abol 1948 pt to help cr Bredenbury with Grendon Bishop and Wacton EP, pt to Edvin Ralph AP, pt to Thornbury AP.[33]

BREDWARDINE

AP *LG* Seq 18. *Parl* Seq 2. *Eccl* Weob. RDn (until 1878), Weob. 1 RDn (1878—98), Weob. RDn (1898—1970). Abol eccl 1970 to help cr Bredwardine with Brobury EP.[34]

BREDWARDINE WITH BROBURY

EP Cr 1970 by union Bredwardine AP, Brobury AP.[34] Weob. RDn (1970—72), Abbeyd. RDn (1972—*).

BREINTON

AP *LG* Grimsw. Hd, Heref PLU, pt Heref Bor/MB (until 1884), pt Heref USD (1875—84), Heref RSD (pt 1875—84, ent 1884—94), Heref RD. Civ bdry: 1884 (the pt in the MB transf to Huntington CP),[35] 1884.[36] *Parl* Seq 5. *Eccl* Seq 9.

BRIDGE SOLLERS

AP *LG* Seq 9. *Parl* Seq 1. *Eccl* Weob. RDn (until 1878), Weob. 1 RDn (1878—98), Weob. RDn (1898—1923), Weston RDn (1923—72), Heref Rural RDn (1972—*).

BRIDSTOW

AP *LG* Worm. Hd, Ross PLU, pt Ross USD, pt Ross RSD, Ross RD (1894—1931), Ross & Whitch. RD (1931—74). Civ bdry: 1884,[37] 1894 (loses the pt in the UD to help cr Ross Urban CP),[38] 1931.[39] *Parl* Seq 3. *Eccl* Seq 4.

BRILLEY

Chap in Kington AP, sep civ identity early, eccl united 1860 with chap Michaelchurch on Arrow (Radnor) in same par to cr Brilley with Michaelchurch on Arrow EP.[40] *LG* Seq 10. *Parl* Seq 1.

BRILLEY WITH MICHAELCHURCH ON ARROW

EP Cr 1860 by union chaps Brilley (Heref), Michaelchurch on Arrow (Radnor), both in Kington AP.[40] Weob. RDn (1860—78), Weob. 3 RDn (1878—98), Kingt. RDn (1898—1923), Weob. RDn (1923—72), Kingt. & Weob. RDn (1972—*).

BRIMFIELD

Chap in Eye AP, sep civ identity early, sep EP 1754.[18] *LG* Seq 25. *Parl* Seq 1. *Eccl* Leom. RDn (1754—1878), Leom. 2 RDn (1878—98), Leom. RDn (1898—*).

BRINSOP

AP *LG* Seq 9. *Parl* Seq 1. *Eccl* Weston RDn (until 1968), Weob. RDn (1968—72). Abol eccl 1972 to help cr Brinsop with Wormesley EP.[41]

BRINSOP WITH WORMESLEY

EP Cr 1972 by union Brinsop AP, Wormesley AP.[41] Weob. RDn (1972), Heref Rural RDn (1972—*).

BROBURY

AP *LG* Seq 9. *Parl* Seq 1. *Eccl* Weob. RDn (until 1878), Weob. 1 RDn (1878—98), Weob. RDn (1898—1970). Abol eccl 1970 to help cr Bredwardine with Brobury EP.[34]

BROCKHAMPTON

Chap in Woolhope AP, sep civ identity early, sep EP 1771.[18] *LG* Seq 7. Civ bdry: 1884.[42] *Parl* Seq 3. *Eccl* [All Saints] Heref RDn (1771—1923), Heref (S) RDn (1923—72), Heref Rural RDn (1972—*).

BROCKHAMPTON

Chap in Bromyard AP, forming together with area Norton single tp of 'Norton with Brockhampton', as such sep CP 1866,[3] qv, an area in that tp/CP considered sep CP 1863 (when sep rated for poor law purposes) as 'Lower Brockhampton' (Brox. Hd, Bromyd. PLU), qv in following entry for civ abol 1894.

CP Cr 1894 by union ent Lower Brockhampton CP and pts Norton with Brockhampton CP, Linton CP, Whitbourne AP.[43] *LG* Bromyd. PLU, RD. *Parl* Leom. Dv/CC (1918—*).

LOWER BROCKHAMPTON

CP Area orig in tp Norton with Brockhampton (sep CP 1866 from Bromyard AP[3]), considered sep CP 1863 (when sep rated for poor law purposes) (Brox. Hd,

Bromyd. PLU), abol 1894 to help cr Brockhampton CP.[43] *Parl* Leom. Dv (1885—1918).

BROMYARD

AP Incl chap Grendon (sep EP 1739,[18] civ comprised of 'Grendon Bishop', 'Grendon Warren', each with sep civ identity early, chap Stanford Bishop (sep civ identity early, sep EP 1745[18]), chap Wacton (sep civ identity early, sep EP 1749[18]), chap Brockhampton, area Norton (forming together single tp of 'Norton with Brockhampton', as such sep CP 1866,[3] an area in that tp/CP considered sep CP as 'Lower Brockhampton' 1863, qv in prev entry), tp Linton (sep CP 1866,[3] pt eccl severed 1891 and transf to Stanford Bishop EP[44]), tp Winslow (sep CP 1866[3]). *LG* Brox. Hd, pt Bromyd. Bor, Bromyd. PLU, RSD, UD (1894—1968), RD (1968—74). Addtl civ bdry alt: 1883,[5] 1884,[12] 1884,[45] 1884,[46] 1884,[47] 1884,[48] 1894 (gains pt Winslow CP as the enlarged area constituted Bromyd. UD).[49] *Parl* Pt Bromyd. Parl Bor (1305 only), Seq 1. *Eccl* Seq 6. Addtl eccl bdry alt: 1882,[14] 1931.[16]

BUCKNELL

AP Main tp mostly Salop (Purslow Hd), pt Heref (Wigm. Hd); incl in Heref (Wigm. Hd) tp Buckton and Coxall (sep CP 1866 in Heref[3]). *LG* Knight. PLU, RSD. Addtl civ bdry alt: 1894 (loses the pt in Heref to Brampton Bryan AP,[31] so that this par ent Salop thereafter, qv for organisation).

BUCKTON AND COXALL

Tp (Heref, Wigm. Hd) in Bucknell AP (o'wise Salop, Purslow Hd), sep CP 1866 in Heref (Bucknell ent Salop thereafter).[3] *LG* Seq 21. *Parl* Seq 1.

BULLINGHAM

AP Prebendal chap not with sep eccl identity but early with sep civ identity, comprised of tps Lower Bullingham, Upper Bullingham (each a sep CP 1866,[3] the chap pec jurisd Bullingham prebend, eccl severed 1747 to help cr Upper and Lower Bullinghope with Grafton EP[18]) so that 'Bullingham' has no sep civ identity after 1866. *LG* Webt. Hd, pt Heref Bor/MB (pt of Upper Bullingham, qv below).

LOWER BULLINGHAM

Tp in prebendal chap Bullingham (qv in prev entry), sep CP 1866,[3] in pec jurisd Bullingham prebend, eccl severed 1747 to help cr Upper and Lower Bullinghope with Grafton EP.[18] *LG* Seq 19. *Parl* Seq 3.

UPPER BULLINGHAM

Tp in prebendal chap Bullingham (qv above), sep CP 1866,[3] in pec jurisd Bullingham prebend, eccl severed 1747 to help cr Upper and Lower Bullinghope with Grafton EP.[18] *LG* Webt. Hd, Heref PLU (soon after 1836[4]—85), pt Heref Bor/MB, pt Heref USD, pt Heref RSD. Abol 1885 the pt in the MB transf to Hereford St Martin AP, the remainder to Grafton CP.[50] *Parl* Ross Dv (1885—1918).

UPPER AND LOWER BULLINGHOPE WITH GRAFTON

EP Cr 1747 by union prebendal chap Bullingham, tp Grafton in Hereford All Saints AP.[18] Pec jurisd

Bullingham prebend (1747—1840s), Heref RDn (1840s—1923), Heref (S) RDn (1923—72), Heref City RDn (1972—*).

BURGHILL

AP *LG* Seq 8. Civ bdry: 1883,[5] 1884.[51] *Parl* Seq 5. *Eccl* Seq 26.

BURRINGTON

AP *LG* Seq 22. Bdry: 1885.[52] *Parl* Seq 1. *Eccl* Clun RDn (Salop AD, until 1878), Ludl. RDn (1878—1923), Wigm. RDn (1923—58), Ludl. RDn (1958—*).

BYFORD

AP *LG* Seq 9. *Parl* Seq 1. *Eccl* Weob. RDn (until 1878), Weob. 1 RDn (1878—98), Weob. RDn (1898—1971). Abol eccl 1971 to help cr Byford and Mansel Gamage EP.[53]

BYFORD AND MANSEL GAMAGE

EP Cr 1971 by union Byford AP, Mansel Gamage EP.[53] Weob. RDn (1971—72), Heref Rural RDn (1972—*).

BYTON

AP *LG* Seq 23. *Parl* Seq 1. *Eccl* Seq 14.

CALLOW

Chap or curacy of Knights Templar, sep civ identity early, early eccl annexed to Dewsall AP to cr Dewsall with Callow EP.[54] *LG* Seq 19. *Parl* Seq 3.

HOW CAPLE

AP *LG* Seq 7. *Parl* Seq 3. *Eccl* Seq 19.

KING'S CAPLE

Chap in Sellack AP, sep civ identity early. *LG* Seq 29. *Parl* Seq 3.

CANON PYON

AP *LG* Seq 9. *Parl* Seq 1. *Eccl* Heref RDn (until 1878), Weston RDn (1878—1965), Weob. RDn (1965—72), Leom. RDn (1972—*).

CASCOB

AP In Radnor (Radnor Bor), incl in Heref (Wigm. Hd) pt tp Litton and Cascob (Prest. PLU [1836], Kingt. PLU [thereafter]), the ent tp transf to Radnor 1832 for parl purposes, 1844 for civ purposes[55] and Cascob ent Radnor thereafter.

CLEHONGER

AP *LG* Seq 19. Civ bdry: 1884.[56] *Parl* Seq 3. *Eccl* Seq 10. Eccl bdry: 1966 (loses the pt in Heref MB to Hereford St Martin AP).[57]

CLIFFORD

AP *LG* Hunt. Hd, Hay PLU, RSD, Bredw. RD (1894—1934), Dore & Bredw. RD (1934—74). *Parl* Seq 2. *Eccl* Seq 20. Eccl bdry: 1853 (cr Hardwick EP).[58]

CLODOCK

AP Incl chap Craswall (sep CP 1866,[3] sep EP 1728 as 'Craswell'[18]), chap Longtown (sep CP 1866,[3] endowed chap a sep benefice and sometimes considered sep EP, the benefice united 1927 with mother par and thereafter eccl 'Clodock with Longtown',[59] qv), chap Llanveynoe (sep CP 1866,[3] endowed chap, sometimes considered sep EP, eccl united 1929 with Craswell EP to cr 'Craswell with Llanveynoe',[60] later called simply 'Craswell'), tp Newton (sep CP 1866,[3] sep EP 1848[61]) so that 'Clodock' has no sep civ identity after 1866. *LG* Ewy. Lacy Hd. *Eccl* Brecknock RDn (until mid 19th cent), Brenock 3 RDn (mid 19th cent—later

19th cent), Weob. RDn (later 19th cent—1878), Abbey Dore RDn (1878—1927).

CLODOCK WITH LONGTOWN
EP Cr 1927 by union Clodock AP, endowed chap Longtown in Clodock AP (sep benefice, sometimes considered sep EP).[59] Abbey Dore RDn (1927—72), Abbeyd. RDn (1972—*).

CODDINGTON
AP *LG* Seq 13. *Parl* Seq 5. *Eccl* Seq 8.

COLLINGTON
AP *LG* Seq 1. *Parl* Seq 1. *Eccl* Seq 6.

COLWALL
AP *LG* Seq 13. *Parl* Seq 5. *Eccl* Seq 8.

COMBE
Tp in Presteigne AP, sep CP 1866.[3] *LG* Seq 23. *Parl* Seq 1.

LITTLE COWARNE
AP Orig sep AP (Frome RDn), abol 1478 ent to Ullingswick AP and thereafter considered its chap (qv for later eccl severing),[62] sep civ identity retained or early gained. *LG* Seq 1. *Parl* Seq 1.

MUCH COWARNE
AP *LG* Seq 1. Civ bdry: 1884,[12] 1884.[13] *Parl* Seq 1. *Eccl* Seq 6. Eccl bdry: 1928.[15]

CRADLEY
AP *LG* Seq 11. Civ bdry: 1897 (loses pt to Mathon Urban CP, Worcs and the enlarged area of the latter renamed 'West Malvern' in that co),[63] 1897 (loses pt to Leigh AP, Worcs).[64] *Parl* Seq 1. *Eccl* Seq 8. Eccl bdry: 1856 (cr Storridge EP).[65]

CRASWALL
Chap in Clodock AP, sep CP 1866,[3] sep EP 1728 as 'Craswell',[18] qv. *LG* Seq 3. *Parl* Seq 3.

CRASWELL
Chap in Clodock AP, sep EP 1728,[18] sep CP 1866 as 'Craswall',[3] qv. *Eccl* Weob. RDn (1728—1878), Weob. 2 RDn (1878—98), Abbey Dore RDn (1898—early 20th cent). Gains early 20th cent endowed chap Llanveynoe in Clodock AP, the union thereafter 'Craswell with Llanveynoe,'[60] later called simply Craswell.

CRASWELL—see prev entry

CRASWELL WITH LLANVEYNOE
EP Cr 1929 by union Craswell EP, endowed chap Llanveynoe in Clodock AP.[60] Abbey Dore RDn (1929—72), Abbeyd. RDn (1972—*). Later called simply 'Craswell'.

CREDENHILL
AP *LG* Seq 8. Civ bdry: 1883,[5] 1884.[51] *Parl* Seq 5. *Eccl* Weob. RDn (until 1878), Weston RDn (1878—1968), Weob. RDn (1968—72), Heref Rural RDn (1972—*).

CROFT
AP Incl tp Newton (sep CP 1866[3]). *LG* Seq 24. *Parl* Seq 1. *Eccl* Leom. RDn (until 1878), Leom. 2 RDn (1878—98), Leom RDn (1898—1973). Abol eccl 1973 to help cr Croft with Yarpole and Lucton EP.[66]

CROFT WITH YARPOLE AND LUCTON
EP Cr 1973 by union Croft AP, Yarpole AP, Lucton EP.[66] Leom. RDn.

CUSOP
AP *LG* Ewy. Lacy Hd, Hay PLU, RSD, Bredw. RD

(1894—1934), Dore & Bredw. RD (1934—74). *Parl* Seq 2. *Eccl* Seq 20.

CWMYOY
AP Mostly Monm (Abergavenny Hd), incl in Heref (Ewy. Lacy Hd) hmlt Bwlch Trewyn (transf to Monm 1832 for parl purposes, 1844 for civ purposes,[55] sep CP 1866 in Monm), tp Fwthog (sep CP 1866 in Heref[3]) so that 'Cwmyoy' ent Monm from 1866.

LITTLE DEWCHURCH
Chap (Archenf. RDn) in Lugwardine AP (Weston RDn), sep civ identity early, eccl severed 1849 to help cr Hentland EP,[67] 'Little Dewchurch' a sep EP 1862 from Hentland EP.[68] *LG* Seq 27. Civ bdry: 1883.[5] *Parl* Seq 3. *Eccl* Archenf. RDn (1862—1923), Heref (S) RDn (1923—1972), Heref Rural RDn (1972—74). Abol eccl 1974 to help cr Little Dewchurch with Aconbury EP.[1]

LITTLE DEWHURCH WITH ACONBURY
EP Cr 1974 by union Little Dewchurch EP, Aconbury AP.[1] Heref Rural RDn.

MUCH DEWCHURCH
AP Prob incl chap Much Birch (sep par by 1621[23]). *LG* Seq 27. *Parl* Seq 3. *Eccl* Seq 3.

DEWSALL
AP Incl chap Callow (orig chap or curacy of Knights Templar, sep civ identity early, early annexed to Dewsall AP to cr Dewsall with Callow EP.[54] *LG* Seq 27. *Parl* Seq 3. *Eccl* Heref RDn.

DEWSALL WITH CALLOW
EP Cr early by union Dewsall AP, chap or curacy Callow (of Knights Templar).[54] Archenf. RDn (cr—1878), Heref RDn (1878—1923), Heref (S) RDn (1923—72), Heref City RDn (1972—*).

DILWYN
AP *LG* Seq 16. Civ bdry: 1884.[24] *Parl* Seq 1. *Eccl* Weston RDn (until 1878), Weob. 1 RDn (1878—98), Weob. RDn (1898—1972), Leom. RDn (1972). Abol eccl 1972 to help cr Dilwyn and Stretford EP.[65]

DILWYN AND STRETFORD
EP Cr 1972 by union Dilwyn AP, Stretford AP.[65] Leom. RDn.

DINEDOR
AP Usual civ spelling; for eccl see 'Dyndor'. *LG* Seq 19. Civ bdry: 1884.[21] *Parl* Seq 3.

DINMORE
Ex-par place, sep CP 1858.[69] *LG* Grimsw. Hd, Heref PLU (1858—1930), RSD, RD. Civ bdry: 1887.[70] *Parl* Seq 5.

DOCKLOW
Chap in Leominster AP, sep civ identity early, sep EP 1745.[18] *LG* Seq 24. Civ bdry: 1883,[5] 1884.[71] *Parl* Seq 1. *Eccl* Leom. RDn (1745—1878), Leom. 2 RDn (1878—98), Leom. RDn (1898—*).

DONNINGTON
AP *LG* Seq 13. Civ bdry: 1885.[9] *Parl* Seq 4. *Eccl* Frome RDn (until 1878), S Frome RDn (1878—98), Ledb. RDn (1898—1955), Forest North RDn (dioc Glouc, 1955[72]—*). Eccl bdry: 1929.[73]

DORMINGTON
AP Incl chap Bartestree (sep CP 1866,[3] sep EP 1729[18] but sep eccl status not sustained, hence this par eccl

'Dormington with Bartestree' until the chap severed 1928 to help cr Lugwardine with Bartestree EP,[19] this par 'Dormington thereafter. *LG* Seq 4. *Parl* Seq 3. *Eccl* Weston RDn (1928—47), Heref (S) RDn (1947—72), Heref Rural RDn (1972—*).

DORMINGTON WITH BARTESTREE
AP Usual eccl spelling until chap Bartestree (for earlier civ and eccl independence [latter not sustained], see prev entry), eccl severed 1928 to help cr Lugwardine with Bartestree EP, the remainder to be 'Dormington'.[19] *Eccl* Weston RDn (until 1898), Heref RDn (1898—1923), Weston RDn (1923—28).

DORSTONE
AP *LG* Seq 18. *Parl* Seq 2. *Eccl* Seq 23 .

DOWNTON
AP *LG* Seq 22. Civ bdry: 1885.[47] *Parl* Seq 1. *Eccl* Clun RDn (until 1878), Ludl. RDn (1878—1923), Wigm. RDn (1923—58), Ludl. RDn (1928—*).

DULAS
Chap in Ewyas Harold AP, sep civ identity early, sep EP 1741.[18] *LG* Seq 17. *Parl* Seq 3. *Eccl* Seq 27.

DYNDOR
AP Usual eccl spelling; for civ see 'Dinedor'. *Eccl* Seq 11.

EARDISLAND
AP *LG* Seq 16. Civ bdry: 1884.[21] *Parl* Seq 1. *Eccl* Seq 15.

EARDISLEY
AP Usual civ spelling; for eccl see followng entry. *LG* Seq 10. Civ bdry: 1884.[74] *Parl* Seq 1.

EARDISLEY WITH BOLLINGHAM
AP Usual eccl spelling; for civ see prev entry. *Eccl* Weob. RDn (until 1878), Weob. 1 RDn (1878—98), Weob. RDn (1898—1964). Abol eccl 1964 to help cr Eardisley with Bollingham and Willersley EP.[75]

EARDISLEY WITH BOLLINGHAM AND WILLERSLEY
EP Cr 1964 by union Eardisley with Bollingham AP, orig area Willersley AP (before union 1926 to cr Letton with Willersley EP, qv).[75] Weob. RDn (1964—72), Kingt. & Weob. RDn (1972—*).

EASTNOR
AP *LG* Seq 13. *Parl* Seq 4. *Eccl* Seq 8.

EATON BISHOP
AP *LG* Webt. Hd, Heref PLU (soon after 1836[4]—1930), RSD, RD. Civ bdry: 1884.[18] *Parl* Seq 3. *Eccl* Seq 10.

EDVIN LOACH
AP Chap (Heref, Brox. Hd) in Clifton upon Teme AP (o'wise Worcs, Doddingtree Hd; eccl, 'Clifton on Teme'), sep civ identity early in Heref, the CP transf to Worcs 1832 for parl purposes, 1844 for civ purposes,[50] the area eccl a united benefice 1625 with Tedstone Wafer AP,[76] but not eccl severed from this par until 1972 when helps cr Edvin Loach with Tedstone Wafer EP.[77] *LG* Bromyd. PLU, RSD. Civ bdry: 1884 (when in Worcs, gains pt Collington AP, Heref).[78] Transf 1893 from Worcs to Heref,[79] and from 1894 in Bromyd. RD. *Parl* Leom. Dv/CC (1918—*).

EDVIN LOACH WITH TEDSTONE WAFER
EP Cr 1972 (united benefice of the 2 existed from 1625[76]) by union Tedstone Wafer AP, chap Edvin Loach in Clifton on Teme AP (Worcs, civ 'Clifton upon Teme').[77] Bromyd. RDn.

EDVIN RALPH
AP *LG* Wolp. Hd, Bromyd. PLU, RSD, RD. Civ bdry: 1884.[11] *Parl* Seq 1. *Eccl* Seq 6. Eccl bdry: 1948,[28] 1963.[80]

EGLETON
Tp in Bishop's Frome AP, sep CP 1866,[3] eccl severed 1879 and transf to Stretton Grandison with Ashperton AP.[81] *LG* Seq 13. *Parl* Seq 5.

ELTON
Chap in Wigmore AP, sep civ identity early, sep EP 1766.[18] *LG* Seq 22. *Parl* Seq 1. *Eccl* Leom. RDn (1766—1878), Leom. 2 RDn (1878—98), Kingsl. RDn (1898—1923), Wigm. RDn (1923—58), Ludl. RDn (1958—*).

EVESBATCH
AP *LG* Seq 11. *Parl* Seq 1. *Eccl* Frome RDn (until 1878), S Frome RDn (1878—98), Bromyd. RDn (1898—1923). Abol eccl 1923 to help cr Evesbatch with Fromes Hill EP.[76]

EVESBATCH WITH FROMES HILL
EP Cr 1923 by union Evesbatch AP, pt Bishop's Frome AP.[82] Bromyd. RDn. Bdry: 1952.[83]

EWYAS HAROLD
AP Incl chap Dulas (sep civ identity early, sep EP 1741[18]). *LG* Seq 17. *Parl* Seq 3. *Eccl* Seq 27.

EYE
AP Incl chap Brimfield (sep civ identity early, sep EP 1754[18]), chap Eyton (sep civ identity early, sep EP 1740[18]), chap Kimbolton (sep civ identity early, sep EP 1745,[18] later called 'Kimbolton with Hammish'), chap Lucton (sep civ identity early, sep EP 1747[18]), chap Middleton on the Hill (sep civ identity early, sep EP 1745[18]), tp Eye, Moreton and Ashton (sep CP 1866[3]), tp Luston (sep CP 1866[3]) so that 'Eye' has no sep civ identity after 1866. *LG* Wolp. Hd. *Eccl* Seq 17. Addtl eccl bdry alt: 1949.[84]

EYE, MORETON AND ASHTON
Tp in Eye AP, sep CP 1866.[3] *LG* Seq 24. Bdry: 1883.[5] *Parl* Seq 1.

EYTON
Chap in Eye AP, sep civ identity early, sep EP 1740.[18] *LG* Seq 24. Civ bdry: 1883.[5] *Parl* Seq 1. *Eccl* Leom. RDn (1740—1878), Leom. 2 RDn (1878—98), Leom. RDn (1898—*). Eccl bdry: 1949.[84]

FELTON
AP *LG* Seq 1. Civ bdry: 1884,[11] 1884,[23] 1884.[85] *Parl* Seq 1. *Eccl* Seq 7.

FORD
Ex-par place, eccl severed 1928 to help cr Hope under Dinmore with Ford EP,[86] the orig area of Ford severed 1961 from the latter to help cr Stoke Prior and Ford EP.[87] *LG* Seq 24. *Parl* Seq 1.

FOWNHOPE
AP Usual civ spelling; for eccl see following entry. *LG* Seq 4. Civ bdry: 1884,[37] 1884.[18] *Parl* Seq 3.

FOWNHOPE WITH FAWLEY
AP Usual eccl spelling; for civ see prev entry. *Eccl* Seq

18.

FOY

AP *LG* Pt Greyt. Hd, pt Worm. Hd, Ross PLU, RSD, RD (1894—1931), Ross & Whitch. RD (1931—74). *Parl* Seq 3. *Eccl* Seq 4.

BISHOP'S FROME

AP Incl tp Egleton (sep CP 1866,[3] eccl severed 1879 and transf to Stretton Grandison with Ashperton AP[81]); usual civ spelling, but eccl 'Bishop's Frome with Fromes Hill' until area Fromes Hill eccl severed 1923 to help cr Evesbatch with Fromes Hill EP,[82] so that this par eccl 'Bishop's Frome with Fromes Hill' before 1923, qv, and 'Bishop's Frome' thereafter. *LG* Seq 11. Addtl civ bdry alt: 1884,[11] 1887.[88] *Parl* Seq 1. *Eccl* Bromyd. RDn (1923—*). Eccl bdry: 1953.[89]

BISHOP'S FROME WITH FROMES HILL

AP Usual eccl spelling until 1923 when area Fromes Hill eccl severed 1923 to help cr Evesbatch with Fromes Hill EP;[82] this par 'Bishop's Frome' for civ purposes and also for eccl purposes after 1923, qv above for organisation and for civ sep tp. *Eccl* Frome RDn (until 1878), S Frome RDn (1878—98), Bromyd. RDn (1898—1923).

CANON FROME

AP *LG* Seq 13. *Parl* Seq 5. *Eccl* Frome RDn (until 1878), S Frome RDn (1878—98), Ledb. RDn (1898—*). Bdry: 1854 (gains Munsley EP,[90] the united par called 'Canon Frome with Munsley' for a while thereafter, later simply 'Canon Frome').

CANON FROME WITH MUNSLEY—see prev entry

CASTLE FROME

AP *LG* Seq 13. Civ bdry: 1887.[91] *Parl* Seq 5. *Eccl* Seq 8. Eccl bdry: 1953.[83]

FWTHOG

Hmlt in Cwmyoy AP, sep CP 1866.[3] *LG* Ewy. Lacy Hd, Abergavenny PLU, RSD. Transf 1891 to Monm.[92] *Parl* Ross Dv (1885—1918).

GANAREW

AP *LG* Seq 28. *Parl* Seq 3. *Eccl* Seq 5.

GARWAY

AP Chap appropriated to Knights Templar, sep par at Dissolution. *LG* Seq 28. *Parl* Seq 3. *Eccl* Archenf. RDn (until 1923), Ross & Archenf. RDn (1923—42), Heref (S) RDn (1942—72), Ross & Archenf. RDn (1972—*).

GOODRICH

AP *LG* Seq 29. Civ bdry: 1884,[25] 1965 (gains pt English Bicknor AP, Glos).[10] *Parl* Seq 3. *Eccl* Seq 5.

GRAFTON

Tp in Hereford All Saints AP, sep CP 1866,[3] eccl severed 1747 to help cr Upper and Lower Bullinghope with Grafton EP.[18] *LG* Seq 19. Bdry: 1885.[44] *Parl* Seq 3.

GRENDON

Chap in Bromyard AP, sep EP 1739[18]; for civ see 2 following entries. Frome RDn (1739—1878), N Frome RDn (1878—98), Bromyd. RDn (1898—1948). Abol 1948 to help cr Bredenbury with Grendon Bishop and Wacton EP.[28]

GRENDON BISHOP

One of two areas (along with Grendon Warren) in chap Grendon in Bromyard AP, the ent area a sep EP 1739 as 'Grendon',[18] qv, each of the 2 areas with sep civ identity early. *LG* Seq 1. *Parl* Seq 1.

GRENDON WARREN

One of two areas (along with Grendon Bishop) in chap Grendon in Bromyard AP, the ent area a sep EP 1739 as 'Grendon',[18] qv, each of the 2 areas with sep civ identity early. *LG* Brox. Hd, Bromyd. PLU, RSD, RD. Abol 1895 to help cr Pencombe with Grendon Warren CP.[93] *Parl* Leom. Dv (1885—1918).

NEW HAMPTON

Ex-par place, sep CP 1858.[64] *LG* Wolp. Hd, Leom. PLU (1858—1930), RSD, RD (1894—1930), Leom. & Wigm. RD (1930—74). *Parl* Seq 1.

HAMPTON BISHOP

AP Incl tp Tupsley (sep CP 1866,[3] sep EP 1866[94]). *LG* Seq 8. Addtl civ bdry alt: 1884,[18] 1884 (gains the pt of Tuplsley CP not in Heref MB).[95] *Parl* Seq 3. *Eccl* Seq 11.

HAMPTON CHARLES

Hmlt in Bockleton AP, sep CP 1866.[3] *LG* Seq 1. *Parl* Seq 1.

HAMPTON WAFER

Ex-par place, sep CP 1858.[64] *LG* Wolp. Hd, Leom. PLU (1858—1930), RSD, RD (1894—1930), Leom. & Wigm. RD (1930—74). *Parl* Seq 1.

HARDWICK

EP Cr 1853 from Clifford AP.[53] Weob. 1 RDn (1853—98), Abbey Dore RDn (1898—1972), Abbeyd. RDn (1972—*).

HAREWOOD

Chap appropriated to Priory of St John of Jerusalem, donative after Dissolution and sep eccl identity not sustained, sep civ identity early. *LG* Seq 29. *Parl* Seq 3.

LOWER HARPTON

Tp (Heref, Wigm. Hd) in Old Radnor AP (o'wise Radnor, Radnor Bor; eccl, 'Old Radnor with Kinnerton'), sep CP 1866 in Heref.[3] *LG* Kingt. PLU, RSD, RD. *Parl* Seq 1.

HATFIELD

Chap in Leominster AP, sep civ identity early, sep EP 1742.[18] *LG* Seq 24. Civ bdry: 1884,[71] 1965 (loses pt to Bockleton AP, Worcs).[10] *Parl* Seq 1. *Eccl* Leom. RDn (1742—1878), Leom. 2 RDn (1878—98), Leom. RDn (1898—*).

HAYWOOD

Ex-par place, sep CP 1858.[64] *LG* Webt. Hd, Heref PLU (1858—1930), RSD, RD. *Parl* Seq 3.

HENTLAND

Chap (Archenf. RDn) in Lugwardine AP (o'wise Weston RDn), sep civ identity early, eccl severed 1849 and united with chap Little Dewchurch in same par to cr 'Hentland' EP,[62] later called 'Hentland with Hoarwithy'. *LG* Seq 29. Civ bdry: 1883,[5] 1884.[32] *Parl* Seq 3. *Eccl* Archenf. RDn (until 1923), Ross & Archenf. RDn (1923—*). Eccl bdry: 1862 (area Little Dewchurch severed as 'Little Dewchurch' EP).[63]

HENTLAND WITH HOARWITHY—see prev entry

HEREFORD

The following have 'Hereford' in their names.

Insofar as any existed at a given time: Heref Bor/MB, PLU, USD. *Parl* Heref Parl Bor (1295—1885), Ross Dv (1885—1918), Heref Dv/CC (1918—*). *Eccl* Heref RDn (until 1923), Heref (City) RDn (1923—72), Heref City RDn (1972—*).

CP1—HEREFORD—Cr 1932 by union pars in Heref MB: CP2, AP1, AP2, AP3, AP4, CP3, Holmer Within CP, Huntington CP, Tupsley CP.[96]

CP2/EP1—HEREFORD ALL SAINTS—Chap in AP2, sep civ identity early, sep EP 1850.[97] Main area pt in Heref Bor/MB, pt in Webt. Hd as was tp Grafton (sep CP 1866[3]). *LG* Heref Bor/MB (pt until 1884 [enlarged pt 1866—84], ent 1884—1932), Heref USD (pt 1875—84, ent 1884—94), pt Heref RSD (1875—84). Addtl civ bdry alt: 1884,[46] 1884 (loses the detached pt not in the MB to help cr Holmer Within CP).[98] Abol civ 1932 to help cr CP1.[96] Eccl bdry: 1902 (help cr EP2).[99]

EP2—HEREFORD HOLY TRINITY—Cr 1902 from Holmer EP, AP3, EP1, AP1.[99]

EP3—HEREFORD ST JAMES—Cr 1869 from EP4.[100]

AP1—HEREFORD ST JOHN THE BAPTIST—Main area pt in Heref Bor/MB, pt in Webt. Hd. *LG* Heref Bor/MB (pt until 1884, ent 1884—1932), Heref USD (pt 1875—84, ent 1884—94), pt Heref RSD (1875—84). Addtl civ bdry alt: 1884,[46] 1884,[44] 1884.[51] Abol civ 1932 to help cr CP1.[96] Eccl bdry: 1902 (help cr EP2).[99]

AP2—HEREFORD ST MARTIN—Main area pt in Heref Bor/MB, pt in Webt. Hd. Incl chap Hereford All Saints (sep civ identity early as CP2, sep EP 1850 as EP1[99]). *LG* Heref Bor/MB (pt until 1884, ent 1884—1932), Heref USD (pt 1875—84, ent 1884—94), pt Heref RSD (1875—84). Addtl civ bdry alt: 1884,[46] 1884,[51] 1885 (gains the pt of Upper Bullingham CP in Heref MB).[44] Abol civ 1932 to help cr CP1.[96] Addtl eccl bdry alt: 1966 (gains the pt of Clehonger AP in Heref MB).[52]

AP3—HEREFORD ST NICHOLAS—Abol civ 1932 to help cr CP1.[96] Eccl bdry: 1902 (help cr EP2).[99]

AP4—HEREFORD ST OWEN—Civ bdry: 1884.[18] Abol civ 1932 to help cr CP1.[96] Abol eccl 1869 to help cr EP4.[101]

AP5—HEREFORD ST PETER—Abol civ 1932 to help cr CP1.[96] Abol eccl 1869 to help cr EP4.[101]

EP4—HEREFORD ST PETER WITH ST OWEN—Cr 1869 by union AP4, AP5.[101] Eccl bdry: 1869 (cr EP3).[100]

CP3—HEREFORD THE VINEYARD—Ex-par place, sep CP 1858.[64] Abol civ 1932 to help cr CP1.[96]

LITTLE HEREFORD
AP *LG* Seq 25. *Parl* Seq 1. *Eccl* Pec jurisd Chancellor of Cathedral (until 1840s), Leom. RDn (1840s—78), Ludl. RDn (1878—98), Burf. RDn (1898—1972), Ludl. RDn (1972—*). Eccl bdry: 1880 (cr Ashford Carbonnell EP).[6]

HOLME LACY
AP Incl chap Ballingham, chap Bolstone (each prob sep civ identity from Reformation, the 2 eccl united then as 'Ballingham and Bolstone' EP[17]). *LG* Seq 19. Addtl civ bdry alt: 1884.[18] *Parl* Seq 3. *Eccl* Archenf. RDn (until 1898), Heref RDn (1898—1923), Heref (S) RDn (1923—72), Heref Rural RDn (1972—*).

HOLMER
AP Incl tp Holmer and Shelwick (pt in Heref Bor/MB, sep CP 1866[3]), chap Huntington (sep CP 1866,[3] not sep eccl hence this par eccl 'Holmer with Huntington', qv) so that 'Holmer' has no sep civ identity 1886—94 (see following entry). *LG* Grimsw. Hd.

CP Cr 1884 from the pt of Holmer and Shelwick CP neither in Heref MB nor transf to Breinton AP.[31] *LG* Grimsw. Hd, Heref PLU, RSD, RD. *Parl* Seq 5.

HOLMER AND SHELWICK
Tp in Holmer AP, sep CP 1866.[3] *LG* Grimsw. Hd, Heref PLU, pt Heref Bor/MB, pt Heref USD, pt Heref RSD. Abol 1884 the pt in the MB to help cr Holmer Within CP, pt to Breinton AP, the remainder cr Holmer CP.[31]

HOLMER WITH HUNTINGTON
AP Usual eccl spelling; for civ and civ sep tp and chap, see 1st 'Holmer' above. *Eccl* Seq 9.

HOLMER WITHIN
CP Cr 1884 by union of the pt of Holmer and Shelwick CP in Heref MB[31] and the detached pt not in the MB of Hereford All Saints CP.[98] *LG* Grimsw. Hd, Heref PLU, MB, USD. Abol 1932 to help cr Hereford CP.[96] *Parl* Heref Dv (1885—1948).

HOPE MANSELL
AP *LG* Seq 7. Civ bdry: 1884 (gains pt Lea Bailey CP, Glos),[102] 1965 (incl loses pt to Drybrook CP and gains pt Mitcheldean AP, both Glos).[10] *Parl* Seq 3. *Eccl* Seq 19.

HOPE UNDER DINMORE
Chap in Leominster AP, sep civ identity early, sep EP 1741.[18] *LG* Seq 24. *Parl* Seq 1. *Eccl* Leom. RDn (until 1878), Leom. 1 RDn (1878—98), Leom. RDn (1898—1928). Abol eccl 1928 to help cr Hope under Dinmore with Ford EP.[87]

EP Reconstitution 1961 of orig area Hope under Dinmore EP after area Ford severed from Hope under Dinmore with Ford EP (cr as in following entry).[87] Weston RDn (1961—72), Heref Rural RDn (1972—*).

HOPE UNDER DINMORE WITH FORD
EP Cr 1928 by union Hope under Dinmore EP, ex-par Ford.[86] Leom. RDn. Abol 1961, orig area of Ford severed to help cr Stoke Prior and Ford EP, the remainder reconstituted as 'Hope under Dinmore' EP.[87]

HUMBER
AP *LG* Seq 24. Civ bdry: 1888.[103] *Parl* Seq 1. *Eccl* Seq 17.

HUNTINGTON
Chap in Holmer AP, sep CP 1866.[3] *LG* Grimsw. Hd, Heref PLU, Bor/MB, USD. Bdry: 1884 (gains the pt of Breinton AP in Heref MB).[30] Abol 1932 to help cr Hereford CP.[96] *Parl* Heref Dv (1885—1948).

HUNTINGTON
Chap in Holmer AP, sep civ identity early. *LG* Seq 10. *Parl* Seq 1.

IVINGTON
EP Cr 1844 from Leominster AP.[104] Leom. RDn

(1844—78), Leom. 1 RDn (178—98), Leom. RDn (1898—*).

KENCHESTER

AP *LG* Seq 8. *Parl* Seq 5. *Eccl* Seq 25.

KENDERCHURCH

Chap in Kentchurch AP, sep civ identity early, sep EP 1750.[18] Sometimes early 'Howton'. *LG* Seq 17. *Parl* Seq 3. *Eccl* Archenf. RDn (1750—1898), Abbey Dore RDn (1898—1972), Abbeyd. RDn (1972—*).

KENTCHURCH

AP Incl chap Kenderchurch (sep civ identity early, sep EP 1750[18]). *LG* Seq 17. *Parl* Seq 3. *Eccl* Seq 1.

KILPECK

AP Chap to Kilpeck Priory, sep par at Dissolution. *LG* Seq 26. *Parl* Seq 3. *Eccl* Archenf. RDn (until 1898), Abbey Dore RDn (1898—1972), Abbeyd. RDn (1972—*).

KIMBOLTON

Chap in Eye AP, sep civ identity early, sep EP 1745,[18] later called 'Kimbolton with Hammish'. *LG* Seq 24. *Parl* Seq 1. *Eccl* Leom. RDn (1745—1878), Leom. 2 RDn (1878—98), Leom. RDn (1898—*).

KIMBOLTON WITH HAMMISH—see prev entry

KING'S PYON

AP *LG* Seq 16. *Parl* Seq 1. *Eccl* As 'Kings Pyon', Weston RDn (until 1878), Weob. 1 RDn (1878—98), Weob. RDn (1898—1972), Leom. RDn (1972—*).

KINGS PYON—see prev entry

KINGSLAND

AP *LG* Seq 15. *Parl* Seq 1. *Eccl* Seq 15. Eccl bdry: 1949.[84]

KINGSTONE

AP *LG* Seq 17. Civ bdry: 1884.[105] *Parl* Seq 3. *Eccl* Seq 10.

KINGTON

AP Main tp in Heref (Hunt. Hd) as was chap Brilley (sep civ identity early, eccl united with chap Michaelchurch on Arrow [Radnor, qv below] to cr Brilley with Michaelchurch on Arrow EP[35]), chap Huntington (sep civ identity early, not sep eccl hence this par eccl 'Kington with Huntington', qv); incl in Radnor (Painscastle Hd) chap Michaelchurch on Arrow (sep civ identity early in Radnor, eccl united 1860 with chap Brilley [Heref, qv above] to cr Brilley with Michaelchurch on Arrow EP[35]). *LG* Kingt. PLU, pt Kingt. USD, pt Kingt. RSD. Abol civ 1894 the pt in the UD cr Kington Urban CP, the remainder cr Kington Rural CP.[106] *Parl* Leom. Dv (1885—1918).

KINGTON WITH HUNTINGTON

AP Usual eccl spelling; for civ and civ and eccl sep chaps (incl 1 in Radnor), see prev entry. *Eccl* Seq 24.

KINGTON RURAL

CP Cr 1894 from the pt of Kington AP not in Kingt. UD.[106] *LG* Kingt. PLU, RD. *Parl* Leom. Dv/CC (1918—*).

KINGTON URBAN

CP Cr 1894 from the pt of Kington AP in Kingt. UD.[106] *LG* Kingt. PLU, UD. *Parl* Leom. Dv/CC (1918—*).

KINNERSLEY

AP *LG* Seq 16. *Parl* Seq 1. *Eccl* Seq 22.

KINSHAM

AP Usual eccl spelling for donative curacy; for civ see 'Upper Kinsham'. *Eccl* Leom. RDn (until 1878), Leom. 2 RDn (1878—98), Kingsl. RDn (1898—1923), Kingt. RDn (1923—72), Kingt. & Weob. RDn (1972—*).

CP Cr 1886 by union Upper Kinsham AP, Lower Kinsham CP.[107] *LG* Wigm. Hd, Kingt. PLU, RSD, RD. *Parl* Leom. Dv/CC (1918—*).

LOWER KINSAM

Tp in Presteigne AP, sep CP 1866.[3] *LG* Wigm. Hd, Prest. PLU (1836), Kingt. PLU (1836—86), RSD. Abol 1886 to help cr Kinsham CP.[107] *Parl* Leom. Dv (1885—1918).

UPPER KINSHAM

AP Usual civ spelling; for eccl (donative curacy), see 'Kinsham'. *LG* Wigm. Hd, Prest. PLU (1836), Kingt. PLU (1836—86), RSD. Abol 1886 to help cr Kinsham CP.[107] *Parl* Leom. Dv (1885—1918).

KNILL

AP *LG* Seq 23. *Parl* Seq 1. *Eccl* Seq 24.

LAYSTERS

Chap (Heref, Wolp. Hd) in Tenbury AP (Worcs, Heref), sep civ identity early in Heref, sep EP 1717 as 'Leysters',[18] qv. *LG* Seq 24. *Parl* Seq 1.

LEA

Chap (Heref, Glos) in Linton AP, sep civ identity early with pt in each co, sep EP early 19th cent.[108] The Heref pt (Greyt. Hd) was tp Lea Upper (sep CP 1866[3]); the Glos pt (St Briavells Hd) was tp Lea Lower (transf to Heref 1832 for parl purposes, 1844 for civ purposes,[50] sep CP 1866 in Heref[3]) so that 'Lea' has no sep civ identity 1866—83 (see following entry). *LG* Greyt. Hd (pt until 1844, ent 1844—66). *Eccl* See entry in Glos.

CP Cr 1883 by union Lea Upper CP, Lea Lower CP (both Heref),[109] pt Lea Bailey CP (Glos).[110] *LG* Greyt. Hd, Ross PLU, RSD, RD (1894—1931), Ross & Whitch. RD (1931—74). Bdry: 1965 (incl gains pt Longhope CP, pt Mitcheldean CP, both Glos).[10] *Parl* Ross Dv (1885—1918), Heref Dv/CC (1918—*).

LEA LOWER

Tp (Glos, St Briavells Hd) in Lea CP (Heref, Glos, qv for early status in Linton AP), transf to Heref 1832 for parl purposes, 1844 (Greyt. Hd) for civ purposes,[50] sep CP 1866 in Heref.[3] *LG* Ross PLU, RSD. Abol 1883 to help cr Lea CP.[109]

LEA UPPER

Tp (Heref, Greyt. Hd) in Lea CP (Heref, Glos, qv for early status in Linton AP), sep CP 1866.[3] *LG* Ross PLU, RSD. Abol 1883 to help cr Lea CP.[109]

LEDBURY

AP Incl chap Aylton (prob sep par at Reformation, sep status noted 1587[15]), chap Little Marcle (sep par by 1535), chap Pixley (sep CP 1866,[3] sep EP 1736[18]), tp Parkhold (sep CP 1866[3]). *LG* Radl. Hd, pt Ledb. Bor, Ledb. PLU, RSD. Addtl civ bdry alt: 1885.[8] Abol civ 1894 the pt constituted Ledb. UD cr Ledbury Urban CP, the remainder to cr 2 CPs of Ledbury Rural,[111] Wellington Heath.[112] *Parl* Pt

Ledb. Parl Bor (1295, 1305 only), Ross Dv (1885—1918). *Eccl* Seq 8. Addtl eccl bdry alt: 1842 (cr Wellington Heath EP),[113] 1929.[73]

LEDBURY RURAL
CP Cr 1894 from pt of the pt of Ledbury AP not constituted Ledb. UD.[111] *LG* Ledb. PLU, RD. *Parl* Heref Dv (1918—48), Leom. CC (1948—*).

LEDBURY TOWN
CP Renaming 1968 of Ledbury Urban CP when Ledb. UD abol and area of par incl in Ledb. RD.[114] *LG* Ledb. RD. *Parl* Leom. CC (1970—*).

LEDBURY URBAN
CP Cr 1894 from the pt of Ledbury AP constituted Ledb. UD.[111] *LG* Ledb. PLU, UD. Renamed 1968 'Ledbury Town' CP when Ledb. UD abol and this par transf to Ledb. RD.[114] *Parl* Heref Dv (1918—48), Leom. CC (1948—70).

LEINTHALL EARLES
EP Chap in Aymestrey AP, sep EP 1756.[18] Leom. RDn (1756—1878), Leom. 1 RDn (1878—98), Kingsl. RDn (1898—1923), Wigm. RDn (1923—37). Abol 1937 to help cr Aymestry with Leinthall Earles EP.[19]

LEINTHALL STARKES
Chap in Aymestrey AP, sep civ identity early, sep EP 1783.[18] *LG* Seq 22. *Parl* Seq 1. *Eccl* Leom. RDn (1783—1878), Leom. 2 RDn (1878—98), Kingsl. RDn (1898—1923), Wigm. RDn (1923—58), Leom. RDn (1958—*).

LEINTWARDINE
AP Mostly Heref (Wigm. Hd): tp Walford, Letton and Newton (sep CP 1866[3]), tp Adforton (sep CP 1866,[3] not sep eccl hence this par eccl 'Leintwardine with Adforton', qv); incl tp Leintwardine North Side (pt Heref [Wigm. Hd], pt Salop [Purslow Hd], sep CP 1866 with pt in ea co[3]), so that 'Leintwardine' has no sep civ identity 1866—95 (see following entry).
CP Name used for Leintwardine North Side CP (Heref, Salop) when made 1895 ent Heref.[2] *LG* Ludl. PLU, Wigm. RD (1894—1930), Leom. & Wigm. RD (1930—74). *Parl* Leom. Dv/CC (1918—*).

LEINTWARDINE NORTH SIDE
Tp in Leintwardine AP, pt Heref (Wigm. Hd), pt Salop (Purslow Hd), sep CP 1866 with pt in ea co.[3] *LG* Ludl. PLU, RSD, pt Wigm. RD (1894—95), pt sep RD in Salop (1894—95). Bdry: 1885.[47] Made 1895 ent Heref.[2] *Parl* Heref pt, Leom. Dv (1885—1918).

LEOMINSTER
AP Incl chap Hatfield (sep civ identity early, sep EP 1742[18]), chap Hope under Dinmore (sep civ identity early, sep EP 1741[18]), chaps Stoke Prior, Docklow (each sep civ identity early, each a sep EP 1745[18]), tp Leominster Borough (in Leom. Bor/MB, sep CP 1866[3]), tp Leominster Out (not in Leom. Bor but in Leom. MB, sep CP 1866[3]) so that 'Leominster' has no sep civ identity after 1866. *LG* Wolp. Hd, Leom. Bor/MB (pt until 1835, ent 1835—66). *Parl* Leom. Parl Bor (pt 1295—1832, ent 1832—67). *Eccl* Leom. RDn (until 1878), Leom. 1 RDn (1878—98), Leom. RDn (1898—*). Addtl eccl bdry alt: 1844 (cr Ivington EP).[104]

LEOMINSTER BOROUGH
Tp in Leominster AP, sep CP 1866.[3] *LG* Wolp. Hd, Leom. PLU, MB, USD. *Parl* Leom. Parl Bor (1295—1885), Seq 1 thereafter.

LEOMINSTER OUT
Tp in Leominster AP (area orig not in Leom. Bor), sep CP 1866.[3] *LG* Wolp. Hd, Leom. PLU, MB (area incl in MB from 1835), USD. *Parl* Leom. Parl Bor (1832—85), Seq 1 thereafter.

LETTON
AP *LG* Pt Stretf. Hd, pt Wolp. Hd, Weob. PLU (soon after 1836[4]—1930), RSD, RD. *Parl* Seq 1. *Eccl* Weob. RDn (until 1878), Weob. 1 RDn (1878—98), Weob. RDn (1898—1926). Abol eccl 1926 to help cr Letton with Willersley EP.[115]
EP Reconstitution 1964 of Letton after orig area Willersley AP severed from Letton with Willersley EP (cr 1926, qv below) to help cr Eardisley with Bollingham and Willersley EP, the remainder to be 'Letton'.[75] Weob. RDn (1964—72), Heref Rural RDn (1972—*).

LETTON WITH WILLERSLEY
EP Cr 1926 by union Letton AP, Willersley AP.[115] Weob. RDn. Abol 1964, orig area Willersley severed to help cr Eardisley with Bollingham and Willersley EP, the remainder reconstituted 'Letton'.[75]

LEYSTERS
Chap (Heref, Wolp. Hd) in Tenbury AP (Worcs, Heref), sep EP 1717,[18] sep civ identity early in Heref as 'Laysters', qv. *Eccl* Burf. RDn (1717—1878), Burf. (W) RDn (1878—98), Burf. RDn (1898—1972), Leom. RDn (1972—*).

LINGEN
AP *LG* Wigm. Hd, Prest. PLU (1836), Kingt. PLU (1836—1930), RSD, Wigm. RD (1894—1930), Leom. & Wigm. RD (1930—74). *Parl* Seq 1. *Eccl* Leom. RDn (until 1878), Leom. 2 RDn (1878—98), Kingt. RDn (1898—1923), Wigm. RDn (1823—58), Kingt. RDn (1958—72), Kingt. & Weob. RDn (1972—*).

LINTON
AP Incl chap Lea (Glos [St Briavells Hd], Heref [Greyt. Hd], sep civ identity early in both cos, qv, sep EP early 19th cent[108]). *LG* Seq 6. *Parl* Seq 3. *Eccl* Seq 5.

LINTON
Tp in Bromyard AP, sep CP 1866,[3] pt eccl severed 1891 and transf to Stanford Bishop EP.[44] *LG* Seq 1. Bdry: 1883,[5] 1884,[11] 1884,[39] 1884,[41] 1894 (incl loses pt to help cr Brockhampton CP).[38] *Parl* Seq 1.

LLANCILLO
AP *LG* Seq 3. *Parl* Seq 3. *Eccl* Seq 27.

LLANDINABO
AP *LG* Seq 29. *Parl* Seq 3. *Eccl* Seq 3.

LLANGARRON—see following entry
LLANGARREN
Chap (Archenf. RDn) in Lugwardine AP (Weston RDn), sep civ identity early, sep EP 1849 as 'Llangarron' incl chap St Weonards in same par.[62] *LG* Seq 29. Civ bdry: 1884,[25] 1885.[66] *Parl* Seq 3. *Eccl* Archenf. RDn (1849—1923), Ross & Archenf. RDn (1923—*). Eccl bdry: 1856 (cr Llangrove

EP),[116] 1879 (cr St Weonards EP).[117]

LLANGROVE

EP Cr 1856 from Llangarren EP.[116] Sometimes early 'Long Grove'. Archenf. RDn (until 1923), Ross & Archenf. RDn (1923—*).

LLANROTHAL

AP Incl chap Welsh Newton (sep civ identity early, sep EP 1798[18]). *LG* Worm. Hd, Monm PLU, RSD, Whitch. RD (1894—1931), Ross & Whitch. RD (1934—74). Addtl civ bdry alt: 1883 (gains pt Dixton Newton AP, Monm).[118] *Parl* Seq 3. *Eccl* Archenf. RDn (until 1923), Ross & Archenf. RDn (1923—39). Abol eccl 1939 to help cr Welsh Newton with Llanrothal EP.[119]

LLANVEYNOE

Chap (sometimes early 'Llanyveyno') in Clodock AP, sep CP 1866,[3] endowed chap, sometimes considered sep EP, eccl united early 20th cent with Craswell EP to cr 'Craswell with Llanveynoe',[55] later called simply 'Craswell'. *LG* Seq 3. *Parl* Seq 3.

LLANWARNE

AP *LG* Seq 29. *Parl* Seq 3. *Eccl* Seq 3.

LLANYVEYNO—see LLANVEYNOE

LONG GROVE—see LLANGROVE

LONGTOWN

Chap in Clodock AP, sep CP 1866,[3] endowed chap a sep benefice and sometimes considered sep EP, the benefice united 1927 with mother par and thereafter eccl 'Clodock with Longtown'.[59] *LG* Seq 3. *Parl* Seq 3.

LUCTON

Chap in Eye AP, sep civ identity early, sep EP 1747.[18] *LG* Seq 24. *Parl* Seq 1. *Eccl* Leom. RDn (until 1878), Leom. 2 RDn (1878—98), Leom. RDn (1898—1973). Abol eccl 1973 to help cr Croft with Yarpole and Lucton EP.[66]

LUDFORD

Chap (Salop [Munslow Hd], Heref [Wolp. Hd]) in Bromfield AP (Salop), sep civ identity early with pt in each co, sep EP 1771.[18] *LG* Ludl. PLU, RSD, pt sep RD in Heref (1894—95). Made 1895 ent Salop.[2] *Parl* Ludl. Parl Bor (ent par [Salop, Heref] 1832—85), pt Leom. Dv (1885—1918). *Eccl* See main entry in Salop.

LUGWARDINE

AP Incl chap Little Dewchurch, chap Hentland (each sep civ identity early, both in Archenf. RDn, the 2 eccl united 1849 as 'Hentland' EP,[67] 'Little Dewchurch' a sep EP 1862 from the latter[68]), chap Llangarren, chap St Weonards (each sep civ identity early, both in Archenf. RDn, the 2 eccl united 1849 as 'Llangarren' EP,[67] 'St Weonards' a sep EP 1879 from the latter[117]). *LG* Seq 12. *Parl* Seq 4. *Eccl* Weston RDn. Abol eccl 1928 to help cr Ludwardine with Bartestree EP.[22]

LUGWARDINE WITH BARTESTREE

EP Cr 1928 by union Ludwardine AP, chap Bartestree in Dormington with Bartestree EP.[22] Weston RDn (1928—72), Heref Rural RDn (1972—*).

LUSTON

Tp in Eye AP, sep CP 1866.[3] *LG* Seq 24. Bdry: 1887.[120] *Parl* Seq 1.

LYONSHALL

AP *LG* Seq 14. *Parl* Seq 1. *Eccl* Seq 24.

MADLEY

AP Incl chap Tyberton (sep civ identity early, not sep eccl hence this par eccl 'Madley with Tyberton', qv in following entry. *LG* Seq 17. *Parl* Seq 3.

MADLEY WITH TYBERTON

AP Usual eccl spelling; for civ and civ sep chap Tyberton, see prev entry. *Eccl* Seq 10.

MANSEL GAMAGE—see MANSELL GAMAGE

MANSEL LACY—see MANSELL LACY

MANSELL GAMAGE

AP *LG* Seq 9. *Parl* Seq 1. *Eccl* As 'Mansel Gamage', Weob. RDn (until 1878), Weob. 1 RDn (1878—98), Weob. RDn (1898—1971). Abol eccl 1971 to help cr Byford and Mansel Gamage EP.[53]

MANSELL LACY

AP *LG* Seq 9. Civ bdry: 1884.[24] *Parl* Seq 1. *Eccl* As 'Mansel Lacy', Seq 21.

LITTLE MARCLE

AP Orig chap in Ledbury AP, sep par by 1535. *LG* Seq 13. *Parl* Seq 4. *Eccl* Seq 8.

MUCH MARCLE

AP Incl tp Yatton (sep CP 1866,[3] not sep eccl hence this par eccl 'Much Marcle with Yatton', qv). *LG* Seq 5. Addtl civ bdry alt: 1884.[121] *Parl* Seq 4.

MUCH MARCLE WITH YATTON

AP Usual eccl spelling; for civ and civ sep tp, see prev entry. *Eccl* Ross RDn (until 1923), Ledb. RDn (1923—*).

MARDEN

AP Incl chap Amberley (sep CP 1866,[3] not sep eccl hence this par eccl 'Marden with Amberley', qv); incl chap Wisteston (sep EP 1728[18]). *LG* Seq 2. Addtl civ bdry alt: 1883,[5] 1884,[85] 1884,[51] 1887.[6] *Parl* Seq 5.

MARDEN WITH AMBERLEY

AP Usual eccl spelling; for civ and civ sep chap, see prev entry. *Eccl* Seq 13.

MARSTON STANNETT

Chap in Pencombe AP, sep EP 1718.[18] Frome RDn (1718—1878), Leom. 2 RDn (1878—98), Bromyd. RDn (1898—1928). Abol eccl 1928 to help cr Pencombe with Marston Stannett EP.[15]

MARSTOW

Chap in Sellack AP, sep civ identity early, sep EP 1777.[18] *LG* Seq 29. Civ bdry: 1884,[37] 1884.[29] *Parl* Seq 3. *Eccl* Archenf. RDn (1777—1923), Ross & Archenf. RDn (1923—*).

MATHON

CP Renaming 1897 of Mathon Rural CP as it is transf from Worcs to Heref.[2] *LG* Ledb. PLU, RD. *Parl* Leom. Dv/CC (1918—*).

MICHAELCHURCH ESCLEY

AP *LG* Seq 3. *Parl* Seq 3. *Eccl* Seq 27.

MIDDLETON ON THE HILL

Chap in Eye, sep civ identity early, sep EP 1745.[18] *LG* Seq 24. *Parl* Seq 1. *Eccl* Leom. RDn (1745—78), Leom. 2 RDn (1878—98), Leom. RDn (1898—*).

MOCCAS

AP *LG* Webt. Hd, Weob. PLU (soon after 1836[4]—1930), RSD, RD. Seq 20. *Parl* Seq 1. *Eccl* Seq 20.

MONKLAND
AP *LG* Seq 15. *Parl* Seq 1. *Eccl* Seq 15.

MONNINGTON ON WYE
AP *LG* Seq 9. *Parl* Seq 1. *Eccl* Seq 21.

MORDIFORD
AP *LG* Seq 4. *Parl* Seq 3. *Eccl* Seq 18.

MORETON JEFFREYS
AP Usual civ spelling; for eccl see 'Morton Jefferies'. *LG* Seq 11. *Parl* Seq 1.

MORETON ON LUGG
AP *LG* Seq 8. Civ bdry: 1883,[5] 1884.[51] *Parl* Seq 5. *Eccl* Pec jurisd Moreton on Lugg (until 1840s), Weston RDn (1840s—78), Heref RDn (1878—98), Weston RDn (1898—1972), Heref Rural RDn (1972—*).

MORTON JEFFRIES
AP Usual eccl spelling; for civ see 'Moreton Jeffreys'. *Eccl* Heref RDn (until 1878), N Frome RDn (1878—98), Bromyd. RDn (1898—*).

MUNSLEY
AP *LG* Seq 13. Civ bdry: 1885,[9] 1885.[10] *Parl* Seq 5. *Eccl* Frome RDn. Abol eccl 1854 to help cr Canon Frome with Munsley EP,[90] later called simply 'Canon Frome'.

NEWTON
Tp in Clodock AP, sep CP 1866,[3] sep EP 1848.[61] *LG* Seq 3. *Parl* Seq 3. *Eccl* Weob. RDn (1848—78), Weob. 2 RDn (1878—98), Abbey Dore RDn (1898—1972), Abbeyd. RDn (1972—*).

NEWTON
Tp in Croft AP, sep CP 1866.[3] *LG* Seq 24. *Parl* Seq 1.

NORTON
CP Cr 1894 from Norton with Brockhampton CP.[43] *LG* Bromyd. PLU, RD. *Parl* Leom. Dv/CC (1918—*).

NORTON CANON
AP *LG* Grimsw. Hd, Weob. PLU (soon after 1836[4]—1930), RSD, RD. *Parl* Seq 1. *Eccl* Seq 22.

NORTON WITH BROCKHAMPTON
Tp in Bromyard AP, sep CP 1866,[3] an area in this tp/CP considered sep CP as 'Lower Brockhampton' 1863, qv. *LG* Brox. Hd, Bromyd. PLU, RSD. Bdry: 1883,[5] 1884,[12] 1884,[88] 1884.[46] Abol 1894 pt to cr Norton CP, pt to Linton CP, pt to Whitchurch CP, the remainder to help cr Brockhampton CP.[43] *Parl* Leom. Dv (1885—1918).

OCLE PYCHARD
AP *LG* Seq 1. Civ bdry: 1887.[122] *Parl* Seq 1. *Eccl* Seq 7.

ORCOP
Priory, sep civ identity erly, no incumbent before 1674, donative until 1860,[123] sep eccl identity sustained. *LG* Seq 26. *Parl* Seq 3. *Eccl* Archenf. RDn (cr—1923), Heref (S) RDn (1923—72), Ross & Archenf. RDn (1972—*).

ORLETON
AP *LG* Seq 24. *Parl* Seq 1. *Eccl* Seq 17.

PARKHOLD
Tp in Ledbury AP, sep CP 1866.[3] *LG* Radl. Hd, Ledb. PLU, RSD. Abol 1884 ent to Pixley AP.[124]

PEMBRIDGE
AP Usual civ spelling; for eccl see following entry. *LG* Seq 14. *Parl* Seq 1.

PEMBRIDGE WITH MOORCOURT
AP Usual eccl spelling; for civ see prev entry. *Eccl* Seq 14.

PENCOMBE
AP Incl chap Marston Stannett (sep EP 1718[18]). *LG* Brox. Hd, Bromyd. PLU, RSD, RD. Abol civ 1895 to help cr Pencombe with Grendon Warren CP.[93] *Parl* Leom. Dv (1885—1918). *Eccl* Frome RDn (until 1878), N Frome RDn (1878—98), Bromyd. RDn (1898—1928). Abol eccl 1928 to help cr Pencombe with Marston Stannett EP.[15]

PENCOMBE WITH GRENDON WARREN
CP Cr 1895 by union Pencombe AP, Grendon Warren AP.[93] *LG* Bromyd. PLU, RD. *Parl* Leom. Dv/CC (1918—*).

PENCOMBE WITH MARSTON STANNETT
EP Cr 1928 by union Pencombe AP, Marston Stannett EP.[15] Bromyd. RDn. Abol 1953 to help cr Pencombe with Marston Stannett and Little Cowarne EP.[125]

PENCOMBE WITH MARSTON STANNETT AND LITTLE COWARNE
EP Cr 1953 by union Pencombe with Marston Stannett EP, area Little Cowarne (orig sep AP, qv for union) from Ullingswick with Little Cowarne EP.[125]

PENCOYD
Chap in Sellack AP, sep civ identity early, sep EP 1765.[18] *LG* Seq 29. *Parl* Seq 3.

PETERCHURCH
AP *LG* Seq 17. *Parl* Seq 3. *Eccl* Seq 23.

PETERSTOW
AP *LG* Seq 29. Civ bdry: 1884.[37] *Parl* Seq 3. *Eccl* Seq 5.

PIPE AND LYDE
AP *LG* Seq 8. Civ bdry: 1883,[5] 1884.[51] *Parl* Seq 5. *Eccl* Seq 13.

PIXLEY
Chap in Ledbury AP, sep civ identity early, sep EP 1736.[18] *LG* Seq 13. Civ bdry: 1965 (gains Parkhold CP).[124] *Parl* Seq 5. *Eccl* Frome RDn (1736—1878), S Frome RDn (1878—98), Ledb. RDn (1898—*).

PRESTEIGNE
AP Pt Radnor (2 wards and tp Discoed, all sep CPs 1866 in Radnor,[3] the tp not sep eccl hence this par eccl 'Presteigne with Discoed', qv); pt Heref (Wigm. Hd, tps Combe, Lower Kinsham, Stapleton, Willey; Rodd, Nash and Little Brampton) (each of the 5 a sep CP 1866 in Heref[3]); incl pt tp Litton and Cascob (in Heref, the ent tp [pt in Cascob AP] transf to Radnor 1832 for parl purposes, 1844 for civ purposes,[55] sep CP 1866 in Radnor[3]) so that 'Presteigne' ent Radnor from 1866.

PRESTEIGNE WITH DISCOED
AP Usual eccl spelling; for civ and civ sep tps and wards, incl pts in Heref and Radnor, see prev entry. *Eccl* Seq 24.

PRESTON ON WYE
AP Webt. Hd, Weob. PLU (1836—1930), RSD, RD. *Parl* Seq 1. *Eccl* Seq 12.

PRESTON WYNNE
Chap in Withington AP, sep CP 1866,[3] sep EP 1734,[18] eccl refounded 1857.[126] *LG* Seq 2. Civ bdry: 1884.[51] *Parl* Seq 5. *Eccl* Herf. RDn (1734—

1898), Weston RDn (1898—1972), Heref RDn (1972—*).

PUDLESTON WITH WHYLE
AP Usual eccl spelling; for civ see following entry. *Eccl* Seq 17.

PUDLESTONE
AP Usual civ spelling; for eccl see prev entry. *LG* Seq 24. *Parl* Seq 1.

PUTLEY
AP *LG* Seq 5. Civ bdry: 1885,[10] 1885.[9] *Parl* Seq 4. *Eccl* Heref RDn (until 1878), S Frome RDn (1878—98), Ledb. RDn (1898—*).

OLD RADNOR
AP Mostly Radnor (Radnor Bor; incl chap Kinnerton, not sep eccl hence this par eccl 'Old Radnor with Kinnerton', qv); incl in Heref tp Lower Harpton (sep CP 1866 in Heref[3]) so that this par ent Radnor from 1866.

OLD RADNOR WITH KINNERTON
AP Usual eccl spelling; for civ sep tp in Heref, see prev entry. *Eccl* Seq 24.

RICHARDS CASTLE
AP Pt Salop (Munslow Hd), pt Heref (Wolp. Hd). *LG* Ludl. PLU, RSD. Made 1889 2 sep CPs, each 'Richards Castle', one in each co.[127] *Parl* Heref pt, Leom. Dv (1885—1918). *Eccl* See entry in Salop.
CP Cr 1889 from the pt in Heref of Richards Castle AP (Salop, Heref).[127] *LG* Ludl. PLU, Wigm. RD (1894—1931), Leom. & Wigm. RD (1931—74). *Parl* Leom. Dv/CC (1918—*).

RODD, NASH AND LITTLE BRAMPTON
Tp in Presteigne AP, sep CP 1866.[3] *LG* Seq 23. *Parl* Seq 1.

ROSS
AP Incl chap Brampton Abbots, chap Weston under Penyard (each a sep par 1671[28]). *LG* Pt Ross Bor, Greyt. Hd, Ross PLU, pt Ross USD, pt Ross RSD. Abol civ 1894 the pt in the UD cr Ross Urban CP, the remainder cr Ross Rural CP.[38] *Parl* Pt Ross Parl Bor (1305 only), Ross Dv (1885—1918). *Eccl* Seq 19. Addtl eccl bdry alt: 1960.[30]

ROSS RURAL
CP Cr 1894 from the pt of Ross AP not in Ross UD.[38] *LG* Ross PLU, RD (1894—1931), Ross & Whitch. RD (1931—74). Bdry: 1905,[128] 1931.[39] *Parl* Heref Dv/CC (1918—*).

ROSS URBAN
CP Cr 1894 by union of the pts in Ross UD of Ross AP, Bridstow AP.[38] *LG* Ross PLU, UD (1894—1931), Ross & Whitch. RD (1931—74). Bdry: 1905,[128] 1931.[39] *Parl* Heref Dv/CC (1918—*).

ROWLSTONE
AP *LG* Seq 3. *Parl* Seq 3. *Eccl* Seq 27.

ST DEVEREUX
AP *LG* Seq 17. *Parl* Seq 3. *Eccl* Seq 2.

ST MARGARET'S
AP *LG* Seq 3. *Parl* Seq 3. *Eccl* Seq 27.

ST WEONARDS
Chap in Lugwardine AP, sep civ identity early, eccl severed 1849 to help cr Llangarren EP,[67] 'St Weonards' a sep EP 1879 from the latter.[117] *LG* Seq 29. *Parl* Seq 3. *Eccl* Archenf. RDn (1879—1923), Heref (S) RDn (1923—72), Ross & Archenf. RDn

(1972—*).

SALTMARSHE
Ex-par place, sep CP 1858.[69] *LG* Brox. Hd, Bromyd. PLU (1858—1930), RSD, RD. *Parl* Seq 1.

UPPER SAPEY
AP *LG* Seq 1. *Parl* Seq 1. *Eccl* Frome RDn (until 1878), Burf. (E) RDn (1878—98), Burf. RDn (1898—1923), Bromyd. RDn (1923—*).

SARNESFIELD
AP *LG* Wolp. Hd, Weob. PLU, RSD, RD. Civ bdry: 1884.[24] *Parl* Seq 1. *Eccl* Seq 22.

SELLACK
AP Incl chap Marstow (sep civ identity early, sometimes early 'Pipe', sep EP 1777[18]), chap Pencoyd (sep civ identity early, sep EP 1765[18]), chap King's Caple (sep civ identity early, not sep eccl hence this par eccl 'Sellack with King's Caple', qv). *LG* Seq 29. Addtl civ bdry alt: 1884.[42] *Parl* Seq 3.

SELLACK WITH KING'S CAPLE
AP Usual eccl spelling; for civ and civ and eccl sep chaps, see prev entry. *Eccl* Seq 4.

SHOBDON
AP *LG* Seq 15. *Parl* Seq 1. *Eccl* Seq 16.

SOLLERS HOPE
AP *LG* Seq 7. *Parl* Seq 3. *Eccl* Seq 19.

STANFORD BISHOP
Chap in Bromyard AP, sep civ identity early, sep EP 1745.[18] *LG* Seq 1. Civ bdry: 1884.[12] *Parl* Seq 1. *Eccl* Frome RDn (1745—1878), N Frome RDn (1878—98), Bromyd. RDn (1898—*). Eccl bdry: 1891 (gains pt tp Linton from Bromyard AP.[44]

STAPLETON
Tp in Presteigne AP, sep CP 1866.[3] *LG* Seq 23. *Parl* Seq 1.

STAUNTON ON ARROW
AP *LG* Pt Stretf. Hd, pt Wigm. Hd, Kingt. PLU, RSD, RD. *Parl* Seq 1. *Eccl* Seq 14.

STAUNTON ON WYE
AP *LG* Grimsw. Hd, Weob. PLU (1836—1930), RSD, RD. *Parl* Seq 1. *Eccl* Seq 21.

STOKE BLISS
AP Pt Worcs (Doddingtree Hd), pt Heref (Brox. Hd). *LG* Tenb. PLU, RSD, sep RD in Heref (1894—97). Made 1897 ent Worcs.[2] *Parl* Leom. Dv (1885—1918). *Eccl* Frome RDn (until 1878), N Frome RDn (1878—98), Burf. RDn (1898—1919); see entry in Worcs for RDns thereafter and for eccl abol of this par in 1973.

STOKE EDITH
AP Incl chap Westhide (sep CP 1866,[3] eccl 'West Hide' and as such eccl severed 1928 to help cr Withington with West Hide EP,[22] so that this par eccl 'Stoke Edith with West Hide' until 1928, 'Stoke Edith' thereafter). *LG* Seq 12. Addtl civ bdry alt: 1884,[8] 1885.[9] *Parl* Seq 3. *Eccl* Ledb. RDn.

STOKE EDITH WIH WEST HIDE
AP Usual eccl spelling until chap West Hide eccl severed 1928 to help cr Withington with West Hide, the remainder 'Stoke Edith' thereafter,[22] qv also for civ and civ sep chap. *Eccl* Weston RDn.

STOKE LACY
AP *LG* Seq 1. Civ bdry: 1884,[12] 1884.[13] *Parl* Seq 1.

Eccl Seq 6. Eccl bdry: 1931,[16] 1953.[89]

STOKE PRIOR

Chap in Leominster AP, sep civ identity early, sep EP 1745.[18] *LG* Seq 24. Civ bdry: 1883,[5] 1888.[103] *Parl* Seq 1. *Eccl* Leom. RDn (1745—1878), Leom. 2 RDn (1878—98), Leom. RDn (1898—1961). Abol eccl 1961 to help cr Stoke Prior and Ford EP.[87]

STOKE PRIOR AND FORD

EP Cr 1961 by union Stoke Prior EP, orig area ex-par Ford (before its union) in Hope under Dinmore with Ford EP.[87] Leom. RDn.

STORRIDGE

EP Cr 1856 from Cradley AP.[65] Frome RDn (1856—78), S Frome RDn (1878—98), Ledb. RDn (1898—*).

STOTTESDEN

AP Mostly Salop (Stottesden Hd), incl in Heref (Wolp. Hd) chap Farlow (transf to Salop 1832 for parl purposes, 1844 for civ purposes,[55] sep CP 1866 in Salop[3]) so that Stottesden ent Salop from 1844, qv for organisation.

STRETFORD

AP *LG* Seq 16. *Parl* Seq 1. *Eccl* Leom. RDn (until 1878), Leom. 1 RDn (1878—98), Kingsl. RDn (1898—1923), Leom. RDn (1923—72). Eccl bdry: 1956.[25] Abol eccl 1972 to help cr Dilwyn and Stretford EP.[65]

STRETTON GRANDISON

AP Incl chap Ashperton (sep civ identity early, not sep eccl hence this par eccl 'Stretton Grandison with Ashperton', qv). *LG* Seq 13. Addtl civ bdry alt: 1884,[8] 1885.[9] *Parl* Seq 5.

STRETTON GRANDISON WITH ASHPERTON

AP Usual eccl spelling; for civ and civ sep chap, see prev entry. *Eccl* Seq 8. Eccl bdry: 1879 (gains tp Egleton from Bishop's Frome AP).[81]

STRETTON SUGWAS

AP *LG* Seq 8. Civ bdry: 1883,[5] 1884.[21] *Parl* Seq 5. *Eccl* Seq 25.

SUTTON

CP Joint rating for poor law purposes of Sutton St Michael AP, Sutton St Nicholas AP. *LG* Brox. Hd, Heref PLU, RSD, RD. Bdry: 1883,[5] 1884,[51] 1884,[85] 1887.[122] *Parl* Seq 5.

SUTTON ST MICHAEL

AP Chap appropriated to Preceptory of Dinmore, sep par from Dissolution.[129] *LG* Brox. Hd, but jointly rated for poor law purposes with Sutton St Nicholas as 'Sutton', qv for civ organisation. *Eccl* Seq 26.

SUTTON ST NICHOLAS

AP *LG* Brox. Hd, but jointly rated for poor law purposes with Sutton St Michael as 'Sutton', qv for civ organisation. *Eccl* Seq 26.

TARRINGTON

AP *LG* Seq 13. *Parl* Seq 5. *Eccl* Weston RDn (until 1898), Ledb. RDn (1898—*).

TEDSTONE DELAMERE

AP *LG* Seq 1. *Parl* Seq 1. *Eccl* Seq 6.

TEDSTONE WAFER

AP Prob orig a sep AP, perhaps an independent chap, sep civ identity retained or early gained, eccl in united benefice from 1625 with Edvin Loach EP

(Heref until 1844, Worcs 1844—93, Heref from 1893) until the 2 eccl united 1972 as Edvin Loach with Tedstone Wafer EP.[77] *LG* Seq 1. *Parl* Seq 1. As united benefice: Frome RDn (1625—1878), N Frome RDn (1878—98), Bromyd. RDn (1898—1972).

TENBURY

AP Chap in Worcs (Doddingtree Hd), incl in Heref (Wolp. Hd) chap Laysters (sep civ identity early in Heref, sep EP 1717[18]), chap Rochford (sep EP 1843,[129] transf to Worcs 1832 for parl purposes, 1844 for civ purposes [Doddingtre Hd], sep CP 1866 in Worcs[3]) so that Tenbury ent Worcs from 1844, qv for organisation.

THORNBURY

AP *LG* Pt Brox. Hd, pt Wolp. Hd, Bromyd. PLU, RSD, RD. Civ bdry: 1883,[5] 1884.[12] *Parl* Seq 1. *Eccl* Seq 6. Eccl bdry: 1948,[33] 1963.[80]

THRUXTON

AP *LG* Seq 17. Civ bdry: 1884.[105] *Parl* Seq 3. *Eccl* Seq 10.

TITLEY

AP LG Wigm. Hd, Kingt. PLU, RSD, RD. *Parl* Seq 1. *Eccl* Leom. RDn (until 1878), Weob. 3 RDn (1878—98), Kingt. RDn (1898—1972), Kingt. & Weob. RDn (1972—*).

TRETIRE WITH MICHAELCHURCH

AP *LG* Seq 29. *Parl* Seq 3. *Eccl* Seq 5.

TREVILLE

Ex-par place, sep CP 1858.[69] *LG* Seq 26. *Parl* Seq 3.

TUPSLEY

Tp in Hampton Bishop AP, sep CP 1866,[3] sep EP 1866.[100] *LG* Grimsw. Hd, Heref PLU, Heref Bor/MB (pt until 1884, ent 1884—1932), Heref USD (pt 1875—84, ent 1884—94), pt Heref RSD (1875—94). Civ bdry: 1884,[51] 1884 (loses the pt not in the MB to Hampton Bishop AP).[95] Abol civ 1932 ent to Hereford CP.[96] *Parl* Ross Dv (1885—1918), Heref Dv (1918—48). *Eccl* Heref RDn (1866—1923), Heref (City) RDn (1923—72), Heref City RDn (1972—*).

TURNASTONE

AP *LG* Seq 17. *Parl* Seq 3. *Eccl* Seq 23.

TYBERTON

Chap in Madley AP, sep civ identity early. *LG* Seq 17. *Parl* Seq 3.

ULLINGSWICK

AP Gains 1478 Little Cowarne AP (sep civ identity regained early) and thereafter the latter eccl a chap in this par so that eccl 'Ullingswick with Little Cowarne' until 1953,[62] qv). *LG* Seq 1. Addtl civ bdry alt: 1884,[12] 1884.[85] *Parl* Seq 1.

EP Reconstitution 1953 as area Little Cowarne severed from Ullingswick with Little Cowarne EP to help cr Pencombe with Marston Stannett and Little Cowarne EP, the remainder to be 'Ullingswick' EP.[125] Weston RDn (1953—72), Heref Rural RDn (1872—*).

ULLINGSWICK WITH LITTLE COWARNE

AP Usual eccl spelling after union 1478 of Ullingswick AP, Little Cowarne AP (the latter sep civ identity regained early).[62] Frome RDn (1478—1878), N

Frome RDn (1878—98), Bromyd. RDn (1898—1953). Abol eccl 1953, the area of Little Cowarne severed to help cr Pencombe with Marston Stannett and Little Cowarne EP, the remainder to be 'Ullingswick' EP.[125]

UPTON BISHOP
AP *LG* Seq 7. Civ bdry: 1884,[121] 1884,[29] 1965 (loses pt to Kempley AP, Glos).[11] *Parl* Seq 3. *Eccl* Seq 19. Eccl bdry: 1960.[30]

VOWCHURCH
AP *LG* Seq 17. *Parl* Seq 3. *Eccl* Seq 23.

WACTON
Chap in Bromyard AP, sep civ identity early, sep EP 1749.[18] *LG* Seq 1. Civ bdry: 1884.[12] *Parl* Seq 1. *Eccl* Frome RDn. Abol eccl 1875 to help cr Bredenbury with Wacton EP.[32]

WALFORD
AP Heref par (Greyt. Hd), incl in Glos chap Ruardean (St Briavells Hd, sep civ identity early in Glos, sep EP 1842[130]). *LG* Newent PLU (1835—36), Ross PLU (1836—1930), RSD, RD (1894—1931), Ross & Whitch. RD (1931—74). Addtl civ bdry alt: 1884,[131] 1884 (gains pt Lea Bailey CP, Glos),[132] 1931.[39] *Parl* Seq 3. *Eccl* Seq 19. Addtl eccl bdry alt: 1845 (help cr Bishop's Wood EP).[26]

WALFORD, LETTON AND NEWTON
Tp in Leintwardine AP, sep CP 1866.[3] *LG* Seq 21. *Parl* Seq 1.

WALTERSTONE
AP LG Seq 3. *Parl* Seq 3. *Eccl* Seq 27.

WELLINGTON
AP *LG* Seq 8. Civ bdry: 1884,[51] 1887.[70] *Parl* Seq 5. *Eccl* Seq 26.

WELLINGTON HEATH
EP Cr 1842 from Ledbury AP.[113] Frome RDn (1842—78), S Frome RDn (1878—98), Ledb. RDn (1898—*).
CP Cr 1894 from pt of the pt of Ledbury AP not in Ledb. UD.[112] *LG* Ledb. PLU, RD. *Parl* Heref Dv (1918—48), Leom. CC (1948—*).

WELSH BICKNOR
AP Monm AP (Skenfreth Hd) transf to Heref (Worm. Hd) 1832 for parl purposes, 1844 for civ purposes.[55] *LG* Monm PLU, RSD, Whitch. RD (1894—1931), Ross & Whitch. RD (1931—74). *Parl* Ross Dv (1885—1918), Heref Dv/CC (1918—*). *Eccl* Seq 4.

WELSH NEWTON
Chap in Llanrothal AP, sep civ identity early, sep EP 1798.[18] *LG* Seq 28. *Parl* Seq 3. *Eccl* Archenf. RDn (1798—1923), Ross & Archenf. RDn (1923—39). Abol eccl 1939 to help cr Welsh Newton and Llanrothal EP.[119]

WELSH NEWTON AND LLANROTHAL
EP Cr 1939 by union Welsh Newton EP, Llanrothal AP (both Heref), Dixton Newton AP (Monm).[119] Ross & Archenf. RDn.

WEOBLEY
AP *LG* Weob. Bor, Seq 16. Civ bdry: 1884.[24] *Parl* Weob. Parl Bor (1295—1306, 1628—1832), Seq 1 thereafter. *Eccl* Seq 22.

WEST HIDE—see following entry

WESTHIDE
Chap in Stoke Edith AP, sep CP 1866,[3] eccl 'West Hide', eccl severed 1928 to help cr Withington with West Hide EP.[22] *LG* Seq 12. Bdry: 1885.[9] *Parl* Seq 4.

WESTON BEGGARD
AP *LG* Seq 12. Civ bdry: 1885.[9] *Parl* Seq 5. *Eccl* Weston RDn. Eccl bdry: 1929.[73] Abol eccl 1971 to help cr Withington with Westhide and Weston Beggard EP.[133]

WESTON UNDER PENYARD
Chap in Ross AP, sep par 1671.[28] *LG* Seq 7. Civ bdry: 1883 (gains pt Lea Bailey CP, Glos),[134] 1965 (gains pt Mitcheldean AP, Glos).[11] *Parl* Seq 3. *Eccl* Seq 19.

WHITBOURNE
AP *LG* Seq 1. Civ bdry: 1894 (incl loses pt to help cr Brockhampton CP).[43] *Parl* Seq 1. *Eccl* Seq 6.

WHITCHURCH
AP *LG* Seq 28. Civ bdry: 1885.[71] *Parl* Seq 3. *Eccl* Seq 5.

WHITNEY
AP *LG* Hunt. Hd, Hay PLU, RSD, Bredw. RD (1894—1934), Kingt. RD (1934—74). *Parl* Seq 1. *Eccl* Seq 22.

WIGMORE
AP Incl chap Elton (sep civ identity early, sep EP 1766[18]). *LG* Seq 22. *Parl* Seq 1. *Eccl* Leom. RDn (until 1878), Leom. 2 RDn (1878—98), Kingsl. RDn (1898—1923), Wigm. RDn (1923—58), Leom. RDn (1958—*).

WILLERSLEY
AP *LG* Seq 10. Civ bdry: 1884.[74] *Parl* Seq 1. *Eccl* Weob. RDn (until 1878), Weob. 1 RDn (1878—98), Weob. RDn (1898—1926). Abol eccl 1926 to help cr Lutton with Withersley EP,[115] qv for severing of area of this par 1964 to help cr Eardisley with Bollingham and Willersley EP.[75]

WILLEY
Tp in Presteigne AP, sep CP 1866.[3] *LG* Wigm. Hd, Prest. PLU (1836), Kingt. PLU (1836—1930), RSD, Wigm. RD (1894—1930), Leom. & Wigm. RD (1930—74). *Parl* Seq 1.

WINFORTON
AP *LG* Seq 10. *Parl* Seq 1. *Eccl* Seq 22.

WINSLOW
Tp in Bromyard AP, sep CP 1866.[3] *LG* Seq 1. Bdry: 1883,[5] 1884,[12] 1884,[48] 1884,[88] 1894 (loses pt to help constitute Bromyd. UD and added to Bromyard AP).[49] *Parl* Seq 1.

WISTESTON
Chap in Marden AP (eccl, 'Marden with Amberley'), sep EP 1728.[18] Weston RDn (1728—1972), Heref Rural RDn (1972—*).

WITHINGTON
AP Incl chap Preston Wynne (sep CP 1866,[3] sep EP 1734,[18] eccl refounded 1857[126]). *LG* Seq 2. *Parl* Seq 5. *Eccl* Heref RDn (until 1898), Weston RDn (1898—1928). Abol eccl 1928 to help cr Withington and West Hide EP.[15]

WITHINGTON AND WEST HIDE
EP Cr 1928 by union Withington AP, chap West Hide in Stoke Edith with West Hide AP.[15] Weston RDn.

Abol 1971 to help cr Withington with Westhide and Weston Beggard EP.[133]

WITHINGTON WITH WESTHIDE AND WESTON BEGGARD

EP Cr 1971 by union Withington and West Hide EP, Weston Beggard AP.[133] Weston RDn (1971—72), Heref Rural RDn (1972—*).

WOLFERLOW

AP *LG* Seq 1. *Parl* Seq 1. *Eccl* Seq 6.

WOOLHOPE

AP Incl chap Brockhampton ([All Saints], sep civ identity early, sep EP 1771[18]). *LG* Seq 5. Addtl civ bdry alt: 1885.[9] *Parl* Seq 4. *Eccl* Seq 11.

WORMBRIDGE

Area appropriated to Knights Templar, donative from Dissolution and sep eccl status sustained, sep civ identity early. *LG* Seq 17. *Parl* Seq 3. *Eccl* Seq 2.

WORMSLEY

AP Priory church, sep par from Dissolution. *LG* Seq 9.

Parl Seq 1. *Eccl* Weob. RDn (until 1878), Weob. 1 RDn (1878—98), Weob. RDn (1898—1923), Weston RDn (1923—46), Weob. RDn (1946—72). Abol eccl 1972 to help cr Brinsop with Wormesley EP.[41]

YARKHILL

AP *LG* Seq 13. Civ bdry: 1885.[9] *Parl* Seq 5. *Eccl* Frome RDn (until 1878), S Frome RDn (1878—98), Ledb. RDn (1898—1923), Weston RDn (1923—71), Ledb. RDn (1971—*). Eccl bdry: 1929.[73]

YARPOLE

AP *LG* Seq 24. Civ bdry: 1887.[120] *Parl* Seq 1. *Eccl* Leom. RDn (until 1878), Leom. 2 RDn (1878—98), Leom. RDn (1898—1973). Abol eccl 1973 to help cr Croft with Yarpole and Lucton EP.[66]

YATTON

Chap in Much Marcle AP, sep CP 1866.[3] *LG* Seq 7. *Parl* Seq 3.

YAZOR

AP *LG* Seq 9. *Parl* Seq 1. *Eccl* Seq 21.

LANCASHIRE

ABBREVIATIONS

Abbreviations peculiar to Lancs follow. Those general abbreviations used throughout the *Guide* are found on pages xvii—xix.

Accr.	Accrington
Amound.	Amounderness
Asht.	Ashton
Blackp.	Blackpool
Clith.	Clitheroe
Copel.	Copeland
Droyl.	Droylsden
Farnw.	Farnworth
Garst.	Garstang
Hasl.	Haslingden
Heyw.	Heyworth
Lanc.	Lancaster
Leyl.	Leyland
Lonsd.	Lonsdale
Lunesd.	Lunesdale
Middl.	Middleton
Morec.	Morecambe
Ormsk.	Ormskirk
Prestw.	Prestwich
Radcl.	Radcliffe
Ramsb.	Ramsbottom
Rawt.	Rawtenstall
Rochd.	Rochdale
Rossend.	Rossendale
Salf.	Salford
S'port.	Southport
Stretf.	Stretford
Ulv.	Ulverston
Warr.	Warrington
W'hough.	Westhoughton

SEQUENCES

An abbreviated entry prefixed by 'Seq' is used in the parochial entries to avoid repeating often the names of superior units of administration. The content of each sequence is shown below.

Local Government Sequences ('LG')

SEQ 1 Amound. Hd, Fylde PLU, RSD, RD
SEQ 2 Amound. Hd, Garst. PLU, RSD, RD
SEQ 3 Amound. Hd, Preston PLU, RSD, RD
SEQ 4 Blackb Hd, PLU, RSD, RD
SEQ 5 Blackb Hd, Burnley PLU, RSD, RD
SEQ 6 Blackb Hd, Clith. PLU, RSD, RD
SEQ 7 Blackb Hd, Preston PLU, RSD, RD
SEQ 8 Leyl. Hd, Chorley PLU, RSD, RD
SEQ 9 Leyl. Hd, Ormsk. PLU, RSD, W Lancs RD
SEQ 10 Leyl. Hd, Preston PLU, RSD, RD
SEQ 11 Leyl. Hd, Wigan PLU, RSD, RD
SEQ 12 Lonsd. Hd, Lanc. PLU, RSD, RD
SEQ 13 Lonsd. Hd, Caton GilbU (until 1869), Lunesd. PLU (1869—1930), RSD, RD
SEQ 14 Lonsd. Hd, Ulv. PLU, RSD, RD (1894—1960), N Lonsd. RD (1960—74)
SEQ 15 Salf. Hd, Chorley PLU, RSD, RD
SEQ 16 W Derby Hd, PLU, RSD, Sefton RD (1894—1932), W Lancs RD (1932—74)
SEQ 17 W Derby Hd, Ormsk. PLU, RSD, W Lancs RD
SEQ 18 W Derby Hd, Prescot PLU, RSD, Whiston RD
SEQ 19 W Derby Hd, Warr. PLU, RSD, RD
SEQ 20 W Derby Hd, Wigan PLU, RSD, RD

139

Parliamentary Sequences ('Parl')

SEQ 1   Clith. Parl Bor (1832—85), Clith. Dv/CC (1885—*)

SEQ 2   N'rn Dv (1832—67), North Dv (1867—85), Blackp. Dv (1885—1918), Fylde Dv (1918—48), S Fylde CC (1948—*)

SEQ 3   N'rn Dv (1832—67), North Dv (1867—85), Chorley Dv/CC (1918—*)

SEQ 4   N'rn Dv (1832—67), North Dv (1867—85), Chorley Dv (1885—1918), Ince Dv (1918—48), W'hough. CC (1948—*)

SEQ 5   N'rn Dv (1832—67), North Dv (1867—85), Chorley Dv (1885—1948), W'hough CC (1948—*)

SEQ 6   N'rn Dv (1832—67), North Dv (1867—85), Lanc. Dv/CC (1885—*)

SEQ 7   N'rn Dv (1832—67), North Dv (1867—85), Lanc. Dv (1885—1948), N Fylde CC (1948—*)

SEQ 8   N'rn Dv (1832—67), North Dv (1867—85), Lanc. Dv (1885—1918), Lonsd. Dv (1918—48), Lanc. CC (1948—*)

SEQ 9   N'rn Dv (1832—67), North Dv (1867—85), N Lonsd. Dv (1885—1918), Lonsd. Dv (1918—48), Lanc. CC (1948—*)

SEQ 10   N'rn Dv (1832—67), North Dv (1867—85), N Lonsd. Dv (1885—1918), Lonsd. Dv (1918—48), Morec. & Lonsd. CC (1948—*)

SEQ 11   N'rn Dv (1832—67), N-E Dv (1867—85), Clith. Dv/CC (1885—*)

SEQ 12   N'rn Dv (1832—67), N-E Dv (1867—85), Darwen Dv/CC (1885—*)

SEQ 13   N'rn Dv (1832—67), N-E Dv (1867—85), Darwen Dv (1885—1918), Clith. Dv/CC (1918—*)

SEQ 14   S'rn Dv (1832—67), S-E Dv (1867—85), Radcl. cum Farnw. Dv (1885—1918), Farnw. Dv/CC (1918—*)

SEQ 15   S'rn Dv (1832—67), S-E Dv (1867—85), W'hough. Dv/CC (1885—*)

SEQ 16   S'rn Dv (1832—67), S-E Dv (1867—85), W'hough. Dv (1885—1918), Chorley Dv/CC (1918—*)

SEQ 17   S'rn Dv (1832—67), S-W Dv (1867—85), Ince Dv/CC (1885—1970), Ince BC (1970—*)

SEQ 18   S'rn Dv (1832—67), S-W Dv (1867—85), Newton Dv/CC (1885—*)

SEQ 19   S'rn Dv (1832—67), S-W Dv (1867—85), Newton Dv (1885—1918), Widnes Dv/CC (1918—*)

SEQ 20   S'rn Dv (1832—67), S-W Dv (1867—85), Ormsk. Dv/CC (1885—*)

SEQ 21   S'rn Dv (1832—67), S-W Dv (1867—85), Ormsk. Dv (1885—1918), Widnes Dv (1918—48), Huyton CC (1948—*)

SEQ 22   S'rn Dv (1832—67), S-W Dv (1867—85), S'port. Dv (1885—1918), Ormsk. Dv/CC (1918—*)

SEQ 23   S'rn Dv (1832—67), S-W Dv (1867—85), Widnes Dv/CC (1885—*)

Ecclesiastical Sequences ('Eccl')

Orig in Lichf and Cov dioc

SEQ 1   Leyl. RDn

SEQ 2   Leyl. RDn (until 1847), N Meols RDn (1847—48), Leyl. RDn (1848—1964), Chorley RDn (1964—*)

SEQ 3   Manch & Blackb RDn (before 1291—before 1535), Manch RDn (before 1535—1850), Bury RDn (1850—51), Prestw. RDn (1851—72), Prestw. & Middl. RDn (1872—1912), Radcl. & Prestw. RDn (1912—*)

SEQ 4   Warr. RDn (until 1847), N Meols RDn (1847—*)

SEQ 5   Warr. RDn (until 1847), N Meols RDn (1847—87), Ormsk. RDn (1887—*)

SEQ 6   Warr. RDn (until 1847), Prescot RDn (1847—*)

SEQ 7   Warr. RDn (until 1847), Winwick RDn (1847—1949), Warr. RDn (1949—*)

Orig in York dioc

SEQ 8   Lanc. RDn (until before 1291), Amound. RDn (before 1291—1852), The Fylde RDn (1852—*)

SEQ 9   Lanc. RDn (until before 1291), Amound. RDn (before 1291—1852), Preston RDn (1852—*)

SEQ 10   Lanc. RDn (until before 1291), Copel. RDn (before 1291—before 1535), Furness & Cartmel RDn (before 1535—1859), Aldingham RDn (1859—83), Ulv. RDn (1883—1970), Furness RDn (1970—*)

SEQ 11   Lanc. RDn (until before 1291), Kirkby Lonsd. & Kendal RDn (before 1291—before 1535), Kendal RDn (before 1535—1848), Tunstall RDn (1848—*)

SEQ 12   Lanc. RDn (until before 1291), Kirkby Lonsd. & Kendal RDn (before 1291—before 1535), Kirkby Lonsd. RDn (before 1535—1848), Tunstall RDn (1848—*)

DIOCESES AND ARCHDEACONRIES

Lancs pars were arranged in Archdeaconries and Rural Deaneries as follows:

BLACKBURN DIOC (1926—*)
Blackburn AD: Accr. RDn, Blackb RDn, Burnley RDn, Chorley RDn (1964—*), Darwen RDn (1964—*), Leyl. RDn, Pendle RDn (1970—*), Whalley RDn
Lanc. AD: Blackp. RDn (1963—*), The Fylde RDn, Garst. RDn, Lanc. RDn, Preston RDn, Tunstall RDn

BRADFORD DIOC (1919—*)
Craven AD: Bolland RDn (1921—*), Craven W'rn RDn (1919—21)

CARLISLE DIOC (1856—*)

Furness AD (1884—1959): Cartmel RDn , Dalton RDn

Westmorland AD (1856—1959): Aldingham RDn (1859—82), Cartmel RDn (1859—1959), Copel. RDn (1856—59), Dalton RDn (1884—1959), Furness & Cartmel RDn (1856—59), Kirkby Lonsd. RDn, Ulv. RDn (1859—84)

Westmorland & Furness AD (1959—):* Cartmel RDn (1959—70), Dalton RDn (1959—70), Furness RDn (1970—*), Kirkby Lonsd. RDn (1959—70), Ulv. RDn (1959—70), Windermere RDn (1970—*)

CHESTER DIOC (1541—1880)

Chester AD: Bangor RDn (1541—1857), Blackb RDn (1541—1844), Leyl. RDn (1541—1844), Manch RDn (1541—1844), Warr. RDn (1541—1844)

Liverp AD (1847—80): N Meols & Ormsk. RDn (1848—80), Prescot RDn, Warr. RDn (1847—80), Wigan RDn (1848—80), Winwick RDn (1848—80)

Macclesfield AD (1880—):* Mottram RDn (1962—*)

Manch AD (1844—47): Amound. RDn, Blackb RDn, Leyl. RDn, Manch RDn, Warr. RDn

Richmond AD (1541—1856): Amound. RDn (1541—1844), Furness & Cartmel RDn, Kendal RDn, Kirkby Lonsd. RDn (1541—1848)

LICHFIELD AND COVENTRY DIOC (until 1541) [before 1837 variously styled 'Lichfield' (until 1075), 'Chester' (1075—1102), 'Coventry' (1102—1128), 'Coventry and Lichfield' (1228—Reformation), 'Lichfield and Coventry' (Reformation—1837)]

Chester AD: Blackb RDn (before 1535—1541), Leyl. RDn, Manch RDn (before 1541—1541), Manch & Blackb RDn (before 1291—before 1535), Warr. RDn

LIVERPOOL DIOC (1880—*)

Liverpool AD: Bootle RDn (1895—*), Childwall RDn (1949—*), W Derby RDn (1949—*), Liverp RDn (1949—*), Liverp North RDn (1880—1949), Liverp South RDn (1880), N Meols RDn (1887—1949), N Meols and Ormsk. RDn (1880—87), Ormsk. RDn (1887—1949), Prescot RDn (1880), Toxteth RDn (1949—*), Walton RDn (1882—*), Wigan RDn (1880—1949), Winwick RDn (1880)

Warrington AD (1880—):* Childwall RDn (1882—1949), W Derby RDn (1902—49), Farnw. RDn (1949—*), Liverp South RDn (1880—1949), N Meols RDn (1949—*), Ormsk. RDn (1949—*), Prescot RDn, Toxteth RDn (1882—1949), Warr. RDn (1949—*), Wigan RDn (1949—*), Winwick RDn (1880—1949)

MANCHESTER DIOC (1847—*)

Blackburn AD (1877—1926): Accr. RDn (1912—26), Blackb RDn, Burnley RDn, Leyl. RDn, Rossend. RDn (1912—26), Whalley RDn

Lancaster AD (1847—1926): Amound. RDn (1847—52), The Fylde RDn (1852—1926), Garst. RDn (1852—1926), Lanc. RDn (1852—1926), Preston RDn (1852—1926), Tunstall RDn (1848—1926)

Manchester AD: Accr. RDn (1866—72), Ardwick RDn (1872—*), Asht. under Lyne RDn (1847—1910), Blackb RDn (1847—77), Bolton le Moors RDn (1847—93), Bolton North RDn (1893—1901), Bolton South RDn (1893—1901), Burnley RDn (1872—77), Bury RDn (1850—1910), Cathedral RDn (1872—*), Cheetham RDn (1872—*), Chorlton RDn (1855—66), Chorlton and Hulme RDn (1866—69), Eccles RDn (1850—66), Eccles & Salf. RDn (1866—72), Heaton RDn (1912—*), Hulme RDn (1869—*), Leigh RDn (1933—*), Leyl. RDn (1847—77), Manch RDn (1847—72), N Meols RDn (1847—48), Oldham RDn (1872—1910), Prestw RDn (1851—72), Prestw. & Middl. RDn (1872—1910), Rochd. RDn (1847—1910), Salf. RDn (1872—*), Stretf. RDn (1933—*), Whalley RDn (1847—77), Withington RDn (1965—*)

Rochdale AD (1910—):* Asht. under Lyne RDn (1910—29), Bolton le Moors RDn, Bury RDn, Deane RDn (1968—*), Farnw. RDn (1968—*), Middl. RDn (1912—*), Oldham RDn, Prestw. & Middl. RDn (1919—12), Radcliffe and Prestw. RDn (1912—*), Rochd. RDn, Rossend. RDn (1927—*), Walmsley RDn (1968—*)

RIPON DIOC (1836—*)

Craven AD: Craven RDn (1836—57), Craven W'rn RDn (1857—1919), Halifax RDn (1857—88)

WAKEFIELD DIOC (1888—*)

Halifax AD: Calder Valley RDn (1967—*), Halifax RDn (1888—1967)

YORK DIOC (until 1541)

Richmond AD: Amound. RDn (before 1291—1541), Copel. RDn (before 1291—before 1535), Furness & Cartmel RDn (before 1535—1541), Kendal RDn (before 1535—1541), Kirkby Lonsd. RDn (before 1535—1541), Kirkby Lonsd. & Kendal RDn (before 1291—before 1535), Lanc. RDn (until before 1291)

THE PARISHES OF LANCASHIRE

ABBEY HEY

EP Cr 1899 from Gorton EP.[1] Ardwick RDn. Bdry: 1902 (help cr North Reddish EP),[2] 1921.[3]

ABRAM

Tp in Wigan AP, sep CP 1866,[4] some eccl parochial rights 1843 (incl pt Hindley EP),[5] 'Abram' ent sep EP 1852.[6] *LG* W Derby Hd, Wigan PLU, Abram USD, UD. Civ bdry: 1957.[7] *Parl* Seq 17. *Eccl* Wigan RDn (1852—*). Eccl bdry: 1878 (help refound Hindley EP),[8] 1899 (exchanges pts with Westleigh EP, dioc Manch),[9] 1905 (cr Bickershaw EP),[10] 1957.[11]

ACCRINGTON

The following have 'Accrington' in their names. Insofar as any existed at a given time: *LG* Blackb Hd, Hasl. PLU, Accr. USD; MB sep noted. *Parl* N'rn Dv (1832—67), N-E Dv (1867—85), Accr. Dv (1885—1918), Accr. Parl Bor/BC (1918—*). *Eccl* Blackb RDn (cr—1847), Whalley RDn (1847—66), Accr. RDn (1866—72), Whalley RDn (1872—1912), Accr. RDn (1912—*).

CP1/EP1—ACCRINGTON [ST JAMES]—Chap in Whalley AP, sep EP 1732,[12] pt eccl severed 1855 to help cr EP2,[12] the remainder refounded 1870 as EP1[13]; the area civ as tp/CP2 until the latter and CP3 civ united 1878 as CP1.[14] *LG* Accr. MB. Civ bdry: 1929 (gains Huncoat CP).[15] Addtl eccl bdry alt: 1871 (cr EP5),[16] 1890 (cr EP6),[17] 1895 (cr EP2),[18] 1928.[19]

CP2—NEW ACCRINGTON—Chap in Whalley AP, sep CP 1866,[4] sep EP 1732 as EP1,[12] qv for later refounding. Abol 1878 to help cr CP1.[14]

CP3—OLD ACCRINGTON—Tp in Whalley AP, sep CP 1866,[4] eccl in chap Altham (sep EP 1723 from Whalley AP[12]). Civ, parl organisation as for CP2.

EP2—ACCRINGTON CHRIST CHURCH—Cr 1855 from EP1.[12] Bdry: 1878 (cr Baxenden EP),[20] 1913 (help cr EP6).[21]

EP3—ACCRINGTON MILNSHAW ST MARY MAGDALENE—Cr 1895 from EP1.[18] Bdry: 1928.[19]

EP4—ACCRINGTON ST ANDREW—Cr 1898 from EP6.[22]

EP5—ACCRINGTON ST JOHN THE EVANGELIST—Cr 1871 from EP1.[16] Bdry: 1913 (help cr EP6),[21] 1928.[19]

EP6—ACCRINGTON ST PAUL—Cr 1913 from EP2, EP5.[21]

EP6—ACCRINGTON ST PETER—Cr 1890 from EP1.[17] Bdry: 1898 (cr EP4).[22]

ADLINGTON

Tp in Standish AP, sep CP 1866,[4] sep EP 1840,[12] eccl refounded 1842.[23] *LG* Leyl. Hd, Chorley PLU, Adlington USD, UD. *Parl* Seq 3. *Eccl* Leyl. RDn (1840—1964), Chorley RDn (1964—*). Eccl bdry: 1959,[24] 1959 (help cr Chorley All Saints EP).[25]

ADMARSH

Chap 'Bleasdale' in Lancaster AP (qv for sep CP 1866) cr a sep EP 1748 as 'Admarsh',[12] sometimes 'Admarsh in Bleasdale'. Amound. RDn (1748—1852), Lanc. RDn (1852—66), Garst. RDn (1866—*).

AIGBURTH

EP Cr 1844 from Garston EP.[26] Warr. RDn (1844—47), Prescot RDn (1847—82), Childwall RDn (1882—*). Bdry: 1855 (help cr Grassendale EP),[27] 1887 (help cr Mossley Hill St Matthew and St James EP),[28] 1964.[29]

AIGHTON, BAILEY AND CHAIGLEY

Hmlt (Lancs, Blackb Hd) in Mitton AP (o'wise Yorks W Riding, Staincliffe & Ewcross Wap), sep CP 1866 in Lancs,[4] the area in Bailey a sep EP 1839 as 'Hurst Green',[12] as such eccl refounded 1870,[30] qv. *LG* Seq 6. Bdry: 1883.[31] *Parl* Seq 13.

AINSDALE

Area in Formby CP/EP, sep CP 1894,[32] sep EP 1906.[33] *LG* Ormsk. PLU, W Lancs RD (1894—1905), Birkdale UD (1905—12), S'port CB (1912—25). Abol civ 1925 ent to Southport CP.[34] *Parl* S'port BC (1918—48). *Eccl* N Meols RDn.

AINSWORTH

Chap (sometimes 'Cockey') in Middleton AP, sep CP 1866,[4] sep EP 1725,[12] eccl refounded 1867.[35] *LG* Salf. Hd, Bury PLU, RSD, RD. Civ bdry: 1894 (gains the pt of Elton CP not in a CB or UD).[36] Abol civ 1933 ent to Radcliffe UD & AP.[37] *Parl* S'rn Dv (1832—67), S-E Dv (1867—85), Heyw. Dv (1885—1918), Farnw. Dv (1918—48). *Eccl* Manch RDn (1725—1847), Bolton le Moors RDn (1847—93), Bolton North RDn (1893—1901), Bolton le Moors RDn (1901—12), Radcl. & Prestw. RDn (1912—29), Bury RDn (1929—64), Radcl. & Prestw. RDn (1964—*).

AINTREE

Tp in Sefton AP, sep CP 1866,[4] sep EP 1878 from Walton on the Hill AP, Sefton AP.[38] *LG* Seq 16. Civ bdry: 1951 (loses pt to Bootle CB [assoc with Lancs] and to Orrell CP).[39] Transf 1974 to Merseyside.[40] *Parl* S'rn Dv (1832—67), S-W Dv (1867—85), Ormsk. Dv (1885—1948), Liverp, Walton BC (1948—*). *Eccl* Liverp N RDn (1878—82), Walton RDn (1882—*). Eccl bdry: 1909 (help cr Fazakerley EP),[41] 1956 (cr Aintree St Giles EP),[42] 1971.[18]

AINTREE ST GILES

EP Cr 1956 from Aintree EP.[42] Walton RDn.

ALDCLIFFE

Tp in Lancaster AP, sep CP 1866.[4] *LG* Lonsd. Hd, Lanc. PLU, RSD, RD. Abol 1935 ent to Lanc. MB & AP.[43] *Parl* N'rn Dv (1832—67), North Dv (1867—85), Lanc. Dv (1885—1948).

ALDINGHAM

AP Incl undivided pt Birkrig Common (Land Common to this par and to Urswick AP, qv). *LG* Seq 14. Transf 1974 to Cumbria.[40] *Parl* Seq 10. *Eccl* Lanc. RDn (until before 1291), Copel. RDn (before 1291—before 1541), Furness & Cartmel RDn (before 1541—1859), Aldingham RDn (1859—83), Dalton RDn (1883—1970), Furness RDn (1970—*). Eccl bdry: 1773 (cr Dendron EP,[12] refounded 1892[44]).

ALKRINGTON

Tp in Prestwich AP, sep CP 1866,[4] eccl severed 1842 to help cr Tonge cum Alkrington EP.[22] *LG* Salf. Hd, Oldham PLU, Middl. & Tonge USD (1875—86), Middl. MB & USD (1886—94). Abol 1894 ent to Middleton AP.[45] *Parl* S'rn Dv (1832—67), S-E Dv (1867—85), Middl. Dv (1885—1918).

ALLERTON

Tp in Childwall AP, sep CP 1866,[4] sep EP 1876.[46] *LG* W Derby Hd, PLU, Allerton USD, UD (1894—1913), Liverp CB (1913—22). Abol civ 1922 ent to Liverpool CP.[47] *Parl* S'rn Dv (1832—67), S-W Dv (1867—85), Widnes Dv (1885—1918); see Part III of the *Guide* for composition of Liverp Parl Bors (1918—48) by wards of the CB. *Eccl* Prescot RDn (1876—82), Childwall RDn (1882—*). Eccl bdry:

1923 (incl help cr Liverpool All Souls, Springwood EP),[48] 1964.[49]

ALLITHWAITE
EP Cr 1866 from Cartmel AP[50]; for civ see following 2 entries. Cartmel RDn (1866—1970), Windermere RDn (1970—*).

LOWER ALLITHWAITE
Tp in Cartmel AP, sep CP 1866[4]; for eccl see 'Allithwaite'. *LG* Lonsd. Hd, Ulv. PLU, pt Grange USD, pt Ulv. RSD, Ulv. RD (1894—1960), N Lonsd. RD (1960—74). Bdry: 1884,[51] 1884,[52] 1884,[53] 1884,[54] 1884,[55] 1884,[56] 1884,[57] 1894 (loses the pt in the UD to help cr Grange CP),[58] 1914,[59] 1927,[60] 1949 (gains Upper Holker CP).[61] Transf 1974 to Cumbria.[40] *Parl* Seq 10.

UPPER ALLITHWAITE
Tp in Cartmel AP, sep CP 1866.[4] Organisation as for Lower Allithwaite, with bdry alt as follows: 1884,[51] 1884,[52] 1884,[53] 1884,[54] 1884,[55] 1884.[57]

ALSTON
Tp in Ribchester AP, sep CP 1866,[4] eccl severed 1727 to help cr Longridge EP,[12] the latter eccl refounded 1861.[62] *LG* Amound. Hd, Preston PLU, RSD (1875—83), Longridge USD (1883—94), UD. *Parl* N'rn Dv (1832—67), North Dv (1867—85), Blackp. Dv (1885—1918), Fylde Dv (1918—48), Clith. CC (1948—*).

ALT
CP Cr 1894 from pt of the pt of Ashton under Lyne AP not in a MB or UD.[63] *LG* Asht. under Lyne PLU, Limehurst RD. Bdry: 1935,[43] 1951 (loses pt to Oldham CB [assoc with Lancs] & CP).[64] Abol 1954 pt to Oldham CB (assoc with Lancs) and CP, pt to Asht. under Lyne MB & AP, pt to Mossley MB & CP.[65] *Parl* Mossley Dv (1918—48), Asht. under Lyne Parl Bor (1948—55). Parl bdry: 1951.[66]

ALTCAR
AP Chap served by monks at Merivale Abbey (Warws), sep par at Dissolution.[67] *LG* Seq 17. Pt transf 1974 to Merseyside as 'Altcar', the pt remaining in Lancs cr 'Great Altcar'.[40] *Parl* S'rn Dv (1832—67), S-W Dv (1867—85), S'port Dv (1885—1918), Ormsk. Dv/CC (1918—70), Crosby BC (1970—*). *Eccl* Seq 4.

GREAT ALTCAR
CP Cr 1974 from the pt of Altcar AP remaining in Lancs.[40]

ALTHAM
Chap in Whalley AP, sep CP 1866,[4] sep EP (incl tps Old Accrington, Clayton le Moors) 1723.[12] *LG* Seq 5. *Parl* N'rn Dv (1832—67), N-E Dv (1867—85), Accr. Dv (1885—1918), Clith. Dv/CC (1918—*). *Eccl* Blackb RDn (1723—47), Whalley RDn (1847—66), Accr. RDn (1866—72), Whalley RDn (1872—1912), Accr. RDn (1912—*). Eccl bdry: 1840 (area of orig tp Clayton le Moors cr 'Clayton le Moors' EP).[68]

AMBLESIDE WITH BRATHAY
EP Cr 1967 by union Ambleside EP (Westm), pt Brathay EP (Lancs).[69] Ambleside RDn.

ANCOATS
The following have 'Ancoats' in their names. Insofar as any existed at a given time: *Eccl* Manch RDn (cr—1855), Chorlton RDn (1855—66), Manch RDn (1866—72), Cathedral RDn (1872—*).

EP1—ANCOATS ALL SOULS—Cr 1858 by union Manchester All Souls EP, pt Manchester AP.[70] Bdry: 1879 (help cr Beswick EP).[71] Abol 1960 to help cr EP3.[72]

EP2—ANCOATS ALL SOULS—Cr 1966 by union EP3, Beswick EP.[73]

EP3—ANCOATS ALL SOULS WITH ST ANDREW—Cr 1960 by union EP1, pt EP4.[72] Abol 1966 to help cr EP2.[73]

EP4—ANCOATS ST ANDREW—Cr 1839 from Manchester AP.[74] Bdry: 1871 (help cr Manchester St James the Less EP),[75] 1928,[76] 1938.[77] Abol 1960 pt to help cr EP3, pt to Manchester St Ann EP.[72]

ANDERTON
Tp in Standish AP, sep CP 1866.[4] *LG* Seq 8. *Parl* Seq 3.

ANFIELD ST COLUMBA
EP Cr 1919 from Walton on the Hill AP, West Derby St John the Baptist EP.[78] Walton RDn. Bdry: 1959.[79]

ANFIELD ST SIMON AND ST JUDE
EP Cr 1896 from Walton on the Hill AP.[24] Walton RDn.

ANGERTON
Ex-par place, sep CP 1858.[80] *LG* Lonsd. Hd, Ulv. PLU (1858—1930), RSD, RD (1894—1960), N Lonsd. RD (1960—74). Transf 1974 to Cumbria.[40] *Parl* Seq 10.

ANGLEZARKE
Tp in Bolton le Moors AP, sep CP 1866.[4] *LG* Seq 15. *Parl* Seq 16.

ARDWICK
The following have 'Ardwick' in their names. Insofar as any existed at a given time: *LG* Salf. Hd, Chorlton PLU, Manch MB (1838—89), CB (1889—96). *Parl* Manch Parl Bor (1832—85), Manch, East Dv Parl Bor (1885—1918). *Eccl* Manch RDn (cr—1855), Chorlton RDn (1855—72), Ardwick RDn (1872—*).

CP1/EP1—ARDWICK [ST THOMAS]—Tp (chap built 1741[81]) in Manchester AP, sep CP 1866,[4] sep EP 1839.[74] Civ bdry: 1883.[31] Abol civ 1896 to help cr South Manchester CP.[82] Eccl bdry: 1856 (cr EP6),[83] 1866 (help cr Gorton St Mark EP),[84] 1869 (help cr EP5).[85] 1955.[86]

EP2—ARDWICK ST BENEDICT—Cr 1880 from Gorton St Mark EP, EP5.[87]

EP3—ARDWICK ST JEROME—Cr 1912 from EP6.[88] Abol 1956 to help cr EP4.[89]

EP4—ARDWICK ST JEROME AND ST SILAS—Cr 1956 by union EP3, EP6.[89] Ardwick RDn (1956—69), Cathedral RDn (1969—*).

EP5—ARDWICK ST MATTHEW—Cr 1869 from EP1, Chorlton on Medlock St Stephen EP.[85] Bdry: 1876 (help cr Longsight St Clement EP),[90] 1880 (help cr EP2).[87] Abol 1968 to help cr Longsight St Matthew with St Clement EP.[85]

EP6—ARDWICK ST SILAS—Cr 1856 from EP1.[83] Bdry: 1912 (cr EP3).[88] Abol 1956 to help cr EP4.[89]

ARKHOLME

Chap in Melling AP, sep EP 1740,[12] eccl refounded 1863,[91] sep CP 1866 as 'Arkholme with Cawood',[4] qv. Kirkby Lonsd. RDn (1740—1848), Tunstall RDn (1848—*).

ARKHOLME WITH CAWOOD

Chap in Melling AP, sep CP 1866,[4] sep EP 1740 as 'Arkholme',[12] as such eccl refounded 1863,[91] qv in prev entry. *LG* Lonsd. Hd, Lunesd. PLU, RSD, RD. *Parl* Seq 8.

ASHTON IN MAKERFIELD

Chap in Winwick AP, sep CP 1845,[92] sep EP 1840 (incl tp Haydock in same par),[12] eccl refounded 1845 from the remainder of the EP as the chap in Downall Green cr 'Ashton in Makerfield Holy Trinity' EP.[93] *LG* W Derby Hd, Wigan PLU, Ashton in Makerfield USD, UD. Civ bdry: 1933,[37] 1957.[7] Transf 1974 pt to Gtr Manch, pt (South Ward) to Merseyside.[40] *Parl* S'rn Dv (1832—67), S-W Dv (1867—85), Newton Dv (1885—1918), Ince Dv/CC (1918—70), Ince BC (1970—*). *Eccl* Warr. RDn (1840—47), Winwick RDn (1847—1920), Wigan RDn (1920—*). Addtl eccl bdry alt: 1864 (orig area of tp Haydock cr 'Haydock' EP),[94] 1931 (help cr Bryn EP),[95] 1935.[96]

ASHTON IN MAKERFIELD HOLY TRINITY

EP Cr 1845 from Ashton in Makerfield EP (the pt of the par not refounded at the same time as 'Ashton in Makerfield').[93] Winwick RDn (1845—1920), Wigan RDn (1920—*). Bdry: 1931 (help cr Bryn EP).[95]

ASHTON UNDER LYNE

The following have 'Ashton under Lyne' in their names. Insofar as any existed at a given time: *LG* Salf. Hd, Asht. under Lyne PLU, Asht. under Lyne MB (pt 1847—94, ent 1894—1974), pt Asht. under Lyne USD, pt Lees USD, pt Audenshaw USD, pt Hurst USD, pt Mossley USD (Lancs, Ches), pt Mossley MB ([Lancs, Ches], 1885—94), pt Stalybridge MB ([Ches, Lancs], 1857—94), pt Stalybr. USD (Ches, Lancs). *Parl* Asht. under Lyne Parl Bor ([Lancs 1832—67; Lancs, Ches 1867—1918], pt 1832—1918 [enlarged pt 1867—85, further enlarged pt 1885—1918], ent 1918—*), pt Oldham Parl Bor (1867—1918), pt S'rn Dv (1832—67), pt Stalybridge Parl Bor ([Ches, Lancs], 1867—1918), pt S-E Dv (1867—85), pt Prestw. Dv (1885—1918). *Eccl* Manch & Blackb RDn (until before 1535), Manch RDn (before 1535—1847), Asht. under Lyne RDn (1847—*).

AP1—ASHTON UNDER LYNE [ST MICHAEL]—

The pt in Stalybridge MB becomes 1889 pt Ches (abol civ 1894 to help cr Stalybridge CP in that co).[97] Addtl civ bdry alt: 1894 (the pt in Lees UD cr Lees CP, the pt in Audenshaw UD cr Audenshaw CP, the pt in Hurst UD cr Hurst CP),[98] 1894 (loses the pt in Mossley MB to help cr Mossley CP),[97] 1894 (the pt not in a MB or UD divided into 7 CPs of Alt, Bardsley, Crossbank, Hartshead, Little Moss, Waterloo, Woodhouses),[63] 1898 (exchanges pts with Dukinfield CP, Ches),[99] 1927,[100] 1954 (incl gains Waterloo CP).[65] Transf 1974 to Gtr Manch.[40]

Parl bdry: 1955.[101] Eccl bdry: 1746 (help cr Hey EP [Lancs, Yorks],[12] refounded 1860 from Lydgate EP [Yorks][102]), 1798 (cr Stalybridge Old St George EP,[12] refounded 1865[104]), 1801 (cr Mossley EP,[12] refounded 1865[104]), 1826 (cr EP4,[12] refounded 1840[105]), 1844 (cr Bardsley EP),[106] 1846 (cr EP1, cr Hurst EP),[27] 1846 (help cr Leesfield EP),[107] 1847 (cr Stalybridge New St George EP),[108] 1866 (help cr EP3),[109] 1879 (help cr EP2).[17]

EP1—ASHTON UNDER LYNE CHRIST CHURCH— Cr 1846 from AP1.[27] Bdry: 1866 (help cr EP3),[109] 1879 (help cr EP2).[17]

EP2—ASHTON UNDER LYNE HOLY TRINITY— Cr 1879 from EP4, AP1, EP1.[17]

EP3—ASHTON UNDER LYNE ST JAMES—Cr 1866 from AP1, EP1, Hurst EP.[109] Bdry: 1974.[110]

EP4—ASHTON UNDER LYNE ST PETER—Cr 1826 from AP1,[12] refounded 1840.[105] Bdry: 1844 (cr Audenshaw EP),[111] 1845,[112] 1879 (help cr EP2),[17] 1921,[3] 1961.[113]

ASHTON UPON RIBBLE ST ANDREW

EP Tp in Preston AP, sep EP 1837,[12] sep CP 1866 as 'Lea, Ashton, Ingol and Cottam',[4] qv. Amound. RDn (1837—52), Preston RDn (1852—*). Bdry: 1929 (help cr Ashton upon Ribble St Michael and All Angels EP),[88] 1972 (cr Ingol EP).[114]

ASHTON UPON RIBBLE ST MICHAEL AND ALL ANGELS

EP Cr 1929 from Ashton upon Ribble St Andrew EP, Preston St Mark EP.[88] Preston RDn.

ASHTON WITH STODDAY

Tp in Lancaster AP, sep CP 1866.[4] *LG* Seq 12. Bdry: 1935.[43] *Parl* Seq 6.

ASHWORTH

Chap in Middleton AP, sep CP 1866,[4] sep EP 1735,[12] eccl refounded 1867.[35] *LG* Salf. Hd, Bury PLU, RSD. Abol civ 1894 ent to Birtle cum Bamford CP.[115] *Parl* S'rn Dv (1832—67), S-E Dv (1867—85), Heyw. Dv (1885—1918). *Eccl* Manch RDn (1735—1850), Bury RDn (1850—1949), Rochd. RDn (1949—*).

ASPULL

Tp (Salf. Hd) in Wigan AP (o'wise W Derby Hd), sep CP 1866,[4] eccl severed 1838 to help cr Haigh and Aspull EP,[116] 'Aspull' a sep EP 1883 from the latter.[117] *LG* Salf. Hd, Wigan PLU, Aspull USD, UD. Transf 1974 to Gtr Manch.[40] *Parl* S'rn Dv (1832—67), S-W Dv (1867—85), W'hough. Dv/CC (1885—*). *Eccl* Wigan RDn. Eccl bdry: 1953 (help cr New Springs EP).[118]

ASTLEY

Chap in Leigh AP, sep CP 1866,[4] sep EP 1722,[12] eccl refounded 1843.[119] *LG* W Derby Hd, Leigh PLU, RSD, RD. Abol civ 1933 ent to Tyldesley with Shakerley CP to help cr Tyldesley UD.[37] *Parl* S'rn Dv (1832—67), S-W Dv (1867—85), Leigh Dv (1885—1918), Stretf. Dv (1918—48). *Eccl* Warr. RDn (1722—1847), Leyl. RDn (1847—50), Eccles RDn (1850—66), Eccles & Salf. RDn (1866—72), Eccles RDn (1872—1933), Leigh RDn (1933—*).

ASTLEY BRIDGE

EP Cr 1844 from Little Bolton EP, Bolton le Moors AP

(pt tp Sharples).[111] Manch RDn (1844—47), Bolton le Moors RDn (1847—93), Bolton North RDn (1893—1901), Bolton le Moors RDn (1901—68), Walmsley RDn (1968—*).

CP Cr 1894 from the pt of Sharples CP in Astley Bridge UD.[120] *LG* Bolton PLU, Astley Bridge UD. Abol 1898 ent to Bolton CB (assoc with Lancs) & CP.[36]

ATHERTON

Chap in Leigh AP, sep CP 1866,[4] pt a sep EP 1722,[12] eccl refounded 1859.[121] *LG* W Derby Hd, Leigh PLU, Atherton USD, UD. Civ bdry: 1894 (help cr Leigh UD & CP).[122] Transf 1974 to Gtr Manch.[40] *Parl* S'rn Dv (1832—67), S-W Dv (1867—85), Leigh Dv (1885—1918), Leigh Parl Bor/BC (1918—*). *Eccl* Warr. RDn (1722—1847), Leyl. RDn (1847—50), Eccles RDn (1850—66), Eccles & Salf. RDn (1866—72), Eccles RDn (1872—1933), Leigh RDn (1933—*). Eccl bdry: 1878 (cr Howe Bridge EP),[87] 1884 (cr Hindsford EP).[123]

AUDENSHAW

EP Cr 1844 from Ashton under Lyne St Peter EP.[111] Manch RDn (1844—47), Asht. under Lyne RDn (1847—*). Bdry: 1845,[124] 1921,[3] 1923 (help cr Audenshaw St Hilda EP),[125] 1961.[113]

CP Cr 1894 from the pt of Asht. under Lyne AP in Audenshaw UD.[98] *LG* Asht. under Lyne PLU, Audenshaw UD. Transf 1974 to Gtr Manch.[40] *Parl* Mossley Dv (1918—48), Droyl. BC (1948—*).

AUDENSHAW ST HILDA

EP Cr 1923 from Audenshaw EP, Denton Christ Church EP, Haughton EP.[125] Asht. under Lyne RDn.

AUGHTON

AP *LG* Seq 17. Civ bdry: 1931,[126] 1956.[127] *Parl* Seq 20. *Eccl* Seq 5. Eccl bdry: 1929 (cr Aughton Christ Church EP).[128]

AUGHTON CHRIST CHURCH

EP Cr 1929 from Aughton AP.[128] Ormsk. RDn.

BACUP

CP Cr 1894 by union of the pts in Bacup MB of Newchurch CP, Spotland CP.[129] *LG* Hasl. PLU, Bacup MB. *Parl* Rossend. Parl Bor/BC (1918—*).

EP Chap in chap Newchurch in Rossendale (sep EP early from Walley AP[130]), 'Bacup' a sep EP 1801 [St John the Evangelist] from Newchurch in Rossendale EP, refounded 1843 from Newchurch in Rossendale EP, Rochdale AP.[131] Blackb RDn (1801—47), Whalley RDn (1847—66), Accr. RDn (1866—72), Burnley RDn (1872—73), Whalley RDn (1873—1912), Rossend. RDn (1912—*). Bdry: 1854 (cr Bacup Christ Church EP),[79] 1866 (help cr Bacup St Saviour EP).[132]

BACUP CHRIST CHURCH

EP Cr 1854 from Bacup EP.[79] RDns as for Bacup, from 1854. Bdry: 1866 (help cr Bacup St Saviour EP).[132]

BACUP ST SAVIOUR

EP Cr 1866 from Bacup EP, Bacup Christ Church EP.[132] RDns as for Bacup, from 1866.

BALDERSTONE

Chap in Blackburn AP, sep CP 1866,[4] sep EP 1741,[12] eccl refounded 1842.[133] *LG* Seq 4. *Parl* Seq 12. *Eccl* Blackb RDn. Eccl bdry: 1891.[134]

BALDERSTONE IN ROCHDALE

EP Cr 1865 from Rochdale AP (pt tp Castleton).[119] Rochd. RDn. Bdry: 1958,[135] 1964 (help cr Kirkholt EP).[136]

BAMBER BRIDGE ST AIDAN

EP Cr 1897 from Bamber Bridge St Saviour EP, Walton le Dale EP.[137] Blackb RDn (1897—1964), Leyl. RDn (1964—*). Bdry: 1957 (help cr Lostock Hall EP).[138]

BAMBER BRIDGE ST SAVIOUR

EP Cr 1842 from Blackburn AP.[133] Blackb RDn (1842—1964), Leyl. RDn (1964—*). Bdry: 1869,[139] 1897 (help cr Bamber Bridge St Aidan EP),[137] 1898 (help cr Leyland St Ambrose EP),[70] 1957 (help cr Lostock Hall EP).[138]

BAMFORD

EP Cr 1881 from Heywood St Luke EP, Heywood St James EP, Bircle EP, Middleton AP.[140] Bury RDn.

BANK QUAY

EP Cr 1884 from Warrington St Paul EP.[141] Winwick RDn (1884—1949), Warr. RDn (1949—*). Now called 'Warrington St Barnabas'.

BANKS—see ST STEPHENS IN THE BANKS

BARDSEA

EP Cr 1854 from Urswick AP.[142] Furness & Cartmel RDn (1854—59), Aldringham RDn (1859—83), Ulv. RDn (1883—1963), Dalton RDn (1963—70), Furness RDn (1970—*). Bdry: 1926.[143]

BARDSLEY

EP Cr 1844 from Ashton under Lyne AP.[106] Manch RDn (1844—47), Asht. under Lyne RDn (1847—*). Bdry: 1957,[144] 1965 (help cr Oldham St Chad, Limeside EP),[145] 1966.[146]

CP Cr 1894 from pt of the pt of Ashton under Lyne AP not in a MB or UD.[63] *LG* Asht. under Lyne PLU, Limehurst RD. Bdry: 1951 (loses pt to Oldham CB [assoc with Lancs] & CP).[64] Abol 1954 pt to Oldham CB (assoc with Lancs) & CP, pt to Asht. under Lyne MB & AP, pt to Failsworth UD & CP.[65] *Parl* Mossley Dv (1918—48), Asht. under Lyne CC (1948—55). Parl bdry: 1951.[66]

BARE

EP Cr 1933 from Poulton EP, Skerton EP, Bolton le Sands AP.[147] Lanc. RDn. Bdry: 1959 (cr Torrisholme EP).[148]

BARLEY WITH WHEATLEY BOOTH

Tp in Whalley AP, sep CP 1866,[4] eccl in chap Newchurch in Pendle (sep EP 1723 from Whalley AP[12]). *LG* Seq 5. *Parl* Seq 11.

BARLOW MOOR

EP Cr 1860 from Didsbury EP.[149] Asht. under Lyne RDn (1860—72), Ardwick RDn (1872—1912), Heaton RDn (1912—65), Withington RDn (1965—*). Bdry: 1875 (help cr Burnage EP),[150] 1882 (help cr Disbury Christ Church, Barlow Moor Road EP),[151] 1927,[135] 1929 (cr Burnage St Nicholas EP).[152]

BARNACRE

EP Cr 1911 from Garstang St Thomas EP, Calder Vale EP, Garstang AP.[153] Garst. RDn.

BARNACRE WITH BONDS

Tp in Garstang AP, sep CP 1866,[4] pt eccl severed 1864 to help cr Calder Vale EP.[154] *LG* Seq 2. Bdry:

1887.[155] *Parl* Seq 7.

BARROW IN FURNESS

The following have 'Barrow in Furness' in their names. Insofar as any existed at a given time: *LG* Lonsd. Hd, Ulv. PLU (soon after 1851[156]—1930), Barrow in Furness MB (pt 1867—81, ent 1881—89), CB (1889—1974), USD (pt 1875—81, pt 1881—94), pt Ulv. RSD (1875—81). *Parl* N'rn Dv (1832—67), North Dv (1867—85), Barrow in Furness Parl Bor/BC (1885—*). *Eccl* Aldingham RDn (cr—1883), Dalton RDn (1883—1970), Furness RDn (1970—*).

CP1/EP1—BARROW IN FURNESS [ST GEORGE]—Isle in Dalton in Furness AP, sep CP 1866,[4] pt a sep EP 1860,[12] eccl refounded 1861 (as 'Barrow St George', later 'Barrow in Furness').[157] Civ bdry: 1878.[158] Transf 1974 to Cumbria.[40] Eccl bdry: 1867 (cr EP3),[159] 1877 (cr EP4, cr EP6, help cr EP5),[160] 1894,[161] 1937.[162]

EP2—BARROW IN FURNESS ST AIDAN—Cr 1967 from Newbarns and Hawcoat EP.[163]

EP3—BARROW IN FURNESS ST JAMES—Cr 1867 from EP1.[159] Bdry: 1877 (help cr EP7).[160]

EP4—BARROW IN FURNESS ST JOHN—Cr 1877 from EP1.[160]

EP5—BARROW IN FURNESS ST LUKE—Cr 1877 from EP1, Dalton in Furness AP.[160] Bdry: 1894,[161] 1937.[162]

EP6—BARROW IN FURNESS ST MARK—Cr 1877 from EP1.[160] Bdry: 1894,[161] 1937.[162]

EP7—BARROW IN FURNESS ST MATTHEW—Cr 1877 from EP3, Newbarns and Hawcoat EP.[160] Bdry: 1894,[161] 1937.[162]

—BARROW IN FURNESS ST PAUL—Name used now for EP cr 1869 as 'Newbarns and Hawcoat', qv.

BARROW ST GEORGE—see BARROW IN FURNESS

BARROWFORD

EP Cr 1845 from Whalley AP.[12] Blackb RDn (1845—47), Whalley RDn (1847—72), Burnley RDn (1872—1970), Pendle RDn (1970—*).

CP Cr 1894 from the pt of Barrowford Booth CP in Barrowford Booth UD.[164] *LG* Burnley PLU, Barrowford UD. *Parl* Nelson & Colne Parl Bor/BC (1918—*).

BARROWFORD BOOTH

Tp in Whalley AP, sep CP 1866,[4] eccl in chap Colne (sep EP 1820 from Whalley AP[12]). *LG* Blackb Hd, Burnley PLU, pt Nelson USD, pt Nelson MB (1890—94), pt Barrowford Booth USD (1892—94), pt Burnley RSD. Abol 1894 the pt in Nelson MB to help cr Nelson CP, the pt in Barrowford Booth UD cr Barrowford CP, the remainder cr Blacko CP.[164] *Parl* N'rn Dv (1832—67), N-E Dv (1867—85), Clith. Dv (1885—1918).

BARTON

Tp in Preston AP, sep CP 1866,[4] perhaps a sep EP 1723,[165] certainly a sep EP 1851,[12] eccl refounded 1856.[166] *LG* Seq 3. Civ bdry: 1894.[167] *Parl* Seq 2. *Eccl* Amound. RDn (1851—52), Preston RDn (1852—1968), Garst. RDn (1968—*). Eccl bdry: 1925 (help cr Bilsborrow EP).[168]

BARTON MOSS

CP Cr 1894 from pt of the pt of Barton upon Irwell CP not in Eccles MB.[169] *LG* Barton upon Irwell PLU, RD. Bdry: 1896.[170] Abol 1933 pt to Eccles MB & CP, pt to Worsley UD & CP.[171] *Parl* Stretf. Dv (1918—48).

BARTON UPON IRWELL

Tp in Eccles AP, sep CP 1866,[4] sep EP 1849,[12] eccl refounded 1867.[172] *LG* Salf. Hd, Chorlton PLU (1837—49), Barton upon Irwell PLU (1849—94); pt Barton, Eccles, Winton and Monton USD (1875—92); pt Eccles MB & USD (1892—94), pt Barton upon Irwell RSD. Civ bdry: 1892 (loses pt to Salf. CB [assoc with Lancs] and to Pendleton CP).[173] Abol civ 1894 the pt in the MB to help cr Eccles CP,[174] the remainder to cr the 3 CPs of Barton Moss,[169] Davyhulme,[175] Irlam.[176] *Parl* S'rn Dv (1832—67), S-E Dv (1867—85), Eccles Dv (1885—1918). *Eccl* Manch RDn (1849—50), Eccles RDn (1850—66), Eccles & Salf. RDn (1866—72), Eccles RDn (1872—1971). Bdry: 1885 (help cr Davyhulme St Mary the Virgin EP),[177] 1902 (help cr Old Trafford St Cuthbert EP),[2] 1964.[178] Abol eccl 1971 to help cr Barton with Peel Green EP.[179]

BARTON WITH PEEL GREEN

EP Cr 1971 by union Peel Green EP, Barton upon Irwell EP.[179] Eccles RDn.

BAXENDEN

EP Cr 1878 from Accrington Christ Church EP.[20] Whalley RDn (1878—1912), Accr. RDn (1912—*).

BECCONSALL

EP Cr 1730 from Croston AP (in area chap Hesketh with Becconsall),[12] sep status not sustained, the area of the ent chap a sep par 1821 as 'Hesketh with Becconsall' EP,[180] qv, from Croston AP.[181] Leyl. RDn.

BEDFORD

Tp in Leigh AP, sep CP 1866,[4] sep EP 1843 as 'Bedford Leigh'[119] but later 'Bedford'. *LG* W Derby Hd, Leigh PLU, USD. Abol civ 1894 to help cr Leigh CP.[122] *Parl* S'rn Dv (1832—67), S-W Dv (1867—85), Leigh Dv (1885—1918). *Eccl* Warr. RDn (1843—50), Leyl. RDn (1850—66), Eccles & Salf. RDn (1866—72), Eccles RDn (1872—1933), Leigh RDn (1933—*). Eccl bdry: 1878 (help cr Glazebury EP).[38]

BEDFORD LEIGH—see prev entry

BELFIELD

EP Cr 1911 from Milnrow EP, Newbold EP.[182] Rochd. RDn.

BELMONT

EP Cr 1861 from Little Bolton EP, Bolton le Moors AP (pt tp Longworth, pt tp Sharples).[183] Bolton le Moors RDn (1861—93), Bolton North RDn (1893—1901), Bolton le Moors RDn (1901—68), Walmsley RDn (1968—*).

CP Cr 1894 from the pt of Sharples CP not in Astley Bridge UD.[120] *LG* Bolton PLU, RD (1894—98), Turton UD (1898—1925). Abol 1925 ent to Turton CP.[184] *Parl* Darwen Dv (1918—48).

BESWICK

Ex-par place (situated in Manchester AP), sep CP 1858,[80] eccl abol 1862 to help cr Bradford EP,[185]

'Beswick' a sep EP 1879 from Bradford EP, Ancoats All Souls EP.[71] *LG* Salf. Hd, Prestw. PLU (1858—96), Manch MB (1838—89), CB (1889—96), USD. Abol civ 1896 to help cr North Manchester CP.[82] *Parl* Manch Parl Bor (1832—85), Manch, East Dv Parl Bor (1885—1918). *Eccl* Cathedral RDn. Abol eccl 1966 to help cr Ancoats All Souls EP.[73]

BEVINGTON
EP Cr 1845 from Liverpool AP.[186] Warr. RDn (1845—47), Liverp North RDn (1847—1929). Bdry: 1904.[187] Abol 1929 to help cr Liverpool St Alban, Bevington EP.[188]

BICKERSHAW
EP Cr 1905 from Abram EP.[10] Wigan RDn.

BICKERSTAFFE
Tp in Ormskirk AP, sep CP 1866,[4] church built 1843 by Earl of Derby and eccl sep thereafter.[189] *LG* Seq 17. Civ bdry: 1931.[126] *Parl* Seq 21. *Eccl* Warr. RDn (1843—47), N Meols RDn (1847—87), Ormsk. RDn (1887—*).

BILLINGE
Chap in Wigan AP (comprised of civ tp of Billinge Higher End, qv for sep civ identity), sep EP 1720 as 'Billinge',[12] as such eccl refounded 1882.[190] Warr. RDn (1720—1847), Wigan RDn (1847—*). Bdry: 1966.[104]

BILLINGE AND WINSTANLEY
CP Cr 1924 by union pars in Billinge UD as latter renamed 'Billinge and Winstanley': Billinge Chapel End CP, Billinge Higher End CP, Winstanley CP.[191] *LG* Wigan PLU, Billinge and Winstanley UD. Transf 1974 pt to Gtr Manch (wards of Billinge Higher End, pt Winstanley [all except detached pt]), pt to Merseyside (remainder).[40] *Parl* Ince CC (1948—70), Ince BC (1970—*).

BILLINGE CHAPEL END
Tp in Wigan AP, sep CP 1866,[4] the area comprising chap Billinge, sep EP 1720 as 'Billinge',[12] as such eccl refounded 1882,[190] qv. *LG* W Derby Hd, Wigan PLU, Billinge USD, UD. Abol 1924 to help cr Billinge and Winstanley UD & CP.[191] *Parl* S'rn Dv (1832—67), S-W Dv (1867—85), Newton Dv (1885—1918), Ince Dv (1918—48).

BILLINGE HIGHER END
Tp in Wigan AP, sep CP 1866,[4] eccl in chap Upholland (sep EP 1643 from Wigan AP,[192] qv for later refounding). Civ and parl organisation as for Billinge Chapel End.

BILLINGTON
Chap in Blackburn AP, sep CP 1866,[4] sep EP 1746 as 'Langho',[12] qv, as such eccl refounded 1842,[133] sometimes called 'Langho Billington'. *LG* Seq 4. *Parl* Seq 12.

BILLINGTON LANGHO—see LANGHO

BILSBORROW
Tp in Garstang AP, sep CP 1866,[4] sep EP 1925 from Barton EP, Garstang AP.[168] *LG* Seq 2. *Parl* Seq 7. *Eccl* Garst. RDn.

BIRCH
EP Cr 1830 from Middleton AP,[12] refounded 1843 from Middleton AP, Heywood St James EP.[193] Manch RDn (1830—50), Bury RDn (1850—72),

Prestw & Middl. RDn (1872—1912), Middl. RDn (1912—*). Bdry: 1896 (help cr Thornham with Gravel Hole EP),[194] 1905 (help cr Hopwood EP),[195] 1964,[196] 1964 (help cr Langley EP).[197]

BIRCH IN RUSHOLME
EP Built *ca* 1580 as chap [St James] in Manchester AP, later Presbyterian chap until 1697,[198] sep EP 1739,[12] eccl refounded 1839,[74] eccl refounded 1854.[199] Manch RDn (1739—1855), Chorlton RDn (1855—72), Ardwick RDn (1872—1912), Heaton RDn (1912—65), Withington RDn (1965—*). Bdry: 1854 (cr Rusholme [Holy Trinity] EP),[199] 1861 (help cr Levenshulme EP),[200] 1878 (help cr Manchester St Chrysostom, Victoria Park EP),[35] 1886 (help cr Birch in Rusholme St Agnes EP [orig as 'Birch St Agnes', later as 'Birch in Rusholme' or 'Birch in Rusholme St Agnes']),[201] 1900 (help cr Ladybarn EP),[202] 1911,[203] 1929.[204]

BIRCH IN RUSHOLME ST AGNES
EP Cr 1886 (orig as 'Birch St Agnes', later as 'Birch in Rusholme' or 'Birch in Rusholme St Agnes') from Birch in Rusholme EP, Levenshulme EP, Longsight EP.[201] Ardwick RDn (1886—1912), Heaton RDn (1912—*). Bdry: 1929,[204] 1957.[205]

BIRCH ST AGNES—see prev entry

BIRCLE
EP Cr 1848 from Middleton AP (tp Birtle cum Bamford, qv for sep civ identity), Bury AP (pt chap Heywood situated in tp Heap [qv for sep civ identity]).[206] Manch RDn (1848—50), Bury RDn (1850—*). Bdry: 1881 (help cr Bamford EP).[140]

BIRKDALE
Tp in North Meols AP, sep CP 1866,[4] sep EP [St James] 1865.[104] *LG* W Derby Hd, Ormsk. PLU, Birkdale USD, UD. Abol civ 1912 ent to S'port. CB (assoc with Lancs) & CP.[207] *Parl* S'rn Dv (1832—67), S-W Dv (1867—85), S'port. Dv (1885—1918). *Eccl* N Meols RDn. Eccl bdry: 1875 (help cr Birkdale St Peter EP),[183] 1896,[113] 1904 (help cr Birkdale St John EP),[208] 1936.[209]

BIRKDALE ST JOHN
EP Cr 1904 from Birkdale EP, Birkdale St Peter EP.[208] N Meols RDn.

BIRKDALE ST PETER
EP Cr 1875 from Birkdale EP, Southport St Paul EP, North Meols AP.[183] N Meols RDn. Bdry: 1904 (help cr Birkdale St John EP).[208]

BIRKRIG COMMON
Land Common to Aldingham AP, Urswick AP. *LG* Ulv. RD (1894—1960), N Lonsd. RD (1960—74). Transf 1974 to Cumbria.[40] *Parl* Lonsd. Dv (1918—48), Morec. & Lonsd. CC (1948—*).

BIRTLE CUM BAMFORD
Tp in Middleton AP, sep CP 1866,[4] sep EP 1840 as 'Bircle' from Middleton AP (tp Birtle cum Bamford), Bury AP (pt chap Heywood situated in tp Heap).[206] *LG* Salf. Hd, Bury PLU, pt Heyw. USD, pt Heyw. MB (1881—94), pt Bury USD, pt Bury MB (1876—89), pt Bury CB (1889—94), pt Bury RSD, Bury RD. Bdry: 1883,[31] 1894 (incl loses the pt in Heyw. MB to help cr Heywood CP, loses the pt in Bury CB to Bury AP, gains Ashworth CP).[115] Abol 1933 pt to Bury CB (assoc with Lancs) & AP,

pt to Rochd. CB (assoc with Lancs) & AP, pt to Heyw. MB & CP.[37] *Parl* S'rn Dv (1832—67), S-E Dv (1867—85), pt Heyw. Dv, pt Bury Parl Bor (1885—1918), Heyw. & Radcl. Dv (1918—48).

BISPHAM

AP Prob orig a sep AP, appropriated to Lanc. Priory and after Dissolution deemed chap in Poulton le Fylde AP until again a sep par 1688.[210] Incl tps Bispham with Norbreck, Layton with Warbreck (each a sep CP 1866[4]) so that 'Bispham' has no sep civ identity after 1866. *LG* Amound. Hd. *Parl* N'rn Dv (1832—67). *Eccl* Amound. RDn (until 1852), The Fylde RDn (1852—1963), Blackp. RDn (1963—*). Eccl bdry: 1837 (cr South Shore Holy Trinity [o'wise 'Blackpool Holy Trinity'] EP,[211] refounded 1871[212]), 1871 (cr Blackpool Christ Church EP),[16] 1911 (help cr Cleveleys EP),[213] 1919 (cr Blackpool St Stephen EP).[21]

BISPHAM

Tp in Croston AP, sep CP 1866,[4] eccl severed 1843 to help cr Mawdersley with Bispham EP.[214] *LG* Seq 9. *Parl* Seq 3.

BISPHAM WITH NORBRECK

Tp in Bispham AP, sep CP 1866.[4] *LG* Amound. Hd, Fylde PLU, pt Blackp. USD (1875—83), pt Blackp. MB (1879—83), Fylde RSD (pt 1875—83, ent 1883—94), Fylde RD (1894—1903), Bispham with Norbreck UD (1903—18). Bdry: 1877,[215] 1883 (loses the pt in the MB & USD to Layton and Warbreck CP),[216] 1894 (loses the pt in the MB to help cr Blackpool CP).[217] Abol civ 1918 ent to Blackp. CB (assoc with Lancs) & CP.[218] *Parl* N'rn Dv (1832—67), North Dv (1867—85), Blackp. Dv (1885—1918), Blackp. Parl Bor (1918—48).

BLACKBURN

The following have 'Blackburn' in their names. Insofar as any existed at a given time: *LG* Blackb Hd, PLU, USD, MB (1851—89), CB (1889—1974). *Parl* Blackb Parl Bor (1832—1918), pt Blackb East Parl Bor, pt Blackb West Parl Bor (1918—55), Blackb BC (1955—*). *Eccl* Manch & Blackb RDn (until before 1535), Blackb RDn (before 1535—*).

AP1—BLACKBURN [ST MARY]—Incl chap Balderstone (sep CP 1866,[4] sep EP 1741,[12] eccl refounded 1842[133]), chap Billington (sep CP 1866,[4] sep EP 1746 as 'Langho',[12] as such eccl refounded 1842,[133] sometimes called 'Langho Billington'), chap Over Darwen (sep CP 1866,[4] sep EP 1719 [St James],[12] the latter divided 1842 into 2 EPs of 'Over Darwen Holy Trinity', 'Over Darwen St James',[133] the pars later called respectively 'Darwen Holy Trinity', 'Darwen St James'), chap Great Harwood (sep CP 1866,[4] sep EP 1735 [incl pt tp Rishton],[12] eccl refounded 1840[219]), chap Salesbury (sep CP 1866[4]), chap Samlesbury (orig an area in chap Walton le Dale,[220] early considered chap in AP1, sep CP 1866,[4] sep EP 1763[12]), chap Tockholes (sep CP 1866,[4] sep EP 1725 [incl pt tp Livesey],[12] eccl refounded 1842[133]), chap Walton le Dale (sep CP 1866,[4] sep EP 1764 [incl tp Cuerdale][12]), tp Clayton le Dale (sep CP 1866[4]), tp Cuerdale (sep

CP 1866,[4] eccl in chap/EP Walton le Dale, qv above), tp Lower Darwen (sep CP 1866,[4] sep EP 1830,[12] eccl refounded 1842[133]), tps Dinckley, Eccleshill, Little Harwood (each of the 3 a sep CP 1866[4]), tp Livesey (sep CP 1866,[4] pt eccl severed 1725 to help cr Tockholes EP,[12] qv above for refounding, a pt of tp Livesey eccl severed 1839 to help cr Feniscowles EP,[12] qv for later refounding, 'Livesey' a sep EP 1877 from Feniscowles EP, Tockholes EP[221]), tp Mellor (sep CP 1866,[4] sep EP 1830,[12] eccl refounded 1842[133]), tps Osbaldeston, Pleasington, Ramsgreave (each of the 3 a sep CP 1866[4]), tp Rishton (sep CP 1866,[4] pt eccl in chap Great Harood [sep EP 1735 from AP1,[12] refounded 1840[219]], pt of tp Rishton eccl severed 1845 to help cr EP14,[222] pt of tp Rishton eccl severed 1866 to help cr EP19,[50] 'Rishton' a sep EP 1874 from Great Harwood EP, EP14, EP19[24]), tp Wilpshire (sep CP 1866[4]), tp Witton (sep CP 1866,[4] sep EP 1842[133]). Addtl civ bdry alt: 1893 (gains the following area in Blackb CB: Little Harwood CP, pt Lower Darwen CP, pt Livesey CP, pt Witton CP),[223] 1901,[224] 1922,[225] 1934 (incl gains Witton CP).[226] Eccl bdry: 1812 (cr EP8,[12] refounded 1842[133]), 1824 (cr EP16,[12] refounded 1842[133]), 1832 (cr EP15,[12] refounded 1842[133]), 1839 (cr Feniscowles EP [incl pt tp Livesey],[12] refounded 1842[133]), 1842 (cr Bamber Bridge St Saviour EP[133]), 1845 (cr EP14 [incl pt tp Rishton]),[222] 1849 (cr EP3),[227] 1860 (cr EP2),[102] 1866 (cr EP19 [incl pt tp Rishton]),[50] 1872 (cr EP1),[228] 1873.[154] Abol eccl 1961 to help cr EP12.[229]

EP1—BLACKBURN ALL SAINTS, NOVA SCOTIA—Cr 1872 from AP1.[228] Bdry: 1884,[230] 1916,[231] 1940.[150]

EP2—BLACKBURN CHRIST CHURCH—Cr 1860 from AP1.[102] Bdry: 1884,[230] 1911,[232] 1916,[231] 1923 (cr EP20).[233]

EP3—BLACKBURN HOLY TRINTY—Cr 1849 from AP1.[227] Bdry: 1904.[234]

EP4—BLACKBURN ST AIDAN—Cr 1925 from Livesey EP, Feniscliffe EP.[213] Blackb RDn (1925—64), Darwen RDn (1964—*).

—BLACKBURN ST ANDREW—Name used now for EP cr 1877 as 'Livesey', qv.

EP5—BLACKBURN ST BARNABAS—Cr 1887 from EP15.[235] Bdry: 1907.[236]

—BLACKBURN ST BARTHOLOMEW—Name used now for EP cr 1911 as 'Ewood', qv.

—BLACKBURN ST FRANCIS—Name used now for EP cr 1893 as 'Feniscliffe', qv.

EP6—BLACKBURN ST GABRIEL—Cr 1928 from EP14, Mellor EP, EP7.[237]

EP7—BLACKBURN ST JAMES—Cr 1875 from EP8, EP15.[85] Bdry: 1899,[9] 1928 (help cr EP6).[237]

EP8—BLACKBURN ST JOHN—Cr 1812 from AP1,[12] refounded 1842.[133] Bdry: 1875 (help cr EP7).[85]

EP9—BLACKBURN ST JUDE—Cr 1914 from EP19.[238]

EP10—BLACKBURN ST LUKE—Cr 1878 from EP16.[239] Abol 1972 to help cr EP11.[240] Bdry: 1940.[150]

EP11—BLACKBURN ST LUKE WITH ST PHILIP—Cr 1972 by union EP10, Griffin EP.[240]

EP12—BLACKBURN ST MARY THE VIRGIN AND ST PAUL—Cr 1961 by union AP1, EP15.[229]

EP13—BLACKBURN ST MATTHEW, HIGHER AUDLEY—Cr 1887 from EP19.[241] Bdry: 1911.[232]

EP14—BLACKBURN ST MICHAEL AND ALL ANGELS—Cr 1845 from AP1 (incl pt tp Rishton).[222] Bdry: 1874 (the orig pt of tp Rishton severed to help cr Bispham EP),[24] 1899,[9] 1904,[234] 1909 (cr EP18),[41] 1930,[242] 1928 (help cr EP6).[237]

EP15—BLACKBURN ST PAUL—Cr 1832 from AP1,[12] refounded 1842.[133] Bdry: 1875 (help cr EP7),[85] 1887 (cr EP5),[235] 1900 (cr EP17).[221] Abol 1961 to help cr EP12.[229]

EP16—BLACKBURN ST PETER—Cr 1824 from AP1,[12] refounded 1842.[133] Bdry: 1873,[154] 1878 (cr EP10).[239]

EP17—BLACKBURN ST SILAS—Cr 1900 from EP15.[221] Bdry: 1940.[150]

EP18—BLACKBURN ST STEPHEN—Cr 1909 from EP14.[41] Bdry: 1930.[242]

EP19—BLACKBURN ST THOMAS—Cr 1866 from AP1 (incl pt tp Rishton).[50] Bdry: 1874 (the orig pt of tp Rishton severed to help cr Rishton EP),[24] 1879 (help cr Knuzden EP),[154] 1887 (cr EP13),[241] 1911,[232] 1914 (cr EP9).[238]

EP20—BLACKBURN THE SAVIOUR—Cr 1923 from EP2.[233] Bdry: 1947.[243]

BLACKLEY

The following have 'Blackley' in their names. Insofar as any existed at a given time: *LG* Salf. Hd, Manch PLU (1840—50), Prestw. PLU (1850—96), RSD (1875—90), Manch CB (1890—96), USD (1890—94). *Parl* S'rn Dv (1832—67), S-E Dv (1867—85), Prestw. Dv (1885—1918). *Eccl* Manch RDn (cr—1851), Bury RDn (1851—72), Cheetham RDn (1872—*).

CP1/EP1—BLACKLEY [ST PETER]—Chap in Manchester AP, sep CP 1866,[4] sep EP 1800,[12] eccl refounded 1839,[74] eccl refounded 1854.[199] Abol civ 1896 to help cr North Manchester CP.[82] Eccl bdry: 1866 (cr EP3),[244] 1900 (help cr EP2),[202] 1925 (help cr EP4),[147] 1958.[245]

EP2—BLACKLEY HOLY TRINITY—Cr 1900 from EP1, Harpurhey Christ Church EP.[202]

EP3—BLACKLEY ST ANDREW—Cr 1866 from EP1.[244] Bdry: 1925 (help cr EP4), 1928.[147]

EP4—BLACKLEY ST PAUL—Cr 1925 from EP1, EP3.[147] Bdry: 1958.[245]

BLACKO

CP Cr 1894 from the pt of Barrowford Booth CP not in a MB or UD.[164] *LG* Burnley PLU, RD. *Parl* Clith. Dv/CC (1918—*).

BLACKPOOL

The following have 'Blackpool' in their names. Insofar as any existed at a given time: *LG* Fylde PLU, Blackp. MB (1894—1904), CB (1904—74). *Parl* Blackp. Parl Bor (1918—48); see Part III of the *Guide* for composition of Blackp. BCs (1948—*) by wards of the CB. *Eccl* Amound. RDn (cr—1852), The Fylde RDn (1852—1963), Blackp. RDn (1963—*).

CP1—BLACKPOOL—Cr 1894 by union of areas in Blackp. MB: Layton with Warbreck CP, pt Bispham with Norbreck CP, pt Marton CP.[217] Bdry: 1897 (gains Foreshore),[246] 1918 (incl gains Bispham with Norbreck UD & CP),[218] 1934,[226] 1955.[247] Parl bdry: 1956.[248]

EP1—BLACKPOOL ALL SAINTS—Cr 1907 from EP4, Marton EP.[249]

EP2—BLACKPOOL CHRIST CHURCH—Cr 1871 from Bispham AP.[16] Bdry: 1900 (cr EP8),[250] 1928 (help cr EP5),[251] 1957 (help cr EP7).[252]

EP3—BLACKPOOL HOLY CROSS, SOUTH SHORE—Cr 1951 from South Shore Holy Trinity EP, Marton EP.[253]

—BLACKPOOL HOLY TRINITY—see SOUTH SHORE HOLY TRINITY

EP4—BLACKPOOL ST JOHN—Cr 1822 from Bispham AP,[12] refounded 1860.[254] Bdry: 1907 (help cr EP1),[249] 1921 (cr EP10),[208] 1928 (help cr EP5),[251] 1957 (help cr EP7).[252]

EP5—BLACKPOOL ST MARK—Cr 1928 from EP2, EP4.[251] Bdry: 1957 (help cr EP7).[252]

EP6—BLACKPOOL ST MARY, SOUTH SHORE—Cr 1951 from South Shore Holy Trinity EP.[255]

EP7—BLACKPOOL ST MICHAEL AND ALL ANGELS—Cr 1957 from Poulton le Fylde AP, EP2, EP4, EP5.[252]

EP8—BLACKPOOL ST PAUL—Cr 1900 from EP2.[250]

EP9—BLACKPOOL ST STEPHEN—Cr 1919 from Bispham AP.[21] Bdry: 1954.[139]

EP10—BLACKPOOL ST THOMAS—Cr 1921 from EP4.[208]

BLACKROD

Chap in Bolton le Moors AP, sep CP 1866,[4] sep EP 1730,[12] eccl refounded 1858.[256] *LG* Salf. Hd, Wigan PLU, Blackrod USD, UD. Transf 1974 to Gtr Manch.[40] *Parl* Seq 15. *Eccl* Manch RDn (1730—1847), Bolton le Moors RDn (1847—93), Bolton North RDn (1893—1901), Bolton le Moors RDn (1901—68), Deane RDn (1968—*).

BLATCHINWORTH AND CALDERBROOK

Tp in Rochdale AP, sep CP 1866.[4] *LG* Salf. Hd, Rochd. PLU, Littleborough USD. Abol 1894 to help cr Littleborough CP.[257] *Parl* S'rn Dv (1832—67), S-E Dv (1867—85), Middl. Dv (1885—1918).

BLAWITH

Chap in Ulverston AP, sep CP 1866,[4] 'Blawith' a sep EP 1745 (pt tp Blawith, pt tp Subberthwaite in same par),[12] eccl refounded 1892,[44] the remainder of tp Blawith severed 1747 to help cr Torver EP,[12] the latter eccl refounded 1892.[83] *LG* Seq 14. Transf 1974 to Cumbria.[40] *Parl* Seq 10. *Eccl* Furness & Cartmel RDn (1745—1859), Ulv. RDn (1859—1970), Furness RDn (1970—*).

BLEASDALE

Chap in Lancaster AP, sep CP 1866,[4] sep EP 1748 as 'Admarsh',[12] qv, sometimes 'Admarsh in Bleasdale'. *LG* Seq 2. *Parl* Seq 7.

BLUNDELLSANDS

EP Cr 1875 from Great Crosby EP.[139] Liverp North RDn (1875—95), Bootle RDn (1895—*). Bdry:

1924 (help cr Blundellsands St Michael EP),[258] 1937,[259] 1971 (cr Hightown EP).[260]

BLUNDELLSANDS ST MICHAEL
EP Cr 1924 from Blundellsands EP, Great Crosby EP, Sefton AP.[258] Bootle RDn.

BOLD
Tp in Prescot AP, sep CP 1866,[4] eccl in Farnworth (chap and bor in tp Widnes in Prescot AP, the chap with some parochial rights from Middle Ages,[261] 'Farnworth' a sep EP 1859 from Prescot AP [incl tp Bold], Widnes EP, Great Sankey EP[262]). *LG* Seq 18. Transf 1974 pt to Merseyside to be 'Bold' CP there, pt to Ches (the pt in Warrington New Town, added to Great Sankey CP).[40] *Parl* Seq 19.

BOLTON
CP Cr 1895 by unions pars in Bolton CB: Rumworth CP, Halliwell CP, Great Bolton CP, Little Bolton CP, Tonge with Haulgh CP.[263] *LG* Bolton PLU, CB. Bdry: 1898 (gains Astley Bridge UD & CP, Breightmet CP, Deane CP, Heaton CP, Middle Hulton CP, Darcy Lever CP, Great Lever CP, Lostock CP, Smithills CP, Tonge CP, pt Over Hulton CP).[36] Transf 1974 to Gtr Manch.[40] *Parl* Bolton Parl Bor (1832—1948), pt Bolton East BC, pt Bolton West BC (1948—*).

GREAT BOLTON
Tp in Bolton le Moors AP, sep CP 1866,[4] sep EP 1880 from Bolton le Moors Holy Trinity EP, Bolton le Moors St Mark EP, Great Lever EP.[264] *LG* Salf. Hd, Bolton PLU, MB (1838—89), CB (1889—95), USD. Abol civ 1895 to help cr Bolton CP.[263] *Parl* Bolton Parl Bor (1832—1918). *Eccl* Bolton le Moors RDn (1880—93), Bolton South RDn (1893—1901), Bolton le Moors RDn (1901—61). Eccl bdry: 1902 (help cr Bolton le Moors St Simon and St Jude EP),[230] 1930.[149] Abol eccl 1961 to help cr Great Lever St Michael with St Bartholomew EP.[265]

LITTLE BOLTON
Chap in Bolton le Moors AP, sep CP 1866,[4] pt a sep EP [All Saints] 1745,[12] eccl refounded 1841.[266] *LG* Salf. Hd, Bolton PLU, MB (pt 1838—85, ent 1885—89), CB (1889—95), Bolton USD (pt 1875—85, ent 1885—94), pt Astley Bridge USD (1875—85), pt Bolton RSD (1875—85). Civ bdry: 1885.[267] Abol civ 1895 to help cr Bolton CP.[263] *Parl* Bolton Parl Bor (pt 1832—67, enlarged pt 1867—85, ent 1885—1918), pt S'rn Dv (1832—67), pt S-E Dv (1867—85). *Eccl* Manch RDn (1745—1847), Bolton le Moors RDn (1847—93), Bolton North RDn (1893—1901), Bolton le Moors RDn (1901—68). Sometimes 'Bolton le Moors All Saints'. Eccl bdry: 1844 (help cr Astley Bridge EP),[111] 1846 (help cr Little Bolton St John EP),[268] 1861 (help cr Belmont EP),[183] 1912 (help cr Tonge Fold EP).[269] Abol eccl 1968 ent to Bolton le Moors AP.[214]

LITTLE BOLTON ST GEORGE
EP Cr 1802 from Bolton le Moors AP,[12] refounded 1841 as 'Bolton le Moors St George' EP,[266] qv. Manch RDn.

LITTLE BOLTON ST JOHN
EP Cr 1846 from Little Bolton EP, Bolton le Moors St George EP.[268] Manch RDn (1846—47), Bolton le Moors RDn (1847—93), Bolton North RDn (1893—

1901), Bolton le Moors RDn (1901—68). Abol 1968 ent to Bolton le Moors AP.[214]

BOLTON ALL SOULS WITH ST JAMES
EP Cr 1968 by union Bolton le Moors All Souls EP, Bolton le Moors St James EP.[270] Bolton le Moors RDn (1968), Walmsley RDn (1968—*).

BOLTON CHRIST CHURCH—see BOLTON LE MOORS CHRIST CHURCH

BOLTON LE MOORS
The following have 'Bolton le Moors' in their names. Insofar as any existed at a given time: *LG* Salf. Hd. *Parl* S'rn Dv (1832—67). *Eccl* Manch & Blackb RDn (until before 1535), Manch RDn (before 1535—1847), Bolton le Moors RDn (1847—93), Bolton North RDn (1893—1901), Bolton le Moors RDn (1901—*).

AP1—BOLTON LE MOORS [ST PETER]—Incl chap Blackrod (sep CP 1866,[4] sep EP 1730,[12] eccl refounded 1858[256]), chap Little Bolton (sep CP 1866,[4] sep EP 1745,[12] eccl refounded 1841[266]), chap Bradshaw (sep CP 1866,[4] sep EP 1737 [incl pt Turton EP],[12] eccl refounded 1853[154]), chap Rivington (sep CP 1866,[4] sep EP 1754[12]), chap Turton (sep CP 1866,[4] sep EP 1719,[12] eccl refounded [after bdry alts, qv] 1881[135]), tp Anglezarke (sep CP 1866[4]), tp Great Bolton (sep CP 1866,[4] sep EP 1880 from EP4, EP9, Great Lever EP[109]), tp Breightmet (sep CP 1866,[4] pt eccl severed 1845 to help refound Tonge EP[83]), tps Edgeworth, Entwisle (each a sep CP 1866[4]), tp Harwood (sep CP 1866,[4] pt eccl severed 1845 to help refound Tonge EP,[83] the remainder cr 1851 'Harwood' EP[271]), tp Darcy Lever (sep CP 1866,[4] eccl severed 1844 to help cr Lever Bridge EP[111]), tp Little Lever (sep CP 1866,[4] sep EP 1793,[12] eccl refounded 1866[272]), tp Longworth (sep CP 1866,[4] pt eccl severed 1741 to help cr Walmsley EP,[12] the remainder eccl severed 1861 to help cr Belmont EP[183]), tp Lostock (sep CP 1866,[4] eccl severed 1860 to help cr Wingates EP[273]), tp Quarlton (sep CP 1866[4]), tp Sharples (sep CP 1866,[4] pt eccl severed 1741 to help cr Walmsley EP[12] [the latter refounded 1844[88]], pt of area of Sharples eccl severed 1844 to help cr Astley Bridge EP,[111] the remainder of the orig area of tp severed 1861 to help cr Belmont EP[183]), tp Tonge with Haulgh (sep CP 1866,[4] pt area Haulgh eccl severed 1844 to help cr Lever Bridge EP,[111] the remainder of the tp cr 1841 'Tonge' EP,[12] eccl refounded 1845 [incl pt tp Breightmet, pt chap Haywood in same par][83]) so that 'Bolton le Moors' has no sep civ identity after 1866. Addtl eccl bdry alt: 1741 (cr Walmsley EP [incl pt tp Longworth, pt tp Sharples, pt Turton EP],[12] refounded 1844[88]), 1802 (cr Little Bolton St George EP,[12] refounded 1841 as Bolton le Moors St George EP[266]), 1841 (cr EP4, cr EP3),[266] 1844 (help cr Bolton Christ Church EP, soon and thereafter called as EP2),[111] 1866 (help cr EP12),[274] 1888,[19] 1912 (help cr Tonge Fold EP),[269] 1968 (gains Little Bolton St John EP, Little Bolton EP),[214] 1973 (gains EP4, EP7, EP9).[275]

—BOLTON LE MOORS ALL SAINTS—Name sometimes used for EP cr 1745 as 'Little Bolton', qv.

EP1—BOLTON LE MOORS ALL SOULS—Cr 1879 from EP8.[186] Abol 1966 to help cr Bolton All Souls with St James EP.[270]

EP2—BOLTON LE MOORS CHRIST CHURCH—Cr 1844 (orig as 'Bolton Christ Church') from AP1 (the pt of the AP in Bolton le Moors MB), EP3,[111] soon and thereafter called 'Bolton le Moors Christ Church'. Bdry: 1866 (help cr EP12).[274] Abol 1933 pt to EP3, pt to EP12.[49]

EP3—BOLTON LE MOORS EMMANUEL—Cr 1841 from AP1.[266] Bdry: 1844 (help cr Bolton Christ Church EP,[111] soon and thereafter called as EP2), 1882 (cr EP15),[151] 1882,[203] 1898,[276] 1933,[49] 1972 (gains EP15).[277]

EP4—BOLTON LE MOORS HOLY TRINITY—Cr 1841 from AP1.[266] Bdry: 1866 (cr EP9),[244] 1880 (help cr Great Bolton EP).[264] Abol 1973 ent to AP1.[275]

EP5—BOLTON LE MOORS ST BARNABAS—Cr 1896 from EP7, EP10, Halliwell St Luke EP.[254] Abol 1971 to help cr EP11.[278]

EP6—BOLTON LE MOORS ST BEDE—Cr 1923 from Deane AP, Daubhill EP.[89] Bolton le Moors RDn (1923—68), Deane RDn (1968—*).

EP7—BOLTON LE MOORS ST GEORGE—Refounding 1841 of Little Bolton St George EP.[266] Bdry: 1846 (help cr Little Bolton St John EP),[268] 1872 (cr EP8),[279] 1875 (cr EP10),[150] 1876 (help cr Halliwell St Luke EP),[280] 1891,[195] 1896 (help cr EP5).[254] Abol 1973 ent to AP1.[275]

EP8—BOLTON LE MOORS ST JAMES—Cr 1872 from EP7.[279] Bdry: 1879 (cr EP1).[186] Abol 1966 to help cr Bolton All Souls with St James EP.[270]

EP9—BOLTON LE MOORS ST MARK—Cr 1866 from EP4.[244] Bdry: 1880 (help cr Great Bolton EP),[264] 1897 (help cr EP13),[144] 1930.[149] Abol 1973 ent to AP1.[275]

EP10—BOLTON LE MOORS ST MATTHEW—Cr 1875 from EP7.[150] Bdry: 1896 (help cr EP5).[254] Abol 1971 to help cr EP11.[278]

EP11—BOLTON LE MOORS ST MATTHEW WITH ST BARNABAS—Cr 1971 by union EP10, EP5.[278]

EP12—BOLTON LE MOORS ST PAUL—Cr 1866 from EP2, AP1.[274] Bdry: 1891,[195] 1933.[49]

EP13—BOLTON LE MOORS ST PHILIP—Cr 1897 from EP9, Daubhill EP.[144] Bdry: 1930.[149]

EP14—BOLTON LE MOORS ST SIMON AND ST JUDE—Cr 1902 from Great Bolton EP, Great Lever EP.[230] Bdry: 1930.[149]

EP15—BOLTON LE MOORS THE SAVIOUR—Cr 1882 from EP3.[151] Bolton South RDn (1882—1901), Bolton le Moors RDn (1901—72). Bdry: 1898.[276] Abol 1972 ent to EP3.[277]

BOLTON LE SANDS

AP Incl chap Over Kellet (sep CP 1866,[4] sep EP 1730[12]), tp Nether Kellet (sep CP 1866[4]), tp Slyne with Hest (sep CP 1866,[4] sep EP 1935 from Bolton le Sands AP, Skerton EP[281]). *LG* Lonsd. Hd, Caton GilbU (until 1869), Lanc. PLU (1869—1930), RSD, RD. Addtl civ bdry alt: 1887.[282] *Parl* Seq 10.

Eccl Seq 11. Eccl bdry: 1933 (help cr Bare EP).[147]

HIGHER BOOTHS

Tp in Whalley AP, sep CP 1866,[4] eccl in chap Haslingden (sep EP 1719 from Whalley AP[12]), pt of the orig area of Higher Booths eccl severed 1846 from Haslingden EP to help cr Lumb EP,[283] 'Higher Booths' a sep EP 1849 from Haslingden EP,[284] sep status of this EP not sustained. *LG* Blackb Hd, Hasl. PLU, pt Rawt. USD (1883—94), pt Rawt. MB (1891—94), pt Hasl. USD, pt Hasl. MB (1891—94), pt Hasl. RSD (1875—83). Abol civ 1894 the pt in Rawt. MB to help cr Rawtenstall CP, the pt in Hasl. MB transf to Haslingden CP.[129] *Parl* N'rn Dv (1832—67), N-E Dv (1867—85), Rossend. Dv (1885—1918). *Eccl* Blackb RDn.

LOWER BOOTHS

Tp in Whalley AP, sep CP 1866,[4] eccl in chap Haslingden (sep EP 1719 from Whalley AP[12]), pt of the orig area of this Lower Booths eccl severed 1846 from Haslingden EP to help cr Lumb EP.[283] Organisation for civ, parl as for Higher Booths, with civ bdry alt 1883 as well.[31]

BOOTLE

The following have 'Bootle' in their names. Insofar as any existed at a given time: *LG* W Derby Hd, PLU, Bootle cum Linacre USD, Bootle cum Linacre MB (1868—89), Bootle CB (1889—1974). *Parl* S'rn Dv (1832—67), S-W Dv (1867—85), Bootle Dv (1885—1918), Bootle Parl Bor/BC (1918—*). *Eccl* Liverp North RDn (cr—1895), Bootle RDn (1895—*).

EP1—BOOTLE CHRIST CHURCH—Cr 1866 from Walton on the Hill AP (pt tp Bootle cum Linacre).[84] Bdry: 1957.[285]

CP1—BOOTLE CUM LINACRE—Tp in Walton on the Hill AP, sep CP 1866,[4] pt incl chap St Mary (erected 1827,[286] not a sep EP until so cr 1913 as EP4[194]), pt eccl severed 1866 to help cr EP2,[287] pt eccl severed 1866 to help cr EP1.[84] Transf 1974 to Merseyside.[40]

EP2—BOOTLE ST JOHN—Cr 1866 from Walton on the Hill AP (pt tp Bootle cum Liancre).[287] Abol 1957 pt to help cr EP5, pt to EP1, pt to Kirkdale St Paul, North Shore EP.[285]

EP3—BOOTLE ST LEONARD—Cr 1890 from Walton on the Hill AP.[17]

EP4—BOOTLE ST MARY—Chap erected 1827[286] in Walton on the Hill AP (in tp Bootle cum Linacre, in area Warr. RDn), sep EP 1913.[194] Abol 1957 to help cr EP5.[285]

EP5—BOOTLE ST MARY WITH ST JOHN—Cr 1957 by union EP4, pt EP2.[285]

EP6—BOOTLE ST MATTHEW—Cr 1892 from Walton on the Hill AP.[83]

BORWICK

Tp in Warton AP, sep CP 1866.[4] *LG* Seq 13. *Parl* Seq 9.

LITTLE BOWLAND

Tp in Whalley AP, sep CP 1866.[4] *LG* Blackb Hd, Clith. PLU (sometimes early rated for poor law purposes with Leagram), RSD, RD. Abol 1935 to help cr Bowland with Leagram CP.[43] *Parl* N'rn Dv (1832—67), N-E Dv (1867—85), Darwen Dv

(1885—1918), Clith. Dv (1918—48).

BOWLAND WITH LEAGRAM
CP Cr 1935 by union Little Bowland CP, Leagram CP.[43] *LG* Clith. RD. *Parl* Clith. CC (1948—*).

BRADFORD
Tp in Manchester AP, sep CP 1866,[4] eccl severed 1840 to help cr Openshaw EP,[288] 'Bradford' a sep EP 1862 by union eccl ex-par Beswick (situated in Manchester AP), and area orig tp Bradford from Openshaw EP.[185] *LG* Salf. Hd, Manch PLU (1840—50), Prestw. PLU (1850—96), Bradford USD (1875—85), Manch MB (1885—89), CB (1889—96), USD (1885—94). Abol civ 1896 to help cr North Manchester CP.[82] *Parl* Manch Parl Bor (1832—85), Manch, East Dv Parl Bor (1885—1918). *Eccl* Manch RDn (1862—72), Cheetham RDn (1872—93), Cathedral RDn (1893—1972). Eccl bdry: 1879 (help cr Beswick EP),[71] 1898 (cr Manchester St Aidan EP),[13] 1905 (help cr Manchester St Paul, Bradford EP).[123] Abol eccl 1972 to help cr Manchester The Resurrection EP.[289]

BRADSHAW
Chap in Bolton le Moors AP, sep CP 1866,[4] sep EP 1737 (incl pt Turton EP),[12] eccl refounded 1853.[154] *LG* Salf. Hd, Bolton PLU, RSD, RD. Abol civ 1898 ent to Turton CP.[36] *Parl* S'rn Dv (1832—67), S-E Dv (1867—85), W'hough. Dv (1885—1918). *Eccl* Manch RDn (1737—1847), Bolton le Moors RDn (1847—93), Bolton North RDn (1893—1901), Bolton le Moors RDn (1901—68), Walmsley RDn (1968—*).

BRATHAY
EP Cr 1836 from Hawkshead AP.[290] Furness & Cartmel RDn (1836—59), Ambleside RDn (1847—1967). Abol 1967 pt to help cr Ambleside with Brathay EP (Westm, Lancs), pt to Hawkshead and Low Wray EP (Lancs), pt to Langdale EP (Westm), pt to Church Coniston EP (Lancs).[69]

BREIGHTMET
Tp in Bolton le Moors AP, sep CP 1866,[4] pt eccl severed 1845 to help cr Tonge EP.[83] *LG* Salf. Hd, Bolton PLU, RSD, RD. Abol 1898 ent to Bolton CB (assoc with Lancs) & CP.[36] *Parl* S'rn Dv (1832—67), S-E Dv (1867—85), W'hough. Dv (1885—1918).

BRETHERTON
Tp in Croston AP, sep CP 1866,[4] sep EP 1843.[214] *LG* Leyl. Hd, Preston PLU (1837—soon after 1837[291]), Chorley PLU (soon after 1837[291]—1930), RSD, RD. *Parl* Seq 3. *Eccl* Leyl. RDn (1843—47), N Meols RDn (1847—48), Leyl. RDn (1848—1964), Chorley RDn (1964—*). Eccl bdry: 1855 (help cr Leyland St James EP).[292]

BRIERCLIFFE
Tp (civ, 'Briercliffe with Extwistle', qv for sep civ identity) in Whalley AP, eccl in chap Burnley (sep EP 1716 from Whalley AP[12]), 'Briercliffe' a sep EP 1843 from Burnley EP.[293] Blackb RDn (1843—47), Whalley RDn (1847—72), Burnley RDn (1872—*). Bdry: 1908 (help cr Burnley St Cuthbert EP).[294]

CP Cr 1894 from the pt of Briercliffe with Extwistle CP not in Burnley CB.[295] *LG* Burnley PLU, RD. *Parl* Clith. Dv/CC (1918—*).

BRIERCLIFFE WITH EXTWISTLE
Tp in Whalley AP, sep CP 1866,[4] eccl in chap Burnley (sep EP 1716 from Whalley AP[12]), 'Briercliffe' a sep EP 1843 from Burnley EP.[293] *LG* Blackb Hd, Burnley PLU, RSD (ent 1875—89, pt 1889—94), pt Burnley CB & USD (1889—94). Abol civ 1894 the pt in the CB transf to Burnley CP, the remainder cr Briercliffe CP.[295] *Parl* N'rn Dv (1832—67), N-E Dv (1867—85), Darwen Dv (1885—1918).

BRIERFIELD
EP Cr 1873 from Little Marsden EP.[154] Burnley RDn (1873—1970), Pendle RDn (1970—*). Bdry: 1881,[209] 1887,[296] 1890.[297]

CP Cr 1894 from the pt of Great and Little Marsden CP in Brierfield UD.[164] *LG* Burnley PLU, Brierfield UD. Bdry: 1897.[298] *Parl* Nelson & Colne Parl Bor/BC (1918—*).

BRINDLE
AP *LG* Seq 8. *Parl* Seq 3. *Eccl* Leyl. RDn (until 1847), Blackb RDn (1847—55), Leyl. RDn (1855—1964), Chorley RDn (1964—*).

BRINDLE HEATH
EP Cr 1923 from Pendleton EP.[105] Salf. RDn. Bdry: 1925 (help cr Claremont EP).[221] Abol 1971 pt to Pendleton EP, pt to Claremont EP, pt to Pendlebury EP.[299]

BROUGHTON
Tp in Manchester AP, sep CP 1866,[4] sep EP [St John] 1854.[199] *LG* Salf. Hd, PLU, USD, MB (pt 1844—53, ent 1853—89), CB (1889—1919). Abol civ 1919 ent to Salford CP.[300] *Parl* Salf. Parl Bor (1832—1918); see Part III of the *Guide* for composition of Salf. Parl Bors (1918—48) by wards of the CB. *Eccl* Bury RDn (1854—66), Eccles & Salf. RDn (1866—72), Salf. RDn (1872—*). Eccl bdry: 1870 (cr Lower Broughton [The Ascension] EP),[301] 1878 (cr Broughton St John the Evangelist EP),[302] 1881 (help cr Lower Broughton St Clement EP).[216]

BROUGHTON
Chap in Preston AP, sep CP 1866,[4] sep EP [St John the Baptist] 1774,[12] eccl refounded 1878.[302] *LG* Seq 3. Civ bdry: 1883,[31] 1934.[226] *Parl* Seq 2. *Eccl* Amound. RDn (1774—1852), Preston RDn (1852—*).

FIELD BROUGHTON
Chap (built 1745[303]) and tp in Cartmel AP, sep EP [St Peter] 1748,[12] eccl refounded 1875,[304] sep CP 1866 as 'Broughton East',[4] qv. *Eccl* Pec jurisd Dean & Chapter of York (until 1836), Furness & Cartmel RDn (1836—59), Cartmel RDn (1859—1970), Windermere RDn (1970—*).

HIGHER BROUGHTON
EP Cr 1879 [St James] from Broughton St John EP.[78] Salf. RDn.

LOWER BROUGHTON
EP Cr 1870 [The Ascension] from Broughton EP.[301] Eccles & Salf. RDn (1870—72), Salf. RDn (1872—*). Bdry: 1881 (help cr Lower Broughton St Clement EP).[216]

LOWER BROUGHTON ST CLEMENT
EP Cr 1881 from Broughton EP, Lower Broughton EP,

Cheetwood EP.[216] Salf. RDn. Abol 1967 to help cr Lower Broughton St Clement with St Matthias EP.[305]

LOWER BROUGHTON ST CLEMENT WITH ST MATTHIAS
EP Cr 1967 by union Lower Broughton St Clement EP, pt Salford St Matthias with St Simon EP.[305] Salf. RDn.

BROUGHTON EAST
Tp and chap (built 1745[322]) in Cartmel AP, sep CP 1866,[4] sep EP 1748 as 'Field Broughton',[12] as such eccl refounded 1875,[304] qv. *LG* Lonsd. Hd, Ulv. PLU, pt Grange USD, pt Ulv. RSD, Ulv. RD (1894—1960), N Lonsd. RD (1960—74). Civ bdry: 1884,[51] 1884,[52] 1884,[53] 1884,[55] 1884,[56] 1894 (loses the pt in the UD to help cr Grange CP),[58] 1914.[59] Transf 1974 to Cumbria.[40] *Parl* Seq 10.

BROUGHTON ST JOHN [THE EVANGELIST]
EP Cr 1878 from Broughton EP.[303] Salf. RDn.

BROUGHTON IN FURNESS
Chap in Kirkby Ireleth AP, sep EP [St Mary Magdalene] 1870,[306] sep CP 1866 as 'Broughton West',[4] qv. Ulv. RDn. Eccl bdry: 1886.[8] Abol 1956 to help cr Broughton in Furness with Woodland EP.[244]

BROUGHTON IN FURNESS WITH WOODLAND
EP Cr 1956 by union Broughton in Furness EP, Woodland EP.[244] Ulv. RDn (1956—70), Furness RDn (1970—*).

BROUGHTON WEST
Chap in Kirkby Ireleth AP, sep CP 1866,[4] sep EP 1870 [St Mary Magdalene] as 'Broughton in Furness',[307] qv. *LG* Seq 14. Bdry: 1935 (exchanges pts with Millom Rural CP, Cumb).[307] Transf 1974 to Cumbria.[40] *Parl* Seq 10.

BRUNSHAW
CP Cr 1894 from the pt of Burnley CP not in Burnley CB.[295] *LG* Burnley PLU, RD. Abol 1911 pt to Burnley CB (assoc with Lancs) & CP, pt to Cliviger CP.[309]

BRYN
EP Cr 1931 from Ashton in Makerfield EP, Ashton in Makerfield St Thomas EP.[95] Wigan RDn.

BRYNING WITH KELLAMERGH
Tp in Kirkham AP, sep CP 1866.[4] *LG* Amound. Hd, Fylde PLU, RSD, RD. Abol 1934 to help cr Bryning with Warton CP.[226] *Parl* N'rn Dv (1832—67), North Dv (1867—85), Blackp. Dv (1885—1918), Fylde Dv (1918—48).

BRYNING WITH WARTON
CP Cr 1934 by union ent Bryning with Kellarmergh CP, pts Lytham St Anne's CP, Ribby with Wrea CP, Warton CP.[226] *LG* Fylde RD. *Parl* S Fylde CC (1948—*).

BULK
Tp in Lancaster AP, sep CP 1866.[4] *LG* Lonsd. Hd, Lanc. PLU, RSD, RD. Abol 1900 pt to Lanc. MB & AP, pt to Quernmore CP.[309] *Parl* Pt Lanc. Parl Bor (1832—67), pt N'rn Dv (1832—67), North Dv (1867—85), Lanc. Dv (1885—1918).

BURNAGE
Tp in Manchester AP, sep CP 1866,[4] pt eccl severed 1853 to help cr Withington EP,[12] the latter refounded 1854,[199] 'Burnage' a sep EP 1875 from Withington EP, Barlow Moor EP.[150] *LG* Salf. Hd, Chorlton PLU, Withington USD, UD (1894—1904), Manch CB (1904—10). Civ bdry: 1883.[31] Abol civ 1910 ent to Manch CB (assoc with Lancs) and to South Manchester CP.[310] *Parl* S'rn Dv (1832—67), S-E Dv (1867—85), Stretf. Dv (1885—1918). *Eccl* Ardwick RDn (1875—1912), Heaton RDn (1912—*). Eccl bdry: 1900 (help cr Ladybarn EP),[202] 1905,[199] 1927,[135] 1929.[204]

BURNAGE ST NICHOLAS
EP Cr 1929 from Barlow Moor EP.[152] Heaton RDn.

BURNLEY
The following have 'Burnley' in their names. Insofar as any existed at a given time: *LG* Black. Hd, Burnley PLU, pt Burnley USD, pt Burnley MB (1861—89 [enlarged pt 1871—89]), Burnley CB (pt 1889—94, ent 1894—1974), pt Burnley RSD. *Parl* N'rn Dv (1832—67), Burnley Parl Bor/BC (1867—*). *Eccl* Blackb RDn (until 1847), Whalley RDn (1847—72), Burnley RDn (1872—*).

CP1/EP1—BURNLEY [ST PETER]—Chap in Whalley AP, sep CP 1866,[4] sep EP 1716 (incl tps Briercliffe with Extwistle, Cliviger, Habergham Eaves, Worsthorne with Hurstwood; also incl 2 civ tp/eccl ex-par areas of Ightenhill Park [eccl, 'Ighton Hill' until eccl abol 1845 to help cr Habergham All Saints EP[124]] and Reedley Hallows, Filly Close and New Laund Booth).[12] Civ bdry: 1894 (the pt not in the CB cr Brunshaw CP, and gains the pts in Burnley CB of Briercliffe with Extwistle CP, Habergham Eaves CP, Ightenhill Park CP; Reedley Hallows, Filly Close and New Laund Booth CP),[295] 1911,[308] 1926.[311] Eccl bdry: 1741 (pt orig area tp Cliviger cr 'Holme in Cliviger' EP,[12] refounded 1843 as 'Holme St John'[293]), 1837 (orig area tp Worsthorne with Hurstwood cr 'Worsthorne' EP,[12] as such refounded 1843[293]), 1843 (orig area tp Briercliffe with Extwistle cr 'Briercliffe' EP, pt orig area tp Habergham Eaves cr 'Habergham Eaves' EP),[293] 1844 (cr EP6),[144] 1845 (the remainder of orig tp Habergham Eaves [not severed in 1843] cr 'Lane Bridge' EP),[124] 1846,[312] 1851,[313] 1869 (cr EP3),[237] 1871,[149] 1879 (help cr EP9),[314] 1880,[315] 1889,[87] 1895,[316] 1898 (help cr EP7),[22] 1962.[317]

EP2—BURNLEY ST ALBAN WITH ST PAUL—Cr 1964 from EP4.[318]

EP3—BURNLEY ST ANDREW—Cr 1869 from EP1.[237] Bdry: 1890,[297] 1898 (help cr EP7),[22] 1908,[319] 1908 (help cr EP5).[294]

EP4—BURNLEY ST CATHERINE—Cr 1897 from EP9.[157] Bdry: 1964 (cr EP2).[318]

EP5—BURNLEY ST CUTHBERT—Cr 1908 from EP3, Briercliffe EP.[294]

EP6—BURNLEY ST JAMES—Cr 1844 from EP1.[144] Bdry: 1846,[312] 1871,[149] 1889,[87] 1895,[316] 1908,[319] 1908 (help cr EP5).[294]

—BURNLEY ST JOHN THE BAPTIST—Name used now for EP cr 1880 as 'Gannow', qv.

EP7—BURNLEY ST MARGARET—Cr 1898 from EP3, EP1.[22] Bdry: 1908.[319]

EP8—BURNLEY ST MARK—Cr 1959 from

Habergham All Saints EP, Gannow EP, Habergham Eaves EP, Habergham Eaves St Matthew the Apostle EP.[320]

EP9—BURNLEY ST STEPHEN—Cr 1879 from Lane Bridge EP, EP1.[314] Bdry: 1897 (cr EP4),[157] 1898,[321] 1962.[317]

BURROW WITH BURROW

Tp in Tunstal AP, sep CP 1866.[4] *LG* Lonsd. Hd, Lunesd. PLU, RSD, RD. *Parl* Seq 8.

BURSCOUGH

Tp in Ormskirk AP, sep CP 1866,[4] sep EP 1844 as 'Burscough Bridge' (incl pt tp Lathom in same par, church in the latter hence this par sometimes 'Lathom St John'),[322] qv. *LG* W Derby Hd, Ormsk. PLU, RSD (1875—94), Lathom & Burscough USD (1894), UD (1894—1931), Ormsk. UD (1931—74). Civ bdry: 1931.[126] *Parl* Seq 21.

BURSCOUGH BRIDGE

Tp in Ormskirk AP, sep EP 1844 (incl pt tp Lathom in same par, church in the latter hence this par sometimes 'Lathom St John'),[322] sep CP 1866 as 'Burscough',[4] qv. Warr. RDn (1844—47), Prescot RDn (1847—82), N Meols RDn (1882—87), Ormsk. RDn (1887—*).

BURTON

AP Usual civ spelling, eccl 'Burton in Kendal'. Westm par (Kendal Wd) incl in Lancs tp Dalton (Lonsd. Hd, sep CP 1866 in Lancs[4]) so that this par ent Westm thereafter. See main entry in Westm.

BURTON IN KENDAL—see prev entry

BURTON WOOD

Chap in Warrington AP, sep EP 1740,[12] eccl refounded 1898,[323] sep CP 1866 as 'Burtonwood',[4] qv. *Eccl* Warr. RDn (1740—1847), Winwick RDn (1847—1949), Warr. RDn (1949—*).

BURTONWOOD

Chap in Warrington AP, sep CP 1866,[4] sep EP 1740 as 'Burton Wood',[12] as such eccl refounded 1898,[324] qv. *LG* Seq 19. Civ bdry: 1933 (loses pt to Warr. CB [assoc with Lancs] & AP).[324] Transf 1974 to Ches.[40] *Parl* Seq 19.

BURY

The following have 'Bury' in their names. Insofar as any existed at a given time: *LG* Bury PLU, USD, MB (1876—89), CB (1889—1974); Hd sep noted. *Parl* Bury Parl Bor (1832—1948), Bury & Radcl. BC (1948—*). *Eccl* Manch & Blackb RDn (until before 1535), Manch RDn (before 1535—1850), Bury RDn (1850—*).

AP1—BURY [ST MARY]—Tp 'Bury' in Salf. Hd as were chap Edenfield (sep EP 1725 incl area Shuttleworth [qv in tp Walmersley cum Shuttleworth below for sep civ status][12]), chap Heywood (civ in tp Heap, 'Heywood' not sep civ until 1894, qv for constituent pars then, pt chap Heywood eccl severed 1720 to cr Heywood St James EP,[12] pt eccl severed 1843 to help refounded Birch EP,[193] another pt of orig chap not in Heywood St James EP eccl severed 1848 to help cr Bircle EP,[206] the remainder of the orig chap of Heywood cr 1864 Heywood St Luke EP[325]), chap Walmersley (sep EP 1741,[12] civ pt of tp Walmersley cum Shuttleworth, qv below for sep

civ status); incl also tp Elton (sep CP 1866,[4] sep EP 1844[326]), tp Heap (sep CP 1866,[4] incl area chap Heywood, qv above for cr of 4 EPs, 'Heap' a sep EP 1864 from Bury AP[325]), tp Tottington Higher End (sep CP 1866,[4] eccl severed 1802 and united with the pt of orig tp Tottington Lower End not in Holcombe EP to cr 'Tottington' EP,[12] the area as such refounded 1844[326]), tp Tottington Lower End (sep CP 1866,[4] pt eccl severed 1725 to help cr Holcombe EP,[12] the latter eccl refounded 1863,[327] the remainder of orig area of the tp eccl severed 1802 to help cr 'Tottington' EP,[12] qv above for refounding), tp Walmersley cum Shuttleworth (sep CP 1866,[4] the area of chap Walmersley in the tp a sep EP 1741,[12] the area of hmlt Shuttleworth eccl severed 1725 to help cr Edenfield EP,[12] 'Shuttleworth' a sep EP 1845 from Edenfield EP [the area of the orig hmlt], Walmersley EP[328]); incl in Blackb Hd tp Cowpe Lench, Newhall Hey and Hall Carr (this single tp a sep CP 1866[4]), tp Musbury (sep CP 1866,[4] sep EP 1844 by union tp Musbury and pts Edenfield EP, Haslingden EP[112]). Addtl civ bdry alt: 1894 (gains the pts in Bury CB of Birtle cum Bamford CP, Elton CP, Heap CP, Pilkington CP, Pilsworth CP, Radcliffe AP, Tottington Lower End CP, Walmersley cum Shuttleworth CP),[115] 1911,[329] 1933,[330] 1933 (incl exchanges pts with Radcl. MB & AP),[37] 1937 (exchanges pts with Whitefield UD & CP).[331] Addtl eccl bdry alt: 1781 (cr EP2,[12] refounded 1859[332]), 1843 (cr EP4),[333] 1866 (cr EP1),[132] 1866 (cr Waterfoot EP),[50] 1867 (help cr EP6),[35] 1873 (help cr EP5),[194] 1965.[334]

EP1—BURY MOST HOLY TRINITY—Cr 1866 from AP1.[132] Bdry: 1957.[335]

EP2—BURY ST JOHN—Cr 1781 from AP1,[12] refounded 1859.[332] Bdry: 1958.[44]

EP3—BURY ST MARK—Cr 1885 from EP4.[317]

EP4—BURY ST PAUL—Cr 1843 from AP1.[333] Bdry: 1867 (help cr EP6),[35] 1885 (cr EP3),[317] 1957.[335]

EP5—BURY ST PETER—Cr 1873 from AP1, Radcliffe AP.[194] Bdry: 1965,[336] 1973.[269]

EP6—BURY ST THOMAS—Cr 1867 from EP4, AP1.[35]

NEW BURY

EP Cr 1866 from Farnworth with Kearsley EP.[272] Bolton le Moors EP (1866—93), Bolton South RDn (1893—1901), Bolton le Moors RDn (1901—68), Farnw. RDn (1968—*). Bdry: 1880 (help cr Dixon Green EP),[42] 1887 (help cr Farnworth St Peter, Bradford Street EP),[337] 1923.[233]

BUTTERWORTH

Tp (incl chap Milnrow [orig oratory], sep EP 1717[12]; see below for civ) in Rochdale AP, sep CP 1866.[4] *LG* Salf. Hd, Rochd. PLU, pt Littleborough USD, pt Milnrow USD, pt Wuerdle & Wardle USD, pt Rochd. USD, pt Rochd. MB (1856—89 [enlarged pt 1872—89]), pt Rochd. CB (1889—94). Abol 1894 the pt in Littleborough UD to help cr Littleborough CP, the pt in Milnrow UD to help cr Milnrow CP, the pt in Wuerdle & Wardle UD to help cr Wardle UD & CP, the pt in the CB to help cr

Rochdale CP.[257] *Parl* S'rn Dv (1832—67), pt Rochd. Parl Bor (1867—1918), pt S-E Dv (1867—85), pt Middl. Dv (1885—1918).

CABUS

Tp in Garstang AP, sep CP 1866.[4] *LG* Seq 2. Bdry: 1887,[155] 1935.[43] *Parl* Seq 7.

CADISHEAD

EP Cr 1925 from 2 Lancs pars (both dioc Manch) of Irlam EP, Flixton AP and from 2 Ches pars (both dioc Chester) of Partington EP, Carrington EP,[338] to be in dioc Manch. Eccles RDn.

CALDER VALE

EP Cr 1864 from Garstang AP (pt tps Claughton, Barnacre with Bonds, Catterall), Admarsh EP.[154] Garst. RDn. Bdry: 1911 (help cr Barnacre EP).[153]

CALDERBROOK

EP Cr 1896 from Littleborough EP.[194] Rochd. RDn.

CANTRIL FARM

EP Cr 1971 from West Derby St Luke EP.[150] W Derby RDn.

CANTSFIELD

Tp in Tunstal AP, sep CP 1866.[4] *LG* Lonsd. Hd, Lunesd. PLU, RSD, RD. *Parl* Seq 8.

CARLETON

Tp in Poulton le Fylde AP, sep CP 1866.[4] *LG* Amound. Hd, Fylde PLU, RSD, RD. Civ bdry: 1887,[215] 1918 (loses pt to Blackp. CB [assoc with Lancs] & CP).[218] Abol 1934 pt to Blackp. CB (assoc with Lancs) & CP, pt to Poulton le Fylde UD & AP, pt to Thornton Clevelys UD and to Thornton CP.[226] *Parl* N'rn Dv (1832—67), North Dv (1867—85), Blackp. Dv (1885—1918), Fylde Dv (1918—48). Parl bdry: 1945.[339]

CARNFORTH

Tp in Warton AP, sep CP 1866,[4] sep EP 1875.[85] *LG* Lonsd. Hd, Lanc. PLU, RSD, Carnforth UD. *Parl* Seq 9. *Eccl* Tunstall RDn.

CARTMEL

AP Incl tp and chap (built 1741[303]) Broughton East (sep CP 1866,[4] sep EP [pec jurisd Dean and Chapter of York, until 1836] 1748 as 'Field Broughton',[12] as such eccl refounded 1875[304]), chap Cartmel Fell (sep CP 1866,[4] sep EP 1718[12]), chap Staveley (sep CP 1866,[4] sep EP 1718,[12] eccl refounded 1876[340]), tps Lower Allithwaite, Upper Allithwaite (each a sep CP 1866,[4] the 2 united 1866 as 'Allithwaite' EP[50]), tp Little Holker (incl Flookburgh Bor, bor status not sustained, 'Lower Holker' a sep CP 1866[4], 'Flookburgh' a sep EP 1723,[12] as such refounded 1879[16]), tp Upper Holker (sep CP 1866,[4] pt eccl severed 1858 and transf to Haverthwaite EP[128]) so that 'Cartmel' has no sep civ identity after 1866. *LG* Lonsd. Hd. *Parl* N'rn Dv (1832—67). *Eccl* Lanc. RDn (until before 1291), Copel. RDn (before 1291—before 1541), Furness & Cartmel RDn (before 1541—1859), Cartmel RDn (1859—1970), Windermere RDn (1970—*). Addtl eccl bdry alt: 1734 (cr Lindale EP),[12] 1884 (pt of Cartmel AP and ent area of eccl ex-par Holme Island situated in this par cr 'Grange Sands' EP).[234]

CARTMEL FELL

Chap in Cartmel AP, sep CP 1866,[4] sep EP 1718.[12] *LG* Seq 14. Civ bdry: 1884,[341] 1884.[56] Transf 1974

to Cumbria.[40] *Parl* Seq 10. *Eccl* Furness & Cartmel RDn (1718—1859), Cartmel RDn (1859—1970), Windermere RDn (1970—73), Kendal RDn (1973—*).

CASTLETON

Tp in Rochdale AP, sep CP 1866,[4] pt eccl severed 1863 to cr Castleton Moor EP,[342] pt eccl severed 1865 to help cr Balderstone EP.[119] *LG* Salf. Hd, Rochd. PLU, pt Heyw. USD, pt Heyw. MB (1881—94), pt Milnrow USD, pt Castleton by Rochd. USD, pt Rochd. USD, Rochd. MB (pt 1856—72, enlarged pt 1872—89), pt Rochd. CB (1889—94). Abol civ 1894 the pt in Heyw. MB to help cr Heywood CP, the pt in Milnrow UD to help cr Milnrow CP,[257] the pt in Castleton by Rochd. UD to help cr Castleton by Rochdale CP,[343] the pt in Rochd. CB to help cr Rochdale CP.[257] *Parl* Pt Rochd. Parl Bor (1832—1918 [enlarged pt 1867—1918]), pt S'rn Dv (1832—67), pt S-E Dv (1867—85), pt Middl. Dv (1885—1918).

CASTLETON ALL SOULS

EP Cr 1896 from Castleton Moor EP.[227] Rochd. RDn (1896—1929), Bury RDn (1929—*). Bdry: 1913 (help cr Rochdale St Aidan, Sudden EP).[344] Now called 'Heywood All Souls'.

CASTLETON BY ROCHDALE

CP Cr 1894 by union of the following in Castleton by Rochd. UD: pt Castleton CP, pt Hopwood CP, pt Thornham CP.[343] *LG* Rochd. PLU, Castleton by Rochd. UD. Renamed 1896 'Castleton, Lancashire' CP.[345]

CASTLETON, LANCASHIRE

CP Renaming 1896 of Castleton by Rochdale CP.[345] *LG* Rochd. PLU, Castleton by Rochdale UD. Abol 1900 pt to Rochd. CB (assoc with Lancs) & CP, pt to Heyw. MB & CP.[176]

CASTLETON MOOR

EP Cr 1863 from Rochdale AP (pt tp Castleton).[342] Rochd. RDn. Bdry: 1896 (cr Castleton All Souls EP, now called 'Heywood All Souls').[227] Bdry: 1913 (help cr Rochdale St Aidan, Sudden EP),[344] 1964 (help cr Kirkholt EP).[136]

CATON

Tp in Lancaster AP, sep CP 1866,[4] sep EP 1737 as 'Caton with Littledale'.[12] qv. *LG* Seq 13. *Parl* Seq 8.

CATON WITH LITTLEDALE

Tp in Lancaster AP, sep EP 1737,[12] sep CP 1866 as 'Caton',[4] qv. *Eccl* Amound. RDn (1737—1852), Lanc. RDn (1852—*).

CATTERALL

Tp in Garstang AP, sep CP 1866,[4] pt eccl severed 1864 to help cr Calder Vale EP.[154] *LG* Seq 2. Bdry: 1887.[155] *Parl* Seq 7.

CHADDERTON

The following have 'Chadderton' in their names. Insofar as any existed at a given time: *LG* Salf. Hd, Oldham PLU, Chadderton USD, UD. *Parl* Oldham Parl Bor (1832—1918), Middl. & Prestw. Dv (1918—48), Oldham West BC (1948—*). *Eccl* Manch. RDn (cr—1847), Rochd. RDn (1847—72), Oldham RDn (1872—1912), Middl. RDn (1912—*).

CP1—CHADDERTON—Tp in Prestwich AP, sep CP 1866, eccl in chap Oldham (sep EP 1746 from Prestwich AP[12]), pt orig area tp Chadderton severed 1835 from Oldham EP to cr Hollinwood EP as the remainder refounded as 'Oldham'.[182] Bdry: 1933 (incl exchanges pts with Manch CB [assoc with Lancs] & AP).[171] Transf 1974 to Gtr Manch.[40]

EP1—CHADDERTON CHRIST CHURCH—Cr 1871 from EP3, Hollinwood EP.[16] Bdry: 1885 (help cr Middleton Junction EP),[317] 1911 (cr EP2),[193] 1927,[346] 1928.[48]

EP2—CHADDERTON EMMANUEL—Cr 1911 from EP1.[193] Bdry: 1927.[346] 1966.[347]

EP3—CHADDERTON ST JOHN—Cr 1844 from Hollinwood EP.[348] Bdry: 1871 (help cr EP1),[16] 1928.[48] Renamed 1945 'Oldham St John Werneth' EP.[139]

EP4—CHADDERTON ST LUKE—Cr 1889 from EP6.[349]

EP5—CHADDERTON ST MARK—Cr 1922 from EP6.[232]

EP6—CHADDERTON ST MATTHEW—Cr 1844 from Hollinwood EP.[348] Bdry: 1885 (help cr Middleton Junction EP),[317] 1889 (cr EP4),[349] 1912,[96] 1922 (cr EP5).[232]

CHARLESTOWN
EP Cr 1860 from Pendleton EP.[254] Eccles RDn (1860—66), Eccles & Salf. RDn (1866—72), Salf. RDn (1872—1973). Bdry: 1888 (cr Pendleton St Barnabas EP),[350] 1972 (help cr Lower Kersal EP).[351] Abol 1973 to help cr Charlestown St George with St Barnabas EP.[352]

CHARLESTOWN ST GEORGE WITH ST BARNABAS
EP Cr 1973 by union Charlestown EP, Pendleton EP.[352] Salf. RDn.

CHARNOCK RICHARD
Tp in Standish AP, sep CP 1866,[4] eccl severed 1717 to help cr Coppull EP,[12] 'Charnock Richard' a sep EP 1861 (incl orig area tp Welsh Whittle, severed 1717 from Standish AP to help cr Coppull EP) from Coppull EP.[304] LG Seq 8. Civ bdry: 1934 (gains Welsh Whittle CP).[226] Parl Seq 3. Eccl Leyl. RDn (1861—1964), Chorley RDn (1964—*). Eccl bdry: 1959,[24] 1959 (help cr Chorley All Saints EP).[25]

CHATBURN
Tp in Whalley AP, sep CP 1866,[4] sep EP 1843 (incl tp Worston in same par).[293] LG Seq 6. Parl Seq 1. Eccl Blackb RDn (1843—47), Whalley RDn (1847—*).

CHEETHAM
The following have 'Cheetham' or 'Cheetham Hill' in their names. Insofar as any existed at a given time: LG Salf. Hd, Manch PLU (1840—50), Prestw. PLU (1850—96), Manch MB (1838—89), CB (1889—96), USD. Parl Manch Parl Bor (1832—85), Manch, N-W Dv Parl Bor (1885—1918). Eccl Manch RDn (cr—1872), Cheetham RDn (1872—*).

CP1—CHEETHAM—Tp and chap (St Mark, built 1794[353]) in Manchester AP, sep CP 1866,[4] pt of the tp which incl the chap a sep EP 1839 as EP4,[74] eccl refounded 1856,[83] qv, pt of tp Cheetham eccl severed 1856 to help cr EP3.[83] This CP abol 1896 to help cr North Manchester CP.[82]

EP1—CHEETHAM ST JOHN THE EVANGELIST—Cr 1872 from EP3.[85]

EP2—CHEETHAM ST SAVIOUR—Cr 1904 from Manchester AP, Cheetwood EP.[140] Abol 1945 ent to Cheetwood EP.[354]

EP3—CHEETHAM HILL ST LUKE—Cr 1856 from Manchester AP (pt tp Cheetham, the pt of tp Crumpsall not severed 1839 to help cr EP4).[83] Bdry: 1859 (help cr Crumpsall EP,[12] refounded 1860[102]), 1863 (help cr Lower Cumpsall EP,[12] refounded 1864[6]), 1872 (cr EP1),[85] 1873.[355]

EP4—CHEETHAM HILL ST MARK—Pt of tp Cheetham (incl the chap [built 1794[353]]) cr a sep EP 1839 (incl pt tp Crumpsall in the same par) as EP4,[353] eccl refounded 1856.[83] Manch RDn (1839—72), Cheetham RDn (1872—*). Bdry: 1859 (help cr Crumpsall EP,[12] refounded 1860[102]), 1901,[241] 1909,[356] 1910 (help cr Crumpsall St Matthew EP).[111]

CHEETWOOD
EP Cr 1874 from Manchester AP.[357] Cathedral RDn. Bdry: 1881,[358] 1881 (help cr Lower Broughton St Clement EP),[216] 1904 (help cr Cheetham St Saviour EP),[140] 1945 (gains Cheetham St Saviour EP).[354]

CHILDWALL
AP Incl chap Garston (sep CP 1866,[4] the orig chap of St Wilfrid in ruins by 16th cent and new chap St Michael erected later,[359] sep EP 1729 [incl pt tp Speke],[12] eccl refounded 1828[75]), chap Hale (sep CP 1866,[4] sep EP 1732 [incl pt tp Speke],[12] eccl refounded 1828[75]), tp Allerton (sep CP 1866,[4] sep EP 1876[46]), tp Halewood (sep CP 1866,[4] sep EP 1845[12]), tp Speke (sep CP 1866,[4] pt eccl severed 1729 to help cr Garston EP [qv for later refounding],[12] the remainder eccl severed 1732 to help cr Hale EP [qv for later refounding],[12] the orig area of tp Speke a sep EP 1875 as 'Speke' from Garston EP, Hale EP[150]), tp Wavertree (sep CP 1866,[4] sep EP 1825,[12] eccl refounded 1828[75]), tp Little Woolton (sep CP 1866,[4] pt eccl severed 1893 to help cr Gateacre EP[360]), tp Much Woolton (sep CP 1866,[4] pt a sep EP 1827,[12] eccl refounded 1828,[75] the remainder of the orig tp severed 1893 to help cr Gateacre EP[360]). LG W Derby Hd, PLU, Childwall USD, UD (1894—1913), Liverp CB (1913—22). Abol civ 1922 ent to Liverpool CP.[47] Parl S'rn Dv (1832—67), S-W Dv (1867—85), Bootle Dv (1885—1918); see Part III of the Guide for composition of Liverp Parl Bors (1918—48) by wards of the CB. Eccl Warr. RDn (until 1847), Prescot RDn (1847—82), Childwall RDn (1882—*). Addtl eccl bdry alt: 1877,[272] 1927 (help refound Knotty Ash St John the Evangelist EP),[346] 1937 (cr Childwall St David EP),[150] 1964.[49]

CHILDWALL ST DAVID
EP Cr 1937 from Childwall AP.[150] Childwall RDn. Bdry: 1964.[49]

CHIPPING
AP Perhaps orig a chap in Preston AP, sep par no later than 13th cent.[361] Incl tp Thornley with Wheatley (sep CP 1866[4]). LG Seq 6. Parl Seq 13. Eccl Seq 9.

CHORLEY

The following have 'Chorley' in their names. Insofar as any existed at a given time: *LG* Leyl. Hd, Chorley Bor, PLU, USD, MB (1881—1974). *Parl* Seq 3. *Eccl* Leyl. RDn (cr—1964), Chorley RDn (1964—*).

CP1/EP1—CHORLEY [ST LAURENCE]—Chap and bor in Croston AP, sep par 1793.[362] Civ bdry: 1934.[363] Eccl bdry: 1835 (cr EP5),[364] 1835 (cr EP3),[134] 1879 (help cr EP4),[83] 1959.[24]

EP2—CHORLEY ALL SAINTS—Cr 1959 from Adlington EP, Charnock Richard EP, EP3.[25]

EP3—CHORLEY ST GEORGE—Cr 1835 from EP1.[134] Bdry: 1879 (help cr EP4),[83] 1959,[24] 1959 (help cr EP2).[25]

EP4—CHORLEY ST JAMES—Cr 1879 from EP3, EP1.[83]

EP5—CHORLEY ST PETER—Cr 1835 from EP1.[364]

CHORLTON CUM HARDY

Chap in Manchester AP, sep CP 1866,[4] sep EP 1723,[12] eccl refounded 1839,[74] eccl refounded 1854.[199] *LG* Salf. Hd, Chorlton PLU, Withington USD, UD (1894—1904), Manch CB (1904—10). Civ bdry: 1883.[31] Abol civ 1910 ent to South Manchester CP.[310] *Parl* S'rn Dv (1832—67), S-E Dv (1867—85), Stretf. Dv (1885—1918). *Eccl* Manch RDn (1723—66), Chorlton & Hulme RDn (1866—72), Hulme RDn (1872—1933), Stretf. RDn (1933—*). Eccl bdry: 1882 (help cr Didsbury Christ Church, Barlow Moor Road EP),[151] 1898 (help cr Chorlton cum Hardy St Werburgh EP),[323] 1930,[365] 1958.[366]

CHORLTON CUM HARDY ST WERBURGH

EP Cr 1898 from Chorlton cum Hardy EP, Fallowfield EP.[323] Hulme RDn (1898—1933), Stretf. RDn (1933—*). Bdry: 1902,[230] 1905,[195] 1916 (help cr Withington St Crispin EP).[110]

CHORLTON ON MEDLOCK

The following have 'Chorlton on Medlock' or 'Chorlton upon Medlock' in their names. Insofar as any existed at a given time: *LG* Salf. Hd, Chorlton PLU, Manch MB (1838—89), CB (1889—96), USD. *Parl* Manch Parl Bor (1832—85), pt Manch, East Parl Bor, pt Manch, South Parl Bor (1885—1918). *Eccl* Manch RDn (cr—1855), Chorlton RDn (1855—66), Chorlton & Hulme RDn (1866—72), Hulme RDn (1872—*).

CP1/EP1—CHORLTON ON/UPON MEDLOCK [ALL SAINTS]—Tp in Manchester AP, sep CP 1866 ('upon'),[4] sep EP 1823,[12] eccl refounded 1839,[367] orig eccl 'upon', later 'on'. Civ bdry: 1883.[31] Abol civ 1896 to help cr South Manchester CP.[82] Eccl bdry: 1859 (help cr Hulme St John EP, cr EP2),[365] 1858 (help cr Moss Side EP),[70] 1861 (cr Hulme St Philip EP),[181] 1885 (cr EP5).[368]

EP2—CHORLTON ON MEDLOCK ST LUKE—Cr 1859 from EP1.[365] Abol 1962 to help cr EP3.[369]

EP3—CHORLTON ON MEDLOCK ST PAUL WITH ST LUKE—Cr 1962 by union EP2, EP7.[369]

EP4—CHORLTON ON MEDLOCK ST STEPHEN—Cr 1856 from EP6 (sometimes early 'Manchester St Saviour').[83] Bdry: 1869 (help cr Ardwick St Matthew EP),[368] 1876 (help cr Longsight St Clement EP).[90] Abol 1971 to help cr Longsight St Luke EP.[370]

—CHORLTON UPON MEDLOCK [ALL SAINTS]—see CP1/EP1

EP5—CHORLTON UPON MEDLOCK ST AMBROSE—Cr 1885 from EP1.[368] Bdry: 1902,[230] 1966,[23] 1967.[322]

EP6—CHORLTON UPON MEDLOCK ST SAVIOUR—Cr 1851 from Manchester AP,[12] refounded 1856.[83] Sometimes early 'Manchester St Saviour'. Bdry: 1856 (cr EP4),[83] 1862 (cr EP7),[321] 1878 (help cr Manchester St Chrysostom, Victoria Park EP),[35] 1955,[86] 1967.[322]

EP7—CHORLTON UPON MEDLOCK ST PAUL—Cr 1862 from EP6.[321] Abol 1962 to help cr EP3.[369]

CHURCH

Tp in Whalley AP, sep CP 1866,[4] sep EP 1723 (incl tps Huncoat, Oswaldtwistle, pt tp Clayton le Moors, all in the same par) as 'Church Kirk',[12] qv. *LG* Blackb Hd, PLU, Church USD, UD. *Parl* N'rn Dv (1832—67), N-E Dv (1867—85), Accr. Dv (1885—1918), Accr. Parl Bor/BC (1918—*).

CHURCH KIRK

Tp in Whalley AP, sep EP 1723 (incl tps Huncoat, Oswaldtwisle, pt tp Clayton le Moors, all in the same par),[12] sep CP 1866 as 'Church',[4] qv. *Eccl* Blackb RDn (1723—1847), Whalley RDn (1847—66), Accr. RDn (1866—72), Whalley RDn (1872—1912), Accr. RDn (1912—*). Eccl bdry: 1885 (cr Oswaldtwistle St Paul EP),[371] 1950,[214] 1966 (help cr Oswaldtwistle All Saints EP).[372]

CHURCH TOWN—see GARSTANG

CLAIFE

Tp in Hawkshead AP, sep CP 1866.[4] *LG* Seq 14. Transf 1974 to Cumbria.[40] *Parl* Seq 10.

CLAREMONT

EP Cr 1925 from Pendlebury EP, Brindle Heath EP, Hope EP.[221] Salf. RDn. Bdry: 1971.[299] Now sometimes called 'Pendleton Holy Angels (Claremont)'.

CLAUGHTON

AP *LG* Seq 13. *Parl* Seq 8. *Eccl* Lanc. RDn (until before 1291), Kirkby Lonsd. & Kendal RDn (before 1291—before 1541), Kirkby Lonsd. RDn (before 1541—1848), Tunstall RDn (1848—1931). Abol eccl 1931 to help cr Hornby with Claughton EP.[50]

CLAUGHTON

Tp in Garstang AP, sep CP 1866,[4] pt eccl severed 1864 to help cr Calder Vale EP.[154] *LG* Seq 2. *Parl* Seq 7.

CLAYTON

Area in Droylsden CP/EP, sep EP 1874,[232] sep CP 1894 (the pt of Droylsden CP in Manch CB).[373] *LG* Prestw. PLU, Manch CB. Abol civ 1896 to help cr North Manchester CP.[82] *Eccl* Ardwick RDn. Eccl bdry: 1905 (help cr Manchester St Paul, Bradford EP),[123] 1913 (help cr Droylsden St Andrew EP),[112] 1921.[3] Abol eccl 1970 to help cr Manchester St Cross with St Paul, Clayton EP.[374]

CLAYTON LE DALE

Tp in Blackburn AP, sep CP 1866.[4] *LG* Seq 4.

Bdry: 1934.[226] *Parl* Seq 12.

CLAYTON LE MOORS

Tp in Whalley AP, sep CP 1866,[4] pt eccl in chap Church Kirk (sep EP 1723 from Whalley AP[12]), pt eccl in chap Altham (sep EP 1723 from Whalley AP[12]), 'Clayton le Moors' a sep EP 1840 from Altham EP.[68] *LG* Blackb Hd, PLU, Clayton le Moors USD, UD. *Parl* N'rn Dv (1832—67), N-E Dv (1867—85), Accr. Dv (1885—1918), Accr. Parl Bor/BC (1918—*). *Eccl* Blackb RDn (1840—47), Whalley RDn (1847—66), Accr. RDn (1866—72), Whalley RDn (1872—1912), Accr. RDn (1912—*).

CLAYTON LE WOODS

Tp in Leyland AP, sep CP 1866.[4] *LG* Seq 8. *Parl* Seq 3.

CLEVELEY

Tp pt in Garstang AP (Amound. Hd), pt in Cockerham AP (Lonsd. Hd), sep CP 1866,[4] the pt in Garstang AP eccl severed and joined to the remainder of orig tp Cleveley to help refound Shireshead EP.[272] *LG* Garst. PLU, RSD, RD. Bdry: 1877,[155] 1887.[375] Abol civ 1935 ent to Forton CP.[43] *Parl* N'rn Dv (1832—67), North Dv (1867—85), Lanc. Dv (1885—1948).

CLEVELEYS

EP Cr 1911 from Thorton EP, Bispham AP.[213] The Fylde RDn (1911—63), Blackp. RDn (1963—*).

CLIFTON

Tp in Eccles AP, sep CP 1866,[4] sep EP 1875.[304] *LG* Salf. Hd, not in a PLU (until 1849), Barton upon Irwell PLU (1849—1930), RSD, RD. Abol civ 1933 pt to Kearsley UD & CP, pt to help cr Swinton & Pendlebury MB & CP.[171] *Parl* S'rn Dv (1832—67), S-E Dv (1867—85), Eccles Dv (1885—1918), Farnw. Dv (1918—48). *Eccl* Eccles RDn. Eccl bdry: 1974 (cr Clifton Green EP).[376]

CLIFTON GREEN

EP Cr 1974 from Clifton EP.[376] Eccles RDn.

CLIFTON WITH SALWICK

Tp in Kirkham AP, sep CP 1866,[4] sep EP 1737 as 'Lund',[12] as such eccl refounded 1840.[377] *LG* Amound. Hd, Flyde PLU, RSD, RD. Abol 1934 pt to help cr Newton with Clifton CP, pt to Hutton CP.[226] *Parl* N'rn Dv (1832—67), North Dv (1867—85), Blackp. Dv (1885—1918), Fylde Dv (1918—48).

CLITHEROE

Tp in Whalley AP, sep CP 1866,[4] sep EP 1723.[12] *LG* Blackp. Hd, Clith. PLU, Bor/MB, USD. Civ bdry: 1895 (gains Clitheroe Castle CP).[378] *Parl* Clith. Parl Bor (1558—1885), Clith. Dv/CC (1885—*). *Eccl* Blackb RDn (1723—1847), Whalley RDn (1847—*). Eccl bdry: 1871 (cr Clitheroe St Paul, Low Moor EP).[379]

CLITHEROE CASTLE

Ex-par place, sep CP 1858.[80] *LG* Blackb Hd, Clith. PLU (1858—95), RSD, RD. Abol civ 1895 ent to Clitheroe CP.[378] *Parl* Clith. Parl. Bor (1832—85), Clith. Dv (1885—1918).

CLITHEROE ST JAMES

EP Cr 1839 from Whalley AP (incl area tp Pendelton).[380] Blackb RDn (1839—47), Whalley RDn (1847—*). Bdry: 1873 (area of orig tp Pendleton severed to help cr Pendleton in Whalley EP),[298] 1953.[381]

CLITHEROE ST PAUL, LOW MOOR

EP Cr 1871 from Clitheroe EP.[379] Whalley RDn. Bdry: 1953.[381]

CLIVIGER

Tp in Whalley AP, sep CP 1866,[4] incl area Holme in Cliviger (not sep civ, eccl in chap Burnley [sep EP 1716 from Whalley AP[12]], pt of the orig tp a sep EP 1741 from Burnley EP as 'Holme in Cliviger',[12] eccl refounded 1843 as 'Holme St John'[298]). *LG* Blackb Hd, Burnley PLU, pt Todmorden USD (primarily Yorks W Riding, and hence pt of that Adm Co 1889), pt Burnley RSD, Burnley RD. Civ bdry: 1894 (the pt in Yorks W Riding, in Todmorden UD, severed to cr Cornholme CP in that co,[382] so that 'Cliviger' ent Lancs thereafter), 1901,[308] 1911 (incl loses pt to Burnley CB [assoc with Lancs] & CP),[309] 1914.[383] *Parl* Seq 13.

CLOUGH FOLD—see RAWTENSTALL ST JOHN, CLOUGH FOLD

CLUBMOOR

EP Cr 1927 from West Derby EP.[3] W Derby RDn.

COCKERHAM

AP Incl chap Ellel (sep CP 1866,[4] pt a sep EP 1734,[12] eccl refounded 1866[384]), pt chap Pilling (sep CP 1866,[4] sep EP 1756[12]), pts tps Cleveley, Forton (each a sep CP 1866,[4] the pts of each tp in this par eccl severed 1858 to help refound Shireshead EP[272]), pt tp Holleth (sep CP 1866[4]), pt tp Thurnham (sep CP 1866[4]). *LG* Seq 12. *Parl* Seq 6. *Eccl* Lanc. RDn (until before 1291), Amound. RDn (before 1291—1852), Garst. RDn (1852—66), Lanc. RDn (1866—*). Addtl eccl bdry alt: 1747 (cr Shireshead EP,[12] refounded 1858 from Ellel EP, Garstang AP [pt tp Cleveley, pt tp Nether Wyresdale], Cockerham AP [pt tp Forton, pt tp Cleveley][272]).

COCKERSAND ABBEY

Ex-par place, sep CP 1858.[80] *LG* Lonsd. Hd, Lanc. PLU (1858—1930), RSD, RD. Civ bdry: 1887.[385] Abol civ 1935 ent to Thurnham CP.[43] *Parl* N'rn Dv (1832—67), North Dv (1867—85), Lanc. Dv (1885—1948).

COLDHURST

EP Cr 1844 from Oldham EP.[348] Manch RDn (1844—47), Rochd. RDn (1847—72), Oldham RDn (1872—*). Bdry: 1892 (help cr Oldham All Saints EP),[44] 1912,[96] 1957.[386]

COLLYHURST

The following have 'Collyhurst' in their names. Insofar as any existed at a given time: *Eccl* Manch RDn (cr—1872), Cheetham RDn (1872—*).

EP1—COLLYHURST ST JAMES—Cr 1874 from Manchester The Albert Memorial Church EP.[387] Abol 1972 to help cr EP4.[388]

EP2—COLLYHURST ST OSWALD—Cr 1856 from Manchester St Michael EP.[83] Bdry: 1860 (help cr Manchester St Catherine EP).[149] Abol 1967 to help cr EP3.[146]

EP3—COLLYHURST ST OSWALD AND ST CATHERINE—Cr 1967 by union EP2, Manchester St Catherine EP.[146] Abol 1972 to help cr EP4.[388]

EP4—COLLYHURST ST SAVIOUR—Cr 1972 by union EP1, EP3, Manchester Albert Memorial Church with Newton Heath St Augustine EP.[388]

COLNE

Tp in Whalley AP, sep CP 1866,[4] sep EP 1820 (incl tp Barrowford Booth, tp Foulridge, pt Trawden, area Great Marsden [civ in tp Great and Little Marsden, qv below], all in same par).[12] *LG* Blackb Hd, Burnley PLU, Colne & Marsden USD (1875—94), Colne USD (1894), UD (1894—95), MB (1895—1974). Civ bdry: 1894 (gains the pt of Great and Little Marsden CP in Colne & Marsden USD,[389] the USD renamed 2 days later 'Colne'),[390] 1935.[43] *Parl* N'rn Dv (1832—67), N-E Dv (1867—85), Clith. Dv (1885—1918), Nelson & Colne Parl Bor/BC (1918—*). *Eccl* Blackb RDn (1820—47), Whalley RDn (1847—72), Burnley RDn (1872—1968), Pendle RDn (1968—*). Eccl bdry: 1836 (help cr Colne Christ Church EP [incl pt area orig tp Trawden]),[12] 1845 (orig area of Great Marsden and an addtl pt of this par severed to cr Great Marsden EP),[124] 1905 (help cr Foulridge EP),[391] 1913 (help cr Colne Holy Trinity EP),[2] 1914.[147]

COLNE CHRIST CHURCH

EP Cr 1836 from Whalley AP, Colne EP (orig area pt tp Trawden, orig area Great Marsden).[12] Blackb RDn (1836—47), Whalley RDn (1847—72), Burnley RDn (1872—1968), Pendle RDn (1968—*). Bdry: 1845 (the pt of orig area tp Trawden cr 'Trawden' EP),[118] 1845 (the orig area Great Marsden severed to help cr Great Marsden EP),[118] 1905 (help cr Foulridge EP).[118]

COLNE HOLY TRINITY

EP Cr 1913 from Great Marsden EP, Colne EP.[2] Burnley RDn (1913—68), Pendle RDn (1968—*).

COLTON

Chap orig in Dalton in Furness AP, then in Hawkshead AP when the latter a sep par 1578 from Dalton in Furness AP,[392] 'Colton' a sep par 1676 from Hawkshead.[393] Sometimes 'Coulton'. *LG* Seq 14. Civ bdry: 1927 (help cr Haverthwaite CP).[394] Transf 1974 to Cumbria.[40] *Parl* Seq 10. *Eccl* Furness & Cartmel RDn (1676—1859), Cartmel RDn (1859—1970), Windermere RDn (1970—*). Eccl bdry: 1724 (cr Finsthwaite EP),[12] 1750 (cr Rusland EP,[12] refounded 1844[395]), 1828 (cr Haverthwaite EP,[12] refounded 1844[395]).

CONISTON

CP Cr 1894 by union Church Coniston CP, pt Hawkshead and Monk Coniston with Skelwith CP.[396] *LG* Ulv. PLU, RD (1894—1960), N Lonsd. RD (1960—74). Transf 1974 to Cumbria.[40] *Parl* Lonsd. Dv (1918—48), Morec. & Lonsd. CC (1948—*).

CHURCH CONISTON

Chap in Ulverston AP, sep CP 1866,[4] sep EP 1730,[12] eccl refounded 1892.[44] *LG* Lonsd. Hd, Ulv. PLU, RSD. Abol civ 1894 to help cr Coniston CP.[396] *Parl* N'rn Dv (1832—67), North Dv (1867—85), N Lonsd. Dv (1885—1918). *Eccl* Furnes & Cartmel RDn (1730—1859), Ulv. RDn (1859—1970), Furness RDn (1970—*). Eccl bdry: 1967.[69]

CONSTABLE LEE

EP Cr 1914 from Rawtenstall EP.[397] Rossend. RDn.

COPP

EP Cr 1723 from St Michael on the Wyre AP (pt area tp Great Eccleston),[12] refounded 1849 from ent tp Great Eccleston, Little Eccleston.[398] Amound. RDn (1723—1852), Garst. RDn (1852—*).

COPPULL

Chap in Standish AP, sep CP 1866,[4] sep EP 1717 (incl tp Charnock Richard, tp Welsh Whittle in same par),[12] eccl refounded 1842.[108] *LG* Seq 8. *Parl* Seq 3. Civ bdry: 1934.[226] *Eccl* Leyl. RDn (1717—1964), Chorley RDn (1964—*). Eccl bdry: 1861 (orig area tps Charnock Richard, Welsh Whittle cr 'Charnock Richard' EP),[304] 1911 (cr Coppull St John the Divine EP),[232] 1959.[24]

COPPULL ST JOHN THE DIVINE

EP Cr 1911 from Coppull EP.[232] Leyl. RDn (1911—64), Chorley RDn (1964—*).

COWPE LENCH, NEWHALL HEY AND HALL CARR

Tp (Blackb Hd) in Bury AP (mainly Salf. Hd), sep CP 1866.[4] *LG* Blackb Hd, Hasl. PLU, Rawt. MB (1891—94), Rawt. USD (pt 1875—83, ent 1883—94), pt Hasl. RSD (1875—83). Abol 1894 to help cr Rawtensall CP.[36] *Parl* N'rn Dv (1832—67), N-E Dv (1867—85), Rossend. Dv (1885—1918).

CRAWSHAWBOOTH

EP Cr 1899 from Goodshaw EP.[386] Whalley RDn (1899—1912), Rossend. RDn (1912—*).

CROFT

CP Cr 1933 from Southworth with Croft CP, Culcheth CP, Woolston with Martinscroft CP.[37] *LG* Warr. RD. *Parl* Newton CC (1948—*). ●

CROFT WITH SOUTHWORTH

Tp in Winwick AP, sep EP 1835,[12] eccl refounded 1844,[399] sep CP 1841 as 'Southworth with Croft',[400] qv. *Eccl* Warr. RDn (1835—47), Winwick RDn (1847—1949), Warr. RDn (1949—*).

CROMPTON

Tp in Prestwich AP, sep CP 1866,[4] eccl in chap Oldham in Prestwich AP, the area eccl severed 1719 from chap Oldham as 'Shaw' EP,[12] as such eccl refounded 1835.[182] *LG* Salf. Hd, Oldham PLU, Crompton USD, UD. Transf 1974 to Gtr Manch.[40] *Parl* Oldham Parl Bor (1832—1918), Royton Dv (1918—48), Heyw. & Royton CC (1948—*).

EAST CROMPTON

EP Cr 1844 from Shaw EP (pt of orig area tp Crompton, qv civ in prev entry).[11] Manch RDn (1844—47), Rochd. RDn (1847—72), Oldham RDn (1872—*). Bdry: 1878 (help cr High Crompton EP).[87]

HIGH CROMPTON

EP Cr 1878 from East Crompton EP, Shaw EP.[87] Oldham RDn.

CRONTON

Tp in Prescot AP, sep CP 1866,[4] eccl in Farnworth (chap and bor in tp Widnes in Prescot AP, the chap with some parochial rights from Middle Ages,[261] 'Farnworth' a sep EP 1859 from Prescot AP [incl tp Cronton], Widnes EP, Great Sankey EP[262]). *LG* Seq 18. Bdry: 1877.[401] Transf 1974 to Merseyside.[40] *Parl* Seq 23.

GREAT CROSBY

Chap in Sefton AP, sep CP 1866,[4] sep EP 1729,[12] pt of the latter eccl severed 1875 to cr Blundellsands EP,[139] the remainder refounded 1875 as 'Great Crosby' EP.[150] *LG* W Derby Hd, PLU, pt Waterloo with Seaforth USD, pt Great Crosby USD, Great Crosby UD (1894—1937), Crosby MB (1937—74). Civ bdry: 1894 (loses the pt in Waterloo with Seaforth UD to cr Waterloo CP),[402] 1932 (incl gains Little Crosby UD & CP),[403] 1956.[404] Transf 1974 to Merseyside.[40] *Parl* S'rn Dv (1832—67), S-W Dv (1867—85), S'port. Dv (1885—1918), Waterloo Dv (1918—48), Crosby BC (1948—*). Parl bdry: 1960.[405] *Eccl* Warr. RDn (1729—1847), Liverp North RDn (1847—95), Bootle RDn (1895—*). Addtl eccl bdry alt: 1877 (help cr Waterloo St John EP),[406] 1901 (help cr Great Crosby St Faith EP),[62] 1924 (help cr Blundellsands St Michael EP).[258]

GREAT CROSBY ST FAITH

EP Cr 1901 from Great Crosby EP, Waterloo Park EP.[62] Bootle RDn.

LITTLE CROSBY

Tp in Sefton AP, sep CP 1866.[4] *LG* W Derby Hd, PLU, Little Crosby USD, UD. Abol 1932 ent to Great Crosby UD & CP.[403] *Parl* S'rn Dv (1832—67), S-W Dv (1867—85), S'port. Dv (1885—1918), Waterloo Dv (1918—48).

CROSSBANK

CP Cr 1894 from pt of the pt of Ashton under Lyne AP not in a MB or UD.[63] *LG* Asht. under Lyne PLU, Limehurst RD. Bdry: 1911.[407] Abol 1914 ent to Lees UD & CP.[408]

CROSSENS

EP Cr 1840 from North Meols AP,[12] refounded 1860.[322] N Meols RDn.

CROSTON

AP Incl chap Chorley (sep par 1793[362]), chap Hesketh with Becconsall ('Becconsall' a sep EP 1730,[12] sep eccl status not sustained, 'Hesketh with Becconsall' a sep par 1721[180]), chap Hoole (sep par 1641[409]), chap Rufford (sep EP 1726,[12] sep par 1793[362]), chap Tarleton (sep par 1821[180]), tp Bispham, tp Mawdesley (each a sep CP 1866,[4] the 2 tps eccl united 1843 to cr Mawdesley with Bispham EP[213]), tp Bretherton (sep CP 1866,[4] sep EP 1843[214]), tp Ulnes Walton (sep CP 1866[4]). *LG* Leyl. Hd, Chorley PLU, Croston USD, UD (1894—1934), Chorley RD (1934—74). Addtl civ bdry alt: 1934.[226] *Parl* Seq 3. *Eccl* Seq 2.

CROXTETH PARK

Ex-par place, sep CP 1858,[80] pt eccl severed 1968 and transf to Knowsley EP.[231] *LG* W Derby Hd, PLU (1862—1928), RSD, Sefton RD. Abol civ 1928 ent to Liverp CB (assoc with Lancs) & CP.[410] *Parl* S'rn Dv (1832—67), S-W Dv (1867—85), Ormsk. Dv (1885—1948).

CRUMPSALL

Tp in Manchester AP, sep CP 1866,[4] eccl in chap (built 1794[353]) Cheetham, pt of tp Crumpsall eccl severed 1839 to help cr Cheetham Hill St Mark EP (qv for refounding),[353] pt eccl severed 1856 to help cr Cheetham Hill St Luke EP,[83] 'Crumpsall' a sep EP 1859 from Cheetham Hill St Mark EP,

Cheetham Hill St Luke EP,[12] refounded 1860.[102] *LG* Salf. Hd, Manch PLU (1840—50), Prestw. PLU (1850—96), Crumpsall USD (1875—90), Manch CB (1890—96), Manch USD (1890—94). Abol civ 1896 to help cr North Manchester CP.[82] *Parl* S'rn Dv (1832—67), S-E Dv (1867—85), Prestw. Dv (1885—1918). *Eccl* Manch RDn (1859—72), Cheetham RDn (1872—*). Eccl bdry: 1863 (help cr Lower Crumpsall EP,[12] refounded 1864[6]), 1901,[241] 1910 (help cr Crumpsall St Matthew EP),[111] 1928.[147]

CRUMPSALL ST MATTHEW

EP Cr 1910 from Crumpsall EP, Cheetham Hill St Mark EP.[111] Cheetham RDn.

LOWER CRUMPSALL

EP Cr 1863 from Cheetham Hill St Luke EP, Crumpsall EP,[12] refounded 1864.[6] Manch RDn (1863—72), Cheetham RDn (1872—*). Bdry: 1873,[355] 1901.[241]

CUERDALE

Tp in Blackburn AP, sep CP 1866,[4] eccl in chap Walton le Dale (sep EP 1764 from Blackburn AP[12]). *LG* Seq 7. Bdry: 1934.[226] Transf 1974 to Ches.[40] *Parl* Seq 13.

CUERDLEY

Tp in Prescot AP, sep CP 1866,[4] eccl in Farnworth (chap and bor in tp Widnes in Prescot AP, the chap with some parochial rights from Middle Ages,[261] 'Farnworth' a sep EP 1859 from Prescot AP [incl tp Cuerdley], Widnes EP, Great Sankey EP[262]). *LG* Seq 19. Bdry: 1920,[411] 1933 (gains pt Norton CP, Ches).[412] *Parl* Seq 18.

CUERDON

Tp in Leyland AP, sep CP 1866.[4] *LG* Seq 8. *Parl* Seq 3.

CULCETH

Tp in Winwick AP, united with tp Kenyon in same par eccl in 1748 to cr 'Newchurch' EP,[12] as such eccl refounded 1844,[399] united civ 1845 with same tp to cr 'Newchurch Kenyon' CP,[92] 'Culceth' a sep CP 1866 from Newchurch Kenyon CP.[4] *LG* W Derby Hd, Leigh PLU, RSD, RD. Abol 1933 pt to help cr Croft CP, pt to help cr Woolston CP, pt to Golborne CP.[37] *Parl* S'rn Dv (1832—67), S-W Dv 1867—85), Leigh Dv (1885—1918), Newton Dv (1918—48). Parl bdry: 1945.[339]

DAISY HILL

EP Cr 1882 from West Houghton EP.[147] Bolton le Moors RDn (1882—93), Bolton South RDn (1893—1901), Bolton le Moors RDn (1901—68), Deane RDn (1968—*).

DALTON

Tp (Lancs, Lonsd. Hd) in Burton AP ([eccl, 'Burton in Kendal'] o'wise Westm, Kendal Wd), sep CP 1866 in Lancs[4] so that Burton ent Westm thereafter. *LG* Kendal PLU, RSD, sep RD in Lancs (1894—95). Transf 1895 to Westm.[413] *Parl* N'rn Dv (1832—67), North Dv (1867—85), N Lonsd. Dv (1885—1918), Westm thereafter.

DALTON

Tp in Wigan AP, sep CP 1866,[4] eccl in chap Upholland (orig priory, sep EP 1643 from Wigan,[133] eccl refounded 1748[12]), 'Dalton' a sep

EP 1870 from Upholland EP.[38] *LG* Seq 20. Civ bdry: 1968.[414] *Parl* S'rn Dv (1832—67), S-W Dv (1867—85), Ormsk. Dv (1885—1948), W'hough. CC (1948—*). *Eccl* Wigan RDn (1870—1949), Ormsk. RDn (1949—*).

DALTON IN FURNESS

AP Incl chap Colton (orig a chap in this par, later chap in Hawkshead AP,[393] qv for sep identities), tp Barrow in Furness (sep CP 1866,[4] pt a sep EP 1860 as 'Barrow in Furness St George',[12] eccl refounded 1861[157]). *LG* Lonsd. Hd, pt Dalton Bor, Ulv. PLU, Dalton in Furness USD, UD. Addtl civ bdry alt: 1878,[158] 1935.[43] Transf 1974 to Cumbria.[40] *Parl* N'rn Dv (1832—67), North Dv (1867—85), N Lonsd. Dv (1885—1918), Lonsd. Dv (1918—48), Barrow in Furness BC (1948—*). *Eccl* Lanc. RDn (until before 1291), Copel. RDn (before 1291—before 1541), Furness & Cartmel RDn (before 1541—1859), Aldingham RDn (1859—83), Dalton RDn (1883—1970), Furness RDn (1970—*). Addtl eccl bdry alt: 1742 (cr Walney EP,[12] refounded 1899 as 'Walney Island',[146] now usually called 'Walney St Mary'), 1743 (cr Rampside EP,[12] refounded 1887[86]), 1869 (cr Newbarns and Hawcort EP,[139] later called 'Barrow in Furness St Paul'), 1872 (cr Lindale with Marton EP),[70] 1874 (cr Ireleth with Askham EP),[24] 1877 (help cr Barrow in Furness St Luke EP),[160] 1895,[23] 1937.[162]

DARWEN

The following have 'Darwen', 'Lower Darwen', or 'Over Darwen' in their names. Insofar as any existed at a given time: *LG* Blackb Hd, PLU; RSD, USD, MB sep noted. *Parl* N'rn Dv (1832—67), N-E Dv (1867—85); thereafter sep noted. *Eccl* Blackb RDn (cr—1964), Darwen RDn (1964—*).

CP1—DARWEN—Cr 1894 by union of the following pars in Darwen MB: ent CP2, ent CP3, pt Eccleshill CP.[415] *LG* Darwen MB. *Parl* Darwen Dv/CC (1918—*).

CP2/EP1—LOWER DARWEN [ST JAMES]—Tp in Blackburn AP, sep CP 1866,[4] sep EP 1830,[12] eccl refounded 1842.[133] *LG* Pt Blackb USD (1875—93), pt Blackb MB (1879—89), pt Blackb CB (1889—93), Darwen USD (pt 1879—93, ent 1893—94), Darwen MB (pt 1879—93, ent 1893—94), pt Blackb RSD (1875—79). Civ bdry: 1893 (loses the pt in the CB to Blackburn AP).[223] Abol civ 1894 ent to help cr CP1.[415] *Parl* Pt Blackb Parl Bor, pt Darwen Dv (1885—1918). Eccl bdry: 1947.[243]

CP3/EP2—OVER DARWEN [ST JAMES]—Chap in Blackburn AP, sep CP 1866,[4] sep EP 1719,[12] eccl divided 1842 into 2 EPs of EP2, EP3.[133] *LG* Over Darwen USD (1875—78), Darwen MB & USD (1878—94). Abol civ 1894 to help cr CP1.[415] *Parl* Darwen Dv (1885—1918). Eccl bdry: 1897.[35] Later called 'Darwen St James'.

EP3—OVER DARWEN HOLY TRINITY—Cr 1842 when EP2 divided into 2 EPs of EP2, EP3.[133] Bdry: 1863 (cr Hoddlesden EP),[91] 1865 (cr Turncroft EP),[71] 1873,[379] 1874 (help cr EP5),[177] 1897,[35] 1904 (cr EP7),[234] 1911 (help cr Ewood EP).[416] Later called 'Darwen Holy Trinity'.

—DARWEN HOLY TRINITY—Name used now for EP cr 1842 as EP3, qv.

EP4—DARWEN ST BARNABAS—Cr 1911 from Turncroft EP.[29]

EP5—DARWEN ST CUTHBERT—Cr 1874 from EP2, EP3, Tockholes EP.[177] Bdry: 1897,[35] 1916.[231]

EP6—DARWEN ST GEORGE—Cr 1904 from EP3.[234]

—DARWEN ST JAMES—Name used now for EP cr 1842 as EP2, qv.

—DARWEN ST JOHN THE EVANGELIST—Name sometimes used now for EP cr 1865 as 'Turncroft', qv.

DAUBHILL

EP Cr 1881 from Deane AP.[154] Bolton le Moors RDn (1881—93), Bolton South RDn (1893—1901), Bolton le Moors RDn (1901—*). Bdry: 1882,[203] 1897 (help cr Bolton le Moors St Philip EP),[144] 1898,[276] 1923 (help cr Bolton le Moors St Bede EP),[89] 1930.[149]

DAVYHULME

CP Cr 1894 from pt of the pt of Barton upon Irwell CP not in Eccles MB.[175] *LG* Barton upon Irwell PLU, RD (1894—1933), Urmston UD (1933—74). Bdry: 1896,[170] 1933.[171] Transf 1974 to Gtr Manch.[40] *Parl* Stretf. Dv/CC (1918—70), Stretf. BC (1970—*). Parl bdry: 1945.[339]

DAVYHULME CHRIST CHURCH

EP Cr 1967 from Davyhulme St Mary the Virgin EP.[417] Stretf. RDn.

DAVYHULME ST MARY THE VIRGIN

EP Cr 1885 from Barton upon Irwell EP, Flixton AP.[177] Eccles RDn (1885—1933), Stretf. RDn (1933—*). Bdry: 1964,[178] 1967 (incl cr Davyhulme Christ Church EP),[417] 1968 (help cr Flixton St John EP).[418]

DEANE

AP Orig chap in Eccles AP, sep par 1541.[419] Incl chap Farnworth (sep CP 1866,[4] sep EP 1750[12]), chap Horwich (sep CP 1866,[4] sep EP 1723,[12] eccl refounded 1854[420]), chap Little Hulton (sep CP 1866,[4] pt a sep EP 1761 as 'Peel',[12] as such refounded 1874,[350] another pt of chap Little Hulton eccl severed 1887 to cr 'Little Hulton' EP[287]), chap Westhoughton (sep CP 1866,[4] sep EP 1719 as 'West Houghton',[12] as such eccl refounded 1859[332]), tp Halliwell (sep CP 1866,[4] sep EP 1808[12]); tp Heaton, tp Rumworth (each a sep CP 1866,[4] pt of each of the 2 tps eccl united 1897 to cr 'Heaton' EP[137]); tps Middle Hulton, Over Hulton (each a sep CP 1866[4]), tp Kearsley (sep CP 1866,[4] eccl severed 1829 to help cr Farnworth with Kearsley EP,[12] as such eccl refounded 1829[421]), so that 'Deane' has no sep civ identity 1866—94 (see following entry). *LG* Salf. Hd. *Parl* S'rn Dv (1832—67). *Eccl* Manch RDn (1541—1847), Bolton le Moors RDn (1847—93), Bolton South RDn (1893—1901), Bolton le Moors RDn (1901—68), Deane RDn (1968—*). Addtl eccl bdry alt: 1848 (cr Halliwell St Paul EP),[12] 1863 (help cr Walkden Moor EP),[49] 1881 (cr Daubhill EP),[154] 1923 (help cr Bolton le Moors St Bede EP).[89]

CP Cr 1894 from the pt of Rumworth CP not in Bolton

CB (assoc with Lancs).[120] *LG* Bolton PLU, RD. Abol 1898 ent to Bolton CB (assoc with Lancs) & CP.[36]

DEARNLEY

EP Cr 1895 from Smallbridge EP, Littleborough EP.[88] Rochd. RDn.

DENDRON

EP Cr 1773 from Aldingham AP,[12] refounded 1892.[44] Furness & Cartmel RDn (1773—1859), Aldingham RDn (1859—83), Dalton RDn (1883—1970), Furness RDn (1970—*). Bdry: 1887 (help refound Rampside EP).[86]

DENTON

Chap in Manchester AP, sep CP 1866,[4] sep EP 1770 (pt tp Denton, pt tp Haughton),[12] orig dedication changed *ca* 1800 from 'St James' to 'St Lawrence',[422] the par eccl refounded 1839,[74] eccl refounded 1846,[21] eccl refounded 1854,[199] the remainder of orig tp Denton cr 1846 'Denton Christ Church' EP.[283] *LG* Salf. Hd, Asht. under Lyne PLU, Denton USD (1875—84), Denton & Houghton USD (1884—94), Denton USD (1894), UD. Civ bdry: 1894 (gains Haughton CP),[423] 1933 (loses pt to Manch CB [assoc with Lancs] & AP),[171] 1937 (exchanges pts with Stockport CB [assoc with Ches] & AP).[411] Transf 1974 to Gtr Manch.[40] *Parl* S'rn Dv (1832—67), S-E Dv (1867—85), Gorton Dv (1885—1918), Mossley Dv (1918—48), Droyl. BC (1948—*). *Eccl* Manch RDn (1770—1847), Asht. under Lyne RDn (1847—1910), Ardwick RDn (1910—*).

DENTON CHRIST CHURCH

EP Cr 1846 from Manchester AP (pt tp Denton, pt tp Haughton).[283] RDns as for Denton, from 1846. Bdry: 1879 (cr Haughton EP,[75] refounded 1881 [incl pt Hyde St George EP, Ches][313]), 1902 (help cr North Reddish EP),[2] 1923 (help cr Audenshaw St Hilda EP).[125]

WEST DERBY

The following have West Derby in their names. Insofar as any existed at a given time: *LG* W Derby Hd, Bor, PLU; USD, RSD, UD, RD, CB sep noted. *Parl* Sep noted. *Eccl* Warr. RDn (cr—1847), Prescot RDn (1847—1902), W Derby RDn (1902—*).

CP1/EP1—WEST DERBY [ST MARY]—Chap and bor in Walton on the Hill AP, sep EP 1810,[12] sep par 1843 by statutory authority,[424] eccl refounded 1847.[264] *LG* Pt W Derby USD, pt W Derby RSD, W Derby UD (1894—95), pt Liverp MB (1835—89), pt Liverp USD (1875—89), Liverp CB (1895—1922). The pt in the Liverp MB becomes 1889 pt Liverp CB. Addtl civ bdry alt: 1895 (the pt not transf to the CB cr CP2).[425] *Parl* Pt Liverp Parl Bor (1832—85), pt S'rn Dv (1832—67), pt S-W Dv (1867—85), pt Liverp Parl Bor, Walton (1885—1918), pt Bootle Dv (1885—1918); see Part III of the *Guide* for composition of Liverp Parl Bors (1918—48) by wards of the CB. Eccl bdry: 1852 (cr Edge Hill St Stephen EP,[336] qv for re-erection), 1854 (cr Fairfield EP),[426] 1863 (cr Edge Hill St Catherine EP),[427] 1872 (cr EP4, later called 'Tue Brook'),[132] 1872 (help cr Liverpool

Christ Church, Kensington EP),[279] 1874 (help cr Walton on the Hill St Margaret, Belmont Road EP),[357] 1875 (cr Stoneycroft EP),[150] 1876 (cr Edge Hill St Jude EP [built 1831 by subscription[428]]),[429] 1881 (cr Edge Hill St Cyprian EP),[355] 1886 (cr Stanley St Ann EP),[201] 1888 (cr Edge Hill St Dunstan, Earle Road EP [privately erected by Earle family[430]]),[431] 1890,[358] 1893,[104] 1905 (cr Edge Hill St Mary EP [built 1813[432]]),[107] 1909 (help cr Fazakerley EP),[41] 1925,[283] 1927 (cr EP3, help refound Knotty Ash St John the Evangelist EP),[346] 1927 (cr Clubmoor EP),[3] 1930 (help cr EP2, help cr Liverpool Norris Green St Christopher EP),[243] 1930 (help cr Liverpool Norris Green Christ Church EP),[433] 1933 (help cr Knotty Ash Holy Spirit EP),[283] 1951 (help cr EP5).[434]

EP2—WEST DERBY THE GOOD SHEPHERD—Cr 1930 from EP1, Fazakerley EP.[243]

CP2—WEST DERBY RURAL—Cr 1895 from the pt of CP1 not transf to Liverp CB (assoc with Lancs).[425] *LG* Sefton RD. Abol 1928 ent to Liverp CB (assoc with Lancs) & CP.[410] *Parl* Ormsk. Dv (1918—48).

EP3—WEST DERBY ST JAMES—Cr 1927 from EP1.[346]

EP4—WEST DERBY ST JOHN THE BAPTIST—Cr 1872 from EP1.[132] Later called 'Tue Brook'. Bdry: 1919 (help cr Anfield St Columba EP),[78] 1925.[283]

—WEST DERBY ST JOHN THE EVANGELIST— Name sometimes used for EP cr 1836 as 'Knotty Ash St John the Evangelist' EP, qv.

EP5—WEST DERBY ST LUKE—Cr 1951 from EP1, Roby EP, Knowsley EP.[434] Bdry: 1968,[231] 1971 (cr Cantril Farm EP).[150]

EP6—WEST DERBY ST NATHANIEL, WINDSOR— Cr 1871 from Toxteth Park St Clement EP.[5] Prescot RDn (1871—82), Liverp South RDn (1882—1902), Toxteth RDn (1902—73). Bdry: 1890.[358] Abol 1973 to help cr Edge Hill St Nathaniel EP.[435]

DIDSBURY

Chap in Manchester AP, sep CP 1866,[4] sep EP 1727,[12] eccl refounded 1839,[74] eccl refounded 1854.[199] *LG* Salf. Hd, Chorlton PLU, Withington USD, UD (1894—1904), Manch CB (1904—10). Civ bdry: 1883.[31] Abol civ 1910 ent to South Manchester CP.[310] *Parl* S'rn Dv (1832—67), S-E Dv (1867—85), Stretf. Dv (1885—1918). *Eccl* Manch RDn (1727—1847), Asht. under Lyne RDn (1847—72), Ardwick RDn (1872—1912), Heaton RDn (1912—65), Withington RDn (1965—*). Eccl bdry: 1860 (cr Barlow Moor EP),[149] 1964 (loses pt to Gatley EP, Ches and dioc Manch).[436]

DIDSBURY CHRIST CHURCH, BARLOW MOOR ROAD

EP Cr 1882 from Barlow Moor EP, Withington EP, Chorlton cum Hardy EP.[151] Ardwick RDn (1882—1912), Heaton RDn (1912—65), Withington RDn (1965—*). Bdry: 1932 (help cr Withington St Christopher EP).[323]

DILWORTH

Tp in Ribchester AP, sep CP 1866,[4] eccl severed 1727 to help cr Longridge EP,[12] the latter eccl refounded 1861.[62] *LG* Blackb Hd, Preston PLU, RSD (1875—83), Longridge USD (1883—94), UD. *Parl* N'rn Dv (1832—67), N-E Dv (1867—85), Darwen Dv (1885—1918), Fylde Dv (1918—48), Clith. CC (1948—*).

DINCKLEY

Tp in Blackburn AP, sep CP 1866.[4] *LG* Seq 4. *Parl* Seq 12.

DITTON

Tp in Prescot AP, sep CP 1866,[4] eccl in Farnworth (chap and bor in tp Widnes in Prescot AP, the chap with some parochial rights from Middle Ages,[261] 'Farnworth' a sep EP 1859 from Prescot AP [incl tp Ditton], Widnes EP, Great Sankey EP[262]), 'Ditton' a sep EP 1875 from Farnworth EP, Whiston EP, Halewood EP.[437] *LG* W Derby Hd, Prescot PLU, RSD, Whiston RD. Civ bdry: 1877.[438] Abol civ 1920 pt to Widnes MB & CP, pt to Tarbock CP.[411] *Parl* S'rn Dv (1832—67), S-W Dv (1867—85), Widnes Dv (1885—1948). *Eccl* Prescot RDn (1859—82), Childwall RDn (1882—1949), Farnw. RDn (1949—*).

DIXON GREEN

EP Cr 1880 from New Bury EP, Farnworth and Kearsley EP.[42] Bolton le Moors RDn (1880—93), Bolton South RDn (1893—1901), Bolton le Moors RDn (1901—68), Farnw. RDn (1968—*). Bdry: 1923.[233]

DOLPHINHOLME

EP Cr 1863 from Ellel EP, Garstang AP.[132] Garst. RDn (1863—66), Lanc. RDn (1866—*).

DOUGLAS

EP Cr 1862 from Eccleston AP.[439] Leyl. RDn (1862—1964), Chorley RDn (1964—*).

DOWNHAM

Tp in Whalley AP, sep CP 1866,[4] sep EP 1723.[12] *LG* Seq 6. *Parl* Seq 1. *Eccl* Blackb RDn (1723—1847), Whalley RDn (1847—*).

DOWNHOLLAND

Tp in Halsall AP, sep CP 1866.[4] *LG* Seq 17. Civ bdry: 1974 (gains the pt of Lydiate CP remaining in Lancs, the remainder transf to Merseyside to be 'Lydiate' CP).[40] *Parl* Seq 20.

DROYLSDEN

Tp in Manchester AP, sep CP 1866,[4] eccl in chap Newton (sep EP 1839 as 'Newton All Saints' from Manchester EP[74]), 'Droylsden' a sep EP 1844 from Newton All Saints EP.[348] *LG* Salf. Hd, Asht. under Lyne PLU, pt Manch MB (1884—89), pt Manch CB (1889—94), pt Manch USD (1884—94), pt Droyl. USD, pt Asht. under Lyne RSD (1875—84), Droyl. UD. Civ bdry: 1883,[31] 1889,[440] 1894 (the pt in the CB cr Clayton CP),[373] 1933 (exchanges pts with Manch CB [assoc with Lancs] & AP),[171] 1954.[65] Transf 1974 to Gtr Manch.[40] *Parl* S'rn Dv (1832—67), S-E Dv (1867—85), Prestw. Dv (1885—1918), Mossley Dv (1918—48), Droyl. BC (1948—55), Asht. under Lyne BC (1955—*). *Eccl* Manch RDn (1844—47), Asht. under Lyne RDn (1847—72), Ardwick RDn (1872—*). Eccl bdry: 1874 (cr

Clayton EP),[232] 1881 (help cr Higher Openshaw EP),[355] 1913 (help cr Droylsden St Andrew EP),[112] 1921,[3] 1961.[113]

DROYLSDEN ST ANDREW

EP Cr 1913 from Droylsden EP, Clayton EP, Higher Openshaw EP.[112] Ardwick RDn.

DUNNERDALE WITH SEATHWAITE

Tp in Kirkby Ireleth AP, sep CP 1866,[4] incl chap Seathwaite ([pec jurisd Dean & Chapter of York, until 1836] sep EP 1738,[12] refounded 1886[233]). *LG* Seq 14. Bdry: 1935 (loses pt to Ulpha CP, Cumb).[307] Transf 1974 to Cumbria.[40] *Parl* Seq 10.

DUNNOCKSHAW

Tp in Whalley AP, sep CP 1866,[4] eccl in chap Haslingden (sep EP 1719 from Whalley AP[12]). *LG* Seq 5. Bdry: 1894,[441] 1935.[43] *Parl* N'rn Dv (1832—67), N-E Dv (1867—85), Rossend. Dv (1885—1918), Clith. Dv/CC (1918—*).

DUTTON

Tp in Ribchester AP, gains 1858 ex-par Stidd,[80] the enlarged area a sep CP 1866 as 'Dutton'.[4] *LG* Seq 7. Addtl civ bdry alt: 1883,[31] 1934.[226] *Parl* Seq 13.

DUXBURY

Tp in Standish AP, sep CP 1866.[4] *LG* Leyl. Hd, Chorlton PLU, RSD, RD. Abol 1934 pt to Coppull CP, pt to Heath Charnock CP, pt to Chorley MB & CP.[226] *Parl* N'rn Dv (1832—67), North Dv (1867—85), Chorley Dv (1885—1948).

EARLESTOWN

EP Cr 1879 from Newton in Makerfield EP.[442] Winwick RDn (1879—1949), Warr. RDn (1949—*). Bdry: 1923.[48]

ECCLES

AP Incl chap Deane (sep par 1541[419]), tp Barton upon Irwell (sep CP 1866,[4] sep EP 1849,[12] eccl refounded 1867[172]), tp Clifton (sep CP 1866,[4] sep EP 1875[304]), tp Pendlebury (sep CP 1866,[4] sep EP 1843[443]), tp and chap (built 1776[444]) Pendleton (sep CP 1866,[4] sep EP 1807[12]), tp Worsley (sep CP 1866,[4] sep EP 1847[428]) so that 'Eccles' has no sep civ identity 1866—94 (see following entry). *LG* Salf. Hd. *Parl* S'rn Dv (1832—67). *Eccl* Manch & Blackb RDn (until before 1535), Blackb RDn (before 1535—1850), Eccles RDn (1850—66), Eccles & Salf. RDn (1866—72), Eccles RDn (1872—*). Addtl eccl bdry alt: 1806 (cr Swinton St Peter EP,[12] refounded 1865[119]), 1861 (help cr Pendlebury Christ Church EP),[157] 1863 (help cr Walkden Moor EP),[49] 1865 (cr Pendleton St Thomas EP),[391] 1866 (cr Weaste St Luke EP),[132] 1866 (cr Hope EP),[445] 1867 (cr Irlam EP),[446] 1869 (cr Patricroft EP),[437] 1880 (help cr Eccles St Andrew EP),[445] 1902 (help cr Old Trafford St Cuthbert EP),[2] 1912.[85]

CP Cr 1894 by union of the pts of the following in Eccles MB: Barton upon Irwell CP, Worsley CP.[174] *LG* Barton upon Irwell PLU, Eccles MB. Bdry: 1933,[171] 1961 (loses pt to Salf. CB [assoc with Lancs] & CP).[447] Transf 1974 to Gtr Manch.[40] *Parl* Eccles Parl Bor/BC (1918—*). Parl bdry: 1964.[448]

ECCLES ST ANDREW

EP Cr 1880 from Eccles AP, Patricroft EP.[445] Eccles RDn. Bdry: 1912,[85] 1912 (help cr Monton EP).[200]

ECCLESHILL

Tp in Blackburn AP, sep CP 1866.[4] *LG* Blackb Hd, PLU, pt Darwen MB & USD (1884—94), Blackb RSD (ent 1875—84, pt 1884—94), Blackb RD. Civ bdry: 1894 (loses the pt in the MB to help cr Darwen CP).[415] *Parl* Seq 13.

ECCLESTON

AP Incl tp Heskin (sep CP 1866[4]), tp Parbold (sep CP 1866[4]), tp Wrightington (sep CP 1866,[4] sep EP 1877[449]). *LG* Seq 8. Transf 1974 to Merseyside.[40] *Parl* Seq 3. *Eccl* Seq 2. Eccl bdry: 1862 (cr Douglas EP).[439]

ECCLESTON

The following have 'Eccleston' in their names. Insofar as any existed at a given time: *LG* Sep noted. *Parl* Sep noted. *Eccl* Warr. RDn (cr—1847), Prescot RDn (1847—*).

CP1/EP1—ECCLESTON [CHRIST CHURCH]—Tp in Prescot AP, sep CP 1866,[4] sep EP 1839.[12] *LG* W Derby Hd, Prescot PLU, pt Prescot USD, pt St Helens MB (1868—89), pt St Helens CB (1889—94), pt St Helens RSD, Whiston RD. Civ bdry: 1894 (loses the pt in Prescot UD to Prescot AP,[450] loses the pt in the CB and an additional pt to help cr St Helens CP[451]), 1899 (loses pt to St Helens CB [assoc with Lancs] & CP),[452] 1932,[453] 1934 (loses pt to St Helens CB [assoc with Lancs] & CP).[363] *Parl* S'rn Dv (1832—67), S-W Dv (1867—85), pt Newton Dv, pt St Helens Parl Bor (1885—1918), Widnes Dv (1918—48), Huyton CC (1948—*). Eccl bdry: 1931 (cr EP2),[454] 1955 (cr Thatto Heath EP),[455] 1961 (cr EP4),[456] 1963.[121]

CP2—GREAT ECCLESTON—Tp in St Michael on Wyre AP, sep CP 1866,[4] pt of the tp cr 1723 'Copp' EP,[12] the remainder of the orig tp, tp Little Eccleston with Larbreck, tp Elswick (both in same par) united eccl 1849 and added to Copp EP to refound the latter.[398] *LG* Seq 2. *Parl* Seq 7.

CP3—LITTLE ECCLESTON WITH LARBRECK—Tp in Kirkham AP, sep CP 1866,[4] eccl severed 1849 to help refound Copp EP.[398] *LG* Seq 1. *Parl* Seq 2.

EP2—ECCLESTON ST LUKE—Cr 1931 from EP1.[454] Bdry: 1963.[121]

EP3—ECCLESTON ST THOMAS—Cr 1839 from Prescot AP.[457] Bdry: 1870 (help cr Ravenhead EP).[314]

EP4—ECCLESTON PARK—Cr 1961 from EP1.[456]

EDENFIELD

Chap (incl area hmlt Shuttleworth in tp Walmersley cum Suttleworth) in Bury AP, sep EP 1725,[12] refounded 1865.[391] Manch RDn (1725—1850), Bury RDn (1850—51), Prestw. RDn (1851—72), Bury RDn (1872—*). Bdry: 1844 (help cr Musbury EP),[112] 1845 (the area of hmlt Shuttleworth severed to help cr Shuttleworth EP),[328] 1927 (help cr Stubbins EP).[269]

EDGE HILL

The following have 'Edge Hill' in their names. Insofar as any existed at a given time: Warr. RDn (cr—1847), Liverp South RDn (1847—82), Toxteth RDn (1882—1902), Liverp South RDn (1902—49), Toxteth RDn (1949—*).

EP1—EDGE HILL ST CATHERINE—Cr 1863 from West Derby EP.[427] Bdry: 1890,[358] 1893.[104] Abol 1973 to help cr EP6.[435]

EP2—EDGE HILL ST CYPRIAN—Cr 1881 from West Derby EP.[355]

EP3—EDGE HILL ST DUNSTAN, EARLE ROAD—Privately erected by Earle family,[430] sep EP 1888 from West Derby EP.[431]

EP4—EDGE HILL ST JUDE—Built by subscription 1831,[428] sep EP 1876 from West Derby EP.[429] Abol 1974 pt to EP5, pt to Everton St Ambrose with St Timothy EP, pt to Liverpool Christ Church, Kensington EP.[458] Sometiems 'West Derby St Jude'.

EP5—EDGE HILL ST MARY—Built 1813,[432] sep EP 1905 from West Derby EP.[107] Bdry: 1974.[458]

EP6—EDGE HILL ST NATHANIEL—Cr 1973 by union EP1, West Derby St Nathaniel, Windsor EP.[435] Bdry: 1974.[11]

EP7—EDGE HILL ST STEPHEN—Built 1851, sep EP 1852 from West Derby EP,[336] taken down for building of railway tunnel and re-erected 1882 on different site.[428] Liverp South RDn (1902—49), Liverp RDn (1949—52). Bdry: 1882,[213] 1890.[358] Abol 1952 to help cr Liverpool St Stephen with St Catherine EP.[110]

EDGESIDE

EP Cr 1887 from Newchurch in Rossendale EP, Lumb EP.[439] Whalley RDn (1887—1912), Rossend. RDn (1912—*).

EDGEWORTH

Tp in Bolton le Moors AP, sep CP 1866.[4] *LG* Salf. Hd, Bolton PLU, RSD, RD (1894—98), Turton UD (1898—1925). Bdry: 1898 (gains Entwistle CP, Quarlton CP).[36] Abol 1925 ent to Turton CP.[184] *Parl* S'rn Dv (1832—67), S-E Dv (1867—85), W'hough. Dv (1885—1918), Darwen Dv (1918—48).

EGTON CUM NEWLAND

Chap in Ulverston AP, sep EP 1793,[12] sep CP 1866 as 'Egton with Newland',[4] qv. Furness & Cartmel RDn (1793—1859), Ulv. RDn (1859—1970), Furness RDn (1970—*).

EGTON WITH NEWLAND

Chap in Ulverston AP, sep CP 1866,[4] sep EP 1793 as 'Egton cum Newland',[12] qv. *LG* Seq 14. Transf 1974 to Cumbria.[40] *Parl* Seq 11.

ELLEL

Tp in Cockerham AP, sep CP 1866,[4] pt a sep EP 1734,[12] eccl refounded 1866,[384] another pt eccl severed 1858 to help refound Shireshead EP.[272] *LG* Seq 12. Civ bdry: 1887,[375] 1962.[459] *Parl* Seq 6. *Eccl* Amound. RDn (1734—1852), Garst. RDn (1852—66), Lanc. RDn (1866—*). Eccl bdry: 1863 (help cr Dolphinholme EP).[132]

ELSTON

Tp in Preston AP, sep CP 1866,[4] eccl in chap Grimsargh (sep EP 1717 from Preston AP,[12] eccl refounded 1875[85]). *LG* Amound. Hd, Preston PLU, RSD, RD. Abol 1934 to help cr Grimsargh CP.[226] *Parl* N'rn Dv (1832—67), North Dv (1867—85), Blackp. Dv (1885—1918), Fylde Dv (1918—48).

ELSWICK

Tp in St Michael on Wyre AP, sep CP 1866,[4] eccl severed 1849 to help refound Copp EP.[398] *LG* Seq 1. *Parl* Seq 2.

ELTON

Tp in Bury AP, sep CP 1866,[4] sep EP 1844.[326] *LG* Salf. Hd, Bury PLU, pt Ramsb. USD (1883—94), pt Bury MB (1876—89), pt Bury CB (1889—94), pt Bury USD, pt Bury RSD (reduced pt 1883—94). Abol civ 1894 the pt in Ramsb. UD to help cr Ramsbottom CP, pt added to Tottington CP (renaming of Tottington Lower End with altered area [qv]), the pt in the CB added to Bury AP, pt transf to Ainsworth CP,[115] pt transf to Radcl. UD & AP.[460] *Parl* Pt Bury Parl Bor (1832—1918), pt S'rn Dv (1832—67), pt S-E Dv (1867—85), pt Heyw. Dv (1885—1918). *Eccl* Manch RDn (1844—50), Bury RDn (1850—51), Prestw. RDn (1851—72), Bury RDn (1872—*). Eccl bdry: 1884 (cr Elton St Stephen EP),[461] 1889 (help cr Walshaw EP),[349] 1915 (help cr Woolfold EP).[462]

ELTON ST STEPHEN

EP Cr 1884 from Elton EP.[461] Bury RDn. Bdry: 1889 (help cr Walshaw EP).[349]

ENTWISTLE

Tp in Bolton le Moors AP, sep CP 1866.[4] *LG* Salf. Hd, Bolton PLU, RSD, RD. Abol 1898 ent to Edgeworth CP.[36] *Parl* S'rn Dv (1832—67), S-E Dv (1867—85), W'hough. Dv (1885—1918).

EUXTON

Chap in Leyland AP, sep CP 1866,[4] sep EP 1729,[12] eccl refounded 1892.[463] *LG* Seq 8. Civ bdry: 1934.[226] *Parl* Seq 3. *Eccl* Leyl. RDn.

EVERTON

The following have 'Everton' in their names. Insofar as any existed at a given time: *LG* W Derby Hd, PLU, Liverp MB/CB, USD. *Parl* Liverp Parl Bor (1832—85), pt Liverp, Everton Parl Bor, pt Liverp, Kirkdale Parl Bor, pt Liverp, Walton Parl Bor (1885—1918); see Part III of the *Guide* for composition of Liverp Parl Bors (1918—48) by wards of the CB. *Eccl* Liverp North RDn (cr—1882), Walton RDn (1882—*).

CP1/EP1—EVERTON [ST GEORGE]—Chap in Walton on the Hill AP, sep CP 1866,[4] the chap proprietary until 1879,[464] pt eccl severed 1878 and transf to EP16,[159] the remainder a sep EP 1881.[465] Abol civ 1922 ent to Liverpool CP.[47] Eccl bdry: 1972 (gains EP8, EP10).[371]

EP2—EVERTON CHRIST CHURCH—Built 1848 by Horsfall family,[466] sep EP 1849 from Walton on the Hill AP.[467] Bdry: 1887,[296] 1887 (cr EP15).[439] Abol 1948 to help cr EP10.[468]

EP3—EVERTON EMMANUEL—Cr 1867 from EP11.[183]

EP4—EVERTON ST AMBROSE—Cr 1872 from EP14.[70] Abol 1939 to help cr EP5.[469]

EP5—EVERTON ST AMBROSE WITH ALL SAINTS—Cr 1939 by union EP4, Liverpool All Saints EP (closed 1937).[469] Abol 1942 to help cr Liverpool St Peter with St Ambrose and All Saints EP.[473]

EP6—EVERTON ST AMBROSE WITH ST TIMOTHY—Cr 1957 by union Liverpool St Peter with St Ambrose and All Saints EP, EP18, EP7.[41] Liverp RDn. Bdry: 1974.[458]

EP7—EVERTON ST AUGUSTINE—Cr 1873 from Walton on the Hill AP.[21] Bdry: 1868 (cr EP18).[113] Abol 1957 to help cr EP6.[41]

EP8—EVERTON ST BENEDICT—Cr 1888 from Walton on the Hill AP, EP16.[147] Abol 1972 ent to EP1.[371]

EP9—EVERTON ST CHAD—Cr 1885 from Walton on the Hill AP, EP12.[10] Abol 1948 to help cr EP10.[468]

EP10—EVERTON ST CHAD WITH CHRIST CHURCH—Cr 1948 by union EP9, EP2.[468] Abol 1972 ent to EP1.[371]

EP11—EVERTON ST CHRYSOSTOM—Cr 1855 from Walton on the Hill AP.[470] Bdry: 1867 (cr EP3),[183] 1890 (cr EP13).[75]

EP12—EVERTON ST CUTHBERT—Cr 1878 from Walton on the Hill AP.[172] Bdry: 1885 (help cr EP9).[10] Abol 1970 to help cr EP16.[471]

—EVERTON ST GEORGE—see EP1

EP13—EVERTON ST JOHN THE EVANGELIST—Cr 1890 from EP11.[75]

EP14—EVERTON ST PETER—Privately erected 1849 from Walton on the Hill EP.[472] Bdry: 1872 (cr EP4).[70] Abol 1942 to help cr Liverpool St Peter with St Ambrose and All Saints EP.[473]

EP15—EVERTON ST POLYCARP—Cr 1887 from EP2.[439]

EP16—EVERTON ST SAVIOUR—Cr 1870 from Walton on the Hill AP.[62] Bdry: 1878,[159] 1888 (help cr EP8).[147] Abol 1970 to help cr EP17.[471]

EP17—EVERTON ST SAVIOUR WITH ST CUTHBERT—Cr 1970 by union EP16, EP12.[471]

EP18—EVERTON ST TIMOTHY—Cr 1868 from EP7.[113] Sometimes 'Liverpool St Timothy'. Abol 1957 to help cr EP6.[41]

EWOOD

EP Cr 1911 from Livesey EP, Feniscliffe EP, Darwen St Cuthbert EP.[416] Blackb RDn (1911—64), Darwen RDn (1964—*). Bdry: 1916.[231] Later called 'Blackburn St Bartholomew'.

FACIT

EP Cr 1867 from Whitworth EP.[474] Rochd. RDn.

FAILSWORTH

Tp in Manchester AP, sep CP 1866,[4] eccl in chap Newton (sep EP 1839 from Manchester AP as 'Newton All Saints'[74]), 'Failsworth' a sep EP 1844 from Newton All Saints EP.[348] *LG* Salf. Hd, Manch PLU (1840—50), Prestw. PLU (1850—1930), Failsworth USD, UD. Civ bdry: 1933 (exchanges pts with Manch CB [assoc with Lancs] & AP),[171] 1954.[65] Transf 1974 to Gtr Manch.[40] *Parl* S'rn Dv (1832—67), S-E Dv (1867—85), Prestw. Dv (1885—1918), Mossley Dv (1918—48), Droyl. BC (1948—55), Manch, Openshaw BC (1955—*). *Eccl* Manch RDn (1844—51), Bury RDn (1851—72), Cheetham RDn (1872—*). Eccl bdry: 1904 (cr Failsworth Holy Trinity EP),[234] 1964.[475]

FAILSWORTH HOLY TRINITY

EP Cr 1904 from Failsworth EP.[234] Cheetham RDn.

FAIRFIELD

EP Cr 1854 from West Derby EP.[426] Prescot RDn (1854—1902), W Derby RDn (1902—*). Bdry: 1872 (help cr Liverpool Christ Church, Kensington EP),[279] 1874 (help cr Walton on the Hill St Margaret, Belmont Road EP),[357] 1891 (cr Liverpool St Philip EP),[315] 1909 (help cr Liverpool St Mark, Edge Lane EP).[35]

FAIRHAVEN

EP Cr 1917 from Lytham AP.[162] The Fylde RDn.

FALINGE

EP Cr 1867 from Rochdale St Alban EP, Spotland EP.[474] Rochd. RDn. Bdry: 1925 (help cr Oakenrod EP).[49]

FALLOWFIELD

EP Cr 1873 from Withington EP.[355] Ardwick RDn (1873—1912), Heaton RDn (1912—65), Withington RDn (1965—*). Bdry: 1898 (help cr Chorlton cum Hardy St Werburgh EP),[323] 1900 (help cr Ladybarn EP),[202] 1905,[195] 1916 (help cr Withington St Crispin EP),[110] 1929.[204]

FARINGTON

Tp in Penwortham AP, sep CP 1866,[4] sep EP 1843.[476] *LG* Seq 10. *Parl* Seq 2. *Eccl* Leyl. RDn. Bdry: 1898 (help cr Leyland St Ambrose EP),[62] 1931 (help cr New Longton EP),[95] 1957 (help cr Lostock Hall EP),[138] 1972 (help cr Penwortham St Leonard EP).[477]

FARLETON

Tp in Melling AP, sep CP 1866,[4] eccl severed 1741 to help cr Hornby EP,[12] the latter eccl refounded 1859.[478] *LG* Lonsd. Hd, Caton GilbU (until 1869), Lunesd. PLU (1869—87), RSD. Abol 1887 to help cr Hornby with Farleton CP.[479] *Parl* N'rn Dv (1832—67), North Dv (1867—85), Lanc. Dv (1885—1918).

FARNWORTH

Chap in Deane AP, sep CP 1866,[4] sep EP 1750,[12] the EP united 1829 with tp Kearsley in same par to cr Farnworth and Kearsley EP.[421] *LG* Salf. Hd, Bolton PLU, Farnworth USD, UD (1894—1939), MB (1939—74). Transf 1974 to Gtr Manch.[40] *Parl* Seq 15. *Eccl* Manch RDn.

FARNWORTH

Chap and bor (status not sustained) in tp Widnes in Prescot AP, some parochial rights from Middle Ages,[261] sep EP 1859 by union pt of tp Widnes (the remainder cr at same time Widnes St Mary EP), pt Prescot AP (tps Bold, Cronton, Cuerdley, Ditton), ent Great Sankey EP (comprised of orig area tps Great Sankey, Penketh, both orig in Prescot AP).[262] Prescot RDn (1859—82), Childwall RDn (1882—1949), Farnw. RDn (1949—*). Bdry: 1859 (help cr Ditton EP),[437] 1875 (area orig Great Sankey EP [area orig tps Great Sankey, Penketh] severed to re-cr Great Sankey EP),[150] 1884 (cr Widnes St Ambrose EP),[123] 1909.[41]

FARNWORTH ALL SAINTS

EP Cr 1913 from Farnworth and Kearsley EP, Dixon Green EP.[2] Bolton le Moors RDn (1913—68), Farnw. RDn (1968—*).

FARNWORTH AND KEARSLEY

EP Cr 1829 by union Farnworth EP (area orig chap in Deane AP), tp Kearsley in Deane AP.[421] Manch RDn (1829—47), Bolton le Moors RDn (1847—93), Bolton South RDn (1893—1901), Bolton le Moors RDn (1901—68), Farnw. RDn (1968—*). Bdry: 1866 (cr New Bury EP),[272] 1872 (cr Kearsley Moor EP),[272] 1880 (help cr Dixon Green EP),[42] 1883 (help cr Prestolee EP),[27] 1898 (help cr Ringley EP),[276] 1887 (help cr Farnworth St Peter, Bradford Street EP),[337] 1913 (help cr Farnworth All Saints EP).[2]

FARNWORTH ST PETER, BRADFORD STREET

EP Cr 1887 from Farnworth and Kearsley EP, New Bury EP.[337] Bolton le Moors RDn (1887—93), Bolton South RDn (1893—1901), Bolton le Moors RDn (1901—68), Farnw. RDn (1968—*). Bdry: 1923.[233]

FAZAKERLEY

Tp in Walton on the Hill AP, sep CP 1866,[4] pt eccl severed 1881 and united with pt Walton on the Hill AP to cr Walton on the Hill St John the Evangelist EP,[355] 'Fazakerley' a sep EP 1909 from Walton on the Hill St John the Evangelist EP, Aintree EP, Kirkby EP, West Derby EP.[41] *LG* W Derby Hd, PLU, RSD, Sefton RD (1894—1905), Liverp CB (1905—22). Abol civ 1922 ent to Liverpool CP.[47] *Parl* S'rn Dv (1832—67), S-W Dv (1867—85), Bootle Dv (1885—1918); see Part III of the *Guide* for composition of Liverp Parl Bors (1918—48) by wards of the CB. *Eccl* Walton RDn. Eccl bdry: 1930 (help cr West Derby The Good Shepherd EP),[243] 1930 (help cr Liverpool Norris Green Christ Church EP),[433] 1971.[18]

FAZAKERLEY ST NATHANAEL

EP Cr 1957 from Walton on the Hill St John the Evangelist EP, Walton on the Hill AP.[480] Walton RDn.

FENCE-IN-PENDLE

EP Cr 1841 from Whalley AP (incl pt eccl ex-par Reedley Hallows, Filly Close and New Laund Booth).[12] Blackb RDn (1841—47), Whalley RDn (1847—72), Burnley RDn (1872—*).

FENISCLIFFE

EP Cr 1893 from Livesey EP, Feniscowles EP.[481] Blackb RDn (1893—1964), Darwen RDn (1964—*). Bdry: 1911 (help cr Ewood EP),[416] 1911,[319] 1925 (help cr Blackburn St Aidan EP).[213] Later called 'Blackburn St Francis'.

FENISCOWLES

EP Cr 1839 from Blackburn AP (incl pt tp Livesey),[12] refounded 1842.[133] Blackb RDn (1839—1964), Darwen RDn (1964—*). Bdry: 1877 (help cr Livesey EP),[221] 1893 (help cr Feniscliffe EP, later called 'Blackburn St Francis').[481]

FINSTHWAITE

EP Cr 1724 from Colton EP.[12] Furness & Cartmel RDn (1724—1858), Cartmel RDn (1859—1970), Windermere RDn (1970—*).

FISHWICK

Tp in Preston AP, sep CP 1866.[4] *LG* Amound. Hd, Preston PLU, Bor/MB/CB, USD. Abol 1894 ent to Preston AP.[482] *Parl* Preston Parl Bor (1832—1918).

FLEETWOOD

EP Cr 1867 from Poulton le Fylde AP.[483] The Fylde

RDn (1867—*).

CP Cr 1894 from the pt of Thornton CP in Fleetwood UD.[217] *LG* Fylde PLU, Fleetwood UD (1894—1933), MB (1933—74). *Parl* Fylde Dv (1918—48), N Fylde CC (1948—*).

FLIXTON
AP Incl tp Urmston (sep CP 1866,[4] sep EP 1868[273]). *LG* Salf. Hd, Chorlton PLU (1837—49), Barton upon Irwell PLU (1849—1930), RSD, RD (1894—1933), Urmston UD (1933—74). Addtl civ bdry alt: 1896,[170] 1920 (exchanges pts with Carrington CP, Ches).[484] Transf 1974 to Gtr Manch.[40] *Parl* S'rn Dv (1832—67), S-E Dv (1867—85), Eccles Dv (1885—1918), Stretf. Dv/CC (1918—70), Stretf. BC (1970—*). Parl bdry: 1945.[339] *Eccl* Manch & Blackb RDn (until before 1535), Manch RDn (before 1535—1855), Eccles RDn (1855—66), Eccles & Salf. RDn (1866—72), Hulme RDn (1872—1933), Stretf. RDn (1933—*). Eccl bdry: 1885 (help cr Davyhulme St Mary the Virgin EP),[177] 1925 (help cr Cadishead EP),[338] 1967,[160] 1968 (help cr Flixton St John EP).[418]

FLIXTON ST JOHN
EP Cr 1968 from Flixton AP, Davyhulme St Mary the Virgin EP, Irlam EP.[418] Stretf. RDn.

FLOOKBURGH
EP Cr 1723 from Cartmel AP,[12] refounded 1879.[16] Furness & Cartmel RDn (1723—1859), Cartmel RDn (1859—1970), Windermere RDn (1970—*).

FORD
CP Cr 1905 from the pt of Orrell and Ford CP not transf to Bootle CB (assoc with Lancs).[485] *LG* W Derby PLU, Sefton RD (1905—32), W Lancs RD (1932—54). Bdry: 1940 (loses pt to Bootle CB [assoc with Lancs] & to Orrell CP).[486] Abol 1954 ent to Litherland UD & CP.[487] *Parl* Ormsk. Dv (1918—48), Crosby BC (1948—60). Parl bdry: 1955.[488]

FORMBY
Chap in Walton on the Hill AP, sep CP 1866,[4] pt a sep EP 1748,[12] eccl refounded 1893,[1] pt of orig chap a sep EP 1888 as 'Formby St Luke'.[24] *LG* W Derby Hd, Ormsk. PLU, RSD, W Lancs RD (1894—1905), Formby UD (1905—74). Civ bdry: 1894 (cr Ainsdale CP).[32] Transf 1974 to Merseyside.[40] *Parl* Seq 23. *Eccl* Warr. RDn (1748—1847), Prescot RDn (1847—54), Liverp North RDn (1854—82), N Meols RDn (1882—*). Eccl bdry: 1906 (cr Ainsdale EP).[33]

FORMBY HOLY TRINITY
EP Cr 1893 from Walton on the Hill AP.[1] N Meols RDn.

FORMBY ST LUKE
EP Cr 1888 from Walton on the Hill AP (pt orig chap Formby).[24] N Meols RDn.

FORTON
Tp pt in Cockerham AP (Lonsd. Hd), pt in Garstang AP (Amound. Hd), sep CP 1866,[4] the pt in Cockerham AP eccl severed 1858 to help refound Shireshead EP.[272] *LG* Garst. PLU, RSD, RD. Bdry: 1935 (gains Cleveley CP, Holleth CP).[43] *Parl* Seq 7.

FOULRIDGE
Tp in Whalley AP, sep CP 1866,[4] eccl in chap Colne (sep EP 1820 from Whalley AP[12]), 'Foulridge' a sep EP 1905 from Colne EP, Colne Christ Church EP.[391] *LG* Seq 5. Civ bdry: 1935.[43] *Parl* N'rn Dv (1832—67), N-E Dv (1867—85), Clith. Dv (ent 1885—1918, pt 1918—48), pt Nelson & Colne Parl Bor (1918—48), Clith. CC (1948—*). *Eccl* Burnley RDn (1905—70), Pendle RDn (1970—*).

FRECKLETON
Tp in Kirkham AP, sep CP 1866,[4] sep EP 1874.[489] *LG* Seq 1. Civ bdry: 1934.[226] *Parl* Seq 2. *Eccl* The Fylde RDn.

FULWOOD
Tp in Lancaster AP, sep CP 1866,[4] sep EP 1865.[10] *LG* Amound. Hd, Preston PLU, Fulwood USD, UD. Civ bdry: 1934 (incl loses pt to Preston CB [assoc with Lancs] & AP),[226] 1952 (loses pt to Preston CB [assoc with Lancs] & AP).[490] *Parl* N'rn Dv (1832—67), North Dv (1867—85), Preston Parl Bor (1885—1948), Preston North BC (1948—*). *Eccl* Preston RDn. Eccl bdry: 1883 (help cr Ribbleton EP),[317] 1916 (help cr Preston St Cuthbert EP).[436]

GANNOW
EP Cr 1880 from Habergham Eaves EP.[42] Burnley RDn. Bdry: 1959 (help cr Burnley St Mark EP).[320] Sometimes called 'Burnley St John the Baptist'.

GARSTANG
AP Incl pt chap Pilling (sep CP 1866,[4] sep EP 1756[12]), tp Barnacre with Bonds, tp Catterall, tp Claughton (each a sep CP 1866,[4] pt of each of the 3 tps eccl severed 1864 to help cr Calder Vale EP[154]), tp Bilsborough (sep CP 1866,[4] sep EP 1925 from Barton EP, Garstang AP[168]), tp Cabus (sep CP 1866[4]), pt tp Cleveley, pt tp Forton (each a sep CP 1866,[4] the pts of each of the 2 tps severed 1858 from Garstang AP [along with the remaining pt of orig tp Cleveley (in Cockerham AP)] to help refound Shireshead EP[272]), pt tp Holleth (sep CP 1866[4]), tp Kirkland, tp Nateby (each a sep CP 1866[4]), tp Winmarleigh (sep CP 1866,[4] pt a sep EP 1876 as 'Winmarleigh'[340]), tp Nether Wyresdale (sep CP 1866,[4] pt eccl severed 1858 to help refound Shireshead EP,[272] pt eccl severed 1880 to cr Scorton EP[491]). *LG* Seq 2. Addtl civ bdry alt: 1887,[155] 1935.[43] *Parl* Seq 7. *Eccl* Sometimes as 'Church Town', Lanc. RDn (until before 1291), Amound. RDn (before 1291—1852), Garst. RDn (1852—*). Addtl eccl bdry alt: 1863 (help cr Dolphinholme EP),[132] 1881 (cr Garstang St Thomas EP).[121]

GARSTANG ST THOMAS
EP Cr 1881 from Garstang AP.[121] Garst. RDn.

GARSTON
Chap (the orig chap of St Wilfrid in ruins by 16th cent and new chap St Michael erected later[359]) in Childwall AP, sep CP 1866,[4] sep EP 1729 (incl pt tp Speke),[12] eccl refounded 1828.[75] *LG* W Derby Hd, PLU, Garston USD, UD (1894—1902), Liverp CB (1902—22). Abol civ 1922 ent to Liverpool CP.[47] *Parl* S'rn Dv (1832—67), S-W Dv (1867—

85), Widnes Dv (1885—1918); see Part III of the *Guide* for composition of Liverp Parl Bors (1885—1918) by wards of the CB. *Eccl* Warr. RDn (1729—1847), Prescot RDn (1847—82), Childwall RDn (1882—1949), Farnw. RDn (1949—*). Eccl bdry: 1844 (cr Aigburth EP),[26] 1855 (help cr Grassendale EP),[27] 1875 (the pt of orig tp Speke in this par severed to help cr Speke EP),[150] 1923 (help cr Liverpool All Souls, Springwood EP),[48] 1964,[49] 1972.[442]

GATEACRE
EP Cr 1893 from Childwall AP (pt tp Little Woolton, pt tp Much Woolton).[360] Childwall RDn (1893—1949), Farnworth RDn (1949—*). Bdry: 1964.[49]

GLASSON
EP Cr 1846 from Lancaster AP.[12] Amound. RDn (1846—52), Lanc. RDn (1852—*).

GLAZEBURY
EP Cr 1878 from Newchurch EP, Bedford EP.[38] Winwick RDn (1879—1949), Warr. RDn (1949—*).

GLODWICK
EP Cr 1844 from Oldham St Peter EP.[348] Manch RDn (1844—47), Rochd. RDn (1847—72), Oldham RDn (1872—1966). Bdry: 1876 (cr Glodwick St Mark EP).[492] Bdry: 1925 (help cr Roundthorn EP).[493] Abol 1966 to help cr Glodwick St Mark with Christ Church EP.[256]

GLODWICK ST MARK
EP Cr 1876 from Glodwick EP.[492] Oldham RDn. Bdry: 1925 (help cr Roundthorne EP).[493] Abol 1966 to help cr Glodwick St Mark with Christ Church EP.[256]

GLODWICK ST MARK WITH CHRIST CHURCH
EP Cr 1966 by union Glodwick EP, Glodwick St Mark EP.[256] Oldham RDn.

GOLBORNE
Tp in Winwick AP, abol civ and eccl 1845 and incl in Lowton CP/EP, 'Golborne' a sep par again 1850 civ and eccl from Lowton CP/EP.[494] *LG* W Derby Hd, Warr. PLU (1837—50), Leigh PLU (1850—1930), RSD, Golborne UD. Civ bdry: 1933 (incl gains Kenyon CP, Lowton CP),[37] 1957,[7] 1969.[495] Transf 1974 pt to Ches (wards of Culceth, Newchurch [area ceases to be a par]), pt to Gtr Manch (wards of Heath Park, Lowton East, Lowton West).[40] *Parl* Seq 18. *Eccl* Winwick RDn (1850—1949), Warr. RDn (1949—*).

GOLDSHAW BOOTH
Tp in Whalley AP, sep CP 1866,[4] eccl in chap Newchurch in Pendle (sep EP 1723 from Whalley AP[12]). *LG* Seq 5. Bdry: 1898,[496] 1904 (help cr Sabden CP),[497] 1935.[43] *Parl* Seq 11.

GOODSHAW
EP Cr 1741 from Whalley AP.[12] Blackb RDn (1741—1847), Whalley RDn (1847—66), Accr. RDn (1866—72), Burnley RDn (1872—93), Whalley RDn (1893—1912), Rossend. RDn (1912—*). Bdry: 1899 (cr Crawshawbooth EP).[386]

GOOSE GREEN
EP Cr 1915 from Highfield EP, Pemberton St Mark Newtown EP, Wigan St James EP.[125] Wigan RDn.

GOOSNARGH
Detached chap and tp in Kirkham AP, sep CP 1866,[4] pt eccl severed 1717 to cr 'Whitechapel' EP,[12] the latter refounded 1846,[498] the remainder of the chap a sep EP 1721 (incl tp Newsham [not sep civ] and tp Whittingham [qv for civ] in same par),[12] eccl refounded 1846.[499] *LG* Seq 3. Civ bdry: 1894.[167] *Parl* Seq 2. *Eccl* Amound. RDn (1721—1852), Garst. RDn (1852—*).

GORTON
The following have 'Gorton' or 'West Gorton' in their names. Insofar as any existed at a given time: *LG* Salf. Hd, Chorlton PLU, Gorton USD (ent 1875—90, pt 1890—94), pt Manch CB & USD (1890—94), Gorton UD (1894—1909), Manch CB (1909—10). *Parl* S'rn Dv (1832—67), S-E Dv (1867—85), pt Manch, South Parl Bor, pt Gorton Dv (1885—1918). *Eccl* Manch RDn (cr—1847), Asht. under Lyne RDn (1847—72), Ardwick RDn (1872—*).

CP1/EP1—GORTON [ST JAMES]—Chap in Manchester AP, sep CP 1866,[4] sep EP 1728 (incl pt chap Newton in same par),[12] eccl refounded 1838,[74] eccl refounded 1854.[199] Civ bdry: 1890 (loses pt to Manch CB [assoc with Lancs] & AP),[500] 1894 (the pt in the CB cr West Gorton CP),[501] 1901 (loses pt to Manch CB [assoc with Lancs] and to South Manchester CP).[502] Abol civ 1910 ent to South Manchester CP.[310] Eccl bdry: 1861 (help cr Levenshulme EP),[200] 1866 (help cr EP3),[84] 1879 (help cr EP2),[75] 1881 (help cr Higher Openshaw EP),[355] 1899 (cr Abbey Hey EP),[1] 1902 (help cr North Reddish EP),[2] 1904 (cr EP5),[234] 1921.[3]

EP2—GORTON ALL SAINTS—Cr 1879 from EP1, EP3.[75] Bdry: 1921.[3] Abol 1968 to help cr EP6.[256]

EP3—GORTON ST MARK—Cr 1866 from EP1, Openshaw EP, Ardwick EP, Longsight EP.[84] Bdry: 1879 (help cr EP2),[75] 1880 (help cr Ardwick St Benedict EP).[87] Abol 1968 to help cr EP6.[256]

EP4—GORTON ST MARY AND ST THOMAS—Cr 1925 from EP5, Kirkmanshulme EP, Birch in Rusholme St Agnes EP, Levenshulme EP.[49]

EP5—GORTON ST PHILIP—Cr 1904 from EP1.[234] Bdry: 1925 (help cr EP4),[49] 1926.[70]

CP2—WEST GORTON—Cr 1894 from the pt of CP1 in Manch CB.[501] Abol 1896 to help cr South Manchester CP.[82]

EP6—WEST GORTON ST MARK WITH ALL SAINTS—Cr 1968 by union EP3, EP2.[256]

GRANGE
CP Cr 1894 by union of the following pts of pars in Grange UD: Lower Allithwaite CP, Upper Allithwaite CP, Broughton East CP.[58] *LG* Ulv. PLU, Grange UD. Bdry: 1914.[59] Transf 1974 to Cumbria.[40] *Parl* Lonsd. Dv (1918—48), Morec. & Lonsd. CC (1948—*).

GRANGE OVER SANDS
EP Cr 1884 from Cartmel AP, ent area of eccl ex-par Holme Island (situated in Cartmel AP).[234] Cartmel RDn (1889—1970), Windermere RDn (1970—*).

GRASSENDALE
EP Cr 1855 from Garston EP, Aigburth EP.[27] Prescot

RDn (1855—82), Childwall RDn (1882—*). Bdry: 1923 (help cr Liverpool All Souls, Springwood EP).[48]

GREENHALGH WITH THISTLETON
Tp in Kirkham AP, sep CP 1866,[4] LG Seq 1. Parl Seq 2.

GREENHEYS
EP Cr 1882 from Moss Side EP, Whalley Range St Margaret EP, Hulme St Mary EP, Hulme St Paul EP.[203] Hulme RDn. Sometimes called 'Manchester St Clement'. Abol 1973 to help cr Moss Side St James with St Clement EP.[275]

GRESSINGHAM
Chap in Lancaster AP, sep CP 1866,[4] sep EP 1725.[12] LG Seq 13. Parl Seq 8. Eccl Amound. RDn (1725—1852), Lanc. RDn (1852—72), Tunstall RDn (1872—*).

GRIFFIN
EP Cr 1881 from Witton EP.[235] Blackb RDn. Bdry: 1940.[150] Abol 1972 to help cr Blackburn St Luke with St Philip EP.[240]

GRIMSARGH
Hmlt in Preston AP, chap erected 1716,[503] sep EP 1717 (incl tp Elston in same par),[12] eccl refounded 1875,[85] civ 'Grimsargh with Brockholes', as such a sep CP 1866 from Preston AP,[4] qv, 'Grimsargh' a sep CP 1934 by union pt Grimsargh with Brockholes CP, ent Elston CP.[226] LG Preston RD. Parl S Fylde CC (1948—*). Eccl Amound. RDn (1717—1852), Preston RDn (1852—*).

GRIMSARGH WITH BROCKHOLES
Hmlt in Preston AP, sep CP 1866,[4] chap erected 1716,[503] sep EP 1717 (incl tp Elston in same par) as 'Grimsargh',[12] as such eccl refounded 1875,[85] qv. LG Amound. Hd, Preston PLU, pt Preston USD, pt Preston MB (1880—89), pt Preston CB (1889—94), pt Preston RSD, Preston RD. Bdry: 1894 (loses the pt in the CB to Preston AP).[482] Abol 1934 pt to help cr Grimsargh CP, pt to Preston CB [assoc with Lancs] & AP.[226] Parl N'rn Dv (1832—67), North Dv (1867—85), pt Preston Parl Bor, pt Blackp. Dv (1885—1918), Fylde Dv (1918—48).

HABERGHAM ALL SAINTS
EP Cr 1845 from pt Padiham EP, pt Habergham Eaves EP, and from ent eccl ex-par Ighton Hill (situated in chap/EP Burnley in Whalley AP).[124] Blackb RDn (1845—47), Whalley RDn (1847—72), Burnley RDn (1872—*). Bdry: 1959 (help cr Burnley St Mark EP).[320]

HABERGHAM EAVES
Tp in Whalley AP, sep CP 1866,[4] eccl in chap Burnley (sep EP 1716 from Whalley AP[12]), pt of the area of the orig tp a sep EP 1843 as 'Habergham Eaves',[293] the remainder of the orig tp cr 1845 'Lane Bridge' EP.[124] LG Blackb Hd, Burnley PLU, pt Burnley USD, pt Burnley MB (1871—89), pt Burnley CB ([area larger than the area prev in the MB] 1889—94), pt Burnley RSD, Burnley RD. Civ bdry: 1894 (loses the pt to Burnley CP, loses pt to help cr Ightenhill CP),[295] 1911 (loses pt to Burnley CB [assoc with Lancs] & CP),[308] 1926 (loses pt to Burnley CB [assoc with Lancs] & CP).[311] Parl N'rn Dv (1832—67), Burnley Parl Bor

(1867—1918), Clith. Dv/CC (1918—*). Eccl Blackb RDn (1843—47), Whalley RDn (1847—72), Burnley RDn (1872—*). Eccl bdry: 1845 (help cr Habergham All Saints EP),[124] 1880,[315] 1880 (help cr Habergham Eaves St Matthew the Apostle EP),[94] 1880 (cr Gannow EP),[42] 1959 (help cr Burnley St Mark EP).[320]

HABERGHAM EAVES ST MATTHEW THE APOSTLE
EP Cr 1880 from Habergahm Eaves EP, Lane Bridge EP.[94] Burnley RDn. Bdry: 1959 (help cr Burnley St Mark EP),[320] 1962.[317]

HAIGH
Tp in Wigan AP, sep CP 1866,[4] eccl severed 1838 to help cr Haigh and Aspull EP.[116] LG Seq 20. Transf 1974 to Gtr Manch.[40] Parl S'rn Dv (1832—67), S-W Dv (1867—85), Ince Dv (1885—1918), Chorley Dv (1918—48), W'hough. CC (1948—*).

HAIGH AND ASPULL
EP Cr 1838 by union tp Haigh (W Derby Hd), tp Aspull (Salf. Hd), both in Wigan AP.[116] Warr. RDn (1838—47), Wigan RDn (1847—*). Bdry: 1883 (cr Aspull EP),[117] 1953 (help cr New Springs EP).[118]

HAIGHTON
Tp in Preston AP, sep CP 1866.[4] LG Seq 3. Parl Seq 2.

HALE
Chap in Childwall AP, sep CP 1866,[4] sep EP 1732 (incl pt tp Speke),[12] eccl refounded 1828.[75] LG Seq 18. Civ bdry: 1952 (loses pt to Liverp CB [assoc with Lancs] & CP).[504] Transf 1974 to Ches.[40] Parl Seq 23. Parl bdry: 1955.[488] Eccl Warr. RDn (1732—1847), Prescot RDn (1847—82), Childwall RDn (1882—1949), Farnw. RDn (1949—*). Eccl bdry: 1875 (the area of pt orig tp Speke severed to help cr Speke EP),[150] 1972.[442]

HALEWOOD
Tp in Childwall AP, sep CP 1866,[4] sep EP 1845.[12] LG Seq 18. Civ bdry: 1920,[411] 1952 (loses pt to Liverp CB [assoc with Lancs] & CP).[504] Transf 1974 to Merseyside.[40] Parl Seq 23. Parl bdry: 1955.[488] Eccl Warr. RDn (1845—47), Prescot RDn (1847—82), Childwall RDn (1882—1949), Farnw. RDn (1949—*). Eccl bdry: 1869 (help cr Whiston EP),[505] 1875 (help cr Ditton EP),[437] 1957 (help cr Hunts Cross EP),[506] 1964,[49] 1972.[442]

HALLIWELL
The following have 'Halliwell' in their names. Insofar as any existed at a given time: LG Salf. Hd, Bolton PLU, pt Bolton MB (1877—89), Bolton CB (pt 1889—94, ent 1894—95), pt Bolton USD (1877—94), Bolton RSD (ent 1875—77, pt 1877—94). Parl S'rn Dv (1832—67), pt Bolton Parl Bor (1867—1918), pt S-E Dv (1867—85), pt W'hough. Dv (1885—1918). Eccl Manch RDn (cr—1847), Bolton le Moors RDn (1847—93), Bolton North RDn (1893—1901), Bolton le Moors RDn (1901—*).

CP1/EP1—HALLIWELL [ST PETER]—Cr 1808 from Deane AP,[12] refounded 1840.[494] Civ bdry: 1894 (the pt not in the CB cr Smithills CP).[120] Abol civ 1895 to help cr Bolton CP.[263] Eccl bdry: 1876 (help cr EP2),[280] 1879 (help cr EP5).[83]

EP2—HALLIWELL ST LUKE—Cr 1876 from EP1, Bolton le Moors St George EP.[280] Bdry: 1896 (help cr Bolton le Moors St Barnabas EP),[254] 1907 (cr EP3).[507]

EP3—HALLIWELL ST MARGARET—Cr 1907 from EP2.[507]

EP4—HALLIWELL ST PAUL—Cr 1848 from Deane AP.[12] Bdry: 1879 (help cr EP5).[83]

EP5—HALLIWELL ST THOMAS—Cr 1879 from EP1, EP4.[83]

HALSALL
AP Incl chap Maghull (sep CP 1866,[4] sep EP 1748,[12] eccl refounded 1923[89]), chap Melling (sep CP 1866,[4] sep EP 1810,[12] eccl refounded 1923[89]), tp Downholland (sep CP 1866[4]), tp Lydiate (sep CP 1866,[4] sep EP 1841,[12] eccl refounded 1844,[125] eccl refounded 1871[16]). *LG* Seq 17. *Parl* Seq 20. *Eccl* Seq 5. Eccl bdry: 1936.[209]

HALTON
AP *LG* Seq 13. Civ bdry: 1900.[309] *Parl* Seq 8. *Eccl* Lanc. RDn (until before 1291), Kirkby Lonsd. & Kendal RDn (before 1291—before 1541), Kendal RDn (before 1541—1848), Tunstall RDn (1848—72), Lanc. RDn (1872—1928), Tunstall RDn (1928—*).

HAMBLETON
Chap in Kirkham AP, sep CP 1866,[4] sep EP 1738,[12] eccl refounded 1846.[508] *LG* Seq 2. *Parl* Seq 7. *Eccl* Amound. RDn (1738—1852), The Fylde RDn (1852—72), Garst. RDn (1872—*).

HAMER
EP Cr 1867 from Smallbridge EP, Wardleworth St James EP, Rochdale AP.[172] Rochd. RDn. Bdry: 1902 (help cr Rochdale Good Shepherd EP).[11]

HAPTON
Tp in Whalley AP, sep CP 1866,[4] eccl in chap Padiham (sep EP 1730 [qv for later refounding] from Whalley AP[12]). *LG* Blackb Hd, Burnley PLU, pt Padiham & Hapton USD, pt Burnley RSD, Burnley RD. Civ bdry: 1894 (the pt in the UD transf to Padiham CP),[164] 1894,[441] 1935.[43] *Parl* N'rn Dv (1832—67), N-E Dv (1867—85), Accr. Dv (1885—1918), Clith. Dv/CC (1918—*).

HARDHORN WITH NEWTON
Tp in Poulton le Fylde AP, sep CP 1866.[4] *LG* Amound. Hd, Fylde PLU, RSD, RD. Bdry: 1934 (incl loses pt to Blackp. CB [assoc with Lancs] & CP).[226] Renamed 1969 'Staining' CP.[509] *Parl* N'rn Dv (1832—67), North Dv (1867—85), Blackp. Dv (1885—1918), Fylde Dv (1918—48), S Fylde CC (1948—70). Parl bdry: 1945.[339]

HARLEY WOOD
EP Cr 1864 from Todmorden EP (Lancs), Cross Stone EP (Yorks W Riding).[433] Halifax RDn (1864—1967), Calder Valley RDn (1967—72). Bdry: 1898 (gains pt Holme St John EP, dioc Manch),[22] 1903 (the pt in Yorks cr Cornholme EP to be dioc Wakef).[50] Abol 1972 ent to Todmorden EP.[510]

HARPURHEY
Tp in Manchester AP, sep CP 1866,[4] sep EP 1844,[12] eccl refounded 1854 (when gains tp Moston in Manchester AP) as 'Harpurhey cum Moston' EP,[199] qv for later refounding 1898 of orig area tp Harpurhey as 'Harpurhey Christ Church'. *LG* Salf. Hd, Manch PLU (1840—50), Prestw. PLU (1850—96), RSD (1875—85), Manch MB (1885—89), CB (1889—96), USD (1885—94). Abol civ 1896 to help cr North Manchester CP.[82] *Parl* Manch Parl Bor (1832—85), Manch, North Parl Bor (1885—1918). *Eccl* Manch RDn (1844—51), Bury RDn (1851—54).

HARPURHEY CHRIST CHURCH
EP Refounding 1898 of the remainder of Harpurhey cum Moston EP after two areas severed: the area of Moston to cr Moston EP, and another pt to cr Harpurhey St Stephen EP.[323] Cheetham RDn. Bdry: 1900 (help cr Blackley Holy Trinity EP),[202] 1903,[50] 1909 (cr Moston St John Ashley Lane EP).[33]

HARPURHEY CUM MOSTON
EP Refounding 1854 of Harpurhey EP when the latter gains tp Moston from Manchester AP.[199] Bury RDn (1854—72), Cheetham RDn (1872—98). Eccl bdry: 1865 (help cr Manchester The Albert Memorial Church EP),[119] 1870 (cr Moston EP).[31] Abol 1898 the area of Moston severed to cr Moston EP, pt to cr Harpurhey St Stephen EP, the remainder refounded as 'Harpurhey Christ Church' EP.[323]

HARPURHEY ST STEPHEN
EP Cr 1898 from Harpurhey cum Moston EP.[323] Cheetham RDn. Bdry: 1903.[50]

HARTSHEAD
CP Cr 1894 from pt of the pt of Ashton under Lyne AP not in a MB or UD.[63] *LG* Asht. under Lyne PLU, Limehurst RD (1894—1935), Asht. under Lyne MB (1935—74). Bdry: 1935.[43] Transf 1974 to Gtr Manch.[40] *Parl* Mossley Dv (1918—48), Asht. under Lyne BC (1948—*).

HARWOOD
Tp in Bolton le Moors AP, sep CP 1866,[4] pt eccl severed 1845 to help cr Tonge EP,[83] the remainder cr 1851 'Harwood' EP.[271] *LG* Salf. Hd, Bolton PLU, RSD, RD. Abol civ 1898 ent to Turton CP.[36] *Parl* S'rn Dv (1832—67), S-E Dv (1867—85), W'hough. Dv (1885—1918). *Eccl* Bolton le Moors RDn (1851—93), Bolton North RDn (1893—1901), Bolton le Moors RDn (1901—68), Walmsley RDn (1968—*).

GREAT HARWOOD
Chap in Blackburn AP, sep CP 1866,[4] sep EP 1735 (incl pt tp Rishton in same par),[12] eccl refounded 1840.[219] *LG* Blackb Hd, PLU, Gt Harwood USD, UD. *Parl* Seq 13. *Eccl* Blackb RDn (1735—1964), Whalley RDn (1964—*). Eccl bdry: 1874 (help cr Rishton EP),[24] 1908 (cr Great Harwood St John EP).[113]

GREAT HARWOOD ST JOHN
EP Cr 1908 from Great Harwood EP.[113] Blackb RDn (1908—64), Whalley RDn (1964—*).

LITTLE HARWOOD
Tp in Blackburn AP, sep CP 1866.[4] *LG* Blackb Hd, PLU, USD, MB (pt 1877—89, ent 1877—89), CB (1889—93). Abol 1893 ent to Blackburn AP.[223] *Parl* N'rn Dv (1832—67), Blackb Parl Bor (pt 1867—85, ent 1885—1918), pt N-E Dv (1867—85).

HASLINGDEN
Chap in Whalley AP, sep CP 1866,[4] sep EP 1719

(incl tps Higher Booths, Lower Booths, Dunnock-shaw, and area eccl ex-par Henheads).[12] *LG* Blackb Hd, Hasl. PLU, pt Hasl. USD, Hasl. MB (pt 1891—94, ent 1894—1974), pt Rawt. USD, pt Rawt. MB (1891—94). Civ bdry: 1894 (loses the pt in Rawt. MB to help cr Rawtenstall CP and gains the following in Hasl. MB: ent Henheads CP, Musbury CP, and pts Higher Booths CP, Lower Booths CP, Tottington Lower End CP, Tottington Higher End CP),[129] 1934.[226] *Parl* N'rn Dv (1832—67), N-E Dv (1867—85), Rossend. Dv (1885—1918), Rossend. Parl Bor/BC (1918—*). *Eccl* Blackb RDn (1719—1847), Whalley RDn (1847—66), Accr. RDn (1866—72), Whalley RDn (1872—1912), Accr. RDn (1912—*). Eccl bdry: 1844 (help cr Musbury EP),[112] 1846 (pt of orig area tp Higher Booths cr Lumb EP),[283] 1849 (remainder of orig area tp Higher Booths [not severed 1846] cr 'Higher Booths' EP,[284] sep status not sustained), 1883 (cr Haslingden Grane EP),[221] 1889 (cr Haslingden St John, Stonefold EP [later called 'Stonefold']),[228] 1894 (cr Laneside EP, sometimes later called 'Haslingden St Peter').[161]

HASLINGDEN GRANE
EP Cr 1883 from Haslingden EP.[221] Whalley RDn (1883—1912), Accr. RDn (1912—*).

HASLINGDEN ST JOHN, STONEFOLD
EP Cr 1889 from Haslingden EP.[228] Whalley RDn (1889—1912), Accr. RDn (1912—*). Later called 'Stonefold'.

HASLINGDEN ST PETER—see LANESIDE

HAUGHTON
Tp in Manchester AP, sep CP 1866,[4] pt eccl severed 1770 to help cr Denton EP,[12] the latter refounded 1839,[74] eccl refounded 1846,[21] eccl refounded 1854,[199] 'Haughton' a sep EP 1879 from Denton EP,[75] refounded 1881 from Denton EP, Hyde St George EP (Ches).[313] *LG* Salf. Hd, Asht. under Lyne PLU, Haughton USD (1875—84), Denton & Haughton USD (1884—94), Denton USD (1894). Abol civ 1894 ent to Denton CP.[423] *Parl* S'rn Dv (1832—67), S-E Dv (1867—85), Gorton Dv (1885—1918). *Eccl* Asht. under Lyne RDn (1879—1910), Ardwick RDn (1910—*). Eccl bdry: 1923 (help cr Audenshaw St Hilda EP).[125]

HAVERTHWAITE
EP Cr 1828 from Colton EP,[12] refounded 1844.[395] Furness & Cartmel RDn (1828—59), Cartmel RDn (1859—1970), Windermere RDn (1970—*). Bdry: 1859.[128]
CP Cr 1927 from Colton CP, Upper Holker CP.[395] *LG* Ulv. PLU, RD (1927—60), N Lonsd. RD (1960—74). Transf 1974 to Cumbria.[40] *Parl* Morec. & Lonsd. CC (1948—*).

HAWKSHAW LANE
EP Cr 1892 from Holcombe EP, Tottington EP, Turton EP.[44] Bury RDn.

HAWKSHEAD
AP Chap in Dalton in Furness AP, perhaps sep par before 1200, sep par certainly in 1578.[392] Incl chap Colton (sep par 1676[393]), chap Satterthwaite (sep CP 1866,[4] sep EP 1741 [incl tps Grizdaleon, Dale Park (neither sep civ) in same par],[12] refounded 1881[465]), tp Claife (sep CP 1866[4]), tp Hawkshead and Monks Coniston with Skelwith (sep CP 1866[4]) so that 'Hawkshead' has no sep civ identity 1866—94 (see following entry). *LG* Lonsd. Hd. *Parl* N'rn Dv (1832—67). *Eccl* Furness & Cartmel RDn (cr—1859), Ambleside RDn (1859—1954). Eccl bdry: 1836 (cr Brathay EP),[290] 1860 (cr Low Wray EP,[12] refounded 1846[511]), 1873 (hmlt Lower Claife [not sep civ] cr Sawrey EP).[379] Abol eccl 1954 to help cr Hawkshead and Low Wray EP.[348]
CP Cr 1894 from Hawkshead and Monk Coniston with Skelwith CP.[396] *LG* Ulv. PLU, RD (1894—1960), N Lonsd. RD (1960—74). Transf 1974 to Cumbria.[40] *Parl* Lonsd. Dv (1918—48), Morec. & Lonsd. CC (1948—*).

HAWKSHEAD AND LOW WRAY
EP Cr 1954 by union Hawkshead AP, Low Wray EP.[348] Ambleside RDn (1954—70), Windermere RDn (1970—*). Bdry: 1967.[69]

HAWKSHEAD AND MONK CONISTON WITH SKELWITH
Tp in Hawkshead AP, sep CP 1866.[4] *LG* Lonsd. Hd, Ulv. PLU, RSD. Abol 1894 pt to cr Hawkshead CP, pt to cr Skelwith CP, pt to help cr Coniston CP.[396] *Parl* N'rn Dv (1832—67), North Dv (1867—85), N Lonsd. Dv (1885—1918).

HAYDOCK
Tp in Winwick AP, sep CP 1845,[92] eccl severed 1840 to help cr Ashton in Makerfield EP,[12] qv for refounding 1845, 'Haydock' a sep EP 1864 from Ashton in Makerfield EP.[94] *LG* W Derby Hd, Warr. PLU, Haydock USD, UD. Civ bdry: 1933.[37] Transf 1974 to Merseyside.[40] *Parl* Seq 18. *Eccl* Winwick RDn (1864—1920), Prescot RDn (1920—*). Eccl bdry: 1910 (cr Haydock St Mark EP),[222] 1923.[48]

HAYDOCK ST MARK
EP Cr 1910 from Haydock EP.[222] Winwick RDn (1910—20), Prescot RDn (1920—*).

HEALEY
EP Cr 1846 from Spotland EP.[512] Manch RDn (1846—47), Rochd. RDn (1847—*). Bdry: 1913.[203]

HEAP
Tp in Bury AP, sep CP 1866,[4] incl area chap Heywood (pt of the chap a sep EP 1720 as 'Heywood St James',[12] pt of the latter severed 1843 to help refound Birch EP,[193] another pt of orig chap not in Heywood St James EP eccl severed 1848 from Bury AP to help cr Bircle EP,[206] the remainder of the orig chap of Heywood cr 1864 Heywood St Luke EP[325]), 'Heap' a sep EP 1864 from Bury AP.[325] *LG* Salf. Hd, Bury PLU, pt Heyw. USD, pt Heyw. MB (1881—94), pt Bury USD, pt Bury MB (1876—89), pt Bury CB (1889—94), pt Bury RSD. Civ bdry: 1883.[31] Abol civ 1894 the pt in Heyw. MB to help cr Heywood CP, the pt in Bury CB transf to Bury AP, pt of the remainder transf to Birtle cum Bamford CP, pt to help cr Unsworth CP.[115] *Parl* S'rn Dv (1832—67), S-E Dv (1867—85), pt Bury Parl Bor, pt Heyw. Dv (1885—1918). *Eccl* Bury RDn.

HEAP BRIDGE
EP Cr 1907 from Heywood St James EP.[513] Bury RDn.

HEAPEY

Chap in Leyland AP, sep CP 1866,[4] sep EP 1739.[12] *LG* Seq 8. *Parl* Seq 3. *Eccl* Leyl. RDn (1739—1847), Blackb RDn (1847—55), Leyl. RDn (1855—1964), Chorley RDn (1964—*).

HEATH CHARNOCK

Tp in Standish AP, sep CP 1866.[4] *LG* Seq 8. Bdry: 1934.[226] *Parl* Seq 3.

HEATON

Tp in Deane AP, sep CP 1866,[4] pt a sep EP 1897 (incl pt tp Rumworth in same par).[137] *LG* Salf. Hd, Bolton PLU, RSD, RD. Abol 1898 ent to Bolton CB (assoc with Lancs) & CP.[36] *Parl* S'rn Dv (1832—67), S-E Dv (1867—85), W'hough. Dv (1885—1918). *Eccl* Bolton South RDn (1897—1901), Bolton le Moors RDn (1901—*).

GREAT HEATON

Tp in Prestwich AP, sep CP 1866.[4] *LG* Salf. Hd, Manch PLU (1840—50), Prestw. PLU (1850—94), RSD (ent 1875—91, pt 1891—94), pt Middl. MB & USD (1891—94). Abol 1894 the pt in the MB transf to Middleton AP,[45] the remainder to Prestwich AP.[514] *Parl* S'rn Dv (1832—67), S-E Dv (1867—85), Prestw. Dv (1885—1918).

LITTLE HEATON

Tp in Prestwich AP, sep CP 1866.[4] *LG* Salf. Hd, Manch PLU (1840—50), Prestw. PLU (1850—94), RSD (ent 1875—91, pt 1891—94), pt Middl. MB & USD (1891—94). Abol 1894 the pt in the MB transf to Middleton AP,[45] the remainder to Prestwich AP.[514] *Parl* S'rn Dv (1832—67), S-E Dv (1867—85), Prestw. Dv (1885—1918).

HEATON MERSEY

EP Cr 1852 from Manchester AP.[315] Asht. under Lyne RDn (1852—72), Ardwick RDn (1872—1912), Heaton RDn (1912—*). Bdry: 1878 (help cr Heaton Moor EP),[239] 1899 (help cr Norris Bank EP),[1] 1927.[135]

HEATON MOOR

EP Cr 1878 from Heaton Norris EP, Heaton Mersey EP.[239] Bdry: 1927.[135] Ardwick RDn (1879—1912), Heaton RDn (1912—*).

HEATON NORRIS

Tp and chap (built 1765[515]) in Manchester AP, sep CP 1866,[4] sep EP [St Thomas] 1770 (incl tp Levenshulme, tp Reddish),[12] eccl refounded 1839,[74] pt of the EP cr 1854 'Heaton Norris Christ Church' and the remainder refounded at the same time as 'Heaton Norris'.[199] *LG* Salf. Hd, Stockport PLU, pt Heaton Norris USD, pt Stockport MB ([Ches, Lancs] 1835—89), pt Stockport CB ([Ches, Lancs 1889—94, ent Ches thereafter] 1889—94), pt Stockport USD (Ches, Lancs), pt Heaton Norris USD, Heaton Norris UD (1894—1913), Stockport CB ([assoc with Ches] 1913—35). Civ bdry: 1894 (loses the pt in Stockport CB to Stockport AP so that Heaton Norris ent Lancs 1894—1913),[516] 1901 (loses pt to Stockport CB [assoc with Ches] & AP),[207] 1913 (loses pt to Manch CB [assoc with Lancs] & to South Manchester CP,[517] as the remainder of Heaton Norris CP transf to Stockport CB [assoc with Ches] to be a constituent par in the latter[518]). Abol 1935 ent to Stockport AP.[519] *Parl*

Stockport Parl Bor ([Ches, Lancs 1832—1918, ent Ches 1918—48] pt until 1918, ent 1918—48); pt in Lancs: S'rn Dv (1832—67), S-E Dv (1867—85), Stretf. Dv (1885—1918). *Eccl* Manch RDn (1770—1847), Asht. under Lyne RDn (1847—72), Ardwick RDn (1872—1912), Heaton RDn (1912—*). Eccl bdry: 1861 (orig area tp Levenshulme severed to help cr Levenshulme EP),[200] 1865 (cr Heaton Reddish EP),[334] 1878 (help cr Heaton Moor EP),[239] 1884 (help cr Reddish EP).[123]

HEATON NORRIS ALL SAINTS

EP Cr 1888 from Heaton Reddish EP, Heaton Norris Christ Church EP.[227] Ardwick RDn (1888—1912), Heaton RDn (1912—*). Bdry: 1891.[426]

HEATON NORRIS CHRIST CHURCH

EP Cr 1854 from Heaton Norris EP as the remainder of the latter refounded as 'Heaton Norris'.[199] Asht. under Lyne RDn (1854—72), Ardwick RDn (1872—1912), Heaton RDn (1912—*). Bdry: 1888 (help cr Heaton Norris All Saints EP),[227] 1891,[426] 1899 (help cr Norris Bank EP).[1]

HEATON REDDISH

EP Cr 1865 from Heaton Norris EP.[334] Asht. under Lyne RDn (1865—72), Ardwick RDn (1872—*). Bdry: 1884 (help cr Reddish EP),[123] 1888 (help cr Heaton Norris All Saints EP).[227]

HEATON WITH OXCLIFFE

Tp in Lancaster AP, sep CP 1866,[4] eccl in chap Overton (sep EP 1715 from Lancaster AP[12]). *LG* Seq 12. Bdry: 1900,[309] 1935.[43] *Parl* Seq 6.

HENHEADS

Tp in Whalley AP, sep CP 1866,[4] eccl ex-par and situated in chap Haslingden (sep EP 1719 from this area and 3 tps in Whalley AP [qv][12]). *LG* Blackb Hd, Hasl. PLU (pt 1875—83, ent 1883—94), pt Hasl. RSD (1875—83), Hasl. MB (1891—94). Abol 1894 ent to Haslingden CP.[129] *Parl* N'rn Dv (1832—67), N-E Dv (1867—85), Accr. Dv (1885—1918).

HESKETH WITH BECCONSALL

Tp in Croston AP, 'Becconsall' a sep EP 1730,[12] sep eccl status of the latter not sustained, 'Hesketh with Becconsall' a sep par 1821.[181] *LG* Seq 9. *Parl* Seq 3. *Eccl* Leyl. RDn (1821—47), N Meols RDn (1847—48), Leyl. RDn (1848—*).

HESKIN

Tp in Eccleston AP, sep CP 1866.[4] *LG* Seq 8. *Parl* Seq 3.

HEY

EP Cr 1746 from Ashton under Lyne AP (Lancs), Lydgate EP (Yorks W Riding),[12] refounded 1860.[102] Manch RDn (1746—1847), Asht. under Lyne RDn (1847—72), Oldham RDn (1872—*). Sometimes 'Lees'. Bdry: 1886 (help cr Scouthead EP [Yorks W Riding, Lancs]).[70]

NEW HEY

EP Cr 1876 from Milnrow EP.[213] Rochd. RDn. Later called 'Newhey'.

NEWHEY—see prev entry

HEYHOUSES

Ex-par place (situated in Whalley AP), sep CP 1858,[80] sep EP 1849 (incl pt tp Read in Whalley AP).[466] *LG* Blackb Hd, Burnley PLU, RSD, RD.

Abol civ 1904 to help cr Sabden CP.[497] *Parl* N'rn Dv (1832—67), N-E Dv (1867—85), Darwen Dv (1885—1918). *Eccl* Whalley RDn (1858—72), Burnley RDn (1872—1912), Whalley RDn (1912—*). Later eccl 'Sabden'.

HEYHOUSES ON THE SEA
EP Cr 1877 from Lytham AP.[406] The Fylde RDn. Later called 'St Anne's on the Sea'. Bdry: 1902 (cr St Anne's on the Sea St Thomas EP),[323] 1966 (cr St Anne's on the Sea St Margaret EP).[520]

HEYSHAM
AP *LG* Lonsd. Hd, Caton GilbU (until 1869), Lanc. PLU (1869—1928), RSD, RD (1894—99), Heysham UD (1899—1928). Abol civ 1928 to help cr Morecambe and Heysham MB & CP.[440] *Parl* N'rn Dv (1832—67), North Dv (1867—85), Lanc. Dv (1885—1948). *Eccl* Lanc. RDn (until before 1291), Kirkby Lonsd. RDn (before 1291—before 1541), Kendal RDn (before 1541—1848), Tunstall RDn (1848—72), Lanc. RDn (1872—*). Bdry: 1919 (cr Sandylands EP).[111]

HEYSIDE
EP Cr 1879 from Royton EP, Lower Moor EP.[245] Oldham RDn. Bdry: 1957.[386]

HEYWOOD
Chap in area tp Heap (qv for sep civ identity 1866) in Bury AP, pt eccl severed 1720 to cr Heywood St James EP,[12] qv, pt of the latter eccl severed 1843 to help refound Birch EP,[193] another pt of orig chap not in Heywood St James EP eccl 1848 severed from Bury AP to help cr Bircle EP,[206] the remainder of the orig chap of Heywood cr 1864 Heywood St Luke EP,[325] qv, 'Heywood' a sep CP 1894 by union of the pts of the following in Heyw. MB: Birtle cum Bamford CP, Castleton CP, Heap CP, Hopwood CP, Pilsowrth CP.[115] *LG* Bury PLU, Heyw. MB. Bdry: 1900 (gains pt Castleton by Rochd. UD and Castleton, Lancashire CP),[176] 1933,[171] 1933 (loses pt to Bury CB [assoc with Lancs] & AP).[37] Transf 1974 to Gtr Manch.[40] *Parl* Heyw. & Radcl. Dv/CC (1918—48), Heyw. & Royton CC (1948—*).

HEYWOOD ST JAMES
EP Cr 1720 from Bury AP (pt of chap Heywood in tp Heap).[12] Manch RDn (1720—1850), Bury RDn (1850—*). Bdry: 1843 (help refound Birch EP),[193] 1881 (help cr Bamford EP),[140] 1902,[2] 1907 (cr Heap Bridge EP).[513]

HEYWOOD ST LUKE
EP Cr 1864 from the remainder of orig chap Heywood (civ in tp Heap) not in Heywood St James EP, Bircle EP, or Birch EP.[325] Bury RDn. Bdry: 1881 (help cr Bamford EP),[140] 1905 (help cr Hopwood EP).[195]

HIGHAM WITH WEST CLOSE BOOTH
Tp in Whalley AP, sep CP 1866,[4] eccl in chap Padiham (sep EP 1730 from Whalley AP,[12] qv for later refounding). *LG* Seq 5. Bdry: 1898,[496] 1904 (help cr Sabden CP).[497] *Parl* Seq 13.

HIGHFIELD
EP Cr 1911 from Pemberton EP, Wigan St James EP.[38] Wigan RDn. Bdry: 1915 (help cr Goose Green EP),[125] 1966.[104]

HIGHTOWN
EP Cr 1971 from Blundellsands EP.[260] Bootle RDn.

HINDLEY
Tp in Wigan AP, sep CP 1866,[4] Puritan chap built 1641, consecr in Church of England 1698 and perhaps sep then,[521] certainly a sep EP 1777,[12] pt of the latter eccl severed 1866 to help cr Hindley St Peter EP,[219] a further pt eccl severed 1843 to cr Abram EP (some parochial rights 1843,[5] the par ent a sep EP 1852[6]), the remainder of Hindley EP enlarged 1878 with a pt of Abram EP and refounded as 'Hindley' EP.[8] *LG* W Derby Hd, Wigan PLU, Hindley USD, UD. Transf 1974 to Gtr Manch.[40] *Parl* S'rn Dv (1832—67), S-W Dv (1867—85), Ince Dv (1885—1918), W'hough. Dv/CC (1918—*). *Eccl* Warr. RDn (cr—1847), Wigan RDn (1847—*). Addtl eccl bdry alt: 1903 (cr Hindley Green EP).[522]

HINDLEY GREEN
EP Cr 1903 from Hindley EP.[522] Wigan RDn.

HINDLEY ST PETER
EP Cr 1866 from Hindley EP.[219] Wigan RDn. Bdry: 1906 (help cr Platt Bridge EP).[523]

HINDSFORD
EP Cr 1884 from Atherton EP.[123] Eccles RDn (1884—1933), Leigh RDn (1933—*).

HODDLESDEN
EP Cr 1863 from Over Darwen EP.[91] Blackb RDn (1863—1964), Darwen RDn (1964—*).

HOGHTON
Tp in Leyland AP, sep CP 1866,[4] sep EP 1835,[12] eccl refounded 1842.[524] *LG* Seq 8. Civ bdry: 1877,[525] 1934.[226] *Parl* Seq 3. *Eccl* Leyl. RDn (1835—47), Blackb RDn (1847—55), Leyl. RDn (1855—*).

HOLCOMBE
EP Cr 1725 from Bury AP (pt tp Tottington Lower End),[12] pt severed 1844 to help cr Ramsbottom EP,[111] the remainder refounded 1863 as 'Holcombe' EP.[526] Manch RDn (1725—1850), Bury RDn (1850—51), Prestw. RDn (1851—72), Bury RDn (1872—*). Bdry: 1892 (help cr Hawkshaw Lane EP).[44]

LOWER HOLKER
Tp (incl Flookburgh Bor, bor status not sustained) in Cartmel AP, sep CP 1866.[4] *LG* Seq 14. Bdry: 1884,[51] 1884,[341] 1884,[54] 1884,[55] 1884,[56] 1884.[57] Transf 1974 to Cumbria.[40] *Parl* Seq 10.

UPPER HOLKER
Tp in Cartmel AP, sep CP 1866,[4] pt eccl severed 1858 and transf to Haverthwaite EP.[128] *LG* Lonsd. Hd, Ulv. PLU, pt Grange USD (1875—84), Ulv. RSD (pt 1875—84, ent 1884—94), Ulv. RD. Bdry: 1884,[51] 1884,[52] 1884,[53] 1884,[55] 1884,[56] 1884,[57] 1927,[60] 1927 (help cr Haverthwaite CP).[394] Abol 1949 ent to Lower Allithwaite CP.[61] *Parl* N'rn Dv (1832—67), North Dv (1867—85), N Lonsd. Dv (1885—1918), Lonsd. Dv (1918—48), Morec. & Lonsd. CC (1948—70).

HOLLETH
Tp pt in Garstang AP (Amound. Hd), pt in Cockerham AP (Lonsd. Hd), sep CP 1866.[4] *LG* Garst. PLU, RSD, RD. Abol 1935 ent to Forton

CP.[43] *Parl* N'rn Dv (1832—67), North Dv (1867—85), Lanc. Dv (1885—1948).

HOLLINFARE
Chap in Winwick AP, sep EP 1722,[12] eccl refounded 1874,[350] the area of the chap the same as tp Rixton cum Glazebrook, qv for sep civ identity 1866. Warr. RDn (1722—1847), Winwick RDn (1847—1949), Warr. RDn (1949—*).

HOLLINWOOD
EP Cr 1835 from Oldham EP (pt orig area tp Chadderton).[182] Manch RDn (1835—47), Rochd. RDn (1847—72), Oldham RDn (1872—*). Bdry: 1844 (cr Chadderton St Matthew EP, cr Chadderton St John EP, help cr Werneth EP),[348] 1871 (help cr Chadderton Christ Church EP),[16] 1927,[346] 1964,[475] 1965 (help cr Oldham St Chad, Limeside EP).[145]

HOLME IN CLIVIGER
EP Area in tp Cliviger in Whalley AP, eccl in chap Burnley (sep EP 1716 from Whalley AP[12]), pt of orig tp a sep EP 1741 from Burnley EP as 'Holme in Cliviger',[12] refounded 1843 as 'Holme St John' EP.[293] Blackb RDn.

HOLME ISLAND
Eccl ex-par area situated in Cartmel AP, abol eccl 1884 to help cr Grange Over Sands EP.[234]

HOLME ST JOHN
EP Refounding 1843 of EP cr 1741 as 'Holme in Cliviger' (see prev entry for orig status and for cr 1741).[293] Blackb RDn (1843—1847), Whalley RDn (1847—72), Burnley RDn (1872—*). Bdry: 1898 (loses pt [the pt in Todmorden MB] to Harley Wood EP [Lancs, Yorks W Riding] and to dioc Wakef).[22]

HOOLE
Chap in Croston AP, sep par 1641.[409] Incl tps Little Hoole, Much Hoole (each a sep CP 1866[4]) so that 'Hoole' has no sep civ identity after 1866. *LG* Leyl. Hd. *Parl* N'rn Dv (1832—67). *Eccl* Leyl. RDn (1641—1847), N Meols RDn (1847—48), Leyl. RDn (1848—*).

LITTLE HOOLE
Tp in Hoole CP, sep CP 1866.[4] *LG* Seq 10. *Parl* Seq 2.

MUCH HOOLE
Organisation as for Little Hoole.

HOPE
EP Cr 1866 from Eccles AP.[445] Eccles & Salf. RDn (1866—72), Eccles RDn (1872—1903), Salf. RDn (1903—*). Bdry: 1925 (help cr Claremont EP),[221] 1971.[299]

HOPWOOD
Tp in Middleton AP, sep CP 1866,[4] sep EP 1905 from Birch EP, Heywood St Luke EP (qv for sep eccl identity earlier of each).[195] *LG* Salf. Hd, Bury PLU, pt Heyw. USD, pt Heyw. MB (1881—94), pt Middl. & Tonge USD (1875—86), pt Middl. MB & USD (1886—94), pt Castleton by Rochd. USD. Abol civ 1894 the pt in Heyw. MB to help cr Heywood CP,[115] the pt in Middl. MB transf to Middleton AP,[45] the pt in Castleton by Rochdale UD to help cr Castleton by Rochdale CP.[169] *Parl* S'rn Dv (1832—67), S-E Dv (1867—85), Middl. Dv (1885—1918). *Eccl* Prestw. & Middl. RDn (1905—12), Middl. RDn (1912—29), Bury RDn

(1929—*).

HORNBY
Chap (incl Hornby Bor, bor status not sustained) in Melling AP, sep CP 1866,[4] sep EP 1741 (incl tp Farleton in same par),[12] eccl refounded 1859 (incl the pt of orig tp Roeburndale in Wray EP).[478] *LG* Lonsd. Hd, Caton GilbU (until 1869), Lunesd. PLU (1869—87), RSD. Abol civ 1887 to help cr Hornby with Farleton CP.[479] *Parl* N'rn Dv (1832—67), North Dv (1867—85), Lanc. Dv (1885—1918). *Eccl* Kirkby Lonsd. RDn (1741—1848), Tunstall RDn (1848—1931). Abol eccl 1931 to help cr Hornby with Claughton EP.[50]

HORNBY WITH CLAUGHTON
EP Cr 1931 by union Hornby EP, Claughton AP.[50] Tunstall RDn.

HORNBY WITH FARLETON
CP Cr 1887 by union Hornby CP, Farleton CP.[479] *LG* Lonsd. Hd, Lunesd. PLU, RSD, RD. *Parl* Lonsd. Dv (1918—48), Lanc. CC (1948—*).

HORWICH
Chap in Deane AP, sep CP 1866,[4] sep EP 1723,[12] eccl refounded 1853.[420] *LG* Salf. Hd, Bolton PLU, Horwich USD, UD. Transf 1974 to Gtr Manch.[40] *Parl* Seq 15. *Eccl* Manch RDn (1723—1847), Bolton le Moors RDn (1847—93), Bolton North RDn (1893—1901), Bolton le Moors RDn (1901—68), Deane RDn (1968—*). Eccl bdry: 1910 (cr Horwich St Catherine EP).[478]

HORWICH ST CATHERINE
EP Cr 1910 from Horwich EP.[478] Bolton le Moors RDn (1910—68), Deane RDn (1968—*).

HOTHERSALL
Tp in Ribchester AP, sep CP 1866.[4] *LG* Seq 3. *Parl* Seq 2.

WEST HOUGHTON
Tp in Deane AP, sep EP 1719,[12] eccl refounded 1859,[332] sep CP 1866 as 'Westhoughton',[4] qv. *Eccl* Manch RDn (1719—1847), Bolton le Moors RDn (1847—93), Bolton South RDn (1893—1901), Bolton le Moors RDn (1901—68), Deane RDn (1968—*). Eccl bdry: 1860 (help cr Wingates EP),[273] 1882 (cr Daisey Hill EP).[147]

HOUGHTON, MIDDLETON AND ARBURY
Tp in Winwick AP, sep CP 1866.[4] *LG* W Derby Hd, Warr. PLU, RSD, RD. Abol 1933 to help cr Winwick CP.[324] *Parl* S'rn Dv (1832—67), S-W Dv (1867—85), Newton Dv (1885—1948).

HOWE BRIDGE
EP Cr 1878 from Atherton EP.[87] Eccles RDn (1878—1933), Leigh RDn (1933—*). Bdry: 1930 (help cr Leigh St John the Evangelist EP).[149]

HOWICK
Tp in Penwortham AP, sep CP 1866.[4] *LG* Leyl. Hd, Preston PLU, RSD, RD. Abol 1934 pt to help cr Lea CP, pt to Penwortham AP.[226] *Parl* N'rn Dv (1832—67), North Dv (1867—85), Blackp. Dv (1885—1918), Fylde Dv (1918—48).

HULME
The following have 'Hulme' in their names. Insofar as any existed at a given time: *LG* Salf. Hd, Chorlton PLU, Manch MB (1838—89), CB (1889—94), USD. *Parl* Manch Parl Bor (1832—85),

Manch, South West Parl Bor (1885—1918). *Eccl*
Manch RDn (cr—1866), Chorlton & Hulme RDn
(1866—72), Hulme RDn (1872—*).

CP1/EP1—HULME [ST GEORGE]—Tp in Manchester AP, sep CP 1866,[4] sep EP 1836,[527] eccl
refounded 1854.[199] Abol civ 1896 to help cr South
Manchester CP.[82] Eccl bdry: 1846 (cr EP6),[528]
1856 (cr EP9,[529] refounded 1858[70]), 1859 (cr
EP7),[365] 1864 (cr EP8),[94] 1869 (cr EP4),[139] 1870
(cr EP11).[13]

EP2—HULME THE ASCENSION—Renaming 1973
of EP10.[116]

EP3—HULME HOLY TRINITY—Cr 1854 from Manchester AP.[199] Bdry: 1859 (help cr EP5),[365] 1861
(help cr EP10).[181]

EP4—HULME ST GABRIEL—Cr 1869 from EP1.[139]
Bdry: 1875,[85] 1958.[366] Abol 1970 ent to EP10.[530]

EP5—HULME ST JOHN—Cr 1859 from EP3,
Chorlton on Medlock EP, Moss Side EP.[365] Abol
1960 ent to EP10.[531]

EP6—HULME ST MARK—Cr 1846 from EP1.[528]
Abol 1950 to help cr EP13.[186]

EP7—HULME ST MARY—Cr 1859 from EP1.[365]
Bdry: 1882 (help cr Greenheys EP).[203] Abol 1955
to help cr Manchester St Mary, Hulme EP.[154]

EP8—HULME ST MICHAEL—Cr 1864 from EP1.[94]
Abol 1967 to help cr EP12.[273]

EP9—HULME ST PAUL—Cr 1856 from EP1,[529]
refounded 1858.[70] Bdry: 1882 (help cr Greenhays
EP).[203] Abol 1955 to help cr Manchester St Mary,
Hulme EP.[154]

EP10—HULME ST PHILIP—Cr 1861 from EP3,
Chorlton on Medlock EP.[181] Bdry: 1960 (gains
EP5),[531] 1966,[23] 1967 (gains EP12),[493] 1970
(gains EP4).[530] Renamed 1973 as EP2.[116]

EP11—HULME ST STEPHEN—Cr 1870 from EP1.[13]
Abol 1950 to help cr EP13.[186]

EP12—HULME ST STEPHEN—Cr 1967 by union
EP8, EP13.[273] Abol 1967 ent to EP10.[493]

EP13—HULME ST STEPHEN WITH ST MARK—Cr
1950 by union EP12, EP6.[186] Abol 1967 to help
cr EP12.[273]

LITTLE HULTON

Chap in Deane AP, sep CP 1866,[4] pt eccl severed
1761 to cr Peel EP,[12] the latter refounded 1874,[350]
'Little Hulton' a sep EP 1887 from Walkden Moor
EP, Deane AP.[287] *LG* Salf. Hd, Bolton PLU, Little
Hulton USD, UD (1894—1933), Worsley UD
(1933—74). *Parl* Seq 14. *Eccl* Eccles RDn (1887—
1968), Farnw. RDn (1968—*).

MIDDLE HULTON

Tp in Deane AP, sep CP 1866.[4] *LG* Salf. Hd,
Bolton PLU, RSD, RD. Abol 1898 ent to Bolton CB
(assoc with Lancs) & CP.[36] *Parl* S'rn Dv (1832—
67), S-E Dv (1867—85), W'hough. Dv
(1885—1918).

OVER HULTON

Tp in Deane AP, sep CP 1866.[4] *LG* Salf. Hd,
Bolton PLU, RSD, RD. Abol 1898 pt to Bolton CB
(assoc with Lancs) & CP, pt to Westhoughton CP.[36]
Parl S'rn Dv (1832—67), S-E Dv (1867—85),
W'hough. Dv (1885—1918).

HUNCOAT

Tp in Whalley AP, sep CP 1866,[4] eccl in chap
Church (sep EP 1723 as 'Church Kirk' from
Whalley AP[12]), 'Huncoat' a sep EP 1910 from
Church Kirk EP.[121] *LG* Blackb Hd, Burnley PLU,
RSD, RD. Abol 1929 ent to Accr. MB & CP.[15] *Parl*
N'rn Dv (1832—67), N-E Dv (1867—85), Accr. Dv
(1885—1918), Clith. Dv (1918—48).

HUNDERSFIELD

EP Cr 1746 from Rochdale AP,[12] sep eccl status not
sustained. Rochd. RDn.

HUNTS CROSS

EP Cr 1957 from Much Woolton EP, Halewood EP,
Speke EP.[506] Farnw. RDn. Bdry: 1964.[49]

HURST

Area in Ashton under Lyne AP, sep EP 1846,[27] sep
CP 1894 from the pt of the AP in Hurst UD.[98] *LG*
Asht. under Lyne PLU, Hurst UD (1894—1927),
Asht. under Lyne MB (1927—74). Transf 1974 to
Gtr Manch.[40] *Parl* Asht. under Lyne Parl Bor/BC
(1918—*). *Eccl* Manch RDn (1846—47), Asht.
under Lyne RDn (1847—*). Eccl bdry: 1866 (help
cr Ashton under Lyne St James EP),[109] 1974.[110]

HURST GREEN

EP Cr 1839 from Mitton AP (in area Bailey in tp
Aighton, Bailey and Chaigley [ent in Lancs, the
remainder of Mitton AP in Yorks W Riding]),[12]
refounded 1870.[30] Craven RDn (1839—57), Craven
RDn, W'rn Dv (1857—1921), Bolland RDn
(1921—*) (dioc Ripon 1839—1919, dioc Bradf
1919—*).

HUTTON

Tp in Penwortham AP, sep CP 1866.[4] *LG* Seq 10.
Bdry: 1934 (incl help cr Lea CP).[226] *Parl* Seq 2.

HUYTON

AP Incl tp Knowsley (sep CP 1866,[4] chap erected orig
Presbyterian, consecr 1830 in Church of England,
sep EP 1844[532]), tp Huyton with Roby (incl Roby
Bor [status not sustained], the tp a sep CP 1866,[4]
'Roby' a sep EP 1853[533]), tp Tarbock (sep CP
1866[4]) so that 'Huyton' has no sep civ identity after
1866. *LG* W Derby Hd. *Parl* S'rn Dv (1832—67).
Eccl Seq 6. Addtl eccl bdry alt: 1869 (help cr
Whiston EP),[505] 1951 (help cr Huyton St George
EP),[534] 1959 (help cr Huyton Quarry EP),[91]
1963.[276]

HUYTON QUARRY

EP Cr 1959 from Huyton AP, Roby EP, Whiston EP.[91]
Prescot RDn.

HUYTON ST GEORGE

EP Cr 1951 from Huyton AP, Knowsley EP.[534] Prescot
RDn.

HUYTON WITH ROBY

Tp (incl Roby Bor [status not sustained]) in Huyton
AP, sep CP 1866,[4] 'Roby' a sep EP 1853 from this
area[533]. *LG* W Derby Hd, Prescot PLU, Huyton
with Roby USD, UD. Bdry: 1877.[535] Transf 1974
to Merseyside.[40] *Parl* S'rn Dv (1832—67), S-W Dv
(1867—85), Widnes Dv (1885—1948), Huyton CC
(1948—*).

IGHTENHILL

CP Cr 1894 by union of the pts not in Burnley CB of
Habergham Eaves CP, Ightenhill Park CP.[295] *LG*

Burnley PLU, RD. Bdry: 1926 (loses pt to Burnley CB [assoc with Lancs] & CP).[310] *Parl* Clith. Dv/CC (1918—*).

IGHTENHILL PARK

Civ tp in Whalley AP, sep CP 1866,[4] eccl ex-par place called 'Ighton Hill' situated in chap Burnley (qv for sep eccl identity 1716), 'Ighton Hill' eccl abol 1845 to help cr Habergham All Saints EP.[124] *LG* Blackb Hd, Burnley PLU, pt Burnley CB & USD (1889—94), Burnley RSD (ent 1875—89, pt 1889—94). Abol civ 1894 the pt in Burnley CB transf to Burnley CP, the remainder to help cr Ightenhill CP.[295] *Parl* N'rn Dv (1832—67), N-E Dv (1867—85), Darwen Dv (1885—1918).

IGHTON HILL

Ex-par place situated in chap Burnley in Whalley AP, eccl abol 1845 to help cr Habergham All Saints EP,[124] civ a tp in Whalley AP called 'Ightenhill Park', qv for sep identity 1866.

INCE BLUNDELL

Tp in Sefton AP, sep CP 1866.[4] *LG* Seq 16. Bdry: 1956.[404] Transf 1974 to Merseyside.[40] *Parl* S'rn Dv (1832—67), S-W Dv (1867—85), S'port. Dv (1885—1918), Ormsk. Dv/CC (1918—70), Crosby BC (1970—*). Parl bdry: 1960.[536]

INCE IN MAKERFIELD

Tp in Wigan AP, sep CP 1866,[4] eccl severed to help cr Wigan St Catherine EP (some parochial rights 1843,[5] ent sep 1854[119]), 'Ince in Makerfield' a sep EP 1862 from Wigan St Catherine EP.[433] *LG* W Derby Hd, Wigan PLU, Ince in Makerfield USD, UD. Transf 1974 to Gtr Manch.[40] *Parl* Seq 17. *Eccl* Wigan RDn. Eccl bdry: 1888 (cr Ince in Makerfield St Mary EP).[147]

INCE IN MAKERFIELD ST MARY

EP Cr 1888 from Ince in Makerfield EP.[147] Wigan RDn. Bdry: 1906 (help cr Platt Bridge EP).[523]

INGOL

EP Cr 1972 from Ashton upon Ribble St Andrew EP.[114] Preston RDn.

INSKIP

Tp in St Michael on Wyre AP, sep EP 1850,[12] sep CP 1866 as 'Inskip with Sowerby',[4] qv. Amound. RDn (1850—52), Garst. RDn (1852—*).

INSKIP WITH SOWERBY

Tp in St Michael on Wyre AP, sep CP 1866,[4] sep EP 1850 as 'Inskip',[12] qv. *LG* Seq 2. *Parl* Seq 7.

IREBY

Tp (Lancs, Lonsd. Hd) in Thornton in Lonsdale AP (o'wise ent Yorks W Riding, Staincliffe Wap), sep CP 1866 in Lancs.[4] *LG* Lonsd. Hd, Lunesd. PLU, RSD, RD. *Parl* Seq 8.

IRELETH WITH ASKAM

EP Cr 1874 from Dalton in Furness AP.[24] Aldingham RDn (1874—83), Dalton RDn (1883—1970), Furness RDn (1970—*).

IRLAM

EP Cr 1867 from Eccles AP.[446] Eccles & Salf. RDn (1867—72), Eccles RDn (1872—*). Bdry: 1925 (help cr Cadishead EP),[338] 1967,[160] 1968 (help cr Flixton St John EP).[418]

CP Cr 1894 from pt of the pt of Barton upon Irwell CP not in Eccles MB.[176] *LG* Barton upon Irwell PLU,

Irlam UD. Bdry: 1896,[170] 1920 (exchanges pts with Carrington CP, Partington CP, both Ches),[484] 1933,[171] 1969.[495] Transf 1974 to Gtr Manch.[40] *Parl* Stretf. Dv (1918—48), Newton CC (1948—*). Parl bdry: 1945.[339]

KEARSLEY

Tp in Deane AP, sep CP 1866,[4] eccl severed 1829 to help cr Farnsworth and Kearsley EP.[421] *LG* Salf. Hd, Bolton PLU, Kearsley USD, UD. Bdry: 1933.[171] Transf 1974 to Gtr Manch.[40] *Parl* Seq 14.

KEARSLEY MOOR

EP Cr 1872 from Farnsworth and Kearsley EP.[132] Bolton le Moors RDn (1872—93), Bolton South RDn (1893—1901), Bolton le Moors RDn (1901—68), Farnw. RDn (1968—*).

NETHER KELLET

Tp in Bolton le Sands AP, sep CP 1866.[4] *LG* Seq 13. *Parl* Seq 9.

OVER KELLET

Chap in Bolton le Sands AP, sep CP 1866,[4] sep EP 1730.[12] *LG* Seq 13. *Parl* Seq 9. *Eccl* Kendal RDn (1730—1848), Tunstall RDn (1848—*).

KENYON

Tp in Winwick AP, united eccl 1748 with tp Culceth in same par to cr 'Newchurch' EP,[12] as such eccl refounded 1844,[399] the orig tp of Kenyon united civ 1845 with tp Culceth to cr 'Newchurch Kenyon' CP,[92] 'Kenyon' a sep CP 1866 from Newchurch Kenyon CP.[4] *LG* W Derby Hd, Warr. PLU (1837—soon after 1837[537]), Leigh PLU (soon after 1837[537]—1930), RSD, RD. Abol civ 1933 ent to Golborne UD & CP.[37] *Parl* S'rn Dv (1832—67), S-W Dv (1867—85), Leigh Dv (1885—1918), Newton Dv (1918—48).

LOWER KERSAL

EP Cr 1972 from Charlestown EP, Kersall Moor EP.[351] Salf. RDn.

KERSALL MOOR

EP Cr 1854 from Manchester AP.[199] Bury RDn (1854—72), Salf. RDn (1872—*). Bdry: 1909,[356] 1947,[243] 1972 (cr Lower Kersal EP).[351]

KIKRBY

Chap in Walton on the Hill AP, sep CP 1866,[4] sep EP 1748,[12] eccl refounded 1872 from Walton on the Hill AP (incl tp [orig ex-par] Simonswood).[70] *LG* W Derby Hd, PLU, RSD, Sefton RD (1894—1922), Whiston RD (1922—58), Kirkby UD (1958—74). Civ bdry: 1956 (exchanges pts with Liverp CB [assoc with Lancs] & CP),[538] 1958,[539] 1969.[540] Transf 1974 to Merseyside.[40] *Parl* S'rn Dv (1832—67), S-W Dv (1867—85), Ormsk. Dv (1885—1918), Widnes Dv (1918—48), Huyton CC (1948—70), Ormsk. CC (1970—*). Parl bdry: 1960.[405] *Eccl* Warr. RDn (1748—1847), Prescot RDn (1847—1902), W Derby RDn (1902—20), Ormsk. RDn (1920—49), Walton RDn (1949—*). Eccl bdry: 1909 (help cr Fazakerley EP),[41] 1971.[18]

KIRKBY IRELETH

AP Incl chap Broughton West (sep CP 1866,[4] sep EP 1870 as 'Broughton in Furness'[306]), chap Seathwaite (sep EP 1738,[12] eccl refounded 1886[233]; the area civ pt of tp Dunnerdale with Seathwaite, qv below for sep civ identity), chap Woodland (sep EP

1731,[12] refounded 1876[75]), tp Dunnerdale with Seathwaite (sep CP 1866,[4] eccl incl chap Seathwaite, qv above for sep eccl identity). *LG* Seq 14. Transf 1974 to Cumbria.[40] *Parl* Seq 10. *Eccl* Pec jurisd Dean & Chapter of York (until 1836), Furness & Cartmel RDn (1836—59), Ulv. RDn (1859—1970), Furness RDn (1970—*).

KIRKDALE

The following have 'Kirkdale' in their names. Insofar as any existed at a given time: *LG* W Derby Hd, Liverp MB/CB, USD. *Parl* Liverp Parl Bor (1832—85), Liverp, Kirkdale Parl Bor (1885—1918); see Part III of the *Guide* for composition of Liverp Parl Bors (1918—48) by wards of the CB. *Eccl* Warr. RDn (cr—1847), Liverp North RDn (1847—1949), Liverp RDn (1949—*).

CP1/EP1—KIRKDALE [ST MARY]—Tp in Walton on the Hill AP, sep CP 1866,[4] sep EP 1844.[42] Abol civ 1922 ent to Liverpool CP.[47] Eccl bdy: 1867,[172] 1868 (cr North Shore EP, sometimes called 'Kirkdale St Paul, North Shore'),[91] 1881 (cr EP2),[541] 1887,[296] 1912 (cr EP3).[397]

EP2—KIRKDALE ST ATHANASIUS—Cr 1881 from EP1.[541] Bdry: 1958 (incl gains Liverpool St Aidan EP).[542]

EP3—KIRKDALE ST LAWRENCE—Cr 1912 from EP1.[397]

—KIRKDALE ST PAUL, NORTH SHORE—Name sometimes used for EP cr 1868 as 'North Shore', qv.

KIRKHAM

AP Incl detached chap and tp Goosnargh (sep CP 1866,[4] pt of tp Goosnargh eccl severed 1717 to cr 'Whitechapel' EP,[12] the latter refounded 1846,[498] the remainder of the chap a sep EP 1721 [incl tp Newsham (not sep civ) and tp Whittingham (qv for civ) in same par],[12] eccl refounded 1846[499]), chap Hambleton (sep CP 1866,[4] sep EP 1738,[12] eccl refounded 1846[508]), chap Lytham (sep par early[189]), chap Ribby with Wrea (sep CP 1866,[4] sep EP 1759 as 'Ribby cum Wrea',[12] as such eccl refounded 1846[543]), chap Singleton (sep CP 1866,[4] sep EP 1754 [areas Great Singleton, Little Singleton, Thistleton (none sep civ)],[12] eccl refounded 1851[544]), chap Warton (sep CP 1866,[4] sep EP 1754,[12] eccl refounded 1846[545]), tp Bryning with Kellamergh (sep CP 1866,[4] tp Clifton with Salwick (sep CP 1866,[4] sep EP 1737 as 'Lund'[12]), tp Little Eccleston with Larbreck (sep CP 1866[4]), tp Freckleton (sep CP 1866,[4] sep EP 1874[489]), tps Greehalgh with Thistleton, Medlar with Wesham, Newton with Scales; Treales, Roseacre and Wharles; Westby with Plumpton, Whittingham (each of the 6 a sep CP 1866[4]), tp Weeton and Preese (sep CP 1866,[4] sep EP 1846 as 'Weeton'[546]). *LG* Amound. Hd, Fylde PLU, pt Kirkham Bor, Kirkham USD, UD. Addtl civ bdry alt: 1935.[43] *Parl* Seq 2. *Eccl* Seq 8. Addtl eccl bdry alt: 1846 (cr Weeton EP),[547] 1858 (cr Treales EP),[548] 1912 (cr Wesham EP).[88]

KIRKHOLT

EP Cr 1964 from Castleton Moor EP, Balderstone in Rochdale EP.[136] Rochd. RDn.

KIRKLAND

Tp in Garstang AP, sep CP 1866.[4] *LG* Seq 2. *Parl* Seq 7.

KIRKMANSHULME

EP Cr 1898 from Longsight EP.[13] Ardwick RDn (1898—1912), Heaton RDn (1912—*). Bdry: 1925 (help cr Gorton St Mary and St Thomas EP),[49] 1957.[205]

KNOTTY ASH HOLY SPIRIT

EP Cr 1933 from Knotty Ash St John the Evangelist EP, West Derby EP.[283] W Derby RDn.

KNOTTY ASH ST JOHN THE EVANGELIST

EP Cr 1836 from Walton on the Hill AP,[306] refounded 1927 from West Derby EP, Childwall AP.[346] Warr. RDn (1836—47), Prescot RDn (1847—1902), W Derby RDn (1902—*). Bdry: 1933 (cr Knotty Ash Holy Spirit EP),[283] 1964.[49] Sometimes 'West Derby St John the Evangelist'.

KNOWSLEY

Tp in Huyton AP, sep CP 1866,[4] the chap built orig Presbyterian, consecr 1830 in Church of England, sep EP 1844.[531] *LG* Seq 18. Civ bdry: 1932,[453] 1958.[540] Transf 1974 to Merseyside.[40] *Parl* Seq 21. Parl bdry: 1960.[536] *Eccl* Warr. RDn (1844—47), Prescot RDn (1847—1920), W Derby RDn (1920—*). Eccl bdry: 1951 (help cr Huyton St George EP),[534] 1951 (help cr West Derby St Luke EP),[434] 1968.[231]

KNUZDEN

EP Cr 1879 from Oswaldtwistle EP, Blackburn St Thomas EP.[154] Whalley RDn (1879—1912), Accr. RDn (1912—67), Blackb RDn (1967—*). Bdry: 1950,[213] 1966 (help cr Oswaldtwistle All Saints EP).[372]

LADYBARN

EP Cr 1900 from Fallowfield EP, Birch in Rusholme EP, Withington EP, Burnage EP.[202] Ardwick RDn (1900—12), Heaton RDn (1912—65), Withington RDn (1965—*). Bdry: 1929.[204]

LANCASTER

The following have 'Lancaster' in their names. Insofar as any existed at a given time: *LG* Lonsd. Hd (pt until 1866, ent from 1866), pt Amound. Hd (until 1866), Lanc. PLU, Bor/MB, USD. *Parl* Lanc. Parl Bor (irregularly 1295—1359, regularly 1547—1867), North Dv (1867—85), Lanc. Dv/CC (1885—*). *Eccl* Lanc. RDn (until before 1291), Amound. RDn (before 1291—1852), Lanc. RDn (1852—*).

AP1—LANCASTER [ST MARY]—Tp 'Lancaster' in Lonsd. Hd as were chap Caton (sep CP 1866,[4] sep EP 1737 as 'Caton with Littledale'[12]), chap Gressingham (sep CP 1866,[4] sep EP 1725[12]), chap Overton (sep CP 1866,[4] sep EP 1715 [incl tps Heaton with Oxcliffe, Middleton][12]), chap Over Wyresdale (sep CP 1866,[4] sep EP 1728 as 'Wyresdale',[12] as such eccl refounded 1867[159]), tps Adcliffe, Ashton with Stodday, Bulk (each a sep CP 1866[4]), tps Heaton with Oxcliffe, Middleton (each a sep CP 1866,[4] both eccl in chap/EP Overton [qv above]), tp Poulton Barre and Torrisholme (sep CP 1866,[4] sep EP 1748 as 'Poulton',[12] as such eccl refounded 1859[332] [the

EP sometimes called 'Poulton le Sands']), tp Quernmore (sep CP 1866,[4] sep EP 1836,[12] eccl refounded 1858[347]), tp Scotforth (sep CP 1866,[4] sep EP 1846 [the tp and an addtl pt of the AP][16]), tp Skerton (sep CP 1866,[4] sep EP 1834[549]), pt tp Thurnham (sep CP 1866[4]); incl in Amound. Hd chap Bleasdale (sep CP 1866,[4] sep EP 1748 as 'Admarsh',[12] sometimes called 'Admarsh in Bleasdale'), chap Stalmine with Staynall (perhaps orig a sep AP,[550] sep CP 1866,[4] sep EP 1714 as 'Stalmine'[12]), tp Fulwood (sep CP 1866,[4] sep EP 1865[10]), tp Myerscough (sep CP 1866[4]), tp Preesall with Hackinsall (sep CP 1866[4]); incl for poor law purposes ex-par Lancaster Castle, so that the area of the latter is gained civ 1858.[80] Addtl civ bdry alt: 1935 (incl gains Aldcliffe EP),[43] 1962.[459] Addtl eccl bdry alt: 1756 (cr EP3,[12] refounded 1842[23]), 1812 (cr EP2,[12] refounded 1842[23]), 1844 (cr EP5),[551] 1846 (cr Glasson EP),[12] 1874 (cr EP1),[177] 1955.[552]

—LANCASTER CASTLE—Ex-par place, in Lanc. Bor/MB, not sep rated for poor law purposes and thus incl 1858 in AP1.[80]

EP1—LANCASTER CHRIST CHURCH—Cr 1874 from AP1.[177] Bdry: 1933.[206]

EP2—LANCASTER ST ANNE—Cr 1812 from AP1,[12] refounded 1842.[23] Bdry: 1955.[552] Abol 1958 to help cr EP4.[553]

EP3—LANCASTER ST JOHN—Cr 1756 from AP1,[12] refounded 1842.[23] Abol 1958 to help cr EP4.[553]

EP4—LANCASTER ST JOHN WITH ST ANNE—Cr 1958 by union EP2, EP3.[553]

EP5—LANCASTER ST THOMAS—Cr 1844 from AP1.[551] Bdry: 1933,[206] 1963.[150]

LANDS COMMON TO LOWICK AND SUBBERTHWAITE
LG Ulv. RD (1894—1960), N Lonsd. RD (1960—74). Transf 1974 to Cumbria.[40] Parl Lonsd. Dv (1918—48), Morec. & Lonsd. CC (1948—*).

LANE BRIDGE
EP Cr 1845 from Whalley AP (pt tp Habergham Eaves [qv for orig status in chap Burnley]).[124] Blackb RDn (1845—47), Whalley RDn (1847—72), Burnley RDn (1872—1962). Bdry: 1851,[313] 1879 (help cr Burnley St Stephen EP),[314] 1880,[315] 1880 (help cr Habergham Eaves St Matthew the Apostle EP),[320] 1880.[321] Abol 1962 pt to Burnley EP, pt to Burnley St Stephen EP, pt to Habergham Eaves St Matthew the Apostle EP.[317]

LANESIDE
EP Cr 1894 from Haslingden EP.[161] Whalley RDn (1894—1912), Accr. RDn (1912—*). Now sometimes called 'Haslingden St Peter'.

LANGHO
EP Chap in Blackburn AP, sep EP 1746,[12] eccl refounded 1842,[133] sep CP 1866 as 'Billington',[4] qv. Blackb RDn (1746—1912), Whalley RDn (1912—*). Bdry: 1936.[71] Sometimes called 'Langho Billington'.

LANGLEY
EP Cr 1964 from Birch EP, Middleton AP, Parkfield in Middleton EP, Rhodes EP.[197] Middl. RDn.

LATCHFORD
Chap in Grappenhall AP, deemed civ ent in Ches, sep CP 1866,[4] deemed eccl pt in Lancs, that pt a sep EP 1796 as 'Latchford St James',[12] eccl refounded 1866 from Grappenhall AP, Thelwall EP (both Ches) and from Warrington AP (Lancs),[84] the pt deemed eccl in Ches a sep EP 1866 from Grappenhall AP as 'Latchford Christ Church',[554] qv in entries for that co. LG Runcorn PLU (1836—45), Warr. PLU (1845—94), Warr. MB (pt 1847—94, ent 1894—98), pt Warr. USD, pt Runc. RSD. Civ bdry: 1884,[555] 1894 (the pt in Ches [the pt not in Warr. MB] cr Latchford Without CP),[556] 1896 (gains pts Appleton CP, Latchford Without CP, Walton Inferior CP, all Ches).[557] Abol civ 1898 ent to Warrington AP.[558] Parl Lancs pt, S'rn Dv (1832—67), S-W Dv (1867—85), Bootle Dv (1885—1918).

LATCHFORD ST JAMES
EP EP cr 1796 from the Lancs pt of chap Latchford (Ches, Lancs) in Grappenhall AP,[12] refounded 1866 from Grappenhall AP, Thelwall EP (both Ches), Warrington AP (Lancs)[84]; for remainder of orig area chap Latchford, see 'Latchford Christ Church' in entries for Ches. For RDns, see entry in Ches.

LATHOM
Chap in Ormskirk AP, sep CP 1866,[4] pt eccl severed 1847 to cr Burscough Bridge EP [sometimes 'Lathom St John'],[322] the remainder cr 1851 'Lathom St James' EP,[12] the latter eccl refounded as such 1860.[254] LG W Derby Hd, Ormsk. PLU, Lathom USD (1875—94), Lathom & Burscough USD (1894), UD (1894—1931), Ormsk. UD (1931—74). Civ bdry: 1914,[559] 1931.[126] Parl Seq 20.

LATHOM ST JAMES
EP Cr 1851 from the pt of tp Lathom in Ormskirk AP not severed 1847 (to cr Burscough Bridge EP),[12] refounded 1860.[254] N Meols RDn (1851—87), Ormsk. RDn (1887—*). Bdry: 1871 (area of hmlt Newburgh in this par severed to cr 'Newburgh' EP).[149]

LATHOM ST JOHN—see BURSCOUGH BRIDGE

LAYTON WITH WARBRECK
Tp in Bispham AP, sep CP 1866.[4] LG Amound. Hd, Fylde PLU, Blackp. USD, MB (1876—94). Bdry: 1883 (gains the pt of Bispham with Norbreck CP in Blackp. MB & USD).[216] Abol 1894 to help cr Blackpool CP.[217] Parl N'rn Dv (1832—67), North Dv (1867—85), Blackp. Dv (1885—1918).

LEA
CP Cr 1934 from Howick CP, Hutton CP, and Lea, Ashton, Ingol and Cottam CP.[226] LG Preston RD. Bdry: 1952 (loses pt to Preston CB [assoc with Lancs] & AP),[490] 1956 (loses pt to Preston CB [assoc with Lancs] & AP).[560] Parl S Fylde CC (1948—*). Parl bdry: 1953,[561] 1960.[562]

LEA, ASHTON, INGOL AND COTTAM
Tp in Preston AP, sep CP 1866,[4] sep EP 1837 as 'Ashton upon Ribble St Andrew'.[12] LG Amound. Hd, Preston PLU, pt Preston USD, pt Preston MB (1880—89), pt [enlarged] Preston CB (1889—94), pt Preston RSD, Preston RD. Civ bdry: 1889

(further pt incl in the CB),[563] 1894 (loses the pt in the CB to Preston AP).[482] Abol 1934 pt to help cr Lea CP, pt to Preston CB (assoc with Lancs) & AP, pt to Fulwood UD & CP, pt to Penwortham AP.[226] *Parl* N'rn Dv (1832—67), North Dv (1867—85), pt Preston Parl Bor, pt Blackp. Dv (1885—1918), Fylde Dv (1918—48).

LEAGRAM
Tp in Whalley AP, sep CP 1866,[4] sometimes early rated for poor law purposes with Little Bowland. *LG* Blackb Hd, Clith. PLU, RSD, RD. Abol 1935 to help cr Bowland with Leagram CP.[43] *Parl* N'rn Dv (1832—67), N-E Dv (1867—85), Darwen Dv (1885—1918), Clith. Dv (1918—48).

LECK
Chap in Tunstal AP, sep CP 1866,[4] sep EP 1737,[12] eccl refounded 1859.[478] *LG* Lonsd. Hd, Lunesd. PLU, RSD, RD. *Parl* Seq 8. *Eccl* Kirkby Lonsd. RDn (1737—1848), Tunstall RDn (1848—*).

LEES
EP Name sometimes used for EP cr 1746 and refounded 1860 as 'Hey', qv.
CP Cr 1894 from the pt of Ashton under Lyne AP in Lees UD.[98] *LG* Asht. under Lyne PLU, Lees UD. Bdry: 1911,[407] 1914 (gains Crossbank CP).[408] Transf 1974 to Gtr Manch.[40] *Parl* Mossley Dv (1918—48), Oldham East BC (1948—*).

LEESFIELD
EP Cr 1846 from Oldham EP, Ashton under Lyne AP.[107] Manch RDn (1846—47), Asht. under Lyne RDn (1847—72), Oldham RDn (1872—*). Bdry: 1925 (help cr Roundthorn EP).[493]

LEIGH
AP Incl chap Astley (sep CP 1866,[4] sep EP 1722,[12] eccl refounded 1843[119]), chap Atherton (sep CP 1866,[4] pt a sep EP 1722,[12] eccl refounded 1859[121]), tp Bedford (sep CP 1866,[4] sep EP 1843 as 'Bedford Leigh', later 'Bedford'[119]), tp West Leigh (sep CP 1866,[4] sep EP 1851 as 'Westleigh St Paul',[12] as such eccl refounded 1892[564]), tp Pennington (sep CP 1866,[4] sep EP 1854[565]), tp Tyldesley cum Shackerley (sep CP 1866,[4] sep EP 1827,[12] refounded 1828[566]) so that 'Leigh' has no sep civ identity 1866—94 (see following entry). *LG* W Derby Hd. *Parl* S'rn Dv (1832—67). *Eccl* Warr. RDn (until 1847), Leyl. RDn (1847—50), Eccles RDn (1850—66), Eccles & Salf. RDn (1866—72), Eccles RDn (1872—1933), Leigh RDn (1933—*). Eccl bdry: 1881 (cr Westleigh St Peter EP),[567] 1930 (help cr Leigh St John the Evangelist EP).[149]
CP Cr 1894 by union of the pars in Leigh UD: Bedford CP, West Leigh CP, Pennington CP, and also pt Atherton CP.[122] *LG* Leigh PLU, USD (1894—99), MB (1899—1974). Bdry: 1969.[495] Transf 1974 to Gtr Manch.[40] *Parl* Leigh Parl Bor/BC (1918—*).

WEST LEIGH
Tp in Leigh AP, sep CP 1866,[4] sep EP 1851 as 'Westleigh St Paul',[12] qv. *LG* W Derby Hd, Leigh PLU, USD. Abol 1894 to help cr Leigh CP.[122] *Parl* S'rn Dv (1832—67), S-W Dv (1867—85), Leigh Dv (1885—1918).

LEIGH ST JOHN THE EVANGELIST
EP Cr 1930 from Leigh AP, Howe Bridge EP.[149]

Eccles RDn (1930—33), Leigh RDn (1933—*).

LEVENSHULME
Tp in Manchester AP, sep CP 1866,[4] eccl severed 1770 to help cr Heaton Norris EP,[12] 'Levenshulme' a sep EP 1861 from Heaton Norris EP (orig area tp Levenshulme), Gorton EP, Birch in Rusholme EP.[200] *LG* Salf. Hd, Chorlton PLU, Levenshulme USD, UD (1894—1909), Manch CB (1909—10). Abol civ 1910 ent to South Manchester CP.[310] *Parl* S'rn Dv (1832—67), S-E Dv (1867—85), Stretf. Dv (1885—1918). *Eccl* Chorlton RDn (1861—72), Ardwick RDn (1872—1912), Heaton RDn (1912—*). Eccl bdry: 1886 (help cr Birch in Rusholme St Agnes EP [orig as 'Birch St Agnes', later 'Birch in Rusholme St Agnes']),[201] 1899 (cr South Levenshulme EP),[146] 1902 (cr Levenshulme St Mark EP),[554] 1925 (help cr Gorton St Mary and St Thomas EP),[49] 1926.[70]

SOUTH LEVENSHULME
EP Cr 1899 from Levenshulme EP.[146] Ardwick RDn (1899—1912), Heaton RDn (1912—*).

LEVENSHULME ST MARK
EP Cr 1902 from Levenshulme EP.[554] Ardwick RDn (1902—12), Heaton RDn (1912—*).

DARCY LEVER
Tp in Bolton le Moors AP, sep CP 1866,[4] eccl severed 1844 to help cr Lever Bridge EP.[111] *LG* Salf. Hd, Bolton PLU, RSD, RD. Abol 1898 ent to Bolton CB (assoc with Lancs) & CP.[36] *Parl* S'rn Dv (1832—67), S-E Dv (1867—85), W'hough. Dv (1885—1918).

GREAT LEVER
Tp in Middleton AP, sep CP 1866,[4] sep EP 1861.[568] *LG* Salf. Hd, Bolton PLU, RSD, RD. Abol civ 1898 ent to Bolton CB (assoc with Lancs) & CP.[36] *Parl* S'rn Dv (1832—67), S-E Dv (1867—85), W'hough. Dv (1885—1918). *Eccl* Bolton le Moors RDn (1861—93), Bolton South RDn (1893—1901), Bolton le Moors RDn (1901—61). Eccl bdry: 1880 (help cr Great Bolton EP),[264] 1902 (help cr Bolton le Moors St Simon and St Jude EP),[230] 1930.[149] Abol eccl 1961 to help cr Great Lever St Michael with St Bartholomew EP.[265]

GREAT LEVER ST MICHAEL WITH ST BARTHOLOMEW
EP Cr 1961 by union Great Lever EP, Great Bolton EP.[265] Bolton le Moors RDn (1961—68), Farnw. RDn (1968—*).

LITTLE LEVER
Tp in Bolton le Moors AP, sep CP 1866,[4] sep EP 1793,[12] eccl refounded 1866.[272] *LG* Salf. Hd, Bolton PLU, Little Lever USD, UD. Transf 1974 to Gtr Manch.[40] *Parl* S'rn Dv (1832—67), S-E Dv (1867—85), W'hough. Dv (1885—1918), Farnw. Dv/CC (1918—*). *Eccl* Manch RDn (1793—1847), Bolton le Moors RDn (1847—93), Bolton South RDn (1893—1901), Bolton le Moors RDn (1901—68), Farnw. RDn (1968—*). Sometimes eccl 'Lever St Matthew'.

LEVER BRIDGE
EP Cr 1844 from Bolton le Moors AP (union tp Darcy Lever, pt of the area of Haulgh in tp Tonge with Haulgh).[111] Manch RDn (1844—47), Bolton le

Moors RDn (1847—93), Bolton North RDn (1893—1901), Bolton le Moors RDn (1901—*). Bdry: 1912 (help cr Tonge Fold EP).[269]

LEYLAND

AP Incl chap Euxton (sep CP 1866,[4] sep EP 1729,[12] eccl refounded 1892[463]), chap Heapey (sep CP 1866,[4] sep EP 1739[12]), tp Clayton le Woods (sep CP 1866[4]), tp Cuerden (sep CP 1866[4]), tp Hoghton (sep CP 1866,[4] sep EP 1835,[12] eccl refounded 1842[521]), tp Wheelton (sep CP 1866[4]), tp Whittle le Woods (sep CP 1866,[4] sep EP 1832,[12] eccl refounded 1842[521]), tp Withnell (sep CP 1866,[4] sep EP 1842[521]). *LG* Leyl. Hd, Chorley PLU, Leyl. USD, UD. Addtl civ bdry alt: 1934.[226] *Parl* Seq 3. *Eccl* Seq 1. Addtl eccl bdry alt: 1855 (help cr Leyland St James EP),[292] 1869,[139] 1888,[19] 1898 (help cr Leyland St Ambrose EP).[62]

LEYLAND ST AMBROSE

EP Cr 1898 from Leyland AP, Whittle le Woods EP, Bamber Bridge St Saviour EP, Farington EP.[62] Leyl. RDn.

LEYLAND ST JAMES

EP Cr 1855 from Leyland AP, Bretherton EP.[292] Leyl. RDn.

LIGHTBOWNE

EP Cr 1911 from Moston EP.[71] Cheetham RDn. Bdry: 1924.[313]

LINDALE

EP Cr 1734 from Cartmel AP.[12] Furness & Cartmel RDn (1734—1859), Cartmel RDn (1859—1970), Windermere RDn (1970—*).

LINDALE WITH MARTON

EP Cr 1872 from Dalton in Furness AP.[70] Aldingham RDn (1872—83), Dalton RDn (1883—1970), Furness RDn (1970—*).

LITHERLAND

The following have 'Litherland' in their names. Insofar as any existed at a given time: *LG* W Derby Hd, PLU, pt Waterloo with Seaforth USD, pt Litherland USD, Litherland UD. *Parl* S'rn Dv (1832—67), S-W Dv (1867—85), Ormsk. Dv (1885—1918), Waterloo Dv (1918—48), Bootle BC (1948—55), Crosby BC (1955—70), Bootle BC (1970—*). Parl bdry: 1955.[488] *Eccl* Warr. RDn (cr—1847), Liverp North RDn (1847—95), Bootle RDn (1895—*).

CP1/EP1—LITHERLAND [CHRIST CHURCH]—Tp in Sefton AP, sep CP 1866,[4] sep EP 1842.[569] Civ bdry: 1894 (the pt in Waterloo with Seaforth UD cr Seaforth CP),[402] 1940 (loses pt to Bootle CB [assoc with Lancs] and to Orrell CP),[486] 1954 (incl gains Ford CP).[487] Transf 1974 to Merseyside.[40] Eccl bdry: 1877 (help cr Waterloo St John EP),[406] 1933.[49] Later called 'Waterloo Christ Church'.

EP2—LITHERLAND ST ANDREW—Cr 1905 from EP5.[342]

EP3—LITHERLAND ST JOHN AND ST JAMES—Cr 1911 from EP5.[212] Bdry: 1956.[416]

EP4—LITHERLAND ST PAUL, HATTON HILL—Cr 1961 from EP5.[570]

EP5—LITHERLAND ST PHILIP—Cr 1871 from Sefton AP.[75] Bdry: 1886,[8] 1905 (cr EP2),[342] 1911

(cr EP3),[212] 1956,[416] 1961 (cr EP4).[570] Sometimes called 'Orrell Hey'.

LITTLEBOROUGH

EP Chap in Rochdale AP, sep EP 1745 (incl pt areas Wuerdle, Wardle [each a pt of the area of tp Wuerdle and Wardle, qv for civ identity from Rochdale AP]),[12] refounded 1859.[235] Manch RDn (1745—1847), Rochd. RDn (1847—*). Bdry: 1841 (loses the orig pt of area Wardle to help cr Wardle St James EP),[235] 1841 (loses the orig pt of area Wuerdle, severed and transf to Smallbridge EP),[296] 1895 (help cr Dearnley EP),[88] 1896 (cr Calderbrook EP),[194] 1900 (cr Shore EP).[132]

CP Cr 1894 by union of the following in Littleborough UD: ent Blatchinworth and Caldebrook CP, pt Butterworth CP, pt Wuerdle and Wardle CP.[257] *LG* Rochd. PLU, Littleborough UD. Transf 1974 to Gtr Manch.[40] *Parl* Royton Dv (1918—48), Heyw. & Royton CC (1948—*).

LIVERPOOL

The following have 'Liverpool' in their names. Details of cr, consecr, acquisition of early pars, unless o'wise noted, from secondary sources.[165] Insofar as any existed at a given time: *LG* W Derby Hd, Liverp Par (poor law purposes), Bor/MB/CB, USD. *Parl* Liverp Parl Bor (1295, 1306, 1547—1885); see Part III of the *Guide* for composition of Liverp Parl Bors/BCs (1885—*) by wards of the MB/CB. *Eccl* Warr. RDn (cr—1847), sep noted (1847—1949), Liverp RDn (1949—*).

CP1/EP1—LIVERPOOL [orig chap ST MARY DEL KEY, from 1356 OUR LADY AND ST NICHOLAS, from 1699 (new church built when made a sep par) ST PETER AND ST NICHOLAS, from 1916 ST NICHOLAS when that church was made the par church in place of St Peter[571]]—Chap in Walton on the Hill AP, sep par 1699.[572] Civ bdry: 1922 (gains the following pars in Liverp CB: Allerton CP, Childwall AP, West Derby CP, Everton CP, Fazakerley CP, Garston CP, Kirkdale CP, Toxteth Park CP, Walton on the Hill AP, Wavertree CP, Little Woolton CP, Much Woolton CP),[47] 1928 (gains Croxteth Park CP, West Derby Rural CP),[410] 1932 (gains Speke CP),[362] 1952,[504] 1956 (exchanges pts with Kirkby UD & CP).[534] Transf 1974 to Merseyside.[40] Parl bdry: 1955,[488] 1960.[532] *Eccl* Liverp North RDn (1847—1949). Eccl bdry: 1734 (cr EP24 [begun 1726 by statutory authority in act of 1715]), 1769 (cr EP35 [begun 1763]), 1773 (consecr EP15 [built by statutory authority 1772, opened 1773]), 1785 (consecr EP26 [built by corporation]), 1792 (cr EP42 [former Baptist chap opened as Church of England 1792]), 1812 (cr EP32 [former Presbyterian chap, consecr 1798 Church of England]),[12] 1814 (cr EP43),[12] 1815 (consecr EP29 [built 1803 by subscription]), 1815 (cr EP14 [privately erected]),[360] 1816 (open EP37), 1826 (open EP34 [begun 1816]), 1829 (cr EP31 [erected 1825—29]), 1831 (consecr EP21), 1831 (cr EP23),[12] 1831 (consecr EP19), 1831 (opening of EP28 [begun 1811]), 1834 (cr EP33 [built 1833—34]), 1839 (cr EP38 [built by subscription]), 1841 (cr EP18), 1841 (opening of EP17), 1841 (cr EP27 [acquired 1841 from Nonconformists]), 1843 (cr EP39 [opened 1841]), 1845 (cr Bevington EP, cr EP2),[186] 1846 (cr EP41 [former Presbyterian chap, consecr 1841 Church of England]),[254] 1847 (cr EP4 [or 'Vauxhall']),[573] 1852,[574] 1858 (cr EP22 [Wesleyan chap acquired 1858 and consecr in Church of England]), 1861 (help cr EP12),[304] 1862 (consecr EP30 [built 1859]), 1866 (cr EP44),[575] 1881 (help cr EP7),[507] 1917,[576] *ca* 1947 (gains EP13),[577] 1949 (gains EP31, EP33),[577] 1958.[542] Abol eccl 1970 to help cr EP10.[578]

EP2—LIVERPOOL ALL SAINTS—Cr 1845 from EP1.[186] Liverp North RDn (1847—82), Walton RDn (1882—1906), Liverp North RDn (1906—39). Closed 1937, abol 1939 to help cr Everton St Ambrose with All Saints.[469]

EP3—LIVERPOOL ALL SOULS, SPRINGWOOD—Cr 1923 from Grassendale EP, Garston EP, Allerton EP.[48] Childwall RDn. Bdry: 1964.[49]

EP4—LIVERPOOL ALL SOULS [VAUXHALL]—Cr 1847 (sometimes early 'Vauxhall') from AP1.[573] Bdry: 1852.[574] Liverp North RDn (1847—1923). Abol 1923 ent to EP18.[579]

EP5—LIVERPOOL CHRIST CHURCH, KENSINGTON—Cr 1872 from West Derby EP, Fairfield EP.[279] Liverp North RDn (1872—82), Walton RDn (1882—1906), Liverp North RDn (1906—49), Toxteth RDn (1949—*). Bdry: 1974.[458]

EP6—LIVERPOOL EDGE LANE ST MARK—Cr 1909 from Fairfield EP, Wavertree St Mary EP, Stoneycroft EP, Stanley St Ann EP.[35] W Derby RDn.

—LIVERPOOL HOLY INNOCENTS—Chap of Myrtle Street Orphanage, sometimes considered sep par because of some baptismal rights, closed 1923.

EP7—LIVERPOOL HOLY TRINITY—Cr 1881 from EP1, EP30.[507] Warr. RDn (until 1847), Liverp North RDn (1847—82), Walton RDn (1882—1906), Liverp North RDn (1906—49). Bdry: 1929 (gains EP30).[580] Bombed May 1941, church closed 1968, par abol 1974.[581]

EP8—LIVERPOOL NORRIS GREEN CHRIST CHURCH—Cr 1930 from Fazakerley EP, West Derby EP.[433] W Derby RDn.

EP9—LIVERPOOL NORRIS GREEN ST CHRISTOPHER—Cr 1930 from West Derby EP.[243] W Derby RDn.

EP10—LIVERPOOL OUR LADY AND ST NICHOLAS WITH ST ANNE—Cr 1970 by union EP1, EP16.[578]

EP11—LIVERPOOL PRINCES PARK ALL SAINTS—Cr 1884 from Walton on the Hill AP, Toxteth Park St Clement EP.[335] Toxteth RDn.

EP12—LIVERPOOL ST AIDAN—Cr 1861 from EP1, Walton on the Hill AP.[304] Liverp North RDn (1861—1949). Bdry: 1867.[172] Abol 1958 ent to Kirkdale St Athanasius EP.[542]

EP13—LIVERPOOL ST ALBAN, BEVINGTON—Cr 1929 by union Bevington EP, EP18.[188] Church bombed 9 May 1941; par abol *ca* 1947 ent to EP1.[577]

EP14—LIVERPOOL ST ANDREW—Cr 1815 (privately erected) from EP1, later abol and incl in Toxteth Park St Andrew when that par cr 1893,[360] qv.

EP15—LIVERPOOL ST ANNE—Built by statutory auth 1772, opened 1773, consecr 1871. Liverp North RDn (1847—82), Walton RDn (1882—1906), Liverp North RDn (1906—39). Bdry: 1917.[576] Abol 1939 to help cr EP16.[91]

EP16—LIVERPOOL ST ANNE WITH ST STEPHEN—Cr 1939 by union EP15, EP42.[91] Abol 1970 to help cr EP10.[578]

EP17—LIVERPOOL ST BARNABAS—Opened 1841 from AP1. Abol *ca* 1892/1893 ent to EP34.[577]

EP18—LIVERPOOL ST BARTHOLOMEW—Cr 1841 from EP1. Bdry: 1881 (help cr EP13),[188] 1923 (gains EP4).[579] Closed 17 Mar 1929, abol ent to EP13.[188]

EP19—LIVERPOOL ST BRIDE—Consecr 1831 from EP1. Liverp South RDn (1847—1949). Abol 1971 to help cr EP20.[582]

EP20—LIVERPOOL ST BRIDE WITH ST SAVIOUR—Cr 1971 by union EP19, EP38.[582] Bdry: 1974.[11]

EP21—LIVERPOOL ST CATHERINE—Consecr 1831 from EP1. Liverp South RDn (1847—1949). Bdry: 1882.[212] Church bombed May 1941; par abol 1952 to help cr EP43.[110]

EP22—LIVERPOOL ST COLUMBA—Wesleyan chap acquired 1858 and consecr in Church of England. Liverp South RDn (1847—1930). Abol 1930 to help cr EP40.[583]

EP23—LIVERPOOL ST DAVID—Cr 1831 from EP1.[12] Welsh church now considered chap of ease, situated now in par of Fairfield.

EP24—LIVERPOOL ST GEORGE—Begun 1726 in EP1 by statutory auth in act of 1715, completed 1734, closed 1897 and demolished. Liverp South RDn (1847—82), Liverp North RDn (1882—97).

EP25—LIVERPOOL ST JAMES THE LESS—Cr 1869 from EP31.[18] Liverp North RDn. Bdry: 1929.[584] Church bombed 12 Apr 1941; par abol 1958 pt to EP1, pt to Kirkdale St Athanasius EP.[542]

EP26—LIVERPOOL ST JOHN—Built by corporation in area EP1, consecr 1785, closed 1898 and demolished. Liverp South RDn (1847—82), Liverp North RDn (1882—98).

EP27—LIVERPOOL ST JOHN THE EVANGELIST—Acquired 1841 from Nonconformists, abandoned 1853.

EP28—LIVERPOOL ST LUKE—Begun 1811, opended 1831 in area EP1. Liverp South RDn.

EP29—LIVERPOOL ST MARK—Built by subscription 1803 in area EP1, consecr 1815. Liverp South RDn (1847—1929). Abol 1929 ent to EP7.[580]

EP30—LIVERPOOL ST MARY MAGDALENE—Built 1859 in area EP1, consecr 1862. Liverp South RDn (1862—82), Walton RDn (1882—1906), Liverp North RDn (1906—29). Bdry: 1881 (help cr EP7).[507] Abol 1929 ent to EP7.[580]

EP31—LIVERPOOL ST MARTIN IN THE FIELDS—Erected 1825—29 in area EP1. Bdry: 1869 (cr EP25).[18] Liverp North RDn (1847—1949). Bdry: 1904,[187] 1929.[584] Church bombed in 1941, demolished Oct 1956; par abol *ca* May 1949 ent to EP1.[577]

EP32—LIVERPOOL ST MATTHEW—Former Presbyterian chap consecr 1798 Church of England, sep EP 1812 from EP1.[12] Liverp North RDn (1847—82), Walton RDn (1882—1906), Liverp North RDn (1906—29). Abol 1929 pt to EP31, pt to EP25.[584]

EP33—LIVERPOOL ST MATTHIAS—Built 1833—34 in area EP1, demolished for railway purposes, reerected 1848 in different site. Liverp North RDn (1847—1949). Church closed 1949; par abol then ent to EP1.[577]

EP34—LIVERPOOL ST MICHAEL—Begun 1816 in area EP1, opened 1826. Bdry: *ca* 1892/1893 (gains EP17).[577] Liverp South RDn.

EP35—LIVERPOOL ST PAUL—Begun 1763 in area EP1, opened 1769, closed 1900.[503]

EP36—LIVERPOOL ST PETER WITH ST AMBROSE AND ALL SAINTS—Cr 1942 by union Everton St Peter EP, Everton St Ambrose with All Saints EP.[473] Abol 1957 to help cr Everton St Ambrose with St Timothy EP.[41]

EP37—LIVERPOOL ST PHILIP—Opened 1816 in area EP1, orig church sold to Salvation Army and new one built in different site, sep EP 1891 from Fairfield EP.[315] Prescot RDn (1847—1902), W Derby RDn (1902—49).

EP38—LIVERPOOL ST SAVIOUR—Built by subscription 1839 in area EP1. Liverp South RDn (1847—1949). Abol 1971 to help cr EP20.[582]

EP39—LIVERPOOL ST SILAS—Opened 1841 in area EP1, consecr 1843. Abol 1930 to help cr EP40.[583]

EP40—LIVERPOL ST SILAS WITH ST COLUMBA AND ST SIMON—Cr 1930 by union EP39, EP22, EP41.[583] Church bombed early May 1941.

EP41—LIVERPOOL ST SIMON—Former Presbyterian chap consecr Church of England 1841, sep EP 1846 from EP1.[254] Liverp South RDn (1847—1930). Abol 1930 to help cr EP40.[583]

EP42—LIVERPOOL ST STEPHEN—Former Baptist chap opened as Church of England 1792, taken down 1871. Liverp North RDn (1847—1939). Abol 1939 to help cr EP16.[91]

—LIVERPOOL ST STEPHEN GROVE STREET—see following entry

EP43—LIVERPOOL ST STEPHEN WITH ST CATHERINE—Cr 1952 by union EP21, Edge Hill St Stephen EP [by time of abol, called 'Liverpool St Stephen Grove Street']).[110] Liverp RDn.

—LIVERPOOL ST THOMAS—Name sometimes used for EP built 1750, sep EP 1814 from EP1 as 'Toxteth Park St Thomas', qv.

—LIVERPOOL ST TIMOTHY—Name sometimes used for EP cr 1868 as 'Everton St Timothy', qv.

EP44—LIVERPOOL ST TITUS—Cr 1866 from EP1.[575] Liverp North RDn. Abol 1904, pt to Bevington EP, pt to EP31.[187]

EP46—LIVERPOOL STANLEY ST PAUL—Cr 1913 from Stanley St Ann EP (sometimes 'Liverpool Stanley St Ann').[194] W Derby RDn.

LIVESEY
Tp in Blacksburn AP, sep CP 1866,[4] pt eccl severed 1725 to help cr Tockholes EP,[12] the latter refounded 1842,[133] another pt severed 1839 to help cr Feniscowles EP,[12] the latter refounded 1842,[133] 'Livesey' a sep EP 1877 from Feniscowles EP, Tockholes EP.[221] *LG* Blackb Hd, PLU, pt Blackb USD (1875—93), pt Blackb MB (1877—89), pt Blackb CB (1889—93), Blackb RSD (pt 1875—93, ent 1893—94), Blackb RD. Civ bdry: 1893 (loses the pt in the CB to Blackburn AP),[223] 1901 (loses pt to Blackb CB [assoc with Lancs] & AP),[224] 1922 (loses pt to Blackb CB [assoc with Lancs] & AP).[225] *Parl* N'rn Dv (1832—67), Blackb Parl Bor (pt 1867—85, ent 1885—1918), pt N-E Dv (1867—85), Darwen Dv/CC (1918—*). *Eccl* Blackb RDn (1877—1964), Darwen RDn (1964—*). Eccl bdry: 1893 (help cr Feniscliffe EP),[328] 1911 (help cr Ewood EP),[416] 1911,[319] 1925 (help cr Blackburn St Aidan EP).[212] Now called 'Blackburn St Andrew'.

LONGRIDGE
EP Cr 1727 from Ribchester AP (tps Alston, Dilworth),[12] refounded 1861.[62] Amound. RDn (1727—1852), Preston RDn (1852—*).

LONGSIGHT
The following have 'Longsight' in their names. Insofar as any existed at a given time: *Eccl* Manch RDn (cr—1855), Chorlton RDn (1855—72), Ardwick RDn (1872—1912), Heaton RDn (1912—*).

EP1—LONGSIGHT [ST JOHN]—Cr 1852 from Manchester AP,[12] refounded 1854.[199] Bdry: 1866 (help cr Gorton St Mark EP),[84] 1878 (help cr Manchester St Chrysostom, Victoria Park EP),[35] 1886 (help cr Birch in Rusholme St Agnes [orig as 'Birch St Agnes', later 'Birch in Rusholme St Agnes']),[201] 1911.[203]

EP2—LONGSIGHT ST CLEMENT—Cr 1876 from Ardwick St Matthew EP, Chorlton on Medlock St Stephen EP.[90] Ardwick RDn (1876—1912), Heaton RDn (1912—56), Ardwick RDn (1956—68). Abol 1968 to help cr EP4.[85]

EP3—LONGSIGHT ST LUKE—Cr 1971 by union EP4, Chorlton on Medlock St Stephen EP.[370] Ardwick RDn.

EP4—LONGSIGHT ST MATTHEW WITH ST CLEMENT—Cr 1968 by union Ardwick St Matthew EP, EP2.[85] Ardwick RD. Abol 1971 to help cr EP3.[370]

LONGTON
Chap in Penwortham AP, sep CP 1866,[4] sep EP 1719.[12] *LG* Seq 10. *Parl* Seq 2. *Eccl* Leyl. RDn.

NEW LONGTON
EP Cr 1931 from Penwortham EP, Farington EP.[95] Leyl. RDn.

LONGWORTH
Tp in Bolton le Moors AP, sep CP 1866,[4] pt eccl severed 1741 to help cr Walmsley EP,[12] the latter refounded 1844,[88] the remainder of tp Longworth severed 1861 to help cr Belmont EP.[183] *LG* Salf. Hd, Bolton PLU, RSD, RD. Abol 1898 ent to

Turton CP.[36] *Parl* S'rn Dv (1832—67), S-E Dv (1867—85), W'hough. Dv (1885—1918).

LOSTOCK

Tp in Bolton le Moors AP, sep CP 1866,[4] eccl severed 1860 to help cr Wingates EP.[273] *LG* Salf. Hd, Bolton PLU, RSD, RD. Abol 1898 ent to Bolton CB (assoc with Lancs) & CP.[36] *Parl* S'rn Dv (1832—67), S-E Dv (1867—85), W'hough. Dv (1885—1918).

LOSTOCK HALL

EP Cr 1957 from Farington EP, Bamber Bridge St Saviour EP, Bamber Bridge St Aidan EP.[138] Leyl. RDn.

LOWER MOOR

EP Cr 1873 from Oldham St James EP.[391] Oldham RDn. Bdry: 1879 (help cr Heyside EP),[245] 1957.[386] Sometimes called 'Oldham St Stephen and All Martyrs, Lower Moor'.

LOWICK

Chap in Ulverston AP, sep CP 1866,[4] sep EP 1743 (incl pt tp Subberthwaite in same par),[12] eccl refounded 1866.[132] *LG* Seq 14. Transf 1974 to Cumbria.[40] *Parl* Seq 11. *Eccl* Furness & Cartmel RDn (1743—1859), Ulv. RDn (1859—1970), Furness RDn (1970—*).

LOWTON

Chap in Winwick AP, sep CP 1866,[4] sep EP 1734.[12] Gains 1845 civ[92] and eccl[399] tp Golborne ('Golborne' sep civ and eccl 1850[494]). *LG* W Derby Hd, Leigh PLU, RSD, RD. Abol civ 1933 ent to Golborne UD & CP.[37] *Parl* S'rn Dv (1832—67), S-W Dv (1867—85), Leigh Dv (1885—1918), Newton Dv (1918—48). *Eccl* Warr. RDn (1734—1847), Winwick RDn (1847—1949), Warr. RDn (1949—*). Eccl bdry: 1862 (cr Lowton St Mary EP).[439]

LOWTON ST MARY

EP Cr 1862 from Lowton EP.[439] Winwick RDn (1862—1949), Warr. RDn (1949—*). Bdry: 1974.[585]

LUMB

EP Cr 1846 from Haslingden EP (pt orig tps Higher Booths, Lower Booths), Newchurch in Pendle EP.[283] Blackb RDn (1846—47), Whalley RDn (1847—66), Accr. RDn (1866—72), Burnley RDn (1872—93), Whalley RDn (1893—1912), Rossend. RDn (1912—*). Bdry: 1887 (help cr Edgeside EP).[238]

LUND

EP Chap in Kirkham AP, sep EP 1737[12]; for civ see 'Clifton with Salwick', as such sep CP 1866.[4] Amound. RDn (1737—1852), The Fylde RDn (1852—*).

LUNT

Tp in Sefton AP, sep CP 1866.[4] *LG* W Derby Hd, PLU, RSD, Sefton RD. Abol 1932 ent to Sefton AP.[403] *Parl* S'rn Dv (1832—67), S-W Dv (1867—85), Ormsk. Dv (1885—1948).

LYDIATE

Tp in Halsall AP, sep CP 1866,[4] sep EP 1841,[12] eccl refounded 1844,[125] eccl refounded 1871.[16] *LG* Seq 17. Civ bdry: 1956.[586] Transf 1974 to Merseyside except for pt remaining in Lancs, the latter transf to Downholland CP.[40] *Parl* Seq 21. *Eccl* Warr. RDn (1841—47), N Meols RDn (1847—87), Ormsk. RDn (1887—*).

LYTHAM

AP Orig chap in Kirkham AP, sep par early.[189] *LG* Amound. Hd, Fylde PLU, pt St Anne's on the Sea USD, pt Lytham USD, Lytham UD (1894—1922), Lytham St Anne's MB (1922—24). Civ bdry: 1894 (loses the pt in St Anne's on the Sea UD to help cr St Anne's on the Sea CP),[217] 1897 (gains foreshore),[246] 1912.[587] Abol civ 1924 to help cr Lytham St Anne's CP.[588] *Parl* N'rn Dv (1832—67), North Dv (1867—85), Blackp. Dv (1885—1918), Black. Parl Bor (1918—48). *Eccl* Lanc. RDn (cr—before 1291), Amound. RDn (before 1291—1852), The Fylde RDn (1852—*). Eccl bdry: 1851 (cr Lytham St John EP),[589] 1877 (cr Heyhouses on the Sea EP, later called 'St Anne's on the Sea'),[406] 1917 (cr Fairhaven EP).[162]

LYTHAM ST ANNE'S

CP Cr 1924 by union of pars in Lytham St Anne's MB: Lytham AP, St Anne's on the Sea CP.[587] Bdry: 1934 (help cr Bryning with Warton CP).[226] *LG* Fylde PLU, Lytham St Anne's MB. Bdry: 1934 (help cr Bryning with Warton CP).[226] *Parl* S Fylde CC (1948—*).

LYTHAM ST JOHN

EP Cr 1851 from Lytham AP.[589] Amound. RDn (1851—52), The Fylde RDn (1852—*).

MAGHULL

Chap in Halsall AP, sep CP 1866,[4] sep EP 1748,[12] eccl refounded 1923.[89] *LG* Seq 17. Civ bdry: 1956.[127] Transf 1974 to Merseyside.[40] *Parl* S'rn Dv (1832—67), S-W Dv (1867—85), Ormsk. Dv/CC (1885—1970), Crosby BC (1970—*). *Eccl* Warr. RDn (1748—1847), N Meols RDn (1847—87), Ormsk. RDn (1887—*).

MANCHESTER

The following have 'Manchester' in their names. Insofar as any existed at a given time: *LG* Salf. Hd, Manch PLU (1840—50), Par (poor law purposes, 1850—1930), Bor (tp Manchester), Newton Bor (tp Newton), Manch MB (1838—89), CB (1889—1974). *Parl* Tp Manchester: Manch Parl Bor (1832—85); tp Newton: Newton Parl Bor (1558—1832); see Part III of the *Guide* for composition of Manch Parl Bors (1885—*) by wards of the MB/CB. *Eccl* Manch & Blackb RDn (until before 1535), Manch RDn (before 1535—1872), sep noted thereafter.

AP1—MANCHESTER [OUR LADY, ST GEORGE AND ST DENYS]—Collegiate 1421—1547, parochial thereafter. Incl chap Birch in Rusholme (built *ca* 1580, later Presbyterian chap until 1697,[198] sep EP 1739,[12] eccl refounded 1839,[74] eccl refounded 1854[199]; for civ see tp Rusholme below), chap Blackley (sep CP 1866,[4] sep EP 1800,[12] eccl refounded 1839,[74] eccl refounded 1854[199]), chap Chorlton cum Hardy (sep CP 1866,[4] sep EP 1723,[12] eccl refounded 1839,[74] eccl refounded 1854[199]), chap Denton (sep CP 1866,[4] sep EP 1770 [pt tp Denton, pt tp Haughton],[12] orig dedication changed *ca* 1800 from 'St James' to 'St Lawrence',[422] eccl refounded 1839,[74] eccl refounded 1846,[21] eccl refounded 1854,[199] the remainder of tp Denton cr 1846 'Denton Christ Church' EP[283]), chap Didsbury (sep CP 1866,[4] sep EP 1727,[12] eccl refounded 1839,[74] eccl refounded 1854[199]), chap Gorton (sep CP 1866,[4] sep EP 1728 [incl pt chap Newton],[12] eccl refounded 1838,[74] eccl refounded 1854[199]), chap and bor Newton (sep CP 1866,[4] pt eccl severed 1728 to help cr Gorton EP,[12] the remainder a sep EP 1839 [incl tp Droylsden, tp Failsworth] as 'Newton All Saints',[74] the areas of the 2 tps severed 1844 to cr the 2 EPs respectively of 'Droylsden', 'Failsworth',[348] the remainder refounded 1854 as 'Newton All Saints'EP[199]), chap ([Holy Trinity] built 1635[590]) and tp Salford (sep CP 1866,[4] sep EP 1839,[74] eccl refounded 1856[83]), chap Stretford (sep CP 1866,[4] sep EP 1717[12]), tp and chap (built 1741[81]) Ardwick (sep CP 1866,[4] sep EP 1741 [St Thomas],[81] eccl refounded 1854[74] the latter divided 1856 into the 2 EPs of Ardwick St Thomas, Ardwick St Silas[74]), tp Bradford (sep CP 1866,[4] eccl severed 1840 to help cr Openshaw EP,[288] the orig area of tp Bradford and orig ex-par Beswick in Openshaw EP severed 1862 to cr 'Bradford' EP[185]), tp Broughton (sep CP 1866,[4] sep EP 1854[199]), tp Burnage (sep CP 1866,[4] pt eccl severed 1853 to help cr Withington EP,[12] the latter refounded 1854,[199] 'Burnage' a sep EP 1845 from Withington EP, Barlow Moor EP[150]), tp and chap (built 1794[353]) Cheetham (sep CP 1866,[4] pt of the tp incl the chap [St Mark] and pt tp Crumpsall a sep EP 1839 as 'Cheetham Hill St Mark',[353] the latter refounded 1856,[83] another pt of orig tp Cheetham eccl severed 1856 to help cr Cheetham Hill St Luke EP[83]), tp Chorlton upon Medlock (sep CP 1866,[4] sep EP 1823,[12] eccl refounded 1839,[367] eccl later called 'Chorlton on Medlock'), tp Crumpsall (sep CP 1866,[4] eccl in chap [built 1794[353]] Cheetham and thus pt eccl severed 1839 to help cr Cheetham Hill St Mark EP,[74] another pt eccl severed 1856 to help cr Cheetham Hill St Luke EP,[83] 'Crumpsall' a sep EP 1859, pt from Cheetham Hill St Mark EP, pt from Cheetham Hill St Luke EP,[12] refounded 1860[102]), tp Droylsden, tp Failsworth (each a sep CP 1866,[4] both eccl in chap Newton and both thus eccl severed 1839 to help cr 'Newton All Saints' EP,[74] 'Droylsden' and 'Failsworth' each a sep EP 1844 from Newton All Saints EP[512]), tp Harpurhey (sep CP 1866,[4] sep EP 1844,[12] eccl refounded 1854 [when gains tp Moston from AP1] as 'Harpurhey cum Moston',[199] the orig area of tp Moston severed 1870 from the latter to cr Moston EP[323]), tp Haughton (sep CP 1866,[4] pt eccl severed 1770 to help cr Denton EP,[21] qv for later refoundings, 'Haughton' a sep EP 1879 from Denton EP[365]), tp and chap (built 1765[515]) Heaton Norris (sep CP 1866,[4] sep EP 1770 [St Thomas] [incl tp Levenshulme, tp Reddish],[12] eccl refounded 1839,[74] pt of the EP cr 1854 'Heaton Norris Christ Church' and the remainder refounded at the same time as

'Heaton Norris'[199]), tp Hulme (sep CP 1866,[4] sep EP 1836,[527] eccl refounded 1854[199]), tp Levenshulme (sep CP 1866,[4] eccl severed 1770 to help cr Heaton Norris EP,[12] the orig area of tp Levenshulme severed 1861 from Heaton Norris EP and united with pt Gorton EP, pt Birch in Rusholme EP to cr 'Levenshulme' EP[200]), tp Moss Side (sep CP 1866,[4] sep EP 1858 from AP1, Chorlton on Medlock EP, Whalley Range St Margaret EP, Withington EP, Rusholme EP[70]), tp Moston (sep CP 1866,[4] eccl severed 1854 to help cr Harpurhey cum Moston EP,[199] 'Moston' a sep EP 1870 from the latter[323]), tp Openshaw (sep CP 1866,[4] sep EP 1840 and eccl ex-par Beswick,[288] the orig area of tp Bradford and ex-par Beswick severed 1862 to cr Bradford EP,[185] the remainder of this par refounded 1864 as 'Openshaw' EP[154]), tp Reddish (sep CP 1866,[4] eccl severed 1770 to help cr Heaton Norris EP,[12] qv above for later refoundings, 'Reddish' a sep EP 1884 from Heaton Reddish EP, Heaton Norris EP[123]), tp Rusholme (sep CP 1866,[4] chap built ca 1580 and later Presbyterian chap until 1697,[198] sep EP 1739 as 'Birch in Rusholme',[12] refounded 1839,[74] the orig EP refounded at same time as new EP 'Rusholme [Holy Trinity]' cr a sep EP from it[199]), tp Withington (sep CP 1866,[4] sep EP 1853,[12] eccl refounded 1854[199]). Addtl civ bdry alt: 1890,[500] 1916 (gains CP1, CP2),[591] 1931 (gains Ches pars of Baguley CP, Northern Etchells CP, Northenden AP),[592] 1933 (incl exchanges pts with Chadderton UD & CP, Droyl. UD & CP, Failsworth UD & CP, Middl. MB & CP).[171] Transf 1974 to Gtr Manch.[40] *Eccl* Addtl eccl bdry alt: 1712 (cr EP6,[593] refounded 1839,[42] refounded 1856[83]), 1756 (cr EP22,[594] refounded 1839[42]), 1793 (cr by license EP13),[595] 1805 (cr Salford St Stephen EP [built 1794[590]],[12] refounded 1856[83]), 1809 (cr EP17,[12] refounded 1839,[42] refounded 1856[83]), 1812 (cr EP27 [built 1765[596]],[12] refounded 1839,[42] refounded 1856,[83] after rebuilt 1878 on a different site often called 'St Paul, New Cross'[596]), 1818 (cr EP15 [opened 1798, later Nonconformist, consecr in Church of England 1818],[12] refounded 1839,[42] refounded 1856[83] [orig 'St George in the Fields' but after rebuilt 1877 on a different site, 'St George Oldham Road'[596]]), 1828 (cr Salford St Philip EP,[75] pt of the latter severed 1858 to help refound Salford Christ Church EP and the remainder refounded as Salford St Philip[70]), 1828 (cr as 'Manchester St Matthew, Campfield' EP,[75] refounded 1858 and thereafter as EP24[597]), 1838 (cr [consecr 1794[595]] EP30,[12] refounded 1858 from same area, addtl pt AP1, pt EP25[70]), 1839 (cr EP19 [built 1769[596]],[12] refounded 1856[83]), 1839 (cr Ancoats St Andrew EP,[74] refounded 1856[83]), 1839 (help cr EP31,[42] refounded 1860[322]), 1839 (cr [consecr 1789[596]] EP26,[42] refounded 1856[83]), 1842 (cr EP3),[22] 1842 (cr Salford St Matthias EP,[598] refounded 1858[70]), 1851 (cr EP36),[12] 1852 (cr Heaton Mersey EP),[315] 1852 (cr Longsight EP,[12] refounded

1854[199]), 1854 (cr EP37),[12] 1854 (cr Hulme Holy Trinity EP, cr Kersal Moor EP),[199] 1854 (cr Whalley Range St Margaret EP),[199] 1856 (cr EP20, EP36),[83] 1856 (cr Chorlton upon Medlock St Saviour EP),[83] 1858 (help cr Ancoats All Souls EP, help refound Moss Side EP),[70] 1874 (cr EP6),[357] 1876,[75] 1881,[358] 1904 (help cr Cheetham St Saviour EP).[140]

CP1—NORTH MANCHESTER—Cr 1896 by union of the following pars in Manch CB and in Prestw. PLU: Beswick CP, Blackley CP, Bradford CP, Cheetham CP, Clayton CP, Crumpsall CP, Harpurhey CP, Moston CP, Newton CP.[82] *LG* Prestw. PLU, Manch CB. Bdry: 1903.[599] Abol 1916 ent to AP1.[591]

CP2—SOUTH MANCHESTER—Cr 1896 by union of the following pars in Manch CB and in Chorlton PLU: Ardwick CP, Chorlton upon Medlock CP, West Gorton CP, Hulme CP, Openshaw CP, Rusholme CP.[82] *LG* Chorlton PLU, Manch CB. Bdry: 1901 (gains pt Gorton UD & CP),[502] 1910 (gains the following pars in Manch CB: Burnage CP, Chorlton cum Hardy CP, Didsbury CP, Gorton CP, Levenshulme CP, Moss Side CP, Withington CP).[310] Abol 1916 ent to AP1.[591]

EP1—MANCHESTER THE ALBERT MEMORIAL CHURCH—Cr 1865 from EP15, Harpurhey cum Moston EP.[119] Cheetham RDn (1872—1968). Bdry: 1874 (cr Collyhurst St James EP),[387] 1889 (help cr Newton Heath St Augustine EP).[87] Abol 1968 to help cr EP2.[256]

EP2—MANCHESTER THE ALBERT MEMORIAL CHURCH WITH NEWTON HEATH ST AUGUSTINE—Cr 1968 by union EP1, Newton Heath St Augustine EP.[256] Cheetham RDn. Abol 1972 to help cr Collyhurst The Saviour EP.[388]

EP3—MANCHESTER ALL SOULS—Cr 1842 from AP1.[22] Manch RDn (1842—55), Chorlton RDn (1855—58). Bdry: 1850 (help cr EP34).[346] Abol 1858 to help cr Ancoats All Souls EP.[465]

EP4—MANCHESTER THE RESURRECTION—Cr 1972 by union Bradford EP, EP5.[289] Cathedral RDn.

EP5—MANCHESTER ST AIDAN—Cr 1898 from Bradford EP.[13] Cathedral RDn. Abol 1972 to help cr EP4.[289]

—MANCHESTER ST ALBAN, CHEETWOOD—see CHEETWOOD

EP6—MANCHESTER ST ANN—Cr 1712 from AP1,[593] refounded 1839,[42] refounded 1856.[83] Cathedral RDn (1872—90). Abol 1890 to help cr EP8.[594]

EP7—MANCHESTER ST ANN—Cr 1943 by union EP25, EP8.[35] Cathedral RDn. Bdry: 1960.[72]

EP8—MANCHESTER ST ANN AND ST MARY—Cr 1890 by union EP6, EP22.[594] Cathedral RDn. Bdry: 1928.[76] Abol 1943 to help cr EP7.[35]

EP9—MANCHESTER ST BARNABAS—Cr 1841 from EP15,[12] refounded 1844.[348] Cathedral RDn (1872—1958). Bdry: 1874 (help cr EP21).[600] Abol 1958 to help cr EP16.[601]

EP10—MANCHESTER ST CATHERINE—Cr 1860 from Redbank EP, EP26, Collyhurst St Oswald EP.[149] Cathedral RDn (1872—1967). Abol 1967 to help cr Collyhurst St Oswald and St Catherine EP.[146]

EP11—MANCHESTER ST CHRYSOSTOM, VICTORIA PARK—Cr 1878 from Birch in Rusholme EP, Longsight EP, Chorlton upon Medlock St Saviour EP.[35] Ardwick RDn (1878—1912), Heaton RDn (1912—65), Withington RDn (1965—*). Bdry: 1878 (help cr Birch in Rusholme EP),[35] 1911.[203]

EP12—MANCHESTER ST CLEMENT [LEVER STREET]—Opened 1793 by license from AP1, never consecrated, site sold and funds therefrom diverted to build Greenheys, Higher Openshaw, Lower Broughton.[595]

—MANCHESTER ST CLEMENT—Name sometimes used for EP cr 1882 as 'Greenheys', qv.

EP13—MANCHESTER ST CROSS WITH ST PAUL, CLAYTON—Cr 1970 by union Clayton EP, EP29.[374] Ardwick RDn.

EP14—MANCHESTER ST CUTHBERT, MILES PLATTING—Cr 1972 by union EP16, Miles Platting St John EP, Miles Platting St Luke EP.[601] Cathedral RDn.

EP15—MANCHESTER ST GEORGE—Opened 1798, later Nonconformist until consecr 1818 Church of England,[596] sep EP 1818 from AP1,[12] refounded 1839,[42] refounded 1856.[83] Orig 'St George in the Fields', but after rebuilt 1877 on a different site, 'St George Oldham Road'.[596] Cathedral RDn (1872—*). Bdry: 1839 (help cr EP31,[42] refounded 1860[322]), 1841 (cr EP9,[12] refounded 1844[348]), 1856 (cr Miles Platting St John EP),[83] 1865 (help cr EP1),[119] 1876.[107] Abol 1958 to help cr EP16.[135]

EP16—MANCHESTER ST GEORGE WITH ST BARNABAS—Cr 1958 by union EP9, EP15.[135] Cathedral RDn. Abol 1972 to help cr EP14.[601]

EP17—MANCHESTER ST JAMES—Cr 1809 from AP1,[12] refounded 1839,[42] refounded 1856.[83] Cathedral RDn (1872—1928). Abol 1928 pt to EP8, pt to Ancoats St Andrew EP.[76]

EP18—MANCHESTER ST JAMES THE LESS—Cr 1871 from EP21, Ancoats St Andrew EP.[75] Cathedral RDn (1872—1937). Bdry: 1876.[75] Abol 1937 pt to help cr EP32, pt to Ancoats St Andrew EP, pt to EP20.[77]

EP19—MANCHESTER ST JOHN—Built 1769,[596] sep par 1839 from AP1.[42] Cathedral RDn (1872—1928). Abol 1928 to help cr EP25.[272]

EP20—MANCHESTER ST JUDE, ANCOATS—Cr 1856 from AP1.[83] Chorlton RDn (1855—66), Manch RDn (1866—72), Cathedral RDn (1872—1958). Bdry: 1871 (help cr EP19),[75] 1937.[77] Abol 1958 to help cr EP35.[602]

EP21—MANCHESTER ST MARTIN—Cr 1874 from EP31, EP9.[600] Sometimes 'Ancoats St Martin'. Cathedral RDn.

EP22—MANCHESTER ST MARY—Cr 1756 from AP1,[594] refounded 1839.[42] Cathedral RDn (1872—90). Abol 1890 to help cr EP8.[594]

EP23—MANCHESTER ST MARY, HULME—Cr 1955 by union Hulme St Paul EP, Hulme St Mary

EP.[154] Hulme RDn.

EP24—MANCHESTER ST MATTHEW—Cr 1828 as 'Manchester St Matthew, Campfield' EP from AP1,[75] refounded 1858 and thereafter 'Manchester St Matthew'.[597] Cathedral RDn (1872—1928). Bdry: 1839 (help cr EP31,[42] refounded 1860[322]). Abol 1928 to help cr EP25.[272]

EP25—MANCHESTER ST MATTHEW AND ST JOHN—Cr 1928 by union EP24, EP19.[272] Cathedral RDn. Abol 1943 to help cr EP7.[35]

—MANCHESTER ST MATTHEW, CAMPFIELD— see EP24

EP26—MANCHESTER ST MICHAEL—Consecr 1789 from AP1,[596] cr a sep EP 1839,[42] refounded 1856.[83] Cathedral RDn (1872—1929). Bdry: 1856 (cr Collyhurst St Oswald EP),[83] 1860 (help cr EP11).[149] Abol 1929 to help cr EP29.[603]

EP27—MANCHESTER ST PAUL—Built 1765, sep EP 1812 from AP1,[12] refounded 1839,[42] refounded 1856.[83] After rebuilt 1878 on a different site, often called 'St Paul, New Cross'. Cathedral RDn (1872—1929). Abol 1929 to help cr EP29.[603]

EP28—MANCHESTER ST PAUL, BRADFORD—Cr 1905 from Bradford EP, Clayton EP.[123] Cathedral RDn. Abol 1970 to help cr EP13.[374]

EP29—MANCHESTER ST PAUL, NEW CROSS, WITH ST MICHAEL, AND ST THOMAS, REDBANK—Cr 1929 by union EP27, EP26, EP37.[603] Cathedral RDn.

EP30—MANCHESTER ST PETER—Consecr 1794,[595] sep EP 1838 from AP1,[12] refounded 1858 from same area enlarged by further pt AP1, pt EP25.[70] Cathedral RDn.

EP31—MANCHESTER ST PETER, OLDHAM ROAD—Cr 1839 from AP1, EP15, EP24,[42] refounded 1860.[322] Cathedral RDn (1872—1927). Bdry: 1874 (help cr EP21).[600] Abol 1927 to help cr EP32.[77]

EP32—MANCHESTER ST PETER OLDHAM ROAD WITH ST JAMES THE LESS— Cr 1937 by union ent EP31, pt EP18.[77] Cathedral RDn.

EP33—MANCHESTER ST PHILIP—Cr 1850 from EP3, Newton All Saints EP.[346] Cathedral RDn. Abol 1958 to help cr EP35.[594]

EP34—MANCHESTER ST PHILIP, BRADFORD ROAD—Cr 1850 from EP3, Newton All Saints EP.[346] Cathedral RDn. Bdry: 1885 (cr Newton Heath St Mark, Holland Street EP).[371] Abol 1958 to help cr EP35.[602]

EP35—MANCHESTER ST PHILIP WITH ST MARK—Cr 1958 by union EP34, EP20, Newton Heath St Mark, Holland Street EP.[602] Cathedral RDn.

—MANCHESTER ST SAVIOUR—Name sometimes used for EP cr 1851 as 'Chorlton upon Medlock St Saviour', qv.

EP36—MANCHESTER ST SIMON AND ST JUDE— Cr 1856 from AP1.[83] Cathedral RDn (1872—*).

EP37—MANCHESTER ST THOMAS REDBANK— Cr 1854 from AP1.[12] Cathedral RDn (1872—1929). Abol 1929 to help cr EP29.[603]

MANSRIGGS

Tp in Ulverston AP, sep CP 1866.[4] LG Seq 14. Transf 1974 to Cumbria.[40] Parl Seq 11.

GREAT MARSDEN

Area in Whalley AP, civ pt of tp Great and Little Marsden (qv for sep civ identity), eccl in chap Colne (sep EP 1820 from Whalley AP[12]), the orig area of Great Marsden eccl severed 1836 to help cr Colne Christ Church EP,[12] the orig area of Great Marsden severed 1845 from the latter and united with a pt of Colne EP to cr 'Great Marsden' EP.[118] Blackb RDn (1845—47), Whalley RDn (1847—72), Burnley RDn (1872—1970), Pendle RDn (1970—*). Bdry: 1902 (help cr Nelson St Philip EP),[604] 1913 (help cr Colne Holy Trinity EP),[2] 1914.[147]

GREAT AND LITTLE MARSDEN

Tp in Whalley AP civ comprised of area Great Marsden, chap Little Marsden, the ent civ area a sep CP 1866 as 'Great and Little Marsden',[4] the area of chap Little Marsden eccl severed 1783 to cr 'Little Marsden' EP,[12] qv below for refounding, the area of Great Marsden eccl in chap Colne (sep EP 1820 from Whalley AP[12]), the orig area of Great Marsden severed 1836 from the latter to help cr Colne Christ Church EP,[12] the orig area of Great Marsden severed 1845 from the latter and united with a pt of Colne EP to cr 'Great Marsden' EP.[124] LG Blackb Hd, Burnley PLU, pt Nelson USD, Nelson MB (1890—94), pt Colne and Marsden USD (1875—94), pt Brierfield USD. Civ bdry: 1894 (the pt in Colne and Marsden UD transf to Colne CP,[389] the UD renamed 2 days later 'Colne').[390] Abol civ 1894 the pt in the MB to help cr Nelson CP, the pt in Brierfield UD cr Brierfield CP.[164] Parl N'rn Dv (1832—67), N-E Dv (1867—85), Clith. Dv (1885—1918).

LITTLE MARSDEN

Chap in Whalley AP, sep EP 1783,[12] pt of the latter eccl severed 1873 to cr Brierfield EP,[154] the remainder refounded 1877 as 'Little Marsden' EP[287]; for civ see 'Great and Little Marsden'. Burnley RDn (1877—1970), Pendle RDn (1970—*). Bdry: 1879 (cr Nelson in Little Marsden EP),[314] 1881,[209] 1902 (help cr Nelson St Philip EP),[604] 1924 (cr Nelson St Bede EP).[111]

MARTON

Chap in Poulton le Fylde AP, sep CP 1866,[4] sep EP 1805,[12] pt of the latter severed 1837 to help cr South Shore Holy Trinity EP,[211] refounded 1871,[212] the remainder of Marton EP eccl refounded 1892 as such.[44] LG Amound. Hd, Fylde PLU, pt St Anne's on the Sea USD, pt Blackp. USD, pt Blackp. MB (1879—94), pt Fylde RSD, Fylde RD. Civ bdry: 1894 (loses the pt in the UD to help cr St Anne's on the Sea CP,[216] loses the pt in the MB to help cr Blackpool CP[216]). Abol civ 1934 pt to Westby with Plumptons CP, pt to Blackp. CB (assoc with Lancs) & CP.[226] Parl N'rn Dv (1832—67), North Dv (1867—85), Blackp. Dv (1885—1918), Fylde Dv (1918—48). Parl bdry: 1945.[339] Eccl Amound. RDn (1805—52), The Fylde RDn (1852—1963), Blackp. RDn (1963—*). Eccl bdry: 1907 (help cr Blackpool All Saints EP),[249] 1951 (help cr

Blackpool Holy Cross, South Shore EP),[253] 1954,[144] 1957 (help cr Mereside EP).[605]

MAWDESLEY

Tp in Croston AP, sep CP 1866,[4] eccl severed 1843 to help cr Mawdesley with Bispham EP,[213] qv. *LG* Seq 8. *Parl* Seq 3.

MAWDESLEY WITH BISPHAM

EP Cr 1843 by union tps Mawdesley, Bispham, both in Croston AP.[213] Leyl. RDn (1843—47), N Meols RDn (1847—48), Leyl. RDn (1848—1964), Chorley RDn (1964—*).

MEARLEY

Tp in Whalley AP, sep CP 1866.[4] *LG* Seq 6. *Parl* Seq 1.

MEDLAR WITH WESHAM

Tp in Kirkham AP, sep CP 1866.[4] *LG* Seq 1. Bdry: 1935.[43] *Parl* Seq 2.

MELLING

AP Incl chap Arkhome with Cawood (sep CP 1866,[4] sep EP 1740 as 'Arkholme',[12] as such eccl refounded 1863[91]), chap and bor Hornby (bor status not sustained, sep CP 1866,[4] sep EP 1741 [incl tp Farleton],[12] eccl refounded 1859 incl the pt of tp Roeburndale severed 1842 to help cr Wray EP[478]), tp Farleton (sep CP 1866,[4] eccl severed 1741 to help cr Hornby EP,[12] qv above for refounding), tp Melling with Wrayton (sep CP 1866[4]), tp Roeburndale, tp Wray with Botton (each a sep CP 1866,[4] pt of the former and the ent latter eccl severed 1842 to help cr Wray EP,[606] 'Wray' refounded 1843,[607] the pt of tp Roeburndale in Wray severed from the latter 1859 to help refound Hornby EP[478]), tp Wennington (sep CP 1866[4]) to that 'Melling' has no sep civ identity after 1866. *LG* Lonsd. Hd. *Parl* N'rn Dv (1832—67). *Eccl* Lanc. RDn (until before 1291), Kirkby Lonsd. & Kendal RDn (before 1291—before 1541), Kirkby Lonsd. RDn (before 1541—1848), Tunstall RDn (1848—*).

MELLING

Chap in Halsall AP, sep CP 1866,[4] sep EP 1810,[12] eccl refounded 1923.[89] *LG* Seq 17. Civ bdry: 1877.[608] Transf 1974 to Merseyside.[40] *Parl* Seq 21. *Eccl* Warr. RDn (1810—47), N Meols RDn (1847—87), Ormsk. RDn (1887—*).

MELLING WITH WRAYTON

Tp in Melling AP, sep CP 1866.[4] *LG* Lonsd. Hd, Lunesd. PLU, RSD, RD. *Parl* Seq 8.

MELLOR

Tp in Blackburn AP, sep CP 1866,[4] sep EP 1830,[12] eccl refounded 1842.[133] *LG* Seq 4. Civ bdry: 1934.[226] *Parl* Seq 13. *Eccl* Blackb RDn. Eccl bdry: 1916,[609] 1928 (help cr Blackburn St Gabriel EP).[237]

NORTH MEOLS

AP Incl tp Birkdale (sep CP 1866,[4] sep EP 1865[104]). *LG* W Derby Hd, Ormsk. PLU, pt S'port. MB (1866—94), pt S'port. USD, pt Ormsk. RSD, W Lancs RD. Addtl civ bdry alt: 1894 (the pt in the MB cr Southport CP),[610] 1900 (loses pt to S'port. CB [assoc with Lancs] & CP),[611] 1936.[612] *Parl* Seq 23. *Eccl* Seq 4. Addtl eccl bdry alt: 1825 (cr Southport Christ Church EP,[12] refounded 1865[104]), 1840 (cr Crossens EP,[12] refounded 1860[322]), 1864 (cr

Southport St Paul EP),[433] 1865 (cr Southport Holy Trinity EP),[104] 1868 (cr St Stephens in the Banks EP, sometimes called 'Southport St Stephens in the Banks' or 'Banks'),[613] 1875 (help cr Birkdale St Peter EP),[304] 1878 (cr Southport All Saints EP),[614] 1905 (cr Southport Emmanuel EP, cr Southport St Simon and St Jude EP),[526] 1906.[33]

MERESIDE

EP Cr 1957 from Marton EP, Weeton EP.[605] The Fylde RDn (1957—63), Blackp. RDn (1963—*).

MICKLEHURST

EP Cr 1962 from Millbrook EP (Ches, dioc Chester), Mossley EP (Lancs, dioc Manch) to be in dioc Chester.[369] Mottram RDn.

MIDDLETON

AP Incl chap Ainsworth (sep CP 1866,[4] sep EP 1725,[12] eccl refounded 1867[35]), chap Ashworth (sep CP 1866,[4] sep EP 1735,[12] eccl refounded 1867[35]), tp Birtle cum Bamford (sep CP 1866,[4] 'Bircle' a sep EP 1848 by union this tp and pt Bury AP [pt chap Heywood, pt tp Heap][206]), tp Hopwood (sep CP 1866,[4] pt eccl severed 1830 to help cr Birch EP [qv for later refounding],[12] 'Hopwood' a sep EP 1905 from Birch EP, Heywood St Luke EP[195]), tp Great Lever (sep CP 1866,[4] sep EP 1861[568]), tps Pilsworth, Thornham (each a sep CP 1866[4]). *LG* Salf. Hd, Oldham PLU, Middl. & Tonge USD (1875—86), Middl. MB (1886—1974), USD (1886—94). Addtl civ bdry alt: 1894 (gains the following in Middl. MB: Alkrington CP, Tonge CP, pt Great Heaton CP, pt Little Heaton CP, pt Hopwood CP, pt Thornham CP),[45] 1933 (incl exchanges pts with Manch CB [assoc with Lancs] & AP).[171] Transf 1974 to Gtr Manch.[40] *Parl* S'rn Dv (1832—67), S-E Dv (1867—85), Middl. Dv (1885—1918), Middl. & Prestw. Dv/CC (1918—70), Middl. & Prestw. BC (1970—*). *Eccl* Manch & Blackb RDn (until before 1535), Manch RDn (before 1535—1850), Bury RDn (1850—72), Prestw. & Middl. RDn (1872—1912), Middl. RDn (1912—*). Addtl eccl bdry alt: 1830 (cr Birch EP [incl pt tp Hopwood],[12] refounded 1843 from Middleton AP, Bury AP),[193] 1846 (help cr Thornham with Gravel Hole EP),[194] 1863 (cr Parkfield in Middleton EP),[426] 1864 (help cr Rhodes EP),[256] 1881 (help cr Bamford EP),[140] 1964,[196] 1964 (help cr Langley EP).[197]

MIDDLETON

Tp in Lancaster AP, sep CP 1866,[4] eccl in chap Overton (sep EP 1715 from Lancaster AP[12]). *LG* Seq 12. *Parl* Seq 6.

MIDDLETON JUNCTION

EP Cr 1885 from Tonge cum Alkrington EP, Chadderton Christ Church EP, Chadderton St Matthew EP.[317] Prestw. & Middl. RDn (1885—1912), Middl. RDn (1912—*).

MILES PLATTING ST JOHN

EP Cr 1856 from Manchester St George EP.[83] Manch RDn (1856—72), Cheetham RDn (1872—1961), Cathedral RDn (1961—72). Abol 1972 to help cr Manchester St Cuthbert, Miles Platting EP.[601]

MILES PLATTING ST LUKE

EP Cr 1876 from Newton All Saints EP.[90] Cheetham

RDn (1876—1961), Cathedral RDn (1961—72). Abol 1972 to help cr Manchester St Cuthbert, Miles Platting EP.[601]

MILNROW

EP Chap (orig an oratory) situated in tp Butterworth in Rochdale AP, sep EP 1717.[12] Manch RDn (1717—1847), Rochd. RDn (1847—*). Bdry: 1867 (help cr Newbold EP),[474] 1876 (cr New Hey EP),[213] 1911 (help cr Belfield EP).[182]

CP Cr 1894 by union of the pts of the following in Milnrow UD: Butterworth CP, Castleton CP.[257] LG Rochd. PLU, Milnrow UD. Transf 1974 to Gtr Manch.[40] Parl Royton Dv (1918—48), Heyw. & Royton CC (1948—*).

MITTON

AP Par in Yorks W Riding (Staincliffe & Ewcross Wap), incl in Lancs (Blackb Hd) tp Aighton, Bailey and Chaigley (sep CP 1866 in Lancs,[4] an area in Bailey a sep EP 1839 as 'Hurst Greeen',[12] refounded 1870[30]) so that Mitton ent Yorks W Riding after 1866, qv.

LITTLE MITTON

CP Cr 1935 from Little Mitton, Henthorn and Coldcoats CP.[43] LG Clith. RD. Parl Clith. CC (1948—*).

LITTLE MITTON, HENTHORN AND COLDCOATS

Tp in Whalley AP, sep CP 1866.[4] LG Blackb Hd, Clith. PLU, RSD, RD. Abol 1935 pt to cr Little Mitton CP, pt to Pendleton CP.[43] Parl Clith. Parl Bor (1832—85), Clith. Dv (1885—1948).

MONTON

EP Cr 1912 from Eccles St Andrew EP, Swinton St Peter EP, Patricroft EP.[200] Eccles RDn.

MOORSIDE

EP Cr 1870 from Oldham St James EP, Waterhead EP.[38] Asht. under Lyne RDn (1870—72), Oldham RDn (1872—*).

MORECAMBE

The following have 'Morecambe' in their names. Insofar as any existed at a given time: LG Lanc. PLU, Morec. MB. Parl Morec. & Lonsd. CC (1948—*). Eccl Lanc. RDn.

CP1—MORECAMBE—Renaming 1924 of Poulton Barre and Torrisholme CP.[615] Abol 1928 to help cr Morecambe and Heysham MB & CP2.[616]

CP2—MORECAMBE AND HEYSHAM—Cr 1928 by union Morec. MB & CP1, Heysham MB & AP.[440] Bdry: 1935,[43] 1965.[617]

—MORECAMBE HOLY TRINITY—Name sometimes used for EP cr 1748 as 'Poulton' (sometimes 'Poulton le Sands'), qv.

EP1—MORECAMBE ST BARNABAS—Cr 1910 from Poulton EP.[618]

—MORECAMBE ST CHRISTOPHER—Name sometimes used for EP cr 1933 as 'Barre', qv.

—EP2—MORECAMBE ST LAURENCE—Cr 1918 from Poulton EP.[201] Bdry: 1959 (help cr Torrisholme EP).[148]

MOSLEY COMMON

EP Cr 1895 from Tyldesley cum Shackerley EP.[88] Eccles RDn (1895—1933), Leigh RDn (1933—*).

LITTLE MOSS

CP Cr 1894 from pt of the pt of Ashton under Lyne AP

not in a MB or UD.[63] LG Asht. under Lyne PLU, Limehurst RD. Abol 1954 pt to Asht. under Lyne MB & AP, pt to Failsworth UD & CP, pt to Droyl. UD & CP.[65] Parl Mossley Dv (1918—48), Asht. under Lyne BC (1948—55).

MOSS SIDE

Tp in Manchester AP, sep CP 1866,[4] sep EP [Christ Church] 1858 from Manchester AP, Chorlton on Medlock EP, Whalley Ridge St Margaret EP, Withington EP, Rusholme EP.[70] LG Salf. Hd, Chorlton PLU, pt Moss Side USD, pt Rusholme USD (1875—85), pt Manch MB (1884—89), pt Manch CB (1889—94), pt Manch USD (1884—94), Moss Side UD (1894—1904), Manch CB (1904—10). Civ bdry: 1894 (gains the pt of Withington CP in Moss Side UD,[619] loses the pt in the CB to Rusholme CP[501]). Abol civ 1910 ent to South Manchester CP.[310] Parl S'rn Dv (1832—67), S-E Dv (1867—85), Manch, South Parl Bor (1885—1918). Eccl Chorlton RDn (1858—66), Chorlton & Hulme RDn (1866—72), Hulme RDn (1872—*). Eccl bdry: 1859 (help cr Hulme St John EP),[365] 1882 (help cr Greenhays EP),[203] 1902,[230] 1905.[195]

MOSS SIDE ST JAMES

EP Cr 1889 from Whalley Range St Edmund EP.[103] Hulme RDn. Bdry: 1902.[230] Abol 1973 to help cr Moss Side St James with St Clement EP.[275]

MOSS SIDE ST JAMES WITH ST CLEMENT

EP Cr 1973 by union Greenhays EP, Moss Side St James EP.[275] Hulme RDn.

MOSSLEY

EP Cr 1801 from Ashton under Lyne AP,[12] refounded 1865.[104] Manch RDn (1801—47), Asht. under Lyne RDn (1847—*). Bdry: 1962 (help cr Micklehurst EP [Ches, Lancs] to be in dioc Chester, gains pt Millbrook EP, Ches, dioc Chester).[369]

CP Cr 1894 by union of the following pars in Mossley MB: pt Ashton under Lyne AP (Lancs), Saddleworth CP (the pt of the par in Yorks W Riding before 1889, in Lancs from 1889), Tintwistle CP (the pt of the par in Ches before 1889, in Lancs from 1889), Stayley CP (the pt of the par in Ches before 1889, in Lancs from 1889).[97] LG Asht. under Lyne PLU, Mossley MB. Civ bdry: 1954.[65] Transf 1974 to Gtr Manch.[40] Parl Mossley Dv (1918—48), Asht. under Lyne BC (1948—*). Parl bdry: 1945,[339] 1955.[101]

MOSSLEY HILL ST BARNABAS

EP Cr 1914 from Mossley Hill St Matthew and St James EP.[238] Childwall RDn.

MOSSLEY HILL ST MATTHEW AND ST JAMES

EP Cr 1875 from Aigburth EP, Wavertree EP, Toxteth Park Christ Church EP.[28] Prescot RDn (1875—82), Childwall RDn (1882—*). Bdry: 1887,[335] 1914 (cr Mossley Hill St Barnabas EP),[238] 1964.[29]

MOSTON

Tp in Manchester AP, sep CP 1866,[4] eccl severed 1854 to help cr Harpurhey cum Moston EP,[199] 'Moston' a sep EP 1870 from Harpurhey cum Moston EP.[323] LG Salf. Hd, Manch PLU (1840—50), Prestw. PLU (1850—96), RSD (1875—90), Manch CB (1890—96), USD (1890—94). Abol civ 1896 to help cr North Manchester CP.[82] Parl S'rn

Dv (1832—67), S-E Dv (1867—85), Prestw. Dv (1885—1918). *Eccl* Cheetham RDn. Eccl bdry: 1911 (help cr Lightbowne EP),[71] 1931 (cr Moston St Chad EP),[620] 1966.[347]

MOSTON ST CHAD

EP Cr 1931 from Moston EP.[620] Cheetham RDn. Bdry: 1966.[347]

MOSTON ST JOHN ASHLEY LANE

EP Cr 1909 from Harpurhey Christ Church EP.[33] Cheetham RDn. Bdry: 1924.[313]

MUSBURY

Tp (Blackb Hd) in Bury AP (mainly Salf. Hd), sep CP 1866,[4] sep EP 1844 by union tp Musbury, pt Edenfield EP, pt Haslingden EP.[112] *LG* Blackb Hd, Hasl. PLU, RSD (1875—83), Hasl. USD (1883—94), MB (1891—94). Abol civ 1894 ent to Haslingden CP.[129] *Parl* N'rn Dv (1832—67), N-E Dv (1867—85), Rossend. Dv (1885—1918). *Eccl* Manch RDn (1844—50), Bury RDn (1850—51), Prestw. RDn (1851—72), Bury RDn (1872—77), Whalley RDn (1877—1912), Accr. RDn (1912—*).

MYERSCOUGH

Tp in Lancaster AP, sep CP 1866.[4] *LG* Seq 2. *Parl* Seq 7.

NATEBY

Tp in Garstang AP, sep CP 1866.[4] *LG* Seq 2. *Parl* Seq 7.

NELSON

CP Cr 1894 by union of the pts of the following in Nelson MB: Great and Little Marsden CP, Barrowford Booth CP.[164] *LG* Burnley PLU, Nelson MB. Bdry: 1896 (gains the pt of Wheatley Carr Booth CP in Nelson MB),[621] 1897,[298] 1935.[43] *Parl* Nelson & Colne Parl Bor/BC (1918—*).

NELSON IN LITTLE MARSDEN

EP Cr 1879 from Little Marsden EP.[314] Burnley RDn (1879—1970), Pendle RDn (1970—*). Bdry: 1902 (help cr Nelson St Philip EP).[604]

NELSON ST BEDE

EP Cr 1924 from Little Marsden EP.[111] Burnley RDn (1924—70), Pendle RDn (1970—*).

NELSON ST PHILIP

EP Cr 1902 from Great Marsden EP, Little Marsden EP, Nelson in Little Marsden EP.[604] Burnley RDn (1902—70), Pendle RDn (1970—*).

NETHERTON

Tp in Sefton AP, sep CP 1866,[4] sep EP 1957.[622] *LG* Seq 16. Civ bdry: 1940 (loses pt to Bootle CB [assoc with Lancs] & to Orrell CP),[43] 1951 (loses pt to Bootle CB [assoc with Lancs] & to Orrell CP),[39] 1968 (loses pt to Bootle CB [assoc with Lancs] & to Orrell CP).[623] Transf 1974 to Merseyside.[40] *Parl* Seq 21. *Eccl* Bootle RDn.

NEW SPRINGS

EP Cr 1953 from Haigh and Aspull EP, Aspull EP.[118] Wigan RDn.

NEWBARNS AND HAWCORT

EP Cr 1869 from Dalton in Furness AP.[139] Aldingham RDn (1869—83), Dalton RDn (1883—1970), Furness RDn (1970—*). Bdry: 1877 (help cr Barrow in Furness St Matthew EP),[160] 1894,[161] 1937,[162] 1967 (cr Barrow in Furness St Aidan EP).[163] Later called 'Barrow in Furness St Paul'.

NEWBOLD

EP Cr 1867 from Rochdale AP, Milnrow EP.[474] Rochd. RDn. Bdry: 1911 (help cr Belfield EP),[182] 1958.[135]

NEWBURGH

EP Cr 1871 from Lathom St James EP (orig hmlt [not sep civ] in chap Lathom).[149] N Meols RDn (1871—87), Ormsk. RDn (1887—*).

NEWCHURCH

Chap in Whalley AP, sep CP 1866,[4] sep EP 1723 (incl tps Barley with Wheatacre Booth, Goldshaw Booth, Old Laund Booth, Roughlee Booth, all in Whalley AP) as 'Newchurch in Pendle',[12] qv. *LG* Blackb Hd, Hasl. PLU, pt Rawt. USD, pt Rawt. MB (1891—94), pt Bacup USD, pt Bacup MB (1882—94). Civ bdry: 1883.[31] Abol civ 1894 the pt in the MB to help cr Rawtenstall CP, the pt in the UD to help cr Bacup CP.[129] *Parl* N'rn Dv (1832—67), N-E Dv (1867—85), Rossend. Dv (1885—1918).

NEWCHURCH

EP Cr 1748 from Winwick AP (tps Newchurch, Culceth [civ united 1845 as 'Newchurch Kenyon',[92] qv]),[12] refounded 1844.[399] Warr. RDn (1748—1847), Winwick RDn (1847—1949), Warr. RDn (1949—*). Bdry: 1878 (help cr Glazebury EP).[38]

NEWCHURCH IN PENDLE

Chap in Whalley AP, sep EP 1723 (incl tps Barley with Wheatacre Booth, Goldshaw Booth, Old Laund Booth, Roughlee Booth, all in Whalley AP),[12] sep CP 1866 as 'Newchurch',[4] qv. Blackb RDn (1723—1847), Whalley RDn (1847—72), Burnley RDn (1872—1970), Pendle RDn (1970—*). Bdry: 1846 (help cr Lumb EP).[283]

NEWCHURCH IN ROSSENDALE

EP Chap in Whalley AP (incl chap Bacup), early sep.[130] Blackb RDn (cr—1847), Whalley RDn (1847—66), Accr. RDn (1866—72), Whalley RDn (1872—1912), Rossend. RDn (1872—1973). Bdry: 1801 (area orig chap Bacup severed to cr Bacup EP,[12] refounded 1843 from Newchurch in Rossendale EP, Rochdale AP[206]), 1866 (help cr Waterfoot EP),[50] 1881,[235] 1887 (help cr Edgeside EP),[439] 1887 (help cr Rawtenstall St John, Clough Fold EP).[241] Abol civ 1973 to help cr Newchurch St Nicholas with St John EP.[624]

NEWCHURCH KENYON

CP Cr 1845 by union tps Kenyon, Culceth in Winwick AP[92]; for union of the 2 tps eccl 1748, see 'Newchurch'. *LG* W Derby Hd. Abol 1866, the area of each orig tp a sep CP as 'Culceth', 'Kenyon',[4] so that this area has no sep civ identity thereafter.

NEWCHURCH ST NICHOLAS WITH ST JOHN

EP Cr 1973 by union Newchurch in Rossendale EP, Rawtenstall St John, Clough Fold EP.[624] Rossend. RDn.

NEWHEY—see NEW HEY

NEWTON

Chap and bor in Manchester AP, sep CP 1866,[4] pt eccl severed 1728 to help cr Gorton EP,[12] qv for later refounding, the remainder of chap Newton and ent tps Droylsden, Failwsowrth in same par cr 1839

'Newton All Saints' EP,[74] the areas of the 2 other tps severed 1844 to cr the 2 EPs of Droylsden, Failsworth,[348] the remainder refounded 1854 as 'Newton All Saints'.[199] *LG* Salf. Hd, Manch PLU (1840—50), Prestw. PLU (1850—96), pt Newton Heath USD (1875—90), pt Prestw. RSD (1875—90), Manch CB (1890—96), USD (1890—94). Abol civ 1896 to help cr North Manchester CP.[82] *Parl* Newton Parl Bor (1558—1832), Manch Parl Bor (1832—85), pt Manch, North Parl Bor, pt Manch, South Parl Bor (1885—1918). *Eccl* As 'Newton All Saints', sometimes 'Newton Heath All Saints', Manch RDn (1839—51), Bury RDn (1851—72), Cheetham RDn (1872—*). Addtl eccl bdry alt: 1850 (help cr Manchester St Philip, Bradford Road EP),[346] 1876 (cr Miles Platting St Luke EP),[90] 1883 (cr Newton Heath St Anne EP),[625] 1906 (cr Newton Heath St Wilfrid EP).[268]

NEWTON ALL SAINTS—see prev entry

NEWTON HEATH
The following have 'Newton Heath' in their names. Insofar as any existed at a given time: *Eccl* Cheetham RDn.

—NEWTON HEATH ALL SAINTS—see NEWTON ALL SAINTS

EP1—NEWTON HEATH ST ANNE—Cr 1883 from Newton EP.[625] Bdry: 1889 (help cr EP2).[87] Abol 1973 to help cr EP5.[626]

EP2—NEWTON HEATH ST AUGUSTINE—Cr 1889 from EP1, Manchester The Albert Memorial Church EP.[87] Abol 1968 to help cr Manchester The Albert Memorial Church with Newton Heath St Augustine EP.[256]

EP3—NEWTON HEATH ST MARK, HOLLAND STREET—Cr 1885 from Manchester St Philip, Bradford Road EP.[371] Cathedral RDn. Abol 1958 to help cr Manchester St Philip with St Mark EP.[602]

EP4—NEWTON HEATH ST WILFRID—Cr 1906 from Newton EP.[268] Abol 1973 to help cr EP5.[626]

EP5—NEWTON HEATH ST WILFRID AND ST ANNE—Cr 1973 by union EP1, EP4.[626]

NEWTON IN MAKERFIELD
Tp (sometimes 'Newton le Willows') and bor in Winwick AP, sep CP 1841,[400] sep EP 1770,[12] eccl refounded 1844.[399] *LG* W Derby Hd, Warr. PLU, Newton in Makerfield Bor, USD, UD (1894—Mar 1939), Newton le Willows UD (Mar—June 1939). Renamed civ 1939 'Newton le Willows'.[627] *Parl* Newton in Makerfield Parl Bor (1559—1832), S'rn Dv (1832—67), S-W Dv (1867—85), Newton Dv (1885—1948). *Eccl* Warr. RDn (1770—1847), Winwick RDn (1847—1949), Warr. RDn (1949—*). Eccl bdry: 1845 (cr Newton in Makerfield St Peter EP),[194] 1879 (cr Earlestown EP).[442]

NEWTON IN MAKERFIELD ST PETER
EP Cr 1845 from Newton in Makerfield EP.[194] Warr. RDn (1845—47), Winwick RDn (1847—1949), Warr. RDn (1949—*). Bdry: 1916 (cr Newton le Willows EP),[429] 1955.[602]

NEWTON LE WILLOWS
EP Cr 1916 from Newton in Makerfield St Peter EP.[429] Winwick RDn (1916—49), Warr. RDn (1949—*).

Bdry: 1955.[602]
CP Renaming 1939 of Newton in Makerfield CP.[627] *LG* Newton le Willows UD. Transf 1974 to Merseyside.[40] *Parl* Newton CC (1948—*).

NEWTON WITH CLIFTON
CP Cr 1934 by union pt Clifton with Salwick CP, pt Newton with Scales CP.[226] *LG* Fylde RD. *Parl* S Fylde CC (1948—*).

NEWTON WITH SCALES
Tp in Kirkham AP, sep CP 1866.[4] *LG* Amound. Hd, Fylde PLU, RSD, RD. Abol 1934 pt to help cr Newton with Clifton CP, pt to Hutton CP.[226] *Parl* N'rn Dv (1832—67), North Dv (1867—85), Blackp. Dv (1885—1918), Fylde Dv (1918—48).

NORDEN
EP Cr 1862 from Spotland EP, Whitworth EP.[628] Rochd. RDn. Bdry: 1913.[203]
CP Cr 1894 from the pt of Spotland CP in Norden UD.[257] *LG* Rochd. PLU, Norden UD. Abol 1933 pt to Rochd. CB (assoc with Lancs) & CP, pt to Heyw. MB & CP.[37] *Parl* Royton Dv (1918—48).

NORRIS BANK
EP Cr 1899 from Heaton Mersey EP, Heaton Norris Christ Church EP.[1] Ardwick RDn (1899—1912), Heaton RDn (1912—*).

NORTH SHORE
EP Cr 1868 from Kirkdale EP.[91] Liverp North RDn (1868—95), Bootle RDn (1895—*). Bdry: 1957,[285] 1958.[543] Sometimes called 'Kirkdale St Paul, North Shore'.

NORTHENDEN
AP Ches par transf 1931 to Manch CB and its area civ abol into Manchester AP,[592] so that the orig area thereafter assoc with Lancs as was the CB. See main entry in Ches, incl the cr of the following EPs after 1931 pt or ent from this par, those EPs sometimes considered Lancs because of the civ change: Benchill (1936), Lawton Moor (1937), Wythenshawe (1960), Newall Green (1960).

NORTHTOWN
CP Cr (orig as 'North Town', later and usually 'Northtown') 1894 from the pt of Padiham CP not in Padiham & Hapton UD.[164] *LG* Burnley PLU, RD. Bdry: 1904 (help cr Sabden CP),[497] 1935.[43] *Parl* Clith. Dv/CC (1918—*).

OAKENROD
EP Cr 1925 from Spotland EP, Rochdale St Alban EP, Falinge EP.[49] Rochd. RDn. Abol 1972 to help cr Rochdale St George with St Alban EP.[299]

OLD LAUND BOOTH
Tp in Whalley AP, sep CP 1866,[4] eccl in chap Newchurch in Pendle (sep EP 1723 from Whalley AP[12]). *LG* Seq 5. Bdry: 1898,[496] 1935 (gains Wheatley Carr Booth CP).[43] *Parl* Seq 12.

OLDHAM
The following have 'Oldham' in their names. Insofar as any existed at a given time: *LG* Salf. Hd, Oldham PLU, MB (1849—89), CB (1889—1974), USD. *Parl* Oldham Parl Bor (1832—1948); see Part III of the *Guide* for composition of Oldham BCs (1948—*) by wards of the CB. *Eccl* Manch RDn (cr—1847), Rochd. RDn (1847—72), Oldham RDn (1872—*).

CP1/EP1—OLDHAM [ST MARY]—Chap (incl tps Chadderton, Compton, Royton in same par) and tp in Prestwich AP, the tp a sep CP 1866,[4] the orig area of tp Compton eccl severed 1719 from the chap as 'Shaw' EP,[12] refounded 1835,[182] the remainder of the area of chap Oldham a sep EP 1746,[12] eccl refounded (after bdry alts noted below) 1835.[182] Civ bdry: 1951,[64] 1954.[65] Transf 1974 to Gtr Manch.[40] Parl bdry: 1951,[66] 1955.[101] Addtl eccl bdry alt: 1757 (orig area tp [chap built 1754[629]] Royton cr 'Royton' EP,[12] refounded 1835[182]), 1815 (cr EP10,[12] refounded 1835[182]), 1835 (pt orig area tp Chadderton cr 'Hollinwood' EP[182]), 1835 (cr EP6),[182] 1844 (cr Coldhurst EP, help cr Werneth EP),[348] 1846 (help cr Leesfield EP),[107] 1873 (cr EP3),[630] 1892 (help cr EP1).[44] Abol eccl 1964 to help cr EP8.[196]

EP1—OLDHAM ALL SAINTS—Cr 1892 from EP1, Coldhurst EP.[44] Sometimes called 'Northmoor'. Bdry: 1957.[386]

EP2—OLDHAM ST AMBROSE—Cr 1929 from EP6, Waterhead EP.[159]

EP3—OLDHAM ST ANDREW—Cr 1873 from EP1.[630]

EP4—OLDHAM ST BARNABAS—Cr 1930 from EP6.[358]

EP5—OLDHAM ST CHAD, LIMESIDE—Cr 1965 from Bardsley EP, Hollinwood EP.[145]

EP6—OLDHAM ST JAMES—Cr 1835 from EP1.[182] Bdry: 1844 (cr Waterhead EP),[144] 1870 (help cr Moorside EP),[38] 1871,[379] 1873 (cr Lower Moor EP, sometimes called 'Oldham St Stephen and All Martyrs, Lower Moor'),[391] 1929 (help cr EP2),[159] 1930 (cr EP4).[358]

EP7—OLDHAM ST JOHN, WERNETH—Renaming 1945 of Chadderton St John EP.[139]

EP8—OLDHAM ST MARY WITH ST PETER—Cr 1964 by union EP1, EP10.[196]

EP9—OLDHAM ST PAUL—Cr 1880 from EP10, Werneth EP.[322] Bdry: 1957,[144] 1967.[146]

EP10—OLDHAM ST PETER—Cr 1815 from EP1,[12] refounded 1835.[182] Bdry: 1844 (cr Glodwick EP, help cr Werneth EP),[348] 1880 (help cr EP9).[322] Abol 1964 to help cr EP8.[196]

—OLDHAM ST STEPHEN AND ALL MARTYRS, LOWER MOOR—see LOWER MOOR

OPENSHAW
Tp in Manchester AP, sep CP 1866,[4] sep EP 1840 (incl area tp Bradford in same par and eccl ex-par Beswick),[288] eccl refounded 1864.[154] LG Salf. Hd, Chorlton PLU, Openshaw USD (1875—90), Manch CB (1890—96), USD (1890—94). Civ bdry: 1883,[31] 1889.[440] Abol civ 1896 to help cr South Manchester CP.[82] Parl S'rn Dv (1832—67), S-E Dv (1867—85), Gorton Dv (1885—1918). Eccl Manch RDn (1840—47), Asht. under Lyne RDn (1847—72), Ardwick RDn (1872—*). Eccl bdry: 1862 (area of orig tp Bradford and eccl ex-par Beswick severed to cr Bradford EP),[185] 1866 (help cr Gorton St Mark EP),[84] 1881 (help cr Higher Openshaw EP),[355] 1921.[3]

HIGHER OPENSHAW
EP Cr 1881 from Openshaw EP, Droylsden EP, Gorton EP.[355] Ardwick RDn. Bdry: 1913 (help cr Droylsden St Andrew EP).[112]

ORDSALL IN SALFORD ST CLEMENT
EP Cr 1879 from Salford St Bartholomew EP, Salford Stowell Memorial Church EP.[328] Salf. RDn. Bdry: 1900 (help cr Ordsall in Salford St Cyprian EP).[368] Abol 1967 to help cr Salford St Clement with St Cyprian, Ordsall EP.[273]

ORDSALL IN SALFORD ST CYPRIAN
EP Cr 1900 from Ordsall in Salford St Clement EP, Stretford EP.[368] Salf. RDn. Abol 1967 to help cr Salford St Clement with St Cyprian, Ordsall EP.[273]

ORFORD ST ANDREW
EP Cr 1964 from Orford St Margaret and All Hallows EP, Winwick AP.[631] Warr. RDn.

ORFORD ST MARGARET AND ALL HALLOWS
EP Cr 1909 from Padgate EP.[259] Winwick RDn (1909—49), Warr. RDn (1949—*). Bdry: 1964 (help cr Orford St Andrew EP).[631]

ORMSKIRK
AP Incl chap Lathom (sep CP 1866,[4] pt cr 1851 Lathom St James EP,[12] refounded 1860,[254] pt of orig area of Lathom and tp Burscough cr 1844 Burscough Bridge EP,[12] refounded 1847,[322] the latter sometimes called 'Lathom St John'), chap (orig) and tp Scarisbrick (sep CP 1866,[4] sep EP 1869[632]), chap (built 1776 by subscription[633]) and tp Skelmersdale (sep CP 1866,[4] sep EP 1782,[12] eccl refounded 1858[256]), tp Bickerstaffe (sep CP 1866,[4] church built 1843 by Early of Derby and eccl sep thereafter[189]), tp Burscough (sep CP 1866,[4] sep EP 1844 as 'Burscough Bridge' [incl pt tp Lathom],[12] refounded 1847[322]). LG W Derby Hd, pt Ormsk. Bor, Ormsk. PLU, USD, UD. Addtl civ bdry alt: 1914,[559] 1931,[592] 1968.[414] Parl Seq 21. Eccl Seq 5.

ORRELL
Tp in Wigan AP, sep CP 1866,[4] sep EP 1922 from Upholland EP, Pemberton EP, Billinge EP.[493] LG W Derby Hd, Wigan PLU, Orrell USD, UD. Transf 1974 to Gtr Manch.[40] Parl Seq 18. Eccl Wigan RDn. Eccl bdry: 1966.[104]

ORRELL
CP Cr 1905 from the pt of Orrell and Ford CP transf to Bootle CB (assoc with Lancs).[485] LG W Derby PLU, Bootle CB. Bdry: 1940,[486] 1951,[39] 1968.[623] Parl Bootle Parl Bor/BC (1918—*).

ORRELL AND FORD
Tp in Sefton AP, sep CP 1866.[4] LG W Derby Hd, PLU, RSD, Sefton RD. Abol 1905 the pt transf to Bootle CB (assoc with Lancs) cr Orrell CP, the remainder cr Ford CP.[485] Parl S'rn Dv (1832—67), S-W Dv (1867—85), Ormsk. Dv (1885—1918).

ORRELL HEY—see LITHERLAND ST PHILIP
OSBALDESTON
Tp in Blackburn AP, sep CP 1866.[4] LG Seq 4. Parl Seq 13.

OSMOTHERLEY
Tp in Ulverston AP, sep CP 1866.[4] LG Seq 14. Transf 1974 to Cumbria.[40] Parl Seq 11.

OSWALDTWISTLE
Tp in Whalley AP, sep CP 1866,[4] eccl in chap Church (sep EP 1723 as 'Church Kirk' from Whalley AP[12]), 'Oswaldtwistle' a sep EP 1865 from

Church Kirk EP.[12] *LG* Blackb Hd, PLU, Oswald-twistle USD, UD. *Parl* N'rn Dv (1832—67), N-E Dv (1867—85), Accr. Dv (1885—1918), Accr. Parl Bor/BC (1918—*). *Eccl* Whalley RDn (1865—66), Accr. RDn (1866—72), Whalley RDn (1872—1912), Accr. RDn (1912—*). Eccl bdry: 1879 (help cr Knuzden EP),[154] 1950,[213] 1966 (help cr Oswald-twistle All Saints EP).[372]

OSWALDTWISTLE ALL SAINTS
EP Cr 1966 from Knuzden EP, Church Kirk EP, Oswaldtwistle EP.[372] Accr. RDn.

OSWALDTWISTLE ST PAUL
EP Cr 1885 from Church Kirk EP.[371] Whalley RDn (1885—1912), Accr. RDn (1912—*). Bdry: 1950.[213]

OUTWOOD
CP Cr 1894 from the pt of Pilkington CP not in a UD.[115] *LG* Bury PLU, RD. Abol 1933 pt to Radcl. MB & AP, pt to Kearsley UD & CP, pt to Whitefield UD & CP.[171] *Parl* Farnw. Dv (1918—48).

OVERTON
Chap in Lancaster AP, sep CP 1866,[4] sep EP 1715 (incl tps Heaton with Oxcliffe, Middleton in the same par).[12] *LG* Seq 12. *Parl* Seq 6. *Eccl* Amound. RDn (1715—52), Lanc. RDn (1852—*). Eccl bdry: 1959 (help cr Torrisholme EP).[148]

PADDINGTON
EP Cr 1846 from Pendleton EP, Salford Christ Church EP.[449] Manch RDn (1846—50), Eccles RDn (1850—66), Eccles & Salf. RDn (1866—72), Salf. RDn (1872—1965). Abol 1965 to help cr Salford St Paul with Christ Church EP.[634]

PADGATE
EP Cr 1838 from Warrington AP.[635] Warr. RDn (1842—47), Winwick RDn (1847—1949), Warr. RDn (1949—*). Bdry: 1909,[41] 1909 (cr Orford St Margaret and All Hallows EP),[259] 1971 (cr Woolston EP).[636]

PADIHAM
Chap in Whalley AP, sep CP 1866,[4] sep EP 1730 (incl tps Hapton, Higham with West Close Booth, Simonstone),[12] pt of Padiham EP severed 1845 to help cr help cr Habergham All Saints EP,[124] the remainder refounded 1868 as 'Padiham'.[27] *LG* Blackb Hd, Burnley PLU, pt Padiham & Hapton USD, pt Burnley RSD, Padiham & Hapton UD (1894—96), Padiham UD (1896—1974). Civ bdry: 1894 (the pt not in the UD cr North Town CP, later called 'Northtown'),[164] 1894 (gains the pt of Hapton CP in the UD),[164] 1896,[637] 1935.[43] *Parl* Seq 14. *Eccl* Blackb RDn (1730—1847), Whalley RDn (1847—72), Burnley RDn (1872—*).

PARBOLD
Tp in Eccleston AP, sep CP 1866.[4] *LG* Seq 11. *Parl* Seq 5.

PARKFIELD IN MIDDLETON
EP Cr 1863 from Middleton AP.[426] Bury RDn (1863—72), Prestw. & Middl. RDn (1872—1912), Middl. RDn (1912—*). Bdry: 1964 (help cr Langley EP).[197]

PARR
Tp in Prescot AP, sep CP 1866,[4] sep EP 1844.[12] *LG* W Derby Hd, Prescot PLU, St Helens MB (1868—89), CB (1889—94), USD. Abol civ 1894 to help cr St Helens CP.[451] *Parl* S'rn Dv (1832—67), S-W Dv (1867—85), St Helens Parl Bor (1885—1918). *Eccl* Warr. RDn (1844—47), Prescot RDn (1847—*).

PARR MOUNT
EP Cr 1863 from St Helens EP.[91] Prescot RDn.

PATRICROFT
EP Cr 1869 from Eccles AP.[437] Eccles & Salf. RDn (1869—72), Eccles RDn (1872—*). Bdry: 1880 (help cr Eccles St Andrew EP),[445] 1912 (help cr Monton EP),[200] 1922 (help cr Winton EP),[493] 1936 (cr Peel Green EP).[638]

PEEL
EP Cr 1761 from Deane AP (pt chap Little Hulton),[12] refounded 1874.[350] Manch RDn (1761—1847), Bolton le Moors RDn (1847—93), Bolton South RDn (1893—1901), Bolton le Moors RDn (1901—68), Farnw. RDn (1968—*).

PEEL GREEN
EP Cr 1936 from Patricroft EP.[638] Eccles RDn. Abol 1971 to help cr Barton with Peel Green EP.[179]

PEMBERTON
Tp in Wigan AP, sep CP 1866,[4] sep EP 1838.[16] *LG* W Derby Hd, Wigan PLU, Pemberton USD, UD (1894—1904), Wigan CB (1904—20). Abol civ 1920 ent to Wigan AP.[639] *Parl* S'rn Dv (1832—67), S-W Dv (1867—85), Ince Dv (1885—1918), Wigan Parl Bor/BC (1918—48). *Eccl* Warr. RDn (1838—47), Wigan RDn (1847—*). Eccl bdry: 1863 (help cr Wigan St James EP),[640] 1871 (help cr Wigan St Andrew EP, sometimes early called 'Scholes'),[16] 1882,[146] 1891 (help cr Pemberton St Mark Newtown EP),[213] 1911 (help cr Highfield EP),[38] 1915 (help cr Goose Green EP),[125] 1922 (help cr Orrell EP).[493]

PEMBERTON ST MARK NEWTOWN
EP Cr 1891 from Pemberton EP, Wigan St Andrew EP, Wigan AP, Wigan St Thomas EP, Wigan St James EP.[213] Wigan RDn.

PENDLEBURY
Tp in Eccles AP, sep CP 1866,[4] sep EP 1843.[443] *LG* Salf. Hd, PLU, Swinton & Pendlebury USD (pt 1875—83, ent 1893—94), pt Salford USD (1875—83), pt Salf. MB (1853—83), Salf. RSD (pt 1875—83, ent 1883—94), Swinton & Pendlebury UD. Civ bdry: 1883.[641] Abol civ 1934 to help cr Swinton & Pendlebury MB & CP.[171] *Parl* Pt Salf. Parl Bor (1832—85), pt S'rn Dv (1832—67), pt S-E Dv (1867—85), Eccles Dv (1885—1918), Eccles Parl Bor (1918—48). *Eccl* Manch RDn (1843—50), Eccles RDn (1850—66), Eccles & Salf. RDn (1866—72), Eccles RDn (1872—1903), Salf. RDn (1903—*). Eccl bdry: 1861 (help cr Pendlebury Christ Church EP),[157] 1868,[24] 1874 (help cr Pendlebury St Augustine EP),[357] 1925 (help cr Claremont EP),[220] 1971.[299]

PENDLEBURY CHRIST CHURCH
EP Cr 1861 from Pendlebury EP, Eccles AP.[157] Eccles RDn (1861—66), Eccles & Salf. RDn (1866—72), Eccles RDn (1872—*). Bdry: 1868,[24] 1874 (help cr Pendlebury St Augustine EP).[357]

PENDLEBURY ST AUGUSTINE

EP Cr 1874 from Pendlebury Christ Church EP, Pendlebury EP.[357] Eccles RDn.

PENDLETON

Tp and chap ([St Thomas] built 1776[445]) in Eccles AP, sep CP 1866,[4] sep EP 1807,[12] eccl refounded 1865.[391] *LG* Salf. Hd, PLU, MB (1853—89), CB (1889—1919), USD (1875—92), RSD (1892—94). Civ bdry: 1883,[641] 1892.[173] Abol civ 1919 ent to Salford CP.[300] *Parl* Salf. Parl Bor (1832—1918); see Part III of the *Guide* for composition of Salf. Parl Bors (1918—48) by wards of the CB. *Eccl* Manch RDn (cr—1850), Eccles RDn (1850—66), Eccles & Salf. RDn (1866—72), Salf. RDn (1872—*). Eccl bdry: 1846 (help cr Paddington EP),[449] 1860 (cr Charlestown EP),[254] 1902 (help cr Pendleton St Ambrose EP),[553] 1903,[522] 1923 (cr Brindle Heath EP),[105] 1971.[299]

PENDLETON

Tp in Whalley AP, sep CP 1866,[4] eccl severed 1839 to help cr Clitheroe St James EP,[380] the orig area of the tp severed 1873 from the latter to help cr Pendleton in Whalley EP.[297] *LG* Seq 6. Bdry: 1904 (help cr Sabden CP),[497] 1935.[43] *Parl* Seq 1.

PENDLETON HALL

Ex-par place, civ abol 1858 ent to Pendelton tp in Whalley AP,[80] eccl abol 1873 to help cr Pendleton in Whalley EP.[297]

PENDLETON IN WHALLEY

EP Cr 1873 from Clitheroe St James EP (incl orig area tp Pendleton, qv in prev entry), eccl ex-par place Pendleton Hall, Whalley AP.[297] Whalley RDn.

PENDLETON ST AMBROSE

EP Cr 1902 from Pendleton EP, Weaste St Luke EP, Salford Christ Church EP.[553] Salf. RDn.

PENDLETON ST BARNABAS

EP Cr 1888 from Charlestown EP.[350] Salf. RDn. Abol 1973 to help cr Charlestown St George with St Barnabas EP.[352]

PENKETH

Tp in Prescot AP, sep CP 1866,[4] eccl severed 1728 to help cr Great Sankey EP,[12] the latter abol 1859 to help cr Farnworth EP,[262] the area of orig tps Penketh, Great Sankey severed 1875 from the latter to cr Great Sankey EP.[150] *LG* Seq 19. Bdry: 1933 (gains pts Acton Grange CP, Moore CP, both Ches).[412] Transf 1974 to Ches.[40] *Parl* Seq 19.

PENNINGTON

AP *LG* Seq 14. Civ bdry: 1935.[43] Transf 1974 to Cumbria.[40] *Parl* Seq 11. *Eccl* Seq 10.

PENNINGTON

Tp in Leigh AP, sep CP 1866,[4] sep EP 1854.[565] *LG* W Derby Hd, Leigh PLU, USD. Abol civ 1894 to help cr Leigh CP.[122] *Parl* S'rn Dv (1832—67), S-W Dv (1867—85), Leigh Dv (1885—1918). *Eccl* Eccles RDn (1854—66), Eccles & Salf. RDn (1866—72), Eccles RDn (1872—1933), Leigh RDn (1933—*). Bdry: 1889,[103] 1974.[585]

PENWORTHAM

AP Incl chap Longton (sep CP 1866,[4] sep EP 1719[12]), tp Farington (sep CP 1866,[4] sep EP 1843[476]), tps Howick, Hutton (each a sep CP 1866[4]). *LG* Leyl. Hd, Penwortham Bor (status not sustained), Preston PLU, RSD (ent 1875—89, pt 1889—94), pt Preston CB & USD (1889—94), Preston RD. Addtl civ bdry alt: 1894 (loses the pt in the CB to Preston AP),[482] 1934.[226] *Parl* N'rn Dv (1832—67), North Dv (1867—85), pt Preston Parl Bor, pt Blackp. Dv (1885—1918), Fylde Dv (1918—48), S Fylde CC (1948—*). *Eccl* Seq 1. Addtl eccl bdry alt: 1931 (help cr New Longton EP),[95] 1972 (help cr Penwortham St Leonard EP).[477]

PENWORTHAM ST LEONARD

EP Cr 1972 from Penwortham AP, Farington EP.[477] Leyl. RDn.

PILKINGTON

Tp in Prestwich AP, sep CP 1866.[4] *LG* Salf. Hd, Bury PLU, pt Bury MB (1885—89), pt Bury CB (1889—94), pt Bury USD (1885—94), pt Whitefield USD (reduced pt June—apptd day 1894), pt Bury RSD (reduced pt 1885—94). Bdry: 1894 (loses pt in Whitefield UD to Radcliffe UD & AP).[460] Abol 1894 the pt in the CB transf to Bury AP, the pt in the UD cr Whitefield CP, pt of the pt not in a CB or UD cr Outwood CP, pt cr Unsworth CP,[115] pt to Radcl. UD & AP.[460] *Parl* S'rn Dv (1832—67), S-E Dv (1867—85), Heyw. Dv (1885—1918).

PILLING

Chap pt in Garstang AP (Amound. Hd), pt in Cockerham AP (Lonsd. Hd), sep CP 1866,[4] sep EP 1756.[12] *LG* Seq 2. Civ bdry: 1883,[31] 1887.[385] *Parl* Seq 7. *Eccl* Amound. RDn (1756—1852), Garst. RDn (1852—*).

PILSWORTH

Tp in Middleton AP, sep CP 1866.[4] *LG* Salf. Hd, Bury PLU, pt Heyw. USD, pt Heyw. MB (1881—94), pt Bury USD, pt Bury MB (1876—89), pt Bury CB (1889—94), pt Bury RSD. Abol 1894 the pt in Heyw. UD to help cr Heywood CP, the pt in the CB transf to Bury AP, the remainder to help cr Unsworth CP.[115] *Parl* S'rn Dv (1832—67), S-E Dv (1867—85), pt Bury Parl Bor, pt Heyw. Dv (1885—1918).

PLATT BRIDGE

EP Cr 1906 from Hindley St Peter EP, Ince in Makerfield St Mary EP.[523] Wigan RDn.

PLEASINGTON

Tp in Blackburn AP, sep CP 1866.[4] *LG* Seq 4. *Parl* Seq 13.

POULTON

Tp in Lancaster AP, sep EP 1748,[12] eccl refounded 1859,[332] sometimes eccl 'Poulton le Sands', or 'Morecambe Holy Trinity', sep CP 1866 as 'Poulton Barre and Torrisholme',[4] qv. Amound. RDn (1748—1852), Lanc. RDn (1852—*). Eccl bdry: 1910 (cr Morecambe St Barnabas EP),[618] 1918 (cr Morecambe St Laurence EP),[201] 1933 (help cr Bare EP),[147] 1959 (help cr Torrisholme EP).[148]

POULTON BARRE AND TORRISHOLME

Tp in Lancaster AP, sep CP 1866,[4] sep EP 1748 as 'Poulton le Sands',[12] eccl refounded 1859,[332] qv. *LG* Lonsd. Hd, Caton GilbU (until 1869), Lanc. PLU (1869—1924), Poulton Barre and Torrisholme USD (later called 'Morecambe' USD), Morec. UD (1894—1902), MB (1902—24). Civ bdry: 1894.[642]

Renamed civ 1924 'Morecambe'.[615] *Parl* N'rn Dv (1832—67), North Dv (1867—85), Blackp. Dv (1885—1918), Lanc. Dv (1918—48).

POULTON LE FYLDE

AP Incl chap Bishpam (prob orig a sep AP, appropriated to Lanc. Priory and after the Dissolution deemed a chap in this par until again a sep par 1688[210]), chap Marton (sep CP 1866,[4] sep EP 1805,[12] pt of the latter severed 1837 to help cr South Shore EP [o'wise 'Blackpool Holy Trinity'],[211] refounded 1871,[212] the remainder of Marton EP eccl refounded as such 1892[44]), tps Carleton, Hardhorn with Newton (each a sep CP 1866[4]), tp Thornton (sep CP 1866,[4] sep EP 1838,[12] eccl refounded 1869[643]). *LG* Amound. Hd, Fylde PLU, RSD, RD (1894—1900), Poulton le Fylde UD (1900—74). Civ bdry: 1934,[226] 1955 (loses pt to Blackp. CB [assoc with Lancs] & CP).[247] *Parl* N'rn Dv (1832—67), North Dv (1867—85), Blackp. Dv (1885—1918), Fylde Dv (1918—48), S Fylde CC (1948—*). Parl bdry: 1956.[248] *Eccl* Seq 8. Eccl bdry: 1954,[139] 1957 (help cr Blackpool St Michael and All Angels EP).[252]

POULTON LE SANDS—see POULTON

POULTON WITH FEARNHEAD

Tp in Warrington AP, sep CP 1866.[4] *LG* Seq 19. Bdry: 1896.[557] Transf 1974 to Ches.[40] *Parl* Seq 19.

PREESALL

EP Cr 1934 from Stalmine EP.[641] Garst. RDn.

PREESALL WITH HACKINSALL

Tp in Lancaster AP, sep CP 1866.[4] *LG* Amound. Hd, Garst. PLU, RSD, RD (1894—1900), Preesall with Hackinsall UD (1900—10), Preesall UD (1910—74). Bdry: 1883.[31] *Parl* Seq 7.

PRESCOT

AP Incl chap Rainford (sep CP 1866,[4] held by Dissenters until 17th cent,[333] sep EP 1869[505]), chap Great Sankey (used after Civil War by Presbyterians, until 1728[106]), tp Penketh (each a sep CP 1866,[4] the 2 severed and united eccl 1728 to cr Great Sankey EP,[150] the latter abol 1859 to help cr Farnworth EP,[262] the area of orig Great Sankey, Penketh eccl severed 1875 from Farnworth EP to re-cr Great Sankey EP[150]), tps Bold, Cronton, Cuerdley, Ditton (each a sep CP 1866,[4] all severed eccl 1859 to help cr Farnworth EP [qv above for earlier status],[262] 'Ditton' a sep EP 1875 from Farnworth EP, Whiston EP, Halewood EP[437]), tp Eccleston (sep CP 1866,[4] sep EP 1839 [Christ Church][12]), tp Parr (sep CP 1866,[4] sep EP 1844[12]), tp Rainhill (sep CP 1866,[4] sep EP 1837[443]), tp Sutton (sep CP 1866,[4] sep EP 1848[462]), tp Whiston (sep CP 1866,[4] sep EP 1869 from Prescot AP, Huyton AP, Halewood EP[505]), tp Widnes (incl area chap and bor Farnworth [bor status not sustained], the chap had some parochial rights from Middle Ages,[261] pt of the orig tp eccl severed 1859 to help cr Farnworth EP [remainder of the EP consists of Great Sankey EP abol for this purpose along with the 4 tps in Prescot of Bold, Cronton, Cuerdley, Ditton] while the remainder cr at the same time 'Widnes St Mary'[262]), tp Windle (sep CP 1866,[4] eccl incl chap St Helens [orig Presbyterian chap, sep EP 1716,[12] refounded 1852[644]]). *LG* W Derby Hd, Prescot PLU, pt Prescot USD, pt (uninhabited) Prescot RSD, Prescot UD. Addtl civ bdry alt: 1894 (loses the uninhabited pt not in the UD to Whiston CP, gains the pt of Eccleston CP in the UD),[450] 1914,[645] 1932.[453] *Parl* Seq 22. *Eccl* Seq 6.

PRESTOLEE

EP Cr 1883 from Prestwich AP, Farnworth and Kearsley EP.[27] Bolton le Moors RDn (1883—93), Bolton South RDn (1893—1901), Bolton le Moors RDn (1901—12), Radcl. & Prestw. RDn (1912—68), Farnw. RDn (1968—*).

PRESTON

The following have 'Preston' in their names. Insofar as any existed at a given time: *LG* Amound. Hd, Preston PLU, Bor/MB/CB, USD. *Parl* Preston Parl Bor (1295—1307, 1326, 1547—1867, pt 1867—1918, ent 1918—48), pt North Dv (1867—85), pt Blackp. Dv (1885—1918), pt Preston North BC, pt Preston South BC (1948—*). *Eccl* Lanc. RDn (until before 1291), Amound. RDn (before 1291—1852), Preston RDn (1852—*).

AP1—PRESTON [ST WILFRID, later ST JOHN]—Perhaps orig incl chap Chipping (sep par no later than 13th cent[361]); incl chap Broughton (sep CP 1866,[4] sep EP 1774[12]), chap Grimsargh (comprised of tps Elston, Grimsargh [each a sep CP 1866,[4] the latter as 'Grimsargh with Bockholes'], 'Grimsargh' a sep EP 1717,[12] eccl refounded 1875[85]), tp Barton (sep CP 1866,[4] perhaps a sep EP 1723,[165] certainly a sep EP 1851,[12] eccl refounded 1856[166]), tps Fishwick, Haighton (each a sep CP 1866[4]), tp Lea, Ashton, Ingol, and Cottam (sep CP 1866,[4] sep EP 1837 as 'Ashton upon Ribble St Andrew'[12]), tp Ribbleton (sep CP 1866,[4] sep EP 1883 from Preston AP, Fulwood EP[317]). Addtl civ bdry alt: 1894 (gains the pts of the following in Preston CB: Grimsargh with Brockholes CP; Lea, Ashton, Ingol, and Cottam CP; Penwortham AP, Ribbelton CP),[482] 1934,[226] 1952,[490] 1956.[560] Parl bdry: 1867 (area south of River Ribble excluded from Parl Bor),[646] 1953,[561] 1960.[562] Addtl eccl bdry alt: 1725 (cr EP6 [early 'New Chapel'],[12] refounded 1844[287]), 1816 (cr EP4,[12] refounded 1844[287]), 1826 (cr EP15,[12] refounded 1843[287]), 1830 (cr EP14,[12] refounded 1843[287]), 1836 (cr EP2),[647] 1838 (cr EP11),[648] 1844 (cr EP7),[287] 1858 (cr EP1),[649] 1859 (cr EP19),[12] 1863 (cr EP10,[12] refounded 1866[650]), 1963 (gains EP2).[349]

EP1—PRESTON ALL SAINTS—Cr 1858 from AP1.[649]

EP2—PRESTON CHRIST CHURCH—Cr 1836 from AP1.[647] Bdry: 1863 (help cr EP10,[12] refounded 1866[650]), 1894 (cr EP18).[384] Abol 1963 ent to AP1.[349]

EP3—PRESTON EMMANUEL—Cr 1871 from EP15.[75] Bdry: 1916 (help cr EP5).[436]

EP4—PRESTON HOLY TRINITY—Cr 1816 from AP1,[12] refounded 1844.[287] Abol 1951 ent to EP6.[227]

EP5—PRESTON ST CUTHBERT—Cr 1916 from Fulwood EP, EP3, EP19.[436]

EP6—PRESTON ST GEORGE—Cr 1725 (early 'New Chapel') from AP1,[12] refounded 1844.[287] Bdry: 1951 (gains EP4).[227]

EP7—PRESTON ST JAMES—Cr 1844 from AP1.[287] Bdry: 1869 (help cr EP16),[259] 1925.[493] Abol 1970 to help cr EP17.[651]

EP8—PRESTON ST JUDE—Cr 1894 from EP14, EP19.[244]

EP9—PRESTON ST LUKE—Cr 1859 from EP14,[12] refounded 1860.[322] Bdry: 1934 (help cr EP13).[315]

EP10—PRESTON ST MARK—Cr 1863 from EP2, EP15,[12] refounded 1866.[650] Bdry: 1929 (help cr Ashton upon Ribble St Michael and All Angels EP).[88]

EP11—PRESTON ST MARY—Cr 1838 from AP1.[648] Bdry: 1869 (help cr EP16),[259] 1884 (cr EP12),[652] 1893,[360] 1925.[493]

EP12—PRESTON ST MATTHEW—Cr 1884 from EP11.[652] Bdry: 1893,[360] 1934.[84]

EP13—PRESTON ST OSWALD—Cr 1934 from EP9, Ribbleton EP.[315]

EP14—PRESTON ST PAUL—Cr 1830 from AP1,[12] refounded 1843.[287] Bdry: 1859 (cr EP9,[12] refounded 1860[322]), 1894 (help cr EP8).[244]

EP15—PRESTON ST PETER—Cr 1826 from AP1,[12] refounded 1844.[287] Bdry: 1863 (help cr EP10,[12] refounded 1866[650]), 1871 (cr EP3).[75]

EP16—PRESTON ST SAVIOUR—Cr 1869 from EP7, EP11.[259] Bdry: 1925.[493] Abol 1970 to help cr EP17.[651]

EP17—PRESTON ST SAVIOUR WITH ST JAMES—Cr 1970 by union EP7, EP16.[651]

EP18—PRESTON ST STEPHEN—Cr 1894 from EP2.[384]

EP19—PRESTON ST THOMAS—Cr 1859 from AP1.[12] Bdry: 1894 (help cr EP8),[244] 1916 (help cr EP5).[436]

PRESTWICH

The following have 'Prestwich' in their names. Insofar as any existed at a given time: *LG* Salf. Hd, Manch PLU (1840—50), Prestw. PLU (1850—1930), USD, UD (1894—1939), MB (1939—74). *Parl* S'rn Dv (1832—67), S-E Dv (1867—85), Prestw. Dv (1885—1918), Middl. & Prestw. Dv/CC (1918—70), Middl. & Prestw. BC (1970—*). *Eccl* Blackb & Manch RDn (until before 1535), Manch RDn (before 1535—1850), Bury RDn (1850—51), Prestw. RDn (1851—72), Prestw. & Middl. RDn (1872—1912), Radcl. & Prestw. RDn (1912—*).

AP1—PRESTWICH [ST MARY]—Incl chap and tp Oldham (sep CP 1866,[4] the chap eccl incl tps Chadderton, Crompton, Royton, the orig area of tp Crompton a sep EP 1719 as 'Shaw',[12] the remainder of chap Oldham a sep EP 1746 as 'Oldham',[12] the orig area of tp [chap built 1754[629]] Royton severed 1757 from Oldham EP as 'Royton' EP [refounded 1835[182]],[350] pt of tp Chadderton severed 1835 from Oldham EP to cr 'Hollinwood' EP,[182] the remainder of Oldham EP refounded 1835 as 'Oldham' after pt severed at the same time to cr 'Oldham St James' EP[182], chap Royton (sep CP 1866,[4] sep EP 1757,[12] eccl

refounded 1835[182]), tp Alkrington, tp Tonge (each a sep CP 1866,[12] eccl severed and united 1842 as 'Tonge cum Alkrington' EP[22]), tp Chadderton (sep CP 1866,[4] pt eccl severed 1835 to help cr Hollinwood EP[182]), tp Crompton (sep CP 1866,[4] sep EP 1719 as 'Shaw',[12] as such eccl refounded 1835[182]), tp Great Heaton, tp Little Heaton (each a sep CP 1866[4]), tp Pilkington (sep CP 1866[4]). Addtl civ bdry alt: 1894,[514] 1903 (loses pt to Manch CB [assoc with Lancs] and to North Manchester CP),[599] 1933 (help cr Swinton and Pendlebury MB & CP).[171] Addtl eccl bdry alt: 1719 (cr Ringley EP,[12] refounded 1898 from AP1, Farnworth and Kearsley EP, Stand EP[276]), 1730 (cr Unsworth EP,[12] refounded 1885[368]), 1829 (cr Stand EP),[600] 1864 (cr Rhodes EP),[256] 1883 (help cr Prestolee EP),[27] 1885 (cr EP3),[368] 1920 (help cr EP2),[648] 1926 (cr EP1).[84]

EP1—PRESTWICH ST GABRIEL—Cr 1926 from AP1.[84]

EP2—PRESTWICH ST HILDA—Cr 1920 from AP1, EP3.[648]

EP3—PRESTWICH ST MARGARET, HOLY-ROOD—Cr 1885 from AP1.[368] Bdry: 1920 (help cr EP2),[648] 1928.[147]

PRIEST HUTTON

Tp in Warton AP, sep CP 1866.[4] *LG* Seq 12. *Parl* Seq 10.

PRINCES PARK

EP Cr 1854 from Toxteth Park St John the Baptist EP.[2] Liverp North RDn (1854—82), Toxteth RDn (1882—*). Bdry: 1867 (help cr Toxteth Park St Silas EP).[183] Sometimes 'Toxteth Park St Paul'.

QUARLTON

Tp in Bolton le Moors AP, sep CP 1866.[4] *LG* Salf. Hd, Bolton PLU, RSD, RD. Abol 1898 ent to Edgeworth CP.[36] *Parl* S'rn Dv (1832—67), S-E Dv (1867—85), W'hough. Dv (1885—1918).

QUERNMORE

Tp in Lancaster AP, sep CP 1866,[4] sep EP 1836,[12] eccl refounded 1858.[347] *LG* Seq 13. Civ bdry: 1900.[309] *Parl* Seq 8. *Eccl* Amound. RDn (1836—52), Lanc. RDn (1852—*).

RADCLIFFE

AP *LG* Salf. Hd, Bury PLU, pt Radcl. USD (enlarged pt June—apptd day 1894), pt Bury USD, pt Bury MB (1876—89), pt Bury CB (1889—94), Radcl. UD (1894—1935), MB (1935—74). Civ bdry: 1894 (the UD & AP gains pt Whitefield UD and Pilkington CP),[460] 1894 (incl loses the pt in the CB to Bury AP),[115] 1896 (loses pt to Whitefield UD & CP),[653] 1911 (loses pt to Bury CB [assoc with Lancs] & AP),[329] 1933 (incl gains Ainsworth CP, exchanges pts with Bury CB [assoc with Lancs] & AP).[37] Transf 1974 to Gtr Manch.[40] *Parl* S'rn Dv (1832—67), S-E Dv (1867—85), pt Bury Parl Bor, pt Heyw. Dv (1885—1918), Heyw. & Radcl. Dv (1918—48), Bury & Radcl. CC (1948—*). *Eccl* Manch & Blackb RDn (until before 1535), Manch RDn (before 1535—1850), Bury RDn (1850—51), Prestw. RDn (1851—72), Prestw. & Middl. RDn (1872—1912), Radcl. & Prestw. RDn (1912—*). Eccl bdry: 1821 (cr Radcliffe St Thomas EP,[12] refounded 1839[654]), 1873 (help cr Bury St Peter EP),[194] 1878 (help cr Radcliffe St Andrew, Black Lane EP),[655] 1973.[269]

RADCLIFFE ST ANDREW, BLACK LANE
EP Cr 1878 from Radcliffe AP, Radcliffe St Thomas EP.[655] Prestw. & Middl. RDn (1878—1912), Radcl. & Prestw. RDn (1912—*).

RADCLIFFE ST THOMAS
EP Cr 1821 from Radcliffe AP,[12] refounded 1839.[654] Manch RDn (1821—50), Bury RDn (1850—51), Prestw. RDn (1851—72), Prestw. & Middl. RDn (1872—1912), Radcl. & Prestw. RDn (1912—*). Bdry: 1878 (help cr Radcliffe St Andrew, Black Lane EP),[655] 1973.[269]

RAINFORD
Chap in Prescot AP, sep CP 1866,[4] held by Dissenters late 17th cent,[333] sep EP 1869.[505] LG W Derby Hd, Prescot PLU, Rainford USD, UD. Transf 1974 to Merseyside.[40] Parl S'rn Dv (1832—67), S-W Dv (1867—85), Newton Dv (1885—1918), Ormsk. Dv/CC (1918—*). Eccl Prescot RDn.

RAINHILL
Tp in Prescot AP, sep CP 1866,[4] sep EP 1837.[443] LG Seq 18. Transf 1974 to Merseyside.[40] Parl Seq 20. Eccl Warr. RDn (1837—47), Prescot RDn (1847—82), Childwall RDn (1882—1902), Prescot RDn (1902—*).

RAMPSIDE
EP Cr 1743 from Dalton in Furness AP,[12] refounded 1887 from Dalton in Furness AP, Dendron EP.[86] Furness & Cartmel RDn (1743—1859), Aldingham RDn (1859—83), Dalton RDn (1883—1970), Furness RDn (1970—*). Bdry: 1895.[23]

RAMSBOTTOM
EP Cr 1844 from Holcombe EP (incl pt area tp Tottington Lower End, orig in Bury AP).[111] Manch RDn (1844—50), Bury RDn (1850—51), Prestw. RDn (1851—72), Bury RDn (1872—*). Bdry: 1876 (help cr Ramsbottom St Andrew EP).[656]

CP Cr 1894 by union of the pts of the following in Ramsb. UD: Elton CP, Tottington Higher End CP, Tottington Lower End CP, Walmersley and Shuttleworth CP.[115] LG Bury PLU, Ramsb. UD. Bdry: 1933 (incl exchanges pts with Bury CB [assoc with Lancs] & AP).[37] Transf 1974 pt to Gtr Manch (wards of Central, East, South West), pt to Lancs (wards of North, Walmersley cum Shuttleworth).[40] Parl Heyw. & Radcl. Dv (1918—48), Rossend. BC (1948—*).

RAMSBOTTOM ST ANDREW
EP Cr 1876 from Ramsbottom EP, Shuttleworth EP.[656] Bury RDn.

RAMSGREAVE
Tp in Blackburn AP, sep CP 1866.[4] LG Seq 4. Bdry: 1922 (loses pt to Blackb CB [assoc with Lancs] & AP).[225] Parl Seq 13.

RAVENHEAD
EP Cr 1870 from St Helens EP, Eccleston St Thomas EP.[314] Prescot RDn.

OUT RAWCLIFFE
Tp in St Michael on Wyre AP, sep CP 1866,[4] sep EP 1840,[12] eccl refounded 1848.[630] LG Seq 2. Parl Seq 7. Eccl Amound. RDn (1840—52), Garst. RDn (1918—48),(1852—*).

UPPER RAWCLIFFE WITH TARNACRE
Tp (incl par church) in St Michael on Wyre AP, sep CP 1866.[4] LG Seq 2. Parl Seq 7.

RAWTENSTALL
EP Cr 1842 from Whalley AP.[12] Blackb RDn (1842—47), Whalley RDn (1847—66), Accr. RDn (1866—72), Whalley RDn (1872—1912), Rossend. RDn (1912—*). Bdry: 1887 (help cr Rawtenstall St John, Clough Fold EP),[241] 1914 (cr Constable Lee EP).[397]

CP Cr 1894 by union of the following in Rawt. MB: ent Cowpe Lench, Newhall Hay and Hall Carr CP and pts of Haslingden CP, Higher Booths CP, Lower Booths CP, Newchurch CP, Tottington Higher End CP.[129] LG Hasl. PLU, Rawt. MB. Parl Rossend. Parl Bor/BC (1918—*).

RAWTENSTALL ST JOHN, CLOUGH FOLD
EP Cr 1887 from Rawtenstall EP, Waterfoot EP, Newchurch in Rossendale EP.[241] Whalley RDn (1887—1912), Rossend. RDn (1912—73). Abol 1973 to help cr Newchurch St Nicholas with St John EP.[624]

READ
Tp in Whalley AP, sep CP 1866,[4] sep EP 1893 as 'Read in Whalley',[1] qv. LG Seq 5. Civ bdry: 1904 (help cr Sabden CP).[497] Parl Seq 14.

READ IN WHALLEY
Tp in Whalley AP, pt eccl severed 1849 to help cr Heyhouses EP,[466] the remainder a sep EP 1893 as 'Read in Whalley',[1] sep CP 1866 as 'Read',[4] qv. Whalley RDn.

REDDISH
Tp in Manchester AP, sep CP 1866,[4] eccl severed 1770 to help cr Heaton Norris EP,[12] 'Reddish' a sep EP 1884 from Heaton Reddish EP, Heaton Norris EP.[123] LG Salf. Hd, Stockport PLU, Reddish USD, UD (1894—1901), Stockport CB ([assoc with Ches] 1901—35). Abol civ 1935 ent to Stockport AP.[519] Parl S'rn Dv (1832—67), S-E Dv (1867—85), Stretf. Dv (1885—1918), Stockport Parl Bor/BC (1918—48). Eccl Ardwick RDn. Eccl bdry: 1902 (help cr North Reddish EP).[2]

NORTH REDDISH
EP Cr 1902 from Reddish EP, Gorton EP, Denton Christ Church EP, Abbey Hey EP.[2] Ardwick RDn. Bdry: 1926.[70]

REEDLEY HALLOWS
CP Cr 1894 from the pt of Reedley Hallows, Filly Close and New Laund Booth CP not in Burnley CB.[295] LG Burnley PLU, RD. Parl Clith. Dv/CC (1918—*).

REEDLEY HALLOWS, FILLY CLOSE AND NEW LAUND BOOTH
Tp in Whalley AP, sep CP 1866,[4] eccl ex-par and situated in chap Burnley (sep EP 1716 from Whalley AP[12]), pt of the orig tp eccl severed 1841 to help cr Fence-in-Pendle EP,[12] the remainder eccl abol 1887 and transf to Brierfield EP.[296] LG Blackb Hd, Burnley PLU (soon after 1837[657]—94), pt Burnley CB & USD (1889—94), Burnley RSD (ent 1875—89, pt 1889—94). Abol civ 1894 the pt in the CB

transf to Burnley CP, the remainder cr Reedley Hallows CP.[295] *Parl* N'rn Dv (1832—67), N-E Dv (1867—85), Darwen Dv (1885—1918).

RHODES

EP Cr 1864 from Middleton AP, Prestwich AP.[256] Prestw. RDn (1864—72), Prestw. & Middl. RDn (1872—1912), Middl. RDn (1912—*). Bdry: 1928,[147] 1964 (help cr Langley EP).[197]

RIBBLETON

Tp in Preston AP, sep CP 1866,[4] sep EP 1883 from Preston AP, Fulwood EP.[317] *LG* Amound. Hd, Preston PLU, pt Preston USD, pt Preston MB (1880—89), pt Preston CB (1889—94), Preston RD. Civ bdry: 1894 (loses the pt in the CB to Preston AP).[482] Abol civ 1934 pt to Preston CB (assoc with Lancs) & AP, pt to Fulwood UD & CP.[226] *Parl* N'rn Dv (1832—67), North Dv (1867—85), pt Preston Parl Bor, pt Blackp. Dv (1885—1918), Fylde Dv (1918—48). *Eccl* Preston RDn. Eccl bdry: 1934 (help cr Preston St Oswald EP),[315] 1934.[84]

RIBBY CUM WREA—see following entry

RIBBY WITH WREA

Chap in Kirkham AP, sep CP 1866,[4] sep EP 1759 as 'Ribby cum Wrea',[12] as such eccl refounded 1846.[544] *LG* Seq 1. Civ bdry: 1934 (incl help cr Bryning with Warton CP),[226] 1935.[43] *Parl* Seq 2. *Eccl* Amound. RDn (1846—52), The Fylde RDn (1852—*). Eccl bdry: 1954.[144]

RIBCHESTER

AP Tp 'Ribchester' in Blackb Hd as were tp Dilworth (sep CP 1866,[4] eccl severed 1727 to help cr Longridge EP,[12] eccl refounded 1861 as noted below), tp Dutton (sep CP 1866[4]); incl ex-par Stidd (situated in tp Dutton, orig chap of Knights of St John of Jerusalem, not sep civ or eccl, abol civ 1858 and transf to area of tp Dutton[80]) so that this par eccl 'Ribchester with Stidd', qv; incl in Amound. Hd tp Alston (sep CP 1866,[4] eccl severed 1727 to help cr Longridge EP,[12] the latter refounded 1861[62]), tp Hothersall (sep CP 1866[4]). *LG* Preston PLU, RSD, RD. Addtl civ bdry alt: 1934.[226] *Parl* Seq 14.

RIBCHESTER WITH STIDD

AP Usual eccl spelling (incl ex-par Stidd, qv in prev entry for earlier status); for civ and civ and eccl sep tps, see prev entry. *Eccl* Seq 9.

RINGLEY

EP Cr 1719 from Prestwich AP,[12] refounded 1898 from Preston AP, Farnworth and Kearsley EP, Stand EP.[276] Manch RDn (1719—1847), Bolton RDn (1847—51), Prestw. RDn (1851—72), Prestw. & Middl. RDn (1872—1912), Radcl. & Prestw. RDn (1912—*).

RISHTON

Tp in Blackburn AP, sep CP 1866,[4] pt eccl in chap Great Harwood (sep EP 1735 from Blackburn EP,[12] eccl refounded 1840[221]), pt of the remainder of the orig tp eccl severed 1845 to help cr Blackburn St Michael and All Angels EP,[222] another pt of orig area eccl severed 1866 to help cr Blackburn St Thomas EP,[50] 'Rishton' a sep EP 1874 from Great Harwood EP, Blackburn St Thomas EP, Blackburn St Michael and All Angels EP.[24] *LG* Blackb Hd,

PLU, RSD (1875—82), Rishton UD (1882—94), UD. Civ bdry: 1934 (loses pt to Blackb CB [assoc with Lancs] & AP).[226] *Parl* N'rn Dv (1832—67), N-E Dv (1867—85), Darwen Dv (1885—1918), Accr. Parl Bor/BC (1918—*).

RIVINGTON

Chap in Bolton le Moors AP, sep CP 1866,[4] sep EP 1754.[12] *LG* Seq 15. *Parl* Seq 17. *Eccl* Manch RDn (1754—1847), Bolton le Moors RDn (1847—93), Bolton North RDn (1893—1901), Bolton le Moors RDn (1901—68), Deane RDn (1968—*).

RIXTON WITH GLAZEBROOK

Tp in Warrington AP, sep CP 1866,[4] the tp comprises the chap of Hollinfare, as such sep EP 1722,[12] eccl refounded 1874.[350] *LG* Seq 19. Civ bdry: 1920 (gains pts Partington CP, Warburton AP, both Ches),[484] 1933 (exchanges pts with Lymm AP, Warburton AP, both Ches),[412] 1969.[495] Transf 1974 to Ches.[40] *Parl* Seq 19. Parl bdry: 1945.[339]

ROBY

EP Cr 1853 from Huyton AP (in area tp Huyton with Roby).[533] Prescot RDn. Bdry: 1951 (help cr West Derby St Luke EP),[434] 1959 (cr Huyton Quarry EP),[91] 1963.[276]

ROCHDALE

The following have 'Rochdale' in their names. Insofar as any existed at a given time: *LG* Pt Yorks W Riding (Agbrigg Wap), pt Lancs (Salf. Hd, pt Rochd. Bor), Rochd. PLU; after dependent units gain sep civ identity 1866 in the 2 cos, 'Rochdale' has no sep civ identity until cr 1894 of CP1 in Rochd. CB (assoc with Lancs). *Parl* Lancs pt, S'rn Dv (1832—67); Rochd. Parl Bor (1918—*). *Eccl* Manch & Blackb RDn (until before 1535), Blackb RDn (before 1535—before 1786), Manch RDn (before 1786—1847), Rochd. RDn (1847—*).

AP1—ROCHDALE [ST CHAD]—Incl in Lancs chap Littleborough (sep EP 1745 [incl pt areas Wuerdle, Wardle, each in tp Wuerdle and Wardle, qv below for sep civ identity],[12] eccl refounded 1859,[235] 'Littleborough' a sep CP 1894, qv for constituent pars), chap Milnrow (orig an oratory, sep EP 1717,[12] 'Milnrow' a sep CP 1894, qv for constituent pars), chap Todmorden (sep EP 1832 as 'Todmorden',[12] 'Walsden' a sep EP 1845 from Todmorden EP,[75] the ent area a sep CP 1866 as 'Todmorden and Walsden'[4]), pt area chap Whitworth (sep EP 1721 from Rochdale AP [incl pt tp Spotland, pt area Wardle in tp Wuerdle and Wardle][12]), tp Blatchinworth and Calderbrook (sep CP 1866[4]), tp Butterworth (sep CP 1866[4]), tp Castleton (sep CP 1866,[4] pt eccl severed 1863 to cr Castleton Moor EP,[342] pt eccl severed 1865 to cr Balderstone in Rochdale EP[119]), tp Spotland (sep CP 1866,[4] pt eccl severed 1721 to help cr Whitworth EP,[12] the remainder a sep EP 1844 as 'Spotland',[125] refounded 1844[125]), tp Wardleworth (sep CP 1866,[4] eccl severed 1844 to cr 2 EPs of Wardleworth St James, Wardleworth St Mary[125]), tp Wuerdle and Wardle (sep CP 1866,[4] pt of area Wuerdle severed 1745 to help cr Littleborough EP,[12] that pt of orig area severed 1841 from Littleborough EP and transf to Smallbridge EP,[195] pt of the area of Wardle eccl severed 1721 to help cr Whitworth EP,[12] pt of the area of Wardle eccl severed 1745 to help cr Littleborough EP,[12] pt of the area of Wardle eccl severed 1843 to cr Smallbridge EP,[12] the latter refounded 1844,[125] the 3 separate pts of Wardle earlier severed in turn severed 1841 from the 3 respective EPs to cr Wardle St James EP,[12] as such eccl refounded 1859[235]); incl in Yorks W Riding chap Saddleworth (sep CP 1866 in Yorks,[4] sep EP 1737[12]); after all units gains sep civ identity, 'Rochdale' has no sep civ identity 1886—94 (see following entry). Addtl eccl bdry alt: 1746 (cr Hundersfield EP,[12] sep eccl status not sustained), 1843 (help refound Bacup EP),[131] 1844 (from area in Yorks, cr 3 EPs of Friar Mere, Dobcross, Lydiate),[125] 1856 (cr EP3),[203] 1866 (help cr Waterfoot EP),[50] 1867 (help cr Hamer EP),[172] 1867 (help cr Newbold EP),[474] 1884,[492] 1895 (help cr EP5),[201] 1972.[299]

CP1—ROCHDALE—Cr 1894 by union of the pts of the following in Rochd. CB (assoc with Lancs): Butterworth CP, Castleton CP, Spotland CP, Wuerdle and Wardle CP, and ent Wardleworth CP.[257] Bdry: 1900 (gains pt Castleton by Rochd. UD and Castleton, Lancashire CP),[176] 1933,[37] Transf 1974 to Gtr Manch.[40]

EP1—ROCHDALE GOOD SHEPHERD—Cr 1902 from Wardleworth St James EP, Hamer EP, Newbold EP.[11]

EP2—ROCHDALE ST AIDAN, SUDDEN—Cr 1913 from EP3, Castleton All Souls EP, Castleton Moor EP.[344] Bdry: 1972.[299]

EP3—ROCHDALE ST ALBAN—Cr 1856 from AP1.[203] Bdry: 1867 (help cr Falinge EP),[474] 1871,[104] 1884,[492] 1895 (help cr EP5),[201] 1913 (help cr EP2),[344] 1925 (help cr Oakenrod EP).[49] Abol 1972 pt to help cr EP4, pt to AP1, pt to EP2.[299]

EP4—ROCHDALE ST GEORGE WITH ST ALBAN—Cr 1972 by union pt EP3, ent Oakenrod EP.[299]

EP5—ROCHDALE ST LUKE, DEEPLISH—Cr 1895 from AP1, EP3.[201]

ROEBURNDALE
Tp in Melling AP, sep CP 1866,[4] pt eccl severed 1841 to help cr Wray EP,[607] the remainder severed 1859 to help refound Hornby EP.[477] LG Lonsd. Hd, Lunesd. PLU, RSD, RD. Parl Seq 8.

ROUGHLEE BOOTH
Tp in Whalley AP, sep CP 1866,[4] eccl in chap Pendle (sep EP 1723 from Whalley AP[12]). LG Seq 5. Bdry: 1935.[43] Parl Seq 12.

ROUNDTHORN
EP Cr 1925 from Leesfield EP, Glodwick EP, Glodwick St Mark EP.[493] Oldham RDn.

ROYTON
Chap in Prestwich AP, sep CP 1866,[4] eccl in chap Oldham (sep EP 1746 from Prestwich AP[12]), 'Royton' a sep EP 1757 from Oldham EP,[12] eccl refounded 1835.[182] LG Salf. Hd, Oldham PLU, Royton USD, UD. Civ bdry: 1894 (gains the pt of Thornham CP in Royton UD),[169] 1933.[171] Transf

1974 to Gtr Manch.[40] Parl Oldham Parl Bor (1832—1918), Royton Dv (1918—48), Heyw. & Royton CC (1948—*). Eccl Manch RDn (1757—1847), Rochd. RDn (1847—72), Oldham RDn (1872—*). Eccl bdry: 1879 (help cr Heyside EP),[245] 1910 (cr Royton St Anne Longsight EP).[618]

ROYTON ST ANNE LONGSIGHT
EP Cr 1910 from Royton EP.[618] Oldham RDn. Bdry: 1912,[96] 1957.[386]

RUFFORD
Chap in Croston AP, sep EP 1726,[12] sep par 1793.[362] LG Seq 9. Parl Seq 3. Eccl Leyl. RDn (1726—1847), N Meols RDn (1847—48), Leyl. RDn (1848—*).

RUMWORTH
Tp in Deane AP, sep CP 1866,[4] pt eccl severed 1897 to help cr Heaton EP.[137] LG Salf. Hd, Bolton PLU, pt Bolton MB (1872—89), Bolton CB (pt 1889—94, ent 1894—95), pt Bolton USD, pt Bolton RSD. Civ bdry: 1894 (the pt not in the CB cr Deane CP).[120] Abol civ 1895 to help cr Bolton CP.[263] Parl S'rn Dv (1832—67), S-E Dv (1867—85), pt Bolton Parl Bor, pt W'hough. Dv (1885—1918).

RUSHOLME
Chap (built at Birch ca 1580, later Presbyterian chap until 1697[198]) and tp in Manchester AP, sep CP 1866,[4] sep EP 1739 as 'Birch in Rusholme',[12] the latter refounded 1839 as 'Holy Trinity at Rusholme',[74] 'Rusholme' [Holy Trinity] a sep EP 1854 from Birch in Rusholme EP.[199] LG Salf. Hd, Chorlton PLU, Rusholme USD (1875—85), Manch MB (1885—89), CB (1889—96). Civ bdry: 1894 (gains the pts in the CB of Moss Side CP, Withington CP).[501] Abol civ 1896 to help cr South Manchester CP.[82] Parl S'rn Dv (1832—67), S-E Dv (1867—85), Stretf. Dv (1885—1918). Eccl Manch RDn (1854—55), Chorlton RDn (1855—66), Chorlton & Hulme RDn (1866—72), Ardwick RDn (1872—1912), Heaton RDn (1912—33), Hulme RDn (1933—*). Eccl bdry: 1858 (help cr Moss Side EP),[70] 1902.[230]

RUSLAND
EP Cr 1750 from Colton EP,[12] refounded 1844.[395] Furness & Cartmel RDn (1750—1859), Cartmel RDn (1859—1970), Windermere RDn (1970—*).

SABDEN
EP Name used now for EP cr 1849 as 'Heyhouses', qv.
CP Cr 1904 by union Heyhouses CP and pts Goldshaw Booth CP, Higham with West Close Booth CP, Northtown CP, Pendleton CP, Read CP, Wiswell CP.[497] LG Burnley PLU, RD. Parl Clith. Dv/CC (1918—*).

SADDLEWORTH
CP Area in York W Riding, civ organisation in Yorks except pt in Mossley USD ([Lancs, Ches until 1881; Lancs, Ches, Yorks W Riding 1881—94] 1881—94), pt in Mossley MB ([Lancs, Ches, Yorks W Riding] 1885—94). The pt in the MB becomes 1889 pt of Lancs (abol 1894 to help cr Mossley CP[97]). For remainder of civ and for parl organisation, see entry in Yorks.

ST ANNE'S ON THE SEA
CP Cr 1894 by union of the pts of the following in St

Anne's on the Sea UD: Lytham AP, Marton CP.[217] *LG* Fylde PLU, St Anne's on the Sea UD (1894—1922), Lytham St Anne's MB (1922—24). Bdry: 1912.[587] Abol 1924 to help cr Lytham St Anne's CP.[588] *Parl* Blackp. Parl Bor (1918—48).

EP Name used now for EP cr 1877 as 'Heyhouses on the Sea', qv.

ST ANNE'S ON THE SEA ST MARGARET

EP Cr 1966 from Heyhouses on the Sea EP.[520] The Fylde RDn.

ST ANNE'S ON THE SEA ST THOMAS

EP Cr 1902 from Heyhouses on the Sea EP.[323] The Fylde RDn.

ST HELENS

EP Orig Prebyterian chap, sep EP 1716 from Prescot AP (pt area tp Windle),[12] refounded 1852.[644] Warr. RDn (1716—1847), Prescot RDn (1847—*). Bdry: 1863 (cr Parr Mount EP),[91] 1870 (help cr Ravenhead EP),[314] 1887 (cr St Helens St Mark EP).[439]

CP Cr 1894 by union of areas in St Helens CB (Parr CP, Sutton CP, pt Eccleston CP, pt Windle CP) and of nearby areas (addtl pts of Eccleston CP, Windle CP).[451] *LG* Prescot PLU, St Helens CB. Bdry: 1899,[452] 1934,[363] 1954.[658] Transf 1974 to Merseyside.[40] *Parl* St Helens Parl Bor/BC (1918—*). Parl bdry: 1955.[488]

ST HELENS ST MARK

EP Cr 1887 from St Helens EP.[439] Prescot RDn.

ST MICHAEL ON WYRE

AP Incl chap Woodplumpton (sep CP 1866,[4] sep EP 1740[12]), tps Great Eccleston, Elswick (each a sep CP 1866,[4] pt of tp Great Eccleston cr 1723 'Copp' EP,[12] the remainder of the tp and tp Elswick eccl united 1849 with Copp EP to refound the latter[398]), tp Inskip with Sowerby (sep CP 1866,[4] sep EP 1850 as 'Inskip'[12]), tp Out Rawcliffe (sep CP 1866,[4] sep EP 1840,[12] eccl refounded 1848[630]), tp Upper Rawcliffe with Tranacre ([incl par church] sep CP 1866[4]) so that 'St Michael on Wyre' has no sep civ identity after 1866. *LG* Amound. Hd. *Parl* N'rn Dv (1832—67). *Eccl* Lanc. RDn (until before 1291), Amound. RDn (before 1291—1852), Garst. RDn (1852—*).

ST STEPHENS IN THE BANKS

EP Cr 1868 from North Meols AP.[613] N Meols RDn. Sometimes called 'Southport St Stephens in the Banks' or 'Banks'.

SALESBURY

Chap in Blackburn AP, sep CP 1866,[4] sep EP 1809,[12] eccl refounded 1842.[133] *LG* Seq 4. *Parl* Seq 13. *Eccl* Blackb RDn. Eccl bdry: 1891,[134] 1916,[609] 1936.[71]

SALFORD

The following have 'Salford' in their names. Insofar as any existed at a given time: *LG* Salf. Hd, PLU, MB (1844—89), CB (1889—1974), USD. *Parl* Salf. Parl Bor (1832—1918), pt Salf. North Parl Bor, pt Salf. South Parl Bor, pt Salf. West Parl Bor (1918—48), pt Salf. East BC, pt Salf. West BC (1948—*). *Eccl* Manch RDn (cr—1850), Eccles RDn (1850—66), Eccles & Salf. RDn (1866—72), Salf. RDn (1872—*).

CP1/EP1—SALFORD [HOLY TRINITY]—Chap (built 1635[590]) in Manchester AP, sep CP 1866,[4] sep EP 1839,[74] eccl refounded 1856.[83] Civ bdry: 1919 (gains Broughton CP, Pendleton CP),[300] 1961.[447] Transf 1974 to Gtr Manch.[40] *Parl* bdry: 1964.[448] Eccl bdry: 1832 (cr EP2,[659] refounded 1858 incl pt EP9[70]), 1842 (cr EP3,[660] refounded 1858[70]), 1846 (cr EP11).[147]

EP2—SALFORD CHRIST CHURCH—Cr 1832 from EP1,[659] eccl refounded 1858 incl pt EP9.[70] Bdry: 1846 (help cr Paddington EP),[449] 1871 (help cr EP13),[104] 1902 (help cr Pendleton St Ambrose EP).[553] Abol 1965 to help cr EP8.[634]

EP3—SALFORD ST BARTHOLOMEW—Cr 1842 from EP1,[660] refounded 1858.[70] Bdry: 1871 (help cr EP13),[104] 1879 (help cr Ordsall in Salford St Clement EP),[328] 1903 (cr EP5).[50]

EP4—SALFORD ST CLEMENT WITH ST CYPRIAN, ORDSALL—Cr 1967 by union Ordsall in Salford St Clement EP, Ordsall in Salford St Cyprian EP.[273]

EP5—SALFORD ST IGNATIUS—Cr 1903 from EP3.[50]

EP6—SALFORD ST MATTHIAS—Cr 1842 from Manchester AP.[598] refounded 1858.[70] Abol 1926 to help cr EP7.[661]

EP7—SALFORD ST MATTHIAS WITH ST SIMON—Cr 1926 by union EP11, EP6.[661] Abol 1967 pt to help cr Lower Broughton St Clement with St Matthias EP, pt to EP10.[305]

EP8—SALFORD ST PAUL WITH CHRIST CHURCH—Cr 1965 by union EP2, Paddington EP.[634]

EP9—SALFORD ST PHILIP—Cr 1828 from Manchester AP,[75] pt severed 1858 to help refound EP2 while the remainder refounded as EP9.[70] Abol 1959 to help cr EP10.[397]

EP10—SALFORD ST PHILIP WITH ST STEPHEN—Cr 1959 by union EP9, EP12.[397] Bdry: 1967.[305]

EP11—SALFORD ST SIMON—Cr 1846 from EP1.[147] Abol 1926 to help cr EP7.[661]

EP12—SALFORD ST STEPHEN—Built 1794,[590] sep EP 1805 from Manchester AP,[12] refounded 1839,[74] refounded 1856.[83] Abol 1959 to help cr EP10.[397]

EP13—SALFORD STOWELL MEMORIAL CHURCH—Cr 1871 from EP2, EP3.[104] Bdry: 1879 (help cr Ordsall in Salford EP),[328] 1902 (help cr Old Trafford St Cuthbert EP).[2]

SAMLESBURY

Chap (orig in area chap Walton le Dale in same par[220]) in Blackburn AP, sep CP 1866,[4] sep EP 1763.[12] *LG* Seq 7. Civ bdry: 1934.[226] *Parl* Seq 14. *Eccl* Blackb RDn (1763—1964), Leyl. RDn (1964—*).

SANDYLANDS

EP Cr 1919 from Heysham AP.[111] Lanc. RDn.

GREAT SANKEY

Chap (used after Civil War by Presbyterians, until 1728[106]) in Prescot AP, sep CP 1866,[4] eccl severed 1728 and united with tp Penketh in same par to cr Great Sankey EP,[12] that EP abol 1858 to help cr Farnworth EP,[262] the area of the orig EP (the 2 tps) severed 1875 from Farnworth EP to re-cr Great Sankey EP.[150] *LG* Seq 19. Civ bdry: 1933 (loses pt to Warr. CB [assoc with Lancs] & AP).[324] Transf 1974 to Ches.[40] *Parl* Seq 19. *Eccl* Warr. RDn (1728—1847), Prescot RDn (1847—58, 1875—82), Childwall RDn (1882—1920), Winwick RDn (1920—49), Farnw. RDn (1949—*).

LITTLE SANKEY
CP Cr 1894 from pt of the pt of Warrington AP not in Warr. MB.[662] *LG* Warr. PLU, RD. Abol 1896 ent to Warrington AP.[557]

SATTERTHWAITE
Chap in Hawkshead AP, sep CP 1866,[4] sep EP 1741 (incl tps Grizdaleon, Dale Park [neither sep civ] in same par),[12] eccl refounded 1881.[465] *LG* Seq 14. Transf 1974 to Cumbria.[40] *Parl* Seq 11. *Eccl* Furness & Carmtel RDn (1741—1859), Windermere RDn (1859—*).

SAWREY
EP Cr 1873 from Hawkshead AP (hmlt Lower Claife [not sep civ]).[379] Ambleside RDn (1873—1970), Windermere RDn (1970—*).

SCARISBRICK
Chap (orig) and tp in Ormskirk AP, sep CP 1866,[4] sep EP 1869.[632] *LG* Seq 17. Civ bdry: 1931.[126] *Parl* Seq 21. *Eccl* N Meols RDn (1869—87), Ormsk. RDn (1887—*).

SCHOLES—see WIGAN ST ANDREW

SCORTON
EP Cr 1880 from Garstang AP (pt chap Nether Wyresdale).[491] Garst. RDn.

SCOTFORTH
Tp in Lancaster AP, sep CP 1866,[4] sep EP 1876 (tp Scotforth and addtl pt Lancaster AP).[16] *LG* Seq 12. Civ bdry: 1900,[309] 1935,[43] 1962.[459] *Parl* Seq 6. *Eccl* Lanc. RDn. Eccl bdry: 1933,[206] 1963.[150]

SCOUTHEAD
EP Cr 1886 from Lydgate EP (Yorks W Riding), Dobcross EP (Yorks W Riding), Hey EP (Lancs, Yorks W Riding).[70] Rochd. RDn (1886—93), Asht. under Lyne RDn (1893—1929), Oldham RDn (1929—*).

SEAFORTH
EP Cr 1816 from Sefton AP,[12] refounded 1870.[314] Warr. RDn (1816—47), Liverp North RDn (1847—95), Bootle RDn (1895—*). Bdry: 1886,[8] 1933.[49]
CP Cr 1894 from the pt of Litherland CP in Waterloo and Seaforth UD.[402] *LG* W Derby PLU, Waterloo and Seaforth UD (1894—1937), Crosby MB (1937—74). Transf 1974 to Merseyside.[40] *Parl* Waterloo Dv (1918—48), Crosby BC (1948—*).

SEATHWAITE
EP Chap in Kirkby Ireleth AP, sep EP 1738 (incl pt tp Dunnerdale with Seathwaite),[12] refounded 1886.[233] Pec jurisd Dean & Chapter of York (until 1836), Furness & Cartmel RDn (1836—59), Ulv. RDn (1859—83), Gosforth RDn (1883—1970), Furness RDn (1970—*).

SEFTON
AP Incl chap Great Crosby (sep CP 1866,[4] sep EP 1729,[12] pt of the latter eccl severed 1875 to cr Blundellsands EP,[139] the remainder refounded soon after in 1875 as 'Great Crosby' EP[150]), tp Aintree (sep CP 1866,[4] sep EP 1878 from this par and from Walton on the Hill AP[38]), tps Little Crosby, Ince Blundell (each a sep CP 1866[4]), tp Litherland (sep CP 1866,[4] sep EP 1842,[569] later called 'Waterloo Christ Church'), tp Lunt (sep CP 1866[4]), tp Netherton (sep CP 1866,[4] sep EP 1957[622]), tps Orrell and Ford, Thornton (each a sep CP 1866[4]). *LG* Seq 16. Addtl civ bdry alt: 1932 (gains Lunt CP),[403] 1940 (loses pt to Bootle CB [assoc with Lancs] & to Orrell CP),[486] 1951 (loses pt to Bootle CB [assoc with Lancs] & to Orrell CP),[39] 1954,[487] 1956,[404] 1968 (loses pt to Bootle CB [assoc with Lancs] & to Orrell CP).[623] Transf 1974 to Merseyside.[40] *Parl* S'rn Dv (1832—67), S-W Dv (1867—85), Ormsk. Dv/CC (1885—1970), pt Crosby BC, pt Ormsk. CC (1970—*). Parl bdry: 1960.[536] *Eccl* Sometimes as 'Sephton', Warr. RDn (until 1847), Liverp North RDn (1847—95), Bootle RDn (1895—*). Addtl eccl bdry alt: 1816 (cr Seaforth EP,[12] refounded 1870[314]), 1871 (cr Litherland St Philip EP),[75] 1924 (help cr Blundellsands St Michael EP).[258]

SEPHTON—see prev entry

SHARPLES
Tp in Bolton le Moors AP, sep CP 1866,[4] pt eccl severed 1741 to help cr Walmsley EP,[12] the latter refounded 1844,[88] pt of the orig tp eccl severed 1844 to help cr Astley Bridge EP,[111] the remainder of the orig area eccl severed 1861 to help cr Belmont EP.[183] *LG* Salf. Hd, Bolton PLU, pt Astley Bridge USD, pt Bolton RSD. Bdry: 1885.[267] Abol 1894 the pt in the UD cr Astley Bridge CP, the remainder cr Belmont CP.[120] *Parl* S'rn Dv (1832—67), pt Bolton Parl Bor (1867—1918), pt S-E Dv (1867—85), pt W'hough. Dv (1885—1918).

SHAW
EP Cr 1719 from Prestwich AP (tp Crompton in area chap Oldham),[12] refounded 1835[182]; for civ see 'Crompton'. Manch RDn (1719—1847), Rochd. RDn (1847—72), Oldham RDn (1872—*). Bdry: 1844 (cr East Crompton EP),[11] 1878 (help cr High Crompton EP).[87]

SHEVINGTON
Tp in Standish AP, sep CP 1866,[4] sep EP 1873.[379] *LG* Seq 11. Transf 1974 to Gtr Manch.[40] *Parl* Seq 4. *Eccl* Leyl. RDn (1873—1964), Chorley RDn (1964—*). Eccl bdry: 1888.[160]

SHIRESHEAD
EP Cr 1747 from Cockerham AP,[12] refounded 1858 from Ellel EP, Garstang AP (pt tp Cleveley, pt tp Nether Wyresdale), Cockerham AP (pt tp Forton, pt tp Cleveley).[272] Amound. RDn (1747—1852), Garst. RDn (1852—66), Lanc. RDn (1866—*).

SHORE
EP Cr 1900 from Littleborough EP.[132] Rochd. RDn.

SHUTTLEWORTH
EP Cr 1845 from Edenfield EP (orig area hmlt Shuttleworth), Walmersley EP.[328] Manch RDn (1845—50), Bury RDn (1850—51), Prestw. RDn (1851—72), Bury RDn (1872—*). Bdry: 1876 (help cr Ramsbottom St Andrew EP),[663] 1927 (help cr Stubbins EP).[269]

SILVERDALE

Chap in Warton AP, sep CP 1866,[4] sep EP 1754 (tp Silverdale, hmlt Lindeth [not sep civ but incl in area tp/CP Warton with Lindeth]),[12] eccl refounded 1871.[78] *LG* Seq 12. Civ bdry: 1935.[43] *Parl* Seq 10. *Eccl* Kendal RDn (1754—1848), Tunstall RDn (1848—*).

SIMONSTONE

Tp in Whalley AP, sep CP 1866,[4] eccl in chap Padiham (sep EP 1730 from Whalley AP,[12] qv for later refounding). *LG* Seq 5. Bdry: 1935.[43] *Parl* Seq 14.

SIMONSWOOD

Tp (orig ex-par) in Walton on the Hill AP, sep CP 1866,[4] eccl severed 1748 to help cr Kirkby EP,[12] the latter refounded 1872.[70] *LG* Seq 17. Bdry: 1877,[608] 1958,[539] 1969.[540] Transf 1974 to Merseyside.[40] *Parl* Seq 21. Parl bdry: 1960.[536]

SINGLETON

EP Chap in Kirkham AP, sep CP 1866,[4] sep EP 1754 (areas Great Singleton, Little Singleton, Thistle Ton [none sep civ]),[12] eccl refounded 1851.[545] *LG* Seq 1. Civ bdry: 1934.[226] *Parl* Seq 2. *Eccl* Amound. RDn (1754—1852), The Fylde RDn (1852—*).

SKELMERSDALE

Chap (built 1776 by subscription[633]) and tp in Ormskirk AP, sep CP 1866,[4] sep EP 1782,[12] eccl refounded 1858.[256] *LG* W Derby Hd, Ormsk. PLU, Skelmersdale USD, UD (1894—1968), Skelmersdale and Holland UD (1968—74). Civ bdry: 1968.[414] *Parl* S'rn Dv (1832—67), S-W Dv (1867—85), Ormsk. Dv (1885—1948), Ince CC (1948—70), Ince BC (1970—*). *Eccl* Warr. RDn (1782—1847), N Meols RDn (1847—87), Ormsk. RDn (1887—*).

SKELWITH

CP Cr 1894 from Hawkshead and Monk Coniston with Skelwith CP.[396] *LG* Ulv. PLU, RD (1894—1960), N Lonsd. RD (1960—74). Transf 1974 to Cumbria.[40] *Parl* Lonsd. Dv (1918—48), Morec. & Lonsd. CC (1948—*).

SKERTON

Tp in Lancaster AP, sep CP 1866,[4] sep EP 1834.[549] *LG* Lonsd. Hd, Lanc. PLU, RSD, RD. Civ bdry: 1894.[642] Abol civ 1900 pt to Lanc. MB & AP, pt to Halton AP, pt to Heaton with Oxcliffe CP, pt to Slyne with Hest CP.[309] *Parl* N'rn Dv (1832—67), North Dv (1867—85), Lanc. Dv (1885—1918). *Eccl* Amound. RDn (1834—52), Lanc. RDn (1852—*). Eccl bdry: 1933 (help cr Bare EP),[147] 1935 (help cr Slyne with Hest EP),[281] 1959 (help cr Torrisholme EP),[629] 1964 (help cr Skerton St Chad EP).[663]

SKERTON ST CHAD

EP Cr 1964 from Skerton EP, Torrisholme EP.[663] Lanc. RDn.

SLYNE WITH HEST

Tp in Bolton le Sands AP, sep CP 1866,[4] sep EP 1935 from Bolton le Sands AP, Skerton EP.[281] *LG* Seq 12. Civ bdry: 1887,[282] 1900,[309] 1935,[43] 1965.[617] *Parl* N'rn Dv (1832—67), North Dv (1867—85), Lanc. Dv (1885—1918), Lonsd. Dv (1918—48), Morec. & Lonsd. CC (1948—*). *Eccl* Tunstall RDn.

SMALLBRIDGE

EP Cr 1843 from Rochdale AP (pt area Wardle in tp Wuerdle and Wardle),[12] refounded 1844.[125] Manch RDn (1843—47), Rochd. RDn (1847—*). Bdry: 1841 (loses the orig pt area Wardle to help cr Wardle St James EP,[12] refounded 1859[235]), 1841 (gains pt tp Wuerdle from Rochdale AP),[296] 1864,[94] 1867 (help cr Hamer EP),[172] 1870 (gains the remaining pt of hmlt Wuerdle from Rochdale AP),[38] 1895 (help cr Dearnley EP).[88]

SMITHILLS

CP Cr 1894 from the pt of Halliwell CP not in Bolton CB[120]; the area of 'Smithills' or 'Smithells' eccl a domestic chap, not sep eccl. *LG* Bolton PLU, RD. Abol 1898 ent to Bolton CB (assoc with Lancs) & CP.[36]

SOUTH SHORE HOLY TRINITY

EP Cr 1837 from Bispham AP, Poulton le Fylde AP, Marton EP,[211] refounded 1871.[212] Amound. RDn (1837—52), The Fylde RDn (1852—1963), Blackp. RDn (1963—*). Bdry: 1921 (cr South Shore St Peter EP [o'wise called 'Blackpool St Peter']),[302] 1951 (help cr Blackpool Holy Cross, South Shore EP,[444] help cr Blackpool St Mary, South Shore EP[277]). O'wise called 'Blackpool Holy Trinity'.

SOUTH SHORE ST PETER

EP Cr 1921 from South Shore Holy Trinity EP.[302] The Fylde RDn (1921—63), Blackp. RDn (1963—*). O'wise called 'Blackpool St Peter'.

SOUTHPORT

The following have 'Southport' in their names. Insofar as any existed at a given time: *LG* Ormsk. PLU, S'port. MB (1894—1905), CB (1905—74). *Parl* S'port. Parl Bor/BC (1918—*). *Eccl* Warr. RDn (cr—1847), N Meols RDn (1847—*).

CP1—SOUTHPORT—Cr 1894 from the pt of North Meols AP in S'port. MB.[610] Bdry: 1900,[611] 1912 (gains Birkdale CP),[207] 1925 (gains Ainsdale CP).[34] Transf 1974 to Merseyside.[40]

EP1—SOUTHPORT ALL SAINTS—Cr 1878 from North Meols AP.[614] Bdry: 1906,[33] 1931 (help cr EP2).[522]

EP2—SOUTHPORT ALL SOULS—Cr 1931 from EP1, EP8.[522]

EP3—SOUTHPORT CHRIST CHURCH—Cr 1825 from North Meols AP,[12] refounded 1865.[104] Bdry: 1872 (help cr EP7),[228] 1888 (cr EP10),[147] 1889.[281] Abol 1969 to help cr EP4.[664]

EP4—SOUTHPORT CHRIST CHURCH WITH ST ANDREW—Cr 1969 by union EP3, EP7.[664]

EP5—SOUTHPORT EMMANUEL—Cr 1905 from North Meols AP.[526]

EP6—SOUTHPORT HOLY TRINITY—Cr 1865 from North Meols AP.[104] Bdry: 1883 (cr EP8).[665]

EP7—SOUTHPORT ST ANDREW—Cr 1872 from EP3, EP9.[228] Bdry: 1889,[281] 1896.[113] Abol 1969 to help cr EP4.[664]

EP8—SOUTHPORT ST LUKE—Cr 1883 from EP6.[665] Bdry: 1931 (help cr EP2).[522]

EP9—SOUTHPORT ST PAUL—Cr 1864 from North Meols AP.[433] Bdry: 1872 (help cr EP7),[228] 1875 (help cr Birkdale St Peter EP),[304] 1896.[113]

EP10—SOUTHPORT ST PHILIP—Cr 1888 from EP3.[147] Bdry: 1896.[113]

EP11—SOUTHPORT ST SIMON AND ST JUDE—Cr 1905 from North Meols AP.[526]

—SOUTHPORT ST STEPHEN IN THE BANKS—see ST STEPHENS IN THE BANKS

SOUTHWORTH WITH CROFT

Tp in Winwick AP, sep CP 1841,[400] sep EP 1844 as 'Croft with Southworth',[399] qv. *LG* W Derby Hd, Warr. PLU, RSD, RD. Abol 1933 pt to help cr Croft CP, pt to help cr Winwick CP.[324] *Parl* S'rn Dv (1832—67), S-W Dv (1867—85), Newton Dv (1885—1948).

SPEKE

Tp in Childwall AP, sep CP 1866,[4] pt eccl severed 1729 to help cr Garston EP,[12] refounded 1828,[75] the remainder of orig tp Speke eccl severed 1732 to help cr Hale EP,[12] refounded 1828,[75] 'Speke' a sep EP 1875 from Garston EP, Hale EP.[150] *LG* W Derby Hd, Prescot PLU, RSD, Whiston RD. Abol 1932 ent to Liverp CB (assoc with Lancs) & CP.[363] *Parl* S'rn Dv (1832—67), S-W Dv (1867—85), Widnes Dv (1885—1948). *Eccl* Prescot RDn (1875—82), Childwall RDn (1882—1949), Farnw. RDn (1949—*). Addtl eccl bdry alt: 1964.[49] Dedication changed 1972 (at same time as bdry alt) from 'All Saints' to 'St Aidan'.[442]

SPEKE ST AIDAN—see prev entry

SPOTLAND

Tp in Rochdale AP, sep CP 1866,[4] pt eccl in chap Whitworth in Rochdale AP, that pt eccl severed 1721 to help cr Whitworth EP,[12] the remainder (and pt area Wardle in tp Wuerdle and Wardle in the same par) cr 1840 Spotland EP,[12] eccl refounded 1844.[125] *LG* Salf. Hd, Rochd. PLU, pt Rochd. MB (1852—89), pt Rochd. CB (1889—94), pt Rochd. USD, pt Norden USD, pt Whitworth USD, pt Bacup USD, pt Bacup MB (1882—94). Abol civ 1894 the pt in the CB to help cr Rochdale CP, the pt in Norden UD cr Norden CP, the pt in Whitworth UD cr Whitworth CP,[257] the pt in the MB to help cr Bacup CP.[129] *Parl* Pt Rochd. Parl Bor (1832—1918 [enlarged pt 1867—1918]), pt S'rn Dv (1832—67), pt S-E Dv (1867—85), pt Heyw. Dv (1885—1918). *Eccl* Manch RDn (1840—47), Rochd. RDn (1847—*). Eccl bdry: 1846 (cr Healey EP),[515] 1862 (help cr Norden EP),[628] 1867 (help cr Falinge EP),[473] 1913,[203] 1925 (help cr Oakenrod EP).[49]

STAINING

CP Renaming 1969 of Hardhorn with Newton CP.[509] *LG* Fylde RD. *Parl* S Fylde CC (1970—*).

STALMINE

Chap (perhaps orig a sep AP[550]) in Lancaster AP, sep EP 1740,[12] sep CP 1866 as 'Stalmine with Staynall',[4] qv. *Eccl* Amound. (1740—1852), Lanc. RDn (1852—66), Garst. RDn (1866—*). Eccl bdry: 1934 (cr Preesall EP).[633]

STALMINE WITH STAYNALL

Chap (perhaps orig a sep AP[550]) in Lancaster AP, sep CP 1866,[4] sep EP 1740 as 'Stalmine',[12] qv. *LG* Seq 2. *Parl* Seq 7.

STALYBRIDGE

EP Cr 1969 by union Stalybridge New St George EP,

Stalybridge Old St George EP.[492] Asht. under Lyne RDn.

STALYBRIDGE NEW ST GEORGE

EP Cr 1847 from Ashton under Lyne AP.[108] Manch RDn (1847), Asht. under Lyne RDn (1847—1969). Bdry: 1965.[336] Abol 1969 to help cr Stalybridge EP.[492]

STALYBRIDGE OLD ST GEORGE

EP Cr 1798 from Ashton under Lyne AP,[12] refounded 1864.[103] Manch RDn (1798—1847), Asht. under Lyne RDn (1847—1969). Bdry: 1965.[336] Abol 1969 to help cr Stalybridge EP.[492]

STAND

EP Cr 1829 from Prestwich AP.[600] Manch RDn (1829—50), Bury RDn (1850—51), Prestw. RDn (1851—72), Prestw. & Middl. RDn (1872—1912), Radcl. & Prestw. RDn (1912—*). Bdry: 1868 (cr Stand Lane EP),[27] 1898 (help refound Ringley EP).[276]

STAND LANE

EP Cr 1868 from Stand EP.[27] Prestw. RDn (1868—72), Prestw. & Middl. RDn (1872—1912), Radcl. & Prestw. RDn (1912—*).

STANDISH

AP Incl chap Coppul (sep CP 1866,[4] sep EP 1717 [incl tp Charnock Richard, tp Welsh Whittle],[12] eccl refounded 1842[108]), tp Adlington (sep CP 1866,[4] sep EP 1840,[12] eccl refounded 1842[23]), tp Anderton (sep CP 1866[4]), tp Charnock Richard (sep CP 1866,[4] eccl severed 1717 to help cr Coppull EP,[12] the latter refounded 1842,[23] 'Charnock Richard' a sep EP 1861 from Coppull EP [area tps Charnock Richard, Welsh Whittle][304]), tp Duxbury (sep CP 1866[4]), tp Heath Charnock (sep CP 1866[4]), tp Shevington (sep CP 1866,[4] sep EP 1873[379]), tp Standish with Langtree (sep CP 1866[4]), tp Welsh Whittle (sep CP 1866,[4] eccl severed 1717 to help cr Coppull EP,[12] qv above for its refounding, the orig area eccl severed from the latter 1861 to help cr Charnock Richard EP[304]), tp Worthington (sep CP 1866[4]) so that 'Standish' has no sep civ identity after 1866. *LG* Leyl. Hd. *Parl* N'rn Dv (1832—67). *Eccl* Leyl. RDn (until 1964), Chorley RDn (1964—*). Addtl eccl bdry alt: 1888,[160] 1960 (loses pt to Wigan St Ann EP, dioc Liverp).[567]

STANDISH WITH LANGTREE

Tp in Standish AP, sep CP 1866.[4] *LG* Leyl. Hd, Wigan PLU, Standish with Langtree USD, UD. Transf 1974 to Gtr Manch.[40] *Parl* Seq 4.

STANLEY ST ANN

EP Cr 1886 from West Derby EP.[201] Prescot RDn (1886—1902), W Derby RDn (1902—*). Bdry: 1909 (help cr Liverpool St Mark, Edge Lane EP),[35] 1913 (cr Liverpool Stanley St Paul EP).[194]

STAVELEY

Chap in Cartmel AP, sep CP 1866,[4] sep EP 1718,[12] eccl refounded 1876.[340] *LG* Seq 14. Civ bdry: 1884,[52] 1884,[56] 1884,[53] 1884,[341] 1884.[51] Transf 1974 to Cumbria.[40] *Parl* Seq 11. *Eccl* Furness & Cartmel RDn (1718—1859), Cartmel RDn (1859—1970), Windermere RDn (1970—*).

STAYLEY

Area ent in Ches, tp in Mottram AP (eccl 'Mottram

in Longendale'), sep CP 1866 in Ches,[4] civ organisation in Ches except for pt Mossley USD ([Lancs, Ches, 1875—81; Lancs, Ches, Yorks W Riding 1881—94] 1881—94), pt Mossley MB ([Lancs, Ches] 1885—94). The pt in Mossley MB becomes 1889 pt of Lancs (that pt abol 1894 to help cr Mossley CP in Lancs[97]). See main entry in Ches for remainder of civ organisation and for parl organisation, incl pt in Stalybridge Parl Bor (Ches, Lancs, 1867—1918).

STIDD
Ex-par area (Blackb Hd) situated in tp Dutton in Ribchester AP, abol civ 1858 to be incl in tp Dutton,[80] not sep eccl so that the par eccl 'Ribchester with Stidd', qv.

STONEFOLD—see HASLINGDEN ST JOHN, STONEFOLD

STONEYCROFT
EP Cr 1875 from West Derby EP.[150] Liverp North RDn (1875—82), Prescot RDn (1882—1902), W Derby RDn (1902—*). Bdry: 1909 (help cr Liverpool St Mark, Edge Lane EP).[35]

STRETFORD
The following have 'Stretford' in their names. Insofar as any existed at a given time: LG Salf. Hd, Chorlton PLU (1837—49), Barton upon Irwell PLU (1849—1930), Stretf. USD, UD (1894—1933), MB (1933—74). Parl S'rn Dv (1832—67), S-E Dv (1867—85), Stretf. Dv (1885—1948), Stretf. BC (1948—*). Eccl Manch RDn (cr—1850), Eccles RDn (1850—55), Manch RDn (1855—66), Chorlton & Hulme RDn (1866—72), Hulme RDn (1872—1933), Stretf. RDn (1933—*).

CP1/EP1—STRETFORD [ST MATTHEW]—Chap in Manchester AP, sep CP 1866,[4] sep EP 1717.[12] Civ bdry: 1933.[171] Transf 1974 to Gtr Manch.[40] Eccl bdry: 1858 (cr Old Trafford St Thomas EP),[70] 1875,[85] 1899 (cr Old Trafford St Hilda EP),[386] 1900 (help cr Ordsall in Salford St Cyprian EP),[368] 1902 (help cr Old Trafford St Cuthbert EP),[2] 1902 (help cr Old Trafford St John EP),[323] 1904 (cr EP2),[161] 1905 (cr EP4),[195] 1930,[365] 1955,[507] 1958.[366]

EP2—STRETFORD ALL SAINTS—Cr 1904 from EP1.[161] Bdry: 1955,[507] 1967.[417]

EP3—STRETFORD ST BRIDE—Cr 1879 from Whalley Range St Margaret EP.[442] Sometimes called 'Old Trafford St Bride'.

EP4—STRETFORD ST PETER—Cr 1905 from EP1.[195] Bdry: 1930,[365] 1955,[507] 1958.[366]

STUBBINS
EP Cr 1927 from Edenfield EP, Shuttleworth EP.[269] Bury RDn.

SUBBERTHWAITE
Tp in Ulverston AP, sep CP 1866,[4] pt eccl severed 1743 to help cr Lowick EP,[12] refounded 1886,[132] the remainder of orig tp Subberthwaite eccl severed 1745 to help cr Blawith EP,[12] refounded 1892.[44] LG Seq 14. Transf 1974 to Cumbria.[40] Parl Seq 11.

SUTTON
Tp in Prescot AP, sep CP 1866,[4] sep EP 1848.[462] LG W Derby Hd, Prescot PLU, St Helens MB (1868—89), CB (1889—94), USD. Abol 1894 to help cr St Helens CP.[451] Parl S'rn Dv (1832—67), S-W Dv (1867—85), St Helens Parl Bor (1885—1918). Eccl Prescot RDn.

SWINTON
CP Cr 1894 from the pt of Worsley CP in Swinton & Pendlebury UD.[174] LG Barton upon Irwell PLU, Swinton & Pendlebury UD. Bdry: 1907.[666] Abol 1934 to help cr Swinton and Pendlebury MB & CP.[171] Parl Eccles Parl Bor (1918—48).

SWINTON AND PENDLEBURY
CP Cr 1934 by union ent Pendlebury CP, ent Swinton CP, pt Clifton CP, pt Prestwich AP.[171] LG Swinton & Pendlebury MB. Civ bdry: 1955.[586] Transf 1974 to Gtr Manch.[40] Parl Eccles BC (1948—*). Parl bdry: 1956.[667]

SWINTON HOLY ROOD
EP Cr 1911 from Swinton St Peter EP.[232] Eccles RDn.

SWINTON ST PETER
EP Cr 1806 from Eccles AP,[12] refounded 1865.[119] Manch RDn (1806—50), Eccles RDn (1850—66), Eccles & Salf. RDn (1866—72), Eccles RDn (1872—*). Bdry: 1911 (cr Swinton Holy Rood EP),[232] 1912 (help cr Monton EP).[200]

TARBOCK
Tp in Huyton AP, sep CP 1866.[4] LG Seq 18. Bdry: 1877,[401] 1877,[438] 1920.[411] Transf 1974 to Merseyside.[40] Parl Seq 24.

TARLETON
Chap in Croston AP, sep par 1821.[180] LG Seq 9. Civ bdry: 1936.[612] Parl Seq 3. Eccl Leyl. RDn (1821—47), N Meols RDn (1847—48), Leyl. RDn (1848—*).

TATHAM
AP LG Seq 13. Parl Seq 8. Eccl Lanc. RDn (until before 1291), Lonsd. & Kendal RDn (before 1291—before 1541), Kirkby Lonsd. RDn (before 1541—1848), Tunstall RDn (1848—*). Eccl bdry: 1737 (cr Tatham Fells EP,[12] refounded 1916[492]), 1955.[86]

TATHAM FELLS
EP Cr 1737 from Tatham AP,[12] refounded 1916.[492] Kirkby Lonsd. RDn (1737—1848), Tunstall RDn (1848—*).

THATTO HEATH
EP Cr 1955 from Eccleston EP.[455] Prescot RDn.

THORNHAM
Tp in Middleton AP, sep CP 1866.[4] LG Salf. Hd, Oldham PLU, pt Middl. & Tonge USD (1875—86), pt Middl. MB & USD (1886—84), pt Royton USD, pt Castleton by Rochd. USD. Abol 1894 the pt in Middl. MB transf to Middleton AP, the pt in Royton UD transf to Royton CP,[45] the pt in Castleton by Rochd. UD to help cr Castleton by Rochdale CP.[169] Parl S'rn Dv (1832—67), S-E Dv (1867—85), Middl. Dv (1885—1918).

THORNHAM ST JAMES
EP Cr 1960 from Thornham with Gravel Hole EP.[668] Rochd. RDn.

THORNHAM WITH GRAVEL HOLE
EP Cr 1896 from Middleton AP, Birch EP.[194] Prestw. & Middl. RDn (1896—1912), Middl. RDn (1912—*). Bdry: 1960 (cr Thornham St James EP).[668]

THORNLEY WITH WHEATLEY
Tp in Chipping AP, sep CP 1866.[4] *LG* Seq 6. *Parl* Seq 14.

THORNTON
Tp in Sefton AP, sep CP 1866.[4] *LG* Seq 16. Civ bdry: 1934,[226] 1956.[404] Transf 1974 to Merseyside.[40] *Parl* S'rn Dv (1832—67), S-W Dv (1867—85), S'port. Dv (1885—1918), Ormsk. Dv/CC (1918—70), Crosby BC (1970—*). Parl bdry: 1960.[405]

THORNTON
Tp in Poulton le Fylde AP, sep CP 1866,[4] sep EP 1838,[12] eccl refounded 1869.[643] *LG* Amound. Hd, Fylde PLU, pt Fleetwood USD (enlarged pt 1882—94), pt Fylde RSD (reduced pt 1882—94), Fylde RD (1894—1900), Thornton UD (1900—27), Thornton Clevelys UD (1927—74). Civ bdry: 1894 (the pt in Fleetwood UD cr Fleetwood CP),[217] 1934,[226] 1935.[43] *Parl* N'rn Dv (1832—67), North Dv (1867—85), Blackp. Dv (1885—1918), Fylde Dv (1918—48), N Fylde CC (1948—*). *Eccl* Sometimes as 'Thornton le Fylde', Amound. RDn (1838—52), The Fylde RDn (1852—*). Eccl bdry: 1911 (help cr Cleveleys EP),[213] 1960 (cr Little Thornton EP).[669]

LITTLE THORNTON
EP Cr 1960 from Thornton EP.[669] The Fylde RDn.

THORNTON IN LONSDALE
AP Mostly in Yorks W Riding (Staincliffe Wap) incl in Lancs tp Ireby (Lonsd. Hd, sep CP 1866 in Lancs[4]) so that this par ent Yorks W Riding thereafter, qv.

THURNHAM
Tp pt in Cockerham AP, pt in Lancaster AP, sep CP 1866.[4] Bdry: 1935 (gains Cockersand Abbey CP).[43] *LG* Seq 12. *Parl* Seq 6.

TINTWISTLE
Area in Ches, tp in Mottram (eccl, 'Mottram in Longendale') AP, sep CP 1866 in Ches,[4] sep EP 1840.[12] Civ organisation in Ches except pt Mossley USD (Lancs, Ches, 1875—81; Lancs, Ches, Yorks W Riding 1881—94), pt Mossley MB ([Lancs, Ches] 1885—94). The pt in Mossley MB becomes 1889 pt Lancs (abol civ 1894 to help cr Mossley CP[97]). See main entry in Ches for remainder of civ organisation, and for parl and eccl organisation.

TOCKHOLES
Chap in Blackburn AP, sep CP 1866,[4] sep EP 1725 (incl pt tp Livesey in same par),[12] eccl refounded 1842.[133] *LG* Seq 4. *Parl* Seq 13. *Eccl* Blackb RDn (1725—1964), Darwen RDn (1964—*). Eccl bdry: 1874 (help cr Darwen St Cuthbert EP),[177] 1877 (help cr Livesey EP).[221]

TODMORDEN
Chap in Rochdale AP, sep EP 1832 as 'Todmorden',[3] 'Walsden' a sep EP 1845 from Todmorden EP,[75] the entire area a sep CP 1866 as 'Todmorden and Walsden',[4] qv in the following entry. Manch RDn (1832—47), Rochd. RDn (1847—1927), Halifax RDn (dioc Wakef, 1927—67), Calder Valley RDn (1967—*). Addtl eccl bdry alt: 1864 (help cr Harley Wood EP [Yorks W Riding, Lancs] to be in dioc Ripon),[433] 1972 (gains Harley Wood EP).[513]

TODMORDEN AND WALSDEN
Chap in Rochdale AP, sep CP 1866 as 'Todmorden and Walsden',[4] 'Todmorden' a sep EP 1832,[12] qv in prev entry, 'Walsden' a sep EP 1845 from Todmorden EP.[75] *LG* Salf. Hd, Todmorden PLU, USD (Yorks W Riding, Lancs), UD (1894—96), MB (1896—97). This par becomes 1889 pt of Yorks W Riding (abol 1897 to help cr Todmorden CP[66]). *Parl* S'rn Dv (1832—67), S-E Dv (1867—85), Middl. Dv (1885—1918). See entry in Yorks for civ and parl organisation thereafter.

TONGE
Tp in Prestwich AP, sep CP 1866,[4] eccl severed 1842 to help cr Tonge cum Alkrington EP.[22] *LG* Salf. Hd, Oldham PLU, Middl. & Tonge USD (1875—86), Middl. MB & USD (1886—94). Abol 1894 ent to Middleton AP.[45] *Parl* S'rn Dv (1832—67), S-E Dv (1867—85), Middl. Dv (1885—1918).

TONGE
CP Cr 1894 from the pt of Tonge with Haulgh CP not in Bolton CP.[120] *LG* Bolton PLU, RD. Abol 1898 ent to Bolton CB (assoc with Lancs) & CP.[36]

TONGE
Tp in Bolton le Moors AP, sep EP 1841,[12] eccl refounded 1845 (orig area and pt tp Breightmet, pt chap Harwood, also in Bolton le Moors AP),[83] sep CP 1866 as 'Tonge with Haulgh',[4] qv. Manch RDn (1841—47), Bolton le Moors RDn (1847—93), Bolton North RDn (1893—1901), Bolton le Moors RDn (1901—68), Walmsley RDn. Bdry: 1886 (cr Tonge Moor EP),[670] 1912 (help cr Tonge Fold EP).[269] Now called 'Breightmet'.

TONGE CUM ALKRINGTON
EP Cr 1842 by union tps Tonge, Alkrington, both in Prestwich AP.[22] Bury RDn (1842—72), Prestw. & Middl. RDn (1872—1912), Middl. RDn (1912—*). Bdry: 1885 (help cr Middleton Junction EP).[317]

TONGE FOLD
EP Cr 1912 from Tonge EP, Tonge Moor EP, Bolton le Moors AP, Lever Bridge EP, Little Bolton EP.[269] Bolton le Moors RDn.

TONGE MOOR
EP Cr 1886 from Tonge EP.[670] Bolton le Moors RDn (1886—93), Bolton North RDn (1893—1901), Bolton le Moors RDn (1901—68), Walmsley RDn (1968—*). Bdry: 1912 (help cr Tonge Fold EP).[269]

TONGE WITH HAULGH
Tp in Bolton le Moors AP, sep CP 1866,[4] pt of area of Haulgh eccl severed 1844 to help cr Lever Bridge EP,[111] the remainder a sep EP 1841 as 'Tonge',[12] eccl refounded 1845 (incl pt tp Breightmet, pt chap Harwood in same par),[83] qv. *LG* Salf. Hd, Bolton PLU, pt Bolton MB (1877—89), Bolton CB (pt 1889—94, ent 1894—95), pt Bolton USD (1877—94), pt Bolton RSD (1875—77). Bdry: 1894 the pt not in the CB cr Tonge CP.[120] Abol 1895 to help cr Bolton CP.[263] *Parl* Pt Bolton Parl Bor (1832—1918), pt S'rn Dv (1832—67), pt S-E Dv (1867—85), pt W'hough. Dv (1885—1918).

TORRISHOLME
EP Cr 1959 from Bare EP, Poulton EP, Morecambe St Lawrence EP, Overton EP, Skerton EP.[148] Lanc. RDn. Bdry: 1964 (help cr Skerton St Chad EP).[663]

TORVER

Chap in Ulverston AP, sep CP 1866,[4] sep EP 1747 (incl pt tp Blawith in same par),[12] eccl refounded 1892.[83] *LG* Seq 14. Transf 1974 to Cumbria.[40] *Parl* Seq 11. *Eccl* Furness & Cartmel RDn (1747—1859), Ulv. RDn (1859—1970), Furness RDn (1970—*).

TOTTINGTON

EP Cr 1802 from Bury AP (ent tp Tottington Higher End, pt tp Tottington Lower End),[12] refounded 1843.[326] Manch RDn (1802—50), Bury RDn (1850—51), Prestw. RDn (1851—72), Bury RDn (1872—*). Bdry: 1844 (help cr Ramsbottom EP),[111] 1889 (help cr Walshaw EP),[551] 1892 (help cr Hawkshaw Lane EP),[44] 1915 (help cr Woolfold EP).[462]

CP Renaming 1894 of Tottington Lower End CP after the latter loses the pts in MBs, CB and UD to other pars in those and gains pt Elton CP (see under 'Tottington Lower End' below).[115] *LG* Bury PLU, RD (1894—99), Tottington UD (1899—1974). Bdry: 1933 (loses pt to Bury CB [assoc with Lancs] & AP).[37] Transf 1974 to Gtr Manch.[40] *Parl* Bury Parl Bor (1918—48), Bury & Radcl. BC (1948—*).

TOTTINGTON HIGHER END

Tp in Bury AP, sep CP 1866,[4] eccl severed 1802 to help cr Tottington EP,[12] the latter refounded 1843.[326] *LG* Salf. Hd, Hasl. PLU, pt Ramsb. USD (1883—94), pt Rawt. USD (1883—94), pt Rawt. MB (1891—94), pt Hasl. USD, pt Hasl. MB (1891—94), pt Hasl. RSD (1875—83). Abol 1894 the pt in Ramsb. USD to help cr Ramsbottom CP,[115] the pt in Rawt. MB to help cr Rawtenstall CP, the pt in Hasl. MB transf to Haslingden CP.[129] *Parl* S'rn Dv (1832—67), S-E Dv (1867—85), Heyw. Dv (1885—1918).

TOTTINGTON LOWER END

Tp in Bury AP, sep CP 1866,[4] pt eccl severed 1725 to help cr Holcombe EP,[12] the latter refounded (after cr of other EPs, qv for details) 1863,[327] pt of orig tp eccl severed 1802 to help cr Tottington EP,[12] the latter refounded 1843.[326] *LG* Salf. Hd, Bury PLU, pt Hasl. USD (1883—94), pt Hasl. MB (1891—94), pt Ramsb. USD, pt Bury USD, pt Bury MB (1876—89), pt Bury CB (1889—94), pt Bury RSD (1875—83). Renamed 1894 'Tottington' CP after loses the pt in Hasl. MB to Haslingden CP, loses the pt in Bury CB to Bury AP, loses the pt in Ramsb. UD to help cr Ramsbottom CP and gains pt Elton CP.[115] *Parl* S'rn Dv (1832—67), S-E Dv (1867—85), pt Bury Parl Bor, pt Heyw. Dv (1885—1918).

TOXTETH PARK

The following have 'Toxteth Park' in their names. Insofar as any existed at a given time: *LG* W Derby Hd, PLU (1837—57), Toxteth Park Par (poor law purposes, 1857—1922), pt Toxteth Park USD, pt Liverp USD, Toxteth Park UD (1894—95), Liverp CB (1895—1922). *Parl* Pt Liverp Parl Bor (1832—85), pt S'rn Dv (1832—67), pt S-W Dv (1867—85), pt Bootle Dv (1885—1918), pt Liverp, E Toxteth Parl Bor, pt Liverp, W Toxteth Parl Bor (1885—1918); see Part III of the *Guide* for compostion of

Liverp Parl Bors (1918—48) by wards of the CB. *Eccl* Warr. RDn (cr—1847), Liverp South RDn (1847—82), Toxteth RDn (1882—*).

CP1—TOXTETH PARK—Ex-par place, sep CP 1858[80]; for eccl see EP9. Abol civ 1922 ent to Liverpool CP.[47]

EP1—TOXTETH PARK CHRIST CHURCH—Cr 1872 from Walton on the Hill AP.[279] Bdry: 1875 (help cr Mossley Hill St Matthew and St James EP),[28] 1887,[335] 1886 (help cr EP3),[162] 1893 (cr EP4),[360] 1899.[386]

EP2—TOXTETH PARK HOLY TRINITY—Cr 1862 from EP9, EP15.[245] Abol 1942 to help cr EP11.[671]

EP3—TOXTETH PARK ST AGNES—Cr 1886 from EP6, EP1.[162] Bdry: 1899.[386]

EP4—TOXTETH PARK ST ANDREW, AIGBURTH ROAD—Cr 1893 from EP1 (incl ent area Liverpool St Andrew EP),[360] 1898.[13]

EP5—TOXTETH PARK ST BEDE—Cr 1887 from EP6.[439]

EP6—TOXTETH PARK ST CLEMENT—Cr 1842 from Walton on the Hill AP.[377] Bdry: 1871 (cr West Derby St Nathaniel, Windsor EP),[5] 1884 (help cr Liverpool Princes Park All Saints EP),[335] 1886 (help cr EP3),[162] 1887 (cr EP5),[439] 1893.[153]

EP7—TOXTETH PARK ST CLEOPAS—Cr 1867 from EP12.[172] Bdry: 1884 (cr EP8),[335] 1887.[13]

EP8—TOXTETH PARK ST GABRIEL—Cr 1884 from EP7.[335]

EP9—TOXTETH PARK ST JAMES—Built 1774, opened 1775 under parl authority,[672] refounded 1844 from Walton on the Hill AP[42]; for civ see CP1. Bdry: 1858 (cr EP15),[239] 1862 (help cr EP2),[245] 1873.[526] Abol 1931 to help cr EP10.[673]

EP10—TOXTETH PARK ST JAMES WITH ST MATTHEW—Cr 1931 by union EP9, EP15.[673] Abol 1942 to help cr EP11.[671]

EP11—TOXTETH PARK ST JAMES WITH ST MATTHEW AND HOLY TRINITY—Cr 1942 by union EP2, EP10.[671]

EP12—TOXTETH PARK ST JOHN THE BAPTIST—Cr 1837 from Walton on the Hill AP.[585] Bdry: 1854 (cr Princes Park EP),[2] 1867 (cr EP7),[172] 1880,[315] 1887.[13] Abol 1939 to help cr EP13.[357]

EP13—TOXTETH PARK ST JOHN THE BAPTIST WITH ST THOMAS—Cr 1939 by union EP12, EP21.[357] Abol 1968 to help cr EP18.[85]

EP14—TOXTETH PARK ST MARGARET—Cr 1893 (as 'Liverpool St Margaret, Toxteth', later as EP14) from Walton on the Hill AP.[113]

EP15—TOXTETH PARK ST MATTHEW—Cr 1858 from EP9.[239] Bdry: 1862 (help cr EP2),[245] 1873.[526] Abol 1931 to help cr EP10.[673]

EP16—TOXTETH PARK ST MICHAEL—Built 1817,[377] sep EP 1898 from Walton on the Hill AP.[22]

—TOXTETH PARK ST PAUL—Name sometimes used for EP cr 1854 as 'Princes Park', qv

EP17—TOXTETH PARK ST PHILEMON—Cr 1874 from EP21.[10] Bdry: 1880.[315] Abol 1958 to help cr EP19.[5]

EP18—TOXTETH PARK ST PHILEMON—Cr 1968

by union EP19, EP13.[85]

EP19—TOXTETH PARK ST PHILEMON WITH ST SILAS—Cr 1958 by union EP17, EP20.[5] Abol 1968 to help cr EP18.[85]

EP20—TOXTETH PARK ST SILAS—Cr 1867 from Princes Park EP, Walton on the Hill AP.[183] Abol 1958 to help cr EP19.[5]

EP21—TOXTETH PARK ST THOMAS—Cr 1842 from Walton on the Hill AP.[674] Bdry: 1874 (cr EP17).[10] Abol 1939 to help cr EP13.[357]

OLD TRAFFORD

The following have 'Old Trafford' in their names. Insofar as any existed at a given time: *Eccl* Chorlton & Hulme RDn (cr—1872), Hulme RDn (1872—1933), Stretf. RDn (1933—*).

EP1—OLD TRAFFORD ST CUTHBERT—Cr 1902 from Stretford St Matthew EP, Barton upon Irwell EP, Salford Stowell Memorial Church EP, Weaste St Luke EP, Eccles AP.[2]

EP2—OLD TRAFFORD ST HILDA—Cr 1899 from Stretford EP.[386] Bdry: 1902 (help cr EP3),[323] 1930,[365] 1958.[366]

EP3—OLD TRAFFORD ST JOHN—Cr 1902 from Whalley Ridge St Margaret EP, Stretford EP, EP2.[323] Bdry: 1930,[365] 1958.[366]

EP4—OLD TRAFFORD ST THOMAS—Cr 1858 from Stretford EP.[70]

TRAWDEN

Tp in Whalley AP, sep CP 1866,[4] eccl in chap Colne (sep EP 1820 from Whalley AP[12]), pt of orig area tp eccl severed 1836 to help cr Colne Christ Church EP,[12] that same pt severed from the latter 1845 to cr 'Trawden' EP.[72] *LG* Blackb Hd, Burnley PLU, Trawden USD, UD. *Parl* N'rn Dv (1832—67), N-E Dv (1867—85), Clith. Dv (1885—1918), Nelson & Colne Parl Bor/BC (1918—*). *Eccl* Blackb RDn (1845—47), Whalley RDn (1847—72), Burnley RDn (1872—1970), Pendle RDn (1970—*).

TREALES

Tp in Kirkham AP, sep EP 1858,[548] sep CP 1866 as 'Treales, Roseacre and Wharles',[4] qv. The Fylde RDn.

TREALES, ROSEACRE AND WHARLES

Tp in Kirkham AP, sep CP 1866,[4] sep EP 1858 as 'Treales',[548] qv. *LG* Seq 1. *Parl* Seq 2.

TUNSTALL

AP Incl chap Leck (sep CP 1866,[4] sep EP 1737,[12] eccl refounded 1859[477]), tp Burrow with Burrow (sep CP 1866[4]), tp Cantsfield (sep CP 1866[4]). *LG* Lonsd. Hd, Lunesd. PLU, RSD, RD. *Parl* Seq 8. *Eccl* Lanc. RDn (until before 1291), Kirkby Lonsd. & Kendal RDn (before 1291—before 1541), Kirkby Lonsd. RDn (before 1541—1848), Tunstall RDn (1848—*).

TUNSTEAD

EP Cr 1853 from Whalley AP,[12] refounded 1868.[675] Blackb RDn (1853—47), Whalley RDn (1847—66), Accr. RDn (1866—72), Whalley RDn (1872—1912), Rossend. RDn (1912—*).

TURNCROFT

EP Cr 1865 from Over Darwen Holy Trinity EP.[71] Blackb RDn (1865—1964), Darwen RDn (1964—

*). Bdry: 1873,[379] 1897,[35] 1911 (cr Darwen St Barnabas EP).[29] Sometimes called 'Darwen St John the Evangelist'.

TURTON

Chap in Bolton le Moors AP, sep CP 1866,[4] pt eccl severed 1737 to help cr Bradshaw EP,[12] qv for refounding, pt of the orig chap eccl severed 1741 to help cr Walmsley EP,[12] qv for refounding, the remainder of the orig chap a sep EP 1719 as 'Turton',[12] eccl refounded 1881.[135] *LG* Salf. Hd, Bolton PLU, Turton USD, UD. Civ bdry: 1898 (gains Bradshaw CP, Harwood CP, Longworth CP),[36] 1925 (gains Belmont CP, Edgeworth CP).[184] Transf 1974 pt (wards of Bradshaw North, Bradshaw South, Bromley Cross, Eagley, pt Egerton) to Gtr Manch to be 'Turton' par in that Metrop Co, pt (remainder: wards of Belmont, Chapeltown, Edgeworth, pt Egerton) to Lancs to be 'North Turton' par in that Non-Metrop Co.[40] *Parl* S'rn Dv (1832—67), S-E Dv (1867—85), W'hough. Dv (1885—1918), Darwen Dv/CC (1918—*). *Eccl* Manch RDn (1719—1847), Bolton le Moors RDn (1847—93), Bolton North RDn (1893—1901), Bolton le Moors RDn (1901—68), Walmsley RDn (1968—*). Bdry: 1892 (help cr Hawkshaw Lane EP).[44]

TWISTON

Tp in Whalley AP, sep CP 1866.[4] *LG* Seq 6. *Parl* Seq 1.

TYLDESLEY CUM SHAKERLEY

Tp in Leigh AP, sep CP 1866,[4] sep EP 1827,[12] eccl refounded 1828.[566] *LG* W Derby Hd, Leigh PLU, Tyldesley with Shakerley USD, UD (1894—1933), Tyldesley UD (1933—74). Civ bdry: 1933 (gains Astley CP to help cr Tyldesley UD).[37] Transf 1974 to Gtr Manch.[40] *Parl* S'rn Dv (1832—67), S-W Dv (1867—85), Leigh Dv (1885—1918), Leigh Parl Bor/BC (1918—*). *Eccl* Warr. RDn (1827—47), Leyl. RDn (1847—50), Eccles RDn (1850—66), Eccles & Salf. RDn (1866—72), Eccles RDn (1872—1933), Leigh RDn (1933—*).

ULVERSTON

AP Incl chap Blawith (sep CP 1866,[4] pt eccl severed 1745 to help cr Blawith EP,[12] refounded 1892,[44] the remainder of the orig chap eccl severed 1747 to help cr Torver EP,[12] refounded 1892[83]), chap Church Coniston (sep CP 1866,[4] sep EP 1730,[12] eccl refounded 1892[44]), chap Egton with Newland (sep CP 1866[4]), chap Lowick (sep CP 1866,[4] sep EP 1743,[12] eccl refounded 1866[132]), chap Torver (sep CP 1866[4]), tps Mansriggs, Osmotherley (each a sep CP 1866[4]), tp Subberthwaite (sep CP 1866,[4] pt eccl severed 1743 to help cr Lowick EP,[12] refounded 1866,[132] the remainder of the orig tp eccl severed 1745 to help cr Blawith EP,[12] refounded 1892[44]). *LG* Lonsd. Hd, pt Ulv. Bor (status not sustained), Ulv. PLU, USD, UD. Transf 1974 to Cumbria.[40] *Parl* Seq 10. *Eccl* Lanc. RDn (until before 1291), Copel. RDn (before 1291—before 1541), Furness & Cartmel RDn (before 1541—1859), Ulv. RDn (1859—*). Addtl eccl bdry alt: 1836 (cr Ulverston Holy Trinity EP),[533] 1926.[143] Abol eccl 1966 to help cr Ulverston St Mary with Holy Trinity EP.[135]

ULVERSTON HOLY TRINITY
EP Cr 1836 from Ulverston AP.[533] Furness & Cartmel RDn (1836—59), Ulv. RDn (1859—1966). Abol 1966 to help cr Ulverston St Mary with Holy Trinity EP.[135]

ULVERSTON ST MARY WITH HOLY TRINITY
EP Cr 1966 by union Ulverston AP, Ulverston Holy Trinity EP.[135] Ulv. RDn (1966—70), Furness RDn (1970—*).

ULNES WALTON
Tp in Croston AP, sep CP 1866.[4] *LG* Seq 8. Bdry: 1934.[226] *Parl* Seq 3.

UNSWORTH
EP Cr 1730 from Prestwich AP,[12] refounded 1885.[368] Manch RDn (1730—1850), Bury RDn (1850—51), Prestw. RDn (1851—72), Prestw. & Middl. RDn (1872—1912), Radcl. & Prestw. RDn (1912—67), Bury RDn (1967—*). Bdry: 1902,[2] 1973.[269]
CP Cr 1894 from the pts of the following not in a UD: Heap CP, Pilsworth CP, Pilkington CP.[115] *LG* Bury PLU, RD. Abol 1933 pt to Middl. MB & AP, pt to Heyw. MB & CP, pt to Whitefield UD & CP,[171] pt to Bury CB (assoc with Lancs) & AP.[37] *Parl* Heyw. & Radcl. Dv (1918—48).

UPHOLLAND
Tp in Wigan AP, sep CP 1866,[4] orig incl priory, sep EP 1643 (incl tp Billinge Higher End, tp Dalton, both in the same par),[192] 'Upholland' eccl refounded 1748,[12] 'Dalton' a sep EP 1870 from this par,[38] the remainder of this par eccl refounded 1882 as 'Upholland'.[190] *LG* W Derby Hd, Wigan PLU, Upholland USD, UD (1894—1968), Skelmersdale and Holland UD (1968—74). *Parl* S'rn Dv (1832—67), S-W Dv (1867—85), Ormsk. Dv (1885—1948), Ince CC (1948—70), Ince BC (1970—*). *Eccl* Warr. RDn (1643—1847), Wigan RDn (1847—1971), Ormsk. RDn (1971—*). Addtl eccl bdry alt: 1922 (help cr Orrell EP).[493]

URMSTON
Tp in Flixton AP, sep CP 1866,[4] sep EP 1868.[273] *LG* Salf. Hd, Chrolton PLU (1837—49), Barton upon Irwell PLU (1849—1930), RSD, Urmston UD. Transf 1974 to Gtr Manch.[40] *Parl* S'rn Dv (1832—67), S-E Dv (1867—85), Eccles Dv (1885—1918), Stretf. Dv (1918—48), Stretf. BC (1948—*).

URSWICK
AP Incl undivided pt Birkrig Common (land common to this par and to Aldringham AP). *LG* Seq 14. Transf 1974 to Cumbria.[40] *Parl* Seq 11. *Eccl* Seq 10. Eccl bdry: 1854 (cr Bardsea EP).[142]

VAUXHALL—see LIVERPOOL ALL SOULS

WALKDEN MOOR
EP Cr 1863 from Eccles AP, Deane AP.[49] Eccles RDn (1863—66), Eccles & Salf. RDn (1866—72), Eccles RDn (1872—1968), Farnw. RDn (1968—*). Bdry: 1887 (help cr Little Hulton EP).[287]

WALMERSLEY
EP Chap situated in tp Walmersley cum Shuttleworth in Bury AP, sep EP 1741.[12] Manch RDn (1741—1850), Bury RDn (1850—51), Prestw. RDn (1851—72), Bury RDn (1872—*). Bdry: 1845 (help cr Shuttleworth EP),[328] 1958.[44]

WALMERSLEY CUM SHUTTLEWORTH
Tp in Bury AP, sep CP 1866,[4] eccl comprised of chap Walmersley (sep EP 1741[12]), hmlt of Shuttleworth (eccl in chap Edenfield [sep EP 1725 from Bury AP[12]], 'Shuttleworth' a sep EP 1845 from Edenfield EP [orig area hmlt Shuttleworth], Walmersley EP[328]). *LG* Salf. Hd, Bury PLU, pt Bury USD, pt Bury MB (1876—89), pt Bury CB (1889—94), pt Ramsb. USD (1883—94), pt Bury RSD (1875—83), Bury RD. Civ bdry: 1894 (incl loses the pt in Ramsb. UD to help cr Ramsbottom CP, loses the pt in Bury CB to Bury AP).[115] Abol 1933 pt to Bury CB (assoc with Lancs) & AP, pt to Ramsbottom UD & CP.[37] *Parl* S'rn Dv (1832—67), S-E Dv (1867—85), pt Bury Parl Bor, pt Heyw. Dv (1885—1918), Heyw. & Radcl. Dv (1918—48).

WALMSLEY
EP Cr 1741 (incl pt tp Longworth, pt tp Sharples) from Bolton le Moors AP, Turton EP,[12] refounded 1844.[88] Manch RDn (1741—1847), Bolton le Moors RDn (1847—93), Bolton North RDn (1893—1901), Bolton le Moors RDn (1901—68), Walmsley RDn (1968—*).

WALNEY
EP Cr 1742 from Dalton in Furness AP,[12] refounded 1899 as 'Walney Island',[146] now usually called 'Walney St Mary'. Furness & Cartmel RDn (1742—1859), Aldingham RDn (1859—83), Dalton RDn (1883—99).

WALNEY ISLAND
EP Refounding 1899 of Walney EP (for cr 1742 see prev entry),[146] now usually called 'Walney St Mary'. Dalton RDn (1899—1970), Furness RDn (1970—*).

WALNEY ST MARY—see prev entry

WALSDEN
EP Cr 1845 from Todmorden EP[75]; civ pt of tp Todmorden and Walsden, qv for sep civ identity 1866 from Rochdale AP. Manch RDn (1845—47), Rochd. RDn (1847—1927), Halifax RDn ([dioc Wakef] 1927—67), Calder Valley RDn (1967—*).

WALSHAW
EP Cr 1889 from Tottington EP, Elton EP, Elton St Stephen EP.[348] Bury RDn. Bdry: 1915 (help cr Woolfold EP).[462]

HIGHER WALTON
EP Cr 1865 from Walton le Dale EP.[71] Blackb RDn (1865—1964), Leyl. RDn (1964—*).

WALTON BRECK
EP Cr 1891 from Walton on the Hill AP.[387] Walton RDn. Bdry: 1959.[79]

WALTON LE DALE
Chap (orig incl area chap Samlesbury,[220] the latter early considered a chap in Blackburn AP) in Blackburn AP, sep CP 1866,[4] sep EP 1764 (incl tp Cuerdale in the same par).[12] *LG* Blackb Hd, Preston PLU, Walton le Dale USD, UD. Civ bdry: 1934.[226] *Parl* N'rn Dv (1832—67), N-E Dv (1867—85), Darwen Dv (1885—1918), Fylde Dv (1918—48), Preston South BC (1948—*). *Eccl* Leyl. RDn (1764—1847), Blackb RDn (1847—1964), Leyl. RDn (1964—*). Eccl bdry: 1865 (cr Higher Walton EP),[71] 1897 (help cr Bamber Bridge St Aidan

EP).[137]

WALTON ON THE HILL

The following have 'Walton on the Hill' in their names. Insofar as any existed at a given time: *LG* W Derby Hd, PLU, pt W Derby USD, pt Walton on the Hill USD, Walton on the Hill UD (1894—95), Liverp CB (1895—1922). *Parl* S'rn Dv (1832—67), S-W Dv (1867—85), pt Liverp, Walton Parl Bor, pt Bootle Dv (1885—1918); see Part III of the *Guide* for composition of Liverp Parl Bors (1918—48) by wards of the CB. *Eccl* Warr. RDn (until 1847), Liverp North RDn (1847—82), Walton RDn (1882—*).

AP1—WALTON ON THE HILL [ST MARY]—Incl chap and bor West Derby (sep EP 1810,[12] sep par 1843 by parl authority,[424] eccl refounded 1847[264]), chap Everton (sep CP 1866,[4] the chap proprietary until 1879,[464] pt eccl severed 1878 and transf to Everton St Saviour EP,[159] the remainder of the orig chap a sep EP 1881 as 'Everton' [St George] [465]), chap Formby (sep CP 1866,[4] pt a sep EP 1748,[12] refounded 1893,[1] pt of the orig chap a sep EP 1888 as 'Formby St Luke'[24]), chap Kirkby, tp (orig ex-par) Simonswood (each a sep CP 1866,[4] the 2 severed and eccl united 1748 as 'Kirkby' EP,[12] as such eccl refounded 1872[70]), chap and bor Liverpool (sep par 1699[572]), tp Bootle cum Linacre (sep CP 1866,[4] the earliest chap [St Mary] erected 1827,[286] pt of the orig area eccl severed 1866 to cr Bootle St John EP,[287] pt eccl severed 1866 to cr Bootle Christ Church EP,[84] 'Bootle St Mary' a sep EP 1913[194]), tp Fazakerley (sep CP 1866,[4] eccl severed and joined 1881 with another pt of AP1 to cr EP1,[355] 'Fazakerley' a sep EP 1909 from 4 pars, qv for composition[41]), tp Kirkdale (sep CP 1866,[4] sep EP 1844[42]), tp (orig ex-par) Simonswood (sep CP 1866,[4] eccl severed 1748 to help cr Kirkby EP,[12] the latter refounded 1872[70]). Abol civ 1922 ent to Liverpool CP.[47] Addtl eccl bdry alt: 1775 (cr Toxteth Park St James EP [built 1774, opened 1775 under parl authority[672], refounded 1844 from this par[42]), 1836 (cr Knotty Ash St John the Evangelist EP,[306] qv for later refounding, sometimes called 'West Derby St John the Evangelist'), 1837 (cr Toxteth Park St John the Baptist EP),[585] 1842 (cr Toxteth Park St Thomas EP),[674] 1842 (cr Toxteth Park St Clement EP),[377] 1849 (cr Everton Christ Church EP [built 1848 by Horsfall family[466]]),[467] 1855 (cr Everton St Chrysostom EP),[470] 1861 (help cr Liverpool St Aidan EP),[304] 1867 (help cr Toxteth Park St Silas EP),[183] 1870 (cr Everton St Saviour EP),[62] 1872 (cr Toxteth Park Christ Church EP),[279] 1873 (cr Everton St Augustine EP),[21] 1874 (help cr EP3),[357] 1878 (cr Everton St Cuthbert EP),[172] 1878 (help cr Aintree EP),[38] 1884 (help cr Liverpool Princes Park All Saints EP),[335] 1885 (help cr Everton St Chad EP),[10] 1886,[8] 1888 (help cr Everton St Benedict EP),[147] 1890 (cr Bootle St Leonard EP),[17] 1891 (cr Walton Breck EP),[387] 1892 (cr Bootle St Matthew EP),[83] 1893 (cr Formby Holy Trinity EP),[1] 1893 (cr Toxteth Park

St Margaret EP),[113] 1893,[153] 1896 (cr Anfield St Simon and St Jude EP),[24] 1898,[13] 1898 (cr Toxteth Park St Michael EP),[22] 1901 (cr EP2),[208] 1919 (help cr Anfield St Columba EP),[78] 1957 (help cr Fazakerley St Nathanael EP).[480]

EP1—WALTON ON THE HILL ST JOHN THE EVANGELIST—Cr 1881 from AP1 (pt tp Fazakerley, addtl pt of AP1).[355] Bdry: 1909 (orig area of tp Fazakerley severed to help cr 'Fazakerley' EP),[41] 1957 (help cr Fazakerley St Nathanael EP).[480]

EP2—WALTON ON THE HILL ST LUKE THE EVANGELIST—Cr 1901 from AP1.[208]

EP3—WALTON ON THE HILL ST MARGARET, BELMONT ROAD—Cr 1874 from AP1, West Derby EP, Fairfield EP.[357] Prescot RDn (1874—82), Walton RDn (1882—1920), W Derby RDn (1920—*).

WARDLE

Area in tp Wuerdle and Wardle (qv for sep civ identity 1866 from Rochdale AP[4]), pt of the area of Wardle eccl severed 1721 to help cr Whitworth EP,[12] pt of the area of Wardle eccl severed 1745 to help cr Littleborough EP,[12] pt of the area of Wardle eccl severed 1843 to cr Smallbridge EP,[12] the latter refounded 1844,[125] the 3 separate pts of Wardle earlier severed in turn severed 1841 from the 3 respective EPs to cr 'Wardle St James' EP,[12] as such eccl refounded 1859,[235] qv.

CP Cr 1894 by union of the pts of the following in Wuerdle & Wardle UD: Butterworth CP, Wuerdle and Wardle CP.[257] *LG* Rochd. PLU, Wardle UD. Transf 1974 to Gtr Manch.[40] *Parl* Royton Dv (1918—48), Heyw. & Royton CC (1948—*).

WARDLE ST JAMES

EP Cr 1841 from Whitworth EP, Littleborough EP, Smallbridge EP (see 'Wardle' above for eccl severing into those 3 EPs from area Wardle in tp Wuerdle and Wardle in Rochdale AP),[12] eccl refounded 1859.[235] Rochd. RDn.

WARDLEWORTH

Tp in Rochdale AP, sep CP 1866,[4] eccl severed 1844 to cr the 2 EPs of Wardleworth St James, Wardleworth St Mary.[125] *LG* Salf. Hd, Rochd. PLU, MB (pt 1856—72, ent 1872—89), CB (1889—94), USD. Abol 1894 to help cr Rochdale CP.[257] *Parl* Rochd. Parl Bor (pt 1832—67, ent 1867—1918), pt S'rn Dv (1832—67).

WARDLEWORTH ST JAMES

EP Cr 1844 from Rochdale AP (pt tp Wardleworth).[125] Manch RDn (1844—47), Rochd. RDn (1847—1973). Bdry: 1864,[94] 1867 (help cr Hamer EP),[172] 1902 (help cr Rochdale Good Shepherd EP).[11] Abol 1973 to help cr Wardleworth St Mary with St James EP.[676]

WARDLEWORTH ST MARY

EP Organisation as for Wardleworth St James, but no bdry alt 1864.

WARDLEWORTH ST MARY WITH ST JAMES

EP Cr 1973 by union Wardleworth St Mary EP, Wardleworth St James EP.[676] Rochd. RDn.

WARRINGTON

The following have 'Warrington' in their names.

Insofar as any existed at a given time: *LG* W Derby Hd, Warr. PLU, MB (pt 1874—94, ent 1894—1900), pt Warr. USD, pt Warr. RSD, Warr. CB (1900—74). *Parl* Warr. Parl Bor (1832—*). *Eccl* Warr. RDn (until 1847), Winwick RDn (1847—1949), Warr. RDn (1949—*).

AP1—WARRINGTON [orig ST ELFIN, now ST HELEN]—Incl chap (built 1605[607]) Burtonwood (sep CP 1866,[4] sep EP 1740 as 'Burton Wood',[12] as such eccl refounded 1898[323]), tp Poulton with Fearnhead (sep CP 1866[4]), tp Rixton with Glazebrook (sep CP 1866,[4] the pt comprising anc chap Hollinfare, as such sep EP 1722,[12] eccl refounded 1874[349]), tp Woolston with Martinscroft (sep CP 1866[4]). Addtl civ bdry alt: 1884 (loses pt to Latchford CP, Ches),[677] 1894 (loses the pt not in the MB, pt to Winwick with Hulme CP, pt to cr Little Sankey CP),[662] 1896 (incl gains Little Sankey CP),[557] 1898 (gains Latchford CP [orig in Ches, then an area ent in Warr. MB]),[678] 1933 (incl gains pts of the following Ches pars: Grappenhall AP, Latchford Without CP, Stockton Heath CP, Walton Inferior CP),[324] 1954.[679] Transf 1974 to Ches.[40] Parl bdry: 1955.[680] Addtl eccl bdry alt: 1757 (cr EP2,[12] refounded 1870 from AP1, EP4[62]), 1838 (cr Padgate EP),[635] 1841 (cr EP4),[22] 1842 (cr EP1),[12] 1866 (help cr Latchford St James EP [Ches, Lancs]),[84] 1874 (help cr EP5),[357] 1888,[19] 1909.[41]

EP1—WARRINGTON CHRIST CHURCH—Cr 1842 from AP1.[12]

EP2—WARRINGTON HOLY TRINITY—Cr 1757 from AP1,[12] refounded 1870 from AP1, EP4.[62]

EP3—WARRINGTON ST ANN—Cr 1864 from EP4.[433]

—WARRINGTON ST BARNABAS—Name used now for EP cr 1884 as 'Bank Quay', qv

EP4—WARRINGTON ST PAUL—Cr 1841 from AP1.[259] Bdry: 1864 (cr EP3),[433] 1870 (help refound EP2),[62] 1874 (help cr EP5),[357] 1884 (cr Bank Quay EP,[141] now called 'Warrington St Barnabas').

EP5—WARRINGTON ST PETER—Cr 1874 from AP1, EP4.[357] Bdry: 1888.[19]

WARTON

AP Incl chap Silverdale (sep CP 1866,[4] sep EP 1754 [incl hmlt Lindeth, not sep civ, in area tp Warton with Lindeth],[12] eccl refounded 1871[78]), tp Borwick (sep CP 1866[4]), tp Carnforth (sep CP 1866,[4] sep EP 1875[85]), tp Priest Hutton (sep CP 1866[4]), tp Warton with Lindeth (sep CP 1866,[4] hmlt Lindeth eccl severed 1754 to help cr Silverdale EP,[12] the latter eccl refounded 1871[78]), tp Yealand Conyers, tp Yealand Redmayne (each a sep CP 1866,[4] the 2 eccl united 1846 as 'Yealand' EP,[159] as such eccl refounded 1867[159]) so that 'Warton' has no sep civ identity 1866—1935 (see following entry). *LG* Pt Warton Bor (status not sustained), Lonsd. Hd. *Parl* N'rn Dv (1832—67). *Eccl* Seq 11.

CP Cr 1935 from Warton with Lindeth CP.[43] *LG* Lanc. RD. *Parl* Morec. & Lonsd. CC (1948—*).

WARTON

Chap in Kirkham AP, sep CP 1866,[4] sep EP 1724,[12] eccl refounded 1846.[546] *LG* Amound. Hd, Fylde PLU, RSD, RD. Abol civ 1934 pt to help cr Bryning with Warton CP, pt to Freckleton CP.[226] *Parl* N'rn Dv (1832—67), North Dv (1867—85), Blackp. Dv (1885—1918), Fylde Dv (1918—48). *Eccl* Amound. RDn (1724—1852), The Fylde RDn (1852—*).

WARTON WITH LINDETH

Tp in Warton AP, sep CP 1866, hmlt Lindeth (not sep civ) eccl severed 1754 to help cr Silverdale EP,[12] the latter refounded 1871.[78] *LG* Lonsd. Hd, Lanc. PLU, RSD. RD. Abol 1935 pt to cr Warton CP, pt to Silverdale CP.[226] *Parl* N'rn Dv (1832—67), North Dv (1867—85), N Lonsd. Dv (1885—1918), Lonsd. Dv (1918—48).

WATERFOOT

EP Cr 1866 from Bury AP, Rochdale AP, Newchurch in Rossendale EP.[50] Prestw. RDn (1866—72), Bury RDn (1872—78), Whalley RDn (1878—1912), Rossend. RDn (1912—*). Bdry: 1881,[235] 1887 (help cr Rawtenstall St John, Clough Fold EP).[241]

WATERHEAD

EP Cr 1844 from Oldham St James EP.[144] Manch RDn (1844—47), Rochd. RDn (1847—72), Oldham RDn (1872—*). Bdry: 1870 (help cr Moorside EP).[38]

WATERLOO

CP Cr 1894 from pt of the pt of Ashton under Lyne AP not in a MB or UD.[63] *LG* Asht. under Lyne PLU, Limehurst RD. Abol 1954 ent to Asht. under Lyne MB & AP.[65] *Parl* Mossley Dv (1918—48), Asht. under Lyne BC (1948—55).

WATERLOO

CP Cr 1894 from the pt of Great Crosby CP in Waterloo with Seaforth UD.[402] *LG* W Derby PLU, Waterloo & Seaforth UD (1894—1937), Crosby MB (1937—74). Bdry: 1932.[403] Transf 1974 to Merseyside.[40] *Parl* Waterloo Dv (1918—48), Crosby BC (1948—*).

WATERLOO CHRIST CHURCH—see LITHERLAND CHRIST CHURCH

WATERLOO PARK

EP Cr 1887 from Waterloo St John EP.[235] Liverp North RDn (1887—95), Bootle RDn (1895—*). Bdry: 1901 (help cr Great Crosby St Faith EP).[62]

WATERLOO ST JOHN

EP Cr 1877 from Litherland EP, Great Crosby EP.[406] Liverp North RDn (1877—95), Bootle RDn (1895—*). Bdry: 1887 (cr Waterloo Park EP).[235]

WAVERTREE

The following have 'Wavertree' in their names. Insofar as any existed at a given time: *LG* W Derby Hd, PLU, Wavertree USD, UD (1894—95), Liverp CB (1895—1922). *Parl* S'rn Dv (1832—67), S-W Dv (1867—85), pt Liverp, Walton Parl Bor, pt Bootle Dv (1885—1918); see Part III of the *Guide* for composition of Liverp Parl Bors (1918—48) by wards of the CB. *Eccl* Warr. RDn (cr—1847), Prescot RDn (1847—82), Childwall RDn (1882—*).

CP1/EP1—WAVERTREE [HOLY TRINITY]—Tp in Childwall AP, sep CP 1866,[4] sep EP 1825,[12] eccl refounded 1828.[75] Abol civ 1922 ent to Liverpool CP.[47] Eccl bdry: 1856 (cr EP3),[564] 1875 (help cr

Mossley Hill St Matthew and St James EP),[28] 1887,[335] 1901 (cr EP2),[70] 1923,[48] 1964.[49]

EP2—WAVERTREE ST BRIDGET—Cr 1901 from EP1.[70] Bdry: 1906 (cr EP4).[368]

EP3—WAVERTREE ST MARY—Cr 1856 from EP1.[564] Bdry: 1909 (help cr Liverpool St Mark, Edge Lane EP).[35]

EP4—WAVERTREE ST THOMAS—Cr 1906 from EP2.[368]

WEASTE ALL SAINTS
EP Cr 1910 from Weaste St Luke EP.[465] Salf. RDn. Abol 1949 to help cr Weaste St Luke with All Saints EP.[140]

WEASTE ST LUKE
EP Cr 1866 from Eccles AP.[335] Eccles & Salf. RDn (1866—72), Eccles RDn (1872—1903), Salf. RDn (1903—49). Bdry: 1902 (help cr Old Trafford St Cuthbert EP),[2] 1902 (help cr Pendleton St Ambrose EP),[553] 1903,[522] 1910 (cr Weaste All Saints EP).[461] Abol 1949 to help cr Weaste St Luke with All Saints EP.[140]

WEASTE ST LUKE WITH ALL SAINTS
EP Cr 1949 by union Weaste St Luke EP, Weaste All Saints EP.[140] Salf. RDn.

WEETON
Tp in Kirkham AP, sep EP 1846,[547] sep CP 1866 as 'Weeton and Preese',[4] qv. *Eccl* Amound. RDn (1846—52), The Fylde RDn (1852—*). Eccl bdry: 1957 (help cr Mereside EP).[605]

WEETON AND PREESE
Tp in Kirkham AP, sep CP 1866,[4] sep EP 1846 as 'Weeton',[547] qv. *LG* Seq 1. *Parl* Seq 2.

WELSH WHITTLE
Tp in Standish AP, sep CP 1866,[4] eccl severed 1717 to help cr Coppull EP,[12] the latter refounded 1842,[23] the orig area of Welsh Whittle eccl severed 1861 from the latter to help cr Charnock Richard EP.[304] *LG* Leyl. Hd, Chorley PLU, RSD, RD. Abol 1934 ent to Charnock Richard CP.[226] *Parl* N'rn Dv (1832—67), North Dv (1867—85), Chorley Dv (1885—1948).

WENNINGTON
Tp in Melling AP, sep CP 1866.[4] *LG* Seq 13. *Parl* Seq 8.

WERNETH
EP Cr 1844 from Oldham EP, Hollinwood EP, Oldham St Peter EP.[347] Manch RDn (1844—47), Rochd. RDn (1847—72), Oldham RDn (1872—*). Bdry: 1880 (help cr Oldham St Paul EP).[322]

WESHAM
EP Cr 1912 from Kirkham AP.[88] The Fylde RDn.

WESTBY WITH PLUMPTON
Tp in Kirkham AP, sep CP 1866.[4] *LG* Seq 1. Bdry: 1934.[226] *Parl* Seq 2.

WESTHOUGHTON
Chap in Deane AP, sep CP 1866,[4] sep EP 1719 as 'West Houghton',[12] as such eccl refounded 1859,[332] qv. *LG* Salf. Hd, Bolton PLU, Westhoughton USD, UD. Civ bdry: 1898.[36] Transf 1974 to Gtr Manch.[40] *Parl* Seq 16.

WESTLEIGH ST PAUL
Tp in Leigh AP, sep EP 1851,[12] eccl refounded 1892,[564] sep CP 1866 as 'West Leigh',[4] qv. *Eccl*

Eccles RDn (1851—1933), Leigh RDn (1933—*).

WESTLEIGH ST PETER
EP Cr 1881 from Leigh AP.[567] Eccles RDn (1881—1933), Leigh RDn (1933—*). Bdry: 1889,[103] 1899 (exchanges pts with Abram EP, dioc Liverp).[9]

WHALLEY
AP Tp 'Whalley' in Blackb Hd as were chap Accrington (sep CP 1866 as 'New Accrington',[4] sep EP 1732 as 'Accrington',[12] pt of the latter severed 1855 to cr Accrington Christ Church EP,[12] the remainder refounded 1870 as 'Accrington'[13]), chap Altham (sep EP 1866,[4] sep EP 1723 [incl tp Old Accrington, pt tp Clayton le Moors][12]), chap Burnley (sep CP 1866,[4] sep EP 1716 [incl tps Briercliffe with Extwistle, Cliviger, Habergham Eaves, Worsthorne with Hurstwood, and two civ tp/eccl ex-par areas of Ightenhill Park (eccl. 'Ighton Hill', qv below for eccl abol 1845); Reedley Hallows, Filly Close and New Laund Booth][12]), chap Church (sep CP 1866,[4] sep EP 1820 as 'Church Kirk' [incl tps Huncoat, Oswaldtwistle, pt tp Clayton le Moors][12]), chap Colne (sep CP 1866,[4] sep EP 1820 [incl tps Barrowford Booth, Foulridge, Trawden, and the area of Great Marsden in tp Great and Little Marsden (see below for cr of EPs of Foulridge, Trawden, Great Marsden)][12]), chap Haslingden (sep CP 1866,[4] sep EP 1719 [incl tps Higher Booths, Lower Booths, Dunnockshaw, and area of eccl ex-par Henheads][12]), chap Little Marsden (civ pt of tp Great and Little Marsden, qv below for sep civ identity 1866, 'Little Marsden' a sep EP 1873,[12] pt of the latter severed 1873 to cr Briercliffe EP,[154] the remainder refounded 1877 as 'Little Marsden'[287]), chap Newchurch (sep CP 1866,[4] sep EP 1723 as 'Newchurch in Pendle' [incl tps Barley with Wheatley Booth, Goldshaw Booth, Old Laund Booth, Roughlee Booth][12]), chap Newchurch in Rossendale (early sep,[130] this chap itself incl chap Bacup, qv for sep eccl identity), chap Padiham (sep CP 1866,[4] sep EP 1730 [incl tps Hapton, Higham with West Close Booth, Simonstone],[12] pt eccl severed 1845 to help cr Habergham All Saints EP,[124] the remainder refounded 1868 as 'Padiham' EP[27]), tp New Accrington (the area of chap Accrington [qv above for eccl status], sep CP 1866 as 'New Accrington'[4]), tp Old Accrington (sep CP 1866,[4] eccl in chap/EP Altham, qv above), tp Barley with Wheatley Booth (sep CP 1866,[4] eccl in chap/EP Newchurch in Pendle, qv above), tp Barrowford Booth (sep CP 1866,[4] eccl in chap/EP Colne, qv above), tp Higher Booths (sep CP 1866,[4] eccl in chap/EP Haslingden, qv above, pt of orig area of the tp severed 1846 from Haslingden EP to help cr Lumb EP,[283] 'Higher Booths' a sep EP 1849 from Haslingden EP[284]), tp Lower Booths (sep CP 1866,[4] eccl in chap/EP Haslingden, qv above, pt of the orig area of the tp severed 1846 from Haslingden EP to help cr Lumb EP[283]), tp Bowland (sep CP 1866[4]), tp Briercliffe with Extwistle (sep CP 1866,[4] eccl in chap/EP Burnley, qv above, 'Briercliffe' a sep EP 1843 from Burnley EP[293]), tp Chatburn (sep CP 1866,[4] sep EP 1843[293]), tp Clayton le Moors (sep CP 1866,[4] pt eccl in chap/EP

Altham, pt eccl in chap Church [eccl, 'Church Kirk'], both qv above, 'Clayton le Moors' a sep EP 1840 from Altham EP[68]), tp and bor Clitheroe (sep CP 1866,[4] sep EP 1723[12]), tp Cliviger (sep CP 1866,[4] eccl in chap/EP Burnley, qv above, pt of area of Cliviger incl area Holme [not sep civ] a sep EP 1741 as 'Holme', [12] the latter eccl refounded 1843[293]), tp Downham (sep CP 1866,[4] sep EP 1723[12]), tp Dunnockshaw (sep CP 1866,[4] eccl in chap/EP Haslingden, qv above), tp Foulridge (sep CP 1866,[4] eccl in chap/EP Colne, qv above, 'Foulridge' a sep EP 1905 from Colne EP, Colne Christ Church EP[391]), tp Goldshaw Booth (sep CP 1866,[4] eccl in chap/EP Newchurch in Pendle, qv above), tp Habergham Eaves (sep CP 1866,[4] eccl in chap/EP Burnley, qv above, 'Habergham Eaves' a sep EP 1843 from Burnley EP[12]), tp Hapton (sep CP 1866,[4] eccl in chap/EP Padiham, qv above), tp Henheads (sep CP 1866,[4] eccl ex-par and situated in area chap/EP Haslingden [qv above]), tp Higham with West Close Booth (sep CP 1866,[4] eccl in chap/ EP Padiham, qv above), tp Huncoat (sep CP 1866,[4] eccl in chap/EP Church, qv above), tp Ightenhill Park (sep CP 1866,[4] eccl ex-par as 'Ighton Park', in area chap/EP Burnley [qv above] until eccl abol 1845 to help cr Habergham All Saints EP[124]), tp Leagrim (sep CP 1866[4]), tp Great and Little Marsden (sep CP 1866,[4] eccl incl chap Little Marsden [sep EP 1783,[12] qv above for later refounding], area Great Marsden [in chap/EP Colne, qv above], the orig area of Great Marsden eccl severed 1836 from Colne EP to help cr Colne Christ Church EP,[12] the orig area of Great Marsden eccl severed 1845 from the latter and united with a pt of Colne EP to cr 'Great Marsden' EP[118]), tp Mearley (sep CP 1866[4]); tp Little Mitton, Henthorn and Coldcoats (sep CP 1866[4]); tp Old Laund Booth (sep CP 1866,[4] eccl in chap/EP Newchurch in Pendle, qv above); tp Oswaldtwistle (sep CP 1866,[4] eccl in chap/EP Church Kirk, qv above, 'Oswald-twistle' a sep EP 1865 from Church Kirk[12]), tp Pendleton (sep CP 1866,[4] eccl severed 1839 to help cr Clitheroe St James EP,[380] the orig area of tp Pendleton severed 1873 from the latter and united with eccl ex-par Pendleton Hall and a further pt of Whalley AP to cr 'Pendleton in Whalley' EP[297]), tp Read (sep CP 1866,[4] pt eccl severed 1849 to help cr Heyhouses EP,[466] the remainder a sep EP 1893 as 'Read in Whalley'[1]); tp Reedley Hallows, Filley Close and New Laund Booth (sep CP 1866,[4] eccl ex-par and situated in chap/EP Burnley, qv above); tp Roughlee Booth (sep CP 1866,[4] eccl in chap/EP Newchurch in Pendle, qv above), tp Simonstone (sep CP 1866,[4] eccl in chap/EP Padiham, qv above), tp Trawden (sep CP 1866,[4] eccl in chap/EP Colne, qv above, pt of orig tp Trawden severed 1836 from the latter to help cr Colne Christ EP,[12] 'Trawden' a sep EP 1845 from Colne Christ Church EP[72]), tp Twiston (sep CP 1866[4]), tp Wheatley Carr Booth (sep CP 1866[4]), tp Wiswell (sep CP 1866[4]), tp Worthstone with Hurstwood (sep CP 1866,[4] eccl in chap/EP Burnley, qv above, 'Worthstone' a sep EP 1837 from Burnley EP,[12] as such eccl refounded

1843[293]), tp Worston (sep CP 1866,[4] eccl severed 1843 to help cr Chatburn EP[293]), tp Yate and Pickup Bank (CP 1866,[4] eccl ex-par); incl area ex-par Heyhouses (sep CP 1858,[80] sep EP 1849[466]); incl in Yorks W Riding (Staincliffe and Ewcross Wap) tp Bowland Forest Low (sep CP 1866 in Yorks[4]) so that 'Whalley' ent Lancs thereafter. *LG* Pt Clith. Bor (tp Clitheroe), Clith. PLU, RSD, RD. *Parl* Clith. Parl Bor (pt [tp Clitheroe] 1558—1832, ent 1832—85), Clith. Dv/CC (1885—*). *Eccl* Manch & Blackb RDn (until before 1535), Blackb RDn (before 1535—1847), Whalley RDn (1847—*). Addtl eccl bdry alt: 1717 (cr Whitewell EP),[12] 1741 (cr Goodshaw EP),[12] 1841 (cr Fence in Pendle EP),[12] 1842 (cr Rawtenstall EP),[12] 1853 (cr Tunstead EP,[12] refounded 1868[675]).

WHALLEY RANGE ST EDMUND

EP Cr 1883 from Whalley Range St Margaret EP.[221] Hulme RDn. Bdry: 1889 (cr Moss Side St James EP),[103] 1916 (help cr Withington St Crispin EP).[110]

WHALLEY RANGE ST MARGARET

EP Cr 1854 from Manchester AP.[199] Manch RDn (1854—55), Chorlton RDn (1855—66), Chorlton & Hulme RDn (1866—72), Hulme RDn (1872—*). Bdry: 1858 (help cr Moss Side EP),[70] 1879 (cr Stretford St Bride EP,[442] sometimes called 'Old Trafford St Bride'), 1882 (help cr Greenheys EP),[203] 1883 (cr Whalley Range St Edmund EP),[221] 1902 (help cr Old Trafford St John EP).[323]

WHEATLEY CARR BOOTH

Tp in Whalley AP, sep CP 1866.[4] *LG* Blackb Hd, Burnley PLU, pt Nelson USD, pt Nelson MB (1890—96), pt Burnley RSD, Burnley RD (pt 1894—96, ent 1896—1935). Bdry: 1896 (loses the pt in the MB to Nelson CP).[621] Abol 1935 ent to Old Laund Booth CP.[43] *Parl* N'rn Dv (1832—67), N-E Dv (1867—85), Clith. Dv (1885—1948).

WHEELTON

Tp in Leyland AP, sep CP 1866.[4] *LG* Seq 8. Bdry: 1899,[681] 1934.[226] *Parl* Seq 3.

WHISTON

Tp in Prescot AP, sep CP 1866,[4] sep EP 1869 from Prescot AP, Huyton AP, Halewood EP.[505] *LG* Seq 18. Civ bdry: 1914,[645] 1932.[307] Transf 1974 to Merseyside.[40] *Parl* Seq 24. *Eccl* Prescot RDn. Eccl bdry: 1875 (help cr Ditton EP),[437] 1959 (help cr Huyton Quarry EP).[91]

WHITECHAPEL

EP Cr 1717 from pt of tp Goosnargh in chap Goosnargh in Kirkham AP,[12] refounded 1846.[498] Amound. RDn (1717—1852), Garst. RDn (1852—*).

WHITEFIELD

CP Cr 1894 from the pt of Pilkington CP in Whitefield UD.[115] *LG* Bury PLU, Whitefield UD. Bdry: 1933,[171] 1937 (exchanges pts with Bury CB [assoc with Lancs] & AP).[331] Transf 1974 to Gtr Manch.[40] *Parl* Heyw. & Radcl. Dv (1918—48), Middl. & Prestw. CC (1948—70), Middl. & Prestw. BC (1970—*).

WHITEWELL

EP Cr 1717 from Whalley AP.[12] Blackb RDn (1717—1847), Whalley RDn (1847—*).

WHITTINGHAM

Tp in Kirkham AP, sep CP 1866,[4] *LG* Seq 3. *Parl* Seq 2.

WHITTINGTON

AP *LG* Lonsd. Hd, Lunesd. PLU, RSD, RD. *Parl* Seq 8. *Eccl* Lanc. RDn (until before 1291), Kirkby Lonsd. & Kendal RDn (before 1291—before 1541), Kirkby Lonsd. RDn (before 1541—1848), Tunstall RDn (1848—*).

WHITTLE LE WOODS

Tp in Leyland AP, sep CP 1866,[4] sep EP 1832,[12] eccl refounded 1842.[524] *LG* Seq 8. *Parl* Seq 3. *Eccl* Leyl. RDn (1832—1964), Chorley RDn (1964—*). Eccl bdry: 1898 (help cr Leyland St Ambrose EP).[62]

WHITWORTH

Chap in Rochdale AP, sep EP 1721 (pt tp Spotland, pt area Wardle in tp Wuerdle and Wardle),[12] refounded 1844.[125] Manch RDn (1721—1847), Rochd. RDn (1847—*). Bdry: 1849 (loses the orig pt area Wardle to help cr Wardle St James EP,[12] refounded 1859[235]), 1862 (help cr Norden EP),[628] 1867 (cr Facit EP).[474]

EP Cr 1894 from the pt of Spotland CP in Whitworth UD.[257] *LG* Rochd. PLU, Whitworth UD. *Parl* Royton Dv (1918—48), Heyw. & Royton CC (1948—*).

WIDNES

The following have 'Widnes' in their names. Insofar as any existed at a given time: *LG* W Derby Hd, Prescot PLU, Widnes USD, MB (1892—1974). *Parl* Seq 24. *Eccl* Prescot RDn (cr—1882), Childwall RDn (1882—1949), Farnw. RDn (1949—*).

CP1—WIDNES—Tp in Prescot AP, sep CP 1866,[4] incl area chap & bor Farnworth (bor status not sustained, chap had some parochial rights from Middle Ages,[261] this pt of the orig tp eccl severed 1859 to help cr 'Farnworth' EP (qv for other constituent tps), the remainder of the orig tp of Widnes cr at same time EP2,[262] qv. Bdry: 1920.[411] Transf 1974 to Ches.[40]

EP1—WIDNES ST AMBROSE—Cr 1884 from Farnworth EP.[123] Bdry: 1909.[41]

EP2—WIDNES ST MARY—Cr 1859 from the pt of the orig tp of Widnes in Prescot AP not cr Farnworth EP (for status of that chap, see above in CP1).[262] Bdry: 1901 (cr EP3).[62]

EP3—WIDNES ST PAUL—Cr 1901 from EP2.[62] Bdry: 1909.[41]

WIGAN

The following have 'Wigan' in their names. Insofar as any existed at a given time: *LG* Wigan PLU, Bor/MB/CB, USD; Hd sep noted. *Parl* Wigan Parl Bor (1295, 1306, 1547—*). *Eccl* Warr. RDn (until 1847), Wigan RDn (1847—*).

AP1—WIGAN [ALL SAINTS]—Tp 'Wigan' in W Derby Hd as were chap Upholland (sep CP 1866,[4] sep EP 1643 [incl tps Billinge Higher End, Dalton, both in this par],[133] eccl refounded 1748,[12] 'Dalton' a sep EP 1870 from Upholland EP,[38] the remainder of this par eccl refounded 1882 as 'Upholland' EP[190]), tp Abram (sep CP 1866,[4] some eccl parochial rights 1843 [incl pt Hindley EP],[5] 'Abram' ent sep EP 1852[6]), tp Billinge Chapel End (sep CP 1866,[4] sep EP 1720 as 'Billinge'[12]), tp Billinge Higher End (sep CP 1866,[4] eccl in chap/EP Upholland [sep EP 1643 from Wigan AP,[192] qv above for later refounding]), tp Dalton (sep CP 1866,[4] eccl in chap/EP Upholland, qv above, 'Dalton' a sep EP 1870 from Upholland EP[38]), tp Haigh (sep CP 1866,[4] eccl severed 1838 to help cr Haigh and Aspull EP,[116] 'Haigh' a sep EP 1883 from Haigh and Aspull EP[117]), tp Hindley (sep CP 1866,[4] Puritan chap built 1641, consecr in Church of England 1698 and perhaps sep then,[521] certainly a sep EP 1777,[12] pt of the latter eccl severed 1866 to help cr Hindley St Peter EP,[219] a further pt eccl severed 1843 to help cr Abram EP [some eccl parochial rights 1843,[5] 'Abram' ent sep 1852[6]], the remainder of this par and a pt of Abram EP refounded 1877 as 'Hindley' EP[8]), tp Ince in Makerfield (sep CP 1866,[4] eccl severed 1843 to help cr EP3 [some parochial rights 1843,[5] ent sep 1854[119]], 'Ince in Makerfield' a sep EP 1862 from EP3[433]), tp Orrell (sep CP 1866,[4] sep EP 1922 from Upholland EP, Pemberton EP, Billinge EP[493]), tp Pemberton (sep CP 1866,[4] sep EP 1838[116]), tp Winstanley (sep CP 1866[4]); incl in Salf. Hd tp Aspull (sep CP 1866,[4] eccl severed 1838 to help cr Haigh and Aspull EP,[116] 'Aspull' a sep EP 1883 from Haigh and Aspull EP[117]). Addtl civ bdry alt: 1920 (gains Pemberton CP).[639] Transf 1974 to Gtr Manch.[40] Addtl eccl bdry alt: 1784 (cr EP4,[12] refounded 1843 with some parochial rights,[5] ent sep 1854[119]), 1852 (cr EP9),[682] 1871 (help cr EP1),[16] 1881 (cr EP7),[302] 1891 (help cr Pemberton St Mark Newtown EP),[213] 1929,[88] 1871 (cr EP1, sometimes early 'Scholes').[16]

EP1—WIGAN ST ANDREW—Cr 1871 from AP1, Pemberton EP.[16] Bdry: 1882,[146] 1891 (help cr Pemberton St Mark Newtown EP),[213] 1907,[614] 1929,[88] 1947 (cr EP2).[243] Sometimes early 'Scholes'.

EP2—WIGAN ST ANNE—Cr 1947 from EP1.[243] Bdry: 1960 (gains pt Standish AP, dioc Blackb).[567]

EP3—WIGAN ST CATHERINE—Cr 1843 from AP1 (incl tp Ince in Makerfield in same par) with some parochial rights,[5] ent sep EP 1854.[119] Bdry: 1862 (area of the incl tp a sep EP as 'Ince in Makerfield'),[433] 1925 (help cr EP8).[146]

EP4—WIGAN ST GEORGE—Cr 1784 from AP1,[12] refounded 1843 with some parochial rights,[5] ent sep EP 1854.[119] Bdry: 1863 (help cr EP5),[640] 1907,[614] 1925 (help cr EP8).[146]

EP5—WIGAN ST JAMES—Cr 1863 from Pemberton EP, EP4, EP9.[640] Bdry: 1891 (help cr Pemberton St Mark Newtown EP),[213] 1911 (help cr Highfield EP),[38] 1915 (help cr Goose Green EP).[125] Abol 1970 to help cr EP6.[683]

EP6—WIGAN ST JAMES WITH ST THOMAS—Cr 1970 by union EP5, EP9.[683]

EP7—WIGAN ST MICHAEL AND ALL ANGELS—Cr 1881 from AP1.[302] Bdry: 1907.[614]

EP8—WIGAN ST STEPHEN—Cr 1925 from EP3, EP4.[146]

EP9—WIGAN ST THOMAS—Cr 1852 from AP1.[682] Bdry: 1863 (help cr EP5),[640] 1891 (help cr Pemberton St Mark Newtown EP),[213] 1907.[614] Abol 1970 to help cr EP6.[683]

WILPSHIRE

Tp in Blackburn AP, sep CP 1866.[4] *LG* Seq 4. *Parl* Seq 13.

WINDLE

Tp (incl chap St Helens, sep EP 1716[12]) in Prescot AP, sep CP 1866.[4] *LG* W Derby Hd, Prescot PLU, pt St Helens MB (1868—89), pt St Helens CB (1889—94), pt St Helens USD, pt Prescot RSD, Whiston RD. Bdry: 1894 (loses the pt in the CB and an addtl pt to help cr St Helens CP),[451] 1934 (loses pt to St Helens CB [assoc with Lancs] & CP),[363] 1954 (loses pt to St Helens CB [assoc with Lancs] & CP).[658] Transf 1974 to Merseyside.[40] *Parl* S'rn Dv (1832—67), S-W Dv (1867—85), pt St Helens Parl Bor, pt Newton Dv (1885—1918), Widnes Dv (1918—48), Hyton CC (1948—*). Parl bdry: [488]

WINDSOR—see WEST DERBY ST NATHANIEL, WINDSOR

WINGATES

EP Cr 1860 from West Houghton EP, Bolton le Moors AP (tp Lostock).[273] Bolton le Moors RDn (1860—93), Bolton South RDn (1893—1901), Bolton le Moors RDn (1901—68), Deane RDn (1968—*).

WINMARLEIGH

Tp in Garstang AP, sep CP 1866,[4] pt of the tp a sep EP 1876.[340] *LG* Seq 2. *Parl* Seq 7. *Eccl* Garst. RDn.

WINSTANLEY

Tp in Wigan AP, sep CP 1866.[4] *LG* W Derby Hd, Wigan PLU, Billinge USD, UD. Abol 1924 to help cr Billinge & Winstanley UD & CP.[191] *Parl* S'rn Dv (1832—67), S-W Dv (1867—85), Newton Dv (1885—1918), Ince Dv (1918—48).

WINTON

EP Cr 1922 from Worsley EP, Patricroft EP.[493] Eccles RDn.

WINWICK

AP Incl (listed by chrolonogical order of civ sep from this par) tp (sometimes 'Newton le Willows') and bor Newton in Makerfield (sep CP 1841,[400] sep EP 1770,[12] eccl refounded 1844[399]), tp Southworth with Croft (sep CP 1841,[400] sep EP 1835 as 'Croft with Southworth',[12] as such eccl refounded 1844[399]); incl tps Culceth, Kenyon (united 1845 as tps in new CP of 'Newchurch Kenyon',[92] the 2 tps having been eccl united 1748 as 'Newchurch' EP,[12] as such eccl refounded 1844,[399] 'Kenyon' and 'Culceth' each a sep CP 1866[4] and therefore 'Newchurch Kenyon' ceases to have sep civ identity), chap Ashton in Makerfield (sep CP 1845,[92] sep EP 1840 [incl tp Haydock in same par],[12] eccl refounded 1845 from the remainder of this EP as the incl chap in Downall Green cr at the same time 'Ashton in Makerfield Holy Trinity' EP[93], tp Haydock (sep CP 1845,[92] eccl in chap/EP Ashton in Makerfield, qv above for cr and later refounding, 'Haydock' a sep EP 1864 from Ashton

in Makerfield EP[94]), chap Lowton, tp Golborne (united civ 1845 as sep CP of 'Lowton',[92] 'Lowton' a sep EP 1734,[12] the EP enlarged 1845 to incl eccl tp Golborne,[399] 'Golborne' a sep EP 1850[494] at which time Lowton, Golborne sep both civ and eccl); tps Houghton, Middleton and Arbury, Winwick with Hulme (each of the 3 a sep CP 1866[4]) so that 'Winwick' has no sep civ identity 1866—1934 (see following entry). *LG* W Derby Hd. *Parl* S'rn Dv (1832—67). *Eccl* Seq 7. Addtl eccl bdry alt: 1964 (help cr Orford St Andrew EP).[631]

CP Cr 1934 from pt Southworth with Croft CP, ent Houghton, Middleton and Arbury CP,[37] pt Winwick with Hulme CP.[324] *LG* Warr. RD. Civ bdry: 1954 (loses pt to Warr. CB [assoc with Lancs] & AP).[679] *Parl* Newton CC (1948—*). Parl bdry: 1955.[680]

WINWICK WITH HULME

Tp in Winwick AP, sep CP 1866.[4] *LG* W Derby Hd, Warr. PLU, RSD, RD. Bdry: 1894 (gains pt of the pt of Warrington AP not in Warr. MB).[662] Abol 1933 pt to Warr. CB (assoc with Lancs) & AP, pt to help cr Winwick CP.[324] *Parl* S'rn Dv (1832—67), S-W Dv (1867—85), Newton Dv (1885—1948).

WISWELL

Tp in Whalley AP, sep CP 1866.[4] *LG* Seq 6. Bdry: 1904 (help cr Sabden CP).[497] *Parl* Seq 1.

WITHINGTON

Tp in Manchester AP, sep CP 1866,[4] sep EP 1853 (incl pt tp Burnage),[12] eccl refounded 1854.[199] *LG* Salf. Hd, Chorlton PLU, pt Moss Side USD, pt Withington USD, pt Rusholme USD (1875—85), pt Manch MB (1884—89), pt Manch CB (1889—94), pt Manch UD, Withington UD (1894—1904), Manch CB (1904—10). Civ bdry: 1883,[31] 1894 (loses the pt in Moss Side UD to Moss Side CP,[619] loses the pt in the CB to Rusholme CP[501]). Abol civ 1910 ent to South Manchester CP.[310] *Parl* S'rn Dv (1832—67), S-E Dv (1867—85), Stretf. Dv (1885—1918). *Eccl* Asht. under Lyne RDn (1853—72), Ardwick RDn (1872—1912), Heaton RDn (1912—65), Withington RDn (1965—*). Eccl bdry: 1858 (help cr Moss Side EP),[70] 1873 (cr Fallowfield EP),[355] 1875 (the pt of orig tp Burnage severed to help cr Burnage EP),[150] 1882 (help cr Disbury Christ Church, Barlow Moor Road EP),[151] 1900 (help cr Ladybarn EP),[202] 1927,[135] 1932 (help cr Withington St Christopher EP).[323]

WITHINGTON ST CHRISTOPHER

EP Cr 1932 from Withington EP, Didsbury Christ Church, Barlow Moor Road EP.[323] Heaton RDn (1932—65), Withington RDn (1965—*).

WITHINGTON ST CRISPIN

EP Cr 1916 from Fallowfield EP, Chorlton cum Hardy St Werburgh EP, Whalley Range St Edmund EP.[110] Heaton RDn (1916—65), Hulme RDn (1965—*). Bdry: 1929.[204]

WITHNELL

Tp in Leyland AP, sep CP 1866,[4] sep EP 1842.[524] *LG* Leyl. Hd, Chorley PLU, RSD (1875—93), Withnell USD (1893—94), UD. Civ bdry: 1877,[525] 1899,[681] 1934.[226] *Parl* N'rn Dv (1832—67), North Dv (1867—85), Chorley Dv (1885—1948), Darwen

CC (1948—55), Chorley CC (1955—*).

WITTON

Tp in Blackburn AP, sep CP 1866,[4] sep EP 1842.[133] *LG* Blackb Hd, PLU (1837—1930), pt Blackb USD (1875—93), pt Blackb MB (1877—89), pt Blackb CB (1889—93), Blackb RSD (pt 1875—93, ent 1893—94), Blackb RD. Civ bdry: 1893 (loses the pt in the CB to Blackburn AP),[223] 1901 (loses pt to Blackb CB [assoc with Lancs] & AP).[224] Abol civ 1934 ent to Blackb CB (assoc with Lancs) & AP.[226] *Parl* N'rn Dv (1832—67), Blackb Parl Bor (pt 1867—85, ent 1885—1918), pt N-E Dv (1867—85). *Eccl* Blackb RDn. Eccl bdry: 1881 (cr Griffin EP),[235] 1907,[236] 1940.[150]

WOODHOUSES

CP Cr 1894 from pt of the pt of Ashton under Lyne AP not in a MB or UD.[63] *LG* Asht. under Lyne PLU, Limehurst RD. Bdry: 1951 (loses pt to Oldham CB [assoc with Lancs] & CP).[64] Abol 1954 pt to Oldham CB (assoc with Lancs) & CP, pt to Failsworth UD & CP.[65] *Parl* Mossley Dv (1918—48), Asht. under Lyne BC (1948—55).

WOODLAND

Chap in Kirkby Ireleth AP, sep EP 1731,[12] eccl refounded 1876.[75] Furness & Cartmel (1731—1859), Ulv. RDn (1859—1956). Bdry: 1886.[8] Abol 1956 to help cr Broughton in Furness with Woodland EP.[244]

WOODPLUMPTON

Chap in St Michael on Wyre AP, sep CP 1866,[4] sep EP 1743.[12] *LG* Seq 3. Civ bdry: 1883.[31] *Parl* Seq 2. *Eccl* Amound. RDn (1743—1852), Garst. RDn (1852—*).

WOOLFOLD

EP Cr 1915 from Elton EP, Tottington EP, Walshaw EP.[462] Bury RDn.

WOOLSTON

CP Cr 1933 from Culceth CP, Woolston with Martinscroft CP.[37] *LG* Warr. RD. *Parl* Newton CC (1948—*). Parl bdry: 1945.[339]

EP Cr 1971 from Padgate EP.[636] Warr. RDn.

WOOLSTON WITH MARTINSCROFT

Tp in Warrington AP, sep CP 1866,[4] *LG* W Derby Hd, Warr. PLU, RSD, RD. Bdry: 1885 (gains pt Thelwall CP, Ches),[684] 1933 (gains pt Lymm AP, exchanges pts with Grappenhall AP, exchanges pts with Thelwall CP, all Ches).[412] Abol 1933 pt to help cr Croft CP, pt to help cr Woolston CP.[37] *Parl* S'rn Dv (1832—67), S-W Dv (1867—85), Newton Dv (1885—1948).

LITTLE WOOLTON

Tp in Childwall AP, sep CP 1866,[4] pt eccl severed 1893 to help cr Gateacre EP.[360] *LG* W Derby Hd, Prescot PLU, Little Woolton USD, UD (1894—1913), Liverp CB (1913—22). Abol 1922 ent to Liverpool CP.[47] *Parl* S'rn Dv (1832—67), S-W Dv (1867—85), Widnes Dv (1885—1918); see Part III of the *Guide* for composition of Liverp Parl Bors (1918—48) by wards of the CB.

MUCH WOOLTON

Tp in Childwall AP, sep CP 1866,[4] pt a sep EP 1827,[12] eccl refounded 1828,[75] the remainder of the orig tp eccl severed 1893 to help cr Gateacre EP.[360]

LG W Derby Hd, Prescot PLU, Much Woolton USD, UD (1894—1913), Liverp CB (1913—22). Civ bdry: 1877.[539] Abol 1922 ent to Liverpool CP.[47] *Parl* S'rn Dv (1832—67), S-W Dv (1867—85), Widnes Dv (1885—1918); see Part III of the *Guide* for composition of Liverp Parl Bors (1918—48) by wards of the CB. *Eccl* Warr. RDn (1827—47), Prescot RDn (1847—82), Childwall RDn (1882—*). Eccl bdry: 1877,[272] 1957 (help cr Hunts Cross EP),[506] 1964.[49]

WORSLEY

Tp in Eccles AP, sep CP 1866,[4] sep EP 1847.[428] *LG* Salf. Hd, not in a PLU (until 1849), Barton upon Irwell PLU (1849—1930), pt Swinton & Pendlebury USD, pt Eccles MB & USD (1892—94), Worsley UD. Civ bdry: 1894 (the pt in Swinton & Pendlebury UD cr Swinton CP, the pt in the MB to help cr Eccles CP),[174] 1907,[666] 1933,[171] 1955.[586] Transf 1974 to Gtr Manch.[40] *Parl* S'rn Dv (1832—67), S-E Dv (1867—85), Eccles Dv (1885—1918), Farnw. Dv/CC (1918—*). Parl bdry: 1956.[667] *Eccl* Manch RDn (1847—50), Eccles RDn (1850—66), Eccles & Salf. RDn (1866—72), Eccles RDn (1872—*). Eccl bdry: 1922 (help cr Winton EP).[493]

WORSTHORNE

Tp in Whalley AP, eccl in chap Burnley (sep EP 1716 from Whalley AP[12]), 'Worsthorne' a sep EP 1837 from Burnley EP,[12] as such eccl refounded 1843,[293] sep CP 1866 from Whalley AP as 'Worsthorne with Hurstwood',[4] qv. Blackb RDn (1837—47), Whalley RDn (1847—72), Burnley RDn (1872—*).

WORSTHORNE WITH HURSTWOOD

Tp in Whalley AP, sep CP 1866,[4] eccl in chap Burnley (sep EP 1716 from Whalley AP[12]), 'Worsthorne' a sep EP 1837,[12] as such eccl refounded 1843,[293] qv. *LG* Seq 5. Bdry: 1914.[517] *Parl* Seq 14.

WORSTON

Tp in Whalley AP, sep CP 1866,[4] eccl severed 1843 to help cr Chatburn EP.[293] *LG* Seq 6. *Parl* Seq 1.

WORTHINGTON

Tp in Standish AP, sep CP 1866.[4] *LG* Seq 11. Transf 1974 to Gtr Manch.[40] *Parl* Seq 5.

WRAY

EP Cr 1842 from Melling EP (tp Wray with Botton, pt tp Roeburndale),[606] refounded 1843.[607] Kirkby Lonsd. RDn (1842—48), Tunstall RDn (1848—*). Bdry: 1859 (the orig area of pt tp Roeburndale severed to help refound Hornby EP),[477] 1955.[86]

LOW WRAY

EP Cr 1860 from Hawkshead EP,[12] eccl refounded 1846.[511] Ambleside RDn. Abol 1954 to help cr Hawkshead and Low Wray EP.[347]

WRAY WITH BOTTON

Tp in Melling AP, sep CP 1866,[4] eccl severed 1842 to help cr Wray EP,[606] qv above for later refounding. *LG* Seq 13. *Parl* Seq 8.

WRIGHTINGTON

Tp in Eccleston AP, sep CP 1866,[4] sep EP 1877.[449] *LG* Seq 11. *Parl* Seq 5. *Eccl* Leyl. RDn (1877—1964), Chorley RDn (1964—*).

WUERDLE AND WARDLE

Tp in Rochdale AP, sep CP 1866,[4] pt of the area of

Wuerdle in chap Littleborough, that area eccl severed 1745 to help cr Littlebough EP,[12] the same area eccl severed 1859 from Littleborough EP and transf to Smallbridge EP,[296] the remainder of the area of Wuerdle eccl severed 1870 and transf to Smallbridge EP[38]; pt of the area of Wardle eccl in chap Whitworth (sep EP 1721 from Rochdale AP[12]), another pt of the area of Wardle eccl severed 1745 to help cr Littleborough EP,[12] the remainder of area Wardle in chap Whitworth eccl severed 1843 to cr Smallbridge EP,[12] the 3 orig areas of Wardle severed 1859 from the 3 respective EPs to cr Wardle St James EP.[235] *LG* Salf. Hd, Rochd. PLU, pt Littleborough USD, pt Wuerdle & Wardle USD, pt Rochd. USD, pt Rochd. MB (1856—89), pt Rochd. CB (1889—94). Abol civ 1894 the pt in Littleborough UD to help cr Littleborough CP, the pt in Wuerdle & Wardle UD to help cr Wardle UD & CP, the pt in the CB to help cr Rochdale CP.[257] *Parl* Pt Rochd. Parl Bor (1832—1918 [enlarged pt 1867—1918]), pt S'rn Dv (1832—67), pt S-E Dv (1867—85), pt Middl. Dv (1885—1918).

WYRESDALE

Chap in Lancaster AP, sep EP 1728,[12] eccl refounded 1867,[159] sep CP 1866 as 'Over Wyresdale',[4] qv. Amound. RDn (1728—1852), Lanc.

RDn (1852—*).

NETHER WYRESDALE

Tp in Garstang AP, sep CP 1866,[4] pt eccl severed 1858 to help refound Shireshead EP, pt eccl severed 1880 to cr Scorton EP.[491] *LG* Seq 2. Bdry: 1887,[155] 1887.[375] *Parl* Seq 7.

OVER WYRESDALE

Chap in Lancaster AP, sep CP 1866,[4] sep EP 1728 as 'Wyresdale',[12] as such eccl refounded 1867,[159] qv. *LG* Seq 12. *Parl* Seq 6.

YATE AND PICKUP BANK

Tp in Whalley AP, sep CP 1866,[4] eccl ex-par. *LG* Seq 4. Civ bdry: 1934.[226] *Parl* Seq 13.

YEALAND

EP Cr 1846 by union tps Yealand Conyers, Yealand Redmayne, both in Warton AP,[12] refounded 1867.[159] Kendal RDn (1846—48), Tunstall RDn (1848—*).

YEALAND CONYERS

Tp in Warton AP, sep CP 1866,[4] eccl severed 1846 to help cr 'Yealand' EP,[12] refounded 1867.[159] *LG* Seq 12. *Parl* Seq 10.

YEALAND REDMAYNE

Tp in Warton AP, sep CP 1866,[4] eccl severed 1846 to help cr 'Yealand' EP,[12] refounded 1867.[159] *LG* Seq 12. *Parl* Seq 10.

LEICESTERSHIRE

ABBREVIATIONS

Abbreviations particular to Leics follow. Those general abbreviations in use throughout the *Guide* are found on pages xvii—xix.

Ashb. (de la Z.)	Ashby (de la Zouch)
Ath.	Atherstone
Barr. upon S.	Barrow upon Soar
Belv.	Belvoir
Bill.	Billesdon
Bosw.	Bosworth
Cast. Don.	Castle Donington
Framl.	Framland
Gart.	Gartree
Gosc.	Goscote
Granth.	Grantham
Guthl.	Guthlaxton
Hall.	Hallaton
Harb.	Harborough
Hinck.	Hinckley
Longb.	Longborough
Loughb.	Loughborough
Lutt.	Lutterworth
Melt.	Melton
Mowb.	Mowbray
Mkt.	Market
Shard.	Shardlow
Spark.	Sparkenhoe
Upp.	Uppingham

SEQUENCES

An abbreviated entry prefixed by 'Seq' is used in the parochial entries to avoid repeating often the names of superior units of administration. The content of each sequence is shown below.

Local Government Sequences ('LG')

SEQ 1 Framl. Hd, Granth. PLU, RSD, Belv. RD (1894—1935), Melt. & Belv. RD (1935—74)

SEQ 2 Framl. Hd, Melt. Mowb. PLU, RSD, RD (1894—1935), Melt. & Belv. RD (1935—74)

SEQ 3 Gart. Hd, Bill. PLU, RSD, RD

SEQ 4 Gart. Hd, Mkt. Harb. PLU, RSD, RD

SEQ 5 Gart. Hd, Upp. PLU, RSD, Hall. RD (1894—1935), Mkt. Harb. RD (1935—74)

SEQ 6 E Gosc. Hd, Barr. upon S. PLU, RSD, RD

SEQ 7 E Gosc. Hd, Bill. PLU, RSD, RD

SEQ 8 E Gosc. Hd, Loughb. PLU, RSD, RD (1894—1935), Barr. upon S. RD (1935—74)

SEQ 9 E Gosc. Hd, Melt. Mowb. PLU, RSD, RD (1894—1935), Melt. & Belv. RD (1935—74)

SEQ 10 W Gosc. Hd, Ashb. de la Z. PLU, RSD, RD

SEQ 11 W Gosc. Hd, Barr. upon S. PLU, RSD, RD

SEQ 12 W Gosc. Hd, Loughb. PLU, RSD, RD (1894—1936), Cast. Don. RD (1936—74)

SEQ 13 W Gosc. Hd, Shard. PLU, RSD, Cast. Don. RD

SEQ 14 Guthl. Hd, Blaby PLU, RSD, RD

SEQ 15 Guthl. Hd, Lutt. PLU, RSD, RD

SEQ 16 Spark. Hd, Ashb. de la Z. PLU, RSD, RD

SEQ 17 Spark. Hd, Blaby PLU, RSD, RD

SEQ 18 Spark. Hd, Hinck. PLU, RSD, RD (1894—1936), Blaby RD (1936—74)

SEQ 19 Spark. Hd, Mkt. Bosw. PLU, RSD, RD

Parliamentary Sequences ('Parl')

SEQ 1 N'rn Dv (1832—85), E'rn Dv (1885—1918), Melt. Dv/CC (1918—*)

SEQ 2 N'rn Dv (1832—85), E'rn Dv (1885—1918), Melt. Dv/CC (1918—70), Harb. CC (1970—*)

SEQ 3 N'rn Dv (1832—85), Mid Dv (1885—1918), Loughb. Dv/CC (1918—*)

SEQ 4 N'rn Dv (1832—85), Mid Dv (1885—1918), Loughb. Dv (1918—48), Melt. CC (1948—*)

SEQ 5 N'rn Dv (1832—85), Mid Dv (1885—1918), Melt. Dv/CC (1918—*)

SEQ 6 N'rn Dv (1832—85), W'rn Dv (1885—1918),

SEQ 7   Loughb. Dv/CC (1918—*)

SEQ 7   S'rn Dv (1832—85), E'rn Dv (1885—1918), Melt. Dv/CC (1918—70), Harb. CC (1970—*)

SEQ 8   S'rn Dv (1832—85), Mid Dv (1885—1918), Bosw. Dv/CC (1918—*)

SEQ 9   S'rn Dv (1832—1918), Harb. Dv/CC (1918—*)

SEQ 10   S'rn Dv (1832—1918), Harb. Dv/CC (1918—70), Blaby CC (1970—*)

SEQ 11   S'rn Dv (1832—1918), Melt. Dv/CC (1918—70), Harb. CC (1970—*)

SEQ 12   S'rn Dv (1832—85), W'rn Dv (1885—1918), Bosw. Dv/CC (1918—*)

SEQ 13   S'rn Dv (1832—85), W'rn Dv (1885—1918), Bosw. Dv (1918—48), Harb. CC (1948—70), Blaby CC (1970—*)

SEQ 14   S'rn Dv (1832—85), W'rn Dv (1885—1918), Harb. Dv/CC (1918—70), Blaby CC (1970—*)

SEQ 15   S'rn Dv (1832—85), W'rn Dv (1885—1918), Loughb. Dv/CC (1918—*)

Ecclesiastical Sequences ('Eccl')

SEQ 1   Akeley RDn (until 1865), E Akeley RDn (1865—*)

SEQ 2   Akeley RDn (until 1865), E Akeley RDn (1865—73), W Akeley RDn (1873—77), E Akeley RDn (1877—*)

SEQ 3   Akeley RDn (until 1865), E Akeley RDn (1865—73), W Akeley RDn (1873—93), S Akeley RDn (1893—*)

SEQ 4   Akeley RDn (until 1865), E Akeley RDn (1865—93), Gosc. II RDn (1893—*)

SEQ 5   Akeley RDn (until 1865), W Akeley RDn (1865—*)

SEQ 6   Akeley RDn (until 1865), W Akeley RDn (1865—93), E Akeley RDn (1893—*)

SEQ 7   Framl. RDn (until 1865), Framl. I RDn (1865—73), Framl. III RDn (1873—77), Framl. II RDn (1877—*)

SEQ 8   Framl. RDn (until 1865), Framl. II RDn (1865—73), Framl. I RDn (1873—*)

SEQ 9   Framl. RDn (until 1865), Framl. II RDn (1865—73), Framl. I RDn (1873—93), Framl. II RDn (1893—1961), Framl. I RDn (1961—*)

SEQ 10   Framl. RDn (until 1865), Framl. III RDn (1865—73), Framl. II RDn (1873—77), Framl. III RDn (1877—1961), Framl. II RDn (1961—*)

SEQ 11   Framl. RDn (until 1865), Framl. III RDn (1865—73), Framl. II RDn (1873—77), Framl. III RDn (1877—93), Gosc. I RDn (1893—*)

SEQ 12   Framl. RDn (until 1865), Framl. IV RDn (1865—73), Framl. I RDn (1873—*)

SEQ 13   Gart. RDn (until 1865), Gart. I RDn (1865—*)

SEQ 14   Gart. RDn (until 1865), Gart. I RDn (1865—73), Gart. III RDn (1873—*)

SEQ 15   Gart. RDn (until 1865), Gart. II RDn (1865—*)

SEQ 16   Gart. RDn (until 1865), Gart. II RDn (1865—73), Gosc. I RDn (1873—*)

SEQ 17   Gosc. RDn (until 1865), Gosc. I RDn (1865—*)

SEQ 18   Gosc. RDn (until 1865), Gosc. I RDn (1865—93), Christianity RDn (1893—*)

SEQ 19   Gosc. RDn (until 1865), Gosc. I RDn (1865—73), Gart. III RDn (1873—*)

SEQ 20   Gosc. RDn (until 1865), Gosc. I RDn (1865—73), Gosc. III RDn (1873—*)

SEQ 21   Gosc. RDn (until 1865), Gosc. I RDn (1865—73), Gosc. II RDn (1893—*)

SEQ 22   Gosc. RDn (until 1865), Gosc. II RDn (1865—*)

SEQ 23   Gosc. RDn (until 1865), Gosc. II RDn (1865—93), E Akeley RDn (1893—*)

SEQ 24   Gosc. RDn (until 1865), Gosc. II RDn (1865—93), Framl. III RDn (1893—1961), Framl. II RDn (1961—*)

SEQ 25   Guthl. RDn (until 1865), Guthl. I RDn (1865—*)

SEQ 26   Guthl. RDn (until 1865), Guthl. I RDn (1865—93), Gart. II RDn (1893—*)

SEQ 27   Guthl. RDn (until 1865), Guthl. I RDn (1865—93), Spark. II RDn (1893—*)

SEQ 28   Guthl. RDn (until 1865), Guthl. I RDn (1865—1928), Spark. III RDn (1928—*)

SEQ 29   Guthl. RDn (until 1865), Guthl. II RDn (1865—*)

SEQ 30   Guthl. RDn (until 1865), Guthl. II RDn (1865—73), Guthl. I RDn (1873—*)

SEQ 31   Guthl. RDn (until 1865), Guthl. II RDn (1865—1928), Spark. II RDn (1928—*)

SEQ 32   Guthl. RDn (until 1865), Guthl. III RDn (1865—1928), Guthl. I RDn (1928—*)

SEQ 33   Guthl. RDn (until 1865), Guthl. III RDn (1865—1928), Guthl. II RDn (1928—*)

SEQ 34   Spark. RDn (until 1865), Spark. I RDn (1865—*)

SEQ 35   Spark. RDn (until 1865), Spark. I RDn (1865—93), S Akeley RDn (1893—*)

SEQ 36   Spark. RDn (until 1865), Spark. I RDn (1865—93), S Akeley RDn (1893—1928), Spark. I RDn (1928—*)

SEQ 37   Spark. RDn (until 1865), Spark. I RDn (1865—93), Spark. II RDn (1893—*)

SEQ 38   Spark. RDn (until 1865), Spark. II RDn (1865—*)

SEQ 39   Spark. RDn (until 1865), Spark. II RDn (1865—93), Spark. I RDn (1893—*)

DIOCESES AND ARCHDEACONRIES

Leics pars were organised in Archdeaconries and Rural Deaneries as follows:

LEICESTER DIOC (1926—*)

Leicester AD: Christianity RDn, Framl. I RDn, Framl. II RDn, Framl. III RDn (1926—61), Gart. I RDn, Gart. II RDn, Gart. III RDn, Gosc. I RDn, Gosc. II RDn

Loughborough AD: E Akeley RDn, S Akeley RDn, W Akeley RDn, Guthl. I RDn, Guthl. II RDn, Guthl. III RDn, Spark. I RDn, Spark. II RDn, Spark. III RDn

LINCOLN DIOC (until 1837)

Leicester AD: Akeley RDn, Christianity RDn, Framl. RDn, Gart. RDn, Gosc. RDn, Guthl. RDn, Spark. RDn

PETERBOROUGH DIOC (1837—1926)

Leicester AD: Akeley RDn (1837—66), E Akeley RDn (1875—1926), S Akeley RDn (1893—26), W Akeley RDn (1875—1926), Akeley I RDn (1866—75), Akeley II RDn (1866—75), Christianity RDn, Framl. RDn (1837—66), Framl. I RDn (1866—1926), Framl. II RDn (1866—1926), Framl. III RDn (1866—1926), Framl. IV RDn (1866—73), Gart. RDn (1837—66), Gart. I RDn (1866—1926), Gart. II RDn (1866—1926), Gart. III RDn, (1873—1926), Gosc. RDn (1837—66), Gosc. I RDn (1866—1921), Gosc. II RDn (1866—1926), Guthl. RDn (1837—66), Guthl. I RDn (1866—1921), Guthl. II RDn (1866—1921), Guthl. III RDn (1866—1921), Spark. RDn (1837—66), Spark. I RDn (1866—1921), Spark. II RDn (1866—1921)

Loughborough AD (1921—26): Guthl. I RDn, Guthl. II RDn, Guthl. III RDn, Spark. I RDn, Spark. II RDn

THE PARISHES OF LEICESTERSHIRE

AB KETTLEBY

AP Incl chap Holwell (sep CP 1866,[1] not sep eccl hence this par eccl 'Ab Kettleby with Holwell', qv). *LG* Seq 2. Addtl civ bdry alt: 1884,[2] 1936 (gains Holwell CP, Wartnaby CP).[3] *Parl* Seq 1.

AB KETTLEBY WITH HOLWELL

AP Usual eccl spelling; for civ and civ sep chap, see prev entry. Framl. RDn (until 1865), Framl. III RDn (1865—73), Framl. II RDn (1873—77), Framl. III RDn (1877—1932). Abol eccl 1932 to help cr Ab Kettleby with Wartnaby and Holwell EP.[4]

AB KETTLEBY WITH WARTNABY AND HOLWELL

EP Cr 1932 by union Ab Kettleby with Holwell AP, pt Grimston with Wartnaby AP (area of Wartnaby CP).[4] Framl. III RDn (1932—61), Framl. II RDn (1961—*).

ALEXTON

AP Usual eccl spelling; for civ see 'Allexton'. *Eccl* Gosc. RDn (until 1865), Gosc. I RDn (1865—73), Gosc. III RDn (1873—1927). Abol eccl 1927 to help cr Alexton with East Norton EP.[5]

EP Cr 1961 when chap East Norton severed from Alexton with East Norton EP to help cr Tugby and East Norton EP, the remainder to be 'Alexton'.[6] Gart. III RDn.

ALEXTON WITH EAST NORTON

EP Cr 1927 by union Alexton AP (civ, 'Allexton'), chap East Norton in Tugby with East Norton AP.[5] Gart. III RDn. Abol 1961 when area East Norton severed to help cr Tugby and East Norton EP, the remainder to be 'Alexton'.[6]

ALLEXTON

AP Usual civ spelling; for eccl see 'Alexton'. *LG* Seq 7. *Parl* Seq 2.

ANSTEY

Chap (pec jurisd Groby, until 1851) in Thurcaston AP, sep CP 1866,[1] sep EP 1866.[7] *LG* Seq 11. Civ bdry: 1884,[8] 1935 (incl loses pt to Leic CB [assoc with Leics] & CP, pt to help cr Glenfields CP),[9] 1936,[10] 1953,[11] 1966 (exchanges pts with Leic CB [assoc with Leics] & CP).[12] *Parl* Seq 5. *Eccl* E Akeley RDn (1866—93), Guthl. I RDn (1893—1928), Spark. III RDn (1928—*). Eccl bdry: 1974.[13]

ANSTEY PASTURES

Ex-par place, sep CP 1858.[14] *LG* W Gosc. Hd, Barr. upon S. PLU (1858—1930), RSD, RD. Abol 1935 pt to Anstey CP, pt to help cr Glenfields CP.[9] *Parl* N'rn Dv (1832—85), Mid Dv (1885—1918), Melt. Dv (1918—48).

APPLEBY

AP Pt Leics (Spark. Hd), pt Derbys (Repley & Gresley Hd). *LG* Ashb. de la Z. PLU, RSD. Abol civ 1889 to cr 2 CPs, one in ea co, each 'Appleby'.[15] *Parl* Leics pt, S'rn Dv (1832—85), W'rn Dv (1885—1918). *Eccl* Spark. RDn (until 1865), Spark. II RDn (1865—73), Spark. I RDn (1873—93), W Akeley RDn (1893—*).

CP Cr 1889 from the Leics pt of Appleby AP (Leics, Derbys).[15] *LG* Ashb. de la Z. PLU, RSD. Renamed 1897 'Appleby Magna South'.[16]

APPLEBY MAGNA

CP Cr 1898 by union Appleby Magna North CP, Appleby Magna South CP.[17] *LG* Ashb. de la Z. PLU, RD. Bdry: 1965 (loses pt to Newton Regis AP, Warws).[18] *Parl* Loughb. Dv/CC (1918—*).

APPLEBY MAGNA NORTH

CP Appleby CP (cr 1889 in Derbys from the pt in that co of Appleby AP) transf 1897 from Derbys to Leics and renamed 'Appleby Magna North'.[16] *LG* Ashb. de la Z. PLU, RD. Abol 1898 to help cr Appleby Magna CP.[17]

APPLEBY MAGNA SOUTH

CP Renaming 1897 of Appleby CP.[16] *LG* Ashb. de la Z. PLU, RD. Abol 1898 to help cr Appleby Magna CP.[17]

ARNESBY

AP *LG* Seq 15. *Parl* Seq 10. *Eccl* Guthl. RDn (until 1865), Guthl. III RDn (1865—1927). Abol eccl 1927 to help cr Arnesby with Shearsby EP.[19]

ARNESBY WITH SHEARSBY

EP Cr 1927 by union Arnesby AP, chap Shearsby in Knaptoft AP.[19] Guthl. III RDn (1927—28), Guthl. I RDn (1928—*).

ASFORDBY

AP *LG* Seq 9. Civ bdry: 1935,[9] 1936 (gains Welby CP).[3] *Parl* Seq 1. *Eccl* Seq 24.

ASHBY DE LA ZOUCH

AP Incl pt chap Blackfordby (sep CP 1866,[1] sep EP 1876,[20] qv for other constituent pars in each case). *LG* W Gosc. Hd, Ashb. de la Z. PLU, pt Ashb. de la Z. USD, pt Ashb. Woulds USD, Ashb. de la Z. UD. Addtl civ bdry alt: 1884 (help cr Ravenstone with Snibstone CP),[21] 1894 (the pt in Ashb. Woulds UD cr Ashby Woulds CP),[22] 1936,[23] 1956.[24] *Parl* Seq 6. *Eccl* Seq 5. Addtl eccl bdry alt: 1840 (cr Ashby de la Zouch Holy Trinity EP,[25] refounded 1860[26]), 1846 (help cr Woodville EP,[25] refounded 1847,[27] qv for other constituent pt from Derbys).

ASHBY DE LA ZOUCH HOLY TRINITY

EP Cr 1840 from Ashby de la Zouch AP.[25] refounded 1860.[26] W Akeley RDn. Bdry: 1876 (help cr Blackfordby EP).[20]

ASHBY FOLVILLE

AP Incl chap Barsby (pec jurisd Manor of Rothley [until 1851], sep CP 1866[1]). *LG* E Gosc. Hd, Melt. Mowb. PLU, RSD, RD (1894—1935), Melt. & Belv. RD (1935—36). Addtl civ bdry alt: 1883,[28] 1884.[2] Abol civ 1936 ent to Gaddesby CP.[3] *Parl* N'rn Dv (1832—85), E'rn Dv (1885—1918), Melt. Dv (1918—48). *Eccl* Seq 17.

ASHBY MAGNA

AP *LG* Seq 15. Civ bdry: 1877.[29] *Parl* Seq 10. *Eccl* Guthl. RDn (until 1865), Guthl. III RDn (1865—1928), Guthl. II RDn (1928—52), Guthl. I RDn (1952—*).

ASHBY PARVA

AP *LG* Seq 15. Civ bdry: 1877,[29] 1877,[30] 1877.[31] *Parl* Seq 10. *Eccl* Seq 29.

ASHBY WOULDS

CP Cr 1894 from the pt of Ashby de la Zouch AP in Ashb. Woulds UD.[22] *LG* Ashb. de la Z. PLU, Ashb. Woulds UD. Bdry: 1897 (help cr Woodville CP, to be in Derbys),[32] 1936,[23] 1956.[24] *Parl* Loughb. Dv/CC (1918—*).

ASTON FLAMVILLE

AP Incl chap Burbage ([earlier, 'Burbage and Sketchley', the latter a hmlt] sep CP 1866 as 'Burbage',[1] not sep eccl hence this par eccl 'Aston Flamville with Burbage', qv). *LG* Seq 18. *Parl* Seq 13.

ASTON FLAMVILLE WITH BURBAGE

AP Usual eccl spelling; for civ and civ sep chap, see prev entry. *Eccl* Guthl. RDn (until 1865), Guthl. II (1865—73), Spark. II RDn (1873—*).

ATTERTON

Hmlt (orig chap, early destroyed) in Witherley AP, sep CP 1866.[1] *LG* Spark. Hd, Ath. PLU (soon after 1836[33]—1930), RSD, Mkt. Bosw. RD. Bdry: 1885.[34] Abol 1935 ent to Witherley AP.[9] *Parl* S'rn Dv (1832—85), W'rn Dv (1885—1918), Bosw. Dv (1918—48).

AYLESTONE

AP Tp 'Aylestone' in Guthl. Hd as was chap Glen Parva (sep CP 1866,[1] eccl severed 1893 to help cr Glen Parva with South Wigston EP[35]); incl in Spark. Hd chap Lubbesthorpe (sep CP 1866,[1] eccl severed 1902 and transf to Enderby AP[36]). *LG* Blaby PLU (1836—92), Leic PLU (1892—96), Leic CB (1892—96), Blaby RSD (1875—92), Leic USD (1892—94). Addtl civ bdry alt: 1885,[37] 1892 (the pt not made pt of Leic CB transf to Lubbesthorpe CP).[38] Abol civ 1896 to help cr Leicester CP.[39] *Parl* S'rn Dv (1832—85), Guthl. I RDn (1865—93), Christianity RDn (1893—*). Addtl eccl bdry alt: 1881 (cr Aylestone Park EP),[40] 1951 (help cr Leicester St Christopher EP),[41] 1962 (help cr Eyres Monsell EP).[42]

AYLESTONE PARK

EP Cr 1881 from Aylestone AP.[40] Guthl. I RDn (1881—93), Christianity RDn (1893—*). Bdry: 1951 (help cr Leicester St Christopher EP).[41]

BAGWORTH

Chap in Thornton AP, sep CP 1866.[1] *LG* Seq 19. Bdry: 1886,[43] 1935 (gains Thornton AP).[9] *Parl* Seq 12.

BARDON

Ex-par place, sep CP 1858,[14] eccl abol 1960 to help cr Copt Oak EP.[44] *LG* Spark. Hd, Ashb. de la Z. PLU (1862—1930) RSD, RD. Bdry: 1893 (gains the pt of Hugglescote and Donington CP not in Coalville USD),[45] 1935,[9] 1936,[23] 1959,[46] 1969.[47] *Parl* S'rn Dv (1832—85), Mid Dv (1885—1918), Bosw. Dv (1918—48), Loughb. CC (1948—*). Parl bdry: 1955,[48] 1972.[49]

BARDON HILL

EP Cr 1918 from Huggglescote with Donington EP.[50] S Akeley RDn. Bdry: 1962,[51] 1962 (help cr Broom Leys EP),[52] 1966.[53]

BARKBY

AP Incl chap Barkby Thorpe, chap North Thurmaston (each a sep CP 1866[1]). *LG* Seq 6. Addtl civ bdry alt: 1897,[54] 1914,[55] 1935.[9] *Parl* Seq 1. *Eccl* Seq 21.

BARKBY THORPE

Chap in Barkby AP, sep CP 1866.[1] *LG* Seq 6. Bdry: 1897.[54] *Parl* Seq 1.

BARKESTONE

AP *LG* Framl. Hd, Bing. PLU, RSD, Belv. RD (1894—1935), Melt. & Belv. RD (1935—36). Abol civ 1936 ent to Redmile AP.[3] *Parl* N'rn Dv (1832—85), E'rn Dv (1885—1918), Melt. Dv (1918—48).

BARLESTONE

Chap in Market Bosworth AP, sep CP 1866,[1] sep EP 1914.[56] *LG* Seq 19. Civ bdry: 1883,[28] 1935.[9] *Parl* Seq 12. *Eccl* Spark. I RDn.

BARROW UPON SOAR

AP Tp 'Barrow upon Soar' in E Gosc. Hd; incl in W. Gosc. Hd chap Woodhouse (sep CP 1866,[1] sep EP

1784,[25] eccl refounded 1868 incl pt ex-par [not sep civ] Beau Manor[57]), hmlt Maplewell Longdale (sep CP 1866[1]), tp Mountsorrel North End (sep CP 1866,[1] eccl in chap and bor Mountsorrel, the pt in this par a sep EP 1868 as 'Mountsorrel St Peter',[57] qv for other constituent par and for pec jurisd), tp Quorndon (sep CP 1866,[1] sep EP 1728 as 'Quorn,'[25] as such eccl refounded 1868[57]). *LG* Pt Mountsorrel Bor, Barr. upon S. PLU, RSD, RD. Addtl civ bdry alt: 1884,[58] 1896.[59] *Parl* Seq 5. *Eccl* Seq 1. Addtl eccl bdry alt: 1839 (help cr Woodhouse Eaves EP,[25] refounded 1844[60]).

BARSBY
Chap (pec jurisd Manor of Rothley, until 1851) in Ashby Folville AP, sep CP 1866.[1] *LG* E Gosc. Hd, Melt. Mowb. PLU, RSD, RD (1894—1935), Melt. & Belv. RD (1935—36). Bdry: 1884,[61] 1884.[2] Abol 1936 ent to Gaddesby CP.[3] *Parl* N'rn Dv (1832—85), E'rn Dv (1885—1918), Melt. Dv (1918—48).

BARTON IN THE BEANS
Tp in Nailstone AP, sep CP 1866.[1] *LG* Spark. Hd, Mkt. Bosw. PLU, RSD, RD. Bdry: 1883,[28] 1886.[43] Abol 1935 ent to Shackerstone AP.[9] *Parl* S'rn Dv (1832—85), W'rn Dv (1885—1918), Bosw. Dv (1918—48).

BARWELL
AP Incl chap Potters Marston, chap Stapleton (each a sep CP 1866,[1] neither sep eccl hence this par eccl 'Barwell with Stapleton and Potters Marston', qv). *LG* Spark. Hd, Hinck. PLU, RSD, RD. Addtl bdry alt: 1920.[62] Abol 1936 ent to Hinck. UD & AP.[19] *Parl* S'rn Dv (1832—85), W'rn Dv (1885—1918), Bosw. Dv (1918—48).

BARWELL WITH STAPLETON AND POTTERS MARSTON
AP Usual eccl spelling; for civ and civ sep chaps, see prev entry. *Eccl* Seq 38.

BEAUMONT LEYS
Ex-par place, sep CP 1858.[14] *LG* W Gosc. Hd, Barr. upon S. PLU (1858—1930), RSD, RD. Bdry: 1892 (gains the pt of Leicester Abbey CP not in Leic CB[38]). Abol civ 1935 pt to Anstey CP, pt to Leic CB (assoc with Leics) & CP, pt to Thurcaston AP.[9] *Parl* N'rn Dv (1832—85), Mid Dv (1885—1918), Melt. Dv (1918—48).

BEEBY
AP *LG* Seq 6. *Parl* Seq 1. *Eccl* Seq 17.

BELGRAVE
AP Tp 'Belgrave' in E Gosc. Hd as was chap Thurmaston (sep EP 1794,[25] sep CP 1866 as 'South Thurmaston'[1]); incl in W Gosc. Hd chap Birstall (sep CP 1866,[1] sep EP 1928[64]). *LG* Barr. upon S. PLU (1837—92), Leic PLU (1892—96), Leic CB (1892—96), pt Barr. upon S. RSD (1875—92), Leic USD (1892—94). Addtl civ bdry alt: 1892 (the pt not in Belgrave USD transf to Beaumont Leys CP).[38] Abol civ 1896 to help cr Leicester CP.[39] *Parl* N'rn Dv (1832—85), E'rn Dv (1885—1918). *Eccl* Seq 18. Addtl eccl bdry alt: 1887 (help cr New Humberstone EP),[65] 1888 (help cr Belgrave St Michael and All Angels EP),[66] 1958 (help cr Stocking Farm EP).[67]

BELGRAVE ST MICHAEL AND ALL ANGELS
EP Cr 1888 from Belgrave AP.[66] Gosc. I RDn (1888—93), Christianity RDn (1893—*). Bdry: 1892,[68] 1906 (help cr Leicester St Alban EP),[69] 1951 (cr Leicester St Gabriel EP).[70]

BELTON
AP *LG* Seq 12. Civ bdry: 1936,[23] 1969.[47] *Parl* Seq 3. Parl bdry: 1972.[49] *Eccl* Seq 3.

BELVOIR
Ex-par place (eccl, 'Belvoir Castle'), sep CP 1858.[14] *LG* Pt Framl. Hd, pt Granth. Soke, Granth. PLU (1861—1930), RSD, Belv. RD (1894—1935), Melt. & Belv. RD (1935—74). Bdry: 1936 (gains Harston AP, Knipton AP),[3] 1965 (loses pt to Denton AP, exchanges pts with Woolsthorpe AP, both Lincs Pts Kestev).[18] *Parl* Seq 1.

BELVOIR CASTLE—see prev entry

BESCABY
Ex-par place, sep CP 1858.[14] *LG* Framl. Hd, Melt. Mowb. PLU (1858—1930), RSD, RD (1894—1935), Melt. & Belv. RD (1935—36). Abol 1936 ent to Sproxton AP.[3] *Parl* N'rn Dv (1832—85), E'rn Dv (1885—1918), Melt. Dv (1918—48).

BILLESDON
AP Incl chap and tp Goadby, chap and tp Rolleston (each a sep CP 1866,[1] neither sep eccl hence this par eccl 'Billesdon cum Goadby and Rolleston', qv). *LG* Seq 3. *Parl* Seq 7.

BILLESDON CUM GOADBY AND ROLLESTON
AP Usual eccl spelling; for civ and civ sep chaps, see prev entry. *Eccl* Gart. RDn (until 1865), Gart. II RDn (1865—73), Gart. III RDn (1873—*).

BILSTONE
Chap in Norton juxta Twycross AP, sep CP 1866.[1] *LG* Spark. Hd, Mkt. Bosw. PLU, RSD, RD. Abol 1935 ent to Shackerstone AP.[9] *Parl* S'rn Dv (1832—85), W'rn Dv (1885—1918), Bosw. Dv (1918—48).

BIRSTALL
Chap in Belgrave AP, sep CP 1866,[1] sep EP 1928.[64] *LG* Seq 11. Civ bdry: 1935 (loses pt to Leic CB [assoc with Leics] & CP),[9] 1966 (exchanges pts with Leic CB [assoc with Leics] & CP).[71] *Parl* Seq 1. *Eccl* Christianity RDn (1928—66), Gosc. II RDn (1966—*). Eccl bdry: 1958 (help cr Stocking Farm EP).[67]

BITTESBY
Lbty (in Leics, orig a chap, early destroyed) in Claybrooke AP (Warws, Leics), sep CP in Leics 1866.[1] *LG* Seq 15. Bdry: 1935 (gains pt Wibtoft CP, pt Willey AP, both Warws).[72] *Parl* Seq 10.

BITTESWELL
AP *LG* Seq 15. *Parl* Seq 10. *Eccl* Seq 29.

BLABY
AP Incl chap Countesthorpe (sep CP 1866,[1] sep EP 1878[73]). *LG* Seq 14. Addtl civ bdry alt: 1935,[9] 1936.[23] *Parl* Seq 10. *Eccl* Seq 25. Addtl eccl bdry alt: 1962.[74]

BLACKFORDBY
Tp pt in Ashby de la Zouch AP, pt in Seal AP, sep CP 1866,[1] sep EP 1876 from Ashby de la Zouch AP, Seal AP, Ashby de la Zouch Holy Trinity EP (all 3 in Leics) and from Woodville EP, Donis-

thorpe EP (both Leics and Derbys) and from ent ex-par place The Boundary (Derbys).[20] *LG* W Gosc. Hd, Ashb. de la Z. PLU, RSD, RD. Civ bdry: 1884,[75] 1897 (help cr Woodville CP, to be in Derbys).[32] Abol civ 1936 pt to Ashb. de la Z. UD & AP, pt to Ashb. Woulds UD & CP.[23] *Parl* N'rn Dv (1832—85), W'rn Dv (1885—1918), Loughb. Dv (1918—48). *Eccl* W Akeley RDn.

BLASTON

AP Orig free chap [St Giles] in Medbourne AP, sep par by early 13th cent.[76] *LG* Seq 5. *Parl* Seq 9. *Eccl* Gart. RDn (until 1865), Gart. I RDn (1865—73), Gart. III RDn (1873—1930). United 1930 with chap Blaston St Michael in Hallaton AP to be 'Blaston' EP.[77]

EP Cr 1930 by union Blaston [St Giles] AP, chap Blaston St Michael in Hallaton AP.[77] Gart. III RDn.

HUSBANDS BOSWORTH

AP *LG* Seq 4. *Parl* Seq 9. *Eccl* Seq 13.

MARKET BOSWORTH

AP Incl chap Carlton (sep CP 1866,[1] sep EP 1868[78]), tp Sutton Cheney (sep CP 1866,[1] sep EP 1860[77]), tp Barlestone (sep CP 1866,[1] sep EP 1914[56]), tp Shenton (sep CP 1866,[1] not sep eccl hence this par eccl 'Market Bosworth with Shenton', qv). *LG* Seq 19. Addtl civ bdry alt: 1883,[28] 1884.[80] *Parl* Seq 12.

MARKET BOSWORTH WITH SHENTON

AP Usual eccl spelling; for civ and civ sep chap and tps, see prev entry. *Eccl* Seq 39. Addtl eccl bdry alt: 1927.[81]

BOTTESFORD

AP *LG* Seq 1. Civ bdry: 1936 (gains Muston AP),[3] 1965 (exchanges pts with Sedgebrook AP, Woolsthorpe AP, both Lincs Pts Kestev).[18] *Parl* Seq 1. *Eccl* Seq 12.

GREAT BOWDEN

AP Incl chap and tp Market Harborough (sep CP 1866,[1] sep EP 1827[25]). *LG* Gart. Hd, Mkt. Harb. PLU, USD, UD. Addtl civ bdry alt: 1924.[82] Abol civ 1927 ent to Market Harborough CP.[83] *Parl* S'rn Dv (1832—1918), Harb. Dv (1918—48). *Eccl* Seq 13. Addtl eccl bdry alt: 1901.[84]

LITTLE BOWDEN

AP Northants par, pt Mkt. Harb. USD (o'wise ent Leics) so that the pt in the USD transf 1889 to Leics.[85] *LG* Mkt. Harb. PLU, UD (pt 1894—96, ent 1896—1927), pt sep RD in Northants (1894—96). Civ bdry: 1896 (loses the pt in Northants [the pt not in the UD] to Great Oxendon AP, Northants, and this par ent Leics thereafter).[86] Abol civ 1927 ent to Market Harborough CP.[83] *Parl* Leics pt, Harb. Dv (1918—48). *Eccl* In dioc Linc until 1541, dioc Peterb 1541—1927, dioc Leic 1927—*: Rothwell RDn (until 1867), Rothwell II RDn (1867—1927), Gart. I RDn (1927—*). Eccl bdry: 1892,[87] 1901,[84] 1920 (cr Little Bowden St Hugh EP).[88]

LITTLE BOWDEN ST HUGH

EP Cr 1920 from Little Bowden AP.[88] Rothwell II RDn (1920—27), Gart. I RDn (dioc Liec, 1927—*).

BRADGATE PARK

Ex-par place (pec jurisd Groby, until 1851), sep CP 1858,[14] bdry alt 1974 for eccl purposes.[13] *LG* W

Gosc. Hd, Barr. upon S. PLU (1858—84), RSD. Abol civ 1884 pt to Ulverscroft CP, pt to Newtown Linford CP, pt to Anstey CP.[8] *Parl* N'rn Dv (1832—85).

BRANSTON

AP *LG* Framl. Hd, Melt. Mowb. PLU, RSD, RD (1894—1935), Melt. & Belv. RD (1935—36). Abol civ 1936 ent to Croxton Kerrial AP.[3] *Parl* N'rn Dv (1832—85), E'rn Dv (1885—1918), Melt. Dv (1918—48). *Eccl* Seq 8.

BRAUNSTONE

Chap in Glenfield AP, sep CP 1866,[1] sep EP 1937.[89] *LG* Spark. Hd, Blaby PLU, RSD, RD. Civ bdry: 1892 (loses the pt transf to Leic CB to Leicester St Mary AP),[38] 1935 (loses pt to Leic CB [assoc with Leics] & CP),[9] 1936,[90] 1966 (exchanges pts with Leic CB [assoc with Leics] & CP).[71] *Parl* S'rn Dv (1832—85), E'rn Dv (1885—1918), Harb. Dv/CC (1918—70), Blaby CC (1970—*). *Eccl* Spark. III RDn. Eccl bdry: 1924 (help cr Leicester The Holy Apostles EP),[91] 1937.[92]

BRAUNSTONE FRITH

Ex-par lbty, sep CP 1858,[14] pt eccl severed 1937 and transf to Braunstone EP.[92] *LG* Spark. Hd, Blaby PLU (1861—1930), RSD, RD. Abol civ 1935 ent to Leic CB (assoc with Leics) & CP.[9] *Parl* S'rn Dv (1832—1918), Harb. Dv (1918—48).

BREEDON ON THE HILL

AP Incl chap and tp Staunton Harrold (sep CP 1866,[1] eccl donative but sep status not sustained), chap Worthington (sep CP 1866,[1] sep EP 1747[25]). *LG* Seq 13. Addtl civ bdry alt: 1936,[23] 1965 (exchanges pts with Medbourne AP, Derbys).[18] *Parl* Seq 3. *Eccl* Seq 5.

BRETINGBY AND WYFORDBY

AP Name used civ in 20th cent (as was at time of civ abol, qv) for AP which was eccl and earlier civ called 'Wyfordby', qv.

BRINGHURST

AP Incl tp Drayton (orig chap, early desecrated, sep CP 1866[1]), chap and tp Great Easton (sep CP 1866,[1] not sep eccl hence this par eccl 'Bringhurst cum Great Easton', qv). *LG* Seq 5. *Parl* Seq 9.

BRINGHURST CUM GREAT EASTON

AP Usual eccl spelling; for civ and civ sep chaps, see prev entry. *Eccl* Seq 14.

BROOKSBY

AP *LG* E Gosc. Hd, Melt. Mowb. PLU, RSD, RD (1894—1935), Melt. & Belv. RD (1935—36). Abol civ 1936 to help cr Hoby with Rotherby CP.[3] *Parl* N'rn Dv (1832—85), E'rn Dv (1885—1918), Melt. Dv (1918—48). *Eccl* Seq 22.

BROOM LEYS

EP Cr 1962 from Whitwick AP, Bardon Hill EP, Copt Oak EP.[52] S Akeley RDn. Bdry: 1966.[53]

NETHER BROUGHTON

AP *LG* Framl. Hd, Melt. Mowb PLU, RSD, RD (1894—1935), Melt. & Belv. RD (1936—36). Abol civ 1936 to help cr Broughton and Old Dalby CP.[3] *Parl* N'rn Dv (1832—85), E'rn Dv (1885—1918), Melt. Dv (1918—48). *Eccl* Framl. RDn (until 1865), Framl. IV RDn (1865—73), Framl. II RDn (1873—77), Framl. III RDn (1877—1961), Framl.

II RDn (1961—*).

BROUGHTON AND OLD DALBY

CP Cr 1936 by union Nether Broughton AP, Old Dalby AP.[3] *LG* Melt. & Belv. RD. Bdry: 1965 (loses pt to Upper Broughton AP, Notts).[18] *Parl* Melt. CC (1948—*).

BROUGHTON ASTLEY

AP *LG* Seq 15. Civ bdry: 1885,[93] 1935.[9] *Parl* Seq 10. *Eccl* Guthl. RDn (until 1865), Guthl. II RDn (1865—1928), Guthl. I RDn (1928—*).

BRUNTINGTHORPE

AP *LG* Seq 15. *Parl* Seq 10. *Eccl* Seq 32.

BUCKMINSTER

AP Incl chap Sewstern (sep CP 1866,[1] not sep eccl hence this par eccl 'Buckminster with Sewstern', qv). *LG* Seq 2. Addtl civ bdry alt: 1884,[94] 1936 (gains Sewstern CP),[3] 1965 (gains pt Colsterworth AP, exchanges pts with Stainby CP, Skillington AP, all Lincs Pts Kestev).[18] *Parl* Seq 1.

BUCKMINSTER WITH SEWSTERN

AP Usual eccl spelling; for civ and civ sep chap, see prev entry. *Eccl* Framl. RDn (until 1865), Framl. I RDn (1865—77), Framl. RDn (1877—*).

BURBAGE

Chap (earlier, 'Burbage and Sketchley') in Aston Flamville AP, sep CP 1866.[1] *LG* Spark. Hd, Hinck. PLU, RSD, RD. Bdry: 1928.[95] Abol 1936 ent to Hinck. UD & AP.[63] *Parl* S'rn Dv (1832—85), W'rn Dv (1885—1918), Bosw. Dv (1918—48).

BURROUGH ON THE HILL

AP *LG* Gart. Hd, Melt. Mowb. PLU, RSD, RD (1894—1935), Melt. & Belv. RD (1935—36). Civ bdry: 1887.[96] Abol civ 1936 ent to Somerby AP.[3] *Parl* N'rn Dv (1832—85), E'rn Dv (1885—1918), Melt. Dv (1918—48). *Eccl* Seq 11.

BURTON AND DALBY

CP Cr 1936 by union Burton Lazars CP, Great Dalby AP, Little Dalby AP.[3] *LG* Melt. & Belv. RD. *Parl* Melt. CC (1948—*).

BURTON LAZARS

Tp in Melton Mowbray AP, sep CP 1866.[1] *LG* Framl. Hd, Melt. Mowb. PLU, RSD, RD (1894—1935), Melt. & Belv. RD (1936—36). Bdry: 1935.[9] Abol 1936 to help cr Burton and Dalby CP.[3] *Parl* N'rn Dv (1832—85), E'rn Dv (1885—1918), Melt. Dv (1918—48).

BURTON ON THE WOLDS

Tp in Prestwold AP, sep CP 1866.[1] *LG* Seq 8. Bdry: 1965 (gains pt Willoughby on the Wolds AP, Notts).[18] *Parl* Seq 4.

BURTON OVERY

AP *LG* Seq 3. *Parl* Seq 11. *Eccl* Seq 15.

BUSHBY

Hmlt in Thurnby AP, sep CP 1866.[1] *LG* Gart. Hd, Bill. PLU, RSD, RD. Abol 1935 ent to Thurnby AP.[9] *Parl* S'rn Dv (1832—85), E'rn Dv (1885—1918), Melt. Dv (1918—48).

CADEBY

AP Incl tp Osbaston (sep CP 1866[1]). *LG* Seq 19. Addtl civ bdry alt: 1884.[80] *Parl* Seq 12. *Eccl* Seq 39.

CARLTON

Chap in Market Bosworth AP, sep CP 1866,[1] sep EP 1868.[78] *LG* Seq 19. *Parl* Seq 12. *Eccl* Spark. II

RDn (1868—93), Spark. I RDn (1893—*). *Eccl* bdry: 1927.[81]

CARLTON CURLIEU

AP Incl chap and tp Ilston on the Hill (sep CP 1866,[1] sep EP 1972 as 'Illston on the Hill',[97] so that this par eccl 'Carlton Curlieu with Illston on the Hill' until 1972, 'Carlton Curlieu' thereafter). *LG* Seq 3. *Parl* Seq 11. *Eccl* Gart. II RDn.

CARLTON CURLIEU WITH ILLSTON ON THE HILL

AP Usual eccl spelling until chap and tp Illston on the Hill (civ, 'Ilston on the Hill', qv) a sep EP 1972,[97] the main pt of the par thereafter 'Carlton Curlieu' EP; for civ and civ sep chap, see prev entry. *Eccl* Gart. RDn (until 1865), Gart. II RDn (1865—1972).

CASTLE DONINGTON

AP *LG* Seq 13. Civ bdry: 1936 (help cr Isley cum Langley CP),[23] 1965 (gains pt Weston upon Trent AP, exchanges pts with Shardlow and Great Wilne CP, Melbourne AP, all Derbys).[18] *Parl* Seq 3. *Eccl* Seq 6.

CATTHORPE

AP *LG* Seq 15. Civ bdry: 1935 (incl loses pt to Newton and Biggin CP, Warws).[72] *Parl* Seq 10. *Eccl* Seq 29.

CHARLEY

Ex-par place, sep CP 1858,[14] eccl abol 1860 to help cr Copt Oak EP.[44] *LG* Seq 12. Bdry: 1885,[98] 1885,[99] 1936.[23] *Parl* Seq 3.

CHARNWOOD FOREST

EP Pt of the area of the forest in pec jurisd Groby (until 1851); 'Charnwood Forest' a sep EP 1852 from Newton Linford AP, Whitwick AP, Sheepshed AP, Woodhouse Eaves EP.[100] Sometimes 'Oaks Church'. Akeley RDn (1852—65), E Akeley RDn (1865—93), S Akeley RDn (1893—*). Bdry: 1860 (help cr Copt Oak EP).[44]

CHARNWOOD FOREST COPT OAK—see COPT OAK

CHARNWOOD FOREST OAKS CHURCH—see CHARNWOOD FOREST

CHILCOTE

CP Derbys par, transf 1897 to Leics.[32] *LG* Ashb. de la Z. PLU, RD. Bdry: 1965 (loses pt to Newton Regis AP, Warws).[101] *Parl* Loughb. Dv/CC (1918—*).

LONG CLAWSON

AP *LG* Framl. Hd, Melt. Mowb. PLU, RSD, RD (1894—1935), Melt. & Belv. RD (1935—36). Abol civ 1936 to help cr Clawson and Harby CP.[3] *Parl* N'rn Dv (1832—85), E'rn Dv (1885—1918), Melt. Dv (1918—48). *Eccl* Framl. RDn (until 1865), Framl. IV RDn (1865—73), Framl. III RDn (1873—1961), Framl. II RDn (1961—*).

CLAWSON AND HARBY

CP Cr 1936 by union Long Clawson AP, Harby AP, Hose AP.[3] *LG* Melt. & Belv. RD. *Parl* Melt. CC (1948—*).

CLAYBROOKE

AP Incl in Warws chap Wibtoft (Knightlow Hd, sep CP 1866 in Warws,[1] not sep eccl hence this par eccl 'Claybrooke with Wibtoft'); incl in Leics lbty (orig chap, early destroyed) Bittesby, tps Great Claybrook, Little Claybrook, hmlt Ullesthorpe, chap Wigston Parva (each a sep CP 1866[1]) so that

'Claybrooke' has no sep civ after 1866 in either co. *LG* Leics pt, Guthl. Hd. *Parl* Leics pt, S'rn Dv (1832—67).

CLAYBROOKE CUM WIBTOFT
AP Usual eccl spelling; for civ and civ sep all units, incl chap Wibtoft in Warws, see prev entry. *Eccl* Seq 29.

CLAYBROOKE MAGNA
Tp in Claybrooke AP, sep CP 1866.[1] *LG* Seq 15. Bdry: 1885.[102] *Parl* Seq 10.

CLAYBROOKE PARVA
Tp in Claybrooke AP, sep CP 1866.[1] *LG* Seq 15. Bdry: 1885,[102] 1925 (gains pt Wibtoft CP, Warws).[72] *Parl* Seq 10.

COALVILLE
EP Cr 1840,[25] refounded soon after in that year from Ibstock AP, Whitwick AP, Packington AP.[103] Spark. RDn (1840—65), Spark. I RDn (1865—93), S Akeley RDn (1893—*). Bdry: 1962.[51]
CP Cr 1894 from Hugglescote and Donnington CP, Ravenstone and Snibston CP, Swannington, Whitwick AP.[104] *LG* Ashb. de la Z. PLU, Coalville UD. Civ bdry: 1912,[105] 1936,[23] 1954,[46] 1969.[47] *Parl* Bosw. Dv/CC (1918—*). Parl bdry: 1955,[48] 1972.[49]

COLD NEWTON
Tp in Lowesby AP, sep CP 1866.[1] *Parl* Seq 2.

COLE ORTON
AP Usual eccl spelling; for civ see following entry. *Eccl* Seq 5. Eccl bdry: 1939.[106]

COLEORTON
AP Usual civ spelling; for eccl see prev entry. *LG* W Gosc. Hd, Ashb. de la Z. PLU (soon after 1836[33]—1930), RSD. RD. Civ bdry: 1884,[107] 1936.[23] *Parl* Seq 6.

CONGERSTON—see following entry
CONGERSTONE
AP Sometimes earlier 'Congerston'. *LG* Spark. Hd, Mkt. Bosw. PLU, RSD, RD. Civ bdry: 1884,[80] 1886.[43] Abol civ 1935 ent to Shakerstone AP.[9] *Parl* S'rn Dv (1832—85), W'rn Dv (1885—1918), Bosw. Dv (1918—48). *Eccl* Seq 36.

COPT OAK
EP Cr 1860 from pts of ex-par Ulverscroft, Marksfield AP, Newtown Linford AP, Woodhouse Eaves EP, Charnwood Forest [Oaks Church] EP, Whitwick AP, and ent ex-par Charley, ex-par Bardon.[44] Sometimes 'Charnwood Forest Copt Oak'. Akeley RDn (1860—65), E Akeley RDn (1865—93), S Akeley RDn (1893—*). Bdry: 1962 (help cr Broom Leys EP).[52]

COSBY
AP *LG* Seq 14. Civ bdry: 1885,[37] 1935.[9] *Parl* Seq 10. *Eccl* Seq 25.

COSSINGTON
AP *LG* Seq 6. Civ bdry: 1935.[9] *Parl* Seq 1. *Eccl* Seq 22.

COSTON
AP Incl undivided pt Lands Common to Coston and Garthorpe. *LG* Framl. Hd, Melt. Mowb. PLU, RSD, RD (1894—1935), Melt. & Belv. RD (1935—36). Abol civ 1936, the par and the undivided pt of

Lands Common to Coston and Garthorpe ent to Garthorpe AP.[3] *Parl* N'rn Dv (1832—85), E'rn Dv (1885—1918), Melt. Dv (1918—48). *Eccl* Framl. RDn (until 1865), Framl. I RDn (1865—77), Framl. II RDn (1877—1961), Framl. I RDn (1961—*).

COTES
Tp in Prestwold AP, sep CP 1866.[1] *LG* Seq 8. *Parl* Seq 4.

COTESBACH
AP *LG* Seq 15. Civ bdry: 1935 (loses pt to Churchover AP, Warws).[72] *Parl* Seq 10. *Eccl* Seq 29.

COUNTESTHORPE
Chap in Blaby AP, sep CP 1866,[1] sep EP 1878.[73] *LG* Seq 14. Civ bdry: 1935,[9] 1936.[23] *Parl* Seq 10. *Eccl* Guthl. I RDn.

CRANOE
AP Perhaps orig dependent on Welham AP,[108] early indept or orig sep. *LG* Seq 4. *Parl* Seq 9. *Eccl* Seq 13.

CROFT
AP *LG* Seq 17. Civ bdry: 1885.[93] *Parl* Seq 10. *Eccl* Seq 27.

CROPSTON
Tp (pec jurisd Groby, until 1851) in Thurcaston AP, sep CP 1866.[1] *LG* W Gosc. Hd, Barr. upon S. PLU, RSD, RD. Abol 1935 ent to Thurcaston AP.[9] *Parl* N'rn Dv (1832—85), Mid Dv (1885—1918), Melt. Dv (1918—48).

SOUTH CROXTON
AP *LG* Seq 6. Civ bdry: 1884,[61] 1884.[2] *Parl* Seq 1. *Eccl* Pec jurisd Manor of Rothley (until 1851), Seq 17 thereafter.

CROXTON KERRIAL
AP *LG* Seq 1. Civ bdry: 1936 (gains Branston AP),[3] 1965 (loses pt to Denton AP, pt to Wyville cum Hungerton AP, both Lincs Pts Kestev).[18] *Parl* Seq 1. *Eccl* Seq 8.

DADLINGTON
Chap in Hinckley AP, sep CP 1866,[1] eccl united 1865 with chap Stoke Goldington in same par to cr Stoke Goldington cum Dadlington EP.[109] *LG* Spark. Hd, Mkt. Bosw. PLU, RSD, RD. Abol civ 1935 ent to Sutton Cheney AP.[9] *Parl* S'rn Dv (1832—85), W'rn Dv (1885—1918), Bosw. Dv (1918—48).

GREAT DALBY
AP *LG* E Gosc. Hd, Melt. Mowb. PLU, RSD, RD (1894—1935), Melt. & Belv. RD (1936—36). Abol civ 1936 to help cr Burton and Dalby CP.[3] *Parl* N'rn Dv (1832—85), E'rn Dv (1885—1918), Melt. Dv (1918—48). *Eccl* Gosc. RDn (until 1865), Gosc. II RDn (1865—93), Gosc. I RDn (1893—*).

LITTLE DALBY
AP *LG* Framl. Hd, Melt. Mowb. PLU, RSD, RD (1894—1935), Melt. & Belv. RD (1935—36). Abol civ 1936 to help cr Burton and Dalby CP.[3] *Parl* N'rn Dv (1832—85), E'rn Dv (1885—1918), Melt. Dv (1918—48). *Eccl* Seq 11.

OLD DALBY
AP *LG* E Gosc. Hd, Melt. Mowb. PLU, RSD, RD (1894—1935), Melt. & Belv. RD (1935—36). Abol civ 1936 to help cr Broughton and Old Dalby CP.[3] *Parl* N'rn Dv (1832—85), E'rn Dv (1885—1918), Melt. Dv (1918—48). *Eccl* Donative, sometimes

'Dalby on the Wolds', Seq 24.

DESFORD

AP *LG* Seq 19. Civ bdry: 1936.[23] *Parl* Seq 12. *Eccl* Seq 28.

DISEWORTH

AP *LG* W Gosc. Hd, Shard. PLU, RSD, Cast. Don. RD. Abol civ 1936 ent to Long Whatton AP.[23] *Parl* N'rn Dv (1832—85), Mid Dv (1885—1918), Loughb. Dv (1918—48).

DISHLEY

AP Curacy appropriated to Garendon Abbey, sometimes called chap, donative of Earl of Rutland[110]; incl hmlt Thorpe Acre and hence civ 'Thorpe Acre and Dishley', qv. *Eccl* Akeley RDn. Eccl bdry: 1850 (cr Thorpe Acre EP).[111] Abol eccl 1921 to help cr Thorpe Acre with Dishley EP.[112]

DONISTHORPE

Hmlt in Church Gresley AP, Measham AP (both Derbys) and in Seal AP, Ashby de la Zouch AP (both Leics), sep EP 1869 as 'Donisthorpe',[113] the area civ united with hmlt Oakthorpe (ent Derbys, Repton and Gresley Hd) in Church Gresley AP, Stretton en le Field AP, Measham AP and the entire area a sep CP 1866 as 'Oakthorpe and Donisthorpe' with pt in ea co,[1] qv. In dioc Lichf 1869—84, dioc S'well 1884—1927, dioc Leic (1927—*): Hartshorne RDn (1869—87), Repton RDn (1887—1927), W Akeley RDn (1927—*). *Eccl* bdry: 1876 (help cr Blackfordby EP [Leics, Derbys]).[20] Now called 'Donisthorpe and Moira'.

DONISTHORPE AND MOIRA—see prev entry

DRAYTON

Tp (orig chap, early desecrated) in Bringhurst AP, sep CP 1866.[1] *LG* Seq 5. *Parl* Seq 9.

FENNY DRAYTON

AP *LG* Spark. Hd, Ath. PLU, RSD, Mkt. Bosw. RD. Civ bdry: 1935 (loses pt to Caldecote AP, pt to Hartshill CP, Mancetter AP, all Warws).[72] Abol civ 1935 ent to Witherley AP.[9] *Parl* S'rn Dv (1832—85), W'rn Dv (1885—1918), Bosw. Dv (1918—48). *Eccl* Seq 37.

DUNTON BASSETT

AP *LG* Seq 15. *Parl* Seq 10. *Eccl* Seq 29.

EARL SHILTON

Chap in Kirkby Mallory AP, sep CP 1866,[1] sep EP 1853.[114] *LG* Spark. Hd, Hinck. PLU, RSD,RD. Civ bdry: 1885.[115] Abol civ 1936 ent to Hinck. UD & AP.[63] *Parl* S'rn Dv (1832—85), W'rn Dv (1885—1918), Bosw. Dv (1918—48). *Eccl* Spark. RDn (1853—65), Spark. II RDn (1865—*).

GREAT EASTON

Chap in Bringhurst AP, sep CP 1866.[1] *LG* Seq 5. *Parl* Seq 9.

EASTWELL

AP *LG* Framl. Hd, Melt. Mowb. PLU, RSD, RD (1894—1935), Melt. & Belv. RD (1935—36). Abol civ 1936 ent to Eaton AP.[3] *Parl* N'rn Dv (1832—85), E'rn Dv (1885—1918), Melt. Dv (1918—48). *Eccl* Framl. RDn (until 1865), Framl. IV RDn (1865—73), Framl. I RDn (1873—77), Framl. II RDn (1877—1961), Framl. I RDn (1961—*).

EATON

AP *LG* Seq 2. Civ bdry: 1936 (gains Eastwell AP, Goadby Marwood AP).[3] *Parl* Seq 1. *Eccl* Seq 12.

EDMONDTHORPE

AP *LG* Framl. Hd, Mkt. Mowb. PLU, RSD, RD (1894—1935), Melt. & Belv. RD (1935—36). Abol civ 1936 ent to Wymondham AP.[3] *Parl* N'rn Dv (1832—85), E'rn Dv (1885—1918), Melt. Dv (1918—48). *Eccl* Framl. RDn (until 1865), Framl. I RDn (1865—73), Framl. III RDn (1873—77), Framl. II RDn (1877—1951). Abol eccl 1951 to help cr Wymondham cum Edmondthorpe EP.[116]

ELLISTOWN

EP Cr 1896 from Hugglescote with Donington EP, Ibstock AP.[35] S Akeley RDn.

ELMERSTHORPE

AP *LG* Seq 18. *Parl* Seq 13. *Eccl* Seq 38.

ENDERBY

AP Tp 'Enderby' in Spark. Hd; incl in Guthl. Hd chap Whetstone (sep civ identity early, sep EP 1867[117]). *LG* Blaby PLU, RSD, RD. Addtl civ bdry alt: 1935.[9] *Parl* Seq 10. *Eccl* Seq 25. Addtl eccl bdry alt: 1902 (gains chap Lubbesthorpe from Aylestone AP).[36]

EVINGTON

AP *LG* Gart. Hd, Bill. PLU, RSD, RD. Civ bdry: 1892 (the pt transf to Leic CB cr North Evington CP).[38] Abol civ 1936 pt to Oadby UD & AP, pt to Leic CB (assoc with Leics) & CP, pt to Stoughton CP.[23] *Parl* S'rn Dv (1832—85), E'rn Dv (1885—1918), Melt. Dv (1918—48). *Eccl* Pec jurisd Manor of Evington (until 1851), Gart. RDn (1851—65), Gart. II RDn (1865—93), Christianity RDn (1893—*). Eccl bdry: 1887 (help cr New Humberstone EP),[65] 1913 (cr Leicester St Philip EP),[118] 1952 (incl help cr Leicester St Chad EP).[119]

NORTH EVINGTON

CP Cr 1892 from the pt of Evington AP in Leic CB.[38] *LG* Leic PLU, CB. Abol 1896 to help cr Leicester CP.[39]

EP Cr 1904 from New Humberstone EP.[118] Christianity RDn. Bdry: 1952 (incl help cr Leicester St Chad EP).[119]

EYE KETTLEBY—see SYSONBY AND EYE KETTLEBY

EYRES MONSELL

EP Cr 1962 from Aylestone AP, Glen Parva with South Wigston EP, Leicester St Christopher EP.[42] Christianity RDn.

FLECKNEY

AP Orig chap in Wistow AP, sep par early and donative.[120] *LG* Seq 4. *Parl* Seq 9. *Eccl* Seq 15.

FOSTON

AP *LG* Guthl. Hd, Blaby PLU, RSD, RD. Abol civ 1935 ent to Kilby AP.[9] *Parl* S'rn Dv (1832—1918), Harb. Dv (1918—48). *Eccl* Seq 30.

FOXTON

AP *LG* Seq 4. Civ bdry: 1935.[9] *Parl* Seq 9. *Eccl* Gart. Hd (until 1865), Gart. II RDn (1865—73), Gart. I RDn (1873—*).

FREAKES GROUND

Ex-par place, sep CP 1858,[14] eccl abol 1904 to help cr Leicester St Augustine New Found Pool EP.[121] *LG* Guthl. Hd, Blaby PLU (1861—92), RSD. Abol civ 1892 ent to Leicester Abbey CP.[38] *Parl* S'rn Dv

(1832—1918).

FREEBY

Chap and tp in Melton Mowbray AP, sep CP 1866.[1]
LG Seq 2. Bdry: 1936 (gains Wyfordby AP [in 20th
cent civ 'Bretingby and Wyfordby', as was at time
of abol], Saxby AP, Stapleford AP).[3] *Parl* Seq 1.

FRISBY

Chap in Galby AP (eccl, 'Gaulby'), sep CP 1866.[1]
LG Seq 3. *Parl* Seq 7.

FRISBY

CP Cr 1936 by union Frisby on the Wreak AP, Kirby
Bellars AP.[3] *LG* Melt. & Belv. RD. *Parl* Melt. CC
(1948—*).

FRISBY ON THE WREAK

AP *LG* E Gosc. Hd, Melt. Mowb. PLU, RSD, RD
(1894—1935), Melt. & Belv. RD (1935—36). Abol
civ 1936 to help cr Frisby CP.[3] *Parl* N'rn Dv
(1832—85), E'rn Dv (1885—1918), Melt. Dv
(1918—48). *Eccl* Gosc. RDn (until 1865), Gosc. II
RDn (1865—1928), Framl. III RDn (1928—61),
Framl. II RDn (1961—*).

FROLESWORTH

AP *LG* Seq 15. *Parl* Seq 10. *Eccl* Seq 29.

GADDESBY

Chap (pec jurisd Manor of Rothley, until 1851) in
Rothley AP, sep civ identity early, sep EP 1874.[122]
LG Seq 9. Civ bdry: 1883,[28] 1936 (gains Ashby
Folville AP, Barsby CP).[3] *Parl* Seq 1. *Eccl* Akeley
II RDn (1874—77), Gosc. I RDn (1877—*).

GALBY

AP Usual civ spelling until 1960; for usual eccl spelling
and civ after renamed 1960,[123] see 'Gaulby'. Incl
chap Frisby (sep CP 1866[1]). *LG* Gart. Hd, Bill.
PLU, RSD, RD (1894—1960). *Parl* S'rn Dv
(1832—85), E'rn Dv (1885—1918), Melt. Dv/CC
(1918—70).

GARENDON

Ex-par place, sep CP 1858,[14] eccl bdry alt 1963.[123]
LG W Gosc. Hd, Loughb. PLU (1862—1930),
RSD, RD. Civ bdry: 1891 (gains the pt of Knight
Thorpe CP not in Loughb. MB).[124] Abol civ 1936
pt to Loughb. MB & AP, pt to Shepshed UD &
AP.[23] *Parl* N'rn Dv (1832—85), Mid Dv (1885—
1918), Loughb. Dv (1918—48).

GARTHORPE

AP Incl undivided pt Lands Common to Coston and
Garthorpe (abol 1936 ent to this par[3]). *LG* Seq 2.
Parl Seq 1. *Eccl* Seq 7.

GAULBY

AP Usual eccl spelling; civ spelling after renaming
1960 of 'Galby', prev civ spelling.[123] *LG* Bill. RD.
Parl Harb. CC (1970—*). *Eccl* Seq 15.

GILMORTON

AP *LG* Seq 15. Civ bdry: 1877.[125] *Parl* Seq 10. *Eccl*
Guthl. RDn (until 1865), Guthl. II RDn (1865—73),
Guthl. III RDn (1873—1928), Guthl. II RDn
(1928—*).

GILROES

Ex-par place, sep CP 1858.[14] *LG* W Gosc. Hd,
Barr. upon S. PLU (1858—1930), RSD, RD. Abol
1935 ent to Leic CB (assoc with Leics) & CP.[9] *Parl*
N'rn Dv (1832—85), Mid Dv (1885—1918), Melt.
Dv (1918—48).

GREAT GLEN

CP Renaming 1958 of Glen Magna AP.[126] *LG* Bill.
RD. *Parl* Harb. CC (1970—*).

GLEN MAGNA

AP Incl chap Stretton Magna (sep CP 1866,[1] eccl
'Great Stretton', not sep eccl hence this par eccl
'Glen Magna cum Great Stretton', qv). *LG* Gart.
Hd, Bill. PLU, RSD, RD. Addtl civ bdry alt:
1936.[23] Renamed civ 1958 'Great Glen'.[126] *Parl*
S'rn Dv (1832—1918), Melt. Dv/CC (1918—70).

GLEN MAGNA CUM GREAT STRETTON

AP Usual eccl spelling; for civ and civ sep chap, see
prev entry. *Eccl* Seq 15.

GLEN PARVA

Chap in Aylestone AP, sep CP 1866,[1] eccl severed
1893 to help cr Glen Parva with South Wigston
EP.[35] *LG* Seq 14. Bdry: 1885,[37] 1928,[127] 1935,[9]
1966 (exchanges pts with Leic CB [assoc with
Leics] & CP).[71] *Parl* Seq 10.

GLEN PARVA WITH SOUTH WIGSTON

EP Cr 1893 from Aylestone AP (chap Glen Parva),
Great Wigston AP.[35] Christianity RDn. Bdry: 1951
(help cr Leicester St Christopher EP),[41] 1962,[74]
1962 (help cr Eyres Monsell EP).[42]

GLENFIELD

AP Incl chap Braunstone (sep CP 1866,[1] sep EP
1937[89]), chap Kirby Muxloe (sep CP 1866,[1] sep EP
1930 incl ent ex-par Leicester Forest East[77]). *LG*
Spark. Hd, Blaby PLU, RSD, RD. Abol civ 1935 to
help cr Glenfields CP.[9] *Parl* S'rn Dv (1832—1918),
Harb. Dv (1918—48). *Eccl* Pec jurisd Groby (until
1851), Seq 28 thereafter. Eccl bdry: 1877 (gains the
3 ex-par places of Glenfield Frith, Kirby Frith,
Leicester Frith),[128] 1959 (help cr Leicester St Aidan
EP).[129]

GLENFIELD FRITH

Ex-par place, sep CP 1858,[14] abol eccl 1877 ent to
Glenfield AP.[128] *LG* Spark. Hd, Blaby PLU
(1861—1930), RSD, RD. Abol civ 1935 to help cr
Glenfields CP.[9] *Parl* S'rn Dv (1832—1918), Harb.
CC (1918—48).

GLENFIELDS

CP Cr 1935 by union ent Glenfield AP, Glenfield Frith
CP, Kirby Frith CP, and pts Anstey CP, Anstey
Pastures CP, Leicester Frith CP, New Parks CP.[9]
LG Blaby RD. Bdry: 1936,[10] 1966 (exchanges pts
with Leic CB [assoc with Leics] & CP).[71] *Parl*
Harb. CC (1948—70), Blaby CC (1970—*).

GLOOSTON

AP Perhaps orig dependent on Welham AP, sep par by
1220.[130] *LG* Seq 4. *Parl* Seq 9. *Eccl* Seq 13.

GOADBY

Chap and tp in Billesdon AP, sep CP 1866.[1] *LG* Seq
3. *Parl* Seq 7.

GOADBY MARWOOD

AP *LG* Framl. Hd, Mkt. Mowb. PLU, RSD, RD
(1894—1935), Melt. & Belv. RD (1935—36). Abol
civ 1936 ent to Eaton AP.[3] *Parl* N'rn Dv (1832—
85), E'rn Dv (1885—1918), Melt. Dv (1918—48).
Eccl Framl. RDn (until 1865), Framl. IV RDn
(1865—75), Framl. III RDn (1875—77), Framl. II
RDn (1877—1961), Framl. I RDn (1961—*).

GOPSALL

Ex-par place (orig cell to Merevale Abbey), sep CP 1858,[14] abol eccl 1956 ent to Twycross EP.[131] *LG* Spark. Hd, Mkt. Bosw. PLU (1861—1930), RSD, RD. Abol civ 1935 ent to Twycross CP.[9] *Parl* S'rn Dv (1832—85), W'rn Dv (1885—1918), Bosw. Dv (1918—48).

EAST GOSCOTE

CP Cr 1967 from Queniborough AP, Ratcliffe on the Wreake AP, Rearsby AP.[132] *LG* Barr. upon S. RD. *Parl* Melt. CC (1970—*).

GRIMSTON

Chap (pec jurisd Rothley) in Rothley AP, sep civ identity early, sep EP 1791.[25] *LG* Seq 9. Civ bdry: 1936 (gains Saxelby AP, Shoby CP).[3] *Parl* Seq 1. *Eccl* Pec jurisd Rothley (until 1851), Akeley RDn (1851—65), Akeley II RDn (1865—72). Gains eccl 1872 chap Warnatby from Rothley AP to cr Grimston with Wartnaby EP.[133]

EP Cr 1932 when area Wartnaby severed from Grimston with Wartnaby EP to help cr Ab Kettleby with Wartnaby and Holwell EP, the remainder to be 'Grimston'.[4] Framl. III RDn (1932—61), Framl. II RDn (1961—*).

GRIMSTON WITH WARTNABY

EP Cr 1872 by union Grimston EP, chap Wartnaby in Rothley AP.[133] Akeley II RDn (1872—73), Framl. II RDn (1877—73), E Akeley RDn (1877—93), Framl. III RDn (1893—1932). Abol eccl 1932, area Wartnaby severed to help cr Ab Kettleby with Wartnaby and Holwell EP, the remainder to be 'Grimston' EP.[4]

GROBY

CP Cr 1896 from Ratby AP.[134] *LG* Mkt. Bosw. PLU, RD. Bdry: 1935,[9] 1936.[135] *Parl* Bosw. Dv/CC (1918—*).

GUMLEY

AP *LG* Seq 4. *Parl* Seq 9. *Eccl* Seq 13.

HALLATON

AP Incl chap Blaston St Michael (not sep civ, eccl severed 1930 to help cr Blaston EP[77]). *LG* Seq 5. *Parl* Seq 9. *Eccl* Seq 14.

HALSTEAD

Tp in Tilton AP, sep CP 1866.[1] *LG* E Gosc. Hd, Bill. PLU, RSD, RD. Abol 1935 ent to Tilton AP.[9] *Parl* N'rn Dv (1832—85), E'rn Dv (1885—1918), Melt. Dv (1918—48).

HARBY

AP *LG* Framl. Hd, Mkt. Mowb. PLU, RSD, RD (1894—1935), Melt. & Belv. RD (1935—36). Abol civ 1936 to help cr Clawson and Harby CP.[3] *Parl* N'rn Dv (1832—85), E'rn Dv (1885—1918), Melt. Dv (1918—48). *Eccl* Framl. RDn (until 1865), Framl. I RDn (1865—73), Framl. III RDn (1873—93), Framl. I RDn (1893—*).

HARSTON

AP *LG* Framl. Hd, Granth. PLU, RSD, Belv. RD (1894—1935), Melt. & Belv. RD (1935—36). Abol 1936 ent to Belvoir CP.[3] *Parl* N'rn Dv (1832—85), E'rn Dv (1885—1918), Melt. Dv (1918—48). *Eccl* Seq 8.

HATHERN

AP *LG* W Gosc. Hd, Loughb. PLU, RSD, RD. Abol

civ 1936 pt to Long Whatton AP, pt to Loughb. MB & AP, pt to Shepshed UD & AP.[23] *Parl* N'rn Dv (1832—85), Mid Dv (1885—1918), Loughb. Dv (1918—48). *Eccl* Seq 1.

HEATHER

AP *LG* Seq 16. Civ bdry: 1936.[23] *Parl* Seq 15. *Eccl* Seq 35.

HEMINGTON

Tp (orig chap, early desecrated) in Lockington AP, sep CP 1866.[1] *LG* W Gosc. Hd, Shard. PLU, RSD, Cast. Don. RD. Abol 1936 ent to Lockington AP.[23] *Parl* N'rn Dv (1832—85), Mid Dv (1885—1918), Loughb. Dv (1918—48).

HIGHAM ON THE HILL

AP *LG* Spark. Hd, Hinck. PLU (soon after 1836[33]—1930), RSD, RD (1894—1936), Mkt. Bosw. RD (1936—74). Civ bdry: 1935 (loses pt to Nuneaton MB & AP, pt to Caldecote AP, both Warws),[72] 1936.[63] *Parl* Seq 12. *Eccl* Seq 38.

HINCKLEY

AP Tp 'Hinckley' in Leics, Spark. Hd, as were chaps Dadlington, Stoke Goldington (each chap a sep CP 1866 in Leics,[1] the 2 united 1865 as Stoke Goldington cum Dadlington EP[109]); incl in Warws, Knightlow Hd, chap (early destroyed) Hydes Pastures (not sep). Prob in 1880s (before census of 1891, but with no explicit order),[136] Hinckley considered ent Leics. *LG* Pt Hinck. Bor, Hinck. PLU, USD, UD. Addtl civ bdry alt: 1920,[62] 1928,[95] 1935 (incl exchanges pts with Nuneaton AP, exchanges pts with Stretton Baskerville AP, gains pt Wolvey AP, all Warws),[72] 1936 (incl gains Barwell AP, Burbage CP, Earl Shilton CP),[63] 1965 (gains pt Stretton Baskerville AP, Warws).[103] *Parl* Seq 12. *Eccl* Seq 38. Addtl eccl bdry alt: 1843 (cr Hinckley Holy Trinity EP).[137]

HINCKLEY HOLY TRINITY

EP Cr 1843 from Hinckley AP.[137] Spark. RDn (1843—65), Spark. II RDn (1865—*).

HOBY

AP *LG* E Gosc. Hd, Mkt. Mowb. PLU, RSD, RD (1894—1935), Melt. & Belv. RD (1935—36). Abol civ 1936 to help cr Hoby with Rotherby CP.[3] *Parl* N'rn Dv (1832—85), E'rn Dv (1885—1918), Melt. Dv (1918—48). *Eccl* Seq 20.

HOBY WITH ROTHERBY

CP Cr 1936 by union Brooksby AP, Hoby AP, Ragdale AP, Rotherby AP.[3] *LG* Melt. & Belv. RD. *Parl* Melt. CC (1948—*).

NEVILL HOLT

Chap (eccl, 'Holt') and tp in Medbourne AP, sep CP 1866.[1] *LG* Seq 5. *Parl* Seq 9.

HOLWELL

Chap in Ab Kettleby AP, sep CP 1866.[1] *LG* Framl. Hd, Mkt. Mowb. PLU, RSD, RD (1894—1935), Melt. & Belv. RD (1935—36). Bdry: 1884.[2] Abol 1936 ent to Ab Kettleby AP.[3] *Parl* N'rn Dv (1832—85), E'rn Dv (1885—1918), Melt. Dv (1918—48).

HORNINGHOLD

AP *LG* Seq 5. *Parl* Seq 9. *Eccl* Seq 14.

HOSE

AP *LG* Framl. Hd, Mkt. Mowb. PLU, RSD, RD (1894—1935), Melt. & Belv. RD (1935—36). Abol

1936 to help cr Clawson and Harby CP.[3] *Parl* N'rn Dv (1832—85), E'rn Dv (1885—1918), Melt. Dv (1918—48). *Eccl* Framl. RDn (until 1865), Framl. IV RDn (1865—73), Framl. III RDn (1873—93), Framl. I RDn (1893—1961), Framl. II RDn (1961—*).

HOTON
Chap in Prestwold AP, sep CP 1866.[1] *LG* Seq 8. *Parl* Seq 4.

HOUGHTON ON THE HILL
AP *LG* Seq 3. *Parl* Seq 7. *Eccl* Gart. RDn (until 1865), Gart. II RDn (1865—93), Gosc. I RDn (1893—1954). Abol eccl 1954 to help cr Houghton on the Hill and Keyham EP.[138]

HOUGHTON ON THE HILL AND KEYHAM
EP Cr 1954 by union Houghton on the Hill AP, chap Keyham in Rothley AP.[138] Gosc. I RDn.

HUGGLESCOTE AND DONINGTON
Chap in Ibstock AP, sep CP 1866,[1] sep EP 1865 as 'Hugglescote with Donington',[139] qv. *LG* Spark. Hd, Ashb. de la Z. PLU, Coalville USD (pt 1892—93, ent 1893—94), Ashb. de la Z. RSD (ent 1875—92, pt 1892—93), Coalville UD. Bdry: 1893 (loses the pt not in the USD to Bardon CP),[45] 1894 (help cr Coalville CP).38[106] Abol 1936 pt to Coalville UD & CP, pt to Ibstock AP.[23] *Parl* S'rn Dv (1832—85), W'rn Dv (1885—1918), Bosw. Dv (1918—48).

HUGGLESCOTE WITH DONINGTON
Chap in Ibstock AP, sep EP 1865,[139] sep CP 1866 as 'Hugglescote and Donington',[1] qv. Spark. I RDn (1865—93), S Akeley RDn (1893—*). Bdry: 1896 (help cr Ellistown EP),[35] 1918 (cr Bardon Hill EP).[50]

HUMBERSTONE
AP *LG* E Gosc. Hd, Bill. PLU, RSD, RD. Civ bdry: 1892 (the pt transf to Leic CB cr West Humberstone CP).[38] Abol civ 1935 ent to Leic CB (assoc with Leics) & CP.[9] *Parl* N'rn Dv (1832—85), E'rn Dv (1885—1918), Melt. Dv (1918—48). *Eccl* Seq 18. Eccl bdry: 1887 (help cr New Humberstone EP),[65] 1952 (help cr Leicester St Chad EP),[119] 1961 (help cr Thurnby Lodge EP),[140] 1967,[141] 1971 (help cr Leicester St Elizabeth, Nether Hall EP).[142]

NEW HUMBERSTONE
EP Cr 1887 from Humberstone AP, Evington AP, Belgrave AP.[65] Gosc. I RDn (1887—93), Christianity RDn (1893—*). Bdry: 1904 (cr North Evington EP),[118] 1972.[143]

WEST HUMBERSTONE
CP Cr 1892 from the pt of Humberstone AP in Leic CB.[38] *LG* Leic PLU, CB. Abol 1896 to help cr Leicester CP.[39]

HUNCOTE
AP Orig AP, not sep after 13th cent and hmlt in Narborough AP,[144] sep CP 1866,[1] sep EP 1904.[145] *LG* Seq 17. Civ bdry: 1935.[9] *Parl* Seq 10. *Eccl* Guthl. I RDn.

HUNGARTON
AP Usual eccl spelling; for civ see 'Hungerton'. *Eccl* Gosc. RDn. Abol eccl 1732 to help cr Hungarton with Twyford and Thorpe Satchville EP.[146]
EP Cr 1925 when Hungarton with Twyford and Thorpe Satchville EP divided into 2 EPs of Hungarton,

Twyford with Thorpe Satchville.[147] Gosc. I RDn. CP Renaming 1947 of Hungerton AP.[148] *LG* Bill. RD. *Parl* Melt. CC (1948—70), Harb. CC (1970—*).

HUNGARTON WITH TWYFORD AND THORPE SATCHVILLE
EP Cr 1732 by union Hungarton AP (civ, 'Hungerton'), Twyford with Thorpe Satchville AP.[146] Gosc. RDn (1732—1865), Gosc. II RDn (1865—73), Gosc. I RDn (1873—1925). Abol 1925, divided into 2 EPs of Hungarton, Twyford with Thorpe Satchville.[147]

HUNGERTON
AP Usual civ spelling until renamed 'Hungarton',[148] the latter the usual eccl spelling, qv. *LG* Pt Gart. Hd, pt E Gosc. Hd, Bill. PLU, RSD, RD. *Parl* Pt N'rn Dv, pt S'rn Dv (1832—85), E'rn Dv (1885—1918), Melt. Dv (1918—48).

IBSTOCK
AP Incl chap Hugglescote and Donington (sep CP 1866,[1] sep EP 1865 as 'Hugglescote with Donington'[139]). *LG* Seq 19. Addtl civ bdry alt: 1936.[23] *Parl* Seq 12. *Eccl* Seq 35. Addtl eccl bdry alt: 1840 (help cr Coalville EP),[105] 1896 (help cr Ellistown EP,[25] refounded soon after in that year[35]).

ILLSTON ON THE HILL
Chap and tp in Carlton Curlieu AP, sep EP 1972,[97] sep CP 1866 as 'Ilston on the Hill',[1] qv in following entry. *Eccl* Gart. II RDn.

ILSTON ON THE HILL
Chap and tp in Carlton Curlieu AP, sep CP 1866,[1] sep EP 1972 as 'Illston on the Hill',[97] qv in prev entry. *LG* Seq 3. *Parl* Seq 7. *Eccl* Gart. II RDn.

ISLEY CUM LANGLEY
CP Cr 1936 by union Isley Walton CP, Langley Priory CP, pt Castle Donington AP.[23] *LG* Cast. Don. RD. *Parl* Loughb. CC (1948—*).

ISLEY WALTON
Chap in Kegworth AP, sep CP 1866.[1] *LG* W Gosc. Hd, Shard. PLU, RSD, Cast. Don. RD. Abol 1936 to help cr Isley cum Langley CP.[23] *Parl* N'rn Dv (1832—85), Mid Dv (1885—1918), Loughb. Dv (1918—48).

KEGWORTH
AP Incl chap Isley Walton (sep CP 1866[1]). *LG* Seq 13. *Parl* Seq 3. *Eccl* Seq 2.

KEYHAM
Chap (pec jurisd Manor of Rothley, until 1851) in Rothley AP, sep CP 1866,[1] eccl severed 1954 to help cr Houghton on the Hill and Keyham EP.[138] *LG* E Gosc. Hd, Bill. PLU (soon after 1835[34]— 1930), RSD, RD. *Parl* Seq 2.

KIBWORTH BEAUCHAMP
AP Incl chap and tp Kibworth Harcourt (sep CP 1866[1]), tp Smeeton Westerby (sep CP 1866,[1] sep EP 1852[149]). *LG* Seq 4. *Parl* Seq 9. *Eccl* Gart. RDn (until 1865), Gart. I RDn (1865—73), Gart. II RDn (1873—*).

KIBWORTH HARCOURT
Chap and tp in Kibworth Beauchamp AP, sep CP 1866.[1] *LG* Seq 4. *Parl* Seq 9.

KILBY
Chap in Wistow AP, sep civ identity early, date sep eccl uncertain,[150] but certainly in 1733.[25] *LG* Seq

14. Civ bdry: 1935 (gains Foston AP).[9] *Parl* Seq 10. *Eccl* Seq 15.

NORTH KILWORTH
AP *LG* Seq 15. *Parl* Seq 10. *Eccl* Seq 33.

SOUTH KILWORTH
AP Organisation as for North Kilworth.

KIMCOTE
AP *LG* Guthl. Hd, Lutt. PLU, RSD, RD. Civ bdry: 1877,[30] 1877,[151] 1877.[125] Abol civ 1898 to help cr Kimcote and Walton CP.[152] *Parl* S'rn Dv (1832—1918). *Eccl* Guthl. RDn (until 1865), Guthl. III RDn (1865—1926). Abol eccl 1926 to help cr Kimcote with Walton EP.[70]

KIMCOTE AND WALTON
CP Cr 1898 by union Kimcote AP, Walton in Knaptoft CP.[152] *LG* Lutt. PLU, RD. *Parl* Harb. Dv/CC (1918—70), Blaby CC (1970—*).

KIMCOTE WITH WALTON
EP Cr 1926 by union Kimcote AP, chap Walton in Knaptoft AP.[70] Guthl. III RDn (1926—28), Guthl. II RDn (1928—*).

KIRBY BELLARS
AP Orig Collegiate. *LG* Framl. Hd, Mkt. Mowb. PLU, RSD, RD (1894—1935). Melt. & Belv. RD (1935—36). Abol civ 1936 to help cr Frisby CP.[3] *Parl* N'rn Dv (1832—85), E'rn Dv (1885—1918), Melt. Dv (1918—48). *Eccl* Framl. RDn (until 1865), Framl. III RDn (1865—73), Framl. II RDn (1873—77), Framl. III RDn (1877—1961), Framl. II RDn (1961—*).

KIRBY FRITH
Ex-par place, sep CP 1858,[14] abol eccl 1877 ent to Glenfield AP.[128] *LG* Spark. Hd, Blaby PLU (1861—1930), RSD, RD. Abol civ 1935 to help cr Glenfields CP.[9] *Parl* S'rn Dv (1832—1918), Harb. Dv (1918—48).

KIRBY MUXLOE
Chap in Glenfield AP, sep CP 1866,[1] sep EP 1930 incl ent ex-par Leicester Forest East.[77] *LG* Seq 17. Civ bdry: 1885,[37] 1904,[153] 1935 (loses pt to Leic CB [assoc with Leics] & CP, gains Leicester Forest East CP),[9] 1966 (loses pt to Leic CB [assoc with Leics] & CP).[71] *Parl* Seq 10. *Eccl* Spark. III RDn.

KIRKBY MALLORY
AP Incl chap Earl Shilton (sep CP 1866,[1] sep EP 1853[114]). *LG* Spark. Hd, Mkt. Bosw. PLU, RSD, RD. Abol civ 1935 pt to Newbold Verdon AP, pt to Peckleton AP.[9] *Parl* S'rn Dv (1832—85), W'rn Dv (1885—1918), Bosw. Dv (1918—48). *Eccl* Seq 38.

KNAPTOFT
AP Tp 'Knaptoft' in Guthl. Hd as were chap and tp Shearsby (sep CP 1866,[1] eccl severed 1927 to help cr Arnesby with Shearsby EP[19]), chap and tp Walton (sep CP 1866 as 'Walton in Knaptoft',[1] eccl severed 1926 to help cr Kimcote with Walton EP[70]); incl in Gart. Hd chap and tp Mowsley (sep CP 1866,[1] sep EP perhaps in 1660 [date 1st registers][154]). *LG* Lutt. PLU, RSD, RD. *Parl* Seq 10. *Eccl* Guthl. RDn (until 1865), Guthl. III RDn (1865—1926), Gart. I RDn (1926—*).

KNIGHT THORPE
Tp in Loughborough AP, sep CP 1866.[1] *LG* W Gosc. Hd, Loughb. PLU, USD, MB (pt 1881—91,

ent 1891—1902). Bdry: 1891 (gains the pt of Thorpe Acre and Dishley AP in Loughb. MB, loses pts not in the MB to Garendon CP, Loughborough AP).[124] Abol 1902 ent to Loughborough AP.[155] *Parl* N'rn Dv (1832—85), Mid Dv (1885—1918).

KNIGHTON
Chap (pec jurisd prebend Leicester St Margaret, until 1851) in Leicester St Margaret AP, sep CP 1866,[1] sep EP [St Mary Magdalen] 1878 from main pt of the tp (3 villages or hmlts of Knighton, South Knighton, Stoneygate).[68] *LG* Guthl. Hd, Blaby PLU (1836—92), Leic PLU (1892—96), Leic CB (1892—96), Leic USD (1892—94), Blaby RSD (1875—92). Civ bdry: 1885,[156] 1892 (loses the area not transf to Leic CB, pt to Oadby AP, pt to Lubbesthorpe CP).[38] Abol civ 1896 to help cr Leicester CP.[39] *Parl* S'rn Dv (1832—1918). *Eccl* Christianity RDn. Eccl bdry: 1917 (cr Knighton St John the Baptist EP),[157] 1951 (help cr Leicester St Christopher EP).[41]

KNIGHTON ST JOHN THE BAPTIST
EP Cr 1917 from Knighton EP.[157] Christianity RDn. Bdry: 1918 (help cr Leicester St James EP),[158] 1930 (help cr Knighton St Michael and All Angels EP).[159]

KNIGHTON ST MICHAEL AND ALL ANGELS
EP Cr 1930 from Knighton St John the Baptist EP, Leicester All Souls EP.[159] Christianity RDn. Bdry: 1931.[160]

KNIPTON
AP *LG* Framl. Hd, Granth. PLU, RSD, Belv. RD (1894—1935), Melt. & Belv. RD (1935—36). Abol civ 1936 ent to Belvoir CP.[3] *Parl* N'rn Dv (1832—98), E'rn Dv (1885—1918), Melt. Dv (1918—48). *Eccl* Seq 8.

KNOLL AND BASSETT HOUSE
Ex-par place, sep CP 1858.[14] *LG* Spark. Hd, Blaby PLU (1861—1909), RSD, RD. Abol civ 1909 ent to Thurlaston AP.[161] *Parl* S'rn Dv (1832—85), W'rn Dv (1885—1918).

KNOSSINGTON
AP *LG* Gart. Hd, Oakham PLU, RSD, Melt. Mowb. RD (1894—1935), Melt. & Belv. RD (1935—74). Civ bdry: 1936 (gains Cold Overton AP).[3] *Parl* N'rn Dv (1832—85), E'rn Dv (1885—1918), Melt. Dv/CC (1918—*).

LANDS COMMON TO COSTON AND GARTHORPE
LG Melt. Mowb. RD (1894—1935), Melt. & Belv. RD (1935—36). Abol 1936 ent to Garthorpe AP as Coston AP, Garthorpe AP, and the Lands Common to them united.[3] *Parl* Melt. Dv (1918—48).

LANGLEY PRIORY
Ex-par place, sep CP 1858.[14] *LG* W Gosc. Hd, Shard. PLU (1861—1930), RSD, Cast. Don. RD. Abol civ 1936 to help cr Isley cum Langley CP.[23] *Parl* N'rn Dv (1832—85), Mid Dv (1885—1918), Loughb. Dv (1918—48).

CHURCH LANGTON
AP Incl tp East Langton, chaps and tps West Langton, Thorpe Langton, Tur Langton (each a sep CP 1866,[1] the 4 jointly rated in Mkt. Harb. PLU as 'Church Langton' but each sep soon thereafter[33]) so that 'Church Langton' has no sep civ identity after

1866. *LG* Gart. Hd. *Parl* S'rn Dv (1832—67). *Eccl* Seq 13.

EAST LANGTON

Tp in Church Langton AP, sep CP 1866,[1] orig rated in Mkt. Harb. PLU with other areas in Church Langton but soon thereafter sep rated.[33] *LG* Seq 4. Bdry: 1885,[162] 1927 (bdry with West Langton CP defined).[163] *Parl* Seq 9.

THORPE LANGTON

Chap and tp in Church Langton AP, sep CP 1866.[1] Organisation and orig/later rating in PLU as for East Langton, except no bdry alt 1927.

TUR LANGTON

Chap and tp in Church Langton AP, sep CP 1866.[1] Organisation and orig/later rating in PLU as for East Langton, except no bdry alts at all.

WEST LANGTON

Chap and tp in Church Langton AP, sep CP 1866.[1] Organisation, orig/later rating in PLU, bdry alts 1883 and 1927 as for East Langton.

LAUGHTON

AP *LG* Seq 4. *Parl* Seq 9. *Eccl* Gart. RDn (until 1865), Gart. II RDn (1865—73), Gart. I RDn (1873—*).

LAUNDE

Ex-par place, sep CP 1858[14]; eccl 'Launde Abbey', eccl abol 1961 ent to Loddington AP.[6] *LG* E Gosc. Hd, Bill. PLU (1858—1930), RSD, RD. *Parl* Seq 2.

LAUNDE ABBEY—see prev entry

LEICESTER

The following have 'Leicester' in their names (entries for Leicester Forest East, Leicester Forest West, Leicester Frith are not included but follow these entries). Insofar as any existed at a given time: *LG* Leic PLU; Hd, Bor/MB, USD, RSD sep noted. *Parl* Sep noted. *Eccl* Christianity RDn.

CP1—LEICESTER—Cr 1896 by union pars in Leic CB: Aylestone AP, Belgrave AP, North Evington CP, West Humberstone CP, Knighton CP, CP2, AP1, CP3, CP4, CP5, CP6, CP7, AP5, AP6, AP7, AP8, AP10.[39] *LG* Leic CB. Civ bdry: 1935 (incl gains Gilroes CP, Humberstone AP, Braunstone Firth CP, exchanges pts with Oadby UD & AP),[9] 1936,[23] 1939 (exchanges pts with Wigston UD and Wigston Magna AP),[164] 1966 (incl exchanges pts with Oadby UD & AP, Wigston UD and Wigston Magna AP, Anstey CP, Birstall CP, Thurmaston CP, Braunstone CP, Glenfields CP, Glen Parva CP),[71] 1969 (exchanges pts with Wigston UD and Wigston Magna AP).[165] *Parl* See Part III of the *Guide* for composition of Leic Parl Bors/BCs (1918—*) by wards of the CB. Parl bdry: 1972.[166]

CP2—LEICESTER ABBEY—Ex-par place, sep CP 1858,[14] pt eccl severed 1904 to help cr EP10,[121] pt eccl severed 1958 to help cr Stocking Farm EP.[67] *LG* W Gosc. Hd, Barr. upon S. PLU (1858—92), Leic PLU (1892—96), Leic CB (1892—96), Barr. upon S. RSD (1875—92), Leic USD (1892—94). Bdry: 1892 (loses the pt not transf to Leic CB to Beaumont Leys CP and gains Freakes Ground CP). Abol civ 1896 to help cr CP1.[39] *Parl* N'rn Dv (1832—85), Mid Dv (1885—1918).

AP1—LEICESTER ALL SAINTS—*LG* Leic Bor/MB/CB, USD. Bdry: 1885.[156] Abol civ 1896 to help cr CP1.[39] *Parl* Leic Parl Bor (1275—1918). Eccl bdry: 1645 (gains AP5).[167]

EP1—LEICESTER ALL SOULS—Cr 1907 from EP8, AP8.[20] Bdry: 1930 (help cr Knighton St Michael and All Angels EP),[159] 1931.[160]

CP3—LEICESTER AUGUSTINE FRIARS—Ex-par place, sep CP 1858.[14] *LG* Leic Bor/MB/CB, USD, PLU (1861—96). Abol 1896 to help cr CP1.[39] *Parl* Leic Parl Bor (1275—1918).

CP4—LEICESTER BLACKFRIARS—Ex-par place, sep CP 1858,[14] abol eccl 1880 ent to AP10.[168] *LG* Leic Bor/MB/CB, USD, PLU (1861—96). Abol civ 1896 to help cr CP1.[39] *Parl* Leic Parl Bor (1275—1918).

CP5—LEICESTER THE CASTLE VIEW—Ex-par place, sep CP 1858.[14] *LG* Guthl. Hd, Leic MB (1835—89), CB (1889—96), USD. PLU. Abol civ 1896 to help cr CP1.[39] *Parl* Leic Parl Bor (1832—1918).

EP2—LEICESTER CHRIST CHURCH—Cr 1843 from AP6.[169] Bdry: 1867 (cr EP20),[68] 1872 (help cr EP19),[170] 1941.[171] Abol 1956 ent to EP20.[172]

EP3—LEICESTER THE HOLY APOSTLES—Cr 1924 from EP5, Braunstone EP.[91] Bdry: 1937.[92]

EP4—LEICESTER HOLY TRINITY—Cr 1838 from AP8.[173] Bdry: 1886.[174]

EP5—LEICESTER THE MARTYRS—Cr 1890 from AP8.[175] Bdry: 1924 (help cr EP3),[90] 1930 (help cr EP9).[176]

CP6—LEICESTER NEW FOUND POOL—Ex-par place, sep CP 1858,[14] eccl severed 1904 to help cr EP10.[121] *LG* Guthl. Hd, Blaby PLU (1861—92), Leic PLU (1892—96), Blaby RSD (1875—92), Leic CB (1892—96), USD (1892—94). Abol civ 1896 to help cr CP1.[39] *Parl* S'rn Dv (1832—1918).

CP7—LEICESTER THE NEWARKE—Lbty, sep CP 1866,[1] abol eccl 1871 ent to AP8.[177] *LG* Surrounded by Leic Bor (brought within by charter of 1599 but sep status not sustained, again a lbty not in a Hd until 1835), Leic PLU, MB (1835—89), CB (1889—96). Abol civ 1896 to help cr CP1.[39] *Parl* Leic Parl Bor (1832—1918).

EP6—LEICESTER ST AIDAN—Cr 1959 from EP9, EP10, Glenfield AP.[129] Bdry: 1971.[178]

EP7—LEICESTER ST ALBAN—Cr 1906 from EP19, Belgrave St Michael and All Angels EP.[69]

EP8—LEICESTER ST ANDREW—Cr 1862 from AP8.[179] Bdry: 1886,[174] 1907 (help cr EP1).[20]

EP9—LEICESTER ST ANNE—Cr 1930 from EP10, EP5, AP8.[176] Bdry: 1959 (help cr EP6),[129] 1971.[178]

AP2—LEICESTER ST AUGUSTINE—Demolished late 11th cent.[180]

EP10—LEICESTER ST AUGUSTINE NEW FOUND POOL—Cr 1904 by union ent ex-par place New Found Pool (civ, CP6), ex-par Freakes Ground, ex-par New Parks (not sep civ), pt ex-par Leicester Abbey (civ, CP2).[121] Bdry: 1930 (help cr EP9),[176] 1930,[159] 1959 (help cr EP 6).[129]

EP11—LEICESTER ST CHAD—Cr 1952 from Evington AP, EP24, North Evington EP, Humberstone AP.[119]

EP12—LEICESTER ST CHRISTOPHER—Cr 1951 from Aylestone AP, Aylestone Park EP, Knighton EP, Glen Parva with South Wigston EP.[41] Bdry: 1962,[74] 1962 (help cr Eyres Monsell EP).[42]

AP3—LEICESTER ST CLEMENT—Exists 1220, given 13th cent to Grey Friars.[180]

AP4—LEICESTER ST COLUMBA—Demolished late 11th cent.[180]

—LEICESTER ST CROSS—see AP7

EP13—LEICESTER ST ELIZABETH, NETHER HALL—Cr 1971 from Humberstone AP, Scraptoft AP.[142]

EP14—LEICESTER ST GABRIEL—Cr 1951 from Belgrave St Michael and All Angels EP.[70] Bdry: 1972.[144]

EP15—LEICESTER ST GEORGE—Cr 1829 from AP6.[181] Bdry: 1854 (cr EP17,[182] refounded same month[159]), 1868 (help cr EP18),[183] 1874 (help cr EP23),[184] 1941.[171] Abol 1971 to help cr EP21.[185]

EP16—LEICESTER ST JAMES—Cr 1918 from EP23, EP24, Knighton St John the Baptist EP.[158]

EP17—LEICESTER ST JOHN—Cr 1854 from EP15,[182] refounded same month.[159]

AP5—LEICESTER ST LEONARD—Orig AP, destroyed 1645 and thereafter in AP1,[167] sep civ identity regained early, eccl refounded 1904.[167] *LG* Pt W Gosc. Hd, pt Leic Bor,[186] Leic PLU, MB (1835—89), CB (1889—96). USD. Abol civ 1896 to help cr CP1.[39] *Parl* Leic Parl Bor (pt 1295—1832, ent 1832—1918).

EP18—LEICESTER ST LUKE, HUMBERSTONE ROAD—Cr 1868 from EP15, EP20.[183] Abol 1941 pt to EP20, EP2, EP15.[171]

AP6—LEICESTER ST MARGARET—Tp 'Leicester St Margaret' pt in Leic Bor, pt in Guthl. Hd; also incl in Guthl. Hd chap Knighton (sep CP 1866,[1] pt a sep EP 1878 [3 villages or hmlts of Knighton, South Knighton, Stoneygate][68]). *LG* Pt Leic Bor, Leic MB (pt 1835 [enlarged by incl of remainder of main tp not prev in Bor]—66, ent 1866—89), CB (1889—96). Addtl civ bdry alt: 1883,[28] 1885.[156] Abol civ 1896 to help cr CP1.[39] *Parl* Main tp: Leic Parl Bor (pt 1295—1832, ent 1832—1918). *Eccl* Pec jurisd prebend St Margaret (until 1851). Addtl eccl bdry alt: 1829 (cr EP15),[181] 1843 (cr EP2),[169] 1872 (help cr EP19),[170] 1874 (help cr EP23),[184] 1890.[187]

EP19—LEICESTER ST MARK THE EVANGELIST—Cr 1872 from AP6, EP2.[170] Bdry: 1892,[68] 1906 (help cr EP7).[69]

AP7—LEICESTER ST MARTIN—Sometimes 'Leicester St Cross'. *LG* Leic Bor/MB/CB, PLU, USD. Abol civ 1896 to help cr CP1.[39] *Parl* Leic Parl Bor (1275—1918). *Eccl* Cathedral upon cr of dioc Leic.

AP8—LEICESTER ST MARY—*LG* Pt Leic Bor,[188] pt Guthl. Hd, Leic PLU, MB (ent par, 1835—89), CB (1889—96), USD. Civ bdry: 1892 (gains the pt of Braunstone CP transf to Leic CB).[37] Abol civ 1896 to help cr CP1.[39] *Parl* Leic Parl Bor (pt 1295—1832, ent 1832—1918). *Eccl* Sometimes 'Leicester St Mary de Castro'. Eccl bdry: 1838 (cr EP4),[173] 1862 (cr EP8),[179] 1871 (gains eccl ex-par The Newarke [civ, CP7]),[177] 1872 (cr EP22),[189] 1880,[92] 1886,[174] 1890 (cr EP5),[175] 1907 (help cr EP1),[20] 1930 (help cr EP9),[176] 1930.[159]

—LEICESTER ST MARY DE CASTRO—see AP8

EP20—LEICESTER ST MATTHEW—Cr 1867 from EP2.[68] Bdry: 1868 (help cr EP18),[183] 1878 (help cr EP25),[190] 1941,[171] 1956 (gains EP2).[172] Abol 1971 to help cr EP21.[185]

EP21—LEICESTER ST MATTHEW AND ST GEORGE—Cr 1971 by union EP20, EP15.[185]

AP9—LEICESTER ST MICHAEL—Exists 1220, not mentioned later and prob demolished end 15th cent.[191]

AP10—LEICESTER ST NICHOLAS—*LG* Leic Bor/ MB/CB, PLU, USD. Abol civ 1896 to help cr CP1.[39] *Parl* Leic Parl Bor (1275—1918). Eccl bdry: 1880 (gains ex-par area CP4).[168]

EP22—LEICESTER ST PAUL—Cr 1872 from AP8.[189]

AP11—LEICESTER ST PETER—Taken down 16th cent.[192]

EP23—LEICESTER ST PETER—Cr 1874 from AP6, EP15.[184] Bdry: 1878 (help cr EP25),[190] 1880,[92] 1918 (help cr EP16).[158]

EP24—LEICESTER ST PHILIP—Cr 1913 from Evington AP.[118] Bdry: 1918 (help cr EP16),[158] 1952 (help cr EP11).[119]

EP25—LEICESTER ST SAVIOUR—Cr 1878 from EP23, EP20.[190]

LEICESTER FOREST EAST

Ex-par place, sep CP 1858,[14] abol eccl 1930 to help cr Kirby Muxloe EP.[77] *LG* Spark. Hd, Blaby PLU, RSD, RD. Civ bdry: 1885.[36] Abol civ 1935 ent to Kirby Muxloe CP.[9] *Parl* S'rn Dv (1832—1918), Harb. Dv (1918—48).

LEICESTER FOREST WEST

Ex-par place, sep CP 1858.[14] *LG* Spark. Hd, Blaby PLU (1861—1930), RSD, RD. *Parl* Seq 10.

LEICESTER FRITH

Ex-par place, sep CP 1858,[14] abol eccl 1877 ent to Glenfield AP.[128] *LG* W Gosc. Hd, Barr. upon S. PLU (1858—1930), RSD, RD. Abol civ 1935 pt to Leic CB (assoc with Leics) & CP, pt to help cr Glenfields CP.[9] *Parl* N'rn Dv (1832—85), Mid Dv (1885—1918), Melt. Dv (1918—48).

LEIRE

AP *LG* Seq 15. Civ bdry: 1877,[31] 1877.[151] *Parl* Seq 10. *Eccl* Seq 33.

LOCKINGTON

AP Incl tp Hemington (orig chap, early desecrated, sep CP 1866[1]). *LG* W Gosc. Hd, Shard. PLU, RSD, RD. Cast. Don. RD. Addtl civ bdry alt: 1884 (gains pt Sawley and Wilsthorpe CP, Derbys),[23] 1936 (gains Hemington CP).[23] Renamed civ 1938 'Lockington-Hemington'.[193] *Parl* N'rn Dv (1832—85), Mid Dv (1885—1918), Loughb. Dv (1918—48). *Eccl* Seq 6.

LOCKINGTON-HEMINGTON

CP Renaming 1938 of Lockington AP (which had gained 1936 Hemington CP).[193] *LG* Cast. Don. RD.

Bdry: 1965 (loses pt to Breaston CP, gains pt Shardlow and Great Wilne CP, both Derbys).[18] *Parl* Loughb. CC (1948—*).

LODDINGTON

AP *LG* Seq 7. *Parl* Seq 2. *Eccl* Seq 19. Eccl bdry: 1961 (gains ex-par Launde Abbey, hence sometimes afterward this par 'Loddington and Launde').[6]

LODDINGTON AND LAUNDE—see prev entry

LOUGHBOROUGH

The following have 'Loughborough' in their names. Insofar as any existed at a given time: *LG* W Gosc. Hd, Loughb. PLU, USD, MB (pt 1888—94, ent 1894—1974). *Parl* Seq 3. *Eccl* Akeley RDn (until 1865), Akeley I RDn (1865—73), E Akeley RDn (1873—*).

AP1—LOUGHBOROUGH—Incl tp Knight Thorpe, hmlt Woodthorpe (each a sep CP 1866[1]). Addtl civ bdry alt: 1891 (gains the pt of Knight Thorpe CP in Lough. MB),[124] 1894 (the pt not in the MB cr Nanpanton CP),[22] 1902 (gains Knight Thorpe CP),[155] 1935,[9] 1936 (incl gains Nanpanton CP, Thorpe Acre and Dishley AP).[23] Eccl bdry: 1838 (cr EP1),[194] 1879 (help cr EP2),[195] 1909 (cr EP3),[196] 1963.[197]

EP1—LOUGHBOROUGH EMMANUEL—Cr 1838 from AP1.[194] Bdry: 1879 (help cr EP2),[195] 1963,[197] 1969 (cr Shelthorpe EP).[198]

EP2—LOUGHBOROUGH HOLY TRINITY—Cr 1879 from EP1, AP1.[195]

EP3—LOUGHBOROUGH ST PETER—Cr 1909 from AP1.[196] Bdry: 1963.[197]

LOWESBY

AP Incl chap Cold Newton (sep CP 1866[1]). *LG* Seq 7. *Parl* Seq 2. *Eccl* Seq 17.

LUBBESTHORPE

Chap in Aylestone AP, sep CP 1866,[1] eccl severed 1902 and transf to Enderby AP.[35] *LG* Seq 17. Bdry: 1885,[37] 1892 (gains the pt not in Leic CB of Aylestone AP, pt of the pt not in Leic CB of Knighton CP),[38] 1935 (incl loses pt to Leic CB [assoc with Leics] & CP),[9] 1936,[23] 1936.[90] *Parl* Seq 10.

LUBENHAM

AP *LG* Seq 4. Civ bdry: 1924,[82] 1935,[9] 1965 (exchanges pts with Marston Trussel AP, gains pt East Farndon AP, both Northants).[18] *Parl* Seq 9. *Eccl* Seq 13.

LUTTERWORTH

AP *LG* Seq 15. Civ bdry: 1935 (exchanges pts with Monks Kirby AP, loses pt to Churchover AP, gains pt Willey AP, all Warws).[72] *Parl* Seq 10. *Eccl* Seq 29.

MAPLEWELL LONGDALE

Hmlt in Barrow upon Soar AP, sep CP 1866.[1] *LG* W Gosc. Hd, Barr. upon S. PLU (1866—84), RSD. Abol 1884 ent to Woodhouse CP.[58] *Parl* N'rn Dv (1832—85).

MAREFIELD

Tp in Tilton AP, sep CP 1866.[1] *LG* Seq 3. *Parl* Seq 2.

MARKET HARBOROUGH

Chap and tp in Great Bowden AP, sep CP 1866,[1] sep EP 1827.[25] *LG* Gart. Hd, Mkt. Harb. PLU,

USD, UD. Civ bdry: 1927 (incl gains Great Bowden AP, Little Bowden AP),[83] 1935,[9] 1965 (gains pt East Farndon AP, Northants).[18] *Parl* Seq 9. *Eccl* Gart. RDn (1827—65), Gart. I RDn (1865—*). Eccl bdry: 1892,[87] 1901.[84]

MARKFIELD

AP *LG* Seq 19. Civ bdry: 1884,[199] 1885,[98] 1935 (incl gains Stanton under Bardon CP).[9] *Parl* Seq 8. *Eccl* Spark. RDn (until 1865), Spark. II RDn (1865—93), S Akeley RDn (1893—1928), Spark. III RDn (1928—*). Eccl bdry: 1860 (help cr Copt Oak EP),[44] 1935 (gains chap Stanton under Bardon from Thornton AP).[200]

MEASHAM

AP In Derbys, transf 1897 to Leics.[32] *LG* Ashb. de la Z. PLU, RD. Bdry: 1936.[23] *Parl* Loughb. Dv/CC (1918—*). *Eccl* In dioc Lichf & Cov (until 1837), dioc Lichf 1837—84, dioc S'well 1884—1927, dioc Leic 1927—*: Repton RDn (until 1846), Lullington RDn (1846—55), Hartshorne RDn (1855—87), Repton RDn (1887—1927), W Akeley RDn (1927—*).

MEDBOURNE

AP Incl free chap Blaston [St Giles] (sep par by early 13th cent[76]), chap and tp Nevill Holt (sep CP 1866,[1] not sep eccl [eccl, 'Holt'] hence this par eccl 'Medbourne with Holt', qv). *LG* Seq 5. *Parl* Seq 9.

MEDBOURNE WITH HOLT

AP Usual eccl spelling; for civ and civ sep chap (civ, 'Nevill Holt') see prev entry. *Eccl* Seq 14.

MELTON MOWBRAY

AP Incl chap and tp Freeby, chap and tp Welby, tps Burton Lazars, Sysonby (each of the 4 a sep CP 1866,[1] none sep eccl hence this par eccl 'Melton Mowbray with Burton Lazars, Freeby, Sysonby and Welby', qv). *LG* Framl. Hd, Mkt. Mowb. PLU, pt Melt. Mowb. USD, pt Melt. Mowb. RSD, Melt. Mowb. UD. Addtl civ bdry alt: 1894 (the pt not in the UD cr Sysonby with Eye Kettleby CP [later called 'Eye Kettleby']),[22] 1930 (gains Sysonby CP),[201] 1935 (incl gains Eye Kettleby CP [cr 1894 as 'Sysonby with Eye Kettleby' EP]).[9] *Parl* Seq 1.

MELTON MOWBRAY WITH BURTON LAZARS, FREEBY, SYSONBY AND WELBY

AP Usual eccl spelling; for civ and civ sep chaps and tps, see prev entry. *Eccl* Framl. RDn (until 1865), Framl. III RDn (1865—73), Framl. II RDn (1873—77), Framl. III RDn (1877—1961), Framl. II RDn (1961—71). Abol eccl 1971 to help cr Melton Mowbray with Thorpe Arnold EP.[202]

MELTON MOWBRAY WITH THORPE ARNOLD

EP Cr 1971 by union Melton Mowbray with Burton Lazars, Freeby, Sysonby and Welby AP, Thorpe Arnold AP.[202] Framl. II RDn.

MEREVALE

AP Pt Warws (Hemlingford Hd), 3 pts in Leics (Spark. Hd). *LG* Ath. PLU, RSD. Civ bdry: 1880 (bdry alt ent in Warws),[203] 1880 (a pt in Leics transf to Norton juxta Twycross CP, Leics),[204] 1885 (incl the remaining 2 pts in Leics lost, transf to Norton juxta Twycross CP, Orton on the Hill CP, both Leics, the remainder during exchange of pts with Sheepy Magna AP, Leics, so that Merevale ent Warws thereafter).[205] *Parl* Leics pt, S'rn Dv (1832—85), W'rn Dv (1885—1918). *Eccl* For RDns, see entry in Warws. Abol eccl 1958 to help cr Merevale with Bentley EP.[206]

MEREVALE WITH BENTLEY
EP Cr 1958 by Merevale AP (Leics, Warws), chap (detached pt of par) Bentley in Shustoke AP (Leics).[206] Polesw. RDn (Birm dioc, 1958—*).

MISTERTON
AP *LG* Seq 15. *Parl* Seq 10. *Eccl* Seq 33.

MOUNTSORREL
Chap (pec jurisd Manor of Rothley, until 1851) and bor pt in Barrow upon Soar AP, pt in Rothley AP, the latter pt a sep EP 1846 as 'Mountsorrel Christ Church'[207] and a sep CP 1866 as 'Mountsorrel South End'[1], qv, the former a sep EP 1868 as 'Mountsorrel St Peter'[57] and a sep CP 1866 as 'Mountsorrel North End'[1], qv.

CP Cr 1884 by union Mountsorrel South End CP and pts Mountsorrel North End CP, Rothley Temple CP.[58] *LG* W Gosc. Hd, Barr. upon S. PLU, RSD, RD. Bdry: 1896,[59] 1935,[9] 1936.[23] *Parl* Melt. Dv/CC (1918—*).

MOUNTSORREL CHRIST CHURCH
EP Cr 1846 from the pt of chap Mountsorrel in Rothley AP[207]; for civ see 'Mountsorrel South End'. Pec jurisd Manor of Rothley (1846—51), Akeley RDn (1851—65), E Akeley RDn (1865—*).

MOUNTSORREL NORTH END
Tp in Barrow upon Soar AP, sep CP 1866[1]; eccl the pt of chap Mountsorrel (pec jurisd Manor of Rothely, until 1851) in this par, sep EP 1868 as 'Mountsorrel St Peter',[57] qv. *LG* W Gosc. Hd, Barr. upon S. PLU, RSD. Abol civ 1884 pt to help cr Mountsorrel CP, pt to Barrow upon Soar AP.[58] *Parl* N'rn Dv (1832—85).

MOUNTSORREL SOUTH END
Tp in Rothley AP, sep CP 1866[1]; eccl the pt of chap Mountsorrel (pec jurisd Manor of Rothley, until 1851) in this par, sep EP 1846 as 'Mountsorrel Christ Church',[207] qv. *LG* W Gosc. Hd, Barr. upon S. PLU, RSD. Abol civ 1884 to help cr Mountsorrel CP.[58] *Parl* N'rn Dv (1832—85).

MOUNTSORREL ST PETER
The pt of chap Mountsorrel (pec jurisd Manor of Rothley, until 1851) in Barrow upon Soar AP, sep EP 1868,[57] sep CP 1866 as 'Mountsorrel North End',[1] qv. E Akeley RDn.

MOWSLEY
Chap and tp in Knaptoft AP, sep CP 1866,[1] sep EP perhaps in 1660 (date 1st registers).[154] *LG* Seq 4. *Parl* Seq 9. *Eccl* Gart. I RDn.

MUSTON
AP *LG* Framl.Hd, Granth. PLU, RSD, Belv. RD (1894—1935), Melt. & Belv. RD (1935—36). Abol civ 1936 ent to Bottesford AP.[3] *Parl* N'rn Dv (1832—85), E'rn Dv (1885—1918), Melt. Dv (1918—48). *Eccl* Seq 8.

NAILSTONE
AP Incl tp Barton in the Beans (sep CP 1866[1]), chap Normanton le Heath (sep CP 1866,[1] sep EP 1852[208]). *LG* Seq 19. Addtl civ bdry alt: 1883,[28] 1886.[43] *Parl* Seq 12. *Eccl* Seq 34. Eccl bdry: 1927.[81]

NANPANTON
CP Cr 1894 from the pt of Loughborough AP not in Loughb. MB.[22] *LG* Loughb. PLU, RD. Abol 1936 ent to Loughb. MB & AP.[23] *Parl* Loughb. Dv (1918—48).

NARBOROUGH
AP Incl hmlt Huncote (orig sep AP, not sep after 13th cent and hmlt in this par,[145] sep CP 1866,[1] sep EP 1904[146]). *LG* Seq 17. Addtl civ bdry alt: 1885,[37] 1935.[9] *Parl* Seq 10. *Eccl* Seq 30.

NEW PARKS
Ex-par place, sep CP 1858.[14] *LG* Guthl. Hd, Blaby PLU (1861—1930), RSD, RD. Abol 1935 pt to help cr Glenfields CP, pt to Leic CB (assoc with Leics) & CP.[9] *Parl* S'rn Dv (1832—1918), Harb. Dv (1918—48).

NEWBOLD VERDON
AP *LG* Seq 19. Civ bdry: 1883,[28] 1886,[43] 1935.[9] *Parl* Seq 12. *Eccl* Seq 34.

NEWTON HARCOURT
Chap in Wistow AP, sep CP 1866.[1] *LG* Gart. Hd, Bill. PLU, RSD, RD. Abol 1936 pt to Wistow AP, pt to Oadby UD & AP.[23] *Parl* S'rn Dv (1832—1918), Melt. Dv (1918—48).

NEWTOWN LINFORD
Chap in Groby AP, sep civ identity early, donative (pec jurisd Groby, until 1851) and sep eccl status sustained. *LG* Seq 11. Civ bdry: 1884,[199] 1884,[96] 1884,[8] 1884,[99] 1935,[9] 1936,[136] 1953,[11] 1968.[11] *Parl* Seq 5. *Eccl* Spark. RDn (1851—65), not in a RDn (1865—93), Guthl. I RDn (1893—1928), Spark. III RDn (1928—*). Eccl bdry: 1839 (help cr Woodhouse Eaves EP,[25] refounded 1844[60]), 1852 (help cr Charnwood Forest [Oaks Church] EP),[100] 1860 (help cr Copt Oak EP),[44] 1974.[13]

NO MAN'S HEATH
Ex-par area, uncertain if within or near junction of any of 3 cos of Derbys, Leics, Warws, or whether in diocs of Worc, Lichf, or Peterb, the area civ abol 1888 ent to Newton Regis AP, Warws,[209] 'No Man's Heath' a sep EP 1873 from ent ex-par area and pt Newton Regis AP, Warws, to be in dioc Lichf, Staff AD, Tamworth RDn.[210]

NORMANTON LE HEATH
Chap in Nailstone AP, sep CP 1866,[1] sep EP 1852.[208] *LG* Seq 16. *Parl* Seq 15. *Eccl* Spark. RDn (1852—65), Spark. I RDn (1865—93), W Akeley RDn (1893—*).

EAST NORTON
Chap in Tugby AP, sep CP 1866,[1] eccl severed 1927 to help cr Alexton with East Norton EP,[5] the area of East Norton severed 1961 from the latter to help cr Tugby and East Norton EP.[5] *LG* Seq 7. *Parl* Seq 2.

KING'S NORTON
AP Incl chap Stretton Parva (sep CP 1866,[1] not sep eccl hence this par eccl 'King's Norton with Stretton Parva', qv). Sometimes early 'Norton by Galby'. *LG* Seq 3. *Parl* Seq 7.

KING'S NORTON WITH STRETTON PARVA
AP Usual eccl spelling; for civ and civ sep chap, see prev entry. *Eccl* Seq 15.

NORTON JUXTA TWYCROSS
AP Incl chap Bilstone (sep CP 1866[1]). *LG* Spark. Hd,
Mkt. Bosw. PLU, RSD, RD. Addtl civ bdry alt:
1880 (gains pt in Leics of Merevale AP [Warws,
Leics]).[204] Abol civ 1935 ent to Twycross AP.[9]
Parl S'rn Dv (1832—85), W'rn Dv (1885—1918),
Bosw. Dv (1918—48). *Eccl* Seq 34. Eccl bdry:
1927.[81]

NOSELEY
AP Orig AP, sep in 1428 but not in 1535, replaced by
chap at Noseley Hall[211] and ex-par thereafter, sep
CP 1858,[14] eccl donative and status sustained. *LG*
Gart. Hd, Bill. PLU (1858—1930), RSD, RD. *Parl*
Seq 7. *Eccl* Gart. RDn (until 1865), Gart. II RDn
(1865—*).

OADBY
AP *LG* Guthl. Hd, Blaby PLU, RSD, RD (1894—
1913), Oadby UD (1913—74). Civ bdry: 1892,[38]
1936 (incl loses pt to Leic CB [assoc with Leics] &
CP),[23] 1966 (exchanges pts with Leic CB [assoc
with Leics] & CP).[71] *Parl* S'rn Dv (1832—1918),
Harb. Dv/CC (1918—55), Leic South-East BC
(1955—70), Harb. CC (1970—*).

OAKTHORPE AND DONISTHORPE
Tp comprised of hmlt Donisthorpe (in Church
Gresley AP, Measham AP [both Derbys] and in
Seal AP, Ashby de la Zouch AP [both Leics] and
hmlt Oakthorpe ([ent Derbys] in Church Gresley
AP, Stretton en le Field AP, Measham AP), the
combined area a sep CP 1866 with pt in ea co,[1] the
same area a sep EP 1869 as 'Donisthorpe',[113] qv.
LG Pt Derbys (Repton and Gresley Hd), pt Leics
(W Gosc. Hd), Ashb. de la Z. PLU, RSD. Prob in
1880s (before census of 1891, but with no explicit
order,[212]) considered ent Derbys, until transf 1897
to Leics,[32] thereafter Ashb. de la Z. RD. Bdry:
1936.[23] *Parl* Leics pt, N'rn Dv (1832—85), W'rn
Dv (1885—1918); after 1918, Loughb. Dv/CC
(1918—*).

ODSTONE
Hmlt (orig chap, early destroyed) in Shackerstone
AP, sep CP 1866.[1] *LG* Spark. Hd, Mkt. Bosw.
PLU, RSD, RD. Abol 1935 ent to Shackerstone
AP.[9] *Parl* S'rn Dv (1832—85), W'rn Dv (1885—
1918), Bosw. Dv (1918—48).

ORTON ON THE HILL
AP Incl chap Twycross (sep civ identity early, sep CP
1839[25]). *LG* Spark. Hd, Mkt. Bosw. PLU, RSD,
RD. Addtl civ bdry alt: 1885 (gains pt in Leics of
Merevale AP [Warws, Leics, the latter ent Warws
after this order]).[205] Abol civ 1935 ent to Twycross
AP.[9] *Parl* S'rn Dv (1832—85), W'rn Dv (1885—
1918), Bosw. Dv (1918—48). *Eccl* Seq 34.

OSBASTON
Tp in Cadeby AP, sep CP 1866.[1] *LG* Seq 19. *Parl*
Seq 12.

OSGATHORPE
AP *LG* W Gosc. Hd, Ashb. de la Z. PLU (soon after
1836[33]—1930), RSD, RD. Civ bdry: 1936,[23]
1969.[47] *Parl* Seq 3. Parl bdry: 1972.[49] *Eccl* Akeley
RDn (until 1865), W Akeley RDn (1865—1928), S
Akeley RDn (1928—*).

COLD OVERTON
AP *LG* Framl. Hd, Oakham PLU, RSD, Melt. Mowb.
RD (1894—1935), Melt. & Belv. RD (1935—36).
Abol civ 1936 ent to Knossington AP.[3] *Parl* N'rn
Dv (1832—85), E'rn Dv (1885—1918), Melt. Dv
(1918—48). *Eccl* Seq 11.

OWSTON
AP Usual eccl spelling; incl tps and former chaps of
Newbold (orig 'Newbold Saucey', 'Newbold Mare-
field'[213]) and therefore later civ 'Owston and
Newbold', qv. *Eccl* Seq 16.

OWSTON AND NEWBOLD
AP Usual civ spelling; for eccl and lesser units, see
prev entry. *LG* Seq 3. *Parl* Seq 2.

PACKINGTON
AP Pt Derbys (Repton & Gresley Hd, until 1884), Leics
(W Gosc. Hd, pt until 1884, ent from 1884: incl
chap Snibston [detached pt not sep civ, civ severed
1884 along with Derbys pt of par to help cr
Ravenstone with Snibston CP[21]], sep EP 1910[214]).
LG Ashb. de la Z. PLU, RSD, RD. Addtl civ bdry
alt: 1936.[23] *Parl* Seq 6. *Eccl* Seq 5. Addtl eccl bdry
alt: 1840 (help cr Coalville EP,[25] refounded soon
after in that year[103]).

PEATLING MAGNA
AP *LG* Seq 15. *Parl* Seq 10. *Eccl* Guthl. RDn. Abol
eccl 1729 to help cr Willoughby Waterless with
Peatling Magna EP.[215]

PEATLING PARVA
AP *LG* Seq 15. *Parl* Seq 10. *Eccl* Seq 32.

PECKLETON
AP *LG* Seq 19. Civ bdry: 1935 (incl gains Stapleton
CP).[9] *Parl* Seq 12. *Eccl* Seq 38.

PICKWELL
AP Usual eccl spelling; for civ and hmlt (orig chap), see
following entry. *Eccl* Seq 16.

PICKWELL WITH LEESTHORPE
AP Usual civ spelling, incl hmlt (orig chap, decayed by
17th cent[216]) Leesthorpe; for eccl see prev entry.
LG Gart. Hd, Melt. Mowb. PLU, RSD, RD
(1894—1935), Melt. & Belv. RD (1935—36). Abol
civ 1936 ent to Somerby AP.[3] *Parl* N'rn Dv
(1832—85), E'rn Dv (1885—1918), Melt. Dv
(1918—48).

PLUNGAR
AP *LG* Framl. Hd, Bing. PLU, RSD, Belv. RD (1894—
1935), Melt. & Belv. RD (1935—36). Abol civ
1936 ent to Redmile AP.[3] *Parl* N'rn Dv (1832—
85), E'rn Dv (1885—1918), Melt. Dv (1918—48).
Eccl Seq 8.

POTTERS MARSTON
Chap in Barwell AP, sep CP 1866.[1] *LG* Seq 17.
Parl Seq 14.

PRESTWOLD
AP Incl chap Hoton, tps Burton on the Wold, Cotes
(each a sep CP 1866,[1] not sep eccl hence this par
eccl 'Preston cum Hoton', qv). *LG* Seq 8. *Parl* Seq
4.

PRESTWOLD CUM HOTON
AP Usual eccl spelling; for civ and civ sep chap and tps,
see prev entry. *Eccl* Donative, Seq 23.

QUENIBOROUGH
AP *LG* Seq 6. Civ bdry: 1967 (help cr East Goscote

CP).[132] *Parl* Seq 1. *Eccl* Seq 21.

QUORN

Chap in Barrow upon Soar AP, sep EP 1728,[25] eccl refounded 1868,[57] sep CP 1866 as 'Quorndon',[1] qv. Akeley RDn (1728—1865), E Akeley RDn (1865—*).

QUORNDON

Chap in Barrow upon Soar AP, sep CP 1866,[1] sep EP 1728 as 'Quorn',[25] as such eccl refounded 1868,[57] qv. *LG* W Gosc. Hd, Barr. upon S. PLU, Quorndon USD, UD (1894—1935), Barr. upon S. RD (1935—74). Civ bdry: 1935,[9] 1936.[217] *Parl* Seq 5.

RAGDALE

AP *LG* E Gosc. Hd, Mkt. Mowb. PLU, RSD, RD (1894—1935), Melt. & Belv. RD (1935—36). Abol civ 1936 to help cr Hoby with Rotherby CP.[3] *Parl* N'rn Dv (1832—85), E'rn Dv (1885—1918), Melt. Dv (1918—48). *Eccl* Seq 22.

RATBY

AP Usual civ spelling; for eccl see following entry. *LG* Seq 19. Civ bdry: 1896 (cr Groby CP),[134] 1904,[154] 1935,[9] 1936.[23] *Parl* Seq 8.

RATBY CUM GROBY

AP Usual eccl spelling; for civ see prev entry. *Eccl* Pec jurisd Groby (until 1851), Seq 28 thereafter.

RATCLIFFE CULEY

Chap in Sheepy Magna AP, sep CP 1866.[1] *LG* Spark. Hd, Ath. PLU (soon after 1836[33]—1930), RSD, Mkt. Bosw. RD. Abol 1935 ent to Witherley AP.[9] *Parl* S'rn Dv (1832—85), W'rn Dv (1885—1918), Bosw. Dv (1918—48).

RATCLIFFE ON THE WREAKE

AP *LG* Seq 6. Civ bdry: 1935,[9] 1967 (help cr East Goscote CP).[132] *Parl* Seq 1. *Eccl* Seq 22.

RAVENSTONE

AP Pt Leics (W Gosc. Hd), pt Derbys (Repton & Gresley Hd). *LG* Ashb. de la Z. PLU, RSD. Reconstituted 1884 as 'Ravenstone with Snibston' when gains pt Ashby de la Zouch AP, hmlt Snibston from Packington AP, and pt in Derbys from Packington AP.[21] *Parl* Leics pt, N'rn Dv (1832—85). *Eccl* In dioc Lichf & Cov until 1837, dioc Lichf 1837—84, dioc S'well 1884—1927, dioc Leic 1927—*: Repton RDn (until 1846), Hartshorne RDn (1846—87), Repton RDn (1887—1927), W Akeley RDn (1927—28), S Akeley RDn (1928—*).

RAVENSTONE WITH SNIBSTON

CP Cr 1884 by union Ravenstone AP, hmlt Snibston in Packington AP, pt Ashby de la Zouch AP.[21] *LG* W Gosc. Hd, Ashb. de la Z. PLU, pt Ashb. de la Z. USD, pt Coalville USD (1892—94), pt Ashb. de la Z. RSD (reduced pt 1892—94), pt Ashb. de la Z. UD (apptd day—18 Dec 1894), Ashb. de la Z. RD (pt apptd day—18 Dec 1894, ent 18 Dec 1894—1974). Bdry: 1894 (loses the pt in Coalville UD to help cr Coalville CP),[104] 1894 ([18 Dec] no bdry alt, but the remainder of the par made ent in Ashb. de la Z. UD),[218] 1912,[105] 1936.[23] *Parl* W'rn Dv (1885—1918), Loughb. Dv/CC (1918—*).

REARSBY

AP *LG* Seq 6. Civ bdry: 1935,[9] 1967 (help cr East Goscote CP).[132] *Parl* Seq 1. *Eccl* Seq 22.

REDMILE

AP *LG* Seq 1. Civ bdry: 1936 (gains Barkstone AP, Plungar AP).[3] *Parl* Seq 1. *Eccl* Seq 8.

ROLLESTON

Chap and tp in Billesdon AP, sep CP 1866.[1] *LG* Seq 3. *Parl* Seq 7.

ROTHERBY

AP *LG* E Gosc. Hd, Mkt. Mowb. PLU, RSD, RD (1894—1935), Melt. & Belv. RD (1835—36). Abol civ 1936 to help cr Hoby with Rotherby CP.[3] *Parl* N'rn Dv (1832—85), E'rn Dv (1885—1918), Melt. Dv (1918—48). *Eccl* Seq 20.

ROTHLEY

AP Tp 'Rothley' in W Gosc. Hd as was pt chap and bor Mountsorrel (the latter a sep EP 1846 as 'Mountsorrel Christ Church,[208] and a sep CP 1866 as 'Mountsorrel South End'[1]); incl in E Gosc. Hd chap Gaddesby (sep civ identity early, sep EP 1874[122]), chap Grimston (sep civ identity early, sep EP 1791[25]), chap Keyham (sep CP 1866,[1] eccl severed 1954 to help cr Houghton on the Hill and Keyham EP[139]), chap Wartnaby (sep CP 1866,[1] eccl severed 1872 and transf to Grimston AP,[133] the latter called 'Grimston with Wartnaby' until area Wartnaby severed 1932 to help cr Ab Kettleby with Wartnaby and Holwell EP[4]), hmlt Wycomb and chap Chadwell (sep CP 1866 as 'Wycomb and Chadwell',[1] eccl called 'Wycombe and Chadwell' and eccl severed 1954 to help cr Scalford with Wycombe and Chadwell EP[138]). *LG* W Gosc. Hd (pt until 1866, ent from 1866), pt E Gosc. Hd (until 1866), pt Mountsorrel Bor, Barr. upon S. PLU, RSD, RD. Addtl civ bdry alt: 1884,[8] 1884,[96] 1912,[219] 1935.[9] *Parl* Seq 5. *Eccl* Pec jurisd Manor of Rothley (until 1851), Seq 4 thereafter.

ROTHLEY TEMPLE

Ex-par place, sep CP 1858.[14] *LG* W Gosc. Hd, Barr. upon S. PLU (1858—84), RSD. Abol civ 1884 pt to Rothley AP, pt to help cr Mountsorrel CP.[58] *Parl* N'rn Dv (1832—85).

SADDINGTON

AP *LG* Seq 4. *Parl* Seq 9. *Eccl* Seq 15.

SALTBY

AP *LG* Framl. Hd, Mkt. Mowb. PLU, RSD, RD (1894—1935), Melt. & Belv. RD (1935—36). Abol civ 1936 ent to Sproxton AP.[3] *Parl* N'rn Dv (1832—85), E'rn Dv (1885—1918), Melt. Dv (1918—48). *Eccl* Seq 9.

SAPCOTE

AP *LG* Seq 18. *Parl* Seq 13. *Eccl* Seq 31.

SAXBY

AP *LG* Framl. Hd, Mkt. Mowb. PLU, RSD, RD (1894—1935), Melt. & Belv. RD (1935—36). Abol civ 1936 ent to Freeby CP.[3] *Parl* N'rn Dv (1832—85), E'rn Dv (1885—1918), Melt. Dv (1918—48). *Eccl* Seq 7.

SAXELBY

AP Usual civ spelling; for eccl see following entry. *LG* E Gosc. Hd, Mkt. Mowb. PLU, RSD, RD (1894—1935), Melt. & Belv. RD (1935—36). Abol civ 1936 ent to Grimston CP.[3] *Parl* N'rn Dv (1832—85), E'rn Dv (1885—1918), Melt. Dv (1918—48).

SAXELBY WITH SHOBY

AP Usual eccl spelling for 'Saxelby' AP (qv for civ) incl ex-par Shoby (orig sep AP, early 'Siwoldby'). *Eccl* Pec jurisd Manor of Rothley (until 1851), Seq 24 thereafter.

SCALFORD

AP *LG* Seq 2. Civ bdry: 1936 (gains Wycomb and Chadwell CP).[3] *Parl* Seq 1. *Eccl* Framl. RDn (until 1865), Framl. IV RDn (1865—73), Framl. III RDn (1873—1954). Abol eccl 1954 to help cr Scalford with Wycombe and Chadwell EP.[138]

SCALFORD WITH WYCOMBE AND CHADWELL

EP Cr 1954 by union Scalford AP, chap Wycombe and Chadwell in Rothley AP.[138] Framl. III RDn (1954—61), Framl. II RDn (1961—*).

SCRAPTOFT

AP *LG* Seq 3. Civ bdry: 1966 (loses pt to Leic CB [assoc with Leics] & CP).[71] *Parl* Seq 7. *Eccl* Gart. RDn (until 1865), Gart. II RDn (1865—93), Gosc. I RDn (1893—*). Eccl bdry: 1961 (help cr Thurnby Lodge EP),[140] 1971 (help cr Leicester St Elizabeth, Nether Hall EP).[142]

SEAGRAVE

AP *LG* Seq 6. *Parl* Seq 1. *Eccl* Seq 22.

SEAL

AP Usual eccl spelling, sometimes 'Nether Seal with Over Seal', sometimes 'Seale'; Nether Seal AP incl chap Over Seal, the latter early destroyed so the two united as tp Over and Nether Seal, qv for status as sep CP 1866.[1] Incl pt chap Blackfordby (sep CP 1866,[1] sep EP 1876,[20] qv for other constituent pars), pt hmlt Donisthorpe (eccl severed 1869 to help cr Donisthorpe EP[113]; civ pt of tp Oakthorpe and Donisthorpe [Leics, Derbys], the latter a sep CP 1866 with pt in both cos[1]) so that once the 3 areas have sep civ status, 'Seal' has no sep civ identity after 1866. *LG* W Gosc. Hd. *Parl* N'rn Dv (1832—67). *Eccl* In dioc Linc until 1837, dioc Peterb 1837—1927, dioc Derby 1927—*: Akeley RDn (until 1865), W Akeley RDn (1865—1927), Repton RDn (1927—*).

NETHER SEAL

CP Orig chap, early destroyed, incl thereafter in tp/CP Over and Nether Seal (eccl, 'Seal'), 'Nether Seal' a sep CP 1894 from the latter.[220] *LG* Ashb. de la Z. PLU, RD. Transf 1897 to Derbys where later called 'Netherseal',[32] qv in that co.

OVER SEAL

CP Orig AP incl area chap Nether Seal, the latter early destroyed and the 2 thereafter tp/CP Over and Nether Seal (eccl, 'Seal'), 'Over Seal' a sep CP 1894 from the latter.[220] *LG* Ashb. de la Z. PLU, RD. Transf 1897 to Derbys where later called 'Overseal'.[32]

OVER SEAL AND NETHER SEAL

Tp comprised of Over Seal AP, chap (early destroyed) Nether Seal, sep CP 1866[1]; for eccl see 'Seal'. *LG* W Gosc. Hd, Ashb. de la Z. PLU, RSD. Bdry: 1884,[75] 1884 (loses pt to Oakthorpe and Donisthorpe CP [Leics, Derbys]).[221] Abol 1894 to cr 2 CPs of 'Nether Seal', 'Over Seal',[220] later after transf 1897 to Derbys called 'Netherseal', 'Overseal'. *Parl* N'rn Dv (1832—85), W'rn Dv

(1885—1918).

SEWSTERN

Chap in Buckminster AP, sep CP 1866.[1] *LG* Framl. Hd, Mkt. Mowb. PLU, RSD, RD (1894—1935), Melt. & Belv. RD (1935—36). Bdry: 1884.[94] Abol 1936 ent to Buckminster AP.[3] *Parl* N'rn Dv (1832—85), E'rn Dv (1885—1918), Melt. Dv (1918—48).

SHACKERSTONE

AP Incl hmlt Odstone (orig chap, early destroyed, sep CP 1866[1]). *LG* Seq 19. Addtl civ bdry alt: 1883,[28] 1886,[43] 1935 (gains Barton in the Beans CP, Bilstone CP, Congerstone AP, Odstone CP).[9] *Parl* Seq 12. *Eccl* Seq 36. Eccl bdry: 1927.[81]

SHANGTON

AP *LG* Seq 4. *Parl* Seq 9. *Eccl* Seq 15.

SHARNFORD

AP *LG* Seq 18. Civ bdry: 1935 (incl gains pt Copston Magna CP, Warws).[72] *Parl* Seq 13. *Eccl* Seq 31.

SHAWELL

AP *LG* Seq 15. Civ bdry: 1935 (loses pt to Newton and Biggin CP, pt to Churchover AP, both Warws).[72] *Parl* Seq 10. *Eccl* Seq 29.

SHEARSBY

Chap and tp in Knaptoft AP, sep CP 1866,[1] eccl severed 1927 to help cr Arnesby with Shearsby EP.[19] *LG* Seq 15. *Parl* Seq 10.

SHEEPSHED

AP Usual eccl spelling until renamed 1971 (incl bdry alt) 'Shepshed',[222] the latter the usual civ spelling, qv. *Eccl* Akeley RDn (until 1865), E Akeley RDn (1865—93), S Akeley RDn (1893—1928), E Akeley RDn (1928—71). Eccl bdry: 1852 (help cr Charnwood Forest [Oaks Church] EP).[100]

SHEEPY

CP Cr 1935 by union Sheepy Magna AP, Sheepy Parva AP, Sibson AP, Upton CP.[9] *LG* Mkt. Bosw. RD. *Parl* Bosw. CC (1948—*).

SHEEPY MAGNA

AP Incl eccl Sheepy Parva AP (no church, sep civ status retained, qv), chap Ratcliffe Culey (sep CP 1866,[1] not sep eccl) hence this par eccl 'Sheepy with Ratcliffe Culey', qv. *LG* Spark. Hd, Ath. PLU, RSD, Mkt. Bosw. RD. Civ bdry: 1885 (exchanges pts with Merevale AP [Warws, Leics] so that the latter ent Warws thereafter).[205] Abol civ 1935 to help cr Sheepy CP.[9] *Parl* S'rn Dv (1832—85), W'rn Dv (1885—1918), Bosw. Dv (1918—48).

SHEEPY PARVA

AP No church, eccl in Sheepy Magna with Ratcliffe Culey AP, sep civ status retained. Organisation as for Sheepy Magna.

SHEEPY WITH RATCLIFFE CULEY

AP Usual eccl spelling, incl Sheepy Magna AP, Sheepy Parva AP (no church, sep civ identity sustained), chap Ratcliffe Culey (sep CP 1866[1]). *Eccl* Seq 34.

SHELTHORPE

EP Cr 1969 from Loughborough Emmanuel EP.[198] E Akeley RDn.

SHENTON

Chap in Market Bosworth AP, sep CP 1866.[1] *LG* Spark. Hd, Mkt. Bosw. PLU, RSD, RD. Abol 1935 ent to Sutton Cheney CP.[9] *Parl* S'rn Dv (1832—

85), W'rn Dv (1885—1918), Bosw. Dv (1918—48).

SHEPSHED

AP Usual civ spelling, eccl spelling after renaming (and bdry alt) 1971 of 'Sheepshed',[222] qv for earlier eccl organisation. *LG* W Gosc. Hd, Loughb. PLU, pt Shepshed USD (1886—94), Loughb. RSD (ent 1875—86, pt 1886—94), Shepshed UD. Civ bdry: 1891,[124] 1894 (the pt not in the UD cr Shepshed Parva CP),[22] 1896 (gains Shepshed Parva CP),[223] 1936.[23] *Parl* Seq 3. *Eccl* E Akeley RDn (1971—*).

SHEPSHED PARVA

CP Cr 1894 from the pt of Shepshed AP (eccl, 'Sheepshed') not in Shepshed UD.[22] *LG* Loughb. PLU, RD. Abol 1896 ent to Shepshed UD & AP.[223]

SHOBY

AP Orig sep par (early 'Siwoldby') in Gosc. RDn, not found after 1428,[224] thereafter deemed ex-par place, sep CP 1858,[14] eccl in Saxelby AP (eccl, 'Saxelby with Shoby'). *LG* E Gosc. Hd, Mkt. Bosw. PLU (1858—1930), RSD, RD (1894—1935), Melt. & Belv. RD (1935—36). Abol civ 1936 ent to Grimston CP.[3] *Parl* N'rn Dv (1832—85), E'rn Dv (1885—1918), Melt. Dv (1918—48).

SIBSON

AP Incl tp Upton (orig chap, early destroyed, sep CP 1866,[1] not sep eccl hence this par eccl 'Sibson cum Upton', qv). *LG* Spark. Hd, Mkt. Bosw. PLU (soon after 1836[33]—1930), RSD, RD. Abol civ 1935 to help cr Sheepy CP.[9] *Parl* S'rn Dv (1832—85), W'rn Dv (1885—1918), Bosw. Dv (1918—48).

SIBSON CUM UPTON

AP Usual eccl spelling; for civ and civ sep tp (orig chap), see prev entry. *Eccl* Seq 34.

SILEBY

AP *LG* Seq 6. *Parl* Seq 1. *Eccl* Seq 22.

SIWOLDBY—see SHOBY

SKEFFINGTON

AP *LG* Seq 7. *Parl* Seq 2. *Eccl* Seq 19.

SLAWSTON

AP *LG* Gart. Hd, Upp. PLU, RSD, Mkt. Harb. RD. *Parl* Seq 9. *Eccl* Seq 13.

SMEETON WESTERBY

Tp in Kibworth Beauchamp AP, sep CP 1866,[1] sep EP 1852.[149] *LG* Seq 4. *Parl* Seq 9. *Eccl* Gart. RDn (until 1865), Gart. II RDn (1865—*).

SNARESTONE

Chap in Swepstone AP, sep civ identity early. *LG* Seq 16. *Parl* Seq 15.

SNIBSTON

EP Chap in Packington AP, not sep civ [but civ severed 1884 to help cr Ravenstone with Snibston CP[21]], sep EP 1910 (detached pt of par).[214] W Akeley RDn (1910—28), S Akeley RDn (1928—*).

SOMERBY

AP *LG* Seq 2. Civ bdry: 1887,[96] 1936 (gains Burrough on the Hill AP, Pickwell with Leesthorpe AP).[3] *Parl* Seq 1. *Eccl* Pt pec jurisd Manor of Rothley (until 1851), remainder and later, Seq 11.

SPROXTON

AP *LG* Seq 2. Civ bdry: 1936 (gains Bescaby CP, Saltby AP, Stonesby AP),[3] 1965 (loses pt to Skillington AP, pt to Stoke Rochford CP, pt to Wyville cum Hungerton AP, all Lincs Pts

Kestev).[18] *Parl* Seq 1. *Eccl* Seq 9.

STANTON UNDER BARDON

Chap (pec jurisd Groby, until 1851) in Thornton AP, sep CP 1866,[1] eccl severed 1935 and transf to Markfield AP.[200] *LG* Spark. Hd, Mkt. Bosw. PLU, RSD, RD. Abol civ 1935 ent to Markfield AP.[9] *Parl* S'rn Dv (1832—85), W'rn Dv (1885—1918), Bosw. Dv (1918—48).

STAPLEFORD

AP *LG* Framl. Hd, Mkt. Mowb. PLU, RSD, RD (1894—1935), Melt. & Belv. RD (1935—36). Abol civ 1936 ent to Freeby CP.[3] *Parl* N'rn Dv (1832—85), E'rn Dv (1885—1918), Melt. Dv (1918—48). *Eccl* Seq 7.

STAPLETON

Chap in Barwell AP, sep CP 1866.[1] *LG* Spark. Hd, Mkt. Bosw. PLU (soon after 1836[33]—1930), RSD, RD. Abol 1935 ent to Peckleton AP.[9] *Parl* S'rn Dv (1832—85), W'rn Dv (1885—1918), Bosw. Dv (1918—48).

STATHERN

AP *LG* Seq 2. *Parl* Seq 1. *Eccl* Framl. RDn (until 1865), Framl. IV RDn (1865—73), Framl. III RDn (1873—77), Framl. I RDn (1877—*).

STAUNTON HAROLD

Chap and tp in Breedon on the Hill AP, sep CP 1866,[1] donative but sep eccl status not sustained. *LG* Seq 10. *Parl* Seq 6. *Eccl* Akeley RDn.

STOCKERSTON

AP *LG* Seq 5. Civ bdry: 1877 (gains the pt of Stoke Dry AP [Rutl, Leics] in Leics and the latter ent Rutl thereafter).[225] *Parl* Seq 9. *Eccl* Seq 14.

STOCKING FARM

EP Cr 1958 from Belgrave AP, Birstall EP, pt eccl ex-par Leicester Abbey.[67] Christianity RDn.

STOKE DRY

AP Pt Leics (Gart. Hd), mostly Rutl (Wrangdyke Hd), the former pt transf 1885 to Stockerston AP, Leics, and the par ent Rutl thereafter).[225] *LG* Upp. PLU, RSD; for later civ organisation see main entry in Rutl. *Parl* Leics pt, S'rn Dv (1832—1918). *Eccl* See entry in Rutl.

STOKE GOLDING

Chap in Hinckley AP, sep CP 1866,[1] eccl united 1865 with chap Dadlington in same par to cr Stoke Golding cum Dadlington EP,[109] qv. *LG* Spark. Hd, Hinck. PLU (orig rated as pt Hinckley AP, sep rated soon after 1836[33]—1930), RSD, RD. Abol civ 1936 pt to Hinck. UD & AP, pt to Higham on the Hill AP.[63] *Parl* S'rn Dv (1832—85), W'rn Dv (1885—1918), Bosw. Dv (1918—48).

STOKE GOLDING CUM DADLINGTON

EP Cr 1865 by union chaps Stoke Golding, Dadlington, each in Hinckley AP.[109] Spark. RDn (1865), Spark. II RDn (1865—*).

STONESBY

AP *LG* Framl. Hd, Mkt. Mowb. PLU, RSD, RD (1894—1935), Melt. & Belv. RD (1935—36). Abol civ 1936 ent to Sproxton AP.[3] *Parl* N'rn Dv (1832—85), E'rn Dv (1885—1918), Melt. Dv (1918—48). *Eccl* Seq 7.

STONEY STANTON

AP *LG* Seq 18. Civ bdry: 1885.[115] *Parl* Seq 13. *Eccl*

Seq 27.

STONTON WYVILLE

AP *LG* Seq 4. *Parl* Seq 9. *Eccl* Seq 13.

STOUGHTON

Chap in Thurnby AP, sep CP 1866.[1] *LG* Seq 3. Civ bdry: 1936,[23] 1966 (loses pt to Leic CB [assoc with Leics] & CP).[71] *Parl* Seq 7.

STRETTON EN LE FIELD

AP Derbys par transf 1897 to Leics.[32] *LG* Ashby de la Z. PLU, RD. Bdry: 1965 (loses pt to Newton Regis AP, Warws).[101] *Parl* Loughb. Dv/CC (1918—*). *Eccl* In dioc Lichf & Cov until 1837, dioc Lichf 1837—84, dioc S'well 1884—1927, dioc Leic 1927—*: Repton RDn (until 1846), Hartshorne RDn (1846—55), Lullington RDn (1855—66), Hartshorne RDn (1866—87), Repton RDn (1887—1927), W Akeley RDn (1927—*).

STRETTON MAGNA

Chap and tp in Glen Magna AP, sep CP 1866[1]; eccl 'Great Stretton', not sep eccl hence that par 'Glen Magna cum Great Stretton'. *LG* Seq 3. Bdry: 1936.[23] *Parl* Seq 7.

STRETTON PARVA

Chap in King's Norton AP, sep CP 1866.[1] *LG* Seq 3. *Parl* Seq 7.

SUTTON CHENEY

Chap in Market Bosworth AP, sep CP 1866,[1] sep EP 1860.[79] *LG* Spark. Hd, Bosw. PLU (soon after 1836[33]—1930), RSD, RD. Civ bdry: 1935 (gains Dadlington CP, Shenton CP).[9] *Parl* Seq 12. *Eccl* Spark. RDn (1860—65), Spark. II RDn (1865—93), Spark. I RDn (1893—*).

SWANNINGTON

Chap in Whitwick AP, sep CP 1866,[1] pt eccl severed 1875 to help cr Whitwick St George EP.[100] *LG* W Gosc. Hd, Ashb. de la Z. PLU, pt Coalville USD (1892—94), Ashb. de la Z. RSD (ent 1875—92, pt 1892—94), Ashb. de la Z. RD. Bdry: 1894 (loses the pt in the UD to help cr Coalville CP),[104] 1912,[105] 1936.[23] *Parl* Seq 6.

SWEPSTONE

AP Incl chap Snarestone (Spark. Hd, sep civ identity early). *LG* Seq 10. *Parl* Seq 6. *Eccl* Akeley RDn (until 1865), W Akeley RDn (1865—*).

SWINFORD

AP *LG* Seq 15. *Parl* Seq 10. *Eccl* Guthl. RDn (until 1865), Guthl. II RDn (1865—93), Guthl. III RDn (1893—1928), Guthl. II RDn (1928—*).

SWITHLAND

AP *LG* Seq 11. Civ bdry: 1912,[219] 1968.[226] *Parl* Seq 5. *Eccl* Pec jurisd Groby (until 1851), Seq 1 thereafter.

SYSONBY

Tp in Melton Mowbray AP, sep CP 1866.[1] *LG* Framl. Hd, Mkt. Mowb. PLU, RSD, RD. Abol 1930 ent to Melt. Mowb. UD & AP.[201] *Parl* N'rn Dv (1832—85), E'rn Dv (1885—1918), Melt. Dv (1918—48).

SYSONBY WITH EYE KETTLEBY

CP Cr 1894 from the pt of Melton Mowbray AP not in Melt. Mowb. UD.[22] *LG* Melt. Mowb. PLU, RD. Later called 'Eye Kettleby' and as such abol 1935 ent to Melt. Mowb. UD & AP.[9] *Parl* Melt. Dv (1918—48).

SYSTON

AP *LG* Seq 6. Civ bdry: 1935.[9] *Parl* Seq 1. *Eccl* Gosc. RDn (until 1865), Gosc. I RDn (1865—93), Gosc. II RDn (1893—*).

THEDDINGWORTH

AP Tp 'Theddingworth' in Leics, Gart. Hd; incl in Northants hmlt Hothorpe (Rothwell Hd, sep CP 1866[1] in Northants) so that Teddingworth ent Leics thereafter. *LG* Mkt. Harb. PLU, RSD, RD. *Parl* Leics pt, Seq 9. *Eccl* Seq 13.

THORNTON

AP Incl chap Bagworth (sep CP 1866, not sep eccl hence this par eccl 'Thornton with Bagworth', qv), chap Stanton under Bardon (sep CP 1866,[1] eccl severed 1935 and transf to Markfield AP[200]). *LG* Spark. Hd, Mkt. Bosw. PLU, RSD, RD. Abol civ 1935 ent to Bagworth CP.[9] *Parl* S'rn Dv (1832—85), W'rn Dv (1885—1918), Bosw. Dv (1918—48).

THORNTON WITH BAGWORTH

AP Usual eccl spelling; for civ, civ sep chaps, eccl transf of a chap, see prev entry. Spark. RDn (until 1865), Spark. II RDn (1865—93), S Akeley RDn (1893—1928), Spark. III RDn (1928—*).

THORPE ACRE

EP Cr 1850 from Dishley AP.[111] Akeley RDn (1850—65), E Akeley RDn (1865—1921). Abol eccl 1921 to help cr Thorpe Acre with Dishley EP.[112]

THORPE ACRE AND DISHLEY

AP Usual civ spelling for Dishley AP (qv for eccl) incl hmlt Thorpe Acre. *LG* W Gosc. Hd, Loughb. PLU, pt Loughb. MB & USD (1888—91), Loughb. RSD (ent 1875—88, pt 1888—91, ent 1891—94), Loughb. RD. Civ bdry: 1891 (incl loses the pt in the MB to Knight Thorpe CP).[124] Abol civ 1936 ent to Loughb. MB & AP.[23] *Parl* N'rn Dv (1832—85), Mid Dv (1885—1918), Loughb. Dv (1918—48).

THORPE ACRE WITH DISHLEY

EP Cr 1921 by union Dishley AP, Thorpe Acre EP.[112] E Akeley RDn. Bdry: 1963,[207] 1971.[222]

THORPE ARNOLD

AP *LG* Framl. Hd, Mkt. Mowb. PLU, RSD, RD (1894—1935), Melt. & Belv. RD (1935—36). Civ bdry: 1935.[9] Abol civ 1936 to help cr Waltham CP.[3] *Parl* N'rn Dv (1832—85), E'rn Dv (1885—1918), Melt. Dv (1918—48). *Eccl* Framl. RDn (until 1865), Framl. I RDn (1865—73), Framl. III RDn (1873—77), Framl. II RDn (1877—93), Framl. III RDn (1893—1961), Framl. II RDn (1961—71). Abol eccl 1971 to help cr Melton Mowbray with Thorpe Arnold EP.[202]

THORPE SATCHVILLE

Chap in Twyford AP, sep CP 1866,[1] the par gains eccl 1732 Twyford AP to cr Hungarton with Twyford and Thorpe Satchville EP,[146] qv for later division into 2 EPs of Hungarton, Twyford with Thorpe Satchville. *LG* E Gosc. Hd, Mkt. Mowb. PLU, RSD, RD (1894—1935), Melt. & Belv. RD (1935—36). Abol civ 1936 to help cr Twyford and Thorpe CP.[3] *Parl* N'rn Dv (1832—85), E'rn Dv (1885—1918), Melt. Dv (1918—48).

THRINGSTONE

Chap in Whitwick AP, sep CP 1866,[1] pt eccl severed 1875 to help cr Whitwick St George EP.[100]

LG W Gosc. Hd, Ashby de la Z. PLU (soon after 1836[33]—1930), RSD, RD. Bdry: 1884.[107] Abol 1936 pt to Coalville UD & CP, pt to Coleorton AP, pt to Osgathorpe AP, pt to Swannington CP, pt to Worthington CP, pt to Belton AP.[23] *Parl* N'rn Dv (1832—85), Mid Dv (1885—1918), Loughb. Dv (1918—48).

THRUSSINGTON
AP *LG* Seq 6. *Parl* Seq 1. *Eccl* Seq 22.

THURCASTON
AP Incl chap Anstey (sep CP 1866,[1] sep EP 1866[7]), tp Cropston (sep CP 1866[1]). *LG* Seq 11. Addtl civ bdry alt: 1912,[219] 1935 (incl gains Cropston CP),[9] 1966 (loses pt to Leic CB [assoc with Leics] & CP).[71] *Parl* Seq 5. *Eccl* Akeley RDn (until 1865), E Akeley RDn (1865—93), Guthl. I RDn (1893—1928), Spark. III RDn (1928—*).

THURLASTON
AP *LG* Seq 17. Civ bdry: 1909 (gains Knoll and Bassett House CP).[90] *Parl* Seq 14. *Eccl* Seq 25.

THURMASTON
Chap in Belgrave AP, sep EP 1794 as 'Thurmaston',[25] sep CP 1866 as 'South Thurmaston',[1] qv. *Eccl* Gosc. RDn (1794—1865), Gosc. I RDn (1865—93), Gosc. II RDn (1893—*).

CP Cr 1903 by union North Thurmaston CP, South Thurmaston CP.[227] *LG* Barr. upon S. PLU, Thurmaston UD (1903—35), Barr. upon S. RD (1935—74). Bdry: 1914,[55] 1935 (loses pt to Leic CB [assoc with Leics] & CP),[9] 1966 (exchanges pts with Leic CB [assoc with Leics] & CP).[71] *Parl* Melt. Dv/CC (1918—*).

NORTH THURMASTON
Chap in Barkby AP, sep CP 1866.[1] *LG* E Gosc. Hd, Barr. upon S. PLU, Thurmaston USD, UD. Abol 1903 to help cr Thurmaston CP.[227] *Parl* N'rn Dv (1832—85), E'rn Dv (1885—1918).

SOUTH THURMASTON
Chap in Belgrave AP, sep CP 1866,[1] sep EP 1794 as 'Thurmaston',[25] qv. *LG*, civ abol, *Parl* as for North Thurmaston.

THURNBY
AP Incl chap Stoughton, hmlt Bushby (each a sep CP 1866,[1] neither sep eccl hence this par eccl 'Thurnby with Stoughton', qv). *LG* Gart. Hd, Bill. PLU (soon after 1835[33]—1930), RSD, RD. Addtl civ bdry: 1935 (loses pt to Leic CB [assoc with Leics] & CP, gains Bushby CP),[9] 1966 (loses pt to Leic CB [assoc with Leics] & CP).[71] *Parl* Seq 7.

THURNBY WITH STOUGHTON
AP Usual eccl spelling; for civ and civ sep chap and hmlt, see prev entry. *Eccl* Seq 15. Eccl bdry: 1961 (help cr Thurnby Lodge EP).[140] Sometimes 'Thurnby cum Stoughton'.

THURNBY LODGE
EP Cr 1961 from Humberstone AP, Scraptoft AP, Thurnby with Stoughton AP.[140] Christianity RDn. Bdry: 1967.[141]

TILTON
AP Usual civ spelling; for eccl see following entry. Tp 'Tilton' in E Gosc. Hd as were hmlt Whatborough, tp Halstead (the latter 2 each a sep CP 1866[1]); incl in Gart. Hd tp Marefield (sep CP 1866[1]). *LG* Bill.

PLU, RSD, RD. Addtl civ bdry alt: 1935 (gains Halstead CP).[9] *Parl* Pt N'rn Dv ([Marefield] 1832—67), S'rn Dv (pt 1832—67, ent 1867—85), E'rn Dv (1885—1918), Melt. Dv/CC (1918—70), Harb. CC (1970—*).

TILTON ON THE HILL
AP Usual eccl spelling; for civ and civ sep tps, hmlt, see prev entry. *Eccl* Seq 17.

TUGBY
AP Tp 'Tugby' in E Gosc. Hd; incl in Gart. Hd chap East Norton (sep CP 1866,[1] eccl severed 1927 to help cr Alexton with East Norton EP,[5] so that this par 'Tugby with East Norton' until 1927, qv, 'Tugby' thereafter. *LG* E Gosc. Hd (pt until 1866, ent from 1866, pt Gart. Hd (until 1866), Bill. PLU, RSD, RD. *Parl* Seq 7. *Eccl* Gart. III RDn. Abol eccl 1961 to help cr Tugby and East Norton EP.[6]

TUGBY AND EAST NORTON
EP Cr 1961 by union Tugby EP, chap East Norton from Alexton with East Norton EP.[6] Gart. III RDn.

TUGBY WITH EAST NORTON
AP Usual eccl spelling until chap East Norton severed 1927 to help cr Alexton with East Norton EP, the remainder to be 'Tugby'.[5] Gosc. RDn (until 1865), Gosc. I RDn (1865—73), Gart. III RDn (1873—1927).

TWYCROSS
Chap in Orton on the Hill AP, sep civ identity early, sep EP 1839.[25] *LG* Seq 19. Civ bdry: 1935 (gains Gopsall CP, Norton juxta Twycross AP, Orton on the Hill AP).[9] *Parl* Seq 12. *Eccl* Spark. RDn (1839—65), Spark. I RDn (1865—*). Eccl bdry: 1956 (gains eccl ex-par Gopsall).[131]

TWYFORD
AP Incl chap Thorpe Satchville (sep CP 1866[1]). *LG* E Gosc. Hd, Melt. Mowb. PLU, RSD, RD (1894—1935), Melt. & Belv. RD (1935—36). Abol civ 1936 to help cr Twyford and Thorpe CP.[3] *Parl* N'rn Dv (1832—85), E'rn Dv (1885—1918), Melt. Dv (1918—48). *Eccl* Gosc. RDn. Abol eccl 1732 to help cr Hungarton with Twyford and Thorpe Satchville EP,[146] qv for later division into 2 EPs of Hungarton, Twyford with Thorpe Satchville.

TWYFORD AND THORPE
CP Cr 1936 by union Twyford AP, Thorpe Satchville CP.[3] *LG* Melt. & Belv. RD. *Parl* Melt. CC (1948—*).

TWYFORD WITH THORPE SATCHVILLE
EP Cr 1925 when Hungarton with Twyford and Thorpe Satchville EP divided into 2 EPs of Hungarton, Twyford with Thorpe Satchville.[147] Gosc. I RDn.

ULLESTHORPE
Hmlt in Claybrooke AP, sep CP 1866.[1] *LG* Seq 15. Bdry: 1877 (exchanges pts with Monks Kirby AP, Warws),[228] 1935 (gains pt Wibtoft CP, Warws).[72] *Parl* Seq 10.

ULVERSCROFT
Ex-par place, sep CP 1858,[14] pt eccl severed 1839 to help cr Woodhouse Eaves EP,[25] refounded 1844,[60] pt of the ex-par place eccl severed 1860 to help cr Copt Oak EP.[44] *LG* Seq 11. Bdry: 1884,[96] 1884,[8] 1968.[226] *Parl* Seq 5.

UPTON

Tp (orig chap, early destroyed) in Sibson AP, sep CP 1866.[1] *LG* Spark. Hd, Mkt. Bosw. PLU, RSD, RD. Abol 1935 to help cr Sheepy CP.[9] *Parl* S'rn Dv (1832—85), W'rn Dv (1885—1918), Bosw. Dv (1918—48).

WALTHAM

CP Cr 1936 by union Thorpe Arnold AP, Waltham on the Wolds AP.[3] *LG* Melt. & Belv. RD. *Parl* Melt. CC (1948—*).

WALTHAM ON THE WOLDS

AP Sometimes early 'Walton on the Wolds'. *LG* Framl. Hd, Mkt. Mowb. PLU, RSD, RD (1894—1935), Melt. & Belv. RD (1935—36). Abol civ 1936 to help cr Waltham CP.[3] *Parl* N'rn Dv (1832—85), E'rn Dv (1885—1918), Melt. Dv (1918—48). *Eccl* Framl. RDn (until 1865), Framl. IV RDn (1865—73), Framl. III RDn (1873—77), Framl. II RDn (1877—*).

WALTON

Chap in Knaptoft AP, eccl severed 1926 to help cr Kimcote with Walton EP[70]; for civ see following entry.

WALTON IN KNAPTOFT

Hmlt in Knaptoft AP, sep CP 1866[1]; for eccl see prev entry. *LG* Guthl. Hd, Lutt. PLU, RSD, RD. Abol 1898 to help cr Kimcote and Walton CP.[152] *Parl* S'rn Dv (1832—1918).

WALTON LE WOLDS

AP Usual eccl spelling; for civ see following entry. *Eccl* Gosc. RDn (until 1865), Gosc. II RDn (1865—93), E Akeley RDn (1893—1953), Gosc. II RDn (1953—*).

WALTON ON THE WOLDS

AP Usual civ spelling; for eccl see prev entry. *LG* Seq 6. *Parl* Seq 5.

WANLIP

AP *LG* Seq 11. *Parl* Seq 1. *Eccl* Seq 4.

WARTNABY

Chap (pec jurisd Manor Rothley, until 1851) in Rothley AP, sep CP 1866,[1] eccl severed 1872 and transf to Grimston AP,[133] the eccl union 'Grimston with Wartnaby' until area Wartnaby eccl severed 1932 to help cr Ab Kettleby with Wartnaby and Howell EP.[4] *LG* E Gosc. Hd, Mkt. Mowb. PLU, RSD, RD (1894—1935), Melt. & Belv. RD (1935—36). Bdry: 1884.[2] Abol 1936 ent to Ab Kettleby AP.[3] *Parl* N'rn Dv (1832—85), E'rn Dv (1885—1918), Melt. Dv (1918—48).

WELBY

Chap and tp in Melton Mowbray AP, sep CP 1866.[1] *LG* Framl. Hd, Mkt. Mowb. PLU, RSD, RD (1894—1935), Melt. & Belv. Dv (1935—36). Bdry: 1935.[9] Abol 1936 ent to Asfordby AP.[3] *Parl* N'rn Dv (1832—85), E'rn Dv (1885—1918), Melt. Dv (1918—48).

WELHAM

AP Perhaps orig incl Cranoe,[108] Glooston[130] (the former early sep, the latter a sep par by 1220). *LG* Seq 4. Civ bdry: 1885.[162] *Parl* Seq 9. *Eccl* Seq 13.

WESTRILL AND STARMORE

Ex-par place, sep CP 1858.[14] *LG* Guthl. Hd, Rugby PLU (1836—95), Lutt. PLU (1895—1930), sep RD

(1894—95), Lutt. RD (1895—1974). *Parl* Seq 10.

WHATBOROUGH

Hmlt in Tilton AP, sep CP 1866.[1] *LG* Seq 7. *Parl* Seq 2.

LONG WHATTON

AP *LG* Seq 12. Civ bdry: 1936 (incl gains Diseworth AP).[23] *Parl* Seq 3. *Eccl* Seq 2.

WHETSTONE

Chap (Guthl. Hd) in Enderby AP (o'wise Spark. Hd), sep civ identity early, sep EP 1867.[117] *LG* Seq 14. *Parl* Seq 10. *Eccl* Guthl. I RDn.

WHITWICK

AP Incl chap Swannington, chap Thringstone (each a sep CP 1866,[1] pt of each eccl severed 1875 to help cr Whitwick St George EP[100]). *LG* W Gosc. Hd, Ashb. de la Z. PLU, Whitwick USD (1875—92), Coalville USD (1892—94), Coalville UD. Addtl civ bdry alt: 1894 (loses pt to help cr Coalville CP).[104] Abol civ 1936 pt to Coalville CP, pt to Charley AP.[23] *Parl* N'rn Dv (1832—85), Mid Dv (1885—1918), Bosw. Dv (1918—48). *Eccl* Seq 3. Addtl eccl bdry alt: 1840 (help cr Coalville EP,[25] refounded soon after in that year[103]), 1852 (help cr Charnwood Forest [Oaks Church] EP),[100] 1860 (help cr Copt Oak EP),[44] 1875 (help cr Whitwick St Andrew EP),[229] 1962,[51] 1962 (help cr Broom Leys EP).[52]

WHITWICK ST ANDREW

EP Cr 1875 from Whitwick St George EP, Whitwick AP.[229] W Akeley RDn (1875—93), S Akeley RDn (1893—*).

WHITWICK ST GEORGE

EP Cr 1875 from Whitwick AP (pt chap Swannington, pt chap Thringstone).[100] Akeley RDn (1875—93), W Akeley RDn (1893—1928), S Akeley RDn (1928—*). Bdry: 1875 (help cr Whitwick St Andrew EP),[229] 1939.[106]

EAST WIGSTON

CP Cr 1894 from the pt of Wigston Magna AP not in Wigston Magna UD.[45] *LG* Blaby PLU, RD. Abol 1935 ent to Wigston UD and to Wigston Magna CP.[9] *Parl* Harb. Dv (1918—48).

GREAT WIGSTON

AP Usual eccl spelling; for civ see following entry. *Eccl* Seq 26. Eccl bdry: 1893 (help cr Glen Parva with South Wigston EP).[35]

WIGSTON MAGNA

AP Usual civ spelling; for eccl see prev entry. *LG* Guthl. Hd, Blaby PLU, RSD, Wigston Magna UD (pt apptd day—31 Dec 1894, ent 31 Dec 1894—1930), Wigston UD (1930—74). Civ bdry: 1894 (31 Dec, the pt not in the UD cr East Wigston CP),[45] 1928,[127] 1935 (incl gains East Wigston CP),[9] 1936 (incl loses pt to Leic CB [assoc with Leics] & CP),[23] 1939 (exchanges pts with Leic CB [assoc with Leics] & CP),[164] 1966 (exchanges pts with Leic CB [assoc with Leics] & CP),[71] 1969 (exchanges pts with Leic CB [assoc with Leics] & CP).[165] *Parl* Seq 9. Parl bdry: 1972.[166]

WIGSTON PARVA

Chap in Claybrooke AP, sep CP 1866.[1] *LG* Guthl. Hd, Lutt. PLU (1835—95), RSD, RD (1894—95), Hinck. PLU (1895—1930), RD (1895—1936),

Blaby RD (1936—74). Bdry: 1935 (gains pt Copston Magna CP, Warws).[72] *Parl* S'rn Dv (1832—1918), Bosw. Dv (1918—48), Harb. CC (1948—70), Blaby CC (1970—*).

WILLESLEY

AP Derbys par transf 1897 to Leics.[32] *LG* Ashb. de la Z. PLU, RD. Abol civ 1936 pt to Ashb. de la Z. UD & AP, pt to Measham AP, pt to Oakthorpe and Donisthorpe CP.[23] *Parl* Loughb. Dv/CC (1918—*). *Eccl* In dioc Lichf & Cov until 1837, dioc Lichf 1837—84, dioc S'well 1884—1927, dioc Leic 1927—*: Repton RDn (until 1846), Hartshorne RDn (1846—55), Lullington RDn (1855—66), Hartshorne RDn (1866—87), Repton RDn (1887—1927), W Akeley RDn (1927—*).

WILLOUGHBY WATERLESS

AP *LG* Guthl. Hd, Lutt. PLU, RSD, RD. Renamed 1966 'Willoughby Waterleys'.[230] *Parl* S'rn Dv (1832—1918), Harb. Dv/CC (1918—70). *Eccl* Guthl. RDn. Abol eccl 1729 to help cr Willoughby Waterless with Peatling Magna EP.[215]

WILLOUGHBY WATERLESS WITH PEATLING MAGNA

EP Cr 1729 by union Willoughby Waterless AP, Peatling Magna AP.[215] Guthl. RDn (1729—1865), Guthl. III RDn (1865—1928), Guthl. I RDn (1928—*).

WILLOUGHBY WATERLEYS

CP Renaming 1966 of Willoughby Waterless AP.[230] *LG* Lutt. RD. *Parl* Blaby CC (1970—*).

WISTOW

AP Tp 'Wistow' in Gart. Hd as were chap Fleckney (sep par early[120]), chap Newton Harcourt (sep CP 1866,[1] not sep eccl hence this par 'Wistow cum Newton Harcourt', qv); incl in Guthl. Hd chap Kilby (sep civ identity early, date of sep eccl status uncertain,[150] certainly in 1733[25]). *LG* Bill. PLU, RSD, RD. Addtl civ bdry alt: 1935.[23] *Parl* Seq 11.

WISTOW CUM NEWTON HARCOURT

AP Usual eccl spelling; for civ and sep chaps, see prev entry. *Eccl* Seq 15.

WITHERLEY

AP Incl hmlt Atterton (orig chap, early destroyed, sep CP 1866[1]). *LG* Spark. Hd, Ath. PLU, RSD, Mkt. Bosw. RD. Addtl civ bdry alt: 1885,[34] 1935 (loses pt to Mancetter AP, Warws),[72] 1935 (incl gains Atterton CP, Ratcliffe Culey CP, Fenny Drayton AP).[9] *Parl* Seq 12. *Eccl* Seq 37.

WITHCOTE

AP *LG* Framl. Hd, Bill. PLU, RSD, RD. *Parl* Seq 2. *Eccl* Framl. RDn (until 1865), Gart. II RDn (1865—73), Gosc. I RDn (1873—*).

WOODHOUSE

Chap in Barrow upon Soar AP, sep CP 1866,[1] sep EP 1784,[25] eccl refounded 1868 from Barrow upon Soar AP, pt ex-par [not sep civ] Beau Manor.[57] *LG* Seq 11. Civ bdry: 1884 (gains Maplewell Longdale CP),[58] 1935,[9] 1936.[23] *Parl* Seq 5. *Eccl* Akeley RDn (1784—1865), E Akeley RDn (1865—*).

WOODHOUSE EAVES

EP Cr 1839,[25] refounded 1844[60] from Barrow upon

Soar AP, Newton Linford AP, ex-par Ulverscroft. Akeley RDn (1839—65), E Akeley RDn (1865—*). Bdry: 1852 (help cr Charnwood Forest [Oaks Church] EP),[100] 1860 (help cr Copt Oak EP).[44]

WOODTHORPE

Hmlt in Loughborough AP, sep CP 1866.[1] *LG* W Gosc. Hd, Loughb. PLU, USD (1875—88), Loughb. RSD (1888—94), RD. Abol 1935 ent to Loughb. MB & AP, pt to Quorndon CP, pt to Woodhouse CP.[9] *Parl* N'rn Dv (1832—85), Mid Dv (1885—1918), Loughb. Dv (1918—48).

WOODVILLE

EP Cr 1846,[25] refounded 1846[27] from Ashby de la Zouch AP (Leics), Hartshorne AP (Derbys); for CP cr 1897 to be in Derbys, incl pt Ashby Woulds CP, see main entry in Derbys. Akeley RDn (1846—65), W Akeley RDn (1865—1927), Repton RDn (dioc Derby, 1927—*). Bdry: 1876 (help cr Blackfordby EP).[20]

WORTHINGTON

Chap in Breedon on the Hill AP, sep CP 1866,[1] sep EP 1747.[25] Sometimes earlier 'Worthington and Newhold.' *LG* W Gosc.Hd, Ashb. de la Z. PLU (soon after 1836[33]—1930), RSD, RD. Civ bdry: 1936.[23] *Parl* Seq 6. *Eccl* Akeley RDn (1747—1865), W Akeley RDn (1865—*).

WYCOMB AND CHADWELL

Area in Rothley AP comprised of hmlt Wycomb, chap Chadwell, sep CP 1866,[1] eccl 'Wycombe and Chadwell' (pec jurisd Manor Rothley, until 1851), the area eccl severed 1954 to help cr Scalford with Wycombe and Chadwell EP.[138] *LG* W Gosc. Hd, Melt. Mowb. PLU, RSD, RD (1894—1935), Melt. & Belv. RD (1935—36). Abol civ 1936 ent to Scalford AP.[3] *Parl* N'rn Dv (1832—85), E'rn Dv (1885—1918), Melt. Dv (1918—48).

WYFORDBY

AP *LG* Framl. Hd, Melt. Mowb. PLU, RSD, RD (1894—1935), Melt. & Belv. RD (1935—36). In 20th cent, civ 'Bretingby and Wyfordby', as such civ abol 1936 ent to Freeby CP.[3] *Parl* N'rn Dv (1832—85), E'rn Dv (1885—1918), Melt. Dv (1918—48). *Eccl* Framl. RDn (until 1865), Framl. I RDn (1865—73), Framl. II RDn (1873—93), Framl. III RDn (1893—1961), Framl. II RDn (1961—*).

WYMESWOLD

AP *LG* Seq 8. Civ bdry: 1965 (gains pt Willoughby on the Wolds AP, Notts).[18] *Parl* Seq 4. *Eccl* Seq 23.

WYMONDHAM

AP *LG* Seq 2. Civ bdry: 1936 (gains Edmondthorpe AP),[3] 1965 (gains pt South Witham AP, Lincs Pts Kestev).[18] *Parl* Seq 1. *Eccl* Framl. RDn (until 1865), Framl. I RDn (1865—73), Framl. III RDn (1873—77), Framl. II RDn (1877—1951). Abol eccl 1951 to help cr Wymondham cum Edmondthorpe EP.[116]

WYMONDHAM CUM EDMONDTHORPE

EP Cr 1951 by union Wymondham AP, Edmondthorpe AP.[116] Framl. II RDn.

LINCOLNSHIRE

ABBREVIATIONS

Abbreviations particular to Lincs follow. Those general abbreviations in use throughout the *Guide* are found on pages xvii—xix.

Asl.	Aslacoe
Asw.	Aswardhurn
Avel.	Aveland
Axh.	Axholme
Belt.	Beltisloe
Bolingbr.	Bolingbroke
Brad. Hav.	Bradley Haverstoe
Branst.	Branston
Caist.	Caistor
Calc.	Calcewaith
Candl.	Candleshoe
Clayp.	Claypole
Corr.	Corringham
Flax.	Flaxwell
Holb.	Holbeach
Gainsb.	Gainsborough
Gart.	Gartree
Glanf.	Glanford
Graff.	Graffoe
Granth.	Grantham
Hav.	Haverstoe
Hornc.	Horncastle
Laff.	Lafford
Longob.	Longoboby
Loved.	Loveden
Ludb.	Ludborough
Mableth.	Mablethorpe
Newk.	Newark
Scunth.	Scunthorpe
Skirb.	Skirbeck
Sleaf.	Sleaford
Spald.	Spalding
Stamf.	Stamford
Uff.	Uffington
Walshcr.	Walshcroft
Winn. & Thr.	Winnibriggs and Threo
Wragg.	Wraggoe
Yarb.	Yarborough

SEQUENCES

An abbreviated entry prefixed by 'Seq' is used in the parochial entries to avoid repeating often the names of superior units of administration. The content of each sequence is shown below.

Local Government Sequences ('LG')

Parts of Holland

SEQ 1   Elloe Wap, Holb. PLU, RSD, E Elloe RD
SEQ 2   Elloe Wap, Spald. PLU, RSD, RD
SEQ 3   Kirton Wap, Boston PLU, RSD, RD
SEQ 4   Kirton Wap, Spald. PLU, RSD, RD
SEQ 5   Skirb. Wap, Boston PLU, RSD, RD

Parts of Kesteven

SEQ 6   Asw. Wap, Sleaf. PLU, RSD, RD (1894—1931), E Kestev RD (1931—74)
SEQ 7   Avel. Wap, Bourne PLU, RSD, RD (1894—1931), S Kestev RD (1931—74)
SEQ 8   Avel. Wap, Sleaf. PLU, RSD, RD (1894—1931), E Kestev RD (1931—74)
SEQ 9   Belt. Wap, Bourne PLU, RSD, RD (1894—

243

SEQ 10   1931), S Kestev RD (1931—74)

SEQ 10   Belt. Wap, Granth. PLU, RSD, RD (1894—1931), W Kestev RD (1931—74)

SEQ 11   Boothby Graff. Wap, Linc. PLU, RSD, Branst. RD (1894—1931), N Kestev RD (1931—74)

SEQ 12   Boothby Graff. Wap, Newk. PLU, RSD, Clayp. RD (1894—1931), N Kestev RD (1931—74)

SEQ 13   Boothby Graff. Wap, Sleaf. PLU, RSD, RD (1894—1931), N Kestev RD (1931—74)

SEQ 14   Flax. Wap, Sleaf. PLU, RSD, RD (1894—1931), E Kestev RD (1931—74)

SEQ 15   Granth. Soke (until 1830s), Loved. Wap (from 1830s), Granth. PLU, RSD, RD (1894—1931), W Kestev RD (1931—74)

SEQ 16   Lang. Wap, Linc. PLU, RSD, Branst. RD (1894—1931), N Kestev RD (1931—74)

SEQ 17   Lang. Wap, Sleaf. PLU, RSD, RD (1894—1931), E Kestev RD (1931—74)

SEQ 18   Loved. Wap, Granth. PLU, RSD, RD (1894—1931), W Kestev RD (1931—74)

SEQ 19   Loved. Wap, Newk. PLU, RSD, Clayp. RD (1894—1931), W Kestev RD (1931—74)

SEQ 20   Ness Wap, Bourne PLU, RSD, RD (1894—1931), S Kestev RD (1931—74)

SEQ 21   Ness Wap, Stamf. PLU, RSD, Uff. RD (1894—1931), S Kestev RD (1831—74)

SEQ 22   Winn. & Thr. Wap, Granth. PLU, RSD, RD (1894—1931), W Kestev RD (1831—74)

SEQ 23   Winn. & Thr. Wap (until 1830s), Loved. Wap (from 1830s), Newk. PLU, RSD, Clayp. RD (1894—1931), W Kestev RD (1931—74)

Parts of Lindsey

SEQ 24   Asl. Wap, Caist. PLU, RSD, RD

SEQ 25   Asl. Wap, Gainsb. PLU, RSD, RD

SEQ 26   Asl. Wap, Linc. PLU, RSD, Welton RD

SEQ 27   Bolingbr. Soke, Boston PLU, RSD, Sibsey RD (1894—1936), Spilsby RD (1936—74)

SEQ 28   Bolingbr. Soke, Hornc. PLU, RSD, RD

SEQ 29   Bolingbr. Soke, Spilsby PLU, RSD, RD

SEQ 30   Brad. Hav. Wap, Caist. PLU, RSD, RD

SEQ 31   Brad. Hav. Wap, Grimsby PLU, RSD, RD

SEQ 32   Brad. Hav. Wap, Louth PLU, RSD, RD

SEQ 33   Calc. Wap, Louth PLU, RSD, RD

SEQ 34   Calc. Wap, Spilsby PLU, RSD, RD

SEQ 35   Candl. Wap, Spilsby PLU, RSD, RD

SEQ 36   Corr. Wap, Gainsb. PLU, RSD, RD

SEQ 37   Gart. Wap, Hornc. PLU, RSD, RD

SEQ 38   Gart. Wap, Louth PLU, RSD, RD

SEQ 39   Hill Hd, Hornc. PLU, RSD, RD

SEQ 40   Hill Hd, Spilsby PLU, RSD, RD

SEQ 41   Hornc. Soke, Boston PLU, RSD, Sibsey RD (1894—1936), Spilsby RD (1936—74)

SEQ 42   Hornc. Soke, Hornc. PLU, RSD, RD

SEQ 43   Lawres Wap, Linc. PLU, RSD, Welton RD

SEQ 44   Louth Esk Hd, Louth PLU, RSD, RD

SEQ 45   Ludb. Wap, Louth PLU, RSD, RD

SEQ 46   Manley Wap, Glanf. Brigg PLU, RSD, RD

SEQ 47   Manley Wap, Thorne PLU, RSD, Isle of Axh. RD

SEQ 48   Walshcr. Wap, Caist. PLU, RSD, RD

SEQ 49   Well Wap, Gainsb. PLU, RSD, RD

SEQ 50   Wragg. Wap, Caist. PLU, RSD, RD

SEQ 51   Wragg. Wap, Hornc. PLU, RSD, RD

SEQ 52   Wragg. Wap, Linc. PLU, RSD, Welton RD

SEQ 53   Wragg. Wap, Louth PLU, RSD, RD

SEQ 54   Yarb. Wap, Caist. PLU, RSD, RD

SEQ 55   Yarb. Wap, Glanf. Brigg PLU, RSD, RD

Parliamentary Sequences ('Parl')

SEQ 1   N'rn Dv (1832—67), North Dv (1867—85), E Lind Dv (1885—1918), Louth Dv/CC (1918—*)

SEQ 2   N'rn Dv (1832—67), North Dv (1867—85), E Lind Dv (1885—1918), Louth Dv (1918—48), Gainsb. CC (1948—*)

SEQ 3   N'rn Dv (1832—67), North Dv (1867—85), N Lind Dv (1885—1918), Brigg Dv/CC (1918—70), Brigg & Scunth. CC (1970—*)

SEQ 4   N'rn Dv (1832—67), North Dv (1867—85), N Lind Dv (1885—1918), Louth Dv/CC (1918—*)

SEQ 5   N'rn Dv (1832—67), North Dv (1867—85), N Lind Dv (1885—1918), Louth Dv (1918—48), Gainsb. CC (1948—*)

SEQ 6   N'rn Dv (1832—67), North Dv (1867—85), W Lind Dv (1885—1918), Gainsb. Dv/CC (1918—*)

SEQ 7   N'rn Dv (1832—67), North Dv (1867—85), W Lind Dv (1885—1918), Louth Dv (1918—48), Gainsb. CC (1948—*)

SEQ 8   N'rn Dv (1832—67), Mid Dv (1867—85), E Lind Dv (1885—1918), Gainsb. Dv/CC (1918—*)

SEQ 9   N'rn Dv (1832—67), Mid Dv (1867—85), E Lind Dv (1885—1918), Hornc. Dv/CC (1918—*)

SEQ 10   N'rn Dv (1832—67), Mid Dv (1867—85), E Lind Dv (1885—1918), Louth Dv/CC (1918—*)

SEQ 11   N'rn Dv (1832—67), Mid Dv (1867—85), E Lind Dv (1885—1918), Louth Dv (1918—48), Gainsb. CC (1948—*)

SEQ 12   N'rn Dv (1832—67), Mid Dv (1867—85), S Lind Dv (1885—1918), Hornc. Dv/CC (1918—*)

SEQ 13   N'rn Dv (1832—67), Mid Dv (1867—85), S Lind Dv (1885—1918), Louth Dv/CC (1918—*)

SEQ 14   N'rn Dv (1832—67), Mid Dv (1867—85), W Lind Dv (1885—1918), Gainsb. Dv/CC (1918—*)

SEQ 15   S'rn Dv (1832—67), Mid Dv (1867—85), N Kestev Dv (1885—1918), [Pts Kestev] Granth. Dv/CC (1918—*)

SEQ 16   S'rn Dv (1832—67), South Dv (1867—85), Holl Dv (1885—1918), [Pts Holl] Holl with Boston Dv/CC (1918—*)

SEQ 17   S'rn Dv (1832—67), South Dv (1867—85), N Kestev Dv (1885—1918), [Pts Kestev] Granth. Dv/CC (1918—*)

SEQ 18   S'rn Dv (1832—67), South Dv (1867—85), N Kestev Dv (1885—1918), [Pts Kestev]

Granth. Dv (1918—48), Rutl & Stamf. CC (1948—*)

SEQ 19 S'rn Dv (1832—67), South Dv (1867—85), N Kestev Dv (1885—1918), [Pts Holl] Holl with Boston Dv/CC (1918—*)

SEQ 20 S'rn Dv (1832—67), South Dv (1867—85), S Kestev Dv (1885—1918), [Pts Kestev] Granth. Dv/CC (1918—*)

SEQ 21 S'rn Dv (1832—67), South Dv (1867—85), S Kestev D (1885—1918), [Pts Kestev] Rutl & Stamf. Dv/CC (1918—*)

Ecclesiastical Sequences ('Eccl')

Orig Linc AD

SEQ 1 Asw. with Laff. RDn (until 1866), Asw. with Laff. 1 RDn (1866—84), Laff. 1 RDn (1884—1910), Laff. (North) RDn (1910—68), Laff. RDn (1968—*)

SEQ 2 Asw. with Laff. RDn (until 1866), Asw. with Laff. 2 RDn (1866—84), Laff. 2 RDn (1884—1910), Laff. (South) RDn (1910—68), Laff. RDn (1968—*)

SEQ 3 Avel. RDn (until 1866), Avel. 1 RDn (1866—1910), Avel. RDn (1910—68), Avel. with Ness & Stamf. RDn (1968—*)

SEQ 4 Avel. RDn (until 1866), Ness 1 RDn (1866—1910), Avel. 1 RDn (1910—68), Laff. RDn (1968—*)

SEQ 5 Avel. RDn (until 1866), Avel. 1 RDn (1866—1910), Laff. (South) RDn (1910—68), Laff. RDn (1968—*)

SEQ 6 Avel. RDn (until 1866), Avel. 2 RDn (1866—1910), Avel. RDn (1910—68), Avel. with Ness & Stamf. RDn (1968—*)

SEQ 7 Belt. RDn (until 1866), Belt. 1 RDn (1866—73), Belt. RDn (1873—*)

SEQ 8 Belt. RDn (until 1866), Belt. 2 RDn (1866—73), Belt. RDn (1873—*)

SEQ 9 Bolingbr. RDn

SEQ 10 Bolingbr. RDn (until 1884), Candl. 1 RDn (1884—1910), Hill (South) RDn (1910—*)

SEQ 11 Calc. RDn (until 1866), Calc. 1 RDn (1866—1910), Calc. (North) RDn (1910—68), Calc. & Candl. RDn (1968—*)

SEQ 12 Calc. RDn (until 1866), Calc. 1 RDn (1866—1910), Calc. (North) RDn (1910—68), Louthesk RDn (1968—*)

SEQ 13 Calc. RDn (until 1866), Calc. 1 RDn (1866—1910), Louthesk (East) RDn (1910—68), Louthesk RDn (1968—*)

SEQ 14 Calc. RDn (until 1866), Calc. 2 RDn (1866—1910), Calc. (South) RDn (1910—68), Calc. & Candl. RDn (1968—*)

SEQ 15 Candl. RDn (until 1866), Candl. 1 RDn (1866—1910), Candl. RDn (1910—68), Calc. & Candl. RDn (1968—*)

SEQ 16 Candl. RDn (until 1866), Candl. 1 RDn (1866—1910), Hill (South) RDn (1910—68), Bolingbr. RDn (1968—*)

SEQ 17 Candl. RDn (until 1866), Candl. 2 RDn (1866—1910), Candl. RDn (1910—68), Calc. & Candl. RDn (1968—*)

SEQ 18 Gart. RDn (until 1866), Hornc. RDn (1866—*)

SEQ 19 Gart. RDn (until 1884), Hornc. RDn (1884—*)

SEQ 20 Gart. RDn (until 1968), Hornc. RDn (1968—*)

SEQ 21 Gart. RDn (until 1866), Hornc. RDn (1866—84), Louthesk & Ludb. 3 RDn (1884—1910), Louthesk (West) RDn (1910—68), Hornc. RDn (1968—*)

SEQ 22 Graff. RDn

SEQ 23 Granth. RDn (until 1866), Granth. 1 RDn (1866—1910), N Granth. RDn (1910—68), Granth. RDn (1968—*)

SEQ 24 Granth. RDn (until 1866), Granth. 1 RDn (1866—1910), N Granth. RDn (1910—68), Loved. RDn (1968—*)

SEQ 25 Granth. RDn (until 1866), Granth. 2 RDn (1866—1910), S Granth. RDn (1910—68), Granth. RDn (1968—*)

SEQ 26 Granth. RDn (until 1866), Granth. 2 RDn (1866—1910), S Granth. RDn (1910—68), Belt. RDn (1968—*)

SEQ 27 Grimsby RDn (until 1866), Grimsby 1 RDn (1866—84), Grimsby 2 RDn (1884—1910), Grimsby (North) RDn (1910—68), Hav. RDn (1968—*)

SEQ 28 Grimsby RDn (until 1866), Grimsby 1 RDn (1866—1910), Grimsby (South) RDn (1910—68), Hav. RDn (1968—*)

SEQ 29 Grimsby RDn (until 1866), Grimsby 1 RDn (1866—1910), Caist. RDn (1910—68), W Wold RDn (1968—*)

SEQ 30 Grimsby RDn (until 1866), Grimsby 1 RDn (1866—1910), Walshcr. (East) RDn (1910—68), Hav. RDn (1968—*)

SEQ 31 Grimsby RDn (until 1866), Grimsby 2 RDn (1866—1910), Grimsby (North) RDn (1910—68), Hav. RDn (1968—*)

SEQ 32 Grimsby RDn (until 1866), Grimsby 2 RDn (1866—1910), Grimsby (South) RDn (1910—68), Hav. RDn (1968—*)

SEQ 33 Grimsby RDn (until 1866), Grimsby 2 RDn (1866—1910), Grimsby & Cleethorpes RDn (1910—*)

SEQ 34 Hill RDn (until 1866), Hill 1 RDn (1866—1910), Hill (North) RDn (1910—68), Bolingbr. RDn (1968—*)

SEQ 35 Hill RDn (until 1866), Hill 1 RDn (1866—1910), Hill (North) RDn (1910—68), Hornc. RDn (1968—*)

SEQ 36 Hill RDn (until 1866), Hill 2 RDn (1866—1910), Hill (South) RDn (1910—68), Bolingbr. RDn (1968—*)

SEQ 37 Holl RDn (until 1866), N Holl 1 RDn (1866—1910), Elloe (West) RDn (1910—*)

SEQ 38 Holl RDn (until 1866), N Holl 1 RDn (1866—1910), Holl (West) RDn (1910—*)

SEQ 39 Holl RDn (until 1866), N Holl 2 RDn (1866—1910), Holl (East) RDn (1910—*)

SEQ 40 Holl RDn (until 1866), S Holl 1 RDn (1866—77), W Elloe RDn (1877—1910), Elloe (West) RDn (1910—*)

SEQ 41   Holl RDn (until 1866), S Holl 2 RDn (1866—77), E Elloe RDn (1877—1910), Elloe (East) RDn (1910—*)

SEQ 42   Hornc. RDn

SEQ 43   Hornc. RDn (until 1866), Gart. RDn (1866—1968), Hornc. RDn (1968—*)

SEQ 44   Hornc. RDn (until 1884), Gart. RDn (1884—1968), Hornc. RDn (1968—*)

SEQ 45   Longob. RDn (until 1968), Graff. RDn (1968—*)

SEQ 46   Louthesk & Ludb. RDn (until 1863), Louthesk & Ludb. 1 RDn (1863—1910), Ludb. RDn (1910—68), Louthesk RDn (1968—*)

SEQ 47   Louthesk & Ludb. RDn (until 1863), Louthesk & Ludb. 2 RDn (1863—66), Louthesk & Ludb. 1 RDn (1866—1910), Louthesk (East) RDn (1910—68), Louthesk RDn (1968—*)

SEQ 48   Louthesk & Ludb. RDn (until 1863), Louthesk & Ludb. 2 RDn (1863—ca 1896), Louthesk & Ludb. 1 RDn (ca 1896—1910), Louthesk (East) RDn (1910—68), Louthesk RDn (1968—*)

SEQ 49   Louthesk & Ludb. RDn (until 1863), Louthesk & Ludb. 3 RDn (1863—1910), Louthesk (West) RDn (1910—68), Louthesk RDn (1968—*)

SEQ 50   Loved. RDn

SEQ 51   Ness RDn (until 1968), Avel. & Ness with Stamf. RDn (1968—*)

SEQ 52   Walshcr. RDn (until 1866), Walshcr. 1 RDn (1866—73), Walshcr. RDn (1873—1910), Walshcr. (East) RDn (1910—68), W Wold RDn (1968—*)

SEQ 53   Walshcr. RDn (until 1866), Walshcr. 1 RDn (1866—73), Walshcr. RDn (1873—1910), Walshcr. (West) RDn (1910—68), W Wold RDn (1968—*)

SEQ 54   Walshcr. RDn (until 1866), Walshcr. 1 RDn (1866—73), Walshcr. RDn (1873—1910), Caist. RDn (1910—68), W Wold RDn (1968—*)

SEQ 55   Walshcr. RDn (until 1866), Walshcr. 2 RDn (1866—73), Walshcr. RDn (1873—1910), Walshcr. (West) RDn (1910—68), W Wold RDn (1968—*)

SEQ 56   Wragg. RDn (until 1968), Hornc. RDn (1968—*)

SEQ 57   Wragg. RDn (until 1968), Lawres RDn (1968—*)

SEQ 58   Wragg. RDn (until 1910), Walshcr. (West) RDn (1910—68), W Wold RDn (1968—*)

SEQ 59   Wragg. RDn (until 1968), W Wold RDn (1968—*)

SEQ 60   Yarb. RDn (until 1863), Yarb. 1 RDn (1863—1910), Yarb. (North) RDn (1910—68), Yarb. RDn (1968—*)

SEQ 61   Yarb. RDn (until 1863), Yarb. 1 RDn (1863—1910), Yarb. (North) RDn (1910—68), Hav. RDn (1968—*)

SEQ 62   Yarb. RDn (until 1863), Yarb. 1 RDn (1863—1910), Yarb. (South) RDn (1910—68), Yarb. RDn (1968—*)

SEQ 63   Yarb. RDn (until 1863), Yarb. 2 RDn (1863—1910), Caist. RDn (1910—68), W Wold RDn (1968—*)

SEQ 64   Yarb. RDn (until 1863), Yarb. 2 RDn (1863—1910), Caist. RDn (1910—68), Yarb. RDn (1968—*)

SEQ 65   Yarb. RDn (until 1863), Yarb. 2 RDn (1863—1910), Grimsby (North) RDn (1910—68), Hav. RDn (1968—*)

SEQ 66   Yarb. RDn (until 1863), Yarb. 2 RDn (1863—1910), Yarb. (South) RDn (1910—68), Yarb. RDn (1968—*)

Orig Stow AD

SEQ 67   Asl. RDn (until 1968), Corr. RDn (1968—*)

SEQ 68   Asl. RDn (until 1968), Lawres RDn (1968—*)

SEQ 69   Corr. RDn

SEQ 70   Corr. RDn (until 1857), Isle of Axh. RDn (1857—*)

SEQ 71   Corr. RDn (until 1968), Manlake RDn (1968—*)

SEQ 72   Lawres RDn (until 1866), Lawres 1 RDn (1866—1910), Lawres (East) RDn (1910—68), Lawres RDn (1968—*)

SEQ 73   Lawres RDn (until 1866), Lawres 1 RDn (1866—1910), Walshcr. (West) RDn (1910—68), W Wold RDn (1968—*)

SEQ 74   Lawres RDn (until 1866), Lawres 2 RDn (1866—ca 1896), Lawres 1 RDn (ca 1896—1910), Corr. RDn (1910—*)

SEQ 75   Lawres RDn (until 1866), Lawres 2 RDn (1866—1910), Lawres (West) RDn (1910—68), Corr. RDn (1968—*)

SEQ 76   Lawres RDn (until 1866), Lawres 2 RDn (1866—1910), Lawres (West) RDn (1910—68), Lawres RDn (1968—*)

SEQ 77   Manlake RDn

SEQ 78   Manlake RDn (until 1884), Corr. RDn (1884—1910), Yarb. (South) RDn (1910—68), Yarb. RDn (1968—*)

SEQ 79   Manlake RDn (until 1863), Isle of Axh. RDn (1863—*)

SEQ 80   Manlake RDn (until 1910), Yarb. (South) RDn (1910—68), Yarb. RDn (1968—*)

DIOCESES AND ARCHDEACONRIES

Lincs pars are in Linc. Dioc. and were organised in Archdeaconries and Rural Deaneries as follows:

LINCOLN AD

Asw. with Laff. RDn (until 1866), Asw. with Laff. 1 RDn (1866—84), Asw. with Laff. 2 RDn (1866—84), Avel. RDn (until 1866), Avel. RDn (1910—68), Avel. 1 RDn (1866—1910), Avel. 2 RDn (1866—1910), Avel. and Ness with Stamf. RDn (1968—*), Belt. RDn (until 1866), Belt. RDn (1873—*), Belt. 1 RDn (1866—73), Belt. 2 RDn (1866—73), Bolingbr. RDn (until 1933), Calc. RDn (until 1866), Calc. 1 RDn (1866—1910), Calc. 2 RDn (1866—1910), Calc. (North) RDn (1910—33), Calc. (South) RDn (1910—68), Candl. RDn (until 1866), Candl. RDn (1910—33), Candl. 1 RDn (1866—1910), Candl. 2 RDn (1866—1910), Christianity RDn, E Elloe RDn (1877—1910), W Elloe RDn (1877—1910), Elloe (East) RDn (1910—*), Elloe (West) RDn (1910—*), Gart. RDn (until 1877), Graff. RDn, Granth. RDn (until 1866), Granth. RDn (1968—*), Granth. 1 RDn (1866—1910), Granth. 2 RDn (1866—1910), N Granth. RDn (1910—68), S Granth. RDn (1910—68), Grimsby RDn (until 1866), Grimsby 1 RDn (1866—1910), Grimsby 2 RD (1866—1910), Hill RDn (until 1866), Hill 1 RDn (1866—1910), Hill 2 RDn (1866—1910), Holl RDn (until 1866), Holl (East) RDn (1910—*), Holl (West) RDn (1910—*), N Holl 1 RDn (1866—1910), N Holl 2 RDn (1866—1910), S Holl 1 RDn (1866—77), S Holl 2 RDn (1866—77), Hornc. RDn (until 1876), Laff. RDn (1968—*), Laff. 1 RDn (1884—1910), Laff. 2 RDn (1884—1910), Laff. (North) RDn (1910—68), Laff. (South) RDn (1884—1910), Longob. RDn (until 1968), Louthesk and Ludb. RDn (until 1863), Louthesk & Ludb. 1 RDn (1863—76), Louthesk & Ludb. 2 RDn (1863—76), Louthesk & Ludb. 3 RDn (1863—76), Loved. RDn, Ness RDn (until 1968), Stamf. RDn (until 1968), Walshcr. RDn (until 1866), Walshcr. RDn (1873—76), Walshcr. 1 RDn (1866—73), Walshcr. 2 RDn (1866—73), Wragg. RDn (until 1876), Yarb. RDn (until 1863), Yarb. 1 RDn (1863—76), Yarb. 2 RDn (1863—76)

LINDSEY AD (1933—*)

Bolingbr. RDn, Caist. RDn, Calc. (North) RDn (1933—68), Calc. & Candl. RDn (1968—*), Candl. RDn (1933—68), Gart. RDn (1933—68), Grimsby (North) RDn (1933—68), Grimsby (South) RDn (1933—68), Grimsby & Cleethorpes RDn, Hav. RDn (1968—*), Hill (North) RDn (1910—68), Hill (South) (1910—68), Hornc. RDn, Louthesk RDn (1968—*), Louthesk (East) RDn (1933—68), Louthesk (West) RDn (1933—68), Ludb. RDn (1933—68)

STOW AD

Asl. RDn (until 1968), Caist. RDn (1910—33), Corr. RDn, Gart. RDn (1877—1933), Grimsby 1 RDn (1876—1910), Grimsby 2 RDn (1876—1910), Grimsby (North) RDn (1910—33), Grimsby (South) RDn (1910—33), Grimsby and Cleethorpes RDn (1910—33), Hill 1 RDn (1877—1910), Hill (North) RDn (1877—1910), Hill (South) RDn (1910—33), Hornc. RDn (1876—1933), Isle of Axh. RDn (1857—*), Lawres RDn (until 1866), Lawres RDn (1968—*), Lawres 1 RDn (1866—1910), Lawres 2 RDn (1866—1910), Lawres (East) RDn (1910—68), Lawres (West) RDn (1910—68), Louthesk (East) RDn (1910—33), Louthesk (West) RDn (1910—33), Louthesk & Ludb. 1 RDn (1876—1910), Louthesk & Ludb. 2 RDn (1876—1910), Louthesk & Ludb. 3 RDn (1876—1910), Ludb. RDn (1910—33), Manlake RDn, Walshcr. RDn (1876—1910), Walshcr. (East) RDn (1910—68), Walshcr. (West) RDn (1910—68), W Wold RDn (1968—*), Wragg. RDn (1876—1968), Yarb. RDn (1968—*), Yarb. 1 RDn (1876—1910), Yarb. 2 RDn (1876—1910), Yarb. (North) RDn (1910—68), Yarb. (South) RDn (1910—68)

THE PARISHES OF LINCOLNSHIRE

ABY WITH GREENFIELD

AP [Pts Lind] *LG* Seq 33. *Parl* Seq 13. *Eccl* Calc. RDn. Abol eccl 1732 to help cr Belleau with Claythorpe, Aby and Greenfield EP.[1]

ADDLETHORPE

AP [Pts Lind] *LG* Seq 35. Civ bdry: 1888,[2] 1926[3] 1960.[4] *Parl* Seq 12. *Eccl* Seq 17.

AISTHORPE

AP [Pts Lind] *LG* Seq 43. *Parl* Seq 14. *Eccl* Lawres RDn. Abol eccl prob 17th—early 18th cent to help cr Aisthorpe with Thorpe in the Fallows EP.[5]

AISTHORPE WITH THORPE IN THE FALLOWS

EP [Pts Lind] Cr prob 17th—early 18th cent by union Aisthorpe AP, Thorpe in the Fallows EP.[5] Lawres RDn (cr—1866), Lawres 2 RDn (1866—1910), Lawres (West) RDn (1910—68), Lawres RDn (1968—*).

ALFORD

AP [Pts Lind] Incl chap Rigsby with Ailby (sep civ identity early, not sep eccl hence this par eccl 'Alford with Rigsby and Ailby', qv). *LG* Calc. Wap, Spilsby PLU, RSD, RD (1894—96), Alford UD (1896—1974). *Parl* Seq 12.

ALFORD WITH RIGSBY AND AILBY

AP [Pts Lind] Usual eccl spelling; for civ and civ sep chap, see prev entry. *Eccl* Seq 14.

ALGAR KIRK

AP [Pts Holl] Usual civ spelling; for eccl see following entry. Incl chap Fosdyke (sep civ identity early, area eccl reduced 1812 when fen allotment severed to help cr Holland Fen EP,[6] the later refounded 1865,[7] the remainder cr 1898 'Fosdyke' EP[8]). *LG* Seq 3. Addtl civ bdry alt: 1880 (help cr Amber Hill CP).[9] *Parl* Seq 16.

ALGARKIRK

AP [Pts Holl] Usual eccl spelling; for civ and civ and eccl sep chap and fen allotment, see prev entry. *Eccl* Seq 38.

ALKBOROUGH

AP [Pts Lind] *LG* Seq 46. Transf 1974 to Humb.[10] *Parl* Seq 3. *Eccl* Seq 77.

ALLINGTON

[Pts Kestev] Single tp for poor law purposes comprised of East Allington CP, West Allington AP. *LG* Winn. & Thr. Wap (until 1830s), Loved. Wap (from 1830s), Newk. PLU, RSD, Clayp. RD (1894—1931), W Kestev RD (1931—74). *Parl* Seq 20.

EAST ALLINGTON

[Pts Kestev] Chap in Sedgebrook AP, sep civ

identity early, jointly rated with West Allington AP as 'Allington', qv, eccl severed 1872 to help cr East Allington with West Allington EP.[11]

EAST ALLINGTON WITH WEST ALLINGTON

EP [Pts Kestev] Cr 1872 by union West Allington AP, chap East Allington in Sedgebrook AP.[11] Granth. 1 RDn (1872—1910), N Granth. RDn (1910—68), Granth. RDn (1968—*).

WEST ALLINGTON

AP [Pts Kestev] Jointly rated for poor law purposes with chap East Allington (in Sedgebrook AP) as 'Allington', qv. Incl orig chap Sedgebrook (sep par by 1535[12]). *Eccl* Granth. RDn (until 1866), Grant. 1 RDn (1866—72). Gains eccl 1872 chap East Allington from Sedgebrook AP to cr East Allington with West Allington EP.[11]

ALTHORPE

AP [Pts Lind] Incl chap Amcotts (sep CP 1866,[13] sep EP 1850[14]), tp Keadby (sep CP 1866,[13] not sep eccl hence this par eccl 'Althorpe with Keadby', qv). *LG* Manley Wap, Thorne PLU, RSD, Isle of Axh. RD. Abol civ 1958 to help cr Keadby with Althorpe CP.[15] *Parl* N'rn Dv (1832—67), North Dv (1867—85), W Lind Dv (1885—1918), Gainsb. Dv/CC (1918—70).

ALTHORPE WITH KEADBY

AP [Pts Lind] Usual eccl spelling; for civ and civ sep chap and tp, see prev entry. *Eccl* Seq 79.

ALVINGHAM

AP [Pts Lind] *LG* Seq 44. *Parl* Seq 1. *Eccl* Seq 47.

AMBER HILL

CP [Pts Holl] Cr 1880 (although rated in Boston PLU from 1862) from 2 pars in Pts Holl (Kirton Wap) of Algar Kirk AP, Sutterton AP, and from 1 par in Pts Kestev (Lang. Wap) of Dogdyke CP to be in Pts Holl.[9] *LG* Kirton Wap, Boston PLU (1862—1930), RSD, RD. Bdry: 1935 (gains pt South Kyme AP, Pts Kestev).[16] *Parl* N Kestev Dv (1885—1918), Holl with Boston Dv/CC (1918—*).

AMCOTTS

[Pts Lind] Chap in Althorpe AP, sep CP 1866,[13] sep EP 1850.[14] *LG* Seq 47. Civ bdry: 1885.[17] Transf 1974 to Humb.[10] *Parl* Seq 6. *Eccl* Manlake RDn (1850—57), Isle of Axh. RDn (1857—*).

ANCASTER

AP [Pts Kestev] *LG* Seq 18. Civ bdry: 1926,[18] 1931.[19] *Parl* Seq 17. *Eccl* Loved. RDn (until 1910), N Granth. RDn (1910—68), Loved. RDn (1968—*).

ANDERBY

AP [Pts Lind] *LG* Seq 34. *Parl* Seq 12. *Eccl* Seq 14.

ANWICK

AP [Pts Kestev] *LG* Seq 14. Civ bdry: 1885.[20] *Parl* Seq 17. *Eccl* Seq 1.

APLEY

AP [Pts Lind] *LG* Seq 52. *Parl* Seq 8. *Eccl* Seq 57.

APPLEBY

AP [Pts Lind] Incl hmlt Raventhorpe (sep CP 1866[13]). *LG* Seq 46. Addtl civ bdry alt: 1919 (help cr Scunthorpe and Frodingham UD & CP).[21] Transf 1974 to Humb.[10] *Parl* Seq 3. *Eccl* Seq 77.

ASGARBY

AP [Pts Kestev] *LG* Asw. Wap, Sleaf. PLU, RSD, RD. Civ bdry: 1885.[20] Abol civ 1931 to help cr Asgarby

and Howell CP.[19] *Parl* S'rn Dv (1832—67), South Dv (1867—85), N Kestev Dv (1885—1918), Granth. Dv (1918—48). *Eccl* Asw. with Laff. RDn. Abol eccl 1737 to help cr Kirkby Laythorpe with Asgarby EP.[22]

ASGARBY

AP [Pts Lind] *LG* Seq 28. Civ bdry: 1880.[23] *Parl* Seq 12. *Eccl* Pec jurisd Dean & Chapter of Linc. (until 1846), Hill RDn (1846—64). Eccl bdry: 1858 (fen allotment in West Fen severed to help cr New Bolingbroke EP).[24] Abol eccl 1864 to help cr Lusby with Asgarby EP.[25]

ASGARBY AND HOWELL

CP [Pts Kestev] Cr 1931 by union Asgarby AP, Howell AP, pt Kirkby la Thorpe AP.[19] *LG* E Kestev RD. *Parl* Granth. CC (1948—*).

ASHBY

[Pts Lind] Tp in Bottesford AP, sep CP 1866.[13] *LG* Manley Wap, Glanf. Brigg PLU, RSD, RD. Abol 1919 pt to help cr Scunth. and Frodingham UD & CP, pt to Burringham CP.[21] *Parl* N'rn Dv (1832—67), North Dv (1867—85), N Lind Dv (1885—1918), Brigg Dv (1918—48).

WEST ASHBY

[Pts Lind] Chap in Horncastle AP, sep civ identity early, sep EP 1816.[6] *LG* Seq 42. Civ bdry: 1880 (help cr Wildmore CP).[26] *Parl* Seq 12. *Eccl* Hornc. RDn. Eccl bdry: 1881 (help cr Wildmore EP [Pts Lind, Pts Kestev, Pts Holl]).[27]

ASHBY BY PARTNEY

AP [Pts Lind] *LG* Seq 35. *Parl* Seq 9. *Eccl* Seq 16.

ASHBY CUM FENBY

AP [Pts Lind] *LG* Seq 31. Transf 1974 to Humb.[10] *Parl* Seq 4. *Eccl* Seq 32.

ASHBY DE LA LAUNDE

AP [Pts Kestev] *LG* Flax. Wap, Sleaf. PLU, RSD, RD. Abol civ 1931 to help cr Ashby de la Launde and Bloxholm CP.[19] *Parl* S'rn Dv (1832—67), South Dv (1867—85), N Kestev Dv (1885—1918), Granth. Dv (1918—48). *Eccl* Seq 1.

ASHBY DE LA LAUNDE AND BLOXHOLM

CP [Pts Kestev] Cr 1931 by union Ashby de la Launde AP, Bloxholm AP.[19] *LG* E Kestev RD. *Parl* Granth. CC (1948—*).

ASHBY PUERORUM

AP [Pts Lind] *LG* Hill Hd, Hornc. PLU, RSD, RD. Abol civ 1936 ent to Somersby AP.[28] *Parl* N'rn Dv (1832—67), Mid Dv (1867—85), S Lind Dv (1885—1918), Hornc. Dv (1918—48). *Eccl* Hill RDn (until 1866), Hill 1 RDn (1866—1910), Hill (North) RDn (1910—68), Hornc. RDn (1968—*).

ASLACKBY

AP [Pts Kestev] *LG* Avel. Wap, Bourne PLU, RSD, RD. Abol civ 1936 pt to help cr Aslackby and Laughton CP, pt to help cr Pointon and Sempringham CP.[19] *Parl* S'rn Dv (1832—67), South Dv (1867—85), S Kestev Dv (1885—1918), Rutl & Stamf. Dv (1918—48). *Eccl* Seq 6.

ASLACKBY AND LAUGHTON

CP [Pts Kestev] Cr 1931 by union pt Aslackby AP, ent Laughton AP.[19] *LG* S Kestev RD. *Parl* Rutl & Stamf. CC (1948—*).

ASTERBY
AP [Pts Lind] *LG* Seq 37. *Parl* Seq 9. *Eccl* Seq 18.

ASWARBY
AP [Pts Kestev] *LG* Asw. Wap, Sleaf. PLU, RSD, RD. Abol civ 1931 pt to help cr Aswarby and Swarby CP, pt to help cr Aunsby and Dembleby CP.[19] *Parl* S'rn Dv (1832—67), South Dv (1867—85), N Kestev Dv (1885—1918), Grant. Dv (1918—48). *Eccl* Asw. with Laff. RDn. Abol eccl 1850 to help cr Aswarby with Searby EP.[29]

ASWARBY AND SWARBY
CP [Pts Kestev] Cr 1931 by union pt Aswarby AP, pt Aunsby AP, ent Swarby AP.[19] *LG* E Kestev RD. *Parl* Rutl & Stamf. CC (1948—*).

ASWARBY WITH SWARBY
EP [Pts Kestev] Cr 1850 by union Aswarby AP, Swarby AP.[29] Asw. with Laff. RDn (1850—66), Asw. with Laff. 2 RDn (1866—84), Laff. 2 RDn (1884—1910), Laff. (South) RDn (1910—68), Laff. RDn (1968—*).

ASWARDBY
AP [Pts Lind] *LG* Seq 40. *Parl* Seq 12. *Eccl* Seq 36.

ATTERBY
[Pts Lind] Tp in Bishop Norton AP, sep CP 1866.[13] *LG* Asl. Wap, Caist. PLU, RSD, RD. Abol 1936 ent to Bishop Norton AP.[28] *Parl* N'rn Dv (1832—67), North Dv (1867—85), W Lind Dv (1885—1918), Louth Dv (1918—48).

AUBOURN
AP [Pts Kestev] Incl pt tp Haddington (sep CP 1866,[13] the pt of the tp in South Hykeham AP eccl severed 1921 and united with this par to cr Aubourn with Haddington EP[30]). *LG* Boothby Wap, Linc. PLU, RSD, Branst. RD. Abol civ 1931 to help cr Aubourn, Haddington and South Hykeham CP.[19] *Parl* S'rn Dv (1832—67), Mid Dv (1867—85), N Kestev Dv (1885—1918), Granth. Dv (1918—48). *Eccl* Graff. RDn.

AUBOURN, HADDINGTON AND SOUTH HYKEHAM
CP [Pts Kestev] Cr 1931 by union Aubourn AP, Haddington AP, South Hykeham AP.[19] *LG* N Kestev RD. *Parl* Granth. CC (1948—*).

AUBOURN WITH HADDINGTON
EP [Pts Kestev] Cr 1921 by union Aubourn AP and the pt of tp Haddington in South Hykeham AP.[30] Graff. RDn.

AUNBY
[Pts Kestev] Hmlt in Careby AP, sep CP 1866.[13] *LG* Belt. Wap, Bourne PLU, RSD, RD. Abol 1931 to help cr Careby, Aunby and Holywell CP.[19] *Parl* S'rn Dv (1832—67), South Dv (1867—85), S Kestev Dv (1885—1918), Rutl & Stamf. Dv (1918—48).

AUNSBY
AP [Pts Kestev] *LG* Asw. Wap, Sleaf. PLU, RSD, RD. Abol civ 1931 pt to help cr Aswarby and Swarby CP, pt to help cr Aunsby and Dembleby CP.[19] *Parl* S'rn Dv (1832—67), South Dv (1867—85), N Kestev Dv (1885—1918), Granth. Dv (1918—48).

AUNSBY AND DEMBLEBY
CP [Pts Kestev] Cr 1931 by union pt Aswarby AP, pt Aunsby AP, ent Dembleby AP, pt Newton AP, ent

Scott Willoughby AP.[19] *LG* E Kestev RD. *Parl* Rutl & Stamf. CC (1948—*).

AUTHORPE
AP [Pts Lind] *LG* Seq 44. Civ bdry: 1883.[31] *Parl* Seq 1. *Eccl* Louthesk & Ludb. RDn (until 1863), Louthesk & Ludb. 3 RDn (1863—1910), Calc. (North) RDn (1910—68), Calc. & Candl. RDn (1968—*).

AYLESBY
AP [Pts Lind] *LG* Seq 31. Tranf 1974 to Humb.[10] *Parl* Seq 4. *Eccl* Seq 31.

BARDNEY
AP [Pts Lind] *LG* Seq 52. *Parl* Seq 8. *Eccl* Seq 57.

BARHOLM
AP [Pts Kestev] Usual civ spelling; for eccl see 'Barholme'. *LG* Ness Wap, Stamf. PLU, RSD, Uff. RD. Abol civ 1931 pt to help cr Barholm and Stowe CP, pt to Baston AP, pt to Langtoft AP, pt to Market Deeping AP.[19] *Parl* S'rn Dv (1832—67), South Dv (1867—85), S Kestev Dv (1885—1918), Rutl & Stamf. Dv (1918—48).

BARHOLM AND STOWE
CP [Pts Kestev] Cr 1931 by union pt Barholm AP, pt Stowe AP.[19] *LG* S Kestev RD. *Parl* Rutl & Stamf. CC (1948—*).

BARHOLME
AP [Pts Kestev] Usual eccl spelling; for civ see 'Barholm'. *Eccl* Ness RDn. Abol eccl 1772 to help cr Barholme with Stowe EP.[32]

BARHOLME WITH STOWE
EP [Pts Kestev] Cr 1772 by union Barholme AP, Stowe AP.[32] Ness RDn (1772—1968), Avel. & Ness with Stamf. RDn (1968—*).

BARKSTON
AP [Pts Kestev] *LG* Granth. Soke (until 1830s), Loved. Wap (from 1830s), Newk. PLU, RSD, Clayp. RD (1894—1931), W Kestev RD (1931—74). *Parl* Seq 20. *Eccl* Seq 24.

EAST BARKWITH
AP [Pts Lind] *LG* Seq 51. *Parl* Seq 9. *Eccl* Seq 59.

WEST BARKWITH
AP [Pts Lind] Organisation as for East Barkwith.

BARLINGS
AP [Pts Lind] *LG* Seq 43. *Parl* Seq 14. *Eccl* Sometimes as 'Barlings and Langworth', Seq 72.

BARNETBY LE WOLD
AP [Pts Lind] *LG* Seq 55. Civ bdry: 1952.[33] Transf 1974 to Humb.[10] *Parl* Seq 3. *Eccl* Seq 62.

BARNOLDBY LE BECK
AP [Pts Lind] *LG* Seq 31. Transf 1974 to Humb.[10] *Parl* Seq 4. *Eccl* Seq 32.

BARROW UPON HUMBER
AP [Pts Lind] *LG* Seq 55. Transf 1974 to Humb.[10] *Parl* Seq 3. *Eccl* Sometimes as 'Barrow upon Humber with New Holland', Seq 60.

BARROWBY
AP [Pts Kestev] *LG* Winn. & Thr. Wap (until 1830s), Loved. Wap (from 1830s), Granth. PLU, RSD, RD (1894—1931), W Kestev RD (1931—74). Civ bdry: 1930,[34] 1931,[19] 1931.[35] *Parl* Seq 20. *Eccl* Seq 25. Eccl bdry: 1955.[36]

BARTON ON HUMBER
AP [Pts Lind] Cr eccl before 1535 by union Barton on Humber St Mary AP, Barton on Humber St Peter

AP; the pars retained or early regained sep civ identity (until 1888) as 'Barton upon Humber St Mary,' 'Barton upon Humber St Peter', qv. *Eccl* Seq 60.

BARTON UPON HUMBER

CP [Pts Lind] Cr 1888 by union Barton upon Humber St Mary AP, Barton upon Humber St Peter AP.[37] *LG* Yarb. Wap, Glanf. Brigg PLU, Barton upon Humber USD, UD. Transf 1974 to Humb.[10] *Parl* Brigg Dv/CC (1918—70), Brigg & Scunth. CC (1970—*).

BARTON UPON HUMBER ST MARY

AP [Pts Lind] *LG* Yarb. Wap, Glanf. Brigg PLU, Barton upon Humber USD. Abol civ 1888 to help cr Barton upon Humber CP.[37] *Parl* N'rn Dv (1832—67), North Dv (1867—85), N Lind Dv (1885—1918). *Eccl* As 'Barton on Humber St Mary', Yarb. RDn. United before 1535 with Barton on Humber St Peter as 'Barton on Humber', qv.

BARTON UPON HUMBER ST PETER

AP [Pts Lind] Organisation as for Barton upon Humber St Mary AP.

BASSINGHAM

AP [Pts Kestev] *LG* Seq 12. *Parl* Seq 15. *Eccl* Seq 22.

BASSINGTHORPE

AP [Pts Kestev] Usual civ spelling; for eccl see following entry. *LG* Belt. Wap, Granth. PLU, RSD, RD. Abol civ 1931 to help cr Bitchfield and Bassingthorpe CP.[19] *Parl* S'rn Dv (1832—67), South Dv (1867—85), S Kestev Dv (1885—1918), Rutl & Stamf Dv (1918—48).

BASSINGTHORPE WITH WESTBY

AP [Pts Kestev] Usual eccl spelling; for civ see prev entry. *Eccl* Seq 7.

BASTON

AP [Pts Kestev] *LG* Seq 20. Civ bdry: 1931.[19] *Parl* Seq 21. *Eccl* Seq 51.

BAUMBER

AP [Pts Lind] *LG* Seq 37. *Parl* Seq 9. *Eccl* Seq 42.

GREAT BEATS

[Pts Holl] Ex-par place, sep CP 1858.[38] *LG* Skirb. Wap, Boston PLU (1862—1906), RSD, RD. Abol civ 1906 ent to Copping Syke CP.[39] *Parl* S'rn Dv (1832—67), South Dv (1867—85), N Kestev Dv (1885—1918).

LITTLE BEATS

[Pts Holl] Ex-par place, sep CP 1858,[38] abol eccl 1881 to help cr Wildmore EP [Pts Lind, Pts Kestev, Pts Holl].[27] In Kirton Wap, organisation o'wise as for Great Beats.

BECKINGHAM

AP [Pts Kestev] Incl chap Stragglethorpe (sep civ identity early, burial rights 1349 but still remained a chap[40]), chap Fenton (burial rights by 1528 but still a chap,[40] sep civ identity early, eccl severed 1932 to help cr Stubton with Fenton EP[41]), the par eccl 'Beckingham with Fenton and Stragglethorpe' until Stragglethorpe eccl severed 1931 to help cr Brant Broughton with Stragglethorpe EP,[42] the remainder of this par eccl 'Beckingham with Fenton' until area Fenton eccl severed 1932 to help cr Stubton with Fenton EP,[41] the remainder thereafter 'Beckingham' until united 1950 with area Fenton in

Stubton with Fenton EP to cr Beckingham with Fenton EP.[43] *LG* Loved. Wap, Newk. PLU, RSD, Clayp. RD (1894—1931), N Kestev RD (1931—74). *Parl* Seq 20. *Eccl* Loved. RDn (1932—50).

BECKINGHAM WITH FENTON

EP [Pts Kestev] Cr 1932 as remainder of Beckingham with Fenton and Stragglethorpe EP when chap Stragglethorpe eccl severed to help cr Brant Broughton with Straggletorpe EP.[42] Loved. RDn. Abol 1932 when area Fenton eccl severed to help cr Stubton with Fenton EP, the remainder to be 'Beckingham'.[41]

EP [Pts Kestev] Cr 1950 by union Beckingham AP, area Fenton in Stubton with Fenton EP.[43] Loved. RDn.

BECKINGHAM WITH FENTON AND STRAGGLE- THORPE

AP [Pts Kestev] Usual eccl spelling; for civ and civ sep chap Stragglethorpe, see 'Beckingham'. *Eccl* Loved. RDn. Abol eccl 1932 when chap Stragglethorpe eccl severed to help cr Brant Broughton with Stragglethorpe EP, the remainder to be 'Beckingham with Fenton'.[42]

BEELSBY

AP [Pts Lind] *LG* Seq 31. Tranf 1974 to Humb.[10] *Parl* Seq 4. *Eccl* Seq 28.

BEESBY IN THE MARSH

AP [Pts Lind] *LG* Seq 33. *Parl* Seq 13. *Eccl* Calc. RDn (until 1866), Calc. 1 RDn (1866—1910), Calc. (North) RDn (1910—31), Calc. (South) RDn (1931—68), Calc. & Candl. RDn (1968—*).

BELCHFORD

AP [Pts Lind] *LG* Seq 37. *Parl* Seq 9. *Eccl* Gart. RDn (until 1866), Hill 2 RDn (1866—84), Hill 1 RDn (1884—1910), Hill (North) RDn (1910—68), Hornc. RDn (1968—*).

BELLEAU

AP [Pts Lind] Incl chap Claythorpe (sep CP 1866,[13] not sep eccl hence this par eccl 'Belleau with Claythorpe', qv in following entry). *LG* Seq 33. Civ bdry: 1888.[44] *Parl* Seq 13.

BELLEAU WITH CLAYTHORPE

AP [Pts Lind] Usual eccl spelling; for civ and civ sep chap Claythorpe, see prev entry. Calc. RDn. Abol eccl 1772 to help cr Belleau with Claythorpe, Aby and Greenfield EP.[1]

BELLEAU WITH CLAYTHORPE, ABY AND GREENFIELD

EP [Pts Lind] Cr 1732 by union Belleau with Claythorpe AP, Aby with Greenfield AP.[1] Calc. RDn (1732—1866), Calc. 1 RDn (1866—1910), Calc. (North) RDn (1910—68), Louthesk RDn (1968—*).

BELTON

AP [Pts Kestev] *LG* Granth. Soke (until 1830s), Loved. Wap (from 1830s), Granth. PLU, RSD, RD. Civ bdry: 1883,[31] 1884.[45] Abol civ 1931 to help cr Belton and Manthorpe CP.[19] *Parl* S'rn Dv (1832—67), South Dv (1867—85), S Kestev Dv (1885—1918), Granth. Dv (1918—48). *Eccl* Sometimes as 'Belton by Grantham', Seq 24. Eccl bdry: 1970.[46]

BELTON

AP [Pts Lind] *LG* Seq 47. Civ bdry: 1968.[18] Transf 1974 to Humb.[10] *Parl* Seq 6. *Eccl* Sometimes as

'Belton by Gainsborough', Seq 70.

BELTON AND MANTHORPE

CP [Pts Kestev] Cr 1931 by union Belton AP, Manthorpe CP.[19] *LG* W Kestev RD. *Parl* Granth. CC (1948—*).

BENINGTON

AP [Pts Holl] *LG* Seq 5. Civ bdry: 1880.[47] *Parl* Seq 16. *Eccl* Seq 39. Eccl bdry: 1885 (help cr Eastville with Midville EP [Pts Lind, Pts Holl]).[48]

LONG BENNINGTON

AP [Pts Kestev] Incl chap Foston (sep civ identity early, not sep eccl hence this par eccl 'Long Bennington with Foston', qv). *LG* Seq 19. Addtl civ bdry alt: 1931 (gains Bennington Grange CP).[19] *Parl* Seq 20.

LONG BENNINGTON WITH FOSTON

AP [Pts Kestev] Usual eccl spelling; for civ and civ sep chap Foston, see prev entry. *Eccl* Loved. RDn (until 1866), Granth. 1 RDn (1866—1910), N Granth. RDn (1910—68), Granth. RDn (1968—*).

BENNINGTON GRANGE

[Pts Kestev] Ex-par place, sep CP 1858.[38] *LG* Loved. Wap, Newk. PLU (1861—1930), RSD, Clayp. RD. Abol civ 1931 ent to Long Bennington AP.[19] *Parl* S'rn Dv (1832—67), South Dv (1867—85), S Kestev Dv (1885—1918), Granth. Dv (1918—48).

BENNIWORTH

AP [Pts Lind] *LG* Seq 51. *Parl* Seq 9. *Eccl* Seq 56.

BICKER

AP [Pts Holl] *LG* Seq 3. Civ bdry: 1935 (loses pt to Great Hale AP, Pts Kestev).[16] *Parl* Seq 19. *Eccl* Seq 38.

BIGBY

AP [Pts Lind] Incl pt chap Glanford Brigg (sep CP 1866,[13] sep EP 1872 as 'Glanford Bridge' from Bigby AP, Wrawby AP[49]). *LG* Yarb. Wap, Caist. PLU, pt Brigg USD (1875—92), Caist. RSD (pt 1875—92, ent 1892—94), Caist. RD. Addtl civ bdry alt: 1892 (loses the pt in the USD to Glanford Brigg CP),[50] 1936.[28] *Parl* Seq 5. *Eccl* Seq 66.

BILLINGBOROUGH

AP [Pts Kestev] *LG* Seq 7. Civ bdry: 1931 (gains Birthorpe CP).[19] *Parl* Seq 21. *Eccl* Seq 3.

BILLINGHAY

AP [Pts Kestev] Incl tp Dogdyke (sep CP 1866[13]), chap and tp Walcott (sep CP 1866 as 'Walcot near Billinghay'[13]), neither sep eccl hence this par eccl 'Billinghay with Walcott and Dogdyke', qv. *LG* Seq 17. *Parl* Seq 15.

BILLINGHAY WITH WALCOT AND DOGDYKE

AP [Pts Kestev] Usual eccl spelling; for civ and civ sep tp and chap and tp, see prev entry. *Eccl* Longob. RDn (until 1884), Laff. 1 RDn (1884—1968), Laff. RDn (1968—*). Eccl bdry: 1948.[51]

BILSBY

AP [Pts Lind] *LG* Seq 34. *Parl* Seq 12. *Eccl* Seq 14.

BINBROOK

CP [Pts Lind] Joint rating for poor law purposes, prob from 1840s, of Binbrook St Gabriel AP, Binbrook St Mary AP (each orig sep rated). *LG* Walshcr. Wap, Louth PLU, RSD, RD. *Parl* Seq 1.

BINBROOK ST GABRIEL

AP [Pts Lind] Orig sep rated for poor, jointly rated prob from 1840s with Binbrook St Mary as 'Binbrook', qv for civ (Walshcr. Wap) and parl organisation. *Eccl* Pec jurisd Dean & Chapter of Linc. Abol eccl 1846 to help cr Binbrook St Mary and St Gabriel EP.[52]

BINBROOK ST MARY

AP [Pts Lind] Organisation as for Binbrook St Gabriel.

BINBROOK ST MARY AND ST GABRIEL

EP [Pts Lind] Cr 1846 by union Binbrook St Gabriel AP, Binbrook St Mary AP.[52] Walshcr. RDn (1846—66), Walshcr. 2 RDn (1866—73), Walshcr. RDn (1873—1910), Walshcr. (East) RDn (1910—68), Hav. RDn (1968—*).

BIRCHWOOD

EP [Pts Kestev] Cr 1969 from Skellinghrorpe EP.[53] Christianity RDn.

BIRTHORPE

[Pts Kestev] Tp in Sempringham AP, sep CP 1866.[13] *LG* Avel. Wap, Bourne PLU, RSD, RD. Abol 1931 ent to Billingborough AP.[19] *Parl* S'rn Dv (1832—67), South Dv (1867—85), S Kestev Dv (1885—1918), Rutl & Stamf. Dv (1918—48).

BISCATHORPE

AP [Pts Lind] *LG* Wragg. Wap, Louth PLU, RSD, RD. Abol civ 1936 ent to Gayton le Wold AP.[28] *Parl* N'rn Dv (1832—67), Mid Dv (1867—85), E Lind Dv (1885—1918), Louth Dv (1918—48). *Eccl* Wragg. RDn (until 1866), Louthesk & Ludb. 3 RDn (1866—1910), Louthesk (West) RDn (1910—68), Hornc. RDn (1968—*).

BITCHFIELD

AP [Pts Kestev] *LG* Belt. Wap, Granth. PLU, RSD, RD. Abol civ 1931 to help cr Bitchfield and Bassingthorpe CP.[19] *Parl* S'rn Dv (1832—67), South Dv (1867—85), S Kestev Dv (1885—1918), Rutl & Stamf. Dv (1918—48). *Eccl* Seq 7.

BITCHFIELD AND BASSINGTHORPE

CP [Pts Kestev] Cr 1931 by union Bitchfield AP, Bassingthorpe AP.[19] *LG* W Kestev RD. *Parl* Rutl & Stamf. CC (1948—*).

BLANKNEY

AP [Pts Kestev] *LG* Seq 17. *Parl* Seq 15. *Eccl* Seq 45.

BLOXHOLM

AP [Pts Kestev] *LG* Flax. Wap, Sleaf. PLU, RSD, RD. Abol civ 1931 to help cr Ashby de la Launde and Bloxholm CP.[19] *Parl* S'rn Dv (1832—67), South Dv (1867—85), N Kestev Dv (1885—1918), Granth. Dv (1918—48). *Eccl* Asw. & Laff. RDn. Abol eccl 1717 to help cr Digby with Bloxholm EP.[22]

BLYBOROUGH

AP [Pts Lind] *LG* Seq 25. *Parl* Seq 6. *Eccl* Asl. RDn (until 1884), Corr. RDn (1884—*).

BLYTON

CP [Pts Lind] Cr 1936 by union Blyton cum Wharton AP, Greenhill and Redhill CP.[28] *LG* Gainsb. RD. *Parl* Gainsb. CC (1948—*).

BLYTON CUM WHARTON

AP [Pts Lind] Corr. Wap, Gainsb. PLU, RSD, RD. Civ bdry: 1886.[54] Abol civ 1936 to help cr Blyton CP.[28] *Parl* N'rn Dv (1832—67), North Dv (1867—85), W Lind Dv (1885—1918), Gainsb. Dv (1918—48). *Eccl* Seq 69.

BOLINGBROKE

AP [Pts Lind] *LG* Seq 29. Civ bdry: 1880 (help cr Wildmore CP),[26] 1880,[26] 1880.[55] *Parl* Seq 12. *Eccl* Bolingb. RDn. Abol eccl 1739 to help cr Bolingbroke with Hareby EP.[56]

NEW BOLINGBOKE

EP [Pts Lind] Cr 1858 from allotments in West Fen of Asgarby AP, Bolingbroke with Hareby EP, Freiston AP, Mavis Enderby AP, Raithby AP, Revesby AP.[24] Bolingb. RDn (1858—1910), Holl (East) RDn (1910—61). Abol 1961 to help cr New Bolingbroke with Carrington EP.[57]

NEW BOLINGBROKE WITH CARRINGTON

EP [Pts Lind] Cr 1961 by union ent New Bolingbroke EP, pt Carrington with Frithville EP (Pts Lind, Pts Holl).[57] Holl (East) RDn.

BOLINGBROKE WITH HAREBY

EP [Pts Lind] Cr 1739 by union Bolingrboke AP, Hareby AP.[56] Bolingb. RDn. Bdry: 1858 (allotment in West Fen eccl severed to help cr New Bolingbroke EP),[26] 1881 (help cr Wildmore EP [Pts Lind, Pts Kestev, Pts Holl]).[27]

BONBY

AP [Pts Lind] *LG* Seq 55. Transf 1974 to Humb.[10] *Parl* Seq 3. *Eccl* Seq 60.

BOOTHBY GRAFFOE

AP [Pts Kestev] *LG* Seq 11. *Parl* Seq 15. *Eccl* Seq 45.

BOOTHBY PAGNELL

AP [Pts Kestev] *LG* Seq 22. Civ bdry: 1931.[19] *Parl* Seq 21. *Eccl* Seq 26.

BOSTON

AP [Pts Holl] *LG* Skirb. Wap, Boston Bor/MB (pt until 1880, ent 1880—1974), Boston PLU, USD (pt 1875—80, ent 1880—94). Civ bdry: 1880,[47] 1880,[55] 1880,[26] 1880,[58] 1900,[59] 1932 (incl gains Skirbeck Quarter CP).[60] *Parl* Pt Boston Parl Bor (1352—53, 1547—1918 [enlarged pt 1832—85, reduced pt 1885—1918]), pt S'rn Dv (1832—67), pt South Dv (1867—85), pt Holl Dv (1885—1918), Pts Holl with Boston Dv/CC (1918—*). *Eccl* Seq 39. Eccl bdry: 1885 (help cr Eastville with Midville EP [Pts Lind, Pts Holl]),[48] 1886 (help cr Carrington with Frithville EP [Pts Lind, Pts Holl]),[61] 1889.[62]

BOSTON ST THOMAS

EP [Pts Holl] Name used now for EP cr 1912 as 'Skirbeck Quarter', qv.

BOTTESFORD

AP [Pts Lind] Incl tps Ashby, Burringham, Holme, Yaddlethorpe, pt tp East Butterwick (each a sep CP 1866[13]). *LG* Seq 46. Addtl civ bdry: 1887 (gains Yaddlethorpe CP).[63] Transf 1974 to Humb.[10] *Parl* Seq 3. *Eccl* Manlake RDn. Eccl bdry: 1861 (help cr Gunhouse with Burringham EP,[64] now called 'Gunness with Burringham'), 1969 (help cr Scunthorpe All Saints EP).[65] Renamed eccl 1973 'Bottesford with Ashby'.[66]

BOTTESFORD WITH ASHBY

EP [Pts Lind] Renaming 1973 of Bottesford AP.[66] Manlake RDn.

BOULTHAM

AP [Pts Kestev] *LG* Boothby Wap, Linc. PLU, RSD, Branst. RD. Abol civ 1920 ent to Linc. CB (assoc with Pts Lind) & CP.[67] *Parl* S'rn Dv (1832—67),

Mid Dv (1867—85), N Kestev Dv (1885—1918), Granth. Dv (1918—48). *Eccl* Graff. RDn (until 1910), Christianity RDn (1910—*). Eccl bdry: 1964 (incl help cr Lincoln St George, Swallowbeck EP).[68]

BOURNE

AP [Pts Kestev] *LG* Avel. Wap, Bourne PLU, RSD, RD (1894—99), Bourne UD (1899—1974). *Parl* Seq 21. *Eccl* Seq 6.

BRACEBOROUGH

AP [Pts Kestev] *LG* Ness Wap, Stamf. PLU, RSD, Uff. UD. Abol civ 1931 to help cr Braceborough and Wilsthorpe CP.[19] *Parl* S'rn Dv (1832—67), South Dv (1867—85), S Kestev Dv (1885—1918), Rutl & Stamf. Dv (1918—48).

BRACEBOROUGH AND WILSTHORPE

CP [Pts Kestev] Cr 1931 by union Braceborough AP, Wilsthorpe CP.[19] *LG* S Kestev RD. *Parl* Rutl & Stamf. CC (1948—*).

BRACEBRIDGE

AP [Linc Lbty & Co of Itself (1410—1840s), Pts Kestev (Boothby Graff. Wap, from 1840s)] *LG* Linc. PLU, RSD, Branst. RD (1894—98), Bracebridge UD (1898—1920). Civ bdry: 1898 (the pt not constituted Bracebridge UD cr Bracebridge Heath CP).[69] Abol civ 1920 ent to Linc. CB (assoc with Pts Lind) & CP.[67] *Parl* N'rn Dv (1832—67), Mid Dv (1867—85), W Lind. Dv (1885—1918), Linc. Parl Bor (1918—48). *Eccl* Longob. RDn (until 1910), Christianity RDn (1910—*). Eccl bdry: 1971 (help cr Bracebridge Heath EP).[70]

BRACEBRIDGE HEATH

CP [Pts Kestev] Cr 1898 from the pt of Bracebridge AP not constituted Bracebridge UD (the area to be in the UD prev in Linc. CB).[69] *LG* Linc. PLU, Branst. RD (1898—1931), N Kestev RD (1931—74). Bdry: 1920 (loses pt to Linc. CB [assoc with Pts Lind] & CP).[67] *Parl* Granth. Dv/CC (1918—*).

EP [Pts Kestev] Cr 1971 from Waddington AP, Bracebridge AP, Canwick AP.[70] Christianity RDn.

BRACEBY

AP [Pts Kestev] *LG* Granth. Soke (until 1830s), Winn. & Thr. Wap (from 1830s), Granth. PLU, RSD, RD. Abol civ 1931 to help cr Braceby and Sapperton CP.[19] *Parl* S'rn Dv (1832—67), South Dv (1867—85), S Kestev RD (1885—1918), Rutl & Stamf. Dv (1918—48). *Eccl* Seq 26.

BRACEBY AND SAPPERTON

CP [Pts Kestev] Cr 1931 by union Braceby AP, Sapperton AP.[19] *LG* W Kestev RD. *Parl* Rutl & Stamf. CC (1948—*).

BRACKENBOROUGH

AP [Pts Lind] Orig status as an AP not certain, church early destroyed and thereafter eccl in Fotherby AP,[71] sep civ identity sustained. *LG* Seq 45. *Parl* Seq 1.

BRADLEY

AP [Pts Lind] *LG* Seq 31. Civ bdry; 1928 (loses pt to Grimsby CB [assoc with Pts Lind] to help cr Grimsby CP).[72] Transf 1974 to Humb.[10] *Parl* Gt Grimsby Parl Bor (1832—1918), Louth Dv/CC (1918—*). *Eccl* Seq 31.

GREAT BRAND END PLOT

[Pts Holl] Ex-par place, sep CP 1858.[38] *LG* Kirton Wap, Boston PLU (1862—91), RSD. Abol civ 1891 ent to Swineshead AP.[73] *Parl* S'rn Dv (1832—67), South Dv (1867—85), N Kestev Dv (1885—1918).

LITTLE BRAND END PLOT

[Pts Holl] Ex-par place, sep CP 1858.[38] Organisation as for Great Brand End Plot.

BRAMPTON

[Pts Lind] Tp (in Well Wap) in Torksey AP (o'wise Lawres Wap), sep CP 1866.[13] *LG* Seq 49. *Parl* Seq 14.

BRANSBY AND STURTON—see STURTON BY STOW

BRANSTON

AP [Linc Lbty and Co of Itself (1410—1840s), Pts Kestev (Langoe Wap, from 1840s)] *LG* Linc. PLU, RSD, Branst. RD. Abol civ 1931 to help cr Branston and Mere CP.[19] *Parl* N'rn Dv (1832—67), Mid Dv (1867—85), N Kestev Dv (1885—1918), Granth. Dv (1918—48). *Eccl* Seq 45.

BRANSTON AND MERE

CP [Pts Kestev] Cr 1931 by union Branston AP, Mere CP.[19] *LG* N Kestev RD. *Parl* Granth. CC (1948—*).

BRANT BROUGHTON

AP [Pts Kestev] *LG* Loved. Wap, Newk. PLU, RSD, Clayp. RD. Abol civ 1931 to help cr Brant Broughton and Stragglethorpe CP.[19] *Parl* S'rn Dv (1832—67), South Dv (1867—85), S Kestev Dv (1885—1918), Granth. Dv (1918—48). *Eccl* Loved. RDn. Abol eccl 1931 to help cr Brant Broughton with Stragglethorpe EP.[42]

BRANT BROUGHTON AND STRAGGLETHORPE

CP [Pts Kestev] Cr 1931 by union Brant Broughton AP, Stragglethorpe CP.[19] *LG* N Kestev RD. *Parl* Granth. CC (1948—*).

BRANT BROUGHTON WITH STRAGGLETHORPE

EP [Pts Kestev] Cr 1931 by union Brant Broughton AP, chap Stragglethorpe in Beckingham with Fenton and Stragglethorpe AP.[42] Loved. RDn.

BRATOFT

AP [Pts Lind] *LG* Seq 35. *Parl* Seq 12. *Eccl* Seq 15.

BRATTLEBY

AP [Pts Lind] *LG* Seq 43. *Parl* Seq 14. *Eccl* Seq 76.

BRAUNCEWELL

AP [Pts Kestev] *LG* Seq 14. *Parl* Seq 17. *Eccl* Asward. with Laff. RDn. Gains eccl 1718 Dunsby AP and the united par thereafter 'Brauncewell with Dunsby',[74] qv.

BRAUNCEWELL WITH DUNSBY

EP [Pts Kestev] Union 1718 of Brauncewell AP, Dunsby AP.[74] Asw. with Laff. RDn (1718—1866), Asw. with Laff. 1 RDn (1866—84), Laff. 1 RDn (1884—1910), Laff. (North) RDn (1910—68), Laff. RDn (1968—*).

BRIGSLEY

AP [Pts Lind] *LG* Seq 31. Transf 1974 to Humb.[10] *Parl* Seq 4. *Eccl* Seq 32.

BRINKHILL

AP [Pts Lind] *LG* Seq 40. *Parl* Seq 12. *Eccl* Seq 36.

BROCKLESBY

AP [Pts Lind] *LG* Seq 54. Civ bdry: 1887.[75] *Parl* Seq 5.

Eccl Yarb. RDn (until 1863), Yarb. 2 RDn (1863—1910), Grimsby (North) RDn (1910—before 1944), Caist. RDn (before 1944—68), Yarb. RDn (1968—*).

BROTHERTOFT

[Pts Holl] Chap in Kirton AP, sep CP 1866,[13] sep EP 1864.[6] *LG* Seq 3. Civ bdry: 1880,[76] 1906 (incl gains Ferry Corner Plot CP, Shuff Fen CP),[39] 1932,[77] 1935 (exchanges pts with Langriville CP, Pts Lind).[78] *Parl* Seq 19. *Eccl* Holl RDn (1864—66), N Holl 1 RDn (1866—1910), Holl (West) RDn (1910—*).

BROUGHTON

AP [Pts Lind] Manley Wap, Glanf. Brigg. PLU, pt Brigg USD (1875—92), Broughton USD (pt 1875—92, ent 1892—94), Broughton UD (1894—1923), Glanf. Brigg RD (1923—74). Civ bdry: 1892 (loses the pt in Brigg USD to Glanf. Brigg CP).[50] Transf 1974 to Humb.[10] *Parl* Seq 3. *Eccl* Seq 80.

BROXHOLME

AP [Pts Lind] *LG* Seq 43. *Parl* Seq 14. *Eccl* Seq 75.

BUCKNALL

AP [Pts Lind] *LG* Seq 37. *Parl* Seq 9. *Eccl* Gart. RDn (until 1866), Hornc. RDn (1866—84), Gart. RDn (1884—1966). Abol eccl 1966 to help cr Bucknall with Tupholme EP.[79]

BUCKNALL WITH TUPHOLME

EP [Pts Lind] Cr 1966 by union Bucknall AP, Tupholme AP.[79] Walshcr. (West) RDn (1966—68), Hornc. RDn (1968—*).

BRUMBY

[Pts Lind] Tp in Frodingham AP, sep CP 1866.[13] *LG* Manley Wap, Glanf. Brigg PLU, Brumby and Frodingham USD, UD. Abol 1919 pt to help cr Scunth. and Frodingham UD & CP, pt to help cr Brumby Rural CP.[21] *Parl* N'rn Dv (1832—67), North Dv (1867—85), N Lind Dv (1885—1918), Brigg Dv (1918—48).

OLD BRUMBY

EP [Pts Lind] Cr 1936 from Frodingham AP.[81] Manlake RDn. Bdry: 1969 (help cr Scunthorpe All Saints EP).[65]

BRUMBY RURAL

CP [Pts Lind] Cr 1919 by union pt Brumby and Frodingham UD (pt Brumby CP, pt Frodingham AP), pt Scunthorpe UD & CP.[21] *LG* Glanf. Brigg PLU, RD. Abol 1936 ent to Gunness CP.[28]

BULLINGTON

[Pts Lind] Chap in Goltho AP, sep CP 1866.[13] *LG* Seq 52. Bdry: 1887.[82] *Parl* Seq 8.

BURGH LE MARSH

AP [Pts Lind] *LG* Seq 35. *Parl* Seq 12. *Eccl* Seq 17.

BURGH ON BAIN

AP [Pts Lind] *LG* Seq 53. *Parl* Seq 10. *Eccl* Wragg. RDn (until 1968), Louthesk RDn (1968—*).

BURRINGHAM

[Pts Lind] Tp in Bottesford AP, sep CP 1866.[13] *LG* Seq 46. Bdry: 1919.[21] Transf 1974 to Humb.[10] *Parl* Seq 3.

BURTON

AP [Pts Lind] Usual civ spelling; for eccl see 'Burton by Lincoln'. *LG* Seq 43. *Parl* Seq 14.

GATE BURTON
AP [Pts Lind] *LG* Seq 49. *Parl* Seq 14. *Eccl* Seq 74.

BURTON BY LINCOLN
AP [Pts Lind] Usual eccl spelling; for civ see 'Burton'. *Eccl* Seq 76.

BURTON COGGLES
AP [Pts Kestev] Usual civ spelling; for eccl see following entry. *LG* Seq 10. *Parl* Seq 21.

BURTON LE COGGLES
AP [Pts Lind] Usual eccl spelling; for civ see prev entry. *Eccl* Seq 7.

BURTON PENWARDINE
AP [Pts Kestev] *LG* Seq 6. *Parl* Seq 17. *Eccl* Seq 2.

BURTON UPON STATHER
AP [Pts Lind] *LG* Pt Corr. Wap, pt Manley Wap, Glanf. Brigg PLU, RSD, RD. Civ bdry: 1887.[63] Transf 1974 to Humb.[10] *Parl* Seq 3. *Eccl* Seq 77.

BURWELL
AP [Pts Lind] Incl chap Walmsgate (Hill Hd, sep civ identity early). *LG* Pt Hill Hd (until Walmsgate sep civ), remainder, Seq 44. *Parl* Seq 1. *Eccl* Louthesk & Ludb. RDn (until 1863), Calc. RDn (1863—66), Calc. 1 RDn (1866—1910), Louthesk (West) RDn (1910—68), Louthesk RDn (1968—*).

BUSLINGTHORPE
AP [Pts Lind] *LG* Lawres Wap, Caist. PLU, RSD, RD. Civ bdry: 1887.[82] *Parl* Seq 11. *Eccl* Seq 73.

BUTTERWICK
AP [Pts Holl] *LG* Seq 5. Civ bdry: 1880,[47] 1932.[77] *Parl* Seq 16. *Eccl* Seq 39. Eccl bdry: 1885 (help cr Eastville with Midville EP [Pts Lind, Pts Holl]).[48]

EAST BUTTERWICK
[Pts Lind] Tp pt in Bottesford AP, pt in Messingham AP, sep CP 1866.[13] *LG* Seq 46. Bdry: 1887.[63] Transf 1974 to Humb.[10] *Parl* Seq 3.

WEST BUTTERWICK
[Pts Lind] Chap in Owston AP, sep CP 1866,[13] sep EP 1845.[83] *LG* Manley Wap, Gainsb. PLU (soon after 1837[84]—1930), RSD, RD (1894—1936), Isle of Axh. RD (1936—74). Civ bdry: 1886.[85] Transf 1974 to Humb.[10] *Parl* Seq 6. *Eccl* Corr. RDn (1845—57), Isle of Axh. RDn (1857—*).

BYARD'S LEAP
[Pts Kestev] Ex-par place, sep CP 1858.[38] *LG* Flax. Wap, Sleaf. PLU (1861—1930), RSD, RD. Abol civ 1931 to help cr Cranwell and Byard's Leap CP.[19] *Parl* S'rn Dv (1832—67), South Dv (1867—85), N Kestev Dv (1885—1918), Granth. Dv (1918—48).

CASTLE BYTHAM
AP [Pts Kestev] *LG* Seq 9. *Parl* Seq 21. *Eccl* Seq 8.

LITTLE BYTHAM
AP [Pts Kestev] *LG* Seq 9. *Parl* Seq 21. *Eccl* Seq 8.

CABOURNE
AP [Pts Lind] *LG* Seq 30. *Parl* Seq 5. *Eccl* Seq 29.

CADNEY
CP [Pts Lind] Cr 1936 by union Cadney cum Howsham AP, Newstead CP.[28] *LG* Glanf. Brigg RD. Bdry: 1967.[86] Transf 1974 to Humb.[10] *Parl* Brigg CC (1948—70), Brigg & Scunth. CC (1970—*).

CADNEY CUM HOWSHAM
AP [Pts Lind] *LG* Yarb. Wap, Glanf. Brigg PLU, RSD, RD. Civ bdry: 1887.[63] Abol civ 1936 to help cr

Cadney CP.[28] *Parl* N'rn Dv (1832—67), North Dv (1867—85), N Lind Dv (1885—1918), Brigg Dv (1918—48). *Eccl* Seq 66.

CAENBY
AP [Pts Lind] *LG* Seq 26. *Parl* Seq 6. *Eccl* Seq 68.

CAISTOR
AP [Pts Lind] Tp 'Caistor' in Yarb. Wap as was chap Clixby (sep CP 1866[13]); incl in Walshcr. Wap chap Holton le Moor (sep CP 1866[13]); neither chap sep eccl hence this par eccl 'Caistor with Holton le Moor and Clixby', qv. *LG* Pt Caist. Bor, Caist. PLU, RSD, RD. *Parl* Seq 5.

CAISTOR WITH HOLTON LE MOOR AND CLIXBY
AP [Pts Lind] Usual eccl spelling; for civ and civ sep chaps, see prev entry. *Eccl* Pec jurisd Prebend of Caist. (until 1846), Seq 63 thereafter.

CALCEBY
AP [Pts Lind] *LG* Seq 34. *Parl* Seq 12. *Eccl* Calc. RDn. Abol eccl 1774 to help cr South Ormsby with Ketsby, Calceby and Driby EP.[87]

CALCETHORPE
AP [Pts Lind] *LG* Seq 44. *Parl* Seq 1. *Eccl* Louthesk & Ludb. RDn (until 1863), Louthesk & Ludb. 1 RDn (1863—1910), Ludb. RDn (1910—25). Abol eccl 1925 to help cr Kelstern with Calcethorpe EP.[88]

CALKWELL
AP [Pts Lind] Usual eccl spelling; for civ see 'Cawkwell'. *Eccl* Seq 18.

CAMMERINGHAM
AP [Pts Lind] *LG* Seq 26. *Parl* Seq 6. *Eccl* Seq 68.

CANDLESBY
AP [Pts Lind] *LG* Seq 35. Civ bdry: 1936.[28] *Parl* Seq 12. *Eccl* Seq 16.

CANWICK
AP [Linc Lbty & Co of Itself (1410—1840s), Pts Kestev (Lang. Wap, from 1840s)] *LG* Linc. PLU, RSD, Branst. RD (1894—1931), N Kestev RD (1931—74). Civ bdry: 1967 (loses pt to Linc. CB [assoc with Pts Lind] & CP).[89] *Parl* N'rn Dv (1832—67), Mid Dv (1867—85), N Kestev Dv (1885—1918), Granth. Dv/CC (1918—*). *Eccl* Seq 45. Eccl bdry: 1971 (help cr Bracebridge Heath EP).[70]

CAREBY
AP [Pts Kestev] Incl hmlt Aunby, chap Holywell (each a sep CP 1866,[13] neither sep eccl hence this par eccl 'Careby with Holywell and Aunby', qv). *LG* Belt. Wap, Bourne PLU, RSD, RD. Abol civ 1931 to help cr Careby, Aunby and Holywell CP.[19] *Parl* S'rn Dv (1832—67), South Dv (1867—85), S Kestev Dv (1885—1918), Rutl & Stamf. Dv (1918—48).

CAREBY, AUNBY AND HOLYWELL
CP [Pts Kestev] Cr 1931 by union Careby AP, Aunby CP, Holywell CP.[19] *LG* S Kestev RD. *Parl* Rutl & Stamf. CC (1948—*).

CAREBY WITH HOLYWELL AND AUNBY
AP [Pts Kestev] Usual eccl spelling; for civ and civ sep hmlt and chap, see 'Careby'. *Eccl* Belt. RDn (until 1866), Belt. 2 RDn (1866—84), Belt. RDn (1884—1910), Ness RDn (1910—68), Belt. RDn (1968—*).

CARLBY
AP [Pts Kestev] *LG* Seq 20. Civ bdry: 1887 (gains pt Essendine CP, Rutl).[90] *Parl* Seq 21. *Eccl* Ness RDn

(until 1866), Belt. 2 RDn (1866—84), Belt. RDn (1884—1910), Ness RDn (1910—*).

CASTLE CARLTON

AP [Pts Lind] *LG* Louth Esk Hd, Louth PLU, RSD, RD. Abol civ 1936 ent to South Reston AP.[28] *Parl* N'rn Dv (1832—67), North Dv (1867—85), E Lind Dv (1885—1918), Louth Dv (1918—48). *Eccl* Louthesk & Ludb. RDn (until 1863), Louthesk & Ludb. 3 RDn (1863—66), Louthesk & Ludb. 2 RDn (1866—*ca* 1896), Louthesk & Ludb. 1 RDn (*ca* 1896—1910), Louthesk (West) RDn (1910—68), Calc. & Candl. RDn (1968—*).

GREAT CARLTON

AP [Pts Lind] *LG* Seq 44. *Parl* Seq 1. *Eccl* Seq 48.

LITTLE CARLTON

AP [Pts Lind] *LG* Seq 44. Civ bdry: 1888.[44] *Parl* Seq 1. *Eccl* Seq 48.

NORTH CARLTON

AP [Pts Lind] *LG* Seq 43. *Parl* Seq 14. *Eccl* Pec jurisd Dean & Chapter of Linc. (until 1846), Seq 76 thereafter.

SOUTH CARLTON

AP [Pts Lind] Organisation as for North Carlton.

CARLTON LE MOORLAND

AP [Pts Kestev] *LG* Seq 12. *Parl* Seq 15. *Eccl* Seq 22.

CARLTON SCROOP

AP [Pts Kestev] Usual civ spelling; for eccl see following entry. *LG* Seq 18. *Parl* Seq 20.

CARLTON SCROOPE

AP [Pts Kestev] Usual eccl spelling; for civ see prev entry. *Eccl* Loved. RDn. Abol eccl 1974 to help cr Carlton Scroope with Normanton EP.[91]

CARLTON SCROOPE WITH NORMANTON

EP [Pts Kestev] Cr 1974 by union Carton Scroope AP, Normanton AP.[91] Loved. RDn.

CARRINGTON

[Pts Lind] Area reclaimed from draining West Fen, sep tp 1812,[92] sep CP 1866,[13] church built 1826,[93] eccl made pt 1881 of Carrington with Frithville EP (Pts Lind, Pts Holl).[61] *LG* Seq 27. Bdry: 1880.[23] *Parl* Seq 12.

CARRINGTON WITH FRITHVILLE

EP [Pts Lind] Cr 1881 by union areas reclaimed from draining West Fen (areas in Pts Lind: ent Carrington EP, ent area Frithville, Hundleby AP, West Keal AP, Kirby on Bain AP [pt tp Tumby], pt Langriville EP, Lusby with Asgarby EP, Sibsey AP, area Westville, pt area Thornton le Fen [in Wildmore Fen], ex-par Frith Bank [in East Fen]; and from areas in Pts Holl: Boston AP, Fishtoft AP, Freiston AP, Leverton AP, Skirbeck AP).[61] Holl RDn (1851—66), N Holl 2 RDn (1866—1910), Holl (East) RDn (1910—61). Abol 1961 pt to help cr Sibsey with Frithville EP, pt to help cr New Bolingbroke with Carrington EP.[57]

CAWKWELL

AP [Pts Lind] Usual civ spelling; for eccl see 'Calkwell'. *LG* Seq 37. *Parl* Seq 9.

LITTLE CAWTHORPE

AP [Pts Lind] *LG* Seq 33. *Parl* Seq 10. *Eccl* Calc. RDn (until 1863), Louthesk & Ludb. 3 RDn (1863—1910), Louthesk (West) RDn (1910—68), Louthesk RDn (1968—*).

CAYTHORPE

AP [Pts Kestev] *LG* Seq 19. *Parl* Seq 17. *Eccl* Seq 50.

CHAPEL HILL

EP [Pts Holl] Cr 1828 from Swineshead AP.[6] Holl RDn (1828—66), N Holl 1 RDn (1866—1910), Holl (West) RDn (1910—48). Abol 1948 to help cr Holland Fen with Chapel Hill EP.[94]

CHAPEL ST LEONARD

[Pts Lind] Area in Mumby AP, sep CP 1896 as 'Chapel St Leonards',[95] qv, sep EP 1826 as 'Chapel St Leonard',[6] as such eccl refounded 1898 from Mumby AP, Hogsthorpe AP.[96] Calc. RDn (1826—66), Calc. 2 RDn (1866—1910), Calc. (South) RDn (1910—68), Calc. & Candl. RDn (1968—*).

CHAPEL ST LEONARDS

[Pts Lind] Area in Mumby AP, sep CP 1896 as 'Chapel St Leonards',[95] sep EP 1826 as 'Chapel St Leonard',[6] qv in prev entry incl later eccl refounding. *LG* Spilsby PLU, RD. Civ bdry: 1936.[28] *Parl* Hornc. Dv/CC (1918—*).

CLAXBY

AP [Pts Lind] *LG* Seq 48. *Parl* Seq 2. *Eccl* Walshcr. RDn. Abol eccl 1740 to help cr Claxby with Normanby le Wold EP.[97]

CLAXBY

AP [Pts Lind] *LG* Seq 34. *Parl* Seq 12. *Eccl* Seq 14.

CLAXBY PLUCKACRE

AP [Pts Lind] *LG* Seq 39. *Parl* Seq 12. *Eccl* Hill RDn (until 1866), Hill 1 RDn (1866—1910), Gart. RDn (1910—68), Hornc. RDn (1968—*).

CLAXBY WITH NORMANBY LE WOLD

EP [Pts Lind] Cr 1740 by union Claxby AP, Normanby le Wold AP.[97] Walshcr. RDn (1740—1866), Walshcr. 1 RDn (1866—73), Walshcr. RDn (1873—1910), Walshcr. (West) RDn (1910—68), W Wold RDn (1968—*).

CLAYPOLE

AP [Pts Kestev] *LG* Seq 19. *Parl* Seq 20. *Eccl* Seq 50.

CLAYTHORPE

[Pts Lind] Chap in Belleau AP, sep CP 1866.[13] *LG* Seq 33. *Parl* Seq 13.

CLEATHAM

[Pts Lind] Tp (in Corr. Wap) in Manton AP (o'wise Manley Wap), sep CP 1866.[13] *LG* Corr. Wap, Glanf. Brigg PLU, RSD, RD. Abol 1936 ent to Manton AP.[28] *Parl* N'rn Dv (1832—67), North Dv (1867—85), W Lind Dv (1885—1918), Brigg Dv (1918—48).

CLEE

AP [Pts Lind] Usual eccl spelling; for civ and civ sep tp, see 'Clee with Weelsby'. *Eccl* Seq 33. Eccl bdry: 1878 (cr New Clee EP),[98] 1898 (cr Grimsby All Saints EP),[30] 1906 (cr New Cleethorpes EP),[99] 1911 (help cr Grimsby St Stephen EP),[100] 1912 (help cr Grimsby St Augustine EP),[101] 1964.[68]

CP [Grimsby CB] Cr 1894 from the pt of Clee with Weelsby AP in Grimsby CP.[102] *LG* Grimsby PLU, CB. Abol 1928 to help cr Grimsby CP as the CB was extended.[72] *Parl* Grimsby Parl Bor (1918—48).

NEW CLEE

EP [Pts Lind] Cr 1878 from Clee AP.[98] Grimsby 2 RDn (1879—1910), Grimsby & Cleethorpes RDn (1910—*). Bdry: 1911 (help cr Grimsby St Stephen

EP),[100] 1913 (help cr Grimsby St Luke EP),[103] 1964.[68]

CLEE WITH WEELSBY
AP [Pts Lind] Usual civ spelling; for eccl see 'Clee'. Incl tp Cleethorpes (sep CP 1866[13]). *LG* Brad. Hav. Wap, Grimsby PLU, Clee with Weelsby USD (ent 1875—89, pt 1889—94), pt Grimsby CB & USD (1889—94). Abol civ 1894 the pt in the CB cr Clee CP, the remainder cr Weelsby CP.[102] *Parl* Gt Grimsby Parl Bor (1832—1918).

CLEETHORPES
[Pts Lind] Tp in Clee with Weelsby AP, sep CP 1866.[13] *LG* Brad. Hav. Wap, Grimsby PLU, Cleethorpe with Thrunscoe USD, UD (1894—1916), Cleethorpes UD (1916—36), MB (1936—74). Bdry: 1922,[104] 1927.[105] Tranf 1974 to Humb.[10] *Parl* Gt Grimsby Parl Bor (1832—1918), Grimsby Parl Bor (1918—48), Louth CC (1948—*).

NEW CLEETHORPES
EP [Pts Lind] Cr 1906 from Clee AP.[99] Grimsby 2 RDn (1906—10), Grimsby & Cleethorpes RDn (1910—*). Bdry: 1964.[68]

CLIXBY
[Pts Lind] Chap (Yarb. Wap) in Caistor AP (o'wise Walshcr. Wap), sep CP 1866.[13] *LG* Yarb. Wap, Caist. PLU, RSD, RD. Abol 1936 ent to Grasby AP.[28] *Parl* N'rn Dv (1832—67), North Dv (1867—85), N Lind Dv (1885—1918), Louth Dv (1918—48).

COATES
AP [Pts Lind] *LG* Asl. Wap, Gainsb. PLU, RSD, RD. Abol civ 1936 ent to Stow AP.[28] *Parl* N'rn Dv (1832—67), North Dv (1867—85), W Lind Dv (1885—1918), Gainsb. Dv (1918—48). *Eccl* Asl. RDn (until 1863), Lawres 2 RDn (1863—1910), Lawres (West) RDn (1910—68), Corr. RDn (1968—*).

GREAT COATES
AP [Pts Lind] *LG* Brad. Hav. Wap, Grimsby PLU, RSD, RD. Civ bdry: 1928 (loses pt to Grimsby CB [assoc with Pts Lind] and to help cr Grimsby CP [as CB was extended]),[72] 1958 (loses pt to Grimsby CB [assoc with Pts Lind] & CP).[106] Abol civ 1968 pt to Grimsby CB (assoc with Pts Lind) & CP, pt to Healing AP.[107] *Parl* Gt Grimsby Parl Bor (1832—1918), Louth Dv/CC (1918—70). Parl bdry: 1960.[108] *Eccl* Seq 31. Eccl bdry: 1964,[68] 1967.[109]

LITTLE COATES
AP [Pts Lind] *LG* Brad. Hav. Wap, Grimsby PLU, RSD, RD. Abol civ 1928 pt to Grimsby CB (assoc with Pts Lind) and to help cr Grimsby CP (as CB was extended), pt to Waltham AP.[72] *Parl* Gt Grimsby Parl Bor (1832—1918), Louth Dv (1918—48). *Eccl* Seq 33. Eccl bdry: 1933 (help cr Little Coates The Good Shepherd EP),[110] 1964,[68] 1967.[109]

LITTLE COATES THE GOOD SHEPHERD
EP [Pts Lind] Cr 1933 from Little Coates AP, Great Grimsby St Paul, West Marsh EP.[110] Grimsby and Cleethorpes RDn. Bdry: 1964.[68] Abol 1969 ent to Great Grimsby AP.[111]

NORTH COATES
AP [Pts Lind] *LG* Seq 32. *Parl* Seq 1. *Eccl* Grimsby RDn (until 1866), Grimsby 2 RDn (1866—1910), Grimsby (South) RDn (1910—68), Louthesk RDn (1968—*).

NORTH COCKERINGTON
AP [Pts Lind] *LG* Seq 44. Civ bdry: 1888.[44] *Parl* Seq 1. *Eccl* Seq 47. Eccl bdry: 1931.[112]

SOUTH COCKERINGTON
AP [Pts Lind] Organisation as for North Cockerington, incl civ and eccl bdry alts.

COLDSTEAD
[Pts Lind] Ex-par place, sep CP 1858.[38] *LG* Wragg. Wap, Linc. PLU (1862—1930), RSD, Welton RD. Abol civ 1936 ent to Newball CP.[28] *Parl* N'rn Dv (1832—67), Mid Dv (1867—85), E Lind Dv (1885—1918), Gainsb. Dv (1918—48).

COLEBY
AP [Pts Kestev] *LG* Seq 11. *Parl* Seq 15. *Eccl* Seq 45.

COLSTERWORTH
AP [Pts Kestev] *LG* Pt Granth. Soke (until 1830s), pt Winn. & Thr. Wap (from 1830s), the remainder Belt. Wap, Grant. PLU, RSD, RD (1894—1931), W Kestev RD (1931—74). Civ bdry: 1965 (loses pt to Buckminster AP, Leics).[113] *Parl* Seq 21. *Eccl* Seq 7.

CONINGSBY
AP [Pts Lind] *LG* Seq 42. Civ bdry: after 1862 (gains civ ex-par Langrick Ferry [sep rated 1862 in Hornc. PLU, sep status not sustained]), 1880 (help cr Wildmore CP),[26] 1880,[114] 1880,[115] 1884,[116] 1884,[117] 1884,[118] 1904.[119] *Parl* Seq 12. *Eccl* Seq 20. Eccl bdry: 1881 (pt of fen allotment eccl severed to help cr Wildmore EP [Pts Lind, Pts Kestev, Pts Holl]).[27]

CONISHOLME
AP [Pts Lind] *LG* Seq 44. *Parl* Seq 1. *Eccl* Seq 47.

COPPING SYKE
[Pts Holl thereafter] Ex-par place, sep CP 1858.[38] *LG* Kirton Wap, Boston PLU (1862—1930), RSD, RD. Bdry: 1906 (incl gains Great Beats CP, Little Beats CP, Seven Acres CP).[39] Abol 1935 ent to Wildmore CP, Pts Lind).[28] *Parl* N'rn Dv (1832—67), Mid Dv (1867—85), N Kestev Dv (1885—1918), Hornc. Dv (1918—48).

CORBY
AP [Pts Kestev] *LG* Seq 9. *Parl* Seq 21. *Eccl* Seq 7.

CORRINGHAM
AP [Pts Lind] *LG* Seq 36. *Parl* Seq 6. *Eccl* Pec jurisd Corr. prebend (until 1846), Seq 69 thereafter.

COUNTHORPE
[Pts Kestev] Hmlt in Creeton AP, sep CP 1866.[13] *LG* Belt. Wap, Bourne PLU, RSD, RD. Abol 1931 to help cr Counthorpe and Creeton CP.[19] *Parl* S'rn Dv (1832—67), South Dv (1867—85), S Kestev Dv (1885—1918), Rutl & Stamf. Dv (1918—48).

COUNTHORPE AND CREETON
CP [Pts Kestev] Cr 1931 by union Counthorpe CP, Creeton AP.[19] *LG* S Kestev RD. *Parl* Rutl & Stamf. CC (1948—*).

COVENHAM ST BARTHOLOMEW
AP [Pts Lind] *LG* Seq 45. Civ bdry: 1887.[120] *Parl* Seq 1. *Eccl* Seq 46.

COVENHAM ST MARY

AP [Pts Lind] Organisation as for Covenham St Bartholomew, incl bdry alt.

COWBIT

[Pts Holl] Chap in Spalding AP, sep civ identity early, church consecr 1486.[121] Sometimes early 'Peakhill'. *LG* Seq 2. Civ bdry: 1883,[31] 1887,[122] 1932.[123] *Parl* Seq 16. *Eccl* Seq 40. Eccl bdry: 1918.[124]

CRANWELL

AP [Pts Kestev] *LG* Flax. Wap, Sleaf. PLU, RSD, RD. Abol civ 1931 to help cr Cranwell and Byard's Leap CP.[19] *Parl* S'rn Dv (1832—67), South Dv (1867—85), N Kestev Dv (1885—1918), Granth. Dv (1918—48). *Eccl* Seq 1.

CRANWELL AND BYARD'S LEAP

CP [Pts Kestev] Cr 1931 by union Cranwell AP, Byard's Leap CP.[19] *LG* E Kestev RD. *Parl* Granth. CC (1948—*).

CREETON

AP [Pts Kestev] Incl hmlt Counthorpe (sep CP 1866,[13] not sep eccl hence this par eccl 'Creeton with Counthorpe', qv). *LG* Belt. Wap, Bourne PLU (soon after 1836[84]—1930), RSD, RD. Abol civ 1931 to help cr Counthorpe and Creeton CP.[19] *Parl* S'rn Dv (1832—67), South Dv (1867—85), S Kestev Dv (1885—1918), Rutl & Stamf. Dv (1918—48).

CREETON WITH COUNTHORPE

AP [Pts Kestev] Usual eccl spelling; for civ and civ sep hmlt, see prev entry. *Eccl* Seq 8.

CROFT

AP [Pts Lind] *LG* Seq 35. *Parl* Seq 12. *Eccl* Seq 17.

CROSBY

[Pts Lind] Tp pt in Flixborough AP, pt in Frodingham AP, sep CP 1866,[13] the pt in the former remains while pt of the pt in the latter AP eccl severed 1861 to help cr Gunhouse with Burringham EP,[64] the remainder of the pt in Frodingham AP eccl severed 1889 to help cr Scunthorpe EP,[125] 'Crosby' a sep EP 1913 from Scunthorpe EP.[126] *LG* Manley Wap, Glanf. Brigg PLU, RSD, RD. Civ bdry: 1887.[63] Abol civ 1919 pt to help cr Scunth. & Frodingham UD & CP, pt to Flixborough AP.[21] *Parl* N'rn Dv (1832—67), North Dv (1867—85), N Lind Dv (1885—1918), Brigg Dv (1918—48). *Eccl* Manlake RDn. Eccl bdry: 1969 (help cr Scunthorpe The Resurrection, Berkeley EP).[127]

CROWLAND

AP [Pts Holl] Orig Abbey church. *LG* Elloe Wap, Peterb PLU, RSD, Crowland RD (1894—1932), Spald. RD (1932—74). *Parl* S'rn Dv (1832—67), South Dv (1867—85), S Kestev Dv (1885—1918), Holl with Boston Dv/CC (1918—*). *Eccl* Seq 40.

CROWLE

AP [Pt Yorks W Riding (Strafford and Tickhill Wap [moorland, uninhabited until late 19th cent]), pt Lincs Pts Lind (Manley Wap), the par considered ent Lincs by census of 1871[128] Incl in Lincs chap Eastoft (sep CP 1866,[13] the chap and another pt in Lincs of the AP eccl severed 1855 to help cr Eastoft EP,[129] qv for other constituent pars). *LG* Thorne

PLU, Crowle USD, UD (1894—1936), Isle of Axh. RD (1936—74). Addtl civ bdry alt: 1968.[18] Transf 1974 to Humb.[10] *Parl* Lincs pt, Seq 6. *Eccl* Seq 79.

CROXBY

AP [Pts Lind] *LG* Walshcr. Wap, Caist. PLU, RSD, RD. Abol civ 1936 ent to Thoresway AP.[28] *Parl* N'rn Dv (1832—67), North Dv (1867—85), E Lind Dv (1885—1918), Louth Dv (1918—48). *Eccl* Seq 52.

CROXTON

AP [Pts Lind] *LG* Seq 55. Transf 1974 to Humb.[10] *Parl* Seq 3. *Eccl* Seq 60.

CULVERTHORPE

[Pts Kestev] Chap in Heydour AP, sep CP 1866.[13] *LG* Asw. Wap, Sleaf. PLU, RSD, RD. Abol 1931 to help cr Culverthorpe and Kelby CP.[19] *Parl* S'rn Dv (1832—67), South Dv (1867—85), N Kestev Dv (1885—1918), Granth. Dv (1918—48).

CULVERTHORPE AND KELBY

CP [Pts Kestev] Cr 1931 by union Culverthorpe CP, Kelby CP.[19] *LG* E Kestev RD. *Parl* Granth. CC (1948—*).

CUMBERWORTH

AP [Pts Lind] *LG* Seq 34. *Parl* Seq 12. *Eccl* Seq 14.

CUXWOLD

AP [Pts Lind] *LG* Bradf. Hav. Wap, Caist. PLU, RSD, RD. Abol civ 1936 ent to Swallow AP.[28] *Parl* N'rn Dv (1832—67), North Dv (1867—85), N Lind Dv (1885—1918), Louth Dv (1918—48). *Eccl* Seq 29.

DALBY

AP [Pts Lind] *LG* Seq 35. *Parl* Seq 12. *Eccl* Pec jurisd Dean & Chapter of Linc. (until 1846), Candl. RDn (1846—66), Hill 2 RDn (1866—95), Candl. 1 RDn (1895—1910), Hill (South) RDn (1910—68), Bolingbr. RDn (1968—*).

DALDERBY

AP [Pts Lind] *LG* Gart. Hd, Hornc. PLU, RSD, RD. Civ bdry: 1880,[115] 1887.[130] Abol civ 1936 ent to Roughton AP.[28] *Parl* N'rn Dv (1832—67), Mid Dv (1867—85), S Lind Dv (1885—1918), Hornc. Dv (1918—48). *Eccl* Gart. RDn. Abol eccl 1731 to help cr Scrivelsby with Dalderby EP.[131]

MARKET DEEPING

AP [Pts Kestev] *LG* Seq 20. Civ bdry: 1931.[19] *Parl* Seq 21. *Eccl* Seq 51.

WEST DEEPING

AP [Pts Kestev] *LG* Seq 21. Civ bdry: 1931.[19] *Parl* Seq 21. *Eccl* Seq 51.

DEEPING FEN

Ex-par area (pt Pts Holl [Elloe Wap], pt Pts Kestev [Ness Wap]) reclaimed by drainage beginning in 1595, made a sep par 1856 as 'Deeping St Nicholas',[132] qv.

DEEPING ST JAMES

AP [Pts Kestev] Sometimes early 'East Deeping'. *LG* Seq 20. Civ bdry: 1931.[19] *Parl* Seq 21. *Eccl* Seq 51.

DEEPING ST NICHOLAS

[Pt Pts Holl (Elloe Wap), pt Pts Kestev (Ness Wap) until 1930, ent Pts Holl from 1930[133]] Ex-par area of 'Deeping Fen' reclaimed by drainage beginning 1595, sep par 1856 as 'Deeping St Nicholas'.[132] *LG* Spald. PLU (1862—1930), RSD, RD. Addtl civ bdry alt: 1932.[123] *Parl* S'rn Dv (1832—67), South

Dv (1867—85), pt Holl Dv, pt S Kestev Dv (1885—1918), Holl with Boston Dv/CC (1918—*). *Eccl* Holl RDn (1856—66), S Holl RDn (1866—84), W Elloe RDn (1884—1910), Elloe (West) RDn (1910—*).

DEMBLEBY
AP [Pts Kestev] *LG* Avel. Wap, Sleaf. PLU, RSD, RD. Abol civ 1931 to help cr Aunsby and Dembleby CP.[19] *Parl* S'rn Dv (1832—67), South Dv (1867—85), N Kestev Dv (1885—1918), Granth. Dv (1918—48). *Eccl* Seq 5.

DENTON
AP [Pts Kestev] *LG* Seq 15. Civ bdry: 1931,[19] 1931,[35] 1965 (gains pt Belvoir CP, pt Croxton Kerrial AP, both Leics).[113] *Parl* Seq 21. *Eccl* Seq 25.

DIGBY
AP [Pts Kestev] *LG* Seq 14. *Parl* Seq 17. *Eccl* Asw. with Laff. RDn. Abol eccl 1717 to help cr Digby with Bloxholm EP.[22]

DIGBY WITH BLOXHOLM
EP [Pts Kestev] Cr 1717 by union Digby AP, Bloxholm AP.[22] Asw. with Laff. RDn (1717—1866), Asw. with Laff. 1 RDn (1866—84), Laff. 1 RDn (1884—1910), Laff. (North) RDn (1910—68), Laff. RDn (1968—*).

DODDINGTON
AP [Pts Kestev] Incl tp Whisby (sep CP 1866,[13] not sep eccl hence this par eccl 'Doddington with Whisby', qv). *LG* Boothby Wap, Linc. PLU, RSD, Branst. RD. Abol civ 1931 to help cr Doddington and Whisby CP.[19] *Parl* S'rn Dv (1832—67), Mid Dv (1867—85), N Kestev Dv (1885—1918), Granth. Dv (1918—48).

DRY DODDINGTON
[Pts Kestev] Chap in Westborough AP, sep civ identity early. *LG* Loved. Wap, Newk. PLU, RSD, Clayp. RD. Abol 1931 to help cr Westborough and Dry Doddington CP.[19] *Parl* S'rn Dv (1832—67), South Dv (1867—85), S Kestev Dv (1885—1918), Granth. Dv (1918—48).

DODDINGTON AND WHISBY
CP [Pts Kestev] Cr 1931 by union Doddington AP, Whisby CP.[19] *LG* N Kestev RD. *Parl* Granth. CC (1948—*).

DODDINGTON WITH WHISBY
AP [Pts Kestev] Usual eccl spelling; for civ and civ sep tp, see 'Doddington'. *Eccl* seq 22.

DOGDYKE
[Pts Kestev] Tp in Billinghay AP, sep CP 1866,[13] eccl ex-par, eccl abol 1881 to help cr Wildmore EP [Pts Lind, Pts Kestev, Pts Holl].[27] *LG* Langoe Wap, Boston PLU (1836—*ca* 1894), Sleaf. PLU (*ca* 1894—1930), RSD, RD (1894—1931), E Kestev RD (1931—74). Civ bdry: 1884,[117] 1884,[116] 1931,[19] 1935 (gains pt Hart's Grounds CP, pt Pelham's Lands CP, both Pts Holl).[17] *Parl* Seq 15.

DONINGTON
AP [Pts Holl] *LG* Kirton Wap, Spald. PLU (soon after 1835[84]—1930), RSD, RD. *Parl* Seq 19. *Eccl* Holl RDn (until 1866), N Holl 1 RDn (1866—1910), Elloe (West) RDn (1910—68), Holl (West) RDn (1968—*).

DONINGTON ON BAIN
AP [Pts Lind] *LG* Seq 38. *Parl* Seq 10. *Eccl* Seq 21.

DORRINGTON
AP [Pts Kestev] *LG* Seq 14. *Parl* Seq 17. *Eccl* Seq 1.

DOWSBY
AP [Pts Kestev] *LG* Seq 7. *Parl* Seq 21. *Eccl* Seq 6.

DRAINAGE MARSH
[Pts Holl] Ex-par place, sep CP 1858.[38] *LG* Kirton Wap, Boston PLU (1862—1906), RSD, RD. Abol civ 1906 ent to Wigtoft AP.[39] *Parl* S'rn Dv (1832—67), South Dv (1867—85), N Kestev Dv (1885—1918).

DRIBY
AP [Pts Lind] *LG* Seq 35. *Parl* Seq 12. *Eccl* Hill RDn. Abol eccl 1774 to help cr South Ormesby with Ketsby, Calceby and Driby EP.[87]

DROVE END
EP [Pts Holl] Cr 1855 from Gedney AP.[134] Holl RDn (1855—66), S Holl RDn (1866—84), E Elloe RDn (1884—1910), Elloe (East) RDn (1910—*).

DUNHOLME
AP [Pts Lind] *LG* Seq 43. *Parl* Seq 14. *Eccl* Pec jurisd Dean & Chapter of Linc. (until 1846), Seq 72 thereafter.

DUNSBY
AP [Pts Kestev] *LG* Seq 7. *Parl* Seq 21. *Eccl* Asw. with Laff. RDn. Abol eccl 1718 to help cr Brauncewell with Dunsby EP.[74]

DUNSTON
AP [Pts Kestev] *LG* Seq 16. *Parl* Seq 15. *Eccl* Seq 45. *Eccl* bdry: 1942.[135]

EAGLE
AP [Pts Kestev] *LG* Boothby Wap, Linc. PLU, RSD, Branst. RD. Civ bdry: 1886 (gains Eagle Woodhouse CP).[136] Abol civ 1931 to help cr Eagle and Swinethorpe CP.[19] *Parl* S'rn Dv (1832—67), Mid Dv (1867—85), N Kestev Dv (1885—1918), Granth. Dv (1918—48). *Eccl* Seq 22.

EAGLE AND SWINETHORPE
CP [Pts Kestev] Cr 1931 by union Eagle AP, Eagle Hall CP, Swinethorpe CP.[19] *LG* N Kestev RD. *Parl* Granth. CC (1948—*).

EAGLE HALL
[Pts Kestev] Ex-par place, sep CP 1858.[38] *LG* Boothby Graff. Wap, Linc. PLU (1862—1930), RSD, Branst. RD. Abol 1931 to help cr Eagle and Swinethorpe CP.[19] *Parl* S'rn Dv (1832—67), Mid Dv (1867—85), N Kestev Dv (1885—1918), Granth. Dv (1918—48).

EAGLE WOODHOUSE
[Pts Kestev] Ex-par place, sep CP 1858.[38] *LG* Boothby Graff. Wap, Linc. PLU (1862—86), RSD. Abol civ 1886 ent to Eagle AP.[136] *Parl* S'rn Dv (1832—67), Mid Dv (1867—85), N Kestev Dv (1885—1918).

EASTOFT
[Pts Lind] Chap and tp in Lincs (Manley Wap) in Crowle AP (Lincs Pts Lind, Yorks W Riding), sep CP 1866 in Lincs,[13] the chap and tp and another pt in Lincs of Crowle AP eccl severed 1855 and united with pt Adlingfleet AP (Yorks W Riding, dioc York) and pt Luddington with Garthorpe AP (Lincs) as 'Eastoft' EP (to be dioc York).[129] *LG* Manley

Wap, Thorne PLU, Crowle USD, Isle of Axh. RD. Civ bdry: 1884 (loses pt to Thorne AP, Yorks W Riding).[137] Transf 1974 to Humb.[10] *Parl* Seq 6. *Eccl* See entry in Yorks.

EASTON
[Pts Kestev] Tp in Stoke CP (qv for constitution in 1776, that par eccl from constitution at same time as an EP 'North and South Stoke with Easton'), 'Easton' a sep CP 1866.[13] *LG* Seq 15. *Parl* Seq 21.

EASTVILLE
[Pts Lind] Tp cr 1812 from East Fen,[92] sep CP 1866,[13] eccl severed 1885 to help cr Eastville with Midville EP (Pts Lind, Pts Holl).[48] *LG* Seq 29. *Parl* Seq 12.

EASTVILLE WITH MIDVILLE
EP [Pts Lind] Cr 1885 from area in East Fen, pt in Pts Lind (area Eastville, area Midville, West Keal AP, Revesby AP, Spilsby EP), pt in Pts Holl (Benington AP, Boston AP, Butterwick AP, Leverton AP).[48] Bolingbr. RDn.

EDENHAM
AP [Pts Kestev] *LG* Seq 9. *Parl* Seq 21. *Eccl* Donative, Belt. RDn (until 1866), Belt. 2 RDn (1866—84), Belt. RDn (1884—1910), Avel. RDn (1910—68), Avel. & Ness with Stamf. RDn (1968—*).

EDLINGTON
AP [Pts Lind] *LG* Seq 37. Civ bdry: 1936.[28] *Parl* Seq 12. *Eccl* Seq 19. Eccl bdry: 1913.[126]

NORTH ELKINGTON
AP [Pts Lind] *LG* Seq 44. *Parl* Seq 1. *Eccl* Louthesk & Ludb. RDn. Abol eccl 1850 to help cr North Elkington with South Elkington EP.[138]

NORTH ELKINGTON WITH SOUTH ELKINGTON
EP [Pts Lind] Cr 1850 by union North Elkington AP, South Elkington AP.[138] Louthesk & Ludb. RDn (1850—63), Louthesk & Ludb. 1 RDn (1863—1910), Ludb. RDn (1910—68), Louthesk RDn (1968—*).

SOUTH ELKINGTON
AP [Pts Lind] Organisation as for North Elkington.

ELSHAM
AP [Pts Lind] *LG* Seq 55. Transf 1974 to Humb.[10] *Parl* Seq 3. *Eccl* Seq 62.

BAG ENDERBY
AP [Pts Lind] *LG* Hill Hd, Hornc. PLU, RSD, RD. Abol civ 1936 ent to Somersby AP.[28] *Parl* N'rn Dv (1832—67), Mid Dv (1867—85), S Lind Dv (1885—1918), Hornc. Dv (1918—48). *Eccl* Seq 34.

MAVIS ENDERBY
AP [Pts Lind] Sometimes 'St Michael's Enderby'. *LG* Seq 29. Civ bdry: 1880 (help cr West Fen CP).[139] *Parl* Seq 12. *Eccl* Seq 9. Eccl bdry: 1858 (allotment in West Fen eccl severed to help cr New Bolingbroke EP).[24]

WOOD ENDERBY
AP [Pts Lind] *LG* Seq 42. Civ bdry: 1880 (help cr Wildmore CP),[26] 1884,[140] 1936 (gains Wilksby AP).[28] *Parl* Seq 12. *Eccl* Seq 44. Eccl bdry: 1881 (help cr Wildmore EP [Pts Lind, Pts Kestev, Pts Holl]).[27]

EPWORTH
AP [Pts Lind] *LG* Seq 47. Civ bdry: 1883,[31] 1884,[45] 1885.[141] Transf 1974 to Humb.[10] *Parl* Seq 6. *Eccl*

Seq 70.

EVEDON
AP [Pts Kestev] *LG* Asw. Wap, Slap. PLU, RSD, RD. Abol civ 1931 to help cr Ewerby and Evedon CP.[19] *Parl* S'rn Dv (1832—67), South Dv (1867—85), N Kestev Dv (1885—1918), Granth. Dv (1918—48). *Eccl* Seq 1.

EWERBY
AP [Pts Kestev] *LG* Asw. Wap, Slap. PLU, RSD. RD. Abol civ 1931 to help cr Ewerby and Evedon CP.[19] *Parl* S'rn Dv (1832—67), South Dv (1867—85), N Kestev Dv (1885—1918), Granth. Dv (1918—48). *Eccl* Seq 1.

EWERBY AND EVEDON
CP [Pts Kestev] Cr 1931 by union Everdon AP, Ewerby AP, Haverholme Priory CP.[19] *LG* E Kestev RD. *Parl* Granth. CC (1948—*).

FALDINGWORTH
AP [Pts Lind] *LG* Seq 43. Civ bdry: 1887.[142] *Parl* Seq 8. *Eccl* Seq 73.

FARFORTH
AP [Pts Lind] Louthesk & Ludb. RDn, united early with Maidenwell AP (no church) to cr Farforth cum Maidenwell AP.[143]

FARFORTH CUM MAIDENWELL
AP [Pts Lind] Cr early by union Farforth AP, Maidenwell AP (no church).[143] *LG* Louth Esk Hd, Louth PLU, RSD, RD. Abol civ 1936 to help cr Maidenwell CP.[28] *Parl* N'rn Dv (1832—67), North Dv (1867—85), E Lind Dv (1885—1918), Louth Dv (1918—48). *Eccl* Louthesk & Ludb. RDn. Abol eccl 1753 to help cr Ruckland with Farforth and Maidenwell EP.[144]

FARLESTHORPE
AP [Pts Lind] *LG* Seq 34. *Parl* Seq 12. *Eccl* Seq 14.

FENTON
[Pts Kestev] Chap in Beckingham AP (burial rights by 1528 but still a chap[40]), sep civ identity early, eccl severed 1932 to help cr Stubton with Fenton EP.[41] *LG* Seq 19. *Parl* Seq 20.

FENTON
[Pts Lind] Tp in Kettlethorpe AP, sep CP 1866.[13] *LG* Seq 49. *Parl* Seq 14.

SOUTH FERRIBY
AP [Pts Lind] *LG* Seq 55. Transf 1974 to Humb.[10] *Parl* Seq 3. *Eccl* Seq 60.

EAST FERRY
[Pts Lind] Chap pt in Owston AP (Manley Wap), pt in Scotton AP (Corr. Wap), sep CP 1866,[13] the area considered eccl in Owston AP, 'East Ferry' eccl severed 1954 to help cr Scotter with East Ferry EP, the remainder (hitherto 'Owston with East Ferry') to be 'Owston'.[145] Incl from 1866 undivided pt of Lands Common to East Ferry and Scotton (abol civ 1934 with pt to each par[28]). *LG* Gainsb. PLU (soon after 1837[84]—1930), RSD, RD. Addtl civ bdry alt: 1885.[146] *Parl* Seq 6.

FERRY CORNER PLOT
[Pts Holl] Ex-par place, sep CP 1858.[38] *LG* Kirton Wap, Boston PLU (1862—1906), RSD, RD. Abol civ 1906 ent to Brothertoft CP.[39] *Parl* S'rn Dv (1832—67), South Dv (1867—85), N Kestev Dv (1885—1918).

FILLINGHAM
AP [Pts Lind] *LG* Seq 25. *Parl* Seq 6. *Eccl* Seq 68.

FIRSBY
AP [Pts Lind] *LG* Seq 35. Civ bdry: 1888.[2] *Parl* Seq 12. *Eccl* [St Andrew] Candl. RDn (until 1866), Candl. 2 RDn (1866—1910), Hill (South) RDn (1910—68), Bolingbr. RDn (1968—*).

EAST FIRSBY
AP [Pts Lind] Orig chap in Ingham, sep par before 1535. Incl tp West Firsby (sep CP 1866[13]). *LG* Asl. Wap, Linc. PLU, RSD, Welton RD. Abol 1936 ent to West Firsby CP.[28] *Parl* N'rn Dv (1832—67), North Dv (1867—85), W Lind Dv (1885—1918), Gainsb. Dv (1918—48). *Eccl* [St James] Asl. RDn. Abol eccl late 18th or early 19th cent to help cr Saxby with Firsby EP.[147]

WEST FIRSBY
[Pts Lind] Tp in East Firsby AP, sep CP 1866.[13] *LG* Seq 26. Bdry: 1936 (gains East Firsby AP).[28] *Parl* Seq 6.

FISHTOFT
AP [Pts Holl] *LG* Seq 5. Civ bdry: 1880,[115] 1880,[58] 1880,[55] 1900,[59] 1932,[77] 1932,[60] 1935 (loses pt to Langriville CP, gains pt Frithville CP, both Pts Lind).[78] *Parl* Seq 16. *Eccl* Seq 39. Eccl bdry: 1881 (help cr Wildmore EP [Pts Lind, Pts Kestev, Pts Holl]),[27] 1886 (help cr Carrington with Frithville EP [Pts Lind, Pts Holl]),[61] 1966.[148]

FISKERTON
AP [Pts Lind] Incl chap Reepham (sep civ identity early, sep eccl prob from 1633 [first registers[149]]). *LG* Seq 43. *Parl* Seq 14. *Eccl* Seq 72. Eccl bdry: 1889.[62]

FLAWFORD
Ex-par place (pt Notts [Newk. Wap], pt Lincs Pts Kestev [Boothby Graff. Wap]), sep CP 1858 with pt in ea co.[38] *LG* Newk. PLU (1866—84), RSD. Abol 1884 the pt in Lincs transf to Stapleford AP in that co, the pt in Notts transf to Barnby in the Willows AP in that co.[150] *Parl* Lincs pt, S'rn Dv (1832—67), Mid Dv (1867—85).

FLEET
AP [Pts Holl] *LG* Seq 1. *Parl* Seq 16. *Eccl* Seq 41. Eccl bdry: 1867 (help cr Holbeach Fen with Gedney Hall EP).[151]

FLIXBOROUGH
AP [Pts Lind] Incl pt tp Crosby (sep CP 1866[13]). *LG* Seq 46. Addtl civ bdry alt: 1919 (incl help cr Scunthorpe and Frodingham UD & CP).[21] Transf 1974 to Humb.[10] *Parl* Seq 3. *Eccl* Seq 77. Eccl bdry: 1895.[96]

FOLKINGHAM
AP [Pts Kestev] Gains early eccl (sep civ identity retained) Loughton AP (church destroyed),[152] hence this par eccl 'Folkingham wth Loughton', qv. Sometimes 'Falkingham'. *LG* Seq 7. *Parl* Seq 21.

FOLKINGHAM WITH LOUGHTON
AP [Kestev] Usual eccl spelling after Folkingham AP gains early Loughton AP (church destroyed).[152] *Eccl* Seq 4.

FOSDYKE
[Pts Holl] Chap in Algar Kirk AP (eccl, 'Algarkirk'), sep civ identity early, area eccl reduced 1812 when fen allotment severed to help cr Holland Fen EP,[7] the latter refounded 1865,[7] 'Fosdyke' a sep EP 1898 from remainder in Algarkirk.[8] *LG* Seq 3. Civ bdry: 1880.[76] *Parl* Seq 16. *Eccl* N Holl 1 RDn (1898—1910), Holl (West) RDn (1910—*).

FOSTON
[Pts Kestev] Chap in Long Bennington AP, sep civ identity early. *LG* Seq 19. *Parl* Seq 20.

FOTHERBY
AP [Pts Lind] Incl eccl Brackenborough (status earlier as AP not certain,[71] sep civ identity sustained) hence this par eccl 'Fotherby and Brackenborough', qv. *LG* Seq 45. *Parl* Seq 1.

FOTHERBY AND BRACKENBOROUGH
AP [Pts Lind] Usual eccl spelling; for earlier status, civ and par organisation, and union of areas of Fotherby AP, Brackenborough, see prev entry. *Eccl* Seq 46.

FRAMPTON
AP [Pts Holl] *LG* Seq 3. Civ bdry: 1887,[116] 1906 (incl gains The Friths CP),[39] 1932.[77] *Parl* Seq 16. *Eccl* Seq 38.

FREISTON
AP [Pts Holl] *LG* Seq 5. Civ bdry: 1880 (help cr West Fen CP, to be in Pts Lind),[139] 1932.[77] *Parl* Seq 16. *Eccl* Seq 39. Eccl bdry: 1858 (allotment in West Fen severed to help cr New Bolingbroke EP),[24] 1886 (help cr Carrington with Frithville EP [Pts Lind, Pts Holl]).[61]

FREISTHORPE
AP [Pts Lind] *LG* Seq 43. Civ bdry: 1887.[142] *Parl* Seq 8. *Eccl* Pec jurisd Dean & Chapter of Linc. (until 1846), Seq 73 thereafter.

FRISKNEY
AP [Pts Lind] *LG* Seq 35. *Parl* Seq 12. *Eccl* Seq 17.

FRITH BANK
[Pts Lind] Ex-par area in East Fen not sep civ, pt eccl severed 1881 to help cr Wildmore EP (Pts Lind, Pts Kestev, Pts Holl),[27] the remainder eccl abol 1886 to help cr Carrington with Frithville EP (Pts Lind, Pts Holl).[61]

THE FRITHS
[Pts Holl] Ex-par place, sep CP 1858.[38] *LG* Kirton Wap, Boston PLU (1866—1906), RSD, RD. Abol 1906 ent to Frampton AP.[39] *Parl* S'rn Dv (1832—67), South Dv (1867—85), Holl Dv (1885—1918).

FRITHVILLE
[Pts Lind] Area reclaimed from West Fen, sep tp 1812,[92] church erected 1812,[153] sep CP 1866,[13] eccl abol 1886 to help cr Carrington with Frithville EP (Pts Lind, Pts Holl).[61] *LG* Seq 27. Bdry: 1880,[58] 1880,[154] 1935 (loses pt to Fishtoft AP, Pts Holl),[78] 1936.[28] *Parl* Seq 12.

FRODINGHAM
AP [Pts Lind] Incl pt chap Gunness (eccl, 'Gunhouse'), pt tp Crosby (each a sep CP 1866,[13] the pts of each in this par eccl severed 1861 to help cr Gunhouse with Burrington EP,[146] the remainder of Crosby severed 1889 to help cr Scunthorpe EP,[125] 'Crosby' a sep EP 1913 from Scunthorpe EP[126]); also incl tps Brumby, Scunthorpe (each a sep CP 1866,[13] each incl 1889 in Scunthorpe EP[125]). *LG* Manley Wap,

Glanf. Brigg PLU, Brumby and Frodingham USD, UD (1894—1919). Abol civ 1919 pt to help cr Scunthorpe and Frodingham UD & CP, pt to help cr Brumby Rural CP.[21] *Parl* N'rn Dv (1832—67), North Dv (1867—85), N Lind Dv (1885—1918), Brigg Dv (1918—48). *Eccl* Seq 77. Addtl eccl bdry alt: 1936 (cr Old Brumby EP),[81] 1969 (help cr Scunthorpe The Resurrection, Berkeley EP),[127] 1969 (help cr Scunthorpe All Saints EP).[65]

FULBECK
AP [Pts Kestev] *LG* Seq 19. Civ bdry: 1883.[31] *Parl* Seq 17. *Eccl* Seq 50.

FULLETBY
AP [Pts Lind] *LG* Seq 39. *Parl* Seq 12. *Eccl* Seq 35.

FULNETBY
[Pts Lind] Chap in Rand AP, sep CP 1866.[13] *LG* Wrangg. Wap, Linc. PLU (soon after 1836[84]—1930), RSD, Welton RD. Civ bdry: 1887.[81] *Parl* Seq 8.

FULSTOW
AP [Pts Lind] Incl chap Marsh Chapel (sep civ identity early, sep EP 1740[6]). *LG* Seq 32. *Parl* Seq 1. *Eccl* Seq 46.

GAINSBOROUGH
[Pts Lind] The following have 'Gainsborough' in their names. Insofar as any existed at a given time: *LG* Corr. Wap, pt Gainsb. Bor, Gainsb. PLU, pt Gainsb. USD, pt Gainsb. RSD, Gainsb. UD (pt 1894—95, ent 1895—1974), pt Gainsb. RD (1894—95). *Parl* Seq 6. *Eccl* Corr. RDn.

AP1—GAINSBOROUGH [ALL SAINTS]—Incl tp Morton (sep CP 1866,[13] sep EP 1846[155]), tps East Stockwith, Walkerith (each a sep CP 1866,[13] eccl united 1846 as 'East Stockwith with Walkerith' EP,[155] lattr called 'East Stockwith'). Addtl civ bdry alt: 1895 (the pt not in the UD cr Thonock CP).[156] Addtl eccl bdry alt: 1844 (cr EP1),[157] 1964.[158]

EP1—GAINSBOROUGH HOLY TRINITY—Cr 1844 from AP1.[157] Bdry: 1882 (cr EP3),[155] 1964.[158] Renamed 1973 as EP2.[42]

EP2—GAINSBOROUGH ST GEORGE—Renaming 1973 of EP1.[42]

EP3—GAINSBOROUGH ST JOHN THE DIVINE—Cr 1882 from EP1.[155] Bdry: 1964.[158]

GARTHORPE
[Pts Lind] Tp in Luddington AP, sep CP 1866.[13] *LG* Manley Wap, Goole PLU, RSD, Isle of Axh. RD. Bdry: 1885.[17] Transf 1974 to Humb.[10] *Parl* Seq 6.

GAUTBY
AP [Pts Lind] Incl chap Ranby (sep civ identity early, sep EP 1775[6]). *LG* Seq 37. *Parl* Seq 9. *Eccl* Seq 19.

GAYTON LE MARSH
AP [Pts Lind] *LG* Seq 33. *Parl* Seq 10. *Eccl* Seq 11.

GAYTON LE WOLD
AP [Pts Lind] *LG* Seq 44. Civ bdry: 1936 (gains Biscathorpe AP, Grimblethorpe CP).[28] *Parl* Seq 1. *Eccl* Louthesk & Ludb. RDn (until 1863), Louthesk & Ludb. 3 RDn (1863—1910), Louthesk (West) RDn (1910—68), Hornc. RDn (1968—*).

GEDNEY
AP [Pts Holl] Incl chap Gedney Hill (sep CP 1866,[13] eccl severed 1867 to help cr Holbeach Fen with

Gedney Hill EP,[148] the latter divided 1956 into 2 EPs of 'Gedney Hill', 'Holbeach Fen'[159]). *LG* Seq 1. Addtl civ bdry alt: 1883,[31] 1884,[160] 1932.[123] *Parl* Seq 16. *Eccl* Seq 41. Addtl eccl bdry alt: 1855 (cr Drove End EP).[134]

GEDNEY HILL
[Pts Holl] Chap in Gedney AP, sep CP 1866,[13] eccl severed 1867 to help cr Holbeach Fen with Gedney Hill EP,[151] the latter divided 1956 into 2 EPs of 'Holbeach Fen', 'Gedney Hill'.[159] *LG* Seq 1. Civ bdry: 1883.[31] *Parl* Seq 16. *Eccl* Elloe (East) RDn.

GIBBET HILL
[Pts Holl] Ex-par place, sep CP 1858.[38] *LG* Kirton Wap, Boston PLU (1862—91), RSD. Abol 1891 ent to Swineshead AP.[73] *Parl* S'rn Dv (1832—67), South Dv (1867—85), N Kestev Dv (1885—1918).

GLANFORD BRIDGE
[Pts Lind] Chap pt in Bigby AP, pt in Wrawby AP, sep EP 1872,[49] sep CP 1866 as 'Glanford Brigg' from both pars,[13] qv. Yarb. 1 RDn (1872—1910), Yarb. (South) RDn (1910—68), Yarb. RDn (1968—*).

GLANFORD BRIGG
[Pts Lind] Chap pt in Bigby AP, pt in Wrawby AP, sep CP 1866,[13] sep EP 1872 as 'Glanford Bridge' from both pars.[49] *LG* Yarb. Wap, Glanf. Brigg PLU, Brigg USD, UD. Civ bdry: 1892 (gains the pts in Brigg USD of Bigby AP, Broughton AP, Scawby AP, Wrawby AP),[50] 1936.[28] Transf 1974 to Humb.[10] *Parl* Seq 3.

GLENTHAM
AP [Pts Lind] *LG* Seq 24. *Parl* Seq 7. *Eccl* Pec jurisd Dean & Chapter of Linc. (until 1846), Seq 68 thereafter.

GLENTWORTH
AP [Pts Lind] *LG* Seq 25. *Parl* Seq 6. *Eccl* Seq 67.

GOLTHO
AP [Pts Lind] Incl chap Bullington (sep CP 1866,[13] not sep eccl hence this par eccl 'Goltho with Bullington', qv). *LG* Seq 52. *Parl* Seq 8.

GOLTHO WITH BULLINGTON
AP [Pts Lind] Usual eccl spelling; for civ and civ sep chap, see prev entry. *Eccl* Sinecure donative, Seq 57.

GREAT GONERBY
AP [Pts Kestev] Orig AP, loses sep identity early and incl in Grantham AP, sep civ identity retained or early regained, sep eccl status regained 1846.[6] *LG* Seq 15. Civ bdry: 1930.[34] *Parl* Seq 20. *Eccl* Granth. RDn (orig, 1846—66), Granth. 1 RDn (1866—1919), N Granth. RDn (1910—68), Granth. RDn (1968—*).

LITTLE GONERBY
CP [Pts Kestev] Cr 1894 from the pt of Manthorpe cum Little Gonerby CP in Granth. MB.[161] *LG* Granth. PLU, MB. Abol 1909 ent to Grantham AP.[162]

GOSBERTON
AP [Pts Holl] *LG* Seq 4. Civ bdry: 1883,[31] 1925,[163] 1932.[116] *Parl* Seq 16. *Eccl* Seq 37. Eccl bdry: 1912 (help cr Gosberton Clough EP).[164]

GOSBERTON CLOUGH
EP [Pts Holl] Cr 1912 from Gosberton AP, Quadring AP, Surfleet AP, Sempringham with Pointon and

Birthorpe AP.[164] Elloe (West) RDn.

GOULCEBY
AP [Pts Lind] *LG* Seq 37. Civ bdry: 1887.[130] *Parl* Seq 9. *Eccl* Seq 18.

GOXHILL
AP [Pts Lind] *LG* Seq 55. Transf 1974 to Humb.[10] *Parl* Seq 3. *Eccl* Seq 60.

GRAINSBY
AP [Pts Lind] *LG* Seq 32. *Parl* Seq 1. *Eccl* Seq 32.

GRAINTHORPE
AP [Pts Lind] *LG* Seq 44. Civ bdry: 1887.[120] *Parl* Seq 1. *Eccl* Louthesk & Ludb. RDn (until 1863), Louthesk & Ludb. 2 RDn (1863—1910), Ludb. RDn (1910—68), Louthesk RDn (1968—*).

GRANGE DE LINGS
[Pts Lind] Ex-par place, sep CP 1858,[38] eccl in Riseholme AP and the latter therefore eccl 'Riseholme and Grange de Lings'. *LG* Lawr. Wap, Linc. PLU (1858—1930), RSD, Welton RD. *Parl* N'rn Dv (1832—67), Mid Dv (1867—85), W Lind Dv (1885—1918), Gainsb. Dv/CC (1918—*).

GRANTHAM
AP [Pts Kestev] Tp 'Grantham' in Granth. Soke (until 1830s), Loved. Wap (thereafter) as were tp Harrowby (sep CP 1866[13]), tp Manthorpe cum Little Gonerby (sep CP 1866,[13] eccl severed 1849 to help cr Manthorpe with Londonthorpe EP[167]); gains eccl soon after 1535 Londonthorpe AP (sep civ identity retained, eccl severed 1849 to help cr Manthorpe with Londonthorpe EP[165]), gains eccl early Great Gonerby AP (sep civ identity early retained or early regained, sep eccl status regained 1846[6]); incl in Winn. & Thr. Wap tp Spittlegate (sep CP 1866,[13] sep EP 1842,[111] eccl refounded 1844,[166] later called 'Grantham St John'); incl in Grant. Soke (until 1830s), Winn. & Thr. Wap (thereafer) chap Sapperton (sep par by 1535[149]). *LG* Granth. PLU, USD. Addtl civ bdry alt: 1909 (gains the other pars in Granth. MB: Little Gonerby CP, Grantham Grange CP, Harrowby Within CP, New Somerby CP, Spittlegate Within CP),[162] 1930.[34] *Parl* Granth. Parl Bor (pt 1467—1867, ent 1867—85), Granth. Dv/CC (1885—*). *Eccl* Seq 23. Addtl eccl bdry alt: 1910 (help cr Grantham St Anne EP),[167] 1955,[36] 1970 (incl gains ex-par Grantham Grange).[46]

GRANTHAM GRANGE
[Pts Kestev] Ex-par place, sep CP 1858,[38] abol eccl 1970 ent to Grantham AP.[46] *LG* Loved. Wap, Granth. PLU (1866—1909), MB (1879—1909), USD. Abol civ 1909 ent to Grantham AP.[162] *Parl* S'rn Dv (1832—67), South Dv (1867—85), S Kestev Dv (1885—1918).

GRANTHAM ST ANNE
EP [Pts Kestev] Cr 1910 from Somerby with Great Humby AP, Grantham AP, Spittlegate EP.[167] Granth. 2 RDn (1910), S Granth. RDn (1910—68), Granth. RDn (1968—*).

GRANTHAM ST JOHN
EP [Pts Kestev] Name used now for EP cr 1842 as 'Spittlegate', qv.

GRASBY
AP [Pts Lind] *LG* Seq 54. Civ bdry: 1936 (gains Clixby

CP).[28] *Parl* Seq 5. *Eccl* Seq 63.

GRAYINGHAM
AP [Pts Lind] *LG* Seq 36. *Parl* Seq 6. *Eccl* Corr. RDn (until 1968), Yarb. RDn (1968—*).

GREATFORD
AP [Pts Kestev] Incl chap Wilsthorpe (sep CP 1866,[13] not sep eccl hence this par eccl 'Greatford with Wilsthorpe', qv). *LG* Seq 21. Addtl civ bdry alt: 1931.[19] *Parl* Seq 21.

GREATFORD WITH WILSTHORPE
AP [Pts Kestev] Usual eccl spelling; for civ and civ sep chap, see prev entry. *Eccl* Seq 51.

GREENHILL AND REDHILL
[Pts Lind] Ex-par place, sep CP 1858,[38] eccl abol 1931 ent to East Stockwith EP (cr 1846 as 'East Stockwith with Walkerwith').[112] *LG* Corr. Wap, Gainsb. PLU (1861—1930), RSD, RD. Abol civ 1936 to help cr Blyton CP.[28] *Parl* N'rn Dv (1832—67), North Dv (1867—85), W Lind Dv (1885—1918), Gainsb. Dv (1918—48).

GREETHAM
AP [Pts Lind] *LG* Seq 39. *Parl* Seq 12. *Eccl* Seq 35.

GREETWELL
AP [Pts Lind] *LG* Seq 43. Civ bdry: 1887,[81] 1936,[28] 1967 (loses pt to Linc. CB [assoc with Pts Lind] & CP).[89] *Parl* Seq 14. *Eccl* Seq 72.

GRIMBLETHORPE
[Pts Lind] Ex-par place, sep CP 1858.[38] *LG* Louth Esk Hd, Louth PLU (1858—1930), RSD, RD. Abol civ 1936 ent to Gayton le Wold AP.[28] *Parl* N'rn Dv (1832—67), North Dv (1967—85), E Lind Dv (1885—1918), Louth Dv (1918—48).

GRIMOLDBY
AP [Pts Lind] *LG* Seq 44. *Parl* Seq 1. *Eccl* Seq 47.

GRIMSBY
[Pts Lind] (until 1889), Grimsby CB (assoc with Pts Lind (1889—1974)] The following have 'Grimsby' or 'Great Grimsby' in their names. Insofar as any existed at a given time: *LG* Brad. Hav. Wap, Gt Grimsby Bor/MB, USD (1875—89), Grimsby PLU, CB, USD (1889—94). *Parl* Gt Grimsby Parl Bor (1295—1918), Grimsby Parl Bor/BC (1918—*). *Eccl* Grimsby RDn (until 1876), Grimsby 2 RDn (1876—1910), Grimsby & Cleethorpes RDn (1910—*).

CP1—GRIMSBY—Cr 1928 by union pars in Grimsby CB (Clee CP, AP1) and pts of pars formerly outside the CB (Bradley AP, Great Coates AP, Little Coates AP, Scartho AP, Weelsby CP).[72] Civ bdry: 1958,[106] 1968.[107] Transf 1974 to Humb.[10] Parl bdry: 1960.[108]

EP1—GRIMSBY ALL SAINTS—Cr 1898 from Clee AP.[30] Bdry: 1913 (help cr EP3),[103] 1913,[168] 1964.[68]

EP2—GRIMSBY ST AUGUSTINE—Cr 1912 from AP1, Clee AP.[101]

EP3—GRIMSBY ST LUKE—Cr 1913 from EP1, EP5, New Clee EP.[103] Abol 1961 to help cr EP6.[45]

EP4—GRIMSBY ST STEPHEN—Cr 1911 from New Clee EP, Clee AP.[100] Bdry: 1964.[68]

AP1—GREAT GRIMSBY [ST MARY AND ST JAMES]—Cr 1586 by union AP2, AP3.[169] Abol civ 1928 to help cr CP1.[72] Eccl bdry: 1871 (cr

EP5),[170] 1907 (cr EP7),[171] 1912 (help cr EP2),[101] 1964,[68] 1969 (gains EP6, Little Coates The Good Shepherd EP).[111]

EP5—GREAT GRIMSBY ST ANDREW—Cr 1871 from AP1.[170] Bdry: 1913 (help cr EP3),[103] 1913.[168] Abol 1961 to help cr EP6.[172]

EP6—GREAT GRIMSBY ST ANDREW AND ST LUKE—Cr 1961 by union EP3, EP5.[172] Bdry: 1964.[68]

AP2—GREAT GRIMSBY ST JAMES—United 1586 with AP3 to cr AP1.[169]

AP3—GREAT GRIMSBY ST MARY—In ruins, united 1586 with AP2 to cr AP1.[169]

EP7—GREAT GRIMSBY ST PAUL, WEST MARSH—Cr 1907 from AP1.[171] Bdry: 1933 (help cr Little Coates The Good Shepherd EP),[110] 1964.[68] Abol 1969 ent to AP1.[111]

LITTLE GRIMSBY
AP [Pts Lind] *LG* Seq 45. *Parl* Seq 1. *Eccl* Seq 46.

GUNBY
AP [Pts Kestev] *LG* Belt. Wap, Granth. PLU, RSD, RD. Civ bdry: 1887.[173] Abol civ 1931 to help cr Gunby and Stainby CP.[19] *Parl* S'rn Dv (1832—67), South Dv (1867—85), S Kestev Dv (1885—1918), Rutl & Stamf. Dv (1918—48). *Eccl* [St Nicholas] Belt. RDn. Abol eccl 1773 to help cr Stainby with Gunby EP.[174]

GUNBY
AP [Pts Lind] *LG* Seq 35. *Parl* Seq 12. *Eccl* [St Peter] Candl. RDn. Abol eccl 1865 to help cr Welton le Marsh with Gunby EP.[175]

GUNBY AND STAINBY
CP [Pts Kestev] Cr 1931 by union Gunby AP, Stainby AP.[19] *LG* W Kestev RD. Bdry: 1965 (exchanges pts with Buckminster AP, Leics).[113] *Parl* Rutl & Stamf. CC (1948—*).

GUNHOUSE WITH BURRINGHAM
EP [Pts Lind] Cr 1861 from Bottesford AP, Frodingham AP (incl pt tp Crosby, pt chap Gunhouse [civ, 'Gunness']), West Halton AP (pt chap Gunhouse [civ, 'Gunness']).[64] Manlake RDn. Now called 'Gunness with Burringham'.

GUNNESS
[Pts Lind] Chap pt in Frodingham AP, pt in West Halton AP, sep CP 1866[13]; for eccl see 'Gunhouse with Burringham'. *LG* Seq 46. Civ bdry: 1936 (gains Brumby Rural CP).[28] Transf 1974 to Humb.[10] *Parl* Seq 3.

GUNNESS WITH BURRINGHAM—see GUNHOUSE WITH BURRINGHAM

HABROUGH
AP [Pts Lind] *LG* Yarb. Wap, Grimsby PLU, RSD, RD. Civ bdry: 1887.[75] Transf 1974 to Humb.[10] *Parl* Seq 3. *Eccl* Seq 65.

HACCONBY
AP [Pts Kestev] Incl chap Stainfield (sep civ identity early, sep EP in 1680 or after[176]). *LG* Seq 7. *Parl* Seq 21. *Eccl* Avel. RDn. Abol eccl 1732 to help cr Morton with Hacconby EP.[177]

HACKTHORN
AP [Pts Lind] *LG* Seq 26. *Parl* Seq 6. *Eccl* Asl. RDn (until 1968), Lawres RDn (1968—73). Abol eccl 1973 to help cr Hackthorne with Cold Hanworth EP.[178]

HACKTHORN WITH COLD HANWORTH
EP [Pts Lind] Cr 1973 by union Hackthorn AP, Cold Hanworth AP.[178] Lawres RDn.

HACEBY
AP [Pts Kestev] *LG* Avel. Wap, Granth. PLU, RSD, RD. Abol civ 1931 to help cr Newton and Haceby CP.[19] *Parl* S'rn Dv (1832—67), South Dv (1867—85), N Kestev Dv (1885—1918), Rutl & Stamf. Dv (1918—48). *Eccl* Avel. RDn (until 1866), Avel. 1 RDn (1866—1910), Avel. RDn (1910—68), Laff. RDn (1968—73). Abol eccl 1973 to help cr Newton and Haceby EP.[178]

HADDINGTON
[Pts Kestev] Tp pt in Aubourn AP, pt in South Hykeham AP, sep CP 1866,[13] the pt in South Hykeham eccl severed 1921 to help cr Aubourn with Haddington EP.[30] *LG* Boothby Graff. Wap, Linc. PLU, RSD, Branst. RD. Abol 1931 to help cr Aubourn, Haddington and South Hykeham CP.[19] *Parl* S'rn Dv (1832—67), Mid Dv (1867—85), N Kestev Dv (1885—1918), Granth. Dv (1918—48).

HAGNABY
AP [Pts Lind] *LG* Seq 29. Civ bdry: 1880,[179] 1896.[95] *Parl* Seq 12. *Eccl* Seq 9.

HAGWORTHINGHAM
AP [Pts Lind] *LG* Seq 39. *Parl* Seq 12. *Eccl* Seq 36.

HAINTON
AP [Pts Lind] *LG* Seq 53. *Parl* Seq 10. *Eccl* Pec jurisd Dean & Chapter of Linc. (until 1846), Seq 59 thereafter.

GREAT HALE
AP [Pts Kestev] Incl tp Little Hale (sep CP 1866[13]). *LG* Seq 6. Addtl civ bdry alt: 1935 (gains pt Bicker AP, Pts Holl).[16] *Parl* Seq 17. *Eccl* Seq 2.

LITTLE HALE
[Pts Kestev] Tp in Great Hale AP, sep CP 1866.[13] *LG* Seq 6. *Parl* Seq 17.

HALL HILLS
[Pts Holl] Ex-par place, sep CP 1858.[38] *LG* Kirton Wap, Boston PLU (1861—1906), RSD, RD. Abol 1906 ent to Skirbeck AP.[39] *Parl* S'rn Dv (1832—67), South Dv (1867—85), Holl Dv (1885—1918).

HALLINGTON
AP [Pts Lind] *LG* Seq 44. Civ bdry: 1936.[28] *Parl* Seq 1. *Eccl* Louthesk & Ludb. RDn. Abol eccl 1770 to help cr Raithby with Hallington EP.[180]

HALTHAM
AP [Pts Lind] *LG* Seq 42. Civ bdry: 1880 (help cr Wildmore CP),[26] 1884.[116] *Parl* Seq 12. *Eccl* Gart. RDn. Abol eccl 1741 to help cr Roughton with Haltham EP.[131]

EAST HALTON
AP [Pts Lind] *LG* Seq 55. Transf 1974 to Humb.[10] *Parl* Seq 3. *Eccl* Seq 61.

WEST HALTON
AP [Pts Lind] Incl pt chap Gunness (sep CP 1866,[13] eccl 'Gunhouse', eccl severed 1861 to help cr Gunhouse with Burringham EP,[67] now called 'Gunness with Burringham'). *LG* Seq 46. Addtl civ bdry alt: 1887.[63] Transf 1974 to Humb.[10] *Parl* Seq 3. *Eccl* Seq 77. Addtl eccl bdry alt: 1895.[96]

HALTON HOLEGATE
   AP [Pts Lind] *LG* Seq 29. *Parl* Seq 12. *Eccl* Seq 10.
HAMERINGHAM
   AP [Pts Lind] *LG* Seq 39. *Parl* Seq 12. *Eccl* Hill RDn.
      Abol eccl before 1717 to help cr Hameringham with
      Scrafield AP.[181]
HAMERINGHAM WITH SCRAFIELD
   EP [Pts Lind] Cr before 1717 by union Hameringham
      AP, Scrafield AP.[181] Hill RDn (cr—1866), Hill 1
      RDn (1866—1910), Hill (North) RDn (1910—61).
      Abol 1961 to help cr Hameringham with Scrafield
      and Winceby EP.[160]
**HAMERINGHAM   WITH   SCRAFIELD   AND
      WINCEBY**
   EP [Pts Lind] Cr 1961 by union Hameringham with
      Scrafield EP, Winceby AP.[57] Hill (North) RDn
      (1961—68), Hornc. RDn (1968—*).
HANNAH CUM HAGNABY
   AP [Pts Lind] *LG* Seq 33. Civ bdry: 1887.[182] *Parl* Seq
      13. *Eccl* Donative, Calc. RDn, gains early Markby
      AP (sep civ identity maintained) and thereafter
      'Hannah cum Hagnaby and Markby',[183] qv.
HANNAH CUM HAGNABY AND MARKBY
   EP [Pts Lind] Union early of Hannah cum Hagnaby
      AP, Markby AP.[183] *Eccl* Calc. RDn (cr—1866),
      Calc. 2 RDn (1866—1910), Calc. (South) RDn
      (1910—68), Calc. & Candl. RDn (1968—*).
COLD HANWORTH
   AP [Pts Lind] *LG* Seq 26. *Parl* Seq 6. *Eccl* Asl. RDn
      (until 1968), Lawres RDn (1968—73). Abol eccl
      1973 to help cr Hackthorn with Cold Hanworth
      EP.[116]
POTTER HANWORTH
   AP [Pts Kestev] *LG* Seq 16. *Parl* Seq 15. *Eccl* Seq 45.
HARDWICK
   [Pts Lind] Tp (Lawres Wap) in Torksey AP (o'wise
      Well Wap), sep CP 1866.[13] *LG* Lawres Wap,
      Gainsb. PLU, RSD, RD. *Parl* Seq 14.
HAREBY
   AP [Pts Lind] *LG* Seq 29. Civ bdry: 1880 (help cr West
      Fen CP).[137] *Parl* Seq 12. *Eccl* Bolingbr. RDn. Abol
      eccl 1739 to help cr Bolingbroke with Hareby EP.[56]
HARLAXTON
   AP [Pts Kestev] *LG* Seq 15. *Parl* Seq 21. *Eccl* Seq 26.
HARMSTON
   AP [Pts Kestev] *LG* Seq 11. *Parl* Seq 15. *Eccl* Seq 45.
HARPSWELL
   AP [Pts Lind] *LG* Seq 25. *Parl* Seq 6. *Eccl* Donative,
      Seq 67.
HARRINGTON
   AP [Pts Lind] *LG* Seq 40. *Parl* Seq 12. *Eccl* Seq 36.
HARROWBY
   [Pts Kestev] Tp in Grantham AP, sep CP 1866.[13] *LG*
      Granth. Soke (until 1830s), Loved. Wap (from
      1830s), Granth. PLU, pt Granth. MB (1879—94), pt
      Granth. USD (1879—94), Granth. RSD (ent 1875—
      79, pt 1879—94). Abol 1894 the pt in the MB cr
      Harrowby Within CP, the remainder cr Harrowby
      Without CP.[161] *Parl* S'rn Dv (1832—67), South Dv
      (1867—85), S Kestev Dv (1885—1918).
HARROWBY WITHIN
   CP [Pts Kestev] Cr 1894 from the pt of Harrowby CP in
      Granth. MB.[161] *LG* Granth. PLU, MB. Abol 1909

ent to Grantham AP.[162]
HARROWBY WITHOUT
   CP [Pts Kestev] Cr 1894 from the pt of Harrowby CP in
      Granth. MB.[161] *LG* Granth. PLU, RD. Bdry:
      1930.[34] Abol 1931 to help cr Londonthorpe and
      Harrowby Without CP.[19] *Parl* Granth. Dv
      (1918—48).
HART'S GROUND
   [Pts Holl] Ex-par place, sep CP 1858,[38] eccl abol
      1948 to help cr Holland Fen with Chapel Hill EP.[94]
      LG Kirton Wap, Boston PLU (soon after 1836[84]—
      1930), RSD, RD. Bdry: 1935 (loses pt to Dogdyke
      CP, Pts Kestev).[16] *Parl* Seq 19.
HATCLIFFE
   AP [Pts Lind] *LG* Seq 31. Transf 1974 to Humb.[10] *Parl*
      Seq 4. *Eccl* Seq 30.
HATTON
   AP [Pts Lind] *LG* Seq 51. *Parl* Seq 9. *Eccl* Seq 56.
HAUGH
   AP [Pts Lind] Sometimes considered ex-par. *LG* Calc.
      Wap, Louth PLU (1858—1930), RSD, RD. *Parl*
      Seq 13.
HAUGHAM
   AP [Pts Lind] *LG* Seq 44. *Parl* Seq 1. *Eccl* Seq 49.
HAVEN BANK
   [Pts Lind] Ex-par place, sep CP 1858.[38] *LG* Hornc.
      Soke, PLU (1861—84), RSD. Abol civ 1884 pt to
      Coningsby AP, pt to Wildmore CP.[118] *Parl* N'rn
      Dv (1832—67), Mid Dv (1867—85).
HAVERHOLME PRIORY
   [Pts Kestev] Ex-par place, sep CP 1858.[38] *LG* Flax.
      Wap, Sleaf. PLU (1861—1930), RSD, RD. Abol
      civ 1931 to help cr Ewerby and Evedon CP.[19] *Parl*
      S'rn Dv (1832—67), South Dv (1867—85), N
      Kestev Dv (1885—1918), Granth. Dv (1918—48).
HAWERBY CUM BEESBY
   AP [Pts Lind] *LG* Seq 31. Transf 1974 to Humb.[10] *Parl*
      Seq 4. *Eccl* Seq 30.
HAWTHORPE WITH BULBY
   [Pts Kestev] Tp (sometimes 'Bulby cum Haw-
      thorpe') consisting of hmlts Hawthorpe, Bulby in
      Irnham AP, sep rated for poor law purposes (in
      Bourne PLU at the time of the union's cr 1836) but
      sep civ identity not sustained and incl again in
      Irnham AP by mid cent.
HAXEY
   AP [Pts Lind] *LG* Manley Wap, Gainsb. PLU, RSD,
      RD (1894—1936), Isle of Axh. RD (1936—74). Civ
      bdry: 1884,[45] 1886,[85] 1936.[28] Transf 1974 to
      Humb.[10] *Parl* Seq 6. *Eccl* Seq 70.
HEALING
   AP [Pts Lind] *LG* Seq 31. Civ bdry: 1968.[107] Transf
      1974 to Humb.[10] *Parl* Seq 4. *Eccl* Seq 27.
HEAPHAM
   AP [Pts Lind] *LG* Seq 36. *Parl* Seq 6. *Eccl* Seq 69.
HECKINGTON
   AP [Pts Kestev] *LG* Seq 6. *Parl* Seq 17. *Eccl* Asw. with
      Laff. RDn (until 1866), Asw. with Laff. 2 RDn
      (1866—84), Laff. 2 RDn (1884—1910), Laff.
      (South) RDn (1910—68). Abol eccl 1968 to help cr
      Heckington with Howell EP.[184]
HECKINGTON WITH HOWELL
   EP [Pts Kestev] Cr 1968 by union Heckington AP,

Howell AP.[184] Laff. (South) RDn (1968), Laff. RDn (1969—*).

HEIGHINGTON
[Pts Kestev] Chap in Washingborough AP, sep CP 1866.[13] *LG* Seq 16. Bdry: 1887.[185] *Parl* Seq 15.

HELPRINGHAM
AP [Pts Kestev] *LG* Seq 6. *Parl* Seq 18. *Eccl* Seq 2.

HENINGBY
AP [Pts Lind] *LG* Seq 37. *Parl* Seq 9. *Eccl* Seq 18.

HEMSWELL
AP [Pts Lind] *LG* Seq 25. *Parl* Seq 6. *Eccl* Seq 67.

HEYDOR—see following entry

HEYDOUR
AP [Pts Kestev] Tp 'Heydour' in Winn. & Thr. Wap; incl in Asw. Wap chaps Culverthorpe, Kelby (each a sep CP 1866,[13] not sep eccl hence this par 'Heydour with Kelby and Culverthorpe', qv). *LG* Granth. PLU, RS, RD (1894—1931), W Kestev RD (1931—74). Later civ called 'Heydor'. *Parl* Seq 17.

HEYDOUR WITH CULVERTHORPE
EP [Pts Kestev] Cr 1951 when area Kelby severed from Heydour with Kelby and Culverthorpe AP to help cr Wilsford with Kelby EP, the remainder to be this par.[186] N Granth. RDn.

HEYDOUR WITH KELBY AND CULVERTHORPE
AP [Pts Kestev] Usual eccl spelling; for civ and civ sep chaps, see prev entry. Pec jurisd Heydour prebend (until 1846), Granth. RDn (1846—66), Granth. 1 RDn (1866—1910), N Granth. RDn (1910—51). Abol eccl 1951, area Kelby severed to help cr Wilsford with Kelby EP, the remainder to be Heydour with Culverthorpe EP.[186]

HIBALDSTOW
AP [Pts Lind] *LG* Seq 46. Civ bdry: 1967.[86] Transf 1974 to Humb.[10] *Parl* Seq 3. *Eccl* Pec jurisd Dean & Chapter of Linc. (until 1846), Seq 78 thereafter.

HOGSTHORPE
AP [Pts Lind] *LG* Seq 34. Civ bdry: 1883,[31] 1888,[187] 1936.[28] *Parl* Seq 12. *Eccl* Seq 14. Eccl bdry: 1898 (help re-cr Chapel St Leonard EP).[96]

HOLBEACH
AP [Pts Holl] *LG* Elloe Wap, Holb. PLU, USD, UD (1894—1932), E Elloe RD (1932—74). *Parl* Seq 16. *Eccl* Seq 41. Eccl bdry: 1867 (help cr Holbeach Fen with Gedney Hill EP),[151] 1869 (cr Holbeach Marsh EP),[188] 1870 (cr Holbeach Hurn EP),[189] 1964.[190]

HOLBEACH FEN
EP [Pts Holl] Cr 1956 from Holbeach Fen with Gedney Hill EP.[159] Elloe (East) RDn.

HOLBECH FEN WITH GEDNEY HILL
EP [Pts Holl] Cr 1867 from Holbeach AP, Fleet AP, Gedney AP (chap Gedney Hill).[151] S Holl 2 RDn (1867—84), E Elloe RDn (1884—1910), Elloe (East) RDn (1910—56). Abol 1956, divided into 2 EPS of Holbeach Fen, Gedney Hill.[159]

HOLBEACH HURN
EP [Pts Holl] Cr 1870 from Holbeach AP.[189] S Holl 2 RDn (1870—84), E Elloe RDn (1884—1910), Elloe (East) RDn (1910—*). Bdry: 1964.[190]

HOLBEACH MARSH
EP [Pts Holl] Cr 1869 from Holbeach AP.[188] S Holl 2 RDn (1869—84), E Elloe RDn (1884—1910), Elloe (East) RDn (1910—*).

HOLDINGHAM
[Pts Kestev] Hmlt in New Sleaford AP, sep CP 1866.[13] *LG* Flax. Wap, Sleaf. PLU, New Sleaf. USD, UD. Bdry: 1888.[191] *Parl* Seq 17.

HOLLAND FEN
EP [Pts Holl] Cr 1812 from fen allotments in Holland Fen of Algarkirk AP, chap Fosdyke in Algar Kirk AP, Sutterton AP, Kirton in Holland AP,[6] refounded 1865.[7] Holl RDn (1812—66), N Holl 1 RDn (1866—1910), Holl (West) RDn (1910—48). Abol 1948 to help cr Holland Fen with Chapel Hill EP.[94]

HOLLAND FEN WITH CHAPEL HILL
EP [Pts Holl] Cr 1948 by union Holland Fen EP, Chapel Hill EP, ex-par areas of Hart's Ground, North Forty Foot Bank, Pelham's Lands.[94] Holl (West) RDn.

HOLME
[Pts Lind] Tp in Bottesford AP, sep CP 1866.[13] *LG* Seq 46. Bdry: 1936 (gains Raventhorpe CP, Twigmoor CP).[28] Transf 1974 to Humb.[10] *Parl* Seq 3.

HOLTON CUM BECKERING
AP [Pts Lind] *LG* Seq 52. *Parl* Seq 8. *Eccl* Wragg. RDn (until 1941), Walshcr. (West) RDn (1941—68), W Wold RDn (1968—*).

HOLTON LE CLAY
AP [Pts Lind] *LG* Seq 32. *Parl* Seq 1. *Eccl* Seq 32.

HOLTON LE MOOR
[Pts Lind] Chap in Caistor AP, sep CP 1866.[13] *LG* Seq 48. *Parl* Seq 2.

HOLYWELL
[Pts Kestev] Chap in Careby AP, sep CP 1866.[13] *LG* Belt. Wap, Bourne PLU, RSD, RD. Abol 1931 to help cr Careby, Aunby and Holywell CP.[19] *Parl* S'rn Dv (1832—67), South Dv (1867—85), S Kestev Dv (1885—1918), Rutl & Stamf Dv (1918—48).

HONINGTON
AP [Pts Kestev] *LG* Winn. & Thr. Wap (until 1830s), Loved. Wap (from 1830s), Granth. PLU, RSD, RD (1894—1931), W Kestev RD (1931—74). *Parl* Seq 20. *Eccl* Granth. RDn (until 1866), Loved. RDn (1866—*).

HORBLING
AP [Pts Kestev] *LG* Seq 7. *Parl* Seq 21. *Eccl* Seq 3.

HORKSTOW
AP [Pts Lind] *LG* Seq 55. Transf 1974 to Humb.[10] *Parl* Seq 3. *Eccl* Seq 60.

HORNCASTLE
AP [Pts Lind] Incl chap West Ashby (sep civ identity early, sep EP 1816[6]), chaps Toynton All Saints, Toynton St Peter (each a sep par by 1535). *LG* Hornc. Soke, PLU, USD, UD. Addtl civ bdry alt: 1880 (help cr Wildmore CP),[27] 1884,[140] 1887,[130] 1936.[28] *Parl* Seq 12. *Eccl* Seq 42. Addtl eccl bdry alt: 1881 (help cr Wildmore EP [Pts Lind, Pts Kestev, Pts Holl]).[27]

HORSINGTON
AP [Pts Lind] *LG* Seq 37. Civ bdry: 1936.[28] *Parl* Seq 9. *Eccl* Seq 20.

(East) RDn (1910—*).

HOUGH ON THE HILL
AP [Pts Kestev] *LG* Seq 18. *Parl* Seq 20. *Eccl* Seq 50.

HOUGHAM
AP [Pts Kestev] Incl chap Marston (sep civ identity early, not sep eccl hence this par eccl 'Hougham with Marston', qv). *LG* Seq 19. *Parl* Seq 20.

HOUGHAM WITH MARSTON
AP [Pts Kestev] Usual eccl spelling; for civ and civ sep chap, see prev entry. *Eccl* Seq 50.

HOWELL
AP [Pts Kestev] *LG* Asw. Wap, Sleaf. PLU, RSD, RD. Civ bdry: 1885.[20] Abol civ 1931 to help cr Asgarby and Howell CP.[19] *Parl* S'rn Dv (1832—67), South Dv (1867—85), N Kestev Dv (1885—1918), Granth. Dv (1918—48). *Eccl* Asw. with Laff. RDn (until 1866), Asw. with Laff. 2 RDn (1866—84), Laff. 2 RDn (1884—1910), Laff. (South) RDn (1910—68). Abol eccl 1968 to help cr Heckington with Howell EP.[184]

HUMBERSTON
AP [Pts Lind] Usual civ spelling; for eccl see following entry. *LG* Seq 31. Civ bdry: 1922,[104] 1968.[107] Transf 1974 to Humb.[10] *Parl* Seq 1.

HUMBERSTONE
AP [Pts Lind] Usual eccl spelling; for civ see prev entry. *Eccl* Seq 32.

HUMBY
CP [Pts Kestev] Cr 1887 by union Little Humby CP, area Great Humby in Somerby AP.[192] *LG* Winn. & Thr. Wap, Granth. PLU, RSD, RD. Abol 1931 to help cr Ropsley and Humby CP.[19] *Parl* Rutl & Stamf. Dv (1918—48).

LITTLE HUMBY
[Pts Kestev] Hmlt in Ropsley AP, sep CP 1866.[13] *LG* Winn. & Thr. Wap, Granth. PLU, RSD. Abol 1887 to help cr Humby CP.[192] *Parl* S'rn Dv (1832—67), South Dv (1867—85), S Kestev Dv (1885—1918).

HUNDLEBY
AP [Pts Lind] Incl chap Spilsby (sep civ identity early, sep EP 1772,[6] sometimes eccl 'Somerby with Eresby'). *LG* Seq 29. Addtl civ bdry alt: 1880 (help cr West Fen CP).[139] *Parl* Seq 12. *Eccl* Bolingbr. RDn (until 1866), Hill 2 RDn (1866—1910), Hill (South) RDn (1910—68), Bolingbr. RDn (1968—*). Addtl eccl bdry alt: 1886 (help cr Carrington with Frithville EP [Pts Lind, Pts Holl]).[61]

HUNGERTON
AP [Pts Kestev] Orig sep AP (Granth. RDn), abol before 1535, united with Wyville AP, the union called civ 'Wyville cum Hungerton', eccl 'Wyville with Hungerton', qv.

HUTTOFT
AP [Pts Lind] *LG* Seq 34. *Parl* Seq 12. *Eccl* Seq 14.

NORTH HYKEHAM
AP [Pts Kestev] *LG* Seq 11. Civ bdry: 1920 (loses pt to Linc. CB [assoc with Pts Lind] & CP).[67] *Parl* Seq 15. *Eccl* Seq 22. Eccl bdry: 1964 (help cr Lincoln St George, Swallowbeck EP).[68]

SOUTH HYKEHAM
AP [Pts Kestev] Incl pt tp Haddington (sep CP 1866,[13] the pt of the tp in this par eccl severed 1921 to help cr Aubourn with Haddington EP[30]). *LG* Boothb.

Graff. Wap, Linc. PLU, RSD, Branst. RD. Abol civ 1931 to help cr Auburn, Haddington and South Hykeham CP.[19] *Parl* S'rn Dv (1832—67), Mid Dv (1867—85), N Kestev Dv (1885—1918), Granth. Dv (1918—48). *Eccl* Seq 22.

IMMINGHAM
AP [Pts Lind] *LG* Yarb. Wap, Grimsby PLU, RSD, RD. Civ bdry: 1887,[193] 1887.[75] Transf 1974 to Humb.[10] *Parl* Seq 4. *Eccl* Seq 65.

INGHAM
AP [Pts Lind] Incl chap East Firsby (sep par by 1535, incl tp West Firby). *LG* Seq 26. *Parl* Seq 6. *Eccl* Seq 68.

INGOLDMELLS
AP [Pts Lind] *LG* Seq 35. Civ bdry: 1888,[2] 1960.[4] *Parl* Seq 12. *Eccl* Seq 17.

INGOLDSBY
AP [Pts Kestev] *LG* Asw. Wap, Granth. PLU, RSD, RD (1894—1931), W Kestev RD (1931—74). *Parl* Seq 21. *Eccl* Asw. with Laff. RDn (until 1866), Belt. 1 RDn (1866—84), Belt. RDn (1884—*).

IRBY
AP [Pts Lind] Usual civ spelling; for eccl see 'Irby on Humber'. *LG* Seq 31. Transf 1974 to Humb.[10] *Parl* Seq 4.

IRBY IN THE MARSH
AP [Pts Lind] *LG* Seq 35. Civ bdry: 1888.[2] *Parl* Seq 12. *Eccl* Seq 15.

IRBY ON HUMBER
AP [Pts Lind] Usual eccl spelling; for civ see 'Irby'. *Eccl* Seq 28.

IRNHAM
AP [Pts Kestev] Incl tp Hawthorpe with Bulby (consisting of hmlts Hawthorpe, Bulby [sometimes 'Bulby cum Hawthorpe'], sep rated for poor law purposes at cr of Bourne PLU in 1836, sep civ identity not sustained and incl again in Irnham AP by mid cent). *LG* Seq 9. *Parl* Seq 21. *Eccl* Seq 7.

KEADBY
[Pts Lind] Tp in Althorpe AP, sep CP 1866.[13] *LG* Manley Wap, Thorne PLU, RSD, Isle of Axh. RD. Abol 1958 to help cr Keadby with Althorpe CP.[15] *Parl* N'rn Dv (1832—67), North Dv (1867—85), W Lind Dv (1885—1918), Gainsb. Dv/CC (1918—70).

KEADBY WITH ALTHORPE
CP [Pts Lind] Cr 1958 by union Keadby CP, Althorpe AP.[15] *LG* Isle of Axh. RD. Transf 1974 to Humb.[10] *Parl* Gainsb. CC (1970—*).

EAST KEAL
AP [Pts Lind] *LG* Seq 29. *Parl* Seq 12. *Eccl* Seq 9.

WEST KEAL
AP [Pts Lind] *LG* Seq 29. Civ bdry: 1880 (help cr West Fen CP),[139] 1880,[194] 1896.[195] *Parl* Seq 12. *Eccl* Seq 9. Eccl bdry: 1885 (help cr Eastville with Midville EP [Pts Lind, Pts Holl]),[48] 1886 (help cr Carrington with Frithville EP [Pts Lind, Pts Holl]).[61]

KEDDINGTON
AP [Pts Lind] *LG* Seq 44. Civ bdry: 1936.[28] *Parl* Seq 1. *Eccl* Seq 46. Eccl bdry: 1878.[196]

KEELBY
AP [Pts Lind] *LG* Seq 54. *Parl* Seq 5. *Eccl* Seq 65.

KEISBY

[Pts Kestev] Tp in Lenton AP, sep CP 1866.[13] *LG* Belt. Wap, Granth. PLU, RSD, RD. Abol 1931 to help cr Lenton Keisby and Osgodby CP.[19] *Parl* S'rn Dv (1832—67), South Dv (1867—85), S Kestev Dv (1885—1918), Rutl & Stamf. Dv (1918—48).

KELBY

[Pts Kestev] Chap in Heydour AP, sep CP 1866,[13] eccl severed 1951 to help cr Wilsford with Kelby EP.[186] *LG* Asw. Wap, Sleaf. PLU, RSD, RD. Abol 1931 to help cr Culvethorpe and Kelby CP.[19] *Parl* S'rn Dv (1832—67), South Dv (1867—85), N Kestev Dv (1885—1918), Granth. Dv (1918—48).

NORTH KELSEY

AP [Pts Lind] *LG* Seq 54. Civ bdry: 1887.[197] *Parl* Seq 5. *Eccl* Pec jurisd Dean & Chapter of Linc. (until 1846), Seq 64 thereafter.

SOUTH KELSEY

[Pts Lind] Union before 1795 of South Kelsey St Mary AP, South Kelsey St Nicholas AP.[198] *LG* Seq 48. *Parl* Seq 2. *Eccl* Walshcr. RDn (cr—1866), Walshcr. 1 RDn (1866—73), Walshcr. RDn (1873—1910), Caist. RDn (1910—68), W Wold RDn (1968—*).

SOUTH KELSEY ST MARY

AP [Pts Lind] Orig sep AP, Walshcr. Wap, Walshcr. RDn, abol before 1795 to help cr South Kelsey CP/EP.[198]

SOUTH KELSEY ST NICHOLAS

AP [Pts Lind] Organisation as for South Kelsey St Mary.

KELSTERN

AP [Pts Lind] *LG* Seq 44. *Parl* Seq 1. *Eccl* Louthesk & Ludb. RDn (until 1863), Louthesk & Ludb. 1 RDn (1863—1910), Ludb. RDn (1910—25). Abol eccl 1925 to help cr Kelstern with Calcethorpe CP.[88]

KELSTERN WITH CALCETHORPE

EP [Pts Lind] Cr 1925 by union Kelstern AP, Calcethorpe AP.[88] Ludb. RDn. Abol 1929 to help cr Kelstern with Calcethorpe and East Wykeham EP.[199]

KELSTERN WITH CALCETHORPE AND EAST WYKEHAM

EP [Pts Lind] Cr 1929 by union Kelstern with Calcethorpe EP, ex-par (orig AP) East Wykeham.[199] Ludb. RDn (1929—68), Louthesk RDn (1969—*).

KETSBY

AP [Pts Lind] Orig sep AP, Hill Hd, Hill RDn, abol 1774 to help cr 'South Ormsby cum Ketsby' CP, 'South Ormesby with Ketsby, Calceby and Driby' EP.[87]

KETTLETHORPE

AP [Pts Lind] Incl tp Fenton (sep CP 1866,[13] not sep eccl hence this par eccl 'Kettlethorpe with Laughterton and Fenton', qv). *LG* Seq 49. Addtl civ bdry alt: 1884 (gains pt Laneham AP, Notts).[200] *Parl* Seq 14.

KETTLETHORPE WITH LAUGHTERTON AND FENTON

AP [Pts Lind] Usual eccl spelling; for civ and civ sep tp, see prev entry. *Eccl* Seq 75.

KEXBY

[Pts Lind] Tp in Upton AP, sep CP 1866.[13] *LG* Well

Wap, Gainsb. PLU (soon after 1837[84]—1930), RSD, RD. *Parl* Seq 14.

KILLINGHOLME

AP [Pts Lind] Incl tps North Killingholme, South Killingholme (each a sep CP 1866[13]) so that 'Killingholme' has no sep civ identity after 1866. *LG* Yarb. Wap. *Parl* N'rn Dv (1832—67). *Eccl* Seq 61.

NORTH KILLINGHOLME

[Pts Lind] Tp in Killingholme AP, sep CP 1866.[13] *LG* Seq 55. Transf 1974 to Humb.[10] *Parl* Seq 3.

SOUTH KILLINGHOLME

[Pts Lind] Status and organisation as for North Killingholme, with bdry alt 1887.[193]

KINGERBY

AP [Pts Lind] *LG* Walshcr. Wap, Caist. PLU, RSD, RD. Abol civ 1936 to help cr Osgodby CP.[28] *Parl* N'rn Dv (1832—67), North Dv (1867—85), E Lind Dv (1885—1918), Louth Dv (1918—48). *Eccl* Seq 53.

EAST KIRKBY

AP [Pts Lind] *LG* Seq 29. *Parl* Seq 12. *Eccl* Seq 9.

KIRKBY CUM OSGODBY

AP [Pts Lind] Incl chap Usselby (sep civ identity early, sep EP 1746[6]). *LG* Walshcr. Wap, Caist. PLU, RSD, RD. Abol civ 1936 to help cr Osgodby CP.[28] *Parl* N'rn Dv (1832—67), North Dv (1867—85), E Lind Dv (1885—1918), Louth Dv (1918—48). *Eccl* Walshcr. RDn. Abol eccl prob late 18th cent to help cr Owersby with Kirkby and Osgodby EP.[147]

KIRKBY GREEN

AP [Pts Kestev] *LG* Longoe Wap, Sleaf. PLU, RSD, RD. Abol civ 1931 ent to Scopwick AP.[19] *Parl* S'rn Dv (1832—67), Mid Dv (1867—85), N Kestev Dv (1885—1918), Granth. Dv (1918—48). *Eccl* Seq 45.

KIRKBY LA THORPE

AP [Pts Kestev] Usual civ spelling; for eccl see following entry. *LG* Seq 6. Civ bdry: 1931 (help cr Asgarby and Howell CP).[19] *Parl* Seq 17.

KIRKBY LAYTHORPE

AP [Pts Kestev] Usual eccl spelling; for civ see prev entry. *Eccl* Asw. with Laff. RDn. Abol eccl 1737 to help cr Kirkby Laythorpe with Asgarsby EP.[22]

KIRKBY LAYTHORPE WITH ASGARBY

EP [Pts Kestev] Cr 1737 by union Kirkby Laythorpe AP, Asgarby AP.[22] *Eccl* Seq 2.

KIRKBY ON BAIN

AP [Pts Lind] Incl tp Tumby (sep CP 1866,[13] pt eccl severed 1881 to help cr Wildmore EP (Pts Lind, Pts Kestev, Pts Holl),[27] the remainder eccl severed 1886 to help cr Carrington with Frithville EP (Pts Lind, Pts Holl).[61] *LG* Seq 37. *Parl* Seq 12. *Eccl* Seq 20.

KIRKBY UNDERWOOD

AP [Pts Kestev] *LG* Seq 7. *Parl* Seq 21. *Eccl* Seq 6.

KIRKSTEAD

AP [Pts Lind] *LG* Seq 37. Civ bdry: 1880.[115] *Parl* Seq 12. *Eccl* Orig Abbey church, donative thereafter, Gart. RDn. Eccl bdry: 1881 (help cr Wildmore EP [Pts Lind, Pts Kestev, Pts Holl]).[27] Abol eccl 1967 to help cr Woodhall Spa and Kirkstead EP.[201]

KIRMINGTON
AP [Pts Lind] *LG* Seq 55. Transf 1974 to Humb.[10] *Parl* Seq 3. *Eccl* Yarb. RDn (until 1863), Yarb. 1 RDn (1863—84), Yarb. 2 RDn (1884—1910), Grimsby (North) RDn (1910—68), Yarb. RDn (1968—*).

KIRMOND LE MIRE
AP [Pts Lind] *LG* Seq 50. *Parl* Seq 11. *Eccl* Wragg. RDn (until 1875), Walshcr. RDn (1875—1910), Walshcr. (East) RDn (1910—68), W Wold RDn (1968—*).

KIRTON
AP [Pts Holl] Incl chap Brothertoft (sep CP 1866,[13] sep EP 1864[6]). *LG* Seq 3. Addtl civ bdry alt: 1906 (incl gain Simon Weir CP, South of the Witham CP),[39] 1932.[77] *Parl* Seq 16.

KIRTON IN HOLLAND
AP [Pts Holl] Usual eccl spelling; for civ and sep chap, see prev entry. *Eccl* Seq 38. Addtl eccl bdry alt: 1812 (fen allotment severed to help cr Holland Fen EP,[6] the latter refounded 1865[7]).

KIRTON IN LINDSEY
AP [Pts Lind] *LG* Corr. Wap, Glanf. Brigg PLU, RSD, RD. Transf 1974 to Humb.[10] *Parl* N'rn Dv (1832—67), North Dv (1867—85), W Lind Dv (1885—1918), Brigg Dv/CC (1918—70), Brigg & Scunth. CC (1970—*). *Eccl* Pec jurisd Sub-Dean of Kirton in Lindsey (until 1846), Corr. RDn (1846—1968), Yarb. RDn (1968—*).

KNAITH
AP [Pts Lind] *LG* Seq 49. Civ bdry: 1884.[202] *Parl* Seq 14. *Eccl* Seq 74.

NORTH KYME
[Pts Kestev] Tp (Langoe Wap) in South Kyme AP (o'wise Asw. Wap), sep CP 1866.[13] *LG* Seq 17. Bdry: 1883,[31] 1896,[203] 1931.[19] *Parl* Seq 15.

SOUTH KYME
AP [Pts Kestev] Incl in Langoe Wap tp North Kyme (sep CP 1866,[13] not sep eccl hence this par eccl 'South Kyme and North Kyme', qv). *LG* Asw. Wap (pt until 1866, ent from 1866), pt Langoe Wap (until 1866), Sleaf. PLU, RSD, RD (1894—1931), E Kestev RD (1931—74). Addtl civ bdry alt: 1931,[19] 1935 (loses pt to Amber Hill CP, Pts Holl).[16] *Parl* Seq 17.

SOUTH KYME AND NORTH KYME
AP [Pts Kestev] Usual eccl spelling; for civ and civ sep tp, see prev entry. *Eccl* Orig priory, Seq 1. Eccl bdry: 1948.[51]

LACEBY
AP [Pts Lind] *LG* Seq 31. Transf 1974 to Humb.[10] *Parl* Gt Grimsby Parl Bor (1832—1918), Louth Dv/CC (1918—*). *Eccl* Seq 27.

LANDS COMMON TO EAST FERRY AND SCOTTON
[Pts Lind] *LG* Gainsb. RD. Abol 1936 pt to each par.[28] *Parl* Gainsb. Dv (1918—48).

LANDS COMMON TO SWINESHEAD AND WIGTOFT
[Pts Holl] *LG* Boston RD. Abol 1932 ent to Wigtoft AP.[77] *Parl* Holl with Boston Dv (1918—48).

LANGRICK FERRY
[Pts Lind] Ex-par place, rated in Hornc. PLU 1862 but sep status not sustained, thereafter incl in Coningsby AP.

LANGRIVILLE
[Pts Lind] Area cr parochial chap 1812 from Wildmore Fen,[92] sep CP 1866,[13] pt eccl severed 1881 to help cr Wildmore EP (Pts Lind, Pts Kestev, Pts Holl),[27] the remainder eccl severed 1881 to help cr Carrington with Frithville EP (Pts Lind, Pts Holl).[61] *LG* Seq 41. Bdry: 1880,[115] 1887,[116] 1904,[117] 1932,[60] 1935 (exchanges pts with Brothertoft CP, gains pt Fishtoft AP, both Pts Holl),[78] 1936.[28] *Parl* Seq 12.

LANGTOFT
AP [Pts Kestev] *LG* Seq 20. Civ bdry: 1931.[19] *Parl* Seq 21. *Eccl* Seq 51.

LANGTON
AP [Pts Lind] *LG* Seq 37. Civ bdry: 1887,[130] 1936.[28] *Parl* Seq 12. *Eccl* Seq 20. Eccl bdry: 1850 (help cr Langton St Andrew (otherwise Woodhall Spa) EP).[204]

LANGTON BY SPILSBY
AP [Pts Lind] *LG* Seq 40. Civ bdry: 1936 (gains Sutterby AP).[28] *Parl* Seq 12. *Eccl* Seq 36.

LANGTON BY WRAGBY
AP [Pts Lind] *LG* Seq 51. *Parl* Seq 9. *Eccl* Seq 56.

LANGTON ST ANDREW (OTHERWISE WOODHALL SPA)
EP [Pts Lind] Cr 1850 from Langton AP, Woodhall AP, Thornton AP, Thimbleby AP.[204] Gart. RDn. Bdry 1913.[126] Abol 1967 to help cr Woodhall Spa and Kirkstead EP.[201]

LAUGHTON
AP [Pts Kestev] Orig AP (Avel. RDn), churchless, thereafter eccl in Folkingham,[151] sep civ identity retained. *LG* Avel. Wap, Bourne PLU, RSD, RD. Abol 1931 to help cr Aslackby and Laughton CP.[19] *Parl* S'rn Dv (1832—67), South Dv (1867—85), S Kestev Dv (1885—1918), Rutl & Stamf Dv (1918—48).

LAUGHTON
[Pts Lind] Tp in Laughton by Gainsborough AP, sep CP 1866.[13] *LG* Seq 36. *Parl* Seq 6.

LAUGHTON BY GAINSBOROUGH
AP [Pts Lind] Incl tp Laughton, hmlt Wildsworth (each a sep CP 1866,[13] neither sep eccl, so that this par has no sep civ identity after 1866 and eccl called 'Laughton with Wildsworth', qv). *LG* Corr. Wap. *Parl* N'rn Dv (1832—67).

LAUGHTON WITH WILDSWORTH
AP [Pts Lind] Usual eccl spelling; for civ and civ sep tp and hmlt, see prev entry. *Eccl* Seq 69.

LEA
AP [Pts Lind] *LG* Seq 36. Civ bdry: 1895 (loses pt to Bole AP, pt to West Burton AP, both Notts).[156] *Parl* Seq 6. *Eccl* Seq 69.

LEADENHAM
AP [Pts Kestev] *LG* Loved. Wap, Sleaf. PLU, RSD, RD (1894—1931), N Kestev RD (1931—74). Civ bdry: 1883.[31] *Parl* Seq 17. *Eccl* Seq 50.

LEAKE
AP [Pts Holl] *LG* Skir. Wap, Boston PLU, RSD. Civ bdry: 1880.[47] Abol civ 1894 to cr 2 CPs of New Leake (to be in Pts Lind), Old Leake (to be in Pts Holl).[205] *Parl* S'rn Dv (1832—67), South Dv

(1867—85), Holl Dv (1885—1918). *Eccl* Seq 39.

NEW LEAKE

CP [Pts Lind] Cr 1894 from the pt of Leake AP to be in Pts Lind.[205] *LG* Spilsby PLU, RD. *Parl* Hornc. Dv/ CC (1918—*).

OLD LEAKE

CP [Pts Holl] Cr 1894 from the pt of Leake AP to be in Pts Holl.[205] *LG* Boston PLU, RD. *Parl* Holl Dv (1918—48), Holl with Boston CC (1948—*).

LEASINGHAM

[Pts Kestev] Cr 1726 as CP/EP by union Leasingham St John the Baptist AP (dilapidated), Leasingham St Andrew AP.[206] Incl hmlt Roxholme (sep CP 1866,[13] not sep eccl hence this par eccl 'Leasingham with Roxholme', qv). *LG* Seq 14. *Parl* Seq 17.

LEASINGHAM ST ANDREW

AP [Pts Kestev] Orig AP (Flax. Wap, Asw. with Laff. RDn), abol 1726 to help cr Leasingham CP/EP (eccl, 'Leasingham with Roxholme').[206]

LEASINGHAM ST JOHN THE BAPTIST

AP [Pts Kestev] Orig AP (Flax. Wap, Asw. with Laff. RDn), dilapidated, abol 1726 to help cr Leasingham CP/EP (eccl, 'Leasingham with Roxholme').[206]

LEASINGHAM WITH ROXHOLME

EP [Pts Kestev] Cr 1726 by union Leasingham St John the Baptist AP, Leasingham St Andrew AP, the union civ 'Leasingham' (qv for civ sep hmlt Roxholme).[206] *Eccl* Seq 1.

LEGBOURNE

AP [Pts Lind] *LG* Seq 33. *Parl* Seq 10. *Eccl* Calc. RDn (until 1863), Louthesk & Ludb. 3 RDn (1863—*ca* 1896), Louthesk & Ludb. 2 RDn (*ca* 1896—1910), Louthesk (West) RDn (1910—68), Louthesk RDn (1968—*).

LEGSBY

AP [Pts Lind] *LG* Seq 50. Civ bdry: 1936 (gains East Torrington AP).[28] *Parl* Seq 11. *Eccl* Seq 58.

LENTON

AP [Pts Kestev] Sometimes 'Lavington'. Incl tps Keisby, Osgodby (each a sep CP 1866[13]). *LG* Belt. Wap, Granth. PLU, RSD, RD. Abol civ 1931 to help cr Lenton Keisby and Osgodby CP.[19] *Parl* S'rn Dv (1832—67), South Dv (1867—85), S Kestev Dv (1885—1918), Rutl & Stamf Dv (1918—48). *Eccl* Seq 7.

LENTON KEISBY AND OSGODBY

CP [Pts Kestev] Cr 1931 by union Lenton AP, Keisby CP, Osgodby CP.[19] *LG* W Kestev RD. *Parl* Rutl & Stamf. CC (1948—*).

LEVERTON

AP [Pts Holl] *LG* Seq 5. Civ bdry: 1880,[47] 1880 (help cr West Fen CP to be in Pts Lind).[139] *Parl* Seq 16. *Eccl* Seq 39. Eccl bdry: 1885 (help cr Eastville with Midville EP [Pts Lind, Pts Holl]),[48] 1886 (help cr Carrington with Frithville EP [Pts Lind, Pts Holl]).[61]

GREAT LIMBER

AP [Pts Lind] Usual civ spelling; for eccl see following entry. *LG* Seq 54. *Parl* Seq 5.

LIMBER MAGNA

AP [Pts Lind] Usual eccl spelling; for civ see prev entry. *Eccl* Seq 64.

LINCOLN

[Co of Itself from 1410] The following have 'Lincoln' in their names. Insofar as any existed at a given time: *LG* Linc. Bor/MB/CB, PLU, USD. *Parl* Linc. Parl Bor (1295—*). *Eccl* Christianity RDn. Deatils of early APs from various sources.[207]

CP1—LINCOLN—Cr 1907 by union pars in Linc. CB: CP2, CP4, CP6, AP12, AP13, AP20, AP25, AP27, AP28, CP7, AP31, AP32, AP34, AP35, AP37, AP38, AP40, CP8, AP44.[208] Civ bdry: 1920 (incl gains Boultham AP, Bracebridge UD & AP [both Pts Kestev]),[67] 1959,[209] 1967.[89] Parl bdry: 1960.[210]

EP1—LINCOLN ALL SAINTS—Cr 1904 from AP44, pt ex-par Monk's Liberty (area CP7).[211]

AP1—LINCOLN ALL SAINTS IN THE BAIL—Pre-Conquest to *ca* 14th cent, last burial 1290.

AP2—LINCOLN ALL SAINTS IN HUNGATE— demolished 1553.

CP2—LINCOLN BISHOP'S PALACE—Ex-par place, sep CP 1858.[38] *LG* Linc. PLU (1861—1907). Abol 1907 to help cr CP1.[208]

CP3—LINCOLN CASTLE DYKINGS—Ex-par place (sometimes 'Lincoln Castle'), sep CP 1858.[38] Abol 1888 ent to AP37.[212]

CP4—LINCOLN COLD BATH HOUSE—Ex-par place, sep CP 1858.[38] *LG* Linc. PLU (1861—1907). Abol 1907 to help cr CP1.[208]

CP5—LINCOLN HOLMES COMMON—Ex-par place, sep CP 1858.[38] *LG* Linc. PLU (1863—1907). Abol 1888 to help cr CP7.[213]

AP3—LINCOLN HOLY CROSS IN WIGFORD— Merged 1549 with AP13.

AP4—LINCOLN HOLY TRINITY—Connected with Grey Friars, abol 1534.

AP5—LINCOLN HOLY TRINITY AT STARFOOT— demolished 1534.

AP6—LINCOLN HOLY TRINITY IN WIGFORD— Merged 1549 with AP38.

—LINCOLN LUNATIC ASYLUM—Ex-par place, not a sep CP.

CP6—LINCOLN MONKS LIBERTY—Ex-par place, sep CP 1858,[38] pt eccl severed 1904 to help cr EP1.[211] Bdry: 1888.[214] Abol civ 1907 to help cr CP1.[208]

EP2—LINCOLN ST ANDREW—Cr 1883 from AP38.[109] Bdry: 1964.[68] Abol 1968 to help cr EP15.[215]

AP7—LINCOLN ST ANDREW IN WIGFORD— Early destroyed, merged 1549 in AP38.

AP8—LINCOLN ST ANDREW UNDER THE HILL—Demolished 15th cent, merged into AP30.

AP9—LINCOLN ST AUGUSTINE—Demolished *ca* 1534.

AP10—LINCOLN ST BARTHOLOMEW—Demolished 1534 but small chapel on site until 1562.

AP11—LINCOLN ST BAVON—Disappeared *ca* 1500.

AP12—LINCOLN ST BENEDICT—Gains 1549 pt AP21. Abol civ 1907 to help cr CP1.[208] Abol eccl 1931 to help cr EP10.[216]

AP13—LINCOLN ST BOTOLPH—Gains 1549 AP3, AP26. Abol civ 1907 to help cr CP1.[208] Addtl eccl bdry alt: 1964.[68]

AP14—LINCOLN ST CLEMENT IN THE BAIL—Disappeared *ca* 14th cent.

AP15—LINCOLN ST CLEMENT IN BUTWERK—Disappeared *ca* 14th—15th cent.

AP16—LINCOLN ST EDMUND—Demolished 15th cent.

AP17—LINCOLN ST EDWARD IN WIGFORD—Abol 1549, pt to AP38, pt to AP27.

AP18—LINCOLN ST FAITH—Disappeared 14th cent.

EP3—LINCOLN ST FAITH—Renaming 1958 of AP30.[83] Abol 1968 to help cr EP4.[184]

EP4—LINCOLN ST FAITH AND ST MARTIN WITH ST PETER AT ARCHES—Cr 1968 by union EP8, EP3.[184]

AP19—LINCOLN ST GEORGE—Demolished 15th cent.

EP5—LINCOLN ST GEORGE, SWALLOWBECK—Cr 1964 from North Hykeham AP, Skellingthorpe AP, Boultham AP.[68] Graff. RDn (1964—68), Christianity RDn (1968—*).

EP6—LINCOLN ST GILES—Cr 1932 from AP40, AP25.[196]

AP20—LINCOLN ST JOHN IN NEWPORT—Abol civ 1907 to help cr CP1.[208] Abol eccl 1841 to help cr EP14.[217]

AP21—LINCOLN ST JOHN IN WIGFORD—Abol 1549, pt to AP12, pt to AP30.

EP7—LINCOLN ST JOHN THE BAPTIST—Cr 1960 from EP14.[218]

AP22—LINCOLN ST JOHN THE POOR—Disappeared *ca* 14th—15th cent.

AP23—LINCOLN ST LAWRENCE—Dissolved *ca* 1549.

AP24—LINCOLN ST LEONARD—Perhaps AP, perhaps prebendal chap, demolished 1534.

AP25—LINCOLN ST MARGARET IN THE CLOSE—Civ bdry: 1888.[219] Abol civ 1907 to help cr CP1.[208] Pec jurisd Dean & Chapter of Linc. (until 1846). Eccl bdry: 1932 (help cr EP6).[196]

AP26—LINCOLN ST MARGARET IN WIGFORD—Abol 1549 ent to AP13.

AP27—LINCOLN ST MARK—Gains 1549 pt AP17. Abol civ 1907 to help cr CP1.[208] Eccl bdry: 1964.[68] Abol eccl 1971 to help cr EP12.[220]

AP28—LINCOLN ST MARTIN—Gains 1549 AP29. Abol civ 1907 to help cr CP1.[208] Abol eccl 1931 to help cr EP8.[216]

EP8—LINCOLN ST MARTIN WITH ST PETER AT ARCHES—Cr 1931 by union AP28, AP37.[216] Abol 1968 to help cr EP4.[184]

EP9—LINCOLN ST MARY BELOW THE HILL—Cr 1899 from AP30.[221] Abol 1931 to help cr EP10.[216]

EP10—LINCOLN ST MARY BELOW THE HILL WITH ST BENEDICT—Cr 1931 by union EP9, AP12.[216] Renamed 1968 as EP11.[184]

AP29—LINCOLN ST MARY CROCKPOOL—Abol 1549 ent to AP28.

AP30—LINCOLN ST MARY LE WIGFORD—Gains 15th cent AP8; gains 1529 pt AP21. Abol civ 1888 to help cr CP7.[213] Addtl eccl bdry alt: 1899 (cr EP9).[221] Renamed 1958 as EP3.[83]

CP7—LINCOLN ST MARY LE WIGFORD WITH HOLMES COMMON—Cr 1888 by union AP30, CP5.[213] Abol 1907 to help cr CP1.[208]

EP11—LINCOLN ST MARY LE WIGFORD WITH ST BENEDICT—Renaming 1968 of EP10.[184] Abol 1971 to help cr EP12.[220]

EP12—LINCOLN ST MARY LE WIGFORD WITH ST BENEDICT AND ST MARK— Cr 1971 by union EP11, AP27.[220]

AP31—LINCOLN ST MARY MAGDALEN IN THE BAIL—Abol civ 1907 to help cr CP1.[208] Pec jurisd Dean & Chapter of Linc (until 1846). Abol eccl 1968 to help cr EP13.[222]

EP13—LINCOLN ST MARY MAGDALEN WITH ST PAUL IN THE BAIL—Cr 1968 by union AP31, AP35.[222]

AP32—LINCOLN ST MICHAEL—Usual civ spelling; usual eccl, 'Lincoln St Michel on the Mount'. Abol civ 1907 to help cr CP1.[208]

—LINCOLN ST MICHAEL ON THE MOUNT—see AP32

AP33—LINCOLN ST MICHAEL IN WIGFORD—Demolished 1534.

AP34—LINCOLN ST NICHOLAS—Civ bdry: 1883.[31] Abol civ 1907 to help cr CP1.[208] Pec jurisd Dean & Chapter of Linc. Abol eccl 1841 to help cr EP14.[217]

EP14—LINCOLN ST NICHOLAS WITH ST JOHN—Cr 1841 by union AP34 (pec jurisd Dean & Chapter of Linc.), AP20.[217] Bdry: 1960 (cr EP7).[218]

AP35—LINCOLN ST PAUL IN THE BAIL—Civ bdry: 1888 (incl gains CP3).[212] Abol civ 1907 to help cr CP1.[208] Eccl bdry: 1874.[223] Abol eccl 1968 to help cr EP13.[222]

AP36—LINCOLN ST PETER AD FONTEM—Collapsed 15th cent.

AP37—LINCOLN ST PETER AT ARCHES—Gains 1549 AP39. Abol civ 1907 to help cr CP1.[208] Abol eccl 1931 to help cr EP8.[216]

AP38—LINCOLN ST PETER AT GOWTS—Gains 1549 AP6, AP7, pt AP17. Abol civ 1907 to help cr CP1.[208] Addtl eccl bdry alt: 1883 (cr EP2),[109] 1964.[68] Abol eccl 1968 to help cr EP15.[215]

EP15—LINCOLN ST PETER AT GOWTS AND ST ANDREW—Cr 1968 by union AP38, EP2.[215]

AP39—LINCOLN ST PETER AT PLEAS—Abol 1549 ent to AP37.

AP40—LINCOLN ST PETER IN EASTGATE—Civ bdry: 1883,[31] 1888,[219] 1888,[214] 1888.[212] Abol civ 1907 to help cr CP1.[208] Eccl bdry: 1937 (help cr EP6).[196]

CP8—LINCOLN SOUTH COMMON—Ex-par place, sep CP 1858.[38] Abol civ 1907 to help cr CP1.[208]

AP41—LINCOLN ST PETER STANTHAKET—Perhaps AP, perhaps monastery, demolished 15th cent.

AP42—LINCOLN ST RUMBOLD—Dissolved late 15th cent.

AP43—LINCOLN ST STEPHEN—Dissolved *ca* 15th cent.

AP44—LINCOLN ST SWITHIN—Abol civ 1907 to help cr CP1.[208] Eccl bdry: 1904 (help cr EP1),[211]

1964.[68]

LINWOOD

AP [Pts Lind] *LG* Seq 48. Civ bdry: 1887.[82] *Parl* Seq 2. *Eccl* Seq 55.

LISSINGTON

AP [Pts Lind] *LG* Seq 50. Civ bdry: 1887.[82] *Parl* Seq 11. *Eccl* Seq 58.

LONDONTHORPE

AP [Pts Kestev] *LG* Granth. Soke (until 1830s), Loved. Wap (from 1830s), Granth. PLU, RSD, RD. Abol civ 1931 to help cr Londonthorpe and Harrowby Without CP.[19] *Parl* S'rn Dv (1832—67), South Dv (1867—85), S Kestev Dv (1885—1918), Granth. Dv (1918—48). *Eccl* Granth. RDn. Sep eccl identity lost soon after 1535 and incl in Grantham AP, eccl severed 1849 from latter to help cr Mablethorpe with Londonthorpe EP.[165]

LONDONTHORPE AND HARROWBY WITHOUT

AP [Pts Kestev] Cr 1931 by union Londonthorpe AP, Harrowby Without CP, Spittlegate Without CP, pt Old Somerby CP.[19] *LG* W Kestev RD. *Parl* Granth. CC (1948—*).

LOUGHTON

AP [Pts Kestev] Orig AP (Avel. RDn), church early destroyed and eccl incl in Folkingham AP as 'Folkingham with Loughton',[152] qv.

LOUTH

AP [Pts Lind] Incl tp Louth Park (sep CP 1866,[13] eccl ex-par, eccl abol 1867 to help cr Louth Holy Trinity EP[225]). *LG* Louth Esk Hd, Louth PLU, Louth Bor/MB (pt until 1866, ent 1866—1974), Louth USD. Addtl civ bdry alt: 1936.[28] *Parl* Pt Louth Parl Bor (1306 only), Seq 1. *Eccl* Seq 49. Eccl bdry: 1863 (cr Louth St Michael EP),[225] 1867 (help cr Louth Holy Trinity EP).[225]

LOUTH HOLY TRINITY

EP [Pts Lind] Cr 1867 from Louth AP, ent eccl ex-par Louth Park.[225] Louthesk & Ludb. 3 RDn (1867—1910), Louthesk (West) RDn (1910—68), Louthesk RDn (1968—*). Bdry: 1878.[196]

LOUTH PARK

[Pts Lind] Civ a tp in Louth CP, sep CP 1866,[13] eccl ex-par, eccl abol 1867 to help cr Louth Holy Trinity EP.[224] *LG* Louth Esk Hd, Louth PLU, RSD, RD. Bdry: 1888.[44] Abol civ 1936 pt to Kedington AP, pt to Louth MB & AP.[28] *Parl* N'rn Dv (1832—67), North Dv (1867—85), E Lind Dv (1885—1918), Louth Dv (1918—48).

LOUTH ST MICHAEL

EP [Pts Lind] Cr 1863 from Louth AP.[225] Louthesk & Ludb. 3 RDn (1863—1910), Louthesk (West) RDn (1910—68), Louthesk RDn (1968—*).

LUDBOROUGH

AP [Pts Lind] *LG* Seq 45. *Parl* Seq 1. *Eccl* Seq 46.

LUDFORD

CP [Pts Lind] Cr 1936 by union Ludford Magna AP, Ludford Parva AP.[28] *LG* Louth RD. *Parl* Louth CC (1948—*).

LUDFORD MAGNA

AP [Pts Lind] Gains early West Wykeham AP (orig sep AP, early destroyed and incl in this par). *LG* Wragg. Wap, Louth PLU, RSD, RD. Civ bdry: 1883,[31] 1888.[44] Abol civ 1936 to help cr Ludford

CP.[28] *Parl* N'rn Dv (1832—67), Mid Dv (1867—85), E Lind Dv (1885—1918), Louth Dv (1918—48). *Eccl* Wragg. RDn. Abol eccl 1845 to help cr Ludford Magna with Ludford Parva EP.[226]

LUDFORD MAGNA WITH LUDFORD PARVA

EP [Pts Lind] Cr 1845 by union Ludford Magna AP, Ludford Parva AP.[226] Wragg. RDn (1845—1910), Walshcr. (East) RDn (1910—68), Louthesk RDn (1968—*).

LUDFORD PARVA

AP [Pts Lind] Organisation as for Ludford Manga, incl bdry alts.

LUDDINGTON

AP [Pts Lind] Incl tp Garthorpe (sep CP 1866,[13] not sep eccl hence this par eccl 'Luddington with Garthorpe', qv). *LG* Manley Wap, Goole PLU, RSD, Isle of Axh. RD. Civ bdry: 1885.[17] Transf 1974 to Humb.[10] *Parl* Seq 6.

LUDDINGTON WITH GARTHORPE

AP [Pts Lind] Usual eccl spelling; for civ and civ sep tp, see prev entry. *Eccl* Seq 79. Eccl bdry: 1855 (help cr Eastoft EP [Lincs Pts Lind, Yorks W Riding]).[129]

LUSBY

AP [Pts Lind] *LG* Seq 28. Civ bdry: 1880.[194] *Parl* Seq 12. *Eccl* Bolingbr. RDn. Abol eccl 1864 to help cr Lusby with Asgarby EP.[25]

LUSBY WITH ASGARBY

EP [Pts Lind] Cr 1864 by union Lusby AP, Asgarby AP.[25] Bolingbr. RDn (1864—84), Hill 2 RDn (1884—1910), Bolingbr. RDn (1910—27), Hill (South) RDn (1927—68), Bolingbr. RDn (1968—*). Bdry: 1886 (help cr Carrington with Frithville EP [Pts Lind, Pts Holl]).[51]

LUTTON

[Pts Holl] Chap in Sutton St Mary AP, sep CP 1866,[13] sep EP 1882 as 'Sutton St Nicholas',[227] qv. *LG* Seq 1. Bdry: 1932.[123] *Parl* Seq 16.

MABLETHORPE

AP [Pts Lind] Orig 2 APs: Mablethorpe St Peter (early lost into the sea, united 1745 with Theddlethorpe AP as 'Theddlethorpe St Helen with Mablethorpe St Peter' EP[228]); Mablethorpe St Mary (united 1660 with Stane AP,[229] the union civ 'Mablethorpe', eccl 'Mablethorpe with Stane',[228] qv). *LG* Calc. Wap, Louth PLU, RSD, RD (1894—96), Mablethorpe UD (1896—1925), Mablethorpe & Sutton UD (1925—74). *Parl* N'rn Dv (1832—67), Mid Dv (1867—85), E Lind Dv (1885—1918), Louth Dv (1918—48), Hornc. CC (1948—*).

MABLETHORPE ST MARY—see MABLETHORPE

MABLETHORPE ST PETER—see MABLETHORPE

MABLETHORPE WITH STANE

EP [Pts Lind] Cr 1660 by union Mablethorpe St Mary AP, Stane AP[229]; the union civ 'Mablethorpe', qv above. *Eccl* Calc. RDn (1660—1866), Calc. 1 RDn (1866—1910), Louthesk (East) RDn (1910—68), Calc. & Candl. RDn (1968—*).

MAIDENWELL

AP [Pts Lind] Louthesk & Ludb. RDn, without a church and early united with Farforth AP as 'Farforth cum Maidenwell',[143] qv.

CP [Pts Lind] Cr 1936 by union Farforth cum

Maidenwell AP, Oxcombe AP, Ruckland AP, Worlaby AP.[28] *LG* Louth RD. *Parl* Louth CC (1948—*).

MALTBY LE MARSH
AP [Pts Lind] *LG* Seq 33. *Parl* Seq 13. *Eccl* Seq 11.

MANBY
AP [Pts Lind] *LG* Seq 44. Civ bdry: 1883.[31] *Parl* Seq 1. *Eccl* Seq 47.

MANTHORPE
[Pts Kestev] Hmlt in Withern AP, sep CP 1866.[13] *LG* Belt. Wap, Bourne PLU, RSD, RD. Abol 1931 to help cr Toft with Lound and Manthorpe CP.[19] *Parl* S'rn Dv (1832—67), South Dv (1867—85), S Kestev Dv (1885—1918), Granth. Dv (1918—48).

CP [Pts Kestev] Cr 1894 from the pt of Manthorpe cum Little Gonerby CP not in Granth. MB.[161] *LG* Granth. PLU, RD. Bdry: 1930.[34] Abol 1931 to help cr Belton and Manthorpe CP.[19] *Parl* Granth. Dv (1918—48).

EP [Pts Kestev] Cr 1970 from Manthorpe with Londonthorpe EP.[46] Granth. RDn.

MANTHORPE CUM LITTLE GONERBY
[Pts Kestev] Tp in Grantham AP, sep CP 1866,[13] eccl severed 1849 to help cr Mablethorpe with Londonthorpe EP.[165] *LG* Granth. Soke (until 1830s), Loved. Wap (from 1830s), Granth. PLU, pt Granth. MB & USD (1879—94), Granth. RSD (ent 1875—79, pt 1879—94). Abol 1894 the pt in the MB cr Little Gonerby CP, the remainder cr Manthorpe CP.[161] *Parl* S'rn Dv (1832—67), South Dv (1867—85), S Kestev Dv (1885—1918).

MANTHORPE WITH LONDONTHORPE
EP [Pts Kestev] Cr 1849 by union tp Manthorpe cum Little Gonerby, area Londonthorpe (orig sep AP, qv), both in Grantham AP.[165] Granth. RDn (1849—66), Granth. 1 RDn (1866—1910), N Granth. RDn (1910—68), Granth. RDn (1968—70). Abol 1970, pt to help cr Welby and Londonthorpe EP, pt to cr Manthorpe EP, pt to Grantham AP, pt to Belton AP.[46]

MANTON
AP [Pts Lind] Incl tp Cleatham (Corr. Wap, sep CP 1866[13]), tp Twigmore (Manley Wap, sep CP 1866[13]). *LG* Manley Wap (main tp and Twigmore, pt until 1866, ent from 1866), pt Corr. Wap (Cleatham, until 1866), Glanf. Brigg PLU, RSD, RD. Addtl civ bdry alt: 1936 (gains Cleatham AP).[28] Transf 1974 to Humb.[10] *Parl* Seq 3. *Eccl* Seq 78.

MAREHAM LE FEN
AP [Pts Lind] *LG* Seq 42. Civ bdry: 1887.[130] *Parl* Seq 12. *Eccl* Seq 44. Eccl bdry: 1881 (help cr Wildmore EP [Pts Lind, Pts Kestev, Pts Holl]).[27]

MAREHAM ON THE HILL
AP [Pts Lind] *LG* Seq 42. Civ bdry: 1880 (help cr Wildmore CP),[26] 1936 (gains Scrafield AP).[28] *Parl* Seq 12. *Eccl* Seq 42. Eccl bdry: 1881 (help cr Wildmore EP [Pts Lind, Pts Kestev, Pts Holl]).[27]

MARKBY
AP [Pts Lind] *LG* Seq 34. Civ bdry: 1887.[182] *Parl* Seq 12. *Eccl* Calcew. RDn. Abol eccl early, ent to Hannah cum Hagnaby AP, the union 'Hannah cum Hagnaby and Markby',[183] qv.

MARSH CHAPEL
[Pts Lind] Chap in Fulstow AP, sep civ identity early, sep EP 1740.[6] *LG* Seq 32. *Parl* Seq 1. *Eccl* Louthesk & Ludb. RDn (1740—1863), Louthesk & Ludb. 2 RDn (1863—1910), Ludb. RDn (1910—68), Louthesk RDn (1968—*).

MARSTON
[Pts Kestev] Chap in Hougham AP, sep civ identity early. *LG* Seq 19. *Parl* Seq 20.

MARTIN
AP [Pts Lind] *LG* Gart. Wap, Hornc. PLU, RSD, RD. Civ bdry: 1880,[115] 1894 (help cr Woodhall Spa CP).[230] Abol civ 1936 ent to Roughton AP.[28] *Parl* N'rn Dv (1832—67), Mid Dv (1867—85), S Lind Dv (1885—1918), Hornc. Dv (1918—48). *Eccl* Sometimes as 'Martin by Horncastle', Seq 43. Eccl bdry: 1881 (help cr Wildmore EP [Pts Lind, Pts Kestev, Pts Holl]),[27] 1913.[126]

MARTIN
[Pts Kestev] Tp in Timberland AP, sep CP 1866,[13] sep EP 1882.[231] *LG* Seq 17. *Parl* Seq 15. *Eccl* Longob. RDn (1882—1968), Graff. RDn (1968—*).

MARTON
AP [Pts Lind] *LG* Seq 49. *Parl* Seq 14. *Eccl* Seq 74.

MELTON ROSS
AP [Pts Lind] Incl chap Scamblesby (sep civ identity early, sep EP 1752[6]). *LG* Seq 55. Civ bdry: 1952.[33] Transf 1974 to Humb.[10] *Parl* Seq 3. *Eccl* Pec jurisd Dean & Chapter of Linc. (until 1846), Seq 62 thereafter.

MERE
AP [Linc. Co of Itself (1410—1840s), Pts Kestev (Langoe Wap) from 1840s] Orig AP (Christianity RDn), church early destroyed,[232] thereafter ex-par, sep CP 1858.[38] *LG* Linc. PLU, RSD, Branst. RD. Abol civ 1931 to help cr Branston and Mere CP.[19] *Parl* N'rn Dv (1832—67), Mid Dv (1867—1918), Granth. Dv (1918—48).

MESSINGHAM
AP [Pts Lind] Incl pt tp East Butterwick (sep CP 1866,[13] not sep eccl hence this par eccl 'Messingham with East Butterwick', qv). *LG* Seq 46. Civ bdry: 1887.[130] Transf 1974 to Humb.[10] *Parl* Seq 3.

MESSINGHAM WITH EAST BUTTERWICK
AP [Pts Lind] Usual eccl spelling; for civ and civ sep pt tp, see prev entry. *Eccl* Seq 77.

METHERINGHAM
AP [Pts Kestev] *LG* Seq 16. *Parl* Seq 15. *Eccl* Seq 45. Eccl bdry: 1942.[135]

MIDVILLE
[Pts Lind] Area in East Fen, sep tp 1812,[92] sep CP 1866,[13] eccl abol 1885 to help cr Eastville with Midville EP (Pts Lind, Pts Holl).[48] *LG* Seq 29. *Parl* Seq 12.

MININGSBY
AP [Pts Lind] *LG* Seq 28. Civ bdry: 1880.[23] *Parl* Seq 12. *Eccl* Seq 9. Eccl bdry: 1858 (fen allotment severed to help cr New Bolingbroke EP).[24]

MINTING
AP [Pts Lind] *LG* Seq 37. *Parl* Seq 9. *Eccl* Seq 18.

MISSON
AP [Pt Notts (Bassetlaw Wap), pt Lincs, Pts Lind

(Manley Wap), made 1886 ent Notts[233]] *LG* Doncaster PLU, RSD. *Parl* Lincs pt, N'rn Dv (1832—67), North Dv (1867—85), N Lind Dv (1885—1918). *Eccl* See main entry in Notts.

MOORBY

AP [Pts Lind] *LG* Seq 42. Civ bdry: 1880 (help cr Wildmore CP),[26] 1884.[140] *Parl* Seq 12. *Eccl* Seq 43. Eccl bdry: 1881 (help cr Wildmore EP [Pts Lind, Pts Kestev, Pts Holl]).[27]

MORTON

[Pts Kestev] Ex-par place, sep CP 1858.[38] *LG* Boothby Graff. Wap, Linc. PLU, RSD, Branst. RD. Abol civ 1931 ent to Thorpe on the Hill AP.[19] *Parl* S'rn Dv (1832—67), Mid Dv (1867—85), N Kestev Dv (1885—1918), Granth. Dv (1918—48).

MORTON

AP [Pts Kestev] *LG* Seq 7. *Parl* Seq 21. *Eccl* Avel. RDn. Abol eccl 1732 to help cr Morton with Hacconby EP.[177]

MORTON

[Pts Lind] Tp in Gainsborough AP, sep CP 1866,[13] sep EP 1846.[155] *LG* Seq 36. *Parl* Seq 6. *Eccl* Corr. RDn.

MORTON WITH HACCONBY

EP [Pts Kestev] Cr 1732 by union Morton AP, Hacconby AP.[177] *Eccl* Avel. RDn (1732—1866), Avel. 2 RDn (1866—1910), Avel. RDn (1910—68), Avel. with Ness & Stamf. RDn (1968—*).

MOULTON

AP [Pts Holl] *LG* Seq 2. *Parl* Seq 16. *Eccl* Seq 40. Eccl bdry: 1890 (cr Moulton St James EP).[234]

MOULTON ST JAMES

EP [Pts Holl] Cr 1890 from Moulton AP.[234] W Elloe RDn (1890—1910), Elloe (West) RDn (1910—*).

MOWN RAKES

[Pts Holl] Ex-par place (sometimes called 'Rakes Farm'), sep CP 1858.[38] *LG* Kirton Wap, Boston PLU (1866—91), RSD. Abol civ 1891 ent to Swineshead AP.[73] *Parl* S'rn Dv (1832—67), South Dv (1867—85), N Kestev Dv (1885—1918).

MUCKTON

AP [Pts Lind] *LG* Seq 44. Civ bdry: 1883.[31] *Parl* Seq 1. *Eccl* Louthesk & Ludb. RDn (until 1863), Calcew. RDn (1863—66), Calcew. 1 RDn (1866—1910), Louthesk (West) RDn (1910—68), Louthesk RDn (1968—*).

MUMBY

AP [Pts Lind] Incl area Chapel St Leonard (sep CP 1896,[95] sep EP 1826 as 'Chapel St Leonards',[6] as such eccl refounded 1898 from Mumby AP, Hogsthorpe AP[96]). *LG* Seq 34. Addtl civ bdry alt: 1883,[31] 1888.[187] *Parl* Seq 12. *Eccl* Seq 14.

MUMBY ST LEONARD—see CHAPEL ST LEONARD

NAVENBY

AP [Pts Kestev] *LG* Seq 11. Civ bdry: 1931 (gains Skinnand AP).[19] *Parl* Seq 15. *Eccl* Seq 45.

NETTLEHAM

AP [Pts Lind] *LG* Seq 43. Civ bdry: 1965 (loses pt to Linc. CB [assoc with Pts Lind] & CP).[89] *Parl* Seq 14. *Eccl* Seq 72.

NETTLETON

AP [Pts Lind] *LG* Seq 54. *Parl* Seq 5. *Eccl* Seq 63.

NEWBALL

[Pts Lind] Hmlt in Stainton by Longworth AP, sep CP 1866.[13] *LG* Seq 52. Bdry: 1887,[81] 1936 (gains Coldstead CP).[28] *Parl* Seq 8.

NEWSTEAD

[Pts Lind] Ex-par place, sep CP 1858.[38] *LG* Manley Wap, Glanf. Brigg PLU (1861—1930), RSD, RD. Abol civ 1936 to help cr Cadney CP.[28] *Parl* N'rn Dv (1832—67), North Dv (1867—85), N Lind Dv (1885—1918), Brigg Dv (1918—48).

NEWTON

AP [Pts Kestev] *LG* Avel. Wap, Sleaf. PLU, RSD, RD. Abol civ 1931 pt to help cr Aunsby and Dembleby CP, pt to help cr Newton and Haceby CP, pt to Osbournby AP.[19] *Parl* S'rn Dv (1832—67), South Dv (1867—85), N Kestev Dv (1885—1918), Granth. Dv (1918—48). *Eccl* Avel. RDn (until 1866), Avel. 1 RDn (1866—1910), Avel. RDn (1910—68), Laff. RDn (1968—73). Abol eccl 1973 to help cr Newton and Haceby EP.[178]

WOLD NEWTON

AP [Pts Lind] *LG* Seq 31. Transf 1974 to Humb.[10] *Parl* Seq 1. *Eccl* Seq 30.

NEWTON AND HACEBY

CP [Pts Kestev] Cr 1931 by union Haceby AP, pt Newton AP.[19] *LG* E Kestev RD. *Parl* Rutl & Stamf. CC (1948—*).

EP [Pts Kestev] Cr 1973 by union Newton AP, Haceby AP.[178] Laff. RDn.

NEWTON BY TOFT

AP [Pts Lind] *LG* Walshcr. Wap, Caist. PLU, RSD, RD. Abol civ 1936 to help cr Toft Newton CP.[28] *Parl* N'rn Dv (1832—67), North Dv (1867—85), E Lind Dv (1885—1918), Louth Dv (1918—48). *Eccl* Seq 55.

NEWTON ON TRENT

AP [Pts Lind] *LG* Seq 49. *Parl* Seq 14. *Eccl* Seq 75.

NOCTON

AP [Pts Kestev] *LG* Seq 16. *Parl* Seq 15. *Eccl* Seq 45.

NORMANBY AND STOW—see STOW

NORMANBY BY SPITAL

AP [Pts Lind] *LG* Seq 26. *Parl* Seq 6. *Eccl* Seq 68.

NORMANBY LE WOLD

AP [Pts Lind] *LG* Seq 48. *Parl* Seq 7. *Eccl* Walshcr. RDn. Abol eccl 1740 to help cr Claxby with Normanby le Wold EP.[97]

NORMANTON

AP [Pts Kestev] *LG* Seq 18. *Parl* Seq 20. *Eccl* Loved. RDn. Abol eccl 1974 to help cr Carlton Scroope with Normanton EP.[91]

NORTH FORTY FOOT BANK

[Pts Holl] Ex-par place, sep CP 1858,[38] eccl abol 1948 to help cr Holland Fen with Chapel Hill EP.[94] *LG* Kirton Wap, Boston PLU (1862—1906), RSD, RD. Abol civ 1906 pt to Brothertoft CP, pt to Pelham's Lands CP.[39] *Parl* S'rn Dv (1832—67), South Dv (1867—85), N Kestev Dv (1885—1918).

NORTHOLME

[Pts Lind] Chap in Wainfleet All Saints AP, sep civ identity early, sep EP 1822 as 'Wainfleet St Thomas',[235] qv. *LG* Candl. Wap, Spilsby PLU, RSD. Abol 1888 ent to Wainfleet All Saints AP.[236] *Parl* N'rn Dv (1832—67), Mid Dv (1868—85), S

Lind Dv (1885—1918).

NORTHORPE
AP [Pts Lind] *LG* Seq 36. Civ bdry: 1936 (gains Southorpe CP).[28] *Parl* Seq 6. *Eccl* Pec jurisd Corr. Prebend (until 1846), Seq 71 thereafter.

BISHOP NORTON
AP [Pts Lind] Incl tp Atterby (sep CP 1866,[13] not sep eccl hence this par eccl 'Bishop Norton with Atterby', qv). *LG* Seq 24. Addtl civ bdry alt: 1936 (gains Atterby CP).[28] *Parl* Seq 7.

BISHOP NORTON WITH ATTERBY
AP [Pts Lind] Usual eccl spelling; for civ and civ sep tp, see prev entry. *Eccl* Pec jurisd Bishop Norton Prebend (until 1846), Seq 68 thereafter.

NORTON DISNEY
AP [Pts Kestev] *LG* Seq 12. *Parl* Seq 15. *Eccl* Seq 22.

ORBY
AP [Pts Lind] *LG* Seq 35. Civ bdry: 1888.[2] *Parl* Seq 12. *Eccl* Seq 15.

ORFORD
[Pts Lind] Ex-par place, not sep rated but added civ 1858 to Stainton le Vale AP in Casit. PLU.[237]

NORTH ORMESBY
AP [Pts Lind] Sometimes 'Nun Ormesby'. *LG* Seq 45. *Parl* Seq 1. *Eccl* Seq 46.

NUN ORMESBY—see NORTH ORMESBY

SOUTH ORMESBY
AP [Pts Lind] Hill Wap, Hill RDn, united eccl 1774 with Ketsby AP, Calceby AP, Driby AP to cr 'South Ormesby cum Ketsby Calceby and Driby' EP, united civ at same time with Ketsby AP to cr 'South Ormesby with Ketsby' CP,[87] qv.

SOUTH ORMESBY CUM KETSBY
CP [Pts Lind] Cr 1774 by union South Ormesby AP, Ketsby AP.[87] *LG* Seq 40. *Parl* Seq 12.

SOUTH ORMESBY WITH KETSBY CALCEBY AND DRIBY
EP [Pts Lind] Cr 1774 by union South Ormesby AP, Ketsby AP, Calceby AP, Driby AP.[87] Hill RDn (1774—1866), Hill 1 RDn (1866—1910), Hill (North) RDn (1910—68), Bolingbr. RDn (1968—*).

OSBOURNBY
AP [Pts Kestev] *LG* Seq 8. Civ bdry: 1931.[19] *Parl* Seq 18. *Eccl* Seq 5.

OSGODBY
[Pts Kestev] Tp in Lenton AP, sep CP 1866.[13] *LG* Belt. Wap, Granth. PLU, RSD, RD. Abol 1931 to help cr Lenton Keisby and Osgodby CP.[19] *Parl* S'rn Dv (1832—67), South Dv (1867—85), S Kestev Dv (1885—1918), Rutl & Stamf. Dv (1918—48).

OSGODBY
CP [Pts Lind] Cr 1936 by union Kirkby cum Osgodby AP, Usselby CP, Kingerby CP.[28] *LG* Casit. RD. *Parl* Gainsb. CC (1948—*).

OWERSBY
AP [Pts Lind] Incl tps North Owersby, South Owersby (each a sep CP 1866[13]) so that 'Owersby' has no sep civ identity 1866—1936 (see following entry). *LG* Walshcr. Wap. *Parl* N'rn Dv (1832—67). *Eccl* Walshcr. RDn. Abol prob late 18th cent to help cr Owersby with Kirkby and Osgodby EP.[147]

CP [Pts Lind] Cr 1936 by union North Owersby CP, South Owersby CP, Thornton le Moor AP.[28] *LG* Caist. RD. *Parl* Gainsb. CC (1948—*).

NORTH OWERSBY
[Pts Lind] Tp in Owersby AP, sep CP 1866.[13] *LG* Walshcr. Wap, Caist. PLU, RSD, RD. Abol 1936 to help cr Owersby CP.[28] *Parl* N'rn Dv (1832—67), North Dv (1867—85), E Lind Dv (1885—1918), Louth Dv (1918—48).

SOUTH OWERSBY
[Pts Lind] Organisation as for North Owersby.

OWERSBY WITH KIRKBY AND OSGODBY
EP [Pts Lind] Cr prob late 18th cent by union Kirkby cum Osgodby AP, Owersby AP.[147] Walshcr. RDn (cr—1866), Walshcr. 1 RDn (1866—73), Walshcr. RDn (1873—1910), Walshcr. (West) RDn (1910—68), W Wold RDn (1968—*).

OWMBY
AP [Pts Lind] *LG* Seq 26. *Parl* Seq 6. *Eccl* Seq 68.

OWSTON
AP [Pts Lind] incl chap West Butterwick (sep CP 1866,[13] sep EP 1845[83]), pt chap East Ferry (sep CP 1866,[13] the area considered eccl in Owston AP, 'East Ferry' eccl severed 1954 to help cr Scotter with East Ferry EP,[145] so that this par 'Owston with East Ferry' until 1954, 'Owston' thereafter). *LG* Manley Wap, Gainsb. PLU (soon after 1837[84]—1930), RSD, RD (1894—1912). Addtl civ bdry alt: 1885.[146] Renamed civ 1912 'Owston Ferry'.[238] *Parl* N'rn Dv (1832—67), North Dv (1867—85), W Lind Dv (1885—1918). *Eccl* Isle of Axh. RDn (1954—*).

OWSTON FERRY
CP [Pts Lind] Renaming 1912 of Owston AP.[238] *LG* Gainsb. PLU, RD (1912—36), Isle of Axh. RD (1936—74). Bdry: 1936.[28] Transf 1974 to Humb.[10] *Parl* Gainsb. Dv/CC (1918—*).

OWSTON WITH EAST FERRY
AP [Pts Lind] Usual eccl spelling; for civ and civ sep chaps see prev entry. *Eccl* Corr. RDn (until 1910), Isle of Axh. RDn (1910—54). Abol eccl 1954, area of chap East Ferry severed to help cr Scotter with East Ferry EP, the remainder to be 'Owston'.[145]

OXCOMBE
AP [Pts Lind] *LG* Hill Hd, Louth PLU, RSD, RD. Abol civ 1936 to help cr Maidenwell CP.[28] *Parl* N'rn Dv (1832—67), Mid Dv (1867—85), S Lind Dv (1885—1918), Louth Dv (1918—48). *Eccl* Seq 34.

PANTON
AP [Pts Lind] *LG* Seq 51. *Parl* Seq 9. *Eccl* Wragg. RDn. Abol eccl 1860 to help cr Wragby with Panton EP.[239]

PARTNEY
AP [Pts Lind] *LG* Seq 35. *Parl* Seq 12. *Eccl* Seq 16.

PELHAM'S LANDS
[Pts Holl] Ex-par place, sep CP 1858,[38] eccl abol 1948 to help cr Holland Fen with Chapel Hill EP.[94] *LG* Kirton Wap, Boston PLU (1862—1930), RSD, RD. Civ bdry: 1880,[240] 1906,[39] 1932,[77] 1935 (loses pt to Dogdyke CP, Pts Kestev).[16] *Parl* Seq 19.

PEPPER GOWT PLOT
[Pts Holl] Ex-par place, sep CP 1858.[38] Sometimes 'Rowlands Marsh'. *LG* Skirb. Wap, Boston PLU (1862—1906), RSD, RD. Abol civ 1906 ent to

Skirbeck AP.[39] *Parl* S'rn Dv (1832—67), South Dv (1867—85), Holl Dv (1885—1918).

PICKWORTH
AP [Pts Kestev] *LG* Avel. Wap, Granth. PLU, RSD, RD (1894—1931), W Kestev RD (1931—74). *Parl* Seq 21. *Eccl* Seq 4.

PILHAM
AP [Pts Lind] *LG* Seq 36. Civ bdry: 1886.[54] *Parl* Seq 6. *Eccl* Seq 69.

PINCHBECK
AP [Pts Holl] *LG* Seq 2. Civ bdry: 1883,[31] 1887,[122] 1932.[123] *Parl* Seq 16. *Eccl* Seq 40. Eccl bdry: 1851 (cr West Pinchbeck EP),[241] 1874 (help cr Spalding St John the Baptist EP),[242] 1877 (help cr Spalding St Paul EP),[109] 1918.[124]

WEST PINCHBECK
EP [Pts Holl] Cr 1851 from Pinchbeck AP.[241] Holl RDn (1851—66), S Holl RDn (1866—84), W Elloe RDn (1884—1910), Elloe (West) RDn (1910—*). Bdry: 1918.[124]

POINTON
[Pts Kestev] Chap in Sempringham AP, sep CP 1866.[13] *LG* Avel. Wap, Bourne PLU, RSD, RD. Abol 1931 to help cr Pointon and Sempringham CP.[19] *Parl* S'rn Dv (1832—67), South Dv (1867—85), S Kestev Dv (1885—1918), Rutl & Stamf. Dv (1918—48).

POINTON AND SEMPRINGHAM
CP [Pts Kestev] Cr 1931 by union pt Askackby AP, ent Pointon AP, ent Sempringham AP.[19] *LG* S Kestev RD. *Parl* Rutl & Stamf. CC (1948—*).

GREAT PONTON
AP [Pts Kestev] *LG* Granth. Soke (until 1830s), Winn. & Thr. Wap (from 1830s), Granth. PLU, RSD, RD (1894—1931), W Kestev RD (1931—74). *Parl* Seq 21. *Eccl* Seq 26.

LITTLE PONTON
AP [Pts Kestev] *LG* Winn. & Thr. Wap, Granth. PLU, RSD, RD. Abol civ 1931 to help cr Little Ponton and Stroxton CP.[19] *Parl* S'rn Dv (1832—67), South Dv (1867—85), S Kestev Dv (1885—1918), Rutl & Stamf. Dv (1918—48). *Eccl* Seq 26.

LITTLE PONTON AND STROXTON
CP [Pts Kestev] Cr 1931 by union Little Ponton AP, Stroxton AP.[19] *LG* W Kestev RD. *Parl* Rutl & Stamf. CC (1948—*).

QUADRING
AP [Pts Holl] *LG* Seq 4. Civ bdry: 1883,[31] 1925.[163] *Parl* Seq 16. *Eccl* Seq 37. Eccl bdry: 1912 (help cr Gosberton Clough EP).[164]

QUARRINGTON
AP [Pts Kestev] *LG* Asw. Wap, Sleaf. PLU, New Sleaf. USD, Sleaf. UD. Civ bdry: 1888.[243] *Parl* Seq 17. *Eccl* Seq 2. Eccl bdry: 1928.[244]

RAITHBY
AP [Pts Lind] *LG* Seq 29. Civ bdry: 1880 (help cr West Fen CP).[139] *Parl* Seq 12. *Eccl* Sometimes as 'Raithby by Spilsby', Seq 9. Eccl bdry: 1858 (allotment in West Fen eccl severed to help cr New Bolingbroke EP).[24]

RAITHBY CUM MALTBY
AP [Pts Lind] *LG* Seq 44. *Parl* Seq 1. *Eccl* Louthesk & Ludb. RDn. Abol eccl 1770 to help cr Raithby with

Hallington EP.[180]

RAITHBY WITH HALLINGTON
EP [Pts Lind] Cr 1770 by union Raithby cum Maltby AP, Hallington AP.[180] Louthesk & Ludb. RDn (1770—1863), Louthesk & Ludb. 3 RDn (1863—1910), Louthesk (West) RDn (1910—68), Louthesk RDn (1968—*).

RANBY
[Pts Lind] Chap in Gautby AP, sep civ identity early, sep EP 1775.[6] *LG* Seq 37. *Parl* Seq 9. *Eccl* Gart. RDn (1775—1866), Hornc. RDn (1866—1928), Wragg. RDn (1928—68), Hornc. RDn (1968—*).

RAND
AP [Pts Lind] Incl chap Fulnetby (sep CP 1866,[13] not sep eccl hence this par eccl 'Rand with Fulnetby', qv). *LG* Seq 52. Addtl civ bdry alt: 1887.[81] *Parl* Seq 8.

RAND WITH FULNETBY
AP [Pts Lind] Usual eccl spelling; for civ and civ sep chap, see prev entry. *Eccl* Seq 57.

MARKET RASEN
AP [Pts Lind] *LG* Walshcr. Wap, Caist. PLU, Market Rasen USD, UD. *Parl* Seq 2. *Eccl* Seq 55. Eccl bdry: 1952.[135]

MIDDLE RASEN
AP [Pts Lind] *LG* Seq 48. Civ bdry: 1887.[82] *Parl* Seq 2. *Eccl* Seq 55. Eccl bdry: 1952.[135]

WEST RASEN
AP [Pts Lind] *LG* Seq 48. *Parl* Seq 2. *Eccl* Seq 55.

NORTH RAUCEBY
AP [Pts Kestev] Incl chap South Rauceby (sep par by 1535). *LG* Seq 14. *Parl* Seq 17. *Eccl* Asw. with Laff. RDn. Gains *ca* 17th cent dilapidated South Rauceby AP,[245] the united par eccl 'North Rauceby with South Rauceby'.

NORTH RAUCEBY WITH SOUTH RAUCEBY
EP [Pts Kestev] Cr 17th cent by union North Rauceby AP, dilapidated South Rauceby AP.[245] *Eccl* Seq 1. Eccl bdry: 1926.[246]

SOUTH RAUCEBY
AP [Pts Kestev] Orig chap in North Rauceby AP, sep par by 1535. *LG* Seq 14. Civ bdry: 1931.[19] *Parl* Seq 17. *Eccl* Asw. with Laff. RDn. Dilapidated, united 17th cent with North Rauceby as 'North Rauceby with South Rauceby'.[245]

EAST RAVENDALE
AP [Pts Lind] Incl chap West Ravendale (perhaps orig AP appropriated to S'well Collegiate Church [Notts], later accounted chap in this par,[247] sep CP 1866[13]). *LG* Seq 31. Transf 1974 to Humb.[10] *Parl* Seq 4. *Eccl* Seq 30.

WEST RAVENDALE
[Pts Lind] Perhaps orig AP appropriated to S'well Collegiate Church (Notts), later accounted chap in East Ravendale AP, sep CP 1866.[13] *LG* Seq 31. Transf 1974 to Humb.[13] *Parl* Seq 4.

RAVENTHORPE
[Pts Lind] Hmlt in Appleby AP, sep CP 1866.[13] *LG* Manley Wap, Glanf. Brigg PLU (soon after 1837[84]—1930), RSD, RD. Abol 1936 ent to Holme CP.[28] *Parl* N'rn Dv (1832—67), North Dv (1867—85), N Lind Dv (1885—1918), Brigg Dv

(1918—48).

REDBOURNE
AP [Pts Lind] *LG* Seq 46. Transf 1974 to Humb.[13] *Parl* Seq 3. *Eccl* Seq 78.

REEPHAM
[Pts Lind] Chap in Fiskerton AP, sep civ identity early, prob sep eccl from 1633 (first registers[149]). *LG* Seq 43. Civ bdry: 1936.[28] *Parl* Seq 14. *Eccl* Seq 72.

NORTH RESTON
AP [Pts Lind] *LG* Seq 44. Civ bdry: 1888.[44] *Parl* Seq 1. *Eccl* Louthesk & Ludb. RDn (until 1863), Louthesk & Ludb. 3 RDn (1863—1910), Louthesk (West) RDn (1910—68), Calc. & Candl. RDn (1968—*).

SOUTH RESTON
AP [Pts Lind] *LG* Seq 33. Civ bdry: 1936 (gains Castle Carlton AP).[28] *Parl* Seq 10. *Eccl* Calc. RDn (until 1866), Calc. 1 RDn (1866—1910), Louthesk (West) RDn (1910—68), Calc. & Candl. RDn (1968—*).

REVESBY
AP [Pts Lind] *LG* Seq 28. Civ bdry: 1880,[47] 1880,[23] 1884,[248] 1887.[130] *Parl* Seq 12. *Eccl* Bolingbr. RDn. Eccl bdry: 1858 (allotment in West Fen eccl severed to help cr New Bolingbroke EP),[24] 1874,[249] 1874,[250] 1885 (help cr Eastville with Midville EP),[48] 1881 (help cr Wildmore EP [Pts Lind, Pts Kestev, Pts Holl]).[27]

RIBY
AP [Pts Lind] *LG* Seq 54. *Parl* Seq 5. *Eccl* Seq 65.

RIGSBY WITH AILBY
[Pts Lind] Chap in Alford AP, sep civ identity early. *LG* Seq 34. *Parl* Seq 12.

RIPPINGALE
AP [Pts Kestev] *LG* Seq 7. *Parl* Seq 21. *Eccl* Seq 6.

RISBY
AP [Pts Lind] Orig AP (Manley Hd, Manlake RDn) united 1717 with Roxby AP to cr Roxby cum Risby CP/EP.[251]

RISEHOLME
AP [Pts Lind] Usual civ spelling; incl eccl ex-par Grange de de Lings hence this par eccl 'Riseholme and Grange de Lings', qv. *LG* Seq 43. Civ bdry: 1965 (loses pt to Linc. CB [assoc with Pts Lind] & CP).[89] *Parl* Seq 14.

RISEHOLME AND GRANGE DE LINGS
AP [Pts Lind] Usual eccl spelling since incl eccl ex-par Grange de Lings; for civ see prev entry. *Eccl* Seq 72.

ROPSLEY
AP [Pts Kestev] Incl hmlt Little Humby (sep CP 1866[13]). *LG* Winn. & Thr. Wap, Granth. PLU, RSD, RD. Addtl civ bdry alt: 1887.[192] Abol civ 1931 to help cr Ropsley and Humby CP.[19] *Parl* S'rn Dv (1832—67), South Dv (1867—85), S Kestev Dv (1885—1918), Rutl & Stamf. Dv (1918—48). *Eccl* Seq 26.

ROPSLEY AND HUMBY
CP [Pts Kestev] Cr 1931 by union Ropsley AP, Humby CP.[19] *LG* W Kestev RD. *Parl* Rutl & Stamf. CC (1948—*).

ROTHWELL
AP [Pts Lind] *LG* Seq 30. *Parl* Seq 5. *Eccl* Seq 29.

ROUGHTON
AP [Pts Lind] *LG* Seq 42. Civ bdry: 1880 (help cr Wildmore CP),[26] 1894 (help cr Woodhall Spa CP),[230] 1936 (gains Dalderby AP, Martin AP).[28] *Parl* Seq 12. *Eccl* Gart. RDn. Abol eccl 1741 to help cr Roughton with Haltham EP.[131]

ROUGHTON WITH HALTHAM
EP [Pts Lind] Cr 1741 by union Roughton AP, Haltham AP.[131] Gart. RDn (1741—1968), Hornc. RDn (1968—*). Eccl bdry: 1881 (help cr Wildmore EP [Pts Lind, Pts Kestev, Pts Holl]),[27] 1913.[126]

ROWSTON
AP [Pts Kestev] *LG* Seq 14. *Parl* Seq 17. *Eccl* Seq 1.

ROXBY
AP [Pts Lind] Orig AP (Manley Wap, Manlake RDn) united 1717 with Risby AP to cr Roxby cum Risby CP/EP.[251]

ROXBY CUM RISBY
[Pts Lind] Cr 1717 as CP/EP by union Roxby AP, Risby AP.[251] *LG* Manley Wap, Glanf. Brigg PLU, Roxby cum Risby USD, UD (1894—1936), Glanf. Brigg RD (1936—74). Transf 1974 to Humb.[10] *Parl* Seq 3. *Eccl* Manlake RDn.

ROXHOLM
AP [Pts Kestev] Hmlt in Leasingham CP (qv for union 1726 of Leasingham St John the Baptist AP, Leasingham St Andrew AP), sep CP 1866.[13] *LG* Seq 14. *Parl* Seq 17.

ROYALTY FARM
[Pts Holl] Ex-par place, sep CP 1858.[38] *LG* Kirton Wap, Boston PLU (1866—91), RSD. Abol civ 1891 ent to Swineshead AP.[73] *Parl* S'rn Dv (1832—67), South Dv (1867—85), N Kestev Dv (1885—1918).

RUCKLAND
AP [Pts Lind] *LG* Louth Esk Hd, Louth PLU, RSD, RD. Abol civ 1936 to help cr Maidenwell CP.[28] *Parl* N'rn Dv (1832—67), North Dv (1867—85), E Lind Dv (1885—1918), Louth Dv (1918—48). *Eccl* Louthesk & Ludb. RDn. Abol eccl 1753 to help cr Ruckland with Farforth and Maidenwell EP.[144]

RUCKLAND WITH FARFORTH AND MAIDENWELL
EP [Pts Lind] Cr 1753 by union Ruckland AP, Farforth cum Maidenwell AP.[144] Louthesk & Ludb. RDn (1753—1866), Hill 1 RDn (1866—1910), Hill (North) RDn (1910—68), Bolingbr. RDn (1968—*).

RUSKINGTON
AP [Pts Kestev] *LG* Flax. Wap, Sleaf. PLU, Ruskington USD, UD (1894—1930), E Kestev RD (1930—74). Civ bdry: 1883,[31] 1885,[20] 1896.[203] *Parl* Seq 17. *Eccl* Seq 1.

SALEBY WITH THORESTHORPE
AP [Pts Lind] *LG* Seq 33. *Parl* Seq 13. *Eccl* Seq 14.

SALMONBY
AP [Pts Lind] *LG* Seq 39. *Parl* Seq 12. *Eccl* Hill RDn (until 1866), Hill 1 RDn (1866—1910), Hill (North) RDn (1910—66). Abol eccl 1966 to help cr Tetford and Salmonby EP.[252]

SALTFLEEBY
EP [Pts Lind] Cr 1973 by union Saltfleetby All Saints AP, Saltfleetby St Peter AP, Saltfleetby St Clement AP.[253] Louthesk RDn.

SALTFLEETBY ALL SAINTS
AP [Pts Lind] *LG* Seq 44. Civ bdry: 1883,[31] 1887.[254] *Parl* Seq 1. *Eccl* Louthesk & Ludb. RDn (until 1863), Louthesk & Ludb. 2 RDn (1863—*ca* 1896), Louthesk & Ludb. 1 RDn (*ca* 1896—1910), Louthesk (East) RDn (1910—68), Louthesk RDn (1969—73). Eccl bdry: 1967.[255] Abol eccl 1973 to help cr Saltfleetby EP.[253]

SALTFLEETBY ST CLEMENT
AP [Pts Lind] Organisation, incl all bdry alts, as for Saltfleetby All Saints.

SALTFLEETBY ST PETER
AP [Pts Lind] Organisation, incl all bdry alts, as for Saltfleetby All Saints, but with addtl eccl bdry alt 1931.[112]

SAPPERTON
AP [Pts Kestev] Orig chap in Grantham AP,[149] sep par by 1535. *LG* Granth. Soke (until 1830s), Winn. & Thr. Wap (from 1830s), Granth. PLU, RSD, RD. Abol civ 1931 to help cr Braceby and Sapperton CP.[19] *Parl* S'rn Dv (1832—67), South Dv (1867—85), S Kestev Dv (1885—1918), Rutl & Stamf. Dv (1918—48). *Eccl* Seq 26.

SAUSTHORPE
AP [Pts Lind] *LG* Seq 40. *Parl* Seq 12. *Eccl* Seq 36.

SAXBY
AP [Pts Lind] Sometimes 'Saxby St Helen'. *LG* Seq 26. *Parl* Seq 6. *Eccl* Asl. RDn. Abol eccl late 18th or early 19th cent to help cr Saxby with Firsby EP.[147]

SAXBY ALL SAINTS
AP [Pts Lind] *LG* Seq 55. Transf 1974 to Humb.[10] *Parl* Seq 3. *Eccl* Seq 60.

SAXBY WITH FIRSBY
EP [Pts Lind] Cr late 18th or early 19th cent by union Saxby AP, East Firsby AP.[147] Asl. RDn (cr—1968), Lawres RDn (1968—*).

SAXILBY WITH INGLEBY
AP [Pts Lind] *LG* Seq 43. *Parl* Seq 14. *Eccl* Seq 75.

SCAMBLESBY
AP [Pts Lind] Chap in Melton Ross AP, sep civ identity early, sep EP 1752.[6] *LG* Seq 37. *Parl* Seq 9. *Eccl* Pec jurisd Dean & Chapter of Linc. (until 1846), Gart. RDn (1846—66), Hill 2 RDn (1866—84), Hornc. RDn (1884—*).

SCAMPTON
AP [Pts Lind] *LG* Seq 43. *Parl* Seq 14. *Eccl* Seq 76.

NORTH SCARLE
AP [Pts Kestev] *LG* Seq 12. *Parl* Seq 15. *Eccl* Seq 22.

SCARTHO
AP [Pts Lind] *LG* Brad. Hav. Wap, Grimsby PLU, RSD, RD. Abol civ 1928 pt to Grimsby CB (assoc with Pts Lind) to help cr Grimsby CP, pt to Waltham AP.[72] *Parl* Gt Grimsby Parl Bor (1832—1918), Louth Dv (1918—48). *Eccl* Seq 33. Eccl bdry: 1964.[68]

SCAWBY
AP [Pts Lind] *LG* Manley Wap, Glanf. Brigg PLU, Brigg USD (1875—92), Glanf. Brigg RSD (pt 1875—92, ent 1892—94), Glanf. Brigg RD. Civ bdry: 1887,[63] 1892 (loses the pt in the USD to Glandford Brigg CP).[50] Transf 1974 to Humb.[10] *Parl* Seq 3. *Eccl* Seq 80.

SCOPWICK
AP [Pts Kestev] *LG* Seq 17. Civ bdry: 1931 (gains Kirkby Green AP).[19] *Parl* Seq 15. *Eccl* Seq 45.

SCOTHERN
AP [Pts Lind] *LG* Seq 43. *Parl* Seq 14. *Eccl* Seq 72.

SCOTTER
AP [Pts Lind] *LG* Seq 36. Civ bdry: 1885,[256] 1936.[28] *Parl* Seq 6. *Eccl* Corr. RDn. Abol eccl 1954 to help cr Scotter with East Ferry EP.[145]

SCOTTER WITH EAST FERRY
EP [Pts Lind] Cr 1954 by union Scotter AP, chap East Ferry in Owston with East Ferry AP (area civ orig pt in Owston, pt in Scotton, qv).[145] Corr. RDn (1954—68), Manlake RDn (1968—*).

SCOTTON
AP [Pts Lind] Incl pt chap East Ferry (sep CP 1866[13]; East Ferry considered eccl ent in Owston AP; see East Ferry for eccl severing 1954 to help cr Scotter with East Ferry EP[145]); Scotton AP incl from 1866 undivided pt Lands Common to East Ferry and Scotton (abol 1936, pt to each par[28]). *LG* Seq 36. Addtl civ bdry alt: 1885.[256] *Parl* Seq 6. *Eccl* Seq 71.

SCRAFIELD
AP [Pts Lind] *LG* Hill Hd, Hornc. PLU, RSD, RD. Abol civ 1936 ent to Mareham on the Hill AP.[28] *Parl* N'rn Dv (1832—67), Mid Dv (1867—85), S Lind Dv (1885—1918), Hornc. Dv (1918—48). *Eccl* Hill RDn. Abol eccl before 1717 to help cr Hameringham with Scrafield EP.[181]

SCREDINGTON
AP [Pts Kestev] *LG* Seq 6. *Parl* Seq 18. *Eccl* Pec jurisd Dean & Chapter of Linc. (until 1846), Seq 2 thereafter.

SCREMBY
AP [Pts Lind] *LG* Seq 35. *Parl* Seq 12. *Eccl* Seq 16.

SCRIVELSBY
AP [Pts Lind] *LG* Seq 37. Civ bdry: 1880,[115] 1887.[130] *Parl* Seq 12. *Eccl* Gart. RDn. Abol eccl 1731 to help cr Scrivelsby with Dalderby EP.[131]

SCRIVELSBY WITH DALDERBY
EP [Pts Lind] Cr 1731 by union Scrivelsby AP, Dalderby AP.[131] Gart. RDn (1731—1866), Hornc. RDn (1866—*). Bdry: 1881 (help cr Wildmore EP [Pts Lind, Pts Kestev, Pts Holl]).[27]

SCUNTHORPE
[Pts Lind] The following have 'Scunthorpe' in their names. Insofar as any existed at a given time: *LG* Manley Wap, Glanf. Brigg PLU, RSD (1875—90), Scunth. USD (1890—94), UD (1894—1919), Scunth. & Frodingham UD (1919—36), Scunth. MB (1936—74). *Parl* N'rn Dv (1832—67), North Dv (1867—85), N Lind Dv (1885—1918), Brigg Dv/CC (1918—70), Brigg. & Scunth. CC (1970—*). *Eccl* Manlake RDn.

CP1/EP1—SCUNTHORPE [ST JOHN THE EVANGELIST]—Tp in Frodingham AP, sep CP 1866,[13] sep EP 1889 by union this tp and also the pt of area Crosby (pt in Flixborough AP, pt in Frodingham AP, not in Gunhouse with Burringham EP or in Flixborough.[125] Abol civ 1919 pt to help cr Scunth. & Frodingham UD & CP3, pt to help cr Brumby Rural CP.[21] Eccl bdry: 1895,[96]

1913 (area Crosby severed to cr Crosby EP),[126] 1969 (help cr EP3).[127]

CP2—SCUNTHORPE—Renaming 1937 of CP3.[257] Transf 1974 to Humb.[10]

EP2—SCUNTHORPE ALL SAINTS—Cr 1969 from Frodingham AP, Old Brumby EP, Bottesford AP.[65]

EP3—SCUNTHORPE THE RESURRECTION, BERKELEY—Cr 1969 from Crosby EP, EP1, Frodingham AP.[127]

CP3—SCUNTHORPE AND FRODINGHAM—Cr 1919 by union pt Brumby and Frodingham UD (pt Brumby CP, pt Frodingham AP), pt Scunth. UD & CP1, and from pts Appleby AP, Ashby CP, Crosby CP, Flixborough AP.[21] Renamed 1937 as CP2.[257]

SEARBY CUM OWNBY
AP [Pts Lind] *LG* Seq 54. Civ bdry: 1887.[197] *Parl* Seq 5. *Eccl* Pec jurisd Dean & Chapter of Linc. (until 1846), Seq 63 thereafter.

SEDGEBROOK
AP [Pts Kestev] Orig chap in West Allington AP,[12] sep par by 1535. Incl chap East Allington (sep civ identity early, jointly rated with West Allington as 'Allington', 'East Allington' eccl severed 1872 to help cr West Allington with East Allington EP,[11] this par which had heretofore been eccl 'Sedgebrook with East Allington' thereafter 'Sedgebrook'). *LG* Winn. & Thr. Wap (until 1830s), Loved. Wap (from 1830s), Newk. PLU, RSD, Clayp. RD (1894—1931), W Kestev RD (1931—74). Addtl civ bdry alt: 1965 (exchanges pts with Bottesford AP, Leics).[113] *Parl* Seq 20. *Eccl* Under successive names and areas as above, Seq 23.

SEDGEBROOK WITH EAST ALLINGTON—see prev entry

SEMPRINGHAM
AP [Pts Kestev] Incl tp Birthorpe, chap Pointon (each a sep CP 1866,[13] neither sep eccl hence this par eccl 'Sempringham wth Pointon and Birthorpe' qv). *LG* Avel. Wap, Bourne PLU, RSD, RD. Abol civ 1931 to help cr Pointon and Sempringham CP.[19] *Parl* S'rn Dv (1832—67), South Dv (1867—85), S Kestev Dv (1885—1918), Rutl & Stamf. Dv (1918—48).

SEMPRINGHAM WITH POINTON AND BIRTHORPE
AP [Pts Kestev] Usual eccl spelling; for civ and civ sep tp and chap, see prev entry. *Eccl* Seq 6. *Eccl* bdry: 1912 (help cr Gosberton Clough EP).[164]

SEVEN ACRES
[Pts Lind] Ex-par place, sep CP 1858.[38] *LG* Hornc. Soke, Boston PLU (soon after 1836[84]—1906), RSD, Sibsey RD. Abol civ 1906 ent to Copping Syke CP.[39] *Parl* N'rn Dv (1832—67), Mid Dv (1867—85), N Kestev Dv (1885—1918).

SHUFF FEN
[Pts Holl] Ex-par place, sep CP 1858.[38] *LG* Skirb. Wap, Boston PLU (1862—1906), RSD, RD. Abol civ 1906 ent to Brothertoft CP.[39] *Parl* S'rn Dv (1832—67), South Dv (1867—85), Holl Dv (1885—1918).

SIBSEY
AP [Pts Lind] *LG* Seq 27. Civ bdry: 1880,[58] 1880,[154]

1936.[28] *Parl* Seq 12. *Eccl* Bolingbr. RDn (until 1866), N Holl 2 RDn (1866—1910), Holl (East) RDn (1910—61). Eccl bdry: 1886 (help cr Carrington with Frithville EP [Pts Lind, Pts Holl]).[61] Abol eccl 1961 to help cr Sibsey with Frithville EP.[57]

SIBSEY WITH FRITHVILLE
EP [Pts Lind] Cr 1961 by union Sibsey AP, pt Carrington with Frithville EP (Pts Lind, Pts Holl).[57] Holl (East) RDn.

SIMON WEIR
[Pts Holl] Ex-par place, sep CP 1858.[38] *LG* Kirton Wap, Boston PLU (1862—1906), RSD, RD. Abol civ 1906 ent to Kirton AP.[39] *Parl* S'rn Dv (1832—67), South Dv (1867—85), Holl Dv (1885—1918).

SIXHILLS
AP [Pts Lind] *LG* Seq 50. *Parl* Seq 11. *Eccl* Seq 59.

SKEGNESS
AP [Pts Lind] *LG* Candl. Wap, Spilsby PLU, RSD (1875—85), Skegness USD (1885—94), UD. Civ bdry: 1926.[3] *Parl* Seq 12. *Eccl* Seq 17. Eccl bdry: 1952.[258]

SKELLINGTHORPE
AP [Pts Kestev] *LG* Seq 11. Civ bdry: 1920 (loses pt to Linc. CB [assoc with Pts Lind] & CP),[67] 1959 (loses pt to Linc. CB [assoc with Pts Lind] & CP),[209] 1967 (loses pt to Linc. CB [assoc with Pts Lind] & CP).[89] *Parl* bdry: 1960.[210] *Eccl* Seq 22. Eccl bdry: 1964 (incl help cr Lincoln St George, Swallowbeck EP),[68] 1969 (cr Birchwood EP).[53]

SKENDLEBY
AP [Pts Lind] *LG* Seq 35. Civ bdry: 1888,[2] 1936.[28] *Parl* Seq 12. *Eccl* Seq 16.

SKIDBROOKE WITH SALTFLEETBY HAVEN
AP [Pts Lind] *LG* Seq 44. *Parl* Seq 1. *Eccl* Seq 47.

SKILLINGTON
AP [Pts Kestev] Incl chaps North Stoke, South Stoke,[259] each a sep par by 1535, united 1776 as 'Stoke'.[260] *LG* Seq 10. Addtl civ bdry alt: 1965 (exchanges pts with Buckminster AP, gains pt Sproxton AP, both Leics).[113] *Parl* Seq 21. *Eccl* Pec jurisd Dean & Chapter of Linc. (until 1846), Seq 7 thereafter.

SKINNAND
AP [Pts Kestev] *LG* Boothby Graff. Wap, Linc. PLU, RSD, Branst. RD. Abol civ 1931 ent to Navenby AP.[19] *Parl* S'rn Dv (1832—67), Mid Dv (1867—85), N Kestev Dv (1885—1918), Granth. Dv (1918—48). *Eccl* Longob. RDn (until 1884), Graffoe RDn (1884—*).

SKIRBECK
AP [Pts Holl] Incl in Kirton Wap hmlt Skirbeck Quarter (sep CP 1866,[13] sep EP 1912,[261] later called 'Boston St Thomas'). *LG* Pt Kirton Wap (Skirbeck Quarter, until 1866), Skirb. Wap (pt until 1866, ent from 1866), Boston PLU, RSD, RD. Addtl civ bdry alt: 1880,[154] 1900,[59] 1906 (incl gains Hall Hills CP, Pepper Gowt Plot CP).[39] Abol civ 1932 pt to Boston MB & AP, pt to Fishtoft AP.[60] *Parl* Pt Boston Parl Bor (1832—1918 [reduced pt 1885—1918]), pt S'rn Dv (1832—67), pt South Dv (1867—85), pt Holl Dv (1885—1918), Holl with Boton Dv (1918—48).

Eccl Seq 39. Addtl eccl bdry alt: 1874 (from pt fen allotment, cr Skirbeck Holy Trinity EP),[262] 1886 (help cr Carrington with Frithville EP [Pts Lind, Pts Holl]),[61] 1966.[148]

SKIRBECK HOLY TRINITY
EP [Pts Holl] Cr 1874 from Skirbeck AP (pt fen allotment).[262] N Holl 2 RDn (1874—1910), Holl (East) RDn (1910—*). Bdry: 1966.[148]

SKIRBECK QUARTER
[Pts Holl] Hmlt (Kirton Wap) in Skirbeck AP (o'wise Skirb. Wap), sep CP 1866,[13] sep EP 1912.[261] *LG* Boston PLU, RSD, RD. Abol civ 1932 ent to Boston MB & AP.[60] *Parl* S'rn Dv (1832—67), South Dv (1867—85), Holl Dv (1885—1948). *Eccl* Holl (East) RDn. Later called 'Boston St Thomas'.

NEW SLEAFORD
AP [Pts Kestev] Incl hmlt Holdingham (sep CP 1866[13]). *LG* Flax. Wap, Sleaf. PLU, New Sleaf. Bor, USD, Sleaf. UD. Addtl civ bdry alt: 1888,[191] 1908.[263] *Parl* Seq 17. *Eccl* Pec jurisd Sleaf. Prebend (until 1846), Seq 2 thereafter. Eccl bdry: 1928.[244]

OLD SLEAFORD
AP [Pts Kestev] Anc, 'Lafford'. *LG* Asw. Wap, Sleaf. PLU, New Sleaf. USD, Sleaf. UD. Civ bdry: 1888,[243] 1908.[263] *Parl* Seq 17. *Eccl* Pec jurisd Sleaf. prebend (until 1846), Seq 2 thereafter. Eccl bdry: 1928.[244]

SNARFORD
AP [Pts Lind] *LG* Seq 43. *Parl* Seq 14. *Eccl* Seq 73.

SNELLAND
AP [Pts Lind] *LG* Seq 52. *Parl* Seq 8. *Eccl* Seq 58.

SNITTERBY
AP [Pts Lind] Orig chap in Waddingham AP (qv for early union of Waddingham St Mary AP, Waddingham St Peter AP)[264] sep civ identity early, sep EP 1866.[265] *LG* Seq 24. *Parl* Seq 5. *Eccl* Manlake RDn (1846—84), Corr. RDn (1884—1910), Yarb. (South) RDn (1910—68), Yarb. RDn (1968—*).

SOMERBY
AP [Pts Kestev] Incl area Great Humby (civ severed from this par 1887 and united to Little Humby CP, the united area [incl addtl bdry alt] renamed 'Humby',[192] 'Great Humby' not sep eccl hence this par eccl 'Somerby with Great Humby', qv). *LG* Winn. & Thr. Wap, Granth. PLU, pt Granth. MB & USD (1879—94), Granth. RSD (ent 1875—79, pt 1879—94). Abol civ 1894 the pt in Granth. MB cr New Somerby CP, the remainder cr Old Somerby CP.[161] *Parl* Pt Granth. Parl Bor (1832—67), pt S'rn Dv (1832—67), South Dv (1867—85), S Kestev Dv (1885—1918).

SOMERBY
AP [Pts Lind] *LG* Seq 54. *Parl* N'rn Dv (1832—67), North Dv (1867—85), S Lind Dv (1885—1918), Louth Dv (1918—48), Gainsb. CC (1948—*). *Eccl* Yarb. RDn (until 1863), Yarb. 2 RDn (1863—1910), Yarb. (South) RDn (1910—68), W Wold RDn (1968—*).

NEW SOMERBY
CP [Pts Kestev] Cr 1894 from the pt of Somerby AP in Granth. MB.[161] *LG* Granth. PLU, MB. Abol 1909 ent to Grantham AP.[162]

OLD SOMERBY
CP [Pts Kestev] Cr 1894 from the pt of Somerby AP not in Granth. MB.[161] *LG* Granth. PLU, RD (1894—1931), W Kestev RD (1931—74). Bdry: 1930,[34] 1931 (incl help cr Londonthorpe and Harrowby Without CP).[19] *Parl* Rutl & Stamf. Dv/CC (1918—*).

SOMERBY WITH GREAT HUMBY
AP [Pts Kestev] Usual eccl spelling; for civ and civ sep area Great Humby, see 1st 'Somerby' above. *Eccl* Seq 26. Eccl bdry: 1910 (help cr Grantham St Anne EP).[167]

NORTH SOMERCOTES
AP [Pts Lind] *LG* Seq 44. *Parl* Seq 1. *Eccl* Seq 47.

SOUTH SOMERCOTES
AP [Pts Lind] *LG* Seq 44. *Parl* Seq 1. *Eccl* Seq 47.

SOMERSBY
AP [Pts Lind] *LG* Seq 39. Civ bdry: 1936 (gains Ashby Puerorum AP, Bag Enderby AP).[28] *Parl* N'rn Dv (1832—67), Mid Dv (1867—85), N Lind Dv (1885—1918), Hornc. Dv/CC (1918—*). *Eccl* Seq 34.

SOTBY
AP [Pts Lind] *LG* Seq 51. *Parl* Seq 9. *Eccl* Seq 56.

SOUTH OF THE WITHAM
[Pts Holl] Ex-par place, sep CP 1858,[38] eccl abol 1881 to help cr Wildmore EP (Pts Lind, Pts Kestev, Pts Holl).[27] *LG* Kirton Wap, Boston PLU (1862—1906), RSD, RD. Abol civ 1906 ent to Kirton AP.[39] *Parl* S'rn Dv (1832—67), South Dv (1867—85), N Kestev Dv (1885—1918).

SOUTHORPE
[Pts Lind] Ex-par place, sep CP 1858.[38] *LG* Corr. Wap, Gainsb. PLU, RSD, RD. Abol 1936 ent to Northorpe AP.[28] *Parl* N'rn Dv (1832—67), North Dv (1867—85), W Lind Dv (1885—1918), Gainsb. Dv (1918—48).

SPALDING
AP [Pts Holl] Incl chap Cowbit (sep civ identity early, church consecr 1486[121]; sometimes early 'Peakhill'). *LG* Elloe Wap, Spald. PLU, USD (ent 1875—87, pt 1887—88, ent 1888—94), pt Spald. RSD (1887—88), Spald. UD. Addtl civ bdry alt: 1883,[31] 1887,[122] 1932.[123] *Parl* Spald. Parl Bor (1328, 1337 only), Seq 16 thereafter. *Eccl* Seq 40. Addtl eccl bdry alt: 1874 (help cr Spalding St John the Baptist EP),[242] 1877 (help cr Spalding St Paul EP),[44] 1918,[124] 1948.[94]

SPALDING ST JOHN THE BAPTIST
EP [Pts Holl] Cr 1874 from Spalding AP, Pinchbeck AP.[242] S Holl 1 RDn (1874—84), W Elloe RDn (1884—1910), Elloe (West) RDn (1910—*).

SPALDING ST PAUL
EP [Pts Holl] Cr 1877 from Spalding AP, Pinchbeck AP, Surfleet AP.[109] S Holl 1 RDn (1877—84), W Elloe RDn (1884—1910), Elloe (West) RDn (1910—*). Bdry: 1948.[94]

SPANBY
AP [Pts Kestev] Chap in Swaton AP, sep civ identity early, sep EP 1681 (1st registers[266]) or later. *LG* Avel. Wap, Sleaf. PLU, RSD, RD. Abol civ 1931 ent to Threckingham AP.[19] *Parl* S'rn Dv (1832—67), South Dv (1867—85), N Kestev Dv (1885—

1918), Granth. Dv (1918—48). *Eccl* Avel. RDn (until 1866), Avel. 1 RDn (1866—1910), Avel. RDn (1910—68), Avel. with Ness & Stamf. RDn (1968—73). Abol eccl 1973 to help cr Swaton with Spanby EP.[178]

SPILSBY

[Pts Lind] Chap in Hundleby AP, sep civ identity early, sep EP 1772,[6] eccl sometimes 'Spilsby with Eresby'. *LG* Seq 29. Civ bdry: 1880.[194] *Parl* Seq 12. *Eccl* Bolingbr. RDn (until 1866), Hill 2 RDn (1866—1910), Hill (South) RDn (1910—68), Bolingbr. RDn (1968—*). Eccl bdry: 1885 (help cr Eastville with Midville EP).[48]

SPITTLEGATE

[Pts Kestev] Tp in Grantham AP, sep CP 1866,[13] sep EP 1842,[111] eccl refounded 1844,[166] later called 'Grantham St John'. *LG* Granth. Soke (until 1830s), Winn. & Thr. Wap (from 1830s), Granth. PLU, RSD (ent 1875—79, pt 1879—94), pt Granth. MB & USD (1879—94). Abol civ 1894 the pt in the MB cr Spittlegate Within CP, the remainder to be Spittlegate Without CP.[161] *Parl* S'rn Dv (1832—67), South Dv (1867—85), S Kestev Dv (1885—1918). *Eccl* Granth. RDn (1842—66), Granth. 1 RDn (1866—1910), N Granth. RDn (1910—68), Granth. RDn (1968—*). Eccl bdry: 1910 (help cr Grantham St Anne EP).[167]

SPITTLEGATE WITHIN

CP [Pts Kestev] Cr 1894 from the pt of Spittlegate CP in Granth. MB.[161] *LG* Granth. PLU, MB. Abol 1909 ent to Grantham AP.[162]

SPITTLEGATE WITHOUT

CP [Pts Kestev] Cr 1894 from the pt of Spittlegate CP not in Granth. MB.[161] *LG* Granth. PLU, RD. Bdry: 1930.[34] Abol 1931 to help cr Londonthorpe and Harrowby Without CP.[19] *Parl* Pt Rutl & Stamf. Dv (main pt, 1918—48), pt Granth. Dv (detached pt surrounded by Granth. MB, 1918—48).

SPRIDLINGTON

AP [Pts Lind] *LG* Seq 26. *Parl* Seq 6. *Eccl* Seq 68.

SPRINGTHORPE

AP [Pts Lind] *LG* Seq 36. *Parl* Seq 6. *Eccl* Seq 69.

STAINBY

AP [Pts Kestev] *LG* Belt. Wap, Granth. PLU, RSD, RD. Abol civ 1931 to help cr Gunby and Stainby CP.[19] *Parl* S'rn Dv (1832—67), South Dv (1867—85), S Kestev Dv (1885—1918), Rutl & Stamf. Dv (1918—48). *Eccl* Belt. RDn. Abol eccl 1773 to help cr Stainby with Gunby EP.[174]

STAINBY WITH GUNBY

EP [Pts Kestev] Cr 1773 by union Stainby AP, Gunby AP.[174] Belt. RDn (1773—1866), Belt. 1 RDn (1866—84), Belt. RDn (1884—*).

STAINFIELD

AP [Pts Lind] Chap in Hacconby AP, sep civ identity early, sep EP in 1680 or after.[176] *LG* Seq 52. *Parl* Seq 8. *Eccl* Wragg. RDn (cr—1968), Lawres RDn (1968—*).

MARKET STAINTON

AP [Pts Lind] *LG* Seq 37. *Parl* Seq 9. *Eccl* Gart. RDn (until 1866), Hornc. RDn (1866—1910), Wragg. RDn (1910—68), Hornc. RDn (1968—*).

STAINTON BY LANGWORTH

AP [Pts Lind] Incl hmlt Newball (sep CP 1866[13]). *LG* Seq 52. *Parl* Seq 8. *Eccl* Seq 57.

STAINTON LE VALE

AP [Pts Lind] *LG* Seq 48. Civ bdry: 1858 (gains ex-par place Orford).[237] *Parl* Seq 2. *Eccl* Seq 52.

STALLINGBOROUGH

AP [Pts Lind] *LG* Yarb. Wap, Grimsby PLU, RSD, RD. Transf 1974 to Humb.[10] *Parl* Seq 4. *Eccl* Yarb. RDn (until 1863), Yarb. 2 RDn (1863—84), Grimsby 2 RDn (1884—1910), Grimsby (North) RDn (1910—68), Hav. RDn (1968—*).

STAMFORD

[Pts Kestev] The following have 'Stamford' in their names. Insofar as any existed at a given time: *LG* Stamf. Bor, PLU, USD. *Parl* Stamf. Parl Bor (1295—1306 irregularly, 1322, 1467—1885), S Kestev Dv (1918—*). *Eccl* Stamf. RDn (until 1968), Avel. & Ness with Stamf. RDn (1968—*). Details of early pars and early unions from various sources.[267]

CP1—STAMFORD—Cr 1930 by union AP1, AP5, AP6, AP7, AP9, Stamford Baron St Martin AP.[34]

AP1—STAMFORD ALL SAINTS—Civ bdry: 1883.[31] Abol civ 1930 to help cr CP1.[34] Abol eccl 1547 to help cr EP1.

EP1—STAMFORD ALL SAINTS WITH ST PETER—Cr 1547 by union AP1, AP12.

AP2—STAMFORD HOLY TRINITY—Early decayed

AP3—STAMFORD ST ANDREW—Abol 1547 to help cr EP5.

AP4—STAMFORD ST CLEMENT—Abol 1547 to help cr EP3.

AP5—STAMFORD ST GEORGE—Civ bdry: 1883.[31] Abol civ 1930 to help cr CP1.[34] Abol eccl 1547 to help cr EP2.

EP2—STAMFORD ST GEORGE WITH ST PAUL—Cr 1547 by union AP5, AP11. Bdry: 1971.[268]

AP6—STAMFORD ST JOHN—Civ bdry: 1883.[31] Abol civ 1930 to help cr CP1.[34] *Eccl* As 'Stamford St John the Baptist', abol 1547 to help cr EP3.

—STAMFORD ST JOHN THE BAPTIST—see AP6

EP3—STAMFORD ST JOHN WITH ST CLEMENT—Cr 1547 by union AP6, AP4. Bdry: 1971.[268]

AP7—STAMFORD ST MARY—Abol civ 1930 to help cr CP1.[34] Abol eccl 1971 to help cr EP4.[268]

EP4—STAMFORD ST MARY AND ST MICHAEL—Cr 1971 by union AP7, pt EP5.[268]

AP8—STAMFORD ST MARY BENNIWERK—Early decayed

AP9—STAMFORD ST MICHAEL—Civ bdry: 1883.[31] Abol civ 1930 to help cr CP1.[34] Abol eccl 1547 to help cr EP5.

AP10—STAMFORD ST MICHAEL CORNSTALL—Early decayed

EP5—STAMFORD ST MICHAEL WITH ST ANDREW AND ST STEPHEN—Cr 1547 by union AP9, AP3, AP13. Abol 1971 pt to help cr EP4, pt to EP3, pt to EP2.[268]

AP11—STAMFORD ST PAUL—Abol 1547 to help cr EP2.

AP12—STAMFORD ST PETER—Abol 1547 to help cr

EP1.

AP13—STAMFORD ST STEPHEN—Abol 1547 to help cr EP5.

AP14—STAMFORD ST THOMAS—Early decayed

STAMFORD BARON ST MARTIN

AP In Northants (Nassaborough Hd; see entry in Northants for incl of AP/hmlt Wothorpe), pt in Stamf. Par Bor (o'wise ent Lincs, from 1832), pt in Stamf. MB (o'wise ent Lincs, from 1835), the pt in the MB made 1889 'Stamford Baron St Martin' par in Lincs Pts Kestev while the pt in Soke Peterb Adm Co cr St Martin Without CP in that co so that this par ent Lincs Pts Kestev thereafter.[102] LG Stamf. PLU, MB. Abol civ 1930 to help cr Stamford CP.[34] Parl Rutl & Stamf. Dv (1918—48). Eccl See entry in Northants.

STANE

AP [Pts Lind] Calc. Wap, Calc. RDn, united 1660 with Mablethorpe St Mary AP, the union civ 'Mablethorpe', eccl 'Mablethorpe with Stane'.[228]

STAPLEFORD

AP [Pts Kestev] LG Seq 12. Civ bdry: 1884 (gains the pt of Flawford CP [Notts, Lincs Pts Kestev] in Lincs).[150] Parl Seq 15. Eccl Seq 22.

GREAT STEEPING

AP [Pts Lind] LG Seq 35. Parl Seq 12. Eccl Candl. RDn (until 1866), Candl. 2 RDn (1866—1910), Hill (South) RDn (1910—68), Bolingbr. RDn (1968—*).

LITTLE STEEPING

AP [Pts Lind] LG Seq 29. Civ bdry: 1888.[2] Parl Seq 12. Eccl Seq 10.

STENIGOT

AP [Pts Lind] LG Seq 38. Parl Seq 10. Eccl Seq 21.

STEWTON

AP [Pts Lind] LG Seq 44. Parl Seq 1. Eccl Seq 49.

STICKFORD

AP [Pts Lind] LG Seq 29. Civ bdry: 1880.[194] Parl Seq 12. Eccl Seq 9.

STICKNEY

AP [Pts Lind] LG Seq 29. Parl Seq 12. Eccl Seq 9.

STIXWOULD

AP [Pts Lind] LG Seq 37. Civ bdry: 1936.[28] Parl Seq 9. Eccl Seq 20.

EAST STOCKWITH

[Pts Lind] Tp in Gainsborough AP, sep CP 1866,[13] eccl severed 1846 to help cr East Stockwith with Walkerwith EP,[155] qv below, the EP latter called 'East Stockwith'. LG Seq 36. Parl Seq 6.

EAST STOCKWITH WITH WALKERWITH

EP [Pts Lind] Cr 1846 by union tp East Stockwith, tp Walkerwith, each in Gainsborough AP,[155] later called 'East Stockwith'. Corr. RDn. Eccl bdry: 1931 (gains ex-par Greenhill and Redhill).[112]

STOKE

[Pts Kestev] Union 1776 of North Stoke AP [St Andrew], South Stoke AP [St Mary],[260] both orig chaps in Skillington AP,[259] each a sep par by 1535. After union, par consists of 3 tps of North Stoke, South Stoke, Easton (each a sep CP 1866[13] so that after 1866 'Stoke' has no sep civ identity, none sep eccl hence this par eccl 'North and South Stoke with Easton', qv). LG Granth. Soke (until 1830s), Winn.

& Thr. Wap (1830s—66). Parl S'rn Dv (1832—67).

NORTH STOKE

AP [Pts Kestev] Orig chap in Skillington AP,[259] sep AP by 1535, united 1776 with South Stoke AP (qv for orig status) to cr 'Stoke',[260] and thereafter a tp in that par (eccl, 'North and South Stoke with Easton'), 'North Stoke' a sep CP 1866.[13] LG Granth. Soke (until 1830s), Winn. & Thr. Wap (from 1830s), Granth. PLU, RSD, RD. Abol 1931 to help cr Stoke Rochford CP.[19] Parl S'rn Dv (1832—67), South Dv (1867—85), S Kestev Dv (1885—1918), Rutl & Stamf. Dv (1918—48).

NORTH AND SOUTH STOKE WITH EASTON

EP [Pts Kestev] Usual eccl spelling for union 1776 of North Stoke AP, South Stoke AP (qv each for earlier status)[260]; for civ see 'Stoke'. Eccl Belt. RDn (1776—1866), Belt. 1 RDn (1866—73), Belt. RDn (1873—*).

SOUTH STOKE

AP [Pts Kestev] Orig chap in Skillington AP,[259] sep AP by 1535, united 1776 with North Stoke (qv for orig status) to cr 'Stoke',[260] and thereafter a tp in that par (eccl, 'North and South Stoke with Easton'), 'South Stoke' a sep CP 1866.[13] Organisation as for North Stoke.

STOKE ROCHFORD

CP [Pts Kestev] Cr 1931 by union North Stoke CP, South Stoke CP, pt Wyville cum Hungerton AP.[19] LG W Kestev RD. Bdry: 1965 (gains pt Spoxton AP, Leics).[113] Parl Rutl & Stamf. CC (1948—*).

STOW

AP [Pts Lind] Incl hmlt Bransby, tp Sturton (united for support of poor as 'Sturton by Stow', sometimes early 'Bransby and Sturton', sep CP 1866 as 'Sturton by Stow'[13]), hmlt Normanby, tp (main pt of par) Stow (united for support of poor as 'Stow', sometimes early 'Normanby and Stow'). Usual civ spelling; for eccl see 'Stow in Lindsey'. LG Seq 49. Addtl civ bdry alt: 1936 (gains Coates AP).[28] Parl Seq 14.

STOW IN LINDSEY

AP [Pts Lind] Usual eccl spelling; for civ and civ sep tp, see prev entry. Eccl Pec jurisd Prebend Stow in Lind (until 1846), Seq 75 thereafter.

STOWE

AP [Pts Kestev] LG Ness Wap, Stamf. PLU, RSD, Uff. RD. Abol civ 1931 pt to help cr Barholm and Stowe CP, pt to Langtoft AP, pt to Market Deeping AP.[19] Parl S'rn Dv (1832—67), South Dv (1867—85), S Kestev Dv (1885—1918), Rutl & Stamf. Dv (1918—48). Eccl Ness RDn. Abol eccl 1772 to help cr Barholm with Stowe EP.[32]

STRAGGLETHORPE

Chap in Beckingham AP, sep civ identity early, burial rights 1349 but still remained a chap,[40] eccl severed 1931 to help cr Brant Broughton with Stragglethorpe EP.[42] LG Loved. Wap, Newk. PLU, RSD, Clayp. RD. Abol civ 1931 to help cr Brant Broughton and Stragglethorpe CP.[19] Parl S'rn Dv (1832—67), South Dv (1867—85), S Kestev Dv (1885—1918), Granth. Dv (1918—48).

STROXTON

AP [Pts Kestev] LG Winn. & Thr. Wap, Granth.PLU,

RSD, RD. Abol civ 1931 to help cr Little Ponton and Stroxton CP.[19] *Parl* S'rn Dv (1832—67), South Dv (1867—85), S Kestev Dv (1885—1918), Rutl & Stamf. Dv (1918—48). *Eccl* Seq 26.

STRUBBY WITH WOODTHORPE
AP [Pts Lind] *LG* Seq 33. *Parl* Seq 13. *Eccl* Pec jurisd Dean & Chapter of Linc. (until 1846), Seq 11 thereafter.

STUBTON
AP [Pts Kestev] *LG* Seq 19. *Parl* Seq 20. *Eccl* Loved. RDn. Abol eccl 1932 to help cr Stubton with Fenton EP.[41]

STUBTON
EP [Pts Kestev] Remainder of Stubton with Fenton EP after area Fenton severed 1950 to help cr Beckingham with Fenton EP.[43] Loved. RDn.

STUBTON WITH FENTON
EP [Pts Kestev] Cr 1932 by union Stubton AP, area Fenton in Beckingham with Fenton EP.[41] Loved. RDn. Abol 1950, area Fenton severed to help cr Beckingham with Fenton EP, the remainder to be 'Stubton'.[43]

GREAT STURTON
AP [Pts Lind] *LG* Seq 37. *Parl* Seq 9. Eccl Gart. RDn (until 1855), Hornc. RDn (1855—*).

STURTON BY STOW
[Pts Lind] Tp for poor law purposes (comprised of tp Sturton, hmlt Bransby, the area sometimes called 'Bransby and Sturton'), sep CP 1866 as 'Sturton by Stow' from Stow AP.[13] *LG* Seq 49. *Parl* Seq 14.

SUDBROOKE
AP [Pts Lind] *LG* Seq 43. *Parl* Seq 14. *Eccl* Seq 72.

SURFLEET
AP [Pts Holl] *LG* Seq 4. Civ bdry: 1883,[31] 1925,[163] 1932.[123] *Parl* Seq 16. *Eccl* Seq 37. Eccl bdry: 1877 (help cr Spalding St Paul EP),[109] 1912 (help cr Gosberton Clough EP).[164]

SUTTERBY
AP [Pts Lind] Candl. Wap, Spilsby PLU, RSD, RD. Abol civ 1936 ent to Langton by Spilsby AP.[28] *Parl* N'rn Dv (1832—67), Mid Dv (1867—85), S Lind Dv (1885—1918), Hornc. Dv (1918—48). *Eccl* Candl. RDn (until 1866), Hill 2 RDn (1866—1910), Hill (South) RDn (1910—68), Bolingbr. RDn (1968—*).

SUTTERTON
AP [Pts Holl] *LG* Seq 3. Civ bdry: 1880 (help cr Amber Hill CP),[9] 1932.[77] *Parl* Seq 16. *Eccl* Seq 38. Eccl bdry: 1812 (fen allotment severed to help cr Holland Fen EP,[6] refounded 1865[7]).

LITTLE SUTTON
CP [Pts Holl] Cr 1894 from the pt of Sutton St Mary AP not in a UD.[102] *LG* Holb. PLU, E Elloe RD. *Parl* Holl with Boston Dv/CC (1918—*).

LONG SUTTON
AP [Pts Holl] Name declared to be correct 1932, rather than 'Long Sutton or Sutton St Mary'.[123] *LG* E Elloe RD. *Parl* Holl with Boston CC (1948—*).

LONG SUTTON OR SUTTON ST MARY
CP [Pts Holl] Cr 1894 from the pt of Sutton St Mary AP in Long Sutton UD.[102] *LG* Holb. PLU, Long Sutton UD. Name declared 1932 to be 'Long Sutton'.[123] *Parl* Holl with Boston Dv (1918—48).

SUTTON BRIDGE
[Pts Holl] Area in Sutton St Mary (sometimes 'Long Sutton') AP, sep EP 1843,[269] sep CP 1894 from the pt of Sutton St Mary AP in Sutton Bridge UD.[102] *LG* Holb. PLU, Sutton Bridge UD (1894—1932), E Elloe RD (1932—74). Civ bdry: 1932,[123] 1954 (gains Central Wingland CP),[270] 1957 (exchanges pts with Terrington St Clement AP, Norfolk).[271] *Parl* Holl with Boston Dv/CC (1918—*). *Eccl* Holl RDn (1843—63), S Holl 2 RDn (1863—84), E Elloe RDn (1884—1910), Elloe (East) RDn (1910—*).

SUTTON IN THE MARSH
AP [Pts Lind] Usual civ spelling; for eccl see following entry. *LG* Calc. Wap, Spilsby PLU, RSD, RD (1894—1925), Mableth. & Sutton UD (1925—74). *Parl* Seq 12.

SUTTON LE MARSH
AP [Pts Lind] Usual eccl spelling; for civ see prev entry. *Eccl* Seq 11.

SUTTON ST EDMUND
[Pts Holl] Chap in Sutton St Mary AP (sometimes 'Long Sutton'), sep CP 1866,[13] sep EP 1744.[6] *LG* Seq 1. Civ bdry: 1884,[160] 1934 (exchanges pts with Parson Drove CP, Isle of Ely).[272] *Parl* Seq 16. *Eccl* Holl RDn (1744—1863), S Holl 2 RDn (1863—84), E Elloe RDn (1884—1910), Elloe (East) RDn (1910—*).

SUTTON ST JAMES
[Pts Holl] Chap in Sutton St Mary AP (sometimes 'Long Sutton'), sep CP 1866,[13] sep EP 1744.[6] *LG* Seq 1. Civ bdry: 1884.[160] *Parl* Seq 16. *Eccl* Holl RDn (1744—1863), S Holl 2 RDn (1863—84), E Elloe RDn (1884—1910), Elloe (East) RDn (1910—*).

SUTTON ST MARY
AP [Pts Holl] Sometimes 'Long Sutton'. Incl chap Lutton (sep CP 1866,[13] sep EP 1882 as 'Sutton St Nicholas'[227]), chaps Sutton St Edmund, Sutton St James (each a sep CP 1866,[13] each a sep EP 1744[6]). *LG* Elloe Wap, Holb. PLU, pt Long Sutton USD, pt Sutton Bridge USD, pt Holb. RSD. Addtl civ bdry alt: 1884.[160] Abol civ 1894 the pt in Long Sutton UD cr Long Sutton or Sutton St Mary CP, the pt in Sutton Bridge UD cr Sutton Bridge CP, the remainder cr Little Sutton CP.[102] *Parl* S'rn Dv (1832—67), South Dv (1867—85), Holl Dv (1885—1918). *Eccl* Seq 41. Addtl eccl bdry alt: 1843 (cr Sutton Bridge EP).[269]

SUTTON ST NICHOLAS
EP [Pts Holl] Chap in Sutton St Mary (sometimes 'Long Sutton') AP, sep EP 1882,[227] sep CP 1866 as 'Lutton',[13] qv. S Holl 2 RDn (1882—84), E Elloe RDn (1882—1910), Elloe (East) RDn (1910—*).

SWABY
AP [Pts Lind] *LG* Seq 33. Civ bdry: 1888.[44] *Parl* Seq 13. *Eccl* Seq 12.

SWALLOW
AP [Pts Lind] *LG* Seq 30. Civ bdry: 1936 (gains Cuxwold AP).[28] *Parl* Seq 5. *Eccl* Seq 29.

SWARBY
AP [Pts Kestev] *LG* Asw. Wap, Sleaf. PLU, RSD, RD. Abol civ 1931 to help cr Aswarby and Swarby CP.[19] *Parl* S'rn Dv (1832—67), South Dv (1867—

85), N Kestev Dv (1885—1918), Granth. Dv (1918—48). *Eccl* Asw. with Laff. RDn. Abol eccl 1850 to help cr Aswarby with Swarby EP.[29]

SWATON

AP [Pts Kestev] Incl chap Spanby (sep civ identity early, sep EP 1681 [1st registers[266]] or later). *LG* Seq 8. *Parl* Seq 18. *Eccl* Avel. RDn (until 1866), Avel. 1 RDn (1866—1910), Avel. RDn (1910—68), Avel. with Ness & Stamf. RDn (1968—73). Abol eccl 1973 to help cr Swaton with Spanby EP.[178]

SWATON WTH SPANBY

EP [Pts Kestev] Cr 1973 by union Swaton AP, Spanby EP.[178] Avel. with Ness & Stamf. RDn.

SWAYFIELD

AP [Pts Kestev] *LG* Seq 9. *Parl* Seq 21. *Eccl* Belt. RDn (until 1866), Belt. 1 RDn (1866—84), Belt. RDn (1884—*).

SWINDERBY

AP [Pts Kestev] *LG* Seq 12. *Parl* Seq 15. *Eccl* Seq 22.

SWINESHEAD

AP [Pts Holl] Incl undivided pts Lands Common to Swineshead and Wigtoft (abol 1932 ent to Wigtoft AP[77]). *LG* Seq 3. Addtl civ bdry alt: 1880,[240] 1891 (gains Great Brand End Plot CP, Little Brand End Plot CP, Gibbett Hills CP, Mown Rakes CP, Royalty Farm CP),[73] 1932.[77] *Parl* Seq 19. *Eccl* Seq 38. Eccl bdry: 1828 (cr Chapel Hill EP).[6]

SWINETHORPE

[Pts Kestev] Ex-par place, sep CP 1858.[38] *LG* Boothby Graff. Wap, Linc. PLU, RSD, Branst. RD. Abol civ 1931 to help cr Eagle and Swinthorpe CP.[19] *Parl* S'rn Dv (1832—67), Mid Dv (1867—85), N Kestev Dv (1885—1918), Granth. Dv (1918—48).

SWINHOPE

AP [Pts Lind] *LG* Seq 30. *Parl* Seq 2. *Eccl* Grimsby RDn (until 1866), Grimsby 1 RDn (1866—1910), Walshcr. (East) RDn (1910—68), Hav. RDn (1968—*).

SWINSTEAD

AP [Pts Kestev] *LG* Seq 9. *Parl* Seq 21. *Eccl* Seq 8.

SYSTON

AP [Pts Kestev] *LG* Seq 24. *Parl* Seq 20. *Eccl* Seq 24.

TALLINGTON

AP [Pts Kestev] *LG* Seq 21. Civ bdry: 1931.[19] *Parl* Seq 21. *Eccl* Seq 51.

TATHWELL

AP [Pts Lind] *LG* Seq 44. *Parl* Seq 1. *Eccl* Seq 49.

TATTERSHALL

AP [Pts Lind] Orig Collegiate. Incl tp Tattershall Thorpe (sep CP 1866[13]). *LG* Seq 37. Addtl civ bdry alt: 1880 (help cr Wildmore CP),[26] 1887.[130] *Parl* Seq 12. *Eccl* Seq 43. Eccl bdry: 1881 (help cr Wildmore EP [Pts Lind, Pts Kestev, Pts Holl]).[27]

TATTERSHALL THORPE

[Pts Lind] Tp in Tattershall AP, sep CP 1866.[13] *LG* Seq 37. Bdry: 1883,[31] 1887.[130] *Parl* Seq 12.

TEALBY

AP [Pts Lind] *LG* Seq 48. *Parl* Seq 2. *Eccl* Seq 55.

TEMPLE BRUER

EP [Pts Kestev] Cr 1879 by union ex-par places of Temple Bruer, Temple Grange.[273] Longob. RDn (1879—1968), Graff. RDn (1968—*).

TEMPLE BRUER WITH TEMPLE HIGH GRANGE

[Pts Kestev] Union for poor law purposes of ex-par places Temple Bruer, Temple Grange (for eccl see prev entry), sep CP 1858.[38] *LG* Pt Flax. Wap, pt Langoe Wap, Sleaf. PLU (1861—1930), RSD, RD (1894—1931), E Kestev RD (1931—74). *Parl* S'rn Dv (1832—67), pt South Dv, pt Mid Dv (1867—85), N Kestev Dv (1885—1918), Granth. Dv/CC (1918—*).

TETFORD

AP [Pts Lind] *LG* Seq 39. *Parl* Seq 12. *Eccl* Hill RDn (until 1866), Hill 1 RDn (1866—1910), Hill (North) RDn (1910—66). Abol eccl 1966 to help cr Tetford and Salmonby EP.[252]

TETFORD AND SALMONBY

EP [Pts Lind] Cr 1966 by union Tetford AP, Salmonby AP.[252] Hill (North) RDn (1966—68), Bolingbr. RDn (1968—*).

TETNEY

AP [Pts Lind] *LG* Seq 32. *Parl* Seq 1. *Eccl* Seq 32.

THEDDLETHORPE

EP [Pts Lind] Cr 1973 by union Theddlethorpe All Saints AP, Theddlethorpe St Helen with Mablethorpe St Peter EP (by then called 'Theddlethorpe St Helen').[253] Louthesk RDn.

THEDDLETHORPE ALL SAINTS

AP [Pts Lind] *LG* Seq 33. Civ bdry: 1883,[31] 1888.[182] *Parl* Seq 10. *Eccl* Calc. RDn (until 1866), Calc. 1 RDn (1866—1910), Louthesk (East) RDn (1910—68), Louthesk RDn (1968—73). Abol eccl 1973 to help cr Theddlethorpe EP.[253]

THEDDLETHORPE ST HELEN

AP [Pts Lind] *LG* Seq 33. Civ bdry: 1883,[31] 1888.[182] *Parl* Seq 10. *Eccl* Calc. RDn. Abol eccl 1745 to help cr Theddlethorpe St Helen with Mablethorpe St Peter EP.[87]

THEDDLETHORPE ST HELEN WITH MABLE- THORPE ST PETER

EP [Pts Lind] Cr 1745 by union Theddlethorpe St Helen AP, Mablethorpe St Peter (lost into the sea) AP.[87] Calc. RDn (1745—1866), Calc. 1 RDn (1866—1910), Louthesk (East) RDn (1910—68), Louthesk RDn (1968—73). Later called 'Theddlethorpe St Helen' and as such abol eccl 1973 to help cr Theddlethorpe EP.[253]

THIMBLEBY

AP [Pts Lind] *LG* Seq 42. Civ bdry: 1880 (help cr Wildmore CP),[26] 1887.[130] *Parl* Seq 12. *Eccl* Seq 18. Eccl bdry: 1850 (help cr Langton St Andrew (otherwise Woodhall Spa) EP),[204] 1881 (help cr Wildmore EP [Pts Lind, Pts Kestev, Pts Holl]),[27] 1913.[126]

THONOCK

CP [Pts Lind] Cr 1895 from the pt of Gainsborough AP not in Gainsb. UD.[156] *LG* Gainsb. PLU, RD. *Parl* Gainsb. Dv/CC (1918—*).

NORTH THORESBY

AP [Pts Lind] *LG* Seq 32. *Parl* Seq 1. *Eccl* Grimsby RDn (until 1863), Louthesk & Ludb. 1 RDn (1863—1910), Ludb. RDn (1910—68), Hav. RDn (1968—*).

SOUTH THORESBY

AP [Pts Lind] *LG* Seq 33. *Parl* Seq 13. *Eccl* Seq 12.

THORESWAY
AP [Pts Lind] *LG* Seq 48. Civ bdry: 1936 (gains Croxby AP).[28] *Parl* Seq 2. *Eccl* Seq 52.

THORGANBY
AP [Pts Lind] *LG* Seq 48. *Parl* Seq 2. *Eccl* Walshcr. RDn (until 1866), Walshcr. 1 RDn (1866—73), Walshcr. RDn (1873—1910), Walshcr. (East) RDn (1910—68), Hav. RDn (1968—*).

THORNTON
AP [Pts Lind] *LG* Seq 37. Civ bdry: 1887,[130] 1936.[28] *Parl* Seq 12. *Eccl* Hornc. RDn (until 1866), Gart. RDn (1866—84), Hornc. RDn (1884—*). Eccl bdry: 1850 (help cr Langton St Andrew (otherwise Woodhall Spa) EP),[204] 1913.[126]

THORNTON CURTIS
AP [Pts Lind] *LG* Seq 55. Transf 1974 to Humb.[10] *Parl* Seq 3. *Eccl* Seq 60.

THORNTON LE FEN
[Pts Lind] Area cr from Wildmore Fen, parochial chap 1812,[31] sep CP 1866,[13] pt eccl severed 1881 to help cr Wildmore EP (Pts Lind, Pts Kestev, Pts Holl),[27] the remainder eccl abol 1881 to help cr Carrington with Frithville EP (Pts Lind, Pts Holl).[61] *LG* Seq 41. Civ bdry: 1880 (help cr Wildmore CP),[26] 1880.[114] *Parl* Seq 12.

THORNTON LE MOOR
AP [Pts Lind] *LG* Walshcr. Wap, Caist. PLU, RSD, RD. Abol civ 1936 to help cr Owersby CP.[28] *Parl* N'rn Dv (1832—67), North Dv (1867—85), E Lind Dv (1885—1918), Louth Dv (1918—48). *Eccl* Seq 54.

THORPE IN THE FALLOWS
AP [Pts Lind] Sometimes 'West Thorpe'. *LG* Seq 43. *Parl* Seq 14. *Eccl* Lawres RDn. Abol eccl prob 17th—early 18th cent to help cr Aisthorpe with Thorpe in the Fallows EP.[5]

THORPE ON THE HILL
AP [Pts Kestev] *LG* Seq 11. Civ bdry: 1931 (gains Morton CP).[19] *Parl* Seq 15. *Eccl* Seq 22.

THORPE ST PETER
AP [Pts Lind] *LG* Seq 29. Civ bdry: 1880,[179] 1888.[2] *Parl* Seq 12. *Eccl* Bolingbr. RDn (until 1884), Candl. 1 RDn (1884—1910), Candl. RDn (1910—68), Calc. & Candl. RDn (1968—*).

THORPE TILNEY
[Pts Kestev] Tp in Timberland AP, sep CP 1866.[13] *LG* Longoe Wap, Sleaf. PLU, RSD, RD. Abol 1931 ent to Timberland AP.[19] *Parl* S'rn Dv (1832—67), Mid Dv (1867—85), N Kestev Dv (1885—1918), Granth. Dv (1918—48).

THRECKINGHAM
AP [Pts Kestev] *LG* Seq 8. Civ bdry: 1931 (gains Spanby AP).[19] *Parl* Seq 18. *Eccl* Seq 4.

THURLBY
AP [Pts Kestev] *LG* Boothby Graff. Wap, Bourne PLU, RSD, RD (1894—1931), S Kestev RD (1931—74). *Parl* S'rn Dv (1832—67), Mid Dv (1867—85), S Kestev Dv (1885—1918), Rutl & Stamf. Dv/CC (1918—*). *Eccl* Sometimes as 'Thurlby by Bourne', pec jurisd Dean & Chapter of Linc. (until 1846), Seq 22 thereafter.

THURLBY
AP [Pts Kestev] *LG* Ness Wap, Newk. PLU, RSD,

Clayp. RD (1894—1931), N Kestev RD (1931—74). *Parl* Seq 17. *Eccl* Seq 51.

TIMBERLAND
AP [Pts Kestev] Incl tp Martin (sep CP 1866,[13] sep EP 1882[231]), tp Thorpe Tilney (sep CP 1866[13]). *LG* Seq 17. Addtl civ bdry alt: 1931 (gains Thorpe Tilney CP).[19] *Parl* Seq 15. *Eccl* Seq 45.

TOFT AND LOUND
[Pts Kestev] Tp in Witham on the Hill AP, sep CP 1866.[13] *LG* Belt. Wap, Bourne PLU, RSD, RD. Abol civ 1931 to help cr Toft with Lound and Manthorpe CP.[19] *Parl* S'rn Dv (1832—67), South Dv (1867—85), S Kestev Dv (1885—1918), Rutl & Stamf. Dv (1918—48).

TOFT NEWTON
CP [Pts Lind] Cr 1936 by union Newton by Toft AP, Toft next Newton AP.[28] *LG* Caist. RD. *Parl* Gainsb. CC (1948—*).

TOFT NEXT NEWTON
AP [Pts Lind] *LG* Walshcr. Wap, Caist. PLU, RSD, RD. Abol civ 1936 to help cr Toft Newton CP.[28] *Parl* N'rn Dv (1832—67), North Dv (1867—85), E Lind Dv (1885—1918), Louth Dv (1918—48). *Eccl* Seq 55.

TOFT WITH LOUND AND MANTHORPE
CP [Pts Kestev] Cr 1931 by union Manthorpe CP, Toft and Lound CP.[19] *LG* S Kestev RD. *Parl* Rutl & Stamf. CC (1948—*).

TORKSEY
AP [Pts Lind] Tp 'Torksey' in Lawres Wap as was tp Hardwick (sep CP 1866[13]); incl in Well Wap tp Brampton (sep CP 1866[13]). *LG* Torksey Bor, Gainsb. PLU, RSD, RD. *Parl* Seq 14. *Eccl* Seq 75.

EAST TORRINGTON
AP [Pts Lind] *LG* Wragg. Wap, Caist. PLU, RSD, RD. Abol civ 1936 ent to Legsby AP.[28] *Parl* N'rn Dv (1832—67), Mid Dv (1867—85), E Lind Dv (1885—1918), Louth Dv (1918—48). *Eccl* Seq 59.

WEST TORRINGTON
AP [Pts Lind] *LG* Seq 51. *Parl* Seq 9. *Eccl* Seq 59.

TOTHILL
AP [Pts Lind] *LG* Seq 33. *Parl* Seq 13. *Eccl* Seq 11.

HIGH TOYNTON
AP [Pts Lind] *LG* Seq 42. Civ bdry: 1880 (help cr Wildmore CP).[26] *Parl* Seq 12. *Eccl* Seq 42.

LOW TOYNTON
AP [Pts Lind] *LG* Seq 42. Civ bdry: 1880 (help cr Wildmore CP).[26] *Parl* Seq 12. *Eccl* Hornc. RDn (until 1866), Hill 1 RDn (1866—84), Hornc. RDn (1884—*). Eccl bdry: 1881 (help cr Wildmore EP [Pts Lind, Pts Kestev, Pts Holl]).[27]

TOYNTON ALL SAINTS
AP [Pts Lind] Chap in Horncastle AP, sep par by 1535. *LG* Seq 29. Civ bdry: 1880 (help cr Wildmore CP),[26] 1888.[2] *Parl* Seq 12. *Eccl* Bolingbr. RDn. Abol eccl 1842 to help cr Toynton All Saints with Toynton St Peter EP.[274]

TOYNTON ALL SAINTS WITH TOYNTON ST PETER
EP [Pts Lind] Cr 1842 by union Toynton All Saints AP, Toynton St Peter AP.[274] Bolingbr. RDn. Bdry: 1881 (help cr Wildmore EP [Pts Lind, Pts Kestev, Pts Holl]).[27]

TOYNTON ST PETER

AP [Pts Lind] Status, organisation, bdry alts, eccl abol as for Toynton All Saints, with addtl civ bdry alt 1880.[114]

TRUSTHORPE

AP [Pts Lind] Calc. Wap, Louth PLU, RSD, RD (1894—1925), Mableth. & Sutton UD (1925—74). *Parl* N'rn Dv (1832—67), Mid Dv (1867—85), S Lind Dv (1885—1918), Louth Dv (1918—48), Hornc. CC (1948—*). *Eccl* Seq 11.

TUMBY

[Pts Lind] Tp in Kirkby on Bain AP, sep CP 1866,[13] pt eccl severed 1881 to help cr Wildmore EP (Pts Lind, Pts Kestev, Pts Holl),[27] the remainder eccl abol 1886 to help cr Carrington with Frithville EP (Pts Lind, Pts Holl).[61] *LG* Seq 37. Civ bdry: 1884.[248] *Parl* Seq 12.

TUPHOLME

AP [Pts Lind] Orig Abbey, sometimes after Dissolution considered ex-par. *LG* Seq 51. *Parl* Seq 9. *Eccl* Walshcr. RDn (until 1866), Walshcr. 2 RDn (1866—73), Walshcr. RDn (1873—1910), Walshcr. (West) RDn (1910—66). Abol eccl 1966 to help cr Bucknall with Tupholme EP.[79]

TWIGMORE

[Pts Lind] Tp in Manton AP, sep CP 1866.[13] *LG* Manley Wap, Glanf. Brigg PLU, RSD, RD. Abol civ 1936 ent to Holme CP.[28] *Parl* N'rn Dv (1832—67), North Dv (1867—85), N Lind Dv (1885—1918), Brigg Dv (1918—48).

TYDD ST MARY

AP [Pts Holl] *LG* Seq 1. Civ bdry: 1897 (loses pt to Central Wingland CP [prev Pts Holl, Norfolk] as the latter reconstituted to be ent Pts Holl, qv),[275] 1932,[123] 1934 (exchanges pts with Tydd St Giles AP, loses pt to Parson Drove CP, both Isle of Ely).[272] *Parl* Seq 16. *Eccl* Seq 41.

UFFINGTON

AP [Pts Kestev] *LG* Seq 21. Civ bdry: 1931.[19] *Parl* Seq 21. *Eccl* Seq 51.

ULCEBY

AP [Pts Lind] *LG* Seq 55. Transf 1974 to Humb.[10] *Parl* Seq 3. *Eccl* Sometimes as 'Ulceby by Barton', Seq 60.

ULCEBY WITH FORDINGTON

AP [Pts Lind] Sometimes early 'Ulceby by Alford'. *LG* Seq 34. *Parl* Seq 12. *Eccl* Seq 14. Eccl bdry: 1970.[276]

UPTON

AP [Pts Lind] Incl tp Kexby (sep CP 1866,[13] not sep eccl hence this par eccl 'Upton with Kexby', qv). *LG* Seq 49. Addtl civ bdry alt: 1884.[202] *Parl* Seq 14.

UPTON WITH KESBY

AP [Pts Lind] Usual eccl spelling; for civ and civ sep tp, see prev entry. *Eccl* Lawres RDn (until 1866), Lawres 2 RDn (1866—1910), Corr. RDn (1910—*).

USSELBY

[Pts Lind] Chap in Kirkby cum Osgodby AP, sep civ identity early, sep EP 1746.[6] *LG* Walshcr. Wap, Caist. PLU, RSD, RD. Abol civ 1936 to help cr Osgodby CP.[28] *Parl* N'rn Dv (1832—67), North Dv

(1867—85), E Lind Dv (1885—1918), Louth Dv (1918—48). *Eccl* Walshcr. RDn (1746—1866), Walshcr. 1 RDn (1866—73), Walshcr. RDn (1873—1910), Walshcr. (West) RDn (1910—68), W Wold RDn (1968—*).

UTTERBY

AP [Pts Lind] *LG* Seq 45. *Parl* Seq 1. *Eccl* Seq 46.

WADDINGHAM

[Pts Lind] Cr early by union Waddingham St Peter AP (Asl. Wap, church early destroyed), Waddingham St Mary AP (Manley Wap),[5] the united par to be in Manley Wap. Incl chap Snitterby (sep civ identity early, sep EP 1866[265]). *LG* Caist. PLU, RSD, RD. *Parl* Seq 5. *Eccl* Seq 78.

WADDINGHAM ST MARY

AP [Pts Lind] Manley Wap, Manlake RDn, united early with Waddingham St Peter AP (church early destroyed) to cr Waddingham CP/EP.[5]

WADDINGHAM ST PETER

AP [Pts Lind] Asl. Wap, Asl. RDn, united early with Waddingham St Mary AP to cr Waddingham CP/EP.[5]

WADDINGTON

AP [Pts Lind] *LG* Linc. Lbty (until 1840s), Boothby Graff. Wap (from 1840s), Linc. PLU, RSD, Branst. RD (1894—1931), N Kestev RD (1931—74). *Parl* N'rn Dv (1832—67), Mid Dv (1867—85), N Kestev Dv (1885—1918), Granth. Dv/CC (1918—*). *Eccl* Seq 45. Eccl bdry: 1971 (help cr Bracebridge Heath EP).[70]

WADDINGWORTH

AP [Pts Lind] *LG* Seq 37. *Parl* Seq 9. *Eccl* Seq 19.

WAINFLEET ALL SAINTS

AP [Pts Lind] Incl chap Northolme (sep civ identity early, sep EP 1822 as 'Wainfleet St Thomas'[235]). *LG* Wainfleet Bor, Seq 35. Civ bdry: 1888 (gains Northolme CP).[236] *Parl* Wainfleet Parl Bor (1337 only), Seq 12 thereafter. *Eccl* Candl. RDn (until 1866), Candl. 2 RDn (1866—1962). Abol eccl 1962 to help cr Wainfleet All Saints and St Thomas EP.[277]

WAINFLEET ALL SAINTS AND ST THOMAS

EP [Pts Lind] Cr 1962 by union Wainfleet All Saints AP, Wainfleet St Thomas AP.[277] Candl. RDn (1962—68), Calc. & Candl. RDn (1968—*).

WAINFLEET ST MARY

AP [Pts Lind] *LG* Wainfleet Bor, Seq 35. *Parl* Wainfleet Parl Bor (1337), Seq 12 thereafter. *Eccl* Seq 17.

WAINFLEET ST THOMAS

[Pts Lind] Chap in Wainfleet All Saints AP, sep EP 1822,[235] sep civ identity early as 'Northolme',[13] qv. *Eccl* Candl. RDn (1822—66), Candl. 2 RDn (1866—1910), Candl. RDn (1910—62). Abol eccl 1962 to help cr Wainfleet All Saints and St Thomas EP.[277]

WAITHE

AP [Pts Lind] *LG* Seq 32. *Parl* Seq 4. *Eccl* Seq 32.

WALCOT

AP [Pts Kestev] Usual eccl spelling; for civ see 'Walcot near Folkingham'. *Eccl* Seq 4.

WALCOT NEAR BILLINGHAY

[Pts Kestev] Chap and tp in Billinghay AP, sep CP

1866.[13] *LG* Seq 17. *Parl* Seq 15.

WALCOT NEAR FOLKINGHAM
AP [Pts Kestev] Usual civ spelling; for eccl see 'Walcot'. *LG* Seq 8. *Parl* S'rn Dv (1832—67), South Dv (1867—85), S Kestev Dv (1885—1918), Granth. Dv (1918—48), Rutl & Stamf. CC (1948—*).

WALESBY
AP [Pts Lind] *LG* Seq 48. *Parl* Seq 2. *Eccl* Seq 53.

WALKERITH
[Pts Lind] Tp in Gainsborough AP, sep CP 1866,[13] eccl severed 1846 to help cr East Stockwith with Walkerith EP,[155] later called 'East Stockwith'. *LG* Seq 36. *Parl* Seq 6.

WALMSGATE
[Pts Lind] Chap (Hill Hd) in Burwell AP (o'wise Louth Esk Wap), sep civ identity early. *LG* Hill Hd, Louth PLU, RSD, RD. *Parl* Seq 10.

WALTHAM
AP [Pts Lind] *LG* Seq 31. Civ bdry: 1928,[72] 1961 (cr New Waltham CP),[278] 1968 (loses pt to Grimsby CB [assoc with Pts Lind] & CP).[107] Transf 1974 to Humb.[10] *Parl* Seq 4. *Eccl* Seq 32.

NEW WALTHAM
CP [Pts Lind] Cr 1961 from Waltham AP.[278] *LG* Grimsby RD. Bdry: 1968 (incl loses pt to Grimsby CB [assoc with Pts Lind] & CP).[107] Transf 1974 to Humb.[10] *Parl* Louth CC (1970—*).

WASHINGBOROUGH
AP [Pts Kestev] Incl chap Heighington (sep CP 1866,[13] not sep eccl hence this par eccl 'Washingborough with Heighington', qv). *LG* Seq 16. Addtl civ bdry alt: 1887.[185] *Parl* Seq 15.

WASHINGBOROUGH WITH HEIGHINGTON
AP [Pts Kestev] Usual eccl spelling; for civ and civ sep chap, see prev entry. *Eccl* Seq 45.

WEELSBY
CP [Pts Lind] Cr 1894 from the pt of Clee with Weelsby AP not in Grimsby CB.[102] Grimsby PLU, RD. Bdry: 1922,[104] 1927,[105] 1928 (loses pt to Grimsby CB [assoc with Pts Lind] to help cr Grimsby CP).[72] Abol 1968 pt to Grimsby CB (assoc with Pts Lind) & CP, pt to Humberston AP, pt to New Waltham CP.[107] *Parl* Louth Dv/CC (1918—70).

WELBOURN
AP [Pts Kestev] *LG* Seq 13. *Parl* Seq 15. *Eccl* Longob. RDn (until 1910), Loved. RDn (1910—*).

WELBY
AP [Pts Kestev] *LG* Seq 22. *Parl* Seq 20. *Eccl* Granth. RDn (until 1866), Belt. RDn (1866—73), Belt. RDn (1873—84), Granth. 1 RDn (1884—1910), N Granth. RDn (1910—68), Granth. RDn (1968—70). Abol eccl 1970 to help cr Welby and Londonthorpe EP.[46]

WELBY AND LONDONTHORPE
EP [Pts Kestev] Cr 1970 by union Welby AP, pt Manthorpe with Londonthorpe EP.[46] Granth. RDn.

WELL
AP [Pts Lind] *LG* Seq 34. *Parl* Seq 12. *Eccl* Seq 14. Eccl bdry: 1970.[277]

WELLINGORE
AP [Pts Kestev] *LG* Seq 13. *Parl* Seq 15. Eccl Pec

jurisd Dean & Chapter of Linc. (until 1846), Seq 45 thereafter.

WELTON
AP [Pts Lind] *LG* Seq 43. *Parl* Seq 14. *Eccl* Pec jurisd Dean & Chapter of Linc. (until 1846), Seq 72 thereafter.

WELTON LE MARSH
AP [Pts Lind] *LG* Seq 35. Civ bdry: 1888,[2] 1936.[28] *Parl* Seq 12. *Eccl* Candl. RDn. Abol eccl 1865 to help cr Welton le Marsh with Gunby EP.[175]

WELTON LE MARSH WITH GUNBY
EP [Pts Lind] Cr 1865 by union Welton le Marsh AP, Gunby AP.[175] Candl. RDn (1865—66), Candl. 1 RDn (1866—84), Candl. 2 RDn (1884—1910), Candl. RDn (1910—68), Calc. & Candl. RDn (1968—*).

WELTON LE WOLD
AP [Pts Lind] *LG* Seq 44. *Parl* Seq 1. *Eccl* Seq 49.

WEST FEN
[Pts Lind] Area reclaimed, sep tp from 1812,[92] sep CP 1880 in Pts Lind, comprised of area from Pts Holl (Freiston AP, Leverton AP) and from Pts Lind (Mavis Enderby AP, Hareby AP, Hundleby AP, West Keal AP, Raithby AP).[139] *LG* Bolingbr. Soke, Spilsby PLU, RSD, RD. *Parl* S'rn Dv (1832—67), Mid Dv (1867—85), S Lind Dv (1885—1918), Hornc. Dv/CC (1918—*).

WESTBOROUGH
AP [Pts Kestev] Incl chap Dry Doddington (sep civ identity early, not sep eccl hence this par eccl 'Westborough with Dry Doddington', qv). *LG* Loved. Wap, Newk. PLU, RSD, Clayp. RD. Abol civ 1931 to help cr Westborough and Dry Doddington CP.[19] *Parl* S'rn Dv (1832—67), South Dv (1867—85), S Kestev Dv (1885—1918), Granth. Dv (1918—48).

WESTBOROUGH AND DRY DODDINGTON
CP [Pts Kestev] Cr 1931 by union Westborough AP, Dry Doddington CP.[19] *LG* W Kestev RD. *Parl* Granth. CC (1948—*).

WESTBOROUGH WITH DRY DODDINGTON
AP [Pts Kestev] Usual eccl spelling; for civ and civ sep chap, see 'Westborough'. *Eccl* Seq 50.

WESTON
AP [Pts Holl] *LG* Seq 2. Civ bdry: 1932.[123] *Parl* Seq 16. *Eccl* Seq 40.

WESTVILLE
[Pts Lind] Tp cr 1812 from West Fen,[92] sep CP 1866,[13] eccl abol 1886 to help cr Carrington with Frithville EP (Pts Lind, Pts Holl).[61] *LG* Seq 27. *Parl* Seq 12.

WHAPLODE
AP [Pts Holl] *LG* Seq 1. *Parl* Seq 16. *Eccl* Holl RDn (until 1866), S Holl 1 RDn (1866—84), E Elloe RDn (1884—1910), Elloe (East) RDn (1910—*). Eccl bdry: 1902 (cr Whaplode Drove EP).[279]

WHAPLODE DROVE
EP [Pts Holl] Cr 1902 from Whaplode AP.[279] W Elloe RDn (1902—10), Elloe (West) RDn (1910—68), Elloe (East) RDn (1968—*).

WHISBY
[Pts Kestev] Tp in Doddington AP, sep CP 1866.[13] *LG* Boothby Graff. Wap, Linc. PLU, RSD, Branst.

RD. Abol 1931 to help cr Doddington and Whisby CP.[19] *Parl* S'rn Dv (1832—67), Mid Dv (1867—85), N Kestev Dv (1885—1918), Granth. Dv (1918—48).

WHITTON

AP [Pts Lind] *LG* Seq 46. Transf 1974 to Humb.[10] *Parl* Seq 3. *Eccl* Seq 77.

WICKENBY

AP [Pts Lind] *LG* Seq 52. *Parl* Seq 8. *Eccl* Seq 58.

WIGTOFT

AP [Pts Holl] Incl undivided pt Lands Common to Swineshead and Wigtoft, abol 1932 ent to this par [addtl bdry alt affecting this par in same order][77]). *LG* Seq 3. Addtl civ bdry alt: 1906 (gains Drainage Marsh CP).[39] *Parl* Seq 16. *Eccl* Seq 38.

WILDMORE

AP [Pts Lind] Area drained from Wildmore Fen, sep parochial chap chap 1812,[92] sep CP 1880 from Thornton le Fen CP, Bolingbroke AP, Coningsby AP, Tattershall AP, West Ashby AP, Wood Enderby AP, Horncastle AP, Mareham on the Hill AP, Moorby AP, Thimbleby AP, High Toynton AP, Low Toynton AP, Toynton All Saints AP, Wilksby AP, Haltham AP, Roughton AP.[26] *LG* Hornc. Soke, PLU, RSD, RD. Civ bdry: 1883,[31] 1884,[116] 1884,[118] 1884,[140] 1935 (gains Copping Syke CP, Pts Holl).[28] *Parl* S Lind Dv (1885—1918), Hornc. Dv/CC (1918—*).

EP [Pts Lind] Cr 1881 from Pts Lind places of West Ashby AP, Bolingbroke AP, Coningsby AP (pt fen allotment), Wood Enderby AP, Horncastle AP, Kirkby on Bain AP (pt tp Tumby), Kirkstead AP, Mareham le Fen AP, Mareham on the Hill AP, Martin AP, Moorby AP, Revesby AP, Roughton with Haltham EP, Scrivelsby with Dalderby EP, Tattershall AP, Thimbleby AP, Low Toynton AP, Toynton All Saints with Toynton St Peter EP, Woodhall AP, pt of ex-par places of Frith Bank (not sep civ), Langriville, Thornton le Fen; from ent Pts Kestev ex-par place of Dogdyke; from Pts Holl places of ent ex-par Little Beats, ent ex-par South of the Witham, and from pt Fishtoft AP.[27] N Holl 2 RDn (1881—1910), Holl (East) RDn (1910—*).

WILDSWORTH

[Pts Lind] Hmlt in Loughton by Gainsborough AP, sep CP 1866.[13] *LG* Seq 36. *Parl* Seq 6.

WILKSBY

AP [Pts Lind] *LG* Hornc. Soke, PLU, RD, RD. Civ bdry: 1880 (help cr Wildmore CP).[26] Abol civ 1936 ent to Wood Enderby AP.[28] *Parl* N'rn Dv (1832—67), Mid Dv (1867—85), S Lind Dv (1885—1918), Hornc. Dv (1918—48). *Eccl* Holl RDn (until 1866), Hill 1 RDn (1866—1910), Gart. RDn (1910—68), Hornc. RDn (1968—*). Eccl bdry: 1874,[249] 1874.[250]

WILLINGHAM

AP [Pts Lind] *LG* Seq 49. *Parl* Seq 14. Eccl [St Helen] Seq 74.

CHERRY WILLINGHAM

AP [Pts Lind] *LG* Seq 43. Civ bdry: 1887.[81] *Parl* Seq 14. *Eccl* [St Peter] Seq 72.

NORTH WILLINGHAM

AP [Pts Lind] *LG* Seq 48. *Parl* Seq 2. *Eccl* Seq 55.

SOUTH WILLINGHAM

AP [Pts Lind] *LG* Seq 53. *Parl* Seq 10. *Eccl* Seq 59.

WILLOUGHBY

AP [Pts Lind] Usual eccl spelling until 1970; for civ see 'Willoughby and Sloothby'. *Eccl* Calc. RDn (until 1866), Calc. 2 RDn (1866—1910), Calc. (North) RDn (1910—68), Calc. & Candl. RDn (1968—70). Renamed eccl 1970 'Willoughby with Sloothby'.[277]

SCOTT WILLOUGHBY

AP [Pts Kestev] *LG* Avel. Wap, Sleaf. PLU, RSD, RD. Abol civ 1931 to help cr Aunsby and Dembleby CP.[19] *Parl* S'rn Dv (1832—67), South Dv (1867—85), N Kestev Dv (1885—1918), Granth. Dv (1918—48). *Eccl* Seq 5.

SILK WILLOUGHBY

AP [Pts Kestev] *LG* Seq 6. *Parl* Seq 17. *Eccl* Seq 2.

WILLOUGHBY AND SLOOTHBY

AP [Pts Lind] Usual civ spelling; eccl, 'Willoughby' until renamed 1970 'Willoughby with Sloothby'.[277] *LG* Seq 34. *Parl* Seq 12.

WILLOUGHBY WITH SLOOTHBY

EP [Pts Lind] Renaming 1970 of Willoughby AP.[277] Calc. & Candl. RDn (1970—*).

WILLOUGHTON

AP [Pts Lind] *LG* Seq 25. *Parl* Seq 6. *Eccl* Seq 67.

WILSFORD

AP [Pts Kestev] *LG* Winn. & Thr. Wap, Sleaf. PLU, RSD, RD (1894—1931), E Kestev RD (1931—74). Civ bdry: 1931.[19] *Parl* Seq 17. *Eccl* Granth. RDn (until 1866), Granth. 1 RDn (1866—1910), N Granth. RDn (1910—51). Eccl bdry: 1926.[246] Abol eccl 1951 to help cr Wilsford with Kelby EP.[186]

WILSFORD WITH KELBY

EP [Pts Kestev] Cr 1951 by union Wilsford AP, chap Kelby in Heydour with Kelby and Culverthorpe AP.[186] Granth. RDn.

WILSTHORPE

[Pts Kestev] Chap in Greatford AP, sep CP 1866.[13] *LG* Ness Wap, Stamf. PLU, RSD, Uff. RD. Abol 1931 to help cr Braceborough and Wilsthorpe CP.[19] *Parl* S'rn Dv (1832—67), South Dv (1867—85), S Kestev Dv (1885—1918), Rutl & Stamf. Dv (1918—48).

WINCEBY

AP [Pts Lind] *LG* Seq 39. *Parl* Seq 12. *Eccl* Hill RDn (until 1866), Hill 1 RDn (1866—1910), Hill (North) RDn (1910—61). Abol eccl 1961 to help cr Hameringham with Scrafield and Winceby EP.[57]

CENTRAL WINGLAND

[Pt Lincs Pts Holl (Elloe Wap), pt Norfolk (Freebridge Marshland Hd)] Ex-par place, sep CP 1858.[38] *LG* Holb. PLU (1867—1930), RSD, pt sep RD in Norfolk (1894—97), E Elloe RD (pt 1894—97, ent 1897—1954). Civ bdry: 1897 (exchanges pts with Terrington St Clement AP, gains pts Walpole St Andrew AP, Walpole St Peter AP, all Norfolk, gains pt Tydd St Giles AP, Pts Holl, and the reconstituted par ent Lincs Pts Holl thereafter).[280] Abol civ 1954 ent to Sutton Bridge CP.[270] *Parl* S'rn Dv (1832—67), South Dv (1867—85), Holl Dv (1885—1918), Holl with Boston Dv/CC (1918—70).

WINTERINGHAM
AP [Pts Lind] *LG* Seq 46. Transf 1974 to Humb.[10] *Parl* Seq 3. *Eccl* Seq 77.

WINTERTON
AP [Pts Lind] *LG* Manley Wap, Glanf. Brigg PLU, Winterton USD, UD (1894—1936), Glanf. Brigg RD (1936—74). Transf 1974 to Humb.[10] *Parl* Seq 3. *Eccl* Seq 77.

WINTHORPE
AP [Pts Lind] *LG* Candl. Wap, Spilsby PLU, RSD, RD. Abol civ 1926 pt to Skegnes UD & AP, pt to Addlethorpe AP.[3] *Parl* N'rn Dv (1832—67), Mid Dv (1867—85), S Lind Dv (1885—1918), Hornc. Dv (1918—48). *Eccl* Seq 17. Eccl bdry: 1952.[258]

WISPINGTON
AP [Pts Lind] *LG* Seq 37. *Parl* Seq 9. *Eccl* Seq 19.

NORTH WITHAM
AP [Pts Kestev] *LG* Seq 10. Civ bdry: 1887.[173] *Parl* Seq 21. *Eccl* Seq 8.

SOUTH WITHAM
AP [Pts Kestev] *LG* Seq 10. Civ bdry: 1965 (loses pt to Wymondham AP, Leics).[113] *Parl* Seq 21. *Eccl* Seq 8.

WITHAM ON THE HILL
AP [Pts Kestev] Incl hmlt Manthorpe, tp Toft and Lound (each a sep CP 1866[13]). *LG* Seq 9. *Parl* Seq 21. *Eccl* Belt. RDn (until 1866), Belt. 2 RDn (1866—84), Belt. RDn (1884—1910), Ness RDn (1910—*).

WITHCALL
AP [Pts Lind] *LG* Seq 44. *Parl* Seq 1. *Eccl* Seq 49.

WITHERN WITH STAIN
AP [Pts Lind] *LG* Seq 33. *Parl* Seq 13. *Eccl* Seq 11.

WOODHALL
AP [Pts Lind] *LG* Seq 37. Civ bdry: 1880,[115] 1887,[130] 1894 (help cr Woodhall Spa CP).[230] *Parl* Seq 12. *Eccl* Seq 43. Eccl bdry: 1850 (help cr Langton St Andrew (otherwise Woodhall Spa) EP),[204] 1881 (help cr Wildmore EP [Pts Lind, Pts Kestev, Pts Holl]),[27] 1913.[126]

WOODHALL SPA
CP [Pts Lind] Cr 1894 from Martin AP, Roughton AP, Woodhall AP[230]; for eccl cr 1850 as 'Langton St Andrew (otherwise Woodhall Spa)' EP, with slightly different constituent pars,[204] see the latter. *LG* Hornc. PLU, RD (1894—98), Woodhall Spa UD (1898—1974). *Parl* Hornc. Dv/CC (1918—*).

WOODHALL SPA AND KIRKSTEAD
EP [Pts Lind] Cr 1967 by union Langton St Andrew (otherwise Woodhall Spa) EP, Kirkstead AP.[201] Gart. RDn (1967—68), Hornc. RDn (1968—*).

WOOLSTHORPE
AP [Pts Kestev] Usual civ spelling; for eccl see following entry. *LG* Seq 22. Civ bdry: 1931,[19] 1965 (exchanges pts with Bottesford AP, Belvoir CP, both Leics).[113] *Parl* Seq 21.

WOOLSTHORPE WITH STAINWORTH
AP [Pts Kestev] Usual eccl spelling; for civ see prev entry. *Eccl* Seq 25.

WOOTTON
AP [Pts Lind] *LG* Seq 55. Transf 1974 to Humb.[10] *Parl* Seq 3. *Eccl* Seq 60.

WORLABY
AP [Pts Lind] *LG* Seq 55. Transf 1974 to Humb.[10] *Parl* Seq 3. *Eccl* Seq 62.

WORLABY
[Pts Lind] Ex-par place, sep CP 1858.[38] *LG* Hill Hd, Louth PLU, RSD, RD. Abol civ 1936 to help cr Maidenwell CP.[28] *Parl* N'rn Dv (1832—67), Mid Dv (1867—85), S Lind Dv (1885—1918), Louth Dv (1918—48).

WRAGBY
AP [Pts Lind] *LG* Seq 51. *Parl* Seq 9. *Eccl* Wragg. RDn. Abol eccl 1860 to help cr Wragby with Panton EP.[239]

WRAGBY WITH PANTON
EP [Pts Lind] Cr 1860 by union Wragby AP, Ponton AP.[239] Wragg. RDn (1860—1968), Hornc. RDn (1968—*).

WRANGLE
AP [Pts Holl] *LG* Seq 5. *Parl* Seq 16. *Eccl* Seq 39.

WRAWBY
AP [Pts Lind] Incl pt chap Glanford Brigg (sep CP 1866,[13] sep EP 1872 as 'Glanford Bridge' from Bigby AP, Wrawby AP[49]). *LG* Yarb. Wap, Glanf. Brigg PLU, RSD (pt 1875—92, ent 1892—94), pt Brigg USD (1875—92), Glanf. Brigg RD. Addtl civ bdry alt: 1892 (losees the pt in Brigg USD to Glanford Brigg CP),[50] 1936.[28] Transf 1974 to Humb.[10] *Parl* Seq 3. *Eccl* Seq 62.

WROOT
AP [Pts Lind] *LG* Seq 47. Transf 1974 to Humb.[10] *Parl* Seq 6. *Eccl* Seq 70.

WYBERTON
AP [Pts Holl] *LG* Seq 3. Civ bdry: 1887,[116] 1906,[39] 1932.[77] *Parl* Seq 16. *Eccl* Seq 38.

EAST WYKEHAM
AP [Pts Lind] Church (Louthesk & Ludb. RDn) early destroyed, considered thereafter ex-par,[280] sep civ identity retained, eccl abol 1929 to help cr Kelstern with Calcethorpe and East Wykeham EP.[199] *LG* Louth Esk Hd, Louth PLU (1858—1930), RSD, RD. *Parl* Seq 1.

WEST WYKEHAM
AP [Pts Lind] Orig sep AP, Wragg. RDn, early destroyed and incl in Ludford Magna AP.

WYHAM WITH CALDEBY
AP [Pts Lind] *LG* Seq 45. *Parl* Seq 1. *Eccl* Louthesk & Ludb. RDn (until 1863), Louthesk & Ludb. 1 RDn (1863—1910), Walshcr. (East) RDn (1910—22), Ludb. RDn (1922—68), Louthesk RDn (1968—*).

WYVILLE
AP [Pts Kestev] Orig sep AP, Granth. RDn, united before 1535 with Hungerton AP, the union civ 'Wyville cum Hungerton', eccl 'Wyville with Hungerton'.

WYVILLE CUM HUNGERTON
AP [Pts Kestev] Usual civ spelling for union before 1535 of Hungerton AP, Wyville AP, the union eccl 'Wyville with Hungerton', qv. *LG* Winn. & Thr. Wap (until 1830s), Loved. Wap (from 1830s), Granth. PLU, RSD, RD (1894—1931), W Kestev RD (1831—74). Civ bdry: 1931 (help cr Stoke Rochford CP),[19] 1965 (gains pt Sproxton AP, pt Croxton Kerrial AP, both Leics).[113] *Parl* Seq 21.

WYVILLE WITH HUNGERTON
  AP [Pts Kestev] Usual eccl spelling for union before
  1535 of Wyville AP, Hungerton AP, the union civ
  'Wyville cum Hungerton', qv. *Eccl* Granth. RDn
  (cr—1866), Granth. 2 RDn (1866—1910), S
  Granth. RDn (1910—68), Belt. RDn (1968—*).

YADDLETHORPE
  [Pts Lind] Tp in Botttesford AP, sep CP 1866.[13] *LG*
  Manley Wap, Glanf. Brigg PLU, RSD. Abol 1887
  ent to Bottesford AP.[63] *Parl* N'rn Dv (1832—67),
  North Dv (1867—85), N Lind Dv (1885—1918).

YARBURGH
  AP [Pts Lind] *LG* Seq 44. *Parl* Seq 1. *Eccl* Seq 46.

NORTHAMPTONSHIRE

ABBREVIATIONS

Abbreviations particular to Northants follow. Those general abbreviations in use throughout the *Guide* are found on pages xvii—xix.

Banb.	Banbury
Brack.	Brackley
Brixw.	Brixworth
Chip. Ward.	Chipping Warden
Culw.	Culworth
Dav.	Daventry
Grett.	Gretton
Gr's Nort.	Green's Norton
Guilsb.	Guilsborough
Hamf.	Hamfordshoe
Hardingst.	Hardingstone
High. Ferr.	Higham Ferrers
Huxl.	Huxloe
K's Cliffe	King's Cliffe
K's Nort.	King's Norton
K's Sutt.	King's Sutton
Kett.	Kettering
Midd. Chen.	Middleton Cheney
Nassab.	Nassaborough
N'htn	Northampton
Navisf.	Navisford
Nob. Gr.	Nobottle Grove
Orl.	Orlingbury
Ound.	Oundle
Oxend.	Oxendon
Poleb.	Polebrook
Pott.	Potterspury
Rothw.	Rothwell
Spel.	Spelhoe
Stamf.	Stamford
Thrap.	Thrapston
Towc.	Towcester
Upp.	Uppingham
Wellingb.	Wellingborough
Willyb.	Willybrook
Wym.	Wymersley

SEQUENCES

An abbreviated entry prefixed by 'Seq' is used in the parochial entries to avoid repeating often the names of superior units of administration. The content of each sequence is shown below.

Local Government Sequences ('LG')

SEQ 1 Cleley Hd, Pott. PLU, RSD, RD (1894—1935), N'htn RD (1935—74)

SEQ 2 Cleley Hd, Pott. PLU, RSD, RD (1894—1935), Towc. RD (1935—74)

SEQ 3 Cleley Hd, Towc. PLU, RSD, RD

SEQ 4 Corby Hd, Kett. PLU, RSD, RD

SEQ 5 Corby Hd, Mkt. Harb. PLU, RSD, Oxend. RD (1894—1935), Kett. RD (1935—74)

SEQ 6 Corby Hd, Ound. PLU, RSD, RD (1894—1935), Ound. & Thrap. RD (1935—74)

SEQ 7 Corby Hd, Upp. PLU, RSD, Grett. RD (1894—1935), Kett. RD (1935—74)

SEQ 8 Corby Hd, Upp. PLU, RSD, Grett. RD (1894—1935), Ound. & Thrap. RD (1935—74)

SEQ 9 Fawsley Hd, Dav. PLU, RSD, RD

SEQ 10 Fawsley Hd, Rugby PLU, RSD, Crick RD (1894—1935), Dav. RD (1935—74)

SEQ 11 Guilsb. Hd, Brixw. PLU, RSD, RD
SEQ 12 Guilsb. Hd, Dav. PLU, RSD, RD
SEQ 13 Guilsb. Hd, Rugby PLU, RSD, Crick RD (1894—1935), Dav. RD (1935—74)
SEQ 14 Hamf. Hd, Wellingb. PLU, RSD, RD
SEQ 15 High. Ferr. Hd, Thrap. PLU, RSD, RD (1894—1935), Ound. & Thrap. RD (1935—74)
SEQ 16 High. Ferr. Hd, Wellingb. PLU, RSD, RD
SEQ 17 Huxl. Hd, Kett. PLU, RSD, RD
SEQ 18 Huxl. Hd, Thrap. PLU, RSD, RD (1894—1935), Ound. & Thrap. RD (1935—74)
SEQ 19 Nassab. Hd, Peterb PLU, RSD, [Soke Peterb 1889—1965, Hunts & Peterb 1965—74] Peterb RD
SEQ 20 Nassab. Hd, Stamf. PLU, RSD, [Soke Peterb 1889—1965, Hunts & Peterb 1965—74] Barnack RD
SEQ 21 Navisf. Hd, Ound. PLU, RSD, RD (1894—1935), Ound. & Thrap. RD (1935—74)
SEQ 22 Navisf. Hd, Thrap. PLU, RSD, RD (1894—1935), Ound. & Thrap. RD (1935—74)
SEQ 23 Nob. Gr. Hd, Brixw. PLU, RSD, RD
SEQ 24 Nob. Gr. Hd, Dav. PLU, RSD, RD
SEQ 25 Nob. Gr. Hd, N'htn PLU, RSD, RD
SEQ 26 Gr's Nort. Hd, Towc. PLU, RSD, RD
SEQ 27 Orl. Hd, Brixw. PLU, RSD, RD
SEQ 28 Orl. Hd, Kett. PLU, RSD, RD
SEQ 29 Orl. Hd, Wellingb. PLU, RSD, RD
SEQ 30 Poleb. Hd, Ound. PLU, RSD, RD (1894—1935), Ound. & Thrap. RD (1935—74)
SEQ 31 Rothw. Hd, Brixw. PLU, RSD, RD
SEQ 32 Rothw. Hd, Kett. PLU, RSD, RD
SEQ 33 Rothw. Hd, Mkt. Harb. PLU, RSD, Oxend. RD (1894—1935), Brixw. RD (1935—74)
SEQ 34 Spel. Hd, Brixw. PLU, RSD, RD
SEQ 35 K's Sutt. Hd, Banb. PLU, RSD, Midd. Chen. RD (1894—1935), Brack. RD (1935—74)
SEQ 36 K's Sutt. Hd, Brack. PLU, RSD, RD
SEQ 37 Towc. Hd, PLU, RSD, RD
SEQ 38 Chip. Ward. Hd, Banb. PLU, RSD, Midd. Chen. RD (1894—1935), Brack. RD (1935—74)
SEQ 39 Chip. Ward. Hd, Brack. PLU, RSD, RD
SEQ 40 Chip. Ward., Dav. PLU, RSD, RD
SEQ 41 Willyb. Hd, Ound. PLU, RSD, RD (1894—1935), Ound. & Thrap. RD (1935—74)
SEQ 42 Willyb. Hd, Stamf. PLU, RSD, Easton on the Hill RD (1894—1935), Ound. & Thrap. RD (1935—74)
SEQ 43 Wym. Hd, Hardingst. PLU, RSD, RD (1894—1935), N'htn RD (1935—74)

Parliamentary Sequences ('Parl')

SEQ 1 N'rn Dv (1832—85), E'rn Dv (1885—1918), Kett. Dv/CC (1918—*)
SEQ 2 N'rn Dv (1832—85), E'rn Dv (1885—1918), Wellingb. Dv/CC (1918—*)
SEQ 3 N'rn Dv (1832—85), Mid Dv (1885—1918), Kett. Dv/CC (1918—*)
SEQ 4 N'rn Dv (1832—85), Mid Dv (1885—1918), Kett. Dv/CC (1918—70), Dav. CC (1970—*)
SEQ 5 N'rn Dv (1832—1918), Kett. Dv/CC (1918—*)
SEQ 6 N'rn Dv (1832—1918), Peterb Dv/CC (1918—70), [Hunts & Peterb] Peterb BC (1970—*)
SEQ 7 N'rn Dv (1832—1918), Peterb Dv (1918—48), Kett. CC (1948—*)
SEQ 8 N'rn Dv (1832—1918), Peterb Dv/CC (1918—70), Wellingb. CC (1970—*)
SEQ 9 N'rn Dv (1832—1918), Wellingb. Dv/CC (1918—*)
SEQ 10 S'rn Dv (1832—85), Mid Dv (1885—1918), Dav. Dv (1918—48), S Northants CC (1948—70), Dav. CC (1970—*)
SEQ 11 S'rn Dv (1832—85), Mid Dv (1885—1918), Kett. Dv/CC (1918—70), Dav. CC (1970—*)
SEQ 12 S'rn Dv (1832—1918), Dav. Dv (1918—48), S Northants CC (1948—70), Dav. CC (1970—*)

Ecclesiastical Sequences ('Eccl')

SEQ 1 Brack. RDn (until 1867), Brack. I RDn (1867—1954), Culw. RDn (1954—70), Brack. RDn (1970—*)
SEQ 2 Brack. RDn (until 1867), Brack. II RDn (1867—77), Brack. RDn (1877—1954), Culw. RDn (1954—70), Brack. RDn (1970—*)
SEQ 3 Brack. RDn (until 1867), Brack. II RDn (1867—77), Brack. III RDn (1877—1954), Brack. RDn (1954—*)
SEQ 4 Brack. RDn (until 1867), Brack. III RDn (1867—77), Brack. II RDn (1877—1954), Towc. RDn (1954—*)
SEQ 5 Dav. RDn
SEQ 6 Haddon RDn (until 1867), Haddon I RDn (1867—1954), Haddon RDn (1954—70), Brixw. RDn (1970—*)
SEQ 7 Haddon RDn (until 1867), Haddon II RDn (1867—1954), Brampton RDn (1954—55), Brixw. RDn (1955—*)
SEQ 8 Haddon RDn (until 1867), Haddon II RDn (1867—1954), Brampton RDn (1954—55), N'htn RDn (1955—*)
SEQ 9 High. Ferr. RDn (until 1867), High. Ferr. I RDn (1867—82), Weldon II RDn (1882—1954), Kett. RDn (1954—*)
SEQ 10 High. Ferr. RDn (until 1867), High. Ferr. II RDn (1867—82), High. Ferr. I RDn (1882—1954), Higham RDn (1954—*)
SEQ 11 High. Ferr. RDn (until 1867), High. Ferr. II RDn (1867—1954), Thrap. RDn (1954—70), Higham RDn (1954—*)
SEQ 12 High. Ferr. RDn (until 1867), High. Ferr. III RDn (1867—82), High. Ferr. I RDn (1882—1954), Higham RDn (1954—*)
SEQ 13 High. Ferr. RDn (until 1867), High. Ferr. III RDn (1867—82), High. Ferr. II RDn (1882—1954), Thrap. RDn (1954—70), Higham RDn (1970—*)
SEQ 14 N'htn RDn (until 1964), Wootton RDn (1964—*)

SEQ 15 Oundle RDn (until 1867), Oundle I RDn (1867—1954), Oundle RDn (1954—*)

SEQ 16 Oundle RDn (until 1867), Oundle II RDn (1867—82), High. Ferr. II RDn (1882—1954), Thrap. RDn (1954—70), Higham RDn (1970—*)

SEQ 17 Oundle RDn (until 1867), Oundle III RDn (1867—77), Oundle I RDn (1877—1954), Oundle RDn (1954—*)

SEQ 18 Peterb RDn (until 1867), Peterb I RDn (1867—1954), Peterb RDn (1954—*)

SEQ 19 Peterb RDn (until 1867), Peterb II RDn (1867—1954), Barnack RDn (1954—*)

SEQ 20 Preston RDn (until 1867), Preston I RDn (1867—1954), Wootton RDn (1954—70), Towc. RDn (1970—*)

SEQ 21 Preston RDn (until 1867), Preston II RDn (1867—73), Preston I RDn (1873—1954), Wootton RDn (1954—70), Towc. RDn (1970—*)

SEQ 22 Preston RDn (until 1867), Preston II RDn (1867—1954), Preston RDn (1954—70), Wootton RDn (1970—*)

SEQ 23 Preston RDn (until 1867), Preston III RDn (1867—73), Preston II RDn (1873—1954), Preston RDn (1954—70), Wootton RDn (1970—*)

SEQ 24 Rothw. RDn (until 1867), Rothw. I RDn (1867—1954), Wellingb. RDn (1954—*)

SEQ 25 Rothw. RDn (until 1867), Rothw. I RDn (1867—1954), Wellingb. RDn (1954—70), N'htn RDn (1970—*)

SEQ 26 Rothw. RDn (until 1867), Rothw. II RDn (1867—1954), Rothw. RDn (1954—70), Kett. RDn (1970—*)

SEQ 27 Rothw. RDn (until 1867), Rothw. III RDn (1867—1954), Brixw. RDn (1954—*)

SEQ 28 Weldon RDn (until 1867), Weldon I RDn (1867—1954), Weldon RDn (1954—70), Corby RDn (1970—*)

SEQ 29 Weldon RDn (until 1867), Weldon II RDn (1867—82), Oundle II RDn (1882—1954), K's Cliffe RDn (1954—60), Barnack RDn (1960—*)

SEQ 30 Weldon RDn (until 1867), Weldon II RDn (1867—82), Oundle II RDn (1882—1954), K's Cliffe RDn (1954—60), Upp. RDn (1960—70), Barnack RDn (1970—*).

DIOCESES AND ARCHDEACONRIES

Northants pars were organised in Archdeaconries and Rural Deaneries as follows:

LINCOLN DIOC (until 1541)
N'htn AD: Brack. RDn, Dav. RDn, Haddon RDn, High. Ferr. RDn, N'htn RD, Ound. RDn, Peterb RDn, Preston RDn, Rothw. RDn, Weldon RDn

PETERB DIOC (from 1541)
N'htn AD: Brack. RDn (1541—1867), Brack. RDn (1954—*), Brack. I RDn (1867—1954), Brack. II RDn (1867—1954), Brack. III RDn (1867—1954), Brack. IV RDn (1867—75), Brampton RDn (1954—55), Brixw. RDn (1954—*), Culw. RDn (1954—70), Dav. RDn, Haddon RDn (1541—1867), Haddon RDn (1954—70), Haddon I RDn (1867—1954), Haddon II RDn (1867—1954), High. Ferr. RDn (1541—1867), High. Ferr I RDn (1867—1954), High. Ferr. II RDn (1867—75), High. Ferr. III RDn (1867—75), N'htn RDn, Ound. RDn (1541—1867), Ound. I RDn (1867—75), Ound. II RDn (1867—75), Ound. III RDn (1867—75), Ound. IV RDn (1867—73), Peterb RDn (1541—1867), Peterb I RDn (1867—75), Peterb II RDn (1867—75), Preston RDn (1541—1867), Preston RDn (1954—70), Preston I RDn (1867—1954), Preston II RDn (1867—1954), Preston III RDn (1867—73), Rothw. RDn (1541—1867), Rothw. RDn (1954—70), Rothw. I RDn (1867—1954), Rothw. II RDn (1867—1954), Rothw. III RDn (1867—1954), Towc. RDn (1954—*), Weldon RDn (1541—1867), Weldon I RDn (1867—75), Weldon II RDn (1867—75), Wellingb. RDn (1954—*), Wootton RDn (1954—*)

Oakham AD (1875—):* Barnack RDn (1954—*), Corby RDn (1970—*), Higham RDn (1954—*), High. Ferr. I RDn (1875—1954), High. Ferr. II RDn (1875—1954), High. Ferr. III RDn (1875—81), Kett. RDn (1954—*), K's Cliffe RDn (1954—60), Ound. RDn (1954—*), Ound. I RDn (1875—1954), Ound. II RDn (1875—1954), Ound. III RDn (1875—77), Peterb RDn (1954—*), Peterb I RDn (1875—1954), Peterb II RDn (1875—1954), Thrap. RDn (1954—70), Weldon RDn (1954—70), Weldon I RDn (1875—1954), Weldon II RDn (1875—1954)

THE PARISHES OF NORTHAMPTONSHIRE

ABINGTON
AP *LG* Spel. Hd, N'htn PLU, RSD, RD (1894—1900), CB (1900—13). Civ bdry: 1900 (the pt not transf to N'htn CB [assoc with Northants] transf to Weston Favell AP),[1] 1902,[2] 1912 (gains the pt of Weston Favell AP transf to N'htn CB [assoc with Northants]).[3] Abol civ 1913 ent to Northampton CP.[4] *Parl* S'rn Dv (1832—85), Mid Dv (1885—1918).

Eccl Seq 8. Eccl bdry: 1907 (help cr Northampton Christ Church EP),[5] 1951 (incl help cr Abington St Alban the Martyr EP).[6]

ABINGTON ST ALBAN THE MARTYR
EP Cr 1951 from Abington AP, Weston Favell AP.[6] Haddon II RDn. Renamed 1954 'Northampton St Alban the Martyr'.[7]

ABTHORPE

Area in Towcester AP, sep par 1737.[8] *LG* Seq 37. Civ bdry: 1956.[9] *Parl* Seq 12. *Eccl* Brack. RDn (until 1867), Brack. III RDn (1867—77), Brack. II RDn (1877—1954), Towc. RDn (1954—*).

GREAT ADDINGTON

AP *LG* Seq 18. *Parl* Seq 8. *Eccl* Seq 10.

LITTLE ADDINGTON

AP *LG* Seq 18. *Parl* N'rn Dv (1832—85), E'rn Dv (1885—1918), Peterb Dv/CC (1918—70), Wellingb. CC (1970—*). *Eccl* Seq 10.

ADSTONE

Chap in Canons Ashby AP, sep CP 1866,[10] sep EP 1867.[11] *LG* Seq 26. *Parl* Seq 12. *Eccl* Brack. II RDn (1867—77), Brack. I RDn (1877—1954), Culw. RDn (1954—56), Towc. RDn (1956—*).

AILSWORTH

[Soke Peterb] Hmlt in Castor AP, sep CP 1866.[10] Transf 1965 to Hunts & Peterb.[12] *LG* Seq 19. *Parl* Seq 6.

ALDERTON

AP *LG* Cleley Hd, Pott. PLU, RSD, RD. Civ bdry: 1883.[13] Abol civ 1935 ent to Grafton Regis AP.[14] *Parl* S'rn Dv (1832—1918), Dav. Dv (1918—48). *Eccl* Preston RDn (until 1867), Preston I RDn (1867—1954), Preston RDn (1954—70), Towc. RDn (1970—*).

ALDWINCLE

CP Cr 1885 by union Aldwincle All Saints AP, Aldwincle St Peter AP.[15] *LG* Huxl. Hd, Thrap. PLU, RSD, RD (1894—1935), Ound. & Thrap. RD (1935—74). *Parl* Peterb Dv/CC (1918—70), Wellingb. CC (1970—*).

ALDWINCLE ALL SAINTS

AP *LG* Huxl. Hd, Thrap. PLU, RSD. Abol civ 1885 to help cr Aldwincle CP.[15] *Parl* N'rn Dv (1832—1918). *Eccl* Ound. RDn. Abol eccl 1879 to help cr Aldwincle All Saints with St Peter EP.[16]

ALDWINCLE ALL SAINTS WITH ST PETER

EP Cr 1879 by union Aldwincle All Saints AP, Aldwincle St Peter AP.[16] Ound. II RDn (1867—82), High. Ferr. II RDn (1882—1954), Thrap. RDn (1954—70), Ound. RDn (1970—*).

ALDWINCLE ST PETER

AP Organisation as for Aldwincle All Saints.

ALTHORP

Ex-par place, sep CP 1858.[17] *LG* Nob. Gr. Hd, Brixw. PLU (1861—1930), RSD, RD. *Parl* Seq 11.

APETHORPE

AP *LG* Seq 41. *Parl* Seq 8. *Eccl* Pec jurisd Nassington. Gains eccl 1836 Woodnewton EP[18] and thereafter 'Apethorpe with Woodnewton', qv.

APETHORPE WITH WOODNEWTON

EP Union 1747 of Apethorpe AP, Woodnewton EP.[18] Pec jurisd Nassington (1747—1851), Ound. RDn (1851—67), Ound. III RDn (1867—77), Ound. I RDn (1877—82), Ound. II RDn (1882—1954), K's Cliffe RDn (1954—60), Ound. RDn (1960—*).

APPLETREE

Hmlt in Aston le Walls AP, sep CP 1866.[10] *LG* Chip. Ward. Hd, Banb. PLU, RSD, Midd. Chen. RD. Abol 1935 ent to Aston le Walls AP.[14] *Parl* S'rn Dv (1832—1918), Dav. Dv (1918—48).

ARMSTON

Hmlt in Polebrook AP, sep CP 1866.[10] *LG* Polebr. Hd, Ound. PLU, RSD, RD. Abol 1935 ent to Polebrook AP.[14] *Parl* N'rn Dv (1832—1918), Peterb Dv (1918—48).

ARTHINGWORTH

AP *LG* Seq 33. *Parl* Seq 4. *Eccl* Rothw. RDn (until 1867), Rothw. II RDn (1867—1954), Rothw. RDn (1954—70), Brixw. RDn (1970—*).

CANONS ASHBY

AP Orig priory church, donative from Dissolution. Incl chap Adstone (sep CP 1866,[10] sep EP 1867[11]). *LG* Gr's Nort. Hd, Dav. PLU, RSD, RD. *Parl* Seq 12. *Eccl* Brack. RDn (until 1867), Brack. II RDn (1867—77), Brack. I RDn (1877—1952), Colw. RDn (1952—70), Brack. RDn (1970—*).

CASTLE ASHBY

AP *LG* Seq 43. *Parl* Seq 10. *Eccl* Preston RDn (until 1867), Preston III RDn (1867—73), Preston II RDn (1873—1954), Wootton RDn (1954—70), Wellingb. RDn (1970—*).

COLD ASHBY

AP *LG* Guilsb. Hd, Brixw. PLU (1836—1930), RSD, RD. *Parl* Seq 11. *Eccl* Seq 6.

MEARS ASHBY

AP *LG* Seq 14. *Parl* Seq 2. *Eccl* Seq 24.

ASHBY ST LEDGERS

AP *LG* Seq 9. *Parl* Seq 10. *Eccl* Seq 5.

ASHLEY

AP *LG* Seq 5. *Parl* Seq 3. *Eccl* Seq 28.

ASHTON

AP Orig chap in Roade AP,[19] sep par by 1535. *LG* Seq 1. *Parl* Seq 12. *Eccl* Seq 21.

ASHTON

Hmlt in Oundle AP, sep CP 1866.[10] *LG* Seq 30. Bdry: 1885.[20] *Parl* Seq 8.

ASHTON

[Soke Peterb] Hmlt in Ufford AP (eccl in chap Bainton in that par), sep CP 1866.[10] *LG* Nassab. Hd, Stamf. PLU, RSD. Bdry: 1883.[21] Abol 1887 ent to Bainton CP.[22] *Parl* N'rn Dv (1832—1918).

ASTON LE WALLS

AP Incl hmlt Appletree (sep CP 1866[10]). *LG* Seq 38. Addtl civ bdry alt: 1884,[23] 1935 (gains Appletree CP).[14] *Parl* Seq 12. *Eccl* Seq 1.

ASTWELL AND FALCOTT

Hmlt in Wappenham AP, sep CP 1866.[10] *LG* K's Sutt. Hd, Brack. PLU, RSD, RD. Bdry: 1885.[24] Abol 1935 ent to Helmdon AP.[14] *Parl* S'rn DV (1832—1918), Dav. Dv (1918—48).

AYNHO

AP Usual civ spelling; for eccl see following entry. *LG* Seq 36. *Parl* Seq 12.

AYNHOE

AP Usual eccl spelling; for civ see prev entry. *Eccl* Seq 3.

BADBY

AP Incl chap Newnham (prob sep par at Reformation), thereafter incl undivided pt Lands Common to Badby and Newnham (abol 1935, pt to each par[14]). *LG* Seq 9. *Parl* Seq 12. *Eccl* Seq 5.

BAINTON

[Soke Peterb] Chap in Ufford AP, sep civ identity

early, not sep eccl (incl eccl hmlt Ashton in same par, qv for sep civ identity). *LG* Seq 20. Bdry: 1883,[21] 1887 (incl gains Ashton CP).[22] Transf 1965 to Hunts & Peterb.[12] *Parl* Seq 6.

BANBURY

AP Pt in Northants (K's Sutt. Hd: tg Neithrop, civ incl in area Warkworth AP, sep CP 1866 to be in Oxon[10]; chap Grimsbury, pec jurisd Banbury, sep CP 1894 to be in Oxon,[25] eccl severed 1846 to help cr South Banbury EP,[26] 'Grimsbury' a sep EP 1921 from South Banbury EP[27]), pt in Oxon (main area, Banb. Hd, Bor/MB), the par ent Oxon from 1894, qv for other civ organisation. *Parl* Northants pt, Banbury Parl Bor (1832—85), S'rn Dv (1885—1918). *Eccl* See main entry in Oxon, incl pec jurisd. Banbury (until 1851).

SOUTH BANBURY

EP Cr 1846 from Banbury AP (Oxon, Northants) incl chap Grimsbury (Norhtants).[27] Deddington RDn (dioc Oxford). See Oxon for bdry alt 1852 (area in Oxon only) and for eccl abol 1967 ent to Banbury AP (by then ent Oxon); addtl eccl bdry alt: 1921 (orig area Grimsbury [Northants] cr 'Grimsbury' EP).[27]

BARBY

AP *LG* Seq 10. *Parl* Seq 10. *Eccl* Seq 5.

BARFORD

AP Orig par or chap (Rothw. RDn) in jurisd Pipewell Abbey, sep par at Dissolution but destroyed after 1625 and thereafter ex-par,[28] sep CP 1858.[17] *LG* Rothw. Hd, Kett. PLU (1862—1930), RSD, RD. Abol 1935 ent to Rushton AP.[29] *Parl* N'rn Dv (1832—85), Mid Dv (1885—1918), Kett. Dv (1918—48).

BARNACK

AP [Soke Peterb] Incl hmlts Pilsgate, Southorpe (each a sep CP 1866[10]). *LG* Seq 20. Addtl civ bdry alt: 1887 (gains Pilsgate CP).[30] Transf 1965 to Hunts & Peterb.[12] *Parl* Seq 6. *Eccl* Seq 19.

BARNWELL

CP Cr 1935 by union Barnwell All Saints AP, Barnwell St Andrew AP.[14] *LG* Ound. & Thrap. RD. *Parl* Peterb CC (1948—70), Wellingb. CC (1970—*).

EP Union 1821 of Barnwell All Saints AP (church in ruins), Barnwell St Andrew AP.[31] Ound. RDn (cr—1867), Ound. III RDn (1867—73), Ound. I RDn (1873—77), Ound. II RDn (1877—1954), K's Cliffe RDn (1954—60), Ound. RDn (1960—*).

BARNWELL ALL SAINTS

AP *LG* Huxl. Hd, Ound. PLU, RSD, RD. Abol civ 1935 to help cr Barnwell CP.[14] *Parl* N'rn Dv (1832—1918), Peterb Dv (1918—48). *Eccl* Ound. RDn. Church in ruins, united 1821 with Barnwell St Andrew AP as 'Barnwell' EP.[31]

BARNWELL ST ANDREW

AP *LG* Poleb. Hd, Ound. PLU, RSD, RD. Remainder of organisation as for Barnwell All Saints.

BARROWDEN AND WAKERLEY

EP Cr 1972 by union Barrowden AP (Rutl), Wakerley AP (Northants).[32] Barnack RDn.

EARLS BARTON

AP *LG* Seq 14. *Parl* Seq 2. *Eccl* Seq 24.

BARTON SEAGRAVE

AP *LG* Huxl. Hd, Kett. PLU, RSD, RD. Abol civ 1935 pt to Kett. UD & AP, pt to help cr Cranford CP.[14] *Parl* N'rn Dv (1832—1918), Kett. Dv (1918—48). *Eccl* Seq 9.

BEANFIELD LAWNS

Ex-par place, sep CP 1858,[17] pt eccl severed 1961 and transf to Cottingham AP,[33] pt eccl severed 1961 to help cr Corby St Peter and St Andrew EP.[34] *LG* Corby Hd, Kett. PLU (1863—1930), RSD, RD. Abol 1935 ent to Cottingham AP.[14] *Parl* N'rn Dv (1832—1918), Kett. Dv (1918—48).

BENEFIELD

AP *LG* Seq 30. Civ bdry: 1885,[20] 1895 (gains the pt of Oundle AP not in Ound. UD).[35] *Parl* Seq 8. *Eccl* Seq 15.

BILLING

CP Cr 1925 by union Great Billing AP, Little Billing AP.[14] *LG* N'htn RD. Civ bdry: 1965 (incl loses pt to N'htn CB [assoc with Northants] & CP),[36] 1969 (loses pt to N'htn CB [assoc with Northants] & CP),[37] 1971 (loses pt to N'htn CB [assoc with Northants] & CP).[38] *Parl* S Northants CC (1948—70), Dav. CC (1970—*). Parl bdry: 1973.[39]

GREAT BILLING

AP *LG* Spel. Hd, N'htn PLU, RSD, RD. Abol civ 1935 to help cr Billing CP.[14] *Parl* S'rn Dv (1832—85), Mid Dv (1885—1918), Kett. Dv (1918—48). *Eccl* Seq 8.

LITTLE BILLING

AP Organisation as for Great Billing.

BLAKESLEY

AP Incl hmlt Woodend (sep CP 1866[10]). *LG* Seq 26. Addtl civ bdry alt: 1883,[40] 1956.[9] *Parl* Seq 12. *Eccl* Brack. RDn (until 1867), Brack. II RDn (1867—1954), Towc. RDn (1954—*).

BLATHERWYCKE

AP United par cr 1448 by union Blatherwycke Holy Trinity AP, Blatherwycke St Mary Magdalene AP (ruins).[41] *LG* Seq 6. Sometimes incl Laxton AP (orig 2 chaps in Rockingham Forest, sep par 1265, later sometimes considered curacy in this par,[42] but sep civ and eccl status sustained). Civ bdry: 1885.[43] *Parl* Seq 8. *Eccl* Weldon RDn (1448—1867), Weldon I RDn (1867—73), Weldon II RDn (1873—82), Ound. II RDn (1882—1954), K's Cliffe RDn (1954—60), Upp. RDn (1960—70), Barnack RDn (1970—*). Eccl bdry: 1948 (gains the pt of ex-par Fineshade in Blatherwycke CP).[44]

BLATHERWYCKE HOLY TRINITY

AP Weldon RDn, abol 1448 to help cr Blatherwycke AP.[41]

BLATHERWYCKE ST MARY MAGDALENE

AP Organisation as for Blatherwycke Holy Trinity.

BLISWORTH

AP *LG* Wym. Hd, Towc. PLU, RSD, RD. *Parl* Seq 12. *Eccl* Seq 21.

BODDINGTON

CP Cr 1935 by union Lower Boddington CP, Upper Boddington CP.[14] *LG* Brack. RD. *Parl* S Northants CC (1948—70), Dav. CC (1970—*).

BODDINGTON

AP Two lordships combined into one par, served by 2

rectors but united by 1291.[45]; for civ see following 2 entries (each with sep civ identity early). *Eccl* Seq 1.

LOWER BODDINGTON
Area in Boddington AP, sep civ identity early. *LG* Chip. Ward. Hd, Banb. PLU, RSD, Midd. Chen. RD. Abol 1935 to help cr Boddington CP.[14] *Parl* S'rn Dv (1832—1918), Dav. Dv (1918—48).

UPPER BODDINGTON
Area in Boddington AP, sep civ identity early. Organisation as for Lower Boddington.

BOONGATE
EP [Soke Peterb] Cr 1857 from Peterborough AP.[46] Peterb RDn (1857—67), Peterb II RDn (1867—73), Peterb I RDn (1873—1954), Peterb RDn (1954—*). Bdry: 1891 (help cr Peterborough All Saints EP),[47] 1933,[48] 1950.[49] Now called 'Peterborough St Mary'.

BOROUGH FEN
[Soke Peterb] Ex-par place, sep CP 1858.[17] *LG* Nassab. Hd, Peterb PLU (1861—1930), RSD, RD. Transf 1965 to Hunts & Peterb.[12] *Parl* Seq 6.

BOUGHTON
AP *LG* Seq 34. Civ bdry: 1900 (gains pt of the pt of Kingsthorpe CP not transf to N'htn CB),[1] 1932 (incl loses pt to N'htn CB [assoc with Northants] & CP),[50] 1965 (loses pt to N'htn CB [assoc with Northants] & CP),[36] 1969 (loses pt to N'htn CB [assoc with Northants] & CP).[37] *Parl* Seq 11. Parl bdry: 1973.[39] *Eccl* Seq 8. Eccl bdry: 1954.[51]

LITTLE BOWDEN
AP *LG* Rothw. Hd, Mkt. Harb. PLU, pt Mkt. Harb. USD (o'wise ent Leics), pt Mkt. Harb. RSD, pt Mkt. Harb. UD (the pt of this par which became 1889 pt sep RD in Northants (1894—96). Civ bdry: 1896 (loses the pt in Northants to Great Oxendon AP, Northants, and 'Little Bowden' ent Leics [Mkt. Harb. UD] thereafter).[52] *Parl* N'rn Dv (1832—85), Mid Dv (1885—1918), thereafter Leics. *Eccl* Rothw. RDn (until 1867), Rothw. II RDn (1867—1926), not in a RDn (when initially transf to dioc Leic, 1926—27), Gartree I RDn (1927—*). Eccl bdry: 1892,[53] 1920 (cr Little Bowden St Hugh EP).[54]

LITTLE BOWDEN ST HUGH
EP Cr 1920 from Little Bowden AP.[54] Rothw. II RDn (1920—26), not in a RDn (when initially transf to dioc Leic, 1926—27), Gartree I RDn (1927—*).

BOZEAT
AP *LG* Seq 16. *Parl* Seq 2. *Eccl* High. Ferr. RDn (until 1867), High. Ferr. III RDn 1867—82), High. Ferr. I RDn (1882—1954), High. RDn (1954—70), Wellingb. RDn (1970—*).

BRACKLEY ST JAMES
Chap in Brackley St Peter AP, sep civ identity early. *LG* K's Sutt. Hd, Brack. Bor, PLU, RSD. Abol 1884 ent to Brackley St Peter AP.[55] *Parl* Brack. Parl Bor (1547—1832), S'rn Dv (1832—85).

BRACKLEY ST PETER
AP Incl chap Brackley St James (sep civ identity early). *LG* K's Sutt. Hd, Brack. Bor, PLU, RSD (1875—86), USD (1886—94), MB (1886—1974). Addtl civ bdry alt: 1884,[56] 1884,[57] 1884 (gains Brackley St James CP),[55] 1935,[14] 1957.[58] *Parl* Brack. Parl Bor (1547—1832), Seq 12 thereafter. *Eccl* Seq 3.

BRADDEN
AP *LG* Seq 26. Civ bdry: 1956.[9] *Parl* Seq 12. *Eccl* Seq 4.

BRAFIELD ON THE GREEN
AP *LG* Seq 43. Civ bdry: 1884,[59] 1971 (loses pt to N'htn CB [assoc with Northants] & CP),[38] 1974 (the main pt remains as a constituent par of S Northants Dist while the pt of the par transf to N'htn Dist ceases to be in a par).[60] *Parl* Seq 10. Parl bdry: 1973.[39] *Eccl* Seq 23.

CHAPEL BRAMPTON
Chap in Church Brampton AP, ruins by 16th cent,[61] sep civ identity early. *LG* Seq 23. *Parl* Seq 11.

CHURCH BRAMPTON
AP Incl chap Chapel Brampton (in ruins by 16th cent,[61] sep civ identity early). *LG* Seq 23. *Parl* Seq 11. *Eccl* Seq 7.

BRAMPTON ASH
AP *LG* Seq 5. *Parl* Seq 3. *Eccl* Seq 28.

BRAUNSTON
AP *LG* Seq 9. *Parl* Seq 12. *Eccl* Seq 5.

BRAYBROOKE
AP *LG* Rothw. Hd, Mkt. Harb. PLU, RSD, Oxend. RD (1894—1935), Kett. RD (1935—74). *Parl* Seq 3. *Eccl* Seq 26.

BRIGSTOCK
AP Incl chap Stanion (sep civ identity early, not sep eccl hence this par eccl 'Brigstock with Stanion', qv). *LG* Corby Hd, Thrap. PLU, RSD, RD (1894—1935), Ound. & Thrap. RD (1935—74). *Parl* Seq 8.

BRIGSTOCK WITH STANION
AP Usual eccl spelling; for civ and civ sep chap, see prev entry. *Eccl* Weldon RDn (until 1867), Weldon II RDn (1867—82), High. Ferr. RDn (1882—1954), Thrap. RDn (1954—63), Weldon RDn (1963—70), Corby RDn (1970—*).

BRINGTON
AP *LG* Seq 23. *Parl* Seq 11. *Eccl* Haddon RDn (until 1867), Haddon II RDn (1867—1954), Brampton RDn (1954—55), Haddon RDn (1955—70), Dav. RDn (1970—*).

BRIXWORTH
AP *LG* Seq 27. *Parl* Seq 4. *Eccl* Seq 27.

BROCKHALL
AP *LG* Seq 24. *Parl* Seq 12. *Eccl* Haddon RDn (until 1867), Haddon I RDn (1867—73), Weedon RDn (1873—1970), Dav. RDn (1970—*).

BROUGHTON
AP *LG* Seq 28. *Parl* Seq 1. *Eccl* Rothw. RDn (until 1867), Rothw. I RDn (1867—1954), Wellingb. RDn (1954—70), Kett. RDn (1970—*).

LONG BUCKBY
AP *LG* Seq 12. Civ bdry: 1884.[62] *Parl* Seq 10. *Eccl* Haddon RDn (until 1867), Haddon II RDn (1867—73), Haddon I RDn (1873—1954), Haddon RDn (1954—72), Brixw. RDn (1972—*).

BUGBROOKE
AP Incl pt area Upper Heyford (sep civ identity early). *LG* Seq 25. *Parl* Seq 10. *Eccl* Haddon RDn (until 1867), Haddon II RDn (1867—73), Weedon RDn

(1873—1970), Dav. RDn (1970—*).

BULWICK

AP *LG* Seq 6. *Parl* Seq 8. *Eccl* Seq 30.

BURTON LATIMER

AP *LG* Huxl. Hd, Kett. PLU, RSD, RD (1894—1923), Burton Latimer UD (1923—74). *Parl* Seq 5. *Eccl* Seq 9.

BYFIELD

AP *LG* Seq 40. Civ bdry: 1884.[63] *Parl* Seq 12. *Eccl* Seq 1.

EAST CARLTON

Orig chap in Cottingham AP, sep par *ca* 1230.[64] Civ bdry: 1885.[65] *LG* Seq 4. *Parl* Seq 5. *Eccl* Seq 28.

CASTOR

AP [Soke Peterb] Incl hmlt Ailsworth (sep CP 1866[10]), chap Sutton (sep CP 1866,[10] sep EP 1851[66]), chap Upton (sep CP 1866,[10] sep EP 1851[66]). *LG* Seq 19. Addtl civ bdry alt: 1956 (exchanges pts with Alwalton AP, Chesterton AP, both Hunts).[67] Transf 1965 to Hunts & Peterb.[12] *Parl* Seq 6. *Eccl* Seq 18.

CATESBY

AP Incl chap Hellidon (sep par early 13th cent[68]). *LG* Pt Catesby Bor, Seq 9. *Parl* Seq 12. *Eccl* Seq 5.

CHALCOMBE

AP *LG* Seq 35. *Parl* Seq 12. *Eccl* Seq 3.

CHARWELTON

AP *LG* Seq 9. *Parl* Seq 12. *Eccl* Seq 5.

CHELVESTON AND CALDECOTT

EP Cr 1967 from Chelveston and Caldecott with Newton Bromswold EP.[69] High. RDn.

CHELVESTON AND CALDECOTT WITH NEWTON BROMSWOLD

EP Cr 1927 by union Newton Bromswold AP, pt Higham Ferrers with Chelveston and Caldecott AP (specified pt of area of Chelveston and Caldecott).[70] High. Ferr. I RDn (1927—54), High. RDn (1954—67). Abol 1967 the area of Newton Bromswold CP severed and united with ex-par Higham Park to cr 'Newton Bromswold' EP, the remainder to be Chelveston and Caldecott EP.[69]

CHELVESTON CUM CALDECOTT

Chap in Higham Ferrers AP, sep civ identity early, eccl severed 1927 except for one pt to help cr Chelveston and Caldecott with Newton Bromswold EP.[70] *LG* Seq 15. Bdry: 1965 (loses pt to Melchbourne and Yelden CP, Beds).[71] *Parl* Seq 2.

CLAY COTON

AP Orig chap in Lilbourne AP, sep par by 1535. Usual eccl spelling; for civ see following entry. *Eccl* Haddon RDn (cr—1867), Haddon I RDn (1867—1954), Haddon RDn (1954—70), Brixw. RDn (1970—72). Abol eccl 1972 to help cr Yelvertoft with Clay Coton EP.[72]

CLAYCOTON

AP Orig chap in Lilbourne AP, sep par by 1535.[69] Usual civ spelling; for eccl see prev entry. *LG* Seq 13. *Parl* Seq 10.

KING'S CLIFFE

AP *LG* Seq 41. Civ bdry: 1965 (gains the pt of Thornhaugh AP, Soke Peterb, not transf to help cr Hunts & Peterb Adm Co).[68] *Parl* Seq 8. *Eccl* Ound. RDn (until 1867), Ound. IV RDn (1867—73), Weldon II RDn (1873—82), Ound. II RDn (1882—

1954), K's Cliffe RDn (1954—60), Barnack RDn (1960—*).

CLIPSTON

AP *LG* Seq 33. *Parl* Seq 4. *Eccl* Seq 27.

CLOPTON

AP *LG* Seq 22. Civ bdry: 1965 (gains pt Winwick AP, loses pt to Broughton and Molesworth CP, both Hunts, pt of the remainder of each help cr Hunts & Peterb Adm Co.[68] *Parl* Seq 8. *Eccl* Ound. RDn (until 1867), Ound. III RDn (1867—73), Ound. I RDn (1873—77), Ound. II RDn (1877—1954), Thrap. RDn (1954—70), Ound. RDn (1970—*).

COGENHOE

AP *LG* Seq 43. Civ bdry: 1884,[60] 1935 (gains Whiston AP),[14] 1971 (loses pt to N'htn CB [assoc with Northants] & CP).[38] *Parl* Seq 10. Parl bdry: 1973.[39] *Eccl* Seq 23.

COLLINGTREE

AP *LG* Seq 43. Civ bdry: 1974 (the pt transf to S Northants Dist severed to help reconstitute Milton Malsor AP in that Dist while the pt transf to N'htn Dist gains pt Courteenhall AP transf to that Dist as reconstituted 'Collingtree').[60] *Parl* Seq 10. *Eccl* Seq 23.

COLLYWESTON

AP *LG* Seq 42. *Parl* Seq 8. *Eccl* Seq 19.

CORBY

AP *LG* Corby Hd, Kett. PLU, RSD, RD (1894—1939), Corby UD (1939—74). Civ bdry: 1939 (gains pt Weldon CP as the enlarged par constituted Corby UD),[73] 1952,[74] 1955,[75] 1967,[76] 1971.[77] *Parl* Seq 5. *Eccl* Weldon RDn (until 1867), Weldon II RDn (1867—82), Weldon I RDn (1882—1954), Weldon RDn (1954—69). Eccl bdry: 1940 (cr Corby St Columba EP),[78] 1961,[33] 1961 (help cr Corby St Peter and St Andrew EP).[34] Renamed 1969 'Corby The Epiphany with St John the Baptist EP.[79]

CORBY THE EPIPHANY WITH ST JOHN THE BAPTIST

EP Renaming 1969 of Corby AP.[79] Weldon RDn (1969—70), Corby RDn (1970—*).

CORBY ST COLUMBA

EP Cr 1940 from Corby AP.[78] Weldon RDn (1940—70), Corby RDn (1970—*). Bdry: 1961.[33]

CORBY ST PETER AND ST ANDREW

EP Cr 1961 from Corby AP, Cottingham AP, Great Oakley AP, pt ex-par Beanfield Lawns.[34] Weldon RDn (1961—70), Corby RDn (1970—*). Bdry: 1970.[80]

COSGROVE

AP *LG* Seq 2. Civ bdry: 1883,[13] 1916,[81] 1951 (incl help cr Old Stratford CP).[82] *Parl* Seq 12. *Eccl* Seq 20.

COTTESBROOKE

AP *LG* Seq 11. *Parl* Seq 11. *Eccl* Seq 6.

COTON

Hmlt (Guilsb. Hd) in Ravensthorpe AP (o'wise Nob. Gr Hd), sep CP 1866.[10] *LG* Guilsb. Hd, Brixw. PLU, RSD, RD. Abol 1935 ent to Ravensthorpe AP.[14] *Parl* S'rn Dv (1832—85), Mid Dv (1885—1918), Kett. Dv (1918—48).

COTTERSTOCK

AP Incl chap Glapthorn (sep civ identity early, sep EP 1922[83] hence this par eccl 'Cotterstock with Glapthorn', qv in following entry). *LG* Seq 41. *Parl* Seq 8.

COTTERSTOCK WITH GLAPTHORN

AP Usual eccl spelling; for civ and civ sep chap, see prev entry. *Eccl* Ound. RDn (until 1867), Ound. I RDn (1867—1922). Abol eccl 1922, chap Glapthorn severed to be a sep par, the remainder to help cr Tansor with Cottestock EP.[83]

COTTINGHAM

AP Incl tp Middleton (sep CP 1866[10]), chap East Carlton (sep par *ca 1230*[61]). *LG* Seq 4. Addtl civ bdry alt: 1935 (gains Beanfield Lawns CP),[14] 1952.[74] *Parl* Seq 5. *Eccl* Seq 28. Addtl eccl bdry alt: 1961,[33] 1961 (help cr Corby St Peter and St Andrew EP),[34] 1970.[80]

COURTEENHALL

AP *LG* Seq 43. Civ bdry: 1884,[57] 1974 (the pt transf to N'htn Dist severed to help reconstitute Collingtree AP in that Dist while the pt transf to S Northants Dist reconstituted as 'Courteenhall').[60] *Parl* Seq 10. *Eccl* Seq 22.

CRANFORD

CP Cr 1935 by union Cranford St Andrew AP, Cranford St John AP, pt Barton Seagrave AP.[14] *LG* Kett. RD. *Parl* Kett. CC (1948—*).

EP Cr 1954 by union Cranford St Andrew AP, Cranford St John AP.[84] Kett. RDn.

CRANFORD ST ANDREW

AP *LG* Huxl. Hd, Kett. PLU, RSD, RD. Civ bdry: 1885.[85] Abol civ 1935 to help cr Cranford CP.[14] *Parl* N'rn Dv (1832—1918), Kett. Dv (1918—48). *Eccl* High. Ferr. RDn (until 1867), High. Ferr. I RDn (1867—82), Weldon II RDn (1882—1954), Kett. RDn (1954). Abol eccl 1954 to help cr Cranford EP.[84]

CRANFORD ST JOHN

AP Organisation and bdry alt as for Cranford St Andrew.

CRANSLEY

AP *LG* Seq 28. *Parl* Seq 1. *Eccl* Seq 26.

GREAT CREATON

AP *LG* Seq 11. Civ bdry: 1884 (gains Little Creaton CP).[86] *Parl* Seq 11. *Eccl* Seq 6.

LITTLE CREATON

Hmlt (Guilsb. Hd) in Spratton AP (o'wise Spel. Hd), sep CP 1866.[10] *LG* Guilsb. Hd, Brixw. PLU, RSD. Abol 1884 ent to Great Creaton AP.[86] *Parl* S'rn Dv (1832—85).

CRICK

AP *LG* Seq 13. *Parl* Seq 10. *Eccl* Seq 6.

CROUGHTON

AP *LG* Seq 36. *Parl* Seq 12. *Eccl* Seq 3.

CULWORTH

AP *LG* Seq 36. *Parl* Seq 12. *Eccl* Seq 1.

DALLINGTON

AP *LG* Nob. Gr. Hd, N'htn PLU, pt Hardingst. USD, pt N'htn RSD, pt Hardingst. UD (1894—95), N'htn RD (pt 1894—95, ent 1895—1932). Civ bdry: 1895 (the pt in Hardingst. UD cr Dallington St James CP),[87] 1900.[1] Abol civ 1932 pt to N'htn CB (assoc with Northants) & CP, pt to Duston AP.[50] *Parl* Pt N'htn Parl Bor (1867—1918), S'rn Dv (ent 1832—67, pt 1867—85), pt Mid Dv (1885—1918), Dav.

Dv (1918—48). *Eccl* Seq 14. Eccl bdry: 1872 (help cr Dallington St James EP),[88] 1964 (cr King's Heath EP).[89]

DALLINGTON ST JAMES

EP Cr 1872 from Dallington AP, Duston AP.[88] N'htn RDn. Renamed 1959 'Northampton St James'.[90]

CP Cr 1895 from the pt of Dallington AP in Hardingst. UD.[87] *LG* N'htn PLU, Hardingst. UD (1895—96), St James (N'htn) UD (1896—1900), N'htn CB (1900—13). Bdry: 1900.[1] Abol 1913 ent to Northampton CP.[4]

DAVENTRY

AP Incl chap Welton (sep par by 1535[19]). *LG* Fawsley Hd, Dav. PLU, Bor/MB, USD. *Parl* Seq 12. *Eccl* Dav. RDn. Addtl eccl bdry alt: 1840 (cr Daventry St James EP).[11] Abol eccl 1973 to help cr Daventry with Norton EP.[91]

DAVENTRY ST JAMES

EP Cr 1840 from Daventry AP.[11] Dav. RDn.

DAVENTRY WITH NORTON

EP Cr 1973 by union Daventry AP, Norton AP.[91] Dav. RDn.

DEANSHANGER

CP Renaming 1948 of Passenham AP.[92] *LG* Towc. RD. Bdry: 1951 (help cr Old Stratford CP),[82] 1956.[9] *Parl* Dav. CC (1970—*).

DEENE

AP Incl hmlt Deenethorpe (sep CP 1866[10]). *LG* Seq 6. Addtl civ bdry alt: 1885.[93] *Parl* Seq 8. *Eccl* Weldon RDn (until 1867), Weldon II RDn (1867—82), Ound. II RDn (1882—1954), K's Cliffe RDn (1954—60), Weldon RDn (1960—70), Corby RDn (1970—*).

DEENETHORPE

Hmlt in Deene AP, sep CP 1866.[10] *LG* Seq 6. Bdry: 1885.[93] *Parl* Seq 8.

DEEPING GATE

[Soke Peterb] Hmlt in Maxey AP, sep CP 1866.[10] *LG* Seq 19. Transf 1965 to Hunts & Peterb.[12] *Parl* Seq 6.

DENFORD

AP Orig sep AP (High. Ferr. RDn), united before 1535 with Ringstead (prob orig sep AP), the union eccl 'Denford with Ringstead', qv, each par retains or soon regains sep civ identity. *LG* Seq 18. *Parl* Seq 8.

DENFORD WITH RINGSTEAD

AP Name for union before 1535 of Denford AP, Ringstead (prob orig sep AP); for civ (sep civ identities retained or early regained), see 'Denford', 'Ringstead'. *Eccl* Seq 11.

DENTON

Chap in Yardley Hastings AP, sep civ identity early, sep EP 1892.[94] *LG* Seq 43. *Parl* Seq 10. *Eccl* Preston II RDn (1892—1954), Preston RDn (1954—70), Wootton RDn (1970—*).

DESBOROUGH

AP *LG* Rothw. Hd, Kett. PLU, RSD (1875—91), Desborough USD (1891—94), UD. *Parl* Seq 5. *Eccl* Seq 26.

DINGLEY

AP *LG* Seq 5. *Parl* Seq 3. *Eccl* Seq 28.

GREAT DODDINGTON
AP *LG* Seq 14. *Parl* Seq 2. *Eccl* Seq 24.
DODFORD
AP *LG* Seq 9. *Parl* Seq 12. *Eccl* Dav. RDn (until 1873), Weldon RDn (1873—1970), Dav. RDn (1970—*).
DRAUGHTON
AP *LG* Seq 31. *Parl* Seq 4. *Eccl* Seq 27.
DUDDINGTON
Chap in Gretton AP, sep civ identity early, prob sep EP 1733 (date 1st registers).[95] *LG* Seq 42. *Parl* Seq 8. *Eccl* Pec jurisd Grett. (until 1851), Weldon RDn (1851—67), Weldon II RDn (1867—1954), K's Cliffe RDn (1954—60), Barnack RDn (1960—*).
DUSTON
AP *LG* Nob. Gr. Hd, N'htn PLU, pt Hardingst. USD, pt N'htn RSD, pt Hardingst. UD (1894—95), N'htn RD (pt 1894—95, ent 1895—1965). Civ bdry: 1895 (the pt in Hardingst. UD cr Duston St James CP),[87] 1900,[1] 1932 (incl loses pt to N'htn CB [assoc with Northants] & CP).[50] Abol civ 1965 pt to N'htn CB (assoc with Northants) & CP, pt to Upton CP, pt to Harlestone AP.[36] *Parl* Pt N'htn Parl Bor (1867—1918), S'rn Dv (ent 1832—67, pt 1867—85), pt Mid Dv (1885—1918), Dav. Dv (1918—48), S Northants CC (1948—70). *Eccl* Seq 14. Eccl bdry: 1872 (help cr Dallington St James EP),[88] 1971 (gains area church Upton from Northampton St Peter with Upton AP [the latter renamed 'Northampton St Peter']).[96]
DUSTON ST JAMES
CP Cr 1895 from the pt of Duston AP in Hardingst. UD.[87] *LG* N'htn PLU, Hardingst. UD (1895—96), St James (N'htn) UD (1896—1900), N'htn CB (1900—13). Bdry: 1900.[1] Abol 1913 ent to Northampton CP.[4]
EASTON BY STANFORD
AP Usual eccl spelling; for civ see 'Easton on the Hill'. *Eccl* Seq 19.
EASTON MAUDIT
AP *LG* Seq 16. *Parl* Seq 2. *Eccl* High. Ferr. RDn (until 1867), High. Ferr. III RDn (1867—82), High. Ferr. I RDn (1882—1954), High. RDn (1954—70), Wellingb. RDn (1970—*).
EASTON NESTON
AP *LG* Seq 3. *Parl* Seq 12. *Eccl* Preston RDn (until 1867), Preston I RDn (1867—1924), Brack. RDn (1924—54), Culw. RDn (1954—70), Towc. RDn (1970—*).
EASTON ON THE HILL
AP Usual civ spelling; for eccl see 'Easton by Stanford'. *LG* Seq 42. *Parl* Seq 8.
ECTON
AP *LG* Seq 14. Civ bdry: 1971 (loses pt to N'htn CB [assoc with Northants] & CP),[38] 1974 (the main pt remains as a constituent par of S Northants Dist while the pt transf to N'htn Dist ceases to be in a par).[60] *Parl* Seq 2. Parl bdry: 1973.[39] *Eccl* Seq 25.
EDGCOTE
AP *LG* Chip. Ward. Hd, Brack. PLU (1835—ca 1894), Banb. PLU (ca 1894—1930), RSD, Midd. Chen. RD (1894—1935), Brack. RD (1935—74). *Parl* Seq 12. *Eccl* Brack. RDn (until 1867), Brack. II RDn (1867—73), Brack. I RDn (1873—1954), Culw.

RDn (1954—70), Brack. RDn (1970—*).
ELKINGTON
AP Orig AP (curacy, Haddon RDn), in ruins by 16th cent and thereafter ex-par,[97] sep civ identity sustained. *LG* Seq 13. *Parl* Seq 10.
ETTON
AP [Soke Peterb] *LG* Seq 19. Transf 1965 to Hunts & Peterb.[12] *Parl* Seq 6. *Eccl* Peterb RDn (until 1867), Peterb II RDn (1867—1954), Barnack RDn (1954—70), Peterb RDn (1970—*).
EVENLEY
AP *LG* Seq 36. Civ bdry: 1957.[58] *Parl* Seq 12. *Eccl* Seq 3.
EVERDON
AP *LG* Seq 9. *Parl* Seq 12. *Eccl* Seq 5.
EYDON
AP *LG* Seq 39. *Parl* Seq 12. *Eccl* Seq 2.
EYE
AP [Soke Peterb] *LG* Seq 19. Transf 1965 to Hunts & Peterb.[12] *Parl* Seq 6. *Eccl* Peterb RDn (until 1867), Peterb I RDn (1867—1954), Peterb RDn (1954—*).
FAR COTTON
Area in Hardingstone AP, sep EP 1875,[98] sep CP 1895 (the pt of the par in Hardingst. UD).[87] *LG* Hardingst. PLU, UD (1895—96), Far Cotton UD (1896—1900), N'htn CB (1900—31). Civ bdry: 1900 (the pt not transf to N'htn CB [assoc with Northants] transf to Hardingstone AP).[1] Abol civ 1932 ent to Northampton CP.[50] *Parl* N'htn Parl Bor (1918—48). *Eccl* N'htn RDn. Eccl bdry: 1960.[99] Renamed 1960 'Northampton St Mary the Virgin' EP.[100]
FARNDISH
AP *LG* Pt Beds (Willey Hd), pt Northants (High. Ferr. Hd), made ent Beds 1832 for parl purposes, 1844 for civ purposes,[101] qv for later civ (incl Wellingb. PLU), parl and eccl organisation.
EAST FARNDON
AP *LG* Seq 33. Civ bdry: 1965 (loses pt to Lubenham AP, Leics).[102] *Parl* Seq 4. *Eccl* Rothw. RDn (until 1867), Rothw. III RDn (1867—1954), Brixw. RDn (1954—67), Rothw. RDn (1967—70), Brixw. RDn (1970—*).
FARTHINGHOE
AP *LG* Seq 36. Civ bdry: 1935 (gains Steane AP),[14] 1957.[58] *Parl* Seq 12. *Eccl* Seq 3.
FARTHINGSTONE
AP *LG* Seq 9. *Parl* Seq 12. *Eccl* Dav. RDn (until 1873), Weedon RDn (1873—1970), Dav. RDn (1970—*).
FAWSLEY
AP *LG* Seq 9. *Parl* Seq 12. *Eccl* Seq 5.
FAXTON
Chap in Lamport AP, sep CP 1866.[10] *LG* Orl. Hd, Brixw. PLU, RSD, RD. Abol 1935 ent to Lamport AP.[14] *Parl* N'rn Dv (1832—85), Mid Dv (1885—1918), Kett. Dv (1918—48).
FINEDON
AP *LG* Huxl. Hd, Finedon Bor (status not sustained), Wellingb. PLU, RSD, Finedon UD. Abol civ 1935 ent to Wellingb. UD & AP.[103] *Parl* N'rn Dv (1832—85), E'rn Dv (1885—1918), Wellingb. Dv (1918—48). *Eccl* High. Ferr. RDn (until 1867), High. Ferr. I RDn (1867—1954), High. RDn

(1954—*).

FINESHADE

Priory church, eccl and civ ex-par from Dissolution, sep CP 1858,[17] abol eccl 1948, the pt in Fineshade CP transf to Wakerley AP, the pt in Blatherwyke AP transf to that par.[44] *LG* Seq 8. Bdry: 1880.[43] *Parl* Seq 8.

FLETTON

AP Ent Hunts (Norman Cross Hd), pt Peterb MB & USD (1874—94), that pt transf 1889 to Soke Peterb Adm Co (1889—94), the par civ abol 1894, the pt in the MB cr Fletton Urban CP in Soke Peterb, the remainder cr Fletton Rural CP in Hunts.[104] See the main entry in Hunts for civ, parl, and eccl organisation. *Parl* Ent Hunts (qv) except pt Peterb Parl Bor (1867—1918).

FLETTON URBAN

CP [Soke Peterb] Cr 1894 from the pt of Fletton AP (orig ent Hunts until this pt in Peterb MB becomes 1889 pt Soke Peterb Adm Co) in Peterb MB.[104] *LG* Peterb PLU, MB. Abol 1929 to help cr Peterborough CP.[105] *Parl* Peterb Dv (1918—48).

FLORE

AP Incl pt area Upper Heyford (sep civ identity early). *LG* Seq 24. *Parl* Seq 10. *Eccl* Haddon RDn (until 1867), Haddon II RDn (1867—73), Weedon RDn (1873—1970), Dav. RDn (1970—*).

FOTHERINGHAY

AP Collegiate church, curacy from Dissolution. *LG* Seq 41. Civ bdry: 1965 (exchanges pts with Elton AP, Hunts [main pt of latter to help cr Hunts & Peterb Adm Co]).[68] *Parl* Seq 8. *Eccl* Ound. RDn (16th cent—1867), Ound. IV RDn (1867—73), Ound. III RDn (1873—77), Ound. I RDn (1877—82), Ound. II RDn (1882—1954), K's Cliffe RDn (1954—57), Ound. RDn (1957—*).

FURTHO

AP *LG* Cleley Hd, Pott. PLU, RSD, RD (1894—1935), Towc. RD (1935—51). Civ bdry: 1883.[13] Abol civ 1951 pt to Cosgrove AP, pt to help cr Old Stratford CP, pt to Potterspury AP.[82] *Parl* S'rn Dv (1832—1918), Dav. Dv (1918—48), S Northants CC (1948—70). *Eccl* Preston RDn (until 1867), Preston I RDn (1867—1921). Abol eccl 1921 to help cr Potterspury with Furtho and Yardley Gobion EP.[106]

GAYTON

AP *LG* Seq 37. *Parl* Seq 12. *Eccl* Seq 4.

GEDDINGTON

AP Incl chap Newton (comprised of 2 tps of Great Newton, Little Newton, each orig with a chap, the 2 united 1449 as a single chap, sep par from Dissolution[107]). *LG* Seq 4. *Parl* Seq 5. *Eccl* Seq 29. Addtl eccl bdry alt: 1973 (gains Newton EP).[108]

GLAPTHORN

Chap in Cotterstock AP, sep civ identity early, sep EP 1922.[83] *LG* Seq 41. *Parl* Seq 8. *Eccl* Ound. I RDn (1922—54), Ound. RDn (1954—*).

GLENDON

AP *LG* Rothw. Hd, Kett. PLU, RSD, RD. Abol civ 1935 ent to Rushton AP.[14] *Parl* N'rn Dv (1832—85), Mid Dv (1885—1918), Kett. Dv (1918—48). *Eccl* Rothw. RDn (until 1867), Rothw. II RDn (1867—1923). Abol eccl 1923 to help cr Rothwell

with Glendon EP.[109]

GLINTON

[Soke Peterb] Chap in Peakirk AP, sep civ identity early, sep EP 1865.[110] *LG* Seq 19. Civ bdry: 1883,[21] 1883.[111] Transf 1965 to Hunts & Peterb.[12] *Parl* Seq 6. *Eccl* Peterb RDn (1865—67), Peterb I RDn (1867—73), Peterb II RDn (1873—1954), Peterb RDn (1954—*).

GRAFTON REGIS

AP *LG* Seq 2. Civ bdry: 1883,[13] 1935 (gains Alderton AP).[14] *Parl* Seq 12. *Eccl* Seq 20.

GRAFTON UNDERWOOD

AP *LG* Seq 17. *Parl* Seq 5. *Eccl* Seq 9.

GREATWORTH

AP *LG* Seq 39. Civ bdry: 1935 (incl gains Stuchbury AP),[14] 1957.[58] *Parl* Seq 12. *Eccl* Seq 3. Eccl bdry: 1940.[112]

GRENDON

AP *LG* Wym. Hd, Wellingb. PLU, RSD, RD. *Parl* S'rn DV (1832—85), E'rn Dv (1885—1918), Wellingb. Dv/CC (1918—*). *Eccl* Preston RDn (until 1867), Preston III RDn (1867—73), Preston II RDn (1873—1954), Wootton RDn (1954—70), Wellingb. RDn (1970—*).

GRETTON

AP *LG* Incl chap Duddington (sep civ identity early, prob sep EP 1733 (date 1st registers[95]). *LG* Seq 7. Civ bdry: 1885 (gains the pt of Thorpe by Water CP [Rutl, Northants] in Northants and the latter ent Rutl thereafter),[113] 1971.[81] *Parl* Seq 7. *Eccl* Pec jurisd Lyddington (until 1851), Seq 31 thereafter.

GUILSBOROUGH

AP Incl hmlt Hollowell (sep CP 1866,[10] sep EP 1850[114]). Main tp sometimes early called 'Guilsborough and Nortoft'. *LG* Seq 11. *Parl* Seq 11. *Eccl* Haddon RDn (until 1867), Haddon I RDn (1867—1954), Haddon RDn (1954—70), Brixw. RDn (1970—72). Abol eccl 1972 to help cr Guilsborough with Hollowell EP.[115]

GUILSBOROUGH WITH HOLLOWELL

EP Cr 1972 by union Guilsborough AP, Hollowell EP.[115] Brixw. RDn.

GUNTHORPE

[Soke Peterb] Hmlt in Paston AP, sep CP 1866.[10] *LG* Nassab. Hd, Peterb PLU, RSD, RD. Bdry: 1883.[21] Abol 1929 to help cr Peterborough CP in Peterb MB.[105] *Parl* N'rn Dv (1832—1918), Peterb Dv (1918—48).

HACKLETON

Hmlt in Piddington AP, sep CP 1866.[10] *LG* Seq 43. Bdry: 1935 (gains Horton AP, Piddington AP, Preston Deanery AP).[14] *Parl* Seq 10.

EAST HADDON

AP *LG* Seq 23. *Parl* Seq 11. *Eccl* Haddon RDn (until 1867), Haddon I RDn (1867—1954), Haddon RDn (1954—70), Brixw. RDn (1970—72). Abol eccl 1972 to help cr East Haddon and Holdenby EP.[116]

EAST HADDON AND HOLDENBY

EP Cr 1972 by union East Haddon AP, Holdenby AP.[116] Brixw. RDn.

WEST HADDON

AP *LG* Seq 12. *Parl* Seq 10. *Eccl* Seq 6.

HANNINGTON

AP *LG* Seq 27. *Parl* Seq 4. *Eccl* Seq Rothw. RDn (until 1867), Rothw. I RDn (1867—1954), Wellingb. RDn (1954—70), Brixw. RDn (1970—*).

HANSLOPE

AP Mostly Bucks (Newport Hd), pt Northants (Cleley Hd), the pt in Northants transf 1894 to Hartwell CP (Northants) and Hanslope ent Bucks thereafter,[117] qv in entries for that co for later civ, parl and ent eccl organisation. *LG* Newport Pagnell PLU, RSD. *Parl* Northants pt, S'rn Dv (1832—1918).

HARDINGSTONE

AP *LG* Wym. Hd, Hardingst. PLU, pt Hardingst. USD, pt Hardingst. RSD, pt Hardingst. UD (1894—95), Hardingst. RD (pt 1894—95, ent 1895—1932), N'htn RD (1932—74). Civ bdry: 1895 (the pt in Hardingst. UD cr Far Cotton UD & CP),[87] 1900 (gains the pt of Far Cotton CP not transf to N'htn CB),[1] 1932 (loses pt to N'htn CB [assoc with Northants] & CP),[50] 1965 (exchanges pts with N'htn CB [assoc with Northants] & CP),[36] 1971 (loses pt to N'htn CB [assoc with Northants] & CP).[38] *Parl* S'rn Dv (ent 1832—67, pt 1867—85), pt N'htn Parl Bor (1867—1918), pt Mid Dv (1885—1918), Dav. Dv (1918—48), S Northants CC (1948—70), Dav. CC (1970—*). Parl bdry: 1973.[39] *Eccl* Seq 14. Eccl bdry: 1875 (cr Far Cotton EP),[98] 1960.[99]

HARDWICK

AP Usual civ spelling; for eccl see following entry. *LG* Seq 29. *Parl* Seq 2.

HARDWYCKE

AP Usual eccl spelling; for civ see prev entry. *Eccl* Seq 24.

HARGRAVE

AP *LG* Seq 15. *Parl* N'rn Dv (1832—1918), Wellingb. Dv/CC (1918—*). *Eccl* Seq 13.

HARLESTONE

AP *LG* Seq 23. Civ bdry: 1965.[36] *Parl* Seq 11. *Eccl* Seq 7.

HARPOLE

AP *LG* Seq 25. Civ bdry: 1971 (incl loses pt to N'htn CB [assoc with Northants] & CP).[38] *Parl* Seq 10. Parl bdry: 1973.[39] *Eccl* Haddon RDn (until 1873), Haddon II RDn (1867—73), Weedon RDn (1873—1970), Dav. RDn (1970—*).

HARRINGTON

AP *LG* Seq 32. *Parl* Seq 3. *Eccl* Rothw. RDn (until 1867), Rothw. II RDn (1867—1954), Rothw. RDn (1954—70), Brixw. RDn (1970—*).

HARRINGWORTH

AP *LG* Seq 8. *Parl* Seq 8. *Eccl* Weldon RDn (until 1867), Weldon II RDn (1867—82), Ound. II RDn (1882—1954), K's Cliffe RDn (1954—55), Upp. RDn (1955—70), Barnack RDn (1970—*).

GREAT HARROWDEN

AP Incl Little Harrowden (sep civ identity early, sep EP 1725[11] but sep eccl status not sustained so that this par sometimes eccl called 'Great Harrowden with Little Harrowden' or 'Harrowden Magna with Harrowden Parva'). *LG* Seq 29. Civ bdry: 1968.[71] *Parl* Seq 2. *Eccl* Seq 24.

LITTLE HARROWDEN

Area in Great Harrowden AP, sep civ identity early, sep EP 1725[11] but sep eccl status not sustained. *LG* Seq 29. *Parl* Seq 2.

HARTWELL

Chap to Abbey of St James near Northampton, in Roade AP, 'Hartwell' a donative with most parochial rights from Dissolution,[118] sep civ identity early, final eccl separation 1790.[11] *LG* Seq 1. Civ bdry: 1880s (gains Salcey and Hartwell Lodges CP),[119] 1894 (gains the pt of Hanslope AP [Bucks, Northants] in Northants and the latter ent Bucks thereafter).[117] *Parl* Seq 12. *Eccl* Preston RDn (until 1867), Preston II RDn (1867—73), Preston I RDn (1873—1954), Wootton RDn (1954—70), Towc. RDn (1970—*).

HASELBECH

AP Usual civ spelling; for eccl see following entry. *LG* Seq 31. *Parl* Seq 4.

HAZELBEECH

AP Usual eccl spelling; for civ see prev entry. *Eccl* Seq 27.

HELLIDON

AP Orig chap in Catesby AP, sep par early 13th cent.[68] *LG* Seq 9. *Parl* Seq 12. *Eccl* Seq 5.

HELMDON

AP *LG* Seq 36. Civ bdry: 1885,[24] 1935 (gains Astwell and Falcott CP),[14] 1956.[9] *Parl* Seq 12. *Eccl* Brack. RDn. Gains soon after 1560 Stuchbury AP[120] so that this par thereafter 'Helmdon with Stuchbury', qv.

HELMDON WITH STUCHBURY

EP Cr soon after 1560 by union Helmdon AP, Stuchbury AP.[120] Brack. RDn (cr—1867), Brack. II RDn (1867—1954), Towc. RDn (1954—64), Brack. RDn (1964—72). Bdry: 1964.[121] Abol eccl 1971 to help cr Helmdon with Stutchbury and Radstone EP.[98]

HELMDON WITH STUCHBURY AND RADSTONE

EP Cr 1971 by union Helmdon with Stuchbury EP, Radstone AP.[98] Brack. RDn.

HELPSTON

AP [Soke Peterb] *LG* Seq 19. Transf 1965 to Hunts & Peterb.[12] *Parl* Seq 6. *Eccl* Peterb RDn (until 1867), Peterb II RDn (1867—1954), Peterb RDn (1954—*).

HEMINGTON

AP *LG* Seq 30. *Parl* Seq 8. *Eccl* Ound. RDn. Abol eccl 1849 to help cr Luddington with Hemington EP.[122]

HEYFORD

AP Usual eccl spelling for area incl Nether Heyford, pt Upper Heyford; see each for sep civ identities. *Eccl* Haddon RDn (until 1867) Haddon II RDn (1867—73), Weedon RDn (1873—1970), Dav. RDn (1970—*).

NETHER HEYFORD

AP Usual civ spelling; for eccl (which incl pt Upper Heyford, qv in following entry for sep civ identity) see prev entry. *LG* Seq 25. *Parl* Seq 10.

UPPER HEYFORD

Area pt in Flore AP, pt in Bugbrooke AP, pt in Nether Heyford AP [the latter area which eccl incl this pt eccl called 'Heyford, qv above'], sep civ identity early. *LG* Seq 25. *Parl* Seq 10.

COLD HIGHAM

AP *LG* Seq 37. Civ bdry: 1883.[21] *Parl* Seq 12. *Eccl* Seq 4.

HIGHAM FERRERS

AP Incl chap Chelveston cum Caldecott (sep civ identity early, eccl severed except for one pt 1927 to help cr Caldecott with Newton Bromswold EP,[70] so that this par eccl 'Higham Ferrers with Chelveston and Caldecott' until 1927, qv, 'Higham Ferrers' thereafter). *LG* High. Ferr. Hd, pt High. Ferr. Bor, Wellingb. PLU, RSD (1875—86), High. Ferr. MB (1886—1974), USD (1886—94). *Parl* Pt High. Ferr. Parl Bor (1558—1832), Seq 2 thereafter. *Eccl* High. Ferr. I RDn (1927—54), High. RDn (1954—*).

HIGHAM FERRERS WITH CHELVESTON AND CALDECOTT

AP Usual eccl spelling; for civ and civ sep chap, see prev entry. *Eccl* High. Ferr. RDn (until 1867), High. Ferr. III RDn (1867—82), High. Ferr. I RDn (1882—1927). Abol eccl 1927, all except specified pt of chap Chelveston cum Caldecott severed to help cr Chelveston and Caldecott with Newton Bromswold EP, the remainder to be 'Higham Ferrers' EP.[70]

HIGHAM PARK

Ex-par place, sep CP 1858,[17] eccl abol 1967 to help cr Newton Bromswold EP.[69] *LG* High. Ferr. Hd, Wellingb. PLU (1862—1930), RSD, RD. Abol 1935 ent to Newton Bromswold AP.[14] *Parl* N'rn Dv (1832—85), E'rn Dv (1885—1918), Wellingb. Dv (1918—48).

HINTON IN THE HEDGES

AP *LG* Seq 36. Civ bdry: 1957.[58] *Parl* Seq 12. *Eccl* Brack. RDn. United before 1535 with Steane AP (the latter gains early sep civ identity) to cr 'Hinton in the Hedges with Steane' EP.

HINTON IN THE HEDGES WITH STEANE

AP Union before 1535 of Hinton in the Hedges AP, Steane AP (the latter gains sep civ identity early). Brack. RDn (before 1535—1867), Brack. IV RDn (1867—77), Brack. III RDn (1877—1954), Brack. RDn (1954—*).

HOLCOT

AP *LG* Hamf. Hd, Brixw. PLU, RSD, RD. *Parl* Seq 4. *Eccl* Seq 27.

HOLDENBY

AP *LG* Seq 23. *Parl* Seq 11. *Eccl* Haddon RDn (until 1867), Haddon II RDn (1867—1954), Brampton RDn (1954—55), Haddon RDn (1955—70), Brixw. RDn (1970—*). Abol eccl 1972 to help cr East Haddon and Holdenby EP.[116]

HOLLOWELL

Hmlt in Guilsborough AP, sep CP 1866,[10] sep EP 1850.[114] *LG* Seq 11. Civ bdry: 1935 (gains Teeton CP).[14] *Parl* Seq 11. *Eccl* Haddon RDn (1850—67), Haddon I RDn (1867—1954), Haddon RDn (1954—70), Brixw. RDn (1970—72). Abol eccl 1972 to help cr Guilsborough with Hollowell EP.[115]

HORTON

AP Incl chap Piddington (sep civ identity early, not sep eccl hence this par eccl 'Horton with Piddington',

qv). *LG* Wym. Hd, Hardingst. PLU, RSD, RD. Bdry: 1884.[59] Abol 1935 ent to Hackleton CP.[14] *Parl* S'rn Dv (1832—85), Mid Dv (1885—1918), Dav. Dv (1918—48).

HORTON WITH PIDDINGTON

AP Usual eccl spelling; for civ and civ sep chap, see prev entry. *Eccl* Seq 23.

HOTHORPE

Hmlt (Northants, Rothw. Hd) in Theddingworth AP (o'wise ent Leics, Gartree Hd), 'Hothorpe' a sep CP 1866 in Northants[10] and Theddingworth ent Leics thereafter. *LG* Rothw. Hd, Mkt. Harb. PLU, RSD, Oxend. RD. Abol 1935 ent to Marston Trussel AP.[14] *Parl* N'rn Dv (1832—85), Mid Dv (1885—1918), Kett. Dv (1918—48).

GREAT HOUGHTON

AP *LG* Seq 43. Civ bdry: 1884,[59] 1965 (loses pt to N'htn CB [assoc w Northants] & CP),[36] 1974 (the pts of Great Houghton AP, Little Houghton AP transf to N'htn Dist reconstituted as 'Great Houghton' in that Dist while the pts of each transf to S Northants Dist reconstituted as 'Little Houghton' in that Dist).[60] *Parl* Seq 10. *Eccl* Seq 23.

HANGING HOUGHTON

Hmlt in Lamport AP, sep CP 1866.[10] *LG* Orl. Hd, Brixw. PLU, RSD, RD. Abol 1935 ent to Lamport AP.[14] *Parl* N'rn Dv (1832—85), Mid Dv (1885—1918), Kett. Dv (1918—48).

LITTLE HOUGHTON

AP *LG* Seq 43. Civ bdry: 1884,[59] 1971 (loses pt to N'htn CB [assoc with Northants] & CP),[38] 1974 (the pts of Great Houghton AP, Little Houghton AP transf to N'htn Dist reconstituted as 'Great Houghton' in that Dist while the pts of ea transf to S Northants Dist reconstituted as 'Little Houghton' in that Dist).[60] *Parl* Seq 10. Parl bdry: 1973.[39] *Eccl* Seq 23.

IRCHESTER

AP *LG* Seq 16. *Parl* Seq 2. *Eccl* Seq 12.

IRTHLINGBOROUGH

AP Orig 2 sep APs (All Saints, St Peter), early united when former in ruins.[123] *LG* Huxl. Hd, Wellingb. PLU, RSD, RD (1894—1901), Irthlingborough UD (1901—74). Civ bdry: 1935.[103] *Parl* Seq 2. *Eccl* Seq 10.

IRTHLINGBOROUGH ALL SAINTS—see prev entry

IRTHLINGBOROUGH ST PETER—See IRTHLING-BOROUGH

ISHAM

AP *LG* Seq 29. *Parl* Seq 2. *Eccl* Rothw. RDn (until 1867), Rothw. I RDn (1867—1954), Wellinbg. RDn (1954—70), Kett. RDn (1970—*).

ISLIP

AP *LG* Seq 18. *Parl* Seq 8. *Eccl* Seq 16.

KELMARSH

Chap in Maidwell AP, sep civ identity early, sep eccl by 1620.[124] *LG* Seq 33. *Parl* Seq 4. *Eccl* Rothw. RDn (cr—1867), Rothw. II RDn (1867—1954), Rothw. RDn (1954—70), Brixw. RDn (1970—*).

KETTERING

The following have 'Kettering' in their names. Insofar as any existed at a given time: *LG* Huxl. Hd,

Kett. PLU, USD, UD (1894—1938), MB (1938—74). *Parl* Seq 1. *Eccl* Seq 9.

AP1—KETTERING [ST PETER AND ST PAUL]—Civ bdry: 1935.[14] Eccl bdry: 1916 (cr EP2, cr EP3),[125] 1916 (cr EP1).[126]

EP1—KETTERING ALL SAINTS—Cr 1916 from AP1.[126]

EP2—KETTERING ST ANDREW—Cr 1916 from AP1.[125]

EP3—KETTERING ST MARY—Cr 1916 from AP1.[125]

KILSBY
AP *LG* Seq 10. *Parl* Seq 10. *Eccl* Seq 5.

KING'S HEATH
EP Cr 1964 from Dallington AP.[89] N'htn RDn (1964—70), Wootton RDn (1970—*).

KINGSTHORPE
Chap in Northampton St Peter AP, sep civ identity early, sep EP 1850.[127] *LG* Spel. Hd, N'htn PLU, RSD (1875—92), Kingsthorpe USD (1892—94), UD (1894—1900), N'htn CB (1900—13). Civ bdry: 1900 (the pt not transf to N'htn CB [assoc with Northants] transf to Boughton AP, Moulton Park CP).[1] Abol civ 1913 ent to Northampton CP.[4] *Parl* Pt N'htn Parl Bor (1867—1918), S'rn Dv (ent 1832—67, pt 1867—85), pt Mid Dv (1885—1918). *Eccl* N'htn RDn. Eccl bdry: 1893 (cr Northampton St Matthew EP),[128] 1907 (cr Northampton Holy Trinity EP),[129] 1954,[51] 1960,[99] 1967 (cr Northampton St David EP).[130]

KISLINGBURY
AP *LG* Seq 25. Civ bdry: 1974 (the pt transf to N'htn Dist severed to help reconstitute Upton CP in that Dist while the pt transf transf to S Northants reconstituted as 'Kislingbury' in that Dist).[60] *Parl* Seq 10. *Eccl* Haddon RDn (until 1867), Haddon II RDn (1867—73), Weedon RDn (1873—1970), Dav. RDn (1970—*).

LAMPORT
AP Incl chap Faxton (sep CP 1866,[10] not sep eccl hence this par eccl 'Lamport with Faxton', qv), hmlt Hanging Houghton (sep CP 1866[10]). *LG* Seq 27. Addtl civ bdry alt: 1935 (gains Faxton CP, Hanging Houghton CP).[14] *Parl* Seq 4.

LAMPORT WITH FAXTON
AP Usual eccl spelling; for civ and civ sep chap and hmlt, see prev entry. *Eccl* Seq 27.

LANDS COMMON TO BADBY AND NEWNHAM
Orig pt Badby AP, common to both when chap Newham gains sep status prob at Reformation, abol 1935 with pt to each.[14] *LG* Dav. RD. *Parl* Dav. Dv (1918—48).

LANDS COMMON TO POTTERSPURY AND YARDLEY GOBION
Areas of Potterspury Lodge Farm, Whittlewood Forest, orig in Potterspury AP, common to both from 1866 when Yardley Gobion a sep CP from Potterspury, the area abol 1935 with pt to each par.[14] *LG* Pott. RD. *Parl* Dav. Dv (1918—48)

LAXTON
AP Orig 2 chaps in Rockingham Forest, sep par 1265, later sometimes considered curacy in Blatherwycke AP,[42] but sep civ and eccl status sustained. *LG* Seq

8. *Parl* Seq 8. *Eccl* Seq 30.

LILBOURNE
AP Incl chap Clay Coton (sep par by 1535). *LG* Seq 13. *Parl* Seq 10. *Eccl* Seq 6.

LILFORD CUM WIGSTHORPE
AP *LG* Huxl. Hd, Ound. PLU, RSD, RD (1894—1935), Ound. & Thrap. RD (1935—74). *Parl* Seq 8. *Eccl* Ound. RDn. No church and incl 1778 in Thorpe Achurch, to cr Thorpe Achurch with Lilford EP,[131] qv.

LITCHBOROUGH
AP *LG* Fawsley Hd, Towc. PLU, RSD, RD. *Parl* Seq 12. *Eccl* Dav. RDn (until 1873), Weedon RDn (1873—1970), Towc. RDn (1970—*).

LODDINGTON
AP *LG* Seq 32. Civ bdry: 1935 (gains Mawsley CP).[14] *Parl* Seq 3. *Eccl* Seq 26.

LONGTHORPE
[Soke Peterb] Area in Peterborough AP, sep EP 1850,[132] sep CP 1908 from Peterborough Without CP.[133] *LG* Peterb PLU, RD. Abol civ 1929 to help cr Peterborough CP in Peterb MB.[105] *Parl* Peterb Dv (1918—48). *Eccl* Peterb RDn (1850—67), Peterb I RDn (1867—1954), Peterb RDn (1954—*). Bdry: 1969 (help cr Peterborough St Jude EP).[134]

LOWICK
AP *LG* Seq 18. Civ bdry: 1935 (gains Slipton AP).[14] *Parl* Seq 8. *Eccl* Seq 16.

LUDDINGTON
AP Pt Northants (Poleb. Hd), pt Hunts (Leightonstone Hd), made 1895 ent Northants.[135] Sometimes civ 'Luddington in the Brook'. *LG* Northants pt, Seq 30. Civ bdry: 1965 (gains pts Great Gidding AP, Winwick AP, both Hunts, the main pt of each of the latter transf to help cr Hunts & Peterb Adm Co).[71] *Parl* Northants pt, Seq 8. *Eccl* Ound. RDn. Abol eccl 1849 to help cr Luddington with Hemington EP.[122]

LUDDINGTON IN THE BROOK—see prev entry
LUDDINGTON IN THE WOLDS—see LUTTON
LUDDINGTON WITH HEMINGTON
EP Cr 1849 by union Luddington AP (Northants, Hunts, sometimes 'Luddington in the Brook'), Hemington AP.[122] *Eccl* Ound. RDn (1849—67), Ound. III RDn (1867—77), Ound. I RDn (1877—1954), Ound. RDn (1954—*).

LUFFIELD ABBEY
Ex-par place, pt Bucks (Buckingham Hd), pt Northants (Gr's Nort. Hd), the Northants pt transf to Silverstone AP, Northants, 1832 for parl purposes, 1844 for civ purposes,[101] so that the area ent Bucks thereafter, qv for sep civ identity 1858 in that co and for later civ, parl and eccl organisation.

LUTTON
AP Pt Northants (Willyb. Hd), pt Hunts (Norman Cross Hd), made 1895 ent Northants.[135] Sometimes 'Luddington in the Wold'. *LG* Northants pt, Seq 41. Civ bdry: 1965 (loses pt to Denton and Caldecote CP, Hunts, to help cr Hunts & Peterb Adm Co).[71] *Parl* Northants pt, Seq 8. *Eccl* Yaxley RDn (Hunts AD). Gains 1447 Washingley AP to cr Lutton and Washingley AP.[136]

LUTTON AND WASHINGLEY

AP Cr 1447 by union Lutton AP (Northants, Hunts), Washingley AP (Hunts).[136] Yaxley RDn (Hunts AD)(until before 1535), Ound. RDn (before 1535—1867), Ound. III RDn (1867—77), Ound. I RDn (1877—1954), Ound. RDn (1954—*).

MAIDFORD

AP *LG* Seq 26. *Parl* Seq 12. *Eccl* Brack. RDn (until 1867), Brack. II RDn (1867—77), Brack. I RDn (1877—1952), Weedon RDn (1952—70), Towc. RDn (1970—*).

MAIDWELL

AP Cr shortly after 1535 by union Maidwell St Mary AP (incl chap Kelmarsh), Maidwell St Peter AP (last presentment in 1535).[137] Incl chap Kelmarsh (sep civ identity early, sep eccl by 1620[124]). *LG* Seq 31. *Parl* Seq 4. *Eccl* Seq 27.

MAIDWELL ST MARY

AP Orig sep AP (Rothw. RDn), gains shortly after 1535 Maidwell St Peter AP to cr 'Maidwell',[124] qv for main pt of par and chap Kelmarsh in it.

MAIDWELL ST PETER

AP Orig sep AP (Rothw. RDn), abol shortly after 1535 (date of presentment to this par) to help cr 'Maidwell' AP,[124] qv.

MARHOLM

AP [Soke Peterb] *LG* Seq 19. Transf 1965 to Hunts & Peterb.[12] *Parl* Seq 6. *Eccl* Seq 18.

MARSTON ST LAWRENCE

AP Incl chap Warkworth (sep civ identity early, not sep eccl hence this par eccl 'Marston St Lawrence with Warkworth', qv). *LG* Seq 36. Addtl civ bdry alt: 1885,[138] 1885,[24] 1935.[14] *Parl* Seq 12.

MARSTON ST LAWRENCE WITH WARKWORTH

AP Usual eccl spelling; for civ and civ sep chap, see prev entry. *Eccl* Seq 3. Eccl bdry: 1940.[112]

MARSTON TRUSSEL

AP *LG* Seq 33. Civ bdry: 1935 (gains Hothorpe CP, Thorpe Lubenham CP),[14] 1965 (exchanges pts with Lubenham AP, Leics).[102] *Parl* Seq 4. *Eccl* Rothw. RDn (until 1867), Rothw. II RDn (1867—1954), Brixw. RDn (1954—67), Rothw. RDn (1967—70), Brixw. RDn (1970—*).

MAWSLEY

Ex-par place, sep CP 1858.[17] *LG* Orl. Hd, Brixw. PLU (1862—1930), RSD, RD. Abol 1935 ent to Luddington AP.[14] *Parl* N'rn Dv (1832—85), Mid Dv (1885—1918), Kett. Dv (1918—48).

MAXEY

AP [Soke Peterb] Incl hmlt Deeping Gate (sep CP 1866[10]). *LG* Seq 19. Addtl civ bdry alt: 1883.[111] Transf 1965 to Hunts & Peterb.[12] *Parl* Seq 6. *Eccl* Peterb RDn (until 1867), Peterb II RDn (1867—1954), Barnack RDn (1954—70), Peterb RDn (1970—*).

MIDDLETON

Tp in Cottingham AP, sep CP 1866.[10] *LG* Seq 4. Bdry: 1885,[65] 1952,[74] 1967.[77] *Parl* Seq 5.

MIDDLETON CHENEY

AP *LG* Seq 35. Civ bdry: 1883,[21] 1884,[139] 1885.[138] *Parl* Seq 12. *Eccl* Brackley RDn (until 1867), Brackley I RDn (1867—73), Brackley IV RDn (1873—77), Brackley III RDn (1877—1954), Brackley RDn (1954—*).

MILTON

AP Usual civ spelling until 1960; for eccl and civ after 1960, see following entry. *LG* Wym. Hd, Hardingst. PLU, RSD, RD (1894—1932), N'htn RD (1932—60). Renamed civ 1960 'Milton Malsor'.[140] *Parl* S'rn Dv (1832—85), Mid Dv (1885—1918), Dav. Dv (1918—48), S Northants CC (1948—70).

MILTON MALSOR

AP Usual eccl spelling, and civ spelling from 1960 when 'Milton' AP civ renamed.[140] *LG* N'htn RD. Civ bdry: 1974 (the pt transf to N'htn Dist severed to help reconstitute Wootton AP in that Dist while the pt transf to S Northants Dist united with the pt of Collingtree AP transf to that Dist as reconstituted 'Milton Malsor').[60] *Parl* Dav. CC (1970—*). *Eccl* Preston RDn (until 1867), Preston II RDn (1867—1954), Preston RDn (1954—70), Wootton RDn (1970—*).

MORETON PINKNEY

AP *LG* Gr's Nort. Hd, Brack. PLU, RSD, RD. *Parl* Seq 12. *Eccl* Brack. RDn (until 1867), Brack. II RDn (1867—77), Brack. I RDn (1877—1954), Culw. RDn (1954—70), Brack. RDn (1970—*).

MOULTON

AP *LG* Seq 34. Civ bdry: 1965 (loses pt to N'htn CB [assoc with Northants] & CP),[36] 1969 (loses pt to N'htn CB [assoc with Northants] & CP).[37] *Parl* Seq 11. Parl bdry: 1973.[39] *Eccl* Seq 8.

MOULTON PARK

Ex-par place, sep CP 1858.[17] *LG* Spel. Hd, Brixw. PLU (1861—1930), RSD, RD. Civ bdry: 1900 (gains pt of Kingsthorpe CP not transf to N'htn CB).[1] Abol 1932 pt to Boughton AP, pt to N'htn CB (assoc with Northants) & CP.[50] *Parl* S'rn Dv (1832—85), Mid Dv (1885—1918), Kett. Dv (1918—48).

NASEBY

AP *LG* Seq 11. *Parl* Seq 11. *Eccl* Haddon RDn (until 1867), Haddon I RDn (1867—73), Rothw. III RDn (1873—1954), Brixw. RDn (1954—*).

NASSINGTON

AP Incl chap Woodnewton (sep civ identity early, pec jurisd Nassington, sep EP 1747[11]), chap Yarwell (sep civ identity early, pec jurisd Nassington, not sep eccl hence this par eccl 'Nassington with Yarwell', qv). *LG* Seq 41. Addtl civ bdry alt: 1965 (gains pt of Thornhaugh CP, Soke Peterb, exchanges pts with Elton AP, Hunts, as remainder of both transf to help cr Hunts & Peterb Adm Co).[71] *Parl* Seq 8.

NASSINGTON WITH YARWELL

AP Usual eccl spelling; for civ and civ and eccl chaps (incl their inclusion in pec jurisd Nassington), see prev entry. *Eccl* Pec jurisd Nassington (until 1851), Ound. RDn (1851—67), Ound. IV RDn (1867—73), Ound. III RDn (1873—77), Ound. I RDn (1877—82), Ound. II RDn (1882—1954), K's Cliffe RDn (1954—60), Ound. RDn (1960—*).

NEWBOROUGH

AP [Soke Peterb] *LG* Seq 19. Civ bdry: 1883,[21] 1883.[111] Transf 1965 to Hunts & Peterb.[12] *Parl* Seq 6. *Eccl* Seq 18.

NEWBOTTLE

AP Usual civ spelling; for eccl see 'Kings Sutton with Charlton'. *LG* K's Sutt. Hd, Brack. PLU, RSD. Abol civ 1885 to help cr Kings Sutton with Newbottle CP.[141] *Parl* S'rn Dv (1832—1918).

CP Cr 1896 from Kings Sutton with Newbottle CP.[142] *LG* Brack. PLU, RD. *Parl* Dav. Dv (1918—48), S Northants CC (1948—70), Dav. CC (1970—*).

NEWBOTTLE WITH CHARLTON

AP Usual eccl spelling; for civ see 1st 'Newbottle' above. *Eccl* Pt pec jurisd Banb. (hmlts Astrop, Charlton, Purston, until 1851), remainder and later, Seq 3.

NEWNHAM

AP Orig chap in Badby AP, prob sep par at Reformation, incl thereafter undivided pt Lands Common to Badby and Newnham (abol 1935 with pt to each par[14]). *LG* Seq 9. *Parl* Seq 12. *Eccl* Seq 5.

NEWTON

AP Orig 2 tps (Great Newton, Litle Newton, each with a chap) united 1449 as chap in Geddington AP, sep par at Dissolution.[107] *LG* Seq 4. Civ bdry: 1967.[77] *Parl* Seq 5. *Eccl* High. Ferr. RDn (cr—1867), High. Ferr. III RDn (1867—82), High. Ferr. I RDn (1882—1954), High. RDn (1954—73). Abol eccl 1973 ent to Geddington AP.[108]

NEWTON BROMSHOLD

AP Usual civ spelling until 1969; for eccl and civ after 1969, see following entry. *LG* High. Ferr. Hd, Wellingb. PLU, RSD, RD. Civ bdry: 1935 (incl gains Higham Park CP),[14] 1965 (gains pt Melchbourne and Yelden CP, Beds).[71] Renamed civ 1969 'Newton Bromshold'.[143] *Parl* N'rn Dv (1832—85), E'rn Dv (1885—1918), Wellingb. Dv/CC (1918—70).

NEWTON BROMSWOLD

AP Usual eccl spelling, civ spelling from 1969 as renaming of 'Newton Bromshold' AP.[143] *LG* Wellingb. RD. *Parl* Wellingb. CC (1970—*). *Eccl* High. Ferr. RDn (until 1867), High. Ferr. III RDn (1867—82), High. Ferr. I RDn (1882—1927). Abol eccl 1927 to help cr Chelveston and Caldecott with Newton Bromswold EP.[70]

EP Cr 1967 by union of the pt of Chelveston and Caldecott with Newton Bromswold EP equal to Newton Bromshold CP, ent eccl ex-par Higham Park.[69] High. RDn.

NORTHAMPTON

The following have 'Northampton' in their names. Insofar as any existed at a given time: *LG* N'htn Bor/MB/CB, PLU, USD. *Parl* N'htn Parl Bor/BC (1295—1970), pt N'htn North BC, pt N'htn South BC (1970—*). *Eccl* N'htn RDn.

CP1—NORTHAMPTON—Cr 1909 by union AP1, CP2, AP3, AP7, AP8.[144] Civ bdry: 1913 (gains the other pars in N'htn CB: Abington AP, Dallington St James CP, Duston St James CP, Far Cotton CP, Kingsthorpe CP),[4] 1932,[50] 1965 (incl loses pt to Wootton AP, exchanges pts with Hardingstone AP),[36] 1969,[37] 1971.[38] Parl bdry: 1973.[39]

AP1—NORTHAMPTON ALL SAINTS— Civ bdry: 1902.[2] Abol civ 1909 to help cr CP1.[144] Eccl

bdry: 1577 (gains AP4),[145] 1589 (gains AP5),[146] 1841 (cr EP10).[147] Abol eccl 1949 to help cr EP1.[148]

EP1—NORTHAMPTON ALL SAINTS WITH ST KATHERINE—Cr 1949 by union AP1, EP10.[148]

EP2—NORTHAMPTON CHRIST CHURCH—Cr 1907 from Abington AP, EP8, EP14.[5]

—NORTHAMPTON HOLY SEPULCHRE—Usual eccl spelling for AP8, qv. Eccl bdry: after 1493 (gains AP6),[146] after 1509 (gains AP2),[149] 1842 (cr EP6),[150] 1877 (help cr EP15),[151] 1879 (help cr EP11).[152] Abol eccl 1965 to help cr EP3.[153]

EP3—NORTHAMPTON HOLY SEPULCHRE WITH ST ANDREW—Cr 1965 by union EP6, AP8.[153]

EP4—NORTHAMPTON HOLY TRINITY—Cr 1907 from EP15, Kingsthorpe EP.[129] Bdry: 1960.[99]

CP2—NORTHAMPTON PRIORY OF ST ANDREW—Ex-par place, sep CP 1858.[17] *LG* N'htn PLU (1861—1909). Bdry: 1885.[154] Abol civ 1909 to help cr CP1.[144]

EP5—NORTHAMPTON ST ALBAN THE MARTYR—Renaming 1954 of Abington St Alban the Martyr EP.[7] Bdry: 1960.[95]

EP6—NORTHAMPTON ST ANDREW—Cr 1842 from AP8.[150]

EP6—NORTHAMPTON ST ANDREW—Cr 1842 from AP8.[150] Abol 1965 to help cr EP3.[153]

AP2—NORTHAMPTON ST BARTHOLOMEW—Last presentation 1509, afterwards in decay and united to AP8.[149]

EP7—NORTHAMPTON ST DAVID—Cr 1967 from Kingsthorpe EP.[130]

AP3—NORTHAMPTON ST EDMUND—Joined *ca* 1411 to AP6, soon afterwards destroyed.[155]

EP8—NORTHAMPTON ST EDMUND—Cr 1846 from AP3 (incl ex-par places not named in order).[156] Bdry:1879 (help cr EP11)[152] 1883 (cr EP14),[157] 1907 (help cr EP2),[5] 1929.[158]

AP3—NORTHAMPTON ST GILES—Civ bdry: 1885,[154] 1902.[2] Abol civ 1909 to help cr CP1.[144] Eccl bdry: 1846 (cr EP8).[156]

AP4—NORTHAMPTON ST GREGORY—Abol 1577 ent to AP1.[145]

EP9—NORTHAMPTON ST JAMES—Renaming 1959 of Dallington St James EP.[90] N'htn RDn (1959—70), Wootton RDn (1970—*).

EP10—NORTHAMPTON ST KATHERINE—Cr 1841 from AP1.[147] Abol 1949 to help cr EP1.[148]

EP11—NORTHAMPTON ST LAWRENCE—Cr 1879 from EP8, AP8.[152]

—NORTHAMPTON ST MARGARET—Perhaps an AP, mentioned 1490 but no recorded institutions.[146]

AP5—NORTHAMPTON ST MARY—Abol 1589 ent to AP1.[145]

EP12—NORTHAMPTON ST MARY THE VIRGIN—Renaming 1960 of Far Cotton EP.[96] N'htn RDn (1960—70), Wootton RDn (1970—*).

EP13—NORTHAMPTON ST MATTHEW—Cr 1893 from Kingsthorpe EP.[128] Bdry: 1951.[6]

AP6—NORTHAMPTON ST MICHAEL—*ca* 1411 (gains AP3).[155] Last presentation in 1493, united afterwards to AP8.[146]

EP14—NORTHAMPTON ST MICHAEL AND ALL ANGELS—Cr 1883 from EP8.[157] Bdry: 1907 (help cr EP2),[5] 1929.[158]

EP15—NORTHAMPTON ST PAUL—Cr 1877 from AP8, Kingsthorpe EP.[151] Bdry: 1907 (help cr EP4),[129] 1960.[95]

AP7—NORTHAMPTON ST PETER—Incl chap (Spel. Hd) Kingsthorpe (sep civ identity early, sep EP 1850[127]), chap Upton (not sep civ, eccl transf 1971 to Duston AP[92] so that this par 'Northampton St Peter' thereafter). Abol civ 1909 to help cr CP1.[144]

—NORTHAMPTON ST PETER WITH UPTON—see AP7

AP8—NORTHAMPTON ST SEPULCHRE—Usual civ spelling; for eccl see 'NORTHAMPTON HOLY SEPULCHRE' above. Civ bdry: 1885,[154] 1902.[2] Abol civ 1909 to help cr CP1.[144]

NORTHBOROUGH
AP [Soke Peterb] LG Seq 19. Civ bdry: 1883.[111] Transf 1965 to Hunts & Peterb.[12] Parl Seq 6. Eccl Peterb RDn (until 1867), Peterb II RDn (1867—1954), Barnack RDn (1954—70), Peterb RDn (1970—*).

NORTON
AP LG Seq 9. Parl Seq 12. Eccl Dav. RDn. Abol eccl 1973 to help cr Daventry with Norton EP.[91]

GREEN'S NORTON
AP Incl chap Whittlebury (which incl hmlt Silverstone; 'Whittlebury', 'Silverstone' each a sep CP 1866 from this par,[10] sep EP 1852 as 'Whittlebury and Silverstone'[159]). LG Seq 26. Parl Seq 12. Eccl Seq 4.

OAKLEY
CP Cr 1935 by union Great Oakley AP, Little Oakley AP.[14] LG Kett. RD. Bdry: 1952,[74] 1955.[75] Abol 1967 pt to Corby UD & AP, pt to Newton AP.[77] Parl Kett. CC (1948—70).

GREAT OAKLEY
AP LG Corby Hd, Kett. PLU, RSD, RD. Abol civ 1935 to help cr Oakley CP.[14] Parl N'rn Dv (1832—1918), Kett. Dv (1918—48). Eccl Weldon RDn (until 1867), Weldon I RDn (1867—85), Weldon II RDn (1885—1954), Kett. RDn (1954—70), Corby RDn (1970—72). Eccl bdry: 1961 (help cr Corby St Peter and St Andrew EP),[34] 1970.[80] Abol eccl 1972 to help cr Great and Little Oakley EP.[160]

GREAT AND LITTLE OAKLEY
EP Cr 1972 by union Great Oakley AP, Little Oakley AP.[160] Corby RDn.

LITTLE OAKLEY
AP LG Organisation as for Great Oakley, except no eccl bdry alt before abol 1972.

OLD
AP Sometimes 'Wold'. LG Seq 27. Parl Seq 4. Eccl Seq 27.

ORLINGBURY
AP LG Seq 29. Parl Seq 2. Eccl Seq 24.

ORTON
Chap in Rothwell AP, sep CP 1866.[10] LG Seq 32. Parl Seq 3.

OUNDLE
AP Incl hmlt Ashton (sep CP 1866,[10] not sep eccl hence this par eccl 'Oundle with Ashton', qv). LG Polebr. Hd, pt Ound. Bor, Ound. PLU, pt Ound. USD, pt Ound. RSD, Ound. UD (pt 1894—95, ent 1895—1974), pt Ound. RD (1894—95). Addtl civ bdry alt: 1885,[20] 1895 (the pt not in Ound. UD transf to Benefield AP).[35] Parl Seq 8.

OUNDLE WITH ASHTON
AP Usual eccl spelling; for civ and civ sep hmlt, see prev entry. Eccl Seq 15.

OVERSTONE
AP LG Spel. Hd, Wellingb. PLU (1835—ca 1894), Brixw. PLU (ca 1894—1930), RSD, RD. Civ bdry: 1969 (loses pt to N'htn CB [assoc with Northants] & CP),[37] 1971 (loses pt to N'htn CB [assoc with Northants] & CP),[38] 1974 (the main pt transf to Dav. Dist to be 'Overstone' in that Dist while the pt transf to N'htn Dist ceases to be in a par).[60] Parl Seq 11. Parl bdry: 1971.[39] Eccl Haddon RDn (until 1867), Haddon II RDn (1867—1924), Rothw. I RDn (1924—1954), Wellingb. RDn (1954—70), N'htn RDn (1970—*).

OXENDON
AP Usual eccl spelling; for civ see following entry. Eccl Rothw. RDn (until 1867), Rothw. I RDn (1867—73), Rothw. II RDn (1873—1954), Rothw. RDn (1954—70), Brixw. RDn (1970—*).

GREAT OXENDON
AP Usual civ spelling; for eccl see prev entry. LG Seq 33. Civ bdry: 1896 (gains the pt of Little Bowden AP in Northants and Little Bowden ent Leics thereafter).[52] Parl Seq 4.

PASSENHAM
AP Usual civ spelling until 1948; for eccl see following entry. LG Cleley Hd, Pott. PLU, RSD, RD (1894—1935), Towc. RD (1935—48). Renamed civ 1948 'Deanshanger'.[92] Parl S'rn Dv (1832—1918), Dav. Dv (1918—48), S Northants CC (1948—70).

PASSENHAM WITH DEANSHANGER
AP Usual eccl spelling; for civ and civ renaming, see prev entry. Eccl Seq 20.

PASTON
AP [Soke Peterb] Incl chap Werrington (sep CP 1866,[10] sep EP 1853 [incl tp Walton in same par][161]), hmlt Gunthorpe (sep CP 1866[10]), hmlt Walton (sep CP 1866,[10] eccl in chap/EP Werrington, qv above, pt of the hmlt eccl severed 1888 from Werrington EP and transf to Paston AP[162]). LG Nassab. Hd, Peterb PLU, RSD, RD. Addtl civ bdry alt: 1883.[21] Abol civ 1929 to help cr Peterborough CP in Peterb MB.[105] Parl N'rn Dv (1832—1918), Peterb Dv (1918—48). Eccl Seq 18. Addtl eccl bdry alt: 1891 (help cr Peterborough All Saints EP),[47] 1950,[49] 1969 (help cr Peterborough St Jude EP).[134]

PATTISHALL
AP LG Seq 37. Civ bdry: 1883,[21] 1883.[40] Parl Seq 12. Eccl Brack. RDn (until 1867), Brack. III RDn (1867—77), Brack. II RDn (1877—1954), Towc. RDn (1954—*).

PAULERSPURY
AP LG Seq 2. Parl Seq 12. Eccl Seq 20.

PEAKIRK
AP [Soke Peterb] Incl chap Glinton (sep civ identity early, sep EP 1865[110]). LG Seq 19. Addtl civ bdry alt: 1883,[21] 1883.[111] Transf 1965 to Hunts &

Peterb.[12] *Parl* Seq 6. *Eccl* Peterb RDn (until 1867), Peterb I RDn (1867—73), Peterb II RDn (1873—1954), Barnack RDn (1954—70), Peterb RDn (1970—*).

PETERBOROUGH

[Northants until 1889, Soke Peterb thereafter] The following have 'Peterborough' in their names. Insofar as any existed at a given time: *LG* Peterb PLU; Bor, MB, USD, RSD sep noted. *Parl* Sep noted. *Eccl* Peterb RDn (until 1867), Peterb II RDn (1867—73), Peterb I RDn (1873—1954), Peterb RDn (1954—*).

AP1—PETERBOROUGH [ST JOHN THE BAPTIST]—*LG* Pt Peterb Bor, pt Peterb MB (enlarged beyond Bor, 1874—94), pt Peterb USD, pt Peterb RSD. Abol civ 1894 the pt in the MB cr CP3, the remaimder cr CP4.[104] *Parl* Peterb Parl Bor (pt 1547—1867 [enlarged pt 1832—67], ent 1867—1918). Eccl bdry: 1850 (cr Longthorpe EP),[132] 1857 (cr Boongate EP, later called 'Peterborough St Mary'),[46] 1859 (cr EP5),[163] 1864,[164] 1869 (help cr EP6),[165] 1894.[166]

CP1—PETERBOROUGH—Cr 1929 by union 4 pars in Peterb MB (CP3, Fletton Urban, CP2, Woodstone Urban) and 6 other pars heretofore outside MB but now incl in it (Gunthorpe CP, Longthorpe CP, Paston AP, CP3, Walton CP, Werrington CP).[105] *LG* Peterb MB. Bdry: 1956 (exchanges pts with Orton Longueville AP, Hunts).[74] *Parl* Peterb CC (1948—70), BC (1970—*).

EP1—PETERBOROUGH ALL SAINTS—Cr 1891 from EP5, Boongate EP, Paston AP, EP6.[47] Bdry: 1933,[48] 1950,[49] 1973 (cr EP2).[167]

EP2—PETERBOROUGH CHRIST THE CARPENTER—Cr 1973 from EP1.[167]

CP2—PETERBOROUGH MINSTER CLOSE PRECINCTS—Ex-par place, sep CP 1858.[17] *LG* Peterb PLU (1861—1929), MB (1874—1929). Abol 1929 to help cr CP1.[105] *Parl* Peterb Parl Bor (1547—1918), Peterb Dv (1918—48).

EP3—PETERBOROUGH ST BARNABAS—Cr 1933 from EP5, EP6.[168]

EP4—PETERBOROUGH ST JUDE—Cr 1969 from Longthorpe EP, Paston AP.[134]

EP5—PETERBOROUGH ST MARK—Cr 1858 from AP1.[163] Bdry: 1864,[164] 1869 (help cr EP6),[165] 1891 (help cr EP1),[47] 1894,[166] 1933 (help cr EP3),[168] 1933.[48]

—PETERBOROUGH ST MARY—name used now for EP cr 1857 as 'Boongate', qv

EP6—PETERBOROUGH ST PAUL—Cr 1869 from EP5, AP1.[165] Bdry: 1891 (help cr EP1),[47] 1894,[166] 1933 (help cr EP5),[168] 1933.[48]

CP3—PETERBOROUGH WITHIN—Cr 1894 from the pt of AP1 in Peterb MB.[104] Abol 1929 to help cr CP1.[105]

CP4—PETERBOROUGH WITHOUT—Cr 1894 from the pt of AP1 not in Peterb MB.[104] *LG* Peterb RD. Abol 1929 to help cr CP1 to be ent Peterb MB.[105]

PIDDINGTON

Chap in Horton AP, sep civ identity early. Incl hmlt Hackleton (sep CP 1866[10]). *LG* Wym. Hd, Hardingst. PLU, RSD, RD. Abol 1935 ent to Hackleton

CP.[14] *Parl* S'rn Dv (1832—85), Mid Dv (1885—1918), Dav. Dv (1918—48).

PILSGATE

[Soke Peterb] Hmlt in Barnack AP, sep CP 1866.[10] *LG* Nassab. Hd, Stamf. PLU, RSD. Abol 1887 ent to Barnack AP.[30] *Parl* N'rn Dv (1832—1918).

PILTON

AP *LG* Seq 21. *Parl* Seq 8. *Eccl* Ound. RDn (until 1867), Ound. I RDn (1867—77), Ound. II RDn (1877—1954), K's Cliffe RDn (1954—60), Ound. RDn (1960—*).

PITSFORD

AP *LG* Seq 34. *Parl* Seq 11. *Eccl* Seq 7.

PLUMPTON

AP *LG* Gr's Nort. Hd, Towc. PLU, RSD, RD. Abol civ 1935 to help cr Weston and Weedon CP.[14] *Parl* S'rn Dv (1832—1918), Dav. Dv (1918—48). *Eccl* Brack. RDn (until 1867), Brack. II RDn (1867—77), Brack. I RDn (1877—1928). Abol eccl 1928 to help cr Lois Weedon with Plumpton EP,[169] later called 'Weedon Lois with Plumpton'.

POLEBROOK

AP Incl hmlt Armston (sep CP 1866[10]). *LG* Seq 30. Addtl civ bdry alt: 1935 (gains Armston CP).[14] *Parl* Seq 8. *Eccl* Ound. RDn (until 1867), Ound. III RDn (1867—73), Ound. I RDn (1873—1954), Ound. RDn (1954—*).

POTTERSPURY

AP Incl hmlt Yardley Gobion (sep CP 1866,[10] sep EP 1864[11] but not sustained, hence this par eccl 'Potterspury with Yardley Gobion', qv); also incl after 1866 undivided pt Lands Common to Potterspury and Yardley Gobion ([Potterspury Lodge Farm, Whittlewood Forest], abol 1935, pt to each par).[14] *LG* Seq 2. Addtl civ bdry alt: 1883,[13] 1916,[81] 1951.[82] *Parl* Seq 12.

POTTERSPURY WITH YARDLEY GOBION

AP Usual eccl spelling; for civ and civ and eccl (not sustained) sep hmlt, see prev entry. Preston RDn (until 1867), Preston I RDn (1867—1921). Abol eccl 1921 to help cr Potterspury with Furtho and Yardley Gobion EP.[106]

POTTERSPURY WITH FURTHO AND YARDLEY GOBION

EP Cr 1921 by union Potterspury with Yardley Gobion AP, Furtho AP.[106] Later called 'Potterspury cum Furtho cum Yardley Gobion'. Preston I RDn (1921—54), Wootton RDn (1954—70), Towc. RDn (1970—*).

PRESTON CAPES

AP *LG* Seq 9. *Parl* Seq 12. *Eccl* Seq 5.

PRESTON DEANERY

AP *LG* Wym. Hd, Hardingst. PLU, RSD, RD. Abol civ 1935 ent to Hackleton CP.[14] *Parl* S'rn Dv (1832—85), Mid Dv (1885—1918), Dav. Dv (1918—48). *Eccl* Seq 23.

PYTCHLEY

AP *LG* Seq 28. Civ bdry: 1935.[14] *Parl* Seq 1. *Eccl* Rothw. RDn (until 1867), Rothw. I RDn (1867—1954), Wellingb. RDn (1954—72), Kett. RDn (1972—*).

QUINTON

AP *LG* Seq 43. *Parl* Seq 10. *Eccl* Seq 22.

RADSTONE
AP *LG* Seq 36. *Parl* Seq 36. *Eccl* Brack. RDn (until 1867), Brack. II RDn (1867—77), Brack. III RDn (1877—1954), Brack. RDn (1954—71). Abol eccl 1971 to help cr Helmdon with Stutchbury and Radstone EP.[98]

RAUNDS
AP *LG* High. Ferr. Hd, Thrap. PLU, RSD, RD (1894—97), Raunds UD (1897—1974). Civ bdry: 1935 (gains Stanwick AP).[14] *Parl* Seq 9. *Eccl* Seq 13.

RAVENSTHORPE
AP Incl hmlt Coton (Guilsb. Hd, sep CP 1866[10]), hmlt Teeton (sep CP 1866[10]). *LG* Nob. Gr. Hd (pt until 1866, ent from 1866), pt Guilsb. Hd (Coton, until 1866), Brixw. PLU, RSD, RD. Addtl civ bdry alt: 1935 (gains Coton CP).[14] *Parl* Seq 11. *Eccl* Seq 6.

RINGSTEAD
AP Prob orig sep AP (High. Ferr. RDn), united before 1535 with Denford AP, the union eccl 'Denford with Ringstead', qv, each par retains or soon regains sep civ identity. *LG* Seq 15. *Parl* Seq 8.

ROADE
AP Incl chap Ashton (sep par by 1535), chap Hartwell (chap to Abbey of St James, Northampton; a donative with most parochial rights from Dissolution,[118] sep civ identity early, final eccl separation 1790[11]). *LG* Cleley Hd, Hardingst. PLU, RSD, RD (1894—1932), N'hth. RD (1932—74). Addtl civ bdry alt: 1884.[59] *Parl* Seq 10. *Eccl* Seq 22.

ROCKINGHAM
AP *LG* Rockingham Bor, Seq 7. Civ bdry: 1952,[74] 1971.[81] *Parl* Seq 7. *Eccl* Weldon RDn (until 1867), Weldon I RDn (1867—1931). Abol eccl 1971 to help cr Rockingham with Caldecote EP.[170]

ROCKINGHAM WITH CALDECOTE
EP Cr 1931 by union Rockingham AP, area Caldecote in Lyddington AP (Rutl, civ 'Liddington', 'Caldecott').[170] Weldon I RDn (1931—54), Weldon RDn (1954—70), Corby RDn (1970—*).

ROTHERSTHORPE
AP *LG* Seq 43. *Parl* Seq 10. *Eccl* Preston RDn (until 1867), Preston II RDn (1867—73), Preston I RDn (1873—1940), Weedon RDn (1940—70), Dav. RDn (1970—*).

ROTHWELL
AP Incl chap Orton (sep CP 1866,[10] not sep eccl hence this par eccl 'Rothwell with Orton', qv). *LG* Rothw. Hd, Bor, Kett. PLU, RSD (1875—91), Rothw. USD (1891—94), UD. *Parl* Seq 3.

ROTHWELL WITH GLENDON
EP Cr 1923 by union Rothwell with Orton AP, Glendon AP.[109] Rothw. II RDn. Abol 1940, area of Glendon severed to help cr Rushton with Glendon EP, the remainder to be Rothwell with Orton EP.[171]

ROTHWELL WITH ORTON
AP Usual eccl spelling; for civ and civ sep chap, see prev entry. Rothw. RDn (until 1867), Rothw. II RDn (1867—1923). Abol eccl 1923 to help cr Rothwell with Glendon EP.[109]
EP Cr 1940 when area Glendon severed from Rothwell with Glendon EP to help cr Rushton with Glendon EP, the remainder to be Rothwell with Orton EP.[171]

Rothw. II RDn (1940—54), Rothw. II RDn (1954—70), Kett. RDn (1970—*).

RUSHDEN
AP *LG* High. Ferr. Hd, Wellingb. PLU, RSD (1875—91), Rushden UD (1891—94), Rushden UD. Civ bdry: 1965 (gains pt Wymington AP, Beds).[102] *Parl* Seq 9. *Eccl* Seq 12. Eccl bdry: 1913 (cr Rushden St Peter EP).[172]

RUSHDEN ST PETER
EP Cr 1913 from Rushden AP.[172] High. Ferr. I RDn (1913—54), High. RDn (1954—*).

RUSHTON
AP Orig 2 sep APS, Rushton All Saints, Rushton St Peter, a united par prob late 16th or in 17th cent.[173] *LG* Seq 32. Civ bdry: 1935 (gains Barford CP, Glendon AP).[14] *Parl* Seq 3. *Eccl* Rothw. RDn (cr—1867), Rothw. II RDn (1867—1940). Abol eccl 1940 to help cr Rushton with Glendon EP.[171]

RUSHTON ALL SAINTS—see RUSHTON

RUSHTON ST PETER—see RUSHTON

RUSHTON WITH GLENDON
EP Cr 1940 by union Rushton AP, area Glendon in Rothwell with Glendon EP.[171] Rothw. II RDn (19400—54), Rothw. RDn (1954—70), Kett. RDn (1970—*).

ST MARTIN WITHOUT
CP [Soke Peterb] Cr 1894 as 'St Martin Without' from the pt of Stamford Baron AP (Northants) in Peterb MB (Soke),[104] later called 'Stamford Barton St Martin's Without'. *LG* Stamf. PLU, Barnack RD. Transf 1965 to Hunts & Peterb.[12] *Parl* Peterb Dv/ CC (1918—70), Peterb BC (1970—*).

SALCEY AND HARTWELL LODGES
Ex-par place (Cleley Hd), neither cr a sep CP 1858 nor made then pt of another par, sep status not sust and incl by 1880s in Hartwell AP.[119]

SCALDWELL
AP *LG* Seq 27. *Parl* Seq 4. *Eccl* Seq 27.

SHUTLANGER
Chap in Stoke Bruern AP, sep CP 1866.[10] *LG* Seq 3. Bdry: 1883.[174] *Parl* Seq 12.

SIBBERTOFT
AP *LG* Seq 33. *Parl* Seq 4. *Eccl* Rothw. RDn (until 1867), Rothw. II RDn (1867—73), Rothw. III RDn (1873—1954), Brixw. RDn (1954—56), Haddon RDn (1956—70), Brixw. RDn (1970—*).

SILVERSTONE
Hmlt in Green's Norton AP, sep civ identity early, eccl in chap Whittlebury in same par, the 2 united 1852 as 'Wittlebury and Silverstone' EP.[159] *LG* Seq 26. Civ bdry: 1844 (gains the pt in Northants of ex-par Luffield Abbey, the remainder ent Bucks thereafter),[101] 1956.[9] *Parl* Seq 12. Parl bdry: 1832 (gains the pt in Northants of ex-par Luffield Abbey, the remainder ent Bucks Parl Co thereafter).[101]

SLAPTON
AP *LG* Seq 26. Civ bdry: 1956.[9] *Parl* Seq 12. *Eccl* Brack. RDn (until 1867), Brack. II RDn (1867—1954), Towc. RDn (1954—*).

SLIPTON
AP *LG* Huxl. Hd, Thrap. PLU, RSD, RD. Civ bdry: 1885.[15] Abol civ 1935 ent to Lowick AP.[14] *Parl* N'rn Dv (1832—1918), Peterb Dv (1918—48). *Eccl*

Seq 16.

SOUTHORPE

[Soke Peterb] Hmlt in Barnack AP, sep CP 1866.[10] *LG* Seq 20. Transf 1965 to Hunts & Peterb.[12] *Parl* Seq 6.

SOUTHWICK

AP *LG* Seq 41. *Parl* Seq 8. *Eccl* Ound. RDn (until 1867), Ound. IV RDn (1867—73), Ound. III RDn (1873—77), Ound. I RDn (1877—82), Ound. II RDn (1882—1954), K's Cliffe RDn (1954—60), Ound. RDn (1960—*).

SPRATTON

AP Incl hmlt Little Creaton (Guilsb. Hd, sep CP 1866[10]). *LG* Spel. Hd (pt until 1866, ent from 1866), pt Guilsb. Hd (Little Creaton, until 1866), Brixw. PLU, RSD, RD. *Parl* Seq 11. *Eccl* Seq 7.

STAMFORD BARON ST MARTIN

AP Orig in Northants (Nassab. Hd), incl hmlt Wothorpe (orig sep AP, appropriated to Stamford Baron Abbey, parochial rights not sustained after Dissoution[175]). Pt in Stamf. MB (o'wise ent Lincs Pts Kestev, 1835—94), that pt becomes 1889 pt Lincs Pts Kestev and then in 1894 cr St Martin Without CP[104] (later called 'Stamford Barton St Martin's Without') so that the remainder as 'Stamford Baron' ent Northants thereafter. *Parl* Pt Stamf. Parl Bor (o'wise ent Lincs Pts Kestev, 1832—85), N'rn Dv (pt 1832—85, ent 1885—1918). *Eccl* Seq 19.

STAMFORD BARON ST MARTIN'S WITHOUT—see ST MARTIN WITHOUT

STANFORD

AP Usual civ spelling; for eccl see following entry. *LG* Seq 13. *Parl* Seq 10.

STANFORD ON AVON

AP Usual eccl spelling; for civ see prev entry. *Eccl* Haddon RDn (until 1867), Haddon I RDn (1867—1926), not in a RDn (when initially transf to dioc Leic, 1926—27), Guthlaxton III RDn (1927—28), Guthlaxton II RDn (1928—*).

STANION

Chap in Brigstock AP, sep civ identity early. *LG* Seq 4. *Parl* Seq 5.

STANWICK

AP *LG* High. Ferr. Hd, Thrap. PLU, RSD, RD. Abol civ 1935 ent to Raunds AP.[14] *Parl* N'rn Dv (1832—85), E'rn Dv (1885—1918), Wellingb. Dv (1918—48). *Eccl* High. Ferr. RDn (until 1867), High. Ferr. II RDn (1867—82), High. Ferr. I RDn (1882—1954), High. RDn (1954—*).

STAVERTON

AP *LG* Seq 9. *Parl* Seq 12. *Eccl* Seq 5.

STEANE

AP *LG* K's Sutt. Hd, Brack. PLU, RSD, RD. Abol civ 1935 ent to Farthinghoe AP.[14] *Parl* S'rn Dv (1832—1918), Dav. Dv (1918—48). *Eccl* Brack. RDn. Abol eccl before 1535 to help cr Hinton in the Hedges AP with Steane AP.

STOKE ALBANY

AP *LG* Seq 5. *Parl* Seq 3. *Eccl* Seq 28.

STOKE BRUERNE

AP Incl chap Shutlanger (sep CP 1866[10]). *LG* Seq 3. Addtl civ bdry alt: 1883.[174] *Parl* Seq 12. *Eccl* Preston RDn (until 1867), Preston I RDn (1867—

73), Brack. III RDn (1873—1954), Brack. RDn (1954—70), Towc. RDn (1970—*).

STOKE DOYLE

AP *LG* Seq 21. *Parl* Seq 8. *Eccl* Ound. RDn (until 1867), Ound. I RDn (1867—77), Ound. II RDn (1877—1954), K's Cliffe RDn (1954—60), Ound. RDn (1960—*).

STONETON

Ex-par place, sep CP 1858.[17] *LG* Chip. Ward. Hd, Southam PLU (1858—1930), RSD, sep RD in Northants (1894—95). Transf 1895 to Warws.[176] *Parl* S'rn Dv (1832—1918), Warws thereafter.

STOWE NINE CHURCHES

AP *LG* Seq 9. Civ bdry: 1884.[177] *Parl* Seq 12. *Eccl* Dav. RDn (until 1873), Weedon RDn (1873—1970), Dav. RDn (1970—*).

OLD STRATFORD

CP Cr 1951 by union pts Cosgrove AP, Deanshanger CP, Furtho AP.[82] *LG* Towc. RD. *Parl* Dav. CC (1970—*).

STRIXTON

AP *LG* Seq 16. Civ bdry: 1884.[178] *Parl* Seq 2. *Eccl* High. Ferr. RDn (until 1867), High. Ferr. III RDn (1867—82), High. Ferr. I RDn (1882—1929). Abol eccl 1929 to help cr Wollaston with Strixton EP.[179]

STUCHBURY

AP *LG* K's Sutt. Hd, Brack. PLU, RSD, RD. Abol civ 1935 ent to Greatworth AP.[14] *Parl* S'rn Dv (1832—1918), Dav. Dv (1918—48). *Eccl* Church destroyed by 1535, last presentation 1560,[120] abol thereafter and incl with Helmsdon AP as 'Helmsdon with Stuchbury', qv.

SUDBOROUGH

AP *LG* Seq 18. *Parl* Seq 8. *Eccl* Seq 16.

SULBY

Ex-par place (orig church or chap appropriated to Sulby Abbey, last institution 1525, demolished and ex-par thereafter[180]), sep CP 1858.[17] *LG* Seq 33. *Parl* Seq 4.

SULGRAVE

AP *LG* Seq 39. Civ bdry: 1956.[9] *Parl* Seq 12. *Eccl* Seq 2.

SUTTON

[Soke Peterb] Chap in Castor AP, sep CP 1866,[10] sep EP 1851.[66] *LG* Seq 19. Transf 1965 to Hunts & Peterb.[12] *Parl* Seq 6. *Eccl* Peterb RDn (1851—67), Peterb I RDn (1867—1954), Peterb RDn (1954—*).

KINGS SUTTON

AP *LG* K's Sutt. Hd, Brack. PLU, RSD. Abol civ 1885 to help cr Kings Sutton with Newbottle CP.[141] *Parl* S'rn Dv (1832—1918). *Eccl* Pec jurisd Banb. (until 1851), Seq 3 thereafter.

CP Cr 1896 from Kings Sutton with Newbottle CP.[142] *LG* Brack. PLU, RD. *Parl* Dav. Dv (1918—48), S Northants CC (1948—70), Dav. CC (1970—*).

KINGS SUTTON WITH NEWBOTTLE

CP Cr 1885 by union Kings Sutton AP, Newbottle AP.[141] *LG* K's Sutt. Hd, Brack. PLU, RSD, RD. Abol 1896 to cr 2 CPs of Kings Sutton, Newbottle.[142]

SUTTON BASSETT

Chap in Weston by Welland AP, sep civ identity early. *LG* Seq 5. *Parl* Seq 3.

SYRESHAM
AP *LG* Seq 36. Civ bdry: 1884,[56] 1884 (incl gains pt Biddlesden AP, Bucks),[57] 1885.[24] *Parl* Seq 12. *Eccl* Brack. RDn (until 1867), Brack. II RDn (1867—1954), Towc. RDn (1954—64), Brack. RDn (1964—*).

SYWELL
AP *LG* Seq 14. *Parl* Seq 2. *Eccl* Seq 25.

TANSOR
AP *LG* Seq 41. *Parl* Seq 8. *Eccl* Ound. RDn (until 1867), Ound. IV RDn (1867—73), Ound. III RDn (1873—77), Ound. I RDn (1877—1922). Abol eccl 1922 to help cr Tansor with Cottestock EP.[83]

TANSOR WITH COTTESTOCK
EP Cr 1922 by union Tansor AP, pt (area Cottestock) Cottestock with Glapthorn AP.[83] Ound. I RDn (1922—54), Ound. RDn (1954—*). Bdry: 1957.[181]

TEETON
Hmlt in Ravensthorpe AP, sep CP 1866.[10] *LG* Nob. Gr. Hd, Brixw. PLU, RSD, RD. Abol 1935 ent to Hollowell CP.[14] *Parl* S'rn Dv (1832—85), Mid Dv (1885—1918), Kett. Dv (1918—48).

THEDDINGWORTH
AP Mostly Leics (Gartree Hd), pt Northants (Rothw. Hd: hmlt Hothorpe, sep CP 1866[10]) so that the par ent Leics from 1866. *Parl* Northants pt, N'rn Dv (1832—67). See main entry in Leics for eccl and all other later organisation.

THENFORD
AP *LG* Seq 36. Civ bdry: 1885.[24] *Parl* Seq 12. *Eccl* Seq 3.

THONBY
AP *LG* Seq 11. *Parl* Seq 11. *Eccl* Seq 6.

THORNHAUGH
AP [Soke Peterb] Incl chap Wansford (sep civ identity early, not sep eccl hence this par eccl 'Thornhaugh with Wansford', qv). *LG* Seq 20. Addtl civ bdry alt: 1887,[182] 1965 (loses pts to King's Cliffe AP, Nassington AP, Yarwell AP, all Northants, the remainder transf to be 'Thornhaugh' in Hunts & Peterb.[71] *Parl* Seq 6.

THORNHAUGH WITH WANSFORD
AP [Soke Peterb] Usual eccl spelling; for civ and civ sep chap, see prev entry. *Eccl* Seq 19.

THORPE ACHURCH
AP *LG* Seq 21. *Parl* Seq 8. *Eccl* Ound. RDn. Gains eccl 1778 Lilford cum Wigsthorpe AP (no church) to cr Thorpe Achurch with Lilford EP.[131]

THORPE ACHURCH WITH LILFORD
EP Cr 1778 by union Thorpe Achurch AP, Lilford cum Wigsthorpe AP (no church).[131] Ound. RDn (cr—1867), Ound. I RDn (1867—73), Ound. II RDn (1873—1954), Thrap. RDn (1954—70), Ound. RDn (1970—*).

THORPE BY WATER
Hmlt (pec jurisd Lyddington, until 1851), in Seaton AP, sep CP 1866.[10] Mostly Rutl (Wrangdyke Hd), pt Northants (Corby Hd). *LG* Upp. PLU, RSD. Bdry: 1885 (the pt in Northants transf to Gretton AP, Northants, and the par ent Rutl thereafter).[113] *Parl* Northants pt, N'rn Dv (1832—1918).

THORPE LUBENHAM
Ex-par place, sep CP 1858.[17] *LG* Rothw. Hd, Mkt.

Harb. PLU (1863—1930), RSD, Oxend. RD. Abol 1935 ent to Marston Trussel AP.[14] *Parl* N'rn Dv (1832—85), Mid Dv (1885—1918), Kett. Dv (1918—48).

THORPE MALSOR
AP *LG* Seq 32. Civ bdry: 1935.[14] *Parl* Seq 3. *Eccl* Seq 26.

THORPE MANDEVILLE
AP *LG* Seq 36. *Parl* Seq 12. *Eccl* Seq 1.

THRAPSTON
AP *LG* Seq 22. *Parl* Seq 8. *Eccl* Seq 16.

THURNING
AP Pt Hunts (Leightonstone Hd), pt Northants (Navisf. Hd), the par made 1895 ent Northants.[135] *LG* Northants pt, Seq 21. Civ bdry: 1965 (gains pt Winwick AP, Hunts, the remainder of the latter to be in Hunts & Peterb Adm Co).[71] *Parl* Northants pt, Seq 8. *Eccl* Leightonstone RDn (until 1863), Leightonstone RDn Second Dv (1863—78), Leightonstone RDn (1878—1929) (all in dioc Ely until 1929, thereafter dioc Peterb:), High. Ferr. II RDn (1928—54), Thrap. RDn (1954—70), Ound. RDn (1970—*).

TIFFIELD
AP *LG* Seq 37. *Parl* Seq 12. *Eccl* Seq 4.

TITCHMARSH
AP *LG* Seq 22. Civ bdry: 1965 (gains pt Bythorn and Keyston CP, Hunts, the remainder of the latter to be Hunts & Peterb Adm Co).[71] *Parl* Seq 8. *Eccl* Seq 16.

TOWCESTER
AP Incl area Abthorpe (sep par 1737[8]). *LG* Towc. Bor, Seq 37. Addtl civ bdry alt: 1956.[9] *Parl* Seq 12. *Eccl* Seq 4.

TWYWELL
AP *LG* Seq 18. Civ bdry: 1885.[15] *Parl* Seq 8. *Eccl* Seq 16.

UFFORD
AP [Soke Peterb] Incl chap Bainton (sep civ identity early, not sep eccl hence this parl eccl 'Ufford with Bainton', qv), hmlt Ashton (sep CP 1866,[10] eccl in chap Bainton). *LG* Seq 20. Addtl civ bdry alt: 1883,[21] 1887.[25] Transf 1965 to Hunts & Peterb.[12] *Parl* Seq 6.

UFFORD WITH BAINTON
AP [Soke Peterb] Usual eccl spelling; for civ and civ sep chap and hmlt, see prev entry. *Eccl* Seq 19.

UPTON
[Soke Peterb] Chap in Castor AP, sep CP 1866,[10] sep EP 1851.[66] *LG* Seq 19. Transf 1965 to Hunts & Peterb.[12] *Parl* Seq 6. *Eccl* Peterb RDn (1851—67), Peterb I RDn (1867—1954), Peterb RDn (1954—*).

UPTON
Chap in Northampton St Peter AP, sep civ identity early. *LG* Seq 25. Bdry: 1965 (incl loses pt to N'htn CB [assoc with Northants] & CP),[36] 1971 (incl loses pt to N'htn CB [assoc with Northants] & CP).[38] *Parl* Seq 10. Parl bdry: 1973.[39]

WADENHOE
AP *LG* Seq 21. *Parl* Seq 8. *Eccl* Ound. RDn (until 1867), Ound. II RDn (1867—82), Ound. RDn (1882—1954), Ound. RDn (1954—*).

WAKERLEY

AP *LG* Seq 8. *Parl* Seq 8. *Eccl* Weldon RDn (until 1867), Weldon II RDn (1867—82), Ound. II RDn (1882—1954), K's Cliffe RDn (1954—60), Upp. RDn (1960—70), Barnack RDn (1970—72). Eccl bdry: 1948 (gains the pt of ex-par Fineshade in Fineshade CP).[44] Abol eccl 1972, united with Barrowden AP (Rutl) to cr Barrowden and Wakerley EP.[32]

WALGRAVE

AP *LG* Seq 27. *Parl* Seq 4. *Eccl* Rothw. RDn (until 1867), Rothw. I RDn (1867—1954), Wellingb. RDn (1954—70), Brixw. RDn (1970—*).

WALTON

[Soke Peterb] Hmlt in Paston AP, sep CP 1866,[10] eccl in chap Werrington in same par (sep EP 1853[161]), pt of the hmlt eccl severed 1888 from Werrington EP and transf to Paston AP.[162] *LG* Nassab. Hd, Peterb PLU, RSD, RD. Abol 1929 to help cr Peterborough CP to be in Peterb MB.[105] *Parl* N'rn Dv (1832—1918), Peterb Dv (1918—48).

WANSFORD

[Soke Peterb] Chap in Thornhaugh AP, sep civ identity early. *LG* Seq 20. Bdry: 1887,[182] 1965 (loses pt to Yarwell AP, Northants, the remainder transf to be 'Wansford' in Hunts & Peterb).[71] *Parl* Seq 6.

WAPPENHAM

AP Incl hmlt Astwell and Falcott (sep CP 1866[10]). *LG* K's Sutt. Hd, Towc. PLU, RSD, RD. Addtl civ bdry alt: 1956.[9] *Parl* Seq 12. *Eccl* Brack. RDn (until 1867), Brack. I RDn (1867—1954), Culw. RDn (1954—58), Towc. RDn (1958—*). Eccl bdry: 1964.[121]

CHIPPING WARDEN

AP *LG* Seq 38. Civ bdry: 1884,[63] 1884.[23] *Parl* Seq 12. *Eccl* Seq 1.

WARKTON

AP *LG* Seq 17. Civ bdry: 1935.[14] *Parl* Seq 5. *Eccl* Seq 9.

WARKWORTH

Chap in Marston St Lawrence AP, sep civ identity early. Civ incl tg Neithrop (sep CP 1866 in Oxon[10]), the tp eccl in Banbury AP (Oxon, Northants until 1894), qv. *LG* Seq 35. Addtl civ bdry alt: 1883,[21] 1884 (loses pt to Bodicote CP, Oxon),[183] 1884.[139] *Parl* Seq 12.

WARMINGTON

AP *LG* Seq 30. Civ bdry: 1965 (loses pt to Elton AP, Hunts, to be in Hunts & Peterb Adm Co).[71] *Parl* Seq 8. *Eccl* Seq 17. Eccl bdry: 1957.[181]

WATFORD

AP *LG* Seq 12. Civ bdry: 1884.[65] *Parl* Seq 10. *Eccl* Seq 6.

WEEDON BEC

AP Usual eccl spelling; for civ before 1935, see 'Weedon Beck'. *Eccl* Dav. RDn (until 1873), Weedon RDn (1873—1970), Dav. RDn (1970—*).

CP Renaming 1935 of Weedon Beck AP.[184] *LG* Dav. RD. *Parl* S Northants CC (1948—70), Dav. CC (1970—*).

WEEDON BECK

AP Usual eccl spelling, civ spelling until renamed 1935

'Weedon Bec',[184] qv. *LG* Fawsley Hd, Dav. PLU, RSD, RD. Civ bdry: 1884.[177] *Parl* S'rn Dv (1832—1918), Dav. Dv (1918—48).

WEEDON LOIS

AP *LG* Gr's Nort. Hd, Towc. PLU, RSD, RD. Abol civ 1935 to help cr Weston and Weedon CP.[14] *Parl* S'rn Dv (1832—1918), Dav. Dv (1918—48). *Eccl* Brack. RDn (until 1867), Brack. I RDn (1867—77), Brack. II RDn (1877—1928). Abol eccl 1928 to help cr Weedon Lois with Plumpton EP, orig called 'Lois Weedon with Plumpton'.[169]

WEEDON LOIS WITH PLUMPTON

EP Cr 1928 by union Plumpton AP, Weedon Lois AP,[169] orig as 'Lois Weedon with Plumpton'. Brack. II RDn (1928—54), Towc. RDn (1954—58), Culw. RDn (1958—70), Brack. RDn (1970—*).

WEEKLEY

AP *LG* Seq 4. Civ bdry: 1935.[14] *Parl* Seq 5. *Eccl* Seq 29.

WELDON

CP Cr 1935 by union Great Weldon AP, Little Weldon CP.[14] *LG* Kett. RD. Bdry: 1939 (loses pt to Corby AP as the enlarged par constituted Corby UD),[73] 1952,[79] 1967.[80] *Parl* Kett. CC (1948—*).

GREAT WELDON

AP Incl hmlt Little Weldon (sep CP 1866[10]). *LG* Corby Hd, Ound. PLU (1835—94), RSD, Kett. PLU (1894—1930), RD. Addtl civ bdry alt: 1885.[93] Abol civ 1935 to help cr Weldon CP.[14] *Parl* N'rn Dv (1832—1918), Kett. Dv (1918—48). *Eccl* Seq 31.

LITTLE WELDON

Hmlt in Great Weldon AP, sep CP 1866.[10] Organisation as for Great Weldon, incl bdry alt, with no sep eccl identity.

WELFORD

AP *LG* Guilsb. Hd, Lutterworth PLU (1835—94), RSD, Mkt. Harb. PLU (1894—1930), Oxend. RD (1894—1935), Brixw. RD (1935—74). *Parl* Seq 11. *Eccl* Seq 6.

WELLINGBOROUGH

The following have 'Wellingborough' in their names. Insofar as any existed at a given time: *LG* Hamf. Hd, Wellingb. PLU, USD, UD. *Parl* Seq 2. *Eccl* Rothw. RDn (until 1867), Rothw. I RDn (1867—1954), Wellingb. RDn (1954—*).

AP1—WELLINGBOROUGH [ALL HALLOWS]— Civ bdry: 1935 (incl gains Finedon UD & AP),[103] 1968.[102] Eccl bdry: 1872 (cr EP1),[185] 1910 (cr EP3),[186] 1964 (cr EP2).[187]

EP1—WELLINGBOROUGH ALL SAINTS—Cr 1872 from AP1.[185] Bdry: 1904 (cr EP5).[188]

EP2—WELLINGBOROUGH ST ANDREW—Cr 1964 from AP1.[187]

EP3—WELLINGBOROUGH ST BARNABAS—Cr 1910 from AP1.[186] Bdry: 1969 (cr EP4).[189]

EP4—WELLINGBOROUGH ST MARK—Cr 1969 from EP3.[189]

EP5—WELLINGBOROUGH ST MARY THE VIRGIN—Cr 1904 from EP1.[188]

WELTON

AP Orig chap in Daventry AP, sep par by 1535.[19] *LG* Seq 9. *Parl* Seq 12. *Eccl* Seq 5.

WERRINGTON

[Soke Peterb] Chap in Paston AP, sep CP 1866,[10] sep EP 1853 (incl hmlt Walton in same par, a sep CP 1866[10]).[161] *LG* Nassab. Hd, Peterb PLU, RSD, RD. Abol civ 1929 to help cr Peterborough CP to be in Peterb MB.[105] *Parl* N'rn Dv (1832—1918), Peterb Dv (1918—48). *Eccl* Peterb RDn (1853—67), Peterb I RDn (1867—1954), Peterb RDn (1954—*). Eccl bdry: 1888 (pt of the hmlt of Walton eccl severed and transf to Paston AP).[162]

WESTON AND WEEDON

CP Cr 1935 by union Plumpton AP, Weedon Lois AP.[14] *LG* Towc. RD. Bdry: 1956.[9] *Parl* S Northants CC (1948—70), Dav. CC (1970—*).

WESTON BY WELLAND

AP Incl chap Sutton Bassett (sep civ identity early, not sep eccl hence this par eccl 'Weston by Welland with Sutton Bassett', qv). *LG* Seq 5. *Parl* Seq 3.

WESTON BY WELLAND WITH SUTTON BASSETT

AP Usual eccl spelling; for civ and civ sep chap, see prev entry. *Eccl* Seq 28.

WESTON FAVELL

AP *LG* Spel. Hd, N'hton PLU, RSD, RD. Civ bdry: 1900 (gains the pt of Abington AP not transf to N'hton CB),[1] 1912 (loses pt to N'hton CB [assoc with Northants] and to Abington AP),[3] 1932 (loses pt to N'hton CB [assoc with Northants] & CP).[50] Abol civ 1965 pt to N'hton CB (assoc with Northants) & CP, pt to Billing CP.[36] *Parl* S'rn Dv (1832—85), Mid Dv (1885—1918), Kett. Dv (1918—48), S Northants CC (1948—70). *Eccl* Seq 8. Eccl bdry: 1951 (incl help cr Abington St Alban the Martyr EP),[6] 1960.[99]

WHILTON

AP *LG* Seq 24. *Parl* Seq 12. *Eccl* Haddon RDn (until 1867), Haddon II RDn (1867—73), Dav. RDn (1873—1969), Haddon RDn (1969—70), Dav. RDn (1970—*).

WHISTON

AP *LG* Wym. Hd, Hardingst. PLU, RSD, RD. Abol civ 1935 ent to Cogenhoe AP.[14] *Parl* S'rn Dv (1832—85), Mid Dv (1885—1918), Dav. Dv (1918—48). *Eccl* Seq 23.

WHITFIELD

AP *LG* Seq 36. Civ bdry: 1885.[24] *Parl* Seq 12. *Eccl* Seq 3.

WHITTLEBURY

Chap in Green's Norton AP, sep civ identity early; eccl incl hmlt Silverstone (sep civ identity early from Green's Norton AP), the combined area a sep EP 1852 as 'Whittlebury and Silverstone'.[159] *LG* Seq 26. *Parl* Seq 12.

WHITTLEBURY AND SILVERSTONE

EP Cr 1852 from chap Whittlebury (incl hmlt Silverstone) in Green's Norton AP[159]; for civ, each sep early, see 'Whittlebury', 'Silverstone'. Brack. RDn (1852—67), Brack. III RDn (1867—77), Brack. II RDn (1877—1954), Towc. RDn (1954—*).

WICK DYKE

AP Preston RDn, abol 1578 to help cr Wicken AP.[190]

WICK HAMON

AP Organisation as for Wick Dyke.

WICKEN

AP Cr 1578 by union Wick Dyke AP, Wick Hamon AP.[190] *LG* Seq 2. Civ bdry: 1956.[9] *Parl* Seq 12. *Eccl* Seq 20.

WILBARSTON

AP *LG* Seq 5. *Parl* Seq 3. *Eccl* Seq 28.

WILBY

AP *LG* Seq 14. *Parl* Seq 2. *Eccl* Seq 24.

WINWICK

AP Pt Hunts (Leightonstone Hd), pt Northants (Poleb. Hd), the par made 1895 ent Hunts.[135] *LG* Ound. PLU, RSD, pt sep RD in Northants (1894—95). *Parl* Northants pt, N'rn Dv (1832—1918). *Eccl* See main entry in Hunts.

WINWICK

AP *LG* Seq 12. *Parl* Seq 10. *Eccl* Haddon RDn (until 1867), Haddon II RDn (1867—73), Haddon I RDn (1873—1954), Haddon RDn (1954—56), Brixw. RDn (1956—*).

WITTERING

AP [Soke Peterb] *LG* Seq 20. Transf 1965 to Hunts & Peterb.[12] *Parl* Seq 6. *Eccl* Seq 19.

WOLLASTON

AP *LG* Seq 16. Civ bdry: 1884.[178] *Parl* Seq 2. *Eccl* High. Ferr. RDn (until 1867), High. Ferr. III RDn (1867—82), High. Ferr. I RDn (1882—1929). Abol eccl 1929 to help cr Wollaston with Strixton EP.[179]

WOLLASTON WITH STRIXTON

EP Cr 1929 by union Wollaston AP, Strixton AP.[179] High. Ferr. I RDn (1929—54), High. RDn (1954—70), Wellingb. RDn (1970—*).

WOODEND

Hmlt in Blakesley AP, sep CP 1866.[10] *LG* Seq 26. Bdry: 1956.[9] *Parl* Seq 12.

WOODFORD

AP Sometimes 'Woodford near Thrapston'. *LG* Seq 18. *Parl* Seq 8. *Eccl* Seq 11.

WOODFORD CUM MEMBRIS

AP *LG* Seq 40. *Parl* Seq 12. *Eccl* Sometimes lately as 'Woodford Halse', Seq 1.

WOODNEWTON

Chap (pec jurisd Nassington) in Nassington AP, sep civ identity early, sep EP 1747[11] (pec jurisd Nassington) but abol 1836 to help cr Apethorpe with Woodnewton EP.[19] *LG* Seq 41. *Parl* Seq 8.

WOODSTON—see following entry

WOODSTONE

AP In Hunts (Norman Cross Hd, usually called 'Woodston'), pt Peterb MB & USD (1874—94) and thus that pt in Soke Peterb 1889—94, the par abol civ 1894, the pt in the MB cr Woodstone Urban CP in the Soke, the remainder cr Woodstone Rural CP in Hunts.[104] See main entry in Hunts. *Parl* Pt Peterb Parl Bor (1867—1918); remainder in Hunts, qv. *Eccl* See main entry in Hunts.

WOODSTONE URBAN

CP [Soke Peterb] Cr 1894 from the pt of Woodstone AP (in Hunts called 'Woodston') in Peterb MB.[104] *LG* Peterb PLU, MB. Abol 1929 to help cr Peterborough CP.[105] *Parl* Peterb Dv (1918—48).

WOOTTON

AP *LG* Seq 43. Civ bdry: 1884,[59] 1965 (gains pt N'hton CB [assoc with Northants] & CP),[36] 1971 (loses pt to N'htn CB [assoc with Northants] & CP).[38] *Parl* Seq 10. Parl bdry: 1973.[39] *Eccl* Seq 23.

WOTHORPE

AP [Soke Peterb] Orig AP appropriated to Stamford Baron Priory, and considered hmlt in Stamford Baron AP, sep CP 1866.[10] *LG* Seq 20. Transf 1965 to Hunts & Peterb.[12] *Parl* Seq 6.

YARDLEY GOBION

Hmlt in Potterspury AP, sep CP 1866,[10] sep EP 1864[11] (Preston RDn) but not sustained, hence the reunited par eccl 'Potterspury with Yardley Gobion'. Incl undivided pt Lands Common to Potterspury and Yardley Gobion [Potterspury Lodge Farm, Whittlewood Forest] (abol 1935, pt to each par[14]). *LG* Seq 2. *Parl* Seq 12.

YARDLEY HASTINGS

AP Incl chap Denton (sep civ identity early, sep EP 1892[94]). *LG* Seq 43. *Parl* Seq 10. *Eccl* Seq 23.

YARWELL

Chap (pec jurisd Nassington) in Nassington AP, sep civ identity early. *LG* Seq 41. Bdry: 1965 (gains pt Thornhaugh AP, pt Wansford CP, both Soke Peterb, gains pt Sibson cum Stibbington CP, Hunts).[71] *Parl* Seq 8.

YELVERTOFT

AP *LG* Seq 13. *Parl* Seq 10. *Eccl* Haddon RDn (until 1867), Haddon I RDn (1867—1954), Haddon RDn (1954—70), Brixw. RDn (1970—72). Abol eccl 1972 to help cr Yelvertoft with Clay Coton EP.[72]

YELVERTOFT WITH CLAY COTON

EP Cr 1972 by union Yelvertoft AP, Clay Coton AP.[72] Brixw. RDn.

NORTHUMBERLAND

ABBREVIATIONS

Abbreviations particular to Northumb follow. Those general abbreviations in use throughout the *Guide* are found on pages xvii—xix.

Alnw.	Alnwick
Ash.	Ashington
Bamb.	Bamburgh
Bedl.	Bedlington
Belf.	Belford
Bell.	Bellingham
Berw.	Berwick
Coq.	Coquetdale
Corbr.	Corbridge
Craml.	Cramlington
Earsd.	Earsdon
Glend.	Glendale
Haltw.	Haltwhistle
Morp.	Morpeth
Newb.	Newburn
Prud.	Prudhoe
Rothb.	Rothbury
Tyned.	Tynedale
Tynem.	Tynemouth
Tynes.	Tyneside
Wansb.	Wansbeck

SEQUENCES

An abbreviated entry prefixed by 'Seq' is used in the parochial entries to avoid repeating often the names of superior units of administration. The content of each sequence is shown below.

Local Government Sequences ('LG')

SEQ 1   Bamb. Wd, Alnw. PLU, RSD, RD
SEQ 2   Bamb. Wd, Belf. PLU, RSD, RD
SEQ 3   Castle Wd, Castle Wd PLU, RSD, RD
SEQ 4   Castle Wd, Morp. PLU, RSD, RD
SEQ 5   Coq. Wd, Alnw. PLU, RSD, RD
SEQ 6   Coq. Wd, Bell. PLU, RSD, RD
SEQ 7   Coq. Wd, Glend. PLU, RSD, RD
SEQ 8   Coq. Wd, Rothb. PLU, RSD, RD
SEQ 9   Glend. Wd, PLU, RSD, RD
SEQ 10   Morp. Wd, PLU, RSD, RD
SEQ 11   Morp. Wd, Alnw. PLU, RSD, RD
SEQ 12   Morp. Wd, Castle Wd PLU, RSD, RD
SEQ 13   Morp. Wd, Rothb. PLU, RSD, RD
SEQ 14   Norhamshire, Berw. PLU, RSD, Norham & Islandshires RD
SEQ 15   Tyned. Wd, Bell. PLU, RSD, RD
SEQ 16   Tyned. Wd, Castle Wd PLU, RSD, RD
SEQ 17   Tyned. Wd, Haltw. PLU, RSD, RD
SEQ 18   Tyned. Wd, Hexham PLU, RSD, RD

Parliamentary Sequences ('Parl')

SEQ 1   N'rn Dv (1832—85), Berw. upon Tweed Dv/ CC (1885—*)
SEQ 2   N'rn Dv (1832—85), Hexham Dv (1885—1918), Berw. upon Tweed Dv/CC (1918—*)
SEQ 3   N'rn Dv (1832—85), Wansb. Dv (1885—1918), Berw. upon Tweed Dv/CC (1918—*)
SEQ 4   N'rn Dv (1832—85), Wansb. Dv (1885—1948), Morp. CC (1948—*)
SEQ 5   S'rn Dv (1832—85), Hexham Dv/CC (1885—*)
SEQ 6   S'rn Dv (1832—85), Hexham Dv (1885—1918), Berw. upon Tweed Dv/CC (1918—*)
SEQ 7   S'rn Dv (1832—85), Tynes. Dv (1885—1918), Wansb. Dv (1918—48), Hexham CC (1948—*)
SEQ 8   S'rn Dv (1832—85), Wansb. Dv (1885—1948), Hexham CC (1948—*)
SEQ 9   S'rn Dv (1832—85), Wansb. Dv (1885—1948), Morp. CC (1948—*)

Ecclesiastical Sequences ('Eccl')

SEQ 1   Alnw. RDn
SEQ 2   Alnw. RDn (until 1845), Rothb. RDn (1845—*)
SEQ 3   Bamb. RDn (until 1845), Alnw. RDn

SEQ 4   Bamb. RDn (until 1899), Glend. RDn (1899—1969), Bamb. & Glend. RDn (1969—*)
SEQ 5   Bamb. RDn (until 1845), Norham RDn (1845—*)
SEQ 6   Corbr. RDn
SEQ 7   Corbr. RDn (until 1845), Bell. RDn (1845—*)
SEQ 8   Corbr. RDn (until 1845), Hexham RDn (1845—*)
SEQ 9   Morp. RDn

DIOCESES AND ARCHDEACONRIES

Northumb pars were arranged in Archdeaconries and Rural Deaneries as follows:

DURHAM DIOC (until 1882)
Lindisfarne AD (1845—82): Alnw. RDn, Bamb. RDn, Morp. RDn, Norham RDn, Rothb. RDn
Northumberland AD: Alnw. RDn (until 1845), Bamb. RDn (until 1845), Bell. RDn (1845—82), Corbr. RDn, Hexham RDn (1845—82), Morp. RDn (until 1845), Newc upon Tyne RDn (until 1877), Newc upon Tyne RDn (E'rn Dv) (1877—82), Newc upon Tyne RDn (N'rn Dv) (1874—77), Newc upon Tyne RDn (S'rn Dv) (1874—77), Newc upon Tyne RDn (W'rn Dv) (1877—82)

NEWCASTLE DIOC (1882—*)
Lindisfarne AD: Alnw. RDn, Bamb. RDn (1882—1969), Bamb. & Glend. RDn (1969—*), Glend. RDn (1899—1969), Morp. RDn, Norham RDn, Rothb. RDn
Northumberland AD: Bedl. RDn (1884—*), Bell. RDn, Corbr. RDn, Hexham RDn, Newc RDn (1884—1967), Newc Central RDn (1967—*), Newc East RDn (1967—*), Newc West RDn (1967—*), Newc upon Tyne RDn (E'rn Dv) (1882—84), Newc upon Tyne RDn (W'rn Dv) (1882—84), Tynem. RDn (1884—*)

THE PARISHES OF NORTHUMBERLAND

ABBERWICK
Tp in Edlingham AP, sep CP 1866.[1] *LG* Coq. Wd, Alnw. PLU, RSD, RD. Abol 1955 ent to Edlingham AP.[2] *Parl* N'rn Dv (1867—85), Berw. upon Tweed Dv/CC (1885—1970).

ACKLINGTON
Tp in Warkworth AP, sep CP 1866,[1] eccl united 1859 with tp Acklington Park in same par and ex-par Brainshaugh to cr Acklington EP.[3] *LG* Seq 11. Civ bdry: 1955 (gains Acklington Park CP, Guyzance CP).[2] *Parl* Seq 3. *Eccl* Alnw. RDn.

ACKLINGTON PARK
Tp in Warkworth AP, sep CP 1866,[1] eccl severed 1859 to help cr Acklington EP.[3] *LG* Morp. Wd, Alnw. PLU, RSD, RD. Abol 1955 ent to Acklington CP.[2] *Parl* N'rn Dv (1867—85), Wansb. Dv (1885—1918), Berw. upon Tweed Dv/CC (1918—70).

ACOMB
Tp in Lee St John AP, sep CP 1866.[1] *LG* Seq 18. *Parl* Seq 5.

EAST ACOMB
Tp in Bywell St Peter AP, sep CP 1866.[1] *LG* Tyned. Wd, Hexham PLU, RSD. Bdry: 1883.[4] Abol 1887 to help cr Bywell CP.[5] *Parl* S'rn Dv (1867—85), Hexham Dv (1885—1918).

ACTON AND OLD FELTON
Tp in Felton AP, sep CP 1866.[1] *LG* Coq. Wd, Alnw. PLU, RSD, RD. Bdry: 1888.[6] Abol 1955 ent to Felton AP.[2] *Parl* N'rn Dv (1867—85), Berw. upon Tweed Dv/CC (1885—1970).

ADDERSTONE
Tp in Bamburgh AP, sep CP 1866,[1] eccl severed 1884 to help refound Lucker EP.[7] *LG* Bamb. Wd, Belf. PLU, RSD, RD. Abol 1955 to help cr Adderstone with Lucker CP.[8] *Parl* N'rn Dv (1867—85), Berw. upon Tweed Dv/CC (1885—1970).

ADDERSTONE WITH LUCKER
CP Cr 1955 by union Adderstone CP, Bradford CP, Lucker CP, Ratchwood CP, Warenford CP.[8] *LG* Belf. RD. *Parl* Berw. upon Tweed CC (1970—*).

AKELD
Tp in Kirknewton AP, sep CP 1866.[1] *LG* Seq 9. Bdry: 1955 (gains Humbleton CP).[9] *Parl* Seq 1.

WEST ALLEN
Chap in chap Allendale (in co palatine of Hexhamshire until latter merged into Northumb 1572,[10] Allendale gains sep civ identity early from Hexham AP, sep EP 1767[11]), 'West Allen' a sep CP 1897,[12] sep EP 1826,[11] from Allendale CP, EP respectively, 'West Allen' eccl refounded 1900 as 'Carr Shield' EP,[13] qv for organisation after 1900. Incl undivided pt Allendale Common (stinted pasture common to Allendale and West Allen). *LG* Hexham PLU, RD. *Parl* Hexham Dv/CC (1918—*). *Eccl* Newc upon Tyne RDn (1826—45), Hexham RDn (1845—1900).

ALLENDALE
Chap in Hexham AP (in co palatine of Hexhamshire until latter merged into Northumb 1572[10]), sep civ identity early, sep EP 1767.[11] Incl chap Allenheads (orig deemed domestic chap in Allendale, later deemed domestic chap in Allendale), chap Allendale St Peter (sep EP 1819,[11] eccl refounded 1900[13]), chap Ninebanks (sep EP 1763,[11] eccl refounded 1900[13]), chap West Allen (sep EP 1826,[11] sep CP 1897,[12] eccl refounded 1900 as 'Carr Shield' EP[13]); incl undivided pt Allendale Common (stinted Pasture [after cr West Allen CP 1897, common to Allendale and West Allen]). *LG* Seq 18. *Parl* Seq 5. *Eccl* Newc upon Tyne RDn (1767—1845), Hexham RDn (1845—*). Addtl eccl bdry alt: 1953 (gains Allendale St Peter

EP).[14]

ALLENDALE COMMON

Stinted pasture in Allendale AP, after cr West Allen CP 1897 (from Allendale[12]) common to Allendale and West Allen. *LG* Hexham PLU, RD. *Parl* Hexham Dv/CC (1918—*).

ALLENDALE ST PETER

EP Chap in Allendale EP (orig chap in Hexham AP, sep civ identity early, sep EP 1767[11]), sep EP 1819,[11] eccl refounded 1900.[13] Newc upon Tyne RDn (1819—45), Hexham RDn (1845—1953). Abol 1953 ent to Allendale EP.[14]

ALLENHEADS

AP Orig sep AP (Newc upon Tyne RDn), sep status lost and thereafter considered chap in Allendale CP/EP (qv for orig status in Hexham AP and in co palatine Hexhamshire).

ALNHAM

AP Incl tps Prendwick, Scrainwood, Unthank (each a sep CP 1866[1]). *LG* Seq 8. Addtl civ bdry alt: 1889,[15] 1955 (gains Prendwick CP, Great Ryle CP, Little Ryle CP, Scainwood CP, Unthank CP).[16] *Parl* Seq 1. *Eccl* Seq 2.

ALNMOUTH

Chap in Lesbury AP, sep CP 1866,[1] sep EP 1877.[17] *LG* Seq 1. Civ bdry: 1888,[6] 1955 (gains High Buston CP).[2] *Parl* Seq 1. *Eccl* Alnw. RDn.

ALNWICK

AP *LG* Coq. Wd, Alnw. PLU, pt Alnw. & Canongate USD, Alnw. & Canongate UD (1894—96), Alnw. UD (1896—1974). Civ bdry: 1894 (the pt not in the USD cr Denwick CP).[18] *Parl* Seq 1. *Eccl* Seq 1. Eccl bdry: 1846 (cr Alnwick St Paul EP),[14] 1860 (help cr South Charlton EP).[19]

ALNWICK ST PAUL

EP Cr 1846 from Alnwick AP.[14] Alnw. RDn.

ALWINTON

AP Incl tp & bor (status not sustained) Harbottle (sep CP 1866[1]), tps Barrow, Biddlestone, Burradon, Clennell, Dueshill, Fairhaugh, Farnham, Linbridge, Linsheeles, Netherton, North Side, Netherton South Side, Peels, Sharperton (each a sep CP 1866[1]); gains *temp* Dissolution in 16th cent Holystone AP (a par appropriated to Holystone Nunnery just as was Alwinton),[20] thereafter civ considered tp in Alwinton until sep CP 1866,[1] eccl the united par 'Alwinton with Holystone', qv. *LG* Seq 8. Addtl civ bdry alt: 1883,[21] 1883,[22] 1955 (gains Barrow CP, Fairhaugh CP, Kidland CP, Linbridge CP, Linsheeles CP).[16] *Parl* Seq 2. *Eccl* Alnw. RDn.

ALWINTON WITH HOLYSTONE

AP Eccl name for union *temp* Dissolution in 16th cent of Alwinton AP, Holystone AP (each prev appropriated to Holystone Nunnery[20]); for civ union, see prev entry. *Eccl* Seq 2.

AMBLE

Tp in Warkworth AP, sep CP 1866,[1] eccl united 1869 with tps Hauxley, Gloster Hill, pt Togston in same par as Amble EP.[23] *LG* Morp. Wd, Alnw. PLU, USD, UD. *Parl* Seq 3. *Eccl* Alnw. RDn. Eccl bdry: 1889 (gains addtl pt tp Togston from Warkworth AP).[24]

ANCROFT

In Durham, transf to Northumb 1832 for parl purposes, 1844 for civ purposes.[25] Chap in Holy Island AP, sep civ identity early, sep EP 1733.[11] *LG* Islandshire, Berw. upon Tweed PLU, RSD, Norham & Islandshire RD. Civ bdry: 1888.[26] *Parl* In Durham until 1832, Seq 1 thereafter. *Eccl* Bamb. RDn (1733—1845), Norham RDn (1845—*). Eccl bdry: 1844 (help cr Scremerston EP).[27]

HIGH ANGERTON

Tp in Hartburn AP, sep CP 1866.[1] *LG* Morp. Wd, PLU, RSD, RD. Abol 1955 ent to Hartburn AP.[28] *Parl* N'rn Dv (1867—85), Wansb. Dv (1885—1948), Morp. CC (1948—70).

LOW ANGERTON

Tp in Hartburn AP, sep CP 1866.[1] Organisation as for High Angerton.

ANICK

Tp in Lee St John AP, sep CP 1866.[1] *LG* Tyned. Wd, Hexham PLU, RSD. Abol 1887 ent to Sandhoe CP.[29] *Parl* S'rn Dv (1867—85), Hexham Dv (1885—1918).

ANICK GRANGE

Tp in Lee St John AP, sep CP 1866.[1] Organisation as for Anick.

APPERLEY

Tp in Bywell St Peter AP, sep CP 1866.[1] *LG* Tyned. Wd, Hexham PLU (1858—87), RSD. Abol 1887 pt to Broomley CP, pt to Mickley CP.[30] *Parl* S'rn Dv (1867—85), Hexham Dv (1885—1918).

ASHINGTON

Tp in Bothal AP, civ united with chap Sheepwash in same par as 'Ashington with Sheepwash' and as such sep CP 1866,[1] qv, the latter civ divided 1896 into 2 CPs of Ashington (incl pt Bothal Demesne CP), Sheepwash[31]; pts eccl united 1888 with pt chap Sheepwash and pt tp Bothal Demesne to cr Ashington EP.[32] *LG* Morp. PLU, Ash. UD. Civ bdry: 1914,[33] 1935 (incl gains Bothal Demesne CP, Sheepwash CP).[34] *Parl* Morp. Parl Bor (1918—48), Morp. CC (1948—*). *Eccl* Morp. RDn. Eccl bdry: 1951.[35]

ASHINGTON AND SHEEPWASH

Single tp in Bothal AP (comprised of tp Ashington, chap Sheepwash), sep CP 1866,[1] eccl united 1888 with tp Bothal Demesne in same par to cr Ashington EP.[32] *LG* Morp. Wd, PLU, RSD, RD. Bdry: 1883.[4] Abol 1896 pt to cr Ashington CP, pt to cr Sheepwash CP.[31] *Parl* N'rn Dv (1867—85), Wansb. Dv (1885—1918).

AYDON

Tp in Corbridge AP, sep CP 1866.[1] *LG* Tyned. Wd, Hexham PLU, RSD, RD. Bdry: 1887.[36] Abol 1955 ent to Corbridge AP.[37] *Parl* S'rn Dv (1867—85), Hexham Dv/CC (1885—1970).

AYDON CASTLE

Tp in Corbridge AP, sep CP 1866.[1] Organisation as for Aydon except no bdry alt.

BACKWORTH

Tp in Earsdon AP, sep CP 1866.[1] *LG* Castle Wd, Tynem. PLU, RSD, RD (1894—97), Earsdon UD (1897—1935). Bdry: 1881.[38] Abol 1935 to help cr Seaton Valley UD & CP.[34] *Parl* S'rn Dv (1867—

85), Wansb. Dv (1885—1948).

BALKWELL

EP Cr 1968 from Tynemouth Percy EP, Tynemouth AP.[39] Tynem. RDn. Bdry: 1969,[40] 1973.[41]

BAMBURGH

AP Incl chap Belford (mostly in Northumb, pt in Durham [see entry under Belford for tps incl and their cos before and after 1844], sep civ identity early, sep EP 1735[11]), chap Beadnell (sep CP 1866,[1] sep EP 1763,[11] eccl refounded 1854[42]), chap Lucker (sep CP 1866,[1] sep EP 1766[11] eccl refounded 1884 by union Lucker and 8 tps next mentioned[7]: tps Adderstone, Hoppen, Mousen, Newham, Newstead, Ratchwood, Warenford, Warenton [each a sep CP 1866,[1] all united eccl 1884 with Lucker to refound Lucker EP[7]]); chap North Sunderland (sep CP 1866,[1] sep EP 1843[43]); tps Bamburgh Castle, Bradford, Budle, Burton, Elford, Fleetham, Glororum, Outchester, Shoreston, Spindlestone, Swinhoe, Tughall (each a sep CP 1866[1]). LG Orig sep franchise 'Bamburghshire', sep status early lost and thereafter incl in Northumb. LG Bamb. Bor (status not sustained), Seq 2. Addtl civ bdry alt: 1887,[44] 1955 (gains Bamburgh Castle CP, Budle CP, Burton CP, Glororum CP).[8] Parl Bamb. Parl Bor (1295 only), Seq 1. Eccl Bamb. RDn (until 1969), Bamb. & Glend. RDn (1969—*).

BAMBURGH CASTLE

Tp in Bamburgh AP, sep CP 1866.[1] LG Bamb. Wd, Belf. PLU, RSD, RD. Abol 1955 ent to Bamburgh AP.[8] Parl N'rn Dv (1867--85), Berw. upon Tweed Dv/CC (1885—1970).

BARDON MILL

CP Cr 1955 by union Ridley CP, Thorngrafton CP.[45] LG Haltw. RD. Parl Hexham CC (1970—*).

BARROW

Tp in Alwinton AP, sep CP 1866.[1] LG Coq. Wd, Rothb. PLU, RSD, RD. Bdry: 1883,[21] 1883.[46] Abol 1955 ent to Alwinton AP.[16] Parl N'rn Dv (1867—85), Hexham Dv (1885—1918), Berw. upon Tweed Dv/CC (1918—70).

BASSINGTON

Tp in Eglingham AP, sep CP 1866.[1] LG Coq. Wd, Alnw. PLU, RSD, RD. Abol 1955 ent to Eglingham AP.[2] Parl N'rn Dv (1867—85), Berw. upon Tweed Dv/CC (1885—1970).

BAVINGTON

CP Cr 1955 by union Great Bavington CP, Little Bavington CP, Hawick CP, Sweethope CP, Thockrington CP.[47] LG Bell. RD. Parl Hexham CC (1970—*).

GREAT BAVINGTON

Tp in Kirkwhelpington AP, sep CP 1866.[1] LG Tyned. Wd, Bell. PLU, RSD, RD. Abol 1955 to help cr Bavington CP.[47] Parl S'rn Dv (1767—85), Hexham Dv/CC (1885—1970).

LITTLE BAVINGTON

Tp in Throckrington AP, sep CP 1866.[1] Organisation as for Great Bavington.

BEADNELL

Chap in Bamburgh AP, sep CP 1866,[1] sep EP 1763,[11] eccl refounded 1854.[42] LG Seq 2. Civ bdry:

1955 (gains Elford CP, Fleetham CP, Swinhoe CP, Tughall CP).[8] Parl Seq 1. Eccl Bamb. RDn (1763—1969), Bamb. & Glend. RDn (1969—*).

BEANLEY

Tp in Eglingham AP, sep CP 1866.[1] LG Coq. Wd, Alnw. PLU, RSD, RD. Abol 1955 ent to Hedgeley CP.[2] Parl N'rn Dv (1867—85), Berw. upon Tweed Dv/CC (1885—1970).

BEARL

Tp in Bywell St Andrew AP, sep CP 1866.[1] LG Tyned. Wd, Hexham PLU, RSD, RD. Bdry: 1883,[4] 1887.[5] Abol 1955 ent to Bywell CP.[37] Parl S'rn Dv (1867—85), Hexham Dv/CC (1885—1970).

BEBSIDE

Tp in Horton AP, sep CP 1866.[1] LG Castle Wd, Tynem. PLU, RSD, RD (1894—1912), Blyth UD (1912—20). Abol 1920 to help cr Blyth CP.[48] Parl S'rn Dv (1867—85), Wansb. Dv (1885—1918), Morp. Parl Bor (1918—48).

BEDLINGTON

AP In Durham until 1844, transf to Northumb 1832 for parl purposes, 1844 for civ purposes.[25] LG Bedlingtonshire, Morp. PLU, Bedlingtonshire USD, UD. Civ bdry: 1883,[4] 1897.[49] Parl In Durham until 1832, Morp. Parl Bor (1832—1948), Blyth BC (1948—*). Eccl Newc upon Tyne RDn (until 1874), Newc upon Tyne RDn (N'rn Dv) (1874—77), Newc upon Tyne RDn (E'rn Dv) (1877—84), Bedl. RDn (1884—*). Eccl bdry: 1863 (cr Cambois EP [tps Cambois, East Sleekburn, pt West Sleekburn, the latter 2 without sep civ identity], cr Choppington EP [tps Choppington, pt West Sleekburn, the latter without sep civ identity]),[50] 1906 (help cr Sleekburn EP).[51]

BELFORD

Chap (pt Durham [Islandshire], pt Northumb [Bamb. Wd]) in Bamburgh AP (o'wise Northumb [Bamb. Wd]), 'Belford' with sep civ identity early, sep EP 1735.[11] Tp 'Belford' in Northumb (Bamb. Wd) as were tps Detchant, Easington, Easington Grange, Middleton (the 4 each a sep CP 1866[1]); incl in Durham (Islandshire) tp Ross; incl (pt Durham, pt Northumb) tp Elwick, the tps of Ross, Elwick each transf ent to Northumb 1832 for parl purposes, 1844 for civ purposes,[25] each a sep CP 1866 in Northumb.[1] LG Seq 2. Addtl civ bdry alt: 1883,[4] 1955 (gains Mousen CP, Warenton CP).[8] Parl Seq 1. Eccl Bamb. RDn (1735—1969), Bamb. & Glend. RDn (1969—*).

BELLINGHAM

Orig chap in Simonburn AP, sep par 1811.[52] Incl tps East Charlton, West Charlton, Leemailing, Nook, Tarretburn (each a sep CP 1866[1]). LG Seq 15. Addtl civ bdry alt: 1886,[53] 1955 (incl help cr Tarset CP).[47] Parl Seq 5. Eccl Corbr. RDn (1811—45), Bell. RDn (1845—*).

BELLISTER

Tp in Haltwhistle AP, sep CP 1866.[1] LG Tyned. Wd, Haltw. PLU, RSD, RD. Abol 1955 ent to Featherstone CP.[45] Parl S'rn Dv (1867—85), Hexham Dv/CC (1885—1970).

BELSAY

Tp in Bolam AP, sep CP 1866.[1] LG Seq 16. Bdry:

1955 (gains Bitchfield CP, Bolam AP, Bolam Vicarage CP, Bradford CP, Gallowhill CP, Harnham CP, Black Heddon CP, Ingoe CP, Newham CP, Shortflatt CP, Trewick CP, Wallridge CP).[54] *Parl* Seq 8.

BELTINGHAM
Chap in Haltwhistle AP, sep EP 1830,[11] eccl refounded 1890 as 'Beltingham with Henshaw',[55] qv. Corbr. RDn (1830—45), Hexham RDn (1845—90).

BELTINGHAM WITH HENSHAW
EP Name at refounding 1890 of Beltingham EP (qv in prev entry for its orig status as a chap in Haltwhisstle AP).[55] Hexham RDn.

BENRIDGE
Tp in Mitford AP, sep CP 1866.[1] *LG* Morp. Wd, PLU, RSD, RD. Bdry: 1935.[34] Abol 1955 ent to Hebron CP.[28] *Parl* N'rn Dv (1867—85), Wansb. Dv (1885—1948), Morp. CC (1948—70).

LONG BENTON
AP Usual eccl spelling; for civ see 'Longbenton'. *Eccl* Newc upon Tyne RDn (until 1845), Newc upon Tyne RDn (S'rn Dv) (1845—77), Newc upon Tyne RDn (E'rn Dv) (1877—84), Bedl. RDn (1884—1954), Newc RDn (1954—67), Newc East RDn (1967—*). Eccl bdry: 1846 (cr Walker EP),[56] 1865 (help cr North Gosforth EP),[57] 1952,[58] 1954 (help cr Wallsend St John EP),[59] 1955 (help cr Newcastle upon Tyne St Francis, High Heaton EP),[60] 1969 (cr Long Benton St Mary Magdalen EP).[40]

LONG BENTON ST MARY MAGDALEN
EP Cr 1969 from Long Benton EP.[40] Newc East RDn.

BENWELL
Usual civ name for chap in chap Newcastle upon Tyne St John (sep civ identity early from Newcastle upon Tyne AP, sep EP 1808[11]), 'Benwell' a sep CP 1866,[1] sep EP 1843,[61] usually as 'Benwell St James', qv. *LG* Castle Wd, Newc upon Tyne PLU, Benwell & Fenham USD, UD (1894—1904), Newc upon Tyne CB (1904—14). Abol civ 1914 to help cr Newcastle upon Tyne CP.[62] *Parl* S'rn Dv (1832—85), Tynes. Dv (1885—1918).

BENWELL ST AIDAN
EP Cr 1896 from Benwell St James EP (civ, 'Benwell').[63] Newc RDn (1896—1967), Newc West RDn (1967—*). Sometimes called 'Newcastle upon Tyne St Aidan'.

BENWELL ST JAMES
Usual eccl spelling for chap in chap Newcastle upon Tyne (the latter in Newcastle upon Tyne AP, sep civ identity early, sep EP 1808[11]), 'Benwell' a sep CP 1866,[1] qv above, sep EP 1843,[61] usually 'Benwell St James'. *Eccl* Newc upon Tyne RDn (1843—74), Newc upon Tyne RDn (S'rn Dv) (1874—77), Newc upon Tyne RDn (W'rn Dv) (1877—84), Newc RDn (1884—1967), Newc West RDn (1967—*). Eccl bdry: 1892 (help cr Newcastle upon Tyne St Augustine EP),[64] 1896 (cr Benwell St Aidan EP),[63] 1918 (cr Scotswood EP),[65] 1926 (help cr Fenham EP).[66]

BERWICK HILL
Tp in Ponteland AP, sep CP 1866.[1] *LG* Castle Wd, Castle Wd PLU, RSD, RD. Abol 1955 ent to Ponteland AP.[54] *Parl* S'rn Dv (1867—85), Wansb. Dv (1885—1948), Hexham CC (1948—70).

BERWICK UPON TWEED
Town in endemic jurisdictional conflict between England and Scotland in Middle Ages, by treaty made indept of both nations in 1551, the accession of James I ending its frontier status; representation in English Parl received earlier (qv below). The following have Berwick upon Tweed in their names. Insofar as any existed at a given time: *LG* Berw. upon Tweed Bor (Co of Itself from 1835[67]), MB, USD, Berw. PLU. *Parl* Berw. upon Tweed Parl Bor (1554—1885), Dv/CC (1885—*). *Eccl* Orig in dioc St Andrews, transf by Edw II to Durham, Bamb. RDn (until 1845), Norham RDn (1845—*).

AP1—BERWICK UPON TWEED [HOLY TRINITY]—Gains early AP2, AP3.[68] Addtl eccl bdry alt: 1859 (cr EP1).[69]

AP2—BERWICK UPON TWEED ST LAWRENCE—early lost.[68]

EP1—BERWICK UPON TWEED ST MARY—Cr 1859 from AP1.[69]

AP3—BERWICK UPON TWEED THE VIRGIN MARY—Removed when walls built 16th cent.[68]

BEWICK
CP Cr 1955 by union New Bewick CP, Old Bewick CP.[9] *LG* Glend. RD. *Parl* Berw. upon Tweed CC (1970—*).

NEW BEWICK
Tp in Eglingham AP, sep CP 1866.[1] *LG* Coq. Wd, Glend. PLU, RSD, RD. Abol 1955 to help cr Bewick CP.[9] *Parl* N'rn Dv (1867—85), Berw. upon Tweed Dv/CC (1885—1970).

OLD BEWICK
Tp in Eglingham AP, sep CP 1866.[1] Organisation as for New Bewick.

BICKERTON
Tp in Rothbury AP, sep CP 1866.[1] *LG* Coq. Wd, Rothb. PLU, RSD, RD. Abol 1955 ent to Hepple CP.[16] *Parl* N'rn Dv (1867—85), Hexham Dv (1885—1918), Berw. upon Tweed Dv/CC (1918—70).

BIDDLESTONE
Tp in Alwinton AP, sep CP 1866.[1] *LG* Seq 8. Bdry: 1883,[21] 1883,[22] 1955 (gains Clennell CP).[16] *Parl* Seq 2.

BIGGE'S QUARTER
Tp in Long Horsley AP, sometimes 'Carlisle's Quarter', sep CP 1866.[1] Incl undivided pt Horsley Moor (common to Bigge's Quarter CP, Fenrother CP, Freeholders' Quarter CP, Riddell's Quarter CP), undivided pt Horsley Common (common to Bigge's Quarter CP, Freeholders' Quarter CP, Riddell's Quarter CP). *LG* Morp. Wd, PLU, RSD, RD. Abol 1955 to help cr Longhorsley CP.[28] *Parl* N'rn Dv (1867—85), Wansb. Dv (1885—1948), Morp. CC (1948—70).

BINGFIELD
Tp in Lee St John AP, sep CP 1866,[1] sep EP 1740,[11] usually eccl 'Bingfield St Mary', qv. *LG* Seq 18. *Parl* Seq 5.

BINGFIELD ST MARY
Usual eccl name for tp in Lee St John AP, sep CP

1866 as 'Bingfield',[1] qv, sep EP 1740 as 'Bingfield St Mary.'[11] Newc upon Tyne RDn (1740—1845), Hexham RDn (1845—80). Eccl refounded 1879 as 'St Oswald in Lee with Bingfield St Mary' by union 6 tps in Lee St John (eccl, 'St John Lee'): Bingfield, Cocklaw, Fallowfield, Hallington, Portgate, Wall,[70] but the latter EP diminished 1888 when 'Bingfield St Mary' EP cr from tps Bingfield, Hallington, Portgate, gtr pt of Cocklaw.[71] Hexham RDn.

BIRLING
Tp in Warkworth AP, sep CP 1866.[1] LG Coq. Wd, Alnw. PLU, RSD, RD. Abol 1955 ent to Warkworth AP.[2] Parl N'rn Dv (1867—85), Berw. upon Tweed Dv/CC (1885—1970).

BIRTLEY
Chap in Chollerton AP, sep CP 1866,[1] sep EP 1764.[11] LG Seq 15. Civ bdry: 1883,[4] 1887,[72] 1955 (incl gains Carrycoats CP).[47] Parl Seq 5. Eccl Corbr. RDn (1764—1845), Bell. RDn (1845—*). Eccl bdry: 1887.[73]

BITCHFIELD
Tp in Stamfordham AP, sep CP 1866.[1] LG Tyned. Wd, Castle Wd PLU, RSD, RD. Abol 1955 ent to Belsay CP.[54] Parl S'rn Dv (1867—85), Hexham Dv/CC (1885—1970).

BLACK CARTS AND RYEHILL
Tp in Simonburn AP, sep CP 1866,[1] eccl severed 1900 to help cr Humshaugh EP.[74] LG Tyned. Wd, Hexham PLU (1858—1930), RSD, RD. Abol 1955 ent to Humshaugh CP.[5] Parl S'rn Dv (1867—85), Hexham Dv/CC (1885—1970).

BLANCHLAND
Orig abbey church, unused after Dissolution and considered chap Shotley in Bywell St Andrew AP (hence sometimes 'Shotley High Quarter'), sep EP 1751,[11] sep CP 1955 as renaming of Shotley High Quarter CP.[37] LG Hexham RD. Parl Hexham CC (1970—*). Eccl Corbr. RDn.

BLENKINSOPP
Tp in Haltwhistle AP, sep CP 1866,[1] eccl severed 1831 to help cr Greenhead EP,[11] the latter eccl refounded 1892.[75] LG Tyned. Wd, Haltw. PLU, RSD, RD. Bdry: 1886.[76] Abol 1955 to help cr Greenhead CP.[45] Parl S'rn Dv (1867—85), Hexham Dv/CC (1885—1970).

BLYTH
CP Cr 1920 by union pars in Blyth UD: Bebside CP, Cowpen CP, Horton CP, Newsham and South Blyth CP.[48] LG Tynem. PLU, Blyth UD (1920—22), MB (1922—74). Bdry: 1935.[34] Parl Blyth BC (1948—*).

BLYTH
EP Chap erected 1751 in chap Earsdon (sep civ identity early from Tynemouth AP, sep EP 1761[11]), the EP of Blyth St Cuthbert cr 1883 from Earsdon EP (area of tp Newsham and South Blyth), Horton EP.[77] Newc upon Tyne RDn (E'rn Dv) (1883—84), Bedl. RDn (1884—*).

BLYTH ST MARY
EP Cr 1896 from Horton EP.[78] Since church located at Cowpen, sometimes 'Cowpen St Mary'. Bedl. RDn.

BOCKENFIELD
Tp in Felton AP, sep CP 1866.[1] LG Morp. Wd, PLU, RSD, RD. Bdry: 1883,[4] 1888.[79] Abol 1955 to help cr Thirston CP.[28] Parl N'rn Dv (1867—85), Wansb. Dv (1885—1948), Morp. CC (1948—70).

BOLAM
AP LG Tp 'Bolam' in Morp. Wd was were tps Bolam Vicarage, Gallowhill (each a sep CP 1866[1]); incl in Castle Wd tp Trewick (sep CP 1866[1]); incl in Tyned. Wd tps Belsay, Bradford, Harnham, Shortflatt (each a sep CP 1866[1]). LG Castle Wd PLU, RSD, RD. Abol civ 1955 ent to Belsay CP.[54] Parl N'rn Dv (1832—85), Wansb. Dv (1885—1948), Morp. CC (1948—70). Eccl Seq 9.

BOLAM VICARAGE
Tp in Bolam AP, sep CP 1866.[1] LG Morp. Wd, Castle Wd PLU, RSD, RD. Abol 1955 ent to Belsay CP.[54] Parl As for Bolam, from 1867.

BOLTON
Tp in Edlingham AP, sep CP 1866.[1] LG Coq. Wd, Alnw. PLU, RSD, RD. Abol 1955 ent to Hedgeley CP.[2] Parl N'rn Dv (1867—85), Berw. upon Tweed Dv/CC (1885—1970).

BOTHAL
AP Incl tps Causey Park, Cockle Park, Earsdon, Earsdon Forest, Fenrother, Hebron, Pegswood, Tritlington (each a sep CP 1866[1]); tp Ashington, chap Sheepwash (civ united as tp 'Ashington and Sheepwash' and as such sep CP 1866[1] [qv for later sep division into CPs of Ashington, Sheepwash], pts eccl united 1888 with pt tp Bothal Demesne as Ashington EP[32]), tp Bothal Demesne (sep CP 1866[1]); tps Lonhghirst, Old Moor (each a sep CP 1866[1], the 2 tps eccl united 1876 as Longhirst EP[80]) so that 'Bothal' has no sep civ identity after 1866. LG Morp. Wd. Parl N'rn Dv (1867—85). Eccl Bamb. RDn (until 1845), Morp. RDn (1845—*).

BOTHAL DEMESNE
Tp in Bothal AP, sep CP 1866,[1] eccl united 1888 with tp Ashington and Sheepwash to cr Ashington EP.[32] LG Morp. Wd, PLU, RSD, RD. Bdry: 1896 (help cr Ashington CP).[31] Abol 1935 ent to Ashington CP.[34] Parl N'rn Dv (1867—85), Wansb. Dv (1885—1948).

BOULMER AND SEATON HOUSE
Tp in Longhoughton AP, sep CP 1866.[1] LG Bamb. Wd, Alnw. PLU, RSD. Abol 1888 ent to Longhoughton AP.[81] Parl N'rn Dv (1867—85), Berw. upon Tweed Dv (1885—1918).

BOWSDEN
CP Cr 1955 from Lowick AP.[9] LG Glend. RD. Parl Berw. upon Tweed CC (1970—*).

BRADFORD
Tp in Bamburgh AP, sep CP 1866.[1] LG Bamb. Wd, Belf. PLU, RSD, RD. Abol 1955 to help cr Adderstone with Lucker CP.[8] Parl N'rn Dv (1867—85), Berw. upon Tweed Dv/CC (1885—1970).

BRADFORD
Tp in Bolam AP, sep CP 1866.[1] LG Tyned. Wd, Castle Wd PLU, RSD, RD. Abol 1955 ent to Belsay CP.[54] Parl S'rn Dv (1867—85), Wansb. Dv (1885—1948), Hexham CC (1948—70).

BRANDON

Tp in Eglingham AP, sep CP 1866.[1] *LG* Coq. Wd, Glend. PLU, RSD, RD. Abol 1955 to help cr Ingram CP.[9] *Parl* N'rn Dv (1867—85), Berw. upon Tweed Dv/CC (1885—1970).

BRANTON

Tp in Eglingham AP, sep CP 1866.[1] *LG* Coq. Wd, Glend. PLU, RSD, RD. Abol 1955 to help cr Ingram CP.[9] *Parl* N'rn Dv (1867—85), Berw. upon Tweed Dv/CC (1885—1970).

BRANXTON

AP *LG* Seq 9. *Parl* Seq 1. *Eccl* Bamb. RDn (until 1845), Norham RDn (1845—99), Glend. RDn (1899—1969), Norham RDn (1969—*). Eccl bdry: 1957.[82]

BRENKLEY

Tp in Dinnington AP, sep CP 1866.[1] *LG* Castle Wd, Castle Wd PLU, RSD, RD. Abol 1955 pt to help cr Brunswick CP, pt to Dinnington CP.[54] *Parl* S'rn Dv (1867—85), Wansb. Dv (1885—1948), Hexham CC (1948—70).

BRINKBURN

CP Cr 1955 by union Brinkburn High Ward CP, Brinkburn Low Ward CP.[16] *LG* Rothb. RD. *Parl* Berw. upon Tweed CC (1970—*).

BRINKBURN CHAPELRY

AP Orig priory church with parochial service; claimed by vicar of Felton as chap in his par,[83] sep civ identity early, eccl independence assured 1767.[11] *LG* Pt Coq. Wd (tps Brinkburn High Ward, Brinkburn Low Ward), pt Morp. Wd (tp Brinkburn South Side) (each tp with sep civ identity 1866[1]) so that 'Brinkburn Chapelry' has no sep civ identity after 1866. *Parl* N'rn Dv (1832—67). *Eccl* Alnw. RDn (until 1899), Rothb. RDn (1899—*).

BRINKBURN HIGH WARD

Tp in Brinkburn Chapelry AP, sep CP 1866.[1] *LG* Coq. Wd, Rothb. PLU, RSD, RD. Bdry: 1889 (gains Brinkburn South Side CP).[84] Abol 1955 to help cr Brinkburn CP.[16] *Parl* N'rn Dv (1867—85), Hexham Dv (1885—1918), Berw. upon Tweed Dv/CC (1918—70).

BRINKBURN LOW WARD

Tp in Brinkburn Chapelry AP, sep CP 1866.[1] Organisation as for Brinkburn High Ward except no bdry alt.

BRINKBURN SOUTH SIDE

Tp in Brinkburn Chapelry AP, sep CP 1866.[1] *LG* Morp. Wd, Rothb. PLU, RSD. Abol 1889 ent to Brinkburn High Ward CP.[84] *Parl* N'rn Dv (1867—85), Wansb. Dv (1885—1918).

BROOME PARK

Tp in Edlingham AP, sep CP 1866.[1] *LG* Coq. Wd, Alnw. PLU, RSD, RD. Abol 1955 ent to Edlingham AP.[2] *Parl* N'rn Dv (1867—85), Berw. upon Tweed Dv/CC (1885—1948).

BROOMHAUGH

Tp in Bywell St Andrew AP, sep CP 1866.[1] *LG* Tyned. Wd, Hexham PLU, RSD, RD. Abol 1955 to help cr Broomhaugh and Riding CP.[37] *Parl* S'rn Dv (1867—85), Hexham Dv/CC (1885—1970).

BROOMHAUGH AND RIDING

CP Cr 1955 by union Broomhaugh CP, Riding CP.[37]

LG Hexham RD. *Parl* Hexham CC (1970—*).

BROOMLEY

Tp pt in Bywell St Peter AP, pt in Ovingham AP, sep CP 1866,[1] the pt in Bywell St Peter eccl severed 1876 to help cr Healey EP.[85] *LG* Tyned. Wd, Hexham PLU, RSD, RD. Bdry: 1883,[4] 1887,[86] 1887.[36] Renamed 1955 'Broomley and Stocksfield'.[87] *Parl* S'rn Dv (1867—85), Hexham Dv/CC (1885—1970).

BROOMLEY AND STOCKSFIELD

CP Renaming 1955 of Broomley CP.[87] *LG* Hexham RD. *Parl* Hexham CC (1970—*).

BROTHERWICK

Tp in Warkworth AP, sep CP 1866.[1] *LG* Coq. Wd, Alnw. PLU, RSD, RD. Abol 1955 ent to Warkworth AP.[2] *Parl* N'rn Dv (1867—85), Berw. upon Tweed Dv/CC (1885—1970).

BROXFIELD

Tp in Embleton AP, sep CP 1866,[1] eccl severed 1903 to help refound Rennington EP.[88] *LG* Bamb. Wd, Alnw. PLU, RSD, RD. Abol 1955 ent to Rennington CP.[2] *Parl* N'rn Dv (1867—85), Berw. upon Tweed Dv/CC (1885—1970).

BRUNSWICK

CP Cr 1955 from Brenkley CP, Dinnington CP, Mason CP, Stannington CP.[54] *LG* Castle Wd RD. Transf 1974 to Tyne & Wear.[89] *Parl* Hexham CC (1970—*).

BRUNTON

Tp in Embleton AP, sep CP 1866.[1] *LG* Bamb. Wd, Alnw. PLU, RSD, RD. Abol 1955 ent to Newton by the Sea AP.[2] *Parl* N'rn Dv (1867—85), Berw. upon Tweed Dv/CC (1885—1970).

EAST BRUNTON

Tp in chap Gosforth (sep civ identity early from Newcastle upon Tyne AP, sep EP 1865[90]), 'East Brunton' a sep CP 1866 from Gosforth CP.[1] *LG* Castle Wd, Castle Wd PLU, RSD, RD. Bdry: 1935.[34] Abol 1955 to help cr Hazlerigg CP.[54] *Parl* S'rn Dv (1867—85), Tynes. Dv (1885—1918), Wansb. Dv (1918—48), Hexham CC (1948—70).

WEST BRUNTON

Tp in chap Gosforth (sep civ identity early from Newcastle upon Tyne AP, sep EP 1865[90]), 'West Brunton' a sep CP 1866 from Gosforth CP.[1] *LG* Castle Wd, Castle Wd PLU, RSD, RD. Bdry: 1935 (loses pt to Newc upon Tyne CB [assoc with Northumb] & CP).[34] Abol 1955 pt to help cr Hazlerigg CP, pt to Woolsington CP.[54] *Parl* As for East Brunton.

BUDLE

Tp in Bamburgh AP, sep CP 1866.[1] *LG* Bamb. Wd, Belf. PLU, RSD, RD. Abol 1955 ent to Bamburgh AP.[8] *Parl* N'rn Dv (1867—85), Berw. upon Tweed Dv/CC (1885—1970).

BULLERS GREEN

Tp in Morpeth AP, sep CP 1866.[1] *LG* Morp. Wd, PLU, USD (1875—88). Abol 1888 pt to Morpeth AP, pt to Newminster Abbey CP.[91] *Parl* Morp. Parl Bor (1832—1918).

BULLOCK'S HALL

Tp in Warkworth AP, sep CP 1866,[1] eccl severed 1863 to help cr Chevington EP.[92] *LG* Morp. Wd,

PLU, RSD, RD. Abol 1955 ent to West Chevington CP.[28] *Parl* N'rn Dv (1867—85), Wansb. Dv (1885—1948), Morp. CC (1948—70).

BURRADON

Tp in Alwinton AP, sep CP 1866,[1] eccl severed 1891 and transf to Killingworth EP.[93] *LG* Coq. Wd, Rothb. PLU, RSD, RD. Abol 1955 to help cr Netherton CP.[16] *Parl* N'rn Dv (1867—85), Hexham Dv (1885—1918), Berw. upon Tweed Dv/CC (1918—70).

BURRADON

Tp in Earsdon AP, sep CP 1866.[1] *LG* Castle Wd, Tynem. PLU, RSD, RD (1894—1912). Abol 1912 ent to Longbenton AP to help cr Longbenton UD.[94] *Parl* S'rn Dv (1867—85), Wansb. Dv (1885—1918).

BURTON

Tp in Bamburgh AP, sep CP 1866.[1] *LG* Bamb. Wd, Belf. PLU, RSD, RD. Abol 1955 ent to Bamburgh AP.[8] *Parl* N'rn Dv (1867—85), Berw. upon Tweed Dv/CC (1885—1970).

HIGH BUSTON

Tp in Warkworth AP, sep CP 1866.[1] *LG* Coq. Wd, Alnw. PLU, RSD, RD. Abol 1955 ent to Alnmouth CP.[2] *Parl* N'rn Dv (1867—85), Berw. upon Tweed Dv/CC (1885—1970).

LOW BUSTON

Tp in Warkworth AP, sep CP 1866.[1] Organisation as for High Buston except abol 1955 ent to Warkworth AP.[2]

BUTTERLAW

Tp in Newburn AP, sep CP 1866.[1] *LG* Castle Wd, Castle Wd PLU, RSD. Abol 1886 ent to Whortlon CP.[95] *Parl* S'rn Dv (1867—85), Tynes. Dv (1885—1918).

BYKER

The following have 'Byker' in their names. Insofar as any existed at a given time: *LG* Castle Wd, Newc upon Tyne MB (1835—89), USD, CB (1889—1914). *Parl* Newc upon Tyne Parl Bor (1832—1918). *Eccl* Newc upon Tyne RDn (until 1874), Newc upon Tyne RDn (S'rn Dv) (1874—77), Newc upon Tyne RDn (W'rn Dv) (1877—84), Newc RDn (1884—1967), Newc East RDn (1967—*).

CP/EP1—BYKER [ST MICHAEL]—Chap in chap Newcastle upon Tyne All Saints (sep civ identity early from Newcastle upon Tyne AP, sep EP 1808[11]), 'Byker' a sep CP 1866,[1] sep EP 1844,[39] eccl refounded 1868.[96] Abol civ 1914 to help cr Newcastle upon Tyne CP.[62] Eccl bdry: 1868 (cr EP2),[97] 1887 (cr EP5),[98] 1900 (cr Newcastle upon Tyne St Gabriel, Heaton EP),[99] 1906 (help cr EP4),[75] 1931 (help cr EP3).[100]

EP2—BYKER ST ANTHONY—Cr 1868 from EP1.[97] Bdry: 1908,[101] 1931 (help cr EP3).[100]

EP3—BYKER ST LAWRENCE—Cr 1931 from EP1, Newcastle upon Tyne St Anne EP.[100]

EP4—BYKER ST MARK—Cr 1906 from EP1, Walker EP.[75] Bdry: 1952.[58]

EP5—BYKER ST SILAS—Cr 1887 from EP1.[98]

BYRNESS

Chap in Elsdon AP, erected 1793, sep EP 1801,[11] refounded 1883 (incl ex-par Ramshope).[102] Newc

upon Tyne RDn (1801—45), Rothb. RDn (1845—1940). Abol 1940 to help cr Horsley with Byrness EP.[103]

BYWELL

CP Cr 1887 by union East Acomb CP, pt Bywell St Andrew AP, pt Bywell St Peter AP.[5] *LG* Tyned. Wd, Hexham PLU, RSD, RD. Bdry: 1955 (gains Bearl CP, Newton CP, Newton Hall CP, Stelling CP, Styford CP).[37] Hexham Dv/CC (1918—*).

BYWELL ST ANDREW

AP Incl chap Shotley (sep civ identity early, incl from *temp* Dissolution Blanchland [orig abbey church, unused from Dissolution, sometimes 'Shotley High Quarter', sep EP 1751 as 'Blanchland',[11] sep CP 1955 as renaming of Shotley High Quarter CP[37]), tps Bearl, Broomhaugh, Riding, Stocksfield Hall, Styford (each a sep CP 1866[1]). *LG* Tyned. Wd, Hexham PLU, RSD. Abol 1887 pt to Bearl CP, pt to Newton Hall CP, pt to help cr Bywell CP.[5] *Parl* S'rn Dv (1832—85), Hexham Dv (1885—1918). *Eccl* Corbr. RDn. Eccl bdry: 1887 (help cr Newton Hall EP),[104] 1931.[19] Renamed eccl 1973 'Riding Mill'.[19]

BYWELL ST PETER

AP Incl chap Whittonstall (sep CP 1866,[1] sep EP 1774[11]), tps East Acomb, Apperley, Newlands, Newton, Stelling (each a sep CP 1866[1]), tp Newton Hall (sep CP 1866,[1] sep EP 1877 from Bywell St Peter AP, Bywell St Andrew AP, Corbridge AP[104]), pt tp Broomley, tps Espershields, High Fotherley, Healey (each a sep CP 1866,[1] Healey EP cr 1876 by union tp Espershields and pts tps Broomley, High Fotherley, Healey[84]). *LG* Tyned. Wd, Hexham PLU, RSD. Abol civ 1887 pt to Newton CP, pt to Newton Hall CP, pt to help cr Bywell CP.[5] *Parl* S'rn Dv (1832—85), Hexham Dv (1885—1918). *Eccl* Seq 6. Eccl bdry: 1931,[19] 1967.[105]

CAISTRON

Tp in Rothbury AP, sep CP 1866.[1] *LG* Coq. Wd, Rothb. PLU, RSD, RD. Abol 1955 ent to Hepple CP.[16] *Parl* N'rn Dv (1867—85), Hexham Dv (1885—1918), Berw. upon Tweed Dv/CC (1918—70).

CALLALY

CP Cr 1955 by union Callaly and Yetlington CP, Lorbottle CP.[16] *LG* Rothb. RD. *Parl* Berw. upon Tweed CC (1970—*).

CALLALY AND YETLINGTON

Tp in Whittingham AP, sep CP 1866.[1] *LG* Coq. Wd, Rothb. PLU, RSD, RD. Abol 1955 to help cr Callaly CP.[16] *Parl* N'rn Dv (1867—85), Berw. upon Tweed Dv/CC (1885—1970).

BLACK CALLERTON

Tp in Newburn AP, sep CP 1866.[1] *LG* Castle Wd, Castle Wd PLU, RSD, RD. Abol 1955 ent to Woolsington CP.[54] *Parl* S'rn Dv (1867—85), Tynes. Dv (1885—1918), Wansb. Dv (1918—48), Hexham CC (1948—70).

HIGH CALLERTON

Tp pt in Newburn AP, pt in Ponteland AP, sep CP 1866.[1] *LG* Castle Wd, Castle Wd PLU, RSD, RD. Abol 1955 ent to Ponteland AP.[54] *Parl* S'rn Dv

(1867—85), Wansb. Dv (1885—1948), Hexham CC (1948—70).

LITTLE CALLERTON

Tp in Ponteland AP, sep CP 1866.[1] *LG*, abol, *Parl* as for High Callerton.

CAMBO

Tp in Hartburn AP, sep EP 1844,[106] sep CP 1866.[1] *LG* Tyned. Wd, Morp. PLU, RSD, RD. Abol 1955 ent to Wallington Demesne CP.[28] *Parl* S'rn Dv (1867—85), Wansb. Dv (1885—1948), Morp. CC (1948—70). *Eccl* Morp. RDn.

CAMBOIS

EP Cr 1863 from Bedlington AP (union tp Cambois, tp East Sleekburn, pt tp West Sleekburn [none with sep civ identity]).[50] Newc upon Tyne RDn (1863—74), Newc upon Tyne RDn (N'rn Dv) (1874—77), Newc upon Tyne RDn (E'rn Dv) (1877—84), Bedl. RDn (1884—*). Bdry: 1906 (help cr Sleekburn EP).[107]

CAMPERDOWN

CP Cr 1899 from Longbenton AP, Weetslade CP.[108] *LG* Tyned. PLU, RD. Abol 1912 ent to help constitute Longbenton UD, added to Longbenton AP.[94]

CAPHEATON

Tp in Kirkwhelpington AP, sep CP 1866.[1] *LG* Seq 16. Bdry: 1955 (gains Kirkheaton AP, East Shaftoe CP, West Shaftoe CP).[54] *Parl* Seq 5.

CARHAM

AP Sometimes considered chap in Kirknewton,[109] but sep AP. *LG* Seq 9. *Parl* Seq 1. *Eccl* Seq 5. Eccl bdry: 1957.[82]

CARR SHIELD

EP Cr 1900 from Allendale EP as refounding of West Allen[13] (the latter a chap and sep EP 1826,[11] sep CP 1897,[12] qv). Hexham RDn. Abol 1967 to help cr Ninebanks and Carrshield EP.[110]

CARTINGTON

Tp in Rothbury AP, sep CP 1866.[1] *LG* Seq 8. Bdry: 1889,[15] 1955 (gains Debdon CP, Intermixed Lands common to Debdon and Snitter CP, Mount Healy CP).[16] *Parl* Seq 2.

CARRYCOATS

Tp in Throckrington AP, sep CP 1866.[1] *LG* Tyned. Wd, Bell. PLU, RSD, RD. Abol 1955 ent to Birtley CP.[47] *Parl* S'rn Dv (1867—85), Hexham Dv/CC (1885—1970).

CATCHERSIDE

Tp in Kirkwhelpington AP, sep CP 1866.[1] *LG* Tyned. Wd, Bell. PLU, RSD, RD. Abol 1955 ent to Kirkwhelpington AP.[47] *Parl* S'rn Dv (1867—85), Hexham Dv (1885—1970).

CAUSEY PARK

Tp in Bothal AP, sep CP 1866.[1] *LG* Morp. Wd, PLU, RSD, RD. Abol 1955 ent to Tritlington CP.[28] *Parl* N'rn Dv (1867—85), Wansb. Dv (1885—1948), Morp. CC (1948—70).

EAST CHARLTON

Tp in chap Bellingham (sep par 1811 from Simonburn AP[52]), 'East Charlton' a sep CP 1866.[1] *LG* Tyned. Wd, Bell. PLU, RSD. Abol 1886 to help cr Bellingham CP.[53] *Parl* S'rn Dv (1867—85), Hexham Dv (1885—1918).

NORTH CHARLTON

Tp in Ellingham AP, sep CP 1866.[1] *LG* Bamb. Wd, Alnw. PLU, RSD, RD. Abol 1955 ent to Eglingham AP.[2] *Parl* N'rn Dv (1867—85), Berw. upon Tweed Dv/CC (1885—1970).

SOUTH CHARLTON

Tp in Ellingham AP, sep CP 1866,[1] sep EP 1860 from Ellingham AP (tp South Charlton), Alnwick AP (pt tp Hulme Park [no sep civ identity]).[19] *LG* Bamb. Wd, Alnw. PLU, RSD, RD. Abol 1955 ent to Eglingham AP.[2] *Parl* N'rn Dv (1867—85), Berw. upon Tweed Dv/CC (1885—1970). *Eccl* Alnw. RDn (1860—1948), Bamb. RDn (1948—69), Bamb. & Glend. RDn (1969—*).

WEST CHARLTON

Tp in chap Bellingham (sep par 1811 from Simonburn AP[52]), 'West Charltn' a sep CP 1866.[1] Organisation as for East Charlton.

CHATHILL

Tp in Ellingham AP, sep CP 1866.[1] *LG* Bamb. Wd, Belf. PLU, RSD, RD. Abol 1955 ent to Ellingham AP.[8] *Parl* N'rn Dv (1867—85), Berw. upon Tweed Dv/CC (1885—1970).

CHATTON

AP Incl chap Doddington (seemingly sep par 1775[111]). *LG* Seq 9. Addtl civ bdry alt: 1955.[9] *Parl* Seq 1. *Eccl* Bamb. RDn (until 1969), Bamb. & Glend. RDn (1969—70). Addtl eccl bdry alt: 1899.[112] Abol eccl 1970 to help cr Chatton with Chillingham EP.[113]

CHATTON WITH CHILLINGHAM

EP Cr 1970 by union Chatton AP, Chillingham AP.[113] Bamb. & Glend. RDn.

CHEESEBURN GRANGE

Tp in Stamfordham AP, sep CP 1866.[1] *LG* Tyned. Wd, Castle Wd PLU, RSD, RD. Abol 1955 to help cr Stamfordham AP.[54] *Parl* S'rn Dv (1867—85), Hexham Dv/CC (1885—1970).

CHEVINGTON

EP Cr 1863 from Warkworth AP (tps East Chevington, West Chevington, Bullock's Hall, Hadston, qv for sep civ identities 1866).[92] Alnw. RDn.

EAST CHEVINGTON

Tp in Warkworth AP, sep CP 1866,[1] eccl severed 1863 to help cr Chevington EP.[92] *LG* Seq 10. Bdry: 1955 (gains Hadston CP).[28] *Parl* Seq 4.

WEST CHEVINGTON

Tp in Warkworth AP, sep CP 1866,[1] eccl severed 1863 to help cr Chevington EP.[92] *LG* Seq 10. Bdry: 1955 (gains Bullock's Hall CP).[28] *Parl* Seq 4.

CHILLINGHAM

AP Incl tps Hepburn, Newtown (each a sep CP 1866[1]). *LG* Seq 9. Civ bdry: 1955 (gains Hepburn CP).[9] *Parl* Seq 1. *Eccl* Bamb. RDn (until 1899), Glend. RDn (1899—1955), Bamb. RDn (1955—69), Bamb. & Glend. RDn (1969—70). Abol eccl 1970 to help cr Chatton with Chillingham EP.[113]

CHIRDON

Tp in Simonburn AP, made tp in Greystead when latter sep par 1811 from Simonburn,[52] 'Chirdon' a sep CP 1866.[1] *LG* Tyned. Wd, Bell. PLU, RSD, RD. Bdry: 1886.[53] Abol 1955 to help cr Greystead CP.[47] *Parl* S'rn Dv (1867—85), Hexham Dv/CC

(1885—1970).

CHIRTON
Tp in Tynemouth AP, sep CP 1866,[1] pt eccl severed 1860 to help cr Tynemouth Percy EP,[19] the remainder eccl severed 1861 to help cr Tynemouth Holy Trinity (orig, 'Western Town') EP.[114] *LG* Castle Wd, Tynem. PLU, MB (1849—1904), USD, CB (1904—08). Bdry: 1881,[115] 1883,[4] 1889.[116] Abol 1908 ent to Tynemouth AP.[117] *Parl* Tynem. Parl Bor (1832—1918).

CHOLLERTON
AP Incl chap Birtley (sep CP 1866,[1] sep EP 1764[11]), detached chap Kirkheaton (appropriated to Hexham Priory, considerd ex-par after Dissolution, new chapel erected 1793 and considered Donative,[118] sep eccl from that time, sep CP 1858[119]). *LG* Seq 18. Addtl civ bdry alt: 1887.[72] *Parl* Seq 5. *Eccl* Corbr. RDn (until 1845), Bell. RDn (1845—*). Eccl bdry: 1887.[73]

CHOPPINGTON
EP Cr 1863 from Bedlington AP (tp Choppington, pt tp West Sleekburn [latter with no sep civ identity]).[50] Newc upon Tyne RDn (1863—74), Newc upon Tyne RDn (N'rn Dv) (1874—77), Newc upon Tyne RDn (E'rn Dv) (1877—84), Bedl. RDn (1884—*). Bdry: 1906 (cr Sleekburn EP).[107]

CLAREWOOD
Tp in Corbridge AP, sep CP 1866.[1] *LG* Tyned. Wd, Hexham PLU, RSD, RD. Bdry: 1887 (gains Halton Shields CP).[120] Abol 1955 to help cr Whittington CP.[37] *Parl* S'rn Dv (1867—85), Hexham Dv/CC (1885—1970).

CLENNEL
Tp in Alwinton AP, sep CP 1866.[1] *LG* Coq. Wd, Rothb. PLU, RSD, RD. Abol 1955 ent to Biddlestone CP.[16] *Parl* N'rn Dv (1867—85), Hexham Dv (1885—1918), Berw. upon Tweed Dv/CC (1918—70).

COANWOOD
Tp in Haltwhistle AP, sep CP 1866.[1] *LG* Seq 17. Bdry: 1955 (gains Lambley AP).[45] *Parl* Seq 5.

COATYARDS
Tp in chap Netherwitton (sep CP 1866,[1] EP 1835 from Hartburn AP[11]), 'Coatyards' a sep CP 1866.[1] *LG* Seq 18. *Parl* Seq 3.

COCKLAW
Tp in Lee St John AP, sep CP 1866,[1] eccl severed 1879 to help cr St Oswald in Lee with Bingfield EP,[70] the gtr pt of orig area severed 1888 from the latter EP to help cr Bingfield St Mary EP.[71] *LG* Seq 18. *Parl* Seq 5.

COCKLE PARK
Tp in Bothal AP, sep CP 1866.[1] *LG* Morp. Wd, PLU, RSD, RD. Abol 1955 ent to Hebron CP.[28] *Parl* N'rn Dv (1867—85), Wansb. Dv (1885—1948), Morp. CC (1948—70).

COLDCOATS
Tp in Ponteland AP, sep CP 1866.[1] *LG* Castle Wd, Castle Wd PLU, RSD, RD. Abol 1955 ent to Ponteland CP.[54] *Parl* S'rn Dv (1867—75), Wansb. Dv (1885—1948), Hexham CC (1948—70).

COLDSMOUTH AND THOMPSON'S WALLS
Tp in Kirknewton AP, sep CP 1866.[1] *LG* Glend.

Wd, PLU, RSD, RD. Abol 1955 ent to Kilham CP.[9] *Parl* N'rn Dv (1867—85), Berw. upon Tweed Dv/CC (1885—1970).

COLDWELL
Tp in Kirkwhelpington AP, sep CP 1866.[1] *LG* Tyned. Wd, Bell. PLU, RSD, RD. Abol 1955 ent to Kirkwhelpington AP.[47] *Parl* S'rn Dv (1867—85), Hexham Dv/CC (1885—1970).

CORBRIDGE
AP Orig four churches, St Andrew now remains; St Mary, St Helen, Holy Trinity early lost and incl within St Andrew.[121] Incl tps Aydon, Aydon Castle, Clarewood, Dilston, Halton, Halton Shields, Thornbrough, Great Whittington, Little Whittington (each a sep CP 1866[1]). *LG* Corbr. Bor (status not sustained), Seq 18. Addtl civ bdry alt: 1887,[36] 1955 (gains Aydon CP, Aydon Castle CP, Dilston CP, Portgate CP, Thornborough CP, Little Whittington CP).[37] *Parl* Corbr. Parl Bor (1295 only), Seq 5. *Eccl* Sometimes as 'Corbridge with Halton', Seq 6. Eccl bdry: 1877 (help cr Newton Hall EP).[104]

CORNHILL ON TWEED
In Durham, transf to Northumb 1832 for parl purposes, 1844 for civ purposes.[25] Chap in Norham AP, sep CP 1866 in Northumb,[1] sep EP 1730.[11] *LG* Seq 14. *Parl* In Durham until 1832, Seq 1 thereafter. *Eccl* Bamb. RDn (1730—1845), Norham RDn (1845—*).

CORRIDGE
Tp in Hartburn AP, sep CP 1866.[1] *LG* Morp. Wd, PLU, RSD, RD. Abol 1955 ent to Wallington Demesne CP.[28] *Parl* N'rn Dv (1867—85), Wansb. Dv (1885—1948), Morp. CC (1948—70).

CORSENSIDE
AP Abol 1312 and united to Holystone AP, sep civ identity regained early, sep eccl status regained 1728.[122] *LG* Seq 15. *Parl* Seq 5. *Eccl* Newc upon Tyne RDn (until 1312 and 1728—1845), Bell. RDn (1845—*).

COUPLAND
Tp in Kirknewton AP, sep CP 1866.[1] *LG* Glend. Wd, PLU, RSD, RD. Abol 1955 pt to Ewart CP, pt to Kirknewton AP.[9] *Parl* N'rn Dv (1867—85), Berw. upon Tweed Dv/CC (1885—1970).

COWGATE
EP Cr 1957 from Gosforth All Saints EP, Fenham EP, Newcastle upon Tyne St Luke the Evangelist EP.[123] Newc RDn (1957—67), Newc West RDn (1967—*).

COWPEN
Tp in Horton AP, sep CP 1866,[1] eccl severed 1896 (the pt of Horton incl Cowpen St Mary) to cr Blyth St Mary EP.[78] *LG* Castle Wd, Tynem. PLU, Cowpen USD (pt 1875—81, ent 1881—94), pt Tynem. RSD (1875—81), Cowpen UD (1894—1907), Blyth UD (1907—20). Abol 1920 to help cr Blyth CP.[48] *Parl* When tp, S'rn Dv (1832—67); as par, Morp. Parl Bor (1867—1948).

COXLODGE
Tp in chap Gosforth (sep civ identity early from Newcastle upon Tyne AP, sep EP 1865[90]), 'Coxlodge' a sep CP 1866.[1] *LG* Castle Wd, Castle Wd PLU, South Gosforth USD, UD (1894—95),

Gosforth UD (1895—1908). Abol 1908 to help cr Gosforth CP.[124] *Parl* S'rn Dv (1867—85), Tynes. Dv (1885—1918).

CRAMLINGTON

Chap in Newcastle upon Tyne AP, sep CP 1866,[1] sep EP 1742.[11] *LG* Castle Wd, Tynem. PLU, Craml. USD, UD (1894—1935). Abol civ 1935 to help cr Seaton Valley UD & CP.[34] *Parl* S'rn Dv (1867—85), Wansb. Dv (1885—1948). *Eccl* Newc upon Tyne RDn (1742—1874), Newc upon Tyne RDn (N'rn Dv (1874—77), Newc upon Tyne RDn (E'rn Dv) (1877—84), Bedl. RDn (1884—*). Eccl bdry: 1846 (help cr Sighill EP),[97] 1969 (help cr Dudley EP).[125]

CRASTER

Tp in Embleton AP, sep CP 1866.[1] *LG* Seq 1. Bdry: 1955 (gains Dunstan CP).[2] *Parl* Seq 1.

CRAWLEY

Tp in Eglingham AP, sep CP 1866.[1] *LG* Coq. Wd, Alnw. PLU, RSD, RD. Abol 1955 ent to Hedgeley CP.[2] *Parl* N'rn Dv (1867—85), Berw. upon Tweed Dv/CC (1885—1970).

CRESSWELL

Tp in Woodhorn AP, sep CP 1866,[1] eccl severed 1836 and united with tp Ellington in same par as Cresswell EP.[126] *LG* Seq 10. *Parl* Seq 4. *Eccl* Morp. RDn. Eccl bdry: 1962.[127] Abol eccl 1971 to help cr Cresswell and Lynemouth EP.[128]

CRESSWELL AND LYNEMOUTH

EP Cr 1971 by union Cresswell EP, Lynemouth EP.[128] Morp. RDn.

CROOKDEAN

Tp in Kirkwhelpington AP, sep CP 1866.[1] *LG* Tyned. Wd, Bell. PLU, RSD, RD. Abol 1955 ent to Kirkwhelpington AP.[47] *Parl* S'rn Dv (1867—85), Hexham Dv/CC (1885—1970).

CROOKHOUSE

Tp in Kirknewton AP, sep CP 1866.[1] *LG* Glend. Wd, PLU, RSD, RD. Abol 1955 ent to Kirknewton AP.[9] *Parl* N'rn Dv (1867—85), Berw. upon Tweed Dv/CC (1885—1970).

CULLERCOATS

Tp in Tynemouth AP, sep CP 1866,[1] eccl severed 1860 and united with pts tps Whitley, Monkseaton (all of each except the pt of Shiremoor in each made pt of Tynemouth Percy EP) to cr Cullercoats [St Paul] EP.[19] *LG* Castle Wd, Tynem. PLU, MB (1849—1904), USD, CB (1904—08). Abol 1908 ent to Tynemouth AP.[117] *Parl* Tynem. Parl Bor (1832—1918). *Eccl* Sometimes as 'Cullercoats St Paul' or as 'Cullercoats, Tynemouth', Newc upon Tyne RDn (1860—74), Newc upon Tyne RDn (N'rn Dv) (1874—77), Newc upon Tyne RDn (E'rn Dv) (1877—84), Tynem. RDn (1884—*). Eccl bdry: 1880 (help cr Cullercoats St George EP),[129] 1927 (cr Monkseaton St Mary EP),[130], 1969.[123]

CULLERCOATS ST GEORGE

EP Cr 1880 from Tynemouth Priory EP, Cullercoats EP.[129] Newc upon Tyne RDn (E'rn Dv) (1880—84), Tynem. RDn (1884—*). Bdry: 1931,[131] 1969,[40] 1973.[41]

DALTON

Tp in Newbourn AP, sep CP 1866.[1] *LG* Tyned.

Wd, Castle Wd PLU, RSD, RD. Abol 1955 to help cr Stamfordham CP.[54] *Parl* S'rn Dv (1867—85), Wansb. Dv (1885—1948), Hexham CC (1948—70).

DARRAS HALL

Tp in Ponteland AP, sep CP 1866.[1] *LG* Castle Wd, Castle Wd PLU, RSD, RD. Abol 1955 ent to Ponteland AP.[54] *Parl* S'rn Dv (1867—85), Wansb. Dv (1885—1948), Hexham CC (1948—70).

DEANHAM

Tp in Hartburn AP, sep CP 1866.[1] *LG* Tyned. Wd, Morp. PLU, RSD, RD. Abol 1955 ent to Wallington Demesne CP.[28] *Parl* S'rn Dv (1867—85), Wansb. Dv (1885—1948), Morp. CC (1948—70).

DEBDON

Tp in Rothbury AP, sep CP 1866.[1] Incl undivided pt Intermixed Lands common to Debdon CP and Snitter CP. *LG* Coq. Wd, Rothb. PLU, RSD. Abol 1889 ent to Rothbury AP.[132] *Parl* N'rn Dv (1867—85), Hexham Dv (1885—1918).

CP Cr 1896 from Rothbury AP.[133] *LG* Rothb. PLU, RD. Abol 1955 ent to Cartington CP.[16] *Parl* Berw. upon Tweed Dv/CC (1918—70).

DELAVAL

EP Cr 1891 from Earsdon AP (tp Hartley, the pt of tp Seaton Delaval not in Sighill EP).[134] Bedl. RDn. Bdry: 1962,[127] 1965.[135]

DENTON

EP Cr 1964 from Sugley EP.[88] Newc RDn (1964—67), Newc West RDn (1967—*).

EAST DENTON

Tp in Newburn AP, sep CP 1866.[1] *LG* Castle Wd, Castle Wd PLU, RSD (1875—93), Newburn USD (1893—94), UD (1894—1935). Abol 1935 pt to Newc upon Tyne CB (assoc with Northumb) & CP, pt to Newburn AP.[34] *Parl* S'rn Dv (1867—85), Tynes. Dv (1885—1918), Wansb. Dv (1918—48).

WEST DENTON

Tp in Newburn AP, sep CP 1866.[1] Organisation as for East Denton.

DENWICK

CP Cr 1894 from the pt of Alnwick AP not in Alnw. & Canongate USD.[18] *LG* Alnw. PLU, RD. *Parl* Berw. upon Tweed Dv/CC (1918—*).

DETCHANT

Tp in Belford AP, sep CP 1866.[1] *LG* Bamb. Wd, Belf. PLU, RSD, RD. Abol 1955 ent to Middleton CP.[8] *Parl* N'rn Dv (1867—85), Berw. upon Tweed Dv/CC (1885—1970).

DILSTON

Tp in Corbridge AP, sep CP 1866.[1] *LG* Tyned. Wd, Hexham PLU, RSD, RD. Bdry: 1887.[36] Abol 1955 ent to Corbridge AP.[37] *Parl* S'rn Dv (1867—85), Hexham Dv/CC (1885—1970).

DINNINGTON

Tp in Ponteland AP, sep par 1818.[52] Incl tps Brenkley, Horton Grange, Mason, pt Prestwick (each a sep CP 1866[1]). *LG* Seq 3. Addtl civ bdry alt: 1883,[4] 1955 (incl help cr Brunswick CP, help cr Hazlerigg CP).[54] Transf 1974 to Tyne & Wear.[89] *Parl* Seq 8. *Eccl* Morp. RDn (1818—45), Newc upon Tyne RDn (1845—74), Newc upon Tyne RDn (S'rn Dv) (1874—77), Newc upon Tyne RDn (W'rn Dv) (1877—84), Bedl. RDn (1884—99), Newc

RDn (1899—1967), Newc Ctrl. RDn (1967—*).

NORTH DISSINGTON

Tp in Newburn AP, sep CP 1866.[1] *LG* Castle Wd, Castle Wd PLU, RSD, RD. Abol 1955 ent to Ponteland AP.[54] *Parl* S'rn Dv (1867—85), Wansb. Dv (1885—1948), Hexham CC (1948—70).

SOUTH DISSINGTON

Tp in Newburn AP, sep CP 1866.[1] Organisation as for North Dissington.

DITCHBURN

Tp in Eglingham AP, sep CP 1866.[1] *LG* Coq. Wd, Alnw. PLU, RSD, RD. Abol 1955 ent to Eglingham AP.[2] *Parl* N'rn Dv (1867—85), Berw. upon Tweed Dv/CC (1885—1970).

DODDINGTON

Chap in Chatton AP, seemingly sep par 1775.[111] Incl tps Ewart, Nesbit (each a sep CP 1866[1]), tps Earle, Humbleton (each a sep CP 1866,[1] each eccl severed 1882 and transf to Wooler AP as Doddington AP eccl gains chap Fenton [orig sep AP, qv] from Wooler AP[136]). *LG* Seq 9. Addtl civ bdry alt: 1955 (gains Nesbit CP).[9] *Parl* Seq 1. *Eccl* Bamb. RDn (1775—1899), Glend. RDn (1899—1969), Bamb. & Glend. RDn (1969—*). Addtl eccl bdry alt: 1889.[112]

DOXFORD

Tp in Ellingham AP, sep CP 1866.[1] *LG* Bamb. Wd, Alnw. PLU, RSD, RD. Abol 1955 ent to Newton by the Sea CP.[2] *Parl* N'rn Dv (1867—85), Berw. upon Tweed Dv/CC (1885—1970).

DUDDO

In Durham, transf to Northumb 1832 for parl purposes, 1844 for civ purposes.[25] Tp in Norham AP, sep CP 1866 in Northumb,[1] sep EP 1865.[137] *LG* Seq 14. Civ bdry: 1878,[138] 1955 (gains Felkington CP, Grindon CP, Twizell CP).[139] *Parl* In Durham until 1832, Seq 1 thereafter. *Eccl* Norham RDn. Abol eccl 1970 to help cr Norham and Duddo EP.[140]

DUDLEY

EP Cr 1969 from Cramlington EP, Killingworth EP, North Gosforth EP, Sighill EP.[125] Bedl. RDn.

DUESHILL

Tp in Alwinton AP, sep CP 1866.[1] *LG* Coq. Wd, Rothb. PLU, RSD. Abol 1889 ent to Holystone AP.[140] *Parl* N'rn Dv (1867—85), Hexham Dv (1885—1918).

DUKE'S HAGG

Tp in Ovingham AP, sep CP 1866.[1] *LG* Seq 18. *Parl* Seq 5.

DUNSTAN

Tp in Embleton AP, sep CP 1866.[1] *LG* Bamb. Wd, Alnw. PLU, RSD, RD. Abol 1955 ent to Craster CP.[2] *Parl* N'rn Dv (1867—85), Berw. upon Tweed Dv/CC (1885—1970).

EACHWICK

Tp in Heddon on the Wall AP, sep CP 1866.[1] *LG* Pt Castle Wd, pt Tyned. Wd, Castle Wd PLU, RSD, RD. Abol 1955 to help cr Stamfordham CP.[54] *Parl* S'rn Dv (1867—85), Wansb. Dv (1885—1948), Hexham CC (1948—70).

EARLE

Tp in chap Doddington (seemingly sep par 1775

from Chatton AP[111]), 'Earle' a sep CP 1866,[1] eccl severed 1882 and transf to Wooler AP.[136] *LG* Seq 9. Bdry: 1955 (incl gains Middleton Hall CP).[9] *Parl* Seq 1.

EARSDON

Chap in Tynemouth AP, sep civ identity early, sep EP 1761.[11] Incl tps Backworth, Holywell (each a sep CP 1866[1]), tp Burradon (sep CP 1866,[1] eccl severed 1891 and transf to Killingworth EP[93]), tp Newsham and South Blyth (sep CP 1866,[1] eccl severed 1883 to help cr Blyth St Cuthbert EP[77]), tp Seghill (sep CP 1866,[1] sep EP 1864 as 'Sighill' by union tp Seghill, pt tp Seaton Delaval, pt Cramlington EP[97]); tp Hartley, tp Seaton Delaval (each a sep CP 1866,[1] ent Hartley and pt Seaton Delaval [the pt not severed 1864 to help cr Sighill EP] united 1891 to cr Delaval EP[134]). *LG* Castle Wd, Tynem. PLU, RSD, RD (1894—97), Earsdon UD (1897—1935). Addtl civ bdry alt: 1881.[142] Abol civ 1935 pt to Tynem. CB (assoc with Northumb) & AP, pt to help cr Seaton Valley UD & CP, pt to Whitley and Monkseaton UD and to Monkseaton CP.[34] *Parl* S'rn Dv (1832—85), Wansb. Dv (1885—1948). *Eccl* Newc upon Tyne RDn (1761—1874), Newc upon Tyne RDn (N'rn Dv) (1874—77), Newc upon Tyne RDn (E'rn Dv) (1877—84), Bedl. RDn (1884—*). Addtl eccl bdry alt: 1883 (help cr Blyth St Cuthbert EP),[77] 1958,[58] 1968 (incl help cr Shiremoor EP).[39]

EARSDON

Tp in Bothal AP, sep CP 1866.[1] *LG* Morp. Wd, PLU, RSD, RD. Abol 1955 ent to Tritlington CP.[28] *Parl* N'rn Dv (1867—85), Wansb. Dv (1885—1948), Morp. CC (1948—70).

EARSDON FOREST

Tp in Bothal AP, sep CP 1866.[1] Organisation as for Earsdon.

EASINGTON

Tp in Belford AP, sep CP 1866.[1] *LG* Seq 2. Bdry: 1883,[4] 1955 (gains Easington Grange CP, Outchester CP, Spindlestone CP).[8] *Parl* Seq 1.

EASINGTON GRANGE

Tp in Belford AP, sep CP 1866.[1] *LG* Bamb. Wd, Belf. PLU, RSD, RD. Bdry: 1883.[4] Abol 1955 ent to Easington AP.[8] *Parl* N'rn Dv (1867—85), Berw. upon Tweed Dv/CC (1885—1970).

EDINGTON

Tp in Mitford AP, sep CP 1866.[1] *LG* Castle Wd, Morp. PLU, RSD, RD. Abol 1955 ent to Mitford AP.[28] *Parl* S'rn Dv (1867—85), Wansb. Dv (1885—1948), Morp. CC (1948—70).

EDLINGHAM

AP Incl tps Abberwick, Bolton, Broome Park, Learchild, Lemmington (each a sep CP 1866[1]). *LG* Seq 5. Addtl civ bdry alt: 1955 (gains Abberwick CP, Broome Park CP, Learchild CP, Lemmington CP).[2] *Parl* Seq 1. *Eccl* Sometimes as 'Edlingham with Bolton', Seq 1.

EGLINGHAM

AP Incl tps Bassington, Beanley, New Bewick, Old Bewick, Brandon, Branton, Crawley, Ditchburn, Harehope, Hedgeley, East Lilburn, West Lilburn, Shipley, Titlington, Wooperton (each a sep CP

1866[1]), undivided pt Plea Piece (until 1866, common to Ilderton AP, Eglingham AP; see Plea Piece for composition 1866—1955). *LG* Seq 5. Addtl civ bdry alt: 1955 (gains Bassington CP, North Charlton CP, South Charlton CP, Ditchburn CP, Harehope CP, Shipley CP).[2] *Parl* Seq 1. *Eccl* Sometimes as 'Eglingham and Old Bewick', Alnw. RDn (until 1845), Bamb. RDn (1845—99), Glend. RDn (1899—1969), Bamb. & Glend. RDn (1969—*).

ELFORD

Tp in Bamburgh AP, sep CP 1866.[1] *LG* Bamb. Wd, Belf. PLU, RSD, RD. Abol 1955 ent to Beadnell CP.[8] *Parl* N'rn Dv (1867—85), Berw. upon Tweed Dv/CC (1885—1970).

ELLINGHAM

AP Incl tps North Charlton, Chathill, Doxford, Preston (each a sep CP 1866[1]); tp South Charlton (sep CP 1866,[1] sep EP 1860 incl pt Alnwick AP [pt tp Hulme Park, not sep civ][19]). *LG* Seq 2. Addtl civ bdry alt: 1955 (gains Chathill CP, Newham CP, Preston CP).[8] *Parl* Seq 1. *Eccl* Bamb. RDn (until 1969), Bamb. & Glend. RDn (1969—*).

ELLINGTON

Tp in Woodhorn AP, sep CP 1866.[1] *LG* Seq 10. Bdry: 1888.[143] *Parl* Seq 4.

ELSDON

AP Incl tps Monkridge, Rochester, Troughend, Woodside (each a sep CP 1866[1]); incl tp Otterburn (sep CP 1866,[1] sep EP 1857,[11] eccl refounded 1921[144]); incl chap Byrness (built 1793, sep EP 1801,[11] eccl refounded 1883[102]). *LG* Seq 8. Addtl civ bdry alt: 1955 (gains Monkridge CP).[16] *Parl* Seq 2. *Eccl* Newc upon Tyne RDn (until 1845), Rothb. RDn (1845—*). Addtl eccl bdry alt: 1883 (cr Horsley EP).[145]

ELSWICK

Tp in chap Newcastle upon Tyne St John (sep civ identity early from Newcastle upon Tyne AP, sep EP 1808[11]), 'Elswick' a sep CP 1866,[1] pt eccl severed 1846 to cr High Elswick St Paul EP,[146] qv, the remainder added 1854 to High Elswick St Paul EP.[147] *LG* Castle Wd, Newc upon Tyne PLU, MB (1835—89), USD, CB (1889—1914). Abol 1914 to help cr Newcastle upon Tyne CP.[62] *Parl* Newc upon Tyne Parl Bor (1832—1918).

HIGH ELSWICK ST PAUL

EP Cr 1846 from Newcastle upon Tyne St John EP (pt tp Elswick; for civ see prev entry).[146] Newc upon Tyne RDn (1846—74), Newc upon Tyne RDn (S'rn Dv) (1874—77), Newc upon Tyne RDn (W'rn Dv) (1877—84), Newc RDn (1884—1967), Newc West RDn (1967—*). Bdry: 1854 (gains the remainder of tp Elswick from Newcastle upon Tyne St John EP,[147] 1868 (cr High Elswick St Philip EP),[148] 1868 (cr Low Elswick EP),[149] 1895 (help cr Newcastle upon Tyne St Mary the Virgin EP).[150]

HIGH ELSWICK ST PHILIP

EP Cr 1868 from High Elswick St Paul EP.[148] RDns as for High Elswick St Paul, from 1868. Bdry: 1892 (help cr Newcastle upon Tyne St Augustine EP).[130]

LOW ELSWICK

EP Cr 1868 from High Elswick St Paul EP.[149] RDns as for High Elswick St Paul, from 1868. Bdry: 1895 (help cr Newcastle upon Tyne St Mary the Virgin EP),[150] 1961.[151]

ELTRINGHAM

Tp in Ovingham AP, sep CP 1866.[1] *LG* Tyned. Wd, Hexham PLU, RSD, RD (1894—1910), Prudhoe UD (1910—74). Bdry: 1883,[4] 1887.[36] *Parl* Seq 5.

ELWICK

Pt in Durham (Islandshire), pt in Northumb (Bamb. Wd), made ent Northumb in 1832 for parl purposes, 1844 for civ purposes.[25] Tp in Norham AP, sep CP 1866.[1] *LG* Belf. PLU, RSD, RD. Abol 1955 ent to Middleton CP.[8] *Parl* Pt Durham, pt Northumb until 1832, N'rn Dv (1832—85), Berw. upon Tweed Dv/CC (1885—1970).

ELYHAUGH

Tp in Felton AP, sep CP 1866.[1] *LG* Coq. Wd, Alnw. PLU, RSD, RD. Bdry: 1935 (help cr Thirston (with Shothaugh) CP).[34] Abol 1955 ent to Felton AP.[2] *Parl* N'rn Dv (1867—85), Berw. upon Tweed Dv/CC (1885—1970).

EMBLETON

AP Incl tps Brunton, Craster, Dunstan, Fallodon, Newton by the Sea, Stamford (each a sep CP 1866[1]); chap Rennington (sep CP 1866,[1] sep EP 1767,[11] eccl refounded 1903 [incl tp Broxfield][88]); tp Broxfield (sep CP 1866,[1] eccl severed 1903 to help refound Rennington EP[88]); chap Rock (sep CP 1866,[1] sep EP 1767,[11] eccl refounded 1903[88]). *LG* Seq 1. *Parl* Seq 1. *Eccl* Seq 1.

ESHOTT

Tp in Felton AP, sep CP 1866.[1] *LG* Morp. Wd, PLU, RSD, RD. Bdry: 1883.[4] Abol 1955 to help cr Thirston CP.[28] *Parl* N'rn Dv (1867—85), Wansb. Dv (1885—1948), Morp. CC (1948—70).

ESPERSHIELDS

Tp in Bywell St Peter AP, sep CP 1866,[1] eccl severed 1876 to help cr Healey EP.[85] *LG* Seq 18. *Parl* Seq 5.

EWART

Tp in chap Doddington (seemingly sep par 1775 from Chatton AP[111]), 'Ewart' a sep CP 1866.[1] *LG* Seq 9. Bdry: 1955 (incl gains Lanton CP, and also Undivided Moor common to Kirknewton and Lanton).[9] *Parl* Seq 1.

EWESLEY

Tp in chap Netherwitton (sep CP 1866 from Hartburn AP,[1] sep EP 1835 but not incl Ewesley so that the latter eccl remains in Hartburn), 'Ewesley' a sep CP 1866.[1] *LG* Morp. Wd, Rothb. PLU, RSD, RD. Abol 1955 ent to Nunnykirk CP.[16] *Parl* N'rn Dv (1867—85), Wansb. Dv (1885—1918), Berw. upon Tweed Dv/CC (1918—48).

FAIRHAUGH

Tp in Alwinton AP, sep CP 1866.[1] *LG* Coq. Wd, Rothb. PLU, RSD, RD. Abol 1955 ent to Alwinton AP.[16] *Parl* N'rn Dv (1867—85), Hexham Dv (1885—1918), Berw. upon Tweed Dv/CC (1918—48).

FAIRNLEY

Tp in Hartburn AP, sep CP 1866.[1] *LG* Tyned. Wd, Rothb. PLU, RSD, RD. Abol 1955 ent to Rothley CP.[16] *Parl* S'rn Dv (1867—85), Hexham Dv

(1885—1918), Berw. upon Tweed Dv/CC (1918—70).

FALLODON

Tp in Embleton AP, sep CP 1866.[1] *LG* Bamb. Wd, Alnw. PLU, RSD, RD. Abol 1955 ent to Newton by the Sea CP.[2] *Parl* N'rn Dv (1867—85), Berw. upon Tweed Dv/CC (1885—1970).

FALLOWFIELD

Tp in Lee St John AP (eccl, 'St John Lee'), sep CP 1866,[1] eccl severed 1879 to help cr St Oswald Lee with Bingfield St Mary EP.[70] *LG* Tyned. Wd, Hexham PLU, RSD, RD. Abol 1955 ent to Wall CP.[37] *Parl* S'rn Dv (1867—85), Hexham Dv/CC (1885—1970).

FALLOWLEES

Tp in Rothbury AP, sep CP 1866.[1] *LG* Coq. Wd, Rothb. PLU, RSD, RD. Abol 1955 ent to Hollinghill CP.[16] *Parl* N'rn Dv (1867—85), Hexham Dv (1885—1918), Berw. upon Tweed Dv/CC (1918—70).

FALSTONE

Chap appropriated to Kirkham Priory, later in ruins and deemed chap in Simonburn, made sep par 1811 comprised of 2 tps of Plashetts and Tynehead, Wellhaugh[152] (each of the tps a sep CP 1866[1]) so that 'Falstone' has no sep civ identity 1866—1955 (see following entry). *LG* Tyned. Wd. *Parl* S'rn Dv (1832—67). *Eccl* Corbr. RDn (1811—45), Bell. RDn (1845—*).

CP Cr 1955 by union Plashetts and Tynehead CP, Thorneyburn CP, Wellhaugh CP.[47] *LG* Bell. RD. *Parl* Hexham CC (1970—*).

FARNE ISLANDS

Ex-par islands in Durham, transf to Northumb 1832 for parl purposes, 1844 for civ purposes.[25] *LG* Not in a Hd, Belf. PLU, not in a RSD or RD but often listed in Belf. RD for convenience's sake. Abol 1955 ent to North Sunderland CP.[8] *Parl* In Durham until 1832, N'rn Dv (1832—85), Berw. upon Tweed Dv/CC (1885—1970).

FARNHAM

Tp in Alwinton AP, sep CP 1866.[1] *LG* Coq. Wd, Rothb. PLU, RSD, RD. Abol 1955 ent to Hepple CP.[16] *Parl* N'rn Dv (1867—85), Hexham Dv (1885—1918), Berw. upon Tweed Dv/CC (1918—70).

FAWDON

Tp in chap Gosforth (sep civ identity early from Newcastle upon Tyne AP, sep EP 1865[90]), 'Fawdon' a sep CP 1866.[1] *LG* Castle Wd, Castle Wd PLU, RSD, RD. Bdry: 1887.[153] Abol 1935 pt to Newc upon Tyne CB (assoc with Northumb) & CP, pt to Gosforth CP.[154] *Parl* S'rn Dv (1867—85), Tynes. Dv (1885—1918), Wansb. Dv (1918—48).

FAWDON AND CLINCH

CP Cr 1884 when Hartside severed from Fawdon, Clinch and Hartside CP to help cr Ingram, Linhope, Greenshawhill and Hartside CP.[155] *LG* Coq. Wd, Glend. PLU, RD. Abol 1955 to help cr Ingram CP.[9] *Parl* Berw. upon Tweed Dv/CC (1885—1970).

FAWDON, CLINCH AND HARTSIDE

Tp in Ingram AP, sep CP 1866.[1] *LG* Coq. Wd, Glen. PLU, RSD. Bdry: 1884.[156] Abol 1884,

Hartside severed to help cr Ingram, Linhope, Greenshawhill and Hartside CP, the remainder reconstituted Fawdon and Clinch.[155] *Parl* N'rn Dv (1867—85).

FAWNS

Tp in Kirkwhelpington AP, sep CP 1866.[1] *LG* Tyned. Wd, Bell. PLU, RSD, RD. Abol 1955 ent to Kirkwhelpington AP.[47] *Parl* S'rn Dv (1867—85), Hexham Dv/CC (1885—1970).

FEATHERSTONE

Tp in Haltwhistle AP, sep CP 1866.[1] *LG* Seq 17. Bdry: 1955 (gains Bellister CP).[45] *Parl* Seq 5.

FELKINGTON

In Durham, transf to Northumb 1832 for parl purposes, 1844 for civ purposes.[25] Tp in Norham AP, sep CP 1866.[1] *LG* Norhamshire, Berw. PLU, RSD, Norham & Islandshires RD. Abol 1955 ent to Duddo CP.[139] *Parl* In Durham until 1832, N'rn Dv (1832—85), Berw. upon Tweed Dv/CC (1885—1970).

FELTON

AP Tp 'Felton' in Coq. Wd as were chap Longframlington (sep CP 1866,[1] sep EP 1891[157]); tps Acton and Old Felton, Elyhaugh, Greens and Glantlees, Swarland (each a sep CP 1866[1]); incl in Morp. Wd tps Bockenfield, Eshott, East and West Thirston with Shothaugh (each a sep CP 1866[1]); vicar of Felton claimed Brinkburn Chapelry in this par, but the latter really a sep AP.[83] *LG* Felton Bor, Seq 5. Addtl civ bdry alt: 1883,[4] 1888,[158] 1935 (help cr Thirston (with Shothaugh) CP),[34] 1955 (gains Acton and Old Felton CP, Elyhaugh CP).[2] *Parl* Seq 1. *Eccl* Morp. RDn (until 1845), Alnw. RDn (1845—*).

FENHAM

Tp in chap Newcastle upon Tyne St Andrew (sep civ identity early from Newcastle upon Tyne AP, sep EP 1808[11]), 'Fenham' a sep CP 1866,[1] sep EP 1926 from Newcastle upon Tyne St Luke the Evangelist EP, Benwell St James EP, Newcastle upon Tyne St Augustine EP.[66] *LG* Castle Wd, Newc upon Tyne PLU, Benwell & Fenham USD, UD (1894—1904), Newc upon Tyne CB (1904—14). Abol civ 1914 to help cr Newcastle upon Tyne CP.[62] *Parl* S'rn Dv (1867—85), Tynes. Dv (1885—1918). *Eccl* Newc RDn (1926—67), Newc West RDn (1967—*). Eccl bdry: 1928,[159] 1936 (help cr Newcastle upon Tyne Holy Cross EP),[131] 1957 (help cr Cowgate EP).[123]

FENROTHER

Tp in Bothal AP, sep CP 1866.[1] Incl undivided pt Horsley Moor (common to Bigge's Quarter CP, Fenrother CP, Freeholders' Quarter CP, Riddell's Quarter CP). *LG* Morp. Wd, PLU, RSD, RD. Abol 1955 ent to Tritlington CP.[28] *Parl* N'rn Dv (1867—859), Wansb. Dv (1885—1948), Morp. CC (1948—70).

FENTON

AP Bamb. RDn, abol 1313 ent to Wooler AP and thereafter considered latter's chap,[160] eccl transf 1882 to Doddington EP.[136]

FENWICK

Tp in Stamfordham AP, sep CP 1866.[1] *LG* Tyned. Wd, Castle Wd PLU, RSD, RD. Abol 1955 to hlp cr Matfen CP.[54] *Parl* S'rn Dv (1867—85), Hexham Dv/CC (1885—1970).

FLEETHAM

Tp in Bamburgh AP, sep CP 1866.[1] *LG* Bamb. Wd, Belf. PLU, RSD, RD. Abol 1955 ent to Beadnell CP.[8] *Parl* N'rn Dv (1867—85), Berw. upon Tweed Dv/CC (1885—1970).

FLOTTERTON

Tp in Rothbury AP, sep CP 1866.[1] *LG* Coq. Wd, Rothb. PLU, RSD, RD. Abol 1955 ent to Snitter CP.[16] *Parl* N'rn Dv (1867—85), Hexham Dv (1885—1918), Berw. upon Tweed Dv (1918—70).

FORD

AP *LG* Seq 9. *Parl* Seq 1. *Eccl* Usually as 'Ford with Etal' (chap Etal erected 1856[161]), Bamb. RDn (until 1845), Norham RDn (1845—99), Glend. RDn (1899—1969), Norham RDn (1969—*).

FORD WITH ETAL—See prev entry

HIGH FOTHERLEY

Tp in Bywell St Peter AP, sep CP 1866,[1] pt eccl severed 1876 to help cr Healey EP.[85] *LG* Seq 18. Bdry: 1883.[4] *Parl* Seq 5.

FREEHOLDERS' QUARTER

Tp in Long Horsley AP (eccl, 'Longhorsley'), sep CP 1866.[1] Incl undivided pt Horsley Moor (common to Bigge's Quarter CP, Fenrother CP, Freeholders' Quarter CP, Riddell's Quarter CP), undivided pt Long Horsley Common (common to Bigge's Quarter CP, Freeholders' Quarter CP, Riddell's Quarter CP). *LG* Morp. Wd, PLU, RSD, RD. Abol 1955 to help cr Longhorsley CP.[28] *Parl* N'rn Dv (1867—85), Wansb. Dv (1885—1948), Morp. CC (1948—70).

GALLOWHILL

Tp in Bolam AP, sep CP 1866.[1] *LG* Morp. Wd, Castle Wd PLU, RSD, RD. Abol 1955 ent to Belsay CP.[54] *Parl* N'rn Dv (1867—85), Wansb. Dv (1885—1948), Morp. CC (1948—70).

GLANTON

Tp in Whittingham AP, sep CP 1866.[1] *LG* Seq 5. Bdry: 1955.[2] *Parl* Seq 1.

GLORORUM

Tp in Bamburgh AP, sep CP 1866.[1] *LG* Bamb. Wd, Belf. PLU, RSD, RD. Abol 1955 ent to Bamburgh AP.[8] *Parl* N'rn Dv (1867—85), Berw. upon Tweed Dv/CC (1885—1970).

GLOSTER HILL

Tp in Warkworth AP, sep CP 1866,[1] eccl severed 1869 to help cr Amble EP.[23] *LG* Morp. Wd, Alnw. PLU, RSD, RD. Abol 1955 ent to Warkworth AP.[2] *Parl* N'rn Dv (1867—85), Wansb. Dv (1885—1918), Berw. upon Tweed Dv/CC (1918—70).

GOSFORTH

Chap in Newcastle upon Tyne AP, sep civ identity early, sep EP 1865 [St Nicholas].[90] Incl tps East Brunton, West Brunton, Coxlodge, Fawdon, South Gosforth, Kenton (each a sep CP 1866[1]); tp North Gosforth (sep EP 1865 [incl pt Long Benton AP][57]) so that 'Gosforth' has no sep civ identity 1866—1908 (see following entry). *LG* Castle Wd. *Parl* S'rn Dv (1832—67). *Eccl* Newc upon Tyne RDn (1865—74), Newc upon Tyne RDn (S'rn Dv) (1874—77), Newc upon Tyne RDn (W'rn Dv)

(1877—84), Newc RDn (1884—1967), Newc Ctrl. RDn (1967—*). Eccl bdry: 1906 (cr Gosforth All Saints EP),[78] 1967.[90]

CP Cr 1908 by union Coxlodge CP, South Gosforth CP.[124] *LG* Castle Wd PLU, Gosforth UD. Bdry: 1935.[34] Transf 1974 to Tyne & Wear.[89] *Parl* Wallsend Parl Bor/BC (1918—*).

NORTH GOSFORTH

Tp in chap Gosforth (sep civ identity early from Newcastle upon Tyne AP, sep EP 1865[90]), 'North Gosforth' a sep CP 1866,[1] sep EP 1865 from Gosforth EP, Long Benton AP.[57] *LG* Seq 3. Civ bdry: 1935,[34] 1959.[162] Transf 1974 to Tyne & Wear.[89] *Parl* Seq 7. *Eccl* Newc upon Tyne RDn (1865—74), Newc upon Tyne RDn (S'rn Dv) (1874—77), Newc upon Tyne RDn (W'rn Dv) (1877—84), Newc RDn (1884—1967), Newc Ctrl. RDn (1967—*). Eccl bdry: 1967,[90] 1969 (help cr Dudley EP).[125]

SOUTH GOSFORTH

Tp in chap Gosforth (sep civ identity early from Newcastle upon Tyne AP, sep EP 1865[90]), 'South Gosforth' a sep CP 1866.[1] *LG* Castle Wd, Castle Wd PLU, South Gosforth USD, UD (1894—95), Gosforth UD (1895—1908). Bdry: 1887.[153] Abol 1908 to help cr Gosforth CP.[124] *Parl* S'rn Dv (1867—85), Tynes. Dv (1885—1918).

GOSFORTH ALL SAINTS

EP Cr 1906 from Gosforth EP.[78] Newc RDn (1906—67), Newc Ctrl. RDn (1967—*). Bdry: 1957 (help cr Cowgate EP),[123] 1967 (cr Kenton EP).[163]

GREENHEAD

EP Cr 1831 from Haltwhistle AP (tps Blenkinsopp, Thirlwall),[11] eccl refounded 1892.[75] Corbr. RDn (1831—45), Hexham RDn (1845—*).

CP Cr 1955 by union Blenkinsopp CP, Wall Town CP.[45] *LG* Haltw. RD. *Parl* Hexham CC (1970—*).

GREENLEIGHTON

Tp in Hartburn AP, sep CP 1866.[1] *LG* Tyned. Wd, Rothb. PLU, RSD, RD. Abol 1955 ent to Hollinghill CP.[16] *Parl* S'rn Dv (1867—85), Hexham Dv (1885—1918), Berw. upon Tweed Dv (1918—70).

GREENS AND GLANTLEES

Tp in Felton AP, sep CP 1866.[1] *LG* Coq. Wd, Alnw. PLU, RSD, RD. Abol 1955 ent to Newton on the Moor CP.[2] *Parl* N'rn Dv (1867—85), Berw. upon Tweed. Dv/CC (1885—1970).

GREY'S FOREST

Tp in Kirknewton AP, sep CP 1866.[1] *LG* Glend. Wd, PLU, RSD, RD. Abol 1955 ent to Kirknewton AP.[9] *Parl* N'rn Dv (1867—85), Berw. upon Tweed Dv/CC (1885—1970).

GREYSTEAD

Tp in Simonburn AP, made sep par 1811 comprised of tps Chirdon, Smalesmouth,[52] the latter each a sep CP 1866[1] so that 'Greystead' has no sep civ identity 1866—1955 (see following entry). *LG* Tyned. Wd. *Parl* S'rn Dv (1832—67). *Eccl* Corbr. RDn (1811—45), Bell. RDn (1845—*).

CP Cr 1955 by union Chirdon CP, Smalesmouth CP.[47] *LG* Bell. RD. *Parl* Hexham CC (1970—*).

GRINDON

In Durham, transf to Northumb 1832 for parl

purposes, 1844 for civ purposes.[25] Tp in Norham AP, sep CP 1866.[1] *LG* Norhamshire, Berw. PLU, RSD, Norham & Islandshires RD. Abol 1955 ent to Duddo CP.[139] *Parl* In Durham until 1832, N'rn Dv (1832—85), Berw. upon Tweed Dv/CC (1885—1970).

GUYZANCE
Tp in Shilbottle AP, sep CP 1866.[1] Sometimes 'Guyson'. *LG* Coq. Wd, Alnw. PLU, RSD, RD. Abol 1955 ent to Acklington CP.[2] *Parl* N'rn Dv (1867—85), Berw. upon Tweed Dv/CC (1885—1970).

HADSTON
Tp in Warkworth AP, sep CP 1866,[1] eccl severed 1863 to help cr Chevington EP.[92] *LG* Morp. Wd, PLU, RSD, RD. Abol 1955 ent to East Chevington CP.[28] *Parl* N'rn Dv (1867—85), Wansb. Dv (1885—1948), Morp. CC (1948—70).

HALLINGTON
Tp in Lee St John AP (eccl, 'St John Lee'), sep CP 1866,[1] eccl severed 1879 to help cr St Oswald in Lee with Bingfield St Mary EP,[70] the area of Hallington eccl severed from the latter 1888 to help cr Bingfield St Mary EP.[71] *LG* Tyned. Wd, Hexham PLU, RSD, RD. Abol 1955 to help cr Whittington CP.[37] *Parl* S'rn Dv (1867—85), Hexham Dv/CC (1885—1970).

HALTON
Tp in Corbridge AP, sep CP 1866.[1] *LG* Tyned. Wd, Hexham PLU, RSD, RD. Abol 1955 to help cr Whittington CP.[37] *Parl* S'rn Dv (1867—85), Hexham Dv/CC (1885—1970).

HALTON SHIELDS
Tp in Corbridge AP, sep CP 1866.[1] *LG* Tyned. Wd, Hexham PLU, RSD. Abol 1887 ent to Clarewood CP.[120] *Parl* S'rn Dv (1867—85), Hexham Dv (1885—1918).

HALTWHISTLE
AP Incl chap Beltingham (sep EP 1830,[11] eccl refounded 1890 as 'Beltingham with Henshaw'[55]); tps Bellister, Coanwood, Featherstone, Hartleyburn, Henshaw, Melkridge, Plenmellor, Ridley, Thorngrafton, Wall Town (each a sep CP 1866[1]); incl tps Blenkinsopp, Thirlwall (each a sep CP 1866,[1] eccl united 1831 to cr Greenhead EP,[11] eccl refounded 1892[75]). *LG* Seq 17. *Parl* Seq 5. *Eccl* Seq 8.

HARBOTTLE
Tp and bor (status not sustained) in Alwinton AP, sep CP 1866.[1] *LG* Seq 8. Bdry: 1883,[4] 1883,[46] 1955 (gains Holystone CP, Peels CP, Sharperton CP).[16] *Parl* Seq 2.

HAREHOPE
Tp in Eglingham AP, sep CP 1866.[1] *LG* Coq. Wd, Alnw. PLU, RSD, RD. Abol 1955 ent to Eglingham AP.[2] *Parl* N'rn Dv (1867—85), Berw. upon Tweed Dv/CC (1885—1970).

LITTLE HARLE
Tp in Kirkwhelpington AP, sep CP 1866.[1] *LG* Tyned. Wd, Bell. PLU, RSD, RD. Abol 1955 ent to Kirkwhelpington AP.[47] *Parl* S'rn Dv (1867—85), Hexham Dv/CC (1885—1970).

WEST HARLE
Tp in Kirkwhelpington AP, sep CP 1866.[1] Organisation as for West Harle.

HARLOW HILL
Tp in Ovingham AP, sep CP 1866.[1] *LG* Tyned. Wd, Castle Wd PLU, RSD, RD. Abol 1955 to help cr Stamfordham CP.[54] *Parl* S'rn Dv (1867—85), Hexham Dv/CC (1885—1970).

HARNHAM
Tp in Bolam AP, sep CP 1866.[1] *LG* Tyned. Wd, Castle Wd PLU, RSD, RD. Abol 1955 ent to Belsay CP.[54] *Parl* S'rn Dv (1867—85), Wansb. Dv (1885—1948), Hexham CC (1948—70).

HARTBURN
AP Tp 'Hartburn' in Morp. Wap as were chap Netherwitton (sep CP 1866[1] [qv for tps incl], sep EP 1835[11]), tps High Angerton, Low Angerton, Corridge, Hartburn Grange, Highlaws, Longwitton, North Middleton, South Middleton, Rothley, East Thornton, West Thornton, Todridge, Whitridge (each a sep CP 1866[1]); incl in Tyned. Wd tps Deanham, Fairnley, Greenleighton, Hartington, Hartington Hall, Harwood, East Shaftoe, West Shaftoe, Wallington Demesne (each a sep CP 1866[1]), tp Cambo (sep CP 1866,[1] sep EP 1844[106]); incl (Morp. Wd) pt tp Longshaws (sep CP 1866[1]). *LG* Tp 'Hartburn': Seq 10. Addtl civ bdry alt: 1955 (gains High Angerton CP, Low Angerton CP, East Thornton CP, West Thornton CP).[28] *Parl* Seq 4. *Eccl* Morp. RDn. Abol eccl 1939 to help cr Hartburn with Meldon EP.[50]

HARTBURN GRANGE
Tp in Hartburn AP, sep CP 1866.[1] *LG* Morp.Wd, PLU, RSD, RD. Abol 1955 ent to Wallington Demesne CP.[28] *Parl* N'rn Dv (1867—85), Wansb. Dv (1885—1948), Morp. CC (1948—70).

HARTBURN WITH MELDON
EP Cr 1939 by union Hartburn AP, Meldon AP.[50] Morp. RDn.

EAST HARTFORD
Tp in Horton AP, sep CP 1866.[1] *LG* Castle Wd, Tynem. PLU, RSD, RD (1894—1912), Craml. UD (1912—35). Bdry: 1912 (gains the pt of Horton CP not transf to Blyth UD as enlarged East Hartford transf to Craml. UD).[94] Abol 1935 to help cr Seaton Valley UD & CP.[34] *Parl* S'rn Dv (1867—85), Wansb. Dv (1885—1948).

WEST HARTFORD
Tp in Horton AP, sep CP 1866.[1] Organisation as for East Hartford, except no civ bdry alt.

HARTINGTON
Tp in Hartburn AP, sep CP 1866.[1] *LG* Tyned. Wd, Rothb. PLU, RSD, RD. Abol 1955 ent to Rothley CP.[16] *Parl* S'rn Dv (1867—85), Hexham Dv (1885—1918), Berw. upon Tweed Dv/CC (1918—70).

HARTINGTON HALL
Tp in Hartburn AP, sep CP 1866.[1] Organisation as for Hartington.

HARTLEY
Tp in Earsdon AP, sep CP 1866,[1] eccl severed 1891 to help cr Delaval EP.[134] *LG* Castle Wd, Tynem. PLU, RSD, RD. Abol 1912 pt to Whitley and

Monkseaton UD and to Monkseaton CP, the remainder to help constitute Seaton Delaval UD, that area transf to Seaton Delaval CP.[94] *Parl* S'rn Dv (1867—85), Wansb. Dv (1885—1918).

HARTLEYBURN
Tp in Haltwhistle AP, sep CP 1866.[1] *LG* Seq 17. *Parl* Seq 5.

HARWOOD
Tp in Hartburn AP, sep CP 1866.[1] *LG* Tyned. Wd, Rothb. PLU, RSD, RD. Abol 1955 ent to Hollinghill CP.[16] *Parl* S'rn Dv (1867—85), Hexham Dv (1885—1918), Berw. upon Tweed Dv/CC (1918—70).

HAUGHTON
Tp in Simonburn AP, sep CP 1866.[1] *LG* Tyned. Wd, Hexham PLU, RSD, RD. Abol 1955 pt to Humshaugh CP, pt to Simonburn AP.[37] *Parl* S'rn Dv (1867—85), Hexham Dv/CC (1885—1970).

HAUXLEY
Tp in Warkworth AP, sep CP 1866,[1] eccl severed 1869 to help cr Amble EP.[23] *LG* Seq 11. *Parl* Seq 3.

HAWICK
Tp in Kirkharle AP, sep CP 1866.[1] *LG* Tyned. Wd, Bell. PLU, RSD, RD. Abol 1955 to help cr Bavington CP.[47] *Parl* S'rn Dv (1867—85), Hexham Dv/CC (1885—1970).

HAWKWELL
Tp in Stamfordham AP, sep CP 1866.[1] *LG* Tyned. Wd, Castle Wd PLU, RSD, RD. Abol 1955 to help cr Stamfordham CP.[54] *Parl* S'rn Dv (1867—85), Hexham Dv/CC (1885—1970).

HAYDON
Chap and bor ('Haydon Bridge', status not sustained) in Warden AP, sep CP 1866,[1] sep EP 1879 as 'Haydon Bridge',[7] qv. *LG* Seq 18. Civ bdry: 1955.[37] *Parl* Seq 5.

HAYDON BRIDGE
Chap and bor ('Haydon Bridge', status not sustained) in Warden AP, sep EP 1879,[7] sep CP 1866 as 'Haydon',[1] qv. *Eccl* Hexham RDn.

HAZLERIGG
CP Cr 1955 by union East Brunton CP, pt West Brunton CP, pt Dinnington CP.[54] *LG* Castle Wd RD. Transf 1974 to Tyne & Wear.[89] *Parl* Hexham CC (1970—*).

HAZON AND HARTLAW
Tp in Shilbottle AP, sep CP 1866.[1] *LG* Coq. Wd, Alnw. PLU, RSD, RD. Abol 1955 ent to Newton on the Moor CP.[2] *Parl* N'rn Dv (1867—85), Berw. upon Tweed Dv/CC (1885—1970).

HEALEY
Tp in Bywell St Peter AP, sep CP 1866,[1] sep EP 1876 by union tps Healey, High Fotherley, pt Bromley, all in Bywell St Peter AP.[85] *LG* Seq 18. Civ bdry: 1883,[4] 1887.[36] *Parl* Seq 5.

HEALEY AND COMBHILL
Tp in Netherwitton AP, sep CP 1866.[1] *LG* Morp. Wd, Rothb. PLU, RSD, RD. Abol 1955 ent to Nunnykirk CP.[16] *Parl* N'rn Dv (1867—85), Wansb. Dv (1885—1918), Berw. upon Tweed Dv/CC (1918—70).

HEATON
Tp in chap Newcastle upon Tyne All Saints (sep civ identity early from Newcastle upon Tyne AP, sep EP 1808[11]), 'Heaton' a sep CP 1866.[1] *LG* Castle Wd, Newc upon Tyne PLU, MB (1835—89), CB (1889—1914), USD. Abol 1914 to help cr Newcastle upon Tyne CP.[62] *Parl* Newc upon Tyne Parl Bor (1832—1918).

HEBRON
Chap in Bothal AP, sep CP 1866.[1] *LG* Seq 10. Bdry: 1955 (gains Benridge CP, Cockle Park CP, High and Low Highlaws CP).[28] *Parl* Seq 4.

BLACK HEDDON
Tp in Stamfordham AP, sep CP 1866.[1] *LG* Tyned. Wd, Castle Wd PLU, RSD, RD. Abol 1955 ent to Belsay CP.[54] *Parl* S'rn Dv (1867—85), Hexham Dv/CC (1885—1970).

EAST HEDDON
Tp pt in Heddon on the Wall AP, pt in Newburn AP, sep CP 1866.[1] *LG* Castle Wd, Castle Wd PLU, RSD, RD. Bdry: 1887,[153] 1935.[34] Abol 1955 ent to Heddon on the Wall AP.[54] *Parl* S'rn Dv (1867—85), Wansb. Dv (1885—1948), Hexham CC (1948—70).

WEST HEDDON
Tp in Heddon on the Wall AP, sep CP 1866.[1] *LG*, civ abol, *Parl* as for Black Heddon.

HEDDON ON THE WALL
AP Tp 'Heddon on the Wall' in Tyned. Wd as were tps West Heddon, Houghton and Close House, Whitchester (each a sep CP 1866[1]); incl in Castle Wd pt tp East Heddon (sep CP 1866[1]); incl (pt Tyned. Wd, pt Castle Wd) tp Eachwick (sep CP 1866[1]). *LG* Seq 16. Addtl civ bdry alt: 1935,[34] 1955 (gains East Heddon CP, West Heddon CP, Houghton and Close House CP, Rudchester CP, Whitchester CP).[54] *Parl* Seq 8. *Eccl* Newc upon Tyne RDn (until 1845), Corbr. RDn (1845—*).

HEDGELEY
Tp in Eglingham AP, sep CP 1866.[1] *LG* Seq 5. *Parl* Seq 1.

HEDLEY
Tp in Ovingham AP, sep CP 1866.[1] *LG* Seq 18. Bdry: 1887.[164] *Parl* Seq 5.

HEDLEY WOODSIDE
Tp in Ovingham AP, sep CP 1866.[1] *LG* Tyned. Wd, Hexham PLU, RSD. Abol 1887 pt to Hedley CP, pt to Medomsley CP, Durham.[164] *Parl* S'rn Dv (1867—85), Hexham Dv (1885—1918).

HENSHAW
Tp in Haltwhistle AP, sep CP 1866.[1] *LG* Seq 17. Bdry: 1883,[4] 1886.[76] *Parl* Seq 5.

HEPBURN
Tp in Chillingham AP, sep CP 1866.[1] *LG* Glend. Wd, PLU, RSD, RD. Abol 1955 ent to Chillingham AP.[9] *Parl* N'rn Dv (1867—85), Berw. upon Tweed Dv/CC (1885—1970).

HEPPLE
Tp in Rothbury AP, sep CP 1866.[1] *LG* Seq 8. Bdry: 1889,[165] 1955 (gains Bickerton CP, Caistron CP, Farnham CP, Woodside CP, Wreighill CP).[16] *Parl* Seq 2.

HEPPLE DEMESNE
Tp in Rothbury AP, sep CP 1866.[1] *LG* Coq. Wd, Rothb. PLU, RSD. Abol 1889 ent to Hepple CP.[165]

Parl N'rn Dv (1867—85), Hexham Dv (1885—1918).

HEPSCOTT

Tp in Morpeth AP, sep CP 1866.[1] *LG* Castle Wd, Morp. PLU, USD (1875—89), RSD (1889—94), RD. Bdry: 1935,[34] 1965.[166] *Parl* Morp. Parl Bor (1832—1948), Morp. CC (1948—*).

HESLEYHURST

Tp in Rothbury AP, sep CP 1866.[1] *LG* Seq 8. Bdry: 1889,[15] 1889.[167] *Parl* Seq 2.

HETHPOOL

Tp in Kirknewton AP, sep CP 1866.[1] *LG* Glend. Wd, PLU, RSD, RD. Abol 1955 ent to Kirknewton AP.[9] *Parl* N'rn Dv (1867—85), Berw. upon Tweed Dv/CC (1885—1970).

HEUGH

Tp in Stamfordham AP, sep CP 1866.[1] *LG* Tyned. Wd, Castle Wd PLU, RSD, RD. Abol 1955 to help cr Stamfordham CP.[54] *Parl* S'rn Dv (1867—85), Hexham Dv/CC (1885—1970).

HEXHAM

AP Independent co palatine comprised of Hexham AP (incl chap Allendale), Lee St John AP, merged 1572 into Northumb.[10] Orig church of St Mary allowed to decay, the priory (St Andrew) then parochial with St Mary (ruins by 16th cent) deemed its chap, St Andrew solely parochial from Dissolution.[168] Incl chap Allendale (sep civ identity early, sep EP 1767[11]), tps Hexhamshire High Quarter, Hexhamshire Low Quarter, Hexhamshire Middle Quarter (each a sep CP 1866,[1] together comprised chap Whitley, as such a sep EP 1763,[11] eccl refounded 1900 [incl pt Shotley EP][169]), tp Hexhamshire West Quarter (sep CP 1866[1]); also incl Moorland (since cr 1866 of CPs for the 4 Quarters, common to them and to Hexham, this pt lost 1955 to help cr Hexhamshire CP[5]). *LG* Tyned. Wd, Hexham PLU, USD (ent 1875—83, pt 1883—94), Hexham UD. Addtl civ bdry alt: 1883,[4] 1935.[34] *Parl* Seq 5. *Eccl* Newc upon Tyne RDn (until 1845), Hexham RDn (1845—*).

HEXHAM ST PETER

AP Prob destroyed 9th cent, disappeared by 1310.[170]

HEXHAMSHIRE

CP Cr 1955 by union Hexhamshire High Quarter CP, Hexhamshire Middle Quarter CP, pt Hexhamshire West Quarter CP, Moorland common to the Townships of Hexham (Hexham AP, Hexhamshire High Quarter CP, Hexhamshire Low Quarter CP, Hexhamshire Middle Quarter CP, Hexhamshire West Quarter CP).[37] *LG* Hexham RD. *Parl* Hexham CC (1970—*).

HEXHAMSHIRE HIGH QUARTER

Tp in Hexam AP, sep CP 1866,[1] eccl pt of chap Whitley (sep EP 1763,[11] eccl refounded 1900,[169] qv). Incl undivided pt of Moorland common to the Townships of Hexham (Hexham AP, Hexhamshire High Quarter CP, Hexhamshire Low Quarter CP, Hexhamshire Middle Quarter CP, Hexhamshire Low Quarter CP). *LG* Tyned. Wd, Hexham PLU, RSD, RD. Abol 1955 to help cr Hexhamshire CP.[37] *Parl* S'rn Dv (1867—85), Hexham Dv/CC (1885—1970).

HEXHAMSHIRE LOW QUARTER

Tp in Hexam AP, sep CP 1866,[1] eccl pt of chap Whitley (sep EP 1763,[11] eccl refounded 1900,[169] qv). Incl undivided pt Moorland common to the Townships of Hexham (for composition, see Hexhamshire High Quarter above). *LG* Seq 18. Bdry: 1955.[37] *Parl* Seq 5.

HEXHAMSHIRE MIDDLE QUARTER

Tp in Hexam AP, sep CP 1866,[1] eccl pt of chap Whitley (sep EP 1763,[11] eccl refounded 1900,[169] qv). Organisation as for Hexhamshire High Quarter.

HEXHAMSHIRE WEST QUARTER

Tp in Hexam AP, sep CP 1866.[1] Incl undivided pt of Moorland common to the Townships of Hexham (for composition see Hexhamshire High Quarter above). *LG* Tyned. Wd, Hexham PLU, RSD, RD. Bdry: 1883,[4] 1935.[34] Abol 1955 pt to Haydon CP, pt to Hexhamshire Low Quarter CP, pt to help cr Hexhamshire CP.[37] *Parl* S'rn Dv (1867—85), Hexham Dv/CC (1885—1970).

HIGHAM DYKES

Tp in Ponteland AP, sep CP 1866.[1] *LG* Castle Wd, Castle Wd PLU, RSD, RD. Abol 1955 ent to Ponteland AP.[54] *Parl* S'rn Dv (1867—85), Wansb. Dv (1885—1948), Hexham CC (1948—70).

HIGHLAWS

Tp in Hartburn AP, sep CP 1866.[1] *LG* Morp. Wd, PLU, RSD, RD. Abol 1955 ent to Wallington Demesne CP.[28] *Parl* N'rn Dv (1867—85), Wansb. Dv (1885—1948), Morp. CC (1948—*).

HIGH AND LOW HIGHLAWS

Tp in Mitford AP, sep CP 1866.[1] *LG* Morp. Wd, PLU, RSD, RD. Bdry: 1935.[34] Abol 1955 ent to Hebron CP.[28] *Parl* N'rn Dv (1867—85), Wansb. Dv (1885—1948), Morp. CC (1948—70).

HIRST

Tp in Woodhorn AP, sep CP 1866.[1] *LG* Morp. Wd, PLU, RSD, RD (1894—96), Ashington UD (1896—1914). Bdry: 1900,[171] 1909.[172] Abol 1914 ent to Ashington CP.[33] *Parl* N'rn Dv (1867—85), Wansb. Dv (1885—1918).

HOLLINGHILL

Tp in Rothbury AP, sep CP 1866.[1] *LG* Seq 8. Bdry: 1889,[15] 1955 (gains Fallowlees CP, Greenleighton CP, Harwood CP).[16] *Parl* Seq 2.

HOLY ISLAND

AP Incl chap Lowick (in Northumb, sep civ identity early, sep EP 1732[11]), remainder of par incl chaps in Durham, transf to Northumb 1832 for parl purposes, 1844 for civ purposes.[25] Incl orig in Durham chap Ancroft (sep civ identity early, sep EP 1733[11]), chap Kyloe (sep civ identity early, sep EP 1738[11]), chap Tweedmouth (sep civ identity early, sep EP 1737[11]). *LG* Islandshire, Holy Island Bor (status not sustained), Berw. PLU, RSD, Norham & Islandshires RD. Addtl civ bdry alt: 1880,[173] 1888.[26] *Parl* In 2 cos until 1832 (as noted above), Seq 1 thereafter. *Eccl* Seq 5.

HOLYSTONE

AP Orig sep AP appropriated to Holystone Nunnery, from Dissolution held with Alwinton (similarly appropriated) eccl as 'Alwinton with Holystone',[20] qv, sep civ identity regained early. Gains 1312 Corsenside AP (sep civ identity regained early, sep eccl status regained 1728[122]). *LG* Coq. Wd, Rothb. PLU, RSD, RD. Addtl civ bdry alt: 1883,[4] 1883,[46] 1889.[141] Abol 1955 ent to Harbottle CP.[16] *Parl* N'rn Dv (1867—85), Hexham Dv (1885—1918), Berw. upon Tweed Dv/CC (1918—70).

HOLYWELL

Tp in Earsdon AP, sep CP 1866.[1] *LG* Castle Wd, Tynem. PLU, RSD, RD (1894—97), Earsdon UD (1897—1935). Abol 1935 to help cr Seaton Valley UD & CP.[34] *Parl* S'rn Dv (1867—85), Wansb. Dv (1885—1948).

HOPPEN

Tp in Bamburgh AP, sep CP 1866,[1] eccl severed 1884 to help refound Lucker EP.[7] *LG* Bamb. Wd, Belf. PLU, RSD. Abol 1887 ent to Lucker CP.[174] *Parl* N'rn Dv (1867—85), Berw. upon Tweed Dv (1885—1918).

HORNCLIFFE

In Durham, transf to Northumb 1832 for parl purposes, 1844 for parl purposes.[25] Tp in Norham AP, sep CP 1866.[1] *LG* Seq 14. Bdry: 1955 (gains Loanend CP, Longridge CP, Norham Mains CP).[139] *Parl* In Durham until 1832, Seq 1 thereafter.

HORSLEY

Tp in Ovingham AP, sep CP 1866,[1] eccl severed 1902 to help cr Wylam EP.[175] *LG* Seq 18. Bdry: 1955 (gains Nafferton CP, Spital CP, Welton CP, Whittle CP).[5] *Parl* Seq 5.

HORSLEY

EP Cr 1883 from Elsdon AP.[145] Rothb. RDn. Abol 1940 to help cr Horsley with Byrness EP.[103]

HORSLEY MOOR

Orig common to Bothal AP, Long Horsley AP, since cr 1866 as CPs of tps Bigge's Quarter, Freeholders' Quarter, Riddell's Quarter from Long Horsley AP and cr 1866 of Fenrother CP from Bothal AP, common to the 4 new CPs. *LG* Morp. PLU, RD. Abol 1955 to help cr Longhorsley CP.[28] *Parl* Wansb. Dv (1918—48), Morp. CC (1948—70).

HORSLEY WITH BYRNESS

EP Cr 1940 by union Byrness EP, Horsley EP.[103] Rothb. RDn.

LONG HORSLEY

AP Usual civ spelling; for eccl see 'Longhorsley'. Incl tps Bigge's Quarter, Freeholders' Quarter, pt Longshaws, Riddell's Quarter, Stanton, Todburn, Wingates, Witton Shields (each a sep CP 1866,[1] so that after 1866 'Long Horsley' has no sep civ identity). Incl undivided pt Morsley Moor (common to Bothal AP and Long Horsley AP; see Horsley Moor for pars to which area common after 1866), undivided pt Long Horsley Common (see Long Horsley Common for pars to which area common after 1866). *LG* Morp. Wd. *Parl* N'rn Dv (1832—67).

LONG HORSLEY COMMON

Orig in Long Horsley AP, since cr 1866 as CPs of tps Bigge's Quarter, Freeholders' Quarter, Riddell's Quarter from Long Horsley AP, common to

those 3 CPs. *LG* Morp. PLU, RD. Abol 1955 to help cr Longhorsley CP.[28] *Parl* as for Horsley Moor.

HORTON

Chap in Woodhorn AP, sep civ identity early, sep EP 1734.[11] Incl tps Bebside, East Hartford, West Hartford (each a sep CP 1866[1]); tp Cowpen (sep CP 1866,[1] the pt [incl the church at Cowpen] cr 1896 'Blyth St Mary' EP[78]). *LG* Castle Wd, Tynem. PLU, RSD, RD (1894—1912), Blyth UD (1912—20). Addtl civ bdry alt: 1912 (loses pt to help cr Blyth CP, pt transf to help constitute Seaton Delaval UD and added to Seaton Delaval CP, pt to East Hartford CP).[94] Abol 1920 to help cr Blyth CP.[48] *Parl* S'rn Dv (1867—85), Wansb. Dv (1885—1918), Morp. Parl Bor (1918—48). *Eccl* Morp. RDn (1734—1874), Newc upon Tyne RDn (N'rn Dv) (1874—77), Newc upon Tyne RDn (E'rn Dv) (1877—84), Bedl. RDn (1884—*). Addtl eccl bdry alt: 1883 (help cr Blyth St Cuthbert EP),[77] 1957 (cr Newsham EP).[176]

HORTON GRANGE

Tp in Dinnington AP, sep CP 1866.[1] *LG* Castle Wd, Castle Wd PLU, RSD, RD. Abol 1955 pt to Dinnington AP, pt to Stannington AP.[54] *Parl* S'rn Dv (1867—85), Wansb. Dv (1885—1948), Hexham CC (1948—70).

HOUGHTON AND CLOSE HOUSE

Tp in Heddon on the Wall AP, sep CP 1866.[1] *LG* Tyned. Wd, Castle Wd PLU, RSD, RD. Abol 1955 ent to Heddon on the Wall AP.[54] *Parl* S'rn Dv (1867—85), Wansb. Dv (1885—1948), Hexham CC (1948—70).

HOWDEN PANNS

EP Cr 1859 from Wallsend EP (the pt of tp Willington not cr Willington EP).[177] Newc upon Tyne RDn (1859—74), Newc upon Tyne RDn (S'rn Dv) (1874—77), Newc upon Tyne RDn (E'rn Dv) (1877—84), Tynem. RDn (1884—*).

HOWICK

AP *LG* Bamb. Wd, Alnw. PLU, RSD, RD. Abol 1955 ent to Longhoughton AP.[2] *Parl* N'rn Dv (1867—85), Berw. upon Tweed Dv/CC (1885—1970). *Eccl* Newc upon Tyne RDn (until 1845), Alnw. RDn (1845—*).

HOWTEL

Tp in Kirknewton AP, sep CP 1866.[1] *LG* Glend. Wd, PLU, RSD, RD. Abol 1955 ent to Kilham CP.[9] *Parl* N'rn Dv (1867—85), Berw. upon Tweed Dv/CC (1885—1970).

HUMBLETON

Tp in chap Doddington (seemingly sep par 1775 from Chatton AP[111]), 'Humbleton' a sep CP 1866,[1] eccl severed 1882 and transf to Wooler AP.[136] *LG* Glend. Wd, PLU, RSD, RD. Abol 1955 ent to Akeld CP.[9] *Parl* N'rn Dv (1867—85), Berw. upon Tweed Dv/CC (1885—1970).

HUMSHAUGH

Orig tp in Simonburn, made chap in same par 1811,[52] sep CP 1866,[1] sep EP 1832,[178] eccl refounded 1900 from Simonburn AP (tp Humshaugh, tp Black Carts and Ryehill, tp Haughton, pt tp Walwick [the last 2 with no sep civ identity]),

Warden AP.[74] *LG* Seq 18. Civ bdry: 1955 (incl gains Black Carts and Ryehill CP, pt Haughton CP, pt Warden CP).[37] *Parl* Seq 5. *Eccl* Corbr. RDn (1832—45), Bell. RDn (1845—*).

ILDERTON

AP Incl tps North Middleton, South Middleton, Middleton Hall, Roddam, Roseden (each a sep CP 1866[1]). Incl undivided pt of Plea Piece (until 1866, common to Ilderton AP, Eglingham AP; after 1866, common to East Lilburn CP, West Lilburn CP, Ilderton AP, Roseden CP). *LG* Seq 7. Addtl civ bdry alt: 1884,[179] 1955 (gains North Middleton CP, South Middleton CP).[9] *Parl* Seq 1. *Eccl* Seq 4.

INGOE

Tp in Stamfordham AP, sep CP 1866.[1] *LG* Tyned. Wd, Castle Wd PLU, RSD, RD. Abol 1955 pt to Belsay CP, pt to help cr Matfen CP.[54] *Parl* S'rn Dv (1867—85), Hexham Dv/CC (1885—1970).

INGRAM

AP Incl tps Fawdon, Clinch and Hartside; Ingram, Linhope and Greenshawhill; Reaveley (each a sep CP 1866,[1] so that 'Ingram' has no sep civ identity 1866—1955 (see following entry). *LG* Coq. Wd. *Parl* N'rn Dv (1832—67). *Eccl* Alnw. RDn (until 1845), Rothb. RDn (1845—99), Glend. RDn (1899—1969), Bamb. & Glend. RDn (1969—*).

CP Cr 1955 by union Ingram, Linhope, Greenshawhill and Hartside CP; Brandon CP, Branton CP, Fawdon and Clinch CP.[9] *LG* Glend. RD. *Parl* Berw. upon Tweed CC (1970—*).

INGRAM, LINHOPE AND GREENSHAWHILL

Tp in Ingram AP, sep CP 1866.[1] *LG* Coq. Wd, Glend. PLU, RSD. Abol 1884 to help cr Ingram, Linhope, Greenshawhill and Hartside CP.[155] *Parl* N'rn Dv (1867—85).

INGRAM, LINHOPE, GREENSHAWHILL AND HARTSIDE

CP Cr 1884 by union Ingram, Linhope and Greenshawhill CP, area of Hartside from Fawdon, Clinch and Hartside CP.[155] *LG* Coq. Wd, Glend. PLU, RSD, RD. Abol 1955 to help cr Ingram CP.[9] *Parl* Berw. upon Tweed Dv/CC (1885—1970).

INTERMIXED LANDS COMMON TO DEBDON AND SNITTER

Orig in Rothbury AP, after cr 1866 of CPs Debdon, Snitter from Rothbury AP, common as noted above. After abol 1889 of Debdon into Rothbury AP,[132] common to Rothbury and Snitter.

INTERMIXED LANDS COMMON TO ROTHBURY AND SNITTER

Cr 1889 when Debdon CP which incl Intermixed Lands Common to Debdon and Snitter abol into Rothbury AP.[132] *LG* Rothb. PLU, RSD, RD. *Parl* Berw. upon Tweed Dv/CC (1918—*).

JESMOND

Tp in chap Newcastle upon Tyne St Andrew (sep civ identity early from Newcastle upon Tyne AP, sep EP 1808[11]), 'Jesmond' sep civ identity early, sep EP 1861.[11] *LG* Castle Wd, Newc upon Tyne PLU, MB (1835—89), USD, CB (1889—1914). Abol 1914 to help cr Newcastle upon Tyne CP.[62] *Parl* Newc upon Tyne Parl Bor (1832—1918). *Eccl* Newc upon Tyne RDn (1861—74), Newc upon Tyne RDn (S'rn Dv) (1874—77), Newc upon Tyne RDn (W'rn Dv) (1877—84), Newc RDn (1884—1967), Newc Ctrl. RDn (1967—*). Eccl bdry: 1889 (cr Newcastle upon Tyne St George EP),[23] 1892 (help cr Shieldfield St Jude EP),[40] 1908 (cr Newcastle upon Tyne St Barnabas EP),[134] 1926 (help cr Jesmond Holy Trinity EP).[180]

JESMOND HOLY TRINITY

EP Cr 1926 from Jesmond EP, Newcastle upon Tyne St George EP.[180] Newc RDn (1926—67), Newc Ctrl. RDn (1967—*).

KEARSLEY

Tp in Stamfordham AP, sep CP 1866.[1] *LG* Tyned. Wd, Castle Wd PLU, RSD, RD. Abol 1955 to help cr Matfen CP.[54] *Parl* S'rn Dv (1867—85), Hexham Dv/CC (1885—1970).

KENTON

Tp in chap Gosforth (sep civ identity early from Newcastle upon Tyne AP, sep EP 1865[90]), 'Kenton' a sep CP 1866,[1] sep EP 1967 from Gosforth All Saints EP.[163] *LG* Castle Wd, Castle Wd PLU, RSD, RD. Civ bdry: 1904 (loses pt to Newc upon Tyne CB [assoc with Northumb] and to Newcastle St Andrew CP).[181] Abol civ 1935 ent to Newc upon Tyne CB (assoc with Northumb) & CP.[154] *Parl* S'rn Dv (1867—85), Tynes. Dv (1885—1918), Wansb. Dv (1918—48). *Eccl* Newc RDn (1967), Newc Ctrl. RDn (1967—*).

KIDLAND

Ex-par place, sep CP 1858.[119] *LG* Coq. Wd, Rothb. PLU, RSD, RD. Civ bdry: 1889.[15] Abol civ 1955 ent to Alwinton CP.[16] *Parl* N'rn Dv (1867—85), Hexham Dv (1885—1918), Berw. upon Tweed Dv/CC (1918—70).

KIELDER

CP Cr 1955 by union pts Plashetts and Tynehead CP, Wellhaugh CP.[47] *LG* Bell. RD. *Parl* Hexham CC (1970—*).

KILHAM

Tp in Kirknewton AP, sep CP 1866.[1] *LG* Seq 9. Bdry: 1955 (gains Coldsmouth and Thompson's Wall CP, Howtel CP, Paston CP).[9] *Parl* Seq 1.

KILLINGWORTH

EP Cr 1865 from Long Benton AP.[182] Newc upon Tyne RDn (1865—74), Newc upon Tyne RDn N'rn Dv (1874—77), Newc upon Tyne RDn (E'rn Dv) (1877—84), Bedl. RDn (1884—*). Bdry: 1891 (gains tp Burradon from Earsdon EP),[93] 1967,[90] 1968 (help cr Shiremoor EP),[39] 1969 (help cr Dudley EP).[125]

KIRKHARLE

AP Incl tp Hawick (sep CP 1866[1]). *LG* Tyned. Wd, Bell. PLU, RSD, RD. Abol civ 1955 ent to Kirkwhelpington AP.[47] *Parl* S'rn Dv (1867—85), Hexham Dv/CC (1885—1970). *Eccl* Seq 7.

KIRKHAUGH

AP *LG* Tyned. Wd, Haltw. PLU, RSD, RD. Abol 1955 to help cr Slaggyford CP.[45] *Parl* S'rn Dv (1867—85), Hexham Dv/CC (1885—1970). *Eccl* Seq 7.

KIRKHEATON

Priory and considered ex-par after Dissolution, new chapel erected 1753 and considered donative,[118] sep eccl from then, sep CP 1858.[119] *LG* Tyned. Wd,

Castle Wd PLU, RSD, RD. Abol 1955 ent to Capheaton CP.[54] *Parl* S'rn Dv (1867—85), Hexham Dv/CC (1885—1970). *Eccl* Corbr. RDn (1753—1845), Hexham RDn (1845—83), Bell. RDn (1883—*).

KIRKLEY

Tp in Ponteland AP, sep CP 1866.[1] *LG* Castle Wd, Castle Wd PLU, RSD, RD. Abol 1955 ent to Ponteland AP.[54] *Parl* S'rn Dv (1867—85), Wansb. Dv (1885—1948), Hexham CC (1948—70).

KIRKNEWTON

AP Incl tps Akeld, Coldsmouth and Thompson's Walls, Coupland, Crookhouse, Grey's Forest, Hethpool, Howtel, Kilham, Lanton (each a sep CP 1866[1]); also incl undivided pt Undivided Moor (since cr 1866 of Lanton, common to Kirknewton and Lanton); Carham sometimes incorrectly considerd a chap in this par,[109] but a sep AP. *LG* Seq 9. Addtl civ bdry alt: 1955 (gains Crookhouse CP, Grey's Forest CP, Hethpool CP, Westnewton CP, Yeavering CP).[9] *Parl* Seq 1. *Eccl* Seq 4. Eccl bdry: 1957.[82]

KIRKWHELPINGTON

AP Incl tps Great Bavington, Capheaton, Catcherside, Coldwell, Crookdean, Fawns, Little Harle, West Harle, West Whelpington (each a sep CP 1866[1]). *LG* Seq 15. Addtl civ bdry alt: 1955 (gains Catcherside CP, Coldwell CP, Crookdean CP, Fawns CP, Little Harle CP, Kirkharle AP, West Harle CP, West Whelpington CP).[47] *Parl* Seq 5. *Eccl* Morp. RDn (until 1845), Bell. RDn (1845—*).

KNARESDALE

AP Usual eccl spelling; for civ see following entry. *Eccl* Seq 8.

KNARESDALE WITH KIRKHAUGH

CP Renaming 1967 of Slaggyford CP.[183] *LG* Haltw. RD. *Parl* Hexham CC (1970—*).

KNARSDALE

AP Usual civ spelling; for eccl see prev entry. *LG* Tyned. Wd, Haltw. PLU, RSD, RD. Abol civ 1955 to help cr Slaggyford CP.[45] *Parl* S'rn Dv (1832—85), Hexham Dv/CC (1885—1970).

KYLOE

Chap in Holy Island AP in co Durham, sep civ identity early in that co, sep EP 1738,[11] the par transf to Northumb 1832 for parl purposes, 1844 for civ purposes.[25] *LG* Islandshire, Berw. PLU, RSD, Norham & Islandshires RD. Civ bdry: 1880.[173] *Parl* In Durham until 1832, Seq 1 thereafter. *Eccl* Bamb. RDn (1738—1845), Norham RDn (1845—*).

LAMBLEY

AP Orig sep AP, approrpiated, in ruins after Dissolution until rebuilt 1885, prev considered a Donative.[184] *LG* Tyned. Wd, Haltw. PLU, RSD, RD. Abol 1955 ent to Coanwood CP.[45] *Parl* S'rn Dv (1867—85), Hexham Dv/CC (1885—1970). *Eccl* Hexham RDn.

LANTON

Tp in Kirknewton AP, sep CP 1866.[1] Incl undivided pt Undivided Moor (common to Kirknewton and Lanton). *LG* Glend. Wd, PLU, RSD, RD. Abol 1955 ent to Ewart CP.[9] *Parl* N'rn Dv (1867—85), Berw. upon Tweed Dv (1885—1970).

LEARCHILD

Tp in Edlingham AP, sep CP 1866.[1] *LG* Coq. Wd, Alnw. PLU, RSD, RD. Abol 1955 ent to Edlingham AP.[2] *Parl* N'rn Dv (1867—85), Berw. upon Tweed Dv/CC (1885—1970).

LEE ST JOHN

AP Pt Co Palatine of Hexhamshire, merged 1572 into Northumb.[10] Usual civ spelling; for eccl see 'St John Lee'. Incl tps West Acomb, Anick, Anick Grange, Sandhoe (each a sep CP 1866[1]); area St Oswald in Lee (sep EP 1733,[11] eccl refounded 1879 as noted below); tp Bingfield (sep CP 1866,[1] sep EP 1740 as 'Bingfield St Mary'[11]); incl tps Cocklaw, Fallowfield, Hallington, Portgate, Wall (each a sep CP 1866,[1] eccl united 1879 with Bingfield St Mary EP, St Oswald in Lee EP to cr St Oswald in Lee with Bingfield St Mary EP,[70] the new par eccl divided 1888 into 2 EPs of Bingfield St Mary [tps Bingfield, Hallington, Portgate, greater pt of Cocklaw], St Oswald in Lee [the remainder][71]). After cr of all CPs, 'Lee St John' has no further civ identity. *LG* Tyned. Wd. *Parl* S'rn Dv (1832—67).

LEE WARD

Tp in Rothbury AP, sep CP 1866.[1] *LG* Coq. Wd, Rothb. PLU, RSD. Abol 1889 pt to Raw CP, pt to Hesleyhurst CP.[167] *Parl* N'rn Dv (1867—85), Hexham Dv (1885—1918).

LEEMAILING

Tp in chap Bellingham (sep par 1811 from Simonburn AP[52]), 'Leemailing' a sep CP 1866.[1] *LG* Tyned. Wd, Bell. PLU, RSD. Abol 1886 ent to Bellingham CP.[53] *Parl* S'rn Dv (1867—85), Hexham Dv (1885—1918).

LEMMINGTON

Tp in Edlingham AP, sep CP 1866.[1] *LG* Coq. Wd, Alnw. PLU, RSD, RD. Abol 1955 ent to Edlingham AP.[2] *Parl* N'rn Dv (1867—85), Berw. upon Tweed Dv/CC (1885—1970).

LESBURY

AP Incl chap Longhoughton (appropriated to Alnwick Abbey, sep par at Dissolution[185]), chap Alnmouth (sep CP 1866,[1] sep EP 1877[17]). *LG* Seq 1. Addtl civ bdry alt: 1888.[6] *Parl* Seq 1. *Eccl* Seq 3.

LILBURN

CP Cr 1955 by union East Lilburn CP, West Lilburn CP, Newtown CP, Plea Piece (common to East Lilburn CP, West Lilburn CP, Ilderton AP, Roseden CP).[9] *LG* Glend. RD. *Parl* Berw. upon Tweed CC (1970—*).

EAST LILBURN

Tp in Eglingham AP, sep CP 1866.[1] Incl undivided pt Plea Piece (1866—1955, common to East Lilburn CP, West Lilburn CP, Ilderton AP, Roseden CP). *LG* Coq. Wd, Glend. PLU, RSD, RD. Abol 1955 to help cr Lilburn CP.[9] *Parl* N'rn Dv (1867—85), Berw. upon Tweed Dv/CC (1885—1970).

WEST LILBURN

Tp in Eglingham AP, sep CP 1866.[1] Organisation as for East Lilburn.

LINBRIDGE

Tp in Alwinton AP, sep CP 1866.[1] *LG* Coq. Wd, Rothb. PLU, RSD, RD. Bdry: 1883,[4] 1889.[15] Abol

1955 ent to Alwinton AP.[16] *Parl* N'rn Dv (1867—85), Hexham Dv (1885—1918), Berw. upon Tweed Dv/CC (1918—70).

LINSHEELES

Tp in Alwinton AP, sep CP 1866.[1] *LG* Coq. Wd, Rothb. PLU, RSD, RD. Bdry: 1883.[21] Abol 1955 ent to Alwinton AP.[16] *Parl* N'rn Dv (1867—85), Hexham Dv (1885—1918), Berw. upon Tweed Dv/CC (1918—70).

LITTLEHOUGHTON

Tp in chap Longhoughton (appropriated to Alnwick Abbey, sep par at Dissolution[185]), 'Littlehoughton' a sep CP 1866.[1] *LG* Coq. Wd, Alnw. PLU, RSD, RD. Abol 1955 ent to Longhoughton AP.[2] *Parl* N'rn Dv (1867—85), Berw. upon Tweed Dv/CC (1885—1970).

LOANEND

In co Durham, transf to Northumb 1832 for parl purposes, 1844 for civ purposes.[25] Tp in Norham AP, sep CP 1866.[1] *LG* Norhamshire, Berw. PLU, RSD, Norham & Islandshires RD. Abol 1955 ent to Horncliffe CP.[139] *Parl* In Durham until 1832, thereafter N'rn Dv (1832—85), Berw. upon Tweed Dv/CC (1885—1970).

LONGBENTON

AP Usual civ spelling; for eccl see 'Long Benton'. *LG* Castle Wd, Tynem. PLU, pt Walker USD, pt Weetslade USD, pt Tynem. RSD, Tynem. RD (1894—1912), Longbenton UD (1912—74). Civ bdry: 1894 (the pt in Weetslade USD cr Weetslade CP, the pt in Walker USD cr Walker CP),[186] 1899 (help cr Camperdown CP),[108] 1904,[181] 1910,[187] 1912 (gains Burradon CP, Camperdown CP as enlarged area constituted Longbenton UD),[94] 1935 (gains Weetslade UD & CP, loses pt to Newc upon Tyne CB [assoc with Northumb] & CP).[34] Transf 1974 to Tyne & Wear.[89] *Parl* S'rn Dv (1832—85), Tynes. Dv (1885—1918), Wallsend Parl Bor (1918—*).

LONGFRAMLINGTON

Chap in Felton AP, sep CP 1866,[1] sep EP 1891.[157] *LG* Seq 8. *Parl* Seq 2. *Eccl* Alnw. RDn (1891—99), Rothb. RDn (1899—*).

LONGHIRST

Tp in Bothal AP, sep CP 1866,[1] sep EP 1876 by union tp Longhirst, pt tp Old Moor in Bothal AP.[80] *LG* Seq 10. Civ bdry: 1955 (gains Old Moor CP).[28] *Parl* Seq 4. *Eccl* Morp. RDn.

LONGHORSLEY

CP Cr 1955 by union Bigge's Quarter CP, Freeholders' Quarter CP, Riddell's Quarter CP, Long Horsley Common (common to Bigge's Quarter CP, Freeholders' Quarter CP, Riddell's Quarter CP), Horsley Moor (common to Bigge's Quarter CP, Freeholders' Quarter CP, Fenrother CP, Riddell's Quarter CP).[28] *LG* Morp. RD. *Parl* Morp. CC (1970—*).

LONGHOUGHTON

AP Chap in Lesbury AP, appropriated to Alnwick Abbey, sep par at Dissolution.[185] Incl tps Boulmer and Seaton House, Littlehoughton (each a sep CP 1866[1]). *LG* Seq 1. Addtl civ bdry alt: 1888 (gains Boulmer and Seaton House CP),[81] 1955 (gains

Howick AP, Littlehoughton CP).[2] *Parl* Seq 1. *Eccl* Seq 3.

LONGRIDGE

In Durham, transf to Northumb 1832 for parl purposes, 1844 for civ purposes.[25] Tp in Norham AP, sep CP 1866.[1] *LG* Norhamshire, Berw. PLU, RSD, Norham & Islandshires RD. Abol 1955 ent to Horncliffe CP.[139] *Parl* In Durham until 1832, N'rn Dv (1832—85), Berw. upon Tweed Dv/CC (1885—1970).

LONGSHAWS

Tp pt in Long Horsley AP, pt in Hartburn AP, sep CP 1866.[1] *LG* Morp. Wd, PLU, RSD, RD. Abol 1955 ent to Meldon AP.[28] *Parl* N'rn Dv (1867—85), Wansb. Dv (1885—1948), Morp. CC (1948—70).

LONGWITTON

Tp in Hartburn AP, sep CP 1866.[1] *LG* Morp. Wd, PLU, RSD, RD. Abol 1955 ent to Netherwitton CP.[28] *Parl* N'rn Dv (1867—85), Wansb. Dv (1885—1948), Morp. CC (1948—70).

LORBOTTLE

Tp in Whittingham AP, sep CP 1866.[1] *LG* Coq. Wd, Rothb. PLU, RSD, RD. Abol 1955 to help cr Callaly CP.[16] *Parl* N'rn Dv (1867—85), Berw. upon Tweed Dv/CC (1885—1970).

LOWICK

Chap in Holy Island AP, sep civ identity early, sep EP 1732.[11] *LG* Seq 9. Civ bdry: 1955 (cr Bowsden CP).[9] *Parl* Seq 1. *Eccl* Bamb. RDn (1732—1845), Norham RDn (1845—*). Eccl bdry: 1899.[112]

LUCKER

Chap in Bamburgh AP, sep CP 1866,[1] sep EP 1766,[11] eccl refounded 1884 by union Lucker EP and 8 tps in Bamburgh AP: Adderstone, Hoppen, Mousen, Newham, Newstead, Ratchwood, Warenford, Warenton.[7] *LG* Bamb. Wd, Belf. PLU, RSD, RD. Civ bdry: 1887 (incl gains Hoppen CP).[174] *Parl* Seq 1. *Eccl* Bamb. RDn (1766—1969), Bamb. & Glend. RDn (1969—*).

LYNEMOUTH

Tp in Woodhorn AP, sep CP 1866,[1] sep EP 1963 as 'Lynmouth',[188] qv. *LG* Seq 10. *Parl* Seq 4.

LYNMOUTH

Tp in Woodhorn AP, sep EP 1963,[188] sep CP 1866 as 'Lynemouth',[1] qv. *Eccl* Morp. RDn. Abol eccl 1971 to help cr Cresswell and Lynemouth EP.[128]

MASON

Tp in tp Dinnington (sep par 1811 from Simonburn AP[52]), 'Mason' a sep CP 1866.[1] *LG* Castle Wd, Castle Wd PLU, RSD, RD. Bdry: 1883.[4] Abol 1955 pt to help cr Brunswick CP, pt to Dinnington CP.[54] *Parl* S'rn Dv (1867—85), Wansb. Dv (1885—1948), Hexham CC (1948—70).

MASTERS CLOSE

Ex-par place, sep CP 1858,[119] eccl united 1866 with tp Mickley in Ovingham AP to cr Mickley CP.[189] *LG* Tyned. Wd, Hexham PLU (1858—87), RSD. Abol 1887 ent to Prudhoe Castle CP.[190] *Parl* S'rn Dv (1867—85), Hexham Dv (1885—1918).

MATFEN

EP Cr 1846 from Stamfordham AP[140]; for civ see 'East Matfen', 'West Matfen'. Corbr. RDn.

CP Cr 1955 by union Fenwick CP, Kearsley CP, East Matfen CP, West Matfen CP, Ryal CP, pt Ingoe CP.[54] *LG* Castle Wd RD. *Parl* Hexham CC (1970—*).

EAST MATFEN

Tp in Stamfordham AP, sep CP 1866 [1]; for eccl see Matfen. *LG* Tyned. Wd, Castle Wd PLU, RSD, RD. Bdry: 1883.[4] Abol 1955 to help cr Matfen CP.[54] *Parl* S'rn Dv (1867—85), Hexham Dv/CC (1885—1970).

WEST MATFEN

Tp in Stamfordham AP, sep CP 1866 [1]; for eccl see Matfen. Organisation as for East Matfen, except no civ bdry alt.

MELDON

AP *LG* Seq 4. Civ bdry: 1955 (gains Longshaws CP, Molesdon CP, Newton Park CP, Newton Underwood CP, Nunriding CP, Pigdon CP, Rivergreen CP, Throphill CP.[28] *Parl* Seq 9. *Eccl* Morp. RDn. Abol eccl 1939 to help cr Hartburn with Meldon EP.[50]

MELKRIDGE

Tp in Haltwhistle AP, sep CP 1866.[1] *LG* Seq 17. Bdry: 1883.[4] *Parl* Seq 5.

MICKLEY

Tp in Ovingham AP, sep CP 1866,[1] sep EP 1727,[11] eccl refounded 1866 (incl gains ex-par Masters Close).[189] *LG* Tyned. Wd, Hexham PLU, RSD, RD (1894—1910), Prudhoe UD (1910—74). Civ bdry: 1883,[4] 1887,[86] 1887.[190] *Parl* Seq 5. *Eccl* Corbr. RDn. Eccl bdry: 1881 (cr Prudhoe EP),[122] 1921,[123] 1931,[19] 1967.[105]

MIDDLETON

Tp in Belford AP, sep CP 1866.[1] *LG* Seq 2. Bdry: 1955 (gains Detchant CP, Elwick CP, Ross CP).[8] *Parl* Seq 1.

NORTH MIDDLETON

Tp in Hartburn AP, sep CP 1866.[1] *LG* Morp. Wd, PLU, RSD, RD. Abol 1955 ent to Wallington Demesne CP.[28] *Parl* N'rn Dv (1867—85), Wansb. Dv (1885—1948), Morp. CC (1948—70).

NORTH MIDDLETON

Tp in Ilderton AP, sep CP 1866.[1] *LG* Coq. Wd, Glend. PLU, RSD, RD. Abol 1955 ent to Ilderton AP.[9] *Parl* N'rn Dv (1867—85), Berw. upon Tweed Dv/CC (1885—1970).

SOUTH MIDDLETON

Tp in Hartburn AP, sep CP 1866.[1] Organisation as for first North Middleton above.

SOUTH MIDDLETON

Tp in Ilderton AP, sep CP 1866.[1] Organisation as for second North Middleton above.

MIDDLETON HALL

Tp in Ilderton AP, sep CP 1866.[1] *LG* Coq. Wd, Glend. PLU, RSD, RD. Abol 1955 ent to Earle CP.[9] *Parl* N'rn Dv (1867—85), Berw. upon Tweed Dv/CC (1885—1970).

MILBOURNE

Tp in Ponteland AP, sep CP 1866.[1] *LG* Castle Wd, Castle Wd PLU, RSD, RD. Abol 1955 ent to Ponteland AP.[54] *Parl* S'rn Dv (1867—85), Wansb. Dv (1885—1948), Hexham CC (1948—70).

MILBOURNE GRANGE

Tp in Ponteland AP, sep CP 1866.[1] Organisation as for Milbourne.

MILFIELD

Tp in Kirknewton AP, sep CP 1866.[1] *LG* Seq 9. *Parl* Seq 1.

MITFORD

AP Incl tps Edington, Molesden (each Castle Wd, each a sep CP 1866[1]), tps Benridge, High and Low Highlaws, Newton Park, Newton Underwood, Nunriding, Pigdon, Spital Hill, Throphill (each Morp. Wd, each a sep CP 1866[1]). *LG* Mitford Bor (status not sustained), Seq 10. Addtl civ bdry alt: 1955 (gains Edlington CP, Spital Hill CP, Tranwell CP).[28] *Parl* Seq 4. *Eccl* Newc upon Tyne RDn (until 1845), Morp. RDn (1845—*).

MOLESDON

Tp in Mitford AP, sep CP 1866.[1] *LG* Castle Wd, Morp. PLU, RSD, RD. Abol 1955 ent to Meldon AP.[28] *Parl* N'rn Dv (1867—85), Wansb. Dv (1885—1948), Morp. CC (1948—70).

MONKRIDGE

Tp in Elsdon AP, sep CP 1866.[1] *LG* Coq. Wd, Rothb. PLU, RSD, RD. Abol 1955 ent to Elsdon AP.[16] *Parl* N'rn Dv (1867—85), Hexham Dv (1885—1918), Berw. upon Tweed Dv/CC (1918—70).

MONKS HOUSE

In Durham, transf to Northumb 1832 for parl purposes, 1844 for civ purposes.[25] Ex-par place, sep CP 1858.[119] *LG* Bamb. Wd, Belf. PLU (1865—1930), RSD, RD. Abol 1955 ent to North Sunderland CP.[8] *Parl* In Durham until 1832, N'rn Dv (1832—85), Berw. upon Tweed Dv/CC (1885—1970).

MONKSEATON

Tp in Tynemouth AP, sep CP 1866,[1] eccl severed 1860, the pt in Shiremoor to help cr Tynemouth Percy EP, the remainder to help cr Cullercoats EP.[19] *LG* Castle Wd, Tynem. PLU, Whitley & Monkseaton USD, UD (1894—1913). Bdry: 1881,[191] 1883,[11] 1912.[94] Abol 1913 to help cr Whitley and Monkseaton CP.[192] *Parl* S'rn Dv (1867—85), Wansb. Dv (1885—1918).

MONKSEATON ST MARY

EP Cr 1927 from Cullercoats EP.[130] Tynem. RDn. Bdry: 1962.[127]

MONKSEATON ST PETER

EP Name used now for EP cr 1860 as 'Tynemouth St Peter' from Tynemouth AP.[193] Newc upon Tyne RDn (1860—74), Newc upon Tyne RDn (N'rn Dv) (1860—74), Newc upon Tyne RDn (E'rn Dv) (1874—77), Newc upon Tyne RDn (E'rn Dv) (1877—84), Tynem. RDn (1884—*). Bdry: 1968.[39]

MOORLAND COMMON TO THE TOWNSHIPS OF HEXHAM (HEXHAM AP, HEXHAMSHIRE HIGH QUARTER CP, HEXHAMSHIRE LOW QUARTER CP, HEXHAMSHIRE MIDDLE QUARTER CP, HEXHAMSHIRE WEST QUARTER CP)

Since cr 1866 of 4 named CPs from Hexham AP, common to the 5. *LG* Pt Hexham UD, pt Hexham RD. Abol 1955 to help cr Hexhamshire CP.[5] *Parl* Hexham Dv/CC (1918—70).

MOOT HALL PRECINCTS

CP Cr 1884 from Newcastle upon Tyne St Nicholas AP.[194] *LG* Not in a PLU or RD until 1935, Newc upon Tyne RD (1935—*). Transf 1974 to Tyne & Wear.[89] *Parl* Wansb. Dv (1918—48), Newc upon Tyne Ctrl. BC (1948—*).

MORPETH

AP Tp 'Morpeth' in Morp. Wd as was chap Ulgham (sep CP 1866,[1] sep EP 1875[195]), tp Bullers Green (sep CP 1866[1]); incl in Castle Wd tps Hepscott, Morpeth Castle, Newminster Abbey, Shilvington, Tranwell and High Church, Twizell (each a sep CP 1866[1]). *LG* Morp. PLU, MB (pt 1835—94, ent 1894—1974), Morp. USD (ent 1875—89, pt 1889—94), pt Morp. RSD (1889—94). Addtl civ bdry alt: 1888,[91] 1894 (the pt not in the MB cr Newminster CP, gains the pts in Morp. MB of Morpeth Castle CP, Newminster Abbey CP, Tranwell and High Church CP),[196] 1935,[34] 1965.[166] *Parl* Morp. Parl Bor (pt 1553—1832, ent 1832—1948), Morp. CC (1948—*). *Eccl* Seq 9.

MORPETH CASTLE

Tp in Morpeth AP, sep CP 1866.[1] *LG* Castle Wd, Morp. PLU, pt Morp. MB (1889—94), Morp. USD (ent 1875—89, pt 1889—94), pt Morp. RSD (1888—94), Morp. RD. Bdry: 1894 (loses the pt in the MB to Morpeth AP).[196] Abol 1935 pt to Morp. MB & AP, pt to Hepscott CP.[154] *Parl* Morp. Parl Bor (1832—1948).

MORWICK

Tp in Warkworth AP, sep CP 1866.[1] *LG* Morp. Wd, Alnw. PLU, RSD, RD. Abol 1955 ent to Warkworth AP.[2] *Parl* N'rn Dv (1867—85), Wansb. Dv (1885—1948), Morp. CC (1948—70).

MOUNT HEALEY

Tp in Rothbury AP, sep CP 1866.[1] *LG* Coq. Wd, Rothb. PLU, RSD, RD. Bdry: 1883,[4] 1896.[133] Abol 1955 ent to Cartington CP.[16] *Parl* N'rn Dv (1867—85), Hexham Dv (1885—1918), Berw. upon Tweed Dv/CC (1918—70).

MOUSEN

Tp in Bamburgh AP, sep CP 1866,[1] eccl severed 1884 to help refound Lucker EP.[7] *LG* Bamb. Wd, Belf. PLU, RSD, RD. Abol 1955 ent to Belford AP.[8] *Parl* N'rn Dv (1867—85), Berw. upon Tweed Dv/CC (1885—1970).

MURTON

Tp in Tynemouth AP, sep CP 1866,[1] eccl severed 1860 to help cr Tynemouth Percy EP.[19] Sometimes 'Moortown'. *LG* Castle Wd, Tynem. PLU, pt Tynem. MB (1881—89), pt Tynem. CB (1889—94), Tynem. RSD (ent 1875—81, pt 1881—94), Tynem. RD (1894—97), Earsdon UD (1897—1935). Bdry: 1881,[115] 1894 (loses the pt in the CB which becomes 'Unnamed' CP).[194] Abol 1935 pt to Tynem. CB & CP, pt to help cr Seaton Valley UD & CP, pt to Whitley & Monkseaton UD & CP.[34] *Parl* S'rn Dv (1867—85), Wansb. Dv (1885—1948).

NAFFERTON

Tp in Ovingham AP, sep CP 1866.[1] *LG* Tyned. Wd, Hexham PLU, RSD, RD. Bdry: 1887.[36] Abol 1955 ent to Horsley CP.[37] *Parl* S'rn Dv (1867—85), Hexham Dv/CC (1885—1970).

NESBIT

Tp in chap Doddington (seemingly sep par 1775 from Chatton AP[111]), 'Nesbit' a sep CP 1866.[1] *LG* Glend. Wd, PLU, RSD, RD. Bdry: 1884.[197] Abol 1955 ent to Doddington CP.[9] *Parl* N'rn Dv (1867—85), Berw. upon Tweed Dv/CC (1885—1970).

NESBITT

Tp in Stamfordham AP, sep CP 1866.[1] *LG* Tyned. Wd, Castle Wd PLU, RSD, RD. Abol 1955 to help cr Stamfordham CP.[54] *Parl* S'rn Dv (1867—85), Hexham Dv/CC (1885—1970).

NETHERTON

CP Cr 1955 by union Burradon CP, Netherton North Side CP, Netherton South Side CP, High and Low Trewhitt CP.[16] *LG* Rothb. RD. *Parl* Berw. upon Tweed CC (1970—*).

NETHERTON NORTH SIDE

Tp in Alwinton AP, sep CP 1866.[1] *LG* Coq. Wd, Rothb. PLU, RSD, RD. Abol 1955 to help cr Netherton CP.[16] *Parl* N'rn Dv (1867—85), Hexham Dv (1885—1918), Berw. upon Tweed Dv/CC (1918—70).

NETHERTON SOUTH SIDE

Tp in Alwinton AP, sep CP 1866.[1] Organisation as for Netherton North Side.

NETHERWITTON

Chap in Hartburn AP, sep CP 1866,[1] sep EP 1835.[11] Incl tps Coatyards, Ewesley, Healey and Combhill, Nunnykirk, Ritton Colt Park, Ritton White House (each a sep CP 1866,[1] the area of each incl in Netherwitton EP). *LG* Seq 10. Civ bdry: 1955 (gains Longwitton CP, Stanton CP, Whitridge CP, Witton Shields CP).[28] *Parl* Seq 4. *Eccl* Morp. RDn.

NEWBIGGIN

Tp in Newburn AP, sep CP 1866.[1] *LG* Castle Wd, Castle Wd PLU, RSD, RD. Abol 1955 ent to Woolsington CP.[54] *Parl* S'rn Dv (1867—85), Tynes. Dv (1885—1918), Wansb. Dv (1918—48), Hexham CC (1948—70).

NEWBIGGIN

Tp in Shotley AP, sep CP 1866.[1] *LG* Tyned Wd, Hexham PLU, RSD. Abol 1887 ent to Shotley High Quarter CP (sometimes 'Blanchland').[198] *Parl* S'rn Dv (1867—85), Hexham Dv (1885—1918).

NEWBIGGIN BY THE SEA

Tp and bor (status not sustained) in Woodhorn AP, sep CP 1866.[1] *LG* Morp. Wd, PLU, Newbiggin by the Sea USD, UD. Bdry: 1910,[199] 1921,[200] 1935 (incl gains North Seaton CP).[34] *Parl* N'rn Dv (1867—85), Wansb. Dv (1885—1948), Morp. CC (1948—*).

NEWBROUGH

Chap and bor (status not sustained) in Warden AP, sep CP 1866.[1] *LG* Seq 18. Bdry: 1955.[5] *Parl* Seq 5.

NEWBURN

AP Tp 'Newburn' in Castle Wd as were tps Black Callerton, Buttlerlaw, East Denton, West Denton, North Dissington, South Dissington, Newbiggin, Newburn Hall, Throckley, Wallbottle, pt tp High Callerton (each a sep CP 1866[1]), tp Sugley (sep CP 1866,[1] sep EP 1887[201]), tp Whorlton (sep CP 1866,[1] sep EP 1900 [incl pt Sugley EP][202]); incl in

Tyned. Wd tp Dalton (sep CP 1866[1]). *LG* Newburn Bor (status not sustained), Castle Wd PLU, RSD (1875—93), Newburn USD (1893—94), UD. Addtl civ bdry alt: 1887,[153] 1935 (incl gains East Denton CP, West Denton CP, Newburn Hall CP, Sugley CP, Throckley CP, Wallbottle CP).[34] Transf 1974 to Tyne & Wear.[89] *Parl* S'rn Dv (1867—85), Tynes. Dv (1885—1918), Wansb. Dv (1918—48), Newc upon Tyne West BC (1948—*). *Eccl* Morp. RDn (until 1845), Newc upon Tyne RDn (1845—74), Newc upon Tyne RDn (S'rn Dv) (1874—77), Newc upon Tyne RDn (W'rn Dv) (1877—84), Newc upon Tyne RDn (1884—1967), Newc West RDn (1967—*).

NEWBURN HALL

Tp in Newburn AP, sep CP 1866.[1] *LG* Castle Wd, Castle Wd PLU, RSD (1875—93), Newburn USD (1893—94), UD (1894—1935). Bdry: 1887.[153] Abol 1935 ent to Newburn AP.[34] *Parl* S'rn Dv (1867—85), Tynes. Dv (1885—1918), Wansb. Dv (1918—48).

NEWCASTLE UPON TYNE

The following have 'Newcastle upon Tyne' in their names. Insofar as any existed at a given time: Newc upon Tyne Co of Itself (from 1400), Bor/MB/CB, PLU, USD. *Parl* Newc upon Tyne Parl Bor (1295—1918); divided (1918—*) into 4 Parl Bors/BCs of Newc upon Tyne Ctrl, Newc upon Tyne East, Newc upon Tyne North, Newc upon Tyne West, for which see Part III of the *Guide*. *Eccl* Unless noted noted otherwise, Newc upon Tyne RDn (until 1874), Newc upon Tyne RDn (S'rn Dv) (1874—77), Newc upon Tyne RDn (W'rn Dv) (1877—84), Newc RDn (1884—1967), Newc Ctrl RDn (1967—*).

AP1—NEWCASTLE UPON TYNE [ST NICHOLAS]—Usually cited without dedication until many chaps gain sep civ identity, thereafter usually 'Newcastle upon Tyne St Nicholas' for both civ and eccl purposes. Incl chap Gosforth (sep civ identity early, sep EP 1865[90]), chap Cramlington (sep CP 1866,[1] sep EP 1742[11]), chap CP2/EP1 (sep civ identity early [comprised of tps Byker, Heaton; see CP2 below], sep EP 1808[11]), chap CP3/EP4 (sep civ identity early [comprised of tps Fenham, Jesmond; see CP3 below], sep EP 1808[11]), chap CP4/EP14 (sep civ identity early [comprised of tps Benwell, Elswick, Westgate; see CP4 below], sep EP 1808[11]). Abol civ 1914 to help cr CP1.[62] Addtl eccl bdry alt: 1877 (help cr EP8),[203] 1892.[204]

CP1—NEWCASTLE UPON TYNE—Cr 1914 by union pars in Newc upon Tyne CB: Benwell CP, Byker CP, Elswick CP, Fenham CP, Heaton CP, Jesmond CP, CP2, CP3, CP4, AP1, Westgate CP.[62] Bdry: 1935 (gains Kenton CP and pts West Brunton CP, East Denton CP, Fawdon CP, Longbenton AP, loses pt to Seaton Valley UD & CP).[34] Transf 1974 to Tyne & Wear.[89]

CP2/EP1—NEWCASTLE UPON TYNE ALL SAINTS—Chap in AP1, sep civ identity early, sep EP 1808.[11] Incl chap Byker (sep civ identity early, sep EP 1844,[39] eccl refounded 1868[96]), tp

Heaton (sep civ identity early, sep EP 1808[11]), chap EP5 (sep EP 1843[205]). Abol civ 1914 to help cr CP1.[62] Addtl eccl bdry alt: 1862 (cr Shieldfield [Christ Church] EP),[206] 1877 (help cr EP8),[203] 1935.[205] Abol eccl 1955 to help cr EP9.[207]

EP2—NEWCASTLE UPON TYNE CHRIST CHURCH—Cr 1969 by union Shieldfield [Christ Church] EP, EP9.[208]

EP3—NEWCASTLE UPON TYNE HOLY CROSS—Cr 1936 from Scotswood EP, Fenham EP.[131] Newc RDn (1936—67), Newc West RDn (1967—*).

CP3/EP4—NEWCASTLE UPON TYNE ST ANDREW—Chap in AP1, sep civ identity early, sep EP 1808.[11] Incl tps Fenham (sep CP 1866,[1] sep EP 1926 but from EP15, Benwell St James EP, EP6[66]), Jesmond (sep civ identity early, sep EP 1861[11]). Civ bdry: 1904.[181] Abol civ 1914 to help cr CP1.[62] Eccl bdry: 1844 (cr EP19),[209] 1892 (cr EP15),[207] 1935.[205]

EP5—NEWCASTLE UPON TYNE ST ANNE—Chap in CP2/EP1 (orig chap in AP1; see CP2/EP1), sep EP 1843.[205] Bdry: 1908,[101] 1931 (help cr Byker St Lawrence EP).[100]

EP6—NEWCASTLE UPON TYNE ST AUGUSTINE—Cr 1892 from Benwell St James EP, High Elswick St Philip EP.[130] Newc RDn (1892—1967), Newc West RDn (1967—*). Bdry: 1926 (help cr Fenham EP).[66]

EP7—NEWCASTLE UPON TYNE ST BARNABAS—Cr 1908 from Jesmond EP.[134]

EP8—NEWCASTLE UPON TYNE ST CUTHBERT—Cr 1877 from EP1, AP1.[203] Abol 1955 to help cr EP9.[207]

EP9—NEWCASTLE UPON TYNE ST CUTHBERT AND ALL SAINTS—Cr 1955 by union EP8, EP1.[207] Abol 1969 to help cr EP2.[208]

EP10—NEWCASTLE UPON TYNE ST FRANCIS, HIGH HEATON—Cr 1955 from EP11, Long Benton AP.[60] Newc RDn (1955—67), Newc East RDn (1967—*).

EP11—NEWCASTLE UPON TYNE ST GABRIEL, HEATON—Cr 1900 from Byker EP.[99] Newc RDn (1900—67), Newc East RDn (1967—*). Bdry: 1952,[58] 1955 (help cr EP10).[60]

EP12—NEWCASTLE UPON TYNE ST GEORGE—Cr 1889 from Jesmond EP.[23] Bdry: 1909 (help cr EP13),[210] 1926 (help cr Jesmond Holy Trinity EP).[180]

EP13—NEWCASTLE UPON TYNE ST HILDA—Cr 1909 from EP12, EP15.[210]

—NEWCASTLE UPON TYNE ST JAMES—See BENWELL ST JAMES

CP4/EP14—NEWCASTLE UPON TYNE ST JOHN—Chap in AP1, sep civ identity early, sep EP 1808.[11] Incl tps Benwell (sep civ identity early, see EP 1843,[61] usually as 'Benwell St James', qv), Elswick (sep CP 1866,[1] pt eccl severed 1846 to cr High Elswick St Paul EP,[146] the remainder transf 1854 to High Elswick St Paul EP[147]), tp Westgate (sep CP 1866[1]). Abol civ 1914 to help cr CP1.[62] Eccl bdry: 1869 (cr EP17),[159] 1892.[204]

EP15—NEWCASTLE UPON TYNE ST LUKE THE

EVANGELIST—Cr 1892 from EP4.[207] Bdry: 1909 (help cr EP13),[210] 1926 (help cr Fenham EP),[66] 1928,[159] 1957 (help cr Cowgate EP).[123]

EP16—NEWCASTLE UPON TYNE ST MARY THE VIRGIN—Cr 1895 from High Elswick St Paul EP, Low Elswick EP.[150] Abol 1961 pt to help cr EP18, pt to Low Elswick EP).[151]

EP17—NEWCASTLE UPON TYNE ST MATTHEW—Cr 1869 from EP14.[159] Abol 1961 pt to help cr EP18, pt to High Elswick St Paul EP.[151]

EP18—NEWCASTLE UPON TYNE ST MATTHEW WITH ST MARY—Cr 1961 by union pt EP16, pt EP17, pt High Elswick St Paul EP.[151] Newc RDn (1961—67), Newc West RDn (1967—*).

EP19—NEWCASTLE UPON TYNE ST PETER—Cr 1844 from EP4.[209] Abol 1935 pt to EP4, pt to EP1.[205]

NEWHAM

Tp in Bamburgh AP, sep CP 1866,[1] eccl severed 1884 to help refound Lucker EP.[7] LG Bamb. Wd, Belf. PLU, RSD, RD. Abol 1955 ent to Ellingham AP.[8] Parl N'rn Dv (1867—85), Berw. upon Tweed Dv/CC (1885—1970).

NEWHAM

Tp in Whalton AP, sep CP 1866.[1] LG Castle Wd, Castle Wd PLU, RSD, RD. Abol 1955 ent to Belsay CP.[54] Parl S'rn Dv (1867—85), Wansb. Dv (1885—1948), Hexham CC (1948—70).

NEWLANDS

Tp in Bywell St Peter AP, sep CP 1866.[1] LG Tyned. Wd, Hexham PLU, RSD, RD. Bdry: 1887.[36] Abol 1955 ent to help reconstitute Shotley Low Quarter CP.[37] Parl S'rn Dv (1867—85), Hexham Dv/CC (1885—1970).

NEWMINSTER

CP Cr 1894 by union of the pts not in Morp. MB of Morpeth AP, Newminster Abbey CP.[196] LG Morp. PLU, RD. Abol 1935 pt to Morpeth AP, pt to Benridge CP, pt to Tranwell CP.[154] Parl Morp. Parl Bor (1918—48).

NEWMINSTER ABBEY

Tp in Morpeth AP, sep CP 1866.[1] LG Castle Wd, Morp. PLU, pt Morp. MB (1835—94), Morp. USD (ent 1875—89, pt 1889—94). Bdry: 1888.[91] Abol 1894 the pt in the MB transf to Morpeth AP, the remainder to help cr Newminster CP.[196] Parl Morp. Parl Bor (1832—1918).

NEWSHAM

EP Cr 1957 from Horton EP.[176] Bedl. RDn.

NEWSHAM AND SOUTH BLYTH

Tp in Earsdon AP, sep CP 1866,[1] eccl severed 1883 to help cr Blyth St Cuthbert EP.[77] LG Castle Wd, Tynem. PLU, S Blyth USD (pt 1875—83, ent 1883—94), pt Tynem. RSD (1875—83), Blyth UD (1894—1920). Abol 1920 to help cr Blyth CP.[48] Parl S'rn Dv (1832—67), Morp. Parl Bor (1867—1948).

NEWSTEAD

Tp in Bamburgh AP, sep CP 1866,[1] eccl severed 1884 to help refound Lucker EP.[7] LG Bamb. Wd, Belf. PLU, RSD, RD. Abol 1955 to help cr Adderstone with Lucker CP.[8] Parl N'rn Dv (1867—85), Berw. upon Tweed Dv/CC (1885—1970).

NEWTON

Tp in Bywell St Peter AP, sep CP 1866.[1] LG Tyned. Wd, Hexham PLU, RSD, RD. Bdry: 1887.[36] 1887.[5] Abol 1955 ent to Bywell CP.[37] Parl S'rn Dv (1867—85), Hexham Dv/CC (1885—1970).

NEWTON BY THE SEA

Tp in Embleton AP, sep CP 1866.[1] LG Seq 1. Bdry: 1955 (gains Brunton CP, Doxford CP, Fallodon CP).[2] Parl Seq 1.

NEWTON HALL

Tp in Bywell St Peter AP, sep CP 1866,[1] sep EP 1877 from Bywell St Peter AP, Bywell St Andrew AP, Ovingham AP, Corbridge AP.[104] LG Tyned. Wd, Hexham PLU, RSD, RD. Bdry: 1883,[4] 1887.[5] Abol 1955 ent to Bywell CP.[37] Parl S'rn Dv (1867—85), Hexham Dv/CC (1885—1970). Eccl Corbr. RDn.

NEWTON ON THE MOOR

Tp in Shilbottle AP, sep CP 1866.[1] LG Seq 5. Bdry: 1883,[11] 1955 (gains Greens and Gantlees CP, Hazon and Hartlew CP, Swarland CP, Whittle CP).[2] Parl Seq 1.

NEWTON PARK

Tp in Mitford AP, sep CP 1866.[1] LG Morp. Wd, PLU, RSD, RD. Abol 1955 ent to Meldon AP.[28] Parl N'rn Dv (1867—85), Wansb. Dv (1885—1948), Morp. CC (1948—70).

NEWTON UNDERWOOD

Tp in Mitford AP, sep CP 1866.[1] Organisation as for Newton Park.

NEWTOWN

Tp in Chillingham AP, sep CP 1866.[1] LG Glend. Wd, PLU, RSD, RD. Abol 1955 to help cr Lilburn CP.[9] Parl N'rn Dv (1867—85), Berw. upon Tweed Dv/CC (1885—1970).

NEWTOWN

Tp in Rothbury AP, sep CP 1866.[1] LG Coq. Wd, Rothb. PLU, RSD, RD. Bdry: 1896.[133] Abol 1955 ent to Tosson CP.[16] Parl N'rn Dv (1867—85), Hexham Dv (1885—1918), Berw. upon Tweed Dv/CC (1918—70).

NINEBANKS

EP Cr 1763 from chap Allendale (sep civ identity early from Hexham AP, sep EP 1767[11]),[11] eccl refounded 1900.[13] Newc upon Tyne RDn (1763—1845), Hexham RDn (1845—1967). Abol 1967 to help cr Ninebanks and Carrshield EP.[110]

NINEBANKS AND CARRSHIELD

EP Cr 1967 by union Ninebanks EP, Carrshield EP.[110] Hexham RDn.

NOOK

Tp in chap Bellingham (sep par 1811 from Simonburn[52]), 'Nook' a sep CP 1866.[1] LG Tyned. Wd, Bell. PLU, RSD. Abol 1886 pt to help cr Bellingham CP, pt to Wark CP.[53] Parl S'rn Dv (1867—85), Hexham Dv (1885—1918).

NORHAM

AP In Durham, transf to Northumb 1832 for parl purposes, 1844 for civ purposes.[25] Incl chap Cornhill on Tweed (sep CP 1866,[1] sep EP 1730[11]); tps Duddo, Felkington, Grindon, Horncliffe, Loanend, Longridge, Norham Mains, Shoreswood, Thornton, Twizell (each a sep CP 1866[1]). LG Seq

14. Addtl civ bdry alt: 1878.[138] *Parl* In Durham until 1832, Seq 1 thereafter. *Eccl* Bamb. RDn (until 1845), Norham RDn (1845—1970). Abol eccl 1970 to help cr Norham and Duddo EP.[140]

NORHAM AND DUDDO

EP Cr 1970 by union Norham AP, Duddo EP.[140] Norham RDn.

NORHAM MAINS

In Durham, transf to Northumb 1832 for parl purposes, 1832 for civ purposes.[25] Tp in Norham AP, sep CP 1866.[1] *LG* Norhamshire, Berw. PLU, RSD, Norham & Islandshires RD. Abol 1955 ent to Horncliffe CP.[139] *Parl* In Durham until 1832, N'rn Dv (1832—85), Berw. upon Tweed Dv/CC (1885—1970).

NUNNYKIRK

Tp in Netherwitton AP, sep CP 1866.[1] *LG* Seq 13. Bdry: 1955 (gains Coatyards CP, Ewesley CP, Healey and Combhill CP, Ritton Colt Park CP, Ritton White House CP, Todburn CP, Wingates CP).[16] *Parl* Seq 3.

NUNRIDING

Tp in Mitford AP, sep CP 1866.[1] *LG* Morp. Wd, PLU, RSD, RD. Abol 1955 ent to Meldon AP.[28] *Parl* N'rn Dv (1867—85), Wansb. Dv (1885—1948), Morp. CC (1948—70).

OGLE

Tp in Whalton AP, sep CP 1866.[1] *LG* Castle Wd, Castle Wd PLU, RSD, RD. Abol 1955 ent to Whalton AP.[54] *Parl* S'rn Dv (1867—85), Wansb. Dv (1885—1948), Hexham CC (1948—70).

OLD MOOR

Tp in Bothal AP, sep CP 1866,[1] pt eccl severed 1876 to help cr Longhirst EP.[80] *LG* Morp. Wd, PLU, RSD, RD. Abol 1955 ent to Longhirst CP.[28] *Parl* N'rn Dv (1867—85), Wansb. Dv (1885—1948), Morp. CC (1948—70).

ORD

CP Cr 1891 from the pt of Tweedmouth CP not in Berw. upon Tweed MB.[211] *LG* Berw. PLU, RSD, Norham & Islandshires RD. Bdry: 1935.[34] *Parl* Berw. upon Tweed Dv/CC (1918—*).

OTTERBURN

Tp in Elsdon AP, sep CP 1866,[1] sep EP 1857,[11] eccl refounded 1921.[144] *LG* Seq 6. Civ bdry: 1955.[47] *Parl* Seq 2. *Eccl* Rothb. RDn.

OUSTON

Tp in Stamfordham AP, sep CP 1866.[1] *LG* Tyned. Wd, Castle Wd PLU, RSD, RD. Abol 1955 to help cr Stamfordham CP.[54] *Parl* S'rn Dv (1867—85), Hexham Dv/CC (1885—1970).

OUTCHESTER

Tp in Bamburgh AP, sep CP 1866.[1] *LG* Bamb. Wd, Belf. PLU, RSD, RD. Abol 1955 ent to Easington CP.[8] *Parl* N'rn Dv (1867—85), Berw. upon Tweed Dv/CC (1885—1970).

OVINGHAM

AP Incl tp Mickley (sep CP 1866,[1] sep EP 1727,[11] eccl refounded 1866 incl ex-par Masters Close[189]); incl tps Dukers Hagg, Eltringham, Harlow Hill, Hedley, Hedley Woodside, Nafferton, Ovington, Prudhoe Castle, Rudchester, Spital, Welton, Whittle, pt tp Broomley (each a sep CP 1866[1]), tps

Horsley, Prudhoe, Wylam (each a sep CP 1866,[1] eccl united 1902 to cr Wylam EP[175]). *LG* Seq 18. *Parl* Seq 5. *Eccl* Seq 6. Eccl bdry: 1931.[19]

OVINGTON

Tp in Ovingham AP, sep CP 1866.[1] *LG* Seq 18. Bdry: 1883,[11] 1887.[36] *Parl* Seq 5.

PASTON

Tp in Kirknewton AP, sep CP 1866.[1] *LG* Glend. Wd, PLU, RSD, RD. Abol 1955 ent to Kilham CP.[9] *Parl* N'rn Dv (1867—85), Berw. upon Tweed Dv/CC (1885—1970).

PAUPERHAUGH

Tp in Rothbury AP, sep CP 1866.[1] *LG* Coq. Wd, Rothb. PLU, RSD. Abol 1889 ent to Raw CP.[212] *Parl* N'rn Dv (1867—85), Hexham Dv (1885—1918).

PEELS

Tp in Alwinton AP, sep CP 1866.[1] *LG* Coq. Wd, Rothb. PLU, RSD, RD. Bdry: 1883.[21] Abol 1955 ent to Harbottle CP.[16] *Parl* N'rn Dv (1867—85), Hexham Dv (1885—1918), Berw. upon Tweed Dv/CC (1918—70).

PEGSWOOD

Tp in Bothal AP, sep CP 1866.[1] *LG* Seq 10. *Parl* Seq 4.

PIGDON

Tp in Mitford AP, sep CP 1866.[1] *LG* Morp. Wd, PLU, RSD, RD. Abol 1955 ent to Meldon AP.[28] *Parl* N'rn Dv (1867—85), Wansb. Dv (1885—1948), Morp. CC (1948—70).

PLASHETTS AND TYNEHEAD

Tp in chap Falstone (chap appropriated to Kirkham Priory, later in ruins and deemed chap in Simonburn AP,[152] made a sep par 1811[52]), 'Plashetts and Tynehead' a sep CP 1866.[1] *LG* Tyned. Wd, Bell. PLU, RSD, RD. Bdry: 1883.[4] Abol 1955 pt to help cr Falstone CP, pt to help cr Kielder CP.[47] *Parl* S'rn Dv (1867—85), Hexham Dv/CC (1885—1970).

PLEA PIECE

Lands orig common to Eglingham AP, Ilderton AP, after cr 1866 of CPs of East Lilburn, West Lilburn from Eglingham AP and cr of Roseden CP from Ilderton AP, common to East Lilburn CP, West Lilburn CP, Ilderton AP, Roseden CP. *LG* Glend. PLU, RD. Abol 1955 to help cr Lilburn CP.[45] *Parl* Berw. upon Tweed Dv/CC (1918—70).

PLENMELLER

Tp in Haltwhistle AP, sep CP 1866.[1] *LG* Tyned. Wd, Haltw. PLU, RSD, RD. Abol 1955 to help cr Plenmeller with Whitfield CP.[45] *Parl* S'rn Dv (1867—85), Hexham Dv/CC (1885—1970).

PLENMELLER WITH WHITFIELD

CP Cr 1955 by union Plenmeller CP, Whitfield AP.[45] *LG* Haltw. RD. *Parl* Hexham CC (1970—*).

PONTELAND

AP Incl tp Dinnington (sep CP 1818[52] to consist of Dinnington and other tps heretofore in Ponteland: Brenkley, Horton Grange, Mason, pt tp Prestwick); incl tps Berwick Hall, pt High Callerton, Little Callerton, Coldcoats, Darras Hall, Higham Dykes, Kirkley, Milbourne, Milbourne Grange, pt tp Prestwick (the pt not transf 1818 to Dinnington) (each a sep CP 1866[1]). *LG* Seq 3. Addtl civ bdry alt:

1955 (gains Berwick Hall CP, High Callerton CP, Little Callerton CP, Coldcoats CP, Darras Hall CP, North Dissington CP, South Dissington CP, Higham Dykes CP, Kirkley CP, Milbourne CP, Milbourne Grange CP, Prestwick CP).[54] *Parl* Seq 8. *Eccl* Morp. RDn (until 1845), Newc upon Tyne RDn (1845—74), Newc upon Tyne RDn (S'rn Dv) (1874—77), Newc upon Tyne RDn (W'rn Dv) (1877—84), Corbr. RDn (1844—99), Newc RDn (1899—1967), Newc West RDn (1967—*).

PORTGATE
Tp in Lee St John AP, sep CP 1866,[1] eccl severed 1879 to help cr St Oswald in Lee with Bingfield St Mary EP,[70] the area of Portgate eccl severed from latter 1888 to help cr Bingfield St Mary EP.[71] *LG* Tyned. Wd, Hexham PLU, RSD, RD. Abol 1955 ent to Corbridge AP.[37] *Parl* S'rn Dv (1867—85), Hexham Dv/CC (1885—1970).

PRENDWICK
Tp in Alnham AP, sep CP 1866.[1] *LG* Coq. Wd, Rothb. PLU, RSD, RD. Abol 1955 ent to Alnham AP.[16] *Parl* N'rn Dv (1867—85), Berw. upon Tweed Dv/CC (1885—1970).

PRESTON
Tp in Ellingham AP, sep CP 1866.[1] *LG* Bamb. Wd, Belf. PLU, RSD, RD. Abol 1955 ent to Ellingham AP.[8] *Parl* N'rn Dv (1867—85), Berw. upon Tweed Dv/CC (1885—1970).

PRESTON
Tp in Tynemouth AP, sep CP 1866,[1] eccl severed 1861 to help refound Tynemouth Western Town EP.[114] *LG* Castle Wd, Tynem. PLU, MB (1849—1904), USD, CB (1904—08). Bdry: 1883,[4] 1889.[116] Abol 1908 ent to Tynemouth AP.[117] *Parl* Tynem. Parl Bor (1832—1918).

PRESTWICK
Tp in Ponteland AP, pt severed 1818 to help cr Dinnington CP,[52] the remainder a sep CP 1866.[1] *LG* Castle Wd, Castle Wd PLU, RSD, RD. Abol 1955 ent to Ponteland AP.[54] *Parl* S'rn Dv (1867—85), Wansb. Dv (1885—1948), Hexham CC (1948—70).

PRUDHOE
Tp in Ovingham AP, sep CP 1866,[1] eccl severed 1902 to help cr Wylam EP.[175] *LG* Tyned. Wd, Hexham PLU, RSD, RD (1894—1910), Prudhoe UD (1910—74). *Parl* Seq 5.

PRUDHOE
EP Cr 1881 [St Mary Magdalene] from Mickley EP.[128] Corbr. RDn.

PRUDHOE CASTLE
Tp in Ovingham AP, sep CP 1866,[1] eccl severed 1902 to help cr Wylam EP.[175] Organisation as for Prudhoe CP (first Prudhoe above), with civ bdry alt 1887 (gains Masters Close CP).[190]

RAMSHOPE
Ex-par place, sep CP 1858.[119] *LG* Coq. Wd, Bell. PLU, RSD. Abol 1886 to help cr Rochester Ward CP.[53] *Parl* N'rn Dv (1867—85), Hexham Dv (1885—1918).

RATCHWOOD
Tp in Bamburgh AP, sep CP 1866,[1] eccl severed 1884 to help refound Lucker EP.[7] *LG* Bamb. Wd,

Belf. PLU, RSD, RD. Abol 1955 to help cr Adderstone with Lucker CP.[8] *Parl* N'rn Dv (1867—85), Berw. upon Tweed Dv/CC (1885—1970).

RAW
Tp in Rothbury AP, sep CP 1866.[1] *LG* Coq. Wd, Rothb. PLU, RSD, RD. Bdry: 1889,[167] 1889.[212] Abol 1955 to help cr Brinkburn CP.[16] *Parl* N'rn Dv (1867—85), Hexham Dv (1885—1918), Berw. upon Tweed Dv/CC (1918—70).

REAVELEY
Tp in Ingram AP, sep CP 1866.[1] *LG* Coq. Wd, Glend. PLU, RSD, RD. Abol 1955 ent to Roddam CP.[9] *Parl* N'rn Dv (1867—85), Berw. upon Tweed Dv/CC (1885—1970).

RENNINGTON
Chap in Embleton AP, sep CP 1866,[1] sep EP 1767,[11] eccl refounded 1903 (incl gains tp Broxfield in Embleton AP).[88] *LG* Seq 1. Civ bdry: 1955 (gains Broxfield CP, Rock CP, Stamford CP).[2] *Parl* Seq 1. *Eccl* Alnw. RDn.

RIDDELL'S QUARTER
Tp in Long Horsley AP, sep CP 1866.[1] Incl undivided pt Horsley Moor (common to Bigge's Quarter CP, Fenrother CP, Freeholders' Quarter CP, Riddell's Quarter CP), undivided pt Long Horsley Moor (common to Bigge's Quarter CP, Freeholders' Quarter CP, Riddell's Quarter CP). *LG* Morp. Wd, PLU, RSD, RD. Abol 1955 to help cr Longhorsley CP.[28] *Parl* N'rn Dv (1867—85), Wansb. Dv (1885—1948), Morp. CC (1948—70).

RIDING
Tp in Bywell St Andrew AP, sep CP 1866.[1] *LG* Tyned. Wd, Hexham PLU, RSD, RD. Abol 1955 to help cr Broomhaugh and Riding CP.[37] *Parl* S'rn Dv (1867—85), Hexham Dv/CC (1885—1970).

RIDING MILL
EP Renaming 1973 of Bywell St Andrew AP.[19] Corbr. RDn.

RIDLEY
Tp in Haltwhistle AP, sep CP 1866.[1] *LG* Tyned. Wd, Haltw. PLU, RSD, RD. Bdry: 1886.[76] Abol 1955 to help cr Bardon Mill CP.[45] *Parl* S'rn Dv (1867—85), Hexham Dv/CC (1885—1970).

RIPLINGTON
Tp in Whalton AP, sep CP 1866.[1] *LG* Castle Wd, Castle Wd PLU, RSD, RD. Abol 1955 ent to Whalton AP.[54] *Parl* S'rn Dv (1867—85), Wansb. Dv (1885—1948), Hexham CC (1948—70).

RITTON COLT PARK
Tp in chap Netherwitton (sep CP 1866 from Hartburn AP,[1] sep EP 1835[11]), 'Ritton Colt Park' a sep CP 1866.[1] *LG* Morp. Wd, Rothb. PLU, RSD, RD. Abol 1955 ent to Nunnykirk CP.[16] *Parl* N'rn Dv (1867—85), Wansb. Dv (1885—1918), Berw. upon Tweed Dv/CC (1918—70).

RITTON WHITE HOUSE
Tp in chap Netherwitton (sep CP 1866 from Hartburn AP,[1] sep EP 1835[11]), 'Ritton White House' a sep CP 1866.[1] Organisation as for Ritton Colt Park.

RIVERGREEN
Ex-par place, sep CP 1858.[119] *LG* Castle Wd, Morp. PLU, RSD, RD. Abol 1955 ent to Meldon

AP.[28] *Parl* S'rn Dv (1867—85), Wansb. Dv (1885—1948), Morp. CC (1948—70).

ROCHESTER

Tp in Elsdon AP, sep CP 1866.[1] *LG* Coq. Wd, Bell. PLU, RSD. Abol 1886 to help cr Rochester Ward CP.[53] *Parl* N'rn Dv (1867—85), Hexham Dv (1885—1918).

CP Cr 1955 by union Rochester Ward CP, pt Troughend CP.[47] *LG* Bell. RD. *Parl* Hexham CC (1970—*).

ROCHESTER WARD

CP Cr 1886 by union Ramshope CP, Rochester CP.[53] *LG* Coq. Wd, Bell. PLU, RSD, RD. Abol 1955 to help cr Rochester CP.[47] *Parl* Hexham Dv/CC (1918—70).

ROCK

Chap in Embleton AP, sep CP 1866,[1] sep EP 1767,[11] eccl refounded 1903.[88] *LG* Bamb. Wd, Alnw. PLU, RSD, RD. Abol 1955 ent to Rennington CP.[2] *Parl* N'rn Dv (1867—85), Berw. upon Tweed Dv/CC (1885—1970). *Eccl* Alnw. RDn.

RODDAM

Tp in Ilderton AP, sep CP 1866.[1] *LG* Seq 7. Bdry: 1955 (gains Reaveley CP, Roseden CP, Woolperton CP).[9] *Parl* Seq 1.

ROSEDEN

Tp in Ilderton AP, sep CP 1866.[1] *LG* Coq. Wd, Glend. PLU, RSD, RD. Bdry: 1884.[179] Abol 1955 ent to Roddam CP.[9] *Parl* N'rn Dv (1867—85), Berw. upon Tweed Dv/CC (1885—1970).

ROSS

In Durham (Islandshire), transf to Northumb (Bamb. Wd) 1832 for parl purposes, 1844 for civ purposes.[25] Tp in chap Belford (mainly in Northumb, sep civ identity early from Bamburgh AP, sep EP 1735[11]), 'Ross' a sep CP 1866.[1] *LG* Belf. PLU, RSD, RD. Abol 1955 ent to Middleton CP.[8] *Parl* N'rn Dv (1867—85), Berw. upon Tweed Dv/CC (1885—1970).

ROTHBURY

AP Incl tps Bickerton, Caiston, Cartington, Debdon, Fallowlees, Flotterton, Hepple, Hepple Demesne, Hesleyhurst, Hollinghill, Lee Ward, Mount Healey, Newtown, Pauperhaugh, Raw, Snitter, Thropton, Great Tosson and Rye Hill, Little Tosson, High and Low Trewhitt, Warton, Whitton, Wreighill (each a sep CP 1866[1]); also incl Intermixed Lands common from 1866 to CPs Debdon, Snitter (after Rothbury gains 1889 ent Debdon CP,[15] common to Rothbury and Snitter). *LG* Rothb. Bor, Coq. Wd, Rothb. PLU, RSD, RD (1894—96), UD (1896—1935), Rothb. RD (1935—74). Addtl civ bdry alt: 1883,[4] 1896.[133] *Parl* Seq 2. *Eccl* Sometimes as 'Rothbury with Thropton and Hepple', Seq 2.

ROTHLEY

Tp in Hartburn AP, sep CP 1866.[1] *LG* Seq 13. Bdry: 1955 (gains Fairnley CP, Hartington CP, Hartington Hall CP).[16] *Parl* Seq 2.

RUDCHESTER

Tp in Ovingham AP, sep CP 1866.[1] *LG* Tyned. Wd, Castle Wd PLU, RSD, RD. Abol 1955 ent to Heddon on the Wall AP.[54] *Parl* S'rn Dv (1867—85), Wansb. Dv (1885—1948), Hexham CC (1948—70).

RYAL

Tp in Stamfordham AP, sep CP 1866.[1] *LG* Tyned. Wd, Castle Wd PLU, RSD, RD. Abol 1955 to help cr Matfen CP.[54] *Parl* S'rn Dv (1867—85), Hexham Dv/CC (1885—1970).

GREAT RYLE

Tp in Whittingham AP, sep CP 1866.[1] *LG* Coq. Wd, Rothb. PLU, RSD, RD. Bdry: 1889.[15] Abol 1955 ent to Alnham AP.[16] *Parl* N'rn Dv (1867—85), Berw. upon Tweed Dv/CC (1885—1970).

LITTLE RYLE

Tp in Whittingham AP, sep CP 1866.[1] Organisation as for Great Ryle except no bdry alt.

ST JOHN LEE

AP Usual eccl spelling; for civ, tps incl in the par (several of which gain sep eccl status), see 'Lee St John'. *Eccl* Newc upon Tyne RDn (until 1845), Hexham RDn (1845—*).

ST OSWALD IN LEE

EP Area in Lee St John AP (eccl, 'St John Lee'), sep EP 1733,[11] eccl refounded 1879 by union 6 tps in Lee St John: Cocklaw, Fallowfield, Hallington, Portgate, Wall, Bingfield (the last a sep EP 1740[11]),[70] thereafter 'St Oswald in Lee with Bingfield St Mary', qv, the latter reduced in area 1888 when Bingfield, Hallington, Portgate, greater pt of Cocklaw severed to cr 'Bingfield St Mary EP',[71] the reduced area thereafter 'St Oswald in Lee'. Hexham RDn.

ST OSWALD IN LEE WITH BINGFIELD ST MARY

EP Cr 1879 when St Oswald in Lee EP refounded to be 6 tps orig in Lee St John AP (eccl, 'St John Lee'): Cocklaw, Fallowfield, Hallington, Portgate, Wall, Bingfield (the last a sep EP 1740[11]).[70] Hexham RDn. Abol 1888, the area of Bingfield, Hallington, Portgate, greater pt of Cocklaw severed to cr 'Bingfield St Mary EP', the remainder to be 'St Oswald in Lee'.[71]

SANDHOE

Tp in Lee St John AP, sep CP 1866.[1] *LG* Seq 18. Bdry: 1883,[4] 1887 (gains Anick CP, Anick Grange CP).[29] *Parl* Seq 5.

SCOTSWOOD

EP Cr 1918 from Benwell St James EP.[65] Newc RDn (1918—67), Newc West RDn (1967—*). Bdry: 1936 (help cr Newcastle upon Tyne Holy Cross EP).[131]

SCRAINWOOD

Tp in Alnham AP, sep CP 1866.[1] *LG* Coq. Wd, Rothb. PLU, RSD, RD. Abol 1955 ent to Alnham AP.[16] *Parl* N'rn Dv (1867—85), Berw. upon Tweed Dv/CC (1885—1970).

NORTH SEATON

Tp in Woodhorn AP, sep CP 1866.[1] *LG* Morp. Wd, PLU, RSD, RD. Bdry: 1900,[171] 1909,[172] 1910.[199] Abol 1935 ent to Newbiggin by the Sea CP.[34] *Parl* N'rn Dv (1867—85), Wansb. Dv (1885—1948).

SEATON DELAVAL

Tp in Earsdon AP, sep CP 1866,[1] pt severed eccl 1846 to help cr Sighill EP,[97] the remainder eccl severed 1891 to help cr Delaval EP.[134] *LG* Castle Wd, Tynem. PLU, RSD, RD (1894—1912), Seaton

Delaval UD (1912—35). Bdry: 1912 (gains pt Hartley CP, pt Horton CP as enlarged area constituted Seaton Delaval UD),[94] 1920 (exchanges pts with Whitley & Monkseaton UD & CP).[213] Abol 1935 pt to help cr Seaton Valley UD & CP, pt to Blyth MB & CP, pt to Whitley & Monkseaton UD & CP.[34] *Parl* S'rn Dv (1867—85), Wansb. Dv (1885—1948).

SEATON VALLEY
CP Cr 1935 by union Backworth CP, Craml. UD & CP, East Hartford CP, West Hartford CP, Holywell CP, Seghill UD & CP, and pts Earsdon UD & CP, Murton CP, Tynem. CB (assoc with Northumb) & CP.[34] *LG* Seaton Valley UD. Bdry: 1969,[214] 1974 (main pt remains in Northumb, pt [wards of Backworth, Earsdon, Shiremoor] transf to Tyne & Wear).[89] *Parl* Blyth BC (1948—*). Parl bdry: 1971.[215]

SEGHILL
Tp in Earsdon AP, sep CP 1866,[1] eccl united 1846 with pt tp Seaton Delaval in same par, pt Cramlington EP as 'Sighill' EP,[97] qv. *LG* Castle Wd, Tynem. PLU, Seghill USD, UD. Abol civ 1935 to help cr Seaton Valley UD & CP.[34] *Parl* S'rn Dv (1867—85), Wansb. Dv (1885—1948).

SELBY'S FOREST
Tp in Kirknewton AP, sep CP 1866.[1] *LG* Glend. Wd, PLU, RSD, RD. Abol 1955 pt to Earle CP, pt to Kirknewton AP.[9] *Parl* N'rn Dv (1867—85), Berw. upon Tweed Dv/CC (1885—1970).

EAST SHAFTOE
Tp in Hartburn AP, sep CP 1866.[1] *LG* Tyned. Wd, Castle Wd PLU, RSD, RD. Abol 1955 ent to Capheaton CP.[54] *Parl* S'rn Dv (1867—85), Wansb. Dv (1885—1948), Hexham CC (1948—70).

WEST SHAFTOE
Tp in Hartburn AP, sep CP 1866.[1] Organisation as for East Shaftoe.

SHARPERTON
Tp in Alwinton AP, sep CP 1866.[1] *LG* Coq. Wd, Rothb. PLU, RSD, RD. Abol 1955 ent to Harbottle CP.[16] *Parl* N'rn Dv (1867—85), Hexham Dv (1885—1918), Berw. upon Tweed Dv/CC (1918—70).

SHAWDON
Tp in Whittingham AP, sep CP 1866.[1] *LG* Coq.Wd, Alnw. PLU, RSD, RD. Abol 1955 ent to Hedgeley CP.[2] *Parl* N'rn Dv (1867—85), Berw. upon Tweed Dv/CC (1885—1970).

SHEEPWASH
CP Cr 1896 from Ashington and Sheepwash CP (for earlier status of chap Sheepwash and for its early civ and eccl organisation, see 'Ashington').[31] *LG* Morp. PLU, RD. Bdry: 1897.[49] Abol 1935 ent to Ashington CP.[34] *Parl* Wansb. Dv (1918—48).

NORTH SHIELDS
Tp in Tynemouth AP, sep CP 1866,[1] pt eccl severed 1860 to cr Tynemouth Low Town EP (later called 'Tynemouth St Peter' or more commonly 'North Shields St Peter'),[19] pt eccl severed 1861 to help refound Tynemouth Western Town EP (later called 'Tynemouth Holy Trinity').[114] *LG* Castle Wd, Tynem. PLU, MB (1849—1904), USD, CB

(1904—08). Abol 1908 ent to Tynemouth AP.[117] *Parl* Tynem. Parl Bor (1832—1918).

SHIELDFIELD [CHRIST CHURCH]
EP Cr 1861,[11] eccl refounded 1862 from Newcastle upon Tyne All Saints EP.[206] Newc upon Tyne RDn (1861—74), Newc upon Tyne RDn (S'rn Dv) (1874—77), Newc upon Tyne RDn (W'rn Dv) (1877—84), Newc RDn (1884—1967), Newc Ctrl. RDn (1967—69). Bdry: 1892 (help cr Shieldfield St Jude EP).[40] Abol 1969 to help cr Newcastle upon Tyne Christ Church EP.[208]

SHIELDFIELD ST JUDE
EP Cr 1892 from Shieldfield EP.[40] Newc RDn (1892—1967), Newc Ctrl. RDn (1967—*).

SHILBOTEL
AP Usual eccl spelling; for civ and tps, see following entry. *Eccl* Seq 1.

SHILBOTTLE
AP Usual civ spelling; for eccl see prev entry. Incl tps Guyzance, Hazon, Newton on the Moor, Whittle, Woodhouse (each a sep CP 1866[1]). *LG* Seq 5. Addtl civ bdry alt: 1955 (gains Woodhouse CP).[2] *Parl* Seq 1.

SHILVINGTON
Tp in Morpeth AP, sep CP 1866.[1] *LG* Castle Wd, Castle Wd PLU, RSD, RD. Abol 1955 ent to Whalton AP.[54] *Parl* S'rn Dv (1867—85), Wansb. Dv (1885—1948), Hexham CC (1948—70).

SHIPLEY
Tp in Eglingham AP, sep CP 1866.[1] *LG* Coq. Wd, Alnw. PLU, RSD, RD. Abol 1955 ent to Eglingham AP.[2] *Parl* N'rn Dv (1867—85), Berw. upon Tweed Dv/CC (1885—1970).

SHIREMOOR
EP Cr 1968 from Earsdon AP, Killingworth EP, Tynemouth Percy EP.[39] Tynem. RDn. For orig area Shiremoor and its eccl organisation in 1860, see Whitley, Monkseaton.

HIGH SHITLINGTON
Tp in chap Wark (sep par 1811 from Simonburn AP[52]), 'High Shitlington' a sep CP 1866.[1] *LG* Tyned. Wd, Bell. PLU, RSD. Abol 1886 ent to Wark CP.[53] *Parl* S'rn Dv (1867—85), Hexham Dv (1885—1918).

LOW SHITLINGTON
Tp in chap Wark (sep par 1811 from Simonburn AP[52]), 'Low Shitlington' a sep CP 1866.[1] Organisation as for High Shitlington.

SHORESTON
Tp in Bamburgh AP, sep CP 1866.[1] *LG* Bamb. Wd, Belf. PLU, RSD, RD. Bdry: 1887.[44] Abol 1955 ent to North Sunderland CP.[8] *Parl* N'rn Dv (1867—85), Berw. upon Tweed Dv/CC (1885—1970).

SHORESWOOD
In Durham, transf to Northumb 1832 for parl purposes, 1844 for civ purposes.[25] Tp in Norham AP, sep CP 1866.[1] *LG* Seq 14. Bdry: 1955 (gains Thornton CP).[139] *Parl* In Durham until 1832, Seq 1 thereafter.

SHORTFLATT
Tp in Bolam AP, sep CP 1866.[1] *LG* Tyned. Wd, Castle Wd PLU, RSD, RD. Abol 1955 ent to Belsay CP.[54] *Parl* S'rn Dv (1867—85), Wansb. Dv

(1885—1948), Hexham CC (1948—70).

SHOTLEY

Chap in Bywell St Andrew AP, sep civ identity early, sep EP 1724.[11] Incl from Dissolution in 16th cent Blanchland (orig abbey church, sep EP 1751,[11] civ considered tp and called 'Shotley High Quarter', as such a sep CP 1866[1]); incl tps Newbiggin, Shotley Low Quarter (each a sep CP 1866[1] so that after 1866 'Shotley' has no sep civ identity. *LG* Tyned. Wd. *Parl* S'rn Dv (1832—67). *Eccl* Corbr. RDn. Eccl bdry: 1900 (help refound Whitley EP).[169]

SHOTLEY HIGH QUARTER

Tp in chap Shotley (sep civ identity early from Bywell St Andrew AP, sep EP 1724[11]), comprised of the area of Blanchland (orig abbey church, sep EP 1751 as 'Blanchland'[11]), 'Shotley High Quarter' a sep CP 1866.[1] *LG* Tyned. Wd, Hexham PLU, RSD, RD. Bdry: 1887 (gains Newbiggin CP).[198] Renamed 1955 'Blanchland'.[37] *Parl* S'rn Dv (1867—85), Hexham Dv/CC (1885—1970).

SHOTLEY LOW QUARTER

Tp in Shotley AP, sep CP 1866.[1] *LG* Seq 18. Bdry: 1955 (reconstituted, gaining Whittonstall CP, Newlands CP).[216] *Parl* Seq 5.

SIGHILL

Tp in Earsdon AP, sep CP 1866 as 'Seghill',[1] qv, sep EP 1846 by union Seghill, pt tp Seaton Delaval in same par, pt Cramlington EP.[97] Newc upon Tyne RDn (1846—74), Newc upon Tyne RDn (N'rn Dv) (1874—77), Newc upon Tyne RDn (E'rn Dv) (1877—84), Bedl. RDn (1884—*). Eccl bdry: 1958,[58] 1965,[135] 1969 (help cr Dudley EP).[125]

SIMONBURN

AP Incl chap Bellingham (sep par 1811 comprised of tps East Charlton, West Charlton, Leemailing, Nook, Tarretburn[52]), chap Falstone (appropriated to Kirkham Priory, later in ruins and deemed chap in this par,[152] sep EP 1724,[11] sep par 1811 comprised of tps Falstone, Plashetts and Tynehead, Wellhaugh[52]), chap Wark (sep par 1811 comrpised of tps High Shitlington, Low Shitlington, Warkburn[52]), tps Thornyburn, Tarset West (civ united 1811 as Thornyburn CP, Tarset West deemed tp in the new par[52]), tps Chirdon, Greystead, Smalesmouth (civ united 1811 as Greystead CP with others deemed tps in the new par[52]), tp Humshaugh (sep CP 1866,[1] eccl retained 1811 in Simonburn but made a chap, sep EP 1900 from Simonburn AP [tps Humshaugh, Black Carts and Ryehill, Haughton, pt tp Walwick, the latter 2 with no sep civ identity], Warden AP[74]); tps Black Carts and Ryehill, Haughton (each a sep CP 1866,[1] each eccl severed 1900 to help cr Humshaugh EP[74]). *LG* Seq 18. *Parl* Seq 5. *Eccl* Seq 7.

SLAGGYFORD

CP Cr 1955 by union Kirkhaugh AP, Knarsdale AP.[45] *LG* Haltw. RD. Renamed 1967 'Knaresdale with Kirkhaugh' CP.[183]

SLALEY

AP *LG* Seq 18. *Parl* Seq 5. *Eccl* Corbr. RDn (until 1884), Hexham RDn (1884—between 1899 and 1957), Corbr. RDn (between 1899 and 1957—*).

SLEEKBURN

EP Cr 1906 from Bedlington AP, Cambois EP, Choppington EP.[107] Bedl. RDn.

SMALESMOUTH

Tp in Simonburn AP, made 1811 pt of Greystead par cr from Simonburn,[52] 'Smalesmouth' a sep CP 1866.[1] *LG* Tyned. Wd, Bell. PLU, RSD, RD. Bdry: 1883.[4] Abol 1955 to help cr Greystead CP.[47] *Parl* S'rn Dv (1867—85), Hexham Dv/CC (1885—1970).

SNITTER

Tp in Rothbury AP, sep CP 1866.[1] Incl 1866—89 undivided pt Intermixed Lands common to Debdon CP and Snitter CP; after abol of Debdon into Rothbury AP, common to Rothbury AP and Snitter CP. *LG* Seq 8. Bdry: 1889,[15] 1955 (gains Flotterton CP, Warton CP).[16] *Parl* Seq 2.

SPINDLESTONE

Tp in Bamburgh AP, sep CP 1866.[1] *LG* Bamb. Wd, Belf. PLU, RSD, RD. Abol 1955 ent to Easington CP.[8] *Parl* N'rn Dv (1867—85), Berw. upon Tweed Dv/CC (1885—1970).

SPITAL

Tp in Ovingham AP, sep CP 1866.[1] *LG* Tyned. Wd, Hexham PLU, RSD, RD. Abol 1955 ent to Horsley CP.[37] *Parl* S'rn Dv (1867—85), Hexham Dv/CC (1885—1970).

SPITAL HILL

Tp in Mitford AP, sep CP 1866.[1] *LG* Morp. Wd, PLU, RSD, RD. Abol 1955 ent to Mitford AP.[28] *Parl* N'rn Dv (1867—85), Wansb. Dv (1885—1948), Morp. CC (1948—70).

SPITTAL

EP Cr 1873 from Tweedmouth EP.[217] Norham RDn.

STAMFORD

Tp in Embleton AP, sep CP 1866.[1] *LG* Bamb. Wd, Alnw. PLU, RSD, RD. Abol 1955 ent to Rennington CP.[2] *Parl* N'rn Dv (1867—85), Berw. upon Tweed Dv/CC (1885—1970).

STAMFORDHAM

AP Incl tps Bitchfield, Cheesburn Grange, Fenwick, Hawkwell, Black Heddon, Heugh, Ingoe, Kearsley, East Matfen, West Matfen, Nesbit, Ouston, Ryall, Wallridge (each a sep CP 1866[1] so that 'Stamfordham' has no sep civ identity 1866—1955 (see following entry). *LG* Tyned. Wd. *Parl* S'rn Dv (1832—67). *Eccl* Morp. RDn (until 1845), Corbr. RDn (1845—*). Eccl bdry: 1846 (cr Matfen EP).[140]

CP Cr 1955 by union Cheesburn Grange CP, Dalton CP, Eachwick CP, Harlow Hill CP, Hawkwell CP, Heugh CP, Nesbitt CP, Ouston CP.[54] *LG* Castle Wd RD. *Parl* Hexham CC (1970—*).

STANNINGTON

AP *LG* Seq 3. Civ bdry: 1955 (incl help cr Brunswick CP),[54] 1969.[214] *Parl* Seq 8. Parl bdry: 1971.[215] *Eccl* Morp. RDn (until 1845), Newc upon Tyne RDn (1845—74), Newc upon Tyne RDn (N'rn Dv) (1877—84), Newc upon Tyne RDn (E'rn Dv) (1877—84), Bedl. RDn (1884—*).

STANTON

Tp in Long Horsley AP, sep CP 1866.[1] *LG* Morp. Wd, PLU, RSD, RD. Abol 1955 ent to Netherwitton CP.[28] *Parl* N'rn Dv (1867—85), Wansb. Dv

(1885—1948), Morp. CC (1948—70).

STELLING

Tp in Bywell St Peter AP, sep CP 1866.[1] *LG* Tyned. Wd, Hexham PLU, RSD, RD. Bdry: 1883,[4] 1887.[86] Abol 1955 ent to Bywell CP.[37] *Parl* S'rn Dv (1867—85), Hexham Dv/CC (1885—1970).

STOCKSFIELD HALL

Tp in Bywell St Andrew AP, sep CP 1866.[1] *LG* Tyned. Wd, Hexham PLU, RSD. Abol 1887 pt to Mickley CP, pt to Broomley CP.[30] *Parl* S'rn Dv (1867—85), Hexham Dv (1885—1918).

STURTON GRANGE

Tp in Warkworth AP, sep CP 1866.[1] *LG* Coq. Wd, Alnw. PLU, RSD, RD. Bdry: 1888.[6] Abol 1955 ent to Warkworth AP.[2] *Parl* N'rn Dv (1867—85), Berw. upon Tweed Dv/CC (1885—1970).

STYFORD

Tp in Bywell St Andrew AP, sep CP 1866.[1] *LG* Tyned. Wd, Hexham PLU, RSD, RD. Abol 1955 ent to Bywell CP.[37] *Parl* S'rn Dv (1867—85), Hexham Dv/CC (1885—1970).

SUGLEY

Chap in Newburn AP, sep CP 1866,[1] sep EP 1887.[201] *LG* Castle Wd, Castle Wd PLU, RSD (1875—93), Newburn USD (1893—94), UD (1894—1935). Abol civ 1935 ent to Newburn AP.[34] *Parl* S'rn Dv (1867—85), Tynes. Dv (1885—1918), Wansb. Dv (1918—48). *Eccl* Newc RDn (1887—1967), Newc West RDn (1967—*). Eccl bdry: 1900 (help cr Whorlton EP),[202] 1957,[123] 1964 (help cr Denton EP).[88]

NORTH SUNDERLAND

Tp in Bamburgh AP, sep CP 1866,[1] sep EP 1843.[43] *LG* Seq 2. Civ bdry: 1955 (gains ex-par Farne Islands, Monks House CP, Shoreston CP).[8] *Parl* Seq 1. *Eccl* Bamb. RDn (1843—1969), Bamb. & Glend. RDn (1969—*).

SWARLAND

Tp in Felton AP, sep CP 1866.[1] *LG* Coq. Wd, Alnw. PLU, RSD, RD. Bdry: 1888.[6] Abol 1955 ent to Newton on the Moor CP.[2] *Parl* N'rn Dv (1867—85), Berw. upon Tweed Dv/CC (1885—1970).

SWEETHOPE

Tp in Thockrington AP, sep CP 1866.[1] *LG* Tyned. Wd, Bell. PLU, RSD, RD. Abol 1955 to help cr Bavington CP.[47] *Parl* S'rn Dv (1867—85), Hexham Dv/CC (1885—1970).

SWINHOE

Tp in Bamburgh AP, sep CP 1866.[1] *LG* Bamb. Wd, Belf. PLU, RSD, RD. Abol 1955 ent to Beadnell CP.[8] *Parl* N'rn Dv (1867—85), Berw. upon Tweed Dv/CC (1885—1970).

TARRETBURN

Tp in chap Bellingham (sep par 1811 from Simonburn[52]), 'Tarretburn' a sep CP 1866.[1] *LG* Tyned. Wd, Bell. PLU, RSD. Abol 1886 pt to help cr Bellingham CP, pt to Tarset West CP.[53] *Parl* S'rn Dv (1867—85), Hexham Dv (1885—1918).

TARSET

CP Cr 1955 by union Tarset West CP, pt Bellingham AP, pt Thorneyburn CP.[47] *LG* Bell. RD. *Parl* Hexham CC (1970—*).

TARSET WEST

Tp in Simonburn AP, united 1811 with tp Thorneyburn in same par to cr Thorneyburn par[52] and thereafter tp in the latter, 'Tarset West' a sep CP 1866.[1] *LG* Tyned. Wd, Bell. PLU, RSD, RD. Bdry: 1883,[4] 1886.[53] Abol 1955 to help cr Tarset CP.[47] *Parl* S'rn Dv (1867—85), Hexham Dv/CC (1885—1970).

THIRLWALL

Tp in Haltwhislte AP, sep CP 1866,[1] eccl severed 1831 to help cr Greenhead EP,[11] eccl refounded 1892.[75] *LG* Seq 17. *Parl* Seq 5.

THIRSTON

CP Cr 1955 by union Bockenfield CP, Eshott CP, Thirston (with Shothaugh) CP.[28] *LG* Morp. RD. *Parl* Morp. CC (1970—*).

EAST AND WEST THIRSTON WITH SHOTHAUGH

Tp in Felton AP, sep CP 1866.[1] *LG* Morp. Wd, PLU, RSD, RD. Bdry: 1883,[4] 1888,[79] 1888.[218] Abol 1935 to help cr Thirston (with Shothaugh) CP.[34] *Parl* N'rn Dv (1867—85), Wansb. Dv (1885—1948).

THIRSTON (WITH SHOTHAUGH)

CP Cr 1935 by union East and West Thirston with Shothaugh CP, pt Elyhaugh CP, pt Felton AP.[34] *LG* Morp. RD. Abol 1955 to help cr Thirston CP.[28] *Parl* Morp. CC (1948—70).

THOCKRINGTON

AP Incl tps Little Bavington, Carrycoates, Sweethorpe (each a sep CP 1866[1]). *LG* Tyned. Wd, Bell. PLU, RSD, RD. Abol 1955 to help cr Bavington CP.[47] *Parl* S'rn Dv (1867—85), Hexham Dv/CC (1885—1970). *Eccl* Newc upon Tyne RDn (until 1845), Bell. RDn (1885—*).

THORNBROUGH

Tp in Corbridge AP, sep CP 1866.[1] *LG* Tyned. Wd, Hexham PLU, RSD, RD. Abol 1955 ent to Corbridge AP.[37] *Parl* S'rn Dv (1867—85), Hexham Dv/CC (1885—1970).

THORNEYBURN

Tp in Simonburn AP, united 1811 with tp Tarset West in same par as Thorneyburn par,[52] Tarset West deemed tp in the new par (sep CP 1866[1]). *LG* Tyned. Wd, Bell. PLU, RSD, RD. Addtl civ bdry alt: 1883.[4] Abol 1955 pt to help cr Falstone CP, pt to help cr Tarset West CP.[47] *Parl* S'rn Dv (1867—85), Hexham Dv/CC (1885—1970).

THORNGRAFTON

Tp in Haltwhistle AP, sep CP 1866.[1] *LG* Tyned. Wd, Haltw. PLU, RSD, RD. Bdry: 1883,[4] 1886.[76] Abol 1955 to help cr Bardon Mill CP.[45] *Parl* S'rn Dv (1867—85), Hexham Dv/CC (1885—1970).

THORNTON

In Durham, transf to Northumb 1832 for parl purposes, 1844 for civ purposes.[25] Tp in Norham AP, sep CP 1866.[1] *LG* Norhamshire, Berw. PLU, RSD, Norham & Islandshires RD. Abol 1955 ent to Shoreswood CP.[139] *Parl* In Durham until 1832, N'rn Dv (1832—85), Berw. upon Tweed Dv/CC (1885—1970).

EAST THORNTON

Tp in Hartburn AP, sep CP 1866.[1] *LG* Morp. Wd, PLU, RSD, RD. Abol 1955 ent to Hartburn AP.[28]

Parl N'rn Dv (1867—85), Wansb. Dv (1885—1948), Morp. CC (1948—70).

WEST THORNTON
Tp in Hartburn AP, sep CP 1866.[1] Organisation as for East Thornton.

THROCKLEY
Tp in Newburn AP, sep CP 1866.[1] *LG* Castle Wd, Castle Wd PLU, RSD (1875—93), Newburn USD (1893—94), UD (1894—1935). Bdry: 1887.[153] Abol 1935 ent to Newburn AP.[34] *Parl* S'rn Dv (1867—85), Tynes. Dv (1885—1918), Wansb. Dv (1918—48).

THROPHILL
Tp in Mitford AP, sep CP 1866.[1] *LG* Morp. Wd, PLU, RSD, RD. Abol 1955 ent to Meldon AP.[28] *Parl* N'rn Dv (1867—85), Wansb. Dv (1885—1948), Morp. CC (1948—70).

THROPTON
Tp in Rothbury AP, sep CP 1866.[1] *LG* Seq 8. Bdry: 1889.[15] *Parl* Seq 2.

TITLINGTON
Tp in Eglingham AP, sep CP 1866.[1] *LG* Coq. Wd, Alnw. PLU, RSD, RD. Abol 1955 ent to Hedgeley CP.[2] *Parl* N'rn Dv (1867—85), Berw. upon Tweed Dv/CC (1885—1970).

TODBURN
Tp in Long Horsley AP, sep CP 1866.[1] *LG* Morp. Wd, Rothb. PLU, RSD, RD. Abol 1955 ent to Nunnykirk CP.[16] *Parl* N'rn Dv (1867—85), Wansb. Dv (1885—1918), Berw. upon Tweed Dv/CC (1918—70).

TODRIDGE
Tp in Hartburn AP, sep CP 1866.[1] *LG* Morp. Wd, PLU, RSD, RD. Abol 1955 ent to Wallington Demesne CP.[28] *Parl* N'rn Dv (1867—85), Wansb. Dv (1885—1948), Morp. CC (1948—70).

TOGSTON
Tp in Warkworth AP, sep CP 1866,[1] pt eccl severed 1869 to help cr Amble EP,[23] addtl pts transf 1889 to Amble EP, Chevington EP.[24] *LG* Seq 11. *Parl* Seq 3.

TOSSON
CP Cr 1889 by union pt Great Tosson and Rye Hill CP, pt Tosson Little CP.[165] *LG* Coq. Wd, Rothb. PLU, RD. Bdry: 1955 (gains Newtown CP, Whitton CP).[16] *Parl* Berw. upon Tweed Dv/CC (1918—*).

GREAT TOSSON AND RYE HILL
Tp in Rothbury AP, sep CP 1866.[1] *LG* Coq. Wd, Rothb. PLU, RSD. Abol 1889 pt to help cr Tosson CP, pt to Hepple CP.[165] *Parl* N'rn Dv (1867—85), Hexham Dv/CC (1885—1918).

TOSSON LITTLE
Tp in Rothbury AP, sep CP 1866.[1] Organisation as for Great Tosson and Rye Hill.

TRANWELL
CP Cr 1894 from the pt of Tranwell and High Church CP not in Morp. MB.[196] *LG* Morp. PLU, RD. Bdry: 1935.[34] Abol 1955 ent to Mitford AP.[28] *Parl* Morp. Parl Bor (1918—48), Morp. CC (1948—70).

TRANWELL AND HIGH CHURCH
Tp in Morpeth AP, sep CP 1866.[1] *LG* Castle Wd, Morp. PLU, pt Morp. MB (1835—94), Morp. USD (ent 1875—89, pt 1889—94), pt Morp. RSD

(1889—94). Abol 1894 the pt in the MB transf to Morpeth AP, the remainder cr Tranwell CP.[196] *Parl* Morp. Parl Bor (1832—1918).

HIGH AND LOW TREWHITT
Tp in Rothbury AP, sep CP 1866.[1] *LG* Coq. Wd, Rothb. PLU, RSD, RD. Abol 1955 to help cr Netherton CP.[16] *Parl* N'rn Dv (1867—85), Hexham Dv (1885—1918), Berw. upon Tweed Dv/CC (1918—70).

TREWICK
Tp in Bolam AP, sep CP 1866.[1] *LG* Castle Wd, Castle Wd PLU, RSD, RD. Abol 1955 ent to Belsay CP.[54] *Parl* S'rn Dv (1867—85), Wansb. Dv (1885—1948), Hexham CC (1948—70).

TRITLINGTON
Tp in Bothal AP, sep CP 1866.[1] *LG* Seq 10. Bdry: 1955 (gains Causey Park CP, Earsdon CP, Earsdon Forest CP, Fenrother CP).[28] *Parl* Seq 4.

TROUGHEND
Tp in Elsdon AP, sep CP 1866.[1] *LG* Coq. Wd, Bell. PLU, RSD, RD. Abol 1955 pt to help cr Rochester CP, pt to Otterburn CP.[47] *Parl* N'rn Dv (1867—85), Hexham Dv (1885—1918), Berw. upon Tweed Dv/CC (1918—70).

TUGHALL
Tp in Bamburgh AP, sep CP 1866.[1] *LG* Bamb. Wd, Belf. PLU, RSD, RD. Abol 1955 ent to Beadnell CP.[8] *Parl* N'rn Dv (1867—85), Berw. upon Tweed Dv/CC (1885—1970).

TWEEDMOUTH
In Durham, transf to Northumb 1832 for parl purposes, 1844 for civ purposes.[25] Chap in Holy Island AP, sep civ identity early, sep EP 1737.[11] *LG* Islandshire, Berw. PLU, Berw. upon Tweed MB (pt 1835—91, ent 1891—1974), Berw. upon Tweed USD (pt 1875—91, ent 1891—94), pt Berw. RSD (1875—91). Civ bdry: 1891 (the pt not in the MB cr Ord CP),[211] 1935.[34] *Parl* Berw. upon Tweed Parl Bor (1832—85), Dv/CC (1885—*). *Eccl* Bamb. RDn (1737—1845), Norham RDn (1845—*). Eccl bdry: 1844 (help cr Scremerston EP).[27]

TWIZELL
Tp in Morpeth AP, sep CP 1866.[1] *LG* Castle Wd, Castle Wd PLU, RSD, RD. Abol 1955 ent to Whalton AP.[54] *Parl* S'rn Dv (1867—85), Wansb. Dv (1885—1948), Hexham CC (1948—70).

TWIZELL
In Durham, transf to Northumb 1832 for parl purposes, 1844 for civ purposes.[25] Tp in Norham AP, sep CP 1866.[1] *LG* Norhamshire, Berw. PLU, RSD, Norham & Islandshires RD. Abol 1955 ent to Duddo CP.[139] *Parl* In Durham until 1832, N'rn Dv (1832—85), Berw. upon Tweed Dv/CC (1885—1970).

TYNEMOUTH
The following have 'Tynemouth' in their names. Insofar as any existed at a given time: *LG* Castle Wd, Tynem. PLU, MB/CB, USD. *Parl* Tynem. Parl Bor/BC (1832—*). *Eccl* Newc upon Tyne RDn (until 1874), Newc upon Tyne RDn (N'rn Dv) (1874—77), Newc upon Tyne RDn (E'rn Dv) (1877—84), Tynem. RDn (1884—*).
AP1—TYNEMOUTH—Orig pt of priory church. Incl

tp Cullercoates (sep CP 1866,[1] eccl severed 1860 and united with pt tp Whitley, pt tp Monkseaton [all of each except the pt of Shiremoor in each made pt of EP2, qv] to cr Cullercoates [St Paul] EP[19]), chap Whitley (sep CP 1866,[1] eccl severed 1860, the pt of Shiremoor incl to help cr EP2, the remainder to help cr Cullercoates [St Paul] EP[19]), tp Monkseaton (sep CP 1866,[1] the pt of Shiremoor incl to help cr EP3, the remainder to help cr Cullercoates [St Paul] EP[19]), chap Earsdon (sep civ identity early, sep EP 1761[11]), tp Murton (sep CP 1866,[1] eccl severed 1860 to help cr EP3[19]), tp Chirton (sep CP 1866,[1] pt eccl severed 1860 to help refound EP3,[19] the remainder severed 1861 to help refound EP5[114]), tp Preston (sep CP 1866,[1] pt eccl severed 1861 to help refound EP5[114]), tp North Shields (sep CP 1866,[1] eccl severed 1860 to cr EP1 [later called 'North Shields St Peter' or 'Tynemouth St Peter'],[193] pt of latter severed 1861 to help refound EP5[114]). Addtl civ bdry alt: 1908 (gains pars in Tynem. CB: Cullercoates CP, Chirton CP, Preston CP, North Shields CP, Unnamed CP),[117] 1935 (exchanges pts with Whitley & Monkseaton UD & CP, loses pt to help cr Seaton Valley UD & CP, gains pt Earsdon UD & CP, gains pt Earsdon UD & Murton CP).[34] Transf 1974 to Tyne & Wear.[89] Addtl eccl bdry alt: 1859 (cr EP5, refounded 1861, qv),[114] 1861 (cr EP3),[114] 1885 (cr EP4),[219] 1931,[220] 1968 (help cr Balkwell EP),[39] 1969.[40]

—TYNEMOUTH HOLY TRINITY—See EP5

EP1—TYNEMOUTH LOW TOWN—Cr 1860 from AP1 (pt tp North Shields).[193] Later called 'Tynemouth St Peter' or more usually 'North Shields St Peter'. Bdry: 1861 (help refound EP5),[114] 1905.[221] Abol 1931 pt to EP5, pt to AP1.[220]

EP2—TYNEMOUTH PERCY—Erected *ca* 1450 in area of future EP3 in AP1, sep EP 1860 (tp Murton, pt tp Chirton, pt Shiremoor [in chap Whitley, tp Monkseaton]).[19] Bdry: 1968 (incl help cr Balkwell EP, help cr Shiremoor EP).[39]

EP3—TYNEMOUTH PRIORY—Cr 1861 from AP1.[114] Incl from *ca* 1450 area of future EP2, qv. Bdry: 1880 (help cr Cullercoats St George EP),[129] 1931.[19]

EP4—TYNEMOUTH ST AUGUSTINE—Cr 1885 from AP1.[219]

—TYNEMOUTH ST PETER—See EP1

EP5—TYNEMOUTH WESTERN TOWN—Cr 1859,[11] eccl refounded 1861 from AP1 (pts tps Chirton, Preston, North Shields [the latter cr 1860 EP1, qv] and pt of AP1 proper).[114] Sometimes 'Tynemouth Holy Trinity'. Bdry: 1905,[221] 1931,[220] 1968.[39]

ULGHAM
    Chap in Morpeth AP, sep CP 1866,[1] sep EP 1875.[195] *LG* Seq 10. *Parl* Seq 4. *Eccl* Morp. RDn.

UNNAMED
CP Cr 1894 from the pt of Murton CP in Tynem. CB.[194] *LG* Tynem. PLU, CB. Abol 1908 ent to Tynemouth AP.[117]

UNDIVIDED MOOR
    Common to Kirknewton AP and Lanton CP. *LG* Glend. PLU, RD. Abol 1955 ent to Ewart CP.[9] *Parl* Berw. upon Tweed Dv/CC (1918—70).

UNTHANK
    Tp in Alnham AP, sep CP 1866.[1] *LG* Coq. Wd, Rothb. PLU, RSD, RD. Abol 1955 ent to Alnham AP.[16] *Parl* N'rn Dv (1867—85), Berw. upon Tweed Dv/CC (1885—1970).

WALKER
CP Cr 1894 from the pt of Longbenton AP in Walker USD.[186] *LG* Tynem. PLU, Walker UD (1894—1904), Newc upon Tyne CB (1904—74). Transf 1974 to Tyne & Wear.[89] *Parl* See Pt III of the *Guide* for composition of Parl Bors/BCs in Newc upon Tyne CB by wards of the CB.

EP Cr 1846 from Long Benton AP (civ, 'Longbenton').[56] Newc upon Tyne RDn (1846—74), Newc upon Tyne RDn (S'rn Dv) (1874—77), Newc upon Tyne RDn (E'rn Dv) (1877—84), Tynem. RDn (1884—99), Newc RDn (1899—1967), Newc East RDn (1967—*). Bdry: 1906 (help cr Byker St Mark EP),[75] 1952,[57] 1966 (help cr Walkergate EP).[222]

WALKERGATE
    EP Cr 1966 from Walker EP.[222] Newc RDn (1966—67), Newc East RDn (1967—*).

WALKMILL
    Tp in Warkworth AP, sep CP 1866.[1] *LG* Coq. Wd, Alnw. PLU, RSD, RD. Bdry: 1888.[6] Abol 1955 ent to Warkworth AP.[2] *Parl* N'rn Dv (1867—85), Berw. upon Tweed Dv/CC (1885—1970).

WALL
    Tp in Lee St John AP, sep CP 1866,[1] eccl severed 1879 to help cr St Oswald in Lee with Bingfield St Mary EP.[70] *LG* Seq 18. Bdry: 1955 (gains Cocklaw CP, Fallowfield CP).[37] *Parl* Seq 5.

WALL TOWN
    Tp in Haltwhistle AP, sep CP 1866.[1] *LG* Tyned. Wd, Haltw. PLU, RSD, RD. Bdry: 1883.[4] Abol 1955 to help cr Greenhead CP.[45] *Parl* S'rn Dv (1867—85), Hexham Dv/CC (1885—1970).

WALLBOTTLE
    Tp in Newburn AP, sep CP 1866.[1] *LG* Castle Wd, Castle Wd PLU, RSD (1875—83), Newburn USD (1875—83), UD (1894—1935). Bdry: 1887.[153] Abol 1935 ent to Newburn AP.[34] *Parl* S'rn Dv (1867—85), Tynes. Dv (1885—1918), Wansb. Dv (1918—48).

WALLINGTON DEMESNE
    Tp in Hartburn AP, sep CP 1866.[1] *LG* Tyned. Wd, Morp. PLU, RSD, RD. Bdry: 1955 (gains Cambo CP, Corridge CP, Deanham CP, Hartburn Grange CP, Highlaws CP, North Middleton CP, South Middleton CP, Todridge CP).[28] *Parl* Seq 9.

WALLRIDGE
    Tp in Stamfordham AP, sep CP 1866.[1] *LG* Tyned. Wd, Castle Wd PLU, RSD, RD. Abol 1955 ent to Belsay CP.[54] *Parl* S'rn Dv (1867—85), Hexham Dv/CC (1885—1970).

WALLSEND
    Chap (Northumb) appropriated to Jarrow Abbey (Durham), at Dissolution made pt of endowment of

Dean & Chapter of Durham, rebuilt *ca* 1807 and sep par then.[223] *LG* Castle Wd, Tynem. PLU, pt Howdon USD, pt Wallsend USD, pt Willington Quay USD, pt Tynem. RSD, Wallsend UD (1894—1901), MB (1901—74). Civ bdry: 1894 (the pt in Willington Quay and the pt in Howdon USD cr Willington Quay CP, the pt in the RSD cr Willington CP),[224] 1910 (incl gains Willington Quay UD & CP, Willington CP).[187] Transf 1974 to Tyne & Wear.[89] *Parl* S'rn Dv (1832—85), Tynes. Dv (1885—1918), Wallsend Parl Bor/BC (1918—*). *Eccl* Newc upon Tyne RDn (1807—74), Newc upon Tyne RDn (S'rn Dv) (1874—77), Newc upon Tyne RDn (E'rn Dv) (1877—84), Tynem. RDn (1884—*). Eccl bdry: 1859 (the tp of Willington [not sep civ] severed to cr 2 EPs of Howden Panns, Willington),[177] 1887 (cr Wallsend St Luke EP),[225] 1905,[93] 1955 (help cr Wallsend St John EP).[58]

WALLSEND ST JOHN
EP Cr 1955 from Wallsend EP, Wallsend St Luke EP, Long Benton AP.[58] Tynem. RDn.

WALLSEND ST LUKE
EP Cr 1887 from Wallsend EP.[225] Tynem. RDn. Bdry: 1905,[93] 1955 (help cr Wallsend St John EP).[58]

WARDEN
AP Incl chap Haydon (also a bor as 'Haydon Bridge', status not sustained, sep CP 1866 as 'Haydon',[1] sep EP 1879 as 'Haydon Bridge'[7]), chap & bor (status not sustained) Newbrough (sep CP 1866,[1] not sep eccl so this par sometimes eccl 'Warden and Newbrough'). *LG* Seq 18. Addtl civ bdry alt: 1955.[37] *Parl* Seq 5. *Eccl* Seq 8. Addtl eccl bdry alt: 1900 (help refound Humshaugh EP).[74]

WARENFORD
Tp in Bamburgh AP, sep CP 1866,[1] eccl severed 1884 to help refound Lucker EP.[7] *LG* Bamb. Wd, Belf. PLU, RSD, RD. Bdry: 1887.[174] Abol 1955 to help cr Adderstone with Lucker CP.[8] *Parl* N'rn Dv (1867—85), Berw. upon Tweed Dv/CC (1885—1970).

WARENTON
Tp in Bamburgh AP, sep CP 1866,[1] eccl severed 1884 to help refound Lucker EP.[7] *LG* Bamb. Wd, Belf. PLU, RSD, RD. Abol 1955 ent to Belford AP.[8] *Parl* N'rn Dv (1867—85), Berw. upon Tweed Dv/CC (1885—1970).

WARK
Chap in Simonburn AP, sep par 1811.[52] Incl tps High Shitlington, Low Shitlington, Warksburn (each a sep CP 1866[1]). *LG* Seq 15. Addtl civ bdry alt: 1883,[4] 1886,[53] 1955.[47] *Parl* Seq 5. *Eccl* Corbr. RDn (1811—45), Bell. RDn (1845—*).

WARKSBURN
Tp in chap Wark (sep par 1811 from Simonburn AP[52]), sep CP 1866.[1] *LG* Tyned. Wd, Bell. PLU, RSD. Abol 1886 ent to Wark CP.[53] *Parl* S'rn Dv (1867—85), Hexham Dv (1885—1918).

WARKWORTH
AP Tp 'Warworth' in Morp. Wd as were tps Bullock's Hall, East Chevington, West Chevington, Hadston (each a sep CP 1866,[1] eccl united 1863 to cr Chevington EP[92]), tp Morwick (sep CP 1866[1]), tps Acklington, Acklington Park (each a sep CP 1866,[1] eccl united 1859 incl ex-par Brainshaugh to cr Acklington EP[3]), tps Amble, Gloster Hill, Hauxley, Togston (each a sep CP 1866,[1] eccl united 1869 [but only pt Togston] to cr Amble EP[23]); incl in Coq. Wd tps Birling, Brotherwick, High Buston, Low Buston, Sturton Grange, Walkmill (each a sep CP 1866[1]). *LG* Pt Newton Bor (status not sustained), pt Warkworth Bor, Alnw. PLU, RSD, RD. Addtl civ bdry alt: 1955 (gains Birling CP, Brotherwick CP, Low Buston CP, Gloster Hill CP, Morwick CP, Sturton Grange CP, Walkmill CP).[2] *Parl* Seq 3. *Eccl* Seq 1. Addtl eccl bdry alt: 1889 (addtl pts tp Togston transf to Amble EP, Chevington EP).[24]

WARTON
Tp in Rothbury AP, sep CP 1866.[1] *LG* Coq. Wd, Rothb. PLU, RSD, RD. Abol 1955 ent to Snitter CP.[16] *Parl* N'rn Dv (1867—85), Hexham Dv (1885—1918), Berw. upon Tweed Dv/CC (1918—70).

WEETSLADE
CP Cr 1894 from the pt of Longbenton AP in Weetslade USD.[186] *LG* Tynem. PLU, Weetslade UD. Bdry: 1899 (help cr Camperdown CP).[108] Abol 1935 ent to Longbenton UD & AP.[34] *Parl* Wallsend Parl Bor (1918—48).

WELLHAUGH
Tp in chap Falstone (orig appropriated to Kirkham Priory, later deemed chap in Simonburn AP, sep par 1811[52]), sep CP 1866.[1] *LG* Tyned. Wd, Bell. PLU, RSD, RD. Bdry: 1883.[4] Abol 1955 pt to help cr Falstone CP, pt to help cr Kielder CP.[47] *Parl* S'rn Dv (1867—85), Hexham Dv/CC (1885—1970).

WELTON
Tp in Ovingham AP, sep CP 1866.[1] *LG* Tyned. Wd, Hexham PLU, RSD, RD. Abol 1955 ent to Horsley CP.[37] *Parl* S'rn Dv (1867—85), Hexham Dv/CC (1885—1970).

WESTGATE
Tp in chap Newcastle upon Tyne St John (sep civ identity early from Newcastle upon Tyne AP, sep EP 1808[11]), 'Westgate' a sep CP 1866.[1] *LG* Castle Wd, Newc upon Tyne PLU, MB (1835—89), USD, CB (1889—1914). Abol 1914 to help cr Newcastle upon Tyne CP.[62] *Parl* Newc upon Tyne Parl Bor (1832—1918).

WESTNEWTON
Tp in Kirknewton AP, sep CP 1866.[1] *LG* Glend. Wd, PLU, RSD, RD. Abol 1955 ent to Kirknewton AP.[9] *Parl* N'rn Dv (1867—85), Berw. upon Tweed Dv/CC (1885—1970).

WHALTON
AP Incl tps Newham, Ogle, Riplington (each a sep CP 1866[1]). *LG* Seq 3. Addtl civ bdry alt: 1955 (gains Ogle CP, Riplington CP, Shilvington CP, Twizell CP).[54] *Parl* Seq 8. *Eccl* Seq 9.

WEST WHELPINGTON
Tp in Kirkwhelpington AP, sep CP 1866.[1] *LG* Tyned. Wd, Bell. PLU, RSD, RD. Abol 1955 ent to Kirkwhelpington AP.[47] *Parl* S'rn Dv (1867—85), Hexham Dv/CC (1885—1970).

WHITCHESTER
Tp in Heddon on the Wall AP, sep CP 1866.[1] *LG* Tyned. Wd, Castle Wd PLU, RSD, RD. Abol 1955

ent to Heddon on the Wall AP.[54] *Parl* S'rn Dv (1867—85), Wansb. Dv (1885—1948), Hexham CC (1948—70).

WHITFIELD

AP *LG* Tyned. Wd, Haltw. PLU, RSD, RD. Abol 1955 to help cr Plenmeller with Whitfield CP.[45] *Parl* S'rn Dv (1867—85), Hexham Dv/CC (1885—1970). *Eccl* Bamb. RDn (until 1845), Hexham RDn (1845—*).

WHITLEY

Chap in Hexham AP (comprised of tps Hexhamshire High Quarter, Hexhamshire Low Quarter, Hexhamshire Middle Quarter [qv for sep civ identity of each 1866[1]]), sep EP 1763,[11] eccl refounded 1900 incl pt Shotley EP.[169] Hexham RDn (1763—1874), Newc upon Tyne RDn (W'rn Dv) (1874—77), Hexham RDn (1877—*).

WHITLEY

Chap in Tynemouth AP, sep CP 1866,[1] eccl severed 1860, the pt of Shiremoor in this area to help cr Tynemouth Percy EP, the remainder to help cr Cullercoats EP.[19] *LG* Castle Wd, Tynem. PLU, Whitley & Monkseaton USD, UD. Bdry: 1881,[191] 1883.[4] Abol 1913 to help cr Whitley and Monkseaton CP.[192] *Parl* S'rn Dv (1867—85), Wansb. Dv (1885—1918).

WHITLEY AND MONKSEATON

CP Cr 1913 by union Whitley CP, Monkseaton CP.[192] *LG* Tynem. PLU, Whitley & Monkseaton UD (1913—44), Whitley Bay UD (1944—54), MB (1954—74). Bdry: 1920 (exchanges pts with Seaton Delaval UD & CP),[213] 1935 (incl exchanges pts with Tynem. CB [assoc with Northumb] & AP),[34] 1974 (pt transf to Tyne & Wear).[89] *Parl* Wansb. Dv (1918—48), Tynem. BC (1948—*).

WHITRIDGE

Tp in Hartburn AP, sep CP 1866.[1] *LG* Morp. Wd, PLU, RSD, RD. Abol 1955 ent to Netherwitton CP.[28] *Parl* N'rn Dv (1867—85), Wansb. Dv (1885—1948), Morp. CC (1948—70).

WHITTINGHAM

AP Incl tps Callaley and Yetlington, Glanton, Lorbottle, Great Ryle, Little Ryle, Shawdon (each a sep CP 1866[1]). *LG* Seq 8. *Parl* Seq 1. *Eccl* Sometimes as 'Whittingham with Glanton', Seq 2.

WHITTINGTON

CP Cr 1955 by union Clarewood CP, Hallington CP, Halton CP, Great Whittington CP.[37] *LG* Hexham RD. *Parl* Hexham CC (1970—*).

GREAT WHITTINGTON

Tp in Corbridge AP, sep CP 1866.[1] *LG* Tyned. Wd, Hexham PLU, RSD, RD. Abol 1955 to help cr Whittington CP.[37] *Parl* S'rn Dv (1867—85), Hexham Dv/CC (1885—1970).

LITTLE WHITTINGTON

Tp in Corbridge AP, sep CP 1866.[1] Organisation as for Great Whittington.

WHITTLE

Tp in Ovingham AP, sep CP 1866.[1] *LG* Tyned. Wd, Hexham PLU, RSD, RD. Abol 1955 ent to Horsley CP.[37] *Parl* S'rn Dv (1867—85), Hexham Dv/CC (1885—1970).

WHITTLE

Tp in Shilbottle AP, sep CP 1866.[1] *LG* Coq. Wd, Alnw. PLU, RSD, RD. Abol 1955 ent to Newton on the Moor AP.[2] *Parl* N'rn Dv (1867—85), Berw. upon Tweed Dv/CC (1885—1970).

WHITTON

Tp in Rothbury AP, sep CP 1866.[1] *LG* Coq. Wd, Rothb. PLU, RSD, RD. Abol 1955 ent to Tosson CP.[16] *Parl* N'rn Dv (1867—85), Hexham Dv (1885—1918), Berw. upon Tweed Dv/CC (1918—70).

WHITTONSTALL

Chap in Bywell St Peter AP, sep CP 1866,[1] sep EP 1774.[11] *LG* Tyned. Wd, Hexham PLU, RSD, RD. Bdry: 1887.[36] Renamed 1955 'Shotley Low Quarter' when gains Newlands CP.[37] *Parl* S'rn Dv (1867—85), Hexham Dv/CC (1885—1970). *Eccl* Corbr. RDn. Eccl bdry: 1921,[123] 1931.[19]

WHORLTON

Tp in Newburn AP, sep CP 1866,[1] sep EP 1900 from Newburn AP, Sugley EP.[202] *LG* Castle Wd, Castle Wd PLU, RSD, RD. Civ bdry: 1935.[34] Abol 1955 ent to Woolsington CP.[54] *Parl* S'rn Dv (1867—85), Tynes. Dv (1885—1918), Wansb. Dv (1918—48), Hexham CC (1948—70). *Eccl* Newc RDn (1900—67), Newc West RDn (1967—*).

WIDDRINGTON

Chap in Woodhorn AP, sep civ identity early, sep EP 1766.[11] *LG* Seq 10. Civ bdry: 1888.[143] *Parl* Seq 4. *Eccl* Morp. RDn. Eccl bdry: 1962.[127]

WILLINGTON

Tp in chap Wallsend (in Jarrow AP, at Dissolution made pt of endowment of Dean & Chapter of Durham, rebuilt 1807 and sep par at that time[223]), 'Willington' a sep CP 1894 from the pt of Wallsend CP not in an USD,[224] eccl divided 1859 into 2 EPs of Willington, Howden Panns.[177] *LG* Tynem. PLU, RD. Abol 1910 ent to Wallsend MB & CP.[187] *Eccl* Newc upon Tyne RDn (1859—74), Newc upon Tyne RDn (S'rn Dv) (1874—77), Newc upon Tyne RDn (E'rn Dv) (1877—84), Tynem. RDn (1884—*).

WILLINGTON QUAY

CP Cr 1894 from the pt of Wallsend CP in Howdon USD and the pt of Wallsend CP in Willington Quay USD.[224] *LG* Tynem. PLU, Willington Quay UD (1894—1910). Abol 1910 ent to Wallsend MB & CP.[187]

WINGATES

Tp in Long Horsley AP, sep CP 1866.[1] *LG* Morp. Wd, Rothb. PLU, RSD, RD. Abol 1955 ent to Nunnykirk CP.[16] *Parl* N'rn Dv (1867—85), Wansb. Dv (1885—1918), Berw. upon Tweed Dv/CC (1918—70).

WITTON SHIELDS

Tp in Long Horsley AP, sep CP 1866.[1] *LG* Morp. Wd, PLU, RSD, RD. Abol 1955 ent to Netherwitton CP.[28] *Parl* N'rn Dv (1867—85), Wansb. Dv (1885—1948), Morp. CC (1948—70).

WOODHORN

AP Incl chap Horton (sep civ identity early, sep EP 1734[11]), chap Widdrington (sep civ identity early, sep EP 1766[11]), tps Cresswell, Ellington (each a sep

CP 1866,[1] eccl united 1836 to cr Cresswell EP[126]), tps Hurst, North Seaton, Woodhorn Demesne (each a sep CP 1866[1]), tp Lynemouth (sep CP 1866,[1] sep EP 1963 as 'Lynmouth'[188]), tp & bor (status not sustained) Newbiggin by the Sea (sep CP 1866[1]). *LG* Morp. Wd, PLU, RSD, RD. Civ bdry: 1913.[226] Abol civ 1935 pt to Ashington CP, pt to Newbiggin by the Sea CP.[34] *Parl* N'rn Dv (1832—85), Wansb. Dv (1885—1948). *Eccl* Sometimes as 'Woodhorn with Newbiggin by the Sea', Seq 9.

WOODHORN DEMESNE

Tp in Woodhorn AP, sep CP 1866.[1] *LG* Morp. Wd, PLU, RSD, RD (1894—1913), Newbiggin by the Sea UD (1913—74). Bdry: 1913 (pt transf to Woodhorn AP, the remainder constituted Newbiggin by the Sea UD).[226] *Parl* Wansb. Dv (1885—1948), Morp. CC (1948—*).

WOODHOUSE

Tp in Shilbottle AP, sep CP 1866.[1] *LG* Coq. Wd, Alnw. PLU, RSD, RD. Abol 1955 ent to Shilbottle AP.[2] *Parl* N'rn Dv (1867—85), Berw. upon Tweed Dv/CC (1885—1970).

WOODSIDE

Tp in Elsdon AP, sep CP 1866.[1] *LG* Coq. Wd, Rothb. PLU, RSD, RD. Bdry: 1889.[165] Abol 1955 ent to Hepple CP.[16] *Parl* N'rn Dv (1867—85), Hexham Dv (1885—1918), Berw. upon Tweed Dv/CC (1918—70).

WOOLER

AP Gains 1313 Fenton AP, the latter thereafter considered chap in this par,[160] eccl severed 1882 and transf to Doddington EP as Wooler eccl gains from Doddington tps Earle, Humbleton.[136] *LG* Seq 9. Civ bdry: 1884.[197] *Parl* Seq 1. *Eccl* Seq 4. Addtl eccl bdry alt: 1899.[114]

WOOLSINGTON

Tp in Newburn AP, sep CP 1866.[1] *LG* Seq 3. Bdry: 1955 (incl gains Black Callerton CP, Newbiggin CP, Whorlton CP).[54] Transf 1974 to Tyne & Wear.[89] *Parl* Seq 7.

WOOPERTON

Tp in Eglingham AP, sep CP 1866.[1] *LG* Coq. Wd, Glend. PLU, RSD, RD. Abol 1955 ent to Roddam CP.[9] *Parl* N'rn Dv (1867—85), Berw. upon Tweed Dv/CC (1885—1970).

WREIGHILL

Tp in Rothbury AP, sep CP 1866.[1] *LG* Coq. Wd, Rothb. PLU, RSD, RD. Abol 1955 ent to Hepple CP.[16] *Parl* N'rn Dv (1867—85), Hexham Dv (1885—1918), Berw. upon Tweed Dv/CC (1918—70).

WYLAM

Tp in Ovingham AP, sep CP 1866,[1] sep EP 1902 from Ovingham AP (tps Prudhoe, Horsley, Wylam).[175] *LG* Seq 18. *Parl* Seq 8. *Eccl* Norham RDn.

YEAVERING

Tp in Kirknewton AP, sep CP 1866.[1] *LG* Glend. Wd, PLU, RSD, RD. Abol 1955 ent to Kirknewton AP.[9] *Parl* N'rn Dv (1867—85), Berw. upon Tweed Dv/CC (1885—1970).

NOTTINGHAMSHIRE

ABBREVIATIONS

Abbreviations particular to Notts follow. Those general abbreviations in use throughout the *Guide* are found on pages xvii—xix.

Basf.	Basford
Basset.	Bassetlaw
Bing.	Bingham
Brox.	Broxtowe
Coll.	Collingham
Gainsb.	Gainsborough
Loughb.	Loughborough
Mansf.	Mansfield
Mist.	Misterton
Newk.	Newark
Nott.	Nottingham
Radf.	Radford
Retf.	Retford
Rushcl.	Rushcliffe
Shard.	Shardlow
Staplef.	Stapleford
Thurg.	Thurgarton
Tuxf.	Tuxford

SEQUENCES

An abbreviated entry prefixed by 'Seq' is used in the parochial entries to avoid repeating often the names of superior units of administration. The content of each sequence is shown below.

Local Government Sequences ('LG')

SEQ 1   Basset. Wap, Gainsb. PLU, RSD, Mist. RD (1894—1935), E Retf. RD (1935—74)
SEQ 2   Basset. Wap, E Retf. PLU, RSD, RD
SEQ 3   Basset. Wap, S'well PLU, RSD, RD
SEQ 4   Basset. Wap, Worksop PLU, RSD, Blyth & Cuckney RD (1894—1925), Worksop RD (1925—74)
SEQ 5   Bing. Wap, PLU, RSD, RD
SEQ 6   Brox. Wap, Basf. PLU, RSD, RD
SEQ 7   Newk. Wap, PLU, RSD, RD
SEQ 8   Newk. Wap, Bing. PLU, RSD, RD
SEQ 9   Newk. Wap, S'well PLU, RSD, RD (1894—1935), Newk. RD (1935—74)
SEQ 10 Rushcl. Wap, Basf. PLU, RSD, RD
SEQ 11 Rushcl. Wap, Bing. PLU, RSD, RD
SEQ 12 Rushcl. Wap, Loughb. PLU, RSD, Leake RD (1894—1935), Basf. RD (1935—74)
SEQ 13 Rushcl. Wap, Shard. PLU, RSD, Staplef. RD (1894—1935), Basf. RD (1935—74)
SEQ 14 Thurg. Wap, Basf. PLU, RSD, RD
SEQ 15 Thurg. Wap, not in a PLU (until 1861), Mansf. PLU (1861—1930), RSD, Skegby RD (1894—1935), S'well RD (1935—74)
SEQ 16 Thurg. Wap, E Retf. PLU, RSD, RD
SEQ 17 Thurg. Wap, S'well PLU, RSD, RD
SEQ 18 Thurg. Wap, S'well PLU, RSD, RD (1894—

1935), Newk. RD (1935—74)

Parliamentary Sequences ('Parl')

SEQ 1   E Retf. Parl Bor (1832—85), Basset. Dv/CC (1885—*)
SEQ 2   E Retf. Parl Bor (1832—85), Basset. Dv (1885—1918), Newk. Dv/CC (1918—*)
SEQ 3   N'rn Dv (1832—85), Mansf. Dv (1885—1918), Brox. Dv/CC (1918—70), Ashfield CC (1970—*)
SEQ 4   N'rn Dv (1832—85), Mansf. Dv (1885—1918), Brox. Dv/CC (1918—70), Beeston CC (1970—*)
SEQ 5   N'rn Dv (1832—85), Mansf. Dv (1885—1948), Newk. CC (1948—*)
SEQ 6   N'rn Dv (1832—85), Rushcl. Dv (1885—1918), Brox.Dv/CC (1918—70), Carlton CC (1970—*)
SEQ 7   N'rn Dv (1832—85), Rushcl. Dv (1885—1948), Brox. CC (1948—70), Beeston CC (1970—*)
SEQ 8   S'rn Dv (1832—85), Mansf. Dv (1885—1948), Newk. CC (1948—*)
SEQ 9   S'rn Dv (1832—85), Newk. Dv/CC (1885—*)
SEQ 10 S'rn Dv (1832—85), Newk. Dv (1885—1918), Basset. Dv/CC (1918—)
SEQ 11 S'rn Dv (1832—85), Newk. Dv (1885—

1948), Carlton CC (1948—70), Rushcl. CC (1970—*)

SEQ 12   S'rn Dv (1832—85), Rushcl. Dv/CC (1885—*)

SEQ 13   S'rn Dv (1832—85), Rushcl. Dv (1885—1918), Brox. Dv (1918—48), Carlton CC (1948—*)

SEQ 14   S'rn Dv (1832—85), Rushcl. Dv (1885—1948), Carlton CC (1948—*)

SEQ 15   S'rn Dv (1832—85), Rushcl. Dv (1885—1918), Newk. Dv (1918—48), Carlton CC (1948—70), Rushcl. CC (1970—*)

Ecclesiastical Sequences ('Eccl')

SEQ 1   Bing. RDn (until 1857), Bing. 1 RDn (1857—77), Bing. RDn (1877—84), S Bing. RDn (1884—*)

SEQ 2   Bing. RDn (until 1857), Bing. 2 RDn (1857—77), Bing. RDn (1877—*)

SEQ 3   Bing. RDn (until 1857), Bing. 3 RDn (1857—77), Bing. RDn (1877—84), W Bing. RDn (1884—*)

SEQ 4   Bing. RDn (until 1857), Bing. 3 RDn (1857—77), Bing. RDn (1877—84), W Bing. RDn (1884—87), S Bing. RDn (1887—*)

SEQ 5   Bing. RDn (until 1857), Bing. 3 RDn (1857—66), Bing. 1 RDn (1866—77), Bing. RDn (1877—84), W Bing. RDn (1884—*)

SEQ 6   Newk. RDn (until 1857), Newk. 1 RDn (1857—77), Newk. RDn (1877—*)

SEQ 7   Newk. RDn (until 1857), Newk. 1 RDn (1857—77), Newk. RDn (1877—84), Coll. RDn (1884—87), Newk. East RDn (1887—1910), Newk. RDn (1910—*)

SEQ 8   Newk. RDn (until 1857), Newk. 1 RDn (1857—77), Newk. RDn (1877—84), Coll. RDn (1884—87), Norwell RDn (1887—*)

SEQ 9   Newk. RDn (until 1857), Newk. 2 RDn (1857—77), Newk. RDn (1877—*)

SEQ 10   Newk. RDn (until 1857), S'well RDn (1857—*)

SEQ 11   Nott. RDn (until 1857), Nott. 1 RDn (1857—77), Nott. RDn (1877—84), Mansf. RDn (1884—*)

SEQ 12   Nott. RDn (until 1857), Nott. 1 RDn (1857—77), Nott. RDn (1877—84), Mansf. RDn (1884—87), Bulwell RDn (1887—*)

SEQ 13   Nott. RDn (until 1857), Nott. 1 RDn (1857—77), Nott. RDn (1877—84), Mansf. RDn (1884—87), Bulwell RDn (1887—1910), Beeston RDn (1910—*)

SEQ 14   Nott. RDn (until 1857), Nott. 1 RDn (1857—77), Nott. RDn (1877—84), Mansf. RDn (1884—1910), Bulwell RDn (1910—*)

SEQ 15   Nott. RDn (until 1857), Nott. 2 RDn (1857—77), Nott. RDn (1877—87), Gedling RDn (1887—*)

SEQ 16   Nott. RDn (until 1857), Nott. 2 RDn (1857—77), Nott. RDn (1877—84), S'well RDn (1884—87), Gedling RDn (1887—*)

SEQ 17   Nott. RDn (until 1857), Nott. 3 RDn (1857—77), Nott. RDn (1877—*)

SEQ 18   Retf. RDn (until 1857), Retf. 1 RDn (1857—77), Retf. RDn (1877—*)

SEQ 19   Retf. RDn (until 1857), Retf. 1 RDn (1857—77), Retf. RDn (1877—87), Bawtry RDn (1887—*)

SEQ 20   Retf. RDn (until 1857), Retf. 2 RDn (1857—77), Retf. RDn (1877—84), Tuxf. RDn (1884—*)

SEQ 21   Retf. RDn (until 1857), Retf. 3 RDn (1857—77), Retf. RDn (1877—*)

SEQ 22   Retf. RDn (until 1857), Retf. 3 RDn (1857—77), Retf. RDn (1877—84), Worksop RDn (1884—*)

SEQ 23   S'well pec jurisd (until 1841), S'well RDn (1841—*)

SEQ 24   S'well pec jurisd (until 1841), S'well RDn (1841—87), Norwell RDn (1887—*)

SEQ 25   S'well pec jursid (until 1841), S'well RDn (1841—57), Retf. 2 RDn (1857—77), Retf. RDn (1877—84), Tuxf. RDn (1884—*)

DIOCESES AND ARCHDEACONRIES

Notts pars were organised in Archdeaconries and Rural Deaneries as follows:

LINCOLN DIOC (1839—84)

Nottingham AD: Bing. RDn (1839—57), Bing. RDn (1877—84), S Bing. RDn (1877—84), W Bing. RDn (1877—84), Bing. 1 RDn (1857—77), Bing. 2 RDn (1857—77), Bing. 3 RDn (1857—77), Coll. RDn (1877—84), Mansf. RDn (1877—84), Newk. RDn (1839—57), Newk. RDn (1877—84), Newk. 1 RDn (1857—77), Newk. 2 RDn (1857—77), Nott. RDn (1839—57), Nott. RDn (1877—84), Nott. 1 RDn (1857—77), Nott. 2 RDn (1857—77), Nott. 3 RDn (1857—77), Retf. RDn (1839—57), Retf. RDn (1877—84), Retf. 1 RDn (1857—77), Retf. 2 RDn (1857—77), Retf. 3 RDn (1857—77), S'well RDn (1841—84), Tuxf. RDn (1877—84), Worksop RDn (1877—84)

SOUTHWELL DIOC (1884—*)

Newark AD (1912—):* Bawtry RDn, Mansf. RDn, Newk. RDn, Retf. RDn, Tuxf. RDn, Worksop RDn

Nottingham AD: Bawtry RDn (1887—1912), Beeston RDn (1910—*), Bing. RDn, S Bing. RDn, W Bing. RDn, Bulwell RDn (1887—*), Coll. RDn (1884—87), Gedling RDn (1887—*), Mansf. RDn (1884—1912), Newk. RDn (1884—1912), Newark East RDn (1887—1910), Norwell RDn (1887—1912), Nott. RDn, Retf. RDn (1884—1912), S'well RDn, Tuxf. RDn (1884—1912), Worksop RDn (1884—1912)

YORK DIOC (until 1839)

Nottingham AD: Bing. RDn, Newk. RDn, Nott. RDn, Retf. RDn

THE PARISHES OF NOTTINGHAMSHIRE

ADBOLTON

AP Bing. Hd, Bing. RDn, abol 1707 ent to Holme Pierrepont AP,[1] the union civ 'Holme Pierrepont', eccl 'Holme Pierrepont with Adbolton'.

ALVERTON

Hmlt in Kilvington AP, sep CP 1866.[2] *LG* Seq 7. *Parl* Seq 9.

ANNESLEY

AP *LG* Seq 6. Civ bdry: 1935.[3] *Parl* Seq 3. *Eccl* Seq 14.

APESTHORPE

AP Usual eccl spelling; for civ see 'Habblesthorpe'. *Eccl* Pec Prebend of Apesthorpe. Abol eccl early to help cr North Leverton with Apesthorpe EP.[4]

ARNOLD

AP *LG* Brox. Wap, Basf. PLU, Arnold USD, UD. Civ bdry: 1933 (loses pt to Nott. [assoc with Notts] CB & CP).[5] *Parl* N'rn Dv (1832—85), Rushcl. Dv (1885—1918), Brox. Dv (1918—48), Carlton CC (1948—*). *Eccl* Seq 15. Eccl bdry: 1896 (help cr Daybrook EP).[6]

ASKHAM

Chap (pec jurisd Dean & Chapter of York, until 1841) in East Drayton AP (eccl, 'East Drayton with Stokeham'), sep civ identity early, sep EP 1866.[7] *LG* Lbty S'well & Scrooby (until 1836/37), Seq 2. Civ bdry: 1935.[3] *Parl* Seq 1. *Eccl* Retf. 2 RDn (1866—77), Retf. RDn (1877—84), Tuxf. RDn (1884—*)

ASLOCKTON

Tp in Whatton AP, sep CP 1866,[2] eccl severed 1867 to help cr Scarrington with Aslockton EP.[8] *LG* Seq 5. *Parl* Seq 11.

ASPLEY

EP Cr 1933 from Radford AP, Bilborough with Strelley EP (by then called 'Bilborough'), Wollaton with Cossall AP (civ, 'Wollaton'), Basford AP, Cinder Hill EP.[9] Nott. RDn. Bdry: 1962.[10]

ATTENBOROUGH

AP Incl chap Bramcote (sep civ identity early, sep EP 1967[11]), hmlt Chilwell (sep CP 1866[2]), tp Toton (sep CP 1866[2]) so that 'Attenborough' has no sep civ identity after 1866; the par eccl 'Attenborough with Bramcote' until 1967, 'Attenborough with Chilwell' thereafter, qv. *LG* Brox. Wap. *Parl* N'rn Dv (1832—67).

ATTENBOROUGH WITH BRAMCOTE

AP Usual eccl name until 1967 (for civ and civ sep chap, tp, hmlt, see prev entry) until chap Bramcote a sep EP 1967,[11] the par thereafter 'Attenborough with Chilwell', qv. *Eccl* Nott. RDn (until 1857), Nott. 2 RDn (1857—77), Nott. RDn (1877—84), Mansf. RDn (1884—87), Bulwell RDn (1887—1910), Beeston RDn (1910—67).

ATTENBOROUGH WITH CHILWELL

EP Renaming 1967 of Attenborough with Bramcote AP (for civ and civ chap, tp, hmlt, see 'Attenborough') after Bramcote made 1967 a sep EP.[11] Beeston RDn.

AUCKLEY

Tp in Finningley AP, pt in Yorks W Riding (Doncaster Soke), pt in Notts (Basset. Wap), sep CP 1866 with pt in each co,[2] the par made 1895 ent Yorks W Riding.[12] *LG* Doncaster PLU, RSD, pt sep RD in Notts (1894—95); for remainder see main entry in Yorks. *Parl* Notts pt, E Retf. Parl Bor (1832—85), Basset. Dv (1885—1918).

AVERHAM

AP Incl tp Staythorpe (sep CP 1866[2]). *LG* Seq 17. Addtl civ bdry alt: 1935.[3] *Parl* Seq 9. *Eccl* Newk. RD. Abol eccl prob late 16th or 17th cent to help cr Averham with Kelham EP.[13]

AVERHAM WITH KELHAM

EP Cr prob late 16th or 17th cent by union Averham AP, Kelham AP.[13] Newk. RDn (cr—1857), Newk. 2 RDn (1857—77), Newk. RDn (1877—*). Eccl bdry: 1940.[14]

AWSWORTH

Chap in Nuthall AP, sep EP 1748,[15] sep CP 1894.[16] *LG* Basf. PLU, RD. *Parl* Rushcl. Dv (1918—48), Brox. CC (1948—70), Beeston CC (1970—*). *Eccl* Nott. RDn (1748—1857), Nott. 1 RDn (1857—77), Nott. RDn (1877—84), Mansf. RDn (1884—87), Bulwell RDn (1887—1910), Beeston RDn (1910—53). Abol eccl 1953 to help cr Awsworth with Cossall EP.[17]

AWSWORTH WITH COSSALL

EP Cr 1953 by union Awsworth EP, chap Cossall in Wollaton with Cossall AP.[17] Beeston RDn. Bdry: 1955.[18]

BABWORTH

AP Incl hmlts Morton, Ranby (neither sep civ). *LG* Seq 2. *Parl* Seq 1. *Eccl* Seq 21. Eccl bdry: 1875 (help cr Scofton with Osberton EP).[19]

BALDERTON

AP Chap in Farndon AP, sep par before 1535. *LG* Seq 7. Civ bdry: 1935.[3] *Parl* Seq 9. *Eccl* Seq 9. Eccl bdry: 1940.[14]

BARNBY MOOR

Tp (Notts, Basset. Wap) in Blyth AP (Notts [Basset. Wap], Yorks W Riding [Strafforth & Tickhill Wap]), sep CP 1866 in Notts.[2] *LG* Seq 2. *Parl* Seq 1.

BARNBY IN THE WILLOWS

AP *LG* Seq 7. Civ bdry: 1884 (gains the pt in Notts of Flawford CP [Notts, Lincs Pts Kestev]).[20] *Parl* Seq 9. *Eccl* Newk. RDn (until 1857), Newk. 1 RDn (1857—77), Newk. RDn (1884—87), Newk. East RDn (1887—1910), Newk. RDn (1910—*).

BARNSTONE—see LANGAR CUM BARNSTONE

BARTON IN FABIS

AP *LG* Seq 10. Civ bdry: 1952.[21] *Parl* Seq 12. *Eccl* Seq 3.

BASFORD

AP *LG* Brox. Wap, Basf. PLU, RSD (1875—77), Nott. MB (1877—89), CB (1889—99), USD (1877—94). Abol civ 1899 ent to Nottingham CP.[22] *Parl* N'rn Dv (1832—85), Nott Parl Bor (1885—1918). *Eccl* Nott. RDn (until 1857), Nott. 1 RDn (1857—77),

Nott. RDn (1877—*). Eccl bdry: 1843 (cr Carrington EP),[23] 1847 (cr New Basford EP),[24] 1897,[25] 1910 (cr Basford St Aidan EP),[26] 1929 (cr Cinder Hill EP, later 'Cinderhill'),[27] 1933 (help cr Aspley EP).[9]

NEW BASFORD
EP Cr 1847 from Basford AP.[24] Nott. RDn (1847—57), Nott. 1 RDn (1857—77), Nott. RDn (1877—*). Bdry: 1897.[25]

BASFORD ST AIDAN
EP Cr 1910 from Basford AP.[26] Nott. RDn. Bdry: 1961 (help cr Bestwood EP).[28]

BATHLEY
Tp in North Muskham AP, sep CP 1866.[2] *LG* Seq 17. *Parl* Seq 9.

BAWTRY WITH AUSTERFIELD
EP Cr 1858 from Blyth AP (union of chaps Bawtry, Austerfield, the only pts of Blyth AP [Notts, Yorks W Riding] in Yorks),[29] to be dioc Linc. Retf. 1 RDn (1858—77), Retf. RDn (1877—87), Bawtry RDn (1887—*). Bdry: 1962.[11]

BECKINGHAM
AP *LG* Lbty S'well & Scrooby (until 1836/37), Seq 1. *Parl* Seq 1. *Eccl* S'well pec jurisd (until 1841), S'well RDn (1841—57), Retf. 1 RDn (1857—77), Retf. RDn (1877—87), Bawtry RDn (1887—*).

BEESTON
AP *LG* Brox. Wap, Basf. PLU, Beeston USD, UD. Civ bdry: 1933 (loses pt to Nott. CB [assoc with Notts] & CP).[5] Abol civ 1935 to help cr Beeston & Staplef. UD & CP.[3] *Parl* N'rn Dv (1832—85), Rushcl. Dv (1885—1948). *Eccl* Seq 13. Eccl bdry: 1958 (incl help cr Lenton Abbey EP).[30]

BEESTON AND STAPLEFORD
CP Cr 1935 by union Beeston UD & AP, Bramcote CP, Stapleford AP, Toton CP, pt Chilwell CP.[3] *LG* Beeston & Staplef. UD. Bdry: 1952.[21] *Parl* Rushcl. CC (1948—70), Beeston CC (1970—*).

BESTHORPE
Chap in South Scarle AP, sep CP 1866.[2] *LG* Seq 7. *Parl* Seq 9.

BESTWOOD
EP Cr 1961 from Bestwood Park EP, Basford St Aidan EP.[28] Bulwell RDn.

BESTWOOD PARK
EP Cr 1874 from Lenton AP (detached pt).[31] Nott. 3 RDn (1874—77), Nott. RDn (1877—87), Gedling RDn (1887—1910), Bulwell RDn (1910—*). Bdry: 1961 (help cr Bestwood EP).[28]

CP Cr 1877 from Lenton AP.[32] *LG* Brox. Wap, Basf. PLU, RSD, RD. Bdry: 1883,[33] 1933 (loses pt to Nott. CB [assoc with Notts] & CP).[5] *Parl* Rushcl. Dv (1885—1918), Brox. Dv/CC (1918—70), Carlton CC (1970—*).

BEVERCOTES
AP Early in ruins and incl in Markham Clinton or West Markham AP,[34] sep identity regained early. *LG* Seq 2. *Parl* Seq 1. *Eccl* Retf. RDn (until 1884), Tuxf. RDn (1884—*).

BILBOROUGH
AP Incl chap Broxtowe (early destroyed, sep EP 1965 from Bilborough with Strelley EP, Cinder Hill [by then called 'Cinderhill'] EP[35]). *LG* Brox. Wap,

Basf. PLU, RSD, RD. Abol civ 1933 ent to Nott. CB (assoc with Notts) & CP.[5] *Parl* N'rn Dv (1832—85), Rushcl. Dv (1885—1948). *Eccl* Nott. RDn. Abol eccl 1838 to help cr Bilborough with Strelley EP,[36] the union later called 'Bilborough'.
EP Name used now for EP cr 1838 as 'Bilborough with Strelley', qv.

BILBOROUGH ST JOHN THE BAPTIST
EP Cr 1962 from Bilborough with Strelley EP (by then called 'Bilborough'), Wollaton EP.[10] Beeston RDn.

BILBOROUGH WITH STRELLEY
EP Cr 1838 by union Bilborough AP, Strelley AP,[36] latter called 'Bilborough'. Nott. RDn (1838—57), Nott. 1 RDn (1857—77), Nott. RDn (1877—84), Mansf. RDn (1884—87), Bulwell RDn (1887—1910), Beeston RDn (1910—*). Bdry: 1933 (help cr Aspley EP),[9] 1934,[37] 1962 (incl help cr Bilborough St John the Baptist EP),[10] 1965 (help cr Broxtowe EP).[35]

BILSTHORPE
AP *LG* Seq 3. *Parl* Seq 2. *Eccl* Retf. RDn (until 1857), S'well RDn (1857—*).

BINGHAM
AP *LG* Seq 5. *Parl* Seq 11. *Eccl* Seq 2.

BLEASBY
AP Incl hmlt Goverton (not sep civ). *LG* Lbty S'well & Scrooby (until 1836/37), Seq 17. *Parl* Seq 9. *Eccl* Seq 23.

BLIDWORTH
AP *LG* Lbty S'well & Scrooby (until 1836/37), Thurg. Wap, Mansf. PLU, RSD, Skegby RD (1894—1935), S'well RD (1935—74). Civ bdry: 1935.[3] *Parl* Seq 5. *Eccl* S'well pec jurisd (until 1841), S'well RDn (1841—1910), Mansf. RDn (1910—*). Eccl bdry: 1955 (help cr Rainworth EP),[38] 1971 (help cr Ravenshead EP).[39]

BLYTH
AP Tp 'Blyth' in Notts (Basset. Wap) as were chap Gamston (sep par by early 14th cent[40]), lordship Hodsock, tps Barnby Moor, Ranskill, Styrrup, Torworth (each of the 5 a sep CP 1866[2]; Ranskill in Lbty S'well & Scrooby [until 1836/37]); incl in Yorks W Riding (Strafforth & Tickhill Wap) chaps Bawtry, Austerfield (each a sep CP 1866 in Yorks,[2] so that Blyth ent Notts thereafter, the 2 chaps eccl severed and united 1858 to cr Bawtry with Austerfield EP in dioc Linc[29]). *LG* Worksop PLU, RSD, Blyth & Cuckney RD (1894—1925), Worksop RD (1925—74). Addtl civ bdry alt: 1883,[41] 1935.[3] *Parl* Notts pt, Seq 1. *Eccl* Retf. RDn (until 1857), Retf. 1 RDn (1857—77), Retf. RDn (1877—84), Worksop RDn (1884—*). Addtl eccl bdry alt: 1875 (help cr Scofton with Osberton EP),[19] 1953 (cr Langold EP),[42] 1959,[43] 1961.[44]

BOLE
AP *LG* Seq 1. Civ bdry: 1895 (gains pt Lea AP, Lincs Pts Lind).[12] *Parl* Seq 1. *Eccl* Pec jurisd Dean & Chapter of York (until 1841), Retf. RDn (1841—57), Retf. 1 RDn (1857—77), Retf. RDn (1877—*).

BOTHAMSALL
AP Chap in Elksley AP, sep civ identity early, sep EP by 1841.[45] Incl area chap Haughton (early in ruins,[46] not sep eccl, sep CP 1866 from Bothamsall

CP[2]).*LG* Seq 2. Civ bdry: 1884.[47] *Parl* Seq 1. *Eccl* Retf. RDn (cr—1857), Retf. 3 RDn (1857—77), Retf. RDn (1877—84), Worksop RDn (1884—1910), Retf. RDn (1910—*).

BOUGHTON
Chap (demolished by 1535) in Kneesall AP, sep civ identity early, sep EP 1866.[7] *LG* Seq 3. *Parl* Seq 2. *Eccl* Retf. RDn (1866—57), Retf. 3 RDn (1857—77), Retf. RDn (1877—84), Worksop RDn (1884—1910), Tuxf. RDn (1910—*). Eccl bdry: 1931.[48]

BRADMORE
Chap (early burned) in Bunny AP, sep civ identity early. *LG* Seq 10. *Parl* Seq 12.

BRAMCOTE
Chap in Attenborough AP (eccl, 'Attenborough with Bramcote' until 1967), sep civ identity early, sep EP 1967 (the remainder of the mother par thereafter 'Attenborough with Chilwell').[11] *LG* Brox. Wap, Shard. PLU, RSD, Staplef. RD. Abol civ 1935 to help cr Beeston & Staplef. UD & CP.[3] *Parl* N'rn Dv (1832—85), Rushcl. Dv (1885—1948). *Eccl* Beeston RDn.

BREWHOUSE YARD
Ex-par place, sep CP 1858,[49] eccl abol 1912 ent to Nottingham St John the Baptist EP.[50] *LG* Brox. Wap, Radf. PLU, RSD (1875—77), Nott. MB (1877—89), CB (1889—97), USD (1877—94). Abol civ 1897 to help cr Nottingham CP.[51] *Parl* N'rn Dv (1832—85), Nott. Parl Bor (1885—1918).

EAST BRIDGFORD
AP *LG* Seq 5. *Parl* Seq 11. *Eccl* Seq 2.

WEST BRIDGFORD
AP Incl tp Gamston (sep CP 1866[2]). *LG* Bing. Wap, Basf. PLU, RSD (ent 1875—77, pt 1877—91), pt W Bridgford USD (1891—94), pt Nott. MB (1877—89), pt Nott. CB (1889—94), pt Nott. USD (1877—94), W Bridgford UD. Addtl civ bdry alt: 1889,[52] 1894 (loses the pt in Nott. CB [assoc with Notts] to Nottingham St Mary AP),[53] 1935 (gains Edwalton CP, South Wilford CP),[3] 1952 (exchanges pts with Nott. CB [assoc with Notts] & CP).[21] *Parl* S'rn Dv (1832—85), pt Nott. Parl Bor (1885—1918), Rushcl. Dv/CC (pt 1885—1918, ent 1918—56), Nott. South BC (1956—70), Rushcl. CC (1970—*). Parl bdry: 1952.[54] *Eccl* Seq 3. Eccl bdry: 1950 (cr Lady Bay EP).[55]

BRINSLEY
Area in Greasley AP, sep EP 1861,[56] sep CP 1896.[57] *LG* Basf. PLU, RD. *Parl* Brox. Dv/CC (1918—70), Beeston CC (1970—*). *Eccl* Nott. 1 RDn (1861—77), Nott. RDn (1877—84), Mansf. RDn (1884—1910), Bulwell RDn (1910—55). Abol eccl 1955 to help cr Brinsley with Underwood EP.[58]

BRINSLEY WITH UNDERWOOD
EP Cr 1955 by union Brinsley EP, pt Selston with Underwood and Westwood AP (area of Underwood), ent ex-par Felley.[56] Bulwell RDn.

BROADHOLME
Hmlt in Thorney AP, sep CP 1866.[2] *LG* Newk. Wap, PLU (soon after 1836[59]—1930), RSD, RD. *Parl* Seq 9.

UPPER BROUGHTON
AP Usual civ spelling; for eccl see following entry. *LG* Bing. Wap, Melton Mowbray PLU, RSD, Bing. RD. Sometimes civ 'Broughton Sulney'. Civ bdry: 1965 (gains pt Broughton and Old Dalby CP, Leics).[60] *Parl* Seq 11.

BROUGHTON SULNEY
AP Usual eccl spelling; for civ see prev entry. *Eccl* Seq 1.

BROXTOWE
Orig chap (early destroyed) in Bilborough AP, sep EP 1965 from Bilborough with Strelley EP (by then called 'Bilborough'), Cinder Hill EP (by then called 'Cinderhill').[35] Beeston RDn.

BUDBY
Tp in Edwinstowe AP, sep CP 1866.[2] *LG* Basset. Wap, S'well PLU, RSD, RD. Abol 1899 to help cr Perlethorpe cum Budby CP.[61] *Parl* E Retf. Parl Bor (1832—85), Basset. Dv (1885—1918).

BULCOTE
Chap in Burton Joyce AP, sep CP 1866.[2] *LG* Seq 17. *Parl* Seq 9.

BULWELL
AP *LG* Brox. Wap, Basf. PLU, RSD (1875—77), Nott. MB (1877—89), CB (1899—99), USD (1877—94). Abol civ 1899 ent to Nottingham CP.[22] *Parl* N'rn Dv (1832—85), Nott. Parl Bor (1885—1918). *Eccl* Nott. RDn (until 1857), Nott. 1 RDn (1857—77), Nott. RDn (1877—87), Bulwell RDn (1887—*). Eccl bdry: 1928 (cr Bulwell St John EP).[62]

BULWELL ST JOHN
EP Cr 1928 from Bulwell AP.[62] Bulwell RDn.

BUNNY
AP Incl chap Bradmore (sep civ identity early, early burned, not sep eccl hence this par eccl 'Bunny with Bradmore', qv). *LG* Seq 10. *Parl* Seq 12.

BUNNY WITH BRADMORE
AP Usual eccl spelling; for civ and civ sep chap, see prev entry. *Eccl* Seq 4.

WEST BURTON
AP *LG* Seq 1. Civ bdry: 1886,[63] 1895 (gains pt Lea AP, Lincs Pts Lind).[12] *Parl* Seq 1. *Eccl* Seq 18.

BURTON JOYCE
AP Incl chap Bulcote (sep CP 1866,[2] not sep eccl hence this par eccl 'Burton Joyce with Bulcote', qv). *LG* Seq 14. *Parl* Seq 14.

BURTON JOYCE WITH BULCOTE
AP Usual eccl spelling; for civ and civ sep chap, see prev entry. *Eccl* Seq 15.

CALVERTON
AP *LG* Seq 14. *Parl* S'rn Dv (1832—85), Newk. Dv (1885—1918), Brox. Dv (1918—48), Carlton CC (1948—*). *Eccl* Seq 23.

CARBURTON
Chap in Edwinstowe AP, sep CP 1866.[2] *LG* Seq 4. *Parl* Seq 1.

CARLTON
EP Cr 1958 from Colwick AP.[64] Gedling RDn.

CARLTON
Hmlt in Gedling AP, sep CP 1866,[2] pt a sep EP 1883 as 'Carlton in the Willows',[65] the remainder a sep EP 1885 as 'Netherfield'.[66] *LG* Thurg. Wap, Basf. PLU, RSD (ent 1875—77, pt 1877—81), pt Carlton USD (1881—94), pt Nott. MB (1877—89), pt Nott. CB (1889—94), pt Nott. USD (1877—94),

Carlton UD. Civ bdry: 1894 (loses the pt in Nott. CB [assoc with Notts] to Nottingham St Mary AP),[53] 1935 (incl gains Gedling AP).[3] *Parl* S'rn Dv (1832—85), pt Nott. Parl Bor (1885—1918), Rushcl. Dv (pt 1885—1918, ent 1918—48), Carlton CC (1948—*).

CARLTON IN LINDRICK
AP *LG* Seq 4. Civ bdry: 1883,[41] 1885.[67] *Parl* Seq 1. *Eccl* Retf. RDn (until 1857), Retf. 1 RDn (1857—77), Retf. RDn (1877—84), Worksop RDn (1884—*). Eccl bdry: 1875 (help cr Scofton with Osberton EP).[19]

CARLTON IN THE WILLOWS
Hmlt Carlton in Gedling AP, sep CP 1866 as 'Carlton',[2] qv, pt a sep EP 1883 as 'Carlton in the Willows',[65] the remainder a sep EP 1885 as 'Netherfield'.[66] *Eccl* Nott. RDn (1883—87), Gedling RDn (1887—*). Eccl bdry: 1927 (help cr Sneinton St Cyprian EP),[64] 1935 (help cr Porchester EP),[68] 1935.[69]

CARLTON ON TRENT
Chap (S'well pec jurisd, until 1841) in Norwell AP, sep CP 1866,[2] sep EP 1874.[70] *LG* Seq 17. *Parl* Seq 9. *Eccl* S'well RDn (1874—84), Coll. RDn (1884—87), Norwell RDn (1887—*).

CARRINGTON
EP Cr 1843 from Basford AP.[23] Nott. RDn (1843—57), Nott. 2 RDn (1857—77), Nott. RDn (1877—*). Bdry: 1877,[71] 1896 (help cr Daybrook EP),[6] 1936 (help cr Sherwood EP).[72]

CAUNTON
AP Incl hmlts Beesthorpe, Knapthorpe (neither sep civ). *LG* Seq 17. Civ bdry: 1877.[73] *Parl* Seq 9. *Eccl* Seq 24.

CAYTHORPE
Tp in Lowdham AP, sep CP 1866.[2] *LG* Seq 17. *Parl* Seq 9.

CHILWELL
Hmlt in Attenborough AP, sep CP 1866.[2] *LG* Brox. Wap, Shard. PLU, RSD, Staplef. RD. Abol 1935 pt to help cr Beeston & Staplef. UD & CP, pt to Clifton with Glapton AP.[3] *Parl* N'rn Dv (1832—85), Rushcl. Dv (1885—1948).

CINDER HILL
EP Cr 1929 from Basford AP.[27] Nott. RDn. Later called 'Cinderhill'. Bdry: 1933 (help cr Aspley EP),[9] 1934,[37] 1965 (help cr Broxtowe EP).[35]

CINDERHILL—see prev entry

CLARBOROUGH
AP Incl hmlts Bolham, Little Gringley, Welham, pt hmlt Moorgate (none sep civ). *LG* Basset. Wap, E Retf. PLU, pt E Retf. USD, pt E Retf. MB (1878—94), pt E Retf. RSD, E Retf. RD. Civ bdry: 1894 (the pt in E Retf. MB cr North Retford CP).[74] *Parl* Seq 1. *Eccl* Seq 16. Eccl bdry: 1933 (cr Retford EP).[75]

CLAYWORTH
AP Incl tp Wiseton (sep CP 1866[2]). *LG* Seq 2. *Parl* Seq 1. *Eccl* Seq 19.

CLIFTON
EP Cr 1971 by union Clifton with Galpton AP, Clifton St Francis EP.[76] W Bing. RDn.

NORTH CLIFTON
AP Incl tp South Clifton (sep CP 1866[2]), hmlt Harby (sep CP 1866,[2] eccl severed 1874 and united with pt tp North Clifton to cr Harby with Swinethorpe EP[77]), hmlt Spalford (sep CP 1866,[2] eccl severed 1875 and united with chap Girton in South Scarle AP [eccl, 'South Scarle with Besthorpe and Girton'][78]). *LG* Newk. Wap, PLU (soon after 1836[59]—1930), RSD, RD. *Parl* Seq 9. *Eccl* Seq 7.

SOUTH CLIFTON
Tp in North Clifton AP, sep CP 1866.[2] *LG* Seq 7. Bdry: 1885.[79] *Parl* Seq 9.

CLIFTON ST FRANCIS
EP Cr 1958 from Clifton with Glapton AP.[80] W Bing. RDn. Abol 1971 to help cr Clifton EP.[76]

CLIFTON WITH GLAPTON
AP *LG* Rushcl. Wap, Basf. PLU, RSD, RD. Civ bdry: 1935.[3] Abol civ 1952 pt to Nott. CB (assoc with Notts) & CP, pt to Beeston & Staplef. UD & CP, pt to Barton in Fabis AP.[21] *Parl* S'rn Dv (1832—85), Rushcl. Dv/CC (1885—1970). Parl bdry: 1952.[54] *Eccl* Bing. RDn (until 1857), Bing. 3 RDn (1857—77), Bing. RDn (1877—84), W Bing. RDn (1884—1971). Eccl bdry: 1958 (cr Clifton St Francis EP).[80] Abol eccl 1971 to help cr Clifton EP.[76]

CLIPSTON
Tp in Plumtree AP, sep CP 1866.[2] *LG* Seq 5. *Parl* Seq 11. Later called 'Clipston-on-the-Wolds'.

CLIPSTONE
Tp in Edwinstowe AP, sep CP 1866.[2] *LG* Seq 3. *Parl* Seq 2.

CLIPSTONE ALL SAINTS
EP Renaming 1957 of New Clipstone EP after bdry alt of latter.[81] Mansf. RDn.

NEW CLIPSTONE
EP Cr 1930 from Edwinstowe with Carburton AP (civ, 'Edwinstowe').[82] Worksop RDn (1930—57), Mansf. RDn (1957). Renamed 1957 'Clipstone All Saints' after bdry alt.[81]

CODDINGTON
Chap in East Stoke AP, sep civ identity early, sep EP prob in 1676 (date 1st registers).[83] *LG* Seq 7. *Parl* Seq 9. *Eccl* Newk. RDn (cr—1857), Newk. 1 RDn (1857—77), Newk. RDn (1877—87), Newk. East RDn (1887—1910), Newk. RDn (1910—*).

COLLINGHAM
CP Cr 1970 by union North Collingham AP, South Collingham AP.[84] *LG* Newk. RD.

NORTH COLLINGHAM
AP *LG* Newk. Wap, PLU, RSD, RD. Abol civ 1970 to help cr Collingham CP.[84] *Parl* Seq 9. *Eccl* Seq 7.

SOUTH COLLINGHAM
AP Organisation as for North Collingham.

CAR COLSTON
AP *LG* Seq 5. *Parl* Seq 11. *Eccl* Seq 2.

COLSTON BASSETT
AP *LG* Seq 5. *Parl* Seq 11. *Eccl* Seq 1.

COLWICK
AP *LG* Thurg. Wap, Basf. PLU, RSD, RD. Civ bdry: 1933 (loses pt to Nott. CB [assoc with Notts] & CP).[5] Abol civ 1935 pt to Carlton UD & CP, pt to Holme Pierrepont AP.[3] *Parl* S'rn Dv (1832—85), Rushcl. Dv (1885—1948). *Eccl* Seq 13. Eccl bdry:

1927 (help cr Sneinton St Cyprian EP),[64] 1958 (cr Carlton EP).[64]

COSSALL

Chap in Wollaton AP, sep civ identity early, eccl severed 1953 to help cr Awsworth with Cossall EP.[17] *LG* Seq 6. *Parl* Seq 7.

COSTOCK

AP *LG* Seq 12. *Parl* Seq 12. *Eccl* Seq 5.

COTGRAVE

AP *LG* Seq 5. Civ bdry: 1896 (gains Lodge on the Wolds CP).[85] *Parl* Seq 11. *Eccl* Bing. RDn (until 1857), Bing. 3 RDn (1857—77), Bing. RDn (1877—*).

COTHAM

AP *LG* Seq 7. *Parl* Seq 9. *Eccl* Seq 9.

COTTAM

Chap in South Leverton AP, sep CP 1866,[2] eccl severed 1876 to help cr Littleborough with Cottam EP.[86] *LG* Seq 2. *Parl* Seq 1.

CROMWELL

AP *LG* Seq 17. *Parl* Seq 9. *Eccl* Seq 8.

CROPWELL BISHOP

AP *LG* Seq 5. Civ bdry: 1935.[3] *Parl* Seq 11. *Eccl* S'well pec jurisd (until 1841), S'well RDn (1841—57), Bing. 2 RDn (1857—77), Bing. RDn (1877—*).

CROPWELL BUTLER

Tp in Tithby AP, sep CP 1866.[2] *LG* Seq 5. Bdry: 1935.[3] *Parl* Seq 11.

CUCKNEY

Tp in Norton Cuckney AP, sep CP 1866.[2] *LG* Seq 4. *Parl* Seq 1.

NORTON CUCKNEY

AP Incl tps Cuckney, Holbeck, Nether Langwith, Norton (each a sep CP 1866[2]) so that 'Norton Cuckney' has no sep civ identity after 1866. *LG* Basset. Wap. *Parl* E Retf. Parl Bor (1832—67). *Eccl* Sometimes as 'Norton Cuckney with Holbeck Woodhouse', Seq 22. Eccl bdry: 1924 (help cr Whaley Thorns EP [Derbys, Notts; see entry in Derbys for the 3 other constituent pars]).[28]

DARLTON

Chap (S'well pec jurisd, until 1841) in Dunham AP, sep civ identity early. *LG* Seq 2. *Parl* Seq 1.

DAYBROOK

EP Cr 1896 from Arnold AP, Carrington EP.[6] Gedling RDn (1896—1910), Nott. RDn (1910—*). Bdry: 1936 (help cr Sherwood EP),[72] 1940.[87]

EAST DRAYTON

AP Incl chap Askham (sep civ identity early, sep EP 1866[7]), chap Stokeham (sep civ identity early, not sep eccl hence this par eccl 'East Drayton with Stokeham', qv). *LG* Seq 2. *Parl* Seq 1.

EAST DRAYTON WITH STOKEHAM

AP Usual eccl spelling; for civ and eccl sep chaps, see prev entry. *Eccl* Pec jurisd Dean & Chapter of York (until 1841), Seq 20 thereafter.

WEST DRAYTON

Chap in East Markham AP, sep civ identity early, sep EP prob in 1632 (date 1st registers).[88] *LG* Seq 2. Civ bdry: 1951.[89] *Parl* Seq 1. *Eccl* Retf. RDn (until 1857), Retf. 2 RDn (1857—77), Retf. RDn (1877—84), Tuxf. RDn (1884—1960), Retf. RDn

(1960—*).

DUNHAM

AP Incl chaps Darlton, Ragnall (each gains sep civ identity early, neither sep eccl hence this par eccl 'Dunham with Darlton and Ragnall', qv). *LG* Seq 2. *Parl* Seq 1.

DUNHAM WITH DARLTON AND RAGNALL

AP Usual eccl spelling; for civ and civ sep chaps, see prev entry. *Eccl* Seq 25.

EAKRING

AP *LG* Seq 3. *Parl* Seq 2. *Eccl* Newk. RDn (until 1857), Retf. 2 RDn (1857—77), Retf. RDn (1877—84), S'well RDn (1884—*).

EASTWOOD

AP *LG* Brox. Wap, Basf. PLU, RSD, RD (1894—96), Eastwood UD (1896—1974). Civ bdry: 1935.[3] *Parl* Seq 4. *Eccl* Seq 14.

EATON

AP *LG* Seq 2. *Parl* Seq 1. *Eccl* S'well pec jurisd (until 1841), S'well RDn (1841—57), Retf. 3 RDn (1857—77), Retf. RDn (1877—*).

EDINGLEY

AP Incl hmlts Greaves Lane, Osmanthorpe (neither sep civ). *LG* Lbty S'well & Scrooby (until 1836/37), Seq 17. Civ bdry: 1884.[90] *Parl* Seq 9. *Eccl* Seq 23.

EDWALTON

Chap in Ruddington AP, sep civ identity early, sep EP 1739.[15] *LG* Rushcl. Wap, Bing. PLU, RSD, RD. Civ bdry: 1889.[52] Abol civ 1935 ent to W Bridgford UD & AP.[3] *Parl* S'rn Dv (1832—85), Rushcl. Dv (1885—1918), Newk. Dv (1918—48). *Eccl* Bing. RDn (1739—1857), Bing. 3 RDn (1857—77), Bing. RDn (1877—84), W Bing. RDn (1884—87), S Bing. RDn (1887—*).

EDWINSTOWE

AP Incl chap Carburton (sep CP 1866,[2] not sep eccl hence this par eccl 'Edwinstowe with Carburton', qv), chap Ollerton (sep CP 1866,[2] sep EP 1888[91]), chap Perlethorpe (sep CP 1866,[2] sep EP 1836[92]), tp Budby, tp Clipstone (each a sep CP 1866[2]), pt hmlt Thoresby (not sep civ). *LG* Seq 3. Addtl civ bdry alt: 1899 (help cr Perlethorpe cum Budby CP),[61] 1957.[93] *Parl* Seq 2.

EDWINSTOWE WITH CARBURTON

AP Usual eccl spelling; for civ and civ sep tps and chaps, see prev entry. *Eccl* Seq 22. Addtl eccl bdry alt: 1877,[94] 1930 (cr New Clipstone EP).[82]

EGMANTON

AP *LG* Seq 3. *Parl* Seq 2. *Eccl* Seq 20.

ELKSLEY

AP Incl chap Bothamsall (sep civ identity early, sep EP by 1841[45]), hmlt Normanton (not sep civ). *LG* Seq 2. *Parl* Seq 1. *Eccl* Retf. RDn (until 1857), Retf. 3 RDn (1857—77), Retf. RDn (1877—84), Worksop RDn (1884—1910), Retf. RDn (1910—*).

ELSTON

AP Incl civ chap Elston (not sep civ, early considered eccl in East Stoke AP, transf 1876 to Elston, the union sometimes thereafter 'Elston with Elston Chapel'[96]). *LG* Seq 9. Civ bdry: 1884.[95] *Parl* Seq 9. *Eccl* Seq 6.

ELSTON

Chap civ in Elston AP, early considered eccl in East

Stoke AP, not sep civ, transf eccl 1876 to Elston AP and the union sometimes thereafter 'Elston with Elston Chapel'.[96]

ELSTON WITH ELSTON CHAPEL—see prev entries

ELTON

AP Usual civ spelling; for eccl see following entry. *LG* Seq 5. *Parl* Seq 11.

ELTON ON THE HILL

AP Usual eccl spelling; for civ see prev entry. *Eccl* Seq 2.

EPPERSTONE

AP *LG* Seq 17. *Parl* Seq 9. *Eccl* Seq 16.

EVERTON

AP Incl tp Scaftworth (sep CP 1866[2]); main tp sometimes early called 'Everton with Harwell'. *LG* Lbty S'well & Scrooby (until 1836/37), Seq 2. *Parl* Seq 1. *Eccl* Seq 19.

FARNDON

AP Incl chap Balderton (sep par before 1535). *LG* Seq 7. Civ bdry: 1884,[97] 1935.[3] *Parl* Seq 9. *Eccl* Seq 9. Eccl bdry: 1940.[14]

FARNSFIELD

AP *LG* Lbty S'well & Scrooby (until 1836/37), Seq 17. Civ bdry: 1877.[98] *Parl* Seq 9. *Eccl* Seq 23.

FELLEY

Ex-par place, sep CP 1858,[49] eccl abol 1955 to help cr Brinsley with Underwood EP.[58] *LG* Seq 6. *Parl* Seq 3.

FINNINGLEY

AP Tp 'Finningley' in Basset. Wap; incl tp Auckley (pt Notts [Basset. Wap], pt Yorks W Riding [Doncaster Soke], sep CP 1866 with pt in each co[2]) so that Finningley ent Notts thereafter. *LG* Doncaster PLU, RSD, E Retf. RD. Transf 1974 to S Yorks.[99] *Parl* Notts pt, Seq 1. *Eccl* Seq 19.

FISKERTON

Tp in Rolleston AP, sep CP 1866.[2] *LG* Thurg. Wap, S'well PLU, RSD. Abol 1884 pt to help cr Fiskerton cum Morton CP, pt to East Stoke AP.[100] *Parl* S'rn Dv (1832—85).

FISKERTON CUM MORTON

CP Cr 1884 by union pt Fiskerton CP, ent Morton CP.[100] *LG* Thurg. Wap, S'well PLU, RSD, RD. *Parl* Newk. Dv/CC (1885—*).

FLAWBOROUGH

Chap in Staunton AP, sep CP 1866.[2] *LG* Seq 8. *Parl* Seq 11.

FLAWFORD

Ex-par place, pt Notts (Newk. Wap), pt Lincs Pts Kestev (Boothby Graffoe Wap), sep CP 1858 with pt in each co.[49] *LG* Newk. PLU (1866—84), RSD. Abol 1884 the pt in Lincs transf to Stapleford AP, Lincs Pts Kestev, the pt in Notts transf to Barnby in the Willows AP, Notts.[20] *Parl* S'rn Dv (1832—85).

FLEDBOROUGH

AP *LG* Seq 16. *Parl* Seq 10. *Eccl* Newk. RDn (until 1857), Newk. 1 RDn (1857—77), Newk. RDn (1877—84), Coll. RDn (1884—87), Tuxf. RDn (1887—*).

FLINTHAM

AP *LG* Seq 5. *Parl* Seq 11. *Eccl* Seq 2.

FOREST TOWN

EP Cr 1936 from Mansfield Woodhouse EP, Mansfield

St Lawrence EP.[101] Mansf. RDn. Bdry: 1955 (help cr Rainworth EP),[38] 1957.[81]

FULWOOD

Ex-par place, sep CP 1858.[49] *LG* Brox. Wap, Mansf. PLU (1861—1930), RSD (ent 1875—83, pt 1883—94), pt Hucknall under Huthwaite USD (1883—94), pt Hucknall under Huthwaite UD (1894—96), Skegby RD (pt 1894—96, ent 1896—1935). Bdry: 1884,[102] 1896 (loses the pt in the UD to Hucknall under Huthwaite CP),[103] 1897.[104] Abol civ 1935 ent to Sutton in Ashfield UD & AP.[3] *Parl* N'rn Dv (1832—85), Mansf. Dv (1885—1948).

GAMSTON

AP Chap in Blyth AP, sep par by early 14th cent.[40] *LG* Seq 2. *Parl* Seq 1. *Eccl* Seq 21.

GAMSTON

Tp in West Bridgford AP, sep CP 1866.[2] *LG* Bing. Wap, Basf. PLU, RSD, RD (1894—1935), Bing. RD (1935—74). Bdry: 1884.[47] *Parl* S'rn Dv (1832—85), Newk. Dv (1885—1918), Rushcl. Dv (1918—48), Carlton CC (1948—70), Rushcl. CC (1970—*).

GEDLING

AP Incl hmlt Carlton (sep CP 1866,[2] pt eccl severed 1883 to cr 'Carlton in the Willows' EP,[65] the remainder a sep EP 1885 as 'Netherfield'[66]), tp Stoke Bardolph (sep CP 1866[2]). *LG* Thurg. Wap, Basf. PLU, RSD, RD. Abol civ 1935 ent to Carlton CP.[3] *Parl* S'rn Dv (1832—85), Rushcl. Dv (1885—1948). *Eccl* Seq 15. Addtl eccl bdry alt: 1935 (help cr Porchester EP).[68]

GIRTON

Chap in South Scarle AP, sep civ identity early, not sep eccl (enlarged 1875 eccl when gains hmlt Spalford in North Clifton AP[78]). *LG* Seq 7. *Parl* Seq 9.

GLAPTON—see CLIFTON WITH GLAPTON

GONALSTON

AP *LG* Seq 17. *Parl* Seq 9. *Eccl* Seq 16.

GOTHAM

AP *LG* Seq 10. *Parl* Seq 12. *Eccl* Seq 3.

GRANBY

AP Incl hmlt Sutton (not sep civ). *LG* Seq 5. *Parl* Seq 11. *Eccl* Seq 2.

GRASSTHORPE

Tp in Marnham AP, sep CP 1866.[2] *LG* Seq 17. *Parl* Seq 9.

GREASLEY

AP Incl chap Kimberley (sep EP 1848,[105] sep CP 1896[57]), hmlts Moorgreen, Newthorpe; Watnall Chahworth and Cantelupe (none sep civ). *LG* Seq 6. Addtl civ bdry alt: 1887,[106] 1887,[107] 1896 (cr Brinsley CP),[56] 1935.[3] *Parl* Seq 4. *Eccl* Seq 14. Addtl eccl bdry alt: 1861 (cr Brinsley EP),[105] 1955.[18]

GRINGLEY ON THE HILL

AP *LG* Seq 2. *Parl* Seq 1. *Eccl* Seq 19.

GROVE

AP *LG* Seq 2. *Parl* Seq 1. *Eccl* Seq 18.

GUNTHORPE

Tp in Lowdham AP, sep CP 1866.[2] *LG* Seq 17. Bdry: 1899.[108] *Parl* Seq 9.

HABBLESTHORPE

AP Usual civ spelling; for eccl see 'Apesthorpe'. *LG* Basset. Wap, E Retf. PLU, RSD. Abol civ 1884 to help cr North Leverton with Habblesthorpe CP.[109] *Parl* E Retf. Parl Bor (1832–85).

HALAM

Chap (S'well pec jurisd, until 1841) in Southwell AP, sep civ identity early, sep EP 1715.[15] *LG* Lbty S'well & Scrooby (until 1836/37), Seq 17. *Parl* Seq 9. *Eccl* S'well RDn (1841–*).

HALLOUGHTON

AP *LG* Lbty S'well & Scrooby (until 1836/37), Seq 17. *Parl* Seq 9. *Eccl* Seq 23.

HARBY

Hmlt in North Clifton AP, sep CP 1866,[2] eccl severed 1874 to help cr Harby with Swinethorpe EP,[77] qv. *LG* Newk. Wap, PLU (soon after 1836[59]–1930), RSD, RD. *Parl* Seq 9.

HARBY WITH SWINETHORPE

EP Cr 1874 from North Clifton AP (incl hmlt Harby).[77] Newk. RDn (1874–77), Coll. RDn (1877–87), Newk. East RDn (1874–1910), Newk. RDn (1910–*).

HARWELL—see EVERTON

HARWORTH

AP Incl hmlts Bircotes, Serlby (neither sep civ). *LG* Seq 4. Addtl civ bdry alt: 1935,[3] 1974 (the pt transf to S Yorks transf to Bawtry CP [prev Yorks W Riding, also transf 1974 to S Yorks]).[99] *Parl* Seq 1. *Eccl* Retf. RDn (until 1857), Retf. 1 RDn (1857–77), Retf. RDn (1877–84), Worksop RDn (1884–87), Bawtry RDn (1887–*). Addtl eccl bdry alt: 1961,[44] 1962.[11]

HAUGHTON

Chap (early in ruins[46]) in chap Bothamsall in Elkesley AP, not sep eccl, sep CP 1866.[2] *LG* Seq 2. *Parl* Seq 1.

HAWKSWORTH

AP *LG* Seq 5. Civ bdry: 1889.[110] *Parl* Seq 11. *Eccl* Seq 2.

HAWTON

AP *LG* Seq 7. Civ bdry: 1935.[3] *Parl* Seq 9. *Eccl* Seq 9. Eccl bdry: 1940,[14] 1961.[30]

HAYTON

AP Incl hmlt Tilne (not sep civ). *LG* Lbty S'well & Scrooby (until 1836/37), Seq 2. *Parl* Seq 1. *Eccl* Seq 18.

HAYWOOD OAKS

Ex-par place, sep CP 1858.[49] *LG* Thurg. Wap, Mansf. PLU (1861–1930), RSD, Skegby RD (1894–1935), S'well RD (1935–74). *Parl* Seq 8.

HEADON CUM UPTON

AP *LG* Seq 2. *Parl* Seq 1. *Eccl* Seq 20.

HICKLING

AP *LG* Seq 5. *Parl* Seq 11. *Eccl* Seq 1.

HOCKERTON

AP *LG* Seq 17. *Parl* Seq 9. *Eccl* Seq 10.

HODSOCK

Lordship (Notts, Basset. Wap) in Blyth AP (Notts [Basset. Wap], Yorks W Riding [Strafforth & Tickhill Wap]), sep CP 1866 in Notts.[2] *LG* Seq 4. Bdry: 1935.[3] *Parl* Seq 1.

HOLBECK

Tp in Norton Cuckney AP, sep CP 1866.[2] *LG* Seq 4. Bdry: 1935 (gains Woodhouse Hall CP).[3] *Parl* Seq 1.

HOLME

Chap (S'well pec jurisd, until 1841) in North Muskham AP, sep civ identity early, eccl severed *ca* 1849 to help cr Langford with Holme EP.[111] *LG* Seq 18. Bdry: 1884.[112] *Parl* Seq 9.

HOLME PIERREPONT

AP Incl hmlts Bassingfield, Lamcote (neither sep civ); gains 1707 Adbolton AP, the union civ 'Holme Pierrepont', eccl 'Holme Pierrepont with Adbolton',[1] qv. *LG* Seq 5. Civ bdry: 1935.[3] *Parl* Seq 11. *Eccl* Bing. RDn.

HOLME PIERREPONT WITH ADBOLTON

EP Cr 1707 by union Holme Pierrepont AP, Adbolton AP,[1] the union eccl 'Holme Pierrepont with Adbolton', civ 'Holme Pierrepont', qv. *Eccl* Bing. RDn (1707–1857), Bing. 2 RDn (1857–77), Bing. RDn (1877–*).

HOVERINGAM

AP *LG* Seq 17. *Parl* Seq 9. *Eccl* Nott. RDn. Abol eccl 1848 to help cr Thurgarton with Hoveringam EP.[113]

HUCKNALL TORKARD

AP *LG* Brox. Wap, Basf. PLU, Hucknall Torkard USD, UD (1894–1916), Hucknall UD (1916–74). Civ bdry: 1935.[3] *Parl* N'rn Dv (1832–85), Rushcl. Dv (1885–1918), Brox. Dv/CC (1918–56), Nott. North BC (1956–70), Ashfield CC (1970–*). *Eccl* Seq 14.

HUCKNALL UNDER HUTHWAITE

Hmlt in Sutton in Ashfield AP, sep CP 1866,[2] sep EP 1906.[114] *LG* Brox. Wap, Mansf. PLU, Hucknall under Huthwaite USD, UD (1894–1907), Huthwaite UD (1907–35). Civ bdry: 1884,[102] 1896 (gains the pt of Fulwood CP in Hucknall under Huthwaite UD),[103] 1897.[104] Abol civ 1935 ent to Sutton in Ashfield UD & AP.[3] *Parl* N'rn Dv (1832–85), Mansf. Dv (1885–1948). *Eccl* Mansf. RDn. Eccl bdry: 1911.[115] Now usually called 'Huthwaite'.

HUTHWAITE—see prev entry

HYSON GREEN

EP Cr 1844 from Lenton AP, Radford AP.[116] Nott. RDn (1841–57), Nott. 3 RDn (1857–77), Nott. RDn (1877–*). Bdry: 1898 (re-cr Nottingham St Stephen EP [qv for earlier demolition of former church]).[19]

IRONVILLE

EP Cr 1850 from Selston with Underwood and Westwood AP (Notts, civ 'Selston') and the Derbys pars of Codnor and Loscoe EP, Pentrich AP, Riddings EP, ent ex-par Codnor Park (after lost pt 1850 to cr Codnor and Loscoe EP),[117] to be dioc Lichf. See main entry in Derbys.

KELHAM

AP *LG* Seq 17. Civ bdry: 1899 (gain Park Leys CP),[118] 1935.[3] *Parl* Seq 9. *Eccl* Newk. RDn. Abol eccl prob late 16th or 17th cent to help cr Averham with Kelham EP.[13]

KERSALL
Tp in Kneesall AP, sep CP 1866.[2] *LG* Seq 17. *Parl* Seq 9.

KEYWORTH
AP *LG* Seq 11. *Parl* Seq 15. *Eccl* Seq 1.

KILVINGTON
AP Incl hmlt Alverton (sep CP 1866[2]). *LG* Seq 7. *Parl* Seq 9. *Eccl* Seq 9.

KIMBERLEY
Chap in Greasley AP, sep EP 1848,[105] sep CP 1896.[57] *LG* Basf. PLU, RD. *Parl* Brox. Dv/CC (1918—70), Beeston CC (1970—*). *Eccl* Nott. RDn (1848—57), Nott. 3 RDn (1857—77), Nott. RDn (1877—84), Mansf. RDn (1884—87), Bulwell RDn (1887—1910), Beeston RDn (1910—*). Eccl bdry: 1955.[18]

KINGSTON ON SOAR
Chap in Ratcliffe on Soar AP, sep civ identity early, sep EP 1762.[15] *LG* Rushcl. Wap, Shard. PLU, RSD, Unnamed RD (1894—1927), Leake RD (1927—35), Basf. RD (1935—74). *Parl* Seq 12. *Eccl* Bing. RDn (1762—1857), Bing. 3 RDn (1857—77), Bing. RDn (1877—84), W Bing. RDn (1884—*).

KINOULTON
AP *LG* Seq 5. *Parl* Seq 11. *Eccl* Pec jurisd Kinoulton (until 1841), Seq 1 thereafter.

EAST KIRKBY
EP Erected as eccl dist 1933 from Kirkby in Ashfield St Thomas EP,[119] no church ever built so dist abol 1961 ent to Kirkby in Ashfield St Thomas EP.[120] Mansf. RDn.

KIRKBY IN ASHFIELD
AP *LG* Brox. Wap, Basf. PLU, RSD, RD (1894—96), Kirkby in Ashfield UD (1896—1974). Civ bdry: 1895 (exchanges pts with Pinxton AP [prev Derbys, Notts] so that Pinxton thereafter ent Derbys),[12] 1935.[3] *Parl* Seq 3. *Eccl* Seq 11. Eccl bdry: 1901 (cr Kirkby Woodhouse EP),[25] 1901 (cr Kirkby in Ashfield St Thomas EP),[121] 1973 (incl loses pt to Pinxton AP, dioc Derby).[122]

KIRKBY IN ASHFIELD ST THOMAS
EP Cr 1901 from Kirkby in Ashfield AP.[121] Mansf. RDn. Bdry: 1933 (cr East Kirkby EP),[119] 1961 (gains East Kirkby EP since no church ever built for that dist).[120]

KIRKBY WOODHOUSE
EP Cr 1901 from Kirkby in Ashfield AP.[25] Mansf. RDn.

KIRKLINGTON
AP *LG* Lbty S'well & Scrooby (until 1836/37), Seq 17. *Parl* Seq 9. *Eccl* Seq 23.

KIRTON
AP *LG* Seq 3. *Parl* Seq 2. *Eccl* Seq 20.

KNEESALL
AP Tp 'Kneesall' in Thurg. Wap, as was tp Kersall (sep CP 1866[2]); incl in Basset. Wap chap Boughton (sep civ identity early, chap demolished by 1535, sep EP 1866[7]), tp Ompton (sep CP 1866[2]). *LG* Thurg. Wap (pt until 1886, ent from 1866), pt Basset. Wap (until 1866), S'well PLU, RSD, RD. *Parl* Pt E Retf. Parl Bor (1832—67), remainder and later, Seq 9. *Eccl* Newk. RDn (until 1857), Retf. 3 RDn (1857—77),

Retf. RDn (1877—84), S'well RDn (1884—87), Norwell RDn (1887—*).

KNEETON
AP *LG* Seq 5. *Parl* Seq 11. *Eccl* Seq 2.

LADY BAY
EP Cr 1950 from West Bridgford AP.[55] W Bing. RDn.

LAMBLEY
AP *LG* Seq 14. *Parl* Seq 13. *Eccl* Seq 15.

LANEHAM
AP *LG* Lbty S'well & Scrooby (until 1836/37), Seq 2. Civ bdry: 1884 (loses pt to Kettlethorpe AP, Lincs Pts Lind).[123] *Parl* Seq 1. *Eccl* Pec jurisd Dean & Chapter of York (until 1841), Seq 20 thereafter.

LANGAR CUM BARNSTONE
AP *LG* Seq 5. *Parl* Seq 11. *Eccl* Bing. RDn (until 1857), Bing. 1 RDn (1857—77), Bing. RDn (1877—84), S Bing. RDn (1884—87), Bing. RDn (1887—*).

LANGFORD
AP *LG* Seq 7. *Parl* Seq 9. *Eccl* Newk. RDn. Abol eccl *ca* 1849 to help cr Langford with Holme EP.[111]

LANGFORD WITH HOLME
EP Cr *ca* 1849 by union Langford AP, chap Holme in North Muskham AP.[111] *Eccl* Newk. 1 RDn (1860—77), Newk. RDn (1877—84), Coll. RDn (1884—87), Newk. East RDn (1887—1910), Newk. RDn (1910—*).

LANGOLD
EP Cr 1953 from Blyth AP.[42] Worksop RDn. Bdry: 1961.[44]

NETHER LANGWITH
Tp in Norton Cuckney AP, sep CP 1866.[2] *LG* Seq 4. *Parl* Seq 1.

LAXTON
AP Sometimes early 'Lexington'. *LG* Basset. Wap, S'well PLU (soon after 1836[59]—1930), RSD, RD. *Parl* Seq 2. *Eccl* Sometimes as 'Laxton with Moorhouse', Seq 8.

EAST LEAKE
AP *LG* Seq 12. *Parl* Seq 12. *Eccl* Seq 3.

WEST LEAKE
AP *LG* Seq 12. *Parl* Seq 12. *Eccl* Seq 3.

LENTON
AP *LG* Brox. Wap, Radf. PLU, RSD (ent 1875—77, pt 1877—94), pt Nott. MB (1877—89), Nott. CB (pt 1899—94, ent 1894—97), pt Nott. USD (1877—94). Civ bdry: 1877 (cr Bestwood Park CP),[32] 1880,[124] 1880,[125] 1894 (loses the pt in the CB [assoc with Notts] to help cr South Wilford CP).[53] Abol civ 1897 to help cr Nottingham CP.[51] *Parl* N'rn Dv (1832—85), pt Nott. Parl Bor, pt Rushcl. Dv (1885—1918). *Eccl* Seq 17. Eccl bdry: 1844 (help cr Hyson Green EP),[116] 1874 (detached pt severed to cr Bestwood Park EP),[31] 1894,[126] 1956 (help cr Wollaton Park EP),[19] 1958 (incl help cr Lenton Abbey EP).[30]

LENTON ABBEY
EP Cr 1958 from Lenton AP, Beeston AP.[30] Nott. RDn.

NORTH LEVERTON
AP *LG* Basset. Wap, E Retf. PLU, RSD. Abol civ 1884 to help cr North Leverton with Habblesthorpe CP.[109] *Parl* E Retf. Parl Bor (1832—85). *Eccl*

S'well pec jurisd. Gains early Apesthorpe AP (civ, 'Habblesthorpe') and thereafter 'North Leverton with Apesthorpe',[4] qv.

NORTH LEVERTON WITH APESTHORPE

EP Cr early by union North Leverton AP, Apesthorpe AP (civ, 'Habblesthorpe').[4] S'well pec jurisd (cr—1841), S'well RDn (1841—84), Tuxf. RDn (1884—87), Retf. RDn (1887—*). Bdry: 1876.[78]

NORTH LEVERTON WITH HABBLESTHORPE

CP Cr 1884 by union North Leverton AP, Habblesthorpe AP (eccl, 'Apesthorpe').[109] *LG* Basset. Wap, E Retf. PLU, RSD, RD. *Parl* Basset. Dv/CC (1885—*).

SOUTH LEVERTON

AP Incl chap Cottam (sep CP 1866,[2] eccl severed 1876 to help cr Littleborough with Cottam EP[86]). *LG* Seq 2. Addtl civ bdry alt: 1885.[127] *Parl* Seq 1. *Eccl* Retf. RDn (until 1857), Retf. 2 RDn (1857—77), Retf. RDn (1877—84), Tuxf. RDn (1884—87), Retf. RDn (1887—*). Eccl bdry: 1876.[78]

LINBY

AP *LG* Seq 6. Civ bdry: 1935.[3] *Parl* Seq 6. *Eccl* Retf. RDn (until 1857), Nott. 1 RDn (1857—77), Nott. RDn (1877—84), Mansf. RDn (1884—1910), Bulwell RDn (1910—*).

LINDHURST

Ex-par place, sep CP 1858,[49] abol eccl 1955 to help cr Rainworth EP.[38] *LG* Seq 15. Bdry: 1894 (gains the pt of Mansforth AP not in Mansf. MB).[128] *Parl* Seq 8.

LITTLEBOROUGH

AP *LG* Basset. Wap, E Retf. PLU, RSD, RD. Abol civ 1935 ent to Sturton le Steeple AP.[3] *Parl* E Retf. Parl Bor (1832—85), Basset. Dv (1885—1948). *Eccl* Retf. RDn. Gains eccl 1876 chap Cottam from South Leverton AP to cr Littleborough with Cottam EP.[86]

EP Cr 1925 when area incl village Cottam severed from Littleborough with Cottam EP to help cr Treswell with Cottam EP, the remainder to be 'Littleborough'.[129] Retf. RDn.

LITTLEBOROUGH WITH COTTAM

EP Cr 1876 by union Littleborough AP, chap Cottam in South Leverton AP.[86] Retf. 2 RDn (cr—77), Retf. RDn (1877—84), Tuxf. RDn (1884—87), Retf. RDn (1887—1925). Bdry: 1876.[78] Abol eccl 1925 when area incl village Cottam eccl severed to help cr Treswell with Cottam EP, the remainder to be 'Littleborough'.[129]

LODGE ON THE WOLDS

Ex-par place, sep CP 1858.[49] *LG* Bing. Wap, PLU (1858—96), RSD, RD. Abol 1896 ent to Cotgrave AP.[85] *Parl* S'rn Dv (1832—85), Newk. Dv (1885—1918).

LOUND

Tp (Lbty S'well & Scrooby, until 1836/37) in Sutton cum Lound AP, sep CP 1866.[2] *LG* Seq 2. Bdry: 1884.[47] *Parl* Seq 1.

LOWDHAM

AP Incl tps Caythorpe, Gunthorpe (each a sep CP 1866,[2] neither sep eccl hence this par eccl 'Lowdham with Gunthorpe and Caythorpe', qv). *LG* Seq 17. Addtl civ bdry alt: 1899.[108] *Parl* Seq 9.

LOWDHAM WITH GUNTHORPE AND CAYTHORPE

AP Usual eccl spelling; for civ and civ sep tps, see prev entry. *Eccl* Seq 16.

MANSFIELD

The following have 'Mansfield' in their names (the entry for Mansfield Woodhouse follows these entries). Insofar as any existed at a given time: *LG* Brox. Wap, Mansf. PLU, USD, MB (pt 1891—94, ent 1894—1974). *Parl* N'rn Dv (1832—85), Mansf. Dv/CC (1885—*). *Eccl* Nott. RDn (until 1857), Nott. 1 RDn (1857—77), Nott. RDn (1877—84), Mansf. RDn (1884—*).

AP1—MANSFIELD [ST PETER AND ST PAUL]—Incl chap Mansfield Woodhouse (sep civ identity early, sep EP 1736[15]), chap Skegby (sep civ identity early, sep EP 1771[15]). Addtl civ bdry alt: 1894 (loses the pt not in the MB to Lindhurst CP),[128] 1935.[3] Addtl eccl bdry alt: 1857 (cr EP2),[130] 1889 (cr EP4),[131] 1921 (cr EP3),[69] 1955 (help cr Rainworth EP).[38]

EP1—MANSFIELD ST AUGUSINE—Cr 1953 from Pleasley Hill EP, EP2.[132]

EP2—MANSFIELD ST JOHN—Cr 1857 from AP1.[130] Bdry: 1897 (cr Pleasley Hill EP),[87] 1953 (help cr EP1).[132]

EP3—MANSFIELD ST LAWRENCE—Cr 1921 from AP1.[69] Bdry: 1936 (help cr Forest Town EP),[101] 1955 (help cr Rainworth EP).[38]

EP4—MANSFIELD ST MARK—Cr 1889 from AP1.[131]

MANSFIELD WOODHOUSE

Chap in Mansfield AP, sep civ identity early, sep EP 1736.[15] *LG* Brox. Wap, Mansf. PLU, Mansf. Woodhouse USD, UD. *Parl* Seq 5. *Eccl* Nott. RDn (1736—1857), Nott. 1 RDn (1857—77), Nott. RDn (1877—84), Mansf. RDn (1884—*). Eccl bdry: 1936 (help cr Forest Town EP).[101]

MAPLEBECK

AP *LG* Seq 17. *Parl* Seq 9. *Eccl* Seq 10.

MAPPERLEY ST JUDE—see NOTTINGHAM ST JUDE

EAST MARKHAM

AP Sometimes 'Great Markham'. Incl chap West Drayton (sep civ identity early, sep EP prob in 1632 [date 1st registers][88]). *LG* Seq 2. Addtl civ bdry alt: 1935,[3] 1951.[89] *Parl* Seq 1. *Eccl* Retf. RDn (until 1857), Retf. 2 RDn (1857—77), Retf. RDn (1877—84), Tuxf. RDn (1884—*).

GREAT MARKHAM—see prev entry

MARKHAM CLINTON OR WEST MARKHAM

AP Gains early Bevercotes AP (early in ruins,[34] sep identity regained early); incl hmlt Milton (not sep civ). *LG* Seq 2. Civ bdry: 1935.[3] *Parl* Seq 1. *Eccl* Seq 20.

MARNHAM

AP Incl tp Grassthorpe (sep CP 1866[2]), hmlt Skegby (not sep civ). *LG* Seq 16. Addtl civ bdry alt: 1885,[79] 1935.[3] *Parl* Seq 10. *Eccl* Seq 8.

MATTERSEY

AP *LG* Seq 2. *Parl* Seq 1. *Eccl* Retf. RDn (until 1857), Retf. 1 RDn (1857—77), Retf. RDn (1877—1968), Bawtry RDn (1968—*).

MEERING

Ex-par place, sep CP 1858.[49] *LG* Thurg. Wap, Newk. PLU (1858—1930), RSD, RD. *Parl* Seq 9.

MISSON

AP *LG* Pt Notts (Basset. Wap), pt Lincs Pts Lind (Manley Wap), made 1886 ent Notts.[133] *LG* Doncaster PLU, RSD, E Retf. RD. *Parl* Notts pt, Seq 1. *Eccl* Seq 19.

MISTERTON

AP Incl tp West Stockwith (sep CP 1866,[2] eccl chap 'Stockwith', pec jurisd Dean & Chapter of York [until 1841], sep EP 1892[134]). *LG* Seq 1. *Parl* Seq 1. *Eccl* Pec jurisd Dean & Chapter of York (until 1841), Retf. RDn (1841—57), Retf. 1 RDn (1857—77), Retf. RDn (1877—87), Bawtry RDn (1887—*).

MORTON

Chap (S'well pec jurisd) in Southwell AP, sep civ identity early, sep EP 1780.[15] *LG* Lbty S'well & Scrooby (until 1836/37), Thurg. Wap, S'well PLU, RSD. Abol civ 1884 to help cr Fiskerton cum Morton CP.[100] *Parl* S'rn Dv (1832—85). *Eccl* S'well pec jurisd (until 1841), S'well RDn (1841—86). Abol eccl 1886 to help cr Rolleston with Morton EP.[133]

NORTH MUSKHAM

AP Incl chap Holme (sep civ identity early), tp Bathley (sep CP 1866[2]). *LG* Seq 17. *Parl* Seq 9. *Eccl* Pt S'well pec jurisd (until 1841), Newk. RDn (pt until 1841, ent 1841—57), S'well RDn (1857—87), Norwell RDn (1887—*).

SOUTH MUSKHAM

AP Incl hmlt Little Carlton (not sep civ). *LG* Seq 17. *Parl* Seq 9. *Eccl* S'well pec jurisd (until 1841), Newk. RDn (1841—57), S'well RDn (1857—87), Norwell RDn (1887—*).

NETHERFIELD

EP Cr 1885 from Gedling AP (the pt of tp Carlton not severed 1883 to cr Carlton in the Willows EP).[66] Nott. RDn (1885—87), Gedling RDn (1887—*).

WEST NEWARK

CP Cr 1894 from the pt of Newark upon Trent AP not in Newk. MB.[136] *LG* Newk. PLU, RD. Abol 1935 ent to Newk. MB & to Newark upon Trent AP.[3] *Parl* Newk. Dv (1918—48).

NEWARK ON TRENT

AP Usual eccl spelling; for civ see 'Newark upon Trent'. *Eccl* Seq 9. Eccl bdry: 1837 (cr Newark on Trent Christ Church EP),[137] 1873 (cr Newark on Trent St Leonard EP),[138] 1940.[14]

NEWARK ON TRENT CHRIST CHURCH

EP Cr 1837 from Newark on Trent AP.[137] Newk. RDn (1837—57), Newk. 2 RDn (1857—77), Newk. RDn (1877—*). Bdry: 1940,[13] 1961.[30]

NEWARK ON TRENT ST LEONARD

EP Cr 1873 from Newark on Trent AP.[138] Newk. 2 RDn (1873—77), Newk. RDn (1877—*).

NEWARK UPON TRENT

AP Usual civ spelling; for eccl see 'Newark on Trent'. *LG* Newk. Wap, PLU, Newk. upon Tr. Bor, Newk. MB (ent 1835—84, pt 1884—94, ent 1894—1974), Newk. USD (ent 1875—77, pt 1877—94), pt Newk. RSD (1877—94). Civ bdry: 1877 (gains the pt of East Stoke AP in Newk. MB),[139] 1884,[97] 1894 (loses the pt not in the MB to cr West Newark CP),[136] 1935 (incl gains West Newark CP).[3] *Parl* Newk. upon Tr. Parl Bor (1673—1885), Newk. Dv/ CC (1885—*).

NEWSTEAD

Ex-par place (orig an Austin priory and thus eccl 'Newstead Priory'), sep CP 1858 as 'Newstead',[49] pt eccl severed 1971 to help cr Ravenshead EP.[39] *LG* Brox. Wap, Basf. PLU, RSD, RD. Civ bdry: 1935.[3] *Parl* Seq 6.

NEWSTEAD PRIORY—see prev entry

NORMANTON ON SOAR

AP *LG* Seq 12. *Parl* Seq 12. *Eccl* Seq 3.

NORMANTON ON TRENT

AP *LG* Seq 16. Civ bdry: 1935.[3] *Parl* Seq 10. *Eccl* Seq 8.

NORMANTON ON THE WOLDS

Tp (Rushcl. Wap) in Plumtree AP (o'wise Bing. Wap), sep CP 1866.[2] *LG* Seq 5. *Parl* Seq 15.

NORTON

Tp in Norton Cuckney AP, sep CP 1866.[2] *LG* Seq 4. *Parl* Seq 1.

NORWELL

AP Incl chap Carlton on Trent (sep CP 1866,[2] sep EP 1874[70]), tp Norwell Woodhouse (sep CP 1866[2]). *LG* Seq 17. Addtl civ bdry alt: 1877,[73] 1935 (gains Norwell Woodhouse CP).[3] *Parl* Seq 9. *Eccl* Seq 24.

NORWELL WOODHOUSE

Tp in Norwell AP, sep CP 1866.[2] *LG* Thurg. Wap, S'well PLU, RSD, RD. Abol 1935 ent to Norwell AP.[3] *Parl* S'rn Dv (1832—85), Newk. Dv (1885—1948).

NOTTINGHAM

The following have 'Nottingham' in their names. Insofar as any existed at a given time: *LG* Nott. Bor (Co of Itself from 1448), Nott. PLU (1836—97), Par (poor law purposes, 1897—1930), Nott. MB/ CB, USD. *Parl* Nott. Parl Bor (1295—1918); Nott. Central Parl Bor/BC (1918—70), Nott. East Parl Bor/BC (1918—70), Nott. North BC (1970—*), Nott. North West BC (1948—70), Nott. South Parl Bor/BC (1918—70), Nott. West Parl Bor (1918— 48), Nott. West BC (1970—*); see Part III of the *Guide* for composition of Nott. Parl Bors/BCs (1918—*) by wards of the CB and other units. *Eccl* Nott. RDn (until 1857), Nott. 3 RDn (1857—77), Nott. RDn (1877—*).

CP1—NOTTINGHAM—Cr 1897 by union AP1, AP2, AP3, Brewhouse Yard CP, Lenton AP, Radford AP, Sneinton CP, Standard Hill CP.[51] Civ bdry: 1899 (gains Basford AP, Bulwell AP, North Wilford CP),[22] 1933 (incl gains Bilborough AP, Wollaton AP),[5] 1952.[21] Parl bdry: 1952.[54]

EP1—NOTTINGHAM ALL SAINTS—Cr 1865 from AP1.[140] Bdry: 1959.[141]

EP2—NOTTINGHAM EMMANUEL—Cr 1886 from EP7.[142] Abol 1972 to help cr EP8.[143]

EP3—NOTTINGHAM HOLY TRINITY—Cr 1859 from AP1.[14] Bdry: 1869 (help cr EP24).[144] Abol 1930 to help cr EP5.[145]

EP4—NOTTINGHAM HOLY TRINITY—Cr 1954 by union EP18, EP5.[146] Abol 1959 pt to AP1, pt to

EP20, pt to EP1.[141]

EP5—NOTTINGHAM HOLY TRINITY WITH ST MARK—Cr 1930 by union EP3, EP17.[145] Abol 1954 to help cr EP4.[146]

EP6—NOTTINGHAM ST ANDREW—Cr 1871 from EP7, EP17.[9]

EP7—NOTTINGHAM ST ANN—Cr 1865 from AP1.[6] Bdry: 1871 (help cr EP6),[9] 1877,[71] 1886 (cr EP2),[142] 1890,[147] 1905 (help cr EP9),[148] 1926 (cr EP15, commonly called 'Mapperley St Jude'),[149] 1935 (help cr Porchester EP),[68] 1935.[69] Abol 1972 to help cr EP8.[143]

EP8—NOTTINGHAM ST ANN WITH EMMANUEL—Cr 1972 by union EP7, EP2.[143]

EP9—NOTTINGHAM ST BARTHOLOMEW—Cr 1905 from EP7, Snenton St Matthias EP.[148]

EP10—NOTTINGHAM ST CATHERINE—Cr 1888 from EP16, EP17, EP19, AP1.[150] Bdry: 1924,[120] 1963.[151] Because bdry alt 1963 transf to this par orig area EP16, this par sometimes thereafter called 'Nottingham St Catherine with St Luke'

—NOTTINGHAM ST CATHERINE WITH ST LUKE—see EP10

—NOTTINGHAM ST CYPRIAN—Name commonly used for EP cr 1927 as 'Sneinton St Cyprian', qv.

EP11—NOTTINGHAM ST GEORGE—Cr 1892 from EP23.[132] Abol 1953 to help cr EP12.[152]

EP12—NOTTINGHAM ST GEORGE WITH ST JOHN THE BAPTIST—Cr 1953 by union EP11, EP14.[152]

EP13—NOTTINGHAM ST JAMES—Church erected 1809 without parochial district assigned.[153] Abol 1953 to help cr EP20.[150]

EP14—NOTTINGHAM ST JOHN THE BAPTIST—Cr 1844 from AP1.[154] Bdry: 1851,[155] 1912 (gains ex-par Brewhouse Yard, ex-par The Park [not sep civ]),[115] 1933 (help cr EP20).[150] Abol 1953 to help cr EP12.[152]

EP15—NOTTINGHAM ST JUDE—Cr 1926 from EP7.[149] Commonly called 'Mapperley St Jude'. Bdry: 1935,[69] 1936 (help cr Sherwood EP).[72]

EP16—NOTTINGHAM ST LUKE—Cr 1863 from AP1.[156] Bdry: 1880 (help cr EP21),[37] 1888 (help cr EP10),[150] 1890.[147] Abol 1924 to help cr EP22.[157]

EP17—NOTTINGHAM ST MARK—Cr 1856 from AP1.[158] Bdry: 1871 (help cr EP6),[9] 1888 (help cr EP10),[150] 1898 (gains area EP24 as latter demolished for railroad construction; see EP24 for later re-cr).[19] Abol 1930 to help cr EP5.[145]

AP1—NOTTINGHAM ST MARY—Incl in Thurg. Wap chap Sneinton (sep civ identity early, sep EP 1771[15]). *LG* Nott. Bor (pt until Sneinton gains sep civ identity, ent thereafter). Addtl civ bdry alt: 1858 (gains civ ex-par The Park),[49] 1894 (gains the pts in Nott. CB of West Bridgford AP, Carlton CP).[53] Abol civ 1897 to help cr CP1.[51] Commonly eccl 'Nottingham St Mary the Virgin'. Addtl eccl bdry alt: 1839 (cr EP19),[159] 1844 (cr EP14),[154] 1851,[155] 1855 (cr EP18),[160] 1856 (cr EP17),[158] 1859 (cr EP3),[15] 1863 (cr EP16),[156] 1865 (cr EP1),[140] 1865 (cr EP7, cr EP23),[6] 1881,[27] 1888 (help cr EP10),[150] 1924,[120] 1959.[141]

—NOTTINGHAM ST MARY THE VIRGIN—see AP1

EP18—NOTTINGHAM ST MATTHEW—Cr 1855 from AP1.[160] Bdry: 1874 (help cr EP25),[161] 1897 (help cr EP24),[144] 1929.[162] Abol 1954 to help cr EP4.[146]

AP2—NOTTINGHAM ST NICHOLAS—Civ bdry: 1877.[163] Abol civ 1897 to help cr CP1.[51] Eccl bdry: 1874 (help cr EP25),[161] 1929.[162]

EP19—NOTTINGHAM ST PAUL—Cr 1839 from AP1.[159] Bdry: 1888 (help cr EP10).[150] Abol 1924 pt to AP1, pt to EP10.[120]

AP3—NOTTINGHAM ST PETER—Civ bdry: 1877.[163] Abol civ 1897 to help cr CP1.[51] Eccl bdry: 1874 (help cr EP25).[151] Abol eccl 1933 to help cr EP20.[150]

EP20—NOTTINGHAM ST PETER WITH ST JAMES—Cr 1933 by union AP3, EP13, pt EP14.[150] Bdry: 1959.[141]

EP21—NOTTINGHAM ST PHILIP—Cr 1880 from EP16.[37] Abol 1924 to help cr EP22.[157]

EP22—NOTTINGHAM ST PHILIP WITH ST LUKE—Cr 1924 by union EP21, EP16.[157] Abol 1963 the former area of EP21 severed to help cr Sneinton St Christopher with St Philip EP, the remainder to EP10.[151]

EP23—NOTTINGHAM ST SAVIOUR—Cr 1865 from AP1.[6] Bdry: 1892 (cr EP11).[132]

EP24—NOTTINGHAM ST STEPHEN—Cr 1869 from EP3, EP18.[144] Church demolished for railroad construction, 'St Stephen' re-cr 1898 from Hyson Green EP and old site added to EP17.[19] Bdry: 1881.[27]

EP25—NOTTINGHAM ST THOMAS—Cr 1874 from EP18, AP2, AP3.[161] Abol 1929 pt to AP2, pt to EP18.[162]

NUTHALL

AP Incl chap Awsworth (sep EP 1748,[15] sep CP 1894[16]). *LG* Seq 6. Addtl civ bdry alt: 1877,[106] 1877.[107] *Parl* Seq 7. *Eccl* Seq 13. Addtl eccl bdry alt: 1934,[37] 1955.[18]

OLDCOTES—see STYRRUP WITH OLDCOTES

OLLERTON

Chap in Edwinstowe AP (eccl 'Edwinstowe with Carburton'), sep CP 1866,[2] sep EP 1888.[91] *LG* Seq 3. Civ bdry: 1957.[93] *Parl* Seq 2. *Eccl* Worksop RDn. Eccl bdry: 1931.[48]

OMPTON

Tp in Kneesall AP, sep CP 1866.[2] *LG* Seq 3. *Parl* Seq 2.

ORDSALL

AP Incl hmlt Thrumpton (not sep civ). *LG* Basset. Wap, E Retf. PLU, USD, MB (1878—1921). Abol civ 1921 ent to East Retford AP.[164] *Parl* E Retf. Parl Bor (1832—85), Basset. Dv (1885—1948). *Eccl* Seq 21.

ORSTON

AP Incl chap Scarrington (sep civ identity early, eccl severed 1867 to help cr Scarrington with Aslockton EP[8]), chap Thoroton (sep civ identity early, not sep eccl hence this par eccl 'Orston with Thoroton', qv). *LG* Seq 5. *Parl* Seq 11.

ORSTON WITH THOROTON

AP Usual eccl spelling; for civ and civ and eccl sep

chaps, see prev entry. *Eccl* Seq 2.

OSBERTON—see SCOFTON WITH OSBERTON

OSSINGTON

AP *LG* Seq 17. *Parl* Seq 9. *Eccl* Seq 8.

OWTHORPE

AP *LG* Seq 5. *Parl* Seq 11. *Eccl* Seq 1.

OXTON

AP *LG* Seq 17. Civ bdry: 1884.[90] *Parl* Seq 9. *Eccl* Seq 23.

PAPPLEWICK

AP *LG* Seq 6. Civ bdry: 1883,[33] 1935.[3] *Parl* Seq 6. *Eccl* Retf. RDn (until 1884), Mansf. RDn (1884—1910), Bulwell RDn (1910—*).

THE PARK

Ex-par place situated in Nottingham St Mary AP (eccl, Nottingham St Mary the Virgin'), incl civ in the latter 1858,[49] abol eccl 1912 to help cr Nottingham St John the Baptist EP.[115]

PARK LEYS

Ex-par place, sep CP 1858.[49] *LG* Thurg. Wap, S'well PLU (1858—99), RSD, RD. Abol 1899 ent to Kelham AP.[118] *Parl* S'rn Dv (1832—85), Newk. Dv (1885—1918).

PERLETHORPE

Chap (incl pt hmlt Thoresby [not sep civ] in Edwinstowe AP, sep CP 1866,[2] sep EP 1836.[92] *LG* Basset. Wap, S'well PLU, RSD, RD. Abol civ 1899 to help cr Perlethorpe cum Budby CP.[61] *Parl* E Retf. Parl Bor (1832—85), Basset. Dv (1885—1918). *Eccl* Retf. RDn (1836—57), Retf. 3 RDn (1857—77), Retf. RDn (1877—84), Worksop RDn (1884—*). Eccl bdry: 1877.[94]

PERLETHORPE CUM BUDBY

CP Cr 1899 by union Perlethorpe CP, Budby CP, pt Edwinstowe AP.[61] *LG* S'well PLU, RD. *Parl* Newk. Dv/CC (1918—*).

PINXTON

AP Derbys par considered most of 19th cent to be ent Derbys (Scarsdale Wap, Mansf. PLU), by 1891 census deemed pt in Notts; pts exchanged 1895 with Kirkby in Ashfield AP (Notts),[12] so that Pinxton ent Derbys thereafter, qv in entries for that co.

PLEASLEY HILL

EP Cr 1897 from Mansfield St John EP.[87] Mansf. RDn. Bdry: 1953 (help cr Mansfield St Augustine EP).[132]

PLUMTREE

AP Tp 'Plumtree' in Bing. Wap as was tp Clipston (sep CP 1866[2]); incl in Rushcl. Wap tp Normanton on the Wolds (sep CP 1866[2]). *LG* Bing. PLU, RSD, RD. *Parl* Seq 15. *Eccl* Seq 4.

PORCHESTER

EP Cr 1935 from Gedling AP, Nottingham St Ann EP, Carlton in the Willows EP.[68] Gedling RDn. Bdry: 1940,[87] 1963 (cr Woodthorpe EP).[165]

RADCLIFFE ON TRENT

AP *LG* Seq 5. Civ bdry: 1935.[3] *Parl* Seq 11. *Eccl* Seq 2.

RADFORD

The following have 'Radford' in their names. Insofar as any existed at a given time: *LG* Brox. Wap, Radf. PLU, RSD (1875—77), Nott. MB (1877—89), CB (1899—97), USD (1877—94). *Parl* N'rn Dv (1832—85), Nott. Parl Bor (1885—1918).

Eccl Nott. RDn (until 1857), Nott. 3 RDn (1857—77), Nott. RDn (1877—*).

AP1—RADFORD [ST PETER]— Civ bdry: 1880,[125] 1880.[124] Abol civ 1897 to help cr Nottingham CP.[51] Eccl bdry: 1844 (help cr Hyson Green EP),[116] 1845 (cr EP1),[165] 1894,[126] 1896 (cr EP2),[167] 1913 (cr EP3),[26] 1933 (help cr Aspley EP).[9]

EP1—NEW RADFORD—Cr 1845 from AP1.[166]

EP2—RADFORD ALL SOULS—Cr 1896 from AP1.[167]

EP3—RADFORD ST MICHAEL AND ALL ANGELS—Cr 1913 from AP1.[26]

RAGNALL

Chap (S'well pec jurisd, until 1841) in Dunham AP, sep civ identity early. *LG* Seq 2. *Parl* Seq 1.

RAINWORTH

EP Cr 1955 from Mansfield St Lawrence EP, Forest Town EP, Mansfield AP, Blidworth AP, and ent ex-par places of Rufford Abbey, Lindhurst.[38] Mansf. RDn.

RAMPTON

AP *LG* Seq 2. *Parl* Seq 1. *Eccl* Seq 25.

RANSKILL

Tp (Notts, Lbty S'well & Scrooby [until 1836/37], Basset. Wap) in Blyth AP (Notts [Basset. Wap], Yorks W Riding [Strafforth & Tickhill Wap]), sep CP 1866 in Notts.[2] *LG* Seq 2. *Parl* Seq 1.

RATCLIFFE ON SOAR

AP Incl chap Kingston on Soar (sep civ identity early, sep EP 1762[15]), chap Thrumpton (sep civ identity early, prob sep EP in 1679 [date 1st registers][168]). *LG* Rushcl. Wap, Shard. PLU, RSD, Unnamed RD (1894—1927), Leake RD (1927—35), Basf. RD (1935—74). *Parl* Seq 12. *Eccl* Seq 5.

RAVENSHEAD

EP Cr 1971 from Sutton in Ashfield AP, Blidworth AP, pt ex-par place Newstead Priory.[39] Mansf. RDn.

REMPSTONE

AP *LG* Seq 12. *Parl* Seq 12. *Eccl* Seq 5.

RETFORD

EP [St Saviour] Cr 1933 from Clarborough AP.[75] Retf. RDn.

EAST RETFORD

AP *LG* Basset. Wap, [E] Retf. Bor, E Retf. PLU, USD, MB. Civ bdry: 1921 (gains the other pars in E Retf. MB: Ordsall AP, West Retford AP, North Retford CP).[164] *Parl* E Retf. Parl Bor (1316, 1572—1885), Basset. Dv/CC (1885—*). *Eccl* [St Swithun] Seq 18.

NORTH RETFORD

CP Cr 1894 from the pt of Clarborough AP in E Retf. MB.[74] *LG* E Retf. PLU, MB. Abol 1921 ent to East Retford AP.[164] *Parl* Basset. Dv (1918—48).

WEST RETFORD

AP *LG* Basset. Wap, E Retf. PLU, USD, MB (1878—1921). Abol civ 1921 ent to East Retford AP.[164] *Parl* E Retf. Parl Bor (1832—85), Basset. Dv (1885—1948). *Eccl* [St Michael the Archangel] Seq 18.

ROLLESTON

AP Incl tp Fiskerton (sep CP 1866[2]). *LG* Seq 17. *Parl* Seq 9. *Eccl* Newk. RDn (until 1857), S'well RDn

(1857—late 1880s). Abol eccl late 1880s to help cr Rolleston with Morton EP.[135]

ROLLESTON WITH FISKERTON AND MORTON— see following entry

ROLLESTON WITH MORTON

EP Cr late 1880s by union Rolleston AP, Morton EP.[135] S'well RDn. Sometimes 'Rolleston with Fiskerton and Morton'.

RUDDINGTON

AP Incl chap Edwalton (sep civ identity early, sep EP 1739[15]), hmlt Flawford (not sep civ). *LG* Seq 10. Addtl civ bdry alt: 1952 (loses pt to Nott. CB [assoc with Notts] & CP).[21] *Parl* Seq 12. Parl bdry: 1952.[54] *Eccl* Seq 3.

RUFFORD

Ex-par place, sep CP 1858,[49] eccl 'Rufford Abbey', eccl abol 1955 to help cr Rainworth EP.[38] *LG* Seq 3. *Parl* Seq 2.

RUFFORD ABBEY—see prev entry

SAUNDBY

AP *LG* Seq 1. *Parl* Seq 1. *Eccl* Seq 18.

SAXONDALE

Tp in Shelford AP, sep CP 1866.[2] *LG* Seq 5. *Parl* Seq 11.

SCAFTWORTH

Tp in Everton AP, sep CP 1866.[2] *LG* Lbty S'well & Scrooby (until 1836/37), Seq 2. *Parl* Seq 1.

SOUTH SCARLE

AP Incl chap Girton (sep civ identity early, not sep eccl but enlarged eccl 1875 when gains hmlt Spalford from North Clifton AP[78]), chap Besthorpe (sep CP 1866[2]) so that this par eccl 'South Scarle with Besthorpe and Girton', qv. *LG* Seq 7. *Parl* Seq 9.

SOUTH SCARLE WITH BESTHORPE AND GIRTON

AP Usual eccl spelling; for civ and civ sep and enlargement of chaps, see prev entry. *Eccl* Seq 7.

SCARRINGTON

Chap in Orston AP, sep civ identity early, eccl united 1867 with tp Aslockton in Whatton AP as 'Scarrington with Aslockton',[8] qv. *LG* Seq 5. *Parl* Seq 11.

SCARRINGTON WITH ASLOCKTON

EP Cr 1867 by union chap Scarrington in Orston AP, tp Aslockton in Whatton AP.[8] Bing. 2 RDn (1867—77), Bing. RDn (1877—*).

SCOFTON WITH OSBERTON

EP Cr 1875 from Worksop AP, Carlton in Lindrick AP, Blyth AP, Babworth AP.[19] Retf. 3 RDn (1875—77), Retf. RDn (1877—84), Worksop RDn (1884—*). Bdry: 1960 (help cr Worksop Priory EP).[169]

SCREVETON

AP *LG* Seq 5. *Parl* Seq 11. *Eccl* Seq 2.

SCROOBY

AP Orig chap (pec jurisd Archbp York) in Sutton cum Lound AP, sep par before 1535. *LG* Lbty S'well & Scrooby (until 1836/37), Seq 2. *Parl* Seq 1. *Eccl* Pec jurisd Archbp York (until 1841), Seq 18 thereafter. Eccl bdry: 1959,[43] 1962.[11]

SELSTON

AP Usual civ spelling; for eccl see following entry. Incl hmlts Bagthorpe, Jackfield (neither sep civ). *LG* Seq 6. *Parl* Seq 3.

SELSTON WITH UNDERWOOD AND WESTWOOD

AP Usual eccl spelling; for civ see prev entry. *Eccl* Nott. RDn (until 1857), Nott. 1 RDn (1857—77), Nott. RDn (1877—84), Mansf. RDn (1884—1910), Bulwell RDn (1910—55). Eccl bdry: 1850 (help cr Ironville EP [Derbys, Notts] to be dioc Lichf).[117] Abol eccl 1955, the area of Underwood eccl severed to help cr Brinsley with Underwood EP, the remainder to be 'Selston with Westwood'.[58]

SELSTON WITH WESTWOOD

EP Cr 1955 when area Underwood eccl severed from Selston with Underwood and Westwood AP to help cr Brinsley with Underwood EP,[58] the remainder to be 'Selston with Westwood'. Bulwell RDn.

SHELFORD

AP Incl tp Saxondale (sep CP 1866[2]), hmlt Newton (not sep civ). *LG* Seq 5. *Parl* Seq 11. *Eccl* Seq 2.

SHELTON

AP *LG* Seq 8. *Parl* Seq 11. *Eccl* Seq 9.

SHERWOOD

EP Cr 1936 from Daybrook EP, Carrington EP, Nottingham St Jude EP.[72] Nott. RDn.

SHIREOAKS

EP Cr 1865 from Worksop AP (Notts), Anston cum Membris AP (Yorks W Riding, civ 'North and South Anston'), to be dioc Linc.[170] Retf. 3 RDn (1865—77), Retf. RDn (1877—84), Worksop RDn (1884—*).

SIBTHORPE

AP Orig Collegiate church. *LG* Seq 8. *Parl* Seq 11. *Eccl* Seq 9.

SKEGBY

Chap in Mansfield AP, sep civ identity early, sep EP 1771.[15] *LG* Brox. Wap, Mansf. PLU, RSD, Skegby RD. Abol civ 1935 ent to Sutton in Ashfield UD & AP.[3] *Parl* N'rn Dv (1832—85), Mansf. Dv (1885—1948). *Eccl* Nott. RDn (1771—1857), Nott. 1 RDn (1857—77), Nott. RDn (1877—84), Mansf. RDn (1884—*).

SNEINTON

The following have 'Sneinton' in their names (EP6 cr as 'Snenton' but incl here as well for completeness); insofar as any existed at a given time: *LG* Thurg. Wap, Radf. PLU, RSD (1875—77), Nott. MB (1877—89), CB (1889—97), USD (1877—94). *Parl* S'rn Dv (1832—85), Nott. Parl Bor (1885—1918). *Eccl* Nott. RDn (cr—1857), Nott. 2 RDn (1857—77), Nott. RDn (1877—*).

CP1/EP1—SNEINTON [ST STEPHEN]—Chap in Nottingham St Mary AP, sep civ identity early, sep EP 1771.[15] Abol civ 1897 to help cr Nottingham CP.[51] Eccl bdry: 1869 (cr EP6),[171] 1888 (help cr EP2),[62] 1911 (cr EP3).[115] Abol eccl 1961 to help cr EP7.[172]

EP2—SNEINTON ST ALBAN—Cr 1888 from EP1, EP6.[62] Abol 1961 to help cr EP7.[172]

EP3—SNEINTON ST CHRISTOPHER—Cr 1911 from EP1.[115] Abol 1963 to help cr EP4.[151]

EP4—SNEINTON ST CHRISTOPHER WITH ST PHILIP—Cr 1963 by union EP3, pt Nottingham St Philip with St Luke EP (area of Nottingham St Philip EP before its abol in 1924).[151]

EP5—SNEINTON ST CYPRIAN—Cr 1927 from EP6,

Carlton in the Willows EP, Colwick AP.[64] Commonly called 'Nottingham St Cyprian'. Bdry: 1935.[69]

EP6—SNENTON ST MATTHIAS—Cr 1869 from EP1[171]; orig spelling less often used later. Bdry: 1888 (help cr EP2),[62] 1890,[147] 1905 (help cr Nottingham St Bartholomew EP),[148] 1927 (help cr EP5),[64] 1935.[69]

EP7—SNEINTON ST STEPHEN WITH ST ALBAN— Cr 1961 by union EP1, EP2.[172]

SNENTON ST MATTHIAS

EP Orig spelling of EP cr 1869, later commonly 'Sneinton St Matthias', qv above.

SOOKHOLME

Tp in Warsop AP, sep CP 1866.[2] LG Basset. Wap, Mansf. PLU, RSD, Skegby RD. Abol 1935 ent to Warsop UD & AP.[3] Parl E Retf. Parl Bor (1832— 85), Basset. Dv (1885—1948).

SOUTHWELL

AP Orig Collegiate church. Incl chap Halam (sep civ identity early, sep EP 1715[15]), chap Morton (sep civ identity early, sep EP 1780[15]), hmlts Easthorpe, Normanton, Westhorpe (none sep civ). LG Lbty S'well & Scrooby (until 1836/37), Seq 17. Addtl civ bdry alt: 1877.[98] Parl Seq 9. Eccl Seq 23. Addtl eccl bdry alt: 1846 (cr Southwell Holy Trinity EP).[173]

SOUTHWELL HOLY TRINITY

EP Cr 1846 from Southwell AP.[173] S'well RDn.

SPALFORD

Hmlt in North Clifton AP, sep CP 1866,[2] eccl severed 1875 and united to chap Girton in South Scarle AP (eccl, 'South Scarle with Besthorpe and Girton').[78] LG Seq 7. Parl Seq 9.

STANDARD HILL

Ex-par place, sep CP 1858.[49] LG Brox. Wap, Basf. PLU (1862—97), RSD (1875—77), Nott. MB (1877—89), CB (1899—97), USD (1877—94). Abol civ 1897 to help cr Nottingham CP.[51] Parl N'rn Dv (1832—85), Nott. Parl Bor (1885—1918), Rushcl. Dv (1918—48).

STANFORD ON SOAR

AP LG Seq 12. Parl Seq 12. Eccl Seq 3.

STANTON ON THE WOLDS

AP LG Seq 11. Parl Seq 15. Eccl Seq 1.

STAPLEFORD

AP LG Brox. Wap, Shard. PLU, RSD, Staplef. RD. Abol civ 1935 to help cr Beeston & Staplef. UD & CP.[3] Parl N'rn Dv (1832—85), Rushcl. Dv (1885— 1948). Eccl Seq 13.

STAUNTON

AP Incl chap Flawborough (sep civ identity early, not sep eccl hence this par eccl 'Staunton with Flawbor-ough', qv), area orig AP 'Staunton Chapel' (appar-ently stood in same churchyard, demolished 1827 when presumably united with Staunton[174]). LG Seq 7. Parl Seq 9.

STAUNTON CHAPEL—see prev entry

STAUNTON WITH FLAWBOROUGH

AP Usual eccl spelling; for civ and civ sep chap, see prev entry. Eccl Seq 9.

STAYTHORPE

Tp in Averham AP, sep CP 1866.[2] LG Seq 17. Parl

Seq 9.

STOCKWITH

Chap (pec jurisd Dean & Chapter of York, until 1841) in Misterton AP, pt a sep EP 1892,[134] civ the tp called 'West Stockwith', as such sep CP 1866,[2] qv. Bawtry RDn.

WEST STOCKWITH

Tp in Misterton AP, sep CP 1866,[2] eccl chap 'Stockwith', pt of the chap a sep EP 1892 as 'Stockwith',[134] qv in prev entry (incl pec jurisd). LG Seq 1. Parl Seq 1.

EAST STOKE

AP Tp 'East Soke' in Thurg. Wap as was chap Elston (sep CP 1866,[2] by 1870s deemed eccl in Elston and that union sometimes thereafter 'Elston with Elston Chapel'[96]); incl in Newk. Wap chap Coddington (sep civ identity early, sep EP prob in 1676 [date 1st registers][83]), chap Syerston (sep civ identity early, not sep eccl hence this par eccl 'East Stoke with Syerston', qv). LG Thurg. Wap (pt until Codd-ington, Syerston gain sep civ identity, ent there-after), pt Newk. Wap (until Coddington, Syerston gain sep civ identity), S'well PLU, pt Newk. upon Tr. Bor, pt Newk. MB (1835—77), pt Newk. USD (1875—77), S'well RSD (pt 1875—77, ent 1877— 94), S'well RD (1894—1935), Newk. RD (1935— 74). Addtl civ bdry alt: 1877 (loses the pt in the MB to Newark upon Trent AP),[139] 1884.[100] Parl Pt Newk. upon Tr. Parl Bor (1673—1885), remainder and later, Seq 9.

EAST STOKE WITH SYERSTON

AP Usual eccl spelling; for civ and civ and eccl sep chaps, see prev entry. Eccl Seq 9. Addtl eccl bdry alt: 1940.[14]

STOKE BARDOLPH

Tp in Gedling AP, sep CP 1866.[2] LG Seq 14. Bdry: 1935.[3] Parl Seq 14.

STOKEHAM

Chap (pec jurisd Dean & Chapter of York, until 1841) in East Drayton AP, sep civ identity early. LG Seq 2. Parl Seq 1.

STRELLEY

AP LG Seq 6. Parl Seq 7. Eccl Nott. RDn. Abol eccl 1838 to help cr Bilbrough with Strelley EP,[36] later called 'Bilborough'.

STURTON LE STEEPLE

AP Sometimes 'Sturton le Clay'. Incl hmlt Fenton (not sep civ). LG Seq 2. Civ bdry: 1886,[63] 1935 (gains Littleborough AP).[3] Parl Seq 1. Eccl Seq 18.

STYRRUP

Tp (Notts. Basset. Wap) in Blyth AP (Notts [Basset. Wap], Yorks W Riding [Strafforth & Tickhill Wap]), sep CP 1866 in Notts.[2] LG Basset. Wap, Worksop PLU, RSD, Blyth & Cuckney RD (1894— 1925), Worksop RD (1925—51). Bdry: 1883.[41] Renamed civ 1951 'Styrrup with Oldcotes'.[175] Parl E Retf. Parl Bor (1832—85), Basset. Dv/CC (1885—1970).

STYRRUP WITH OLDCOTES

CP Renaming 1951 of Styrrup CP.[175] LG Worksop RD. Parl Basset. CC (1970—*).

SUTTON

Tp (Lbty S'well & Scrooby, until 1836/37) in

Sutton cum Lound AP, sep CP 1866.[2] *LG* Seq 2. Bdry: 1884.[47] *Parl* Seq 1.

SUTTON BONINGTON

Single tp rated for poor law purposes comprised of 2 APs of Sutton Bonington St Anne, Sutton Bonington St Michael.[176] *LG* Seq 12. *Parl* Seq 12.

SUTTON BONINGTON ST ANNE

AP Rushcl. Wap, civ jointly rated with Sutton Bonington St Michael AP as 'Sutton Bonington',[176] qv. *Eccl* Seq 3.

SUTTON BONINGTON ST MICHAEL

AP Ruchcl. Wap, civ jointly rated with Sutton Bonington St Anne AP as 'Sutton Bonington',[176] qv. *Eccl* Seq 3.

SUTTON CUM LOUND

AP Incl chap Scrooby (pec jurisd Archbp York, sep par before 1535), tps Lound, Sutton (each a sep CP 1866[2]) so that after 1866 'Sutton cum Lound' has no civ identity. *LG* Lbty S'well & Scrooby (until 1836/37), Basset. Wap. *Parl* E Retf. Parl Bor (1832—67). *Eccl* Seq 18.

SUTTON IN ASHFIELD

AP Incl hmlt Hucknall under Huthwaite (sep CP 1866,[2] sep EP 1906[114]). *LG* Brox. Wap, Mansf. PLU, Sutton in Ashfield USD, UD. Addtl civ bdry alt: 1884,[102] 1935 (incl gains Fulwood CP, Huthwaite UD & Hucknall under Huthwaite CP, Skegby CP, Teversal AP).[3] *Parl* N'rn Dv (1832—85), Mansf. Dv/CC (1885—1970), Ashfield CC (1970—*). *Eccl* Seq 11. Addtl eccl bdry alt: 1910 (cr Sutton in Ashfield St Michael and All Angels EP),[177] 1911,[115] 1971 (help cr Ravenshead EP).[39]

SUTTON IN ASHFIELD ST MICHAEL AND ALL ANGELS

EP Cr 1910 from Sutton in Ashfield AP.[177] Mansf. RDn.

SUTTON ON TRENT

AP *LG* Seq 17. *Parl* Seq 9. *Eccl* Seq 8.

SWINETHORPE—see HARBY WITH SWINETHORPE

SYERSTON

Chap in East Stoke AP, sep civ identity early. *LG* Seq 9. Bdry: 1884.[95] *Parl* Seq 9.

TEVERSAL

AP *LG* Brox. Wap, Mansf. PLU, RSD, Skegby RD. Abol civ 1935 ent to Sutton in Ashfield UD & AP.[3] *Parl* N'rn Dv (1832—85), Mansf. Dv (1885—1948). *Eccl* Seq 11.

THORNEY

AP Incl hmlts Broadholme, Wigsley (each a sep CP 1866,[2] neither sep eccl hence this par eccl 'Thorney with Wigsley and Broadholme', qv). *LG* Newk. Wap, PLU (soon after 1836[59]—1930), RSD, RD. *Parl* Seq 9.

THORNEY WITH WIGSLEY AND BROADHOLME

AP Usual eccl spelling; for civ and civ sep hmlts, see prev entry. *Eccl* Seq 7.

THOROTON

Chap in Orston AP, sep civ identity early. *LG* Seq 5. Civ bdry: 1889.[111] *Parl* Seq 11.

THORPE

AP Sometimes civ 'Thorpe near Newark'. *LG* Newk. Wap, S'well PLU, RSD, RD (1894—1935), Newk. RD (1935—74). *Parl* Seq 9. *Eccl* Seq 9.

THORPE IN THE GLEBE

AP Sometimes 'Thorpe Bochart'. *LG* Seq 12. *Parl* Seq 12. *Eccl* Bing. RDn. Church early destroyed, thereafter eccl in Wysall AP.

THRUMPTON

Chap in Ratcliffe on Soar, sep civ identity early, prob sep EP in 1679 (date 1st registers).[168] *LG* Seq 10. *Parl* Seq 12. *Eccl* Seq 3.

THURGARTON

AP *LG* Seq 17. *Parl* Seq 9. *Eccl* Nott. RDn. Abol eccl 1848 to help cr Thurgarton with Hoveringham EP.[113]

THURGARTON WITH HOVERINGHAM

EP Cr 1848 by union Thurgarton AP, Hoveringham AP.[113] Nott. RDn (1848—57), Nott. 2 RDn (1857—77), Nott. RDn (1877—84), S'well RDn (1884—*).

TITHBY

AP Incl tp Cropwell Butler (sep CP 1866,[2] not sep eccl hence this par eccl 'Tythby with Cropwell Butler', qv). *LG* Seq 5. *Parl* Seq 11.

TOLLERTON

AP *LG* Seq 5. *Parl* Seq 11. *Eccl* Seq 4.

TORWORTH

Tp (Notts, Basset. Wap) in Blyth AP (Notts [Basset. Wap], Yorks W Riding [Strafforth & Tickhill Wap]), sep CP 1866 in Notts.[2] *LG* Seq 2. *Parl* Seq 1.

TOTON

Tp in Attenborough AP, sep CP 1866.[2] *LG* Brox. Wap, Shard. PLU, RSD, Staplef. RD. Abol 1935 to help cr Beeston & Staplef. UD & CP.[3] *Parl* N'rn Dv (1832—85), Rushcl. Dv (1885—1948).

TRESWELL

AP *LG* Seq 2. *Parl* Seq 1. *Eccl* Pec jurisd Dean & Chapter of York (early period only), thereafter Retf. RDn (until 1857), Retf. 2 (1857—77), Retf. RDn (1877—84), Tuxf. RDn (1884—1925). Abol eccl 1925 to help cr Treswell with Cottam EP.[129]

TRESWELL WITH COTTAM

EP Cr 1925 by union Treswell AP, pt Littleborough with Cottam AP (incl village Cottam).[129] Tuxf. RDn.

TROWELL

AP *LG* Seq 6. *Parl* Seq 7. *Eccl* Orig pec jurisd Dean & Chap of York but not later, Seq 13 thereafter.

TUXFORD

AP *LG* Seq 2. Civ bdry: 1935.[3] *Parl* Seq 1. *Eccl* Seq 18.

TYTHBY WITH CROPWELL BUTLER

AP Usual eccl spelling; for civ and civ sep tp, see 'Tithby'. *Eccl* Seq 2.

UNDERWOOD—see SELSTON WITH UNDERWOOD AND WESTWOOD

UPTON

AP *LG* Lbty S'well & Scrooby (until 1836/37), Seq 17. *Parl* Seq 9. *Eccl* Seq 23.

UPTON—see HEADON CUM UPTON

WALESBY

AP *LG* Seq 3. *Parl* Seq 2. *Eccl* Seq 20.

WALKERINGHAM

AP *LG* Seq 1. *Parl* Seq 1. *Eccl* Seq 19.

WALLINGWELLS

Ex-par place, pt in Notts (Basset. Wap), pt in Yorks

W Riding (uninhabited, Doncaster Soke), sep CP 1858 with pt in each co,[49] eccl abol 1841 to help cr Woodsetts EP (Yorks W Riding, Notts) to be in dioc York,[178] 'Wallingwells' made 1895 ent Notts.[12] *LG* Worksop PLU (1862—1930), RSD, pt sep RD in Yorks W Riding (1894—95), Blyth & Cuckney RD (pt 1894—95, ent 1895—1925), Worksop RD (1925—74). Civ bdry: 1883,[41] 1885.[67] *Parl* Notts pt, Seq 1.

WARSOP
AP Incl tp Sookholme (sep CP 1866,[2] not sep eccl hence this par 'Warsop with Sookholme', qv). *LG* Basset. Wap, Mansf. PLU, Warsop USD, UD. Addtl civ bdry alt: 1935 (gains Sookholme CP).[3] *Parl* Seq 1.

WARSOP WITH SOOKHOLME
AP Usual eccl spelling; for civ and civ sep tp, see prev entry. *Eccl* Retf. RDn (until 1857), Retf. 3 RDn (1857—77), Retf. RDn (1877—84), Mansf. RDn (1884—*).

WELBECK
Ex-par place, sep CP 1858.[49] *LG* Basset. Wap, Worksop PLU (1862—1930), RSD, RD. *Parl* Seq 1.

WELLOW
AP *LG* Seq 3. *Parl* Seq 12. *Eccl* Seq 22.

WESTON
AP *LG* Seq 17. *Parl* Seq 9. *Eccl* Seq 8.

WESTWOOD—see SELSTON WITH UNDERWOOD AND WESTWOOD

WHALEY THORNS
EP Cr 1924 from Notts par of Norton Cuckney AP and from Derbys pars of Bolsover AP, Scarcliffe AP, Upper Langwith AP to be in Derby AD.[28] See main entry in Derbys.

WHATTON
AP Incl tp Aslockton (sep CP 1866,[2] eccl severed 1867 to help cr Scarrington with Aslockton EP[8]). *LG* Seq 5. *Parl* Seq 11. *Eccl* Seq 2.

NORTH WHEATLEY
AP *LG* Seq 2. *Parl* Seq 1. *Eccl* Pec jurisd Westminster Abbey (until Dissolution), Retf. RDn (Dissolution—1841), S'well RDn (1841—57), Retf. 1 RDn (1857—77), Retf. RDn (1877—*). Eccl bdry: 1883 (gains South Wheatley AP).[179]

SOUTH WHEATLEY
AP *LG* Seq 2. *Parl* Seq 1. *Eccl* S'well pec jurisd (until 1841), S'well RDn (1841—57), Retf. 1 RDn (1857—77), Retf. RDn (1877—83). Church ruined in 1883 and par to North Wheatley AP.[179]

WIDMERPOOL
AP *LG* Seq 11. *Parl* Seq 15. *Eccl* Bing. RDn (until 1857), Bing. 3 RDn (1857—77), Bing. RDn (1877—84), S Bing. RDn (1884—*).

WIGSLEY
Hmlt in Thorney AP, sep CP 1866.[2] *LG* Newk. Wap, PLU (soon after 1836[59]—1930), RSD, RD. *Parl* Seq 9.

WILFORD
AP *LG* Rushcl. Wap, Basf. PLU, pt Nott. MB (1877—89), pt Nott. CB (1889—94), pt Nott. USD (1877—94), Basf. RSD (ent 1875—77, pt 1877—94). Abol civ 1894 the pt in the CB (assoc with Notts) cr North

Wilford CP, the remainder united with the pt of Lenton AP not in the CB to cr South Wilford CP.[53] *Parl* S'rn Dv (1832—85), pt Nott. Parl Bor, pt Rushcl. Dv (1885—1918). *Eccl* Seq 3. Eccl bdry: 1914 (cr North Wilford EP).[66]

NORTH WILFORD
CP Cr 1894 from the pt of Wilford AP in Nott. CB.[53] *LG* Basf. PLU, Nott. CB. Abol 1899 ent to Nottingham CP.[22]

EP Cr 1914 from Wilford AP.[66] W Bing. RDn.

SOUTH WILFORD
CP Cr 1894 by union of the pts not in Nott. CB (assoc with Notts) of Wilford AP, Lenton AP.[53] *LG* Basf. PLU, RD. Abol 1935 ent to W Bridgford UD & AP.[3] *Parl* Rushcl. Dv (1918—48).

WILLOUGHBY ON THE WOLDS
AP *LG* Seq 12. Civ bdry: 1965 (loses pt to Burton on the Wolds CP, Leics).[60] *Parl* Seq 12. *Eccl* Seq 1.

WINKBURN
AP *LG* Seq 17. *Parl* Seq 9. *Eccl* Seq 10.

WINTHORPE
AP *LG* Seq 7. Civ bdry: 1884.[112] *Parl* Seq 9. *Eccl* Seq 6.

WISETON
Tp in Clayworth AP, sep CP 1866.[2] *LG* Seq 2. *Parl* Seq 1.

WIVERTON HALL
Ex-par place, sep CP 1858.[49] *LG* Bing. Wap, PLU (1858—1930), RSD, RD. *Parl* Seq 11.

WOLLATON
AP Incl chap Cossall (sep civ identity early, not sep eccl until 1953 so that this par eccl 'Wollaton with Cossall' until then, qv, the chap eccl severed 1953 to help cr Awsworth with Cossall EP,[17] the remainder to be 'Wollaton' EP). *LG* Brox. Wap, Basf. PLU, RSD, RD. Abol civ 1933 ent to Nott. CB (assoc with Notts) & CP.[5] *Parl* N'rn Dv (1832—85), Rushcl. Dv (1885—1948).

EP Cr 1953 when chap Cossall severed from Wollaton with Cossall AP, the remainder to be 'Wollaton'.[17] Beeston RDn. Bdry: 1956 (help cr Wollaton Park EP),[19] 1958,[30] 1962 (incl help cr Bilborough St John the Baptist EP).[10]

WOLLATON PARK
EP Cr 1956 from Lenton AP, Wollaton AP.[19] Nott. RDn.

WOLLATON WITH COSSALL
AP Usual eccl spelling; for civ and civ sep chap, see 'Wollaton'. *Eccl* Nott. RDn (until 1857), Nott. 1 RDn (1857—77), Nott. RDn (1877—87), Bulwell RDn (1887—1910), Beeston RDn (1910—53). Eccl bdry: 1933 (help cr Aspley EP).[95] Abol eccl 1953, chap Cossall eccl severed to help cr Awsworth with Cossall EP, the remainder to be 'Wollaton' EP.[17]

WOODBOROUGH
AP *LG* Lbty S'well & Scrooby (until 1836/37), Seq 14. *Parl* Seq 13. *Eccl* S'well pec jurisd (until 1841), S'well RDn (1841—87), Gedling RDn (1887—*).

WOODHOUSE HALL
Ex-par place, sep CP 1858.[49] *LG* Basset. Wap, Worksop PLU (1862—1930), RSD, Blyth & Cuckney RD (1894—1925), Worksop RD (1925—35). Abol 1935 ent to Holbeck CP.[3] *Parl* E Retf.

Parl Bor (1832—85), Basset. Dv (1885—1948).

WOODSETTS

EP Cr 1841 from ent ex-par Wallingwells (Notts, Yorks W Riding), tp Woodsetts in Anston cum Membris EP, area Gildingwells from Letwell with Gildingwells EP (both Yorks W Riding) to be dioc York.[178] See entry in Yorks.

WOODTHORPE

EP Cr 1963 from Porchester EP.[165] Gedling RDn.

WORKSOP

The following have 'Worksop' in their names. Insofar as any existed at a given time: *LG* Basset. Wap, Worksop PLU, USD, UD (1894—1931), MB (1931—74). *Parl* Seq 1. *Eccl* Retf. RDn (until 1857), Retf. 3 RDn (1857—77), Retf. RDn (1877—84), Worksop RDn (1884—*).

AP1—WORKSOP [ST MARY AND ST CUTHBERT]—Incl hmlts Clumber, Gateford, Kilton, Radford, pt hmlt Hardwick (none sep civ), hmlt Manton (not sep civ, eccl in area EP3). Eccl bdry: 1865 (help cr Shireoaks EP [Yorks W Riding, Notts]),[170] 1867 (cr EP2),[180] 1875 (help cr Scofton with Osberton EP),[19] 1912,[157] 1913 (help cr EP1).[181] Abol eccl 1960 to help cr Worksop Priory EP.[169]

EP1—WORKSOP ST ANNE—Cr 1913 from AP1, EP2.[181]

EP2—WORKSOP ST JOHN—Cr 1867 from AP1.[180] Bdry: 1912,[157] 1913 (help cr EP1).[181]

EP3—WORKSOP ST PAUL—Cr 1968 from Worksop Priory EP.[81]

WORKSOP PRIORY

EP Cr 1960 by union Worksop AP, pt Scofton with Osberton EP.[169] Worksop RDn. Bdry: 1968 (cr Worksop St Paul EP).[81]

WYSALL

AP *LG* Seq 12. *Parl* Seq 12. *Eccl* Seq 1. Gains eccl early (sep civ status maintained) Thorpe in the Glebe AP (church early destroyed).

RUTLAND

ABBREVIATIONS

Abbreviations particular to Rutl follow. Those general abbreviations in use throughout the *Guide* are found on pages xvii—xix.

Alst.	Alstow
Mart.	Martinsley
Oakh.	Oakham
Stamf.	Stamford
Upp.	Uppingham
Wrangd.	Wrangdyke

SEQUENCES

An abbreviated entry prefixed by 'Seq' is used in the parochial entries to avoid repeating often the names of superior units of administration. The content of each sequence is shown below.

Local Government Sequences ('LG')

SEQ 1 Alst. Hd, Oakh. PLU, RSD, RD
SEQ 2 East Hd, Oakh. PLU, RSD, RD
SEQ 3 East Hd, Stamf. PLU, RSD, Ketton RD
SEQ 4 Mart. Hd, Oakh. PLU, RSD, RD
SEQ 5 Mart. Hd, Upp. PLU, RSD, RD
SEQ 6 Oakh. Soke, Oakh. PLU, RSD, RD
SEQ 7 Oakh. Soke, Upp. PLU, RSD, RD
SEQ 8 Wrangd. Hd, Upp. PLU, RSD, RD

Parliamentary Sequences ('Parl')

SEQ 1 Rutl Parl Co (until 1918), Northants Parl Co (Rutl & Stamf Dv/CC, 1918—*)

Ecclesiastical Sequences ('Eccl')

SEQ 1 Alst. Hd RDn (until 1842), Rutl RDn (1842—67), Rutl I RDn (1867—1954), Oakh. RDn (1954—70), Rutl RDn (1970—*)
SEQ 2 East Hd RDn (until 1842), Rutl RDn (1842—67), Rutl II RDn (1867—1954), Ketton RDn (1954—63), Barnack RDn (1963—*)
SEQ 3 Rutl (or Mart. Hd) RDn (until 1842), Rutl RDn (1842—67), Rutl III RDn (1867—1954), Upp. RDn (1954—70), Rutl RDn (1970—*)
SEQ 4 Wrangd. Hd RDn (until 1842), Rutl RDn (1842—67), Rutl III RDn (1867—1954), Upp. RDn (1954—70), Rutl RDn (1970—*)
SEQ 5 Wrangd. Hd RDn (until 1842), Rutl RDn (1842—67), Rutl IV RDn (1867—73), Rutl III RDn (1873—1954), Upp. RDn (1954—70), Rutl RDn (1970—*)

DIOCESES AND ARCHDEACONRIES

Rutl pars were organised in Archdeaconries and Rural Deaneries as follows:

LINCOLN DIOC (until 1541)
Northampton AD: Alst. Hd RDn, East Hd RDn, Oakh. Soke RDn, Rutl (or Mart. Hd) RDn, Wrangd. Hd RDn

PETERBOROUGH DIOC (1541—*)
Northampton AD (1541—1875): Alst. Hd RDn (1541—1842), East Hd RDn (1541—1842), Rutl RDn (1842—67), Rutl I RDn (1867—75), Rutl II RDn (1867—75), Rutl III RDn (1867—75), Rutl IV RDn (1867—73), Rutl (or Mart. Hd) RDn (until 1842), Wrangd. Hd RDn (1541—1842)
Oakham AD (1875—):* Barnack RDn (1963—*), Ketton RDn (1954—63), Oakh. RDn (1954—70), Rutl RDn (1970—*), Rutl I RDn (1875—1954), Rutl II RDn (1875—1954), Rutl III RDn (1875—1954), Upp. RDn (1954—70)

THE PARISHES OF RUTLAND

Rutl pars were transf 1974 to Leicestershire Non-Metrop Co.

ASHWELL
AP *LG* Seq 1. *Parl* Seq 1. *Eccl* Seq 1.

AYSTON
AP *LG* Seq 5. *Parl* Seq 1. *Eccl* Seq 3.

BARLEYTHORPE
CP Renaming 1894 of Deanshold with Barleythorpe CP after latter loses pt to Oakham Lordship CP (the latter then renamed 'Oakham').[1] *LG* Oakh. PLU, RD. *Parl* Rutl & Stamf. Dv/CC (1918—*).

BARROW
Chap in Cottesmore AP, sep CP 1866.[2] *LG* Seq 1. *Parl* Seq 1.

BARROWDEN
AP *LG* Seq 8. *Parl* Seq 1. *Eccl* Wrangd. Hd RDn (until 1842), Rutl RDn (1842—67), Rutl IV RDn (1867—73), Rutl III RDn (1873—1954), Upp. RDn (1954—70), Barnack RDn (1970—72). Abol eccl 1972, united with Wakerley AP (Northants) to cr Barrowden and Wakerley EP.[3]

BARROWDEN AND WAKERLEY
EP Cr 1972 by union Barrowden AP (Rutl), Wakerley AP (Northants).[3] Barnack RDn.

BEAUMONT CHASE
Ex-par place, sep CP 1858.[4] *LG* Mart. Hd, Upp. PLU (1861—1930), RSD, RD. Bdry: 1885,[5] 1885.[6] *Parl* Seq 1.

BELTON
Chap in Wardley AP, sep civ identity early. *LG* Seq 7. *Parl* Seq 1.

BISBROOKE
AP *LG* Seq 8. *Parl* Seq 1. *Eccl* Seq 4.

BRAUNST0N
Chap in Hambleton AP (o'wise ent Mart. Hd), sep civ identity early, eccl severed 1884 to help cr Braunston with Brooke EP.[7] *LG* Seq 6. *Parl* Seq 1.

BRAUNSTON WITH BROOKE
EP Cr 1884 by union chap Braunston in Hambleton AP, chap Brooke in Oakham AP.[7] Rutl I RDn (1884—1954), Oakh. RDn (1954—70), Rutl RDn (1970—*).

BROOKE
Chap in Oakham AP, sep civ identity early, eccl severed 1884 to help cr Braunston with Brooke EP.[7] *LG* Seq 6. *Parl* Seq 1.

BURLEY
AP *LG* Seq 1. *Parl* Seq 1. *Eccl* Seq 1.

CALDECOTT
Chap (pec jurisd Lyddington, until 1851) in Lyddington AP (eccl, 'Lyddington'), sep civ identity early, eccl 'Caldecote' and as such severed 1931, united with Rockingham AP (Northants) to cr Rockingham with Caldecote EP.[8] *LG* Seq 8. *Parl* Seq 1.

GREAT CASTERTON
AP Gains before 1535 Pickworth AP (in ruins [latter gains sep civ identity early] hence this par eccl 'Great Casterton with Pickworth', qv). *LG* Seq 3. *Parl* Seq 1. *Eccl* East Hd RDn.

GREAT CASTERTON WITH PICKWORTH
AP Usual eccl spelling for union before 1535 of Great Casterton AP, Pickworth AP (in ruins, latter gains sep civ identity early, qv). *Eccl* Seq 2.

LITTLE CASTERTON
AP *LG* Seq 3. *Parl* Seq 1. *Eccl* Seq 2.

CLIPSHAM
AP *LG* Oakh. Soke, Stamf. PLU, RSD, Ketton RD. *Parl* Seq 1. *Eccl* Oakh. Soke RDn (until 1842), Rutl RDn (1842—67), Rutl II RDn (1867—73), Rutl I RDn (1873—1954), Oakh. RDn (1954—70), Rutl RDn (1970—*).

COTTESMORE
AP Incl chap Barrow (sep CP 1866[2]). *LG* Seq 1. *Parl* Seq 1. *Eccl* Seq 1.

EDITH WESTON
AP *LG* Seq 4. *Parl* Seq 1. *Eccl* Rutl (or Mart. Hd) RDn (until 1842), Rutl RDn (1842—67), Rutl IV RDn (1867—73), Rutl II RDn (1873—1954), Ketton RDn (1954—63), Oakh. RDn (1963—70), Rutl RDn (1970—72). Abol eccl 1972 to help cr Edith Weston with Normanton EP.[9]

EDITH WESTON WITH NORMANTON
EP Cr 1972 by union Edith Weston AP, Normanton AP.[9] Rutl RDn.

EGLETON
Chap in Oakham AP, sep civ identity early, eccl severed 1930 to help cr Hambleton with Egleton EP.[10] *LG* Seq 6. *Parl* Seq 1.

EMPINGHAM
AP *LG* Seq 2. *Parl* Seq 1. *Eccl* Pec jurisd Empingham (until 1851), Rutl RDn (1851—67), Rutl II RDn (1867—1954), Ketton RDn (1954—63), Oakh. RDn (1963—70), Rutl RDn (1970—*).

ESSENDINE
Chap in Ryhall AP, sep civ identity early. *LG* Seq 3. Bdry: 1887 (loses pt to Carlby AP, Lincs Pts Kestev).[11] *Parl* Seq 1.

EXTON
AP *LG* Seq 1. *Parl* Seq 1. *Eccl* Alst. Hd RDn (until 1842), Rutl RDn (1842—67), Rutl II RDn (1867—70). Gains 1870 Horn AP (in ruins by 15th cent) to cr Exton and Horn EP.[12]

EXTON AND HORN
EP Cr 1870 by union Exton AP, Horn AP (in ruins by 15th cent).[12] Rutl II RDn (1870—1954), Ketton RDn (1954—63), Oakh. RDn (1963—70), Rutl RDn (1970—*).

GLASTON
AP *LG* Seq 8. *Parl* Seq 1. *Eccl* Seq 4.

GREETHAM
AP *LG* Seq 1. *Parl* Seq 1. *Eccl* Seq 1.

GUNTHORPE
Tp in Oakham AP, sep CP 1866.[2] *LG* Seq 6. *Parl* Seq 1.

HAMBLETON
AP Tp 'Hambleton' in Mart. Hd; incl in Oakh. Soke chap Braunston (sep civ identity early, sep EP

1884[7]). *LG* Tp 'Hambleton': Seq 4. *Parl* Seq 1. *Eccl* Rutl. (or Mart. Hd) RDn (until 1842), Rutl RDn (1842—67), Rutl I RDn (1867—1930). Abol eccl 1930 to help cr Hambleton with Egleton EP.[10]

HAMBLETON AND EGLETON

EP Renaming 1972 of Hambleton with Egleton EP.[13] Rutl RDn.

HAMBLETON WITH EGLETON

EP Cr 1930 by union Hambleton AP, chap Egleton in Oakham AP.[10] Rutl I RDn (1930—54), Oakh. RDn (1954—70), Rutl RDn (1970—72). Bdry: 1960.[14] Renamed 1972 'Hambleton and Egleton'.[13]

HORN

AP *LG* Seq 1. *Parl* Seq 1. *Eccl* Alst. Hd RDn (until 1842), Rutl RDn (1842—67), Rutl. II RDn (1867—70). Church in ruins by 15th cent, abol eccl 1870 to help cr Exton and Horn EP.[12]

KETTON

AP Tp 'Ketton' in East Hd; incl in Wrangd. Hd chap Tixover (sep civ identity early). *LG* Stamf. PLU, RSD, Ketton RD. *Parl* Seq 1. *Eccl* Pec jurisd Ketton (until 1851), Rutl RDn (1851—67), Rutl II RDn (1867—1954), Ketton RDn (1954—63), Barnack RDn (1963—*).

LANGHAM

Chap in Oakham AP, sep par perhaps as early as 13th cent but not sustained, sep civ identity early, sep EP *ca* 1900—13.[15] *LG* Seq 6. *Parl* Seq 1. *Eccl* Rutl I RDn (cr—1954), Oakh. RDn (1954—70), Rutl RDn (1970—*).

LEIGHFIELD

Ex-par place, sep CP 1858.[4] *LG* Oakh. Soke, PLU (1861—1930), RSD, RD. *Parl* Seq 1.

LIDDINGTON

AP Usual civ spelling. Incl chap Caldecott (sep civ identity identity early, eccl 'Caldecote', eccl severed 1931 to help cr Rockingham with Caldecote EP[8] hence this par eccl 'Lyddington with Caldecote' until then, 'Lyddington' thereafter, qv). *LG* Seq 8. Addtl civ bdry alt: 1885.[6] *Parl* Seq 1.

NORTH LUFFENHAM

AP *LG* Seq 8. *Parl* Seq 1. *Eccl* Wrangd. Hd RDn (until 1842), Rutl RDn (1842—67), Rutl. IV RDn (1867—73), Rutl II RDn (1873—1954), Ketton RDn (1954—63), Oakh. RDn (1963—70), Rutl RDn (1970—*).

SOUTH LUFFENHAM

AP *LG* Seq 8. *Parl* Seq 1. *Eccl* Wrangd. Hd RDn (until 1842), Rutl RDn (1842—67), Rutl IV RDn (1867—73), Rutl II RDn (1873—1954), Ketton RDn (1954—56), Upp. RDn (1956—70), Rutl RDn (1970—*).

LYDDINGTON

EP Cr 1931 when chap Caldecote severed from Lyddington with Caldecote AP (Rutl) and united with Rockingham AP (Northants) to cr Rockingham with Caldecote EP, the remainder to be 'Lyddington'.[8] Rutl III RDn (1931—54), Upp. RDn (1954—70), Rutl RDn (1970—*).

LYDDINGTON WITH CALDECOTE

AP Usual eccl spelling; for civ and civ sep chap Caldecott (civ spelling), see 'Liddington'. *Eccl* Pec jurisd Lyddington (until 1851), Rutl RDn (1851—

67), Rutl III RDn (1867—1931). Abol eccl 1931, chap Caldecote eccl severed and united with Rockingham AP (Northants) to cr Rockingham with Caldecote EP, the remainder to be 'Lyddington'.[8]

LYNDON

AP *LG* Seq 4. *Parl* Seq 1. *Eccl* Rutl (or Mart. Hd) RDn (until 1842), Rutl RDn (1842—67), Rutl IV RDn (1867—73), Rutl III RDn (1873—1935), Rutl I RDn (1935—54), Oakh. RDn (1954—70), Rutl RDn (1970—*).

MANTON

AP *LG* Seq 4. *Parl* Seq 1. *Eccl* Rutl (or Mart. Hd) RDn (until 1842), Rutl RDn (1842—67), Rutl IV RDn (1867—73), Rutl I RDn (1873—86). Abol eccl 1886 to help cr Manton with Martinsthorpe EP.[16]

MANTON WITH MARTINSTHORPE

EP Cr 1886 by union Manton AP, Martinsthorpe AP.[16] Rutl I RDn (1886—1954), Oakh. RDn (1954—70), Rutl RDn (1970—*). Bdry: 1960.[14]

MARTINSTHORPE

AP *LG* Seq 4. *Parl* Seq 1. *Eccl* Rutl (or Mart. Hd) RDn (until 1842), Rutl RDn (1842—67), Rutl IV RDn (1867—73), Rutl I RDn (1873—86). Par church early destroyed and sinecure, eccl abol 1886 to help cr Manton with Martinsthorpe EP.[16]

MORCOTT

AP *LG* Seq 8. *Parl* Seq 1. *Eccl* Seq 5.

NORMANTON

AP *LG* Seq 4. *Parl* Seq 1. *Eccl* Rutl (or Mart. Hd) RDn (until 1842), Rutl RDn (1842—67), Rutl IV RDn (1867—73), Rutl II RDn (1873—1954), Ketton RDn (1954—63), Oakh. RDn (1963—70), Rutl RDn (1970—72). Abol eccl 1972 to help cr Edith Weston with Normanton EP.[9]

OAKHAM

AP Incl chap Barleythorpe (not sep civ or eccl, civ in manor/CP Oakham Deanshold with Barleythorpe until latter renamed 1894 'Barleythorpe' after bdry alt[1]), chap Brooke (sep civ identity early, eccl severed 1884 to help cr Braunston with Brooke EP[7]), chap Egleton (sep civ identity early, eccl severed 1930 to help cr Hambleton with Egleton EP[10]), chap Langham (sep par perhaps as early as 13th cent but not sustained, sep civ identity early, sep EP *ca* 1900—13[15]), tp Gunthorpe, manor Oakham Deanshold with Barleythorpe, manor Oakham Lordship (each of the 3 a sep CP 1866[2]) so that 'Oakham' has no sep civ identity 1866—94 (see following entry). *LG* Oakh. Soke, Bor. *Parl* Rutl Parl Co (1832—67). *Eccl* Oakh. Soke RDn (until 1842), Rutl RDn (1842—67), Rutl I RDn (1867—1954), Oakh. RDn (1954—70), Rutl RDn (1970—*).

CP Renaming 1894 of Oakham Lordship CP after gains pt Oakham Deanshold with Barleythorpe CP (the latter then renamed 'Barleythorpe').[1] *LG* Oakh. PLU, RD (1894—1911), UD (1911—74). *Parl* Rutl & Stamf. Dv/CC (1918—*).

OAKHAM DEANSHOLD WITH BARLEYTHORPE

Manor in Oakham AP, sep CP 1866.[2] *LG* Oakh. Soke, PLU, RSD. Renamed 1894 'Barleythorpe' after loses pt to Oakham Lordship CP (the latter then renamed 'Oakham').[1] *Parl* Rutl Parl Co

(1832—1918).

OAKHAM LORDSHIP

Manor in Oakham AP, sep CP 1866.[2] *LG* Oakh. Soke, PLU, RSD. Renamed 1894 'Oakham' after gains pt Oakham Deanshold with Barleythorpe CP (the latter than renamed 'Barleythorpe').[1] *Parl* Rutl Parl Co (1832—1918).

MARKET OVERTON

AP *LG* Seq 1. *Parl* Seq 1. *Eccl* Seq 1.

PICKWORTH

AP In ruins and incl in Great Casterton AP before 1535, sep civ identity early (for eccl see 'Great Casterton with Pickerton'). *LG* Seq 3. *Parl* Seq 1. *Eccl* East Hd RDn.

PILTON

AP *LG* Seq 8. *Parl* Seq 1. *Eccl* Seq 5.

PRESTON

AP *LG* Seq 5. *Parl* Seq 1. *Eccl* Seq 3.

RIDLINGTON

AP *LG* Seq 5. *Parl* Seq 1. *Eccl* Seq 3.

ROCKINGHAM WITH CALDECOTE

EP Cr 1931 by union Rockingham AP (Northants), chap Caldecote in Lyddington with Caldecote AP (civ, 'Liddington', 'Caldecott').[8] Weldon I RDn (1931—54), Weldon RDn (1954—70), Corby RDn (1970—*).

RYHALL

AP Incl chap Essendine (sep civ identity early, not sep eccl hence this par eccl 'Ryhall with Essendine', qv). *LG* Seq 3. *Parl* Seq 1.

RYHALL WITH ESSENDINE

AP Usual eccl spelling; for civ and civ sep chap, see prev entry. *Eccl* Seq 2.

SEATON

AP Incl hmlt Thorpe by Water (only pt of par in pec jurisd Lyddington [until 1851], the hmlt mostly Rutl, pt Leics [no houses or inhabitants], Gartree Hd, sep CP 1866 with pt in both cos,[2] not sep eccl hence this par eccl 'Seaton with Thorpe', qv). *LG* Seq 8. *Parl* Seq 1.

SEATON WITH THORPE

AP Usual eccl spelling; for civ and civ sep hmlt, see prev entry. *Eccl* Seq 4.

STOKE DRY

AP *LG* Pt Leics (Gartree Hd, until 1885), Rutl (Wrangd. Hd, pt until 1885, ent thereafter), Upp. PLU, RSD, RD. Civ bdry: 1885 (loses the pt in Leics to Stockerston AP, Leics, and the par ent Rutl thereafter).[6] *Parl* Rutl pt, Seq 1. *Eccl* Seq 4.

STRETTON

AP *LG* Seq 1. *Parl* Seq 1. *Eccl* Alst. Hd RDn (until

1842), Rutl RDn (1842—67), Rutl II RDn (1867—73), Rutl I RDn (1873—1954), Oakh. RDn (1954—70), Rutl RDn (1970—*).

TEIGH

AP *LG* Seq 1. *Parl* Seq 1. *Eccl* Seq 1.

THISTLETON

AP *LG* Seq 1. *Parl* Seq 1. *Eccl* Seq 1.

THORPE BY WATER

Hmlt (pec jurisd Lyddington, until 1851) in Seaton AP, sep CP 1866.[2] *LG* Pt Leics (Gartree Hd, no houses or inhabitants, until 1885), Rutl (Wrangd. Hd, pt until 1885, ent thereafter), Upp. PLU, RSD, RD. Bdry: 1885 (incl loses the pt in Northants to Gretton AP, Northants, and the par ent Rutl thereafter).[6] *Parl* Rutl pt, Seq 1.

TICKENCOTE

AP *LG* Seq 2. *Parl* Seq 1. *Eccl* Seq 2.

TINWELL

AP *LG* Seq 3. *Parl* Seq 1. *Eccl* Seq 2.

TIXOVER

Chap (pec jurisd Ketton, until 1851) in Ketton AP, sep civ identity early. *LG* Wrangd. Hd, Stamf. PLU, RSD, Ketton RD. *Parl* Seq 1.

UPPINGHAM

AP *LG* Pt Mart. Hd, pt Wrangd. Hd, Upp. PLU, RSD, RD. Civ bdry: 1885,[5] 1885.[6] *Parl* Seq 1. *Eccl* Seq 3.

WARDLEY

AP Incl chap Belton (sep civ identity early, not sep eccl hence this par eccl 'Wardley with Belton', qv). *LG* Seq 7. *Parl* Seq 1.

WARDLEY WITH BELTON

AP Usual eccl spelling; for civ and civ sep chap, see prev entry. *Eccl* Oakh. Soke RDn (until 1842), Rutl RDn (1842—67), Rutl III RDn (1867—1954), Upp. RDn (1954—70), Rutl RDn (1970—*).

WHISSENDINE

AP *LG* Seq 1. *Parl* Seq 1. *Eccl* Seq 1.

WHITWELL

AP *LG* Seq 1. *Parl* Seq 1. *Eccl* East Hd RDn (until 1842), Rutl RDn (1842—67), Rutl IV RDn (1867—73), Rutl II RDn (1873—82), Rutl II RDn (1882—1954), Ketton RDn (1954—63), Oakh. RDn (1963—70), Rutl RDn (1970—*).

WING

AP *LG* Seq 5. *Parl* Seq 1. *Eccl* Rutl (or Mart. Hd) RDn (until 1842), Rutl RDn (1842—67), Rutl IV RDn (1867—73), Rutl III RDn (1873—1954), Upp. RDn (1954—70), Rutl RDn (1970—*).

SHROPSHIRE

ABBREVIATIONS

Abbreviations particular to Salop follow. Those general abbreviations in use throughout the *Guide* are found on pages xvii—xix.

Alb.	Albrighton
Bewd.	Bewdley
Bps. Cast.	Bishop's Castle
Bradf.	Bradford
Bridgn.	Bridgnorth
Brim.	Brimstree
Burf.	Burford
Ch. Strett.	Church Stretton
Chirb.	Chirbury
Cleob. Mort.	Cleobury Mortimer
Cond.	Condover
Drayt.	Drayton
Edgm.	Edgmond
Ellesm.	Ellesmere
Franch.	Franchise
Knight.	Knighton
Ludl.	Ludlow
Mkt. Drayt.	Market Drayton
Munsl.	Munslow
Newpt.	Newport
Osw.	Oswestry
Pimh.	Pimhill
Pontesb.	Pontesbury
Pursl.	Purslow
Sev.	Severn
Shrewsb.	Shrewsbury
Shropsh.	Shropshire
Stott.	Stottesdon
Tenb.	Tenbury
Wellingt.	Wellington
Wenl.	Wenlock
Whitch.	Whitchurch
Wrockw.	Wrockwardine

SEQUENCES

An abbreviated entry prefixed by 'Seq' is used in the parochial entries to avoid repeating often the names of superior units of administration. The content of each sequence is shown below.

Local Government Sequences ('LG')

SEQ 1 N Bradf. Hd, Mkt. Drayt. PLU, RSD, Drayt. RD (1894—1966), Mkt. Drayt. RD (1966—74)

SEQ 2 N Bradf. Hd, Wem PLU, RSD, RD (1894—1967), N Shropsh. RD (1967—74)

SEQ 3 S Bradf. Hd, Atcham PLU, RSD, RD

SEQ 4 S Bradf. Hd, Newpt. PLU, RSD, RD (1894—1934), Wellingt. RD (1934—74)

SEQ 5 S Bradf. Hd, Wellingt. PLU, RSD, RD

SEQ 6 Brim. Hd, Brigdn. PLU, RSD, RD

SEQ 7 Brim. Hd, Shifnal PLU, RSD, RD

SEQ 8 Cond. Hd, Atcham PLU, RSD, RD

SEQ 9 Cond. Hd, Ch. Strett. PLU, RSD, RD (1894—1934), Atcham RD (1934—74)

SEQ 10 Ford Hd, Atcham PLU, RSD, RD

SEQ 11 Munsl. Hd, Ch. Strett. PLU, RSD, RD (1894—1934), Ludl. RD (1934—74)

SEQ 12 Munsl. Hd, Ludl. PLU, RSD, RD

SEQ 13 Osw. Hd, PLU, RSD, RD

SEQ 14 Overs Hd, Cleob. Mort. PLU, RSD, RD (1894—1934), Ludl. RD (1934—74)

SEQ 15 Overs Hd, Tenb. PLU, RSD, Burf. RD (1894—1934), Ludl. RD (1934—74)

SEQ 16 Pimh. Hd, Ellesm. PLU, RSD, RD (1894—

1967), N Shropsh. RD (1967—74)

SEQ 17   Pursl. Hd, Clun PLU, RSD, RD (1894—1967), Clun & Bps. Cast. RD (1967—74)

SEQ 18   Pursl. Hd, Knight. PLU, RSD, Teme RD (1894—1934), Clun RD (1934—67), Clun & Bps. Cast. RD (1967—74)

SEQ 19   Shrewsb. Lbty (until 1836), Alb. Dv (from 1836), Wem PLU, RSD, RD (1894—1967), N Shropsh. RD (1967—74)

SEQ 20   Stott. Hd, Bridgn. PLU, RSD, RD

SEQ 21   Stott. Hd, Cleob. Mort. PLU, RSD, RD (1894—1934), Bridgn. RD (1934—74)

SEQ 22   Stott. Hd, Cleob. Mort. PLU, RSD, RD (1894—1934), Ludl. RD (1934—74)

SEQ 23   Stott. Hd, Ludl. PLU, RSD, RD

SEQ 24   Wenl. Franch. (until 1836), Brim. Hd (from 1836), Shifnal PLU, RSD, RD

Parliamentary Sequences ('Parl')

SEQ 1   N'rn Dv (1832—1918), Osw. Dv/CC (1918—*)

SEQ 2   N'rn Dv (1832—1918), Shrewsb. Dv/CC (1918—*)

SEQ 3   N'rn Dv (1832—1918), The Wrekin Dv/CC (1918—*)

SEQ 4   N'rn Dv (1832—85), Mid Dv (1885—1918), Shrewsb. Dv/CC (1918—*)

SEQ 5   N'rn Dv (1832—85), Mid Dv (1885—1918), The Wrekin Dv/CC (1918—*)

SEQ 6   N'rn Dv (1832—85), W'rn Dv (1885—1918), Osw. Dv/CC (1918—*)

SEQ 7   S'rn Dv (1832—1918), Ludl. Dv/CC (1918—*)

SEQ 8   S'rn Dv (1832—85), N'rn Dv (1885—1918), The Wrekin Dv/CC (1918—*)

SEQ 9   S'rn Dv (1832—85), W'rn Dv (1885—1918), Ludl. Dv (118—48), Shrewsb. CC (1948—*)

SEQ 10   S'rn Dv (1832—85), W'rn Dv (1885—1918), Shrewsb. Dv/CC (1918—*)

Ecclesiastical Sequences ('Eccl')

Orig Heref Dioc:

SEQ 1   Bridgn. pec jurisd (until 1846), Newpt. RDn (1846), Bridgn. RDn (1846—*)

SEQ 2   Burf. RDn (until 1878), Burf. (West) RDn (1878—98), Burf. RDn (1898—1972), Ludl. RDn (1972—*)

SEQ 3   Burf. RDn (until 1878), Burf. (West) RDn (1878—98), Stott. RDn (1898—1955), Burf. RDn (1955—72), Ludl. RDn (1972—*)

SEQ 4   Clun & Wenl. RDn (until 1842), Clun RDn (1842—98), Bps. Cast. RDn (1898—1923), Stokesay RDn (1923—72), Clun Forest RDn (1972—*)

SEQ 5   Clun & Wenl. RDn (until 1842), Clun RDn (1842—1972), Clun Forest RDn (1972—*)

SEQ 6   Clun & Wenl. RDn (until 1842), Wenl. RDn (1842—78), Wenl. (1) RDn (1878—98), Ch. Strett. RDn (1898—1923), Cond. RDn (1923—*)

SEQ 7   Clun & Wenl. RDn (until 1842), Wenl. RDn (1842—78), Wenl. (1) RDn (1878—98), Ch. Strett. RDn (1898—1923), Ludl. RDn (1923—*)

SEQ 8   Clun & Wenl. RDn (until 1842), Wenl. RDn (1842—78), Wenl. (1) RDn (1878—98), Ch. Strett. RDn (1898—1923), Stokesay RDn (1923—72), Cond. RDn (1972—*)

SEQ 9   Clun & Wenl. RDn (until 1842), Wenl. RDn (1842—78), Wenl. (1) RDn (1878—98), Ch. Strett. RDn (1898—1923), Wenl. RDn (1923—72), Ludl. RDn (1972—*)

SEQ 10   Clun & Wenl. RDn (until 1842), Wenl. RDn (1842—78), Wenl. (2) RDn (1878—98), Wenl. RDn (1898—1972), Telford Sev. Gorge RDn (1972—*)

SEQ 11   Ludl. RDn

SEQ 12   Pontesb. RDn (until 1878), Pontesb. (1) RDn (1878—98), Pontesb. RDn (1898—*)

SEQ 13   Ponteb. RDn (until 1878), Pontesb. (1) RDn (1878—98), Montg RDn (1898—1923), Ponteb. RDn (1923—*)

SEQ 14   Stott. RDn (until 1898), Bridgn. RDn (1898—*)

SEQ 15   Stott. RDn (until 1955), Bridgn. RDn (1955—*)

SEQ 16   Stott. RDn (until 1955), Burf. RDn (1955—72), Ludl. RDn (1972—*)

Orig Lichf. dioc:

SEQ 17   Newpt. RDn (until 1859), Edgm. RDn (1859—*)

SEQ 18   Newpt. RDn (until 1837), Shifnal RDn (1837—*)

SEQ 19   Salop RDn (until 1837), Cond. RDn (1837—*)

SEQ 20   Salop RDn (until 1837), Ellesm. RDn (1837—*)

SEQ 21   Salop RDn (until 1837), Shrewsb. RDn (1837—*)

SEQ 22   Salop RDn (until 1837), Wellingt. RDn (1837—59), Wrockw. RDn (1859—*)

SEQ 23   Salop RDn (until 1837), Wem RDn (1837—1962), Wem & Whitch. RDn (1962—*)

Orig St Asaph dioc:

SEQ 24   Marchia RDn (until 1844), Osw. RDn (1844—*)

DIOCESES AND ARCHDEACONRIES

Salop pars were organised in Archdeaconries and Rural Deaneries as follows:

HEREFORD DIOC

Ludl. AD (1876—):* Bewd. RDn (1898—1919), Bps. Cast. RDn (1898—1923), Bridgn. RDn, Burf. RDn (1876—78), Burf. RDn (1898—1972), Burf. (East) RDn (1878—98), Burf. (West) RDn (1878—98), Ch. Strett. RDn (1898—1923), Clun RDn (1876—1972), Clun Forest RDn (1972—*), Cond. RDn (1905—*), Ludl. RDn, Montg RDn (1898—1923), Pontesb. RDn (1876—78), Pontesb. RDn (1898—*), Pontesb. (1) RDn (1878—98), Pontesb. (2) RDn (1878—98), Stokesay RDn (1923—72), Stott. RDn (1876—1955), Telford Sev. Gorge RDn (1972—*), Wenl. RDn (1876—78), Wenl. RDn (1898—1972), Wenl. (1) RDn (1878—98), Wenl. (2) RDn (1878—98)

Salop AD (until 1876): Bridgn. RDn (1846—76), Burf. RDn, Clun RDn (1842—76), Clun & Wenl. RDn (until 1842), Ludl. RDn, Pontesb. RDn, Stott. RDn, Wenl. RDn (1842—76)

LICHFIELD DIOC (from 1837)

Salop AD: Cond. RDn (1837—1905), Edgm. RDn (1859—*), Ellesm. RDn (1837—*), Hodnet RDn (1859—*), Mkt. Drayt. RDn (1837—59), Newpt. RDn (until 1859), Osw. RDn (1920—*), Salop RDn (until 1837), Shifnal RDn (1837—*), Shrewsb. RDn (1837—*), Wellingt. RDn (1837—59), Wem RDn (1837—1962), Wem & Whitch. RDn (1962—*), Whitch. RDn (1863—1962), Wrockw. RDn (1859—*)

Stafford AD: Brewood RDn (1851—94), Eccleshall (1851—1923), Lapley & Trysull (until 1851), Newcastle & Stone RDn (until 1851), Trysull (1851—1905)

LICHFIELD AND COVENTRY (styled LICHFIELD 1053—1075, CHESTER 1075—1102, COVENTRY 1102—1128, COVENTRY AND LICHFIELD 1228—Reformation, LICHFIELD AND COVENTRY Reformation—1837)

Salop AD: Newpt. RDn, Salop RDn

ST ASAPH DIOC

Montg AD (1844—1920): Llangollen RDn (1844—90), Montg RDn (1844—81), Osw. RDn

St Asaph AD (until 1844): Marchia RDn

Wrexham AD (1890—1924): Llangollen RDn

THE PARISHES OF SHROPSHIRE

ABDON
AP *LG* Seq 12. Civ bdry: 1884,[1] 1967.[2] *Parl* Seq 7. *Eccl* Seq 7.

ACTON BURNELL
AP Incl tp Ruckley and Langley ([incl area chap Langley] sep CP 1866[3]). *LG* Acton Burnell Bor (status not sustained), Seq 8. *Parl* Seq 10. *Eccl* Seq 19.

ACTON ROUND
Chap in Much Wenlock AP, sep CP 1866,[3] sep EP 1731.[4] *LG* Seq 20. *Parl* Seq 7. *Eccl* Clun & Wenl. RDn (1731—1842), Wenl. RDn (1842—78), Wenl. (2) RDn (1878—98), Wenl. RDn (1898—1972), Bridgn. RDn (1972—*).

ACTON SCOTT
AP *LG* Seq 11. *Parl* Seq 7. *Eccl* Seq 8.

ADDERLEY
AP *LG* Seq 1. Civ bdry: 1883,[5] 1934 (gains Tittenley CP).[6] *Parl* Seq 1. *Eccl* Newpt. RDn (until 1837), Mkt. Drayt. RDn (1837—59), Hodnet RDn (1859—63), Whitch. RDn (1863—84), Hodnet RDn (1884—*).

ALBERBURY
AP Main tp in Salop (Ford Hd), a sep CP 1866 as 'Alberbury Lower Quarter'[3]; incl also in Salop (Ford Hd) chap Wollaston (sep CP 1866 in Salop,[3] sep EP 1733 as 'Great Wollaston',[4] as such eccl refounded 1864 [incl area in Montg][7]); incl in Montg chap Criggion (Caus Hd, sep CP 1866 in Montg,[3] sep EP 1769,[4] eccl refounded 1864[7]), tp

Bauseley (Deythur Hd, sep CP 1866 in Montg[3]), tps Middletown, Uppington (each Caus Hd, each a sep CP 1866 in Montg[3]) so that 'Alberbury' has no sep civ identity after 1866. *Parl* Salop pt, S'rn Dv (1832—67). *Eccl* Seq 12.

ALBERBURY LOWER QUARTER
Main tp (Salop, Ford Hd) in Alberbury AP (Salop, Montg), sep CP 1866 in Salop.[3] *LG* Atcham PLU, RSD. Abol 1886 to help cr Alberbury with Cardeston CP.[8] *Parl* S'rn Dv (1832—85), W'rn Dv (1885—1918).

ALBERBURY WITH CARDESTON
CP Cr 1886 by union Alberbury Lower Quarter CP, Cardeston AP (both Salop), pt Bauseley CP (Montg).[8] *LG* Ford Hd, Atcham PLU, RSD, RD. Bdry: 1967.[2] *Parl* Shrewsb. Dv/CC (1918—*).

ALBRIGHTON
AP *LG* Alb. Bor (status not sustained), Seq 7. Civ bdry: 1934.[6] *Parl* Seq 8. *Eccl* Seq 18. Eccl bdry: 1973.[9]

ALBRIGHTON
Chap in Shrewsbury St Mary AP, sep CP 1866,[3] sep EP 1738,[4] eccl refounded 1860.[10] *LG* Pimh. Hd (until 1836), Alb. Dv (from 1836), Atcham PLU, RSD, RD. Civ bdry: 1934.[6] Abol civ 1967 pt to Astley CP, pt to Shrewsb. MB & CP, pt to Pimhill CP.[2] *Parl* N'rn Dv (1832—1918), Shrewsb. Dv/CC (1918—70). *Eccl* Salop RDn (1738—1837), Wem RDn (1837—1930), Shrewsb. RDn (1930—*).

ALVELEY
AP Incl Lbty Romsley (Bridgn. Lbty & Bor, until 1836,

Stott. Hd from 1836, sep CP 1866[3]). *LG* Stott. Hd (pt until 1836, ent from 1836), pt Bridgn. Lbty ([Romsley] until 1836), Bridgn. PLU, RSD, RD. *Parl* Pt Bridgn. Parl Bor ([Romsley] 1832—67), remainder and later, Seq 7. *Eccl* Seq 1. Eccl bdry: 1870 (help cr Tuck Hill EP [Salop, Staffs]).[11]

ANNSCROFT
EP Cr 1872 from Condover AP, Shrewsbury St Chad AP, Meole Brace AP.[12] Cond. RDn (1872—1972), Pontesb. RDn (1972—*).

ASH
EP Cr 1844 from Whitchurch AP.[13] Mkt. Drayt. RDn (1844—59), Hodnet RDn (1859—63), Whitch. RDn (1863—1962), Wem & Whitch. RDn (1962—*).

ASHFORD BOWDLER
Chap in Bromfield AP, sep civ identity early, sep EP 1735.[4] *LG* Seq 12. *Parl* Seq 7. *Eccl* Ludl. RDn. Eccl bdry: 1928.[14]

ASHFORD CARBONELL
Chap (Salop, pt Munsl. Hd, pt Stott. Hd, pec jurisd Chancellor of Heref [until 1846]) in Little Hereford AP (o'wise ent Heref, Wolphy Hd), sep civ identity early in Salop (later civ, 'Ashford Carbonel'), sep EP 1748,[4] eccl refounded 1880.[15] *LG* Ludl. PLU, RSD, RD. *Parl* Seq 7. *Eccl* Ludl. RDn. Eccl bdry: 1928.[14]

ASTLEY
Chap in Shrewsbury St Mary AP, sep CP 1866,[3] sep EP 1860.[16] *LG* Shrewsb. Lbty (until 1836), Alb. Dv (from 1836), Atcham PLU, RSD, RD. Civ bdry: 1967.[2] *Parl* Seq 2. *Eccl* Wem RDn (1860—1966), Wem & Whitch. RDn (1966—*).

ASTLEY ABBOTS
Chap in Morville AP, sep civ identity early (later civ 'Astley Abbotts'), prob a sep EP 1561 (date 1st registers).[17] *LG* Seq 20. *Parl* Bridgn. Parl Bor (1832—85), S'rn Dv (1885—1918), Ludl. Dv/CC (1885—*). *Eccl* Stott. RDn (cr—1898), Bridgn. RDn (1898—*).

ASTON BOTTERELL
AP *LG* Seq 21. Civ bdry: 1967.[18] *Parl* Seq 7. *Eccl* Seq 15.

ASTON EYRE
Chap & tp in Morville AP, sep CP 1866,[3] sep EP 1748,[4] sep eccl status not sustained and thereafter incl in Morville AP. *LG* Seq 20. *Parl* Seq 7. *Eccl* Stott. RDn.

ATCHAM
AP *LG* Seq 3. Civ bdry: 1885,[18] 1885,[20] 1934,[6] 1967.[2] *Parl* Seq 2. *Eccl* Seq 21.

BADGER
AP *LG* Seq 24. *Parl* Much Wenl. Parl Bor (1468—1832), Wenl. Parl Bor (1832—85), N'rn Dv (1885—1918), The Wrekin Dv/CC (1918—*). *Eccl* Clun & Wenl. RDn (until 1842), Wenl. RDn (1842—78), Wenl. (2) RDn (1878—98), Bridgn. RDn (1898—1905), Shifnal RDn (1905—*).

BARROW
AP *LG* Wenl. Franch & Much Wenl. Bor, Madeley PLU, Wenl. MB (1835—1966), USD, Bridgn. RD (1966—74). Civ bdry: 1934.[6] Reconstituted 1966 (enlarged area) as Wenl. MB abol (qv for details), the altered area to be in Bridgn. RD.[18] *Parl* Much

Wenl. Parl Bor (1468—1832), Wenl. Parl Bor (1832—85), S'rn Dv (1885—1918), Wenl. Dv (1918—48), Ludl. CC (1948—*). *Eccl* Seq 10.

BASCHURCH
AP Incl chap Petton (sep civ identity early, prob a sep EP 1695 [date 1st registers][21]), chap and tp Little Ness (sep CP 1866,[3] sep EP 1911[22]). *LG* Baschurch Bor (status not sustained), Seq 16. Addtl civ bdry alt: 1934 (help cr Pimhill CP).[6] *Parl* Seq 6. *Eccl* Seq 20. Eccl bdry: 1857 (cr Weston Lullingfield EP).[23]

BATTLEFIELD
AP Orig Collegiate, parochial from Dissolution. *LG* Shrewsb. Lbty (until 1836), Alb. Dv (from 1836), Atcham PLU, RSD, RD. Abol civ 1934 pt to Albrighton CP, pt to Shrewsb. MB & CP.[6] *Parl* N'rn Dv (1832—1918), Shrewsb. Dv (1918—48). *Eccl* Seq 21. Eccl bdry: 1875.[24]

BAYSTON HILL
EP Cr 1843 from Shrewsbury St Julian AP, Condover AP,[4] refounded 1844.[25] Shrewsb. RDn.
CP Cr 1967 by union pt Shrewsb. MB & CP, pt Condover AP.[2] *LG* Atcham RD. *Parl* Shrewsb. CC (1970—*).

BECKBURY
AP *LG* Seq 24. *Parl* Much Wenl. Parl Bor (1468—1832), Wenl. Parl Bor (1832—85), N'rn Dv (1885—1918), The Wrekin Dv/CC (1918—*). *Eccl* Clun & Wenl. RDn (until 1842), Wenl. RDn (1842—78), Wenl. (2) RDn (1878—98), Bridgn. RDn (1898—1905), Shifnal RDn (1905—*).

BEDSTONE
AP *LG* Seq 18. Civ bdry: 1884.[26] *Parl* Seq 7. *Eccl* Seq 5.

BENTHALL
Chap in Much Wenlock AP, sep civ identity early, sep EP 1735.[4] *LG* Wenl. Franch. (until 1836), Much Wenl. Bor, Madeley PLU, Wenl. MB (1835—1966), USD. Abol civ 1966 as area Wenl. MB abol (qv for details).[18] *Parl* Much Wenl. Parl Bor (1468—1832), Wenl. Parl Bor (1832—85), Mid Dv (1885—1918), The Wrekin Dv (1918—48), Ludl. CC (1948—70). *Eccl* Clun & Wenl. RDn (1735—1842), Wenl. RDn (1842—78), Wenl. (2) RDn (1878—98), Wenl. RDn (1898—1972), Telford Sev. Gorge RDn (1972—*).

BERRINGTON
AP *LG* Seq 8. Civ bdry: 1885,[20] 1967.[2] *Parl* Seq 10. *Eccl* Salop RDn (until 1837), Cond. RDn (1837—1930). Abol eccl 1930 to help cr Berrington with Betton Strange EP.[27]

BERRINGTON WITH BETTON STRANGE
EP Cr 1930 by union Berrington AP, Betton Strange EP.[27] Cond. RDn.

LITTLE BERWICK
EP Cr 1852 from Shrewsbury St Mary AP.[28] Shrewsb. RDn. Bdry: 1963 (incl help cr Harlescott EP).[29]

BETTON STRANGE
EP Cr 1860 from Shrewsbury St Chad AP.[30] Shrewsb. RDn (1860—1929), Cond. RDn (1929—30). Abol 1930 to help cr Berrington with Betton Strange EP.[27]

BETTWS Y CRWYN

Chap in Clun AP, sep civ identity early, sep EP 1764.[4] *LG* Seq 18. Civ bdry: 1967.[2] *Parl* Seq 7. *Eccl* Clun & Wenl. RDn (1764—1842), Clun RDn (1842—1972), Clun Forest RDn (1972—*).

BICTON

Chap in Shrewsbury St Chad AP, sep EP 1810,[4] eccl refounded 1853 from Shrewsbury St Chad AP, Shrewsbury St Alkmund AP,[31] sep CP 1885 from Shrewsbury St Alkmund AP, Shrewsbury St Julian AP, Shrewsbury St Chad AP.[20] *LG* Ford Hd, Atcham PLU, RSD, RD. Civ bdry: 1901 (gains Unnamed CP [formerly pt of Meole Brace AP]),[32] 1934,[6] 1967.[2] *Parl* Shrewsb. Dv/CC (1918—*). *Eccl* Salop RDn (1810—37), Shrewsb. RDn (1837—*).

BILLINGSLEY

AP Orig chap in Morville AP, sep par by 1535. *LG* Seq 20. *Parl* Seq 7. *Eccl* Seq 15.

BISHOP'S CASTLE

The following have 'Bishop's Castle' in their names. Insofar as any existed at a given time: *LG* Pursl. Hd, Clun PLU; Bor/MB, USD, RSD, RD sep noted. *Parl* Before 1832 sep noted; S'rn Dv (1832—1918), Ludl. Dv/CC (1918—*). *Eccl* Seq 4.

AP1—BISHOP'S CASTLE—Incl 2 areas of Bishop's Castle Borough, Bishop's Castle Out (the areas respectively within and without Bps. Cast. Bor, each a sep CP 1866[3] as CP3, CP4, respectively, so that AP1 has no sep civ identity 1866—84 [see following entry]). *Parl* Pt Bps. Cast. Parl Bor (1573—1832).

CP1—BISHOP'S CASTLE—Cr 1884 by union CP2, CP3.[33] *LG* Pt Bps. Cast. MB & USD (1885—94), Clun RSD (ent 1884—85, pt 1885—94). Abol 1894 the pt in the MB cr CP6, the remainder cr CP5.[34]

CP2—BISHOP'S CASTLE—Renaming 1967 of CP6 as Bps. Cast. MB abol and its constituent par made pt of Clun & Bps. Cast. RD.[2] *LG* Clun & Bps. Cast. RD.

CP3—BISHOP'S CASTLE BOROUGH—The area of AP1 in Bps. Cast. Bor, sep CP 1866.[3] *LG* Bps. Cast. Bor. Abol 1884 to help cr CP1.[33]

CP4—BISHOP'S CASTLE OUT—The area of AP1 not in Bps. Cast. Bor, sep CP 1866.[3] Abol 1884 to help cr CP1.[33]

CP5—BISHOP'S CASTLE RURAL—Cr 1894 from the pt of CP1 not in Bps. Cast. MB.[34] *LG* Clun RD. Abol 1934 pt to cr Colebatch CP, the remainder to Lydham AP.[6]

CP6—BISHOP'S CASTLE URBAN—Cr 1894 from the pt of CP1 in Bps. Cast. MB.[34] *LG* Bps. Cast. MB. Renamed 1967 as CP2 as the MB abol and its constituent par transf to Clun & Bps. Cast. RD.[2]

BITTERLEY

AP Gains before 1535 Upper Ledwich AP. Incl chap Middleton (not sep) so that this par eccl 'Bitterley with Middleton', qv. *LG* Pt Overs Hd, pt Munsl. Hd, Ludl. PLU, RSD, RD. Civ bdry: 1884.[35] *Parl* Seq 7.

BITTERLEY WITH MIDDLETON

AP Usual eccl spelling; for civ see prev entry. *Eccl* Seq

11. Eccl bdry: 1844 (help cr Knowbury EP),[36] 1879 (help cr Cleeton EP).[37]

BOBBINGTON

Chap (pec jurisd Bridgn.) in Claverley AP (o'wise ent Staffs, S Seisdon Hd), 'Bobbington' pt Staffs (S Seisdon Hd), pt Salop (Brim. Hd), sep civ identity early with pt in ea co, made 1895 ent Staffs,[38] sep EP 1726.[4] *LG* Seisdon PLU, RSD, pt sep RD in Salop (1894—95). *Parl* Salop pt, S'rn Dv (1832—1918). *Eccl* See main entry in Staffs for organisation in RDns; incl eccl bdry alt: 1870 (help cr Tuck Hill EP [Salop, Staffs]).[11]

BOLAS MAGNA

AP *LG* Seq 5. *Parl* Seq 3. *Eccl* Seq 17.

BONINGALE

Chap in Stockton AP, sep civ identity early, sep EP 1857.[39] *LG* Seq 7. Civ bdry: 1934.[6] *Parl* Seq 8. *Eccl* Shifnal RDn.

BORASTON

Chap in Burford, sep CP 1866,[3] eccl in Burford 1st Portion, Nash with Boraston AP. *LG* Seq 15. Bdry: 1884.[40] *Parl* Seq 7.

BOSCOBEL

Ex-par place, sep CP 1858.[41] *LG* Brim. Hd, Shifnal PLU (1858—1930), RSD, RD. *Parl* Seq 8.

BOURTON

EP Chap in Much Wenlock AP, sep EP 1770.[4] Clun & Wenl. RDn (1770—1842), Wenl. RDn (1842—78), Wenl. (2) RDn (1878—98), Wenl. RDn (1898—1926). Abol 1926 to help cr Much Wenlock with Bourton EP.[42]

BRIDGNORTH

CP Cr 1967 by union pars in Bridgn. MB (Oldbury Ap, Quatford AP, Bridgnorth St Leonard AP, Bridgnorth St Mary Magdalen AP) as area of MB abol and this new par made pt of Bridgn. RD.[2] *LG* Bridgn. RD. *Parl* Ludl. CC (1970—*).

BRIDGNORTH ST LEONARD

AP *LG* Bridgn. Lbty & Bor (until 1836), Bridgn. MB (1835—1967), PLU, USD. Civ bdry: 1883.[43] Abol civ 1967 to help cr Bridgnorth CP to be in Bridgn. RD.[2] *Parl* Bridgn. Parl Bor (1295—1885), S'rn Dv (1832—1918), Ludl. Dv/CC (1918—70). *Eccl* Seq 1.

BRIDGNORTH ST MARY MAGDALEN

AP Organisation as for Bridgnorth St Leonard AP, with addtl civ bdry alt 1934.[6]

BROMFIELD

AP Tp 'Bromfield' in Munsl. Hd as were chap Ashford Bowdler (sep civ identity early, sep EP 1735[4]), chap Halford (sep CP 1866,[3] sep EP 1844[4]); incl also chap Ludford (pt Salop [Munsl. Hd], pt Heref [Wolphy Hd], sep civ identity early with pt in ea co, sep EP 1771[4]). *LG* Tp 'Bromfield': Seq 12. Addtl civ bdry alt: 1884,[1] 1934.[6] *Parl* Pt Ludl. Parl Bor (1832—85), remainder and later, Seq 7. *Eccl* Seq 11.

BROMPTON AND RHISTON

Tp (Salop, Chirb. Hd) in Churchstoke AP (o'wise Montg, Caus Hd), sep CP 1866 in Salop.[3] *LG* Montg PLU, RSD, Chirb. RD (1894—1934), Clun RD (1934—67), Clun & Bps. Cast. RD (1967—74). *Parl* S'rn Dv (1832—67), W'rn Dv (1885—1918),

Ludl. Dv/CC (1918—*).

BROSELEY

AP Sometimes early 'Burwardsley'. Incl chap Linley (sep civ identity early, prob a sep EP 1700 [date 1st registers[44]]). *LG* Wenl. Franch. (until 1836), Much Wenl. Bor, Madeley PLU, Wenl. MB (1835—1966), Broseley USD (1875—89), Wenl. USD (1889—94), Bridgn. RD (1966—74). *Parl* Much Wenl. Parl Bor (1468—1832), Wenl. Parl Bor (1832—85), Mid Dv (1885—1918), The Wrekin Dv (1918—48), Ludl. CC (1948—*). *Eccl* Seq 10. Addtl eccl bdry alt: 1790 (cr Jackfield EP,[4] refounded 1862[45]).

BROUGHTON

Chap in Shrewsbury St Mary AP, sep civ identity early, sep EP 1718.[4] *LG* Seq 19. *Parl* Seq 1. *Eccl* Salop RDn (1718—1837), Wem RDn (1837—1962), Wem & Whitch. RDn (1962—*).

BUCKNELL

AP Tp 'Bucknell' mostly Salop (Pursl. Hd), pt Heref (Wigmore Hd); incl in Heref tp Buckton and Coxall (Wigmore Hd, sep CP 1866 in Heref,[3] the tp not sep eccl hence this par eccl 'Bucknell and Buckton', qv in following entry). *LG* Knight. PLU, RSD, Teme RD (1894—1934), Clun RD (1934—67), Clun & Bps. Cast. RD (1967—74). Addtl civ bdry alt: 1884,[26] 1894 (loses the pt in Heref to Brampton Brayan AP, Heref, and this par ent Salop thereafter).[46] *Parl* Salop pt, Seq 7.

BUCKNELL AND BUCKTON

AP Usual eccl spelling; for civ and for civ sep tp in Heref, see prev entry. *Eccl* Seq 5.

BUILDWAS

AP *LG* S Bradf. Hd, Madeley PLU (1836—95), RSD, RD (1894—95), Atcham PLU (1895—1930), RD (1895—1974). *Parl* Seq 4. *Eccl* Pec jurisd Buildwas Abbey (until Dissolution), Newpt. RDn (Dissolution—1837), Wellingt. RDn (1837—59), Wrockw. RDn (1859—*).

BURFORD

AP Usual civ spelling; for eccl see following 3 entries. Incl chaps Boraston, Nash, Whitton (each a sep CP 1866[3]). *LG* Burford Bor (status not sustained), Seq 15. Addtl civ bdry alt: 1884,[40] 1965 (gains pt Tenbury AP, Worcs).[47] *Parl* Seq 7.

BURFORD 1ST PORTION, NASH WITH BORASTON
WHITTON, BURFORD 2ND PORTION
BURFORD 3RD PORTION

3 sep eccl benefices and pars (so sep before 1851[48]) forming pt of single AP of 'Burford' for civ purposes, qv. *Eccl* Each of the 3, Seq 2. Eccl bdry: 1929 (affecting only Burford 3rd Portion).[49]

BURWARTON

AP *LG* Seq 20. *Parl* Seq 7. *Eccl* Stott. RDn (until 1955), Bridgn. RDn (1955—72). Abol eccl 1972 to help cr Burwarton with Cleobury North EP.[50]

BURWARTON WITH CLEOBURY NORTH

EP Cr 1972 by union Burwarton AP, Cleobury North AP.[50] Bridgn. RDn.

CAKEMORE—see HALESOWEN

CALVERHALL

EP Chap in Prees AP, sep EP 1726,[4] refounded 1858.[51] Salop RDn (1726—1837), Mkt. Drayt. RDn

(1837—59), Hodnet RDn (1859—63), Whitch. RDn (1863—1928). Bdry: 1891.[52] Abol eccl 1928 to help cr Ightfield with Calverhall EP.[53]

CARDESTON

AP *LG* Ford Hd, Atcham PLU, RSD. Abol civ 1886 to help cr Alberbury with Cardeston CP.[8] *Parl* S'rn Dv (1832—85), W'rn Dv (1885—1918). *Eccl* Seq 12.

CARDINGTON

AP *LG* Munsl. Hd, Ch. Strett. PLU, RSD, RD (1894—1934), Atcham RD (1934—74). Civ bdry: 1934,[6] 1967.[2] *Parl* S'rn Dv (1832—1918), Ludl. Dv (1918—48), Shrewsb. CC (1948—*). *Eccl* Seq 12.

CAYNHAM

AP *LG* Seq 23. *Parl* Seq 7. *Eccl* Seq 11. Eccl bdry: 1844 (help cr Knowbury EP).[36]

CHELMARSH

AP *LG* Seq 20. *Parl* Seq 7. *Eccl* Seq 14. Eccl bdry: 1956.[54]

CHERRINGTON

Tp in Edgmond AP, sep CP 1866,[3] eccl severed 1863 to help cr Tibberton EP.[55] *LG* Seq 4. *Parl* Seq 3.

CHESWARDINE

AP In Staffs *temp* Domesday Book, later considered in Salop. *LG* Seq 1. Civ bdry: 1883.[56] *Parl* Seq 1. *Eccl* Ecclesh. RDn (Staffs AD, until 1861), Hodnet RDn (1861—*). Eccl bdry: 1857 (help cr Sambrook EP).[57]

CHETTON

AP Incl chap Loughton (sep CP 1866,[3] the chap and a further pt of Chetton eccl transf 1895 to Wheathill AP,[58] the latter thereafter 'Wheathill with Loughton'). *LG* Seq 20. *Parl* Seq 7. *Eccl* Seq 14.

CHETWYND

AP *LG* S Bradf. Hd, Newpt. PLU, pt Newpt USD (1893—94), Newpt. RSD (ent 1875—93, pt 1893—94). Civ bdry: 1880,[59] 1880,[60] 1883.[56] Abol civ 1894 the pt in the UD cr Chetwynd Urban CP, the remainder cr Chetwynd Rural CP.[61] *Parl* N'rn Dv (1832—1918). *Eccl* Seq 17. Eccl bdry: 1857 (help cr Sambrook EP).[57]

CP Name used by 1930s (after abol of Chetwynd Urban CP 1896 left this the only 'Chetwynd' par) for CP cr 1894 as 'Chetwynd Rural', qv for civ organisation until 1934, parl organisation until 1948. *LG* Wellingt. RD (1934—74). Bdry: 1965 (loses pt to Fortron AP, Staffs).[47] *Parl* The Wrekin CC (1948—*).

CHETWYND ASTON

Tp in Edgmond AP, sep CP 1866.[3] *LG* S Bradf. Hd, Newpt. PLU, pt Newpt. USD (1893—94), Newpt. RSD (ent 1875—93, pt 1893—94). Abol 1894 the pt in the UD cr Chetwynd Aston Urban AP, the remainder cr Chetwynd Aston Rural CP.[61] *Parl* N'rn Dv (1832—1918).

CP Name used by 1930s (after abol of Chetwynd Aston Urban CP 1896 left this the only 'Chetwynd Aston' par) for CP cr 1894 as 'Chetwynd Aston Rural', qv for civ organisation until 1934, parl organisation until 1948. *LG* Wellingt. RD (1934—74). Bdry: 1934.[6] *Parl* The Wrekin CC (1948—*).

CHETWYND ASTON RURAL

CP Cr 1894 from the pt of Chetwynd Aston CP not in

Newp. UD.[61] *LG* Newp. PLU, RD. By 1930s called 'Chetwynd Aston' (after abol of Chetwynd Aston Urban CP 1896 left this the only 'Chetwynd Aston' par), qv for civ organisation after 1934, parl organisation after 1948. *Parl* The Wrekin Dv (1918—48).

CHETWYND ASTON URBAN
CP Cr 1894 from the pt of Chetwynd Aston CP in Newpt. UD.[61] *LG* Newpt. PLU, UD. Abol 1896 ent to Newport AP.[62]

CHETWYND RURAL
CP Cr 1894 from the pt of Chetwynd AP not in Newpt. UD.[61] *LG* Newpt. PLU, RD. By 1930s called 'Chetwynd' (after abol of Chetwynd Urban 1896 left this the only 'Chetwynd' par), qv for civ organisation after 1934, parl organisation after 1948. *Parl* The Wrekin Dv (1918—48).

CHETWYND URBAN
CP Cr 1894 from the pt of Chetwynd AP in Newpt. UD.[61] *LG* Newpt. PLU, UD. Abol 1896 ent to Newport AP.[62]

CHIRBURY
AP *LG* Chirb. Hd, Montg PLU, RSD, Chirb. RD (1894—1934), Clun RD (1934—67), Clun & Bps. Cast. RD (1967—74). *Parl* S'rn Dv (1832—85), W'rn Dv (1885—1918), Ludl. Dv/CC (1918—*). *Eccl* Pontesb. RDn (until 1878), Pontesb. (2) RDn (1878—98), Montg RDn (1898—1923), Pontesb. RDn (1923—*). Eccl bdry: 1845 (help cr Middleton EP as ptly independent,[63] fully independent 1850[64]), 1859 (cr Marton EP).[65]

CHURCH ASTON
Chap in Edgmond AP, sep CP 1866,[3] sep EP 1860.[66] *LG* S Bradf. Hd, Newpt. PLU, pt Newpt. USD (1893—94), Newpt. RSD (ent 1875—93, pt 1893—94). Abol civ 1894 the pt in the UD cr Church Aston Urban CP, the remainder cr Church Aston Rural CP.[61] *Parl* N'rn Dv (1832—1918). *Eccl* Edgm. RDn.

CP Name used by 1930s for CP cr 1894 as 'Chetwynd Aston Rural' (after abol 1896 of Church Aston Urban CP left this the only 'Church Aston' par), qv for civ organisation before 1934, parl organisation before 1948. *LG* Wellingt. RD. Bdry: 1934.[6] *Parl* The Wrekin CC (1948—*).

CHURCH ASTON RURAL
CP Cr 1894 from the pt of Church Aston CP not in Newpt. UD.[61] *LG* Newpt. PLU, RD. Called by 1930s 'Church Aston' (after abol 1896 of Church Aston Urban CP left this the only 'Church Aston' par), qv for civ organisation after 1934, parl organisation after 1948. *Parl* The Wrekin Dv (1918—48).

CHURCH ASTON URBAN
CP Cr 1894 from the pt of Church Aston CP in Newpt. UD.[61] *LG* Newpt. PLU, RD. Abol 1896 ent to Newport AP.[62]

CHURCHSTOKE
AP Montg par (pt Caus Hd, pt Montg Hd) incl in Salop tp Brompton and Rhiston (Chirb. Hd, sep CP 1866 in Salop[3]) so that 'Churchstoke' ent Montg thereafter. Eccl bdry: 1845 (help cr Middleton EP as ptly independent,[63] fully independent 1850[64]).

CHURTON—see CHURCH PULVERBACH

CLAVERLEY
AP Tp 'Claverley' in Brim. Hd; incl chap Bobbington (pt Staffs [S Seisdon Hd], pt Salop [Brim. Hd], sep civ identity early with pt in ea co,[3] pec jurisd Bridgn. [until 1846], sep EP 1726[4]). *LG* Tp 'Claverley': Seq 6. Addtl civ bdry alt: 1967.[2] *Parl* Seq 7. *Eccl* Seq 1. Eccl bdry: 1870 (help cr Tuck Hill EP [Salop, Staffs]).[11]

CLEE—see followng entry

CLEE ST MARGARET
AP Usual civ spelling, eccl 'Clee'. *LG* Seq 12. Civ bdry: 1967 (gains Cold Weston AP).[2] *Parl* Seq 7. *Eccl* Seq 11.

CLEETON
EP Cr 1879 from Bitterley with Middleton AP, Farlow EP, Doddington EP.[37] Ludl. RDn (1879—98), Stott. RDn (1898—1955), Ludl. RDn (1955—72), Bridgn. RDn (1972—*). Bdry: 1928.[67]

CLEOBURY MORTIMER
AP *LG* Cleob. Mort. Bor (status not sustained), Seq 22. Civ bdry: 1877,[68] 1939.[69] *Parl* Seq 7. *Eccl* Seq 3. Eccl bdry: 1848 (help cr Doddington EP,[4] refounded 1848[70]).

CLEOBURY NORTH
AP *LG* Seq 20. *Parl* Seq 7. *Eccl* Stott. RDn (until 1955), Bridgn. RDn (1955—72). Abol eccl 1972 to help cr Burwarton with Cleobury North EP.[50]

CLIVE
Chap in Shrewsbury St Mary AP, sep CP 1866,[3] sep EP 1753,[4] eccl refounded 1860.[10] *LG* Shrewsb. Lbty (until 1836), Alb. Dv (from 1836), Wem PLU, RSD, RD (1894—1967), N Shropsh. RD (1967—74). Civ bdry: 1967.[2] *Parl* Seq 1. *Eccl* Seq 23.

CLUN
AP In Salop until 1536, Montg 1536—46, primarily Salop thereafter. Usual civ spelling; for eccl see following entry. Main tp in Pursl. Hd as were chap Bettws y Crwyn (sep civ identity early, sep EP 1764[4]), chap Edgton (sep civ identity early, prob a sep EP 1722 [date 1st registers][71]), chap Llanfair Waterdine (sep civ identity early, sep EP 1790[4]), chap Sibdon Carwood (sep civ identity early, prob a sep 1582 [date 1st registers][72]); incl also chap Mainstone (Salop [Pursl. Hd], incl in Montg tp Castlewright [Montg Hd, sep CP 1866 in Montg[3]], 'Mainstone' gains sep civ identity early with pt in each co, prob a sep EP 1590[73]), so that Clun ent Salop from 1866. *LG* Main tp: Clun Bor (status not sustained), Seq 17. *Parl* Seq 7.

CLUN WITH CHAPEL LAWN
AP Usual eccl spelling; for civ and civ and eccl sep chaps, see prev entry. *Eccl* Seq 5. Eccl bdry: 1849 (cr Newcastle EP).[74]

CLUNBURY
AP Usual civ spelling; for eccl see following entry. *LG* Seq 17. Civ bdry: 1967.[2] *Parl* Seq 7.

CLUNBURY WITH CLUNTON
AP Usual eccl spelling; for civ see prev entry. *Eccl* Seq 5.

CLUNGUNFORD
AP *LG* Seq 17. Civ bdry: 1884,[75] 1967.[2] *Parl* Seq 7. *Eccl* Seq 5.

COALBROOKDALE

EP Cr 1851 from Madeley AP, Ironbridge EP, Dawley Parva EP.[76] Wenl. RDn (1851—78), Wenl. (2) RDn (1878—98), Wenl. RDn (1898—1972), Telford Sev. Gorge RDn (1972—*).

COCKSHUTT

Chap in Ellesmere AP, sep EP 1742,[4] sep CP 1896 from Ellesmere Rural CP.[77] *LG* Ellesm. PLU, RD (1894—1967), N Shropsh. RD (1967—74). Bdry: 1967.[2] *Parl* Osw. Dv/CC (1918—*). *Eccl* Salop RDn (1742—1837), Ellesm. RDn (1837—*).

COLEBATCH

CP Cr 1934 from Bishop's Castle Rural CP.[6] *LG* Clun RD (1934—67), Clun & Bps. Cast. RD (1967—74). *Parl* Ludl. CC (1948—*).

COLEHAM—see SHREWSBURY HOLY TRINITY

CONDOVER

AP Incl chap Longnor (sep civ identity early, some independent eccl rights from 16th cent,[78] sep EP 1739[4]). *LG* Seq 8. Addtl civ bdry alt: 1934,[6] 1967 (incl loses pt to help cr Bayston Hill CP, gains ent Stapleton AP).[2] *Parl* Seq 10. *Eccl* Seq 19. Eccl bdry: 1843 (help cr Bayston Hill EP,[4] eccl refounded 1844[25]), 1845 (cr Dorrington EP),[79] 1872 (help cr Annscroft EP).[12]

CORELEY

AP *LG* Seq 22. *Parl* Seq 7. *Eccl* Seq 2. Eccl bdry: 1848 (help cr Doddington EP,[4] refounded 1848[70]), 1929.[49]

COUND

AP Incl chap Cressage (sep CP 1866,[3] sep EP 1864[7]). *LG* Seq 8. *Parl* Seq 10. *Eccl* Seq 19.

CRESSAGE

Chap in Cound AP, sep CP 1866,[3] sep EP 1844.[7] *LG* Seq 8. Civ bdry: 1885.[18] *Parl* Seq 10. *Eccl* Cond. RDn.

CRIFTINS

EP Cr 1872 from Dudleston EP, Ellesmere AP.[80] Ellesm. RDn.

CRUCKTON—see PONTESBURY 1st AND 2nd PORTIONS WITH CRUXTON

CULMINGTON

AP *LG* Seq 12. Civ bdry: 1883.[43] *Parl* Seq 7. *Eccl* Seq 11.

DAWLEY MAGNA

Chap in Shifnal AP, sep civ identity early, sep EP 1779 (incl area chap Malins Lee, also in Shifnal AP).[4] *LG* S Bradf. Hd, Madeley PLU, Dawley USD, UD. Civ bdry: 1934,[6] 1966.[18] *Parl* Seq 5. *Eccl* Newpt. RDn (1779—1837), Shifnal RDn (1837—*). Eccl bdry: 1843 (area of Malins Lee severed to cr Malins Lee EP),[81] 1844 (cr Dawley Parva EP).[82]

DAWLEY PARVA

EP Cr 1844 from Dawley Magna EP.[82] Shifnal RDn. Bdry: 1851 (help cr Coalbrookdale EP).[76]

DEUXHILL

AP United before 1535 with Glazeley AP, sep civ identity retained or early regained, the union eccl 'Glazeley and Deuxhill', qv. *LG* Wenl. Lbty (until 1836), Brim. Hd (1836—by 1841), Stott. Hd (by 1841 and later), Bridgn. PLU, RSD, RD. *Parl* Much Wenl. Parl Bor (1468—1832), Wenl. Parl

Bor (1832—85), S'rn Dv (1885—1918), Ludl. Dv/CC (1918—*). *Eccl* Stott. RDn.

DIDDLEBURY

AP *LG* Seq 12. Ex-par place of Skirmage adjacent, sep rated 1865 in Ludl. PLU, sep status not sustained and incl thereafter in this par. Civ bdry: 1883,[43] 1884,[1] 1967.[2] *Parl* Seq 7. *Eccl* Ludl. RDn. Gains eccl 1926 the pt of Holdgate AP in Diddlebury CP to cr Diddlebury with Bouldon EP.[83]

DIDDLEBURY WITH BOULDON

EP Cr 1926 by union Diddlebury AP, the pt of Holdgate AP in Diddlebury CP.[83] Ludl. RDn.

DINMORE

Ex-par place, sep CP 1858.[41] *LG* Pursl. Hd, Clun PLU (1862—84), RSD. Abol 1884 ent to Lydbury North AP.[84] *Parl* S'rn Dv (1832—85).

DITTON PRIORS

AP Pt Wenl. Franch. (until 1836), pt Much Wenl. Bor, Munsl. Hd (pt [Ruthall and Ashfield, not sep] until 1836, ent from 1836), Bridgn. PLU, Wenl. MB (1835—89), USD (1875—89), RSD (1889—94), RD. Civ bdry: 1967.[2] *Parl* Much Wenl. Parl Bor (1468—1832), Wenl. Parl Bor (1832—85), S'rn Dv (1885—1918), Ludl. Dv/CC (1918—*). *Eccl* Seq 15.

DODDINGTON

EP Cr 1848 from Cleobury Mortimer AP, Coreley AP,[4] refounded 1848.[70] Stott. RDn (1848—1955), Burf. RDn (1955—72), Ludl. RDn (1972—*). Bdry: 1879 (help cr Cleeton EP).[37] Sometimes early 'Clee Hill St John'.

DODINGTON

EP Cr 1849 from Whitchurch AP.[85] Mkt. Drayt. RDn (1849—59), Hodnet RDn (1859—63), Whitch. RDn (1863—70s). Sep status not sustained and incl again from 1870s in Whitchurch AP.

DONINGTON

AP *LG* Seq 7. *Parl* Seq 8. *Eccl* Seq 18.

DONINGTON WOOD

EP Cr 1808 from Lilleshall AP,[4] refounded 1850.[84] Salop RDn (1809—37), Newpt. RDn (1837—59), Edgm. RDn (1859—*).

DORRINGTON

EP Cr 1845 from Condover AP.[79] Cond. RDn.

DOWLES

AP *LG* Stott. Hd, Kidderminster PLU, RSD, sep RD in Salop (1894—95). Transf 1895 to Worcs.[87] *Parl* S'rn Dv (1832—1918), Worcs thereafter. *Eccl* Burf. RDn (until 1878), Burf. (East) RDn (1878—98), Bewdley RDn (1898—1926), Kidderminster RDn (dioc Worc, 1926—40). Abol eccl 1940 to help cr Ribbesford with Bewdley EP.[88]

LITTLE DRAYTON

EP Cr 1848 from Market Drayton AP.[89] Mkt. Drayt. RDn (1848—59), Hodnet RDn (1859—*).

MARKET DRAYTON

AP Usual eccl spelling (and after reconstitution 1914, civ, qv in following entry); for civ before 1914, see 'Drayton in Hales'. *Eccl* Salop RDn (until 1837), Mkt. Drayt. RDn (1837—59), Hodnet RDn (1859—*). Eccl bdry: 1848 (cr Little Drayton EP),[89] 1857 (cr Hales EP).[90]

CP Cr 1914 from the pt of Drayton in Hales AP

constituted Mkt. Drayt. UD.[91] *LG* Mkt. Drayt. PLU, Mkt. Drayt. UD (1914—66), Mkt. Drayt. RD (1966—74). Bdry: 1965 (gains pt Tyrley CP, Staffs).[47] *Parl* Osw. Dv/CC (1918—*).

DRAYTON IN HALES

AP Usual civ spelling until reconstitution 1914 (qv below); for usual eccl and for civ after 1914, see 'Market Drayton'. Main tp in Salop (N Bradf. Hd, and Mkt. Drayt. Bor [status not sustained]); incl in Staffs tp Tyrley (N Pirehill Hd, sep CP 1866 in Staffs[3]) so that 'Drayton in Hales' ent Salop thereafter. *LG* Mkt. Drayt. PLU, RSD, Drayt. RD. Abol civ 1914 the pt to help constitute Mkt. Drayt. UD cr Market Drayton CP, pt cr Sutton upon Tern CP, pt to Moreton Say CP, pt to Norton in Hales AP.[91] *Parl* N'rn Dv (1832—1918).

DUDLESTON

Chap and tp in Ellesmere AP, sep EP 1715.[4] Salop RDn (1715—1837), Ellesm. RDn (1837—*). Bdry: 1872 (help cr Criftins EP).[80]

EARDINGTON

Tp in Quatford AP, sep CP 1866.[3] *LG* Seq 20. *Parl* Bridgn. Parl Bor (1832—85), S'rn Dv (1885—1918), Ludl. Dv/CC (1918—*).

EAST HAMLET

Hmlt in Stanton Lacy AP, sep CP 1884,[35] eccl severed 1880 and transf to Ludlow AP.[92] *LG* Munsl. Hd, Ludl. PLU (1884—1930), RSD, RD. Bdry: 1901,[93] 1934.[6] *Parl* S'rn Dv (1885—1918), Ludl. Dv/CC (1918—*).

EASTHOPE

AP *LG* Munsl. Hd, Ch. Strett. PLU, RSD, RD (1894—1934), Bridgn. RD (1934—74). *Parl* Seq 7. *Eccl* Seq 9.

EATON CONSTANTINE

AP Sometimes early called 'free chap'. *LG* S Bradf. Hd, Atcham PLU, RSD, RD. Civ bdry: 1885.[18] Abol civ 1934 ent to Leighton AP.[6] *Parl* N'rn Dv (1832—85), Mid Dv (1885—1918), Shrewsb. Dv (1918—48). *Eccl* Seq 22.

EATON UNDER HAYWOOD

AP *LG* Wenl. Franch. (until 1836), Munsl. Hd (from 1836), Ch. Strett. PLU, RSD, RD (1894—1934), Ludl. RD (1934—74). Civ bdry: 1883,[43] 1883,[94] 1967.[2] *Parl* Much Wenl. Parl Bor (1468—1832), Wenl. Parl Bor (1832—85), S'rn Dv (1885—1918), Ludl. Dv/CC (1918—*). *Eccl* Seq 8.

EDGMOND

AP Incl chap Church Aston (sep CP 1866,[3] sep EP 1860[66]), chap Tibberton (sep CP 1866,[3] sep EP 1863 [incl tp Cherrington][55]), tp Cherrington (sep CP 1866,[3] eccl severed 1863 to help cr Tibberton EP[55]), tp Chetwynd Aston (sep CP 1866[3]). *LG* Seq 4. Addtl civ bdry alt: 1880.[60] *Parl* Seq 3. *Eccl* Seq 17. Eccl bdry: 1857 (help cr Sambrook EP).[57]

EDGTON

Chap in Clun AP, sep civ identity early, prob a sep EP 1722 (date 1st registers).[71] *LG* Seq 17. Civ bdry: 1884 (gains Horderley Hall CP).[95] *Parl* Seq 7. *Eccl* Clun & Wenl. RDn (cr—1842), Clun RDn (1842—98), Bps. Cast. RDn (1898—1923), Stokesay RDn (1923—32), Clun RDn (1932—72), Clun Forest RDn (1972—*).

EDSTASTON

EP Cr 1850 from Wem AP.[96] Wem RDn (1850—1962), Wem & Whitch. RDn (1962—*). Bdry: 1961.[97]

ELLESMERE

AP In Marches of Wales until 1536, primarily Salop thereafter. Main tp in Salop (Pimh. Hd) as were chap Cockshutt (sep EP 1742,[4] sep CP 1896 from Ellesmere Rural CP,[77] qv), chap and tp Dudleston (sep EP 1715[4]); incl in Marches, then Wales (Flints, Maylor Hd) chap Penley (sep CP 1866 in Flints,[3] sep EP 1745,[4] eccl refounded 1902[98]) so that Ellesmere ent Salop thereafter. *LG* Pt Ellesm. Bor, Ellesm. PLU, pt Ellesm. USD, pt Ellesm. RSD. Addtl civ bdry alt: 1879,[99] 1879,[100] 1883.[43] Abol civ 1894 the pt in the UD cr Ellesmere Urban CP, the remainder cr Ellesmere Rural CP.[101] *Parl* N'rn Dv (1832—85), W'rn Dv (1885—1918). *Eccl* Seq 20. Addtl eccl bdry alt: 1865 (help cr Welsh Frankton EP),[102] 1869 (cr Lyneal cum Colemere EP),[103] 1872 (help cr Criftins EP).[80]

ELLESMERE RURAL

CP Cr 1894 from the pt of Ellesmere AP not in Ellesm. UD.[101] *LG* Ellesm. PLU, RD (1894—1967), N Shropsh. RD (1967—74). Bdry: 1896 (cr Cockshutt CP[77] from area chap Cockshutt [sep EP 1742 from Ellesmere AP,[4] qv]), 1934,[6] 1967 (incl help cr Selattyn and Gobowen CP).[2] *Parl* Osw. Dv/CC (1918—*).

ELLESMERE URBAN

CP Cr 1894 from the pt of Ellesmere AP in Ellesm. UD.[101] *LG* Ellesm. PLU, UD (1894—1967), N Shropsh. RD (1967—74). Bdry: 1934.[6] *Parl* Osw. Dv/CC (1918—*).

CHILD'S ERCALL

AP Sometimes 'Ercall Parva'. *LG* Seq 1. *Parl* Seq 1. *Eccl* Seq 17.

ERCALL MAGNA

AP Sometimes 'High Ercall'. *LG* Seq 5. Civ bdry: 1884.[104] *Parl* Seq 3. *Eccl* Seq 22. Eccl bdry: 1827 (cr Rowton EP,[105] refounded 1859[106]).

EYTON ON THE WEALD MOORS

AP Earlier called 'Eyton upon the Weald Moors'. *LG* Seq 5. Civ bdry: 1884,[104] 1884,[33] 1905,[107] 1934.[6] *Parl* Seq 5. *Eccl* Newpt. RDn (until 1837), Wellingt. RDn (1837—59), Wrockw. RDn (1859—*).

FAR FOREST

EP Cr 1845 from Ribbesford AP, Rock AP (both Worcs), Stottesdon AP (Salop).[108] For RDns see entry in Worcs.

FARLOW

Chap (Heref, Wolphy Hd) in Stottesdon AP (o'wise ent Salop), the chap transf to Salop (Stott. Hd) 1832 for civ purposes, 1844 for parl purposes,[109] sep CP 1866 in Salop,[3] sep EP 1854.[110] *LG* Cleob. Mort. PLU, RSD, RD (1894—1934), Bridgn. RD (1934—74). Civ bdry: 1877,[111] 1967.[2] *Parl* From 1832, Seq 7. *Eccl* Stott. RDn (1854—1955), Ludl. RDn (1955—72), Bridgn. RDn (1972—*). Eccl bdry: 1879 (help cr Cleeton EP),[37] 1928.[67]

FAULS

EP Cr 1856 from Prees AP.[112] Mkt. Drayt. RDn

(1856—59), Hodnet RDn (1859—63), Whitch. RDn (1863—1962), Wem & Whitch. RDn (1962—*). Bdry: 1871.[113]

WEST FELTON
AP In Marches of Wales until 1536, Salop thereafter. *LG* Seq 13. *Parl* Seq 6. *Eccl* Salop RDn (until 1837), Ellesm. RDn (1837—1923), Osw. RDn (1923—*).

FITZ
AP *LG* Pimh. Hd (until 1836), Alb. Dv (from 1836), Atcham PLU, RSD, RD. Abol civ 1934 pt to Mountford CP, pt to help cr Pimhill CP.[6] *Parl* N'rn Dv (1832—85), W'rn Dv (1885—1918), Shrewsb. Dv (1885—1948). *Eccl* Seq 21. Eccl bdry: 1860 (help cr Leaton EP).[114]

FORD
AP *LG* Seq 10. Civ bdry: 1885,[18] 1967.[2] *Parl* Seq 10. *Eccl* Seq 12.

FRODESLEY
AP *LG* Seq 8. *Parl* Seq 10. *Eccl* Seq 19.

GLAZELEY
AP Orig sep AP united before 1535 with Deuxhill AP, retains or regains early sep civ identity, the union eccl 'Glazeley and Deuxhill', qv. *LG* Seq 20. *Parl* Seq 7. *Eccl* Stott. RDn.

GLAZELEY AND DEUXHILL
AP Union before 1535 of Glazeley AP, Deuxhill AP, the union eccl as here, each constituent par retains or regains early sep civ identity, qv for each. Stott. RDn (union—1898), Bridgn. RDn (1898—*).

GREETE
AP Sometimes early civ 'Greet'. *LG* Seq 15. Civ bdry: 1884.[40] *Parl* Seq 7. *Eccl* Seq 2.

GRINSHILL
AP *LG* Seq 19. Civ bdry: 1967.[2] *Parl* Seq 1. *Eccl* Seq 23.

HABBERLEY
AP *LG* Ford Hd, Atcham PLU, RSD, RD. Abol civ 1967 ent to Pontesbury AP.[2] *Parl* S'rn Dv (1832—85), W'rn Dv (1885—1918), Shrewsb. Dv (1918—48). *Eccl* Seq 12.

HADLEY
EP Cr 1857 from Wellington AP,[4] refounded 1858.[115] Wellingt. RDn (1857—59), Wrockw. RDn (1859—*).
CP Cr 1898 from Wellington Rural CP.[116] *LG* Wellingt. PLU, RD. Civ bdry: 1903,[117] 1905,[107] 1934 (incl help cr Oakengates CP in enlarged Oakengates UD).[6] *Parl* The Wrekin Dv/CC (1918—*).

HADNALL
Chap in Myddle AP, sep CP 1866,[3] sep EP 1742,[4] eccl refounded 1856.[118] *LG* Shrewsb. Lbty (until 1836), Alb. Dv (from 1836), Ellesm. PLU, RSD, RD (1894—1934), Wem RD (1934—67), N Shropsh. RD (1967—74). Civ bdry: 1934,[6] 1967.[2] *Parl* Seq 1. *Eccl* Salop RDn (1742—1837), Wem RDn (1837—1962), Wem & Whitch. RDn (1962—*).

HALES
EP Cr 1857 from Market Drayton AP.[90] Mkt. Drayt. RDn (1857—59), Hodnet RDn (1859—*).

HALESOWEN
AP Main tp in Salop (Brim. Hd) as were tps Cakemore,

Hasbury, Hawne, Hill, Illey, Lapal, Ridgacre, Warley Salop (all transf along with main tp to Worcs 1832 for civ purposes, 1844 for civ purposes [Halfshire Hd],[109] each a sep CP 1866 in Worcs[3]), tp Hunnington (transf to Worcs at same time as others, sep CP 1866 in Worcs,[3] eccl in chap St Kenelm), tp Oldbury (transf to Worcs at same time as others, sep CP 1866 in Worcs,[3] sep EP 1715,[4] eccl refounded 1841[119]), tp Romsley (transf to Worcs at same time as others, sep CP 1866 in Worcs,[3] eccl in chap St Kenelm until 'Romsley' a sep EP 1841[119]); incl in Worcs (Halfshire Hd) chap Cradley (sep CP 1866,[3] sep EP 1812,[4] eccl refounded 1841[120]), chap Frankley (sep civ identity early, sep EP 1860[4]), hmlt Lutley, hmlt Warley Wigorn (each a sep CP 1866[3]) so that Halesowen ent Worcs from 1844, qv for later civ and parl organisation. *Parl* Salop pt, S'rn Dv (1832—67). *Eccl* See main entry in Worcs. Eccl bdry: see entries in Worcs, incl cr 1841 of The Quinton EP and later EPs cr from it.[119]

HALFORD
Chap in Bromfield AP, sep CP 1866,[3] sep EP 1844.[4] *LG* Seq 12. *Parl* Seq 7. *Eccl* Ludl. RDn. Abol eccl 1886 to help cr Sibdon Carwood with Halford EP.[121]

GREAT HANWOOD
AP *LG* Shrewsb. Lbty (until 1836), Ford Hd (from 1836), Atcham PLU, RSD, RD. Civ bdry: 1934,[6] 1948,[122] 1967.[2] *Parl* Seq 10. *Eccl* Seq 12.

HARLESCOTT
EP Cr 1963 from Shrewsbury St Alkmund AP, Uffington AP, Little Berwick EP.[30] Shrewsb. RDn.

HARLEY
AP *LG* Seq 8. Civ bdry: 1883.[43] *Parl* Seq 10. *Eccl* Seq 19.

HASBURY—see HALESOWEN

HAUGHTON DEMESNE
Ex-par place, sep CP 1858.[41] *LG* S Bradf. Hd (until 1836), Alb. Dv (from 1836), Atcham PLU (1858—85), RSD. Abol civ 1885 ent to Uffington AP.[123] *Parl* N'rn Dv (1832—1918).

HAWNE—see HALESOWEN

HEATH
Chap and tp (Munsl. Hd) in Stoke St Milborough AP (o'wise Wenl. Franch., until 1836), sep CP 1866.[3] *LG* Seq 12. Civ bdry: 1884.[1] *Parl* Seq 7.

HENGOED
EP Cr 1854 from Selattyn AP, Whittington AP.[124] Osw. RDn. Bdry: 1896.[125]

LITTLE HEREFORD
AP Heref par incl in Salop chap Ashford Carbonel (pt Munsl. Hd, pt Stott. Hd, pec jurisd Chancellor of Heref [until 1846], sep civ identity early in Salop, sep EP 1748[4]) so that Little Hereford ent Heref thereafter, qv.

HIGHLEY
AP *LG* Seq 21. *Parl* Seq 7. *Eccl* Seq 14.

HILL—see HALESOWEN

HILL END
Ex-par place, sep CP 1858.[41] *LG* Pursl. Hd, Clun PLU (1862—84), RSD. Abol civ 1884 ent to Lydbury North AP.[84] *Parl* S'rn Dv (1832—85).

HINSTOCK
AP *LG* Seq 1. Civ bdry: 1880.[59] *Parl* Seq 1. *Eccl* Seq 17.

HODNET
AP Incl chap Moreton Say (sep civ identity early, prob a sep EP [as 'Moreton Saye'] 1690 [date 1st registers][126]), chap Weston under Redcastle (sometimes early 'Weston and Whixhill under Redcastle', sep CP 1866,[3] not sep eccl hence this par eccl 'Hodnet with Weston under Redcastle', qv). *LG* Seq 1. *Parl* Seq 1.

HODNET WITH WESTON UNDER REDCASTLE
AP Usual eccl spelling; for civ and civ and eccl sep chaps, see prev entry. *Eccl* Salop RDn (until 1837), Mkt. Drayt. RDn (1837—59), Hodnet RDn (1859—*).

HOLDGATE
AP *LG* Munsl. Hd, Ludl. PLU, RSD, RD. Civ bdry: 1883,[43] 1884,[1] 1884.[127] Abol civ 1967 pt to Munslow AP, pt to Tugford AP.[2] *Parl* S'rn Dv (1832—1918), Ludl. Dv/CC (1918—*). *Eccl* Seq 9.

HOPE
EP Cr 1859 from Worthen AP, the EP in both Salop and Montg as was mother par.[128] Pontesb. RDn (1859—78), Pontesb. (1) RDn (1878—98), Montg RDn (1898—1923), Pontesb. RDn (1923—*).

HOPE BAGOT
AP *LG* Seq 23. *Parl* Seq 7. *Eccl* Burf. RDn (until 1972), Ludl. RDn (1972—*).

HOPE BOWDLER
AP *LG* Seq 11. Civ bdry: 1967.[2] *Parl* Seq 7. *Eccl* Clun & Wenl. RDn (until 1842), Wenl. RDn (1842—78), Wenl. (1) RDn (1878—98), Ch. Strett. RDn (1898—1923), Stokesay RDn (1923—72), Cond. RDn (1972—*).

HOPESAY
AP *LG* Seq 17. Civ bdry: 1967.[2] *Parl* Seq 7. *Eccl* Seq 5.

HOPTON CANGEFORD
Chap in Stanton Lacy AP, sep civ identity early, sep EP 1784.[4] *LG* Seq 12. Civ bdry: 1884,[1] 1884.[129] *Parl* Seq 7. *Eccl* Ludl. RDn.

HOPTON CASTLE
AP *LG* Seq 17. Civ bdry: 1884.[75] *Parl* Seq 7. *Eccl* Seq 5.

HOPTON WAFERS
AP *LG* Civ bdry: 1877,[68] 1939,[69] 1967 (incl gains Woodhouse CP).[2] *Parl* Seq 7. *Eccl* Seq 3.

HORDERLEY HALL
Ex-par place, sep CP 1858.[41] *LG* Pursl. Hd, Clun PLU (1862—84), RSD. Abol civ 1884 ent to Edgton CP.[95] *Parl* S'rn Dv (1832—85).

HORDLEY
AP *LG* Seq 16. *Parl* Seq 6. *Eccl* Salop RDn (until before 1535), Newpt. RDn (before 1535—1837), Ellesm. RDn (1837—*).

HUGHLEY
AP *LG* Wenl. Franch. (until 1836), Much Wenl. Bor, Atcham PLU, Wenl. MB (1835—89), USD (1875—89), Atcham RSD (1889—94), RD. *Parl* Much. Wenl. Parl Bor (1468—1832), Wenl. Parl Bor (1832—85), W'rn Dv (1885—1918), Shrewsb. Dv/CC (1918—*). *Eccl* Clun & Wenl. RDn (until

1842), Wenl. RDn (1842—78), Wenl. (1) RDn (1878—98), Ch. Strett. RDn (1898—1923), Wenl. RDn (1923—*).

HUNNINGTON—see HALESOWEN

HYSSINGTON
AP Montg par (Montg Hd) incl in Salop (Chirb. Hd) tp Mucklewick (sep CP 1866[3] in Salop) so that Hyssington ent Montg thereafter. *Parl* Salop pt, S'rn Dv (1832—67).

IGHTFIELD
AP *LG* N Bradf. Hd, Wem PLU (1836—54), Whitch. PLU (1854—1930), RSD, RD (1894—1934), Drayt. RD (1934—66), Mkt. Drayt. RD (1966—74). Civ bdry: 1934.[6] *Parl* Seq 1. *Eccl* Salop RDn (until 1837), Mkt. Drayt. RDn (1837—59), Hodnet RDn (1859—63), Whitch. RDn (1863—1928). Abol eccl 1928 to help cr Ightfield with Calverhall EP.[53]

IGHTFIELD WITH CALVERHALL
EP Cr 1928 by union Ightfield AP, Calverhall EP.[53] Whitch. RDn (1928—62), Wem & Whitch. RDn (1962—*).

ILLEY—see HALESOWEN

IRONBRIDGE
EP Cr 1845 from Madeley AP.[130] Wenl. RDn (1845—78), Wenl. (2) RDn (1878—98), Wenl. RDn (1898—1972), Telford Sev. Gorge RDn (1972—*). Bdry: 1851 (help cr Coalbrookdale EP).[76]

JACKFIELD
EP Cr 1790 from Broseley AP,[4] refounded 1862.[45] Clun & Wenl. RDn (1790—1842), Wenl. RDn (1842—78), Wenl. (2) RDn (1878—98), Wenl. RDn (1898—1972), Telford Sev. Gorge RDn (1972—*).

KEMBERTON
AP *LG* Seq 7. Civ bdry: 1966.[18] *Parl* Seq 8. *Eccl* Seq 18.

KENLEY
AP *LG* Seq 8. *Parl* Seq 10. *Eccl* Seq 19.

KETLEY
EP Cr 1844 from Wellington AP,[4] refounded 1880.[131] Wellingt. RDn (1844—59), Wrockw. RDn (1859—*).

KINLET
AP *LG* Seq 21. Civ bdry: 1883.[132] *Parl* Seq 7. *Eccl* Seq 16.

KINNERLEY
AP In Marches of Wales until 1536, Salop thereafter. *LG* Seq 13. Civ bdry: 1926,[133] 1967.[2] *Parl* Seq 6. *Eccl* Seq 24. Eccl bdry: 1941 (help cr Knockin with Maesbrook EP).[134]

KINNERSLEY
AP Usual civ spelling until 1970s; for eccl and for civ spelling from 1970s, see 'Kynnersley'. *LG* Seq 5. Civ bdry: 1884,[104] 1905.[107] *Parl* Seq 3.

KNOCKIN
AP In Marches of Wales until 1536, Salop thereafter. *LG* Seq 13. *Parl* Seq 6. *Eccl* Marchia RDn (until 1844), Osw. RDn (1844—1941). Abol eccl 1941 to help cr Knockin with Maesbrook EP.[134]

KNOCKIN WITH MAESBROOK
EP Cr 1941 by union ent Knockin AP, pt Kinnerley AP.[134] Osw. RDn.

KNOWBURY
EP Cr 1844 from Bitterley with Middleton AP, Caynham AP.[36] Ludl. RDn.

KYNNERSLEY
AP Usual eccl spelling and usual civ spelling from 1970s; for civ and parl organisation, see 'Kinnersley'. *Eccl* Salop RDn (until before 1535), Newpt. RDn (before 1535—1859), Edgm. RDn (1859—*).

LAPAL—see HALESOWEN

LAWLEY
EP Cr 1867 from Wellington AP, Little Wenlock AP.[55] Wrockw. RDn.

LEATON
EP Cr 1860 from Shrewsbury St Mary AP, Fitz AP, Preston Gobalds EP.[114] Shrewsb. RDn. Bdry: 1973.[9]

UPPER LEDWICH
AP Orig sep AP (Ludl. RDn), no longer sep by 1535 and incl in Bitterley AP.

LEE BROCKHURST
Chap in Wem AP, sep civ identity early, sep EP 1777.[4] *LG* Seq 2. *Parl* Seq 1. *Eccl* Salop RDn (1777—1837), Wem RDn (1837—1962), Wem & Whitch. RDn (1962—*).

LEEBOTWOOD
AP *LG* Seq 9. Civ bdry: 1967.[2] *Parl* Seq 9. *Eccl* Seq 19.

LEIGHTON
AP *LG* Seq 3. Civ bdry: 1885,[19] 1934 (gains Eaton Constantine AP).[6] *Parl* Seq 4. *Eccl* Seq 22.

LEINTWARDINE
AP Heref par (Wigmore Hd; see entry in Heref for 3 tps in that co; eccl, 'Leintwardine with Adforton') incl tp Leintwardine (North Side) (pt Heref [Wigmore Hd], pt Salop [Pursl. Hd], sep CP 1866 with pt in each co[3]); because all 4 tps gain sep civ identity 1866, 'Leintwardine' has no sep civ identity 1866—1895 (see following entry). *Parl* Salop pt, S'rn Dv (1832—67).

LEINTWARDINE (NORTH SIDE)
Tp (pt Heref [Wigmore Hd], pt Salop [Pursl. Hd]) in Leintwardine AP (o'wise ent Heref [Wigmore Hd]), sep CP 1866 with pt in each co.[3] *LG* Ludl. PLU, RSD, pt sep RD in Salop (1894—95). Civ bdry alt: 1885 (affecting only Heref areas).[135] The par made 1895 ent Heref, where there called 'Leintwardine'.[87] *Parl* S'rn Dv (1832—1918).

LILLESHALL
AP *LG* Seq 4. Civ bdry: 1898 (cr St George CP, later called 'St George's').[136] *Parl* Seq 5. *Eccl* Seq 17. Eccl bdry: 1808 (cr Donington Wood EP,[4] refounded 1850[86]), 1861 (help cr Pain's Lane EP,[13] soon afterward's called 'St George's').

LINLEY
Chap in Broseley AP, sep civ identity early, prob a sep EP 1700 (date 1st registers).[44] *LG* Wenl. Franch. (until 1836), Much Wenl. Bor, Madeley PLU, Wenl. MB (1835—1966), USD. Civ bdry: 1934.[6] Abol 1966 as Wenl. MB abol (qv for details).[18] *Parl* Much Wenl. Parl Bor (1468—1832), Wenl. MB (1832—85), S'rn Dv (1885—1918), The Wrekin Dv/CC (1918—*). *Eccl* Clun &

Wenl. RDn (cr—1842), Wenl. RDn (1842—78), Wenl. (2) RDn (1878—98), Wenl. RDn (1898—1930), Bridgn. RDn (1930—*).

LLANFAIR WATERDINE
Chap in Clun AP, sep CP 1866,[3] sep EP 1751.[4] *LG* Seq 18. Civ bdry: 1967.[2] *Parl* Seq 7. *Eccl* Clun & Wenl. RDn (1751—1842), Clun RDn (1842—1972), Clun Forest RDn (1972—*).

LLANSILIN
AP In Marches of Wales until 1536, thereafter mainly in Denb, but incl in Salop (Osw. Hd) tp Sychtyn (sep CP 1866 in Salop[3]) so that Llansilin ent Denb thereafter. Eccl bdry: 1844 (help cr Rhydycroseau EP [Salop, Denb]),[137] 1877 (incl loses pt to Rhydycroseau EP [Salop, Denb]),[138] 1879 (loses pt to Rhydycroseau EP [Salop, Denb]).[139]

LLANYBLODWEL
AP In Marches of Wales until 1536, primarily Salop thereafter, a further pt (Aber Tanat) transf 1543 from Wales to Salop. By 1970s, civ 'Llanyblodwell'. *LG* Seq 13. Civ bdry: 1934.[6] *Parl* Seq 6. *Eccl* Marchia RDn (until 1844), Llangollen RDn (1844—81), Osw. RDn (1881—*). Eccl bdry: 1844 (help cr Rhydycroseau EP [Salop, Denb]).[137]

LLANYBLODWELL—see prev entry

LLANYMYNECH
AP In Marches of Wales until 1536, thereafter primarily Salop (Osw. Hd), incl tp Carreghova (Denb [Chirk Hd], transf to Montg [Deythur Hd] 1832 for parl purposes, 1844 for civ purposes[109], Carreghova a sep CP 1866 in Montg[3]) so that Llanymynech ent Salop thereafter. *LG* Osw. PLU, RSD, RD. Abol civ 1967 to help cr Llanymynech and Pant CP.[2] *Parl* N'rn Dv (1832—85), W'rn Dv (1885—1918), Osw. Dv/CC (1918—70). *Eccl* Seq 24.

LLANYMYNECH AND PANT
CP Cr 1967 by union ent Llanymynech AP, pt Oswestry Rural CP.[2] *LG* Osw. RD. *Parl* Osw. CC (1970—*).

THE LODGE
EP Cr 1870 from St Martin's AP.[141] Llangollen RDn (1870—1923), Osw. RDn (1923—*). Later called 'Weston Rhyn'.

LONGDON UPON TERN
Chap (pec jurisd donative of Lilleshall Abbey, until Dissolution, thereafter Lichf dioc, Salop RDn) in Pontebsury AP, sep civ identity early, sep EP 1746 as 'Pontebsury Hamlet of Longden',[4] qv. *LG* Seq 5. *Parl* Seq 3.

LONGFORD
AP *LG* Seq 4. Civ bdry: 1880.[142] *Parl* Seq 3. *Eccl* Seq 17.

LONGNOR
Chap in Condover AP, sep civ identity early, some independent eccl rights from 16th cent,[78] sep EP 1739.[4] *LG* Seq 9. Civ bdry: 1934,[6] 1967.[2] *Parl* Seq 9. *Eccl* Salop RDn (cr—1837), Cond. RDn (1837—*).

LOPPINGTON
AP *LG* Pimh. Hd, Wem PLU, RSD, RD (1894—1967), N Shropsh. RD (1967—74). Civ bdry: 1967.[2] *Parl* Seq 1. *Eccl* Seq 23.

LOUGHTON

Chap in Chetton AP, sep CP 1866,[3] eccl transf (incl further pt of Chetton AP) 1895 to Wheathill AP.[58] *LG* Stott. Hd, Cleob. Mort. PLU, RSD, RD (1894—1934), Ludl. RD (1934—67). Abol civ 1967 ent to Wheathill AP.[2] *Parl* S'rn Dv (1832—1918), Ludl. Dv/CC (1918—70).

LUDFORD

Chap in Bromfield AP, the chap pt Salop (Munsl. Hd), pt Heref (Wolphy Hd), sep civ identity early with pt in ea co, made 1895 ent Salop,[87] sep EP 1771.[4] *LG* Ludl. PLU, sep RD in Heref (1894—95), Ludl. RD (pt 1894—95, ent 1895—1974). Civ bdry: 1901,[93] 1934.[6] *Parl* Ludl. Parl Bor (ent par [Salop, Heref] 1832—85), pt S'rn Dv (1885—1918), Ludl. Dv/CC (1918—*). *Eccl* Ludl. RDn. Eccl bdry: 1928.[14]

LUDLOW

AP In 19th cent civ called 'Ludlow St Lawrence'. *LG* Munsl. Hd, Ludl. Bor, PLU, MB (1835—1967), USD, Ludl. RD (1967—74). Civ bdry: 1901 (incl gains Ludlow Castle CP),[93] 1934.[6] *Parl* Ludl. Parl Bor (1461—1885), Ludl. Dv/CC (1885—*). *Eccl* Seq 11. Eccl bdry: 1880 (incl gains area East Hamlet from Stanton Lacy AP).[92]

LUDLOW CASTLE

Ex-par place, sep CP 1858.[41] *LG* Munsl. Hd, Ludl. PLU (1862—1901), RSD, RD. Abol civ 1901 ent to Ludl. MB & CP.[93] *Parl* Ludl. Parl Bor (1832—1918).

LUDLOW ST LAWRENCE—see LUDLOW

LYDBURY NORTH

AP Incl chap Norbury (sep civ identity early, eccl severed 1894 to help cr Myndtown and Norbury EP[143]). *LG* Seq 17. Addtl civ bdry alt: 1884 (gains Hill End CP, Old Church Moor CP, Dinmore CP).[84] *Parl* Seq 7. *Eccl* Seq 4.

LYDHAM

AP Salop par incl in Montg tp Aston (Montg Hd, sep CP 1866 in Montg[3]) so that Lydham ent Salop thereafter. *LG* Salop pt, Lydham Bor (status not sustained), Seq 17. Addtl civ bdry alt: 1884 (gains the pt in Salop [uninhabited] of Snead AP [Montg, Salop, ent Montg thereafter]),[144] 1934.[6] *Parl* Salop pt, Seq 7. *Eccl* Seq 4.

LYNEAL CUM COLEMERE

EP Cr 1869 from Ellesmere AP.[103] Ellesm. RDn.

MADELEY

AP *LG* Wenl. Franch. (until 1836), Madeley Bor (status not sustained) Much Wenl. Bor (thereafter), Madeley PLU, USD (1875—89), Wenl. MB (1835—1966), USD (1889—94). Abol civ 1966 as Wenl. MB abol (qv for details).[18] *Parl* Much Wenl. Parl Bor (1468—1832), Wenl. Parl Bor (1832—85), Mid Dv (1885—1918), The Wrekin Dv (1918—48), Ludl. CC (1948—70). *Eccl* Seq 10. Eccl bdry: 1845 (cr Ironbridge EP),[130] 1851 (help cr Coalbrookdale EP).[76]

MAINSTONE

Chap in Clun AP, sep civ identity early; incl in Montg tp Castlewright (Montg Hd, sep CP 1866 in Montg[3]) so that Mainstone ent Salop from 1866, prob a sep EP 1590 (date 1st registers).[73] *LG* Tp 'Mainstone': Seq 17. *Parl* Salop pt, Seq 7. *Eccl* Clun & Wenl. RDn (cr—1842), Clun RDn (1842—98), Bps. Cast. RDn (1898—1923), Stokesay RDn (1923—72), Clun Forest RDn (1972—*).

MALINS LEE

EP Chap in Shifnal AP, eccl severed 1779 to help cr Dawley Magna EP,[4] 'Malins Lee' a sep EP 1843 from Dawley Magna EP.[81] Shifnal RDn.

MARTON

EP Cr 1859 from Chirbury AP.[65] Pontesb. RDn (1859—78), Pontesb. (2) RDn (1878—98), Montg RDn (1898—1923), Pontesb. RDn (1923—*). Sometimes called 'Marton-in-Chirbury'.

MELVERLEY

AP In Marches of Wales until 1536, Salop thereafter. *LG* Osw. Hd, Atcham PLU, RSD, RD (1894—1934), Osw. RD (1934—74). Civ bdry: 1926.[133] *Parl* N'rn Dv (1832—85), W'rn Dv (1885—1918), Shrewsb. Dv (1918—48), Osw. CC (1948—*). *Eccl* Seq 24.

MEOLE BRACE

AP *LG* Shrewsb. Lbty (until 1836), Cond. Hd (from 1836), Shrewsb. Incorp for poor (1784—1870), PLU (1870—71), Atcham PLU (1871—1930), pt Shrewsb. MB (1835—94 [reduced pt 1885—94], pt Shrewsb. USD (1875—85 [reduced pt 1885—94]), Atcham RSD (pt 1875—94 [enlarged pt 1885—94]), Atcham RD. Civ bdry: 1885 (incl loses nearly all of the pt in Shrewsb. MB to Shrewsbury St Julian AP),[20] 1894 (the 2 acre pt of the par not affected in the bdry alt of 1885 cr 2 sep CPs, each 'Unnamed' CP, one in the MB, one in Atcham RD).[144] Abol civ 1934 pt to Condover AP, pt to Great Hanwood AP, pt to Shrewsb. MB & CP.[6] *Parl* Pt Shrewsb. Parl Bor (1832—85), pt S'rn Dv (1832—85), pt W'rn Dv (1885—1918), Shrewsb. Dv (1918—48). *Eccl* Pontesb. RDn (until 1878), Pontesb. (1) RDn (1878—98), Pontesb. RDn (1898—1905), Shrewsb. RDn (1905—*). Eccl bdry: 1872 (help cr Annscroft EP).[12]

MIDDLETON

EP Cr from Chirbury AP (Salop), Churchstoke AP (Montg, Salop) as ptly independent 1845,[63] fully independent 1850.[64] Pontesb. RDn (cr—1878), Pontesb. (2) RDn (1878—98), Montg RDn (1898—1923), Pontesb. RDn (1923—*). Sometimes called 'Middleton-in-Chirbury'.

MIDDLETON SCRIVEN

AP *LG* Seq 20. *Parl* Seq 7. *Eccl* Stott. RDn (until 1898), Bridgn. RDn (1898—1927), Stott. RDn (1927—55), Bridgn. RDn (1955—*).

MILSON

AP Orig sep AP, united before 1535 with Neen Sollars AP, each par retains or gains early sep civ identity, the union eccl 'Neen Sollars with Milson', qv. *LG* Seq 14. *Parl* Seq 7. *Eccl* Burf. RDn.

MINSTERLEY

Chap in Westbury AP, sep CP 1866,[3] sep EP 1814,[4] eccl refounded 1910.[145] *LG* Seq 10. Civ bdry: 1934,[6] 1967.[2] *Parl* Seq 10. *Eccl* Pontesb. RDn (1814—78), Pontesb. (1) RDn (1878—98), Pontesb. RDn (1898—*).

MONKHOPTON

Chap in Much Wenlock AP, sep civ identity early, sep EP 1747,[4] sep eccl identity not sustained, incl again in Much Wenlock AP until eccl severed 1970 to help cr Upton Cressett with Monk Hopton EP.[146] *LG* Wenl. Franch. (until 1836), Much Wenl. Bor, Wenl. MB (1835—89), USD (1875—89), Bridgn. PLU, RSD (1889—94), RD. Civ bdry: 1883.[147] *Parl* Much Wenl. Parl Bor (1468—1832), Wenl. Parl Bor (1832—85), S'rn Dv (1885—1918), Ludl. Dv/CC (1918—*). *Eccl* Clun & Wenl. RDn.

MONTFORD

AP *LG* Pimh. Hd, Atcham PLU, RSD, RD. Civ bdry: 1934 (incl gains Shrawardine AP, loses pt to help cr Pimhill CP).[6] *Parl* N'rn Dv (1832—85), W'rn Dv (1885—1918), Shrewsb. Dv/CC (1918—*). *Eccl* Seq 21.

MORE

AP *LG* Seq 17. *Parl* Seq 7. *Eccl* Seq 4.

MORETON CORBET

AP *LG* Seq 2. Civ bdry: 1883,[43] 1934,[6] 1967.[2] *Parl* Seq 1. *Eccl* Seq 23.

MORETON SAY

Chap in Hodnet AP, sep civ identity early, prob a sep EP (as 'Moreton Saye') 1690 (date 1st registers).[126] *LG* Seq 1. Civ bdry: 1883,[5] 1914.[91] *Parl* Seq 1. *Eccl* Salop RDn (cr—1837), Mkt. Drayt. RDn (1837—59), Hodnet RDn (1859—*). Eccl bdry: 1891.[52]

MORETON SAYE—see prev entry

MORVILLE

AP Incl chap Astley Abbots (sep civ identity early [later civ 'Astley Abbotts'], prob a sep EP 1561 [date 1st registers][17]), chap Aston Eyre (sep CP 1866,[3] sep EP 1748,[4] sep eccl status not sustained and thereafter considered a chap in this par hence this par eccl 'Morville with Aston Eyre', qv), chap Billingsley (sep par by 1535). *LG* Seq 20. *Parl* Seq 7.

MORVILLE WITH ASTON EYRE

AP Usual eccl spelling; for civ and civ and eccl sep chaps, see prev entry. *Eccl* Seq 14.

MUCKLEWICK

Tp (Salop, Chirb. Hd) in Hyssington AP (o'wise Montg [Montg Hd]), sep CP 1866 in Salop[3] and Hyssington ent Montg thereafter. *LG* Clun PLU (orig rated in Hyssington, sep rated soon thereafter[148]), RSD. Abol 1884 ent to Shelve AP.[144] *Parl* S'rn Dv (1832—85).

MUCKLESTONE

AP Staffs par (N Pirehill Hd) incl in Salop chap Woore (N Bradf. Hd, sep CP 1866 in Salop[3] so that Mucklestone ent Staffs thereafter, Woore a sep EP 1760,[4] eccl refounded 1842[149]).

MUNSLOW

AP *LG* Seq 12. Civ bdry: 1883,[43] 1884,[129] 1967.[2] *Parl* Pt Much Wenl. Parl Bor (1468—1832), pt Wenl. Parl Bor (1832—85), remainder and later, Seq 7. *Eccl* Seq 7. Gains eccl between 1291 and 1535 Thonglands AP.

MYDDLE

AP Incl chap Hadnall (Shrewsb. Lbty [until 1836], Alb. Dv [from 1836], sep CP 1866,[3] sep EP 1742,[4] eccl refounded 1856[118]). *LG* Pimh. Hd (pt [all except Hadnall] until 1866, ent from 1866), Ellesm. PLU, RSD, RD (1894—1967), N Shropsh. RD (1967—74). Addtl civ bdry alt: 1934.[6] *Parl* Seq 1. *Eccl* Seq 23.

MYNDTOWN

AP *LG* Seq 17. Civ bdry: 1883.[150] *Parl* Seq 7. *Eccl* Clun & Wenl. RDn (until 1842), Clun RDn (1842—94). Abol eccl 1894 to help cr Myndtown and Norbury EP.[143]

MYNDTOWN AND NORBURY

EP Cr 1894 by union Myndtown AP, chap Norbury in Lydbury North AP.[143] Clun RDn (1894—98), Bps. Cast. RDn (1898—1923), Stokesay RDn (1923—72), Clun Forest RDn (1972—*).

NASH

Chap in Burford AP, sep CP 1866,[3] eccl 1 of 3 sep eccl benefices and pars (so sep before 1851[48]) in Burford AP as 'Burford 1st Portion, Nash with Boraston', qv. *LG* Seq 15. Civ bdry: 1884.[40] *Parl* Seq 7.

NEEN SAVAGE

AP *LG* Seq 21. *Parl* Seq 7. *Eccl* Seq 16.

NEEN SOLLARS

AP Orig sep AP, united before 1535 with Milton AP, each par retains or regains early sep civ identity, the union eccl 'Neen Sollars with Milson', qv. *LG* Seq 14. *Parl* Seq 7.

NEEN SOLLARS WITH MILSON

AP Union before 1535 of Neen Sollars AP, Milson AP, each retains or regains early sep civ identity, both qv. *Eccl* Seq 2.

NEENTON

AP *LG* Seq 20. Civ bdry: 1967.[2] *Parl* Seq 7. *Eccl* Seq 15.

GREAT NESS

AP Sometimes early 'Nestrange'. *LG* Pimh. Hd, Ellesm. PLU, RSD, RD (1894—1967), Atcham RD (1967—74). Civ bdry: 1967.[2] *Parl* N'rn Dv (1832—85), W'rn Dv (1885—1918), Osw. Dv/CC (1918—70), Shrewsb. CC (1970—*). *Eccl* Salop RDn (until 1837), Ellesm. RDn (1837—1973). Abol eccl 1973 to help cr Great Ness with Little Ness EP.[151]

GREAT NESS WITH LITTLE NESS

EP Cr 1973 by union Great Ness AP, Little Ness EP.[151] Ellesm. RDn.

LITTLE NESS

Chap and tp in Baschurch AP, sep CP 1866,[3] sep EP 1911.[22] *LG, Parl* as for Great Ness except no civ bdry alt 1967. *Eccl* Ellesm. RDn. Abol eccl 1973 to help cr Great Ness with Little Ness EP.[151]

NEWCASTLE

EP Cr 1849 from Clun with Chapel Lawn AP.[74] Clun RDn (1849—1972), Clun Forest RDn (1972—*).

NEWPORT

AP *LG* Newpt. Bor (status not sustained), S Bradf. Hd, Newpt. PLU, USD, UD. Civ bdry: 1896 (gains the other pars in Newpt. UD: Chetwynd Urban CP, Chetwynd Aston Urban CP, Church Aston Urban CP),[62] 1965 (gains pt Forton AP, Staffs).[47] *Parl* Seq 3. *Eccl* Seq 17.

NEWTOWN

Chap in Wem AP, consecr 1663,[152] sep EP 1745,[4]

refounded 1861.[153] Newpt. RDn (1745—1837), Wem RDn (1837—1962), Wem & Whitch. RDn (1962—*).

NORBURY

Chap in Lydbury North AP, sep civ identity early, eccl severed 1894 to help cr Myndtown and Norbury EP.[143] *LG* Seq 17. Civ bdry: 1883.[150] *Parl* Seq 7.

NORTON IN HALES

AP *LG* Seq 1. Civ bdry: 1914.[91] *Parl* Seq 1. *Eccl* Salop RDn (until 1837), Mkt. Drayt. RDn (1837—59), Hodnet RDn (1859—*).

OAKENGATES

EP Cr 1853 from Wombridge AP, Shifnal AP,[4] refounded 1855.[154] Newpt. RDn (1853—59), Edgm. RDn (1859—*). Bdry: 1859.[155]

CP Cr 1934 by union areas in Oakengates UD (St George's CP, Wombridge AP, Wrockwardine Wood CP, pt Priorslee CP), areas outside the UD (pt Hadley CP, pt Shifnal AP, pt Wellington Rural CP).[6] *LG* Oakengates UD. Bdry: 1966.[18] *Parl* The Wrekin CC (1948—*).

OLD CHURCH MOOR

Ex-par place, sep CP 1858.[41] *LG* Pursl. Hd, Clun PLU (1862—84), RSD. Abol 1884 ent to Lydbury North AP.[84] *Parl* S'rn Dv (1832—85).

OLDBURY

AP *LG* Stott. Hd, Bridgn. PLU, RSD, RD (1894—1934), Bridgn. MB (1934—67). Abol civ 1967 to help cr Bridgnorth CP to be in Bridgn. RD.[2] *Parl* Bridgn. Parl Bor (1832—85), S'rn Dv (1885—1918), Ludl. Dv/CC (1918—70). *Eccl* Seq 14.

OLDBURY—see HALESOWEN

ONIBURY

AP *LG* Seq 12. Civ bdry: 1879,[156] 1967.[2] *Parl* Seq 7. *Eccl* Seq 11.

OSWESTRY

AP In Marches of Wales until 1536, Salop thereafter. Incl 2 areas Oswestry Town (in Osw. Bor), Oswestry Rural (each a sep CP 1866[3]) so that 'Oswestry' has no sep civ identity 1866—1967 (see following entry). *LG* Osw. Hd. *Parl* N'rn Dv (1832—67). *Eccl* [St Mary] Seq 24. Eccl bdry: 1842 (cr Trefonen EP, cr Oswestry Holy Trinity EP),[157] 1844 (help cr Rhydycroseau EP [Salop, Denb]).[137]

CP Renaming 1967 of Oswestry Urban CP as Osw. MB abol and its constituent par transf to Osw. RD.[2] *LG* Osw. RD. *Parl* Osw. CC (1970—*).

OSWESTRY HOLY TRINITY

EP Cr 1842 from Oswestry AP.[157] Marchia RDn (1842—44), Osw. RDn (1844—*).

OSWESTRY RURAL

The pt of Oswestry AP not in Osw. Bor/MB, sep CP 1866.[3] *LG* Osw. Hd, PLU, RSD, RD. Bdry: 1967 (incl help cr Llanymynech and Pant CP, gains Sychtyn CP).[2] *Parl* Seq 6.

OSWESTRY TOWN

The pt of Oswestry AP in Osw. Bor/MB, sep CP 1866.[3] *LG* Osw. Hd, PLU, MB, USD. Called from 1880s 'Oswestry Urban', qv. *Parl* N'rn Dv (1832—85).

OSWESTRY URBAN

CP Name used from 1880s for 'Oswestry Town' CP, qv

in prev entry. *LG* Osw. Hd, PLU, MB, USD. Bdry: 1934.[6] Renamed 1967 'Oswestry' as Osw. MB abol and its constituent par transf to Osw. RD.[2] *Parl* W'rn Dv (1885—1918), Osw. Dv/CC (1918—70).

PAIN'S LANE

EP Cr 1861 as 'Pain's Lane' from Lilleshall AP, Wrockwardine Wood EP, Shifnal AP,[13] soon afterwards called 'St George's', qv.

PATTINGHAM

AP Staffs par (S Seisdon Hd), incl in Salop tp Rudge (Stott. Hd, sep CP 1866 in Salop[3]) so that Pattingham ent Staffs thereafter.

PETTON

AP Chap in Baschurch AP, sep civ identity early, prob a sep EP 1695 (date 1st registers).[21] *LG* Seq 16. *Parl* Seq 6. *Eccl* Salop RDn (cr—1837), Ellesm. RDn (1837—*).

PIMHILL

CP Cr 1934 by union Preston Gubbals CP and pts Baschurch AP, Montford AP, Fitz AP, Shrewsbury St Alkmund AP.[6] *LG* Atcham RD. Bdry: 1967.[2] *Parl* Shrewsb. CC (1970—*).

PITCHFORD

AP *LG* Seq 8. *Parl* Seq 10. *Eccl* Seq 19.

PONTESBURY

AP Usual civ spelling; for eccl and for chap and hmlt (civ and eccl), see following 3 entries and 'Longdon upon Tern'. *LG* Pt Shrewsb. Lbty [area Little Hanwood, not sep] (until 1836), Ford Hd (pt until 1836, ent from 1836), Atcham PLU, RSD, RD. Civ bdry: 1884,[158] 1885,[19] 1885,[20] 1934,[6] 1948,[159] 1967 (incl gains Habberley AP).[2] *Parl* Seq 10.

PONTESBURY 1st AND 2nd PORTIONS WITH CRUCKTON

PONTESBURY 3rd PORTION

PONTESBURY HAMLET OF LONGDEN

AP Each of the 3 a sep EP forming pt of Pontesbury (the first two a part of AP, 3rd a chap [qv for organisation in pec jurisd, sep EP 1746 from the AP,[4] sep civ identity early as Longdon upon Tern]); for civ see 'Pontesbury', 'Longdon upon Tern'. *Eccl* Each of the 3, Seq 12.

POSENHALL

Ex-par place, sep CP 1858.[41] *LG* Wenl. Franch. (until 1836), Much. Wenl. Bor, Madeley PLU, Wenl. MB (1835—66), USD. Abol civ 1966 as Wenl. MB abol (qv for details).[18] *Parl* Much Wenl. Parl Bor (1468—1832), Wenl. Parl Bor (1832—85), S'rn Dv (1885—1918), The Wrekin Dv (1918—48), Ludl. CC (1948—70).

CHURCH PREEN

AP Early status as par uncertain.[160] *LG* Seq 8. *Parl* Seq 10. *Eccl* Seq 9.

PREES

AP Incl chap Calverhall (sep EP 1726,[4] refounded 1856[51]), chap Preston Gubbals (sep CP 1866,[3] sep EP 1746 as 'Preston Gobalds',[4] qv), area Whixall (sep CP 1894,[161] sep EP 1776[4]). *LG* Seq 2. Addtl civ bdry alt: 1934.[159] *Parl* Seq 1. *Eccl* Pec jurisd Prebend of Prees (until 1846), Mkt. Drayt. RDn (1846—59), Hodnet RDn (1859—63), Whitch. RDn (1863—1962), Wem & Whitch. RDn (1962—*). Addtl eccl bdry alt: 1856 (cr Fauls EP),[112] 1859,[162]

1871,[113] 1961.[97]

PRESTON GOBALDS—see following entry

PRESTON GUBBALS

Chap in Prees AP, sep CP 1866,[3] sep EP 1746 as 'Preston Gobalds'.[4] *LG* Shrewsb. Lbty (until 1836), Alb. Dv (from 1836), Atcham PLU, RSD, RD. Abol civ 1934 to help cr Pimhill CP.[6] *Parl* N'rn Dv (1832—1918), Shrewsb. Dv (1918—48). *Eccl* Salop RDn (1746—1837), Wem RDn (1837—1962), Wem & Whitch. RDn (1962—73). Eccl bdry: 1860 (help cr Leaton EP).[114] Abol eccl 1973 pt to Leaton EP, pt to Albrighton AP.[9]

PRESTON UPON THE WEALD MOORS

AP Sometimes called early 'free chapel'. *LG* Seq 5. Civ bdry: 1884,[104] 1884 (help cr Wrockwardine Wood CP),[163] 1884.[33] *Parl* Seq 5. *Eccl* Seq 17.

PRIORS LEE

Chap and tp in Shifnal AP, sep EP 1720,[4] eccl refounded 1863,[164] sep CP 1898 as 'Priorslee',[165] qv in following entry. Newpt. RDn (1720—1837), Shifnal RDn (1837—*).

PRIORSLEE

Chap and tp in Shifnal AP, sep CP 1898,[154] sep EP 1720 as 'Priors Lee',[4] as such eccl refounded 1863,[74] qv in prev entry. *LG* Shifnal PLU, Oakengates UD. Abol 1934 pt to Dawley UD and to Dawley Magna AP, pt to help cr Oakengates CP.[6] *Parl* The Wrekin Dv (1918—48).

CHURCH PULVERBACH

AP Sometimes early 'Churton'. *LG* Seq 8. *Parl* Seq 10. *Eccl* Pontesb. RDn (until 1878), Pontesb. (1) RDn (1878—98), Pontesb. RDn (1898—1972), Cond. RDn (1972—*).

QUATFORD

AP Incl tp Eardington (Stott. Hd, sep CP 1866[3]). *LG* Pt Quatford Bor (912—1101, status not sustained), pt Bridgn. Lbty and Bor (thereafter, until 1835), pt Stott. Hd ([Eardington] until 1866), Bridgn. MB (pt 1835—66, ent 1866—1967), Bridgn. PLU, USD. Abol civ 1967 to help cr Bridgnorth CP to be in Bridgn. RD.[2] *Parl* Bridgn. Parl Bor (pt 1295—1832, ent [incl Eardington] 1832—85), S'rn Dv (1885—1918), Ludl. Dv/CC (1918—70). *Eccl* Seq 1. Eccl bdry: 1956.[54]

QUATT

AP In Staffs *temp* Domesday Book, Salop thereafter. Incl tp Quatt Malvern (Stott. Hd, sep CP 1866[3]), tp Quatt Jarvis (Bridgn. Lbty [until 1836] and Bor, Stott. Hd [from 1836], Bridgn. MB 1835—66, sep CP 1866[3]) so that 'Quatt' has no sep civ identity after 1866 even though orig rated in Bridgn. PLU (the 2 tps sep rated soon after[148]). *Parl* Pt (Quatt Jarvis) Bridgn. Parl Bor (1295—1867), pt S'rn Dv (1832—67). *Eccl* Lapley & Trysull RDn (until 1851), Trysull RDn (1851—1905), Bridgn. RDn (1905—*).

QUATT JARVIS

Tp in Quatt AP, sep CP 1866.[3] *LG* Bridgn. Lbty (until 1836), Bor, Stott. Hd (from 1836), Bridgn. MB (1835—1934), Bridgn. PLU (soon after 1836[148]—1930), USD. Abol 1934 ent to Quatt Malvern CP.[6] *Parl* Bridgn. Parl Bor (1295—1885), S'rn Dv (1885—1918), Ludl. Dv (1918—48).

QUATT MALVERN

Tp in Quatt AP, sep CP 1866.[3] *LG* Stott. Hd, Bridgn. PLU (soon after 1836[148]—1930), RSD, RD. Bdry: 1934 (gains Quatt Jarvis CP).[6] *Parl* Seq 7.

THE QUINTON—see HALESOWEN

RATLINGHOPE

AP Orig Priory church. *LG* Seq 17. Civ bdry: 1967.[2] *Parl* Seq 7. *Eccl* Pontesb. RDn (until 1878), Clun RDn (1878—98), Bps. Cast. RDn (1898—before 1957), Stokesay RDn (before 1957—1972), Clun Forest RDn (1972—*).

RHYDYCROSEAU

EP Cr 1844 from Llanyblodwel AP, Oswestry AP, Selattyn AP (each Salop), Llansilin AP (Denb), hence pt in ea co.[137] Marchia RDn (1844), Llangollen RDn (1844—81), Osw. RDn (1881—*). Bdry: 1877 (gains pt Llansilin AP, Denb),[138] 1871 (gains pt Llansilin AP, Denb).[139]

RICHARD'S CASTLE

AP Pt Heref (Wolphy Hd), pt Salop (Munsl. Hd), becomes 1889 2 sep CPs, each 'Richard's Castle', one in each co (the one in Salop sometimes early called 'Richard's Castle (Salop)'). *LG* Richard's Castle Bor (status not sustained), Ludl. PLU, RSD. *Parl* Salop pt, S'rn Dv (1832—1918). *Eccl* Seq 11. Eccl bdry: 1928.[14]

CP Cr 1889 from the pt in Salop of Richard's Castle AP (Heref, Salop). Sometimes early called 'Richard's Castle (Salop)'. *LG* Ludl. PLU, RD. *Parl* Ludl. Dv/CC (1918—*).

RIDGACRE—see HALESOWEN

RODINGTON

AP *LG* Seq 5. Civ bdry: 1884.[104] *Parl* Seq 3. *Eccl* Seq 22.

ROMSLEY

Lbty in Alveley AP, sep CP 1866.[3] *LG* Bridgn. Lbty & Bor (until 1836), Stott. Hd (from 1836), Bridgn. PLU, RSD, RD. *Parl* Bridgn. Parl Bor (1832—85), S'rn Dv (1885—1918), Ludl. Dv/CC (1918—*).

ROMSLEY—see HALESOWEN

ROWTON

EP Cr 1827 from Ercall Magna AP,[105] refounded 1859.[106] Salop RDn (1827—37), Wellingt. RDn (1837—59), Wrockw. RDn (1859—*).

RUCKLEY AND LANGLEY

Tp (incl area chap Langley) in Acton Burnell AP, sep CP 1866.[3] *LG* Seq 8. *Parl* Seq 10.

RUDGE

Tp (Salop, Stott. Hd) in Pattingham AP (o'wise Staffs, S Seisdon Hd), sep CP 1866 in Salop.[3] *LG* Sesidon PLU (1836—95), RSD, Bridgn. PLU (1895—1930), not in a RD (1894—95), Bridgn. RD (1895—1974). Bdry: 1967.[2] *Parl* Seq 7.

RUSHBURY

AP *LG* Seq 11. Civ bdry: 1883,[94] 1967.[2] *Parl* Seq 7. *Eccl* Seq 8.

RUYTON OF THE ELEVEN TOWNS

AP In Marches of Wales until 1536, Salop thereafter.[166] *LG* Ruyton Bor (status not sustained), Seq 13. By time of census of 1971, civ 'Ruyton XI Towns'. *Parl* Seq 6. *Eccl* Seq 20.

RUYTON XI TOWNS—see prev entry

ST GEORGE—see following entry (civ)

ST GEORGE'S

EP Cr 1861 as 'Pain's Lane' from Lilleshall AP, Wrockwardine Wood EP, Shifnal EP,[13] soon afterwards called 'St George's'. Shifnal RDn.

CP Cr 1898 (orig as 'St George') from Lilleshall AP,[136] later called 'St George's'. *LG* Newpt. PLU, Oakengates UD. Abol 1934 to help cr Oakengates CP.[6] *Parl* The Wrekin Dv (1918—48).

ST MARTIN'S

AP In Marches of Wales until 1536, Salop thereafter. *LG* Seq 13. Civ bdry: 1897 (cr Weston Rhyn CP),[167] 1967.[2] *Parl* Seq 6. *Eccl* Marchia RDn (until 1844), Osw. RDn (1844—81), Llangollen RDn (1881—1920), Osw. RDn (1920—*). Eccl bdry: 1870 (cr The Lodge EP, later called 'Weston Rhyn').[141]

SAMBROOK

EP Cr 1857 from Cheswardine AP, Chetwynd AP, Edgmond AP.[57] Newpt. RDn (1857—59), Edgmond RDn (1859—*).

SELATTYN

AP In Marches of Wales until 1536, Salop thereafter. *LG* Osw. Hd, PLU, RSD, RD. Civ bdry: 1934.[6] Abol civ 1967 pt to help cr Selattyn and Gobowen CP, pt to Whittington AP.[2] *Parl* N'rn Dv (1832—85), W'rn Dv (1885—1918), Osw. Dv/CC (1918—70). *Eccl* Seq 24. Eccl bdry: 1844 (help cr Rhydycroseau EP [Salop, Denb]),[137] 1854 (help cr Hengoed EP).[124]

SELATTYN AND GOBOWEN

CP Cr 1967 by union pts Selattyn AP, Ellesmere Rural CP, Whittington AP.[2] *LG* Osw. RD. *Parl* Osw. CC (1970—*).

SHAWBURY

AP *LG* Pt Shrewsb. Lbty (until 1836), pt Pimh. Hd (until 1836), N Bradf. Hd (pt until 1836, ent from 1836), Wem PLU, RSD, RD (1894—1967), N Shropsh. RD (1967—74). Civ bdry: 1883,[43] 1934,[6] 1967.[2] *Parl* Seq 1. *Eccl* Seq 23.

SHEINTON

AP *LG* Stott. Hd, Atcham PLU, RSD, RD. *Parl* Seq 10. *Eccl* Seq 19.

SHELTON AND OXON

EP Cr 1855 from Shrewsbury St Chad AP.[168] Shrewsb. RDn. Bdry: 1957.[169]

SHELVE

AP *LG* Chirb. Hd, Clun PLU, RSD, RD (1894—1967), Clun & Bps. Cast. RD (1967—74). Civ bdry: 1884 (gains Mucklewick CP).[144] *Parl* S'rn Dv (1832—85), W'rn Dv (1885—1918), Ludl. Dv/CC (1918—*). *Eccl* Seq 13.

SHERIFF HALES

AP Usual civ spelling until by time of census of 1971 called 'Sheriffhales'; for eccl see below. In Staffs *temp* Domesday Book, primarily Salop thereafter. Tp 'Sheriff Hales' pt Salop (S Bradf. Hd), pt Staffs (Cottlestone Hd), the par made 1895 ent Salop;[87] incl in Salop chap Woodcote (sep CP 1866,[3] not sep eccl so that this par eccl 'Sheriffhales (with Woodcote)', qv). *LG* Shifnal PLU, RSD, RD. Addtl civ bdry alt: 1965 (loses pt to Blymhill AP, Staffs).[47] *Parl* Salop pt, Seq 3.

SHERIFFHALES—see prev entry

SHERIFFHALES (WITH WOODCOTE)

AP Usual eccl spelling; for civ and status chap, see 'Sheriff Hales'. Lapley & Trysull RDn (until 1851), Brewood RDn (1851—94) (both Stafford AD), Edgm. RDn (1894—*).

SHIFNAL

AP Incl chap Dawley Magna (sep civ identity early, sep EP 1779 [incl area chap Malins Lee][4]), chap Malins Lee (eccl severed 1779 to help cr Dawley Magna EP,[4] 'Malins Lee' a sep EP 1843 from Dawley Magna[81]), chap and tp Priors Lee (sep EP 1720,[4] eccl refounded 1863,[164] sep CP 1898 as 'Priorslee'[165]). *LG* Shifnal Bor (status not sustained), Seq 7. Addtl civ bdry alt: 1934 (help cr Oakengates CP in an enlarged Oakengates UD),[6] 1966.[18] *Parl* Seq 8. *Eccl* Seq 18. Addtl eccl bdry alt: 1853 (help cr Oakengates EP,[154] refounded 1855[154]), 1861 (help cr Pain's Lane EP, soon afterwards called 'St George's').[13]

SHIPTON

Chap in Much Wenlock AP, sep civ identity early, sep EP 1779.[4] *LG* Wenl. Franch. (until 1836), pt Much Wenl. Bor, Munsl. Hd (from 1836), Ch. Strett. PLU, pt Wenl. MB (1835—89), pt Wenl. USD (1875—89), Ch. Strett. RSD (pt 1875—89, ent 1889—94), RD (1894—1934), Bridgn. RD (1934—74). Civ bdry: 1883.[147] *Parl* Pt Much. Wenl. Parl Bor (1468—1832), Wenl. Parl Bor ([ent area] 1832—85), S'rn Dv (1885—1918), Ludl. Dv/CC (1918—*). *Eccl* Clun & Wenl. RDn (1779—1842), Wenl. RDn (1842—78), Wenl. (1) RDn (1878—98), Ch. Strett. RDn (1898—1923), Wenl. RDn (1923—72), Ludl. RDn (1972—*).

SHRAWARDINE

AP *LG* Pimh. Hd, Atcham PLU, RSD, RD. Abol civ 1934 ent to Montford AP.[6] *Parl* N'rn Dv (1832—85), W'rn Dv (1885—1918), Shrewsb. Dv (1918—48). *Eccl* Pontesb. RDn (dioc Heref, until 1851), Shrewsb. RDn (dioc Lichf, 1851—*).

SHREWSBURY

The following have 'Shrewsbury' in their names. Insofar as any existed at a given time: *LG* Shrewsb. Lbty, Incorp (poor law purposes, 1784—1870), PLU (1870—71), Atcham PLU (1871—1930); Bor/ MB, USD, RSD sep noted. *Parl* Sep noted before 1918; Shrewsb. Dv/ CC (1918—*). *Eccl* Salop RDn (until 1837), Shrewsb. RDn (1837—*).

CP1—SHREWSBURY—Cr 1924 by union CP2, AP3, AP5, AP6.[170] *LG* Shrewsb. MB. Bdry: 1934 (incl gains Sutton AP),[6] 1967 (incl help cr Bayston Hill CP to be in Atcham RD).[2]

EP1—SHREWSBURY ALL SAINTS—Cr 1881,[4] refounded 1883 from EP6.[16]

AP1—SHREWSBURY HOLY CROSS—Sometimes early 'Shrewsbury Abbey'. United before 1786 with AP4 as CP2/EP3,[171] qv.

EP2—SHREWSBURY HOLY CROSS—Eccl re-cr 1857 as EP3 divided into 2 EPs of EP2, EP6.[172]

CP2/EP3—SHREWSBURY HOLY CROSS WITH ST GILES—Union before 1786 of AP1, AP4.[171] *LG* Shrewsb. MB (1835—1924), USD. Abol civ 1924 to help cr CP1.[170] *Parl* Shrewsb. Parl Bor (1832—

1918). Abol eccl 1857 to re-cr orig constituent areas as EP2, EP6.[172]

EP4—SHREWSBURY HOLY TRINITY—Cr 1840 from AP5.[173] Sometimes early 'Coleham Holy Trinity'.

AP2—SHREWSBURY ST ALKMUND—Pt Shrewsb. Bor/MB (until 1885), pt Alb. Dv (from 1836), pt Ford Hd (from 1836), pt Shrewsb. USD (1875—85), Shrewsb. RSD (pt 1875—85, ent 1885—94), Atcham RD. Civ bdry: 1885 (incl help cr Bicton CP, gains pt AP6 and loses the pt in the MB to AP6).[20] Abol civ 1934 pt to CP1 and the MB, pt to Albrighton CP, pt to help cr Pimhill CP, pt to Uffington AP.[6] Parl Pt Shrewsb. Parl Bor (1295—1918), pt N'rn Dv (1832—1918). Eccl bdry: 1837 (cr EP5),[122] 1853 (help refound Bicton EP),[31] 1875,[24] 1957,[169] 1963 (incl help cr Harlescott EP).[29]

AP3—SHREWSBURY ST CHAD—Incl chap Bicton (sep EP 1810,[4] eccl refounded 1853 from AP3, AP2,[31] sep CP 1885 from AP3, AP2, AP5[20]). LG Shrewsb. Bor/MB (pt until 1885, ent 1885—1924), pt Alb. Dv (1836—85), pt Cond. Hd (from 1836), pt Ford Hd (from 1836), Shrewsb. USD (pt 1875—85, ent 1885—94), pt Shrewsb. RSD (1875—85). Addtl civ bdry alt: 1885 (incl made ent in the MB),[20] 1901 (gains Unnamed CP [formerly pt of Meole Brace AP]).[32] Abol civ 1924 to help cr CP1.[170] Parl As for AP2. Addtl eccl bdry alt: 1855 (cr Shelton and Oxon EP),[168] 1860 (cr Betton Strange EP),[30] 1872 (help cr Annscroft EP),[12] 1957.[169]

EP5—SHREWSBURY ST GEORGE—Cr 1837 from AP2.[122]

AP4—SHREWSBURY ST GILES—Abol before 1786 to help cr CP2/EP3.[171]

EP6—SHREWSBURY ST GILES—Re-cr 1857 when EP3 divided into 2 EPs of EP2, EP6.[172]

AP5—SHREWSBURY ST JULIAN—Orig royal free chap (royal pec jurisd, until 1548) and par. LG Shrewsb. Bor/MB (pt until 1885, ent 1885—1924), pt Ford Hd (from 1836), pt Cond. Hd (from 1836), Shrewsb. USD (pt 1875—85, ent 1885—94), pt Shrewsb. RSD (1875—85). Civ bdry: 1885 (incl loses pt to help cr Bicton CP, gains most of the pt in the MB of Meole Brace AP, and the altered area made ent in the MB).[20] Abol civ 1924 to help cr CP1.[170] Parl As for AP2. Eccl bdry: 1840 (cr EP4, sometimes early called 'Coleham Holy Trinity'),[173] 1843 (help cr Bayston Hill EP,[4] refounded 1844[25]).

AP6—SHREWSBURY ST MARY—Incl chap Albrighton ([Pimh. Hd until 1836, Alb. Dv 1836—66] sep CP 1866,[3] sep EP 1738,[4] eccl refounded 1860[10]), chap Astley ([Shrewsb. Lbty until 1836, Alb. Dv 1836—66] sep CP 1866,[3] sep EP 1860[16]), chap Broughton ([Pursl. Hd] sep civ identity early, sep EP 1718[4]), chap Clive ([Shrewsb. Lbty until 1836, Alb. Dv 1836—66] sep CP 1866,[3] sep EP 1753,[4] eccl refounded 1860[12]). LG Shrewsb. Bor/MB (pt until 1885 [enlarged pt 1835—85], ent 1885—1924), Shrewsb. USD (pt 1875—85, ent 1885—94), pt

Shrewsb. RSD (1875—85). Addtl civ bdry alt: 1885 (incl loses pt to AP2 and gains the pt of AP2 in the MB as the altered area made ent in the MB).[20] Abol civ 1924 to help cr CP1.[170] Parl Pt Shrewsb. Parl Bor (1295—1918 [enlarged pt 1832—1918]), pt N'rn Dv (1832—1918). Eccl Royal pec jurisd (until 1846). Addtl eccl bdry alt: 1835 (cr EP7,[4] eccl refounded 1852 as ptly independent,[28] fully independent 1854[174]), 1852 (cr Little Berwick EP),[28] 1860 (help cr Leaton EP),[114] 1875.[24]

EP7—SHREWSBURY ST MICHAEL—Cr 1835 from AP6,[4] eccl refounded 1852 as ptly independent,[28] fully independent 1854[174]). Bdry: 1881 (cr EP1,[4] refounded 1883[16]), 1957.[169]

SIBDON CARWOOD
Chap in Clun AP, sep civ identity early, prob a sep EP 1582 (date 1st registers).[72] LG Pursl. Hd, Ch. Strett. PLU, RSD, RD (1894—1934), Ludl. RD (1934—74). Parl Seq 7. Eccl Clun & Wenl. RDn (cr—1842), Clun RDn (1842—86). Abol eccl 1886 to help cr Sibdon Carwood with Halford EP.[121]

SIBDON CARWOOD WITH HALFORD
EP Cr 1886 by union Sibdon Carwood EP, Halford EP.[121] Stokesay RDn (1886—98), Bps Cast. RDn (1898—1923), Stokesay RDn (1923—72), Cond. RDn (1972—*).

SIDBURY
AP LG Seq 20. Parl Seq 7. Eccl Seq 15.

SILVINGTON
AP LG Overs Hd, Cleob. Mort. PLU, RSD, RD (1894—1934), Ludl. RD (1934—67). Abol civ 1967 ent to Wheathill AP.[2] Parl S'rn Dv (1832—1918), Ludl. Dv/CC (1918—70). Eccl Ludl. RDn (until 1898), Stott. RDn (1898—1955), Ludl. RDn (1955—72), Bridgn. RDn (1972—*).

SKIRMAGE
Ex-par place, sep rated 1865 in Ludl. PLU, sep status not sustained and incl thereafter in Diddlebury AP.

SMETHCOTT
AP LG Seq 9. Parl Seq 9. Eccl Seq 19.

SNEAD
AP Montg par (Montg Hd) with an uninhabited pt in Salop (Pursl. Hd), the pt in Salop transf 1884 to Lydham AP (Salop) so that Snead ent Montg thereafter.[144] LG Clun PLU, RSD. Parl S'rn Dv (1832—85).

STANTON LACY
AP Incl chap Hopton Cangeford (sep civ identity early, sep EP 1784[4]), hmlt East Hamlet (sep CP 1884,[35] eccl severed 1880 and transf to Ludlow AP[92]). LG Seq 12. Addtl civ bdry alt: 1879,[156] 1884.[1] Parl Pt Ludl. Parl Bor (1832—85), remainder and later, Seq 7. Eccl Seq 11.

STANTON LONG
AP LG Munsl. Hd, Bridgn. PLU, RSD, RD. Civ bdry: 1883,[43] 1884.[127] Parl Seq 7. Eccl Clun & Wenl. RDn (until 1842), Wenl. RDn (1842—78), Wenl. (1) RDn (1878—98), Ch. Strett. RDn (1898—1923), Wenl. RDn (1923—72), Cond. RDn (1972—*).

STANTON ON HINE HEATH—see following entry

STANTON UPON HINE HEATH
AP *LG* Seq 2. *Parl* Seq 1. *Eccl* Sometimes as 'Stanton on Hine Heath', Seq 23.

STAPLETON
AP *LG* Cond. Hd, Atcham PLU, RSD, RD. Abol civ 1967 ent to Condover AP.[2] *Parl* S'rn Dv (1832—85), W'rn Dv (1885—1918), Shrewsb. Dv/CC (1918—70). *Eccl* Seq 19.

STIRCHLEY
AP *LG* S Bradf. Hd, Madeley PLU, RSD, RD (1894—95), Shifnal RD (1895—1966). Civ bdry: 1934.[6] Abol civ 1966 ent to Dawley UD and to Dawley Magna AP.[18] *Parl* N'rn Dv (1832—85), Mid Dv (1885—1918), The Wrekin Dv/CC (1918—70). *Eccl* Seq 18.

STOCKTON
AP Incl chap Boningale (sep civ identity early, sep EP 1857[39]). *LG* Brim. Hd, Shifnal PLU, RSD, RD (1894—1967), Bridgn. RD (1967—74). *Parl* S'rn Dv (1832—85), N'rn Dv (1885—1918), The Wrekin Dv/CC (1918—70), Ludl. CC (1970—*). *Eccl* Seq 18.

STOKE ST MILBOROUGH
AP Tp 'Stoke St Milborough' in Wenl. Franch; incl in Munsl. Hd chap Heath (sep CP 1866,[3] not sep eccl hence this par eccl 'Stoke St Milborough with Heath', qv). *LG* Ludl. PLU, RSD, RD. Addtl civ bdry alt: 1884.[1] *Parl* Much Wenl. Parl Bor (1468—1832), Wenl. Parl Bor (1832—85), S'rn Dv (1885—1918), Ludl. Dv/CC (1918—*).

STOKE ST MILBOROUGH WITH HEATH
AP Usual eccl spelling; for civ and civ sep chap, see prev entry. *Eccl* Seq 11.

STOKE UPON TERN
AP *LG* Seq 1. *Parl* Seq 1. *Eccl* Salop RDn (until 1837), Mkt. Drayt. RDn (1837—59), Hodnet RDn (1859—*). Sometimes eccl 'Stoke on Tern'.

STOKESAY
AP *LG* Seq 12. Civ bdry: 1967.[2] *Parl* Seq 7. *Eccl* Ludl. RDn (until 1923), Stokesay RDn (1923—72), Cond. RDn (1972—*).

STOTTESDON
AP Incl in Heref chap Farlow (Wolphy Hd, transf to Salop 1832 for parl purposes, 1844 for civ purposes,[109] sep CP 1866 in Salop,[3] sep EP 1854[110]). *LG* Pt Stott. Bor (status not sustained), Stott. Hd (pt until 1844, ent from 1844), Cleob. Mort. PLU, RSD, RD (1894—1934), Bridgn. RD (1934—74). Addtl civ bdry alt: 1877,[111] 1883,[132] 1967.[2] *Parl* From 1832, Seq 7. *Eccl* Seq 15. Addtl eccl bdry alt: 1845 (help cr Far Forest EP [Worcs, Salop]).[108]

STOWE
AP *LG* Seq 18. *Parl* Seq 7. *Eccl* Seq 5.

ALL STRETTON
CP Cr 1899 from pt of the pt of Church Stretton AP not constituted Ch. Strett. UD.[175] *LG* Ch. Strett. PLU, RD (1899—1934), Atcham RD (1934—74). Bdry: 1934.[6] *Parl* Ludl. Dv (1918—48), Shrewsb. CC (1948—*).

CHURCH STRETTON
AP Usual civ spelling; for eccl see following entry. *LG* Munsl. Hd, Ch. Strett. PLU, RSD, RD (1894—99), UD (1899—1966), Ludl. RD (1966—74). Civ bdry:

1899 (the pt not constituted Ch. Strett. UD cr 2 CPs of All Stretton CP, Little Stretton CP),[175] 1934,[6] 1966 (gains Little Stretton CP as Ch. Strett. UD abol and enlarged area transf to Ludl. RD),[18] 1967.[2] *Parl* Seq 7.

CHURCH STRETTON WITH ALL STRETTON AND LITTLE STRETTON
AP Usual eccl spelling; for civ and for cr of 2 CPs of All Stretton, Little Stretton, see prev entry. *Eccl* Seq 8.

LITTLE STRETTON
CP Cr 1899 from pt of the pt of Church Stretton AP not constituted Ch. Strett. UD.[175] *LG* Ch. Strett. PLU, RD (1899—1934), Ludl. RD (1934—66). Bdry: 1934.[6] Abol 1966 ent to Church Stretton AP as Ch. Strett. UD abol and the enlarged area transf to Ludl. RD.[18] *Parl* Ludl. Dv/CC (1918—70).

SUTTON
AP *LG* Shrewsb. Lbty (until 1836), Cond. Hd (from 1836), Atcham PLU, RSD, RD. Abol civ 1934 ent to Shrewsb. MB & CP.[6] *Parl* S'rn Dv (1832—85), W'rn Dv (1885—1918), Shrewsb. Dv (1918—48). *Eccl* Pontesb. RDn (until 1878), Pontesb. (1) RDn (1878—98), Pontesb. RDn (1898—1905), Shrewsb. RDn (1905—*).

SUTTON MADDOCK
AP *LG* Brim. Hd, Shifnal PLU, RSD, RD (1894—1967), Bridgn. RD (1967—74). Civ bdry: 1966.[18] *Parl* S'rn Dv (1832—85), N'rn Dv (1885—1918), The Wrekin Dv/CC (1918—70), Ludl. CC (1970—*). *Eccl* Seq 18.

SUTTON UPON TERN
CP Cr 1914 from pt of the pt of Drayton in Hales AP not constituted Mkt. Drayt. UD and CP.[91] *LG* Mkt. Drayt. PLU, Drayt. RD (1894—1966), Mkt. Drayt. RD (1966—74). Bdry: 1965 (gains pt Tyrley CP, Staffs).[47] *Parl* Osw. Dv/CC (1918—*).

SYCHTYN
Tp (Salop, Osw. Hd) in Llansilin AP (o'wise Denb, Chirk Hd), sep CP 1866 in Salop.[3] *LG* Osw. PLU, RSD, RD. Abol 1967 ent to Oswestry Rural CP.[2] *Parl* N'rn Dv (1832—85), W'rn Dv (1885—1918), Osw. Dv/CC (1918—70).

TASLEY
AP *LG* Seq 20. *Parl* Bridgn. Parl Bor (1832—85), S'rn Dv (1885—1918), Ludl. Dv/CC (1918—*). *Eccl* Seq 14.

THONGLANDS
AP Orig sep AP (Wenl. RDn), disappears between 1291 and 1535 and thereafter incl in Munslow AP.

TIBBERTON
Chap and tp in Edgmond AP, sep CP 1866,[3] sep EP 1863 (incl tp Cherrington in same par).[55] *LG* Seq 4. *Parl* Seq 3. *Eccl* Edgm. RDn.

TILSTOCK
Chap in Whitchurch AP, sep EP 1718,[4] refounded 1824.[13] Salop RDn (1718—1837), Mkt. Drayt. RDn (1837—59), Hodnet RDn (1859—63), Whitch. RDn (1863—1962), Wem & Whitch. RDn (1962—*). Eccl bdry: 1859.[162]

TITTENLEY
CP Ches par transf 1895 to Salop.[87] *LG* Mkt. Drayt. PLU, sep RD in Ches (1894—95), Drayt. RD

(1895—1934). Abol civ 1934 ent to Adderley AP.[6] *Parl* Osw. Dv (1918—48).

TONG
AP Orig Collegiate. *LG* Seq 7. *Parl* Seq 8. *Eccl* Seq 18.

TREFONEN
EP Cr 1842 from Oswestry AP.[157] Marchia RDn (1842—44), Osw. RDn (1844—*).

TRELYSTAN
EP Chap (Montg, Caus Hd) in Worthen AP (Salop [Chirb. Hd], Montg [Caus Hd]), sep CP 1866 in Montg,[3] sep EP 1853.[176] Pontesb. RDn (1853—78), Pontesb. (2) RDn (1878—98), Montg RDn (1898—1923), Pontesb. RDn (1923—*).

TUCK HILL
EP Cr 1870 from Alveley AP, Claverley AP (both Salop), Bobbington EP (Staffs, Salop), Enville AP (Staffs).[11] Bridgn. RDn.

TUGFORD
AP *LG* Seq 12. Civ bdry: 1884,[1] 1967.[2] *Parl* Seq 7. *Eccl* Clun & Wenl. RDn (until 1842), Wenl. RDn (1842—78), Wenl. (1) RDn (1878—98), Ch. Strett. RDn (1898—1923), Ludl. RDn (1923—26), Wenl. RDn (1926—72), Ludl. RDn (1972—*).

UFFINGTON
AP *LG* S Bradf. Hd (until 1836), Alb. Dv (from 1836), Atcham PLU, RSD, RD. Civ bdry: 1885 (gains Haughton Demesne CP),[123] 1934,[6] 1967.[2] *Parl* Seq 2. *Eccl* Seq 21. Eccl bdry: 1963 (help cr Harlescott EP).[29]

UNNAMED
CP Pt of the 2 acre pt of Meole Brace AP not affected by bdry alt 1885 (qv above) remains in Shrewsb. MB, becomes 1894 'Unnamed' CP.[144] *LG* Atcham PLU, Shrewsb. MB. Abol 1901 ent to Shrewsbury St Chad AP.[32]

UNNAMED
CP Pt of the 2 acre pt of Meole Brace AP not affected by bdry alt 1885 (qv above) remains outside Shrewsb. MB, in Atcham RSD, becomes 1894 'Unnamed' CP.[144] *LG* Atcham PLU, RD. Abol 1901 ent to Bicton AP.[32]

UPPINGTON
AP *LG* Seq 3. Civ bdry: 1885.[19] *Parl* Seq 4. *Eccl* Salop RDn (until 1837), Wellingt. RDn (1837—59), Wrockw. RDn (1859—*). Eccl bdry: 1874.[177]

WATERS UPTON
AP Sometimes early 'Upton Parva'. *LG* Seq 5. Civ bdry: 1884.[104] *Parl* Seq 3. *Eccl* Seq 17.

UPTON CRESSETT
AP *LG* Seq 20. *Parl* Seq 7. *Eccl* Stott. RDn (until 1898), Bridgn. RDn (1898—1970). Abol eccl 1970 to help cr Upton Cressett with Monk Hopton EP.[146]

UPTON CRESSETT WITH MONK HOPTON
EP Cr 1970 by union Upton Cressett AP, chap Monk Hopton (civ, 'Monkhopton') in Much Wenlock AP.[146] Bridgn. RDn.

UPTON MAGNA
AP Incl chap Withington (sep civ identity early, sep EP 1738[4]). *LG* Seq 3. Civ bdry: 1967.[2] *Parl* Seq 2. *Eccl* Seq 22.

WARLEY SALOP—see HALESOWEN
WELLINGTON
AP *LG* S Bradf. Hd, Wellingt. PLU, pt Wellingt. USD,

pt Wellingt. RSD. Civ bdry: 1884.[104] Abol civ 1894 the pt in the UD cr Wellington Urban CP, the remainder cr Wellington Rural CP.[62] *Parl* N'rn Dv (1832—85), Mid Dv (1885—1918). *Eccl* Seq 22. Eccl bdry: 1844 (cr Ketley EP,[4] refounded 1880[131]), 1857 (cr Hadley EP,[4] refounded 1858[115]), 1859 (cr Wellington Christ Church EP),[178] 1867 (help cr Lawley EP),[55] 1874,[179] 1874.[177]

WELLINGTON CHRIST CHURCH
EP Cr 1859 from Wellington AP.[178] Wellingt. RDn (1859), Wrockw. RDn (1859—*).

WELLINGTON RURAL
CP Cr 1894 from the pt of Wellington AP not in Wellingt. UD.[62] *LG* Wellingt. PLU, RD. Bdry: 1898 (cr Hadley CP),[116] 1903,[117] 1934 (incl help cr Oakengates CP in an enlarged Oakengates UD),[6] 1966 (incl help reconstitute Little Wenlock CP).[18] *Parl* Osw. Dv/CC (1918—*).

WELLINGTON URBAN
CP Cr 1894 from the pt of Wellington AP in Wellingt. UD.[62] *LG* Wellingt. PLU, UD. Bdry: 1903,[117] 1934.[6] *Parl* The Wrekin Dv/CC (1918—*).

WELSH FRANKTON
EP Cr 1865 from Whittington AP, Ellesmere AP.[102] Montg RDn (1865—1920), Osw. RDn (1920—*).

WELSHAMPTON
AP *LG* Seq 16. Civ bdry: 1879,[99] 1879,[100] 1967.[2] *Parl* Seq 6. *Eccl* Seq 20.

WEM
AP Incl chap Edstaston (sep EP 1850[96]), chap Newtown (consecr 1663,[152] sep EP 1745,[4] refounded 1861[153]), chap Lee Brockhurst (sep civ identity early, sep EP 1777[4]). *LG* Pt Pimh. Hd, pt N Bradf. Hd, Wem PLU, RSD, RD. Abol civ 1900 the pt to constitute Wem UD cr Wem Urban CP, the remainder cr Wem Rural CP.[180] *Parl* N'rn Dv (1832—1918). *Eccl* Salop RDn (until before 1535), Newpt. RDn (before 1535—1837), Wem RDn (1837—1962), Wem & Whitch. RDn (1962—*). Addtl eccl bdry alt: 1961.[97]

WEM RURAL
CP Cr 1900 from the pt of Wem AP not constituted Wem UD.[180] *LG* Wem PLU, RD (1900—67), N Shropsh. RD (1967—74). Bdry: 1934.[6] *Parl* Ows. Dv/CC (1918—*).

WEM URBAN
CP Cr 1900 from the pt of Wem AP constituted Wem UD.[180] *LG* Wem PLU, UD (1900—67), N Shropsh. RD (1967—74). Bdry: 1934.[6] *Parl* Osw. Dv/CC (1918—*).

WENLOCK
MB Consisted 1966 of pars of Barrow, Benthall, Broseley, Linley, Madeley, Posenhall, Little Wenlock, Much Wenlock, Willey. The MB abol 1966, pt of its constituent area transf to Dawley UD & to Dawley Magna AP, pt (enlarged area) to help refound Barrow CP, pt (reduced area) to help refound Broseley CP, pt (reduced area) to help refound Much Wenlock CP, pt (reduced area) to help reconstitute Little Wenlock AP.[18]

LITTLE WENLOCK
AP *LG* Wenl. Franch. (until 1836), Much Wenl. Bor, Madeley PLU, Wenl. MB (1835—1966), USD,

Wellingt. RD (1966—74). Reconstituted 1966 (enlarged area, incl gains pt Wellington Rural CP) to be in Wellingt. RD as Wenl. MB abol (qv for details).[18] *Parl* Much Wenl. Parl Bor (1468—1832), Wenl. Parl Bor (1832—85), Mid Dv (1885—1918), The Wrekin Dv (1918—48), Ludl. CC (1948—70), The Wrekin CC (1970—*). *Eccl* Seq 10. Eccl bdry: 1867 (help cr Lawley EP).[55]

MUCH WENLOCK

AP Incl chap Acton Round (sep CP 1866,[3] sep EP 1731[4]), chap Benthall (sep CP 1866,[3] sep EP 1735[4]), chap Bourton (sep EP 1770[4]), chap Monkhopton (sep civ identity early, sep EP 1747,[4] sep eccl status not sustained, eccl severed 1970 to help cr Upton Cressett with Monk Hopton EP[146]), chap Shipton (sep civ identity early, sep EP 1779[4]). *LG* Wenl. Franch. (until 1836), Much Wenl. Bor, Madeley PLU, Wenl. MB (1835—1966), Much Wenlock USD (1875—89), Wenlock USD (1889—94), Bridgn. RD (1967—74). Addtl civ bdry alt: 1883.[43] Reconstituted 1966 (reduced area) to be in Bridgn. RD as Wenl. MB abol (qv for details).[18] *Parl* Much Wenl. Parl Bor (1468—1832), Wenl. Parl Bor (1832—85), S'rn Dv (1885—1918), The Wrekin Dv (1918—48), Ludl. CC (1948—*). *Eccl* Clun & Wenl. RDn (until 1842), Wenl. RDn (1842—78), Wenl. (2) RDn (1878—98), Wenl. RDn (1898—1926). Abol eccl 1926 to help cr Much Wenlock with Bourton EP.[42]

MUCH WENLOCK WITH BOURTON

EP Cr 1926 by union Much Wenlock AP, Bourton EP.[42] Wenl. RDn (1926—72), Cond. RDn (1972—*).

WENTNOR

AP *LG* Seq 17. Civ bdry: 1967.[2] *Parl* Seq 7. *Eccl* Seq 4.

WESTBURY

AP Incl chap Minsterley (sep CP 1866,[3] sep EP 1814,[4] eccl refounded 1910[145]), Caus Bor (status not sustained, no sep civ identity). *LG* Pt Caus Bor, Seq 10. Addtl civ bdry alt: 1934,[6] 1967.[2] *Parl* Seq 10. *Eccl* Seq 12. Addtl eccl bdry alt: 1863 (cr Yockleton EP).[30]

COLD WESTON

AP *LG* Munsl. Hd, Ludl. PLU, RSD, RD. Abol civ 1967 ent to Clee St Margaret AP.[2] *Parl* S'rn Dv (1832—1918), Ludl. Dv/CC (1918—70). *Eccl* Seq 11.

WESTON LULLINGFIELD

EP Cr 1857 from Baschurch AP.[23] Ellesm. RDn.

WESTON RHYN

CP Cr 1897 from St Martin's AP.[167] *LG* Osw. PLU, RD. *Parl* Osw. Dv/CC (1918—*).

EP Name used now for EP cr 1870 from St Martin's AP as 'The Lodge',[141] qv.

WESTON AND WIXHILL UNDER REDCASTLE—see following entry

WESTON UNDER REDCASTLE

Chap in Hodnet AP, sep CP 1866 (sometimes early 'Weston and Wixhill under Redcastle').[3] *LG* Seq 2. *Parl* Seq 1.

WHEATHILL

AP *LG* Seq 22. Civ bdry: 1967 (gains Loughton CP,

Silvington AP).[2] *Parl* Seq 7. *Eccl* Stott. RDn. Abol eccl 1895 to help cr Wheathill with Loughton EP.[58]

WHEATHILL WITH LOUGHTON

EP Cr 1895 by union Wheathill AP, chap Loughton and further pt of Chetton AP.[58] Stott. RDn (1895-1955), Bridgn. RDn (1955—*).

WHITCHURCH

AP Tp 'Whitchurch' in N Bradf. Hd as was chap Tilstock (sep EP 1718,[4] refounded 1814[13]); incl in Ches (Nantwich Hd) chap Marbury (sep EP 1870[39]; the chap civ consisted of tp Marbury with Quoisley [in 20th cent, 'Marbury cum Quoisley], tp Norbury [each a sep CP 1866 in Ches[3]]), tp Wirswall (sep CP 1866 in Ches[3]) so that Whitchurch ent Salop after 1866. *LG* Whitch. Incorp for poor (1792—1854), PLU (1854—1930), pt Whitch. & Doddington USD, pt Whitch. RSD. Abol civ 1894 the pt in the UD cr Whitchurch Urban CP, the remainder cr Whitchurch Rural CP.[181] *Parl* Salop pt, N'rn Dv (1832—1918). *Eccl* Salop RDn (until 1837), Mkt. Drayt. RDn (1837—59), Hodnet RDn (1859—63), Whitch. RDn (1863—1962), Wem & Whitch. RDn (1962—*). Addtl eccl bdry alt: 1844 (cr Ash EP),[13] 1849 (cr Dodington EP,[85] sep status not sustained and incl again from 1870s in Whitchurch).

WHITCHURCH RURAL

CP Cr 1894 from the pt of Whitchurch AP not in Whitch. & Doddington UD.[181] *LG* Whitch. PLU, RD (1894—1934), Wem RD (1934—67), N Shropsh. RD (1967—74). Bdry: 1934.[6] *Parl* Osw. Dv/CC (1918—*).

WHITCHURCH URBAN

CP Cr 1894 from the pt of Whitchurch AP in Whitch. & Doddington UD.[181] *LG* Whitch. PLU, Whitch. & Doddington UD (1894—95), Whitch. UD (1895—1967), N Shropsh. RD (1967—74). Bdry: 1934,[6] 1965 (loses pt to Marbury cum Quoisley CP [orig, 'Marbury with Quoisley'], Ches).[46] *Parl* Osw. Dv/CC (1918—*).

WHITTINGTON

AP In Marches of Wales until 1536, Salop thereafter. *LG* Seq 13. Civ bdry: 1883,[43] 1934,[6] 1967 (incl help cr Selattyn and Gobowen CP).[2] *Parl* Seq 6. *Eccl* Dioc Lichf (until *temp* Henry II), then dioc St Asaph: Marchia RDn (*temp* Henry II—1844), Montg RDn (1844—1920), Osw. RDn (1920—*). Eccl bdry: 1854 (help cr Hengoed EP),[124] 1865 (help cr Welsh Frankton EP),[102] 1896.[125]

WHITTON

Chap in Burford AP, sep CP 1866,[3] eccl in 'Whitton Burford 2nd Portion' AP, qv under 'Burford' above. *LG* Seq 15. Bdry: 1884.[40] *Parl* Seq 7.

WHIXALL

Area in Prees AP, sep EP 1776,[4] sep CP 1894.[161] *LG* Wem PLU, RD (1894—1967), N Shropsh. RD (1967—74). *Parl* Osw. Dv/CC (1918—*). *Eccl* Salop RDn (1776—1837), Mkt. Drayt. RDn (1837—59), Hodnet RDn (1859—63), Whitch. RDn (1863—1962), Wem & Whitch. RDn (1962—*).

WILLEY

AP *LG* Wenl. Franch. (until 1836), Much. Wenl. Bor, Madeley PLU, Wenl. MB (1835—1966), USD.

Abol civ 1966 as Wenl. MB abol (qv for details).[18]
Parl Much Wenl. Parl Bor (1468—1832), Wenl. Parl Bor (1832—85), S'rn Dv (1885—1918), The Wrekin Dv (1918—48), Ludl. CC (1948—70). *Eccl* Seq 10.

WISTANSTOW
AP *LG* Pt Pursl. Hd, pt Munsl. Hd, Ch. Strett. PLU, RSD, RD (1894—1934), Ludl. RD (1934—74). *Parl* Seq 7. *Eccl* Ludl. RDn (until 1841), Clun RDn (1841—98), Bps. Cast. RDn (1898—1923), Stokesay RDn (1923—72), Cond. RDn (1972—*).

WITHINGTON
Chap in Upton Magna AP, sep civ identity early, sep EP 1738.[4] *LG* Seq 3. *Parl* Seq 2. *Eccl* Salop RDn (1738—1837), Wellingt. RDn (1837—59), Wrockw. RDn (1859—*). Eccl bdry: 1874.[179]

WOLLASTON
Chap (Salop, Ford Hd) in Alberbury AP (Montg [pt Caus Hd, pt Deythur Hd], Salop [Ford Hd]), sep CP 1866 in Salop,[3] sep EP 1733 as 'Great Wollaston', qv,[4] as such eccl refounded 1864 [Salop, Montg].[7] *LG* Seq 10. Civ bdry: 1934,[6] 1967.[2] *Parl* Seq 10.

GREAT WOLLASTON
Chap (Salop, Ford Hd) in Alberbury AP (Montg [pt Caus Hd, pt Deythur Hd], Salop [Ford Hd]), sep EP 1733,[4] eccl refounded 1864 [Salop, Montg],[7] sep CP 1866 in Salop as 'Wollaston',[3] qv. *Eccl* Pontesb. RDn (1733—1878), Pontesb. (1) RDn (1878—98), Pontesb. RDn (1898—*).

WOMBRIDGE
AP *LG* S Bradf. Hd, Wellingt. PLU, RSD, RD (1894—98), Oakengates UD (1898—1934). Abol civ 1934 to help cr Oakengates CP.[6] *Parl* N'rn Dv (1832—85), Mid Dv (1885—1918), The Wrekin Dv (1918—48). *Eccl* Pec jurisd Wombridge Priory (until Dissolution), Salop RDn (Dissolution—1837), Newpt. RD (1837—59), Edgm. RDn (1859—*). Eccl bdry: 1853 (help cr Oakengates EP,[4] refounded 1855[154]), 1859.[155]

WOODCOTE
Chap and tp (Salop, S Bradf. Hd) in Sheriff Hales AP (Salop [S Bradf. Hd], Staffs [W Cuttlestone ·Hd]), sep CP 1866 in Salop.[3] *LG* Seq 4. Bdry: 1880,[142] 1936 (exchanges pts with Gnosall AP, Staffs).[182] *Parl* Seq 3.

WOODHOUSE
Ex-par place, sep CP 1858.[41] *LG* Stott. Hd, Cleob. Mort. PLU (1862—1930), RSD, RD (1894—1934), Ludl. RD (1934—67). Abol civ 1967 ent to Hopton Wafers AP.[2] *Parl* S'rn Dv (1832—1918), Ludl. Dv/ CC (1918—70).

WOOLSTASTON
AP *LG* Seq 9. *Parl* Seq 9. *Eccl* Seq 6.

WOORE
Chap (Salop, N Bradf. Hd) in Mucklestone AP (o'wise ent Staffs, N Pirehill Hd), sep CP 1866 in Salop,[3] so that Mucklestone ent Staffs thereafter, sep EP 1760,[4] eccl refounded 1842.[149] *LG* Seq 1. *Parl* Seq 1. *Eccl* Newcastle & Stone RDn (1760—1851), Eccleshall RDn (1851—1923) (both Stafford AD), Hodnet RDn (Salop AD, 1923—*).

WORFIELD
AP In Staffs *temp* Domesday Book, in Salop thereafter. *LG* Seq 6. Civ bdry: 1934.[6] *Parl* Seq 7. *Eccl* Lapley & Trysull RDn (until 1851), Trysull RDn (1851—1905) (both Stafford AD), Bridgn. RDn (1905—*).

WORTHEN
AP Pt Salop (Chirb. Hd), pt Montg (Caus Hd: chap Trelystan [sep CP 1866 in Montg,[3] sep EP 1853[176]], tps Rhosgoch, Leighton [each a sep CP 1866 in Montg[3]]) so that Worthen ent Salop thereafter. *LG* Montg PLU, RSD, Chirb. RD (1894—1934), Clun RD (1934—67), Clun & Bps. Cast. RD (1967—74). Addtl civ bdry alt: 1884,[158] 1934,[6] 1967.[2] *Parl* S'rn Dv (1832—85), W'rn Dv (1885—1918), Ludl. Dv/CC (1918—*). *Eccl* Seq 13. Addtl eccl bdry alt: 1859 (cr Hope EP [Salop, Montg]).[128]

WROCKWARDINE
AP Incl tp Wrockwardine Wood (sep CP 1884,[183] sep EP 1834[171]). *LG* Seq 5. Addtl civ bdry alt: 1884,[104] 1884,[162] 1903,[117] 1934.[6] *Parl* Seq 5. *Eccl* Salop RDn (until 1837), Newpt. RDn (1837—59), Wrockw. RDn (1859—*).

WROCKWARDINE WOOD
Tp in Wrockwardine AP, sep CP 1884 (incl pt Eyton on the Weald Moor AP, pt Preston upon the Weald Moors AP),[183] sep EP 1834.[162] *LG* S Bradf. Hd, Wellingt. PLU (1884—1930), RSD, RD (1894—98), Oakengates UD (1898—1934). Abol civ 1934 to help cr Oakengates CP.[6] *Parl* N'rn Dv (1832—85), Mid Dv (1885—1918), The Wrekin Dv (1918—48). *Eccl* Salop RDn (1834—37), Newpt. RDn (1837—59), Wrockw. RDn (1859—*). Eccl bdry: 1861 (help cr Pain's Lane EP,[13] soon afterwards called 'St George's').

WROXETER
AP *LG* Seq 3. Civ bdry: 1885,[19] 1967.[2] *Parl* Seq 4. *Eccl* Seq 22.

YOCKLETON
EP Cr 1863 from Westbury AP.[30] Pontesb. (1) RDn (1863—98), Pontesb. RDn (1898—*).

STAFFORDSHIRE

ABBREVIATIONS

Abbreviations particular to Staffs follow. Those general abbreviations in use throughout the *Guide* are found on pages xvii—xix.

Alst.	Alstonfield
Ashb.	Ashbourne
Brew.	Brewood
Bromw.	Bromwich
Burt.	Burton
Congl.	Congleton
Cutt.	Cuttlestone
Ecclesh.	Eccleshall
Handsw.	Handsworth
Kingswinf.	Kingswinford
Mayf.	Mayfield
Mkt. Dray.	Market Drayton
Newc.	Newcastle
Offl.	Offlow
Penkr.	Penkridge
Pir.	Pirehill
Seisd.	Seisdon
Shif.	Shifnal
Smethw.	Smethwick
Staff.	Stafford
Tamw.	Tamworth
Totm.	Totmanslow
Tr.	Trent
Tutb.	Tutbury
Uttox.	Uttoxeter
Wednesb.	Wednesbury
Wolverh.	Wolverhampton

SEQUENCES

An abbreviated entry prefixed by 'Seq' is used in the parochial entries to avoid repeating often the names of superior units of administration. The content of each sequence is shown below.

Local Government Sequences ('LG')

SEQ 1   E Cutt. Hd, Penkr. PLU (1836—70s), Cannock PLU (1870s—1930), RSD, RD

SEQ 2   E Cutt. Hd, Staff. PLU, RSD, RD

SEQ 3   W Cutt. Hd, Newport PLU, RSD, Gnosall RD (1894—1934), Staff. RD (1934—74)

SEQ 4   W Cutt. Hd, Penkr. PLU (1836—70s), Cannock PLU (1870s—1930), RSD, RD

SEQ 5   W Cutt. Hd, Shif. PLU, RSD, Unnamed RD (1894—1934), Cannock RD (1934—74)

SEQ 6   W Cutt. Hd, Staff. PLU, RSD, RD

SEQ 7   N Offl. Hd, Burt. upon Tr. PLU, RSD, Tutb. RD

SEQ 8   N Offl. Hd, Lichf PLU, RSD, RD

SEQ 9   N Offl. Hd, Tamw. PLU, RSD, RD (1894—1934), Lichf RD (1934—74)

SEQ 10   N Offl. Hd, Uttox. PLU, RSD, RD

SEQ 11   S Offl. Hd, Lichf PLU, RSD, RD

SEQ 12   S Offl. Hd, Tamw. PLU, RSD, RD (1894—1934), Lichf RD (1934—74)

SEQ 13   N Pir. Hd, Mkt. Dray. PLU, RSD, Blore Heath RD (1894—1932), Newc. under Lyme RD (1932—74)

SEQ 14   N Pir. Hd, Newc. under Lyme PLU, RSD, RD

SEQ 15   N Pir. Hd, Newport PLU, RSD, Gnosall RD (1894—1934), Staff. RD (1934—74)

SEQ 16   N Pir. Hd, Stone PLU, RSD, RD

SEQ 17   S Pir. Hd, Staff. PLU, RSD, RD

SEQ 18   S Pir. Hd, Stone PLU, RSD, RD

SEQ 19   N Seisd. Hd, Seisd. PLU, RSD, RD

SEQ 20   S Seisd. Hd, Seisd. PLU, RSD, RD

SEQ 21   N Totm. Hd, Cheadle PLU, RSD, RD

SEQ 22   N Totm. Hd, Leek PLU, RSD, RD

SEQ 23   S Totm. Hd, Ashb. PLU, RSD, Mayf. RD (1894—1934), Uttox. RD (1934—74)

SEQ 24   S Totm. Hd, Cheadle PLU, RSD, RD

SEQ 25   S Totm. Hd, Leek PLU, RSD, RD
SEQ 26   S Totm. Hd, Uttox. PLU, RSD, RD

Parliamentary Sequences ('Parl')

SEQ 1   N'rn Dv (1832—67), East Dv (1867—85), Burt. Dv/CC (1885—*)

SEQ 2   N'rn Dv (1832—67), East Dv (1867—85), Lichf Dv (1885—1948), Lichf & Tamw CC (1948—*)

SEQ 3   N'rn Dv (1832—67), North Dv (1867—85), Burt. Dv/CC (1885—*)

SEQ 4   N'rn Dv (1832—67), North Dv (1867—85), Handsw. Dv (1885—1918), Staff. Dv (1918—48), Staff. & Stone CC (1948—*)

SEQ 5   N'rn Dv (1832—67), North Dv (1867—85), Handsw. Dv (1885—1918), Stone Dv (1918—48), Staff. & Stone CC (1948—*)

SEQ 6   N'rn Dv (1832—67), North Dv (1867—85), Leek Dv/CC (1885—*)

SEQ 7   N'rn Dv (1832—67), North Dv (1867—85), Leek Dv (1885—1918), Burt. Dv/CC (1918—*)

SEQ 8   N'rn Dv (1832—67), North Dv (1867—85), Leek Dv (1885—1918), Stone Dv (1918—48), Burt. CC (1948—*)

SEQ 9   N'rn Dv (1832—67), North Dv (1867—85), Leek Dv (1885—1918), Stone Dv (1918—48), Leek CC (1948—*)

SEQ 10   N'rn Dv (1832—67), North Dv (1867—85), N-W'rn Dv (1885—1918), Stone Dv (1918—48), Newc. under Lyme BC (1948—*)

SEQ 11   N'rn Dv (1832—67), West Dv (1867—85), Burt. Dv/CC (1885—*)

SEQ 12   N'rn Dv (1832—67), West Dv (1867—85), W'rn Dv (1885—1918), Staff. Dv (1918—48), Staff. & Stone CC (1948—*)

SEQ 13   N'rn Dv (1832—67), West Dv (1867—85), W'rn Dv (1885—1918), Stone Dv (1918—48), Staff. & Stone CC (1948—*)

SEQ 14   S'rn Dv (1832—67), East Dv (1867—85), Lichf Dv (1885—1948), Lichf & Tamw. CC (1948—*)

SEQ 15   S'rn Dv (1832—67), West Dv (1867—85), Handsw. Dv (1885—1918), Staff. Dv (1918—48), Staff. & Stone CC (1948—*)

SEQ 16   S'rn Dv (1832—67), West Dv (1867—85), Kingswinf. Dv (1885—1918), Cannock Dv (1918—48), Brierley Hill CC (1948—70), S W Staffs CC (1970—*)

SEQ 17   S'rn Dv (1832—67), West Dv (1867—85), W'rn Dv (1885—1918), Cannock Dv/CC (1918—70), S W Staffs CC (1970—*)

SEQ 18   S'rn Dv (1832—67), West Dv (1867—85), W'rn Dv (1885—1918), Staff. Dv (1918—48), Cannock CC (1948—70), S W Staffs CC (1970—*)

SEQ 19   S'rn Dv (1832—67), West Dv (1867—85), W'rn Dv (1885—1918), Staff. Dv (1918—48), Staff. & Stone CC (1948—*)

Ecclesiastical Sequences ('Eccl')

SEQ 1   Alton & Leek RDn (until 1851), Alst. RDn (1851—*)

SEQ 2   Alton & Leek RDn (until 1851), Cheadle RDn (1851—*)

SEQ 3   Alton & Leek RDn (until 1851), Uttox. RDn (1851—*)

SEQ 4   Lapley & Trysull RDn (until 1851), Brew. RDn (1851—94), Penkr. RDn (1894—*)

SEQ 5   Lapley & Trysull RDn (until 1851), Ecclesh. RDn (1851—*)

SEQ 6   Lapley & Trysull RDn (until 1851), Himley RDn (1851—*)

SEQ 7   Lapley & Trysull RDn (until 1851), Trysull RDn (1851—*)

SEQ 8   Lichf pec jurisd (until 1836), Newc. & Stone RDn (1836—51), Ecclesh. RDn (1851—*)

SEQ 9   Newc. RDn (until early 14th cent), Newc. & Stone RDn (early 14th cent—1851), Newc. under Lyme RDn (1851—*)

SEQ 10   Staff. RDn (until early 14th cent), Newc. & Stone RDn (early 14th cent—1851), Ecclesh. RDn (1851—*)

SEQ 11   Staff. RDn (until early 14th cent), Newc. & Stone RDn (early 14th cent—1851), Stone RDn (1851—61), Trentham RDn (1861—*)

SEQ 12   Tamw. & Tutb. RDn (until 1851), Lichf RDn (1851—*)

SEQ 13   Tamw. & Tutb. RDn (until 1851), Tamw. RDn (1851—*)

SEQ 14   Tamw. & Tutb. RDn (until 1851), Tutb. RDn (1851—*)

SEQ 15   Tamw. & Tutb. RDn (until 1851), Walsall RDn (1851—*)

DIOCESES AND ARCHDEACONRIES

Staffs pars were organised in Archdeaconries and Rural Deaneries as follows:

BIRMINGHAM DIOC (1905—*)
Birmingham AD: Edgbaston RDn (1929—*), Handsw. RDn, Harborne RDn (1905—29), Smethw. RDn (1929—66), Warley (1966—*)

LICHFIELD DIOC (1837—*)
Staff. AD: Alst. RDn (1851—77), Brew. RDn (1851—94), Cheadle RDn (1851—77), Ecclesh. RDn (1851—77), Handsw. RDn (1851—1906), Himley RDn (1851—*), Lapley & Trysull RDn (1837—51), Leek RDn (1851—77), Leek & Alton RDn (1837—51), Lichf RDn (1851—*), Newc. & Stone RDn (1837—51), Newc. under Lyme RDn (1851—77), Penkr. RDn (1851—*), Rugeley RDn (1851—*), Staff. RDn (1851—*), Stoke upon Tr. RDn (1837—51), Tamw. RDn (1851—*), Tamw. & Tutb. RDn (1837—51), Trentham RDn (1851—77), Trysull RDn (1851—*), Tutb. RDn (1851—*), Uttox.

RDn (1851—77), Walsall RDn (1851—*),
Wednesb. RDn (1894—*), W Bromw. RDn
(1894—*), Wolverh. RDn (1851—*)

Stoke on Tr. AD (1877—):* Alst. RDn, Cheadle RDn,
Ecclesh. RDn, Hamley RDn (1894—1920), Leek
RDn, Newc. under Lyme RDn, Stoke (North) RDn
(1962—*), Trentham RDn, Uttox. RDn

LICHFIELD AND COVENTRY (styled LICHFIELD
1053—1075, CHESTER 1075—1102, COVEN-
TRY 1102—1128, COVENTRY AND LICH-
FIELD 1228—Reformation, LICHFIELD AND
COVENTRY Reformation—1837)

Staff. AD: Lapley & Trysull RDn, Leek & Alton RDn,
Newc. RDn (until early 14th cent), Newc. & Stone
RDn (early 14th cent—1851), Staff. RDn (until
early 14th cent), Tamw. & Tutb. RDn

THE PARISHES OF STAFFORDSHIRE

ACTON TRUSSELL—see following entry

ACTON TRUSSELL AND BEDNALL
Orig 2 chaps and tps of Acton Trussell (pec jurisd
prebend Whittington), Bednall (sometimes reputed
to have been in Cannock AP, generally considered
in Baswich AP), each in Baswich AP (eccl,
'Berkswich with Walton'), sep par by 1671 with
each chap with all rights of a par church,[1] sep status
of the 2 not sustained, thereafter deemed joint tp in
Baswich AP, sep CP 1866 as 'Acton Trussell and
Bednall',[2] sep EP 1776 as 'Acton Trussell with
Bednall'.[3] *LG* Seq 1. Civ bdry: 1934.[4] *Parl* Seq 18.
Eccl Pt pec jurisd Whittington (until 1836), Newc.
& Stone RDn (pt 1776—1836, ent 1836—51),
Penkr. RDn (1851—*).

ACTON TRUSSELL WITH BEDNALL—see prev entry

ADBASTON
AP *LG* Seq 15. Civ bdry: 1934.[4] *Parl* Seq 4. *Eccl* Pec
jurisd Dean of Lichf (until 1846), Seq 8 thereafter.

ALDRIDGE
AP Incl chap Great Barr (sep CP 1866,[2] sep EP 1847[5]).
LG S Offl. Hd, Walsall PLU, RSD, RD (1894—
1934), Aldridge UD (1934—66). For civ abol 1966,
see Aldridge UD. *Parl* S'rn Dv (1832—67), East
Dv (1867—85), Handsw. Dv (1885—1918), Lichf
Dv (1918—48), Lichf & Tamw. CC (1948—55),
Walsall South BC (1955—70). *Eccl* Seq 15.

UD Aldridge UD comprised of the following pars:
Aldridge AP, Great Barr CP, Pelsall CP, Rushall
AP, the area cr 1934, qv in Part II of the *Guide*. The
UD abol 1966 (incl its constituent pars) pt to
Walsall CB (assoc with Staffs) & CP, pt to W
Bromw. CB (assoc with Staffs) & AP, pt to help cr
Aldridge-Brownhills UD & CP, pt to Cannock UD
& AP, pt to Shenstone AP.[6] *Parl* See constituent
pars.

ALDRIDGE-BROWNHILLS
CP Cr 1966 by union pts Aldridge UD (qv in prev entry
for constituent pars), Brownhills UD (qv for
constituent pars), Hammerwich CP, Shenstone AP
(all Staffs), Walsall CB (assoc with Staffs) & CP,
Birm CB (assoc with Warws) & AP, Sutton
Coldfield MB & AP (Warws).[6] *LG* Aldridge-
Brownhills UD. Transf 1974 to W Midlands.[7] *Parl*
Aldridge-Brownhills BC (1970—*).

ALREWAS
AP Incl chaps (each in pec jurisd prebend Alrewas)
Edingale (sep civ identity early, sep EP 1824[3]),
Pipe Ridware (sep civ identity early, sep EP 1726[3]),
tps Fradley, Orgreave (each a sep CP 1866[2]). *LG* Pt

Alrewas Bor, Seq 8. Addtl civ bdry alt: 1883,[8] 1885
(incl gains Fradley CP, Orgreave CP, Alrewas
Hays CP),[9] 1934.[4] *Eccl* Pec jurisd prebend Alrewas
(until 1846), Seq 12 thereafter.

ALREWAS HAYS
Ex-par place, sep CP 1858.[10] *LG* N Offl. Hd, Lichf
PLU (1858—85), RSD. Abol civ 1885 ent to
Alrewas AP.[9] *Parl* N'rn Dv (1832—67), East Dv
(1867—85), Lichf Dv (1885—1918).

ALSAGERS BANK
EP Cr 1932 from Chesterton AP, Audley AP.[11] Newc.
under Lyme RDn.

ALSTONFIELD
AP Incl chap Longnor (sep CP 1866,[2] sep EP 1737 [incl
pt tps Fawfieldhead, Heathylee, Hollinsclough, all
in same par],[3] eccl refounded 1902[12]), chap
Quarnford (sep CP 1866,[2] sep EP 1752 [incl pt tp
Heathylee, pt tp Hollinsclough, both in same par],[3]
eccl refounded 1902[12]), tp Warslow and Elkstones
(single tp comprised of chaps Warslow, Elkstones,
the tp a sep CP 1866,[2] 'Warslow' a sep EP 1785
[incl pt tp Fawfieldhead in the same par],[3] 'Elkstone' a sep EP 1785,[3] the 2 EPs united 1902 to help
refound 'Warslow EP',[12] the union later called
'Warslow and Elkstone'), tp Fawfieldhead (sep CP
1866,[2] pt in chap/EP Longnor, qv above for cr and
refounding, pt eccl severed 1785 to help cr Warslow
EP,[3] qv for later refounding), tps Heathylee,
Hollinsclough (each a sep CP 1866,[2] pt of each eccl
in chap/EP Longnor, qv above for cr and refounding, pt of each in chap/EP Quarnford, qv above for
cr and refounding). *LG* N Totm. Hd, Alst. GilbU
(until 1869), Ashb. PLU (1869—1930), RSD,
Mayf. RD (1894—1934), Leek RD (1934—74).
Addtl civ bdry alt: 1934.[4] *Parl* Seq 9. *Eccl* Seq 1.

ALTON
AP Incl tp Cotton (sep CP 1866,[2] sep EP 1796,[3] sep
eccl status not sustained, the area eccl severed 1932
to help cr Oakamoor with Cotton EP[13]), tp
Denstone (sep CP 1866,[2] sep EP 1860 by union this
tp, pt Ellastone AP (tp Prestwood), pt Rocester
AP[14]), tp Farley (sep CP 1866[2]). *LG* Alton Bor, Seq
24. Addtl civ bdry alt: 1883,[8] 1896,[15] 1934.[4] *Parl*
Seq 9. *Eccl* Seq 2.

AMBLECOTE
Hmlt (Staffs, S Seisd. Hd) in Oldswinford AP
(o'wise ent Worcs [Halfshire Hd]; eccl, 'Old
Swinford'), 'Amblecote' a sep CP 1866 in Staffs[2]
(and Oldswinford ent Worcs thereafter), sep EP
1845 (incl tp Wollaston [Worcs] in same par),[16] eccl

refounded 1860.[17] *LG* Stourbridge PLU, RSD, Kingswinf. RD (1894—98), Amblecote UD (1898—1966). Civ bdry: 1936.[18] Abol civ 1966 pt to Dudley CB (as the CB becomes assoc with Staffs) & AP, pt to Stourbridge MB & CP, Worcs).[6] *Parl* S'rn Dv (1832—67), West Dv (1867—85), Kingswinf. Dv (1885—1948), Brierley Hill CC (1948—70). *Eccl* Kidderminster RDn (1844—1907), Swinford RDn (1907—*) (both dioc Worc). Eccl bdry: 1860 (area of orig tp Wollaston [Worcs] severed and also area in Staffs to cr Wollaston EP).[19]

AMINGTON

EP Cr 1864 from Tamworth AP,[3] sep status not sustained and reunited with Tamworth by 1870s.[20] Tamw. RDn.

ANSLOW

Tp in Rolleston AP, sep CP 1866,[2] sep EP 1861 from Rolleston AP, Tutbury AP.[21] *LG* Seq 7. Civ bdry: 1883,[8] 1934.[4] *Parl* Seq 1. *Eccl* Tutb. RDn. Eccl bdry: 1884 (help cr Rangemore EP),[22] 1899,[23] 1940.[24]

ARLEY

AP Usual eccl spelling; for civ see following entry. *Eccl* Pec jurisd Dean & Chapter of Lichf (until 1846), Lapley & Trysull RDn (1846—51), Trysull RDn (1851—1905), Kidderminster RDn (dioc Worc, 1905—*).

UPPER ARLEY

AP Usual civ spelling; for eccl see prev entry. *LG* S Seisd. Hd, Kidderminster PLU, RSD, sep RD in Staffs (1894—95). Transf 1895 to Worcs.[25] *Parl* S'rn Dv (1832—67), West Dv (1867—85), Kingswinf. Dv (1885—1918); see Worcs for parl organisation thereafter.

ARMITAGE

AP *LG* Seq 11. Civ bdry: 1934.[4] *Parl* Seq 14. *Eccl* Pec jurisd prebend Hansacre (until 1846), Tamw. & Tutb. RDn (1846—51), Rugeley RDn (1851—*).

ASHLEY

AP *LG* N Pir. Hd, Mkt. Dray. PLU (soon after 1836[26]—1930), RSD, Blore Heath RD (1894—1932), Newc. under Lyme RD (1932—74). Civ bdry: 1932.[27] *Parl* Seq 5. *Eccl* Newc. & Stone RDn (until 1851), Ecclesh. RDn (1851—*).

ASTON

EP Cr 1846 from Stone AP.[3] Newc. & Stone RDn (1846—51), Stone RDn (1851—61), Trentham RDn (1861—*).

LITTLE ASTON

EP Cr 1876 from Shenstone AP, Stonnal EP (both Staffs), Hill EP (Warws) to be dioc Lichf.[28] Lichf RDn. Bdry: 1918 (help cr Streetly EP),[29] 1974.[30]

AUDLEY

AP Incl tp and bor Betley (sep civ identity early, sep EP 1717[3]), area Talke (sep EP 1741,[3] eccl refounded 1859,[31] orig as 'Talke o' the Hill', but later called 'Talke', as such a sep CP 1932 from Audley AP at its civ abol[27]). *LG* Pt Betley Bor, N Pir. Hd, Newc. under Lyme PLU, pt Audley USD, pt Kidsgrove USD, Audley UD. Addtl civ bdry alt: 1894 (the pt in Kidsgrove UD cr Hardings Wood CP).[32] Abol civ 1932 pt to help cr Audley Rural CP, pt to Madeley AP, pt to cr Talke CP.[28] *Parl* N'rn Dv (1832—67), North Dv (1867—85), N-W'rn Dv (1885—1918), Newc. under Lyme Parl Bor (1918—48). *Eccl* Seq 9. Addtl eccl bdry alt: 1846 (help cr Chesterton EP),[33] 1932 (help cr Alsagers Bank EP).[11]

AUDLEY RURAL

CP Cr 1932 from Audley AP, Keele CP, Madeley AP.[27] *LG* Newc. under Lyme RD. *Parl* Newc. under Lyme CC (1948—70), BC (1970—*).

BAGNALL

Chap in Stoke upon Trent AP, sep CP 1896 from Stoke Rural CP,[34] eccl severed 1716 to help cr Bucknall EP,[3] 'Bagnall' a sep EP 1736 from Bucknall EP,[3] sep eccl status of Bagnall not sustained and the reunited par thereafter 'Bucknall cum Bagnall', qv. *LG* Stoke on Tr. PLU (1896—1922), Stoke and Wolstanton PLU (1922—30), Stoke upon Tr. RD (1896—1922), Leek RD (1922—74). Civ bdry: 1965 (incl exchanges pts with Stoke on Tr. CB [assoc with Staffs] & AP).[35] *Parl* Leek Dv/CC (1918—*). *Eccl* Newc. & Stone RDn.

BALTERLEY

Tp (Staffs, N Pir. Hd) in Barthomley AP (o'wise ent Ches, Nantwich Hd), sep CP 1866 in Staffs and Barthomley ent Ches thereafter.[2] *LG* Seq 14. Bdry: 1965 (exchanges pts with Weston CP, loses pt to Chorlton CP, both Ches).[6] *Parl* Seq 10.

BARLASTON

AP *LG* Seq 18. Addtl civ bdry alt: 1930 (loses pt to Stoke on Tr. CB [assoc with Staffs] & AP),[36] 1932,[27] 1965 (exchanges pts with Stoke on Tr. CB [assoc with Staffs] & AP).[35] *Parl* Seq 13. *Eccl* Newc. & Stone RDn (until 1851), Trentham RDn (1851—*). Addtl eccl bdry alt: 1948 (help cr Meir Heath EP).[37]

GREAT BARR

Chap and tp in Aldridge AP, sep CP 1866,[2] sep EP 1849.[5] *LG* S Offl. Hd, Walsall PLU, RSD, RD (1894—1934), Aldridge UD (1934—66). Civ bdry: 1931 (loses pt to Walsall CB [assoc with Staffs] & AP,[38] loses pt to W Bromw. CB [assoc with Staffs] & AP,[39] loses pt to Sutton Coldfield MB & AP, Warws[40]). For civ abol 1966, see Aldridge UD. *Parl* S'rn Dv (1832—67), East Dv (1867—85), Handsw. Dv (1885—1918), Lichf Dv (1918—48), Lichf & Tamw. CC (1948—55), Walsall South BC (1955—70). *Eccl* Tamw. & Tutb. RDn (1849—51), Walsall RDn (1851—*). Eccl bdry: 1918 (help cr Streetly EP).[29]

BARTHOMLEY

AP Ches par (Nantwich Hd), incl in Staff tp Balterley (N Pir. Hd, sep CP 1866 in Staffs[2]) and Barthomley ent Ches thereafter, qv for organisation.

BARTON UNDER NEEDWOOD

Chap in Tatenhill AP, sep CP 1866,[2] sep EP 1796,[3] eccl refounded 1881.[13] *LG* Seq 7. Civ bdry: 1886,[41] 1934.[4] *Parl* Seq 1. *Eccl* Tamw. & Tutb. RDn (1796—1851), Tutb. RDn (1851—*). Eccl bdry: 1895 (help cr Needwood EP).[42]

BASFORD

EP Cr 1915 from Wolstanton AP (Staffs), Hartshill EP

(Warws) to be dioc Lichf.[43] Stoke upon Tr. RDn (1915—62), Newc. under Lyme RDn (1962—*). Bdry: 1934.[44]

BASWICH

AP Usual civ spelling; for eccl see 'Berkswich with Walton'. Tp 'Baswich' sometimes early called 'Baswich, Milford and Walton'. Incl chaps and tps Acton Trussell, Bednall (Bednall sometimes reputed to have been in Cannock AP, generally considered in Baswich AP) (sep par by 1671 with each chap with all rights of a par church,[1] sep status of the 2 not sustained, thereafter deemed joint tp in Baswich AP, 'Acton Trussell and Bednall' a sep CP 1866,[2] 'Acton Trussell with Bednall' a sep EP 1776[3]), tp Brocton (sep CP 1866[2]). *LG* Seq 2. Addtl civ bdry alt: 1885,[45] 1934.[4] *Parl* Seq 19.

BEDNALL

Chap and tp (sometimes reputed to have been chap in Cannock AP, generally considered in Baswich AP) in Baswich AP (eccl, 'Berkswich with Walton'); for civ organisation, for early sep eccl status (not sustained), and for later eccl status, see 'Baswich,' 'Acton Trussell and Bednall', 'Acton Trussell with Bednall'.

BENTLEY

Tp in Wolverhampton AP, sep CP 1866,[2] eccl severed 1912 to help cr Willenhall St Giles EP,[46] 'Bentley' a sep EP 1958 from the latter.[47] *LG* S Offl. Hd, Walsall PLU, RSD, RD. Civ bdry: 1931 (loses pt to Walsall CB [assoc with Staffs] & AP).[38] Abol civ 1934 pt to Darlaston AP, pt to Short Heath CP.[4] *Parl* S'rn Dv (1832—67), East Dv (1867—85), Handsw. Dv (1885—1918), Cannock Dv (1918—48). *Eccl* Wolverh. RDn.

BERKSWICH WITH WALTON

AP Usual eccl spelling; for civ and civ and eccl sep chaps and tps, see 'Baswich'. *Eccl* Pec jurisd Whittington (until 1846), Newc. & Stone RDn (1846—51), Staff. RDn (1851—*).

BETLEY

Tp and Bor in Audley AP, sep civ identity early, sep EP 1717.[3] *LG* Betley Bor, Seq 14. Civ bdry: 1965 (gains pt Blakenall CP, Checkley cum Wrinehill CP, both Ches).[6] *Parl* Seq 10. *Eccl* Newc. & Stone RDn (1717—1851), Newc. under Lyme RDn (1851—*).

BEWDLEY

Ex-par place incl in Staffs in 15th cent although usually considered in Worcs, status in Worcs asserted by statute 1543[48]; for status (incl eccl status as chap in Ribbesford) and later organisation, see entry in Worcs.

BIDDULPH

AP *LG* N Pir. Hd, Congleton PLU, RSD (1875—82), Biddulph USD (1882—94), UD. Civ bdry: 1934.[4] *Parl* Seq 6. *Eccl* Newc. RDn (until early 14th cent), Stone RDn (early 14th cent—1851), Leek RDn (1851—*). Eccl bdry: 1843 (help cr Mowcop EP,[3] refounded 1844),[49] 1864 (help cr Biddulph Moor EP),[50] 1921 (cr Knypersley EP).[51]

BIDDULPH MOOR

EP Cr 1864 from Biddulph AP, Horton AP.[50] Leek RDn.

BILSTON

Chap and tp in Wolverhampton AP, sep CP 1866,[2] sep EP 1723.[3] *LG* N Seisd. Hd, Wolverh. PLU, Bilston USD, UD (1894—1933), MB (1933—66). Civ bdry: 1934.[4] Abol civ 1966 pt to Walsall CB (assoc with Staffs) & CP, pt to W Bromw. CB (assoc with Staffs) & AP, pt to Wolverh. CB (assoc with Staffs) & AP.[6] *Parl* Wolverh. Parl Bor (1832—1918), Wolverh. Bilston Parl Bor (1918—48), Bilston BC (1948—70). *Eccl* Lapley & Trysull RDn (1723—1851), Wolverh. RDn (1851—*). Eccl bdry: 1837 (help cr Ettingshall EP),[52] 1845 (help cr Moxley EP),[53] 1845 (cr Bilston St Luke EP),[54] 1959,[55] 1972 (gains Bilston St Luke EP).[56]

BILSTON ST LUKE

EP Cr 1845 from Bilston EP.[54] Lapley & Trysull RDn (1845—51), Wolverh. RDn (1851—1972). Abol 1972 ent to Bilston EP.[56]

BILSTON ST MARY

EP Cr 1848 from Wolverhampton AP.[57] Lapley & Trysull RDn (1848—51), Wolverh. RDn (1851—*). Bdry: 1865 (help cr Bradley EP),[58] 1918.[59]

BIRCHES HEAD

EP Cr 1954 from Northwood EP.[60] Stoke upon Tr. RDn (1954—62), Stoke North RDn (1962—*).

BIRCHFIELD

EP Cr 1865 from Handsworth AP.[54] W Bromw. RDn (1865—66), Handsw. RDn (1866—*). Bdry: 1926 (help cr Witton EP [Staffs, Warws]).[61]

BISHOPS WOOD

EP Cr 1852 from Brewood AP.[62] Brew. RDn (1852—94), Penkr. RDn (1894—*).

BLACKHEATH

EP Cr 1869 from The Quinton EP, Halesowen AP (both Worcs), Rowley Regis AP (Staffs) to be dioc Worc.[63] For RDns see entry in Worcs.

BLAKENALL

EP Cr 1861 from Wolverhampton St John EP, Wolverhampton St Paul EP, Sedgley AP,[3] refounded 1862.[50] Wolverh. RDn. Bdry: 1938 (help cr Rough Hills EP),[64] 1959.[24] Now called 'Wolverhampton St Luke'.

BLAKENALL HEATH

EP Cr 1873 from Bloxwich AP.[65] Walsall RDn.

BLITHFIELD

AP *LG* S Pir. Hd, Uttox. PLU (soon after 1837[26]—1930), RSD, RD. Civ bdry: 1934.[4] *Parl* Seq 11. *Eccl* Staff. RDn (until early 14th cent), Newc. & Stone RDn (early 14th cent—1851), Rugeley RDn (1851—*).

BLORE

AP Usual civ spelling; for eccl see 'Blore Ray'. Incl pt chap Calton (sep CP 1866,[2] sep EP 1902 [qv for other constituent pars])[66]), tp Blore with Swinscoe (sep CP 1866[2]) so that 'Blore' has no sep civ identity after 1866. Perhaps also incl chap Okeover (qv for uncertain status). *LG* N Totm. Hd. *Parl* N'rn Dv (1832—67).

BLORE RAY

AP Usual eccl spelling; for civ and civ sep chap and tp, see prev entry. *Eccl* Alton & Leek RDn (until 1851), Alst. RDn (1851—1946). Abol eccl 1946 to help cr Ilam with Blore Ray and Okeover EP.[67]

BLORE WITH SWINSCOE

Tp in Blore AP (eccl, 'Blore Ray') sep CP 1866.[2] *LG* N Totm. Hd, Ashb. PLU, RSD, Mayf. RD (1894—1934), Cheadle RD (1934—74). *Parl* Seq 9.

BLOXWICH

EP Cr 1810 from Walsall AP,[3] refounded 1842.[68] Tamw. & Tutb. RDn (1810—51), Walsall RDn (1851—*). Bdry: 1873 (cr Blakenall Heath EP).[65]

BLURTON

Chap in Trentham AP, sep EP 1721,[3] eccl refounded 1832.[69] Newc. & Stone RDn (1721—1851), Trentham RDn (1851—*). Bdry: 1849 (help cr Forsbrook EP),[70] 1852 (cr Normancot EP),[71] 1853 (cr Dresden EP,[3] refounded 1867,[72] sometimes called 'Redbank'), 1948 (help cr Meir Heath EP).[37]

BLYMHILL

AP *LG* Seq 5. Civ bdry: 1934,[4] 1966 (gains pt Sheriffhales AP, earlier 'Sheriff Hales', Salop).[6] *Parl* Seq 18. *Eccl* Seq 4.

BOBBINGTON

Chap (pt Staffs [S Seisd. Hd], pt Salop [Brimstree Hd] in Calverley AP, sep civ identity early, sep EP 1726,[3] the par made 1895 ent Staffs.[73] *LG* Seisd. PLU, RSD, RD. *Parl* Staffs pt, Seq 16. *Eccl* Pec jurisd Bridgnorth (Salop, until 1846), Bridgnorth RDn (dioc Heref, 1846—1905 [Salop AD 1846—76, Ludlow AD 1876—1905], Trysull RDn (dioc Lichf, 1905—*). Eccl bdry: 1870 (help cr Tuck Hill EP [Salop, Staffs]).[51]

BRADLEY

AP Sometimes 'Bradley near Stafford'. *LG* Seq 6. Civ bdry: 1885,[74] 1934.[4] *Parl* Seq 19. *Eccl* Lapley & Trysull RDn (until 1851), Penkr. RDn (1851—*).

BRADLEY

EP Cr 1865 [St Martin] from Bilston St Mary EP, Coseley EP.[58] Wolverh. RDn.

BRADLEY IN THE MOORS

Chap in Rocester AP, sep civ identity early, sep EP 1744 as 'Bradley le Moors',[3] qv in following entry. *LG* S Totm. Hd, Cheadle PLU, RSD, RD. Abol civ 1934 pt to Alton AP, pt to Croxden AP.[4] *Parl* N'rn Dv (1832—67), North Dv (1867—85), Leek Dv (1885—1918), Stone Dv (1918—48).

BRADLEY LE MOORS

Chap in Rocester AP, sep EP 1744,[3] sep civ identity early as 'Bradley in the Moors', qv in prev entry. *Eccl* Alton & Leek RDn (1744—1851), Newc. & Stone RDn (1851—66), Cheadle RDn (1866—*).

BRADNOP AND CAWDRY

Tp in Leek AP, sep CP 1866,[2] eccl severed 1862 to help refound Onecote EP as 'Onecote cum Bradnop'.[50] *LG* Seq 22. Bdry: 1934.[4] *Parl* Seq 6.

BRAMSHALL

AP *LG* S Totm. Hd, Uttox. PLU, RSD, RD. Abol civ 1934 pt to Uttoxeter Rural CP, pt to Uttox. UD & AP.[4] *Parl* N'rn Dv (1832—67), North Dv (1867—85), Burt. Dv (1885—1948). *Eccl* Seq 3.

BRANSTON

Tp in Burton upon Trent AP, sep CP 1866,[2] eccl severed 1825 to help cr Burton upon Trent Christ Church EP,[3] eccl refounded 1845,[75] 'Branstone' a

sep EP 1870 from the latter,[51] qv. *LG* N Offl. Hd, Burt. upon Tr. PLU, pt Burt. upon Tr. MB (1878—89), pt Burt. upon Tr. USD (1878—94), Burt. upon Tr. RSD (ent 1875—78, pt 1878—94), Tutb. RD. Civ bdry: 1894 (loses the pt in Burt. upon Tr. MB to Burton Extra CP).[76] *Parl* Seq 1.

EP Renaming 1958 of Branstone EP.[47] Tutb. RDn.

BRANSTONE

EP Cr 1870 from Burton upon Trent Christ Church EP (for earlier status and sep civ identity of tp 'Branston', sep prev entry).[51] Tutb. RDn. Bdry: 1898 (help cr Burton upon Trent All Saints EP),[77] 1916 (help cr Shobnall EP, now called 'Burton upon Trent St Aidan'),[78] 1940.[24] Renamed eccl 1958 'Branston'.[47]

BRERETON

EP Cr 1838 from Rugeley AP,[3] refounded 1843 with most parochial rights,[79] remainder of rights gained 1852.[80] Tamw. & Tutb. RDn (1838—51), Rugeley RDn (1851—*). Bdry: 1870 (help cr Hednesford EP).[81]

CP Cr 1894 from the pt of Rugeley AP not in Rugeley UD.[82] *LG* Lichf PLU, RD. Abol civ 1934 pt to Cannock UD & CP, pt to Rugeley UD & AP, pt to Armitage AP, the remainder cr Brindley Heath EP.[76] *Parl* Lichf Dv (1918—48).

BREWOOD

AP *LG* Brewood Bor, Seq 1. Civ bdry: 1934,[4] 1966 (exchanges pts with Wolverh. CB [assoc with Staffs] & AP).[35] *Parl* Seq 18. *Eccl* Pec jurisd Dean of Lichf (until 1846), Lapley & Trysull RDn (1846—51), Brew. RDn (1851—94), Penkr. RDn (1894—*). Eccl bdry: 1852 (cr Bishopswood EP),[62] 1858 (cr Coven EP),[83] 1869 (help cr Gailey cum Hatherton EP).[84]

BRIERLEY HILL

EP Cr 1842 from Kingswinford AP.[51] Lapley & Trysull RDn (1842—51), Himley RDn (1851—*). Bdry: 1844 (cr Brockmoor EP, cr Quarry Bank EP),[85] 1930 (loses pt to Dudley St Augustine, Holly Hall EP, Worcs, dioc Worcs).[86]

CP Cr 1894 from the pt of Kingswinford AP in Brierley Hill UD.[87] *LG* Stourbridge PLU, Brierley Hill UD. Bdry: 1936[18]; see also alt in civ and in parl bdry 1954 affecting the UD, in the following entry. For civ abol 1966, see Brierley Hill UD. *Parl* Kingswinf. Dv (1918—48), Brierley Hill CC (1948—70).

UD Brierley Hill UD comprised of the following pars: Brierley Hill CP, Kingswinford AP, Quarry Bank CP. Civ bdry: 1954 (loses pt to Dudley CB [assoc with Worcs] & AP).[88] The UD abol 1966 pt to Stourbridge MB & CP (Worcs), pt to Dudley CB (as CB becomes assoc with Staffs) & AP, pt to help cr Warley CB (assoc with Worcs) & CP, pt to Himley AP, pt to Kinver AP (both Staffs).[6] Parl bdry: 1955.[89]

BRINDLEY HEATH

CP Cr 1934 from the pt of Brereton CP not transf to Cannock UD & AP or to Rugeley UD & AP or to Armitage AP.[4] *LG* Lichf RD. *Parl* Lichf & Tamw. CC (1948—70), Cannock CC (1970—*).

BROCKMOOR

EP Cr 1844 from Brierley Hill EP.[85] Lapley & Trysull RDn (1844—51), Himley RDn (1851—*).

BROCTON

Tp in Baswich AP (eccl, 'Berkswich with Walton'), sep CP 1866.[2] *LG* Seq 2. Bdry: 1885,[45] 1934.[4] *Parl* Seq 19.

ABBOT'S BROMLEY

AP *LG* Abbot's Bromley Bor, S Pir. Hd, Uttox. PLU, RSD, RD. *Parl* Seq 11. *Eccl* Staff. RDn (until early 14th cent), Newc. & Stone RDn (early 14th cent—before 1535), Tamw. & Tutb. RDn (before 1535—1851), Rugeley RDn (1851—*). Eccl bdry: 1874 (help cr Hoar Cross EP).[90]

KING'S BROMLEY

AP Chap appropriated to Alrewas Priory, sep par from Dissolution.[91] *LG* Seq 8. Civ bdry: 1922 (gains King's Bromley Hays CP),[92] 1934.[4] *Parl* Seq 2. *Eccl* Pec jurisd Dean & Chapter of Lichf (until 1846), Seq 12 thereafter.

KING'S BROMLEY HAYS

Ex-par place, sep CP 1858.[10] *LG* N Offl. Hd, Lichf PLU (1858—1922), RSD, RD. Abol civ 1922 ent to King's Bromley AP.[92] *Parl* N'rn Dv (1832—67), East Dv (1867—85), Lichf Dv (1885—1948).

WEST BROMWICH

The following have 'West Bromwich' in their names. Insofar as any existed at a given time: *LG* S Offl. Hd, W Bromw. PLU, USD, MB (1882—89), CB, USD. *Parl* S'rn Dv (1832—67), Wednesbury Parl Bor (1867—85), W Bromw. Parl Bor/BC (1885—1970), pt W Bromw. South West BC, pt W Bromw. North East BC (1970—*). *Eccl* Tamw. & Tutb. RDn (until 1851), Handsw. RDn (1851—94), W Bromw. RDn (1894—*).

AP1—WEST BROMWICH [ALL SAINTS]—Perhaps orig pt of Handsworth AP but sep par by 12th cent.[93] Civ bdry: 1897,[94] 1928 (gains pt Perry Barr UD & CP,[95] as most of the remainder [qv] transf to be 'Perry Barr' CP in Birm CB [assoc with Warws]96), 1931 (loses pt to Walsall CB [assoc with Staffs] & AP),[38] 1931,[39] 1931,[97] 1966 (incl exchanges pts with Walsall CB [assoc with Staffs] & AP, exchanges pts with Birm CB [assoc with Warws] & AP, gains pt Smethw. CB [assoc with Staffs] & CP, loses pt to help cr Warley CB [assoc with Worcs] & CP).[6] Transf 1974 to W Midlands.[7] Eccl bdry: 1837 (cr EP1),[98] 1841 (cr EP4),[3] 1844 (cr Hill Top EP),[99] 1875 (help cr Wednesbury St Paul, Wood Green EP),[61] 1879 (help cr EP5),[100] 1937 (help cr EP6),[101] 1969.[102]

EP1—WEST BROMWICH CHRIST CHURCH—Cr 1837 from AP1.[98] Bdry: 1858 (cr EP9,[3] refounded 1861103), 1879 (help cr EP7),[104] 1879 (help cr EP5),[100] 1900 (cr EP10).[105]

EP2—WEST BROMWICH THE GOOD SHEPHERD—Cr 1910 from EP7, EP4.[106] Abol 1966 pt to help cr EP3, pt to EP4.[77]

EP3—WEST BROMWICH THE GOOD SHEPHERD WITH ST JOHN—Cr 1966 by union pt EP2, ent EP7.[77]

EP4—WEST BROMWICH HOLY TRINITY—Cr 1841 from AP1.[3] Bdry: 1910 (help cr EP2),[106]

1966.[77]

EP5—WEST BROMWICH ST ANDREW—Cr 1879 from AP1, EP1, EP9, Hill Top EP.[100]

EP6—WEST BROMWICH ST FRANCIS—Cr 1937 from AP1, Wednesbury St Paul, Wood Green EP.[101] Bdry: 1969.[102]

—WEST BROMWICH ST JAMES—Name used now for EP cr 1844 as 'Hill Top', qv.

EP7—WEST BROMWICH ST JOHN THE EVANGELIST—Cr 1879 from EP1.[104] Bdry: 1910 (help cr EP2).[106] Abol 1966 to help cr EP3.[77]

EP8—WEST BROMWICH ST PAUL, GOLDS HILL—Cr 1887 from Hill Top EP.[81]

EP9—WEST BROMWICH ST PETER—Cr 1858 from EP1,[3] refounded 1861.[103] Bdry: 1879 (help cr EP5).[100]

EP10—WEST BROMWICH ST PHILIP—Cr 1900 from EP1.[105]

BROOM

AP Staffs par (S Seisd. Hd), transf to Worcs 1832 for parl purposes, 1844 for civ purposes (Halfshire Hd).[107] *LG* Kidderminster PLU. For remainder of civ and parl organisation, and for all eccl organisation, see entry in Worcs.

BROUGHTON

EP Cr 1787 from Ecclesall AP,[3] refounded 1907 from Croxton EP (an EP cr 1857 from Ecclesall AP, qv).[108] Newc. & Stone RDn (1787—1851), Ecclesall RDn (1851—*). Bdry: 1921.[109]

BROWN EDGE

Area in Norton in the Moors (chap in Stoke on Trent AP, sep civ identity early, sep EP 1729 as 'Norton le Moors'3), 'Brown Edge' a sep EP 1844 from Norton le Moors EP,[99] sep CP 1965.[6] *LG* Leek RD. *Parl* Leek CC (1970—*). *Eccl* Alton & Leek RDn (1844—51), Leek RDn (1851—*).

BROWNHILLS

UD Brownhills UD comprised of the following pars: Hammerwich (1894—96), Norton Canes, Ogley Hay (1894—96, ent 1896—1966), Shire Oak, Walsall Wood. The UD abol 1966 pt to help cr Aldridge-Brownhills UD & CP, pt to Cannock UD & AP, pt to Hammerwich CP.[6] *Parl* See constituent pars.

BUCKNALL

Chap in Stoke upon Trent AP, sep EP 1716 (incl chap Bagnall in same par),[3] 'Bagnall' a sep EP 1736 from the latter[3] but does not sustain sep eccl identity, the reunited EP refounded 1849 as 'Bucknall cum Bagnall',[110] qv in following entry. Newc. & Stone RDn.

BUCKNALL CUM BAGNALL

EP Refounding 1849 of reunited EP (see prev entry for sep status of Bagnall EP from Bucknall EP, both orig in Stoke upon Trent AP).[110] Newc. & Stone RDn (1807—51), Stoke upon Tr. RDn (1851—1920), Leek RDn (1920—62), Stoke upon Tr. RDn (1962—*). Bdry: 1902,[111] 1964 (help cr Werrington EP).[112]

BURNTWOOD

Hmlt in Lichfield St Michael AP, sep EP 1821 as 'Burntwood',[3] as such eccl refounded 1845,[65] sep CP 1866 as 'Burntwood, Edial and Woodhouses',[2] qv in following entry, until renamed 1929 'Burnt-wood' after bdry alt.[113] *LG* Lichf RD. Civ bdry: 1934,[4] 1966.[6] *Parl* Lichf & Tamw. CC (1948—*). *Eccl* Tamw. & Tutb. RDn (1845—51), Lichf RDn (1851—*). Eccl bdry: 1867 (help cr Chasetown EP).[114]

BURNTWOOD, EDIAL AND WOODHOUSES
Hmlt in Lichfield St Michael AP, sep CP 1866,[2] sep EP 1821 as 'Burntwood,'[3] as such eccl refounded,[65] qv in prev entry. *LG* S Offl. Hd, Lichf PLU, RSD, RD. Civ bdry: 1879.[115] Renamed civ 1929 'Burnt-wood'.[113] *Parl* S'rn Dv (1832—67), East Dv (1867—85), Lichf Dv (1885—1948).

BURSLEM
Chap in Stoke upon Trent AP, some parochial rights from 16th cent, sep civ identity early, sep EP 1849.[110] *LG* N Pir. Hd, Wolstanton & Burslem PLU (1838—1922), Stoke and Wolstanton PLU (1922—30), Burslem MB (pt 1878—94 [enlarged pt 1891—94], ent 1894—1910), pt Burslem USD (1878—91 [enlarged pt 1891—94]), Wolstanton & Burslem RSD (ent 1875—78, pt 1878—94 [reduced pt 1891—94]), Stoke on Tr. CB (1910—22). Civ bdry: 1894 (the pt not in the MB cr Milton CP).[116] Abol civ 1922 ent to Stoke on Trent AP.[117] *Parl* Stoke upon Tr. Parl Bor (pt 1832—67, ent 1867—85), pt N'rn Dv (1832—67); pt Hanley Parl Bor, pt Stoke upon Trent Parl Bor (1885—1918); see Part III of the *Guide* for composition of Stoke on Tr. Parl Bors (1918—48) by wards of the CB. *Eccl* Newc. & Stone RDn (1809—51), Stoke upon Tr. RDn (1851—94), Hanley RDn (1894—1920), Stoke upon Tr. RDn (1920—62), Stoke North RDn (1962—*). Eccl bdry: 1809 (cr Burslem St Paul EP,[3] refounded 1845[118]), 1844 (cr Sneyd EP),[119] 1844,[120] 1845 (cr Cobridge EP),[118] 1941.[106]

BURSLEM ST PAUL
EP Cr 1809 from Burslem AP,[3] refounded 1845.[118] Newc. & Stone RDn (1809—51), Stoke upon Tr. RDn (1851—94), Hanley RDn (1894—1920), Stoke upon Tr. RDn (1920—62), Stoke North RDn (1962—*). Bdry: 1881 (help cr Tunstall St Mary the Virgin EP).[121]

BURSLEM ST WERBURGH
EP Cr 1939 from Sneyd EP.[122] Stoke upon Tr. RDn (1939—62), Stoke North RDn (1962—*). Bdry: 1958.[123]

BURTON EXTRA
Tp in Burton upon Trent AP, sep CP 1866.[2] *LG* N Offl. Hd, Burt. upon Tr. PLU, MB (1878—89), CB (1889—1904), RSD (1875—78), USD (1878—94). Bdry: 1887,[41] 1894 (gains the pt of Branston CP in Burt. upon Tr. CB [assoc with Staffs]).[76] Abol 1904 ent to Burton upon Trent AP.[124] *Parl* N'rn Dv (1832—67), East Dv (1867—85), Burt. Dv (1885—1918).

BURTON UPON TRENT
The following have 'Burton upon Trent' in their names. Insofar as any existed at a given time: *LG* Burt. upon Tr. PLU, USD, MB (1878—89), CB; Hds and Bor sep noted. *Parl* Staffs pt, Seq 1. *Eccl* Tamw. & Tutb. RDn (until 1851), Tutb. RDn (1851—*).

AP1—BURTON UPON TRENT [ST MOWDEN]—Tp
'Burton upon Trent' in Staffs (N Offl. Hd, Burton upon Tr. Bor) as were tp Branston (sep CP 1866,[2] eccl severed 1825 [incl pt main tp] to help cr EP2,[3] eccl refounded 1845,[75] 'Branstone' a sep EP 1870 from EP2,[51] eccl renamed 1958 'Bran-ston'[47]), tp Burton Extra (sep CP 1866[2]), tps Horninglow, Stretton (each a sep CP 1866,[2] both eccl severed 1825 to help cr EP3,[3] the latter eccl refounded 1842,[125] 'Horninglow' a sep EP 1867 from EP3,[126] 'Stretton' a sep EP 1844 from EP3,[3] refounded 1873 as 'Stretton cum Wetmoor'[127]); incl in Derbys (Repton & Greasley Hd) tp Winshill (sep CP 1866 in Derbys,[2] eccl severed 1825 to help cr EP3,[3] the latter refounded 1842,[125] 'Winshill' a sep EP 1867 from EP3[126]), incl eccl chap and tp Chilcote (civ in Derbys, qv for sep civ identity 1866 in Derbys; lost eccl early to Clifton Campville, the union 'Clifton Campville with Chilcote' qv). 'Burton upon Trent' thus ent Staffs from 1866. Addtl civ bdry alt: 1886,[41] 1904 (gains the other CPs in Burt. upon Tr. CB: Burton Extra CP, Horninglow CP, Stapenhill CP, Winshill CP),[124] 1934 (gains pt Bretby CP, Derbys).[128] Addtl eccl bdry alt: 1873 (help cr EP5),[129] 1969 (incl gains EP3).[130]

EP1—BURTON UPON TRENT ALL SAINTS—Cr
1898 from EP2, Branstone EP.[77]

EP2—BURTON UPON TRENT CHRIST CHURCH—
Cr 1825 from AP1 (incl tp Branston),[3] refounded 1845.[75] Bdry: 1870 (area of tp Branston severed to cr 'Branstone' EP,[51] renamed 1958 'Bran-ston'[47]), 1873 (help cr EP5),[129] 1898 (help cr EP1),[77] 1916 (help cr Shobnall EP, now called 'Burton upon Trent St Aidan').[78]

EP3—BURTON UPON TRENT HOLY TRINITY—Cr
1825 from AP1 (incl Staffs tps Horninglow, Stretton, Derbys tp Winshill, all in AP1),[3] refounded 1842.[125] Bdry: 1844 (cr Stretton EP,[3] refounded 1873 as 'Stretton cum Wetmoor'[127]), 1867 (area of tps Horninglow, Winshill each severed to cr respectively Horninglow EP, Winshill EP),[126] 1873 (help cr EP5).[129] Abol 1969 ent to AP1.[130]

—BURTON UPON TRENT ST AIDAN—Name used
now for EP cr 1916 as 'Shobnall', qv.

EP4—BURTON UPON TRENT ST CHAD—Cr 1903
from Horninglow EP.[131]

EP5—BURTON UPON TRENT ST PAUL—Cr 1873
from AP1, EP3, EP2.[129]

BUSHBURY
AP Tp 'Bushbury' in N Seisd. Hd; incl in E Cutt. Hd tp Essington (sep CP 1866,[2] sep EP 1934 from Bushbury AP, Wednesfield EP[132]). *LG* N Seisd. Hd (pt until 1866, ent from 1866), pt E Cutt. Hd (until 1866), Penkr. PLU (1836—70s), Cannock PLU (1870s—1930), RSD, RD. Addtl civ bdry alt: 1927 (loses pt to Wolverh. CB [assoc with Staffs] & AP),[133] 1933 (loses pt to Wolverh. CB [assoc with Staffs] & AP).[134] Abol civ 1934 pt to Brewood AP, pt to Featherstone CP.[4] *Parl* S'rn Dv (1832—67), West Dv (1867—85), Kingswinf. Dv (1885—1918), Cannock Dv (1918—48). *Eccl* Lapley & Trysull

RDn (until 1851), Brew. RDn (1851—94), Wolverh. RDn (1894—*). Addtl eccl bdry alt: 1953 (cr Oxley EP),[135] 1964 (help cr Wednesfield St Gregory the Great EP).[136]

BUTTERTON

Chap in Mayfield AP, sep CP 1866,[2] sep EP 1775.[3] *LG* S Totm. Hd, Alst. GilbU (until 1869), Leek PLU (1869—1930), RSD, RD. Civ bdry: 1934.[4] *Parl* Seq 6. *Eccl* Alton & Leek RDn (1775—1851), Alst. RDn (1851—*).

BUTTERTON

EP Cr 1845 from Trentham AP, Stoke upon Trent AP, Swynnerton AP,[3] refounded 1845.[53] Newc. & Stone RDn (1845—51), Trentham RDn (1851—1940). Abol 1940 to help cr Newcastle under Lyme with Butterton EP.[137]

CALDMORE

EP Cr 1872 from Walsall AP.[138] Walsall RDn. Bdry: 1902 (cr Walsall Palfrey EP),[109] 1939 (help cr Walsall St Gabriel EP).[139] Now called 'Walsall St Michael'.

CALDON—see CAULDON

CALTON

Chap in Blore AP (eccl, 'Blore Ray'), Mayfield AP, Waterfall AP, sep CP 1866,[2] sep EP 1902 from those 3 APs and from Croxden AP.[66] *LG* P N Totm. Hd (the area orig in Blore AP), pt S Totm. Hd (the remainder), Ashb. PLU, RSD, Mayf. RD. Civ bdry: 1886.[140] Abol civ 1934 to help cr Waterhouses CP.[4] *Parl* N'rn Dv (1832—67), North Dv (1867—85), Leek Dv (1885—1948). *Eccl* Alst. RDn. Eccl bdry: 1917.[141]

CALWICH

Tp in Ellastone AP, sep CP 1866.[2] *LG* S Totm. Hd, Ashb. PLU, RSD, Mayf. RD. Abol 1934 ent to Ellastone AP.[4] *Parl* N'rn Dv (1832—67), North Dv (1867—85), Leek Dv (1885—1918), Stone Dv (1918—48).

CANNOCK

AP Prob dependent on Penkr. Collegiate Church and therefore in Penkridge AP (if dependent on College), sep par at Dissolution.[142] Incl tp Great Wyrley (sep CP 1866,[2] sep EP 1845,[3] eccl refounded 1846[143]), tp Huntington (sep CP 1866[2]); sometimes reputed to have incl chap Bednall, the latter generally considered in Baswich AP (eccl, 'Berkswich with Walton'), qv. *LG* E Cutt. Hd, Penkr. PLU (1836—70s), Cannock PLU (1870s—1930), USD, UD. Addtl civ bdry alt: 1934,[4] 1966.[35] *Parl* S'rn Dv (1832—67), West Dv (1867—85), W'rn Dv (1885—1918), Cannock Dv/CC (1918—*). *Eccl* Pec jurisd Dean & Chapter of Lichf (until 1846), Lapley & Trysull RDn (1846—51), Rugeley RDn (1851—*). Addtl eccl bdry alt: 1840 (help cr Gentleshaw EP),[144] 1870 (help cr Hednesford EP),[81] 1905.[145]

CANWELL

Ex-par place, sep CP 1858,[10] sep EP 1927.[146] *LG* S Offl. Hd, Tamw. PLU (soon after 1836[26]—1930), RSD, RD. Civ bdry: 1896.[147] Abol civ 1934 ent to Hints AP.[4] *Parl* S'rn Dv (1832—67), East Dv (1867—85), Lichf Dv (1885—1948). *Eccl* Lichf RDn.

CASTLE CHURCH

AP Orig chap in Stafford St Mary Collegiate Church with all rights except burial, that right gained in 1573 and completely independent thereafter.[148] *LG* E Cutt. Hd, Staff. PLU, MB (pt 1835—94 [enlarged pt 1876—94]), pt Staff. USD (enlarged pt 1876—94), pt Staff. RSD (reduced pt 1876—94), Staff. RD. Civ bdry: 1894 (loses the pt in the MB to Stafford St Mary and St Chad CP as the latter renamed 'Stafford' CP),[149] 1917,[150] 1934.[4] *Parl* Staff. Parl Bor (pt 1832—67, ent 1867—1918), pt S'rn Dv (1832—67), Staff. Dv (1918—48), Staff. & Stone CC (1948—*). *Eccl* Pec jurisd royal free chap of Stafford St Mary (until 1846), Newc. & Stone RDn (1846—51), Staff. RDn (1851—*). Eccl bdry: 1844 (cr Forebridge EP),[151] 1962 (help cr Rickerscote EP).[152]

CASTLE TOWN

EP Cr 1867 from Forebridge EP.[46] Staff. RDn. Bdry: 1936.[153] Now called 'Stafford St Thomas'.

CAULDON

Chap (sometimes early 'Caldon') in Irlam AP, sep civ identity early, sep EP 1748.[3] *LG* N Totm. Hd, Cheadle PLU, RSD, RD. Abol civ 1934 to help cr Waterhouses CP.[4] *Parl* N'rn Dv (1832—67), North Dv (1867—85), Leek Dv (1885—1918), Stone Dv (1918—48). *Eccl* Alton & Leek RDn (1748—1851), Alst. RDn (1851—*).

CAVERSWALL

AP *LG* N Totm. Hd, Cheadle PLU, pt East Vale USD (1875—83), pt Longton MB & USD (1883—94), pt Cheadle RSD, Cheadle RD. Civ bdry: 1883,[8] 1894 (the pt in the MB cr East Vale CP),[154] 1922 (incl loses pt to Stoke on Tr. CB [assoc with Staffs] & AP),[117] 1934,[4] 1965 (exchanges pts with Stoke on Tr. CB [assoc with Staffs] & AP).[35] *Parl* N'rn Dv (1832—67), pt Stoke upon Tr. Parl Bor (1867—1918 [area of the East Vale Local Government Dist/ USD, then in Longton MB]), pt North Dv (1867—85), pt Leek Dv (1885—1918), Stone Dv (1918—48), Leek CC (1948—*). *Eccl* Seq 2. Eccl bdry: 1899 (help cr Longton St Mary and St Chad EP),[155] 1902,[111] 1926 (help cr Meir EP),[156] 1964 (help cr Werrington EP),[112] 1964.[157]

CHAPEL AND HILL CHORLTON

Chap in Eccleshall AP, sep CP 1866,[2] sep EP 1743 as 'Chapel Chorlton',[3] qv. *LG* Seq 14. Bdry: 1932.[27] *Parl* Seq 10.

CHAPEL CHORLTON

Chap in Eccleshall AP, sep EP 1743,[3] sep CP 1866 as 'Chapel and Hill Chorlton',[2] qv. Newc. & Stone RDn (1743—1851), Ecclesh. RDn (1851—*).

CHARTLEY HOLME

Ex-par place, sep CP 1858.[10] *LG* S Pir. Hd, Staff. PLU (1858—1930), RSD, RD. Abol civ 1934 ent to Stowe AP.[4] *Parl* N'rn Dv (1832—67), West Dv (1867—85), W'rn Dv (1885—1918), Staff. Dv (1918—48).

CHASETOWN

EP Cr 1867 from Burntwood EP, Ogley Hall EP, Hammerwich EP.[114] Lichf RDn.

CHEADLE

AP *LG* Seq 24. Civ bdry: 1883,[8] 1896 (help cr

Oakamoor CP).[158] *Parl* Seq 9. *Eccl* Seq 2. Eccl bdry: 1833 (cr Oakamoor EP,[3] refounded 1864[159]), 1847 (cr Freehay EP).[160]

CHEBSEY

AP Incl tp Cold Norton (sep CP 1866[2]). *LG* Seq 18. Addtl civ bdry alt: 1932 (gains Cold Norton CP).[27] *Parl* N'rn Dv (1832—67), West Dv (1867—85), Handsw. Dv (1885—1918), Stone Dv (1918—48), Staff. & Stone CC (1948—*). *Eccl* Seq 10.

CHECKLEY

AP *LG* Seq 24. Civ bdry: 1883,[8] 1893,[161] 1934.[4] *Parl* Seq 9. *Eccl* Seq 3. Eccl bdry: 1844 (cr Upper Tean EP),[162] 1897 (help cr Foxt with Whiston EP).[163]

CHEDDLETON

AP Orig sep AP (Alton & Leek RDn), considered before 1535 a chap in Leek AP,[164] sep civ identity early, sep EP 1721.[3] Incl tp Consall (sep CP 1866[2]). *LG* N Totm. Hd, Cheadle PLU, RSD, RD. Civ bdry: 1934.[4] *Parl* Seq 9. *Eccl* Alton & Leek RDn (1721—1851), Leek RDn (1851—*). Eccl bdry: 1862 (cr Wetley Rocks EP).[3]

CHELL

CP Cr 1894 from pt of the rural pt of Wolstanton AP.[113] *LG* Wolstanton PLU, RD (1894—1904), Smallthorne UD (1904—22). Civ bdry: 1899,[165] 1904.[166] Abol 1922 ent to Stoke on. Tr. CB (assoc with Staffs) & AP.[117] *Parl* Leek Dv (1918—48).

EP Cr 1925 from Newchapel EP.[167] Newc. under Lyme RDn (1825—62), 1966.[168]

CHESLYN HAY

Ex-par place, sep CP 1858.[10] *LG* Seq 1. Civ bdry: 1934.[4] *Parl* Seq 17.

CHESTERTON

EP Cr 1846 from Audley EP, Wolstanton AP.[33] Newc. & Stone RDn (1846—51), Newc. under Lyme RDn (1851—*). Bdry: 1932 (help cr Alsagers Bank EP).[11]

CP Cr 1894 from pt of the rural pt of Wolstanton AP.[113] *LG* Wolstanton and Burslem PLU (1894—1922), Stoke and Wolstanton PLU (1922—30), Wolstanton RD (1894—1904), Wolstanton United UD (1904—32). Abol 1932 ent to Newc. under Lyme MB & AP.[169] *Parl* Newc. under Lyme Parl Bor (1918—48).

CHESWARDINE

AP In Staffs *temp* Domesday Book, thereafter in Salop, qv for main entry.

CHURCH EATON

AP *LG* Church Eaton Bor, W Cutt. Hd, Penkr. PLU (1836—70s), Cannock PLU (1870s—1930), RSD, Gnosall RD (1894—1934), Staff. RD (1934—74). Civ bdry: 1934.[4] *Parl* Seq 19. *Eccl* Lapley & Trysull RDn (until 1851), Penkr. RDn (1851—94), Staff. RDn (1894—*).

CLAYTON

CP Cr 1896 from Stoke Rural CP,[170] Trentham AP.[171] *LG* Newc. under Lyme PLU, RD. Bdry: 1921,[172] 1927.[173] Abol 1932 ent to Newc. under Lyme AP.[169] *Parl* Stone Dv (1918—48).

EP Cr 1969 from Newcastle under Lyme with Butterton EP.[23] Newc. under Lyme RDn.

CLENT

AP In Worcs *temp* Domesday Book, soon thereafter

considered in Staffs (S Seisd. Hd),[174] transf to Worcs 1832 for parl purposes, 1844 for civ purposes (Halfshire Hd).[107] Incl in Staffs chap Rowley Regis (sep civ identity early in Staffs, sep EP 1848[175]). *LG* Bromsgrove PLU. For remainder of civ and parl organisation, and for all eccl organisation, see entry in Worcs.

CLIFTON CAMPVILLE AND HAUNTON

AP Usual civ spelling (Haunton a hmlt, orig a chap, not sep civ); for eccl see following entry. Incl chap Harlaston (sep CP 1866,[2] sep EP 1846[176]). *LG* Seq 9. *Parl* Seq 2.

CLIFTON CAMPVILLE WITH CHILCOTE

AP Usual eccl spelling after Clifton Campville AP gains early eccl chap and tp Chilcote (civ in Derbys, qv for sep civ identity 1866 in Derbys); for civ, see prev entry. *Eccl* Seq 13. Addtl eccl bdry alt: by end of 18th cent (gains eccl Statfold AP [church of prebend (sometimes 'Stotfold') of Cathedral Chapter of Lichf, sep civ identity retained, sometimes eccl claimed to be in Lichfield St Mary AP but unused except for burials and eccl in this par]),[177] 1967.[178]

CODSALL

Orig chap in Tettenhall AP,[179] sep civ identity early, sep EP 1756.[3] *LG* Seq 20. Civ bdry: 1966.[6] *Parl* Seq 16. *Eccl* Lapley & Trysull RDn (until 1851), Brew. RDn (1851—94), Penkr. RDn (1894—*). Eccl bdry: 1962.[180]

COLTON

AP *LG* Colton Bor, S Pir. Hd, Lichf PLU, RSD, RD. Civ bdry: 1883,[8] 1885,[181] 1934.[4] *Parl* N'rn Dv (1832—67), West Dv (1867—85), Lichf Dv (1885—1948), Lichf & Tamw. CC (1948—*). *Eccl* Newc. & Stone RDn (until before 1535), Tamw. & Tutb. RDn (before 1535—1851), Rugeley RDn (1851—*).

COLWICH

AP Incl chap Fradswell (sep CP 1866,[2] sep EP 1851[182]). *LG* S Pir. Hd, Staff. PLU, RSD, RD. Addtl civ bdry alt: 1883,[8] 1885,[181] 1885,[45] 1886,[183] 1934.[4] *Parl* Seq 12. *Eccl* Pec jurisd Dean & Chapter of Lichf (until 1846), Tamw. & Tutb. RDn (1846—51), Rugeley RDn (1851—*). Addtl eccl bdry alt: 1848 (help cr Hixon EP),[184] 1854 (help cr Great Haywood EP).[185]

CONSALL

Tp in Cheddleton AP (orig sep AP, considered before 1535 a chap in Leek AP, sep civ identity early, sep EP 1721[3]), 'Consall' a sep CP 1866.[2] *LG* Seq 21. Bdry: 1934.[4] *Parl* Seq 9.

COPPENHALL

Chap in Penkridge AP, sep CP 1866,[2] sep EP 1744.[3] *LG* Seq 1. *Parl* Seq 18. *Eccl* Lapley & Trysull RDn (1744—1851), Penkr. RDn (1851—*). Eccl bdry: 1958.[186]

COBRIDGE

EP Cr 1845 from Burslem AP.[118] Newc. & Stone RDn (1845—51), Stoke upon Tr. RDn (1851—94), Hanley RDn (1894—1920), Stoke upon Tr. RDn (1920—62), Stoke North RDn (1862—*). Bdry: 1865 (help cr Milton EP),[122] 1941,[106] 1955 (incl cr Sneyd Green EP).[187]

COSELEY
Area in Sedgley AP, sep EP 1832,[141] sep CP 1903 from the pt of Sedgley AP in Coseley UD.[188] *LG* Dudley PLU, Coseley UD. Civ bdry: 1929 (loses pt to Dudley CB [assoc with Worcs] & AP),[189] 1954 (loses pt to Dudley CB [assoc with Worcs] & AP).[88] Abol civ 1966 pt to Dudley CB (as CB becomes assoc with Staffs) & AP, pt to W Bromw. CB (assoc with Staffs) & AP, pt to Walsall CB (assoc with Staffs) & CP, pt to Wolverh. CB (assoc with Staffs) & AP.[6] *Parl* Wolverh. Bilston Parl Bor (1918—48), Bilston BC (1948—70). Parl bdry: 1955.[89] *Eccl* Lapley & Trysull RDn (until 1851), Himley RDn (1851—*). Eccl bdry: 1865 (help cr Bradley [St Martin] EP),[58] 1873 (help cr Sedgley St Mary the Virgin EP),[190] 1884 (help cr West Coseley EP).[191]

COSELEY ST CHAD
EP Renaming 1956 of West Coseley EP.[192] Himley RDn.

WEST COSELEY
EP Cr 1884 from Coseley EP, Sedgley EP.[191] Himley RDn. Renamed 1956 'Coseley St Chad'.[192]

COTES HEATH
EP Cr 1844 from Eccleshall AP (incl pt tp Aspley, pt tp Slindon, both in same par, neither sep civ).[193] Newc. & Stone RDn (1844—51), Ecclesh. RDn (1851—*).

COTTON
Tp in Alton AP, sep CP 1866,[2] sep EP 1796,[3] sep eccl status not sustained, the area eccl severed 1932 from Alton AP to help cr Oakamoor with Cotton EP.[13] *LG* Seq 24. Civ bdry: 1883,[8] 1896 (help cr Oakamoor CP).[158] *Parl* Seq 9.

COVEN
EP Cr 1858 from Brewood AP.[83] Brew. RDn (1858—94), Penkr. RDn (1894—*).

CRADLEY HEATH—see REDDAL HILL
CRESSWELL
AP Orig sep AP, unused by 1633 and thereafter ex-par, sep CP 1858,[10] eccl abol 1930 to help cr Seighford with Derrington and Cresswell EP.[194] *LG* S Pir. Hd, Staff. PLU (1858—1930), RSD, RD. Civ bdry: 1917,[150] 1934.[4] *Parl* Seq 12.

CROSS HEATH
EP Cr 1952 from Wolstanton AP, Newcastle under Lyme St George EP.[195] Newc. under Lyme RDn.

CROXALL
AP Tp 'Croxall' pt in Derbys (Repton and Gresley Hd), pt in Staffs (N Offl. Hd), the par made 1895 ent Staffs[25]; incl in Derbys (Repton and Gresley Hd) tp Catton (sep CP 1866 in Derbys[2]). *LG* Tamw. PLU, RSD, pt sep RD in Derbys (1894—95), Tamw. RD (pt 1894—95, ent 1895—1934). Abol civ 1934 ent to Edingale CP.[4] *Parl* Staffs pt, N'rn Dv (1832—67), East Dv (1867—85), Lichf Dv (1885—1948). *Eccl* See entry in Derbys; incl eccl bdry alt 1899 (loses pt to Edingale EP).[196]

CROXDEN
AP Uncertain if orig sep AP, prob so after Dissolution.[197] *LG* Seq 26. Addtl civ bdry alt: 1883 (loses pt to Doveridge AP, Derbys),[8] 1886,[140] 1934.[4] *Parl* Seq 7. *Eccl* Sometimes as 'Croxden with Hollington', Alton & Leek RDn (until 1851), Uttox.

RDn (1851—*). Eccl bdry: 1902 (help cr Calton EP).[66]

CROXTON
EP Cr 1857 from Eccleshall AP.[198] Ecclesh. RDn. Bdry: 1907 (help refound Broughton St Peter EP).[108]

CURBOROUGH AND ELMHURST
Tp (N Offl. Hd) in Lichfield St Chad AP (o'wise Staff. Bor/MB), sep CP 1866.[2] *LG* Seq 8. Bdry: 1879.[114] *Parl* Seq 2.

DARLASTON
AP *LG* S Offl. Hd, Walsall PLU, Darlaston USD, UD. Civ bdry: 1883,[8] 1934,[4] 1934 (gains pt Walsall CB [assoc with Staffs] & CP),[199] 1937.[200] Abol civ 1966 pt to Walsall CB (assoc with Staffs) & CP, pt to Wolverh. CB (assoc with Staffs) & AP.[6] *Parl* S'rn Dv (1832—67), Wednesb. Parl Bor/BC (1867—1970). *Eccl* Tamw. & Tutb. RDn (until 1851), Walsall RDn (1851—94), Wednesb. RDn (1894—*). Eccl bdry: 1844 (cr Darlaston St George EP),[201] 1845 (help cr Moxley EP),[53] 1872 (help cr Darlaston All Saints EP),[202] 1973 (gains Darlaston St George EP).[203]

DARLASTON ALL SAINTS
EP Cr 1872 from Darlaston AP, Wednesbury AP.[202] Walsall RDn (1872—94), Wednesb. RDn (1894—*).

DARLASTON ST GEORGE
EP Cr 1845 from Darlaston AP.[201] Tamw. & Tutb. RDn (1844—51), Walsall RDn (1851—94), Wednesb. RDn (1894—1973). Abol 1973 ent to Darlaston AP.[203]

DENSTONE
Tp in Alton AP, sep CP 1866,[2] sep EP 1860 from Alston AP (tp Denston), Ellastone AP (tp Prestwood), Rocester AP.[14] *LG* S Totm. Hd, Cheadle PLU, RSD, RD (1894—1934), Uttox. RD (1934—74). Civ bdry: 1896,[15] 1934 (gains Prestwood CP).[4] *Parl* Seq 8. *Eccl* Cheadle RDn (1860—94), Uttox. RDn (1894—*).

DERRINGTON
EP Area in Seighford AP (existed before 16th cent, rebuilt 1845[204]), sep EP 1847.[3] Newc. & Stone RDn (1847—51), Staff. RDn (1851—1930). Abol 1930 to help cr Seighford with Derrington and Creswell EP.[194]

DILHORNE
AP *LG* Seq 21. Civ bdry: 1896 (cr Forsbrook CP).[205] *Parl* Seq 9. *Eccl* Seq 2. Eccl bdry: 1849 (help cr Forsbrook EP).[70]

DRAYCOTT IN THE CLAY
Tp in Hanbury AP, sep CP 1866.[2] *LG* Seq 10. Civ bdry: 1934.[4] *Parl* Seq 1.

DRAYCOTT IN THE MOORS
AP Usual civ spelling; for ecccl see following entry. *LG* Seq 24. *Parl* Seq 9.

DRAYCOTT LE MOORS
AP Usual eccl spelling; for civ see prev entry. *Eccl* Newc. & Stone RDn (until 1851), Cheadle RDn (1851—*).

MARKET DRAYTON—see DRAYTON IN HALES
DRAYTON BASSETT
AP Pt Staffs (S Offl. Hd), pt Warws (Hemlingford Hd),

the par made 1895 ent Staffs.[25] *LG* Tamw. PLU,
RSD, pt sep RD in Warws (1894—95), Tamw. RD
(pt 1894—95, ent 1895—1934), Lichf RD (1934—
74). Civ bdry: 1896,[147] 1934.[4] *Parl* Staffs pt, Seq
14. *Eccl* Seq 13.

DRAYTON IN HALES

AP Salop par (N Bradford Hd), sometimes 'Market
Drayton', incl in Staffs tp Tyrley (sep CP 1866 in
Staffs[2]) so that this par ent Salop thereafter, qv.

DRESDEN

EP Cr 1853 from Blurton EP,[3] refounded 1867.[72]
Trentham RDn (1853—94), Stoke upon Tr. RDn
(1894—*). Sometimes called 'Redbank'.

DUDLEY

AP Worcs par [St Thomas] (gains 1182 Dudley St
James[206]). In Dudley CB (assoc with Worcs 1889—
1966, assoc with Staffs 1966—74). See entry in
Worcs for organisation and cr of many civ and eccl
units before 1966 and for parl organisation before
1970. Civ bdry: 1966 (as transf to become assoc
with Staffs, gains from Staffs pt Amblecote UD &
CP, pt Brierley Hill UD [qv for constituent pars], pt
Coseley UD & CP, pt Sedgley UD & CP, pt Rowley
Regis MB & CP, pt Tipton UD & AP, pt Himley
AP, pt Kinver CP; gains from Worcs pt Stourbridge
MB & CP; loses pt to help cr Warley CB [assoc with
Worcs]).[199] *LG* Dudley CB. Transf 1974 to W
Midlands.[7] *Parl* Dudley East BC, Dudley West BC
(1970—*). *Eccl* Dudley RDn.

DUDLEY CASTLE HILL

Ex-par place, sep CP 1858.[10] *LG* Although in
Dudley MB (1865—89), excluded from Dudley CB
and thereafter in Staffs (Dudley RD, 1894—1929)
until civ abol 1929 ent to Dudley CB (assoc with
Worcs) & AP.[189] *LG* Dudley PLU (1867—1929).
Parl Dudley Parl Bor (1918—48).

DUNSTALL

Tp in Tattenhill AP, sep CP 1866,[2] sep EP 1852,[3]
eccl refounded 1854.[207] *LG* Seq 7. Civ bdry:
1886,[41] 1896,[208] 1934.[4] *Parl* Seq 1. *Eccl* Tutb.
RDn. Eccl bdry: 1884 (help cr Rangemore EP).[22]

DUNSTON

Chap in Penkridge AP, sep CP 1866,[2] sep EP
1824.[3] *LG* Seq 1. Civ bdry: 1934.[4] *Parl* Seq 18.
Eccl Lapley & Trysull RDn (1824—51), Penkr.
RDn (1851—*).

ECCLESHALL

AP Incl chap Chapel and Hill Chorlton (sep CP 1866,[2]
sep EP 1743 as 'Chapel Chorlton'[3]). *LG* Ecclesh.
Bor, Seq 16. Addtl civ bdry alt: 1932.[27] *Parl* Seq 5.
Eccl Pec jurisd prebend Ecclesh. (until 1846), Seq 8
thereafter. Addtl eccl bdry alt: 1787 (cr Broughton
EP,[3] refounded 1907 from Croxton EP[108] [an EP cr
1857 from Eccleshall EP, qv]), 1844 (cr Cotes
Heath EP [incl pt tp Aspley, pt tp Slindon, neither
sep civ]),[193] 1857 (cr Croxton EP),[198] 1895.[84]

EDENSOR

EP Cr 1846 from Longton EP.[209] Newc. & Stone RDn
(1846—51), Stoke upon Tr. RDn (1851—*).

EDINGALE

Chap (pec jurisd prebend Alrewas) in Alrewas AP,
sep civ identity early, sep EP 1824.[3] *LG* Seq 9. Civ
bdry: 1934 (incl gains Croxall AP).[4] *Parl* Seq 2.

Eccl Pec jurisd Alrewas (until 1846), Tamw. &
Tutb. RDn (1846—51), Tamw. RDn (1851—*).
Eccl bdry: 1899 (gains pt Croxall AP [orig Derbys,
Staffs] dioc S'well).[196]

ELFORD

AP *LG* S Offl. Hd, Lichf PLU, RSD, RD. Civ bdry:
1934.[4] *Parl* Seq 14. *Eccl* Seq 13. Eccl bdry:
1967.[178]

ELKSTONE

Chap in Alstonfield AP, sep EP 1785[3]; jointly rated
with chap Warslow in same par as single tp
'Warslow and Elkstones', qv for sep civ identity
1866. Alton & Leek RDn (1785—1851), Alst. RDn
(1851—1902). Abol 1902 to help refound Warslow
EP,[12] the union later called 'Warslow and
Elkstone'.

ELLASTONE

AP Incl tps Calwich, Ramshorn, Wootton (each a sep
CP 1866[2]), tp Prestwood (sep CP 1866,[2] eccl
severed 1860 to help cr Denstone EP[14]), tp Stanton
(sep CP 1866,[2] sep EP 1849[3] but sep status not
sustained and continues eccl in this par so that this
par eccl sometimes 'Ellastone with Stanton'). *LG*
Seq 23. Addtl civ bdry alt: 1934 (gains Calwich
CP).[4] *Parl* Seq 8. *Eccl* Seq 3.

ELLASTONE WITH STANTON—see prev entry

ELLENHALL

AP *LG* S Pir. Hd, Staff. PLU (soon after 1836[26]—
1930), RSD, RD. Civ bdry: 1885 (gains Ranton
Abbey CP).[210] *Parl* N'rn Dv (1832—67), West Dv
(1867—85), Handsw. Dv (1885—1918), Staff. Dv
(1918—48), Staff. & Stone CC (1948—*). *Eccl*
Newc. & Stone RDn (until 1851), Ecclesh. RDn
(1851—*).

ENDON

Chap in Leek AP, sep EP 1720,[3] later called 'Endon
with Stanley'; for civ see 'Endon, Longsdon and
Stanley'. Alton & Leek RDn (1720—1851), Leek
RDn (1851—*).

ENDON AND STANLEY

CP Cr 1894 when Endon, Longsdon and Stanley CP
divided into 2 CPs of Longsdon, Endon and
Stanley.[211] *LG* Leek PLU, RD. Bdry: 1934.[4] *Parl*
Leek Dv/CC (1918—*).

ENDON, LONGSDON AND STANLEY

Chap in Leek AP, sep CP 1866,[2] sep EP 1720 as
'Endon',[3] qv. *LG* N Totm. Hd, Leek PLU, RSD.
Abol civ 1894 to cr 2 CPs of Longsdon, Endon and
Stanley.[211] *Parl* N'rn Dv (1832—67), North Dv
(1867—85), Leek Dv (1885—1918).

ENVILLE

AP *LG* Seq 20. *Parl* Seq 16. *Eccl* Seq 7. Eccl bdry:
1870 (help cr Tuck Hill EP [Salop, Staffs]).[51]

ESSINGTON

Tp (E Cutt. Hd) in Bushbury AP (o'wise N Seisd.
Hd), sep CP 1866,[2] sep EP 1934 from Bushbury
AP, Wednesfield EP.[130] *LG* Seq 1. Civ bdry: 1966
(incl exchanges pts with Walsall CB [assoc with
Staffs] & CP, loses pt to Wolverh. CB [assoc with
Staffs] & AP).[6] *Parl* Seq 17. *Eccl* Wolverh. RDn.
Eccl bdry: 1964 (help cr Wednesfield St Gregory
the Great EP),[136] 1964.[212]

ETRURIA
EP Cr 1844 from Shelton EP.[119] Newc. & Stone RDn (1844—51), Stoke upon Tr. RDn (1851—94), Hanley RDn (1894—1920), Stoke upon Tr. RDn (1920—*). Bdry: 1845.[53]

ETTINGSHALL
EP Cr 1837 from Sedgley AP, Wolverhampton AP, Bilston EP.[52] Lapley & Trysull RDn (1837—51), Himley RDn (1851—94), Wolverh. RDn (1894—*). Bdry: 1938 (help cr Rough Hills EP),[64] 1959.[55]

FAREWELL
AP Usual eccl spelling; for civ see following entry. Eccl Pec jurisd Dean & Chapter of Lichf (1527—1846), Tamw. & Tutb. RDn (1846—51), Lichf RDn (1851—*).

FAREWELL AND CHORLEY
AP Usual civ spelling; for eccl see prev entry. LG Seq 11. Civ bdry: 1879,[114] 1885.[9] Parl Seq 14.

FARLEY
Tp in Alton AP, sep CP 1866.[2] LG Seq 24. Bdry: 1883,[8] 1896 (help cr Oakamoor CP).[158] Parl Seq 9.

FAWFIELDHEAD
Tp in Alstonfield AP, sep CP 1866,[2] pt eccl in chap Longnor (sep EP 1737,[3] refounded 1902[213]), pt eccl severed 1785 to help cr Warslow EP,[3] refounded 1902 (incl gains Elkstone EP).[12] LG Seq 22. Bdry: 1934.[4] Parl Seq 6.

FAZELEY
Tp (Staffs, S Offl. Hd) in Tamworth AP (Staffs, Warws until 1866, ent Staffs thereafter), sep CP 1866,[2] sep EP 1813,[3] eccl refounded 1842.[68] LG Seq 12. Civ bdry: 1932,[214] 1934.[4] Parl Seq 14. Eccl Tamw. & Tutb. RDn (1813—51), Tamw. RDn (1851—*).

FEATHERSTONE
Tp in Wolverhampton AP, sep CP 1866.[2] LG Seq 1. Bdry: 1934,[4] 1966 (gains pt Wolverh. CB [assoc with Staffs] & AP).[6] Parl Seq 18.

FENTON
Area in Stoke upon Trent AP, pt eccl severed 1802 to help cr Longton EP,[3] the latter refounded 1839,[215] the remainder of the area of Fenton cr 1841 'Fenton' EP,[216] 'Fenton' a sep CP 1894 from the pt of Stoke upon Trent AP in Fenton UD.[154] LG Stoke on Tr. PLU, Fenton UD (1894—1910), Stoke on Tr. CB (1910—22). Civ bdry: 1910.[217] Abol civ 1922 ent to Stoke on Trent AP.[117] Parl Stoke on Tr. Parl Bor (1918—48). Eccl Newc. & Stone RDn (1842—51), Stoke on Tr. RDn (1851—*). Eccl bdry: 1886,[218] 1921.[219]

FIELD
Tp in Leigh AP, sep CP 1866.[2] LG S Totm. Hd, Uttox. PLU (soon after 1837[26]—1930), RSD, RD. Abol 1934 ent to Leigh AP.[4] Parl N'rn Dv (1832—67), North Dv (1867—85), Burt. Dv (1885—1948).

FISHERWICK
Tp in chap Lichfield St Michael (sep civ identity early from Lichfield St Mary AP, sep EP 1729[3]), 'Fisherwick' a sep CP 1866.[2] LG Seq 8. Bdry: 1934 (incl gains Tamhorn CP).[4] Parl Seq 2.

FLORENCE
CP Cr 1894 from the pt of Trentham AP in Longton MB.[154] LG Stoke on Tr. PLU, Longton MB. Abol

1896 ent to Longton CP.[220]

FOREBRIDGE
EP Cr 1844 from Castle Church AP.[151] Newc. & Stone RDn (1844—51), Staff. RDn (1851—*). Bdry: 1867 (cr Castle Town EP),[46] 1917,[221] 1962 (help cr Rickerscote EP).[152] Now called 'Stafford St Paul'.

FORSBROOK
EP Cr 1849 from Dilhorne AP, Blurton EP.[70] Alton & Leek RDn (1849—51), Cheadle RDn (1851—*).
CP Cr 1896 from Dilhorne AP.[205] LG Cheadle PLU, RD. Bdry: 1934,[4] 1965 (gains pt Stoke on Tr. CB [assoc with Staff] & AP).[35] Parl Stone Dv (1918—48), Leek CC (1948—*).

FORTON
AP LG Seq 3. Civ bdry: 1934,[4] 1965 (loses pt to Newport UD & AP, gains pt Chetwynd CP, both Salop).[6] Parl Seq 15. Eccl Seq 5.

FOSTON AND SCROPTON
The sole tp in Scropton AP (area Foston ent Derbys [Appletree Hd], area Scopton pt Derbys [Appletree Hd], pt Staffs [N Offl. Hd], pt but not all of the area in Derbys transf to Staffs 1832 for parl purposes, 1844 for civ purposes[107]), 'Foston and Scropton' a sep CP 1866 with pt in each co[2] so that 'Scropton' has no sep civ identity thereafter; for eccl see 'Scropton'. LG Burt. upon Tr. PLU, RSD. Bdry: 1885,[222] 1890 (loses the pt in Staffs to Staffs pars of Tutbury AP, Tatenhill AP, Yoxall AP so that 'Foston and Scropton' ent Derbys thereafter).[223] Parl Staffs pt, N'rn Dv (1832—67), East Dv (1867—85), Burt. Dv (1885—1918).

FOXT WITH WHISTON
EP Cr 1897 from Ipstones EP, Checkley AP, Kingsley AP.[163] Cheadle RDn.

FRADLEY
Tp in Alrewas AP, sep CP 1866.[2] LG N Offl. Hd, Lichf PLU, RSD. Bdry: 1883.[8] Abol 1885 ent to Alrewas AP.[9] Parl N'rn Dv (1832—67), East Dv (1867—85), Lichf Dv (1885—1918).

FRADSWELL
Chap in Colwich AP, sep CP 1866,[2] sep EP 1851.[182] LG Seq 17. Parl Seq 12. Eccl Stone RDn (1851—61), Staff. RDn (1861—94), Uttox. RDn (1894—1923), Staff. RDn (1923—*).

FREEFORD
Ex-par place, sep CP 1858.[10] LG N Offl. Hd, Lichf PLU (1858—1930), RSD, RD. Abol 1934 ent to Swinfen and Packington CP.[4] Parl N'rn Dv (1832—67), East Dv (1867—85), Lichf Dv (1885—1918).

FREEHAY
EP Cr 1847 from Cheadle AP.[160] Alton & Leek RDn (1847—51), Cheadle RDn (1851—*).

FULFEN
Ex-par place, sep CP 1858.[10] LG N Offl. Hd, Lichf PLU (1858—1930), RSD, RD. Civ bdry: 1879.[114] Abol civ 1934 pt to Streethay CP, pt to Whittington AP.[199] Parl N'rn Dv (1832—67), East Dv (1867—85), Lichf Dv (1885—1918).

FULFORD
Chap in Stone AP, sep EP 1774,[3] sep CP 1897 from Stone Rural CP.[224] LG Stone PLU, RD. Civ bdry: 1932,[27] 1965 (exchanges pts with Stoke on Tr. CB [assoc with Staffs] & AP).[35] Parl Stone Dv (1918—

48), Staff. & Stone CC (1948—*). *Eccl* Newc. & Stone RDn (1774—1851), Stone RDn (1851—61), Trentham RDn (1861—*). Eccl bdry: 1948 (help cr Meir Heath EP).[37]

GAILEY CUM HATHERTON
EP Cr 1869 from Penkridge AP, Wolverhampton AP, Brewood AP.[84] Penkr. RDn.

GAYTON
AP *LG* Seq 17. *Parl* Seq 12. *Eccl* Newc. & Stone RDn (until 1851), Stone RDn (1851—61), Staff. RDn (1861—*).

GENTLESHAW
EP Cr 1840 from Longdon AP, Cannock AP.[144] Tamw. & Tutb. RDn (until 1851), Lichf RDn (1851—*). Bdry: 1870 (help cr Hednesford EP).[81]

GNOSALL
AP Orig Norman royal free chap, then Collegiate and parochial.[225] *LG* Seq 3. Civ bdry: 1885,[74] 1934,[4] 1936 (exchanges pts with Woodcote CP, Salop).[226] *Parl* Seq 19. *Eccl* Sometimes as 'Gnosall with Knightley', Seq 5. Eccl bdry: 1845 (cr Moreton EP).[186]

GOLDENHILL
Area in Wolstanton AP, sep EP 1842,[3] sep CP 1894 from pt of the rural pt of Wolstanton AP.[116] *LG* Wolstanton & Burslem PLU, Wolstanton RD (1894—1904), Stoke on Tr. CB (1904—22). Civ bdry: 1904.[166] Abol 1922 ent to Stoke on Trent AP.[117] *Parl* See Part III of the *Guide* for composition of Stoke upon Tr. Parl Bors (1885—1918) by wards of the CB. *Eccl* Sometimes as 'Golden Hill', Newc. & Stone RDn (1842—51), Newc. under Lyme RDn (1851—1920), Stoke upon Tr. RDn (1920—62), Stoke North RDn (1962—*). Eccl bdry: 1853 (help cr Kidsgrove EP,[3] refounded the same year[227]).

GORNAL
EP Cr 1824 from Sedgley AP,[3] refounded 1832.[141] Lapley & Trysull RDn (1824—51), Himley RDn (1851—*). Now called 'Lower Gornal'.

LOWER GORNAL—see prev entry

UPPER GORNAL
EP Cr 1844 from Sedgley AP.[228] Lapley & Trysull RDn (1844—51), Himley RDn (1851—*). Bdry: 1864,[114] 1931 (loses pt to Dudley St Edmund EP).[229]

GRATWICH
AP *LG* S Totm. Hd, Uttox. PLU, RSD, RD. Abol civ 1934 ent to Kingston AP.[4] *Parl* N'rn Dv (1832—67), North Dv (1867—85), Burt. Dv (1885—1948). *Eccl* Seq 3. Eccl bdry: 1939.[23]

GRINDON
AP *LG* N Totm. Hd, Alst. GilbU (until 1869), Leek PLU (1869—1930), RSD, RD. *Parl* Seq 6. *Eccl* Seq 1.

HAMMERWICH
Chap in chap Lichfield St Michael (sep civ identity early from Lichfield St Mary AP, sep EP 1729[3]), 'Hammerwich' a sep CP 1866,[2] sep EP 1737,[3] eccl refounded 1860.[58] *LG* S Offl. Hd, Lichf PLU, Brownhills USD, UD (1894—96), Lichf RD (1896—1974). Civ bdry: 1934 (gains Ogley Hay Rural CP),[4] 1966 (incl help cr Aldridge-Brownhills

CP).[6] *Parl* Seq 14. *Eccl* Tamw. & Tutb. RDn (1737—1851), Lichf RDn (1851—*). Eccl bdry: 1854 (help refound Ogley Hey EP),[186] 1867 (help cr Chasetown EP).[114]

HAMSTEAD
EP Cr 1894 from Perry Barr EP, Handsworth AP.[230] Handsw. RDn. Bdry: 1964 (cr Hamstead St Bernard EP).[231]

HAMSTEAD ST BERNARD
EP Cr 1964 from Hamstead EP.[231] Handsw. RDn.

HANBURY
AP Incl chap Marchington (sep CP 1866,[2] sep EP 1739,[3] eccl refounded 1862[232]), chap Newborough (sep CP 1866,[2] sep EP 1784,[3] eccl refounded 1862[232]), tp Draycott in the Clay (sep CP 1866[2]), tp Marchington Woodlands (sep CP 1866,[2] sep EP 1859,[3] eccl refounded 1860[19]). *LG* Seq 7. Addtl civ bdry alt: 1934.[4] *Parl* Seq 1. *Eccl* Seq 14. Addtl eccl bdry alt: 1895 (help cr Needwood EP),[42] 1899.[233]

HANDSWORTH
The following have 'Handsworth' in their names. Insofar as as existed at a given time: *LG* S Offl. Hd, W Bromw. PLU (1836—1911), Birm PLU (1911—12), pt Handsw. USD, pt W Bromw. RSD, Handsw. UD (1894—1911), Birm CB (assoc with Warws) (1911—30). *Parl* S'rn Dv (1832—67), East Dv (1867—85), Handsw. Dv (1885—1918); see Part III of the *Guide* for composition of Birm Parl Bors (1918—48) by wards of the CB. *Eccl* Tamw. & Tutb. RDn (until 1851), W Bromw. RDn (1851—66), Handsw. RDn (1866—*).

AP1—HANDSWORTH [ST MARY]—Perhaps incl West Bromwich (sep par by 12th cent[93]). Civ bdry: 1894 (the pt not in the UD cr Perry Barr UD & CP).[234] Abol civ 1930 ent to Birmingham AP.[235] Eccl bdry: 1854 (cr EP2),[12] 1861 (cr EP3),[236] 1862 (cr Perry Barr EP),[237] 1865 (cr Birchfield EP),[236] 1894 (help cr Hamstead EP),[230] 1914 (help cr EP1).[14]

EP1—HANDSWORTH ST ANDREW—Cr 1914 from AP1, EP2.[14]

EP2—HANDSWORTH ST JAMES—Cr 1854 from AP1.[12] Bdry: 1907 (help cr EP4),[108] 1914 (help cr EP1).[14]

EP3—HANDSWORTH ST MICHAEL—Cr 1861 from AP1.[236] Bdry: 1907 (help cr EP4).[108]

EP4—HANDSWORTH ST PETER—Cr 1907 from EP2, EP3.[108]

HANFORD
EP Cr 1828 from Trentham AP,[3] refounded 1832.[69] Newc. & Stone RDn (1828—51), Trentham RDn (1851—*). Bdry: 1843 (help cr Mowcop EP),[3] 1853 (help cr Kidsgrove EP,[3] refounded the same year[227]), 1853 (help cr Silverdale EP,[3] refounded 1855 as 'Silverdale and Knutton Heath'[84]).

HANLEY
Tp in Stoke upon Trent AP, sep EP 1740,[3] eccl refounded 1891 (at time of cr Hanley St Jude),[238] this tp and pt tp Shelton (both in Stoke upon Trent) constituted 1857 Hanley MB, 'Hanley' a sep CP 1894 from the pt of Stoke upon Trent AP in Hanley CB.[154] *LG* Stoke on Tr. PLU, Hanley CB (1894—1910), Stoke on Tr. CB (1910—22). Civ bdry:

1905.[239] Abol civ 1922 ent to Stoke on Trent AP.[117] *Parl* Stoke upon Tr. Parl Bor (1918—48). *Eccl* Newc. & Stone RDn (1740—1851), Stoke upon Tr. RDn (1851—94), Hanley RDn (1894—1920), Stoke upon Tr. RDn (1920—41). Eccl bdry: 1845 (cr Northwood EP, cr Wellington EP),[218] 1913 (help cr Hanley All Saints EP).[240] Abol eccl 1941 to help cr Hanley with Hope EP.[241]

HANLEY ALL SAINTS
EP Cr 1913 from Wellington EP, Hanley EP, Shelton EP.[240] Stoke upon Tr. RDn.

HANLEY ST JUDE
EP Cr 1895 from Stoke upon Trent AP.[242] Stoke upon Tr. RDn. Bdry: 1921.[219]

HANLEY ST LUKE—see WELLINGTON

HANLEY WITH HOPE
EP Cr 1941 by union Hanley EP, Hope EP.[241] Stoke upon Tr. RDn (1941—62), Stoke North RDn (1962—*).

HARBORNE
The following have 'Harborne' in their names. Insofar as any existed at a given time: *LG* S Offl. Hd, Kings Norton PLU, pt Harborne USD (1875—91), Birm CB (assoc with Warws, pt 1891—94, ent 1894—1912), pt Smethw. USD, pt Birm USD (1891—94). *Parl* S'rn Dv (1832—67), East Dv (1867—85), Handsw. Dv (1885—1918). *Eccl* Pec jurisd Dean & Chapter of Lichf (until 1846), Tamw. & Tutb. RDn (1846—51), W Bromw. RDn (1851—66), Handsw. RDn (1866—1905), Harborne RDn (1905—29), sep noted thereafter.

AP1—HARBORNE—Incl in Warws chap Edgbaston (sep par no later than 1658[243]). Civ bdry: 1894 (the pt in Smethw. MB cr Smethwick CP).[154] Abol civ 1912 ent to Birmingham AP.[244] *Eccl* Edgbaston RDn (1929—*). Eccl bdry: 1842 (cr Smethwick EP, cr EP1),[245] 1858 (cr EP4,[3] refounded 1859 as EP2[246]), 1933 (help cr EP3),[144] 1958 (help cr Quinton Road West EP [Worcs, Staffs]).[99]

EP1—NORTH HARBORNE [HOLY TRINITY]—Cr 1842 from AP1.[245] Smethw. RDn (1929—66), Warley RDn (1966—*). Bdry: 1860 (cr West Smethwick EP),[19] 1893 (help cr Smethwick St Michael and All Angels EP),[247] 1903 (cr Smethwick St Stephen EP),[248] 1909 (cr Smethwick St Alban EP).[126] This par sometimes called 'Smethwick Holy Trinity'.

EP2—HARBORNE HEATH—Refounding 1859 of EP4.[246] Edgbaston RDn (1929—*). Bdry: 1906 (gains pt Edgbaston St Augustine EP, Warws).[152]

EP3—HARBORNE ST FAITH AND ST LAWRENCE—Cr 1933 from AP1, The Quinton EP (Worcs).[144] Edgbaston RDn.

EP4—HARBORNE ST JOHN THE BAPTIST—Cr 1858 from AP1,[3] refounded 1859 as EP2,[246] qv.

HARDINGS WOOD
CP Cr 1894 from the pt of Audley AP in Kidsgrove UD.[32] *LG* Newc. under Lyme PLU, Kidsgrove UD. Bdry: 1932.[27] *Parl* Leek Dv/CC (1918—*).

HARLASTON
Chap in Clifton Campville and Haunton AP (eccl, 'Clifton Campville'), sep CP 1866,[2] sep EP 1846.[176] *LG* Seq 9. Civ bdry: 1934 (incl gains Haselour CP).[4] *Parl* Seq 2. *Eccl* Tamw. & Tutb. RDn (1846—51), Tamw. RDn (1851—*). Eccl bdry: 1967.[178]

HASELOUR
Chap (pec jurisd prebend of Lichf Chapter), civ ex-par, sep CP 1858,[10] claimed eccl 1832 to be pt of Lichfield St Michael EP but declared to be eccl ex-par,[118] eccl abol 1968 pt to Harlaston EP, pt to Elford AP.[178] *LG* N Offl. Hd, Lichf PLU (1858—1930), RSD, RD. Abol civ 1934 ent to Harlaston CP.[4] *Parl* N'rn Dv (1832—67), East Dv (1867—85), Lichf Dv (1885—1948).

HATHERTON
Tp in Wolverhampton AP, sep CP 1866.[2] *LG* Seq 1. *Parl* Seq 18.

HAUGHTON
AP *LG* Seq 6. Civ bdry: 1885,[74] 1934.[4] *Parl* Seq 19. *Eccl* Lapley & Trysull RDn (until before 1535), Newc. & Stone RDn (before 1535—1851), Staff. RDn (1851—*).

GREAT HAYWOOD
EP Cr 1854 from Colwich AP, Stowe AP.[185] Rugeley RDn.

HEATH TOWN—see HEATHTOWN
HEATH TOWN—see WEDNESFIELD HEATH
HEATHTOWN
CP Cr 1894 as 'Heath Town', later called 'Heathtown' from the pt of Wednesfield CP in Heath Town (or Wednesfield Heath) UD.[154] *LG* Wolverh. PLU, Heathtown UD (orig 'Heath Town'). Abol 1927 ent to Wolverh. CB (assoc with Staffs) & AP.[133] *Parl* Wolverh. Parl Bor (1918—48).

HEATHYLEE
Tp in Alstonfield AP, sep CP 1866,[2] pt eccl in chap Longnor (sep EP 1737,[3] refounded 1902,[12] qv for other constituent areas), pt eccl in chap Quarnford (sep EP 1752,[3] refounded 1902[12] qv for other constituent areas). *LG* Seq 22. Bdry: 1934.[4] *Parl* Seq 6.

HEATON
Tp in Leek AP, sep CP 1866,[2] eccl in chap Rushton (sep EP 1726 from Leek AP,[3] eccl refounded 1865[249]). *LG* Seq 22. *Parl* Seq 6.

HEDNESFORD
EP Cr 1870 from Cannock AP, Rugeley AP, Brereton EP, Gentleshaw EP.[81] Rugeley RDn. Bdry: 1951.[145]

HILDERSTONE
CP Cr 1897 from Stone Rural CP.[250] *LG* Stone PLU, RD. *Parl* Stone Dv (1918—48), Staff. & Stone CC (1948—*).

EP Cr 1833 from Stone AP.[251] Newc. & Stone RDn (1833—51), Stone RDn (1851—61), Trentham RDn (1861—*).

HILL TOP
EP Cr 1844 from West Bromwich AP.[99] Tamw. & Tutb. RDn (1844—51), Handsw. RDn (1851—94), W Bromw. RDn (1894—*). Bdry: 1879 (help cr West Bromwich St Andrew EP),[100] 1887 (cr West Bromwich St Paul, Golds Hill EP).[81] Now called 'West Bromwich St James'.

HILTON
Tp in Wolverhampton AP, sep CP 1866.[2] *LG* Seq 1. *Parl* Seq 17.

HIMLEY
AP *LG* Seq 19. Civ bdry: 1966 (incl loses pt to Dudley CB [as CB becomes assoc with Staffs] & AP).[6] *Parl* Seq 16. *Eccl* Seq 6.

HINTS
AP *LG* Seq 12. Civ bdry: 1934 (gains Canwell CP).[4] *Parl* Seq 14. *Eccl* Pec jurisd prebend Hansacre (until 1846), Tamw. & Tutb. RDn (1846—51), Lichf RDn (1851—*).

HIXON
EP Cr 1848 from Colwich AP, Stowe AP.[184] Newc. & Stone RDn (1848—51), Rugeley RDn (1851—*).

HOAR CROSS
EP Cr 1874 from Yoxall AP, Abbot's Bromley AP, Hamstall Ridware AP, Newborough EP.[90] Lichf RDn (1874—1924), Tutb. RDn (1924—*).

HOLLINSCLOUGH
Tp in Alstonfield AP, sep CP 1866,[2] pt eccl in chap Longnor (sep EP 1737,[3] refounded 1902,[12] qv for other constituent areas), pt in chap Quarnford (sep EP 1752,[3] refounded 1902,[12] qv for other constituent areas). *LG* Seq 22. *Parl* Seq 6.

HOPE
EP Cr 1845 from Shelton EP.[218] Newc. & Stone RDn (1845—51), Stoke upon Tr. RDn (1851—94), Hanley RDn (1894—1920), Stoke upon Tr. RDn (1920—41). Bdry: 1914.[252] Abol 1941 to help cr Hanley with Hope EP.[241]

HOPTON AND COTON
Tp (pt Staff. Bor/MB & USD, pt S Pir. Hd) in Stafford St Mary AP (civ, 'Stafford St Mary and St Chad'), sep CP 1866.[2] *LG* Staff. PLU, pt Staff. RSD, Staff. RD. Bdry: 1886 (loses the pt in the MB to Stafford St Mary and St Chad CP),[253] 1917.[150] *Parl* Seq 12.

HOPWAS HAYS
Hmlt in Tamworth AP, sep CP 1866,[2] eccl ex-par, abol eccl 1967 ent to Whittington AP.[178] *LG* S Offl. Hd, Tamw. PLU (1865—1930), RSD, RD. Abol civ 1934 ent to Wiggington CP.[4] *Parl* S'rn Dv (1832—67), East Dv (1867—85), Lichf Dv (1885—1948).

HORNINGLOW
Tp in Burton upon Trent AP, sep CP 1866,[2] eccl severed 1821 to help cr Burton upon Trent Christ Church EP,[3] the latter refounded 1845,[75] 'Horninglow' a sep EP 1867 from the latter.[126] *LG* N Offl. Hd, Burt. upon Tr. PLU, pt Burt. upon Tr. USD, pt Burt. upon Tr. MB (1878—89), Burt. upon Tr. CB (pt 1889—94, ent 1894—1904), pt Burt. upon Tr. RSD. Civ bdry: 1886,[41] 1894 (the pt not in the CB cr Outwoods CP).[76] Abol civ 1904 ent to Burton upon Trent AP.[124] *Parl* N'rn Dv (1832—67), East Dv (1867—85), Burt. Dv (1885—1918). *Eccl* Tutb. RDn. Eccl bdry: 1903 (cr Burton upon Trent St Chad EP),[56] 1916 (help cr Shobnall EP, now called 'Burton upon Trent St Aidan').[78]

HORTON
Uncertain early status, perhaps sep AP, prob chap in Leek AP,[75] sep civ identity early, sep EP no later than 1745.[3] *LG* Seq 22. Reconstituted 1934, loses pt to Biddulph UD & AP, loses pt to Endon and Standon CP, gains ent Rudyard CP,[4] the reconstituted area named 'Horton'.[254] *Parl* Seq 6. *Eccl* Alton & Leek RDn (cr—1851), Leek RDn (1851—*). Eccl bdry: 1864 (help cr Biddulph Moor EP).[50]

HUNTINGTON
Tp in Cannock AP, sep CP 1866.[2] *LG* Seq 1. *Parl* Seq 18.

ILAM
AP Incl chap Cauldon (sometimes early 'Caldon', sep civ identity early, sep EP 1748[3]), prob incl chap Okeover (early status uncertain, prob in this par, perhaps in Blore [eccl, 'Blore Ray'],[255] sep civ identity early, eccl independent as donative); incl Sheen (prob orig a sep AP, granted 1541 to Burt. upon Tr. Collegiate Church, by 1552 deemed chap in this par,[256] sep civ identity early, sep EP 1743[3]). *LG* N Totm. Hd, Ashb. PLU, RSD, Mayf. RD (1894—1934), Leek RD (1934—74). Addtl civ bdry alt: 1886 (gains Musden Grange CP),[257] 1934 (incl help cr Waterhouses CP).[4] *Parl* Seq 9. *Eccl* Alton & Leek RDn (until 1851), Alst. RDn (1851—1946). Addtl eccl bdry alt: 1917.[141] Abol eccl 1946 to help cr Ilam with Blore Ray and Okeover EP.[67]

ILAM WITH BLORE RAY AND OKEOVER
EP Cr 1946 by union Ilam AP, Blore Ray AP, Okeover EP.[67] Alst. RDn.

INGESTRE
AP *LG* Seq 17. *Parl* Seq 12. *Eccl* Pec jurisd royal free chap of Stafford St Mary (until 1846), Newc. & Stone RDn (1846—51), Staff. RDn (1851—*).

IPSTONES
Chap with cure of souls, called 1553 chap in Leek AP,[258] sep civ identity early, sep EP 1720.[3] *LG* Seq 21. Civ bdry: 1893,[161] 1934.[4] *Parl* Seq 9. *Eccl* Newc. & Stone RDn (1720—1851), Leek RDn (1851—*). Eccl bdry: 1897 (help cr Foxt with Whiston EP).[163]

KEELE
Chap in Wolstanton AP, sep civ identity early, sep EP 1774.[3] *LG* Seq 14. Civ bdry: 1894,[259] 1921,[172] 1927,[173] 1932 (help cr Audley Rural CP),[27] 1932.[169] *Parl* Seq 10. *Eccl* Newc. & Stone RDn (1774—1851), Newc. under Lyme RDn (1851—*). Eccl bdry: 1843 (help cr Mowcop EP,[3] refounded 1844[49]), 1853 (help cr Kidsgrove EP,[3] refounded the same year[227]), 1853 (help cr Silverdale EP,[3] refounded 1855 as 'Silverdale and Knutton Heath' EP[84]).

KIDSGROVE
EP Cr 1853 from Wolstanton AP, Goldenhill EP, Keele EP, Hanford EP, Talke EP,[3] refounded the same year.[227] Newc. under Lyme RDn.

CP Cr 1894 from the pt of Wolstanton AP in Kidsgrove UD.[116] *LG* Wolstanton & Burslem PLU (1894—1922), Stoke & Wolstanton PLU (1922—30), Wolstanton RD (1894—1904), Kidsgrove UD (1904—74). Bdry: 1904,[166] 1932,[27] 1965 (incl exchanges pts with Stoke on Tr. CB [assoc with Staffs] & AP),[35] 1965 (exchanges pts with Church Lawton AP, Odd Rode CP, both Ches).[6]

KINGSLEY
AP *LG* Pt N Totm. Hd, pt S Totm. Hd, Cheadle PLU, RSD, RD. Civ bdry: 1883,[8] 1896 (help cr Oakamoor CP),[158] 1934.[4] *Parl* Seq 9. *Eccl* Seq 2. Eccl bdry: 1897 (help cr Foxt with Whiston EP).[163]

KINGSTANDING ST LUKE
EP Cr 1933 from Perry Barr EP.[207] Handsw. RDn. Bdry: 1948 (incl loses pt to Boldmere EP, Warws),[143] 1966,[260] 1967 (cr Kingstanding St Mark EP).[261]

KINGSTANDING ST MARK
EP Cr 1967 from Kingstanding St Luke EP.[261] Handsw. RDn.

KINGSTON
AP Usual civ spelling; for eccl see following entry. *LG* Seq 26. Civ bdry: 1934 (gains Gratwich AP).[4] *Parl* Seq 3.

KINGSTONE
AP Usual eccl spelling; for civ see prev entry. *Eccl* Seq 3. Eccl bdry: 1939.[23]

KINGSWINFORD
AP *LG* N Seisd. Hd, Stourbridge PLU, pt Brierley Hill USD, pt Quarry Bank USD, pt Stourbridge RSD, Kingswinf. RD (1894—1934), Brierley Hill UD (1934—66). Civ bdry: 1894 (the pt in Brierley Hill UD cr Brierley Hill CP, the pt in Quarry Bank UD cr Quarry Bank CP),[87] 1934.[4] For civ abol 1966, see Brierley Hill UD. *Parl* S'rn Dv (1832—67), pt Dudley Parl Bor (primarily Worcs, 1867—1918 [areas of EPs of Brierley Hill, Pensett, Brockmoor, Quarry Bank (the latter 2 cr from Brierley Hill]), pt West Dv (1867—85), pt Kingswinf. Dv (1885—1948), Brierley Hill CC (1948—70). *Eccl* Seq 6. Eccl bdry: 1842 (cr Brierley Hill EP),[51] 1844 (cr Pensett EP),[85] 1846 (cr Kingswinford St Mary EP).[262]

KINGSWINFORD ST MARY
EP Cr 1846 from Kingswinford AP.[262] Lapley & Trysull RDn (1846—51), Himley RDn (1851—*).

KINVASTON
Tp in Wolverhampton AP, sep CP 1866.[2] *LG* E Cutt. Hd, Penkr. PLU (1836—70s), Cannock PLU (1870s—1930), RSD, RD. Abol 1934 ent to Penkridge AP.[4] *Parl* S'rn Dv (1832—67), West Dv (1867—85), W'rn Dv (1885—1918), Staff. Dv (1918—48).

KINVER
AP Sometimes early 'Kinfare'. *LG* Kinver Bor, Seq 20. Addtl civ bdry alt: 1934,[4] 1966 (incl loses pt to Dudley CB [as CB becomes assoc with Staffs] & AP).[6] *Parl* Seq 16. *Eccl* Seq 7.

KNUTTON
EP Cr 1875 from Silverdale and Knutton Heaton EP, Wolstanton AP.[114] Newc. under Lyme RD.

KNYPERSLEY
EP Cr 1921 from Biddulph AP.[51] Leek RDn.

LANE END
EP Cr 1866 from Longton EP.[263] Stoke upon Tr. RDn. Bdry: 1899 (help cr Longton St Mary and St Chad EP),[155] 1902.[111] 1921.[219] Sometimes 'Longton St John the Baptist'.

LANE END AND LONGTON—see LONGTON

LAPLEY
AP *LG* Seq 4. Civ bdry: 1934.[4] *Parl* Seq 18. *Eccl* Sometimes as 'Lapley with Wheaton Aston', Lapley & Trysull RDn (until 1851), Penkr. RDn (1851—*).

LEEK
AP Incl in N Totm Hd: Cheddleton (orig sep AP, considered before 1535 a chap to this par,[164] sep civ identity early, sep EP 1721[3]), chap Endon, Longdon and Stanley (sep CP 1866,[2] sep EP 1720 as 'Endon',[3] later called 'Endon with Stanley'), prob incl chap Horton (uncertain early status, perhaps sep AP, prob chap in Leek AP,[75] sep civ identity early, sep EP no later than 1745[3]), chap Ipstones (chap with cure of souls, called 1533 chap in this par,[258] sep civ identity early, sep EP 1720[3]), chap Onecote (sep CP 1866,[2] sep EP 1783,[3] eccl refounded 1862 when gains tp Bradnop and Cawdry[50]), chap Rushton (sep EP 1726,[3] refounded 1865,[249] comprised of 3 tps Heaton, Rushton James, Rushton Spenser [each a sep CP 1866 from Leek[2]] and hmlt Rushton Marsh [not sep civ]), tp Bradnop and Cawdry (sep CP 1866,[2] eccl severed 1862 to help refound Onecote EP as 'Onecote cum Bradnop'[50]), tp Leek and Lowe, tp Tittesworth (each a sep CP 1866,[2] the latter and pt of the former eccl severed 1845 to cr Leek St Luke EP[53]), tp Leekfrith (sep CP 1866,[2] pt eccl severed 1724 to help cr Meerbrook EP,[3] the latter refounded 1859[100]); incl in S Totm. Hd tp and manor Rudyard (sep CP 1866[2]); because the units cited have sep civ identity by 1866, 'Leek' has no sep civ identity 1866—94 (see following entry). *LG* Pt Leek Bor. *Parl* N'rn Dv (1832—67). *Eccl* Alton & Leek RDn (until 1851), Leek RDn (1851—*). Addtl eccl bdry alt: 1724 (help cr Meerbrook EP [incl pt tp Leekfrith],[3] refounded 1859[100]), 1889 (help cr Leek All Saints Compton EP),[108] 1906 (help cr Longsdon EP).[264]

6 CP Cr 1894 by union of the pts in Leek UD of Leek and Lowe CP, Leekfrith CP, Tittesworth CP.[265] *LG* Leek PLU, UD. Bdry: 1934 (incl gains Lowe CP).[4] *Parl* Leek Dv/CC (1918—*).

LEEK ALL SAINTS COMPTON
EP Cr 1889 from Leek St Luke EP, Leek AP.[108] Leek RDn. Bdry: 1906 (help cr Longsdon EP).[264]

LEEK AND LOWE
Tp in Leek AP, sep CP 1866,[2] pt eccl severed 1845 to help cr Leek St Luke EP.[53] *LG* N Totm. Hd, Leek PLU, pt Leek USD, pt Leek RSD, Leek RD. Bdry: 1883,[8] 1894 (incl loses the pt in Leek UD to cr Leek CP).[265] Renamed 1895 'Lowe'.[266] *Parl* N'rn Dv (1832—67), North Dv (1867—85), Leek Dv (1885—1918).

LEEK ST LUKE
EP Cr 1845 from Leek AP (tp Tittesworth, pt tp Leek and Lowe).[53] Alton & Leek RDn (1845—51), Leek RDn (1851—*). Bdry: 1889 (help cr Leek All Saints Compton EP).[108]

LEEKFRITH
Tp in Leek AP, sep CP 1866,[2] pt eccl severed 1724 to help cr Meerbrook EP,[3] the latter refounded 1859.[100] *LG* N Totm. Hd, Leek PLU, pt Leek USD, pt Leek RSD, Leek RD. Civ bdry: 1883,[8] 1894

(loses the pt in the UD to help cr Leek CP),[265] 1934.[4] *Parl* Seq 6.

LEIGH

AP Incl tp Field (sep CP 1866[2]). *LG* Seq 26. Addtl civ bdry alt: 1934 (gains Field CP).[4] *Parl* Seq 3. *Eccl* Seq 3.

LICHFIELD

The following have 'Lichfield' in their names. Insofar as any existed at a given time: *LG* Lichf Co of Itself (1556—1889), Bor/MB, PLU, USD. *Parl* Lichf Parl Bor (1305, 1311—27, 1353, 1553—*), Lichf Dv (1885—1948), Lichf & Tamw. CC (1948—*). *Eccl* Pec jurisd Dean and Chapter of Lichf (until 1846), Tamw. & Tutb. RDn (1846—51), Lichf RDn (1851—*).

EP1—LICHFIELD CHRIST CHURCH—Cr 1848 from EP2.[267]

CP1—LICHFIELD THE CLOSE—Ex-par place, sep CP 1858.[10]

CP2—LICHFIELD THE FRIARY—Ex-par place, sep CP 1858.[10] Lichf PLU (1858—1930). Abol civ 1934 ent to CP3.[4]

AP1—LICHFIELD ST CHAD—Sometimes early 'Stow'. Tp 'Lichfield St Chad' in Lichf Bor/MB; incl in N Offl. Hd tp Curborough and Elmhursrt (sep CP 1866[2]) so that this par pt Bor/MB until 1866, ent thereafter. *Parl* Lichf Parl Bor (pt 1305, 1311—27, 1353, 1553—1867, ent 1867—85), pt N'rn Dv (1832—67); Lichf Dv (1885—1948), Lichf. & Tamw. CC (1948—*).

AP2—LICHFIELD ST MARY—Incl chap CP3/EP2 (sep civ identity early, sep EP 1729[3]).

CP3/EP2—LICHFIELD ST MICHAEL—Chap in AP2, sep civ identity early, sep EP 1729.[3] Tp 'Lichfield St Michael' in Lichf Bor/MB; incl in N Offl. Hd tps Fisherwick, Streethay (each a sep CP 1866[2]); incl in S Offl. Hd chap Hammerwich (sep CP 1866,[2] sep EP 1737,[3] eccl refounded 1860[58]), hmlt Burntwood, Edial and Woodhouses (sep CP 1866,[2] sep EP 1821 as 'Burntwood',[3] as such eccl refounded 1845[65]), tp Pipehill (sep CP 1866[2]), tp Wall (sep CP 1866,[2] sep EP 1843,[3] eccl refounded 1845[65]) so that this par pt Lichf Bor/MB until 1866, reduced pt 1866—94, ent thereafter. Chap Haselour claimed 1832 to be pt of this par, declared instead to be ex-par,[118] qv for later eccl abol. Addtl civ bdry alt: 1894 (gains the pt of Pipehill CP in Lichf MB),[82] 1896 (loses the pt not in Lichf MB to Swinfen and Packington CP),[268] 1934 (gains CP2).[4] *Parl* As for AP1. Addtl eccl bdry alt: 1848 (cr EP1),[267] 1967.[178]

LONDONDERRY

EP Cr 1929 from The Quinton EP, Oldbury EP (both Worcs), Smethwick EP, Smethwick St Alban EP (both Staffs).[159] Smethw. RDn (1929—66), Warley RDn (1966—*).

LONGDON

AP *LG* Seq 11. Civ bdry: 1934.[4] *Parl* Seq 14. *Eccl* Pec jurisd prebend Longdon (until 1846), Seq 12 thereafter. Eccl bdry: 1840 (help cr Gentleshaw EP).[144]

LONGNOR

Chap in Alstonfield AP, sep CP 1866,[2] sep EP 1737 (incl pt tps Fawfieldhead, Heathylee, Hollinsclough, all in Alstonfield AP),[3] eccl refounded 1902.[12] *LG* Seq 22. Addtl civ bdry alt: 1934.[4] *Parl* Seq 6. *Eccl* Alton & Leek RDn (1737—1851), Alst. RDn (1851—66), Leek RDn (1866—84), Alst. RDn (1884—*).

LONGSDON

CP Cr 1894 when Endon, Longsdon and Stanley CP divided into 2 CPs of Longsdon, Endon and Stanley.[211] *LG* Leek PLU, RD. Bdry: 1934.[4] *Parl* Leek Dv/CC (1918—*).

EP Cr 1906 from Leek All Saints Compton EP, Leek AP.[264] Leek RDn.

LONGTON

Chap in Stoke upon Trent AP, rebuilt 1762 by statutory authority, later used by Dissenters and reconsecr 1792 in Church of England,[269] sep EP 1802,[3] eccl refounded 1839,[270] civ tp 'Lane End and Longton', constituted 1865 Longton MB, the area of the tp & MB civ enlarged 1884 from area of Stoke upon Trent AP,[271] 'Longton' a sep CP 1894 from the pt of Stoke on Trent AP in Longton MB.[154] *LG* Stoke on Tr. PLU, Longton MB (1894—1910), Stoke on Tr. CB (1910—22). Civ bdry: 1896 (gains Normancot CP, Florence CP, East Vale CP).[220] Abol civ 1922 ent to Stoke on Trent AP.[117] *Parl* Stoke upon Tr. Parl Bor (1918—48). *Eccl* Newc. & Stone RDn (cr—1851), Stoke upon Tr. RDn (1851—*). Eccl bdry: 1846 (cr Edensor EP),[209] 1866 (cr Lane End EP,[263] sometimes called 'Longton St John the Baptist'), 1964.[157]

LONGTON ST JOHN THE BAPTIST—see LANE END

LONGTON ST MARY AND ST CHAD

EP Cr 1899 from Lane End EP, Caverswall EP.[155] Stoke upon Tr. RDn.

LOWE

CP Renaming 1895 of Leek and Lowe CP.[266] *LG* Leek PLU, RD. Abol 1934 ent to Leek UD & CP.[4] *Parl* Leek Dv (1918—48).

MADELEY

AP *LG* Seq 14. Civ bdry: 1932 (incl help cr Audley Rural CP).[27] *Parl* Seq 10. *Eccl* Newc. RDn (until early 14th cent), Newc. & Stone RDN (early 14th cent—1851), Trentham RDn (1851—1924), Newc. under Lyme RDn (1924—*).

MAER

AP *LG* Seq 14. Civ bdry: 1932.[27] *Parl* Seq 10. *Eccl* Seq 8.

MARCHINGTON

Chap in Hanbury AP, sep CP 1866,[2] sep EP 1739,[3] eccl refounded 1862.[232] *LG* Seq 10. Civ bdry: 1934.[4] *Parl* Seq 1. *Eccl* Tamw. & Tutb. RDn (1739—1851), Tutb. RDn (1851—1962), Uttox. RDn (1962—*). Eccl bdry: 1895 (help cr Needwood EP).[42]

MARCHINGTON WOODLANDS

Tp in Hanbury AP, sep CP 1866,[2] sep EP 1859,[3] eccl refounded 1860.[19] *LG* N Offl. Hd, Uttox. PLU, RSD, RD. Abol civ 1934 pt to Marchington CP, pt to Newborough CP, pt to Hanbury AP, pt to Tatenhill AP, pt to Anslow CP.[4] *Parl* N'rn Dv (1832—67), East Dv (1867—85), Burt. Dv (1885—1948). *Eccl* Tutb. RDn (1859—1962), Uttox. RDn

(1962—*). Eccl bdry: 1895 (help cr Needwood EP).[42]

MARSTON

Chap in Stafford St Mary AP, all parochial rights 1548 except burials,[255] sep civ identity early, sep EP 1777 (incl tp Whitgreave in same par) as 'Marston with Whitgreaves',[3] 'Whitgreaves' a sep EP 1846 from the latter which then becomes 'Marston' EP.[271] *LG* Seq 17. Civ bdry: 1884,[25] 1885,[45] 1934 (incl gains Yarlet CP).[4] *Parl* Seq 12. *Eccl* Newc. & Stone RDn. Abol eccl 1850 to help cr Marston with Whitgreave EP.[272]

MARSTON ON DOVE WITH SCROPTON

EP Cr 1974 by union Marston upon Dove AP (Derbys), Scropton AP (Staffs) to be dioc Derby.[273] Longford RDn.

MARSTON WITH WHITGREAVE

EP Cr 1850 by union Marston EP, Whitgreave EP.[272] Newc. & Stone RDn (1850—51), Staff. RDn (1851—*).

MAYFIELD

AP Incl chap Butterton (sep CP 1866,[2] sep EP 1775[3]), pt chap Calton (sep CP 1866,[2] sep EP 1902 [qv for other constituent pars][66]), chap Wetton (sep par early, before 1535), tp Woodhouses (sep CP 1866[2]). *LG* Seq 23. *Parl* Seq 8. *Eccl* Seq 3.

MEERBROOK

EP Cr 1724 from Leek AP (incl pt tp Leekfrith),[3] refounded 1859.[100] Alton & Leek RDn (1724—1851), Leek RDn (1851—*).

MEIR

EP Cr 1926 from Caverswall AP, Normancot EP.[156] Cheadle RDn.

MEIR HEATH

EP Cr 1948 from Blurton EP, Barlaston AP, Oulton EP, Fulford EP, Normancot EP.[37] Stoke upon Tr. RDn.

MILTON

EP Cr 1865 from Norton le Moors EP, Cobridge EP.[122] Leek RDn. Bdry: 1966.[168]

CP Cr 1894 from the pt of Burslem CP not in Burslem MB.[116] *LG* Wolstanton PLU, RD (1894—1904), Smallthorne UD (1904—22). Bdry: 1896,[274] 1905.[248] Abol 1922 pt to Stoke on Tr. CB (assoc with Staffs) & AP, pt to Norton in the Moors CP.[117] *Parl* Leek Dv (1918—48).

MILWICH

AP *LG* Seq 18. *Parl* Seq 13. *Eccl* Staff. RDn (until early 14th cent), Newc. & Stone RDn (early 14th cent—1851), Staff. RDn (1851—*).

MORETON

EP Cr 1845 from Gnosall AP.[186] Newc. & Stone RDn (1845—51), Ecclesh. RDn (1851—1924), Staff. RDn (1924—*).

MOWCOP

EP Cr 1843 from Wolstanton AP, Keele EP, Hanford EP, Biddulph AP,[3] refounded 1844.[49] Newc. & Stone RDn (1843—51), Newc. under Lyme RDn (1851—1962), Stoke North RDn (1962—*).

MOXLEY

EP Cr 1845 from Darlaston AP, Wednesbury AP, Bilston EP.[53] Tamw. & Tutb. RDn (1845—51), Walsall RDn (1851—94), Wednesb. RDn

(1894—*).

MUCKLESTONE

AP Incl in Salop chap Woore (N Bradf. Hd, sep CP 1866 in Salop[2] so that Mucklestone ent Staffs thereafter, Woore a sep EP 1760,[3] eccl refounded 1842[275]). *LG* N Pir. Hd (pt until 1866, ent from 1866), Mkt. Dray. PLU, RSD, Blore Heath RD (1894—1932), Newc. under Lyme RD (1932—74). Addtl civ bdry alt: 1932.[27] *Parl* Staffs pt, Seq 10. *Eccl* Seq 8.

MUSDEN GRANGE

Ex-par place, sep CP 1858.[10] *LG* S Totm. Hd, Ashb. PLU (1861—86), RSD. Abol civ 1886 ent to Ilam AP.[257] *Parl* N'rn Dv (1832—67), North Dv (1867—85), Leek Dv (1885—1918).

NEEDWOOD

EP Cr 1895 from Tutbury AP, Hanbury AP, Marchington Woodlands EP, Marchington AP, Newborough EP, Yoxall AP, Rangemore EP, Barton under Needwood EP, Scropton AP (Staffs, Derbys until 1866, ent Staffs thereafter).[42] Tutb. RDn.

NEWBOROUGH

Chap in Hanbury AP, sep CP 1866,[2] sep EP 1784,[3] eccl refounded 1862.[232] *LG* Seq 10. Civ bdry: 1934.[4] *Parl* Seq 1. *Eccl* Tamw. & Tutb. RDn (1784—1851), Tutb. RDn (1851—*). Eccl bdry: 1874 (help cr Hoar Cross EP),[90] 1895 (help cr Needwood EP).[42]

NEWCASTLE UNDER LYME

Chap in Stoke upon Trent AP, sep civ identity early, sep EP 1849.[110] *LG* S Pir. Hd (until 1834), N Pir. Hd (from 1834), Newc. under Lyme Bor/MB, PLU, USD. Civ bdry: 1878,[276] 1894 (gains the pt of Trentham AP in Newc. under Lyme MB),[259] 1921,[172] 1927,[173] 1932 (incl gains Wolstanton AP, Silverdale CP, Clayton CP, Chesterton CP),[169] 1965 (exchanges pts with Stoke on Tr. CB [assoc with Staffs] & AP).[35] *Parl* Newc. under Lyme Parl Bor/BC (1355—*). *Eccl* [St Giles] Newc. & Stone RDn (1849—51), Newc. under Lyme RDn (1851—1940). Eccl bdry: 1832 (cr Newcastle under Lyme St George EP,[3] refounded 1844[242]), 1875.[24] Abol eccl 1940 to help cr Newcastle under Lyme with Butterton EP.[137]

NEWCASTLE UNDER LYME ST GEORGE

EP Cr 1832 from Newcastle under Lyme AP,[3] refounded 1844.[242] Newc. & Stone RDn (1832—51), Newc. under Lyme RDn (1851—*). Bdry: 1875,[24] 1905 (help cr Newcastle under Lyme St Paul EP),[277] 1952 (incl help cr Cross Heath EP).[195]

NEWCASTLE UNDER LYME ST PAUL

EP Cr 1905 from Newcastle under Lyme St George EP, Penkhull EP.[277] Newc. under Lyme RDn. Bdry: 1967.[221]

NEWCASTLE UNDER LYME WITH BUTTERTON

EP Cr 1940 by union Newcastle under Lyme AP, Butterton EP.[137] Newc. under Lyme RDn. Bdry: 1961,[278] 1966 (cr The Westlands EP),[279] 1967,[221] 1969 (incl cr Clayton EP).[23]

NEWCHAPEL

EP Cr 1715 from Wolstanton AP (incl areas Tunstall, Ravenscliffe, Chell),[3] refounded 1846.[153] Newc. & Stone RDn (1715—1851), Newc. under Lyme RDn

(1851—1962), Stoke North RDn (1962—*). Bdry: 1925 (cr Chell EP).[167] Sometimes early called 'Wolstanton St James New Chapel' or 'New Chapel'.

CP Cr 1894 from the pt of the pt of Wolstanton AP not in a UD.[116] *LG* Wolstanton & Burslem PLU (1894—1922), Stoke & Wolstanton PLU (1922—30), Wolstanton RD (1894—1904), Kidsgrove UD (1904—74). Bdry: 1922 (loses pt to Stoke on Tr. CB [assoc with Staffs] & AP).[117] *Parl* Leek Dv/CC (1918—*).

NORBURY

AP Incl tp Weston Jones (sep CP 1866[2]). *LG* Seq 3. Addtl civ bdry alt: 1934.[4] *Parl* Seq 15. *Eccl* Seq 5.

NORMANCOT

EP Cr 1852 from Blurton EP.[71] Trentham RDn (1852—94), Stoke upon Tr. RDn (1894—*). Bdry: 1926 (help cr Meir EP),[156] 1948 (help cr Meir Heath EP).[37]

CP Cr 1894 from the pt of Stone AP in Longton MB.[154] *LG* Stoke on Tr. PLU, Longton MB. Abol 1896 ent to Longton CP.[220]

NORTHWOOD

EP Cr 1845 from Hanley EP.[218] Newc. & Stone RDn (1845—51), Stoke upon Tr. RDn (1851—94), Hanley RDn (1894—1920), Stoke upon Tr. RDn (1920—62), Stoke North RDn (1962—*). Bdry: 1954 (cr Birches Head EP),[60] 1955.[187]

COLD NORTON

Tp in Chebsey AP, sep CP 1866.[2] *LG* S Pir. Hd, Stone PLU, RSD, RD. Abol 1932 ent to Chebsey AP.[27] *Parl* N'rn Dv (1832—67), West Dv (1867—85), Handsw. Dv (1885—1918), Stone Dv (1918—48).

NORTON CANES

AP Sometimes 'Norton under Cannock'. *LG* S Offl. Hd, Penkr. PLU, Brownhills USD, UD. Civ bdry: 1934.[4] See Brownhills UD for its abol 1966 (incl constituent pars).[6] *Parl* S'rn Dv (1832—67), East Dv (1867—85), Lichf Dv (1885—1918), Cannock Dv/CC (1918—55), Walsall North BC (1955—70). *Eccl* Pec jurisd Dean & Chapter of Lichf (until 1846), Newc. & Stone RDn (1846—51), Rugeley RDn (1851—*). Eccl bdry: 1954 (help cr Ogley Hay EP).[186]

NORTON IN THE MOORS

Chap in Stoke upon Trent AP, sep civ identity early, sep EP 1779 as 'Norton le Moors' (incl area Brown Edge),[3] eccl refounded 1849,[110] qv in following entry, sometimes eccl 'Norton on the Moors'. Incl hmlt Smallthorne (sep CP 1894 from the pt of Norton in the Moors CP in Smallthorne UD,[265] sep EP 1859 from Norton le Moors EP[31]). *LG* N Pir. Hd, Leek PLU, pt Smallthorne USD, pt Leek RSD, Leek RD. Addtl civ bdry alt: 1896,[274] 1922 (incl loses pt to Stoke on Tr. CB [assoc with Staffs] & AP).[117] Abol civ 1965 pt to Stoke on Tr. CB (assoc with Staffs) & AP, pt to Bagnall CP, pt to cr Brown Edge CP.[35] *Parl* N'rn Dv (1832—67), North Dv (1867—85), N-W'rn Dv (1885—1918), Leek Dv/CC (1918—70).

NORTON LE MOORS

Chap in Stoke on Trent AP, sep EP 1779 (incl area Brown Edge),[3] eccl refounded 1849,[110] sometimes eccl 'Norton on the Moors', sep civ identity early as 'Norton in the Moors', qv in prev entry (incl civ hmlt Smallthorne). Alton & Leek RDn (1779—1851), Leek RDn (1851—*). Eccl bdry: 1844 (cr Brown Edge EP),[99] 1859 (cr Smallthorne EP),[31] 1865 (help cr Milton EP),[122] 1966.[168]

NORTON UNDER CANNOCK—see NORTON CANES

OAKAMOOR

EP Cr 1833 from Cheadle AP,[3] refounded 1864.[159] Alton & Leek RDn (1833—51), Cheadle RDn (1851—1932). Abol 1932 to help cr Oakamoor with Cotton EP.[13]

CP Cr 1896 from Cheadle AP, Cotton CP, Farley CP, Kingsley AP.[158] *LG* Cheadle PLU, RD. *Parl* Stone Dv (1918—48), Leek CC (1948—*).

OAKAMOOR WITH COTTON

EP Cr 1932 by union Oakamoor EP, pt area Alton AP (area of tp Cotton, the area a sep EP 1796 but not sustained, qv).[13] Cheadle RDn.

OCKER HILL

EP Cr 1845 from Tipton AP.[54] Tamw. & Tutb. RDn (1845—51), Handsw. RDn (1851—94), Wednesb. RDn (1894—*). Now called 'Tipton St Mark'.

HIGH OFFLEY

AP *LG* Seq 15. Civ bdry: 1934.[4] *Parl* Seq 4. *Eccl* Pec jurisd prebend Otley (until 1846), Seq 8 thereafter. Eccl bdry: 1974.[280]

OGLEY HAY

Ex-par place, sep CP 1858,[10] sep EP 1852,[3] eccl refounded 1854[186] from ent ex-par Ogley Hay and pts of Norton Canes AP, Hammerwich EP, Stonnall EP, Walsall Wood EP, the EP later called 'Ogley Hay with Brownhills'. *LG* S Offl. Hd, Lichf PLU (soon after 1836[26]—1930), pt Brownhills USD, pt Lichf RSD, Brownhills UD (pt 1894—96, ent 1896—1966). Civ bdry: 1896 (the pt not in the UD cr Ogley Hay Rural CP).[281] See Brownhills UD for its abol 1966 (incl constituent pars).[6] *Parl* S'rn Dv (1832—67), East Dv (1867—85), Lichf Dv (1885—1918), Cannock Dv/CC (1918—55), Walsall North BC (1955—70). *Eccl* Lichf RDn. Eccl bdry: 1867 (help cr Chasetown EP),[114] 1910.[282]

OGLEY HAY RURAL

CP Cr 1896 from the pt of Ogley Hay CP not in Brownhills UD.[281] *LG* Lichf PLU, RD. Abol 1934 ent to Hammerwich CP.[4] *Parl* Lichf Dv (1918—48).

OGLEY HAY WITH BROWNHILLS—see OGLEY HAY

OKEOVER

Donative, early status as par uncertain, perhaps in Blore AP (eccl, 'Blore Ray'), prob in Ilam AP,[255] sep civ identity early, eccl independent as donative. *LG* N Totm. Hd, Ashb. PLU, RSD, Mayf. RD (1894—1934), Uttox. RD (1934—74). Civ bdry: 1916 (gains Woodhouses CP).[283] *Parl* Seq 8. *Eccl* Alton & Leek RDn (until 1851), Alst. RDn (1851—1946). Abol eccl 1946 to help cr Ilam with Blore Ray and Okeover EP.[67]

OLD HILL

EP Cr 1876 from Reddal Hill EP.[284] Kidderminster RDn (1877—80), Dudley RDn (1880—*) (both dioc

Worc).

OLD SWINFORD—see following entry

OLDSWINFORD

AP Worcs par (eccl, 'Old Swinford'), incl in Staffs tp Amblecote (S Seisd. Hd, sep CP 1866 in Staffs,[2] sep EP 1844 [incl Worcs tp Wollaston in same par, qv for sep eccl identity 1860][16]) so that this par ent Worcs thereafter, qv.

ONECOTE

Chap in Leek AP, sep CP 1866,[2] sep EP 1783,[3] eccl refounded 1862 as 'Onecote cum Bradnop' when gains tp Bradnop and Cawdry from Leek AP.[50] LG Seq 22. Civ bdry: 1934.[4] Parl Seq 6. Eccl Alton & Leek RDn (1783—1851), Leek RDn (1851—62).

ONECOTE CUM BRADNOP

EP Refounding 1862 of Onecote EP when gains tp Bradnop and Cawdry from Leek AP.[50] Leek RDn.

ORGREAVE

Tp in Alrewas AP, sep CP 1866.[2] LG N Offl. Hd, Lichf PLU, RSD. Abol 1885 ent to Alrewas AP.[9] Parl N'rn Dv (1832—67), East Dv (1867—85), Lichf Dv (1885—1918).

OULTON

EP Cr 1879 from Stone Christ Church EP, Stone AP.[285] Trentham RDn. Bdry: 1948 (help cr Meir Heath EP).[37]

OUTWOODS

CP Cr 1894 from the pt of Horninglow CP not in Burt. upon Tr. CB.[76] LG Burt. upon Tr. PLU, Tutb. RD. Parl Burt. Dv/CC (1918—*).

OXLEY

EP Cr 1953 from Bushbury AP.[135] Wolverh. RDn.

PALFREY—see WALSALL PALFREY

PATSHULL

AP LG S Seisd. Hd, Shif. PLU, RSD, Seisd. RD. Parl Seq 16. Eccl Lapley & Trysull RDn (until 1851), Trysull RDn (1851—*).

PATTINGHAM

AP Staffs par (S Seisd. Hd) incl in Salop tp Rudge (Stottesdon Hd, sep CP 1866 in Salop[2]) so that this par ent Staffs thereafter. LG Seisd. PLU, RSD, RD. Parl Staffs pt, Seq 16. Eccl Seq 7.

PELSALL

Chap in Wolverhampton AP, sep CP 1866,[2] sep EP 1766.[3] LG S Offl. Hd, Walsall Bor, PLU, RSD, RD (1894—1934), Aldridge UD (1934—66). For civ abol 1966, see Aldridge UD. Parl S'rn Dv (1832—67), East Dv (1867—85), Handsw. Dv (1885—1918), Lichf Dv (1918—48), Lichf & Tamw. CC (1948—55), Walsall South BC (1955—70). Eccl Lapley & Trysull RDn (1766—1851), Walsall RDn (1851—*).

PENKHULL

Tp in Stoke upon Trent AP, sep EP 1845[3]; not sep civ, a detached pt incl in Newc. under Lyme MB (1832—78) and Parl Bor (1832—85), that pt civ severed 1878 and transf to Trentham AP.[267] Newc. & Stone RDn (1845—51), Stoke upon Tr. RDn (1851—*). Bdry: 1905 (help cr Newcastle under Lyme St Paul EP),[277] 1967.[221]

PENKRIDGE

AP Orig chap in Penkridge Collegiate Church, sep par 1551.[286] Tp 'Penkridge' (and pt in Penkr. Bor) in E Cutt. Hd as was Cannock (prob incl in this par if dependent on the College, sep par at Dissolution[142]), chap Coppenhall (sep CP 1866,[2] sep EP 1744[3]), chap Dunston (sep CP 1866,[2] sep EP 1824[3]), chap Shareshill (sep par 1551 [incl tp Saredon, qv for sep civ identity 1866][286]); incl in W Cutt. Hd chap Stretton (sep CP 1866,[2] all parochial rights from Dissolution except burial,[287] sep EP 1722[3]). LG Pt Penkr. Bor, Penkr. PLU (1836—70s), Cannock PLU (1870s—1930), RSD, RD. Addtl civ bdry alt: 1934 (incl gains Kinvaston CP).[4] Parl Seq 18. Eccl Pec jurisd Penkr. (until 1846), Lapley & Trysull RDn (1846—51), Penkr. RDn (1851—*). Addtl eccl bdry alt: 1869 (help cr Gailey cum Hatherton EP).[84]

PENN

AP Incl tp Lower Penn (sep CP 1866[2]), tp Upper Penn (sep CP 1866,[2] pt of the tp cr 1859 'Upper Penn' EP[31]) so that 'Penn' has no sep civ identity after 1866. LG N Seisd. Hd. Parl S'rn Dv (1832—67). Eccl Seq 7. Addtl eccl bdry alt: 1965.[288]

LOWER PENN

Tp in Penn AP, sep CP 1866.[2] LG Seq 19. Bdry: 1934,[4] 1966 (incl exchanges pts with Wolverh. CB [assoc with Staffs] & AP).[6] Parl Seq 16.

UPPER PENN

Tp in Penn AP, sep CP 1866,[2] pt of the tp cr 1859 'Upper Penn' EP.[31] LG N Seisd. Hd, Seisd. PLU, RSD, RD. Civ bdry: 1927 (loses pt to Wolverh. CB [assoc with Staffs] & AP),[133] 1933 (loses pt to Wolverh. CB [assoc with Staffs] & AP).[134] Abol civ 1934 ent to Wombourn AP.[4] Parl S'rn Dv (1832—67), West Dv (1867—85), Kingswinf. Dv (1885—1918), Cannock Dv (1918—48). Eccl Trysull RDn. Eccl bdry: 1965.[288] Renamed eccl 1966 'Penn Fields'.[77]

PENN FIELDS

EP Renaming 1966 of Upper Penn EP.[77] Trysull RDn.

PENSETT

EP Cr 1844 from Kingswinford AP.[85] Lapley & Trysull RDn (1844—51), Himley RDn (1851—*).

PERRY BARR

Area in Handsworth AP, sep CP 1894 from the pt of Handsworth AP not in Handsw. UD,[234] sep EP 1862.[237] LG W Bromw. PLU (1894—1928), Perry Barr UD (1894—1928), Birm PLU (1928—30), CB (1928—30). Civ bdry: 1928 (loses pt to W Bromw. CB [assoc with Staffs] & AP,[95] pt to Sutton Coldfield MB & AP [Warws],[289] the remainder transf to be 'Perry Barr' CP in Birm CB [assoc with Warws]96). See entry in Warws for civ abol 1930. Parl Lichf Dv (1918—48). Eccl W Bromw. RDn (1862—66), Handsw. RDn (1866—*). Eccl bdry: 1894 (help cr Hamstead EP),[230] 1933 (cr Kingstanding St Luke EP),[207] 1948 (incl loses pt to Boldmere EP, Warws),[143] 1957 (cr Perry Beaches EP).[290]

PERRY BEACHES

EP Cr 1957 from Perry Barr EP.[290] Handsw. RDn.

PIPEHILL

Tp (pt Lichf. Bor/MB & USD, pt S Offl. Hd) in chap Lichfield St Michael (sep civ identity early from Lichfield St Mary AP, sep EP 1729[3]), 'Pipehill' a sep CP 1866.[2] Sometimes 'Pipe Hill'.

LG Lichf PLU, pt Lichf RSD. Bdry: 1879.[115] Abol 1894 the pt in the MB transf to Lichfield St Michael CP, the remainder to Wall CP.[82] *Parl* S'rn Dv (1832—67), East Dv (1867—85), Lichf Dv (1885—1918).

PLECK AND BESCOT
EP Cr 1860 from Walsall AP.[291] Walsall RDn. Bdry: 1881.[292] Now called 'Walsall St John'.

PORTHILL
EP Cr 1913 from Wolstanton AP.[293] Newc. under Lyme RDn.

PRESTWOOD
Tp in Ellastone AP, sep CP 1866,[2] eccl severed 1860 to help cr Denstone EP.[14] *LG* S Totm. Hd, Ashb. PLU, RSD, Mayf. RD. Abol civ 1934 ent to Denstone CP.[4] *Parl* N'rn Dv (1832—67), North Dv (1867—85), Leek Dv (1885—1918), Stone Dv (1918—48).

QUARNFORD
Chap in Alstonfield AP, sep CP 1866,[2] sep EP 1752 (incl pt tp Heathylee, pt tp Hollinsclough, both in Alstonfield AP),[3] eccl refounded 1902.[12] *LG* Seq 22. *Parl* Seq 6. *Eccl* Alton & Leek RDn (1752—1851), Alst. RDn (1851—*).

QUARRY BANK
EP Cr 1844 from Brierley Hill EP.[85] Lapley & Trysull RDn (1844—51), Himley RDn (1851—*).

CP Cr 1894 from the pt of Kingswinford AP in Quarry Bank UD.[87] *LG* Stourbridge PLU, Quarry Bank UD (1894—1934), Brierley Hill UD (1934—66). For civ abol 1966, see Brierley Hill UD. *Parl* Kingswinf. Dv (1918—48), Brierley Hill CC (1948—70).

QUINTON ROAD WEST
EP Cr 1958 from The Quinton EP (Worcs), Harborne AP (Staffs).[99] Edgbaston RDn.

RAMSHORN
Tp in Ellastone AP, sep CP 1866.[2] *LG* Seq 23. *Parl* Seq 8.

RANGEMORE
EP Cr 1884 from pt of the Staffs pt of Scropton AP (Staffs, Derbys until 1866, ent Staffs thereafter) and from Tatenhill AP, Tutbury AP, Anslow EP, Dunstall EP.[22] Tutb. RDn. Bdry: 1895 (help cr Needwood EP),[42] 1899.[23]

RANTON
AP Sometimes 'Ronton'. *LG* Seq 17. *Parl* Seq 12. *Eccl* Newc. & Stone RDn (until 1851), Staff. RDn (1851—94), Ecclesh. RDn (1894—*).

RANTON ABBEY
Ex-par place, sep CP 1858.[10] *LG* S Pir. Hd, Staff. PLU (1858—85), RSD. Abol civ 1885 ent to Ellenhall AP.[210] *Parl* N'rn Dv (1832—67), West Dv (1867—85), W'rn Dv (1885—1918).

REDBANK—see DRESDEN

REDDAL HILL
EP Cr 1844 from Rowley Regis AP.[85] Kidderminster RDn (1844—80), Dudley RDn (1880—*) (both dioc Worc). Bdry: 1876 (cr Old Hill EP).[284] Sometimes called 'Cradley Heath'.

RICKERSCOTE
EP Cr 1962 from Castle Church AP, Forebridge EP.[152] Staff. RDn.

HAMSTALL RIDWARE
AP *LG* Seq 8. Civ bdry: 1883,[8] 1934.[4] *Parl* Seq 2. *Eccl* Tamw. & Tutb. RDn (until 1851), Rugeley RDn (1851—*). Eccl bdry: 1874 (help cr Hoar Cross EP).[90]

MAVESYN RIDWARE
AP *LG* Seq 8. Civ bdry: 1934 (incl gains Pipe Ridware AP).[4] *Parl* Seq 2. *Eccl* Pec jurisd prebend Alrewas (until 1846), Tamw. & Tutb. RDn (1846—51), Rugeley RDn (1851—*).

PIPE RIDWARE
Chap (pec jurisd prebend Alrewas) in Alrewas AP, sep civ identity early, sep EP 1726.[3] *LG* N Offl. Hd, Lichf PLU, RSD, RD. Abol civ 1934 ent to Mavesyn Ridware AP.[4] *Parl* N'rn Dv (1832—67), East Dv (1867—85), Lichf Dv (1885—1948). *Eccl* Pec jurisd prebend Alrewas (until 1846), Tamw. & Tutb. RDn (1846—51), Rugeley RDn (1851—*).

ROCESTER
AP Incl chap Bradley in the Moors (sep civ identity early, sep EP 1744 as 'Bradley le Moors'[3]), chap Waterfall (sep par early with curates[294]). *LG* Seq 26. Addtl civ bdry alt: 1896,[15] 1934.[4] *Parl* Seq 7. *Eccl* Seq 3. Addtl eccl bdry alt: 1860 (help cr Denstone AP).[14]

ROLLESTON
AP Staffs par considered in 19th cent and earlier to be ent Staffs, a small pt without population deemed later to be in Derbys, the latter transf 1903 to Marston on Dove AP (Derbys) and Rolleston ent Staffs thereafter.[295] Incl tp Anslow (sep CP 1866,[2] sep EP 1861 from Rolleston AP, Tutbury AP[21]). *LG* Staffs pt, Seq 7. Civ bdry: 1883,[8] 1896,[208] 1934.[4] *Parl* Staffs pt, Seq 1. *Eccl* Seq 14.

RONTON—see RANTON

ROUGH HILLS
EP Cr 1938 from Blakenall EP, Ettingshall EP, Sedgley AP.[64] Wolverh. RDn. Bdry: 1959.[55] Now called 'Wolverhampton St Martin'.

ROWLEY REGIS
Chap (Staffs, N Seisd. Hd) in Clent AP (in Worcs *temp* Domesday Book, soon thereafter considered in Staffs [N Seisd. Hd], transf to Worcs 1832 for parl purposes, 1844 for civ purposes[107]), sep civ identity early in Staffs, sep EP 1848.[175] *LG* Dudley PLU, Rowley Regis USD, UD (1894—1933), MB (1933—66). Civ bdry: 1954 (loses pt to Dudley CB [assoc with Worcs] & AP).[88] Abol civ 1966 pt to Dudley CB (as CB becomes assoc with Staffs) & AP, pt to W Bromw. CB (assoc with Staffs) & AP, pt to help cr Warley CB (assoc with Worcs) & CP, pt to Halesowen MB & AP, Worcs.[6] *Parl* S'rn Dv (1832—67), pt Dudley Parl Bor (primarily Worcs, 1867—1918 [area of Reddal Hill EP]), pt West Dv (1867—85), pt Kingswinf. Dv (1885—1948), Rowley Regis & Tipton BC (1948—70). Parl bdry: 1955.[89] *Eccl* Kidderminster RDn (1848—80), Dudley RDn (1880—1905) (both dioc Worc), not in a RDn (when transf to dioc Birm, July—Aug 1905), Harb. RDn (Aug. 1905—29), Smethw. RDn (1929—66), Warley RDn (1966—*). Eccl bdry: 1844 (cr Reddall Hill EP),[85] 1869 (help cr Blackheath EP [Worcs, Staffs]),[63] 1879 (help cr

Tiverdale EP, to be dioc Lichf),[296] 1959 (loses pt to Rounds Green EP, Worcs, dioc Birm).[297]

RUDYARD

Tp and manor in Leek AP, sep CP 1866.[2] *LG* S Totm. Hd, Leek PLU, RSD, RD. Abol 1934 ent to help reconstitute Horton CP.[4] *Parl* N'rn Dv (1832—67), North Dv (1867—85), Leek Dv (1885—1948).

RUGELEY

AP *LG* E Cutt. Hd, Lichf PLU, pt Rugeley USD, pt Lichf RSD, Rugeley UD. Civ bdry: 1894 (the pt not in the UD cr Brereton CP),[82] 1934.[4] *Parl* S'rn Dv (1832—67), West Dv (1867—85), Lichf Dv (1885—1948), Lichf & Tamw. CC (1948—70), Cannock CC (1970—*). *Eccl* Pec jurisd Dean & Chapter of Lichf (until 1846), Tamw. & Tutb. RDn (1846—51), Rugeley RDn (1851—*). Eccl bdry: 1838 (cr Brereton EP,[3] refounded 1843 with most parochial rights,[79] remainder of rights gained 1852[80]), 1870 (help cr Hednesford EP).[81]

RUSHALL

AP *LG* S Offl. Hd, Walsall PLU, RSD (ent 1875—90, pt 1890—94), pt Walsall CB & USD (1890—94), Walsall RD (1894—1934), Aldridge UD (1934—66). Civ bdry: 1894 (loses the pt in the CB to help cr Walsall CP),[298] 1931 (loses pt to Walsall CB [assoc with Staffs] & CP).[38] For civ abol 1966, see Aldridge UD. *Parl* S'rn Dv (1832—67), pt Walsall Parl Bor (1867—1918), pt East Dv (1867—85), pt Handsw. Dv (1885—1918), Lichf Dv (1918—48), Lichf & Tamw. CC (1948—55), Walsall South BC (1955—70). *Eccl* Seq 15. Eccl bdry: 1925 (help cr Walsall St Mark EP).[299]

RUSHTON

EP Chap in Leek AP (comprised of 3 tps of Heaton, Rushton James, Ruston Spencer [each a sep CP 1866 from Leek AP[2]], and of hmlt Rushton Marsh [not sep civ]), sep EP 1726,[3] eccl refounded 1865.[249] Alton & Leek RDn (1726—1851), Leek RDn (1851—*). Later called 'Rushton Spencer'.

CP Cr 1934 by union Rushton James CP, Rushton Spencer CP.[4] *LG* Leek RD. *Parl* Leek CC (1948—*).

RUSHTON JAMES

Tp in Leek AP, sep CP 1866,[2] the tp eccl in chap Rushton (qv for sep eccl status 1726 and eccl refounding). *LG* N Totm. Hd, Leek PLU, RSD, RD. Abol 1934 to help cr Rushton CP.[4] *Parl* N'rn Dv (1832—67), North Dv (1867—85), Leek Dv (1885—1948).

RUSHTON SPENCER

Tp in Leek AP, civ and eccl status, organisation, abol as for Rushton James. The name 'Rushton Spencer' sometimes used for 'Rushton' EP, qv.

SALT—see following entry

SALT AND ENSON

Tp (a union early *temp* Eliz I of chap Salt, chap Enson[300]) in Stafford St Mary AP, sep CP 1866 as 'Salt and Enson',[2] sep EP 1843 as 'Salt',[3] the EP now called 'Stafford St James'. *LG* Seq 17. Civ bdry: 1885,[45] 1934.[4] *Parl* Seq 12. *Eccl* Newc. & Stone RDn (1843—51), Staff. RDn (1851—*).

SANDON

AP *LG* Seq 18. Civ bdry: 1932.[27] *Parl* Seq 13. *Eccl* Staff. RDn (until early 14th cent), Newc. & Stone RDn (early 14th cent—1851), Stone RDn (1851), Staff. RDn (1851—*).

SAREDON

Tp in chap Shareshill (sep par 1551 from Penkridge AP[286]), 'Saredon' a sep CP 1866.[2] *LG* Seq 1. Civ bdry: 1934.[4] *Parl* Seq 18.

SCROPTON

AP Consisted of sole tp Foston and Scropton (area Foston ent Derbys [Appletree Hd], area Scropton pt Derbys [Appletree Hd], pt Staffs [N Offl. Hd], pt but not all of the area in Derbys transf to Staffs 1832 for parl purposes, 1844 for civ purposes,[107] the tp a sep CP 1866 with pt in each co[2]) so that 'Scropton' has no sep civ identity after 1866. *LG* Burt. upon Tr. PLU. *Parl* Staffs pt, N'rn Dv (1832—67). *Eccl* Donative, Derby RDn (until 1846), Willington RDn (1846—47), Cubley RDn (1847—87), Longford RDn (dioc Lichf and Cov until 1837, dioc Lichf 1837—84, dioc S'well 1884—1927, dioc Derby 1927—*). Eccl bdry alt ent from Staffs pts: 1884 (help cr Rangemore EP),[22] 1895 (help cr Needwood EP).[42] Abol eccl 1974 to help cr Marston on Dove with Scropton EP.[273]

SEDGLEY

AP Incl area Coseley (sep EP 1832,[141] sep CP 1903 from the pt of Sedgley AP in Coseley UD[188]). *LG* N Seisd. Hd, Dudley PLU, pt Upper Sedgley USD (1875—87), pt Sedgley USD (1887—94), pt Coseley USD, pt Dudley RSD, Sedgley UD (pt 1894—1903, ent 1903—66), pt Coseley UD (1894—1903). Addtl civ bdry alt: 1883,[8] 1954 (loses pt to Dudley CB [assoc with Worcs] & AP).[88] Abol civ 1966 pt to Dudley CB (as CB becomes assoc with Staffs) & AP, pt to Wolverh. CB (assoc with Staffs) & AP, pt to Himley AP.[6] *Parl* Wolverh. Parl Bor (1832—1918), Wolverh. Bilston Parl Bor (1918—48), Bilston BC (1948—70). Parl bdry: 1955.[89] *Eccl* Lapley & Trysull RDn (until 1851), Himley RDn (1851—*). Addtl eccl bdry alt: 1824 (cr Gornal EP,[3] refounded 1832[141]), 1837 (help cr Ettingshall EP),[52] 1844 (cr Upper Gornal EP),[228] 1861 (help cr Blakenall EP,[3] refounded 1862[50]), 1864,[114] 1873 (help cr Sedgley St Mary the Virgin EP),[190] 1884 (help cr West Coseley EP),[191] 1938 (help cr Rough Hills EP),[64] 1959.[55]

SEDGLEY ST MARY THE VIRGIN

EP Cr 1873 from Sedgley AP, Coseley EP.[190] Himley RDn. Bdry: 1959.[55]

SEIGHFORD

AP Incl area Derrington (existed before 16th cent, rebuilt 1845,[204] sep EP 1847[3]). *LG* Seq 17. Civ bdry: 1917,[150] 1934 (gains Worston CP).[4] *Parl* Seq 12. *Eccl* Staff. RDn (until early 14th cent), Newc. & Stone RDn (early 14th cent—1851), Staff. RDn (1851—1930). Abol eccl 1930 to help cr Seighford with Derrington and Cresswell EP.[194]

SEIGHFORD WITH DERRINGTON AND CRESS-WELL

EP Cr 1930 by union Seighford AP, Derrington EP, Cresswell AP.[194] Staff. RDn. Bdry: 1936.[153]

SHARESHILL

AP Chap in Penkridge AP, sep par 1551.[286] Incl tp

Saredon (sep CP 1866[2]). *LG* Seq 1. Addtl civ bdry alt: 1934.[4] *Parl* Seq 18. *Eccl* Royal pec jurisd of Penkr. (until 1846), Lapley & Trysull RDn (1846—51), Brew. RDn (1851—94), Penkr. RDn (1894—*). Eccl bdry: 1958.[301]

SHEEN
AP Prob orig AP, granted 1541 to Burt. upon Tr. Collegiate Church, by 1552 deemed chap in this par,[256] sep civ identity early, sep EP 1743.[3] *LG* Seq 25. Civ bdry: 1934.[4] *Parl* Seq 6. *Eccl* Seq 1.

SHELTON
EP Cr 1843 from Stoke upon Trent AP.[249] Newc. & Stone RDn (1844—51), Stoke upon Tr. RDn (1851—94), Hanley RDn (1894—1920), Stoke upon Tr. RDn (1920—*). Bdry: 1844 (cr Etruria EP),[119] 1845 (cr Hope EP),[218] 1913 (help cr Hanley All Saints EP),[240] 1948 (loses pt to Yardley AP, Worcs, and gains pt Olton EP, Warws).[302]

SHENSTONE
AP *LG* S Offl. Hd, Lichf PLU, pt Brownhills USD, pt Lichf RSD, Lichf RD. Civ bdry: 1894 (the pt in the UD cr Shire Oak CP),[82] 1911,[303] 1931 (loses pt to Sutton Coldfield MB & AP, Warws),[40] 1957,[304] 1966 (incl help cr Aldridge-Brownhills UD & CP, exchanges pts with Sutton Coldfield MB & AP, Warws).[6] *Parl* Seq 14. *Eccl* Seq 12. Eccl bdry: 1823 (cr Stonnall EP,[3] refounded 1845[109]), 1876 (help cr Little Aston EP [Staffs, Warws]),[28] 1974.[30]

SHERIFF HALES
AP Mostly Salop (S Bradford Hd), pt Staffs (W Cutt. Hd), the par made 1895 ent Salop.[25] The par in Salop civ called 'Sheriff Hales' until, by 1971 census, 'Sheriffhales'; for usual eccl, see below. Incl in Salop chap Woodcote (sep CP 1866 in Salop,[3] not sep eccl hence this par eccl 'Sheriffhales (with Woodcote)', qv in following entry. *LG* Shif. PLU, RSD, pt sep RD in Staffs (1894—95); for remainder and later, see entry in Salop. *Parl* Staffs pt, S'rn Dv (1832—67), West Dv (1867—1918).

SHERIFFHALES—see prev entry

SHERIFFHALES (WITH WOODCOTE)
AP Usual eccl spelling; for civ name in Salop and Staffs, civ and parl organisation, and civ sep chap, see prev entry. *Eccl* Lapley & Trysull RDn (until 1851), Brew. RDn (1851—94), Edgmond RDn (Salop AD, 1894—*).

SHIRE OAK
CP Cr 1894 from the pt of Shenstone AP in Brownhills UD.[82] *LG* Lichf PLU, Brownhills UD. Bdry: 1911.[303] For civ abol 1966, see Brownhills UD. *Parl* Cannock Dv/CC (1918—55), Walsall North BC (1955—70).

SHOBNALL
EP Cr 1916 from Horninglow EP, Burton upon Trent Christ Church EP, Branstone EP.[78] Tutb. RDn. Bdry: 1940.[24] Now called 'Burton upon Trent St Aidan'.

SHORT HEATH
CP Cr 1894 from the pt of Willenhall CP in Short Heath UD[154]; for eccl see 'Willenhall Holy Trinity'. *LG* Wolverh. PLU, Short Heath UD (1894—1934), Willenhall UD (1934—74). Bdry: 1895,[305] 1934.[4] For civ abol 1966, see Willenhall UD. *Parl*

Wolverh. East Parl Bor (1918—48), Wednesb. BC (1948—70).

SILVERDALE
EP Cr 1853 from Wolstanton AP, Keele EP, Hanford EP.[3] Newc. under Lyme RDn. Refounded 1855 as 'Silverdale and Knutton Heath' from same pars,[84] qv.
CP Cr 1894 from pt of the pt of Wolstanton AP not in a UD.[116] *LG* Wolstanton & Burslem PLU (1894—1922), Stoke & Wolstanton PLU (1922—30), Wolstanton RD (1894—1904), Wolstanton United UD (1904—32). Abol 1932 ent to Newc. under Lyme MB & AP.[169] *Parl* Newc. under Lyme Parl Bor (1918—48).

SILVERDALE AND KNUTTON HEATH
EP Refounding 1885 from Wolstanton AP, Keele EP, Hanford EP[84] of EP cr 1853 from the same pars as 'Silverdale'.[3] Newc. under Lyme RDn. Bdry: 1875 (help cr Knutton EP).[114]

SMALLTHORNE
Hmlt in Norton in the Moors (sep civ identity early from Stoke upon Trent AP, sep EP 1779 as 'Norton le Moors' EP[3]), 'Smallthorne' a sep EP 1859 from Norton le Moors EP,[31] sep CP 1894 from the pt of Norton in the Moors CP in Smallthorne UD.[265] *LG* Leek PLU, Smallthorne UD. Abol civ 1922 ent to Stoke on Tr. CB (assoc with Staffs) & AP.[117] *Parl* Leek Dv (1918—48). *Eccl* Leek RDn (1859—1962), Stoke North RDn (1962—*). Eccl bdry: 1966.[168]

SMETHWICK
The following have 'Smethwick' in their names. Insofar as any existed at a given time: *LG* King's Norton PLU, Smethw. UD (1894—99), MB (1899—1907), CB (1907—66). *Parl* Smethw. Parl Bor/BC (1918—70). *Eccl* Tamw. & Tutb. RDn (cr—1851), W Bromw. RDn (1851—66), Handsw. RDn (1866—1905), Harborne RDn (1905—29), Smethw. RDn (1929—66), Warley RDn (1966—*).
CP1—SMETHWICK—Cr 1894 from the pt of Harborne AP in Smethw. UD.[154] Bdry: 1897 (loses pt to W Bromw. CB [assoc with Staffs] & AP).[93] For abol 1966, see following entry for CB.
MB/CB—SMETHWICK—Constituted of CP1 (1894—1966), Warley Wood CP (1928—66). Abol 1966 pt to W Bromw. CB (assoc with Staffs) & AP, pt to Birm CB (assoc with Warws) & AP, pt to help cr Warley CB (assoc with Worcs) & CP.[6]
EP1—SMETHWICK—Cr 1842 from Harborne AP.[245] Bdry: 1856 (cr EP5),[306] 1892 (cr EP4),[307] 1893 (help cr EP7),[247] 1902 (cr EP3),[308] 1929 (help cr Londonderry EP),[160] 1970.[309]
—SMETHWICK HOLY TRINITY—see NORTH HARBORNE
EP2—SMETHWICK ST ALBAN—Cr 1909 from North Harborne EP.[21] Bdry: 1929 (help cr Londonderry EP).[160]
EP3—SMETHWICK ST CHAD—Cr 1902 from EP1.[308] Abol 1970 pt to EP1, pt to help cr EP6.[309]
EP4—SMETHWICK ST MARY—Cr 1892 from EP1.[307]
EP5—SMETHWICK ST MATTHEW—Cr 1856 from EP1.[306] Bdry: 1893 (help cr EP7).[247] Abol 1970

to help cr EP6.[309]

EP6—SMETHWICK ST MATTHEW WITH ST CHAD—Cr 1970 by union EP5, pt EP3.[309]

EP7—SMETHWICK ST MICHAEL AND ALL ANGELS—Cr 1893 from EP1, EP5, North Harborne EP.[247]

EP8—SMETHWICK ST STEPHEN—Cr 1903 from North Harborne EP.[248]

EP9—WEST SMETHWICK [ST PAUL]—Cr 1860 from North Harborne EP.[20]

SNEYD

EP Cr 1844 from Burslem EP.[119] Newc. & Stone RDn (1844—51), Stoke upon Tr. RDn (1851—94), Hanley RDn (1894—1920), Stoke upon Tr. RDn (1920—62), Stoke North RDn (1962—*). Bdry: 1844,[120] 1939 (cr Burslem St Werburgh EP),[122] 1958.[123]

SNEYD GREEN

EP Cr 1955 from Cobridge EP.[187] Stoke upon Tr. RDn (1955—62), Stoke North RDn (1962—*).

STAFFORD

The following have 'Stafford' in their names. Insofar as any existed at a given time: *LG* S Pir. Hd, Staff. PLU, USD; Bor/MB sep noted. *Parl* Sep noted. *Eccl* Pec jurisd Dean & Chapter of Lichf (until 1846), Newc. & Stone RDn (1846—51), Staff. RDn (1851—*).

CP1—STAFFORD—Renaming 1894 of CP2 when its bdry extended to incl the pt of Castle Church AP in Staff. MB.[149] Bdry: 1917,[150] 1934.[4] *Parl* Staff. Dv (1918—48), Staff. & Stone CC (1948—*).

EP1—STAFFORD CHRIST CHURCH—Cr 1844 from AP2.[271]

AP1—STAFFORD ST CHAD—*LG* Staff. Bor/MB. Civ jointly rated with AP2 as CP2, qv, sep eccl identity retained. *Parl* Staff Parl Bor (see CP2).

—STAFFORD ST JAMES—Name used now for EP cr 1843 as 'Salt' qv.

EP2—STAFFORD ST JOHN—Cr 1928 from AP2.[221]

AP2—STAFFORD ST MARY—Orig royal free chap (its own pec jurisd)/Collegiate. *LG* Tp 'Stafford St Mary' in Staff. Bor/MB as was pt tp Hopton and Coton (see below); incl in S Pir. Hd chap Marston (all parochial rights 1548 except burials,[255] sep civ identity early, sep EP 1777 [incl tp Whitgreave] as 'Marston with Whitgreave',[3] 'Whitgreave' a sep EP 1844 from the latter which then becomes 'Marston' EP[271]), tp Hopton and Copton ([pt in Staff. Bor/MB] sep CP 1866[2]), tp Salt and Enson (a union early *temp* Eliz I of chap Salt, chap Enson, both in this par, sep CP 1866 as 'Salt and Enson',[2] sep EP 1843 as 'Salt',[3] the EP now called Stafford St James'), tp Whitgreave (sep CP 1866,[2] in chap Marston and thus pt of cr 1777 of 'Marston with Whitgreave' EP,[3] 'Marston' a sep EP when 'Whitgreave' a sep EP 1844 from the latter[271]). Jointly rated civ with AP1 as CP2, qv. *Parl* Pt Staf. Parl Bor (see CP2). Addtl eccl bdry alt: 1844 (cr EP1),[271] 1928 (cr EP2).[221]

CP2—STAFFORD ST MARY AND ST CHAD—Joint rating for civ purposes of AP1 (ent in Staff. Bor/MB), AP2 (pt in Staff. Bor/MB until 1866, ent thereafter), qv for civ and eccl sep chaps and tps.

Addtl civ bdry alt: 1886 (gains the pt of Hopton and Coton CP in Staff. MB).[253] Renamed 1894 as CP1 when gains the pt of Castle Church AP in Staff. MB.[149] *Parl* Staff. Parl Bor (pt 1295—1867, ent 1867—1918).

—STAFFORD ST PAUL—Name used now for EP cr 1844 as 'Forebridge', qv.

—STAFFORD ST THOMAS—Name used for for EP cr 1867 as 'Castle Town', qv.

STANDON

AP *LG* Seq 16. Civ bdry: 1932.[27] *Parl* Seq 5. *Eccl* Seq 10. Eccl bdry: 1921.[109]

STANTON

Tp in Ellastone AP, sep CP 1866,[2] sep EP 1849[3] but sep eccl status not sustained and Stanton contines eccl in Ellastone AP. *LG* Seq 23. *Parl* Seq 8. *Eccl* Alton & Leek RDn.

STAPENHILL

AP Derbys par, pt in Burt. upon Tr. MB (o'wise ent Staffs, 1878—89), pt Burt. upon Tr. CB (1889—94), pt Burt. upon Tr. USD (1878—94). Civ bdry: 1894 (the pt in Derbys transf pt to Bretby CP, pt to Drakelow CP [both Derbys] and thus 'Stapenhill' ent Burt. upon Tr. CB).[76] Abol civ 1904 ent to Burton upon Trent AP.[124] See entry in Derbys for earlier civ and parl organisation and for ent eccl organisation.

STATFOLD

AP Church of prebend (sometimes 'Stotfold') in Cathedral Chapter of Lichf, sep civ identity retained, sometimes eccl claimed to be in Lichfield St Mary AP but unused except for burials by ent 18th cent and eccl incl by then in Clifton Campville with Chilcote AP.[177] *LG* S Offl. Hd, Tamw. PLU, RSD, RD. Abol civ 1934 ent to Thorpe Constantine AP.[4] *Parl* S'rn Dv (1832—67), East Dv (1867—85), Lichf Dv (1885—1918).

STOKE ON TRENT

AP Usual civ name from 1920s, prev civ and eccl 'Stoke upon Trent'. For sake of completeness, all entered here together. Early status greatly dependent upon the potteries.[310] Incl chap Bagnall (eccl severed 1716 to help cr Bucknall EP,[3] 'Bagnall' a sep EP 1736 from Bucknall EP,[3] sep eccl status not sustained, 'Bucknall cum Bagnall' eccl refounded 1849 from this par,[110] 'Bagnall' a sep CP 1896 from Stoke Rural CP[34]), chap Bucknall (sep EP 1716 [incl chap Bagnall in same par, qv above for later sep eccl status][3]), chap Burslem (some parochial rights from 16th cent, sep civ identity early, sep EP 1849[112]), chap Longton (rebuilt 1762 by statutory authority, later used by Dissenters and re-consecr 1792 in Church of England,[269] sep EP 1802 [incl area Fenton],[3] eccl refounded 1839,[215] civ as tp 'Lane End and Longton', the tp constituted 1865 Longton MB, the area of the tp & MB civ enlarged 1884 from area of Stoke upon Trent AP,[270] 'Longton' a sep CP 1894 from the pt of Stoke upon Trent AP in Longton MB[154]), chap and bor Newcastle under Lyme (sep civ identity early, sep EP 1849[110]), chap Norton in the Moors (sep civ identity early, sep EP 1729 as 'Norton le Moors',[3] eccl refounded 1849,[110] sometimes eccl 'Norton on the Moors'), chap Whitmore (sep civ identity early, sep EP 1725,[3] eccl refounded 1849[110]), area Fenton (pt eccl severed 1802 to help cr Longton EP,[3] the latter refounded 1839,[215] the remainder of the area of Fenton cr 1841 'Fenton' EP,[215] 'Fenton' a sep CP 1894 from the pt of Stoke upon Trent AP in Fenton UD[154]), tp Hanley (sep EP 1740,[3] eccl refounded 1891 [at time of cr Hanley St Jude],[238] the area of tp Hanley and pt tp Shelton constituted 1878 Hanley MB, 'Hanley' a sep CP 1894 from the pt of AP1 in Hanley CB),[154] tp Penkhull (not sep civ, a detached pt incl in Newc. under Lyme MB [1835—78] and in Newc. under Lyme Parl Bor [1832—85], that pt civ severed 1878 and transf to Trentham AP[276]), tp Shelton (not sep civ, pt incl in constitution 1878 of Hanley MB and thus made pt of Hanley CP when constituted 1894, the remainder incl in constitution 1874 of Stoke on Tr. MB). *LG* N Pir. Hd, Stoke upon Tr. PLU (1836—1922), Stoke & Wolstanton PLU (1922—30), pt Newc. under Lyme Bor (until Newcastle under Lyme gains sep civ identity), pt Hanley MB (1857—89), pt Hanley CB (1889—94), pt Longton MB (1865—94), Stoke on Tr. MB (pt 1874—94, ent 1894—1910), pt Longton MB (1878—94), pt Burslem MB (1878—94), pt each in Hanley USD, Longton USD, Stoke on Tr. USD, Fenton USD; pt in Burslem USD (1878—94), pt Stoke on Tr. RSD (reduced pt 1878—94), Stoke on Tr. CB (1910—74). Made a city in 1925. Addtl civ bdry alt: 1883,[8] 1894 (the pt in Hanley CB cr Hanley CP, the pt in Longton MB cr Normancot CP, the pt in Fenton UD cr Fenton CP, the pt not in a CB, MB or UD cr Stoke Rural CP),[154] 1922 (incl gains all the pars in the CB which had been cr 1910: Burslem CP, Fenton CP, Goldenhill CP, Hanley CP, Longton CP, Tunstall CP, and also area outside the CB incl pt Smallthorne UD [ent Chell CP, pt Milton CP, ent Smallthorne CP]),[117] 1930,[36] 1965 (incl exchanges pts with Kidsgrove UD & CP, with Newc. under Lyme MB & AP, with Bagnall AP, with Caverswall AP, with Fulford CP, with Swynnerton AP, and loses pt to Forsbrook CP).[35] Transf 1974 to Staffs.[7] *Parl* Pt Stoke upon Tr. Parl Bor (1832—85 [all except the detched pt of tp Penkhull]), pt Newc. under Lyme Parl Bor (1832—85 [the detached pt of tp Penkhull]); pt Hanley Parl Bor (1885—1918 [tp Hanley, pt tp Shelton, the area of Hanley MB]), pt Stoke upon Tr. Parl Bor (1885—1918 [the remainder of the par]); see Part III of the *Guide* for composition of Stoke on Tr. Parl Bors/BCs (1918—*) by wards of the CB. *Eccl* Newc. RDn (until early 14th cent), Newc. & Stone RDn (early 14th cent—1851), Stoke upon Tr. RDn (1851—*). Addtl eccl bdry alt: 1843 (cr Shelton EP),[249] 1844 (cr Trent Vale EP),[99] 1845 (cr Penkhull EP),[3] 1845 (help cr Butterton EP,[3] refounded 1845[53]), 1886,[218] 1895 (cr Hanley St Jude EP),[242] 1967.[221]

STOKE RURAL

CP Cr 1894 from the pt of Stoke upon Trent AP not in a CB, MB or UD.[154] *LG* Stoke on Tr. PLU, RD. Bdry: 1896 (cr Bagnall CP),[34] 1896 (help cr Clayton CP),[170] 1910.[217] Abol civ 1922 pt to Stoke

on Tr. CB (assoc with Staffs) & AP, pt to Caverswall AP.[117] *Parl* Leek Dv (1918—48).

STOKE UPON TRENT—see STOKE ON TRENT

STONE

AP Incl chap Fulford (sep EP 1774,[3] sep CP 1897 from Stone Rural CP[224]). *LG* S Pir. Hd, Stone Bor, PLU, pt Longton MB & USD (1884—94), pt Stone USD, pt Stone RSD (reduced pt 1889—94), Stone UD. Civ bdry: 1894 (the pt not in a MB or UD cr Stone Rural CP),[311] 1932,[27] 1956.[312] *Parl* Seq 13. *Eccl* Seq 11. Eccl bdry: 1833 (cr Hilderstone EP),[251] 1840 (cr Stone Christ Church EP),[3] 1846 (cr Aston EP),[3] 1879 (help cr Oulton EP).[285]

STONE CHRIST CHURCH

EP Cr 1840 from Stone AP.[3] Newc. & Stone RDn (1849—51), Stone RDn (1851—61), Trentham RDn (1861—*). Bdry: 1879 (help cr Oulton EP),[285] 1882 (cr Tittensor EP).[186]

STONE RURAL

CP Cr 1894 from the pt of Stone AP not in Stone UD.[311] *LG* Stone PLU, RD. Bdry: 1897 (cr Hilderstone CP),[250] 1897 (cr Fulford CP [see 'Fulford' for early status as chap in Stone AP and for sep eccl identity]),[224] 1922 (loses pt to Stoke on Tr. CB [assoc with Staffs] & AP),[117] 1932,[27] 1956.[312] *Parl* Stone Dv (1918—48), Staff. & Stone CC (1948—*).

STONNALL

EP Cr 1823 from Shenstone AP,[3] refounded 1845.[109] Tamw. & Tutb. RDn (1823—51), Lichf RDn (1851—*). Bdry: 1854 (help cr Ogley Hall EP),[186] 1876 (help cr Little Aston EP [Staffs, Warws] to be dioc Lichf),[28] 1884.[68]

STOW—see LICHFIELD ST CHAD

STOWE

AP *LG* Seq 17. Civ bdry: 1883,[8] 1885,[45] 1886,[183] 1934 (incl gains Chartley Holme CP).[4] *Parl* Seq 12. *Eccl* Sometimes as 'Stowe by Chartley', Staff. RDn (until early 14th cent), Newc. & Stone RDn (early 14th cent—1851), Stone RDn (1851—61), Staff. RDn (1861—94), Uttox. RDn (1894—*). Eccl bdry: 1848 (help cr Hixon EP),[184] 1854 (help cr Great Haywood EP).[185]

STRAMSHALL

EP Cr 1853 from Uttoxeter AP,[3] refounded 1854.[262] Uttox. RDn.

STREETHAY

Tp in chap Lichfield St Michael (sep civ identity early from Lichfield St Mary AP, sep EP 1729[3]), 'Streethay' a sep CP 1866 from Lichfield St Michael CP.[2] *LG* Seq 8. Bdry: 1879,[115] 1885,[199] 1934.[4] *Parl* Seq 2.

STREETLY

EP Cr 1918 from Great Barr EP, Little Aston EP (Staffs, Warws).[29] Walsall RDn.

STRETTON

Tp (Staffs, N Offl. Hd) in Burton upon Trent AP (Staffs, Derbys), sep CP 1866 in Staffs,[2] eccl severed 1825 to help cr Burton upon Trent Holy Trinity EP,[3] the latter refounded 1842,[125] 'Stretton' a sep EP 1844 from Burton upon Trent Holy Trinity EP,[3] refounded 1873 as 'Stretton cum Wetmoor'.[127] *LG* Seq 7. *Parl* Seq 1. *Eccl* Tamw. & Tutb. RDn

(1844—51), Tutb. RDn (1851—73).

STRETTON

Chap in Penkridge AP, sep CP 1866,[2] all parochial rights from Dissolution except burial,[287] sep EP 1722.[3] LG Seq 4. Parl Seq 18. Eccl Lapley & Trysull RDn (1722—1851), Penkr. RDn (1851—*).

STRETTON CUM WETMOOR

EP Refounding 1873 of Stretton EP,[127] qv in earlier entry (1st Stretton above) for cr and earlier organisation. Tutb. RDn. Bdry: 1969.[130]

SWINDON

Lbty in Wombourn AP, sep EP 1867,[72] sep CP 1896.[313] LG S Seisd. PLU, RD. Parl Cannock Dv (1918—48), S W Staffs CC (1948—*). Eccl Trysull RDn.

SWINFEN AND PACKINGTON

Hmlts Swinfen, Packington, both in Weeford AP, united for civ purposes and as 'Swinfen and Packington' a sep CP 1866.[2] LG Seq 11. Bdry: 1896 (gains the pt of Lichfield St Michael CP not in Lichf MB),[268] 1934 (gains Freeford CP).[4] Parl Seq 14.

SWYNNERTON

AP LG Seq 16. Civ bdry: 1932,[27] 1965 (exchanges pts with Stoke on Tr. CB [assoc with Staffs] & AP).[35] Parl Seq 5. Eccl Seq 11. Eccl bdry: 1845 (help cr Butterton EP,[3] eccl refounded 1845[53]).

SYERSCOTE

Tp in Tamworth AP, sep CP 1866.[2] LG N Offl. Hd, Tamw. PLU, RSD, RD. Abol 1934 ent to Thorpe Constantine AP.[4] Parl N'rn Dv (1832—67), East Dv (1867—85), Lichf Dv (1885—1948).

TALK O' THE HILL—see following entry

TALKE

Area in Audley AP, sep EP 1741,[3] eccl refounded 1859,[31] orig as 'Talk o' the Hill' but later 'Talke', as such sep CP 1932 from Audley AP.[27] LG Kidsgrove UD. Parl Leek CC (1948—*). Eccl Newc. & Stone RDn (1741—1851), Newc. under Lyme RDn (1851—*). Eccl bdry: 1853 (help cr Kidsgrove EP,[3] refounded the same year[227]).

TAMHORN

Ex-par place, sep CP 1858,[10] eccl abol 1967 ent to Whittington AP.[178] LG N Offl. Hd, Lichf PLU (1858—1930), RSD, RD. Abol civ 1934 ent to Fisherwick CP.[4] Parl N'rn Dv (1832—67), East Dv (1867—85), Lichf Dv (1885—1948).

TAMWORTH

AP Tp 'Tamworth' (the orig area Tamw. Bor) in Staffs (N Offl. Hd) as was tp Syerscote (sep CP 1866[2]); incl in Staffs (S Offl. Hd) chap Wiggington ([civ and eccl incl hmlt Hopwas] sep CP 1866,[2] sep EP 1778,[3] eccl refounded 1856[314]), tp Fazeley (sep CP 1866,[2] sep EP 1813,[3] eccl refounded 1842[68]), hmlt Hopwas Hays (sep CP 1866,[2] eccl ex-par, eccl abol 1967 ent to Whittington AP[178]); incl in Warws (Hemlingford Hd) chap Wilncote (sep EP 1770 [incl lbty Tamworth Castle],[3] the area civ tp 'Wilncote and Castle Liberty' [Hemlingford Hd], as such a sep CP 1866 in Warws[2]), tp Amington and Stoneydelph, tp Bolehall and Glascote (each a sep CP 1866 in Warws[2]), lbty Tamworth Castle (sep CP 1866 in Warws,[2] eccl in chap Wilncote as above) so that 'Tamworth' ent Staffs after 1866. LG Tamw.

PLU, pt Tamw. Bor, Tamw. MB (ent par [incl areas in Warws until 1866]), Tamw. USD. Addtl civ bdry alt: 1894 (gains the pts in Tamw. MB of Tamworth Castle CP, Bolehall and Glascote CP, both Warws),[315] 1932 (incl gains pt Amington and Stoneydelph CP, Bolehall and Glascote CP, Wilncote and Castle Liberty CP, all Warws),[214] 1965 (gains 2 ent pars of Amington CP, Glascote CP, and pts of Dordon CP, Kingsbury AP, Polesworth AP, Shuttington AP, Wilncote and Castle Liberty CP, all Warws).[316] Parl Tamw. Parl Bor (tp Tamworth, 1563—1832; ent par [incl pts in Warws] 1832—85), Lichf Dv (1885—1948), Lichf & Tamw. CC (1948—*). Eccl Usually as 'Tamworth with Glascote and Hopwas' until 1967, Seq 13. Addtl eccl bdry alt: 1864 (cr Amington EP,[3] sep eccl status not sustained and incl again in Tamworth AP by 1870s[43]).

TATENHILL

AP Incl chap Barton under Needwood (sep CP 1866,[2] sep EP 1796,[3] eccl refounded 1881[13]), chap Wychnor (sep CP 1866,[2] sep EP 1792,[3] eccl refounded 1881[13]), tp Dunstall (sep CP 1866,[2] sep EP 1852,[3] eccl refounded 1854[207]). LG Seq 7. Addtl civ bdry alt: 1886,[41] 1890,[223] 1896,[208] 1934.[4] Parl Seq 1. Eccl Seq 14. Addtl eccl bdry alt: 1884 (help cr Rangemore EP),[22] 1899,[23] 1940.[24]

UPPER TEAN

EP Cr 1844 from Checkley AP.[162] Alton & Leek RDn (1844—51), Uttox. RDn (1851—1924), Cheadle RDn (1924—*).

TEDDESLEY HAY

Ex-par place, sep CP 1858.[10] LG E Cutt. Hd, Penkr. PLU (1858—70s), Cannock PLU (1870s—1930), RSD, RD. Parl S'rn Dv (1832—67), West Dv (1867—85), W'rn Dv (1885—1918), Staff. Dv (1918—48), Cannock CC (1948—*).

TETTENHALL

AP Orig Collegiate. Usual civ spelling; for eccl see following entry. Tp 'Tettenhall' pt N Seisd. Hd, pt S Seisd. Hd; incl in S Seisd. Hd chap Codsall[179] (sep civ identity early, sep EP 1756[3]). LG Seisd. PLU, pt Tettenhall USD (1883—94), Seisd. RSD (ent 1875—83, pt 1883—94), Tettenhall UD. Addtl civ bdry alt: 1894 (the pt not in the UD cr Wrottesley CP),[317] 1934.[4] Abol civ 1966 pt to Wolverh. CB (assoc with Staffs) & AP, pt to Codsall CP, pt to Lower Penn CP, pt to Wrottesley CP.[6] Parl S'rn Dv (1832—67), West Dv (1867—85), Kingswinf. Dv (1885—1918), Cannock Dv (1918—48), Brierley Hill CC (1948—70).

TETTENHALL REGIS

AP Usual eccl spelling; for civ and civ and eccl sep chap, see prev entry. Eccl Pec jurisd royal free chap of Tettenhall (until 1846), Lapley & Trysull RDn (1846—51), Trysull RDn (1851—*). Addtl eccl bdry alt: 1868 (cr Tettenhall Wood EP),[318] 1962.[180]

TETTENHALL WOOD

EP Cr 1868 from Tettenhall Regis AP (civ, 'Tettenhall').[318] Trysull RDn. Bdry: 1962.[180]

THORPE CONSTANTINE

AP LG Seq 9. Civ bdry: 1934 (incl gains Statfold AP, Syerscote CP).[4] Parl Seq 2. Eccl Seq 13.

TILLINGTON

Ex-par place, sep CP 1858.[10] *LG* S Pir. Hd, Staff. PLU (1858—1917), RSD, RD. Civ bdry: 1884.[25] Abol civ 1917 pt to Staff. MB & CP, pt to Creswell AP.[150] *Parl* N'rn Dv (1832—67), West Dv (1867—85), W'rn Dv (1885—1918).

TIPTON

The following have 'Tipton' in their names. Insofar as any existed at a given time: *LG* S Offl. Hd, Dudley PLU, Tipton USD, UD (1894—1938), MB (1938—66). *Parl* S'rn Dv (1832—67), Wednesb. Parl Bor (1867—1948), Rowley Regis & Tipton BC (1948—70). *Eccl* Pec jurisd prebend Prees (until 1846), Tamw. & Tutb. RDn (1846—51), Handsw. RDn (1851—94), Wednesb. RDn (1894—*).

AP1—TIPTON [ST MARTIN]—Civ bdry: 1934 (exchanges pts with Dudley CB [assoc with Worcs] & AP).[4] Abol civ 1966 pt to Dudley CB (as CB becomes assoc with Staffs) & AP, pt to W Bromw. CB (assoc with Staffs) & AP, pt to help cr Warley CB (assoc with Worcs) & CP.[6] Eccl bdry: 1842 (cr EP3,[3] refounded 1853,[319] sometimes called 'Tipton Green'), 1845 (cr Ocker Hill EP, now called 'Tipton St Mark'),[54] 1854 (cr EP1),[191] 1879 (help cr Tividale EP).[296]

EP1—TIPTON ST JOHN—Cr 1854 from AP1.[191] Bdry: 1870.[320]

—TIPTON ST MARK—Name used now for EP cr 1845 as 'Ocker Hill', qv.

EP2—TIPTON ST MATTHEW—Cr 1881 from EP3.[321]

—TIPTON ST MICHAEL—Name sometimes used now for EP cr 1879 as 'Tividale', qv.

EP3—TIPTON ST PAUL—Cr 1842 from AP1,[3] refounded 1853.[319] Bdry: 1870,[320] 1881 (cr EP2).[321] Sometimes called 'Tipton Greeen'.

TITTENSOR

EP Cr 1882 from Stone Christ Church EP.[186] Trentham RDn.

TITTESWORTH

Tp in Leek AP, sep CP 1866,[2] eccl severed 1845 to help cr Leek St Luke EP.[53] *LG* N Totm. Hd, Leek PLU, pt Leek USD, pt Leek RSD, Leek RD. Bdry: 1883,[8] 1894 (incl loses the pt in Leek UD to help cr Leek CP),[265] 1934.[4] *Parl* Seq 6.

TIVIDALE

EP Cr 1879 from Tipton AP (dioc Lichf), Rowley Regis AP (dioc Worc) to be dioc Lichf.[296] Handsw. RDn (1879—94), Wednesb. RDn (1894—*). Bdry: 1921 (gains pt Kate's Hill EP, Worcs, dioc Worc).[322] Now sometimes called Tipton St Michael'.

TIXALL

AP *LG* Seq 17. Civ bdry: 1934.[4] *Parl* Seq 12. *Eccl* Pec jurisd royal free chap of Stafford St Mary (until 1846), Newc. & Stone RDn (1846—51), Staff. RDn (1851—*).

TRENT VALE

EP Cr 1844 from Stoke upon Trent AP.[99] Newc. & Stone RDn (1844—51), Stoke upon Tr. RDn (1851—*). Bdry: 1961.[278]

TRENTHAM

AP Incl chap Blurton (sep EP 1721,[3] eccl refounded

1832[69]). *LG* N Pir. Hd, Stone PLU, pt Longton MB & USD (1884—94), pt Newc. under Lyme MB & USD (1878—94), Stone RSD (ent 1875—78, pt 1878—94 [reduced pt 1884—94]), Stone RD. Civ bdry: 1878 (gains a detached pt of area Penkhull [not sep civ] in Stoke upon Trent AP and thus thereafter pt Newc. under Lyme MB),[276] 1883,[8] 1894 (loses the pt in Newc. under Lyme MB to Newcastle under Lyme AP, loses pt to Keele CP,[259] the pt in Longton MB cr Florence CP[154]), 1896 (help cr Clayton CP),[171] 1922 (loses pt to Stoke upon Tr. CB [assoc with Staffs] & AP),[117] 1930 (loses pt to Stoke upon Tr. CB [assoc with Staffs] & AP).[36] Abol civ 1932 pt to Barlaston AP, pt to Swynnerton AP, pt to Whitmore CP.[27] *Parl* N'rn Dv (1832—67), North Dv (1867—85); pt Newc. under Lyme Parl Bor, pt N-W'rn Dv (1885—1918); Stone Dv (1918—48). *Eccl* Newc. RDn (until early 14th cent), Newc. & Stone RDn (early 14th cent—1851), Trentham RDn (1851—*). Addtl eccl bdry alt: 1828 (cr Hanford EP),[3] refounded 1832[69]), 1845 (help cr Butterton EP,[3] refounded 1845[53]), 1969.[23]

TRYSULL

Chap in Wombourn AP, sep EP 1888,[323] sep CP 1866 as 'Trysull and Seisdon',[2] qv. Trysull RDn.

TRYSULL AND SEISDON

Chap in Wombourn AP, sep CP 1866,[2] sep EP 1866 as 'Trysull',[323] qv. *LG* Seq 20. Civ bdry: 1900 (gains Woodford Grange CP).[324] *Parl* Seq 16.

TUCK HILL

EP Cr 1870 from Alveley AP, Claveley AP (both Salop), Bobbington EP (Staffs, Salop), Enville AP (Staffs).[51] See main entry in Salop.

TUNSTALL

Area in Wolstanton AP, sep CP 1894 from the pt of Wolstanton in Tunstall UD,[116] sep EP 1837 as 'Tunstall Christ Church'.[186] *LG* Wolstanton PLU, Tunstall UD (1894—1910), Stoke on. Tr. CB (1910—22). Civ bdry: 1899,[165] 1904.[166] Abol civ 1922 ent to Stoke upon Trent AP.[117] *Parl* Stoke on Tr. Parl Bor (1918—48).

TUNSTALL CHRIST CHURCH

EP Area in Wolstanton AP, sep EP 1837,[186] sep CP 1894 as 'Tunstall' from the pt of the AP in Tunstall UD,[116] qv. Newc. & Stone RDn (1837—51), Stoke upon Tr. RDn (1851—94), Hanley RDn (1894—1920), Stoke upon Tr. RDn (1920—62), Stoke North RDn (1962—*). Bdry: 1881 (help cr Tunstall St Mary the Virgin EP).[121]

TUNSTALL ST MARY THE VIRGIN

EP Cr 1881 from Tunstall Christ Church EP, Wolstanton AP, Burslem St Paul EP.[121] Stoke upon Tr. RDn (1881—94), Hanley RDn (1894—1920), Stoke upon Tr. RDn (1920—62), Stoke North RDn (1962—*). Bdry: 1914.[252]

TUTBURY

AP *LG* Pt Tutb. Bor, perhaps pt in New Borough Bor,[325] Seq 7. Civ bdry: 1883,[8] 1890,[326] 1934.[4] *Parl* Seq 1. *Eccl* Seq 14. Eccl bdry: 1861 (help cr Anslow EP),[21] 1884 (help cr Rangemore EP),[22] 1895 (help cr Needwood EP),[42] 1899.[233]

TYRLEY
>Tp (Staffs, N Pir. Hd) in Drayton in Hales AP (o'wise Salop, N Bradford Hd), sep CP 1866 in Staffs[2] and Drayton in Hales ent Salop thereafter. *LG* Seq 13. Bdry: 1932,[27] 1965 (loses pt to Sutton upon Tern CP, Salop).[6] *Parl* Seq 10.

UTTOXETER
>AP *LG* S Totm. Hd, Uttox. Bor, PLU, RSD, RD (1894—96), UD (1896—1974). Civ bdry: 1883,[8] 1896 (the pt not constituted Uttox. UD cr Uttoxeter Rural CP),[327] 1934,[4] 1967.[328] *Parl* Seq 3. *Eccl* Alton & Leek RDn (until 1851), Uttox. RDn (1851—*). Eccl bdry: 1853 (cr Stramshall EP,[3] refounded 1854[262]), 1939.[23]

UTTOXETER RURAL
>CP Cr 1896 from the pt of Uttoxeter AP not constituted Uttox. UD.[327] *LG* Uttox. PLU, RD. Bdry: 1934,[4] 1967.[328] *Parl* Burt. Dv/CC (1918—*).

EAST VALE
>CP Cr 1894 from the pt of Caverswall AP in Longton MB.[154] *LG* Stoke on Tr. PLU, Longton MB. Abol 1896 ent to Longton CP.[220]

WALL
>Tp in chap Lichfield St Michael (sep civ identity AP, sep civ identity early from Lichfield St Mary AP, sep EP 1729[3]), 'Wall' a sep CP 1866 from Lichfield St Michael EP,[2] sep EP 1843,[3] eccl refounded 1845.[65] *LG* Seq 11. Civ bdry: 1879,[115] 1894,[82] 1934,[4] 1957.[304] *Parl* Seq 14. *Eccl* Tamw. & Tutb. RDn (1843—51), Lichf RDn (1851—*). Eccl bdry: 1910.[282]

WALSALL
>The following have 'Walsall' in their names. Insofar as any existed at a given time: *LG* S Offl. Hd, Walsall PLU; Bor/MB/CB, USD sep noted. *Parl* Sep noted for 1832—67; thereafter, Walsall Parl Bor/BC (1867—1955), pt Walsall North BC, pt Walsall South BC (1955—70). *Eccl* Tamw. & Tutb. RDn (until 1851), Walsall RDn (1851—*).

>AP1—WALSALL [ST MATTHEW]—Incl chap Wednesbury (sep par by 1535), tps CP2, CP3 (each a sep CP 1866[2]) so that 'Walsall' has no sep civ identity 1866—94 (see following entry). *LG* Pt Walsall Bor/MB. *Parl* Pt Walsall Parl Bor, pt S'rn Dv (1832—67). Addtl eccl bdry alt: 1810 (cr Bloxwich EP,[3] refounded 1842[68]), 1842 (cr EP6,[3] refounded 1845[329]), 1845 (cr EP8),[329] 1860 (cr Pleck and Bescot EP),[291] 1872 (cr Caldmore EP),[138] 1875 (help cr EP5),[330] 1878 (cr EP3),[331] 1911,[332] 1939 (help cr EP2),[139] 1964.[252]

>CP1—WALSALL—Cr 1894 by union of the following areas in Walsall CB: ent CP2, pt CP3, pt Rushall AP.[298] *LG* Walsall CB. Bdry: 1931 (incl gains pt W Bromw. CB [assoc with Staffs] & AP),[38] 1934 (loses pt to Darlaston UD & AP),[199] 1966 (incl exchanges pts with W Bromw. CB [assoc with Staffs] & AP, Essington CP, help cr Aldridge-Brownhills UD & CP).[6] Transf 1974 to W Midlands.[7]

>CP2—WALSALL BOROUGH—Tp in AP1, sep CP 1866.[2] *LG* Walsall MB/CB, USD. Abol 1894 to help cr CP1.[298] *Parl* S'rn Dv (1832—67), Walsall Parl Bor (1867—1918).

>CP3—WALSALL FOREIGN—Tp in AP1, sep CP 1866.[2] *LG* Pt Walsall CB (1890—94), pt Walsall USD, pt Brownhills USD. Abol 1894 the pt in Brownhills UD cr CP4, the remainder to help cr CP1.[298] *Parl* S'rn Dv (1832—67), East Dv (1867—85), Handsw. Dv (1885—1918).

>EP1—WALSALL ST ANDREW—Cr 1889 from EP6.[67]

>EP2—WALSALL ST GABRIEL—Cr 1939 from AP1, Caldmore EP, EP7, Wednesbury St Paul, Wood Green EP.[139]

>EP3—WALSALL ST GEORGE—Cr 1878 from AP1.[331] Bdry: 1911,[332] 1925 (help cr EP4).[299] Abol 1964 pt to EP5, pt to AP1.[252]

>—WALSALL ST JOHN—Name used now for EP cr 1860 as 'Pleck and Bescot'. qv.

>EP4—WALSALL ST MARK—Cr 1925 from Rushall AP, EP3, EP6.[299] Abol 1973 pt to EP5, pt to EP6.[333]

>—WALSALL ST MICHAEL—Name used now for EP cr 1872 as 'Caldmore', qv.

>EP5—WALSALL ST PAUL—Cr 1875 from AP1, EP6.[330] Bdry: 1928,[320] 1964,[252] 1973.[333]

>EP6—WALSALL ST PETER—Cr 1842 from AP1,[3] refounded 1845.[329] Bdry: 1875 (help cr EP5),[330] 1889 (cr EP1),[67] 1925 (help cr EP4),[299] 1928,[320] 1973.[333]

>EP7—WALSALL PALFREY [ST MARY AND ALL SAINTS]—Cr 1902 from Caldmore EP.[109] Bdry: 1939 (help cr EP2).[139] Sometimes 'Palfrey'.

>CP4/EP8—WALSALL WOOD [ST JOHN]—Cr eccl 1845 from AP1,[329] cr civ 1894 from the pt of CP3 in Brownhills UD.[298] *LG* Brownhills UD. For civ abol 1966, see Brownhills UD. *Parl* Cannock Dv/CC (1918—55), Walsall North BC (1955—70). Eccl bdry: 1854 (help cr Ogley Hey EP),[186] 1884.[68]

WARLEY WOODS
>CP Cr 1928 from Oldbury UD & CP, Worcs, to be in Smethw. CB (assoc with Staffs).[334] *LG* W Bromw. PLU, Smethw. CB. For civ abol 1966, see Smethw. CB. *Parl* Smethw. CC (1948—70).

WARSLOW—see following entry

WARSLOW AND ELKSTONES
>Single tp comprised of chaps Warslow, Elkstone (each in Alstonfield AP), the tp a sep CP 1866 as 'Warslow and Elkstones',[2] 'Warslow' a sep EP 1785 (incl pt tp Fawfieldhead in same par),[3] 'Elkstone' a sep EP 1785,[3] the 2 EPS united 1902 to refound Warslow EP,[12] the union later called 'Warslow and Elkstone'. *LG* N Totm. Hd, Leek PLU, RSD, RD. Civ bdry: 1934.[4] *Parl* Seq 6. *Eccl* Under the successive names, Alton & Leek RDn (1785—1851), Alst. RDn (1851—*).

WARSLOW AND ELKSTONE—see prev entry

WATERFALL
>AP Orig chap in Rocester AP, sep par early with curates.[295] Incl pt chap Calton (sep CP 1866,[2] sep EP 1902 [qv for other constituent pars][241]). *LG* S Totm. Hd, Ashb. PLU, RSD, Mayf. RD. Abol civ 1934 to help cr Waterhouses CP.[4] *Parl* N'rn Dv (1832—67), North Dv (1867—85), Leek Dv (1885—1918), Stone Dv (1918—48). *Eccl* Alton &

Leek RDn (until 1851), Alst. RDn (1851—*).

WATERHOUSES

CP Cr 1934 by union ent Calton CP, ent Cauldon CP, ent Waterfall AP, pt Ilam AP.[4] *LG* Cheadle RD. *Parl* Leek CC (1948—*).

WEDNESBURY

The following have 'Wednesbury' in their names. Insofar as any existed at a given time: *LG* S Offl. Hd, W Bromw. PLU, Wednesb. USD, MB (1886—1966). *Parl* S'rn Dv (1832—67), Wednesb. Parl Bor/BC (1867—1970). *Eccl* Tamw. & Tutb. RDn (until 1851), Walsall RDn (1851—94), Wednesb. RDn (1894—*).

AP1—WEDNESBURY [ST BARTHOLOMEW]—Orig chap in Walsall AP, sep par by 1535. Civ bdry: 1931 (loses pt to Walsall CB [assoc with Staffs] & CP,[38] loses pt to W Bromw. CB [assoc with Staffs] & AP,[39] gains pt W Bromw. CB [assoc with Staffs] & AP[97]). Abol civ 1966 pt to Walsall CB (assoc with Staffs) & AP, pt to W Bromw. CB (assoc with Staffs) & CP.[6] Eccl bdry: 1843 (cr EP1,[3] refounded 1844[119]), 1844 (cr EP2),[119] 1845 (help cr Moxley EP),[53] 1872 (help cr Darlaston All Saints EP),[202] 1875 (help cr EP3),[61] 1881,[293] 1912.[159]

EP1—WEDNESBURY ST JAMES—Cr 1843 from AP1,[3] refounded 1844.[119]

EP2—WEDNESBURY ST JOHN—Cr 1844 from AP1.[119]

EP3—WEDNESBURY ST PAUL, WOOD GREEN—Cr 1875 from AP1, West Bromwich AP.[61] Bdry: 1881,[293] 1912,[102] 1937 (help cr West Bromwich St Francis EP),[101] 1939 (help cr Walsall St Gabriel EP),[139] 1969.[102]

WEDNESFIELD

Chap in Wolverhampton AP, sep CP 1866,[2] sep EP 1755.[3] *LG* S Offl. Hd, Wolverh. PLU, pt Wednesfield USD, pt Heath Town (or Wednesfield Heath) USD, Wednesfield UD. Civ bdry: 1894 (the pt in Heath Town (or Wednesfield Heath) UD cr Heath Town CP, later called 'Heathtown'),[154] 1895,[305] 1933 (loses pt to Wolverh. CB [assoc with Staffs] & AP).[134] Abol civ 1966 pt to Walsall CB (assoc with Staffs) & CP, pt to Wolverh. CB (assoc with Staffs) & AP, pt to Essington CP.[6] *Parl* Wolverh. Parl Bor (1832—1918), Wolverh. East Parl Bor (1918—48), Wednesb. BC (1948—55), Cannock CC (1955—70). *Eccl* Lapley & Trysull RDn (1755—1851), Wolverh. RDn (1851—*). Eccl bdry: 1852 (cr Wednesfield Heath EP,[3] refounded 1853[168]), 1934 (help cr Essington EP),[132] 1964 (help cr Wednesfield St Gregory the Great EP),[136] 1965.[335]

WEDNESFIELD ST GREGORY THE GREAT

EP Cr 1964 from Wednesfield EP, Bushbury AP, Essington EP.[136] Wolverh. RDn.

WEDNESFIELD HEATH

EP Cr 1852 from Wednesfield EP,[3] refounded 1853.[168] Wolverh. RDn. Bdry: 1965.[335] Sometimes called 'Heath Town'.

WEEFORD

AP Incl hmlts Swinfen, Packington (united for civ purposes and as 'Swinfen and Packington' a sep CP

1866[2]). *LG* Seq 11. Addtl civ bdry alt: 1966 (gains pt Sutton Coldfield MB & AP, Warws).[6] *Parl* Seq 14. *Eccl* Pec jurisd Dean & Chapter of Lichf (until 1846), Seq 12 thereafter.

WELLINGTON

EP Cr 1845 from Hanley EP.[218] Newc. & Stone RDn (1845—51), Stoke upon Tr. RDn (1851—94), Hanley RDn (1894—1920), Stoke upon Tr. RDn (1920—62), Stoke North RDn (1962—*). Bdry: 1913 (help cr Hanley All Saints EP).[240] Now called 'Hanley St Luke'.

WERRINGTON

EP Cr 1964 from Caverswall AP, Wetley Rocks EP, Bucknall cum Bagnall EP.[112] Cheadle RDn.

THE WESTLANDS

EP Cr 1966 from Newcastle under Lyme with Butterton EP.[279] Newc. under Lyme RDn.

WESTON JONES

Tp in Norbury AP, sep CP 1866.[2] *LG* W Cutt. Hd, Newport PLU, RSD, Gnosall RD. Abol 1934 pt to Adbaston CP, pt to Norbury CP, pt to High Offley CP.[4] *Parl* S'rn Dv (1832—67), West Dv (1867—85), Handsw. RDn (1885—1918), Staff. Dv (1918—48).

WESTON UNDER LIZARD

AP *LG* Seq 5. *Parl* Seq 18. *Eccl* Seq 4.

WESTON UNDER TRENT

AP *LG* Seq 17. Civ bdry: 1934.[4] *Parl* Seq 12. *Eccl* Staff. RDn (until early 14th cent), Newc. & Stone RDn (early 14th cent—1851), Stone RDn (1851—61), Staff. RDn (1861—*).

WETLEY ROCKS

EP Cr 1862 from Cheddleton EP (qv for earlier status).[3] Leek RDn. Bdry: 1964 (help cr Werrington EP).[112]

WETTON

AP Orig chap in Mayfield AP, sep par early, before 1535. *LG* S Totm. Hd, Alst. GilbU (until 1869), Alst. PLU (1869—1930), Mayf. RD (1894—1934), Leek RD (1934—74). Civ bdry: 1934.[4] *Parl* Seq 9. *Eccl* Alton & Leek RDn (until 1851), Alst. RDn (1851—*).

WHITGREAVE

Tp in Stafford St Mary AP, sep CP 1866,[2] eccl in chap Marston (sep EP 1777 as 'Marston with Whitgreave'[3]), 'Whitgreave' a sep EP 1844 from the latter [which becomes 'Marston']).[271] *LG* Seq 17. *Parl* Seq 12. *Eccl* Newc. & Stone RDn. Abol eccl 1850 to help cr Marston with Whitgreave EP.[272]

WHITMORE

Chap in Stoke upon Trent AP, sep civ identity early, sep EP 1725,[3] eccl refounded 1849.[110] *LG* Seq 14. Civ bdry: 1932.[27] *Parl* Seq 10. *Eccl* Newc. & Stone RDn (1725—1851), Trentham RDn (1851—*).

WHITTINGTON

AP *LG* Seq 8. Civ bdry: 1934.[4] *Parl* Seq 2. *Eccl* Pec jurisd Dean & Chapter of Lichf (until 1846), Seq 12 thereafter. Eccl bdry: 1967 (gains ex-par places of Tamhorn, Hopwas Hays).[178]

WIGGINGTON

Chap (incl civ and eccl hmlt Hopwas) in Tamworth AP, sep CP 1866,[2] sep EP 1778,[3] eccl refounded

1856.[314] *LG* Seq 12. Civ bdry: 1932,[214] 1934 (incl gains Hopwas Hays CP).[4] *Parl* Seq 14. *Eccl* Tamw. & Tutb. RDn (1778—1851), Tamw. RDn (1851—*).

WILLENHALL

The following have 'Willenhall' in their names. Insofar as any existed at a given time: *LG* S Offl. Hd, Wolverh. PLU, pt Willenhall USD, pt Short Heath USD, Willenhall UD. *Parl* Wolverh. Parl Bor (1832—1918), Willenhall East Parl Bor (1918—48), Wednesb. BC (1948—70). *Eccl* Lapley & Trysull RDn (until 1851), Wolverh. RDn (1851—*).

CP1—WILLENHALL—Chap and tp in Wolverhampton AP, sep CP 1866,[2] pts eccl severed 1846 to help cr EP1 and to help cr EP4,[247] pt eccl severed 1912 to help cr EP3.[46] Civ bdry: 1894 (the pt in Short Heath UD cr Short Heath CP),[154] 1934,[4] 1937.[200] For civ abol 1966, see following entry for the UD.

UD—WILLENHALL—Consisted of CP1 (1894—1966), Short Heath (1934—66). Abol civ 1966, pt to Walsall CB (assoc with Staffs) & AP, pt to Wolverh. CB (assoc with Staffs) & AP, pt to Essington CP.[6]

EP1—WILLENHALL HOLY TRINITY—Cr 1846 from Wolverhampton AP (pt tp Willenhall).[247] Walsall RDn (1894—1924), Wolverh. RDn (1924—*). Bdry: 1860 (cr EP2),[3] 1964.[212]

EP2—WILLENHALL ST ANN—Cr 1860 from EP1.[3] Bdry: 1964.[212]

EP3—WILLENHALL ST GILES—Cr 1912 from Wolverhampton AP (tp Bentley, pt tp Willenhall).[46] Bdry: 1958 (cr Bentley EP).[47]

EP4—WILLENHALL ST STEPHEN—Cr 1846 from Wolverhampton AP (pt tp Willenhall).[247]

WINSHILL

Tp (Derbys, Repton and Gresley Hd) in Burton upon Trent AP (Staffs, Derbys), sep CP 1866 in Derbys,[2] eccl severed 1825 to help cr Burton upon Trent Holy Trinity EP,[3] the latter refounded 1842,[125] 'Winshill' a sep EP 1867 from Burton upon Trent Holy Trinity EP.[126] *LG* Burt. upon Tr. PLU, pt Burt. upon Tr. MB (1878—89), Burt. upon Tr. CB (pt 1889—94, ent 1894—1909), pt Burt. upon Tr. USD (1878—94), Burt. upon Tr. RSD (ent 1875—78, pt 1878—94). Civ bdry: 1894 (loses the pt not in the CB [assoc with Staffs] to Newton Solney AP, Derbys,[223] and 'Winshill' ent in the CB until abol civ 1904 ent to Burton upon Trent AP.[124] See entry in Derbys for parl and eccl organisation.

WITTON

EP Cr 1926 from Birchfield EP (Staffs), Aston juxta Birmingham AP (Warws, dioc Birm) to be dioc Lichf.[61] Handsw. RDn.

WOLLASTON

Tp (Worcs, Halfshire Hd) in Oldswinford AP (Worcs, Staffs until 1866, ent Worcs thereafter; eccl, 'Old Swinford'), eccl severed 1860 to help cr Amblecote EP (o'wise Staffs, qv above),[16] 'Wollaston' a sep EP 1860 from Amblecote EP.[20] Kidderminster RDn (1860—1907), Swinford RDn (1907—*) (both dioc Worc).

WOLSTANTON

AP Incl chap Keele (sep civ identity early, sep EP 1774[3]), area Goldenhill (sep EP 1842,[3] sep CP 1894 from pt of the rural pt of this par[116]), area Tunstall (sep CP 1894 from the pt of the par in Tunstall UD,[116] sep EP 1837 as 'Tunstall Christ Church'[186]). *LG* N Pir. Hd, Wolstanton & Burslem PLU (1838—1922), Stoke & Wolstanton PLU (1922—30), pt Kidsgrove USD, pt Tunstall USD, pt Wolstanton RSD, Wolstanton RD (1894—1904), Wolstanton United UD (1904—32). Addtl civ bdry alt: 1894 (the pt in Kidsgrove UD cr Kidsgrove CP, the rural pt severed to cr the 5 CPs of Chesterton, Silverdale, Newchapel, Chell, Goldenhill [qv above], the pt in Tunstall UD cr Tunstall CP [qv above]).[116] Abol civ 1932 ent to Newc. under Lyme MB & AP.[169] *Parl* Pt Stoke upon Tr. Parl Bor (1832—85 [ville Rushton Grange, hmlt Sneyd, tp Tunstall, none sep civ], pt N'rn Dv (1832—67), pt North Dv (1867—85); pt Hanley Parl Bor (1885—1918 [ville Rushton Grange, hmlt Sneyd]), pt Newc. under Lyme Parl Bor (1885—1918 [tp Tunstall]), pt N-W'rn Dv (1885—1918); Newc. under Lyme Parl Bor (1918—48). *Eccl* Newc. RDn (until early 14th cent), Newc. & Stone RDn (early 14th cent—1851), Newc. under Lyme RDn (1851—*). Addtl eccl bdry alt: 1715 (cr Newchapel EP [incl areas Tunstall, Ravenscliffe, Chell],[3] refounded 1846,[153] sometimes early called 'Wolstanton St James New Chapel' or 'New Chapel'), 1843 (cr Mowcop EP,[3] refounded 1844[49]), 1846 (help cr Chesterton EP),[33] 1853 (help cr Kidsgrove EP,[3] refounded same year[227]), 1853 (help cr Silverdale EP,[3] refounded 1855 as 'Silverdale and Knutton Heath'[84]), 1875 (help cr Knutton EP),[114] 1881 (help cr Tunstall St Mary the Virgin EP),[121] 1913 (cr Porthill EP),[294] 1915 (help cr Basford EP),[43] 1934,[44] 1952 (incl help cr Cross Heath EP).[195]

WOLSTANTON ST JAMES—see NEWCHAPEL

WOLVERHAMPTON

The following have 'Wolverhampton' in their names. Insofar as any existed at a given time: *LG* Pt Wolverh. Bor, Wolverh. PLU, MB (1849—89), CB (1889—1974), USD; Hds sep noted. *Parl* Wolverh. Parl Bor (1832—1918); pt Wolverh. Bilston Parl Bor, pt Wolverh. East Parl Bor, pt Wolverh. North Parl Bor (1918—48); pt Wolverh. North East BC (1948—*), pt Wolverh. South West BC (1948—*), pt Wolverh. South East BC (1970—*). *Eccl* Pec jurisd royal free chap of Wolverh. (until 1846), Lapley & Trysull RDn (1846—51), Wolverh. RDn (1851—*).

AP1—WOLVERHAMPTON [ST PETER]—Orig royal free chap, independent early. Tp 'Wolverhampton' (and Wolverh. Bor) in N Seisd. Hd as was chap and tp Bilston (sep CP 1866,[2] sep EP 1723[3]); incl in E Cutt. Hd tps Featherstone, Hatherton, Hilton, Kinvaston (each a sep CP 1866[2]); incl in S Offl. Hd chap Pelsall (sep CP 1866,[2] sep EP 1766[3]), chap Wednesfield (sep CP 1866,[2] sep EP 1755[3]), chap and tp Willenhall (sep CP 1866,[2] pts eccl severed 1846 to cr 2 EPs of Willenhall Holy Trinity, Willenhall St Stephen,[247] pt eccl severed

1912 and united with tp Bentley to cr Willenhall St Giles EP[46]), tp Bentley (sep CP 1866,[2] eccl severed 1912 to help cr Willenhall St Giles EP,[3] 'Bentley' a sep EP 1958 from Willenhall St Giles EP[47]). *LG* N Seisd. Hd (pt until 1866, ent from 1866), pt E Cutt. Hd (until 1866), pt pt S Offl. Hd (until 1866), pt Wolverh. Bor (tp Wolverhampton, chap Pelsall, tp Bentley). Addtl civ bdry alt: 1927 (incl gains Heath Town (or Wednesfield Heath) UD & CP),[133] 1933,[134] 1966 (incl loses pt to Walsall CB [assoc with Staffs] & CP, loses pt to Featherstone CP, loses pt to help cr Wombourne CP, exchanges pts with Brewood AP, Lower Penn CP, Wrottesley CP).[6] Transf 1974 to W Midlands.[7] Addtl eccl bdry alt: 1834 (cr EP5),[336] 1837 (help cr Ettingshall EP),[52] 1843 (cr EP6,[3] refounded 1844[337]), 1843 (cr EP10),[338] 1844 (cr EP12),[339] 1846 (cr EP11),[340] 1846 (cr EP9),[340] 1847,[341] 1848 (cr Bilston St Mary EP),[57] 1869 (help cr Gailey cum Hatherton EP),[84] 1871 (cr EP3),[278] 1871 (cr EP7),[3] 1884,[342] 1905,[279] 1912 (pt united with tp Bentley [qv above] to cr Willenhall St Giles EP),[46] 1955,[343] 1958,[301] 1973 (gains EP2).[203]

EP1—WOLVERHAMPTON ALL SAINTS—Cr 1881 from EP7.[344]

EP2—WOLVERHAMPTON CHRIST CHURCH—Cr 1876 from EP3, EP10.[28] Bdry: 1897.[288] Abol 1973 ent to AP1.[203]

EP3—WOLVERHAMPTON ST ANDREW—Cr 1871 from AP1.[278] Bdry: 1876 (help cr EP2),[28] 1897,[288] 1904.[279]

EP4—WOLVERHAMPTON ST CHAD—Cr 1909 from EP12.[287]

EP5—WOLVERHAMPTON ST GEORGE—Cr 1834 from AP1.[336]

EP6—WOLVERHAMPTON ST JAMES—Cr 1843 from AP1,[3] refounded same year.[337] Abol 1955 pt to AP1, pt to EP14.[343]

EP7—WOLVERHAMPTON ST JOHN—Cr 1871 from AP1.[3] Bdry: 1861 (help cr Blakenall EP,[3] refounded 1862,[50] later called 'Wolverhampton St Luke'), 1881 (cr EP1),[344] 1973 (gains EP12).[345]

EP8—WOLVERHAMPTON ST JUDE—Cr 1869 from EP9.[213] Bdry: 1894.[14]

—WOLVERHAPTON ST LUKE—Name used now for EP cr 1861 as 'Blakenall'. qv.

EP9—WOLVERHAMPTON ST MARK—Cr 1846 from AP1.[340] Bdry: 1847,[341] 1869 (cr EP8),[213] 1894.[14]

—WOLVERHAMPTON ST MARTIN—Name used now for EP cr 1938 as 'Rough Hill', qv.

EP10—WOLVERHAMPTON ST MARY—Cr 1843 from AP1.[338] Bdry: 1876 (help cr EP2),[28] 1884,[342] 1909 (cr EP13).[331]

EP11—WOLVERHAMPTON ST MATTHEW—Cr 1846 from AP1.[340] Bdry: 1965.[335]

EP12—WOLVERHAMPTON ST PAUL—Cr 1844 from AP1.[339] Bdry: 1861 (help cr Blakenall EP,[3] refounded 1862,[50] later called 'Wolverhmapton St Luke'), 1909 (cr EP4).[287] Abol 1973 ent to EP7.[345]

EP13—WOLVERHAMPTON ST STEPHEN—Cr

1909 from EP10.[331] Bdry: 1955.[343]

WOMBOURN
AP Incl chap Trysull and Seisdon (sep CP 1866,[2] sep EP 1888 as 'Trysull'[323]), lbty Swindon (sep EP 1867,[72] sep CP 1896[313]). *LG* S Seisd. Hd, Seisd. PLU, RSD, RD. Addtl civ bdry alt: 1934 (incl gains Upper Penn EP).[4] Abol civ 1966 pt to Wolverh. CB (assoc with Staffs) & AP, pt to help cr Wombourne CP.[6] *Parl* S'rn Dv (1832—67), West Dv (1867—85), Kingswinf. Dv (1885—1918), Cannock Dv (1918—48), Brierley Hill CC (1948—70). *Eccl* Now as 'Wombourne', Seq 7.

WOMBOURNE
CP Cr 1966 by union pt Wombourn AP, pt Wolverh. CB (assoc with Staffs) & AP.[6] *LG* S Seisd. RD. *Parl* S W Staffs CC (1970—*).

WOODFORD GRANGE
Ex-par place, sep CP 1858.[10] *LG* S Seisd. Hd, Seisd. PLU (1861—1900), RSD, RD. Abol civ 1900 ent to Trysull and Seisdon CP.[324] *Parl* S'rn Dv (1832—67), West Dv (1867—85), Kingswinf. Dv (1885—1918).

WOODHOUSES
Tp in Mayfield AP, sep CP 1866.[2] *LG* S Totm. Hd, Ashb. PLU, RSD, Mayf. RD. Abol 1916 ent to Okeover CP.[283] *Parl* N'rn Dv (1832—67), North Dv (1867—85), Leek Dv (1885—1918).

WOOTTON
Tp in Ellastone AP, sep CP 1866.[2] *LG* Seq 23. *Parl* Seq 8.

WORSTON
Ex-par place, sep CP 1858.[10] *LG* S Pir. Hd, Staff. PLU (1858—1930), RSD, RD. Abol civ 1934 ent to Seighford AP.[4] *Parl* N'rn Dv (1832—67), West Dv (1867—85), W'rn Dv (1885—1918), Staff. Dv (1918—48).

WROTTESLEY
CP Cr 1894 from the pt of Tettenhall AP not in Tettenhall UD.[317] *LG* Seisd. PLU, RD. Bdry: 1927 (loses pt to Wolverh. CB [assoc with Staffs] & AP),[133] 1934,[4] 1966 (incl exchanges pts with Wolverh. CB [assoc with Staffs] & AP).[6] *Parl* Cannock Dv (1918—48), Brierley Hill CC (1948—70), S W Staffs CC (1970—*).

WYCHNOR
Chap in Tattenhill AP, sep CP 1866,[2] sep EP 1792,[3] eccl refounded 1881.[13] *LG* Seq 7. Civ bdry: 1934.[4] *Parl* Seq 1. *Eccl* Tamw. & Tutb. RDn (1792—1851), Lichf RDn (1851—*).

GREAT WYRLEY
Tp in Cannock AP, sep CP 1866,[2] sep EP 1845,[3] eccl refounded 1846.[143] *LG* Seq 1. Civ bdry: 1934.[4] *Parl* S'rn Dv (1832—67), West Dv (1867—85), Lichf Dv (1885—1918), Cannock Dv/CC (1918—*). *Eccl* Lapley & Trysull RDn (1846—51), Rugeley RDn (1851—*).

YARLET
Ex-par place, sep CP 1858.[10] *LG* S Pir. Hd, Staff. PLU (1858—1930), RSD, RD. Abol civ 1934 ent to Marston CP.[4] *Parl* N'rn Dv (1832—67), West Dv (1867—85), W'rn Dv (1885—1918), Staff. Dv (1918—48).

YOXALL
AP *LG* N Offl. Hd, Lichf PLU, RSD, RD (1894—1934), Tutb. RD (1934—74). Civ bdry: 1883,[8] 1934.[4] *Parl* Seq 2. *Eccl* Seq 12. Eccl bdry: 1874 (help cr Hoar Cross EP),[88] 1895 (help cr Needwood EP).[42]

WARWICKSHIRE

ABBREVIATIONS

Abbreviations particular to Warws follow. Those general abbreviations in use throughout the *Guide* are found on pages xvii—xix.

Alc.	Alcester
Ath.	Atherstone
Bag.	Baginton
Banb.	Banbury
Barl.	Barlinchway
Bedw.	Bedworth
Bord.	Bordesley
Cast. Bromw.	Castle Bromwich
Chip. Nort.	Chipping Norton
Colesh.	Coleshill
Dass. Mag.	Dassett Magna
Dunch.	Dunchurch
Edgb.	Edgbaston
Farnb.	Farnborough
Folesh.	Foleshill
Handsw.	Handsworth
Harb.	Harborne
Heml.	Hemlingford
Hinck.	Hinckley
K's Nort.	King's Norton
Kenil.	Kenilworth
Kinet.	Kineton
Kingt.	Kington
Knight.	Knighton
Leam.	Leamington
Lutt.	Lutterworth
Merid.	Meriden
Northf.	Northfield
Nun.	Nuneaton
Polesw.	Polesworth
Shipst.	Shipston
Smethw.	Smethwick
Solih.	Solihull
Ston.	Stonleigh
Stratf.	Stratford
Sutt. Coldf.	Sutton Coldfield
Tamw.	Tamworth
Warw.	Warwick
Yard.	Yardley

SEQUENCES

An abbreviated entry prefixed by 'Seq' is used in the parochial entries to avoid repeating often the names of superior units of administration. The content of each sequence is shown below.

Local Government Sequences ('LG')

SEQ 1 Barl. Hd, Alc. PLU, RSD, RD
SEQ 2 Barl. Hd, Stratf. on Avon PLU, RSD, RD
SEQ 3 Barl. Hd, Warw. PLU, RSD, RD
SEQ 4 Heml. Hd, Ath. PLU, RSD, RD
SEQ 5 Heml. Hd, Merid. PLU, RSD, RD

SEQ 6 Heml. Hd, Solih. PLU, RSD, RD (1894—1932), Merid. RD (1932—74)
SEQ 7 Heml. Hd, Tamw. PLU, RSD, RD (1894—1964), Ath. RD (1964—74)
SEQ 8 Kingt. Hd, Banb. PLU (1836—1930), Farnb. RD (1894—1932), Southam RD (1932—74)
SEQ 9 Kingt. Hd, Chip. Norton PLU, RSD, Brailes

RD (1894—1931), Shipst. on Stour RD (1931—74)

SEQ 10 Kingt. Hd, Shipst. on Stour, PLU, RSD, Brailes RD (1894—1931), Shipst. on Stour RD (1931—74)

SEQ 11 Kingt. Hd, Southam PLU, RSD, RD

SEQ 12 Kingt. Hd, Stratf. on Avon PLU, RSD, RD

SEQ 13 Kingt. Hd, Warw. PLU, RSD, RD

SEQ 14 Knight. Hd, Folesh. PLU, RSD, RD (1894—1932), Rugby RD (1932—74)

SEQ 15 Knight. Hd, Hinck. PLU (1836—between 1896/1900), RSD, Nun. PLU (between 1896/1900—1930), RD (1894—1932), Rugby RD (1932—74)

SEQ 16 Knight. Hd, Lutt. PLU, RSD, Monks Kirkby RD (1894—1932), Rugby RD (1932—74)

SEQ 17 Knight. Hd, Nun. PLU, RSD, RD (1894—1932), Rugby RD (1932—74)

SEQ 18 Knight. Hd, Rugby PLU, RSD, RD

SEQ 19 Knight. Hd, Southam PLU, RSD, RD

SEQ 20 Knight. Hd, Warw. PLU, RSD, RD

Parliamentary Sequences ('Parl')

SEQ 1 N'rn Dv (1832—1918), Nun. Dv/CC (1918—70), Merid. CC (1970—*)

SEQ 2 N'rn Dv (1832—1918), Tamw. Dv (1918—45), Sutt. Coldf. Dv/CC (1945—70), Merid. CC (1970—*)

SEQ 3 N'rn Dv (1832—85), N-E'rn Dv (1885—1918), Nun. Dv/CC (1918—70), Merid. CC (1970—*)

SEQ 4 N'rn Dv (1832—85), N-E'rn Dv (1885—1918), Nun. Dv (1918—45), Rugby Dv/CC (1945—*)

SEQ 5 N'rn Dv (1832—85), N-E'rn Dv (1885—1918), Nun. Dv (1918—45), Sutt. Coldf. Dv/CC (1945—55), Merid. CC (1955—*)

SEQ 6 N'rn Dv (1832—85), N-E'rn Dv (1885—1918), Rugby Dv/CC (1918—*)

SEQ 7 N'rn Dv (1832—85), N-E'rn Dv (1885—1918), Tamw. Dv (1918—48), Sutt. Coldf. CC (1948—70), Merid. CC (1970—*)

SEQ 8 N'rn Dv (1832—85), S-E'rn Dv (1885—1918), Rugby Dv/CC (1918—*)

SEQ 9 S'rn Dv (1832—85), N-E'rn Dv (1885—1918), Rugby Dv (1918—48), Stratf. CC (1948—70), Stratf. on Avon CC (1970—*)

SEQ 10 S'rn Dv (1832—85), S-E'rn Dv (1885—1918), Rugby Dv/CC (1918—*)

SEQ 11 S'rn Dv (1832—85), S-E'rn Dv (1885—1918), Rugby Dv (1918—48), Stratf. CC (1948—70), Stratf. on Avon CC (1970—*)

SEQ 12 S'rn Dv (1832—85), S-E'rn Dv (1885—1918), Warw. & Leam. Dv/CC (1918—*)

SEQ 13 S'rn Dv (1832—85), S-W'rn Dv (1885—1918), Rugby Dv (1918—48), Stratf. CC (1948—70), Stratf. on Avon CC (1970—*)

SEQ 14 S'rn Dv (1832—85), S-W'rn Dv (1885—1918), Warw. & Leam. Dv/CC (1918—*)

SEQ 15 S'rn Dv (1832—85), S-W'rn Dv (1885—

1918), Warw. & Leam. Dv (1918—48), Stratf. CC (1948—70), Stratf. on Avon CC (1970—*)

Ecclesiastical Sequences ('Eccl')

Orig Cov AD

SEQ 1 Arden RDn (until 1854), Ath. RDn (1854—1963), Nun. RDn (1863—*)

SEQ 2 Arden RDn (until 1854), Colesh. RDn (1854—92), Cov RDn (1892—1907), Kenilw. RDn (1907—*)

SEQ 3 Arden RDn (until 1854), Colesh. RDn (1854—60), Sutt. Coldf. RDn (1860—*)

SEQ 4 Arden RDn (until 1854), Polesw. RDn (1854—*)

SEQ 5 Arden RDn (until 1854), Polesw. RDn (1854—92), Colesh. RDn (1892—1905), Sutt. Coldf. RDn (1905—57), Colesh. RDn (1957—*)

SEQ 6 Arden RDn (until 1854), Solih. RDn (1854—*)

SEQ 7 Arden RDn (until 1854), Solih. RDn (1854—60), Ath. RDn (1860—1963), Nun. RDn (1963—*)

SEQ 8 Arden RDn (until 1854), Solih. RDn (1854—92), Cov RDn (1892—1907), Kenilw. RDn (1907—*)

SEQ 9 Cov RDn (until 1854), Monks Kirby RDn (1854—1963), Bedw. RDn (1963—*)

SEQ 10 Cov RDn (until 1854), Rugby RDn (1854—1907), Rugby with Dunch. RDn (1907—21), Rugby RDn (1921—*)

SEQ 11 Marton RDn (until 1854), Bag. RDn (1854—1921), Dunch. RDn (1921—*)

SEQ 12 Marton RDn (until 1854), Dunch. RDn (1854—1907), Rugby with Dunch. RDn (1907—21), Dunch. RDn (1921—*)

SEQ 13 Marton (until 1854), Rugby RDn (1854—1907), Rugby with Dunch. RDn (1907—21), Rugby RDn (1921—*)

SEQ 14 Marton RDn (until 1854), Southam RDn (1854—*)

SEQ 15 Ston. RDn (until 1854), Cov RDn (1854—1907), Kenilw. RDn (1907—*)

SEQ 16 Ston. RDn (until 1854), Dass. Mag. RDn (1854—*)

SEQ 17 Ston. RDn (until 1854), Leam. RDn (1854—*)

Orig Worc AD

SEQ 18 Kinet. RDn (until 1861), N Kinet. RDn (1861—1921), Kinet. RDn (1921—63), Dass. Mag. RDn (1963—*)

SEQ 19 Kinet. RDn (until 1861), N Kinet. RDn (1861—1921), Kinet. RDn (1921—63), Stratf. on Avon RDn (1963—*)

SEQ 20 Kinet. RDn (until 1861), S Kinet. RDn (1861—1921), Shipst. RDn (1921—*)

SEQ 21 Warw. RDn

SEQ 22 Warw. RDn (until 1861), Alc. RDn (1861—*)

DIOCESES AND ARCHDEACONRIES

Warws pars were arranged in Archdeaconries and Rural Deaneries as follows:

BIRMINGHAM DIOC (1905—*)

Aston AD (1906—):* Aston RDn, E Birm RDn (1906—57), Bord. RDn, Colesh. RDn (1957—*), Polesw. RDn, Solih. RDn, Sutt. Coldf. RDn, Yard. (1957—*)

Birm AD: Aston RDn (1905—06), Birm RDn (1905), E Birm RDn (1905—06), Birm Central RDn (1905—57), Birm City RDn (1957—*), Bord. RDn, Colesh. RDn, Edgb. RDn, Handsw. RDn, Harb. RDn (1905—29), K's Nort. RDn, Mosley RDn (1957—*), Northf. RDn (1905), Polesw. RDn (1905—06), Smethw. RDn (1929—66), Solih. RDn (1905—06), Sutt. Coldf. RDn (1905—06), Warley RDn (1957—*)

COVENTRY DIOC (1918—*)

Cov AD: Ath. RDn (1918—63), Bag. RDn (1918—21), Bedw. RDn (1963—*), Cov RDn (1918—63), Cov East RDn (1963—*), Cov North RDn (1963—*), Cov South RDn (1963—*), Dass. Mag. RDn (1918—21), Dewchurch RDn (1921—*), Kenilw. RDn, Leam. RDn (1918—21), Monks Kirby RDn (1918—63), Nun. RDn (1963—*), Rugby RDn (1921—*), Rugby & Dewchurch RDn (1918—21), Southam RDn (1918—21)

Warw. AD: Alc. RDn, Dass. Mag. RDn (1921—*), Kinet. RDn (1921—63), N Kinet. RDn (1918—21), S Kinet. RDn (1918—21), Leam. RDn (1921—*), Shipst. RDn (1921—*), Southam RDn (1921—*), Stratf. on Avon RDn (1963—*), Warw. RDn

LICHFIELD AND COVENTRY DIOC (until 1837) [before 1837 variously styled 'Lichfield' (until 1075), 'Chester' (1075—1102), 'Coventry' (1102—1128), 'Coventry and Lichfield' (1228—Reformation), 'Lichfield and Coventry' (Reformation—1837)]

Cov AD: Arden RDn, Cov RDn, Marton RDn, Ston. RDn

WORCESTER DIOC (1837—1918)

Birm AD (1892—1905): Aston RDn, Birm RDn, Colesh. RDn, Northf. RDn, Polesw. RDn, Sutt. Coldf. RDn, Solih. RDn

Cov AD: Arden RDn (1837—54), Ath. RDn (1854—1918), Bag. RDn (1854—1918), Birm RDn (1854—92), Colesh. RDn (1854—92), Cov RDn, Dass. Mag. RDn (1854—1918), Dunch. RDn (1854—1907), Kenilw. RDn (1907—18), Leam. RDn (1854—1907), Marton RDn (1837—54), Monk's Kirby RDn (1854—1918), Polesw. RDn (1854—92), Rugby RDn (1854—1907), Rugby and Dunch. RDn (1907—18), Southam RDn (1854—1918), Sutt. Coldf. RDn (1869—92), Solih. RDn (1854—92), Ston. RDn (1837—54)

Warw. AD (1910—18): Alc. RDn, N Kinet. RDn, S. Kinet. RDn, Warw. RDn

Worcester AD: Alc. RDn (1861—1910), N Kinet. RDn, S Kinet. RDn, Warw. RDn

THE PARISHES OF WARWICKSHIRE

ADMINGTON
CP Glos par transf 1935 to Warws.[1] *LG* Stratf. on Avon RD. *Parl* Stratf. CC (1948—70), Stratf. on Avon CC (1970—*).

ALCESTER
AP *LG* Alc. Bor (status not sustained beyond 18th cent[2]), Seq 1. Civ bdry: 1949 (gains Oversley CP),[3] 1965 (loses pt to Inkberrow AP, Worcs).[4] *Parl* Alc. Parl Bor (1275 only), Seq 16. *Eccl* Warw. RDn (until 1861), Alc. RDn (1861—76). Abol eccl 1876 to help cr Alcester with Weethley EP.[5]

ALCESTER WITH WEETHLEY
EP Cr 1876 by union Alcester AP, chap Weethley in Kinwarton AP.[5] Alc. RDn.

ALDERMINSTER
AP Worcs par transf 1931 to Warws.[6] *LG* Stratf. on Avon RD. *Parl* Stratf. CC (1948—70), Stratf. on Avon CC (1970—*). *Eccl* See entry in Worcs.

ALLESLEY
AP Orig chap in Coventry St Michael AP, sep par 1249.[7] *LG* Knight. Hd, Merid. PLU, RSD, RD. Civ bdry: 1928 (loses pt to Cov CB [assoc with Warws] & CP),[8] 1932 (loses pt to Cov CB [assoc with Warws] & CP),[9] 1956 (exchanges pts with Cov CB [assoc with Warws] & CP),[10] 1965 (loses pt to Cov CB [assoc with Warws] & CP).[11] Transf 1974 to W Midlands.[12] *Parl* N'rn Dv (1832—85), N-E'rn Dv (1885—1918), Tamw. Dv (1918—45), Sutt. Coldf. Dv/CC (1945—55), Merid. CC (1955—*). Parl bdry: 1960.[13] *Eccl* Cov RDn (until 1907), Kenilw. RDn (1907—63), Cov North RDn (1963—*). Eccl bdry: 1876 (cr Allesley St Andrew, Eastern Green EP),[14] 1957,[15] 1959 (incl cr Allesley Park EP).[16]

ALLESLEY ST ANDREW, EASTERN GREEN
EP Cr 1876 from Allesley AP.[14] Cov RDn (1876—1907), Kenilw. RDn (1907—63), Cov South RDn (1963—*). Bdry: 1957.[15]

ALLESLEY PARK
EP Cr 1959 from Allesley AP.[16] Kenilw. RDn (1959—63), Cov South RDn (1963—*).

GREAT ALNE
Chap in Kinwarton AP, sep civ identity early. *LG* Seq 1. *Parl* Seq 15.

ALVESTON
AP Orig chap (pec jurisd Hampton Lucy) in Hampton Lucy AP, sep par 1269.[17] *LG* Barl. Hd, Stratf. on Avon PLU, RSD, RD (1894—1924), MB (1924—74). *Parl* Seq 15. *Eccl* Pec jurisd Hampton Lucy

(until 1851), Kinet. RDn (1851—61), N Kinet. RDn (1861—1921), Kinet. RDn (1921—63), Stratf. on Avon RDn (1963—*).

AMINGTON

CP Cr 1935 from Amington and Stoneydelph CP.[18] *LG* Tamw. RD. Bdry: 1956,[19] 1958.[20] Abol 1965 ent to Tamw. MB & AP, Staffs.[21] *Parl* Sutt. Coldf. CC (1948—60), Merid. CC (1960—70).

AMINGTON AND STONEYDELPH

Tp (Warws, Heml. Hd) in Tamworth AP (Staffs, Warws until 1866, ent Staffs thereafter), sep CP 1866 in Warws.[22] *LG* Tamw. PLU, RSD, RD. Bdry: 1932 (loses pt to Tamw. MB & AP, Staffs).[23] Abol 1935 pt to cr Amington CP, pt to Wilnecote and Castle Liberty CP.[18] *Parl* Tamw. Parl Bor ([Staffs, Warws], 1832—85), N'rn Dv (1885—1918), Tamw. Dv (1918—45).

ANSLEY

AP *LG* Seq 4. *Parl* Seq 3. *Eccl* Seq 7.

ANSTY

AP Chap in Bulkington AP, appropriated to Cov Priory and considered sep par *ca* 1410 with Shilton (orig chap in Bulkington AP) as its chap[24] (the latter with sep civ identity early from Ansty, sep EP 1754[25]). *LG* Cov Co of Itself (1452—1842), Knight. Hd (from 1842), Folesh. PLU, RSD, RD (1894—1932), Rugby RD (1932—74). Addtl civ bdry alt: 1932,[9] 1932,[26] 1965 (gains pt Cov CB [assoc with Warws] & CP).[11] *Parl* N'rn Dv (1832—85), N-E'rn Dv (1885—1918), Nun. Dv (1918—45), Rugby Dv/ CC (1945—*). *Eccl* Seq 9.

ARLEY

AP *LG* Seq 17. *Parl* Seq 5. *Eccl* Seq 7.

ARROW

AP Incl hmlt Oversley (sep CP 1866[22]). *LG* Seq 1. Civ bdry: 1965 (loses pt to Inkberrow AP, Worcs).[4] *Parl* Seq 15. *Eccl* Seq 22.

ASHOW

AP Orig chap in Leek Wootton AP, sep par between 1198—1215.[27] *LG* Seq 20. *Parl* Seq 12. *Eccl* Seq 15.

ASHTED

EP Cr 1853 from Aston juxta Birmingham AP (civ, 'Aston').[28] Arden RDn (1853—54), Birm RDn (1854—1892), Aston RDn (1892—1905), E Birm RDn (1905—57), Birm City RDn (1957—70). Bdry: 1907.[29] Abol 1970 ent to Duddeston cum Nechells EP, by then called 'Duddeston St Matthew EP'.[30]

ASTLEY

AP At one time Collegiate. *LG* Seq 17. Civ bdry: 1932.[26] *Parl* Seq 5. *Eccl* Seq 1. Eccl bdry: 1937.[31]

ASTON

AP Usual civ spelling; for eccl see 'Aston juxta Birmingham' (incl all EPs in addition to chap and hmlt from this par). Incl chap Castle Bromwich (sep CP 1894, qv below, donative early augmented,[32] sep EP 1878[33]), hmlt Water Orton (sep CP 1894, qv below, sep EP 1732,[25] eccl refounded 1871[34]). *LG* Heml. Hd, Aston PLU (1836—1911), pt Birm MB (1838—89), pt Aston Manor USD, pt Aston RSD (reduced pt 1891—94), Birm PLU (1911—12), CB (pt 1889—94 [enlarged pt 1891—94], ent 1894—

1912). Civ bdry: 1894 (the pt in Aston Manor UD cr Aston Manor CP, main pt remains as 'Aston' par in Birm CB [assoc with Warws], the remaining area not in the UD or CB cr 3 CPs of Castle Bromwich, Erdington, Water Orton).[35] Abol civ 1912 ent to Birmingham AP.[36] *Parl* Pt Birm Parl Bor (1832—1918), pt Aston Manor Parl Bor (1885—1918), pt N'rn Dv (1832—1918).

ASTON BROOK

EP Cr 1864 from Aston juxta Birmingham AP (civ, 'Aston'), Lozells St Silas EP, Duddeston cum Nechells EP.[37] Sutt. Coldf. RDn (1864—92), Aston RDn (1892—1971). Bdry: 1907,[29] 1950.[38] Abol 1971 to help cr Aston juxta Birmingham St Peter and St Paul EP.[39]

ASTON CANTLOW

AP *LG* Seq 1. *Parl* Seq 15. *Eccl* Seq 22. Eccl bdry: 1863 (help cr Wilmcote EP).[40]

ASTON JUXTA BIRMINGAM

AP Usual eccl spelling; for civ and civ and eccl sep chap and hmlt, see 'Aston'. Arden RDn (until 1854), Colesh. RDn (1854—60), Sutt. Coldf. RDn (1860—92), Aston RDn (1892—1971). Addtl eccl bdry alt: 1841 (cr Ward End EP,[41] refounded 1870[42]), 1842 (cr Duddeston cum Nechells EP, later called 'Duddeston St Matthew'),[43] 1846 (from area Bordesley, cr Bordesley St Andrew EP),[44] 1848 (cr Saltley EP),[45] 1848 (cr Bordesley Holy Trinity EP,[25] refounded 1864[46]), 1853 (cr Ashted EP),[28] 1853 (cr Lozells St Silas EP),[47] 1858 (cr Erdington EP),[48] 1864 (help cr Aston Brook EP),[37] 1867 (cr Sparkbrook Christ Church EP),[49] 1886 (cr Deritend St Basil EP),[50] 1890 (cr Deritend St John EP),[51] 1906 (cr Aston juxta Birmingham St James EP),[52] 1929 (help cr Gravelly Hill EP),[53] 1971 (cr Perry Common EP).[39] Abol eccl 1971 to help cr Aston juxta Birmingham St Peter and St Paul EP.[39]

ASTON JUXTA BIRMINGHAM ST JAMES

EP Cr 1906 from Aston juxta Birmingham AP (civ, 'Aston').[52] Aston RDn.

ASTON JUXTA BIRMINGHAM ST PETER AND ST PAUL

EP Cr 1971 by union Aston juxta Birmingham AP (civ, 'Aston'), Aston Brook EP.[39] Aston RDn.

ASTON MANOR

CP Cr 1894 from the pt of Aston AP in Aston Manor UD.[35] *LG* Aston PLU (1894—1911), Aston Manor UD (1894—1903), MB (1903—11), Birm PLU (1911—12), CB (1911—12). Abol 1912 ent to Birmingham AP.[36]

ATHERSTONE

Tp and bor in Mancetter AP, sep CP 1866,[22] sep EP 1825,[25] eccl refounded 1851.[54] *LG* Ath. Bor, Seq 4. *Parl* Seq 3. *Eccl* Arden RDn (1825—54), Ath. RDn (1854—1963), Nun. RDn (1963—*).

ATHERSTONE ON STOUR

AP *LG* Seq 12. *Parl* Seq 15. *Eccl* Seq 19.

ATTLEBOROUGH

EP Cr (partly independent) 1843 from Nuneaton AP,[55] fully independent 1854.[56] Arden RDn (1843—54), Ath. RDn (1854—1953), Nun. RDn (1963—*).

AUSTREY
AP *LG* Seq 7. *Parl* Seq 2. *Eccl* Seq 4.

BADDESLEY CLINTON
AP Orig chap in Hampton in Arden AP, sep par bef 1298.[57] *LG* Heml. Hd, Solih. PLU, RSD, RD (1894—1932), Warw. RD (1932—74). *Parl* N'rn Dv (1832—1918), Tamw. Dv (1918—45), Warw. & Leam. Dv/CC (1945—*). *Eccl* Seq 6.

BADDESLEY ENSOR
Chap in Polesworth AP, sep civ by 1666,[58] sep EP 1760.[25] *LG* Seq 4. *Parl* Seq 3. *Eccl* Seq 4.

BAGINTON
AP Orig chap in Stoneleigh AP, sep par *temp* John.[59] *LG* Seq 20. Civ bdry: 1932,[26] 1932 (incl loses pt to Cov CB [assoc with Warwes] & CP),[9] 1956 (exchanges pts with Cov CB [assoc with Warws] & CP),[10] 1965 (incl exchanges pts with Cov CB [assoc with Warws] & CP).[11] *Parl* Seq 12. Parl bdry: 1960.[13] *Eccl* Ston. RDn (until 1854), Bag. RDn (1854—1921), Dunch. RDn (1921—70), Cov South RDn (1970—*).

BALSALL
Chap in Hampton in Arden AP, sep CP 1866,[22] sep EP 1863 as 'Temple Balsall',[60] qv. *LG* Seq 6. Civ bdry: 1932,[61] 1964 (loses pt to Solih. MB & to Solihull Urban CP as revised area of latter constituted Solih. CB [assoc with Warws]).[62] Transf 1974 to W Midlands.[12] *Parl* Seq 2.

TEMPLE BALSALL
Chap in Hampton in Arden AP, sep EP 1863,[60] sep CP 1866 as 'Balsall',[22] qv. *Eccl* Solih. RDn (1863—92), Cov RDn (1892—1905), not in a RDn (July—Aug 1905 when first in dioc Birm), Solih. RDn (Aug 1905—*). Eccl bdry: 1959 (cr Balsall Common EP).[63]

BALSALL COMMON
EP Cr 1959 from Temple Balsall EP.[63] Solih. RDn.

BALSALL HEATH
CP Cr 1894 from the pt of King's Norton CP (Worcs) in Birm CB.[64] *LG* Kings Norton PLU (1894—1911), Birm PLU (1911—12), CB. Abol 1912 ent to Birmingham AP.[36]

BARCHESTON
AP *LG* Seq 10. Civ bdry: 1884.[65] *Parl* Seq 13. *Eccl* Seq 20.

BARFORD
AP *LG* Seq 13. Civ bdry: 1954.[66] *Parl* Seq 14. *Eccl* Eccl bdry: 1955.[67]

BARSTON
Chap in Berkswell AP, sep civ identity early, sep EP 1893.[68] *LG* Seq 6. Civ bdry: 1964 (gains pt Solih. MB & Solihull Urban CP as revised latter area constituted Solih. CB [assoc with Warws]).[62] Transf 1974 to W Midlands.[12] *Parl* Seq 2. *Eccl* Cov RDn (1893—1907), Kenilw. RDn (1907—19), Solih. RDn (1919—*).

BARTON ON THE HEATH
AP *LG* Seq 9. *Parl* Seq 13. *Eccl* Seq 20.

BAXTERLEY
AP *LG* Seq 4. *Parl* Seq 3. *Eccl* Seq 4.

BEARLEY
AP Chap in Wootton Wawen AP, sep par from Dissolution.[69] *LG* Seq 2. *Parl* Seq 15. *Eccl* Seq 21.

BEAUDESERT
AP *LG* Seq 2. Civ bdry: 1922,[70] 1957.[71] *Parl* Seq 15. *Eccl* Seq 21. Eccl bdry: 1915 (gains Henley in Arden EP).[72]

BEAUSALE
Chap (not sep eccl, eccl enlarged 1893[73]) and hmlt in Hatton AP, sep CP 1866.[22] *LG* Seq 3. Civ bdry: 1931.[74] *Parl* Seq 14.

BEDWORTH
AP *LG* Knight. Hd, Folesh. PLU, RSD, RD (1894—1928), Bedw. UD (1928—74). Civ bdry: 1932,[26] 1965 (loses pt to Cov CB [assoc with Warws] & CP).[11] *Parl* N'rn Dv (1832—85), N-E'rn Dv (1885—1918), Nun. Dv/CC (1918—*). *Eccl* Seq 9.

BENTLEY
Chap and hmlt in Shustoke AP, sep CP 1866,[22] detached pt eccl severed 1958 to help cr Merevale with Bentley EP (Warws, Leics).[42] *LG* Seq 4. *Parl* Seq 3.

BERKSWELL
AP Incl chap Barston (sep civ identity early, sep EP 1893[68]). *LG* Seq 5. Addtl civ bdry alt: 1928 (loses pt to Cov CB [assoc with Warws] & CP),[8] 1965 (loses pt to Cov CB [assoc with Warws] & CP).[11] Transf 1974 to W Midlands.[12] *Parl* Seq 7. *Eccl* Seq 8. Addtl eccl bdry alt: 1957,[15] 1965.[75]

BICKENHILL
AP *LG* Seq 5. Civ bdry: 1877,[76] 1932,[61] 1958,[77] 1964 (exchanges pts with Solih. MB & Solihull Urban CP as revised area of latter constituted Solih. CB [assoc with Warws]),[62] 1966 (exchanges pts with Birm CB [assoc with Warws] & AP),[4] 1970.[78] Transf 1974 to W Midlands.[12] *Parl* Seq 2. *Eccl* Arden RDn (until 1854), Solih. RDn (1854—92), Colesh. RDn (1892—1905), Solih. RDn (1905—*). Eccl bdry: 1908 (help cr Olton EP).[79]

BICKMARSH
CP Cr 1894 from the pt of Welford AP (Glos, Warws) in Warws and Welford ent Glos thereafter.[80] *LG* Stratf. on Avon PLU, RD. Pt transf 1931 to Dorsington AP (as that Glos par transf to be in Warws), the remainder transf to be 'Bickmarsh' par in Worcs.[6] *Parl* Warw. & Leam. Dv (1918—48).

BIDFORD ON AVON
AP *LG* Seq 1. *Parl* Seq 15. *Eccl* Sometimes as 'Bidford on Avon with Broom', Seq 22.

BILLESLEY
AP *LG* Seq 2. *Parl* Seq 15. *Eccl* Seq 22.

BILTON
AP *LG* Knight. Hd, Rugby PLU, RSD, RD. Abol civ 1932 pt to Rugby UD & AP, pt to Dunchurch AP.[61] *Parl* N'rn Dv (1832—85), S-E'rn Dv (1885—1918), Rugby Dv (1918—45). *Eccl* Marton RDn (until 1854), Dunch. RDn (1854—1907), Rugby & Dunch. RDn (1907—21), Rugby RDn (1921—*). Eccl bdry: 1867 (cr New Bilton EP).[81]

NEW BILTON
EP Cr 1867 from Bilton AP.[81] Dunch. RDn (1867—1907), Rugby with Dunch. RDn (1907—21), Rugby RDn (1921—*). Bdry: 1947.[82]

BINLEY
Chap in Coventry Holy Trinity AP, sep civ identity early, donative and sep eccl status sustained.[83] *LG*

Knight. Hd, Folesh. PLU, RSD, RD (1894—1932), Rugby RD (1932—61). Civ bdry: 1932,[25] 1932 (loses pt to Cov CB [assoc with Warws] & CP),[9] 1956 (exchanges pts with Cov CB [assoc with Warws] & CP).[10] Renamed civ 1961 'Binley Woods'.[84] *Parl* N'rn Dv (1832—85), N-E'rn Dv (1885—1918), Nun. Dv (1918—45), Rugby Dv/CC (1945—70). Parl bdry: 1960.[13] *Eccl* Ston. RDn (until 1860), Monks Kirkby RDn (1860—92), Bag. RDn (1892—1921), Cov RDn (1921—63), Cov East RDn (1963—*). Eccl bdry: 1957.[15]

BINLEY WOODS
CP Renaming 1961 of Binley CP.[84] *LG* Rugby RD. Bdry: 1965 (loses pt to Cov CB [assoc with Warws] & CP).[11] *Parl* Rugby CC (1970—*).

BINTON
AP *LG* Seq 2. *Parl* Seq 15. *Eccl* Seq 22.

BIRDINGBURY
AP Sometimes early 'Birbury'. *LG* Seq 18. *Parl* Seq 10. *Eccl* Seq 14.

BIRMINGHAM
The following have 'Birmingham' in their names. Insofar as any existed at a given time: *LG* Heml. Hd, Birm Par (poor law purposes, 1783—1930), Bor, MB (1838—89), CB (1889—1974), USD. *Parl* Birm Parl Bor (1832—85); see Part III of the *Guide* for composition of Birm Parl Bors/BCs (1885—*) by wards of the MB/CB. *Eccl* Arden RDn (until 1854), Birm RDn (1854—1905); sep noted thereafter.

AP1—BIRMINGHAM [ST MARTIN]—Civ bdry: 1891 (incl gains pt Harborne AP, Staffs and pt King's Norton CP, Worcs),[85] 1909 (gains Quinton CP, Worcs),[86] 1911 (gains pt Kings Norton CP, pt Northfield AP, both Worcs),[87] 1912 (gains the following pars in Birm CB: Aston AP, Aston Manor CP, Balsall Heath CP, Edgbaston AP, Erdington AP, Harborne AP, Quinton CP, Yardley AP, and from the following pars in Worcs in a Separate RD administered by Bromsgrove RD Council: King's Norton CP, Northfield AP),[36] 1930 (gains within CB Handsworth AP and Perry Barr CP),[88] 1931,[89] 1964 (exchanges pts with Solih. MB & Solihull Urban CP as revised area of latter constituted Solih. CB [assoc with Warws]),[62] 1966 (gains pt Smethw. CB [assoc with Staffs] & CP, exchanges pts with W Bromwich CB & AP [assoc with Staffs], gains from Staffs pt Aldridge UD [see entry in that co for its constituent pars], exchanges pts with Halesowen MB & AP, Worcs, gains pt Bromsgrove UD & AP, Worcs, exchanges pts with Sutton Coldfield MB & AP, Bickenhill AP, both Warws).[4] Transf 1974 to W Midlands.[12] *Eccl* Central Birm (1905—57), Birm City RDn (1957—*). Eccl bdry: 1708 (cr EP29),[90] 1778 (cr EP25,[91] refounded 1841[92]), 1830 (cr EP16),[93] 1834 (cr EP1),[51] 1834 (cr EP32),[94] 1841 (cr EP4),[95] 1843 (cr EP19),[96] 1843 (cr EP21),[97] 1845 (help cr EP17),[98] 1847 (cr EP10),[99] 1854 (cr Ladywood St John EP),[100] 1861 (cr EP9),[101] 1865 (help cr EP5),[102] 1869 (help cr EP15),[103] 1900,[91] 1939,[99] 1958 (gains EP15),[104] 1970,[30] 1971

(gains EP17).[105]

EP1—BIRMINGHAM ALL SAINTS—Cr 1834 from AP1.[51] Handsw. RDn (1905—57), Birm City RDn (1957—73). Bdry: 1872 (cr EP12),[106] 1890 (cr EP11),[107] 1902 (help cr EP28).[98] Abol 1973 to help cr EP3.[108]

EP2—BIRMINGHAM BISHOP LATIMER MEMORIAL CHURCH—Cr 1905 from EP11, EP12.[109] Handsw. RDn (1905—63). Bdry: 1964.[110] Abol 1973 to help cr EP3.[108]

EP3—BIRMINGHAM BISHOP LATIMER WITH ALL SAINTS—Cr 1973 by union EP1, EP2, EP11.[108] Birm City RDn.

EP4—BIRMINGHAM BISHOP RYDER—Cr 1841 from AP1.[95] Central Birm RDn (1905—57), Birm City RDn (1957—70). Bdry: 1939,[99] 1951.[111] Abol 1970 pt to Duddleston St Matthew EP, pt to AP1, pt to EP29.[30]

EP5—BIRMINGHAM CHRIST CHURCH—Cr 1865 from AP1, EP29.[102] Abol 1899 ent to EP29.[112]

EP6—BIRMINGHAM CHRIST CHURCH, SUMMERFIELD—Cr 1885 from Ladywood St John EP.[44] Edgb. RDn (1905—*). Bdry: 1906,[113] 1964.[110]

EP7—BIRMINGHAM IMMANUEL—Cr 1865 from EP32.[114] Edgb. RDn (1905—39). Abol 1939 to help cr EP33.[14]

EP8—BIRMINGHAM ST ASAPH—Cr 1869 from EP32.[115] Edgb. RDn (1905—58). Abol 1958 ent to EP19.[104]

EP9—BIRMINGHAM ST BARNABAS—Cr 1861 from AP1.[101] Edgb. RDn (1905—56). Bdry: 1901.[116] Abol 1956 ent to Ladywood St John EP.[117]

EP10—BIRMINGHAM ST BARTHOLOMEW—Cr 1847 from AP1.[99] Central Birm RDn (1905—39). Bdry: 1869 (help cr EP15).[103] Abol 1939 pt to EP29, pt to EP15, pt to AP1, pt to EP4.[99]

EP11—BIRMINGHAM ST CHRYSOSTOM—Cr 1890 from EP1.[107] Handsw. RDn (1905—73). Bdry: 1905 (help cr EP2).[109] Abol 1973 to help cr EP3.[108]

EP12—BIRMINGHAM ST CUTHBERT—Cr 1872 from EP1.[106] Handsw. RDn (1905—64). Bdry: 1905 (help cr EP2).[109] Abol 1964 pt to EP2, pt to EP6.[110]

EP13—BIRMINGHAM ST DAVID—Cr 1866 from EP19.[118] Central Birm RDn (1905—58). Abol 1958 ent to EP19.[104]

EP14—BIRMINGHAM ST EDWARD—Cr 1899 from EP31, EP22.[119] Aston RDn (1905—42). Abol 1942 to help cr EP24.[40]

EP15—BIRMINGHAM ST GABRIEL—Cr 1869 from EP10, AP1.[103] Central Birm RDn (1905—57), Birm City RDn (1957—58). Bdry: 1939.[99] Abol 1958 ent to AP1.[104]

EP16—BIRMINGHAM ST GEORGE—Cr 1830 from AP1.[93] Central Birm RDn (1905—57), Birm City RDn (1957—*). Bdry: 1844 (cr EP31),[120] 1856 (cr EP22),[121] 1949 (gains EP24, EP22),[122] 1950.[38]

—BIRMINGHAM ST JOHN, LADYWOOD—see LADYWOOD ST JOHN

EP17—BIRMINGHAM ST JUDE—Cr 1845 from AP1, EP29.[98] Central Birm RDn (1905—57), Birm City RDn (1957—71). Bdry: 1885.[123] Abol 1971 ent to AP1.[105]

EP18—BIRMINGHAM ST LAWRENCE—Cr 1868 from Duddleston cum Nechells EP.[60] E Birm RDn (1905—51). Abol 1951 pt to Duddleston cum Nechells EP (by then called 'Duddleston St Matthew'), pt to EP4.[111]

EP19—BIRMINGHAM ST LUKE—Cr 1843 from AP1.[96] Edgb. RDn (1905—57), Birm City RDn (1957—*). Bdry: 1866 (cr EP13),[118] 1958 (gains EP8, EP13),[104] 1969 (incl gains EP33),[124] 1972.[125]

EP20—BIRMINGHAM ST MARGARET—Cr 1876 from Ladywood St John EP.[126] Edgb. RDn (1905—56). Abol 1956 ent to Ladywood St John EP.[118]

EP21—BIRMINGHAM ST MARK—Cr 1843 from AP1.[97] Sometimes called 'Duddeston St Mark'. Central Birm RDn (1905—47). Bdry: 1902 (help cr EP28).[98] Abol 1947 to help cr EP26.[127]

EP22—BIRMINGHAM ST MATTHIAS—Cr 1856 from EP16.[122] Central Birm RDn (1905—49). Bdry: 1874 (cr EP30),[128] 1899 (help cr EP14).[119] Abol 1949 ent to EP16.[121]

EP23—BIRMINGHAM ST NICHOLAS—Cr 1869 from EP31.[115] Aston RDn (1905—42). Abol 1942 to help cr EP24.[40]

EP24—BIRMINGHAM ST NICHOLAS WITH ST EDWARD—Cr 1942 by union EP23, EP14.[40] Aston RDn. Abol 1949 ent to EP16.[121]

EP25—BIRMINGHAM ST PAUL—Cr 1778 from AP1,[91] refounded 1841.[92] Central Birm RDn (1905—47). Bdry: 1900.[91] Abol 1947 to help cr EP26.[127]

EP26—BIRMINGHAM ST PAUL AND ST MARK—Cr 1947 by union EP25, EP21.[127] Central Birm RDn (1947—57), Birm City RDn (1957—*). Bdry: 1969.[129]

EP27—BIRMINGHAM ST PETER—Cr 1847 from EP29.[130] Abol 1899 ent to EP29.[131]

EP28—BIRMINGHAM ST PETER—Cr 1902 from EP1, EP21.[98] Handsw. RDn (1905—57), Birm City RDn (1957—*). Bdry: 1969.[129]

EP29—BIRMINGHAM ST PHILIP—Cr 1708 from AP1.[90] Cathedral from 1905. Central Birm RDn (1905—57), Birm City RDn (1957—*). Bdry: 1845 (help cr EP17),[98] 1845 (help cr EP17),[98] 1847 (cr EP27),[130] 1865 (help cr EP5),[102] 1899 (gains EP5),[112] 1899 (gains EP27),[131] 1901,[116] 1939,[99] 1970.[30]

EP30—BIRMINGHAM ST SAVIOUR—Cr 1874 from EP22.[128] Central Birm RDn (1905—57), Birm City RDn (1957—68). Abol 1968 ent to Lozells St Silas EP.[132]

EP31—BIRMINGHAM ST STEPHEN—Cr 1844 from EP16.[120] Aston RDn (1905—50). Bdry: 1869 (cr EP23),[115] 1899 (help cr EP14).[119] Abol 1950 pt to Aston Brook EP, pt to EP16.[38]

EP32—BIRMINGHAM ST THOMAS—Cr 1834 from AP1.[94] Edgb. RDn (1905—39). Bdry: 1865 (cr EP7),[114] 1869 (cr EP8).[115] Abol 1939 to help cr EP33.[14]

EP33—BIRMINGHAM ST THOMAS AND IMMANUEL—Cr 1939 by union EP32, EP7.[14] Edgb. RDn (1939—57), Birm City RDn (1957—69). Abol 1969 ent to EP19.[124]

BISHOPSTON
Chap in Stratford on Avon AP, sep EP 1737.[25] Kinet. RDn (1737—1861), N Kinet. RDn (1861—1921), Kinet. RDn (1921—63). Abol 1963 to help cr Stratford on Avon with Bishopston EP.[133]

BLACKDOWN
EP Cr 1894 from the pt of Lillington AP not in Royal Leam. Spa MB.[64] LG Warw. PLU, RD. Parl Warw. & Leam. Dv/CC (1918—*).

BOLDMERE
EP Cr 1858 from Sutton Coldfield AP.[134] Colesh. RDn (1858—60), Sutt. Coldf. RDn (1860—*). Bdry: 1923 (cr Wylde Green EP),[113] 1948 (gains pt Perry Barr CP, pt Kingstanding St Luke EP, both orig Staffs),[135] 1954 (cr Sutton Coldfield St Columba EP),[136] 1971.[135]

BOLEHALL AND GLASCOTE
Tp (Warws, Heml. Hd) in Tamworth AP (Staffs, Warws until 1866, ent Staffs thereafter), sep CP 1866 in Warws.[22] LG Tamw. PLU, pt Tamw. MB & USD (1890—94), Tamw. RSD (ent 1875—90, pt 1890—94), RD. Bdry: 1894 (gains pt of the pt of Tamworth Castle CP not in Tamw. MB, Staffs, loses its own pt in that MB to Tamworth AP, Staffs),[137] 1932 (loses pt to Tamw. MB & AP, Staffs),[23] 1956.[19] Renamed 1957 'Glascote'.[138] Parl Tamw. Parl Bor ([Staffs, Warws], 1832—85), N'rn Dv (1885—1918), Tamw. Dv (1918—45), Sutt. Coldf. Dv/CC (1945—70).

BORDESLEY
The following have 'Bordesley' in their names. Insofar as any existed at a given time: Arden RDn (cr—1854), Birm RDn (1854—92), Aston RDn (1892—1905), Bord. RDn (1905—*).

EP1—BORDESLEY [HOLY TRINITY]—Cr 1848 from Aston juxta Birmingham AP (civ, 'Aston'),[25] refounded 1864.[46] Bdry: 1846 (before cr of this par, pt area severed to cr EP4),[44] 1871 (cr EP2),[34] 1875 (cr Small Heath EP),[103] 1896.[139] Abol 1967 pt to Sparkbrook Christ Church EP, pt to EP4, pt to Small Heath St Aidan EP, pt to Sparkbrook St Agatha EP, pt to EP2.[140]

—BORDESLEY ST AIDAN—see SMALL HEATH ST AIDAN

EP2—BORDESLEY ST ALBAN THE MARTYR—Cr 1871 from EP1.[34] Bdry: 1900 (help cr EP6),[141] 1967,[140] 1969.[129] Abol 1973 to help cr EP3.[142]

EP3—BORDESLEY ST ALBAN AND ST PATRICK—Cr 1973 by union EP2, pt EP6.[142]

EP4—BORDESLEY ST ANDREW—Cr 1846 from area EP1 before latter a sep par from Aston juxta Birmingham AP (civ, 'Aston').[44] Bdry: 1889 (cr EP5),[143] 1967.[140]

—BORDESLEY ST BENEDICT—Name used now for EP cr 1910 as 'Small Heath St Benedict', qv.

EP5—BORDESLEY ST OSWALD—Cr 1889 from EP4.[143] Bdry: 1896,[139] 1907,[29] 1910 (cr Small Heath St Benedict EP, now called 'Bordesley St

Benedict'),[144] 1924 (help cr Small Heath St Gregory EP).[145]

EP6—BORDESLEY ST PATRICK—Cr 1900 from EP2 and from Worcs EPs of Balsall Heath, Balsall Heath St Thomas in the Moors.[141] Abol 1973 pt to help cr EP3, pt to Balsall Heath St Paul EP.[142]

BORDESLEY GREEN

EP Cr 1928 from Ward End EP.[146] E Birm RDn (1928—57), Yard. RDn (1957—*).

BOURTON ON DUNSMORE

AP More recently civ 'Burton and Draycote'. *LG* Seq 18. *Parl* Seq 8. *Eccl* Seq 12.

BRAILES

AP Incl chap Tanworth (sep par by 1202[147]). *LG* Seq 10. *Parl* Seq 13. *Eccl* Seq 20.

BRANDON AND BRETFORD

Hmlt (incl area Bretford Bor, status not sustained) in Wolston AP, sep CP 1866.[22] *LG* Seq 18. Bdry: 1965 (incl gains pt Cov CB [assoc with Warws] & CP).[11] *Parl* Seq 6.

BRINKLOW

AP Orig chap in Smite AP (Smite subsumed into Combe Abbey and from Dissolution ex-par place as 'Combe Fields'[148]), appropriated to Kenilw. Priory and early considered sep.[149] *LG* Brinklow Bor (status not sustained), Knight. Hd, Rugby PLU (soon after 1836[150]—1930), RSD, RD. *LG* Seq 18. Civ bdry: 1885 (gains Monks Riding CP).[151] *Parl* Seq 6. *Eccl* Seq 10.

BROWNSOVER

Chap in Clifton upon Dunsmore AP, sep CP 1866.[22] *LG* Knight. Hd, Rugby PLU, RSD, RD. Abol 1932 pt to Rugby UD & AP, pt to Churchover AP, pt to Clifton upon Dunsmore AP.[61] *Parl* N'rn Dv (1832—85), S-E'rn Dv (1885—1918), Rugby Dv (1918—45).

BUBBENHALL

AP *LG* Seq 20. *Parl* Seq 12. *Eccl* Seq 11.

BUDBROOKE

AP *LG* Seq 3. Civ bdry: 1931.[74] *Parl* Seq 14. *Eccl* Seq 21.

BULKINGTON

AP Incl chap Ryton on Dunsmore (made prebendal 1249 and sep par thereafter[152]), chap Shilton (orig chap in this par, from *ca* 1410 considered chap in Anstey AP,[24] 'Shilton' sep civ identity early from Anstey, sep EP 1754[25]). *LG* Knight. Hd, Nun. PLU, Bulkington USD (ent 1875—83, pt 1883—94), pt Nun. RSD (1883—94), Bulkington UD (1894—1932), Rugby RD (1932—38), Bedworth UD (1938—74). Addtl civ bdry alt: 1883,[153] 1938,[154] 1938.[155] *Parl* N'rn Dv (1832—85), N-E'rn Dv (1885—1918), Rugby Dv (1918—45), Nun. Dv/CC (1945—*). *Eccl* Seq 9.

BURMINGTON

Chap in Great Wolford AP, sep civ identity early, sep eccl no later than 1634.[156] *LG* Seq 10. Civ bdry: 1884.[65] *Parl* Seq 13. *Eccl* Kinet. RDn (cr—1861), S Kinet. RDn (1861—1921), Shipst. RDn (1921—*).

BURNLEY LANE

EP Cr 1966 from Ward End EP.[157] Yard. RDn.

BURTON AND DRAYCOTE—see BOURTON ON DUNSMORE

BURTON HASTINGS

AP *LG* Knight. Hd, Hinck. PLU (soon after 1836[150]—between 1896/1900), RSD, Nun. PLU (between 1896/1900—1930), RD (1894—1932), Rugby RD (1932—74). Civ bdry: 1885,[158] 1938.[154] *Parl* Seq 4. *Eccl* Arden RDn (until 1854), Monks Kirby RDn (1854—1963), Bedw. RDn (1963—*).

BUSHWOOD

Tp in Old Stratford AP, sep CP 1866.[22] *LG* Barl. Hd, Solih. PLU, RSD, RD (1894—1932), Warw. RD (1932—74). *Parl* S'rn Dv (1832—85), S-W'rn Dv (1885—1918), Tamw. Dv (1918—48), Warw. & Leam. CC (1948—*).

CALDECOTE

AP *LG* Heml. Hd, Nun. PLU, RSD, RD (1894—1932), Ath. RD (1932—74). Civ bdry: 1931,[159] 1935 (gains pt Fenny Drayton AP, pt Higham on the Hill AP, both Leics).[160] *Parl* Seq 3. *Eccl* Seq 1.

CAMP HILL WITH GALLEY COMMON

EP Renaming 1959 of Galley Common EP when gains pt Nuneaton St Mary the Virgin EP.[118] Ath. RDn (1959—1963), Nun. RDn (1963—*).

CASTLE BROMWICH

Chap in Aston AP (eccl, 'Aston juxta Birmingham'), sep CP 1894 from pt of the pt of Aston AP not in Birm CB or Aston Manor UD,[35] eccl donative early augmented,[32] eccl refounded 1878.[33] *LG* Aston PLU, Cast. Bromw. RD (1894—1912), Merid. RD (1912—74). Civ bdry: 1931 (incl loses pt to Birm CB [assoc with Warws] & AP),[89] 1966 (incl exchanges pts with Birm CB [assoc with Warws] & AP),[4] 1970.[78] Transf 1974 to W Midlands.[12] *Parl* Tamw. Dv (1918—45), Sutt. Coldf. Dv/CC (1948—70), Merid. CC (1970—*). *Eccl* Arden RDn (cr—1854), Colesh. RDn (1854—60), Sutt. Coldf. RDn (1860—92), Aston RDn (1892—1957), Colesh. RDn (1957—*). Eccl bdry: 1958 (cr Shard End EP),[127] 1964 (incl help cr Hodge Hill EP),[161] 1968 (cr Castle Bromwich St Clement EP).[162]

CASTLE BROMWICH ST CLEMENT

EP Cr 1968 from Castle Bromwich EP.[162] Colesh. RDn.

CASTLE VALE

EP Cr 1968 from Curdworth AP.[163] Sutt. Coldf. RDn.

CHADSHUNT

Prebendal chap in Bishop's Itchington AP, sep civ identity early incl chap Gaydon (Gaydon sep civ identity early from this par), the 2 areas united 1879 as 'Gaydon with Chadshunt' EP,[164] qv. *LG* Seq 11. *Parl* Seq 9.

CHAPEL ASCOTE

Orig pt of Hodnell AP (incl area orig church), depopulated 15th cent and considered ex-par thereafter,[165] sep CP 1858.[166] *LG* Knight. Hd, Southam PLU (1858—1930), RSD, RD. *Parl* Seq 11.

CHARLECOTE

AP Orig chap in Hampton Lucy AP, dependent on Kenilw. Priory, sep early but independence disputed.[167] *LG* Seq 12. Civ bdry: 1886.[168] *Parl* Seq 13. *Eccl* Seq 19.

CHELMSLEY WOOD

CP Cr 1970 from Coleshill AP, Kingshurst CP.[78] *LG* Merid. RD. Transf 1974 to W Midlands.[12]

EP Cr 1972 from Coleshill AP, Marston Green EP, Tile Cross EP.[169] Colesh. RDn.

CHERINGTON

AP *LG* Seq 10. *Parl* Seq 13. *Eccl* Seq 20. Eccl bdry: 1910 (gains hmlt Stourton from Whichford AP).[170]

CHESTERTON

AP *LG* Seq 11. *Parl* Seq 13. *Eccl* Ston. RDn (until 1854), Southam RDn (1854—60), Leam. RDn (1860—1921), Kinet. RDn (1921—63), Dass. Mag. RDn (1963—*).

CHEYLESMORE

EP Cr 1957 from Coventry St Anne EP, Stivichall EP.[171] Cov RDn (1957—63), Cov South RDn (1963—*).

CHILVERS COTON

AP *LG* Heml. Hd, Nun. PLU, Chilvers Coton USD (1875—93), Nun. & Chilvers Coton USD (1893—94), UD (1894—1907), Nun. MB (1907—20). Civ bdry: 1885.[172] Abol civ 1920 ent to Nuneaton AP.[173] *Parl* N'rn Dv (1832—85), N-E'rn Dv (1885—1918), Nun. Dv (1918—45). *Eccl* Seq 1. Eccl bdry: 1937.[31]

CHURCHOVER

AP *LG* Seq 18. Civ bdry: 1932,[61] 1935 (gains pt Cotesbach AP, pt Lutterworth AP, pt Shawell AP, all Leics).[160] *Parl* Seq 8. *Eccl* Seq 10.

CLAVERDON

AP Incl chap Norton Lindsey (sep civ identity early, sep EP 1771,[25] sep eccl status not sustained hence this par eccl 'Claverdon with Norton Lindsey' until area chap Norton Lindsey and area hmlt Langley eccl severed 1925 to help cr Wolverton with Norton Lindsey EP,[174] this par 'Calverdon' thereafter), hmlt Langley (sep CP 1866,[22] eccl severed 1925 to help cr Wolverton with Norton Lindsey EP[174]). *LG* Seq 2. *Parl* Seq 15. *Eccl* Warw. RDn (1925—*).

CALVERDON WITH NORTON LINDSEY

AP Usual eccl spelling until chap Norton Lindsey (qv in prev entry for earlier sep eccl status, not sustained, and for sep civ identity of this par), hmlt Langley both severed 1925 to help cr Wolverton with Norton Lindsey EP,[174] this par eccl 'Claverdon' thereafter, qv. *Eccl* Warw. RDn.

CLAYBROOKE

AP Incl in Warws chap Wibtoft (Knight. Hd, sep CP 1866,[22] not sep eccl hence this par eccl 'Claybrooke with Wibtoft', qv in Leics for eccl organisation); incl in Leics (Guthlaxton Hd) lbty (orig chap, early destroyed) Bittesby, tps Great Claybrooke, Little Claybrooke, hmlt Ullesthorpe, chap Wigston Parva (each a sep CP 1866 in Leics[22]) so that 'Claybrooke' has no sep civ identity after 1866 in either co. *Parl* Warws pt, N'rn Dv (1832—67).

CLAYBROOKE WITH WIBTOFT—see prev entry

CLAYDON WITH MOLLINTON

EP Cr 1851 by union chap Claydon (ent Oxon), chap Mollington (Oxon, Warws), both in Cropredy AP (o'wise ent Oxon),[175] to be dioc Oxford (Deddington RDn), the par divided 1863 into the 2 EPs of Claydon, Mollington.[176]

CLIFFORD CHAMBERS

AP Glos par transf 1931 to Warws.[6] *LG* Stratf. on Avon RD. *Parl* Stratf. CC (1948—70), Stratf. on Avon CC (1970—*).

CLIFTON UPON DUMSMORE

AP Incl chap Rugby (sep par by 1291[177]), chap Brownsover, hmlt Newton and Biggin (each a sep CP 1866[22]). *LG* Seq 18. Addtl civ bdry alt: 1932.[61] *Parl* Seq 8. *Eccl* Seq 13.

COLESHILL

AP Incl chap Lea Marston (sep par at Reformation[178]), chap Nether Whitacre, chap Over Whitacre (each prob sep par at Reformation[179]). *LG* Pt Colesh. Bor, Seq 5. Addtl civ bdry alt: 1932,[25] 1956 (cr Kingshurst CP),[180] 1958,[77] 1970 (incl help cr Chelmsley Wood CP, help cr Fordbridge CP).[78] *Parl* Seq 2. *Eccl* Seq 5. Addtl eccl bdry alt: 1939 (help cr Marston Green EP),[181] 1957 (cr Kingshurst EP),[182] 1972 (help cr Chelmsley Wood EP).[169]

COMBE FIELDS

Orig 'Smite' AP (incl chap Brinkow, qv for sep identity), subsumed into Combe Abbey and from Dissolution considered ex-par 'Combe Fields',[148] sep CP 1858.[166] *LG* Seq 18. Civ bdry: 1932,[25] 1932.[9] *Parl* Seq 6.

COMBROOK

Chap in Kineton AP, sep CP 1866,[22] sep EP 1853 as 'Combrooke'.[183] *LG* Seq 12. *Parl* S'rn Dv (1832—85), N'rn Dv (1885—1918), Rugby Dv (1918—48), Stratf. CC (1948—70), Stratf. on Avon CC (1970—*). *Eccl* Kinet. RDn. Reconstituted 1858 as 'Combrooke with Compton Verney' when gains ex-par (orig AP, qv) Compton Verney.[184]

COMBROOKE—see prev entry

COMBROOKE WITH COMPTON VERNEY

EP Cr 1858 by union Combrooke EP, ex-par (orig AP, qv) Compton Verney.[184] Kinet. RDn (1858—61), N Kinet. RDn (1861—1963), Dass. Mag. RDn (1963—*).

FENNY COMPTON

AP Areas Hodnell, Watergall in Hodnell AP (depopulated 15th cent) at first considered in this par and later detached, then considered ex-par, qv. *LG* Seq 11. *Parl* Seq 11. *Eccl* Seq 16.

LITTLE COMPTON

AP Glos par (Deerhurst Hd) situated in Warws to which transf 1832 for parl purposes, 1844 for civ purposes.[185] *LG* After 1844, Seq 9. *Parl* After 1832, Seq 14. *Eccl* See entry in Glos.

LONG COMPTON

AP *LG* Seq 9. *Parl* Seq 13. *Eccl* Seq 20.

COMPTON VERNEY

AP Orig AP (Kinet. RDn), prebendal for canon at Collegiate Curch of Warwick St Mary, priv chap from Dissolution and eccl abol 1858 ent to Combrooke EP which was henceforth called 'Combrooke with Compton Verney',[184] qv. *LG* Seq 12. *Parl* Seq 9.

COMPTON WYNYATES

AP *LG* Seq 10. *Parl* Seq 13. *Eccl* Seq 20.

COPSTON MAGNA

Chap and hmlt in Monks Kirby AP, sep CP 1866.[22] *LG* Seq 16. Civ bdry: 1935 (loses pt to Sharnford

AP, Wigston Parva CP, both Leics).[160] *Parl* Seq 6.

CORLEY
AP *LG* Seq 5. *Parl* Seq 2. *Eccl* Cov RDn (until 1854), Solih. RDn (1854—60), Ath. RDn (1860—1907), Monks Kirby RDn (1907—21), Cov RDn (1821—63), Bedw. RDn (1963—*). Eccl bdry: 1957.[15]

COSFORD
Hmlt in Newbold on Avon AP, sep CP 1866.[22] *LG* Seq 18. Bdry: 1932.[61] *Parl* Seq 8.

COUGHTON
AP Incl hmlt Sambourn (sep CP 1866,[22] not sep eccl hence this par eccl 'Coughton with Sambourn', qv). *LG* Seq 1. *Parl* Seq 15.

COUGHTON WITH SAMBOURN
AP Usual eccl spelling; for civ and civ sep chap, see prev entry. *Eccl* Seq 22.

COUNDON
Tp in Coventry St Michael AP, sep CP 1866,[22] eccl severed 1848 to help cr Keresley with Coundon EP.[186] *LG* Knight. Hd, Merid. PLU, RSD, RD. Bdry: 1928 (loses pt to Cov CB [assoc with Warws] & CP).[8] Abol 1932 pt to Cov CB (assoc with Warws) & CP, pt to Keresley CP.[9] *Parl* N'rn Dv (1832—85), N-E'rn Dv (1885—1918), Tamw. Dv (1918—45).

COVENTRY
The following have 'Coventry' in their names. Insofar as any existed at a given time: *LG* Cov Incorp (poor law purposes); Hd, Bor/MB/CB, USD, Co of Itself sep noted. *Parl* Sep noted (represented before 1832: 1295—1306, 1315, 1346, 1353, 1472—77, 1529—1832). *Eccl* Cov RDn (until 1963), sep noted (1963—*).

CP1—COVENTRY—Cr 1900 by union of pars in Cov CB: CP2, CP4.[187] *LG* Cov CB. Bdry: 1928 (incl gains CP3, CP5, Stoke AP, Stoke Heath CP),[8] 1932,[26] 1956 (incl exchanges pts with Allesley AP, Baginton AP, Binley CP, Stoneligh AP),[10] 1965 (loses pt to help cr Binley Woods CP, exchanges pts with Shilton CP, loses pt to Ansty AP, loses pt to Brandon and Bretford CP).[11] Transf 1974 to W Midlands.[12] *Parl* Cov Parl Bor (1918—48); see Part III of the *Guide* for composition of Cov BCs (1948—*) by wards of the CB. Parl bdry: 1960.[13]

EP1—COVENTRY ALL SAINTS—Cr 1869 from EP13, AP1, AP2.[103] Cov East RDn (1963—70). Bdry: 1930 (help cr EP5),[188] 1957.[15] Abol 1970 pt to EP13, pt to help cr EP6.[189]

EP2—COVENTRY CHRIST CHURCH GREY FRIARS—Cr 1900 from AP2.[141] Abol 1957 ent to AP1.[15]

EP3—COVENTRY EAST—Cr 1973 by union EP6, EP11, EP13.[190] Cov East RDn.

AP1—COVENTRY HOLY TRINITY—Tp 'Coventry Holy Trinity' in Cov Bor, Cov Co of Itself (1452—1842); incl in Knight. Hd chap Binley (sep civ identity early, donative and sep eccl status sustained[83]), hmlt Willenhall (sep CP 1866[22]). *LG* Pt Cov MB (1835—89), pt Cov CB (1889—94), pt Cov USD, pt Cov RSD. Addtl civ bdry alt: 1884.[191] Abol civ 1894 the pt in the CB cr CP2, the remainder cr CP3.[64] *Parl* Cov Parl Bor (pt

until 1867 [dates before 1832 noted above], ent 1867—1918), pt N'rn Dv (1832—67). *Eccl* Cov North RDn (1963—*). Eccl bdry: 1842 (cr EP13),[192] 1868 (help cr EP1, help cr EP11),[103] 1912 (cr Radford EP, now called 'Coventry St Nicholas'),[193] 1940,[194] 1957 (incl gains EP2),[15] 1958 (cr Willenhall with Whitley EP).[195]

CP2—COVENTRY HOLY TRINITY WITHIN—Cr 1894 from the pt of AP1 in Cov CB.[64] *LG* Cov CB. Bdry: 1899.[196] Abol 1900 to help cr CP1.[187]

CP3—COVENTRY HOLY TRINITY WITHOUT—Cr 1894 from the pt of AP1 not in Cov CB.[64] *LG* Cov RD. Abol 1928 ent to Cov CB (assoc with Warws) & to CP1.[8] *Parl* Nun. Dv (1918—45).

EP4—COVENTRY ST ALBAN STOKE HEATH—Cr 1939 from Wyken AP.[197] Cov East RDn (1963—*).

EP5—COVENTRY ST ANNE—Cr 1930 from AP2, EP1.[188] Cov East RDn (1963—70). Bdry: 1940,[194] 1957 (help cr Cheylesmore EP),[171] 1957,[15] 1959.[198] Abol 1970 to help cr EP6.[189]

EP6—COVENTRY ST ANNE AND ALL SAINTS—Cr 1970 by union EP5, pt EP1.[189] Cov East RDn. Abol 1973 to help cr EP3.[190]

—COVENTRY ST CHAD—Name used now for EP cr 1957 as 'Woodend', qv.

EP7—COVENTRY ST FRANCIS OF ASSISI NORTH RADFORD—Cr 1952 from Radford EP, Holbrooks EP.[199] Cov North RDn (1863—*).

EP8—COVENTRY ST GEORGE—Cr 1935 from EP9, Keresley and Coundon EP, Radford EP.[200] Cov North RDn. Bdry: 1959.[16]

EP9—COVENTRY ST JOHN [THE BAPTIST]—Orig hospital, civ in AP2. Cov North RDn (1963—*). Bdry: 1844 (cr EP14),[201] 1935 (help cr EP8).[200]

—COVENTRY ST LUKE—name used now for EP cr 1935 as 'Holbrooks', qv.

EP10—COVENTRY ST MARGARET—Cr 1913 from Stoke EP, EP13.[145] Cov East RDn (1963—*). Bdry: 1957.[15]

EP11—COVENTRY ST MARK—Cr 1869 from AP1, AP2, EP13.[103] Cov East RDn (1963—73). Bdry: 1957.[15] Abol 1973 to help cr EP3.[190]

EP12—COVENTRY ST MARY MAGDALEN—Cr 1926 from EP14, AP2.[202] Cov South RDn (1963—*).

AP2—COVENTRY ST MICHAEL—Tp 'Coventry St Michael' in Cov Bor; incl in Knight. Hd chap Allesley (sep par 1249[7]), chap Exhall (sep par at Reformation[203]); incl in Cov Co of Itself (1452—1842), Knight. Hd (from 1842) chap Foleshill (sep par from 1552 but independence early disputed[204]), chap Stivichall (sep civ identity early, sep EP 1739[25]), chap Stoke (sep par prob at beginning of reign Eliz I, sep status disputed,[205] recognised 1595 as independent[206]), chap Wyken (sep par by 1547[207]); incl pt in Cov Co of Itself, pt in Knight. Hd chap Sowe (first called sep par early 17th cent,[208] later called 'Walsgrave on Sowe'); incl hmlt Keresley (Cov Co), tp Coundon (Knight. Hd) (each a sep CP 1866,[22] eccl united 1848 as 'Keresley with Coundon' EP[186]). Civ incl area Coventry St John (orig hospital; for eccl see EP9).

LG Pt Cov MB (1835—89), pt Cov CB (1889—94), pt Cov USD, pt Cov RSD. Addtl civ bdry alt: 1884.[191] Abol civ 1894 the pt in the CB cr CP4, the remainder cr CP5.[64] *Parl* Cov Parl Bor (pt until 1867 [dates before 1832 noted above], ent 1867—1918), pt N'rn Dv (1832—67). *Eccl* Cov North RDn (1963—*). Addtl eccl bdry alt: 1869 (help cr EP1, help cr EP11),[103] 1900 (cr EP2),[141] 1922 (help cr Earlsdon EP),[209] 1926 (help cr EP12),[202] 1930 (help cr EP5),[188] 1957.[15]

CP4—COVENTRY ST MICHAEL WITHIN—Cr 1894 from the pt of AP2 in Cov CB.[64] *LG* Cov CB. Abol 1900 to help cr CP1.[187]

CP5—COVENTRY ST MICHAEL WITHOUT—Cr 1894 from the pt of AP2 not in Cov CB.[64] *LG* Cov RD. Abol 1928 ent to Cov CB (assoc with Warws) & to CP1.[8] *Parl* Nun. Dv (1918—45).

—COVENTRY ST NICHOLAS—Name used now for EP cr 1912 as 'Radford', qv.

EP13—COVENTRY ST PETER—Cr 1842 from AP1.[192] Cov East RDn (1963—73). Bdry: 1869 (help cr EP1, help cr EP11),[103] 1913 (help cr EP10),[145] 1957,[15] 1970.[189] Abol 1973 to help cr EP3.[190]

EP14—COVENTRY ST THOMAS—Cr 1844 from EP9.[201] Cov North RDn (1963—*). Bdry: 1922 (help cr Earsldon EP),[209] 1926 (help cr EP12).[202]

CROPREDY
AP Mostly Oxon (Banbury Hd, qv for 3 chaps), incl chap Mollington (pt Oxon [only pt in Bloxham Hd], pt Warws [Kingt. Hd], the latter a sep CP 1866 with pt in each co[22] so that Cropredy ent Oxon thereafter, 'Mollington' eccl severed 1853, united with chap Claydon [Oxon] in same par to cr Claydon with Mollington EP,[210] the latter area divided 1863 into the 2 EPs of Claydon, Mollington[211]). *LG* Banb. PLU. *Parl* Warws pt, S'rn Dv (1832—67). See main entry in Oxon for other organisation and for pars cr from chaps in that co.

CUBBINGTON
AP Orig chap in Leek Wootton AP, sep par by 1331.[212] *LG* Seq 20. *Parl* Seq 12. *Eccl* Seq 17.

CURDWORTH
AP Incl hmlt Minworth (sep CP 1866[22]). *LG* Heml. Hd, Aston PLU (1836—1911), RSD, Cast. Bromw. RD (1894—1912), Merid. PLU (1911—30), RD (1912—74). Addtl civ bdry alt: 1883,[213] 1966.[4] *Parl* Seq 2. *Eccl* Seq 3. Eccl bdry: 1968 (cr Castle Vale EP).[163]

AVON DASSETT
AP Sometimes early 'Dassett Parva'. *LG* Seq 8. *Parl* Seq 11. *Eccl* Seq 16.

BURTON DASSETT
AP Sometimes early 'Dassett Magna'. *LG* Seq 11. *Parl* Seq 11. *Eccl* Seq 16.

DERITEND ST BASIL
EP Cr 1886 from Aston juxta Birmingham AP (civ, 'Aston').[50] Birm RDn (1886—92), Aston RDn (1892—1905), Central Birm RDn (1905—40). Bdry: 1896.[214] Abol 1940 to help cr Deritend St John and St Basil EP.[215]

DERITEND ST JOHN
EP Cr 1890 from Aston juxta Birmingham AP (civ, 'Aston').[51] RDns (from 1890), abol as for Deritend St Basil.

DERITEND ST JOHN AND ST BASIL
EP Cr 1940 by union Deritend St John EP, Deritend St Basil EP.[215] Central Birm RDn (1940—57), Birm City RDn (1957—*). Bdry: 1969.[129]

DORDON
CP Cr 1948 from Polesworth AP.[216] *LG* Ath. RD. Bdry: 1965 (loses pt to Tamw. MB & AP, Staffs).[21] *Parl* Merid. CC (1970—*).
EP Cr 1933 from Polesworth AP.[217] Polesw. RDn.

DORRIDGE
EP Cr 1967 from Solihull AP, Nuthurst cum Hockley Heath EP, Packwood AP, Knowle EP.[218] Solih. RDn.

DORSINGTON
AP Glos par transf 1931 to Warws (gains at same time pt Bickmarsh CP, Warws, as remainder of that par transf to be 'Bickmarsh' par in Worcs).[6] *LG* Stratf. on Avon RD. *Parl* Stratf. CC (1948—70), Stratf. on Avon CC (1970—*).

DOSTHILL AND WOOD END
EP Cr 1959 from Kingsbury AP.[219] Polesw. RDn.

DRAYTON BASSETT
AP Pt Staffs (N Offlow Hd), pt Warws (Heml. Hd), the par made 1895 ent Staffs.[220] *LG* Tamw. PLU, RSD, pt sep RD in Warws (1894—95). *Parl* Warws pt, N'rn Dv (1832—1918). For remainder of civ and parl, and for ent eccl organisation, see entry in Staffs.

DUDDESTON CUM NECHELLS
EP Cr 1842 from Aston juxta Birmingham AP (civ, 'Aston').[43] Arden RDn (1842—54), Birm RDn (1854—92), Aston RDn (1892—1905), E Birm RDn (1905—57), Birm City RDn (1957—*). Bdry: 1864 (help cr Aston Brook EP),[37] 1860 (cr Nechells St Clement EP),[109] 1868 (cr Birmingham St Lawrence EP),[60] 1869 (cr Duddeston St Anne EP),[221] 1951 (incl gains Duddeston St Anne EP, gains Nechells St Catherine EP),[111] 1970 (incl gains Ashted EP).[29] More recently called 'Duddeston St Matthew'.

DUDDESTON ST ANNE
EP Cr 1869 from Duddeston cum Nechells EP.[221] Birm RDn (1869—92), Aston RDn (1892—1905), E Birm RDn (1905—51). Bdry: 1907.[28] Abol 1951 ent to Duddeston cum Nechells EP.[111]

DUDDESTON ST MATTHEW—see DUDDESTON CUM NECHELLS

DUNCHURCH
AP Incl tp Thurlaston (sep CP 1866[22]). *LG* Seq 18. *Parl* Seq 8. *Eccl* Seq 12.

EARLSDON
EP Cr 1922 from Coventry St Michael AP, Coventry St Thomas EP.[209] Cov RDn (1922—63), Cov South RDn (1963—*).

EARLSWOOD
EP Name used now for EP cr 1843 (ptly independent), 1848 (fully independent) as 'Tanworth Salter's Street', qv.

EASENHALL
Hmlt in Monks Kirby AP, sep CP 1866.[22] *LG* Knight. Hd, Rugby PLU (soon after 1836[150]—1930), RSD, RD. *Parl* Seq 6.

EATHORPE

Hmlt in Wappenbury AP, sep CP 1866.[22] *LG* Seq 20. *Parl* Seq 12.

EATINGTON

AP Usual civ spelling until renamed 1948 'Ettington'[222]; for usual eccl, see following entry. *LG* Kingt. Hd, Stratf. on Avon PLU, RSD, RD. *Parl* S'rn Dv (1832—85), S-W'rn Dv (1885—1918), Rugby Dv (1918—48), Stratf. CC (1948—70).

LOWER EATINGTON, OTHERWISE ETTINGTON

AP Usual eccl spelling; for civ until renamed 1948, see prev entry; for civ after 1948, see 'Ettington'. *Eccl* Seq 19.

EDGBASTON

The following have 'Edgbaston' in their names. Insofar as any existed at a given time: *LG* Heml. Hd, Birm MB (1838—89), CB (1889—1912), USD, PLU (1911—12), K's Nort. PLU (1836—1911). *Parl* Birm Parl Bor (1832—85); see Part III of the *Guide* for composition of Birm Parl Bors (1885—1918) by wards of the MB. *Eccl* Arden RDn (until 1854), Birm RDn (1854—1905), Edgb. RDn (1905—*).

CP1/EP1—EDGBASTON [ST BARTHOLOMEW]—Orig chap (Warws) in Harborne AP (o'wise Staffs, S Offlow Hd), sep par in Warws no later than 1658.[223] Abol civ 1912 ent to Birmingham AP.[36] *Eccl* bdry: 1832 (cr EP5,[224] refounded 1852[225]), 1838 (cr EP3,[226] refounded 1852[227]), 1889 (cr EP2),[228] 1903 (cr EP6),[229] 1972.[125]

EP2—EDGBASTON ST AUGUSTINE—Cr 1889 from EP1.[228] Bdry: 1906 (incl loses pt to Harborne Heath EP, Staffs, dioc Birm),[117] 1908,[230] 1920 (cr EP4).[231]

EP3—EDGBASTON ST GEORGE—Cr 1838 from EP1,[226] refounded 1952.[227] Bdry: 1908.[230]

EP4—EDGBASTON ST GERMAIN—Cr 1920 from EP2.[231]

EP5—EDGBASTON ST JAMES—Cr 1832 from EP1,[224] refounded 1852.[225] Birm City RDn (1957—72). Abol 1972 pt to EP1, pt to Birmingham St Luke EP.[125]

EP6—EDGBASTON ST MARY AND ST AMBROSE—Cr 1903 from EP1.[229] Bdry: 1958 (incl gains pt Balsall Heath St Thomas in the Moors EP and exchanges pts with Moseley St Anne EP, both Worcs),[125] 1969.[120]

ELMDON

AP *LG* Heml. Hd, Solih. PLU, RSD, RD. Abol 1932 pt to help cr Solih. UD and to help cr Solihull Urban CP, pt to Bickenhill AP.[64] *Parl* N'rn Dv (1832—1918), Tamw. Dv (1918—45). *Eccl* Seq 6. Eccl bdry: 1966.[157]

EMSCOTE

EP Cr 1867 from Warwick St Nicholas EP.[101] Warw. RDn. Now called 'Warwick All Saints'.

ERDINGTON

Chap in Aston AP (eccl 'Aston juxta Birmingham'), sep EP 1858 [St Barnabas],[48] sep CP 1894 from the pt of Aston AP neither in Birm CB nor in Aston Manor UD.[35] *LG* Aston PLU (1836—1911), Erdington UD (1894—1911), Birm PLU (1911—12), Birm CB (1911—12). Abol 1912 ent to Birmingham

AP.[36] *Eccl* Sutt. Coldf. RDn (1858—92), Aston RDn (1892—*). Eccl bdry: 1907,[29] 1929 (help cr Garvelly Hill EP),[53] 1930 (cr Pype Hayes EP),[232] 1962 (cr Short Heath EP),[233] 1968 (help cr Erdington St Chad EP).[234]

ERDINGTON ST CHAD

EP Cr 1968 from Erdington EP, Pype Hayes EP.[234] Aston RDn.

ETTINGTON

CP Renaming 1948 of Eatington AP (eccl, 'Lower Eatington, otherwise Ettington').[222] *LG* Stratf. on Avon RD. *Parl* Stratf. on Avon CC (1970—*).

EXHALL

AP Chap in Coventry St Michael AP, sep par at Reformation.[203] *LG* Cov Co of Itself (1452—1842), Knight. Hd (from 1842), Folesh. PLU, RSD, RD. Civ bdry: 1883,[158] 1885.[235] Abol civ 1932 pt to Cov CB (assoc with Warws) & CP, pt to Bedw. UD & AP.[26] *Parl* N'rn Dv (1832—85), N-E'rn Dv (1885—1918), Nun. Dv (1918—45). *Eccl* Cov RDn (until 1854), Bag. RDn (1854—92), Monks Kirby RDn (1892—1963), Bedw. RDn (1963—*). Eccl bdry: 1908 (help cr Longford EP),[236] 1935 (help cr Holbrooks EP,[200] now called 'Coventry St Luke'), 1957,[15] 1958.[237]

EXHALL

AP Chap in Salford Priors AP, sep par early incl from Reformation chap Wixford,[238] hence the par eccl thereafter 'Exhall with Wixford otherwise Wigglesford', qv. *LG* Seq 1. *Parl* Seq 15.

EXHALL WITH WIXFORD OTHERWISE WIGGLESFORD

AP Chap in Salford Priors AP, sep par early, civ as 'Exhall', qv, incl from Reformation chap Wixford,[238] hence eccl thereafter as here. *Eccl* Seq 22.

FARNBOROUGH

AP *LG* Seq 8. *Parl* Seq 11. *Eccl* Seq 16.

FILLONGLEY

AP *LG* Seq 5. Civ bdry: 1895 (gains Kinwalsey CP).[239] *Parl* Seq 7. *Eccl* Arden RDn (until 1854), Solih. RDn (1854—60), Ath. RDn (1860—1907), Monks Kirby RDn (1907—21), Ath. RDn (1921—63), Nun. RDn (1963—*).

FINHAM

EP Cr 1938 from Stoneleigh AP.[240] Kenilw. RDn (1938—63), Cov South RDn (1963—*). Bdry: 1967.[241]

FLETCHAMSTEAD

EP Cr 1963 from Westwood EP.[242] Cov South RDn.

FOLESHILL

AP Chap in Coventry St Michael AP, sep par from 1552 but independence early disputed.[204] *LG* Cov Co of Itself (1452—1842), Knight. Hd (from 1842), Folesh. PLU, RSD, RD. Civ bdry: 1883,[158] 1885,[235] 1899 (loses pt to Cov CB [assoc with Warws] and to Coventry Holy Trinity Within CP),[196] 1928 (loses pt to Cov CB [assoc with Warws] & CP).[8] Abol civ 1932 pt to Cov CB (assoc with Warws) & CP, pt to Bedw. UD & AP.[26] *Parl* N'rn Dv (1832—85), N-E'rn Dv (1885—1918), Nun. Dv (1918—45). *Eccl* Cov RDn (until 1854), Monks Kirby RDn (1854—1963), Cov North RDn

(1963—*). Eccl bdry: 1842 (cr as partly independent Foleshill St Paul EP,[243] 1845 as fully independent[244]), 1908 (help cr Longford EP),[236] 1956 (help cr Woodend EP).[245]

FOLESHILL ST PAUL
EP Cr 1842 as partly independent from Foleshill AP,[243] 1845 as fully independent.[244] Cov RDn (1842—54), Monks Kirby RDn (1854—1907), Cov RDn (1907—63), Cov North RDn (1963—*). Bdry: 1935 (help cr Holbrooks EP,[200] now called 'Coventry St Luke'), 1957.[15]

FORDBRIDGE
CP Cr 1970 from Coleshill AP, Kingshurst CP.[78] LG Merid. RD. Transf 1974 to W Midlands.[12]

FOUR OAKS
EP Cr 1920 from Hill EP.[15] Sutt. Coldf. RDn.

FRANKTON
AP LG Seq 18. Parl Seq 8. Eccl Merton RDn (until 1841), Cov RDn (1841—54), Dunch. RDn (1854—1907), Rugby with Dunch. RDn (1907—21), Dunch. RDn (1921—*).

FULBROOK
AP Orig sep AP (Warw. RDn), last presentment 1543 and called free chap, demolished but sep civ identity retained, eccl in Sherborne AP.[246] LG Seq 2. Parl Seq 15.

GALLEY COMMON
EP Cr 1952 from Stockingford EP, Nuneaton St Mary the Virgin EP.[247] Ath. RDn. Renamed 1959 'Camp Hill with Galley Common' when gains pt Nuneaton St Mary the Virgin EP.[118]

GARRETT'S GREEN
EP Cr 1967 from Yardley AP (Worcs), Sheldon AP (Warcs).[248] Colesh. RDn.

GAYDON
Chap in Chadshunt (prebendal chap in Bishop's Itchington AP, sep civ identity early incl chap Gaydon [Gaydon gains sep civ identity early from Chadshunt], the two united eccl 1879 as 'Gaydon with Chadshunt' EP,[164] qv). LG Seq 11. Parl Seq 10.

GAYDON WITH CHADSHUNT
EP Cr 1879 by union chap Chadshunt (sep civ identity early from Bishop's Itchington with Gaydon as its chap), chap Gaydon.[164] Dass. Mag. RDn.

GLASCOTE
CP Renaming 1957 of Bolehall and Glascote CP.[138] LG Tamw. RD. Bdry: 1958.[20] Abol 1965 ent to Tamw. MB & AP, Staffs.[21]

GOSPEL LANE
EP Cr 1964 from Warws pars of Olton EP, Shirley EP, and from Worcs par of Acocks Green EP.[249] Solih. RDn. Bdry: 1972 (incl loses pt to Acocks Green EP, Worcs).[250]

GRANDBOROUGH
AP LG Seq 18. Parl Seq 10. Eccl Seq 12.

GRAVELLY HILL
EP Cr 1929 from Erdington EP, Aston juxta Birmingham AP (civ, 'Aston').[53] Aston RDn. Bdry: 1934 (cr Stockland Green EP).[251]

GRENDON
AP LG Seq 4. Parl Seq 1. Eccl Seq 4.

GUY'S CLIFFE
Orig hermitage and chap,[252] ex-par from Dissolution, sep CP 1858.[166] LG Knight. Hd, Warw. PLU (1862—1930), RSD, RD. Parl Seq 12.

HALFORD
AP LG Seq 10. Parl Seq 13. Eccl Seq 20.

HAMPTON IN ARDEN
AP Incl chap Baddesley Clinton (sep par before 1298[57]), chap Balsall (sep CP 1866,[22] sep EP 1863 as 'Temple Balsall'[60]), chap Knowle (sep CP 1866,[22] sep EP 1726,[25] refounded 1859[253]), hmlt Kinwasley, hmlt (orig chap, early destroyed) Nuthurst (each a sep CP 1866[22]). LG Seq 5. Addtl civ bdry alt: 1932 (incl help cr Solihull Urban CP to constitute Solih. UD).[26] 1964 (exchanges pts with Solih. MB and Solihull Urban CP as revised area constituted Solih. CB [assoc with Warws]).[62] Transf 1974 to W Midlands.[12] Parl Seq 2. Eccl Seq 6. Addtl eccl bdry alt: 1878 (help cr Nuthurst cum Hockley Heath EP).[148]

HAMPTON LUCY
AP Sometimes 'Bishop's Hampton'. Incl chap Alveston (sep par 1269,[17]), chap Charlecote (dependent on Kenilw. Priory, sep early but independence disputed[162]), chap Wasperton (which incl chap Packwood, each a sep par by 1535,[254] although Packwood often described as eccl dependent on Wasperton,[255] Packwood with certain sep civ identity early, sep eccl status certain by 1786[25]). LG Seq 2. Parl Seq 15. Eccl Pec jurisd Hampton Lucy (1st mention 1593—1851), Seq 19 thereafter.

HANDSWORTH
AP Staffs par transf 1911 to be in Birm CB (assoc with Warws).[36] LG Birm PLU, CB. Abol 1930 ent to Birmingham AP.[88] Parl See Part III of the Guide for composition of Birm Parl Bors (1918—48) by wards of the CB. Eccl See entry in Staffs.

HARBORNE
AP Staffs par (S Offlow Hd) incl in Warws chap Edgbaston (Heml. Hd, sep par no later than 1658[223]). LG K's Nort. PLU (1836—1911), Birm PLU (1911—12), pt Harb. USD (1875—91), pt Smethw. USD. Made 1891 pt Birm CB & USD (assoc with Warws), and when in 1894 the remainder in Staffs (in Smethw. UD) cr Smethwick CP (see entry in Staffs), 'Harborne' ent Birm CB 1894—1912. Abol civ 1912 ent to Birmingham AP.[36] For other civ organisation, and for parl and eccl, see entry in Staffs.

HARBOROUGH MAGNA
AP LG Seq 18. Parl Seq 6. Eccl Cov RDn (until 1854), Rugby RDn (1854—1907), Rugby with Dunch. RDn (1907—21), Rugby RDn (1921—*).

HARBURY
AP LG Seq 19. Parl Seq 11. Eccl Ston. RDn (until 1854), Leam. RDn (1854—1907), Southam RDn (1907—*).

HARTSHILL
Hmlt in Mancetter AP, sep CP 1866,[22] sep EP 1842,[25] eccl refounded 1848.[256] LG Seq 4. Civ bdry: 1935 (gains pt Fenny Drayton AP, Leics).[160] Parl Seq 3. Eccl Arden RDn (1848—54), Ath. RDn (1854—1963), Nun. RDn (1963—*).

HASELEY

AP *LG* Seq 3. *Parl* Seq 14. *Eccl* Seq 21.

HASELOR

AP *LG* Seq 1. *Parl* Seq 15. *Eccl* Seq 22.

HATTON

AP Incl hmlt Beausale (sep CP 1866,[22] not sep eccl, eccl enlarged 1893[73]), hmlt Shrewley (sep CP 1866[22]). *LG* Seq 3. *Parl* Seq 14. *Eccl* Seq 21.

HEADLESS CROSS

EP Cr 1850 from Ipsley AP (Warws, Worcs), Tardebigge AP (Worcs, Warws until 1844, ent Worcs from 1844), Feckenham AP (Worcs).[257] Warw. RDn (1850—61), Alc. RDn (1861—1907), Bromsgrove RDn (1907—*). Bdry: 1924 (gains pt of Worcs pars of Feckenham AP, Ipsley AP, Redditch EP, loses pt to Worcs par of Tardebigge AP, all dioc Worc),[253] 1950 (help cr Astwood Bank with Crabbs Cross EP [Worcs, Warws, dioc Worc]).[258]

HENLEY IN ARDEN

Tp and bor in Wootton Wawen AP, sep EP 1747,[25] sep CP 1957 from Beaudesert AP, Wootton Wawen AP.[71] *LG* Straf. on Avon RD. *Parl* Straf. on Avon CC (1970—*). *Eccl* Warw. RDn. Abol eccl 1915 ent to Beaudesert AP.[72]

HILL

EP Cr 1853 from Sutton Coldfield AP.[28] Arden RDn (1853—54), Colesh. RDn (1854—60), Sutt. Coldf. RDn (1860—*). Bdry: 1920 (cr Four Oaks EP).[15]

HILLMORTON

AP *LG* Knight. Hd, Rugby PLU, RSD, RD. Abol civ 1932 pt to Rugby UD & AP, pt to Clifton upon Dunsmore AP.[61] *Parl* N'rn Dv (1832—85), S-E'rn Dv (1885—1918), Rugby Dv (1918—45). *Eccl* Seq 13. Eccl bdry: 1940.[31]

HINCKLEY

AP Leics par (Sparkenhoe Hd) incl in Warws chap Hyde (Knight. Hd, chap early destroyed and the area later considered hmlt 'Hydes Pastures', no sep civ or eccl identity), the par considered ent Leics by 1880s without explicit order.[259] See main entry in Leics.

HOBS MOAT

EP Cr 1966 from Solihull AP, Sheldon AP, Olton EP.[260] Solih. RDn.

HOCKLEY HEATH

CP Cr 1964 from a pt of Solih. MB and Solihull Urban CP not constituted Solih. CB.[62] *LG* Straf. on Avon RD. Transf 1974 to W Midlands.[12] *Parl* Straf. on Avon CC (1970—*).

HODGE HILL

EP Cr 1964 from Castle Bromwich EP, Ward End EP.[161] Colesh. RDn.

HODNELL

AP Orig AP, depopulated 15th cent, incl areas Hodnell, Watergall (both at first considered in Fenny Compton AP and later detached), Chapel Ascote (incl area orig church), Wills Pastures, each of the 4 considered thereafter ex-par tps,[160] 'Hodnell' a sep CP 1858,[166] 'Hodnell' eccl severed 1930 to help cr Ladbroke and Radbourn EP.[261] *LG* Knight. Hd, Southam PLU (1858—1930), RSD, RD. *Parl* Seq 11.

HOLBROOKS

EP Cr 1935 from Foleshill St Peter EP, Radford EP, Exhall EP.[200] Cov RDn (1935—63), Cov North RDn (1963—*). Bdry: 1952 (help cr Coventry St Francis of Assisi North Radford EP).[199] Now called 'Coventry St Luke'.

HONILEY

AP *LG* Seq 3. *Parl* Seq 14. *Eccl* Arden RDn (until 1854), Cov RDn (1854—1907), Kenilw. RDn (1907—21), Warw. RDn (1921—*).

HONINGTON

AP *LG* Seq 10. *Parl* Seq 13. *Eccl* Seq 20.

HUNNINGHAM

AP Orig chap in Wappenbury AP, sep par by 1535.[262] *LG* Seq 20. *Parl* Seq 12. *Eccl* Marton RDn (until 1854), Leam. RDn (1854—*).

IDLICTOE

AP *LG* Seq 10. *Parl* Seq 13. *Eccl* Seq 20.

ILMINGTON

AP *LG* Pt Glos (Kiftsgate Hd), pt Warws (Kingt. Hd), Shipst. on Stour PLU, RSD, Brailes RD (1894—1931), Shipst. on Stour RD (1931—74). Civ bdry: 1894 (loses the pt in Glos to Admington CP in that co and Ilmington ent Warws thereafter).[263] *Parl* Warws pt, Seq 15. *Eccl* Seq 20.

IPSLEY

AP Pt Warws (Barl. Hd), pt Worcs (Halfsh. Hd: pt hmlt Crabbs Cross, hmlt Headless Cross, the areas eccl severed 1850 to help cr Headless Cross EP[257]; the area civ in Redditch USD [o'wise ent Worcs] hence this par pt Worcs 1889—94 [see bdry alt 1894 below]). *LG* Alc. PLU, pt Redditch USD, pt Alc. RSD, Alc. RD. Civ bdry: 1894 (the pt in Worcs, Redditch UD, or Upper Ipsley CP in Worcs and 'Ipsley' ent Warws 1894—1931).[64] Transf 1931 to Worcs and to Redditch UD.[6] *Parl* S'rn Dv (1832—85), S-W'rn Dv (1885—1918), Warw. & Leam. Dv (1918—45). *Eccl* Warw. RDn (until 1861), Alc. RDn (1861—1907), Bromsgrove RDn (1907—33). Abol eccl 1933 pt to Redditch St George EP, pt to Redditch St Stephen EP, both Worcs.[264]

BISHOP'S ITCHINGTON

AP Incl chap Chadshunt (prebendal chap by 1341 in this par, sep civ identity early incl chap Gaydon [Gaydon sep civ identity early from Chadshunt], the two areas united 1879 as 'Gaydon with Chadshunt' EP[164]). *LG* Seq 19. *Parl* Seq 11. *Eccl* Ston. RDn (until 1841), Marton RDn (1841—54), Dass. Mag. RDn (1854—*).

LONG ITCHINGTON

AP *LG* Seq 19. *Parl* Seq 11. *Eccl* Seq 14.

KENILWORTH

AP Orig chap in Stoneleigh AP, sep AP by mid 13th cent.[265] *LG* Kenilw. Bor, Knight. Hd, Warw. PLU, Kenilw. USD, UD. Civ bdry: 1931,[74] 1932.[26] *Parl* Seq 12. *Eccl* Seq 15. Eccl bdry: 1854 (cr Kenilworth St John the Evangelist EP).[266]

KENILWORTH ST JOHN THE EVANGELIST

EP Cr 1854 from Kenilworth AP.[266] Cov RDn (1854—1907), Kenilw. RDn (1907—*). Bdry: 1962.[267]

KERESLEY

Hmlt in Coventry St Michael AP, sep civ identity early, eccl united 1848 with tp Coundon in same par as 'Keresley with Coundon' EP,[186] qv. *LG* Cov Co of Itself (1452—1842), Knight. Hd (from 1842), Folesh. PLU, RSD, RD (1894—1932), Merid. RD (1932—74). Bdry: 1932 (incl loses pt to Cov CB [assoc with Warws] & CP),[9] 1965 (loses pt to Cov CB [assoc with Warws] & CP).[11] Transf 1974 to W Midlands.[12] *Parl* N'rn Dv (1832—85), N-E'rn Dv (1885—1918), Nun. Dv (1918—45), Sutt. Coldf. Dv/CC (1945—70), Merid. CC (1970—*).

KERESLEY WITH COUNDON
EP Cr 1848 by union hmlt Keresley, tp Coundon (both in Coventry St Michael AP).[186] Cov RDn (1848—1963), Cov North RDn (1963—*). Bdry: 1935 (help cr Coventry St George EP),[200] 1957,[15] 1958.[249]

KINETON
AP Sometimes 'Kington' (the name used for the Hd). Incl chap Combrook (sep CP 1866,[22] sep EP 1853 as 'Combrooke',[183] qv for later union). *LG* Pt Kinet. Bor, Seq 12. *Parl* S'rn Dv (1832—85), N'rn Dv (1885—1918), Warw. & Leam. Dv (1918—48), Stratf. CC (1948—70), Stratf. on Avon CC (1970—*). *Eccl* Seq 18.

KINGSBURY
AP *LG* Seq 7. Civ bdry: 1954,[268] 1965 (incl loses pt to Tamw. MB & AP, Staffs).[21] *Parl* Seq 2. *Eccl* Arden RDn (until 1854), Polesw. RDn (1854—92), Colesh. RDn (1892—1905), Polesw. RDn (1905—*). Eccl bdry: 1959 (cr Dosthill and West End EP).[219]

KINGSHURST
EP Cr 1957 from Coleshill AP.[182] Sutt. Coldf. RDn (1957), Colesh. RDn (1957—*).

CP Cr 1956 from Coleshill AP.[180] *LG* Merid. RD. Civ bdry: 1966 (loses pt to Birm CB [assoc with Warws] & AP),[4] 1970 (incl help cr Chelmsley Wood CP, help cr Fordbridge CP).[78] Transf 1974 to W Midlands.[12] *Parl* Merid. CC (1970—*).

KINWARTON
AP Incl chap Weethley (sep civ identity early, eccl severed 1876 and transf to Alcester AP,[5] the latter thereafter called 'Alcester with Weethley'), chap Great Alne (sep civ identity early, not sep eccl hence this par eccl 'Kinwarton with Great Alne', qv). *LG* Seq 1. *Parl* Seq 15.

KINWARTON WITH GREAT ALNE
AP Usual eccl spelling; for civ and civ and eccl changes in chaps, see prev entry. *Eccl* Seq 22.

KINWASLEY
Hmlt in Hampton in Arden AP, sep CP 1866.[22] *LG* Heml. Hd, Merid. PLU, RSD, RD. Abol 1895 ent to Fillongley AP.[251] *Parl* N'rn Dv (1832—85), N-E'rn Dv (1885—1918).

KNOWLE
Chap in Hampton in Arden AP, sep CP 1866,[22] sep EP 1726,[25] eccl refounded 1859.[253] *LG* Heml. Hd, Solih. PLU, RSD, RD. Abol civ 1932 pt to help cr Solih. UD and help cr Solihull Urban CP.[26] *Parl* N'rn Dv (1832—1918), Tamw. Dv (1918—45). *Eccl* Arden RDn (1726—1854), Solih. RDn (1854—*). Eccl bdry: 1895,[269] 1941,[270] 1967 (help cr Dorridge EP),[218] 1966.[271]

LADBROKE
AP *LG* Seq 19. *Parl* Seq 11. *Eccl* Marton RDn (until 1854), Southam RDn (1854—1930). Abol eccl 1930 to help cr Ladbroke with Radbourn EP.[261]

LADBROKE WITH RADBOURN
EP Cr 1930 by union Ladbroke AP, Radbourn AP (no church; for civ see 2 ex-par places of Lower Radbourn, Upper Radbourn), and ex-par Hodnell.[261] Southam RDn.

LADYWOOD ST JOHN
EP Cr 1854 from Birmingham AP.[100] Arden RDn (1854), Birm RDn (1854—1905), Edgb. RDn (1905—57), Birm City RDn (1957—*). Bdry: 1876 (cr Birmingham St Margaret EP),[122] 1885 (cr Birmingham Christ Church, Summerfield EP),[44] 1956 (gains Birmingham St Barnabas EP, Birmingham St Margaret EP).[117]

LANGLEY
Hmlt in Claverdon AP, sep CP 1866,[22] eccl severed 1925 to help cr Wolverton with Norton Lindsey EP.[174] *LG* Seq 2. *Parl* Seq 15.

LAPWORTH
AP *LG* Kingt. Hd (until 1833), Barl. Hd (from 1833), Solih. PLU, RSD, RD (1894—1932), Warw. RD (1932—74). Civ bdry: 1932 (incl help cr Solihull Urban CP to constitute Solih. UD),[26] 1964.[62] *Parl* S'rn Dv (1832—85), S-W'rn Dv (1885—1918), Tamw. Dv (1918—48), Warw. & Leam. CC (1948—*). *Eccl* Kinet. RDn (until 1861), S Kinet. RDn (1861—1905), not in a RDn (July—Aug 1905 when first transf to Birm dioc), Solih. RDn (Aug 1905—*). Eccl bdry: 1909,[267] 1966.[271]

CHURCH LAWFORD
AP *LG* Seq 18. *Parl* Seq 8. *Eccl* Cov RDn (until 1854), Rugby RDn (1854—1907), Rugby with Dunch. RDn (1907—21), Rugby RDn (1921—*).

LITTLE LAWFORD
Hmlt in Newbold on Avon AP, sep CP 1866.[22] *LG* Seq 18. Civ bdry: 1932.[61] *Parl* Seq 8.

LONG LAWFORD
Hmlt in Newbold on Avon, sep CP 1866.[22] Organisation as for Little Lawford.

LEA HALL
EP Cr 1968 from Tile Cross EP (Warws), Yardley AP (Worcs).[272] Colesh. RDn.

LEAMINGTON
CP Cr 1902 by union pars in Royal Leam. Spa MB: Leamington Priors AP, Lillington AP, New Milverton CP.[273] *LG* Warw. PLU, Royal Leam. Spa MB. Bdry: 1931,[74] 1953.[274] *Parl* Warw. & Leam. Dv/CC (1918—*).

SOUTH LEAMINGTON
EP Cr 1875 from Leamington Priors AP.[45] Leam. RDn. Bdry: 1957.[275]

LEAMINGTON HASTINGS
AP *LG* Seq 18. *Parl* Seq 10. *Eccl* Marton RDn (until 1854), Dunch. RDn (1854—1907), Southam RDn (1907—21), Dunch. RDn (1921—*).

LEAMINGTON PRIORS
The following have 'Leamington Priors' in their names. Insofar as any existed at a given time: *LG* Knight. Hd, Warw. PLU, Royal Leam. Spa MB (1875—1902), USD. *Parl* S'rn Dv (1832—85), S-E'rn Dv (1885—1918). *Eccl* Ston. RDn (until 1854), Leam. RDn (1854—*).

AP1—LEAMINGTON PRIORS [ALL SAINTS]—Orig

chap in Leek Wootton AP, sep par by 1291.[276] Abol civ 1902 to help cr Leamington CP.[273] Eccl bdry: 1840 (cr EP2),[277] 1875 (cr South Leamington EP),[45] 1900 (cr EP1),[278] 1957.[275]

EP1—LEAMINGTON PRIORS HOLY TRINITY—Cr 1900 from AP1.[278] Bdry: 1957.[275]

—LEAMINGTON PRIORS ST MARK—Name used now for EP cr 1875 as 'New Milverton', qv.

EP2—LEAMINGTON PRIORS ST MARY—Cr 1840 from AP1.[277] Bdry: 1878 (cr EP3),[126] 1957.[275]

EP3—LEAMINGTON PRIORS ST PAUL—Cr 1878 from EP2.[126] Bdry: 1957.[275]

LEEK WOOTTON
AP Incl chap Ashow (sep par between 1198—1215[27]), chap Cubbington (sep par by 1331[212]), chap Leamington Priors (sep par by 1291[276]), chap Lillington (sep par by 1291[279]), chap Milverton (sep par by 1535[280]). *LG* Seq 20. Addtl civ bdry alt: 1931,[74] 1932.[26] *Parl* Seq 12. *Eccl* Ston. RDn (until 1854), Cov RDn (1854—92), Leam. RDn (1892—1907), Kenilw. RDn (1907—*). Addtl eccl bdry alt: 1962.[267]

LIGHTHORNE
AP *LG* Seq 11. *Parl* Seq 9. *Eccl* Seq 18.

LILLINGTON
AP Orig chap in Leek Wootton AP, sep par by 1291.[279] *LG* Knight. Hd, Warw. PLU, Lillington USD (1875—90), Royal Leam. Spa MB (pt 1890—94, ent 1894—1902), pt Warw. RSD (1890—94). Civ bdry: 1894 (the pt not in the MB cr Blackdown CP).[64] Abol civ 1902 to help cr Leamington CP.[273] *Parl* S'rn Dv (1832—85), S-E'rn Dv (1885—1918). *Eccl* Seq 17. Eccl bdry: 1957.[275]

LONGFORD
EP Cr 1908 from Foleshill AP, Walsgrave on Sowe EP, Exhall AP.[236] Monks Kirby RDn (1908—63), Bedw. RDn (1963—70), Cov North RDn (1970—*).

LOXLEY
AP *LG* Seq 2. *Parl* S'rn Dv (1832—85), S-W'rn Dv (1885—1918), Rugby Dv (1918—48), Stratf. CC (1948—70), Stratf. on Avon CC (1970—*). *Eccl* Seq 19.

LOZELLS ST PAUL
EP Cr 1881 from Lozells St Silas EP.[281] Sutt. Coldf. RDn (1881—92), Aston RDn (1892—*).

LOZELLS ST SILAS
EP Cr 1853 from Aston juxta Birmingham AP (civ, 'Aston').[47] Arden RDn (1853—54), Colesh. RDn (1854—60), Sutt. Coldf. RDn (1860—92), Aston RDn (1892—*). Bdry: 1864 (help cr Aston Brook EP),[37] 1881 (cr Lozells St Paul EP),[281] 1968 (gains Birmingham St Saviour EP).[128]

LUDDINGTON
Chap and hmlt in Old Stratford AP, sep civ 1664 incl area Drayton (not sep civ) in same par.[282] *LG* Seq 2. *Parl* Seq 15.

MANCETTER
AP Incl tp and bor Atherstone (sep CP 1866,[22] sep EP 1825,[25] eccl refounded 1851[54]), hmlt Hartshill (sep CP 1866,[22] sep EP 1842,[25] eccl refounded 1848[256]), hmlt Oldbury (sep CP 1866[22]). *LG* Seq 4. Addtl civ bdry alt: 1935 (gains pt Fenny Drayton AP, pt

Witherley AP, both Leics).[160] *Parl* Seq 3. *Eccl* Seq 1.

MANEY
EP Cr 1907 from Sutton Coldfield AP.[283] Sutt. Coldf. RDn. Bdry: 1971.[135]

BUTLERS MARSTON
AP *LG* Seq 10. *Parl* Seq 9. *Eccl* Seq 19.

LEA MARSTON
Chap in Coleshill AP, sep par at Reformation.[178] *LG* Seq 5. Civ bdry: 1880.[284] *Parl* Seq 2. *Eccl* Arden RDn (cr—1854), Colesh. RDn (1854—60), Sutt. Coldf. RDn (1860—1957), Colesh. RDn (1957—63). Abol eccl 1963 ent to Nether Whitacre AP.[253]

LONG MARSTON
AP Par 'Marston Sicca' in Glos transf 1931 to Warws where called 'Long Marston'.[6] *LG* Stratf. on Avon RD. *Parl* Stratf. CC (1948—70), Stratf. on Avon CC (1970—*). For civ and parl organisation before 1931, and for all eccl organisation, see 'Marston Sicca' in Glos.

PRIORS MARSTON
Chap in Priors Hardwick AP, sep civ identity early, sep EP 1860.[285] *LG* Seq 11. *Parl* Seq 11. *Eccl* Southam RDn.

MARSTON GREEN
EP Cr 1939 from Sheldon AP, Coleshill AP.[181] Colesh. RDn. Bdry: 1956 (cr Tile Cross EP),[286] 1966,[287] 1972 (help cr Chelmsley Wood EP).[80]

MARTON
AP *LG* Seq 18. *Parl* Seq 10. *Eccl* Marton RDn (until 1854), Leam. RDn (1854—60), Southam RDn (1860—*).

MAXSTOKE
AP *LG* Seq 5. *Parl* Seq 2. *Eccl* Seq 5.

MEREVALE
Orig chap outside Merevale Abbey, civ ex-par from Dissolution,[288] sep civ identity early, eccl donative and sep status sustained. Pt Leics (Sparkenhoe Hd), pt Warws (Heml. Hd). *LG* Ath. PLU, RSD. Civ bdry: 1880 (Warws territory only),[284] 1880 (loses pt in Leics to Norton juxta Twycross AP, Leics),[289] 1885 (loses pt in Leics to Orton on the Hill AP, Leics, and exchanges pts [incl loses remaining pt in Leics] to Sheepy Magna AP, Leics, so that Merevale ent Warws thereafter (Ath. RD).[290] *Parl* Warws pt, N'rn Dv (1832—85), N-E'rn Dv (1885—1918); thereafter ent Warws, Nun. Dv/CC (1918—55), Merid. CC (1955—*). *Eccl* Arden RDn (until 1854), Polesw. RDn (1854—1958). Abol eccl 1958 to help cr Merevale with Bentley EP.[291]

MEREVALE WITH BENTLEY
EP Cr 1958 by union chap and hmlt Bentley (detached pt Shustoke AP), Merevale AP (Warws, Leics).[291] Polesw. RDn.

MERIDEN
AP *LG* Seq 5. Transf 1974 to W Midlands.[12] *Parl* Seq 7. *Eccl* Seq 8.

MIDDLETON
AP *LG* Heml. Hd, Tamw. PLU, RSD, RD (1894—1964), Merid. RD (1964—74). Civ bdry: 1966.[21] *Parl* Seq 2. *Eccl* Donative, Arden RDn (until 1854), Colesh. RDn (1854—60), Sutt. Coldf. RDn (1960—*).

MILCOTE

CP Cr 1894 from the pt of Weston on Avon AP (Glos, Warws) in Warws and the latter ent Glos thereafter.[80] *LG* Stratf. on Avon RD. *Parl* Warw. & Leam. Dv (1918—48), Stratf. CC (1948—70), Stratf. on Avon CC (1970—*).

MILVERTON

AP Chap in Leek Wootton AP, sep par by 1535.[280] *LG* Knight. Hd, Warw. PLU, Milverton USD (1875—90), pt Royal Leam. Spa MB & USD (1890—94), pt Warw. RSD (1890—94). Abol civ 1894 the pt in the MB cr New Milverton CP, the remainder cr Old Milverton CP.[64] *Parl* S'rn Dv (1832—85), S-E'rn Dv (1885—1918). *Eccl* Arden RDn (until 1854), Leam. RDn (1854—*). Eccl bdry: 1875 (cr New Milverton EP),[194] 1957.[275]

NEW MILVERTON

EP Cr 1875 from Milverton AP.[194] Leam. RDn. Bdry: 1893,[102] 1957.[275] Now called 'Leamington Priors St Mark'.

CP Cr 1894 from the pt of Milverton AP in Royal Leam. Spa MB.[64] *LG* Warw. PLU, Royal Leam. Spa MB. Abol 1902 to help cr Leamington CP.[273]

OLD MILVERTON

CP Cr 1894 from the pt of Milverton AP not in Royal Leam. Spa MB.[64] *LG* Warw. PLU, RD. *Parl* Warw. & Leam. Dv/CC (1918—*).

MINWORTH

Hmlt in Curdworth AP, sep CP 1866.[22] *LG* Heml. Hd, Aston PLU (1836—1911), RSD, Cast. Bromw. RD (1894—1912), Merid. PLU (1911—30), RD (1912—31). Bdry: 1883.[213] Abol 1931 pt to Birm CB (assoc with Warws) & AP, pt to Sutt. Coldf. MB & AP, pt to Castle Bromwich CP.[89] *Parl* N'rn Dv (1832—1918), Tamw. Dv (1918—45).

MOLLINGTON

Chap (pec jurisd Banbury, until 1846) in Cropredy AP (o'wise ent Oxon), pt in Oxon (Bloxham Hd), pt in Warws (Kingt. Hd), sep CP 1866 with pt in ea co,[22] eccl severed 1851 to help cr Claydon with Mollington EP[176] to be dioc Oxford (Deddington RDn), the latter divided 1863 into 2 EPs of Claydon, Mollington.[176] *LG* Banbury PLU, RSD. Became 1889 2 CPs of 'Mollington', one in ea co,[292] the CP in Warws abol 1895 ent to the other in Oxon, the combined 'Mollington' to be ent Oxon.[293] *Parl* Warws pt, S'rn Dv (1832—85), S-E'rn Dv (1885—1918). *Eccl* See entry in Oxon.

MONKS KIRBY

AP Perhaps incl chap Withybrook (sep par by 1205[294]); incl chap and hmlt Copston Magna, hmlts Easenhall, Pailton, Stretton under Fosse (each a sep CP 1866[22]). *LG* Seq 16. Addtl civ bdry alt: 1877 (loses pt to Ullesthorpe CP, Leics),[295] 1935 (exchanges pts with Lutterworth AP, Leics).[160] *Parl* Seq 6. *Eccl* Seq 9.

MONKS RIDING

Ex-par place, sep CP 1858.[166] *LG* Knight. Hd, Rugby PLU (1862—85), RSD. Abol civ 1885 ent to Brinklow AP.[151] *Parl* N'rn Dv (1832—85), N-E'rn Dv (1885—1918).

MORETON MORRELL

AP *LG* Seq 12. *Parl* Seq 13. *Eccl* Seq 19.

MORTON BAGOT

AP *LG* Seq 1. *Parl* Seq 15. *Eccl* Warw. RDn (until 1861), Alc. RDn (1861—1972). Abol eccl 1971 to help cr Spernall, Morton Bagot and Oldberrow EP.[296]

NAPTON ON THE HILL

AP *LG* Seq 19. *Parl* Seq 11. *Eccl* Seq 14.

NECHELLS ST CATHERINE

EP Cr 1879 from Nechells St Clement EP.[297] Birm RDn (1879—92), Aston RDn (1892—1905), E Birm RDn (1905—51). Bdry: 1907.[29] Abol 1951 ent to Duddeston cum Nechells EP (by that time called 'Duddleston St Matthew').[111]

NECHELLS ST CLEMENT

EP Cr 1860 from Duddeston cum Nechells EP.[109] Birm RDn (1860—92), Aston RDn (1892—1905), E Birm RDn (1905—57), Aston RDn (1957—*). Bdry: 1879 (cr Nechells St Catherine EP),[297] 1907.[29]

NEWBOLD ON AVON

AP Incl hmlts Cosford, Little Lawford, Long Lawford (each a sep CP 1866[22]). *LG* Knight. Hd, Rugby PLU, RSD, RD. Abol civ 1932 pt to Rugby UD & AP, pt to Harborough Magna AP.[61] *Parl* N'rn Dv (1832—85), S-E'rn Dv (1885—1918), Rugby Dv (1918—45). *Eccl* Cov RDn (until 1854), Dunch. RDn (1854—1907), Rugby with Dunch. RDn (1907—21), Rugby RDn (1921—*). Eccl bdry: 1947.[82]

NEWBOLD PACEY

AP *LG* Seq 12. *Parl* Seq 13. *Eccl* Seq 19.

KINGS NEWNHAM

AP Sometimes early 'Newnham Regis'. *LG* Seq 18. *Parl* Seq 8. *Eccl* Cov RDn (until 1854), Rugby RDn (1854—1907), Rugby with Dunch. RDn (1907—21), Rugby RDn (1921—*).

NEWTON AND BIGGIN

Chap and hmlt in Clifton upon Dunsmore AP, sep CP 1866.[22] *LG* Seq 18. Bdry: 1932,[61] 1935 (gains pt Catthorpe AP, pt Shawell AP, both Leics).[160] *Parl* Seq 8.

NEWTON REGIS

AP *LG* Seq 7. Civ bdry: 1888 (gains ex-par No Mans Heath [qv below for uncertain location in cos]),[298] 1965 (gains pt Appleby Magna CP, pt Chilcote CP, pt Stretton en le Field AP, both Leics).[4] *Parl* Seq 2. *Eccl* Seq 4. Eccl bdry: 1873 (help cr No Man's Heath EP [qv below for uncertain location in diocs] to be dioc Lichf).[299]

NO MANS HEATH

Ex-par area (uncertain if within or near junction of any of the 3 cos of Derbys, Leics, Warws, or whether in diocs of Worc, Lichf, or Peterb, sep CP 1858 (Heml. Hd),[166] rated in Tamw. PLU (1861—88), the CP civ abol 1888 ent to Newton Regis AP,[298] 'No Man's Heath' a sep EP 1873 from ent ex-par area and pt Newton Regis AP (Warws), to be dioc Lichf.[299] *Parl* N'rn Dv (1832—1918). See entry in Derbys for organisation in dioc Lichf.

NO MAN'S HEATH—see prev entry

NORTON LINDSEY

Chap in Claverdon AP, sep civ identity early, sep EP 1771,[25] sep eccl status not sustained, eccl severed 1925 (along with hmlt Langley also in same par) to help cr Wolverton with Norton Lindsey EP.[174] *LG* Seq 3. *Parl* Seq 14. *Eccl* Warw. RDn.

NUNEATON
AP *LG* Heml. Hd, Nun. PLU, USD (1875—93), Nun. & Chilvers Coton USD (1893—94), UD (1894—1907), Nun. MB (1907—74). Civ bdry: 1885,[172] 1904,[282] 1930 (gains Chilvers Coton AP),[173] 1931 (incl gains Weddington AP),[159] 1935 (exchanges pts with Hinck. UD & AP, gains pt Higham on the Hill AP, both Leics),[160] 1938.[155] *Parl* N'rn Dv (1832—85), N-E'rn Dv (1885—1918), Nun. Dv/CC (1918—70), Nun. BC (1970—*). *Eccl* Seq 1. Eccl bdry: 1843 (cr as ptly indepdendent Attenborough EP, Stockingford EP),[55] 1854 (each of the 2 EPS ptly independent 1843 made fully independent),[56] 1878 (cr Nuneaton St Mary the Virgin EP).[148]

NUNEATON ST MARY THE VIRGIN
EP Cr 1878 from Nuneaton AP.[148] Ath. RDn (1878—1963), Nun. RDn (1963—*). Bdry: 1952 (help cr Galley Common EP),[247] 1959 (help refound Galley Common EP as 'Camp Hill with Galley Common' when gains pt of this par EP).[117]

NUTHURST
Chap (early destroyed) then hmlt in Hampton in Arden AP, sep CP 1866.[22] *LG* Heml. Hd, Solih. PLU, RSD, RD. Abol 1932 pt to help cr Solih. UD and to help cr Solihull Urban CP, pt to Tamworth AP.[26] *Parl* N'rn Dv (1832—85), S-W'rn Dv (1885—1918), Tamw. Dv (1918—45).

NUTHURST CUM HOCKLEY HEATH
EP Cr 1878 from Hampton in Arden AP, Tanworth AP, Tanworth Salter's Street EP.[148] Solih. RDn. Bdry: 1909,[267] 1966,[271] 1967 (help cr Dorridge EP).[218]

OFFCHURCH
AP *LG* Seq 20. *Parl* Seq 12. *Eccl* Seq 17.

OLDBERROW
AP Worcs par transf 1896 to Warws.[300] *LG* Alc. PLU, RD. *Parl* Warw. & Leam. Dv (1918—48), Stratf. CC (1948—70), Stratf. on Avon CC (1970—*). *Eccl* Warw. RDn (until 1861), Alc. RDn (1861—1972). Abol eccl 1972 to help cr Spernall, Morton Bagot and Oldberrow EP.[296]

OLDBURY
Hmlt in Mancetter AP, sep CP 1866.[22] *LG* Seq 4. *Parl* Seq 3.

OLTON
EP Cr 1908 from Bickenhill AP, Solihull AP.[79] Solih. RDn. Bdry: 1948 (incl loses pt to Yardley AP, Worcs, and pt to Shelton EP, Staffs),[301] 1966,[157] 1966 (help cr Hobs Moat EP),[260] 1966 (help cr Gospel Lane EP [Worcs, Warws]),[249] 1972.[250]

OVERSLEY
Hmlt in Arrow AP, sep CP 1866.[22] *LG* Barl. Hd, Alc. PLU, RSD, RD. Abol 1949 ent to Alcester AP.[3] *Parl* S'rn Dv (1832—85), S-W'rn Dv (1885—1918), Warw. & Leam. Dv (1918—48), Stratf. CC (1948—70).

OXHILL
AP *LG* Seq 10. Civ bdry: 1885.[302] *Parl* Seq 9. *Eccl* Seq 20.

GREAT PACKINGTON
AP *LG* Seq 5. *Parl* Seq 7. *Eccl* Seq 2.

LITTLE PACKINGTON
AP *LG* Seq 5. *Parl* Seq 7. *Eccl* Seq 2.

PACKWOOD
Chap (within area chap Hampton Lucy in same par) in Wasperton AP , each chap a sep par by 1535[254] although Packwood often described as eccl dependent on Wasperton[255]), certain sep civ identity early, sep eccl status certain by 1786.[25] *LG* Kingt. Hd (until 1833), Barl. Hd (from 1833), Solih. PLU, RSD, RD. Abol civ 1932 pt to help cr Solih. UD and help cr Solihull Urban CP, pt to Lapworth AP.[26] *Parl* S'rn Dv (1832—85), S-W'rn Dv (1885—1918), Tamw. Dv (1918—45). *Eccl* Arden RDn (1786—1854), Solih. RDn (1854—*). Eccl bdry: 1895,[269] 1966,[271] 1967 (help cr Dorridge EP).[218]

PAILTON
Hmlt in Monks Kirby AP, sep CP 1866.[22] *LG* Seq 16. *Parl* Seq 6.

PERRY BARR
CP Staffs par (qv for sep eccl status) in Perry Barr UD, transf 1928, the main pt to be 'Perry Barr' par in Birm CB (assoc with Warws),[303] the remainder transf to Sutton Coldfield MB & AP, Warws.[304] *LG* Birm PLU, CB. Abol 1930 ent to Birmingham AP.[88]

PERRY COMMON
EP Cr 1971 from Aston juxta Birmingham AP (civ, 'Aston').[39] Aston RDn.

PILLERTON HERSEY
AP Incl Pillerton Priors (perhaps orig sep par or chap in this par, sep civ identity early, not sep eccl after burned 1672,[305] so that this par eccl 'Pillerton Hersey with Pillerton Priors', qv). *LG* Seq 10. *Parl* Seq 9.

PILLERTON HERSEY WITH PILLERTON PRIORS
AP Usual eccl spelling; for civ and uncertain status of Pillerton Priors, see prev and following entry. *Eccl* Seq 19.

PILLERTON PRIORS
Perhaps orig sep par or perhaps chap in Pillerton Hersey AP, sep civ identity early, not sep eccl after burned 1672.[305] *LG* Seq 10. *Parl* Seq 9.

PINLEY
Tp in Rowington AP, sep CP 1866.[22] *LG* Barl. Hd, Warw. PLU, RSD. Abol 1886 ent to Rowington AP.[306] *Parl* S'rn Dv (1832—85), S-W'rn Dv (1885—1918).

POLESWORTH
AP Incl chap Baddesley Ensor (sep civ by 1666,[58] sep EP 1760[25]). *LG* Seq 4. Addtl civ bdry alt: 1935,[18] 1948 (cr Dordon CP),[216] 1965 (loses pt to Tamw. MB & AP, Staffs).[21] *Parl* Seq 1. *Eccl* Seq 4. Eccl bdry: 1849 (cr Warton EP),[307] 1856 (help refound Wilnecote EP),[308] 1933 (cr Dordon EP).[216]

POTTERS GREEN
EP Cr 1964 from Walsgrave on Sowe EP, Woodend EP.[309] Cov East RDn.

PRESTON BAGOT
AP *LG* Seq 2. *Parl* Seq 15. *Eccl* Seq 21.

PRESTON ON STOUR
AP Glos par transf 1931 to Warws.[6] *LG* Stratf. on Avon RD. *Parl* Stratf. CC (1948—70), Stratf. on Avon

CC (1970—*). *Eccl* Campden RDn ([see entry in Glos for successive diocs] until 1920), Stratf. on Avon RDn ([dioc Cov] 1920—*).

PRINCETHORPE
Tp in tp Stretton on Dunsmore (sep civ identity early from Wolston AP [incl tp Princethorpe]), 'Princethorpe' a sep CP 1866 from Stretton on Dunsmore CP,[22] the areas eccl united 1696 as 'Stretton upon Dunsmore and Princethorpe'.[310] *LG* Seq 18. *Parl* Seq 8.

PRIORS HARDWICK
AP Incl chap Priors Marston, chap Lower Shuckburgh (each sep civ identity early, each a sep EP 1860[285]). *LG* Seq 11. *Parl* Seq 11. *Eccl* Ston. RDn (until 1854), Southam RDn (1854—*).

PYPE HAYES
EP Cr 1930 from Erdington EP.[232] Aston RDn. Bdry: 1968 (help cr Erdington St Chad EP).[234]

QUINTON
AP Glos par transf 1935 to Warws gaining at same time Clopton CP (also transf from Warws).[1] *LG* Stratf. on Avon RD. *Parl* Stratf.CC (1948—70), Stratf. on Avon CC (1970—*).

QUINTON
CP Sometimes 'The Quinton' (usual eccl spelling) or 'Christ Church at the Quinton' (variant eccl spelling). Worcs par (Stourbridge PLU; qv for eccl organisation) transf 1909 to be par in Birm CB (assoc with Warws).[86] *LG* Birm PLU (1911—12), CB (1909—12). Abol 1912 ent to Birmingham AP.[36]

RADBOURNE
AP Orig AP, no church and civ considered 2 ex-par places of Lower Radbourn, Upper Radbourn (each a sep CP 1858,[166] qv). *Eccl* Marton RDn (until 1854), Southam RDn (1854—1930). Abol eccl 1930 to help cr Ladbroke with Radbourne EP.[261]

LOWER RADBOURN
Civ ex-par place, pt of orig AP Radbourne (no church, qv for eccl), sep CP 1858.[166] *LG* Knight. Hd, Southam PLU (1858—1930), RSD, RD. *Parl* Seq 11.

UPPER RADBOURN
Status and organisation as for Lower Radbourn.

RADFORD
EP Cr 1912 from Coventry Holy Trinity EP.[193] Cov RDn (1912—63), Cov North RDn (1963—*). Bdry: 1935 (help cr Coventry St George EP, help cr Holbrooks EP, the latter now called 'Coventry St Luke'),[200] 1952 (help cr Coventry St Francis of Assisi, North Radford EP),[199] 1957.[15] Now called 'Coventry St Nicholas'.

RADFORD SEMELE
AP *LG* Seq 20. *Parl* Seq 12. *Eccl* Seq 17.

RADWAY
AP *LG* Seq 8. *Parl* Seq 9. *Eccl* Seq 16.

RATLEY
AP Usual eccl spelling; for civ see following entry. *Eccl* Seq 16.

RATLEY AND UPTON
AP Usual civ spelling; for eccl see prev entry. *LG* Seq 8. *Parl* Seq 11.

ROWINGTON
AP Incl tp Pinley (sep CP 1866[22]). *LG* Seq 3. Addtl civ bdry alt: 1886 (gains Pinley CP),[306] 1886.[311] *Parl* Seq 14. *Eccl* Seq 21. Eccl bdry: 1893.[73]

RUGBY
AP Orig chap in Clifton upon Dunsmore AP, sep par by 1291.[177] *LG* Knight. Hd, Rugby Bor, PLU, USD, UD (1894—1932), MB (1932—74). Civ bdry: 1932.[61] *Parl* Seq 8. *Eccl* Seq 13. Eccl bdry: 1856 (cr Rugby St Matthew EP),[25] 1940.[31]

RUGBY ST MATTHEW
EP Cr 1856 from Rugby AP.[25] Rugby RDn (1856—1907), Rugby with Dunch. RDn (1907—21), Rugby RDn (1921—*).

RYTON ON DUNSMORE
AP Orig chap in Bulkington AP, made prebendal 1249 and sep thereafter.[152] *LG* Seq 18. Civ bdry: 1965 (loses pt to Cov CB [assoc with Warws] & CP).[11] *Parl* Seq 8. *Eccl* Ston. RDn (until 1854), Bag. RDn (1854—1921), Dunch. RDn (1921—*).

SALFORD PRIORS
AP Incl chap Exhall (sep civ identity early, incl eccl from Reformation chap Wixford [orig chap in Salford Priors, sep civ identity early from that par][238] hence this par eccl thereafter 'Exhall with Wixford otherwise Wigglesford', itself with sep civ identity early). *LG* Seq 1. *Parl* Seq 15. *Eccl* Seq 22.

SALTLEY
EP Cr 1848 from Aston juxta Birmingham AP.[45] Arden RDn (1848—54), Colesh. RDn (1854—60), Sutt. Coldf. RDn (1860—92), Aston RDn (1892—1905), E Birm RDn (1905—57), Yard. RDn (1957—*). Bdry: 1907,[29] 1907 (cr Washwood Heath EP),[312] 1929 (help cr Shaw Hill EP).[313]

SAMBOURN
Hmlt in Coughton AP, sep CP 1866.[22] *LG* Seq 1. Bdry: 1963,[314] 1965 (loses pt to Inkberrow AP, pt to Redditch UD & CP, both Worcs).[4] *Parl* Seq 15. By 1971 census, called 'Sambourne'.

SAMBOURNE—see prev entry

SECKINGTON
AP *LG* Seq 7. *Parl* Seq 2. *Eccl* Seq 4.

SHARD END
EP Cr 1958 from Castle Bromwich EP.[123] Colesh. RDn.

SHAW HILL
EP Cr 1929 from Saltley EP, Ward End EP, Washwood Heath EP.[313] E Birm RDn (1929—57), Yard. RDn (1957—*).

SHELDON
AP *LG* Heml. Hd, Merid. PLU, RSD, RD. Civ bdry: 1931 (loses pt to Birm CB [assoc with Warws] and AP).[89] Abol civ 1932 pt to Solih. UD and to help cr Solihull Urban CP, pt to Coleshill AP.[26] *Parl* N'rn Dv (1832—1918), Tamw. Dv (1918—45). *Eccl* Arden RDn (until 1854), Polesw. RDn (1854—92), Colesh. RDn (1892—1905), Solih. RDn (1905—57), Colesh. RDn (1957—*). Eccl bdry: 1939 (help cr Marston Green EP),[181] 1966,[157] 1966 (help cr Hobs Moat EP),[260] 1967 (help cr Garrett's Green EP, o'wise Worcs).[248]

SHERBOURNE
AP *LG* Seq 3. Civ bdry: 1931.[74] *Parl* Seq 14. *Eccl*

Warw. RDn. Gains eccl after 1543 Fulbrook AP (sep civ identity retained, last presentment 1543, thereafter in this par) to cr 'Sherbourne with Fulbrook' EP[246]).

SHERBOURNE WITH FULBROOK
EP Cr after 1543 by union Sherbourne AP, Fulbrook AP.[246] Warw. RDn.

SHILTON
Chap in Bulkington AP, considered 1410 chap to Ansty (itself a chap in Bulkington, considered *ca* 1410 a sep par[24]), 'Shilton' sep civ identity early from Ansty, sep EP 1754.[25] *LG* Seq 14. Civ bdry: 1932,[26] 1932,[9] 1938,[159] 1956 (gains pt Cov CB [assoc with Warws] & CP),[10] 1965 (exchanges pts with Cov CB [assoc with Warws] & CP).[11] *Parl* Seq 4. *Eccl* Marton RDn (1754—1854), Monks Kirby RDn (1854—1963), Bedw. RDn (1963—*).

SHIPSTON ON STOUR
CP Worcs par transf 1931 to Warws.[6] *LG* Shipst. on Stour RD. *Parl* Stratf. CC (1948—70), Stratf. on Avon CC (1970—*). *Eccl* See entry in Worcs.

SHIRLEY
EP Cr 1843 from Solihull AP.[128] Arden RDn (1843—54), Solih. RDn (1854—*). Bdry: 1962 (loses pt to Yardley Wood EP, Worcs),[315] 1966 (help cr Gospel Lane EP [Worcs, Warws]),[249] 1972.[250]

SHORT HEATH
EP Cr 1962 from Erdington EP.[233] Aston RDn.

SHOTTSWELL
AP *LG* Kingt. Hd, Banb. PLU (1835—1930), RSD, Farnb. RD. *Parl* Seq 11. *Eccl* Seq 16.

SHREWLEY
Hmlt in Hatton AP, sep CP 1866.[22] *LG* Seq 3. *Parl* Seq 14.

LOWER SHUCKBURGH
Chap in Priors Hardwick AP, sep civ identity early, sep EP 1860.[285] *LG* Seq 11. *Parl* Seq 11. *Eccl* Southam RDn. Gains early 20th cent Upper Shuckburgh AP.[316]

UPPER SHUCKBURGH
AP *LG* Seq 19. *Parl* Seq 11. *Eccl* Donative, Marton RDn (until 1854), Southam RDn (1854—early 20th cent). Abol early 20th cent ent to Lower Shuckburgh EP.[316]

SHUSTOKE
AP Incl chap and hmlt Bentley (sep CP 1866,[22] detached area eccl severed 1958 to help cr Merevale with Bentley EP [Warws, Leics][291]). *LG* Seq 5. *Parl* Seq 2. *Eccl* Seq 5.

SHUTTINGTON
AP *LG* Seq 7. Civ bdry: 1965 (loses pt to Tamw. MB & AP).[21] *Parl* Seq 2. *Eccl* Seq 4.

SMALL HEATH
EP Cr 1875 [All Saints] from Bordesley EP.[103] Birm RDn (1875—92), Aston RDn (1892—1905), Bord. RDn (1905—49). Bdry: 1897 (cr Small Heath St Aidan EP),[75] 1907,[317] 1924 (help cr Small Heath St Gregory EP).[145] Abol 1949 pt to Small Heath St Aidan EP, pt to Small Heath St Gregory EP.[318]

SMALL HEATH ST AIDAN
EP Cr 1897 as 'Bordesley St Aidan' from Small Heath EP,[75] soon called 'Small Heath St Aidan'. Aston RDn (1897—1905), Bord. RDn (1905—*). Bdry:

1907,[317] 1949,[318] 1967.[140]

SMALL HEATH ST BENEDICT
EP Cr 1910 from Bordesley St Oswald EP.[144] Bord. RDn (1910—57), Yard. RDn (1957—*). Now called 'Bordesley St Benedict'.

SMALL HEATH ST GREGORY
EP Cr 1924 from Small Heath EP, Bordesley St Oswald EP.[145] Bord. RDn. Bdry: 1949.[318]

SMITE
AP Orig sep AP (Cov RDn) incl chap Brinklow (qv for sep identity), subsumed into Combe Abbey and from Dissolution considered ex-par as 'Combe Fields',[148] as such sep CP 1858,[166] qv.

SNITTERFIELD
AP *LG* Seq 2. *Parl* Seq 15. *Eccl* Seq 21.

SOLIHULL
AP *LG* Heml. Hd, Solih. PLU, RSD, RD. Civ bdry: 1877,[76] 1931 (loses pt to Birm CB [assoc with Warws] and AP).[89] Abol civ 1932 pt to help cr Solih. UD and help cr Solihull Urban CP, pt to Hampton in Arden AP, pt to Tanworth AP.[26] *Parl* N'rn Dv (1832—1918), Tamw. Dv (1918—45). *Eccl* Seq 6. Eccl bdry: 1843 (cr Shirley EP),[128] 1853 (help cr Withall EP, o'wise Worcs),[319] 1908 (help cr Olton EP),[79] 1941,[270] 1966 (help cr Hobs Moat EP),[260] 1966,[157] 1967 (help cr Dorridge EP).[218]

SOLIHULL URBAN
CP Cr 1932 to constitute Solih. UD by union pts Elmdon AP, Hampton in Arden AP, Knowle CP, Lapworth AP, Nuthurst CP, Packwood AP, Sheldon AP, Solihull AP, Tanworth AP.[26] *LG* Solih. UD (1932—54), MB (1954—64), CB (1964—74). Bdry: 1964 (loses pt to Barston CP, pt to cr Hockley Heath CP, pt to Lapworth AP; gains pt Balsall CP; loses pt to Wythall CP, Worcs; exchanges pts wth Birm CB [assoc with Warws] & AP, Bickenhill AP, Hampton in Arden AP, as new area constituted Solih. CB [assoc with Warws]).[62] Transf 1974 to W Midlands.[12] *Parl* Solih. Dv/CC (1945—70), Solih. BC (1970—*).

SOUTHAM
AP *LG* Southam Bor, Seq 19. *Parl* Seq 11. *Eccl* Seq 14.

SOWE—see WALSGRAVE ON SOWE

SPARKBROOK CHRIST CHURCH
EP Cr 1867 from Aston juxta Birmingham (civ, 'Aston') AP.[49] Sutt. Coldf. RDn (1867—92), Aston RDn (1892—1906), Bord. RDn (1906—*). Bdry: 1902 (cr Sparkbrook St Agatha EP),[320] 1908 (gains pt Sparkhill St John the Evangelist EP, Worcs, dioc Birm),[321] 1928 (cr Sparkbrook Emmanuel EP),[174] 1967.[140]

SPARKBROOK EMMANUEL
EP Cr 1928 from Sparkbrook Christ Church EP.[174] Bord. RDn.

SPARKBROOK ST AGATHA
EP Cr 1902 from Sparkbrook Christ Church EP.[320] Aston RDn (1902—06), Bord. RDn (1906—*). Bdry: 1967.[140]

SPERNALL
AP *LG* Seq 1. *Parl* Seq 16. *Eccl* Warw. RDn (until 1861), Alc. RDn (1861—1972). Abol eccl 1972 to help cr Spernall, Morton Bagot and Oldberrow

EP.[296]

SPERNALL, MORTON BAGOT AND OLDBERROW
EP Cr 1972 by union Oldberrow AP (orig Worcs), Morton Bagot AP, Spernall AP.[296] Alc. RDn.

STIVICHALL
Chap in Coventry St Michael AP, sep civ identity early, sep EP 1739.[25] *LG* Cov Co of Itself (1452—1842), Knight. Hd (from 1842), Warw. PLU, RSD, RD. Civ bdry: 1928 (loses pt to Cov CB [assoc with Warws] & CP).[8] Abol civ 1932 pt to Cov CB (assoc with Warws) & CP, pt to Baginton AP.[26] *Parl* N'rn Dv (1832—85), N-E'rn Dv (1885—1918), Warw. & Leam. Dv (1918—45). *Eccl* Cov RDn (1739—1854), Bag. RDn (1854—1921), Cov RDn (1921—63), Cov South RDn (1963—*). Bdry: 1957 (help cr Cheylesmore EP),[171] 1967.[241]

STOCKINGFORD
EP Cr from Nuneaton AP as ptly independent 1843,[55] fully independent 1854.[56] Arden RDn (1843—54), Ath. RDn (1854—1963), Nun. RDn (1963—*). Bdry: 1937,[31] 1952 (help cr Galley Common EP).[247]

STOCKLAND GREEN
EP Cr 1933 from Gravelly Hall EP.[251] Aston RDn.

STOCKTON
AP *LG* Seq 19. *Parl* Seq 11. *Eccl* Marton RDn (until 1854), Dass. Mag. RDn (1854—84), Southam RDn (1884—*).

STOKE
AP Orig chap in Coventry St Michael AP, sep par prob beginning reign Eliz I, sep status disputed,[205] recognised 1595 as independent.[206] *LG* Cov Co of Itself (1452—1842), Knight. Hd (from 1842), Folesh. PLU, RSD, RD. Civ bdry: 1899 (loses pt to Cov CB [assoc with Warws] and to Coventry Holy Trinity Within CP).[196] Abol civ 1928 ent to Cov CB (assoc with Warws) & CP.[8] *Parl* N'rn Dv (1832—67), Cov Parl Bor (1867—1918), Rugby Dv (1918—45). *Eccl* Cov RDn (cr—1854), Bag. RDn (1854—1907), Cov RDn (1907—63), Cov East RDn (1963—*). Eccl bdry: 1913 (help cr Coventry St Margaret EP),[145] 1959.[198]

STOKE HEATH
CP Cr 1920 from Wyken AP.[322] *LG* Folesh. PLU, RD. Abol 1928 ent to Cov CB (assoc with Warws) & CP.[8]

STONELEIGH
AP Incl chap Baginton (sep par *temp* John[59]), chap Kenilworth (sep par mid 13th cent[265]). *LG* Seq 20. Civ bdry: 1928 (loses pt to Cov CB [assoc with Warws] & CP),[8] 1932,[26] 1932 (loses pt to Cov CB [assoc with Warws] & CP),[9] 1956 (exchanges pts with Cov CB [assoc with Warws] & CP),[10] 1965 (exchanges pts with Cov CB [assoc with Warws] & CP).[11] *Parl* Seq 12. Parl bdry: 1960.[14] *Eccl* Seq 15. Eccl bdry: 1846 (cr Westwood EP),[323] 1938 (cr Finham EP).[240]

STONETON
CP Northants par transf 1895 to Warws.[324] *LG* Southam PLU (1858—1930), RD. *Parl* Rugby Dv (1918—48), Stratf. CC (1948—70), Stratf. on Avon CC (1970—*).

STOURTON
Hmlt in Whichford AP, sep CP 1866,[22] eccl severed 1910 and transf to Cherington AP.[170] *LG* Seq 10. *Parl* Seq 13.

OLD STRATFORD
AP Usual civ spelling; for eccl see 'Stratford on Avon'. Incl chap Bishopton (not sep civ, sep EP 1737[25]), chap & hmlt Luddington (sep civ 1664 incl area Drayton [not sep civ] in same par[282]), hmlt Bushwood, tp Stratford on Avon (each a sep CP 1866[22]). *LG* Barl. Hd, Stratf. on Avon PLU, pt Stratf. on Avon Bor/MB, pt Stratf. on Avon USD, pt Stratf. on Avon RSD. Abol civ 1894 the pt in the MB cr Old Stratford Within CP, the remainder cr Old Stratford and Drayton CP.[80] *Parl* S'rn Dv (1832—85), S-W'rn Dv (1885—1918).

OLD STRATFORD AND DRAYTON
CP Cr 1894 from the pt of Old Stratford AP not in Stratf. on Avon MB.[80] *LG* Stratf. on Avon PLU, RD. *Parl* Warw. & Leam. Dv (1918—48), Stratf. CC (1948—70), Stratf. on Avon CC (1970—*).

OLD STRATFORD WITHIN
CP Cr 1894 from the pt of Old Stratford AP in Stratf. on Avon MB.[80] *LG* Stratf. on Avon PLU, MB. *Parl* Warw. & Leam. Dv (1918—48), Stratf. CC (1948—70), Stratf. on Avon CC (1970—*).

STRATFORD ON AVON
AP Usual eccl spelling; for civ and civ and eccl sep chap, hmlts and tp, see 'Old Stratford'. *Eccl* Kinet. RDn (until 1861), N Kinet. RDn (1861—1921), Kinet. RDn (1921—63). Eccl bdry: 1863 (help cr Wilmcote EP).[40] Abol eccl 1963 to help cr Stratford on Avon with Bishopton EP.[133]

CP Tp in Old Stratford AP (for eccl, see prev entry), sep CP 1866.[22] *LG* Barl. Hd, Stratf. on Avon PLU, Bor/MB, USD. *Parl* Seq 15.

STRATFORD ON AVON WITH BISHOPTON
EP Cr 1963 by union Stratford on Avon AP, Bishopton EP.[133] Kinet. RDn (1963), Stratf. on Avon RDn (1963—*).

STRETTON BASKERVILLE
AP *LG* Seq 15. Civ bdry: 1935 (incl exchanges pts with Hinck. UD & AP, Leics),[160] 1965 (loses pt to Hinck. UD & AP, Leics).[4] *Parl* Seq 4. *Eccl* Cov RDn (until 1860), Ath. RDn (1860—1907), Monks Kirby RDn (1907—63), Bedw. RDn (1963—*).

STRETTON ON DUNSMORE
Hmlt in Wolston AP, sep civ identity early (incl tp Princethorpe [sep CP 1866 from this par[22]]), sep EP 1696 as 'Stretton upon Dunsmore and Princethorpe'.[310] *LG* Seq 18. *Parl* Seq 8.

STRETTON ON FOSSE
AP Orig chap (Warws, Kingt. Hd) in Blockley AP (o'wise Worcs, Oswaldslow Hd), sep par by 14th cent.[325] *LG* Seq 10. *Parl* Seq 15. *Eccl* Sometimes as 'Stretton on Fosse with Ditchford', Blockley RDn (dioc Worc, cr—1919), S Kinet. RDn (1919—21), Shipst. RDn (1921—*).

STRETTON UNDER FOSSE
Hmlt in Monks Kirby AP, sometimes early 'Stretton under Fosse and Newbold Revel', sep CP 1866.[22] *LG* Seq 16. *Parl* Seq 6.

STRETTON UPON DUNSMORE AND PRINCE-THORPE

EP Cr 1696 from Stretton on Dunsmore (qv for civ) and the tp of Princethorpe incl within it, both orig pt Wolston AP.[206] Cov RDn (1696—1854), Bag. RDn (1854—1921), Dunch. RDn (1921—*).

STUDLEY

AP *LG* Seq 1. Civ bdry: 1963,[314] 1969 (loses pt to Redditch UD & CP, Worcs).[326] *Parl* Seq 15. Parl bdry: 1971.[327] *Eccl* Sometimes as 'Studley with Mappleborough', Seq 22.

SUTTON COLDFIELD

AP *LG* Heml. Hd, Aston PLU, RSD (1875—85), MB (1885—1974), USD (1885—94). Civ bdry: 1928 (gains pt Perry Barr UD & CP, Staffs,[304] as remainder of latter transf to be 'Perry Barr' par in Birm CB [assoc with Warws][303]), 1931 (gains pt Shenstone AP, pt Great Barr CP, both Staffs),[328] 1931,[89] 1966 (incl exchanges pts with Birm CB [assoc with Warws] and AP, gains pt Shenstone AP, Staffs).[4] Transf 1974 to W Midlands.[12] *Parl* N'rn Dv (1832—1918), Tamw. Dv (1918—45), Sutt. Coldf. Dv/CC (1945—70), Sutt. Coldf. BC (1970—*). *Eccl* Seq 3. Eccl bdry: 1845 (cr Walmley EP,[329] refounded 1846[330]), 1853 (cr Hill EP),[28] 1858 (cr Boldmere EP),[134] 1907 (cr Maney EP),[283] 1959 (help cr Sutton Coldfield St Chad EP).[331]

SUTTON COLDFIELD ST CHAD

EP Cr 1959 from Sutton Coldfield AP, Walmley EP.[331] Sutt. Coldf. RDn.

SUTTON COLDFIELD ST COLUMBA

EP Cr 1954 from Boldmere EP.[136] Sutt. Coldf. RDn. Bdry: 1971.[135]

SUTTON UNDER BRAILES

AP Glos par (Westminster Hd) transf to Warws (Kingt. Hd) 1832 for parl purposes, 1844 for civ purposes.[185] *LG* From 1844, Seq 10. *Parl* From 1832, Seq 13. *Eccl* Stow RDn (Glouc AD [see Glos for successive diocs], until 1919), S Kinet. RDn (1919—21), Shipst. RDn (1921—*).

BISHOPS TACHBROOK

AP *LG* Pt Kingt. Hd, pt Knight. Hd, Warw. PLU, RSD, RD. *Parl* Seq 14. *Eccl* Seq 17.

TAMWORTH

AP Tp 'Tamworth' (the orig area Tamw. Bor) in Staffs (N Offlow Hd) as was tp Syerscote; incl in Staffs (S Offlow Hd) chap Wiggington, tp Fazeley, hmlt Hopwas Hays (for sep civ [all by 1866] and eccl status of these, see entry in Staffs); incl in Warws (Heml. Hd) chap Wilncote (sep EP 1770 [incl lbty Tamworth Castle],[25] the area civ tp 'Wilncote and Castle Liberty', as such sep CP 1866 in Warws[22]), tp Amington and Stoneydelph, tp Bolehall and Glascote (each a sep CP 1866 in Warws[22]), lbty Tamworth Castle (sep CP 1866 in Warws,[3] eccl in chap Wilncote as above) so that 'Tamworth' ent Staffs after 1866. See entry in Staffs for other civ, parl, eccl organisation and bdry alts.

TAMWORTH CASTLE

Ltby (Warws, Heml. Hd) in Tamworth AP (Staffs, Warws until 1866, ent Staffs thereafter, sep CP 1866,[22] eccl in chap Wilncote (sep EP 1770 from Tamworth AP[25]). *LG* Tamw. PLU, pt Tamw. MB & USD (1890—94), Tamw. RSD (ent 1875—90, pt 1890—94). Abol civ 1894 the pt in the MB to Tamworth AP, Staffs, pt of the remainder to Bolehall and Glascote CP, pt to Wilncote and Castle Liberty CP, both Warws.[137] *Parl* Tamw. Parl Bor (1832—85), N'rn Dv (1885—1918).

TANWORTH

AP Orig chap in Brailes AP, sep par by 1202.[145] *LG* Kingt. Hd (until 1833), Barl. Hd (from 1833), Solih. PLU, RSD, RD (1894—1932), Stratf. on Avon RD (1932—67). Civ bdry: 1895,[332] 1932 (incl help cr Solihull Urban CP to constitute Solih. UD).[26] Renamed civ 1967 'Tanworth in Arden'.[333] *Parl* S'rn Dv (1832—85), S-W'rn Dv (1885—1918), Tamw. Dv (1918—48), Stratf. CC (1948—70). *Eccl* Warw. RDn (until 1861), Alc. RDn (1861—92), Solih. RDn (1892—*). Eccl bdry: 1770 (cr Wilncote EP,[25] refounded 1856 from Tanworth AP, Polesworth AP[308]), 1843 (cr as ptly independent Tanworth Salter's Street EP,[334] fully independent 1848[45]), 1878 (help cr Nuthurst cum Hockley Heath EP).[143]

TANWORTH IN ARDEN

CP Renaming 1965 of Tanworth AP.[333] *LG* Warw. RD. *Parl* Warw. & Leam. CC (1970—*).

TANWORTH SALTER'S STREET

EP Cr from Tanworth AP 1843 as ptly independent,[334] fully independent 1848.[45] Warw. RDn (1843—61), Alc. RDn (1861—92), Solih. RDn (1892—*). Bdry: 1878 (help cr Nuthurst cum Hockley Heath EP).[143] Now called 'Earlswood'.

TARDEBIGGE

AP Medieval status in Warws, Staffs, Worcs varied at different times,[335] thereafter ent Worcs (Halfshire Hd) except for tp Tutnall and Cobley (Barl. Hd, transf to Worcs 1832 for parl purposes, 1844 for civ purposes (Halfshire Hd)[185] so that Tardebigge ent Worcs from 1844; see entry in Worcs for its chap and tps in Worcs (each with sep civ identity 1866, so that 'Tardebigge' has no sep civ identity after 1866), for eccl organisation (sometimes as 'Tardebigge with Webheath'), and for eccl bdry alts in addition to the following which affects Warws: 1850 (help cr Headless Cross EP [Worcs, Warws]).[257]

TEMPLE GRAFTON

AP *LG* Seq 2. *Parl* Seq 15. *Eccl* Seq 22.

THURLASTON

Tp in Dunchurch AP, sep CP 1866.[22] *LG* Seq 18. *Parl* Seq 8.

TIDMINGTON

CP Worcs par transf 1931 to Warws.[6] *LG* Shipst. on Stour RD. *Parl* Stratf. CC (1948—70), Stratf. on Avon CC (1970—*).

TILE CROSS

EP Cr 1956 from Marston Green EP.[286] Colesh. RDn. Bdry: 1966,[287] 1972 (cr Chelmsley Wood EP [Warws], help cr Lea Hall EP [Warws, Worcs]).[169]

TILE HILL

EP Cr 1958 from Westwood EP.[14] Kenilw. RDn (1958—63), Cov South RDn (1963—*).

TREDINGTON

AP Worcs par transf 1931 to Warws.[6] *LG* Shipst. on

Stour RD. *Parl* Stratf. CC (1948—70), Stratf. on Avon CC (1970—*).

TYSOE

AP *LG* Seq 10. *Parl* Seq 9. *Eccl* Seq 20.

UFTON

AP *LG* Seq 19. *Parl* Seq 11. *Eccl* Seq 14.

ULLENHALL

Chap and hmlt in Wootton Wawen AP, sep EP 1861,[336] sep CP 1957 from Wootton Wawen CP, Beaudesert AP.[71] *LG* Stratf. on Avon RD. *Parl* Stratf. on Avon CC (1970—*). *Eccl* Alc. RDn.

WALMLEY

EP Cr 1845 from Sutton Coldfield AP,[329] refounded 1846.[330] Arden RDn (1845—54), Colesh. RDn (1854—60), Sutt. Coldf. RDn (1860—*). Bdry: 1959 (help cr Sutton Coldfield St Chad EP).[331]

WALSGRAVE ON SOWE

Chap in Coventry St Michael AP, sep par early 17th cent as 'Sowe',[208] later called 'Walsgrave on Sowe'. *LG* Pt Cov Co of Itself (1452—1842), Knight. Hd (pt until 1842, ent from 1842), Folesh. PLU, RSD, RD. Civ bdry: 1928 (loses pt to Cov CB [assoc with Warws] & CP).[8] Abol civ 1932 pt to Cov CB (assoc with Warws) & CP, pt to Ansty AP,[9] pt to Bedw. UD & AP, pt to Shilton CP, pt to Combe Fields CP.[26] *Parl* N'rn Dv (1832—85), N-E'rn Dv (1885—1918), Nun. Dv (1918—45). *Eccl* Cov RDn (cr—1854), Bag. RDn (1854—1921), Cov RDn (1921—63), Cov East RDn (1963—*). Eccl bdry: 1908 (help cr Longford EP),[236] 1957 (help cr Woodend EP),[245] 1964 (incl help cr Potters Green EP).[309]

WALTON D'EIVILE

AP Orig chap in Wellesbourne AP, ptly independent 14th cent, sep par by 1535, united 1633 to Wellesbourne AP and not civ thereafter,[337] sep EP 1841 from Wellesbourne AP.[25] *LG* Kingt. Hd. *Eccl* Kinet. RDn (orig, 1841—61), N Kinet. RDn (1861—1921), Kinet. RDn (1921—63), Stratf. on Avon RDn (1963—*).

WAPPENBURY

AP Incl chap Hunningham (sep par by 1535[262]), hmlt Eathorpe (sep CP 1866[22]). *LG* Seq 20. *Parl* Seq 12. *Eccl* Marton RDn (until 1854), Dunch. RDn (1854—1907), Leam. RDn (1907—*).

WARD END

EP Cr 1841 from Aston juxta Birmingham (civ, 'Aston') AP,[41] eccl refounded 1870.[42] Arden RDn (1841—54), Colesh. RDn (1854—60), Sutt. Coldf. RDn (1870—92), Aston RDn (1892—1905), E Birm RDn (1905—57), Yard. RDn (1957—*). Bdry: 1928 (cr Bordesley Green EP),[146] 1929 (help cr Shaw Hill EP),[313] 1964 (incl help cr Hodge Hill EP),[161] 1966 (cr Burney Lane EP).[157]

WARMINGTON

AP *LG* Seq 8. *Parl* Seq 11. *Eccl* Seq 16.

WARTON

EP Cr 1849 from Polesworth AP.[307] Arden RDn (1849—54), Polesw. RDn (1854—*).

WARWICK

The following have 'Warwick' in their names. Insofar as any existed at a given time: Knight. Hd. Warw. Bor/MB, PLU, USD. *Parl* Warw. Parl Bor (1295—1918), Warw. & Leam. Dv/CC (1918—*). *Eccl* Warw. RDn.

CP1—WARWICK—Cr 1921 by union AP1, AP2.[338] Bdry: 1931.[74]

—WARWICK ALL SAINTS—Name used now for EP cr 1867 as 'Emscote' qv.

AP1—WARWICK ST MARY—Abol civ 1921 to help cr CP1.[338] Eccl bdry: 1844 (cr EP1).[339]

AP2—WARWICK ST NICHOLAS—Abol civ 1921 to help cr CP1.[338] Eccl bdry: 1861 (cr Emscote EP, now called 'Warwick All Saints'),[101] 1957.[275]

EP1—WARWICK ST PAUL—Cr 1844 from AP1.[339]

WASHWOOD HEATH

EP Cr 1907 from Saltley EP.[312] E Birm RDn (1907—57), Yard. RDn (1957—*). Bdry: 1929 (help cr Shaw Hill EP).[313]

WASPERTON

AP Incl chap Hampton Lucy ([which in turn incl area chap Packwood], each chap a sep par by 1535[254] although Packwood often described as eccl dependent on Wasperton,[255] Packwood certain sep civ identity early, sep eccl status certain by 1786[25]). *LG* Seq 13. Civ bdry: 1954.[66] *Parl* Seq 14. *Eccl* Seq 19. Eccl bdry: 1955.[67]

WATER ORTON

Hmlt in Aston AP (eccl, 'Aston juxta Birmingham'), sep CP 1894 from pt of the pt of Aston AP neither in Birm CB (assoc with Warws) nor in Aston Manor UD,[35] sep EP 1732,[25] eccl refounded 1871.[34] *LG* Aston PLU, Cast. Bromw. RD (1894—1912), Merid. RD (1912—74). Civ bdry: 1966,[4] 1970.[78] *Parl* Tamw. Dv (1918—45), Sutt. Coldf. Dv/CC (1945—55), Merid. CC (1955—*). *Eccl* Arden RDn (1732—1854), Colesh. RDn (1854—60), Sutt. Coldf. RDn (1860—92), Aston RDn (1892—1905), Sutt. Coldf. RDn (1905—57), Colesh. RDn (1957—*).

WATERGALL

Orig pt of Hodnell AP (depopulated 15th cent), at first considered in Fenny Compton AP but later detached and considered ex-par,[165] sep CP 1858.[166] *LG* Knight. Hd, Southam PLU (1858—1930), RSD, RD. *Parl* Seq 11.

WEDDINGTON

AP *LG* Heml. Hd, Nun. PLU, RSD, RD. Civ bdry: 1904.[340] Abol civ 1931 ent to Nun. MB & AP.[159] *Parl* N'rn Dv (1832—85), N-E'rn Dv (1885—1918), Nun. Dv (1918—48). *Eccl* Seq 1.

WEETHLEY

Chap in Kinwarton AP, sep civ identity early, eccl severed 1876 and transf to Alcester AP.[5] *LG* Seq 1. Bdry: 1965 (loses pt to Inkberrow AP, Worcs).[4] *Parl* Seq 15.

WELFORD

AP Pt Glos (Deerhurst Hd), pt Warws (Barl. Hd). *LG* Stratf. on Avon PLU, RSD. Civ bdry: 1894 (the pt in Warws cr Bickmarsh CP in Warws so that Welford ent Glos 1894—1931).[80] Transf 1931 to Warws and thereafter called 'Welford on Avon' (Stratf. on Avon RD).[6] *Parl* Warws pt (until 1918): S'rn Dv (1832—85), S-W'rn Dv (1885—1918); again in Warws (from 1948): Stratf. CC (1948—70), Stratf. on Avon CC (1970—*). *Eccl* See entry in Glos.

WELFORD ON AVON—see prev entry

WELLESBOURNE

AP Incl chap Walton D'Eivile (ptly independent 14th cent, sep par by 1535, united 1633 to Wellesbourne AP and not sep civ thereafter,[337] sep EP 1841[25]), tps Wellesbourne Hastings and Walton, Wellesbourne Mountford (each a sep CP 1866[22]) so that 'Wellesbourne' has no sep civ identity 1866—1952 (qv in following entry). *LG* Kingt. Hd. *Parl* S'rn Dv (1832—67). *Eccl* Seq 19.

CP Cr 1952 by union Wellesbourne Hastings and Walton CP, Wellesbourne Mountford CP.[341] *LG* Stratf. on Avon RD. *Parl* Stratf. on Avon CC (1970—*).

WELLESBOURNE HASTINGS AND WALTON

Tp in Wellesbourne AP, sep CP 1866.[22] *LG* Kingt. Hd, Stratf. on Avon PLU, RSD, RD. Abol 1952 to help cr Wellesbourne CP.[341] *Parl* S'rn Dv (1832—85), S-W'rn Dv (1885—19118), Rugby Dv (1918—48), Stratf. CC (1948—70).

WELLESBOURNE MOUNTFORD

Tp in Wellesbourne AP, sep CP 1866.[22] Organisation as for Wellesbourne Hastings and Walton, with bdry alt 1886[168] which former did not have.

WESTON ON AVON

AP Pt Glos (Kiftsgate Hd), pt Warws (Barl. Hd). *LG* Stratf. on Avon PLU, RSD. Civ bdry: 1894 (the pt in Warws cr Milcote CP in Warws so that Weston on Avon ent Glos 1894—1931).[80] Transf 1931 to Warws (Stratf. on Avon RD).[6] *Parl* Warws pt (until 1918): S'rn Dv (1832—85), S-W'rn Dv (1885—1918); again in Warws (from 1948): Stratf. CC (1948—70), Stratf. on Avon CC (1970—*). *Eccl* See entry in Glos.

WESTON UNDER WETHERLEY

AP *LG* Seq 20. *Parl* Seq 12. *Eccl* Ston. RDn (until 1854), Bag. RDn (1854—1907), Leam. RDn (1907—*).

WESTWOOD

EP Cr 1846 from Stoneleigh AP.[323] Ston. RDn (1846—60), Cov RDn (1860—1907), Kenilw. RDn (1907—63), Cov South RDn (1963—*). Bdry: 1957,[15] 1958 (cr Tile Hill EP),[14] 1964 (cr Fletchamstead EP),[242] 1965.[75]

WHATCOTE

AP *LG* Seq 10. *Parl* Seq 13. *Eccl* Seq 20.

WHICHFORD

AP Incl hmlt Stourton (sep CP 1866,[22] eccl severed 1910 and transf to Cherington AP[170]). *LG* Seq 10. *Parl* Seq 13. *Eccl* Seq 20.

NETHER WHITACRE

AP Orig chap in Coleshill AP, prob sep par at Reformation.[179] *LG* Seq 5. Civ bdry: 1965.[21] *Parl* Seq 2. *Eccl* Seq 5. Eccl bdry: 1963 (gains Lea Marston AP).[253]

OVER WHITACRE

AP Orig chap in Coleshill AP, prob sep par at Reformation.[179] *LG* Seq 5. *Parl* Seq 2. *Eccl* Seq 5.

WHITCHURCH

AP *LG* Seq 12. *Parl* Seq 15. *Eccl* Seq 19.

WHITLEY

EP Cr 1965 when Willenhall with Whitley EP divided into 2 EPS of Willenhall, Whitley.[342] Cov East RDn.

WHITNASH

AP *LG* Seq 20. Civ bdry: 1953.[274] *Parl* Seq 12. *Eccl* Seq 17. Eccl bdry: 1957.[275]

WIBTOFT

Chap (Warws, Knight. Hd) in Claybrooke AP (o'wise Leics, Guthlaxton Hd), sep CP 1866 in Warws.[22] *LG* Seq 16. Bdry: 1935 (loses pt to Bittesby CP, pt to Claybrooke Parva CP, pt to Ullesthorpe CP, all Leics).[160] *Parl* Seq 6.

WILLENHALL

Tp in Coventry Holy Trinity AP, sep CP 1866,[22] eccl severed 1958 to cr Willenhall with Whitley EP,[195] the latter divided 1965 into 2 EPs of Willenhall, Whitley.[342] *LG* Knight. Hd, Folesh. PLU, RSD, RD. Abol civ 1932 pt to Cov CB (assoc with Warws) & CP, pt to Baginton AP.[9] *Parl* N'rn Dv (1832—85), N-E'rn Dv (1885—1918), Nun. Dv (1918—45). *Eccl* Cov East RDn (1965—*).

WILLENHALL WITH WHITLEY

EP Cr 1958 from Coventry Holy Trinity AP (tp Willenhall).[195] Cov RDn (1958—63), Cov East RDn (1963—65). Divided 1965 into 2 EPs of Willenhall, Whitley.[342]

WILLEY

AP *LG* Seq 16. Civ bdry: 1935 (loses pt to Bittesby CP, pt to Lutterworth AP, both Leics).[160] *Parl* Seq 6. *Eccl* Cov RDn (until 1854), Rugby RDn (1854—92), Monks Kirby RDn (1892—1963), Bedw. RDn (1963—65), Rugby RDn (1965—*).

WILLOUGHBY

AP *LG* Seq 18. *Parl* Seq 8. *Eccl* Seq 12.

WILLS PASTURES

Orig pt Hodnell AP (depopulated 15th cent) and later considered ex-par,[165] sep CP 1858.[166] Sometimes 'Lower Hodnell'. *LG* Knight. Hd, Southam PLU (1858—1930), RSD, RD. *Parl* Seq 11.

WILMCOTE

EP Cr 1863 from Aston Cantlow AP, Stratford on Avon AP.[40] Alc. RDn.

WILNECOTE—see following entry

WILNECOTE AND CASTLE LIBERTY

Chap (Warws, Heml. Hd [eccl incl lbty Tamworth Castle, qv above for civ status]) Wilnecote (civ, tp 'Wilnecote and Castle Liberty') in Tamworth AP (Staffs [N Offlow Hd, S Offlow Hd], Warws [Heml. Hd]), the tp a sep CP 1866 in Warws,[22] the chap a sep EP 1770,[25] eccl refounded 1856 from Tamworth AP, Polesworth AP.[308] *LG* Tamw. PLU, RSD, RD (1894—1964), Ath. RD (1964—65). Civ bdry: 1894 (gains pt of the pt of Tamworth Castle CP not in Tamw. MB),[137] 1932 (loses pt to Tamw. MB & AP, Staffs),[23] 1935.[18] Abol 1965 pt to Tamw. MB & AP, Staffs, pt to Kingsbury AP, pt to Shuttington AP (last 2 in Warws).[21] *Parl* Tamw. Parl Bor ([Staffs, Warws] 1832—85), N'rn Dv (1885—1918), Tamw. Dv (1918—45), Sutt. Coldf. Dv/CC (1945—55), Merid. CC (1955—70).

WISHAW

AP *LG* Heml. Hd, Aston PLU, RSD, Cast. Bromw. RD (1894—1912), Merid. RD (1912—74). Civ bdry: 1966.[4] *Parl* Seq 2. *Eccl* Seq 3.

WITHYBROOK

AP Perhaps orig chap in Monks Kirby AP, sep par by 1205.[294] *LG* Seq 14. *Parl* Seq 4. *Eccl* Cov RDn (until 1854), Monks Kirby RDn (1854—1963), Bedw. RDn (1963—*).

WIXFORD

Chap in Salford Priors AP, sep civ identity early, eccl in Exhall AP since Reformation,[238] that par eccl thereafter 'Exhall with Wixford otherwise Wigglesford'. *LG* Seq 1. *Parl* Seq 16.

WOLFHAMPCOTE

AP *LG* Seq 18. *Parl* Seq 10. Eccl Marton RDn (until 1854), Dunch. RDn (1854—1907), Southam RDn (1907—*).

WOLFORD

AP Usual eccl spelling; for civ and sep chap and hmlt, see following entry. *Eccl* Seq 20.

GREAT WOLFORD

AP Usual civ spelling; for eccl see prev entry. Incl chap Burmington (sep civ identity early, sep eccl no later than 1634[156]), hmlt Little Wolford (sep CP 1866[22]). *LG* Seq 10. Addtl civ bdry at: 1885.[343] *Parl* Seq 13.

LITTLE WOLFORD

Hmlt in Great Wolford AP (eccl, 'Wolford'), sep CP 1866.[22] *LG* Seq 10. *Parl* Seq 13.

WOLSTON

AP Incl hmlt Stretton on Dunsmore (sep civ identity early, incl tp Princethorpe [the latter a sep CP 1866 from Stretton on Dunsmore[22]], united 1696 as 'Stretton upon Dunsmore and Princethorpe' EP[310]), hmlt Brandon and Bretford ([incl Bretford Bor, status not sustained] sep CP 1866[22]). *LG* Seq 18. *Parl* Seq 8. *Eccl* Seq 11.

WOLVERTON

AP Sometimes early 'Wolverdinton'. *LG* Seq 2. *Parl* Seq 15. *Eccl* Warw. RDn. Abol eccl 1925 to help cr Wolverton with Norton Lindsey EP.[174]

WOLVERTON WITH NORTON LINDSEY

EP Cr 1925 by union Wolverton AP, areas chap Norton Lindsey, hmlt Langley, both in Claverdon with Norton Lindsey AP.[174] Warw. RDn.

WOLVEY

AP *LG* Seq 15. Civ bdry: 1883,[153] 1885,[158] 1935 (incl loses pt to Hinck. UD & AP, Leics),[160] 1938.[154]

Parl Seq 4. *Eccl* Seq 9.

WOODEND

EP Cr 1957 from Foleshill AP, Wyken AP, Walsgrave on Sowe EP.[245] Cov RDn (1957—63), Cov East RDn (1963—*). Bdry: 1964 (incl help cr Potters Green EP).[309] Now called 'Coventry St Chad'.

WOOTTON WAWEN

AP Incl chap Bearley (sep par at Dissolution[69]), tp and Bor Henley in Arden (sep EP 1747,[25] sep CP 1957 with pt from this par [qv for other constituent pars][71]), chap and hmlt Ullenhall (sep EP 1861,[336] sep CP 1957 with pt from this par[71]). *LG* Seq 2. Addtl civ bdry alt: 1895,[332] 1922.[70] *Parl* Seq 15. *Eccl* Seq 22.

WORMLEIGHTON

AP *LG* Seq 11. *Parl* Seq 11. *Eccl* Seq 16.

WROXALL

AP Orig priory church. *LG* Seq 3. Civ bdry: 1886.[311] *Parl* Seq 14. *Eccl* Seq 21. Eccl bdry: 1893.[73]

WYKEN

AP Orig chap in Coventry St Michael AP, sep par by 1547.[207] *LG* Cov Co of Itself (1452—1842), Knight. Hd (from 1842), Folesh. PLU, RSD, RD. Civ bdry: 1884,[191] 1920 (cr Stoke Heath CP).[322] Abol civ 1932 pt to Cov CB (assoc with Warws) & CP, pt to Combe Fields CP.[9] *Parl* N'rn Dv (1832—85), N-E'rn Dv (1885—1918), Nun. Dv (1918—48). *Eccl* Cov RDn (cr—1854), Monks Kirby RDn (1854—92), Bag. RDn (1892—1921), Cov RDn (192—63), Cov East RDn (1963—*). Eccl bdry: 1939 (cr Coventry St Alban Stoke Heath EP),[197] 1957 (help cr Woodend EP).[245]

WYLDE GREEN

EP Cr 1923 from Boldmere EP.[113] Sutt. Coldf. RDn.

WYTHALL

EP Cr 1755 from Bromsgrove AP (Worcs),[25] refounded 1853 from Kings Norton EP, Alvechurch AP (both Worcs), Solihull AP (Warws).[319] See entry in Worcs for RDns.

YARDLEY

AP Worcs par (Solih. PLU) transf 1911 to be in Birm CB (1911—12) and Birm PLU (1911—12). Abol civ 1912 ent to Birmingham AP.[34] See main entry in Worcs.

WESTMORLAND

ABBREVIATIONS

Abbreviations particular to Westm follow. Those general abbreviations in use throughout the *Guide* are found on pages xvii—xix.

Ambles.	Ambleside
Appl.	Appleby
Bown.	Bowness
Grasm.	Grasmere
Lonsd.	Lonsdale
Penr.	Penrith
Winderm.	Windermere

SEQUENCES

An abbreviated entry prefixed by 'Seq' is used in the parochial entries to avoid repeating often the names of superior units of administration. The content of each sequence is shown below.

Local Government Sequences ('LG')

SEQ 1 East Wd, East Wd PLU, RSD, E Westm RD (1894—1935), N Westm RD (1935—74)

SEQ 2 Kendal Wd, Kendal PLU, RSD, S Westm RD

SEQ 3 Lonsd. Wd, Kendal PLU, RSD, S Westm RD

SEQ 4 West Wd, West Wd PLU, RSD, RD (1894—1935), N Westm RD (1935—74)

Parliamentary Sequences ('Parl')

Westm was undivided for parl purposes before 1885 and after 1918.

SEQ 1 Appl. Dv (1885—1918)

SEQ 2 Kendal Dv (1885—1918)

Ecclesiastical Sequences ('Eccl')

Orig in Carlisle dioc

SEQ 1 Westm RDn (until 1859), Appl. RDn (1859—82), Appl. & Kirkby Stephen RDn (1882—1970), Appl. RDn (1970—*)

SEQ 2 Westm RDn (until 1859), Kirkby Stpehen RDn (1859—82), Appl. & Kirkby Stephen RDn (1882—1970), Appl. RDn (1970—*)

SEQ 3 Westm RDn (until 1859), Lowther RDn (1859—1970), Appl. RDn (1970—*)

Orig in York (until 1541)

SEQ 4 Kendal RDn (until 1859), Ambles. RDn (1859—1970), Winderm. RDn (1970—*)

SEQ 5 Kendal RDn (until 1859), Kirkby Lonsd. RDn (1859—1970), Kendal RDn (1970—*)

DIOCESES AND ARCHDEACONRIES

Westm pars were organised in Archdeaconries and Rural Deaneries as follows:

CARLISLE DIOC
Carlisle AD: Appl. RDn (1859—82), Appl. RDn (1970—*), Appl. & Kirkby Stephen RDn (1882—1970), Greystoke RDn (1859—82), Kirkby Stephen RDn (1859—82), Lowther RDn (1859—1970), Penr. RDn (1970—*), Penr. West RDn (1882—1926), Westm RDn (until 1856)
Westmorland AD (1856—1959): Ambles. RDn (1859—1959), Kendal RDn, Kirkby Lonsd. RDn, Westm RDn (1856—59)

Westmorland and Furness AD (1959—):* Ambles. RDn (1959—70), Kirkby Lonsd. RDn (1959—70), Winderm. RDn (1970—*)

CHESTER DIOC (1541—1856)
Richmond AD: Kendal RDn, Kirkby Lonsd. RDn

YORK DIOC (until 1541)
Richmond AD: Kendal RDn (before 1535—1541), Kirkby Lonsd. RDn (before 1535—1541) Kirkby Lonsd. and Kendal (before 1291—before 1535)

THE PARISHES OF WESTMORLAND

Westm pars were transf 1974 to help cr Cumbria Non-Metrop Co.

AMBLESIDE

Chap pt in Grasmere AP, pt in Windermere AP (each orig a chap in Kendal AP, each a sep par at the Reformation[1]), 'Ambleside' a sep CP 1866,[2] sep EP 1746,[3] eccl refounded 1863.[4] *LG* Kendal Wd, PLU, Ambles. USD, UD (1894—1935), Lakes UD (1935—74). Civ bdry: 1886,[5] 1894 (gains the pt of Applethwaite CP in Ambles. UD).[6] *Parl* Seq 1. *Eccl* Kendal RDn (1746—1859), Ambles. RDn (1859—1967). Abol eccl 1967 to help cr Ambleside with Brathay EP.[7]

AMBLESIDE WITH BRATHAY

EP Cr 1967 by union Ambleside EP (Westm), pt Brathay EP (Lancs).[7] Ambles. RDn (1967—70), Winderm. RDn (1970—*).

APPLEBY

CP Cr 1894 from the pt of Appleby St Laurence AP in Appl. MB.[6] *LG* East Wd PLU, Appl. MB. Bdry: 1908 (gains Bongate CP).[8]

EP Cr 1972 by union Appleby St Laurence AP, Appleby St Michael AP, Murton cum Hilton EP.[9] Appl. RDn.

APPLEBY ST LAURENCE

AP *LG* East Wd, East Wd PLU, pt Appl. MB & USD (1885—94), East Wd RSD (ent 1875—85, pt 1885—94). Abol civ 1894 the pt in Appl. MB to cr Appleby CP, the remainder to cr the 2 CPs of Colby, Hoff.[6] *Parl* Appl. Parl Bor (1295—1832), Appl. Dv (1885—1918). *Eccl* Westm RDn (until 1859), Appl. RDn (1859—82), Appl. & Kirkby Stephen RDn (1882—1970), Appl. RDn (1970—72). Abol eccl 1972 to help cr Appleby EP.[9]

APPLEBY ST MICHAEL

AP Usual eccl spelling; for civ see following entry. *Eccl* RDns as for Appleby St Laurence. Eccl bdry: 1863 (cr Murton cum Hilton EP [tps Murton, Hilton, neither with sep civ identity at that time]).[10] Abol eccl 1972 to help cr Appleby EP.[9]

APPLEBY ST MICHAEL OR BONGATE

AP Usual civ spelling; for eccl see prev entry. *LG* East Wd, East Wd PLU, pt Appl. MB & USD (1885—94), East Wd RSD (ent 1875—85, pt 1885—94). Abol civ 1894 the pt in the MB to cr Bongate CP, the remainder to cr the 2 CPs of Crackenthorpe, Murton.[6] *Parl* As for Appleby St Laurence.

APPLETHWAITE

Tp in Windermere AP (orig chap in Kendal AP, sep par at Reformation[1]), 'Applethwaite' a sep CP 1866,[2] eccl within area of chap Troutbeck (in Windermere AP, consecr 1562,[11] sep EP 1747[3]), 'Applethwaite' a sep EP 1836 from Troutbeck EP,[3] eccl refounded 1856.[12] *LG* Kendal Wd, PLU, pt Winderm. USD, pt Ambles. USD, pt Bown. on Winderm. USD. Abol civ 1894 the pt in Winderm. USD to cr Windermere CP, the pt in Ambles. USD transf to Ambleside CP, the pt in Bown. on Winderm. USD to help cr Bowness on Windermere CP.[6] *Parl* Appl. Dv (1885—1918). *Eccl* Kendal

RDn (1836—59), Ambles. RDn (1859—1970), Winderm. RDn (1970—*). Now called 'Windermere St Mary'. Eccl bdry: 1882 (help refound Troutbeck EP),[13] 1888 (help cr Windermere St John EP),[14] 1960.[15]

ARNSIDE

Hmlt in Beetham AP, sep EP 1870,[16] sep CP 1897.[17] *LG* Kendal PLU, S Westm RD. *Eccl* Kirkby Lonsd. RDn (1870—1970), Kendal RDn (1970—*).

ASBY

AP Incl undivided pt Bank Moor (common to Asby AP and Crosby Ravensworth AP, abol 1935 ent to the latter[18]). *LG* Seq 1. Addtl civ bdry alt: 1883.[19] *Parl* Seq 1. *Eccl* Seq 1.

ASKHAM

AP *LG* Seq 4. *Parl* Seq 1. *Eccl* Seq 3.

BAMPTON

AP *LG* Seq 4. *Parl* Seq 1. *Eccl* Seq 3.

BANK MOOR

Moor common to Asby AP and Crosby Ravensworth AP. *LG* West Wd RD. Abol 1935 ent to Crosby Ravensowrth AP.[18]

BARBON

Chap in Kirkby Lonsdale AP, sep CP 1866,[1] sep EP 1738.[3] *LG* Seq 3. *Parl* Seq 2. *Eccl* Kirkby Lonsd. RDn (1738—1970), Kendal RDn (1970—*).

BARTON

AP Incl chap Martindale (sep CP 1866,[1] sep EP 1748[3]), chap Patterdale (sep CP 1866,[2] sep EP 1743,[3] eccl refounded 1866[20]), tps High Barton, Sockbridge, Low Winder, Yanwath and Eamont Bridge (each of the 4 a sep CP 1866[2]), moor Barton Fell (orig in Barton AP, after 1866 comon to High Barton CP and Sockbridge CP, common 1894—1935 to Sockbridge CP and Barton CP, the area abol 1935 ent to Barton CP[18]) so that 'Barton' has no sep civ identity 1866—94 (see following entry). *LG* West Wd. *Eccl* Westm RDn (until 1859), Penr. RDn (1859—82), Penr. West RDn (1882—1926), Penr. RDn (1926—*). Eccl bdry: 1905 (cr Pooley Bridge EP),[21] 1957.[22]

CP Cr 1894 by union High Barton CP, Low Winder CP.[6] Incl undivided pt Barton Fell (moor orig in Barton AP, after 1866 common to High Barton CP and Sockbridge CP, after 1894 common to Sockbridge CP and Barton CP, the area abol 1935 ent to Barton CP[18]). *LG* West Wd PLU, RD (1894—1935), N Westm RD (1935—74).

HIGH BARTON

Tp in Barton AP, sep CP 1866.[2] Incl undivided pt Barton Fell (moor orig in Barton AP, after 1866 common to High Barton CP and Sockbridge CP). *LG* West Wd, West Wd PLU, RSD. Bdry: 1883,[19] 1888.[23] Abol 1894 (incl undivided pt Barton Fell) to help cr Barton CP.[6] *Parl* Appl. Dv (1885—1918).

BARTON FELL

Moor orig in Barton AP, after 1866 common to High Barton CP and Sockbridge CP, common

1894—1935 to Sockbridge CP and Barton CP.[18] *LG* West Wd RD. Abol 1935 ent to Barton CP.[18]

BEETHAM
AP Incl chap & tp Witherslack (sep CP 1866,[2] sep EP 1748 [incl tp Meathop and Ulpha],[3] eccl refounded 1891[24]), hmlt Arnside (sep EP 1870,[16] sep CP 1897[17]), tp Meathop and Ulpha (sep CP 1866,[2] eccl in chap/EP Witherslack, qv above), tps Farleton, Haverback (each a sep CP 1866[2]). *LG* Seq 2. Addtl civ bdry alt: 1935 (gains Farleton CP),[18] 1935 (gains Haverbrack CP).[25] *Parl* Seq 2. *Eccl* Seq 5.

BOLTON
Chap in Morland AP, sep CP 1866,[1] sep EP 1745.[3] *LG* Seq 4. *Parl* Seq 1. *Eccl* Westm RDn (1745—1859), Lowther RDn (1859—82), Appl. & Kirkby Stephen RDn (1882—1970), Appl. RDn (1970—*).

BONGATE
CP Cr 1894 from the pt of Appleby St Michael or Bongate AP in Appl. MB.[6] *LG* East Wd PLU, Appl. MB. Abol 1908 ent to Appleby CP.[8] *Parl* Appl. Dv (1885—1918).

BOWNESS ON WINDERMERE
CP Cr 1894 from the pts in Winderm. UD of Applethwaite CP, Undermillbeck CP.[6] *LG* Kendal PLU, Bown. on Winderm. UD (1894—1905), Winderm. UD (1905—74). Bdry: 1935.[18]

BROUGH
AP Orig chap and bor (as 'Market Brough' status not sustained) in Kirkby Stephen AP, sep par at Reformation (usual eccl spelling 'Brough under Stainmore', qv in following entry).[26] Incl chap Stainmore (sep CP 1866,[2] sep EP 1721[3]), tps Hillbeck, Brough Somerby (each a sep CP 1866[2]). *LG* Seq 1. Addtl civ bdry alt: 1883.[19] *Parl* Seq 1.

BROUGH UNDER STAINMORE
AP Orig chap in Kirkby Stephen AP, sep par at Reformation.[26] Usual eccl spelling; for civ and sep chap and tps in the par, see prev entry. Westm RDn (cr—1859), Kirkby Stephen RDn (1859—82), Appl. & Kirkby Stephen RDn (1882—1970), Appl. RDn (1970—73). Abol eccl 1973 to help cr Brough with Stainmore EP.[27]

BROUGH WITH STAINMORE
EP Cr 1973 by union Brough under Stainmore AP, Stainmore EP.[27] Appl. RDn.

BROUGHAM
AP *LG* Seq 4. Civ bdry: 1935.[18] *Parl* Seq 1. *Eccl* Westm RDn (until 1859), Penr. RDn (1859—82), Penr. East RDn (1882—1926), Penr. RDn (1926—57), Lowther RDn (1957—70), Penr. RDn (1970—*). Eccl bdry: 1957.[22]

BURNESIDE
Chap in Kendal AP, sep EP 1772 (tps Strickland Ketel, Strickland Roger [each a sep CP 1866, qv]),[3] eccl refounded 1929.[28] Kendal RDn.

BURTON
AP Usual civ spelling; for eccl see following entry. Tp 'Burton' in Westm (Kendal Wd) as were tp Holme (sep CP 1866,[2] sep EP 1843[29]), tp Preston Patrick (sep CP 1866,[2] sep EP 1722[3]), hmlt Holmescales (civ united with chap Old Hutton in Kendal AP as 'Old Hutton and Holmescales', as such a sep CP 1866[2]); incl in Lancs (Lonsd. Hd) tp Dalton (sep CP

1866 in Lancs[2]), so that 'Burton' ent Westm thereafter). *LG* Kendal PLU, RSD, S Westm RD. *Parl* Westm pt, Seq 2.

BURTON IN KENDAL
AP Usual eccl spelling (as opposed to 'Burton in Lonsdale' in Lancs); for civ and sep tps and hmlt, see prev entry. *Eccl* Seq 5.

CASTERTON
Orig chap (early in ruins and later tp) in Kirkby Lonsdale AP, sep CP 1866,[2] sep EP 1862,[3] eccl refounded 1864.[30] *LG* Seq 3. *Parl* Seq 2. *Eccl* Kirkby Lonsd. RDn (1862—1970), Kendal RDn (1970—*).

CLIBURN
AP *LG* Seq 4. *Parl* Seq 1. *Eccl* Seq 3.

CLIFTON
AP *LG* Seq 4. Civ bdry: 1935.[18] *Parl* Seq 1. *Eccl* Westm RDn (until 1859), Lowther RDn (1859—1970), Penr. RDn (1970—*). Eccl bdry: 1957.[22]

COLBY
CP Cr 1894 from pt of the pt of Appleby St Laurence AP not in Appl. MB.[6] *LG* East Wd PLU, E Westm RD (1894—1935), N Westm RD (1935—74).

CRACKENTHORPE
CP Cr 1894 from pt of the pt of Appleby St Michael or Bongate AP not in Appl. MB.[6] *LG* East Wd PLU, E Westm RD (1894—1935), N Westm RD (1935—74).

CROOK
Chap & tp in Kendal AP, orig one chap with Winster[31] (in Windermere AP, the latter orig a chap in Kendal AP, Windermere a sep par at Reformation, qv), 'Crook' eccl in Winster when a sep EP 1718,[3] 'Crook' a sep EP 1748 from Winster EP,[3] eccl refounded 1929,[28] 'Crook' a sep CP 1866.[2] *LG* Seq 2. Civ bdry: 1935,[18] 1951.[32] *Parl* Seq 2. *Eccl* Kendal RDn.

CROSBY GARRETT
AP Incl tp Little Musgrave (sep CP 1866[2]). *LG* Seq 1. *Parl* Seq 1. *Eccl* Seq 2.

CROSBY RAVENSWORTH
AP Incl undivided pt Bank Moor (common to Asby AP and Crosby Ravensworth AP, abol 1935 ent to this par[18]), undivided pt of Lands Common to Orton AP and Crosby Ravensworth AP (abol 1935, pt to this par[18]). *LG* Seq 4. *Parl* Seq 1. *Eccl* Seq 3.

CROSSCAKE
Chap in Heversham AP, sep EP 1756 (incl tp Sedgwick in same par),[3] refounded 1877.[33] Kendal RDn (1756—1859), Kirkby Lonsd. RDn (1859—1970), Kendal RDn (1970—*).

CROSTHWAITE
Chap in Heversham AP, sep EP 1718,[3] eccl refounded 1869[34]; for civ see following entry. Kendal RDn (1718—1859), Kirkby Lonsd. RDn (1859—1919), Kendal RDn (1919—*).

CROSTHWAITE AND LYTH
Chap Crosthwaite (for sep eccl status see prev entry) and tp Lyth in Heversham AP formed one unit for civ purposes and as 'Crosthwaite and Lyth' sep CP 1866.[2] *LG* Seq 2. Bdry: 1886.[35] *Parl* Seq 2.

DALTON
Tp in Burton AP (eccl, 'Burton in Kendal'), the only

pt of the AP in Lancs (Lonsd. Hd), sep civ identity 1866 in Lancs,[2] transf 1895 to Westm.[36] *LG* Kendal PLU, sep RD in Lancs (1894—95), S Westm RD (1895—1974). *Parl* In Lancs (until 1918), Westm thereafter.

DILLICAR
Hmlt in Kendal AP, sep CP 1866.[2] *LG* Seq 3. *Parl* Seq 2.

DOCKER
Tp in Kendal AP, sep CP 1866.[2] *LG* Seq 2. *Parl* Seq 2.

DUFTON
AP *LG* Seq 1. *Parl* Seq 1. *Eccl* Seq 1.

FARLETON
Tp in Beetham AP, sep CP 1866.[2] *LG* Kendal Wd, PLU, RSD, S Westm RD. Abol 1935 ent to Beetham AP.[18] *Parl* Kendal Dv (1885—1918).

FAWCETT FOREST
Tp pt in Kendal AP (Kendal Wd), pt in Orton AP (East Wd), sep CP 1866,[2] eccl in chap Selside EP (in Kendal AP, 'Selside' a sep EP 1772[3]). *LG* Kendal PLU, RSD, S Westm RD. Bdry: 1935.[18] *Parl* Kendal Dv (1885—1918).

FIRBANK
Chap in Kirkby Lonsdale AP, sep CP 1866,[2] orig one chap with Killington[37] until Firbank a sep EP 1721.[3] *LG* Seq 3. *Parl* Seq 2. *Eccl* Kirkby Lonsd. RDn (1721—1925), Ewecross RDn (dioc Bradf [united benefice with Howgill in Yorks], 1925—26), Sedbergh RDn (dioc Bradf, 1926—*).

GRASMERE
AP Chap in Kendal AP, sep par at Reformation.[1] Incl pt chap Ambleside (sep CP 1866,[2] sep EP 1746,[3] eccl refounded 1863[4]), chap Langdales (sep CP 1866,[2] sep EP 1744 as 'Langdale' [incl pt tp Rydal and Loughrigg],[3] eccl refounded 1863[4]), chap Rydal (sep EP 1826,[3] eccl refounded 1886,[38] sep CP 1866 as 'Rydal and Loughrigg',[2] pt of area of latter eccl in Langdale chap/EP as noted above). *LG* Kendal Wd, PLU, Grasm. USD (ent 1875—83, pt 1883—91, ent 1891—94), pt Kendal RSD (1883—91), Grasm. UD (1894—1935), Lakes UD (1935—74). Addtl civ bdry alt: 1883.[19] *Parl* Seq 1. *Eccl* Seq 4. Addtl eccl bdry alt: 1940.[39]

NETHER GRAVESHIP
Tp in Kendal AP, sep CP 1866.[2] *LG* Kendal Wd, PLU, MB, USD. Bdry: 1880,[40] 1880.[41] Abol 1908 ent to Kendal AP.[42] *Parl* Kendal Parl Bor (1832—85), Kendal Dv (1885—1918).

GRAYRIGG
Chap (anc chap, rebuilt 1708[43]) & tp in Kendal AP, sep CP 1866,[2] sep EP 1722.[3] *LG* Seq 2. Civ bdry: 1935.[18] *Parl* Seq 2. *Eccl* Kendal RDn.

HARTLEY
Tp in Kirkby Stephen AP, sep CP 1866.[2] *LG* Seq 1. Bdry: 1911 (areas determined and altered for this par and for Westm pars of Kaber CP, Winton CP, and for Yorks N Riding par of Muker CP).[44] *Parl* Seq 1.

HAVERBRACK
Tp in Beetham AP, sep CP 1866.[2] *LG* Kendal Wd, PLU, RSD, S Westm RD. Abol 1935 ent to Beetham AP.[25] *Parl* Kendal Dv (1885—1918).

HELSINGTON
Chap (anc chap, rebuilt 1726[45]) & tp in Kendal AP, sep CP 1866,[2] sep EP 1728.[3] *LG* Seq 2. Civ bdry: 1880,[41] 1935,[18] 1970.[46] *Parl* Seq 2. *Eccl* Kendal RDn.

HEVERSHAM
AP Incl chap Crosthwaite (sep EP 1718,[3] eccl refounded 1869,[34] one civ unit with tp Lyth in same par and as 'Crosthwaite and Lyth' sep CP 1866[2]), chap Crosscake (sep EP 1756 [incl tp Sedgwick],[3] refounded 1877[33]), tp Levens (sep CP 1866,[2] sep EP 1836[47]), tp Sedgwick (sep CP 1866,[2] eccl in chap/EP Crosscake as noted above), area Milnthorpe (sep EP 1839,[3] civ incl with main area Heversham as 'Heversham with Milnthorpe' and as such CP 1866[2]), tp (orig chap, in ruins from Dissolution[48]) Stainton, tps Hincaster, Preston Richard (the last 3 each a sep CP 1866[2]) so that 'Heversham' has no sep civ identity 1866—1896 (see following entry). *LG* Kendal Wd. *Eccl* Seq 5. Addtl eccl bdry alt: 1873.[49]
CP Cr 1896 from Heversham with Milnthorpe CP.[50] *LG* Kendal PLU, S Westm RD.

HEVERSHAM WITH MILNTHORPE
Tp in Heversham AP (main area of par and area Milnthorpe [for sep eccl identity of latter, see Milnthorpe], sep CP 1866.[2] *LG* Kendal Wd, PLU, RSD, S Westm RD. Abol 1896 to cr the 2 CPs of Heversham, Milnthorpe.[50] *Parl* Kendal Dv (1885—1918)

HILLBECK
Tp in Brough AP, sep CP 1866.[2] *LG* Seq 1. Bdry: 1883.[19] *Parl* Seq 1.

HINCASTER
Tp in Heversham AP, sep CP 1866.[2] *LG* Seq 2. Bdry: 1883.[19] *Parl* Seq 2.

HOFF
CP Cr 1894 from pt of the pt of Appleby St Laurence AP not in Appl. MB.[6] *LG* East Wd PLU, E Westm RD (1894—1935), N Westm RD (1935—74).

HOLME
Tp in Burton AP, sep CP 1866,[2] sep EP 1843.[29] *LG* Seq 2. *Parl* Seq 2. *Eccl* Kendal RDn (1843—59), Kirkby Lonsd. RDn (1859—1970), Kendal RDn (1970—*).

HUGILL
Chap in Kendal AP, sep CP 1866,[2] eccl in chap Staveley in same par (sep EP 1723[3]), 'Hugill' a sep EP 1743 from Staveley EP,[3] eccl refounded 1929 as 'Ings',[28] the latter a name often used earlier for this par. *LG* Seq 2. *Parl* Seq 2. *Eccl* Kendal RDn.

NEW HUTTON
Tp and chap (built 1739[51]) in Kendal AP, sep CP 1866,[2] sep EP 1739.[3] *LG* Seq 2. Civ bdry: 1883,[19] 1886,[35] 1897.[52] *Parl* Seq 2. *Eccl* Kendal RDn.

OLD HUTTON
Tp and chap (built 1628[51]) in Kendal AP, sep EP 1737,[3] civ united with hmlt Holmescales in Burton AP and as 'Old Hutton and Holmescales' sep CP 1866,[2] qv. *Eccl* Kendal RDn.

OLD HUTTON AND HOLMESCALES
Civ union of tp and chap (built 1628[51]) Old Hutton in Kendal AP (for eccl identity, see prev entry),

hmlt Holmescales in Burton AP, the union a sep CP 1866.[2] *LG* Seq 2. *Parl* Kendal Dv (1885—1918).

HUTTON ROOF

Chap in Kirkby Lonsdale AP, sep CP 1866,[2] sep EP 1743.[3] *LG* Seq 3. *Parl* Seq 2. *Eccl* Kirkby Lonsd. RDn. Abol eccl 1926 to help cr Hutton Roof with Lupton EP.[53]

HUTTON ROOF WITH LUPTON

EP Cr 1926 by union Hutton Roof EP, tp and chap Lupton in Kirkby Lonsdale AP.[53] Kirkby Lonsd. RDn (1926—70), Kendal RDn (1970—*).

INGS

EP Refounding 1929 of Hugill EP (Hugill orig a chap in Kendal AP, sep CP 1866,[2] eccl in chap Staveley in Kendal AP until Hugill a sep EP 1743[3]).[28] Kendal RDn.

KABER

Tp in Kirkby Stephen AP, sep CP 1866.[2] *LG* Seq 1. Bdry: 1883,[19] 1911 (areas determined and altered for this par and for Westm pars of Hartley CP, Winton CP, and for Yorks N Riding par of Muker CP).[44] *Parl* Seq 1.

KENDAL

AP Sometimes 'Kirkby Kendal'. Tp 'Kendal' and all chaps and tp in Kendal Wd except for hmlt Dillicar (Lonsd. Wd, sep CP 1866[2]); incl in Kendal Wd chap Burneside (sep EP 1722 [incl tps Strickland Ketel, Strickland Roger],[3] eccl refounded 1929[28]), chap & tp Crook (sep CP 1866,[2] orig one chap with Winster[31] [sep EP 1718 from chap/AP Windermere[3]], 'Crook' a sep EP 1748 from Winster EP,[3] refounded 1929[28]), chap Grasmere (prob sep par at Reformation[1] [qv for inclusion and later independence of pt chap Ambleside, chap Langdales (eccl, 'Langdale'), chap Rydal (civ, 'Rydal and Loughrigg')], chap Windermere (sep par at Reformation[54] [qv for inclusion and later independence of pt chap Ambleside, tp Applethwaite, chap Troutbeck, pt tp Undermillbeck, chap Winster (orig one chap with Crook, for which see below)], chap (anc, rebuilt 1708[43]) and tp Grayrigg (sep CP 1866,[2] sep EP 1708[3]), tp and chap (built 1722[45]) Helsington (sep CP 1866,[2] sep EP 1728[3]), chap Hugill (orig in chap Staveley and incl in it when latter a sep EP 1723,[3] 'Hugill' a sep EP 1743[3] [often as 'Ings', eccl refounded 1929 as 'Ings'[28]]), tp and chap (built 1739[45]) New Hutton (sep CP 1866,[2] sep EP 1739[3]), tp and chap (built 1628[51]) Old Hutton (sep EP 1737,[3] civ united with hmlt Holmescales in Burton AP and as 'Old Hutton with Holmescales', as such sep CP 1866[1]), chap & tp Kentmere (sep CP 1866,[2] sep EP 1735[3]), chap & tp Longsleddale (sep CP 1866,[2] sep EP 1735[3]), chap (anc chap, in ruins and rebuilt 1735[55]) & tp Natland (sep CP 1866,[2] sep EP 1746[3]), tp & chap (built just before augmentation[54]) Selside (sep EP 1772 [incl tp Fawcett Forest],[3] civ called 'Whitwell and Selside' and as such sep CP 1866[2]), chap and tp Skelsmergh (sep CP 1866,[2] sep EP 1871 [incl tp Patton, pt tp Scalthwaiterigg, Hay and Hutton in the Hay][56]), chap Staveley (sep EP 1723,[3] eccl refounded 1929,[28] civ comprised of the 2 tps of Nether Staveley, Over Staveley, each a sep CP 1866[2]), chap Underbarrow (anc chap rebuilt

1708,[57] sep EP 1708,[3] eccl refounded 1929,[28] eccl excludes area tp Bradleyfield but civ united with the latter and as 'Underbarrow and Bradleyfield' a sep CP 1866[2]), chap and tp Winster (sep CP 1866,[2] orig one chap together with Crook in chap/AP Windermere, sep EP 1718,[3] 'Crook' severed 1748 from the latter as a sep EP 1748[3]), tp Docker (sep CP 1866[2]), pt tp Fawcett Forest (sep CP 1866,[2] the tp eccl in Selside as noted above), tp Nether Graveship (sep CP 1866[2]), tp Kirkland (sep CP 1866[2]), tp Lambrigg (sep CP 1866,[2] eccl in Skelsmergh as noted above incl refounding); tp Scalthwaiterigg, Hay and Hutton in the Hay (sep CP 1866,[2] pt eccl severed 1871 to help cr Skelsmergh EP[56]); tps Strickland Ketel, Strickland Roger (each a sep CP 1866,[2] both eccl incl in Burnside as noted above), pt tp Undermillbeck (sep CP 1866[2]), tp Whitwell and Selside (sep CP 1866[2]; for eccl see Selside above). *LG* Kendal PLU, Bor/MB, USD. Addtl civ bdry alt: 1880,[45] 1908 (gains Nether Graveship CP, Kirkland CP),[42] 1919,[58] 1935.[18] *Parl* Kendal Parl Bor (1832—85), Kendal Dv (1885—1918). *Eccl* Seq 4. Addtl eccl bdry alt: 1738 (cr Kendal St George EP,[3] refounded 1848[59]), 1739 (cr Kendal St Thomas EP),[3] 1872,[60] 1960.[61]

KENDAL ST GEORGE

EP Cr 1738 from Kendal AP,[3] refounded 1848.[59] Kendal RDn. Bdry: 1960.[61]

KENDAL ST THOMAS

EP Cr 1739 from Kendal AP.[3] Kendal RD. Bdry: 1960.[61]

KENTMERE

Chap and tp in Kendal AP, sep CP 1866,[2] sep EP 1735.[3] *LG* Seq 2. *Parl* Seq 2. *Eccl* Kendal RDn.

KILLINGTON

Chap in Kirkby Lonsdale AP, orig one chap with Firbank[37] until the latter a sep EP 1721,[3] 'Killington' a sep CP 1866,[1] sep EP 1748.[3] *LG* Seq 3. *Parl* Seq 2. *Eccl* Kirkby Lonsd. RDn (1748—1951), Sedbergh RDn (dioc Bradf [because united benefice with Sedbergh in Yorks], 1951—*).

KIRKBY KENDAL—See KENDAL

KIRKBY LONSDALE

AP Incl chap Casterton (early in ruins and later tp, sep CP 1866,[2] sep EP 1862,[3] eccl refounded 1864[30]), chap Firbank, chap Killington (the last 2 orig one chap together,[37] 'Firbank' a sep EP 1721,[3] 'Killington' a sep EP 1748,[3] each a sep CP 1866[2]), chap Hutton Roof (sep CP 1866,[2] sep EP 1743[3]), tp and chap (built *ca* 1728[62]) Mansergh (sep CP 1866,[2] sep EP 1728,[3] eccl refounded 1866[63]), tp and chap (built 1634[64]) Middleton (sep CP 1866,[2] sep EP 1732[3]), tp Lupton (sep CP 1866,[2] eccl severed 1926 to help cr Hutton Roof with Lupton EP[53]), tp Barbon (sep CP 1866,[2] sep EP 1738[3]). *LG* Lonsd. Wd, Kendal PLU, Kirkby Lonsd. USD, UD (1894—1935), S Westm RD (1935—74). *Parl* Seq 2. *Eccl* Kirkby Lonsd. RDn (until 1970), Kendal RDn (1970—*).

KIRKBY STEPHEN

AP Incl chap Brough (sep par at Reformation[26]), chap Mallerstang (forest, chap rebuilt 1663,[65] sep EP 1721,[3] sep CP 1866[2]), tp and chap (built 1663[65])

Soulby (sep CP 1866,[2] sep EP 1766,[3] eccl refounded 1874[66]), chap and tp Smardale, tps Hartley, Kaber, Nateby, Waitby, Wharton, Winton (the last 7 each a sep CP 1866[2]). *LG* Seq 1. *Parl* Seq 2. *Eccl* Seq 2. Addtl eccl bdry alt: 1971 (gains Mallerstang EP).[67]

KIRKBY THORE
AP Incl chap Milburn (sep CP 1866,[2] sep EP 1753[3]), chap Temple Sowerby (sep CP 1866,[2] sep EP 1753[3]). *LG* Seq 1. *Parl* Seq 1. *Eccl* Seq 1.

KIRKLAND
Tp in Kendal AP, sep CP 1866.[2] *LG* Kendal Wd, PLU, MB, USD. Abol 1908 ent to Kendal AP.[42] *Parl* Kendal Parl Bor (1832—85), Kendal Dv (1885—1918).

LAMBRIGG
Tp in Kendal AP, sep CP 1866.[2] *LG* Seq 2. *Parl* Seq 2.

LANDS COMMON TO ORTON AND CROSBY RAVENSWORTH
LG West Wd RD. Abol 1935 pt to Orton AP, pt to Crosby Ravensworth AP, pt to Shap Rural CP.[18]

LANGDALE
Usual eccl spelling for chap in Grasmere AP (orig chap in Kendal AP, sep par at Reformation[1]), 'Langdale' a sep EP 1744 (incl pt tp Rydal and Loughrigg),[3] eccl refounded 1863 in same area,[4] sep CP 1866 as 'Langdales',[2] qv. *Eccl* Kendal RDn (1744—1859), Ambles. RDn (1859—1970), Winderm. RDn (1970—*). Eccl bdry: 1967 (gains pt Brathay EP, Lancs).[7]

LANGDALES
Usual civ spelling for chap in Grasmere AP (orig chap in Kendal AP, sep par at Reformation[1]), 'Langdales' a sep CP 1866,[2] 'Langdale' a sep EP 1744,[3] qv in prev entry for area, refounding. *LG* Kendal Wd, PLU, RSD, S Westm RD (1894—1935), Lakes UD (1935—74). *Parl* Seq 1.

LEVENS
Tp in Heversham AP, sep CP 1866,[2] sep EP 1836.[47] *LG* Seq 2. Civ bdry: 1883,[19] 1886,[35] 1970.[46] *Parl* Seq 2. *Eccl* Kendal RDn (1836—59), Kirkby Lonsd. RDn (1859—1919), Kendal RDn (1919—*). Eccl bdry: 1918.[68]

LONGSLEDDALE
Chap and tp in Kendal AP, sep CP 1866,[2] sep EP 1712.[3] *LG* Seq 2. *Parl* Seq 2. *Eccl* Kendal RDn.

LOWTHER
AP *LG* Seq 4. *Parl* Seq 1. *Eccl* Seq 3.

LUPTON
Chap and tp in Kirkby Lonsdale AP, sep CP 1866,[2] eccl severed 1926 to help cr Hutton Roof with Lupton EP.[53] *LG* Seq 3. *Parl* Seq 2.

MALLERSTANG
Chap (forest, anc chap rebuilt 1663[65]) in Kirkby Stephen AP, sep CP 1866,[2] sep EP 1721.[3] *LG* Seq 1. *Parl* Seq 1. *Eccl* Westm RDn (1721—1859), Kirkby Stephen RDn (1859—82), Appl. & Kirkby Stephen RDn (1882—1970), Appl. RDn (1970—71). Abol eccl 1971 ent to Kirkby Stephen AP.[67]

MANSERGH
Tp and chap (built 1728[62]) in Kirkby Lonsdale AP, sep CP 1866,[2] sep EP 1728,[3] eccl refounded

1866.[63] *LG* Seq 3. *Parl* Seq 2. *Eccl* Kirkby Lonsd. RDn (1728—1970), Kendal RDn (1970—*).

MARDALE
Chap in Shap AP, sep EP 1748.[3] Westm RDn (1748—1859), Lowther RDn (1859—1970), Appl. RDn (1970—*).

MARTINDALE
Chap in Barton AP, sep CP 1866,[2] sep EP 1748.[3] *LG* Seq 4. *Parl* Seq 1. *Eccl* Westm RDn (1748—1859), Lowther RDn (1859—82), Penr. West RDn (1882—1926), Penr. RDn (1926—*).

LONG MARTON
AP *LG* Seq 1. *Parl* Seq 1. *Eccl* Seq 1.

KING'S MEABURN
Tp in Newland AP, sep CP 1866.[2] *LG* Seq 4. *Parl* Seq 1.

MEATHOP AND ULPHA
Tp in Beetham AP, sep CP 1866,[2] eccl in chap Witherslack (sep EP 1748 from Beetham AP,[3] refounded 1891[24]). *LG* Seq 2. *Parl* Seq 2.

MIDDLETON
Tp and chap (built 1634[64]) in Kirkby Lonsdale AP, sep CP 1866,[2] sep EP 1732.[3] *LG* Seq 3. *Parl* Seq 2. *Eccl* Kirkby Lonsd. RDn (1732—1970), Kendal RDn (1970—*).

MILBURN
Chap in Kirkby Thore AP, sep CP 1866,[2] sep EP 1753.[3] *LG* Seq 1. *Parl* Seq 1. *Eccl* Westm RDn (1753—1859), Appl. RDn (1859—82), Appl. & Kirkby Stephen RDn (1882—1970), Appl. RDn (1970—*).

MILNTHORPE
Area in Heversham AP, sep EP 1839,[3] forms with main pt of Heversham a single tp 'Heversham with Milnthorpe' and as such a sep CP 1866,[2] qv, 'Milnthorpe' a sep CP 1896 from Heversham with Milnthorpe CP.[50] *LG* Kendal PLU, S Westm RD. *Eccl* Kendal RDn (1839—59), Kirkby Lonsd. RDn (1859—1970), Kendal RDn (1970—*).

MORLAND
AP Incl chap Bolton (sep CP 1866,[2] sep EP 1745[3]), chap (anc chap, rebuilt late 17th cent[69]) and tp Thrimby (sep EP 1741 [incl tps Great Strickland, Little Strickland],[3] eccl refounded 1870[70]), tps Great Strickland, Little Strickland (each a sep CP 1866,[2] each eccl in chap/EP Thrimby as noted above), tps King's Meaburn, Newby, Sleagill (each a sep CP 1866[2]). *LG* Seq 4. Addtl civ bdry alt: 1888.[23] *Parl* Seq 1. *Eccl* Seq 3.

MURTON
CP Cr 1894 from pt of the pt of Appleby St Michael or Bongate AP not in Appl. MB[6]; for eccl see following entry. *LG* East Ward PLU, E Westm RD (1894—1935), N Westm RD (1935—74).

MURTON CUM HILTON
EP Cr 1863 from Appleby St Michael AP (tps Murton, Hilton, neither with sep civ identity at that time; for Murton later see prev entry).[10] Appl. RDn (1863—82), Appl. & Kirkby Stephen RDn (1882—1970), Appl. RDn (1970—72). Abol 1972 to help cr Appleby EP.[9]

MUSGRAVE
CP Cr 1894 by union Great Musgrave AP, Little

Musgrave CP.[6] *LG* East Ward PLU, E Westm RD (1894—1935), N Westm RD (1935—74).

GREAT MUSGRAVE

AP *LG* East Wd, East Ward PLU, RSD. Civ bdry: 1883.[19] Abol civ 1894 to help cr Musgrave CP.[6] *Parl* Appl. Dv (1885—1918). *Eccl* Seq 2.

LITTLE MUSGRAVE

Tp in Crosby Garrett AP, sep CP 1866.[2] *LG* East Wd, East Ward PLU, RSD. Abol 1894 to help cr Musgrave CP.[6] *Parl* Appl. Dv (1885—1918).

NATEBY

Tp in Kirkby Stephen AP, sep CP 1866.[2] *LG* Seq 1. *Parl* Seq 1.

NATLAND

Chap (in ruins, rebuilt 1735[55]) in Kendal AP, sep CP 1866,[2] sep EP 1746.[3] *LG* Seq 2. Civ bdry: 1935.[18] *Parl* Seq 2. *Eccl* Kendal RDn.

NEWBIGGIN [ST EDMUND]

AP *LG* Seq 1. *Parl* Seq 1. *Eccl* Seq 1.

NEWBIGGIN-ON-LUNE—See following entry

NEWBIGGIN ST AIDAN

EP Cr 1893 from Ravenstonedale AP.[71] Appl. & Kirkby Stephen RDn (1893—1970), Appl. RDn (1970—*). Sometimes 'Newbiggin-on-Lune'.

NEWBY

Tp in Morland AP, sep CP 1866.[2] *LG* Seq 4. *Parl* Seq 1.

ORMSIDE

AP *LG* Seq 1. Civ bdry: 1883.[19] *Parl* Seq 1. *Eccl* Seq 1.

ORTON

AP Incl pt tp Fawcett Forest (sep CP 1866[2]), undivided pt Land Common to Orton AP and Crosby Ravensworth AP [abol 1935, pt to Orton AP, pt to Crosby Ravensworth AP, pt to Shap Rural CP[18]]), tp Tebay (sep EP 1884,[72] sep CP 1897[17]). *LG* Seq 1. Addtl civ bdry alt: 1935.[18] *Parl* Seq 1. *Eccl* Seq 3.

PATTERDALE

Chap in Barton AP, sep CP 1866,[2] sep EP 1743,[3] eccl refounded 1866.[20] *LG* West Wd, West Ward PLU, RSD, RD (1894—1935), Lakes UD (1935—74). *Parl* Seq 1. *Eccl* Westm RDn (1743—1859), Greystoke RDn (1859—82), Penr. West RDn (1882—1926), Penr. RDn (1926—*).

PATTON

Tp in Kendal AP, sep CP 1866,[2] eccl severed 1871 to help cr Skelsmergh EP.[64] *LG* Seq 2. *Parl* Seq 2.

POOLEY BRIDGE

EP Cr 1905 from Barton AP.[21] Penr. West RDn (1905—26), Penr. RDn (1926—*).

PRESTON PATRICK

Tp in Barton AP, sep CP 1866,[1] EP 1722.[3] *LG* Seq 2. *Parl* Seq 2. *Eccl* Kendal RDn (1722—1859), Kirkby Lonsd. RDn (1859—1970), Kendal RDn (1970—*). Eccl bdry: 1873.[49]

PRESTON RICHARD

Tp in Heversham AP, sep CP 1866.[2] *LG* Seq 2. *Parl* Seq 2.

RAVENSTONEDALE

AP LG Seq 1. *Parl* Seq 1. *Eccl* Seq 2. Eccl bdry: 1893 (cr Newbiggin St Aidan EP).[71]

RYDAL

Chap in Grasmere AP (orig chap in Kendal AP, sep par at Reformation[1]), sep EP 1826,[3] eccl refounded 1886[38]; area of chap incl in but smaller than tp Rydal and Loughrigg (the latter a sep CP 1866,[2] qv in following entry). *Eccl* Kendal RDn (1826—59), Ambles. RDn (1859—1970), Winderm. RDn (1970—*). Eccl bdry: 1940.[50]

RYDAL AND LOUGHRIGG

Tp in Gramere AP (orig chap in Kendal AP, sep par at Reformation[1]) incl chap Rydal (sep CP 1866,[2] sep EP 1826 from pt of this tp,[3] eccl refounded 1886,[38] qv in prev entry). *LG* Kendal Wd, PLU, pt Grasm. USD (1875—83), Kendal RSD (pt 1875—83, ent 1883—94), S Westm RD (1894—1935), Lakes UD (1935—74). Bdry: 1883,[19] 1886.[5] *Parl* Seq 1.

SCALTHWAITERIGG

CP Cr 1897 from Scalthwaiterigg, Hay and Hutton in the Hay CP.[52] *LG* Kendal PLU, S Westm RD. Bdry: 1919,[58] 1935.[18]

SCALTHWAITERIGG, HAY AND HUTTON IN THE HAY

Tp in Kendal AP, sep CP 1866,[2] pt eccl severed 1871 to help cr Skelsmergh CP.[52] *LG* Kendal Wd, PLU, RSD, S Westm RD. Bdry: 1883,[19] 1886.[35] Abol 1897 pt to cr Scalthwaiterigg CP, pt to New Hutton CP.[52] *Parl* Kendal Dv (1885—1918).

SEDGWICK

Tp in Heversham AP, sep CP 1866,[2] eccl in chap Crosscake in same par (sep EP 1756,[3] eccl refounded 1877[33]). *LG* Seq 2. *Parl* Seq 2.

SELSIDE

Chap in Kendal AP, built just before augmentation,[54] sep EP (incl tp Fawcett Forest) 1772[3]; for civ see 'Whitwell and Selside', 'Fawcett Forest'. Kendal RDn.

SHAP

AP Incl chap Mardale (sep EP 1748[3]), chap Swindale (sep EP 1744[3]). *LG* West Wd, West Ward PLU, RSD, RD. Abol civ 1905, the pt constituted Shap UD to cr Shap Urban CP, the remainder to cr Shap Rural CP.[74] *Parl* Appl. Dv (1885—1918). *Eccl* Westm RDn (until 1859), Lowther RDn (1859—1929). Abol eccl 1929 to help cr Shap with Swindale EP.[73]

CP Renaming 1935 of Shap Urban CP.[18] *LG* N Westm RD.

SHAP RURAL

CP Cr 1905 from the pt of Shap AP not constituted Shap UD.[74] *LG* West Ward PLU, RD (1905—35), N Westm RD (1935—74).

SHAP URBAN

CP Cr 1905 from the pt of Shap AP constituted Shap UD.[74] *LG* West Wd PLU, Shap UD. Renamed 1935 'Shap' CP.[18]

SHAP WITH SWINDALE

EP Cr 1929 by union Shap AP, Swindale EP.[20] Lowther RDn (1929—70), Appl. RDn (1970—*).

SKELSMERGH

Chap & tp in Kendal AP, sep CP 1866,[2] eccl incl area tp Patton, 'Skelsmergh' a sep EP 1871 by union Skelsmergh, Patton, pt tp Scalthwaiterigg, Hay and Hutton in the Hay, all in Kendal AP.[64] *LG* Seq 2. Civ bdry: 1935.[18] *Parl* Seq 2. *Eccl* Kendal RDn. Eccl bdry: 1872,[60] 1960.[61]

SLEAGILL
Tp in Morland AP, sep CP 1866.[2] LG Seq 4. Bdry: 1888.[23] Parl Seq 1.

SMARDALE
Chap & tp in Kirkby Stephen AP, sep CP 1866.[2] LG East Wd, East Wd PLU, RSD. Abol 1894 ent to Waitby CP.[6] Parl Appl. Dv (1885—1918).

SOCKBRIDGE
Tp in Barton AP, sep CP 1866.[2] Incl undivided pt Barton Fell (orig in Barton AP, from 1866—94 common to High Barton CP and Sockbridge CP, from 1894—1935 common to Sockbridge CP and Barton CP, abol 1935 ent to Barton CP[18]). LG Seq 4. Addtl bdry alt: 1883,[19] 1888.[23] Parl Seq 1.

SOULBY
Tp and chap (built 1663[65]) in Kirkby Stephen AP, sep CP 1866,[2] sep EP 1766,[3] eccl refounded 1874.[66] LG Seq 1. Parl Seq 1. Eccl Westm RDn (1766—1859), Kirkby Stephen RDn (1859—82), Appl. & Kirkby Stephen RDn (1882—1970), Appl. RDn (1970—*).

BROUGH SOWERBY
Tp in Brough AP, sep CP 1866.[2] LG Seq 1. Bdry: 1883.[19] Parl Seq 1.

TEMPLE SOWERBY
Chap in Kirkby Thore AP, sep CP 1866,[2] sep EP 1753.[3] LG Seq 1. Parl Seq 1. Eccl Westm RDn (1753—1859), Appl. RDn (1859—82), Appl. & Kirkby Stephen RDn (1882—1970), Appl. RDn (1970—*).

STAINMORE
Chap in Brough AP, sep CP 1866,[2] sep EP 1721.[3] LG Seq 1. Civ bdry: 1883.[19] Parl Seq 1. Eccl Westm RDn (1721—1859), Kirkby Stephen RDn (1859—82), Appl. & Kirkby Stephen RDn (1882—1970), Appl. RDn (1970—73). Abol 1973 to help cr Brough with Stainmore EP.[27]

STAINTON
Chap (in ruins from Dissolution[48]) in Heversham AP, sep CP 1866.[2] LG Seq 2. Parl Seq 2.

STAVELEY
Chap in Kendal AP, sep CP 1866,[2] sep EP 1723 (incl areas chap Hugill, tps Nether Staveley, Over Staveley [qv for sep civ identities]),[3] eccl refounded 1929.[28] Kendal RDn. Eccl bdry: 1732 (area Hughill [sometimes called 'Ings'] severed to cr 'Hughill' EP, qv for refounding later as 'Ings').[28]

NETHER STAVELEY
Tp in Kendal AP, sep CP 1866,[2] eccl incl in chap/EP Staveley (qv in prev entry). LG Seq 2. Bdry: 1951.[32] Parl Seq 2.

OVER STAVELEY
Organisation as for Nether Staveley, but no bdry alt 1951.

GREAT STRICKLAND
Tp in Morland AP, sep CP 1866,[2] eccl in chap Thrimby in that par, eccl severed 1741 to help cr Thrimby EP,[3] the latter eccl refounded 1870.[70] LG Seq 4. Parl Seq 1.

LITTLE STRICKLAND
Organisation as for Great Strickland.

STRICKLAND KETEL
Tp in chap Burneside (sep EP 1722 from Kendal AP,[3] eccl refounded 1929[28]), 'Strickland Ketel' a sep CP 1866.[2] LG Seq 2. Bdry: 1883,[19] 1935,[18] 1951.[32] Parl Seq 2.

STRICKLAND ROGER
Organisation as for Strickland Ketel, except bdry alt only in 1883.[19]

SWINDALE
Chap in Shap AP, sep EP 1744.[3] Westm RDn (1744—1859), Lowther RDn (1859—1929). Abol 1929 to help cr Shap with Swindale EP.[73]

TEBAY
Tp in Orton AP, sep CP 1897,[17] sep EP 1884.[72] LG East Wd, East Wd PLU, RSD, E Westm RD (1897—1935), N Westm RD (1935—74). Civ bdry: 1935.[18] Eccl Lowther RDn (1884—1970), Appl. RDn (1970—*).

THRIMBY
Chap (anc chap rebuilt late 17th cent[69]) and tp in Morland AP, sep CP 1866,[2] sep EP 1741 (incl tps Great Strickland, Little Strickland in same par).[3] LG Seq 4. Parl Seq 1. Eccl Westm RDn (1741—1859), Lowther RDn (1859—1970), Appl. RDn (1970—*).

TROUTBECK
Chap (consecr 1562[11]) in Windermere AP (orig in Kendal AP, sep par at Reformation[54]), sep CP 1866,[2] sep EP 1747 (incl tp Applethwaite in same par),[3] eccl refounded 1856,[12] eccl refounded 1882 from most of orig area of Troutbeck, pt orig area Applethwaite.[13] LG Seq 1. Civ bdry: 1935.[18] Parl Seq 1. Eccl Kendal RDn (1747—1859), Ambles. RDn (1859—1970), Winderm. RDn (1970—*).

UNDERBARROW
Chap (anc chap rebuilt 1708[57]) in Kendal AP, sep EP 1725[3] excluding area Bradleyfield, eccl refounded 1929,[28] civ incl Bradleyfield and as 'Underbarrow and Bradleyfield' a sep CP 1866,[2] qv. Eccl Kendal RDn.

UNDERBARROW AND BRADLEYFIELD
Chap (anc chap rebuilt 1708[57]) in Kendal AP, sep EP 1725[3] excluding area Bradleyfield (see prev entry), civ incl Bradleyfield and sep CP 1866.[2] LG Seq 2. Bdry: 1935,[18] 1951.[32] Parl Seq 2.

UNDERMILLBECK
Tp pt in Windermere AP (sep par at Reformation from Kendal AP[54]), pt in Kendal AP, sep CP 1866.[2] LG Kendal Wd, PLU, pt Bown. on Winderm. USD, pt Kendal RSD, S Westm RD. Bdry: 1894 (loses the pt in the USD to help cr Bowness on Windermere CP).[6] Abol 1935 pt to Winderm. UD & Bowness on Windermere CP, pt to Crook CP.[18] Parl Appl. Dv (1885—1918).

WAITBY
Tp in Kirkby Stephen AP, sep CP 1866.[2] LG Seq 1. Bdry: 1894 (gains Smardale CP).[6] Parl Seq 1.

WARCOP
AP LG Seq 1. Civ bdry: 1883.[19] Parl Seq 1. Eccl Seq 2.

WHARTON
Tp in Kirkby Stephen AP, sep CP 1866.[2] LG Seq 1. Parl Seq 1.

WHINFELL
Tp in Kendal AP, sep CP 1866.[2] LG Seq 2. Bdry: 1935.[18] Parl Seq 2.

WHITWELL AND SELSIDE

Tp and chap (erected just before augmention[54]) in Kendal AP, sep EP 1772 as 'Selside',[3] sep CP 1866 as 'Whitwell and Selside'.[2] *LG* Seq 2. *Parl* Seq 2.

LOW WINDER

Tp in Barton AP, sep CP 1866.[2] *LG* West Wd, W Ward PLU, RSD. Bdry: 1883,[19] 1888.[23] Abol 1894 to help cr Barton CP.[6] *Parl* Appl. Dv (1885—1918).

WINDERMERE

AP Orig chap in Kendal AP, sep par at Reformation.[54] Incl pt chap Ambleside (sep sep CP 1866,[2] sep EP 1746,[3] eccl refounded 1863[4]), chap Troutbeck (sep CP 1866,[2] sep EP 1747 [incl tp Applethwaite][3]), chap Winster (orig one chap with chap Crook in Kendal AP, 'Winster' a sep EP 1718[3]), tp Applethwaite (sep CP 1866,[2] eccl in chap/EP Troutbeck, qv above,[3] 'Applethwaite' a sep EP 1836 from Troutbeck EP,[3] eccl refounded 1856[12]), pt tp Undermillbeck (sep CP 1866[2]) so that 'Windermere' has no sep civ identity 1866—94 (see following entry). *LG* Kendal Wd. *Eccl* Seq 4. Addtl eccl bdry alt: 1888 (help cr Windermere St John EP).[14]

CP Cr 1894 from the pt of Applethwaite CP in Winderm. UD.[6] *LG* Kendal PLU, Winderm. UD. Bdry: 1935.[18]

WINDERMERE ST JOHN

EP Cr 1888 from Windermere AP, Applethwaite EP.[14] Ambles. RDn (1888—1970), Winderm. RDn (1970—*).

WINDERMERE ST MARY

EP Name used now for EP cr 1836 as 'Applethwaite', qv.

WINSTER

Area in Windermere AP (sep par at Reformation from Kendal AP[54]), orig one chap with chap and tp Crook in Kendal AP, 'Winster' a sep EP 1718.[3] Kendal RDn.

WINTON

Tp in Kirkby Stephen AP, sep CP 1866.[2] *LG* Seq 1. Bdry: 1883,[19] 1911 (areas determined and altered for this par and for Westm pars of Hartley CP, Keber CP, and for Yorks N Riding par of Muker CP).[44] *Parl* Seq 1.

WITHERSLACK

Chap and tp in Beetham AP, sep CP 1866,[2] sep EP 1748 (incl tp Meathop and Ulpha),[3] eccl refounded 1891.[24] *LG* Seq 2. *Parl* Seq 2. *Eccl* Kendal RDn (1748—1859), Kirkby Lonsd. RDn (1859—1919), Kendal RDn (1919—*). Eccl bdry: 1918.[68]

YANWATH AND EAMONT BRIDGE

Tp in Barton AP, sep CP 1866.[2] *LG* Seq 4. *Parl* Seq 1.

WORCESTERSHIRE

ABBREVIATIONS

Abbreviations particular to Worcs follow. Those general abbreviations in use throughout the *Guide* are found on pages xvii—xix.

Alc.	Alcester
Bewd.	Bewdley
Black.	Blackenhurst
Bord.	Bordesley
Bromsgr.	Bromsgrove
Bromyd.	Bromyard
Burf.	Burford
Cleob. Mort.	Cleobury Mortimer
Dodd.	Doddingtree
Droitw.	Droitwich
Edgb.	Edgbaston
Evesh.	Evesham
Feck.	Feckenham
Halfsh.	Halfshire
Handsw.	Handsworth
Harb.	Harborne
K's Nort.	King's Norton
Kidderm.	Kidderminster
Kinet.	Kineton
Lindr.	Lindridge
Malv.	Malvern
Northf.	Northfield
Oldb.	Oldbury
Osw.	Oswaldslow
Persh.	Pershore
Sev.	Severn
Smethw.	Smethwick
Solih.	Solihull
Stourbr.	Stourbridge
Stourpt.	Stourport
Stratf.	Stratford
Swinf.	Swinford
Tenb.	Tenbury
Tewksb.	Tewksbury
Winch.	Winchcomb
Yard.	Yardley

SEQUENCES

An abbreviated entry prefixed by 'Seq' is used in the parochial entries to avoid repeating often the names of superior units of administration. The content of each sequence is shown below.

Local Government Sequences ('LG')

SEQ 1   Black. Hd, Eveshm. PLU, RSD, RD

SEQ 2   Dodd. Hd, Cleob. Mort. PLU, RSD, Rock RD (1894—1933), Tenb. RD (1933—74)

SEQ 3   Dodd. Hd, Martley PLU, RSD, RD

SEQ 4   Dodd. Hd, Tenb. PLU, RSD, RD

SEQ 5   Halfsh. Hd, Bromsgr. PLU, RSD, RD

SEQ 6   Halfsh. Hd, Droitw. PLU, RSD, RD

SEQ 7   Halfsh. Hd, Kidderm. PLU, RSD, RD

SEQ 8   Osw. Hd, Bromsgr. PLU, RSD, RD

SEQ 9   Osw. Hd, Droitw. PLU, RSD, RD

SEQ 10   Osw. Hd, Evesh. PLU, RSD, RD

SEQ 11   Osw. Hd, Martley PLU, RSD, RD

SEQ 12   Osw. Hd, Persh. PLU, RSD, RD

SEQ 13   Osw. Hd, Tenb. PLU, RSD, RD

SEQ 14   Osw. Hd, Tewksb. PLU, RSD, RD (1894—1933), Evesh. RD (1933—74)

SEQ 15   Osw. Hd, Tewksb. PLU, RSD, RD (1894—1933), Persh. RD (1933—74)

SEQ 16 Osw. Hd, Upton upon Sev. PLU, RSD, RD
SEQ 17 Persh. Hd, PLU, RSD, RD
SEQ 18 Persh. Hd, Martley PLU, RSD, RD (1894—1936), Blaby RD (1936—74)
SEQ 19 Persh. Hd, Upton upon Sev. PLU, RSD, RD

Parliamentary Sequences ('Parl')

SEQ 1 E'rn Dv (1832—1918), Kidderm. Dv (1918—48), Bromsgr. CC (1948—70), Bromsgr. & Redditch CC (1970—*).

SEQ 2 E'rn Dv (1832—85), N'rn Dv (1885—1918), Stourbr. Dv (1918—48), Oldb. & Halesowen BC (1948—70), Halesowen & Stourbr. BC (1970—*)

SEQ 3 E'rn Dv (1832—85), S'rn Dv (1885—1918), Evesh. Dv (1918—48), S Worcs CC (1948—*).

SEQ 4 E'rn Dv (1832—85), W'rn Dv (1885—1918), Evesh. Dv (1918—48), S Worcs CC (1948—*)

SEQ 5 W'rn Dv (1832—1918), Bewd. Dv (1918—48), Kidderm. CC (1948—*)

SEQ 6 W'rn Dv (1832—1918), Bewd. Dv (1918—48), S Worcs CC (1948—*)

SEQ 7 W'rn Dv (1832—1918), Evesh. Dv (1918—48), Worc BC (1948—*)

SEQ 8 W'rn Dv (1832—1918), Evesh. Dv (1918—48), S Worcs CC (1948—*)

SEQ 9 W'rn Dv (1832—85), Mid Dv (1885—1918), Kidderm. Dv/CC (1918—*)

SEQ 10 W'rn Dv (1832—85), Mid Dv (1885—1918), Kidderm. Dv (1918—48), Bromsgr. CC (1948—70), Bromsgr. & Redditch CC (1970—*)

SEQ 11 W'rn Dv (1832—85), Mid Dv (1885—1918), Stourbr. Dv (1918—48), Dudley BC (1948—70), Halesowen & Stourbr. BC (1970—*)

SEQ 12 W'rn Dv (1832—85), S'rn Dv (1885—1918), Bewd. Dv (1918—48), S Worcs CC (1948—*)

SEQ 13 Droitw. Parl Bor (1832—85), Mid Dv (1885—1918), Evesh. Dv (1918—48), Worc BC (1948—*)

SEQ 14 Droitw. Parl Bor (1832—85), W'rn Dv (1885—1918), Evesh. Dv (1918—48), Worc BC (1948—*)

Ecclesiastical Sequences ('Eccl')

Orig Worc dioc:

SEQ 1 Droitw. RDn
SEQ 2 Droitw. RDn (until 1892), Bromsgr. RDn (1892—*)
SEQ 3 Droitw. RDn (until 1880), Northf. RDn (1880—92), Bromsgr. RDn (1892—*)
SEQ 4 Evesh. RDn
SEQ 5 Kidderm. RDn
SEQ 6 Kidderm. RDn (until 1907), Swinf. RDn (1907—73), Stourbr. RDn (1974—*)
SEQ 7 Persh. RDn
SEQ 8 Persh. RDn (until 1861), Bredon RDn (1861—1973), Persh. RDn (1974—*)
SEQ 9 Persh. RDn (until 1861), Bredon RDn (1861—1973), Upton RDn (1974—*)
SEQ 10 Persh. RDn (until 1861), Evesh. RDn (1861—*)
SEQ 11 Persh. RDn (until 1907), Feck. RDn (1907—73), Persh. RDn (1974—*)
SEQ 12 Persh. RDn (until 1862), Feck. RDn (1962—73), Persh. RDn (1974—*)
SEQ 13 Persh. RDn (until before 1535), Powyke RDn (before 1535—1861), Upton RDn (1861—*)
SEQ 14 Powyke RDn (until 1973), Malv. RDn (1974—*)
SEQ 15 Powyke RDn (until 1861), Upton RDn (1861—*)
SEQ 16 Worc RDn (until 1861), Worc West RDn (1861—1921), Martley RDn (1921—73), Martley & Worc West RDn (1974—*)
SEQ 17 Worc RDn (until 1861), Worc West RDn (1861—1921), Mitton RDn (1921—73), Stourpt. RDn (1974—*)
SEQ 18 Worc RDn (until 1861), Worc West RDn (1861—1921), Outer Worc RDn (1921—26), Martley RDn (1926—73), Martley & Worc West RDn (1974—*)

Orig Heref dioc:

SEQ 19 Burf. RDn (until 1878), Burf. (East) RDn (1878—98), Bewd. RDn (1898—1926), Kidderm. RDn (1926—*)
SEQ 20 Burf. RDn (until 1878), Burf. (East) RDn (1878—98), Bewd. RDn (1898—1926), Lindr. RDn (1926—73), Stourpt. RDn (1974—*)

DIOCESES AND ARCHDEACONRIES

Worcs pars were organised in Archdeaconries and Rural Deaneries as follows:

BIRMINGHAM DIOC (1905—*)
Aston AD (1906—):* Bord. RDn, Coleshill RDn (1957—*), Solih. RDn, Yard. RDn (1957—*)
Birmingham AD: Bord. RDn (1905—06), Edgb. RDn (1957—*), Harb. RDn (1905—29), K's Nort. RDn, Moseley RDn (1957—*), Northf. RDn (1905), Smethw. RDn (1929—66), Solih. RDn (1905—06), Warley RDn (1966—*)

COVENTRY DIOC (1918—*)
Warwick AD: S Kinet. RDn (1918—21), Shipston RDn (1921—*)

GLOUCESTER DIOC (1919—*)
Glouc AD: Campden RDn (1919—*), Glouc North RDn (1952—*), Stow RDn (1919—*), Tewk. RDn (1919—*)

HEREFORD DIOC
> *Hereford AD:* Bromyd. RDn (1919—*), Ledb. RDn (1905—*)
>
> *Ludlow AD (1876—1919):* Bewd. RDn (1898—1919), Burf. RDn (1876—78), Burf. (East) RDn (1878—98), Burf. (West) RDn (1878—98)
>
> *Salop AD (until 1876):* Burf. RDn, Stottesden RDn (until 1840s)

OXFORD DIOC (1919—*)
Oxford AD: Chipping Norton RDn (1919—*)

WORCESTER DIOC
> *Dudley AD (1921—*):* Bewd. RDn (1921—26), Bromsgr. RDn, Droitw. RDn, Dudley RDn, Kidderm. RDn, Lindr. RDn (1926—73), Mitton RDn (1921—73), Stourbr. RDn (1974—*), Stourpt. RDn (1974—*), Swinf. RDn (1921—73)

Worcester AD: Alc. RDn (1861—1910), Bewd. RDn (1919—21), Blockley RDn (until 1918), Bredon RDn (1861—1973), Bromsgr. RDn (1892—1921), Droitw. RDn (until 1921), Dudley RDn (1880—1921), Evesh. RDn, Feck. RDn (1861—1910), Feck. RDn (1919—73), Kidderm. RDn (until 1921), Kinet. RDn (until 1861), S Kinet. RDn (1861—1918), Malv. RDn (1974—*), Martley RDn (1921—73), Martley & Worc West RDn (1974—*), Mitton RDn (1921—73), Northf. RDn (1880—92), Persh. RDn (until 1910), Powyke RDn (until 1973), Stourpt. RDn (1974—*), Swinf. RDn (1907—73), Upton RDn (1861—*), Worc RDn (until 1861), Worc RDn (1926—73), Inner Worc RDn (1921—26), Outer Worc RDn (1921—26), Worc East RDn (1861—1921), Worc East RDn (1974—*), Worc West RDn (1861—1921)

THE PARISHES OF WORCESTERSHIRE

Worcs pars (except those noted below as transf to help cr W Midlands Metrop Co)
transf 1974 to help cr Hereford & Worcester Non-Metrop Co

ABBERLEY
AP *LG* Seq 3. Civ bdry: 1884,[1] 1885.[2] *Parl* Seq 5. *Eccl* Burf. RDn (until 1878), Burf. (East) RDn (1878—98), Bewd. RDn (1898—1926), Mitton RDn (1926—73), Stourpt. RDn (1974—*).

ABBERTON
AP *LG* Seq 17. *Parl* Seq 3. *Eccl* Seq 11.

ABBOTS MORTON
AP *LG* Black. Hd, Alc. PLU, RSD, Feck. RD (1894—1933), Evesh. RD (1933—74). *Parl* Seq 3. *Eccl* Persh. RDn (until 1861), Feck. RDn (1861—1957). Abol eccl 1957 to help cr Rous Lench and Abbots Morton EP.[3]

ACOCKS GREEN
EP Cr 1867 from Yardley AP.[4] Kidderm. RDn (1867—80), Northf. RDn (1880—1905), Solih. RDn (1905—57), Yard. RDn (1957—*). Bdry: 1907,[5] 1913,[6] 1931 (help cr Tyseley EP),[7] 1966,[8] 1972.[9]

ACTON BEAUCHAMP
AP *LG* Dodd. Hd, Bromyd. PLU, RSD, RD. Transf 1897 to Heref.[10] *Parl* W'rn Dv (1832—1918). *Eccl* Powyke RDn (until 1919), Bromyd. RDn (dioc Heref, 1919—*).

ALDERMINSTER
AP *LG* Persh. Hd, Stratf. on Avon PLU, RSD, Shipst. on Stour RD. Transf 1931 to Warws.[11] *Parl* E'rn Dv (1832—85), S'rn Dv (1885—1918), Evesh. Dv (1918—48). *Eccl* Kinet. RDn (until 1861), N Kinet. RDn (1861—1921), Kinet. RDn (1921—63), Stratf. on Avon RDn (1963—*)

ALDINGTON
Hmlt in Badsey AP, sep CP 1866.[12] *LG* Seq 1. Bdry: 1921,[13] 1933.[14] *Parl* Seq 3.

ALFRICK
Chap in Suckley AP, sep CP 1866,[12] eccl severed 1912 to help cr Alfrick and Lulsey EP.[15] *LG* Seq 3. Civ bdry: 1884,[16] 1894.[17] *Parl* Seq 5.

ALFRICK AND LULSEY
EP Cr 1912 by union chap Alfrick, chap Lulsey, both in Suckley AP.[15] Powyke RDn (1912—21), Outer Worc RDn (1921—26), Martley RDn (1926—73), Martley & Worc West RDn (1974—*).

ALLENS CROSS
EP Cr 1938 from Northfield AP, Rubery EP.[18] K's Nort. RDn. Bdry: 1965.[19]

ALVECHURCH
AP *LG* Alvechurch Bor, Seq 8. Civ bdry: 1930,[20] 1933,[14] 1966 (incl loses pt to Birm CB [assoc with Warws] & AP).[21] *Parl* E'rn Dv (1832—1918), Kidderm. Dv (1918—48), Bromsgr. CC (1948—70), Bromsgr. & Redditch CC (1970—*). *Eccl* Droitw. RDn (until 1880), Northf. RDn (1880—92), Bromsgr. RDn (1892—*). Eccl bdry: 1853 (help refound Withyall EP),[22] 1913 (loses pt to The Lickey EP, dioc Birm).[23]

AMBLECOTE
Hmlt (Staffs, S Seisdon Hd) in Oldswinford AP (o'wise ent Worcs, Halfsh. Hd; eccl, 'Old Swinford'), sep CP 1866 in Staffs[12] and Oldswinford ent Worcs thereafter, sep EP 1845 from Old Swinford AP (incl area Worcs tp Wollaston),[24] eccl refounded 1860.[25] For civ and for organisation in RDns, see entry in Staffs. Eccl bdry: 1860 (area of tp Wollaston eccl severed to cr Wollaston EP).[26]

ARELEY KINGS
AP Orig chap in Martley AP, sep par by 1535 although 17th cent references to its continued dependence.[27] *LG* Dodd. Hd, Martley PLU, RSD, RD. Civ bdry: 1920.[28] Abol civ 1933 pt to Astley AP, pt to Stourpt. UD & CP.[14] *Parl* W'rn Dv (1832—1918), Bewd. Dv (1918—48). *Eccl* Worc RDn (until 1861), Worc West RDn (1861—1921), Mitton RDn (1921—*).

ARLEY
AP Usual eccl spelling for Staffs par transf civ 1895 to Worcs[27]; for RDns see entry in Staffs, and for civ and parl organisation in Worcs after 1895, see following entry.

UPPER ARLEY
AP Usual civ spelling for Staffs par transf civ 1895 to Worcs[29]; for eccl see prev entry. *LG* Kidderm. PLU, RD. Civ bdry: 1933.[14] *Parl* Kidderm. Dv/CC (1918—*).

ASHTON UNDER HILL
CP Glos par transf 1931 to Worcs.[11] *LG* Evesh. RD. Bdry: 1965 (gains pt Dumbleton AP, Glos).[21] *Parl* S Worcs CC (1948—*).

ASTLEY
AP *LG* Seq 3. Civ bdry: 1933,[14] 1953.[30] *Parl* Seq 5. *Eccl* Seq 17.

ASTON MAGNA
Hmlt in Blockley AP, sep EP 1747.[31] Blockley RDn (1747—1921), Campden RDn (dioc Glouc, 1921—*).

ASTON SOMERVILLE
AP Glos par transf 1931 to Worcs.[11] *LG* Evesh. RD. *Parl* S Worcs CC (1948—*). *Eccl* See entry in Glos.

ASTWOOD BANK WITH CRABBS CROSS
EP Cr 1950 from Feckenham AP (Worcs), Headless Cross EP (Worcs, Warws).[32] Bromsgr. RDn.

BADSEY
AP Orig chap to Evesh. Abbey, sep par from Dissolution.[33] Incl hmlt Aldington (sep CP 1866,[12] not sep eccl hence this par eccl 'Badsey with Aldington', qv). *LG* Seq 1. Addtl civ bdry alt: 1921,[13] 1933,[14] 1949.[34] *Parl* Seq 3.

BADDSEY WITH ALDINGTON
AP Usual eccl spelling; for civ and civ sep hmlt, see prev entry. *Eccl* Seq 4. Eccl bdry: 1967.[35]

BALSALL HEATH
EP Cr 1853 [St Paul] from Kings Norton EP.[22] Droitw. RDn (1853—80), Northf. RDn (1880—1905), K's Nort. RDn (1905—57), Moseley RDn (1957—*). Bdry: 1884 (cr Balsall Heath St Thomas in the Moors EP),[36] 1900 (help cr Bordesley St Patrick EP [Warws, Worcs]),[37] 1905 (cr Balsall Heath St Barnabas EP),[38] 1973.[39]

BALSALL HEATH ST BARNABAS
EP Cr 1905 from Balsall Heath EP.[38] RDns as for Balsall Heath, from 1905.

BALSALL HEATH ST THOMAS IN THE MOORS
EP Cr 1884 from Balsall Heath EP.[36] RDns as for Balsall Heath, 1884—1958. Bdry: 1900 (help cr Bordesley St Patrick EP [Warws, Worcs]).[37] Abol 1958 pt to Edgbaston St Mary and St Ambrose EP, Warws, pt to Moseley St Anne EP, Worcs.[18]

BARBOURNE
EP Cr 1862 from Claines EP,[40] refounded 1863.[41] E Worc RDn (1862—1921), Inner Worc RDn (1921—26), Worc RDn (1926—73), Worc East RDn (1974—*).

BARNT GREEN
EP Cr 1922 from The Lickey EP.[42] K's Nort. RDn.

BARTLEY GREEN
EP Cr 1956 from Weoley Castle EP.[43] K's Nort. RDn. (1956—57), Edgb. RDn (1957—*).

BATSFORD
AP Pt Glos (Kiftsgate Hd), pt Worcs (Osw. Hd). *LG* Shipston on Stour PLU, RSD, pt sep RD in Worcs (1894—96). Civ bdry: 1896 (the par made ent Glos).[44] *Parl* Worcs pt, E'rn Dv (1832—85), W'rn Dv (1885—1918). For remainder and eccl organisation, see entry in Glos.

BAYTON
AP *LG* Seq 2. Civ bdry: 1877.[45] *Parl* W'rn Dv (1832—1918), Bewd. Dv (1918—48), Kidderm. CC (1948—*). *Eccl* Burf. RDn. Abol eccl 1669 to help cr Mamble with Bayton EP.[46]

BECKFORD
AP Glos par transf 1931 to Worcs.[11] *LG* Winch. RD (1931—33), Evesh. RD (1933—74). Civ bdry: 1965 (exchanges pts with Teddington AP, gains pt Ashchurch AP, gains pt Dumbleton AP, all Glos).[21] *Parl* S Worcs CC (1948—*). *Eccl* See entry for 'Beckford with Ashton under Hill' in entries for Glos.

BEDWARDINE ST JOHN
AP Orig chap in Wick Episcopi (the latter orig a chap in Worcester St Helen AP, sep par 1283), Wick Episcopi abandoned and Bedwardine St John (eccl, 'Worcester St John the Baptist, Bedwardine') consecr 1371 as the par church.[47] *LG* Osw. Hd, Worc PLU, pt Worc MB (1835—89 [enlarged pt 1885—89]), pt Worc CB (1889—94), pt Worc USD (enlarged pt 1885—94), pt Worc RSD (reduced pt 1885—94). Abol civ 1894 the pt in the CB cr Worcester St John Bedwardine City CP, the remainder cr Worcester St John Bedwardine County CP.[48] *Parl* Pt Worc Parl Bor (1832—1918 [enlarged pt 1867—1918]), pt W'rn Dv (1832—1918).

BEDWARDINE ST MICHAEL
AP Incl Bishop's Palace and Cathedral churchyard (pec jurisd Dean & Chapter of Worc, the greater pt of the latter transf eccl 1910 to Worcester St Helen AP[49]). *LG* In the Cathedral lbty in Worc and not in the Bor, Worc PLU, MB (1835—89), CB (1889—98), USD. Abol civ 1898 to help cr Worcester CP.[50] *Parl* Worc Parl Bor (1832—1918). *Eccl* Worc RDn (until 1861), Worc East RDn (1861—1921), Inner Worc RDn (1921—26), Worc RDn (1926—*).

BELBROUGHTON
AP *LG* Seq 5. Civ bdry: 1933.[14] *Parl* Seq 10. *Eccl* Seq 6.

BENGEWORTH
AP Sometimes 'Evesham St Peter, Bengeworth'. Orig chap to Evesh. Abbey, sep par early. *LG* Blackh. Hd, Evesh. PLU, MB (from 1605), USD. Abol civ 1924 to help cr Evesham CP.[51] *Parl* Evesh. Parl Bor (1603—1885), S'rn Dv (1885—1918), Evesh. Dv (1918—48). *Eccl* Seq 4. Eccl bdry: 1967.[35]

BENTLEY PAUNCEFOOT
Tp (Worcs, Halfsh. Hd) in Tardebrigge AP (Worcs, Warws until 1844, ent Worcs thereafter), sep CP 1866.[12] *LG* Bromsgr. PLU (orig rated in Tardebrigge AP, sep rated soon after[52]—1930), RSD, RD. Bdry: 1933,[14] 1966.[50] *Parl* Seq 1.

BEOLEY

AP *LG* Persh. Hd, K's Nort. PLU (1836—1911), pt (uninhabited) Redditch USD, pt Kings Norton RSD, Kings Norton RD (1894—98), Bromsgr. PLU (1911—30), K's Nort. and Northf. UD (1898—1911), sep RD (administered by Bromsgr. RD Council, 1911—12), Bromsgr. RD (1912—74). Civ bdry: 1894 (the pt in the UD cr Unnamed CP),[53] 1966.[54] *Parl* Seq 1. *Eccl* Seq 3.

BERROW

AP Orig chap (pec jurisd Dean & Chapter of Worc) in Overbury AP, sep par by 1535.[55] *LG* Seq 16. Civ bdry: 1883.[56] *Parl* Seq 12. *Eccl* Seq 13. Eccl bdry: 1912 (help cr Hollybush EP [Worcs, Heref]),[57] 1964.[58]

BESFORD

Chap in Pershore St Andrew AP, sep CP 1866,[12] eccl severed 1865 to help cr Defford cum Besford EP.[59] *LG* Seq 17. *Parl* Seq 3.

BEWDLEY

Ex-par place sometimes considered in Staffs in 15th cent although usually considered in Worcs, status in Worcs confirmed by statute 1543,[60] made *temp* Henry VI a chap of Ribbesford AP,[61] sep CP 1866,[12] sep EP 1853.[62] *LG* Dodd. Hd, Bewd. Bor/ MB, Kidderm. PLU. Civ bdry: 1881,[1] 1933.[14] *Parl* W'rn Dv (1832—67), Bewd. Parl Bor (1867—85), W'rn Dv (1885—1918), Bewd. Dv (1918—48), Kidderm. CC (1948—*). *Eccl* Burf. RDn (1853—78), Burf. (East) RDn (1878—98), Bewd. RDn (1898—1926), Kidderm. RDn (1926—40). Abol eccl 1940 to help cr Ribbesford with Bewdley EP.[63]

BICKMARSH

CP Warws par transf 1931 to Worcs (after pt transf to Dorsington AP, Glos, as that enlarged par transf to Warws).[11] *LG* Evesh. RD. *Parl* S Worcs CC (1948—*).

BILLESLEY COMMON

EP Cr 1937 from Yardley Wood EP, Moseley St Agnes EP, Kings Heath EP.[64] K's Nort. RDn (1937—57), Moseley RDn (1957—*). Bdry: 1952,[65] 1962 (incl gains pt Shirley EP, Warws),[26] 1963.[66] Sometimes called 'Billesley Holy Cross'.

BIRLINGHAM

AP Orig chap in Nafford AP, Nafford early in ruins and Birlingham then the par church,[67] the par thereafter civ 'Birlingham', eccl 'Birlingham with Nafford', qv below. *LG* Seq 17. *Parl* Seq 3. *Eccl* Seq 7.

BIRLINGHAM WITH NAFFORD—see prev entry

BIRTSMORTON

AP *LG* Seq 19. *Parl* Seq 12. *Eccl* Seq 15. Eccl bdry: 1964.[58]

BISHAMPTON

AP *LG* Seq 12. *Parl* Seq 3. *Eccl* Seq 11.

BLACKHEATH

EP Cr 1869 from The Quinton EP, Halesowen AP (both Worcs), Rowley Regis EP (Staffs).[68] Kidderm. RDn (1869—80), Dudley RDn (1880—1919), Harb. RDn (1919—29), Smethw. RDn (1929—66), Warley RDn (1966—*). Bdry: 1959.[69]

BLOCKLEY

AP Tp 'Blockley' in Worcs (Osw. Hd) as was hmlt Aston Magna (sep EP 1747[31]; incl in Warws (Kington Hd) chap Stretton on the Fosse (some sep rights from 1351, completely indepdendent by end 14th cent[70]) and Blockley ent Worcs thereafter. *LG* Shipst. on Stour PLU, RSD, RD. Transf 1931 to Glos.[11] *Parl* E'rn Dv (1832—85), S'rn Dv (1885—1918), Evesh. Dv (1918—48). *Eccl* Blockley RDn (until 1919), Campden RDn (dioc Glouc, 1919—*).

BOCKLETON

AP Tp 'Bockleton' in Worcs (Dodd. Hd); incl in Heref (Broxash Hd) hmlt Hampton Charles (sep CP 1866 in Heref[12]) so that 'Bockleton' ent Worcs thereafter. *LG* Tenb. PLU, RSD, RD. Civ bdry: 1965 (gains pt Hatfield CP, Heref).[21] *Parl* Worcs pt, Seq 5. *Eccl* Burf. RDn (until 1878), Burf. (West) RDn (1878—98), Burf. RDn (1898—1972), Leominster RDn (1972—*)

BOURNVILLE

EP Cr 1926 from Selly Oak St Mary EP, Kings Norton EP, Cotteridge EP.[71] K's Nort. RDn (1926—57), Moseley RDn (1957—*). Bdry: 1933.[72]

BRADLEY

EP Cr 1862 from Fladbury AP.[73] Feck. RDn (1862—1973), Droitw. RDn (1974—*).

BRANDWOOD

EP Cr 1963 from Kings Norton EP, Hazelwell EP.[74] K's Nort. RDn.

BRANSFORD

Chap perhaps orig in Powick AP,[75] certainly later in Leigh AP, sep CP 1866 from the latter.[12] *LG* Seq 18. Bdry: 1884,[16] 1933.[14] *Parl* Seq 5.

BREDICOT

AP *LG* Seq 12. *Parl* Seq 8. *Eccl* Worc RDn (until 1861), Worc East RDn (1861—1921), Droitw. RDn (1921—27). Abol eccl 1927 to help cr Tibberton with Bredicot EP.[76]

BREDON

AP Incl chap Welland (sep par perhaps by 1300[77]), detached chap Cutsdean (sep CP 1866,[12] eccl severed 1912 and transf to Temple Guiting AP, Glos, to help cr Temple Guiting with Cutsdean EP[78]), chap Bredon's Norton (perhaps sep par by 1300,[77] sep status not sustained hence this par eccl 'Bredon with Bredon's Norton', qv, 'Bredon's Norton' a sep CP 1866[12]). *LG* Seq 15. Addtl civ bdry alt: 1966 (loses pt to Tewksbury MB & AP, Glos).[21] *Parl* Seq 3.

BREDON'S NORTON

Chap in Bredon AP, perhaps sep par by 1300,[77] sep status not sustained, 'Bredon's Norton' a sep CP 1866.[12] *LG* Seq 15. *Parl* Seq 3.

BREDON WITH BREDON'S NORTON

AP Usual eccl spelling; for chaps and their status, and for civ and parl organisation, see 'Bredon'. *Eccl* Seq 8. Addtl eccl bdry alt: 1964 (loses pt to Tewsbury Holy Trinity EP, Glos).[79]

BRETFORTON

AP *LG* Seq 1. Civ bdry: 1933.[14] *Parl* Seq 3. *Eccl* Seq 4.

BRICKLEHAMPTON

Chap in Pershore St Andrew AP, sep CP 1866,[12] eccl severed 1922 to help cr Elmley Castle with Bricklehampton EP.[80] *LG* Seq 17. *Parl* Seq 3.

BROADHEATH

EP Cr 1910 from Hallow EP; Worcester St John the

Baptist, Bredwardine AP; Wichenford AP.[81] W Worc RDn (1910—21), Outer Worc RDn (1921—26), Martley RDn (1926—73), Martley & Worc West RDn (1974—*).

CP Cr 1952 from Cotheridge AP, North Hallow CP, Worcester St John Bedwardine County CP.[82] *LG* Martley RD. *Parl* Kidderm. CC (1970—*).

BROADWAS
AP *LG* Seq 11. Civ bdry: 1884,[83] 1884.[16] *Parl* Seq 5. *Eccl* Pec jurisd Prior and Chapter of Worc (until 1851), Seq 18 thereafter.

BROADWATERS
EP Cr 1952 from Kidderminster AP, Wolverley AP, Kidderminster St George EP.[84] Kidderm. RDn.

BROADWAY
AP *LG* Broadway Bor, Persh. Hd, Evesh. PLU, RSD, RD. Civ bdry: 1933,[14] 1966 (gains pt Willersey AP, loses pt to Chipping Campden AP, both Glos).[21] *Parl* Seq 3. *Eccl* Campden RDn (until *ca* 1840), Evesh. RDn (*ca* 1840—*).

BROMSGROVE
AP Incl chap Grafton Manor (sep early 13th cent as expar,[85] sep CP 1858,[86] abol eccl 1908 to help cr Dodford EP[87]), chap Kings Norton (sep civ identity early, sep EP 1846[88]). *LG* Halfsh. Hd, Bromsgr. PLU, pt Bromsgr. Town USD, pt Bromsgr. Country USD, Bromsgr. Town UD (1894—96), Bromsgr. UD (1896—1974). Addtl civ bdry alt: 1880,[89] 1883,[56] 1894 (gains the pt in Bromsgr. Town UD of Grafton Manor CP, loses the pt in Bromsgr. Country UD to cr North Bromsgrove CP),[90] 1933 (incl gains Stoke in Bromsgrove CP).[14] *Parl* Seq 1. *Eccl* Seq 2. Addtl eccl bdry alt: 1755 (cr Wythall EP,[31] qv for constituent pars at refounding 1853), 1767 (cr Moseley EP,[31] refounded 1853 from Kings Norton EP[91]), 1844 (cr Catshill EP),[92] 1858 (help cr The Lickey EP),[93] 1875 (cr Bromsgrove All Saints EP).[94]

NORTH BROMSGROVE
CP Cr 1894 from the pt of Bromsgrove AP in Bromsgr. Country UD.[90] *LG* Bromsgr. PLU, Bromsgr. Country UD (1894—96), N Bromsgr. UD (1896—1933). Abol 1933 pt to Bromsgr. UD & AP, pt to Alvechurch AP, pt to Belbroughton AP, pt to help cr Dodford with Grafton CP, pt to Romsley CP, pt to Tutnall and Chobley CP.[14] *Parl* Kidderm. Dv (1918—48).

BROMSGROVE ALL SAINTS
EP Cr 1875 from Bromsgrove AP.[94] Droitw. RDn (1875—92), Bromsgr. RDn (1892—*). Bdry: 1913 (loses pt to The Lickey EP, dioc Birm).[21]

BROMSGROVE CHRIST CHURCH—see CATSHILL
BROOM
AP Staffs par (S Seisdon Hd) transf to Worcs 1832 for parl purposes, 1844 for civ purposes (Halfsh. Hd).[92] Usual civ spelling; for eccl and for civ after 1953, see following entry. *LG* Kidderm. PLU, RSD, RD. Reconstituted 1953 as 'Broome' CP when gains pt Chaddesley Corbett AP.[30] *Parl* W'rn Dv (1832—85), Mid Dv (1885—1918), Kidderm. Dv/CC (1918—70).

BROOME
AP Usual eccl spelling; for civ before 1953 and orig

status in Staffs, see prev entry. *Eccl* Seq 6.

CP Reconstitution 1953 of Broom AP when gains pt Chaddesley Corbett AP.[30] *LG* Kidderm. RD. *Parl* Kidderm. CC (1970—*).

BROUGHTON HACKETT
AP *LG* Seq 17. *Parl* Seq 4. *Eccl* Persh. RDn (until 1880s), E Worc RDn (1880s—1921), Outer Worc RDn (1921—26), Droitw. RDn (1926—34), Persh. RDn (1934—*).

BUSHLEY
Chap (Worcs, Persh. Hd) in Tewksbury AP (o'wise Glos, Tweskbury Hd), sep civ identity in Worcs (Tewksbury ent Glos thereafter), eccl donative, sep par no later than 1817.[31] *LG* Seq 19. Civ bdry: 1965 (gains pt Forthampton AP, Glos).[21] *Parl* Seq 12. *Eccl* Seq 15.

CAKEMORE
Tp (Salop, Brimstree Hd) in Halesowen AP (Worcs [Halfsh. Hd], Salop [Brimstree Hd] until 1844, ent Worcs thereafter), transf from Salop to Worcs 1832 for parl purposes, 1844 (Halfsh. Hd) for civ purposes,[95] sep CP 1866.[12] *LG* Stourbr. PLU, RSD, Halesowen RD. Abol 1919 to help cr Hill and Cakemore CP.[96] *Parl* E'rn Dv (1832—85), N'rn Dv (1885—1918), Stourbr. Dv (1918—48).

CASTLE MORTON—see following entry
CASTLEMORTON
Chap in Longdon AP, sep civ identity early, sep EP 1880 as 'Castle Morton'.[97] *LG* Seq 19. *Parl* Seq 12. *Eccl* Upton on Sev. RDn. Eccl bdry: 1912 (help cr Hollybush EP [Worcs, Heref]).[57]

CATSHILL
EP Cr 1844 from Bromsgrove AP.[92] Droitw. RDn (1844—92), Bromsgr. RDn (1892—*). Bdry: 1858 (help cr The Lickey EP),[93] 1908 (help cr Dodford EP),[85] 1913 (exchanges pts with The Lickey EP, dioc Birm).[21]

CHACELEY
Chap in Longdon AP, sep civ identity early, sep EP 1760.[31] *LG* Persh. Hd, Tewksb. PLU, RSD, RD. Transf 1931 to Glos.[11] *Parl* W'rn Dv (1832—85), S'rn Dv (1885—1918), Bewd. Dv (1918—48). *Eccl* Powyke RDn (1760—1861), Upton on Sev. RDn (1861—1919), Tewksb. RDn (dioc Glouc, 1919—*).

CHADDESLEY CORBETT
AP Incl chap Rushock (sep par by 1535[98]), chap Stone (sep par by 1535[99]). *LG* Seq 7. Addtl civ bdry alt: 1933,[14] 1953 (help cr Broome CP).[30] *Parl* Seq 9. *Eccl* Seq 5.

CHARLTON
Hmlt in Cropthore AP, sep CP 1866,[12] sep EP 1882.[100] *LG* Seq 12. Civ bdry: 1950.[101] *Parl* Seq 3. *Eccl* Feck. RDn (1882—92), Persh. RDn (1892—*).

CHILD'S WICKHAM
AP Glos par transf 1931 to Worcs.[11] *LG* Evesh. RD. *Parl* S Worcs CC (1948—*). *Eccl* See entry in Glos for RDns and for eccl renaming 1973.

CHRIST CHURCH AT THE QUINTON—see THE QUINTON
CHURCHILL
AP Sometimes 'Churchill in Halfshire'. *LG* Halfsh. Hd,

Kidderm. PLU, RSD, RD. Abol civ 1933 to help cr Churchill and Blakedown CP.[14] *Parl* W'rn Dv (1832—85), Mid Dv (1885—1918), Kidderm. Dv (1918—48). *Eccl* Kidderm. RDn (until 1907), Swinf. RDn (1907—21), Kidderm. RDn (1921—*). Eccl bdry: 1888.[102]

CHURCHILL
AP Sometimes 'Churchill in Oswaldslow'. Orig chap in Worcester St Helen AP, sep par by 1269.[103] *LG* Seq 12. *Parl* Seq 8. *Eccl* Persh. RDn (until 1892), Worc East RDn (1892—1921), Outer Worc (1921—26). Abol eccl 1924 to help cr White Ladies Aston with Churchill EP.[104]

CHURCHILL AND BLAKEDOWN
CP Cr 1933 by union ent Churchill AP, pts Hagley AP, Kidderminster Foreign CP.[14] *LG* Kidderm. RD. *Parl* Kidderm. CC (1948—*).

CLAINES
AP Orig chap in Worcester St Helen AP, sep par from 13th cent.[105] Incl tp Whistones (sep CP 1866[12]). *LG* Osw. Hd, Droitw. PLU, pt Worc MB ([incl tp Whistones before sep par] 1835—85 [reduced pt 1866—85 after Whistones sep]), pt Worc USD, pt Worc RSD. Addtl civ bdry alt: 1880.[87] Abol civ 1885 the pt in the MB cr South Claines CP, the remainder cr North Claines CP.[106] *Parl* Pt Droitw. Parl Bor (1832—85), pt Worc Parl Bor (1867—1918), pt W'rn Dv (1832—1918 [reduced pt 1867—1918]). *Eccl* Worc RDn (until 1861), Worc East RDn (1861—1921), Inner Worc RDn (1921—26), Worc RDn (1926—73), Worc East RDn (1974—*). Eccl bdry: 1862 (cr Claines St George EP,[107] now called 'Worcester St George'), 1862 (cr Barbourne EP,[40] refounded 1863[41]), 1866 (help cr Worcester Holy Trinty EP),[108] 1875 (cr Worcester The Tything EP),[71] 1883 (cr Rainbow Hill EP),[109] 1895,[110] 1912.[111]

NORTH CLAINES
CP Cr 1885 from the pt of Claines AP not in Worc MB.[106] *LG* Osw. Hd, Droitw. PLU, RSD, RD. Bdry: 1914 (loses pt to Worc CB [assoc with Worcs] & CP),[112] 1931 (loses pt to Worc CB [assoc with Worcs] & CP),[113] 1952 (incl loses pt to Worc CB [assoc with Worcs] & CP).[114] *Parl* Evesh. Dv (1918—48), Worc BC (1948—*). Parl bdry: 1952 (does not affect constituency).[115]

SOUTH CLAINES
CP Cr 1885 from the pt of Claines AP in Worc MB.[106] *LG* Osw. Hd, Droitw. PLU, Worc MB (1885—89), CB (1889—98), USD. Abol 1898 to help cr Worcester CP.[50]

CLAINES ST GEORGE
EP Cr 1862 from Claines AP.[107] Worc East RDn (1862—1921), Inner Worc RDn (1921—26), Worc RDn (1926—73), Worc East RDn (1974—*). Now called 'Worcester St George'.

CLENT
AP In Worcs *temp* Domesday Book, soon thereafter considered in Staffs (S Seisdon Hd),[116] transf to Worcs 1832 for parl purposes, 1844 for civ purposes (Halfsh. Hd).[95] Incl in Staffs chap Rowley Regis (sep civ identity early in Staffs, sep EP 1848[117]). *LG* After 1844, Seq 5. *Parl* After 1832,

Seq 10. *Eccl* Kidderm. RDn[118] (until 1907), Swinf. RDn (1907—73), Stourbr. RDn (1974—*).

CLEEVE PRIORS
AP *LG* Seq 10. *Parl* Seq 3. *Eccl* Seq 10.

CLIFTON ON TEME
AP Usual eccl spelling; for civ and chaps, see following entry. *Eccl* Burf. RDn (until 1878), Burf. (East) RDn (1878—98), Bromsgr. RDn (1898—1919), Worc West RDn (1919—21), Martley RDn (1921—73), Martley & Worc West RDn (1974—*).

CLIFTON UPON TEME
AP Usual civ spelling; for eccl see prev entry. Tp & bor 'Clifton upon Teme' in Worcs (Dodd. Hd) as was chap Lower Sapey (or 'Sapey Prichard' perhaps a sep par as early as 1291, sep civ identity early, all eccl rights except burial until completely independent 18th cent[119]); incl in Heref (Bromyard Hd) chap Edvin Loach (sep civ identity early in Heref [so that Clifton upon Teme ent Worcs thereafter], 'Edvin Loach' transf to Worcs 1832 for parl purposes, 1844 for civ purposes [Dodd. Hd],[95] the area of the orig chap eccl severed 1972 to help cr Edvin Loach with Tedstone Wafer EP[120] [the united benefice of Edvin Loach with Tedstone Wafer had existed from 1625]). *LG* Tp Clifton upon Teme: Clifton upon Teme Bor, Seq 3. *Parl* Seq 5.

COFTON HACKETT
Chap in Northfield AP, sep civ identity early, sep EP 1866,[121] eccl refounded 1871.[122] *LG* Seq 5. Civ bdry: 1911,[123] 1966 (incl exchanges pts with Birm CB [assoc with Warws] & CP).[21] *Parl* Seq 1. *Eccl* Northf. RDn (1866—92), Bromsgr. RDn (1892—1919), K's Nort. RDn (1919—*). Eccl bdry: 1966 (help cr West Heath EP),[124] 1972.[125]

GREAT COMBERTON
AP *LG* Seq 17. *Parl* Seq 3. *Eccl* Seq 7.

LITTLE COMBERTON
AP Organisation as for Great Comberton.

CONDERTON
Hmlt in Overbury AP, sep CP 1866.[12] *LG* Seq 1 *Parl* Seq 3.

COOKLEY
EP Cr 1849 from Wolverley AP.[126] Kidderm. RDn.

COTHERIDGE
AP *LG* Seq 3. Civ bdry: 1884,[127] 1884,[83] 1884,[16] 1952 (help cr Broadheath CP).[82] *Parl* Seq 5. *Eccl* Worc RDn (until 1861), Worc West RDn (1861—1921), Outer Worc RDn (1921—24). Abol eccl 1924 to help cr Cotheridge with Crown East EP.[128]

COTHERIDGE WITH CROWN EAST
EP Cr 1924 by union Cotheridge AP, pt Worcester St John the Baptist, Bedwardine AP.[128] Outer Worc RDn (1924—26), Martley RDn (1926—73), Martley & Worc West RDn (1974—*). Bdry: 1953,[129] 1967 (help cr Dines Green EP).[130]

COTTERIDGE
EP Cr 1916 from Kings Norton EP.[131] K's Nort. RDn. Bdry: 1926 (help cr Bournville EP).[71] Sometimes called 'The Cotteridge'.

COWLEIGH
EP Cr 1876 from Mathon St James EP (Worcs, Heref).[132] Powyke RDn. Abol 1973 to help cr Malvern Link with Cowleigh EP.[74]

CRADLEY

Chap (Worcs, Halfsh. Hd) in Halesowen AP, sep CP 1866 (Worcs [Halfsh. Hd], Salop [Brimstree Hd] until 1844, ent Worcs thereafter), sep CP 1866,[12] sep EP 1812,[31] eccl refounded 1841.[133] LG Stourbr. PLU, RSD, Halesowen RD (1894—1925), UD (1925—36), MB (1936—74). Transf 1974 to W Midlands.[134] Parl W'rn Dv (1832—85), N'rn Dv (1885—1918), Stourbr. Dv (1918—48), Oldb. & Halesowen BC (1948—70), Halesowen & Stourbr. BC (1970—*). Eccl Kidderm. RDn (1841—80), Dudley RDn (1880—*).

EARL'S CROOME

AP Usual eccl spelling; for civ see following entry. Eccl Seq 9.

EARLS CROOME

AP LG Seq 16. Civ bdry: 1884.[135] Parl Seq 12.

HILL CROOME

AP LG Seq 16. Parl Seq 12. Eccl Seq 9.

CROOME D'ABITOT

AP LG Seq 16. Parl Seq 12. Eccl Persh. RDn (until 1861), Bredon RDn (1861—1973). After gains 1771 Pirton AP[136] usually called 'Croome d'Abitot with Pirton' but by 20th cent called simply 'Croome d'Abitot' and as such eccl abol 1973 to help cr Severn Stoke with Croome d'Abitot EP.[137]

CROOOME D'ABITOT WITH PIRTON—see prev entry

CROPTHORNE

AP Incl hmlt Netherton (sep CP 1866[12]), hmlt Charlton (sep CP 1866,[12] sep EP 1882[100]). LG Seq 12. Addtl civ bdry alt: 1950.[101] Parl Seq 3. Eccl Persh. RDn (until 1861), Feck. RDn (1861—92), Persh. RDn (1892—*).

CROWLE

AP Incl chap Huddington (orig chap in Worcester St Helen AP, early considered chap in this par, sep par prob in 1570 from this par[138]). LG Seq 9. Parl Seq 7. Eccl Persh. RDn (until 1880s), E Worc RDn (1880s—1921), Droitw. RDn (1921—*).

CRUTCH

Ex-par place, sep CP 1858.[86] LG Halfsh. Hd, Droitw. PLU (1858—1930), RSD, RD. Abol civ 1933 ent to Hampton Lovett AP.[14] Parl Droitw. Parl Bor (1832—85), Mid Dv (1885—1918), Evesh. Dv (1918—48).

CUTSDEAN

Chap (detached) in Bredon AP, sep CP 1866,[12] eccl severed 1912 and transf to Temple Guiting AP, Glos, to help cr Temple Guiting with Cutsdean EP.[78] LG Osw. Hd, Winch. PLU, RSD, RD. Tranf 1931 to Glos.[11] Parl E'rn Dv (1832—85), S'rn Dv (1885—1918), Evesh. Dv (1918—48).

DAYLESFORD

AP LG Osw. Hd, Stow on the Wold PLU, RSD, RD. Transf 1931 to Glos.[11] Parl E'rn Dv (1832—85), S'rn Dv (1885—1918), Evesh. Dv (1918—48). Eccl Blockley RDn (until 1919), Chipping Norton RDn (dioc Oxford, 1919—*).

DEFFORD

Chap in Pershore St Andrew AP, sep CP 1866,[12] eccl severed 1865 to help cr Defford cum Besford EP.[59] LG Seq 17. Parl Seq 3.

DEFFORD CUM BESFORD

EP Cr 1865 by union chaps Defford, Besford, both in Pershore St Andrew AP.[59] Persh. RDn.

DINES GREEN

EP Cr 1967 from Worcester St Clement AP, Cotheridge with Crown East EP.[130] Worc RDn (1967—73), Martley & Worc West RDn (1974—*).

DODDENHAM

AP Orig chap to Worc Priory, sep par at Dissolution.[139] LG Seq 3. Civ bdry: 1894.[17] Parl Seq 5. Eccl Worc RDn. Abol eccl ca 1665 to help cr Knightwick with Doddenham EP.[139]

DODDERHILL

AP Incl chap Elmbridge (sep CP 1866,[12] sep EP 1877[140]), chap Westwood Park (ex-par 1178,[141] chap with all parochial rights before Dissolution but not sustained thereafter,[142] sep CP 1858[86]), area Dodderhill In Liberties (the area of the par in Droitw. Bor/MB, sep CP 1866[12]). LG Halfsh. Hd, Droitw. PLU, pt Droitw. Bor/MB (Dodderhill In Liberties, until 1866), Droitw. RSD, RD. Addtl civ bdry alt: 1880,[87] 1884 (gains Paper Mills CP),[143] 1934.[14] Parl Droitw. Parl Bor (pt 1554—1832, ent 1832—85), Mid Dv (1885—1918), Evesh. Dv (1918—48), Worc BC (1948—*). Eccl Seq 1. Addtl eccl bdry alt: 1888 (cr Wychbold EP),[144] 1908 (help cr Dodford EP).[85]

DODDERHILL IN LIBERTIES

Area (in Droitw. Bor/MB) in Dodderhill AP, sep CP 1866.[12] LG Halfsh. Hd, Droitw. Bor/MB, PLU. Abol 1884 pt to Droitwich St Andrew AP, pt to Droitwich St Nicholas AP, pt to Droitwich St Peter AP.[145] Parl Droitw. Parl Bor (1867—85).

DODFORD

EP Cr 1908 from Bromsgrove AP, Dodderhill AP, Upton Warren AP, Catshill EP, ent ex-par Grafton Manor.[85] Bromsgr. RDn.

DODFORD WITH GRAFTON

CP Cr 1933 by union pt Grafton Manor CP, pt North Bromsgrove CP.[14] LG Bromsgr. RD. Parl Bromsgr. CC (1948—70), Bromsgr. & Redditch CC (1970—*).

DORMSTON

AP Orig chap to Studley Priory, sep par at Dissolution.[146] LG Seq 17. Parl Seq 3. Eccl Persh. RDn (until 1861), Feck. RDn (1861—1973), Persh. RDn (1974—*).

DOVERDALE

AP LG Seq 6. Parl Seq 13. Eccl Kidderm. RDn (until 1880s), Droitw. RDn (1880s—1921), Mitton RDn (1921—30), Martley RDn (1930—73), Martley & Worc West RDn (1974—*).

DOWLES

AP Salop par transf 1895 to Worcs.[29] LG Kidderm. PLU, RD. Abol civ 1933 pt to Bewd. MB & CP, pt to Kidderminster Foreign CP, pt to Upper Arley AP.[14] Parl Kidderm. Dv (1918—48). Eccl Burf. RDn (until 1878), Burf. (East) RDn (1878—98), Bewd. RDn (1898—1926), Kidderm. RDn (1926—40). Abol eccl 1940 to help cr Ribbesford with Bewdley EP.[63]

DRAKES BROUGHTON AND WADBOROUGH

CP Cr 1958 from Pershore CP.[147] LG Persh. Hd. Parl

S Worcs CC (1970—*).

DROITWICH

The following have 'Droitwich' in their names. Insofar as any existed at a given time: *LG* Halfsh. Hd, Droitw. PLU, Bor/MB, USD. *Parl* Droitw. Parl Bor (1554—1885), Mid Dv (1885—1918), Evesh. Dv (1918—48), Worc BC (1948—*). *Eccl* Droitw. RDn.

CP1—DROITWICH—Cr 1920 by union AP1, AP3, AP4, Land Common to Droitwich St Andrew and St Peter (The Wrangling Division).[148] Bdry: 1933 (incl gains Unnamed CP),[14] 1968.[149]

EP1—DROITWICH—Cr 1972 by union EP2, AP3, AP4.[150]

AP1—DROITWICH ST ANDREW—Gains 1662 AP2, the union civ called as AP1, eccl as EP2.[148] Addtl civ bdry alt: 1880,[87] 1884.[145] Abol civ 1920 to help cr CP1.[148]

EP2—DROITWICH ST ANDREW WITH ST MARY WITTON—Cr 1662 when AP1 gains AP2 (in decay 14th cent).[151] Abol 1972 to help cr EP1.[150]

AP2—DROITWICH ST MARY DE WITTON—In decay 14th cent, abol 1662 ent to AP1, the union civ called as AP1, eccl as EP2.[151]

AP3—DROITWICH ST NICHOLAS—Civ bdry: 1880,[152] 1880,[153] 1880,[87] 1880,[145] 1884 (gains Marlborough in the Vines CP),[153] 1884.[145] Abol civ 1920 to help cr CP1.[148] Abol eccl 1972 to help cr EP1.[150]

AP4—DROITWICH ST PETER—Civ bdry: 1884.[145] Abol civ 1920 to help cr CP1.[148] Abol eccl 1972 to help cr EP1.[150]

DUDLEY

The following have 'Dudley' in their names. Insofar as any existed at a given time: *LG* Halfsh. Hd, Dudley Bor, MB (1865—89), CB (1889—1974 [assoc with Worcs 1889—1966, assoc with Staffs 1966—74]), PLU, USD. *Parl* Dudley Parl Bor/MB (1295, 1832—1970); Dudley East BC, Dudley West BC (1970—*). *Eccl* Kidderm. RDn (until 1880), Dudley RDn (1880—*).

AP1—DUDLEY [ST THOMAS]—Gains 1882 AP2.[154] Addtl civ bdry alt: 1929 (gains ent Dudley Castle CP, pt Coseley CP, both Staffs),[155] 1934 (exchanges pts with Tipton UD & CP, Staffs),[156] 1954 (gains pt Brierley Hill UD [qv in Staffs for constituent pars]), pt Coseley UD & CP, pt Rowley Regis MB & CP, pt Sedgley UD & AP, all Staffs),[157] 1966 (as CB becomes assoc with Staffs, gains from Worcs pt Stourbr. MB & CP; gains from Staffs pt Amblecote UD & CP, pt Brierley Hill UD [qv in Staffs for constituent pars], pt Coseley UD & CP, pt Sedgley UD & AP, pt Rowley Regis MB & CP, pt Tipton UD & AP, pt Himley AP, pt Kinver AP).[21] Eccl bdry: 1844 (cr EP4, cr Eve Hill EP [now called 'Dudley St James'], cr Kate's Hill EP, cr Netherton St Andrew EP),[158] 1866,[159] 1876 (cr EP6),[160] 1884 (cr EP2),[161] 1931.[7] Abol eccl 1969 to help cr EP1.[162]

CP1—DUDLEY CASTLE—Ex-par place, eccl and sometimes civ 'Dudley Castle Hill', sep CP 1858,[86] abol eccl 1931 ent to EP4.[7] *LG* Although in Dudley MB 1865—89, excluded from the CB and in Staffs (Dudley RD, 1889—1929) until abol civ 1929 ent to Dudley CB (assoc with Worcs) & AP1.[155] *Parl* W'rn Dv (1832—67), Dudley Parl Bor (1867—1948).

—DUDLEY CASTLE HILL—see prev entry

EP1—DUDLEY (ST THOMAS AND ST LUKE)—Cr 1969 by union AP1, EP6.[162]

EP2—DUDLEY ST AUGUSTINE, HOLLY HALL—Cr 1884 from AP1.[161] Bdry: 1930 (gains pt Brierley Hill EP, Staffs, dioc Lichf),[163] 1931.[7]

EP3—DUDLEY ST BARNABAS—Cr 1969 from EP6, Eve Hill EP (now called 'Dudley St James').[164]

EP4—DUDLEY ST EDMUND—Cr 1844 from AP1.[158] Bdry: 1866,[159] 1931 (incl gains eccl ex-par Dudley Castle Hill, gains pt Upper Gornall EP, Staffs),[7] 1935 (cr EP5).[93]

EP5—DUDLEY ST FRANCIS—Cr 1935 from EP4.[93]

AP2—DUDLEY ST JAMES—Abol 1182 ent to AP1.[154]

—DUDLEY ST JAMES—Name used now for EP cr 1844 as 'Eve Hill', qv.

EP6—DUDLEY ST LUKE—Cr 1876 from AP1.[160] Bdry: 1931,[7] 1969 (help cr EP3).[164] Abol 1969 to help cr EP1.[162]

DUDLEY WOOD

EP Cr 1950 from Netherton St Andrew EP.[165] Dudley RDn

EASTHAM

AP Incl chap Hanley Child (sometimes 'Lower Hanley', sep CP 1866,[12] eccl severed 1909 and united with area Hanley William in the same par to cr Hanley William with Hanley Child EP[166]), chap Orleton (sep CP 1866,[12] this par eccl 'Eastham with Orleton' until the chap eccl severed 1923 to to help cr Stanford on Teme with Orleton EP,[167] the par 'Eastham' thereafter). *LG* Seq 4. Addtl civ bdry alt: 1884.[168] *Parl* Seq 5. *Eccl* Burf. RDn (until 1878), Burf. (West) RDn (1878—98), Bewd. RDn (1898—1921), Martley RDn (1921—26), Lindr. RDn (1926—73), Stourpt. RDn (1974—*). Addtl eccl bdry alt: 1560 (gains eccl [sep civ identity retained] Hanley William AP [no change in name of par thereafter], the orig area eccl severed 1909 and united with chap Hanley Child [qv above] to cr Hanley William with Hanley Child EP[166]).

EASTHAM WITH ORLETON—see prev entry

ECKINGTON

AP *LG* Seq 17. *Parl* Seq 3. *Eccl* Persh. RDn (until 1861), Bredon RDn (1861—80s), Persh. RDn (1880s—*).

EDVIN LOACH

Chap (Heref, Bromyard Hd) in Clifton upon Teme AP (o'wise ent Worcs, Dodd Hd.; eccl, 'Clifton on Teme'), sep civ identity early in Heref (so that Clifton upon Teme ent Worcs thereafter), 'Edvin Loach' transf to Worcs 1832 for parl purposes, 1844 for civ purposes (Dodd. Hd),[95] the area of the orig chap eccl severed 1972 to help cr Edvin Loach with Tedstone Wafer EP[120] (the united benefice of Edvin Loach with Tedstone Wafer had existed from 1625). *LG* Bromyard PLU, RSD. Civ bdry: 1884 (loses pt to Collington AP, Heref).[169] Transf 1893 to Heref.[170] *Parl* W'rn Dv (1832—1918), Heref before and after.

EDVIN LOACH AND TEDSTONE WAFER

EP Cr 1972 (the united benefice for the 2 had existed from 1625) by union chap Edvin Loach in Clifton on Teme AP (civ, 'Clifton upon Teme'; see prev entry for organisation in different cos), Tedstone Wafer (prob an orig AP, perhaps an independent chap) (Heref).[120] Bromyd. RDn.

ELDERSFIELD

AP Orig chap in Longdon AP, sep par prob *ca* 1232—33.[171] *LG* Seq 19. Civ bdry: 1931 (gains pt Forthampton AP, Glos),[11] 1965 (gains pt Chaceley AP, pt Forthampton AP, pt Staunton AP, loses pt to Redmarley d'Abitot AP, all Glos).[21] *Parl* Seq 12. *Eccl* Seq 15.

ELMBRIDGE

Chap in Dodderhill AP, sep CP 1866,[12] sep EP 1877.[140] *LG* Seq 6. *Parl* Seq 13. *Eccl* Droitw. RDn.

ELMLEY CASTLE

AP *LG* Seq 12. *Parl* Seq 4. *Eccl* Persh. RD. Abol eccl 1972 to help cr Elmley Castle with Bricklehampton EP.[80]

ELMLEY CASTLE WITH BRICKLEHAMPTON

EP Cr 1922 by union Elmley Castle AP, chap Bricklehampton in Pershore St Andrew AP.[80] Persh. RDn.

ELMLEY LOVETT

AP *LG* Seq 6. Civ bdry: 1884.[152] *Parl* W'rn Dv (1832—85), Mid Dv (1885—1918), Evesh. Dv (1918—48), Worc BC (1948—*). *Eccl* Kidderm. RDn (until 1921), Mitton RDn (1921—30), Droitw. RDn (1930—*).

EVE HILL

EP Cr 1844 from Dudley AP.[158] Kidderm. RDn (1844—80), Dudley RDn (1880—*). Bdry: 1931,[7] 1969 (help cr Dudley St Barnabas EP).[164] Now called 'Dudley St James'.

EVENLODE

AP *LG* Osw. Hd, Stow on the Wold PLU, RSD, RD. Transf 1931 to Glos.[11] *Parl* E'rn Dv (1832—85), S'rn Dv (1885—1918), Evesh. Dv (1918—48). *Eccl* Blockley RDn (until 1919), Stow RDn (dioc Glouc, 1919—*).

EVESHAM

The following have 'Evesham' in their names. Insofar as any existed at a given time: *LG* Black. Hd, Evesh. Bor/MB, PLU, USD. *Parl* Evesh. Parl Bor (1604—1885), S'rn Dv (1885—1918), Evesh. Dv (1918—48), S Worcs CC (1948—*). *Eccl* Evesh. RDn.

CP1—EVESHAM—Cr 1924 by union CP2, CP3, Bengeworth AP.[51] Bdry:1933 (incl gains Great and Little Hampton AP).[14]

CP2—EVESHAM ALL SAINTS—Orig chap to Evesh. Abbey, sep civ from Dissolution, forms single EP with chap St Lawrence as EP1,[172] qv. Abol civ 1924 to help cr CP1.[51]

EP1—EVESHAM ALL SAINTS WITH ST LAWRENCE—Union eccl of 2 chaps of All Saints, St Lawrence (for civ, see CP2, CP3), each orig chap to Evesh. Abbey.[172]

CP3—EVESHAM ST LAWRENCE—Orig chap to

Evesh. Abbey, sep civ identity early, forms single EP with chap All Saints as EP1,[172] qv. Abol civ 1924 to help cr CP1.[51]

FAR FOREST

EP Cr 1845 from Ribbesford AP, Rock with Heightington AP (both Worcs), Stottesdon AP (Salop).[18] Burf. RDn (1845—78), Burf. (East) RDn (1878—98), Bewd. RDn (1898—1926), Kidderm. RDn (1926—*).

FECKENHAM

AP *LG* Halfsh. Hd, Alc. PLU, pt Redditch PLU, pt Alc. RSD, Feck. RD (1894—1933), Redditch UD (1933—74). Civ bdry: 1894 (the pt in the UD cr Feckenham Urban CP),[173] 1930.[20] *Parl* E'rn Dv (1832—85), S'rn Dv (1885—1918), Evesh. Dv (1918—48), Bromsgr. CC (1948—70), Bromsgr. & Redditch UD (1970—*). *Eccl* Persh. RDn (until 1861), Feck. RDn (1861—1973), Droitw. RDn (1974—*). Eccl bdry: 1850 (help cr Headless Cross EP [Warws, Worcs]),[174] 1924,[66] 1950 (help cr Astwood Bank with Crabbs Cross EP).[32]

FECKENHAM URBAN

CP Cr 1894 from the pt of Feckenham AP in Redditch UD.[173] *LG* Alc. PLU, Redditch UD. Bdry: 1930.[20] *Parl* Kidderm. Dv (1918—48), Bromsgr. CC (1948—70), Bromsgr. & Redditch CC (1970—*).

FINSTALL

EP Cr 1868 from Stoke Prior AP.[175] Droitw. RDn (1868—92), Bromsgr. RDn (1892—*).

FLADBURY

AP Incl chap Stock and Bradley, chap Throckmorton, chap Wyre Piddle, hmlt Ab Lench, hmlt Hill and Moor (each a sep CP 1866[12]). *LG* Seq 12. *Parl* Seq 3. *Eccl* Persh. RDn (until 1861), Feck. RDn (1861—1921), Persh. RDn (1921—*). Eccl bdry: 1862 (cr Bradley EP).[73]

FLYFORD FLAVELL

AP *LG* Seq 17. *Parl* Seq 3. *Eccl* Seq 11.

FOLEY PARK

EP Cr 1936 from Kidderminster St John the Baptist EP.[176] Kidderm. RDn. Now called 'Kidderminster Holy Innocents'.

FRANKLEY

Chap (Worcs, Halfsh. Hd) in Halesowen AP (Worcs, Salop until 1844, ent Worcs thereafter), sep civ identity early in Worcs, sep EP 1860.[31] *LG* Seq 5. Civ bdry: 1966 (loses pt to Birm CB [assoc with Warws] & AP).[21] *Parl* W'rn Dv (1832—85), N'rn Dv (1885—1918), Kidderm. Dv (1918—48), Bromsgr. CC (1948—70), Bromsgr. & Redditch CC (1970—*). *Eccl* Kidderm. RDn (1860—80), Northf. RDn (1880—1905), K's Nort. RDn (1905—*).

GARRETT'S GREEN

EP Cr 1967 from Yardley AP (Worcs), Sheldon AP (Warws).[177] Coleshill RDn.

GOSPEL LANE

EP Cr 1966 from Hall Green St Peter EP (Worcs), Olton EP, Shirley EP (boths Warws).[178] Solih. RDn. Bdry: 1972.[9]

GRAFTON FLYFORD

AP *LG* Seq 17. *Parl* Seq 3. *Eccl* Seq 12.

GRAFTON MANOR

Orig chap in Bromsgrove AP, sep early 13th cent as ex-par,[85] sep CP 1858,[86] abol eccl 1908 to help cr Dodford EP.[87] *LG* Halfsh. Hd, Bromsgr. PLU (1863—1930), pt Bromsgr. Town USD, pt Bromsgr. RSD, Bromsgr. RD. Civ bdry: 1880,[89] 1894 (loses the pt in the UD to Bromsgrove AP).[90] Abol civ 1933 pt to help cr Dodford with Grafton CP, pt to Bromsgr. UD & AP.[14] *Parl* E'rn Dv (1832—85), Mid Dv (1885—1918), Kidderm. Dv (1918—48).

GRIMLEY

AP Incl chap Hallow (sep civ identity early, sep EP 1876[179]). *LG* Seq 11. *Parl* Seq 5. *Eccl* Seq 18.

GUARLFORD

Hmlt in Great Malvern AP (the area of the latter not in Great Malv. UD), sep CP 1894,[180] sep EP 1866 from Great Malvern AP, Madresfield AP.[7] *LG* Upton upon Sev. PLU, RD. Civ bdry: 1933.[14] *Parl* Bewd. Dv (1918—48), S Worcs CC (1948—*). *Eccl* Powyke RDn (1867—1973), Malv. RDn (1974—*).

HADZOR

AP *LG* Seq 6. Civ bdry: 1880.[89] *Parl* Seq 13. *Eccl* Droitw. RDn (until 1864), Worc East RDn (1864—92), Droitw. RDn (1892—1973). Abol eccl 1973 to help cr Hadzor with Oddingley EP.[181]

HADZOR WITH ODDINGLEY

EP Cr 1972 by union Hadzor AP, Oddingley AP.[181] Droitw. RDn.

HAGLEY

AP *LG* Seq 5. Civ bdry: 1933 (incl help cr Churchill and Blakedown CP),[14] 1966.[21] *Parl* Seq 10. *Eccl* Seq 6. Eccl bdry: 1888.[102]

HALESOWEN

AP Tp 'Halesowen' in Salop (Brimstree Hd) as were tps Cakemore, Hasbury, Hawne, Hill, Illey, Lapal, Ridgacre, Warley Salop (all transf along with tp Halesowen to Worcs 1832 for parl purposes, 1844 for civ purposes [Halfsh. Hd],[95] each a sep CP 1866 in Worcs[12]), tp Hunnington (transf to Worcs at same time as others, sep CP 1866 in Worcs,[12] eccl in chap St Kenelm), tp Oldbury (transf to Worcs at same time as others, sep CP 1866 in Worcs,[12] sep EP 1715,[31] eccl refounded 1841[133]), tp Romsley (transf to Worcs at same time as others, sep CP 1866 in Worcs,[12] eccl in chap St Kenelm until 'Romsley' a sep EP 1841[133]); incl in Worcs (Halfsh. Hd) chap Cradley (sep CP 1866,[12] sep EP 1812,[31] eccl refounded 1841[133]), chap Frankley (sep civ identity early, sep EP 1860[31]), hmlt Lutley, hmlt Warley Wigorn (each a sep CP 1866[12]) so that Halesowen ent Worcs from 1844. *LG* Halesowen Bor, Stourbr. PLU, RSD, Halesowen RD (1894—1925), UD (1925—36), MB (1936—74). Addtl civ bdry alt: 1894,[182] 1922,[183] 1933,[14] 1966 (incl gains pt Rowley Regis MB & CP, Staffs, loses pt to help cr Warley CB [assoc with Worcs] & CP, exchanges pts with Birm CB [assoc with Warws] & AP).[21] Transf 1974 to W Midlands.[134] *Parl* E'rn Dv (1832—85), N'rn Dv (1885—1918), Stourbr. Dv (1918—48), Oldb. & Halesowen BC (1948—70), Halesowen & Stourbr. BC (1970—*). *Eccl*

Kidderm. RDn (until 1880s), Dudley RDn (1880s—*). Addtl eccl bdry alt: 1841 (cr The Quinton EP),[133] 1846 (cr Langley EP),[184] 1869 (help cr Blackheath EP).[68]

HALL GREEN [MARSTON CHAPEL]

EP Cr 1907 from Yardley AP.[185] Solih. RDn (1907—57), Coleshill RDn (1957—*). Bdry: 1966,[4] 1966.[8] By 1950s, called 'Marston Green'.

HALL GREEN ST PETER

EP Cr 1962 from Yardley Wood EP.[150] Solih. RDn. Bdry: 1966,[8] 1966 (help cr Gospel Lane EP [Warws, Worcs]).[178]

HALLOW

Chap in Grimley AP, sep civ identity early, sep EP 1876.[31] *LG* Osw. Hd, Martley PLU, RSD. Abol civ 1885 the pt to be in the MB cr South Hallow CP, the remainder cr North Hallow CP.[104] *Parl* Pt Worc Parl Bor (1867—1918), W'rn Dv (ent 1832—67, pt 1867—1918). *Eccl* W Worc RDn (1876—1921), Inner Worc RDn (1921—26), Worc RDn (1926—56), Martley RDn (1956—73), Martley & Worc West RDn (1974—*). Eccl bdry: 1910 (help cr Broadheath EP).[81]

CP Renaming 1952 of North Hallow CP.[186] *LG* Martley RD. *Parl* Kidderm. CC (1970—*).

NORTH HALLOW

CP Cr 1885 from the pt of Hallow CP not to be in Worc MB (for the remainder, see following entry).[104] *LG* Osw. Hd, Martley PLU, RSD, RD. Bdry: 1952 (incl help cr Broadheath CP).[82] Renamed 1952 'Hallow' CP.[186] *Parl* Bewd. Dv (1918—48), Kidderm. CC (1948—*).

SOUTH HALLOW

CP Cr 1885 from the pt of Hallow CP to be in Worc MB (for the remainder, see prev entry).[104] *LG* Osw. Hd, Martley PLU, Worc MB (1885—89), CB (1889—98), USD. Abol 1898 to help cr Worcester CP.[50]

GREAT AND LITTLE HAMPTON

AP Orig chap in Evesh. Abbey, sep par at Dissolution.[187] *LG* Black. Hd, Evesh. PLU, RSD, RD. Abol civ 1933 ent to Evesh. MB & CP.[14] *Parl* E'rn Dv (1832—85), S'rn Dv (1885—1918), Evesh. Dv (1918—48). *Eccl* Seq 4.

HAMPTON LOVETT

AP *LG* Seq 6. Civ bdry: 1880,[89] 1884,[152] 1933 (incl gains Crutch CP).[14] *Parl* Seq 13. *Eccl* Seq 1.

HANBURY

AP *LG* Seq 9. Civ bdry: 1880.[89] *Parl* Pt Droitw. Parl Bor (1832—85 [enlarged pt 1867—85]), pt E'rn Dv (1832—85 [reduced pt 1867—85]), Mid Dv (1885—1918), Evesh. Dv (1918—48), Worc BC (1948—*). *Eccl* Seq 1.

HANLEY

CP Cr 1933 by union pt Hanley Child CP, ent Hanley William AP.[14] *LG* Tenb. RD. *Parl* Kidderm. CC (1948—*).

HANLEY CASTLE

AP Sometimes early 'Potters Hanley'. *LG* Persh. Hd, Upton upon Sev. PLU, pt Great Malv. USD (Mar—apptd day 1894), Upton upon Sev. RSD (ent 1875—Mar 1894, pt Mar—apptd day 1894), Upton upon Sev. RD. Civ bdry: 1894 (the pt in the UD cr South

Malvern CP),[180] 1896 (loses pt to South Malvern CP as enlarged area of latter renamed 'Malvern Wells' CP),[188] 1898.[189] *Parl* Seq 12. *Eccl* Seq 15. Eccl bdry: 1836 (cr Malvern Wells EP).[190]

HANLEY CHILD
Chap (sometimes 'Lower Hanley') in Eastham AP, sep CP 1866,[12] eccl severed 1909 to help cr Hanley William with Hanley Child EP.[166] *LG* Dodd. Hd, Tenb. PLU, RSD, RD. Civ bdry: 1884.[168] Abol civ 1933 pt to help cr Hanley CP, pt to help cr Kyre CP.[14] *Parl* W'rn Dv (1832—1918), Bewd. Dv (1918—48).

HANLEY WILLIAM
AP *LG* Dodd. Hd, Tenb. PLU, RSD, RD. Abol civ 1933 to help cr Hanley CP.[14] *Parl* W'rn Dv (1832—1918), Bewd. Dv (1918—48). *Eccl* Burf. RDn. Abol eccl 1560 ent to Eastham AP, the orig area of Hanley William eccl severed 1909 from the latter to help cr Hanley William with Hanley Child EP.[163]

HANLEY WILLIAM WITH HANLEY CHILD
EP Cr 1909 by union area Hanley William (qv in prev entry) in Eastham AP, chap Hanley Child in same par.[166] Bewd. RDn (1909—21), Martley RDn (1921—26), Lindr. RDn (1926—73). Abol 1973 to help cr Stoke Bliss with Kyre Wyard, Hanley William and Hanley Child EP.[191]

HARTLEBURY
AP Tp 'Hartlebury' in Osw. Hd; incl in Halfsh. Hd hmlt Upper Mitton (sep CP 1866[12]). *LG* Osw. Hd (pt until 1866, ent from 1866), pt Halfsh. Hd (until 1866), Droitw. PLU, RSD, RD. Addtl civ bdry alt: 1920,[28] 1933.[14] *Parl* W'rn Dv (1832—1918), Evesh. Dv (1918—48), Worc BC (1948—*). *Eccl* Kidderm. RDn (until 1921), Mitton RDn (1921—73), Stourpt. RDn (1974—*). Eccl bdry: 1877,[192] 1904 (help cr Wilden EP).[193]

HARVINGTON
AP *LG* Seq 10. *Parl* Seq 3. *Eccl* Persh. RDn (until 1861), Feck. RDn (1861—1907), Evesh. RDn (1907—*).

HASBURY
Tp (Salop, Brimstree Hd) in Halesowen AP (Worcs, Salop until 1844, ent Worcs thereafter), transf to Worcs 1832 for parl purposes, 1844 for civ purposes (Halfsh. Hd),[95] sep CP 1866 in Worcs.[12] *LG* Stourbr. PLU, RSD, Halesowen RD (1894—1925), UD (1925—36), MB (1936—74). Bdry: 1894.[182] Transf 1974 to W Midlands.[134] *Parl* After 1832, Seq 2.

HAWNE
Tp (Salop, Brimstree Hd) in Halesowen AP (Worcs, Salop until 1844, ent Worcs thereafter), transf to Worcs 1832 for parl purposes, 1844 for civ purposes (Halfsh. Hd).[95] Organisation, civ bdry alt, transf 1974 as for Hasbury.

HAY MILL
EP Cr 1878 from Yardley AP.[4] Northf. RDn (1878—1905), Bord. RDn (1905—57), Yard. RDn (1957—*). Bdry: 1948.[19]

HAZELWELL
EP Cr 1932 from Kings Norton EP, Stirchley EP, Kings Heath EP.[194] K's Nort. RDn (1932—57), Moseley RDn (1957—*). Bdry: 1963,[73] 1963 (help

cr Brandwood EP).[71]

HEADLESS CROSS
EP Cr 1850 from pt (hmlt Headless Cross, pt hmlt Crabbs Cross) of the pt in Worcs of Ipsley AP (Warws, Worcs), Tardebigge AP (medieval location in Warws, Staffs differed at different times, thereafter Warws, Worcs until 1844, ent Worcs from 1844).[174] Warw. RDn (1850—51), Alc. RDn (1851—1907), Bromsgr. RDn (1907—*). Bdry: 1924,[66] 1950 (incl help cr Astwood Bank with Crabbs Cross EP).[32]

HIGHTERS HEATH
EP Cr 1938 from Yardley Wood EP.[195] K's Nort. RDn (1938—57), Moseley RDn (1957—*). Bdry: 1962.[26]

HILL
Tp (Salop, Brimstree Hd) in Halesowen AP (Worcs, Salop until 1844, ent Worcs thereafter), transf to Worcs 1832 for parl purposes, 1844 for civ purposes (Halfsh. Hd),[95] sep CP 1866 in Worcs.[12] *LG* Stourbr. PLU, RSD, Halesowen RD. Abol 1919 to help cr Hill and Cakemore CP.[96] *Parl* From 1844, E'rn Dv (1832—85), N'rn Dv (1885—1918), Stourbr. Dv (1918—48).

HILL AND CAKEMORE
CP Cr 1919 by union Hill CP, Cakemore CP.[96] *LG* Stourbr. PLU, Halesowen RD (1919—25), UD (1925—36), MB (1936—74). Bdry: 1933.[14] Transf 1974 to W Midlands.[134] *Parl* Oldb. & Halesowen BC (1948—70), Halesowen & Stourbr. BC (1970—*).

HILL AND MOOR
Hmlt in Fladbury AP, sep CP 1866.[12] *LG* Seq 12. *Parl* Seq 3.

HILLHAMPTON
Hmlt in Martley AP, sep CP 1866.[12] *LG* Seq 3. *Parl* Seq 5.

HIMBLETON
AP *LG* Seq 9. Civ bdry: 1884 (gains Shell CP).[196] *Parl* Seq 13. *Eccl* Feck. RDn (until 1880s), Droitw. RDn (1880s—*).

HINDLIP
AP Orig chap in Worcester St Helen AP, sep par by 1269.[197] *LG* Seq 9. Civ bdry: 1880,[89] 1952 (incl loses pt to Worc CB [assoc with Worcs] & CP).[114] *Parl* Droitw. Parl Bor (1832—85), W'rn Dv (1885—1918), Evesh. Dv (1918—48), Worc BC (1948—*). Parl bdry: 1952 (does not affect constituency).[115] *Eccl* Worc RDn (until 1861), Worc East RDn (1861—1921), Outer Worc RDn (1921—26), Droitw. RDn (1926—73), Worc East RDn (1974—*). Eccl bdry: 1895,[110] 1966 (incl help cr Warndon St Wulstan EP).[198]

HINTON ON THE GREEN
AP Glos par transf 1931 to Worcs.[11] *LG* Evesh. RD. *Parl* S Worcs CC (1948—*). *Eccl* Campden RDn (until 1907), Tewkesb. RDn (1907—19) (dioc Worc until 1541, dioc Glouc 1541—1836, dioc Glouc & Bristol 1836—97, dioc Glouc 1897—1919), Evesh. RDn (1919—*).

HOLDFAST
Hmlt in Ripple AP, sep CP 1866,[12] eccl severed 1863 to help cr Queenhill with Holdfast EP.[199] *LG*

Seq 16. *Parl* Seq 12.

HOLLYBUSH

EP Cr 1912 from Castle Morton EP, Berrow AP (both Worcs), Eastnor AP, Ledbury AP (both Heref).[57] Upton RDn. Bdry: 1964.[58]

HOLT

AP Orig chap in Worcester St Helen AP, sep par by 1269.[200] Incl chap Little Witley (sep CP 1866[12]). *LG* Seq 1. *Parl* Seq 5. *Parl* Seq 18.

HONEYBOURNE

CP Cr 1953 by union Church Honeybourne AP, Cow Honeybourne CP.[201] *LG* Evesh. RD. Bdry: 1966 (exchanges pts with Weston Subedge AP, Glos).[21] *Parl* S Worcs CC (1948—*).

CHURCH HONEYBOURNE

AP Incl chap Cow Honeybourne (Glos, Kiftsgate Hd, sep civ identity early in Glos, eccl united early to Church Honeybourne, union reaffirmed 1885[202] so that this par eccl 'Church Honeybourne with Cow Honeybourne', qv). *LG* Black. Hd, Evesh. PLU, RSD, RD. Abol civ 1953 to help cr Honeybourne CP.[201] *Parl* E'rn Dv (1832—85), S'rn Dv (1885—1918), Evesh Dv (1918—48), S Worcs CC (1948—70).

CHURCH HONEYBOURNE WITH COW HONEY-BOURNE

AP Usual eccl spelling; for civ and civ sep chap (in Glos), see prev entry. *Eccl* Evesh. RDn (until 1919), Campden RDn (dioc Glouc, 1919—*).

COW HONEYBOURNE

Chap (Glos, Kiftsgate Hd) in Church Honeybourne AP (o'wise Worcs, Black. Hd), sep civ identity early in Glos, eccl united early to Church Honeybourne, union reaffirmed 1885.[202] For civ and parl before 1931, see entry in Glos; transf 1931 to Worcs.[11] *LG* After 1931, Evesh. RD. Abol civ 1953 to help cr Honeybourne CP.[201] *Parl* S Worcs CC (1948—70).

HUDDINGTON

Chap orig in Worcester St Helen AP, early considered chap in Crowle AP, sep par prob in 1570 from the latter.[138] *LG* Seq 9. *Parl* Seq 7. *Eccl* Persh. RDn (until 1880s), Droitw. RDn (1880s—*).

HUNNINGTON

Tp (Salop, Brimstree Hd) in Halesowen AP (Worcs, Salop until 1844, ent Worcs thereafter), transf to Worcs 1832 for parl purposes, 1844 for civ purposes (Halfsh. Hd),[95] sep CP in Worcs,[12] eccl in chap St Kenelm. *LG* Bromsgr. PLU, RSD, RD. Bdry: 1922,[183] 1933.[14] *Parl* E'rn Dv (1832—85), N'rn Dv (1885—1918), Kidderm. Dv (1918—48), Bromsgr. CC (1948—70), Bromsgr. & Redditch CC (1970—*).

ICOMB

AP Tp 'Icomb' in Glos (Slaughter Hd); incl in Worcs (Osw. Hd) tp Church Icomb (transf to Glos 1832 for parl purposes, 1844 for civ purposes [Slaughter Hd],[95] sep CP 1866 in Glos[12]) so that Icomb ent Glos from 1844. See entries in Glos for all organisation.

ILLEY

Tp (Salop, Brimstree Hd) in Halesowen AP (Worcs, Salop until 1844, ent Worcs thereafter), transf to Worcs 1832 for parl purposes, 1844 for civ purposes (Halfsh. Hd),[95] sep CP 1866 in Worcs.[12] *LG* Stourbr. PLU, RSD, Halesowen RD (1894—1925), UD (1925—36), MB (1936—74). Bdry: 1911.[123] Transf 1974 to W Midlands.[134] *Parl* Seq 2.

INKBERROW

AP *LG* Osw. Hd, Alc. PLU, RSD, Feck. RD (1894—1933), Evesh. RD (1933—74). Civ bdry: 1965 (gains pt Alcester AP, pt Arrow AP, pt Sambourne CP, pt Weethley CP, all Warws).[21] *Parl* Seq 3. *Eccl* Persh. RDn (until 1861), Feck. RDn (1861—1973), Evesh. RDn (1974—*).

IPSLEY

AP Mostly Warws (Barlinchway Hd), pt Worcs (pt hmlt Crabbs Cross, hmlt Headless Cross, the 2 areas eccl severed 1850 to help cr Headless Cross EP [Worcs, Warws],[174] the area civ in Redditch UD [o'wise ent Worcs], that area cr 1894 Upper Redditch UD to be in the UD in Worcs,[173] so that 'Ipsley' ent Warws 1894—1931, the par transf 1931 to Worcs.[11] *LG* Alc. PLU, pt Redditch USD, pt Alc. RSD, Redditch UD (1931—74). *Parl* In Warws before 1948; Bromsgr. CC (1948—70), Bromsgr. & Redditch CC (1970—*). *Eccl* Warw. RDn (until 1861), Alc. RDn (1861—1907), Bromsgrove RDn (1907—33). Eccl bdry: 1924.[66] Abol eccl 1933, pt to Redditch St George EP, pt to Redditch EP.[203]

UPPER IPSLEY

CP Cr 1894 from the pt of Ipsley AP (Warws) in Redditch UD (o'wise ent Worcs) to be in Worcs.[173] *LG* Alc. PLU, Redditch UD. *Parl* Kidderm. Dv (1918—48), Bromsgr. CC (1948—70), Bromsgr. & Redditch CC (1970—*).

KATE'S HILL

EP Cr 1844 from Dudley AP.[158] Kidderm. RDn. Bdry: 1921 (loses tp to Tividale EP [Staffs, dioc Lichf]),[204] 1931.[7]

KEMERTON

AP Glos par transf 1931 to Worcs.[11] *LG* Tewksb. RD (1931—33), Evesh. RD (1933—74). *Parl* S Worcs CC (1948—*).

KEMPSEY

AP Incl chap Norton juxta Kempsey (sep civ identity early, sep EP 1781[31]), chap Stoulton (sep civ identity early, sep EP 1794[31]). *LG* Seq 16. *Parl* W'rn Dv (1832—1918), Bewd. Dv (1918—48), S Worcs CC (1948—*). *Eccl* Prebendal, Worc RDn (until 1861), Worc East RDn (1861—1921), Inner Worc RDn (1921—26), Worc RDn (1926—71), Bredon RDn (1971—73), Upton RDn (1974—*). Addtl eccl bdry alt: 1967.[205]

KENSWICK

Orig chap in chap/AP Knightwick (chap appropriated to Worc Priory, sep par by 1535[139]) 'Kenswick' in ruins by late 18th cent and considered ex-par, sep CP 1858,[86] eccl severed 1908 and transf to Wichenford AP,[139] the area so transf incl 1910 in cr of Broadheath EP from Wichenford AP.[81] *LG* Osw. Hd, Martley PLU (1861—1930), RSD, RD. Civ bdry: 1952.[82] *Parl* Seq 5.

KIDDERMINSTER

The following have 'Kidderminster' in their names. Insofar as any existed at a given time: *LG* Halfsh.

Hd, Kidderm. PLU; Bor/MB, USD, RSD sep noted. *Parl* Sep noted. *Eccl* Kidderm. RDn.

AP1—KIDDERMINSTER [ST MARY]—Incl tp Kidderminster Borough (in Bor, sep CP 1866 as CP1[12]), tp Kidderminster Foreign (not in Bor, sep CP 1866 as CP2[12]), tp Lower Mitton (sep CP 1866,[12] sep EP 1844,[108] sometimes called 'Stourport') so that AP1 has no sep civ identity after 1866. *LG* Pt Kidderm. Bor, pt Kidderm. MB ([enlarged pt, incl pt Kidderminster Foreign] 1836—66). *Parl* Pt Kidderm. Parl Bor (1295, 1832—67), pt Bewd. Parl Bor (1832—67). Addtl eccl bdry alt: 1844 (cr Wribbenhall EP),[108] 1867 (cr EP1, EP2),[206] 1952 (help cr Broadwaters EP).[84]

CP1—KIDDERMINSTER BOROUGH—Tp in AP1, sep CP 1866.[12] *LG* Kidderm. Bor/MB, USD. Bdry: 1894 (gains the pt in Kidderm. MB of CP2),[207] 1912,[208] 1933.[14] *Parl* Kidderm. Parl Bor (1832—1918), Kidderm. Dv/CC (1918—*).

CP2—KIDDERMINSTER FOREIGN—Tp in AP1, sep CP 1866.[12] *LG* Pt Kidderm. MB (1835—94), pt Kidderm. USD, pt Kidderm. RSD. Bdry: 1894 (loses the pt in the MB to CP1),[207] 1901 (cr Wribbenhall CP),[209] 1912,[208] 1933 (incl help cr Churchill and Blakedown CP).[14] *Parl* Pt Kidderm. Parl Bor (1832—1918 [enlarged pt 1867—1918]), pt Bewd. Parl Bor (1867—85), pt Mid Dv (1885—1918), Kidderm. Dv/CC (1918—*).

—KIDDERMINSTER THE HOLY INNOCENTS—Name used now for EP cr 1936 as 'Foley Park', qv.

EP1—KIDDERMINSTER ST GEORGE—Cr 1867 from AP1.[206] Bdry: 1952 (help cr Broadwaters EP).[84]

EP2—KIDDERMINSTER ST JOHN THE BAPTIST—Cr 1867 from AP1.[206] Bdry: 1885,[210] 1936 (cr Foley Park EP, now called 'Kidderminster The Holy Innocents').[176]

KINGS HEATH
EP Cr 1863 from Moseley EP, Kings Norton EP.[211] Droitw. RDn (1863—80), Northf. RDn (1880—1905), K's Nort. RDn (1905—57), Moseley RDn (1957—*). Bdry: 1932 (help cr Hazelwell EP),[194] 1963.[66]

KINGS NORTON
Chap in Bromsgrove AP, sep civ identity early, sep EP 1846.[88] *LG* Halfsh. Hd, Kings Norton PLU (1836—1911), Bromsgr. PLU (1911—12), pt Birm CB & USD (1891—94), Kings Norton RSD (ent 1875—91, pt 1891—94), Kings Norton RD (1894—98), Kings Norton & Northf. UD (1898—1911), sep RD (administered by Bromsgr. RD Council, 1911—12). Civ bdry: 1894 (the pt in the CB cr Balsall Heath CP to be in Birm CB [assoc with Warws]),[212] 1911 (loses pt to Birm CB [assoc with Warws] & AP, pt to Cofton Hackett CP, pt to cr Wythall CP).[123] Abol civ 1912 ent to Birmingham CB (assoc with Warws) & AP.[213] *Parl* E'rn Dv (1832—1918). *Eccl* Droitw. RDn (1846—80), Northf. RDn (1880—1905), K's Nort. RDn (1905—*). Eccl bdry: 1849 (help cr Yardley Wood EP),[214] 1853

(refound Moseley EP [cr 1767 from Bromsgrove AP[31]]),[91] 1853 (cr Balsall Heath EP, help cr Wythall EP [Worcs, Warws]),[22] 1863 (help cr Kings Heath EP),[211] 1912 (help cr Stirchley EP),[215] 1916 (cr Cotteridge EP),[131] 1926 (help cr Bournville EP),[71] 1932 (help cr Hazelwell EP),[194] 1957 (cr Longbridge EP),[41] 1963,[66] 1963 (help cr Brandwood EP),[74] 1966 (help cr West Heath EP).[124]

KINGTON
AP *LG* Halfsh. Hd, Persh. PLU, RSD, RD. *Parl* E'rn Dv (1832—85), S'rn Dv (1885—1918), Evesh. Dv (1918—48), S Worcs CC (1948—*). *Eccl* Persh. RDn (until 1861), Feck. RDn (1861—1973), Persh. RDn (1974—*).

KINGTON ON TEME
Chap in Lindridge AP, sep CP 1866,[12] sep EP 1843.[216] *LG* Seq 13. *Parl* Seq 5. *Eccl* Burf. RDn (1843—78), Burf. (West) RDn (1878—98), Burf. RDn (1898—1919), Bewd. RDn (1919—21), Martley RDn (1921—26), Lindr. RDn (1926—73), Stourpt. RDn (1974—*).

KNIGHTWICK
AP Orig chap appropriated to Worc Priory, sep par by 1535.[139] Incl chap Kenswick (in ruins by late 18th cent and considered ex-par, sep CP 1858,[86] eccl severed 1908 and transf to Wichenford AP,[139] the area so transf incl 1910 in cr of Broadheath EP from Wichenford AP[81]). *LG* Seq 11. *Parl* Seq 5. *Eccl* Worc RDn. Abol ca 1655 to help cr Knightwick with Doddenham AP.[139]

KNIGHTWICK WITH DODDENHAM
EP Cr ca 1655 by union Knightwick AP, Doddenham AP.[139] *Eccl* Seq 17.

KYRE
CP Cr 1933 by union ent Kyre Magna AP, pt Hanley Child CP.[14] *LG* Tenb. RD. *Parl* Kidderm. CC (1948—*).

KYRE MAGNA
AP Orig chap in Tenbury AP, sep par by 1535.[217] Perhaps orig incl Kyre Parva but that hmlt in Stoke Bliss AP (o'wise Heref, Broxash Hd) by 1655.[218] Usual civ spelling; for eccl see 'Kyre Wyard'. *LG* Dodd. Hd, Tenb. PLU, RSD, RD. Abol civ 1933 to help cr Kyre CP.[14] *Parl* W'rn Dv (1832—1918), Bewd. Dv (1918—48).

KYRE PARVA
Hmlt (Worcs, Dodd. Hd) perhaps orig in Kyre Magna AP (eccl, 'Kyre Wyard') but in Stoke Bliss AP (o'wise Heref, Broxash Hd) by 1655,[218] sep CP 1866 in Worcs.[12] *LG* Tenb. PLU, RSD, RD. Abol 1933 ent to Stoke Bliss AP (transf 1897 from Heref to Worcs, qv).[14] *Parl* W'rn Dv (1832—1918), Bewd. Dv (1918—48).

KYRE WYARD
AP Usual eccl spelling; for civ, orig status as chap, and civ and parl organisation, see 'Kyre Magna'. *Eccl* Burf. RDn (until 1878), Burf. (West) RDn (1878—98), Burf. RDn (1898—1919), Bewd. RDn (1919—21), Martley RDn (1921—26), Lindr. RDn (1926—73). Abol eccl 1973 to help cr Stoke Bliss with Kyre Wyard, Hanley William and Hanley Child EP.[191]

LAND COMMON TO DROITWICH ST ANDREW AND DROITWICH ST PETER (THE WRANGLING DIVISION)
  LG Droitw. MB. Abol 1920 to help cr Droitwich CP.[148] *Parl* Evesh. Dv (1918—48).

LANGLEY
  EP Cr 1846 from Halesowen AP (Worcs, Salop until 1844, ent Worcs thereafter).[184] Kidderm. RDn (1846—80), Dudley RDn (1880—Mar 1905), not in a RDn (Mar—Aug 1905, when first transf to dioc Birm), Harb. RDn (Aug 1905—29), Smethw. RDn (1926—66), Warley RDn (1966—*). Bdry: 1905 (cr Rounds Green EP),[219] 1959.[69]

LANGLEY
  EP Cr 1969 [St John] from Oldbury EP.[220] Warley RDn.

LAPAL
  Tp (Salop, Brimstree Hd) in Halesowen AP (Worcs, Salop until 1844, ent Worcs thereafter), transf to Worcs 1832 for parl purposes, 1844 for civ purposes (Halfsh. Hd),[95] sep CP 1866 in Worcs.[12] *LG* Stourbr. PLU, RSD, Halesowen RD (1894—1925), UD (1925—36), MB (1936—74). Transf 1974 to W Midlands.[134] *Parl* From 1832, Seq 2.

LEA HALL
  EP Cr 1968 from Yardley AP (Worcs), Tile Cross EP (Warws).[221] Coleshill RDn.

LEIGH
  AP Incl chap Bransford (perhaps orig in Powick AP,[75] later or orig in this par, sep CP 1866 from this par,[12] not sep eccl hence this par eccl 'Leigh with Bransford', qv). *LG* Persh. Hd, Martley PLU, pt Malv. Link USD, pt Martley RSD, Martley RD. Addtl civ bdry alt: 1884,[16] 1894 (the pt in the UD cr Malvern Link CP),[180] 1897 (gains Cradley AP, Heref),[10] 1933.[14] *Parl* Seq 5.

LEIGH WITH BRANSFORD
  AP Usual eccl spelling; for civ and civ sep chap, see prev entry. *Eccl* Seq 14. Eccl bdry: 1844 (help cr Mathon St James EP [Worcs, Heref]),[65] 1845 (cr Link EP [sometimes called 'Malvern Link'],[222] refounded 1846[223]).

AB LENCH
  Tp (sometimes 'Hob Lench') in Fladbury AP, sep CP 1866.[12] *LG* Osw. Hd, Evesh. PLU, RSD, RD. Abol 1933 ent to Church Lench AP.[14] *Parl* E'rn Dv (1832—85), S'rn Dv (1885—1918), Evesh. Dv (1918—48).

CHURCH LENCH
  AP *LG* Mostly Halfsh. Hd, pt Black. Hd, Evesh. PLU, RSD, RD. Civ bdry: 1933 (gains Ab Lench CP).[14] *Parl* Seq 3. *Eccl* Persh. RDn (until 1861), Feck. RDn (1861—1973), Evesh. RDn (1974—*).

ROUS LENCH
  AP *LG* Seq 10. *Parl* Seq 3. *Eccl* Persh. RDn (until 1861), Feck. RDn (1861—1957). Abol eccl 1957 to help cr Rous Lench and Abbots Morton EP.[3]

ROUS LENCH AND ABBOTS MORTON
  EP Cr 1957 by union Rous Lench AP, Abbots Morton AP.[3] Feck. RDn (1957—73), Evesh. RDn (1974—*).

THE LICKEY
  EP Cr 1858 from Bromsgrove AP, Catshill EP.[93]

Droitw. RDn (1858—92), Bromsgr. RDn (1892—Mar 1905), not in a RDn (Mar—Aug 1905, when first transf to dioc Birm), K's Nort. RDn (1905—*). Bdry: 1913 (exchanges pts with Bromsgrove AP and with Catshill EP and gains pt Tradebigge AP, Alvechurch AP, all dioc Worc),[23] 1922 (cr Burnt Green EP),[42] 1933 (cr Rubery EP).[224]

LINDRIDGE
  AP Incl chap Knighton on Teme, chap Pensax (each a sep CP 1866,[12] each a sep EP 1843[216]). *LG* Seq 13. *Parl* Seq 5. *Eccl* Seq 20. Addtl eccl bdry alt: 1879.[225]

LINK
  EP Cr 1845 from Leigh AP,[222] refounded 1846.[223] Powyke RDn. Sometimes called 'Malvern Link'. Abol 1973 to help cr Malvern Link with Cowleigh EP.[74]

LITTLETON—see following 2 entries

NORTH AND MIDDLE LITTLETON
  AP Orig 1 AP as 'Littleton' but by 1535 2 EPs of 'North and Middle Littleton', 'South Littleton'. *LG* Seq 1. Civ bdry: 1886.[226] *LG* Seq 3. *Eccl* Seq 4.

SOUTH LITTLETON
  AP Orig status and organisation as for North and Middle Littleton, incl bdry alt 1886 and adding civ bdry alt 1933.[14]

LONDONDERRY
  EP Cr 1929 from The Quinton EP, Oldbury EP (both Worcs), Smethwick EP, Smethwick St Alban EP (both Staffs) to be dioc Birm.[227] Smethw. RDn (1929—66), Warley RDn (1966—*).

LONGBRIDGE
  EP Cr 1957 from Kings Norton EP.[41] K's Nort. RDn. Bdry: 1966 (help cr West Heath EP),[124] 1972.[125]

LONGDON
  AP Incl chap Castlemorton (sep civ identity early, sep EP 1880[97]), chap Chaceley (sep civ identity early, sep EP 1760[31]), chap Eldersfield (sep par prob *ca* 1232—33[171]). *LG* Seq 19. *Parl* Seq 12. *Eccl* Seq 15.

LULSLEY
  Chap in Suckley AP, sep CP 1866,[12] eccl severed 1912 to help cr Alfrick and Lulsley EP.[15] *LG* Seq 3. Civ bdry: 1884,[127] 1894.[17] *Parl* Seq 5.

LUTLEY
  Hmlt (Worcs, Halfsh. Hd) in Halesowen AP (Worcs, Salop until 1844 ent Worcs thereafter), sep CP 1866.[12] *LG* Stourbr. PLU, RSD, Halesowen RD (1894—1925), UD (1925—36), MB (1936—74). Transf 1974 to W Midlands.[134] *Parl* Seq 2.

LYE
  Tp in Oldswinford AP (eccl, 'Old Swinford'), sep CP 1866,[12] sep EP (sometimes called 'The Lye') 1839,[228] eccl refounded 1841.[229] *LG* Halfsh. Hd, Stourbr. PLU (orig rated in Oldwinford, sep rated soon after 1836[52]—1930), RSD, RD (1894—97), Lye & Wollescote UD (1897—1933), Stourbr. MB (1933—74). Transf 1974 to W Midlands.[134] *Parl* W'rn Dv (1832—85), N'rn Dv (1885—1918), Stourbr. Dv (1918—48), Dudley BC (1948—70), Halesowen & Stourbr. BC (1970—*). *Eccl* Kidderm. RDn (1839—1907), Swinf. RDn (1907—73), Stourbr. RDn (1974—*). Eccl bdry: 1873 (help cr Stamber Mill EP),[230] 1873,[231] 1930,[232] 1965

484 THE PARISHES OF ENGLAND

(help cr Wollescote EP).[233]

MADRESFIELD
AP *LG* Seq 19. Civ bdry: 1884,[234] 1933.[14] *Parl* Seq 6. *Eccl* Seq 14. Eccl bdry: 1866 (help cr Guarlford EP).[7]

GREAT MALVERN
AP Incl chap Newland (sep CP 1866,[12] sep EP 1728[31]), hmlt Guarlford (sep CP 1894 from the pt of this par not in Great Malv. UD,[180] sep EP 1866 by union of this hmlt and pt Madresfield AP[7]). *LG* Persh. Hd, Upton upon Sev. PLU, pt Great Malvern USD (enlarged pt Mar—apptd day 1894), pt Upton upon Sev. RSD (reduced pt Mar—apptd day 1894), Great Malv. UD (1894—98), Malv. UD (1898—1974). Addtl civ bdry alt: 1884,[234] 1933.[14] *Parl* Seq 6. *Eccl* Seq 14. Addtl eccl bdry alt: 1869 (cr Great Malvern Holy Trinity EP),[235] 1872 (cr Great Malvern Christ Church EP),[236] 1895,[237] 1926 (cr Wyche EP).[238]

GREAT MALVERN CHRIST CHURCH
EP Cr 1872 from Great Malvern AP.[236] Powyke RDn (1872—1973), Malv. RDn (1974—*).

GREAT MALVERN HOLY TRINITY
EP Cr 1869 from Great Malvern AP.[235] Powyke RDn (1869—1973), Malv. RDn (1974—*).

LITTLE MALVERN
AP Priory church, sep par from Dissolution.[239] *LG* Seq 16. Civ bdry: 1900.[240] *Parl* Seq 12. *Eccl* Seq 14.

SOUTH MALVERN
CP Cr 1894 from the pt of Hanley Castle AP in Great Malv. UD.[180] *LG* Upton upon Sev. PLU, Great Malv. UD. Renamed 1896 'Malvern Wells' when gains pt Hanley Castle AP.[188]

WEST MALVERN
CP Cr 1897 as renaming of area cr by union Mathon Urban CP (Worcs), pt Cradley CP (Heref), to be ent Worcs.[241] *LG* Ledbury PLU, Malv. Link UD (1897—98), Malv. UD (1898—1974). *Parl* Bewd. Dv (1918—48), S Worcs CC (1948—*).
EP Name used now for EP cr 1844 as 'Mathon St James', qv.

MALVERN LINK
EP Name sometimes used for EP cr 1845 as 'Link', qv (incl eccl abol 1973).
CP Cr 1894 from the pt of Leigh AP in Malv. Link UD.[180] *LG* Upton upon Sev. PLU, Malv. Link UD (1894—98), Malv. UD (1898—1974). Bdry: 1933.[14] *Parl* Bedw. Dv (1918—48), S Worcs CC (1948—*).

MALVERN LINK WITH COWLEIGH
EP Cr 1973 by union Link EP (sometimes called 'Malvern Link'), Cowleigh EP.[74] Powyke RDn (1973), Malv. RDn (1974—*).

MALVERN WELLS
EP Cr 1836 from Hanley Castle AP.[190] Powyke RDn (1836—1973), Malv. RDn (1974—*). Bdry: 1895.[237]
CP Renaming 1896 of South Malvern CP when gains pt Hanley Castle AP.[188] *LG* Upton upon Sev. PLU, Great Malv. UD (1896—98), Malv. UD (1898—1974). Bdry: 1898,[189] 1898,[242] 1900.[240] *Parl* Bewd. Dv (1918—48), S Worcs CC (1948—*).

MAMBLE
AP *LG* Seq 2. Civ bdry: 1877.[243] *Parl* Seq 5. *Eccl* Burf. RDn. Abol eccl 1669 to help cr Mamble with Bayton EP.[46]

MAMBLE WITH BAYTON
EP Cr 1669 by union Mamble AP, Bayton AP.[46] Burf. RDn (1669—1878), Burf. (East) RDn (1878—98), Bewd. RDn (1898—1926), Lindr. RDn (1926—73), Stourpt. RDn (1974—*).

MARLBOROUGH IN THE VINES
Ex-par place, sep CP 1858.[86] *LG* Halfsh. Hd, Droitw. PLU (1858—84), MB (1835—84), USD. Abol civ 1884 ent to Droitwich St Nicholas AP.[153] *Parl* Droitw. Parl Bor (1832—85).

MARTIN HUSSINGTREE
AP *LG* Persh. Hd, Droitw. PLU, RSD, RD. *Parl* Seq 14. *Eccl* Droitw. RDn (through 1973), Worc East RDn (1974—*). Eccl bdry: 1895.[110]

MARSTON CHAPEL or MARTSON GREEN—see HALL GREEN [MARSTON CHAPEL]

MARTLEY
AP Incl chap Areley Kings (sep par by 1535 although 17th cent references to its dependence[27]), hmlt Hillhampton (sep CP 1866[12]). *LG* Seq 3. *Parl* Seq 5. *Eccl* Seq 16.

MATHON
AP *LG* Persh. Hd, Ledbury PLU, pt Mathon USD (1875—92), pt Malv. Link UD (1892—94), pt Ledbury RSD. Abol civ 1894 the pt in the UD cr Mathon Urban CP, the remainder cr Mathon Rural CP.[244] *Parl* W'rn Dv (1832—1918). *Eccl* Powyke RDn (until 1905), Ledbury RDn (dioc Heref, 1905—*). Eccl bdry: 1844 (help cr Mathon St James EP).[65]

MATHON RURAL
CP Cr 1894 from the pt of Mathon AP not in Malv. Link UD.[244] *LG* Ledbury PLU, sep RD in Worcs (1894—97). Transf 1897 to Heref.[10]

MATHON ST JAMES
EP Cr 1844 from Mathon AP, Leigh AP (both Worcs) and from Cradley AP, Colwall AP (both Heref), to be dioc Worc.[65] Powyke RDn (1844—73), Malv. RDn (1974—*). Bdry: 1876 (help cr Cowleigh EP [Worcs, Heref]).[132] Later called 'West Malvern'.

MATHON URBAN
CP Cr 1894 from the pt of Mathon AP in Malv. Link UD.[244] *LG* Ledbury PLU, Malv. Link UD. Abol 1897, united with pt Cradley AP, Heref, and the enlarged par renamed 'West Malvern' CP, to be ent in Worcs.[241]

LOWER MITTON
Tp in Kidderminster AP, sep CP 1866,[12] sep EP 1844 (sometimes as 'Stourport').[108] *LG* Halfsh. Hd, Kidderm. PLU, Lower Mitton USD (1875—89), Stourpt. USD (1889—94), UD (1894—1928). Civ bdry: 1920.[28] Abol civ 1928 to help cr Stourport CP.[245] *Parl* Bewd. Parl Bor (1832—85), Mid Dv (1885—1918), Bewd. Dv (1918—48). *Eccl* Kidderm. RDn (1844—1921), Mitton RDn (1921—73), Stourpt. RDn (1974—*). Eccl bdry: 1885,[210] 187,[192] 1904 (help cr Wilden EP).[193]

UPPER MITTON
Hmlt (Halfsh. Hd) in Hartlebury AP (o'wise Osw.

Hd), sep CP 1866.[12] *LG* Droitw. PLU, RSD, RD (1894—97), Stourpt. UD (1897—1928). Abol 1928 to help cr Stourport CP.[245] *Parl* W'rn Dv (1832—67), Bewd. Parl Bor (1867—85), Mid Dv (1885—1918), Bewd. Dv (1918—48).

MOSELEY
EP Cr 1767 from Bromsgrove AP,[31] refounded 1853 from Kings Norton EP (itself a sep EP 1846 from Bromsgrove AP[88]).[91] Droitw. RDn (1767—1880), Northf. RDn (1880—1905), K's Nort. RDn (1905—57), Moseley RDn (1957—*). Bdry: 1863 (help cr Kings Heath EP),[211] 1875 (cr Moseley St Anne EP),[246] 1879,[247] 1912 (help cr Stirchley EP),[215] 1914 (help cr Moseley St Agnes EP).[92]

MOSELEY ST AGNES
EP Cr 1914 from Moseley EP, Yardley Wood EP.[92] K's Nort. RDn (1914—57), Moseley RDn (1957—*). Bdry: 1937 (help cr Billesley Common EP),[63] 1962.[26]

MOSELEY ST ANNE
EP Cr 1875 from Moseley EP.[246] Droitw. RDn (1875—80), Northf. RDn (1880—1905), K's Nort. RDn (1905—57), Moseley RDn (1957—*). Bdry: 1958 (incl exchanges pts with Edgbaston St Mary and St Ambrose EP, Warws).[18]

NAFFORD
AP Orig AP (Persh. RDn) incl chap Birlingham, the par church early in ruins and the chap made the par church,[67] the par thereafter civ 'Birlingham', eccl 'Birlingham with Nafford'.

NAUNTON BEAUCHAMP
AP *LG* Seq 17. *Parl* Seq 3. *Eccl* Seq 7.

NETHERTON
Hmlt in Cropthorne AP, sep CP 1866.[12] *LG* Seq 12. *Parl* Seq 3.

NETHERTON ST ANDREW
EP Cr 1844 from Dudley AP.[158] Persh. RDn (1844—61), Kidderm. RDn (1861—80), Dudley RDn (1880—*). Bdry: 1931,[7] 1950 (cr Dudley Wood EP).[165]

NEWLAND
Chap in Great Malvern AP, sep CP 1866,[12] sep EP 1728.[31] *LG* Seq 19. *Parl* Seq 6. *Eccl* Powyke RDn (1728—1973), Malv. RDn (1974—*).

NORTHFIELD
AP Incl chap Cofton Hackett (sep civ identity early, sep EP 1866,[121] eccl refounded 1871[122]). *LG* Halfsh. Hd, Kings Norton PLU (1836—1911), RSD, RD (1894—98), Kings Norton & Northf. UD (1898—1911), Bromsgr. PLU (1911—12), sep RD (administered by Bromsgr. RD Co Council, 1911—12). Civ bdry: 1911 (loses pt to Birm CB [assoc with Warws] & AP, pt to Cofton Hackett CP, pt to Illey CP).[123] Abol civ 1912 ent to Birm CB (assoc with Warws) & AP.[213] *Parl* E'rn Dv (1832—1918). *Eccl* Droitw. RDn (until 1880), Northf. RDn (1880—1905), K's Nort. RDn (1905—*). Addtl eccl bdry alt: 1862 (cr Selly Oak St Mary EP),[248] 1933 (help cr Weoley Castle EP),[61] 1938 (help cr Allens Cross EP),[18] 1965,[19] 1965 (help cr Shenley Green EP),[249] 1966 (help cr West Heath EP).[125]

NORTON
EP Cr [St Michael and St George] 1953 from Old

Swinford AP (civ, 'Oldswinford'), Stourbridge St Thomas EP.[250] Swinf. RDn (1953—73), Stourbr. RDn (1974—*).

NORTON AND LENCHWICK
AP *LG* Seq 1. *Parl* Seq 3. *Eccl* Seq 4.

NORTON JUXTA KEMPSEY
Chap in Kempsey AP, sep civ identity early, sep EP 1781.[31] *LG* Seq 12. Civ bdry: 1885.[251] *Parl* Seq 8. *Eccl* Worc RDn (1781—1861), Worc East RDn (1861—1921), Outer Worc RDn (1921—26), Worc RDn (1926—61). Abol eccl 1961 to help cr Norton with Whittington EP.[252]

NORTON WITH WHITTINGTON
EP Cr 1961 by union Norton juxta Kempsey EP, pt Worcester St Martin AP.[252] Worc RDn (1961—73), Worc East RDn (1974—*). Bdry: 1967.[205]

ODDINGLEY
AP *LG* Seq 9. *Parl* Seq 13. *Eccl* Worc RDn (until 1861), Worc East RDn (1861—92), Droitw. RDn (1892—1973). Abol eccl 1973 to help cr Hadzor with Oddingley EP.[181]

OFFENHAM
AP Orig chap in Evesh. Priory, sep par at Dissolution.[253] *LG* Seq 1. Civ bdry: 1933,[14] 1949.[34] *Parl* Seq 3. *Eccl* Seq 4. Eccl bdry: 1967.[35]

OLD WOOD
EP Cr 1856 from Tenbury AP (Worcs), Laysters EP, Middleton on the Hill EP (both Heref).[254] Burf. RDn (1856—78), Burf. (West) RDn (1878—98), Burf RDn (1898—1972), Ludlow RDn (1972—*). Now called 'Tenbury St Michael and All Angels'.

OLDBERROW
AP *LG* Black. Hd, Alc. PLU, RSD, sep RD in Worcs (1894—96). Transf 1896 to Warws.[255] *Parl* E'rn Dv (1832—1918). *Eccl* See entry in Warws for RDns and for eccl abol 1972.

OLDBURY
Tp (Salop, Brimstree Hd) in Halesowen AP (Worcs, Salop until 1844, ent Worcs thereafter), transf to Worcs (Halfsh. Hd) 1832 for parl purposes, 1844 for civ purposes,[95] sep CP 1866 in Worcs,[12] sep EP 1715.[31] *LG* Oldb. PLU, USD, UD (1894—1935), MB (1935—66). Civ bdry: 1884 (incl help cr Warley CP),[256] 1895 (gains the pt in Oldb. UD of Warley CP),[257] 1908 (gains Warley CP),[258] 1928 (cr Warley Woods CP to be in Smethw. CB [assoc with Staffs]),[259] 1933.[14] Abol civ 1966 pt to W Bromwich CB (assoc with Staffs) & AP, pt to help cr Warley CP (assoc with Worcs) & CP), pt to Halesowen MB & AP.[21] *Parl* E'rn Dv (1832—85), N'rn Dv (1885—1918), Stourbr. Dv (1918—48), Oldb. & Halesowen BC (1948—70). *Eccl* Stottesdon RDn (dioc Heref, until 1841), Kidderm. RDn (dioc Worc, 1841—80), Dudley RDn (1880—Mar 1905), not in a RDn (Mar—Aug 1905, when 1st transf to dioc Birm), Harb. RDn (Aug 1905—1929), Smethw. RDn (1929—66), Warley RDn (1966—*). Eccl bdry: 1969 (cr Langley [St John] EP).[220]

OLDSWINFORD
AP Usual civ spelling; for eccl organisation and for cr of EPs other than those below, see 'Old Swinford' in entries below for 'S'. Tp 'Oldswinford' in Worcs

(Halfsh. Hd) as were tp Lye (sep CP 1866,[12] sep EP 1839 [sometimes 'The Lye'],[228] eccl refounded 1841[229]), tp Stourbridge (sep CP 1866,[12] sep EP 1862[260]), tp Upper Swinford (sep CP 1866[12]), tp Wollescote (sep CP 1866,[12] sep EP 1965 from Old Swinford AP and 3 others pars [qv][233]), tp Wollaston (sep CP 1866,[12] eccl severed 1860 to help cr Amblecote EP [qv below][25]); incl in Staffs (S Seisdon Hd) hmlt Amblecote (sep CP 1866 in Staffs,[12] sep EP 1845 [incl Worcs tp Wollaston (qv above)],[24] eccl refounded 1860[25]) so that 'Oldswinford' has no sep civ identity after 1866. *LG* Oldswinford sep rated for poor law purposes 1836 as were Stourbridge and Amblecote; remainder of tps sep rated soon after 1836 and 'Oldswinford' thereafter has no sep poor law identity. *Parl* Worcs pt, W'rn Dv (1832—67).

OMBERSLEY

AP *LG* Seq 9. *Parl* Seq 7. *Eccl* Worc RDn (until 1861), Worc East RDn (1861—1921), Outer Worc RDn (1921—26), Martley RDn (1926—73), Martley & Worc West RDn (1974—*).

ORLETON

Chap in Eastham AP, sep CP 1866,[12] eccl severed 1923 to help cr Stanford on Teme with Orleton EP.[167] *LG* Dodd. Hd, Tenb. PLU, RSD, RD. Abol civ 1933 to help cr Stanford with Orleton CP.[14] *Parl* W'rn Dv (1832—1918), Bewd. Dv (1918—48).

OVERBURY

AP Incl chap Berrow (pec jurisd Dean & Chapter of Worc, sep par by 1535[55]), hmlt Washbourne (transf to Glos 1832 for parl purposes, 1844 for civ purposes [Kiftsgate Hd],[95] sep CP 1866 in Glos[12]); also incl chap Teddington, hmlt Conderton (each a sep CP 1866 in Worcs,[12] neither sep eccl hence this par eccl 'Overbury with Alstone, Teddington and Little Washbourne', qv). *LG* Seq 14. *Parl* Seq 3.

OVERBURY WITH ALSTONE, TEDDINGTON AND LITTLE WASHBOURNE

AP Usual eccl spelling; for civ, change in cos and civ sep hmlt and chap, see prev entry. *Eccl* Seq 8.

PAPER MILLS

Ex-par area, sep CP 1858.[86] *LG* Halfsh. Hd, Droitw. PLU (1858[261]—84), RSD. Abol civ 1884 ent to Dodderhill AP.[143] *Parl* E'rn Dv (1832—85).

PEBWORTH

AP Glos par transf 1931 to Worcs.[11] *LG* Evesh. RD. *Parl* S Worcs (1948—*). *Eccl* See entry in Glos for eccl organisation and eccl abol 1964.

PEDMORE

AP *LG* Halfsh. Hd, Bromsgr. PLU, RSD, RD (1894—1933), Stourbr. MB (1933—74). Civ bdry: 1929.[262] Transf 1974 to W Midlands.[134] *Parl* W'rn Dv (1832—85), Mid Dv (1885—1918), Kidderm. Dv (1918—48), Dudley BC (1948—70), Halesowen & Stourbr. BC (1970—*). *Eccl* Kidderm. RDn (until 1907), Swinf. RDn (1907—73), Stourbr. RDn (1974—*). *Eccl* bdry: 1965 (help cr Wollescote EP).[233]

PENDOCK

AP *LG* Osw. Hd, Tewksb. PLU, RSD, RD (1894—1933), Upton upon Sev. RD (1933—74). Civ bdry: 1883,[55] 1965 (exchanges pts with Redmarley

d'Abitot AP, Glos).[21] *Parl* W'rn Dv (1832—85), S'rn Dv (1885—1918), Bewd. Dv (1918—48), S Worcs CC (1948—*). *Eccl* Seq 15.

PENSAX

Chap in Lindridge AP, sep CP 1866,[12] sep EP 1843.[216] *LG* Osw. Hd, Martley PLU, RSD, RD (1894—1933), Tenb. RD (1933—74). *Parl* W'rn Dv (1832—1918), Bewd. Dv (1918—48), Kidderm. CC (1948—*). *Eccl* Burf. RDn (1843—78), Burf. (East) RDn (1878—98), Bewd. RDn (1898—1926), Lindr. RDn (1926—73), Stourpt. RDn (1974—*). *Eccl* bdry: 1879.[225]

PEOPLETON

AP *LG* Seq 17. *Parl* Seq 3. *Eccl* Seq 7.

PERSHORE

CP Cr 1949 by union Pershore Holy Cross AP, Pershore St Andrew AP.[263] *LG* Persh. RD. Bdry: 1955,[264] 1958 (cr Drakes Broughton and Wadborough CP).[147] *Parl* S Worcs CC (1970—*).

PERSHORE HOLY CROSS

AP Orig pt of Persh. Abbey, sep par from Dissolution. Incl chap Strensham (sep par by 1535[265]), chap Upton Snodbury (sep par by 1535[265]). *LG* Persh. Hd, PLU, RSD, RD. Addtl civ bdry alt: 1883,[55] 1885.[251] Abol civ 1949 to help cr Pershore CP.[263] *Parl* Persh. Parl Bor (1295 only), E'rn Dv (1832—85), S'rn Dv (1885—1918), Evesh. Dv (1918—48), S Worcs CC (1948—70). *Eccl* Persh. RDn. Abol eccl 1729 to help cr Pershore St Andrew with Pershore Holy Cross EP.[266]

PERSHORE ST ANDREW

AP Incl chaps Besford, Defford (each a sep CP 1866,[12] the 2 eccl united 1865 to cr Defford cum Besford EP[58]), chap Bricklehampton (sep CP 1866,[12] eccl severed 1922 to help cr Elmley Castle with Bricklehampton EP[80]), tp Pinvin (sep CP 1866[12]), tp Wick (sep CP 1866,[12] sep EP 1727[31]). *LG* Persh. Hd, PLU, RSD, RD. Addtl civ bdry alt: 1883.[55] Abol civ 1949 to help cr Pershore CP.[263] *Parl* Organisation as for Pershore Holy Cross. *Eccl* Persh. RDn. Abol eccl 1729 to help cr Pershore St Andrew with Pershore Holy Cross EP.[266]

PERSHORE ST ANDREW WITH PERSHORE HOLY CROSS

EP Cr 1729 by union Pershore St Andrew AP, Pershore Holy Cross AP.[266] Persh. RDn. Bdry: 1922 (help cr Stoulton with Drake's Broughton EP).[80]

NORTH PIDDLE

AP *LG* Seq 17. *Parl* Seq 3. *Eccl* Seq 12.

PINVIN

Chap in Pershore St Andrew AP, sep CP 1866.[12] *LG* Seq 17. Bdry: 1955.[267] *Parl* Seq 3.

PIRTON

AP *LG* Seq 17. *Parl* Seq 3. *Eccl* Worc RDn. Abol eccl 1771 to help cr Croome d'Abitot with Pirton EP,[136] by 20th cent called 'Croome d'Abitot', qv for eccl abol 1973.

POWICK

AP Perhaps incl chap Bransford (either orig or early in Leigh AP,[75]) sep CP 1866 from Leigh[12]). *LG* Seq 19. *Parl* Seq 6. *Eccl* Seq 14.

QUEENHILL

Chap (Persh. Hd) in Ripple AP (o'wise Osw. Hd),

sep CP 1866,[12] eccl severed 1863 to help cr Queenhill with Holdfast EP.[199] *LG* Seq 19. *Parl* Seq 12.

QUEENHILL WITH HOLDFAST

EP Cr 1863 by union chap Queenhill, hmlt Holdfast, both in Ripple AP.[199] Bredon RDn (1863—92), Upton RDn (1892—*).

QUINTON

CP Renaming between 1891 and 1901 of Ridgacre CP.[268] *LG* Stourbr. PLU (renaming—1911), RSD, Halesowen RD (renaming—1909), Birm CB (1909—12), PLU (1911—12). See entry in Warws for civ abol of Quinton 1912 ent to Birmingham AP.

THE QUINTON

EP Cr 1841 from Halesowen AP.[133] Kidderm. RDn (1841—80), Dudley RDn (1880—Mar 1905), not in a RDn (Mar—Aug 1905, when 1st transf to dioc Birm), Harb. RDn (Aug 1905—29), Edgb. RDn (1929—*). Bdry: 1869 (help cr Blackheath EP),[68] 1929 (help cr Londonderry EP [Worcs, Staffs]),[227] 1930 (cr Warley Woods EP),[269] 1933 (help cr Harborne St Faith and St Laurence EP),[270] 1959 (help cr Quinton Road West EP [Worcs, Staffs]). Sometimes 'Christ Church at The Quinton'.

QUINTON ROAD WEST

EP Cr 1958 from The Quinton EP, Harborne AP (Staffs).[223] Edgb. RDn.

RAINBOW HILL

EP Cr 1883 from Claines AP.[109] Worc East RDn (1883—1921), Inner Worc RDn (1921—26), Worc RDn (1926—73), Worc East RDn (1974—*). Bdry: 1912,[111] 1952 (help cr Tollandine EP),[271] 1966 (help cr Wardon St Wulfstan EP),[198] 1967.[272]

REDDITCH

Chap (Worcs, Halfsh. Hd) in Tardebigge AP (Worcs, Warws until 1844, ent Worcs thereafter), sep CP 1866,[12] sep EP 1855.[93] *LG* Bromsgr. PLU (soon after 1836[273]—1930), pt Redditch RSD (1875—91), Redditch USD (pt 1875—91, ent 1891—94), Redditch UD. Civ bdry: 1894 (the pt prev not in the USD cr North Redditch CP and gains the pt of Webheath CP in the UD),[90] 1904 (gains Unnamed CP [former pt Beoley, in the area of the UD]),[274] 1930,[20] 1933,[14] 1965 (gains pt Sambourne CP, Warws),[21] 1966,[54] 1969 (gains pt Studley AP, Warws).[275] *Parl* Seq 1. *Eccl* Droitw. RDn (1855—80), Northf. RDn (1880—92), Bromsgr. RDn (1892—*). Eccl bdry: 1902 (cr Redditch St George EP),[276] 1924,[66] 1933,[203] 1950.[32]

NORTH REDDITCH

CP Cr 1894 from the pt of Redditch CP prev not in Redditch USD.[90] *LG* Bromsgr. PLU, RD. Bdry: 1930.[20] Abol 1933 ent to Tutnall and Cobley CP.[14] *Parl* Kidderm. Dv (1918—48).

REDDITCH ST GEORGE

EP Cr 1902 from Redditch EP.[276] Bromsgr. RDn. Bdry: 1933.[203]

REDMARLEY D'ABITOT

AP *LG* Osw. Hd, Newent PLU, RSD, Unnamed RD (administered by Newent RD Council, Glos, 1894—1931). Transf 1931 to Glos.[11] *Parl* W'rn Dv (1832—85), S'rn Dv (1885—1918), Bewd. Dv (1918—48). *Eccl* Seq 15.

REDNALL

EP Cr 1957 from Rubery EP.[277] K's Nort. RDn. Bdry: 1972.[125]

RIBBESFORD

AP Incl chap and bor Bewdley (orig ex-par place sometimes considered in Staffs in 15th cent although usually considered in Worcs, status in Worcs confirmed by statute 1543,[60] made *temp* Henry VI a chap of Ribbesford AP,[60] sep CP 1866,[12] sep EP 1853[61]). *LG* Dodd. Hd, pt Bewd. Bor/MB (until 1866), Kidderm. PLU, RSD, RD. *Parl* Bewd. Parl Bor (pt 1606—1832, ent 1832—85), W'rn Dv (1885—1918), Kidderm. Dv/CC (1918—*). *Eccl* Burf. RDn (until 1878), Burf. (East) RDn (1878—98), Bewd. RDn (1898—1926), Kidderm. RDn (1926—40). Eccl bdry: 1845 (help cr Far Forest EP [Worcs, Salop]),[18] 1853 (cr Bewdley St Anne EP).[61] Abol eccl 1940 to help cr Ribbesford with Bewdley EP.[62]

RIBBESFORD WITH BEWDLEY

EP Cr 1940 by union Dowles AP (Salop until 1895, Worcs thereafter), Ribbesford AP, Bewdley EP (both Worcs).[62] Kidderm. RDn.

RIDGACRE

Tp (Salop, Brimstree Hd) in Halesowen AP (Worcs, Salop until 1844, ent Worcs thereafter), transf to Worcs 1832 for parl purposes, 1844 for civ purposes (Halfsh. Hd), sep CP 1866 in Worcs.[12] *LG* Stourbr. PLU, RSD. Bdry: 1884 (incl help cr Warley CP).[256] Renamed between 1891 and 1901 'Quinton' CP.[268] *Parl* From 1832, E'rn Dv (1832—85), N'rn Dv (1885—1918).

RIPPLE

AP Tp 'Ripple' in Osw. Hd as was hmlt Holdfast (sep CP 1866[12]); incl in Persh. Hd chap Queenhill (sep CP 1866[12]) (the chap and hmlt eccl severed and united 1863 as 'Queenhill with Holdfast'.[199] *LG* Osw. Hd (pt until 1866, ent from 1866), pt Persh. Hd (until 1866), Upton upon Sev. PLU, RSD, RD. Addtl civ bdry alt: 1884,[135] 1884 (loses pt to Twyning AP, Glos).[278] *Parl* Seq 12. *Eccl* Seq 9.

ROCHFORD

Chap in Tenbury AP (Heref, Wolphy Hd), the chap transf to Worcs 1832 for parl purposes, 1844 for civ purposes (Dodd. Hd),[95] sep CP 1866 in Worcs,[12] sep EP 1843.[279] *LG* From 1844, Seq 4. *Parl* From 1832, Seq 5. *Eccl* Burf. RDn (1843—78), Burf. (West) RDn (1878—98), Burf. RDn (1898—1921), Martley RDn (1921—26), Lindr. RDn (1926—73), Stourpt. RDn (1974—*).

ROCK

AP Sometimes 'Aka'. Usual civ spelling as 'Rock'; for eccl see following entry. *LG* Dodd. Hd, Cleob. Mort. PLU, RSD, Rock RD (1894—1933), Kidderm. RD (1933—74). Civ bdry: 1881,[1] 1885,[2] 1933.[14] *Parl* Seq 5.

ROCK WITH HEIGHTINGTON

AP Usual eccl spelling; for civ see prev entry. *Eccl* Seq 19. Eccl bdry: 1845 (help cr Far Forest EP [Worcs, Salop]).[18]

ROMSLEY

Tp (Salop, Brimstree Hd) in Halesowen AP (Worcs, Salop until 1844, ent Salop thereaftrer), transf to

Worcs 1832 for parl purposes, 1832 for civ purposes (Halfsh. Hd),[95] sep CP 1866 in Worcs.[12] *LG* From 1844, Seq 5. Bdry: 1933.[14] *Parl* From 1832, E'rn Dv (1832—85), N'rn Dv (1885—1918), Kidderm. Dv (1918—48), Bromsgr. CC (1948—70), Bromsgr. & Redditch CC (1970—*).

ROUNDS GREEN
EP Cr 1905 from Langley EP.[219] Not in a RDn (May—Aug 1905), Harb. RDn (Aug 1905—29), Smethw. RDn (1929—66), Warley RDn (1966—*). Bdry: 1959 (incl gains pt Rowley Regis EP, Staffs).[69]

RUBERY
EP Cr 1933 from The Lickey EP.[224] K's Nort. RDn. Bdry: 1957 (cr Rednall EP).[277]

RUSHOCK
AP Orig chap in Chaddesley Corbett AP, sep par by 1535.[98] *LG* Seq 7. *Parl* Seq 9. *Eccl* Kidderm. RDn (cr—1929), Droitw. RDn (1929—*).

ST THOMAS IN THE MOORS—see BALSALL HEATH ST THOMAS IN THE MOORS

SALWARPE
AP Incl hmlt Chawson (sep CP 1894 as 'Unnamed' CP [the pt of Salwarpe in Droitw. MB]).[53] *LG* Halfsh. Hd, Droitw. PLU, pt Droitw. MB & USD (1880—94), Droitw. RSD (ent 1875—80, pt 1880—94). Civ bdry: 1880,[89] 1933,[14] 1968.[149] *Parl* Seq 13. *Eccl* Seq 1.

LOWER SAPEY
AP Orig chap (sometimes 'Sapey Prichard') in Clifton upon Teme AP, perhaps a sep par as early as 1291, sep civ identity early, all eccl rights except burial until completely independent 18th cent.[119] *LG* Dodd. Hd, Bromyard PLU (1836—*ca* 1894), RSD, Martley PLU (*ca* 1894—1930), RD. *Parl* Seq 5. *Eccl* Seq 16.

SEDGEBERROW
AP *LG* Seq 10. *Parl* Seq 3. *Eccl* Seq 10.

SELLY HILL
EP Cr 1892 from Selly Oak St Mary EP.[280] Northf. RDn (1892—1905), K's Nort. RDn (1905—57), Moseley RDn (1957—*).

SELLY OAK ST MARY
EP Cr 1862 from Northfield AP.[248] Droitw. RDn (1862—80), Northf. RDn (1880—1905), K's Nort. RDn (1905—57), Edgb. RDn (1957—*). Bdry: 1892 (cr Selly Hill EP),[280] 1911 (cr Selly Oak St Wulstan EP),[276] 1926 (help cr Bournville EP),[71] 1933 (help cr Weoley Castle EP).[61]

SELLY OAK ST WULSTAN
EP Cr 1911 from Selly Oak St Mary EP.[276] K's Nort. RDn (1911—57), Moseley RDn (1957—*).

SEVERN STOKE
AP *LG* Seq 19. *Parl* Seq 12. *Eccl* Worc RDn (until 1861), Worc East RDn (1861—80s), Bredon RDn (1880s—1973). Abol eccl 1973 to help cr Severn Stoke with Croome d'Abitot EP.[137]

SEVERN STOKE WITH CROOME D'ABITOT
EP Cr 1973 by union Severn Stoke AP, Croome d'Abitot with Pirton EP (by 20th cent called simply 'Croome d'Abitot').[137] Bredon RDn (1973), Upton RDn (1974—*).

SHELL
Ex-par place, sep CP 1858.[86] *LG* Osw. Hd, Droitw.

PLU (1858—84), RSD. Abol civ 1884 ent to Himbleton AP.[196] *Parl* Droitw. Parl Bor (1832—85).

SHELSLEY BEAUCHAMP
AP Incl hmlt Shelsey Kings (sep CP 1866[12]). *LG* Seq 3. *Parl* Seq 5. *Eccl* Worc RDn (until 1861), Worc West RDn (1861—1921), Martley RDn (1921—72). Abol eccl 1972 to help cr The Shelsleys EP.[281]

SHELSLEY KINGS
Hmlt in Shelsley Beauchamp AP, sep CP 1866.[12] *LG* Seq 3. *Parl* Seq 5.

SHELSLEY WALSH
AP *LG* Seq 3. *Parl* Seq 5. *Eccl* Burf. RDn (until 1878), Burf. (East) RDn (1878—98), Bewd. RDn (1898—1905), W Worc RDn (1905—21), Martley RDn (1921—72). Abol eccl 1972 to help cr The Shelsleys EP.[281]

THE SHELSLEYS
EP Cr 1972 by union Shelsley Beauchamp AP, Shelsley Walsh AP.[281] Martley RDn (1972—73), Martley & Worc West RDn (1974—*).

SHENLEY GREEN
EP Cr 1965 from Weoley Castle EP, Northfield AP.[249] K's Nort. RDn.

SHIPSTON ON STOUR
Chap in Tredington AP, sep CP/EP 1719 (eccl incl Tidmington, a chap in Tredington AP which civ became sep at that time).[282] *LG* Osw. Hd, Shipst. on Stour PLU, RSD, RD. Transf 1931 to Warws.[11] *Parl* E'rn Dv (1832—85), S'rn Dv (1885—1918), Evesh. Dv (1918—48). *Eccl* Seq 22.

SHRAWLEY
AP *LG* Seq 3. *Parl* Seq 5. *Eccl* Seq 17.

SPARKHILL ST JOHN THE EVANGELIST
EP Cr 1894 from Yardley AP.[283] Northf. RDn (1894—1905), Bord. RDn (1905—*). Bdry: 1907,[185] 1908 (loses pt to Sparkbrook Christ Church EP, Warws),[87] 1911 (cr Springfield EP),[276] 1913,[6] 1931 (help cr Tyseley EP).[7]

SPETCHLEY
AP Orig chap in Worcester St Mary AP, sep par by 1291.[284] *LG* Seq 12. Civ bdry: 1952.[114] *Parl* Seq 8. *Eccl* Worc RDn (until 1861), Worc East RDn (1861—1921), Outer Worc RDn (1921—26), Persh. RDn (1926—*).

SPRINGFIELD
EP Cr 1911 from Sparkhill St John the Evangelist EP.[276] Bord. RDn (1911—57), Moseley RDn (1957—*). Bdry: 1931 (help cr Tyseley EP).[7]

STAMBER MILL
EP Cr 1873 from Lye EP, Stourbridge EP, Old Swinford AP.[230] Kidderm. RDn (1873—1907), Swinf. RDn (1907—73), Stourbr. RDn (1974—*). Bdry: 1930,[232] 1965 (help cr Wollescote EP).[233]

STANFORD ON TEME
AP *LG* Dodd. Hd, Martley PLU, RSD, RD. Abol civ 1933 to help cr Stanford with Orleton CP.[14] *Parl* W'rn Dv (1832—1918), Bewd. Dv (1918—48). *Eccl* Burf. RDn (until 1878), Burf. (East) RDn (1878—98), Bewd. RDn (1898—1921), Martley RDn (1921—23). Abol eccl 1923 to help cr Stanford on Teme with Orleton EP.[167]

STANFORD ON TEME WITH ORLETON
EP Cr 1923 by union Stanford on Teme AP, chap Orleton in Eastham AP.[167] Martley RDn (1923—26), Lindr. RDn (1926—73), Stourbr. RDn (1974—*).

STANFORD WITH ORLETON
CP Cr 1933 by union Orleton CP, Stanford on Teme AP.[14] *LG* Tenb. RD. *Parl* Kidderm. CC (1948—*).

STAUNTON
AP *LG* Persh. Hd, Newent PLU, RSD Unnamed RD (administered by Newent RD Council, Glos, 1894—1931). Transf 1931 to Glos.[11] *Parl* W'rn Dv (1832—85), S'rn Dv (1885—1918), Bewd. Dv (1918—48). *Eccl* Powyke RDn (until 1861), Upton RDn (1861—1952), Glouc North RDn (dioc Glouc, 1952—*).

STECHFORD
EP Cr 1932 from Yardley AP.[91] Solih. RDn (1932—57), Yard. RDn (1957—*).

STIRCHLEY
EP Cr 1912 from Kings Norton EP, Moseley EP.[215] K's Nort. RDn. Bdry: 1932 (help cr Hazelwell EP).[194]

STOCK AND BRADLEY
Chap in Fladbury AP, sep CP 1866.[12] *LG* Seq 9. *Parl* E'rn Dv (1832—85), Mid Dv (1885—1918), Kidderm. Dv (1918—48), Worc BC (1948—*).

STOCKTON ON TEME
AP *LG* Dodd. Hd, Martley PLU, RSD, RD (1894—1931), Tenb. RD (1933—74). *Parl* Seq 5. *Eccl* Burf. RDn (until 1878), Burf. (East) RDn (1878—98), Bewd. RDn (1898—1926), Lindr. RDn (1926—73), Stourpt. RDn (1974—*).

STOKE BLISS
AP In Heref (Brockash Hd) incl in Worcs hmlt Kyre Parva (Dodd. Hd [perhaps orig in Kyre Magna AP but in Stoke Bliss (o'wise Heref, Broxash Hd) by 1655[218]], sep CP 1866 in Worcs[12]) so that 'Stoke Bliss' ent Heref 1866—97 until transf 1897 to Worcs.[10] *LG* Tenb. PLU, RSD, sep RD in Heref (1894—97), Tenb. RD (1897—1974). Addtl civ bdry alt: 1933 (gains Kyre Parva CP).[14] *Parl* Worcs pt, W'rn Dv (1832—67), Bewd. Dv (1918—48), Kidderm. CC (1948—*). *Eccl* Burf. RDn (until 1878), Froome (North) (1878—98), Bewd. RDn (1898—1921), Martley RDn (1921—26), Lindr. RDn (1926—73). Abol eccl 1973 to help cr Stoke Bliss with Kyre Wyard, Hanley William and Hanley Child EP.[191]

STOKE BLISS WITH KYRE WYARD, HANLEY WILLIAM AND HANLEY CHILD
EP Cr 1973 by union Stoke Bliss AP, Kyre Wyard AP (civ, 'Great Wyard'), Hanley William with Hanley Child EP.[191] Lindr. RDn (1973), Stourpt. RDn (1974—*).

STOKE IN BROMSGROVE
CP Cr 1894 from the pt (uninhabited) of Stoke Prior AP in Bromsgr. Town UD.[34] *LG* Bromsgr. PLU, Bromsgr. Town UD (1894—96), Bromsgr. UD (1896—1933). Abol 1933 ent to Bromsgrove AP.[14] *Parl* Kidderm. Dv (1918—48).

STOKE PRIOR
AP *LG* Osw. Hd, Bromsgr. PLU, pt (uninhabited) Bromsgr. Town USD, pt Bromsgr. RSD, Bromsgr. RD. Civ bdry: 1894 (the pt in the UD cr Stoke in Bromsgrove CP),[53] 1933.[14] *Parl* Pt Droitw. Parl Bor (1867—85), E'rn Dv (ent 1832—67, pt 1867—85), Mid Dv (1885—1918), Kidderm. Dv (1918—48), Bromsgr. CC (1948—70), Bromsgr. & Redditch CC (1970—*). *Eccl* Droitw. RDn (until 1921), Bromsgr. RDn (1921—*). Eccl bdry: 1868 (cr Finstall EP).[175]

STONE
AP Orig chap in Chaddesley AP, sep par by 1535.[99] *LG* Seq 7. Civ bdry: 1933.[14] *Parl* Seq 9. *Eccl* Seq 5.

STOULTON
Tp in Kempsey AP, sep civ identity early, sep EP 1794.[31] *LG* Seq 12. Civ bdry: 1885.[251] *Parl* Seq 8. *Eccl* Worc RDn (1794—1861), Worc East RDn (1861—80s), Persh. RDn (1880s—1922). Abol eccl 1922 to help cr Stoulton with Drake's Broughton EP.[80]

STOULTON WITH DRAKE'S BROUGHTON
EP Cr 1922 by union Stoulton EP, pt Pershore St Andrew with Pershore Holy Cross EP.[80] Persh. RDn.

STOURBRIDGE
Tp in Oldswinford AP (eccl, 'Old Swinford'), sep CP 1866,[12] sep EP 1862.[260] *LG* Halfsh. Hd, Stourbr. PLU, USD, UD. Civ bdry: 1966 (incl loses pt to Dudley CB [as the CB becomes assoc with Staffs] & CP).[21] Transf 1974 to W Midlands.[134] *Parl* W'rn Dv (1832—85), Mid Dv (1885—1918), Stourbr. Dv (1918—48), Dudley BC (1948—70), Halesowen & Stourbr. BC (1970—*). *Eccl* Kidderm. RDn (1862—1907), Swinf. RDn (1907—73), Stourbr. RDn (1974—*). Eccl bdry: 1873 (help cr Stamber Mill EP).[230]

STOURBRIDGE ST THOMAS
EP Cr 1866 from Old Swinford AP (civ, 'Oldswinford').[285] Kidderm. RDn (1866—1907), Swinf. RDn (1907—73), Stourbr. RDn (1974—*). Bdry: 1930,[232] 1953 (help cr Norton EP).[250]

STOURPORT
CP Cr 1928 by union Lower Mitton CP, Upper Mitton CP.[245] *LG* Kidderm. PLU, Stourpt. UD. Bdry: 1933.[14] Renamed 1934 'Stourport-on-Severn' CP.[286]

STOURPORT-ON-SEVERN
CP Renaming 1934 of Stourport CP.[286] *LG* Stourpt.-on-Sev. UD. Bdry: 1953.[30] *Parl* Kidderm. CC (1948—*).

STRENSHAM
AP Orig chap in Pershore Holy Cross AP (pt of Persh. Abbey at Dissolution), sep par by 1535.[265] *LG* Seq 17. *Parl* Seq 3. *Eccl* Seq 9.

SUCKLEY
AP Incl chap Alfrick, chap Lulsley (each a sep CP 1866,[12] the 2 united eccl 1912 as 'Alfrick and Lulsey' EP[15]). *LG* Seq 3. *Parl* Seq 5. *Eccl* Seq 14.

OLD SWINFORD
AP Usual eccl spelling; for civ organisation, status in 2 cos, and civ and eccl sep tps and hmlt, see 'Oldswinford'. *Eccl* Seq 6. Addtl eccl bdry alt: 1866 (cr Stourbridge St Thomas EP),[285] 1873,[231] 1873 (help cr Stamber Mill EP),[230] 1953 (help cr

Norton EP).[250]

UPPER SWINFORD
Tp in Oldswinford AP (eccl, 'Old Swinford'), sep CP 1866.[12] *LG* Halfsh. Hd, Stourbr. PLU (orig rated in Oldswinford, sep rated soon after 1836[52]—1930), RSD, Halesowen RD (1894—95), Stourbr. UD (1895—1914), MB (1914—74). Transf 1974 to W Midlands.[134] *Parl* W'rn Dv (1832—85), Mid Dv (1885—1918), Stourbr. Dv (1918—48), Dudley BC (1948—70), Halesowen & Stourbr. BC (1970—*).

TARDEBIGGE
AP Medieval status in Warws, Staffs, Worcs varied at different times,[287] thereafter ent Worcs (Halfsh. Hd) except for tp Tutall and Cobley (Warws, Barlinchway Hd, transf to Worcs 1832 for parl purposes, 1844 for civ purposes (Halfsh. Hd)[95]; incl in Worcs chap Redditch (sep CP 1866,[12] sep EP 1855[93]), tps Bentley Pauncefoot, Webheath (each a sep CP 1866[12]) so that Tardebigge ent Worcs 1844—66 and has no sep civ identity after 1866. *LG* Hds noted above; 'Tardebigge' was sep rated for poor law purposes at cr of Bromsgr. PLU but each of the 4 units sep rated soon after 1836 and 'Tardebigge' no longer had sep poor law status.[52] *Parl* From 1844, E'rn Dv (1832—67). *Eccl* Sometimes as 'Tardebigge with Webheath', Seq 2. Addtl eccl bdry alt: 1850 (help cr Headless Cross EP [Warws, Worcs]),[174] 1913 (loses pt to The Lickey EP, dioc Birm),[23] 1924,[66] 1950.[32]

TEDDINGTON
Chap in Overbury AP, sep CP 1866.[12] *LG* Osw. Hd, Tewksb. PLU, RSD, RD. Transf 1931 to Glos.[11] *Parl* E'rn Dv (1832—85), S'rn Dv (1885—1918), Evesh. Dv (1918—48).

TENBURY
AP Tp 'Tenbury' (Tenb. Bor) in Worcs (Dodd. Hd) as was chap Kyre Magna (eccl, 'Kyre Wyard', sep par by 1535[217]); incl in Heref (Wolphy Hd) chap Rochford (transf to Worcs 1832 for parl purposes, 1844 for civ purposes [Dodd. Hd] sep CP 1866 in Worcs[12]) so that Tenbury ent Worcs from 1844. *LG* Tenb. PLU, RSD, RD. Addtl civ bdry alt: 1965 (loses pt to Burford AP, Salop).[21] *Parl* From 1844, Seq 5. *Eccl* Sometimes later as 'Tenbury Wells', Burf. RDn (until 1878), Burf. (West) RDn (1878—98), Burf. RDn (1898—1972), Ludlow RDn (1972—*). Addtl eccl bdry alt: 1856 (help cr Old Wood EP [Worcs, Heref]).[254]

TENBURY ST MICHAEL AND ALL ANGELS
EP Name used now for EP cr 1856 as 'Old Wood' (Worcs, Heref), qv.

TENBURY WELLS—see TENBURY

THROCKMORTON
Chap in Fladbury AP, sep CP 1866.[12] *LG* Seq 12. *Parl* Seq 3.

TIBBERTON
AP *LG* Seq 9. *Parl* Seq 7. *Eccl* Worc RDn (until 1861), Worc East RDn (1861—1921), Droitw. RDn (1921—27). Abol eccl 1927 to help cr Tibberton with Bredicot EP.[76]

TIBBERETON WITH BREDICOT
EP Cr 1927 by union Tibberton AP, Bredicot AP.[76] Droitw. RDn.

TIDMINGTON
Chap in Tredington AP, sep CP 1719, eccl severed at the same time to help cr Shipston on Stour EP.[283] *LG* Osw. Hd, Shipst. on Stour PLU, RSD, RD. Transf 1931 to Warws.[11] *Parl* E'rn Dv (1832—85), S'rn Dv (1885—1918), Evesh. Dv (1918—48).

TOLLANDINE
EP Cr 1952 from Rainbow Hill EP, Worcester Holy Trinity EP.[271] Worc RDn (1952—73), Worc East RDn (1974—*).

TREDINGTON
AP Incl chap Shipston on Stour, chap Tidmington (each a sep CP 1719, the 2 eccl severed and united at the same time to cr Shipston on Stour EP[282]). *LG* Osw. Hd, Shipst. on Stour PLU, RSD, RD. Transf 1931 to Warws.[11] *Parl* E'rn Dv (1832—85), S'rn Dv (1885—1918), Evesh. Dv (1918—48). *Eccl* Kinet. RDn (until 1861), S Kinet. RDn (1861—1921), Shipston RDn (1921—*) (dioc Cov, from 1918).

TUTNALL AND COBLEY
Tp (Warws, Barlinchway Hd) in Tardebigge AP (Worcs, Warws until 1844, ent Worcs thereafter), the tp transf to Worcs 1832 for parl purposes, 1844 for civ purposes (Halfsh. Hd), sep CP 1866 in Worcs.[12] *LG* Bromsgr. PLU (orig rated in Tardebigge, sep rated soon after 1836[52]—1930), RSD, RD. Bdry: 1933 (incl gains North Redditch CP).[14] *Parl* Seq 1.

TYSELEY
EP Cr 1931 from Sparkhill EP, Acocks Green EP, Springfield EP.[7] Bord. RDn.

UNNAMED
EP Cr 1894 from the pt (uninhabited) of Beoley AP in Redditch UD.[53] *LG* Kings Nort. PLU, Redditch UD. Abol 1904 ent to Redditch CP.[274]

UNNAMED
CP Cr 1894 from the pt (hmlt Chawson, not sep civ) of Salwarpe AP in Droitw. MB.[53] *LG* Droitw. PLU, MB. Abol 1933 ent to Droitwich CP.[14] *Parl* Evesh. Dv (1918—48).

UPTON SNODBURY
AP Orig chap in Pershore Holy Cross (itself pt of Persh. Abbey, sep par at Dissolution), 'Upton Snodbury' a sep par by 1535.[265] *LG* Osw. Hd (until 1760), Persh. Hd (from 1760) and Seq 17 thereafter. *Parl* Seq 4. *Eccl* Seq 7.

UPTON UPON SEVERN
AP *LG* Osw. Hd (until 1760), Persh. Hd (from 1760), Upton upon Sev. PLU, RSD, RD. *Parl* Seq 12. *Eccl* Seq 15.

UPTON WARREN
AP *LG* Seq 6. Civ bdry: 1880,[89] 1883,[56] 1933.[14] *Parl* E'rn Dv (1832—85), Mid Dv (1885—1918), Evesh. Dv (1918—48), Worc BC (1948—*). *Eccl* Droitw. RDn (until 1921), Bromsgr. RDn (1921—64), Droitw. RDn (1964—*). Eccl bdry: 1908 (help cr Dodford EP).[87]

WARLEY
CP Cr 1884 by union Warley Salop CP, pt Warley Wigorn CP, pt Ridgacre CP, pt Oldbury CP.[256] *LG* Halfsh. Hd, W Bromwich PLU, pt Oldbury USD, pt W Bromwich RSD, pt Oldbury UD (1894—95), Unnamed RD. Civ bdry: 1895 (loses the pt in

Oldbury UD to Oldbury CP).[257] Abol 1908 ent to Oldbury MB & CP.[258] *Parl* W'rn Dv (1885—1918).

CP Cr 1966 when Warley CB constituted from following areas: pt Birm CB & AP (assoc with Warws), pt Dudley CB & AP (as reconstituted CB becomes assoc with Staffs), pt Smethwick CB & CP (assoc with Staffs), pt W Bromwich CB & AP (assoc with Staffs); pt Halesowen MB & AP, pt Oldbury MB & CP, both Worcs; pt Brierley Hill UD (qv in entries for Staffs for constituent pars), pt Rowley Regis MB & CP, pt Tipton MB & AP, all Staffs.[21] *LG* Warley CB. Transf 1974 to W Midlands.[134] *Parl* Pt Warley East BC, pt Warley West BC (1970—*).

WARLEY SALOP
Tp (Salop, Brimstree Hd) in Halesowen AP (Worcs, Salop until 1844, ent Worcs thereafter), the tp transf to Worcs 1832 for parl purposes, 1844 for civ purposes (Halfsh. Hd),[95] sep CP 1866 in Worcs.[12] *LG* W Bromwich PLU, RSD. Abol 1884 to help cr Warley CP.[256] *Parl* From 1844, E'rn Dv (1832—85).

WARLEY WIGORN
Tp (Worcs, Halfsh. Hd) in Halesowen AP (Worcs, Salop until 1844, ent Worcs thereafter), sep CP 1866.[12] *LG* W Bromwich PLU, RSD. Abol 1884 to help cr Warley CP.[256] *Parl* E'rn Dv (1832—85).

WARLEY WOODS
CP Cr 1938 from Oldbury CP to be in Smethw. CB (assoc with Staffs).[259] See entry in Staffs.

EP Cr 1930 from The Quinton EP.[269] Edgb. RDn (1930—66), Warley RDn (1966—*).

WARNDON
AP Orig chap in Worcester St Helen AP, sep par by 1300.[288] *LG* Seq 9. Civ bdry: 1880,[89] 1952 (incl loses pt to Worc CB [assoc with Worcs] & CP).[114] *Parl* Pt Droitw. Parl Bor (1832—85), remainder and later, Seq 7. Parl bdry: 1952 (does not affect constituency).[115] *Eccl* Worc RDn (until 1861), Worc East RDn (1861—1921), Outer Worc RDn (1921—26), Persh. RDn (1926—27), Droitw. RDn (1927—*). Eccl bdry: 1966 (incl help cr Warndon St Wulstan EP).[198]

WARNDON ST WULSTAN
EP Cr 1966 from Rainbow Hill EP, Hindlip AP, Warndon AP.[198] Worc East RDn.

WEBHEATH
Tp (Worcs, Halfsh. Hd) in Tardebigge AP (Worcs, Warws until 1844, ent Worcs thereafter), sep CP 1866.[12] *LG* Bromsgr. PLU (orig rated in Tardebigge, sep rated soon after 1836[52]—1930), pt Redditch USD, pt Bromsgr. RSD, Bromsg. RD. Bdry: 1894 (loses the pt in the UD to Redditch CP),[90] 1930.[20] Abol 1933 pt to Bentley Pauncefoot CP, pt to Tutnall and Cobley CP, pt to Redditch CP.[14] *Parl* E'rn Dv (1832—85), Mid Dv (1885—1918), Kidderm. Dv (1918—48).

WELLAND
AP Orig chap in Bredon AP, sep par by 1300.[77] *LG* Seq 16. Civ bdry: 1898.[242] *Parl* Seq 12. *Eccl* Seq 13.

WEOLEY CASTLE
EP Cr 1933 from Northfield AP, Selley Oak St Mary EP.[62] K's Nort. RDn (1933—57), Edgb. RDn (1957—*). Bdry: 1956 (cr Bartley Green EP),[43]

1965,[19] 1965 (help cr Shenley Green EP).[249]

WEST HEATH
EP Cr 1966 from Kings Norton EP, Northfield AP, Longbridge EP, Cofton Hackett EP.[124] K's Nort. RDn.

WESTWOOD
CP Renaming 1937 of Westwood Park CP.[289] *LG* Droitw. RD. Bdry: 1968.[149] *Parl* Worc BC (1948—*).

WESTWOOD PARK
Orig chap in Dodderhill AP, ex-par 1178,[141] chap with full parochial rights before Dissolution but not sustained thereafter,[142] sep CP 1858.[86] *LG* Halfsh. Hd, Droitw. PLU (1858—1930), RSD, RD. Renamed 1937 'Westwood'.[289] *Parl* E'rn Dv (1832—85), Mid Dv (1885—1918), Evesh. Dv (1918—48), Worc BC (1948—70).

WHISTONES
Tp in Claines AP, sep CP 1866.[12] *LG* Osw. Hd, Worc PLU, MB (1835—89), CB (1889—98), USD. Abol 1898 to help cr Worcester CP.[50] *Parl* Worc Parl Bor (1832—1918).

WHITE LADIES ASTON
AP Sometimes early 'Aston Episcopi' or 'Bishop's Aston'. *LG* Seq 12. *Parl* Seq 8. *Eccl* Worc RDn (until 1861), Worc East RDn (1861—1921), Persh. RDn (1921—24). Abol eccl 1924 to help cr White Ladies Aston with Churchill EP.[104]

WHITE LADIES ASTON WITH CHURCHILL
EP Cr 1924 by union White Ladies Aston AP, Churchill AP.[104] Persh. RDn.

WHITTINGTON
Chap in Worcester St Helen AP, early transf to Worcester St Peter the Great AP from which a sep CP 1866,[12] eccl severed and transf 1910 to Worcester St Helen AP.[290] *LG* Seq 12. Bdry: 1883,[56] 1884,[291] 1931 (loses pt to Worc CB [assoc with Worcs] & CP),[113] 1933,[14] 1952 (loses pt to Worc CB [assoc with Worcs] & CP).[114] *Parl* Seq 8. Parl bdry: 1952.[115]

WICHENFORD
AP Orig chap in Worcester St Helen AP, sep par at Dissolution.[292] *LG* Seq 11. Civ bdry: 1884,[127] 1952.[82] *Parl* Seq 5. *Eccl* Seq 18. Eccl bdry: 1908 (gains ex-par [orig chap, qv] Kenswick),[139] 1910 (cr Broadheath EP [incl area of Kenswick gained 1908]).[81]

WICK
Chap in Pershore St Andrew AP, sep CP 1866,[12] sep EP 1727.[31] *LG* Seq 17. Civ bdry: 1883,[56] 1955.[264] *Parl* Seq 3. *Eccl* Persh. RDn.

WICK EPISCOPI
AP Orig chap in Worcester St Helen AP (incl chap Bedwardine St John), sep par 1283 (Worc RDn), the par church abandoned and chap consecr 1371 as par church of 'Bedwardine St John' (eccl, 'Worcester St John the Baptist, Bedwardine'),[47] qv.

WICKHAMFORD
AP Orig chap to Evesh. Abbey, sep par at Dissolution.[293] *LG* Seq 1. *Parl* Seq 3. *Eccl* Seq 4.

WILDEN
EP Cr 1904 from Lower Mitton EP, Hartlebury AP.[193] Kidderm. RDn (1904—21), Mitton EP (1921—73),

Stourpt. RDn (1974—*).

GREAT WITLEY

AP *LG* Seq 3. *Parl* Seq 5. *Eccl* Seq 17.

LITTLE WITLEY

Chap in Holt AP, sep CP 1866.[12] *LG* Seq 11. *Parl* Seq 5.

WOLLASTON

Tp in Oldswinford AP (eccl, 'Old Swinford'), sep CP 1866,[12] eccl severed 1845 to help cr Amblecote EP,[28] 'Wollaston' a sep EP 1860 from Amblecote EP.[26] *LG* Halfsh. Hd, Stourbr. PLU (orig rated in Oldswinford, sep rated soon after 1836[52]—1930), RSD, UD (1894—1914), MB (1914—74). Transf 1974 to W Midlands.[134] *Parl* Seq 11. *Eccl* Kidderm. RDn (1860—1907), Swinf. RDn (1907—73), Stourbr. RDn (1974—*). Eccl bdry: 1930.[232]

WOLLESCOTE

Tp in Oldswinford AP (eccl, 'Old Swinford'), sep CP 1866,[12] pt eccl severed 1873 and transf to Lye EP,[231] 'Wollescote' a sep EP 1965 from Lye EP, Stamber Mill EP, Old Swinford AP, Pedmore AP.[233] *LG* Halfsh. Hd, Stourbr. PLU (orig rated in Oldswinford, sep rated soon after 1836[52]—1930), RSD, Halesowen RD (1894—97), Lye & Wollescote UD (1897—1933), Stourbr. MB (1933—74). Civ bdry: 1929.[262] Transf 1974 to W Midlands.[134] *Parl* Seq 11. *Eccl* Swinf. RDn (1965—73), Stourbr. RDn (1974—*).

WOLVERLEY

AP *LG* Pt Halfsh. Hd (area Kingsford, not sep civ), pt Osw. Hd, Kidderm. PLU, RSD, RD. Civ bdry: 1912,[208] 1933.[14] *Parl* W'rn Dv (ent 1832—67, pt 1878—85), pt Kidderm Parl Bor (1867—1918), pt Mid Dv (1918—48), Kidderm. Dv/CC (1918—*). *Eccl* Kidderm. RDn. Eccl bdry: 1849 (cr Cookley EP),[126] 1952 (help cr Broadwaters EP).[84]

WORCESTER

The following have 'Worcester' in their names. Insofar as any existed at a given time: *LG* Worc Bor/MB/CB, USD. *Parl* Worc Parl Bor (1295—*). *Eccl* Worc RDn (until 1861), sep noted thereafter.

CP1—WORCESTER—Cr 1898 by union of the pars in Worc CB: Bedwardine St Michael AP, South Claines AP, South Hallow CP, AP1, CP2, CP3, AP2, AP3, AP4, AP5, CP4, CP6, AP9, CP8, AP11, Whistones CP.[50] Bdry: 1914,[112] 1931,[113] 1952.[114] Transf 1974 to Worcs.[134] Parl bdry: 1952.[115]

AP1—WORCESTER ALL SAINTS—Abol civ 1898 to help cr CP1.[50] *Eccl* Worc West RDn (1861—1921), Inner Worc RDn (1921—26), Worc RDn (1926—73), Worc East RDn (1974—*).

CP2—WORCESTER BLOCKHOUSE—Ex-par place, sep CP 1858,[86] eccl severed 1844 to help cr EP3.[108] *LG* Worc PLU (1858—1930). Abol civ 1898 to help cr CP1.[50]

CP3—WORCESTER COLLEGE PRECINCTS—Ex-par place, sep CP 1858.[86] Incl area AP8, the Cathedral not a sep civ unit. Worc PLU (1858—98). Abol civ 1898 to help cr CP1.[50]

EP1—WORCESTER HOLY TRINITY—Cr 1866 from AP7, Claines AP.[108] Worc East RDn (1866—1921), Inner Worc RDn (1921—26), Worc RDn

(1926—73), Worc East RDn (1974—*). Bdry: 1912,[111] 1925 (help cr Tolladine EP),[271] 1966,[294] 1967.[272]

AP2—WORCESTER ST ALBAN—Orig chap in AP8, sep par by 1206.[295] Abol civ 1898 to help cr CP1.[50] *Eccl* Organisation as for AP1.

AP3—WORCESTER ST ANDREW—Area appropriated to Worc Priory, sep par at Dissolution.[295] Abol civ 1898 to help cr CP1.[50] *Eccl* Organisation as for AP1.

AP4—WORCESTER ST CLEMENT—Free chap appropriated to Worc Priory, sep par at Dissolution.[295] *LG* Pt Worc Bor, pt Osw. Hd, ent Worc MB/CB, USD. Abol civ 1898 to help cr CP1.[50] *Eccl* Worc West RDn (1861—1921), Inner Worc RDn (1921—26), Worc RDn (1926—73), Martley & Worc West RDn (1974—*). Eccl bdry: 1953,[129] 1967 (help cr Dines Green EP).[130]

—WORCESTER ST GEORGE—Name used now for EP cr 1862 as 'Claines St George', qv.

AP5—WORCESTER ST HELEN—Orig in AP8, sep par by 10th cent.[296] Incl orig in Osw. Hd chap Churchill (sep par by 1269[103]), chap Claines (sep par from 13th cent[105]), chap Hindlip (sep par by 1269[197]), chap Holt (sep par by 1269[200]), chap Huddington (early considered chap in Crowle AP, sep from latter prob in 1570[138]), chap Warndon (sep par by 1300[288]), chap Whittington (early transf to AP10[290]), chap Wichenford (sep par at Dissolution[292]), chap Wick Episcopi (incl chap Bedwardine St John, 'Wick Episcopi' sep par 1283 but later abandoned and the chap consecr 1371 as the par church, eccl as AP6, civ as 'Bedwardine St John', qv[47]). Abol civ 1898 to help cr CP1.[50] *Eccl* Organisation as for AP1. Addtl eccl bdry alt: 1910.[49]

AP6—WORCESTER ST JOHN THE BAPTIST, BEDWARDINE—Orig chap in Wick Episcopi (itself a chap in AP5, sep par 1283 but later abandoned), the chap consecr 1371 as the par church, eccl as AP6, civ as 'Bedwardine St John', qv.[47] *Eccl* Organisation as for AP4. Eccl bdry: 1910 (help cr Broadheath EP),[81] 1924 (help cr Cotheridge with Crown East EP).[128]

CP4—WORCESTER ST JOHN BEDWARDINE CITY—Cr 1894 from the pt of Bedwardine St John AP in Worc CB.[48] Abol civ 1898 to help cr CP1.[50]

CP5—WORCESTER ST JOHN BEDWARDINE COUNTY—Cr 1894 from the pt of Bedwardine St John AP not in Worc CB.[48] *LG* Martley RD. Bdry: 1914 (loses pt to Worc CB [assoc with Worcs] & CP),[112] 1931 (loses pt to Worc CB [assoc with Worcs] & CP),[113] 1952 (help cr Broadheath CP).[82] *Parl* Bewd. Dv (1918—48), Kidderm. CC (1948—*).

EP2—WORCESTER ST MARK IN THE CHERRY ORCHARD—Cr 1955 from AP10.[297] Worc RDn (1955—73), Worc East RDn (1974—*).

AP7—WORCESTER ST MARTIN—*LG* Osw. Hd, pt Worc MB (1835—89 [enlarged pt 1885—89]), pt Worc CB (1889—94), pt Worc USD (enlarged pt 1885—94), pt Worc RSD (reduced pt 1885—94).

Abol civ 1894 the pt in the CB cr CP6, the remainder CP7.[48] *Parl* Pt Worc Parl Bor (1832–1918 [enlarged pt 1867–1918]), pt W'rn Dv (1832–1918 [reduced pt 1867–1918]). *Eccl* Worc East RDn (1861–1921), Inner Worc RDn (1921–26), Worc RDn (1926–73), Worc East RDn (1974–*). Eccl bdry: 1866 (help cr EP1),[108] 1910 (gains chap Whittington from AP10),[290] 1912,[111] 1961 (help cr Norton with Whittington EP),[252] 1966.[294]

CP6—WORCESTER ST MARTIN CITY—Cr 1894 from the pt of AP7 in Worc CB.[48] Abol 1898 to help cr CP1.[50]

CP7—WORCESTER ST MARTIN COUNTY—Cr 1894 from the pt of AP7 not in Worc CB.[48] *LG* Worc PLU, Droitw. RD. Bdry: 1931 (loses pt to Worc CB [assoc with Worcs] & CP).[113] Abol 1952 pt to Worc CB (assoc with Worcs) & CP, pt to Warndon AP, pt to Spetchley AP.[114] *Parl* Evesh. Dv (1918–48), Worc BC (1948–70).

AP8—WORCESTER ST MARY [CATHEDRAL]— Eccl ex-par; civ not sep but incl in area CP3). Incl chap AP2 (sep par by 1206[295]), chap AP5 (sep par by 10th cent,[296]) qv for cr of many chaps as sep APs later), chap Spetchley (sep par by 1291[284]).

AP9—WORCESTER ST NICHOLAS—Abol civ 1898 to help cr CP1.[50] *Eccl* Organisation as for AP7.

EP3—WORCESTER ST PAUL—Cr 1844 from AP10 and ent ex-par area Worcester Blockhouse (area of CP2).[108] Organisation as for AP7, from 1861. Bdry: 1912.[111]

AP10—WORCESTER ST PETER THE GREAT—Incl in Osw. Hd chap Whittington (orig in AP5, early transf to this par and sep CP 1866 from it,[12] eccl severed 1910 and transf to AP7,[290] qv for cr 1961 of Norton with Whittington EP). *LG* Pt Osw. Hd, pt Worc MB (1835–89), pt Worc CB (1889–94), pt Worc USD, pt Worc RSD. Addtl civ bdry alt: 1883,[56] 1885.[291] Abol civ 1894 the pt in the CB cr CP8, the remainder cr CP9.[48] *Parl* Pt Worc Parl Bor (1832–1918 [enlarged pt 1867–1918]), pt W'rn Dv (1832–1918 [reduced pt 1867–1918]). *Eccl* Worc West RDn (1861–92), Worc East RDn (1892–1921), Inner Worc RDn (1921–26), Worc RDn (1926–73), Worc East RDn (1974–*). Addtl eccl bdry alt: 1844 (help cr EP3),[108] 1955 (cr EP2).[297]

CP8—WORCESTER ST PETER THE GREAT CITY—Cr 1894 from the pt of AP10 in Worc CB.[48] Abol civ 1898 to help cr CP1.[50]

CP9—WORCESTER ST PETER THE GREAT COUNTY—Cr 1894 from the pt of AP10 not in Worc CB.[48] Worc PLU, Persh. RD. Bdry: 1931 (loses pt to Worc CB [assoc with Worcs] & CP),[113] 1933.[14] *Parl* Evesh. Dv (1918–48), S Worcs CC (1948–*).

AP11—WORCESTER ST SWITHIN—Abol civ 1898 to help cr CP1.[50] *Eccl* Organisation as for AP7. Eccl bdry: 1966.[294]

EP4—WORCESTER THE TYTHING—Cr 1875 from Claines AP.[71] Organisation as for AP7, from 1875.

WRIBBENHALL

EP Cr 1844 from Kidderminster AP.[108] Kidderm. RDn.

CP Cr 1901 from Kidderminster Foreign CP.[209] *LG* Kidderm. PLU, RD (1901–33), Bewd. MB (1933–74). Bdry: 1933 (exchanges pts with Kidderminster Foreign CP, loses pt to Stourpt. UD & CP as the area of this par so altered transf to Bewd. MB as one of its constituent pars.[14] *Parl* Kidderm. Dv/CC (1918–*).

WYCHBOLD

EP Cr 1888 from Dodderhill AP.[144] Droitw. RDn.

WYCHE

EP Cr 1926 from Great Malvern AP.[238] Powyke RDn (1926–73), Malv. RDn (1974–*).

WYRE PIDDLE

Tp in Fladbury AP, sep CP 1866.[12] *LG* Seq 12. Bdry: 1956.[267] *Parl* Seq 3.

WYTHALL

EP Cr 1755 from Bromsgrove AP,[31] refounded 1853 from Kings Norton EP, Alvechurch AP (both Worcs), Solihull AP (Warws).[22] Droitw. RDn (1755–1880), Northf. RDn (1880–1905), K's Nort. RDn (1905–*).

CP Cr 1911 from pt of the pt of Kings Norton CP not transf to Birm CB (assoc with Warws)) & AP.[123] *LG* Bromsgr. PLU, RD. Bdry: 1964 (gains pt Solih. MB & AP, Warws as the altered area [qv in Warws for details] constituted Solih. CB),[298] 1966 (loses pt to Birm CB [assoc with Warws] & AP).[21] *Parl* Kidderm. Dv (1918–48), Bromsgr. CC (1948–70), Bromsgr. & Redditch CC (1970–*).

YARDLEY

AP *LG* Persh. Hd (until 1760), Halfsh. Hd (from 1760), Solih. PLU (1836–1911), RSD, Yard. RD (1894–1911), Birm CB (1911–12), PLU (1911–12). Abol civ 1912 ent to Birmingham AP.[213] *Parl* E'rn Dv (1832–1918). *Eccl* Kidderm. RDn (until 1880), Northf. RDn (1880–1905), Solih. RDn (1905–57), Yard. RDn (1957–*). Eccl bdry: 1849 (help cr Yardley Wood EP),[213] 1867 (cr Acocks Green EP),[4] 1878 (cr Hay Mill EP),[4] 1879,[247] 1894 (cr Sparkhill St John the Evangelist EP),[283] 1907 (cr Hall Green [Marston Chapel] EP),[185] 1932 (cr Stetchford EP),[91] 1948 (incl gains pt Shelton EP, Staffs and gains pt Olton EP, Warws),[19] 1956 (cr South Yardley EP),[40] 1967 (help cr Garretts Green EP [Worcs, Warws]),[177] 1968 (help cr Lea Hall EP [Worcs, Warws]).[221]

SOUTH YARDLEY

EP Cr 1956 from Yardley AP, Kings Norton EP.[40] Solih. RDn (1956–57), Yard. RDn (1957–*).

YARDLEY WOOD

EP Cr 1849 from Yardley AP, Kings Norton EP.[213] Kidderm. RDn (1849–80), Northf. RDn (1880–1905), K's Nort. RDn (1905–57), Moseley RDn (1957–*). Bdry: 1914 (help cr Moseley St Agnes EP),[92] 1937 (help cr Billesley Common EP),[64] 1938 (cr Highters Heath EP),[195] 1952,[65] 1962 (incl gains pt Shirley EP, Warws),[26] 1962 (cr Hall Green St Peter EP).[150]

YORKSHIRE

ABBREVIATIONS

Abbreviations particular to Yorks follow. Those general abbreviations in use throughout the *Guide* are found on pages xvii—xix.

Agb.	Agbrigg
Aireb.	Aireborough
Allert.	Allerton
Almondb.	Almondbury
Aysg.	Aysgath
Bark. Ash	Barkstone Ash
Bev.	Beverley
Birdf.	Birdforth
Boroughbr.	Boroughbridge
Bowl.	Bowling
Bp'thorpe	Bishopthorpe
Bridl.	Bridlington
Brigh.	Brighouse
Buckr.	Buckrose
Castlef.	Castleford
Catt.	Catterick
Darl.	Darlington
Derw.	Derwent
Dewsb.	Dewsbury
Dick.	Dickering
Donc.	Doncaster
Driff.	Driffield
Eas.	Easingwold
Escr.	Escrick
Ewecr.	Ewecross
Gill.	Gilling
Gt Ouseb.	Great Ouseburn
Guisb.	Guisborough
Hallik.	Hallikeld
Haltemp.	Haltemprice
Handsw.	Handsworth
Harrog.	Harrogate
Harth.	Harthill
Head.	Headingley
Helm.	Helmsley
Hemsw.	Hemsworth
Hold.	Holderness
Holmf.	Holmfirth
Howdensh.	Howdenshire
Hudd.	Huddersfield
Keigh.	Keighley
Kingst.	Kingston
Kiv. Pk.	Kiverton Park
Knar.	Knaresborough
Langb.	Langbaurgh
Leyb.	Leyburn
Lonsd.	Lonsdale
Middlesb.	Middlesbrough
Moors.	Moorside
N'allert.	Northallerton
Nidd.	Nidderdale
Norm.	Normanton
Osg.	Osgoldcross
Ouseb.	Ouseburn

Patr.	Patrington
Penist.	Penistone
Pick.	Pickering
Pockl.	Pocklington
Pontef.	Pontefract
Richm.	Richmond
Rotherh.	Rotherham
Rothw.	Rothwell
Ryed.	Ryedale
Scarb.	Scarborough
Scul.	Sculcoates
Settr.	Settrington
Sherb.	Sherburn
Silkst.	Silkstone
Skirl.	Skirlaugh
Skyr.	Skyrack
Spenb.	Spenborough
Stancl. & Ewc.	Stanciffe & Ewcross
Stancr.	Stancross
Stock.	Stockton
Stokes.	Stokesley
Straff. & Tick.	Strafforth & Tickhill
Tadc.	Tadcaster
Weigh.	Weighton
Wensleyd.	Wensleydale
Wentw.	Wentworth
Wethb.	Wetherby
Wharfed.	Wharfedale

SEQUENCES

An abbreviated entry prefixed by 'Seq' is used in the parochial entries to avoid repeating often the names of superior units of administration. The content of each sequence is shown below.

Local Government Sequences ('LG')

East Riding
SEQ 1   Buckr. Wap, Driff. PLU, RSD, RD
SEQ 2   Buckr. Wap, Malton PLU, RSD, Norton RD
SEQ 3   Buckr. Wap, Pockl. PLU, RSD, RD
SEQ 4   Buckr. Wap, Pockl. PLU, RSD, RD (1894—1935), Norton RD (1935—74)
SEQ 5   Dick. Wap, Bridl. PLU, RSD, RD
SEQ 6   Dick. Wap, Driff. PLU, RSD, RD
SEQ 7   Dick. Wap, Scarb. PLU, RSD, Sherb. RD (1894—1935), Bridl. RD (1935—74)
SEQ 8   Dick. Wap, Scarb. PLU, RSD, Sherb. RD (1894—1935), Norton RD (1935—74)
SEQ 9   Hath. Wap, Bev. PLU, RSD, RD
SEQ 10   Hath. Wap, Driff. PLU, RSD, RD
SEQ 11   Hath. Wap, Howden PLU, RSD, RD
SEQ 12   Hath. Wap, Pockl. PLU, RSD, RD
SEQ 13   Hold. Wap, Bev. PLU, RSD, RD
SEQ 14   Hold. Wap, Bridl. PLU, RSD, RD
SEQ 15   Hold. Wap, Patr. PLU, RSD, RD (1894—1935), Hold. RD (1935—74)
SEQ 16   Hold. Wap, Skirl. PLU, RSD, RD (1894—1935), Hold. RD (1935—74)
SEQ 17   Howdensh. Wap, Howden PLU, RSD, RD
SEQ 18   Kingst. upon Hull Co, Scul. PLU, RSD, RD (1894—1935), Bev. RD (1935—74)
SEQ 19   Ouse & Derw. Wap, Selby PLU, RSD, Riccall RD (1894—1935), Derw. RD (1935—74)
SEQ 20   Ouse & Derw. Wap, York PLU, RSD, Escr. RD (1894—1935), Derw. RD (1935—74)

North Riding
SEQ 21   Allert. Wap, Darl. PLU, RSD, Croft RD
SEQ 22   Allert. Wap, N'allert. PLU, RSD, RD
SEQ 23   Allert. Wap, Thirsk PLU, RSD, RD
SEQ 24   Birdf. Wap, Eas. PLU, RSD, RD
SEQ 25   Birdf. Wap, Helm. PLU, RSD, RD
SEQ 26   Birdf. Wap, N'allert. PLU, RSD, RD
SEQ 27   Birdf. Wap, Thirsk PLU, RSD, RD
SEQ 28   Bulmer Wap, Eas. PLU, RSD, RD
SEQ 29   Bulmer Wap, Malton PLU, RSD, RD
SEQ 30   Bulmer Wap, Gt Ouseb. GilbU (until 1854), PLU (1854—1930), Eas. RD
SEQ 31   Bulmer Wap, York PLU, RSD, Eas. RD
SEQ 32   Bulmer Wap, York PLU, RSD, Flaxton RD
SEQ 33   E Gill. Wap, Darl. PLU, RSD, Croft RD
SEQ 34   E Gill. Wap, N'allert. PLU, RSD, RD
SEQ 35   E Gill. Wap, Richm. PLU, RSD, RD
SEQ 36   E Gill. Wap, Thirsk PLU, RSD, RD
SEQ 37   W Gill. Wap, Reeth PLU, RSD, RD
SEQ 38   W Gill. Wap, Richm. PLU, RSD, RD
SEQ 39   W Gill. Wap, Teesdale PLU, RSD, Startforth

RD

SEQ 40	Hallik. Wap, Bedale PLU, RSD, RD
SEQ 41	Hallik. Wap, Gt Ouseb. GilbU (until 1854), PLU (1854—1930), Thirsk RD
SEQ 42	Hallik. Wap, Gt Ouseb. GilbU (until 1854), Ripon PLU (1854—1930), RSD, Wath RD
SEQ 43	Hallik. Wap, not in a PLU (until 1852), Ripon PLU (1852—1930), RSD, Bedale RD
SEQ 44	Hallik. Wap, not in a PLU (until 1852), Ripon PLU (1852—1930), Wath RD
SEQ 45	Hallik. Wap, Thirsk PLU, RSD, RD
SEQ 46	E Hang Wap, Bedale PLU, RSD, RD
SEQ 47	E Hang Wap, Leyb. PLU, RSD, RD
SEQ 48	E Hang Wap, Leyb. PLU (1837—39), Bedale PLU (1839—1930), RSD, RD
SEQ 49	E Hang Wap, N'allert. PLU (1837—39), Bedale PLU (1939—1930), RSD, RD
SEQ 50	E Hang Wap, Richm. PLU, RSD, RD
SEQ 51	W Hang Wap, not in a PLU (until 1869), Aysg. PLU (1869—1930), RSD, RD
SEQ 52	W Hang Wap, Bainbridge GilbU (until 1869), Aysg. PLU (1869—1930), RSD, RD
SEQ 53	W Hang Wap, Leyb. PLU, RSD, RD
SEQ 54	W Hang Wap, Richm. PLU, RSD, RD
SEQ 55	Langb. Lbty, Guisb. PLU, RSD, RD (1894—1932), Whitby RD (1932—74)
SEQ 56	Langb. Lbty, Stock. PLU (1837—75), Middlesb. PLU (1875—1930), RSD, RD (1894—1932), Stokes. RD (1932—74)
SEQ 57	Langb. Lbty, Stock. PLU (1837—75), Middlesb. PLU (1875—1930), RSD, Stokes. RD
SEQ 58	Langb. Lbty, Stokes. PLU, RSD, RD
SEQ 59	Langb. Lbty, Whitby PLU, RSD, RD
SEQ 60	Pick. Lythe Wap, Malton PLU, RSD, RD
SEQ 61	Pick. Lythe Wap, Pick. PLU, RSD, RD
SEQ 62	Pick. Lythe Wap, Scarb. PLU, RSD, RD
SEQ 63	Ryed. Wap, Helm. PLU, RSD, RD
SEQ 64	Ryed. Wap, Helm. PLU (1837—48), Kirkby Moors. PLU (1848—1930), RSD, RD
SEQ 65	Ryed. Wap, Malton PLU, RSD, RD
SEQ 66	Ryed. Wap, Pick. PLU, RSD, RD (1894—1934), Kirkby Moors. RD (1934—74)
SEQ 67	Whitby Strand Lbty, Scarb. PLU, RSD, RD
SEQ 68	Whitby Strand Lbty, Whitby PLU, RSD, RD

West Riding

SEQ 69	Agb. Wap, Wakef PLU, RSD, RD
SEQ 70	Ainsty (W Riding until 1449 and from 1836, indept jurisd 1449—1836), Barwick GilbU (until 1869), Tadc. PLU (1869—1930), RSD, RD
SEQ 71	Ainsty (W Riding until 1449 and from 1836, indept jurisd 1449—1836), Barwick GilbU (until 1869), Wethb. PLU (1869—1930), RSD, RD
SEQ 72	Ainsty (W Riding until 1449 and from 1836, indept jurisd 1449—1836), Gt Ouseb. GilbU (until 1854), PLU (1854—1930), RSD, RD (1894—1938), Nidd. RD (1938—74)
SEQ 73	Ainsty (W Riding until 1449 and from 1836, indept jurisd 1449—1836), not in a PLU (until 1862), Tadc. PLU (1862—1930), RSD, RD
SEQ 74	Ainsty (W Riding until 1449 and from 1836, indept jurisd 1449—1836), not in a PLU (until 1861), Wethb. PLU (1861—1930), RSD, RD
SEQ 75	Bark. Ash Wap, Gt Preston GilbU (until 1862), Pontef. PLU (1862—1930), RSD, RD (1894—1938), Osg. RD (1938—74)
SEQ 76	Bark. Ash Wap, Gt Preston GilbU (until 1869), Pontef. PLU (1869—1930), RSD, RD (1894—1938), Osg. RD (1938—74)
SEQ 77	Bark. Ash Wap, Gt Preston GilbU (until 1862), Tadc. PLU (1862—1930), RSD, RD
SEQ 78	Bark. Ash Wap, Gt Preston GilbU (until 1869), Tadc. PLU (1869—1930), RSD, RD
SEQ 79	Bark. Ash Wap, Gt Preston GilbU (until 1869), Selby PLU (1869—1930), RSD, RD
SEQ 80	Bark. Ash Wap, Selby PLU, RSD, RD
SEQ 81	Bark. Ash Wap, not in a PLU (until 1862), Tadc. PLU (1862—1930), RSD, RD
SEQ 82	Claro Wap, Barwick GilbU (until 1869), Gt Ouseb. PLU (1869—1930), RSD, RD (1894—1938), Nidd. RD (1938—74)
SEQ 83	Claro Wap, Carlton GilbU (until 1869), Wharfed. PLU (1869—1930), RSD, RD
SEQ 84	Claro Wap, not in a PLU (until 1854), Knar. PLU (1854—1930), RSD, RD (1894—1938), Nidd. RD (1938—74)
SEQ 85	Claro Wap, Gt Ouseb. GilbU (until 1854), PLU (1854—1930), RSD, RD (1894—1938), Nidd. RD (1938—74)
SEQ 86	Claro Wap, not in a PLU (until 1854), Gt Ouseb. PLU (1854—1930), RSD, RD (1894—1938), Nidd. RD (1938—74)
SEQ 87	Claro Wap, Gt Ouseb. GilbU (until 1854), Knar. PLU (1854—1930), RSD, RD (1894—1938), Nidd. RD (1938—74)
SEQ 88	Claro Wap, Gt Ouseb. GilbU (until 1854), not in a PLU (1854—61), Wethb. PLU (1861—1930), RSD, RD
SEQ 89	Claro Wap, Pateley Br. PLU, RSD, RD (1894—1937), Ripon & Pateley Br. RD (1937—74)
SEQ 90	Claro Wap, not in a PLU (until 1852), Ripon PLU (1852—1930), RSD, RD (1894—1937), Ripon & Pateley Br. RD (1937—74)
SEQ 91	Claro Wap, not in a PLU (until 1861), Wethb. PLU (1861—1930), RSD, RD
SEQ 92	Claro Wap, not in a PLU (until 1861), Wharfed. PLU (1861—1930), RSD, RD
SEQ 93	Donc. Soke, PLU, RSD, RD
SEQ 94	Osg. Wap, Donc. PLU, RSD, RD
SEQ 95	Osg. Wap, Goole PLU, RSD, RD
SEQ 96	Osg. Wap, not in a PLU (until 1850), Hemsw. PLU (1850—1930), RSD, RD
SEQ 97	Osg. Wap, not in a PLU (until 1862), Pontef. PLU (1862—1930), RSD, RD (1894—1938), Osg. RD (1938—74)
SEQ 98	Osg. Wap, Gt Preston GilbU (until 1862), Pontef. PLU (1862—1930), RSD, RD (1894—1938), Osg. RD (1938—74)
SEQ 99	Osg. Wap, Gt Preston GilbU (until 1869), Pontef. PLU (1869—1930), RSD, RD (1894—1938), Osg. RD (1938—74)
SEQ 100	Ripon Lbty, PLU, RSD, RD (1894—1938), Ripon & Pateley Br. RD (1938—74)

SEQ 101   Ripon Lbty, Pateley Br. PLU, RSD, RD (1894—1938), Ripon & Pateley Br. RD (1938—74)

SEQ 102   Skyr. Wap, Calton GilbU (until 1869), Wethb. PLU (1869—1930), RSD, RD

SEQ 103   Skyr. Wap, Calton GilbU (until 1861), Wharfed. PLU (1861—1930), RSD, RD

SEQ 104   Skyr. Wap, Calton GilbU (until 1869), Wharfed. PLU (1869—1930), RSD, RD

SEQ 105   Skyr. Wap, Gt Preston GilbU (until 1869), Tadc. PLU (1869—1930), RSD, RD

SEQ 106   Skyr. Wap, not in a PLU (until 1862), Tadc. PLU (1862—1930), RSD, RD

SEQ 107   Skyr. Wap, not in a PLU (until 1861), Wethb. PLU (1861—1930), RSD, RD

SEQ 108   Staincl. & Ewc. Wap, Clith. PLU, RSD, Bowland RD

SEQ 109   Staincl. & Ewc. Wap, Keigh. PLU, RSD, RD (1894—1938), Skipton RD (1938—74)

SEQ 110   Staincl. & Ewc. Wap, Sedb. PLU, RSD, RD

SEQ 111   Staincl. & Ewc. Wap, Settle PLU, RSD, RD

SEQ 112   Staincl. & Ewc. Wap, Skipton PLU, RSD, RD

SEQ 113   Staincr. Wap, not in a PLU (until 1850), Hemsw. PLU (1850—1930), RSD, RD

SEQ 114   Stancr. Wap, not in a PLU (until 1849), Penist. PLU (1849—1930), RSD, RD

SEQ 115   Staincr. Wap, Wortley PLU, RSD, RD

SEQ 116   Staincr. Wap, Wortley PLU (1838—49), Penist. PLU (1849—1930), RSD, RD

SEQ 117   Straff. & Tick. Wap, Donc. PLU, RSD, RD

SEQ 118   Straff. & Tick. Wap, not in a PLU (until 1850), Hemsw. PLU (1850—1930), RSD, RD

SEQ 119   Straff. & Tick. Wap, Rotherh. PLU, RSD RD

SEQ 120   Straff. & Tick. Wap, Thorne PLU, RSD, RD

SEQ 121   Straff. & Tick. Wap, Worksop PLU, RSD, Kiv. Pk RD

Parliamentary Sequences ('Parl')

East Riding

SEQ 1   E Riding (1832—85), Buckr. Dv (1885—1948), Bev. CC (1948—55), Howden CC (1955—*)

SEQ 2   E Riding (1832—85), Buckr. Dv (1885—1948), Bridl. CC (1948—*)

SEQ 3   E Riding (1832—85), Buckr. Dv (1885—1948), Bridl. CC (1948—55), Howden CC (1955—*)

SEQ 4   E Riding (1832—85), Hold. Dv (1885—1948), Bev. CC (1948—55), Haltemp. CC (1955—*)

SEQ 5   E Riding (1832—85), Hold. Dv (1885—1948), Bridl. CC (1948—*)

SEQ 6   E Riding (1832—85), Howdensh. Dv (1885—1948), Bev. CC (1948—55), Haltemp. CC (1955—*)

SEQ 7   E Riding (1832—85), Howdensh. Dv (1885—1948), Howden CC (1948—*)

SEQ 8   E Riding (1832—85), Howdensh. Dv (1885—1918), Hold. Dv (1918—48), Bev. CC (1948—55), Haltemp. CC (1955—*)

North Riding

SEQ 9   N Riding (1832—85), Clev Dv/CC (1885—1970), Clev & Whitby CC (1970—*)

SEQ 10   N Riding (1832—85), Clev Dv (1885—1948), Richm. CC (1948—*)

SEQ 11   N Riding (1832—85), Clev Dv (1885—1918), Richm. Dv/CC (1918—*)

SEQ 12   N Riding (1832—85), Clev Dv (1885—1918), Scarb. & Whitby Dv/CC (1918—70), Clev & Whitby CC (1970—*)

SEQ 13   N Riding (1832—85), Richm. Dv/CC (1885—*)

SEQ 14   N Riding (1832—85), Richm. Dv (1885—1918), Thirsk & Malton Dv/CC (1918—*)

SEQ 15   N Riding (1832—85), Richm. Dv (1885—1948), Thirsk & Malton CC (1948—*)

SEQ 16   N Riding (1832—85), Thirsk & Malton Dv/CC (1885—*)

SEQ 17   N Riding (1832—85), Thirsk & Malton Dv (1885—1918), Richm. Dv/CC (1918—*)

SEQ 18   N Riding (1832—85), Thirsk & Malton Dv (1885—1918), Richm. Dv (1918—48), Thirsk & Malton CC (1948—*)

SEQ 19   N Riding (1832—85), Whitby Dv (1885—1918), Scarb. & Whitby Dv/CC (1918—70), Clev & Whitby CC (1970—*)

SEQ 20   N Riding (1832—85), Whitby Dv (1885—1918), Scarb. & Whitby Dv/CC (1918—70), Scarb. CC (1970—*)

SEQ 21   N Riding (1832—85), Whitby Dv (1885—1918), Thirsk & Malton Dv/CC (1918—*)

SEQ 22   N Riding (1832—85), Whitby Dv (1885—1918), Thirsk & Malton Dv/CC (1918—70), Scarb. CC (1970—*)

SEQ 23   N Riding (1832—85), Thirsk & Malton Dv (1885—1918), Bark. Ash Dv/CC (1918—*)

West Riding

SEQ 24   W Riding (1832—67), E'rn Dv of W Riding (1867—85), Bark. Ash Dv/CC (1885—*)

SEQ 25   W Riding (1832—67), E'rn Dv of W Riding (1867—85), Bark. Ash Dv (1885—1948), Norm. CC(1948—*)

SEQ 26   W Riding (1832—67), E'rn Dv of W Riding (1867—85), Bark. Ash Dv (1885—1918), Pontef. Dv (1918—48), Goole CC (1948—*)

SEQ 27   W Riding (1832—67), E'rn Dv of W Riding (1867—85), Osg. Dv (1885—1918), Don Valley Dv/CC (1918—*)

SEQ 28   W Riding (1832—67), E'rn Dv of W Riding (1867—85), Osg. Dv (1885—1918), Hemsw. Dv/CC (1918—*)

SEQ 29   W Riding (1832—67), E'rn Dv of W Riding (1867—85), Osg. Dv (1885—1918), Pontef. Dv (1918—48), Goole CC (1948—*)

SEQ 30   W Riding (1832—67), E'rn Dv of W Riding (1867—85), Otley Dv (1885—1918), Pudsey & Otley Dv (1918—48), Ripon CC (1948—*)

SEQ 31   W Riding (1832—67), E'rn Dv of W Riding (1867—85), Otley Dv (1885—1918), Shipley Dv/CC (1918—*)

SEQ 32   W Riding (1832—67), E'rn Dv of W Riding (1867—85), Otley Dv (1885—1918), Skipton

Dv/CC (1918—*)

SEQ 33 W Riding (1832—67), E'rn Dv of W Riding (1867—85), Ripon Dv/CC (1885—*)

SEQ 34 W Riding (1832—67), E'rn Dv of W Riding (1867—85), Ripon Dv/CC (1885—*)

SEQ 35 W Riding (1832—67), E'rn Dv of W Riding (1867—85), Ripon Dv (1885—1918), Bark. Ash Dv/CC (1918—*)

SEQ 36 W Riding (1832—67), E'rn Dv of W Riding (1867—85), Ripon Dv (1885—1948), Harrog. CC (1948—*)

SEQ 37 W Riding (1832—67), E'rn Dv of W Riding (1867—85), Sowerby Dv/CC (1885—*)

SEQ 38 W Riding (1832—67), E'rn Dv of W Riding (1867—85), Spen Valley Dv (1885—1948), Brigh. & Spenb. CC (1948—*)

SEQ 39 W Riding (1832—67), N'rn Dv of W Riding (1867—85), Keigh. Dv (1885—1948), Keigh. BC (1948—*)

SEQ 40 W Riding (1832—67), N'rn Dv of W Riding (1867—85), Keigh. Dv (1885—1918), Skipton Dv/CC (1918—*)

SEQ 41 W Riding (1832—67), N'rn Dv of W Riding (1867—85), Skipton Dv/CC (1885—*)

SEQ 42 W Riding (1832—67), S'rn Dv of W Riding (1867—85), Barnsley Dv (1885—1918), Hemsw. Dv/CC (1918—*)

SEQ 43 W Riding (1832—67), S'rn Dv of W Riding (1867—85), Barnsley Dv (1885—1918), Hemsw. Dv (1918—48), Wakef BC (1948—*)

SEQ 44 W Riding (1832—67), S'rn Dv of W Riding (1867—85), Donc. Dv (1885—1918), Don Valley Dv/CC (1918—*)

SEQ 45 W Riding (1832—67), S'rn Dv of W Riding (1867—85), Donc. Dv (1885—1948), Don Valley CC (1948—*)

SEQ 46 W Riding (1832—67), S'rn Dv of W Riding (1867—85), Donc. Dv (1885—1918), Don Valley Dv (1918—48), Dearne Valley CC (1948—*)

SEQ 47 W Riding (1832—67), S'rn Dv of W Riding (1867—85), Donc. Dv (1885—1918), Don Valley Dv (1918—48), Goole CC (1948—*)

SEQ 48 W Riding (1832—67), S'rn Dv of W Riding (1867—85), Donc. Dv (1885—1918), Rother Valley Dv/CC (1918—*)

SEQ 49 W Riding (1832—67), S'rn Dv of W Riding (1867—85), Hallamshire Dv (1885—1918), Penist. Dv/CC (1918—*)

SEQ 50 W Riding (1832—67), S'rn Dv of W Riding (1867—85), Holmf. Dv (1885—1918), Penist. Dv/CC (1918—*)

SEQ 51 W Riding (1832—67), S'rn Dv of W Riding (1867—85), Holmf. Dv (1885—1918), Penist. Dv/CC (1918—55), Colne Valley CC (1955—*)

SEQ 52 W Riding (1832—67), S'rn Dv of W Riding (1867—85), Morley Dv (1885—1918), Batley & Morley Parl Bor/BC (1918—*)

SEQ 53 W Riding (1832—67), S'rn Dv of W Riding (1867—85), Norm. Dv (1885—1918), Rothw. Dv (1918—48), Norm. CC (1948—*)

SEQ 54 W Riding (1832—67), S'rn Dv of W Riding

(1867—85), Norm. Dv (1885—1918), Rothw. Dv (1918—48), Wakef BC (1948—*)

Ecclesiastical Sequences ('Eccl')

Orig York dioc, East Riding AD

SEQ 1 Buckr. RDn (until 1857), E Buckr. RDn (1857—66), Buckr. RDn (1866—*)

SEQ 2 Buckr. RDn (until 1857), E Buckr. RDn (1857—66), Buckr. RDn (1866—1922), Hath. RDn (1922—*)

SEQ 3 Buckr. RDn (until 1857), E Buckr. RDn (1857—66), Buckr. RDn (1866—87), Settr. RDn (1887—1922), Buckr. RDn (1922—*)

SEQ 4 Dick. RDn (until 1857), N Dick. RDn (1857—66), Scarb. RDn (1866—*)

SEQ 5 Dick. RDn (until 1862), N Dick. RDn (1862—66), Scarb. RDn (1866—87), Bridl. RDn (1887—*)

SEQ 6 Dick. RDn (until 1862), N Dick. RDn (1862—66), Scarb. RDn (1866—87), Buckr. RDn (1887—1922), Bridl. RDn (1922—*)

SEQ 7 Dick. RDn (until 1862), S Dick. RDn (1862—66), Bridl. RDn (1866—*)

SEQ 8 Dick. RDn (until 1857), S Harth. RDn (1857—62), S Dick. RDn (1862—66), Bridl. RDn (1866—*)

SEQ 9 Hath. & Hull RDn (until 1857), W Buckr. RDn (1857—66), Pockl. RDn (1866—*)

SEQ 10 Hath. & Hull RDn (until 1857), N Hath. RDn (1857—66), Hath. RDn (1866—*)

SEQ 11 Hath. & Hull RDn (until 1857), S Hath. RDn (1857—66), Bev. RDn (1866—*)

SEQ 12 Hath. & Hull RDn (until 1857), S Hath. RDn (1857—66), Howden RDn (1866—1916), Kingst. upon Hull RDn (1916—*)

SEQ 13 Hath. & Hull RDn (until 1857), W Hath. RDn (1857—66), Howden RDn (1866—*)

SEQ 14 Hath. & Hull RDn (until 1857), W Hath. RDn (1857—66), Weigh. RDn (1866—*)

SEQ 15 Hold. RDn (until 1849), N Hold. RDn (1849—66), Hornsea RDn (1866—1916), N Hold. RDn (1916—*)

SEQ 16 Hold. RDn (until 1849), S Hold. RDn (1849—66), Hedon RDn (1866—1916), S Hold. RDn (1916—*)

Orig York dioc, Clev AD

SEQ 17 Bulmer RDn

SEQ 18 Bulmer RDn (until 1862), Eas. RDn (1862—*)

SEQ 19 Bulmer RDn (until 1896), Escr. RDn (1896—*)

SEQ 20 Bulmer RDn (until 1862), Thirsk RDn (1862—*)

SEQ 21 Clev RDn (until 1862), Guisb. RDn (1862—78), Middlesb. RDn (1878—1924), Guisb. RDn (1924—*)

SEQ 22 Clev RDn (until 1862), Guisb. RDn (1862—78), Whitby RDn (1878—*)

SEQ 23 Clev RDn (until 1862), N'allert. RDn (1862—*)

SEQ 24 Clev RDn (until 1862), Stokes. RDn

(1862—*)

SEQ 25   Clev RDn (until 1862), Stokes. RDn (1862—78), Middlesb. RDn (1878—*)

SEQ 26   Riddal RDn (until 1862), Helm. RDn (1862—*)

SEQ 27   Riddal RDn (until 1862), Helm. RDn (1862—1928), Malton RDn (1928—*)

SEQ 28   Riddal RDn (until 1862), Malton RDn (1862—1928), Pick. RDn (1928—*)

Orig York dioc, West Riding AD

SEQ 29   Ainsty RDn (until 1820), New Ainsty RDn (1820—36), City of York & Ainsty RDn (1836—62), Ainsty RDn (1862—*)

SEQ 30   Ainsty RDn (until 1820), New Ainsty RDn (1820—36), City of York & Ainsty RDn (1836—38), Pontef. RDn (1838—57), Wethb. RDn (1857—*)

SEQ 31   Ainsty RDn (until 1820), New Ainsty RDn (1820—36), City of York & Ainsty RDn (1836—62), Tadc. RDn (1862—71), Bp'thorpe RDn (1871—96), Ainsty RDn (1896—*)

SEQ 32   Ainsty RDn (until 1820), New Ainsty RDn (1820—36), City of York & Ainsty RDn (1836—62), Tadc. RDn (1862—71), Selby RDn (1871—*)

SEQ 33   Ainsty RDn (until 1820), New Ainsty RDn (1820—36), City of York & Ainsty RDn (1836—62), Tadc. RDn (1862—71), Selby RDn (1871—1921), Tadc. RDn (1921—*)

SEQ 34   Ainsty RDn (until 1820), Old Ainsty RDn (1820—36), City of York & Ainsty RDn (1836—38), Pontef. RDn (1838—*)

SEQ 35   Craven RDn (until 1857), Craven RDn, N'rn Dv (1857—1921), Settle RDn (1921—71), Bowl. & Horton RDn (1971—*)

SEQ 36   Craven RDn (until 1857), Craven RDn, N'rn Dv (1857—1921), Skipton RDn (1921—*)

SEQ 37   Craven RDn (until 1857), Craven RDn, W'rn Dv (1857—1905), Craven RDn, E'rn Dv (1905—21), Skipton RDn (1921—*)

SEQ 38   Craven RDn (until 1857), Craven RDn, W'rn Dv (1857—1921), Bolland RDn (1921—*)

SEQ 39   Craven RDn (until 1857), Craven RDn, W'rn Dv (1857—1905), Craven RDn, E'rn Dv (1905—21), Skipton RDn (1921—*)

SEQ 40   Donc. RDn

SEQ 41   Donc. RDn (until 1838), Pontef. RDn (1838-57), Silkst. RDn (1857—1927), Bansley RDn (1927—*)

SEQ 42   Donc. RDn (until 1857), Rotherh. RDn (1857—*)

SEQ 43   Donc. RDn (until 1857), Rotherh. RDn (1857—1927), Handsw. RDn (1927—42), Laughton RDn (1942—*)

SEQ 44   Donc. RDn (until 1857), Rotherh. RDn (1857—1942), Laughton RDn (1942—*)

SEQ 45   Donc. RDn (until 1871), Snaith RDn (1871—*)

SEQ 46   Donc. RDn (until 1871), Wath RDn (1871—*)

SEQ 47   Pontef. RDn (until 1857), Dewsb. RDn (1857—*)

SEQ 48   Pontef. RDn (until 1857), Dewsb. RDn (1857—66), Birstall RDn (1866—83), Dewsb. RDn (1883—*)

SEQ 49   Pontef. RDn (until 1857), Hudd. RDn (1857—1968), Almondb. RDn (1968—*)

SEQ 50   Pontef. RDn (until 1857), Wakef RDn (1857—*)

Orig York dioc, Chester dioc (1541—1836), Ripon dioc thereafter; orig Richmn AD

SEQ 51   Boroughbr. RDn (until 1870), Knar. RDn (1870—1971), Harrog. RDn (1971—*)

SEQ 52   Boroughbr. RDn (until 1971), Ripon RDn (1971—*)

SEQ 53   Catt. RDn (until 1857), Catt. East RDn (1857—1928), Bedale RDn (1928—*)

SEQ 54   Catt. RDn (until 1857), Catt. West RDn (1857—1928), Wensleyd. RDn (1928—*)

SEQ 55   Catt. RDn (until 1857), Ripon RDn (1857—77), Masham RDn (1877—1905), Ripon RDn (1905—*)

SEQ 56   Kirkby Lonsd. RDn (until 1849), Clapham RDn (1849—1921), Ewecr. RDn (1921—*)

SEQ 57   Richm. RDn (until 1857), Richm. East RDn (1857—*)

SEQ 58   Richm. RDn (until 1857), Richm. West RDn (1857—*)

SEQ 59   Richm. RDn (until 1857), Richm. West RDn (1857—63), Richm. North RDn (1863—*)

DIOCESES AND ARCHDEACONRIES

Yorks pars were organised in Archdeaconries and Rurarl Deaneries as follows:

BRADFORD DIOC (1919—*)

Bradford AD (1921—):* Airedale RDn (1971—*), Bowl. RDn (1921—71), Bowl. & Horton RDn (1971—*), Bradf RDn (1921—71), Calverley RDn, Horton RDn (1921—71), Otley RDn

Craven AD: Bolland RDn (1921—*), Bradf RDn (1919—21), Clapham RDn (1919—21), S Craven RDn (1921—*), Craven RDn, E'rn Dv (1919—21), Craven RDn, N'rn Dv (1919—21), Craven RDn, S'rn Dv (1919—21), Craven RDn, W'rn Dv (1919—21), Ewecr. RDn (1921—*), Otley RDn (1919—21), Sedbergh RDn (1926—71), Settle RDn (1926—71), Skipton RDn (1921—*)

CHESTER DIOC (1541—1836)

Richmond AD: Boroughbr. RDn, Catt. RDn, Richm. RDn

MANCHESTER DIOC (1847—*)

Manchester AD: Ashton under Lyne RDn (1847—

1929), Oldham RDn (1929—*), Manch. RDn (1847—72), Rochdale RDn (1872—81)

RIPON DIOC (1836—*)
Craven AD (1836—1919): Birstall RDn (1866—88), Bradf RDn (1857—1919), Craven RDn (1836—57), Craven RDn, E'rn Dv (1905—19), Craven RDn, N'rn Dv (1857—1919), Craven RDn, S'rn Dv (1857—1919), Craven RDn, W'rn Dv (1857—1919), Dewsb. RDn (1857—88), Halifax RDn (1857—88), Hudd. RDn (1857—88), Leeds RDn (1857—94), Otley RDn (1857—94), Pontef. RDn (1836—57), Silkst. RDn (1857—88), Wakef RDn (1857—88), Wethb. RDn (1857—94), Whitkirk RDn (1861—94)
Leeds AD (1921—):* Allert. RDn (1971—*), Armley RDn (1971—*), Boroughbr. RDn, Harrog. RDn (1971—*), Head. RDn (1971—*), Knar. RDn, Leeds RDn, Wethb. RDn, Whitkirk RDn
Richmond AD: Amound. RDn (1836—44), Bedale RDn (1928—*), Boroughbr. RDn (1836—94), Catt. RDn (1836—57), Catt. East RDn (1857—1928), Catt. West RDn (1857—1928), Clapham RDn (1849—94), Kirkby Lonsd. RDn (1836—49), Knar. RDn (1870—94), Masham RDn (1877—1905), Nidderdale RDn (1905—21), Richm. RDn (1836—57), Richm. East RDn (1857—*), Richm. North RDn (1863—*), Richm. West RDn (1857—*), Ripon RDn (1849—94), Ripon RDn (1921—*), Wensleyd. RDn (1928—*)
Ripon AD (1894—1921): Boroughbr. RDn, Clapham RDn (1894—1919), Knar. RDn, Leeds RDn, Otley RDn, Ripon RDn, Wethb. RDn, Whitkirk RDn

SHEFFIELD DIOC (1914—*)
Doncaster AD: Donc. RDn, Snaith RDn, Wath RDn
Sheffield AD: Attercliffe RDn (1942—*), Eccleshall RDn (1942—*), Ecclesfield RDn, Hallam RDn (1942—*), Handsw. RDn (1927—42), Laughton RDn (1942—*), Rotherh. RDn, Sheff RDn (1914—42), Tankersley RDn (1942—*)

WAKEFIELD DIOC (1888—*)
Halifax AD: Almondb. RDn (1968—*), Birstall RDn (1888—1927), Blackmoorfoot RDn (1968—*), Brigh. & Elland RDn (1967—*), Calder Valley RDn (1967—*), Dewsb. RDn (1888—1927), Halifax RDn, Hudd. RDn (1927—*), Kirkburton RDn (1968—*)
Huddersfield AD (1888—1927): Hemsw. RDn (1919—27), Hudd. RDn, Pontef. RDn (1919—27), Silkst. RDn, Wakef RDn
Pontefract AD (1927—):* Barnsley RDn, Birstall RDn,

Chevet RDn (1973—*), Dewsb. RDn, Pontef. RDn, Wakef RDn

YORK DIOC
Cleveland AD: Bulmer RDn (until 1913), Clev RDn (until 1862), Eas. RDn (1862—1913), Guisb. RDn (1862—78), Guisb. RDn (1924—*), Helm. RDn (1862—*), Malton RDn (1862—*), Middlesb. RDn (1878—*), N'allert. RDn (1862—*), Pick. RDn (1928—*), Riddal RDn (until 1862), Ripon RDn (until 1836), Stokes. RDn (1862—*), Thirsk RDn (1862—*), Whitby RDn (1878—*)
Doncaster AD (1913—14): Donc. RDn, Snaith RDn, Wath RDn
East Riding AD: Bev. RDn (1866—*), Bridl. RDn (1866—*), Buckr. RDn (until 1857), Buckr. RDn (1866—1936), E Buckr. RDn (1857—66), W Buckr. RDn (1857—66), Dick. RDn (until 1862), N Dick. RDn (1862—66), S Dick. RDn (1862—66), Escr. RDn (1896—1913), Harthill RDn (1866—*), N Harthill RDn (1857—66), S Harthill RDn (1857—66), W Harthill RDn (1857—66), Harthill & Hull RDn (until 1857), Hedon RDn (1866—1916), Hold. RDn (until 1849), N Hold. RDn (1849—66), N Hold. RDn (1916—*), S Hold. RDn (1849—66), S Hold. RDn (1916—*), Hornsea RDn (1866—1916), Howden RDn (1866—*), Kingst. upon Hull RDn (1869—*), Pockl. RDn (1866—1936), Scarb. RDn (1866—*), Settr. RDn (1887—1922), Weigh. RDn (1866—1936)
Richmond AD (until 1541): Boroughbr. RDn, Catt. RDn, Richm. RDn
Sheffield AD (1884—1914): Ecclesfield RDn, Rotherh. RDn, Sheff RDn, Wath RDn (1884—1913)
York AD (1928—):* Ainsty RDn, Buckr. RDn (1936—*), Bulmer RDn, Eas. RDn, Escr. RDn, Pockl. RDn (1936—*), Selby RDn, Tadc. RDn, Weigh. RDn (1936—*), City of York RDn
York and West Riding AD (until 1928): Ainsty RDn (until 1820), Ainsty RDn (1862—1928), New Ainsty RDn (1820—62), Old Ainsty RDn (1820—62), Bp'thorpe RDn (1871—96), Bulmer RDn (1913—28), Craven RDn (until 1836), Donc. RDn (until 1913), Eas. RDn (1913—28), Ecclesfield RDn (1862—84), Escr. RDn (1913—28), Hemsw. RDn (1916—19), Pontef. RDn (until 1836), Pontef. RDn (1857—1919), Rotherh. RDn (1857—84), Selby RDn (1862—1928), Sheff RDn (1862—84), Snaith RDn (1871—1913), Tadc. RDn (1862—71), Tadc. RDn (1922—28), Wath RDn (1871—84), City of York RDn (until 1836), City of York RDn (1862—1928), City of York and Ainsty RDn (1836—62)

THE PARISHES OF YORKSHIRE

ABBEYDALE
EP [W Riding] Cr 1895 from Sharrow EP, Sheffield St Barnabas EP.[1] Sheff RDn (1895—1942), Ecclesall RDn (1942—*). Sometimes 'Sheffield St Peter, Abbeydale'.

HIGH ABBOTSIDE
[N Riding] Tp in Aysgarth AP, sep CP 1866.[2] Incl undivided pt Abbotside Common (undivided moor common to High Abbotside, Low Abbotside, abol 1934 pt to each CP).[3] *LG* Seq 52. Addtl civ bdry alt: 1886.[4] Transf 1974 to N Yorks.[5] *Parl* Seq 14.

LOW ABBOTSIDE

[N Riding] Organisation as for High Abbotside.

ABBOTSIDE COMMON

[N Riding] Undivided moor in Aysgarth AP, after 1866 common to High Abbotside, Low Abbotside. *LG* Aysg. RD. Abol 1934 pt to High Abbotside CP, pt to Low Abbotside CP.[3] *Parl* Thirsk & Malton Dv (1918—48).

ABERFORD

AP [W Riding] Incl tps Parlington, Sturton Grange (each a sep CP 1866[2]). *LG* Seq 106. *Parl* Seq 24. *Eccl* Ainsty RDn (until 1820), New Ainsty RDn (1820—57), Pontef. RDn (1857—1914). Gains eccl 1914 tp Lotherton cum Aberford in Sherburn in Elmet AP to cr Aberford with Lotherton EP.[6]

ABERFORD WITH LOTHERTON

EP [W Riding] Cr 1914 by union Aberford AP, tp Lotherton cum Aberford in Sherburn in Elmet AP.[6] Pontef. RDn (1914—16), Selby RDn (1916—21), Tadc. RDn (1921—*).

ACASTER MALBIS

AP [Ainsty (W Riding until 1449 and from 1836, indept jurisd 1449—1836). Tp 'Acaster Malbis' in Ainsty; incl (pt in Ainsty, pt in E Riding [Ouse & Derw. Wap]) pt chap Naburn (qv for other mother pars, sep CP 1866[2] so that 'Acaster Malbis' ent W Riding thereafter, 'Naburn' a sep EP 1842[7]). *LG* York PLU, RSD, Bp'thorpe RD (1894—1937), Tadc. RD (1937—74). Transf 1974 to N Yorks.[5] *Parl* Pt N Riding (the pt in Ainsty), pt E Riding (1832—67), N Riding (1867—85), Thirsk & Malton Dv (1885—1918), [W Riding for parl purposes thereafter] Bark. Ash Dv/CC (1918—*). *Eccl* Pec jurisd Selby (1440—1539), Ainsty RDn (1539—1820), New Ainsty RDn (1820—62), Tadc. RDn (1862—71), Bp'thorpe RDn (1871—96), Ainsty RDn (1896—*). Addtl eccl bdry alt: 1880s.[8]

ACASTER SELBY

[W Riding] Tp (W Riding until 1449 and from 1836, indept jurisd 1449—1836) in Stillingfleet AP (o'wise E Riding), sep CP 1866,[2] sep EP 1772,[9] eccl refounded 1850.[10]. *LG* Seq 70. Transf 1974 to N Yorks.[5] *Parl* Seq 23. *Eccl* Bulmer RDn (1772—1862), Tadc. RDn (1862—71), Bp'thorpe RDn (1871—96), Ainsty RDn (1896—1971). Eccl bdry: 1875 (gains tp Appleton Roebuck from Bolton Percy AP).[11] Renamed eccl 1971 'Appleton Roebuck with Acaster Selby'.[12]

ACKLAM

AP [E Riding] Chap in Stainton AP, sep civ identity early, sep EP 1770 as 'East Acklam',[9] qv. Incl tps Acklam with Barthorpe, Leavening (each a sep CP 1866[2]) so that 'Acklam' has no sep civ identity 1866—1935 (see following entry). *LG* Buckr. Wap. *Parl* E Riding (1832—67).

CP [E Riding] Renaming 1935 of Acklam with Barthorpe CP.[13] *LG* Norton RD. Transf 1974 to N Yorks.[5] *Parl* Bev. CC (1948—55), Howden CC (1955—*).

EAST ACKLAM

AP [E Riding] Chap in Stainton AP, sep civ identity early as 'Acklam', qv also its tps incl, sep EP 1770.[9] *Eccl* Pec jurisd Chancellor of Cathedral of York (until 1836), Buckr. RDn (1836—57), W Buckr. RDn (1857—66), Pockl. RDn (1866—1930), Buckr. RDn (1930—71). Renamed 1971 'Acklam and Leaving'.[14]

WEST ACKLAM

AP [N Riding] Domesday church, later sometimes described as a chap in Stainton AP, sep status maintained.[15] Incl Middlesbrough (cell in Whitby Abbey, in West Acklam after Dissolution, sep civ identity early, sep EP 1744[9]). *LG* Langb. Lbty, Stock. PLU (1837—75), Middlesb. PLU (1875—1930), pt Middlesb. MB (1887—89), pt Middlesb. CB (1889—94), pt Middlesb. USD (1887—94), Middlesb. RSD (pt 1875—87, ent 1887—94), Middlesb. RD. Addtl civ bdry alt: 1883,[16] 1887,[17] 1894 (loses the pt in Middlesb. CB [assoc with N Riding] to Middlesbrough CP),[18] 1913.[19] Abol civ 1932 pt to Middlesb. CB (assoc with N Riding) & CP, pt to Hemlington CP, pt to Marton AP.[20] *Parl* N Riding (1832—85), pt Middlesb. Parl Bor (1885—1918), Clev Dv (pt 1885—1918, ent 1918—48). *Eccl* Clev RDn (until 1862), Stokes. RDn (1862—78), Middlesb. RDn (1878—*). Addtl eccl bdry alt: 1872 (help cr Middblesbrough St Paul EP),[21] 1879 (help cr Middlesbrough All Saints EP),[22] 1900,[23] 1936 (help cr Middlesbrough St Oswald EP),[24] 1939 (help cr Middlesbrough St Martin EP),[25] 1950 (help cr Middlesbrough St Chad EP),[26] 1969.[27]

ACKLAM AND LEAVENING

EP [E Riding] Renaming 1971 of East Acklam AP.[14] Buckr. RDn.

ACKLAM WITH BARTHORPE

[E Riding] Tp in Acklam AP, sep CP 1866.[2] *LG* Buckr. Wap, Malton PLU, RSD, Norton RD. Renamed 1935 'Acklam'.[13] *Parl* E Riding (1832—85), Buckr. Dv (1885—1948).

ACKTON

[W Riding] Tp in Featherstone AP, sep CP 1866.[2] *LG* Agb. Wap, Barwick GilbU (until 1869), Pontef. PLU (1869—1930), Featherstone USD, UD. Abol 1938 to help cr Ackton and Snydale CP.[28] *Parl* W Riding (1832—67), S'rn Dv of W Riding (1867—85), Norm. Dv (1885—1948).

ACKTON AND SNYDALE

CP [W Riding] Cr 1938 by union ent Ackton CP, pt Snydale CP.[28] *LG* Featherstone UD. Transf 1974 to W Yorks.[5] *Parl* Pontef. BC (1948—70), Pontef. & Castlef. BC (1970—*).

ACKWORTH

AP [W Riding] *LG* Seq 96. Transf 1974 to W Yorks.[5] *Parl* Seq 28. *Eccl* Pontef. RDn. Eccl bdry: 1876 (help cr East Hardwick EP).[29]

ACOMB

AP [Ainsty (W Riding until 1449 and from 1836, indept jurisd 1449—1836] Incl pt tp Dringhouses (sep CP 1866,[2] sep EP 1853 [qv for constituent pars][30]), pt tp Knapton (sep CP 1866[2]). *LG* York PLU (1837—54), Gt Ouseb PLU (1854—1930), RSD, RD. Abol civ 1937 pt to Askham Bryan AP, pt to York CB (not assoc with a Riding) & CP.[31] *Parl* N Riding (1832—85), Thirsk & Malton Dv (1885—1918), [W

Riding for parl purposes thereafter] Bark. Ash Dv (1918—48). *Eccl* Pec jurisd Treasurer of York (early dissolved), contentious pec jurisd Dean & Chapter of York, Ainsty RDn (early—1820), New Ainsty RDn (1820—62), Ainsty RDn (1862—1919), York RDn (1919—*). Addtl eccl bdry alt: 1938 (cr Acomb Holy Redeemer EP),[32] 1968 (help cr Acomb Moor EP).[33]

ACOMB HOLY REDEEMER

EP [W Riding] Cr 1938 from Acomb AP.[32] York RDn.

ACOMB MOOR

EP [W Riding] Cr 1968 from Acomb AP, Dringhouses EP.[33] York RDn.

ADDINGHAM

AP [W Riding] Tp 'Addingham' in Staincl. & Ewc. Wap; incl in Claro Wap pt tp Beamsley (sep CP 1866[2]). *LG* Skipton PLU, RSD, RD. Transf 1974 to W Yorks.[5] *Parl* Seq 41. *Eccl* Craven RDn (until 1857), Craven RDn, S'rn Dv (1857—94), Otley RDn (1894—1921), Skipton RDn (1921—35), Otley RDn (1935—*).

ADEL

AP [W Riding] lncl tp Adel cum Eccup (sep CP 1866[2]), tp Arthington (sep CP 1866,[2] sep EP 1865[34]) so that 'Adel' has no sep civ identity after 1866. *LG* Skyr. Wap. *Parl* W Riding (1832—67). *Eccl* Ainsty RDn (until 1820), Old Ainsty RDn (1820—57), Wethb. RDn (1857—61), Whitkirk RDn (1861—94), Leeds RDn (1894—1971), Head. RDn (1971—*). Addtl eccl bdry alt: 1846 (help cr Woodside EP),[35] 1964 (cr Cookridge EP),[36] 1967.[37]

ADEL CUM ECCUP

[W Riding] Tp 'Adel cum Eccup' in Adel AP, sep CP 1866.[2] *LG* Skyr. Wap, Carlton GilbU (until 1869), Wharfed. PLU (1869—1930), RSD, RD. Bdry: 1926 (loses pt to Leeds CB [assoc with W Riding] & AP).[38] Abol 1928 ent to Leeds CB (assoc with W Riding) & AP.[39] *Parl* W Riding (1832—67), E'rn Dv of W Riding (1867—85), Bark. Ash Dv (1885—1918), Pudsey & Otley Dv (1918—48).

ADLINGFLEET

AP [W Riding] Incl tps Fockerby, Haldenby (each a sep CP 1866[2]). *LG* Seq 95. Transf 1974 to Humb.[5] *Parl* Seq 29. *Eccl* Pec jurisd Selby (1440—1539), Pontef. RDn (1539—1838), New Ainsty RDn (1838—57), Pontef. RDn (1857—62), Selby RDn (1862—71), Snaith RDn (1871—1952). Eccl bdry: 1885 (help cr Eastoft EP [Lincs Pts Lind, Yorks W Riding] to be dioc York).[40] Abol eccl 1952 to help cr Whitgift with Adlingfleet EP.[41]

ADWICK LE STREET

AP [W Riding] Incl tp Harpole (sep CP 1866[2]). *LG* Straff. & Tick. Wap, Donc. PLU, RSD, RD (1894—1915), Adwick le Street UD (1915—74). Addtl civ bdry alt: 1883,[42] 1915 (gains Skellow CP, pts Brodsworth AP, Owston AP as enlarged par constituted the UD).[43] Transf 1974 to S Yorks.[5] *Parl* Seq 45. *Eccl* Seq 40. Eccl bdry: 1914 (help cr Woodlands EP).[44]

ADWICK UPON DEARNE

AP [W Riding] LG Seq 117. Civ bdry: 1938.[28] Transf 1974 to S Yorks.[5] *Parl* Seq 44. *Eccl* Seq 46.

AGGLETHORPE WITH COVERHAM

[N Riding] Tp in Coverham AP, sep CP 1866.[2] *LG* Seq 53. Transf 1974 to N Yorks.[5] *Parl* Seq 14.

AIKE

[E Riding] Tp pt in Lockington AP (Harth. Wap), pt in Beverley St John AP (area of this pt in Bev. Lbty), sep CP 1866.[2] *LG* Bev. PLU, RSD, RD. Abol 1935 ent to Lockington AP.[13] *Parl* E Riding (1832—85), Hold. Dv (1885—1948).

AINDERBY MIERS WITH HOLTBY

[N Riding] Tp in Hornby AP, sep CP 1866.[2] *LG* Seq 46. Transf 1974 to N Yorks.[5] *Parl* Seq 15.

AINDERBY QUERNHOW

[N Riding] Tp in Pickhill AP, sep CP 1866.[2] *LG* Seq 45. Transf 1974 to N Yorks.[5] *Parl* Seq 16.

AINDERBY STEEPLE

AP [N Riding] lncl tps Morton upon Swale, Thrintoft, Warlaby (each a sep CP 1866[2]). *LG* Seq 34. Transf 1974 to N Yorks.[5] *Parl* Seq 14. *Eccl* Richm. RDn (until 1857), Richm. East RDn (1857—1928), Bedale RDn (1928—*).

AIREBOROUGH

CP [W Riding] Cr 1937 by union pts Esholt CP, Guiseley AP, Hawksworth CP, Menston CP, Otley AP, Rawdon CP, Yeadon CP.[31] *LG* Aireb. UD. Transf 1974 to W Yorks.[5] *Parl* Pudsey BC (1948—*).

AIREDALE WITH FRYSTON

EP [W Riding] Cr 1930 by union pt Ferry Fryston AP, pt Pontefract All Saints EP, ent Glass Houghton EP.[45] Pontef. RDn. Bdry: 1962.[46]

AIRMYN

[W Riding] Chap in Snaith AP, sep CP 1866,[2] sep EP 1728.[9] *LG* Osg. Wap, Goole PLU, pt Goole USD, pt Goole RSD, Goole RD. Civ bdry: 1894 (loses the pt in Goole UD to Goole CP).[47] Transf 1974 to Humb.[5] *Parl* Seq 29. *Eccl* Pec jurisd Selby (1440—1539), pec jurisd Snaith (1539—1836), Pontef. RDn (1836—38), New Ainsty RDn (1838—57), Pontef. RDn (1857—62), Selby RDn (1862—71), Snaith RDn (1871—*). Eccl bdry: 1905 (help refound Goole EP).[48]

AIRTON

[W Riding] Tp in Kirkby in Malham Dale AP, sep CP 1866.[2] *LG* Seq 111. Bdry: 1938.[28] Transf 1974 to N Yorks.[5] *Parl* Seq 41.

AIRYHOLME WITH HOWTHORPE AND BAXTON HOWE

[N Riding] Tp in Hovingham AP, sep CP 1866.[2] *LG* Seq 65. Transf 1974 to N Yorks.[5] *Parl* Seq 16.

AISKEW

[N Riding] Tp in Bedale AP, sep CP 1866.[2] *LG* Seq 49. Transf 1974 to N Yorks.[5] *Parl* Seq 15.

AISLABY

[N Riding] Tp in Middleton AP, sep CP 1866.[2] *LG* Seq 61. Bdry: 1883,[16] 1887.[49] Transf 1974 to N Yorks.[5] *Parl* Seq 22.

AISLABY

[N Riding] Chap in Whitby AP, sep CP 1866,[2] sep EP 1768,[9] eccl refounded 1865.[50] *LG* Seq 59. Civ bdry: 1932.[51] Transf 1974 to N Yorks.[5] *Parl* Seq 19. *Eccl* Clev RDn (1768—1862), Guisb. RDn (1862—78), Whitby RDn (1878—*).

AISMUNDERBY WITH BONDGATE

[W Riding] Tp in Ripon AP, sep CP 1866.[2] *LG* Ripon Lbty, not in a PLU (until 1852), Ripon PLU (1852—94), pt Ripon MB (1835—94), pt Ripon USD, pt Ripon RSD. Bdry: 1883.[52] Abol 1894 the pt in the MB transf to Ripon AP, the remainder to help cr Littlethorpe CP.[53] *Parl* Pt Ripon Parl Bor (1832—85), pt W Riding (1832—67), pt E'rn Dv of W Riding (1867—85), Ripon Dv (1885—1918).

AKEBAR

[N Riding] Tp in Finghall AP, sep CP 1866.[2] *LG* Seq 53. Transf 1974 to N Yorks.[5] *Parl* Seq 14.

ALDBOROUGH

AP [Pt N Riding (Halik. Wap: pt tp Lower Dunsforth, pt tp Upper Dunsforth cum Branton Green, tp Ellenthorpe [each a sep CP 1866[2]; for Dunsforth eccl, see below]); pt W Riding (Claro Wap: tp and bor 'Aldborough', chap and bor Boroughbridge [sep CP 1866,[2] sep EP 1720,[9] eccl refounded 1866[54]; claimed to be in pec jurisd Dean & Chapter of York], chap Hampsthwaite [early 13th cent considered a chap in this par, sep par soon thereafter], pt tps Lower Dunsforth, Upper Dunsforth cum Branton Green, Humberton, Milby [each pt in N Riding, pt in W Riding, each a sep CP 1866[2]], tp Minskip [sep CP 1866[2]], tp Roecliffe [sep CP 1866,[2] sep EP 1844[55]], chap Dunsforth [sep EP 1782,[9] eccl refounded 1867,[56] in pec jurisd Dean & Chapter of York until 1836; for civ, see Lower Dunsforth, Upper Dunsforth cur Branton Green, above)]]. *LG* After cr of CPs 1866 from this par, Aldborough ent W Riding (Claro Wap), not in a PLU (until 1854), Gt Ouseb. PLU (1854—1930), RSD, RD. Abol civ 1938 ent to Boroughbridge CP.[28] *Parl* Pt Aldborough Parl Bor (1558—1832), pt Boroughbridge Parl Bor (1553—1832); after 1832, pt N Riding, pt W Riding (1832—67), N'rn Dv of W Riding (1867—85), Ripon Dv (1885—1918). *Eccl* Pec jurisd Dean & Chapter of York (until 1836), Boroughbr. RDn (1836—1971), Ripon RDn (1971—*). Addtl eccl bdry alt: 1941,[27] 1973 (gains Dunsforth EP).[57]

ALDBROUGH

AP [E Riding] Gains early (if did not aready incl) chap (sometimes 'church') Colden Parva (later swallowed by sea[58]) hence this par sometimes eccl 'Aldbrough with Colden Parva'. Incl also pt tp Great and Little Cowdens, tp East Newton, pt tp West Newton with Burton Constable (each a sep CP 1866[2]). *LG* Seq 16. Addtl civ bdry alt: 1885,[59] 1935 (gains East Newton CP).[13] Transf 1974 to Humb.[5] *Parl* Seq 5. *Eccl* Hold. RDn (until 1849), N Hold. RDn (1849—66), Hornsea RDn (1866—1916) N Hold. RDn (1916—*). Eccl bdry: 1962.[60]

ALDBROUGH

[N Riding] Tp in Stanwick AP, sep CP 1866.[2] *LG* Seq 38. Transf 1974 to N Yorks.[5] *Parl* Seq 14.

ALDBROUGH WITH COLDEN PARVA—see first ALDBROUGH above

ALDFIELD

[W Riding] Tp in Ripon AP, sep CP 1866,[2] sep EP 1724 incl tp Studley Roger as 'Aldfield with Studley', qv.[9] *LG* Seq 90. Transf 1974 to N Yorks.[5]

Parl Seq 33.

ALDFIELD WITH STUDLEY

EP [W Riding] Cr 1724 by union tp Aldfield, tp Studley Roger, each in Ripon AP.[9] Pec jurisd Lbty Ripon (1724—1836), Boroughbr. RDn (1836—49), Ripon RDn (1849—*).

ALDWARK

[N Riding] Tp in Alne AP, sep CP 1866.[2] *LG* Seq 28. *Parl* Seq 16.

ALLERSTON

[N Riding] Chap in Pickering AP, united 1252 with chap Ebberston in same par as sep EP 'Ebberston with Allerston',[61] qv, 'Ebberston' and 'Allerston' each sep civ identity early. *LG* Seq 61. Transf 1974 to N Yorks.[5] *Parl* Seq 20.

ALLERTHORPE

[E Riding] Chap (in pec jurisd Dean of York) in Pocklington AP, united 1252 with chap Thornton in same par as sep EP 'Thornton with Allerthorpe',[62] qv, 'Thornton' and 'Allerthorpe' each sep civ identity early. Incl tp Waplington (sep CP 1866[2]). *LG* Seq 12. Addtl civ bdry alt: 1935 (gains Waplington CP).[13] Transf 1974 to Humb.[5] *Parl* Seq 7.

ALLERTON

[W Riding] Tp in Bradford AP, sep CP 1866,[2] eccl severed 1828 to help cr Wilsden cum Allerton EP,[63] qv, 'Allerton' a sep EP 1890 from Wilsden cum Allerton EP.[64] *LG* Morley Wap, Bradf PLU (1837—48), N Bierley PLU (1848—98), Allert. USD (1875—82), Bradf MB (1882—89), Bradf CB (1889—98), Bradf USD (1882—94). Abol civ 1898 ent to Bradf CB (assoc with W Riding) & AP.[65] *Parl* W Riding (1832—67), E'rn Dv of W Riding (1867—85); see Part III of the *Guide* for composition of Bradf Parl Bors (1885—1918) by wards of the MB. *Eccl* Bradf RDn (1890—1921), Horton RDn (1921—71), Airedale RDn (1971—*). Eccl bdry: 1924 (help cr Bradford St Saviour EP),[66] 1927,[67] 1967.[68]

CHAPEL ALLERTON

[W Riding] Chap in Leeds AP, sep CP 1866,[2] sep EP 1719.[9] *LG* Leeds Bor/MB/CB, USD, Carlton GilbU (until 1869), Leeds PLU (1869—1904). Abol civ 1904 ent to Leeds AP.[69] *Parl* Leeds Parl Bor (1832—85); see Part III of the *Guide* for composition of Leeds Parl Bors (1885—1918) by wards of the MB. *Eccl* Ainsty RDn (1719—1820), Old Ainsty RDn (1820—36), Pontef. RDn (1836—57), Leeds RDn (1857—1971), Allert. RDn (1971—*). Eccl bdry: 1847 (help cr Meanwood EP),[70] 1895 (help cr Leeds St Aidan EP),[71] 1902,[72] 1910 (help refound Roundhay EP),[73] 1967.[37]

MOOR ALLERTON

EP [W Riding] Cr 1860 from Leeds AP.[9] Leeds RDn (1860—1971), Allert. RDn (1971—*). Bdry: 1910 (help refound Roundhay EP),[73] 1954,[37] 1967.[37]

ALLERTON BYWATER

[W Riding] Tp in Kippax AP, sep CP 1866,[2] sep EP 1867.[74] *LG* Skyr. Wap, Gt Preston GilbU (until 1869), Tadc. PLU (1869—1930), RSD, RD. Civ bdry: 1884,[75] 1938.[28] Abol civ 1939 ent to Garforth UD & AP.[76] *Parl* W Riding (1832—67), N'rn Dv of

W Riding (1867—85), Osg. Dv (1885—1918), Bark. Ash Dv (1918—48). *Eccl* Wakef RDn (1867—94), Whitkirk RDn (1894—*).

ALLERTON MAULEVERER

AP [W Riding] Incl pt tp Allerton Mauleverer with Hopperton, ent tp Clareton (each a sep CP 1866[2]) so that after 1866 'Allerton Maulever' has no sep civ identity. *LG* Claro Wap. *Parl* W Riding (1832—67). *Eccl* Boroughbr. RDn (until 1971), Ripon RDle (1971). Eccl bdry: 1924 (help refound Arkendale EP).[77] Abol eccl 1971 to help cr Whixley with Green Hammerton EP.[78]

ALLERTON MAULEVERER WITH HOPPERTON

[W Riding] Tp pt in Allerton Mauleverer AP, pt in Whixley AP, sep CP 1866.[2] *LG* Seq 86. Transf 1974 to N Yorks.[5] *Parl* Seq 36.

ALMONDBURY

AP [W Riding] Incl chap South Crosland (sep CP 1866,[2] sep EP 1839,[9] eccl refounded 1843[79]), chap Honley (sep CP 1866,[2] sep EP 1729 as 'Honley with Brockholes',[9] eccl refounded 1876 as 'Honley'[29]), chap Linthwaite (sep CP 1866,[2] sep EP 1833,[9] eccl refounded 1843[79]), chap Lockwood (sep CP 1866,[2] sep EP 1831,[9] eccl refounded 1843[79]), pt chap Marsden (sep EP 1742,[9] eccl refounded 1868[80]; the pt of this chap in Almondbury a sep tp/CP 1866 as 'Marsden in Almondbury',[2] [the remainder sep tp/CP 1866 as 'Marsden in Huddersfield',[2] qv]), chap Meltham (sep CP 1866,[2] sep EP 1874[81]), chap Netherthong (sep CP 1866,[2] sep EP 1831,[9] eccl refounded 1843[79]), tps Austonley, Lingards (each a sep CP 1866[2]), tp Farnley Tyas (sep CP 1866,[2] sep EP 1840,[9] eccl refounded 1897[56]), tp Holme (sep CP 1866,[2] sep EP 1842 as 'Holme Bridge',[9] as such eccl refounded 1843[79]), tp Marsden in Almondbury (the pt of chap Marsden in this par, qv above for eccl status, sep CP 1866[2]), tp Upperthong (sep CP 1866,[2] sep EP 1846[82]). *LG* Agb. Wap, Hudd. PLU, Almondb. Bor, Hudd. MB (1868—89), CB (1889—1924,) USD. Abol civ 1924 ent to Hudd. CB (assoc with W Riding) & AP.[83] *Parl* W Riding (1832—67), Hudd. Parl Bor (1867—1948). *Eccl* Pontef. RDn (until 1857), Hudd. RDn (1857—1968), Almondb. RDn (1968—*). Addtl eccl bdry alt: 1845 (help cr Meltham Mills EP),[84] 1846 (cr Milnsbridge EP),[85] 1848 (cr Armitage Bridge EP),[86] 1857.[87]

ALNE

AP [N Riding] lncl tps Aldwark, Flawith, Tholthorpe, Tollerton, Youlton (each a sep CP 1866[2]). *LG* Seq 28. Transf 1974 to N Yorks.[5] *Parl* Seq 16. *Eccl* As 'Alne with Aldwark', pec jurisd Treasurer of Cathedral of York (all except Youlton, until 1547), Seq 18 thereafter.

ALNE WITH ALDWARK—see prev entry

ALTOFTS

[W Riding] Tp in Normanton AP, sep CP 1866,[2] sep EP 1878.[88] *LG* Agb. Wap, Gt Preston GilbU (until 1869), Wakef PLU (1869—1930), Altofts USD, UD. Abol 1938 ent to Norm. UD & AP.[28] *Parl* W Riding (1832—67), S'rn Dv of W Riding (1867—85), Norm. Dv (1885—1948). *Eccl* Pontef.

RDn (1878—1927), Wakef RDn (1927—73), Chevet RDn (1973—*). Eccl bdry: 1944.[89]

ALVERTHORPE

EP [W Riding] Cr 1826 from Wakfield AP, incl area Wrenthorpe[9] (for civ status of latter see 'Stanley cum Wrenthorpe' [Wrenthorpe a sep EP 1875 from this par[90]]), 'Alverthorpe' eccl refounded 1830[91]; for civ see 'Alverthorpe with Thornes'. Pontef. RDn (1826—57), Wakef RDn (1857—*). Bdry: 1861 (help cr Westgate Common EP,[9] refounded 1862,[92] now called 'Wakefield St Michael'), 1913,[93] 1934 (help cr Lupset EP).[94]

CP [W Riding] Cr 1894 from the pt of Alverthorpe with Thornes CP not in Wakef MB.[95] *LG* Wakef PLU, RD. Bdry: 1895,[96] 1899,[97] 1900,[98] 1901,[99] 1902 (cr Lupset CP).[100] Renamed 1916 'Kirkhamgate'.[101] *Parl* Rothw. Dv (1918—48).

ALVERTHORPE WITH THORNES

[W Riding] Tp in Wakefield AP, sep CP 1866[2]; for eccl see 'Alverthorpe', 'Thornes'. *LG* Agb. Wap, Wakef PLU, pt Wakef MB (1848—94), pt Wakef USD, pt Wakef RSD. Bdry: 1883,[52] 1884.[102] Abol 1894 the pt in the MB transf to Wakefield AP, the remainder cr Alverthorpe CP.[95] *Parl* Pt Wakef Parl Bor (1832—1918), pt W Riding (1832—67), pt S'rn Dv of W Riding (1867—85), pt Norm. Dv (1885—1918).

ALWOODLEY

[W Riding] Tp in Harewood AP, sep CP 1866.[2] *LG* Skyr. Wap, Barwick GilbU (until 1861), Wharfed. PLU (1861—1928), RSD, RD. Abol 1928 ent to Leeds CB (assoc with W Riding) & AP.[39] *Parl* W Riding (1832—67), E'rn Dv of W Riding (1867—85), Bark. Ash Dv (1885—1918), Pudsey & Otley Dv (1918—48).

AMOTHERBY

[N Riding] Chap in Appleton le Street AP, sep CP 1866.[2] *LG* Seq 65. Transf 1974 to N Yorks.[5] *Parl* Seq 16.

AMPLEFORTH

AP [N Riding] Tp 'Ampleforth St Peter' in Ryed. Wap; incl in Birdf. Wap tp Ampleforth Birdforth (each a sep CP 1866[2]) so that 'Ampleforth' has no sep civ identity 1866—87 (see following entry). *Parl* N Riding (1832—67). *Eccl* Pec jurisd Ampleforth Prebend (until 1836), Seq 26 thereafter.

CP [N Riding] Cr 1887 by union Ampleforth St Peter CP, Ampleforth Birdforth CP, Ampleforth Oswaldkirk CP, pt Oswaldkirk AP.[103] *LG* Pt Ryed. Wap, pt Birdf. Wap, Helm. PLU, RSD, RD. Transf 1974 to N Yorks.[5] *Parl* Thirsk & Malton Dv/CC (1918—*).

AMPLEFORTH BIRDFORTH

[N Riding] Tp (Birdf. Wap) in Ampleforth AP (o'wise Ryed. Wap), sep CP 1866.[2] *LG* Helm. PLU, RSD. Abol 1887 to help cr Ampleforth CP.[103] *Parl* N Riding (1832—85), Whitby Dv (1885—1918).

AMPLEFORTH OSWALDKIRK

[N Riding] Tp in Oswaldkirk AP, sep CP 1866.[2] *LG* Ryed. Wap, Helm. PLU, RSD, RD. Abol 1887 to help cr Ampleforth CP.[103] *Parl* N Riding (1832—85), Whitby Dv (1885—1918).

AMPLEFORTH ST PETER

[N Riding] Tp 'Ampleforth St Peter' in Ampleforth AP, organisation as for Ampleforth Birdforth except this tp in Ryed. Wap.

ANGRAM

[W Riding] Tp in Long Marston AP, sep CP 1866,[2] *LG* Seq 74. Transf 1974 to N Yorks.[5] *Parl* Seq 23.

ANGRAM GRANGE

[N Riding] Tp in Coxwold AP, sep CP 1866.[2] *LG* Seq 24. Transf 1974 to N Yorks.[5] *Parl* Seq 16.

ANLABY

[E Riding] Tp pt in Hessle AP, pt in Kirk Ella AP, sep CP 1866,[2] sep EP 1902 from Kirk Ella AP, Hessle AP, Cottingham AP, North Ferriby AP.[104] *LG* Kingst. upon Hull Co, Scul. PLU, RSD, RD. Civ bdry: 1930 (loses pt to Kingst. upon Hull CB [assoc with E Riding] and to Sculcoates AP).[105] Abol civ 1935 pt to Kingst. upon Hull CB (assoc with E Riding) and to Sculcoates AP, pt to Haltemp. UD & CP.[13] *Parl* E Riding (1832—85), Howdensh. Dv (1885—1948). *Eccl* Howden RDn (1902—16), Kingst. upon Hull RDn (1916—*). Eccl bdry: 1951 (cr Hull St Mark, Anlaby Common EP),[106] 1959.[107]

NORTH AND SOUTH ANSTON

[W Riding] Area comprised of chaps North Anston, South Anston, each in Laughton en le Morthen AP, sep civ identity together early as 'North and South Anston', sep EP 1786 usually as 'Anston cum Membris',[108] qv. Incl tp Woodsetts (sep CP 1866,[2] sep EP 1841 by union tp Woodsetts, area Gildingwells in Letwell with Gildingwells EP, ex-par place Wallingwells[109]). *LG* Seq 121. Transf 1974 to S Yorks.[5] *Parl* Seq 48.

ANSTON CUM MEMBRIS

[W Riding] Area comprised of chaps North Anston, South Anston, each in Laughton en le Morthen AP, sep EP 1736 usually as 'Anston cum Membris',[108] sep civ identity early as 'North and South Anston', qv in prev entry (incl tp Woodsetts). Pec jurisd Laughton en le Morthen (until 1484), pec jurisd Chancellor of York (1484—1836), Donc. RDn (1836—57), Rotherh. RDn (1857—1927), Handsw. RDn (1927—42), Laughton RDn (1942—*). Eccl bdry: 1865 (help cr Shireoaks EP [Notts, Yorks]).[110]

APPLETON

[N Riding] Tp in Catterick AP, sep CP 1866.[2] *LG* Seq 50. Transf 1974 to N Yorks.[5] *Parl* Seq 14.

APPLETON LE MOORS

[N Riding] Tp in Lastingham AP, sep CP 1866,[2] sep EP 1868 by union pt tp Appleton le Moors, pt Spaunton Moor (area of Appleton Common).[111] Incl undivided pt Spaunton Moor (qv for other pars to which common, abol 1934 incl pt to this par [other areas also transf by same order to this par][3]). *LG* Ryed. Wap, Pick. PLU (1837—soon after 1848[112]), Kirkby Moors. PLU (soon after 1848[112]—1930), RSD, RD. Transf 1974 to N Yorks.[5] *Parl* Seq 21. *Eccl* Helm. RDn.

APPLETON LE STREET

AP [N Riding] Incl chap Amotherby, tps Broughton, Hildenley, Swinton (each a sep CP 1866[2]). *LG* Seq 65. Transf 1974 to N Yorks.[5] *Parl* Seq 16. *Eccl* As

'Appleton le Street with Amotherby', Seq 27.

APPLETON LE STREET WITH AMOTHERBY—see prev entry

APPLETON ROEBUCK

[W Riding] Tp in Bolton Percy AP, sep CP 1866,[2] eccl severed 1875 and transf to Acaster Selby EP (see following entry for later renaming of the enlarged par).[11] *LG* Seq 70. Transf 1974 to N Yorks.[5] *Parl* Seq 23.

APPLETON ROEBUCK WITH ACASTER SELBY

EP [W Riding] Renaming 1971 of Acaster Selby EP (which had in 1875 gained tp Appleton Roebuck, as in prev entry).[64] Ainsty RDn.

APPLETON UPON WISKE—see following entry

APPLETON WISKE

[N Riding] Chap in Great Smeaton AP, sep CP 1866,[2] sep EP 1869 as 'Appleton upon Wiske'[113] in Richm. East RDn, the order of 1869 revoked 1872[114] and the area thereafter eccl a chap in Great Smeaton. *LG* Langb. Lbty, N'allert. PLU, RSD, RD. Transf 1974 to N Yorks.[5] *Parl* Seq 11.

APPLETREEWICK

[W Riding] Tp in Burnsall AP, sep CP 1866,[2] pt eccl severed 1860 to help refound Greenhow Hill EP.[68] *LG* Seq 112. Transf 1974 to N Yorks.[5] *Parl* Seq 41.

ARDEN

[N Riding] Tp in Hawnby AP, sep CP 1866,[2] sep EP 1733.[9] *LG* Seq 25. Transf 1974 to N Yorks.[5] *Parl* Seq 16.

ARDSLEY

[W Riding] Tp in Darfield AP, sep CP 1866,[2] sep EP 1843,[9] eccl refounded 1844.[115] *LG* Staincr. Wap, Barnsley PLU, RSD (1875—92), Ardsley USD (1892—94), UD (1894—1921). Abol civ 1921 ent to Barnsley CB (assoc with W Riding) & CP.[116] *Parl* W Riding (1832—67), E'rn Dv of W Riding (1867—85), Barnsley Dv (1885—1918), Hemsw. Dv (1918—48). *Eccl* Donc. RDn (1843—71), Wath RDn (1871—*). Eccl bdry: 1955.[117]

ARDSLEY EAST

AP [W Riding] *LG* Agb. Wap, Wakef PLU, RSD, RD (1894—95), Ardsley East and West UD (1895—1937). Abol civ 1937 pt to Morley MB & CP, pt to Stanley UD & CP.[31] *Parl* W Riding (1832—67), S'rn Dv of W Riding (1867—85), Morley Dv (1885—1918), Rothw. Dv (1918—48). *Eccl* Seq 50.

ARDSLEY WEST

AP [W Riding] Orig cell in Nostell Priory; sometimes 'Woodkirk'. *LG* Agb. Wap, Wakef PLU, RSD (ent 1875—91, pt 1891—94), pt Morley MB & USD (1891—94), Wakef RD (1894—95), Ardsley East and West UD (1895—1937). Civ bdry: 1894 (loses the pt in Morley MB to Morley CP).[118] Abol civ 1937 ent to Morley MB & CP.[21] *Parl* As for Ardsley East. *Eccl* Pontef. RDn (until 1857), Dewsb. RDn (1857—66), Birstall RDn (1866—83), Dewsb. RDn (1883—*). Eccl bdry: 1913.[119]

ARGAM

AP [E Riding] Orig chap in Hunmanby AP, sep par 1269[120]; usual eccl spelling 'Ergham', qv. *LG* Dick. Wap, Bridl. PLU, RSD, RD. Abol civ 1935 ent to Grindale CP.[13] *Parl* E Riding (1832—85),

Buckr. Dv (1885—1948).

ARKENDALE
[W Riding] Chap pt in Knaresborough AP, pt in Farnham AP, sep CP 1866,[2] sep EP 1736,[9] eccl refounded 1924 from Knaresborough AP, Farnham AP, Goldsborough AP, Allerton Mauleverer AP, Marton cum Grafton AP.[77] *LG* Seq 85. Transf 1974 to N Yorks.[5] *Parl* Seq 36. *Eccl* Boroughbr. RDn (1736—1870), Knar. RDn (1870—1971), Harrog. RDn (1971—*).

ARKENGARTHDALE
[N Riding] Chap in Startforth AP, sep civ identity early, sep EP 1733.[9] *LG* Seq 37. Transf 1974 to N Yorks.[5] *Parl* Seq 14. *Eccl* Richm. RDn (1733—1857), Richm. West RDn (1857—*).

ARKSEY
AP [W Riding] Area comprised of 2 tps, Arksey and Bentley, so that 'Arksey' is usual eccl spelling, civ 'Bentley with Arksey', qv. *Eccl* Seq 40. Eccl bdry: 1898 (cr Bentley EP),[121] 1958,[122] 1958 (incl help cr New Bentley EP).[123]

ARMITAGE BRIDGE
EP [W Riding] Cr 1848 from Almondbury AP.[86] Pontef. RDn (1848—57), Hudd. RDn (1857—1968), Almondb. RDn (1968—*).

ARMLEY
[W Riding] Chap in Leeds AP, sep CP 1866,[2] sep EP 1729.[9] *LG* Skyr. Wap, Leeds Bor/MB/CB, Carlton GilbU (until 1869), Bramley PLU (1896—1904). Abol civ 1904 to help cr Armley and Bramley CP.[124] *Parl* Leeds Parl Bor (1832—85); see Part III of the *Guide* for composition of Leeds Parl Bors (1885—1918) by wards of the MB. *Eccl* Ainsty RDn (1729—1820), Old Ainsty RDn (1820—36), Pontef. RDn (1836—57), Leeds RDn (1857—1971), Armley RDn (1971—72). Eccl bdry: 1867 (help cr Upper Armley EP),[125] 1887 (help cr New Wortley St Mary of Bethany, Tong Road EP),[126] 1967.[127] Renamed 1972 'Armley St Bartholomew' EP.[128]

UPPER ARMLEY
EP [W Riding] Cr 1867 from Bramley EP, Kirkstall EP, Armley EP.[125] Leeds RDn (1867—1971), Armley RDn (1971—*). Bdry: 1967.[127]

ARMLEY AND BRAMLEY
CP [W Riding] Cr 1904 by union Armley CP, Bramley CP, Farnley CP, Wortley CP.[124] *LG* Bramley PLU, Leeds CB. Abol 1925 ent to Leeds AP.[129] *Parl* See Part III of the *Guide* for composition of Leeds Parl Bors (1918—48) by wards of the CB.

ARMLEY HALL
EP [W Riding] Cr 1872 from New Wortley EP.[90] Leeds RDn. Bdry: 1903.[130] Abol 1953 to help cr New Wortley St Mary with Armley Hall EP.[131]

ARMLEY ST BARTHOLOMEW
EP [W Riding] Renaming 1972 of Armley EP.[128] Armley RDn.

ARMTHORPE
AP [W Riding] *LG* Seq 117. Civ bdry: 1936 (loses pt to Donc. CB [assoc with W Riding] & AP).[132] Transf 1974 to S Yorks.[5] *Parl* Seq 44. *Eccl* Seq 40. Eccl bdry: 1952,[133] 1952 (help cr Wheatley Hills EP).[134]

ARNCLIFFE
AP [W Riding] Incl chap Halton Gill (sep CP 1866,[2] sep EP 1775[9]), tps Buckden, Hawkswick, Litton (each a sep CP 1866[2]). *LG* Seq 111. Addtl civ bdry alt: 1883,[52] 1884.[135] Transf 1974 to N Yorks.[5] *Parl* Seq 41. *Eccl* Seq 36. Addtl eccl bdry alt: 1765 (cr Hubberholme EP),[9] 1842 (help cr Stainforth EP).[136]

ARRATHORNE
[N Riding] Tp pt in Patrick Brompton AP, pt in Hornby AP, sep CP 1866,[2] the pt in Patrick Brompton AP eccl severed 1930 and transf to Hornby AP so that the area of Arrathorne CP ent in Hornby AP.[137] *LG* Seq 47. Bdry: 1934.[3] Transf 1974 to N Yorks.[5] *Parl* Seq 14.

ARTHINGTON
[W Riding] Tp in Adel AP, sep CP 1866,[2] sep EP 1865.[34] *LG* Seq 104. Civ bdry: 1937 (incl loses pt to Leeds CB [assoc with W Riding] & AP).[31] Transf 1974 to W Yorks.[5] *Parl* Seq 30. *Eccl* Otley RDn (1865—1921), Knar. RDn (1921—71), Harrog. RDn (1971—*).

ASENBY
[N Riding] Tp in Topcliffe AP, sep CP 1866.[2] *LG* Hallik. Wap, not in a PLU (until soon after 1852[112]), Ripon PLU (soon after 1852[112]—1930), RSD. Wath RD. Transf 1974 to N York.[5] *Parl* Seq 16.

ASKE
[N Riding] Tp in Easby AP, sep CP 1866.[2] *LG* Seq 38. Transf 1974 to N Yorks.[5] *Parl* Seq 14.

ASKERN
[W Riding] Tp in Campsall AP, sep CP 1866,[2] sep EP 1852.[138] *LG* Osg. Wap, Donc. PLU, Askern USD (1875—81), Donc. RSD (1881—94), RD. Civ bdry: 1883.[42] Transf 1974 to S Yorks.[5] *Parl* Seq 27. *Eccl* Donc. RDn.

ASKHAM BRYAN
AP [W Riding] *LG* Seq 70. Civ bdry: 1937,[31] 1957 (loses pt to Yorks CB [not assoc with a Riding] & CP).[139] Transf 1974 to N Yorks.[5] *Parl* Seq 23. Parl bdry: 1960.[140] *Eccl* Seq 29. Eccl bdry: 1967.[141]

ASKHAM RICHARD
AP [Ainsty (W Riding until 1449 and from 1836, indept jurisd 1449—1836)] *LG* York PLU, RSD, Bp'thorpe RD (1894—1937), Tadc. RD (1937—74). Transf 1974 to N Yorks.[5] *Parl* Seq 23. *Eccl* Seq 29.

ASKRIGG
[N Riding] Chap in Aysgarth AP, sep CP 1866,[2] sep EP 1739.[9] *LG* Seq 52. Civ bdry: 1883,[16] 1886.[4] Transf 1974 to N Yorks.[5] *Parl* Seq 14. *Eccl* Catt. RDn (1739—1857), Catt. West RDn (1857—1928), Wensleyd. RDn (1928—*).

ASKWITH
[W Riding] Tp in Weston AP, sep CP 1866.[2] *LG* Seq 83. Bdry: 1937.[31] Transf 1974 to N Yorks.[5] *Parl* Seq 30.

ASSELBY
[E Riding] Tp in Howden AP, sep CP 1866.[2] *LG* Seq 17. Bdry: 1880 (help cr Bishopsoil CP),[142] 1935.[13] Transf 1974 to Humb.[5] *Parl* Seq 7.

ASTON CUM AUGHTON
AP [W Riding] Incl pt tp Ulley (sep CP 1866,[2] sep EP 1852[143]). *LG* Seq 119. Civ bdry: 1967 (exchanges

pts with Sheff CB [assoc with W Riding] & AP and gains pt Beighton AP, Derbys).[144] Transf 1974 to S Yorks.[5] *Parl* Seq 55. *Eccl* Seq 43.

ATHERSLEY

EP [W Riding] Cr 1973 from Carlton EP, Monk Bretton EP.[145] Barnsley RDn.

ATTERCLIFFE

EP [W Riding] Cr 1844 when Attercliffe cum Darnall EP divided into 2 EPs of Attercliffe, Darnall,[88] 'Attercliffe' refounded 1849.[146] Donc. RDn (1844—57), Rotherh. RDn (1857—62), Sheff RDn (1862—1942), Attercliffe RDn (1942—46). Bdry: 1845 (cr 3 EPs of Brightside, Pitsmoor, Wicker),[147] 1874 (help cr Carbrook EP),[148] 1882 (help cr Attercliffe Emmanuel EP).[149] Abol 1946 to help cr Attercliffe with Carbrook EP.[150]

EP [W Riding] Cr 1963 by union Attercliffe with Carbrook EP; Sheffield St Clement, Newhall EP.[67] Attercliffe RDn.

ATTERCLIFFE CUM DARNALL

[W Riding] Chap in Sheffield AP, sep CP 1866,[2] sep EP 1731,[9] the latter abol 1844 into the 2 EPs of Attercliffe, Darnall[88] (Attercliffe refounded 1849[146]). *LG* Straff. & Tick. Wap, Sheff PLU, MB (1843—89), CB (1889—1902), USD. Abol civ 1902 ent to Sheffield AP.[151] *Parl* Sheff Parl Bor (1832—85); see Part III of the *Guide* for composition of Sheff Parl Bors (1885—1918) by wards of the MB. *Eccl* Donc. RDn.

ATTERCLIFFE EMMANUEL

EP [W Riding] Cr 1882 from Brightside All Saints EP, Brightside EP, Attercliffe EP, Sheffield Park EP.[149] Sheff RDn (1882—1942), Attercliffe RDn (1942—*).

ATTERCLIFFE WITH CARBROOK

EP [W Riding] Cr 1946 by union Attercliffe EP, Carbrook EP.[150] Attercliffe RDn. Abol 1963 to help cr Attercliffe EP.[67]

ATWICK

AP [E Riding] *LG* Seq 16. Transf 1974 to Humb.[5] *Parl* Seq 5. *Eccl* Seq 15.

AUBURN

[E Riding] Chap in Carnaby AP, inhabitants told to attend chap Fraisthorpe in same par, the 2 united 1731 as 'Auburn with Fraisthorpe' EP,[152] qv, 'Fraisthorpe' a sep EP 1824[9] and this par thereafter eccl 'Auburn'; the hmlt of Auburn civ pt in Carnaby AP, pt in Bridlington AP, sep CP 1866.[2] *LG* Dick. Wap, Bridl. PLU, RSD, RD. Abol civ 1896 to help cr Fraisthorpe with Auburn and Wilsthorpe CP.[153] *Parl* E Riding (1832—85), Buckr. Dv (1885—1918). *Eccl* Dick. RDn (1824—62), S Dick. RDn (1862—66), Bridl. RDn (1866—*).

AUBURN WITH FRAISTHORPE

EP [E Riding] Cr 1731 when 2 chaps Auburn, Fraisthorpe, each in Carnaby AP, united as sep EP.[152] Dick. RDn. Abol 1824 when Fraisthorpe a sep EP,[9] the remainder to be 'Auburn' EP.

AUCKLEY

[Pt Notts (Bassetlaw Wap), pt Yorks (W Riding, Donc. Soke), made 1895 ent Yorks W Riding[154]] Tp in Finningley AP (Notts, Yorks), sep CP 1866 with pt in ea co.[2] *LG* Donc. PLU. RSD, pt sep RD

in Notts (1894—95), Donc. RD (pt 1894—95, ent 1895—1974). Transf 1974 to S Yorks.[5] *Parl* Yorks pt, W Riding (1832—67), S'rn Dv of W Riding (1867—85), Donc. Dv (1885—1918), Don Valley Dv/CC (1918—*).

AUGHTON

AP [E Riding] Incl tp Laytham, pt tps Gribthorpe, Spaldington (each a sep CP 1866[2]), chap East Cottingwith (sep CP 1866,[2] not sep eccl hence this par usually eccl 'Aughton with East Cottingwith', qv). *LG* Harth. Wap, Howden PLU, RSD, RD. Abol civ 1935 to help cr Ellerton CP.[13] *Parl* E Riding (1832—85), Howdensh. Dv (1885—1948).

AUGHTON WITH EAST COTTINGWITH

AP [E Riding] Usual eccl name; for civ and civ sep tp and pt tps, chap, see prev entry. *Eccl* Seq 14.

AUSTERFIELD

[W Riding] Chap (Yorks, Straff. & Tick. Wap) in Blyth AP (Notts [Bassetlaw Wap], Yorks), sep CP 1866 in Yorks,[2] eccl severed 1858 and united with chap Bawtry (only other pt of Blyth in Yorks) to cr Bawtrey with Austerfield EP,[155] qv, to be in dioc Linc. *LG* Seq 117. Transf 1974 to S Yorks.[5] *Parl* Seq 44.

AUSTHORPE

[W Riding] Tp pt in Whitkirk AP, pt in Garsforth AP, sep CP 1866.[2] *LG* Skyr. Wap, Gt Preston GilbU (until 1862), Tadc. PLU (1862—1930), RSD, RD. Civ bdry: 1928 (loses pt to Leeds CB [assoc with W Riding] & AP),[141] 1937 (loses pt to Leeds CB [assoc with W Riding] & AP),[31] 1957 (loses pt to Leeds CB [assoc with W Riding] & AP).[156] Transf 1974 to W Yorks.[5] *Parl* Seq 24. Parl bdry: 1960.[140]

AUSTONLEY

[W Riding] Tp in Almondbury AP, sep CP 1866.[2] *LG* Agb. Wap, Hudd. PLU, Austonley USD (ent 1875—86, pt 1886—94), pt Holmf. USD (1886—94), Holmf. UD. Bdry: 1883,[52] 1886,[157] 1894 (gains the pt of Holme CP and the pt of Upperthong CP in Austonley UD).[158] Abol 1921 to help cr Holmfirth CP.[159] *Parl* W Riding (1832—67), S'rn Dv of W Riding (1867—85), Holmf. Dv (1885—1918), Colne Valley Dv (1918—48).

AUSTWICK

[W Riding] Tp in Clapham AP, sep CP 1866,[2] sep EP 1843 by union gtr pt tp Austwick, ent tp Lawland, both in Clapham AP,[9] eccl refounded 1879.[22] *LG* Seq 111. Civ bdry: 1883,[52] 1884.[135] Transf 1974 to N Yorks.[5] *Parl* Seq 41. *Eccl* Kirkby Lonsd. RDn (1843—49), Clapham RDn (1849—1921), Ewecr. RDn (1921—*).

AYSGARTH

AP [N Riding] Incl chap Askrigg (sep CP 1866,[2] sep EP 1739[9]), chap Hawes (sep CP 1866,[2] sep EP 1739[9]), tps High Abbotside, Low Abbotside, Bainbridge, Bishopdale, Burton cum Walden, Carperby cum Thoresby, Newbiggin, Thorlaby, Thornton Rust (each a sep CP 1866[2]); also incl Abbotside Common (undivided moor, after 1866 common to High Abbotside, Low Abbotside). *LG* Seq 52. Transf 1974 to N Yorks.[5] *Parl* Seq 14. *Eccl* Seq 54. Addtl eccl bdry alt: 1736 (cr Stalling Busk EP),[9] 1737 (cr

Lunds EP),[9] 1748 (cr Hadraw EP).[9]

AYTON

AP [N Riding] Usual civ spelling; for eccl see 'Great Ayton'. Incl chap Nunthorpe (sep CP 1866,[2] sep EP 1790,[9] eccl refounded 1925 from Great Ayton EP, Marton AP, Ormesby AP[160]), tps Great Ayton, Little Ayton (each a sep CP 1866[2]) so that after 1866 'Ayton' has no sep civ identity. *LG* Langb. Lbty. *Parl* N Riding (1832—67).

EAST AYTON

[N Riding] Tp in Seamer AP, sep CP 1866.[2] *LG* Seq 62. Transf 1974 to N Yorks.[5] *Parl* Seq 20.

GREAT AYTON

AP [N Riding] Usual eccl spelling; for civ and civ sep chap and tps, see 'Ayton'. *Eccl* Clev RDn (until 1862), Stokes. RDn (1862—80). Gains eccl 1880 tp Easby from Stokesley AP to cr Great Ayton with Easby EP.[161]

GREAT AYTON

[N Riding] Tp in Ayton AP (eccl, 'Great Ayton'), sep CP 1866.[2] *LG* Seq 58. Bdry: 1883.[16] Transf 1974 to N Yorks.[5] *Parl* Seq 11.

GREAT AYTON WITH EASBY

EP [N Riding] Cr 1880 by union Great Ayton AP (civ, 'Ayton'), tp Easby in Stokesley AP.[161] Stokes. RDn.

LITTLE AYTON

[N Riding] Tp in Ayton AP (eccl, 'Great Ayton'), sep CP 1866.[2] *LG* Seq 58. Bdry: 1932.[20] Transf 1974 to N Yorks.[5] *Parl* Seq 11.

WEST AYTON

[N Riding] Tp in Hutton Buscel AP, sep CP 1866.[2] *LG* Seq 62. Bdry: 1887.[162] Transf 1974 to N Yorks.[5] *Parl* Seq 20.

AZERLEY

[W Riding] Tp pt in Kirkby Malzeard AP, pt in Ripon AP, sep CP 1866,[2] the pt in Ripon AP eccl severed 1863 to help cr Winksley cum Grantley EP.[163] Incl undivided pt Lands Common to Azerley and Laverton (abol 1937 incl pt to this par [addtl bdry alt affecting this par made in same order][31]). *LG* Seq 90. Addtl bdry alt: 1883.[52] Transf 1974 to N Yorks.[5] *Parl* Seq 33.

BADSWORTH

AP [W Riding] Incl tps Thorpe Audlin, Upton (each a sep CP 1866[2]). *LG* Seq 96. Transf 1974 to W Yorks.[5] *Parl* Seq 28. *Eccl* Donc. RDn (until 1857), Pontef. RDn (1857—*). Eccl bdry: 1880.[164]

BAGBY

[N Riding] Tp in Kirby Knowle AP, sep CP 1866.[2] *LG* Birdf. Wap, Thirsk PLU (soon after 1837[112]—1930), RSD, RD. Bdry: 1883,[16] 1888.[165] Transf 1974 to N Yorks.[5] *Parl* Seq 16.

BAILDON

[W Riding] Chap in Otley AP, sep CP 1866,[2] sep EP 1719,[9] eccl refounded 1869.[71] *LG* Skyr. Wap, Carlton GilbU (until 1869), Wharfed. PLU (1869—1930), Baildon USD, UD. Civ bdry: 1937.[31] Transf 1974 to W Yorks.[5] *Parl* Seq 31. *Eccl* Ainsty RDn (1719—1820), Old Ainsty RDn (1820—36), Pontef. RDn (1836—57), Otley RDn (1857—94), Bradf RDn (1894—1921), Calverley RDn (1921—71), Airedale RDn (1971—*).

BAINBRIDGE

[N Riding] Tp in Aysgarth AP, sep CP 1866.[2] Incl undivided pt Land near Horton Gill Bridge (common to Bainbridge and Hawes, abol 1934 ent to Bainbridge[3]), undivided pt Wether Fell (common to Bainbridge and Hawes, abol 1934 ent to Hawes[3]), undivided pt Mossdale Moor (common to Bainbridge and Hawes, abol 1934 ent to Hawes[3]). *LG* Seq 52. Addtl civ bdry alt: 1883,[16] 1886,[4] 1934.[3] Transf 1974 to N Yorks.[5] *Parl* Seq 14.

BAINTON

AP [E Riding] Incl tp Neswick (sep CP 1866[2]). *LG* Seq 10. Addtl civ bdry alt: 1935 (gains Neswick CP).[13] Transf 1974 to Humb.[5] *Parl* Seq 3. *Eccl* Seq 10.

BALBY WITH HEXTHORPE

[W Riding] Tp in Doncaster AP, sep CP 1866,[2] sep EP 1846 (tp Balby with Hexthorpe, pt tp 'Doncaster').[166] *LG* Donc. Soke, Donc. PLU, RSD, RD (1894—95), Balby with Hexthorpe UD (1895—1914). Abol civ 1914 ent to Donc. MB and AP.[167] *Parl* W Riding (1832—67), S'rn Dv of W Riding (1867—85), Donc. Dv (1885—1918). *Eccl* Donc. RDn. Eccl bdry: 1858 (help er Doncaster St James EP,[9] eccl refounded 1864[137]), 1900 (help cr Doncaster St Jude EP),[168] 1930.[169] Sometimes called 'Doncaster St John the Evangeist'.

BALDERSBY

[N Riding] Tp in Topcliffe AP, sep CP 1866,[2] sep EP 1859.[170] *LG* Seq 42. Transf 1974 to N Yorks.[5] *Parl* Seq 16. *Eccl* Bulmer RDn (1859—62), Thirsk RDn (1862—*).

BALK

[N Riding] Tp in Kirby Knowle AP, sep CP 1866.[2] *LG* Seq 27. Transf 1974 to N Yorks.[5] *Parl* Seq 16.

BALKHOLME

[E Riding] Tp in Howden AP, sep CP 1866.[2] *LG* Howden Wap, PLU, RSD, RD. Bdry: 1880,[171] 1880.[172] Abol 1935 pt to Kilpin CP, pt to Eastrington AP, pt to help cr Gilberdyke CP.[13] *Parl* E Riding (1832—85), Howdensh. Dv (1885—1918).

BALNE

[W Riding] Tp in Snaith AP, sep CP 1866,[2] sep EP 1855.[173] *LG* Seq 97. Bdry: 1883.[52] Transf 1974 to N Yorks.[5] *Parl* Seq 29. *Eccl* Pontef. RDn (1855—62), Selby RDn (1862—71), Snaith RDn (1871—*).

BANK NEWTON

[W Riding] Tp in Gargrave AP, sep CP 1866.[2] *LG* Seq 112. Transf 1974 to N Yorks.[5] *Parl* Seq 41.

BANKFOOT

EP [W Riding] Cr 1850 from Bradford AP, Buttershaw EP.[174] Pontef. RDn (1850—57), Bradf RDn (1857—1921), Bowl. RDn (1921—71), Bowl. & Horton RDn (1971—*).

BARDEN

[N Riding] Tp in Hauxwell, sep CP 1866.[2] *LG* Seq 53. Transf 1974 to N Yorks.[5] *Parl* Seq 14.

BARDEN

[W Riding] Tp in Skipton AP, sep CP 1866,[2] eccl severed 1814 to help cr Bolton Abbey EP,[9] the latter eccl refounded 1864.[175] *LG* Seq 112. Transf 1974 to N Yorks.[5] *Parl* Seq 41.

BARDSEY

AP [W Riding] Incl tps Bardsey cum Rigton, Wothersome, pt tp Wyke (each a sep CP 1866[2]) so that after 1866 'Bardsey' has no sep civ identity. *LG* Skyr. Wap. *Parl* W Riding (1832—67). *Eccl* Seq 30.

BARDSEY CUM RIGTON

[W Riding] Tp 'Bardsey cum Rigton' in Bardsey AP, sep CP 1866.[2] *LG* Skyr. Wap, Gt Preston GilbU (until 1861), Wethb. PLU (1861—1930), RSD, RD. Transf 1974 to W Yorks.[5] *Parl* Seq 24.

BARFORTH

[N Riding] Tp pt in Forcett AP, pt in Stanwick AP, sep CP 1866.[2] *LG* Seq 39. Bdry: 1884.[176] Transf 1974 to Durham.[5] *Parl* Seq 14.

BARKISLAND

[W Riding] Tp in Halifax AP, incl area Ripponden (the latter a sep EP 1724,[9] refounded 1878[177]), 'Barkisland' a sep CP 1866,[2] eccl incl 1724 in Elland cum Stainland and Fixby EP[178], the latter reaugmented 1739 as 'Elland'[9] but usually called 'Elland with Greetland' until 'Greetland' a sep EP 1862,[138] the remainder still called 'Elland' (incl area Barkisland), 'Barkisland' a sep EP 1855 from Elland,[9] eccl refounded 1858.[179] *LG* Morley Wap, Halifax PLU, Barkisland USD, UD. Abol civ 1937 to help cr Ripponden UD & CP.[31] *Parl* W Riding (1832—67), E'rn Dv of W Riding (1867—85), Sowerby Dv (1885—1948). *Eccl* Halifax RDn (1855—1967), Brigh. & Elland RDn (1967—*). Eccl bdry: 1938.[180]

BARKSTON

[W Riding] Tp pt in Saxton AP, pt in Sherburn in Elmet AP, sep CP 1866.[2] *LG* Bark. Ash Wap, Barwick GilbU (until 1869), Tadc. PLU (1869—1930), RSD, RD. Bdry: 1883.[52] Transf 1974 to N Yorks.[5] *Parl* Seq 24.

BARLBY

[E Riding] Chap in Hemingbrough AP, sep CP 1866,[2] sep EP 1726.[9] *LG* Ouse & Derw. Wap, Selby PLU, pt Selby USD (1881—83), Selby RSD (ent 1875—81, pt 1881—83, ent 1883—94), Riccall RD (1894—1935), Derw. RD (1935—74). Civ bdry: 1883 (loses the pt in the USD to Selby AP, W Riding),[181] 1935 (gains Osgodby CP).[13] Transf 1974 to N Yorks.[5] *Parl* Seq 7. *Eccl* Pec jurisd Dean & Chapter of Durham (until 1836), Bulmer RDn (1836—96), Escr. RDn (1896—*).

BARLOW

[W Riding] Chap (donative, no sep eccl status sustained) in Brayton AP, sep CP 1866.[2] *LG* Seq 80. Transf 1974 to N Yorks.[5] *Parl* Seq 24.

BARMBY MARSH

[E Riding] Chap in Howden AP, sep EP 1796,[9] eccl refounded 1864,[182] sep CP 1866 as 'Barmby on the Marsh',[2] qv. *Eccl* Pec jurisd Dean & Chapter of Durham (until 1836), Harth. & Hull RDn (1836—57), W Harth. RDn (1857—66), Howden RDn (1866—*).

BARMBY MOOR

AP [E Riding] Sometime eccl spelling of Barmby on the Moor, qv below.

CP [E Riding] Renaming 1935 of Barmby on the Moor AP.[13] *LG* Pockl. RD. Transf 1974 to Humb.[5] *Parl* Bev. CC (1948—55), Howden CC (1955—*).

BARMBY ON THE MARSH

[E Riding] Chap in Howden AP, sep CP 1866,[2] sep EP 1796 'Barmby Marsh',[9] qv, as such eccl refounded 1864.[183] *LG* Seq 17. Civ bdry: 1880 (help cr Bishopsoil CP,[142] 1935.[13] Transf 1974 to Humb.[5] *Parl* Seq 7.

BARMBY ON THE MOOR

AP [E Riding] Orig chap in Pocklington AP, sep par 1252,[183] eccl held as one with Fangfoss from 1586 until Fangfoss a sep EP 1747.[9] *LG* Harth. Wap, Pockl. PLU, RSD, RD. Civ bdry: 1901.[184] Renamed civ 1935 'Barmby Moor'.[13] *Parl* E Riding (1832—85), Howdensh. Dv (1885—1948). *Eccl* Sometimes as 'Barmby Moor', pec jurisd Barmby Moor Prebend, later pec jurisd Dean of York (until 1836), Harth. & Hull RDn (1836—57), W Buckr. RDn (1857—66), Pockl. RDn (1866—*). Eccl bdry: 1960.[122]

BARMSTON

AP [E Riding] Incl pt chap Ulrome (sep CP 1866,[2] sep EP before 1835.[185] *LG* Seq 14. Addtl civ bdry 1935.[13] Transf 1974 to Humb.[5] *Parl* Seq 2. *Eccl* Hold. RDn (until 1849), N Hold. RDn (1849—66), Hornsea RDn (1866—87), Bridl. RDn (1887—1929). Abol eccl 1929 to help cr Barmston with Fraisthorpe EP.[186]

BARMSTON WITH FRAISTHORPE

EP [E Riding] Cr 1929 by union Barmston AP, chap Fraisthorpe (qv for earlier sep eccl status) in Carnaby AP.[186] Bridl. RDn.

BARNBROUGH

AP [W Riding] Incl pt tp Bilham (sep CP 1866[2]). *LG* Straff. & Tick. Wap, Donc. PLU, RSD, RD. Addtl civ bdry alt: 1883.[42] Renamed civ 1951 'Barnburgh'.[187] *Parl* W Riding (1832—67), S'rn Dv of W Riding (1867—85), Donc. Dv (1885—1918), Don Valley Dv/CC (1918—70). *Eccl* Seq 46.

BARNBURGH

CP [W Riding] Renaming 1951 of Barnbrough AP.[187] *LG* Donc. RD. Transf 1974 to S Yorks.[5] *Parl* Don Valley CC (1970—*).

BARNBY

[N Riding] Tp in Lythe AP, sep CP 1866,[2] pt eccl severed 1868 to help cr Ugthorpe EP.[188] *LG* Seq 59. Bdry: 1884.[189] Transf 1974 to N Yorks. *Parl* Seq 9.

BARNBY DUN WITH KIRK SANDALL

CP [W Riding] Cr 1921 by union Barnby upon Don AP, Kirk Sandall AP.[190] *LG* Donc. PLU, RD. Bdry: 1936 (loses pt to Donc. CB [assoc with W Riding] & AP),[132] 1956 (cr Edenthorpe CP).[98] Transf 1974 to S Yorks.[5] *Parl* Don Valley CC (1948—*).

BARNBY UPON DON

AP [W Riding] Incl tp Thorpe in Balne (sep CP 1866[2]), pt tp Burghwallis (sep CP 1866[2]), tp Stainforth (sep CP 1866,[2] sep EP 1884,[191] qv for other constituent pars). *LG* Straff. & Tick. Wap, Donc. PLU, RSD, RD. Addtl civ bdry alt: 1883.[42] Abol civ 1921 to help cr Barnby Dun with Kirk Sandall CP.[190] *Parl* W Riding (1832—67), S'rn Dv of W Riding (1867—85), Donc. Dv (1885—1918), Don Valley

Dv (1918—48). *Eccl* Sometimes as 'Barnby Dun' Seq 40.

BARNINGHAM

AP [N Riding] Incl tps Hope, Scargill, pt tp Newsham (each of the 3 a sep CP 1866[2]). *LG* Seq 39. Transf 1974 to Durham.[5] *Parl* Seq 14. *Eccl* Seq 59.

BARNOLDSWICK

AP [W Riding] Sometimes 'Gill'. Incl tps Brogden, Coates, Salterforth (each a sep CP 1866[2]). *LG* Staincl. & Ewc. Wap, Skipton PLU, RSD (1875—90), Barnoldswick USD (1890—94), UD. Addtl civ bdry alt: 1923 (gains Coates CP).[192] Transf 1974 to Lancs.[5] *Parl* Seq 41. *Eccl* Seq 39.

BARNSLEY

[W Riding] The following have 'Barnsley' in their names. Insofar as any existed at a given time: *LG* Staincr. Wap, Barnsley PLU, MB (1869—1913), USD, CB (1913—74). *Parl* W Riding (1832—67), S'rn Dv of W Riding (1867—85), Barnsley Dv (1885—1918), Barnsley Parl Bor/BC (1918—*). *Eccl* Donc. RDn (until 1838), Pontef. RDn (1838—57), Silkst. RDn (1857—1927), Barnsley RDn (1927—*).

CP1/EP1—BARNSLEY [ST MARY]—Chap in Silkstone AP, sep CP 1866,[2] sep EP 1718.[9] Civ bdry: 1921,[116] 1938.[28] Transf 1974 to S Yorks.[5] Eccl bdry: 1881 (help cr EP5),[193] 1933.[194]

EP2—BARNSLEY ST EDWARD THE CONFESSOR—Cr 1903 from EP4, EP3.[195]

EP3—BARNSLEY ST GEORGE—Cr 1823 from Silkstone AP,[9] refounded 1831.[196] Bdry: 1844 (cr EP4),[197] 1903 (help cr EP2),[195] 1912,[198] 1933.[194]

EP4—BARNSLEY ST JOHN—Cr 1844 from EP3.[197] Bdry: 1903 (help cr EP2),[195] 1912.[198] Abol 1972 to help cr EP6.[199]

EP5—BARNSLEY ST PETER—Cr 1881 from EP1.[193] Abol 1972 to help cr EP6.[199]

EP6—BARNSLEY ST PETER AND ST JOHN THE BAPTIST—Cr 1972 by union EP4, EP5.[199]

BARTON

[N Riding] Tp pt in Gilling AP, pt in Stanwick AP, sep CP 1866,[2] the pt in Stanwick a sep EP 1754 ([St Cuthbert] incl tp Newton Morrell),[9] the pt in Gilling a sep EP 1732 (St Mary),[9] qv, the 2 EPs united 1840 as 'Barton'.[200] *LG* Pt E Gill. Wap, pt W Gill. Wap, Darl. PLU, RSD, Croft RD. Transf 1974 to N Yorks.[5] *Parl* Seq 14. *Eccl* Richm. RDn (1840—57), Richm. East RDn (1857—*). Eccl bdry: 1930.[201]

BARTON LE STREET

AP [N Riding] Tp 'Barton le Street' in Ryed. Wap as was tp Butterwick (sep CP 1866,[2] sep EP 1790[9]); incl in Bulmer Wap tp Coneysthorpe (sep CP 1866[2]). *LG* Ryed. Wap (ent from 1866), Malton PLU, RSD, RD. Transf 1974 to N Yorks.[5] *Parl* Seq 14. *Eccl* Seq 27.

BARTON LE WILLOWS

[N Riding] Tp in Crambe AP, sep CP 1866.[2] *LG* Seq 29. Transf 1974 to N Yorks.[5] *Parl* Seq 16.

BARTON ST CUTHBERT

EP [N Riding] Cr 1754 from the pt of Barton tp in Stanwick EP.[9] Richm. RDn. United 1840 with Barton St Mary EP as Barton EP.[200]

BARTON ST MARY

EP [N Riding] Cr 1732 by union ent tp Newton Morrell and the pt of Barton tp in Gilling AP.[9] Richm. RDn. United 1840 with Barton St Cuthbert EP as Barton EP.[200]

BARUGH

[W Riding] Tp in Darton AP, sep CP 1866.[2] *LG* Staincr. Wap, Barnsley PLU, Darton USD, UD. Abol 1938 ent to Darton AP.[28] *Parl* W Riding (1832—67), S'rn Dv of W Riding (1867—85), Barnsley Dv (1885—1918), Hemsw. Dv (1918—48).

BARUGHS AMBO

[N Riding] Tp in Kirkby Misperton AP, sep CP 1866.[2] *LG* Seq 61. Transf 1974 to N Yorks.[5] *Parl* Seq 22.

BARWICK IN ELMET

AP [W Riding] Incl tp Roundhay (sep CP 1866,[2] sep EP 1843,[9] eccl refounded 1910 [qv for constituent pars at that time][73]). *LG* Skyr. Wap, not in a PLU (until 1862), Tadc. PLU (1862—1930), RSD, RD. Addtl civ bdry alt: 1884,[75] 1912 (loses pt to Leeds CB [assoc with W Riding] & AP),[202] 1937 (exchanges pts with Leeds CB [assoc with W Riding] & AP),[31] 1957 (loses pt to Leeds CB [assoc with W Riding] & AP).[156] Renamed civ 1970 'Barwick in Elmet and Scholes.'[203] *Parl* Seq 24. Parl bdry: 1960.[140] *Eccl* Ainsty RDn (until 1820), New Ainsty RDn (1820—36), Pontef. RDn (1836—57), Wethb. RDn (1857—61), Whitkirk RDn (1861—*). Eccl bdry: 1849 (cr Manston EP),[146] 1939 (help cr Leeds The Epiphany, Gipton EP),[204] 1967,[127] 1972 (incl cr Roundhay St John EP).[205]

BARWICK IN ELMET AND SCHOLES

CP [W Riding] Renaming 1970 of Barwick in Elmet AP.[203] *LG* Tadc. RD. Transf 1974 to W Yorks.[5]

BASHALL EAVES

[W Riding] Tp in Mitton AP, sep CP 1866.[2] *LG* Seq 108. Transf 1974 to Lancs.[5] *Parl* Seq 41.

BATLEY

AP [W Riding] Tp 'Batley' in Agb. Wap as was area of Morley (orig AP, usurped by Presbyterian trustees and thereafter in this par,[206] sep CP 1866,[2] sep EP 1831,[9] eccl refounded 1832[85]); incl in Morley Wap chap Gildersome (sep CP 1866,[2] sep EP 1789,[9] eccl refounded 1832[85]), tp Churwell (sep CP 1866[2]). *LG* Ent Agb. Wap (from 1866), Dewsb. PLU, Batley MB (1868—1974), USD. Addtl civ bdry alt: 1910,[207] 1937.[31] Transf 1974 to W Yorks.[5] *Parl* W Riding (1832—67), pt Dewsb. Parl Bor (1867—1918), pt S'rn Dv of W Riding (1867—85), pt Morley Dv (1885—1918), Batley & Morley Parl Bor/BC (1918—*). *Eccl* Seq 48. Addtl eccl bdry alt: 1868 (cr Staincliffe EP, sometimes called 'Staincliffe Christ Church, Batley'),[208] 1869 (cr Batley St Thomas EP),[209] 1871 (help cr Brownhill EP),[210] 1878 (help cr Morley St Paul, Townend EP),[211] 1880 (help cr Carlinghow EP),[212] 1892 (help cr Bruntcliffe EP),[213] 1911 (cr Purlwell EP),[214] 1911.[215]

BATLEY CARR

EP [W Riding] Cr 1841 from Dewsbury AP,[9] refounded 1842.[30] Pontef. RDn (1841—57),

Dewsb. RDn (1857—*). Bdry: 1867 (help cr
Dewsbury St Mark EP),[74] 1868,[208] 1901,[216]
1913.[119]

BATLEY ST THOMAS
EP [W Riding] Cr 1869 from Batley AP.[209] Birstall
RDn (1869—83), Dewsb. RDn (1883—*). Bdry:
1911.[215]

BATTYEFORD
EP [W Riding] Cr 1841 from Mirfield AP.[217] Pontef.
RDn (1841—57), Dewsb. RDn (1857—83), Birstall
RDn (1883—1927), Dewsb. RDn (1927—*). Bdry:
1881 (help cr Eastthorpe EP).[218]

BAWTRY
[W Riding] Chap (Yorks, Straff. & Tick. Wap) in
Blyth AP (Notts [Bassetlaw Wap], Yorks [Straff. &
Tick. Wap] until 1866, ent Notts thereafter), sep CP
1866 in Yorks,[2] eccl severed 1858 and united with
chap Austerfield (only other pt of Blyth in Yorks) to
cr Bawtry with Austerflield EP[155] to be in dioc
Linc. LG Seq 117. Transf 1974 to S Yorks (gaining
at same time the pt of Hanworth AP [Notts] also
transf to S Yorks].[5] Parl Seq 44.

BAWTRY WITH AUSTERFIELD
EP [W Riding] Cr 1858 by unions chaps Bawtry,
Austerfield (the only pts of Blyth AP [Notts, Yorks]
in Yorks),[155] to be in dioc Linc. Retford RDn
(1858—87), Bawtry RDn (1887—*). Eccl bdry:
1962.[219]

BAY HALL
EP [W Riding] Cr 1852 from Huddersfield AP,[9]
refounded 1853 from Huddersfield AP,
Huddersfield Holy Trinity EP.[220] Pontef. RDn
(1852—57) Hudd. RDn (1857—*). Bdry: 1871
(help cr Huddersfield St Andrew EP),[21] 1895 (help
cr Bradley EP),[221] 1932 (cr Birkby EP).[222] Now
usually called 'Huddersfield St John the Evangelist'.

BEADLAM
[W Riding] Tp in Helmsley AP, sep CP 1866,[2] pt
eccl severed 1882 and transf to Kirkdale AP,[223] the
remainder eccl severed 1898 to help cr Pockley cum
Eastmoors EP.[121] LG Seq 63. Transf 1974 to N
Yorks.[5] Parl Seq 21.

BEAL OR BEAGHALL
[W Riding] Tp in Kellington AP, sep CP 1866.[2] LG
Seq 99. Transf 1974 to N Yorks.[5] Parl Seq 29.

BEAMSLEY
CP [W Riding] Cr 1886 by union pt Beamsley in
Addingham CP, pt Beamsley in Skipton CP.[224] LG
Claro Wap, Skipton PLU, RSD, RD. Transf 1974
to N Yorks.[5] Parl Skipton Dv/CC (1918—*).

BEAMSLEY IN ADDINGHAM
[W Riding] Cr 1866 from the pt of Beamsley tp in
Addingham AP.[2] LG Claro Wap, Carlton GilbU
(until 1869), Skipton PLU (1869—86), RSD. Bdry:
1883.[52] Abol 1886 pt to help cr Beamsley CP, pt to
Hazlewood with Storiths CP.[224] Parl W Riding
(1832—67) E'rn Dv of W Riding (1867—85), Otley
Dv (1885—1918).

BEAMSLEY IN SKIPTON
[W Riding] Cr 1866 from the pt of Beamsley tp in
Skipton AP.[2] Organisation as for Beamsley in
Addingham CP.

BECKWITHSAW
EP [W Riding] Cr 1887 from Pannal AP, Low
Harrogate EP, ex-par Haverah Park.[225] Wethb.
RDn (1887—1921), Knar. RDn (1921—71),
Harrog. RDn (1971—*). Bdry: 1957.[226]

BEDALE
AP [N Riding] Tp 'Bedale' in E Hang Wap as were tps
Aiskew, Burrill with Cowling, Crakenhall, Firby,
pt tp Patrick Brompton, ent hmlt Rand Grange (each
a sep CP 1866[2]); incl in Hallik. Wap tp Langthorpe
(sep CP 1866[2]), tps Crakenhall, Langthorne (eccl
united 1841 as 'Crakenhall' EP,[182] sometimes later
'Crakenhall with Langthorne'). LG E Hang Wap (pt
until 1866, ent from 1866), pt Hallik. Wap (until
1866), N'allert. PLU (1837—39), Bedale PLU
(1839—1930), RSD, RD. Transf 1974 to N Yorks.[5]
Parl Seq 15. Eccl Seq 53.

BEEFORD
AP [E Riding] Incl chap Lissett, tp Dunnington (each a
sep CP 1866[2]). LG Hold. Wap, Driff. PLU, RSD,
RD. Addtl civ bdry alt: 1935 (gains Gembling
CP),[13] 1953.[227] Transf 1974 to Humb.[5] Parl Seq 3.
Eccl Usually as 'Beeford with Lissett and Dunn-
ington', Seq 15.

BEEFORD WITH LISSETT AND DUNNINGTON—see
prev entry

BEESTON
[W Riding] Tp in Leeds AP, sep CP 1866,[2] sep EP
1723.[9] LG Leeds Bor/MB/CB, Carlton GilbU (until
1869), Holbeck PLU (1869—1904), Leeds USD.
Abol civ 1904 ent to Holbeck CP.[124] Parl Leeds
Parl Bor (1832—85); see Part III of the Guide for
composition of Leeds Parl Bors (1885—1918) by
wards of the MB. Eccl Ainsty RDn (1723—1820),
Old Ainsty RDn (1820—36), Pontef. RDn (1836—
57), Leeds RDn (1857—1971), Armley RDn
(1971—*). Eccl bdry: 1902 (help cr Holbeck St
Edward King and Martyr EP),[119] 1967.[127]

BEESTON HILL
EP [W Riding] Cr 1872 from Holbeck EP, Hunslet St
Mary EP.[228] Leeds RDn (1872—1971), Armley
RDn (1971—*). Bdry: 1885 (help refound Hunslet
EP),[229] 1902 (help cr Holbeck St Edward King and
Martyr EP),[119] 1905 (help cr Beeston Hill The Holy
Spirit EP),[149] 1967.[127]

BEESTON HILL THE HOLY SPIRIT
EP [W Riding] Cr 1905 from Beeston Hill EP, Hunslet
Moor EP.[149] Leeds RDn (1905—71) Armley RDn
(1971—*). Bdry: 1967.[127]

BELBY
[E Riding] Tp in Howden AP, sep CP 1866.[2] LG
Howden Wap, PLU, RSD, RD. Bdry: 1880.[230]
Abol 1935 ent to Kilpin CP.[13] Parl E Riding
(1832—85), Howdensh. Dv (1885—1948).

BELLASIZE
[E Riding] Tp in Eastrington AP, sep CP 1866.[2] LG
Howden Wap, PLU, RSD, RD. Bdry: 1880 (help cr
Bishopsoil CP),[142] 1880.[171] Abol 1935 pt to
Blacktoft CP, pt to Eastrington AP, pt to help cr
Gilberdyke CP.[13] Parl E Riding (1832—85),
Howdensh. Dv (1885—1948).

BELLERBY
[N Riding] Tp in Spennithorne AP, sep CP 1866,[2]

sep EP 1770,[9] eccl refounded 1848.[231] *LG* Seq 53. Transf 1974 to N Yorks.[5] *Parl* Seq 14. *Eccl* Catt. RDn (1770—1857), Catt. West RDn (1857—1928), Wensleyd. RDn (1928—*).

BEMPTON

AP [E Riding] Orig chap in Bridlngton priory, sep par from 1441 (donative).[232] *LG* Seq 5. Civ bdry: 1935 (incl gains Buckton CP).[13] Transf 1974 to Humb.[5] *Parl* Seq 2. *Eccl* Seq 5. Eccl bdry: 1919 (gains tp Buckton from Bridlington AP).[233]

BEN RHYDDING

EP [W Riding] Cr 1912 from Ilkley AP, Burley EP.[234] Otley RDn.

BENINGBROUGH

[N Riding] Tp in Newton upon Ouse AP, sep CP 1866.[2] *LG* Seq 30. Transf 1974 to N Yorks.[5] *Parl* Seq 16.

BENNINGHOLME AND GRANGE

[E Riding] Tp in Swine AP, sep CP 1866,[2] eccl severed 1867 to help cr Skirlaugh EP.[235] *LG* Hold. Wap, Skirl. PLU, RSD, RD. Bdry: 1885.[59] Abol 1935 ent to Swine AP.[13] *Parl* E Riding (1832—85), Hold. Dv (1885—1948).

BENTHAM

AP [W Riding] Incl chap Ingleton (sep CP 1866,[2] sep EP 1757[9]). *LG* Seq 111. Transf 1974 to N Yorks.[5] *Parl* Seq 41. *Eccl* Seq 56. Addtl eccl bdry alt: 1737 (cr Ingleton Fell EP,[9] refounded 1864 as 'Chapel le Dale' EP [incl gains pt Ingleton EP][236]), 1872 (cr Bentham St Margaret EP).[228]

BENTHAM ST MARGARET

EP [W Riding] Cr 1872 from Bentham AP.[228] Clapham RDn (1872—1921), Ewecr. RDn (1921—*).

BENTLEY

EP [W Riding] Cr 1898 from Arksey AP (civ, 'Bentley with Arksey', qv). Donc. RDn. Bdry: 1940 (help cr Doncaster St Leonard and St Jude EP),[237] 1958,[122] 1958 (help cr New Bentley EP).[123]

NEW BENTLEY

EP [W Riding] Cr 1958 from Bentley EP, Arksey AP (civ, 'Bentley with Arksey', qv).[123] Donc. RDn.

BENTLEY WITH ARKSEY

AP [W Riding] Comprised of 2 tps, Arksey and Bentley, usual civ spelling as above, usual eccl 'Arksey', qv for eccl organisation and for cr EPs from this par. *LG* Straff. & Tick. Wap, Donc. PLU, RSD, RD (1894—1911), Bentley with Arksey UD (1911—74). Civ bdry: 1936 (loses pt to Donc. CB [assoc with W Riding] & AP),[132] 1954.[238] Transf 1974 to S Yorks.[5] *Parl* Seq 45.

BESSINGBY

AP [E Riding] *LG* Dick. Wap, Bridl. PLU, pt Bridl. USD, pt Bridl. RSD, Bridl. RD. Civ bdry: 1894 (loses the pt in the UD to Bridlington AP, gains the pt of Hilderthorpe CP not in the UD),[239] 1923.[240] Abol civ 1935 pt to Bridl. MB & AP, pt to Carnaby AP.[13] *Parl* E Riding (1832—85), Buckr. Dv (1885—1948). *Eccl* Seq 7.

BESWICK

[E Riding] Chap in Kilnwick AP, sep CP 1866,[2] sep EP 1824.[9] *LG* Seq 9. Civ bdry: 1935 (gains Kilnwick AP).[13] Transf 1974 to Humb.[5] *Parl* Seq 4. *Eccl* Harth. & Hull RDn (1824—57), N Harth. RDn

(1857—66), Harth. RDn (1866—*).

BEVERLEY

[E Riding] The following have 'Beverley' in their names. Insofar as any existed at a given time: *LG* Harth. Wap, Bev. PLU; Bor, MB, USD sep noted. *Parl* Sep noted. *Eccl* Pec jurisd Bev. (until 1836), Harth. & Hull RDn (1836—57), S Harth. RDn (1857—66), Bev. RDn (1866—*).

CP1—BEVERLEY—Cr 1936 by union AP2, AP3, AP4.[241] *LG* Bev. MB. Transf 1974 to Humb.[5] *Parl* Bev. CC (1948—55), Haltemp. CC (1955—*).

AP1—BEVERLEY ST JOHN [MINSTER]—Pt in Harth. Wap/Bev. Bor (uninhabited); pt Hold. Wap (tp Eske [sep CP 1866[2]]); pt Bev. Lbty (remainder: tps Storkhill and Sandholme, Thearne, Tickton and Hull Bridge, Weel, Woodmansey and Beverley Parks, pt tp Aike, pt tp Molescroft [each a sep CP 1866[2]]) so that after 1866 AP1 has no sep civ identity. *Parl* E Riding (1832—67). *Eccl* Eccl united prob 1546 with AP2 as EP1,[242] each retaining sep civ identity.

EP1—BEVERLEY ST JOHN WITH ST MARTIN—Cr prob 1546 by union AP1, AP2,[242] sometimes called 'Beverley St John with St Martin and Tickton'.

AP2—BEVERLEY ST MARTIN—*LG* Bev. Bor/MB,USD. Civ bdry: 1883.[243] Abol civ 1936 to help cr CP1.[241] *Parl* Bev. Parl Bor (1295—1306, 1563—1870), E Riding (1870—85), Hold. Dv (1885—1948). *Eccl* United prob 1546 with AP1 to cr EP1,[242] each retaining sep civ identity.

AP3—BEVERLEY ST MARY—Orig chap, sep par 1325, eccl united 1667 with AP4 to cr EP2,[244] each retaining sep civ identity. *LG* Bev. Bor/MB, USD. Abol civ 1936 to help cr CP1.[241] *Parl* As for AP2.

EP2—BEVERLEY ST MARY WITH ST NICHOLAS—Cr 1667 by union AP3, AP4,[244] each retaining sep civ identity.

AP4—BEVERLEY ST NICHOLAS—*LG* Bev. Bor/MB, USD. Civ bdry: 1883.[243] Abol civ 1936 to help cr CP1.[241] *Parl* As for AP2. *Eccl* Eccl united 1667 with AP3 to cr EP2.[244]

BEWERLEY

[W Riding] Tp in Ripon AP, sep CP 1866,[2] pt eccl severed 1858 to help cr Greenhow Hill EP,[9] the latter eccl refounded 1860 (qv for constituent pars then incl some area from this par).[68] *LG* Seq 89. Transf 1974 to N Yorks.[5] *Parl* Seq 33.

BEWHOLME

CP [E Riding] Cr 1935 by union Bewholme and Nunkeeling AP, Bonwick CP, Dunnington CP.[13] *LG* Hold. RD. Transf 1974 to Humb.[5] Parl Bridl. CC (1948—*).

BEWHOLME AND NUNKEELING

AP [E Riding] Usual civ spelling; for eccl see 'Nunkeeling and Bewholme'. *LG* Hold. Wap, Skirl. PLU, RSD, RD. Abol civ 1935 to help cr Bewholme CP.[13] *Parl* E Riding (1832—85), Hold. Dv (1885—1948).

BICKERTON

[Ainsty (W Riding until 1449 and from 1836, indept

jurisd 1449—1836)] Tp in Bilton AP, sep CP 1866.[2] *LG* Gt Ouseb. GilbU (until 1854), not in a PLU (1854—61), Wethb. PLU (1861—1930), RSD, RD. Bdry: 1883.[52] Abol 1937 ent to Bilton AP.[31] *Parl* N Riding (1832—85), Thirsk & Malton Dv (1885—1918), [W Riding for parl purposes thereafter] Bark. Ash Dv (1918—48).

BIELBY

[E Riding] Orig chap in Pocklington AP, united with chap Hayton in same par 1252,[245] the par civ 'Hayton' in which Bielby deemed a chap (sep CP 1866 from Hayton[2]), eccl 'Hayton with Bielby' (pec jurisd Dean of York), qv. *LG* Seq 12. Transf 1974 to Humb.[5] *Parl* Seq 7.

BIERLEY

EP [W Riding] Tp in Bradford AP, sep EP 1825,[9] eccl refounded 1864,[246] sep CP 1866 as 'North Bierley',[2] qv. Pontef. RDn (1825—57), Bradf RDn (1857—1921), Bowl. RDn (1921—71), Bowl. & Horton RDn (1971—*). Bdry: 1877 (help cr Oakenshaw cum Woodlands EP),[168] 1927,[67] 1965.[247]

NORTH BIERLEY

[W Riding] Tp in Bradford AP, sep CP 1866,[2] sep EP 1825 as 'Bierley',[9] as such eccl refounded 1864,[246] qv. *LG* Morley Wap, Bradf PLU (1837—48), N Bierley PLU (1848—1930), N Bierley USD, UD (1894—99), Bradf CB (1899—1974). Transf 1974 to W Yorks.[5] *Parl* W Riding (1832—67), E'rn Dv of W Riding (1867—85); see Part III of the *Guide* for composition of Bradf Parl Bors/BCs (1885—*) by wards of the MB/CB.

BIGGIN

[W Riding] Tp in Church Fenton AP (eccl, 'Kirk Fenton'), sep CP 1866.[2] *LG* Bark. Ash Wap, Selby PLU (soon after 1837[111])—1930), RSD, RD (1894—1934), Tadc. RD (1937—74). Transf 1974 to N Yorks.[5] *Parl* Seq 24.

BILBROUGH

AP [W Riding] *LG* Seq 70. Transf 1974 to N Yorks.[5] *Parl* Seq 23. *Eccl* Ainsty RDn (until 1820), New Ainsty RDn (1820—62), Tadc. RDn (1862—71), Bp'thorpe RDn (1871—96), Ainsty RDn (1896—*).

BILHAM

[W Riding] Tp pt in Barnbrough AP, pt in Hooton Pagnell AP, sep CP 1866.[2] *LG* Straff. & Tick. Wap, Donc. PLU, RSD, RD. Abol 1920 ent to Hooton Pagnell AP.[248] *Parl* W Riding (1832—67), S'rn Dv of W Riding (1867—85), Donc. Dv (1885—1918), Don Valley Dv (1918—48).

BILLINGLEY

[W Riding] Tp in Darfield AP, sep CP 1866.[2] *LG* Straff. & Tick. Wap, Barnsley PLU, RSD, RD (1894—1938), Hemsworth RD (1938—74). Transf 1974 to S Yorks.[5] *Parl* W Riding (1832—67), S'rn Dv of W Riding (1867—85), Barnsley Dv (1885—1918), Wentw. Dv (1918—48), Hemsworth CC (1948—*).

BILSDALE

EP [N Riding] Cr 1745 from Helmsley AP,[9] refounded 1898 incl pt Hawnby AP.[121] Riddal RDn (1745—1862), Helm. RDn (1862—1916), Stokes. RDn (1916—58), Helm. RDn (1958—*).

BILSDALE MIDCABLE

[N Riding] Tp in Hawnby AP, sep CP 1866.[2] *LG* Ryed. Wap, Stokes. PLU (1848—1930), RSD, RD. Transf 1974 to N Yorks.[5] *Parl* N Riding (1832—85), Whitby Dv (1885—1918), Richm. Dv/CC (1918—*).

BILSDALE, WEST SIDE

[N Riding] Tp in Hawnby AP, sep CP 1866.[2] *LG* Seq 25. Transf 1974 to N Yorks.[5] *Parl* Seq 16.

BILTON

AP [Ainsty (W Riding until 1449 and from 1836, indept jurisd 1449—1836)] Incl tp Bickerton (sep CP 1866[2]), tp Tockwith (sep CP 1866,[2] sep EP 1866,[9] eccl refounded 1867[125]). *LG* Barwick GilbU (until 1869), Wethb. PLU (1869—1930), RSD, RD. Addtl civ bdry alt: 1883,[52] 1937.[31] Renamed 1965 'Bilton in Ainsty'.[249] *Parl* N Riding (1832—85), Thirsk & Malton Dv (1885—1918), [W Riding for parl purposes thereafter] Bark. Ash Dv/CC (1918—70). *Eccl* Pec jurisd Bilton prebend (until 1836), Seq 29 thereafter.

BILTON

[E Riding] Chap in Swine AP, sep CP 1866,[2] sep EP 1794 (incl tps Bilton, Wyton Ganstead, all in Swine),[9] eccl refounded 1867.[250] *LG* Seq 16. Civ bdry: 1930 (loses pt to Kingst. upon Hull CB [assoc with E Riding] and to Sculcoates AP),[251] 1935 (incl gains Ganstead CP, Wyton CP, loses pt to Kingst. upon Hull CB [assoc with E Riding] and to Sculcoates AP),[13] 1955 (loses pt to Kingst. upon Hull CB [assoc with E Riding] and to Sculcoates AP),[252] 1968 (loses pt to Kingst. upon Hull CB [assoc with E Riding] and to Sculcoates AP).[253] Transf 1974 to Humb.[5] *Parl* Seq 5. Parl bdry: 1956.[254] *Eccl* Hold. RDn (1794—1849), S Hold. RDn (1849—57), N Hold. RDn (1857—62), Bev. RDn (1862—71), Hedon RDn (1871—1916), Hold. RDn (1916—*). Eccl bdry: 1952,[255] 1960.[256]

BILTON

CP [W Riding] Cr 1894 from the pt of Bilton with Harrogate CP not in Harrog. MB.[257] *LG* Knar. PLU, RD. Bdry: 1896 (cr Starbeck CP),[258] 1900.[238] Abol 1938 pt to Harrog. MB & CP, pt to Knar. UD & AP.[28] *Parl* Ripon Dv (1918—48).

BILTON

EP [W Riding] Cr 1857 from Bilton with Harrogate EP.[259] Boroughbr. RDn (1857—70), Knar. RDn (1870—1971), Harrog. RDn (1971—*).

BILTON IN AINSTY

CP [W Riding] Renaming 1956 of Bilton AP.[249] *LG* Wethb. RD. Transf 1974 to N Yorks.[5] *Parl* Bark. Ash CC (1970—*).

BILTON WITH HARROGATE

[W Riding] Chap in Knaresborough AP, sep CP 1866,[2] sep EP 1829,[260] often eccl called 'High Harrogate Christ Church'. *LG* Claro Wap, not in a PLU (until 1854), Knar. PLU (1854—94), pt Harrog. MB (1884—94), pt Harrog. USD (enlarged pt 1884—94), pt Knar. RSD (reduced pt 1884—94). Civ bdry: 1883,[52] 1888.[261] Abol civ 1894 the pt in Harrog. MB to help cr Harrogate CP,[262] the remainder cr Bilton CP.[257] *Parl* W Riding (1832—67), N'rn Dv of W Riding (1867—85), Ripon Dv

(1885—1918). *Eccl* Boroughbr. RDn (1829—70), Knar. RDn (1870—*). Eccl bdry: 1857 (cr Bilton EP),[259] 1869 (cr High Harrogate St Peter EP),[109] 1898 (cr Harrogate St Luke EP),[52] 1911 (help cr Starbeck EP),[263] 1957.[226]

BINGLEY
   AP [W Riding] Tp 'Bingley' sometimes called 'Bingley and Micklethwaite', name not sustained and 'Bingley' regularly used later. Incl tp Morton (sep CP 1866,[2] sep EP 1845 incl pt tp Bingley[264]) *LG* Skyr. Wap, Bingley Bor, Keigh. PLU, pt Bingley Local Govt Dist, pt Keigh. MB (1882—94), pt Keigh. USD, Keigh. RSD (pt 1875—94 [reduced pt 1882—94]), Bingley UD. Addtl civ bdry alt: 1894 (loses the pt in Keigh. MB,[265] the remainder of the par not in Bingley Local Govt Dist cr Bingley Outer UD & CP,[257] the remaining urban pt to be Bingley UD), 1898 (gains Bingley Outer UD & CP),[266] 1938 (incl gains Wilsden CP).[28] Transf 1974 to W Yorks.[5] *Parl* Seq 31. *Eccl* Craven RDn (until 1857), Craven RDn, S'rn Dv (1857—1921), S Craven RDn (1921—35), Calverley RDn (1935—71), Airedale RDn (1971—*). Addtl eccl bdry alt: 1844 (help cr Ingrow with Hainworth EP),[267] 1846 (help cr Cullingworth EP),[268] 1869 (cr Bingley Holy Trinity EP),[209] 1911 (help cr Cross Roads cum Lees EP),[269] 1930 (help cr Harden EP).[270]

BINGLEY HOLY TRINITY
   EP [W Riding] Cr 1869 from Bingley AP.[209] Craven RDn, S'rn Dv (1869—1921), S Craven RDn (1921—35), Calverley RDn (1935—71), Airedale RDn (1971—*). Bdry: 1887 (cr Cottingley EP).[92]

BINGLEY OUTER
   CP [W Riding] Cr 1894 from the pt of Bingley AP neither in Keigh. MB nor Bingley Local Govt Dist.[257] *LG* Keigh. PLU, Bingley Outer UD. Bdry: 1895,[271] 1896.[272] Abol 1898 ent to Bingley UD & AP.[266]

BIRCHENCLIFFE
   EP [W Riding] Cr 1877 from Lindley EP, Longwood EP, Elland EP.[141] Hudd. RDn.

BIRDFORTH
   [N Riding] Chap in Coxwold AP, sep CP 1866,[2] sep EP 1739.[9] *LG* Birdf. Wap, Thirsk PLU (soon after 1837[111]—1930), RSD, RD. Transf 1974 to N Yorks.[5] *Parl* Seq 16. *Eccl* Eas. RDn.

BIRDSALL
   AP [E Riding] *LG* Seq 2. Civ bdry: 1935 (gains North Grimston AP).[23] Transf 1974 to N Yorks.[5] *Parl* Seq 1. *Eccl* Buckr. RDn (until 1857), E Buckr. RDn (1857—66), Buckr. RDn (1866—87), Settr. RDn (1887—1922), Buckr. RDn (1922—*).

BIRKBY
   AP [N Riding] Incl chap Hutton Bonville (sep CP 1866,[2] sep EP 1740[9]), tp Little Smeaton (sep CP 1866[2]). *LG* Seq 22. Transf 1974 to N Yorks.[5] *Parl* Seq 14. *Eccl* Pec jurisd Bp Durham (until 1836), Clev RDn (1836—62), N'allert. RDn (1862—1964), Richm. East RDn (1964—*).

BIRKBY
   EP [W Riding] Cr 1932 from Bay Hall EP (commonly called 'Huddersfield St John').[222] Hudd. RDn.

BIRKBY ST CUTHBERT
   EP [W Riding] Cr 1932 from Huddersfield St John EP.[222] Hudd. RDn.

BIRKENSHAW
   CP [W Riding] Cr 1894 from the pt of Gomersal CP in Birkenshaw UD.[257] *LG* Dewsb. PLU, Birkenshaw UD. Abol 1937 ent to Spenb. UD & to Gomersal CP.[31] *Parl* Spen Valley Dv (1918—48).

BIRKENSHAW CUM HUNSWORTH
   EP [W Riding] Cr 1834 from Birstall AP,[9] refounded 1842.[273] Pontef. RDn (1834—57), Dewsb. RDn (1857—66), Birstall RDn (1866—*). Bdry: 1877 (help cr Oakenshaw cum Woodlands EP).[168]

BIRKIN
   AP [W Riding] Incl tps Chapel Haddesley, West Haddesley, Temple Hirst, Hirst Courtney (each a sep CP 1866,[2] the four tps eccl united 1855 to cr Haddesley EP[274]). *LG* Seq 75. Addtl civ bdry alt: 1883.[52] Transf 1974 to N Yorks.[5] *Parl* Seq 26. *Eccl* Ainsty RDn (until 1820), New Ainsty RDn (1820—57), Pontef. RDn (1857—1924), Selby RDn (1924—*).

BIRSTALL
   AP [W Riding] Incl chap Cleckheaton (sep CP 1866,[2] sep EP 1732,[9] eccl refounded 1842[273]), chap Drighlington (sep CP 1866,[2] sep EP 1817,[9] eccl refounded 1847[275]), chap Liversedge (sep CP 1866,[2] sep EP 1817,[9] eccl refounded 1860[250]), chap Tong (sep CP 1866,[2] sep EP 1720[9]), tp Gomersal (sep CP 1866,[2] pt 1846 made Gomersal EP[276]), tp Heckmondwike (sep CP 1866,[2] sep EP 1837,[9] eccl refounded 1842[273]), tp Hunsworth (sep CP 1866[2]; for eccl see Birkenshaw cum Hunsworth, below), tp Wyke (sep CP 1866,[2] sep EP 1844[197]), so that 'Birstall' has no sep civ identity 1866—94 (see following entry). *LG* Morley Wap. *Parl* W Riding (1832—67). *Eccl* Pontef. RDn (until 1857), Dewsb. RDn (1857—66), Birstall RDn (1866—*). Addtl eccl bdry alt: 1834 (cr Birkenshaw cum Hunsworth EP,[9] refounded 1842[273]), 1846,[277] 1847 (help cr Robert Town EP, cr Whitechapel EP),[275] 1862 (cr Tong Street EP),[9] 1871 (help cr Brownhill EP).[210]
   CP [W Riding] Cr 1894 from the pt of Gomersal CP in Birstall UD.[257] *LG* Dewsb. PLU, Birstall UD. Abol 1937 ent to Batley MB & AP.[31] *Parl* Spen Valley Dv (1918—48).

BIRSTWITH
   [W Riding] Tp in Hampsthwaite AP, sep CP 1866,[2] sep EP 1857.[9] *LG* Claro Wap, Pateley Br. PLU (soon after 1837[111]—1930), RSD, RD (1894—1937), Ripon & Pateley Br. RD (1937—74). Transf 1974 to N Yorks.[5] *Parl* Seq 33. *Eccl* Otley RDn (1857—70), Knar. RDn (1870—1905), Nidd. RDn (1905—71), Harrog. RDn (1971—*). Eccl bdry: 1952.[278]

BISHOP INGS
   [N Riding] Eccl ex-par place, abol 1873 ent to Leake AP.[279]

BISHOP WILTON
   AP [E Riding] Incl tps Bishop Wilton with Belthorpe, Bolton, Youlthorpe with Gowthorpe (each a sep CP 1866[2]) so that 'Bishop Wilton' has no sep civ identity 1866—1935 (see following entry). *LG*

Harth. Wap. *Parl* E Riding (1832—67). *Eccl* Pec
jurisd Wilton prebend (until 1241), pec jurisd
Treasurer of York (1241—1836), Seq 9 thereafter.
CP [E Riding] Cr 1935 by union ent Youlthorpe with
Gowthorpe CP and pts Bishop Wilton with Bel-
thorpe CP, Bolton CP.[13] *LG* Pockl. RD. Transf
1974 to Humb.[5] *Parl* Bev. CC (1948—55),
Howdensh. CC (1955—*).

BISHOP WILTON WITH BELTHORPE
[E Riding] Tp in Bishop Wilton AP, sep CP 1866.[2]
LG Harth. Wap, Pockl. PLU, RSD, RD. Abol 1935
pt to help cr Bishop Wilton CP, pt to help cr
Millington CP.[13] *Parl* E Riding (1832—85),
Howdensh. Dv (1885—1948).

BISHOPDALE
[N Riding] Tp in Aysgarth AP, sep CP 1866.[2] *LG*
Seq 51. Transf 1974 to N Yorks.[5] *Parl* Seq 14.

HIGH AND LOW BISHOPSIDE
[W Riding] Chap in Ripon AP, sep CP 1866.[2] *LG*
Seq 101. Bdry: 1937.[31] Transf 1974 to N Yorks.[5]
Parl Seq 34.

BISHOPSOIL
CP [E Riding] Cr 1880 by union pts Asselby CP,
Barmby on the Marsh AP, Bellasize CP, Blacktoft
CP, Cotness CP, Eastrington AP, Gilberdike CP,
Knedlington CP, Laxton CP, Metham CP, Yok-
efleet CP.[142] *LG* Howdensh. Wap, PLU, RSD, RD.
Abol 1935 to help cr Gilberdyke CP.[13] *Parl*
Howdensh. Dv (1885—1948).

BISHOPTHORPE
AP [Ainsty (W Riding until 1449 and from 1836, indept
jurisd 1449—1836)] Incl pt tp Dringhouses (sep CP
1866[2]; sep EP 1853 but no pt from this par). *LG*
York PLU, RSD, Bp'thorpe RD (1894—1937),
Tadc. RD (1937—74). Addtl civ bdry alt: 1937
(loses pt to York CB [not assoc with a Riding] &
CP).[31] Transf 1974 to N Yorks.[5] *Parl* Seq 23. *Eccl*
Seq 31.

BISHOPTON
[W Riding] Tp in Ripon AP, sep CP 1866.[2] *LG*
Ripon Lbty, not in a PLU (until 1852), Ripon PLU
(1852—1900), RSD, RD. Abol 1900 pt to Ripon
MB & AP, pt to Clotherholme CP.[280] *Parl* W
Riding (1832—67), E'rn Dv of W Riding (1867—
85), Ripon Dv (1885—1918).

BLACKSHAW
CP [W Riding] Cr 1894 from the pt of Stansfield CP not
in a UD.[257] *LG* Todm. PLU, RD (1894—1939),
Hepton RD (1939—74). Bdry: 1896 (gains the pt of
Stansfield CP not constituted pt Todmorden
MB).[281] Transf 1974 to W Yorks.[5] *Parl* Sowerby
Dv/CC (1918—*).

BLACKTOFT
[E Riding] Chap in Brantingham AP, sep civ
identity early, sep EP 1776.[9] Incl tp Scalby (sep CP
1866[2]). *LG* Seq 17. Addtl civ bdry alt: 1880,[282]
1880 (help cr Bishopsoil CP),[142] 1880,[283] 1935 (incl
gains Faxfleet CP).[13] Transf 1974 to Humb.[5] *Parl*
Seq 7. *Eccl* Pec jurisd Dean & Chapter of Durham
(1776—1836), Harth. & Hull RDn (1836—57), W
Harth. RDn (1857—66), Howden RDn (1866—*).
Eccl bdry: 1895 (help cr Newport EP).[284]

BLAXTON
[W Riding] Tp (Yorks, Claro Wap) in Finningley
AP (mainly Notts [Bassetlaw Wap], pt Yorks
[Donc. Soke] until 1866, ent Notts thereafter), sep
CP 1866 in Yorks.[2] *LG* Seq 93. Transf 1974 to S
Yorks.[5] *Parl* Seq 44.

BLUBBERHOUSES
[W Riding] Tp in Fewston AP, sep CP 1866.[2] *LG*
Seq 92. Bdry: 1883.[52] Transf 1974 to N Yorks.[5]
Parl Seq 30.

BLYTH
AP Tp 'Blyth' in Notts (Bassetlaw Wap) as were chap
Gamston (sep par by early 14th cent[285]), lordship
Hodstock, tps Barnby Moor, Ranskill, Styrrup,
Torworth (each of the 5 a sep CP 1866[2]); incl in
Yorks W Riding (Straff. & Tick. Wap) chap
Austerfield, chap and bor Bawtry (each a sep CP
1866,[2] the 2 chaps eccl severed and united 1858 to
cr Bawtry with Austerfield EP in dioc Linc[155]) so
that 'Blyth' ent Notts after 1866. See main entry in
Notts.

BOLDRON
[N Riding] Tp in Startforth AP, sep CP 1866.[2] *LG*
Seq 39. Bdry: 1883.[52] Transf 1974 to Durham.[5]
Parl Seq 14.

BOLSTERSTONE
EP [W Riding] Cr 1721 from Ecclesfield AP.[9] Donc.
RDn (1721—1857), Rotherh. RDn (1857—62),
Ecclesfield RDn (1862—1942), Tankersley RDn
(1942—*). Bdry: 1917 (help cr Stocksbridge EP),[46]
1964.[82]

BOLTBY
[N Riding] Tp in Felixkirk AP, sep CP 1866.[2] *LG*
Seq 27. Bdry: 1887.[286] Transf 1974 to N Yorks.[5]
Parl Seq 16.

BOLTON
[E Riding] Tp in Bishop Wilton AP, sep CP 1866.[2]
LG Harth. Wap, Pockl. PLU, RSD, RD. Abol 1935
pt to help cr Bishop Wilton CP, pt to Fangfoss CP.[13]
Parl E Riding (1832—85), Howdensh. Dv
(1885—1948).

BOLTON
EP [N Riding] Cr 1748 from Wensley AP[9]; sometimes
'Castle Bolton', qv for civ status. Catt. RDn
(1748—1857), Catt. West RDn (1857—1928),
Wensleyd. RDn (1928—*).

BOLTON
[W Riding] Tp in Calverley AP, sep CP 1866.[2] *LG*
Morley Wap, Bradf PLU (1837—48), N Bierley
PLU (1848—98), Bradf MB (1882—89), Bradf
USD, CB (1889—98). Abol 1898 ent to Bradford
AP.[65] *Parl* W Riding (1832—67), E'rn Dv of W
Riding (1867—85); see Part III of the *Guide* for
composition of Bradf Parl Bors (1885—1918) by
wards of the MB.

BOLTON ABBEY
[W Riding] Tp in Skipton AP, sep CP 1866,[2] sep EP
1814 (tps Bolton Abbey, Hazlewood with Storiths,
Barden, Halton East),[9] eccl refounded 1864.[175] *LG*
Seq 112. Transf 1974 to N Yorks.[5] *Parl* Seq 41.
Eccl Craven RDn (1814—57), Craven RDn, S'rn
Dv (1857—94), Otley RDn (1894—1905), Craven
RDn, E'rn Dv (1905—21), Skipton RDn (1921—*).

BOLTON BY BOWLAND

AP [W Riding] *LG* Seq 108. Civ bdry: 1938.[28] Transf 1974 to Lancs.[5] *Parl* Seq 41. *Eccl* Seq 38. Eccl bdry: 1918.[287]

BOLTON ON SWALE—see BOLTON UPON SWALE

BOLTON PERCY

AP [Ainsty (W Riding until 1449 and from 1836, indept jurisd 1449—1836)] lncl tp Appleton Roebuck (sep CP 1866,[2] eccl severed 1875 and transf to Acaster Selby EP [qv for later renaming][11]), tps Colton, Steeton, pt tp Kirkby Wharfe and North Milford (each of the 3 a sep CP 1866[2]). *LG* Seq 70. Transf 1974 to N Yorks.[5] *Parl* Seq 23. *Eccl* Seq 31.

BOLTON ST JAMES

EP [W Riding] Cr 1878 from Calverley AP.[198] Bradf RDn (1878—1921) Calverley RDn (1921—66). Bdry: 1927,[288] 1934 (help cr Wrose EP),[46] 1956.[187] Abol 1966 to help cr Bolton St James with St Chrysostom EP.[289]

BOLTON ST JAMES WITH ST CHRYSOSTOM

EP [W Riding] Cr 1965 by union Bolton St James EP, Bradford St Chrysostom EP.[289] Calverley RDn.

BOLTON UPON DEARNE

AP [W Riding] *LG* Straff. & Tick. Wap, Donc. PLU, RSD, RD (1894—99), Bolton upon Dearne UD (1899—1937). Abol civ 1937 to help cr Dearne UD & CP.[31] *Parl* W Riding (1832—67), S'rn Dv of W Riding (1867—85), Donc. Dv (1885—1918), Don Valley Dv (1918—48). *Eccl* Seq 46. Eccl bdry: 1916 (cr Goldthorpe EP).[290]

BOLTON UPON SWALE

[N Riding] Chap in Catterick AP, sep CP 1866,[2] sep EP 1781 (tps Bolton upon Swale, Ellerton upon Swale [Ellerton upon Swale had been cr a sep EP 1732,[9] but sep eccl status not sustained], Kiplin, Scorton, Uckerby, Whitwell),[9] the EP more recently called 'Bolton on Swale'. *LG* Seq 35. Transf 1974 to N Yorks.[5] *Parl* Seq 14. *Eccl* Catt. RDn (1781—1857), Catt. East RDn (1857—63), Richm. North RDn (1863—66), Richm. West RDn (1866—*).

BONWICK

[E Riding] Tp in Skipsea AP, sep CP 1866.[2] *LG* Hold. Wap, Skirl. PLU, RSD, RD. Abol 1935 to help cr Bewholme CP.[13] *Parl* E Riding (1832—85), Hold. Dv (1885—1948).

BOOSBECK AND MOORHOLM

EP [N Riding] Cr 1901 from Skelton in Cleveland AP.[216] Middlesb. RDn (1901—24), Guisb. RDn (1924—*).

BORDLEY

[W Riding] Tp in Burnsall AP, sep CP 1866.[2] *LG* Staincl. & Ewc. Wap, Skipton PLU (soon after 1837[111]—1930), RSD. RD. Transf 1974 to N Yorks.[5] *Parl* Seq 41.

BOROUGHBRIDGE

[W Riding] Chap and bor in Aldborough AP, sep CP 1866,[2] sep EP 1722,[9] eccl refounded 1866.[54] *LG* Boroughbr. Bor, Seq 86. Civ bdry: 1938.[28] Transf 1974 to N Yorks.[5] *Parl* Boroughbr. Parl Bor (1553—1832), Seq 36 thereafter. *Eccl* Claimed in pec jurisd Dean & Chapter of York, Seq 19. Eccl bdry: 1941.[27]

BORROWBY

[N Riding] Tp in Leake AP, sep CP 1866.[2] *LG* Seq 22. Bdry: 1888 (gains Gueldable CP).[291] Transf 1974 to N Yorks.[5] *Parl* Seq 14.

BORROWBY

[N Riding] Tp in Lythe AP, sep CP 1866,[2] eccl severed 1868 to help cr Ugthorpe EP.[188] *LG* Seq 59. Transf 1974 to N Yorks.[5] *Parl* Seq 19.

BOSSALL

AP [N Riding] Incl chap Claxton, tp Sand Hutton (each a sep CP 1866,[2] the 2 eccl united 1861 to cr Sand Hutton EP[292]), tp Harton (sep CP 1866[2]), pt tp Flaxton (sep CP 1866,[2] sep EP 1861 from this par only[292]), tp Bossall with Buttercrambe (sep CP 1866[2]), so that 'Bossall' has no sep civ identity after 1866; usual eccl name, 'Bossall with Buttercrambe', qv. *LG* Bulmer Wap. *Parl* N Riding (1832—67).

BOSSALL WITH BUTTERCRAMBE

AP [N Riding] Usual eccl spelling; for civ and sep chaps and tps civ and eccl, see prev entry for time before 1866, the following entry thereafter. *Eccl* Seq 17.

BOSSALL WITH BUTTERCRAMBE

[N Riding] Tp in Bossall AP (eccl, 'Bossall with Buttercrambe'), sep CP 1866.[2] *LG* Seq 32. Transf 1974 to N Yorks.[5] *Parl* Seq 16.

BOSTON SPA

EP [W Riding] Cr 1816 from Bramham AP,[9] eccl refounded 1852,[293] eccl refounded 1853.[294] Pec jurisd Dean & Chapter of York (until 1836), New Ainsty RDn (1836—62), Tadc. RDn (1862—71), Selby RDn (1871—1921), Tadc. RDn (1921—*).

CP [W Riding] Cr 1896 from Clifford with Boston CP.[295] *LG* Wethb. PLU, RD. Transf 1974 to W Yorks.[5] *Parl* Bark. Ash CC (1918—*).

BOWES

AP [N Riding] Chap appropriated to St Leonard's Hospital York, sep par by 1535.[296] Incl tp Gilmonby (sep CP 1866[2]). *LG* Seq 39. Addtl civ bdry alt: 1883.[52] Transf 1974 to Durham.[5] *Parl* Seq 14. *Eccl* Seq 59.

BOWLAND FOREST HIGH

[W Riding] Tp in Slaidburn AP, sep CP 1866.[2] *LG* Seq 108. Transf 1974 to Lancs.[5] *Parl* Seq 41.

BOWLAND FOREST LOW

[W Riding] Tp in Whalley AP, sep CP 1866.[2] *LG* Seq 108. Bdry: 1938.[28] Transf 1974 to Lancs.[5] *Parl* Seq 41.

BOWLING

[W Riding] The following have 'Bowling' in their names. Insofar as any existed at a given time: *LG* Morley Wap, Bradf PLU, MB (1847—89), USD, CB (1889—98). *Parl* Bradf Parl Bor (1832—85); see Part III of the *Guide* for composition of Bradf Parl Bors (1885—1918) by wards of the MB. *Eccl* Pontef. RDn (until 1857), Bradf RDn (1857—1921), Bowl. RDn (1921—71), Bowl. & Horton RDn (1971—*).

CP/EP1—BOWLING [ST BARTHOLOMEW]—Tp in Bradford AP, sep CP 1866,[2] sep EP 1843,[297] eccl refounded 1865,[298] eccl refounded 1873.[21] Abol civ 1898 ent to Bradford AP.[65] Abol eccl 1940 to help cr EP2.[299]

EP2—BOWLING ST BARTHOLOMEW AND ST LUKE—Cr 1940 by union EP1, Bradford St Luke EP.[299] Abol 1965 pt to Bierley EP, pt to EP3.[247]

EP3—BOWLING ST JOHN—Cr 1862 from Bradford AP,[9] refounded 1865.[298] Bdry: 1927,[67] 1965,[247] 1966.[300]

EP4—BOWLING ST STEPHEN—Cr 1860 from Bradford AP.[301] Bdry: 1868,[208] 1871,[21] 1903 (help cr Bradford St Oswald, Chapel Green EP).[302]

BOYNTON
AP [E Riding] *LG* Seq 5. Bdry: 1935 (gains Easton CP).[13] Transf 1974 to Humb.[5] *Parl* Seq 2. *Eccl* Seq 7.

BRACEWELL
AP [W Riding] *LG* Seq 112. Transf 1974 to Lancs.[5] *Parl* Seq 41. *Eccl* Seq 39.

BRACKEN
[E Riding] Tp in Kilnwick AP, sep CP 1866.[2] *LG* Harth. Wap, Driff. PLU, RSD, RD. Abol 1935 ent to Watton AP.[13] *Parl* E Riding (1832—85), Buckr. Dv (1885—1948).

BRACKENHOLME WITH WOODHALL
[E Riding] Tp in Hemingbrough AP, sep CP 1866.[2] *LG* Ouse & Derw. Wap, Howden PLU, RSD, RD. Abol 1935 ent to Hemingbrough AP.[13] *Parl* E Riding (1832—85), Howdensh. Dv (1885—1918).

BRADFIELD
[W Riding] Chap in Ecclesfield AP, sep CP 1866,[2] sep EP 1720.[9] *LG* Straff. & Tick. Wap, Wortley PLU, pt Stocksbridge USD, pt Wortley RSD, Wortley RD. Civ bdry: 1894 (loses the pt in Stocksbridge UD to help cr Stocksbridge CP),[303] 1901 (loses pt to Sheff CB [assoc with W Riding] & AP),[304] 1914 (the pt transf to Sheff CB [assoc with W Riding] cr Bradfield Urban CP),[178] 1930,[305] 1938 (loses pt to Sheff CB [assoc with W Riding] & AP).[306] Transf 1974 to S Yorks.[5] *Parl* Seq 49. *Eccl* Donc. RDn (1720—1857), Rotherh. RDn (1857—62), Ecclesfield RDn (1862—1942), Tankersley RDn (1942—*).

BRADFIELD URBAN
CP [W Riding] Cr 1914 from the pt of Bradfield CP made pt of Sheff CB (assoc with W Riding).[178] *LG* Sheff PLU, CB. Abol 1933 ent to Sheffield AP.[307] *Parl* See Part III of the *Guide* for composition of Sheff Parl Bors (1918—48) by wards of the CB.

BRADFORD
[W Riding] The following have 'Bradford' in their names. Insofar as any existed at a given time: *LG* Morley Wap, Bradf PLU (1837—98), Par (poor law purposes, 1898—1930), MB (1847—89), CB (1889—1974), USD. *Parl* Bradf Parl Bor (1832—85); see Part III of the *Guide* for composition of Bradf Parl Bors/BCs (1885—*) by wards of the MB/CB. *Eccl* Pontef. RDn (until 1857), Bradf RDn (1857—1971); sep noted (1971—*).

AP1—BRADFORD [ST PETER]—Incl chap Haworth (sep CP 1866,[2] sep EP 1864[308]), chap Horton (sep CP 1866,[2] sep EP 1810,[9] pt of latter eccl severed 1854 to cr EP11,[302] pt of Horton EP eccl severed 1858 to help cr EP4,[285] the remainder eccl

refounded 1863 as 'Great Horton' EP[309]), chap Thornton (sep CP 1866,[2] sep EP 1760[9]), tps Allerton, Wilsden (each a sep CP 1866,[2] the 2 eccl united 1828 as 'Wilsden cum Allerton' EP,[63] pt area Wilsden eccl severed 1846 from latter as Cullingworth EP[285]), tp North Bierley (sep CP 1866,[2] sep EP 1825 as 'Bierley',[9] as such eccl refounded 1864[246]), tp Bowling (sep CP 1866,[2] sep EP 1843,[297] eccl refounded 1865,[298] eccl refounded 1873[21]), tp Clayton (sep CP 1866,[2] pt eccl severed 1854 to help cr Queen's Head EP,[256] the remainder cr 1858 Clayton EP[160]), tp Eccleshill (sep CP 1866,[2] sep EP 1858[310]), tps Heaton, Shipley (each a sep CP 1866,[2] the 2 eccl united 1828 as 'Shipley cum Heaton' EP,[63] the area of tp Heaton eccl severed 1865 from latter to cr Heaton St Barnabas EP[311]), tp Manningham (sep CP 1866,[2] pt a sep EP 1846[166]). Addtl civ bdry alt: 1898 (gains the following CPs in Bradf CB: Allerton, Bolton, Bowling, Heaton, Horton, Manningham, Thornbury, Tyersall).[65] Transf 1974 to W Yorks.[5] *Parl* Parl bdry: 1956.[312] *Eccl* Calverley RDn (1971—*). Addtl eccl bdry alt: 1720 (cr Wibsey EP,[9] refounded 1881[313]), 1810 (cr Horton All Saints EP,[9] refounded 1864[273]), 1816 (cr EP1,[9] refounded 1841,[314] refounded 1863[111]), 1842 (cr Buttershaw EP),[315] 1842 (cr EP10),[316] 1844 (cr Manningham St Jude EP),[1] 1850 (cr Bankfoot EP),[174] 1851 (help cr Shelf EP),[137] 1858,[317] 1860 (cr Bowling St Stephen EP),[301] 1861 (help cr Laister Dyke EP),[193] 1862 (cr Bowling St John EP),[9] 1863 (cr EP16),[111] 1864 (cr EP12),[175] 1865 (incl cr EP3),[35] 1868,[208] 1868 (help cr EP13),[318] 1871,[21] 1878 (cr EP5),[319] 1891 (cr EP6),[297] 1894 (cr EP7),[109] 1903 (help cr EP14),[302] 1924,[89] 1927,[285] 1959 (help cr Buttershaw St Aidan EP).[320]

EP1—BRADFORD CHRIST CHURCH—Cr 1816 from AP1,[9] refounded 1841,[316] refounded 1863.[111] Abol 1922 to help cr EP2.[321]

EP2—BRADFORD CHRIST CHURCH WITH ST THOMAS—Cr 1922 by union EP1, EP16.[321] Abol 1927 pt to AP1, pt to EP6.[285]

EP3—BRADFORD HOLY TRINITY—Cr 1865 from AP1.[35] Bdry: 1927.[174] Abol 1966 pt to EP7, pt to Bowling EP.[300]

EP4—BRADFORD ST ANDREW—Cr 1850 from Horton EP, EP11 (both in orig area tp Horton).[285] Bdry: 1902 (help cr EP8),[322] 1906 (help cr EP17).[323] Abol 1966 to help cr EP9.[324]

EP5—BRADFORD ST AUGUSTINE—Cr 1878 from AP1.[318] Sometimes 'Undercliffe'. Calverley RDn (1971—*). Bdry: 1927.[285]

EP6—BRADFORD ST CHRYSOSTOM—Cr 1891 from AP1.[297] Bdry: 1927.[285] Abol 1966 to help cr Bolton St James with St Chrysostom EP.[289]

EP7—BRADFORD ST CLEMENT—Cr 1894 from AP1, Laister Dyke EP.[109] Calverley RDn (1971—*). Bdry: 1927,[67] 1966.[300]

EP8—BRADFORD ST COLUMBA, HORTON—Cr 1902 from Great Horton EP, Horton All Saints EP, EP4.[322] Abol 1966 to help cr EP9.[324]

EP9—BRADFORD ST COLUMBA WITH ST

ANDREW—Cr 1966 by union EP4, EP8, pt Manningham St Mary Magdalene with St Michael and All Angels EP.[324] Bowl. & Horton RDn (1971—*).

EP10—BRADFORD ST JAMES—Cr 1842 from AP1.[316] Abol 1965 ent to Horton All Saints EP.[325]

EP11—BRADFORD ST JOHN—Cr 1854 from Horton EP.[302] Bdry: 1858 (help cr EP4),[285] 1858.[317] Abol 1965 ent to Horton All Saints EP.[325]

EP12—BRADFORD ST LUKE—Cr 1864 from AP1.[175] Bdry: 1927.[285] Abol 1940 to help cr Bowling St Bartholomew and St Luke EP.[299]

EP13—BRADFORD ST MICHAEL AND ALL ANGELS—Cr 1868 from AP1, EP16.[318] Bdry: 1927.[285] Abol 1958 to help cr Manningham St Mary Magdalene with St Michael and All Angels EP.[322]

EP14—BRADFORD ST OSWALD, CHAPEL GREEN—Cr 1903 from Bowling St Stephen EP, Great Horton EP, AP1.[302] Sometimes 'Little Horton'. Bowl. & Horton RDn (1971—*).

EP15—BRADFORD ST SAVIOUR—Cr 1924 from Girlington EP, Allerton EP.[66] Bdry: 1927.[285] Renamed 1966 'Fairweather Green'.[285]

EP16—BRADFORD ST THOMAS—Cr 1863 from AP1.[111] Bdry: 1868 (help cr EP13).[318] Abol 1922 to help cr EP2.[321]

EP17—BRADFORD ST WILFRID, LIDGET GREEN—Cr 1906 from Great Horton EP, EP4.[323] Bowl. & Horton RDn (1971—*).

WEST BRADFORD
  [W Riding] Tp in Mitton AP, sep CP 1866.[2] LG Seq 108. Transf 1974 to Lancs.[5] Parl Seq 41.

BRADLEY
  EP [W Riding] Cr 1895 from Huddersfield Christ Church, Woodhouse EP, Bay Hall EP, Kirkheaton AP.[221] Hudd. RDn.

BRADLEY'S BOTH
  [W Riding] Tp in Kildwick AP, sep CP 1866.[2] LG Seq 112. Transf 1974 to N Yorks.[5] Parl Seq 41.

BRADSHAW
  EP [W Riding] Name used now for EP cr 1843 as 'Ovenden', qv.

BRAFFERTON
  AP [N Riding] Tp 'Brafferton' in Bulmer Wap as was tp Helperby (sep CP 1866,[2] not sep eccl but in pec jurisd Dean & Chapter of York until 1836); incl in Hallik. Wap tp Thornton Bridge (sep CP 1866[2]). LG After 1866, Seq 28. Transf 1974 to N Yorks.[5] Parl Seq 16. Eccl Seq 18.

BRAITHWELL
  AP [W Riding] Incl tp Bramley (sep CP 1866,[2] sep EP 1956 [qv for 6 other constituent pars then and for other bdry alt affecting Braithwell][215]) so that this par eccl 'Braithwell with Bramley' before 1956, 'Braithwell' thereafter. LG Seq 117. Transf 1974 to S Yorks.[5] Parl Seq 44. Eccl Seq 42.

BRAITHWELL WITH BRAMLEY—see prev entry

BRAMHAM
  AP [W Riding] Incl tp Bramham cum Oglethorpe (sep CP 1866[2]), pt tp Clifford cum Boston (sep CP 1866[2]; Boston alone in area pec jurisd Dean & Chapter of York, with 2 EPs cr, 'Boston Spa' in 1816,[9] eccl refounded 1852[293] and 1853,[294] 'Clifford' in 1842,[9] eccl refounded 1853[294]) so that 'Bramham' has no sep civ identity after 1866. LG Bark. Ash Wap. Parl W Riding (1832—67). Eccl Pec jurisd Bramham prebend (until 1540), pec jurisd Dean & Chapter of York (1540—1836), New Ainsty RDn (1836—62), Tadc. RDn (1862—71), Selby RDn (1871—1921), Tadc. RDn (1921—*).

BRAMHAM CUM OGLETHORPE
  [W Riding] Tp in Bramham AP sep CP 1866.[2] LG Bark. Ash Wap, Barwick GilbU (until 1869), Wethb. PLU (1869—1930), RSD, RD. Transf 1974 to W Yorks.[5] Parl Seq 24.

BRAMHOPE
  [W Riding] Tp in Otley AP, sep CP 1866,[2] sep EP 1882.[326] LG Seq 103. Bdry: 1937 (incl gains pt Leeds CB [assoc with W Riding] & AP).[31] Transf 1974 to W Yorks.[5] Parl Seq 30. Eccl Otley RDn (1882—1921), Knar. RDn (1921—71), Head. RDn (1971—*).

BRAMLEY
  [W Riding] Chap in Leeds AP, sep CP 1866,[2] sep EP 1730.[9] LG Skyr. Wap, Leeds Bor/MB/CB, USD, Bramley PLU. Abol civ 1904 to help cr Armley and Bramley CP.[124] Parl Leeds Parl Bor (1832—85); see Part III of the Guide for composition of Leeds Parl Bors (1885—1918) by wards of the MB. Eccl Ainsty RDn (1730—1820), Old Ainsty RDn (1820—36), Pontef. RDn (1836—57), Leeds RDn (1857—1971), Armley RDn (1971—*). Eccl bdry: 1847 (cr Stanningley EP,[9] refounded 1862[263]), 1867 (help cr Upper Armley EP),[125] 1950,[327] 1967,[127] 1968.[328]

BRAMLEY
  [W Riding] Tp in Braithwell AP, sep CP 1866,[2] sep EP 1956 from Braithwell AP, Conisbrough AP, Dalton EP, Maltby AP, Ravensfield EP, Stainton AP, Wickersley AP.[215] LG Seq 119. Civ bdry: 1886,[65] 1937.[31] Transf 1974 to S Yorks.[5] Parl Seq 55. Eccl Rotherh. RDn.

BRAMPTON
  CP [W Riding] Renaming 1894[329] of the remainder of Brampton Bierlow CP after the pt in Wath upon Dearne UD cr West Melton CP.[257] LG Rotherh. PLU, RD. Renamed 1897 'Brampton Bierlow'.[330]

BRAMPTON BIERLOW
  [W Riding] Tp in Wath upon Dearne AP, sep CP 1866,[2] sep EP 1856.[331] LG Straff. & Tick. Wap, Rotherh. PLU, pt Wath upon Dearne USD, pt Rotherh. RSD. Civ bdry: 1881,[332] 1881,[333] 1883.[52] Abol civ 1894 the pt in the UD cr West Melton CP, the remainder renamed 'Brampton'.[329] Parl W Riding (1832—67), S'rn Dv of W Riding (1867—85), Hallamshire Dv (1885—1918). Eccl Rotherh. RDn (1856—71), Wath RDn (1871—*). Eccl bdry: 1930,[334] 1955.[117]

  CP [W Riding] Renaming 1897 of Brampton CP.[330] LG Rotherh. PLU, RD. Bdry: 1936,[132] 1939.[76] Transf 1974 to S Yorks.[5] Parl Wentw. Dv (1918—48), Rother Valley CC (1948—*).

BRAMPTON EN LE MORTHEN
  [W Riding] Tp in Treeton AP, sep CP 1866.[2] LG

Straff. & Tick. Wap, Rotherh. PLU, RSD, RD. Abol 1923 to help cr Thurcroft CP.[151] *Parl* W Riding (1832—67), S'rn Dv of W Riding (1867—85), Rotherh. Dv (1885—1918), Rother Valley Dv (1918—48).

BRANDESBURTON
AP [E Riding] Incl tp Moor Town (sep CP 1866[2]). *LG* Seq 16. Addtl civ bdry alt: 1885,[335] 1895,[336] 1935 (gains Hempholme CP, Moor Town CP).[13] Transf 1974 to Humb.[5] *Parl* Seq 5. *Eccl* Pec jurisd Bev. (until 1836), Seq 15 thereafter.

BRANDSBY
AP [N Riding] Usual eccl spelling; for civ see following entry. *Eccl* Seq 18. Eccl bdry: 1960 (gains chap Yearsley [Yearsley had been cr a sep EP 1855,[9] sep eccl status not sustained] from Coxwold AP).[337]

BRANDSBY CUM STEARSBY
AP [N Riding] Usual civ spelling; for eccl and eccl bdry alt, see prev entry. *LG* Seq 28. Transf 1974 to N Yorks.[5] *Parl* Seq 16.

BRANSDALE
CP [N Riding] Cr 1934 by union Bransdale, West Side CP, pt Farndale, Low Quarter CP, pt Farndale, West Side CP.[3] *LG* Kirkby Moors. RD. Transf 1974 to N Yorks.[5] *Parl* Thirsk & Malton CC (1948—*).

BRANSDALE CUM FARNDALE
EP [N Riding] Cr 1873 from Kirkdale with Nawton AP (area of tp Farndale East [not sep civ]), Lastingham AP, Kirkby Moorside AP (incl area tps Farndale, Low Quarter and Farndale, West Side).[21] Helm. RDn. Abol 1973 to help cr Kirkbymoorside with Gillamoor, Farndale and Bransdale EP.[338]

BRANSDALE, WEST SIDE
[N Riding] Tp in Kirkdale AP, sep CP 1866.[2] *LG* Ryed. Wap, Helm. PLU (1837—48), Kirkby Moors. PLU (1848—1930), RSD, RD. Abol 1934 to help cr Bransdale CP.[3] *Parl* N Riding (1832—85), Whitby Dv (1885—1918), Thirsk & Malton Dv (1918—48).

BRANTINGHAM
AP [E Riding] Incl chap Blacktoft (sep civ identity early, sep EP 1776[9]), tp Ellerker (sep CP 1866,[2] no sep eccl identity [see below for eccl severance] hence this par eccl 'Brantingham with Ellerker' until 1968, qv). *LG* Pt Harth. Wap, pt Howden Wap, Bev. PLU, RSD, RD. Addtl civ bdry alt: 1935.[13] Transf 1974 to Humb.[5] *Parl* Seq 6.
EP [E Riding] Cr 1968 when tp Ellerker eccl severed from Bantingham with Ellerker AP (civ, 'Brantingham'; see above) to help cr South Cave and Ellerker EP, the remainder to be 'Brantingham'.[339] Howden RDn.

BRANTINGHAM WITH ELLERKER
AP [E Riding] Usual eccl spelling; for civ and civ sep chap and tp, see 'Brantingham'. *Eccl* Pec jurisd Dean & Chapter of Durham (until 1836), Harth. & Hull RDn (1836—57), S Harth. RDn (1857—66), Howden RDn (1866—1968). Abol eccl 1968, tp Ellerker eccl severed to help cr South Cave and Ellerker EP, the remainder to be 'Brantingham'.[339]

BRAWBY
[N Riding] Tp in Salton AP, sep CP 1866.[2] *LG* Seq

65. Transf 1974 to N Yorks.[5] *Parl* Seq 21.

BRAYTON
AP [W Riding] Incl tp Barlow (sep CP 1866,[2] orig donative chap, sep status not sustained so that this par eccl 'Brayton with Barlow', qv), tp Burn (sep CP 1866[2]), tps Gateforth, Hambleton (each a sep CP 1866,[2] Hambleton and pt Gateforth eccl united 1914 to cr Gateforth cum Hambleton EP[340]), tp Thorpe Willoughby (sep CP 1866[2]). *LG* Seq 80. Addtl civ bdry alt: 1883 (loses pt to Cliffe cum Lund CP, E Riding),[341] 1894.[342] Transf 1974 to N Yorks.[5] *Parl* Seq 24.

BRAYTON WITH BARLOW
AP [W Riding] Usual eccl spelling; for civ and civ and eccl sep tps, see prev entry. *Eccl* Pec jurisd Selby (until 1836), New Ainsty RDn (1836—57), Pontef. RDn (1857—62), Selby RDn (1862—*). Addtl eccl bdry alt: 1972.[214]

BREARTON
[W Riding] Tp pt in Knaresborough AP, pt in Ripley AP, sep CP 1866,[2] sep EP 1841 (tp Brearton, ex-par Walkingham with Occaney),[9] eccl refounded 1866[23] (pt in Ripley not mentioned in orders).*LG* Seq 84. Civ bdry: 1888.[261] Transf 1974 to N Yorks.[5] *Parl* Seq 36. *Eccl* Boroughbr. RDn (1841—70), Knar. RDn (1870—1971), Harrog. RDn (1971—*). Eccl bdry: 1951.[343]

BREIGHTON AND GUNBY
[E Riding] Tp in Bubwith AP, sep CP 1866.[2] *LG* Harth. Wap, Howden PLU, RSD, RD. Abol 1935 ent to Bubwith AP.[13] *Parl* E Riding (1832—85), Howdensh. Dv (1885—1948).

WEST BRETTON
[W Riding] Chap & tp pt (Agb. Wap) in Sandal Magna AP, pt (Staincr. Wap) in Silkstone AP, sep CP 1866.[2] *LG* Wakef PLU, RSD, RD. Transf 1974 to W Yorks.[5] *Parl* Seq 54.

BREWERY FIELD
EP [W Riding] Cr 1851 from Hunslet EP, Holbeck EP.[344] Pontef. RDn (1851—57), Leeds RDn (1857—1901). Bdry: 1885 (help refound Hunslet EP).[229] Abol 1901 to help cr Leeds St John the Evangelist and St Barnabas EP.[345]

BRIDLINGTON
AP [E Riding] Incl area chap Bempton (orig chap in Bridlington priory, sep par [donative] from 1441[232]), chap Grindall (sep CP 1866,[2] sep EP 1749[9]), chap & tp Sewerby cum Marton (sep CP 1866,[2] sep EP 1850 as 'Sewerby with Marton'[346]), chap Speeton (sep CP 1866,[2] sep EP 1734[9]), tp Buckton (sep CP 1866,[2] eccl severed 1919 and transf to Bempton AP[233]), hmlt Easton (sep CP 1866[2]), tp Hilderthorpe (sep CP 1866[2]), tp Wilsthorpe (sep CP 1866[2]). *LG* Dick. Wap, Bridl. PLU, USD, UD (1894—99), MB (1899—1974). Addtl civ bdry alt: 1894 (gains the pts in Bridl. MB of Bessingby AP, Sewerby cum Marton CP),[239] 1923 (incl gains Hilderthorpe CP),[240] 1935.[13] Transf 1974 to Humb.[5] *Parl* Seq 2. *Eccl* Seq 7. Eccl bdry: 1842 (cr Bridlington Quay EP,[9] refounded 1843[194]).

BRIDLINGTON EMMANUEL
EP [E Riding] Cr 1916 from Bridlington Quay EP.[347]

Bridl. RDn.

BRIDLINGTON QUAY

EP [E Riding] Cr 1842 from Bridlington AP,[9] refounded 1843.[194] Dick. RDn (1842—62) S Dick. RDn (1862—66), Bridl. RDn (1866—*). Bdry: 1870,[213] 1874 (cr Bridlington Quay Holy Trinity EP),[82] 1916 (cr Bridlington Emmanuel EP).[347]

BRIDLINGTON QUAY HOLY TRINITY

EP [E Riding] Cr 1874 from Bridlington Quay EP.[82] Bridl. RDn.

BRIERLEY

[W Riding] Tp in Felkirk AP, sep CP 1866.[2] *LG* Seq 113. Bdry: 1888,[348] 1916.[349] Transf 1974 to S Yorks.[5] *Parl* Seq 42.

BRIGHAM

[E Riding] Tp in Foston on the Wolds AP, sep CP 1866.[2] *LG* Dick. Wap, Driff. PLU, RSD, RD. Bdry: 1884.[350] Abol 1935 to help cr Foston CP.[13] *Parl* E Riding (1832—85), Buckr. Dv (1885—1948).

BRIGHOUSE

EP [W Riding] Cr 1836 from Lightcliffe EP,[9] eccl refounded 1849.[351] Pontef. RDn (1836—57), Halifax RDn (1857—1967), Brigh. & Elland RDn (1967—*). Bdry: 1894.[323]

CP [W Riding] Cr 1894 from the pt of Hipperholme with Brighouse CP in Brigh. MB.[257] Halifax PLU, Brigh. MB. Bdry: 1915 (gains Rastrick CP),[352] 1937 (incl loses pt to Hudd. CB [assoc with W Riding] & AP, gains Hipperholme UD & CP, Norwood Green and Coley CP).[31] Transf 1974 to W Yorks.[5] *Parl* Elland Dv (1918—48), Brigh. & Spenb. BC (1948—*).

BRIGHTSIDE

EP [W Riding] Cr 1845 from Attercliffe EP.[147] Donc. RDn (1845—57), Rotherh. RDn (1857—62), Sheff RDn (1862—1942), Ecclesfield RDn (1942—*). Bdry: 1848 (cr Brightside All Saints EP),[353] 1877 (help cr Wincobank EP),[303] 1882 (help cr Attercliffe Emmanuel EP),[149] 1902 (help cr Sheffield St Cuthbert EP),[354] 1907 (cr Sheffield St Clement Newhall EP),[211] 1918 (help cr Brightside St Margaret EP),[355] 1936 (help cr Shiregreen EP).[24]

BRIGHTSIDE ALL SAINTS

EP [W Riding] Cr 1848 from Brightside EP.[353] Donc. RDn (1848—57), Rotherh. RDn (1857—62), Sheff RDn (1862—1942), Ecclesfield RDn (1942—*). Bdry: 1882 (help cr Attercliffe Emmanuel EP).[149]

BRIGHTSIDE BIERLOW

[W Riding] Tp in Sheffield AP, sep CP 1866,[2] sep EP 1869.[356] *LG* Straff. & Tick. Wap, Sheff PLU, MB (1843—89), CB (1889—1902), USD. Abol 1902 ent to Sheffield AP.[151] *Parl* Sheff Parl Bor (1832—85); see Part III of the *Guide* for composition of Sheff Parl Bors (1885—1918) by wards of the MB. *Eccl* Sheff RDn (1869—1942), Ecclesfield RDn (1942—*).

BRIGHTSIDE ST MARGARET

EP [W Riding] Cr 1918 from Brightside EP, Wincobank EP.[355] Sheff RDn (1918—42), Ecclesfield RDn (1942—*).

BRIGNALL

AP [N Riding] *LG* Seq 39. Transf 1974 to Durham.[5]

Parl Seq 14. *Eccl* Richm. RDn (until 1857), Richm. West RDn (1857—63), Richm. North RDn (1863—1929). Abol eccl 1929 to help cr Rokeby and Brignall EP.[357]

BRINSWORTH

[W Riding] Tp in Rotherham AP, sep CP 1866,[2] sep EP 1903 from Rotherham AP, Whiston AP.[195] *LG* Straff. & Tick. Wap, Rotherh. PLU, pt Rotherh. MB & USD (1879—94), Rotherh. RSD (ent 1875—79, pt 1879—94), Rotherh. RD. Civ bdry: 1883,[358] 1894 (loses the pt in Rotherh. MB to Rotherham AP),[359] 1912,[360] 1921 (loses pt to Sheff CB [assoc with W Riding] and to Tinsley CP),[361] 1936 (loses pt to Rotherh. CB [assoc with W Riding] & AP).[132] Transf 1974 to S Yorks.[5] *Parl* Seq 55. *Eccl* Rotherh. RDn.

BRODSWORTH

AP [W Riding] *LG* Seq 117. Civ bdry: 1915 (loses pt to Adwick le Street AP as the latter [enlarged, qv] constituted Adwick le Street UD).[43] Transf 1974 to S Yorks.[5] *Parl* Seq 44. *Eccl* Seq 40. Eccl bdry: 1914 (help cr Woodlands EP),[44] 1940 (help cr Doncaster St Leonard and St Jude EP).[237]

BROGDEN

[W Riding] Tp in Barnoldswick AP, sep CP 1866.[2] *LG* Staincl. & Ewc. Wap, Skipton PLU, RSD, RD. Transf 1974 to Lancs.[5] *Parl* Seq 41.

BROMPTON

AP [N Riding] Incl tps Sawdon, Troutsdale (each a sep CP 1866[2]), pt chap Snainton (sep CP 1866,[2] not sep eccl hence this par eccl 'Brompton with Snainton', qv). *LG* Seq 62. Addtl civ bdry alt: 1886 (gains Sawdon CP).[176] Transf 1974 to N Yorks.[5] *Parl* Seq 20.

BROMPTON

[N Riding] Chap in Northallerton AP, sep CP 1866,[2] sep EP 1841,[9] eccl refounded 1843.[362] *LG* Seq 22. Civ bdry: 1934.[3] Transf 1974 to N Yorks.[5] *Parl* N'allert. Parl Bor (1298, 1640—1885), Richm. Dv (1885—1918), Thirsk & Malton Dv/CC (1918—*). *Eccl* Pec jurisd Dean & Chapter of Durham (until 1836), Clev RDn (1836—62), N'allert. RDn (1862—1957). Abol eccl 1957 to help cr Brompton with Deighton EP.[74]

BROMPTON ON SWALE

[N Riding] Tp in Easby AP, sep CP 1866.[2] *LG* Seq 35. Transf 1974 to N Yorks.[5] *Parl* Seq 14.

BROMPTON WITH DEIGHTON

EP [N Riding] Cr 1957 by union Brompton EP, chap Deighton in Northallerton AP.[74] N'allert. RDn.

BROMPTON WITH SNAINTON

AP [N Riding] Usual eccl spelling; for civ and civ sep tps and pt chap Snainton, see first 'Brompton' above. *Eccl* Seq 28.

BROOMFLEET

[E Riding] Tp in South Cave AP, sep CP 1866,[2] sep EP 1862 (incl tp Faxfleet, so that this par later 'Broomfleet with Faxfleet').[136] *LG* Harth. Wap, Howden PLU, South Cave & Wallingfen USD (ent 1875—80, pt 1880—94), pt Howden RSD (1880—94), Howden RD. Civ bdry: 1880.[230] Transf 1974 to Humb.[5] *Parl* Seq 7. *Eccl* Bev. RDn (1862—66), Howden RDn (1866—*).

BROOMFLEET WITH FAXELEET—see prev entry
BROTHERTON
AP Incl tps Byram cum Poole, Sutton (each a sep CP 1866[2]). *LG* Seq 76. Transf 1974 to N Yorks.[5] *Parl* Seq 29. *Eccl* Pec jurisd Dean & Chapter of York (tp 'Brotherton' and not the other tps, until 1836), New Ainsty RDn (1836—57), Pontef. RDn (1857—*).
BROTTON
[N Riding] Tp in Skelton AP, sep CP 1866,[2] sep EP 1868 (tps Brotton, Skinningrove).[188] *LG* Langb. Lbty, Guisb. PLU, Brotton USD (1875—84), Skelton & Brotton USD (1884—94), UD. Civ bdry: 1934.[363] Transf 1974 to Clev.[5] *Parl* Seq 9. *Eccl* Guisb. RDn (1868—78), Middlesb. RDn (1878—1924), Guisb. RDn (1924—*). Eccl bdry: 1952 (help cr Carlin How with Skinningrove EP, later 'Carlin How').[364]
BROUGH
[N Riding] Tp in Catterick AP, sep CP 1866.[2] *LG* Seq 50. Transf 1974 to N Yorks.[5] *Parl* Seq 14.
BROUGHTON
AP [W Riding] Incl hmlt Elslack (sep CP 1866,[2] not sep eccl hence this par eccl 'Broughton with Elslack', qv). *LG* Seq 112. Transf 1974 to N Yorks.[5] *Parl* Seq 41.
BROUGHTON
[N Riding] Tp in Appleton le Street AP, sep CP 1866.[2] *LG* Seq 65. Bdry: 1934.[3] Transf 1974 to N Yorks.[5] *Parl* Seq 16.
BROUGHTON
[N Riding] Tp in Kirby in Cleveland AP, sep CP 1866.[2] *LG* Seq 58.Transf 1974 to N Yorks.[5] *Parl* Seq 11.
BROUGHTON WITH ELSLACK
AP [W Riding] Usual eccl spelling; for civ and civ sep hmlt Elslack, see first 'Broughton' above. *Eccl* Seq 37.
BROWNHILL
EP [W Riding] Cr 1871 from Batley AP, Birstall AP.[210] Birstall RDn (1871—83), Dewsb. RDn (1883—*). Bdry: 1880 (help cr Carlinghow EP).[198]
BROXA
[N Riding] Tp in Hockness AP, sep CP 1866.[2] *LG* Seq 67. Transf 1974 to N Yorks.[5] *Parl* Seq 20.
BRUNTCLIFFE
EP [W Riding] Cr 1892 from Morley EP, Morley St Paul Townend EP, Batley AP.[215] Dewsb. RDn (1892—1927), Birstall RDn (1927—*). Bdry: 1913.[119]
BUBWITH
AP [E Riding] Incl tps Breighton cum Gunby, Foggathorpe, Harlthorpe, Willitoft, pts tps Gribthorpe, Spaldington (each a sep CP 1866[2]). *LG* Seq 11. Addtl civ bdry alt: 1935 (gains Breighton and Gunby CP, Willitoft CP).[13] Transf 1974 to Humb.[5] *Parl* Seq 7. *Eccl* Orig but not later in pec jurisd Dean & Chapter of York, Seq 14 thereafter.
BUCKDEN
[W Riding] Tp in Arncliffe AP, sep CP 1866.[2] *LG* Seq 112. Transf 1974 to N Yorks.[5] *Parl* Seq 41.
BUCKTON
[E Riding] Chap & tp in Bridlington AP, sep CP 1866,[2] eccl severed 1919 and transf to Bempton

AP.[233] *LG* Dick. Wap, Bridl. PLU, RSD, RD. Abol 1913 ent to Bempton AP.[13] *Parl* E Riding (1832—85), Buckr. Dv (1885—1948).
BUGTHORPE
AP [E Riding] Incl chap Stockton on the Forest (sep civ identity early, sep EP 1738[9]). *LG* Seq 3. Transf 1974 to Humb.[5] *Parl* Seq 7. *Eccl* Pec jurisd Bugthorpe prebend (until 1836), Seq 9 thereafter.
BULL FORT
[E Riding] Ex-par place, not mentioned in acts and schedules until later 20th century, sometimes 'Bull Sand Fort'. *LG* Hold. RD (1935—74). Transf 1974 to Humb.[5] *Parl* Bridl. CC (1948—*).
BULMER
AP [N Riding] Incl tps Henderskelf, Welburn (each a sep CP 1866[2]). *LG* Seq 29. Transf 1974 to N Yorks.[5] *Parl* Seq 16. *Eccl* Usually as 'Bulmer with Welburn and Castle Howard', Seq 17.
BULMER WITH WELBURN AND CASTLE HOWARD—see prev entry
BURGHWALLIS
AP [W Riding] (The AP incl pt tp Sutton and only pt tp of Burghwallis [the latter mainly in Osg. Wap, extended into other pars: into Barnby upon Don AP in Straff. & Tick. Wap, and into Owston AP in Osg. Wap], Sutton a sep CP 1866[2]). *LG* Donc. PLU, RSD, RD. Civ bdry: 1883.[42] Transf 1974 to S Yorks.[5] *Parl* W Riding (1832—67), pt N'rn Dv, pt S'rn Dv (because of area of Burghwallis tp, 1867—85), Osg. Dv (1885—1918), Don Valley Dv/CC (1918—*). *Eccl* Seq 40.
BURLEY
EP [W Riding] Refounding 1856 of Burley in Wharfedale EP (incl tp Menstone).[351] Pontef. RDn (1856—57), Otley RDn (1857—*). Bdry: 1876 (cr Menstone with Woodhead EP),[365] 1912 (help cr Ben Rhydding EP).[234]
BURLEY
EP [W Riding] Cr 1793 from Headingley cum Burley EP (the pt consisting of hmlt Burley),[9] refounded 1849.[54] Ainsty RDn (1793—120), Old Ainsty RDn (1820—36), Pontef. RDn (1856—57), Leeds RDn (1857—1971), Head. RDn (1971—*). Bdry: 1850,[366] 1887 (help cr Leeds All Hallows EP),[126] 1902,[364] 1911 (cr Leeds St Margaret EP),[367] 1967.[127]
BURLEY IN WHARFEDALE
[W Riding] Tp in Otley AP, sep CP 1866,[2] sep EP 1793 as 'Burley in Wharfedale',[9] eccl refounded 1856 as 'Burley'.[351] *LG* Skyr. Wap, Carlton GilbU (until 1869), Wharfed. PLU (1869—1930), Burley in Wharfed. USD, UD (1894—1937). Abol civ 1937 ent to Ilkley UD & AP.[31] *Parl* W Riding (1832—67), N'rn Dv of W Riding (1867—85), Otley Dv (1885—1948). *Eccl* Ainsty RDn (1792—1920), Old Ainsty RDn (1820—36), Pontef. RDn (1836—56).
BURMANTOFTS
EP [W Riding] Cr 1851 from Leeds AP.[344] Pontef. RDn (1851—57), Leeds RDn (1857—1901). Bdry: 1877 (cr Leeds St Alban the Martyr EP),[369] 1890 (help cr Burmantofts St Agnes EP).[370] Abol 1901 to help cr Burmantofts St Stephen and St Agnes EP.[371]

BURMANTOFTS ST AGNES

EP [W Riding] Cr 1890 from Burmantofts EP, Leeds AP.[370] Leeds RDn. Abol 1901 to help cr Burmantofts St Stephen and St Agnes EP.[371]

BURMANTOFTS ST STEPHEN AND ST AGNES

EP [W Riding] Cr 1901 by union Burmantofts EP, Burmantofts St Agnes EP.[371] Leeds RDn (1901–71), Allert. RDn (1971–*). Bdry: 1939 (help cr Leeds The Epiphany, Gipton EP).[204]

BURN

[N Riding] Tp in Brayton AP, sep CP 1866.[2] *LG* Seq 80. Transf 1974 to N Yorks.[5] *Parl* Seq 24.

BURNBY

AP [E Riding] *LG* Harth. Wap, Pockl. PLU, RSD, RD. Abol 1935 ent to Hayton AP.[13] *Parl* E Riding (1832–85), Howdensh. Dv (1885–1948). *Eccl* Seq 14.

BURNESTON

AP [N Riding] Incl tps Carthorpe; Exelby, Leeming and Newton; Gatenby, Theakston, pt tp Swainby with Allerthorpe (each a sep CP 1866[2]). *LG* Seq 40. Transf 1974 to N Yorks.[5] *Parl* Seq 18. *Eccl* Catt. RDn (until 1857), Catt. East RDn (1857–1928), Bedale RDn (1928–73), Wensleyd. RDn (1973–*). Eccl bdry: 1755 (cr Leeming EP,[9] refounded 1880[68]), 1921.[221]

BURNISTON

[N Riding] Tp in Scalby AP, sep CP 1866.[2] *LG* Seq 62. Bdry: 1883,[16] 1887.[162] Transf 1974 to N Yorks.[5] *Parl* Seq 20.

BURNSALL

AP [W Riding] Incl chap Conistone with Kilnsey, tp Rylstone (each a sep CP 1866,[2] eccl united 1867 as Rylstone with Conistone EP[368]), tp Appletreewick (sep CP 1866,[2] pt eccl severed 1860 to help refound Greenhow Hill EP[68]), tps Bordley, Cracoe, Hartlington, Hetton, Thorpe (each a sep CP 1866[2]); also incl Burnsall and Thorpe Fell, after 1866 common to Burnsall AP and to Thorpe CP (abol 1938, pt to each par[28]). *LG* Staincl. & Ewc. Wap, Skipton PLU (soon after 1837[112]–1930), RSD, RD. Transf 1974 to N Yorks.[5] *Parl* Seq 41. *Eccl* Seq 36.

BURNSALL AND THORPE FELL

[W Riding] Land Common to Burnsall AP, after 1866 common to Burnsall AP and to Thorpe CP. *LG* Skipton RD. Abol 1938 pt to Burnsall AP, pt to Thorpe CP.[28] *Parl* Skipton Dv (1918–48).

BURRILL WITH COWLING

[N Riding] Tp in Bedale AP, sep CP 1866.[2] *LG* Seq 48. Transf 1974 to N Yorks.[5] *Parl* Seq 15.

BURSTWICK

AP [E Riding] Chap in Skeckling AP, sep civ identity early, sep EP between 1869 and 1871.[372] Incl tp Burstwick with Skeckling, pt tp Ryhill and Camerton (each a sep CP 1866[2]) so that 'Burstwick' has no sep civ identity 1866–1935 (see following entry). *LG* Hold. Wap. *Parl* E Riding (1832–67). *Eccl* Hedon RDn. Loses 1954 pt to Hedon AP, gains tp Thorgumbald from Paull with Thorgumbald AP (the remainder of latter to be 'Paull') to cr 'Burstwick with Thorgumbald' EP.[373] CP [E Riding] Cr 1935 by union pts Burstwick with Skeckling CP, Ryhill and Camerton CP.[13] *LG*

Hold. RD. Bdry: 1964.[374] Transf 1974 to Humb.[5] *Parl* Bridl. CC (1948–*).

BURSTWICK WITH SKECKLING

[E Riding] Tp in Burstwick AP, sep CP 1866.[2] *LG* Hold. Wap, Patr. PLU (soon after 1836[112]–1930), RSD, RD. Abol 1935 pt to Preston AP, pt to help cr Burstwick CP.[13] *Parl* E Riding (1832–85), Hold. Dv (1885–1948).

BURSTWICK WITH THORGUMBALD

EP [E Riding] Cr 1954 by union pt Burstwick AP, tp Thorgumbald in Paull with Thorgumbald AP.[373] S Hold. RDn.

BISHOP BURTON

AP [E Riding] *LG* Seq 9. Transf 1974 to Humb.[5] *Parl* Seq 4. *Eccl* Orig but not later in pec jurisd Dean & Chapter of York, Seq 11 thereafter.

BLACK BOURTON—see BOURTON IN LONSDALE

CHERRY BOURTON

AP [E Riding] *LG* Seq 9. Transf 1974 to Humb.[5] *Parl* Seq 4. *Eccl* Pec jurisd Bev. (until 1836), Seq 11 thereafter.

NORTH BURTON—see BURTON FLEMING

WEST BURTON—see BURTON CUM WALDEN

BURTON AGNES

AP [E Riding] Incl chap Foxholes (appropriated to York St Mary Abbey early 12th cent and sep par thereafter[375]), tp Harpham (sep CP 1866,[2] perhaps sep parochial rights 17th–18th cents,[376] sep eccl status not sustained hence this par usually eccl 'Burton Agnes with Harpham', qv), tps Gransmoor, Haisthorpe, Thornholme (each a sep CP 1866[2]). *LG* Seq 5. Addtl civ bdry alt: 1884,[377] 1935 (gains Gransmoor CP, Thornholme CP).[13] Transf 1974 to Humb.[5] *Parl* Seq 2.

BURTON AGNES WITH HARPHAM

AP [E Riding] Usual eccl spelling (Harpham perhaps had sep parochial rights 17th–18th cents,[376] sep eccl status not sustained); for civ and civ sep chap and tps, see prev entry. *Eccl* Seq 7.

BURTON CONSTABLE

CP [E Riding] Cr 1935 by union Marton CP, West Newton with Burton Constable CP.[13] *LG* Hold. RD. Bdry: 1952.[378] Transf 1974 to Humb.[5] *Parl* Bridl. CC (1948–*).

BURTON CUM WALDEN

[N Riding] Tp in Aysgarth AP, sep CP 1866.[2] Sometimes 'West Burton'. *LG* Seq 52. Bdry: 1886.[4] Transf 1974 to N Yorks.[5] *Parl* Seq 14.

BURTON FLEMING

AP [E Riding] Orig chap in Hunmanby AP, sep par 1269.[379] Sometimes 'North Burton', name declared 1920 to be 'Burton Fleming'.[380] *LG* Seq 5. Transf 1974 to Humb.[5] *Parl* Seq 2. *Eccl* Dick. RDn (until 1857), N Dick. RDn (1857–58). Gains eccl 1858 chap Fordon in Hunmanby AP to cr Burton Fleming with Fordon EP.[381]

BURTON FLEMING WITH FORDON

EP [E Riding] Cr 1858 by union Burton Fleming AP, chap Fordon in Hunmanby AP.[381] N Dick. RDn (1858–66), Scarb. RDn (1866–1922), Bridl. RDn (1922–*).

BURTON IN LONSDALE

[W Riding] Chap & tp in Thornton in Lonsdale AP,

sep CP 1866,[2] sep EP 1823,[9] eccl refounded 1867.[361] Sometimes 'Black Bourton'. *LG* Seq 111. Bdry: 1883.[52] Transf 1974 to N Yorks.[5] *Parl* Seq 41. *Eccl* Kirkby Lonsd. RDn (1823—49), Clapham RDn (1849—1921), Ewecr. RDn (1921—*).

BURTON LEONARD
AP [W Riding] *LG* Seq 87. Transf 1974 to N Yorks.[5] *Parl* Seq 36. *Eccl* Pec jurisd Dean & Chapter of York (until 1836), Boroughbr. RDn (1836—70), Knar. RDn (1870—1956), Ripon RDn (1956—*).

BURTON PIDSEA
AP [E Riding] *LG* Hold. Wap, Patr. PLU (soon after 1836[112]—1930), RSD, RD (1894—1935), Hold. RD (1935—74). Transf 1974 to Humb.[5] *Parl* Seq 5. *Eccl* Pec jurisd Dean & Chapter of York (until 1836), Seq 16 thereafter.

BURTON SALMON
[W Riding] Tp in Monk Frystone AP, sep CP 1866.[2] *LG* Seq 76. Transf 1974 to N Yorks.[5] *Parl* Seq 26.

BURTON UPON URE
[N Riding] Tp in Masham AP, sep CP 1866.[2] *LG* E Hang Wap, Bedale PLU, Masham USD, UD (1894—1934), Masham RD (1934—74). Bdry: 1883,[16] 1886.[382] Transf 1974 to N Yorks.[5] *Parl* Seq 14.

BURYTHORPE
AP [E Riding] *LG* Seq 2. Civ bdry: 1935 (gains Eddlethorpe CP, Kennythorpe CP, Menethorpe CP).[13] Transf 1974 to N Yorks.[5] *Parl* Seq 1. *Eccl* Buckr. RDn (until 1857), W Buckr. RDn (1857—66), Pockl. RDn (1866—87), Settr. RDn (1887—1922), Buckr. RDn (1922—*).

GREAT BUSBY
[N Riding] Tp in Stokesley AP, sep CP 1866.[2] *LG* Seq 58. Transf 1974 to N Yorks.[5] *Parl* Seq 11.

LITTLE BUSBY
[N Riding] Organisation as for Great Busby.

BUSLINGTHORPE
EP [W Riding] Cr 1849 from Woodhouse EP, Little London EP, Leeds AP.[54] Pontef. RDn (1849—57), Leeds RDn (1857—1955). Bdry: 1869 (help cr Sheepscar St Clement EP,[383] 1883 (help cr Potter Newton EP),[113] 1902.[368] Abol 1955 ent to Woodhouse EP.[384]

BUTTERSHAW
EP [W Riding] Cr 1842 from Bradford AP.[315] Pontef. RDn (1842—57), Bradf RDn (1857—1921), Bowl. RDn (1921—71), Bowl. & Bradf RDn (1971—*). Bdry: 1850 (help cr Blackfoot EP),[174] 1924,[89] 1959 (help cr Buttershaw St Aidan EP),[320] 1967.[194]

BUTTERSHAW ST AIDAN
EP [W Riding] Cr 1959 from Bradford AP, Great Horton EP, Clayton EP, Shelf EP, Buttershaw EP.[320] Horton RDn (1959—71), Bowl. & Horton RDn (1971—*).

BUTTERWICK
[N Riding] Tp in Barton le Street AP, sep CP 1866.[2] *LG* Seq 65. Transf 1974 to N Yorks.[5] *Parl* Seq 16.

BUTTERWICK
[E Riding] Tp in Foxholes AP (orig chap in Burton Agnes AP, qv), sep CP 1866,[2] sep EP 1790.[9] *LG* Dick. Wap, Driff. PLU, RSD, RD. Abol civ 1935

to help cr Foxholes CP.[13] *Parl* E Riding (1832—85), Buckr. Dv (1885—1948). *Eccl* Dick. RDn (1790—1857), N Dick. RDn (1857—66), Scarb. RDn (1866—87), Buckr. RDn (1887—1922), Scarb. RDn (1922—47). Abol eccl 1947 to help cr Foxholes with Butterwick EP.[22]

OLD BYLAND
AP [N Riding] *LG* Seq 25. Transf 1974 to N Yorks.[5] *Parl* Seq 16. *Eccl* Seq 26.

BYLAND ABBEY
[N Riding] Tp in Coxwold AP, sep CP 1866.[2] *LG* Birdf. Wap, Helm. PLU, RSD. Abol 1887 to help cr Byland with Wass CP.[385] *Parl* N Riding (1832—85), Thirsk & Malton Dv (1885—1918).

BYLAND WITH WASS
CP [N Riding] Cr 1887 by union Byland Abbey CP, Wass CP.[385] *LG* Birdf. Wap, Helm. PLU, RSD, RD. Transf 1974 to N Yorks.[5] *Parl* Thirsk & Malton Dv/CC (1918—*).

BYRAM CUM POOLE
[W Riding] Tp in Brotherton AP, sep CP 1866.[2] *LG* Bark. Ash Wap, Gt Preston GilbU (until 1862), Pontef. PLU (1862—91), RSD. Abol 1891 to help cr Byram cum Sutton CP.[386] *Parl* W Riding (1832—67), N'rn Dv of W Riding (1867—85), Bark. Ash Dv (1885—1918).

BYRAM CUM SUTTON
CP [W Riding] Cr 1891 by union Byram cum Poole CP, Sutton CP.[386] *LG* Pontef. PLU, RSD, RD (1894—1938), Osg. RD (1938—74). Transf 1974 to N Yorks.[5] *Parl* Pontef. Dv (1918—48), Goole CC (1948—*).

CADEBY
[W Riding] Tp in Sprotbrough AP, sep CP 1866.[2] *LG* Seq 117. Bdry: 1921 (loses pt to Conisbrough AP as latter [enlarged] constituted Conisbrough UD).[387] Transf 1974 to S Yorks.[5] *Parl* Seq 44.

CALDBERGH WITH EAST SCRAETON
[N Riding] Tp in Coverham AP, sep CP 1866.[2] *LG* Seq 53. Transf 1974 to N Yorks.[5] *Parl* Seq 13.

CALDWELL
[N Riding] Tp in Stanwick AP, sep CP 1866,[2] sep EP 1840.[9] *LG* Seq 38. Transf 1974 to N Yorks.[5] *Parl* Seq 14. *Eccl* Richm. RDn (1840—57), Richm. West RDn (1857—*).

CALTON
[W Riding] Tp in Kirkby in Malham Dale AP, sep CP 1866.[2] *LG* Seq 112. Transf 1974 to N Yorks.[5] *Parl* Seq 41.

CALVERLEY
AP [W Riding] lncl chap Idle (sep CP 1866,[2] sep EP 1717,[9] eccl refounded 1878[337]), chap Pudsey (sep CP 1866,[2] sep EP 1733,[9] eccl refounded 1878[337]), tp Bolton (sep CP 1866[2]), tp Calverley with Farsley (sep CP 1866,[2] 'Farsley' a sep EP 1844[73]) so that 'Calverley' has no sep civ identity 1866—94 (see following entry). *LG* Morley Wap. *Parl* W Riding (1832—67). *Eccl* Pontef. RDn (1717—1857), Bradf RDn (1857—1921), Calverley RDn (1921—*). Addtl eccl bdry alt: 1878 (cr Bolton St James EP),[198] 1913 (help cr Thornbury EP),[93] 1959 (incl help cr Woodhall EP).[320]
CP [W Riding] Cr 1894 from the pt of Calverley with

Farsley CP in Calverley UD.[257] *LG* N Bierley PLU, Calverley UD. Abol 1937 ent to Pudsey MB & CP.[31] *Parl* Pudsey & Otley Dv (1918—48).

CALVERLEY WITH FARSLEY

[W Riding] Tp in Calverley AP, sep CP 1866.[2] *LG* Morley Wap, Bradf PLU (1837—48), N Bierley PLU (1848—94), pt Calverley USD (reduced pt 1882—94), pt Farsley USD, pt Bradf MB ([hmlt Thornbury, not sep civ], 1882—89), pt Bradf USD (1882—94), pt Bradf CB (1889—94). Abol 1894 the pt in Farsley UD cr Farsley CP, the pt in Calverley CP cr Calvery CP, the pt in Bradf CB cr Thornbury CP.[257] *Parl* W Riding (1832—67), E'rn Dv of W Riding (1867—85), pt Pudsey Dv, pt Bradf Parl Bor (1885—1918).

CAMBLESFORTH

[W Riding] Tp in Drax AP, sep CP 1866.[2] *LG* Seq 80. Bdry: 1883,[52] 1883.[388] Transf 1974 to N Yorks.[5] *Parl* Seq 24.

CAMPSALL

AP [W Riding] Incl tp Askern (sep CP 1866,[2] sep EP 1852[138]), tp Fenwick (sep CP 1866,[2] sep EP 1852[138]), pt tp Moss (sep CP 1866,[2] sep EP 1875 from 5 pars [incl Fenwick EP, orig in this par, qv][11]), tp Norton (sep CP 1866[2]), pt tp Sutton (sep CP 1866[2]). *LG* Osg. Wap, Donc. PLU, RSD, RD. Addtl civ bdry alt: 1883.[42] Abol 1938 ent to Norton CP.[28] *Parl* W Riding (1832—67), N'rn Dv of W Riding (1867—85), Osg. Dv (1885—1918), Don Valley Dv (1918—48).

CANTLEY

AP [W Riding] *LG* Seq 117. Civ bdry: 1936 (loses pt to Donc. CB [assoc with W Riding] & AP),[132] 1951 (loses pt to Donc. CB [assoc with W Riding] & AP).[389] Transf 1974 to S Yorks.[5] *Parl* Seq 44. Parl bdry: 1951.[390] *Eccl* Seq 40.

CARBROOK

EP [W Riding] Cr 1874 from Attercliffe EP, Darnall EP.[148] Sheff RDn (1874—1942), Attercliffe RDn (1942—46). Abol 1946 to help cr Attercliffe with Carbrook EP.[150]

CARLETON

AP [W Riding] Usual civ spelling; for eccl see 'Carleton in Craven'. *LG* Seq 112. Civ bdry: 1894 (cr Lothersdale CP).[349] Transf 1974 to N Yorks.[5] *Parl* Seq 41.

CARLETON

[W Riding] Tp in Pontefract AP, sep CP 1866,[2] sep EP 1869.[109] *LG* Osg. Wap, Gt Preston GiblU (until 1869), Pontef. PLU (1869—1930), RSD, RD. Abol 1937 ent to Pontefract AP.[31] *Parl* Pontef. Parl Bor (1832—1918), Pontef. Dv (1918—48). *Eccl* Pontef. RDn. Eccl bdry: 1956.[149]

CARLETON IN CRAVEN

AP [W Riding] Usual eccl spelling; for civ see first 'Carleton' above. *Eccl* Seq 37. Eccl bdry: 1844 (help cr Lothersdale EP).[247]

CARLIN HOW—see following entry

CARLIN HOW WITH SKINNINGROVE

EP [N Riding] Cr 1952 from Brotton EP, Lofthouses EP.[368] Guisb. RDn. Later simply 'Carlin How'.

CARLINGHOW

EP [W Riding] Cr 1880 from Brownhill EP, Staincliffe

EP, Batley AP.[198] Dewsb. RDn.

CARLTON

[N Riding] Prob orig chap in Rudby in Cleveland AP, perhaps sep par early 17th cent,[391] sep civ identity early, sep EP no later than 1726.[9] *LG* Seq 58. Transf 1974 to N Yorks.[5] *Parl* Seq 11. *Eccl* Clev RDn (cr—1862), N'allert. RDn (1862—1916), Stokes. RDn (1916—*).

CARLTON

[W Riding] Tp in Guiseley AP, sep CP 1866.[2] *LG* Seq 104. Transf 1974 to W Yorks. *Parl* Seq 30.

CARLTON

[W Riding] Tp in Royston AP, sep CP 1866,[2] sep EP 1881.[117] *LG* Staincr. Wap, Barnsley PLU, RSD, RD. Abol civ 1938 pt to Royston AP, pt to Barnsley CB (assoc with W Riding) & CP.[28] *Parl* W Riding (1832—67), S'rn Dv of W Riding (1867—85), Barnsley Dv (1885—1918), Hemsw. Dv (1918—48). *Eccl* Hemsw. RDn (1881—1927), Barnsley RDn (1927—*). Eccl bdry: 1957,[299] 1973 (help cr Athersley EP).[145]

CARLTON

[W Riding] Chap (in pec jurisd Selby, 1440—1539) in Snaith AP, sep CP 1866,[2] sep EP 1834.[9] *LG* Seq 80. Civ bdry: 1883.[388] Transf 1974 to N Yorks.[5] *Parl* Seq 24. *Eccl* Pontef. RDn (1834—62), Selby RDn (1862—71), Snaith RDn (1871—*).

CARLTON HIGHDALE

[N Riding] Tp ln Coverham AP, sep CP 1866.[2] *LG* Seq 53. Bdry: 1883.[16] Transf 1974 to N Yorks.[5] *Parl* Seq 14.

CARLTON HUSTHWAITE

[N Riding] Chap (not sep eccl, orig pec jurisd Husthwaite prebend) in Husthwaite AP, sep CP 1866.[2] *LG* Seq 24. Transf 1974 to N Yorks.[5] *Parl* Seq 16.

CARLTON MINIOTT

[N Riding] Chap pt in Thirsk AP, pt in Kirby Knowle AP, sep CP 1866,[2] sep EP 1747.[9] *LG* Seq 27. Transf 1974 to N Yorks.[5] *Parl* Seq 16. *Eccl* Bulmer RDn (1747—1862), Thirsk RDn (1862—*).

CARLTON TOWN

[N Riding] Tp in Coverham AP, sep CP 1866,[2] sep EP 1726,[9] sep eccl status not sustained. *LG* Seq 53. Transf 1974 to N Yorks.[5] *Parl* Seq 13.

CARNABY

AP [E Riding] Orig chap in Hunmanby AP, sep par before 1268.[392] Incl chaps Auburn, Fraisthorpe (each a sep CP 1866 [hmlt Auburn pt in Carnaby AP, pt in Bridlington AP],[2] inhabitants of Auburn told to attend chap Fraisthorpe, the 2 a sep EP 1731 as 'Auburn with Fraisthorpe',[152] 'Fraisthorpe' a sep EP 1824 [the remainder to be Auburn EP] but sep eccl status not sustained and later considered in Carnaby AP, eccl severed 1929 to help cr Barmston with Fraisthorpe EP.[186] *LG* Seq 5. Addtl civ bdry alt: 1935 (incl gains Haisthorpe CP).[13] Transf 1974 to Humb.[5] *Parl* Seq 2. *Eccl* Dick. RDn (until 1862), S Dick. RDn (1862—66), Bridl. RDn (1866—*).

CARPERBY CUM THORESBY

[N Riding] Tp in Aysgarth AP, sep CP 1866.[2] *LG* Seq 51. Transf 1974 to N Yorks.[5] *Parl* Seq 14.

CARR HOUSE AND ELM FIELD

[W Riding] Ex-par place, sep CP 1858.[393] *LG* Straff. & Tick. Wap, Donc. PLU (1862—1914), RSD, RD. Abol 1914 ent to Donc. MB & AP.[167] *Parl* W Riding (1832—67), S'rn Dv of W Riding (1867—85), Donc. Dv (1885—1918).

CARTHORPE

[N Riding] Tp in Burneston AP, sep CP 1866.[2] *LG* Seq 40. Transf 1974 to N Yorks.[5] *Parl* Seq 18.

CARTWORTH

[W Riding] Tp in Kirkburton AP, sep CP 1866,[2] pt eccl severed 1858 to help refound Holmfirth EP.[293] *LG* Agb. Wap, Hudd. PLU, pt Cartworth USD (1875—84), pt Scholes USD (1875—86), pt Austonley USD (1886—94), pt Holmf. USD (1884—94), Holmf. UD (1894—1921). Bdry: 1883,[52] 1886.[151] Abol 1921 to help cr Holmfirth CP.[159] *Parl* W Riding (1832—67), S'rn Dv of W Riding (1867—85), Holmf. Dv (1885—1918), Colne Valley Dv (1918—48).

CARVER STREET—see SHEFFIELD ST MATTHEW, CARVER STREET

CASTLE BOLTON

[N Riding] Chap in Wensley AP, sep CP 1866,[2] sep EP 1748 as 'Bolton',[9] qv. *LG* Seq 53. Transf 1974 to N Yorks.[5] *Parl* Seq 14.

CASTLEFORD

AP [W Riding] Incl tp Glass Houghton (sep CP 1866,[2] sep EP 1923[188]). *LG* Osg. Wap, Gt Preston GilbU (until 1869), Pontef. PLU (1869—1930), Castlef. USD, UD (1894—1955), MB (1955—74). Addtl civ bdry alt: 1937 (incl gains Glass Houghton CP),[31] 1938.[306] Transf 1974 to W Yorks.[5] *Parl* W Riding (1832—67), E'rn Dv of W Riding (1867—85), Osg. Dv (1885—1918), Norm. Dv (1918—48), Pontef. BC (1948—70), Pontef. & Castlef. BC (1970—*). *Eccl* Ainsty RDn (until 1820), New Ainsty RDn (1820—57), Pontef. RDn (1857—*). Addtl eccl bdry alt: 1924 (cr Smawthorne EP, later called 'Castleford St Michael and All Angels').[89]

CASTLEFORD ST MICHAEL AND ALL ANGELS

EP [W Riding] Name used now for EP cr 1924 as 'Smawthorne', qv.

CASTLEY

[W Riding] Tp in Leathley AP, sep CP 1866.[2] *LG* Seq 92. Bdry: 1883.[52] Transf 1974 to N Yorks.[5] *Parl* Seq 30.

CATCLIFFE

[W Riding] Tp in Rotherham AP, sep CP 1866.[2] *LG* Seq 119. Bdry: 1901 (loses pt to Sheff CB [assoc with W Riding] & AP).[394] Transf 1974 to S Yorks.[5] *Parl* Seq 55.

CATFOSS

[E Riding] Tp in Sigglesthorpe AP, sep CP 1866.[2] *LG* Hold. Wap, Skirl. PLU, RSD, RD. Abol 1935 to help cr Seaton CP.[13] *Parl* E Riding (1832—85), Hold. Dv (1885—1918).

CATTAL

[W Riding] Tp in Hunsingore AP, sep CP 1866.[2] *LG* Seq 82. Transf 1974 to N Yorks.[5] *Parl* Seq 36.

CATTERICK

AP [N Riding] Tp 'Catterick' in E Hang Wap as was chap Hipswell (sep CP 1866,[2] sep EP 1738,[9] eccl refounded 1897 [incl pt Patrick Brompton AP, pt tp Scotton[247]], pt tp Scotton (sep CP 1866,[2] eccl severed 1897 to help refound Hipswell EP[247]), tps Appleton, Brough, Colburn, Killerby, Tunstall (each a sep CP 1866,[2] none sep eccl hence this par eccl 'Catterick with Tunstall', qv); incl in E Gill Wap chap Bolton upon Swale, tps Ellerton upon Swale (sep EP 1732,[9] sep eccl status not sustained), Kiplin, Scorton, Uckerby, Whitwell (each a sep CP 1866,[2] the 6 eccl united 1781 to cr 'Bolton upon Swale' EP,[9] eccl refounded 1885[347]); incl in W Hang Wap pt chap Hudswell (sep CP 1866,[2] sep EP 1739[9]). *LG* Richm. PLU, RSD, RD. Transf 1974 to N Yorks.[5] *Parl* Pt Richm. Parl Bor (chap Hipswell, until gains sep civ identity), remainder and later, Seq 14.

CATTERICK AND TUNSTALL

AP [N Riding] Usual eccl spelling; for civ and civ and eccl sep chaps and tps, see prev entry. *Eccl* Catt. RDn (until 1857), Catt. East RDn (1857—63), Richm. North RDn (1863—66), Richm. West RDn (1866—*). Addtl eccl bdry alt: 1939,[395] 1958.[396]

CATTERTON

[Ainsty (W Riding until 1449 and from 1836, indept jurisd 1449—1836)] Tp in Tadcaster AP, sep CP 1866.[2] *LG* Seq 70. Transf 1974 to N Yorks.[5] *Parl* Seq 23.

CATTON

AP [E Riding] Pt Harth. Wap (chap Full Sutton [sep par early 13th cent[241]], tps High Catton, Low Catton, East Stamford Bridge [each a sep CP 1866[2]]), pt Ouse & Derw. Wap (tp Kexby [sep CP 1866,[2] sep EP 1853[64]], tp West Stamford Bridge with Scoreby [sep CP 1866[2]]) so that 'Catton' has no sep civ identity after 1866; because area Stamford Bridge has no sep eccl identity, this par eccl 'Catton with Stamford Bridge', qv. *Parl* E Riding (1832—67).

CP [N Riding] Cr 1935 by union High Catton CP, Low Catton CP.[13] *LG* Pockl. RD. Transf 1974 to Humb.[5] *Parl* Bev. CC (1948—55), Howdensh. CC (1955—*).

CATTON

[N Riding] Tp in Topcliffe AP, sep CP 1866.[2] *LG* Seq 27. Transf 1974 to N Yorks.[5] *Parl* Seq 16.

HIGH CATTON

[E Riding] Tp in Catton AP, sep CP 1866.[2] *LG* Harth. Wap, Pockl. PLU, RSD, RD. Abol 1935 to help cr Catton CP.[13] *Parl* E Riding (1832—85), Howdensh. Dv (1885—1948).

LOW CATTON

[E Riding] Organisation as for High Catton.

CATTON WITH STAMFORD BRIDGE

AP [E Riding] Usual eccl spelling; for civ and civ and eccl sep chap and tps, see Catton AP. *Eccl* Seq 9.

CATWICK

AP [E Riding] *LG* Seq 16. Transf 1974 to Humb.[5] *Parl* Seq 5. *Eccl* Hold. RDn (until 1849), S Hold. RDn (1849—57), S Harth. RDn (1857—66), Hornsea RDn (1866—1916), N Hold. RDn (1916—56), Bev. RDn (1956—*).

CAUNTLEY WITH DOWBIGGIN

EP [W Riding] Cr 1856 from Sedbergh AP.[311] Clapham RDn (1856—1921), Ewecr. RDn (1921—26),

Sedbergh RDn (1926—71), Ewecr. RDn (1971—74). Abol 1974 to help cr Sedbergh, Cauntley and Garsdale EP.[397]

NORTH CAVE

AP [E Riding] lncl tps North Cave with Everthorpe and Drewton, South Cliffe (each a sep CP 1866[2]) so that 'North Cave' has no sep civ identity 1866—1935 (see following entry). *LG* Harth. Wap. *Parl* E Riding (1832—67). *Eccl* Harth. & Hull RDn (until 1857), S Harth. RDn (1857—66), Bev. RDn (1866—71), Howden RDn (1871—87). Eccl bdry: 1875.[398] Gains eccl 1887 tp North Cliffe from Sancton AP[399] so that this par 'North Cave with Cliffe' thereafter, qv.

CP [E Riding] Cr 1935 from North Cave with Everthorpe and Drewton CP.[13] *LG* Howden RD. Transf 1974 to Humb.[5] *Parl* Bev. CC (1948—55), Howdensh. CC (1955—*).

NORTH CAVE WITH CLIFFE

EP [E Riding] Cr 1887 by union North Cave AP (eccl incl tp South Cliffe), tp North Cliffe from Santon AP.[399] Howden RDn.

NORTH CAVE WITH EVERTHORPE AND DREWTON

[E Riding] Tp in North Cave AP, sep CP 1866.[2] *LG* Harth. Wap, Howden PLU, RSD, RD. Abol 1935 pt to cr North Cave CP, pt to Hotham AP, pt to South Cave AP.[13] *Parl* E Riding (1832—85), Howdensh. Dv (1885—1948).

SOUTH CAVE

AP [E Riding] Incl tp Broomfleet, tp Faxfleet (each a sep CP 1866,[2] eccl united 1862 as 'Broomfleet' EP,[136] the latter later called 'Broomfleet with Faxfleet'). *LG* Harth. Wap, Bev. PLU, South Cave & Wallingfen USD, Bev. RD. Civ bdry: 1935.[13] Transf 1974 to Humb.[5] *Parl* Seq 6. *Eccl* Pec jurisd S Cave prebend (until 1549), pec jurisd Dean & Chapter of York (1549—1836), Harth. & Hull RDn (1836—57), S Harth. RDn (1857—62), Bev. RDn (1862—66), Howden RDn (1866—1968). Abol eccl 1968 to help cr South Cave and Ellerker EP.[339]

SOUTH CAVE AND ELLERKER

EP [E Riding] Cr 1968 by union South Cave AP, pt Brantingham with Ellerker AP.[339] Howden RDn.

CAWOOD

[W Riding] Chap in Wistow AP, sep civ identity early, sep EP 1810.[9] *LG* Seq 80. Transf 1974 to N Yorks.[5] *Parl* Seq 24. *Eccl* Seq 32. Eccl bdry: 1963.[400]

CAWTHORN

[N Riding] Tp in Middleton AP, sep CP 1866.[2] *LG* Seq 61. Transf 1974 to N Yorks.[5] *Parl* Seq 22.

CAWTHORNE

[W Riding] Chap in Silkstone AP, sep par 1608.[401] *LG* Seq 114. Transf 1974 to S Yorks.[5] *Parl* Seq 50. *Eccl* Donc. RDn (1608—1838), Pontef. RDn (1838—57), Silkst. RDn (1857—1927), Barnsley RDn (1927—*). Eccl bdry: 1869 (help cr Hoyland Swaine EP).[109]

CAWTON

[N Riding] Tp in Gilling AP, sep CP 1866.[2] *LG* Seq 63. Transf 1974 to N Yorks.[5] *Parl* Seq 21.

CAYTON

CP [N Riding] Cr 1886 by union Osgodby CP, Cayton with Deepdale and Killerby CP.[402] *LG* Pick. Lythe Wap, Scarb. PLU, RSD, RD. Bdry: 1886,[403] 1934,[3] 1953.[404] Transf 1974 to N Yorks.[5] *Parl* Scarb. & Whitby Dv/CC (1918—70), Scarb. CC (1970—*).

CAYTON WITH DEEPDALE AND KILLERBY

[N Riding] Tp in Seamer AP, sep CP 1866,[2] not sep eccl hence that par eccl 'Seamer with Cayton and East Ayton' until divided eccl 1961 into 2 EPs of 'Seamer with East Ayton', 'Cayton with Eastfield'.[396] *LG* Pick. Lythe Wap, Scarb. PLU, RSD. Abol 1886 to help cr Cayton CP.[402] *Parl* N Riding (1832—85), Whitby Dv (1885—1918).

CAYTON WITH EASTFIELD

EP [N Riding] Cr 1961 when Seamer with Cayton and East Ayton AP (see 'Seamer' for civ division and organisation) divided into 2 EPs of Cayton with Eastfield, Seamer with East Ayton.[39] Scarb. RDn.

CHAPEL LE DALE

EP [W Riding] Refounding 1864 of EP cr 1737 as 'Ingleton Fell', incl in 1864 pt lngleton EP.[405] Clapham RDn (1864—1921), Ewecr. RDn (1921—*).

CHAPELTHORPE

EP [W Riding] Cr 1735 from Sandal Magna AP,[9] eccl refounded 1843.[406] Pontef. RDn (1735—1857), Wakef RDn (1857—1973), Chevet RDn (1973—*).

CHAPELTOWN

EP [W Riding] Cr 1844 from Ecclesfield AP.[55] Donc. RDn (1844—62), Ecclesfield RDn (1862—1942), Tankersley RDn (1942—*). Bdry: 1925 (help cr Mortomley EP).[407]

CHARLESTOWN

EP [W Riding] Cr 1862 from Copley EP.[92] Halifax RDn.

CHEAPSIDES

[E Riding] Ex-par place, sep CP 1858,[393] eccl severed 1895 to help cr Newport EP.[284] *LG* Howden Wap, PLU (1858—92), RSD. Abol 1892 ent to Scalby CP.[408] *Parl* E Riding (1832—85), Howdensh. Dv (1885—1918).

CHEVET

[W Riding] Tp in Royston AP, sep CP 1866.[2] *LG* Staincr. Wap, Wakef PLU (soon after 1837[112]—1930), RSD, RD. Transf 1974 to W Yorks.[5] *Parl* Seq 54.

CHURWELL

[W Riding] Tp in Batley AP, sep CP 1866.[2] *LG* Morley Wap, Carlton GilbU (until 1869), Holbeck PLU (1869—1930), Churwell USD (1875—91), Morley MB (1891—1937), Morley USD (1891—94). Abol 1937 ent to Morley CP.[31] *Parl* W Riding (1832—67), E'rn Dv of W Riding (1867—85), Pudsey Dv (1885—1918), Batley & Morley Parl Bor (1918—48).

CLAPHAM

AP [W Riding] Incl tp Austwick, tp Lawkland (each a sep CP 1866,[2] the gtr pt of former and ent latter eccl united 1843 to cr 'Austwick' EP,[9] eccl refounded 1879[22]), tp Clapham cum Newby (sep CP 1866[2]) so that 'Clapham' has no sep civ identity after 1866. *LG* Staincl. & Ewc. Wap. *Parl* W Riding (1832—67). *Eccl* Seq 56.

CLAPHAM CUM NEWBY
[W Riding] Tp in Clapham AP, sep CP 1866.[2] *LG* Seq 111. Transf 1974 to N Yorks.[5] *Parl* Seq 41.

CLARETON
[W Riding] Tp in Allerton Mauleverer AP, sep CP 1866.[2] *LG* Claro Wap, Gt Ouseb. GilbU (orig rated together with Coneythorpe, in this union until 1854), Gt Ouseb. PLU (1854—88), RSD. Abol 1888 to help cr Coneythorpe and Clareton CP.[409] *Parl* W Riding (1832—67), N'rn Dv of W Riding (1867—85), Ripon Dv (1885—1918).

CLAXTON
[N Riding] Chap in Bossall AP, sep CP 1866,[2] eccl severed 1861 to help cr Sand Hutton EP.[292] *LG* Seq 32. Transf 1974 to N Yorks.[5] *Parl* Seq 16.

CLAYTON
[W Riding] Tp in Bradford AP, sep CP 1866,[2] pt eccl severed 1845 to help cr Queen's Head EP,[256] the remainder cr 1858 'Clayton' EP.[121] *LG* Morley Wap, Bradf PLU (1837—48), N Bierley PLU (1848—1930), pt Clayton USD, pt Queensbury USD, Clayton UD (1894—1930), Bradf CB (1930—74). Civ bdry: 1894 (loses the pt in Queensbury UD to help cr Queensbury CP).[410] Transf 1974 to W Yorks.[5] *Parl* W Riding (1832—67), E'rn Dv of W Riding (1867—85), Shipley Dv (1885—1918); see Part III of the *Guide* for composition of Bradf Parl Bors/BCs (1918—*) by wards of the CB. *Eccl* Bradf RDn (1858—1921), Horton RDn (1921—71), Bowl. & Horton RDn (1971—*). Eccl bdry: 1959 (help cr Buttershaw St Aidan EP).[320]

CLAYTON WEST
[W Riding] Tp in High Hoyland AP, sep CP 1866.[2] *LG* Staincr. Wap, not in a PLU (until 1849), Penist. PLU (1849—1930), Clayton West USD, UD (1894—1938), Denby Dale UD (1938—74). Transf 1974 to W Yorks.[5] *Parl* Seq 51.

CLAYTON WITH FRICKLEY
AP [W Riding] Orig Frickley AP with Clayton chap, few inhabitants in Frickley, name as above used from 1810 when so augmented as a perpetual curacy.[411] *LG* Straff. & Tick. Wap, Donc. PLU, RSD, RD. Civ bdry: 1908.[207] Transf 1974 to S Yorks.[5] *Parl* Seq 44. *Eccl* Seq 46.

CLEASBY
[N Riding] Chap in Stanwick AP, sep civ identity early, sep EP 1715.[9] *LG* Seq 33. Civ bdry: 1883,[52] 1967 (gains pt Blackwell CP, Durham).[412] Transf 1974 to N Yorks.[5] *Parl* Seq 14. *Eccl* Richm. RDn (1715—1857), Richm. East RDn (1857—*). Eccl bdry: 1958.[413]

CLECKHEATON
[W Riding] Chap in Birstall AP, sep CP 1866,[2] sep EP 1732,[9] eccl refounded 1842.[273] *LG* Morley Wap, Bradf PLU (1837—48), N Bierley PLU (1848—1930), Cleckheaton USD, UD (1894—1915), Spenb. UD (1915—55), MB (1955—74). Civ bdry: 1937 (incl gains Hunsworth CP).[31] Transf 1974 to W Yorks.[5] *Parl* Seq 38. *Eccl* Pontef. RDn (1732—1857), Dewsb. RDn (1857—66), Birstall

RDn (1866—*). Eccl bdry: 1858,[414] 1888,[74] 1878 (help cr Cleckheaton St Luke EP),[415] 1900,[188] 1929 (help cr Scholes EP).[416]

CLECKHEATON ST LUKE
EP [W Riding] Cr 1878 from Whitechapel EP, Cleckheaton EP, Liversedge EP.[415] Birstall RDn.

CLIFFE
CP [E Riding] Cr 1935 by union Cliffe cum Lund CP, South Duffield CP.[13] *LG* Derw. RD. Transf 1974 to N Yorks.[5] *Parl* Bev. CC (1948—55), Howdensh. CC (1955—*).

CLIFFE
[N Riding] Tp in Manfield AP, sep CP 1866.[2] *LG* W Gill. Wap, Darl. PLU, RSD, Croft RD. Transf 1974 to N Yorks.[5] *Parl* Seq 14.

NORTH CLIFFE
[E Riding] Tp in Sancton AP, sep CP 1866,[2] eccl severed 1887 to help cr North Cave with Cliffe EP.[399] *LG* Harth. Wap, Pockl. PLU, RSD, RD. Bdry: 1884.[417] Abol 1935 ent to South Cliffe CP.[13] *Parl* E Riding (1832—85), Howdensh. Dv (1885—1948).

SOUTH CLIFFE
[E Riding] Tp in North Cave AP, sep CP 1866.[2] *LG* Seq 12. Bdry: 1935 (gains North Cliffe CP).[13] Transf 1974 to Humb.[5] *Parl* Seq 7.

CLIFFE CUM LUND
[E Riding] Tp in Hemingbrough AP, sep CP 1866.[2] *LG* Ouse & Derw. Wap, Selby PLU, RSD, Riccall RD. Bdry: 1888 (gains pt Brayton AP, pt Drax AP, both W Riding).[341] Abol 1935 pt to Hemimgbrough AP, pt to help cr Cliffe CP.[13] *Parl* E Riding (1832—85), Howdensh. Dv (1885—1948).

CLIFFORD
CP [W Riding] Cr 1896 from Clifford with Boston CP.[295] *LG* Wethb. PLU, RD. Transf 1974 to W Yorks.[5] *Parl* Bark. Ash Dv/CC (1918—*).

CLIFFORD
EP [W Riding] Cr 1842 from Bramham AP,[9] refounded 1842[294]; for civ see following entry. New Ainsty RDn (1842—62), Tadc. RDn (1862—71), Selby RDn (1871—1921), Tadc. RDn (1921—*).

CLIFFORD WITH BOSTON
[W Riding] Tp pt in Bramham AP, pt in Collingham AP, sep CP 1866[2]; for eccl see prev entry. *LG* Bark. Ash Wap, Barwick GilbU (until 1869), Wethb. PLU (1869—96), RSD, RD. Abol 1896 to cr the 2 CPs of Clifford, Boston Spa.[295] *Parl* W Riding (1832—67), N'rn Dv of W Riding (1867—85), Bark. Ash Dv (1885—1918).

CLIFTON
[N Riding] Tp pt in York St Michael le Belfry AP, pt in York St Olave, Marygate AP, sep CP 1866[2]; for eccl see 'Clifton St Philip and St James'. *LG* Bulmer Wap, York PLU, pt York MB (1884—89), pt York CB (1889—94), pt York USD (1884—94), York RSD (ent 1875—84, pt 1884—94). Abol 1894 the pt in the CB cr Clifton Within CP, the remainder cr Clifton Without CP in N Riding.[418] *Parl* N Riding (1832—85), pt York Parl Bor, pt Thirsk & Malton Dv in N Riding (1885—1918).

CLIFTON
[W Riding] Chap in Dewsbury AP, sep CP 1866,[2]

eccl severed 1742 to help cr Hartshead cum Clifton EP,[9] 'Clifton' a sep EP 1887 from the latter (remainder to be 'Hartshead').[419] *LG* Morley Wap, Halifax PLU, RSD, RD. Abol 1937 pt to Brigh. MB & CP, pt to Spenb. UD & to Cleckheaton CP, pt to Spenb. UD & to Liversedge CP.[31] *Parl* W Riding (1832—67), E'rn Dv of W Riding (1867—85), Spen Valley Dv (1885—1918), Elland Dv (1918—48). *Eccl* Birstall RDn (1887—1913), Halifax RDn (1913—27), Birstall RDn (1927—54), Halifax RDn (1954—1967), Brigh. & Elland RDn (1967—*).

CLIFTON

EP [W Riding] Cr 1937 from Rotherham AP.[420] Rotherh. RDn. Bdry: 1950 (help cr Herringthorpe EP),[212] 1952,[322] 1952.[421]

CLIFTON ST PHILIP AND ST JAMES

EP [N Riding] Cr 1871 from York St Michael le Belfry AP, York St Olave with St Giles EP, York St Thomas EP[326]; for civ see 1st 'Clifton' above. City of York RDn. Bdry: 1930 (help cr York St Luke EP),[263] 1961.[44]

CLIFTON UPON URE

[N Riding] Tp in Thornton Watlass AP, sep CP 1866.[2] *LG* Seq 48. Transf 1974 to N Yorks.[5] *Parl* Seq 15.

CLIFTON WITH NORWOOD

[W Riding] Tp in Fewston AP, sep CP 1866.[2] *LG* Claro Wap, not in a PLU (until 1861), Wharfed. PLU (1861—1930), RSD, RD. Renamed 1950 'Norwood'.[422] *Parl* W Riding (1832—67), N'rn Dv of W Riding (1867—85), Otley Dv (1885—1918), Pudsey & Otley Dv (1918—48), Ripon CC (1948—70).

CLIFTON WITHIN

CP [York CB] Cr 1894 from the pt of Clifton CP (ent N Riding before pt incl in CB 1884) in York CB.[418] *LG* York PLU, CB. Abol 1900 to help cr York CP.[423]

CLIFTON WITHOUT

CP [N Riding] Cr 1894 from the pt of Clifton CP not in York CB.[418] *LG* York PLU, Flaxton RD. Bdry: 1934 (loses pt to York CB [not assoc with a Riding] & CP),[3] 1968 (loses pt to York CB [not assoc with a Riding] & CP).[424] Transf 1974 to N Yorks.[5] *Parl* Thirsk & Malton Dv/CC (1918—*).

CLINT

[W Riding] Tp in Ripley AP, sep CP 1866.[2] *LG* Claro Wap, Pateley Br. PLU (soon after 1837[112]—1930), RSD, RD (1894—1937), Ripon & Pateley Br. RD (1937—74). Transf 1974 to N Yorks. *Parl* Seq 33.

CLIVIGER

Tp in Whalley AP, all in Lancs, pt Todmorden USD (o'wise Yorks W Riding) and hence pt in that admin co 1889, the Yorks pt severed 1894 to cr Cornholme CP.[425] See main entry in Lancs for other organisation of Cliviger.

CLOTHERHOLME

[W Riding] Tp in Ripon AP, sep CP 1866.[2] *LG* Seq 100. Bdry: 1900.[280] Transf 1974 to N Yorks.[5] *Parl* Seq 34.

CLOUGHTON

[N Riding] Chap in Scalby AP, sep CP 1866,[2] sep

EP 1874 (incl tp Staintondale [qv for sep civ identity] in same par).[148] *LG* Seq 62. Civ bdry: 1883,[16] 1887.[168] Transf 1974 to N Yorks.[5] *Parl* Seq 20. *Eccl* Scarb. RDn. Eccl bdry: 1914 (help cr Ravenscar EP),[168] 1932.[138]

COATES

[W Riding] Tp in Barnoldswick AP, sep CP 1866.[2] *LG* Staincl. & Ewc. Wap, Skipton PLU, RSD, RD. Abol 1923 ent to Barnoldswick UD & AP.[192] *Parl* W Riding (1832—67), N'rn Dv of W Riding (1867—85), Skipton Dv (1885—1948).

COATHAM

CP [N Riding] Cr 1899 from Kirkleatham AP.[426] *LG* Guisb. PLU, Redcar UD. Bdry: 1920.[427] Abol 1921 ent to Redcar CP.[428] *Parl* Clev Dv (1918—48).

EAST COATHAM

EP [N Riding] Cr 1854 from Kirkleatham AP.[368] Clev RDn (1854—62), Stokes. RDn (1862—78), Middlesb. RDn (1878—1924), Guisb. RDn (1924—*). Bdry: 1927 (help cr Dormanstown EP).[284]

COLBURN

[N Riding] Tp in Catterick AP, sep CP 1866.[2] *LG* Seq 50. Transf 1974 to N Yorks.[5] *Parl* Seq 6.

COLD KIRBY

[N Riding] Chap in Easingwold AP, sep civ identity early, sep EP 1737.[9] *LG* Seq 25. Transf 1974 to N Yorks.[5] *Parl* Seq 16. *Eccl* Seq 26.

COLDEN PARVA

[E Riding] Anc chap sometimes called 'church', swallowed up by sea, name retained eccl in 'Aldbrough with Colden Parva', qv.

COLEY

EP [W Riding] Cr 1749 from Halifax AP (incl pt tp Northowran).[9] Pontef. RDn (1749—1857), Halifax RDn (1857—1967), Brigh. & Elland RDn (1967—*). Bdry: 1855 (cr Haley Hill EP, later called 'Halifax All Souls'),[166] 1909 (help cr Northowram EP).[429]

COLLINGHAM

AP [W Riding] Incl pt tp Clifford with Boston (sep CP 1866[2]; 'Clifton' EP 1842 ent from the pt in Bramham AP, qv), tp Micklethwaite (sep CP 1866[2]). *LG* Seq 102. Addtl civ bdry alt: 1885,[430] 1937.[31] Transf 1974 to W Yorks.[5] *Parl* Seq 24. *Eccl* Seq 30.

COLNE VALLEY

CP [W Riding] Cr 1937 by union Marsden UD & CP, Scammonden UD & CP, Slaithwaite UD & CP, pt Linthwaite UD & CP, pt Golcar UD & CP.[31] *LG* Colne Valley UD. Transf 1974 to W Yorks.[5] *Parl* Colne Valley CC (1948—*).

COLSTERDALE

CP [N Riding] Cr 1894 from the pt of Healy with Sutton CP not in Masham UD.[431] *LG* Leyb. PLU, RD (1894—1934), Masham RD (1934—74). Bdry: 1934.[3] Transf 1974 to N Yorks.[5] *Parl* Richm. Dv/CC (1918—*).

COLTON

[Ainsty (W Riding until 1449 and from 1836, indept jurisd 1449—1836)] *LG* Seq 73. Transf 1974 to N Yorks.[5] *Parl* Seq 23.

COMMONDALE

[N Riding] Tp in Guisborough AP, sep CP 1866.[2]

LG Seq 55. Transf 1974 to N Yorks.[5] *Parl* Seq 12.

CONEYSTHORPE

[N Riding] Tp in Barton le Street AP, sep CP 1866.[2] *LG* Seq 29. Transf 1974 to N Yorks.[5] *Parl* Seq 16.

CONEYTHORPE

[W Riding] Tp in Goldsborough AP, sep CP 1866.[2] *LG* Claro Wap, Gt Ouseb. GilbU (until 1854), PLU (1854—88), RSD. Abol 1888 to help cr Coneythorpe and Clareton CP.[409] *Parl* W Riding (1832—67), N'rn Dv of W Riding (1867—85), Ripon Dv (1885—1918).

CONEYTHORPE AND CLARETON

CP [W Riding] Cr 1888 by union Coneythorpe CP, Clareton CP.[409] *LG* Claro Wap, Gt Ouseb. PLU, RSD, RD (1894—1938), Nidd. RD (1938—74). Transf 1974 to N Yorks.[5] *Parl* Ripon Dv (1918—48), Harrog. CC (1948—*).

CONISBROUGH

AP [W Riding] *LG* Staincl. & Ewc. Wap, Donc. PLU, RSD, RD (1894—1921) Conisbrough UD (1921—74). Civ bdry: 1881,[432] 1883,[42] 1921 (gains pts Cadeby CP, Denaby CP, loses pt to cr Conisbrough Parks CP, the remainder constituted Conisbrough UD).[387] Transf 1974 to S Yorks.[5] *Parl* Seq 46. *Eccl* Seq 40. Eccl bdry: 1898 (help cr Denaby Main EP),[63] 1953,[433] 1954 (help cr New Edlington EP),[434] 1956 (incl help cr Bramley EP).[215]

CONISBROUGH PARKS

CP [W Riding] Cr 1921 from the pt of Conisbrough AP (o'wise enlarged, qv) not transf from Donc. RD to constitute Conisbrough UD.[387] *LG* Donc. RD. Bdry: 1938.[76] Transf 1974 to S Yorks.[5] *Parl* Don Valley CC (1948—*).

CONISTON

[E Riding] Tp in Swine AP, sep CP 1866.[2] *LG* Seq 16. Bdry: 1935 (gains Thirtleby CP).[13] Transf 1974 to Humb.[5] *Parl* Seq 5.

CONISTON

[W Riding] Tp in Gargrave AP, sep CP 1866 as 'Coniston Cold',[2] qv, sep EP 1840,[9] eccl refounded 1847 from Gargrave AP, Kirkby Malham AP.[435] Craven RDn (1840—57), Craven RDn, N'rn Dv (1857—1921), Settle RDn (1921—71), Bowland RDn (1971—*). Bdry: 1930.[210]

CONISTON COLD

[W Riding] Tp in Gargrave CP, sep CP 1866,[2] sep EP 1840 as 'Coniston',[9] qv incl later eccl refounding. *LG* Seq 112. Bdry: 1938.[28] Transf 1974 to N Yorks.[5] *Parl* Seq 41.

CONISTONE WITH KILNSEY

[W Riding] Chap in Burnsall AP, sep CP 1866[2]; for eccl see 'Rylstone with Conistone'. *LG* Seq 112. Transf 1974 to N Yorks.[5] *Parl* Seq 41.

CONONLEY

[W Riding] Tp in Kildwick AP, sep CP 1866,[2] sep EP 1871 as 'Cononley with Bradle',[296] qv. *LG* Staincl. & Ewc. Wap, Skipton PLU (soon after 1837[112]—1930), RSD, RD. Transf 1974 to N Yorks.[5] *Parl* Seq 41.

CONONLEY WITH BRADLEY

[W Riding] Tp in Kildwick AP, sep EP 1871,[296] sep CP 1866 as 'Cononley',[2] qv. *Eccl* Craven RDn, S'rn Dv (1871—1921), S Craven RDn (1921—*).

CONSTABLE BURTON

[N Riding] Chap in Finghall AP, sep CP 1866.[2] *LG* Seq 53. Transf 1974 to N Yorks.[5] *Parl* Seq 14.

COOKRIDGE

EP [W Riding] Cr 1964 from Adel AP.[36] Leeds RDn (1964—71), Head. RDn (1971—*). Bdry: 1967.[127]

COPGROVE

AP [W Riding] *LG* Seq 86. Transf 1974 to N Yorks.[5] *Parl* Seq 36. *Eccl* Seq 51. Eccl bdry: 1951.[343]

COPLEY

EP [W Riding] Cr 1866 from Elland EP, Sowerby Bridge EP, Salterhebble EP.[436] Halifax RDn. Bdry: 1862 (cr Charlestown EP).[92]

COPMANTHORPE

[Ainsty (W Riding until 1449 and from 1836, indept jurisd 1449—1836)] Chap (pec jurisd Dean & Chapter of York, until 1836) in York St Mary Bishophill Junior AP, sep CP 1866,[2] sep EP 1844 by union this chap, chap Upper Poppleton in the same par,[437] Upper Poppleton eccl severed 1866 to help cr Nether Poppleton with Upper Poppleton EP.[438] *LG* York PLU, RSD, Bp'thorpe RD (1894—1937), Tadc. RD (1937—74). Transf 1974 to N Yorks.[5] *Parl* Seq 23. *Eccl* City of York RDn (1844—61), Ainsty RDn (1861—71), Bp'thorpe RDn (1871—96), Ainsty RDn (1896—*). Bdry: 1967.[141]

CORNHOLME

CP [W Riding] Cr 1894 from the pt of Cliviger CP (the pt of the par [ent Lancs] in Todmorden USD [o'wise in in Yorks W Riding] which became 1889 pt Yorks W Riding).[425] *LG* Todmorden PLU, UD (1894—96), MB (1896—97). Abol 1897 to help cr Todmorden CP.[439]

EP [W Riding] Cr 1903 from Harley Wood EP (Yorks W Riding, Lancs).[436] Halifax RDn (1903—67), Calder Valley RDn (1967—*).

COTCLIFFE

[N Riding] Ex-par place, sep CP 1858,[393] eccl abol 1873 ent to Leake AP.[279] *LG* Seq 22. Transf 1974 to N Yorks.[5] *Parl* Seq 14.

COTHERSTONE

[N Riding] Tp in Romandkirk AP, sep CP 1866.[2] *LG* Seq 39. Transf 1974 to Durham.[5] *Parl* Seq 14.

COTNESS

[E Riding] Tp in Howden AP, sep CP 1866,[2] eccl severed 1858 to help refound Laxton EP.[440] *LG* Howdensh. Wap, PLU, RSD, RD. Bdry: 1880 (help cr Bishopsoil CP),[142] 1880.[230] Abol 1935 pt to Laxton CP, pt to Eastrington AP, pt to Howden AP.[13] *Parl* E Riding (1832—85), Howdensh. Dv (1885—1948).

COTTAM

[E Riding] Chap in Langtoft AP, sep CP 1866.[2] *LG* Seq 6. Bdry: 1935 (gains Cowlam AP).[13] Transf 1974 to Humb.[5] *Parl* Seq 3.

COTTINGHAM

AP [E Riding] Incl chap Skidby (some parochial rights from 16th cent,[441] sep civ identity early, sep EP 1858,[9] eccl refounded 1859[442]), pt tp Willerby (sep CP 1866[2]). *LG* Harth. Wap, Scul. PLU, Cottingham USD (ent 1875—83, pt 1883—94), pt Kingst. upon Hull MB (1883—89), pt Kingst. upon

Hull CB (1889—94), pt Kingst. upon Hull USD (1883—94). Addtl civ bdry alt: 1879,[443] 1883.[243] Abol civ 1894 the pt in the CB cr Cottingham Within CP, the remainder cr Cottingham Without CP (after abol 1898 of Cottingham Within, called simply 'Cottingham').[444] *Parl* E Riding (1832—85), pt Howdensh. Dv (1885—1918); see Part III of the *Guide* for composition of Kingst. upon Hull Parl Bors (1885—1918) by wards of the MB (incl pt of this par). *Eccl* Harth. & Hull RDn (until 1857), S Harth. RDn (1857—66), Howden RDn (1866—87), Kingst. upon Hull RDn (1887—*). Addtl eccl bdry alt: 1862 (help cr Newland St John EP),[35] 1902 (help cr Anlaby EP),[104] 1937 (cr Hull St Alban EP),[246] 1959.[107]

CP [E Riding] Name used for CP cr 1894 as 'Cottingham Without' after abol 1898 of Cottingham Within CP, qv. *LG* Scul. PLU, Cottingham UD. Bdry: 1930 (loses pt to Kingst. upon Hull CB [assoc with E Riding] & to Sculcoates AP).[251] Abol 1935 pt to Kingst. upon Hull CB (assoc with E Riding) & to Sculcoates AP, pt to Haltemp. UD & CP.[13] *Parl* Hold. Dv (1918—48).

COTTINGHAM WITHIN

CP [Kingst. upon Hull CB] Cr 1894 from the pt of Cottingham AP (orig ent E Riding) in Kingst. upon Hull CB.[444] *LG* Scul. PLU, Kingst. upon Hull CB. Bdry: 1897 (gains pt Cottingham Without CP).[445] Abol 1898 ent to Sculcoates AP.[446]

COTTINGHAM WITHOUT

CP [E Riding] Cr 1894 from the pt of Cottingham AP in Cottingham UD and not in Kingst. upon Hull CB.[444] *LG* Scul. PLU, Cottingham UD. Bdry: 1897 (loses pt to Kingst. upon Hull CB [assoc with E Riding] & to Cottingham Within CP).[445] After abol 1898 of Cottingham Within CP, this par called simply 'Cottingham', qv.

COTTINGLEY

EP [W Riding] Cr 1887 from Bingley Holy Trinity EP.[92] Craven RDn, S'rn Dv (1887—1921), Calverley RDn (1921—71), Airedale RDn (1971—*). Bdry: 1921.[197]

COTTINGWITH

CP [E Riding] Cr 1935 by union East Cottingwith CP, Storwood CP.[13] *LG* Pockl. RD. Transf 1974 to Humb.[5] *Parl* Bev. CC (1948—55), Howdensh. CC (1955—*).

EAST COTTINGWITH

[E Riding] Chap in Aughton AP, sep CP 1866.[2] *LG* Harth. Wap, Pockl. PLU, RSD, RD. Abol 1935 to help cr Cottingwith CP.[13] *Parl* E Riding (1832—85), Howdensh. Dv (1885—1918).

COULTON

[N Riding] Tp in Hovingham AP, sep CP 1866.[2] *LG* Seq 63. Transf 1974 to N Yorks.[5] *Parl* Seq 21.

COVERHAM

AP [N Riding] Incl tps Agglethorpe with Coverham, Caldbergh with East Scrafton, Carlton, Carlton Highdale, Melmerby, West Scrafton (each a sep CP 1866,[2] Carlton a sep EP 1726[9] but sep eccl status not sustained) so that 'Coverham' has no sep civ identity after 1866. *LG* W Hang Wap. *Parl* N Riding (1832—67). *Eccl* Seq 54. Eccl bdry: 1735

(cr Horsehouse EP).[9]

GREAT AND LITTLE COWDENS

[E Riding] Tp (sometimes early 'Cowdens Ambo') pt in Aldbrough AP, pt in Mappleton AP, sep CP 1866.[2] *LG* Hold. Wap, Skirl. PLU, RSD, RD. Abol 1935 to help cr Mappleton CP.[13] *Parl* E Riding (1832—85), Hold. Dv (1885—1948).

COWGILL

EP [W Riding] Area incl in Dent EP when latter cr 1742 from Sedbergh AP,[9] 'Cowgill' a sep EP 1864 from Dent EP,[9] refounded 1865 as 'Kirkwaite',[264] the latter renamed 1869 'Cowgill'.[400] Clapham RDn (1864—65, 1869—1921), Ewecr. RDn (1921—26), Sedbergh RDn (1926—*).

COWICK

EP [W Riding] Cr 1855 (orig as 'East Cowick') from Snaith AP,[173] later called 'Cowick'. Pontef. RDn (1855—62), Selby RDn (1862—71), Snaith RDn (1871—*).

EAST COWICK—see prev entry

COWLAM

AP [E Riding] *LG* Buckr. Wap, Driff. PLU, RSD, RD. Abol civ 1935 ent to Cottam CP.[13] *Parl* E Riding (1832—85), Buckr. Dv (1885—1948). *Eccl* Buckr. RDn (until 1857), E Buckr. RDn (1857—66), Buckr. RDn (1866—1922), Harth. RDn (1922—29), Buckr. RDn (1929—63), Harth. RDn (1963—*).

COWLING

[W Riding] Tp in Kildwick AP, sep CP 1866,[2] sep EP 1844.[117] *LG* Staincl. & Ewc. Wap, Skipton PLU (soon after 1837[112]—1930), RSD, RD. Transf 1974 to N Yorks.[5] *Parl* Seq 40. *Eccl* Craven RDn (1844—57), Craven RDn, S'rn Dv (1857—1921), S Craven RDn (1921—*).

COWESBY

AP [N Riding] Incl pt tp Kepwick (sep CP 1866[2]). *LG* Seq 27. Transf 1974 to N Yorks.[5] *Parl* Seq 16. *Eccl* Pec jurisd Bp Durham (until 1836), Clev RDn (1836—62), N'allert. RDn (1862—1936), Thirsk RDn (1936—*).

COWTHORPE

AP [W Riding] *LG* Claro Wap, Wethb. PLU, RSD, RD. Civ bdry: 1885.[179] Abol civ 1937 ent to Tockwith CP.[31] *Parl* W Riding (1832—67), N'rn Dv of W Riding (1867—85), Bark. Ash Dv (1885—1948). *Eccl* Ainsty RDn (until 1820), New Ainsty RDn (1820—36), Pontef. RDn (1836—1925), Wethb. RDn (1925—*).

EAST COWTON

AP [N Riding] *LG* Seq 34. Transf 1974 to N Yorks.[5] *Parl* Seq 14. *Eccl* Seq 57.

NORTH COWTON

[N Riding] Tp in Gilling AP, sep CP 1866,[2] eccl severed 1783 to help cr South Cowton EP.[9] *LG* Seq 35. Transf 1974 to N Yorks.[5] *Parl* Seq 14.

SOUTH COWTON

[N Riding] Tp in Gilling AP, sep CP 1866,[2] sep EP 1783 (tps North Cowton, South Cowton).[9] *LG* Seq 34. Transf 1974 to N Yorks.[5] *Parl* Seq 14. *Eccl* Richm. RDn (1783—1857), Richm. East RDn (1857—*).

COXWOLD

AP [N Riding] Perhaps orig incl Husthwaite (possibly an AP, appropriated to Newburgh Priory, sep early[448]), incl chap Birdforth (sep CP 1866,[2] sep EP 1739[9]), chap Kilburn (sep civ identity early [qv for chap, tps, hmlt in it and their later sep identities], sep EP 1732[9]), tps Angram Grange, Byland Abbey, Newburgh, Oulston, Thornton cum Baxby, Wildon Grange (each a sep CP 1866[2]), tp Yearsley (sep CP 1866,[2] sep EP 1855,[9] sep eccl status not sustained, eccl severed 1960 and transf to Brandsby AP[337]), pt tp Kepwick (sep CP 1866,[2] qv for eccl status). *LG* Seq 24. Transf 1974 to N Yorks. *Parl* Seq 16. *Eccl* Seq 18.

CRACOE

[W Riding] Tp in Burnsall AP, sep CP 1866.[2] *LG* Seq 112. Transf 1974 to N Yorks.[5] *Parl* Seq 41.

CRAKEHALL

[N Riding] Tp in Bedale AP, sep CP 1866,[2] sep EP 1840 (tps Crakehall, Langthorne, so that later sometimes called 'Crakehall with Langthorne').[362] *LG* Seq 49. Transf 1974 to N Yorks.[5] *Parl* Seq 15. *Eccl* Bedale RDn. Eccl bdry: 1930 (help cr Patrick Brompton with Hunton EP).[137]

CRAKEHALL WITH LANGTHORNE—see prev entry

CRAMBE

AP [N Riding] lncl tp Barton le Willows (sep CP 1866[2]). *LG* Seq 29. Transf 1974 to N Yorks.[5] *Parl* Seq 16. *Eccl* Bulmer RDn (until 1964), Malton RDn (1964—*).

CRATHORNE

AP [N Riding] *LG* Seq 58. Transf 1974 to N Yorks.[5] *Parl* Seq 11. *Eccl* Seq 24.

CRAYKE

AP [In Durham, transf to Yorks N Riding 1832 for parl purposes, 1844 for civ purposes[449]] *LG* After 1844, Seq 28. Transf 1974 to N Yorks.[5] *Parl* Seq 16. *Eccl* Pec jurisd Bp Durham (until 1836), Seq 18 thereafter.

CRIDING STUBBS

[W Riding] Tp pt in Womersley AP, pt in Darrington AP, sep CP 1866.[2] *LG* Seq 97. Transf 1974 to N Yorks.[5] *Parl* Seq 29.

CRIGGLESTONE

[W Riding] Tp in Sandal Magna AP, sep CP 1866.[2] *LG* Seq 69. Bdry: 1951 (loses pt to Wakef CB [assoc with W Riding] & AP).[450] Transf 1974 to W Yorks.[5] *Parl* Seq 54.

CROFT

AP [N Riding] Incl tp Dalton upon Tees (only pt of this par in pec jurlsd Dean & Chapter of York), pts tps Great Smeaton, Stapleton (each of the 3 a sep CP 1866[2]). *LG* E Gill. Wap, Darl. PLU, RSD, RD. Civ bdry: 1879.[451] Renamed civ 1971 'Croft on Tees'.[452] *Parl* Seq 6. *Eccl* Seq 57. Eccl bdry: 1930,[201] 1958.[413]

CROFT ON TEES

CP [N Riding] Renaming 1971 of Croft AP.[452] *LG* Croft RD. Transf 1974 to N Yorks.[5]

CROFTON

AP [W Riding] *LG* Agb. Wap, Gt Preston GilbU (until 1869), Wakef PLU (1869—1930), RSD, RD. Transf 1974 to W Yorks.[5] *Parl* Seq 53. *Eccl* Ainsty

RDn (until 1820), New Ainsty RDn (1820—57), Pontef. RDn (1857—89), Wakef RDn (1889—1973), Chevet RDn (1973—*).

CROOKES ST THOMAS

EP [W Riding] Cr 1848 from Sheffield AP,[453] refounded 1849.[454] Donc. RDn (1848—57), Roth-erh. RDn (1857—62), Sheff RDn (1862—1942), Hallam RDn (1942—*). Sometimes 'Sheffield St Thomas'. Bdry: 1879 (help cr Ranmoor EP),[218] 1908 (cr Crookes St Timothy EP),[36] 1962.[455]

CROOKES ST TIMOTHY

EP [W Riding] Cr 1908 from Crookes St Thomas EP.[36] Sheff RDn (1908—42), Hallam RDn (1942—*).

CROPTON

[N Riding] Tp in Middleton AP, sep CP 1866.[2] *LG* Seq 61. Bdry: 1887.[49] Transf 1974 to N Yorks.[5] *Parl* Seq 22.

CROSBY

[N Riding] Tp in Leake AP, sep CP 1866.[2] *LG* Seq 22. Transf 1974 to N Yorks.[5] *Parl* Seq 14.

SOUTH CROSLAND

[W Riding] Chap in Almondbury AP, sep CP 1866,[2] sep EP 1839,[9] eccl refounded 1843.[79] *LG* Agb. Wap, Hudd. PLU, S Crosland USD, UD. Civ bdry: 1883.[52] Abol civ 1938 pt to Hudd. CB (assoc with W Riding) & AP, pt to Holmf. UD & CP, pt to Meltham UD & CP.[28] *Parl* W Riding (1832—67), S'rn Dv of W Riding (1867—85), Colne Valley Dv (1885—1948). *Eccl* Pontef. RDn (1839—57), Hudd. RDn (1857—1968), Blackmoor Foot RDn (1968—*). Eccl bdry: 1858 (help cr Helme EP).[456]

CROSLAND MOOR

EP [W Riding] Cr 1897 from Lockwood EP, Milns-bridge EP, Rashcliffe EP.[310] Hudd. RDn (1897—1968), Blackmoorfoot RDn (1968—*).

CROSS GREEN

EP [W Riding] Cr 1963 by union Leeds St Saviour EP, Leeds St Hilda EP.[308] Leeds RDn (1963—71) Whitkirk RDn (1971—*). Bdry: 1967.[127]

CROSS ROADS CUM LEES

EP [W Riding] Cr 1911 from Ingrow with Hanworth EP, Haworth EP, Bingley AP.[269] Craven RDn, S'rn Dv (1911—21), S Craven RDn (1921—*).

CROSS STONE

EP [W Riding] Cr 1810 from Halifax AP (tp Stansfield).[9] Pontef. RDn (1810—57), Halifax RDn (1857—1967), Calder Valley RDn (1967—*). Bdry: 1864 (help cr Harley Wood EP [Yorks W Riding, Lancs]).[457]

CROWLE

AP [Mostly Lincs Pts Lind (Manley Wap), pt Yorks W Riding (Straff. & Tick. Wap [moorland, uninhabit-ed until late 19th cent], the par considered ent Lincs by census of 1871[460]] See main entry in Lincs for chap Eastoft in Lincs and for all organisation.

CUDWORTH

[W Riding] Tp in Royston AP, sep CP 1866,[2] eccl severed 1843 to help cr Monk Bretton EP,[331] 'Cudworth' a sep EP 1893 from Monk Bretton EP.[368] *LG* Staincr. Wap, Barnsley PLU, RSD, RD (1894—1900), Cudworth UD (1900—74). Transf 1974 to S Yorks.[5] *Parl* Seq 42. *Eccl* Pontef. RDn (1893—1916), Hemsworth RDn (1916—27),

Barnsley RDn (1927—*).

CULLINGWORTH

EP [W Riding] Cr 1846 from Bingley AP (pt hmlt Harden, not sep civ), Wilsden cum Allerton EP.[268] Craven RDn (1846—57), Craven RDn, S'rn Dv (1857—1921), S Craven RDn (1921—*).

CUMBERWORTH

[W Riding] Chap and tp pt in High Hoyland AP, pt in Silkstone AP, some parochial rights from 1627,[459] sep CP 1866,[2] sep EP 1865,[9] sometimes as 'Cumberworth with Denby Dale'. *LG* Staincr. Wap, Hudd. PLU, pt Skelmanthorpe USD (1875—76), Cumberworth USD (pt 1875—76, ent 1876—85, pt 1885—94), pt Denby USD (1885—94), Denby & Cumberworth UD (1894—1938), Denby Dale UD (1938—74). Civ bdry: 1876 (gains the pt of Cumberworth Half CP in Cumberworth USD, loses the pt in Skelmanthorpe USD to Cumberworth Half CP as the latter [as altered] renamed 'Skelmanthorpe'),[460] 1883,[52] 1885.[461] Transf 1974 to W Yorks.[5] *Parl* Seq 51. *Eccl* Silkst. RDn (1865—1913), Hudd. RDn (1913—68), Kirkburton RDn (1968—*).

CUMBERWORTH HALF

[W Riding] Tp pt in Emley AP, pt in Kirkburton AP, sep CP 1866.[2] *LG* Agb. Wap, Hudd. PLU, pt Cumberworth USD, pt Skelmanthorpe USD. Abol 1876, the pt in Cumberworth USD transf to Cumberworth CP, gains from the latter its pt in Skelmanthorpe USD, the enlarged remainder renamed 'Skelmanthorpe'.[460] *Parl* W Riding (1832—67), S'rn Dv of W Riding (1867—85).

CUNDALL

AP [N Riding] *LG* Pt Hallik. Wap (tp Cundall with Leckby [sep CP 1866[2]], tp Norton le Clay [sep CP 1866,[2] sep EP 1743[9]]), pt Birdf.Wap (pt tp Fawdington [sep CP 1866[2]]), so that 'Cundall' has no sep civ identity after 1866. *Parl* N Riding (1832—67). *Eccl* Seq 52.

CUNDALL WITH LECKBY

[N Riding] Tp in Cundall AP, sep CP 1866.[2] *LG* Hallik. Wap, Ripon PLU (soon after 1852[112]—1930), RSD, Wath RD. Transf 1974 to N Yorks.[5] *Parl* Seq 16.

DACRE

[W Riding] Tp in Ripon AP, sep CP 1866,[2] sep EP 1839,[9] eccl refounded 1862 from Pateley Bridge EP.[457] *LG* Seq 89. Transf 1974 to N Yorks.[5] *Parl* Seq 33. *Eccl* Boroughbr. RDn (1839—49), Ripon RDn (1849—1905), Nidd. RDn (1905—71), Ripon RDn (1971—*).

DAIRYCOATES

EP [E Riding] Cr 1906 from Kingston upon Hull St John the Baptist, Newington EP.[462] Kingst. upon Hull RDn. Abol 1969 to help cr Newington and Dairycoates EP.[228]

DALBY

AP [N Riding] Usual eccl spelling; for civ see following entry. *Eccl* Bulmer RDn (until 1862), Eas. RDn (1862—1928), Malton RDn (1928—*).

DALBY WITH SKEWSBY

AP [N Riding] Usual civ spelling; for eccl see prev entry. *LG* Seq 28. Transf 1974 to N Yorks.[5] *Parl*

Seq 16.

DALE HEAD

EP [W Riding] Cr 1871 from Slaidburn AP.[21] Craven RDn, W'rn Dv (1871—1921), Bolland RDn (1921—38). Abol 1938 pt to Slaidburn AP, pt to Tossside EP.[463]

DALE TOWN

[N Riding] Tp in Hawnby AP, sep CP 1866.[2] *LG* Birdf. Wap, Helm. PLU (soon after 1837[112]—1930), RSD, RD. Transf 1974 to N Yorks.[5] *Parl* Seq 16.

DALLAGHILL

EP [N Riding] Cr 1844 from Kirkby Malzeard AP.[133] Catt. RDn (1844—57), Ripon RDn (1857—77), Masham RDn (1877—1905), Ripon RDn (1905—*). Sometimes early 'Dallowgill'.

DALTON

[N Riding] Tp in Kirkby Ravensworth AP, sep CP 1866,[2] sep EP 1841,[9] sep eccl status not sustained. *LG* Seq 38. Transf 1974 to N Yorks.[5] *Parl* Seq 14.

DALTON

[N Riding] Tp in Topcliffe AP, sep CP 1866.[2] *LG* Seq 27. Bdry: 1883,[16] 1888.[165] Transf 1974 to N Yorks. *Parl* Seq 16.

DALTON

[W Riding] Tp in Kirkheaton AP, sep CP 1866.[2] *LG* Agb. Wap, Hudd. PLU, MB (1868—89), CB (1889—1924), USD. Abol 1924 ent to Huddersfield AP.[83] *Parl* W Riding (1832—67), Hudd. Parl Bor (1867—1948).

DALTON

[W Riding] Tp pt in Thrybergh AP, pt in Rotherham AP, sep CP 1866,[2] sep EP 1849 from Thrybergh AP, Rotherham AP, Ecclesfield AP.[464] *LG* Seq 119. Civ bdry: 1881,[465] 1881,[432] 1936 (loses pt to Rotherh. CB [assoc with W Riding] & AP).[132] Transf 1974 to S Yorks.[5] *Parl* Seq 55. *Eccl* Donc. RDn (1849—57), Rotherh. RDn (1857—*). Eccl bdry: 1950 (help cr Herringthorpe EP),[212] 1952,[466] 1956 (incl help cr Bramley EP).[214]

NORTH DALTON

AP [E Riding] *LG* Seq 10. Transf 1974 to Humb.[5] *Parl* Seq 3. *Eccl* Seq 10.

SOUTH DALTON

AP [E Riding] *LG* Harth. Wap, Bev. PLU, RSD, RD. Abol 1935 to help cr Dalton Holme CP.[13] *Parl* E Riding (1832—85), Hold. Dv (1885—1948). *Eccl* Pec jurisd Bev. (until 1836), Harth. & Hull RDn (1836—57), S Harth. RDn (1857—62). Abol 1862 to help cr South Dalton and Holme on the Wolds EP.[467]

SOUTH DALTON AND HOLME ON THE WOLDS

EP [E Riding] Cr 1862 by union South Dalton AP, Holme on the Wolds AP.[467] S Harth. RDn (1862—66), Bev. RDn (1866—*).

DALTON HOLME

CP [E Riding] Cr 1935 by union Holme on the Wolds AP, South Dalton AP.[13] *LG* Bev. RD. Transf 1974 to Humb.[5] *Parl* Bev. CC (1948—55), Haltemp. CC (1955—*).

DALTON UPON TEES

[N Riding] Tp (orig but not later in pec jurisd Dean & Chapter of York) in Croft AP, sep CP 1866.[2] *LG*

Seq 33. Transf 1974 to N Yorks.[5] *Parl* Seq 14.

DANBY

AP [N Riding] Usual civ spelling; for eccl see following entry. Incl chap Glaisdale (sep CP 1866,[2] sep EP 1741[9]); also incl from 1866 undivided pt Land Common to Danby and Glaisdale (abol 1929 with pt to each par[468]). *LG* Seq 55. Transf 1974 to N Yorks.[5] *Parl* Seq 19.

DANBY WITH CASTLETON

AP [N Riding] Usual eccl spelling; for civ and civ and eccl sep chap Glaisdale, see prev entry. *Eccl* Clev RDn (until 1862), Guisb. RDn (1862—67), Stokes. RDn (1878—1919), Whitby RDn (1919—36), Stokes. RDn (1936—58), Whitby RDn (1958—*).

DANBY WISKE

AP [N Riding] Incl chap Yafforth (sep CP 1866,[2] no sep eccl identity hence this par eccl 'Danby Wiske with Yafforth', qv). *LG* Seq 34. Transf 1974 to N Yorks.[5] *Parl* Seq 14.

DANBY WISKE WITH YAFFORTH

AP [N Riding] Usual eccl spelling; for civ and civ sep chap Yafforth, see prev entry. *Eccl* Richm. RDn (until 1857), Richm. East RDn (1857—1965). Abol eccl 1965 to help cr Danby Wiske with Yafforth and Hutton Bonville EP.[469]

DANBY WISKE WITH YAFFORTH AND HUTTON BONVILLE

EP [N Riding] Cr 1965 by union Danby Wiske with Yafforth AP, Hutton Bonville EP.[469] Richm. East RDn.

DANTHORPE

[E Riding] Tp in Humbleton AP, sep CP 1866.[2] *LG* Hold. Wap, Skirl. PLU, RSD, RD. Abol 1935 ent to Elstronwick CP.[13] *Parl* E Riding (1832—85), Hold. Dv (1885—1948).

DARFIELD

AP [W Riding] Tp 'Darfield' in Straff. & Tick. Wap as were tps Billingley, Great Houghton, Little Houghton (each a sep CP 1866,[2]), tp Wombwell (sep CP 1866,[2] donative, sep EP 1864[277]); incl in Staincr. Wap chap Worsbrough (sep CP 1866,[2] sep EP 1722[470]), tp Ardsley (sep CP 1866,[2] sep EP 1843,[9] eccl refounded 1844[115]). *LG* Barnsley PLU, RSD, RD (1894—96), Darfield UD (1896—1974). Transf 1974 to S Yorks.[5] *Parl* W Riding (1832—67), S'rn Dv of W Riding (1867—85), Barnsley Dv (1885—1918), Wentw. Dv (1918—48), Colne Valley CC (1948—*). *Eccl* Seq 46.

DARLEY

EP [W Riding] Cr 1968 from Thornthwaite EP.[73] Nidd. RDn (1968—71), Ripon RDn (1971—*).

DARNALL

EP [W Riding] Cr 1844 from Attercliffe cum Darnall EP (the remainder to be 'Attercliffe').[88] Donc. RDn (1844—57), Rotherh. RDn (1857—62), Sheff RDn (1862—1927), Handsw. RDn (1927—42), Attercliffe RDn (1942—*). Bdry: 1874 (help cr Carbrook EP),[148] 1909 (cr Darnall St Alban EP),[471] 1933.[214]

DARNALL ST ALBAN

EP [W Riding] Cr 1909 from Darnall EP.[471] RDns as for Darnall, from 1909.

DARRINGTON

AP [W Riding] Incl tp Stapleton, pt tp Cridling Stubbs (each a sep CP 1866[2]). *LG* Seq 99. Transf 1974 to W Yorks.[5] *Parl* Seq 29. *Eccl* Ainsty RDn (until 1820), New Ainsty RDn (1820—57), Pontef. RDn (1857—*). Eccl bdry: 1880.[164]

DARTON

AP [W Riding] Incl tps Barugh, Kexborough (each a sep CP 1866[2]). *LG* Staincr. Wap, Barnsley PLU, Darton USD, UD. Addtl civ bdry alt: 1938,[28] 1959.[472] Transf 1974 to S Yorks.[5] *Parl* W Riding (1832—67), S'rn Dv of W Riding (1867—85), Barnsley Dv (1885—1918), Barnsley Parl Bor/BC (1918—*). Parl bdry: 1960.[473] *Eccl* Seq 41. Eccl bdry: 1849 (cr Gawber EP),[309] 1928 (help cr Staincross EP).[325]

DEARNE

CP [W Riding] Cr 1937 by union Bolton upon Dearne UD & AP, Thurnscoe UD & AP, pt Barnbrough AP.[31] *LG* Dearne UD. Transf 1974 to S Yorks.[5] *Parl* Hemsw. CC (1948—*).

DEIGHTON

[E Riding] Tp in Escrick AP, sep CP 1866.[2] *LG* Seq 20. Transf 1974 to N Yorks.[5] *Parl* Seq 7.

DEIGHTON

[N Riding] Chap (pec jurisd Dean & Chapter of Durham) in Northallerton AP, sep CP 1866.[2] *LG* Seq 22. Transf 1974 to N Yorks.[5] *Parl* Seq 14.

KIRK DEIGHTON

AP [W Riding] Incl tp North Deighton, pt tp Spofforth with Stockeld (each a sep CP 1866[2]). *LG* Claro Wap, Barwick GilbU (until 1869), Wethb. PLU (1869—1930), RSD, RD. Transf 1974 to N Yorks.[5] *Parl* Seq 24. *Eccl* Ainsty RDn (until 1820), New Ainsty RDn (1820—36), Pontef. RDn (1836—57), Wethb. RDn (1857—1971). Abol eccl 1971 to help cr Spofforth with Kirk Deighton EP.[78]

NORTH DEIGHTON

[W Riding] Tp in Kirk Deighton AP, sep CP 1866.[2] *LG* Seq 91. Transf 1974 to N Yorks. *Parl* Seq 24.

DENABY

[W Riding] Tp in Mexborough AP, sep CP 1866.[2] *LG* Seq 117. Bdry: 1921 (loses pt to Conisbrough AP as latter [enlarged] constituted Conisbrough UD).[387] Transf 1974 to S Yorks.[5] *Parl* W Riding (1832—67), S'rn Dv of W Riding (1867—85), Rotherh. Dv (1885—1918), Don Valley Dv/CC (1918—*).

DENABY MAIN

EP [W Riding] Cr 1898 from Conisbrough AP, Mexborough AP.[63] Donc. RDn.

DENBY

[W Riding] Tp in Penistone AP, sep CP 1866,[2] sep EP 1738,[9] eccl refounded 1854.[311] *LG* Staincr. Wap, not in a PLU (until 1849), Penist. PLU (1849—1930), Denby USD (ent 1875—85, pt 1885—94, pt Penist. RSD (1885—94), Denby UD (1894), Denby & Cumberworth UD (1894—1938), Denby Dale UD (1938—74). Civ bdry: 1883,[52] 1885,[460] 1915.[461] Transf 1974 to W Yorks.[5] *Parl* Seq 51. *Eccl* Donc. RDn (1738—1838), Pontef. RDn (1838—57), Silkst. RDn (1857—1927), Hudd. RDn (1927—68), Kirkburton RDn (1968—*).

DENHOLME

CP [W Riding] Cr 1894 from the pt of Thornton CP in Denholme UD.[257] *LG* N Bierley PLU, Denholme UD. Transf 1974 to W Yorks.[5] *Parl* Keigh. Dv (1918—48), Keigh. BC (1948—*).

DENHOLME GATE

EP [W Riding] Cr 1846 from Thornton EP.[208] Pontef. RDn (1846—57), Bradf RDn (1857—1921), Horton RDn (1921—59), S Craven RDn (1959—*).

DENSHAW

EP [W Riding] Cr 1864 from Friar Mere EP.[326] Ashton under Lyne RDn (1864—72), Rochdale RDn (1872—81), Ashton under Lyne RDn (1881—1929), Oldham RDn (1929—*).

DENT

[W Riding] Chap in Sedbergh AP, sep CP 1866,[2] sep EP 1742 (incl area Cowgill),[9] eccl refounded 1865.[264] *LG* Seq 110. Transf 1974 to Cumbria.[5] *Parl* Seq 41. *Eccl* Kirkby Lonsd. RDn (1742—1849), Clapham RDn (1849—1921), Ewecr. RDn (1921—26), Sedbergh RDn (1926—*). Eccl bdry: 1864 (cr Cowgill EP,[9] refounded 1865 as 'Kirkthwaite',[9] renamed 1869 'Cowgill'[400]).

DENTON

[W Riding] Chap in Otley AP, sep CP 1866,[2] sep EP 1868.[474] *LG* Seq 83. Civ bdry: 1937.[31] Transf 1974 to N Yorks.[5] *Parl* Seq 30. *Eccl* Donative, Otley RDn (1868—1969). Abol eccl 1969 to help cr Weston with Denton EP.[475]

DERRINGHAM BANK

EP [E Riding] Cr 1935 from Newington EP.[476] Kingst. upon Hull RDn. Bdry: 1959.[107] Later called 'Kingston upon Hull The Ascension'.

DEWSBURY

[W Riding] The following have 'Dewsbury' in their names. Insofar as any existed at a given time: *LG* Waps sep noted; Dewsb. PLU, MB (1862—1913), USD, CB (1913—74). *Parl* W Riding (1832—67), Dewsb. Parl Bor/BC (1867—*). *Eccl* Pontef. RDn (until 1857), Dewsb. RDn (1857—*).

AP1—DEWSBURY [ALL SAINTS]—Tp 'Dewsbury' in Agb. Wap as was tp Ossett cum Gawthorpe (sep CP 1866,[2] sep EP 1718,[9] eccl refounded 1858[247]), tp Soothill (sep CP 1866[2]); incl in Morley Wap chap Clifton, chap Hartshead (each a sep CP 1866,[2] eccl united 1742 as 'Hartshead with Clifton' EP,[9] the latter divided 1887 into 2 EPs of Clifton, Hartshead[419]). Addtl civ bdry alt: 1910,[207] 1925 (gains the following in Dewsb. CB: Ravensthorpe CP, Soothill Nether CP, Thornhill AP).[477] Transf 1974 to W Yorks.[5] Addtl eccl bdry alt: 1826 (cr Hanging Heaton EP,[9] refounded 1842[30]), 1828 (cr EP1,[9] refounded 1885 from EP5, EP2[30]), 1828 (cr Earls Heaton EP,[9] refounded 1842[30]), 1828 (cr EP5,[9] refounded 1842[30]), 1841 (cr Batley Carr EP,[9] refounded 1842[30]), 1849 (cr EP6),[146] 1859 (help cr Thornhill EP),[478] 1867 (help cr EP2),[74] 1879 (help cr EP4),[326] 1968 (gains EP4).[73]

EP1—DEWSBURY ST JOHN THE BAPTIST, DAW GREEN—Cr 1885 from EP5, EP2.[347] Abol 1965 to help cr EP3.[234]

EP2—DEWSBURY ST MARK—Cr 1867 from Batley Carr EP, AP1.[74] Bdry: 1868,[208] 1885 (help refound EP1),[347] 1901,[216] 1913.[119]

EP3—DEWSBURY ST MATTHEW AND ST JOHN THE BAPTIST—Cr 1965 by union EP1, EP6.[234]

EP4—DEWSBURY ST PHILIP—Cr 1879 from AP1, Hanging Heaton EP, Earls Heaton EP.[326] Bdry: 1935.[479] Abol 1968 ent to AP1.[73]

EP5—DEWSBURY MOOR [ST JOHN]—Cr 1828 from AP1,[9] refounded 1842.[30] Bdry: 1885 (help refound EP1),[347] 1901,[216] 1913.[119]

EP6—DEWSBURY WEST TOWN [ST MATTHEW]—Cr 1849 from AP1.[146] Bdry: 1901.[216] Abol 1965 to help cr EP3.[234]

DINNINGTON

AP [W Riding] (Tp of Dinnington pt in Dinnington AP, pt in Laughton en le Morthen AP). *LG* Straff. & Tick. Wap, Worksop PLU, RSD, Kiv. Pk. RD. Abol civ 1954 to help cr Dinnington St John's CP.[480] *Parl* W Riding (1832—67), S'rn Dv of W Riding (1867—85), Donc. Dv (1885—1918), Rother Valley Dv/CC (1918—70). *Eccl* Seq 44.

DINNINGTON ST JOHN'S

CP [W Riding] Cr 1954 by union Dinnington AP, St John's with Throapham CP.[480] *LG* Kiv. Pk. RD. Transf 1974 to S Yorks.[5] *Parl* Rother Valley CC (1970—*).

OVER DINSDALE

[N Riding] Tp (Yorks N Riding, Allert. Wap) in Sockburn AP (Durham [Stock. Ward], Yorks N Riding [Allert. Wap] until 1866, ent Durham thereafter), sep CP 1866 in Yorks.[2] *LG* Seq 21. Transf 1974 to N Yorks.[5] *Parl* Seq 11.

DISHFORTH

[N Riding] Chap in Topcliffe AP, sep CP 1866,[2] sep EP 1747.[9] *LG* Seq 42. Transf 1974 to N Yorks.[5] *Parl* Seq 16. *Eccl* Bulmer RDn (1747—1862), Thirsk RDn (1862—*).

DOBCROSS

EP [W Riding] Cr 1797 from Rochdale AP (Lancs, Yorks W Riding until 1866, ent Lancs thereafter),[9] refounded 1844.[481] Manch RDn (1797—1847), Ashton under Lyne RDn (1847—72), Rochdale RDn (1872—81), Ashton under Lyne RDn (1881—1929), Oldham RDn (1929—*). Bdry: 1886 (help cr Scouthead EP [Yorks, Lancs] to be dioc Manch).[479]

DODWORTH

[W Riding] Tp in Silkstone AP, sep CP 1866,[2] sep EP 1848.[86] *LG* Staincr. Wap, Barnsley PLU, Dodworth USD, UD. Civ bdry: 1938.[28] Transf 1974 to S Yorks.[5] *Parl* W Riding (1832—67), S'rn Dv of W Riding (1867—85), Holmf. Dv (1885—1918), Wentw. Dv (1918—48), Penist. CC (1948—*). *Eccl* Pontef. RDn (1848—57), Silkst. RDn (1857—1927), Barnsley RDn (1927—*).

DONCASTER

[W Riding] The following have 'Doncaster' in their names. Insofar as any existed at a given time: *LG* Donc. PLU, MB (1835—1927), USD, CB (1927—74); Wap, Bor sep noted. *Parl* W Riding (1832—67), S'rn Dv of W Riding (1867—85), Donc. Dv (1885—1918), Donc. Parl Bor/BC (1918—*). *Eccl* Donc. RDn.

AP1—DONCASTER [ST GEORGE]—Tp 'Doncaster'

in Donc. Bor; incl in Donc. Soke tp Balby with Hexthorpe (sep CP 1866,[2] sep EP 1846 by union this tp, pt tp Doncaster[166]), tp Loversall (sep civ identity early, sep EP 1766[9]), tp Long Sandall, hmlt Wheatley (each a sep CP 1866[2]); incl in Straff. & Tick. Wap tp Langthwaite with Tilts (sep CP 1866[2]). Addtl civ bdry alt: 1914 (gains Balby with Hexthorpe UD & CP, Wheatley UD & CP, Carr House and Elmfield CP),[167] 1936,[132] 1951 (gains pt Cauntley AP).[439] Transf 1974 to S Yorks.[5] Parl bdry: 1951.[390] Addtl eccl bdry alt: 1846 (cr EP1),[293] 1858 (help cr EP2),[145] 1899 (cr EP5),[308] 1914 (help cr Woodlands EP).[44]

EP1—DONCASTER CHRIST CHURCH—Cr 1846 from AP1.[293] Bdry: 1858 (help cr EP2,[9] refounded 1864[145]), 1940 (cr EP6).[482]

—DONCASTER ST AIDAN—Name sometimes used now for EP cr 1952 as 'Wheatley Hills', qv

EP2—DONCASTER ST JAMES—Cr 1858,[9] refounded 1864 from AP1, EP1, Balby with Hexthorpe EP.[145] Bdry: 1900 (help cr EP3).[168]

EP3—DONCASTER ST JUDE—Cr 1900 from EP2, Balby with Hexthorpe EP.[168] Bdry: 1930.[169]

EP4—DONCASTER ST LEONARD AND ST JUDE—Cr 1940 from Brodsworth AP, Spotbrough AP, Bentley EP.[237]

EP5—DONCASTER ST MARY—Cr 1899 from AP1.[308] Bdry: 1952 (help cr Wheatley Hills EP).[134]

EP6—DONCASTER INTAKE—Cr 1940 from EP1.[482] Bdry: 1952 (help cr Wheatley Hills EP),[134] 1952.[483]

DORMANSTOWN
EP [N Riding] Cr 1927 from Kirkleatham AP, East Coatham EP.[284] Middlesb. RDn.

DOWNHOLME
AP [N Riding] Incl tps Ellerton Abbey, Stainton, Walburn (each a sep CP 1866[2]). LG Seq 54. Addtl civ bdry alt: 1883.[16] Transf 1974 to N Yorks.[5] Parl Seq 14. Eccl Catt. RDn (until 1857), Richm. West RDn (1857—*).

DRAUGHTON
[W Riding] Tp in Skipton AP, sep CP 1866.[2] LG Seq 112. Transf 1974 to N Yorks.[5] Parl Seq 41.

DRAX
AP [W Riding] Incl tps Camblesforth, Long Drax, Newland (each a sep CP 1866[2]). LG Drax Bor (status not sustained), Seq 80. Addtl civ bdry alt: 1883,[52] 1883 (loses pt to Cliffe cum Lund CP, E Riding).[341] Transf 1974 to N Yorks.[5] Parl Seq 24. Eccl Ainsty RDn (until 1820), New Ainsty RDn (1820—57), Pontef. RDn (1857—62), Selby RDn (1862—71), Snaith RDn (1871—*).

LONG DRAX
[W Riding] Tp in Drax AP, sep CP 1866.[2] LG Seq 80. Transf 1974 to N Yorks.[5] Parl Seq 24.

DRIFFIELD
CP [E Riding] Cr 1935 by union pts Emswell with Little Driffield CP, Great Driffield AP, Skerne AP.[13] LG Driff. UD. Transf 1974 to Humb.[5] Parl Bridl. CC (1948—55), Howden CC (1955—*).

GREAT DRIFFIELD
AP [E Riding] Incl chap Little Driffield (sep CP 1866,[2]

sep EP 1821[9]), tp Emswell with Kellythorpe (sep CP 1866[2]). LG Harth. Wap, Driff. PLU, Gt Driff. USD (ent 1875—83, pt 1883—85, ent 1885—94), pt Driff. RSD (1883—85), Driff. UD. Addtl civ bdry alt: 1883,[243] 1885 (the pt gained 1883 from Little Driffield CP [not in the USD] made pt of Gt Driff. USD).[484] Abol civ 1935 pt to Nafferton AP, pt to help cr Driff. UD & CP.[13] Parl E Riding (1832—85), Buckr. Dv (1885—1948). Eccl Pec jurisd Driff. prebend (until 1485), pec jurisd Precentor of York (1485—1836), Harth. & Hull RDn (1836—57), N Harth. RDn (1857—66), Harth. RDn (1866—*).

LITTLE DRIFFIELD
[E Riding] Chap in Great Driffield AP, sep CP 1866,[2] sep EP 1821.[9] LG Harth. Wap, Driff. PLU, RSD. Civ bdry: 1883.[243] Abol civ 1885 pt to Great Driffield AP, pt to help cr Emswell with Little Driffield CP.[484] Parl E Riding (1832—85), Buckr. Dv (1885—1918). Eccl Pec jurisds and RDns as for Great Driffield.

DRIGHLINGTON
[W Riding] Chap in Birstall AP, sep CP 1866,[2] sep EP 1817,[9] eccl refounded 1847.[275] LG Morley Wap, Bradf PLU (1837—48), N Bierley PLU (1848—1930), Drighlington USD, UD. Abol civ 1937 ent to Morley MB & CP.[31] Parl W Riding (1832—67), E'rn Dv of W Riding (1867—85), Pudsey Dv (1885—1918), Spen Valley Dv (1918—48). Eccl Pontef. RDn (1817—57), Dewsb. RDn (1857—66), Birstall RDn(1866—*).

DRINGHOE, UPTON AND BROUGH
[E Riding] Tp in Skipsea AP, sep CP 1866.[2] LG Hold. Wap, Bridl. PLU, RSD, RD. Abol 1935 ent to Skipsea AP.[13] Parl E Riding (1832—85), Hold. Dv (1885—1918), Buckr. Dv (1918—48).

DRINGHOUSES
[Ainsty (W Riding until 1449 and from 1836, indept jurisd 1449—1836)] Tp pt in Acomb AP, pt in York Holy Trinity Micklegate AP, pt in York St Mary Bishophill Senior AP, pt in Bishopthorpe AP, sep CP 1866,[2] sep EP 1853 from York Holy Trinity Micklegate AP, York St Mary Bishophill Senior AP, Acomb AP.[30] LG York PLU, pt York MB (1884—89), pt York CB (1889—94), pt York USD (1884—94), York RSD (ent 1875—84, pt 1884—94). Civ bdry: 1888.[485] Abol civ 1894 the pt in York CB cr Dringhouses Within CP, the remainder cr Dringhouses Without CP.[418] Parl N Riding (1832—85), pt York Parl Bor, pt Thirsk & Malton Dv (1885—1918). Eccl City of York RDn (1853—62), Ainsty RDn (1862—71), Bp'thorpe RDn (1871—96), Ainsty RDn (1896—1936), City of York RDn (1936—*). Eccl bdry: 1968 (help cr Acomb Moor EP).[33]

DRINGHOUSES WITHIN
CP [York CB] Cr 1894 from the pt of Dringhouses CP (ent W Riding before 1889) in York CB.[418] LG York PLU, CB. Abol 1900 to help cr York CP.[423]

DRINGHOUSES WITHOUT
CP [W Riding] Cr 1894 from the pt of Dringhouses CP not in York CB.[418] LG York PLU, Bp'thorpe RD. Abol 1937 pt to York CB (not assoc with a Riding)

& CP, pt to Askham Bryan AP.[31] *Parl* Bark. Ash Dv (1918—48).

DRYPOOL

[E Riding] The following have 'Drypool' in their names. Insofar as any existed at a given time: *LG* Hold. Wap, Scul. PLU, Kingst. upon Hull MB/CB, USD. *Parl* Kingst. upon Hull Parl Bor (1832—85); see Part III of the *Guide* for composition of Kingst. upon Hull Parl Bors (1885—1918) by wards of the MB. *Eccl* Hold. RDn (until 1849), S Hold. RDn (1849—57), S Harth. RDn (1857—62), Bev. RDn (1862—69), Kingst. upon Hull RDn (1869—*).

CP1/EP1—DRYPOOL [ST ANDREW]—Area in Sutton and Stoneferry AP (anc chap in Wawne AP, then Collegiate, sep par from Dissolution), sep civ identity early, sep EP 1766.[9] Incl tps Southcoates (sep CP 1866[2]). Abol civ 1898 ent to Sculcoates.[445] Eccl bdry: 1879 (cr EP5),[278] 1917 (cr EP4),[486] 1927 (help cr Sutton in Holderness EP),[487] 1935.[77] Abol eccl 1951 to help cr EP2.[488]

EP2—DRYPOOL ST ANDREW AND ST PETER—Cr 1951 by union EP1, EP5.[488] Bdry: 1954 (incl help cr Kingston upon Hull Southcoates EP).[489] Renamed 1961 as EP3.[490]

EP3—DRYPOOL ST COLUMBA WITH ST ANDREW AND ST PETER—Renaming 1961 of EP2.[490]

EP4—DRYPOOL ST JOHN—Cr 1917 from AP1.[486] Bdry: 1935.[77]

EP5—DRYPOOL ST PETER—Cr 1879 from AP1.[278] Abol 1951 to help cr EP2.[488]

NORTH DUFFIELD

[E Riding] Tp in Skipwith AP, sep CP 1866.[2] *LG* Seq 19. Bdry: 1935 (gains Menthorpe cum Bowthorpe CP).[13] Transf 1974 to N Yorks.[5] *Parl* Seq 7.

SOUTH DUFFIELD

[E Riding] Tp in Hemingbrough AP, sep CP 1866.[2] *LG* Ouse & Derw. Wap, Selby PLU, RSD, Riccall RD. Abol 1935 pt to help cr Cliffe CP, pt to help cr Wressle CP.[13] *Parl* E Riding (1832—85), Howdensh. Dv (1885—1948).

DUGGLEBY

[E Riding] Tp in Kirby Grindalythe AP, sep CP 1866.[2] *LG* Buckr. Wap, Malton PLU, RSD, Norton RD. Abol 1935 ent to Kirby Grindalythe AP.[13] *Parl* E Riding (1832—85), Buckr. Dv (1885—1948).

DUNFORD

CP [W Riding] Cr 1938 by union pts Fulstone CP, Hepworth CP, Holme CP, Scholes CP, Thurlstone CP.[28] *LG* Penist. RD. Transf 1974 to S Yorks.[5] *Parl* Penist. CC (1948—*).

DUNKESWICK

[W Riding] Tp in Harewood AP, sep CP 1866.[2] *LG* Claro Wap, Carlton GilbU (until 1869), Wethb. PLU (1869—1930), RSD, RD. Bdry: 1883.[52] Abol 1937 ent to Harewood AP.[31] *Parl* W Riding (1832—67), N'rn Dv of W Riding (1867—85), Bark. Ash Dv (1885—1948).

DUNNINGTON

AP [E Riding] Incl tp Grimston (sep CP 1866[2]). *LG* Seq 20. Addtl civ bdry alt: 1935 (gains Grimston CP).[13] Transf 1974 to N Yorks.[5] *Parl* Seq 7. *Eccl* Pec jurisd Dunnington prebend (early abol), Bulmer RDn (thereafter—1896), Escr. RDn (1896—1916), Bulmer RDn (1916—*).

DUNNINGTON

[E Riding] Tp in Beeford AP, sep CP 1866.[2] *LG* Hold. Wap, Skirl. PLU, RSD, RD. Abol 1935 to help cr Bewholme CP.[13] *Parl* E Riding (1832—85), Hold. Dv (1885—1948).

DUNSFORTH

EP [W Riding, N Riding] Chap in Aldborough AP, sep CP 1782,[9] eccl refounded 1867[56]; for civ see following 2 entries. Pec jurisd Dean & Chapter of York (until 1836), Boroughbr. RDn (1836—1971), Ripon RDn (1971—73). Abol 1973 ent to Aldborough AP.[57]

LOWER DUNSFORTH

[Pt W Riding (Claro Wap), pt N Riding (Hallik. Wap) until 1895, ent W Riding thereafter[491]] Tp in Aldborough AP (W Riding, N Riding), sep CP 1866[2]; for eccl see prev entry. *LG* Gt Ouseb. GilbU (until 1854), PLU (1854—1930), RSD, pt sep RD in N Riding (1894—95), Gt Ouseb. RD (W Riding, pt 1894—95, ent 1895—1938), Nidd. RD (1938—60). Abol 1960 to help cr Dunsforths CP.[492] *Parl* Pt W Riding, pt N Riding (1832—67), pt N Riding, pt N'rn Dv of W Riding (1867—85), pt Thirsk & Malton Dv (N Riding, 1885—1918), Ripon Dv (W Riding, pt 1885—1918, ent 1918—48), Harrog. CC (1948—70).

UPPER DUNSFORTH WITH BRANTON GREEN

[Pt W Riding (Claro Wap), pt N Riding (Hallik. Wap) until 1895, ent W Riding thereafter[491]] Tp in Aldborough AP (W Riding, N Riding), pt in Great Ouseburn AP (N Riding), sep CP 1866[2]; for eccl see 'Dunsforth'. Civ, parl organisation as for Lower Dunsforth except abol civ 1960 pt to help cr Dunsforths CP, pt to Great Ouseburn AP, pt to Marton cum Grafton AP.[492]

DUNSFORTHS

CP [W Riding] Cr 1960 by union Lower Dunsforth CP, pt Upper Dunsforth with Branton Green CP.[492] *LG* Nidd. RD. Transf 1974 to N Yorks.[5] *Parl* Harrog. CC (1970—*).

DYERS HILL

EP [W Riding] Cr 1846 from Sheffield AP.[493] Donc. RDn (1846—57), Rotherh. RDn (1857—62), Sheff RDn (1862—1942), Attercliffe RDn (1942—49). Bdry: 1879,[494] 1929.[416] Abol 1949 pt to Sheffield St John EP, pt to Sheffield St Aidan with St Luke EP.[495]

EARBY

CP [W Riding] Cr 1909 from Thornton in Craven AP.[496] *LG* Skipton PLU, Earby UD. Transf 1974 to Lancs.[5] *Parl* Skipton Dv/CC (1918—*).

EP [W Riding] Cr 1923 from Thornton in Craven AP, Kelbrook EP.[497] Skipton RDn. Bdry: 1924.[27]

EARSWICK

[N Riding] Tp pt in Huntington AP, pt in Strensall AP, sep CP 1866.[2] *LG* Seq 32. Bdry: 1934.[3] Transf 1974 to N Yorks.[5] *Parl* Seq 16.

NEW EARSWICK

CP [N Riding] Cr 1934 from Huntington AP.[3] *LG* Flaxton RD. Transf 1974 to N Yorks.[5] *Parl* Thirsk & Malton CC (1948—*).

EASBY
AP [N Riding] Tp 'Easby' in W Gill. Wap as were tps Aske, Skeeby (each a sep CP 1866[2]); incl in E Gill. Wap tp Brompton on Swale (sep CP 1866[2]); incl in W Hang Wap pt tp Hudswell (sep CP 1866[2]). *LG* Richm. PLU, RSD, RD. Transf 1974 to N Yorks.[5] *Parl* Pt Richm. Parl Bor (1585—1885), remainder and later, Seq 14. *Eccl* Seq 58. Eccl bdry: 1939.[396]

EASBY
[N Riding] Tp in Stokesley AP, sep CP 1866,[2] eccl severed 1880 to help cr Great Ayton with Easby EP.[161] *LG* Seq 58. Transf 1974 to N Yorks.[5] *Parl* Seq 11.

EASINGTON
AP [E Riding] Incl tp Out Newton (sep CP 1866[2]). *LG* Seq 15. Bdry: 1935 (gains Kilnsea AP, Out Newton CP).[13] Transf 1974 to Humb.[5] *Parl* Seq 5. *Eccl* Seq 16.

EASINGTON
AP [N Riding] Incl chap Liverton (sep CP 1866,[2] sep EP 1923[498]). *LG* Langb. Lbty, Guisb. PLU, pt Loftus USD, pt Guisb. RSD, Guisb. RD (1894—1932), Loftus UD (1932—74). Civ bdry: 1932.[51] Transf 1974 to Clev.[5] *Parl* N Riding (1832—85), Whitby Dv (1885—1918), Clev Dv/CC (1918—70), Clev & Whitby CC (1970—*). *Eccl* Clev RDn (until 1862), Guisb. RDn (1862—78), Whitby RDn (1878—1916), Middlesb. RDn (1916—24), Guisb. RDn (1924—*).

EASINGTON
[W Riding] Tp in Slaidburn AP, sep CP 1866.[2] *LG* Seq 108. Bdry: 1938.[499] Transf 1974 to Lancs.[5] *Parl* Seq 41.

EASINGWOLD
AP [N Riding] Incl chap Cold Kirby (sep civ identity early, sep EP 1737[9]), chap Raskelf (sep CP 1866,[2] sep EP 1744 as 'Raskelfe'[9]). *LG* Seq 28. Transf 1974 to N Yorks.[5] *Parl* Seq 16. *Eccl* Seq 18.

EASTBURN
[E Riding] Tp in Kirkburn AP, sep CP 1866.[2] *LG* Harth. Wap, Driff. PLU, RSD, RD. Abol 1935 to help cr Kirkburn CP.[13] *Parl* E Riding (1832—85), Buckr. Dv (1885—1948).

EASTOFT
[W Riding] Chap and tp (Lincs Pts Lind, Manley Wap) in Crowle AP (Lincs Pts Lind [Manley Wap], Yorks W Riding [Straff. & Tick. Wap]), sep CP 1866 in Lincs,[2] eccl severed 1855 and united with pt Adlingfleet AP (Yorks W Riding, dioc York) and pt Luddington with Garthorpe AP (Lincs) as 'Eastoft' EP, to be dioc York.[40] *LG* Seq 95. Civ bdry: 1884.[500] Transf 1974 to Humb.[5] *Parl* Seq 29. *Eccl* Pontef. RDn (1855—62), Selby RDn (1862—71), Snaith RDn (1871—*).

EASTON
[E Riding] Hmlt in Bridlington AP, sep CP 1866.[2] *LG* Dick. Wap, Bridl. PLU, RSD, RD. Abol 1935 ent to Boynton AP.[13] *Parl* E Riding (1832—85), Buckr. Dv (1885—1948).

EASTRINGTON
AP [E Riding] Incl tps Bellasize, Gilberdike, Newport Wallingfen, Portington and Cavil (each a sep CP 1866[2]). *LG* Seq 17. Addtl civ bdry alt: 1880,[142] 1880,[172] 1935 (incl gains Portington and Cavil CP).[13] Transf 1974 to Humb.[5] *Parl* Seq 7. *Eccl* Pec jurisd Dean & Chapter of Durham (until 1836), Seq 13 thereafter. Eccl bdry: 1895 (help cr Newport EP).[284]

EASTTHORPE
EP [W Riding] Cr 1881 from Mirfield AP, Battyeford EP.[218] Birstall RDn (1881—1927), Dewsb. RDn (1927—*).

EASTWOOD
EP [W Riding] Cr 1844 from Keighley AP.[197] Craven RDn (1844—57), Craven RDn, S'rn Dv (1857—1921), S Craven RDn (1921—*). Bdry: 1954.[489]

EASTWOOD
EP [W Riding] Cr 1875 from Rotherham AP.[90] Rotherh. RDn. Bdry: 1952.[421]

EAVESTONE
[W Riding] Tp in Ripon AP, sep CP 1866,[2] eccl severed 1743 to help cr Sawley EP,[9] eccl refounded 1863.[163] *LG* Seq 100. Transf 1974 to N Yorks.[5] *Parl* Seq 34.

EBBERSTON
[N Riding] Chap in Pickering AP, united 1252 with chap Allerston in same par as 'Ebberston with Allerston',[61] 'Ebberston', 'Allerston' each gain sep civ identity early. Incl pt chap Snaiton (sep CP 1866[2]). *LG* Seq 61. Addtl civ bdry alt: 1886.[501] Transf 1974 to N Yorks.[5] *Parl* Seq 20.

EBBERSTON WITH ALLERSTON
AP [N Riding] Chaps Ebberston, Allerston, each in Pickering AP, eccl united 1252 to form this par,[61] 'Ebberston' 'Alleston' each gain sep civ identity early, qv for organisation and for civ sep pt chap Snainton (from Ebberston). *Eccl* Seq 28.

ECCLESALL
CP [W Riding] Cr 1904 by union of the following in Sheff CB: Ecclesall Bierlow CP, Heeley CP, Nether Hallam CP, Upper Hallam CP, Norton Within CP.[502] *LG* Sheff PLU, CB. Bdry: 1928 (gains pts of following, all in Derbys: Derwent CP, Dore CP, Hathersage AP, Outseats CP, Totley CP).[503] Abol 1933 ent to Sheffield AP.[504] *Parl* See Part III of the *Guide* for composition of Sheff Parl Bors (1918—48) by wards of the CB.

ECCLESALL BIERLOW
[W Riding] Chap in Sheffield AP, sep CP 1866,[2] sep EP 1746,[9] eccl refounded 1849.[146] *LG* Straff. & Tick. Wap, Ecclesall Bierlow PLU, Sheff MB (1843—89), CB (1889—1904), USD. Civ bdry: 1877,[505] 1879.[506] Abol civ 1904 to help cr Ecclesall CP.[502] *Parl* Sheff Parl Bor (1832—85); see Part III of the *Guide* for composition of Sheff Parl Bors (1885—1918) by wards of the MB. *Eccl* Donc. RDn (1746—1857), Rotherh. RDn (1857—62), Sheff RDn (1862—1942), Ecclesall RDn (1942—*). Eccl bdry: 1870 (help cr Sharrow EP),[213] 1899 (help cr Endcliffe EP),[507] 1907 (cr Sheffield St Oswald EP),[211] 1959.[508]

ECCLESFIELD
AP [W Riding] Incl chap Bradfield (sep CP 1866,[2] sep EP 1720[9]). *LG* Straff. & Tick. Wap, Wortley PLU, RSD, RD. Addtl civ bdry alt: 1881,[38] 1901 (loses pt to Sheff CB [assoc with W Riding] & AP),[304] 1921

(loses pt to Sheff CB [assoc with W Riding] to cr Ecclesfield Urban CP),[361] 1930,[124] 1930,[305] 1957,[509] 1967 (exchanges pts with Sheff CB [assoc with W Riding] & AP).[144] Transf 1974 to S Yorks.[5] *Parl* Seq 49. *Eccl* Donc. RDn (until 1857), Rotherh. RDn (1857—62), Ecclesfield RDn (1862—*). Addtl eccl bdry alt: 1721 (cr Bolderstone EP),[9] 1741 (cr Midhope EP),[9] 1841 (cr Wadsley EP),[510] 1843 (cr Stannington EP),[194] 1844 (cr Chapeltown EP),[54] 1849 (help cr Dalton EP),[464] 1877 (help cr Wincobank EP),[301] 1884,[466] 1895 (cr Hillsborough and Wadsley Bridge EP,[115] refounded 1939 [qv for constituent pars at that time][407]), 1902 (help cr Sheffield St Cuthbert EP),[354] 1910 (cr Grenoside EP),[23] 1938 (help cr Sheffield St Leonard, Norwood EP),[511] 1939 (help cr Sheffield St Cecilia, Parsons Cross EP),[512] 1941 (help cr Shiregreen St James and St Christopher EP),[513] 1948,[514] 1973 (cr Sheffield St Paul Wordsworth Avenue EP).[515]

ECCLESFIELD URBAN

CP [W Riding] Cr 1921 from the pt of Ecclesfield AP made pt of Sheff CB.[361] *LG* Sheff PLU, CB. Abol 1933 ent to Sheffield AP.[307]

ECCLESHILL

[W Riding] Tp in Bradford AP, sep CP 1866,[2] sep EP 1858.[310] *LG* Morley Wap, Carlton GilbU (until 1869), N Bierley PLU (1869—1930), Eccleshill USD, UD (1894—99), Bradf CB (1899—1974). Transf 1974 to W Yorks.[5] *Parl* W Riding (1832—67), E'rn Dv of W Riding (1867—85), Shipley Dv (1885—1918); see Part III of the *Guide* for composition of Bradf Parl Bors/BCs (1918—*) by wards of the CB. *Eccl* Bradf RDn (1858—1921), Calverley RDn (1921—*). Eccl bdry: 1911 (cr Greengates EP),[365] 1956.[516]

EDDLETHORPE

[E Riding] Tp in Westow AP, sep CP 1866.[2] *LG* Buckr. Wap, Malton PLU, RSD, Norton RD. Abol 1935 ent to Burythorpe AP.[13] *Parl* E Riding (1832—85), Buckr. Dv (1885—1918).

EDENTHORPE

CP [W Riding] Cr 1956 from Barnby Dun with Kirk Sandall CP.[517] *LG* Donc. RD. Transf 1974 to S Yorks.[5] *Parl* Don Valley CC (1970—*).

EDLINGTON

AP [W Riding] *LG* Seq 117. Civ bdry: 1939.[76] Transf 1974 to S Yorks.[5] *Parl* Seq 44. *Eccl* Seq 40. Eccl bdry: 1953,[433] 1954 (help cr New Edlington EP),[434] 1967 (gains New Edlington EP).[21]

NEW EDLINGTON

EP [W Riding] Cr 1954 from Edlington AP, Conisbrough AP, Warmsworth AP.[434] Donc. RDn. Abol 1967 ent to Edlington EP.[21]

GREAT EDSTONE

AP [N Riding] Incl tp North Holme (sep CP 1866[2]). *LG* Seq 64. Bdry: 1934.[3] Transf 1974 to N Yorks.[5] *Parl* Seq 21. *Eccl* Seq 26.

LITTLE EDSTONE

[N Riding] Tp in Sinnington AP, sep CP 1866.[2] *LG* Seq 64. Bdry: 1934.[3] Transf 1974 to N Yorks. *Parl* Seq 21.

EGGBOROUGH

[W Riding] Tp in Kellington AP, sep CP 1866.[2] *LG*

Seq 97. Transf 1974 to N Yorks.[5] *Parl* Seq 29.

EGGLESTONE ABBEY

[N Riding] Tp in Startforth AP, sep CP 1866.[2] *LG* Seq 39. Transf 1974 to Durham.[5] *Parl* Seq 14.

EGTON

[N Riding] Tp in Lythe AP, sep civ identity early, sep EP 1807.[9] *LG* Seq 59. Transf 1974 to N Yorks.[5] *Parl* Seq 19. *Eccl* Clev RDn (1807—62), Guisb. RDn (1862—78), Whitby RDn (1878—*). Eccl bdry: 1852 (help refound Grosmont EP).[258]

ELDON

EP [W Riding] Cr 1846 from Sheffield AP.[493] Donc. RDn (1846—57), Rotherh. RDn (1857—62), Sheff RDn (1862—1940). Abol 1940 pt to Sheffield St Matthew EP, pt to Gillcar EP.[518]

KIRK ELLA

AP [E Riding] (Tp 'Kirk Ella' pt in Kirk Ella AP, pt in North Ferriby AP; Kirk Ella AP also incl pt of main tps of North Ferriby AP, Hessle AP). Incl pt tps Anlaby (sep CP 1866,[2] sep EP 1902 [qv for constituent pars at that time][104]), West Ella, Swanland (each a sep CP 1866[2]), pt tp Willerby (sep CP 1866[2]). *LG* Kingst. upon Hull Co, Scul. PLU, RSD, RD. Addtl civ bdry alt: 1878,[519] 1883.[243] Abol civ 1935 pt to Skidby CP, pt to Kingst. upon Hull CB (assoc with E Riding) and to Sculcoates AP, pt to Haltemp. UD & CP.[13] *Parl* E Riding (ent 1832—67, pt 1867—85), pt Kingst. upon Hull Parl Bor (1867—85), Howdensh. Dv (pt 1885—1918, ent 1918—48); see Part III of the *Guide* for composition of Kingst. upon Hull Parl Bors (1885—1918) incl pt of this par. *Eccl* Seq 12. Addtl eccl bdry alt: 1879 (help cr Kingston upon Hull St John the Baptist, Newington EP).[520]

WEST ELLA

[E Riding] Tp pt in Kirk Ella AP, pt in North Ferriby AP, sep CP 1866.[2] *LG* Kingst. upon Hull Co, Scul. PLU, RSD, RD. Bdry: 1878,[519] 1883.[243] Abol 1935 ent to Haltemp. UD & CP.[13] *Parl* E Riding (1832—85), Howdensh. (1885—1948).

ELLAND

[W Riding] Chap in Halifax AP, eccl severed (incl area tp Soyland) 1724 to help cr Elland cum Stainland and Fixby EP,[178] although reaugmented 1739 as 'Elland',[9] usually 'Elland with Greetland' until 1862 when Greetland cr from the latter EP, 'Elland' thereafter[138]; for civ see Elland with Greetland. Halifax RDn (1862—1967) Brigh. & Elland RDn (1967—*). Bdry: 1848 (pt orig area tp Soyland cr Soyland EP),[231] 1855 (cr Barkisland EP,[9] eccl refounded 1858[179]), 1866 (help cr Copley EP),[436] 1869 (help re-cr Sowerby Bridge EP),[521] 1877 (help cr Birchencliffe EP),[141] 1879,[137] 1881 (re-cr Rastrick EP).[522]

ELLAND CUM STAINLAND AND FIXBY

EP [E Riding] Cr 1724 by union places in Halifax AP: chaps Elland, Rastrick (sep EP 1720,[9] until incl in this par, eccl re-cr 1881[522]), areas Brighouse, Greetland, Old Lindley, pt tp Barkisland, tps Norland, Rishworth, Soyland, Stainland (for civ see Barkisland, Elland with Greetland, Fixby, Hipperholme and Brighouse, Norland, Rishworth, Soyland, Stainland and Old Lindley).[178] Pontef.

RDn (1724—1857), Halifax RDn (1857—62). Although re-augmented 1739 as 'Elland',[9] usually 'Elland with Greetland' until cr 1862 of Greeetland EP,[138] thereafter 'Elland', qv. Addtl eccl bdry alt before 1862: 1732 (area Warley eccl severed to help cr Luddendon EP),[9] 1749 (help cr Lightcliffe [area Hipperholme with Brighouse, pt tp Northowram] EP),[9] eccl refounded 1846[523]), 1843 (cr Stainland EP),[351] 1855 (cr Barkisland EP,[9] eccl refounded 1858[179]), 1869 (help re-cr Sowerby Bridge EP[521]).

ELLAND WITH GREETLAND
EP [W Riding] See prev entry.
CP [W Riding] Tp in Halifax AP, sep CP 1866.[2] *LG* Morley Wap, Halifax PLU, pt Elland USD, pt Greetland USD, pt Halifax RSD. Abol 1894 the pt in Elland UD cr Elland CP, the pt in Greetland UD cr Greetland UD, the remainder cr Upper Greetland CP.[257] *Parl* W Riding (1832—67), E'rn Dv of W Riding (1867—85), Elland Dv (1885—1918).

ELLENTHORPE
[N Riding] Tp in Aldborough AP, sep CP 1866.[2] *LG* Hallik. Wap, not in a PLU (until 1854), Gt Ouseb. PLU (1854—1930), RSD, Thirsk RD. Transf 1974 to N Yorks.[5] *Parl* Seq 16.

ELLERBECK
[N Riding] Tp in Osmotherley AP, sep CP 1866.[2] *LG* Seq 22. Transf 1974 to N Yorks.[5] *Parl* Seq 14.
CP [W Riding] Cr 1894 from the pt of Elland with Greetland CP in Elland UD.[257] *LG* Halifax PLU, Elland RD. Bdry: 1937 (incl gains Upper Greetland CP, Greetland UD & CP).[31] Transf 1974 to W Yorks.[5] *Parl* Elland Dv (1918—48), Sowerby CC (1948—*).

ELLERBURNE
[N Riding] Chap in Pickering AP, eccl united 1252 with chap Wilton in same par to cr 'Ellerburne with Wilton'; civ called 'Ellerburne', Wilton considered a chap within the area (sep CP 1866,[2] sep EP 1755[9] but sep eccl status not sustained); also incl tp Farnaby (sep CP 1866[2]) so that 'Ellerburne' has no sep civ identity after 1866. *LG* Pick. Lythe Wap. *Parl* N Riding (1832—67). *Eccl* Pec jurisd Dean of York (until 1836), Riddal RDn (1836—62), Malton RDn (1862—1928), Pick. RDn (1928—34). Abol eccl 1934 to help cr Thornton Dale with Ellerburne and Wilton EP.[524]

ELLERBURNE WITH WILTON—see prev entry
ELLERBY
[E Riding] Tp in Swine AP, sep CP 1866.[2] *LG* Seq 16. Bdry: 1952.[378] Transf 1974 to Humb.[5] *Parl* Seq 5.

ELLERBY
[N Riding] Tp in Lythe AP, sep CP 1866,[2] eccl severed 1868 to help cr Ugthorpe EP.[188] *LG* Seq 59. Transf 1974 to N Yorks.[5] *Parl* Seq 19.

ELLERKER
[E Riding] Tp (pec jurisd Dean & Chapter of Durham) in Brantingham AP, sep CP 1866,[2] not sep eccl hence usual eccl 'Brantingham with Ellerker' until Ellerker eccl severed 1968 to help cr South Cave and Ellerker EP (the remainder to be 'Brantingham').[337] *LG* Howdensh. Wap, Bev. PLU, RSD, RD. Bdry: 1935.[13] Transf 1974 to Humb.[5]

Parl E Riding (1832—85), Howdensh. Dv (1885—1948), Bev. CC (1948—55), Haltemp. CC (1955—*).

ELLERTON
CP [E Riding] Cr 1935 by union Aughton AP, Ellerton Priory AP.[13] *LG* Howden RD. Transf 1974 to Humb.[5] *Parl* Bev. CC (1948—55), Howden CC (1955—*).

ELLERTON ABBEY
[N Riding] Tp in Downholme AP, sep CP 1866.[2] *LG* W Hang Wap, Richm. PLU (1837—40), Reeth PLU (1840—1930), RSD, RD. Transf 1974 to N Yorks.[5] *Parl* Seq 14.

ELLERTON PRIORY
AP [E Riding] *LG* Harth. Wap, Howden PLU, RSD, RD. Abol 1935 to help cr Ellerton CP.[13] *Parl* E Riding (1832—85), Howdensh. Dv (1885—1918). *Eccl* Seq 14.

ELLERTON UPON SWALE
[N Riding] Tp in Catterick AP, sep CP 1866,[2] sep EP 1732,[9] sep eccl status not sustained, made pt 1781 of Bolton upon Swale EP,[9] the latter refounded 1885.[347] *LG* Seq 35. Transf 1974 to N Yorks.[5] *Parl* Seq 14.

ELLENSTRING
[N Riding] Tp in Masham AP, sep CP 1866.[2] *LG* E Hang Wap, Leyb. PLU, Masham USD, UD (1894—1934), Masham RD (1934—74). Bdry: 1883,[16] 1886,[525] 1886,[526] 1934 (incl help cr Healey CP).[363] Transf 1974 to N Yorks.[5] *Parl* Seq 14.

ELLINGTONS
[N Riding] Tp in Maham AP, sep CP 1866.[2] *LG* E Hang Wap, Leyb. PLU, Masham USD, UD (1894—1934), Masham RD (1934—74). Bdry: 1883,[527] 1886,[526] 1934.[3] Transf 1974 to N Yorks.[5] *Parl* Seq 14.

ELLOUGHTON
AP [E Riding] Incl hmlt Elloughton with Brough (sep CP 1866[2]; 13th cent attempt to cr Brough on Humber Bor seemingly unsuccessful[528]), chap and tp Wauldby (sep CP 1866,[2] eccl severed 1904 and transf to Welton AP[529]) so that 'Elloughton' has no sep civ identity 1866—1935 (see following entry). *LG* Harth. Wap. *Parl* E Riding (1832—67). *Eccl* Pec jurisd Wetwang prebend (until 1836), Harth. & Hull RDn (1836—57), S Harth. RDn (1857—66), Howden RDn (1866—*).
CP [E Riding] Renaming 1935 of Elloughton with Brough CP.[13] *LG* Bev. RD. Transf 1974 to Humb.[5] *Parl* Bev. CC (1948—55), Haltemp. CC (1955—*).

ELLOUGHTON WITH BROUGH
[E Riding] Hmlt in Elloughton AP, sep CP 1866.[2] *LG* Harth. Wap, Bev. PLU, RSD, RD. Renamed 1935 'Elloughton'.[13] *Parl* E Riding (1832—85), Howdensh. Dv (1885—1948).

ELDMIRE WITH CRAKEHILL
[N Riding] Tp in Topcliffe AP, sep CP 1866.[2] *LG* Seq 27. Bdry: 1883.[16] Transf 1974 to N Yorks. *Parl* Seq 16.

NORTH ELMSALL
[W Riding] Tp in South Kirkby AP, sep CP 1866.[2] *LG* Seq 96. Transf 1974 to W Yorks.[5] *Parl* Seq 28.

SOUTH ELMSALL

[W Riding] Tp in South Kirkby AP, sep CP 1866,[2] sep EP 1911 (tps South Elmsall, Hamphall Stubbs in same par).[37] *LG*, 1974 transf, *Parl* as for North Elmsall. *Eccl* Pontef. RDn (1911—16), Hemsw. RDn (1916—27), Pontef. RDn (1927—*). Eccl bdry: 1933,[413] 1969.[478]

ELSECAR

EP [W Riding] Cr 1844 from Wath upon Dearne AP.[530] Donc. RDn (1844—57), Rotherh. RDn (1857—71), Wath RDn (1871—1942), Tankersley RDn (1942—*).

ELSLACK

[W Riding] Tp in Broughton AP, sep CP 1866.[2] *LG* Staincl. & Ewc. Wap, Skipton PLU (soon after 1837[112]—1930), RSD, RD. Transf 1974 to N Yorks.[5] *Parl* Seq 41.

ELSTRONWICK

[E Riding] Tp in Humbleton AP, sep CP 1866.[2] *LG* Seq 16. Bdry: 1935 (gains Danthorpe CP, Lelley CP).[13] Transf 1974 to Humb.[5] *Parl* Seq 5.

ELVINGTON

AP [E Riding] *LG* Seq 20. Transf 1974 to N Yorks.[5] *Parl* Seq 7. *Eccl* Seq 19.

EMBSAY WITH EASTBY

[W Riding] Tp in Skipton AP, sep CP 1866,[2] sep EP 1854,[9] eccl refounded 1855.[516] *LG* Seq 112. Transf 1974 to N Yorks.[5] *Parl* Seq 41. *Eccl* Craven RDn (1854—57), Craven RDn, W'rn Dv (1857—1905), Craven RDn, E'rn Dv (1905—21), Skipton RDn (1921—*).

EMLEY

AP [W Riding] Incl pt tp Cumberworth Half (sep CP 1866[2]). *LG* Agb. Wap, Wakef PLU, Emley USD, UD (1894—1938), Denby Dale UD (1938—74). Transf 1974 to W Yorks.[5] *Parl* W Riding (1832—67), S'rn Dv of W Riding (1867—85), Norm. Dv (1885—1918), Rothw. Dv (1918—48), Penist. CC (1948—55), Colne Valley CC (1955—*). *Eccl* Pontef. RDn (until 1857), Silkst. RDn (1857—1913), Wakef RDn (1913—27), Hudd. RDn (1927—68), Kirkburton RDn (1968—*). Eccl bdry: 1840 (help cr Scissett EP).[394]

EMSWELL WITH LITTLE DRIFFIELD

CP [E Riding] Cr 1885 by union Emswell with Kellythorpe CP, pt Little Driffield CP.[484] *LG* Harth. Wap, Driff. PLU, RSD, RD. Abol 1935 pt to help cr Garton CP, pt to help cr Kirkburn CP, pt to help cr Driffield UD & CP.[13] *Parl* Buckr. Dv (1885—1918).

EMSWELL WITH KELLYTHORPE

[E Riding] Tp in Great Driffield AP, sep CP 1866.[2] *LG* Harth. Wap, Driff. PLU, RSD. Abol 1885 to help cr Emswell with Little Driffield CP.[484] *Parl* E Riding (1832—85), Buckr. Dv (1885—1918).

ENDCLIFFE

EP [W Riding] Cr 1899 from Broomhall EP, Ecclesall Bierlow EP, Sharrow EP.[507] Sheff RDn (1899—1942), Ecclesall RDn (1942—*). Bdry: 1959,[508] 1962.[455]

EPPLEBY

[N Riding] Tp in Forcett CP, sep CP 1866.[2] *LG* Seq 38. Transf 1974 to N Yorks.[5] *Parl* Seq 14.

ERGHAM

AP [E Riding] Orig chap in Hunmanby AP, sep par 1269.[120] Usual eccl spelling; for civ see 'Argam'. *Eccl* Dick. RDn (until 1862), N Dick. RDn (1862—65), Bridl. RDn (1865—70). Abol eccl 1870 to help cr Grindale and Ergham EP.[531]

ERRINGDEN

[W Riding] Tp in Halifax AP, sep CP 1866,[2] sep EP 1844 as 'Halifax St John in the Wilderness'.[532] *LG* Morley Wap, Todmorden PLU, pt Hebden Bridge USD (enlarged pt 1891—94), pt Mytholmroyd USD (1891—94), pt Todmorden RSD (1875—94 [reduced pt 1891—94]), Todmorden RD (1894—1939), Hepton RD (1939—74). Bdry: 1894 (loses the pt in Hebden Bridge UD to help cr Hebden Bridge CP,[450] loses the pt in Mytholmroyd UD to help cr Mytholmroyd CP[533]), 1937.[31] Transf 1974 to W Yorks.[5] *Parl* Seq 37.

ERYHOLME

[N Ridlng] Chap in Gilling AP, sep CP 1866,[2] sep EP 1801.[9] *LG* Seq 33. Transf 1974 to N Yorks.[5] *Parl* Seq 14. *Eccl* Richm. RDn (1801—57), Richm. East RDn (1857—*).

ESCRICK

AP [E Riding] Incl tp Deighton (sep CP 1866[2]). *LG* Seq 20. Transf 1974 to N Yorks.[5] *Parl* Seq 7. *Eccl* Seq 19.

ESHOLT

[W Riding] Tp in Otley AP, sep CP 1866,[2] sep EP 1853,[534] sometimes eccl 'Esholt with Hawksworth'. *LG* Skyr. Wap, not in a PLU (until 1861), Wharfed. PLU (1861—1930), RSD, RD. Abol 1937 pt to Bradf CB (assoc with W Riding) & to Idle CP, pt to help cr Aireb. UD & CP, pt to Baildon UD & CP.[31] *Parl* W Riding (1832—67), N'rn Dv of W Riding (1867—85), Otley Dv (1885—1918), Shipley Dv (1918—48). *Eccl* Pontef. RDn (1853—57), Otley RDn (1857—*).

ESHTON

[W Riding] Tp in Gargrave AP, sep CP 1866.[2] *LG* Seq 112. Bdry: 1938.[28] Transf 1974 to N Yorks.[5] *Parl* Seq 41.

ESKDALESIDE

[N Riding] Tp in Whitby AP, sep CP 1866,[2] sep EP (sometimes as 'Sleights') 1735.[9] *LG* Whitby Strand Lbty, Whitby PLU, RSD. Abol civ 1885 to help cr Eskdaleside cum Ugglebarnby CP.[534] *Parl* N Riding (1832—85), Whitby Dv (1885—1918). *Eccl* Clev RDn (1735—1862), Guisb. RDn (1862—72). Abol prob 1872 to help cr Eskdaleside with Ugglebarnby EP.[535]

ESKDALESIDE CUM UGGLEBARNBY

CP [N Riding] Cr 1885 by union Eskdaleside CP, Ugglebarnby CP.[534] *LG* Whitby Strand Lbty, Whitby PLU, RSD, RD. Transf 1974 N Yorks.[5] *Parl* Scarb. & Whitby Dv/CC (1918—70), Clev & Whitby CC (1970—*).

ESKDALESIDE WITH UGGLEBARNBY

EP [N Riding] Union prob 1872 of Eskdaleside EP, Ugglebarnby EP.[535] Guisb. RDn (1872—78), Whitby RDn (1878—*).

ESKE

[E Riding] Tp in Beverley St John AP, sep CP

1866.[2] *LG* Hold. Wap, Bev. PLU, RSD, RD. Abol 1935 to help cr Tickton CP.[13] *Parl* E Riding (1832—85), Hold. Dv (1885—1948).

ESTON
[N Riding] Chap in Ormesby AP, comprised of tps Eston, Normanby (each a sep CP 1866 from Ormesby[2]), sep EP 1772,[9] sometimes 'Eston with Normanby'. *LG* Langb. Lbty, Guisb. PLU (1837—75), Middlesb. PLU (1875—1930), RSD (1875—84), Eston USD (1884—94), UD. Addtl civ bdry alt: 1915 (gains Normanby CP as South Bank in Normanby UD abol),[105] 1921.[536] Abol civ 1968 pt to help cr Teesside CB (assoc with N Riding) & CP, pt to Guisb. UD & AP.[537] *Parl* N Riding (ent 1832—67, pt 1867—85), pt Middlesb. Parl Bor (1867—1918), Clev Dv/CC (pt 1885—1918, ent 1918—70). *Eccl* Stokes. RDn (1772—1878), Middlesb. RDn (1878—*). Eccl bdry: 1898 (cr South Bank EP),[121] 1917 (help cr Grangetown EP),[464] 1925.[493]

ETTON
AP [E Riding] *LG* Seq 9. Transf 1974 to Humb.[5] *Parl* Seq 4. *Eccl* Seq 11.

EVERINGHAM
AP [E Riding] *LG* Seq 12. Civ bdry: 1935 (gains Harswell AP).[13] Transf 1974 to Humb. *Parl* Seq 7. *Eccl* Seq 14.

EXELBY, LEEMING AND NEWTON
[N Riding] Tp in Burneston AP, sep CP 1866.[2] *LG* Seq 40. Transf 1974 to N Yorks.[5] *Parl* Seq 15.

FACEBY
[N Riding] Chap in chap Whorlton (sep civ identity early from Rudby in Cleveland AP, sep EP 1766[9]), sep CP 1866,[2] sep EP 1792.[9] *LG* Seq 58. Transf 1974 to N Yorks.[5] *Parl* Seq 11. *Eccl* Clev RDn (1792—1862), N'allert. RDn (1862—1916), Stokes. RDn (1916—*).

FADMOOR
[N Riding] Tp in Kirkby Moorside AP, sep CP 1866.[2] *LG* Seq 64. Bdry: 1883,[16] 1887,[538] 1934.[3] Transf 1974 to N Yorks.[5] *Parl* Seq 21.

FAIRBURN
[W Riding] Orig chap, later tp[539] in Ledsham AP, sep CP 1866.[2] *LG* Seq 76. Bdry: 1938.[28] Transf 1974 to N Yorks.[5] *Parl* Seq 29.

FAIRWEATHER GREEN
EP [W Riding] Renaming 1966 of Bradford St Saviour EP.[288] Horton RDn (1966—71), Airedale RDn (1971—*) Bdry: 1967.[68]

FALSGRAVE
[N Riding] Tp in Scarborough AP, sep CP 1866,[2] sep EP 1873.[540] *LG* Pick. Lythe Wap, Scarb. Bor/MB, PLU, USD. Abol civ 1890 ent to Scarborough AP.[541] *Parl* N Riding (1832—85), Whitby Dv (1885—1918). *Eccl* Scarb. RDn. Eccl bdry: 1893 (cr Scarborough St James EP),[542] 1904 (cr Scarborough St Saviour EP),[543] 1951 (help cr Scarborough St Luke EP).[544] Abol 1973 to help cr Scarborough St Saviour with All Saints EP.[545]

FANGFOSS
AP [E Riding] Chap in Pocklington AP, sep par 1252, eccl held with Barmby on the Moor from 1568 until sep eccl status regained 1747,[9] sep civ identity

retained. *LG* Seq 12. Civ bdry: 1935.[13] Transf 1974 to Humb.[5] *Parl* Seq 7. *Eccl* Pec jurisd Prebend of Barmby Moor, later pec jurisd Dean of York (until 1836), Harth. & Hull RDn (1836—57), W Buckr. RDn (1857—66), Pockl. RDn (1866—*).

FARLINGTON
[N Riding] Chap in Sheriff Hutton AP, sep CP 1866,[2] eccl severed 1836 and transf to Marton cum Moxby AP.[546] *LG* Seq 28. Bdry: 1887.[547] Transf 1974 to N Yorks.[5] *Parl* Seq 16.

FARMANBY
[N Riding] Tp in Ellerburn AP, sep CP 1866.[2] *LG* Pick. Lythe Wap, Pick. PLU, RSD. Abol 1887 ent to Thornton Dale AP.[548] *Parl* N Riding (1832—85), Whitby Dv (1885—1918).

FARNDALE, EAST SIDE
[N Riding] Tp in Lastingham AP, sep CP 1866.[2] *LG* Seq 64. Transf 1974 to N Yorks.[5] *Parl* Seq 21.

FARNDALE, LOW QUARTER
[N Riding] Tp in Kirkby Moorside AP, sep CP 1866,[2] eccl severed 1873 to help cr Bransdale cum Farndale EP.[21] *LG* Ryed. Wap, Helm. PLU (1837—48), Kirkby Moors. PLU (1848—1930), RSD, RD. Abol 1934 pt to help cr Bransdale CP, pt to Farndale, West Side CP.[3] *Parl* N Riding (1832—85), Whitby Dv (1885—1918), Thirsk & Malton Dv (1918—48).

FARNDALE, WEST SIDE
[N Riding] Tp in Kirkby Moorside AP, sep CP 1866,[2] eccl severed 1873 to help cr Bransdale cum Farndale EP.[21] *LG* Seq 64. Bdry: 1934 (incl help cr Bransdale CP).[3] Transf 1974 to N Yorks.[5] *Parl* Seq 21.

FARNHAM
AP [W Riding] Incl pt chap Arkendale (sep CP 1866,[2] sep EP 1736,[9] eccl refounded 1924 [qv for constituent pars then][77]), pt tp Ferrensby, tp Scotton (each a sep CP 1866[2]). *LG* Seq 87. Transf 1974 to N Yorks.[5] *Parl* Seq 36. Eccl Boroughbr. RDn (until 1870), Knar. RDn (1870—1971), Harrog. RDn (1971—73). Renamed eccl 1973 'Farnham with Scotton'.[549]

FARNHAM WITH SCOTTON
EP [W Riding] Renaming 1973 of Farnham AP.[549] Harrog. RDn.

FARNHILL
[W Riding] Tp in Kildwick AP, sep CP 1866.[2] *LG* Seq 112. Transf 1974 to N Yorks.[5] *Parl* Seq 41.

FARNLEY
[W Riding] Chap in Leeds AP, sep CP 1866,[2] sep EP 1723,[9] eccl refounded 1851.[41] *LG* Skyr. Wap, Leeds Bor/MB/CB, USD, Carlton GilbU (until 1869), Bramley PLU (1869—1904). Abol civ 1904 to help cr Armley and Bramley CP.[124] *Parl* Leeds Parl Bor (1832—85); see Part III of the *Guide* for composition of Leeds Parl Bors (1885—1918) by wards of the MB. *Eccl* Ainsty RDn (1723—1820), Old Ainsty RDn (1820—36), Pontef. RDn (1836—57), Leeds RDn (1857—1971), Armley RDn (1971—*). Eccl bdry: 1967.[127]

FARNLEY
[W Riding] Tp in Otley AP, sep CP 1866,[2] sep EP 1746.[9] *LG* Seq 92. Civ bdry: 1927.[550] Transf 1974

to N Yorks.[5] *Parl* Seq 30. *Eccl* Ainsty RDn (1746—1820), Old Ainsty RDn RDn (1820—36), Pontef. RDn (1836—57), Otley RDn (1857—*). Eccl bdry: 1926,[327] 1950.[551]

FARNLEY TYAS
[W Riding] Tp in Almondbury AP, sep CP 1866,[2] sep EP 1840,[9] eccl refounded 1897.[56] *LG* Agb. Wap, Hudd. PLU, Farnley Tyas USD, UD. Abol civ 1925 to heIp cr Thurstonland and Farnley Tyas UD & CP.[552] *Parl* W Riding (1832—67), S'rn Dv of W Riding (1867—85), Holmf. Dv (1885—1918), Colne Valley Dv (1918—48). *Eccl* Pontef. RDn (1840—57), Hudd. RDn (1857—1968), Almondb. RDn (1968—*).

FARSLEY
EP [W Riding] Cr 1844 from Calverley AP.[73] Pontef. RDn (1844—57), Bradf RDn (1857—1921), Calverley RDn (1921—*). Bdry: 1959 (incl help cr Woodhall EP).[320]
CP [W Riding] Cr 1894 from the pt of Calverley with Farsley CP in Farsley UD.[257] *LG* N Bierley PLU, Farsley UD. Abol 1937 ent to Pudsey MB & CP.[31] *Parl* Pudsey & Otley Dv (1918—48).

FAWDINGTON
[N Riding] Tp pt in Cundall AP, pt in Brafferton AP, sep CP 1866.[2] *LG* Birdf. Wap, Thirsk PLU (soon after 1837[112]—1930), RSD, RD. Transf 1974 to Yorks.[5] *Parl* Seq 16.

FAXFLEET
[E Riding] Tp in South Cave AP, sep CP 1866,[2] eccl severed 1862 to help cr Broomfleet EP,[136] later called 'Broomfleet with Faxfleet'. *LG* Harth. Wap, Howden PLU, RSD, RD. Abol 1935 ent to Blacktoft CP.[13] *Parl* E Riding (1832—85), Howdensh. Dv (1885—1948).

FEARBY
[N Riding] Tp in Masham AP, sep CP 1866.[2] *LG* E Hang Wap, Leyb. PLU, Masham USD, UD (1894—1934), Masham RD (1934—74). Bdry: 1883,[16] 1886,[525] 1886,[526] 1934 (incl help cr Healey CP).[3] Transf 1974 to N Yorks.[5] *Parl* Seq 14.

FEATHERSTONE
AP [W Riding] Tp 'Featherstone' in Osg. Wap as was tp Purston Jaglin (sep CP 1866,[2] sep EP 1875 as 'Purston Jaglin cum South Featherstone'[11]); incl in Agb. Wap tp Ackton (sep CP 1866[2]), tp Whitwood (sep CP 1866,[2] pt eccl severed 1865 to help cr Whitwood Mere EP,[553] the eccl remainder cr 1866 'Whitwood' EP[471]). *LG* Barwick GilbU (until 1869), Pontef. PLU (1869—1930), Featherstone USD, UD. Addtl civ bdry alt: 1938.[28] Transf 1974 to W Yorks.[5] *Parl* W Riding (1832—67), E'rn Dv of W Riding (1867—85), Osg. Dv (1885—1918), Norm. Dv (1918—48), Pontef. BC (1948—70), Pontef. & Castlef. BC (1970—*). *Eccl* Ainsty RDn (until 1820), New Ainsty RDn (1820—57), Pontef. RDn (1857—*). Addtl eccl bdry alt: 1904 (help cr Mickletown EP).[300]

FELIXKIRK
AP [N Riding] Incl tps Boltby, Sutton under Whitstone Cliffe, Thirlby (each a sep CP 1866,[2] neither with sep eccl identity hence this par eccl 'Felixkirk with Boltby', qv). *LG* Seq 27. Transf 1974 to N Yorks.[5]

Parl Seq 16.

FELIXKIRK WITH BOLTBY
AP [N Riding] Usual eccl spelling; for civ and civ sep tps, see prev entry, *Eccl* Seq 20.

FELKIRK
AP [W Riding] Incl tps Brierly, Havercroft with Cold Hiendley, South Hiendley, Shafton (each a sep CP 1866[2] [none with sep eccl identity hence this par eccl sometimes 'Felkirk with Brierley']) so that 'Felkirk' has no sep civ identity after 1866. *LG* Staincr. Wap. *Parl* W Riding (1832—67). *Eccl* Donc. RDn (until 1857), Rotherh. RDn (1857—62), Pontef. RDn (1862—84), Hemsw. RDn (1884—1927), Barnsley RDn (1927—*). Eccl bdry: 1876 (help cr Ryhill EP),[29] 1902 (cr Grimethorpe EP).[364]

FELKIRK WITH BRIERLEY—see prev entry

FELLISCLIFFE
[W Riding] Tp in Hampsthwaite AP, sep CP 1866.[2] *LG* Seq 84. Transf 1974 to N Yorks.[5] *Parl* Seq 36.

CHURCH FENTON
AP [W Riding] Usual civ spelling; for eccl see following entry. Incl tps Biggin, Little Fenton (each a sep CP 1866[2]). *LG* Bark. Ash Wap, Barwick GilbU (until 1869), Tadc. PLU (1869—1930), RSD, RD. Addtl civ bdry alt: 1883.[52] Transf 1974 to N Yorks.[5] *Parl* Seq 24.

KIRK FENTON
AP [W Riding] Usual eccl spelling; for civ and civ sep tps, see prev entry. *Eccl* Pec jurisd Fenton prebend (until 1836), New Ainsty RDn (1836—62), Tadc. RDn (1862—71), Selby RDn (1871—1921), Tadc. RDn (1921—*).

LITTLE FENTON
[W Riding] Tp in Church Fenton AP (eccl, 'Kirk Fenton'), sep CP 1866.[2] *LG* Bark. Ash Wap, Selby PLU (soon after 1837[112]—1930), RSD, RD (1894—1937), Tadc. RD (1937—74). Transf 1974 to N Yorks.[5] *Parl* Seq 24.

FENWICK
[W Riding] Tp in Campsall AP, sep CP 1866,[2] sep EP 1852.[138] *LG* Seq 94. Transf 1974 to S Yorks.[5] *Parl* Seq 27. *Eccl* Donc. RDn. Eccl bdry: 1875 (help cr Moss EP).[11]

FERRENSBY
[W Riding] Tp pt in Farnham AP, pt in Knaresborough AP, sep CP 1866.[2] *LG* Seq 84. Transf 1974 to N Yorks.[5] *Parl* Seq 36.

NORTH FERRIBY
AP [E Riding] (Tp 'North Ferriby' pt in North Ferriby AP, pt in Kirk Ella AP; North Ferriby AP also incl pt of main tp of Kirk Ella AP). Incl chap Kingston upon Hull St Mary (most parochial rights 1333, sep civ identity early, final eccl independence 1868[554]), pt tps West Ella, Swanland, Thirlby (each a sep CP 1866[2]), pt tp Willerby (sep CP 1866[2]). *LG* Seq 18. Addtl civ bdry alt: 1878.[519] Transf 1974 to Humb.[5] *Parl* E Riding (ent 1832—67, pt 1867—85), pt Kingst. upon Hull Parl Bor (1867—85), Howdensh. Dv (pt 1885—1918, ent 1918—48), Bev. CC (1948—55), Haltemp. CC (1955—*); see Part III of the *Guide* for composition of Kingst. upon Hull Parl Bors (1885—1918) incl pt of this par. *Eccl* Seq 12.

Eccl bdry: 1879 (help cr Kingston upon Hull St John the Baptist, Newington EP),[300] 1902 (help cr Anlaby EP).[104]

FEWSTON

AP [W Riding] Incl tps Blubberhouses, Clifton with Norwood, Great Timble (each a sep CP 1866[2]), tp Thruscross (sep CP 1866,[2] sep EP 1875[11]). *LG* Seq 92. Transf 1974 to N Yorks.[5] *Parl* Seq 30. *Eccl* Seq 34.

FILEY

AP [Pt E Riding (Dick. Wap: tp 'Filey'), pt N Riding (Pick. Lythe Wap: tps Gristhorpe, Lebberston [each a sep CP 1866[2]]), ent E Riding (from 1866)] *LG* Scarb. PLU (soon after 1837[112]—1930), Filey USD, UD. Addtl civ bdry alt: 1935.[13] Transf 1974 to N Yorks.[5] *Parl* Pt E Riding, pt N Riding (1832—67), thereafter ent E Riding, Seq 2. *Eccl* Dick. RDn (until 1857), N Dick. RDn (1857—66), Scarb. RDn (1866—*).

FIMBER

[E Riding] Chap (pec jurisd Wetwang prebend, until 1836) in Wetwang AP, sep CP 1866,[2] eccl severed 1923 and transf to Fridaythorpe AP.[555] *LG* Seq 1. Bdry: 1935 (gains Towthorpe CP).[13] Transf 1974 to Humb. *Parl* Seq 3.

FINGHALL

AP [N Riding] Incl chap Burton Constable, tps Akebar, Hutton Hang, pt tp Newton le Willows (each a sep CP 1866[2]). *LG* Seq 53. Transf 1974 to N Yorks.[5] *Parl* Seq 14. *Eccl* Seq 54.

FINNINGLEY

AP [Mostly Notts (Bassetlaw Wap), pt Yorks W Riding (Donc. Soke: tp Blaxton, pt tp Auckey [each a sep CP 1866[2]]) so that Finningley ent Notts thereafter] *Parl* Pt W Riding (1832—67). See main entry in Notts for civ, other parl, and eccl organisation.

FIRBECK

AP [W Riding] Orig chap in Laughton en le Morthen AP (in pec jurisd Laughton en le Morthen prebend), annexed 1484 to pec jurisd Chancellor of York and considered sep par thereafter. *LG* Seq 121. Transf 1974 to S Yorks.[5] *Parl* Seq 48. *Eccl* Pec jurisds as noted (until 1836), Donc. RDn (1836—57), Rotherh. RDn (1857—1942), Laughton RDn (1942—*).

FIRBY

[E Riding] Tp in Westow AP, sep CP 1866.[2] *LG* Seq 2. Bdry: 1935 (gains Kirkham CP).[13] Transf 1974 to N Yorks.[5] *Parl* Seq 1.

FIRBY

[N Riding] Tp in Bedale AP, sep CP 1866.[2] *LG* Seq 49. Transf 1974 to N Yorks.[5] *Parl* Seq 15.

FISHLAKE

AP [W Riding] Incl chap Sykehouse (sep CP 1866,[2] sep EP 1830,[9] eccl refounded 1860[553]). *LG* Seq 120. Addtl civ bdry alt: 1883,[52] 1884,[556] 1884,[557] 1884.[558] Transf 1974 to S Yorks.[5] *Parl* Seq 47. *Eccl* Seq 45. Addtl eccl bdry alt: 1884 (help cr Stainforth EP),[316] 1887.[559]

FITLING

[E Riding] Tp in Humbleton AP, sep CP 1866.[2] *LG* Hold. Wap, Skirkl. PLU, RSD, RD. Abol 1935 to help cr East Garton CP.[13] *Parl* E Riding (1832—85), Hold. Dv (1885—1948).

FIXBY

[W Riding] Tp in Halifax AP, sep CP 1866,[2] eccl severed 1724 to help cr Elland cum Stainland and Fixby EP,[178] although re-augmented as 'Elland',[9] usually 'Elland with Greetland' until cr 1862 of Greetland EP,[138] thereafter 'Elland'. *LG* Morley Wap, Halifax PLU, RSD, RD. Bdry: 1883.[52] Abol 1937 pt to Hudd. CB (assoc with W Riding) & AP, pt to Brigh. MB & CP, pt to Elland UD & CP.[31] *Parl* W Riding (1832—67), E'rn Dv of W Riding (1867—85), Elland Dv (1885—1948).

FLAMBOROUGH

AP [E Riding] *LG* Seq 5. Civ bdry: 1935.[13] Transf 1974 to Humb.[5] *Parl* Seq 2. *Eccl* Seq 7.

FLASBY WITH WINTERBURN

[W Riding] Tp in Gargrave AP, sep CP 1866.[2] *LG* Seq 112. Transf 1974 to N Yorks.[5] *Parl* Seq 41.

FLAWITH

[N Riding] Tp in Alne AP, sep CP 1866.[2] *LG* Seq 28. Transf 1974 to N Yorks.[5] *Parl* Seq 16.

FLAXBY

[W Riding] Tp in Goldsborough AP, sep CP 1866.[2] *LG* Seq 84. Transf 1974 to N Yorks.[5] *Parl* Seq 36.

FLAXTON

[N Riding] Tp pt in Bossall AP, pt in Foston AP, sep CP 1866,[2] sep EP 1861 from Bossall AP.[560] *LG* Seq 32. Transf 1974 to N Yorks.[5] *Parl* Seq 16. *Eccl* Bulmer RDn.

FLINTON

[E Riding] Tp in Humbleton AP, sep CP 1866.[2] *LG* Hold. Wap, Skirl. PLU, RSD, RD. Abol 1935 ent to Humbleton AP.[13] *Parl* E Riding (1832—85), Hold. Dv (1885—1948).

FLOCKTON

[W Riding] Chap in Thornhill AP, sep CP 1866,[2] sep EP 1731,[9] eccl refounded 1860 as 'Flockton cum Denby Grange' by union Flockton EP, pt Thornhill AP (pt tp Shitlington), pt Kirkheaton AP (hmlt Denby Grange),[68] qv. *LG* Agb. Wap, Wakef PLU, Flockton USD, UD (1894—1938), Kirkburton UD (1938—74). Transf 1974 to W Yorks.[5] *Parl* W Riding (1832—67), S'rn Dv of W Riding (1867—85), Norm. Dv (1885—1918), Rothw. Dv (1918—48), Colne Valley CC (1948—55), Hudd. East BC (1955—*). *Eccl* Pontef. RDn (1731—1857), Dewsb. RDn (1857—60).

FLOCKTON CUM DENBY GRANGE

EP [W Riding] Refounding 1860 of Flockton EP by union Flockton EP, pt Thornhill AP (pt tp Shitlington), pt Kirkheaton AP (hmlt Denby Grange).[68] Dewsb. RDn (1860—1913), Wakef RDn (1913—68), Kirkburton RDn (1968—*). Bdry: 1878 (help cr Middlestown EP).[198]

FOCKERBY

[W Riding] Tp in Adlingfleet AP, sep CP 1866.[2] *LG* Seq 95. Bdry: 1884.[500] Transf 1974 to Humb.[5] *Parl* Seq 29.

FOGGATHORPE

[E Riding] Tp in Bubwith AP, sep CP 1866.[2] *LG* Seq 11. Bdry: 1935 (gains Gribthorpe CP, Harlthorpe CP, Laytham CP),[13] 1957.[561] Transf 1974 to Humb.[5] *Parl* Seq 7.

FOLKTON

AP [E Riding] *LG* Seq 7. Transf 1974 to N Yorks.[5] *Parl* Seq 2. *Eccl* Seq 4.

FOLLIFOOT

[W Riding] Tp in Spofforth AP, sep CP 1866.[2] *LG* Seq 84. Bdry: 1938.[28] Transf 1974 to N Yorks.[5] *Parl* Seq 36.

FORCETT

AP [N Riding] Orig AP, perhaps once dependent on Gilling AP, granted as church to York St Mary Abbey, eccl treated thereafter as chap to Gilling AP,[562] sep civ identity maintained or regained early, sep EP 1843 as 'Forcett with Carkin' from Gilling AP,[9] as such eccl refounded 1898,[63] qv. Incl tp Carkin (jointly rated with tp 'Forcett' as 'Forcett with Carkin', qv), pt tp Barforth (detached pt, hmlt Little Hutton, 'Barforth' a sep CP 1866[2]), tp Eppleby (sep CP 1866[2]), tp Ovington (sep CP 1866,[2] eccl severed 1899 and transf to Wycliffe AP[563]) so that 'Forcett' has no sep civ identity after 1866. *LG* W Gill. Wap. *Parl* N Riding (1832—67).

FORCETT WITH CARKIN

[N Riding] Civ a joint tp, union tp 'Forcett' AP and tp Carkin (for early status of Forcett AP and civ and eccl sep other tps, see prev entry); eccl, sep EP 1843 from Gilling AP,[9] eccl refounded 1898.[63] *LG* Seq 38. Transf 1974 to N Yorks.[5] *Parl* Seq 14. *Eccl* Richm. RDn (1843—57), Richm. West RDn (1857—94), Richm. East RDn (1894—*). Eccl bdry: 1918 (incl gains area East Layton CP from Melsonby AP, Stanwick AP),[564] 1955.[565]

FORDON

[E Riding] Chap in Hunmanby AP, sep CP 1866,[2] eccl severed 1858 to help cr Burton Fleming with Fordon EP.[381] *LG* Dick. Wap, Bridl. PLU, RSD, RD. Abol 1935 ent to Wold Newton AP.[13] *Parl* E Riding (1832—85), Buckr. Dv (1885—1948).

FOSTON

CP [E Riding] Cr 1935 by union Brigham AP, Foston on the Wolds AP.[13] *LG* Driff. RD. Bdry: 1953.[227] Transf 1974 to Humb.[5] *Parl* Bridl. CC (1948—55), Howden CC (1955—*).

FOSTON

AP [N Riding] lncl tp Thornton le Clay (sep CP 1866[2]), pt tp Flaxton on the Moor (sep CP 1866,[2] sep EP 1861 [but ent from Bossall AP][292]). *LG* Seq 29. Addtl civ bdry alt: 1889.[566] Transf 1974 to N Yorks.[5] *Parl* Seq 16. *Eccl* Seq 17.

FOSTON ON THE WOLDS

AP [E Riding] Incl tps Brigham, Gembling, Great Kelk (each a sep CP 1866[2]); orig incl chap Little Kelk (long considered ex-par, sep CP 1858,[393] abol eccl 1929 ent to Cowthorpe AP[567]). *LG* Dick. Wap, Driff. PLU, RSD, RD. Abol 1935 to help cr Foston CP.[13] *Parl* E Riding (1832—85), Buckr. Dv (1885—1948). *Eccl* Dick. RDn (until 1857), S Dick. RDn (1857—66), Scarb. RDn (1866—87), Harthill RDn (1887—*).

FOUNTAINS EARTH

[W Riding] Tp in Kirkby Malzeard AP, sep CP 1866.[2] *LG* Seq 89. Transf 1974 to N Yorks.[5] *Parl* Seq 33.

FOXHOLES

AP [E Riding] Orig chap in Burton Agnes AP, appropriated to York St Mary Abbey early 12th cent and considered parochial thereafter.[375] Incl chap Butterwick (sep CP 1866,[2] sep EP 1790[9]), tp Foxholes with Boythorpe (sep CP 1866[2]) so that 'Foxholes' has no sep civ identity 1866—1935 (see following entry). *LG* Dick. Wap. *Parl* E Riding (1832—67). *Eccl* Dick. RDn (until 1857), N Dick. RDn (1857—66), Scarb. RDn (1866—87), Buckr. RDn (1887—1922), Scarb. RDn (1922—47). Abol eccl 1947 to help cr Foxholes with Butterwick EP.[22]

CP [E Riding] Cr 1935 by union Butterwick CP, Foxholes with Boythorpe CP.[13] *LG* Norton RD. Transf 1974 to N Yorks.[5] *Parl* Bev. CC (1948—55), Howden CC (1955—*).

FOXHOLES WITH BOYTHORPE

[E Riding] Tp in Foxholes AP, sep CP 1866.[2] *LG* Dick. Wap, Driff. PLU, RSD, RD. Abol 1935 to help cr Foxholes CP.[13] *Parl* E Riding (1832—85), Buckr. Dv (1885—1948).

FOXHOLES WITH BUTTERWICK

EP [E Riding] Cr 1947 by union Foxholes AP, Butterwick EP.[22] Scarb. RDn (1947—72), Harth. RDn (1972—*).

FRAISTHORPE

[E Riding] Chap in Carnaby AP, inhabitants of Auburn chap in same par told to attend this chap, the 2 a sep EP 1731 as 'Auburn with Fraisthorpe',[9] 'Fraisthorpe' a sep EP 1824 (the remainder to be 'Auburn' EP),[9] sep eccl status not sustained and considered eccl in Carnaby AP, sep CP 1866,[2] eccl severed 1929 to help cr Barmston with Fraisthorpe EP.[186] *LG* Dick. Wap, Bridl. PLU, RSD, RD. Abol civ 1896 to help cr Fraisthorpe with Auburn and Wilsthorpe CP.[153] *Parl* E Riding (1832—85), Buckr. Dv (1885—1918). *Eccl* Dick. RDn.

FRAISTHORPE WITH AUBURN AND WILSTHORPE

CP [E Riding] Cr 1896 by union Fraisthorpe CP, Auburn CP, Wilsthorpe CP.[153] *LG* Bridl. PLU, RD. Abol 1935 pt to Bridl. MB & AP, pt to Bempton AP.[13] *Parl* Buckr. Dv (1918—48).

FRIARMERE

EP [W Riding] Cr 1795 from Rochdale AP (Lancs, Yorks W Riding until 1866, ent Lancs thereafter),[9] refounded 1844.[481] Manch RDn (1795—1847), Ashton under Lyne RDn (1847—72), Rochdale RDn (1872—81), Ashton under Lyne RDn (1881—*). Bdry: 1864 (cr Denshaw EP).[326]

FRICKLEY—see CLAYTON WITH FRICKLEY

FRIDAYTHORPE

AP [E Riding] *LG* Buckr. Wap, Pockl. PLU, RSD, RD (1894—1935), Driff. RD (1935—74). Transf 1974 to Humb.[5] *Parl* E Riding (1832—85), Buckr. Dv (1885—1918), Howdensh. Dv (1918—48), Bridl. CC (1948—55), Howden CC (1955—*). *Eccl* Pec jurisd Wetwang prebend (until 1836), Buckr. RDn (1836—57), E Buckr. RDn (1857—66), Buckr. RDn (1866—87), Settr. RDn (1887—1922), Buckr. RDn (1922—61). Eccl bdry: 1923 (gains chap Fimber from Wetwang AP).[555] *Eccl* name declared 1961 to be 'Fridaythorpe with Fimber'.[568]

FRIDAYTHORPE WITH FIMBER

EP [E Riding] Name of Fridaythorpe AP eccl declared 1961 to be 'Fridaythorpe with Fimber' (see prev entry for eccl gain chap Fimber).[568] Settr. RDn. Bdry: 1968.[44]

FRIEZELAND

EP [W Riding] Cr 1848 from Saddleworth EP, Lydgate EP (both Yorks), Staley EP (Ches).[86] Ashton under Lyne RDn (1848—72), Rochdale RDn (1872—81), Ashton under Lyne RDn (1881—1929), Oldham RDn (1929—*). Bdry: 1876 (help cr Greenfield EP).[29]

FRIZINGHALL

EP [W Riding] Cr 1910 from Heaton St Barnabas EP.[476] Bradf RDn (1910—71), Airedale RDn (1971—*). Bdry: 1927.[288]

NORTH FRODINGHAM

AP [E Riding] LG Hold. Wap, Driff. PLU, RSD, RD. Transf 1974 to Humb.[5] Parl Seq 3. Eccl Hold. RDn (until 1849), N Hold. RDn (1849—66), Hornsea RDn (1866—87), Harth. RDn (1887—*).

SOUTH FRODINGHAM

[E Riding] Tp in Owthorne AP, sep CP 1866.[2] LG Hold. Wap, Patr. PLU, RSD, RD. Abol 1935 to help cr Rimswell CP.[13] Parl E Riding (1832—85), Hold. Dv (1885—1948).

FERRY FRYSTON

AP [W Riding] (Tp Ferry Fryston pt in Ferry Fryston AP, pt in Pontefract AP). LG Osg. Wap, Barwick GilbU (until 1869), Pontef. PLU (1869—1930), RSD, RD. Abol 1937 pt to Pontef. MB & AP, pt to Castlef. UD & AP, pt to Knottingley UD & CP, pt to Fairburn CP.[28] Parl Pontef. Parl Bor (1832—1918), Pontef. Dv (1918—48). Eccl Ainsty RDn (until 1820), New Ainsty RDn (1820—57), Pontef. RDn (1857—1930). Abol eccl 1930 to help cr Airedale with Fryston EP.[45]

MONK FRYSTON

[W Riding] Chap in Wistow AP, sep civ identity early, sep EP 1815.[9] Incl tps Burton Salmon, Hillam (each a sep CP 1866[2]). LG Seq 75. Addtl civ bdry alt: 1883,[52] 1937.[31] Transf 1974 to N Yorks.[5] Parl Seq 26. Eccl Pec jurisd Selby (1440—1539), pec jurisd Wistow (1539—1836), Old Ainsty RDn (1836—57), Pontef. RDn (1857—62), Tadc. RDn (1862—71), Selby RDn (1871—*). Eccl bdry: 1859 (help cr South Milford EP).[300]

FRYTON

[N Riding] Tp in Hovingham AP, sep CP 1866.[2] LG Seq 65. Transf 1974 to N Yorks. Parl Seq 16.

FULFORD

[E Riding] Chap in York St Olave, Marygate AP (after 1586, eccl 'York St Olave with St Giles'), comprised civ of tp Gate Fulford, pt tp Water Fulford (each a sep CP 1866[2]), the name 'Fulfords Ambo' used sometimes civ after 1828 for this ent area until 2 tps sep civ identity 1866, 'Fulford' a sep EP 1746,[9] some eccl dependence perhaps remaining until 1825.[569] LG Ouse & Derw. Wap. Parl E Riding (1832—67). Eccl City of York RDn (1828—62), York RDn (1862—71), Bp'thorpe RDn (1871—96), City of York RDn (1896—*).

CP [E Riding] Renaming 1935 of Water Fulford CP.[13]

LG Derw. RD. Transf 1974 to Humb.[5] Parl Bev. CC (1948—55), Howden CC (1955—*).

GATE FULFORD

[E Riding] Tp in chap Fulford (sometimes civ after 1828 'Fulfords Ambo'; for eccl separation from York St Olave with St Giles, see prev entry), sep CP 1866.[2] LG Ouse & Derw. Wap, York PLU, pt York MB (1884—89), York CB (pt 1889—94, ent 1894—1900), pt York USD (1884—94), York RSD (ent 1875—84, pt 1884—94). Bdry: 1894 (loses the pt not in York CB [not assoc with any Riding] to Water Fulford CP).[51] Abol 1900 to help cr York CP.[423] Parl E Riding (1832—85), pt York Parl Bor, pt Howdensh. Dv (1885—1918).

WATER FULFORD

[E Riding] Tp pt in chap Fulford (sometimes civ after 1828 'Fulfords Ambo'; for eccl separation chap Fulford from York St Olave with St Giles, see 'Fulford'), pt in Heslington St Paul AP, pt in York St Martin, Micklegate AP, sep CP 1866.[2] LG Ouse & Derw. Wap, York PLU, RSD, Escr. RD. Bdry: 1894 (gains the pt of Gate Fulford CP not in York CB).[51] Renamed 1935 'Fulford' CP.[13] Parl E Riding (1832—85), Howdensh. Dv (1885—1948).

FULFORDS AMBO—see FULFORD

FULL SUTTON

AP [E Riding] Chap in Catton AP, sep par early 13th cent.[241] LG Seq 12. Transf 1974 to Humb.[5] Parl Seq 7. Eccl Harth. & Hull RDn (until 1857), W Buckr. RDn (1857—66), Pockl. RDn (1866—*).

FULSTONE

[W Riding] Tp in Kirkburton AP, sep CP 1866,[2] pt eccl severed 1858 to help refound Holmfirth EP.[293] LG Agb. Wap, Hudd. PLU, pt Scholes USD, pt Fulstone USD, pt Holmf. USD (1884—94), pt Hepworth USD (1886—94), Fulstone UD (1894—95), New Mill UD (1895—1938). Bdry: 1883,[52] 1886,[157] 1894 (loses the pt in Scholes UD to cr Scholes CP),[158] 1895.[570] Abol 1938 pt to Holmf. UD & CP, pt to help cr Dunford CP.[28] Parl W Riding (1832—67), S'rn Dv of W Riding (1867—85), Holmf. Dv (1885—1918), Colne Valley Dv (1918—48).

FULWOOD

EP [W Riding] Cr 1839 from Sheffield AP.[9] Donc. RDn (1839—57), Rotherh. RDn (1857—62), Sheff RDn (1862—1942), Hallam RDn (1942—*). Bdry: 1879 (help cr Ranmoor EP),[218] 1962.[455]

FURSLEY

EP [W Riding] Cr 1723 from Leeds AP,[9] Ainsty RDn, sep status not sustained.

FYLINGDALES

[N Riding] Chap in Whitby AP, sep civ identity early, sep EP 1786.[9] Incl undivided pt Fylingdales Moor (Land Common to Hawsker with Stainsacre and Fylingdales). LG Seq 68. Transf 1974 to N Yorks.[5] Parl Seq 19. Eccl Clev RDn (1723—1862), Guisb. RDn (1862—78), Whitby RDn (1878—*). Eccl bdry: 1914 (help cr Ravenscar EP).[168]

FYLINGDALES MOOR

[N Riding] Land in Whitby AP, after sep civ identity of chap Fylingdales, tp Hawsker cum Stainsacre, common to those two CPs. LG Whitby

RD. Transf 1974 to N Yorks.[5] *Parl* Scarb. & Whitby Dv/CC (1918—70), Clev & Whitby CC (1970—*).

GANSTEAD

[E Riding] Tp in Swine AP, sep CP 1866,[2] eccl in chap Bilton in same par (sep EP 1794,[9] eccl refounded 1867[250]). *LG* Hold. Wap, Skirl. PLU, RSD, RD. Abol 1935 ent to Bilton CP.[13] *Parl* E Riding (1832—85), Hold. Dv (1885—1948).

GANTHORPE

[N Riding] Tp in Terrington AP, sep CP 1866.[2] *LG* Seq 29. Transf 1974 to N Yorks.[5] *Parl* Seq 16.

GANTON

AP [E Riding] *LG* Seq 8. Transf 1974 to N Yorks.[5] *Parl* Seq 1. *Eccl* Seq 4.

GARFORTH

AP [W Riding] Incl pt tp Austhorpe (sep CP 1866[2]). *LG* Skyr. Wap, Gt Preston GilbU (until 1869), Tadc. PLU (1869—1930), RSD, RD (1894—1908), Garforth UD (1908—74). Addtl civ bdry alt: 1939 (gains Allerton Bywater CP, Kippax AP).[76] Transf 1974 to W Yorks.[5] *Parl* Seq 24. *Eccl* Ainsty RDn (until 1820), New Ainsty RDn (1820—36), Pontef. RDn (1836—57), Wakef RDn (1857—94), Whitkirk RDn (1894—*).

GARGRAVE

AP [W Riding] Incl tps Bank Newton, Eshton, Flasby with Winterburn (each a sep CP 1866[2]), tp Coniston Cold (sep CP 1866,[2] sep EP 1840 as 'Coniston',[9] eccl refounded as such 1847 pt from Gargrave AP, pt from Kirkby Malham AP[435]). *LG* Seq 112. Addtl civ bdry alt: 1938.[28] Transf 1974 to N Yorks.[5] *Parl* Seq 41. *Eccl* Seq 35. Addtl eccl bdry alt: 1930.[210]

GARRISON SIDE

[E Riding] Ex-par place, sep CP 1858.[393] *LG* Kingst. upon Hull Co, Scul. PLU (1858—98), Kingst. upon Hull MB (1835—89), CB (1889—98), USD. Abol 1898 ent to Sculcoates AP.[446] *Parl* Kingst. upon Hull Parl Bor (1832—85); see Part III of the *Guide* for composition of Kingst. upon Hull Parl Bors (1885—1918) by wards of the MB.

GARRISTON

[N Riding] Tp in Hauxwell AP, sep CP 1866.[2] *LG* Seq 53. Transf 1974 to N Yorks.[5] *Parl* Seq 14.

GARSDALE

[W Riding] Chap in Sedbergh AP, sep CP 1866,[2] sep EP 1734.[9] *LG* Seq 110. Transf 1974 to Cumbria.[5] *Parl* Seq 41. *Eccl* Kirkby Lonsd. RDn (1734—1849), Clapham RDn (1849—1921), Ewecr. RDn (1921—26), Sedbergh RDn (1926—71), Ewecr. RDn (1971—74). Abol eccl 1974 to help cr Sedbergh, Cauntley and Garsdale EP.[471]

GARTON

AP [E Riding] Incl pt tps Garton with Grimston, Owstwick (each a sep CP 1866,[2] neither with sep eccl identity hence this par eccl 'Garton in Holderness with Grimston', qv) so that 'Garton' has no sep civ identity after 1866. *LG* Hold. Wap. *Parl* E Riding (1832—67).

GARTON

CP [E Riding] Cr 1935 by union Garton on the Wolds AP, pt Emswell with Little Driffield CP.[13] *LG* Driff. RD. Transf 1974 to Humb.[5] *Parl* Bridl. CC

(1948—55), Howden CC (1955—*).

EAST GARTON

CP [E Riding] Cr 1935 by union Fitling AP, Garton with Grimston CP.[13] *LG* Hold. RD. Transf 1974 to Humb.[5] *Parl* Bridl. CC (1948—*).

GARTON IN HOLDERNESS WITH GRIMSTON

AP [E Riding] Usual eccl spelling; for civ and civ sep tps, see 'Garton'. *Eccl* Seq 16.

GARTON ON THE WOLDS

AP [E Riding] *LG* Dick. Wap, Driff. PLU, RSD, RD. Abol civ 1935 to help cr Garton CP.[13] *Parl* E Riding (1832—85), Buckr. Dv (1885—1918). *Eccl* Dick. RDn (until 1857), N Harth. RDn (1857—66), Harth. RDn (1866—*).

GARTON WITH GRIMSTON

[E Riding] Tp pt in Garston AP, pt in Roos AP, sep CP 1866.[2] *LG* Hold. Wap, Skirl. PLU, RSD, RD. Abol 1935 to help cr East Garton CP.[13] *Parl* E Riding (1832—85), Hold. Dv (1885—1948).

GATEFORTH

[W Riding] Tp in Brayton AP, sep CP 1866,[2] sep EP 1914 as 'Gateforth Hambleton' by union pt of this tp, tp Hambleton also in Brayton AP,[340] qv. *LG* Seq 80. Transf 1974 to N Yorks.[5] *Parl* Seq 24.

GATEFORTH CUM HAMBLETON

EP [W Riding] Cr 1914 by union pt tp Gateforth, tp Hambleton, both in Brayton AP.[340] Selby RDn.

GATENBY

[N Riding] Tp in Burneston AP, sep CP 1866.[2] *LG* Seq 40. Transf 1974 to N Yorks.[5] *Parl* Seq 18.

GAWBER

EP [W Riding] Cr 1849 from Darton AP.[309] Pontef. RDn (1849—57), Silkst. RDn (1857—1927), Barnsley RDn (1927—*).

GAWTHORPE AND CHICKENLEY HEATH

EP [W Riding] Cr 1901 from Ossett cum Gawthorpe EP, Earls Heaton EP, Hanging Heaton EP.[284] Dewsb. RDn.

GAYLES

[N Riding] Tp in Kirkby Ravensworth AP, sep CP 1866.[2] *LG* Seq 38. Transf 1974 to N Yorks.[5] *Parl* Seq 14.

GEMBLING

[E Riding] Tp in Foston on the Wolds AP, sep CP 1866.[2] *LG* Dick. Wap, Driff. PLU, RSD, RD. Abol 1935 ent to Beeford AP.[13] *Parl* E Riding (1832—85) Buckr. Dv (1885—1918).

GIGGLESWICK

AP [W Riding] Incl tp Langcliffe (sep CP 1866,[2] sep EP 1851[293]), tp Rathmell (sep CP 1866,[2] sep EP 1841,[9] eccl refounded 1842 from Giggleswick AP, Long Preston AP[196]), tp Settle (sep CP 1866,[2] sep EP 1838[560]), tp Stainforth (sep CP 1866,[2] sep EP 1842 from this and 3 other pars [qv][136]). *LG* Seq 111. Addtl civ bdry alt: 1912.[571] Transf 1974 to N Yorks.[5] *Parl* Seq 41. *Eccl* Seq 35.

GILBERDIKE

[E Riding] Tp in Eastrington AP, sep CP 1866,[2] eccl ex-par as 'Gilberdike Mill', severed 1895 to help cr Newport EP.[284] *LG* Howdensh. Wap, Howden PLU, RSD, RD. Bdry: 1880 (help cr Bishopsoil CP),[142] 1880.[171] Abol 1935 pt to Eastrington AP, pt to help cr Gilberdyke CP.[13] *Parl*

E Riding (1832—85), Howdensh. Dv (1885—1948).

GILBERDIKE MILL—see prev entry

GILBERDYKE

CP [E Riding] Cr 1935 by union Bishopsoil CP, pts Balkholme CP, Blacktoft CP, Gilberdike CP, Kilpin CP, Scalby CP, Yokefleet CP.[13] *LG* Howden RD. Bdry: 1957.[561] Transf 1974 to Humb.[5] *Parl* Bev. CC (1948—55), Howden CC (1955—*).

GILDERSOME

[W Riding] Chap in Batley AP, sep CP 1866,[2] sep EP 1789,[9] eccl refounded 1832.[85] *LG* Morley Wap, Bramley PLU, Gildersome USD, UD. Abol 1937 ent to Morley MB & CP.[31] *Parl* W Riding (1832—67), E'rn Dv of W Riding (1867—85), Pudsey Dv (1885—1918), Spen Valley Dv (1918—48). *Eccl* Pontef. RDn (1789—1857), Dewsb. RDn (1857—66), Birstall RDn (1866—83), Dewsb. RDn (1883—1927), Birstall RDn (1927—*).

GILDINGWELLS

[W Riding] Tp in area St John's with Throapham (sep civ identity early from Laughton en le Morthen AP, sep EP 1742[9]), sep CP 1866,[2] eccl severed 1768 from Throapham St John's EP to help cr Letwell with Gildingwells EP,[9] area Gildingwells eccl severed 1841 from the latter to help cr Woodsetts EP, the remainder of the latter to be 'Letwell'.[572] *LG* Seq 121. Transf 1974 to S Yorks.[5] *Parl* Seq 48.

GILLAMOOR

[N Riding] Tp in Kirkby Moorside AP, sep CP 1866.[2] *LG* Seq 64. Bdry: 1883,[16] 1887,[538] 1934.[3] Transf 1974 to N Yorks.[5] *Parl* Seq 21.

GILLCAR

EP [W Riding] Cr 1866 from Sheffield AP.[54] Sheff RDn (1866—1942), Ecclesall RDn (1942—*). Bdry: 1962.[455] Now usually called 'Sheffield St Silas'.

GILLING

AP [N Riding] Tp 'Gilling' in E Gill. Wap as were chap Barton (comprised of areas of tp Newton Morrell, pt tp Barton, pt tp Stapleton [each a sep CP 1866[2]], the ent area a sep EP 1732 as 'Barton St Mary'[9] [the remainder of Barton in Stanwick AP, sep EP 1754 as 'Barton St Cuthbert'[9]; the 2 EPs united 1840 as 'Barton' EP[201]]), chap South Cowton (sep CP 1866,[2] sep EP 1783 incl area tp North Cowton[9]), chap Eryholme (sep CP 1866,[2] sep EP 1801[9]), chap Forcett (orig AP, perhaps once dependent on Gilling AP, granted as church to York St Mary Abbey, eccl treated thereafter as chap to Gilling AP,[562] sep civ identity maintained or regained early, sep EP 1843 as 'Forcett with Carkin',[9] as such eccl refounded 1898[63]; Forcett incl tp Carkin [with which jointly rated as 'Forcett with Carkin'], pt tp Barforth, tp Eppleby, tp Ovington; for civ and eccl separation of latter, see Forcett), tp North Cowton (sep CP 1866,[2] eccl severed 1783 to help cr South Cowton EP[9]); incl in W Gill. Wap tp Hutton Magna (sep CP 1866,[2] sep EP 1783[9]), tp West Layton (sep CP 1866[2]), pt tp Stanwick St John (sep CP 1866[2]). *LG* Richm. PLU, RSD, RD. Transf 1974 to N Yorks.[5] *Parl* Seq 14. *Eccl* Seq 58.

GILLING

AP [N Riding] Incl tps Cawton, Gilling East, Grimston (each a sep CP 1866[2]) so that 'Gilling' has no sep civ identity after 1866. *LG* Ryed. Wap. *Parl* N Riding (1832—67). *Eccl* Seq 26.

GILLING EAST

[N Riding] Tp in Gilling AP, sep CP 1866.[2] *LG* Seq 63. Transf 1974 to N Yorks.[5] *Parl* Seq 21.

GILMONBY

[N Riding] Tp in Bowes AP, sep CP 1866.[2] *LG* Seq 39. Transf 1974 to Durham.[5] *Parl* Seq 14.

GIRLINGTON

EP [W Riding] Cr 1860 from Manningham EP.[301] Bradf RDn (1860—1971), Airedale RDn (1971—*). Bdry: 1910 (help cr Manningham St Chad EP),[416] 1911,[365] 1924 (help cr Bradford St Saviour EP),[66] 1927.[67]

GIRSBY

[N Riding] Tp (Yorks N Riding, Allert. Wap) in Sockburn AP (Durham [Stock. Ward], Yorks N Riding [Allert. Wap] until 1866, ent Durham thereafter), sep CP 1866 in Yorks.[2] *LG* Seq 21. Transf 1974 to N Yorks.[5] *Parl* Seq 11.

GISBURN

AP [W Riding] Incl tp Gisburn Forest (sep CP 1866,[2] sep EP 1839 as 'Houghton (or Tosside)',[9] eccl refounded 1870 as 'Tosside'[213]), tp Middop (sep CP 1866,[9] sep EP 1741[9]), tps Horton, Nappa, Newsholme, Paythorne, Rimington, Swinden (each a sep CP 1866[2]). *LG* Seq 108. Addtl civ bdry alt: 1938.[28] Transf 1974 to Lancs.[5] *Parl* Seq 41. *Eccl* Seq 38.

GISBURN FOREST

[W Riding] Tp in Gisburn AP, sep CP 1866,[2] sep EP 1739 as 'Houghton (or Tosside)',[9] eccl refounded 1870 as 'Tosside'.[213] *LG* Seq 108. Bdry: 1938.[28] Transf 1974 to Lancs.[5] Seq 41.

GIVENDALE

[W Riding] Tp in Ripon AP, sep CP 1866,[2] eccl (pec jurisd Dean of York) in chap Skelton (sep EP 1749 from Ripon AP,[9] eccl refounded 1815 as 'Skelton cum Newby'[11]). *LG* Seq 100. Transf 1974 to N Yorks.[5] *Parl* Seq 34.

GREAT GIVENDALE WITH GRIMTHORPE

AP [E Riding] Orig chap in Pocklington AP, sep par 1252.[573] Incl chap Millington with Little Givendale (sep CP 1866,[2] sep EP 1870[574]). *LG* Harth. Wap, Pockl. PLU, RSD, RD. Abol civ 1935 to help cr Millington CP.[13] *Parl* E Riding (1832—85), Howdensh. Dv (1885—1948). *Eccl* Harth. & Hull RDn (until 1857), W Buckr. RDn (1857—62), Pockl. RDn (1862—*).

GLAISDALE

[N Riding] Chap in Danby AP, sep CP 1866,[2] sep EP 1741.[9] Incl undivided pt Land Common to Danby and Glaisdale (abol 1929 with pt to each par[468]). *LG* Seq 59. Transf 1974 to N Yorks.[5] *Parl* Seq 19. *Eccl* Clev RDn (1741—1862), Guisb. RDn (1862—78), Whitby RDn (1878—*). Eccl bdry: 1967.[139]

GLASS HOUGHTON

[W Riding] Tp in Castleford AP, sep CP 1866,[2] sep EP 1923.[188] *LG* Osg. Wap, Gt Preston GilbU (until

1869), Pontef. PLU (1869—1930), RSD, RD. Abol 1937 ent to Castlef. UD & AP.[31] *Parl* W Riding (1832—67), N'rn Dv of W Riding (1867—85), Osg. Dv (1885—1918), Pontef. Dv (1918—48). *Eccl* Pontef. RDn. Abol eccl 1930 to help cr Airedale with Fryston EP.[45]

GLEADLESS
EP [W Riding] Cr 1881 from Handsworth AP.[536] Rotherh. RDn (1881—1927), Handsw. RDn (1927—42), Attercliffe RDn (1942—*). Bdry: 1938 (help cr Sheffield St Paul Arbourthorne EP),[575] 1941 (help cr Sheffield St Catherine Richmond Road EP),[576] 1974 (help cr Gleadless Valley EP [Derbys, Yorks W Riding]).[577]

GLEADLESS VALLEY
EP [W Riding] Cr 1974 from Norton AP (Derbys), Heeley EP, Gleadless EP (both Yorks W Riding).[577] Attercliffe RDn.

GLUSBURN
[W Riding] Tp in Kildwick AP, sep CP 1866.[2] *LG* Seq 112. Transf 1974 to N Yorks.[5] Parl Seq 40.

GOATHLAND
[N Riding] Chap in Pickering AP, sep CP 1866,[2] sep EP 1745.[9] *LG* Pick. Lythe Wap, Whitby PLU, RSD, RD. Transf 1974 to N Yorks.[5] *Parl* Seq 19. *Eccl* Pec jurisd Dean of York (until 1836), Riddal RDn (1836—62), Guisb. RDn (1862—78), Whitby RDn (1878—*).

GOLCAR
[W Riding] Chap in Huddersfield AP, sep CP 1866,[2] sep EP 1836,[9] eccl refounded 1843.[37] *LG* Agb. Wap, Hudd. PLU, Golcar USD, UD. Abol civ 1937 pt to Hudd. CB (assoc with W Riding) & AP, pt to help cr Colne Valley UD & CP.[31] *Parl* W Riding (1832—67), S'rn Dv of W Riding (1867—85), Colne Valley Dv (1885—1948). *Eccl* Pontef. RDn (1836—57), Hudd. RDn (1857—1968), Blackmoorfoot RDn (1968—*).

GOLDSBOROUGH
AP [W Riding] Incl tps Coneythorpe, Flaxby (each a sep CP 1866[2]). *LG* Seq 87. Transf 1974 to N Yorks.[5] *Parl* Seq 36. *Eccl* Seq 51. Eccl bdry: 1924 (help refound Arkendale EP).[77]

GOLDTHORPE
EP [W Riding] Cr 1916 from Bolton upon Dearne AP.[290] Wath RDn.

GOMERSAL
[W Riding] Tp in Birstall AP, sep CP 1866,[2] sep EP 1846 from pt tp Gomersal.[160] *LG* Morley Wap, Dewsb. PLU, pt Gomersal USD, pt Birstall USD, pt Birkenshaw USD, Gomersal UD (1894—1915), Spenb. UD (1915—55), MB (1955—74). Civ bdry: 1894 (loses the pt in Birkenshaw UD to cr Birkenshaw CP, loses the pt in Birstall UD to cr Birstall CP),[257] 1937 (gains Birkenshaw CP).[31] Transf 1974 to W Yorks.[5] *Parl* Seq 38. *Eccl* Pontef. RDn (1846—57), Dewsb. RDn (1857—66), Birstall RDn (1866—*). Eccl bdry: 1846,[277] 1900.[188]

GOODMANHAM
AP [E Riding] *LG* Seq 12. Transf 1974 to Humb.[5] *Parl* Seq 7. *Eccl* Pec jurisd Dean & Chapter of York (orig but not later), Seq 14 thereafter.

GOOLE
[W Riding] Chap and tp in Snaith AP, sep CP 1866,[2] sep EP (prev as chap, pec jurisd Selby [1440—1539], pec jurisd Snaith [1539—1836]) 1849,[247] eccl refounded 1905 incl pt Airmyn EP.[48] *LG* Osg. Wap, Goole PLU, pt Goole USD, pt Goole RSD, Goole UD (1894—1933), MB (1933—74). Civ bdry: 1894 (reconstituted by union of pts of following pars in Goole UD: Airmyn CP, Goole CP, Hook CP, losing the pt not in the UD to help cr Goole Fields CP).[47] *Parl* Seq 29. *Eccl* New Ainsty RDn (1849—57), Pontef. RDn (1857—62), Selby RDn (1862—71), Snaith RDn (1871—*). Eccl bdry: 1905.[48]

GOOLE FIELDS
CP [W Riding] Cr 1894 by union of the pts of Goole CP, Hook CP not made pt of reconstituted Goole UD & CP.[47] *LG* Goole PLU, RD. Transf 1974 to Humb.[5] *Parl* Pontef. Dv (1918—48), Goole CC (1948—*).

GOWDALL
[W Riding] Tp in Snaith AP, sep CP 1866.[2] *LG* Seq 95. Transf 1974 to Humb.[5] *Parl* Seq 29.

GOXHILL
AP [E Riding] *LG* Hold. Wap, Skirl. PLU, RSD, RD. Abol 1935 to help cr Hatfield CP.[13] *Parl* E Riding (1832—85), Hold. Dv (1885—1948). *Eccl* Hold. RDn (until 1849), N Hold. RDn (1849—66), Hornsea RDn (1866—1916), N Hold. RDn (1916—38). Abol eccl 1938 to help cr Hornsea with Goxhill EP.[27]

GRANGETOWN
EP [N Riding] Cr 1917 from Eston EP, Wilton EP.[464] Middlesb. RDn.

GRANSMOOR
[E Riding] Tp in Burton Agnes AP, sep CP 1866.[2] *LG* Dick. Wap, Bridl. PLU, RSD, RD. Bdry: 1884.[377] Abol 1935 ent to Burton Agnes AP.[378] *Parl* E Riding (1832—85), Buckr. Dv (1885—1948).

GRANTLEY
[W Riding] Tp in Ripon AP, sep CP 1866,[2] eccl severed 1740 to help cr Winksley cum Grantley EP,[9] as such eccl refounded 1863.[163] *LG* Seq 100. Transf 1974 to N Yorks.[5] *Parl* Seq 34.

GRASSINGTON
[W Riding] Tp in Linton AP, sep CP 1866.[2] *LG* Seq 112. Transf 1974 to N Yorks.[5] *Parl* Seq 41.

GREASBROUGH
[W Riding] Chap in Rotherham AP, sep CP 1866,[2] sep EP 1718,[9] eccl refounded 1849.[323] *LG* Straff. & Tick. Wap, Rotherh. PLU, pt Greasbrough USD, pt Rotherh. MB (1871—89), pt Rotherh. CB (1889—94), pt Rotherh. USD, Greasbrough UD. Civ bdry: 1894 (loses the pt in Rotherh. CB [assoc with W Riding] to Rotherham AP).[359] Abol civ 1936 pt to Rotherh. CB (assoc with W Riding) & AP, pt to Rawmarsh UD & AP, pt to Wentworth CP.[132] *Parl* W Riding (1832—67), S'rn Dv of W Riding (1867—85), Rotherh. Dv (1885—1918), Rotherh. Parl Bor (1918—48). *Eccl* Donc. RDn (1718—57), Rotherh. RDn (1857—71), Wath RDn (1871—87), Rotherh. RDn (1887—*). Eccl bdry: 1865 (help cr

Masborough St John EP),[578] 1869 (help cr Park Gate EP),[209] 1969 (help cr Kimberworth Park EP).[579]

GREENFIELD
EP [W Riding] Cr 1876 from Saddleworth EP, Friezland EP.[29] Rochdale RDn (1876—81), Ashton under Lyne RDn (1881—1929), Oldham RDn (1929—*).

GREENGATES
EP [W Riding] Cr 1911 from Eccleshill EP.[365] Bradf RDn (1911—21), Calverley RDn (1921—*). Bdry: 1956.[516]

GREENHOW HILL
EP [W Riding] Cr 1858 from Ripon AP,[9] eccl refounded 1860 from Ripon AP (pt tp Bewerley), Burnsall AP (pt tp Appletreewick), Thornthwaite with Padside EP.[68] Ripon RDn (1858—1905), Nidd. RDn (1905—71), Ripon RDn (1971—*).

GREETLAND
EP [W Riding] Cr 1862 from Elland with Greetland EP (usual name then for EP cr as 'Elland cum Stainland and Fixby', qv for earlier organisation; after 1862 the former par less this area called 'Elland').[138] Halifax RDn (1862—1967), Brigh. & Elland RDn (1967—73). Bdry: 1879,[137] 1886 (cr West Vale EP).[56] Abol 1973 to help cr Greetland and West Vale EP.[580]
CP [W Riding] Cr 1894 from the pt of Elland with Greetland CP in Greetland UD.[257] LG Halifax PLU, Greetland UD. Bdry: 1902 (loses pt to Halifax CB [assoc with W Riding] & AP).[581] Abol 1937 ent to Elland UD & CP.[31] Parl Elland Dv (1918—48).

UPPER GREETLAND
CP [W Riding] Cr 1894 from the pt of Elland with Greetland CP not in an UD.[257] LG Halifax PLU, RD. Abol 1937 ent to Elland UD & CP.[31] Parl Elland Dv (1918—48).

GREETLAND AND WEST VALE
EP [W Riding] Cr 1973 by union West Vale EP, Greetland EP.[580] Brigh. & Elland RDn.

GRENOSIDE
EP [W Riding] Cr 1910 from Ecclesfield AP.[23] Ecclesfield RDn. Bdry: 1939 (help cr Sheffield St Cecilia, Parsons Cross EP),[512] 1939 (help refound Hilsborough and Wadsley Bridge EP),[407] 1948.[514]

GREWELTHORPE
[W Riding] Tp in Kirkby Malzeard AP, sep CP 1866,[2] sep EP 1848.[86] Incl undivided pt Land Common to Grewelthorpe, Kirkby Malzeard and Laverton (abol 1937 ent to Laverton CP [other civ bdry alt in same order affecting Grewelthorpe][31]). LG Seq 90. Addtl civ bdry alt: 1883.[52] Transf 1974 to N Yorks.[5] Parl Seq 33. Eccl Ripon RDn (1848—77), Masham RDn (1877—1905), Ripon RDn (1905—*).

GRIBTHORPE
[E Riding] Tp pt in Aughton AP, pt in Bubwith AP, sep CP 1866.[2] LG Harth. Wap, Howden PLU, RSD, RD. Abol 1935 ent to Foggathorpe CP.[13] Parl E Riding (1832—85), Howdensh. Dv (1885—1948).

GRIMETHORPE
EP [W Riding] Cr 1902 from Felkirk AP.[364] Pontef. RDn (1902—16), Hemsw. RDn (1916—27), Barnsley RDn (1927—*).

GRIMSTON
[E Riding] Tp in Dunnington AP, sep CP 1866.[2] LG Ouse & Derw. Wap, York PLU, RSD, Escr. RD. Abol 1935 ent to Dunnington AP.[13] Parl E Riding (1832—85), Howdensh. Dv (1885—1948).

GRIMSTON
[N Riding] Tp in Gilling AP, sep CP 1866.[2] LG Seq 63. Transf 1974 to N Yorks.[5] Parl Seq 21.

GRIMSTON
[W Riding] Tp in Kirkby Wharfe AP, sep CP 1866.[2] LG Seq 81. Transf 1974 to N Yorks.[5] Parl Seq 24.

NORTH GRIMSTON
AP [E Riding] LG Buckr. Wap, Malton PLU, RSD, Norton RD. Abol civ 1935 ent to Birdsall AP.[13] Parl E Riding (1832—85), Buckr. Dv (1885—1948). Eccl Pec jurisd Langtoft prebend (until 1836), Seq 3 thereafter.

GRINDALE
[E Riding] Chap (orig pec jurisd Grindale prebend, early abol) in Bridlington AP, sep CP 1866,[2] sep EP 1749.[9] LG Seq 5. Civ bdry: 1935 (gains Argam AP).[13] Transf 1974 to Humb.[5] Parl Seq 2. Eccl Dick. RDn (1749—1862), N Dick. RDn (1862—65), Bridl. RDn (1865—70). Abol eccl 1870 to help cr Grindale and Ergham EP.[531]

GRINDALE AND ERGHAM
EP [E Riding] Cr 1870 by union Grindale EP, Ergham AP (civ, 'Argam').[531] Birdl. RDn.

GRINDLETON
[W Riding] Chap in Mitton AP, sep CP 1866,[2] sep EP 1741,[9] eccl refounded 1844 from Mitton AP, ex-par place Sawley.[582] LG Seq 108. Civ bdry: 1938.[28] Transf 1974 to Lancs.[5] Parl Seq 41. Eccl Craven RDn (1741—1857), Craven RDn, W'rn Dv (1857—1921), Bolland RDn (1921—*).

GRINTON
AP [N Riding] Tp 'Grinton' in W Hang Wap; incl in W Gill. Wap tp Melbecks (sep CP 1866,[2] sep EP 1838[583]), tp Mucker (sep CP 1866,[2] sep EP 1719,[9] eccl refounded 1843[334]), tp Reeth (sep CP 1866[2]). LG Richm. PLU (1837—40), Reeth PLU (1840—1930), RSD, RD. Transf 1974 to N Yorks.[5] Parl Seq 14. Eccl Catt. RDn (until 1857), Richm. West RDn (1857—1960). Abol eccl 1960 to help cr Grinton with Marrick EP.[138]

GRINTON WITH MARRICK
EP [N Riding] Cr 1960 by union Grinton AP, Marrick AP.[138] Richm. West RDn.

GRISTHORPE
[N Riding] Tp in Filey AP, sep CP 1866.[2] LG Seq 62. Transf 1974 to N Yorks.[5] Parl Seq 20.

GROSMONT
EP [N Riding] Cr 1850 from Lythe AP,[9] refounded 1852 from Lythe AP (hmlt Newbiggin, not sep civ), Whitby AP, Pickering AP, Egton EP.[258] Clev RDn (1850—62), Guisb. RDn (1862—78), Whitby RDn (1878—*).

GUELDABLE

[N Riding] Tp in Leake AP, sep CP 1866.[2] *LG* Birdf. Wap, N'allert. PLU, RSD. Abol 1888 ent to Borrowby CP.[289] *Parl* N Riding (1832—85), Thirsk & Malton Dv (1885—1918).

GUISBOROUGH

AP [N Riding] Incl chap Upleatham (sep civ identity early, sep EP 1786[9]), tps Commondale, Hutton Lowcross, Pinchingthorpe, Tocketts (each a sep CP 1866[2]). *LG* Langb. Lbty, Guisb. PLU, USD, UD. Addtl civ bdry alt: 1968 (incl help cr Teesside CB [assoc with N Riding] & CP).[537] Transf 1974 to Clev.[5] *Parl* Seq 9. *Eccl* Seq 21. Addtl eccl bdry alt: 1967.[141]

GUISELEY

AP [W Riding] Incl chap Horsforth (sep CP 1866,[2] sep EP 1747,[9] eccl refounded 1906[407]), chap Rawdon (sep CP 1866,[2] sep EP 1743[9]), tp Carlton (sep CP 1866[2]), tp Yeadon (sep CP 1866,[2] sep EP 1845[584]). *LG* Skyr. Wap, not in a PLU (until 1861), Wharfed. PLU (1861—1930), Guiseley USD, UD. Abol civ 1937 pt to Ilkley UD & AP, pt to help cr Aireb. UD & CP.[31] *Parl* W Riding (1832—67), N'rn Dv of W Riding (1867—85), Otley Dv (1885—1918), Shipley Dv (1918—48). *Eccl* Seq 34.

GUNTHWAITE

[W Riding] Tp in Penistone AP, sep CP 1866.[2] *LG* Staincr. Wap, not in a PLU (until 1849), Penist. PLU (1849—1930), Gunthwaite & Ingbirchworth USD, UD. Bdry: 1915.[461] Abol 1938 to help cr Gunthwaite and Ingbirchworth CP.[28] *Parl* W Riding (1832—67), S'rn Dv of W Riding (1867—85), Holmf. Dv (1885—1918), Penist. Dv (1918—48).

GUNTHWAITE AND INGBIRCHWORTH

CP [W Riding] Cr 1938 by union Gunthwaite CP, Ingbirchworth CP.[28] *LG* Penist. RD. Transf 1974 to S Yorks.[5] *Parl* Penist. CC (1948—*).

GREAT HABTON

[N Riding] Tp in Kirkby Misperton AP, sep CP 1866.[2] *LG* Seq 60. Transf 1974 to N Yorks.[5] *Parl* Seq 21.

LITTLE HABTON

[N Riding] Organisation as for Great Habton.

HACKFORTH

[N Riding] Tp in Hornby AP, sep CP 1866.[2] *LG* Seq 49. Transf 1974 to N Yorks.[5] *Parl* Seq 15.

HACKNESS

AP [N Riding] Incl chap Harwood Dale (sep CP 1866,[2] not sep eccl hence this par eccl 'Hackness with Harwood Dale', qv), tps Broxa, Silpho, Suffield cum Everley (each a sep CP 1866[2]). *LG* Seq 67. Transf 1974 to N Yorks.[5] *Parl* Seq 20.

HACKNESS WITH HARWOOD DALE

AP [N Riding] Usual eccl spelling; for civ, civ sep chap Harwood Dale and other tps, see prev entry. *Eccl* Seq 4.

HADDLESEY

EP [W Riding] Cr 1855 from Birkin AP (tps Chapel Haddlesey, West Haddlesey, Temple Hirst, Hirst Courtnay).[274] Pontef. RDn (1855—1924), Selby RDn (1924—*).

CHAPEL HADDLESEY

[W Riding] Tp in Birkin AP, sep CP 1866,[2] eccl severed 1855 to help cr Haddlesey EP.[274] *LG* Seq 80. Bdry: 1883.[52] Transf 1974 to N Yorks.[5] *Parl* Seq 24.

WEST HADDLESEY

[W Riding] Tp in Birkin AP, sep CP 1866,[2] eccl severed 1855 to help cr Haddlesey EP.[274] *LG* Seq 79. Bdry: 1883.[52] Transf 1974 to N Yorks. *Parl* Seq 24.

HAISTHORPE

[E Riding] Tp in Burton Agnes AP, sep CP 1866.[2] *LG* Dick. Wap, Bridl. PLU, RSD, RD. Abol 1935 ent to Carnaby AP.[13] *Parl* E Riding (1832—85), Buckr. Dv (1885—1948).

HALDENBY

[W Riding] Tp in Adlingfleet AP, sep CP 1866.[2] *LG* Seq 95. Bdry: 1884.[500] Transf 1974 to Humb.[5] *Parl* Seq 29.

HALEY HILL

EP [W Riding] Cr 1855 from Coley EP (pt orig tp Northowram in Halifax AP).[166] Halifax RDn. Now called 'Halifax All Souls'.

HALIFAX

[W Riding] The following have 'Halifax' in their names. Insofar as any existed at a given time: *LG* Morley Wap, Halifax Bor, PLU, MB (1848—89), CB (1889—1974), USD. *Parl* Halifax Parl Bor/BC (1832—*). *Eccl* Pontef. RDn (until 1857), Halifax RDn (1857—1967); sep noted (1967—*).

AP1—HALIFAX [ST JOHN THE BAPTIST]—Incl chap Elland (sep CP 1866,[2] eccl severed 1724 to help cr Elland cum Stainland and Fixby EP[178] [qv below]), chap Rastrick (sep CP 1866,[2] sep EP 1720,[9] eccl abol 1724 to help cr Elland cum Stainland and Fixby EP[178] [qv below], 'Rastrick' a sep EP 1881 from Elland EP[522]), tp Barkisland (sep CP 1866,[2] pt eccl severed 1724 to cr Ripponden EP[9] [refounded 1878[308]], the remainder eccl severed 1724 to help cr Elland cum Stainland and Fixby EP[178] [qv below], 'Barkisland' a sep EP 1855 from Elland with Greetland EP,[9] eccl refounded 1858[247]), tp Erringden (sep CP 1866,[2] sep EP 1844 as EP8[585]), tp Fixby (sep CP 1866,[2] eccl severed 1724 to help cr Elland cum Stainland and Fixby EP[178] [qv below; Fixby remains in Elland EP after 1862]), tp Heptonstall (sep CP 1866,[2] sep EP 1749[9]), tp Hipperholme with Brighouse (sep CP 1866,[2] area of Brighouse eccl severed 1724 to help cr Elland cum Stainland and Fixby EP[178] [qv below], pt eccl severed 1749 from the latter to help cr Lightcliffe EP,[9] 'Brighouse' a sep EP 1836 from Lightcliffe EP,[9] as Brighouse eccl refounded 1849[351]), tp Langfield (sep CP 1866[2]), tp Midgley (sep CP 1866,[2] eccl severed 1732 to help cr Luddenden EP[9]), tp Norland (sep CP 1866,[2] eccl severed 1719 to help cr Sowerby Bridge EP,[9] the latter eccl abol 1724 to help cr Elland cum Stainland and Fixby EP[178] [Sowerby Bridge refounded 1869 from Elland EP[521]], 'Norland' a sep EP 1877 from Sowerby Bridge EP[301]), tp Northowram (sep CP 1866,[2] pt eccl severed 1749 to cr Coley EP,[9] pt eccl severed 1749 to help cr Lightcliffe EP,[9] pt eccl severed 1845 to help cr Queen's Head EP,[9] 'Northowram' a sep EP 1909 from Coley EP, Lightcliffe EP[429]), tp Ovenden (sep CP 1866,[2] pt eccl severed 1718 to cr Illingworth EP,[9] the remainder a sep EP 1843 as 'Ovenden',[586] later called 'Bradshaw'), tp Rishworth (sep CP 1866,[2] eccl severed 1724 to help cr Elland cum Stainland and Fixby EP[178] [qv below; Rishworth remains in Elland EP after 1862]), tp Shelf (sep CP 1866,[2] sep EP 1851 from pt tp Shelf, pt Bradford AP[137]), tp Skircoat (sep CP 1866,[2] pt eccl severed 1845 to cr Kings Cross EP, pt to help cr Salterhebble EP[587]), tp Southowram (sep CP 1866,[2] sep EP 1793 as EP3,[9] the latter sometimes 'Briers Chapel', pt of latter eccl severed 1845 and united with pt tp Skircoat [see above] to cr Salterhebble EP,[587] the remainder of EP3 refounded 1887 as such[126]), tp Sowerby (sep CP 1866,[2] sep EP 1720,[9] eccl refounded 1848[231] and 1890[12]), tp Soyland (sep CP 1866,[2] eccl severed 1724 to help cr Elland cum Stainland and Fixby EP[177] [qv below], pt orig tp eccl severed 1848 from Elland with Greetland EP to cr Sowerby St Mary EP[231]), tp Stainland with Old Lindley (sep CP 1866,[2] eccl severed 1724 to help cr Elland cum Stainland and Fixby EP[177] [qv below], 'Stainland' a sep EP 1843 from Elland with Greetland EP[351]), tp Stansfield (sep CP 1866,[2] sep EP 1810 as 'Cross Stone'[9]), tp Wadsworth (sep CP 1866[2]), tp Warley (sep CP 1866,[2] eccl severed 1719 to help cr Sowerby Bridge EP,[9] the area of Warley eccl severed 1732 from Sowerby Bridge EP to help cr Luddenden EP,[9] the area of Warley eccl severed 1869 from the latter to help re-cr Sowerby Bridge EP,[521] 'Warley' a sep EP 1878 from Sowerby Bridge EP[429]); 'Elland cum Stainland and Fixby' EP re-augmented 1739 as 'Elland' but usually called 'Elland with Greetland' until Greetland a sep EP 1862,[138] 'Elland' thereafter; see 'Elland with Greetland', 'Elland' for successive alterations in area and for cr of many separate EPs. Addtl civ bdry alt: 1894 (gains the pts of the following in Halifax CB: Skircoat CP, Ovenden CP, Northowram CP, Southowram CP [the latter 2 orig intended to be 'North Ward' CP, 'Southowram Ward' CP[410] but that order superseded by this]),[588] 1899 (gains Skircoat CP),[589] 1900 (gains Warley UD & CP, Northowram UD & CP),[590] 1902,[581] 1912,[591] 1928 (gains pt Southowram UD & CP, loses pt to Sowerby UD & CP).[592] Transf 1974 to W Yorks.[5] *Eccl* Halifax RDn (1967—*). Addtl eccl bdry alt: 1732 (help cr Luddenden EP [areas of Sawley (not sep civ) and tp Midgely from this AP], area tp Warley from Elland cum Stainland and Fixby EP), 1810 (cr EP2,[9] refounded 1862[136]), 1840 (cr EP6,[9] refounded 1843[351]), 1842 (cr Sowerby St George EP,[9] refounded 1843[351]), 1844 (cr Hebden Bridge EP),[585] 1845 (help cr Queen's Head EP),[256] 1855 (cr Mount Pellon EP).[593]

EP1—HALIFAX ALL SOULS—Name used now for EP cr 1855 as 'Haley Hill', qv.

EP2—HALIFAX HOLY TRINITY—Cr 1810 from AP1,[9] refounded 1862.[136] Halifax RDn (1967—

*). Bdry: 1912.[594]

EP3—HALIFAX ST ANN IN THE GROVE—Cr 1793 from AP1,[9] pt eccl severed 1845 to cr Salterhebble EP,[587] the remainder refounded 1887 as EP3[126]; for civ see 'Southowram'. Brigh. & Elland RDn (1967—*). Sometimes early 'Briers Chapel', sometimes later 'Southowram'.

EP4—HALIFAX ST AUGUSTINE—Cr 1876 from AP1.[595] Halifax RDn (1967—*). Bdry: 1912 (help cr EP5).[596]

EP5—HALIFAX ST HILDA—Cr 1912 from Mount Pellon EP, Kings Cross EP, EP4, Warley EP.[596] Halifax RDn (1967—*).

EP6—HALIFAX ST JAMES—Cr 1840 from AP1,[9] refounded 1843.[351] Bdry: 1871 (cr EP9),[213] 1876 (cr EP4),[595] 1878 (help cr Ovenden St George EP).[586] Abol 1953 to help cr EP7.[593]

EP7—HALIFAX ST JAMES AND ST MARY—Cr 1953 by union EP6, EP9.[593] Halifax RDn (1967—*).

EP8—HALIFAX ST JOHN IN THE WILDERNESS—Cr 1844 from AP1.[585] Calder Valley RDn (1967—*). Sometimes 'Cragg Vale'.

EP9—HALIFAX ST MARY—Cr 1871 from EP6.[213] Abol 1953 to help cr EP7.[593]

NETHER HALLAM

[W Riding] Tp in Sheffield AP, sep CP 1866.[2] *LG* Straff. & Tick. Wap, Ecclesall Bierlow PLU, Sheff MB (1843—89), CB (1889—1904), USD. Bdry: 1877,[505] 1879,[597] 1880 (hmlt Heeley in this par cr a sep CP).[430] Abol 1904 to help cr Ecclesall CP.[502] *Parl* Sheff Parl Bor (1832—85); see Part III of the *Guide* for composition of Sheff Parl Bors (1885—1918) by wards of the MB.

UPPER HALLAM

[W Riding] Organisation as for Nether Hallam CP, except only bdry alt 1879.[506]

HALSAM

AP [E Riding] *LG* Seq 15. Transf 1974 to Humb.[5] *Parl* Seq 5. *Eccl* Pec jurisd Bev. (until 1836), Seq 16 thereafter.

HALTEMPRICE

[E Riding] Ex-par place, sep CP 1858.[393] *LG* Kingst. upon Hull Co, Scul. PLU (1862—1930), RSD, RD (1894—1935), Haltemp. UD (1935—74). Bdry: 1935 (incl gains Hessle UD & CP, West Ella CP).[13] Transf 1974 to Humb.[5] *Parl* E Riding (1832—85), Howdensh. Dv (1885—1948), Kingst. upon Hull, Haltemp. BC (1948—55), Haltemp. CC (1955—*).

WEST HALTON

[W Riding] Tp in Long Preston AP, sep CP 1866.[2] *LG* Seq 111. Transf 1974 to N Yorks.[5] *Parl* Seq 41.

HALTON EAST

[W Riding] Tp in Skipton AP, sep CP 1866,[2] eccl severed 1841 to help cr Bolton Abbey EP,[9] the latter refounded 1864.[175] *LG* Seq 112. Transf 1974 to N Yorks.[5] *Parl* Seq 41.

HALTON GILL

[W Riding] Chap in Arncliffe AP, sep CP 1866,[2] sep EP 1775.[9] *LG* Seq 111. Transf 1974 to N Yorks.[5] *Parl* Seq 41. *Eccl* Craven RDn (1775—1857), Craven RDn, N'rn Dv (1857—1921),

Skipton RDn (1921—*).

HAMBLETON

[W Riding] Tp in Brayton AP, sep CP 1866,[2] united eccl 1914 with pt tp Gateforth in same par to cr Gateforth cum Hambleton EP.[340] *LG* Seq 79. Transf 1974 to N Yorks.[5] *Parl* Seq 24.

GREEN HAMMERTON

[W Riding] Tp in Whixley AP, sep CP 1866.[2] *LG* Seq 85. Transf 1974 to N Yorks.[5] *Parl* Seq 36.

KIRK HAMMERTON

AP [Pt Ainsty (W Riding until 1449 and from 1836, indept jurisd 1449—1836: tp Winstrop [sep CP 1866[2]]), W Riding (pt until 1866, Claro Wap: tp 'Kirk Hammerton'; ent Claro Wap from 1866), Gt Ouseb. GilbU (until 1854), PLU (1854—1930), RSD, RD (1894—1938), Nidd. RD (1938—74). Transf 1974 to N Yorks.[5] *Parl* Pt W Riding, pt N Riding (1832—67), N'rn Dv of W Riding (1867—85), Ripon Dv (1885—1948), Harrog. CC (1948—*). *Eccl* Donc. RDn (until 1838), Boroughbr. RDn (1838—70), Knar. RDn (1870—1905), Boroughbr. RDn (1905—71), Ripon RDn (1971—*).

HAMPHALL STUBBS

[W Riding] Tp in South Kirkby AP, sep CP 1866,[2] eccl severed 1911 to help cr South Elmsall EP.[37] *LG* Straff. & Tick. Wap, Hemsw. PLU (soon after 1850[112]—1930), RSD, RD. Abol 1938 ent to Hampole CP.[499] *Parl* W Riding (1832—67), S'rn Dv of W Riding (1867—85), Donc. Dv (1885—1918), Rother Valley Dv (1918—48).

HAMPOLE

[W Riding] Tp in Adwick le Street AP, sep CP 1866.[2] *LG* Seq 117. Bdry: 1938.[28] Transf 1974 to S Yorks.[5] *Parl* Seq 44.

HAMPSTHWAITE

AP [W Riding] Early 13th cent considered a chap in Aldborough AP, sep par soon after. Incl tp Birstwith (sep CP 1866,[2] sep EP 1857[9]), tp Thornwaite with Padside (sep CP 1866,[2] 'Thornwaite' a sep EP 1744,[9] eccl refounded 1855[598]), tps Felliscliffe, Menwith with Darley (each a sep CP 1866[2]). *LG* Seq 84. Addtl civ bdry alt: 1883.[52] Transf 1974 to N Yorks.[5] *Parl* Seq 36. *Eccl* Boroughbr. RDn (until before 1535), Ainsty RDn (before 1535—1820), Old Ainsty RDn (1820—30), Pontef. RDn (1830—57), Otley RDn (1857—70), Knar. RDn (1870—1905), Nidd. RDn (1905—71), Harrog. RDn (1971—*).

HANDSWORTH

AP [W Riding] *LG* Straff. & Tick. Wap, Sheff PLU (soon after 1837[112]—1930), Handsworth USD, UD (1894—1921), Sheff CB (1921—38). Civ bdry: 1901 (loses pt to Sheff CB [assoc with W Riding] & AP).[304] Abol 1938 pt to Sheff CB (assoc with W Riding) & AP, pt to Orgreave CP.[306] *Parl* W Riding (1832—67), S'rn Dv of W Riding (1867—85), Hallamshire Dv (1885—1918), Rother Valley Dv (1918—48). *Eccl* Pec jurisd Laughton en le Morthen prebend (until 1485), pec jurisd Chancellor of York (1485—1836), Donc. RDn (1836—57), Rotherh. RDn (1857—1927), Handsw. RDn (1927—42), Attercliffe RDn (1942—*). Eccl bdry: 1878 (cr Handsworth Woodhouse EP),[198] 1881 (cr Gleadless

EP),[536] 1933,[214] 1941 (help cr Sheffield St Catherine Richmond Road EP).[599]

HANDSWORTH WOODHOUSE

EP [W Riding] Cr 1878 from Handsworth AP.[198] Rotherh. RDn (1878—1927), Handsw. RDn (1927—42), Attercliffe RDn (1942—*).

HANLITH

[W Riding] Tp in Kirkby in Malham Dale AP, sep CP 1866.[2] *LG* Seq 111. Transf 1974 to N Yorks.[5] *Parl* Seq 41.

HARDEN

EP [W Riding] Cr 1930 from Bingley AP, Wilsden cum Allerton EP.[270] Horton RDn. Abol 1960 to help cr Harden and Wilsden EP.[575]

HARDEN AND WILSDEN

EP [W Riding] Cr 1960 by union Harden EP, Wilsden cum Allerton EP.[575] S Craven RDn.

HARDRAW

EP [N Riding] Cr 1748 from Aysgarth AP.[9] Catt. RDn (1748—1857), Catt. West RDn (1857—1928), Wensleyd. RDn (1928—*).

EAST HARDWICK

[W Riding] Tp in Pontefract AP, sep CP 1866,[2] sep EP 1876 incl pt Ackworth AP.[29] *LG* Seq 97. Transf 1974 to W Yorks.[5] *Parl* Seq 29. *Eccl* Pontef. RDn.

WEST HARDWICK

[W Riding] Tp in Wragby AP, sep CP 1866.[2] *LG* Seq 96. Bdry: 1938.[28] Transf 1974 to W Yorks.[5] *Parl* Seq 28.

HAREWOOD

AP [W Riding] Tp 'Harewood' in Skyr. Wap as were tps Alwoodley, East Keswick, Weardley, Wigton, pt tp Wyke (the last 5 each a sep CP 1866[2]); incl in Claro Wap tp Dunkeswick (sep CP 1866[2]), tp Weeton (sep CP 1866,[2] sep EP 1852[71]). *LG* Harewood Bor, Carlton GilbU (until 1869), Wethb. PLU (1869—1930), RSD, RD. Addtl civ bdry alt: 1937.[31] Transf 1974 to W Yorks.[5] *Parl* Seq 24. *Eccl* Ainsty RDn (until 1820), New Ainsty RDn (1820—38), Pontef. RDn (1838—57), Wethb. RDn (1857—61), Whitkirk RDn (1861—94), Wethb. RDn (1894—*).

HARLEY WOOD

EP [W Riding] Cr 1864 from Cross Stone EP (Yorks), Todmorden EP (Lancs).[457] Halifax RDn (1864—1967), Calder Valley RDn (1967—72). Bdry: 1898 (gains pt Holme St John EP [Lancs, dioc Manch] from area of Todmorden MB),[476] 1903 (cr Cornholme EP).[436] Abol 1972 ent to Todmorden EP (Lancs).[600]

EAST HARLSEY

AP [N Riding] Disputed early whether AP or subordinated to Ingleby Arncliffe AP,[601] sep status sustained. *LG* Seq 26. Transf 1974 to N Yorks.[5] *Parl* Seq 14. *Eccl* Seq 23.

WEST HARLSEY

[N Riding] Tp in Osmotherley AP, sep CP 1866.[2] *LG* Seq 22. Transf 1974 to N Yorks.[5] *Parl* Seq 14.

HARLTHORPE

[E Riding] Tp in Bubwith AP, sep CP 1866.[2] *LG* Harth. Wap, Howden PLU, RSD, RD. Abol 1935 ent to Foggathorpe CP.[13] *Parl* E Riding (1832—85), Howdensh. Dv (1885—1948).

HARMBY

[N Riding] Tp in Spennithorne AP, sep CP 1866.[2] *LG* Seq 53. Transf 1974 to N Yorks.[5] *Parl* Seq 14.

HAROME

[N Riding] Chap in Helmsley AP, sep CP 1866,[2] sep EP 1863.[160] *LG* Seq 63. Transf 1974 to N Yorks.[5] *Parl* Seq 21.

HARPHAM

[E Riding] Chap and tp in Burton Agnes AP, perhaps with sep parochial rights 17th—18th cent,[376] sep CP 1866,[2] sep eccl status not sustained. *LG* Seq 6. Bdry: 1884,[377] 1935 (gains Lowthorpe AP, Ruston Parva AP).[13] Transf 1974 to Humb.[5] *Parl* Seq 3.

HARROGATE

[W Riding] The following have 'Harrogate' in their names. Insofar as any existed at a given time: *LG* Knar. PLU, Harrog. MB. *Parl* Ripon Dv (1918—48), Harrog. CC (1948—*). *Eccl* Boroughbr. RDn (cr—1870), Knar. RDn (1870—1971), Harrog. RDn (1971—*).

EP1—HARROGATE ST LUKE—Cr 1898 from Bilton with Harrogate EP (commonly called 'High Harrogate Christ Church').[284]

EP2—HARROGATE ST MARK—Cr 1898 from Pannal AP, EP5, EP4.[284] Bdry: 1957.[565]

EP3—HARROGATE ST WILFRID—Cr 1904 from EP4, EP5.[119]

—HIGH HARROGATE CHRIST CHURCH—Name commonly used for EP cr 1829 as 'Bilton with Harrogate', qv.

EP4—HIGH HARROGATE ST PETER—Cr 1869 from Bilton with Harrogate EP (commonly called 'High Harrogate Christ Church').[109] Boroughbr. RDn (1869—70). Bdry: 1898 (help cr EP2),[284] 1904 (help cr EP3).[119]

EP5—LOW HARROGATE—Cr 1816 from Pannal AP,[9] refounded 1830.[602] Boroughbr. RDn (1816—57), Wethb. RDn (1857—94), Knar. RDn (1894—1971). Bdry: 1887 (help cr Beckwithshaw EP),[225] 1898 (help cr EP2),[284] 1904 (help cr EP3),[119] 1957.[565]

HARSWELL

AP [E Riding] *LG* Harth. Wap, Pockl. PLU, RSD, RD. Abol 1935 ent to Everingham AP.[13] *Parl* E Riding (1832—85), Howdensh. Dv (1885—1918). *Eccl* Seq 14.

HARTHILL

AP [W Riding] Usual eccl spelling; for civ see following entry. *Eccl* Seq 43.

HARTHILL WITH WOODALL

AP [W Riding] Usual civ spelling; for eccl see prev entry. *LG* Seq 121. Civ bdry: 1885.[603] Transf 1974 to S Yorks.[5] *Parl* Seq 48.

HARTLINGTON

[N Riding] Tp in Burnsall AP, sep CP 1866.[2] *LG* Seq 112. Transf 1974 to N Yorks.[5] *Parl* Seq 41.

HARTOFT

[N Riding] Tp in Middleton AP, sep CP 1866.[2] *LG* Seq 61. Bdry: 1887.[49] Transf 1974 to N Yorks.[5] *Parl* Seq 22.

HARTON

[N Riding] Tp in Bossall AP, sep CP 1866.[2] *LG* Seq

32. Transf 1974 to N Yorks.[5] *Parl* Seq 16.

HARTSHEAD

[W Riding] Chap in Dewsbury AP, sep CP 1866 (orig rated for poor law purposes with chap Clifton in same par, sep rated soon thereafter[112]), eccl united 1742 with Clifton as 'Hartshead cum Clifton',[9] qv, the latter divided 1887 into 2 EPs of Hartshead, Clifton.[419] *LG* Morley Wap, Halifax PLU, RSD, RD. Abol civ 1937 pt to Brigh. MB & CP, pt to Spenb. UD and to Liversedge CP.[31] *Parl* W Riding (1832—67), E'rn Dv of W Riding (1867—85), Spen Valley Dv (1885—1918), Elland Dv (1918—48). *Eccl* Birstall RDn. Bdry: 1929 (help cr Scholes EP).[416]

HARTSHEAD CUM CLIFTON

EP [W Riding] Cr 1742 by union chaps Hartshead, Clifton, each in Dewsbury AP.[9] Pontef. RDn (1742—1857), Dewsb. RDn (1857—87). Abol eccl 1887, divided into 2 EPs of Hartshead, Clifton.[419]

HARTWITH CUM WINSLEY

[W Riding] Chap in Kirkby Malzeard AP, sep CP 1866,[2] sep EP 1752,[9] eccl refounded 1861.[284] *LG* Seq 89. Transf 1974 to N Yorks.[5] *Parl* Seq 36. *Eccl* Pec jurisd Masham prebend (until 1836), Catt. RDn (1836—57), Ripon RDn (1857—1905), Nidd. RDn (1905—71) Ripon RDn (1971—*).

HARWOOD DALE

[N Riding] Chap in Hackness AP, sep CP 1866.[2] *LG* Seq 67. Bdry: 1887.[162] Transf 1974 to N Yorks.[5] *Parl* Seq 20.

HATFIELD

CP [E Riding] Cr 1935 by union Goxhill AP, Great Hatfield CP, Little Hatfield CP.[13] *LG* Hold. RD. Transf 1974 to Humb.[5] *Parl* Bridl. CC (1948—*).

HATFIELD

AP [W Riding] Incl chap Thorne (appropriated early to Lewes Priory, early independent[604]), pt tp Stainforth (sep CP 1866,[2] sep EP 1884,[191] qv for other constituents pars then). *LG* Seq 120. Addtl civ bdry alt: 1883,[52] 1884,[556] 1884,[557] 1938.[28] Transf 1974 to S Yorks.[5] *Parl* Seq 47. *Eccl* Seq 40. Addtl eccl bdry alt: 1887.[559]

GREAT HATFIELD

[E Riding] Tp pt in Mappleton AP, pt in Sigglesthorne AP, sep CP 1866.[2] *LG* Hold. Wap, Skirl. PLU, RSD, RD. Abol 1935 to help cr Hatfield CP.[13] *Parl* E Riding (1832—85), Hold. Dv (1885—1948).

LITTLE HATFIELD

[E Riding] Tp in Sigglesthorne AP, sep CP 1866.[2] Organisation as for Great Hatfield.

HAUXWELL

AP [N Riding] Incl tps Barden, Garriston, East Hauxwell, West Hauxwell (each a sep CP 1866[2]) so that 'Hauxwell' has no sep civ identity after 1866.[2] *LG* W Hang Wap. *Parl* N Riding (1832—67). *Eccl* Seq 54.

EAST HAUXWELL

[N Riding] Tp in Hauxwell AP, sep CP 1866.[2] *LG* Seq 53. Transf 1974 to N Yorks.[5] *Parl* Seq 14.

WEST HAUXWELL

[N Riding] Organisation as for East Hauxwell.

HAVERAH PARK

[W Riding] Ex-par place, sep CP 1858,[393] eccl reduced 1887 when pt eccl severed to help cr Beckwithshaw EP.[225] *LG* Seq 84. Transf 1974 to N Yorks.[5] *Parl* Seq 36.

HAVERCROFT WITH COLD HIENDLEY

[W Riding] Tp in Felkirk AP, sep CP 1866.[2] *LG* Seq 113. Transf 1974 to W Yorks.[5] *Parl* Seq 42.

HAWES

[N Riding] Chap in Aysgarth AP, sep CP 1866,[2] sep EP 1739.[9] Incl undivided pt Land near Horton Gill Bridge (common to Bainbridge and Hawes [each orig in Aysgarth], abol 1934 ent to Bainbridge CP3[3]), undivided pt Mossdale Moor, undivided pt Wether Fell (each of the last 2 common to Bainbridge and Hawes, both abol 1934 ent to Hawes CP3[3]). *LG* Seq 52. Addtl civ bdry alt: 1883,[16] 1886.[4] Transf 1974 to N Yorks.[5] *Parl* Seq 14. *Eccl* Catt. RDn (1739—1857), Catt. West RDn (1857—1928), Wensleyd. RDn (1928—*).

HAWKSWICK

[W Riding] Tp in Arncliffe AP, sep CP 1866.[2] *LG* Seq 111. Bdry: 1883,[52] 1884.[135] Transf 1974 to N Yorks.[5] *Parl* Seq 41.

HAWKSWORTH

[W Riding] Tp in Otley AP, sep CP 1866,[2] eccl severed 1853 to help cr Esholt EP,[534] sometimes 'Esholt with Hawksworth'. *LG* Skyr. Wap, Carlton GilbU (until 1869), Wharfed. PLU (1869—1930), RSD, RD. Abol 1937 pt to Baildon UD & CP, pt to help cr Aireb. UD & CP, pt to Ilkley UD & AP.[31] *Parl* W Riding (1832—67), N'rn Dv of W Riding (1867—85), Otley Dv (1885—1918), Shipley Dv (1918—48).

HAWKSWORTH WOOD

EP [W Riding] Cr 1936 from Kirkstall EP, Woodside EP.[188] Leeds RDn (1936—71), Head. RDn (1971—*). Bdry. 1967.[127]

HAWNBY

AP [N Riding] Incl tp Arden (sep CP 1866,[2] sep EP 1733[9]), tps Bilsdale, West Side; Dale Town, Snilesworth (each of the 3 a sep CP 1866[2]). *LG* Seq 25. Transf 1974 to N Yorks.[5] *Parl* Seq 16. *Eccl* Clev RDn (until 1862), Helm. RDn (1862—*). Addtl eccl bdry alt: 1898 (help re found Bilsdale EP).[121]

HAWORTH

[W Riding] Chap in Bradford AP, sep CP 1866,[2] sep EP 1864.[308] *LG* Morley Wap, Keigh. PLU, pt Haworth USD, pt Oxenhope USD, pt Oakworth USD, Haworth UD. Civ bdry: 1894 (the pt in Oxenhope USD cr Oxenhope CP, the pt in Oakworth USD cr Stanbury CP),[257] 1896.[271] Abol civ 1938 ent to Keigh. MB & AP.[31] *Parl* W Riding (1832—67), E'rn Dv of W Riding (1867—85), Keigh. Dv (1885—1948). *Eccl* Bradf RDn (1864—1921), S Craven RDn (1921—*). Eccl bdry: 1845 (cr Oxenhope EP),[91] 1911 (help cr Cross Roads cum Leeds EP).[269]

HAWSKER

EP [N Riding] Cr 1878 from Whitby AP (the gtr pt of tp Hawsker with Stainsacre, qv for civ).[594] Whitby RDn. Bdry: 1955.[197]

HAWSKER WITH STAINSACRE

[N Riding] Tp in Whitby AP, sep CP 1866,[2] gtr pt eccl severed 1878 to cr Hawsker EP,[594] qv. Incl undivided pt Fylingdales Moor (Land Common to Hawsker with Stainsacre and Fylingdales). *LG* Whitby Strand Lbty, Whitby PLU, pt Whitby USD, pt Whitby RSD, Whitby RD. Bdry: 1894 (the pt in Whitby UD cr Helredale CP),[431] 1932.[51] Transf 1974 to N Yorks.[5] *Parl* Seq 19.

HAXBY

[N Riding] Chap (pec jurisd Strensall prebend, until 1836) in Strensall AP, sep CP 1866,[2] sep EP 1863.[83] *LG* Seq 32. Transf 1974 to N Yorks.[5] *Parl* Seq 16. *Eccl* Eas. RDn (1863—1936), City of York RDn (1936—*).

HAYTON

AP [E Riding] Orig chap in Pocklington AP, united with chap Bielby in same par 1252,[245] the par civ 'Hayton' in which Bielby deemed a chap (sep CP 1866[2]), eccl 'Hayton with Bielby' (pec jurisd Dean of York), qv. *LG* Seq 12. Addtl civ bdry alt: 1935 (gains Burnby AP, Thorpe le Street CP).[13] Transf 1974 to Humb.[5] *Parl* Seq 7.

HAYTON WITH BIELBY

AP [E Riding] *Eccl* name used after union 1252 of chaps Hayton, Bielby, each in Pocklington AP (for civ see prev entry).[245] Pec jurisd Dean of York (1252—1836), Harth. & Hull RDn (1836—57), W Harth. RDn (1857—66), Weigh. RDn (1866—*).

HAZLEWOOD WITH STORITHS

[W Riding] Tp in Skipton AP, sep CP 1866,[2] eccl severed 1814 to help cr Bolton Abbey EP,[9] the latter eccl refounded 1864.[175] *LG* Claro Wap, Skipton PLU, RSD, RD. Bdry: 1883,[52] 1886.[224] Transf 1974 to N Yorks.[5] *Parl* Seq 32.

HEADINGLEY

[W Riding] Chap Headingley cum Burley (qv for civ organisation) a sep EP 1717 from Leeds AP,[9] divided eccl 1793 to cr 2 EPs of Burley, Headingley. Ainsty RDn (1793—1820), Old Ainsty RDn (1820—36), Pontef. RDn (1836—57), Leeds RDn (1857—1971), Head. RDn (1971—*). Bdry: 1846 (help cr Meanwood EP),[70] 1846 (help cr Woodside EP),[35] 1866 (help cr Wrangthorn EP),[55] 1967.[127]

FAR HEADINGLEY

EP [W Riding] Cr 1868 from Leeds AP.[290] Leeds RDn (1868—1971), Head. RDn (1971—*). Bdry: 1967.[127] Sometimes 'Leeds St Chad'.

HEADINGLEY CUM BURLEY

[W Riding] Chap in Leeds AP, sep CP 1866,[2] sep EP 1717,[9] divided eccl 1793 into 2 EPs of Headlngley, Burley,[9] qv. *LG* Skyr. Wap, Leeds Bor/MB/CB, Carlton GilbU (until 1869), Leeds PLU (1869—1904), USD. Abol civ 1904 ent to Leeds AP.[69] *Parl* Leeds Parl Bor (1832—85); see Part III of the *Guide* for composition of Leeds Parl Bors (1885—1918) by wards of the MB. *Eccl* Ainsty RDn.

HEALAUGH

AP [Ainsty (W Riding until 1449 and from 1836, indept jurisd 1449—1836)] *LG* Seq 3. Transf 1974 to N Yorks.[5] *Parl* Seq 23. *Eccl* Seq 29.

HEALEY

EP [W Riding] Cr 1849 from Kirkby Malzeard AP.[401] Ripon RDn (1849—77), Masham RDn (1877—1905), Ripon RDn (1905—*).

CP [W Riding] Cr 1934 by union pts Ellingstring CP, Fearby CP, Healey with Sutton CP, Masham Moor CP.[3] LG Masham RD. Transf 1974 to N Yorks.[5] Parl Richm. CC (1948—*).

HEALEY WITH SUTTON

[N Riding] Tp in Masham AP, sep CP 1866.[2] LG E Hang Wap, Leyb. PLU, Masham USD (ent 1875—86), pt Masham RSD (1886—94), Masham UD. Bdry: 1883,[16] 1886,[525] 1886,[526] 1894 (the pt not in Masham UD cr Colsterdale CP).[431] Abol 1934 pt to help cr Healey CP, pt to Ilton cum Pott CP.[3] Parl N Riding (1832—85), Richm. Dv (1885—1948).

HEATON

[W Riding] Tp in Bradford AP, sep CP 1866,[2] eccl severed 1828 to help cr Shipley cum Heaton EP,[63] area of the tp eccl severed from the latter 1865 to cr Heaton St Barnabas EP,[311] qv. LG Morley Wap, Bradf PLU (1837—48), N Bierley PLU (1848—1930), Heaton USD (1875—82), Bradf MB (1882—89), CB (1889—98), USD (1882—94). Abol 1898 ent to Bradford AP.[65] Parl W Riding (1832—67), E'rn Dv of W Riding (1867—85); see Part III of the Guide for composition of Bradf Parl Bors (1885—1918) by wards of the MB.

EARLS HEATON

EP [W Riding] Cr 1828 from Dewsbury AP,[9] refounded 1842.[30] Pontef. RDn (1828—57), Dewsb. RDn (1857—*). Bdry: 1879 (help cr Dewsbury St Philip EP),[326] 1901 (help cr Gawthorpe and Chickenley Heath EP).[284]

HANGING HEATON

EP [W Riding] Cr 1826 from Dewsbury AP,[9] refounded 1842.[30] RDns and bdry alts as for Earls Heaton, with addtl bdry alt 1935.[479]

HEATON ST BARNABAS

EP [W Riding] Cr 1865 when area of tp Heaton (qv for civ) severed from Shipley cum Heaton EP.[311] Bradf RDn (1865—1971), Airedale RDn (1971—*). Bdry: 1874,[605] 1910 (cr Frizinghall EP),[476] 1921,[197] 1927,[288] 1959 (cr Heaton St Martin EP).[606]

HEATON ST MARTIN

EP [W Riding] Cr 1959 from Heaton St Barnabas EP.[606] Bradf RDn (1959—71), Airedale RDn (1971—*).

HEBDEN

[W Riding] Tp in Linton AP, sep CP 1866.[2] LG Seq 112. Transf 1974 to N Yorks.[5] Parl Seq 41.

HEBDEN BRIDGE

EP [W Riding] Area of Hebden Bridge in Halifax AP eccl reduced 1844 to cr Mytholmroyd EP (qv for constituent pars at refounding 1846),[9] the remainder cr 1844 a sep EP of 'Hebden Bridge'.[586] Pontef. RDn (1844—57), Halifax RDn (1857—1967), Calder Valley RDn (1967—*). Bdry: 1968.[90]

CP [W Riding] Cr 1894 by union of pts of the following in Hebden Bridge UD: Erringden CP, Heptonstall CP, Stansfield CP, Wadsworth AP.[450] LG Todmorden PLU, Hebden Bridge UD. Abol 1937 to help cr Hebden Royd UD & CP.[31] Parl Sowerby Dv (1918—48).

HEBDEN ROYD

CP [W Riding] Cr 1937 by union Hebden Bridge UD & CP, Mytholmroyd UD & CP.[31] LG Hebden Royd UD. Transf 1974 to W Yorks.[5] Parl Sowerby CC (1948—*).

HECK

[W Riding] Tp in Snaith AP, sep CP 1866.[2] LG Seq 97. Bdry: 1883,[52] 1889.[607] Transf 1974 to N Yorks.[5] Parl Seq 29.

HECKMONDWIKE

[W Riding] Tp in Birstall AP, sep CP 1866,[2] sep EP 1837,[9] eccl refounded 1842.[273] LG Morley Wap, Dewsb. PLU, Heckmondwike USD, UD. Transf 1974 to W Yorks.[5] Parl W Riding (1832—67), E'rn Dv of W Riding (1867—85), Spen Valley Dv (1885—1948), Dewsb. BC (1948—55), Brigh. & Spenb. CC (1955—*). Eccl Pontef. RDn (1837—57), Dewsb. RDn (1857—66), Birstall RDn (1866—*). Eccl bdry: 1934.[94]

HEDON

[E Riding] Chap in Preston AP, sep civ identity early, sep EP 1814.[608] LG Hold. Wap, Scul. PLU, Hedon Bor, MB (1861—1974), USD. Civ bdry: 1935,[13] 1964.[374] Transf 1974 to Humb.[5] Parl Hedon Parl Bor (1295, 1547—1832), Seq 5 thereafter. Eccl Hold. RDn (1814—49), S Hold. RDn (1849—66), Hedon RDn (1866—1916), S Hold. RDn (1916—*). Eccl bdry: 1954.[373]

HEELEY

EP [W Riding] Cr 1846 from Sheffield AP.[493] Donc. RDn (1846—57), Rotherh. RDn (1857—62), Sheff RDn (1862—1942), Attercliffe RDn (1942—*). Bdry: 1879,[472] 1921 (help cr Sheffield St Aidan EP),[609] 1929,[416] 1974 (help cr Gleadless Valley EP [Derbys, Yorks W Riding]).[577]

CP [W Riding] Hmlt orig in Sheffield AP, after 1866 in Nether Hallam CP, 'Heeley' a sep CP 1880 from the latter.[430] LG Straff. & Tick. Wap, Ecclesall Bierlow PLU, Sheff MB (1880—89), CB (1889—1904) USD. Abol 1904 ent to help cr Ecclesall CP.[502] Parl See Part III of the Guide for composition of Sheff Parl Bors (1885—1918) by wards of the MB.

HELLIFIELD

[W Riding] Tp in Long Preston AP, sep CP 1866,[2] sep EP 1912.[193] LG Seq 111. Bdry: 1938.[28] Transf 1974 to N Yorks.[5] Parl Seq 41. Eccl Craven RDn, N'rn Dv (1912—21), Settle RDn (1921—*).

HELME

EP [W Riding] Cr 1858 from Meltham EP, South Crosland EP, Meltham Mills EP.[479] Hudd. RDn (1858—1968), Blackmoorfoot RDn (1968—*).

HELMSLEY

AP [N Riding] Incl chap Bilsdale Midcable (sep CP 1866,[2] sep EP 1745 as 'Bilsdale',[9] as such eccl refounded 1898 [incl pt Hawnby AP, addtl pt of this par][121]), chap Harome (sep CP 1866,[2] sep EP 1863[160]), chap Pockley (sep CP 1866,[2] sep EP 1898 as 'Pockley cum Eastmoors' incl the pt of tp Bedlam in same par not transf 1882 [qv to Kirkdale[121]]), tp Bedlam (sep CP 1866,[2] pt eccl severed 1882 and transf to Kirkdale AP,[223] the remainder united 1898 with chap Pockley to help cr Pockley cum Eastmoors EP[121]), tps Laskill Pasture, Rievaulx, Sproxton, pt tp Nunnington (each a sep CP 1866,[2] none with sep eccl identity hence this par eccl 'Helmsley with Sproxton, Rievaulx and Carlton', qv). *LG* Seq 63. Transf 1974 to N Yorks.[5] *Parl* Seq 21.

HELMSLEY WITH SPROXTON, RIEVAULX AND CARLTON

AP [N Riding] Usual eccl spelling; for civ and sep chaps and tps civ and eccl, see prev entry. *Eccl* Seq 26.

GATE HELMSLEY

AP [N Riding] *LG* Seq 32. Transf 1974 to N Yorks.[5] *Parl* Seq 16. *Eccl* Pec jurisd Osbaldwick prebend (until 1836), Seq 17 thereafter.

UPPER HELMSLEY

AP [N Riding] Organisation as for Gate Helmsley except not in pec jurisd.

HELPERBY

[N Riding] Tp (in pec jurisd Dean & Chapter of York, until 1836) in Brafferton AP, sep CP 1866.[2] *LG* Seq 30. Transf 1974 to N Yorks.[5] *Parl* Seq 16.

HELPERTHORPE

AP [E Riding] *LG* Buckr. Wap, Driff. PLU, RSD, RD. Abol civ 1935 to help cr Luttons CP.[13] *Parl* E Riding (1832—85), Buckr. Dv (1885—1948). *Eccl* Pec jurisd Dean & Chapter of York (until 1836), Buckr. RDn (1836—57), E Buckr. RDn (1857—58), Buckr. RDn (1874—*). Gains eccl 1858 tp Luttons Ambo from Weaverthorpe AP,[610] then called 'Helperthorpe with Luttons Ambo' until Luttons Ambo severed 1874 as sep EP,[611] the remainder 'Helperthorpe' thereafter.

HELPERTHORPE WITH LUTTONS AMBO

EP [E Riding] Cr 1858 when Helperthorpe AP gains tp Luttons Ambo from Weaverthorpe AP.[610] E Buckr. RDn (1862—66), Buckr. RDn (1866—74). Abol 1874 when Luttons Ambo severed as sep EP,[611] the remainder to be 'Helperthorpe'.

HELREDALE

CP [N Riding] Cr 1894 from the pt of Hawsker with Stainsacre CP in Whitby UD.[431] *LG* Whitby PLU, UD. Abol 1925 ent to Whitby AP.[612] *Parl* Scarb. & Whitby Dv (1918—48).

HEMINGBROUGH

AP [E Riding] Incl chap Barlby (sep CP 1866,[2] sep EP 1726[9]), tps Brackenholme cum Woodhall, Cliffe cum Lund, South Duffield, Osgodby, pt tp Menthorpe cum Bowthorpe (each of the 5 a sep CP 1866[2]). *LG* Ouse & Derw. Wap, Howden PLU, RSD, RD (1894—1935), Derw. RD (1935—74). Addtl civ bdry alt: 1935 (incl gains Brackenholme with Woodhall CP).[13] Transf 1974 to N Yorks.[5] *Parl* Seq 7. *Eccl* Pec jurisd Dean & Chapter of Durham (until 1836), Seq 19 thereafter.

HEMLINGTON

[N Riding] Tp in Stainton AP, sep CP 1866.[2] *LG* Langb. Lbty, Stokes. PLU (1837—75), Middlesb. PLU (1875—1930), RSD, RD (1894—1932), Stokes. RD (1932—68). Bdry: 1932 (incl loses pt to Middlesb. CB [assoc with N Riding] & CP).[20] Abol

1968 to help cr Teesside CB (assoc with N Riding) & CP.[537] *Parl* N Riding (1832—85), Clev Dv (1885—1948), Richm. CC (1948—70).

HEMPHOLME

[E Riding] Tp in Leven AP, sep CP 1866.[2] *LG* Hold. Wap, Skirl. PLU, RSD, RD. Bdry: 1885.[335] Abol 1935 ent to Brandesburton AP.[13] *Parl* E Riding (1832—85), Hold. Dv (1885—1948).

HEMSWORTH

AP [W Riding] *LG* Staincr. Wap, Hemsw. PLU, RSD, RD (1894—1921), UD (1921—74). Transf 1974 to W Yorks.[5] *Parl* Seq 42. *Eccl* Donc. RDn (until 1857), Pontef. RDn (1857—1916), Hemsw. RDn (1916—27), Pontef. RDn (1927—*). Eccl bdry: 1921 (cr Kinsley EP).[522]

HENDERSKELF

[N Riding] Tp in Bulmer AP, sep CP 1866.[2] *LG* Seq 29. Transf 1974 to N Yorks.[5] *Parl* Seq 16.

HENSALL

[W Riding] Tp in Snaith AP, sep CP 1866,[2] sep EP 1855 from Snaith AP, Kellington AP.[173] *LG* Seq 97. Civ bdry: 1883,[52] 1889.[613] Transf 1974 to N Yorks.[5] *Parl* Seq 29. *Eccl* Pontef. RDn (1855—62), Selby RDn (1862—71), Snaith RDn (1871—*).

HEPTONSTALL

[W Riding] Tp in Halifax AP, sep CP 1866,[2] sep EP 1747.[9] *LG* Morley Wap, Todmorden PLU, pt Hebden Bridge USD, pt Todmorden RSD, Todmorden RD (1894—1939), Hepton RD (1939—74). Civ bdry: 1894 (loses the pt in Hebden Bridge UD to help cr Hebden Bridge CP).[450] Transf 1974 to W Yorks.[5] *Parl* Seq 37. *Eccl* Pontef. RDn (1747—57), Halifax RDn (1857—1967), Calder Valley RDn (1967—*). Eccl bdry: 1846 (help refound Mytholmroyd EP),[614] 1968.[90]

HEPWORTH

[W Riding] Tp in Kirkburton AP, sep CP 1866,[2] pt eccl severed 1858 to help refound Holmfirth EP,[294] the remainder cr 1864 'Hepworth' EP.[246] *LG* Agb. Wap, Hudd. PLU, pt Scholes USD (enlarged pt 1886—94), pt Holmf. USD (1884—94), pt Hepworth USD, Hepworth UD (1894—95), New Mill UD (1895—1938). Civ bdry: 1883,[531] 1886,[157] 1894 (loses the pt in Scholes UD to help cr Scholes CP),[158] 1895.[570] Abol civ 1938 pt to Holmf. UD & CP, pt to help cr Dunford CP.[28] *Parl* W Riding (1832—67), S'rn Dv of W Riding (1867—85), Holmf. Dv (1885—1918), Colne Valley Dv (1918—48). *Eccl* Hudd. RDn (1864—1968), Kirkburton RDn (1968—*).

HERRINGTHORPE

EP [W Riding] Cr 1950 from Whiston AP, Wickersley AP, Dalton EP, Clifton EP.[212] Rotherh. RDn.

HESLERTON

AP [E Riding] Incl tp East Heslerton, pt tps West Heslerton, Yedingham (the first two each a sep CP 1866[2]; Yedingham AP comprised of pt tp Yedingham, pt tp West Heslerton) so that 'Heslerton' has no sep civ identity 1866—1935 (see following entry); this par usually eccl 'West Heslerton' with East Heslerton considered its chap until East Heslerton a sep EP 1879,[615] the remainder eccl called 'Heslerton' thereafter. *LG* Buckr. Wap. *Parl*

E Riding (1832—67). *Eccl* Buckr. RDn (1879—87), Settr. RDn (1887—1922), Buckr. RDn (1922—*).

CP [E Riding] Cr 1935 by union East Heslerton CP, West Heslerton CP.[13] *LG* Norton RD. Transf 1974 to N Yorks.[5] *Parl* Bev. CC (1948—55), Howden CC (1955—*).

EAST HESLERTON

[E Riding] Tp in Heslerton AP (eccl considered chap in the par eccl called 'West Heslerton'), sep CP 1866,[2] sep EP 1879 (the eccl remainder 'Heslerton' thereafter).[615] *LG* Buckr. Wap, Malton PLU, RSD, Norton RD. Abol civ 1935 to help cr Heslerton CP.[13] *Parl* E Riding (1832—85), Buckr. Dv (1885—1948). *Eccl* Buckr. RDn (1879—87), Settr. RDn (1887—1922), Buckr. RDn (1922—*).

WEST HESLERTON

AP [E Riding] Usual eccl spelling, with East Heslerton considered its chap until a sep EP 1879,[615] the eccl remainder 'Heslerton' thereafter, qv for eccl after 1879 and for all civ organisation. *Eccl* Buckr. RDn.

CP [E Riding] Tp pt in Heslerton AP (for eccl, see prev entry), pt in Yedingham AP, sep CP 1866.[2] *LG* Buckr. Wap, Malton PLU, RSD, Norton RD. Bdry: 1889.[566] Abol 1935 to help cr Heslerton CP.[13] *Parl* E Riding (1832—85), Buckr. Dv (1885—1948).

HESLINGTON

EP [E Riding] Cr *ca* 1860s by union Heslington St Paul AP, Heslington St Lawrence EP.[616] Bulmer RDn (1860s—96), Escr. RDn (1896—*). Bdry: 1869 (pt of this EP, situated in York St Lawrence AP, eccl severed 1869 and made pt of this EP),[617] 1971.[225]

CP [E Riding] Cr 1885 by union Heslington St Paul AP, Heslington St Lawrence CP.[616] *LG* Ouse & Derw. Wap, York PLU, RSD, Escr. RD (1894—1935), Derw. RD (1935—74). Bdry: 1935 (gains Langwith CP),[13] 1968 (loses pt to York CB [not assoc with a Riding] & CP).[424] Transf 1974 to N Yorks.[5] *Parl* Howdensh. Dv (1918—48), Bev. CC (1948—55), Howden CC (1955—*).

HESLINGTON ST LAWRENCE

[E Riding] Tp in York St Lawrence AP, sep CP 1866,[2] sep EP 1740.[9] *LG* Ouse & Derw. Wap, York PLU, RSD. Abol civ 1885 to help cr Heslington CP.[616] *Parl* E Riding (1832—85), Howdensh. Dv (1885—1918). *Eccl* Pec jurisd Ampleforth prebend (until 1836), Bulmer RDn (1836—60s). Abol eccl *ca* 1860s to help cr Heslington EP.[617]

HESLINGTON ST PAUL

AP [E Riding] *LG* Ouse & Derw. Wap, York PLU, RSD. Abol civ 1885 to help cr Heslington CP.[616] *Parl*, *Eccl* as for Heslington St Lawrence.

HESSAY

[W Riding] Tp in Moor Monkton AP, sep CP 1866.[2] *LG* Seq 72. Transf 1974 to N Yorks.[5] *Parl* Seq 23.

HESSLE

AP [E Riding] (Tp Hessle pt in Hessle AP, pt in Kirk Ella AP). Incl chap Kingston upon Hull Holy Trinity (some parochial rights by 14th cent, being used parochially by 1548, sep independence ent by 1661[618];in jurisd Kingst. upon Hull Bor), pt tp Anlaby (sep CP 1866,[2] sep EP 1902 [qv for other 3 constituent pars then][104]). *LG* Pt Kingst. upon Hull

Bor (until Kingston upon Hull Holy Trinity sep civ identity), Kingst. upon Hull Co, Scul. PLU, pt Kingst. upon Hull MB (1883—89), pt Kingst. upon Hull CB (1889—94), pt Kingst. upon Hull USD (1883—94), Scul. RSD (ent 1875—83, pt 1883—94). Abol civ 1894 the pt in the CB cr Hessle Within CP, the remainder cr Hessle Without CP.[443] *Parl* E Riding (1832—85), pt Hold. Dv (1885—1918) and see Part III of the *Guide* for composition of Kingst. upon Hull Parl Bors (1885—1918, incl pt of this par) by wards of the MB. *Eccl* Harth. & Hull RDn (until 1857), S Harth. RDn (1857—66), Howden RDn (1866—1916), Kingst. upon Hull RDn (1916—*). Addtl eccl bdry alt: 1916 (cr Kingston upon Hull St Nicholas, Anlaby EP),[619] 1961.[44]

CP [E Riding] Renaming 1899 of Hessle Without CP when it was constituted Hessle UD.[446] *LG* Scul. PLU, Hessle UD. Bdry: 1930 (loses pt to Kings. upon Hull CB [assoc with E Riding] and to Sculcoates AP).[251] Abol 1935 ent to Haltemprice CP to help constitute Haltemp. UD.[13] *Parl* Howdensh. Dv (1918—48).

HESSLE

[W Riding] Tp in Wragby AP, sep CP 1866.[2] *LG* Osg. Wap, Hemsw. PLU, RSD. Abol 1888 to help cr Hessle and Hill Top CP.[348] *Parl* W Riding (1832—67), N'rn Dv of W Riding (1867—85), Osg. Dv (1885—1918).

HESSLE AND HILL TOP

CP [W Riding] Cr 1888 by union Hessle CP, Hill Top CP, pt Wintersett CP.[348] *LG* Osg. Wap, Hemsw. PLU, RSD, RD. Transf 1974 to W Yorks.[5] *Parl* Hemsw. Dv/CC (1918—*).

HESSLE WITHIN

CP [Kingst. upon Hull CB] Cr 1894 from the pt of Hessle AP (o'wise E Riding) in Kingst. upon Hull CB.[443] *LG* Scul. PLU, Kingst. upon Hull CB. Abol 1898 ent to Sculcoates AP.[446]

HESSLE WITHOUT

CP [E Riding] Cr 1894 from the pt of Hessle AP not in Kingst. upon Hull CB.[443] *LG* Scul. PLU, RD. Renamed 1899 'Hessle' when constituted Hessle UD.[446]

HETTON

[W Riding] Tp in Burnsall AP, sep CP 1866.[2] *LG* Seq 112. Transf 1974 to N Yorks.[5] *Parl* Seq 41.

BRIDGE HEWICK

[W Riding] Tp in Ripon AP, sep CP 1866.[2] *LG* Seq 100. Transf 1974 to N Yorks.[5] *Parl* Seq 34.

COPT HEWICK

[W Riding] Organisation as for Bridge Hewick.

HEWORTH

[N Riding] Tp pt in York St Cuthbert, St Helen on the Walls and All Saints Peasholm CP, pt in York St Olave, Marygate AP, pt in York St Saviour AP, sep CP 1866[2]; for eccl see 'York Holy Trinity, Heworth'. *LG* Bulmer Wap, York PLU, pt York MB (1884—89), pt York CB (1889—94), pt York USD (1884—94), York RSD (ent 1875—84, pt 1884—94). Abol 1894 the pt in the CB (not assoc with a Riding) cr Heworth Within CP, the remainder cr Heworth Without CP.[51] *Parl* N Riding (1832—85), pt York Parl Bor, pt Thirsk & Malton

Dv (1885—1918).

HEWORTH WITHIN

CP [York CB] Cr 1894 from the pt of Heworth CP (o'wise N Riding) in York CB.[51] *LG* York PLU, CB. Abol 1900 to help cr York CP.[423]

HEWORTH WITHOUT

CP [N Riding] Cr 1894 from the pt of Heworth CP not in York CB.[51] *LG* York PLU, Flaxton RD. Bdry: 1934 (loses pt to York CB [not assoc with a Riding] & CP),[3] 1968 (exchanges pts with York CB [not assoc with a Riding] & CP).[418] Transf 1974 to N Yorks.[5] *Parl* Thirsk & Malton Dv/CC (1918—*).

HICKLETON

AP [W Riding] Incl chap Marr (sep par by 1535[620]). *LG* Seq 117. Civ bdry: 1883.[42] Transf 1974 to S Yorks.[5] *Parl* Seq 44. *Eccl* Seq 46.

SOUTH HIENDLEY

[W Riding] Tp in Felkirk AP, sep CP 1866.[2] *LG* Seq 113. Transf 1974 to W Yorks.[5] *Parl* Seq 42.

HIGHTOWN

EP [W Riding] Cr 1911 from Liversedge EP.[578] Birstall RDn.

HILDENLEY

[N Riding] Tp in Appleton le Street AP, sep CP 1866.[2] *LG* Seq 65. Transf 1974 to N Yorks.[5] *Parl* Seq 16.

HILDERTHORPE

[E Riding] Tp in Bridlington AP, sep CP 1866.[2] *LG* Dick. Wap, Bridl. PLU, MB (1889—1923), pt Bridl. USD, pt Bridl. RSD. Bdry: 1894 (loses the pt not in the UD to Bessingby AP).[239] Abol 1923 ent to Bridlington AP.[240] *Parl* E Riding (1832—85), Buckr. Dv (1885—1948).

HILL TOP

[W Riding] Tp in Wragby AP, sep CP 1866.[2] *LG* Osg. Wap, Hemsw. PLU, RSD. Abol 1888 to help cr Hessle and Hill Top CP.[348] *Parl* W Riding (1832—67), N'rn Dv of W Riding (1867—85), Osg. Dv (1885—1918).

HILLAM

[W Riding] Tp in Monk Fryston AP, sep CP 1866.[2] *LG* Seq 75. Bdry: 1883.[52] Transf 1974 to N Yorks.[5] *Parl* Seq 26.

HILLSBOROUGH AND WADSLEY BRIDGE

EP [W Riding] Cr 1895 from Wadsley EP, Ecclesfield AP,[115] refounded 1939 from Ecclesfield AP, Pitsmoor EP, Grenoside EP.[407] Ecclesfield RDn (1895—1942), Hallam RDn (1942—*). Bdry: 1899,[507] 1963.[621]

HILSTON

AP [E Riding] *LG* Hold. Wap, Patr. PLU, RSD, RD. Abol civ 1935 ent to Roos AP.[13] *Parl* E Riding (1832—85), Hold. Dv (1885—1948). *Eccl* Seq 16.

HILTON

[N Riding] Chap in Rudby in Cleveland AP, sep civ identity early, see EP 1749.[622] *LG* Seq 58. Transf 1974 to Clev.[5] *Parl* Seq 11. *Eccl* Clev RDn (1749—1862), Stokes. RDn (1862—*).

HINDERWELL

AP [N Riding] Incl chap Roxby (sep CP 1866,[2] not sep eccl hence this par eccl 'Hinderwell with Roxby', qv). *LG* Langb. Lbty, Whitby PLU, Hinderwell USD, UD (1894—1923), Whitby UD (1923—74).

Transf 1974 to N Yorks.[5] *Parl* N Riding (1832—85), Whitby Dv (1885—1918), Clev Dv (1918—48), Scarb. & Whitby CC (1948—70), Clev & Whitby CC (1970—*).

HINDERWELL WITH ROXBY

AP [N Riding] Usual eccl spelling; for civ and civ sep chap Roxby, see prev entry. *Eccl* Seq 22.

HIPPERHOLME

CP [W Riding] Cr 1894 from the pt of Hipperholme with Brighouse CP in Hipperholme UD.[257] *LG* Halifax PLU, Hipperholme UD. Bdry: 1899.[623] Abol 1937 ent to Brigh. MB & CP.[31] *Parl* Elland Dv (1918—48).

HIPPERHOLME WITH BRIGHOUSE

[W Riding] Tp in Halifax AP, sep CP 1866[2]; area of Brighouse eccl severed 1724 to help cr Elland cum Stainland and Fixby EP,[178] re-augmented 1739 as 'Elland'[9] but usually called 'Elland with Greetland', area of Brighouse eccl severed 1749 from the latter to help cr Lightcliffe EP,[9] 'Brighouse' a sep EP 1836 from Lightcliffe EP,[9] eccl refounded 1849.[351] *LG* Morley Wap, Halifax PLU, pt Brigh. USD, pt Hipperholme USD, pt Brigh. MB (1893—94), pt Halifax RD. Abol 1894 the pt in Brigh. MB cr Brighouse CP, the pt in Hipperholme UD cr Hipperholme CP, the remainder cr Norwood Green and Coley CP.[257] *Parl* W Riding (1832—67), E'rn Dv of W Riding (1867—85), Elland Dv (1885—1918).

HIPSWELL

[N Riding] Chap in Catterick AP, sep CP 1866,[2] sep EP 1738,[9] eccl refounded 1897 from Catterick AP, Patrick Brompton AP (pt tp Scotton).[247] *LG* Seq 50. Addtl civ bdry alt: 1883,[16] 1888.[624] Transf 1974 to N Yorks.[5] *Parl* Pt Richm. Parl Bor (1585—1885), remainder and later, Seq 14. *Eccl* Catt. RDn (1738—1857), Catt. East RDn (1857—63), Richm. North RDn (1863—66), Richm. West RDn (1866—*). Eccl bdry: 1958.[396]

TEMPLE HIRST

[W Riding] Tp in Birkin AP, sep CP 1866,[2] eccl severed 1855 to help cr Haddlesey EP.[274] *LG* Seq 80. Transf 1974 to N Yorks.[5] *Parl* Seq 24.

HIRST COURTNEY

[W Riding] Organisation as for Temple Hirst.

HOLBECK

[W Riding] Chap in Leeds AP, sep CP 1866,[2] sep EP 1719.[9] *LG* Skyr. Wap, Leeds Bor/MB/CB, USD, Leeds Guardians (for poor, 1844—62), Holbeck Par (for poor, 1862—69), PLU (1869—1925). Civ bdry: 1883,[52] 1896,[322] 1904 (gains Beeston CP).[124] Abol civ 1925 ent to Leeds AP.[129] *Parl* Leeds Parl Bor (1832—85); see Part III of the *Guide* for composition of Leeds Parl Bors (1885—1948) by wards of the MB/CB. *Eccl* Ainsty RDn (1719—1820), Old Ainsty RDn (1820—36), Pontef. RDn (1836—57), Leeds RDn (1857—1971), Armley RDn (1971—*). Eccl bdry: 1847 (cr Little Holbeck EP),[625] 1851 (help cr Brewery Field EP),[344] 1872 (help cr Beeston Hill EP),[90] 1885 (help refound Hunslet [St Cuthbert] EP),[229] 1902 (help cr Holbeck St Edward King and Martyr EP),[119] 1957 (gains New Wortley EP),[626] 1967 (gains Holbeck St Edward King and Martyr EP),[194] 1967.[127]

LITTLE HOLBECK

EP [W Riding] Cr 1847 from Holbeck EP.[625] Pontef. RDn (1847—57), Leeds RDn (1857—1901). Abol 1901 to help cr Leeds St John the Evangelist with St Barnabas EP.[345]

HOLBECK ST EDWARD KING AND MARTYR

EP [W Riding] Cr 1902 from Holbeck EP, Beeston EP, Beeston Hill EP.[119] Leeds RDn. Abol 1967 ent to Holbeck EP.[194]

HOLGATE

[Ainsty (W Riding until 1449 and from 1836, indept jurisd 1449—1836)] Tp in York St Mary Bishopshill Junior AP, sep CP 1866[2]; for eccl see 'York St Paul, Holgate'. LG York PLU, MB (1884—89), CB (1889—1900), USD (1884—94), RSD (1875—84). Abol 1900 to help cr York CP.[423] Parl N Riding (1832—85), York Parl Bor (1885—1918).

HOLLISCROFT

EP [W Riding] Cr 1846 from Sheffield AP.[493] Donc. RDn (1846—57), Rotherh. RDn (1857—62), Sheff RDn (1862—1939). Bdry: 1849.[593] Abol 1939 pt to Sheffield AP, pt to Sheffield St George EP.[627]

HOLLYM

AP [E Riding] Orig chap in Withernsea, later considered the mother par to which Withernsea a chap and tp (sep CP 1866[2]), the par eccl 'Hollym and Withernsea', qv, until eccl divided 1968 into 2 EPs of Hollym, Withernsea[601]; this par also incl pt tp Holmpton, remainder of which constitutes Holmpton AP. LG Seq 15. Addtl civ bdry alt: 1935.[13] Transf 1974 to Humb.[5] Parl Seq 5. Eccl S Hold. RDn.

HOLLYM AND WITHERNSEA

AP [E Riding] Usual eccl spelling until 1968 when divided into 2 EPs of Hollym, Withernsea[598]; for civ and orig arrangement of mother par and chap, for civ organisation and civ sep chap, see prev entry. Eccl Hold. RDn (until 1849), S Hold. RDn (1849—66), Hedon RDn (1866—1916), S Hold. RDn (1916—68).

HOLME

[N Riding] Tp in Pickill AP, sep CP 1866.[2] LG Seq 23. Transf 1974 to N Yorks.[5] Parl Seq 16.

HOLME

[W Riding] Tp in Almondbury AP, sep CP 1866; for eccl see 'Holme Bridge'. LG Agb. Wap, Hudd. PLU, Holme USD (ent 1875—86, pt 1886—94), pt Austonley USD (1886—94), Holme UD. Bdry: 1883,[52] 1886,[151] 1894 (loses the pt in Austonley UD to Austonley CP and loses pt to cr South Holme CP),[158] 1895 (loses pt to Scholes USD & CP and gains South Holme CP).[570] Abol 1938 pt to Holmf. UD & CP, pt to help cr Dunford CP.[28] Parl W Riding (1832—67), S'rn Dv of W Riding (1867—85), Holmf. Dv (1885—1918), Colne Valley Dv (1918—48).

NORTH HOLME

[N Riding] Tp in Great Edstone AP, sep CP 1866.[2] LG Seq 64. Transf 1974 to N Yorks.[5] Parl Seq 21.

SOUTH HOLME

[N Riding] Tp in Hovingham AP, sep CP 1866.[2] LG Seq 65. Transf 1974 to N Yorks.[5] Parl Seq 16.

SOUTH HOLME

CP [W Riding] Cr 1894 from Holme CP.[158] LG Hudd. PLU, Holme UD. Abol 1895 ent to Holme CP.[570]

HOLME BRIDGE

EP [W Riding] Cr 1842 from Almondbury AP,[9] refounded 1843[79]; for civ see 2nd 'Holme' above. Pontef. RDn (1842—57), Hudd. RDn (1857—1968), Almondb. RDn (1968—*). Bdry: 1876 (help cr Wilshaw EP),[29] 1904.[400]

HOLME IN SPALDING MOOR

AP [E Riding] Usual eccl spelling; for civ see 'Holme upon Spalding Moor'. Eccl Seq 14.

HOLME ON THE WOLDS

AP [E Riding] LG Harth. Wap, Bev. PLU, RSD, RD. Abol civ 1935 to help cr Dalton Holme CP.[13] Parl E Riding (1832—85), Hold. Dv (1885—1948). Eccl Pec jurisd Holme prebend (until 1836), Harth. & Hull RDn (1836—57), N Harth. RDn (1857—62). Abol eccl 1862 to help cr South Dalton with Holme on the Wolds EP.[467]

HOLME UPON SPALDING MOOR

AP [E Riding] Usual civ spelling; for eccl see 'Holme in Spalding Moor'. LG Seq 11. Bdry: 1957.[561] Transf 1974 to Humb.[5] Parl Seq 7.

HOLMFIRTH

EP [W Riding] Cr 1726 from Kirkburton AP (pt tps Cartworth, Fulstone, Hepworth, Wooldale),[9] refounded 1858.[294] Pontef. RDn (1726—1857), Hudd. RDn (1857—1968), Almondb. RDn (1968—*). Bdry: 1904.[400]

CP [W Riding] Cr 1921 by union of pars in Holmf. UD: Austonley CP, Cartworth CP, Netherthong CP, Upperthong CP, Wooldale CP.[159] LG Hudd. PLU, Holmf. UD. Bdry: 1938.[28] Transf 1974 to W Yorks.[5] Parl Colne Valley CC (1948—*).

HOLMPTON

AP [E Riding] (Tp Holmpton pt in Holmpton AP, pt in Hollym AP). LG Seq 15. Transf 1974 to Humb.[5] Parl Seq 5. Eccl Seq 16.

HOLTBY

AP [N Riding] Incl pt tps Warthill Copyhold, Warthill Freehold (each a sep CP 1866[2]). LG Seq 32. Transf 1974 to N Yorks.[5] Parl Seq 16. Eccl Pec jurisd Dean & Chapter of Durham (until 1836), Seq 17 thereafter.

HOLWICK

[N Riding] Tp in Romaldkirk AP, sep CP 1866.[2] LG Seq 39. Bdry: 1884 (gains pt Middleton in Teesdale AP, Durham,[176] gains pt Newbiggin CP, Durham[547]). Transf 1974 to Durham.[5] Parl Seq 14.

HONLEY

[W Riding] Chap in Almondbury AP, sep CP 1866,[2] sep EP 1729 as 'Honley with Brockholes',[9] qv, refounded 1876 as 'Honley' after the 3 reductions in area noted in following entry.[29] LG Agb. Wap, Hudd. PLU, Honley USD, UD. Civ bdry: 1897,[628] 1912.[629] Abol civ 1938 ent to Holmf. UD & CP.[28] Parl W Riding (1832—67), S'rn Dv of W Riding (1867—85), Colne Valley Dv (1885—1948). Eccl Hudd. RDn (1876—1968), Almondb. RDn (1968—*).

HONLEY WITH BROCKHOLES

EP [W Riding] Chap 'Honley' in Almondbury (qv for civ) AP, sep EP 1729 as 'Honley with Brockholes'. Pontef. RDn (1739—1857), Hudd. RDn (1857—76). Bdry: 1831 (help cr Netherthong EP,[9] refounded 1843[79]), 1839 (help cr South Crosland EP,[9] refounded 1843[79]), 1845 (help cr Meltham Mills EP).[84] The remaining area eccl refounded 1876 as 'Honley',[29] qv.

HOOD GRANGE

[N Riding] Hmlt in Kilburn AP, sep CP 1866.[2] LG Seq 27. Transf 1974 to N Yorks.[5] Parl Seq 16.

HOOK

[W Riding] Chap (pec jurisd Selby 1440—1539, pec jurisd Snaith 1539—1836) in Snaith AP, sep CP 1866,[2] sep EP 1798.[9] LG Osg. Wap, Goole PLU, pt Goole USD, pt Goole RSD, Goole RD. Civ bdry: 1894 (loses the pt in the UD to help reconstitute Goole CP, loses pt to help cr Goole Fields CP).[47] Transf 1974 to Humb.[5] Parl Seq 29. Eccl Pontef. RDn (1836—38), New Ainsty RDn (1838—57), Pontef. RDn (1857—62), Selby RDn (1862—71), Snaith RDn (1871—*).

HOOTON LEVITT

[W Riding] Tp in Maltby AP, sep CP 1866.[2] LG Seq 119. Transf 1974 to S Yorks.[5] Parl Seq 48.

HOOTON PAGNELL

AP [W Riding] Incl tp Bilham (sep CP 1866[2]).LG Seq 117. Addtl civ bdry alt: 1920 (gains Bilham CP, Stotfold CP).[248] Transf 1974 to S Yorks.[5] Parl Seq 44. Eccl Seq 46.

HOOTON ROBERTS

AP [W Riding] LG Seq 119. Transf 1974 to S Yorks.[5] Parl Seq 55. Eccl Donc. RDn (until 1857), Rotherh. RDn (1857—71), Wath RDn (1871—1927), Rotherh. RDn (1927—*).

HOPE

[N Riding] Tp in Barningham AP, sep CP 1866.[2] LG Seq 39. Transf 1974 to Durham.[5] Parl Seq 14.

UPPER HOPTON

EP [W Riding] Cr 1860 from Mirfield AP, Kirkheaton AP.[301] Dewsb. RDn (1860—83), Birstall RDn (1883—1927), Dewsb. RDn (1927—*).

HORBURY

[W Riding] Chap in Wakefield AP, sep CP 1866,[2] sep EP 1717.[9] LG Agb. Wap, Wakef PLU, Horbury USD, UD. Transf 1974 to W Yorks.[5] Parl Seq 54. Eccl Pontef. RDn (1717—1857), Wakef RDn (1857—*). Eccl bdry: 1882 (help cr Horbury Bridge EP),[130] 1890 (cr Horbury Junction EP).[630]

HORBURY BRIDGE

EP [W Riding] Cr 1882 from Horbury EP, Middlestown EP, Thornhill AP.[130] Dewsb. RDn (1882—1913), Wakef RDn (1913—*).

HORBURY JUNCTION

EP [W Riding] Cr 1890 from Horbury EP.[630] Wakef RDn.

HORNBY

AP [N Riding] Incl tp Ainderby Meyers with Holtby, tp Hackforth, pt tp Arrathorne (each a sep CP 1866[2]), pt tp Hunton (sep CP 1866,[2] sep EP 1794[9]). LG Seq 47. Transf 1974 to N Yorks.[5] Parl Seq 11. Eccl Pec jurisd Dean & Chapter of York (until 1836), Seq 53

thereafter. Eccl bdry: 1930 (so alt that ent area Arrathorne CP in this par eccl, incl gains pt Patrick Brompton AP, help cr Patrick Brompton with Hunton EP).[137]

HORNBY

[N Riding] Tp in Great Smeaton AP, sep CP 1866.[2] LG Seq 22. Transf 1974 to N Yorks.[5] Parl Seq 14.

HORNSEA

AP [E Riding] LG Hold. Wap, Skirl. PLU, Hornsea USD, UD. Transf 1974 to Humb.[5] Parl Seq 5. Eccl Hold. RDn (until 1849), N Hold. RDn (1849—66), Hornsea RDn (1866—1916), N Hold. RDn (1916—38). Abol eccl 1938 to help cr Hornsea with Goxhill EP.[27]

EP [E Riding] Renaming 1972 of Hornsea with Goxhill EP when Goxhill severed to help cr Mappleton with Goxhill EP.[631] N Hold. RDn.

HORNSEA WITH GOXHILL

EP [E Riding] Cr 1939 by union Hornsea AP, Goxhill EP.[27] N Hold. RDn. Abol 1972 when Goxhill severed to help cr Mappleton with Goxhill EP, the remainder renamed 'Hornsea'.[631]

HORSEHOUSE

EP [N Riding] Cr 1735 from Coverham AP.[9] Catt. RDn (1735—1857), Catt. West RDn (1857—1928), Wensleyd. RDn (1928—*).

HORSFORTH

[W Riding] Chap in Guiseley AP sep CP 1866,[2] sep EP 1747,[9] eccl refounded 1906.[407] LG Skyr. Wap, Carlton GilbU (until 1861), Wharfed. PLU (1861—1930), Horsforth USD, UD. Civ bdry: 1937 (incl loses pt to Leeds CB [assoc with W Riding] & AP).[31] Transf 1974 to W Yorks.[5] Parl W Riding (1832—67), N'rn Dv of W Riding (1867—85), Pudsey Dv (1885—1918), Pudsey & Otley Dv (1918—48), Pudsey BC (1948—*). Eccl Ainsty RDn (1747—1820), Old Ainsty RDn (1820—36), Pontef. RDn (1820—57), Otley RDn (1857—1921), Leeds RDn (1921—71), Head. RDn (1971—*). Eccl bdry: 1846 (help cr Woodside EP),[35] 1967.[127]

HORTON

[W Riding] Chap in Bradford AP, sep CP 1866,[2] sep EP 1810.[9] LG Morley Wap, Bradf PLU, MB (1847—89), CB (1889—98), USD. Abol 1898 ent to Bradford AP.[65] Parl Bradf Parl Bor (1832—85); see Part III of the Guide for composition of Bradf Parl Bors (1885—1918) by wards of the MB. Eccl Pontef. RDn (1810—57), Bradf RDn (1857—63). Bdry: 1854 (cr Bradford St John EP).[302] Refounded 1863 as'Great Horton' EP,[309] qv.

HORTON

[W Riding] Tp in Gisburn AP, sep CP 1866.[2] LG Seq 108. Transf 1974 to Lancs.[5] Parl Seq 41.

GREAT HORTON

EP [W Riding] Refounding 1863 of Horton EP.[309] Bradf RDn (1863—1921), Horton RDn (1921—71), Bowl. & Horton RDn (1971—*). Bdry: 1880,[47] 1902 (help cr Bradford St Columba, Horton EP),[322] 1903 (help cr Bradford St Oswald, Chapel Green EP).[302] 1906 (help cr Bradford St Wilfrid, Lidget Green EP),[323] 1959 (help cr Buttershaw St Aidan EP).[320]

LITTLE HORTON—see BRADFORD ST OSWALD, CHAPEL GREEN

HORTON ALL SAINTS

EP [W Riding] Cr 1810 from Bradford AP,[9] refounded 1864.[273] Bradf RDn (1810—1921), Horton RDn (1921—71), Bowl. & Horton RDn (1971—*). Bdry: 1842 (help cr Bradford St Columba, Horton EP),[288] 1965 (gains Bradford St James EP, Bradford St John EP).[325]

HORTON IN RIBBLESDALE

AP [W Riding] *LG* Seq 111. Transf 1974 to N Yorks. *Parl* Seq 41. *Eccl* Craven RDn (until 1857), Craven RDn, N'rn Dv (1857—1921), Settle RDn (1921—71), Bowl. & Horton RDn (1971—*). Eccl bdry: 1842 (help cr Stainforth EP).[136]

HOTHAM

AP [E Riding] *LG* Seq 11. Civ bdry: 1935 (incl help cr Newbald CP).[13] Transf 1974 to Humb.[5] *Parl* Seq 7. *Eccl* Harth. & Hull RDn (until 1866), Bev. RDn (1866—71), Howden RDn (1871—*).

GREAT HOUGHTON

[W Riding] Tp in Darfield AP, sep CP 1866.[2] *LG* Seq 118. Transf 1974 to S Yorks.[5] *Parl* Seq 42.

LITTLE HOUGHTON

[W Riding] Organisation as for Great Houghton.

HOVINGHAM

AP [N Riding] Tp 'Hovingham' in Ryed. Wap as was tp East Ness (sep CP 1866,[2] pt eccl severed 1931 and transf to Nunnington AP[632]), tps Airyholme with Howthorpe and Baxton Howe, Coulton, Fryton, South Holmne, Wath (each of the last 5 a sep CP 1866[2]); incl in Bulmer Wap tp Scackleton (sep CP 1866[2]). *LG* Malton PLU, RSD, RD. Transf 1974 to N Yorks.[5] *Parl* Seq 16. *Eccl* Seq 27.

HOWDEN

AP [E Riding] Orig Collegiate. Incl chap Barmby on the Marsh (sep CP 1866,[2] sep EP 1796 as 'Barmby Marsh',[9] as such eccl refounded 1864[182]), chap Laxton (sep CP 1866,[2] sep EP 1785 [incl tps Cotness, Metham, Saltmarshe, Yokefleet],[9] eccl refounded 1858[440]), tps Cotness, Metham, Saltmarshe, Yokefleet (each a sep CP 1866,[2] each eccl severed 1785 to help cr Laxton EP,[9] qv for refounding 1858), tps Asselby, Balkholme, Belby, Kilpin, Knedlington, Skelton, Thorpe (each a sep CP 1866[2]). *LG* Howden Bor, Seq 17. Addtl civ bdry alt: 1880,[633] 1880,[171] 1935.[13] Transf 1974 to Humb.[5] *Parl* Seq 7. *Eccl* Pec jurisd Dean & Chapter of Durham (until 1836), Harth. & Hull RDn (1836—62), Weigh. RDn (1862—66), Howden RDn (1866—*). Addtl eccl bdry alt: 1895 (help cr Newport EP).[284]

HOWE

[N Riding] Tp in Pickhill AP, sep CP 1866.[2] *LG* Seq 45. Transf 1974 to N Yorks.[5] *Parl* Seq 16.

HOWGILL

EP [W Riding] Cr 1737 from Sedbergh AP.[9] Kirkby Lonsd. RDn (1737—1849), Clapham RDn (1849—1921), Ewecr. RDn (1921—26), Sedbergh RDn (1926—71), Ewecr. RDn (1971—*).

HOWGRAVE

[N Riding] Tp in Kirklington AP, sep CP 1866.[2] *LG* Seq 43. Bdry: 1935 (gains pt Nunwick with Howgrave CP, Yorks W Riding).[634] Transf 1974 to N Yorks.[5] *Parl* Seq 18.

HOWSHAM

[E Riding] Tp in Scrayingham AP, sep CP 1866,[2] sep EP 1860[9] but sep eccl status not sustained. *LG* Seq 2. Transf 1974 to N Yorks.[5] *Parl* Seq 1.

HIGH HOYLAND

AP [W Riding] Incl tp Clayton West (sep CP 1866[2]), pt chap and tp Cumberworth (some parochial rights from 1627,[459] sep CP 1866,[2] sep EP 1865,[9] sometimes as 'Cumberworth with Denby Dale'). *LG* Seq 114. Transf 1974 to S Yorks.[5] *Parl* Seq 50. *Eccl* Donc. RDn (until 1838), Pontef. RDn (1838—57), Silkst. RDn (1857—1927), Hudd. RDn (1927—68), Kirkburton RDn (1968—*). Addtl eccl bdry alt: 1840 (cr Scissett EP),[394] 1913.[365]

NETHER HOYLAND

EP [W Riding] Chap in Wath upon Dearne AP, sep CP 1866 as 'Hoyland Nether',[2] qv, sep EP 1741.[635] Donc. RDn (1741—57), Rotherh. RDn (1857—71), Wath RDn (1871—1942), Tankersley RDn (1942—*). Bdry: 1916 (cr Nether Hoyland St Andrew EP).[636]

NETHER HOYLAND ST ANDREW

EP [W Riding] Cr 1916 from Nether Hoyland EP.[636] Wath RDn (1916—42), Tankersley RDn (1942—*).

HOYLAND NETHER

[W Riding] Chap in Wath upon Dearne AP, sep CP 1866,[2] sep EP 1741 as 'Nether Hoyland',[635] qv. *LG* Straff. & Tick. Wap, Barnsley PLU, RSD (1875—90), Hoyland Nether USD (1890—94), UD. Bdry: 1938,[28] 1939.[76] Transf 1974 to S Yorks.[5] *Parl* W Riding (1832—67), S'rn Dv of W Riding (1867—85), Hallamshire Dv (1885—1918), Wentw. Dv (1918—48), Penist. CC (1948—*).

HOYLAND SWAINE

[W Riding] Tp in Silkstone AP, sep CP 1866,[2] sep EP 1869 incl pt Cawthorne EP.[109] *LG* Staincr. Wap, Wortley PLU (1838—49), Penist. PLU (1849—1930), Hoyland Swaine USD, UD. Abol civ 1937 ent to Penist. UD & AP.[28] *Parl* W Riding (1832—67), S'rn Dv of W Riding (1867—85), Holmf. Dv (1885—1918), Penist. Dv (1918—48). *Eccl* Silkst. RDn (1869—1927) Barnsley RDn (1927—*). Eccl bdry: 1933.[194]

HUBBERHOLME

EP [W Riding] Cr 1765 from Arncliffe AP.[9] Craven RDn (1765—1857), Craven RDn, N'rn Dv (1857—1921), Skipton RDn (1921—*).

HUBY

[N Riding] Tp in Sutton on the Forest AP, sep CP 1866.[2] *LG* Seq 28. Transf 1974 to N Yorks.[5] *Parl* Seq 16.

HUDDERSFIELD

[W Riding] The following have 'Huddersfield' in their names. Insofar as any existed at a given time: *LG* Agb. Wap, Hudd. PLU, MB (1868—89), CB (1889—1974), USD. *Parl* Hudd. Parl Bor (1832—1948); see Part III of the *Guide* for composition of Hudd. BCs (1948—*) by wards of the CB. *Eccl* Pontef. RDn (until 1857), Hudd. RDn (1857—*).

AP1—HUDDERSFIELD [ST PETER]—Incl chap Golcar (sep CP 1866,[2] sep EP 1836,[9] eccl refounded 1843[37]), chap Lindley cum Quarmby (sep CP 1866,[2] 'Lindley' a sep EP 1831,[9] eccl refounded 1843[37]), chap Longwood (sep CP 1866,[2] sep EP 1749,[9] eccl refounded 1843[37]), pt chap Marsden (the pt in this par sep CP 1866 as 'Marsden in Huddersfield',[2] 'Marsden' a sep EP 1742 [incl pt Almondbury AP],[9] eccl refounded 1868[80]), chap Scammonden (sep CP 1866,[2] sep EP 1718,[9] eccl refounded 1862[136]), chap Slaithwaite (sep CP 1866,[2] sep EP 1718[9]). Addtl civ bdry alt: 1924 (gains the following pars in Hudd. CB: Almondbury AP, Dalton CP, Lindley cum Quarmby CP, Lockwood CP, Longwood CP),[83] 1937,[31] 1938.[28] Transf 1974 to W Yorks.[5] Addtl eccl bdry alt: 1825 (cr EP2,[9] refounded 1845[344]), 1831 (cr Paddock EP,[9] refounded 1865[89]), 1844 (cr EP1),[637] 1852 (cr Bay Hall EP,[9] commonly called later 'Huddersfield St John', refounded 1853[220]), 1859 (cr EP7),[638] 1859 (cr EP5),[284] 1871 (help cr EP3),[21] 1888 (cr EP4),[259] 1926 (gains EP4).[639] Abol eccl 1956 to help cr EP6.[568]

EP1—HUDDERSFIELD CHRIST CHURCH, WOODHOUSE—Cr 1844 from AP1.[637] Bdry: 1895 (help cr Bradley EP).[221]

EP2—HUDDERSFIELD HOLY TRINITY—Cr 1825 from AP1,[9] refounded 1845.[344] Bdry: 1852 (help cr Bay Hall EP,[9] commonly called later 'Huddersfield St John', refounded 1853[220]).

EP3—HUDDERSFIELD ST ANDREW—Cr 1871 from AP1, Bay Hall EP.[21]

—HUDDERSFIELD ST JOHN—Name commonly used for EP cr 1852 as 'Bay Hall', qv for organisation and later refounding.

EP4—HUDDERSFIELD ST MARK—Cr 1888 from AP1.[259] Abol 1926 ent to AP1.[639]

EP5—HUDDERSFIELD ST PAUL—Cr 1859 from AP1.[284] Abol 1956 to help cr EP6.[568]

EP6—HUDDERSFIELD ST PETER AND ST PAUL—Cr 1956 by union AP1, EP5.[568]

EP7—HUDDERSFIELD ST THOMAS—Cr 1859 from AP1.[638]

HUDDLESTON CUM LUMBY
[W Riding] Tp in Sherburn in Elmet AP, sep CP 1866,[2] pt eccl severed 1859 to help cr South Milford EP.[300] LG Bark. Ash Wap, not in a PLU (until 1862), Tadc. PLU (1862—1930), RSD, RD. Bdry: 1883.[52] Abol 1937 pt to help cr Huddleston with Newthorpe CP, pt to South Milford CP, pt to Monk Fryston CP.[31] Parl W Riding (1832—67), N'rn Dv of W Riding (1867—85), Bark. Ash Dv (1885—1918), Don Valley Dv (1918—48).

HUDDLESTON WITH NEWTHORPE
CP [W Riding] Cr 1937 by union Huddleston cum Lumby CP, Newthorpe CP.[31] LG Tadc. RD. Transf 1974 to N Yorks.[5] Parl Bark. Ash CC (1948—*).

HUDSWELL
[N Riding] Chap pt in Catterick AP, pt in Easby CP, sep CP 1866,[2] sep EP 1739.[9] LG Seq 54. Civ bdry: 1883,[16] 1888.[624] Transf 1974 to N Yorks.[5] Parl Seq 14. Eccl Catt. RDn (1737—1857), Catt. East RDn (1857—63), Richm. North RDn (1863—66), Richm. West RDn (1866—*). Eccl bdry: 1939.[395]

HUGGATE
AP [E Riding] LG Seq 12. Transf 1974 to Humb.[5] Parl Seq 7. Eccl Harth. & Hull RDn (until 1857), N Harth. RDn (1857—66), Harth. RDn (1866—1954), Pockl. RDn (1954—*).

HULL
[E Riding] The six pars below were cr with 'Hull' in their names rather than the more common 'Kingston upon Hull'. Although the organisation given for each below is complete, they are listed again under 'Kingston upon Hull' for completeness of reference in one place.

HULL ST ALBAN
EP [E Riding] Cr 1937 from Cottingham AP, Newland St John EP.[246] Kingst. upon Hull RDn.

HULL ST MARK
EP [E Riding] Cr 1844 from Sutton AP (civ, 'Sutton and Stoneferry').[188] Harth. & Hull RDn (1844—57), S Harth. RDn (1857—62), Bev. RDn (1862—69), Kingst. upon Hull RDn (1869—1957). Bdry: 1904 (help cr Wilmington EP).[543] Abol 1957 to help cr Kingston upon Hull St Saviour and St Mark EP.[640]

HULL ST MARK, ANLABY COMMON
EP [E Riding] Cr 1951 from Anlaby EP.[106] Kingst. upon Hull RDn.

HULL ST MARTIN
EP [E Riding] Cr 1938 from Newington The Transfiguration EP, Kingston upon Hull St Nicholas, Anlaby EP.[137] Kingst. upon Hull RDn.

HULL ST STEPHEN
EP [E Riding] Cr 1859 from Kingston upon Hull Holy Trinity EP.[288] S Harth. RDn (1859—62), Bev. RDn (1862—69), Kingst. upon Hull RDn (1869—1957). Bdry: 1868 (help cr Kingston upon Hull St John EP),[290] 1874 (help cr Kingston upon Hull St Jude EP).[148] Abol 1957 to help cr Kingston upon Hull St Jude with St Stephen EP.[641]

NORTH HULL
EP [E Riding] Cr 1950 from Newland St John EP.[642] Kingst. upon Hull RDn.

HUMBERTON
[Tp pt in Kirby on the Moor AP (N Riding, Hallik. Wap), pt in Alborough AP (W Riding, Claro Wap), sep CP 1866 with pt in both Ridings[2]] LG Gt Ouseb. GilbU (until 1854), PLU (1854—95), RSD, Thirsk PLU (1895—1930), pt sep RD in W Riding (1894—95), Thirsk RD (pt 1894—95, ent 1895—1974). Made 1895 ent N Riding.[591] Parl Pt N Riding (1832—85), pt W Riding (1832—67), pt N'rn Dv of W Riding (1867—85), pt Ripon Dv in W Riding (1885—1918), Thirsk & Malton Dv/CC in N Riding (pt 1885—1918, ent 1918—*).

HUMBLETON
AP [E Riding] Incl tps Danthorpe, Elstronwick (sometimes 'Elsternwick'), Fitling, Flinton (each a sep CP 1866,[2] no sep eccl identities hence this par eccl 'Humbleton with Elsternwick', qv). LG Seq 16. Bdry: 1935 (gains Flinton CP).[13] Transf 1974 to Humb.[5] Parl Seq 5.

HUMBLETON WITH ELSTERNWICK
AP [E Riding] Usual eccl spelling; for civ and civ sep tps, see prev entry. Eccl Seq 16.

HUNDERTHWAITE

[N Riding] Tp in Romaldkirk AP, sep CP 1866.[2] *LG* Seq 39. Bdry: 1883,[52] 1884.[176] Transf 1974 to Durham.[5] *Parl* Seq 14.

HUNMANBY

AP [E Riding] Incl chap Argam (eccl, 'Ergham', sep par 1269[120]), chap Burton Fleming (sep par 1269,[379] sometimes called 'North Burton'), chap Carnaby (sep par before 1268[379]), chap Muston (sep par 1269[643]), chap Reighton (sep par 1269[644]), chap Wold Newton (sep par 1269[643]), tp Fordon (sep CP 1866,[2] eccl severed 1858 to help cr Burton Fleming with Fordon EP[381]). *LG* Seq 5. Transf 1974 to N Yorks.[5] *Parl* Seq 2. *Eccl* Seq 4.

HUNSHELF

[W Riding] Tp in Penistone AP, sep CP 1866.[2] *LG* Staincr. Wap, Wortley PLU (1838—49), Penist. PLU (1849—1930), pt Stockbridge USD, pt Penist. RSD, Penist. RD. Transf 1974 to S Yorks.[5] *Parl* Seq 50.

HUNSINGORE

AP [W Riding] Incl tps Cattal, Great Ribston with Walshford (each a sep CP 1866[2]). *LG* Seq 82. Transf 1974 to N Yorks.[5] *Parl* Seq 36. *Eccl* Boroughbr. RDn (until 1925), Wethb. RDn (1925—*).

HUNSLET

[W Riding] The following have 'Hunslet' in their names. Insofar as any existed at a given time: *LG* Skyr. Wap, Leeds Bor/MB/CB, USD, Guardians (for poor, 1844—62), Hunslet Par (for poor, 1862—69), PLU (1869—1925). *Parl* Leeds Parl Bor (1832—85); see Part III of the *Guide* for composition of Leeds Parl Bors (1885—1948) by wards of the MB/CB. *Eccl* Ainsty RDn (cr—1820), Old Ainsty RDn (1820—36), Pontef. RDn (1836—57), Leeds RDn (1857—1971), Armley RDn (1971—*).

CP1/EP1—HUNSLET [ST CUTHBERT] —Chap in Leeds AP, sep CP 1866,[2] sep EP 1719,[9] eccl refounded 1885 from EP4, Beeston Hill EP, Holbeck EP, Brewery Field EP.[229] Civ bdry: 1883,[52] 1896,[645] 1920 (gains Middleton CP).[646] Abol civ 1925 ent to Leeds AP.[129] Eccl bdry: 1851 (cr Brewery Field EP, cr Pottery Field EP [the latter sometimes later called 'Hunslet St Jude']).[344] Abol 1955 to help cr EP5.[647]

—HUNSLET ST JUDE—Name sometimes used for EP cr 1851 as 'Pottery Field', qv.

EP2—HUNSLET ST MARY—Cr 1847 from Leeds AP.[70] Bdry: 1868 (cr EP4),[474] 1870 (cr EP3),[284] 1872 (help cr Beeston Hill EP),[90] 1901 (help cr Stourton EP),[366] 1951 (gains EP3, Pottery Field EP [the latter sometimes called 'Hunslet St Jude']),[141] 1967,[127] 1971 (gains Leeds Christ Church with Holbeck St John and St Barnabas EP),[648] 1973 (gains Stourton EP).[354]

EP3—HUNSLET ST SILAS—Cr 1870 from EP2.[284] Abol 1951 ent to EP2.[141]

EP4—HUNSLET MOOR—Cr 1868 from EP2.[474] Bdry: 1885 (help refound EP1),[229] 1905 (help cr Beeston Hill The Holy Spirit EP).[149] Abol 1955 to help cr EP5.[647]

EP5—HUNSLET MOOR ST PETER WITH ST CUTHBERT—Cr 1955 by union EP4, EP1.[647] Bdry: 1967.[127]

HUNSWORTH

[W Riding] Tp in Birstall AP, sep CP 1866.[2] *LG* Morley Wap, Bradf PLU (1837—48), N Bierley PLU (1848—1930), Hunsworth USD, UD. Abol 1937 ent to Spenb. UD and to Cleckheaton CP.[31] *Parl* W Riding (1832—67) E'rn Dv of W Riding (1867—85), Pudsey Dv (1885—1918), Spen Valley Dv (1918—48).

HUNTINGTON

AP [N Riding] Incl tp Earswick, pt tp Towthorpe (each a sep CP 1866[2]). *LG* Seq 32. Addtl civ bdry alt: 1934 (incl loses pt to York CB [not assoc with a Riding] & CP and loses pt to cr New Earswick CP),[3] 1968 (loses pt to York CB [not assoc with a Riding] & CP).[418] Transf 1974 to N Yorks.[5] *Parl* Seq 16. *Eccl* Bulmer RDn (until 1862), Eas. RDn (1862—1928), City of York RDn (1928—*). Addtl eccl bdry alt: 1937,[246] 1961,[521] 1967.[127]

HUNTON

[N Riding] Tp pt in Hornby AP (E Hang Wap), pt in Patrick Brompton AP (W Hang Wap), sep CP 1866,[2] sep EP 1794.[9] *LG* Leyb. PLU, RSD, RD. Transf 1974 to N Yorks.[5] *Parl* Seq 14. *Eccl* Catt. RDn (1794—1857), Catt. East RDn (1857—1930). Abol eccl 1930 to help cr Patrick Brompton with Hunton EP.[137]

HUNTWICK WITH FOULBY AND NOSTELL

[W Riding] Tp in Wragby AP sep CP 1866.[2] *LG* Osg. Wap, Hemsw. PLU (soon after 1850[112]—1930), RSD, RD. Bdry: 1888,[348] 1888,[649] 1938.[28] Transf 1974 to W Yorks.[5] *Parl* Seq 28.

HURST GREEN

EP [W Riding, Lancs] Cr 1839 from Mitton AP (incl the area in Lancs [Blackburn Hd] of Bailey in tp Aighton, Bailey and Chaigley [the only pt of Mitton in Lancs]),[9] refounded 1870.[180] Craven RDn (1839—57), Craven RDn, W'rn Dv (1857—1921), Bolland RDn (1921—*).

HUSTHWAITE

AP [N Riding] Perhaps orig AP, perhaps orig chap in Coxwold AP, appropriated to Newburgh Priory, sep early.[447] Incl chap Carlton Husthwaite (sep CP 1866,[2] not sep eccl hence this par eccl 'Husthwaite with Carlton', qv). *LG* Seq 24. Addtl civ bdry alt: 1883,[16] 1887.[547] Transf 1974 to N Yorks.[5] *Parl* Seq 16.

HUSTHWAITE WITH CARLTON

AP [N Riding] Usual eccl spelling; for civ and civ sep chap Carlton Husthwaite, see prev entry. *Eccl* Pec jurisd Husthwaite prebend (until 1836), Bulmer RDn (1836—62), Eas. RDn (1862—*).

HUTTON BONVILLE

[N Riding] Chap in Birkby AP, sep CP 1866,[2] sep EP 1740.[9] *LG* Seq 22. Transf 1974 to N Yorks.[5] *Parl* Seq 14.

HUTTON BUSCEL

AP [N Riding] Incl tp West Ayton (sep CP 1866[2]). *LG* Seq 62. Addtl civ bdry alt: 1883,[16] 1887.[162] Transf 1974 to N Yorks.[5] *Parl* Seq 20. *Eccl* Seq 28.

HUTTON CONYERS

[N Riding] Ex-par place, sep CP 1858.[393] *LG*

Allert. Wap, Gt Ouseb. GilbU (until 1854), Ripon PLU (1854—1930), RSD, Wath RD. Transf 1974 to N Yorks.[5] *Parl* Seq 16.

HUTTON CRANSWICK

AP [E Riding] Incl tps Rotsea, Sunderlandwick (each a sep CP 1866[2]). *LG* Seq 10. Addtl civ bdry alt: 1884,[350] 1935 (gains Rotsea CP, Sunderlandwick CP).[13] Transf 1974 to Humb.[5] *Parl* Seq 3. *Eccl* Seq 10.

HUTTON HANG

[N Riding] Tp in Finghall AP, sep CP 1866.[2] *LG* Seq 53. Transf 1974 to N Yorks.[5] *Parl* Seq 14.

HUTTON LE HOLE

[N Riding] Tp in Lastingham AP, sep CP 1866.[2] Incl undivided pt Spaunton Moor (qv for pars to which common, abol 1934 incl pt to this par [same order with addtl bdry alt for this par][3]). *LG* Seq 64. Transf 1974 to N Yorks.[5] *Parl* Seq 21.

HUTTON LOWCROSS

[N Riding] Tp in Guisborough AP, sep CP 1866.[2] *LG* Langb. Lbty, Guisb. PLU, RSD, RD (1894—1932), UD (1932—74). Transf 1974 to Clev.[5] *Parl* Seq 9.

HUTTON MAGNA

[N Riding] Tp in Gilling AP, sep CP 1866,[2] sep EP 1783.[9] *LG* Seq 39. Transf 1974 to Durham.[5] *Parl* Seq 13. *Eccl* Richm. RDn (1783—1857), Richm. West RDn (1857—94), Richm. North RDn (1894—*).

HUTTON MULGRAVE

[N Riding] Tp in Lythe AP, sep CP 1866,[2] eccl severed 1868 to help cr Ugthorpe EP.[188] *LG* Seq 59. Bdry: 1884.[189] Transf 1974 to N Yorks.[5] *Parl* Seq 19.

HUTTON RUDBY

[N Riding] Tp in Rudby in Cleveland AP, sep CP 1866.[2] *LG* Seq 58. Bdry: 1883.[16] Transf 1974 to N Yorks.[5] *Parl* Seq 11.

HUTTON SESSAY

[N Riding] Tp in Sessay AP, sep CP 1866.[2] *LG* Seq 23. Transf 1974 to N Yorks.[5] *Parl* Seq 16.

HUTTON WANDESLEY

[W Riding] Tp in Long Marston AP, sep CP 1866.[2] *LG* Seq 71. Transf 1974 to N Yorks.[5] *Parl* Seq 23.

HUTTONS AMBO

AP [N Riding] *LG* Seq 29. Transf 1974 to N Yorks.[5] *Parl* Seq 16. *Eccl* Pec jurisd Dean & Chapter of York (until 1836), Bulmer RDn (1836—1928), Malton RDn (1928—*).

IDLE

[W Riding] Chap in Calverley AP, sep CP 1866,[2] sep EP 1717,[9] eccl refounded 1878.[337] *LG* Morley Wap, Bradf PLU (1837—48), N Bierley PLU (1848—1930), pt Idle USD, pt Windhill USD (1875—91), pt Shipley USD (1891—94), Idle UD (1894—99), Bradf CB (1899—1974). Civ bdry: 1894 (loses the pt in Shipley UD to Shipley CP),[557] 1937,[31] 1955 (loses pt to Shipley UD & CP).[650] Transf 1974 to W Yorks.[5] *Parl* W Riding (1832—67), N'rn Dv of W Riding (1867—85), Shipley Dv (1885—1918); see Part III of the *Guide* for composition of Bradf Parl Bors/BCs (1918—*) by wards of the CB. *Eccl* Pontef. RDn (1717—1857),

Bradf RDn (1857—1921), Calverley RDn (1921—*). Eccl bdry: 1870 (cr Windhill EP),[284] 1923 (cr Idle St John EP),[113] 1934 (help cr Wrose EP).[46]

IDLE ST JOHN

EP [W Riding] Cr 1923 from Idle EP.[113] Calverley RDn. Bdry: 1956.[516] Renamed 1963 'Thorpe Edge'.[288]

ILKLEY

AP [W Riding] Tp 'Ilkley' in Skyr. Wap; incl in Claro Wap tps Middleton, Nesfield with Langbar (each a sep CP 1866[2]). *LG* Carlton GilbU (until 1869), Wharfed. PLU (1869—1930), Ilkley USD, UD. Addtl civ bdry alt: 1937.[31] Transf 1974 to W Yorks.[5] *Parl* Seq 30. *Eccl* Craven RDn (until 1857), Craven RDn, S'rn Dv (1857—94), Otley RDn (1894—*). Eccl bdry: 1879 (cr Ilkley St Margaret EP),[651] 1912 (help cr Ben Rhydding EP).[234]

ILKLEY ST MARGARET

EP [W Riding] Cr 1879 from Ilkley AP.[651] Craven RDn, S'rn Dv (1879—94), Otley RDn (1894—*).

ILLINGWORTH

EP [W Riding] Cr 1718 from Halifax AP (pt tp Ovenden).[9] Pontef. RDn (1718—1857), Halifax RDn (1857—*). Bdry: 1878 (help cr Ovenden St George EP).[587]

ILTON CUM POTT

[N Riding] Tp in Masham AP, sep CP 1866.[2] *LG* E Hang Wap, Leyb. PLU (soon after 1837[112]—1930), Masham USD, UD (1894—1934), RD (1934—74). Bdry: 1883,[16] 1886,[201] 1886,[525] 1934.[3] Transf 1974 to N Yorks.[5] *Parl* Seq 14.

INGBIRCHWORTH

[W Riding] Tp in Penistone AP, sep CP 1866.[2] *LG* Staincr. Wap, Wortley PLU (1838—49), Penist. PLU (1849—1930), Gunthwaite and Ingbirchworth USD, UD. Abol 1938 to help cr Gunthwaite and Ingbirchworth CP.[28] *Parl* W Riding (1832—67), S'rn Dv of W Riding (1867—85), Holmf. Dv (1885—1918), Penist. Dv (1918—48).

INGERTHORPE

[W Riding] Tp in Ripon AP, sep CP 1866.[2] *LG* Ripton Lbty, not in a PLU (until 1852), Ripon PLU (1852—1930), RSD, RD. Abol 1937 ent to Markington with Wallerthwaite CP.[31] *Parl* W Riding (1832—67), E'rn Dv of W Riding (1867—85), Ripon Dv (1885—1948).

INGLEBY ARNCLIFFE

AP [N Riding] Disputed whether East Harsley AP a chap in this par,[601] but its sep status sustained. *LG* Seq 58. Transf 1974 to N Yorks.[5] *Parl* Seq 11. *Eccl* Seq 23.

INGLEBY BARWICK

[N Riding] Tp in Stainton AP, sep CP 1866.[2] *LG* Seq 56. Transf 1974 to Clev.[5] *Parl* Seq 10.

INGLEBY GREENHOW

AP [N Riding] *LG* Seq 58. Transf 1974 to N Yorks.[5] *Parl* Seq 11. *Eccl* Seq 24.

INGLETON

[W Riding] Chap in Bentham AP, sep CP 1866,[2] sep EP 1757.[9] *LG* Seq 111. Transf 1974 to N Yorks.[5] *Parl* Seq 41. *Eccl* Kirkby Lonsd. RDn (1757—1849), Clapham RDn (1849—1921),

Ewecr. RDn (1921—*).

INGLETON FELL

EP [W Riding] Cr 1737 from Bentham AP.[9] Kirbky Lonsd. RDn (1737—1849), Clapham RDn (1849—64). Refounded 1864 as 'Chapel le Dale' EP, qv, when gains pt Ingleton EP.[405]

INGROW WITH HAINWORTH

EP [W Riding] Cr 1844 from Keighley AP, Bingley AP.[267] Craven RDn (1844—57), Craven RDn, S'rn Dv (1857—1921), S Craven RDn (1921—*). Bdry: 1882 (help cr Keighley St Peter EP),[421] 1885,[652] 1911 (help cr Cross Roads cum Lees EP),[269] 1954.[489]

IRTON

[N Riding] Tp in Seamer AP, sep CP 1866.[2] *LG* Seq 62. Bdry: 1934.[3] Transf 1974 to N Yorks. *Parl* Seq 20.

KEARBY WITH NETHERBY

[W Riding] Tp in Kirkby Overblow AP, sep CP 1866.[2] *LG* Seq 91. Transf 1974 to N Yorks.[5] *Parl* Seq 24.

KEIGHLEY

AP [W Riding] *LG* Staincl. & Ewc. Wap, Keigh. PLU, pt Keigh. USD, pt Oakworth USD, Keigh. MB (pt 1882—94, ent 1894—1974). Civ bdry: 1894 (gains the pt of Bingley AP in Keigh. MB,[229] and loses the pt in Oakworth UD to cr Oakworth CP[257]), 1895,[271] 1938.[28] Transf 1974 to W Yorks.[5] *Parl* W Riding (1832—67), N'rn Dv of Riding (1867—85), Keigh. Dv (1885—1948), Keigh. BC (1948—*). *Eccl* Craven RDn (until 1857), Craven RDn, S'rn Dv (1857—1921), S Craven RDn (1921—*). Eccl bdry: 1844 (help cr Ingrow with Hainworth EP),[267] 1844 (cr Eastwood EP, cr Oakworth EP),[197] 1882 (help cr Keighley St Peter EP),[421] 1883 (cr Lawkholme EP),[486] 1885,[652] 1954,[489] 1973 (gains Lawkholme EP).[653]

KEIGHLEY ST PETER

EP [W Riding] Cr 1882 from Keighley AP, Ingrow with Hainworth AP.[421] Craven RDn, S'rn Dv (1882—1921), S Craven RDn (1921—54). Abol 1954 pt to Keighley AP, pt to Ingrow with Hainworth EP.[489]

KELBROOK

EP [W Riding] Cr 1842 from Thornton in Craven AP.[9] Craven RDn (1842—57), Craven RDn, W'rn Dv (1857—1905), Craven RDn, E'rn Dv (1905—21), Skipton RDn (1921—*). Bdry: 1923 (help cr Earby EP),[497] 1924.[27] Sometimes 'Kelbrooke'.

KELFIELD

[E Riding] Tp in Stillingfleet AP, sep CP 1866.[2] *LG* Seq 19. Transf 1974 to N Yorks.[5] *Parl* Seq 7.

KELK

CP [E Riding] Cr 1935 by union Great Kelk CP, Little Kelk CP.[13] *LG* Driff. RD. Transf 1974 to Humb.[5] *Parl* Bridl. CC (1948—55), Howden CC (1955—*).

GREAT KELK

[E Riding] Tp in Foston on the Wolds AP, sep CP 1866.[2] *LG* Dick. Wap, Driff. PLU, RSD, RD. Abol 1935 to help cr Kelk CP.[13] *Parl* E Riding (1832—85), Buckr. Dv (1885—1948).

LITTLE KELK

[E Riding] Orig chap in Foston on the Wolds AP,

long considered ex-par, sep CP 1858,[393] eccl united 1729 to Lowthorpe AP.[567] *LG, Parl* organisation as for Great Kelk.

KELLINGTON

AP [W Riding] Incl tps Beal or Beaghall, Eggborough, Whitley (each a sep CP 1866[2]). *LG* Seq 97. Transf 1974 to N Yorks.[5] *Parl* Seq 29. *Eccl* Sometimes as 'Kellngton with Whitley', Pontef. RDn (until 1820), New Ainsty RDn (1820—57), Pontef. RDn (1857—*). Eccl bdry: 1855 (help cr Hensall EP).[173]

KENNYTHORPE

[E Riding] Tp in Langton AP, sep CP 1866.[2] *LG* Buckr. Wap, Malton PLU, RSD, Norton RD. Abol 1935 ent to Burythorpe AP.[13] *Parl* E Riding (1832—85), Buckr. Dv (1885—1948).

KEPWICK

[N Riding] Tp pt in Leake AP, pt in Cowsby AP, pt in Over Silton (chap in chap Kilburn, the latter sep civ identity early from Coxwold AP, sep EP 1732[9]), sep CP 1866.[2] *LG* Seq 27. Transf 1974 to N Yorks.[5] *Parl* Seq 16.

EAST KESWICK

[W Riding] Tp in Harewood AP, sep CP 1866.[2] *LG* Skyr. Wap, Barwick GilbU (until 1861), Wethb. PLU (1861—1930), RSD, RD. Transf 1974 to W Yorks.[5] *Parl* Seq 24.

KETTLEWELL

AP [W Riding] Usual eccl spelling; for civ see following entry. *Eccl* Seq 36.

KETTLEWELL WITH STARBOTTON

AP [W Riding] Usual civ spelling; for eccl see prev entry. *LG* Seq 112. Transf 1974 to N Yorks.[5] *Parl* Seq 41.

KEXBOROUGH

[W Riding] Tp in Darton AP, sep CP 1866.[2] *LG* Staincr. Wap, not in a PLU (until 1849), Penist. PLU (1849—1930), Darton USD, UD. Abol 1938 ent to Darton AP.[28] *Parl* W Riding (1832—67), S'rn Dv of W Riding (1867—85), Barnsley Dv (1885—1918), Barnsley Parl Bor (1918—48).

KEXBY

[E Riding] Tp in Catton AP, sep CP 1866,[2] sep EP 1853.[64] *LG* Seq 20. Bdry: 1935.[13] Transf 1974 to N Yorks.[5] *Parl* Seq 7. *Eccl* Harth. & Hull RDn (1853—57), W Buckr. RDn (1857—66), Pockl. RDn (1866—*).

KEYINGHAM

AP [E Riding] *LG* Seq 15. Transf 1974 to Humb.[5] *Parl* Seq 5. *Eccl* Seq 16.

KILBURN

[N Riding] Chap in Coxwold AP, sep civ identity early, sep EP 1732.[9] Incl chap Over Silton (sep civ identity early, sep EP 1757[9]; this chap incl pt tp Kepwick [sep CP 1866[2]]), hmlt Hood Grange, tps Olstead, Thorpe le Willows, Wass (each of the last 4 a sep CP 1866[2]). *LG* Seq 27. Transf 1974 to N Yorks.[5] *Parl* Seq 16. *Eccl* Bulmer RDn (1732—1862), Thirsk RDn (1862—*).

KILDALE

AP [N Riding] *LG* Seq 58. Transf 1974 to N Yorks.[5] *Parl* Seq 11. *Eccl* Seq 24.

KILDWICK

AP [W Riding] Incl chap Silsden (sep CP 1866,[2] sep EP

1720,[9] eccl refounded 1898[121]), tps Bradleys Both, Cononley (each a sep CP 1866,[2] sep EP 1871 as 'Cononley with Bradley'[28]), tp Cowling (sep CP 1866,[2] sep EP 1844[117]), tps Farnhill, Glusburn (each a sep CP 1866[2]), tp Steeton with Eastburn (sep CP 1866,[2] sep EP 1881 [incl detached pt tp Sutton] as 'Steeton'[218]), tp Stirton with Thorlby (sep CP 1866[2]), tp Sutton (sep CP 1866,[2] the main pt sep EP 1870 as 'Sutton',[180] the detached pt eccl severed 1881 to help cr Steeton EP[218]). *LG* Seq 112. Transf 1974 to W Yorks.[5] *Parl* Seq 41. *Eccl* Craven RDn (until 1857), Craven RDn, S'rn Dv (1857—1921), S Craven RDn (1921—*). Addtl eccl bdry alt: 1844 (help cr Lothersdale EP).[247]

KILHAM
AP [E Riding] *LG* Seq 6. Transf 1974 to Humb.[5] *Parl* Seq 3. *Eccl* Pec jurisd Dean of York (until 1836), Dick. RDn (1836—57), N Harth. RDn (1857—62), Bridl. RDn (1862—87), Buckr. RDn (1887—1922), Harth. RDn (1922—*).

KILLERBY
[N Riding] Tp in Catterick AP, sep CP 1866.[2] *LG* Seq 49. Transf 1974 to N Yorks.[5] *Parl* Seq 15.

KILLINGHALL
[W Riding] Tp in Ripley AP, sep CP 1866,[2] sep EP 1879 from Ripley AP, Knaresborough AP.[228] *LG* Seq 84. Civ bdry: 1883,[52] 1938.[28] Transf 1974 to N Yorks.[5] *Parl* Seq 36. *Eccl* Knar. RDn (1879—1971), Harrog. RDn (1971—*).

KILNHURST
EP [W Riding Cr 1869 from Swinton EP, Rawmarsh AP.[301] Rotherh. RDn (1869—71), Wath RDn (1871—*). Bdry: 1958.[654]

KILNSEA
AP [E Riding] *LG* Hold. Wap, Patr. PLU, RSD, RD. Abol civ 1935 ent to Easington AP.[13] *Parl* E Riding Dv (1885—1948). *Eccl* Seq 16.

KILNWICK
AP [E Riding] Incl chap Beswick (sep CP 1866,[2] sep EP 1834[9]), tps Bracken, Lockington in Kilnwick (each a sep CP 1866[2]). *LG* Harth. Wap, Bev. PLU, RSD, RD. Abol civ 1935 ent to Beswick CP.[13] *Parl* E Riding (1832—85), Buckr. Dv (1885—1918), Hold. Dv (1918—48). *Eccl* Seq 10.

KILNWICK PERCY
AP [E Riding] *LG* Harth. Wap, Pockl. PLU, RSD, RD. Abol civ 1935 ent to Nunburnholme AP.[13] *Parl* E Riding (1832—85), Howdensh. Dv (1885—1948). *Eccl* Pec jurisd Dean of York (until 1836), Harth. & Hull RDn (1836—57), W Buckr. RDn (1857—66), Pockl. RDn (1866—1948). Abol eccl 1948 to help cr Pocklington with Yapham cum Meltonby and Owsthorpe and Kilnwick Percy EP.[655]

KILPIN
[E Riding] Tp in Howden AP, sep CP 1866.[2] *LG* Seq 17. Bdry: 1880,[172] 1880,[171] 1935 (incl gains Belby CP).[13] Transf 1974 to Humb.[5] *Parl* Seq 7.

KILTON
[N Riding] Tp in Skelton AP, sep CP 1866,[2] pt eccl severed 1868 to help cr Brotton EP.[188] *LG* Langb. Lbty, Guisb. PLU, Brotton USD (1875—84), Skelton & Brotton USD (1884—94), UD. Bdry: 1883,[16] 1886.[656] Transf 1974 to Clev.[5] *Parl* Seq 9.

NORTH KILVINGTON
[N Riding] Tp in Thornton le Street AP, sep CP 1866.[2] *LG* Seq 23. Transf 1974 to N Yorks.[5] *Parl* Seq 16.

SOUTH KILVINGTON
AP [N Riding] Incl tps Thornborough, Upsail (each a sep CP 1866[2]). *LG* Seq 27. Transf 1974 to N Yorks.[5] *Parl* Seq 16. *Eccl* Seq 20.

KIMBERWORTH
[W Riding] Tp in Rotherham AP, sep CP 1866,[2] sep EP 1844.[596] *LG* Straff. & Tick. Wap, Rotherh. PLU, MB (ent 1871—83, pt 1883—89), pt Rotherh. CB (1889—94), Rotherh. USD (ent 1875—83, pt 1883—94), pt Rotherh. RSD (1883—94). Civ bdry: 1883.[52] Abol civ 1894 the pt in the CB transf to Rotherham AP, the remainder transf to Wentworth CP.[359] *Parl* W Riding (1832—85), S'rn Dv of W Riding (1867—85), Rotherh. Dv (1885—1918). *Eccl* Donc. RDn (1844—57), Rotherh. RDn (1857—*). Eccl bdry: 1877 (help cr Wincobank EP),[301] 1916 (cr Masborough St Paul EP),[413] 1969 (help cr Kimberworth Park EP).[579]

KIMBERWORTH PARK
EP [W Riding] Cr 1969 from Kimberworth EP, Greasbrough EP, Rotherham AP, Thorpe Hesley EP.[579] Rotherh. RDn.

KING CROSS
EP [W Riding] Cr 1845 from Halifax AP (pt tp Skircoat, pt main tp Halifax).[657] Pontef. RDn (1845—57), Halifax RDn (1857—*). Bdry: 1912 (help cr Halifax St Hilda EP),[596] 1912.[594]

KINGSTON UPON HULL
[E Riding] The following have 'Kingston upon Hull' in their names. Incl in the list are six pars cr with the less common place name 'Hull'; although they were presented above under 'Hull' they are repeated here, in alphabetical order by dedication, for completeness of reference. Insofar as any par existed at a given time: *LG* Hull PLU; Bor/MB/CB, USD sep noted. *Parl* Kingst. upon Hull Parl Bor (1832—85); see Part III of the *Guide* for composition of Kingst. upon Hull Parl Bors/BCs (1885—*) by wards of the MB/CB. *Eccl* Harth. & Hull RDn (until 1857), S Harth. RDn (1857—62), Bev. RDn (1862—69), Kingst. upon Hull RDn (1869—*).

—KINGSTON UPON HULL THE ASCENSION—
Name used now for EP cr 1935 as 'Derringham Bank', qv.

—KINGSTON UPON HULL CHARTER HOUSE—
Ex-par place, abol eccl 1885 to help cr EP21.[598]

EP1—KINGSTON UPON HULL CHRIST CHURCH—Cr 1950 by union Sculcoates Christ Church EP, EP21.[658] Abol 1962 to help cr EP19.[46]

AP1—KINGSTON UPON HULL HOLY TRINITY—Chap in Hessle AP, some parochial rights by 14th cent, being used parochially by 1548, ent independent by 1661.[618] *LG* Kingst. upon Hull Bor. Jointly rated with CP2 for poor as CP1, qv for later civ organisation. Eccl bdry: 1792 (refound EP15),[9] 1859 (cr EP23),[288] 1862 (cr EP11,[9] refounded 1864[405]), 1868 (help cr EP17),[290] 1872 (cr EP16),[211] 1874 (cr EP5),[605] 1874 (cr EP6),[36]

1874 (help cr EP9),[148] 1882 (cr EP25),[659] 1885 (help cr EP21),[598] 1957 (gains EP6, EP11, EP25).[660]

CP1—KINGSTON UPON HULL HOLY TRINITY AND ST MARY—Joint rating for poor law of AP1, CP2. *LG* Kingst. upon Hull MB/CB, USD. Transf 1974 to Humb.[5]

EP2—KINGSTON UPON HULL ST AIDAN SOUTHCOATES—Cr 1954 from Drypool St Andrew and St Peter EP, Sutton in Holderness EP, Marfleet AP.[489]

EP3—HULL ST ALBAN—Cr 1937 from Cottingham AP, Newland St John EP.[246]

EP4—KINGSTON UPON HULL ST AUGUSTINE—Cr 1897 from Newland St John EP as 'Newland St Augustine',[661] soon after called as EP4. Bdry: 1969.[576]

EP5—KINGSTON UPON HULL ST BARNABAS—Cr 1874 from AP1.[605] Abol 1971 to help cr EP17.[236]

EP6—KINGSTON UPON HULL ST JAMES—Cr 1874 from AP1.[36] Abol 1957 ent to AP1.[660]

EP7—KINGSTON UPON HULL ST JOHN—Cr 1868 from AP1, Sculcoates AP, EP23.[290]

EP8—KINGSTON UPON HULL ST JOHN THE BAPTIST, NEWINGTON—Cr 1879 from Kirk Ella AP, North Ferriby AP.[630] Bdry: 1906 (cr Newington The Transfiguration EP, soon after called as EP26, cr Dairycoates EP).[462] Howden RDn (1879—1887), Kingst. upon Hull RDn (1887—*). Abol 1969 to help cr Newington with Dairycoates EP.[228]

EP9—KINGSTON UPON HULL ST JUDE—Cr 1874 from AP1, EP23.[148] Abol 1957 to help cr EP10.[662]

EP10—KINGSTON UPON HULL ST JUDE WITH ST STEPHEN—Cr 1957 by union EP9, EP23.[641] Abol 1973 to help cr EP24.[662]

EP11—KINGSTON UPON HULL ST LUKE—Cr 1862 from AP1,[9] refounded 1864.[405] Abol 1957 ent to AP1.[660]

EP12—HULL ST MARK—Cr 1844 from Sutton AP (civ, 'Sutton and Stoneferry').[188] Bdry: 1904 (help cr Wilmington EP).[543] Abol 1957 to help cr EP22.[640]

EP13—HULL ST MARK, ANLABY COMMON—Cr 1951 from Anlaby EP.[106]

EP14—HULL ST MARTIN—Cr 1938 from Newington The Transfiguration EP, EP18.[137]

CP2/EP15—KINGSTON UPON HULL ST MARY—Chap in North Ferriby AP, most parochial rights 1333, sep civ identity early, final eccl independence 1868.[554] *LG* Kingst. upon Hull Bor. Jointly rated with AP1 for poor as CP1, qv for later civ organisation.

EP16—KINGSTON UPON HULL ST MATTHEW—Cr 1872 from AP1.[211] Abol 1971 to help cr EP17.[236]

EP17—KINGSTON UPON HULL ST MATTHEW WITH ST BARNABAS—Cr 1971 by union EP16, EP5.[236]

EP18—KINGSTON UPON HULL ST NICHOLAS, ANLABY—Cr 1916 from Hessle AP.[619] Bdry:

1938 (help cr EP14),[137] 1961,[44] 1934.[420]

EP19—KINGSTON UPON HULL ST PAUL WITH CHRIST CHURCH SCULCOATES—Cr 1962 by union Sculcoates St Paul EP, EP1.[46] Abol 1969 to help cr EP2.[14]

EP20—KINGSTON UPON HULL ST PAUL SCULCOATES WITH CHRIST CHURCH AND ST SILAS—Cr 1969 by union EP19, Sculcoates St Silas EP.[14]

EP21—KINGSTON UPON HULL ST PHILIP—Cr 1885 from Sculcoates AP, AP1, ex-par place Kingston upon Hull Charter House.[598] Abol 1950 to help cr EP1.[46]

EP22—KINGSTON UPON HULL ST SAVIOUR AND ST MARK—Cr 1957 by union Wilmington EP, EP12.[640]

EP23—HULL ST STEPHEN—Cr 1859 from AP1.[288] Bdry: 1868 (help cr EP7),[290] 1874 (help cr EP9).[148] Abol 1957 to help cr EP10.[641]

EP24—KINGSTON UPON HULL ST STEPHEN SCULCOATES—Cr 1973 by union EP10, Sculcoates AP.[662]

EP25—KINGSTON UPON HULL ST THOMAS—Cr 1882 from AP1.[659] Abol 1957 ent to AP1.[660]

EP26—KINGSTON UPON HULL THE TRANSFIGURATION—Cr 1906 from EP8, as 'Newington The Transfiguration',[462] soon after called as EP26. Bdry: 1934,[420] 1935 (cr Derringham Bank EP, later call 'Kingston upon Hull The Ascension'),[476] 1938 (help cr EP14).[137]

EP27—NORTH HULL—Cr 1950 from Newland St John EP.[631]

KINGTHORPE

[N Riding] Tp in Pickering AP, sep CP 1866.[2] *LG* Seq 61. Transf 1974 to N Yorks.[5] *Parl* Seq 20.

KINSLEY

EP [W Riding] Cr 1921 from Hemsworth AP.[522] Hemsw. RDn (1921—27), Pontef. RDn (1927—*).

KIPLIN

[N Riding] Tp in Catterick AP, sep CP 1866[2]; eccl in chap Bolton upon Swale in Catterick AP (sep EP 1781,[9] eccl refounded 1881[347]). *LG* Seq 34. Transf 1974 to N Yorks.[5] *Parl* Seq 14.

KIPPAX

AP [W Riding] Incl tp Allerton Bywater (sep CP 1866,[2] sep EP 1867[74]), tp Great and Little Preston, pt tp Ledstone (each a sep CP 1866[2]). *LG* Skyr. Wap, Gt Preston GilbU (until 1869), Tadc. PLU (1869—1930), RSD, RD. Addtl civ bdry alt: 1884.[75] Abol civ 1939 ent to Garforth UD & AP.[76] *Parl* W Riding (1832—67), N'rn Dv of W Riding (1867—85), Osg. Dv (1885—1918), Bark. Ash Dv (1918—48). *Eccl* Ainsty RDn (until 1820), New Ainsty RDn (1820—38), Pontef. RDn (1838—57), Wakef. RDn (1857—94), Whitkirk RDn (1894—*).

KIRBY GRINDALYTHE

AP [E Riding] Incl tps Duggleby, Thirkleby (each a sep CP 1866[2]). *LG* Seq 2. Addtl civ bdry alt: 1935 (gains Duggleby CP, Thirkleby CP).[13] Transf 1974 to N Yorks.[5] *Parl* Seq 1. *Eccl* Buckr. RDn (until 1857), E Buckr. RDn (1857—66), Buckr. RDn (1866—*).

KIRBY HALL

[W Riding] Tp in Little Ouseburn AP, sep CP 1866.[2] *LG* Seq 85. Transf 1974 to N Yorks.[5] *Parl* Seq 36.

KIRBY HILL

[N Riding] Tp in Kirby on the Moor AP, sep CP 1866.[2] *LG* Seq 41. Transf 1974 to N Yorks.[5] *Parl* Seq 16.

KIRBY HILL

[N Riding] Tp in Kirkby Ravensworth AP, sep CP 1866.[2] *LG* Seq 38. Bdry: 1883.[16] 1888.[624] Transf 1974 to N Yorks.[5] *Parl* Seq 13.

KIRBY IN CLEVELAND

AP [N Riding] Incl tp Broughton (sep CP 1866[2]). *LG* Seq 58. Transf 1974 to N Yorks.[5] *Parl* Seq 11. *Eccl* Seq 24.

KIRBY KNOWLE

AP [N Riding] Incl chap Bagby with Islebeck (sep CP 1866[2]), pt chap Carlton Miniott (sep CP 1866,[2] sep EP 1747[9]), tp Balk (sep CP 1866[2]). *LG* Seq 27. Transf 1974 to N Yorks.[5] *Parl* Seq 16. *Eccl* Seq 20.

KIRBY MISPERTON

AP [N Riding] Incl tps Barughs Ambo, Great Habton, Little Habton, Ryton (each a sep CP 1866[2]). *LG* Seq 61. Transf 1974 to N Yorks.[5] *Parl* Seq 22. *Eccl* Seq 28.

KIRBY ON THE MOOR

AP [N Riding] Incl pt chap Marton le Moor (sep CP 1866,[2] sep EP 1731[9]), tps Kirby Hill, Langthorpe (each a sep CP 1866[2]), pt tps Humberton, Milby (each a sep CP 1866[2]) so that 'Kirby on the Moor' has no sep civ identity after 1866. *LG* Hallik. Wap. *Parl* N Riding (1832—67). *Eccl* Seq 52.

KIRBY SIGSTON

AP [N Riding] Sometimes early 'Sigston'. Incl tps Sowerby under Cotcliffe, Winton, pt tp Thimbleby (each of the 3 a sep CP 1866[2]). *LG* Seq 22. Transf 1974 to N Yorks.[5] *Parl* Seq 14. *Eccl* Pec jurisd Dean and Chapter of Durham (until 1836), Seq 23 thereafter.

KIRBY UNDERDALE

AP [E Riding] *LG* Seq 3. Bdry: 1935.[13] Transf 1974 to Humb.[5] *Parl* Seq 7. *Eccl* Seq 9.

KIRBY WISKE

AP [N Riding] Usual civ spelling; for eccl see 'Kirkby Wiske'. *LG* Tp 'Kirby Wiske' in E Gill. Wap as were tps Maunby, Newby Wiske (the last 2 each a sep CP 1866[2]); incl in Birdf. Wap tp Newsham with Breckenbrough (sep CP 1866[2]). *LG* Thirsk PLU, RSD, RD. Transf 1974 to N Yorks.[5] *Parl* Seq 16.

KIRK BRAMWITH

AP [W Riding] Incl pt tp Moss (sep CP 1866,[2] sep EP 1875 from this and 4 other pars, qv[11]). *LG* Seq 94. Addtl civ bdry alt: 1883.[387] Transf 1974 to S Yorks.[5] *Parl* Seq 27. *Eccl* Seq 40.

KIRKBURN

AP [E Riding] Incl tps Eastburn, Kirkburn and Battleburn, Southburn, Tibthorpe (each a sep CP 1866[2]) so that 'Kirkburn' has no sep civ identity 1866—1935 (see following entry). *LG* Harth. Wap. *Parl* E Riding (1832—67). *Eccl* Seq 10.

CP [E Riding] Cr 1935 by union Eastburn CP, Kirkburn and Battleburn CP, Southburn CP, pt Emswell with Little Driffield CP.[13] *LG* Driff. RD. Transf 1974 to Humb.[5] *Parl* Bridl. CC (1948—55), Howden CC (1955—*).

KIRKBURN AND BATTLEBURN

[E Riding] Tp in Kirkburn AP, sep CP 1866.[2] *LG* Harth. Wap, Driff. PLU, RSD, RD. Abol 1935 to help cr Kirkburn CP.[13] *Parl* E Riding (1832—85), Buckr. Dv (1885—1948).

KIRKBURTON

AP [W Riding] Incl tps Cartworth, Fulstone, Wooldale (each a sep CP 1866,[2] pt of each eccl severed 1726 to help cr Holmfirth EP,[9] the latter refounded 1858[294]), tp Hepworth (sep CP 1866,[2] pt eccl severed 1864 to help cr Holmfirth EP,[9] refounded as noted above, the remainder a sep EP 1864 as 'Hepworth'[246]), tp Shelley (sep CP 1866,[2] sep EP 1868[149]), tp Shepley (sep CP 1866,[2] sep EP 1849[166]), tp Thurstonland (sep CP 1866[2]), pt tp Cumberworth Half (sep CP 1866[2]). *LG* Agb. Wap, Hudd. PLU, Kirkburton USD, UD. Addtl civ bdry alt: 1938.[28] Transf 1974 to W Yorks.[5] *Parl* W Riding (1832—67) S'rn Dv of W Riding (1867—85), Holmf. Dv (1885—1918), Penist. Dv (1918—48), Colne Valley CC (1948—55), Hudd. East BC (1955—*). *Eccl* Pontef. RDn (until 1857), Hudd. RDn (1857—1968), Kirkburton RDn (1968—*). Addtl eccl bdry alt: 1834 (cr New Mill EP,[9] refounded 1844[94]).

SOUTH KIRKBY

AP [W Riding] Tp 'South Kirkby' in Osg. Wap as were chap Skelbrooke (sep CP 1866,[2] sep EP 1728[9]), tp North Elmsall (sep CP 1866[2]), tp South Elmsall (sep CP 1866,[2] sep EP 1911 incl tp Hamphall Stubbs[37]); incl in Straff. & Tick. Wap tp Hamphall Stubbs (sep CP 1866,[2] eccl severed 1911 to help cr South Elmsall EP[37]). *LG* Not in a PLU (until 1850), Hemsw. PLU (1850—1930), RSD, RD. Transf 1974 to W Yorks.[5] *Parl* Seq 28. *Eccl* Donc. RDn (until 1871), Pontef. RDn (1871—1916), Hemsw. RDn (1916—27), Pontef. RDn (1927—*). Addtl eccl bdry alt: 1933,[413] 1969.[478]

KIRKBY FLEETHAM

AP [N Riding] *LG* Seq 49. Transf 1974 to N Yorks.[5] *Parl* Seq 15. *Eccl* Seq 53.

KIRKBY IN MALHAM DALE

AP [W Riding] Usual civ spelling; for eccl see following entry. Incl tps Airton, Calton, Hanlith, Kirkby Malham, Malham, Malham Moor, Otterburn, Scosthorp (each a sep CP 1866[2]) so that 'Kirkby in Malham Dale' has no sep civ identity after 1866. *LG* Staincl. & Ewc. Wap. *Parl* W Riding (1832—67).

KIRKBY MALHAM

AP [W Riding] Usual eccl spelling; for civ and civ sep tps, see prev entry. *Eccl* Seq 35. Eccl bdry: 1847 (help refound Coniston EP),[435] 1842 (help cr Stainforth EP).[136]

KIRKBY MALHAM

[W Riding] Tp in Kirkby in Malham Dale AP, sep CP 1866.[2] *LG* Seq 111. Transf 1974 to N Yorks.[5] *Parl* Seq 41.

KIRKBY MALZEARD

AP [W Riding] Incl chap Hartwith cum Winsley (sep

CP 1866,[2] sep EP 1742[9]), tp Grewelthorpe (sep CP 1866,[2] sep EP 1848[86]), tps Fountains Earth, Laverton, Down Stonebeck, Upper Stonebeck (each a sep CP 1866[2]), pt tp Azerley (sep CP 1866[2]), undivided pt Lands Common to Grewelthorpe, Kirkby Malzeard and Laverton (abol 1937 ent to Laverton CP [another civ bdry alt in same order affecting Kirkby Malzeard][31]). *LG* Seq 90. Addtl civ bdry alt: 1883.[52] Transf 1974 to N Yorks.[5] *Parl* Seq 33. *Eccl* Pec jurisd Masham prebend (until 1836), Seq 55 thereafter. Addtl eccl bdry alt: 1743 (cr Middlesmoor EP,[9] refounded 1863[493]), 1844 (cr Dallaghill EP [o'wise Dallowgill], cr Mickley EP, cr Ramsgill EP),[133] 1849 (cr Healey EP).[401]

KIRKBY MOORSIDE
AP [N Riding] Usual civ spelling; for eccl see 'Kirkbymoorside'. Incl tps Fadmoor, Gillamoor (each a sep CP 1866[2]), tps Farndale, Low Quarter, Farndale, West Side (each a sep CP 1866,[2] both eccl severed 1873 and united with tp [not sep civ] Bransdale East in this par to help cr Bransdale cum Farndale EP[21]). *LG* Kirkby Moorside Bor, Seq 64. Addtl civ bdry alt: 1883,[16] 1887,[538] 1934.[3] Transf 1974 to N Yorks.[5] *Parl* Seq 21.

KIRKBY OVERBLOW
AP [W Riding] Incl chap Stainburn (sep CP 1866,[2] sep EP 1775,[9] eccl refounded 1871[21]), tp Rigton (sep CP 1866,[2] eccl severed 1910 and transf to Stainburn EP[197]), tps Kearby with Netherby, Sicklinghall (each a sep CP 1866[2]). *LG* Claro Wap, Carlton GilbU (until 1861), Wethb. PLU (1861—1930), RSD, RD. Addtl civ bdry alt: 1937,[31] 1938.[28] Transf 1974 to N Yorks.[5] *Parl* Seq 35. *Eccl* Ainsty RDn (until 1820), New Ainsty RDn (1820—38), Pontef. RDn (1838—57), Wethb. RDn (1857—*). Addtl eccl bdry alt: 1957.[226]

KIRKBY RAVENSWORTH
AP [N Riding] Incl tp Dalton (sep CP 1866,[2] sep EP 1841[9]), tp Ravensworth (sep CP 1866,[2] sep EP 1841[9]), tps Gayles, Kirby Hill, New Forest, Whashton, pt tp Newsham (each a sep CP 1866[2]) so that 'Kirkby Ravensworth' has no sep civ identity after 1866. *LG* W Gill. Wap. *Parl* N Riding (1832—67). *Eccl* Seq 58. Addtl eccl bdry alt: 1918.[564]

KIRKBY WHARFE
AP [W Riding] Incl tps Grimston, Ulleskelf, pt tp Kirkby Wharfe and North Milford (each a sep CP 1866[2]) so that 'Kirkby Wharfe' has no sep civ identity after 1866. *LG* Bark. Ash Wap. *Parl* W Riding (1832—67). *Eccl* Pec jurisd Wetwang prebend (until 1836), Seq 33 thereafter.

KIRKBY WHARFE AND NORTH MILFORD
[W Riding] Tp pt in Bolton Percy AP, pt in Kirkby Wharfe AP, sep CP 1866.[2] *LG* Seq 77. Transf 1974 to N Yorks.[5] *Parl* Seq 24.

KIRKBY WISKE
AP [N Riding] Usual eccl spelling; for civ and civ sep tps, see 'Kirby Wiske'. *Eccl* Sometimes as 'Kirkby Wiske with Maunby', Richm. RDn (until 1857), Richm. East RDn (1857—1928), Bedale RDn (1928—*). Eccl bdry: 1962 (loses pt to South Otterington AP, dioc York).

KIRKBYMOORSIDE
AP [N Riding] Usual eccl spelling; for civ and civ and eccl sep tps, see 'Kirkby Moorside'. *Eccl* Riddal RDn (until 1862), Helm. RDn (1862—1973). Abol eccl 1973 to help cr Kirkbymoorside with Gillamoor, Farndale and Bransdale EP.[338]

KIRKBYMOORSIDE WITH GILLAMOOR, FARNDALE AND BRANSDALE
EP [N Riding] Cr 1973 by union Kirkbymoorside AP (civ, 'Kirkby Moorside'), Bransdale cum Farndale EP.[338] Helm. RDn.

KIRKDALE
AP [N Riding] Incl tps Bransdale, West Side; Muscoates, Nawton, Skiplam, Welburn, Wombleton (each a sep CP 1866[2]) so that 'Kirkdale' has no sep civ identity after 1866; for usual eccl spelling and for eccl bdry alt, see 'Kirkdale with Nawton'. *LG* Ryed. Wap. *Parl* N Riding (1832—67).

KIRKDALE WITH NAWTON
AP [N Riding] Usual eccl spelling; for civ and civ sep tps, see prev entry. *Eccl* Seq 26. Eccl bdry: 1873 (area of tp Farndale East [not sep civ] eccl severed to help cr Bransdale cum Farndale EP),[21] 1882.[223]

KIRKHAM
[E Riding] Tp in Westow AP, sep CP 1866.[2] *LG* Buckr. Wap, Malton PLU, RSD, Norton RD. Abol 1935 ent to Firby CP.[13] *Parl* E Riding (1832—85), Buckr. Dv (1885—1948).

KIRKHAMGATE
CP [W Riding] Renaming 1916 of Alverthorpe CP.[101] *LG* Wakef PLU, RD. Abol 1937 ent to Stanley UD & CP.[31] *Parl* Rothw. Dv (1918—48).

KIRKHEATON
AP [W Riding] Incl tp Lepton (sep CP 1866,[2] sep EP 1870[9]), tps Dalton, Upper Whitley (each a sep CP 1866[2]). *LG* Agb. Wap, Hudd. PLU, Kirkheaton USD, UD. Abol civ 1938 pt to Hudd. CB (assoc with W Riding) & AP, pt to Kirkburton UD & AP.[28] *Parl* W Riding (1832—67), S'rn Dv of W Riding (1867—85), Holmf. Dv (1885—1918), Spen Valley Dv (1918—48). *Eccl* Seq 49. Addtl eccl bdry alt: 1860 (hmlt Denby Grange [not sep civ] severed to help refound Flockton EP as 'Flockton cum Denby Grange'),[68] 1860 (help cr Upper Hopton EP),[301] 1864 (cr Mold Green EP),[246] 1895 (help cr Bradley EP),[221] 1963 (help cr Rawthorpe EP).[287]

KIRKLEATHAM
AP [N Riding] Incl chap Wilton (sep civ identity early, sep EP 1850[9]). *LG* Langb. Lbty, Guisb. PLU, RSD, Kirkleatham USD, UD (1894—99), Guisb. RD (1899—1932), Guisb. UD (1932—74). Addtl civ bdry alt: 1899 (the pt transf to Redcar UD cr Coatham CP),[426] 1920.[427] Transf 1974 to Clev.[5] *Parl* Seq 9. *Eccl* Clev RDn (until 1862), Stokes. RDn (1862—78), Middlesb. RDn (1878—1924), Guisb. RDn (1924—*). Addtl eccl bdry alt: 1854 (cr East Coatham EP),[368] 1927 (help cr Dormanstown EP).[284]

KIRKLINGTON
AP [Pt N Riding (Hallik. Wap: tps Howgrave, Kirklington cum Upsland, Sutton Howgrave, East Tanfield [each a sep CP 1866[2]]), pt W Riding (Ripon Lbty: pt tp Nunwick cum Howgrave [sep CP

1866^2])] *LG* After 1866 'Kirklington' has no sep civ identity. *Parl* Pt N Riding, pt W Riding (1832—67). *Eccl* Catt. RDn (until 1857), Catt. East RDn (1857—1928), Bedale RDn (1928—73), Wensleyd. RDn (1973—*).

KIRKLINGTON CUM UPSLAND

[N Riding] Tp in Kirklington AP, sep CP $1866.^2$ *LG* Hallik. Wap, Bedale PLU (soon after 1839^{112}—1930), Kirklington cum Upsland USD, UD (1894—1934), Bedale RD (1934—74). Transf 1974 to N Yorks.[5] *Parl* Seq 18.

KIRKSTALL

EP [W Riding] Cr 1831 from Leeds AP.[218] Old Ainsty RDn (1831—36), Pontef. RDn (1836—57), Leeds RDn (1857—1971), Head. RDn (1971—*). Bdry: 1846 (help cr Woodside EP),[35] $1850,^{366}$ 1867 (help cr Upper Armley EP),[125] 1936 (help cr Hawksworth Wood EP),[188] $1967.^{127}$

KIRKTHWAITE

EP [W Riding] Area in chap Dent (sep EP 1742 from Sedbergh AP,[9] qv for civ), sep EP 1864 as 'Cowgill',[9] refounded 1865 as 'Kirkthwaite' EP.[264] Clapham RDn. Renamed 1869 'Cowgill'.[447]

KNAPTON

[E Riding] Tp in Wintringham AP, sep CP $1866,^2$ sep EP 1742.[9] *LG* Buckr. Wap, Malton PLU, RSD, Norton RD. Abol civ 1935 ent to Scampston CP.[13] *Parl* E Riding (1832—85), Buckr. Dv (1885—1948). *Eccl* Buckr. RDn (1742—1857), E Buckr. RDn (1857—66), Buckr. RDn (1866—87), Settr. RDn (1887—1922), Buckr. RDn (1922—*).

KNAPTON

[Ainsty (W Riding until 1449 and from 1836, indept jurisd 1449—1836]). Tp pt in Acomb AP, pt in York Holy Trinity Mickelgate AP (pt of the area not in York Bor/MB/CB), sep CP $1866.^2$ *LG* Gt Ouseb. GilbU (until 1854), PLU (1854—1930), RSD, RD (1894—1938), Nidd. RD (1938—74). Bdry: 1937 (loses pt to York CB [not assoc with a Riding] & CP).[31] Transf 1974 to N Yorks.[5] *Parl* Seq 23.

KNARESBOROUGH

AP [W Riding] Incl pt chap Arkendale (sep CP $1866,^2$ sep EP 1736,[9] eccl refounded 1924 from this and 4 other pars,[77] qv), chap Bilton with Harrogate (sep CP $1866,^2$ sep EP 1829,[260] eccl usually called 'High Harrogate Christ Church'), pt tp Ferrensby, tp Scriven with Tentergate (each a sep CP 1866^2). *LG* Claro Wap, Knar. PLU, pt Knar. & Tentergate USD, pt Harrog. USD (1875—88), pt Harrog. MB (1884—88), pt Knar. RSD, Knar. & Tentergate USD (1894—95), Knar. UD (1895—1974). Addtl civ bdry alt: 1894 (the pt not in Knar. & Tentergate UD cr Knaresborough Outer CP),[257] 1895 (gains Tentergate CP),[663] $1904,^{664}$ $1938.^{28}$ Transf 1974 to N Yorks.[5] *Parl* W Riding (1832—67), pt E'rn Dv of W Riding, pt Knar. Parl Bor (1867—85), Ripon Dv (1885—1948), Harrog. CC (1948—*). *Eccl* Pec jurisd Knaresborough with Bickhill prebend (until 1836), Seq 51 thereafter. Addtl eccl bdry alt: 1866 (cr Knaresborough Holy Trinity EP),[97] 1879 (help cr Killinghall EP),[278] 1911 (help cr Starbeck EP).[263]

KNARESBOROUGH HOLY TRINITY

EP [W Riding] Cr 1866 from KnaresboroughAP.[97] Boroughbr. RDn (1866—70), Knar. RDn (1870—1971), Harrog. RDn (1971—*).

KNARESBOROUGH OUTER

CP [W Riding] Cr 1894 from the pt of Knaresborough AP not in Knar. & Tentergate UD.[257] *LG* Knar. PLU, RD (1894—1938), Nidd. RD (1938—74). Bdry: $1904,^{664}$ $1938.^{28}$ Transf 1974 to N Yorks.[5] *Parl* Ripon Dv (1918—48), Harrog. CC (1948—*).

KNAYTON WITH BRAWITH

[N Riding] Tp in Leake AP, sep CP $1866.^2$ *LG* Seq 23. Transf 1974 to N Yorks.[5] *Parl* Seq 14.

KNEDLINGTON

[E Riding] Tp in Howden AP, sep CP $1866.^2$ *LG* Howdens. Wap, Howden PLU, RSD, RD. Bdry: 1880 (help cr Bishopsoil CP),[142] $1880,^{634}$ 1895 (loses pt to Newland CP, Yorks W Riding).[665] Abol 1935 pt to Asselby CP, pt to Kilpin CP, pt to Eastrington AP, pt to Howden AP.[13] *Parl* E Riding (1832—85), Howdensh. Dv (1885—1948).

KNOTTINGLEY

[W Riding] Chap in Pontefract AP, sep CP $1866,^2$ sep EP 1725.[9] *LG* Osg. Wap, not in a PLU (until 1862), Pontef. PLU (1862—1930), RSD (1875—92), Knottingley USD (1892—94), UD. Civ bdry: $1937.^{31}$ Transf 1974 to W Yorks.[5] *Parl* Seq 29. *Eccl* Ainsty RDn (1725—1820), New Ainsty RDn (1820—57), Pontef. RDn (1857—*). Eccl bdry: 1846 (cr East Knottingley EP),[516] 1941 (gains East Knottingley EP).[62]

EAST KNOTTINGLEY

EP [W Riding] Cr 1846 from Knottingley EP.[516] Pontef. RDn. Abol 1941 ent to Knottingley EP.[630]

LAISTER DYKE

EP [W Ridinge] Cr 1861 from Bradford AP, Pudsey EP.[193] Bradf RDn (1861—1921), Calverley RDn (1921—*). Bdry: $1865,^{35}$ 1894 (help cr Bradford St Clement EP),[109] 1913 (help cr Thornbury EP),[93] $1927,^{67}$ $1959.^{320}$

LAITHKIRK

EP [N Riding] Cr 1844 from Romaldkirk AP.[637] Richm. RDn (1844—57), Richm. West RDn (1857—63), Richm. North RDn (1863—*).

LAND COMMON TO DANBY AND GLAISDALE

[N Riding] *LG* See sep pars for Hd, PLU. Pt Whitby RD, pt Guisb. RD. Abol 1929 pt to Danby AP, pt to Glaisdale CP.[468] *Parl* Scarb. & Whitby Dv (1918—48).

LAND NEAR HORTON GILL BRIDGE

[N Riding] Land Common to Bainbridge CP and to Hawes CP. *LG* Aysg. RD. Abol 1934 ent to Bainbridge CP.[3] *Parl* Richm. Dv (1918—48).

LANDMOTH CUM CATTO

[N Riding] Tp in Leake AP, sep CP $1866.^2$ *LG* Seq 22. Transf 1974 to N Yorks.[5] *Parl* Seq 14.

LANDS COMMON TO AZERLEY AND LAVERTON

[W Riding] *LG* Ripon RD. Abol 1937 pt to Azerley AP, pt to Laverton CP.[31] *Parl* Ripon Dv (1918—48).

LANDS COMMON TO GREWELTHORPE, KIRKBY MALZEARD AND LAVERTON

[W Riding] *LG* Ripon RD. Abol 1937 ent to

Laverton CP.[31] *Parl* Ripon Dv (1918—48).

LANGCLIFFE

[W Riding] Tp in Giggleswick AP, sep CP 1866,[2] sep EP 1851.[294] *LG* Seq 111. Civ bdry: 1912.[571] Transf 1974 to N Yorks.[5] *Parl* Seq 41. *Eccl* Craven RDn (1851—57), Craven RDn, N'rn Dv (1857—1921), Settle RDn (1921—71), Bowl. RDn (1971—*).

LANGFIELD

[W Riding] Tp in Halifax AP, sep CP 1866.[2] *LG* Morley Wap, Todmorden PLU, USD, UD (1894—96), MB (1896—97). Abol 1897 to help cr Todmorden CP.[666] *Parl* W Riding (1832—67), E'rn Dv of W Riding (1867—85), Sowerby Dv (1885—1918).

LANGSETT

[W Riding] Tp in Penistone AP, sep CP 1866.[2] *LG* Seq 116. Transf 1974 to S Yorks.[5] *Parl* Seq 50.

LANGSETT ROAD

EP [W Riding] Cr 1879 from Sheffield St Philip EP.[630] Sheff RDn (1879—1942), Hallam RDn (1942—*). Bdry: 1969.[494]

LANGTHORNE

[N Riding] Tp in Bedale AP, sep CP 1866,[2] eccl severed 1840 to help cr Crakenhall EP,[540] the latter sometimes called 'Crakenhall with Langthorne'. *LG* Hallik. Wap, N'allert, PLU (1837—39), Bedale PLU (1839—1930), RSD, RD. Transf 1974 to N Yorks.[5] *Parl* Seq 15.

LANGTHORPE

[N Riding] Tp in Kirby on the Moor AP, sep CP 1866.[2] *LG* Seq 41. Transf 1974 to N Yorks. *Parl* Seq 16.

LANGTHWAITE WITH TILTS

[W Riding] Tp in Doncaster AP, sep CP 1866.[2] *LG* Straff. & Tick. Wap, Donc. PLU, RSD. Abol 1883 pt to Adwick le Street AP, pt to Thorpe in Balne CP.[42] *Parl* W Riding (1832—67), S'rn Dv of W Riding (1867—85).

LANGTOFT

AP [E Riding] Incl chap Cottam (sep CP 1866,[2] no sep eccl identity hence this par eccl 'Langtoft with Cottam', qv). *LG* Seq 6. Transf 1974 to Humb.[5] *Parl* Seq 3.

LANGTOFT WITH COTTAM

AP [E Riding] Usual eccl spelling; for civ and civ sep chap Cottam, see prev entry. *Eccl* Pec jurisd Langtoft prebend (until 1836), Dick. RDn (1836—57), S Dick. RDn (1857—66), Scarb. RDn (1866—87), Buckr. RDn (1887—1922), Harth. RDn (1922—*).

LANGTON

AP [E Riding] Incl tp Kennythorpe (sep CP 1866[2]). *LG* Seq 2. Transf 1974 to N Yorks.[5] *Parl* Seq 1. *Eccl* Buckr. RDn (until 1857), E Buckr. RDn (1857—66), Buckr. RDn (1866—87), Settr. RDn (1887—1922), Buckr. RDn (1922—*).

GREAT LANGTON

[N Riding] Tp in Langton upon Swale AP, sep CP 1866.[2] *LG* Seq 34. Transf 1974 to N Yorks.[5] *Parl* Seq 14.

LITTLE LANGTON

[N Riding] Organisation as for Great Langton, with

civ bdry alt 1888.[667]

LANGTON UPON SWALE

AP [N Riding] Incl tps Great Langton, Little Langton (each a sep CP 1866[2]) so that 'Langton upon Swale' has no sep civ identity after 1866. *LG* N Gill. Wap. *Parl* N Riding (1832—67). *Eccl* Seq 57.

LANGWITH

[E Riding] Tp (pec jurisd Dean & Chapter of York, until 1836) in Wheldrake AP, sep CP 1866.[2] *LG* Ouse & Derw. Wap, York PLU, RSD, Escr. RD. Abol 1935 ent to Heslington CP.[13] *Parl* E Riding (1832—85), Howdensh. Dv (1885—1948).

LARTINGTON

[N Riding] Tp in Romandkirk AP, sep CP 1866.[2] *LG* Seq 39. Transf 1974 to Durham.[5] *Parl* Seq 14.

LASKILL PASTURE

[N Riding] Tp in Helmsley AP, sep CP 1866.[2] *LG* Seq 63. Transf 1974 to N Yorks.[5] *Parl* Seq 21.

LASTINGHAM

AP [N Riding] incl tp Appleton le Moor (sep CP 1866,[2] sep EP 1868 incl pt Spanton Moor [area of Appleton Common][111]), tp Farndale, East Side (sep CP 1866,[2] eccl severed 1873 to help cr Bransdale cum Farndale EP[21]), tp Hutton le Hole (sep CP 1866[2]), tp Rosedale, West Side (sep CP 1866,[2] eccl severed 1739 to help cr Rosedale EP,[9] confirmed 1876[668]), pt tp Spaunton (sep CP 1866[2]), undivided pt Spaunton Moor (qv for other pars to which common, abol 1934 incl pt to this par [other bdry alt in same order also affecting Lastingham][3]). *LG* Seq 66. Transf 1974 to N Yorks.[5] *Parl* Seq 21. *Eccl* Seq 26.

LAUGHTON EN LE MORTHEN

AP [W Riding] incl chaps North Anston, South Anston (sep civ identity early as 'North and South Anston', sep EP 1786 usually as 'Anston cum Membris'[108]), chap Firbeck (sep civ identity early, sep EP 1768[9]), chap Thorpe Salvin (sep civ identity early, sep EP 1775[9]), chap Wales (sep civ identity early, sep EP 1723[9]), pt tp Dinnington (sep CP 1866[2]), area St John's with Throapham (sep civ identity early, sep EP 1742[9] but sep status not sustained; this area incl chap Letwell, tp Gildingwells, each a sep CP 1866,[2] the 2 eccl severed 1768 as 'Letwell with Gildingwells' EP,[9] the area of Gildingwells severed 1841 from the latter to help cr Woodsetts EP, the remainder to be 'Letwell' EP[572]). *LG* Straff. & Tick. Wap, Rotherh. PLU, RSD, RD. Abol civ 1923 to help cr Thurcroft CP.[151] *Parl* W Riding (1832—67), S'rn Dv of W Riding (1867—85), Donc. Dv (1885—1918), Rother Valley Dv (1918—48). *Eccl* Sometimes as 'Laughton en le Morthen with Throapham', pec jurisd Laughton en le Morthen (until 1484), pec jurisd Chancellor of York (1484—1836), Seq 44 thereafter. Addtl eccl bdry alt: 1948 (help cr Thurcroft EP).[669]

LAUGHTON EN LE MORTHEN WITH THROAPHAM—see prev entry

LAVERTON

[W Riding] Tp in Kirkby Malzeard AP, sep CP 1866.[2] Incl undivided pt Lands Common to Azerley and Laverton (abol 1937 incl pt to this par[31]), undivided pt Lands Common to Grewelthorpe,

Kirkby Malzeard and Laverton (abol 1937 ent to this par[31]). *LG* Seq 90. Addtl civ bdry alt: 1883,[52] 1938 (in addition to pts cited above).[31] Transf 1974 to N Yorks.[5] *Parl* Seq 33.

LAWKHOLME

EP [W Riding] Cr 1883 from Keighley AP.[486] Craven RDn, S'rn Dv (1883—1921), S Craven RDn (1921—73). Bdry: 1954.[489] Abol 1973 ent to Keighley AP.[653]

LAWKLAND

[W Riding] Tp in Clapham AP, sep CP 1866,[2] eccl severed 1843 to help cr Austwick EP,[9] the latter refounded 1879.[22] *LG* Seq 111. Bdry: 1883,[52] 1884.[135] Transf 1974 to N Yorks.[5] *Parl* Seq 41.

LAXTON

[E Riding] Chap in Howden AP, sep CP 1866,[2] sep EP 1785 (eccl comprised of tps Cotness, Laxton, Metham, Saltmarshe, Yokefleet, qv for civ identities),[9] eccl refounded 1858.[440] *LG* Seq 17. Bdry: 1880 (help cr Bishopsoil CP),[142] 1880,[230] 1935.[13] Transf 1974 to Humb.[5] *Parl* Seq 7. *Eccl* Pec jurisd Dean & Chapter of Durham (1785—1836), Harth. & Hull RDn (1836—57), W Harth. RDn (1857—66), Howden RDn (1866—*).

LAYTHAM

[E Riding] Tp in Aughton AP, sep CP 1866.[2] *LG* Harth. Wap, Howden PLU, RSD, RD. Abol 1935 ent to Foggathorpe CP.[13] *Parl* E Riding (1832—85), Howdensh. Dv (1885—1948).

EAST LAYTON

[N Riding] Tp pt in Melsonby AP, pt in Stanwick AP, sep CP 1866,[2] the detached pts which constituted East Layton CP eccl severed 1918 and transf to Forcett EP.[564] *LG* Seq 38. Bdry: 1888.[624] Transf 1974 to N Yorks.[5] *Parl* Seq 14.

WEST LAYTON

[N Riding] Tp in Gilling AP, sep CP 1866.[2] *LG* Seq 38. Bdry: 1888.[624] Transf 1974 to N Yorks.[5] *Parl* Seq 14.

LAZENBY

[N Riding] Ex-par place, sep CP 1858.[393] *LG* Seq 22. Bdry: 1934.[3] Transf 1974 to N Yorks.[5] *Parl* N'allert. Parl Bor (1298, 1640—1885), Richm. Dv (1885—1918), Thirsk & Malton Dv/CC (1918—*).

LEAD

[W Riding] Tp in Ryther AP, sep CP 1866,[2] eccl severed 1912 to help cr Saxton with Lead EP.[670] *LG* Seq 81. Transf 1974 to N Yorks.[5] *Parl* Seq 24.

LEAKE

AP [N Riding] Tp 'Leake' in Allert. Wap as were tps Borrowby, Crosby, Knayton with Brawith, Landmoth cum Catto (each of the last 4 a sep CP 1866[2]); incl in Birdf. Wap chap Nether Silton (sep CP 1866,[2] eccl severed 1935 to help cr Over Silton with Nether Silton EP[671]), tp Gueldable (sep CP 1866[2]), pt tp Kepwick (sep CP 1866[2]). *LG* N'allert. PLU, RSD, RD. Addtl civ bdry alt: 1934.[3] Transf 1974 to N Yorks.[5] *Parl* Seq 14. *Eccl* As 'Leake with Nether Silton' until eccl severance of Nether Silton, 'Leake' thereafter, pec jurisd Bp of Durham (tp Leake and chap only, until 1836), Clev RDn (1836—62), Thirsk RDn (1862—1967). Addtl eccl bdry alt: 1873 (gains ex-par places Cotcliffe, Bishop

Ings).[279] Abol eccl 1967 to help cr Leake with Over and Nether Silton and Kepwick EP.[508]

LEAKE WITH NETHER SILTON—see prev entry

LEAKE WITH OVER AND NETHER SILTON AND KEPWICK

EP [N Riding] Cr 1967 by union Leake AP, Over Silton with Nether Silton EP.[508] Thirsk RDn.

LEATHLEY

AP [W Riding] Incl tp Castley (sep CP 1866[2]). *LG* Claro Wap, Carlton GilbU (until 1861), Wharfed. PLU (1861—1930), RSD, RD. Addtl civ bdry alt: 1883.[52] Transf 1974 to N Yorks.[5] *Parl* Seq 30. *Eccl* Seq 34. Eccl bdry: 1926 (gains area tp Lindley [orig sep EP 1831,[9] sep status not sustained] from Otley AP).[551]

LEAVENING

[E Riding] Tp in Acklam AP, sep CP 1866.[2] *LG* Seq 2. Transf 1974 to N Yorks.[5] *Parl* Seq 1.

CASTLE LEAVINGTON

[N Riding] Tp in Kirk Leavington AP, sep CP 1866.[2] *LG* Seq 57. Transf 1974 to Clev.[5] *Parl* Seq 11.

KIRK LEAVINGTON

AP [N Riding] Incl chap and bor Yarm (sep civ identity early, sep EP 1865[9]), tps Castle Leavington, Picton, Low Worsall (each a sep CP 1866[2]). Usual civ spelling; for eccl see following entry. *LG* Pt Yarm Bor (until Yarm gains sep civ identity), Seq 57. Transf 1974 to Clev.[5] *Parl* Seq 11.

KIRK LEVINGTON

AP [N Riding] Usual eccl spelling; for civ, civ and eccl sep chap and tps, see prev entry. *Eccl* Seq 24.

LEBBERSTON

[N Riding] Tp in Filey AP, sep CP 1866.[2] *LG* Seq 62. Transf 1974 to N Yorks.[5] *Parl* Seq 20.

LECONFIELD

AP [E Riding] Incl tp Leconfield and Arram, pt tp Molescroft (each a sep CP 1866[2]) so that 'Leconfield' has no sep civ identity 1866—1935 (see following entry). *LG* Harth. Wap. *Parl* E Riding (1832—67). *Eccl* Pec jurisd Bev. (until 1836), Harth. & Hull RDn (1836—57), N Harth. RDn (1857—66), Harth. RDn (1866—81), Bev. RDn (1881—*).

CP [E Riding] Cr 1935 by union Leconfield and Arram CP, Scorborough AP.[13] *LG* Bev. RD. Transf 1974 to Humb.[5] *Parl* Bev. CC (1948—55), Haltemp. CC (1955—*).

LECONFIELD AND ARRAM

[E Riding] Tp in Leconfield AP, sep CP 1866.[2] *LG* Harth. Wap, Bev. PLU, RSD, RD. Abol 1935 to help cr Leconfield CP.[13] *Parl* E Riding (1832—85), Hold. Dv (1885—1948).

LEDSHAM

AP [W Riding] Incl pt tp Fairburn (orig chap,[539] later tp, sep CP 1866,[2] no sep eccl identity hence this par eccl 'Ledsham with Fairburn', qv), pt tp Ledston (sep CP 1866[2]). *LG* Seq 78. Transf 1974 to W Yorks.[5] *Parl* W Riding (1832—67), E'rn Dv of W Riding (1867—85), Osg. Dv (1885—1918), Bark. Ash Dv/CC (1918—*).

LEDSHAM WITH FAIRBURN

AP [W Riding] Usual eccl spelling; for civ, and for civ

sep tps, see prev entry. *Eccl* Ainsty RDn (until 1820), New Ainsty RDn (1820—57), Pontef. RDn (1857—1916), Selby RDn (1916—*).

LEDSTON

[W Riding] Tp pt in Ledsham AP, pt in Kippax AP, sep CP 1866.[2] *LG* Pt Bark. Ash Wap (pt in Ledsham), pt Skyr. Wap (pt in Kippax), Gt Preston GilbU (until 1869), Pontef. PLU (1869 and only brief time later), Tadc. PLU (soon after 1869—1930), RSD, RD. Transf 1974 to W Yorks.[5] *Parl* W Riding (1832—67), N'rn Dv of W Riding (1867—85), Osg. Dv (1885—1918), Bark. Ash CC (1918—*).

LEEDS

[W Riding] The following have 'Leeds' in their names. Insofar as any existed at a given time: *LG* Skyr. Wap, Leeds Bor/MB/CB, USD, Guardians (for poor, 1844—69), Leeds PLU (1869—1912), Par (for poor, 1912—30). *Parl* Leeds Parl Bor (1832—85); see Part III of the *Guide* for composition of Leeds Parl Bors/BCs (1885—*) by wards of the MB/CB. *Eccl* Ainsty RDn (until 1820), Old Ainsty RDn (1820—36), Pontef. RDn (1836—57), Leeds RDn (1857—1971), sep noted (1971—*).

AP1—LEEDS [ST PETER]—Incl chap Chapel Allerton (sep CP 1866,[2] sep EP 1719[9]), chap Armley (sep CP 1866,[2] sep EP 1729[9]), chap Beeston (sep CP 1866,[2] sep EP 1739[9]), chap Bramley (sep CP 1866,[2] sep EP 1730[9]), chap Farnley (sep CP 1866,[2] sep EP 1723,[9] eccl refounded 1851[41]), chap Headingley cum Burley (sep CP 1866,[2] sep EP 1717,[9] divided eccl 1793 into 2 EPs of Headingley, Burley [area of hmlt Burley],[9] Burley eccl refounded 1849[54]), chap Holbeck (sep CP 1866,[2] sep EP 1719[9]), chap Hunslet (sep CP 1866,[2] sep EP 1719,[9] eccl refounded 1885 from Hunslet Moor EP, Beeston Hill EP, Holbeck EP, Brewery Field EP[229]), chap Wortley (sep CP 1866,[2] sep EP 1814[9]), tp Potter Newton (sep CP 1866,[2] sep EP 1883 from this par, Sheepscar St Clement EP, Buslingthorpe EP[113]), pt tp Seacroft (sep CP 1866,[2] sep EP 1846 ent from Whitkirk EP, qv), pt tp Templenewsham (sep CP 1866[2]). Addtl civ bdry alt: 1904 (gains Chapel Allerton CP, Headingley cum Burley CP, Potter Newton CP),[69] 1912 (incl gains Roundhay CP, Seacroft CP, Shadwell CP),[202] 1925 (gains following CPs in Leeds CB: Armley and Bramley, Holbeck, Hunslet, Osmondthorpe),[129] 1926,[38] 1928 (incl gains Templenewsham CP, Alwoodley CP, Adel cum Eccup CP),[39] 1937 (incl exchanges pts with Barwick in Elmet AP and loses pt to Bramhope CP),[31] 1957 (gains pts Austhorpe CP, Barwick in Elmet AP).[156] Transf 1974 to W Yorks.[5] Parl bdry: 1960.[473] *Eccl* Allert. RDn (1971—*). Addtl eccl bdry alt: 1723 (cr Fursley EP[9] [sep eccl status not sustained]), 1749 (cr EP9,[672] refounded 1885[553]), 1801 (consecr of EP17, orig a Dissenters' chap[673]), 1814 (cr EP25,[9] refounded 1866[54]), 1829 (cr EP23,[9] refounded 1862[136]), 1831 (cr Woodhouse EP, sometimes called 'Leeds St Mark's, Woodhouse'),[536] 1831 (cr Kirkstall EP),[218] 1837 (cr EP5,[9] refounded 1861[299]), 1838

(cr EP15),[674] 1845 (help cr EP26),[675] 1845 (cr EP20),[676] 1846 (cr EP27),[229] 1846 (cr Little London EP, later called 'Leeds St Matthew'),[107] 1847 (cr EP3),[127] 1847 (cr Hunslet St Mary EP),[70] 1849 (help cr Buslingthorpe EP),[54] 1850 (cr Sheepscar St Luke EP,[9] refounded 1861[67]), 1851 (help cr Burmantofts EP),[334] 1860 (cr Moor Allerton EP),[9] 1865 (cr Leylands EP),[298] 1868 (cr Far Headingley EP, sometimes later called 'Leeds St Chad'),[290] 1869 (help cr Sheepscar St Clement EP),[383] 1890 (help cr Burmantofts St Agnes EP),[370] 1895 (help cr EP10),[71] 1918 (gains EP14),[677] 1918 (gains EP29, EP23),[678] 1957 (gains EP19),[626] 1967.[127]

EP1—LEEDS ALL HALLOWS—Cr 1887 from Burley EP, EP15.[126] Bdry: 1902.[364] Abol 1955 to help cr EP2.[300]

EP2—LEEDS ALL HALLOWS WITH ST SIMON—Cr 1955 by union EP1, EP28.[300] Head. RDn (1971—*). Bdry: 1967.[127]

EP3—LEEDS ALL SAINTS—Cr 1847 from AP1.[127] Whitkirk RDn (1971—*). Bdry: 1877 (cr EP14),[598] 1932 (help cr Osmondthorpe EP),[138] 1941 (gains EP11),[93] 1967.[127]

EP4—LEEDS ALL SOULS—Cr 1881 from Little London EP (later called 'Leeds St Matthew'), Woodhouse EP.[647] Head. RDn (1971—*).

EP5—LEEDS CHRIST CHURCH—Cr 1837 from AP1,[9] refounded 1861.[299] Abol 1937 to help cr EP6.[679]

EP6—LEEDS CHRIST CHURCH WITH HOLBECK ST JOHN AND ST BARNABAS—Cr 1937 by union EP5, EP21.[679] Bdry: 1967.[127] Abol 1971 ent to Hunslet St Mary EP.[648]

EP7—LEEDS EMMANUEL—Cr 1881 from EP15.[313] Head. RDn (1971—*). Bdry: 1887.[126]

EP8—LEEDS THE EPIPHANY, GIPTON—Cr 1939 from Barwick in Elmet AP, Burmantofts St Stephen and St Agnes EP.[204] Allert. RDn. Bdry: 1967.[127]

EP9—LEEDS HOLY TRINITY—Cr 1749 from AP1,[9] refounded 1885.[553] Bdry: 1901 (gains EP25).[371] Abol 1959 ent to EP20.[680]

EP10—LEEDS ST AIDAN—Cr 1895 from AP1, Chapel Allerton EP, Potter Newton EP, Sheepscar St Clement EP.[71] Allert. RDn (1971—*). Bdry: 1926 (cr EP30),[247] 1967.[127]

EP11—LEEDS ST ALBAN THE MARTYR—Cr 1877 from Burmantofts EP.[369] Bdry: 1940 (help cr EP13).[299] Abol 1941 ent to EP3.[93]

EP12—LEEDS ST ANDREW—Cr 1844 from EP15.[117] Bdry: 1869 (cr EP28),[521] 1902.[364] Abol 1959 ent to EP15.[596]

—LEEDS ST CHAD—Name sometimes used for EP cr 1868 as 'Far Headingley', qv.

EP13—LEEDS ST CYPRIAN, HAREHILLS—Cr 1940 from Burmantofts St Stephen and St Agnes EP, EP11.[299] Allert. RDn (1971—*). Bdry: 1967.[127]

EP14—LEEDS ST EDMUND—Cr 1877 from EP3.[598] Abol 1918 ent to AP1.[677]

EP15—LEEDS ST GEORGE—Cr 1838 from AP1.[674] Head. RDn (1971—*). Bdry: 1844 (cr EP12),[117]

1845 (cr EP26),[675] 1881 (cr EP7),[313] 1887 (help cr EP1),[126] 1901 (gains EP26),[371] 1959 (gains EP12),[596] 1967.[127]

EP16—LEEDS ST HILDA—Cr 1885 from EP28.[320] Bdry: 1932 (help cr Osmondthorpe EP).[138] Abol 1963 to help cr Cross Green St Saviour and St Hilda EP.[308]

EP17—LEEDS ST JAMES—Consecr 1801, earlier Dissenters' chap and purchased, sep eccl status not sustained.[673]

EP18—LEEDS ST JOHN AND ST BARNABAS, BELLE ISLE—Cr 1938 from Middleton EP, Stourton EP.[575] Armley RDn (1971—*). Bdry: 1967,[127] 1968.[339]

EP19—LEEDS ST JOHN THE BAPTIST, NEW TOWN—Cr 1868 from EP24.[605] Abol 1957 ent to AP1.[626]

EP2O—LEEDS ST JOHN THE EVANGELIST—Cr 1845 from AP1.[676] Allert. RDn (1971—*). Bdry: 1959 (gains EP9),[680] 1967.[127]

EP21—LEEDS ST JOHN THE EVANGELIST WITH ST BARNABAS—Cr 1901 by union Little Holbeck EP, Brewery Field EP.[345] Abol 1937 to help cr EP6.[679]

EP22—LEEDS ST MARGARET—Cr 1911 from Burley EP.[367] Head. RDn (1971—*). Bdry: 1967.[127]

—LEEDS ST MARK'S, WOODHOUSE—Name sometimes used for EP cr 1831 as 'Woodhouse', qv.

EP23—LEEDS ST MARY—Cr 1829 from AP1,[9] refounded 1862.[136] Sometimes 'Quarry Hill'. Bdry: 1868 (cr EP19).[613] Abol 1918 ent to AP1.[678]

EP24—LEEDS ST MATTHEW—Name used now for EP cr 1846 as 'Little London'.[107] Allert. RDn (1971—*).

EP25—LEEDS ST PAUL—Cr 1814 from AP1, refounded 1866.[54] Abol 1901 ent to EP9.[371]

EP26—LEEDS ST PHILIP—Cr 1845 from EP15, AP1.[675] Abol 1901 ent to EP15.[371]

EP27—LEEDS ST SAVIOUR—Cr 1846 from AP1.[225] Bdry: 1885 (cr EP16).[320] Abol 1963 to help cr Cross Green St Saviour and St Hilda EP.[308]

EP28—LEEDS ST SIMON—Cr 1869 from EP12.[521] Bdry: 1902.[364] Abol 1955 to help cr EP2.[300]

EP29—LEEDS ST THOMAS AND ST LUKE—Cr 1904 by union Sheepscar St Luke EP, Leylands EP.[681] Abol 1918 ent to AP1.[678]

EP30—LEEDS ST WILFRID—Cr 1926 from EP10.[247] Allert. RDn (1971—*). Bdry: 1967.[127]

EP31—LEEDS ST WILFRID, HALTON—Cr 1939 from Whitkirk AP.[682] Whitkirk RDn. Bdry: 1967.[127]

LEEMING

EP [N Riding] Cr 1755 from Burneston AP, refounded 1880.[68] Catt. RDn (1755—1857), Catt. East RDn (1857—1928), Bedale RDn (1928—*) Bdry: 1921.[221]

LELLEY

[E Riding] Tp in Preston AP, sep CP 1866.[2] LG Hold. Wap, Skirl. PLU, RSD, RD. Abol 1935 ent to Elstronwick CP.[13] Parl E Riding (1832—85), Hold. Dv (1885—1948).

LEPPINGTON

[E Riding] Tp in Scrayingham AP, sep CP 1866.[2] LG Buckr. Wap, Malton PLU, RSD, Norton RD. Abol 1935 ent to Scrayingham AP.[13] Parl E Riding (1832—85), Buckr. Dv (1885—1948).

LEPTON

[W Riding] Tp in Kirkheaton AP, sep CP 1866,[2] pt of the tp a sep EP 1870 as 'Lepton'.[483] LG Agb. Wap, Hudd. PLU, Lepton USD, UD. Abol civ 1938 pt to Hudd. CB (assoc with W Riding) & AP, pt to Kirkburton UD & AP.[28] Parl W Riding (1832—67), S'rn Dv of W Riding (1867—85), Holmf. Dv (1885—1918), Spen Valley Dv (1918—48). Eccl Hudd. RDn (1870—1968), Kirkburton RDn (1968—*).

LETWELL

[W Riding] Chap (in pec jurisd Laughton en le Morthen until 1448, pec jurisd Chancellor of York 1448—1836) in area St John's with Throapham (sep civ identity early from Laughton en le Morthen AP, sep EP 1742[9] but sep eccl status not sustained), 'Letwell' a sep CP 1866,[2] eccl severed 1768 and united with tp Gildingwells in same par to cr 'Letwell with Gildingwells' EP,[9] the area of Gildingwells severed 1841 from the latter to help cr Woodsetts EP, the remainder to be 'Letwell' EP.[572] LG Seq 121. Transf 1974 to S Yorks.[5] Parl Seq 48. Eccl Donc. RDn (1841—57), Rotherh. RDn (1857—*).

LEVEN

AP [E Riding] Incl tp Hempholme (sep CP 1866[2]). LG Seq 13. Addtl civ bdry alt: 1895.[336] Transf 1974 to Humb.[5] Parl Seq 4. Eccl Pec jurisd Bev. (until 1836), Hold. RDn (1836—49), N Hold. RDn (1849—62), Bev. RDn (1862—71), Hornsea RDn (1871—1916), N Hold. RDn (1916—36), Bev. RDn (1936—*).

LEVISHAM

AP [N Riding] LG Seq 61. Transf 1974 to N Yorks.[5] Parl Seq 20. Eccl Riddal RDn (until 1862), Malton RDn (1862—1916). Bdry: 1866 (help cr Newton upon Rawcliffe EP).[249] Gains eccl 1916 chap Lockton from Middleton with Cropton and Lockton AP to cr Levisham with Lockton EP.[683]

LEVISHAM WITH LOCKTON

EP [N Riding] Cr 1916 by union Levisham AP, chap Lockton from Middleton with Cropton and Lockton AP.[683] Malton RDn (1916—28), Pick. RDn (1928—*).

LEYBURN

[N Riding] Tp in Wensley AP, sep CP 1866,[2] sep EP 1955.[288] LG Seq 53. Transf 1974 to N Yorks.[5] Parl Seq 14. Eccl Wensleyd. RDn.

LEYLANDS

EP [W Riding] Cr 1865 from Leeds AP.[298] Leeds RDn. Abol 1904 to help cr Leeds St Thomas and St Luke EP.[298]

LIGHTCLIFFE

[W Riding] Cr 1749 from Elland cum Stainland and Fixby EP (area Hipperholme with Brighouse, pt tp Northowram),[9] eccl refounded 1846.[523] Pontef. RDn (1749—1857), Halifax RDn (1857—1967), Brigh. & Elland RDn (1967—*). Bdry: 1894,[323]

1909 (help cr Northowram EP).[429]

LILLINGS AMBO

[N Riding] Tp in Sheriff Hutton AP, sep CP 1866.[2] *LG* Seq 32. Transf 1974 to N Yorks.[5] *Parl* Seq 16.

LINDLEY

[W Riding] Tp in Otley AP, sep CP 1866,[2] sep EP 1831,[9] sep eccl status not sustained and eccl severed 1926 and transf to Leathley AP.[551] *LG* Seq 92. Transf 1974 to N Yorks.[5] *Parl* Seq 30.

LINDLEY

[W Riding] Chap in Huddersfield AP, sep EP 1831,[9] eccl refounded 1843,[37] sep CP 1866 as 'Lindley cum Quarmby',[2] qv. Pontef. RDn (1831—57), Hudd. RDn (1857—*). Bdry: 1877 (help cr Birchencliffe EP).[141]

LINDLEY CUM QUARMBY

[W Riding] Chap in Huddersfield AP, sep CP 1866,[2] sep EP 1831 as 'Lindley',[9] as such eccl refounded 1843,[37] qv. *LG* Agb. Wap, Hudd. PLU, MB (1868—89), CB (1889—1924), USD. Bdry: 1883.[52] Abol 1924 ent to Huddersfield AP.[83] *Parl* W Riding (1832—67), Hudd. Parl Bor (1867—1948).

LINDRICK WITH STUDLEY ROYAL AND FOUN-TAINS

[W Riding] Ex-par place, sep CP 1858.[393] *LG* Seq 90. Bdry: 1938.[28] Transf 1974 to N Yorks.[5] *Parl* Seq 33.

LINGARDS

[W Riding] Tp in Almondbury AP, sep CP 1866.[2] *LG* Agb. Wap, Hudd. PLU, Slaithwaite USD, UD. Abol 1896 ent to Slaithwaite CP.[684] *Parl* W Riding (1832—67), S'rn Dv of W Riding (1867—85), Colne Valley Dv (1885—1918).

LINTHORPE

[N Riding] Tp in Middlesbrough AP, sep CP 1866,[2] sep EP 1897 from Middlesbrough St John the Evangelist EP, Marton AP[685]; this EP sometimes later 'Middlesbrough St Barnabas'. *LG* Langb. Lbty, Stock. PLU (1837—75), Middlesb. PLU (1875—1913), pt Middlesb. MB (1866—94), pt Middlesb. USD, pt Middlesb. RSD, pt Stock. on Tees MB (o'wise Durham, 1889—95). Civ bdry: 1883,[16] 1887,[17] 1894 (loses the pt in Middlesb. CB to Middlesbrough CP),[18] 1895 (loses the pt in Stock. on Tees MB to Stockton on Tees AP, Durham).[686] Abol civ 1913 pt to Middlesbrough CP, pt to West Acklam AP.[19] *Parl* N Riding (ent 1832—67, pt 1867—85), pt Middlesb. Parl Bor (1867—1918), pt Clev Dv (1885—1918). *Eccl* Middlesb. RDn. Eccl bdry: 1900,[23] 1901 (help cr Middlesbrough St Aidan EP),[216] 1902 (help cr Middlesbrough St Cuthbert EP),[336] 1902,[119] 1925,[493] 1936 (help cr Middlesbrough St Oswald EP),[24] 1939 (help cr Middlesbrough St Martin EP),[195] 1967.[113]

LINTHWAITE

[W Riding] Chap in Almondbury AP, sep CP 1866,[2] sep EP 1833,[9] eccl refounded 1843.[79] *LG* Agb. Wap, Hudd. PLU, Linthwaite USD, UD. Abol civ 1937 pt to Hudd. CB (assoc with W Riding) & AP, pt to help cr Colne Valley UD & CP.[31] *Parl* W Riding (1832—67), pt Hudd. Parl Bor

(1867—1918), pt S'rn Dv of W Riding (1867—85), Colne Valley Dv (pt 1885—1918, ent 1918—48). *Eccl* Pontef. RDn (1833—57), Hudd. RDn (1857—1968), Blackmoorfoot RDn (1968—*).

LINTON

AP [W Riding] Usual civ spelling; for eccl see 'Linton in Craven'. Incl tps Grassington, Hebden, Thresfield (each a sep CP 1866[2]). *LG* Seq 112. Transf 1974 to N Yorks.[5] *Parl* Seq 41.

LINTON

[W Riding] Tp in Spofforth AP, sep CP 1866,[2] eccl severed 1877 and transf to Wetherby EP.[126] *LG* Claro Wap, Wethb. PLU, RSD, RD. Abol 1937 pt to Collingham AP, pt to Wetherby CP.[31] *Parl* W Riding (1832—67), N'rn Dv of W Riding (1867—85), Bark. Ash Dv (1885—1948).

LINTON IN CRAVEN

AP [W Riding] Usual eccl spelling; for civ and civ sep tps, see 1st 'Linton' above. *Eccl* Seq 36.

LINTON UPON OUSE

[N Riding] Tp in Newton upon Ouse AP, sep CP 1866.[2] *LG* Seq 28. Transf 1974 to N Yorks.[5] *Parl* Seq 16.

LISSETT

[E Riding] Tp in Beeford AP, sep CP 1866.[2] *LG* Hold. Wap, Bridl. PLU, RSD, RD. Abol 1935 ent to Ulrome CP.[13] *Parl* E Riding (1832—85), Buckr. Dv (1885—1948).

LITTLETHORPE

CP [W Riding] Cr 1894 by union Whitcliffe with Thorpe CP, the pt of Aismunderby with Bundgate CP not in Ripon MB, pt Ripon MB & AP.[53] *LG* Ripon PLU, RD (1894—1938), Ripon & Pateley Br. RD (1938—74). Bdry: 1900.[280] Transf 1974 to N Yorks.[5] *Parl* Ripon Dv/CC (1918—*).

LITTON

[W Riding] Tp in Arncliffe AP, sep CP 1866.[2] *LG* Seq 111. Transf 1974 to N Yorks.[5] *Parl* Seq 41.

LIVERSEDGE

[W Riding] Chap in Birstall AP, sep CP 1866,[2] sep EP 1817,[9] eccl refounded 1860 from the pt of the EP not severed 1847 or 1858 (see below).[250] *LG* Morley Wap, Dewsb. PLU, Liversedge USD, UD (1894—1915), Spenb. UD (1915—55), MB (1955—74). Civ bdry: 1937.[31] Transf 1974 to W Yorks.[5] *Parl* Seq 38. *Eccl* Pontef. RDn (1817—57), Dewsb. RDn (1857—83), Birstall RDn (1883—*). Eccl bdry: 1847 (help cr Robert Town EP),[275] 1858,[414] 1878 (help cr Cleckheaton St Luke EP),[415] 1900,[188] 1911 (cr Hightown EP),[578] 1934.[94]

LIVERTON

[N Riding] Chap in Easington AP, sep CP 1866,[2] sep EP 1923.[498] *LG* Langb. Lbty, Guisb. PLU, pt Loftus USD, pt Guisb. RSD, Loftus UD. Transf 1974 to Clev.[5] *Parl* Seq 9. *Eccl* Middlesb. RDn (1923—24), Guisb. RDn (1924—*).

LOCKINGTON

AP [E Riding] (Tp Lockington pt in this AP, pt in Kilnwick AP [the latter sep CP 1866 as 'Lockington in Kilnwick'[2]]). Incl pt tp Aike (sep CP 1866[2]). *LG* Seq 9. Addtl civ bdry alt: 1883,[243] 1894 (gains Lockington in Kilnwick CP),[687] 1935 (gains Aike CP).[13] Transf 1974 to Humb.[5] *Parl* Seq 4. *Eccl*

Harth. & Hull RDn (until 1857), N Harth. RDn (1857—66), Harth. RDn (1866—87), Bev. RDn (1887—*).

LOCKINGTON IN KILNWICK

[E Riding] The pt of tp Lockington (o'wise in Lockington AP) in Kilnwick AP, sep CP 1866.[2] *LG* Harth. Wap, Bev. PLU, RSD. Bdry: 1883.[243] Abol 1894 ent to Lockington AP.[687] *Parl* E Riding (1832—85), Hold. Dv (1885—1918).

LOCKTON

[N Riding] Chap in Middleton AP, sep CP 1866,[2] eccl formed pt 'Middleton with Cropton and Lockton' until Lockton eccl severed 1916 to help cr Levisham with Lockton EP.[683] *LG* Seq 61. Transf 1974 to N Yorks.[5] *Parl* Seq 20.

LOCKWOOD

[W Riding] Chap in Almondbury AP, sep CP 1866,[2] sep EP 1831,[9] eccl refounded 1843.[79] *LG* Agb. Wap, Hudd. PLU, MB (1868—89), CB (1889—1924), USD. Civ bdry: 1883.[52] Abol civ 1924 ent to Huddersfield AP.[83] *Parl* W Riding (1832—67), Hudd. Parl Bor (1867—1948). *Eccl* Pontef. RDn (1831—57), Hudd. RDn (1857—1968), Almondb. RDn (1968—*). Eccl bdry: 1865 (cr Rashcliffe EP),[311] 1873 (cr Newsome EP),[21] 1897 (help cr Crosland Moor EP).[319]

LOFTHOUSE

EP [W Riding] Cr 1843 from Rothwell AP[278]; for civ see 'Lofthouse with Carlton'. Pontef. RDn (1843—57), Wakef RDn (1857—94), Whitkirk RDn (1894—*). Bdry: 1952 (help cr Carlin How with Skinningrove EP, later called 'Carlin How'),[364] 1968.[339]

CP [W Riding] Cr 1937 by union Lofthouse with Carlton CP, Thorpe CP.[31] *LG* Rothw. UD. Transf 1974 to W Yorks.[5] *Parl* Norm. CC (1948—*).

LOFTHOUSE WITH CARLTON

[W Riding] Tp in Rothwell AP, sep CP 1866[2]; for eccl see prev entry. *LG* Agb. Wap, Wakef PLU (soon after 1837[112]—1930), Rothw. USD (1892—94), UD. Bdry: 1883.[284] Abol 1937 to help cr Lofthouse CP.[31] *Parl* W Riding (1832—67), S'rn Dv of W Riding (1867—85), Morley Dv (1885—1918) Rothw. Dv (1918—48).

LOFTUS

AP [N Riding] Sometimes 'Lofthouse'. *LG* Langb. Lbty, Guisb. PLU, pt Loftus USD, pt Guisb. RSD, Loftus UD. Bdry: 1921.[688] Transf 1974 to Clev.[5] *Parl* Seq 9. *Eccl* Clev. RDn (until 1862), Guisb. RDn (1862—78), Whitby RDn (1878—1929), Guisb. RDn (1929—*).

LONDESBOROUGH

AP [E Riding] Constituent tp called 'Londesborough with Easthorpe', qv for civ and parl organisation 1866—1935. *LG* Harth. Wap. *Parl* E Riding (1832—67). *Eccl* Seq 14.

CP [E Riding] Renaming of Londesborough with Easthorpe CP.[13] *LG* Pockl. RD. Transf 1974 to Humb.[5] *Parl* Bev. CC (1948—55), Howden CC (1955—*).

LONDESBOROUGH WITH EASTHORPE

[E Riding] Name for the constituent tp of Londesborough AP, used for civ purposes from 1866. *LG* Harth. Wap, Pockl. PLU, RSD, RD. Renamed 1935 'Londesborough'.[13] *Parl* E Riding (1832—85), Howdensh. Dv (1885—1948).

LITTLE LONDON

EP [W Riding] Cr 1846 from Leeds AP, Woodhouse EP.[107] Later called 'Leeds St Matthew'. Pontef. RDn (1846—57), Leeds RDn (1857—1971), Allert. RDn (1971—*). Bdry: 1849 (help cr Buslingthorpe EP),[54] 1881 (help cr Leeds All Souls EP),[647] 1967.[127]

LONGWOOD

[W Riding] Chap in Huddersfield AP, sep CP 1866,[2] sep EP 1799,[9] eccl refounded 1843.[37] *LG* Agb. Wap, Hudd. PLU, Longwood USD (1875—90), Hudd. CB (1890—1924), Hudd. USD (1890—94). Civ bdry: 1913.[689] Abol civ 1924 ent to Huddersfield AP.[83] *Parl* W Riding (1832—67), Hudd. Parl Bor (pt 1867—1918, ent 1918—48), pt S'rn Dv of W Riding (1867—85), pt Colne Valley Dv (1885—1918). *Eccl* Pontef. RDn (1799—1857), Hudd. RDn (1857—1968), Blackmoorfoot RDn (1968—*). Eccl bdry: 1877 (help cr Birchencliffe EP).[141]

LOTHERSDALE

[W Riding] Area in Carleton AP (eccl 'Carleton in Craven'), sep CP 1894,[349] sep EP 1844 incl pt Kildwick AP.[247] *LG* Skipton PLU, RD. Transf 1974 to N Yorks.[5] *Parl* Skipton Dv/CC (1918—*). *Eccl* Craven RDn (1844—57), Craven RDn, W'rn Dv (1857—1905), Craven RDn, E'rn Dv (1905—21), Skipton RDn (1921—*).

LOTHERTON CUM ABERFORD

[W Riding] Tp in Sherburn in Elmet AP, sep CP 1866,[2] eccl severed 1908 to help cr Aberford with Lotherton EP.[6] *LG* Seq 77. Transf 1974 to W Yorks.[5] *Parl* Seq 24.

LOVERSALL

[W Riding] Tp in Doncaster AP, sep civ identity early, sep EP 1766.[9] *LG* Seq 93. Civ bdry: 1936 (loses pt to Donc. CB [assoc with W Riding] & AP).[132] Transf 1974 to S Yorks.[5] *Parl* Seq 44. *Eccl* Donc. RDn.

LOW MOOR

EP [W Riding] Cr 1858 from Wibsey AP, orig dedication 'St Mark',[339] dedication changed 1963 to 'Holy Trinity'.[287] Bradf RDn (1858—1921), Bowl. RDn (1921—71), Bowl. & Horton RDn (1971—*). Bdry: 1882,[326] 1927,[67] 1967.[194]

LOWTHORPE

AP [E Riding] Collegiate, sep par from Dissolution.[690] Incl chap Ruston Parva (appropriated to Lowthorpe Collegiate Church, sep par from Dissolution[690]). *LG* Dick. Wap, Driff. PLU, RSD, RD. Abol civ 1935 ent to Harpham CP.[13] *Parl* E Riding (1832—85), Buckr. Dv (1885—1948). *Eccl* Dick. RDn (until 1857), N Harth. RDn (1857—62), S Dick. RDn (1862—66), Bridl. RDn (1866—*). Eccl bdry: 1929 (gains ex-par place [orig chap in Foston on the Wolds AP] Little Kelk).[567]

LUDDENDEN

EP [W Riding] Cr 1732 from Halifax AP (tps Midgley, Warley, tp Sawley [the last not sep for civ purposes later]).[9] Pontef. RDn (1732—1857), Halifax RDn

(1857—1967), Calder Valley RDn (1967—). Bdry: 1846 (help cr Mytholmroyd EP),[614] 1873 (help cr Luddenden Foot EP),[655] 1869 (help re-cr Sowerby Bridge EP [area of tp Warley]),[521] 1969.[27]

LUDDENDEN FOOT

EP [W Riding] Cr 1873 from Luddenden EP, Sowerby EP, Sowerby Bridge EP.[676] Halifax RDn (1873—1967), Calder Valley RDn (1967—*).

CP [W Riding] Cr 1894 by union of the pts in Luddenden Foot UD of Sowerby CP, Warley CP, Northowram EP.[691] LG Halifax PLU, Luddenden Foot UD. Abol 1937 to help cr Sowerby Bridge UD & CP.[31] Parl Sowerby Dv (1918—48).

LUND

AP [E Riding] LG Seq 9. Transf 1974 to Humb.[5] Parl E Riding (1832—85), Buckr. Dv (1885—1918), Howdensh. Dv (1918—48), Bev. CC (1948—55), Haltemp. CC (1955—*). Eccl Seq 10.

LUNDS

EP [N Riding] Cr 1737 from Aysgarth AP.[9] Catt. RDn (1737—1857), Catt. West RDn (1857—1928), Wensleyd. RDn (1928—*).

LUNDWOOD

EP [W Riding] Cr 1957 from Monk Bretton EP.[692] Barnsley RDn.

LUNEDALE

[N Riding] Tp in Romandkirk AP, sep CP 1866.[2] LG Seq 39. Bdry: 1883.[28] Transf 1974 to Durham.[5] Parl Seq 14.

LUPSET

CP [W Riding] Cr 1902 from Alverthorpe CP.[100] LG Wakef PLU, RD (1902—21), CB (1921—25). Bdry: 1921 (loses pt to Ossett MB & CP as remainder of Lupset transf to Wakef CB [assoc with W Riding]).[693] Abol 1925 ent to Wakefield AP.[694] Parl Rothw. Dv (1918—48).

EP [W Riding] Cr 1934 from Westgate Common EP, Thornes EP, Alverthorpe EP.[94] Wakef RDn.

LUTTONS

CP [E Riding] Cr 1935 by union Helperthorpe AP, Luttons Ambo CP.[13] LG Norton RD. Transf 1974 to N Yorks.[5] Parl Bev. CC (1948—55), Howden CC (1955—*).

LUTTONS AMBO

[E Riding] Tp in Weaverthorpe AP, sep CP 1866,[2] eccl severed 1858 to help cr Helperthorpe with Luttons Ambo EP,[610] 'Luttons Ambo' severed from latter 1874 to be sep EP.[611] LG Buckr. Wap, Driff. PLU, RSD, RD. Abol 1935 to help cr Luttons CP.[13] Parl E Riding (1832—85), Buckr. Dv (1885—1948). Eccl Buckr. RDn.

LYDGATE

EP [W Riding] Cr 1793 from Rochdale AP,[9] refounded 1844.[481] Manch RDn (1793—1847), Ashton under Lyne RDn (1847—72), Rochd. RDn (1872—93), Ashton under Lyne RDn (1893—1929), Oldham RDn (1929—*). Bdry: 1847 (help cr Friezeland EP [Yorks, Ches]),[86] 1860 (help refound Hey EP [Lancs, Yorks W Riding]),[695] 1869 (help cr Roughtown EP),[696] 1886 (help cr Scouthead EP [Yorks, Lancs]).[479]

LYTHE

AP [N Riding] Incl tp Egton (sep civ identity early, sep

EP 1807[9]), tp Barnby (sep CP 1866,[2] pt eccl severed 1868 to help cr Ugthorpe EP[188]), tps Ellerby, Hutton Mulgrave, Mickleby, Newton Mulgrave, Ugthorpe (each a sep CP 1866,[2] the 5 eccl united 1868 with pt tp Barnby and with tp Borrowby in Leake AP to cr Ugthorpe EP[188]. LG Seq 59. Addtl civ bdry alt: 1884,[13] 1932.[51] Transf 1974 to N Yorks.[5] Parl Seq 19. Eccl Seq 22. Addtl eccl bdry alt: 1850 (cr Grosmont EP,[9] eccl refounded 1852 [tp Newbiggin (not sep civ) from this par and pts of other pars, qv]).[258]

MALHAM

[W Riding] Tp in Kirkby in Malham Dale AP, sep CP 1866.[2] LG Seq 111. Transf 1974 to N Yorks.[5] Parl Seq 41.

MALHAM MOOR

[W Riding] Organisation as for Malham.

MALIN BRIDGE

EP [W Riding] Cr 1933 from Wadsley EP, Stannington EP, Walkley EP, Owlerton EP.[89] Ecclesfield RDn (1933—42), Hallam RDn (1942—*). Bdry: 1953.[654]

MALTBY

[N Riding] Tp in Stainton AP, sep CP 1866.[2] LG Seq 56. Bdry: 1968 (incl help cr Teesside CB [assoc with N Riding] & CP).[537] Transf 1974 to Clev.[5] Parl Seq 10.

MALTBY

AP [W Riding] Incl tp Hooton Levitt (sep CP 1866[2]). LG Straff. & Tick. Wap, Rotherh. PLU, RSD, RD (1894—1924), Maltby UD (1924—74). Addtl civ bdry alt: 1937.[31] Transf 1974 to S Yorks.[5] Parl Seq 48. Eccl Seq 42. Addtl eccl bdry alt: 1956 (incl help cr Bramley EP).[215]

MALTON

CP [N Riding] Cr 1896 by union New Malton CP, Old Malton AP.[527] LG Malton PLU, UD. Transf 1974 to N Yorks.[5] Parl Thirsk & Malton Dv/CC (1918—*).

NEW MALTON

[N Riding] Area in Old Malton AP, sep civ identity early, eccl comprised of 2 chaps of New Malton St Leonard, New Malton St Michael (each a sep EP 1855,[697] the 2 eccl united 1928 as 'New Malton' EP[698]). LG Ryed. Wap, New Malton Bor, Malton PLU, USD, UD. Abol 1896 to help cr Malton CP.[589] Parl Malton Parl Bor (1295, 1298, 1640—1885), Thirsk & Malton Dv (1885—1918). Eccl Malton RDn.

NEW MALTON ST LEONARD

EP [N Riding] Chap in area New Malton, in Old Malton AP, sep EP 1855[697]; for civ see 'New Malton'. Riddal RDn (1855—62), Malton RDn (1862—1928). Abol 1928 to help cr New Malton EP.[698]

NEW MALTON ST MICHAEL

EP [N Riding] Organisation as for New Malton St Leonard.

OLD MALTON

AP [N Riding] Incl area New Malton (sep bor, sep civ identity early; eccl comprised of 2 chaps New Malton St Leonard, New Malton St Michael, each a sep EP 1855,[697] the 2 eccl united 1928 as 'New

Malton' EP[698]). *LG* Ryed. Wap, pt New Malton Bor, Malton PLU, USD, UD. Abol 1896 to help cr Malton CP.[527] *Parl* Malton Parl Bor (pt until New Malton gained sep civ identity [see 'New Malton' above], Malton Parl Bor (area of this par, 1832—85), Thirsk & Malton Dv (1885—1918). *Eccl* Riddal RDn (until 1862), Malton RDn (1862—*).

MANFIELD
AP [N Riding] Tp 'Manfield' in E Gill. Wap; incl in W Gill. Wap tp Cliffe (sep CP 1866[2]). *LG* Darl. PLU, RSD, Croft RD. Transf 1974 to N Yorks.[5] *Parl* Seq 14. *Eccl* Seq 57.

MANNINGHAM
[W Riding] The following have 'Manningham' in their names. Insofar as any existed at a given time: *LG* Morley Wap, Bradf PLU, MB (1847—89), CB (1889—98), USD. *Parl* Bradf Parl Bor (1832—85); see Part III of the *Guide* for composition of Bradf Parl Bors (1885—1918) by wards of the MB. *Eccl* Pontef. RDn (cr—1857), Bradf RDn (1857—1971), Airedale RDn (1971—*).

CP1/EP1—MANNINGHAM [ST PAUL]—Tp in Bradford AP, sep CP 1866,[2] sep EP 1846 (pt tp Manningham).[166] Abol civ 1898 ent to Bradford AP.[65] Eccl bdry: 1860 (cr Girlington EP),[301] 1873,[636] 1875 (cr EP5),[90] 1881 (cr EP4),[137] 1910 (help cr EP2),[416] 1911,[365] 1927.[288] Abol eccl 1968 pt to help cr EP8, pt to EP4, pt to EP2.[328]

EP2—MANNINGHAM ST CHAD—Cr 1910 from EP1, Girlington EP.[416] Bdry: 1927,[288] 1968.[328]

EP3—MANNINGHAM ST JUDE—Cr 1846 from Bradford AP.[1] Bdry: 1865,[35] 1878 (cr EP6),[198] 1927,[288] 1959.[596] Abol 1968 to help cr EP8.[328]

EP4—MANNINGHAM ST LUKE—Cr 1881 from EP1.[137] Bdry: 1968.[328]

EP5—MANNINGHAM ST MARK—Cr 1875 from EP1.[90] Bdry: 1927.[288] Abol 1959 pt to EP1, pt to EP3.[596]

EP6—MANNINGHAM ST MARY MAGDALENE—Cr 1878 from EP3.[198] Bdry: 1927.[288] Abol 1958 to help cr EP7.[322]

EP7—MANNINGHAM ST MARY MAGDALENE WITH ST MICHAEL AND ALL ANGELS— Cr 1958 by union EP6, Bradford St Michael and All Angels EP.[322] Bdry: 1966 (help cr Bradford St Columba with St Andrew EP).[324]

EP8—MANNINGHAM ST PAUL WITH ST JUDE— Cr 1968 by union EP1, EP3.[328]

MANSTON
EP [W Riding] Cr 1849 from Barwick in Elmet AP.[146] Pontef. RDn (1849—57), Wethb. RDn (1857—61), Whitkirk RDn (1861—*). Bdry: 1873.[636]

MAPPLETON
AP [E Riding] Incl pt tps Great and Little Cowdens (sometimes 'Cowdens Ambo'), Great Hatfield, Withernwick (remainder of last constitutes Withernwick AP) (each of the first 2 a sep CP 1866[2]), tp Mappleton and Rowlstone (the main tp, sep CP 1866 by this name[2]) so that 'Mappleton' has no sep civ identity 1866—1935 (see following entry). *LG* Hold. Wap. *Parl* E Riding (1832—67). *Eccl* Pec jurisd Archdeacon of E Riding, contentious pec jurisd with Dean & Chapter of York (until 1836),

Hold. RDn (1836—49), N Hold. RDn (1849—66), Hornsea RDn (1866—1916), N Hold. RDn (1916—72). Eccl bdry: 1962.[60] Abol eccl 1972 to help cr Mappleton with Goxhill EP.[630]

CP [E Riding] Cr 1935 by union Great and Little Cowdens CP, Mappleton and Rowlston CP.[13] *LG* Hold. RD. Transf 1974 to Humb.[5] *Parl* Bridl. CC (1948—*).

MAPPLETON AND ROWLSTON
[E Riding] Tp in Mappleton AP, sep CP 1866.[2] *LG* Hold. Wap, Skirl. PLU, RSD, RD. Abol 1935 to help cr Mappleton CP.[13] *Parl* E Riding (1832—85), Hold. Dv (1885—1948).

MAPPLETON WITH GOXHILL
EP [E Riding] Cr 1972 by union Mappleton AP, area of Goxhill from Hornsea with Goxhill EP, area of Hatfield CP from Sigglesthorne AP.[630] N Hold. RDn.

MARFLEET
AP [E Riding] Anc chap, appropriated to religious house and sep from Dissolution.[699] *LG* Hold. Wap. Scul. PLU, RSD (1875—83), Kingst. upon Hull MB (1883—89), CB (1889—98), USD (1883—94). Abol civ 1898 ent to Sculcoates AP.[446] *Parl* E Riding (1832—85); see Part III of the *Guide* for composition of Hull Parl Bors (1885—1918) by wards of the MB. *Eccl* Hold. RDn (until 1849), S Hold. RDn (1849—62), Bev. RDn (1862—71), Kingst. upon Hull RDn (1871—*). Eccl bdry: 1952,[255] 1954 (help cr Kingston upon Hull St Aidan Southcoates EP).[489]

MARISHES
[N Riding] Tp in Pickering AP, sep CP 1866[2]; sometimes early 'Pickering Marishes'. *LG* Seq 61. Bdry: 1883,[16] 1887.[700] Transf 1974 to N Yorks.[5] *Parl* Seq 20.

MARKET WEIGHTON
AP [E Riding] Incl chap Shipton (sep CP 1866 as 'Shipton Thorpe',[2] sep EP 1849 as 'Shipton',[9] eccl united 1876 with chap Thorpe le Street in Nunburnholme AP to cr Shipton Thorpe EP[701]), tp Market Weighton and Arras (sep CP 1866[2]) so that 'Market Weighton' has no sep civ identity 1866—1935 (see following entry). *LG* Harth. Wap. *Parl* E Riding (1832—67). *Eccl* Pec jurisd Weigh. prebend (until 1836), Seq 14 thereafter.

CP [E Riding] Renaming 1935 of Market Weighton and Arras CP.[13] *LG* Pockl. RD. Transf 1974 to Humb.[5] *Parl* Bev. CC (1948—55), Howden CC (1955—*).

MARKET WEIGHTON AND ARRAS
[E Riding] Tp in Market Weighton AP, sep CP 1866.[2] *LG* Harth. Wap, Pockl. PLU, RSD, RD. Renamed 1935 'Market Weighton'.[13] *Parl* E Riding (1832—85), Howdensh. Dv (1885—1918).

MARKINGFIELD HALL
[W Riding] Ex-par place, sep CP 1858.[393] *LG* Ripon Lbty, not in a PLU (until 1866), Ripon PLU (1866—1930), RSD, RD (1894—1938), Ripon & Pateley Br. RD (1938—74). Transf 1974 to N Yorks.[5] *Parl* Seq 34.

MARKINGTON
EP [W Riding] Cr 1844 from Ripon AP[507]; for civ see following entry. Boroughbr. RDn (1844—49),

Ripon RDn (1849—*).

MARKINGTON WITH WALLERTHWAITE

[W Riding] Tp in Ripon AP, sep CP 1866[2]; for eccl see prev entry. *LG* Ripon Lbty, Gt Ouseb. GilbU (until 1854), Ripon PLU (1854—1930), RSD, RD (1894—1938), Ripon & Pateley Br. RD (1938—74). Bdry: 1937.[31] Transf 1974 to N Yorks.[5] *Parl* Seq 34.

MARR

AP [W Riding] Chap in Hickleton AP, sep par by 1535.[620] *LG* Seq 117. Transf 1974 to S Yorks.[5] *Parl* Seq 44. *Eccl* Seq 40.

MARRICK

AP [N Riding] *LG* W Gill. Wap, Richm. PLU (1837—40), Reeth PLU (1840—1930), RSD, RD. Transf 1974 to N Yorks.[5] *Parl* Seq 14. *Eccl* Richm. RDn (until 1857), Richm. West RDn (1857—1960). Abol eccl 1960 to help cr Grinton with Marrick EP.[138]

MARSDEN

[W Riding] Chap pt in Huddersfield AP, pt in Marsden AP, sep EP 1742,[9] eccl refounded 1868[80]; comprised of 2 tps, each a sep CP 1866,[2] 'Marsden in Huddersfield' and 'Marsden in Almondbury', qv. *Eccl* Pontef. RDn (1742—1857), Hudd. RDn (1857—1968), Blackmoorfoot RDn (1968—*).

CP [W Riding] Cr 1898 by union pars in Marsden UD: Marsden in Almondbury CP, Marsden in Huddersfield CP.[702] *LG* Hudd. PLU, Marsden UD. Abol 1937 to help cr Colne Valley UD & CP.[31] *Parl* Colne Valley Dv (1918—48).

MARSDEN IN ALMONDBURY

[W Riding] Tp in chap Marsden (qv for sep eccl status), in Almondbury AP, sep CP 1866.[2] *LG* Agb. Wap, Hudd. PLU, Marsden in Almondb. USD (1875—82), Marsden USD (1882—94), UD (1894—98). Abol 1898 to help cr Marsden CP.[702] *Parl* W Riding (1832—67), S'rn Dv of W Riding (1867—85), Colne Valley Dv (1885—1918).

MARSDEN IN HUDDERSFIELD

[W Riding] Tp in chap Marsden (qv for sep eccl status), in Huddersfield AP, sep CP 1866.[2] *LG* Agb. Wap, Hudd. PLU, Marsden in Hudd. USD (1875—82), Marsden USD (1882—94), UD (1894—98). Abol 1898 to help cr Marsden CP.[702] *Parl* As for Marsden in Almondbury.

MARSKE

AP [N Riding] Usual civ spelling (sometimes 'Markse by the Sea'; for eccl see 'Marske in Cleveland'). Incl tp Redcar (sep CP 1866,[2] sep EP 1830,[9] eccl refounded 1867 from Marske AP, Upleatham EP[471]). *LG* Langb. Lbty, Guisb. PLU, pt Redcar USD (1875—86), pt Saltburn by the Sea USD, pt Guisb. RSD, Guisb. RD (1894—1932), Saltburn and Marske by the Sea UD (1932—74). Addtl civ bdry alt: 1883,[16] 1886,[656] 1886,[703] 1894 (loses the pt in Saltburn by the Sea UD to cr Saltburn by the Sea CP),[431] 1932,[51] 1968 (help cr Teesside CB [assoc with N Riding] & CP).[537] Transf 1974 to Clev.[5] *Parl* Seq 9.

MARSKE

AP [N Riding] Sometimes 'Marske near Richmond'. *LG* Seq 38. Transf 1974 to N Yorks.[5] *Parl* Seq 14.

Eccl Seq 58.

MARSKE IN CLEVELAND

AP [N Riding] Usual eccl spelling; for civ organisation and for civ and eccl sep tp, see 1st 'Marske' above. *Eccl* Clev RDn (until 1862), Stokes. RDn (1862—78), Middlesb. RDn (1878—1924), Guisb. RDn (1924—*). Addtl eccl bdry alt: 1873 (cr Saltburn by the Sea EP),[21] 1952,[351] 1955.[457]

LONG MARSTON

AP [Ainsty (W Riding until 1449 and from 1836, indept jurisd 1449—1836)] Incl tps Angram, Hutton Wandesley (each a sep CP 1866[2]). *LG* Seq 71. Transf 1974 to N Yorks.[5] *Parl* Seq 23. *Eccl* Seq 29.

MARTON

[E Riding] Tp in Swine AP, sep CP 1866,[2] eccl severed 1867 to help cr Skirlaugh EP.[235] *LG* Hold. Wap, Skirl. PLU, RSD, RD. Abol 1935 to help cr Burton Constable CP.[13] *Parl* E Riding (1832—85), Hold. Dv (1885—1948).

MARTON

AP [N Riding] Sometimes 'Marton in Cleveland'. *LG* Langb. Lbty, Stokes. PLU (1837—75), Middlesb. PLU (1875—1930), pt Middlesb. MB (1866—89), pt Middlesb. CB (1889—94), pt Middlesb. USD, pt Middlesb. RSD, Middlesb. RD (1894—1932), Stokes. RD (1932—68). Civ bdry: 1894 (loses the pt in Middlesb. CB [assoc with N Riding] to Middlesbrough CP),[18] 1913 (loses pt to Middlesb. CB [assoc with N Riding] & CP),[3] 1929 (loses pt to Middlesb. CB [assoc with N Riding] & CP),[704] 1932 (incl loses pt to Middlesb. CB [assoc with N Riding] & CP).[20] Abol civ 1968 to help cr Teesside CB (assoc with N Riding) & CP.[537] *Parl* N Riding (1832—85), Clev Dv (1885—1948), Richm. CC (1948—70). *Eccl* Clev RDn (until 1862), Stokes. RDn (1862—78), Middlesb. RDn (1878—*). Eccl bdry: 1897 (help cr Linthorpe EP, later sometimes 'Middlesbrough St Barnabas'),[685] 1899,[351] 1925 (help refound Nunthorpe EP),[160] 1936 (help cr Middlesbrough St Oswald EP).[24]

MARTON

[N Riding] Tp in Sinnington AP, sep CP 1866.[2] *LG* Seq 61. Bdry: 1887.[49] Transf 1974 to N Yorks.[5] *Parl* Seq 22.

MARTON CUM GRAFTON

AP [W Riding] *LG* Seq 85. Civ bdry: 1960.[705] Transf 1974 to N Yorks.[5] *Parl* Seq 36. *Eccl* Pec jurisd prebend Knar. (early dissolved), Seq 52 thereafter. Eccl bdry: 1924 (help refound Arkendale EP).[77]

MARTON CUM MOXBY

AP [N Riding] Sometimes 'Marton in the Forest'. *LG* Seq 28. Civ bdry: 1883,[16] 1887.[547] Transf 1974 to N Yorks.[5] *Parl* Seq 16. *Eccl* Seq 18. Eccl bdry: 1836 (gains chap Farlington from Sheriff Hutton AP),[546] 1930.[657]

MARTON IN CRAVEN

AP [W Riding] Usual eccl spelling; for civ see 'Martons Both'. *Eccl* Seq 39.

MARTON LE MOOR

[N Riding] Chap pt in Topcliffe AP, pt in Kirby on the Moor AP, sep CP 1866,[2] sep EP 1731.[9] *LG* Seq 42. Transf 1974 to N Yorks.[5] *Parl* Seq 16. *Eccl* Bulmer RDn (1731—1862), Thirsk RDn (1862—*).

MARTONS BOTH

AP [W Riding] Usual civ spelling; for eccl see 'Marton in Craven'. *LG* Seq 112. Transf 1974 to N Yorks.[5] *Parl* Seq 41.

MASBOROUGH ST JOHN

EP [W Riding] Cr 1865 from Rotherham AP, Greasborough EP,[578] orig as 'Masborough St John the Evangelist'. Rotherh. RDn. Bdry: 1895 (cr Northfield EP).[706]

MASBOROUGH ST PAUL

EP [W Riding] Cr 1916 from Kimberworth EP.[413] Rotherh. RDn.

MASHAM

AP [N Riding] Incl tps Burton upon Ure, Ellingstring, Ellingstons, Fearby, Healy with Sutton, Ilton cum Pott, Swinton with Warthermarske (each a sep CP 1866[2]); also incl Nutwith and Roomer Common (waste area, common stinted pasture, abol 1934 ent to Swinton with Warthermarske CP[3]). *LG* E Hang Wap, Bedale PLU, Masham USD, UD (1894–1934), RD (1934–74). Addtl civ bdry alt: 1883,[16] 1886,[382] 1886,[525] 1934.[3] Transf 1974 to N Yorks.[5] *Parl* Seq 14. *Eccl* Pec jurisd Masham prebend (until 1836), Seq 55 thereafter.

MASHAM MOOR

[N Riding] Undivided moor. *LG* Masham UD. Abol 1934 pt to Colsterdale CP, pt to help cr Healey CP, pt to Ilton cum Pott CP.[3] *Parl* Richm. Dv (1918–48).

MAUNBY

[N Riding] Tp in Kirby Wiske AP, sep CP 1866.[2] *LG* Seq 36. Transf 1974 to N Yorks.[5] *Parl* Seq 16.

MEANWOOD

EP [W Riding] Cr 1847 from Chapel Allerton EP, Headingley EP.[70] Pontef. RDn (1847–57), Leeds RDn (1857–1971), Head. RDn (1971–*) Bdry: 1954,[127] 1967.[127]

MEAUX

[E Riding] Tp in Wawne AP, sep CP 1866.[2] *LG* Hold. Wap, Bev. PLU, RSD, RD. Abol 1935 ent to Wawne AP.[13] *Parl* E Riding (1832–85), Hold. Dv (1885–1948).

MELBECKS

[N Riding] Tp in Grinton AP, sep CP 1866,[2] sep EP 1841.[584] *LG* W Gill. Wap, Reeth PLU, RSD, RD. Transf 1974 to N Yorks.[5] *Parl* Seq 14. *Eccl* Catt. RDn (1841–57), Richm. West RDn (1857–*).

MELBOURNE

[E Riding] Tp in Thornton AP, sep CP 1866.[2] *LG* Seq 12. Transf 1974 to Humb.[5] *Parl* Seq 7.

MELMERBY

[N Riding] Tp in Coverham AP, sep CP 1866.[2] *LG* Seq 53. Transf 1974 to N Yorks.[5] *Parl* Seq 14.

MELMERBY

[N Riding] Tp in Wath AP, sep CP 1866.[2] *LG* Seq 44. Transf 1974 to N Yorks.[5] *Parl* Seq 16.

MELSONBY

AP [N Riding] Incl pt tp East Layton (sep CP 1866,[2] eccl severed 1918 from this par and from Stanwick AP and transf to Forcett EP[564]). *LG* Seq 38. Transf 1974 to N Yorks.[5] *Parl* Seq 14. *Eccl* Pec jurisd Dean of York (until 1836), Seq 57 thereafter.

MELTHAM

[W Riding] Chap in Almondbury AP, sep CP 1866,[2] pt eccl severed 1858 to help cr Helme EP,[521] pt eccl severed 1876 to help cr Wilshaw EP,[29] the remainder sep EP 1874 as 'Meltham'.[81] *LG* Agb. Wap, Hudd. PLU, Meltham USD, UD. Civ bdry: 1897,[628] 1938.[28] Transf 1974 to W Yorks.[5] *Parl* W Riding (1832–67), S'rn Dv of W Riding (1867–85), Colne Valley Dv/CC (1885–*). *Eccl* Hudd. RDn (1874–1968), Blackmoorfoot RDn (1968–*).

MELTHAM MILLS

EP [W Riding] Cr 1845 from Almondbury AP, Honley EP.[84] Pontef. RDn (1845–57), Hudd. RDn (1857–1968), Blackmoorfoot RDn (1968–*). Bdry: 1858 (help cr Helme EP),[479] 1876 (help cr Wilshaw EP).[29]

MELTON

[E Riding] Chap in Welton AP, sep CP 1866.[2] *LG* Howdensh. Wap, Scul. PLU, RSD, RD. Bdry: 1888.[707] Abol 1935 ent to Welton AP.[13] *Parl* E Riding (1832–85), Howdensh. Dv (1885–1948).

HIGH MELTON

AP [W Riding] Sometimes earlier 'Melton on the Hill'. *LG* Seq 117. Transf 1974 to S Yorks.[5] *Parl* Seq 44. *Eccl* Seq 40.

WEST MELTON

CP [W Riding] Cr 1894 from the pt of Brampton Bierlow CP in Wath upon Dearne UD.[329] *LG* Rotherh. PLU, Wath upon Dearne UD. Abol 1923 ent to Wath upon Dearne AP.[708] *Parl* Wentw. Dv (1918–48).

MENETHORPE

[E Riding] Tp in Westow AP, sep CP 1866.[2] *LG* Buckr. Wap, Malton PLU, RSD, Norton RD. Abol 1935 ent to Burythorpe AP.[13] *Parl* E Riding (1832–85), Buckr. Dv (1885–1948).

MENSTON

[W Riding] Tp in Otley AP, sep CP 1866,[2] eccl severed 1793 to help cr Burley in Wharfedale EP,[9] the latter refounded 1856 as Burley EP (see following entry for cr 1876 of Menston with Woodhead EP from the latter).[354] *LG* Skyr. Wap, Carlton GilbU (until 1869), Wharfed. PLU (1869–1930), RSD, RD. Abol 1937 pt to help cr Aireb. UD & CP, pt to Ilkley UD & AP, pt to Otley UD & AP.[31] *Parl* W Riding (1832–67), N'rn Dv of W Riding (1867–85), Otley Dv (1885–1918), Shipley Dv (1918–48).

MENSTON WITH WOODHEAD

EP [W Riding] Cr 1876 from Burley EP[365]; for civ see prev entry. Otley RDn.

MENTHORPE CUM BOWTHORPE

[E Riding] Tp pt in Hemingbrough AP, pt in Skipwith AP, sep CP 1866.[2] *LG* Ouse & Derw. Wap, Howden PLU, RSD, RD. Abol 1935 ent to North Duffield CP.[13] *Parl* E Riding (1832–85), Howdensh. Dv (1885–1948).

METHAM

[E Riding] Tp in Howden AP, sep CP 1866,[2] eccl severed 1858 to help refound Laxton EP.[440] *LG* Howdensh. Wap, Howden PLU, RSD, RD. Bdry: 1880 (help cr Bishopsoil CP),[142] 1880,[230] 1880.[709]

Abol 1935 pt to Laxton CP, pt to Howden AP, pt to Eastrington AP.[13] *Parl* E Riding (1832—85), Howdensh. Dv (1885—1948).

METHLEY

AP [W Riding] *LG* Agb. Wap, Gt Preston GilbU (until 1869), Pontef. PLU (1869—1930), Methley USD, UD. Abol civ 1937 pt to Rothw. UD & AP, pt to Castlef. UD & AP.[31] *Parl* W Riding (1832—67). S'rn Dv of W Riding (1867—85), Norm. Dv (1885—1948). *Eccl* Pontef. RDn (until 1857), Wakef RDn (1857—94), Whitkirk RDn (1894—1972). Eccl bdry: 1865 (help cr Whitwood Mere EP),[553] 1904 (help cr Mickletown EP).[300] Abol eccl 1972 to help cr Methley with Mickletown EP.[659]

METHLEY WITH MICKLETOWN

EP [W Riding] Cr 1972 by union Methley AP, Mickletown EP.[659] Whitkirk RDn.

MENWITH WITH DARLEY

[W Riding] Tp in Hampsthwaite AP, sep CP 1866.[2] *LG* Seq 89. *Parl* Seq 33.

MEXBOROUGH

AP [W Riding] Incl Ravensfield (pec jurisd Archdeacon of York, origins unsure, prob chap in this par,[710] sep civ identity early, sep EP 1743[9]), pt chap Swinton (sep CP 1866,[2] sep EP 1718[9]), tp Denaby (sep CP 1866[2]). *LG* Straff. & Tick. Wap, Donc. PLU, Mexborough USD, UD. Addtl civ bdry alt: 1883,[42] 1883,[711] 1938.[28] Transf 1974 to S Yorks.[5] *Parl* Seq 46. *Eccl* Pec jurisd Archdeacon of York (until 1836), Seq 46 thereafter. Addtl eccl bdry alt: 1898 (help cr Denaby Main EP),[63] 1974.[77]

MICKLEBY

[N Riding] Tp in Lythe AP, sep CP 1866,[2] eccl severed 1868 to help cr Ugthorpe EP.[188] *LG* Seq 59. Transf 1974 to N Yorks.[5] *Parl* Seq 19.

MICKLEFIELD

[W Riding] Tp (orig chap) in Sherburn in Elmet AP (eccl, 'Sherburn in Elmet with Lotherton'), sep CP 1866,[2] sep EP 1886.[113] *LG* Seq 78. Transf 1974 to W Yorks.[5] *Parl* Seq 24. *Eccl* Selby RDn.

MICKLETHWAITE

[W Riding] Tp in Collingham AP, sep CP 1866.[2] *LG* Skyr. Wap, Wethb. PLU (1861—1930), RSD, RD. Abol 1937 ent to Wetherby CP.[31] *Parl* W Riding (1832—67), N'rn Dv of W Riding (1867—85), Bark. Ash Dv (1885—1948).

MICKLETON

[N Riding] Tp in Romaldkirk AP, sep CP 1866.[2] *LG* Seq 39. Bdry: 1883.[285] Transf 1974 to Durham.[5] *Parl* Seq 14.

MICKLETOWN

EP [W Riding] Cr 1904 from Methley AP, Featherstone AP, Swillington AP.[300] Whitkirk RDn. Abol 1972 to help cr Methley with Mickletown EP.[659]

MICKLEY

EP [N Riding] Cr 1844 from Kirkby Malzeard AP.[133] Catt. RDn (1844—57), Ripon RDn (1857—77), Masham RDn (1877—1905), Ripon RDn (1905—*).

MIDDLEHAM

AP [N Riding] *LG* Seq 53. Transf 1974 to N Yorks.[5] *Parl* Seq 14. *Eccl* Royal pec (1481—1836), Catt. RDn (1836—66), Catt. West RDn (1866—1928),

Wensleyd. RDn (1928—*).

MIDDLESBROUGH

[N Riding] The following have 'Middlesbrough' in their names. Insofar as any existed at a given time: *LG* Langb. Lbty, Stock. PLU (1837—75), Middlesb. PLU (1875—1930), MB (1835—89), CB (1889—1967), USD. *Parl* N Riding (1832—67), Middlesb. Parl Bor (1867—1918); see Part III of the *Guide* for composition of Middlesb. East Parl Bor/BC, Middlesb. West Parl Bor/BC (1918—70) by wards of the CB. *Eccl* Clev RDn (cr—1862), Stokes. RDn (1862—78), Middlesb. RDn (1878—*).

CP1/EP1—MIDDLESBROUGH [ST HILDA]—Cell in Whitby Abbey, in West Acklam AP after Dissolution, sep civ identity early, sep EP 1744.[9] Incl tp Linthorpe (sep CP 1866,[2] sep EP 1897 from EP10, Marton AP[685]). Addtl civ bdry alt: 1883,[16] 1887,[17] 1894 (gains the pts in Middlesb. CB of West Acklam AP, Linthorpe CP, Marton AP, Normanby CP, Ormesby AP),[18] 1913,[19] 1929,[704] 1932.[20] Abol civ 1968 to help cr Teesside CB (assoc with N Riding) & CP.[537] Addtl eccl bdry alt: 1864 (cr EP10).[405] Abol eccl 1963 to help cr EP9.[250]

EP2—MIDDLESBROUGH ALL SAINTS—Cr 1879 from EP10, EP13, West Acklam AP.[22] Bdry: 1901 (help cr EP4),[216] 1902,[521] 1903 (help cr EP6),[436] 1925,[493] 1972 (gains EP9).[82]

EP3—MIDDLESBROUGH THE ASCENSION—Cr 1966 from Ormesby AP, North Ormesby EP.[712]

EP4—MIDDLESBROUGH ST AIDAN—Cr 1901 from Linthorpe EP, EP13, EP10, EP2.[216] Bdry: 1925,[493] 1967.[113]

—MIDDLESBROUGH ST BARNABAS—Name sometimes used for EP cr 1897 as 'Linthorpe', qv.

EP5—MIDDLESBROUGH ST CHAD—Cr 1950 from EP12, West Acklam AP.[26]

EP6—MIDDLESBROUGH ST COLUMBA—Cr 1903 from EP2.[436] Bdry: 1921,[213] 1925,[493] 1940.[11] Abol 1966 to help cr EP7.[273]

EP7—MIDDLESBROUGH ST COLUMBA WITH ST PAUL—Cr 1966 by union EP6, EP13 (all except pt transf 1967 to EP8 by supplementary order, qv).[273]

EP8—MIDDLESBROUGH ST CUTHBERT—Cr 1902 from EP13, EP10, Linthorpe EP.[364] Bdry: 1925,[493] 1939 (help cr EP11),[25] 1967 (gains pt of EP13 orig transf 1966 to help cr EP7).[713]

EP9—MIDDLESBROUGH ST HILDA WITH ST PETER—Cr 1963 by union EP1, EP14.[250] Abol 1972 ent to EP2.[82]

EP10—MIDDLESBROUGH ST JOHN THE EVANGELIST—Cr 1864 from EP1.[405] Bdry: 1872 (help cr EP13),[22] 1874 (cr EP14),[508] 1879 (help cr EP2),[22] 1897 (help cr Linthorpe EP, later sometimes 'Middlesbrough St Barnabas' EP),[685] 1899,[351] 1900,[23] 1901 (help cr EP4),[216] 1902 (help cr EP8),[364] 1921,[213] 1925.[493]

EP11—MIDDLESBROUGH ST MARTIN—Cr 1939 from Linthorpe EP, EP8, West Acklam AP.[25]

EP12—MIDDLESBROUGH ST OSWALD—Cr 1936

from Linthorpe EP, Marton AP, West Acklam AP.[24] Bdry: 1950 (help cr EP5).[26]

EP13—MIDDLESBROUGH ST PAUL—Cr 1872 from EP10, West Acklam AP.[21] Bdry: 1879 (help cr EP2),[22] 1901 (help cr EP4),[216] 1902,[521] 1902 (help cr EP8),[364] 1925,[493] 1940.[11] Abol 1966 to help cr EP7,[273] but supplementary order 1967 transf pt to EP8.[713]

EP14—MIDDLESBROUGH ST PETER—Cr 1874 from EP10.[508] Bdry: 1925.[493] Abol 1963 to help cr EP9.[250]

EP15—MIDDLESBROUGH ST THOMAS—Cr 1951 from North Ormesby EP.[714]

MIDDLESMOOR

EP [W Riding] Cr 1743 from Kirkby Malzeard AP,[9] pt severed 1844 to help cr Ramsgill EP,[133] the remainder refounded 1863 as 'Middlesmoor'.[493] Pec jurisd Masham prebend (until 1836), Ripon RDn (1836—77), Masham RDn (1877—1905), Nidd. RDn (1905—71), Ripon RDn (1971—*).

MIDDLESTOWN

EP [W Riding] Cr 1878 from Thornhill AP, Flockton cum Denby Grange EP.[198] Dewsb. RDn (1878—1913), Wakef RDn (1913—*). Bdry: 1882 (help cr Horbury Bridge EP).[130]

MIDDLETHORPE

[Ainsty (W Riding until 1449 and from 1836, indept jurisd 1449—1836)] Tp in York St Mary Bishophill Senior AP, sep CP 1866.[2] LG York PLU, pt York MB (1884—89), pt York CB (1889—1900), pt York USD (1884—94), York RSD (ent 1875—84, pt 1884—94). Abol 1894 the pt in the CB cr Middlethorpe Within CP, the remainder cr Middlethorpe Without CP.[51] Parl N Riding (1832—85), pt York Parl Bor, pt Thirsk & Malton Dv (1885—1918).

MIDDLETHORPE WITHIN

CP [York CB] Cr 1894 from the pt of Middlethorpe CP (o'wise W Riding) in York CB.[51] LG York PLU, CB. Abol 1900 to help cr York CP.[423]

MIDDLETHORPE WITHOUT

CP [W Riding] Cr 1894 from the pt of Middlethorpe CP not in York CB.[51] LG York PLU, Bp'thorpe RD. Abol 1937 ent to York CB (not assoc with a Riding) & CP.[31] Parl Bark. Ash Dv (1918—48).

MIDDLETON

CP [E Riding] Renaming 1935 of Middleton on the Wolds AP.[13] LG Driff. RD. Transf 1974 to Humb.[5] Parl Bridl. CC (1948—55), Howden CC (1955—*).

MIDDLETON

AP [N Riding] Incl chap Cropton (sep CP 1866[2]), chap Lockton (sep CP 1866,[2] eccl severed 1916 to help cr Levisham with Lockton EP[683]), chap Rosedale, East Side (sep CP 1866,[2] eccl severed 1739 to help cr Rosedale EP,[9] confirmed 1876[653]), tps Aislaby, Cawthorn, Hartoft, Middleton, Wrelton (each a sep CP 1866[2]); also incl eccl ex-par place Turnhill (sep CP 1858[393] but sep civ status not sustained, sep eccl status not sustained). This par eccl called 'Middleton with Cropton and Lockton' until 1916, 'Middleton with Cropton' thereafter, qv. LG Seq 61. Civ bdry: 1883,[16] 1887,[715] 1887.[49] Transf 1974 to N Yorks.[5] Parl Seq 22.

MIDDLETON

[W Riding] Tp in Ilkley AP, sep CP 1866.[2] LG Seq 83. Transf 1974 to N Yorks.[5] Parl Seq 30.

MIDDLETON

[W Riding] Tp in Rothwell AP, sep CP 1866,[2] sep EP 1849.[146] LG Agb. Wap, Gt Preston GilbU (until 1869), Hunslet PLU (1869—1920), RSD, RD. Abol civ 1920 ent to Leeds CB (assoc with W Riding) & to Hunslet CP.[646] Parl W Riding (1832—67), S'rn Dv of W Riding (1867—85), Morley Dv (1885—1918), Rothw. Dv (1918—48). Eccl Pontef. RDn (1849—57), Wakef RDn (1857—94), Whitkirk RDn (1894—1971), Armley RDn (1971—*). Eccl bdry: 1901 (help cr Stourton EP),[366] 1935 (cr Middleton St Cross EP),[133] 1938 (help cr Leeds St John and St Barnabas, Belle Isle EP),[575] 1967,[127] 1968.[339]

MIDDLETON ON THE WOLDS

AP [E Riding] LG Harth. Wap, Driff. PLU, RSD, RD. Renamed civ 1935 'Middleton'.[13] Parl E Riding (1832—85), Buckr. Dv (1885—1948). Eccl Pec jurisd Bev. (until 1836), Seq 10 thereafter.

MIDDLETON QUERNHOW

[N Riding] Chap in Wath AP, sep CP 1866.[2] LG Seq 44. Transf 1974 to N Yorks.[5] Parl Seq 16.

MIDDLETON ST CROSS

EP [W Riding] Cr 1935 from Middleton EP.[133] Whitkirk RDn (1935—71), Armley RDn (1971—*). Bdry: 1968.[339]

MIDDLETON TYAS

AP [N Riding] Tp 'Middleton Tyas' sometimes early called 'Middleton Tyas with Kneeton', the shorter form more often and later used. Incl tp Moulton (orig a chap, dilapidated by 16th cent, new chap built later but not sep eccl, area a sep CP 1866[2]). LG Seq 35. Transf 1974 to N Yorks.[5] Parl Seq 14. Eccl Seq 57.

MIDDLETON UPON LEVEN

[N Riding] Chap in Rudby in Cleveland AP, sep CP 1866,[2] sep EP 1740[9] but sep eccl status not sustained. LG Seq 58. Transf 1974 to N Yorks.[5] Parl Seq 11. Eccl Clev RDn.

MIDDLETON WITH CROPTON

AP [N Riding] Name used after 1916 (see following entry for earlier) for eccl purposes; for civ and for civ and eccl sep chaps and tps, see 2nd 'Middleton' above. Eccl Malton RDn (1916—28), Pick. RDn (1928—*).

MIDDLETON WITH CROPTON AND LOCKTON

AP [N Riding] Usual eccl name; for civ and civ and eccl sep chaps and tps, see 2nd 'Middleton' above. Eccl Riddal RDn (until 1862), Malton RDn (1862—1916). Loses chap Lockton 1916 to help cr Levisham with Lockton EP, the remainder to be 'Middleton with Cropton',[683] qv in prev entry.

MIDDOP

[W Riding] Tp in Gisburn AP, sep CP 1866.[2] LG Seq 108. Transf 1974 to Lancs.[5] Parl Seq 41.

MIDGLEY

[W Riding] Tp in Halifax AP, sep CP 1866,[2] eccl severed 1732 to help cr Luddenden EP.[9] LG Morley Wap, Halifax PLU, pt Midgley USD (reduced pt 1891—94), pt Mytholmroyd USD (1891—94), pt

Luddenden Foot USD, Midgley UD. Bdry: 1894 (loses the pt in Mytholmroyd UD to help cr Mytholmroyd CP,[563] loses the pt in Luddenden Foot UD to help cr Luddenden Foot CP[691]). Abol 1939 pt to Wadsworth CP, pt to Sowerby Bridge UD & CP.[77] *Parl* W Riding (1832—67), E'rn Dv of W Riding (1867—85), Sowerby Dv (1885—1948).

MIDHOPE
EP [W Riding] Cr 1741 from Ecclesfield AP.[9] Donc. RDn (1741—1857), Rotherh. RDn (1857—62), Ecclesfield RDn (1862—1914), Silkst. RDn (1914—27), Barnsley RDn (1927—*).

MILBY
[Tp pt in Aldborough AP (W Riding, Claro Wap), pt in Kirby on the Moor AP (N Riding, Hallik. Wap), sep CP 1866[2] with pt in both Ridings] *LG* Gt Ouseb. GilbU (until 1854), PLU (1854—95), RSD, Thirsk PLU (1895—1930), pt sep RD in W Riding (1894—95), Thirsk RD (pt 1894—95, ent 1895—1974). Made 1895 ent N Riding.[492] Transf 1974 to N Yorks.[5] *Parl* Pt N Riding (1832—85), pt W Riding (1832—67), pt N'rn Dv of W Riding (1867—85), pt Ripon Dv (1885—1918), Thirsk & Malton Dv/CC (pt 1885—1918, ent 1918—*).

SOUTH MILFORD
[W Riding] Tp in Sherburn in Elmet AP, sep CP 1866,[2] sep EP 1859 by union of this tp, addtl area from tp Sherburn in Elmet, pt tp Huddlestone cum Lumby in the same par, pt Fryston EP.[299] *LG* Seq 78. Civ bdry: 1937.[31] Transf 1974 to N Yorks.[5] *Parl* Seq 24. *Eccl* New Ainsty RDn (1857—62), Tadc. RDn (1862—71), Selby RDn (1871—*).

MILLHOUSES
EP [W Riding] Cr 1930 from Sheffield St Oswald EP.[210] Sheff RDn (1930—42), Ecclesall RDn (1942—*). Bdry: 1959.[508]

MILLINGTON
CP [E Riding] Cr 1935 by union Great Givendale with Grimthorpe CP, Millington with Little Givendale CP, Ousethorpe CP, pt Bishop Wilton with Belthorpe CP.[13] *LG* Pockl. RD. Transf 1974 to Humb.[5] *Parl* Bev. CC (1948—55), Howden CC (1955—*).

MILLINGTON WITH LITTLE GIVENDALE
[E Riding] Chap in Great Givendale with Grimthorpe AP (qv for orig status), sep CP 1866,[2] sep EP 1870.[574] *LG* Harth. Wap, Pockl. PLU, RSD, RD. Abol civ 1935 to help cr Millington CP.[13] *Parl* E Riding (1832—85), Howdensh. Dv (1885—1948). *Eccl* Pec jurisd Dean of York (until 1836), Harth. & Hull RDn (1836—57), W Buckr. RDn (1857—66), Pockl. RDn (1866—*).

MILNSBRIDGE
EP [W Riding] Cr 1846 from Almondbury AP.[85] Pontef. RDn (1846—57), Hudd. RDn (1857—1968), Blackmoorfoot RDn (1968—*). Bdry: 1897 (help cr Crosland Moor EP).[319]

MINSKIP
[W Riding] Tp in Aldborough AP, sep CP 1866.[2] *LG* Claro Wap, Gt Ouseb. GilbU (until 1854), PLU (1854—1930), RSD, RD. Abol 1938 ent to Boroughbridge CP.[28] *Parl* W Riding (1832—67), N'rn Dv of W Riding (1867—85), Ripon Dv (1885—1948).

MIRFIELD
AP [W Riding] *LG* Agb. Wap, Dewsb. PLU, pt Mirfield USD, pt Ravensthorpe USD, Mirfield UD. Civ bdry: 1894 (the pt in Ravensthorpe UD cr Ravensthorpe CP),[257] 1895.[716] Transf 1974 to W Yorks.[5] *Parl* W Riding (1832—67), pt Dewsb. Parl Bor (1867—1918), pt S'rn Dv of W Riding (1867—85), pt Morley Dv (1885—1918), Spen Valley Dv (1918—48), Dewsb. BC (1948—*). *Eccl* Seq 48. Eccl bdry: 1841 (cr Battyeford EP),[217] 1860 (help cr Upper Hopton EP),[301] 1870 (cr Ravensthorpe EP),[405] 1881 (help cr Eastthorpe EP).[218]

MITTON
AP [Pt in Lancs (Blackb. Hd), pt in Yorks W Riding (Staincl. & Ewc. Wap) until 1866, ent Yorks W Riding thereafter] Incl in Lancs tp Aighton, Bailey and Chaigley (sep CP 1866 in Lancs,[2] the area of Bailey eccl severed 1839 along with pt tp Mitton to cr Hurst Green EP,[9] eccl refounded 1870[180]); remainder in Yorks W Riding (Staincl. & Ewc. Wap): chap Grindleton (sep CP 1866,[2] sep EP 1741,[9] eccl refounded 1844 from this par, Sawley ex-par place[582]), chap Waddington (sep CP 1866,[2] sep EP 1739[9]), tps Bashall Eaves, West Bradford, Great Mitton (each a sep CP 1866[2]) so that 'Mitton' has no sep civ identity after 1866. *Parl* Yorks pt, W Riding (1832—67). *Eccl* Seq 38.

GREAT MITTON
[W Riding] Tp in Mitton AP, sep CP 1866.[2] *LG* Seq 108. Transf 1974 to Lancs.[5] *Parl* Seq 41.

MOLD GREEN
EP [W Riding] Cr 1864 from Kirkheaton AP.[246] Hudd. RDn (1864—1968), Almondb. RDn (1968—*). Bdry: 1963 (help cr Rawthorpe EP).[287]

MOLESCROFT
[E Riding] Tp pt in Leconfield (Harth. Wap), pt in Beverley St John AP (Bev. Lbty), sep CP 1866.[2] *LG* Bev. PLU, RSD, RD. Transf 1974 to Humb.[5] *Parl* Bev. Parl Bor (1832—70), Seq 4 thereafter.

MONK BRETTON
[W Riding] Tp in Royston AP, sep CP 1866,[2] sep EP 1843 incl tp Cudworth in same par.[331] *LG* Staincr. Wap, Barnsley PLU, Monk Bretton USD, UD. Abol civ 1921 ent to Barnsley CB (assoc with W Riding) & CP.[209] *Parl* W Riding (1832—67), S'rn Dv of W Riding (1867—85), Barnsley Dv (1885—1918), Barnsley Parl Bor (1918—48). *Eccl* Donc. RDn (1843—57), Rotherh. RDn (1857—62), Pontef. RDn (1862—1916), Hemsw. RDn (1916—27), Barnsley RDn (1927—*). Eccl bdry: 1893 (the orig area of tp Cudworth severed to cr Cudworth EP),[188] 1957 (cr Lundwood EP),[692] 1973 (incl help cr Athersley EP).[145]

MONKHILL
[W Riding] Tp in Pontefract AP, sep CP 1866.[2] *LG* Osg. Wap, not in a PLU (until 1862), Pontef. PLU (1862—92), Pontef. MB (1875—92), Pontef. USD. Abol 1892 ent to Pontefract AP.[717] *Parl* Pontef. Parl Bor (1832—1918).

BISHOP MONKTON
[W Riding] Chap in Ripon AP, sep CP 1866,[2] sep EP 1746 (incl tp Westwick in same par),[9] eccl refounded 1863.[163] *LG* Seq 41. Transf 1974 to N

Yorks.[5] *Parl* Seq 28. *Eccl* Pec jurisd Lbty Ripon (until 1836), Boroughbr. RDn (1836—49), Ripon RDn (1849—*). Eccl bdry: 1866.[627]

MOOR MONKTON

AP [Ainsty (W Riding until 1449 and from 1836, indept jurisd 1449—1836)] Incl tp Hessay (sep CP 1866[2]). *LG* Seq 72. Addtl civ bdry alt: 1888.[718] Transf 1974 to N Yorks.[5] *Parl* Seq 23. *Eccl* Seq 29.

NUN MONKTON

AP [W Riding] Orig nunnery, sep par from Dissolution. *LG* Seq 86. Civ bdry: 1888.[718] Transf 1974 to N Yorks.[5] *Parl* Seq 36. *Eccl* Seq 52.

MOOR TOWN

[E Riding] Tp in Brandesburton AP, sep CP 1866.[2] *LG* Hold. Wap, Skirl. PLU, RSD, RD. Abol 1935 ent to Brandesburton AP.[13] *Parl* E Riding (1832—85), Hold. Dv (1885—1948).

MOORENDS

EP [W Riding] Cr 1956 from Thorne AP.[719] Snaith RDn.

MOORFIELDS

EP [W Riding] Cr 1846 from Sheffield AP.[493] Donc. RDn (1846—57), Rotherh. RDn (1857—62), Sheff RDn (1862—1938). Abol 1938 to help cr Sheffield (The Cathedral Benefice) EP.[720]

MOORSHOLM

[N Riding] Tp in Skelton AP, sep CP 1866.[2] *LG* Langb. Lbty, Guisb. PLU, Skelton in Clev USD (1875—84), Skelton & Brotton USD (1884—94), UD. Bdry: 1886.[656] Transf 1974 to Clev.[5] *Parl* Seq 9.

MORLEY

AP [W Riding] Orig sep AP, usurped by Presbyterian trustees and thereafter in Batley AP, sep CP 1866,[2] sep EP 1831,[9] eccl refounded 1832.[85] *LG* Agb. Wap, Dewsb. PLU, Morley USD, MB (1884—1974). Civ bdry: 1894 (gains the pt of Ardsley West CP in Morley MB),[118] 1937.[31] Transf 1974 to W Yorks.[5] *Parl* W Riding (1832—67), S'rn Dv of W Riding (1867—85), Morley Dv (1885—1918), Batley & Morley Parl Bor/BC (1918—*). *Eccl* Pontef. RDn (until 1857), Dewsb. RDn (1857—66), Birstall RDn (1866—83), Dewsb. RDn (1883—1927), Birstall RDn (1927—*). Eccl bdry: 1878 (help cr Morley St Paul Townend EP),[211] 1892 (help cr Bruntcliffe EP).[655]

MORLEY ST PAUL TOWNEND

EP [W Riding] Cr 1878 from Morley EP, Batley AP.[211] Dewsb. RDn (1878—1927), Birstall RDn (1927—*). Bdry: 1892 (help cr Bruntcliffe EP),[655] 1913.[119]

MORTOMLEY

EP [W Riding] Cr 1925 from Chapeltown EP, Tankersley AP.[407] Ecclesfield RDn (1925—42), Tankersley RDn (1942—*).

MORTON

[N Riding] Tp in Ormesby AP, sep CP 1866.[2] *LG* Langb. Lbty, Guisb. PLU, RSD, RD (1894—1932), UD (1932—74). Bdry: 1968 (help cr Teesside CB [assoc with N Riding] & CP).[5] Transf 1974 to Clev.[5] *Parl* Seq 9.

MORTON

[W Riding] Tp (sometimes earlier 'East and West Morton') in Bingley AP, sep CP 1866,[2] sep EP 1845 incl pt tp Bingley.[244] *LG* Skyr. Wap, Keigh. PLU, RSD, RD. Civ bdry: 1895.[271] Abol civ 1938 ent to Keigh. MB & AP.[28] *Parl* W Riding (1832—67), N'rn Dv of W Riding (1867—85), Otley Dv (1885—1918), Keigh. Dv (1918—48). *Eccl* Craven RDn (1845—57), Craven RDn, S'rn Dv (1857—1921), Craven RDn (1921—*). Eccl bdry: 1874 (cr Riddlesden EP).[168]

MORTON UPON SWALE

[N Riding] Tp in Ainderby Steeple AP, sep CP 1866.[2] *LG* Seq 34. Transf 1974 to N Yorks.[5] *Parl* Seq 14.

MOSS

[W Riding] Tp pt in Campsall AP, pt in Kirk Bramwith AP, sep CP 1866,[2] sep EP 1875 from Fenwick EP (orig in Campsall AP, qv), Burghwallis AP, Owston AP, Kirk Sandall AP, Kirk Bramwith AP.[11] *LG* Seq 94. Civ bdry: 1883.[42] Transf 1974 to S Yorks.[5] *Parl* Seq 27. *Eccl* Donc. RDn.

MOSSDALE MOOR

[N Riding] Land Common to Bainbridge and to Hawes. *LG* Aysg. RD. Abol 1934 ent to Hawes CP.[3] *Parl* Richm. Dv (1918—48).

MOULTON

[N Riding] Chap in Middleton Tyas AP, church dilapidated by 16th cent, new chap built later but not sep eccl,[721] this area then considered a tp, sep CP 1866.[2] *LG* Seq 35. Transf 1974 to N Yorks.[5] *Parl* Seq 14.

MOUNT PELLON

EP [W Riding] Cr 1855 from Halifax AP.[593] Halifax RDn. Bdry: 1912 (help cr Halifax St Hilda EP),[596] 1927.[67]

MUKER

[N Riding] Tp in Grinton AP, sep CP 1866,[2] sep EP 1719,[9] eccl refounded 1843.[334] *LG* Seq 37. Civ bdry: 1911 (areas determined and altered for this par and for Westm pars of Hartley CP, Kaber CP, Winton CP).[722] Transf 1974 to N Yorks.[5] *Parl* Seq 14. *Eccl* Catt. RDn (1719—1857), Richm. West RDn (1857—*).

MURTON

[N Riding] Ex-par place, sep CP 1858.[393] *LG* Birdf. Wap, Helm. PLU (soon after 1837[112]—1930), RSD, RD. Transf 1974 to N Yorks.[5] *Parl* Seq 16.

MURTON

[N Riding] Chap (pec jurisd Strensall prebend until 1836) in Osbaldwick AP, sep CP 1866.[2] *LG* Seq 32. Transf 1974 to N Yorks.[5] *Parl* Seq 16.

MUSCOATES

[N Riding] Tp in Kirkdale AP, sep CP 1866.[2] *LG* Seq 64. Bdry: 1887.[538] Transf 1974 to N Yorks.[5] *Parl* Seq 21.

MUSTON

AP [E Riding] Orig chap in Nunmanby AP, sep par 1269.[643] *LG* Seq 7. Civ bdry: 1935.[13] Transf 1974 to N Yorks.[5] *Parl* Seq 2. *Eccl* Seq 4.

MYTHOLMROYD

EP [W Riding] Cr 1840 from area Hebden Bridge in Halifax AP,[9] refounded 1846 from Heptonstall EP, Luddenden EP, Sowerby EP.[614] Pontef. RDn (1840—57), Halifax RDn (1857—1967), Calder Valley RDn (1967—*).

CP [W Riding] Cr 1894 by union pts of following in Mytholmroyd UD: Erringden CP, Midgley CP, Sowerby CP, Wadsworth CP.[533] *LG* Todmorden PLU, Mytholmroyd UD. Abol 1937 to help cr Hebden Royal UD & CP.[31] *Parl* Sowerby Dv (1918—48).

MYTON ON SWALE
AP [N Riding] *LG* Seq 28. Transf 1974 to N Yorks.[5] *Parl* Seq 16. *Eccl* Seq 18.

NABURN
[Chap of Naburn pt in Ainsty (W Riding until 1449 and from 1836, indept jurisd 1449—1836), pt in E Riding (Ouse & Derw. Wap)] Chap pt in Acaster Malbis AP, pt in York St George AP, the latter from 1586 eccl York St Denys and St George,[723] sep CP 1866,[2] sep EP 1842.[7] *LG* York PLU, RSD, Escr. RD (1894—1935), Derw. RD (1935—74). Transf 1974 to N Yorks.[5] *Parl* Pt E Riding, pt N Riding (1832—85), pt Thirsk & Malton Dv (1885—1918), Howdensh. Dv (pt 1885—1918, ent 1918—48), Howden CC (1948—*). *Eccl* City of York RDn (1842—62), Tadc. RDn (1862—71), Bp'thorpe RDn (1871—96), Escr. RDn (1896—*).

NAFFERTON
AP [E Riding] Incl tp Wansford (sep CP 1866,[2] sep EP 1907[724]). *LG* Seq 6. Addtl civ bdry alt: 1884,[350] 1935.[13] Transf 1974 to Humb.[5] *Parl* Seq 3. *Eccl* Dick. RDn (until 1857), N Harth. RDn (1857—66), Scarb. RDn (1866—87), Harth. RDn (1887—*).

NAPPA
[W Riding] Tp in Gisburn AP, sep CP 1866.[2] *LG* Seq 111. Transf 1974 to N Yorks.[5] *Parl* Seq 41.

NAWTON
[N Riding] Tp in Kirkdale AP, sep CP 1866.[2] *LG* Seq 64. Bdry: 1887.[538] Transf 1974 to N Yorks.[5] *Parl* Seq 21.

NEEPSEND
EP [W Riding] Cr 1868 from Pitsmoor EP.[208] Sheff RDn (1868—1942), Ecclesfield RDn (1942—52). Abol 1952 to help cr Wicker with Neepsend EP.[725]

NESFIELD WITH LANGBAR
[W Riding] Tp in Ilkley AP, sep CP 1866.[2] *LG* Seq 83. Transf 1974 to N Yorks.[5] *Parl* Seq 30.

NESS
CP [N Riding] Cr 1887 by union East Ness CP, West Ness CP.[726] *LG* Ryed. Wap, Kirkby Moors. PLU, RSD, RD. Transf 1974 to N Yorks.[5] *Parl* Thirsk & Malton Dv/CC (1918—*).

EAST NESS
[N Riding] Tp in Hovingham AP, sep CP 1866,[2] pt eccl severed 1931 and transf to Nunnington AP.[632] *LG* Ryed. Wap, Kirkby Moors. PLU (soon after 1848[112]—1930), RSD. Abol 1887 to help cr Ness CP.[726] *Parl* N Riding (1832—85), Whitby Dv (1885—1918).

WEST NESS
[N Riding] Tp in Stonegrave AP, sep CP 1866,[2] pt eccl severed 1931 and transf to Nunnington AP.[632] Organisation as for East Ness.

NESWICK
[E Riding] Tp in Bainton AP, sep CP 1866.[2] *LG* Harth. Wap, Driff. PLU, RSD, RD. Abol 1935 ent to Bainton AP.[13] *Parl* E Riding (1832—85), Buckr.

Dv (1885—1948).

NETHERTHONG
[W Riding] Chap in Almondbury AP, sep CP 1866,[2] sep EP 1831,[9] eccl refounded 1843 incl pt Honley with Brockholes EP.[79] *LG* Agb. Wap, Hudd. PLU, Netherthong USD, UD (1894—1912), Holmf. UD (1912—21). Civ bdry: 1897,[628] 1912 (gains pt Honley CP as enlarged Netherthong CP transf to Holmf. UD).[629] Abol civ 1921 to help cr Holmfirth CP.[159] *Parl* W Riding (1832—67), S'rn Dv of W Riding (1867—85), Holmf. Dv (1885—1918), Colne Valley Dv (1918—48). *Eccl* Pontef. RDn (1831—57), Hudd. RDn (1857—1968), Almondb. RDn (1968—*). Eccl bdry: 1857,[87] 1876 (help cr Wilshaw EP).[29]

NETHERTHORPE ST ANN
EP [W Riding] Cr 1884 from Sheffield AP.[466] Sheff RDn. Abol 1941 to help cr Sheffield St Philip and St Ann EP.[93]

NETHERTHORPE ST STEPHEN
[W Riding] Cr 1859 from Sheffield St Peter EP, Sheffield St George EP.[647] Sheff RDn. Abol 1941 to help cr Sheffield St George with St Stephen EP.[727]

NEW FOREST
[N Riding] Tp in Kirkby Ravensworth AP, sep CP 1866.[2] *LG* Seq 38. Transf 1974 to N Yorks.[5] *Parl* Seq 14.

NEW MILL
EP [W Riding] Cr 1834 from Kirkburton AP,[9] refounded 1844.[9] Pontef. RDn (1834—57), Hudd. RDn (1857—1968), Kirkburton RDn (1968—*).

NEW VILLAGE
[E Riding] Ex-par place, orig incl ex-par area Wallingfen (sometimes 'Newport Wallingfen'), sep CP 1858,[393] eccl abol 1895 to help cr Newport EP.[284] *LG* Harth. Wap, Howden PLU, RSD. Civ bdry: 1880.[171] Renamed 1881 'Wallingfen'.[728] *Parl* E Riding (1832—85).

NEWBALD
AP [E Riding] Usual civ spelling; for eccl see 'North Newbald'. Incl tps North Newbald, South Newbald (each a sep CP 1866[2]) so that 'Newbald' has no sep civ identity 1866—1935 (see following entry). *LG* Harth. Wap. *Parl* E Riding (1832—67).

CP [E Riding] Cr 1935 by union North Newbald CP, South Newbald CP, pt Hotham AP.[13] *LG* Bev. RD. Transf 1974 to Humb.[5] *Parl* Bev. CC (1948—55), Haltemp. CC (1955—*).

NORTH NEWBALD
AP [E Riding] Usual eccl spelling; for civ and civ sep tps, see Newbald AP. *Eccl* Pec jurisd Newbald prebend (until 1836), Harth. & Hull RDn (1836—57), S Harth. RDn (1857—66), Bev. RDn (1866—87), Weigh. RDn (1887—1916), Howden RDn (1916—*).

CP [E Riding] Tp in Newbald AP, sep CP 1866.[2] *LG* Harth. Wap, Bev. PLU, RSD, RD. Abol 1935 to help cr Newbald CP.[13] *Parl* E Riding (1832—85), Hold. Dv (1885—1918).

SOUTH NEWBALD
[E Riding] Tp in Newbald AP, sep CP 1866.[2] *LG* Harth. Wap, Bev. PLU, RSD, RD. Abol 1935 to

help cr Newbald CP.[13] *Parl* E Riding (1832—85), Howdensh. Dv (1885—1918), Hold. Dv (1918—48).

NEWBIGGIN

[N Riding] Tp in Aysgarth AP, sep CP 1866.[2] *LG* Seq 51. Bdry: 1883.[527] Transf 1974 to N Yorks. *Parl* Seq 14.

NEWBURGH

[N Riding] Tp in Coxwold AP, sep CP 1866.[2] *LG* Seq 24. Transf 1974 to N Yorks.[5] *Parl* Seq 16.

NEWBY

[N Riding] Tp in Scalby AP, sep CP 1866,[2] sep EP 1951.[729] *LG* Pick. Lythe Wap, Scarb. PLU, RSD, RD. Abol civ 1886 ent to Throxenby CP.[730] *Parl* N Riding (1832—85), Whitby Dv (1885—1918). *Eccl* Now usually as 'Scarborough St Mark', Scarb. RDn. Eccl bdry: 1958.[322]

NEWBY

[N Riding] Tp pt in Seamer CP/EP, pt in Stokesley AP, sep CP 1866.[2] *LG* Seq 58. Bdry: 1932,[20] 1968 (help cr Teesside CB [assoc with N Riding] & CP).[537] Transf 1974 to N Yorks.[5] *Parl* Seq 11.

NEWBY WISKE

[N Riding] Tp in Kirby Wiske AP, sep CP 1866.[2] *LG* Seq 36. Transf 1974 to N Yorks.[5] *Parl* Seq 14.

NEWBY WITH MULWITH

[W Riding] Tp in Ripon AP, sep CP 1866,[2] eccl in chap Skelton (sep EP 1749 from Ripon,[9] eccl refounded 1815 as 'Skelton cum Newby',[11] as such refounded 1875[11]). *LG* Seq 100. Transf 1974 to N Yorks.[5] *Parl* Seq 34.

NEWELL WITH CLIFTON

[W Riding] Tp in Otley AP, sep CP 1866.[2] *LG* Seq 92. Bdry: 1897,[731] 1903,[732] 1927.[550] Transf 1974 to N Yorks.[5] *Parl* Seq 30.

NEWHOLM WITH DUNSLEY

[N Riding] Tp in Whitby AP, sep CP 1866.[2] *LG* Seq 68. Bdry: 1932.[51] Transf 1974 to N Yorks. *Parl* Seq 19.

NEWINGTON

CP [E Riding] Cr 1877 from Swanland CP[733]; for eccl see 'Kingston upon Hull St John the Baptist, Newington'. *LG* Harth. Wap, Scul. PLU, RSD (1877—83), Kingst. upon Hull MB (1883—89), CB (1889—98), USD (1883—94). Bdry: 1878.[519] Abol 1898 ent to Sculcoates AP.[446] *Parl* See Part III of the *Guide* for composition of Kingst. upon Hull Parl Bors (1885—1918) by wards of the MB.

NEWINGTON THE TRANSFIGURATION

EP [E Riding] Cr 1906 from Kingston upon Hull St John the Baptist, Newington EP,[462] the new EP soon after called 'Kingston upon Hull The Transfiguration', qv.

NEWINGTON WITH DAIRYCOATES

EP [E Riding] Cr 1969 by union Kingston upon Hull St John the Baptist, Newington EP, Dairycoates EP.[228] Kingst. upon Hull RDn.

NEWLAND

[W Riding] Tp in Drax AP, sep CP 1866.[2] *LG* Bark. Ash Wap, Selby PLU, RSD, RD. Bdry: 1895 (gains pt Knedlington CP, Yorks E Riding).[665] Transf 1974 to N Yorks.[5] *Parl* Seq 24.

NEWLAND ST AUGUSTINE

EP [E Riding] Cr 1897 from Newland St John EP,[661] the new EP soon after called 'Kingston upon Hull St Augustine', qv.

NEWLAND ST JOHN

EP [E Riding] Cr 1862 from Cottingham AP, Skidby EP.[35] Bev. RDn (1862—69), Kingst. upon Hull RDn (1869—*). Sometimes later 'North Cottingham St John'. Bdry: 1897 (cr Newland St Augustine EP, soon after called 'Kingston upon Hull St Augustine'),[661] 1937 (help cr Hull St Alban EP),[246] 1950 (cr North Hull EP).[642]

NEWLAND WITH WOODHOUSE MOOR

[W Riding] Ex-par place, sep CP 1858.[393] *LG* Seq 69. Transf 1974 to W Yorks.[5] *Parl* W Riding (1832—67), S'rn Dv of W Riding (1867—85), Norm. Dv (1885—1948), Wakef BC (1948—55), Norm. CC (1955—*).

NEWPORT

EP [E Riding] Cr 1895 from Blacktoft EP, Howden AP, Eastrington AP, and ex-par places Gilberdike Mill (civ, 'Gilberdike'), Cheapsides, New Village, Market Weighton Canal.[284] Howden RDn.

CP [E Riding] Cr 1935 by union Scalby CP, Wallingfen CP.[13] *LG* Howden RD. Transf 1974 to Humb.[5] *Parl* Bev. CC (1948—55), Howden CC (1955—*).

NEWSHAM

[N Riding] Tp pt in Barningham AP, pt in Kirkby Ravensworth AP, sep CP 1866.[2] *LG* Seq 38. Transf 1974 to N Yorks.[5] *Parl* Seq 14.

NEWSHAM WITH BRECKENBROUGH

[N Riding] Tp in Kirby Wiske AP, sep CP 1866.[2] *LG* Seq 27. Transf 1974 to N Yorks.[5] *Parl* Seq 16.

NEWSHOLME

[W Riding] Tp in Gisburn AP, sep CP 1866.[2] *LG* Seq 108. Transf 1974 to Lancs.[5] *Parl* Seq 41.

NEWSOME

EP [W Riding] Cr 1873 from Lockwood EP.[21] Hudd. RDn (1873—1968), Almondb. RDn (1968—*).

NEWTHORPE

[W Riding] Tp in Sherburn in Elmet AP, sep CP 1866.[2] *LG* Bark. Ash Wap, not in a PLU (until 1862), Tadc. PLU (1862—1930), RSD, RD. Abol 1937 to help cr Huddleston with Newthorpe CP.[31] *Parl* W Riding (1832—67), N'rn Dv of W Riding (1867—85), Bark. Ash Dv (1885—1918), Don Valley Dv (1918—48).

NEWTON

[N Riding] Chap in Rudby in Cleveland AP, sep civ identity early, sep EP 1735 as 'Newton in Cleveland',[9] qv. *LG* Langb. Lbty, Guisb. PLU, RSD, RD (1894—1932), UD (1932—74). Transf 1974 to Clev.[5] *Parl* Seq 9.

NEWTON

[N Riding] Chap in Pickering AP, sep CP 1866,[2] sep EP (qv) 1866 as 'Newton upon Rawcliffe' from Pickering AP, Levisham AP.[249] *LG* Seq 61. Bdry: 1883,[16] 1887,[49] 1887.[700] Transf 1974 to N Yorks.[5] *Parl* Seq 20.

NEWTON

[W Riding] Tp in Slaidburn AP, sep CP 1866.[2] *LG* Seq 108. Bdry: 1938.[28] Transf 1974 to Lancs. *Parl* Seq 41.

EAST NEWTON
[E Riding] Tp in Aldbrough AP, sep CP 1866.[2] *LG*
Hold. Wap, Skirl. PLU, RSD, RD. Abol 1935 ent
to Aldbrough AP.[13] *Parl* E Riding (1832—85),
Hold. Dv (1885—1948).
EAST NEWTON AND LAYSTHORP
[N Riding] Tp pt in Oswaldkirk AP, pt in
Stonegrave AP, sep CP 1866.[2] *LG* Seq 63. Transf
1974 to N Yorks.[5] *Parl* Seq 21.
OUT NEWTON
[E Riding] Tp in Easington AP, sep CP 1866.[2] *LG*
Hold. Wap, Patr. PLU, RSD, RD. Abol 1935 ent
to Easington AP.[13] *Parl* E Riding (1832—85), Hold.
Dv (1885—1948).
WEST NEWTON WITH BURTON CONSTABLE
[E Riding] Tp pt in Aldbrough AP, pt in Swine AP,
sep CP 1866.[2] *LG* Hold. Wap, Skirl. PLU, RSD,
RD. Abol 1935 to help cr Burton Constable CP.[13]
Parl E Riding (1832—85), Hold. Dv (1885—1948).
NEWTON IN CLEVELAND
EP [N Riding] Chap in Rudby in Cleveland AP, sep EP
1735,[9] sep civ identity early as 'Newton', qv (1st
'Newton' above). *Eccl* Clev RDn (1735—1862),
Stokes. RDn (1862—*).
NEWTON KYME
AP [Ainsty (W Riding until 1449 and from 1836, indept
jurisd 1449—1836)] Usual eccl spelling; usual civ
'Newton Kyme cum Toulston'. *LG* Seq 70. Transf
1974 to N Yorks.[5] *Parl* Seq 24. *Eccl* Seq 33.
NEWTON KYME CUM TOULSTON—see prev entry
NEWTON LE WILLOWS
[N Riding] Tp pt in Patrick Brompton AP (E Hang
Wap), pt in Finghall AP (W Hang Wap), sep CP
1866.[2] *LG* Leyb. PLU, RSD, RD. Transf 1974 to N
Yorks.[5] *Parl* Seq 13.
NEWTON MORRELL
[N Riding] Tp in Gilling AP, sep CP 1866[2]; eccl in
chap Barton in same par, Newton Morrell eccl
severed 1732 to help cr Barton St Mary EP.[9] *LG*
Seq 33. Transf 1974 to N Yorks.[5] *Parl* Seq 14.
NEWTON MULGRAVE
[N Riding] Tp in Lythe AP, sep CP 1866,[2] eccl
severed 1868 to help cr Ugthorpe EP.[188] *LG* Seq 59.
Transf 1974 to N Yorks.[5] *Parl* Seq 19.
NEWTON UPON DERWENT
[E Riding] Tp in Wilberfoss AP, sep CP 1866.[2] *LG*
Harth. Wap, Pockl. PLU, RSD, RD. Abol 1935 ent
to Wilberfoss AP.[13] *Parl* E Riding (1832—85),
Howdensh. Dv (1885—1948).
NEWTON UPON OUSE
AP [N Riding] Incl tps Bennington, Linton upon Ouse
(each a sep CP 1866[2]). *LG* Bulmer Wap, Eas. PLU
(soon after 1837[112]—1930), RSD, RD. Transf 1974
to N Yorks.[5] *Parl* Seq 16. *Eccl* Seq 18.
NEWTON UPON RAWCLIFFE
EP [N Riding] Chap in Pickering AP, sep CP 1866 as
'Newton',[2] qv (2nd 'Newton' above), sep EP 1866
from Pickering AP, Levisham AP.[249] *Eccl* Malton
RDn (1866—1928), Pick. RDn (1928—*).
NIDD
AP [W Riding] *LG* Pt Claro Wap. pt Ripon Lbty, Knar.
PLU, RSD, RD (1894—1938), Nidd. RD (1938—
74). Transf 1974 to N Yorks.[5] *Parl* W Riding

(1832—67), pt N'rn Dv of W Riding, pt E'rn Dv of
W Riding (1867—85), Ripon Dv (1885—1948),
Harrog. CC (1948—*). *Eccl* Seq 51.
NORLAND
[W Riding] Tp in Halifax AP, sep CP 1866,[2] eccl
severed 1719 to help cr Sowerby Bridge EP,[9] the
latter abol 1724 to help cr Elland cum Stainland and
Fixby EP,[9] although re-augmented 1739 as 'Elland'
usually called 'Elland with Greetland' until
Greetland a sep EP 1863,[138] 'Elland' thereafter (incl
Norland), Sowerby Bridge EP (incl Norland) re-cr
1869 from Elland,[521] 'Norland' a sep EP 1877 from
Sowerby Bridge EP.[301] *LG* Morley Wap, Halifax
PLU, pt Sowerby Bridge USD, pt Halifax RSD,
Halifax RD. Civ bdry: 1894 (loses the pt in
Sowerby Bridge UD to help cr Sowerby Bridge
CP).[734] Abol civ 1937 to help cr Sowerby Bridge
UD & CP.[31] *Parl* W Riding (1832—67), E'rn Dv of
W Riding (1867—85), Sowerby Dv (1885—1948).
Eccl Halifax RDn. Abol eccl 1923 to help cr
Sowerby Bridge with Norland EP.[735]
NORMANBY
AP [N Riding] Incl tp Thornton Risebrough (sep CP
1866[2]). *LG* Ryed. Wap, Pick. PLU (1837—soon
after 1848[112]), Kirkby Moors. PLU (soon after
1848[112]—1930), RSD, RD (1894—1934), Pick. RD
(1934—74). Transf 1974 to N Yorks.[5] *Parl* Seq 22.
Eccl Seq 26.
NORMANBY
[N Riding] Tp in Ormesby AP, sep CP 1866,[2] eccl
in chap Eston in same par (sep EP 1772[9]). *LG*
Lanbg. Lbty, Guisb. PLU (1837—75), Middlesb.
PLU (1875—1930), pt South Bank in Normanby
USD (1875—88), pt Normanby USD (1888—94), pt
Middlesb. MB (1866—89), pt Middlesb. CB
(1889—94), pt Middlesb. USD, Normanby UD.
Bdry: 1894 (loses the pt in Middlesb. CB to
Middlesbrough CP).[18] Abol 1915 ent to Eston UD
& CP.[105] *Parl* N Riding (ent 1832—67, pt 1867—
85), pt Middlesb. Parl Bor (1867—1918), pt Clev
Dv (1885—1918).
NORMANTON
AP [W Riding] Incl tp Altofts (sep CP 1866,[2] sep EP
1878[88]), tp Snydale (sep CP 1866[2]). *LG* Agb. Wap,
Barwick GilbU (until 1869), Wakef PLU (1869—
1930), Normanton USD, UD. Addtl civ bdry alt:
1906,[736] 1938 (gains Altofts UD & CP).[28] Transf
1974 to W Yorks.[5] *Parl* W Riding (1832—67), S'rn
Dv of W Riding (1867—85), Norm. Dv/CC
(1885—*). *Eccl* Ainsty RDn (until 1820), New
Ainsty RDn (1820—57), Pontef. RDn (1857—
1927), Wakef RDn (1927—73), Chevet RDn
(1973—*). Addtl eccl bdry alt: 1929 (help cr
Sharlston EP).[595]
NORTHALLERTON
AP [N Riding] Incl chap Brompton (sep CP 1866,[2] sep
EP 1841,[9] eccl refounded 1843[362]), chap Deighton
(sep CP 1866,[2] eccl severed 1957 to help cr
Brompton with Deighton EP7[4]), chap High Worsall
(sep CP 1866,[2] sep EP 1719[9]), tp Romanby (sep CP
1866[2]), pt tp Thornton le Beans (sep CP 1866[2]). *LG*
Allert. Wap, N'allert. Bor, PLU, USD, UD. Transf
1974 to N Yorks.[5] *Parl* N'allert. Parl Bor (pt 1298,

1640—1867 [tp Northallerton, Brompton, Roman-by], ent 1867—85), remainder and later, Seq 14. *Eccl* Pec jurisd Dean & Chapter of Durham (until 1836), Seq 23 thereafter.

NORTHFIELD

EP [W Riding] Cr 1895 from Masborough St John EP.[706] Rotherh. RDn.

NORTHOWRAM

[W Riding] Tp in Halifax AP, sep CP 1866,[2] pt eccl severed 1749 to help cr Coley EP, pt eccl severed same year to help cr Lightcliffe EP,[9] pt eccl severed 1845 to help cr Queen's Head EP,[166] pt eccl severed 1855 from Coley EP to cr Haley Hill EP,[166] 'Northowram' EP cr 1909 from Coley EP, Lightcliffe EP.[429] *LG* Morley Wap, Halifax PLU, pt Northowram USD, pt Queensbury USD, pt Halifax MB (1848—89), pt Halifax CB (1889—94), pt Halifax USD, Northowram UD. Civ bdry: 1894 (loses the pt in Halifax CB to Halifax AP [this pt orig intended to be 'North Ward CP',[737] this order superseded]),[588] 1894 (loses the pt in Queensbury USD to help cr Queensbury CP).[410] Abol civ 1900 ent to Halifax AP.[590] *Parl* Pt Halifax Parl Bor (1832—1918), pt W Riding (1832—67), pt E'rn Dv of W Riding (1867—85), pt Elland Dv (1885—1918). *Eccl* Halifax RDn (1909—67), Brigh. & Elland RDn (1967—*).

NORTON

AP [E Riding] *LG* Buckr. Wap, Malton PLU, RSD (1875—90), Norton USD (1890—94), UD. Transf 1974 to N Yorks.[5] *Parl* Malton Parl Bor (o'wise ent E Riding, 1832—85), remainder and later, Seq 1. *Eccl* Seq 3. Eccl bdry: 1742 (cr Sutton EP,[9] sep status lost *ca* 1860s—70s).

NORTON

[W Riding] Tp in Campsall AP, sep CP 1866.[2] *LG* Seq 94. Bdry (gains Campsall AP, Sutton CP).[28] Transf 1974 to S Yorks.[5] *Parl* W Riding (1832—67), Nrn Dv of W Riding (1867—85), Osg. Dv (1885—1918), Donc. Dv/CC (1918—*).

NORTON CONYERS

[N Riding] Chap in Wath AP, sep CP 1866.[2] *LG* Allert. Wap, not in a PLU (until 1852), Ripon PLU (1852—1930), RSD, Wath RD. Transf 1974 to N Yorks.[5] *Parl* Seq 16.

NORTON LE CLAY

[N Riding] Tp in Cundall AP, sep CP 1866,[2] sep EP 1743.[9] *LG* Seq 41. Transf 1974 to N Yorks.[5] *Parl* Seq 16. *Eccl* Boroughbr. RDn (1743—1971), Ripon RDn (1971—*).

NORTON WITHIN

CP [Sheff CB] Cr 1901 by union pt Beauchief CP, pt Norton AP (both Derbys) to be in Sheff CB.[304] *LG* Wakef PLU, Sheff CB. Abol 1904 to help cr Ecclesall CP.[502]

NORWOOD

CP [W Riding] Renaming 1950 of Clifton with Norwood CP.[422] *LG* Wharfed. RD. Transf to N Yorks.[5] *Parl* Ripon CC (1955—*).

NORWOOD GREEN AND COLEY

CP [W Riding] Cr 1894 from the pt of Hipperholme with Brighouse CP not in a MB or UD.[19] *LG* Halifax PLU, RD. Abol 1937 ent to Brigh. MB &

CP.[31] *Parl* Elland Dv (1918—48).

NOTTON

[W Riding] Tp in Royston AP, sep CP 1866.[2] *LG* Staincr. Wap, Barnsley PLU, RSD, RD (1894—1938), Wakef RD (1938—74). Bdry: 1938.[28] Transf 1974 to W Yorks.[5] *Parl* Seq 43.

NUNBURNHOLME

AP [E Riding] Incl tp Thorpe le Street (sep CP 1866,[2] eccl severed 1876 to help cr Shipton Thorpe EP).[701] *LG* Seq 12. Addtl civ bdry alt: 1935 (gains Kilnwick Percy AP).[13] Transf 1974 to Humb.[5] *Parl* Seq 7. *Eccl* Seq 14.

NUNKEELING AND BEWHOLME

AP [E Riding] Usual eccl spelling; for civ see 'Bewholme and Nunkeeling'. *Eccl* Hold. RDn (until 1849), N Hold. RDn (1849—66), Hornsea RDn (1866—1916), N Hold. RDn (1916—*).

NUNNINGTON

AP [N Riding] (Nunnington tp pt in this AP, pt in Helmsley AP, pt in Stonegrave AP). *LG* Seq 64. Transf 1974 to N Yorks.[5] *Parl* Seq 21. *Eccl* Riddal RDn (until 1862), Helm. RDn (1862—*). Eccl bdry: 1931 (gains tp West Ness, pt tp East Ness [both in Hovingham AP] and addtl pt Hovingham AP).[632]

NUNTHORPE

AP [N Riding] Chap in Ayton AP (eccl, 'Great Ayton'), sep CP 1866,[2] sep EP 1790,[9] eccl refounded 1925 from Great Ayton AP, Marton AP, Ormesby AP.[160] *LG* Seq 58. Civ bdry: 1968 (help cr Teesside CB [assoc with N Riding] & CP).[537] Transf 1974 to Clev.[5] *Parl* Seq 11. *Eccl* Clev RDn (l790—1862), Stokes. RDn (1862—*).

NUNWICK CUM HOWGRAVE

[Pt N Riding (in Kirklington AP, Hallik. Wap), pt W Riding (in Ripon AP, Ripon Lbty), made 1895 ent W Riding[492]] Tp, sep CP 1866.[2] *LG* Ripon PLU, RSD, RD (pt 1894—95, ent 1895—1938), pt sep RD in N Riding (1894—95), Ripon & Pateley Br. RD (1938—74). Civ bdry: 1894 (loses pt to Sutton Howgrave CP, Yorks N Riding),[738] 1895 (loses remainder in N Riding, as noted, pt to Sutton Howgrave CP, pt to Howgrave CP, both Yorks N Riding).[634] Transf 1974 to N Yorks.[5] *Parl* Pt N Riding (1832—85), pt Thirsk & Malton Dv (1885—1918), the pt in W Riding and ent pt after 1918, Seq 34.

NUTHILL

AP [E Riding] Orig AP, early demolished, incl in Skeckling AP and in chap Burstwick in that par.[739]

NUTWITH AND ROOMER COMMON

[N Riding] Waste area, common stinted pasture. *LG* Masham UD. Abol 1934 ent to Swinton with Warthermarske CP.[3] *Parl* Thirsk & Malton Dv (1918—48).

OAKENSHAW CUM WOODLANDS

EP [W Riding] Cr 1877 from Bierley EP, Whitechapel EP, Wyke EP, Birkenshaw cum Hunsworth EP, Wibsey EP.[168] Bradf RDn (1877—1921), Bowl. RDn (1921—71), Bowl. & Horton RDn (1971—*).

OAKWORTH

EP [W Riding] Cr 1844 from Keighley AP.[197] Craven RDn (1844—57), Craven RDn, S'rn Dv (1857—

1921), S Craven RDn (1921—*).

CP [W Riding] Cr 1894 from the pt of Keighley AP in Oakworth UD.[257] *LG* Keighley PLU, Oakworth UD. Bdry: 1895.[271] *Parl* Keigh. Dv (1918—48).

OLDSTEAD

[N Riding] Tp in Kilburn AP, sep CP 1866.[2] *LG* Seq 25. Transf 1974 to N Yorks.[5] *Parl* Seq 16.

ORGREAVE

[W Riding] Tp in Rotherham AP, sep CP 1866.[2] *LG* Seq 119. Bdry: 1938 (incl loses pt to Sheff CB [assoc with W Riding] & AP).[306] Transf 1974 to S Yorks.[5] *Parl* Seq 55.

ORMESBY

AP [N Riding] Incl tps Morton, Upsall (each a sep CP 1866[2]), tps Normanby, Eston (each a sep CP 1866,[2] together comprised chap Eston [sep EP 1772[9]]). *LG* Langb. Lbty, Guisb. PLU (1837—75), Middlesb. PLU (1875—1930), pt Middlesb. MB (1866—89), pt Middlesb. CB (1889—94), pt Middlesb. USD, pt Middlesb. RSD, Ormesby UD (1894—1913), Middlesb. RD (1913—32), Stokes. RD (1932—68). Addtl civ bdry alt: 1894 (loses the pt in Middlesb. CB to Middlesbrough CP),[18] 1913 (loses pt to Middlesb. CB [assoc with N Riding] & CP, the remainder transf to Middlesb. RD),[19] 1932 (loses pt to Middlesb. CB [assoc with N Riding] & CP).[20] Abol civ 1968 pt to Guisb. UD & AP, pt to help cr Teesside CB (assoc with N Riding) & CP.[537] *Parl* N Riding (ent 1832—67, pt 1867—85), pt Middlesb. Parl Bor (1867—1918), Clev Dv (pt 1885—1918, ent 1918—48), Richm. CC (1948—70). *Eccl* Seq 25. Addtl eccl bdry alt: 1871 (cr North Ormesby EP),[259] 1925 (help refound Nunthorpe EP),[160] 1951 (help cr Middlesbrough St Thomas EP),[714] 1966 (help cr Middlesbrough The Ascension EP).[712]

NORTH ORMESBY

EP [N Riding] Cr 1871 from Ormesby AP.[259] Stokes. RDn (1871—78), Middlesb. RDn (1878—*). Bdry: 1925,[493] 1951 (help cr Middlesbrough St Thomas EP),[714] 1966 (help cr Middlesbrough The Ascension EP).[712]

OSBALDWICK

AP [N Riding] Incl chap Murton (pec jurisd Strensall prebend until 1836, sep CP 1866[2]). *LG* Seq 32. Addtl civ bdry alt: 1934 (loses pt to York CB [not assoc with a Riding] & CP),[3] 1968 (loses pt to York CB [not assoc with a Riding] & CP).[418] Transf 1974 to N Yorks.[5] *Parl* Seq 16. *Eccl* Pec jurisd Strensall prebend (until 1836), Seq 17 thereafter. Addtl eccl bdry alt: 1936 (help cr York St Hilda EP),[24] 1937.[246]

OSGODBY

[E Riding] Tp in Hemingbrough AP, sep CP 1866.[2] *LG* Ouse & Derw. Wap, Selby PLU, RSD, Riccall RD. Abol 1935 ent to Barlby CP.[13] *Parl* E Riding (1832—85), Howdensh. Dv (1885—1948).

OSGODBY

[N Riding] Tp in Seamer AP, sep CP 1866.[2] *LG* Pick. Lythe Wap, Scarb. PLU, RSD, RD. Abol 1886 to help cr Cayton CP.[402] *Parl* N Riding (1832—85), Whitby Dv (1885—1918).

OSMONDTHORPE

EP [W Riding] Cr 1932 from Leeds All Saints EP,

Leeds St Hilda EP.[138] Leeds RDn (1932—71), Whitkirk RDn (1971—*).

CP [Leeds CB] Cr 1894 from the pt of Templenewsham CP in Leeds CB.[504] *LG* Hunslet PLU, Leeds CB. Abol 1925 ent to Leeds AP.[129] *Parl* See Part III of the *Guide* for composition of Leeds Parl Bors (1918—48) by wards of the CB.

OSMOTHERLEY

AP [N Riding] Incl tps Ellerbeck, West Harsley, pt tp Thimbleby (each a sep CP 1866[2]). *LG* Seq 22. Transf 1974 to N Yorks.[5] *Parl* Seq 14. *Eccl* Pec jurisd Bp Durham (until 1836), Seq 23 thereafter.

OSSETT

CP [W Riding] Renaming civ 1890 of Ossett cum Gawthorpe CP at time of cr Ossett MB.[740] *LG* Dewsb. PLU, Ossett MB, USD. Bdry: 1901,[99] 1921.[694] Transf 1974 to W Yorks.[5] *Parl* Batley & Morley Parl Bor (1918—48), Dewsb. BC (1948—*).

SOUTH OSSETT

EP [W Riding] Cr 1846 from Ossett cum Gawthorpe EP.[741] Pontef. RDn (1846—57), Dewsb. RDn (1857—*). Bdry: 1901.[115]

OSSETT CUM GAWTHORPE

[W Riding] Tp in Dewsbury AP, sep CP 1866,[2] sep EP 1718,[9] pt of latter eccl severed 1846 to cr South Ossett EP,[741] the remainder refounded 1858 as Ossett cum Gawthorpe EP.[247] *LG* Agb. Wap, Dewsb. PLU, Ossett cum Gawthorpe USD. Renamed 1890 'Ossett' at time of cr Ossett MB.[740] *Parl* W Riding (1832—67), S'rn Dv of W Riding (1867—85), Morley Dv (1885—1918). *Eccl* Pontef. RDn (1718—1857), Dewsb. RDn (1857—*). Addtl eccl bdry alt: 1901 (help cr Gawthorpe and Chickenley Heath EP),[284] 1901.[115]

OSWALDKIRK

AP [N Riding] Incl tp Ampleforth Oswaldkirk, pt tp East Newton and Laysthorp (each a sep CP 1866[2]). *LG* Sep 63. Civ bdry: 1887 (help cr Ampleforth CP).[103] Transf 1974 to N Yorks.[5] *Parl* Seq 21. *Eccl* Seq 26.

OTLEY

AP [W Riding] Tp 'Otley' in Skyr. Wap as were chap Basildon (sep CP 1866,[2] sep EP 1719,[9] eccl refounded 1869[71]), chap Burley in Wharfedale, tp Menston (each a sep CP 1866,[2] eccl united 1793 as 'Burley in Wharfedale' EP,[9] the latter eccl refounded 1856 as 'Burley' EP[351]), tp Bramhope (sep CP 1866[2]), tps Esholt, Hawksworth (each a sep CP 1866,[2] eccl united 1853 as 'Esholt' EP,[534] sometimes called 'Esholt with Hawksworth'); incl in Claro Wap chap Denton (sep CP 1866[2]), tp Farnley (sep CP 1866,[2] sep EP 1746[9]), tp Lindley (sep CP 1866,[2] sep EP 1831,[9] sep eccl status not sustained, area eccl severed 1926 and transf to Leathley AP[551]), tp Newell with Clifton (sep CP 1866[2]). *LG* Carlton GilbU (until 1869), Wharfed. PLU (1869—1930), Otley Bor, USD, UD. Addtl civ bdry alt: 1897,[731] 1903,[732] 1927,[550] 1937 (incl help cr Aireb. UD & CP).[31] Transf 1974 to W Yorks.[5] *Parl* Seq 30. *Eccl* Seq 41.

OTTERBURN

[W Riding] Tp in Kirkby in Malham Dale AP, sep

CP 1866.[2] *LG* Seq 111. Bdry: 1938.[28] Transf 1974 to N Yorks.[5] *Parl* Seq 41.

NORTH OTTERINGTON

AP [N Riding] Tp 'North Otterington' in Allert. Wap as was pt tp Thornton le Beans (sep CP 1866,[2] eccl severed 1961 to help cr Thornton le Street with Thornton le Moor and Thornton le Beans EP[742]); incl in Birdf. Wap tp Thornton le Moor (sep CP 1866,[2] eccl severed 1961 as for Thornton le Beans, qv above). *LG* N'allert. PLU, RSD, RD. Transf 1974 to N Yorks.[5] *Parl* Seq 14. *Eccl* Called 'North Otterington with Thornton le Moor and Thornton le Beans' until 1961 (qv in following entry).

NORTH OTTERINGTON WITH THORNTON LE MOOR AND THORNTON LE BEANS

AP [N Riding] Usual eccl spelling; for civ and civ sep tps, see prev entry. *Eccl* Pec jurisd Bp Durham (until 1836), Clev RDn (1836—62), N'allert. RDn (1862—66), Thirsk RDn (1866—1916), N'allert. RDn (1916—61). Abol eccl 1961, the 2 tps eccl severed to help cr Thornton le Street with Thornton le Moor and Thornton le Beans EP, the remainder to help cr North and South Otterington EP.[742]

NORTH AND SOUTH OTTERINGTON

EP [N Riding] Cr 1961 by union South Otterington AP, the remainder of North Otterington with Thornton le Moor and Thornton le Beans AP when tps Thornton le Moor and Thornton le Beans severed to help cr Thornton le Street with Thornton le Moor and Thornton le Beans EP.[742] N'allert. RDn.

SOUTH OTTERINGTON

AP [N Riding] *LG* Seq 27. Transf 1974 to N Yorks.[5] *Parl* Seq 16. *Eccl* Bulmer RDn (until 1862), Thirsk RDn (1862—1916), N'allert. RDn (1916—61). Abol 1961 to help cr North and South Otterington EP.[742]

OTTRINGHAM

[E Riding] *LG* Seq 15. Transf 1974 to Humb.[5] *Parl* Seq 5. *Eccl* Pec jurisd Bev. (until 1836), Seq 16 thereafter.

OUGHTIBRIDGE

EP [W Riding] Cr 1868 from Wadsley EP.[290] *Eccl*esfield RDn (1868—1942), Tankersley RDn (1942—*).

OULSTON

[N Riding] Tp in Coxwold AP, sep CP 1866.[2] *LG* Seq 24. Transf 1974 to N Yorks.[5] *Parl* Seq 16.

OULTON

EP [W Riding] Cr 1960 from Rothwell AP[63]; for civ see following entry. Whitkirk RDn.

OULTON WITH WOODLESFORD

[W Riding] Tp in Rothwell AP, sep CP 1866,[2] 'Oulton' a sep EP 1869,[63] 'Woodlesford' a sep EP 1869.[743] *LG* Agb. Wap, Wakef PLU (1837—69), Hunslet PLU (1869—1930), RSD, RD. Bdry: 1883,[52] 1884.[276] Abol 1937 ent to Rothw. UD & AP.[31] *Parl* W Riding (1832—67), S'rn Dv of W Riding (1867—85), Norm. Dv (1885—1918), Rothw. Dv (1918—48).

GREAT OUSEBURN

AP [W Riding] Incl pt tp Upper Dunsforth cum Branton Green (sep CP 1866,[2] qv for pt of the CP in N Riding). *LG* Claro Wap, Gt Ouseb. GilbU (until

1854), PLU (1854—1930), RSD, RD (1894—1938), Nidd. RD (1938—74). Addtl civ bdry alt: 1886,[718] 1960.[705] Transf 1974 to N Yorks.[5] *Parl* W Riding (1832—67), N'rn Dv of W Riding (1867—85), Ripon Dv (1885—1948), Harrog. CC (1948—*). *Eccl* Seq 52.

LITTLE OUSEBURN

AP [W Riding] Incl tps Kirby Hall, Thorpe Underwoods, Widdington (each a sep CP 1866[2]). *LG* Seq 85. Transf 1974 to N Yorks.[5] *Parl* Seq 36. *Eccl* Pec jurisd Precentor of York Cathedral (until 1836), Seq 52 thereafter.

OUSEFLEET

[W Riding] Tp in Whitgift AP, sep CP 1866.[2] *LG* Seq 95. Transf 1974 to Humb. *Parl* Seq 29.

OUSETHORPE

[E Riding] Tp in Pocklington AP, sep CP 1866.[2] *LG* Harth. Wap, Pockl. PLU, RSD, RD. Abol 1935 to help cr Millington CP.[13] *Parl* E Riding (1832—85), Howdensh. Dv (1885—1948).

OUTWOOD

EP [W Riding] Cr 1861 from Stanley EP.[258] Wakef RDn. Bdry: 1913.[93]

CP [W Riding] Cr 1894 from pt of the pt of Stanley cum Wrenthorpe CP not in Wakef MB.[307] *LG* Wakef PLU, RD (1894—99), Stanley UD (1899—1937). Bdry: 1895.[96] Abol 1937 pt to Wakef CB (assoc with W Riding) & AP, pt to Stanley CP.[13] *Parl* Rothw. Dv (1918—48).

OVENDEN

[W Riding] Tp in Halifax AP, sep CP 1866,[2] pt eccl severed 1718 to help cr Illingworth EP,[9] the remainder a sep EP 1843,[351] later usually called 'Bradshaw'. *LG* Morley Wap, Halifax PLU, pt Ovenden USD (1875—92), Halifax USD (pt 1875—92, ent 1892—94), Halifax MB (pt 1848—92, ent 1892—94). Abol civ 1894 ent to Halifax AP.[588] *Parl* W Riding (1832—67), pt Halifax Parl Bor (1867—1918), pt E'rn Dv of W Riding (1867—85), pt Elland Dv (1885—1918). *Eccl* Pontef. RDn (1843—57), Halifax RDn (1857—*).

OVENDEN ST GEORGE

EP [W Riding] Cr 1878 from Illingworth EP, Halifax St James EP.[587] Halifax RDn. Bdry: 1927.[67]

OVERTON

AP [N Riding] Incl tp Shipton (sep CP 1866[2]); also incl pt of tp Skelton of Skelton AP. Usual civ spelling; for eccl see following entry. *LG* Seq 31. Transf 1974 to N Yorks.[5] *Parl* Seq 16.

OVERTON WITH SHIPTON

AP [N Riding] Usual eccl spelling; for civ and civ sep tps, see prev entry. *Eccl* Bulmer RDn (until 1862), Eas. RDn (1862—1962). Bdry: 1878.[744] Abol eccl 1962 to help cr Shipton with Overton EP.[455]

OVINGTON

[N Riding] Tp in Forcett AP (qv for status), sep CP 1866,[2] eccl severed 1899 and transf to Wycliffe AP.[563] *LG* Seq 39. Transf 1974 to Durham.[5] *Parl* Seq 14.

OWLERTON

EP [W Riding] Cr 1876 from Sheffield St Philip EP.[194] Sheff RDn (1876—1942), Hallam RDn (1942—*). Bdry: 1933 (help cr Malin Bridge EP),[89] 1953.[495]

OWSTON

AP [W Riding] Incl tp Skellow (sep CP 1866[2]), pt tp Burghwallis (remainder constitutes Burghwallis AP). *LG* Seq 94. Civ bdry: 1883,[42] 1915 (loses pt to Adwick le Street AP as the latter [enlarged] constituted Adwick le Street UD).[43] Transf 1974 to S Yorks.[5] *Parl* Seq 27. *Eccl* Seq 40.

OWSTWICK

[E Riding] Tp pt in Garston AP, pt in Roos AP, sep CP 1866.[2] *LG* Hold. Wap, Patr. PLU, RSD, RD. Abol 1935 ent to Roos AP.[13] *Parl* E Riding (1832—85), Hold. Dv (1885—1948).

OWTHORNE

AP [E Riding] Incl tps South Frodingham, Rimswell, Waxholme (each a sep CP 1866[2]). *LG* Hold. Wap, Patr. PLU, RSD, RD. Addtl civ bdry alt: 1891 (reconstituted, exchanging pts with Withernsea CP),[745] 1911.[746] Abol civ 1935 pt to Rimswell CP, pt to Hollym AP.[13] *Parl* E Riding (1832—85), Hold. Dv (1885—1948). *Eccl* Sometimes as 'Owthorne and Rimswell', Seq 16.

OXENHOPE

EP [W Riding] Cr 1845 from Haworth EP.[91] Pontef. RDn (1845—57), Bradf RDn (1857—1921), S Craven RDn (1921—*).

CP [W Riding] Cr 1894 from the pt of Haworth CP in Oxenhope UD.[257] *LG* Keigh. PLU, Oxenhope UD. Abol 1938 ent to Keigh. MB & AP.[28] *Parl* Keigh. Dv (1918—48).

OXSPRING

[W Riding] Tp in Penistone AP, sep CP 1866.[2] *LG* Seq 116. Transf 1974 to S Yorks.[5] *Parl* Seq 50.

OXTON

[Ainsty (W Riding until 1449 and from 1836, indept jurisd 1449—1836)] Tp in Tadcaster AP, sep CP 1866.[2] *LG* Seq 73. Transf 1974 to N Yorks.[5] *Parl* Seq 23.

PADDOCK

EP [W Riding] Cr 1831 from Huddersfield AP,[9] refounded 1856.[89] Pontef. RDn (1831—57), Hudd. RDn (1857—*).

PANNAL

AP [W Riding] *LG* Claro Wap, Knar. PLU, pt Harrog. USD (enlarged pt 1888—94), pt Harrog. MB (1884—94), pt Knar. RSD, Knar. RD (1894—1938), Nidd. RD (1938—74). Civ bdry: 1894 (loses the pt in the MB to help cr Harrogate CP),[262] 1888,[261] 1900,[242] 1938.[28] Transf 1974 to N Yorks.[5] *Parl* Seq 36. *Eccl* Ainsty RDn (until 1820), Old Ainsty RDn (1820—36), Pontef. RDn (1836—57), Wethb. RDn (1857—1921), Knar. RDn (1921—71), Harrog. RDn (1971—*). *Eccl* bdry: 1887 (help cr Beckwithshaw EP),[225] 1898 (help cr Harrogate St Mark EP).[284]

PARK GATE

EP [W Riding] Cr 1869 from Rawmarsh AP, Greasbrough EP.[209] Wath RDn (1869—87), Rotherh. RDn (1887—1960). Abol 1960 to help cr Rawmarsh and Parkgate EP.[288]

PARLINGTON

[W Riding] Tp in Aberford AP, sep CP 1866.[2] *LG* Seq 106. Transf 1974 to W Yorks.[5] *Parl* Seq 24.

PATELEY BRIDGE

EP [W Riding] Cr 1811 from Ripon AP.[9] Pec jurisd Lbty Ripon (until 1836), Boroughbr. RDn (1836—49), Ripon RDn (1849—1905), Nidd. RDn (1905—71), Ripon RDn (1971—*). Bdry: 1862 (refound Dacre EP [orig sep EP 1839 from Ripon, qv]).[457]

PATRICK BROMPTON

AP [N Riding] Pt of tp 'Patrick Brompton' in E Hang Wap as were tp Newton le Willow (sep CP 1866[2]), pt tp Arrathorne (sep CP 1866[2]), pt tp Scotton (sep CP 1866,[2] pt eccl severed 1897 to help refound Hipswell EP[247]); incl in W Hang Wap chap Hunton (sep CP 1866,[2] sep EP 1794[9]). Remainder of tp 'Patrick Brompton' in Bedale AP. *LG* Leyb. PLU, RSD, RD. Transf 1974 to N Yorks.[5] *Parl* Seq 14. *Eccl* Catt. RDn (until 1857), Catt. East RDn (1857—1928), Bedale RDn (1928—30). Abol eccl 1930 pt to help cr Patrick Brompton with Hunton EP, pt to Hornby AP.[137]

PATRICK BROMPTON WITH HUNTON

EP [N Riding] Cr 1930 by union pt Patrick Brompton AP, pt Hornby AP, pt Crakenhall EP.[137] Bedale RDn.

PATRINGTON

AP [E Riding] *LG* Seq 15. Bdry: 1935 (gains Winestead AP).[13] Transf 1974 to Humb.[5] *Parl* Seq 5. *Eccl* Pec jurisd Bev. (until 1836), Seq 16 thereafter.

PAULL

AP [E Riding] Incl tp Thorngumbald, pt tp Ryhill and Camerton (each a sep CP 1866[2]). Usual civ spelling; for eccl see 'Paull with Thorngumbald'. *LG* Seq 15. Transf 1974 to Humb.[5] *Parl* Seq 5.

EP [E Riding] Cr 1954 when tp Thorngumbald eccl severed from Paull with Thorngumbald AP (usual eccl spelling) to help cr Burstwick with Thorngumbald EP, the remainder to be Paull EP.[374] Hold. RDn.

PAULL WITH THORNGUMBALD

AP [E Riding] Usual eccl spelling; for civ and civ sep tps, see 'Paull'. *Eccl* Hold. RDn (until 1849), S Hold. RDn (1849—66), Hedon RDn (1866—1916), S Hold. RDn (1916—54). Abol 1954, area of tp Thorngumbald severed to help cr Burstwick with Thorngumbald EP, the remainder to be 'Paull' EP.[374]

PAYTHORNE

[W Riding] Tp in Gisburn AP, sep CP 1866.[2] *LG* Seq 108. Transf 1974 to Lancs.[5] *Parl* Seq 41.

PENISTONE

AP [W Riding] Incl tp Denby (sep CP 1866,[2] sep EP 1738,[9] eccl refounded 1854[311]), tp Thurlstone (sep CP 1866,[2] sep EP 1906[462]), tps Gunthwaite, Hunshelf, Ingbirchworth, Langsett, Oxspring (each a sep CP 1866[2]). *LG* Staincr. Wap, Wortley PLU (1838—49), Penist. PLU (1849—1930), USD, UD. Addtl civ bdry alt: 1938 (gains Hoyland Swaine UD & CP, pt Thurlstone UD & CP).[28] Transf 1974 to S Yorks.[5] *Parl* Seq 50. *Eccl* Seq 41. Addtl eccl bdry alt: 1917 (help cr Stocksbridge EP),[46] 1964.[82]

PICKERING

AP [N Riding] Incl chaps Allerston, Ebberston (united 1252 as 'Ebberston with Allerston',[61] 'Ebberston', 'Allerston' each gain sep civ identity early), chaps

Ellerburne, Wilton (united 1252 as 'Ellerburne with Wilton'; the par civ 'Ellerburne' with Wilton considered a chap [sep CP 1866[2]], eccl called 'Ellerburne' after 1755 when Wilton a sep EP[9]), chap Goathland (sep CP 1866,[2] sep EP 1745[9]), chap Newton (sep CP 1866,[2] sep EP 1866 as 'Newton upon Rawcliffe' from Pickering AP, Levisham AP[747]), tps Kingthorpe, Marishes (each a sep CP 1866,[2] the latter sometimes early 'Pickering Marishes'). *LG* Pick. Lythe Wap, Pick. PLU, Bor (status not sustained), USD, UD. Addtl civ bdry alt: 1883,[26] 1887,[49] 1887.[700] Transf 1974 to N Yorks.[5] *Parl* Pt Pick. Parl Bor (1295 only), Seq 20. *Eccl* Pec jurisd Dean of York (until 1836), Seq 28 thereafter. Addtl eccl bdry alt: 1852 (help refound Grosmont EP).[258]

PICKERING MARISHES—see MARISHES

PICKHILL

AP [N Riding] *LG* Pt Hallik. Wap (tps Ainderby Quernhow, Howe, Pickhill with Roxby, Sinderby, pt tp Swainby with Allerthrope [each a sep CP 1866[2]]), pt Allert. Wap (tp Holme [sep CP 1866[2]]) so that 'Pickhill' has no sep civ identity after 1866. *Parl* N Riding (1832—67). *Eccl* Seq 53.

PICKHILL WITH ROXBY

[N Riding] Tp in Pickhill AP, sep CP 1866.[2] *LG* Seq 45. Transf 1974 to N Yorks.[5] *Parl* Seq 16.

PICTON

[N Riding] Tp in Kirk Leavington AP, sep CP 1866.[2] *LG* Langb. Lbty, Stock. PLU (soon after 1837[112]—75), Middlesb. PLU (1875—1930), RSD, Stokes. RD. Transf 1974 to N Yorks.[5] *Parl* Seq 11.

PINCHINTHORPE

[N Riding] Tp in Guisborough AP, sep CP 1866.[2] *LG* Langb. Lbty, Guisb. PLU, RSD, RD (1894—1932), UD (1932—74). Transf 1974 to Clev.[5] *Parl* Seq 9.

PITSMOOR

EP [W Riding] Cr 1845 from Attercliffe AP.[147] Donc. RDn (1845—57), Rotherh. RDn (1857—62), Sheff RDn (1862—1942), Attercliffe RDn (1942—71). Bdry: 1846,[320] 1868 (cr Neepsend EP),[208] 1902 (help cr Sheffield St Cuthbert EP),[354] 1938 (help cr Sheffield St Leonard, Norwood EP),[511] 1939 (help cr Sheffield St Cecilia, Parsons Cross EP),[513] 1939 (help refound Hillsborough and Wadsley Bridge EP).[407] Abol 1973 to help cr Pitsmoor with Wicker EP.[456]

PITSMOOR WITH WICKER

EP [W Riding] Cr 1973 by union Pitsmoor EP, Wicker with Neepsend EP.[456] *Eccl*esfield RDn.

PLOMPTON

[W Riding] Tp in Spofforth AP, sep CP 1866.[2] *LG* Seq 84. Bdry: 1938.[28] Transf 1974 to N Yorks. *Parl* Seq 36.

POCKLEY

[N Riding] Chap in Helmsley AP, sep CP 1866[2]; for eccl see 'Pockley cum Eastmoors'. *LG* Seq 63. Transf 1974 to N Yorks.[5] *Parl* Seq 21.

POCKLEY CUM EASTMOORS

EP [N Riding] Cr 1898 from Helmsley AP (tp Pockley, hmlt Eastmoors [not sep civ], pt tp Bedlam)[121]; for civ see prev entry. Helm. RDn.

POCKLINGTON

AP [E Riding] Incl chaps Barmby on the Moor, Fangfoss (each a sep par 1252,[183] each retains sep civ identity, eccl held together 1568—1747, Fangfoss a sep EP 1747[9]), chaps Great Givendale, Millington (united as sep par 1252 as 'Great Givendale with Grimthorpe'[573]), chaps Hayton, Bielby (united as sep par 1252, eccl as 'Hayton with Bielby',[248] civ 'Hayton' from which Bielby a sep CP 1866[2]), chaps Thornton, Allerthorpe (united as sep par 1252, eccl as 'Thornton with Allerthorpe',[62] 'Thornton', 'Allerthorpe' sep civ identity early from latter), tps Ousethorpe, Yapham cum Meltonby (each a sep CP 1866[2]). Usual civ 'Pocklington'; usual eccl 'Pockington with Yapham cum Meltonby and Owsthorpe', qv. *LG* Harth. Wap, Pockl. Bor, PLU, RSD (1875—93), USD (1893—94), UD (1894—1935), RD (1935—74). Addtl civ bdry alt: 1895.[184] Transf 1974 to Humb.[5] *Parl* Seq 7.

POCKLINGTON WITH YAPHAM CUM MELTONBY AND OWSTHORPE

AP [E Riding] Usual eccl spelling; for civ and civ and eccl sep tps and chaps, see prev entry. *Eccl* Pec jurisd Dean of York (until 1836), Harth. & Hull RDn (1836—57), W Buckr. RDn (1857—62), Pockl. RDn (1862—1948). Abol eccl 1948 to help cr Pocklington with Yapham cum Meltonby and Oswthorpe and Kilnwick Percy EP.[655]

POCKLINGTON WITH YAPHAM CUM MELTONBY AND OWSTHORPE AND KILNWICK PERCY

EP [E Riding] Cr 1948 by union Kilnwick Percy AP, Pocklington with Yapham cum Meltonby and Owsthorpe AP.[655] Pockl. RDn. Bdry: 1960.[122]

POLLINGTON

[W Riding] Tp in Snaith AP, sep CP 1866.[2] *LG* Seq 95. Bdry: 1883.[52] Transf 1974 to Humb.[5] *Parl* Seq 29.

PONTEFRACT

AP [W Riding] Incl chap Knottingley (sep CP 1866,[2] sep EP 1725[9]), tp Carleton (sep CP 1866,[2] sep EP 1869[109]), tp East Hardwick (sep CP 1866,[2] sep EP 1876[29]), tp Monkhill, tp Tanshelf, pt tp Ferry Fryston (each a sep CP 1866[2]). *LG* Osg. Wap, not in a PLU (until 1862), Pontef. PLU (1862—1930), Bor/MB, USD. Addtl civ bdry alt: 1883,[52] 1889,[728] 1892 (gains Monkhill CP),[717] 1920 (gains Pontefract Park CP, Tanshelf CP),[65] 1937 (incl gains Carleton CP).[31] Transf 1974 to W Yorks.[5] *Parl* Pontef. Parl Bor (1295, 1298, 1620—1918), Pontef. Dv (1918—48), Pontef. BC (1948—70), Pontef. & Castlef. BC (1970—*). *Eccl* Ainsty RDn (until 1820), New Ainsty RDn (1820—57), Pontef. RDn (1857—*). Addtl eccl bdry alt: 1838 (cr Pontefract All Saints EP),[141] 1956.[149]

PONTEFRACT ALL SAINTS

EP [W Riding] Cr 1838 from Pontefract AP.[141] New Ainsty RDn (1838—57), Pontef. RDn (1857—1930). Bdry: 1930 (help cr Airedale with Fryston EP),[45] 1956.[149]

PONTEFRACT PARK

[W Riding] Ex-par place, sep CP 1858.[393] *LG* Osg. Wap, Barwick GilbU (until 1869), Pontef PLU

(1869—1920), MB (1875—1920), USD. Bdry: 1889.[748] Abol 1920 ent to Pontefract AP.[65] *Parl* Pontef. Parl Bor (1295, 1298, 1620—1918), Pontef. Dv (1918—48).

POOL

[W Riding] Tp in Otley AP, sep CP 1866,[2] sep EP 1749,[9] eccl refounded 1879.[494] *LG* Seq 103. Transf 1974 to W Yorks.[5] *Parl* Seq 30. *Eccl* Ainsty RDn (1749—1820), Old Ainsty RDn (1820—36), Pontef. RDn (1836—57), Otley RDn (1857—1921), Knar. RDn (1921—71), Harrog. RDn (1971—*).

NETHER POPPLETON

AP [Ainsty (W Riding until 1449 and from 1836, indept jurisd 1449—1836)] Incl pt chap Upper Poppleton (sep CP 1866,[2] eccl severed 1844 to help cr Copmanthorpe EP[437]). *LG* Seq 72. Addtl civ bdry alt: 1883.[52] Transf 1974 to N Yorks.[5] *Parl* Seq 23. *Eccl* Ainsty RDn (until 1820), New Ainsty RDn (1820—62), Ainsty RDn (1862—66). Abol eccl 1866 to help cr Nether Poppleton with Upper Poppleton EP.[438]

NETHER POPPLETON WITH UPPER POPPLETON

EP [W Riding] Cr 1866 by union Nether Poppleton AP, area Upper Poppleton from Copmanthorpe EP.[438] Ainsty RDn (1866—71), Bp'thorpe RDn (1871—81), Ainsty RDn (1881—*).

UPPER POPPLETON

[Ainsty (W Riding until 1449 and from 1836, indept jurisd 1449—1836)] Chap pt in York St Mary Bishopshill Junior AP, pt in Nether Poppleton AP, sep CP 1866,[2] eccl severed 1844 to help cr Copmanthorpe EP,[437] the area of the orig chap eccl severed 1866 from the latter to help cr Nether Poppleton with Upper Poppleton EP.[438] *LG* York PLU (1837—54), Gt Ouseb. PLU (1854—1930), RSD, RD (1894—1938), Nidd. RD (1938—74). Bdry: 1883.[52] Transf 1974 to N Yorks.[5] *Parl* Seq 23.

POTTER NEWTON

[W Riding] Tp in Leeds AP, sep CP 1866,[2] sep EP 1883 from Leeds AP, Sheepscar St Clement EP, Buslingthorpe EP.[113] *LG* Skyr. Wap, Carlton GilbU (until 1869), Leeds PLU (1869—1904), Bor/MB/CB, USD. Civ bdry: 1894 (gains the pt of Seacroft CP in Leeds CB).[504] Abol civ 1904 ent to Leeds AP.[69] *Parl* Leeds Parl Bor (1832—85); see Part III of the *Guide* for composition of Leeds Parl Bors (1885—1918) by wards of the MB. *Eccl* Leeds RDn (1883—1971), Allert. RDn (1971—*). Eccl bdry: 1895 (help cr Leeds St Aidan EP),[71] 1967.[127]

POTTERY FIELD

EP [W Riding] Cr 1851 from Hunslet EP.[344] Pontef. RDn (1851—57), Leeds RDn (1857—1954). Sometimes 'Hunslet St Jude EP'. Abol 1954 ent to Hunslet St Mary EP.[141]

POTTO

[N Riding] Tp in chap Whorlton (sep civ identity early from Rudby in Cleveland AP, sep EP 1766[9]), sep CP 1866.[2] *LG* Seq 58. Bdry: 1883.[16] Transf 1974 to N Yorks.[5] *Parl* Seq 11.

PORTINGTON AND CAVIL

[E Riding] Tp in Eastrington AP, sep CP 1866.[2] *LG* Howdensh. Wap, Howden PLU, RSD, RD. Bdry: 1880.[171] Abol 1935 ent to Eastrington AP.[13] *Parl* E

Riding (1832—85), Howdensh. Dv (1885—1948).

PRESTON

AP [E Riding] Usual civ spelling; for eccl see following entry. Incl chap and bor Hedon (sep civ identity early, sep EP 1814[608]), tp Lelley (sep CP 1866[2]). *LG* Hold. Wap, Scul. PLU, RSD, RD (1894—1935), Hold. RD (1935—74). Civ bdry: 1935,[13] 1968 (loses pt to Kingst. upon Hull CB [assoc with E Riding] and to Sculcoates AP).[253] Transf 1974 to Humb.[5] *Parl* Seq 5.

GREAT AND LITTLE PRESTON

[W Riding] Tp in Kippax AP, sep CP 1866.[2] *LG* Seq 105. Transf 1974 to W Yorks.[5] *Parl* Seq 25.

LONG PRESTON

AP [W Riding] Incl tps West Halton, Wigglesworth (each a sep CP 1866[2]), tp Hellifield (sep CP 1866,[2] sep EP 1912[389]). *LG* Seq 111. Transf 1974 to N Yorks.[5] *Parl* Seq 41. *Eccl* Craven RDn (until 1857), Craven RDn, W'rn Dv (1857—63), Craven RDn, N'rn Dv (1863—1921), Settle RDn (1921—71), Bowl. RDn (1971—*). Addtl eccl bdry alt: 1842 (help refound Rathmell EP),[196] 1926.[68]

PRESTON IN HOLDERNESS

AP [E Riding] Usual eccl spelling; for civ and civ and eccl sep chap and tp, see 'Preston'. *Eccl* Pec jurisd Sub-Dean of York (until 1836), Seq 16 thereafter.

PRESTON UNDER SOAR

[N Riding] Tp in Wensley AP, sep CP 1866.[2] *LG* Seq 53. Transf 1974 to N Yorks.[5] *Parl* Seq 14.

PUDSEY

[W Riding] Chap in Calverley AP, sep CP 1866,[2] sep EP 1733,[9] eccl refounded 1878.[432] *LG* Morley Wap, Bradf PLU (1837—48), N Bierley PLU (1848—1930), Pudsey USD (ent 1875—82, pt 1882—94), pt Bradf MB (1882—89), pt Bradf CB (1889—94), pt Bradf USD (1882—94), Pudsey UD (1894—1900), MB (1900—74). Civ bdry: 1894 (loses the pt in Bradf CB [assoc with W Riding] to cr Tyersall CP),[257] 1937 (loses pt to Leeds CB [assoc with W Riding] & AP, gains Calverley UD & CP, gains Farsley UD & CP).[31] Transf 1974 to W Yorks.[5] *Parl* W Riding (1832—67), E'rn Dv of W Riding (1867—85), pt Bradf Parl Bor, pt Pudsey Dv (1885—1918), Pudsey & Otley Dv (1918—48), Pudsey BC (1948—*). *Eccl* Pontef. RDn (1733—1857), Bradf RDn (1857—1921), Calverley RDn (1921—*). Eccl bdry: 1846 (cr Pudsey St Paul EP),[749] 1861 (help cr Laister Dyke EP),[193] 1865,[35] 1959 (incl help cr Woodhall EP),[492] 1967.[127]

PUDSEY ST PAUL

EP [W Riding] Cr 1864 from Pudsey EP.[749] Bradf RDn (1864—1921), Calverley RDn (1921—*). Bdry: 1959.[320]

PURLWELL

EP [W Riding] Cr 1911 from Batley AP.[214] Dewsb. RDn. Bdry: 1913.[119]

PURSTON CUM SOUTH FEATHERSTONE

EP [W Riding] Cr 1875 from Featherstone AP[716]; for civ see following entry. Pontef. RDn.

PURSTON JAGLIN

[W Riding] Tp in Featherstone AP, sep CP 1866,[2] sep EP 1875 as 'Purston cum South Featherstone',[721] qv. *LG* Osg. Wap, Barwick GilbU (until

1869), Pontef. PLU (1869—1930), Featherstone USD, UD. Abol civ 1938 ent to Featherstone AP.[31] *Parl* W Riding (1832—67), N'rn Dv of W Riding (1867—85), Osg. Dv (1885—1918), Pontef. Dv (1918—48).

QUEEN'S HEAD
EP [W Riding] Cr 1845 from Bradford AP (pt tp Clayton), Halifax AP (pt tp Northowram).[256] Pontef. RDn (1845—57), Halifax RDn (1857—94), Bradf RDn (1894—1921), Horton RDn (1921—71), Bowl. & Horton RDn (1971—72). Renamed 1972 'Queensbury' EP.[320]

QUEENSBURY
CP [W Riding] Cr 1894 by union of the pts of Clayton CP, Northowram CP in Queensbury UD.[410] *LG* Halifax PLU, Queensbury UD. Abol 1937 to help cr Queensbury & Shelf UD & CP.[31] *Parl* Elland Dv (1918—48).

EP [W Riding] Renaming 1972 of Queen's Head EP.[320] Bowl. & Horton RDn.

QUEENSBURY AND SHELF
CP [W Riding] Cr 1937 by union Queensbury UD & CP, Shelf UD & CP.[31] *LG* Queensbury & Shelf UD. Transf 1974 to W Yorks.[5] *Parl* Brigh. & Spenb. BC (1948—55), Bradf South BC (1955—*).

RAINTON WITH NEWBY
[N Riding] Tp in Topcliffe AP, sep CP 1866.[2] *LG* Seq 42. Transf 1974 to N Yorks.[5] *Parl* Seq 16.

RAISTHORPE AND BURDALE
[E Riding] Tp in Wharram Percy AP, sep CP 1866.[2] *LG* Buckr. Wap, Malton PLU, RSD, Norton RD. Abol 1935 to help cr Wharram CP.[13] *Parl* E Riding (1832—85), Buckr. Dv (1885—1948).

RAMSGILL
EP [N Riding] Cr 1844 from Middlesmoor EP.[133] Catt. RDn (1844—57), Ripon RDn (1857—77), Masham RDn (1877—1905), Nidd. RDn (1905—71), Ripon RDn (1971—*).

RAND GRANGE
[N Riding] Hmlt in Bedale AP, sep CP 1866.[2] *LG* Seq 49. Transf 1974 to N Yorks.[5] *Parl* Seq 15.

RANMOOR
EP [W Riding] Cr 1879 from Fulwood EP, Crookes St Thomas EP, Broomhall EP.[218] Sheff RDn (1879—1942), Hallam RDn (1942—*). Bdry: 1962.[191]

RASHCLIFFE
EP [W Riding] Cr 1865 from Lockwood EP.[311] Hudd. RDn. Bdry: 1897 (help cr Crosland Moor EP).[319]

RASKELF
[N Riding] Chap in Easingwold AP, sep CP 1866,[2] sep EP 1744 as 'Raskelfe',[9] qv. *LG* Seq 28. Transf 1974 to N Yorks.[5] *Parl* Seq 16.

RASKELFE
[N Riding] Chap in Easingwold AP, sep EP 1744,[9] sep CP 1866 as 'Raskelf',[2] qv in prev entry. *Eccl* Bulmer RDn (1744—1862), Eas. RDn (1862—*).

RASTRICK
[W Riding] Chap in Halifax AP, sep CP 1866,[2] sep EP 1720,[9] abol eccl 1724 to help cr Elland cum Stainland and Fixby EP,[178] the latter re-augmented 1739 as 'Elland' but usually called 'Elland with Greetland' until Greetland a sep EP 1862,[138] thereafter 'Elland' incl area Rastrick, 'Rastrick' re-

cr a sep EP 1881 from Elland EP.[522] *LG* Morley Wap, Halifax PLU, Rastrick USD (1875—93), Brigh. MB (1893—1915), Brigh. USD (1893—94). Abol civ 1915 ent to Brighouse CP.[352] *Parl* W Riding (1832—67), E'rn Dv of W Riding (1867—85), Elland Dv (1885—1918). *Eccl* Pontef. RDn (1720—24), Halifax RDn (1881—1967), Brigh. & Elland RDn (1967—*). *Eccl* bdry: 1916 (cr Rastrick St John EP).[268]

RASTRICK ST JOHN
EP [W Riding] Cr 1916 from Rastrick EP.[268] Halifax RDn (1916—67), Brigh. & Elland RDn (1967—*).

RATHMEL IN CRAVEN
[W Riding] Tp in Giggleswick AP, sep CP 1866 as 'Rathmell',[2] qv, sep EP 1841 as 'Rathmel in Craven',[9] as such eccl refounded 1842 from Giggleswick AP, Long Preston AP.[196] *Eccl* Craven RDn (1841—57), Craven RDn, N'rn Dv (1857—1921), Settle RDn (1921—*). Eccl bdry: 1926.[691]

RATHMELL
[W Riding] Tp in Giggleswick AP, sep CP 1866,[2] sep EP 1841 as 'Rathmel in Craven',[9] qv, as such eccl refounded 1842 from Giggleswick AP, Long Preston AP.[196] *LG* Seq 111. Civ bdry: 1938.[28] Transf 1974 to N Yorks.[5] *Parl* Seq 41.

RAVENFIELD
[W Riding] Origins unsure, prob chap in Mexborough AP,[750] sep civ identity early, sep EP 1743.[9] *LG* Seq 119. Transf 1974 to S Yorks.[5] *Parl* Seq 55. *Eccl* Pec jurisd Archdeacon of York (until 1836), Donc. RDn (1836—57), Rotherh. RDn (1857—*). Eccl bdry: 1956 (incl help cr Bramley EP).[215]

RAVENSCAR
EP [N Riding] Cr 1914 from Cloughton EP, Fylingdales EP.[168] Scarb. RDn.

RAVENSRODD
AP [E Riding] Sometimes 'Ravenser', 'Ravensbury', or 'Ravenspurn'. Orig AP, swallowed into sea & Humber estuary. *LG* Hold. Wap. *Parl* Ravensrodd Parl Bor (1304, 1326—27, 1337 only).

RAVENSTHORPE
[W Riding] Area in Mirfield AP, sep EP 1870,[405] sep CP 1894 from the pt of Mirfield AP in Ravensthorpe UD.[257] *LG* Dewsb. PLU, Ravensthorpe UD (1894—1910), Dewsb. MB (1910—13), CB (1913—25). Civ bdry: 1895.[11] Abol civ 1925 ent to Dewsbury AP.[477] *Parl* Dewsb. Parl Bor (1918—48). *Eccl* Birstall RDn (1870—1927), Dewsb. RDn (1927—*).

RAVENSWORTH
[N Riding] Tp in Kirkby Ravensworth AP, sep CP 1866.[2] *LG* Seq 38. Bdry: 1883,[16] 1888.[624] Transf 1974 to N Yorks.[5] *Parl* Seq 14.

RAWCLIFFE
[N Riding] Tp pt in York St Michael le Belfrey AP, pt in York St Olave, Marygate AP, sep CP 1866.[2] *LG* Seq 32. Bdry: 1934.[3] Transf 1974 to N Yorks.[5] *Parl* Seq 16.

RAWCLIFFE
[W Riding] Tp (pec jurisd Selby [1440—1539], pec jurisd Snaith [1539—1836]) in Snaith AP, sep CP 1866,[2] sep EP 1813.[9] *LG* Seq 95. Civ bdry: 1884.[500] Transf 1974 to Humb.[5] *Parl* Seq 29. *Eccl*

Pontef. RDn (1836—38), New Ainsty RDn (1838—57), Pontef. RDn (1857—62), Selby RDn (1862—71), Snaith RDn (1871—*).

RAWDON

[W Riding] Chap in Guisley AP, sep CP 1866,[2] sep EP 1743.[9] *LG* Skyr. Wap, Carlton GilbU (until 1869), Wharfed. PLU (1869—1930), Rawdon USD, UD. Abol 1937 pt to help cr Aireb. UD & CP, pt to Bradf CB (assoc with W Riding) and to Idle CP, pt to Horsforth UD & CP.[31] *Parl* W Riding (1832—67), N'rn Dv of W Riding (1867—85), Pudsey Dv (1885—1918), Pudsey & Otley Dv (1918—48). *Eccl* Ainsty RDn (1743—1820), Old Ainsty RDn (1820—36), Pontef. RDn (1836—57), Otley RDn (1857—*).

RAWMARSH

AP [W Riding] *LG* Straff. & Tick. Wap, Rotherh. PLU, Rawmarsh USD, UD. Civ bdry: 1886,[751] 1936 (incl loses pt to Rotherh. CB [assoc with W Riding] & AP).[132] Transf 1974 to S Yorks.[5] *Parl* W Riding (1832—67), S'rn Dv of W Riding (1867—85), Rotherh. Dv (1885—1918), Rotherh. Parl Bor (1918—48), Rother Valley CC (1948—*). *Eccl* Donc. RDn (until 1857), Rotherh. RDn (1857—71), Wath RDn (1871—87), Rotherh. RDn (1887—1960). Eccl bdry: 1860 (help cr Kilnhurst EP),[301] 1869 (help cr Park Gate EP),[209] 1958.[654] Abol eccl 1960 to help cr Rawmarsh with Parkgate EP.[288]

RAWMARSH WITH PARKGATE

EP [W Riding] Cr 1960 by union Rawmarsh AP, Park Gate EP.[288] Rotherh. RDn.

RAWTHORPE

EP [W Riding] Cr 1963 from Kirkheaton AP, Mold Green EP.[287] Hudd. RDn (1963—68), Almondb. RDn (1968—*).

REDCAR

[N Riding] Tp in Marske AP, sep CP 1866,[2] sep EP 1830,[9] eccl refounded 1867 from Marske AP, Upleatham EP.[471] *LG* Langb. Lbty, Guisb. PLU, Redcar USD, UD (1894—1922), MB (1922—68). Civ bdry: 1883,[16] 1886,[704] 1921 (gains Coatham CP),[428] 1932.[51] Abol civ 1968 pt to help cr Teesside CB (assoc with N Riding) & CP, pt to Saltburn and Marske by the Sea UD & CP.[537] *Parl* N Riding (1832—85), Clev Dv/CC (1885—1970). *Eccl* Clev RDn (1830—62), Stokes. RDn (1862—78), Middlesb. RDn (1878—1924), Guisb. RDn (1924—*). Eccl bdry: 1955.[457]

REDMIRE

[N Riding] Chap in Wensley AP, sep CP 1866,[2] sep EP 1748.[9] *LG* Seq 53. Transf 1974 to N Yorks.[5] *Parl* Seq 14. *Eccl* Catt. RDn (1748—1857), Catt. West RDn (1857—1928), Wensleyd. RDn (1928—*).

REEDNESS

[W Riding] Tp in Whitgift AP, sep CP 1866.[2] *LG* Osg. Wap, Goole PLU, RSD. Abol 1884 to help cr Swinefleet and Reedness CP.[752] *Parl* W Riding (1832—67), N'rn Dv of W Riding (1867—85).

CP [W Riding] Cr 1894 from Swinefleet and Reedness CP.[753] *LG* Goole PLU, RD. Transf 1974 to Humb.[5] *Parl* Pontef. Dv (1918—48), Goole CC (1948—*).

REETH

[N Riding] Tp in Grinton AP, sep CP 1866.[2] *LG* W Gill. Wap, Richm. PLU (1837—40), Reeth PLU (1840—1930), RSD, RD. Transf 1974 to N Yorks.[5] *Parl* Seq 14.

REIGHTON

AP [E Riding] Orig chap in Hunmanby AP, sep par 1269.[644] *LG* Seq 5. Civ bdry: 1935 (incl gains Speeton CP).[13] Transf 1974 to N Yorks.[5] *Parl* Seq 2. *Eccl* Seq 5.

GREAT RIBSTON WITH WALSHFORD

[W Riding] Tp in Hunsingore AP, sep CP 1866.[2] *LG* Seq 82. Transf 1974 to N Yorks.[5] *Parl* Seq 36.

LITTLE RIBSTON

[W Riding] Tp in Spofforth AP, sep CP 1866.[2] *LG* Seq 88. Transf 1974 to N Yorks.[5] *Parl* Seq 24.

RICCALL

AP [E Riding] *LG* Seq 19. Civ bdry: 1883 (loses pt to Wistow AP, Yorks W Riding).[754] Transf 1974 to N Yorks.[5] *Parl* Seq 7. *Eccl* Pec jurisd Riccall prebend (until 1836), Seq 19 thereafter.

RICHMOND

AP [N Riding] *LG* W Gill. Wap, Richm. PLU, Bor/MB, USD. Transf 1974 to N Yorks.[5] *Parl* Richm. Parl Bor (1585—1885), Richm. Dv/CC (1885—*). *Eccl* Richm. RDn (until 1857), Richm. West RDn (1857—1954). Eccl bdry: 1755 (cr Richmond Holy Trinity EP).[9] Abol eccl 1954 to help cr Richmond St Mary and Holy Trinity EP.[489]

RICHMOND HOLY TRINITY

EP [N Riding] Cr 1755 from Richmond AP.[9] Richm. RDn (1755—1857), Richm. West RDn (1857—1954). Abol 1954 to help cr Richmond St Mary and Holy Trinity EP.[489]

RICHMOND ST MARY AND HOLY TRINITY

EP [N Riding] Cr 1954 by union Richmond AP, Richmond Holy Trinity EP.[489] Richm. West RDn.

RIDDLESDEN

EP [W Riding] Cr 1874 from Morton EP.[168] Craven RDn, S'rn Dv (1874—1921), S Craven RDn (1921—*).

RIEVAULX

[N Riding] Tp in Helmsley AP, sep CP 1866.[2] *LG* Seq 63. Transf 1974 to N Yorks. *Parl* Seq 21.

RIGTON

[W Riding] Tp in Kirkby Overblow AP, sep CP 1866.[2] *LG* Claro Wap, Carlton GilbU (until 1861), Wethb. PLU (1861—1930), RSD, RD. Bdry: 1938.[28] Renamed 1962 'North Rigton' CP.[755] *Parl* W Riding (1832—67), N'rn Dv of W Riding (1867—85), Ripon Dv (1885—1918), Bark. Ash Dv/CC (1918—70).

NORTH RIGTON

CP [W Riding] Renaming 1962 of Rigton CP.[755] *LG* Wethb. RD. Transf 1974 to N Yorks.[5] *Parl* Bark. Ash CC (1970—*).

RILLINGTON

AP [E Riding] Incl chap Scampston (sep CP 1866,[2] sep EP 1766,[9] eccl refounded 1864[756]). *LG* Seq 2. Transf 1974 to N Yorks.[5] *Parl* Seq 1. *Eccl* Seq 3.

RIMINGTON

[W Riding] Tp in Gisburn AP, sep CP 1866.[2] *LG* Seq 108. Transf 1974 to Lancs.[5] *Parl* Seq 41.

RIMSWELL

[E Riding] Tp in Owthorne AP, sep CP 1866.[2] *LG* Seq 15. Bdry: 1935 (incl gains South Frodingham CP, Waxholme CP).[13] Transf 1974 to Humb.[5] *Parl* Seq 5.

RIPLEY

AP [W Riding] Incl pt tp Brearton (sep CP 1866,[2] sep EP 1841[9] but refounded 1866 ent from Knaresborough AP[23]), tp Clint (sep CP 1866[2]), tp Killinghall (sep CP 1866,[2] sep EP 1879 from Ripley AP, Knaresborough AP[278]), pt tp Nidd (remainder of this tp, constituting Nidd AP, in Claro Wap). *LG* Seq 84. Transf 1974 to N Yorks.[5] *Parl* Seq 36. *Eccl* Boroughbr. RDn (until 1870), Knar. RDn (1870—1905), Nidd. RDn (1905—71), Ripon RDn (1971—*). Addtl eccl bdry alt: 1952.[278]

RIPON

AP [W Riding] Tp 'Ripon' in Ripon Lbty as were chap High and Low Bishopside (sep CP 1866[2]), chap Bishop Monkton (sep CP 1866,[2] sep EP 1746 [incl tp Westwick],[9] eccl refounded 1863[163]), chap Sawley (sep CP 1866,[2] sep EP 1743 [incl tp Eavestone],[9] eccl refounded 1863[163]), chap Skelton (sep CP 1866,[2] sep EP 1749 [incl tp Newby with Mulwick],[9] eccl refounded 1815 as 'Skelton cum Newby'[11]), tp Eavestone (sep CP 1866,[2] eccl in chap/EP Sawley as noted above), tp Grantley (sep CP 1866,[2] eccl severed 1740 and united with other tps in Ripon AP but in Claro Wap [qv below] to help cr Winksley cum Grantley EP,[9] the latter refounded 1863[163]), tp Markington with Wallerthwaite (sep CP 1866,[2] 'Markington' a sep EP 1844[507]), tp Newby with Mulwith (sep CP 1866,[2] eccl in chap/EP Skelton as noted above), tp Sharow (sep CP 1866,[2] sep EP 1826,[9] eccl refounded 1829[757]), tp North Stainley with Sleningford (sep CP 1866,[2] 'North Stainley' a sep EP 1842,[9] as such eccl refounded 1844[188]), tp Bishop Thornton (sep CP 1866,[2] sep EP 1748,[9] eccl refounded 1863 [incl ex-par Warsill][163]), tp Westwick (sep CP 1866,[2] eccl in chap/EP Bishop Monkton as noted above), tps Aismunderby with Bondgate, Bishopston, Clotherholme, Givendale, Bridge Hewick, Copt Hewick, Ingerthorpe, Sutton Grange, Whitcliffe with Thorpe (each a sep CP 1866[2]), pt tp Nunwick with Howgrave (the remainder in Yorks N Riding, qv, sep CP 1866[2] with pt in each Riding); incl in Claro Wap tps Aldfieid, Studley Roger (each a sep CP 1866,[2] eccl united 1724 as Aldfield with Studley EP[9]), tp Bewerley (sep CP 1866,[2] pt eccl severed 1858 to help cr Greenhow Hill EP,[9] the latter eccl refounded 1860 from this and other pars,[68] qv), tp Dacre (sep CP 1866,[2] sep EP 1839,[9] eccl refounded 1862 from Pateley Bridge EP[457]), tps Skedling, Winksley (each a sep CP 1866,[2] eccl severed 1740 and united with pt tp Azerley in this Wap and tp Grantley in Ripon Lbty to cr Winksley cum Grantley EP,[9] the latter eccl refounded 1863[163]), pt tp Azerley (sep CP 1866,[2] eccl severed 1740 to help cr Winksley cum Grantley EP as noted). *LG* Not a PLU (until 1852), Ripon PLU (1852—1930), Ripon Bor/MB, USD. Addtl civ bdry alt: 1894 (gains the pt of Aismunderby with Bondgate CP in

Ripon MB, loses pt to help cr Littlethorpe CP),[53] 1900.[280] Transf 1974 to N Yorks.[5] *Parl* Ripon Parl Bor (1295, 1307, 1337, 1553—1885), Ripon Dv/CC (1885—*). *Eccl* Pec jurisd Lbty Ripon (until 1836), Boroughbr. RDn (1836—49), Ripon RDn (1849—*). Addtl eccl bdry alt: 1811 (cr Pateley Bridge EP),[9] 1853 (cr Ripon Holy Trinity EP).[196]

RIPON HOLY TRINITY

EP [W Riding] Cr 1853 from Ripon AP.[196] Ripon RDn.

RIPPONDEN

[W Riding] Area in tp Barkisland in Halifax AP, eccl severed 1724 as sep EP,[9] eccl refounded 1878,[177] sep CP 1937 by union Barkisland UD & CP, Rishworth UD & CP, Sowerby UD & CP, Soyland UD & CP.[31] *LG* Ripponden UD. Transf 1974 to W Yorks.[5] *Parl* Sowerby CC (1948—*). *Eccl* Pontef. RDn (1724—1857), Halifax RDn (1857—*). Eccl bdry: 1881 (help cr Thorpe St John the Divine EP),[758] 1970.[680]

RISE

AP [E Riding] *LG* Seq 16. Civ bdry: 1952.[759] Transf 1974 to Humb.[5] *Parl* Seq 5. *Eccl* Pec jurisd Bev. (until 1836), Seq 15 thereafter.

RISHWORTH

[W Riding] Tp in Halifax AP, sep CP 1866,[2] eccl severed 1724 to help cr Elland cum Stainland and Fixby EP,[177] re-augmented 1739 as 'Elland'[9] but usually called 'Elland with Greetland' until Greetland a sep EP 1862,[138] 'Elland' thereafter (incl area Rishworth). *LG* Morley Wap, Halifax PLU, Rishworth USD, UD. Abol 1937 to help cr Ripponden UD & CP.[31] *Parl* W Riding (1832—67), E'rn Dv of W Riding (1867—85), Sowerby Dv (1885—1948).

RISTON

CP [E Riding] Cr 1935 by union Long Riston AP, North Skirlaugh, Rowton and Arnold CP.[13] *LG* Hold. RD. Bdry: 1952.[759] Transf 1974 to Humb.[5] *Parl* Bridl. CC (1948—*).

LONG RISTON

AP [E Riding] *LG* Hold. Wap, Skirl. PLU, RSD, RD. Civ bdry: 1885.[335] Abol civ 1935 to help cr Riston CP.[13] *Parl* E Riding (1832—85), Hold. Dv (1885—1948). *Eccl* Hold. RDn (until 1849), N Hold. RDn (1849—66), Hornsea RDn (1866—1916), N Hold. RDn (1916—*).

ROBERT TOWN

EP [W Riding] Cr 1847 from Birstall AP, Liversedge EP.[275] Pontef. RDn (1847—57), Dewsb. RDn (1857—66), Birstall RDn (1866—*). Bdry: 1934.[94]

ROCHDALE

AP [Mostly Lancs (Salford Hd), pt Yorks W Riding (Agb. Wap, until 1866)] Incl in Yorks (Agb. Wap) chap Saddleworth (sep CP 1866,[2] sep EP 1737[9]) so that Rochdale ent Lancs thereafter; see main entry in Lancs for other units and for all organisation. Eccl bdry alt (affecting areas in Yorks): 1793 (cr Lydgate EP,[9] eccl refounded 1844[481]), 1796 (cr Friarmere EP,[9] refounded 1844[481]), 1797 (cr Dobcross EP,[9] refounded 1844[447]).

ROECLIFFE

[W Riding] Tp in Aldborough AP, sep CP 1866,[2]

sep EP 1844.[55] *LG* Seq 86. Transf 1974 to N Yorks.[5] *Parl* Seq 36. *Eccl* Boroughbr. RDn (1844—1971), Ripon RDn (1971—*).

ROKEBY

AP [N Riding] *LG* Seq 39. Transf 1974 to Durham.[5] *Parl* Seq 14. *Eccl* Richm. RDn (until 1857), Richm. West RDn (1857—63), Richm. North RDn (1863—1929). Abol eccl 1929 to help cr Rokeby and Brignall EP.[357]

ROKEBY AND BRIGNALL

EP [N Riding] Cr 1929 by union Rokeby AP, Brignall AP.[357] Richm. North RDn.

ROMALDKIRK

AP [N Riding] Incl tps Cotherstone, Holwick, Hunderthwaite, Lartington, Lunedale, Mickleton (each a sep CP 1866[2]). *LG* Seq 39. Addtl civ bdry alt: 1883,[52] 1884.[176] Transf 1974 to Durham.[5] *Parl* Seq 14. *Eccl* Seq 59. Eccl bdry: 1844 (cr Laithkirk EP).[471]

ROMANBY

[N Riding] Tp in Northallerton AP, sep CP 1866.[2] *LG* Seq 22. Transf 1974 to N Yorks.[5] *Parl* N'allert. Parl Bor (1298, 1640—1885), Richm. Dv (1885—1918), Thirsk & Malton Dv/CC (1918—*).

ROOKWITH

[N Riding] Tp in Thornton Watlass AP, sep CP 1866.[2] *LG* Seq 48. Transf 1974 to N Yorks.[5] *Parl* Seq 15.

ROOS

AP [E Riding] Incl pt tp Garton with Grimston, pt tp Owstwick (each a sep CP 1866[2]). *LG* Seq 15. Addtl civ bdry alt: 1935 (gains Hilston CP, Owstwick CP, Tunstall AP).[13] Transf 1974 to Humb.[5] *Parl* Seq 5. *Eccl* Seq 16.

ROSEDALE

EP [N Riding] Cr 1739 from Lastingham AP, Middleton AP,[9] confirmed 1876[668]; for civ, see tp 'Rosedale, West Side' from the former par, tp 'Rosedale, East Side' from the latter. Riddal RDn (1739—1862), Helm. RDn (1862—1928), Pick. RDn (1928—*).

ROSEDALE, EAST SIDE

[N Riding] Tp in Middleton AP, sep CP 1866[2]; for eccl see prev entry. *LG* Seq 61. Transf 1974 to N Yorks.[5] *Parl* Seq 22.

ROSEDALE, WEST SIDE

[N Riding] Tp in Lastingham AP, sep CP 1866[2]; for eccl see 'Rosedale'. Incl undivded pt Spaunton Moor (qv for other pars to which common; abol 1934 lncl pt to this par [another bdry alt in same order affected this par as well][3]). *LG* Ryed. Wap, Pick. PLU, RSD, RD. Transf 1974 to N Yorks.[5] *Parl* Seq 22.

ROSSINGTON

AP [W Riding] *LG* Seq 93. Transf 1974 to S Yorks.[5] *Parl* Seq 44. *Eccl* Retford RDn (until 1856 [Nottingham AD, dioc York (until 1836), dioc Linc (1836—56)]), Donc. RDn (1856—*). Eccl bdry: 1955 (cr New Rossington EP).[760]

NEW ROSSINGTON

EP [W Riding] Cr 1955 from Rossington AP.[760] Donc. RDn.

ROTHERHAM

AP [W Riding] Incl chap Greasbrough (sep CP 1866,[2] sep EP 1718,[9] eccl refounded 1849[323]), chap Tinsley (decayed by 16th cent, rebuilt 17th cent, sep CP 1866,[2] sep EP 1718[9]), tp Brinsworth (sep CP 1866,[2] sep EP 1903 from Rotherham AP, Whiston AP[195]), tp Catcliffe (sep CP 1866[2]), pt tp Dalton (sep CP 1866,[2] sep EP 1849 [qv for constituent pars incl this AP][464]), tp Kimberworth (sep CP 1866,[2] sep EP 1844[596]), tp Orgreave (sep CP 1866[2]), pt tp Whiston (remainder constitutes Whiston AP). *LG* Straff. & Tick. Wap, Rotherh. PLU, MB (1871—1902), USD, CB (1902—74). Addtl civ bdry alt: 1919 (exchanges pts with Sheff CB [assoc with W Riding] and Tinsley CP),[312] 1921 (loses pt to Sheff CB [assoc with W Riding] and to Tinsley CP),[361] 1936 (incl exchanges pts with Wentworth CP),[132] 1967 (loses pt to Sheff CB [assoc with W Riding] & AP).[144] Transf 1974 to S Yorks.[5] *Parl* W Riding (1832—67), S'rn Dv of W Riding (1867—85), Rotherh. Dv (1885—1918), Rotherh. Parl Bor/BC (1918—*). *Eccl* Seq 42. Addtl eccl bdry alt: 1865 (help cr Masborough St John EP),[578] 1875 (cr Eastwood EP),[90] 1937 (cr Clifton EP),[420] 1952,[322] 1969 (help cr Kimberworth Park EP).[579]

ROTHWELL

AP [W Riding] Incl tp Lofthouse with Carlton (sep CP 1866,[2] 'Lofthouse' a sep EP 1843[278]), tp Middleton (sep CP 1866,[2] sep EP 1849[146]), tp Oulton with Woodlesford (sep CP 1866,[2] 'Woodlesford' a sep EP 1869,[743] 'Oulton' a sep EP 1960[416]), tp Thorpe (sep CP 1866[2]). *LG* Agb. Wap, Carlton GilbU (until 1869), Hunslet PLU (1869—1930), Rothwell USD, UD. Addtl civ bdry alt: 1883,[52] 1884,[276] 1937.[31] Transf 1974 to W Yorks.[5] *Parl* Seq 53. *Eccl* Pontef. RDn (until 1857), Wakef RDn (1857—94), Whitkirk RDn (1894—*). Addtl eccl bdry alt: 1968.[339]

ROTSEA

[E Riding] Tp in Hutton Cranswick AP, sep CP 1866.[2] *LG* Harth. Wap, Driff. PLU, RSD, RD. Abol 1935 ent to Hutton Cranswick AP.[13] *Parl* E Riding (1832—85), Buckr. Dv (1885—1948).

ROUGHTOWN

EP [W Riding] Cr 1869 from Lydgate EP (Yorks), the pt in Yorks of Friezeland EP (prev pt Ches, pt Yorks, ent Ches thereafter).[696] Ashton under Lyne RDn.

ROUNDHAY

[W Riding] Tp in Barwick in Elmet AP, sep CP 1866,[2] sep EP 1843,[9] eccl refounded 1910 from Moor Allerton EP, Chapel Allerton AP, Barwick in Elmet AP, Shadwell EP.[73] *LG* Skyr. Wap, Gt Preston GilbU (until 1869), Leeds PLU (1869—1912), RSD, RD. Abol civ 1912 ent to Leeds AP.[202] *Parl* W Riding (1832—85), N'rn Dv of W Riding (1867—85), Bark. Ash Dv (1885—1918). *Eccl* Old Ainsty RDn (1843—57), Wethb. RDn (1857—61), Whitkirk RDn (1861—between 1967 and 1971), Leeds RDn (between 1967 and 1971—71), Allert. RDn (1971—*). Eccl bdry: 1967.[127]

ROUNDHAY ST JOHN

EP [W Riding] Cr 1972 from Barwick in Elmet AP.[205]

Allert. RDn.

EAST ROUNTON

[N Riding] Chap in Rudby in Cleveland AP, sep CP 1866,[2] sep EP 1747,[9] sep eccl status not sustained, eccl severed 1912 and transf to help cr West Rounton with East Rounton EP.[670] *LG* Seq 58. Transf 1974 to N Yorks.[5] *Parl* Seq 11.

WEST ROUNTON

AP [N Riding] *LG* Seq 22. Transf 1974 to N Yorks.[5] *Parl* Seq 14. *Eccl* Pec jurisd Dean & Chapter of Durham (until 1836), Clev RDn (1836—62), N'allert. RDn (1862—1912). Abol eccl 1912 to help cr West Rounton with East Rounton EP.[670]

WEST ROUNTON WITH EAST ROUNTON

EP [N Riding] Cr 1912 by union West Rounton AP, chap East Rounton in Rudby in Cleveland AP.[670] N'allert. RDn.

ROUTH

AP [E Riding] *LG* Seq 13. Transf 1974 to Humb.[5] *Parl* Seq 4. *Eccl* Hold. RDn (until 1849), N Hold. RDn (1849—66), Hornsea RDn (1866—1916), N Hold. RDn (1916—36), Bev. RDn (1936—*).

ROWLEY

AP [E Riding] *LG* Seq 9. Transf 1974 to Humb.[5] *Parl* Seq 8. *Eccl* Harth. & Hull RDn (until 1857), S Harth. RDn (1857—66), Bev. RDn (1866—87), Howden RDn (1887—*).

ROXBY

[N Riding] Tp in Hinderwell AP, sep CP 1866.[2] *LG* Seq 59. Bdry: 1932.[51] Transf 1974 to N Yorks.[5] *Parl* Seq 19.

ROYSTON

AP [W Riding] Incl chap Woolley (sep CP 1866,[2] sep EP 1721[9]), tp Carlton (sep CP 1866,[2] sep EP 1881[117]), tp Chevet (sep CP 1866[2]), tp Cudworth, tp Monk Bretton (each a sep CP 1866,[2] eccl united 1843 as 'Monk Bretton' EP,[331] 'Cudworth' a sep EP 1883 from the latter[368]), tp Notton (sep CP 1866[2]). *LG* Staincr. Wap, Barnsley PLU, RSD, RD (1894—96), Royston UD (1896—1974). Addtl civ bdry alt: 1938.[28] Transf 1974 to S Yorks.[5] *Parl* W Riding (1832—67), S'rn Dv of W Riding (1867—85), Barnsley Dv (1885—1918), Hemsw. Dv/CC (1918—55), Wakef BC (1955—*). *Eccl* Donc. RDn (until 1857), Rotherh. RDn (1857—62), Pontef. RDn (1862—1919), Hemsw. RDn (1919—27), Barnsley RDn (1927—*). Addtl eccl bdry alt: 1876 (help cr Ryhill EP),[29] 1929 (help cr Staincross EP),[325] 1957.[299]

RUDBY IN CLEVELAND

AP [N Riding] Incl Carlton (prob orig chap in this par, perhaps sep par early 17th cent, sep civ identity early, sep EP no later than 1726[9]), chap Faceby (sep civ identity early, eccl in chap/EP Whorlton [qv below], 'Faceby' a sep EP 1792 from Whorton EP[9]), chap Hilton (sep civ identity early, sep EP 1749[622]), chap Middleton upon Leven (sep CP 1866,[2] sep EP 1740,[9] sep eccl status not sustained), chap Newton (sep civ identity early, sep EP 1735[9]), chap East Rounton (sep CP 1866,[2] sep EP 1747,[9] sep eccl status not sustained, eccl severed 1912 to help cr West Rounton with East Rounton EP[670]), chap Seamer (sep civ identity early, sep EP 1728[9]),

chap Whorlton (sep civ identity early, sep EP 1766[9] [eccl incl chap Faceby in this AP until latter a sep EP 1792, qv above]), tps Hutton Rudby, Sexhow, Skutterskelfe (each a sep CP 1866[2]). *LG* Seq 58. Addtl civ bdry alt: 1883.[730] Transf 1974 to N Yorks.[5] *Parl* Seq 11. *Eccl* Sometimes as 'Rudby in Cleveland with Middleton', Seq 24.

RUDSTON

AP [E Riding] *LG* Seq 5. Transf 1974 to Humb.[5] *Parl* Seq 2. *Eccl* Seq 7.

RUFFORTH

AP [Ainsty (W Riding until 1449 and from 1836, indept jurusd 1449—1836)] *LG* Seq 72. Transf 1974 to N Yorks.[5] *Parl* Seq 23. *Eccl* Ainsty RDn (until 1820), New Ainsty RDn (1820—62), Ainsty RDn (1862—71), Bp'thorpe RDn (1871—81), Ainsty RDn (1881—*).

RUSTON PARVA

AP [E Riding] Orig chap in Lowthorpe AP, appropriated to Lowthorpe Collegiate Church, 'Ruston Parva' a sep par from Dissolution.[690] *LG* Dick. Wap, Driff. PLU, RSD, RD. Abol civ 1935 ent to Harpham CP.[13] *Parl* E Riding (1832—85), Buckr. Dv (1885—1948). *Eccl* Seq 8.

RUSWARP

[N Riding] Tp in Whitby AP, sep CP 1866,[2] sep EP 1870 (pt tp Ruswarp).[370] *LG* Whitby Strand Lbty, Whitby PLU, USD, UD. Abol civ 1925 ent to Whitby AP.[612] *Parl* N Riding (1832—85), Whitby Dv (1885—1918), Scarb. & Whitby Dv (1918—48). *Eccl* Guisb. RDn (1870—78), Whitby RDn (1878—*).

RYHILL

[W Riding] Tp in Wragby AP, sep CP 1866,[2] sep EP 1876 from Wragby AP (tp Ryhill, gtr pt tp Wintersett), Royston AP, Felkirk AP.[29] *LG* Seq 113. Transf 1974 to W Yorks.[5] *Parl* Seq 42. *Eccl* Pontef. RDn (1876—1927), Wakef RDn (1927—73), Chevet RDn (1973—*).

RYHILL AND CAMERTON

[E Riding] Tp pt in Burstwick AP, pt in Paull AP, sep CP 1866.[2] *LG* Hold. Wap, Patr. PLU, RSD, RD. Abol 1935 pt to help cr Burstwick CP, pt to Thorngumbald CP.[13] *Parl* E Riding (1832—85), Hold. Dv (1885—1948).

RYLSTONE

[W Riding] Tp in Burnsall AP, sep CP 1866[2]; for eccl see following entry. *LG* Seq 112. Transf 1974 to N Yorks.[5] *Parl* Seq 41.

RYLSTONE WITH CONISTONE

EP [W Riding] Cr 1876 from Burnsall AP (chap Conistone with Kilnsey, tp Rylstone).[368] Craven RDn, N'rn Dv (1876—1921), Skipton RDn (1921—*).

RYTHER

AP [W Riding] Incl tp Lead (sep CP 1866,[2] eccl severed 1912 to help cr Saxton with Lead EP[670]), tp Ryther cum Ossendyke (sep CP 1866[2]) so that 'Ryther' has no sep civ identity after 1866. *LG* Bark. Ash Wap. *Parl* W Riding (1832—67). *Eccl* Seq 32. Addtl eccl bdry alt: 1963.[400]

RYTHER CUM OSSENDYKE

[W Riding] Tp in Ryther AP, sep CP 1866.[2] *LG* Seq

78. Transf 1974 to N Yorks.[5] *Parl* Seq 24.

RYTON

[N Riding] Tp in Kirby Misperton AP, sep CP 1866.[2] *LG* Seq 60. Transf 1974 to N Yorks.[5] *Parl* Seq 21.

SADDLEWORTH

[W Riding] Chap (Yorks, Agb. Wap) in Rochdale AP (o'wise ent Lancs), sep CP 1866 in Yorks,[2] sep EP 1737.[9] *LG* Saddleworth GilbU (until 1853), PLU (1853—1930), pt Quickmere Middle Division USD, pt Upper Mill USD, pt Mossley MB (o'wise ent Lancs, 1885—94), pt Saddleworth RSD, Saddleworth RD (1894—1900), UD (1900—74). Civ bdry: 1894 (loses the pt in Quickmere Middle Division UD to cr Springhead CP, the pt in Mossley MB to help cr Mossley CP [to be ent Lancs], the pt in Upper Mill UD to cr Upper Mill CP),[491] 1900 (gains Upper Mill UD & CP),[761] 1937 (gains Springhead UD & CP).[31] Transf 1974 to Gtr Manch.[5] *Parl* W Riding (1832—67), S'rn Dv of W Riding (1867—85), Colne Valley Dv/CC (1885—*). *Eccl* Manch RDn (until 1848), Ashton under Lyne RDn (1848—72), Rochdale RDn (1872—81), Ashton under Lyne RDn (1881—1929), Oldham RDn (1929—*) (dioc Chester/Manch). Eccl bdry: 1848 (help cr Friezeland EP [Yorks, Ches until 1869, qv]),[86] 1876 (help cr Greenfield EP).[29]

ST JOHN'S WITH THROAPHAM

[W Riding] Area in Laughton en le Morthen AP, sep civ identity early, sep EP 1742[9] but sep status not sustained. Incl chap Letwell, tp Gildingwells (each a sep CP 1866,[2] the 2 eccl severed 1768 as 'Letwell with Gildingwells' EP,[9] the area of Gildingwells severed 1841 to help cr Woodsetts EP, the remainder to be 'Letwell'[572]). *LG* Straff. & Tick. Wap, Worksop PLU, RSD, Kiv. Pk RD. Abol 1954 to help cr Dinnington St John's CP.[480] *Parl* W Riding (1832—67), S'rn Dv of W Riding (1867—85), Donc. Dv (1885—1918), Rother Valley Dv/CC (1918—70).

ST MARTIN

[N Riding] Ex-par place, sep CP 1858.[393] *LG* Seq 50. Transf 1974 to N Yorks.[5] *Parl* Richm. Parl Bor (1585—1885), Richm. Dv/CC (1885—*).

SALTBURN BY THE SEA

[N Riding] Area in Marske AP, sep EP 1873,[21] sep CP 1894 from the pt of Marske AP in Saltburn by the Sea UD.[431] *LG* Guisb. PLU, Saltburn by the Sea UD (1894—1932), Salthurn and Marske by the Sea UD (1932—74). Civ bdry: 1934.[363] Transf 1974 to Clev.[5] *Parl* Clev Dv/CC (1918—70), Clev & Whitby CC (1970—*). *Eccl* Stokes. RDn (1873—78), Middlesb. RDn (1878—1924), Guisb. RDn (1924—*). Eccl bdry: 1952.[351]

SALTERFORTH

[W Riding] Tp in Barnoldswick AP, sep CP 1866.[2] *LG* Seq 112. Transf 1974 to Lancs.[5] *Parl* Seq 41.

SALTERHEBBLE

EP [W Riding] Cr 1845 from Halifax AP (pt tp Skircoat), Halifax St Anne in the Grove EP.[657] Pontef. RDn (1845—57), Halifax RDn (1857—*). Bdry: 1866 (help cr Copley EP),[436] 1891 (cr Salterhebble St Jude EP),[297] 1915 (cr Siddal EP).[762]

SALTERHEBBLE ST JUDE

EP [W Riding] Cr 1891 from Salterhebble EP.[297] Halifax RDn. Bdry: 1912.[594]

SALTMARSHE

[E Riding] Tp in Howden AP, sep CP 1866,[2] eccl severed 1858 to help refound Laxton EP.[440] *LG* Howdensh. Wap, Howden PLU, RSD, RD. Bdry: 1880,[709] 1880,[171] 1880.[172] Abol 1935 pt to Laxton CP, pt to Howden AP.[13] *Parl* E Riding (1832—85), Howdensh. Dv (1885—1948).

SALTON

AP [N Riding] Incl tp Brawby (sep CP 1866[2]). *LG* Ryed. Wap, Kirkby Moors. PLU (soon after 1848[112]—1930), RSD, RD. Transf 1974 to N Yorks.[5] *Parl* Seq 21. *Eccl* Pec jurisd Salton prebend (until 1836), Seq 27 thereafter.

SANCTON

AP [E Riding] Incl tp North Cliffe (sep CP 1866,[2] eccl severed 1887 to help cr North Cave with Cliffe EP[399]), tp Sancton and Houghton (main tp, sep CP as such 1866[2]) so that 'Sancton' has no sep civ identity 1866—1935 (see following entry). *LG* Harth. Wap. *Parl* E Riding (1832—85). *Eccl* Harth. & Hull RDn (until 1857), S Harth. RDn (1857—66), Bev. RDn (1866—71), Weigh. RDn (1871—*). Addtl eccl bdry alt: 1875.[398]

CP [E Riding] Renaming 1935 of Sancton and Houghton CP.[13] *LG* Pockl. RD. Transf 1974 to Humb.[5] *Parl* Bev. CC (1948—55), Howden CC (1955—*).

SANCTON AND HOUGHTON

[E Riding] Main tp in Sancton AP, as such sep CP 1866.[2] *LG* Harth. Wap, Pockl. PLU, RSD, RD. Bdry: 1884.[417] Renamed 1935 'Sancton'.[13] *Parl* E Riding (1832—85), Howdensh. Dv (1885—1948).

SAND HUTTON

[N Riding] Tp in Bossall AP, sep CP 1866,[2] sep EP 1861 by union tp Sand Hutton, chap Claxton, both in Bossall AP.[292] *LG* Seq 32. Transf 1974 to N Yorks.[5] *Parl* Seq 16. *Eccl* Bulmer RDn.

SAND HUTTON

[N Riding] Tp in Thirsk AP, sep CP 1866,[2] sep EP 1753.[9] *LG* Seq 27. Transf 1974 to N Yorks.[5] *Parl* Seq 16. *Eccl* Bulmer RDn (1753—1862), Thirsk RDn (1862—*).

SANDAL MAGNA

AP [W Riding] Incl pt chap and tp West Bretton, tps Crigglestone, Walton (each a sep CP 1866[2]). *LG* Agb. Wap, Wakef PLU, Sandal Magna USD, UD (1894—1909), Wakef MB (1909—15), CB (1915—25). Abol civ 1925 ent to Wakefield AP.[694] *Parl* W Riding (1832—67), S'rn Dv of W Riding (1867—85), pt Norm. Dv (1885—1918), Wakef Parl Bor (pt 1885—1918, ent 1918—48). *Eccl* Pontef. RDn (until 1857), Wakef RDn (1857—1973), Chevet RDn (1973—*). Eccl bdry: 1735 (cr Chapelthorpe EP,[9] refounded 1843[406]), 1876 (help cr Ryhill EP),[29] 1903 (cr Sandal Magna St Catherine EP).[36]

SANDAL MAGNA ST CATHERINE

EP [W Riding] Cr 1903 from Sandal Magna AP.[36] Wakef RDn (1903—73), Chevet RDn (1973—*).

KIRK SANDALL

AP [W Riding] Somtimes early 'Sandall Parva' or

'Little Sandall'. *LG* Straff. & Tick. Wap, Donc. PLU, RSD, RD. Civ bdry: 1886 (gains Long Sandall CP).[763] Abol civ 1921 to help cr Barnby Don with Kirk Sandall CP.[190] *Parl* W Riding (1832—67), S'rn Dv of W Riding (1867—85), Donc. Dv (1885—1918), Don Valley Dv (1918—48). *Eccl* Donc. RDn. Eccl bdry: 1875 (help cr Moss EP),[11] 1952,[522] 1952 (help cr Wheatley Hills EP).[134]

LONG SANDALL

[W Riding] Tp in Doncaster AP, sep CP 1866.[2] *LG* Donc. Soke, PLU, RSD. Abol 1886 ent to Kirk Sandall AP.[763] *Parl* W Riding (1832—67), S'rn Dv of W Riding (1867—85), Donc. Dv (1885—1918).

SAWDON

[N Riding] Tp in Brompton AP, sep CP 1866.[2] *LG* Pick. Lythe Wap, Scarb. PLU, RSD. Abol 1886 ent to Brompton AP.[176] *Parl* N Riding (1832—85), Whitby Dv (1885—1918).

SAWLEY

[W Riding] Ex-par place, sep CP 1858,[393] eccl abol 1844 to help refound Grindleton EP.[582] *LG* Seq 108. Bdry: 1938.[28] Transf 1974 to Lancs.[5] *Parl* Seq 41.

SAWLEY

[W Riding] Tp in Ripon AP, sep CP 1866,[2] sep EP 1743 (tps Sawley, Eavestone, both in Ripon),[9] eccl refounded 1863.[163] *LG* Seq 100. Civ bdry: 1937.[31] Transf 1974 to N Yorks.[5] *Parl* Seq 34. *Eccl* Pec jurisd Lbty Ripon (until 1836), Boroughbr. RDn (1836—49), Ripon RDn (1849—*).

SAXTON

AP [W Riding] Incl pt tp Barkston, tps Saxton with Scarthingwell, Towton (each a sep CP 1866[2]) so that 'Saxton' has no sep civ identity after 1866. *LG* Bark. Ash Wap. *Parl* W Riding (1832—67). *Eccl* Ainsty RDn (until 1820), New Ainsty RDn (1820—62), Tadc. RDn (1862—71), Selby RDn (1871—1912). Eccl bdry: 1884.[764] Gains 1912 tp Lead from Ryther AP to cr Saxton with Lead EP,[670] qv below.

SAXTON WITH LEAD

EP [W Riding] Cr 1912 by union Saxton AP, tp Lead from Ryther AP.[670] Sometimes called 'Saxton with Towton and Lead'. Tadc. RDn.

SAXTON WITH SCARTHINGWELL

[W Riding] Tp in Saxton AP, sep CP 1866.[2] *LG* Seq 78. Transf 1974 to N Yorks.[5] *Parl* Seq 24.

SCACKLETON

[N Riding] Tp in Hovingham AP, sep CP 1866.[2] *LG* Seq 29. Transf 1974 to N Yorks.[5] *Parl* Seq 16.

SCAGGLETHORPE

[E Riding] Tp in Settrington AP, sep CP 1866.[2] *LG* Seq 2. Transf 1974 to N Yorks.[5] *Parl* Seq 1.

SCALBY

[E Riding] Tp in Blacktoft AP, sep CP 1866.[2] *LG* Howdensh. Wap, Howden PLU, RSD, RD. Bdry: 1880,[282] 1880,[283] 1892 (gains Cheapsides CP).[408] Abol 1935 pt to Blacktoft CP, pt to help cr Giiberdyke CP, pt to help cr Newport CP.[13] *Parl* E Riding (1832—85), Howdensh. Dv (1885—1948).

SCALBY

AP [N Riding] Incl chap Cloughton, tp Staintondale (each a sep CP 1866,[2] eccl united 1874 as

Cloughton EP[148]), tps Burniston, Newby, Throxenby (each a sep CP 1866[2]). *LG* Pick. Lythe Wap, Scarb. PLU, RSD, RD (1894—1902), Scalby UD (1902—74). Addtl civ bdry alt: 1880,[283] 1883,[16] 1887,[162] 1909 (gains Throxenby CP),[765] 1914.[766] Transf 1974 to N Yorks.[5] *Parl* Seq 20. *Eccl* Seq 4. Addtl eccl bdry alt: 1932,[138] 1951 (help cr Scarborough St Luke EP).[544]

SCAMMONDEN

[W Riding] Chap in Huddersfield AP, sep CP 1866,[2] sep EP 1718,[9] sometimes early 'Deanhead', eccl refounded 1862.[136] *LG* Agb. Wap, Hudd. PLU, Scammonden USD, UD. Abol civ 1937 to help cr Colne Valley UD & CP.[31] *Parl* W Riding (1832—67), S'rn Dv of W Riding (1867—85), Colne Valley Dv (1885—1948). *Eccl* Pontef. RDn (1718—1857), Hudd. RDn (1857—1938). Abol eccl 1938 pt to help cr Slaithwaite with East Scammonden EP, pt to Barkisland EP (the united benefice cr at that time called 'Barkisland with West Scammonden').[180]

SCAMPSTON

[E Riding] Chap in Rillington AP, sep CP 1866,[2] sep EP 1766,[9] eccl refounded 1864.[756] *LG* Seq 2. Civ bdry: 1889,[767] 1935 (incl gains Knapton CP).[13] Transf 1974 to N Yorks.[5] *Parl* Seq 1. *Eccl* Buckr. RDn (1766—1857), E Buckr. RDn (1857—66), Buckr. RDn (1866—87), Settr. RDn (1887—1922), Buckr. RDn (1922—*).

SCARBOROUGH

[N Riding] The following have 'Scarborough' in their names. Insofar as any existed at a given time: *LG* Pick. Lythe Wap, Scarb. Bor/MB, PLU, USD. *Parl* Seq 20. *Eccl* Dick. RDn (until 1857), N Dick. RDn (1857—66), Scarb. RDn (1866—*).

AP1—SCARBOROUGH [ST MARY]—Incl tp Falsgrave (sep CP 1866,[2] sep EP 1873[676]). Addtl civ bdry alt: 1890 (gains Falsgrave CP),[541] 1914,[766] 1934,[3] 1953.[404] Transf 1974 to N Yorks.[5] Eccl incl chap Christ Church, hence this par eccl often 'Scarborough St Mary with Christ Church'. Addtl eccl bdry alt: 1844 (cr EP9),[70] 1862 (cr EP6,[9] refounded 1863[768]), 1882 (cr EP1),[326] 1932 (cr EP2).[522] Abol eccl 1965 to help cr EP5.[258]

EP1—SCARBOROUGH HOLY TRINITY—Cr 1882 from AP1.[326]

EP2—SCARBOROUGH ST COLUMBA—Cr 1932 from AP1.[522] Bdry: 1958.[322]

EP3—SCARBOROUGH ST JAMES—Cr 1893 from Falsgrave EP.[542]

EP4—SCARBOROUGH ST LUKE—Cr 1951 from Falsgrave EP, Scalby EP, Seamer with Cayton and East Ayton AP.[544]

—SCARBOROUGH ST MARK—Name used now for EP cr as 'Newby', qv

—SCARBOROUGH ST MARY WITH CHRIST CHURCH—see AP1

EP5—SCARBOROUGH ST MARY WITH CHRIST CHURCH, ST PAUL AND ST THOMAS—Cr 1965 by union AP1, EP9.[258]

EP6—SCARBOROUGH ST MARTIN ON THE HILL—Cr 1862 from AP1,[9] refounded 1863.[768]

EP7—SCARBOROUGH ST SAVIOUR—Cr 1904

from Falsgrave EP.[543] Abol 1973 to help cr EP8.[545]

EP8—SCARBOROUGH ST SAVIOUR WITH ALL SAINTS—Cr 1973 by union EP7, Falsgrave EP.[545]

EP9—SCARBOROUGH ST THOMAS—Cr 1844 from AP1.[70] Abol 1965 to help cr EP5.[258]

SCARCROFT
[W Riding] Tp in Thorner AP, sep CP 1866.[2] *LG* Seq 107. Transf 1974 to W Yorks.[5] *Parl* Seq 24.

SCARGILL
[N Riding] Tp in Barningham AP, sep CP 1866.[2] *LG* Seq 39. Transf 1974 to Durham.[5] *Parl* Seq 14.

SCAWTON
AP [N Riding] *LG* Seq 63. Transf 1974 to N Yorks.[5] *Parl* Seq 21. *Eccl* Seq 26.

SCHOLES
CP [W Riding] Cr 1894 by union of the pts of the following in Scholes UD: Fulstone CP, Hepworth CP, Wooldale CP.[158] *LG* Hudd. PLU, Scholes UD (1894—95), New Mill UD (1895—1938). Bdry: 1895.[570] Abol 1938 pt to Holmf. UD & CP, pt to help cr Dunford CP.[28] *Parl* Colne Valley Dv (1918—48).

EP [W Riding] Cr 1929 from Whitechapel EP, Cleckheaton EP, Hartshead EP.[416] Birstall RDn.

SCISSETT
EP [W Riding] Cr 1840 from High Hoyland AP, Emley AP.[394] Pontef. RDn (1840—57), Silkst. RDn (1857—1927), Hudd. RDn (1927—68), Kirkburton RDn (1968—*). Bdry: 1900 (cr Skelmanthorpe EP),[297] 1913.[365]

SCORBOROUGH
AP [E Riding] *LG* Harth. Wap, Bev. PLU, RSD, RD. Abol civ 1935 to help cr Leconfield CP.[13] *Parl* E Riding (1832—85), Hold. Dv (1885—1948). *Eccl* Pec jurisd Bev. (until 1836), Harth. & Hull RDn (1836—57), N Harth. RDn (1857—66), Harth. RDn (1866—81), Bev. RDn (1881—*).

SCORTON
[N Riding] Tp in Catterick AP, sep CP 1866[2]; eccl in chap Bolton upon Swale (sep EP 1781 from Catterick AP,[9] eccl refounded 1881[347]). *LG* Seq 35. Bdry: 1888.[624] Transf 1974 to N Yorks.[5] *Parl* Seq 14.

SCOSTHROP
[W Riding] Tp in Kirkby in Malham Dale AP, sep CP 1866.[2] *LG* Seq 111. Transf 1974 to N Yorks.[5] *Parl* Seq 41.

SCOTTON
[N Riding] Tp pt in Catterick AP, pt in Patrick Brompton AP, sep CP 1866,[2] pt eccl severed 1897 to help refound Hipswell EP.[247] *LG* Seq 50. Bdry: 1934.[3] Transf 1974 to N Yorks.[5] *Parl* Seq 14.

SCOTTON
[W Riding] Tp in Farnham AP, sep CP 1866.[2] *LG* Seq 10. Transf 1974 to N Yorks.[5] *Parl* Seq 36.

SCOUTHEAD
EP [W Riding] Cr 1886 from Lydgate EP, Dobcross EP (both Yorks), Hey EP (Lancs) to be dioc Manch.[479] Rochdale RDn (1886—93), Ashton under Lyne RDn (1893—1929), Oldham RDn (1929—*).

WEST SCRAFTON
[N Riding] Tp in Coverham AP, sep CP 1866.[2] *LG* Seq 53. Transf 1974 to N Yorks.[5] *Parl* Seq 14.

SCRAYINGHAM
AP [E Riding] Incl tp Howsham (sep CP 1866,[2] sep EP 1860,[9] sep eccl status not sustained), tp Leppington (sep CP 1866[2]). *LG* Buckr. Wap, Pockl. PLU, RSD, RD. Addtl civ bdry alt: 1935 (gains Leppington CP).[13] Transf 1974 to N Yorks.[5] *Parl* E Riding (1832—85), Buckr. Dv (1885—1918), Howdensh. Dv (1918—48), Bev. CC (1948—55), Howden CC (1955—*). *Eccl* Sometimes as 'Scrayingham with Howsham and Leppington', Seq 9.

SCRIVEN
CP [W Riding] Cr 1894 from the pt of Scriven with Tentergate CP not in Knar. & Tentergate UD.[257] *LG* Knar. PLU, RD (1894—1938), Nidd. RD (1938—74). Bdry: 1904,[664] 1938.[28] Transf 1974 to N Yorks.[5] *Parl* Ripon Dv (1918—48), Harrog. CC (1948—*).

SCRIVEN WITH TENTERGATE
[W Riding] Tp in Knaresborough AP, sep CP 1866.[2] *LG* Claro Wap, Knar. PLU, pt Knar. & Tentergate USD, pt Harrrog. USD (1875—88), pt Harrog. MB (1884—88), pt Knar. RSD. Bdry: 1883,[52] 1888.[261] Abol 1894 the pt in the UD cr Tentergate CP, the remainder cr Scriven CP.[257] *Parl* W Riding (1832—67), pt Knar. Parl Bor, pt E'rn Dv of W Riding (1867—85), Ripon Dv (1885—1918).

SCRUTON
AP [N Riding] *LG* Seq 49. Transf 1974 to N Yorks.[5] *Parl* Seq 15. *Eccl* Seq 53.

SCULCOATES
[E Riding] The following have 'Sculcoates' in their names. Insofar as any existed at a given time: *LG* Harth. Wap, Scul. PLU, Kingst. upon Hull Co, MB/CB, USD. *Parl* Kingst. upon Hull Parl Bor (1832—85); see Part III of the *Guide* for composition of Kingst. upon Hull Parl Bors/BCs (1885—*) by wards of the MB/CB. *Eccl* Harth. & Hull RDn (until 1857), S Harth. RDn (1857—62), Bev. RDn (1862—69), Kingst. upon Hull RDn (1869—*).

AP1—SCULCOATES [ALL SAINTS]—Civ bdry: 1898 (gains the following pars in Kingst. upon Hull CB: Cottingham Within CP, Drypool CP, Garrison Side CP, Hessle Within CP, Marfleet AP, Newington CP, Southcoates CP, Sutton Within CP),[446] 1930,[251] 1935,[13] 1968.[253] Transf 1974 to Humb.[5] Parl bdry: 1956.[259] Eccl bdry: 1844 (cr EP3),[188] 1868 (help cr Kingston upon Hull St John EP),[290] 1873 (cr EP2),[313] 1885 (help cr Kingston upon Hull St Philip EP),[598] 1886 (cr EP1).[625] Abol eccl 1973 to help cr Kingston upon Hull St Stephen Sculcoates EP.[662]

EP1—SCULCOATES CHRIST CHURCH—Cr 1886 from AP1.[625] Abol 1962 to help cr Kingston upon Hull Christ Church EP.[658]

EP2—SCULCOATES ST MARY—Cr 1873 from AP1.[313]

EP3—SCULCOATES ST PAUL—Cr 1844 from AP1.[188] Bdry: 1871 (cr EP4),[298] 1897,[56] 1898.[476] Abol 1962 to help cr Kingston upon Hull St Paul with Christ Church Sculcoates EP.[46]

EP4—SCULCOATES ST SILAS—Cr 1871 from EP3.[298] Bdry: 1898.[476] Abol 1969 to help cr Kingston upon Hull St Paul Sculcoates with Christ Church and St Silas EP.[14]

SEACROFT

[W Riding] Tp pt in Whitkirk AP, pt in Leeds AP (hmlt Colcotes, not sep civ), sep CP 1866,[2] sep EP 1846 from Whitkirk AP alone.[82] *LG* Skyr. Wap, Barwick GilbU (until 1869), Leeds PLU (1869—1912), pt Leeds Bor/MB, pt Leeds CB (1889—94), pt Leeds USD, pt Leeds RSD, Leeds RD. Civ bdry: 1885,[769] 1894 (loses the pt in Leeds CB [assoc with W Riding] ent to Potter Newton CP).[504] Abol civ 1912 ent to Leeds CB (assoc with W Riding) & AP.[202] *Parl* W Riding (1832—67), pt Leeds Parl Bor (1832—85), pt E'rn Dv of W Riding (1867—85), pt Bark. Ash Dv (1885—1918); see Part III of the *Guide* for composition of Leeds Parl Bors (1885—1918) by wards of the MB (incl pt of this par). *Eccl* Pontef. RDn (1846—57), Wethb. RDn (1857—61), Whitkirk RDn (1861—*). Eccl bdry: 1873,[636] 1967,[127] 1972.[205]

SEAMER

AP [N Riding] Incl tps East Ayton, Cayton with Deepdale and Killerby, Irton, Osgodby (each a sep CP 1866[2]). Usual civ spelling; for eccl see 'Seamer with Cayton and East Ayton'. *LG* Seq 62. Civ bdry: 1934,[3] 1953.[404] Transf 1974 to N Yorks.[5] *Parl* Seq 20.

SEAMER

[N Riding] Chap in Rudby in Cleveland AP, sep civ identity early, sep EP 1728.[9] Incl pt tp Newby (sep CP 1866[2]). *LG* Seq 58. Transf 1974 to N Yorks.[5] *Parl* Seq 11. *Eccl* Clev RDn (1728—1862), Stokes. RDn (1862—*).

SEAMER WITH EAST AYTON

EP [N Riding] One of 2 EPs cr 1961 when Seamer with Cayton and East Ayton AP (qv in following entry) divided.[396] Scarb. RDn.

SEAMER WITH CAYTON AND EAST AYTON

AP [N Riding] Usual eccl spelling; for civ and civ sep tps, see 1st 'Seamer' above. *Eccl* Dick. RDn (until 1857), N Dick. RDn (1857—66), Scarb. RDn (1866—1961). Eccl bdry: 1951 (help cr Scarborough St Luke EP).[544] Divided 1961 into 2 EPs of Cayton with Eastfield, Seamer with East Ayton.[396]

SEATON

CP [E Riding] Cr 1935 by union Catfoss CP, Seaton and Wassand CP.[13] *LG* Hold. RD. Transf 1974 to Humb.[5] *Parl* Bridl. CC (1948—*).

SEATON AND WASSAND

[E Riding] Tp in Sigglesthorne AP, sep CP 1866.[2] *LG* Hold. Wap, Skirl. PLU, RSD, RD. Abol 1935 to help cr Seaton CP.[13] *Parl* E Riding (1832—85), Hold. Dv (1885—1948).

SEATON ROSS

AP [E Riding] *LG* Seq 12. Civ bdry: 1957.[561] Transf 1974 to Humb.[5] *Parl* Seq 7. *Eccl* Seq 14.

SEDBERGH

AP [W Riding] Incl chap Dent (sep CP 1866,[2] sep EP 1742 [incl area Cowgill],[9] 'Cowgill' eccl a sep par 1864 from Dent,[9] 'Dent' eccl refounded 1865[264]),

chap Garsdale (sep CP 1866,[2] sep EP 1734[9]). *LG* Seq 110. Transf 1974 to Cumbria.[5] *Parl* Seq 41. *Eccl* Kirkby Lonsd. RDn (until 1849), Clapham RDn (1849—1921), Ewecr. RDn (1921—26), Sedbergh RDn (1926—74). Addtl eccl bdry alt: 1737 (cr Howgill EP),[9] 1854 (cr Cauntley with Dowbiggin EP).[311] Abol eccl 1974 to help cr Sedbergh, Cauntley and Garsdale EP.[397]

SEDBERGH, CAUNTLEY AND GARSDALE

EP [W Riding] Cr 1974 by union Sedbergh AP, Cauntley with Dowbiggin EP, Garsdale EP.[397] Ewecr. RDn.

SELBY

AP [W Riding] *LG* Bark. Ash Wap, Selby PLU, USD, UD. Civ bdry: 1883 (gains pt Barlby CP, E Riding).[181] Transf 1974 to N Yorks.[5] *Parl* Seq 24. *Eccl* Pec jurisd Selby (1409—1836), New Ainsty RDn (1836—62), Selby RDn (1862—*). Eccl bdry: 1867 (cr Selby St James EP),[287] 1972.[214]

SELBY ST JAMES

EP [W Riding] Cr 1867 from Selby AP.[287] Selby RDn.

SESSAY

AP [N Riding] Incl tp Hutton Sessay (sep CP 1866[2]). *LG* Seq 23. Transf 1974 to N Yorks.[5] *Parl* Seq 16. *Eccl* Seq 20.

SETTLE

[W Riding] Tp in Giggleswick AP, sep CP 1866,[2] sep EP 1838.[560] *LG* Seq 111. Transf 1974 to N Yorks.[5] *Parl* Seq 41. *Eccl* Craven RDn (until 1857), Craven RDn, N'rn Dv (1857—1921), Settle RDn (1921—71), Bowl. RDn (1971—*).

SETTRINGTON

AP [E Riding] Incl tp Scagglethorpe (sep CP 1866[2]). *LG* Seq 2. Transf 1974 to N Yorks.[5] *Parl* Seq 1. *Eccl* Buckr. RDn (until 1857), W Buckr. RDn (1857—66), Buckr. RDn (1866—87), Settr. RDn (1887—1922), Buckr. RDn (1922—*).

SEWERBY CUM MARTON

[E Riding] Chap & tp in Bridlington AP, sep CP 1866,[2] sep EP 1849 as 'Sewerby with Marton',[349] qv. *LG* Dick. Wap, Bridl. PLU, pt Bridl. USD, pt Bridl. RSD, Bridl. RD. Civ bdry: 1894 (loses the pt in Bridl. UD to Bridlington AP),[239] 1923.[240] Abol civ 1935 pt to Bempton AP, pt to Bridl. MB & AP.[13] *Parl* E Riding (1832—85), Buckr. Dv (1885—1948).

SEWERBY WITH MARTON

[E Riding] Chap & tp in Bridlington AP, sep EP 1850,[346] sep CP 1866 as 'Sewerby cum Marton',[2] qv. *Eccl* Dick. RDn (1849—66), S Dick. RDn (1862—66), Bridl. RDn (1866—*). Eccl bdry: 1870.[213]

SEXHOW

[N Riding] Tp in Rudby in Cleveland AP, sep CP 1866.[2] *LG* Seq 58. Transf 1974 to N Yorks.[5] *Parl* Seq 11.

SHADWELL

[W Riding] Tp in Thorner AP, sep CP 1866,[2] sep EP 1843,[9] eccl refounded 1844.[188] *LG* Skyr. Wap, Barwick GilbU (until 1869), Wethb. PLU (1869—1930), RSD, RD. Civ bdry: 1883,[52] 1885.[179] Abol civ 1912 ent to Leeds CB (assoc with W Riding) & AP.[202] *Parl* W Riding (1832—67), N'rn Dv of W

Riding (1867—85), Bark. Ash Dv (1885—1918). *Eccl* Pontef. RDn (1843—57), Wethb. RDn (1857—61), Whitkirk RDn (1861—1971), Allert. RDn (1971—*). Eccl bdry: 1910 (help refound Roundhay EP),[73] 1967,[127] 1972.[78]

SHAFTON

[W Riding] Tp in Felkirk AP, sep CP 1866.[2] *LG* Seq 113. Bdry: 1888,[348] 1916.[349] Transf 1974 to S Yorks.[5] *Parl* W Riding (1832—67), S'rn Dv of W Riding (1867—85), Barnsley Dv (1885—1918), Hemsw. RDn (1918—*).

SHARLSTON

[W Riding] Tp in Warmfield AP, sep CP 1866,[2] sep EP 1929 from Warmfield AP, Normanton AP.[595] *LG* Seq 69. Transf 1974 to W Yorks.[5] *Parl* Seq 53. *Eccl* Wakef RDn (1929—73), Chevet RDn (1973—*).

SHAROW

[W Riding] Tp in Ripon AP, sep CP 1866,[2] sep EP 1826,[9] eccl refounded 1829.[757] *LG* Seq 100. Civ bdry: 1900.[280] Transf 1974 to N Yorks.[5] *Parl* Seq 34. *Eccl* Pec jurisd Lbty Ripon (until 1836), Boroughbr. RDn (1836—49), Ripon RDn (1849—*).

SHARROW

EP [W Riding] Cr 1870 from Ecclesall Bierlow EP, Sheffield St Mary EP.[213] Sheff RDn (1870—1942), Ecclesall RDn (1942—*). Bdry: 1877 (help cr Sheffield St Barnabas EP),[275] 1895 (help cr Abbeydale EP),[1] 1899 (help cr Endcllffe EP),[507] 1959.[508]

SHEEPSCAR ST CLEMENT

EP [W Riding] Cr 1869 from Buslingthorpe EP, Leeds AP.[383] Leeds RDn (1869—1971), Allert. RDn (1971—*). Bdry: 1883 (help cr Potter Newton EP),[113] 1895 (help cr Leeds St Aidan EP),[71] 1902,[364] 1967.[127]

SHEEPSCAR ST LUKE

EP [W Riding] Cr 1850 from Leeds AP,[9] refounded 1861.[67] Leeds RDn (1850—1904). Abol 1904 to help cr Leeds St Thomas and St Luke EP.[681]

SHEFFIELD

[W Riding] The following have 'Sheffield' in their names. Insofar as any existed at a given time: *LG* Straff. & Tick. Wap, Sheff PLU, MB (1843—89), CB (1889—1974), USD. *Parl* Sheff Parl Bor (1832—85); see Part III of the *Guide* for composition of Sheff Parl Bors/BCs (1885—*) by wards of the MB/CB. *Eccl* Donc. RDn (until 1857), Rotherh. RDn (1857—62), Sheff RDn (1862—1942); sep noted (1942—*).

AP1—SHEFFIELD [ST PETER AND ST PAUL]—Incl chap Attercliffe cum Darnall (sep CP 1866,[2] sep EP 1731,[9] the latter eccl abol 1844 and divided into 2 EPs of Attercliffe, Darnall,[88] Attercliffe refounded 1849[146]), tp Brightside Bierlow (sep CP 1866,[2] sep EP 1869[356]), tp Ecclesall Bierlow (sep CP 1866,[2] sep EP 1746,[9] eccl refounded 1849[146]), tp Nether Hallam (sep CP 1866,[2] incl area Heeley [sep CP 1880[430]; see below for eccl]), tp Upper Hallam (sep CP 1866[2]). Addtl civ bdry alt: 1901,[304] 1902 (gains Attercliffe cum Darnall CP, Brightside Bierlow

CP),[157] 1921 (incl gains pt Rotherh. CB [assoc with W Riding] & AP and gains Handsworth UD & AP),[361] 1933 (gains Bradfield Urban CP, Ecclesfield Urban CP, Ecclesall CP, Tinsley CP),[503] 1934 (gains area from Derbys: ent Beauchief CP, ent Dore CP, pt Norton AP, pt Totley CP),[770] 1938,[306] 1967 (incl gains pt Rotherh. CB [assoc with W Riding] & AP, exchanges pts with Aston cum Aughton AP and with Ecclesfield AP, and gains pts of Derbys pars: Beighton AP, Eckington AP, Holmesfield CP, Killamarsh AP, Dronfield UD & AP).[144] Transf 1974 to S Yorks.[5] Addtl eccl bdry alt: 1823 (cr EP12,[9] refounded 1848[323]), 1833 (cr EP22,[9] refounded 1848[323]), 1839 (cr Fulwood EP[9]), 1846 (cr 5 EPs of Moorfields, Holliscroft, Eldon, Dyers Hill, Heeley [qv above for civ], the last soon thereafter called as EP30),[493] 1847 (cr EP18, sometimes early called 'Carver Street'),[294] 1848 (cr EP15, EP9, EP25),[323] 1848 (cr Crookes St Thomas EP,[453] refounded 1849,[241] sometimes called 'Sheffield St Thomas'), 1859 (cr Netherthorpe St Stephen EP),[661] 1866 (cr Gillcar EP,[54] sometimes later called 'Sheffield St Silas'), 1867 (help cr EP27[175]), 1867 (cr EP23[125]), 1884 (cr Netherthrope St Anne EP),[466] 1937,[258] 1939.[627] Reconstituted as EP1 when gains sequentially (1938) Moorfields EP,[720] (1938) EP22,[399] (1948) EP12.[771]

EP1—SHEFFIELD (THE CATHEDRAL BENEFICE)—Reconstitution of AP1 when gains sequentially 1938 Moorfields EP,[720] 1938 EP22,[720] 1948 EP12.[771] Attercliffe RDn (1942—*).

EP2—SHEFFIELD ST AIDAN—Cr 1921 from EP30.[609] Attercliffe RDn (1942—49). Bdry: 1929 (cr EP29),[762] 1929.[416] Abol 1949 to help cr EP3.[495]

EP3—SHEFFIELD ST AIDAN WITH ST LUKE—Cr 1949 by union EP2, pt Dyers Hill EP.[495] Attercliffe RDn.

EP4—SHEFFIELD ST BARNABAS—Cr 1877 from EP15, Sharrow EP.[275] Ecclesall RDn (1942—*). Bdry: 1895 (help cr Abbeydale EP).[1]

—SHEFFIELD ST BARTHOLOMEW—Name used now for EP cr 1879 as 'Langsett Road', qv

EP5—SHEFFIELD ST CATHERINE RICHMOND ROAD—Cr 1941 from Handsworth AP, Handsworth Woodhouse EP, Gleadless EP.[576] Handsw. RDn (1941—42), Attercliffe RDn (1942—*).

EP6—SHEFFIELD ST CECILIA, PARSONS CROSS—Cr 1939 from Ecclesfield AP, Grenoside EP, Pitsmoor EP.[512] Ecclesfield RDn (1939—*). Bdry: 1948.[514]

EP7—SHEFFIELD ST CLEMENT NEWHALL—Cr 1907 from Brightside EP.[211] Attercliffe RDn (1942—63). Abol 1963 to help cr Attercliffe EP.[67]

EP8—SHEFFIELD ST CUTHBERT—Cr 1902 from Brightside EP, Pitsmoor EP, Ecclesfield AP.[354] Ecclesfield RDn (1942—*). Bdry: 1936 (help cr Shiregreen EP).[24]

EP9—SHEFFIELD ST GEORGE—Cr 1848 from

AP1.[323] Bdry: 1859 (help cr Netherthorpe St Stephen EP),[647] 1876,[772] 1878,[433] 1964.[493] Abol 1941 to help cr EP11.[727]

EP10—SHEFFIELD ST GEORGE—Cr 1964 by union EP11, pt EP26.[493] Hallam RDn. Bdry: 1939.[627]

EP11—SHEFFIELD ST GEORGE WITH ST STEPHEN—Cr 1941 by union EP9, Netherthorpe St Stephen EP.[727] Ecclesall RDn (1942—64). Abol 1964 pt to help cr EP28, pt to help cr EP10.[493]

EP12—SHEFFIELD ST JAMES—Cr 1823 from AP1,[9] refounded 1848.[323] Bdry: 1878.[773] Abol 1948 to help reconstitute AP1 as EP1.[771]

EP13—SHEFFIELD ST LEONARD, NORWOOD—Cr 1938 from Ecclesfield AP, Pitsmoor EP.[511] Ecclesfield RDn (1942—*).

EP14—SHEFFIELD ST MARK BROOMHALL—Cr 1867 from AP1.[125] Hallam RDn (1942—*). Bdry: 1880 (help cr EP19).[309]

EP15—SHEFFIELD ST MARY—Cr 1848 from AP1.[323] Ecclesall RDn (1942—46). Bdry: 1867 (help cr EP27),[175] 1870 (help cr Sharrow EP),[213] 1877 (help cr EP4),[275] 1880 (help cr EP18).[309] Abol 1946 to help cr EP16.[497]

EP16—SHEFFIELD ST MARY WITH ST SIMON—Cr 1946 by union EP15, EP27.[774] Ecclesall RDn. Abol 1951 to help cr EP17.[497]

EP17—SHEFFIELD ST MARY WITH ST SIMON WITH ST MATTHIAS—Cr 1951 by union EP16, EP19.[497] Ecclesall RDn.

EP18—SHEFFIELD ST MATTHEW—Cr 1847 from AP1. Sometimes early 'Carver Street'. Ecclesall RDn (1942—*). Bdry: 1849.[593]

EP19—SHEFFIELD ST MATTHIAS—Cr 1880 from EP15, EP14.[309] Ecclesall RDn (1942—51). Abol 1951 to help cr EP17.[497]

EP20—SHEFFIELD ST NATHANAEL—Cr 1912 from EP25.[400] Hallam RDn (1942—*). Bdry: 1962.[191]

EP21—SHEFFIELD ST OSWALD—Cr 1907 from Ecclesall Bierlow EP.[211] Ecclesall RDn (1942—*). Bdry: 1930 (cr Millhouses EP),[210] 1959.[508]

EP22—SHEFFIELD ST PAUL—Cr 1833 from AP1,[9] refounded 1848.[323] Bdry: 1846 (cr Heeley EP, later called as EP30).[293] Abol 1938 to help reconstitute AP1 as EP1.[720]

EP23—SHEFFIELD ST PAUL ARBOURTHORNE—Cr 1938 from EP29, Gleadless EP, EP30.[575] Attercliffe RDn (1942—*).

EP24—SHEFFIELD ST PAUL WORDSWORTH AVENUE—Cr 1973 from Ecclesfield AP.[515] Ecclesfield RDn.

—SHEFFIELD ST PETER—Name sometimes used for EP cr 1895 as 'Abbeydale', qv

EP25—SHEFFIELD ST PHILIP—Cr 1848 from AP1.[323] Bdry: 1810 (cr Walkley EP),[515] 1876 (cr Owlerton EP),[194] 1879 (cr Langsett Road EP, now called 'Sheffield St Bartholomew'),[630] 1912 (cr EP20).[400] Abol 1941 to help cr EP26.[93]

EP26—SHEFFIELD ST PHILIP AND ST ANN—Cr 1941 by union EP25, Netherthorpe St Ann EP.[93] Hallam RDn (1942—64). Abol 1964 pt to help cr EP28, pt to help cr EP10.[493]

—SHEFFIELD ST SILAS—Name used now for EP cr 1866 as 'Gillcar', qv

EP27—SHEFFIELD ST SIMON—Cr 1867 from AP1, EP15.[175] Ecclesall RDn. Abol 1946 to help cr EP16.[774]

EP28—SHEFFIELD ST STEPHEN WITH ST PHILIP AND ST ANN—Cr 1964 by union EP11, EP26.[493] Hallam RDn. Bdry: 1969.[494]

EP29—SHEFFIELD ST SWITHUN—Cr 1929 from EP2.[762] Attercliffe RDn (1942—*). Bdry: 1938 (help cr EP23).[575]

—SHEFFIELD ST THOMAS—Name sometimes used for EP cr 1849 as 'Crookes St Thomas', qv

EP30—SHEFFIELD PARK—Cr 1846 from EP22 as 'Heeley',[293] later called 'Sheffield Park' or 'Sheffield Park St John the Evangelist'. Attercliffe RDn (1942—*). Bdry: 1882 (help cr Attercliffe Emmanuel EP),[149] 1921 (help cr EP2),[609] 1938 (help cr EP23),[575] 1949.[495]

SHELF

[W Riding] Tp in Halifax AP, sep CP 1866,[2] sep EP 1851 from Halifax AP, Bradford AP.[137] LG Morley Wap, Halifax PLU, Shelf USD, UD. Abol civ 1937 to help cr Queensbury & Shelf UD & CP.[31] Parl W Riding (1832—67), E'rn Dv of W Riding (1867—85), Elland Dv (1885—1948). Eccl Pontef. RDn (1851—57), Halifax RDn (1857—94), Bradf RDn (1894—1921), Bowl. RDn (1921—71), Bowl. & Horton RDn (1971—*). Eccl bdry: 1927,[67] 1959 (help cr Buttershaw St Aidan EP),[320] 1967.[194]

SHELLEY

[W Riding] Tp in Kirkburton AP, sep CP 1866,[2] sep EP 1868.[149] LG Agb. Wap, Hudd. PLU, Shelley USD, UD. Abol civ 1938 ent to Kirkburton UD & AP.[28] Parl W Riding (1832—67), S'rn Dv of W Riding (1867—85), Holmf. Dv (1885—1918), Penist. Dv (1918—48). Eccl Hudd. RDn (1868—1968), Kirkburton RDn (1968—*).

SHEPLEY

[W Riding] Tp in Kirkburton AP, sep CP 1866,[2] sep EP 1849.[166] LG Agb. Wap, Hudd. PLU, Shepley USD, UD. Abol civ 1938 ent to Kirkburton UD & AP.[28] Parl W Riding (1832—67), S'rn Dv of W Riding (1867—85), Holmf. Dv (1885—1918), Penist. Dv (1918—48). Eccl Pontef. RDn (1849—57), Hudd. RDn (1857—1968), Kirkburton RDn (1968—*).

SHERBURN

AP [W Riding] LG Buckr. Wap, Scarb. PLU, RSD, Sherburn RD (1894—1935), Norton RD (1935—74). Transf 1974 to N Yorks.[5] Parl Seq 1. Eccl Seq 3.

SHERBURN IN ELMET

[W Riding] Incl pt tp Barkston (sep CP 1866[2]), tp Huddleston and Lumby (sep CP 1866,[2] pt eccl severed 1859 to help cr South Milford EP[300]), tp Lotherton cum Aberford (sep CP 1866,[2] eccl severed 1914 to help cr Aberford with Lotherton EP[6]), tp Micklefield (orig chap, in pec jurisd Fenton prebend, until 1836; sep CP 1866,[2] sep EP 1886[113]), tp South Milford (sep CP 1866,[2] sep EP 1859 by union this tp, addtl pt tp 'Sherburn in Elmet', pt tp Huddleston cum Lumby, pt Monk Fryston EP[300]), tp Newthorpe (sep CP 1866[2]). LG

Seq 78. Transf 1974 to N Yorks.[5] *Parl* Seq 24. *Eccl* Pec jurisd Fenton prebend (until 1836), New Ainsty RDn (1836—62), Tadc. RDn (1826—71), Selby RDn (1871—1921), Tadc. RDn (1921—*). Addtl eccl bdry alt: 1888.[764]

SHERIFF HUTTON

AP [N Riding] Incl chap Farlington (sep CP 1866,[2] eccl severed 1836 and united with Marton cum Moxby AP[546]), tps Lillings Ambo, Sheriff Hutton with Cornbrough, Stittenham (each a sep CP 1866[2]) so that 'Sheriff Hutton' has no sep civ identity after 1866. *LG* Bulmer Wap. *Parl* N Riding (1832—67). *Eccl* Seq 18.

SHERIFF HUTTON WITH CORNBROUGH

[N Riding] Tp in Sheriff Hutton AP, sep CP 1866.[2] *LG* Seq 29. Transf 1974 to N Yorks.[5] *Parl* Seq 16.

SHIPLEY

[W Riding] Tp in Bradford AP, sep CP 1866,[2] eccl severed 1828 to help cr Shipley cum Heaton EP.[63] *LG* Morley Wap, Bradf PLU (1837—48), N Bierley PLU (1848—1930), Shipley USD, UD. Civ bdry: 1894 (gains the pt of Idle CP in Shipley UD),[557] 1937 (exchanges pts with Bradf CB [assoc with W Riding] & Idle CP),[31] 1935 (gains pt Bradf CB [assoc with W Riding] & Idle CP).[650] Transf 1974 to W Yorks.[5] *Parl* W Riding (1832—67), E'rn Dv of W Riding (1867—85), Shipley Dv/CC (1885—*). Parl bdry: 1956.[312]

SHIPLEY CUM HEATON

EP [W Riding] Cr 1828 by union tps Shipley, Heaton, each in Bradford AP.[63] Pontef. RDn (1828—57), Bradf RDn (1857—1921), Calverley RDn (1921—71), Airedale RDn (1971—*). Bdry: 1865 (cr Heaton St Barnabas EP),[311] 1874,[605] 1910 (cr Shipley St Peter EP).[647]

SHIPLEY ST PETER

EP [W Riding] Cr 1910 from Shipley cum Heaton EP.[647] Bradf RDn (1910—21), Calverley RDn (1921—71), Airedale RDn (1971—*). Bdry: 1921.[197]

SHIPTON

[E Riding] Chap in Market Weighton AP, sep CP 1866 as 'Shipton Thorpe',[2] qv, sep EP 1849 as 'Shipton',[9] eccl abol 1876, united with chap Thorpe le Street in Nunburnholme AP to cr Shipton Thorpe EP.[701] *Eccl* Weigh. RDn.

SHIPTON

[N Riding] Tp in Overton AP, sep CP 1866.[2] *LG* Seq 30. Transf 1974 to N Yorks.[5] *Parl* Seq 16.

SHIPTON THORPE

[E Riding] Chap in Market Weighton AP, sep CP 1866,[2] sep EP 1849 as 'Shipton',[9] the latter abol 1876, united with chap Thorpe le Street in Nunburnholme AP as 'Shipton Thorpe' EP.[701] *LG* Seq 12. Transf 1974 to Humb.[5] *Parl* Seq 7. *Eccl* Weigh. RDn.

SHIPTON WITH OVERTON

EP [N Riding] Renaming 1962 of Overton with Shipton AP.[455] Eas. RDn.

SHIREGREEN ST HILDA

EP [W Riding] Cr 1936 from Sheffield St Cuthbert EP, Wincobank EP, Brightside EP.[24] Ecclesfield RDn.

SHIREGREEN ST JAMES AND ST CHRISTOPHER

EP [W Riding] Cr 1941 from Ecclesfield AP, Wincobank EP.[513] Ecclesfield RDn. Bdry: 1948.[514]

SHIREOAKS

EP Cr 1865 from Worksop AP (Notts), Anston cum Membris AP (Yorks W Riding, civ 'North and South Anston') to be dioc Linc.[110] For RDns see entry in Notts.

SHITLINGTON—see SITLINGTON

SICKLINGHALL

[W Riding] Tp in Kirkby Overblow AP, sep CP 1866.[2] *LG* Seq 88. Transf 1974 to N Yorks.[5] *Parl* Seq 24.

SIDDAL

EP [W Riding] Cr 1915 from Salterhebble EP.[762] Halifax RDn.

SIGGLESTHORNE

AP [E Riding] Incl tps Catfoss, Little Hatfield, Seaton and Wassand, pt tp Great Hatfield (each a sep CP 1866[2]). *LG* Seq 16. Transf 1974 to Humb.[5] *Parl* Seq 5. *Eccl* Seq 15. Eccl bdry: 1962,[60] 1972 (loses area of Hatfield CP [qv for composition] to help cr Mappleton with Goxhill EP).[630]

SILKSTONE

AP [W Riding] Incl chap Barnsley (sep CP 1866,[2] sep EP 1718[9]), pt chap & tp West Bretton (sep CP 1866[2]), chap Cawthorne (sep par 1608[401]), pt chap & tp Cumberworth (some parochial rights from 1627,[459] eccl sometimes 'Cumberworth with Denby Dale', 'Cumberworth' a sep CP 1866[2]), tp Dodsworth (sep CP 1866,[2] sep EP 1848[86]), tp Hoyland Swaine (sep CP 1866,[2] sep EP 1869 incl pt Cawthorne EP[109]), tp Stainbrough (sep CP 1866[2]), tp Thurgoland (sep CP 1866,[2] sep EP 1844[188]). *LG* Seq 114. Addtl civ bdry alt: 1938.[28] Transf 1974 to S Yorks.[5] *Parl* Seq 50. *Eccl* Seq 41. Addtl eccl bdry alt: 1823 (cr Barnsley St George EP,[9] refounded 1831[196]).

SILPHO

[N Riding] Tp in Hackness AP, sep CP 1866.[2] *LG* Seq 67. Bdry: 1887.[16] Transf 1974 to N Yorks.[5] *Parl* Seq 20.

SILSDEN

[W Riding] Chap in Kildwick AP, sep CP 1866,[2] sep EP 1720,[9] eccl refounded 1898.[49] *LG* Staincl. & Ewc. Wap, Carlton GilbU (until 1869), Skipton PLU (1869—1930), Silsden USD, UD. Civ bdry: 1896.[775] Transf 1974 to W Yorks.[5] *Parl* W Riding (1832—67), N'rn Dv of W Riding (1867—85), Skipton Dv (1885—1918), Keigh. Dv (1918—48), Keigh. BC (1948—*). *Eccl* Craven RDn (1720—1857), Craven RDn, S'rn Dv (1857—1921), S Craven RDn (1921—*).

NETHER SILTON

[N Riding] Chap (in pec jurisd Bp Durham, until 1836) in Leake AP, sep CP 1866,[2] eccl severed 1935 to help cr Over Silton with Nether Silton EP.[670] *LG* Seq 26. Bdry: 1934.[3] Transf 1974 to N Yorks.[5] *Parl* Seq 17.

OVER SILTON

[N Riding] Chap in chap Kilburn (sep civ identity early from Coxwold AP, sep EP 1732[9]), 'Over Silton' a sep CP 1866,[2] sep EP 1757 from Kilburn

EP.[9] Incl pt tp Kepwick (sep CP 1866[2]). *LG* Seq 26. Transf 1974 to N Yorks.[5] *Parl* Seq 17. *Eccl* Bulmer RDn (1757—1862), N'allert. RDn (1862—1935). Abol eccl 1935 to help cr Over Silton with Nether Silton EP.[670]

OVER SILTON WITH NETHER SILTON

EP [N Riding] Cr 1935 by union Over Silton EP, chap Nether Silton in Leake with Nether Silton AP.[670] Thirsk RDn. Abol 1967 to help cr Leake with Over and Nether Silton and Kepwick EP.[508]

SINDERBY

[N Riding] Tp in Pickhill AP, sep CP 1866.[2] *LG* Seq 45. Transf 1974 to N Yorks.[5] *Parl* Seq 16.

SINNINGTON

AP [N Riding] Tp 'Sinnington' in Pick. Lythe Wap as was tp Marton (sep CP 1866[2]); incl in Ryed. Wap tp Little Edstone (sep CP 1866[2]). *LG* Pick. PLU, RSD, RD. Addtl civ bdry alt: 1887.[49] Transf 1974 to N Yorks.[5] *Parl* Seq 22. *Eccl* Riddal RDn (until 1862), Helm. RDn (1862—1928), Pick. RDn (1928—*).

SITLINGTON

[W Riding] Tp in Thornhill AP, early called 'Shitlington', name as above used from 1930s, sep CP 1866,[2] pt eccl severed 1860 to help refound Flockton EP as 'Flockton cum Denby Grange'.[68] *LG* Seq 69. Transf 1974 to W Yorks.[5] *Parl* Seq 54.

SKEEBY

[N Riding] Tp in Easby AP, sep CP 1866.[2] *LG* Seq 38. Transf 1974 to N Yorks.[5] *Parl* Seq 14.

SKEFFLING

AP [E Riding] *LG* Seq 15. Transf 1974 to Humb.[5] *Parl* Seq 5. *Eccl* Seq 16.

SKELBROOKE

[W Riding] Chap in South Kirkby AP, sep CP 1866,[2] sep EP 1728.[9] *LG* Osg. Wap, Hemsw. PLU, RSD, RD. Abol civ 1938 ent to Hampole CP.[28] *Parl* W Riding (1832—67), N'rn Dv of W Riding (1867—85), Osg. Dv (1885—1918), Hemsw. Dv (1918—48). *Eccl* Donc. RDn (1728—1871), Pontef. RDn (1871—1922), Donc. RDn (1922—*).

SKELDING

[W Riding] Tp (sometimes 'Skelden') in Ripon AP, sep CP 1866,[2] eccl severed 1740 to help cr Winksley cum Grantley EP,[9] the latter refounded 1863.[575] *LG* Seq 90. Transf 1974 to N Yorks.[5] *Parl* Seq 33.

SKELLOW

[W Riding] Tp in Owston AP, sep CP 1866.[2] *LG* Osg. Wap, Donc. PLU, RSD, RD. Abol 1915 ent to Adwick le Street AP to help constitute Adwick le Street UD.[43] *Parl* W Riding (1832—67), N'rn Dv of W Riding (1867—85), Osg.Dv (1885—1918).

SKELMANTHORPE

CP [W Riding] Renaming 1876 of Cumberworth Half CP after latter's bdry alt with Cumberworth CP.[460] *LG* Agb. Wap, Hudd. PLU, Skelmanthorpe USD, UD (1894—1938), Denby Dale UD (1938—74). Transf 1974 to W Yorks.[5] *Parl* Holmf. Dv (1885—1918), Penist. Dv/CC (1918—55), Colne Valley CC (1955—*).

EP [W Riding] Cr 1900 from Scissett EP.[297] Silkst. RDn (1900—13), Hudd. RDn (1913—68),

Kirkburton RDn (1968—*).

SKELTON

[E Riding] Tp in Howden AP, sep CP 1866.[2] *LG* Howdensh. Wap, Howden PLU, RSD, RD. Bdry: 1880,[171] 1880.[172] Abol 1935 pt to Howden AP, pt to Kilpin CP, pt to Eastrington AP.[13] *Parl* E Riding (1832—85), Howdensh. Dv (1885—1948).

SKELTON

AP [N Riding] Incl tps Brotton, Kilton, Skinningrove (each a sep CP 1866,[2] the AP augmented 1713 as 'Skelton with Brotton'[9]; orig areas of Brotton, Skinnigrove, pt Kilton eccl severed 1868 to cr 'Brotton' EP[188]), tps Moorseholm, Stanghow (each a sep CP 1866[2]). Usual civ spelling; for eccl see 'Skelton in Cleveland'. *LG* Langb. Lbty, Skelton Bor (status not sustained), Guisb. PLU, Skelton in Clev USD (1875—84), Skelton & Brotton USD (1884—94), UD. Addtl civ bdry alt: 1883,[16] 1886,[656] 1934.[363] Transf 1974 to Clev.[5] *Parl* Seq 9.

SKELTON

AP [N Riding] Sometimes 'Skelton by York'. (Tp Skelton pt in Skelton AP, pt in Overton AP). *LG* Seq 32. Civ bdry: 1934.[3] Transf 1974 to N Yorks.[5] *Parl* Seq 16. *Eccl* Pec jurisd Treasurer of York (until 1547), Seq 18 thereafter. Eccl bdry: 1878.[744]

SKELTON

[W Riding] Chap in Ripon AP, sep CP 1866,[2] sep EP 1749 (incl 3 tps comprising Skelton chap: Skelton, Newby with Mulwith, Givendale, all in Ripon AP),[9] eccl refounded 1815 as 'Skelton cum Newby',[11] qv, the latter eccl refounded 1875.[11] *LG* Seq 41. Transf 1974 to N Yorks.[5] *Parl* Seq 34. *Eccl* Pec jurisd Lbty Ripon (until 1815).

SKELTON CUM NEWBY

EP [W Riding] Refounding 1815 of Skelton EP (qv for earlier status and composition),[11] again refounded 1875.[11] Pec jurisd Lbty Ripon (1815—36), Boroughbr. RDn (1836—49), Ripon RDn (1849—*).

SKELTON IN CLEVELAND

AP [N Riding] Usual eccl spelling; for civ, civ and eccl sep tps, and for earlier augmentation as 'Skelton with Brotton', see 2nd 'Skelton' above. *Eccl* Seq 21. Addtl eccl bdry alt: 1901 (cr Boosbeck and Moorholm EP).[216]

SKELTON WITH BROTTON—see 2nd Skelton above

SKERNE

AP [E Riding] *LG* Seq 10. Civ bdry: 1935 (loses pt to help constitute Driffield UD & CP, gains Wansford CP).[13] Transf 1974 to Humb.[5] *Parl* Seq 3. *Eccl* Seq 10.

SKIDBY

[E Riding] Chap in Cottingham AP, some parochial rights from 16th cent,[441] sep civ identity early, sep EP 1858,[9] eccl refounded 1859.[442] *LG* Seq 9. Civ bdry: 1879,[444] 1935.[13] Transf 1974 to Humb.[5] *Parl* Seq 8. *Eccl* S Harth. RDn (1858—66), Howden RDn (1866—87), Kingst. upon Hull RDn (1887—*). Eccl bdry: 1862 (help cr Newland St John EP).[35]

SKINNINGROVE

[N Riding] Tp in Skelton AP, sep CP 1866,[2] eccl severed 1868 to help cr Brotton EP.[188] *LG* Langb. Lbty, Guisb. PLU, Loftus USD, UD. Bdry: 1921.[688] Transf 1974 to Clev.[5] *Parl* Seq 9.

SKIPLAM

[N Riding] Tp in Klrkdale AP, sep CP 1866,[2] *LG* Seq 64. Bdry: 1887.[538] Transf 1974 to N Yorks.[5] *Parl* Seq 21.

SKIPSEA

AP [E Riding] Incl pt chap Ulrome (sep CP 1866,[2] sep EP before 1835[185]), tp Bonwick (sep CP 1866[2]); tp Dringhoe, Upton and Brough (sep CP 1866[2]). *LG* Skipsea Bor (status not sustained), Seq 14. Addtl civ bdry alt: 1935 (gains Dringhoe, Upton and Brough CP).[13] Transf 1974 to Humb.[5] *Parl* E Riding (1832—85), Hold. Dv (1885—1918), Buckr. Dv (1918—48), Bridl. CC (1948—*). *Eccl* Seq 15.

SKIPTON

AP [W Riding] Tp 'Skipton' in Staincl. & Ewc. Wap as were tps Barden, Bolton Abbey, Halton East (each a sep CP 1866,[2] each eccl severed 1814 and united with tp Hazlewood with Storiths in Claro Wap to cr Bolton Abbey EP,[9] eccl refounded 1864[175]), tp Draughton (sep CP 1866[2]), tp Embsay with Eastby (sep CP 1866,[2] sep EP 1854, eccl refounded 1855[516]); incl in Claro Wap tp Beamsley (sep CP 1866[2]), tp Hazlewood with Storiths (sep CP 1866,[2] eccl severed 1814 to help cr Bolton Abbey,[9] eccl refounded 1864[175]). *LG* Skipton Bor, PLU, USD, UD. Addtl civ bdry alt: 1937.[31] Transf 1974 to N Yorks.[5] *Parl* Seq 41. *Eccl* Seq 37. Addtl eccl bdry alt: 1840 (cr Skipton Christchurch EP).[776]

SKIPTON CHRISTCHURCH

EP [W Riding] Cr 1840 from Skipton AP.[776] Craven RDn (1840—57), Craven RDn, W'rn Dv (1857—1905), Craven RDn, E'rn Dv (1905—21), Skipton RDn (1921—*).

SKIPTON ON SWALE

[N Riding] Tp in Topcliffe AP, sep CP 1866,[2] sep EP 1842.[9] *LG* Seq 27. Transf 1974 to N Yorks.[5] *Parl* Seq 16. *Eccl* Bulmer RDn (1842—62), Thirsk RDn (1862—*).

SKIPWITH

AP [E Riding] Incl tp North Duffield, pt tp Menthorpe with Bowthorpe (each a sep CP 1866[2]). *LG* Seq 19. Transf 1974 to N Yorks.[5] *Parl* Seq 7. *Eccl* Pec jurisd Dean & Chapter of Durham (until 1836), Seq 19 thereafter.

SKIRCOAT

[W Riding] Tp in Halifax AP, sep CP 1866,[2] pt eccl severed 1845 to cr King Cross EP, pt to help cr Salterhebble EP.[657] *LG* Morley Wap, Halifax PLU, pt Sowerby Bridge USD, pt Halifax MB (1848—89), pt Halifax CB (1889—94), pt Halifax USD, pt Halifax RSD, Halifax RD. Bdry: 1894 (loses the pt in Halifax CB to Halifax AP,[588] loses the pt in Sowerby Bridge UD to help cr Sowerby Bridge CP[734]). Abol 1899 ent to Halifax CB (assoc with W Riding) & AP.[589] *Parl* W Riding (1832—67), pt Halifax Parl Bor (1867—1918), pt E'rn Dv of W Riding (1867—85), pt Sowerby Dv (1885—1918).

SKIRLAUGH

EP [E Riding] Cr 1867 from Swine AP (chap South Skirlaugh, tps Benningholme and Grange, Marton, North Skirlaugh, Rowton and Arnold).[235] Hornsea RDn (1867—1916), N Hold. RDn (1916—*).

CP [E Riding] Renaming 1935 of South Skirlaugh CP.[13] *LG* Hold. RD. Bdry: 1952.[759] Transf 1974 to Humb.[5] *Parl* Bridl. CC (1948—*).

NORTH SKIRLAUGH, ROWTON AND ARNOLD

[E Riding] Tp in Swine AP, sep CP 1866,[2] eccl severed 1867 to help cr Skirlaugh EP.[235] *LG* Hold. Wap, Skirl. PLU, RSD, RD. Bdry: 1885.[335] Abol 1935 to help cr Riston CP.[13] *Parl* E Riding (1832—85), Hold. Dv (1885—1918).

SOUTH SKIRLAUGH

[E Riding] Tp in Swine AP, sep CP 1866,[2] eccl severed 1867 to help cr Skirlaugh EP.[235] *LG* Hold. Wap, Skirl. PLU, RSD, RD. Bdry: 1885.[59] Renamed 1935 'Skirlaugh'.[13] *Parl* E Riding (1832—85), Hold. Dv (1885—1918).

SKIRPENBECK

AP [E Riding] *LG* Seq 3. Transf 1974 to Humb.[5] *Parl* Seq 7. *Eccl* Buckr. RDn (until 1857), W Buckr. RDn (1857—62), Pockl. RDn (1862—*).

SKUTTERSKELFE

[N Riding] Tp pt in Rudby in Cleveland AP, pt in Stokesley AP, sep CP 1866.[2] *LG* Seq 58. Transf 1974 to N Yorks.[5] *Parl* Seq 11.

SLAIDBURN

AP [W Riding] Incl tps Bowland Forest High, Easington, Newton (each a sep CP 1866[2]). *LG* Seq 108. Addtl civ bdry alt: 1938.[28] Transf 1974 to Lancs.[5] *Parl* Seq 41. *Eccl* Seq 38. Addtl eccl bdry alt: 1871 (cr Dale Head EP),[21] 1938.[463]

SLAITHWAITE

[W Riding] Tp in Huddersfield AP, sep CP 1866,[2] sep EP 1718.[9] *LG* Agb. Wap, Hudd. PLU, Slaithwaite USD, UD. Civ bdry: 1896 (gains Lingards CP).[684] Abol civ 1937 ent to help cr Colne Valley UD & CP.[31] *Parl* W Riding (1832—67), S'rn Dv of W Riding (1867—85), Colne Valley Dv (1885—1948). *Eccl* Pontef. RDn (1718—1857), Hudd. RDn (1857—1938). Abol ecccl 1938 to help cr Slaithwaite with East Scammonden EP.[180]

SLAITHWAITE WITH EAST SCAMMONDEN

EP [W Riding] Cr 1938 by union Slaithwaite EP, pt Scammonden EP.[180] Hudd. RDn (1938—68), Blackmoorfoot RDn (1968—*).

SLEDMERE

AP [E Riding] Sometimes 'Sledmere with Croom'. *LG* Seq 1. Transf 1974 to Humb.[5] *Parl* Seq 3. *Eccl* Seq 2.

SLINGSBY

AP [N Riding] *LG* Seq 65. Transf 1974 to N Yorks.[5] *Parl* Seq 16. *Eccl* Seq 27.

SMAWTHORNE

EP [W Riding] Cr 1924 from Castleford AP.[89] Later called 'Castleford St Michael and All Angels'. Pontef. RDn. Bdry: 1962.[46]

GREAT SMEATON

AP [N Riding] Pt tp 'Great Smeaton' in E Gill. Wap (remainder in Croft AP); incl in Allert. Wap tp Hornby (sep CP 1866[2]); incl in Langb. Lbty chap Appleton Wiske (sep CP 1866,[2] sep EP 1869 as 'Appleton upon Wiske',[113] the order of 1869 revoked 1872[114] and the area thereafter eccl a chap in this par). *LG* N'allert. PLU, RSD, RD. Addtl civ bdry alt: 1879.[452] Transf 1974 to N Yorks.[5] *Parl* Seq 11. *Eccl* Seq 57.

KIRK SMEATON

AP [W Riding] *LG* Seq 96. Transf 1974 to W Yorks.[5] *Parl* Seq 28. *Eccl* Donc. RDn (until 1857), Pontef. RDn (1857—*). Eccl bdry: 1880.[164]

LITTLE SMEATON

[N Riding] Tp in Birkby AP, sep CP 1866.[2] *LG* Seq 22. Transf 1974 to N Yorks.[5] *Parl* Seq 14.

LITTLE SMEATON

[W Riding] Tp in Womersley AP, sep CP 1866.[2] *LG* Seq 96. Bdry: 1883,[52] 1888.[348] Transf 1974 to W Yorks.[5] *Parl* Seq 28.

SNAINTON

[N Riding] Chap pt in Brompton AP, pt in Ebberston AP, sep CP 1866.[2] *LG* Seq 62. Bdry: 1886.[501] Transf 1974 to N Yorks.[5] *Parl* Seq 20.

SNAITH

AP [W Riding] Tp 'Snaith' in Osg. Wap as were chap Airmyn (sep CP 1866,[2] sep EP 1728[9]), chap & tp Goole (sep CP 1866,[2] sep EP 1849[247]), chap Hook (sep CP 1866,[2] sep EP 1798[9]), chap Rawcliffe (sep CP 1866,[2] sep EP 1813[9]), tp Balne (sep CP 1866,[2] sep EP 1855[173]), tps Gowdall, Heck (each a sep CP 1866[2]), tp Hensall (sep CP 1866,[2] sep EP 1855 from Snaith AP, Kellington AP[173]), tps Pollington, Snaith and Cowick (each a sep CP 1866,[2] 'Cowick' a sep EP 1855,[173] orig as 'East Cowick' but later 'Cowick'); incl in Bark Ash. Wap chap Carlton (sep CP 1866,[2] sep EP 1834[9]) so that 'Snaith' has no sep civ identity after 1866. *Parl* W Riding (1832—67). *Eccl* Tp 'Snaith' and all chaps, pec jurisd Selby (1440—1539), pec jurisd Snaith (1539—1836), Pontef. RDn (1836—38), New Ainsty RDn (1838—57), Pontef. RDn (1857—62), Selby RDn (1862—71), Snaith RDn (1871—*).

SNAITH AND COWICK

[W Riding] Tp in Snaith AP, sep CP 1866,[2] Cowick a sep EP 1855,[173] orig as 'East Cowick', later as 'Cowick'. *LG* Seq 95. Bdry: 1844.[500] Transf 1974 to Humb.[5] *Parl* Seq 29.

SNAPE

[N Riding] Tp in Well AP, sep CP 1866.[2] *LG* Seq 46. Bdry: 1886,[382] 1904.[777] Transf 1974 to N Yorks.[5] *Parl* Seq 15.

SNEATON

AP [N Riding] *LG* Seq 68. Transf 1974 to N Yorks.[5] *Parl* Seq 19. *Eccl* Clev RDn (until 1862), Guisb. RDn (1862—78), Whitby RDn (1878—*).

SNILESWORTH

[N Riding] Tp in Hawnby AP, sep CP 1866.[2] *LG* Birdf. Wap, Helm. PLU (soon after 1837[112]—1930), RSD, RD. Transf 1974 to N Yorks.[5] *Parl* Seq 16.

SNYDALE

[W Riding] Tp in Normanton AP, sep CP 1866.[2] *LG* Agb. Wap, Gt Preston GilbU (until 1862), Pontef. PLU (1862—1930), Featherstone USD, UD. Bdry: 1906.[736] Abol 1938 pt to help cr Ackton and Snydale CP, pt to Huntwick with Foulby and Nostell CP.[31] *Parl* W Riding (1832—67), S'rn Dv of W Riding (1867—85), Norm. Dv (1885—1948).

SOCKBURN

AP [Pt Durham (Stock. Wd), pt Yorks N Riding (Allert. Wap: tps Over Dinsdale, Girsby [each a sep CP 1866[2]]), ent Durham from 1866] See main entry in Durham for organisation.

SOOTHILL

[W Riding] Tp in Dewsbury AP, sep CP 1866.[2] *LG* Agb. Wap, Dewsb. PLU, pt Soothill Nether USD, pt Soothill Upper USD. Abol 1894 to cr 2 CPs of Soothill Nether, Soothill Upper, to coincide with the respective UDs.[257] *Parl* W Riding (1832—67), pt Dewsb. Parl Bor (1867—1918), pt S'rn Dv of W Riding (1867—85), pt Morley Dv (1885—1918).

SOOTHILL NETHER

CP [W Riding] Cr 1894 from the pt of Soothill CP in Soothill Nether UD.[257] *LG* Dewsb. PLU, Soothill Nether UD (1894—1910), Dewsb. MB (1910—13), CB (1913—25). Abol 1925 ent to Dewsbury AP.[477] *Parl* Dewsb. Parl Bor (1918—48).

SOOTHILL UPPER

CP [W Riding] Cr 1894 from the pt of Soothill CP in Soothill Upper UD.[257] *LG* Dewsb. PLU, Soothill Upper UD. Abol 1910 pt to Batley MB & AP, pt to Dewsb. MB & AP.[207]

SOUTH BANK

EP [N Riding] Cr 1898 from Eston EP.[121] Middlesb. RDn. Bdry: 1925.[493]

SOUTHBURN

[E Riding] Tp in Kirkburn AP, sep CP 1866.[2] *LG* Harth. Wap, Driff. PLU, RSD, RD. Abol 1935 ent to help cr Kirkburn CP.[13] *Parl* E Riding (1832—85), Buckr. Dv (1885—1948).

SOUTHCOATES

[E Riding] Tp in Drypool CP (qv for sep identity from Sutton and Stoneferry AP), sep CP 1866.[2] *LG* Hold. Wap, Scul. PLU, Kingst. upon Hull MB (1835—89), CB (1889—984 USD. Abol 1898 ent to Sculcoates AP.[446] *Parl* Kingst. upon Hull Parl Bor (1832—85); see Part III of the *Guide* for composition of Kingst. upon Hull Parl Bors (1885—1918) by wards of the MB.

SOUTHOWRAM

[W Riding] Tp in Halifax AP, sep CP 1866,[2] sep EP 1793 as 'Halifax St Ann in the Grove',[9] sometimes 'Briers Chapel', pt eccl severed 1845 from the latter to help cr Salterhebble EP.[657] *LG* Morley Wap, Halifax PLU, pt Halifax MB (1848—94), pt Southowram USD, pt Halifax USD, Southowram UD. Bdry: 1894 (loses the pt in Halifax CB to Halifax AP [orig intended to be 'Southowram Ward' CP,[737] this order superseded]],[588]), 1912 (loses pt to Halifax CB [assoc with W Riding] & AP),[591] 1928 (loses pt to Halifax CB [assoc with W Riding] & AP).[592] Abol 1937 pt to Brigh. MB & CP, pt to Elland UD & CP.[31] *Parl* Pt Halifax Parl Bor (1832—1918), pt W Riding (1832—67), pt E'rn Dv of W Riding (1867—85), Elland Dv (pt 1885—1918, ent 1918—48).

SOWERBY

[N Riding] Tp in Thirsk AP, sep CP 1866,[2] sep EP 1763.[9] *LG* Seq 27. Civ bdry: 1934.[3] Transf 1974 to N Yorks.[5] *Parl* Seq 16. *Eccl* Bulmer RDn (1763—1862), Thirsk RDn (1862—*).

SOWERBY

[W Riding] Tp in Halifax AP, sep CP 1866,[2] sep EP 1720 [St Peter],[9] eccl refounded 1848[231] and

1890.[12] *LG* Morley Wap, Halifax PLU, pt Sowerby USD, pt Sowerby Bridge USD, pt Luddenden Foot USD, pt Mytholmroyd USD (1891—94), Sowerby UD. Civ bdry: 1894 (loses the pt in Sowerby Bridge UD to help cr Sowerby Bridge CP,[352] loses the pt in Luddenden Foot UD to help cr Luddenden Foot CP,[691] loses the pt in Mytholmroyd UD to help cr Mytholmroyd CP[778]), 1926 (gains Sowerby Bridge UD & CP),[779] 1928 (gains pt Halifax CB [assoc with W Riding] & AP).[592] Abol civ 1937 pt to help cr Ripponden UD & CP, pt to help cr Sowerby Bridge UD & CP.[31] *Parl* W Riding (1832—67), E'rn Dv of W Riding (1867—85), Sowerby Dv (1885—1948). *Eccl* Pontef. RDn (1720—1857), Halifax RDn (1857—*). Eccl bdry: 1846 (help cr Mytholmroyd EP),[614] 1848 (help cr Sowerby St Mary EP),[231] 1873 (help cr Luddenden Foot EP),[676] 1881 (help cr Thorpe St John the Divine EP),[758] 1923,[407] 1941,[21] 1972 (gains Sowerby St George EP, Sowerby St Mary EP, Thorpe St John the Divine EP).[780]

SOWERBY ST GEORGE

EP [W Riding] Cr 1842 from Halifax AP, refounded 1843.[351] Halifax RDn (1857—1972). Bdry: 1923,[407] 1941.[21] Abol 1972 ent to Sowerby EP.[780]

SOWERBY ST MARY

EP [W Riding] Cr 1848 from Elland with Greetland EP (pt orig tp Soyland).[231] Pontef. RDn (1848—57), Halifax RDn (1857—1972). Bdry: 1881 (help cr Thorpe St John the Divine EP),[758] 1923,[407] 1970.[680] Abol 1972 ent to Sowerby EP.[780]

SOWERBY BRIDGE

EP [W Riding] Cr 1719 from Halifax AP (tps Norland, Warley),[9] abol 1724 to help cr Elland cum Stainland and Fixby EP,[178] the latter re-augmented 1739 as 'Elland'[9] but usually called 'Elland with Greetland' until Greetland a sep EP 1862,[138] the remainder (incl tp Norland) 'Elland' thereafter, the area of tp Warley eccl severed 1732 from Elland with Greetland EP to help cr Luddenden EP,[9] 'Sowerby Bridge' EP re-cr 1869 from Elland EP (orig area Norland), Luddenden EP (orig area Warley).[521] Pontef. RDn (1719—24), Halifax RDn (1869—1923). Bdry: 1866 (help cr Copley EP),[436] 1873 (help cr Luddenden Foot EP),[676] 1877 (cr Norland EP),[301] 1878 (cr Warley EP),[429] 1912.[594] Abol 1923 to help cr Sowerby Bridge with Norland EP.[735]

CP [W Riding] Cr 1894 by union of the pts of the following in Sowerby Bridge UD: Norland CP, Skircoat CP, Sowerby CP, Warley CP.[734] *LG* Halifax PLU, Sowerby Bridge UD. Abol 1926 ent to Sowerby UD & CP.[779] *Parl* Sowerby Dv (1918—48).

CP [W Riding] Cr 1937 by union Luddenden Foot UD & CP, pt Sowerby UD & CP, ent Norland CP.[31] *LG* Sowerby Bridge UD. Bdry: 1939.[76] Transf 1974 to W Yorks.[5] *Parl* Sowerby CC (1948—*).

SOWERBY BRIDGE WITH NORLAND

EP [W Riding] Cr 1923 by union Sowerby Bridge EP, Norland EP.[735] Halifax RDn.

SOWERBY UNDER COTCLIFFE

[N Riding] Tp in Kirby Sigston AP, sep CP 1866.[2]

LG Seq 22. Transf 1974 to N Yorks.[5] *Parl* Seq 14.

SOYLAND

[W Riding] Tp in Halifax AP, sep CP 1866,[2] eccl severed 1724 to help cr Elland cum Stainland and Fixby EP,[178] the latter re-augmented 1739 as 'Elland'[9] but usually called 'Elland with Greetland' until Greetland a sep EP 1862,[141] 'Soyland' a sep EP (pt orig tp) 1848 from Elland with Greetland EP.[231] *LG* Morley Wap, Halifax PLU, Soyland USD, UD. Abol civ 1937 to help cr Ripponden UD & CP.[31] *Parl* W Riding (1832—67), E'rn Dv of W Riding (1867—85), Sowerby Dv (1885—1948).

SPALDINGTON

[E Riding] Tp pt in Aughton AP, pt in Bubwith AP, sep CP 1866.[2] *LG* Seq 11. Bdry: 1957.[561] Transf 1974 to Humb.[5] *Parl* Seq 7.

SPAUNTON

[N Riding] Tp in Lastingham AP, sep CP 1866.[2] Incl undivided pt Spaunton Moor (qv for other pars to which common; abol 1934 incl pt to this par [addtl bdry alt in the same order affecting this par][3]). *LG* Seq 66. Transf 1974 to N Yorks.[5] *Parl* Seq 21.

SPAUNTON MOOR

[N Riding] Area orig in Lastingham AP, after 1866 common to Appleton le Moors CP, Hutton le Hole CP (both in Kirkby Moors. RD), also to Lastingham AP; Rosedale, West Side CP; Spaunton CP (the last 3 in Pick. RD). Abol civ 1934 with pt to each of the 5 pars[3]; pt (Appleton Common) eccl severed 1868 to help cr Appleton le Moors EP.[111]

SPEETON

[E Riding] Chap in Bridlington AP, sep CP 1866,[2] sep EP 1734.[9] *LG* Dick. Wap, Bridl. PLU, RSD, RD. Abol civ 1935 ent to Reighton AP.[13] *Parl* E Riding (1832—85), Buckr. Dv (1885—1948). *Eccl* Dick. RDn (1734—1857), N Dick. RDn (1857—66), Scarb. RDn (1866—87), Bridl. RDn (1887—*).

SPENNITHORNE

AP [N Riding Incl tp Bellerby (sep CP 1866,[2] sep EP 1770,[9] eccl refounded 1848[231]), tp Harmby (sep CP 1866[2]). *LG* Seq 53. Transf 1974 to N Yorks.[5] *Parl* Seq 14. *Eccl* Seq 54.

SPOFFORTH

AP [W Riding] Incl tp Follifoot (sep CP 1866[2]), tp Linton (sep CP 1866,[2] eccl severed 1887 and transf to Wetherby EP[126]), tps Plompton, Little Ribston, pt tp Spofforth with Stockeld (each a sep CP 1866[2]), tp Wetherby (sep CP 1866,[2] sep EP 1776,[9] eccl refounded 1869[71]) so that 'Spofforth' has no sep civ identity after 1866. *LG* Claro Wap. *Parl* W Riding (1832—67). *Eccl* Ainsty RDn (until (1820), Old Ainsty RDn (1820—36), Pontef. RDn (1836—57), Wethb. RDn (1857—1971). Addtl eccl bdry alt: 1957.[226] Abol eccl 1971 to help cr Spofforth with Kirk Deighton EP.[623]

SPOFFORTH WITH KIRK DEIGHTON

EP [W Riding] Cr 1971 by union Spofforth AP, Kirk Deighton AP.[623] Harrog. RDn.

SPOFFORTH WITH STOCKELD

[W Riding] Tp pt in Kirk Deighton AP, pt in Spofforth AP, sep CP 1866.[2] *LG* Seq 91. Transf

1974 to N Yorks.[5] *Parl* Seq 24.

SPOTBROUGH

AP [W Riding] Incl tp Cadeby (sep CP 1866[2]). Tp 'Spotbrough' early sometimes called 'Spotbrough with Cusworth'. *LG* Seq 117. Addtl civ bdry alt: 1954.[781] Transf 1974 to S Yorks.[5] *Parl* Seq 44. *Eccl* Seq 40. Eccl bdry: 1940 (help cr Doncaster St Leonard and St Jude EP).[237]

SPRINGHEAD

CP [W Riding] Cr 1894 from the pt of Saddleworth CP in Quickmere Middle Division UD.[491] *LG* Saddleworth PLU, Quickmere Middle Division UD (1894—95), Springhead UD (1895—1937). Bdry: 1900.[782] Abol 1937 ent to Saddleworth UD & CP.[31] *Parl* Colne Valley Dv (1918—48).

SPROATLEY

AP [E Riding] *LG* Seq 16. Transf 1974 to Humb.[5] *Parl* Seq 5. *Eccl* Seq 16.

SPROXTON

[N Riding] Tp in Helmsley AP, sep CP 1866.[2] *LG* Seq 63. Transf 1974 to N Yorks.[5] *Parl* Seq 21.

STAINBROUGH

[W Riding] Tp and donative chap in Silkstone AP, sep CP 1866,[2] sep eccl identity early. *LG* Staincr. Wap, Barnsley PLU, RSD, RD (1894—1938), Penist. RD (1938—74). Transf 1974 to S Yorks.[5] *Parl* W Riding (1832—67), S'rn Dv of W Riding (1867—85), Holmf. Dv (1885—1918), Wentw. Dv (1918—48), Penist. CC (1948—*). *Eccl* Donc. RDn (until 1838), Pontef. RDn (1838—57), Silkst. RDn (1857—1927), Barnsley RDn (1927—*).

STAINBURN

[W Riding] Chap in Kirkby Overblow AP, sep CP 1866,[2] sep EP 1775,[9] eccl refounded 1871.[21] *LG* Seq 92. Transf 1974 to N Yorks.[5] *Parl* Seq 30. *Eccl* Ainsty RDn (1775—1820), Old Ainsty RDn (1820—36), Pontef. RDn (1836—57), Wethb. RDn (1857—61), Otley RDn (1861—1921), Knar. RDn (1921—71), Harrog. RDn (1971—*). Eccl bdry: 1910 (gains tp Ripton from Kirkby Overblow AP),[197] 1957.[226]

STAINCLIFFE

EP [W Riding] Cr 1868 from Batley AP.[208] Sometimes 'Staincliffe Christ Church, Batley'. Birstall RDn (1868—83), Dewsb. RDn (1883—*). Bdry: 1880 (help cr Carlinghow EP),[198] 1913.[119]

STAINCROSS

EP [W Riding] Cr 1928 from Darton AP, Royston AP.[325] Barnsley RDn.

STAINFORTH

[W Riding] Tp pt in Barnby upon Don AP, pt in Hatfield AP, sep CP 1866,[2] sep EP 1884 from Barnby upon Don AP, Hatfield AP, Thorne AP, Fishlake AP.[316] *LG* Seq 120. Civ bdry: 1883,[52] 1884,[556] 1884.[557] Transf 1974 to S Yorks.[5] *Parl* Seq 47. *Eccl* Donc. RDn.

STAINFORTH

[W Riding] Tp in Giggleswick AP, sep CP 1866,[2] sep EP 1842 [St Peter] from Giggleswick AP, Arncliffe AP, Horton in Ribblesdale AP, Kirkby Malham AP (civ, 'Kirkby in Malham Dale').[136] *LG* Seq 111. Civ bdry: 1938.[28] Transf 1974 to N Yorks.[5] *Parl* Seq 41. *Eccl* Craven RDn (1842—57),

Craven RDn, N'rn Dv (1857—1921), Settle RDn (1921—71), Bowl. RDn (1971—*).

STAINLAND—see following entry

STAINLAND WITH OLD LINDLEY

[W Riding] Tp in Halifax AP, sep CP 1866,[2] eccl severed 1724 to help cr Elland cum Stainland and Fixby EP,[178] the latter re-augmented 1739[9] as 'Elland' but usually called 'Elland with Greetland' until Greetland a sep EP 1862,[138] 'Stainland' a sep EP 1843 from Elland with Greetland EP.[351] *LG* Morley Wap, Halifax PLU, Stainland USD, UD. Civ bdry: 1913 (loses pt to Hudd. CB [assoc with W Riding] and to Longwood CP).[689] Abol civ 1937 pt to Hudd. CB (assoc with W Riding) & AP, pt to Elland UD & CP.[31] *Parl* W Riding (1832—67), E'rn Dv of W Riding (1867—85), Elland Dv (1885—1948). *Eccl* As 'Stainland', Pontef. RDn (1843—57), Halifax RDn (1857—1967), Brigh. & Elland RDn (1967—*).

NORTH STAINLEY—See following entry

NORTH STAINLEY WITH SLENINGFORD

[W Riding] Tp in Ripon AP, sep CP 1866,[2] sep EP 1842 as 'North Stainley',[9] as such eccl refounded 1844.[188] *LG* Seq 100. Transf 1974 to N Yorks.[5] *Parl* Seq 34. *Eccl* As 'North Stainley', Boroughbr. RDn (1842—49), Ripon RDn (1849—*).

SOUTH STAINLEY

AP [W Riding] Usual eccl spelling; for civ see following entry. *Eccl* Seq 51.

SOUTH STAINLEY WITH CAYTON

AP [W Riding] Usual civ spelling; for eccl see prev entry. *LG* Seq 84. Transf 1974 to N Yorks.[5] *Parl* Seq 36.

STAINTON

AP [N Riding] Incl chap Thornaby (sep CP 1866,[2] sometimes early civ 'Thornaby with South Stockton', sep EP 1844[783]), tps Hemlington, Ingleby Barwick, Maltby (each a sep CP 1866[2]); sometimes reputed to have incl West Acklam as a chap, but the latter a Domesday church and sep status sustained,[15] qv. Usual civ spelling; for eccl see 'Stainton in Cleveland'. *LG* Langb. Lbty, Stock. PLU (1837—75), Middlesb. PLU (1875—1930), RSD, RD (1894—1934), Stokes. RD (1934—68). Abol civ 1968 pt to help cr Teesside CB (assoc with N Riding) & CP, pt to Maltby CP.[537] *Parl* Seq 10.

STAINTON

[N Riding] Tp in Downholme AP, sep CP 1866.[2] *LG* Seq 54. Bdry: 1883.[52] Transf 1974 to N Yorks.[5] *Parl* Seq 14.

STAINTON

AP [W Riding] *LG* Seq 117. Civ bdry: 1886,[784] 1886,[785] 1924 (loses pt [cr Stainton Urban CP] to help constitute Maltby UD).[771] Transf 1974 to S Yorks.[5] *Parl* Seq 44. *Eccl* Seq 40. Eccl bdry: 1956 (incl help cr Bramley EP).[215]

STAINTON IN CLEVELAND

AP [N Riding] Usual eccl spelling; for civ and civ sep chap and tps, see 1st 'Stainton' above. *Eccl* Seq 24. Addtl eccl bdry alt: 1969.[27]

STAINTON URBAN

CP [W Riding] Cr 1924 from the pt of Stainton AP transf from Donc. RD to help constitute Maltby

UD.[786] *LG* Donc. PLU, Maltby UD. Transf 1974 to S Yorks.[5] *Parl* Rother Valley CC (1948—*).

STAINTONDALE

[N Riding] Tp in Scalby AP, sep CP 1866[2]; eccl in chap Cloughton (sep EP 1874 from Scalby AP[148]). *LG* Seq 62. Transf 1974 to N Yorks.[5] *Parl* Seq 20.

STALLING BUSK

EP [N Riding] Cr 1736 from Aysgarth AP.[9] Catt. RDn (1736—1857), Catt. West RDn (1857—1928), Wensleyd. RDn (1928—*).

STAMFORD BRIDGE

CP [E Riding] Cr 1935 by union East Stamford Bridge CP, pt West Stamford Bridge with Scoreby CP.[13] *LG* Pockl. RD. Transf 1974 to Humb.[5] *Parl* Bev. CC (1948—55), Howden CC (1955—*).

EAST STAMFORD BRIDGE

[E Riding] Tp in Catton AP, sep CP 1866.[2] *LG* Harth. Wap, Pockl. PLU, RSD, RD. Abol 1935 to help cr Stamford Bridge CP.[13] *Parl* E Riding (1832—85), Howdensh. Dv (1885—1948).

WEST STAMFORD BRIDGE WITH SCOREBY

[E Riding] Tp in Catton AP, sep CP 1866.[2] *LG* Ouse & Derw. Wap, York PLU, RSD, Escr. RD. Abol 1935 to Kexby CP, pt to help cr Stamford Bridge CP.[13] *Parl* E Riding (1832—85), Howdensh. Dv (1885—1948).

STANBURY

CP [W Riding] Cr 1894 from the pt of Haworth CP in Oakworth UD.[257] *LG* Keigh. PLU, Oakworth UD. Abol 1938 ent to Keigh. MB & AP.[28] *Parl* Keigh. Dv (1918—48).

STANCILL WITH WELLINGLEY AND WILSECK

[W Riding] Tp in Tickhill AP, sep CP 1866.[2] *LG* Straff. & Tick. Wap, Donc. PLU, RSD. Abol 1886 pt to Wadworth AP, pt to Stainton AP.[785] *Parl* W Riding (1832—67), S'rn Dv of W Riding (1867—85), Donc. Dv (1885—1918).

STANGHOW

[N Riding] Tp in Skelton AP, sep CP 1866.[2] *LG* Langb. Lbty, Guisb. PLU, Skelton in Clev USD (1875—84), Skelton & Brotton USD (1884—94), UD. Bdry: 1883,[16] 1886.[656] Transf 1974 to Clev.[5] *Parl* Seq 9.

STANLEY

EP [W Riding] Cr 1826 from Wakefield AP (pt of tp Stanley cum Wrenthorpe, qv below for civ),[9] eccl refounded 1830.[91] Pontef. RDn (1826—57), Wakef RDn (1857—*). Bdry: 1861 (cr Outwood EP),[258] 1877,[464] 1944.[89]

CP [W Riding] Cr 1894 from pt of the pt of Stanley cum Wrenthorpe CP not in Wakef MB.[307] *LG* Wakef PLU, RD (1894—99), Stanley UD (1899—1974). Bdry: 1895,[96] 1936 (incl loses pt to Wakef CB [assoc with W Riding] & AP),[132] 1937 (incl gains Kirkhamgate CP).[31] Transf 1974 to W Yorks.[5] *Parl* Rothw. Dv (1918—48), Norm. CC (1948—*).

STANLEY CUM WRENTHORPE

[W Riding] Tp in Wakefield AP, sep CP 1866,[2] 'Stanley' a sep EP 1826,[9] eccl refounded 1830,[91] qv, 'Wrenthorpe' eccl severed 1826 to help cr Alverthorpe EP,[9] the latter eccl refounded 1830,[91] 'Wrenthorpe' a sep EP 1875 from Alverthorpe

EP,[90] qv. *LG* Agb. Wap, Wakef PLU, pt Wakef MB (1848—94), pt Wakef USD, pt Wakef RSD. Abol 1894 the pt in Wakef MB transf to Wakefield AP, the remainder to cr the 2 CPs of Stanley, Outwood.[307] *Parl* Pt Wakef Parl Bor (1832—1918), pt W Riding (1832—67), pt S'rn Dv of W Riding (1867—85), pt Norm. Dv (1885—1918).

STANNINGLEY

EP [W Riding] Cr 1847 from Bramley EP,[9] refounded 1862.[263] Pontef. RDn (1847—57), Leeds RDn (1857—1971), Armley RDn (1971—*). Bdry: 1967,[127] 1968.[328]

STANNINGTON

EP [W Riding] Cr 1843 from Ecclesfield AP.[195] Donc. RDn (1843—57), Rotherh. RDn (1857—62), Ecclesfield RDn (1862—1942), Hallam RDn (1942—*). Bdry: 1933 (help cr Malin Bridge EP).[89]

STANSFIELD

[W Riding] Tp in Halifax AP, sep CP 1866,[2] sep EP 1810 as 'Cross Stone',[9] qv. *LG* Morley Wap, Todmorden PLU, pt Hebden Bridge USD, pt Todmorden USD, Todmorden UD (1894—96), Todmorden MB (1896—97). Bdry: 1894 (incl loses the pt in Hebden Bridge UD to help cr Hebden Bridge CP),[257] 1896.[281] Abol civ 1897 to help cr Todmorden CP.[439] *Parl* W Riding (1832—67), E'rn Dv of W Riding (1867—85), Sowerby Dv (1885—1948).

STANWICK

AP [N Riding] Incl chap Cleasby (sep civ identity early, sep EP 1715[9]), tp Aldbrough, pt tp Barforth (each a sep CP 1866[2]), pt tp Barton (sep CP 1866,[2] the pt of the tp in this par eccl severed 1754 to cr 'Barton St Cuthbert' EP[9]), tp Caldwell (sep CP 1866,[2] sep EP 1840[9]), pt tp East Layton (sep CP 1866,[2] eccl severed 1918 [incl pt in Melsonby AP] and transf to Forcett EP[564]), pt tp Stanwick St John (sep CP 1866[2]) so that 'Stanwick' has no sep civ identity after 1866. *LG* W Gill. Wap. *Parl* N Riding (1832—67). *Eccl* Richm. RDn (until 1857), Richm. East RDn (1857—1973). Addtl eccl bdry alt: 1955.[5] Renamed eccl 1973 'Stanwick with Aldbrough'.[787]

STANWICK ST JOHN

[N Riding] Tp pt in Stanwick AP, pt in Richmond AP, sep CP 1866.[2] *LG* Pt E Gill. Wap (area in Richmond), pt W Gill. Wap (area in Stanwick), Richm. PLU, RSD, RD. Transf 1974 to N Yorks.[5] *Parl* Seq 14.

STANWICK WITH ALDBROUGH

EP [N Riding] Renaming 1973 of Stanwick AP.[787] Richm. East RDn.

STAPLETON

[N Riding] Tp pt in Croft AP, pt in Gilling AP, sep CP 1866,[2] the pt in Gilling eccl severed 1732 to help cr Barton St Mary EP.[9] *LG* Seq 33. Bdry: 1883.[52] Transf 1974 to N Yorks.[5] *Parl* Seq 14.

STAPLETON

[W Riding] Tp in Darrington AP, sep CP 1866.[2] *LG* Seq 98. Transf 1974 to N Yorks. *Parl* Seq 29.

STARBECK

CP [W Riding] Cr 1896 from Bilton CP.[258] *LG* Knar. PLU, RD. Bdry: 1900.[238] Abol 1938 ent to Harrog. MB & CP.[28] *Parl* Ripon Dv (1918—48).

EP [W Riding] Cr 1911 from Bilton with Harrogate EP (commonly 'High Harrogate Christ Church'), Knaresborough AP.[263] Knar. RDn (1911—71), Harrog. RDn (1971—*).

STARTFORTH

AP [N Riding] Incl chap Arkengarthdale (sep civ identity early, sep EP 1733[9]), tps Boldron, Egglestone Abbey (each a sep CP 1866[2]). *LG* Seq 39. Transf 1974 to Durham.[5] *Parl* Seq 14. *Eccl* Seq 59.

STAVELEY

AP [W Riding] *LG* Seq 86. Transf 1974 to N Yorks.[5] *Parl* Seq 36. *Eccl* Seq 51.

STEETON

[W Riding] Tp in Bolton Percy AP, sep CP 1866.[2] *LG* Seq 70. Transf 1974 to N Yorks.[5] *Parl* Seq 23.

STEETON—see following entry

STEETON WITH EASTBURN

[W Riding] Tp in Kildwick AP, sep CP 1866,[2] sep EP 1881 as 'Steeton' from Kildwick AP (this tp), Sutton EP.[218] *LG* Seq 109. Civ bdry: 1883,[52] 1896.[775] Transf 1974 to W Yorks.[5] *Parl* Seq 39. *Eccl* As 'Steeton', Craven RDn, S'rn Dv (1881—1921), S Craven RDn (1921—*).

STILLINGFLEET

AP [Pt E Riding (Ouse & Derw. Wap: tps Kelfield, Stillingfleet with Moreby [each a sep CP 1866[2]]), pt Ainsty (W Riding until 1449 and from 1836, indept jurisd 1449—1836: tp Acaster Selby [sep CP 1866,[2] sep EP 1772,[9] eccl refounded 1850[10]])] so that 'Stillingfleet' has no sep civ identity 1866—1935 (see following entry). *Parl* Pt E Riding, pt N Riding (1832—67). *Eccl* Seq 18.

CP [E Riding] Renaming 1935 of Stillingfleet with Moresby CP.[13] *LG* Derw. RD. Transf 1974 to N Yorks.[5] *Parl* Bev. CC (1948—55), Howden CC (1955—*).

STILLINGFLEET WITH MOREBY

[E Riding] Tp in Stillingfleet AP, sep CP 1866.[2] *LG* Ouse & Derw. Wap, York PLU, RSD, Escr. RD. Renamed 1935 'Stillingfleet' CP.[13] *Parl* E Riding (1832—85), Howdensh. Dv (1885—1948).

STILLINGTON

AP [N Riding] *LG* Seq 28. Transf 1974 to N Yorks.[5] *Parl* Seq 16. *Eccl* Pec jurisd Stillington prebend (until 1836), Seq 18 thereafter.

STIRTON WITH THORLBY

[W Riding] Tp in Kildwick AP, sep CP 1866.[2] *LG* Seq 112. Bdry: 1937.[31] Transf 1974 to N Yorks.[5] *Parl* Seq 41.

STITTENHAM

[N Riding] Tp in Sheriff Hutton AP, sep CP 1866.[2] *LG* Seq 29. Transf 1974 to N Yorks.[5] *Parl* Seq 16.

STOCKSBRIDGE

CP [W Riding] Cr 1894 by union of the pts of the following in Stocksbridge UD: Hunshelf CP, Bradfield CP.[46] *LG* Wortley PLU, Stocksbridge UD. Bdry: 1937.[31] Transf 1974 to S Yorks.[5] *Parl* Penist. Dv/CC (1918—*).

EP [W Riding] Cr 1917 from Bolsterstone EP, Penistone EP.[46] Ecclesfield RDn (1917—42), Tankersley RDn (1942—*). Bdry: 1964.[82]

STOCKTON ON THE FOREST

[N Riding] Chap in Bugthorpe AP, sep civ identity early, sep EP 1738.[9] *LG* Seq 32. Transf 1974 to N Yorks.[9] *Parl* Seq 16. *Eccl* Pec jurisd Bugthorpe prebend (until 1836), Bulmer RDn (1836—*). Eccl bdry: 1967.[127]

STOKESLEY

AP [N Riding] Incl tps Great Busby, Little Busby (each a sep CP 1866[2]), tp Easby (sep CP 1866,[2] eccl severed 1880 to help cr Great Ayton with Easby EP[161]), pt tps Newby, Skutterskelfe (each a sep CP 1866[2]), tp Westerdale (sep civ identity early, sep EP 1858[788]). *LG* Stokesley Bor, Seq 58. Addtl civ bdry alt: 1883.[16] Transf 1974 to N Yorks.[5] *Parl* Seq 11. *Eccl* Seq 24.

DOWN STONEBECK

[W Riding] Tp in Kirkby Malzeard AP, sep CP 1866.[2] *LG* Seq 89. Transf 1974 to N Yorks.[5] *Parl* Seq 33.

UPPER STONEBECK

[W Riding] Organisation as for Down Stonebeck.

STONEGRAVE

AP [N Riding] Incl tp West Ness (sep CP 1866,[2] eccl severed 1931 and transf to Nunnington AP[632]), pt tp East Newton and Laysthorp (sep CP 1866[2]), pt tp Nunnington (remainder constitutes Nunnington AP). *LG* Seq 63. Transf 1974 to N Yorks.[5] *Parl* Seq 21. *Eccl* Seq 26.

STORKHILL AND SANDHOLME

[E Riding] Tp in Beverley St John AP, sep CP 1866.[2] *LG* Bev. Lbty, PLU, RSD, RD. Abol 1935 to help cr Tickton CP.[13] *Parl* Bev. Parl Bor (1832—70), E Riding (1870—85), Hold. Dv (1885—1948).

STORTHWAITE—see STORWOOD

STORWOOD

[E Riding] Tp (sometimes 'Storthwaite') in Thornton AP, sep CP 1866.[2] *LG* Harth. Wap, Pockl. PLU, RSD, RD. Abol 1935 to help cr Cottingwith CP.[13] *Parl* E Riding (1832—85), Howdensh. Dv (1885—1948).

STOTFOLD

[W Riding] Ex-par place, sep CP 1858.[393] *LG* Straff. & Tick. Wap, Donc. PLU, RSD, RD. Abol 1920 ent to Hooton Pagnell AP.[248] *Parl* W Riding (1832—67), S'rn Dv of W Riding (1867—85), Donc. Dv (1885—1918), Don Valley Dv (1918—48).

STOURTON

EP [W Riding] Cr 1901 from Middleton EP, Woodlesford EP, Hunslet St Mary EP.[366] Leeds RDn (1901—71), Armley RDn (1971—73). Bdry: 1938 (help cr Leeds St John and St Barnabas, Belle Isle EP),[575] 1967.[127] Abol 1973 ent to Hunslet St Mary EP.[354]

STRENSALL

AP [N Riding] Incl chap Haxby (pec jurisd as for tp Strensall, sep CP 1866,[2] sep EP 1863[292]), pt tps Earswick, Towthorpe (each a sep CP 1866[2]). *LG* Seq 32. Transf 1974 to N Yorks.[5] *Parl* Seq 16. *Eccl* Pec jurisd Strensall prebend (until 1836), Seq 18 thereafter.

STUDLEY ROGER

[W Riding] Tp in Ripon AP, sep CP 1866,[2] eccl

severed 1724 to help cr Aldfield with Studley EP.[9] *LG* Seq 90. Transf 1974 to N Yorks.[5] *Parl* Seq 33.

STURTON GRANGE

[W Riding] Tp in Aberford AP, sep CP 1866.[2] *LG* Seq 106. Transf 1974 to W Yorks.[5] *Parl* Seq 24.

STUTTON WITH HAZLEWOOD

[W Riding] Ex-par place, sep CP 1858.[393] *LG* Seq 81. Transf 1974 to N Yorks.[5] *Parl* Seq 24.

SUTTON CUM EVERLEY

[N Riding] Tp in Hackness AP, sep CP 1866.[2] *LG* Seq 67. Transf 1974 to N Yorks.[5] *Parl* Seq 20.

SUNDERLANDWICK

[E Riding] Tp in Hutton Cranswick AP, sep CP 1866.[2] *LG* Harth. Wap, Driff. PLU, RSD, RD. Bdry: 1884.[350] Abol 1935 ent to Hutton Cranswick AP.[13] *Parl* E Riding (1832—85), Buckr. Dv (1885—1948).

SUNK ISLAND

[E Riding] Ex-par land reclaimed *temp* Chas I from River Humber, church erected 1800.[789] *LG* Seq 15. Transf 1974 to Humb.[5] *Parl* Seq 5. *Eccl* Harth. & Hull RDn (*ca* 1800—57), S Harth. RDn (1857—66), Hornsea RDn (1866—1916), N Hold. RDn (1916—49), S Hold. RDn (1949—*).

SUTTON

AP [E Riding] Chap in Wawne AP, then Collegiate, sep par from Dissolution. Incl area Drypool (sep civ identity early, sep EP 1766[9]). Usual eccl spelling; for civ see 'Sutton and Stoneferry'. *Eccl* Hold. RDn (until 1849), S Hold. RDn (1849—62), Bev. RDn (1862—71), Kingst. upon Hull RDn (1871—*). Addtl eccl bdry alt: 1844 (cr Hull St Mark EP),[189] 1904 (help cr Wilmington EP),[543] 1927 (help cr Sutton in Holderness EP),[487] 1960.[256]

SUTTON

EP [E Riding] Cr 1742 from Norton AP.[9] Buckr. RDn (1742—1857), E Buckr. RDn (1857—66), Buckr. RDn (1866—sep status lost). Sep status lost *ca* 1860s—70s.

SUTTON

[W Riding] Tp in Brotherton AP, sep CP 1866.[2] *LG* Bark. Ash Wap, Barwick GilbU (until 1869), Pontef. PLU (1869—91), RSD. Abol 1891 to help cr Byram cum Sutton CP.[386] *Parl* W Riding (1832—67), N'rn Dv of W Riding (1867—85), Bark. Ash Dv (1885—1918).

SUTTON

[W Riding] Tp pt in Campsall AP, pt in Burghwallis AP, sep CP 1866.[2] *LG* Osg. Wap, Donc. PLU, RSD, RD. Abol 1938 ent to Norton CP.[28] *Parl* W Riding (1832—67), N'rn Dv of W Riding (1867—85), Osg. Dv (1885—1918), Don Valley Dv (1918—48).

SUTTON

[W Riding] Tp in Kildwick AP, sep CP 1866,[2] main pt a sep EP 1870,[181] the detached pt eccl severed 1881 to help cr Steeton EP.[600] *LG* Seq 109. Bdry: 1883.[52] Transf 1974 to N Yorks.[5] *Parl* Seq 39. *Eccl* Sometimes as 'Sutton in Craven', Craven RDn, S'rn Dv (1870—1921), S Craven RDn (1921—*).

SUTTON AND STONEFERRY

AP [E Riding] Chap in Wawne, then Collegiate, sep par from Dissolution. Usual civ spelling; for eccl and

for civ and eccl sep area Drypool, see 1st 'Sutton' above. *LG* Hold. Wap, Scul. PLU, pt Kingst. upon Hull MB (1835—89), pt Kingst. upon Hull CB (1889—94), pt Kingst. upon Hull USD, pt Scul. RSD. Abol civ 1894 the pt in the CB (assoc with E Riding) to cr Sutton Within CP, the remainder to cr Sutton Without CP,[443] the latter soon called 'Sutton on Hull'. *Parl* Pt Kingst. upon Hull Parl Bor (1832—85), pt E Riding (1832—85), pt Hold. Dv (1885—1918); see Part III of the *Guide* for composition of Kingst. upon Hull Parl Bors (1885—1918) by wards of the MB, incl pt of this par.

SUTTON GRANGE

[W Riding] Tp in Ripon AP, sep CP 1866.[2] *LG* Seq 100. Transf 1974 to N Yorks.[5] *Parl* Seq 34.

SUTTON HOWGRAVE

[N Riding] Tp in Kirklington AP, sep CP 1866.[2] *LG* Seq 43. Bdry: 1894 (gains pt Nunwick with Howgrave CP, Yorks W Riding),[738] 1895 (gains pt Nunwick with Howgrave CP, Yorks W Riding).[634] Transf 1974 to N Yorks.[5] *Parl* Seq 18.

SUTTON IN CRAVEN—see 5th SUTTON above

SUTTON IN HOLDERNESS

EP [E Riding] Cr 1927 from Sutton AP, Drypool EP.[487] Kingst. upon Hull RDn. Bdry: 1954 (incl help cr Kingston upon Hull St Aidan Southcoates EP),[489] 1960.[256] Sometimes 'Sutton in Holderness St Michael, Marfleet'.

SUTTON ON DERWENT

AP [E Riding] Usual eccl spelling; for civ see 'Sutton upon Derwent'. *Eccl* Harth. & Hull RDn (until 1857), W Harth. RDn (1857—66), Weigh. RDn (1866—87), Pockl. RDn (1887—1973), Escr. RDn (1973—*).

SUTTON ON HULL

CP [E Riding] Cr 1894 as 'Sutton Without' CP from the pt of Sutton and Stoneferry AP not in Kingst. upon Hull CB,[443] soon after called 'Sutton on Hull'. *LG* Scul. PLU, RD. Bdry: 1930 (loses pt to Kingst. upon Hull CB [assoc with E Riding] and to Sculcoates AP).[251] Abol 1935 pt to Kingst. upon Hull CB (assoc with E Riding) and to Sculcoates AP, pt to Wawne AP.[13] *Parl* Hold. Dv (1918—48).

SUTTON ON THE FOREST

AP [N Riding] Incl tp Huby (sep CP 1866[2]). *LG* Seq 28. Civ bdry: 1883.[16] Transf 1974 to N Yorks.[5] *Parl* Seq 16. *Eccl* Seq 18. Eccl bdry: 1930.[657]

SUTTON UNDER WHITSTONE CLIFFE

[N Riding] Tp in Felixkirk AP, sep CP 1866.[2] *LG* Seq 27. Bdry: 1934.[3] Transf 1974 to N Yorks.[5] *Parl* Seq 16.

SUTTON UPON DERWENT

AP [E Riding] Usual civ spelling; for eccl see 'Sutton on Derwent'. *LG* Seq 12. Transf 1974 to Humb.[5] *Parl* Seq 7.

SUTTON WITHIN

CP [Kingst. upon Hull CB] Cr 1894 from the pt of Sutton and Stoneferry AP (o'wise E Riding) in Kingst. upon Hull CB.[443] *LG* Scul. PLU, Kingst. upon Hull CB. Abol 1898 ent to Sculcoates AP.[446]

SUTTON WITHOUT—see SUTTON ON HULL

SWAINBY WITH ALLERTHORPE

[N Riding] Tp pt in Pickhill AP, pt in Burneston

AP, sep CP 1866.[2] *LG* Seq 40. Transf 1974 to N Yorks.[5] *Parl* Seq 18.

SWANLAND

[E Riding] Tp pt in Kirk Ella AP, pt in North Ferriby AP, sep CP 1866.[2] *LG* Seq 18. Bdry: 1883,[243] 1877 (cr Newington CP),[733] 1935.[13] Transf 1974 to Humb.[5] *Parl* Seq 6.

SWILLINGTON

AP [W Riding] *LG* Seq 105. Civ bdry: 1937 (loses pt to Leeds CB [assoc with W Riding] & AP).[31] Transf 1974 to W Yorks.[5] *Parl* Seq 25. *Eccl* Ainsty RDn (until 1820), New Ainsty RDn (1820—38), Pontef. RDn (1838—57), Wakef RDn (1857—94), Whitkirk RDn (1894—*). Eccl bdry: 1904 (help cr Mickletown EP).[300]

SWINDEN

[W Riding] Tp in Gisburn AP, sep CP 1866.[2] *LG* Seq 111. Transf 1974 to N Yorks.[5] *Parl* Seq 41.

SWINE

AP [E Riding] Incl chap Bilton, tps Ganstead, Wyton (each a sep CP 1866,[2] the 3 comprised the chap, sep EP 1794 as 'Bilton',[9] eccl refounded 1867[250]), chap South Skirlaugh, tps Benningholme and Grange, Marton; North Skirlaugh, Rowton and Arnold (each a sep CP 1866,[2] the 4 comprised the chap, sep EP 1867 as 'Skirlaugh'[235]), tps Coniston, Ellerby, Thirtleby, pt tp West Newton with Burton Constable (each a sep CP 1866[2]). *LG* Seq 16. Addtl civ bdry alt: 1935 (gains Benningholme and Grange CP).[13] Transf 1974 to Humb.[5] *Parl* Seq 5. *Eccl* Seq 15.

SWINEFLEET

[W Riding] Chap in Whitgift AP, sep CP 1866,[2] sep EP 1753.[9] *LG* Osg. Wap, Goole PLU, RSD. Abol 1884 to help cr Swinefleet and Reedness CP.[752] *Parl* W Riding (1832—67), N'rn Dv of W Riding (1867—85). *Eccl* Pec jurisd Selby (1440—1539), pec jurisd Snaith (1539—1836), Pontef. RDn (1836—38), Old Ainsty RDn (1838—57), Pontef. RDn (1857—62), Selby RDn (1862—71), Snaith RDn (1871—*).

CP [W Riding] Cr 1894 from Swinefleet and Reedness CP.[753] *LG* Goole PLU, RD. Transf 1974 to Humb.[5] *Parl* Pontef. Dv (1918—48), Goole CC (1948—*).

SWINEFLEET AND REEDNESS

CP [W Riding] Cr 1884 by union Swinefleet CP, Reednesss CP.[752] *LG* Osg. Wap, Goole PLU, RSD. Abol 1894 to cr the 2 CPs of Swinefleet, Reedness.[753] *Parl* Osg. Dv (1885—1918).

SWINTON

[N Riding] Tp in Appleton le Street AP, sep CP 1866.[2] *LG* Seq 65. Bdry: 1934.[3] Transf 1974 to N Yorks.[5] *Parl* Seq 16.

SWINTON

[W Riding] Chap pt in Wath upon Dearne AP, pt in Mexborough AP, sep CP 1866,[2] sep EP 1718.[9] *LG* Straff. & Tick. Wap, Rotherh. PLU, Swinton USD, UD. Civ bdry: 1883,[714] 1886,[751] 1938.[28] Transf 1974 to S Yorks.[5] *Parl* W Riding (1832—67), S'rn Dv of W Riding (1867—85), Rotherh. Dv (1885—1918), Rother Valley Dv (1918—48), Deane Valley CC (1948—*). *Eccl* Donc. RDn (1718—1857), Rotherh. RDn (1857—62), Sheff RDn (1862—71),

Wath RDn (1871—*). Eccl bdry: 1860 (help cr Kilnhurst EP),[301] 1974.[77]

SWINTON WITH WARTHERMARSKE

[N Riding] Tp in Masham AP, sep CP 1866.[2] *LG* E Hang Wap, Bedale PLU, Masham USD, UD (1894—1934), RD (1934—74). Bdry: 1883,[16] 1886,[382] 1886,[525] 1934.[3] Transf 1974 to N Yorks.[5] *Parl* Seq 14.

SYKEHOUSE

[W Riding] Chap in Fishlake AP, sep CP 1866,[2] sep EP 1830,[9] eccl refounded 1860.[553] *LG* Seq 120. Civ bdry: 1883,[52] 1884.[558] Transf 1974 to S Yorks.[5] *Parl* Seq 47. *Eccl* Donc. RDn (1830—71), Snaith RDn (1871—*). Eccl bdry: 1887.[559]

TADCASTER

AP [Pt Ainsty (W Riding until 1449 and from 1836, indept jurisd 1449—1836: tps Catterton, Oxton, Tadcaster East [each a sep CP 1866[2]]), pt W Riding (Bark Ash. Wap: tp Tadcaster West [sep CP 1866[2]]) so that 'Tadcaster' has no sep civ identity after 1866. *Parl* W Riding (1832—67). *Eccl* Seq 33.

TADCASTER EAST

[Ainsty (W Riding until 1449 and from 1836, indept jurisd 1449—1836)] Tp in Tadcaster AP, sep CP 1866.[2] *LG* Seq 70. Transf 1974 to N Yorks.[5] *Parl* Seq 23.

TADCASTER WEST

[W Riding] Tp in Tadcaster AP, sep CP 1866.[2] *LG* Seq 81. Transf 1974 to N Yorks.[5] *Parl* Seq 24.

EAST TANFIELD

[N Riding] Tp in Kirkington AP, sep CP 1866.[2] *LG* Seq 22. Transf 1974 to N Yorks.[5] *Parl* Seq 18.

WEST TANFIELD

AP [N Riding] *LG* Seq 43. Transf 1974 to N Yorks.[5] *Parl* Seq 18. *Eccl* Catt. RDn (until 1857), Catt. East RDn (1857—1928), Ripon RDn (1928—*).

TANKERSLEY

AP [W Riding] Incl chap Wortley (sep CP 1866,[2] sep EP 1740[9]). *LG* Seq 115. Civ bdry: 1938,[28] 1957.[509] Transf 1974 to Gtr Manch.[5] *Parl* Seq 49. *Eccl* Donc. RDn (until 1857), Rotherh. RDn (1857—62), Ecclesfield RDn (1862—1942), Tankersley RDn (1942—*). Eccl bdry: 1925 (help cr Mortomley EP).[407]

TANSHELF

[W Riding] Tp in Pontefract AP, sep CP 1866.[2] *LG* Osg. Wap, Gt Preston GilbU (until 1862), Pontef. PLU (1862—1930), Pontef. MB (1875—1920), USD. Bdry: 1883,[52] 1889.[748] Abol 1920 ent to Pontefract AP.[65] *Parl* Pontef. Parl Bor (1832—1918), Pontef. Dv (1918—48).

TEESSIDE

CP [Teesside CB] Cr 1968 by union Middlesb. CB (assoc with N Riding) & CP, pt Yorks N Riding (pt Eston UD & CP, pt Guisb. UD [pts Kirkleatham AP, Morton CP, Wilton CP], pt Redcar MB & CP, pt Saltburn and Markse by the Sea UD and Marske AP, ent Hemlington CP, ent Marton AP, pts Maltby CP, Newby CP, Nunthorpe CP, Ormsesby UD & AP, Stainton AP), pt Durham (Stock. on Tees MB & AP, pts Carlton CP, Elston CP, Grindon AP, Norton AP, Preston on Tees CP).[537] *LG* Teesside CB. Transf 1974 to Clev.[5] *Parl* See Part III of the

Guide for composition of Teesside BCs (1970—*) by wards of the CB.

TEMPLENEWSHAM

[W Riding] Tp pt in Whitkirk AP, pt in Leeds AP (hmlt Osmondthorpe), sep CP 1866.[2] *LG* Skyr. Wap, Carlton GilbU (until 1869), Hunslet PLU (1869—1928), pt Leeds Bor/MB, pt Leeds CB (1889—94), pt Leeds USD, pt Hunslet RSD, Hunslet RD. Bdry: 1894 (loses the pt in the CB to cr Osmondthorpe CP),[504] 1925 (gains Thorpe Stapleton CP).[790] Abol 1928 ent to Leeds CB (assoc with W Riding) & AP.[39] *Parl* Pt Leeds Parl Bor (1832—85), pt W Riding (1832—67), pt N'rn Dv of W Riding (1867—85), pt Bark. Ash Dv (1885—1918); see Part III of the *Guide* for composition of Leeds Parl Bors (1885—1918) by wards of the MB, incl pt of this par.

TENTERGATE

CP [W Riding] Cr 1894 from the pt of Scriven and Tentergate CP in Knar. & Tentergate UD.[257] *LG* Knar. PLU, Knar. & Tentergate UD. Abol 1895 ent to Knaresborough AP.[663]

TERRINGTON

AP [N Riding] Incl tps Ganthorpe, Terrington with Wigganthorpe (each a sep CP 1866[2]) so that 'Terrington' has no sep civ identity after 1866. *LG* Bulmer Wap. *Parl* N Riding (1832—67). *Eccl* Bulmer RDn (until 1862), Eas. RDn (1862—1928), Malton RDn (1928—*).

TERRINGTON WITH WIGGANTHORPE

[N Riding] Tp in Terrington AP, sep CP 1866.[2] *LG* Seq 29. Transf 1974 to N Yorks.[5] *Parl* Seq 16.

THEAKSTON

[N Riding] Tp in Burneston AP, sep CP 1866.[2] *LG* Seq 40. Transf 1974 to N Yorks.[5] *Parl* Seq 18.

THEARNE

[E Riding] Tp in Beverley St John AP, sep CP 1866.[2] *LG* Harth. Wap, Bev. Lbty, Bev. PLU, RSD, RD. Abol 1935 to help cr Woodmamsey CP.[13] *Parl* Bev. Parl Bor (1832—70), E Riding (1870—85), Hold. Dv (1885—1948).

THIMBLEBY

[N Riding] Tp pt in Osmotherley AP, pt in Kirby Sigston AP, sep CP 1866.[2] *LG* Seq 22. Transf 1974 to N Yorks.[5] *Parl* Seq 14.

THIRKLEBY

[E Riding] Tp in Kirby Grindalythe AP, sep CP 1866.[2] *LG* Buckr. Wap, Malton PLU, RSD, Norton RD. Abol 1935 ent to Kirby Grindalythe AP.[13] *Parl* E Riding (1832—85), Buckr. Dv (1885—1948).

THIRKLEBY

AP [N Riding] *LG* Seq 27. Transf 1974 to N Yorks.[5] *Parl* Seq 16. *Eccl* Seq 20.

THIRLBY

[N Riding] Tp in Felixkirk AP, sep CP 1866.[2] *LG* Seq 27. Bdry: 1887.[286] Transf 1974 to N Yorks.[5] *Parl* Seq 16.

THIRN

[N Riding] Tp in Thornton Watlass AP, sep CP 1866.[2] *LG* Seq 48. Transf 1974 to N Yorks.[5] *Parl* Seq 15.

THIRSK

AP [N Riding] Incl pt chap Carlton Miniott (sep CP 1866, sep EP 1747[9]), chap Sand Hutton (sep CP 1866,[2] sep EP 1753[9]), chap Sowerby (sep CP 1866,[2] sep EP 1763[9]). *LG* Thirsk Bor, Seq 27. Addtl civ bdry alt: 1934.[3] Transf 1974 to N Yorks.[5] *Parl* Thirsk Parl Bor (1553—1885), Thirsk & Malton Dv/CC (1885—*). *Eccl* Seq 20.

THIRTLEBY

[E Riding] Tp in Swine AP, sep CP 1866.[2] *LG* Hold. Wap, Skirl. PLU, RSD, RD. Abol 1935 ent to Coniston CP.[13] *Parl* E Riding (1832—85), Hold. Dv (1885—1948).

THIXENDALE

[E Riding] Tp in Wharram Percy AP, sep CP 1866,[2] sep EP 1872.[67] *LG* Seq 4. Civ bdry: 1935.[13] Transf 1974 to N Yorks.[5] *Parl* Seq 7. *Eccl* Pockl. RDn (1872—1961), Buckr. RDn (1961—*). Eccl bdry: 1968.[44]

THOLTHORPE

[N Riding] Tp in Alne AP, sep CP 1866.[2] *LG* Seq 28. Transf 1974 to N Yorks.[5] *Parl* Seq 16.

THORLABY

[N Riding] Tp in Aysgarth AP, sep CP 1866.[2] *LG* Seq 52. Bdry: 1883,[16] 1886.[4] Transf 1974 to N Yorks.[5] *Parl* Seq 14.

THORGANBY

AP [E Riding] Usual eccl spelling; for civ until 1935 see 'Thorganby with West Cottingwith'. *Eccl* Seq 19.

CP [E Riding] Renaming civ 1935 of Thorganby with West Cottingwth AP.[13] *LG* Derw. RD. Transf 1974 to N Yorks.[5] *Parl* Bev. CC (1948—55), Howden CC (1955—*).

THORGANBY WITH WEST COTTINGWITH

AP [E Riding] Usual civ spelling; for eccl see 'Thorganby'. *LG* Ouse & Derw. Wap, York PLU, RSD, Escr. RD. Renamed civ 1935 'Thorganby'.[13] *Parl* E Riding (1832—85), Howdensh. Dv (1885—1948).

THORGUMBALD

[E Riding] Tp in Paull AP, sep CP 1866,[2] eccl severed 1954 to help cr Burstwick with Thorgumbald EP.[373] *LG* Seq 15. Bdry: 1935.[13] Transf 1974 to Humb.[5] *Parl* Seq 5.

THORMANBY

AP [N Riding] *LG* Seq 28. Civ bdry: 1887 (gains pt Stockton on Tees AP, Durham).[501] Transf 1974 to N Yorks.[5] *Parl* Seq 16. *Eccl* Seq 18.

THORNABY

[N Riding] Chap in Stainton AP, sep CP 1866,[2] sep EP 1844.[783] Sometimes early civ 'Thornaby with South Stockton'. *LG* Langb. Lbty, Stock. PLU (1837—75), Middlesb. PLU (1875—1930), S Stock. USD (1875—92), Thornaby on Tees MB (1892—1968), USD (1892—94). Civ bdry: 1887 (gains pt Stockton on Tees AP, Durham).[791] Abol civ 1968 to help cr Teesside CB (assoc with N Riding) & CP.[548] *Parl* N Riding (1832—85), Clev Dv (1885—1918), Stock. on Tees Parl Bor (1918—48), Middlesb. West BC (1948—70). *Eccl* Clev RDn (1844—62), Stokes. RDn (1862—78), Middlesb. RDn (1878—1972). Eccl bdry: 1895 (help cr Thornaby on Tees EP [Yorks N Riding, Durham]),[115] 1969.[27] Abol eccl 1972 ent to

Thornaby on Tees EP.[792]

THORNABY ON TEES

EP [N Riding, Durham] Cr 1895 from Thornaby EP (Yorks N Riding), Stockton upon Tees AP (Durham) to be dioc York.[115] Middlesb. RDn. Bdry: 1969,[27] 1972 (gains Thornaby EP).[792]

THORNBOROUGH

[N Riding] Tp in South Kilvington AP, sep CP 1866.[2] *LG* Seq 27. Transf 1974 to N Yorks.[5] *Parl* Seq 16.

THORNBURY

CP [Bradf CB] Cr 1894 from the pt of Calverley with Farsley CP in Bradf CB.[257] *LG* Bradf PLU, CB. Abol 1898 ent to Bradford AP.[65]

EP [W Riding] Cr 1918 from Laister Dyke EP, Calverley AP.[93] Bradf RDn (1918—21), Calverley RDn (1921—*). Bdry: 1927,[67] 1959 (help cr Woodhall EP).[320]

THORNE

AP [W Riding] Orig chap in Hatfield AP, appropriated to Lewes Priory, sep par early.[604] *LG* Seq 120. Civ bdry: 1883,[52] 1884,[556] 1884,[557] 1884,[558] 1884 (gains pt Eastoft CP, Lincs Pts Lind),[500] 1938.[28] Transf 1974 to S Yorks.[5] *Parl* Seq 47. *Eccl* Seq 45. Eccl bdry: 1884 (help cr Stainforth EP),[192] 1887,[559] 1956 (cr Moorends EP).[719]

THORNER

AP [W Riding] Incl tp Scarcroft (sep CP 1866[2]), tp Shadwell (sep CP 1866,[2] sep EP 1843,[9] eccl refounded 1844[189]). *LG* Seq 102. Addtl civ bdry alt: 1883,[52] 1884.[75] Transf 1974 to W Yorks.[5] *Parl* Seq 24. *Eccl* Ainsty RDn (until 1820), New Ainsty RDn (1820—38), Pontef. RDn (1838—57), Wethb. RDn (1857—61), Whitkirk RDn (1861—*).

THORNES

EP [W Riding] Cr 1840 from Wakefield AP,[9] refounded 1841[625]; for civ see 'Alverthorpe with Thornes'. Pontef. RDn (1840—57), Wakef RDn (1857—1957). Bdry: 1861 (help cr Westgate Common EP,[9] refounded 1862,[92] later called 'Wakefield St Michael'), 1874 (help cr Wakefield Christ Church EP),[148] 1878,[415] 1934 (help cr Lupset EP).[94] Abol 1957 to help cr Thornes St James and Christ Church EP.[793]

THORNES ST JAMES AND CHRIST CHURCH

EP [W Riding] Cr 1957 by union Thornes EP, Wakefield Christ Church EP.[793] Wakef RDn.

THORNHILL

AP [W Riding] Incl chap Flockton (sep CP 1866,[2] sep EP 1731,[9] eccl refounded 1860 as 'Flockton cum Denby Grange' by union Flockton EP, pt Thornhill AP [pt tp Sitlington], pt Kirkheaton AP [hmlt Denby Grange][68]), tp Sitlington (sep CP 1866,[2] called 'Shitlington' until 1930s, 'Sitlington' thereafter, pt eccl severed 1860 to help cr Flockton cum Denby Grange EP,[68] as noted above), tp Whitley Lower (sep CP 1866,[2] sep EP 1848[794]). *LG* Agb. Wap, Dewsb. PLU, Thornhill USD, UD (1894—1910), Dewsb. MB (1910—13), CB (1913—25). Addtl civ bdry alt: 1896 (gains Whitley Lower CP).[795] Abol civ 1925 ent to Dewsbury AP.[477] *Parl* W Riding (1832—67), Dewsb. Parl Bor (pt 1867—1918, ent 1918—48), pt S'rn Dv of W Riding (1867—85), pt

Morley Dv (1885—1918). *Eccl* Seq 47. Addtl eccl bdry alt: 1859 (help cr Thornhill Lees EP),[478] 1878 (help cr Middlestown EP),[199] 1882 (help cr Henbury Bridge EP).[130]

THORNHILL LEES

EP [W Riding] Cr 1859 from Thornhill AP, Dewsbury AP.[478] Dewsb. RDn.

THORNTHWAITE—see following entry

THORNTHWAITE WITH PADSIDE

[W Riding] Tp in Hampsthwaite AP, sep CP 1866,[2] sep EP 1744 as 'Thornthwaite',[9] as such eccl refounded 1866.[598] *LG* Seq 89. Transf 1974 to N Yorks.[5] *Parl* Seq 33. *Eccl* As 'Thornthwaite', Ainsty RDn (1744—1820), Old Ainsty RDn (1820—38), Pontef. RDn (1838—57), Otley RDn (1857—70), Knar. RDn (1870—1905), Nidd. RDn (1905—71), Ripon RDn (1971—*). Eccl bdry: 1860 (help refound Greenhow Hill EP),[68] 1968 (cr Darley EP).[195]

THORNHOLME

[E Riding] Tp in Burton Agnes AP, sep CP 1866.[2] *LG* Dick. Wap, Bridl. PLU, RSD, RD. Bdry: 1884.[377] Abol 1935 ent to Burton Agnes AP.[3] *Parl* E Riding (1832—85), Buckr. Dv (1885—1948).

THORNTON

AP [E Riding] Chap (in pec jurisd Dean of York) in Pocklington AP, united 1252 with chap Allerthorpe in same par as sep EP 'Thornton with Allerthorpe',[62] later called 'Thornton with Allerthorpe and Melbourne', qv, 'Thornton' and 'Allerthorpe' each sep civ identity early. Incl tps Melbourne, Storthwaite (each a sep CP 1866[2]). *LG* Seq 12. Transf 1974 to Humb.[5] *Parl* Seq 7.

THORNTON

[W Riding] Chap in Bradford AP, sep CP 1866,[2] sep EP 1760,[9] pt of latter severed 1846 to cr Denholme Gate EP,[208] the remainder eccl refounded 1867 as 'Thornton'.[67] *LG* Morley Wap, Bradf PLU (1837—48), N Bierley PLU (1848—1930), pt Thornton USD, pt Denholme Gate USD (1875—87), pt Denholme USD (1887—94), Thornton UD (1894—99), Bradf CB (1899—1974). Civ bdry: 1894 (loses the pt in Denholme UD to cr Denholme CP).[257] Transf 1974 to W Yorks.[5] *Parl* W Riding (1832—67), E'rn Dv of W Riding (1867—85), Keigh. Dv (1885—1918); see Part III of the *Guide* for composition of Bradf Parl Bors/ BCs (1918—*) by wards of the CB. *Eccl* Pontef. RDn (1760—1857), Bradf RDn (1857—1921), Horton RDn (1921—71), Airedale RDn (1971—*).

BISHOP THORNTON

[W Riding] Chap in Ripon AP, sep CP 1866,[2] sep EP 1748,[9] eccl refounded 1863 incl ex-par Warsill.[162] *LG* Seq 101. Transf 1974 to N Yorks.[5] *Parl* Seq 34. *Eccl* Pec jurisd Lbty Ripon (until 1836), Boroughbr. RDn (1836—49), Ripon RDn (1849—*).

THORNTON CUM BAXBY—see THORNTON ON THE HILL

THORNTON DALE

AP [N Riding] *LG* Seq 61. Civ bdry: 1887 (gains Farmanby CP).[548] Transf 1974 to N Yorks.[5] *Parl* Seq 20. *Eccl* Riddal RDn (until 1862), Malton RDn

(1862—1928), Pick. RDn (1928—34). Abol 1934 to help cr Thornton Dale with Ellerburne and Wilton EP.[524]

THORNTON DALE WITH ELLERBURNE AND WILTON

EP [N Riding] Cr 1934 by union Thornton Dale AP, Ellerburne with Wilton AP.[524] Pick. RDn.

THORNTON IN CRAVEN

AP [W Riding] *LG* Seq 112. Civ bdry: 1909 (cr Earby CP).[496] Transf 1974 to N Yorks.[5] *Parl* Seq 41. *Eccl* Seq 39. Eccl bdry: 1842 (cr Kelbrook EP),[9] 1923 (cr Earby EP).[497]

THORNTON IN LONSDALE

AP [Pt W Riding (tp 'Thornton in Lonsdale'; chap & tp Burton in Lonsdale [sep CP 1866,[2] sep EP 1823,[9] eccl refounded 1867[74]]), pt Lancs (tp Ireby [sep CP 1866[2]]). *LG* Settle PLU, RSD, RD. Addtl civ bdry alt: 1883.[52] Transf 1974 to N Yorks.[5] *Parl* Seq 41. *Eccl* Seq 56.

THORNTON LE BEANS

[N Riding] Tp pt in Northallerton AP, pt in North Otterington AP, sep CP 1866,[2] eccl severed 1961 to help cr Thornton le Street with Thornton le Moor and Thornton le Beans EP.[742] *LG* Seq 22. Transf 1974 to N Yorks.[5] *Parl* Seq 14.

THORNTON LE CLAY

[N Riding] Tp in Foston AP, sep CP 1866.[2] *LG* Seq 29. Bdry: 1889.[566] Transf 1974 to N Yorks. *Parl* Seq 16.

THORNTON LE MOOR

[N Riding] Tp in North Otterington AP, sep CP 1866,[2] eccl severed 1961 to help cr Thornton le Street with Thornton le Moor and Thornton le Beans EP.[742] *LG* Seq 27. Transf 1974 to N Yorks.[5] *Parl* Seq 16.

THORNTON LE STREET

AP [N Riding] Incl tp North Kilvington (sep CP 1866[2]). *LG* Seq 23. Transf 1974 to N Yorks.[5] *Parl* Seq 16. *Eccl* Pec jurisd Bp Durham (until 1836), Clev RDn (1836—62), Thirsk RDn (1862—1916), N'allert. RDn (1916—61). Abol eccl 1961 to help cr Thornton le Street with Thornton le Moor and Thornton le Beans EP.[742]

THORNTON LE STREET WITH THORNTON LE MOOR AND THORNTON LE BEANS

EP [N Riding] Cr 1961 by union Thornton le Street AP, pt North Otterington with Thornton le Moor and Thornton le Beans AP (the 2 tps in the par).[742] N'allert. RDn.

THORNTON ON THE HILL

[N Riding] Tp (sometimes 'Thornton cum Baxby') in Coxwold AP, sep CP 1866.[2] *LG* Seq 24. Bdry: 1883,[16] 1887.[547] Transf 1974 to N Yorks.[5] *Parl* Seq 16.

THORNTON RISEBROUGH

[N Riding] Tp in Normanby AP, sep CP 1866.[2] *LG* Ryed. Wap, Pick. PLU (1837—soon after 1848[112]), Kirkby Moors. PLU (soon after 1848[112]—1930), RSD, RD (1894—1934), Pick. RD (1934—74). Bdry: 1887.[715] Transf 1974 to N Yorks.[5] *Parl* Seq 22.

THORNTON RUST

[N Riding] Tp in Aysgarth AP, sep CP 1866.[2] *LG*

Seq 51. Transf 1974 to N Yorks.[5] *Parl* Seq 14.

THORNTON STEWARD

AP [N Riding] *LG* Seq 53. Civ bdry: 1886.[526] Transf 1974 to N Yorks.[5] *Parl* Seq 14. *Eccl* Seq 54.

THORNTON WATLASS

AP [N Riding] Incl tps Clifton upon Ure, Rookwith, Thirn (each a sep CP 1866[2]). *LG* Seq 49. Transf 1974 to N Yorks.[5] *Parl* Seq 15. *Eccl* Seq 53.

THORNTON WITH ALLERTON

AP [E Riding] Cr 1252 by union chaps Thornton, Allerton, each in Pocklington AP,[62] 'Thornton', 'Allerton' each with sep civ identity early, qv. *Eccl* Pec jurisd Dean of York (until 1836), Seq 9 thereafter.

THORNVILLE

[W Riding] Tp in Whixley AP, sep CP 1866.[2] *LG* Seq 82. Transf 1974 to N Yorks.[5] *Parl* Seq 36.

THORP ARCH

AP [W Riding] *LG* Seq 71. Civ bdry: 1883,[52] 1885.[180] Transf 1974 to W Yorks.[5] *Parl* Seq 23. *Eccl* Ainsty RDn (until 1820), New Ainsty RDn (1820—62), Tadc. RDn (1862—71), Selby RDn (1871—1921), Tadc. RDn (1971—*).

THORPE

[E Riding] Tp in Howden AP, sep CP 1866.[2] *LG* Howdensh. Wap, Howden PLU, RSD, RD. Bdry: 1880.[230] Abol 1935 pt to Kilpin CP, pt to Eastrington AP.[13] *Parl* E Riding (1832—85), Howdensh. Dv (1885—1948).

THORPE

[W Riding] Tp in Burnsall AP, sep CP 1866.[2] Incl undivided pt Burnsall and Thorpe Fell (orig in Burnsall AP, abol 1938 pt to Burnsall AP, pt to this par[28]). *LG* Seq 112. Transf 1974 to N Yorks.[5] *Parl* Seq 41.

THORPE

[W Riding] Tp in Rothwell AP, sep CP 1866.[2] *LG* Agb. Wap, Wakef PLU, RSD (1875—92), Rothw. USD (1892—94), UD. Abol 1937 to help cr Lofthouse CP.[31] *Parl* W Riding (1832—67), S'rn Dv of W Riding (1867—85), Morley Dv (1885—1918), Rothw. Dv (1918—48).

THORPE AUDLIN

[W Riding] Tp in Badsworth AP, sep CP 1866.[2] *LG* Seq 96. Transf 1974 to W Yorks.[5] *Parl* Seq 28.

THORPE BASSETT

AP [E Riding] *LG* Seq 2. Civ bdry: 1889.[767] Transf 1974 to N Yorks.[5] *Parl* Seq 1. *Eccl* Seq 3.

THORPE EDGE

EP [W Riding] Renaming 1963 of Idle St John EP.[288] Calverley RDn.

THORPE HESLEY

EP [W Riding] Cr 1841 from Wath upon Dearne AP.[9] Donc. RDn (1841—57), Rotherh. RDn (1857—62), Ecclesfield RDn (1862—1942), Rotherh. RDn (1942—*). Bdry: 1969 (help cr Kimberworth Park EP).[579]

THORPE IN BALNE

[W Riding] Tp in Barnby upon Don AP, sep CP 1866.[2] *LG* Seq 117. Bdry: 1883.[42] Transf 1974 to S Yorks.[5] *Parl* Seq 44.

THORPE LE STREET

[E Riding] Tp in Nunburnholme AP, sep CP 1866,[2]

eccl severed 1876 to help cr Shipton Thorpe EP.[701] *LG* Harth. Wap, Pockl. PLU, RSD, RD. Abol 1935 ent to Hayton AP.[13] *Parl* E Riding (1832—85), Howdensh. Dv (1885—1948).

THORPE LE WILLOWS

[N Riding] Tp in Kilburn AP, sep CP 1866.[2] *LG* Seq 5. Transf 1974 to N Yorks.[5] *Parl* Seq 15.

THORPE ST JOHN THE DIVINE

EP [W Riding] Cr 1881 from Sowerby EP, Sowerby St Mary EP, Ripponden EP.[758] Halifax RDn. Bdry: 1923,[407] 1970.[680] Abol 1972 ent to Sowerby EP.[780]

THORPE SALVIN

[W Riding] Chap in Laughton en le Morthen AP, sep civ identity early, sep EP 1775.[9] *LG* Seq 121. Transf 1974 to S Yorks.[5] *Parl* Seq 48. *Eccl* Donc. RDn (1775—1857), Rotherh. RDn (1857—1927), Handsw. RDn (1927—42), Laughton RDn (1942—*).

THORPE STAPLETON

[W Riding] Tp in Whitkirk AP, sep CP 1866.[2] *LG* Skyr. Wap, not in a PLU (until 1869), Hunslet PLU (1869—1925), RSD, RD. Abol 1925 ent to Templenewsham CP.[790] *Parl* W Riding (1832—67), N'rn Dv of W Riding (1867—85), Bark. Ash Dv (1885—1918), Rothw. Dv (1918—48).

THORPE UNDERWOODS

[W Riding] Tp in Little Ouseburn AP, sep CP 1866.[2] *LG* Seq 86. Bdry: 1886.[718] Transf 1974 to N Yorks.[5] *Parl* Seq 36.

THORPE WILLOUGHBY

[W Riding] Tp in Brayton AP, sep CP 1866.[2] *LG* Seq 80. Transf 1974 to N Yorks.[5] *Parl* Seq 24.

THRESFIELD

[W Riding] Tp in Linton AP, sep CP 1866.[2] *LG* Seq 112. Transf 1974 to N Yorks.[5] *Parl* Seq 41.

THRINTOFT

[N Riding] Tp in Ainderby Steeple AP, sep CP 1866.[2] *LG* Seq 34. Bdry: 1888.[796] Transf 1974 to N Yorks.[5] *Parl* Seq 14.

THROXENBY

[N Riding] Tp in Scalby AP, sep CP 1866.[2] *LG* Pick. Lythe Wap, Scarb. PLU, RSD, RD. Bdry: 1883,[16] 1886 (gains Newby CP).[730] Abol 1909 ent to Scalby AP.[738] *Parl* N Riding (1832—85), Whitby Dv (1885—1918).

THRUSCROSS

[W Riding] Tp in Fewston AP, sep CP 1866,[2] sep EP 1875.[11] *LG* Seq 89. Transf 1974 to N Yorks.[5] *Parl* W Riding (1832—67), E'rn Dv of W Riding (1867—85), Otley Dv (1885—1918), Ripon Dv/CC (1918—*). *Eccl* Otley RDn (1875—1905), Nidd. RDn (1905—71), Ripon RDn (1971—*).

THRYBERGH

AP [W Riding] Incl pt tp Dalton (sep CP 1866,[2] sep EP 1849 from Thrybergh AP, Rotherham AP, Ecclesfield AP[464]). *LG* Seq 119. Transf 1974 to S Yorks.[5] *Parl* Seq 55. *Eccl* Seq 42. Addtl eccl bdry alt: 1952.[466]

THURCROFT

CP [W Riding] Cr 1923 by union Brampton en le Morthen CP, Laughton en le Morthen AP.[151] *LG* Rotherh. PLU, RD. Transf 1974 to S Yorks.[5] *Parl* Rother Valley CC (1948—*).

EP [W Riding] Cr 1948 from Laughton en le Morthen AP, Ulley EP.[669] Laughton RDn.

THURGOLAND

[W Riding] Tg in Silkstone AP, sep CP 1866,[2] sep EP 1844.[189] *LG* Seq 116. Transf 1974 to S Yorks.[5] *Parl* Seq 50. *Eccl* Pontef. RDn (1844—57), Silkst. RDn (1857—1927), Barnsley RDn (1927—*).

THURLSTONE

[W Riding] Tp in Penistone AP, sep CP 1866,[2] sep EP 1906.[462] *LG* Staincr. Wap, Wortley PLU (1837—49), Penist. PLU (1849—1930), Thurlstone USD, UD. Abol civ 1938 pt to help cr Dunford CP, pt to Penist. UD & AP.[28] *Parl* W Riding (1832—67), S'rn Dv of W Riding (1867—85), Holmf. Dv (1885—1918), Penist. Dv (1918—48). *Eccl* Silkst. RDn (1906—27), Barnsley RDn (1927—*).

THURNSCOE

AP [W Riding] *LG* Straff. & Tick. Wap, Donc. PLU, RSD, RD (1894—1908), Thurnscoe UD (1908—37). Civ bdry: 1908.[207] Abol civ 1937 to help cr Dearne UD & CP.[31] *Parl* W Riding (1832—67), S'rn Dv of W Riding (1867—85), Donc. Dv (1885—1918), Wentw. Dv (1918—48). *Eccl* Seq 46. Eccl bdry: 1935 (cr Thurnscoe St Hilda EP).[479]

THURNSCOE ST HILDA

EP W Riding] Cr 1935 from Thurnscoe AP.[479] Wath RDn.

THURSTONLAND

[W Riding] Tp in Kirkburton AP, sep CP 1866,[2] sep EP 1871.[21] *LG* Agb. Wap, Hudd. PLU, Thurstonland USD, UD. Abol civ 1925 to help cr Thurstonland & Farnley Tyas UD & CP.[552] *Parl* W Riding (1832—67), S'rn Dv of W Riding (1867—85), Holmf. Dv (1885—1918), Colne Valley Dv (1918—48). *Eccl* Hudd. RDn (1871—1968), Kirkburton RDn (1968—*).

THURSTONLAND AND FARNLEY TYAS

CP [W Riding] Cr 1925 by union Thurstonland UD & CP, Farnley Tyas UD & CP.[552] *LG* Hudd. PLU, Thurstonland & Farnley Tyas UD. Abol 1938 pt to Holmf. UD & CP, pt to Kirkburton UD & AP.[28]

THWING

AP [E Riding] *LG* Seq 5. Transf 1974 to Humb.[5] *Parl* Seq 2. *Eccl* Seq 6.

TIBTHORPE

[E Riding] Tp in Kirkburn AP, sep CP 1866.[2] *LG* Seq 10. Transf 1974 to Humb.[5] *Parl* Seq 3.

TICKHILL

AP [W Riding] Incl tp Stancill with Wellingley and Wilseck (sep CP 1866[2]). *LG* Straff. & Tick. Wap, Donc. PLU, Tickhill Bor, pt Tickhill USD, pt Donc. RSD, Tickhill UD. Addtl civ bdry alt: 1894 (the pt not in Tickhill UD cr Tickhill Outer CP),[257] 1896 (gains Tickhill Outer CP).[797] Transf 1974 to S Yorks.[5] *Parl* Seq 44. *Eccl* Seq 40.

TICKHILL OUTER

CP [W Riding] Cr 1894 from the pt of Tickhill AP not in Tickhill UD.[257] *LG* Donc. PLU, RD. Abol 1895 ent to Tickhill UD & AP.[797]

TICKTON

CP [E Riding] Cr 1935 by union Eske CP, Storkhill and Sandholme CP, Tickton and Hull Bridge CP, Weel CP.[13] *LG* Bev. RD. Transf 1974 to Humb.[5] *Parl*

Bev. CC (1948—55), Haltemp. CC (1955—*).

TICKTON AND HULL BRIDGE

[E Riding] Tp in Beverley St John AP, sep CP 1866.[2] *LG* Harth. Wap, Bev. Lbty, Bev. PLU, RSD, RD. Abol 1935 to help cr Tickton CP.[13] *Parl* Bev. Parl Bor (1832—70), E Riding (1870—85), Hold. Dv (1885—1948).

GREAT TIMBLE

[W Riding] Tp in Fewston AP, sep CP 1866.[2] *LG* Seq 92. Bdry: 1883.[52] Transf 1974 to N Yorks. *Parl* Seq 30.

LITTLE TIMBLE

[W Riding] Tp in Otley AP, sep CP 1866.[2] *LG* Seq 92. Transf 1974 to N Yorks.[5] *Parl* Seq 30.

TINSLEY

[W Riding] Chap in Rotherham AP, decayed in 16th cent, rebuilt in 17th, sep CP 1866,[2] sep EP 1718.[9] *LG* Straff. & Tick. Wap, Rotherh. PLU, RSD, RD (1894—1912), Sheff CB (1912—33). Civ bdry: 1883,[52] 1901 (loses pt to Sheff CB [assoc with W Riding] & AP),[304] 1912 (loses pt to Brinsworth CP, the remainder transf as 'Tinsley' CP to Sheff CB),[360] 1919 (exchanges pts with Rotherh. CB [assoc with W Riding] & AP),[312] 1921 (incl gains pt Rotherh. CB [assoc with W Riding] & AP).[361] Abol civ 1933 ent to Sheffield AP.[307] *Parl* W Riding (1832—67), S'rn Dv of W Riding (1867—85), Rotherh. (1885—1918); see Part III of the *Guide* for composition of Sheff Parl Bors (1918—48) by wards of the CB. *Eccl* Donc. RDn (1718—1857), Rotherh. RDn (1857—1942), Attercliffe RDn (1942—*).

TOCKETTS

[N Riding] Tp in Guisborough AP, sep CP 1866.[2] *LG* Langb. Lbty, Guisb. PLU, RSD, RD (1894—1932), UD (1932—74). Transf 1974 to Clev.[5] *Parl* Seq 9.

TOCKWITH

[Ainsty (W Riding until 1449 and from 1836, indept jurisd 1449—1836)] Tp in Bilton AP, sep CP 1866,[2] sep EP 1866,[9] eccl refounded 1867.[125] *LG* Seq 71. Civ bdry: 1885,[179] 1937.[31] Transf 1974 to N Yorks.[5] *Parl* Seq 23. *Eccl* Ainsty RDn.

TODMORDEN

[Lancs, civ in Yorks W Riding from 1897] Chap (Lancs, Salford Hd) in Rochdale AP (Lancs, Yorks W Riding until 1866, ent Lancs thereafter), sep EP 1832 as 'Todmorden',[9] 'Walsden' a sep EP 1845 from Todmorden EP,[798] the ent area a sep CP 1866 in Lancs as 'Todmorden and Walsden',[2] qv in following entry for early organisation incl pt in Todmorden MB, the CP abol 1897 and united with the 3 Yorks W Riding CPs of Cornholme, Langfield, Stansfield (the other constituent pars in Todmorden MB) to cr 'Todmorden' CP, to be in Yorks W Riding.[439] *LG* Todmorden PLU, MB. Civ bdry: 1937.[31] Transf 1974 to W Yorks.[5] *Parl* Sowerby Dv/CC (1918—*). *Eccl* Halifax RDn (1832—1967), Calder Valley RDn (1967—*). Eccl bdry: 1864 (help cr Harley Wood EP),[457] 1972 (gains Harley Wood EP).[600]

TODMORDEN AND WALSDEN

[Lancs, civ in Yorks W Riding from 1889] Tp (Lancs, Salford Hd) in Rochdale AP (Lancs, Yorks W Riding until 1866, ent Lancs thereafter), sep CP 1866 in Lancs.[2] *LG* Todmorden PLU, USD, UD (1894—96), MB (1896—97). Abol 1897 to help cr Todmorden CP.[439] *Parl* See entry in Lancs.

TODWICK

AP [W Riding] *LG* Seq 121. Transf 1974 to S Yorks.[5] *Parl* Seq 48. *Eccl* Seq 43.

TOLLERTON

[N Riding] Tp (pec jurisd Treasurer of Cathedral of York, until 1836) in Alne AP, sep CP 1866.[2] *LG* Seq 30. Transf 1974 to N Yorks.[5] *Parl* Seq 16.

TONG

[W Riding] Chap in Birstall AP, sep CP 1866,[2] sep EP 1720.[9] *LG* Morley Wap, Bradf PLU (1837—48), N Bierley PLU (1848—1930), Tong USD, UD (1894—99), Bradf CB (1899—1974). Transf 1974 to W Yorks.[5] *Parl* W Riding (1832—67), E'rn Dv of W Riding (1867—85), Pudsey Dv (1885—1918); see Part III of the *Guide* for composition of Bradf Parl Bors/BCs (1918—*) by wards of the CB. *Eccl* Pontef. RDn (1720—1857), Dewsb. RDn (1857—66), Birstall RDn (1866—1920), Bradf RDn (1920—21), Bowl. RDn (1921—71), Calverley RDn (1971—*). Eccl bdry: after 1927 (presumably gains Tong Street EP).[799]

TONG STREET

EP [W Riding] Cr 1862 from Birstall AP.[9] Birstall RDn (1862—1927), Dewsb RDn (1927—after 1927). Sep status lost after 1927, presumably ent to Tong EP.[799]

TOPCLIFFE

AP [N Riding] Usual civ spelling; for eccl see following entry. Tp 'Topcliffe' in Birdf. Wap as were tps Catton, Dalton, Edlmire with Crakehill (each a sep CP 1866[2]), tp Skipton with Swale (sep CP 1866,[2] sep EP 1842[9]); incl in Hallik. Wap chap Dishforth (sep CP 1866, sep EP 1747[9]), pt chap Marton le Moor (sep CP 1866,[2] sep EP 1731[9]), tps Asenby, Rainton with Newby (each a sep CP 1866[2]), tp Baldersby (sep CP 1866,[2] sep EP 1859[170]). *LG* Thirsk PLU, RSD, RD. Addtl civ bdry alt: 1883.[16] Transf 1974 to N Yorks.[5] *Parl* Seq 16.

TOPCLIFFE WITH DALTON

AP [N Riding] Usual eccl spelling; for civ and civ and eccl sep chaps and tps, see prev entry. *Eccl* Orig but not later pec jurisd Dean & Chapter of York, Seq 20.

TOSSIDE

CP [W Riding] Ex-par place, sep CP 1858.[393] *LG* Staincl. & Ewc. Wap, Settle PLU, RSD, RD. Abol 1938 pt to Wigglesworth CP, pt to Bolton by Bowland AP.[28] *Parl* W Riding (1832—67), N'rn Dv of W Riding (1867—85), Skipton Dv (1885—1948).

EP [W Riding] The tp Gisburn Forest in Gisburn AP (qv for civ) sep EP 1739 as 'Houghton (or Tosside)',[9] eccl refounded 1870 as 'Tosside' EP.[213] Craven RDn, W'rn Dv (1870—1921), Bolland RDn (1921—*). Bdry: 1918,[287] 1938.[463]

TOWTHORPE

[E Riding] Tp in Wharram Percy AP, sep CP 1866.[2] *LG* Buckr. Wap, Driff. PLU, RSD, RD.

Abol 1935 ent to Fimber CP.[13] *Parl* E Riding (1832—85), Buckr. Dv (1885—1948).

TOWTHORPE

[N Riding] Tp pt in Huntington AP, pt in Strensall AP, sep CP 1866.[2] *LG* Seq 32. Transf 1974 to N Yorks.[5] *Parl* Seq 16.

TOWTON

[W Riding] Tp in Saxton AP, sep CP 1866.[2] *LG* Seq 81. Transf 1974 to N Yorks.[5] *Parl* Seq 24.

TREETON

AP [W Riding] lncl tp Brampton en le Morthen (sep CP 1866[2]), pt tp Ulley (sep CP 1866,[2] sep EP 1852[143]). *LG* Seq 119. Addtl civ bdry alt: 1877.[358] Transf 1974 to S Yorks.[5] *Parl* Seq 55. *Eccl* Seq 42.

TROUTSDALE

[N Riding] Tp in Brompton AP, sep CP 1866.[2] *LG* Seq 62. Transf 1974 to N Yorks.[5] *Parl* Seq 20.

TUNSTALL

AP [E Riding] Usual civ spelling; for eccl see 'Tunstall in Holderness'. *LG* Hold. Wap, Patr. PLU, RSD, RD. Abol civ 1935 ent to Roos AP.[13] *Parl* E Riding (1832—85), Hold. Dv (1885—1948).

TUNSTALL

[N Riding] Tp in Catterick AP, sep CP 1866.[2] *LG* Seq 50. Transf 1974 to N Yorks.[5] *Parl* Seq 14.

TUNSTALL IN HOLDERNESS

AP [E Riding] Usual eccl spelling; for civ see 1st 'Tunstall' above. *Eccl* Pec jurisd Sub-Chanter of Cathedral of York (until 1836), Seq 16 thereafter.

TURNHILL

[N Riding] Ex-par place, sep CP 1858[393] but sep civ and eccl status not sustained, incl for both purposes in Middleton AP. *LG* Pick. Lythe Wap, Pick. PLU.

TYERSALL

CP [W Riding] Cr 1894 from the pt of Pudsey CP in Bradf CB.[257] *LG* Bradf PLU, CB. Abol 1898 ent to Bradford AP.[65]

UCKERBY

[N Riding] Tp in Catterick AP, sep CP 1866[2]; eccl in chap Bolton upon Swale (sep EP 1781 from Catterick AP,[9] eccl refounded 1885[347]). *LG* Seq 35. Bdry: 1888.[624] Transf 1974 to N Yorks.[5] *Parl* Seq 14.

UGGLEBARNBY

[N Riding] Chap in Whitby AP, sep CP 1866,[2] sep EP 1748.[9] *LG* Whitby Strand Lbty, Whitby PLU, RSD. Abol civ 1885 to help cr Eskdaleside cum Ugglebarnby CP.[534] *Parl* N Riding (1832—85), Whitby Dv (1885—1918). *Eccl* Clev RDn (1748—1862), Guisb. RDn (1862—72). Abol prob 1872 to help cr Eskdaleside with Ugglebarnby EP.[535]

UGTHORPE

[N Riding] Tp in Lythe AP, sep CP 1866,[2] sep EP 1868 by union tps Ugthorpe, Ellerby, Hutton Mulgrave, Mickleby, Newton Mulgrave, pt tp Barnby, pt main tp Lythe (all in Lythe AP), tp Borrowby (in Leake AP).[188] *LG* Seq 59. Transf 1974 to N Yorks.[5] *Parl* Seq 19. *Eccl* Guisb. RDn (1868—78), Whitby RDn (1878—*).

ULLESKELF

[W Riding] Tp (in pec jurisd Wetwang prebend) in Kirkby Wharfe AP, sep CP 1866.[2] *LG* Bark. Ash Wap, Barwick GilbU (until 1869), Tadc. PLU

(1869—1930), RSD, RD. Transf 1974 to N Yorks.[5] *Parl* Seq 24.

ULLEY

[W Riding] Tp pt in Aston cum Aughton AP, pt in Treeton AP, sep CP 1866,[2] sep EP 1852 from the 2 APs.[143] *LG* Seq 119. Transf 1974 to S Yorks.[5] *Parl* Seq 55. *Eccl* Donc. RDn (1852—57), Rotherh. RDn (1857—1942), Laughton RDn (1942—*). Eccl bdry: 1948 (help cr Thurcroft EP).[669]

ULROME

[E Riding] Tp pt in Barmston AP, pt in Skipsea AP, sep CP 1866,[2] sep EP before 1835.[185] *LG* Seq 14. Civ bdry: 1935 (incl gains Lissett CP).[13] Transf 1974 to Humb.[5] *Parl* Seq 2. *Eccl* Hold. RDn (cr— 1849), N Hold. RDn (1849—66), Hornsea RDn (1866—1916), Hold. RDn (1916—*).

UNDERCLIFFE—see BRADFORD ST AUGUSTINE

UPLEATHAM

[N Riding] Chap in Guisborough AP, sep civ identity early, sep EP 1786.[9] *LG* Langb. Lbty, Guisb. PLU, pt Redcar USD (1875—86), Guisb. RSD (pt 1875—86, ent 1886—94), Guisb. RD (1894—1932), Guisb. UD (1932—74). Civ bdry: 1883,[16] 1886,[656] 1886.[703] Transf 1974 to Clev.[5] *Parl* Seq 9. *Eccl* Clev RDn (1786—1862), Stokes. RDn (1862—78), Middlesb. RDn (1878—1924), Guisb. RDn (1924—*). Eccl bdry: 1867 (help refound Redcar EP).[471]

UPPER MILL

CP [W Riding] Cr 1894 from the pt of Saddleworth CP in Upper Mill UD.[491] *LG* Saddleworth PLU, Upper Mill UD. Abol 1900 ent to Saddleworth CP to help constitute Saddleworth UD.[761]

UPPERTHONG

[W Riding] Tp in Almondbury AP, sep CP 1866,[2] sep EP 1846.[82] *LG* Agb. Wap, Hudd. PLU, Upperthong USD (1875—84), Holmf. USD (ent 1884—86, pt 1886—94), pt Austonley USD (1886—94), Holm. UD (1894—1921). Civ bdry: 1883,[52] 1886,[157] 1894 (loses the pt in Austonley UD to Austonley CP).[158] Abol 1921 to help cr Holmfirth CP.[159] *Parl* W Riding (1832—67), S'rn Dv of W Riding (1867—85), Holmf. Dv (1885— 1918), Colne Valley Dv (1918—48). *Eccl* Pontef. RDn (1846—57), Hudd. RDn (1857—1968), Almondb. RDn (1968—*). Eccl bdry: 1876 (help cr Wilshaw EP).[29]

UPSALL

[N Riding] Tp in South Kilvington AP, sep CP 1866.[2] *LG* Seq 27. Transf 1974 to N Yorks.[5] *Parl* Seq 16.

UPSALL

[N Riding] Tp in Ormesby AP, sep CP 1866.[2] *LG* Langb. Lbty, Guisb. PLU, RSD, RD (1894— 1932), Guisb. UD (1932—74). Transf 1974 to Clev.[5] *Parl* Seq 9.

UPTON

[W Riding] Tp in Badsworth AP, sep CP 1866.[2] *LG* Seq 96. Transf 1974 to W Yorks.[5] *Parl* Seq 28.

WADDINGTON

[W Riding] Chap in Mitton AP, sep CP 1866,[2] sep EP 1739.[9] *LG* Seq 108. Transf 1974 to Lancs.[5] *Parl* Seq 41. *Eccl* Craven RDn (1739—1857), Craven

RDn, W'rn Dv (1857—1921), Bolland RDn (1921—*).

WADSLEY

EP [W Riding] Cr 1841 from Ecclesfield AP.[510] Donc. RDn (1841—62), Ecclesfield RDn (1862—1942), Hallam RDn (1942—*). Bdry: 1868 (cr Oughtibridge EP),[290] 1884,[466] 1895 (help cr Hillsbrough and Wadsley Bridge EP,[115] qv for later refounding), 1899,[507] 1933 (help cr Malin Bridge EP).[89]

WADSWORTH

[W Riding] Tp in Halifax AP, sep CP 1866.[2] *LG* Morley Wap, Todmorden PLU, pt Hebden Bridge USD (both enlarged and reduced in sep areas 1891—94), pt Mytholmroyd USD (1891—94), pt Todmorden RSD (1891—94), Todmorden RD (1894—1939), Hepton RD (1939—74). Bdry: 1886,[785] 1894 (loses the pt in Hedben Bridge CP to help cr Hebden Bridge CP,[450] loses the pt in Mytholmroyd UD to help cr Mytholmroyd CP),[533] 1939.[76] Transf 1974 to W Yorks.[5] *Parl* W Riding (1832—67), E'rn Dv (1867—85), Donc. Dv (1885—1918), Sowerby Dv (1918—48).

WADWORTH

AP [W Riding] *LG* Seq 117. Civ bdry: 1886.[52] Transf 1974 to S Yorks.[5] *Parl* W Riding (1832—67), S'rn Dv of W Riding (1867—85), Sowerby Dv (1885—1918), Don Valley Dv/CC (1918—*). *Eccl* Pcc jurisd S Cave prebend (until 1549), pec jurisd Wadworth prebend (1549—1836), Seq 40 thereafter.

WAKEFIELD

[W Riding] The following have 'Wakefield' in their names. Insofar as any existed at a given time: *LG* Agb. Wap, Wakef PLU, MB (1848—1915), USD, CB (1915—74). *Parl* Wakef Parl Bor/BC (1832—*). *Eccl* Pontef. RDn (until 1857), Wakef RDn (1857—*).

AP1—WAKEFIELD [ALL SAINTS]—Incl chap Horbury (sep CP 1866,[2] sep EP 1717[9]), tp Alverthorpe with Thornes (sep CP 1866,[2] sep EP 1826 [incl area Wrenthorpe],[9] eccl refounded 1830 as 'Alverthorpe',[91] 'Wrenthorpe' a sep EP 1875 from Alverthorpe EP[90]), tp Stanley cum Wrenthorpe (sep CP 1866,[2] Wrenthorpe eccl in Alverthorpe with Thornes/Alverthorpe EP as noted above, sep EP 1830 as noted above; remainder of area a sep EP 1862 as 'Stanley',[9] eccl refounded 1830[91]). Addtl civ bdry alt: 1884,[12] 1894 (gains the pts in Wakef MB of Alverthorpe with Thornes CP, Stanley cum Wrenthorpe CP),[800] 1895,[96] 1900,[98] 1901,[99] 1925 (gains Lupset CP, Sandal Magna AP),[694] 1936,[132] 1951.[801] Addtl eccl bdry alt: 1816 (cr EP5,[9] refounded 1844[637]), 1844 (cr EP2),[802] 1844 (cr EP3, EP6),[803] 1956.[804]

EP1—WAKEFIELD CHRIST CHURCH—Cr 1874 from Thornes EP, EP2.[148] Bdry: 1878.[415] Abol 1957 to help cr Thornes St James and Christ Church EP.[793]

EP2—WAKEFIELD HOLY TRINITY—Cr 1844 from AP1.[802] Bdry: 1874 (help cr EP1),[148] 1876,[493] 1878.[415] Abol 1956 pt to AP1, pt to EP6.[804]

EP3—WAKEFIELD ST ANDREW—Cr 1844 from AP1.[803] Bdry: 1877,[464] 1944.[89] Abol 1968 to help cr EP4.[288]

EP4—WAKEFIELD ST ANDREW AND ST MARY—Cr 1968 by union EP3, EP6.[288]

EP5—WAKEFIELD ST JOHN—Cr 1816 from AP1,[9] refounded 1844.[637] Bdry: 1913,[93] 1944.[89]

EP6—WAKEFIELD ST MARY—Cr 1844 from AP1.[803] Bdry: 1876,[493] 1956.[804] Abol 1968 to help cr EP4.[288]

WALBURN

[N Riding] Tp in Downholme AP, sep CP 1866.[2] *LG* Seq 54. Transf 1974 to N Yorks.[5] *Parl* Seq 14.

WALDEN STUBBS

[W Riding] Tp in Womersley AP, sep CP 1866.[2] *LG* Seq 96. Bdry: 1888.[348] Transf 1974 to W Yorks.[5] *Parl* Seq 28.

WALES

[W Riding] Chap in Laughton en le Morthen AP, sep civ identity early, sep EP 1723.[9] *LG* Seq 121. Civ bdry: 1877,[358] 1885,[605] 1967 (loses pt to Sheff CB [assoc with W Riding] & AP, gains pt Beighton CP, Derbys).[144] Transf 1974 to S Yorks.[5] *Parl* Seq 48. *Eccl* Pec jurisd Laughton en le Morthen prebend (until 1484), pec jurisd Chancellor of York (1484—1836), Donc. RDn (1836—57), Rotherh. RDn (1857—1929), Handsw. RDn (1929—42), Laughton RDn (1942—*).

WALKINGHAM HILL WITH OCCANEY

[W Riding] Ex-par place, sep CP 1858,[393] eccl severed 1866 to help refound Brearton EP.[23] *LG* Seq 84. Transf 1974 to N Yorks.[5] *Parl* Seq 36.

WALKINGTON

AP [E Riding] *LG* Pt Harth. Wap, pt Howdensh. Wap, Bev. PLU, RSD, RD. Transf 1974 to Humb.[5] *Parl* Seq 4. *Eccl* Pec jurisd Dean & Chapter of Durham (until 1836), Harth. & Hull RDn (1836—57), W Harth. RDn (1857—62), Bev. RDn (1862—*).

WALKLEY

EP [W Riding] Cr 1870 from Sheffield St Phillp EP.[515] Sheff RDn (1870—1942), Hallam RDn (1942—*). Bdry: 1933 (help cr Malin Bridge EP),[89] 1969.[494]

WALLINGFEN

CP [E Riding] Renaming 1881 of New Village CP.[728] *LG* Howdensh. Wap, Howden PLU, S Cave & Wallingfen USD (ent 1875—80, pt 1880—94), pt Howden RSD (1880—94), Howden RD. Abol 1935 to help cr Newport CP.[13] *Parl* Howdensh. Dv (1885—1948).

WALLINGWELLS

[Pt Notts (Bassetlaw Wap), pt Yorks W Riding (uninhabited, Donc. Soke)] Ex-par place, sep CP 1858,[393] eccl abol 1841 to help cr Woodsetts EP,[572] made 1895 civ ent Notts.[154] *LG* Worksop PLU (1862—95), RSD, pt sep RD in Yorks W Riding (1894—95). *Parl* Yorks pt, W Riding (1832—67), S'rn Dv of W Riding (1867—85), Rotherh. Dv (1885—1918); for remainder see entry in Notts.

WALTON

AP [Ainsty (W Riding until 1449 and from 1836, indept jurisd 1449—1836)] (Tp Walton pt in Walton AP, pt in Wighill AP). *LG* Seq 71. Civ bdry: 1883,[52] 1885.[179] Transf 1974 to W Yorks.[5] *Parl* Seq 23. *Eccl* Ainsty RDn (until 1820), New Ainsty RDn

(1820—62), Ainsty RDn (1862—1921), Tadc. RDn (1921—*).

WALTON

[W Riding] Tp in Sandal Magna AP, sep CP 1866.[2] *LG* Seq 69. Transf 1974 to W Yorks.[5] *Parl* Seq 54.

WANSFORD

[E Riding] Tp in Nafferton AP, sep CP 1866,[2] sep EP 1907.[724] *LG* Dick. Wap, Driff. PLU, RSD, RD. Civ bdry: 1884.[350] Abol civ 1935 ent to Skerne AP.[13] *Parl* E Riding (1832—85), Buckr. Dv (1885—1948). *Eccl* Harth. RDn.

WAPLINGTON

[E Riding] Tp in Allerthorpe CP (qv for earlier status), sep CP 1866.[2] *LG* Harth. Wap, Pockl. PLU, RSD, RD. Abol 1935 ent to Allerthorpe CP.[13] *Parl* E Riding (1832—85), Howdensh. Dv (1885—1948).

WARLABY

[N Riding] Tp in Ainderby Steeple AP, sep CP 1866.[2] *LG* Seq 34. Transf 1974 to N Yorks.[5] *Parl* Seq 14.

WARLEY

[W Riding] Tp in Halifax AP, sep CP 1866,[2] eccl severed 1719 to help cr Sowerby Bridge EP,[9] the area of Warley eccl severed 1732 from the latter to help cr Luddenden EP,[9] again severed 1869 from Luddenden EP to help re-cr Sowerby Bridge EP,[521] 'Warley' a sep EP 1878 from Sowerby Bridge EP.[429] *LG* Morley Wap, Halifax PLU, pt Warley USD, pt Luddenden Foot USD, pt Sowerby Bridge USD, Warley UD. Civ bdry: 1894 (loses the pt in Luddenden Foot UD to help cr Luddenden Foot CP,[691] loses the pt in Sowerby Bridge UD to help cr Sowerby Bridge CP[734]). Abol civ 1900 ent to Halifax CB (assoc with W Riding) & AP.[590] *Parl* W Riding (1832—67), E'rn Dv of W Riding (1867—85), Sowerby Dv (1885—1918). *Eccl* Halifax RDn. Eccl bdry: 1912 (help cr Halifax St Hilda EP),[596] 1969.[27]

WARMFIELD

AP [W Riding] Usual eccl spelling; for civ and for civ and eccl sep tp, see following entry. *Eccl* Sometimes as 'Kirkthorpe', Ainsty RDn (until 1820), New Ainsty RDn (1820—57), Pontef. RDn (1857—89), Wakef RDn (1889—1973), Chevet RDn (1973—*).

WARMFIELD CUM HEATH

AP [W Riding] Usual civ spelling; for eccl see prev entry. Incl tp Sharleston (sep CP 1866,[2] sep EP 1929 from this par, Normanton AP[595]). *LG* Seq 69. Addtl civ bdry alt: 1937.[31] Transf 1974 to W Yorks.[5] *Parl* Seq 53.

WARMSWORTH

AP [W Riding] *LG* Seq 117. Civ bdry: 1936 (loses pt to Donc. CB [assoc with W Riding] & AP),[132] 1936.[76] Transf 1974 to S Yorks.[5] *Parl* Seq 44. *Eccl* Seq 40. Eccl bdry: 1930,[169] 1954 (help cr New Edlington EP).[434]

WARSILL

[W Riding] Ex-par place, sep CP 1858,[393] eccl severed 1863 to help refound Bishop Thornton EP.[162] *LG* Seq 101. Transf 1974 to N Yorks. *Parl* Seq 34.

WARTER

AP [E Riding] *LG* Seq 12. Transf 1974 to Humb.[5] *Parl* Seq 7. *Eccl* Harth. & Hull RDn (until 1857), N Harth. RDn (1857—66), Harth. RDn (1866—1936), Pockl. RDn (1936—*).

WARTHILL

AP [N Riding] Incl pt tp Warthill Copyhold, pt tp Warthill Freehold (each a sep CP 1866[2]) so that 'Warthill' has no sep civ identity 1866—1925 (see following entry). *LG* Bulmer Wap. *Parl* N Riding (1832—67). *Eccl* Pec jurisd Warthill prebend (until 1836), Seq 17 thereafter.

CP [N Riding] Cr 1925 by union Warthill Copyhold CP, Warthill Freehold CP.[805] *LG* York PLU, Flaxton RD. Transf 1974 to N Yorks.[5] *Parl* Thirsk & Malton CC (1948—*).

WARTHILL COPYHOLD

[N Riding] Tp pt in Warthill AP, pt in Holtby AP, sep CP 1866.[2] *LG* Bulmer Wap, York PLU (soon after 1837[112]—1930), RSD, Flaxton RD. Abol 1925 to help cr Warthill CP.[805] *Parl* N Riding (1832—85), Thirsk & Malton Dv (1885—1948).

WARTHILL FREEHOLD

[N Riding] Organisation as for Warthill Copyhold.

WASS

[N Riding] Tp in Kilburn AP, sep CP 1866.[2] *LG* Birdf. Wap, Helm. PLU, RSD. Abol 1887 to help cr Byland with Wass CP.[385] *Parl* N Riding (1832—85), Thirsk & Malton Dv (1885—1918).

WATH

AP [N Riding] Tp 'Wath' in Hallik. Wap as were chap Middleton Quernhow, tp Melmerby (each a sep CP 1866[2]); incl in Allert. Wap chap Norton Conyers (sep CP 1866[2]). *LG* Not in a PLU (until 1852), Ripon PLU (1852—1930), RSD, Wath RD. Transf 1974 to N Yorks.[5] *Parl* Seq 16. *Eccl* Seq 53.

WATH

[N Riding] Tp in Hovingham AP, sep CP 1866.[2] *LG* Seq 65. Transf 1974 to N Yorks.[5] *Parl* Seq 16.

WATH UPON DEARNE

AP [W Riding] Incl chap Hoyland Nether (sep CP 1866,[2] sep EP 1741 as 'Nether Hoyland'[635]), pt chap Swinton (sep CP 1866,[2] sep EP 1718[9]), chap Wentworth (sep CP 1866,[2] sep EP 1718[9]), tp Brampton Bierlow (sep CP 1866,[2] sep EP 1856[331]). *LG* Straff. & Tick. Wap, Rotherh. PLU, pt Wath upon Dearne USD, pt Rotherh. RSD, Wath upon Dearne UD. Addtl civ bdry alt: 1881,[332] 1881,[333] 1883,[52] 1923 (gains West Melton CP),[708] 1938.[28] Transf 1974 to S Yorks.[5] *Parl* W Riding (1832—67), S'rn Dv of W Riding (1867—85), Hallamshire Dv (1885—1918), Wentw. Dv (1918—48), Dearne Valley CC (1948—*). *Eccl* Donc. RDn (until 1857), Rotherh. RDn (1857—71), Wath RDn (1871—*). Addtl eccl bdry alt: 1841 (cr Thorpe Hesley EP),[9] 1844 (cr Elsecar EP),[530] 1930.[334]

WATTON

AP [E Riding] *LG* Seq 10. Civ bdry: 1935 (gains Bracken CP).[13] Transf 1974 to Humb.[5] *Parl* Seq 3. *Eccl* Seq 10.

WAULDBY

[E Riding] Chap & tp in Elloughton AP, sep CP 1866,[2] eccl severed 1904 and transf to Welton

AP.[529] *LG* Harth. Wap, Scul. PLU, RSD, RD. Abol 1935 ent to Welton AP.[13] *Parl* E Riding (1832—85), Howdensh. Dv (1885—1948).

WAWNE

AP [E Riding] Sometimes formerly 'Waghen'. Incl chap Sutton and Stoneferry (later Collegiate, sep par from Dissolution, eccl as 'Sutton'; incl area Drypool, qv for sep status), tp Meaux (sep CP 1866[2]). *LG* Seq 13. Addtl civ bdry alt: 1935 (incl gains Meaux CP),[13] 1968 (loses pt to Kingst. upon Hull CB [assoc with E Riding] and to Sculcoates AP).[253] Transf 1974 to Humb.[5] *Parl* Seq 4. *Eccl* Pec jurisd Chancellor of York (until 1836), Hold. RDn (1836—49), N Hold. RDn (1849—66), Hornsea RDn (1866—1916), N Hold. RDn (1916—36), Bev. RDn (1936—69), Kingst. upon Hull RDn (1969—*).

WAXHOLME

[E Riding] Tp in Owthorne AP, sep CP 1866.[2] *LG* Hold. Wap, Patr. PLU, RSD, RD. Abol 1935 ent to Rimswell CP.[13] *Parl* E Riding (1832—85), Hold. Dv (1885—1948).

WEARDLEY

[W Riding] Tp in Harewood AP, sep CP 1866.[2] *LG* Skyr. Wap, Gt Preston GilbU (until 1861), Wethb. PLU (1861—1930), RSD, RD. Abol 1937 ent to Harewood AP.[31] *Parl* W Riding (1832—67), N'rn Dv of W Riding (1867—85), Bark. Ash Dv (1885—1948).

WEAVERTHORPE

AP [E Riding] Incl tp Luttons Ambo (sep CP 1866,[2] eccl severed 1858 to help cr Helperthorpe with Luttons Ambo EP,[610] the latter abol 1874 to cr the 2 EPs of Helperthorpe, Luttons Ambo[611]). *LG* Buckr. Wap, Driff. PLU, RSD, RD (1894—1935), Norton RD (1935—74). Transf 1974 to N Yorks.[5] *Parl* Seq 1. *Eccl* Pec jurisd Dean & Chapter of York (until 1836), Seq 1 thereafter.

WEEL

[E Riding] Tp in Beverley St John AP, sep CP 1866.[2] *LG* Harth. Wap, Bev. Lbty, PLU, RSD, RD. Abol 1935 to help cr Tickton CP.[13] *Parl* Bev. Parl Bor (1832—70), E Riding (1870—85), Hold. Dv (1885—1948).

WEETON

[W Riding] Tp in Harewood AP, sep CP 1866,[2] sep EP 1852.[71] *LG* Claro Wap, Carlton GilbU (until 1869), Wethb. PLU (1869—1930), RSD, RD. Civ bdry: 1883.[52] Transf 1974 to N Yorks.[5] *Parl* Seq 35. *Eccl* Pontef. RDn (1852—57), Wethb. RDn (1857—61), Whitkirk RDn (1861—70), Otley RDn (1870—1921), Knar. RDn (1921—71), Harrog. RDn (1971—*).

WELBURN

[N Riding] Tp in Bulmer AP, sep CP 1866.[2] *LG* Seq 29. Transf 1974 to N Yorks.[5] *Parl* Seq 16.

WELBURN

[N Riding] Tp in Kirkdale AP, sep CP 1866.[2] *LG* Seq 64. Bdry: 1887.[538] Transf 1974 to N Yorks.[5] *Parl* Seq 21.

WELBURY

AP [N Riding] *LG* Seq 26. Transf 1974 to N Yorks.[5] *Parl* Seq 14. *Eccl* Seq 23.

WELL

AP [N Riding] Incl tp Snape with Thorpe (sep CP 1866[2]). *LG* Seq 46. Addtl civ bdry alt: 1886,[382] 1904.[777] Transf 1974 to N Yorks.[5] *Parl* Seq 15. *Eccl* Catt. RDn (until 1857), Catt. East RDn (1857—1928), Bedale RDn (1928—73). Renamed eccl 1973 'Well with Snape'.[563]

WELL WITH SNAPE

EP [N Riding] Renaming 1973 of Well AP.[563] Ripon RDn.

WELTON

AP [E Riding] Incl chap Melton (sep CP 1866,[2] not sep eccl hence this par sometimes eccl 'Welton with Melton'). *LG* Howdensh. Wap, Scul. PLU, RSD, RD (1894—1935), Bev. RD (1935—74). Addtl civ bdry alt: 1888,[707] 1935 (gains Melton CP, Wauldby CP).[13] Transf 1974 to Humb.[5] *Parl* Seq 6. *Eccl* Pec jurisd Dean & Chapter of Durham (until 1836), Harth. & Hull RDn (1836—57), S Harth. RDn (1857—66), Howden RDn (1866—1916), Kingst. upon Hull RDn (1916—*). Eccl bdry: 1904 (gains chap Wauldby from Elloughton AP).[529]

WELWICK

AP [E Riding] *LG* Seq 15. Transf 1974 to Humb.[5] *Parl* Seq 5. *Eccl* Pec jurisd Bev. (until 1836), Seq 16 thereafter.

WENSLEY

AP [N Riding] Incl chap Castle Bolton (sep CP 1866,[2] sep EP 1748 as 'Bolton'[9]), chap Redmire (sep CP 1866,[2] sep EP 1748[9]), tp Leyburn (sep CP 1866,[2] sep EP 1955[288]), tp Preston under Soar (sep CP 1866[2]). *LG* Seq 53. Transf 1974 to N Yorks.[5] *Parl* Seq 14. *Eccl* Seq 54.

WENTWORTH

[W Riding] Chap in Wath upon Dearne AP, sep CP 1866,[2] sep EP 1718.[9] *LG* Straff. & Tick. Wap, Rotherh. PLU, pt Rotherh. MB & USD (1883—94), Rotherh. RSD (ent 1875—83, pt 1883—94), Rotherh. RD. Civ bdry: 1883,[52] 1894 (loses the pt in the MB to Rotherham AP),[359] 1936 (incl exchanges pts with Rotherh. CB [assoc with W Riding] & AP),[132] 1938.[28] Transf 1974 to S Yorks.[5] *Parl* W Riding (1832—67), S'rn Dv of W Riding (1867—85), Hallamshire Dv (1885—1918), Wentw. Dv (1918—48), Rother Valley CC (1948—*). *Eccl* Donc. RDn (1718—1857), Rotherh. RDn (1857—71), Wath RDn (1871—*). Eccl bdry: 1955.[117]

WEST VALE

EP W Riding] Cr 1886 from Greetland EP.[56] Halifax RDn (1886—1967), Brig. & Elland RDn (1967—73). Abol 1973 to help cr Greetland and West Vale EP.[580]

WESTERDALE

[N Riding] Tp in Stokesley AP, sep civ identity early, sep EP 1858.[788] *LG* Seq 55. Transf 1974 to N Yorks.[5] *Parl* Seq 12. *Eccl* Stokes. RDn (1858—1919), Whitby RDn (1919—36), Stokes. RDn (1936—58), Whitby RDn (1958—*).

WESTGATE COMMON

EP [W Riding] Cr 1862 from Alverthorpe EP, Thornes EP.[92] Wakef RDn Bdry. 1901,[115] 1913,[92] 1934 (help cr Lupset EP).[94] Now called 'Wakefield St Michael'.

WESTON
 AP [W Riding] Incl tp Askwith (sep CP 1866[2]). *LG* Claro Wap, Wharfed. PLU (soon after 1861[112]—1930), RSD, RD. Transf 1974 to N Yorks.[5] *Parl* Seq 30. *Eccl* Ainsty RDn (until 1820), Old Ainsty RDn (1820—36), Pontef. RDn (1836—57), Otley RDn (1857—1969). Abol eccl 1969 to help cr Weston with Denton EP.[475]

WESTON WITH DENTON
 EP [W Riding] Cr 1969 by union Weston AP, Denton EP.[475] Otley RDn.

WESTOW
 AP [E Riding] Incl tps Eddlethorpe, Firby, Kirkham, Menethorpe (each a sep CP 1866[2]). *LG* Seq 2. Transf 1974 to N Yorks.[5] *Parl* Seq 1. *Eccl* Buckr. RDn (until 1857), W Buckr. RDn (1857—66), Pockl. RDn (1866—1916), Settr. RDn (1916—22), Buckr. RDn (1922—*).

WESTWICK
 [W Riding] Tp in Ripon AP, sep CP 1866,[2] eccl in chap Bishop Monkton (sep EP 1746 from Ripon AP,[9] eccl refounded 1863[163]). *LG* Ripon Lbty, not in a PLU (until 1854), Gt Ouseb. PLU (1854—1930), RSD, RD (1894—1938), Nidd. RD (1938—74). Transf 1974 to N Yorks.[5] *Parl* W Riding (1832—67), E'rn Dv of W Riding (1867—85), Ripon Dv (1885—1948), Harrog. CC (1948—*).

WETHER FELL
 [N Riding] Land Common to Bainbridge and to Hawes. *LG* Aysg. RD. Abol 1934 ent to Hawes CP.[3] *Parl* Richm. Dv (1918—48).

WETHERBY
 [W Riding] Tp in Spofforth AP, sep CP 1866,[2] sep EP 1776,[9] eccl refounded 1869.[71] *LG* Seq 91. Civ bdry: 1937.[31] Transf 1974 to W Yorks.[5] *Parl* Seq 24. *Eccl* Ainsty RDn (1776—1820), New Ainsty RDn (1820—36), Pontef. RDn (1836—57), Wethb. RDn (1857—*). Eccl bdry: 1887 (gains tp Linton from Spofforth AP).[126]

WETWANG
 AP [E Riding] Incl chap Fimber (sep CP 1866,[2] eccl severed 1923 and transf to Fridaythorpe AP[555]). *LG* Seq 1. Transf 1974 to Humb.[5] *Parl* Seq 3. *Eccl* As 'Wetwang with Fimber' until 1923, 'Wetwang' thereafter, pec jurisd Wetwang prebend (until 1836), Buckr. RDn (1836—57), N Harth. RDn (1857—66), Harth. RDn (1866—*).

WETWANG WITH FIMBER—see prev entry

WHALLEY
 AP [Mostly Lancs (Blackburn Hd), pt W Riding (Staincl. & Ewc. Wap: tp Bowland Forest Low [sep CP 1866[2]]), ent Lancs from 1866] See main entry in Lancs.

WHARRAM
 CP [E Riding] Cr 1935 by union Raisthorpe and Burdale CP, Wharram le Street AP, Wharram Percy AP.[13] *LG* Norton RD. Transf 1974 to N Yorks.[5] *Parl* Bev. CC (1948—55), Howden CC (1955—*).

WHARRAM LE STREET
 AP [E Riding] *LG* Buckr. Wap, Malton PLU, RSD, Norton RD. Abol civ 1935 to help cr Wharram CP.[13] *Parl* E Riding (1832—85), Buckr. Dv

(1885—1948). *Eccl* Pec jurisd Bramham (early), then pec jurisd Dean & Chapter of York (until 1836), Buckr. RDn (1836—57), E Buckr. RDn (1857—66), Buckr. RDn (1866—1919), Settr. RDn (1919—22), Buckr. RDn (1922—71). Abol eccl 1971 to help cr Wharram Percy with Wharram le Street EP.[806]

WHARRAM PERCY
 AP [E Riding] Incl tps Raisthorpe and Burdale, Towthorpe (each a sep CP 1866[2]), tp Thixendale (sep CP 1866,[2] sep EP 1872[67]). *LG*, civ abol, *Parl*, RDns (except not in a pec jurisd), eccl abol as for Wharram le Street, with eccl bdry alt 1968.[44]

WHARRAM PERCY WITH WHARRAM LE STREET
 EP [E Riding] Cr 1971 by union Wharram Percy AP, Wharram le Street AP.[806] Buckr. RDn.

WHASHTON
 [N Riding] Tp in Kirkby Ravensworth AP, sep CP 1866.[2] *LG* Seq 38. Bdry: 1883,[16] 1888.[624] Transf 1974 to N Yorks.[5] *Parl* Seq 14.

WHEATLEY
 [W Riding] Hmlt in Doncaster AP, sep CP 1866[2]; for eccl see following entry. *LG* Donc. Soke, PLU, RSD, RD (1894—1900), Wheatley UD (1900—14). Abol 1900 ent to Donc. MB & AP.[167] *Parl* W Riding (1832—67), S'rn Dv of W Riding (1867—85), Donc. Dv (1885—1918).

WHEATLEY HILLS
 EP [W Riding] Cr 1952 from Doncaster St Mary EP, Doncaster Intake EP, Kirk Sandall AP, Armthorpe AP; for civ see prev entry. Donc. RDn. Sometimes 'Doncaster St Aidan'.

WHELDRAKE
 AP [E Riding] Incl tp Langwith (sep CP 1866,[2] not sep eccl but the only pt of the par in pec jurisd Dean & Chapter of York, until 1836). *LG* Seq 20. Transf 1974 to N Yorks.[5] *Parl* Seq 7. *Eccl* Seq 19. Eccl bdry: 1971.[225]

WHENBY
 AP [N Riding] *LG* Seq 28. Transf 1974 to N Yorks.[5] *Parl* Seq 16. *Eccl* Bulmer RDn (until 1862), Eas. RDn (1862—1928), Malton RDn (1928—*).

WHISTON
 AP [W Riding] (Tp Whiston pt in Whiston AP, pt in Rotherham AP). *LG* Straff. & Tick. Wap, Rotherh. PLU, pt Rotherh. MB (1871—94), pt Rotherh. USD, pt Rotherh. RSD, Rotherh. RD. Civ bdry: 1894 (loses the pt in Rotherh. MB to Rotherham AP),[359] 1936 (loses pt to Rotherh. CB [assoc with W Riding] & AP).[132] Transf 1974 to S Yorks.[5] *Parl* Seq 55. *Eccl* Seq 42. Eccl bdry: 1903 (help cr Brinsworth EP),[195] 1950 (help cr Herringthorpe EP),[212] 1952.[322]

WHITBY
 AP [N Riding] Tp 'Whitby' in Whitby Stand Lbty as were chap Eskdaleside (sep CP 1866,[2] sep EP 1735[9]), chap Fylingdales (sep civ identity early, sep EP 1786[9]), chap Ugglebarnby (sep CP 1866,[2] sep EP 1748[9]), tp Hawsker with Stainsacre (sep CP 1866,[2] gtr pt eccl severed 1878 to cr 'Hawsker' EP[594]), tp Newholm with Dunsley (sep CP 1866[2]), tp Ruswarp (sep CP 1866,[2] pt a sep EP 1870 as 'Ruswarp'[370]); incl in Langb. Lbty chap Aislaby

(sep CP 1866,[2] sep EP 1768[9]). *LG* Whitby PLU, Bor, USD, UD. Addtl civ bdry alt: 1925 (gains Helredale CP, Ruswarp CP),[612] 1932.[51] Transf 1974 to N Yorks.[5] *Parl* Seq 19. *Eccl* Seq 22. Addtl eccl bdry alt: 1852 (help refound Grosmont EP),[258] 1955.[197]

WHITCLIFFE WITH THORPE
[W Riding] Tp in Ripon AP, sep CP 1866.[2] *LG* Ripon Lbty, not in a PLU (until 1852), Ripon PLU (1852—94), RSD. Bdry: 1883.[52] Abol 1894 to help cr Littlethorpe CP.[53] *Parl* W Riding (1832—67), E'rn Dv of W Riding (1867—85), Ripon Dv (1885—1918).

WHITECHAPEL
EP W Riding] Cr 1847 from Birstall AP.[275] Pontef. RDn (1847—57), Dewsb. RDn (1857—66), Birstall RDn (1866—*). Bdry: 1858,[414] 1877 (help cr Oakenshaw cum Woodlands EP),[168] 1878 (help cr Cleckheaton St Luke EP),[415] 1888,[614] 1929 (help cr Scholes EP).[416]

WHITGIFT
AP [W Riding] Incl chap Swinefleet (sep CP 1866,[2] pec jurisd as for main pt below, sep EP 1753[9]), tps Ousefleet, Reedness (each a sep CP 1866[2]). *LG* Seq 95. Transf 1974 to Humb.[5] *Parl* Seq 29. *Eccl* Pec jurisd Selby (1440—1539), pec jurisd Snaith (1539—1836), Hold. RDn (1836—49), N Hold. RDn (1849—57), Pontef. RDn (1857—62), Selby RDn (1862—71), Snaith RDn (1871—1952). Abol eccl 1952 to help cr Whitgift with Adlingfleet EP.[41]

WHITGIFT WITH ADLINGFLEET
EP [W Riding] Cr 1952 by union Whitgift AP, Adlingfleet AP.[41] Snaith RDn.

WHITKIRK
AP [W Riding] Incl tp Thorpe Stapleton, pt tps Austhorpe, Templenewsham (each a sep CP 1866[2]), pt tp Seacroft (sep CP 1866,[2] sep EP 1846[82]) so that 'Whitkirk' has no sep civ identity after 1866. *LG* Skyr. Wap. *Parl* W Riding (1832—67). *Eccl* Ainsty RDn (until 1820), New Ainsty RDn (1820—38), Pontef. RDn (1838—57), Wethb. RDn (1857—61), Whitkirk RDn (1961—*). Addtl eccl bdry alt: 1939 (cr Leeds St Wilfrid, Halton EP),[682] 1967.[127]

WHITLEY
[W Riding] Tp in Kellington AP, sep CP 1866.[2] *LG* Seq 97. Transf 1974 to N Yorks.[5] *Parl* Seq 29.

WHITLEY LOWER
[W Riding] Tp in Thornhill AP, sep CP 1866,[2] sep EP 1848.[794] *LG* Agb. Wap. Dewsb. PLU, Thornhill USD, UD. Abol civ 1896 ent to Thornhill AP.[795] *Parl* W Riding (1832—67), S'rn Dv of W Riding (1867—85), Morley Dv (1885—1918). *Eccl* Pontef. RDn (1848—57), Dewsb. RDn (1857—*).

WHITLEY UPPER
[W Riding] Tp in Kirkheaton AP, sep CP 1866.[2] *LG* Agb. Wap, Hudd. PLU, Whitley Upper USD, UD. Abol 1938 ent to Kirkburton UD & AP.[28] *Parl* W Riding (1832—67), S'rn Dv of W Riding (1867—85), Holmf. Dv (1885—1918), Spen Valley Dv (1918—48).

WHITWELL
[N Riding] Tp in Catterick AP, sep CP 1866,[2] eccl in chap Bolton upon Swale (sep EP 1781 from

Catterick AP,[9] eccl refounded 1885[347]). *LG* Seq 34. Transf 1974 to N Yorks.[5] *Parl* Seq 14.

WHITWELL ON THE HILL
[N Riding] Ex-par place, sep CP 1858,[393] sep EP 1861.[67] *LG* Seq 29. Transf 1974 to N Yorks.[5] *Parl* Seq 16. *Eccl* Bulmer RDn (1861—1964), Malton RDn (1964—*).

WHITWOOD
[W Riding] Tp in Featherstone AP, sep CP 1866,[2] pt eccl severed 1865 to help cr Whitwood Mere EP,[553] the remainder a sep EP 1866 as 'Whitwood'.[471] *LG* Agb. Wap, Barwick GilbU (until 1869), Pontef. PLU (1869—1930), Whitwood USD, UD. Abol civ 1937 pt to Rothw. UD & AP, pt to Castlef. UD & AP.[31] *Parl* W Riding (1832—67), S'rn Dv of W Riding (1867—85), Norm. Dv (1885—1948). *Eccl* Pontef. RDn. Eccl bdry: 1974 (gains Whitwood Mere EP).[807]

WHITWOOD MERE
EP [W Riding] Cr 1865 from Featherstone AP (pt tp Whitwood), Methley AP.[553] Pontef. RDn. Abol 1974 ent to Whitwood EP.[807]

WHIXLEY
AP [W Riding] Incl tps Green Hammerton, Thornville, pt tp Allerton Mauleverer with Hopperton (each a sep CP 1866[2]). *LG* Seq 85. Transf 1974 to N Yorks.[5] *Parl* Seq 36. *Eccl* Boroughbr. RDn (until 1971), Ripon RDn (1971). Abol 1971 to help cr Whixley with Green Hammerton EP.[623]

WHIXLEY WITH GREEN HAMMERTON
EP [W Riding] Cr 1971 by union Whixley AP, Allerton Mauleverer AP.[623] Ripon RDn.

WHORLTON
[N Riding] Chap in Rudby in Cleveland AP, sep civ identity early, sep EP 1766.[9] Incl chap Faceby (sep CP 1866,[2] sep EP 1792[9]), tp Potto (sep CP 1866[2]). *LG* Seq 58. Transf 1974 to N Yorks.[5] *Parl* Seq 11. *Eccl* Clev RDn (1766—1862), N'allert. RDn (1862—1916), Stokes. RDn (1916—*).

WIBSEY
EP [W Riding] Cr 1720 from Bradford AP,[9] refounded 1881.[313] Pontef. RDn (1720—1857), Bradf RDn (1857—1921), Bowl. RDn (1921—63). Bdry: 1858 (cr Low Moor EP),[339] 1877 (help cr Oakenshaw cum Woodlands EP).[168] Renamed 1963 'Low Moor Holy Trinity'.[287]

WICKER
EP [W Riding] Cr 1845 from Attercliffe EP.[147] Donc. RDn (1845—62), Sheff RDn (1862—1942), Ecclesfield RDn (1942—52). Bdry: 1846.[320] Abol 1952 to help cr Wicker with Neepsend EP.[725]

WICKER WITH NEEPSEND
EP [W Riding] Cr 1952 by union Wicker EP, Neepsend EP.[725] Ecclesfield RDn. Abol 1973 to help cr Pitsmoor with Wicker EP.[456]

WICKERSLEY
AP [W Riding] *LG* Seq 119. Transf 1974 to S Yorks.[5] *Parl* Seq 55. *Eccl* Seq 42. Eccl bdry: 1950 (help cr Herringthorpe EP),[212] 1956 (incl help cr Bramley EP).[215]

WIDDINGTON
[W Riding] Tp in Little Ouseburn AP, sep CP 1866.[2] *LG* Seq 85. Transf 1974 to N Yorks.[5] *Parl*

Seq 36.

WIGGINTON
AP [N Riding] *LG* Seq 32. Transf 1974 to N Yorks.[5] *Parl* Seq 16. *Eccl* Pec jurisd Treasurer of York Cathedral (until 1836), Bulmer RDn (1836—62), Eas. RDn (1862—1936), City of York RDn (1936—*).

WIGGLESWORTH
[W Riding] Tp in Long Preston AP, sep CP 1866.[2] *LG* Seq 111. Bdry: 1938.[28] Transf 1974 to N Yorks.[5] *Parl* Seq 41.

WIGHILL
AP [Ainsty (W Riding until 1449 and from 1836, indept jurisd 1449—1836)] Incl pt tp Walton (remainder constitutes Walton AP). *LG* Seq 74. Transf 1974 to N Yorks.[5] *Parl* Seq 23. *Eccl* Ainsty RDn (until 1820), New Ainsty RDn (1820—62), Ainsty RDn (1862—1921), Tadc. RDn (1921—27), Ainsty RDn (1927—*).

WIGTON
[W Riding] Tp in Harewood AP, sep CP 1866.[2] *LG* Skyr. Wap, Barwick GilbU (until 1869), Wethb. PLU (1869—1930), RSD, RD. Abol 1937 pt to Harewood AP, pt to Leeds CB (assoc with W Riding) & AP.[31] *Parl* W Riding (1832—67), N'rn Dv of W Riding (1867—85), Bark. Ash Dv (1885—1948).

WILBERFOSS
AP [E Riding] Incl tp Newton upon Derwent (sep CP 1866[2]). *LG* Seq 12. Addtl civ bdry alt: 1935 (gains Newton upon Derwent CP).[13] *Parl* Seq 7. *Eccl* Seq 9.

WILDON GRANGE
[N Riding] Tp in Coxwold AP, sep CP 1866.[2] *LG* Seq 24. Transf 1974 to N Yorks.[5] *Parl* Seq 16.

WILLERBY
AP [E Riding] *LG* Seq 8. Transf 1974 to N Yorks.[5] *Parl* Seq 1. *Eccl* Seq 4.

WILLERBY
[E Riding] Tp pt in Cottingham AP, pt in Kirk Ella AP, pt in North Ferriby AP, sep CP 1866.[2] *LG* Pt Harth. Wap, pt Kingst. upon Hull Co, Scul. PLU, RSD, RD. Bdry: 1878.[520] Abol 1935 pt to Kingst. upon Hull CB (assoc with E Riding) and to Sculcoates AP, pt to help constitute Haltemp. UD and to Haltemprice CP, pt to Skidby CP.[13] *Parl* E Riding (1832—85), Howdensh. Dv (1885—1948).

WILLITOFT
[E Riding] Tp in Bubwith AP, sep CP 1866.[2] *LG* Harth. Wap, Howden PLU, RSD, RD. Abol 1935 ent to Bubwith AP.[13] *Parl* E Riding (1832—85), Howdensh. Dv (1885—1948).

WILMINGTON
EP [E Riding] Cr 1904 from Hull St Mark EP, Sutton AP.[543] Kingst. upon Hull RDn. Abol 1957 to help cr Kingston upon Hull St Saviour and St Mark EP.[640]

WILSDEN
[W Riding] Tp in Bradford AP, sep CP 1866,[2] eccl severed 1828 to help cr Wilsden cum Allerton EP.[63] *LG* Morley Wap, Bradf PLU (1837—48), N Bierley PLU (1848—1930), Wilsden USD, UD (1894—98), Bingley UD (1898—1938). Abol 1938 ent to Bingley AP.[28] *Parl* W Riding (1832—67), E'rn Dv of W Riding (1867—85), Keigh. Dv (1885—1918), Shipley Dv (1918—48).

WILSDEN CUM ALLERTON
EP [W Riding] Cr 1828 by union tps Wilsden, Allerton, each in Bradford AP.[63] Pontef. RDn (1828—57), Bradf RDn (1857—1921), Horton RDn (1921—60). Bdry: 1846 (help cr Cullingworth EP),[268] 1890 (cr Allerton EP),[64] 1930 (cr Harden EP).[270] Abol 1960 to help cr Harden and Wilsden EP.[575]

WILSHAW
EP [W Riding] Cr 1876 from Meltham Mills EP, Meltham EP, Netherthong EP, Upperthong EP, Holme Bridge EP.[29] Hudd. RDn (1876—1968), Blackmoorfoot RDn (1968— *).

WILSTHORPE
[E Riding] Tp in Bridlington AP, sep CP 1866.[2] *LG* Dick. Wap, Bridl. PLU, RSD, RD. Abol 1896 to help cr Fraisthorpe with Auburn and Wilsthorpe CP.[153] *Parl* E Riding (1832—85), Buckr. Dv (1885—1918).

WILSTROP
[Ainsty (W Riding until 1449 and from 1836, indept jurisd 1449—1836)] Tp in Kirk Hammerton AP, sep CP 1866.[2] *LG* Seq 71. Transf 1974 to N Yorks.[5] *Parl* Seq 23.

WILTON
[N Riding] Chap in Pickering AP, eccl united 1252 with chap Ellerburne in same par to cr 'Ellerburne with Wilton', Wilton thereafter considered a chap in Ellerburne, sep CP 1866,[2] sep EP 1755[9] but sep eccl status not sustained. *LG* Seq 61. Transf 1974 to N Yorks.[5] *Parl* Seq 20.

WILTON
[N Riding] Tp in Kirkleatham AP, sep civ identity early, sep EP 1850.[9] *LG* Langb. Lbty, Guisb. PLU, RSD, RD (1894—1932), Guisb. UD (1932—74). Civ bdry: 1921,[536] 1932,[51] 1968 (help cr Teesside CB [assoc with N Riding] & CP).[537] Transf 1974 to Clev.[5] *Parl* Seq 9. *Eccl* Clev RDn (1850—62), Stokes. RDn (1862—78), Middlesb. RDn (1878—1924), Guisb. RDn (1924—*). Eccl bdry: 1917 (help cr Grangetown EP).[464]

WINCOBANK
EP [W Riding] Cr 1877 from Ecclesfield AP, Brightside EP, Kimberworth EP.[301] Ecclesfield RDn. Bdry: 1918 (help cr Brightside St Margaret EP),[258] 1936 (help cr Shiregreen EP),[24] 1941 (help cr Shiregreen St James and St Christopher EP).[514]

WINDHILL
EP [W Riding] Cr 1870 from Idle EP.[284] Bradf RDn (1870—1921), Calverley RDn (1921—71), Airedale RDn (1971—*). Bdry: 1934 (help cr Wrose EP).[46]

WINESTEAD
AP [E Riding] *LG* Hold. Wap, Patr. PLU, RSD, RD. Abol civ 1935 ent to Patrington AP.[13] *Parl* E Riding (1832—85), Hold. Dv (1885—1948). *Eccl* Seq 16.

WINKSLEY
[W Riding] Tp in Ripon AP, sep CP 1866,[2] sep EP 1740.[9] *LG* Seq 90. Transf 1974 to N Yorks.[5] *Parl* Seq 33. *Eccl* Pec jurisd Lbty Ripon (until 1836), Boroughbr. RDn (1836—49), Ripon RDn (1849—63). Refounded 1863 as 'Winksley cum Grantley'

when enlarged,[163] qv in following entry.

WINKSLEY CUM GRANTLEY
EP [W Riding] Refounding 1863 of Winksley EP (see prev entry) by union orig area tps Winksley, Grantley, Skelding, pt Azerley, all in Ripon AP.[163] Boroughbr. RDn (1863—49), Ripon RDn (1849—*).

WINTERSETT
[W Riding] Tp in Wragby AP, sep CP 1866,[2] pt eccl severed 1876 to help cr Ryhill EP.[29] LG Staincr. Wap, Hemsw. PLU, RSD, RD (1894—1938), Wakef RD (1938—74). Bdry: 1883,[52] 1888 (help cr Hessle with Hill Top CP).[348] Transf 1974 to W Yorks.[5] Parl Seq 43.

WINTON
[N Riding] Tp in Kirby Sigston AP, sep CP 1866.[2] LG Seq 22. Transf 1974 to N Yorks.[5] Parl Seq 14.

WINTRINGHAM
AP [E Riding] Incl chap Knapton (sep CP 1866,[2] sep EP 1742[9]). LG Seq 2. Addtl civ bdry alt: 1935.[13] Parl Seq 1. Eccl Seq 3.

WISTOW
AP [W Riding] Incl chap Cawood (sep civ identity early, sep EP 1810[9]), chap Monk Fryston (sep civ identity early, sep EP 1815[9]). LG Seq 80. Addtl civ bdry alt: 1883 (gains pt Riccall AP, E Riding).[754] Transf 1974 to N Yorks.[5] Parl Seq 24. Eccl Pec jurisd Wistow prebend (until 1836), Seq 32 thereafter.

WITHERNSEA
[E Riding] Withernsea orig AP with chap Hollym, later Hollym considered the mother par and Withernsea the chap and tp, the par eccl 'Hollym and Withernsea' until eccl divided 1968 into 2 EPs of Hollym, Withernsea,[598] 'Withernsea' a sep CP 1866.[2] LG Hold. Wap, Patr. PLU, RSD, RD (1894—98), Withernsea UD (1898—1974). Civ bdry: 1891 (reconstituted, exchanging pts with Owthorne AP),[745] 1911.[746] Transf 1974 to Humb.[5] Parl Seq 5. Eccl S Hold. RDn.

WITHERNWICK
AP [E Riding] (Tp Withernwick pt in this par, pt in Mappleton AP). LG Seq 16. Civ bdry: 1885.[59] Transf 1974 to Humb.[5] Parl Seq 5. Eccl Pec jurisd Holme prebend (until 1836), Seq 15 thereafter. Eccl bdry: 1962.[60]

EAST WITTON
AP [N Riding] Incl tps East Witton Within, East Witton Without (each a sep CP 1866[2]) so that 'East Witton' has no sep civ identity after 1866. LG W Hang Wap. Parl N Riding (1832—67). Eccl Seq 54.

EAST WITTON WITHIN
[N Riding] Tp in East Witton AP, sep CP 1866.[2] LG Seq 53. Bdry: 1883,[16] 1886.[525] Transf 1974 to N Yorks.[5] Parl Seq 14.

EAST WITTON WITHOUT
[N Riding] Organisation as for East Witton Within, incl bdry alts.

WEST WITTON
AP [N Riding] LG Seq 53. Transf 1974 to N Yorks.[5] Parl Seq 13. Eccl Seq 54.

WOLD NEWTON
AP [E Riding] Chap in Hunmanby AP, sep par 1269.[643]

LG Seq 5. Civ bdry: 1935 (gains Fordon CP).[13] Transf 1974 to Humb.[5] Parl Seq 2. Eccl Seq 6.

WOMBLETON
[N Riding] Tp in Kirkdale AP, sep CP 1866.[2] LG Seq 64. Bdry: 1887.[71] Transf 1974 to N Yorks. Parl Seq 21.

WOMBWELL
[W Riding] Tp in Darfield AP, sep CP 1866,[2] sep EP 1864.[246] LG Straff. & Tick. Wap, Barnsley PLU, Wombwell USD, UD. Civ bdry: 1939.[76] Transf 1974 to S Yorks.[5] Parl W Riding (1832—67), S'rn Dv of W Riding (1867—85), Barnsley Dv (1885—1918), Wentw. Dv (1918—48), Dearne Valley CC (1948—*). Eccl Donc. RDn (1864—71), Wath RDn (1871—*).

WOMERSLEY
AP [W Riding] Incl tps Little Smeaton, Walden Stubbs, pt tp Cridling Stubbs (each a sep CP 1866[2]). LG Seq 98. Addtl civ bdry alt: 1883.[52] Transf 1974 to N Yorks.[5] Parl Seq 29. Eccl Ainsty RDn (until 1820), New Ainsty RDn (1820—57), Pontef. RDn (1857—*). Eccl bdry: 1880.[164]

WOODHALL
EP [W Riding] Cr 1959 from Thornbury EP, Calverley AP, Farsley EP, Pudsey EP.[320] Calverley RDn.

WOODHOUSE
EP [W Riding] Cr 1831 from Leeds AP.[536] Old Ainsty RDn (1831—36), Pontef. RDn (1836—57), Leeds RDn (1857—1971), Head. RDn (1971—*). Bdry: 1846 (help cr Little London EP, later called 'Leeds St Matthew'),[107] 1849 (help cr Buslingthorpe EP),[54] 1866 (help cr Wrangthorne EP),[55] 1881 (help cr Leeds All Souls EP),[647] 1887,[126] 1955 (gains Buslingthorpe EP),[384] 1967.[127] Sometimes 'Leeds St Mark's Woodhouse'.

WOODHOUSE CHRIST CHURCH—see HUDDERSFIELD CHRIST CHURCH, WOODHOUSE

WOODKIRK—see ARDSLEY WEST

WOODLANDS
EP [W Riding] Cr 1913 from Adwick le Street AP, Brodsworth AP, Doncaster AP.[44] Donc. RDn.

WOODLESFORD
EP [W Riding] Cr 1869 from Rothwell AP[743]; for civ see 'Oulton with Woodlesford'. Wakef RDn (1869—94), Whitkirk RDn (1894—*). Bdry: 1901 (help cr Stourton EP),[366] 1967.[127]

WOODMANSEY
CP [E Riding] Cr 1935 by union Thearne CP, Woodmansey and Beverley Parks CP.[13] LG Bev. RD. Transf 1974 to Humb.[5] Parl Bev. CC (1948—55), Haltemp. CC (1955—*).

WOODMANSEY AND BEVERLEY PARKS
[E Riding] Tp in Beverley St John AP, sep CP 1866.[2] LG Harth. Wap, Bev. Lbty, PLU, RSD, RD. Abol 1935 to help cr Woodmansey CP.[13] Parl Bev. Parl Bor (1832—70), E Riding (1870—85), Hold. Dv (1885—1948).

WOODSETTS
[W Riding] Tp in North and South Anston CP (qv for earlier status in Laughton en le Morthen AP; eccl 'Anston cum Membris'), sep CP 1866,[2] sep EP 1841 by union this tp, area Gildingwells from Letwell with Gildingwells EP (the remainder of the

latter to be 'Letwell'), ex-par Wallingwells (Notts, Yorks).[572] *LG* Seq 121. Transf 1974 to S Yorks.[5] *Parl* Seq 48. *Eccl* Donc. RDn (1841—57), Rotherh. RDn (1857—1927), Handsw. RDn (1927—42), Laughton RDn (1942—*).

WOODSIDE

EP [W Riding] Cr 1846 from Horsforth EP, Adel AP, Headingley EP, Kirkstall EP.[35] Pontef. RDn (1846—66), Otley RDn (1866—1921), Leeds RDn (1921—71), Head. RDn (1971—*). Bdry: 1936 (help cr Hawksworth Wood EP),[188] 1967.[127]

WOOLDALE

[W Riding] Tp in Kirkburton AP, sep CP 1866,[2] pt eccl severed 1858 to help refound Holmfirth EP.[293] *LG* Agb. Wap, Hudd. PLU, pt Wooldale USD (1875—84), pt Holmf. USD (1884—94), pt Scholes USD (enlarged pt 1886—94), pt Fulstone USD (1886—94), pt Hepworth USD (1883—94), Holmf. UD. Bdry: 1883,[52] 1886,[157] 1894 (loses the pt in Fulstone UD to Fulstone CP, loses the pt in Scholes UD to help cr Scholes CP),[158] 1895.[570] Abol 1921 to help cr Holmfirth CP.[159] *Parl* W Riding (1832—67), S'rn Dv of W Riding (1867—85), Holmf. Dv (1885—1918), Colne Valley Dv (1918—48).

WOOLLEY

[W Riding] Chap in Royston AP, sep CP 1866,[2] sep EP 1721.[9] *LG* Staincr. Wap, Barnsley PLU, RSD, RD (1894—1938), Wakef RD (1938—74). Civ bdry: 1938,[28] 1957.[472] Transf 1974 to W Yorks.[5] *Parl* Seq 43. Parl bdry: 1960.[473] *Eccl* Donc. RDn (1721—1857), Pontef. RDn (1857—89), Wakef RDn (1889—1973), Chevet RDn (1973—*).

HIGH WORSALL

[N Riding] Chap in Northallerton AP, sep CP 1866,[2] sep EP 1719.[9] *LG* Allert. Wap, Stock. PLU (1837—75), Stokes. PLU (1875—1930), RSD, RD. Civ bdry: 1878.[808] *Parl* Seq 11. *Eccl* Pec jurisd Dean & Chapter of Durham (until 1836), Clev. RDn (1836—62), N'allert. RDn (1862—1936), Stokes. RDn (1936—*).

LOW WORSALL

[N Riding] Tp in Kirk Leavington AP, sep CP 1866.[2] *LG* Seq 57. Transf 1974 to N Yorks.[5] *Parl* Seq 11.

WORSBOROUGH

[W Riding] Chap in Darfield AP, sep CP 1866,[2] sep EP 1722.[9] *LG* Staincr. Wap, Barnsley PLU, Worsborough USD, UD (1894—1956), Worsbrough UD (1956—74). Civ bdry: 1921 (loses pt to Barnsley CB [assoc with W Riding] & CP),[116] 1938 (incl loses pt to Barnsley CB [assoc with W Riding] & CP),[28] 1939.[46] Transf 1974 to S Yorks.[5] *Parl* W Riding (1832—67), S'rn Dv of W Riding (1867—85), Holmf. Dv (1885—1918), Wentw. Dv (1918—48), Barnsley BC (1948—*). *Eccl* Donc. RDn (1722—1857), Rotherh. RDn (1857—71), Wath RDn (1871—1942), Tankersley RDn (1942—*). Eccl bdry: 1861 (cr Worsbrough Dale EP),[809] 1908 (cr Worsborough Bridge EP).[621]

WORSBOROUGH ST THOMAS AND ST JAMES

EP [W Riding] Cr 1955 by union Worsborough Dale EP, pt Worsborough Bridge EP.[117] Tankersley RDn. Renamed 1972 'Worsbrough St Thomas and St James'.[259]

WORSBOROUGH BRIDGE

EP [W Riding] Cr 1903 from Worsborough EP.[621] Wath RDn (1908—42), Tankersley RDn (1942—55). Abol 1955 pt to Worsborough Common EP, pt to help Worsborough St Thomas and St James EP.[117]

WORSBOROUGH COMMON

EP [W Riding] Cr 1917 from Worsborough Dale EP.[810] Wath RDn (1917—42), Takersley RDn (1942—*). Bdry: 1955.[117]

WORSBOROUGH DALE

EP [W Riding] Cr 1861 from Worsborough EP.[809] Rotherh. RDn (1861—71), Wath RDn (1871—1942), Tankersley RDn (1942—55). Bdry: 1917 (cr Worsborough Common EP).[810] Abol 1955 pt to help cr Worsborough St Thomas and St John EP, pt to Ardsley EP.[117]

WORSBROUGH ST THOMAS AND ST JAMES

EP [W Riding] Renaming 1972 of Worsborough St Thomas and St James EP.[259] Tankersley RDn.

WORTLEY

[W Riding] Chap in Leeds AP, sep CP 1866,[2] sep EP 1814.[9] *LG* Skyr. Wap, Carlton GilbU (until 1869), Bramley PLU (1869—1904), Leeds Bor/ MB/CB, USD. Abol civ 1904 to help cr Armley and Bramley CP.[124] *Parl* Leeds Parl Bor (1832—85); see Part III of the *Guide* for composition of Leeds Parl Bors (1885—1918) by wards of the MB. *Eccl* Ainsty RDn (1814—20), Old Ainsty RDn (1820—36), Pontef. RDn (1836—57), Leeds RDn (1857—*). Eccl bdry: 1851 (cr New Wortley EP),[344] 1868 (help cr Wortley-de-Leeds EP).[318]

WORTLEY

[W Riding] Chap in Tankersley AP, sep CP 1866,[2] sep EP 1740.[9] *LG* Seq 115. Civ bdry: 1938.[28] Transf 1974 to Gtr Manch.[5] *Parl* Seq 49. *Eccl* Donc. RDn (1740—1857), Rotherh. RDn (1857—62), Ecclesfield RDn (1862—1942), Tankersley RDn (1942—*).

WORTLEY-DE-LEEDS

EP [W Riding] Cr 1868 from Wortley EP.[318] Leeds RDn (1868—1971), Armley RDn (1971—*). Bdry: 1903,[130] 1967.[127]

NEW WORTLEY

EP [W Riding] Cr 1851 from Wortley EP.[344] Pontef. RDn (1851—57), Leeds RDn (1857—1957). Bdry: 1872 (cr Armley Hall EP),[90] 1887 (help cr New Wortley St Mary of Bethany, Tong Road EP),[126] 1903,[130] 1953 (help cr New Wortley St Mary with Armley Hall EP).[131] Abol 1957 ent to Holbeck EP.[626]

EP [W Riding] Renaming 1972 of New Wortley St Mary with Armley Hall EP.[128] Armley RDn.

NEW WORTLEY ST MARY OF BETHANY, TONG ROAD

EP [W Riding] Cr 1887 from New Wortley EP, Armley EP.[126] Leeds RDn. Abol 1953 to help cr New Wortley St Mary with Armley Hall EP.[131]

NEW WORTLEY ST MARY WITH ARMLEY HALL

EP [W Riding] Cr 1953 by union New Wortley St Mary of Bethany, Tong Road EP, Armley Hall EP, pt New Wortley EP.[131] Leeds RDn (1953—71),

Armley RDn (1971—72). Bdry: 1967.[127] Renamed 1972 'New Wortley'.[128]

WOTHERSOME

[W Riding] Tp in Bardsey AP, sep CP 1866.[2] *LG* Seq 107. Bdry: 1885.[179] Transf 1974 to W Yorks.[5] *Parl* Seq 24.

WRAGBY

AP [W Riding] *LG* Pt Osg. Wap (tps West Hardwick, Hessle, Hill Top, Huntwick with Foulby and Nostell [each a sep CP 1866[2]]), pt Staincr. Wap (tp Ryhill, tp Wintersett [each a sep CP 1866,[2] 'Ryhill' a sep EP 1876 by union tp Ryhill, gtr pt tp Wintersett, and pts Royston AP, Felkirk AP, Sandal Magna AP[29]]) so that 'Wragby' has no sep civ identity after 1866. *Parl* W Riding (1832—67). *Eccl* Pontef. RDn (until 1927), Wakef RDn (1927—73), Chevet RDn (1973—*).

WRANGTHORN

EP [W Riding] Cr 1866 from Headingley EP, Woodhouse EP.[55] Leeds RDn (1866—1971), Head. RDn (1971—*). Bdry: 1902,[364] 1967.[127]

WRELTON

[N Riding] Tp in Middleton AP, sep CP 1866.[2] *LG* Seq 61. Bdry: 1883,[16] 1887.[49] Transf 1974 to N Yorks.[5] *Parl* Seq 22.

WRENTHORPE

EP [W Riding] Cr 1875 from Alverthorpe EP.[90] Wakef RDn. Bdry: 1913.[93]

WRESSELL

AP [E Riding] Usual civ spelling; for eccl see following entry. *LG* Harth. Wap, Howden PLU (soon after 1837[112]—1930), RSD, RD. Abol 1935 to help cr Wressle CP.[13] *Parl* E Riding (1832—85), Howdensh. Dv (1885—1948).

WRESSLE

AP [E Riding] Usual eccl spelling; for civ see prev entry. *Eccl* Seq 13.

CP [E Riding] Cr 1935 by union Wressle AP, pt South Duffield CP.[13] *LG* Howden RD. Transf 1974 to Humb.[5] *Parl* Bev. CC (1948—55), Howden CC (1955—*).

WROSE

EP [W Riding] Cr 1934 from Idle EP, Bolton St James EP.[46] Calverley RDn.

WYCLIFFE

AP [N Riding] Usual eccl spelling; for civ see following entry. *Eccl* Seq 59. Eccl bdry: 1899 (gains tp Ovington from Forcett with Carkin EP).[563]

WYCLIFFE WITH THORPE

AP [N Riding] Usual civ spelling; for eccl see prev entry. *LG* Seq 39. Civ bdry: 1884.[176] Transf 1974 to Durham.[5] *Parl* Seq 14.

WYKE

[W Riding] Tp pt in Bardsey AP, pt in Harewood AP, sep CP 1866.[2] *LG* Skyr. Wap, Barwick GilbU (until 1869), Wethb. PLU (1869—1930), RSD, RD. Abol 1937 ent to Harewood AP.[31] *Parl* W Riding (1832—67), N'rn Dv of W Riding (1867—85), Bark. Ash Dv (1885—1948).

WYKE

[W Riding] Tp in Birstall AP, sep CP 1866,[2] sep EP 1844.[197] *LG* Morley Wap, Bradf PLU (1837—48), N Bierley PLU (1848—1930), N Bierley USD, UD (1894—99), Bradf CB (1899—1974). Civ bdry: 1899 (loses pt to Hipperholme CP as the remainder transf to Bradf CB [assoc with W Riding]).[623] Transf 1974 to W Yorks.[5] *Parl* W Riding (1832—67), E'rn Dv of W Riding (1867—85), Spen Valley Dv (1885—1918); see Part III of the *Guide* for composition of Bradf Parl Bors/BCs (1918—*) by wards of the CB. *Eccl* Pontef. RDn (1844—57), Bradf RDn (1857—89), Birstall RDn (1889—1913), Halifax RDn (1913—21), Bowl. RDn (1921—71), Bowl. & Horton RDn (1971—*). Eccl bdry: 1877 (help cr Oakenshaw cum Woodlands EP),[168] 1882,[326] 1927.[67]

WYKEHAM

AP [N Riding] *LG* Seq 62. Civ bdry: 1883.[16] Transf 1974 to N Yorks.[5] *Parl* Seq 20. *Eccl* Seq 28.

WYTON

[E Riding] Tp in Swine AP, sep CP 1866[2]; eccl in chap Bilton (sep EP 1794 from Swine AP,[9] eccl refounded 1867[98]). *LG* Hold. Wap, Skirl. PLU, RSD, RD. Abol 1935 ent to Bilton CP.[13] *Parl* E Riding (1832—85), Hold. Dv (1885—1948).

YAFFORTH

[N Riding] Chap in Danby Wiske AP, sep CP 1866.[2] *LG* Seq 34. Bdry: 1888.[667] Transf 1974 to N Yorks.[5] *Parl* Seq 14.

YAPHAM

CP [E Riding] Renaming 1935 of Yapham cum Meltonby CP.[13] *LG* Pockl. RD. Transf 1974 to Humb.[5] *Parl* Bev. CC (1948—55), Howden CC (1955—*).

YAPHAM CUM MELTONBY

[E Riding] Tp (in pec jurisd Dean of York until 1836) in Pocklington AP, sep CP 1866.[2] *LG* Harth. Wap, Pockl. PLU, RSD, RD. Renamed 1935 'Yapham'.[13] *Parl* E Riding (1832—85), Howdensh. Dv (1885—1948).

YARM

AP [N Riding] Chap in Kirk Leavington AP, sep civ identity early, sep EP 1865.[9] *LG* Yarm Bor, Seq 57. Civ bdry: 1878.[808] Transf 1974 to Clev.[5] *Parl* Seq 11. *Eccl* Clev. RDn (until 1862), Stokes. RDn (1862—*).

YEADON

[W Riding] Tp in Guiseley AP, sep CP 1866,[2] sep EP 1845.[585] *LG* Skyr. Wap, not in a PLU (until 1861), Wharfed. PLU (1861—1930), Yeadon USD, UD. Abol civ 1937 pt to Bradf CB (assoc with W Riding) & to Idle CP, pt to help cr Aireb. UD & CP.[31] *Parl* W Riding (1832—67), N'rn Dv of W Riding (1867—85), Otley Dv (1885—1918), Pudsey & Otley Dv (1918—48). *Eccl* Pontef. RDn (1845—57), Otley RDn (1857—*). Eccl bdry: 1896 (cr Yeadon St Andrew EP).[553]

YEADON ST ANDREW

EP [W Riding] Cr 1896 from Yeadon EP.[553] Otley RDn.

YEARSLEY

[N Riding] Tp in Coxwold AP, sep CP 1866,[2] sep EP 1855[9] but sep eccl status not sustained, eccl severed 1960 and transf to Brandsby AP.[337] *LG* Seq 24. Transf 1974 to N Yorks.[5] *Parl* Seq 16. *Eccl* Bulmer RDn (1855—66), Eas. RDn (1866—sep status lost).

YEDINGHAM

AP [E Riding] (Tp Yedingham pt in this par, pt in Heslerton AP). Incl pt tp West Heslerton (sep CP 1866[2]). *LG* Seq 2. Addtl civ bdry alt: 1889.[566] Transf 1974 to N Yorks.[5] *Parl* Seq 1. *Eccl* Seq 3.

YOKEFLEET

[E Riding] Tp in Howden AP, sep CP 1866,[2] eccl severed 1858 to help refound Laxton EP.[440] *LG* Howdensh. Wap, Howden PLU, RSD, RD. Bdry: 1880,[230] 1880 (help cr Bishopsoil CP).[142] Abol 1935 pt to Blacktoft CP, pt to Howden AP, pt to help cr Gilberdyke CP.[13] *Parl* E Riding (1832—85), Howdensh. Dv (1885—1948).

YORK

[Not in a Riding but area expanded into all Ridings; York CB not assoc with a Riding] The following have 'York' in their names. Insofar as any existed at a given time: *LG* York Bor/MB/CB, PLU, USD. *Parl* York Parl Bor/BC (1295—*). *Eccl* City of York RDn.

CP1—YORK—Cr 1900 by union AP2, AP3, CP3, AP5, AP6, AP7, CP4, CP5, AP8, AP11, CP6, AP13, AP15, AP16, AP20, AP21, AP23, AP24, AP25, AP26, CP7, AP28, AP29, AP30, AP33, AP34, AP35, AP36, AP37, AP38, AP39, AP40, AP41, AP42, Clifton Within CP, Dringhouses Within CP, Gate Fulford CP, Heworth Within CP, Holgate CP, Middlethorpe Within CP.[423] Civ bdry: 1934 (gains pts of pars in Yorks N Riding: Clifton Without CP, Heworth Without CP, Huntington AP, Osbaldwick AP),[3] 1937 (gains pts of pars in Yorks W Riding: Acomb AP, Bishopthorpe AP, Knapton CP, and ent Middlethorpe Without CP, Dringhouses Without CP),[31] 1957 (gains pt Askham Bryan AP, Yorks W Riding),[139] 1968 (gains pt Heslington CP, Yorks E Riding, gains pts of pars in Yorks N Riding: Clifton Without CP, Huntington AP, Osbaldwick AP, and exchanges pts with Heworth Without CP, Yorks N Riding).[418] Transf 1974 to N Yorks.[5] *Parl* bdry: 1960.[140]

AP1—YORK ALL SAINTS, FISHERGATE—Cell of Whitby Abbey, parochial status uncertain.[811]

AP2—YORK ALL SAINTS NORTH STREET—Abol civ 1900 to help cr CP1.[423]

AP3—YORK ALL SAINTS PAVEMENT—Abol civ 1900 to help cr CP1.[423] Abol eccl 1586 to help cr EP2.[812]

EP1—YORK ALL SAINTS PAVEMENT AND ST CRUX WITH ST SAVIOUR—Cr 1954 by union EP3, AP41.[275]

EP2—YORK ALL SAINTS PAVEMENT WITH ST PETER THE LITTLE—Cr 1586 by union AP3, AP39.[812] Abol 1885 to help cr EP3.[275]

EP3—YORK ALL SAINTS PAVEMENT WITH ST PETER THE LITTLE AND ST CRUX—Cr 1885 by union EP2, AP11.[811] Abol 1954 to help cr EP1.[275]

AP4—YORK ALL SAINTS PEASEHOLME—Abol 1586 to help cr EP10/CP6.[812]

CP2—YORK CASTLE—Ex-par place, sep CP 1858[393]; situated in area of AP30 but not in the Bor/MB/CB.

CP3—YORK DAVY HALL—Ex-par place, sep CP 1858.[393] Abol 1900 to help cr CP1.[423]

AP5—YORK HOLY TRINITY GOODRAMGATE—Abol civ 1900 to help cr CP1.[423] Abol eccl 1586 to help cr EP26.[812]

EP4—YORK HOLY TRINITY, HEWORTH—Cr 1870 from AP41, EP21, EP10.[483] Bdry: 1936 (help cr EP12),[24] 1937,[246] 1961.[29]

AP6—YORK HOLY TRINITY, KING'S COURT—Abol civ 1900 to help cr CP1.[423] Abol eccl 1886 to help cr EP23.[813]

AP7—YORK HOLY TRINITY MICKLEGATE—Incl in Ainsty (W Riding until 1449 and from 1836, indept jurisd 1449—1836) pt tp Dringhouses (sep CP 1866,[2] sep EP 1853, qv for consitituent pars at that time), pt tp Knapton (sep CP 1866[2]) so that AP7 ent York MB/CB 1866—1900. Abol civ 1900 to help cr CP1.[423] *Parl* York Parl Bor (pt 1295—1867, ent 1867—1918), pt N Riding (1832—67). Eccl bdry: 1928 (help cr EP8).[222] Abol eccl 1934 to help cr EP5.[813]

EP5—YORK HOLY TRINITY WITH ST JOHN MICKLEGATE—Cr 1934 by union EP5, AP23.[813] Abol 1953 to help cr EP6.[107]

EP6—YORK HOLY TRINITY WITH ST JOHN MICKLEGATE AND ST MARTIN CUM ST GREGORY—Cr 1953 by union EP5, EP17.[107]

CP4—YORK MINSTER YARD WITH BEDDERN—Ex-par place, sep CP 1858.[393] Abol 1900 to help cr CP1.[423]

CP5—YORK MINT YARD—Ex-par place, sep CP 1858,[393] eccl abol 1879 ent to AP34.[773] Abol 1900 to help cr CP1.[423]

AP8—YORK ST ANDREW—Abol civ 1900 to help cr CP1.[423] Pec jurisd Dean & Chapter of York. Abol eccl 1586 ent to AP41.[812]

—YORK ST ANDREW, FISHERGATE—Gilbertine priory, parochial status uncertain.[811]

EP7—YORK ST BARNABAS—Cr 1912 from EP22.[814]

AP9—YORK ST BENET—Derelict before 1338.[811]

EP8—YORK ST CHAD—Cr 1928 from AP29, AP7.[222]

AP10—YORK ST CLEMENT—Priory church used parochially,[811] abol 1586 ent to AP29.[812]

AP11—YORK ST CRUX—Abol civ 1900 to help cr CP1.[423] Abol eccl 1885 to help cr EP2.[811]

AP12—YORK ST CUTHBERT—Incl in N Riding (Bulmer Wap) pt tp Heworth (for sep identity see CP6). Abol 1586 to help cr EP10/CP6.[812]

EP9—YORK ST CUTHBERT PEASHOLME—Cr 1966 by union EP10, pt EP26.[618]

EP10/CP6—YORK ST CUTHBERT, ST HELEN ON THE WALLS AND ALL SAINTS PEASHOLME—Cr 1586 by union AP12, AP4, AP18, AP31 (eccl 'York St Cuthbert with St Helen on the Walls and All Saints Peasholme').[812] Incl in N Riding (Bulmer Wap) pt tp Heworth (sep CP 1866[2]). Addtl civ bdry alt: 1888.[815] Abol civ 1900 to help cr CP1.[423] Eccl bdry: 1870 (help cr EP4),[483] 1937.[246] Abol eccl 1966 to help cr EP9.[618]

—YORK ST CUTHBERT WITH ST HELEN ON THE WALLS AND ALL SAINTS PEASHOLME—see prev entry

AP13—YORK ST DENNIS—Eccl, 'York St Denys'. Abol civ 1900 to help cr CP1.[423] Abol eccl 1586 to help cr EP11.[812]

—YORK ST DENYS—see prev entry

EP11—YORK ST DENYS WITH ST GEORGE—Cr 1586 by union AP13, AP15.[812] Bdry: 1842 (cr Naburn EP [for sep civ identity see AP15]).[7]

AP14—YORK ST EDWARD—Abol 1586 ent to AP36.[812]

AP15—YORK ST GEORGE—Incl pt chap Naburn (this pt in Ainsty, in W Riding until 1449 and from 1836, indept jurisd 1449—1836, sep civ identity early, sep EP 1842 from EP11, Acaster Malbis AP,[7] qv). Abol civ 1900 to help cr CP1.[423] Abol eccl 1586 to help cr EP11.[812]

AP16—YORK ST GILES—Civ, 'York St Giles in the Suburbs'. Pt N Riding (Bulmer Wap, until 1884), York Bor/MB (pt until 1884, ent 1884—89), York CB (1889—1900), York USD (pt 1875—84, ent 1884—94), pt York RSD (1875—84). Civ bdry: 1888.[816] Abol civ 1900 to help cr CP1.[423] *Parl* As for AP7. Abol eccl 1586 to help cr EP21.[812]

—YORK ST GILES IN THE SUBURBS—see prev entry

AP17—YORK ST GREGORY—Abol 1586 to help cr EP17.[812]

AP18—YORK ST HELEN, ALDWARK—Sometimes 'York St Helen on the Walls'. Abol 1586 to help cr EP10/CP6.[812]

AP19—YORK ST HELEN, FISHERGATE—Abol 1586 ent to AP36.[812]

AP20—YORK ST HELEN, STONEGATE—Abol civ 1900 to help cr CP1.[423] Abol eccl 1954 to help cr EP16.[489]

EP12—YORK ST HILDA—Cr 1936 from EP4, Osbaldwick AP, EP13.[24]

AP21—YORK ST JOHN, DELPIKE—Eccl 'York St John Del Pyke'. Abol civ 1900 to help cr CP1.[423] Pec jurisd Dean & Chapter of York. Abol eccl 1586 to help cr EP26.[812]

—YORK ST JOHN DEL PYKE—see prev entry

AP22—YORK ST JOHN, HUNGATE—Orig pec jurisd Dean & Chapter of York. Abol 1586 ent to AP41.[812]

AP23—YORK ST JOHN MICKLEGATE—Eccl 'York St John, Ouse Bridge End'; pec jurisd Dean & Chapter of York (until 1836). Abol civ 1900 to help cr CP1.[423] Abol eccl 1934 to help cr EP5.[813]

—YORK ST JOHN, OUSE BRIDGE END—see prev entry

AP24—YORK ST LAWRENCE—Incl in E Riding (Ouse & Derw. Wap) tp Heslington St Lawrence (sep CP 1866,[2] sep EP 1740[9]), pt Heslington St Paul AP, after *ca* 1860s pt of Heslington EP (eccl severed 1869 from this par and transf to Heslington EP).[617] Abol civ 1900 to help cr CP1.[423] *Parl* York Parl Bor (pt 1295—1867, ent 1867—1918), pt E Riding (1832—67). Abol eccl 1885 to help cr EP13.[817]

EP13—YORK ST LAWRENCE WITH ST NICHOLAS—Cr 1885 by union AP24, AP36.[817] Bdry: 1936 (help cr EP12).[24]

EP14—YORK ST LUKE—Cr 1930 from EP21, Clifton St Philip and St James EP.[263] Bdry: 1960.[44]

AP25—YORK ST MARGARET—Abol civ 1900 to help cr CP1.[423] Abol eccl 1586 to help cr EP15.[812]

EP15—YORK ST MARGARET WITH ST PETER LE WILLOWS—Cr 1586 by union AP25, AP38.[812]

AP26—YORK ST MARTIN, CONEY STREET—Civ, 'York St Martin le Grand'. Abol civ 1900 to help cr CP1.[423] Pec jurisd Dean & Chapter of York (until 1836). Abol eccl 1954 to help cr EP16.[489]

EP16—YORK ST MARTIN CONEY STREET WITH ST HELEN STONEGATE—Cr 1954 by union AP26, AP20.[489]

—YORK ST MARTIN LE GRAND—see AP26

AP27—YORK ST MARTIN, MICKLEGATE—Abol 1586 to help cr EP17/CP7.[812]

EP17/CP7—YORK ST MARTIN MICKLEGATE WITH ST GREGORY—Cr 1586 by union AP17, AP27.[812] Abol civ 1900 to help cr CP1.[423] Abol eccl 1953 to help cr EP6.[107]

—YORK ST MARY AD VALVAS—not parochial, demolished *ca* 1360.[811]

AP28—YORK ST MARY BISHOPHILL JUNIOR—Incl in Ainsty (W Riding until 1449 and from 1836, sep jurisd 1449—1836) chap Copmanthorpe, pt chap Upper Poppleton (each a sep CP 1866,[2] each pec jurisd Dean & Chapter of York [until 1836], 'Copmanthorpe' a sep EP 1844 by union of the 2 chaps,[437] area of Upper Poppleton eccl severed from latter 1866 to help cr Nether Poppleton with Upper Poppleton EP[438]), tp Holgate (sep CP 1866,[2] sep EP 1855 as EP22[245]). Abol civ 1900 to help cr CP1.[423] *Parl* York Parl Bor (pt 1295—1867, ent 1867—1918), pt W Riding (1832—67). Pec jurisd Dean & Chapter of York (until 1836). Addtl eccl bdry alt: 1885.[818]

AP29—YORK ST MARY BISHOPHILL SENIOR—Incl in Ainsty (W Riding until 1449 and from 1836, indept jurisd 1449—1836) pt tp Dringhouses (sep CP 1866,[2] sep EP 1853,[30] qv for constituent pars then incl pt of this par), tp Middlethorpe (sep CP 1866[2]). Abol civ 1900 to help cr CP1.[423] *Parl* As for AP28. Eccl bdry: 1586 (gains AP10),[812] 1885,[818] 1928 (help cr EP8).[222] Renamed eccl 1971 as EP18.[121]

EP18—YORK ST MARY BISHOPHILL SENIOR WITH ST CLEMENT—Renaming 1971 of AP29.[121]

AP30—YORK ST MARY, CASTLEGATE—Incl area York Castle (sep CP 1858,[393] not in York Bor/MB/CB). Abol civ 1900 to help cr CP1.[423] Abol eccl 1936 to help cr EP19.[464]

EP19—YORK ST MARY CASTLEGATE WITH ST MICHAEL SPURRIERGATE—Cr 1936 by union AP30, AP35.[464]

AP31—YORK ST MARY, LAYERTHORPE—Orig pec jurisd Dean & Chapter of York). Abol 1586 to help cr EP10/CP6.[812]

AP32—YORK ST MARY, WALMGATE—Abol 1308 ent to AP38.[811]

AP33—YORK ST MAURICE—Sometimes 'York St Maurice, Monkgate'. Abol civ 1900 to help cr CP1.[423] Orig pec jurisd Fenton prebend, later pec jurisd Dean & Chapter of York. Abol eccl 1586 to help cr EP26.[812]

AP34—YORK ST MICHAEL LE BELFREY—Incl in N Riding (Bulmer Wap) pt tp Clifton (sep CP 1866,[2] sep EP 1871 as 'Clifton St Philip and St James',[326] qv for constituent pars then incl AP34), pt tp Rawcliffe (sep CP 1866[2]). Addtl civ bdry alt: 1888.[816] Abol civ 1900 to help cr CP1.[423] *Parl* As for AP7. Pec jurisd Dean & Chapter of York (until 1836). Addtl eccl bdry alt: 1586 (gains AP42),[812] 1855 (help cr EP24),[698] 1879 (gains ex-par area York Mint Yard [sep civ as CP5]).[773] Abol eccl 1966 to help cr EP20.[819]

EP20—YORK ST MICHAEL-LE-BELFREY AND TRINITY IN GOODRAMGATE—Cr 1966 by union AP34, pt EP26.[819]

AP35—YORK ST MICHAEL, SPURRIERGATE—Abol civ 1900 to help cr CP1.[423] Abol eccl 1936 to help cr EP19.[464]

—YORK ST MICHAEL WITHOUT WALMGATE—Early parochial status uncertain, demolished 14th cent.[811]

AP36—YORK ST NICHOLAS—Hospital chap used parochially.[811] Abol civ 1900 to help cr CP1.[423] Pec jurisd Dean & Chapter of York (not orig but later, until 1836). Eccl bdry: 1586 (gains AP14, AP19).[812] Abol eccl 1885 to help cr EP13.[817]

AP37—YORK ST OLAVE, MARYGATE—Incl in E Riding (Ouse & Derw. Wap) chap Fulford sep EP 1746 from EP21[9] [qv below, some eccl dependence perhaps remaining until 1746[569]], the area civ comprised of tp Gate Fulford, pt tp Water Fulford [each a sep CP 1866[2]], the name 'Fulfords Ambo' used sometimes civ after 1828 for this ent area until 2 tps sep civ identity 1866); incl in N Riding (Bulmer Wap) pt tp Clifton (sep CP 1866,[2] sep EP 1871 as 'Clifton St Philip and St James' from EP21 and other pars,[326] qv below), pt tp Rawcliffe (sep CP 1866[2]), pt tp Heworth (sep CP 1866,[2] sep eccl 1870 as EP4 from EP21 and other pars,[483] qv). Abol civ 1900 to help cr CP1.[423] Abol eccl 1586 to help cr EP21.[812]

EP21—YORK ST OLAVE WITH ST GILES—Cr 1586 by union AP37, AP16.[812] Incl chap Fulford (sep civ status and dependent tps as in AP37, sep EP 1746[9] but some eccl dependence perhaps remaining until 1825[569]), pt tp Clifton (sep civ as in AP37, sep EP 1871 as 'Clifton St Philip and St James' from this and other pars,[326] qv), pt tp Rawcliffe (sep civ as in AP37), pt tp Heworth (sep civ as in AP37, sep eccl 1870 as EP4 from this and

other pars,[483] qv). Addtl eccl bdry alt: 1855 (help cr EP24),[698] 1930 (help cr EP14).[263]

EP22—YORK ST PAUL, HOLGATE—Cr 1855 from AP28[245]; for civ see 'Holgate'. Bdry: 1912 (cr EP7).[814] Later usually called simply 'York St Paul'.

AP38—YORK ST PETER LE WILLOWS—Bdry: 1308 (gains AP32).[811] Abol civ 1900 to help cr CP1.[423] Abol eccl 1586 to help cr EP15.[812]

AP39—YORK ST PETER THE LITTLE—Abol civ 1900 to help cr CP1.[423] Abol eccl 1586 to help cr EP2.[812]

—YORK ST PHILIP AND ST JAMES—Name sometimes used for EP cr 1871 as 'Clifton St Phllip and St James', qv.

AP40—YORK ST SAMPSON—Abol civ 1900 to help cr CP1.[423] Pec jurisd Dean & Chapter of York (until 1836). Abol eccl 1886 to help cr EP23.[813]

EP23—YORK ST SAMPSON WITH HOLY TRINITY, KING'S COURT—Cr 1886 by union AP40, AP6.[813]

AP41—YORK ST SAVIOUR—Incl in N Riding (Bulmer Wap) pt tp Heworth (sep CP 1866,[2] sep eccl 1870 as EP4 from this and other pars,[483] qv above). Addtl civ bdry alt: 1888.[815] Abol civ 1900 to help cr CP1.[423] *Parl* As for AP7. Pec jurisd Dean & Chapter of York (until 1836). Eccl bdry: 1586 (gains AP8, AP22).[812] Abol eccl 1954 to help cr EP1.[275]

—YORK ST STEPHEN—Early parochial status uncertain, demolished 14th cent.[811]

EP24—YORK ST THOMAS—Cr 1855 from EP21, AP5 (area of orig AP33), AP34.[698] Abol 1966 to help cr EP25.[820]

EP25—YORK ST THOMAS WITH ST MAURICE—Cr 1966 by union EP24, pt EP26.[820]

AP42—YORK ST WILFRID—Abol civ 1900 to help cr CP1.[423] Pec jurisd Dean & Chapter of York. Abol eccl 1586 ent to AP34.[812]

EP26—YORK TRINITY IN GOODRAMGATE WITH ST JOHN DELPIKE AND ST MAURICE WITHOUT MONKBAR—Cr 1586 by union AP5, AP21, AP33.[812] (AP33 was in pec jurisd Dean & Chapter of York). Bdry: 1855 (from orig area AP33, help cr EP24).[698] Abol 1966 pt to help cr EP25, pt to help cr EP20, pt to help cr EP9.[618]

YOULTHORPE WITH GOWTHORPE

[E Riding] Tp in Bishop Wilton AP, sep CP 1866.[2] Harth. Wap, Pockl. PLU, RSD, RD. Abol 1935 to help cr Bishop Wilton CP.[13] *Parl* E Riding (1832—85), Howdensh. Dv (1885—1948).

YOULTON

[N Riding] Tp in Alne AP, sep CP 1866.[2] *LG* Seq 30. Transf 1974 to N Yorks.[5] *Parl* Seq 16

Part II: Local Government Units

CHESHIRE

ALTERATIONS IN COUNTY BOUNDARIES

As noted by year below, Ches pars gained territory from or lost it to pars in adjoining cos or county boroughs, or were entirely transferred to them. Details of these alterations are noted in Part I of the *Guide* under Cheshire.

ANCIENT COUNTY (until 1889: Hds, Bors, MBs, PLUs, RSDs, USDs)
1866 Barthomley, Dodleston, Malpas, Whitchurch. *1884* Latchford. *1885* Thelwall.

ADMINISTRATIVE COUNTY (1889—1974: Hds,[1] PLUs, MBs, RDs, UDs, with assoc CBs of Birkenhead, Chester, Stockport, Wallasey [1913—74])
1889 Higher Bebington, Birkenhead, Brinnington, Cheadle, Chester, Claughton with Grange, Disley, Latchford, Oxton, Stayley, Stockport, Tranmere. *1895* Tittenley. *1896* Appleton, Latchford Without, Threapwood, Walton Inferior. *1898* Lower Bebington, Dukinfield. *1899* Blacon cum Crabwall, Chester Castle. *1901* Bredbury, Brinnington, Cheadle, Hazel Grove and Bramhall. *1913* Wallasey. *1920* Carrington, Partington, Warburton. *1928* Bidston cum Ford, Landican, Moreton, Prenton, Thingwall. *1931* Baguley, Northern Etchells, Northenden. *1933* Acton Grange, Arrowe, Bidston cum Ford, Grappenhall, Latchford Without, Lymm, Moore, Noctorum, Saughall Massie, Stockton Heath, Thelwall, Upton by Birkenhead, Walton Inferior, Warburton, Woodchurch.

1935 Hazel Grove and Bramhall. *1936* Blacon cum Crabwall, Great Boughton, Bredbury, Claverton, Disley, Hoole, Kettleshulme, Marlston cum Lache, Marple, Newton by Chester, Norton, Little Saughall, Taxal, Yeardsley cum Whaley. *1952* Bredbury and Romiley. *1954* Hoole, Upton by Chester. *1965* Blakenhall, Checkley cum Wrinehill, Chorlton, Church Lawton, Marbury with Quoisley, Odd Rode, Weston.

NON-METROPOLITAN COUNTY (from 1974: Dists)
Altrincham, Barnston, Bebington and Bromborough, Bowdon, Bredbury and Romiley, Brimstage, Burtonwood, Caldy, Carrington, Cheadle and Gatley, Croft, Cuerdley, Dukinfield, Dunham Massey, Eastham, Frankby, Gayton, Golborne, Grange, Greasby, Hale, Hale, Hazel Grove and Bramhall, Heswall cum Oldfield, Hoylake cum West Kirby, Hyde, Irby, Longendale, Marple, Partington, Penketh, Pensby, Poulton cum Spital, Poulton cum Fearnhead, Raby, Ringway, Rixton with Glazebrook, Sale, Great Sanky, Stalybridge, Storeton, Thornton Hough, Thurstaston, Tintwistle, Warburton, Widnes, Winwick, Woolston.

ASSOCIATED COUNTY BOROUGHS AND COUNTY OF ITSELF

BIRKENHEAD CB
Bdry: 1928,[2] 1933.[3] Transf 1974 to Merseyside.[4]

CHESTER CO OF ITSELF (from *ca* 1121/1129 and more continuously from 1238/29), CB
Bdry: 1899,[5] 1936,[6] 1954.[7] Transf 1974 to Ches.[4]

STOCKPORT CB
Bdry: 1901,[8] 1913,[9] 1935,[10] 1936,[6] 1937,[11] 1952.[12] Transf 1974 to Gtr Manch.[4]

WALLASEY CB
Cr 1913 when Wall. MB constituted a CB.[13] Bdry: 1928,[14] 1933.[3] Transf 1974 to Merseyside.[4]

HUNDREDS[1]

BROXTON HD
Agden (from 1866), Aldford, Aldersey (from 1866), Bache,[1] pt Backford (until 1866), Barton (from 1866), Bickerton (from 1866), Bickley (from 1866), Great Boughton[15] (from 1866), Bradley (from 1866), Broxton (from 1866), Buerton (from 1866), Bulkeley (from 1866), pt Bunbury (until 1866), Burwardsley (from 1866), Caldecott (from 1866), Carden (from 1866), Caughall (from 1866), pt Chester St Mary on the Hill (until 1866), pt Chester St Oswald (until 1866), Chidlow (from 1866), Cholmondeley (from 1866), Chorlton (from 1866), Chowley (from 1866), Christleton, Churton by Aldford (from 1866), Churton by Farndon (from 1866), Churton Heath (from 1866), Claverton (from 1858), Clutton (from 1866),

Coddington, Cotton Abbotts (from 1866), Cotton Edmunds (from 1866), Crewe (from 1866), Cuddington (from 1866), Dodleston (pt until 1866, ent from 1866), Duckington (from 1866), Eaton (from 1866), Eccleston, Edge (from 1866), Edgerley (from 1866), Egerton (from 1866), Farndon, Golborne Bellow (from 1866), Golborne David (from 1866), Grafton (from 1866), Hampton (from 1866), Handley, Harthill, Hatton (from 1866), Hoole (from 1866), Horton (from 1866), Huntington (from 1866), Huxley (from 1866), Kings Marsh (from 1858), Lower Kinnerton (from 1866), Larkton (from 1866), Lea Newbold (from 1866), Littleton (from 1866), Macefen (from 1866), Malpas (pt until 1866, ent from 1866), Marlston cum Lache (from 1866), Moston (from 1866), Newton by

637

Chester (from 1866), Newton by Malpas (from 1866), Newton by Tattenhall (from 1866), Oldcastle (from 1866), Overton (from 1866), Picton (from 1866), Plemstall (pt until 1866, ent from 1866), Poulton (from 1866), Pulford, Rowton (from 1866), Saighton (from 1866), Shocklach (until 1866), Church Shocklach (from 1866), Shocklach Oviatt (from 1866), Foulk Stapleford (from 1866), Stockton (from 1866), Stretton (from 1866), Guilden Sutton, pt Tarvin (until 1866), Tattenhall, pt Threapwood (from 1858), Tilston, Mickle Trafford (from 1866), Tushingham cum Grindley (from 1866), Upton by Chester (from 1866), Waverton, Wervin (from 1866), Wigland (from 1866), Wychough (from 1866)

BUCKLOW HD

Acton Grange (from 1866), Agden (from 1866), Altrincham[15] (from 1866), Anderton (from 1866), Antrobus (from 1866), Appleton (from 1866), Ashley (from 1866), Ashton upon Mersey, Aston by Budworth (from 1866), Aston by Sutton (from 1866), Aston Grange (from 1866), Baguley (from 1866), Barnton (from 1866), Bartington (from 1866), Bexton (from 1866), Bollington (from 1866), Bowdon,[15] Great Budworth (pt until 1866, ent from 1866), Carrington (from 1866), Clifton (from 1866), Cogshall (from 1866), Comberbach (from 1866), Crowley (from 1866), Daresbury (from 1866), Dunham Massey (from 1866), Dutton (from 1866), Grappenhall, Hale (from 1866), Halton (from 1866), Hatton (from 1866), Keckwick (from 1866), Knutsford (until 1866), Knutsford Nether (from 1866), Knutsford Over (from 1866), Latchford[15] (from 1866), High Legh (from 1866), Little Leigh (from 1866), Lymm, Marbury (from 1866), Marston (from 1866), Marthall cum Warford (from 1866), Mere (from 1866), Millington (from 1866), Mobberley, Moore (from 1866), Newton by Daresbury (from 1866), Norton (from 1866), Ollerton (from 1866), Partington (from 1866), Peover Inferior (from 1866), Peover Superior (from 1866), Pickmere (from 1866), Plumley (from 1866), Preston on the Hill (from 1866), Rostherne (pt until 1866, ent from 1866), Runcorn, Sale (from 1866), Seven Oaks (from 1866), Stockham (from 1866), Stretton (from 1866), Sutton (from 1866), Tabley Inferior (from 1866), Tabley Superior (from 1866), Tatton (from 1866), Thelwall (from 1866), Timperley (from 1866), Toft (from 1866), Walton Inferior (from 1866), Walton Superior (from 1866), Warburton, Weston (from 1866), Higher Whitley (from 1866), Lower Whitley (from 1866), Wincham (from 1866)

EDDISBURY HD

Acton (from 1866), Alpraham (from 1866), Alvanley (from 1866), Ashton (from 1866), Barrow, Beeston (from 1866), pt Great Budworth (until 1866), Little Budworth, Bunbury (pt until 1866, ent from 1866), Burton by Tarvin (from 1866), Calveley (from 1866), pt Chester St Oswald (until 1866), Clotton Hoofield (from 1866), Crowton (from 1866), Cuddington (from 1866), Darnhall (from 1866), Delamere (from 1812), Duddon (from 1866), Dunham on the Hill (from 1866), Eaton (from 1866), Eddisbury (from 1866), Elton (from 1866), Frodsham, Frodsham Lordship (from 1866), Hapsford (from 1866), Hartford (from 1866),

Haughton (from 1866), Helsby (from 1866), Hockenhull (from 1866), Horton cum Peel (from 1866), Iddinshall (from 1866), Ince, Kelsall (from 1866), Kingsley (from 1866), Kingswood (from 1866), Manley (from 1866), Marton (from 1866), pt Middlewich (until 1866), Mouldsworth (from 1866), Newton by Frodsham (from 1866), Norley (from 1866), Castle Northwich (from 1866), Oakmere (from 1866), Onston (from 1866), Low Oulton (from 1866), Over, Peckforton (from 1866), pt Plemstall (until 1866), Prior's Heys (from 1858), Ridley (from 1866), Rushton (from 1866), Spurstow (from 1866), Bruen Stapleford (from 1866), Tarporley, Tarvin (pt until 1866, ent from 1866), Thornton le Moors, Tilstone Fearnall (from 1866), Tiverton (from 1866), Bridge Trafford (from 1866), Wimbolds Trafford (from 1866), Utkinton (from 1866), Wallerscoat (from 1866), Wardle (from 1866), Weaver (from 1866), Weaverham cum Milton, Wettenhall (from 1866), Whitegate (until 1866), Willington (from 1858), Winnington (from 1866)

MACCLESFIELD HD

Adlington (from 1866), Alderley (until 1866), Nether Alderley (from 1866), Over Alderley (from 1866), pt Astbury (until 1866), Birtles (from 1866), Bollinfee (from 1866), Bollington (from 1866), Bosden (from 1877), Bosley (from 1866), Bramhall (from 1866), Bredbury (from 1866), Brinnington[15] (from 1866), Butley (from 1866), Capesthorne (from 1866), Cheadle[15] (until 1866), Cheadle[15] (from 1879), Cheadle Buckley[15] (1866—79), Cheadle Moseley[15] (1866—79), Chelford (from 1866), Chorley (from 1866), Disley (from 1866), Dukinfield[15] (from 1866), Northern Etchells (from 1866), Stockport Etchells (from 1866), Fallibroome (from 1866), Fulshaw (from 1866), Gawsworth, Godley[15] (from 1866), Handforth (from 1877), Handforth cum Bosden (1866—77), Hattersley (from 1866), Henbury cum Pexall (from 1866), Hollingworth (from 1866), Hurdsfield[15] (from 1866), Hyde[15] (from 1866), Kettleshulme (from 1866), Lyme Handley (from 1866), Macclesfield[15] (from 1866), Macclesfield Forest (from 1866), Marple (from 1866), Marton (from 1866), Matley (from 1866), Mottram, Mottram St Andrew (from 1866), Newton (from 1866), Newton[15] (from 1866), Norbury (from 1866), Northenden, Offerton (from 1866), Pott Shrigley (from 1866), Pownall Fee[15] (from 1866), Poynton (1866—80), Poynton with Worth (from 1866), Prestbury,[15] Rainow (from 1866), North Rode (from 1866), Romiley (from 1866), pt Rostherne (until 1866), Siddington (from 1866), Snelson (from 1866), Somerford Booths (from 1866), Stayley[15] (from 1866), Stockport,[15] Sutton (from 1866), Taxal, Tintwistle (from 1866), Torkington (from 1866), Tytherington (from 1866), Upton (from 1866), Great Warford (from 1866), Werneth[15] (from 1866), Wildboarclough (from 1866), Wilmslow (until 1866), Wincle (from 1866), Lower Withington (from 1866), Old Withington (from 1866), Woodford (from 1866), Worth (1866—80), Yeardlsey cum Whalley (from 1866)

NANTWICH HD

Acton, Alsager (from 1866), Alvaston (from 1866), Aston juxta Mondrum (from 1866), Audlem, Austerson (from 1866), Baddiley, Baddington (from 1866), Barthomley (pt until 1866, ent from 1866), Basford (from 1866), Batherton (from 1866), Betchton (from 1866), Blakenhall (from 1866), Bridgemere (from 1866), Brindley (from 1866), Broomhall (from 1866), Buerton (from 1866), Burland (from 1866), Checkley cum Wrinehill (from 1866), Cholmondeston (from 1866), Chorley (from 1866), Chorlton (from 1866), Coole Pilate (from 1866), Coppenhall (until 1866), Church Coppenhall (from 1866), Monks Coppenhall[15] (from 1866), Crewe (from 1866), Dodcott cum Wilkesley (from 1866), Doddington (from 1866), Edleston (from 1866), Faddiley (from 1866), Hankelow (from 1866), Haslington (from 1866), Hassall (from 1866), Hatherton (from 1866), Henhull (from 1866), Hough (from 1866), Hunsterson (from 1866), Hurleston (from 1866), Lea (from 1866), Leighton (from 1866), Marbury with Quoisley (from 1866), Church Minshull, Nantwich, Newhall (from 1866), Norbury (from 1866), Poole (from 1866), Rope (from 1866), pt Sandbach (until 1866), Shavington cum Gresty (from 1866), Sound (from 1866), Stapeley (from 1866), Stoke (from 1866), Tittenley (from 1866), Walgherton (from 1866), Weston (from 1866), pt Whitchurch (until 1866), Willaston (from 1866), Wirswall (from 1866), Wistaston, Woodcott (from 1866), Woolstanwood (from 1866), Worleston (from 1866), Wrenbury cum Frith, Wybunbury

NORTHWICH HD

Allostock (from 1866), Arclid (from 1866), pt Astbury[15] (until 1866), Birches (from 1866), Blackden (from 1866), Bostock (from 1866), Bradwall (from 1866), Brereton cum Smethwick, pt Great Budworth (until 1866), Buglawton (from 1866), Byley (from 1866), Clive (from 1866), Congleton[15] (from 1866), Cotton (from 1866), Cranage (from 1866), Croxton (from 1866), Davenham, Davenport (from 1866), Eaton (from 1866), Eaton (from 1866), Elton (from 1866), Goostrey cum Barnshaw (from 1866), Church Hulme (from 1866), Hulme Walfield (from 1866), Hulse (from 1866), Kermincham (from 1866), Kinderton cum Hulme (from 1866), Lach Dennis (from 1866), Church Lawton, Leese (from 1866), Leftwich (from 1866), Lostock Gralam (from 1866), Middlewich (pt until 1866, ent from 1866), Minshull Vernon (from 1866), Mooresbarrow cum Parme (from 1866), Moreton cum Alcumlow (from 1866), Moston (from 1866), Moulton (from 1866), Newbold Astbury (from 1866), Newhall (from 1866), Newton (from 1866), Northwich (from 1866), Occlestone (from 1866), Odd Rode (from 1866), Nether Peover (from 1866), Radnor (from 1866), Ravenscroft (from 1866), Rudheath (from 1866), Sandbach (pt until 1866, ent from 1866), Shipbrook (from 1866), Shurlach (from 1866), Smallwood (from 1866), Somerford (from 1866), Sproston (from 1866), Stanthorne (from 1866), Stublach (from 1866), Sutton (from 1866), Swettenham, Tetton (from 1866), Twenlow (from 1866), Warmingham, Wharton (from 1866), Whatcroft (from 1866), Wheelock (from 1866), Wimboldsley (from 1866), Witton cum Twanbrooks (from 1866)

WIRRAL HD

Arrowe (from 1866), Backford (pt until 1866, ent from 1866), Barnston (from 1866), Bebington (until 1866), Higher Bebington[15] (from 1866), Lower Bebington (from 1866), Bidston cum Ford, Birkenhead[15] (from 1866), Blacon cum Crabwall (from 1866), Brimstage (from 1866), Bromborough, Burton, Caldy (from 1866), Caldy (from 1866), Capenhurst (from 1866), Chorlton by Backford (from 1866), pt Chester Holy Trinity (until 1866), pt Chester St Mary on the Hill (until 1866), Claughton with Grange[15] (from 1866), Croughton (from 1866), Eastham, Frankby (from 1866), Gayton (from 1866), Grange (from 1866), Greasby (from 1866), Heswall cum Oldfield, Hoose (from 1866), Hooton (from 1866), Irby (from 1866), West Kirby, Landican (from 1866), Lea by Backford (from 1866), Ledsham (from 1866), Leighton (from 1866), Liscard (from 1866), Great Meolse (from 1866), Little Meolse (from 1866), Mollington Banastre (from 1866), Mollington Tarrant (from 1866), Moreton (from 1866), Ness (from 1866), Neston (until 1866), Great Neston (from 1866), Little Neston (from 1866), Netherpool (from 1866), Newton with Larton (from 1866), Noctorum (from 1866), Overpool (from 1866), Oxton[15] (from 1866), Pensby (from 1866), Poulton cum Spital (from 1866), Poulton cum Seacombe (from 1866), Prenton (from 1866), Puddington (from 1866), Raby (from 1866), Great Saughall (from 1866), Little Saughall (from 1866), Saughall Massie (from 1866), Shotwick, Shotwick Park (from 1858), Stanlow (from 1858), Great Stanney (from 1858), Little Stanney (from 1866), Stoke, Storeton (from 1866), Great Sutton (from 1866), Little Sutton (from 1866), Thingwall (from 1866), Childer Thornton (from 1866), Thornton Hough (from 1866), Thurstaston, Tranmere[15] (from 1866), Upton by Birkenhead, Wallasey, Whitby (from 1866), Willaston (from 1866), Woodbank (from 1866), Woodchurch

BOROUGHS

Units with some degree of burghal character[16] are denominated 'Bor'. Those which did not sustain that status until the 19th cent are in italics. MBs were established by the Municipal Corporations Act, 1835,[17] or by later charter.

ALTRINCHAM BOR, MB (1937[18]—74)
Bor: Altrincham (from 1866), pt Bowdon (until 1866)
MB: Altrincham
ASHTON UNDER LYNE MB (1847[19]—1974) [Lancs (qv for principal pt), Ches (1847—89)]
pt Dukinfield (1847—98)

BEBINGTON MB (1937[18]—74)
Bebington and Bromborough, Brimstage, Eastham, Poulton cum Spital, Raby, Storeton, Thornton Hough
BIRKENHEAD MB (1877[20]—89), CB (1889—1974)
pt Higher Bebington (1877—94), Birkenhead, Claughton with Grange (1877—98), Landican (1928—

33), Oxton (1877—98), Prenton (1928—33), Rock Ferry (1894—98), Thingwall (1928—33), Tranmere (1877—98)

CHESTER BOR/MB/CB
pt Great Boughton (1835—84), Chester (1884—1974), Chester Abbey Precincts (until 1884), Chester Holy Trinity (pt until 1866, ent 1866—84), Chester St Bridget (until 1884), Chester St John the Baptist (pt until 1866, ent 1866—84), Chester St Martin (until 1884), Chester St Mary on the Hill (pt until 1866, ent 1866—84), Chester St Michael (until 1884), Chester St Olave (until 1884), Chester St Oswald (pt until 1866, ent 1866—84), Chester St Peter (until 1884), Spital Boughton (until 1884)

CONGLETON BOR/MB
pt Astbury (until 1866), Congleton (1866—1974)

CREWE MB[21] (1877[22]—1974)
pt Church Coppenhall (1892—94), Monks Coppenhall, pt Shavington cum Gresty (1892—94), pt Wistaston (1892—94)

DUKINFIELD MB (1899[23]—1974)
Dukinfield

ELLESMERE PORT MB (1955[24]—74)
Ellesmere Port, Hooton, Great Sutton, Little Sutton, Childer Thornton

FRODSHAM BOR
Frodsham

HALTON BOR
pt Runcorn

HYDE MB (1881[25]—1974)
Godley (1881—1923), Hyde, Newton (1881—1923), pt Werneth (1881—94)

KNUTSFORD BOR
pt Knutsford

MACCLESFIELD BOR/MB
pt Hurdsfield (1835—94), Macclesfield (1866—1974),

pt Prestbury (until 1866), pt Sutton (1835—94)

MALPAS BOR
pt Malpas

MIDDLEWICH BOR
pt Middlewich

MOSSLEY MB (1885[26]—1974) [Lancs, Ches (1885—89), Yorks W Riding (1885—89)]
pt Stayley[27]

NANTWICH BOR
pt Nantwich

NORTHWICH BOR
pt Great Budworth

OVER BOR
pt Over

SALE MB (1935[28]—74)
Ashton upon Mersey (1935—36), Sale

STALYBRIDGE[29] MB (1857[30]—1974 [Ches, *Lancs (1857—94)*]
pt Ashton under Lyne (1857—94 [enlarged pt 1881—94]), pt Dukinfield (1857—94), pt Stayley (1857—94 [enlarged pt 1881—94]), Stalybridge (1894—1974)

STOCKPORT BOR/MB/CB [Ches, *Lancs (1835—94)*]
pt Brinnington (until 1894), pt Cheadle (until 1866), pt Cheadle (1879—94), pt Cheadle Bulkeley (1866—79), pt Cheadle Moseley (1866—79), *pt Heaton Norris (1835—94)*, Stockport

TARPORLEY BOR
pt Tarporley

WALLASEY MB (1910[31]—13), CB (1913[13]—74)
Liscard (1910—12), Poulton cum Seacomb (1910—12), Wallasey

WARRINGTON MB (1847—1900), CB (1900—74) [Lancs (qv for details and principal pt), Ches (1847—94)]
pt Latchford (1847—94), pt Thelwall (1847—84)

POOR LAW UNIONS

In Ches Poor Law County:[32]

ALTRINCHAM PLU (1836—95[33])
Agden, Altrincham, Ashley, Ashton upon Mersey, Aston by Budworth, Baguley, Bexton, Bollington, Bollinfee, Bowdon, Carrington, Dunham Massey, Northern Etchells, Fulshaw (1836—94), Hale, Handforth cum Basen, Knutsford Nether, Knutsford Over, High Legh, Lymm, Marthall cum Warford, Mere, Millington, Mobberley, Northenden, Ollerton, Partington, Peover Inferior, Peover Superior, Pickmere, Plumley, Pownall Fee (1836—94), Rostherne, Sale, Styal (1894—95), Tabley Inferior, Tabley Superior, Tatton, Timperley, Toft, Unnamed (1894—95), Warburton, Wilmslow (1894—95)

BIRKENHEAD PLU (1891—1930)
Bidston cum Ford, Birkenhead, Claughton with Grange (1891—98), Liscard (1891—1912), Noctorum, Oxton (1891—98), Poulton cum Seacombe (1891—1912), Tranmere (1891—98), Wallasey

GREAT BOUGHTON PLU (1837—71) (Ches, Flints)
Aldersey, Aldford, Ashton, Bache, Backford (soon after 1837[34]—71), Barrow,[35] Barton, Blacon cum Crabwall (soon after 1837[34]—71), Great Boughton,

Broxton, Buerton, Burton by Tarvin, Caldecott, Capenhurst, Carden, Caughall, Chorlton by Backford, Chowley, Christleton, Churton by Aldford, Churton by Farndon, Churton Heath, Clotton Hoofield, Clutton, Coddington, Cotton Abbotts, Cotton Edmunds, Crewe, Croughton, Dodleston[36] (1837—53), Duckington (1837—53), Duddon, Dunham on the Hill, Eaton (1837—53), Eccleston (1837—53), Edge (1837—53), Edgerley, Elton, Farndon, Golborne Bellow, Golborne David, Grafton, Handley, Hapsford, Harthill, Hatton, Hockenhull, Hoole, Horton, Horton cum Peel, Huntington, Huxley, Iddinshall, Ince, Kelsall, Kings Marsh, Lower Kinnerton (1837—53), Lea by Backford, Lea Newbold, Littleton, Marlston cum Lache (1837—53), Mollington Banastre, Mollington Tarrant, Moston, Mouldsworth, Newton by Chester, Newton by Tattenhall, Picton, Poulton (1837—53), Prior's Heys (1858—71), Pulford (1837—53), Rowton, Saighton, Great Saughall (1837—53), Little Saughall (1837—53), Shotwick (1837—53), Shotwick Park (1837—53), Stanlow, Great Stanney, Little Stanney, Bruen Stapleford, Foulk Stapleford, Stoke, Stretton, Guilden Sutton, Tarvin, Tattenhall, Thornton le Moors, Tilston,

Bridge Trafford, Mickle Trafford, Wimbolds Trafford, Upton by Chester, Waverton, Wervin, Willington, Woodbank (1837—53)

BUCKLOW PLU (1895[33]—1930)

Agden, Altrincham, Ashley, Ashton upon Mersey, Aston by Budworth, Baguley, Bexton, Bollington, Bolinfee, Bowdon, Carrington, Dunham Massey, Northern Etchells, Hale, Knutsford, High Legh, Lymm, Marthall cum Warford, Mere, Millington, Mobberley, Northenden, Ollerton, Partington, Peover Inferior, Peover Superior, Pickmere, Plumley, Ringway (1900—30), Rostherne, Sale, Styal, Tabley Inferior, Tabley Superior, Tatton, Timperley, Toft, Unnamed, Warburton, Wilmslow

CHESTER INCORP FOR POOR (1762[37]—1869), PLU (1869—1930) [Ches, Flints (1871—1930)]

Bache (1871—1930), Backford (1871—1930), Blacon cum Crabwall (1871—1930), Great Boughton (1871—1930), Capenhurst (1871—1930), Caughall (1871—1930), Chester (1884—1930), Chester Castle (1869—1930), Chester Holy Trinity (1762—1884), Chester St Bridget (1762—1884), Chester St John the Baptist (1762—1884), Chester St Martin (1762—1884), Chester St Mary on the Hill (1762—1884), Chester St Michael (1762—1884), Chester St Olave (1762—1884), Chester St Peter (1762—1884), Chorlton by Backford (1871—1930), Christleton (1871—1930), Claverton (1871—1930), Croughton (1871—1930), Dodleston (1871—1930), Dunham on the Hill (1871—1930), Eaton (1871—1930), Eccleston (1871—1930), Elton (1871—1930), Hapsford (1871—1930), Hoole (1871—1930), Hoole Village (1894—1930), Ince (1871—1930), Lower Kinnerton (1871—1930), Lea by Backford (1871—1930), Littleton (1871—1930), Marlstone cum Lache (1871—1930), Mollington (1901—30), Mollington Banastre (1871—1901), Mollington Tarrant (1871—1901), Moston (1871—1930), Newton by Chester (1871—1930), Picton (1871—1930), Poulton (1871—1930), Pulford (1871—1930), Great Saughall (1871—1930), Little Saughall (1871—1930), Shotwick (1871—1930), Shotwick Park (1871—1930), Stanlow (1871—1911), Great Stanney (1871—1930), Little Stanney (1871—1930), Stoke (1871—1930), Thornton le Moors (1871—1930), Bridge Trafford (1871—1930), Mickle Trafford (1871—1930), Wimbolds Trafford (1871—1930), Upton by Chester (1871—1930), Wervin (1871—1930), Woodbank (1871—1930)

CONGLETON PLU (Ches, Staffs)

Alsager, Arclid, Betchton, Blackden, Bradwall, Brereton cum Smethwick, Buglawton, Congleton, Cotton, Cranage, Davenport, Elton, Goostrey cum Barnshaw, Hassall, Church Hulme, Hulme Walfield, Kerminacham, Church Lawton, Leese, Moreton cum Alcumlow, Moston, Newbold Astbury, Odd Rode, Radnor (1837—95), Sandbach, Smallwood, Somerford, Somerford Booths, Somerford, Swettenham, Tetton, Twemlow, Wheelock

MACCLESFIELD PLU

Adlington, Nether Alderley, Over Alderley, Alderley Edge (1894—1930), Birtles, Bollington, Bosley, Butley, Capesthorne, Chelford, Chorley, Eaton, Fallibroome, Gawsworth, Henbury cum Pexall, Hurdsfield, Kerridge (1894—1900), Kettleshulme, Lyme Handley, Macclesfield, Macclesfield Forest, Marton, Mottram St Andrew, Newton, Pott Shrigley, Poynton (1836—80), Poynton with Worth (1880—1930), Prestbury, Rainow, North Rode, Siddington, Snelson, Sutton, Taxal, Tytherington, Upton, Great Warford, Wildboarclough, Wincle, Lower Withington, Old Withington, Woodford, Worth (1836—80), Yeardsley cum Whaley

NANTWICH PLU

Acton, Alpraham, Alvaston (1837—99), Aston juxta Mondrum, Audlem, Austerson, Baddiley, Baddington, Barthomley, Basford, Batherton, Beeston (1837—92), Bickerton, Bickley (1837—53), Blakenhall, Bridgemere, Brindley, Broomhall, Buerton, Bulkeley, Burland, Bunbury, Burwardsley (1837—92), Calveley, Checkley cum Wrinehill, Cholmondeley, Cholmondeston, Chorley, Chorlton, Coole Pilate, Church Coppenhall, Monks Coppenhall, Crewe, Dodcott cum Wilkesley, Doddington, Eaton (1837—94), Edleston, Egerton, Faddiley, Hampton (1837—53), Hankelow, Haslington, Hatherton, Haughton, Henhull, Hough, Hunsterson, Hurleston, Larkton (1837—53), Lea, Leighton, Macefen (1837—53), Marbury with Quoisley (1837—53), Church Minshull, Minshull Vernon, Nantwich, Newhall, Norbury (1837—53), Peckforton, Poole, Ridley, Rope, Rushton (1837—94), Shavington cum Gresty, Sound, Spurstow, Stapeley, Stoke, Tarporley (1837—94), Tiverton (1837—92), Tilstone Fearnall (1837—92), Tushingham cum Grindley (1837—53), Utkinton (1837—94), Walgherton, Wardle, Warmingham, Weston, Wettenhall, Willaston, Wirswall (1837—53), Wistaston, Woodcott, Woolstanwood, Worleston, Wrenbury cum Frith, Wybunbury

NORTHWICH PLU

Acton, Allostock, Anderton, Barnton, Birches (1836—92), Bostock, Little Budworth, Byley, Clive, Cogshall, Comberbach, Crowton, Croxton (1836—92), Cuddington, Darnhall, Davenham, Delamere, Eaton, Eddisbury, Hartford, Hulse (1836—92), Kinderton (1894—1930), Kinderton cum Hulme (1836—94), Lach Dennis, Little Leigh, Leftwich, Lostock Gralam, Marbury, Marston, Marton, Middlewich, Minshall Vernon, Mooresbarrow cum Parme (1836—92), Moulton, Newhall (1836—92), Newton (1836—94), Northwich, Castle Northwich (1836—94), Oakmere, Occlestone (1836—92), Onston (1836—92), Low Oulton (1836—92), Over, Nether Peover, Ravenscroft (1836—92), Rudheath, Shipbrook (1836—92), Shurlach (1836—92), Sproston, Stanthorne, Stublach (1836—92), Sutton (1836—92), Unnamed (1894—1930), Unnamed (1894—1930), Wallerscoat (1836—92), Weaver (1836—92), Weavenham cum Milton, Wharton, Whatcroft, Wimboldsley, Wincham, Winnington, Witton cum Twambrooks (1836—94)

RUNCORN PLU

Acton Grange, Alvanley, Antrobus, Appleton, Aston by Sutton, Aston Grange, Bartington, Great Budworth, Clifton, Crowley, Daresbury, Dutton, Frodsham, Frodsham Lordship, Grappenhall (1836—45), Halton, Hatton, Helsby, Keckwick, Kingsley, Kingswood, Latchford (1836—45), Latchford Without (1894—1930), Manley, Moore, Newton by Daresbury, Newton by Frodsham, Norley, Norton, Preston on the Hill, Runcorn, Seven Oaks, Stockham, Stockton Heath (1897—1930), Stretton, Sutton, Thelwall (1836—45), Walton Inferior, Walton Superior, Weston, Higher Whitley, Lower Whitley

STOCKPORT PLU (Ches, Lancs)
Bosden (1877—1930), Bramhall (1837—1900), Bredbury, Brinnington (1837—1920), Cheadle (1879—1930), Cheadle Bulkley (1837—79), Cheadle Moseley (1837—79), Compstall (1897—1930), Stockport Etchells, Handforth (1877—1930), Handforth cum Bosden (1837—77), Hazel Grove and Bramhall (1900—30), Hyde, Marple, Norbury (1837—1900), Offerton (1837—1900), Reddish, Romiley, Stockport, Torkington (1837—1900), Werneth (1837—97)

TARVIN PLU (1871—1930)
Aldersey, Aldford, Ashton, Barrow, Barton, Beeston (1892—1930), Broxton, Buerton, Burton by Tarvin, Burwardsley (1892—1930), Caldecott, Carden, Chowley, Churton by Aldford, Churton by Farndon, Churton Heath, Clotton Hoofield, Clutton, Coddington, Cotton Abbotts, Cotton Edmunds, Crewe, Duddon, Eaton (1894—1930), Edgerley, Farndon, Golborne Bellow, Golborne David, Grafton, Handley, Harthill, Hatton, Hockenhull, Horton, Horton cum Peel, Huntington, Huxley, Iddinshall, Kelsall, Kings Marsh, Lea Newbold, Mouldsworth, Newton by Tattenhall, Prior's Heys, Rowton, Rushton (1894—1930), Saighton, Church Shocklach (1894—1930), Shocklach Oviatt (1894—1930), Bruen Stapleford, Foulk Stapleford, Stretton, Guilden Sutton, Tarporley (1894—1930), Tarvin, Tattenhall, Tilston, Tilstone Fearnall (1892—1930), Tiverton (1892—1930), Utkinton (1894—1930), Waverton, Willington

WIRRAL PLU
Arrowe, Barnston, Higher Bebington (1836—1922), Lower Bebington (1836—1922), Bebington and Bromborough (1922—30), Bidston cum Ford (1836—91), Birkenhead (1836—69), Brimstage, Bromborough (1894—1922), Burton, Caldy, Claughton with Grange (1836—91), Eastham, Ellesmere Port (1911—30), Frankby, Gayton, Grange, Greasby, Heswall cum Oldfield, Hoose (1836—94), Hooton, Hoylake cum West Kirby (1894—1930), Irby, West Kirby (1836—94), Landican, Ledsham, Leighton (1836—94), Liscard (1836—91), Great Melose (1836—94), Little Melose (1836—94), Moreton (1836—1928), Ness, Great Neston (1836—94), Little Neston (1836—94), Neston cum Parkgate (1894—1930), Netherpool (1836—1911),

Newton with Larton (1836—89), Noctorum (1836—91), Overpool (1836—1911), Oxton (1836—91), Pensby, Poulton cum Seacombe (1836—91), Poulton cum Spital, Prenton, Puddington, Raby, Rock Ferry (1894—98), Saughall Massie, Storeton, Great Sutton, Little Sutton, Thingwall, Childer Thornton, Thornton Hough, Thurstaston, Tranmere (1836—91), Upton by Birkenhead, Wallasey (1836—91), Whitby, Willaston, Woodchurch

In Other Poor Law Counties:

ASHTON UNDER LYNE PLU (Lancs, Ches)
Dukinfield, Godley (1837—1923), Hattersley, Hollingworth, Matley, Newton (1837—1923), Mottram, Stalybridge (1894—1930), Stayley[27] (1837—94), Tintwistle

HAWARDEN PLU (1853—1930 [Flints, Ches (until 1871)])
Claverton, Dodleston, Eaton, Eccleston, Lower Kinnerton, Marlston cum Lache, Poulton, Pulford, Great Saughall, Little Saughall, Shotwick, Shotwick Park, Woodbank

HAYFIELD PLU (Derbys, Ches)
Disley[38]

MARKET DRAYTON PLU (orig 'Drayton') [Salop, Ches (1836—95)]
Tittenley[39]

WARRINGTON PLU (Lancs, Ches)
Grappenhall (1845—1930), Latchford[40] (1845—1930), Thelwall (1845—1930)

WEM PLU (Salop, Ches [1836—66])
Whitchurch[41]

WHITCHURCH PLU (Salop, Ches [1853—1930]) [all pars below in the PLU 1853—1930 unless o'wise noted])
Agden, Bickley, Bradley, Chidlow, Chorlton, Cuddington, Duckington, Edge, Hampton, Larkton, Macefen, Malpas, Marbury with Quoisley, Newton by Malpas, Norbury, Oldcastle, Stockton, Threapwood[42] (1894—1930), Tushingham cum Grindley, Wigland, Wirswall, Wychough

WREXHAM PLU (Denbigh, Ches [1837—94])
Agden (1837—53), Bradley (1837—53), Chidlow (1837—53), Chorlton (1837—53), Cuddington (1837—53), Malpas (1837—53), Newton by Malpas (1837—53), Oldcastle (1837—53), Overton (1837—53), Church Shocklach, Shocklach Oviatt, Stockton (1837—53), Threapwood[41] (1837—53), Wigland (1837—53), Wychough (1837—53)

SANITARY DISTRICTS

ALDERLEY EGDE USD (5 Sept[43]—Apptd day 1894)
pt Bollinfee, pt Chorley, pt Fulshaw

ALSAGER USD (Jan[44]—Apptd day 1894)
Alsager

ALTRINCHAM RSD
same as PLU for Ches pars less Altrincham, Bollinfee, Bowdon (ent 1875—83, pt 1883—94), Fulshaw, Lymm, Pownall Fee, Sale

ALTRINCHAM USD
Altrincham

ASHTON UNDER LYNE RSD
same as PLU for Ches pars less Dukinfield, Godley, Hollingworth, Mottram, Neeton, Stayley

ASHTON UNDER LYNE USD (Lancs, Ches)
pt Dukinfield

HIGHER BEBINGTON USD
pt Higher Bebington

LOWER BEBINGTON USD
Lower Bebington

BIRKENHEAD RSD
  same as PLU less Birkenhead, Claughton with Grange, Liscard, Oxton, Poulton cum Seacombe, Tranmere, Wallasey

BIRKENHEAD USD (1877[20]—94)
  pt Higher Bebington, Birkenhead, Claughton with Grange, Oxton, Tranmere

BOLLINGTON USD
  pt Bollington

BOWDON USD
  Bowdon (ent 1875—83, pt 1883—94)

BREDBURY AND ROMILEY USD
  Bredbury, Romiley

BROMBOROUGH USD
  Bromborough

BUGLAWTON USD
  Buglawton

CHEADLE AND GATELEY USD (1886[45]—94)
  pt Cheadle, Stockport Etchells

CHESTER RSD
  same as PLU less pars and pts of pars in Chester USD

CHESTER USD
  pt Great Boughton (1875—84), Chester (1884—94), Chester Abbey Precincts (1875—84), Chester Holy Trinity (1875—84), Chester St Bridget (1875—84), Chester St John the Baptist (1875—84), Chester St Martin (1875—84), Chester St Mary on the Hill (1875—84), Chester St Michael (1875—84), Chester St Olave (1875—84), Chester St Oswald (1875—84), Chester St Peter (1875—84), Spital Boughton (1875—84)

CHORLEY USD (1875—5 Sept 1894[43])
  pt Bollinfee, pt Chorley, pt Fulshaw, pt Pownall Fee (1875—88)

CONGLETON RSD
  same as PLU less Buglawton, Congleton

CONGLETON USD
  Congleton

CREWE USD[21] (1877[22]—94)
  pt Church Coppenhall (1892—94), Monks Coppenhall, pt Shavington cum Gresty (1892—94), pt Wistaston (1892—94)

DUKINFIELD USD
  pt Dukinfield

HAWARDEN RSD
  same as PLU for Ches pars

HAYFIELD RSD
  same as PLU for the Ches par

HOOLE USD
  pt Hoole

HYDE USD (1881[25]—94 [Ches, Lancs (1881—94)])
  Godley (1881—94), Hyde, Newton (1881—94), pt Werneth (1881—94)

WEST KIRBY AND HOYLAKE USD (1891[46]—94)
  pt Grange, Hoose, West Kirby, Great Melose, Little Melose

LYMM USD
  Lymm

MACCLESFIELD RSD
  same as PLU less pt Bollington, Cheadle (pt 1879—86, ent 1886—94), pt Cheadle Bukleley (1875—79), pt Cheadle Moseley (1875—79), pt Chorley, pt Hurdsfield, Macclesfield, pt Sutton, Yeardsley cum Whaley

MACCLESFIELD USD
  pt Hurdsfield, Macclesfield, pt Sutton

MARPLE USD
  Marple

MIDDLEWICH USD[47]
  pt Byley (1893—94), pt Kinderton with Hulme (enlarged pt 1893—94), Middlewich, pt Newton (enlarged pt 1893—94)

MOSSLEY USD (*Lancs*, Ches [1875—85], *Yorks W Riding* [1885—94])
  pt Ashton under Lyne (Lancs), pt Saddleworth (Yorks W Riding, 1885—94), pt Staley,[27] pt Tintwwistle

NANTWICH RSD
  same as PLU less pt Church Coppenhall (1892—94), Monks Coppenhall, Eaton, Nantwich, Rushton, pt Shavington cum Gresty (1892—94), Tarporley, Utkinton, pt Wistaston (1892—94)

NANTWICH USD
  Nantwich

NESTON AND PARKGATE USD
  Leighton, Great Neston, Little Neston

NEW MILLS USD (Derbys, Ches)
  Disley[38]

NORTHWICH USD
  same as PLU less pt Byley (1893—94), pt Hartford, pt Kinderton with Hulme (enlarged pt 1893—94), pt Leftwich, Middlewich, pt Newton (enlarged pt 1893—94), Northwich, Castle Northwich, Over, Sandbach, Wharton, pt Winnington, Witton cum Twambrooks

NORTHWICH USD
  pt Hartford, pt Leftwich, Northwich, Castle Northwich, Wharton, pt Winnington, Witton cum Twanbrooks

RUNCORN RSD
  same as PLU less pt Halton (1875—83), Runcorn

RUNCORN USD
  pt Halton (1875—83), Runcorn

SALE USD
  Sale

SANDBACH USD
  Sandbach

STALYBRIDGE USD (*Lancs*, Ches)
  pt Ashton under Lyne (Lancs), pt Dukinfield, pt Staley[27] (1875—94 [enlarged pt 1881—94])

STAYLEY USD (1875—81[29])
  pt Stayley[27]

STOCKPORT RSD
  same as PLU for Ches pars less pt Brinnington, Bredbury, pt Cheadle (1886—94), Stockport Etchells (1886—94), Hyde, Marple, Romiley, Stockport, pt Werneth

STOCKPORT USD (Ches, Lancs)
  pt Brinnington, pt Cheadle, Stockport

TARPORLEY USD
  Eaton, Rushton, Tarporley, Utkinton

TARVIN RSD
  same as PLU less the pars in Chester USD and less Eaton, Rushton, Tarporley, Utkinton

WALLASEY USD
  Liscard, Poulton cum Seacombe, Wallasey

WARRINGTON RSD
  same as PLU for Ches pars

WARRINGTON USD (Lancs, Ches)
  pt Chelwall (1875—84), pt Thelwall
WILMSLOW USD
  pt Bollinfee (1888—94), pt Fulshaw, pt Pownall Fee
  (1875—88)
WINSFORD USD
  Over, Wharton
WIRRAL RSD
  same as PLU less Higher Bebington (pt 1875—77, ent
  1877—94), Lower Bebington, Birkenhead (1877—91),

Bromborough, Claughton with Grange (1877—91), pt
Grange (1891—94), Hoose (1891—94), West Kirby
(1891—94), Leighton, Liscard (1875—91), Great
Meolse (1891—94), Little Meolse (1891—94), Great
Neston, Little Neston, Oxton (1877—91), Poulton cum
Seacombe (1875—91), Tranmere (1877—91), Wallasey
(1875—91)
YEARDSLEY CUM WHALEY USD
  Yeardsley cum Whaley

ADMINISTRATIVE COUNTY

For MBs and the associated CB see BOROUGHS

ALDERLEY EDGE UD
  Alderley Edge, Bollinfee (1894—1936)
ALSAGER UD
  Alsager
ALTRINCHAM RD (1894—95[33])
  Agden, Ashley, Ashton upon Mersey, Aston by
  Budworth, Baguley, Bexton, Bollington, Carrington,
  Dunham Massey, Northern Etchells, Hale, Knutsford
  Nether, Knutsford Over, High Legh, Marthall cum
  Warford, Mere, Millington, Mobberley, Northenden,
  Ollerton, Partington, Peover Inferior, Peover Superior,
  Pickmere, Plumley, Rostherne, Styal, Tabley Inferior,
  Tabley Superior, Tatton, Timperley, Toft, Unnamed,
  Warburton
ALTRINCHAM UD (1894—1937[18])
  Altrincham
ASHTON UPON MERSEY UD (1895[48]—1930[49])
  Ashton upon Mersey
BEBINGTON UD (1933[3]—37[18])
  Bebington and Bromborough, Brimstage, Eastham,
  Poulton cum Spital, Raby, Storeton, Thornton Hough
HIGHER BEBINGTON UD (1894—1922[50])
  Higher Bebington
LOWER BEBINGTON UD (1894—1922[50])
  Lower Bebington
BEBINGTON AND BROMBOROUGH UD
  (1922[50]—33[3])
  Bebington and Bromborough
BOLLINGTON UD
  Bollington
BOWDON UD
  Bowdon
BREDBURY AND ROMILEY UD
  Bredbury (1894—1936), Bredbury and Romiley
  (1936—74), Romiley (1894—1936)
BROMBOROUGH UD (1894—1933[50])
  Bromborough
BUCKLOW RD (1895[33]—1974)
  Agden, Ashley, Aston by Budworth, Baguley (1894—
  1931), Bexton, Bollington, Carrington, Dunham
  Massey, Northern Etchells (1895—1931), Hale (1895—
  1900), High Legh, Marthall (1951—74), Marthall cum
  Warford (1895—1951), Mere, Millington, Mobberley,
  Northenden (1895—1931), Ollerton, Partington,
  Peover Inferior, Peover Superior, Pickmere, Plumley,
  Ringway (1900—74), Rostherne, Styal (1895—1936),
  Tabley Inferior, Tabley Superior, Tatton, Timperley

(1895—1936), Toft, Unnamed (1895—1936),
Warburton, Little Warford (1951—74)
BUGLAWTON UD (1894—1936[51])
  Buglawton
CHEADLE AND GATLEY UD
  Cheadle (1894—1930), Cheadle and Gateley (1930—
  74), Stockport Etchells (1894—1930)
CHESTER RD
  Aldford (1936—74), Bache, Backford, Barrow (1936—
  74), Blacon cum Crabwall (1894—1936), Great
  Boughton, Buerton (1936—74), Capenhurst, Caughall,
  Chester Castle, Chorlton by Backford, Christleton,
  Churton Heath (1936—74), Claverton, Croughton,
  Dodleston, Dunham on the Hill, Eaton, Eccleston,
  Elton, Hapsford, Hoole Village, Huntington (1936—
  74), Ince (1894—1933), Lower Kinnerton, Lea by
  Backford, Lea Newbold (1936—74), Ledsham (1933—
  74), Littleton, Marlston cum Lache, Mollington
  (1901—74), Mollington Banastre (1894—1901), Mollington Tarrant (1894—1901), Moston, Newton by
  Chester (1894—1936), Picton, Poulton, Puddington
  (1933—74), Pulford, Rowton (1936—74), Saighton
  (1936—74), Saughall (1948—74), Great Saughall
  (1894—1948), Little Saughall (1894—1948), Shotwick,
  Shotwick Park, Stanlow (1894—1911), Great Stanney
  (1894—1910), Little Stanney, Stoke, Guilden Sutton
  (1936—74), Thornton le Moors, Bridge Trafford,
  Mickle Trafford, Wimbolds Trafford, Upton by Chester, Wervin, Woodbank
COMPSTALL UD (1902[52]—36[6])
  Compstall
CONGLETON RD
  Arclid, Betchton, Blackden (1894—1936), Bradwall,
  Brereton (1936—74), Brereton cum Smethwick (1894—
  1936), Cotton (1894—1936), Cranage, Davenport
  (1894—1936), Elton (1894—1970), Goostrey (1936—
  74), Goostrey cum Barnshaw (1894—1936), Hassall,
  Church Hulme, Hulme Walfield, Kermincham (1894—
  1936), Church Lawton, Leese (1894—1936), Moreton
  cum Alcumlow, Moston (1894—1936), Moston
  (1970—74), Newbold Astbury, Odd Rode, Radnor
  (1894—95), Smallwood, Somerford, Somerford
  Booths, Swettenham, Tetton (1894—1970), Twemlow,
  Wheelock (1894—1936)
DISLEY RD
  Disley

DUKINFIELD UD (1894—99[23])
  Dukinfield (pt 1894—98, ent 1898—99)
ELLESMERE PORT UD (1933[3]—55[24])
  Ellesmere Port, Hooton (1933—50), Ince (1933—50), Great Stanney (1933—50), Great Sutton (1933—50), Little Sutton (1933—50), Childer Thornton (1933—50)
ELLESMERE PORT AND WHITBY UD (1902[53]—33[3])
  Ellesmere Port (1911—33), Netherpool (1910—11), Overpool (1910—11), Great Stanney (1910—33), Stanlow (1910—11), Whitby (1902—11)
HALE UD (1900[54]—74)
  Hale
HANDFORTH UD (1904[55]—36[51])
  Handforth
HAZEL GROVE AND BRAMHALL UD (1900[56]—74)
  Hazel Grove and Bramhall
HOLLINGWORTH UD (1894—1936[51])
  Hollingworth
HOOLE UD (1894—1954[7])
  Hoole
HOYLAKE UD (1933[3]—74)
  Caldy, Frankby, Grange, Greasby, Hoylake cum West Kirby
HOYLAKE AND WEST KIRBY UD (1897[57]—1933[3])
  Hoylake cum West Kirby
WEST KIRBY AND HOYLAKE UD (1894—97[57])
  Hoylake cum West Kirby
KNUTSFORD UD (1895[58]—1974)
  Knutsford
LONGENDALE UD (1936[51]—74)
  Longendale
LYMM UD
  Lymm
MACCLESFIELD RD
  Adlington, Nether Alderley, Over Alderley, Birtles (1894—1936), Bosley, Butley (1894—1936), Capesthorne (1894—1936), Chelford, Chorley, Eaton, Fallibroome (1894—1936), Gawsworth, Henbury (1936—74), Henbury cum Pexall (1894—1936), Hurdsfield, Kerridge (1894—1900), Kettleshulme, Lyme Handley, Macclesfield Forest, Marton, Mottram St Andrew, Newton (1894—1936), Pott Shrigley, Poynton with Worth, Prestbury, Rainow, North Rode, Siddington, Snelson, Sutton, Taxal (1894—1936), Tytherington (1894—1936), Upton (1894—1936), Great Warford, Wilboarclough, Wincle, Withington (1936—74), Lower Withington (1894—1936), Old Withington (1894—1936), Woodford (1894—1939)
MALPAS RD (1894—1936[51])
  Agden, Bickley, Bradley, Chidlow, Chorlton, Cuddington, Duckington, Edge, Hampton, Larkton, Macefen, Malpas, Marbury with Quoisley, Newton by Malpas, Norbury, Oldcastle, Overton, Stockton, Threapwood (pt 1894—96, ent 1896—1936), Tushingham cum Grindley, Wigland, Wirswall, Wychough
MARPLE UD
  Marple
MIDDLEWICH UD
  Middlewich
MOTTRAM IN LONGENDALE UD (1894—1936[51])
  Mottram

NANTWICH RD
  Acton, Alpraham, Alvaston (1894—99), Aston juxta Mondrum, Audlem, Austerson, Baddiley, Baddington, Barthomley, Basford, Batherton, Bickerton, Blakenhall, Bridgemere, Brindley, Broomhall, Buerton, Bulkeley, Bunbury, Burland, Calveley, Checkley cum Wrinehill, Choldmondeley, Cholmondeston, Chorley, Chorlton, Coole Pilate, Church Coppenhall (1894—1936), Crewe, Dodcott cum Wilkesley, Doddington, Edleston, Egerton, Faddiley, Hankelow, Haslington, Hatherton, Haughton, Henhull, Hough, Hunsterson, Hurleston, Lea, Leighton, Marbury with Quoisley (1936—74), Church Minshull, Minshull Vernon, Newhall, Norbury (1936—74), Peckforton, Poole, Ridley, Rope, Shavington cum Gresty, Sound, Spurstow, Stapeley, Stoke, Walgherton, Wardle, Warmingham, Weston, Wettenhall, Willaston, Wirswall (1936—74), Wistaston, Woodcott, Woolstanwood, Worleston, Wrenbury cum Frith, Wybunbury
NANTWICH UD
  Nantwich
NESTON UD (1933[3]—74)
  Burton, Ness, Neston cum Parkgate, Willaston
NESTON AND PARKGATE UD (1894—1933[3])
  Neston cum Parkgate
NORTHWICH RD
  Acton (1894—1967), Acton Bridge (1967—74), Allostock, Anderton, Barnton, Bostock, Little Budworth, Byley, Clive (1894—1936), Cogshall (1894—1936), Comberbach, Crowton, Cuddington, Darnhall, Davenham, Delamere, Eaton (1894—1936), Eddisbury (1894—1936), Hartford, Kinderton (1894—1936), Lach Dennis, Leftwich (1894—1936), Little Leigh, Lostock Gralam, Marbury, Marston, Marton, Moulton, Oakmere, Nether Peover, Rudheath, Rushton (1936—74), Sproston, Stanthorne, Tarporley (1936—74), Unnamed (1894—1936), Utkinton (1936—74), Weaverham cum Milton, Whatcroft, Wimboldsley, Wincham, Winnington (1894—1936)
NORTHWICH UD
  Northwich
RUNCORN RD
  Acton Grange (1894—1936), Alvanley, Antrobus, Appleton, Aston (1936—74), Aston by Sutton (1894—1936), Aston Grange (1894—1936), Bartington (1894—1936), Great Budworth, Clifton (1894—1936), Crowley (1894—1936), Daresbury, Dutton, Frodsham, Frodsham Lordship (1894—1936), Grappenhall, Halton (1894—1967), Hatton, Helsby, Keckwick (1894—1936), Kingsley, Kingswood (1894—1936), Land Common to Frodsham and Frodsham Lordship (1894—1936), Latchford Without (1894—1936), Manley, Moore, Newton by Daresbury (1894—1936), Newton by Frodsham (1894—1936), Norley, Norton (1894—1967), Preston Brook (1936—74), Preston on the Hill (1894—1936), Seven Oaks (1894—1936), Stockham (1894—1936), Stockton Heath (1897—1974), Stretton, Sutton, Thelwall (1894—1936), Walton (1936—74), Walton Inferior (1894—1936), Walton Superior (1894—1936), Weston (1894—1936), Whitley (1936—74), Higher Whitley (1894—1936), Lower Whitley (1894—1936)

RUNCORN UD
  Runcorn
SALE UD (1894—1935[28])
  Ashton upon Mersey (1930—35), Sale
SANDBACH UD
  Sandbach
STOCKPORT RD (1894—1904[55])
  Bosden (1894—1900), Bramhall (1894—1900), Brinnington (1894—1902), Compstall (1897—1902), Handforth, Norbury (1894—1900), Offerton (1894—1900), Torkington (1894—1900), Werneth (1894—97)
TARPORLEY UD (1894—1936[51])
  Eaton, Rushton, Tarporley, Utkinton
TARVIN RD
  Agden (1936—74), Aldersey, Aldford (1894—1936), Ashton, Barrow (1894—1936), Barton, Beeston, Bickley (1936—74), Bradley (1936—74), Broxton, Buerton (1894—1936), Burton by Tarvin, Burwardsley, Caldecott, Carden, Chidlow (1936—74), Chorlton (1936—74), Chowley, Churton by Aldford, Churton by Farndon, Churton Heath (1894—1936), Clotton Hoofield, Clutton, Coddington, Cotton Abbotts, Cotton Edmunds, Crewe, Cuddington (1936—74), Duckington (1936—74), Duddon, Edge (1936—74), Edgerley, Farndon, Golborne Bellow, Golborne David, Grafton, Hampton (1936—74), Handley, Harthill, Hatton, Hockenhull, Horton, Horton cum Peel, Huntington (1894—1936), Huxley, Iddinshall, Kelsall, Kings Marsh, Larkton (1936—74), Lea Newbold, Macefen (1936—74), Malpas (1936—74), Mouldsworth, Newton by Malpas (1936—74), Newton by Tattenhall, Oldcastle (1936—74), Overton (1936—74), Prior's Heys, Rowton (1894—1936), Saighton (1894—1936), Church Shocklach, Shocklach Oviatt,

Bruen Stapleford, Foulk Stapleford, Stockton (1936—74), Stretton, Guilden Sutton (1894—1936), Tarvin, Tattenhall, Threapwood (1936—74), Tilston, Tilstone Fearnall, Tiverton, Tushingham cum Grindley (1936—74), Waverton, Wigland (1936—74), Willington, Wychough (1936—74)
TINTWISTLE RD
  Hattersley (1894—1936), Matley (1894—1936), Tintwistle
WALLASEY UD (1894—1910[31])
  Liscard, Poulton cum Seacombe, Wallasey
WILMSLOW UD
  Wilmslow
WINSFORD UD
  Over (1894—1936), Unnamed (1894—1936), Wharton (1894—1936), Winsford (1936—74)
WIRRAL RD (1894—1933)
  Arrowe, Barnston, Bidston cum Ford, Brimstage, Burton, Caldy, Eastham, Frankby, Gayton, Grange, Greasby, Heswall cum Oldfield, Hooton, Irby, Landican (1894—1928), Ledsham, Moreton (1894—1928), Ness, Netherpool (1894—1910), Noctorum (1894—1933), Overpool (1894—1910), Pensby, Poulton cum Spital, Prenton (1894—1928), Puddington, Raby, Saughall Massie, Storeton, Great Sutton, Little Sutton, Thingwall (1894—1928), Childer Thornton, Thornton Hough, Thurstaston, Upton by Birkhead, Whitby (1894—1902), Willaston, Woodchurch
WIRRAL UD
  Barnston, Gayton, Heswall cum Oldfield, Irby, Pensby, Thurstaston
YEARDSLEY CUM WHALEY UD (1894—1936[59])
  Yeardsley cum Whaley

NON-METROPOLITAN COUNTY

As constituted 1 Apr 1974, defined in terms of Adm Co units as of 31 Mar.

CHESTER DIST
  CB (assoc with Ches): Chester CB
  from Ches: Chester RD, Tarvin RD
CONGLETON DIST
  Alsager UD, Congleton MB, Congleton RD, Middlewich UD, Sandbach UD
CREWE AND NANTWICH DIST
  Crewe MB, Nantwich RD, Nantwich UD
ELLESMERE PORT DIST
  Ellesmere Port MB, Neston UD
HALTON DIST
  from Ches: pt Runcorn RD (Daresbury, Moore, Preston Brook), Runcorn UD
  from Lancs: pt Whiston RD (Hale), Widnes MB
MACCLESFIELD DIST
  Alderley Edge UD, Bollington UD, pt Bucklow RD (Agden, Ashley, Aston by Budworth, Bexton, Bollington, High Legh, Marthall, Mere, Millington,

Mobberley, Ollerton, Peover Inferior, Peover Superior, Pickmere, Plumley, Rostherne, Tabley Inferior, Tabley Superior, Tatton, Toft, Little Warford), Disley RD, Knutsford UD, Macclesfield MB, Macclesfield RD, Wilmslow UD
VALE ROYAL DIST
  Northwich RD, Northwich UD, pt Runcorn RD (the pars neither in Halton Dist nor in Warrington Dist), Winsford UD
WARRINGTON DIST
  CB (assoc with Lancs): Warrington
  from Ches: Lymm UD, pt Runcorn RD (Appleton, Grappenhall, Harton, Stockton Heath, Stretton, Walton)
  from Lancs: pt Golborne UD (wards of Culcheth, Newchurch), Warrington RD, pt Whiston RD (pt Bold[60], Hale)

CLEVELAND NON-METROPOLITAN COUNTY

As constituted 1 Apr 1974, defined in terms of Adm Co units as of 31 Mar.

HARTLEPOOL DIST
CB (assoc with Durham): Hartlepool CB
from Durham: pt Stockton RD (Brierton, Claxton, Dalton Piercy, Elwick, Elwick Hall, Greatham, Hart, Newton Bewley)
LANGBAURGH DIST
CB (assoc with Yorks N Riding): pt Teesside CB (wards of Coatham, Eston Grange, Kirkleatham, Ormesby, Redcar, South Bank)
from Yorks N Riding: Guisborough UD, Loftus UD, Saltburn and Marske by the Sea UD, Skelton and Brotton UD
MIDDLESBROUGH DIST
CBs (assoc with Yorks N Riding): pt Teesside CB (the area neither in Langbaurgh Dist nor in Stockton-on-Tees Dist)
from Yorks N Riding: pt Stokesley RD (Nunthorpe)
STOCKTON-ON-TEES DIST
CB (assoc with Yorks N Riding): pt Teesside CB (wards of Billingham East, Billingham West, Grangefield, Hartburn, Mile House, North End, Norton, Stockton South, Thornaby East, Thornaby West)
from Durham: pt Stockton RD (the pars not in Hartlepool Dist)
from Yorks N Riding: pt Stokesley RD (Hilton, Ingleby Barwick, Castle Levington, Kirk Levington, Maltby, Yarm)

CUMBERLAND

ALTERATIONS IN COUNTY BOUNDARIES

As noted by year below, Cumb pars gained territory from or lost it to pars in adjoining cos or county boroughs, or were entirely transferred to them. Details of these alterations are noted in Part I of the *Guide* under Cumberland.

ANCIENT COUNTY (until 1889: Wds, Bors, MBs, PLUs, RSDs, USDs)
No bdry alt

ADMINISTRATIVE COUNTY (1899—1974: Wds,[1] PLUs, MBs, RDs, UDs with assoc CB of Carlisle CB [1914—74])
1914 Carlisle. *1935* Millom Without, Ulpha. *1951*

Beaumont, Cummersdale, Kingmoor, St Cuthbert Without, Stanwix, Wetheral.

(Cumb was abol 1974 to help constitute Cumbria Non-Metrop Co).

ASSOCIATED COUNTY BOROUGH

CARLISLE CB (1914—74)
Cr 1914 when Carlisle MB constituted a CB.[2] Bdry: 1951.[3]

WARDS [1]

ALLERDALE ABOVE DERWENT WD
Above Derwent (from 1866), Arlecdon, Beckermet St Bridget, Beckermet St John, Birker and Austhwaite (from 1866), Blindbothel (from 1866), Bootle, Borrowdale (from 1866), Brackenthwaite (from 1866), Brigham,[4] Buttermere (from 1866), Cleator, Great Clifton (from 1866), Little Clifton (from 1866), Cloffocks[4] (from 1858), Cockermouth (from 1866), Corney, pt Crosthwaite (until 1866), Dean, Distington, Drigg and Carleton, Eaglesfield (from 1866), Egremont,[4] Embleton (from 1866), Ennerdale and Kinniside (from 1866), Eskdale and Wasdale (from 1866), Gosforth, Greysouthern (from 1866), Haile, Harrington, Hensingham (from 1866), Irton, Low Keekle (1858—81), Lamplugh, Lorton, Loweswater, Lowside Quarter (from 1866), Millom, Moresby, Mosser (from 1866), Muncaster, Parton (from 1866), Ponsonby, Preston Quarter (from 1866), Rottington (from 1866), St Bees, Salter and Eskett (from 1858), Sandwith (from 1866), Setmurthy (from 1866), Stainburn (from 1866), Ulpha (from 1866), Waberthwaite, Nether Wasdale (from 1866), Weddicar (from 1866), Whicham, Whinfell (from 1866), Whitbeck, Whitehaven (from 1866), Winscales (from 1866), Workington,[4] Wythop (from 1866)

ALLERDALE BELOW DERWENT WD
Allhallows, Aspatria (until 1866), Aspatria and Brayton (from 1866), Bassenthwaite, Bewaldeth and Snittlegarth (from 1866), Blennerhasset and Kirkland (from 1866), Blindcrake Isel and Redmaine (from 1866), Bolton (until 1866), Bolton High (1866—87), Bolton Low (1866—87), Boltons (from 1887), Bothel and Threapland (from 1866), Bridekirk, Briery Cottages (from 1858), Bromfield (pt until 1866, ent from 1866), Great Broughton (from 1866), Little Broughton (from 1866), Caldbeck, Camerton, Castlerigg St John's and Wythburn (from 1866), Crosscanonby, pt Crosthwaite (until 1866), Dearham, Dovenby (from 1866), Ellenborough and Ewanrigg (from 1866), Flimby, Gilcrux, Hayton and Mealo (from 1866), Holme Abbey (from 1866), Holme Low (from 1866), Holme Cultram (until 1866), Holme East Waver (from 1866), Holme St Cuthbert (from 1866), Ireby (until 1866), High Ireby (from 1866), Low Ireby (from 1866), Isel (until 1866), Isel Old Park (from 1866), Keswick (from 1866), Langrigg and Mealrigg (from 1866), Mosedale (from 1866), West Newton and Allonby (from 1866), Oughterside and Allerby (from 1866), Papcastle (from 1866), Plumbland, Ribton (from 1866), Seaton (from 1866), Skiddaw (from 1858), Sunderland (from 1866), Tallentire (from 1866), Torpenhow (until 1866), Torpenhow and Whitrigg (from 1866), Uldale, Underskiddaw (from 1866), Westward

CUMBERLAND WD
Aikton, Beaumont, Blencogo (from 1866), pt Bromfield (until 1866), Bowness, Burgh by Sands, Caldewgate[4] (from 1866), pt Carlisle St Mary[4] (until 1866), Cummersdale[4] (from 1866), Dalston, Dundraw (from 1866), Grinsdale, Kirkandrews upon Eden, Kirkbampton, Kirkbride, Orton, Oulton (from 1866), Rickergate[4] (from 1866), Rockcliffe, pt St Cuthbert Without[4] (from 1866), Sebergham, pt Stanwix,[4] Thursby, pt Warwick, Waverton (from 1866), pt Wetheral, Wigton (until 1887), Wigton cum Woodside (from 1887), Woodside Quarter (1866—87), Wreay (from 1866)

ESKDALE WD
Arthuret, Askerton (from 1866), Bellbank (from 1866), Bewcastle, Brampton, Burtholme (from 1866),

Carlatton (from 1858), Castle Carrock, Crosby upon Eden, Cumrew, Cumwhitton, Nether Denton, Upper Denton, Farlam, Geltsdale (from 1858), Hethersgill (from 1866), Irthington, Kingmoor (from 1858), Kingwater (from 1866), Kirkandrews Middle (from 1866), Kirkandrews Moat (from 1866), Kirkandrews Nether (from 1866), Kirkandrews upon Esk (until 1866), Kirklinton (until 1866), Kirklington Middle (from 1866), Lanercost (until 1866), Midgeholme (from 1858), Nichol Forest (from 1866), Scaleby, Solport (from 1866), pt Stanwix,[4] Stapleton, Trough (from 1866), Walton, pt Warwick, Waterhead (from 1866), Westlinton (from 1866), pt Wetheral

LEATH WD

Addingham (until 1866), Ainstable, Alston with Garragill, Berrier and Murrah (from 1866), Bowscale (from 1866), pt Carlisle St Mary[4] (until 1866), Castle Sowerby, Catterlen (from 1866), Croglin, Culgaith (from 1866), Dacre, Edenhall, Gamblesby (from 1866), Glassonby (from 1866), Greystoke, Hesket in the Forest, Hunsonby and Winskill (from 1866), Hutton in the Forest, Hutton John (from 1866), Hutton Roof (from 1866), Hutton Soil (from 1866), Kirkland (until 1866), Kirkland and Blencarn (from 1866), Kirkoswald, Langwathby, Lazonby, Matterdale (from 1866), Melmerby, Middlesceugh and Braithwaite (from 1866), Mungrisdale (from 1866), Newton Reigny, Ousby, Penrith,[4] Plumpton Wall (from 1866), Renwick, Great Salkeld, Little Salkeld (from 1866), Skelton, Skirwith (from 1866), Staffield (from 1866), Threlkeld (from 1866), Watermillock (from 1866)

BOROUGHS

Units with some degree of burghal character[5] are denominated 'Bor'. Those which did not sustain that status until the 19th cent are in italics. MBs were established by the Municipal Corporations Act, 1835,[6] or by later charter.

CARLISLE BOR/MB[7] (1835—1914), CB (1914[2]—74)
Botchergate (1894—1904), Caldewgate (pt 1835—94, ent 1894—1904), Carlisle (1904—74), pt Carlisle St Mary (until 1866), pt Carlisle St Cuthbert (until 1866), pt Cummersdale (1887—94), Eaglesfield Abbey (until 1904), Rickergate (1835—1904), St Mary Within (1866—1904), pt St Cuthbert Without (1866—94), pt Stanwix (1887—94)

COCKERMOUTH BOR
pt Brigham

EGREMONT BOR
Egremont

GREYSTOKE BOR
pt Greystoke

KESWICK BOR
pt Crosthwaite

NEWTON ARLOSH BOR (from 1305[8]; sometimes 'Kirkby Johannis')
pt Holme Cultram

PENRITH BOR
Penrith

SKINBURNESS BOR (1301—05[8])
pt Holme Cultram

WAVERMOUTH BOR (1300—01[8])
pt Holme Cultram

WHITEHAVEN MB (1894[9]—1974)
Preston Quarter (1894—96), Whitehaven

WORKINGTON MB (1883[10]—1974)
Cloffocks (1883—1934), Harrington (1934—74), Workington (pt 1883—94, ent 1894—1974)

POOR LAW UNIONS

In Cumb Poor Law County:[11]

ALSTON WITH GARRIGILL PLU
Alston with Garrigill

BOOTLE PLU
Birker and Austhwaite, Bootle, Corney, Drigg and Carleton, Eskdale and Wasdale, Irton, Millom, Millom Rural (1894—1930), Muncaster, Seascale (1901—30), Ulpha, Waberthwaite, Whicham, Whitbeck

BRAMPTON PLU
Askerton, Brampton, Burtholme, Carlatton (1861—1930), Castle Carrock, Cumrew, Cumwhitton, Nether Denton, Upper Denton, Farlam, Geltsdale (1861—1930), Irthington, Kingwater, Midgeholme (1861—1930), Walton, Waterhead

CARLISLE PLU
Beaumont, Belle Vue (1894—1912), Botchergate (1894—1904), Burgh by Sands, Caldewgate (1838—1904), Carlisle (1904—30), Crosby upon Eden, Cummersdale, Dalston, Eaglesfield Abbey (1862—1904), Grinsdale, Kingmoor, Kirkandrews upon Eden, Orton, Rickergate, Rockcliffe, St Cuthbert Within (1838—1904), St Cuthbert Without, St Mary Within (1838—1904), Stanwix, Warwick, Wetheral, Wreay

COCKERMOUTH PLU
Above Derwent (soon after 1838[12]—1930), Bassenthwaite, Bewaldeth and Snittlegarth, Blindbothel, Blindcrake Isel and Redmaine, Bothel and Threapland, Borrowdale, Brackenthwaite, Bridekirk, Briery Cottages (1858—1930), Brigham, Broughton (1898—1930), Great Broughton (1838—98), Little Broughton (1838—98), Broughton Moor (1898—1930), Buttermere, Camerton, Castlerigg St John's and Withyburn (soon after 1838[12]—1930), Great Clifton, Little Clifton, Cloffocks (1858—1930), Cockermouth, Crosscanonby (soon after 1838[12]—1930), Dean, Dearham, Dovenby, Eaglesfield, Ellenborough and Ewanrigg (1838—1928), Embleton, Flimby, Gilcrux, Greysouthern, Isel Old Park, Keswick, Lorton, Low-

eswater, Maryport (1928—30), Mosser, Netherall (1894—1928), Oughterside and Allenby, Papcastle, Plumbland, Ribton, Seaton, Setmurthy, Skiddaw (1862—1930), Stainburn, Sunderland, Tallentire, Underskiddaw, Whinfell, Winscales, Workington, Workington Rural (1894—1930), Wythop

LONGTOWN PLU

Arthuret, Bellbank, Bewcastle, Hethersgill, Kirkandrews Middle, Kirkandrews Moat, Kirkandrews Nether, Kirklington Middle, Nichol Forest, Scaleby, Solport, Stapleton, Trough, Westlinton

PENRITH PLU

Ainstable, Berrier and Murrah, Bowscale, Castle Sowerby, Catterlen, Croglin, Culgaith, Dacre, Edenhall, Gamblesby, Glassonby, Greystoke, Hesket in the Forest, Hunsonby and Winskill, Hutton in the Forest, Hutton John, Hutton Roof, Hutton Soil, Kirkland and Blencarn, Kirkoswald, Langwathby, Lazonby, Matterdale, Melmerby, Middlesceugh and Braithwaite, Mosedale, Mungrisdale, Newton Reigny, Ousby, Penrith, Plumpton Wall, Renwick, Great Salkeld, Little Salkeld, Skelton, Skirwith, Staffield, Threlkeld, Watermillock

WHITEHAVEN PLU

Arlecdon, Beckermet St Bridget, Beckermet St John, Cleator, Distington, Egremont, Ennerdale and Kinniside, Gosforth, Haile, Harrington, Hensingham, Low Keekle (1873—81), Lamplugh, Lowside Quarter, Moresby, Parton, Ponsonby, Preston Quarter (1838—96), Preston Quarter (1896—1930), Preston Quarter Rural (1894—96), Rottington, St Bees, Salter and Eskett (1861—1930), Sandwith, Seascale (1897—1901), Nether Wasdale, Weddicar, Whitehaven

WIGTON PLU

Aikton, Allhallows, Allonby (1894—1930), Aspatria and Brayton, Blencogo, Blennerhassett and Kirkland, Bolton High (1837—87), Bolton Low (1837—87), Boltons (1887—1930), Bowness (soon after 1837[12]—1930), Bromfield, Caldebeck, Dundraw, Hayton and Mealo, Holme Abbey, Holme East Waver, Holme Low, Holme St Cuthbert, High Ireby, Low Ireby, Kirkbampton (soon after 1837[12]—1930), Kirkbride, Langrigg and Mealrigg, West Newton and Allonby (1837—94), Oulton, Sebergham, Thursby, Torpenhow and Whitrigg, Uldale, Waverton, Westnewton (1894—1930), Westward, Wigton (1837—87), Wigton (1894—1930), Wigton cum Woodside (1887—94), Woodside (1894—1930), Woodside Quarter (1837—87)

SANITARY DISTRICTS

ALSTON WITH GARRIGILL RSD
same as PLU

ARLECDON AND FRIZINGTON USD (1882[13]—94)
pt Arlecdon

ASPATRIA USD (1892[14]—94)
Aspatria and Brayton

BOOTLE RSD
same as PLU less pt Millom

BRAMPTON USD
same as PLU

CARLISLE RSD
same as PLU less pars and pts of pars in Carlisle USD

CARLISLE USD[7]
Caldewgate, pt Cummersdale (1887—94), Eaglesfield Abbey, Rickergate, St Cuthbert Within, pt St Cuthbert Without, St Mary Within, pt Stanwix (1887—94)

CLEATOR MOOR USD
Cleator

COCKERMOUTH RSD
same as PLU less pt Castlerigg St John's and Wythburn, Cloffocks (1882—94), Cockermouth, pt Crosscanonby, pt Ellenborough and Ewanrigg, Keswick, pt Workington

COCKERMOUTH USD
Cockermouth

EGREMONT USD[15]
pt Beckermet St John (1890—94), Egremont

HARRINGTON USD (1891[16]—94)
Harrington

HOLME CULTRAM USD
Holme Abbey, Holme East Waver, Holme Low, Holme St Cuthbert, Skinburness Marsh

KESWICK USD
pt Castlerigg St John's and Wythburn, Keswick

LONGTOWN RSD
same as PLU

MARYPORT USD
pt Crosscanonby, pt Ellenborough and Ewanrigg

MILLOM USD
pt Millom

PENRITH RSD
same as PLU less Penrith

PENRITH USD
Penrith

WHITEHAVEN RSD
same as PLU less pt Arlecdon (1882—94), pt Beckermet St John (1890—94), Cleator, Egremont, Harrington (1891—94), pt Preston Quarter, Whitehaven

WHITEHAVEN USD
pt Preston Quarter, Whitehaven

WIGTON RSD
same as PLU less Aspatria and Brayton (1892—94), Holme Abbey, Holme East Waver, Holme Low, Holme St Cuthbert, Skinburness Marsh, pt Wigton (1875—87), pt Wigton cum Woodside (1887—94), pt Woodside Quarter (1875—87)

WIGTON USD
pt Wigton (1875—87), pt Wigton cum Woodside (1887—94), pt Woodside Quarter (1875—87)

WORKINGTON USD[10]
pt Cloffocks (1882—94), pt Workington

ADMINISTRATIVE COUNTY

For MBs and the associated CB see BOROUGHS

ALSTON WITH GARRIGILL RD
Alston with Garrigill

ARLECDON AND FRIZINGTON UD[17] (1894—1934[17])
Arlecdon

ASPATRIA UD (1894—1934[18])
Aspatria and Brayton

BOOTLE RD (1894—1934[19])
Birker and Austhwaite, Bootle, Corney, Drigg and Carleton, Eskdale and Wasdale, Irton, Millom Rural, Muncaster, Seascale (1901—34), Ulpha, Waberthwaite, Whicham, Whitbeck

BORDER RD (1934[19]—74)
Arthuret, Askerton, Beaumont, Bewcastle, Brampton, Burgh by Sands, Burtholme, Carlatton, Castle Carrock, Cummersdale, Cumrew, Cumwhitton, Dalston, Nether Denton, Upper Denton, Farlam, Geltsdale, Hethersgill, Irthington, Kingmoor, Kingwater, Kirkandrews, Kirklinton Middle, Midgeholme, Nichol Forest, Orton, Rockcliffe, Scaleby, St Cuthbert Without, Solport, Stanwix (1934—66), Stanwix Rural (1966—74), Stapleton, Walton, Waterhead, Westlinton, Wetheral

BRAMPTON RD (1894—1934[19])
Askerton, Brampton, Burtholme, Carlatton, Castle Carrock, Cumrew, Cumwhitton, Nether Denton, Upper Denton, Farlam, Geltsdale, Irthington, Kingwater, Midgeholme, Walton, Waterhead

CARLISLE RD (1894—1934[19])
Beaumont, Belle Vue (1894—1912), Burgh by Sands, Crosby upon Eden, Cummersdale, Dalston, Grinsdale, Kingmoor, Kirkandrews upon Eden, Orton, Rockcliffe, St Cuthbert Without, Stanwix, Warwick, Wetheral, Wreay

CLEATOR MOOR UD (1894—1934[19])
Cleator

COCKERMOUTH RD
Above Derwent, Bassenthwaite, Bewaldeth and Snittlegarth, Blindbothel, Blindcrake Isel and Redmaine (1894—1934), Borrowdale, Bothel and Threapland, Brackenthwaite (1894—1934), Bridekirk, Brigham, Broughton (1898—1974), Great Broughton (1894—98), Little Broughton (1894—98), Broughton Moor (1898—1974), Buttermere, Camerton, Castlerigg St John's and Wythburn, Great Clifton, Little Clifton, Crosscanonby, Dean, Dearham, Dovenby (1894—1934), Eaglesfield (1894—1934), Embleton, Flimby (1894—1934), Gilcrux, Greysouthern, Isel Old Park (1894—1934), Lorton, Loweswater, Mosser (1894—1934), Oughterside and Allerby, Papcastle, Plumbland, Ribton (1894—1934), Seaton, Setmurthy, Skiddaw (1894—1934), Stainburn (1894—1934), Sunderland (1894—1934), Tallentire (1894—1934), Underskiddaw, Whinfell (1894—1934), Winscales, Workington Rural (1894—1934), Wythop

COCKERMOUTH UD
Cockermouth

EGREMONT UD (1894—1934[19])
Egremont

ENNERDALE RD (1934[19]—74)
Arlecdon and Frizington, Beckermet St Bridget, Beckermet St John, Cleator Moor, Distington, Egremont, Ennerdale and Kinniside, Gosforth, Haile, Lamplugh, Lowca, Lowside Quarter, Moresby, Parton, Ponsonby, Rottington, St Bees, Nether Wasdale, Weddicar

HARRINGTON UD (1894—1934[19])
Harrington

HOLME CULTRAM UD (1894—1934[19])
Holme Abbey, Holme East Waver, Holme Low, Holme St Cuthbert, Skinburness Marsh

KESWICK UD[20]
Keswick

LONGTOWN RD (1894—1934[19])
Arthuret, Bellbank, Bewcastle, Hethersgill, Kirkandrews Middle, Kirkandrews Moat, Kirkandrews Nether, Kirklinton Middle, Nichol Forest, Scaleby, Solport, Stapleton, Trough, Westlinton

MARYPORT UD[21]
Ellenborough and Ewanrigg (1894—1928), Flimley (1934—74), Maryport (1928—74), Netherhall (1894—1928)

MILLOM RD (1934—74[19])
Bootle, Drigg and Carleton, Eskdale, Irton, Millom, Millom Without, Muncaster, Seascale, Ulpha, Waberthwaite, Whicham

MILLOM UD (1894—1934[19])
Millom

PENRITH RD
Ainstable, Berrier and Murrah (1894—1934), Bowscale (1894—1934), Castle Sowerby, Catterlen, Croglin (1894—1934), Culgaith, Dacre, Edenhall (1894—1934), Gamblesby (1894—1934), Glassonby, Greystoke, Hesket (1934—74), Hesket in the Forest (1894—1934), Hunsonby (1934—74), Hunsonby and Winskill (1894—1934), Hutton (1934—74), Hutton in the Forest (1894—1934), Hutton John (1894—1934), Hutton Roof (1894—1934), Hutton Soil (1894—1934), Kirkland and Blencarn (1894—1934), Kirkoswald, Langwathby, Lazonby, Matterdale, Melmerby (1894—1934), Middlesceugh and Braithwaite (1894—1934), Mosedale (1894—1934), Mungrisdale, Newton Reigny (1894—1934), Ousby, Plumpton Wall (1894—1934), Renwick (1894—1934), Great Salkeld, Little Salkeld (1894—1934), Skelton, Skirwith (1894—1934), Staffield (1894—1934), Threlkeld, Watermillock (1894—1934)

PENRITH UD
Penrith

WHITEHAVEN RD (1894—1934[19])
Beckermet St Bridget, Beckermet St John, Distington, Ennerdale and Kinniside, Gosforth, Haile, Hensingham, Lamplugh, Lowside Quarter, Moresby, Parton, Ponsonby, Preston Quarter (1894—96), Preston Quarter (1896—1934), Preston Quarter Rural (1894—96), Rottington, St Bees, Salter and Eskett, Sandwith, Seascale (1897—1901), Nether Wasdale, Weddicar

WIGTON RD

Aikton, Allhallows, Allonby, Aspatria (1934—74), Blencogo (1894—1934), Blennerhassett and Kirkland (1894—1934), Blennerhassett and Torpenhow (1934—74), Boltons, Bowness, Bromfield, Caldbeck, Dundraw, Hayton and Mealo, Holme Abbey (1934—74), Holme East Waver (1934—74), Holme Low (1934—74), Holme St Cuthbert (1934—74), Ireby (1934—74), High Ireby (1894—1934), Low Ireby (1894—1934), Kirkbampton, Kirkbride, Langrigg and Mealrigg (1894—1934), Oulton (1894—1934), Sebergham, Silloth (1934—74), Skinburness Marsh (1934—74), Thursby, Torpenhow and Whitrigg (1894—1934), Uldale (1894—1934), Waverton, Westnewton, Westward, Wigton (1934—74), Woodside

WIGTON UD (1894—1934[19])

Wigton

CUMBRIA NON-METROPOLITAN COUNTY

As constituted 1 Apr 1974, defined in terms of Adm Co units as of 31 Mar.

ALLERDALE DIST
from Cumb: Cockermouth RD, Cockermouth UD, Keswick UD, Maryport UD, Wigton RD (incl Skinburness Marsh), Workington MB

BARROW-IN-FURNESS DIST
CB (assoc with Lancs): Barrow in Furness CB
from Lancs: Dalton in Furness MB

CARLISLE DIST
CB (assoc with Cumb): Carlisle CB
from Cumb: Border RD

COPELAND DIST
from Cumb: Ennerdale RD, Millom RD, Whitehaven MB

EDEN DIST
from Cumb: Alston with Garrigill RD, Pentrith RD, Penrith UD
from Westm: Appleby MB, pt Lakes UD (ward of Patterdale), North Westmorland RD

SOUTH LAKELAND DIST
from Lancs: Grange UD, North Lonsdale RD, Ulverston RD
from Westm: Kendal MB, pt Lakes UD (the areas not in Eden Dist), South Westmorland RD, Windermere UD
from Yorks W Riding: Sedbergh RD

DERBYSHIRE

ALTERATIONS IN COUNTY BOUNDARIES

As noted by year below, Derbys pars gained territory from or lost it to pars in adjoining cos or county boroughs, or were entirely transferred to them. Details of these alterations are noted in Part I of the *Guide* under Derbyshire.

ANCIENT COUNTY (until 1889: Hds, Bors, MBs, PLUs, RSDs, USDs)

1844 Glossop, Scropton. *1866* Burton upon Trent, Church Gresley, Measham, Scropton. *1883* Doveridge. *1884* Oakthorpe and Donisthorpe, Packington, Ravenstone, Sawley and Wilsthorpe. *1886* Barton Blount. *1887* Clifton and Compton, Mapleton, Snelston, Thorpe. *1888* No Man's Heath.

ADMINISTRATIVE COUNTY (1889—1974: Hds,[1] PLUs, MBs, RDs, UDs, with assoc CB of Derby)

1889 Appleby, Little Chester, Derby All Saints, Derby St Alkmund, Derby St Michael, Derby St Peter, Derby St Werburgh, Disley, Litchurch, Stapenhill, Winshill. *1890* Foston and Scropton, Littleover, Markeaton, Normanton. *1895* Croxall, Pinxton. *1897* Appleby, Chilcote, Measham, Netherseal, Oakthorpe and Donisthorpe, Overseal, Stretton en le Field, Willesley, Woodville. *1901* Alvaston and Boulton, Beauchief, Chaddesden, Normanton, Norton, Osmaston, Spondon.

1903 Rolleston. *1928* Alvaston and Boulton, Chaddesden, Darley Abbey, Littleover, Markeaton, Mickleover, Normanton, Sinfin Moor, Spondon. *1929* Derwent, Dore, Hathersage, Outseats, Totley. *1934* Beauchief, Bretby, Chaddesden, Dore, Mackworth, Markeaton, Norton, Spondon, Totley. *1936* Hartington Upper Quarter, Ludworth, Mellor, New Mills, Whaley Bridge. *1965* Breaston, Melbourne, Shardlow and Great Wilne, Weston upon Trent. *1967* Beighton, Dronfield, Eckington, Holmesfield, Killamarsh. *1968* Allestree, Alvaston and Boulton, Aston upon Trent, Breadsall, Chaddesden, Chellaston, Darley Abbey, Duffield, Elvaston, Findern, Littleover, Mackworth, Mickleover, Quarndon, Radbourne, Sinfin and Arleston, Sinfin Moor, Spondon, Swarkestone, Twyford and Stenson.

NON-METROPOLITAN COUNTY (from 1974: Dists)

1974 Tintwistle.

ASSOCIATED COUNTY BOROUGH

DERBY CB

Bdry: 1890,[2] 1901,[3] 1928,[4] 1934,[5] 1968.[6]

HUNDREDS[1]

APPLETREE HD

Alderwasley (from 1866), Alkmonton (from 1866), Ash (from 1866), pt Ashbourne (until 1866), Ashleyhay (from 1866), Atlow (from 1866), Barton Blount, Bearwardcote (from 1866), Belper (from 1866), Hungry Bentley (from 1866), Biggin (from 1866), Boyleston, pt Bradborne (until 1866), Bradley, Brailsford, Breadsall, Church Broughton, Burnaston (from 1866), Chaddesden, Cubley, Dalbury Lees, Doveridge, Duffield, Edlaston and Wyaston, Etwall, pt Foston and Scropton[7] (from 1866), Hargate Manor (1858—85), Hatton (from 1866), Hazlewood (from 1866), Heage (from 1866), Hilton (from 1866), Holbrook (from 1866), Hollington (from 1866), Hoon (from 1866), Hulland (from 1866), Hulland Ward (from 1866), Hulland Ward Intakes (from 1866), Idridgehay and Alton (from 1866), Kedleston, pt Kirk Hallam, Longford, Mapperley (from 1866), Marston Montgomery, Marston on Dove, Mercaston (from 1866), Muggington (pt until 1866, ent from 1866), Norbury and Roston, Osmaston, Osleton and Thurvaston (from 1866), Radbourne, Ravensdale Park (from 1866), Rodsley (from 1866), Shirley, Shottle and

Postern (from 1866), Sinfin and Arleston (from 1866), Snelston, Somersal Herbert, Spondon, Stanley (from 1866), Sturston (from 1866), Stydd (1866—86), Sudbury, Sutton on the Hill, Trusley, Turnditch (from 1866), Twyford and Stenson (from 1866), Windley (from 1866), pt Wirksworth (until 1866), Yeaveley (from 1866), Yeldersley (from 1866)

HIGH PEAK HD

Abney and Abney Grange (from 1866), Ashford (from 1866), Aston (from 1866), Bakewell,[8] Bamford (from 1866), Baslow and Bubnell (from 1866); Beard, Thornsett, Ollerset and Whittle (1866—85); Beeley (from 1866), Birchover (from 1866), Blackwell (from 1866), Bradwell (from 1866), Brough and Shatton (from 1866), Brushfield (from 1866), Buxton (from 1866), Calver (from 1866), Castleton,[8] Chapel en le Frith, Chatsworth (from 1858), Chelmorton (from 1866); Chinley, Bugsworth and Brownside (from 1866); Curbar (from 1866), Darley (pt until 1866, ent from 1866), Derwent (from 1866), Edale (from 1866), Edensor, Eyam, Eyam Woodlands (from 1866), Fairfield (from 1866), Fernilee (from 1866), Flagg (from 1866), Foolow (from 1866), Froggatt (from

654

1866), Glossop,[8] Gratton (from 1866), Grindlow (from 1866), Nether Haddon (from 1866), Over Haddon (from 1866), Harthill (from 1866), Hassop (from 1866), Hathersage, Hayfield (from 1866), Hazlebadge (from 1866), Highlow (from 1866), Hope, Hope Woodlands (from 1866), Great Hucklow (from 1866), Little Hucklow (from 1866), Ivonbrook Grange (from 1866), Litton (from 1866), Great Longstone (from 1866), Little Longstone (from 1866), Ludworth and Chisworth (from 1866), Mellor (from 1866), Monyash (from 1866), New Mills (from 1885), Offerton (from 1866), Outseats (from 1866), Nether Padley (from 1866), Peak Forest (from 1866), Pilsley (from 1866), Rowland (from 1866), Great Rowsley (from 1866), Sheldon (from 1866), Stanton (from 1866), Stoke (from 1866), Stony Middleton (from 1866), Taddington (from 1866), Thornhill (from 1866), Tideswell, Wardlow (from 1866), Wheston (from 1866), Winster (from 1866), pt Wirksworth (until 1866), Wormhill (from 1866), Youlgreave (pt until 1866, ent from 1866)

MORLESTON AND LITCHURCH HD

Allestree, Alvaston (1866—84), Alvaston and Boulton (from 1884), pt Ashbourne (until 1866), Aston upon Trent, Barrow upon Trent, Boulton (until 1884), Breaston (from 1866), Little Chester[8] (from 1866), Clifton and Compton (from 1866), Codnor and Loscoe (from 1866), Codnor Park (from 1858), Crich (pt until 1866, ent from 1866), Dale Abbey, Denby, pt Derby St Alkmund, pt Derby St Michael (until 1877), Draycott and Church Wilne (from 1866), Little Eaton (from 1866), Long Eaton (from 1866), Egginton, Elvaston, Findern (from 1866), Kirk Hallam, West Hallam, Heanor, Hopwell (from 1866), Horsley, Horsley Woodhouse (from 1866), Ilkeston,[8] Kilburn (from 1866), Kirk Langley, Litchurch[8] (from 1866), Littleover (from 1866), Mackworth, Markeaton (from 1866), Mickleover, Morley, pt Muggington (until 1866), Ockbrook, Pentrich, Quarndon, Ripley (from 1866), Risley (from 1866), Sandiacre, Sawley (until 1866), Sawley and Wilsthorpe (from 1866), Shardlow and Great Wilne (from 1866), Shipley (from 1866), Smalley (from 1866), Stanton by Dale, Weston Underwood (from 1866), Weston upon Trent, Willington

REPTON AND GRESLEY HD

pt Appleby, The Boundary (from 1858), Bretby (from 1866), pt Burton upon Trent (until 1866), Caldwell (from 1866), Calke, Catton (from 1866), Chellaston, Chilcote (from 1866), Coton in the Elms (from 1866), pt Croxall, Derby Hills (from 1858), Drakelow (from 1866), Foremark, Castle Gresley (from 1866), Church Gresley, Harthshorne, Ingleby (from 1866), Linton

(from 1866), Lullington, Measham, Melbourne, Newton Solney, Normanton, pt Oakthorpe and Donisthorpe (from 1866), Osmaston, pt Packington (until 1884), pt Ravenstone (until 1884), Repton, Rosliston, Smisby, Stanton and Newhall (from 1866), Stanton by Bridge, Stapenhill, Stretton en le Field, Swadlincote (from 1866), Swarkestone, Ticknall, Walton upon Trent, Willesley, Winshill (from 1866)

SCARSDALE HD

Alfreton, Ashover (pt until 1866, ent from 1866), Ault Hucknall, Barlborough, Barlow (from 1871), Great Barlow (1866—71), Little Barlow (1866—71), Beauchief (from 1858), Beighton, Blackwell, Bolsover, Brackenfield (from 1866), Brampton, Brimington (from 1866), Calow (from 1866), Chesterfield,[8] Clay Lane (from 1866), Clowne, Coal Aston (from 1866), pt Crich (until 1866), Dore (from 1866), Dronfield, Eckington, Elmton, Glapwell (from 1866), Hasland (from 1866), Heath, Holmesfield (from 1866), Killamarsh, Upper Langwith, Morton, Newbold and Dunston (from 1866), South Normanton, Temple Normanton (from 1866), Norton, Pilsley (from 1866), Pinxton,[9] Pleasley, Scarcliffe, Shirebrook (from 1866), Shirland and Higham, Staveley, Stretton (from 1866), Sutton cum Duckmanton, Tapton (from 1866), Tibshelf, Totley (from 1866), Tupton (from 1866), Unstone (from 1866), Walton (from 1866), Wessington (from 1866), Whittington, Whitwell, Wingerworth, North Wingfield, South Wingfield, Woodthorpe (from 1866)

WIRKSWORTH HD

Aldwark (from 1866), Ashbourne,[8] pt Ashover (until 1866), Ballidon (from 1866), Fenny Bentley, Bonsall, Bradbourne (pt until 1866, ent from 1866), Brassington (from 1866), Callow (from 1866), Carsington, pt Crich (until 1866), Cromford (from 1866), pt Darley (until 1866), Dethick and Lea (from 1866), Eaton and Alsop (from 1866), Elton (from 1866), Hartington (until 1866), Hartington Middle Quarter (from 1866), Hartington Nether Quarter (from 1866), Hartington Town Quarter (from 1866), Hartington Upper Quarter (from 1866), Hognaston, Hopton and Griffe Grange (from 1858), Ible (from 1866), Kirk Ireton, Ireton Wood (from 1866), Kniveton, Lea Hall (from 1866), Mapleton, Matlock, Middleton and Smerrill (from 1866), Middleton by Wirksworth (from 1866), Newton Grange (from 1866), Offcote and Underwood (from 1866), Parwich, Tansley (from 1866), Thorpe, Tissington, Wensley and Snitterton (from 1866), Wirksworth[8] (pt until 1866, ent from 1866), pt Youlgreave (until 1866)

BOROUGHS

Units with some degree of burghal character[10] are denominated 'Bor'. Those which did not sustain that status until the 19th cent are in italics. MBs were established by the Municipal Corporations Act, 1835,[11] or by later charter.

ASHBOURNE BOR
pt Ashbourne
BAKEWELL BOR
Bakewell

BURTON UPON TRENT MB (1878[12]—89) [Staffs, Derbys until 1889, ent CB (assoc with Staffs) thereafter]
Stapenhill[13] (pt 1878—94, ent 1894—1904), Winshill[13]

(pt 1878—94, ent 1894—1904)

BUXTON MB (1917[14]—74)

Burbage, Buxton, Fairfield

CASTLETON BOR

Castleton

CHESTERFIELD BOR/MB[15]

pt Brampton (1892—94), Chesterfield, Hasland (1892—94), pt Newbold and Dunston (1892—94), pt Walton (1892—94)

DERBY BOR/MB/CB[16]

Little Chester (1877—98), Derby (1898—1974), Derby All Saints (until 1898), Derby St Alkmund (pt until 1894, ent 1894—98), Derby St Michael (pt until 1877, ent 1877—98), Derby St Peter (pt until 1877, ent 1877—98), Derby St Werburgh (pt until 1877, ent 1877—98), Litchurch (1877—98), New Normanton (1890—98), Rowditch (1890—98)

GLOSSOP MB (1866[17]—1974)

Glossop (pt 1866—94, ent 1894—1974)

ILKESTON MB (1887[18]—1974)

Ilkeston

WIRKSWORTH BOR

Wirksworth

POOR LAW UNIONS

In Derbys Poor Law County:[19]

ASHBOURNE PLU (Derbys, Staffs)

Alkmonton, Ashbourne, Atlow, Ballidon, Fenny Bentley, Hungry Bentley, Biggin, Bonsall, Bradbourne, Bradley, Brailsford, Brassington, Callow, Carsington, Clifton and Compton, Eaton and Alsop, Edlaston and Wyaston, Hartington Nether Quarter, Hartington Town Quarter, Hognaston, Hollington, Hopton and Griffe Grange (1858—1930), Hulland, Hullard Ward, Hulland Ward Intakes, Ible, Kirk Ireton, Kniveton, Lea Hall, Longford, Mapleton, Mercaston, Middleton by Wirksworth, Newton Grange, Offcote and Underwood, Osmaston, Parwich, Rodsley, Shirley, Snelston, Sturston, Stydd (1840—86), Thorpe, Tissington, Yeaveley, Yeldersley

BAKEWELL PLU

Abney and Abney Grange, Aldwark, Ashford, Bakewell, Baslow and Bubnell, Beeley, Birchover, Blackwell (soon after 1838[20]—1930), Bradwell (soon after 1838[20]—1930), Brushfield, Calver, Chatsworth (1861—1930), Chelmorton, Cromford, Curbar, Darley, Edensor, Elton (soon after 1838[20]—1930), Eyam, Eyam Woodlands, Flagg, Foolow, Froggatt, Gratton, Grindlow, Nether Haddon (1861—1930), Over Haddon, Harthill, Hartington Middle Quarter, Hassop, Hathersage, Hazlebadge, Highlow, Great Hucklow, Little Hucklow, Ivonbrook Grange, Litton, Great Longstone, Little Longstone, Matlock, Matlock Bath (1894—1930), Middleton and Smerrill, Monyash, Offerton (soon after 1838[20]—1930), Outseats (soon after 1838[20]—1930), Nether Padley, Pilsley, Rowland (soon after 1838[20]—1930), Great Rowsley, Sheldon, Stanton, Stoke, Stony Middleton, Taddington (soon after 1838[20]—1930), Tansley (soon after 1838[20]—1930), Tideswell, Wardlow, Wensley and Snitterton, Wheston, Winster, Youlgreave (soon after 1838[20]—1930)

BELPER PLU

Alderwasley, Alfreton, Allestree (soon after 1837[20]—1930), Ashleyhay, Belper, Crich, Denby, Dethick and Holloway (1897—1930), Dethick and Lea (1837—97), Duffield, Hazlewood, Heage, Holbrook, Horsley, Horsley Woodhouse, Idridgehay and Alton, Ireton Wood (1837—89), Kedleston, Kilburn, Kirk Langley, Mackworth, Mapperley, Markeaton, Milford (1897—1930), Morley, Muggington (soon after 1837[20]—86), Pentrich, Quarendon, Ravensdale Park (soon after 1837[20]—1930), Ripley, Rowditch (1890—98), Shottle and Postern, Smalley, Turnditch, Weston Underwood, Windley, South Wingfield, Wirksworth

CHAPEL EN LE FRITH PLU

Aston, Bamford, Brough and Shatton, Burbage (1894—1930), Buxton, Castleton, Chapel en le Frith; Chinley, Bugsworth and Brownside; Derwent, Edale, Fairfield, Green Fairfield (1917—30), Fernilee, Hartington Upper Quarter, Hope, Hope Woodlands, Kingsterndale (1894—1930), Peak Forest, Thornhill, Wormhill (soon after 1837[20]—1930)

CHESTERFIELD PLU

Ashover, Barlow (1871—1930), Great Barlow (1837—71), Little Barlow (1837—71), Bolsover, Brackenfield, Brampton, Brimington, Calow, Chesterfield, Clay Lane, Coal Aston, Dronfield, Dronfield Woodhouse (1894—1930), Eckington, Egstow (1894—1930), Hasland, Heath, Holmesfield, Killamarsh, Morton, Newbold and Dunston (1837—1920), Temple Normanton, Pilsley, Shirland and Higham, Staveley, Stretton, Sutton cum Duckmanton, Tapton (1837—1920), Tupton, Unstone, Walton, Wessington, Whittington (1837—1920), Wingerworth, North Wingfield, Woodthorpe

DERBY PLU

Little Chester (1837—98), Darley Abbey (1894—1930), Derby (1898—1930), Derby All Saints (1837—98), Derby St Alkmund (1837—98), Derby St Michael (1837—98), Derby St Peter (1837—98), Derby St Werburgh (1837—98), Litchurch (1837—98)

GLOSSOP PLU

Charlesworth (1894—1930), Chisworth (1896—1930), Glossop, Ludworth (1896—1930), Ludworth and Chisworth (1837—94)

HAYFIELD PLU (Derbys, Ches)

Beard, Thornsett, Ollersett and Whittle (1837—85); Disley,[21] Hayfield, Mellor, New Mills (1885—1930), Newtown (1894—1930)

SHARDLOW PLU[22] (Derbys, Leics, Notts)

Alvaston (1837—84), Alvaston and Boulton (1884—1930), Aston upon Trent, Barrow upon Trent, Boulton (1837—84), Breadsall, Breaston, Chaddesden, Chellaston, Dale Abbey, Derby Hills, Draycott and Church Wilne, Little Eaton, Long Eaton, Elvaston, Kirk Hallam, West Hallam, Hopwell, Littleover, Melbourne, Normanton (1837—1928), New Normanton (1890—98), Ockbrook, Osmaston (1837—

1902), Osmaston (1894—1902), Risley, Sandiacre, Sawley and Wilsthorpe, Shardlow and Great Wilne, Sinfin and Arleston (soon after 1837[20]—1930), Sinfin Moor (1861—1930), Spondon, Stanley, Stanton by Bridge, Stanton by Dale, Swarkestone, Unnamed (1894—97), Weston upon Trent

In Other Poor Law Counties:

ASHBY DE LA ZOUCH PLU (Leics, Derbys)

Appleby[23] (1836—89), Appleby[23] (1889—97), The Boundary (1858—1930), Calke, Hartshorne, Measham, Netherseal[24] (1894—1930), Oakthorpe and Donisthorpe,[25] Overseal[26] (1894—1930), Packington,[27] Ravenstone[27] (1836—84), Smisby, Stretton en le Field, Ticknall, Willesley,[28] Woodville (1897—1930)

BASFORD PLU (Notts, Derbys)

Codnor and Loscoe, Codnor Park, Heanor, Ilkeston, Shipley

BURTON UPON TRENT PLU (Staffs, Derbys)

Ash (soon after 1837[20]—1930), Barton Blount (soon after 1837[20]—1930), Bearwardcote (soon after 1837[20]—1930), Bretby, Church Broughton, Burnaston, Caldwell, Catton (soon after 1837[20]—1930), Coton in the Elms, Dalbury Lees, Drakelow, Egginton, Etwall, Findern, Foremark, Foston and Scropton,[7] Castle Gresley, Church Gresley, Hargate Manor (1862—85), Hatton, Hilton, Hoon, Ingleby, Linton, Lullington, Marston on Dove, Mickleover, Newton Solney, Osleton and Thurvaston (soon after 1837[20]—1930), Radbourne, Repton, Rosliston, Stanton and Newhall, Stapenhill,[13] Sutton on the Hill, Swadlincote, Trusley, Twyford and Stenson, Walton upon Trent, Willington, Winshill[13]

ECCLESALL-BIERLOW PLU (Yorks W Riding, Derbys)

Beauchief, Dore, Norton, Totley

MANSFIELD PLU (Notts, Derbys)

Ault Hucknall, Blackwell, Glapwell (soon after 1836[20]—1930), Upper Langwith, South Normanton, Pinxton,[9] Pleasley, Scarcliffe, Shirebrook (1903—30), Tibshelf

ROTHERHAM PLU (Yorks W Riding, Derbys)

Beighton

TAMWORTH PLU (Staffs, Derbys [until 1895])

Chilcote,[29] Croxall[30]

UTTOXETER PLU (Staffs, Derbys)

Boyleston, Cubley (soon after 1837[20]—1930), Doveridge, Marston Montgomery (soon after 1837[20]—1930), Norbury and Roston (soon after 1837[20]—1930), Somersal Herbert, Sudbury

WORKSOP PLU (Notts, Derbys, Yorks W Riding)

Barlborough, Clowne, Elmton, Whitwell

SANITARY DISTRICTS

ALFRETON USD[31]

Alfreton (pt 1875—88, ent 1888—94)

ALVASTON AND BOULTON USD

Alvaston (1875—84), Alvaston and Boulton (1884—94), Boulton (1875—84), pt Elvaston (1884—94)

ASHBOURNE RSD

same as PLU less Ashbourne, Bonsall, pt Clifton and Compton, pt Offcote and Underwood, pt Sturston

ASHBOURNE USD

Ashbourne, pt Clifton and Compton, pt Offcote and Underwood, pt Sturston

ASHBY DE LA ZOUCH RSD

same as PLU for Derbys pars

BAKEWELL RSD

same as PLU less Bakewell, Baslow and Bubnell, Darley, Matlock, Wensley and Snitterton

BAKEWELL USD

Bakewell

BASFORD RSD

same as PLU for Derbys pars less Heanor, Ilkeston

BASLOW AND BUBNELL USD

Baslow and Bubnell

BELPER RSD

same as PLU less Alfreton (pt 1875—88, ent 1888—94), Belper, Heage, pt Markeaton (1875—90), pt Ripley, Wirksworth

BELPER USD

Belper

BOLSOVER USD (1893[32]—94)

Bolsover

BONSALL USD

Bonsall

BRAMPTON AND WALTON USD[15]

Brampton (ent 1875—92, pt 1892—26 Mar 1894, ent 26 Mar—apptd day 1894), Walton (ent 1875—92, pt 1892—26 Mar 1894, ent 26 Mar—apptd day 1894)

BURTON UPON TRENT RSD

same as PLU for Derbys pars less Church Gresley, Stanton and Newhall, Swadlincote

BUXTON USD

pt Buxton, pt Fairfield, pt Fernilee, pt Hartington Upper Quarter

CHAPEL EN LE FRITH RSD

same as PLU less pt Buxton, Fairfield, pt Fernilee, pt Hartington Upper Quarter, pt Wormhill

CHESTERFIELD RSD

same as PLU less Bolsover (1893—94), Brampton, Chesterfield, Clay Lane, pt Dronfield, pt Hasland (1892—26 Mar 1894), pt Morton (1875—83), Newbold and Dunston, pt Pilsley, Walton, Whittington, pt North Wingfield (1875—83), pt Woodthorpe

CHESTERFIELD USD[15]

pt Brampton (1892—94), Chesterfield, pt Hasland (1892—26 Mar 1894), pt Newbold and Dunston (1892—26 Mar 1894), pt Walton (1892—26 Mar 1894)

CLAY CROSS USD (1893[33]—94)

Clay Lane, pt Pilsley, pt Woodthorpe

CLAY LANE USD (1875—93[33])

Clay Lane, pt Morton (1875—83), pt Pilsley, pt North Wingfield (1875—83), pt Woodthorpe

NORTH DARLEY USD

Darley

SOUTH DARLEY USD

Wensley and Snitterton

DERBY RSD
pt Derby St Alkmund

DERBY USD[16]
Little Chester, Derby All Saints, pt Derby St Alkmund, Derby St Michael, Derby St Peter, Derby St Werburgh, Litchurch, pt Littleover (1875—90), pt Markeaton (1875—90), pt Normanton (1875—90), New Normanton (1890—94), Rowditch (1890—94)

DRONFIELD USD
pt Dronfield

LONG EATON USD
Long Eaton

ECCLESAL BIERLOW RSD
same as PLU for Derbys pars

FAIRFIELD USD
pt Fairfield, pt Wormhill

GLOSSOP RSD
same as PLU less pt Glossop

GLOSSOP USD
pt Glossop

HAYFIELD RSD
same as PLU for Derbys pars less Beard, Thornsett, Ollersett and Whittle (1875—85); pt Disley,[21] New Mills (1885—94)

HEAGE USD
Heage

HEANOR USD
Heanor

ILKESTON USD
Ilkeston

MANSFIELD RSD
same as PLU for Derbys pars

MATLOCK USD
pt Matlock

MATLOCK BATH AND SCARTHIN NICK USD
pt Maltock

NEW MILLS USD (Derbys, *Ches*)
Beard, Thornsett, Ollersett and Whittle (1875—85); pt Disley,[21] New Mills (1885—94)

NEWBOLD AND DUNSTON USD[15]
Newbold and Dunston (ent 1875—92, pt 1892—26 Mar 1894, ent 26 Mar—apptd day 1894)

RIPLEY USD
pt Ripley

SHARDLOW RSD
same as PLU for Derbys pars less Alvaston (1875—84), Alvaston and Boulton (1884—94), Boulton (1875—84), Long Eaton, pt Elvaston (1884—94), pt Littleover (1875—90), pt Normanton (1875—90)

SWADLINCOTE DISTRICT USD
Church Gresley, Stanton and Newhall, Swadlincote

UTTOXETER RSD
same as PLU for Derbys pars

WHITTINGTON USD
Whittington

WIRKSWORTH USD
Wirksworth

WORKSOP RSD
same as PLU for Derbys pars

ADMINISTRATIVE COUNTY

For MBs and the associated CB see BOROUGHS.

ALFRETON UD
Alfreton

ALVASTON AND BOULTON UD (1894—1934[34]**)**
Alvaston and Boulton, Unnamed (1894—97)

ASHBOURNE RD
Alkmonton, Atlow, Ballidon, Fenny Bentley, Hungry Bentley, Biggin, Boyleston (1934—74), Bradbourne, Bradley, Brailsford, Brassington, Callow, Carsington, Clifton and Compton, Cubley (1934—74), Doveridge (1934—74), Eaton and Alsop, Edlaston and Wyaston, Hartington Nether Quarter, Hartington Town Quarter, Hognaston, Hollington, Hopton and Griffe Grange, Hulland, Hulland Ward, Hulland Ward Intakes (1894—1934), Ible, Kirk Ireton, Kniveton, Lea Hall, Longford, Mapleton, Marston Montgomery (1934—74), Mercaston, Middleton by Wirksworth (1894—1934), Newton Grange, Norbury and Roston (1934—74), Offcote and Underwood, Osmaston, Parwich, Rodsley, Shirley, Snelston, Somersal Herbert (1934—74), Sturston (1894—1934), Sudbury (1934—74), Thorpe, Tissington, Yeaveley, Yeldersley

ASHBOURNE UD
Ashbourne

BAKEWELL RD
Abney and Abney Grange, Aldwark, Ashford (1894—1953), Ashford in the Water (1953—74), Baslow and Bubnell (1934—74), Beeley, Birchover, Blackwell, Bradwell, Brushfield, Calver, Chatsworth, Chelmorton, Cromford (1894—1924), Curbar, Edensor, Elton, Eyam, Eyam Woodlands, Flagg, Foolow, Froggatt, Gratton, Grindlow, Nether Haddon, Over Haddon, Harthill, Hartington Middle Quarter, Hassop, Hathersage, Hazlebadge, Highlow, Great Hucklow, Little Hucklow, Ivonbrook Grange, Litton, Great Longstone, Little Longstone, Middleton and Smerrill, Monyash, Offerton, Outseats, Nether Padley, Pilsley, Rowland, Great Rowsley,[35] Sheldon, Stanton, Stoke, Stony Middleton, Taddington, Tansley (1894—1924), Tideswell, Wardlow, Wheston, Winster, Youlgreave

BAKEWELL UD
Bakewell

BASFORD AND BUBNELL UD (1894—1934[34]**)**
Baslow and Bubnell

BELPER RD
Alderwasley, Allestree (1894—1968), Ashleyhay, Crich, Darley Abbey (1894—1968), Denby, Dethick and Holloway (1897—1974), Dethick and Lea (1894—97), Duffield, Hazlewood, Holbrook, Horsley, Horsley Woodhouse, Idridgehay and Alton, Kedleston, Kilburn, Kirk Langley, Mackworth, Mapperley, Markeaton (1894—1934), Milford (1897—1934), Morley (1894—1934), Pentrich, Quarndon, Ravensdale Park, Shipley (1934—74), Shottle and Postern, Smalley, Turnditch,

Weston Underwood, Windley, South Wingfield

BELPER UD
Belper, Milford (1934—74)

BLACKWELL RD
Ault Hucknall, Blackwell, Glapwell, Upper Langwith (1894—1935), South Normanton, Pinxton, Pleasley, Scarcliffe, Shirebrook (1903—74), Tibshelf

BOLSOVER UD
Bolsover

BONSALL UD (1894—1934[34])
Bonsall

BRAMPTON AND WALTON UD (1894—1935[36])
Brampton, Walton

BUXTON UD (1894—1917[14])
Burbage, Buxton, pt Fairfield

CHAPEL EN LE FRITH RD
Aston, Bamford, Brough and Shatton, Castleton, Chapel en le Frith, Charlesworth (1934—74); Chinley, Bugsworth and Brownside; Chisworth (1934—74), Derwent, Edale, Green Fairfield (1917—74), Fernilee (1894—1936), Hartington Upper Quarter, Hayfield (1934—74), Hope, Hope Woodlands, Kingsterndale, Ludworth (1934—36), Mellor (1934—36), Peak Forest, Thornhill, Wormhill

CHESTERFIELD RD
Ashover, Barlow, Beighton (1894—1967), Brackenfield, Brampton (1935—74), Brimington, Calow, Coal Aston (1894—1935), Dronfield Woodhouse (1894—1935), Eckington, Hasland, Heath, Holmesfield, Killamarsh, Morton, Temple Normanton, Pilsley, Shirland and Higham, Staveley (1894—1935), Stretton, Sutton cum Duckmanton, Tapton (1894—1920), Tupton, Unstone, Walton (1935—74), Wessington, Wingerworth, North Wingfield, Woodthorpe (1894—1935)

CLAY CROSS UD
Clay Cross (1935—74), Clay Lane (1894—1935), Egstow (1894—1935)

CLOWNE RD
Barlborough, Clowne, Elmton, Whitwell

NORTH DARLEY UD (1894—1934[34])
Darley

SOUTH DARLEY UD (1894—1934[34])
Wensley and Snitterton

SOUTH EAST DERBYSHIRE RD (1959[37]—74)
Alvaston and Boulton (1959—68), Aston upon Trent, Barrow upon Trent, Breadsall, Breaston, Chaddesden (1959—68), Chellaston (1959—68), Dale Abbey, Derby Hills, Draycott and Church Wilne, Little Eaton, Elvaston, West Hallam, Hopwell, Littleover (1959—68), Melbourne, Morley, Ockbrook, Risley, Sandiacre, Shardlow and Great Wilne, Sinfin and Arleston (1959—68), Sinfin Moor (1959—68), Spondon (1959—68), Stanley, Stanton by Bridge, Stanton by Dale, Swarkestone, Weston upon Trent

DRONFIELD UD
Dronfield

LONG EATON UD
Long Eaton

FAIRFIELD UD (1894—1917[14])
pt Fairfield

GLOSSOP DALE RD (1894—1934[34])
Charlesworth, Chisworth (1896—1934), Ludworth

(1896—1934), Ludworth and Chisworth (1894—96)

HARTSHORN AND SEALS RD (1894—1934[34])
The Boundry, Calke, Hartshorne, Netherseal (1897—1934), Overseal (1897—1934), Smisby, Ticknall, Woodville (1897—1934)

HAYFIELD RD (1894—1934[34])
Hayfield, Mellor

HEAGE UD (1894—1934[34])
Heage

HEANOR UD[38]
Codnor and Loscoe (1899—1974), Heanor

MATLOCK UD (1894—1924[39])
Matlock

MATLOCK UD (1934[34]—74)
Bonsall, Cromford, Darley, Matlock, Matlock Bath, Tansley, Wensley and Snitterton

MATLOCK BATH AND SCARTHIN NICK UD (1894—1924[39])
Matlock Bath

THE MATLOCKS UD (1924[39]—34[34])
Cromford, Matlock, Matlock Bath, Tansley

NEW MILLS UD
New Mills, Newtown (1894—1934)

NEWBOLD AND DUNSTON UD (1894—1911[40])
Newbold and Dunston

NORTON RD (1894—1934[34])
Beauchief, Dore, Norton, Totley

REPTON RD
Ash, Barton Blount, Bearwardcote, Bretby, Church Broughton, Burnaston, Caldwell, Calke (1934—74), Catton, Coton in the Elms, Dalbury Lees, Drakelow, Egginton, Etwall, Findern, Foremark, Foston and Scropton, Castle Gresley, Hartshorne (1934—74), Hatton, Hilton, Hoon, Ingleby, Linton, Lullington, Marston on Dove, Mickleover (1894—1968), Netherseal (1934—74), Newton Solney, Osleston and Thurvaston, Overseal (1934—74), Radbourne, Repton, Rosliston, Smisby (1934—74), Sutton on the Hill, Ticknall (1934—74), Trusley, Twyford and Stenson, Walton upon Trent, Willington, Woodville (1934—74)

RIPLEY UD
Heage (1934—74), Ripley

SHARDLOW RD (1894—1959[37])
Alvaston and Boulton (1934—59), Aston upon Trent, Barrow upon Trent, Breadsall, Breaston, Chaddesden, Chellaston, Dale Abbey, Derby Hills, Draycott and Church Wilne, Little Eaton, Elvaston, Kirk Hallam (1894—1934), West Hallam, Hopwell, Littleover, Melbourne, Morley (1934—59), Normanton (1894—1928), Ockbrook, Osmaston (1894—1902), Risley, Sandiacre, Sawley and Wilsthorpe (1894—1934), Shardlow and Great Wilne, Sinfin and Arleston, Sinfin Moor, Spondon, Stanley, Stanton by Bridge, Stanton by Dale, Swarkestone, Weston upon Trent

STAVELEY UD (1935[36]—74)
Staveley

SUDBURY RD (1894—1934[34])
Boyleston, Cubley, Doveridge, Marston Montgomery, Norbury and Roston, Somersal Herbert, Sudbury

SWADLINCOTE UD (1951[41]—74)
Church Gresley, Stanton and Newhall, Swadlincote

SWADLINCOTE DISTRICT UD (1894—1951[41])
Church Gresley, Stanton and Newhall, Swadlincote

UNNAMED RD (administered by Basford UD, Notts, 1894—1934[34])
  Codnor and Loscoe (1894—99), Codnor Park, Shipley
WHALEY BRIDGE UD (1936[42]—74)
  Whaley Bridge
WHITTINGTON UD (1894—1911[37])
  Whittington

WHITTINGTON AND NEWBOLD UD (1911[40]—20[43])
  Newbold and Dunston, Whittington
WIRKSWORTH UD
  Wirksworth

NON-METROPOLITAN COUNTY

As constituted 1 Apr 1974, defined in terms of Adm Co units as of 31 Mar.

AMBER VALLEY DIST
  Alfreton UD, Belper RD, Belper UD, Heanor UD, Ripley UD
BOLSOVER DIST
  Blackwell RD, Bolsover UD, Clowne RD
CHESTERFIELD DIST
  pt Chesterfield RD (Brimington), Chesterfield MB, Staveley UD
DERBY DIST
  CB (assoc with Derbys): Derby CB
NORTH EAST DERBYSHIRE DIST
  Chesterfield RD (all except the par in Chesterfield Dist), Clay Cross UD, Dronfield UD
SOUTH DERBYSHIRE DIST
  pt South East Derbyshire RD (the pars not in Erewash Dist), Repton RD, Swadlincote UD
WEST DERBYSHIRE DIST
  Ashbourne RD, Ashbourne UD, Bakewell RD, Bakewell UD, Matlock UD, Wirksworth UD
EREWASH DIST
  pt South East Derbyshire RD (Breadall, Breaston, Dale Abbey, Draycott and Church Wilne, Little Eaton, West Hallam, Hopwell, Morley, Ockbrook, Risley, Sandiacre, Stanley, Stanton by Dale
HIGH PEAK DIST
  from Ches: Tintwistle RD
  from Derbys: Buxton MB, Chapel en le Frith RD, Glossop MB, New Mills UD, Whaley Bridge UD

COUNTY DURHAM

ALTERATIONS IN COUNTY BOUNDARIES

As noted by year below, Durham pars gained territory from or lost it to pars in adjoining cos or county boroughs, or were entirely transferred to them. Details of these alterations are noted in Part I of the *Guide* under Durham.

ANCIENT COUNTY[1] (until 1889: Wds, Bors, MBs, PLUs, RSDs, USDs)

1844 Ancroft, Bedlington, Belford,[2] Crayke, Farne Islands, Holy Island,[3] Kyloe, Monks House, Norham,[4] Tweedmouth. *1884* Middleton in Teesdale, Newbiggin. *1887* Medomsley, Stockton on Tees.

ADMINISTRATIVE COUNTY (1889—1974: Wds,[5] PLUs, MBs, RDs, UDs, with assoc CBs of Darlington [1915—74], Gateshead, Hartlepool [1967—74], West Hartlepool [1902—67], South Shields, Sunderland)

1889 Bishopwearmouth, Bishopwearmouth Panns, Gateshead, Heworth, Ryhope, South Shields, Monkwearmouth, Monkwearmouth Shore, Sunderland, Westoe. *1895* Bishopwearmouth Without, Monkwearmouth Without. *1901* Harton. *1902* West Hartlepool, Seaton Carew. *1915* Cockerton, Darlington, Haughton le Skerne. *1921* Boldon, Harton, Whitburn. *1928* Bishopwearmouth Without, Ford, Fulwell, Ryhope, Silksworth, Southwick, Tunstall, Whitburn. *1930* Archdeacon Newton, Blackwell, Haughton le Skerne, Whessoe. *1932* Seaton, Stranton, Throston Rural.

1933 Lamesley, Whickham. *1936* Boldon, Ford, Jarrow, Lamesley, Monkton, Silksworth, Whickham, Whitburn. *1951* Boldon, Ford, Herrington, Hylton, Silksworth. *1953* Dalton Piercy, Greatham, Seaton. *1954* Heworth. *1967* Blackwell, Boldon, Brierton, Burdon, Great Burdon, Low Coniscliffe, Dalton Piercy, Elwick, Ford, Greatham, Hart, Herrington, Houghton le Spring, Hurworth, Hylton, Offerton, Ryhope, Seaton, Silksworth. *1968* Billingham, Carlton, Elton, Grindon, Norton, Preston on Tees, Stockton on Tees.

NON-METROPOLITAN COUNTY (from 1974: Dists)

1974 Aislaby, Newton Bewley, South Biddick, Birtley, Blaydon, Boldon, Brierton, Burdon, Carlton, Claxton, Dalton Piercy, Egglescliffe, Elton, Elwick, Elwick Hall, Greatham, Grindon, Harraton, Hart, Hebburn, Hetton, Heworth, Houghton le Spring, Jarrow, Lamesley, Newsham, Long Newton, Preston on Tees, Redmarshall, Ryton, Warden Law, Washington, Whickham, Whitton, Wolviston.

ASSOCIATED COUNTY BOROUGHS

DARLINGTON CB
Cr 1915 when Darlington MB constituted a CB.[6] Bdry: 1930,[7] 1967.[8] Transf 1974 to Co Durham.[9]

GATESHEAD CB
Bdry: 1933,[10] 1936,[11] 1954.[12] Transf 1974 to Tyne & Wear.[9]

HARTLEPOOL CB (1967—74)
Cr 1967 by union West Hartlepool CB, Hartlepool MB, other pars and pts of pars (see Part I of the *Guide* under 'Hartlepool').[13] Transf 1974 to Clev.[9]

WEST HARTLEPOOL CB (1902—67)
Cr 1902 when West Hartlepool MB constituted a CB.[14] Bdry: 1932,[15] 1953.[16] Abol 1967 to help cr Hartlepool CB.[13]

SOUTH SHIELDS CB
Bdry: 1901,[17] 1921,[18] 1936,[11] 1951.[19] Transf 1974 to Tyne & Wear.[9]

SUNDERLAND CB
Bdry: 1895,[20] 1928,[21] 1936,[22] 1951,[23] 1967.[24] Transf 1974 to Tyne & Wear.[9]

WARDS[1]

BEDLINGTONSHIRE[25] (transf 1844 to Northumb)
Bedlington

CHESTER WD
Barmston (from 1866), Benfieldside (from 1866), Billingside (from 1866), Birtley (from 1866), Boldon, Chester le Street (pt until 1829, reduced pt 1829—66,[26] ent from 1866), Chopwell (from 1866), Collierley (from 1866), Conside and Knitsley (from 1866), Crawcrook (from 1866), Ebchester, Edmondbyers, Edmondsley (from 1866), Gateshead,[27] Greencroft (from 1866), Harraton (from 1866), Harton (from 1866), Healeyfield (from 1866); Hedworth, Monkton and Jarrow[27] (from 1866); Heworth (from 1866), Hunstanworth, Iveston (from 1866), Jarrow (until 1866), Kimblesworth[28] (until 1829), Kyo (from 1866), Lamesley (from 1866), Lanchester (pt until 1829, reduced pt 1829—66,[29] ent from 1866), Langley (from 1866), Medomsley (from 1866), Monkwearmouth[30] (until 1829), Muggleswick, Ouston (from 1866), Pelton (from 1866), Ryton, Ryton Woodside (from 1866), pt St Oswald[31] (until 1829), Satley (from 1866), South Shields[27] (from 1866), Stella (from 1866), Tanfield (from 1866), Urpeth (from 1866), Usworth (from 1866), Waldridge (from 1866), Washington, Westoe[27] (from 1866), Whickham, Whitburn, Winlaton, Witton Gilbert (until 1829)

DARLINGTON WD

Archdeacon Newton (from 1866), Auckland St Andrew,[27] Auckland St Helen, Bishop Auckland (1866—86), Bishop Auckland and Pollard's Lands (from 1886), West Auckland (from 1866), Aycliffe (until 1866), Great Aycliffe (from 1866), School Aycliffe (from 1866), Barmpton (from 1866), Barnard Castle (from 1866), North Bedburn (from 1866), South Bedburn (from 1866), Binchester (from 1866), Blackwell (from 1866), Bolam (from 1866), Brafferton (from 1866), Brancepeth[32] (until 1829), Great Burdon (from 1866), Byers Green (from 1866), Chilton (from 1866), Cleatlam (from 1866), Coatham Mundeville[33] (from 1866), Coatsay Moor (1866—84), Cockerton[27] (from 1866), Cockfield, Coniscliffe (until 1866), High Coniscliffe (from 1866), Low Coniscliffe (from 1866), Cornsay (from 1866), Coundon (from 1866), Coundon Grange, Darlington,[27] Denton (from 1866), Low Dinsdale (from 1829), Eggleston (from 1866), Eldon (from 1866), Escomb, Evenwood and Barony (from 1866), Forest and Frith (from 1866), Gainford,[27] Hamsterley, Haughton le Skerne[27] (pt until 1829,[33] ent from 1829), Headlam (from 1866), Heighington, Hilton (from 1866), Houghton le Side (from 1866), Hunwick and Helmington (from 1866), Hurworth[34] (from 1829), Ingleton (from 1866), Killerby (from 1866), pt Lanchester (until 1866), Langleydale and Shotton (from 1866), Langton (from 1866), Lynesack and Softley (from 1866), Marwood (1866—84), Merrington (ent until 1829, pt 1829—66[35]), Middlestone (from 1866), Middleton in Teesdale, Middridge (from 1866), Middridge Grange (from 1866), Morton Palms[33] (from 1866), Morton Tinmouth (from 1866), Neasham[34] (from 1866), Newbiggin (from 1866), Newfield (from 1866), Newton Cap (from 1866), Old Park (from 1866), Piercebridge (from 1866), Pollard's Lands (1866—86), Preston le Skerne (from 1866), Raby with Keverstone (from 1866), Redworth (from 1866), Sadberge[33] (from 1829), pt St Oswald[36] (until 1829), Shildon (from 1866), pt Sockburn[37] (from 1829), Staindrop, Stanhope, Streatlam and Stainton (from 1866), Summerhouse (from 1866), East Thickley (from 1866), Tudhoe (from 1866), Wackerfield (from 1866), Walworth (from 1866), Westerton (from 1866), Westwick (from 1866), Whessoe (from 1866), Whitworth, Whorlton (from 1866), Windlestone (from 1866), Winston, Witton le Wear, Wolsingham, Woodham (from 1866), Woodland (from 1866)

DURHAM WD (from 1829[38])

Bishop Middleham,[39] Brancepeth,[32] Brandon and Byshottles (from 1866), Broom (from 1866), Cassop[40] (1866—86), Cassop cum Quarrington (from 1886), pt Chester le Street[26] (1829—66), Cornforth[39] (from 1866), Coxhoe[40] (until 1866), Crook and Billy Row (from 1866), Crossgate[27] (from 1866), Durham Castle and Precincts[41] (from 1858), Durham College[41] (from 1858), Durham Magdalen Place[41] (from 1858), Durham St Mary le Bow,[27] Durham St Mary the Less,[27] Durham St Nicholas,[27] Elvet[27] (from 1866), Esh (from 1866), Ferryhill (from 1866), Framwellgate[27] (from 1866), Garmondsway Moor[39] (from 1866), Hedleyhope (from 1866), Helmington Row (from 1866), Hett (from 1866), pt Houghton le Spring[42] (1829—66), pt Kelloe[40] (1829—66), Kimblesworth[28] (from 1858), pt Lanchester (1829—66), Mainsforth[39] (from 1866), pt Merrington (1829—66), Moor House[42] (from 1866), Moorsley[42] (from 1866), Pittington,[43] Plawsworth (from 1866), Quarrington[40] (1866—86), St Giles,[27] St Oswald[27] (1829—66), Shadforth[43] (from 1866), Sherburn[43] (from 1866), Sherburn House[41] (from 1858), Shincliffe (from 1866), Stockley (from 1866), Sunderland Bridge (from 1866), Thrislington[39] (from 1866), Whitwell House[41] (from 1858), Willington (from 1866), Witton Gilbert

EASINGTON WD

South Biddick (from 1866), Bishopwearmouth,[27] Bishopwearmouth Panns[27] (from 1866), Burdon (from 1866), Burnmoor (from 1866), Castle Eden, pt Chester le Street[26] (until 1866), Cocken (from 1866), Cold Hesledon (from 1866), Dalton le Dale, Dawdon (from 1866), Durham Castle and Precincts[41] (until 1829), Durham College[41] (until 1829), Durham Magdalen Place[41] (until 1829), Durham St Mary le Bow[27] (until 1829), Durham St Mary the Less[27] (until 1829), Durham St Nicholas[27] (until 1829), Easington, Great Eppleton (from 1866), Little Eppleton (from 1866), Ford (from 1866), Fulwell[30] (from 1866), pt Hart (until 1866), Haswell (from 1866), Hawthorn (from 1866), East and Middle Herrington (from 1866), West Herrington (from 1866), Hetton le Hole (from 1866), Houghton le Spring[42] (ent until 1829, pt 1829—66, ent from 1866), Hutton Henry (from 1866), Kelloe (ent until 1829, pt 1829—66,[40] ent from 1866), Lambton[26] (from 1866), Great Lumley[26] (from 1866), Little Lumley[26] (from 1866), Monk Hesledon, Monkwearmouth[27] (from 1829), Monkwearmouth Shore[27] (from 1866[30]), Morton Grange (from 1866), East Murton (from 1866), Nesbitt (from 1866), Newbottle (from 1866), Offerton (from 1866), Penshaw (from 1866), Pittington[43] (until 1829), East Rainton (from 1866), West Rainton (from 1866), Ryhope[27] (from 1866), St Giles[27] (until 1829), pt St Oswald[27] (until 1829[36]), Seaham, Seaton with Slingley (from 1866), Sheraton with Hulam (from 1866), Sherburn House[42] (until 1829), Shotton (from 1866), Silksworth (from 1866), Sunderland,[27] Thornley (from 1866), Thorpe Bulmer (from 1866), Trimdon, Tunstall (from 1866), Warden Law (from 1866), Whitwell House[42] (until 1829), Wingate (from 1866)

ISLANDSHIRE (transf 1844 to Northumb)

Ancroft, pt Belford, *Farne Islands*, Holy Island, Kyloe, *Monks House*, Tweedmouth

NORHAMSHIRE (transf 1844 to Northumb)

Norham

STOCKTON WD

Aislaby (from 1866), Cowpen Bewley (from 1866), Newton Bewley (from 1866), Billingham, Bishop Middleham[39] (until 1829), Bishopton, Bradbury (from 1866), Brierton (from 1866), Butterwick and Oldacres (from 1866), Carlton (from 1866), Claxton (from 1866), Crayke (until 1844), Dalton Piercy (from 1866), Low Dinsdale (until 1829), Egglescliffe, Elstob (from 1866), Elton, Elwick (from 1866), Elwick Hall, Embleton (from 1866), Fishburn (from 1866), Foxton and Shotton (from 1866), Greatham, Grindon, Hart[27] (pt until 1866, ent from 1866), East Hartburn (from

1866), Hartlepool,[27] pt Haughton le Skerne[33] (until 1829), Hurworth[34] (until 1829), Middleton St George, Mordon (from 1866), East and West Newbiggin (from 1866), Newsham (from 1866), Long Newton, Norton, Preston on Tees (from 1866), Redmarshall, Seaton Carew[27] (from 1866), Sedgefield, pt Sockburn[37] (until 1829), Great Stainton, Little Stainton (from 1866), Stillington (from 1866), Stockton on Tees,[27] Stranton,[27] Throston[27] (from 1866), Whitton (from 1866), Wolviston (from 1866)

BOROUGHS

Units with some degree of burghal character[44] are denominated 'Bor'. Those which did not sustain that status until the 19th cent are in italics. MBs were established by the Municipal Corporations Act, 1835,[45] or by later charter.

BISHOP AUCKLAND BOR
pt Auckland St Andrew
BARNARD CASTLE BOR
Gainford
CROSSGATE BOR—see DURHAM OLD BOROUGH
DARLINGTON BOR, MB[46] (1867[47]—1915), CB (1915[6]—74)
pt Cockerton (1872—94), Darlington, Harrowgate Hill (1894—1907), pt Haughton le Skerne (1872—94)
DURHAM MB (1835—1974)
Crossgate (pt 1835—94, ent 1894—1916), Durham (1916—74), Durham Castle and Precincts (1835—1916), Durham College (1835—1916), Durham Magdalen Place (1835—1916), Durham St Mary le Bow [North Bailey] (1835—1916), Durham St Mary the Less [South Bailey] (1835—1916), Durham St Nicholas (1835—1916), Elvet (pt 1835—94, ent 1894—1916), Framwellgate (pt 1835—94, ent 1894—1916), St Giles (pt 1835—94, ent 1894—1916), pt St Oswald (1835—66)
DURHAM AND FRAMWELLGATE BOR (1565[48]—1835)
Durham St Nicholas, pt St Oswald [Framwellgate]
DURHAM BISHOP'S BOR[49] (until 1565[48])
Durham St Nicholas, pt St Oswald [Framwellgate]
(DURHAM CASTLE JURISDICTION [not a Bor but seat of Palatinate, until 1835])
Durham St Mary le Bow [North Bailey], Durham St Mary the Less [South Bailey]
DURHAM OLD BOR (or CROSSGATE BOR)[49] (until 1835)
pt St Oswald
ELVET BARONY AND BOR[50] (until 1835)
pt St Oswald [Elvet]
FRAMWELLGATE BOR (until 1565[48])
pt St Oswald [pt Framwellgate]
GATESHEAD BOR[51]/MB/CB
Gateshead, pt Heworth (1835—94), Heworth Within (1894—1907)

HARTLEPOOL BOR, MB (1850[52]—1967), CB (1967[13]—74)
Bor: pt Hart (until Hartlepool gains sep civ identity), Hartlepool (thereafter)
MB[53]/CB: Hartlepool, Middleton (1894—1936), pt Stranton (1883—94), Throston (pt 1883—94, ent 1894—1936)
WEST HARTLEPOOL MB[53] (1887[54]—1902), CB (1902[14]—67[13])
West Hartlepool (1894—1967), Seaton Carew (pt 1887—94, ent 1894—1921), pt Stranton (1887—94)
JARROW MB[55] (1875[56]—1974)
pt Hedworth, Monkton and Jarrow (1875—94 [enlarged pt 1884—94]); Jarrow (1894—1974)
ST GILES BOR
St Giles
SOUTH SHIELDS MB (1850[57]—89), CB (1889—1974)
South Shields, Westoe (1850—97)
STOCKTON BOR, STOCKTON ON TEES MB[58] (1835—1968[59]) [ent Durham until 1889; pt Durham, pt *Yorks N Riding* (1889—94), ent Durham thereafter]
Bor: pt Stockton on Tees
MB/CB: pt *Linthorpe (1889—94)*, Stockton on Tees (pt 1835—89, ent 1889—1967)
SUNDERLAND BOR/MB[60]/CB (earlier, 'Wearmouth Bor')
Bor: Sunderland (from 1719), pt Bishopwearmouth (until 1719)
MB/CB: Bishopwearmouth (pt 1835—94, ent 1894—97), Bishopwearmouth Panns (1835—97), Monkwearmouth (ent 1835—87, pt 1887—94, ent 1894—97), Monkwearmouth Shore (1835—97), pt Ryhope (1867—94), Ryhope Within (1894—97), Sunderland
TEESIDE CB (1968[57]—74)—see entry in Yorks
WEARMOUTH BOR—see SUNDERLAND

POOR LAW UNIONS

In Durham Poor Law County:[61]
AUCKLAND PLU
Bishop Auckland (1837—86), Bishop Auckland (1894—1930), Bishop Auckland and Pollard's Lands (1886—94), West Auckland, Auckland St Andrew, Auckland St Helen, North Bedburn, South Bedburn, Binchester, Bolam, Byers Green, Coundon, Coundon Grange, Crook and Billy Row, Eldon, Escomb, Evenwood and Barony, Hamsterley, Helmington Row, Hunwick and Helmington, Lynesack and Softley, Merrington, Merrington Lane (1894—1930), Middlestone, Middridge, Middridge Grange, Newfield, Newton Cap, Old Park, Pollard's Lands (1837—86), Pollard's Lands (1894—1930), Shildon, East Thickley, Westerton, Whitworth, Whitworth Without (1894—1930), Windlestone, Witton le Wear

CHESTER LE STREET PLU

Barmston, South Biddick, Birtley, Burnmoor, Chester le Street, Cocken, Edmondsley, Harraton, Lambton, Lamesley, Great Lumley, Little Lumley, Ouston, Pelton, Plawsworth, Urpeth, Usworth, Waldridge, Washington, Witton Gilbert

DARLINGTON PLU (Durham, Yorks N Riding)

Archdeacon Newton, Great Aycliffe, School Aycliffe, Barmpton, Blackwell, Brafferton, Great Burdon, Coatham Mundeville, Coatsay Moor (1837—84), Cockerton (1837—1915), High Coniscliffe, Low Coniscliffe, Darlington, Denton, Low Dinsdale, Harrowgate Hill (1894—1907), Haughton le Skerne, Heighington, Houghton le Side, Hurworth, Killerby, Middleton St George, Morton Palms, Neasham, Piercebridge, Redworth, Sadberge, Sockburn, Summerhouse, Walworth, Whessoe

DURHAM PLU

Bearparck (1894—1930), Belmont (1894—1930), Brancepeth, Brandon and Byshottles, Broom, Cassop (1837—87), Cassop cum Quarrington (1887—1930), Coxhoe, Crossgate (1837—1916), Durham (1916—30), Durham Castle and Precincts (1862—1916), Durham College (1862—1916), Durham Magdalen Place (1862—1916), Durham St Mary le Bow [North Bailey] (1837—1916), Durham St Mary the Less [South Bailey] (1837—1916), Durham St Nicholas (1837—1916), Elvet (1837—1916), Framwellgate (1837—1916), Framwellgate Moor (1894—1930), Hett, Kimblesworth, Neville's Cross (1894—1930), Pittington, Quarrington (1837—87), St Giles (1837—1916), St Oswald's (1895—1930), Shadforth, Sherburn, Sherburn House, Shincliffe, Stockley, Sunderland Bridge, Tudhoe, Whitwell House (1862—1930), Willington

EASINGTON PLU

Burdon, Castle Eden, Cold Hesledon, Dalton le Dale, Dawdon, Easington, Haswell, Hawthorn, Hutton Henry, Kelloe, Monk Hesleden, East Murton, Nesbitt, Seaham, Seaton with Slingley, Sheraton with Hulam, Shotton, Thornley, Wingate

GATESHEAD PLU

Chopwell, Crawcrook (1836—1914), Gateshead, Heworth, Heworth Within (1894—1907), Ryton, Ryton Woodside (1836—1914), Stella, Whickham, Winlaton

HARTLEPOOL PLU (1859—1930)

Brierton, Claxton, Dalton Piercy, Elwick, Elwick Hall, Greatham, Hart, Hartlepool, West Hartlepool (1894—1930), Middleton (1894—1930), Seaton (1894—1930), Seaton Carew, Stranton, Thorpe Bulmer, Throston, Throston Rural (1894—1930)

HOUGHTON LE SPRING PLU

Great Eppleton, Little Eppleton, East and Middle Herrington, West Herrington, Hetton le Hole, Houghton le Spring, Moor House, Moorsley, Morton Grange, Newbottle, Offerton, Penshaw, East Rainton, West Rainton, Silksworth, Warden Law

LANCHESTER PLU

Benfieldside, Billingside (1837—87), Collierley, Consett (1894—1930), Conside and Knitsley (1837—94), Cornsay, South Cornsay (1894—1930), Craghead

(1896—1930), Ebchester, Esh, Greencroft, Greencroft Within (1896—1930), Healeyfield, Hedleyhope, Iveston, Knitsley (1894—1930), Kyo, Lanchester, Langley, Medomsley, South Moor (1894—1916), Muggleswick, Oxhill (1894—1916), Satley, Stanley (1894—1930), Tanfield

SEDGEFIELD PLU

Bishop Middleham, Bishopton, Bradbury, Butterwick and Oldacres, Chilton, Cornforth, Elstob, Embleton, Ferryhill, Fishburn, Foxton and Shotton, Garmondsway Moor, Mainsforth, Mordon, East and West Newbiggin, Preston le Skerne, Sedgefield, Low Spennymoor (1894—1930), Great Stainton, Little Stainton, Stillington, Thrislington, Trimdon, Woodham

SOUTH SHIELDS PLU

Boldon, Boldon Colliery (1895—1930), Harton (1836—1921), Hebburn (1894—1930); Hedworth, Monkton and Jarrow (1836—94); Jarrow (1894—1930), Monkton (1894—1930), South Shields, Westoe (1836—97), Whitburn

STOCKTON PLU (Durham, Yorks N Riding)

Aislaby, Cowpen Bewley, Newton Bewley, Billingham, Brierton (1837—59), Carlton, Claxton (1837—59), Dalton Piercy (1837—59), Egglescliffe, Elton, Elwick (1837—59), Elwick Hall (1837—59), Greatham (1837—59), Grindon, Hart (1837—59), East Hartburn (1837—1913), Hartlepool (1837—59), Newsham, Long Newton, Norton, Preston on Tees, Redmarshall, Seaton Carew (1837—59), Stockton on Tees, Stranton (1837—59), Thorpe Bulmer (1837—59), Throston (1837—59), Whitton, Wolviston

SUNDERLAND PLU

Bishopwearmouth (1836—97), Bishopwearmouth Panns (1836—97), Bishopwearmouth Without (1894—1930), Ford, Fulwell (1836—1928), Hylton, Monkwearmouth (1836—97), Monkwearmouth Shore (1836—97), Monkwearmouth Without (1894—95), Ryhope, Ryhope Within (1894—97), Southwick (1836—1928), Sunderland, Tunstall

TEESDALE PLU (Durham, Yorks N Riding)

Barnard Castle, Cleatlam, Cockfield, Eggleston, Forest and Frith, Gainford, Headlam, Hilton, Ingleton, Langleydale and Shotton, Langton, Marwood (1837—84), Marwood (1894—1930), Middleton in Teesdale, Morton Tinmouth, Newbiggin, Raby with Keverstone, Staindrop, Streatlam and Stainton, Wackerfield, Westwick, Whorlton, Winston, Woodland

WEARDALE PLU

Edmondbyers, Hunstanworth, Stanhope, Stanhope Urban (1894—1930), Tow Law (1894—1930), Wolsingham

In Other Poor Law Counties:

BELFORD PLU[62] (Northumb, Durham until 1844, ent Northumb thereafter)

Elwick, Ross

BERWICK PLU (Northumb, Durham [until 1844])

Ancroft, Cornhill on Tweed, Duddo, Felkington, Grindon, Holy Island, Horncliffe, Kyloe, Loanend, Longridge, Norham, Normam Mains, Shoreswood, Thornton, Tweedmouth, Twizell

SANITARY DISTRICTS

AUCKLAND RSD

same as PLU less Bishop Auckland (1875—86), pt Bishop Auckland and Pollard's Lands (1886—94), pt Pollard's Lands (1875—86), Shildon, East Thickley, pt Whitworth

BISHOP AUCKLAND USD

pt Bishop Auckland (1875—86), pt Bishop Auckland and Pollard's Lands (1886—94), pt Pollard's Lands (1875—86)

BARNARD CASTLE USD[63] (Durham, *Yorks N Riding*)

Barnard Castle (ent 1875—84, pt 1884—94), pt Marwood (1875—84), *pt Startforth (1875—89)*

BENFIELDSIDE USD

pt Benfieldside, pt Ebchester (1875—83)

BLAYDON USD

Chopwell, Stella, Winlaton

BRANDON AND BYSHOTTLES USD

Brandon and Byshottles

CHESTER LE STREET RSD

same as PLU

CONSETT USD

pt Conside and Knitsley, pt Ebchester (1875—83), pt Iveston

DARLINGTON RSD

same as PLU for Durham pars less pt Cockerton, Darlington, pt Haughton le Skerne

DARLINGTON USD

pt Cockerton, Darlington, pt Haughton le Skerne

DAWDON USD—see SEAHAM HARBOUR

DURHAM RSD

same as PLU less Brandon and Byshottles, pt Crossgate, Durham Castle and Precincts, Durham College, Durham Magdalen Place, Durham St Mary le Bow [North Bailey], Durham St Mary the Less [South Bailey], Durham St Nicholas, pt Elvet, pt Framwellgate, pt St Giles, Stockley (1881—94), Willington (1881—94)

DURHAM USD

pt Crossgate, Durham Castle and Precincts, Durham College, Durham Magdalen Place, Durham St Mary the Less [North Bailey], Durham St Mary the Less [South Bailey], Durham St Nicholas, pt Elvet, pt Frammwellgate, pt St Giles

EASINGTON RSD

same as PLU less Dawdon

FELLING USD

pt Heworth

GATESHEAD RSD (1883—94)

pt Whickham [only rural area; otherwise ent urban]

GATESHEAD USD

Gateshead, pt Heworth

HARTLEPOOL RSD

same as PLU less Hartlepool, pt Seaton Carew, pt Stranton, pt Throston

HARTLEPOOL USD[53]

Hartlepool, pt Stranton (1883—94), pt Throston (1883—94)

WEST HARTLEPOOL USD[53]

pt Seaton Carew (enlarged pt 1883—94), pt Stranton (1883—94)

HEBBURN USD

pt Hedworth, Monkton and Jarrow

HOUGHTON LE SPRING RSD

same as PLU less Houghton le Spring

HOUGHTON LE SPRING USD

Houghton le Spring

JARROW USD[55]

pt Hedworth, Monkton and Jarrow (enlarged pt 1884—94)

LANCHESTER RSD[63]

same as PLU less pt Benfieldside, pt Conside and Knitsley, pt Cornsay, pt Ebchester (1875—83), pt Hedleyhope, Iveston, pt Kyo (1892—94), pt Lanchester (1892—94), pt Medomsley, pt Tanfield (1883—94 [enlarged pt 1892—94])

LEADGATE USD[64]

pt Iveston (enlarged pt 1888—94), pt Medomsley

MIDDLETON IN STRANTON USD (1875—83[53]**)**

pt Stranton

RYTON USD

Crawcrook, Ryton, Ryton Woodside

SEAHAM HARBOUR USD (earlier, 'DAWDON' USD)

Dawdon

SEATON CAREW USD (1875—83[53]**)**

pt Seaton Carew

SEDGEFIELD RSD

same as PLU

SOUTH SHIELDS RSD

same as PLU less pt Harton (1887); pt Hedworth, Monkton and Jarrow; South Shields, Westoe

SOUTH SHIELDS USD

South Shields, Westoe

SHILDON AND EAST THICKLEY USD

Shildon, East Thickley

SOUTHWICK ON WEAR USD[65]

pt Harton (1887), Southwick (ent 1875—87, pt 1887, ent 1887—94)

SPENNYMOOR USD

pt Whitworth

STANHOPE USD

pt Stanhope

STANLEY USD (1892[66]**—94)**

pt Kyo, pt Lanchester, pt Tanfield

STOCKTON RSD

same as PLU less pt Stockton on Tees

STOCKTON ON TEES USD (Durham, *Yorks N Riding*)

pt Linthorpe (1889—94), Stockton on Tees (pt 1875—89, ent 1889—94)

SUNDERLAND RSD

same as PLU less pt Bishopwearmouth, Bishopwearmouth Panns, pt Monkwearmouth, Monkwearmouth Shore, pt Ryhope, Southwick (ent 1875—87, pt 1887, ent 1887—94), Sunderland

SUNDERLAND USD

pt Bishopwearmouth, Bishopwearmouth Panns, pt Monkwearmouth, Monkwearmouth Shore, pt Ryhope, Sunderland

TEESDALE RSD

same as PLU for Durham pars less Barnard Castle (ent 1875—84, pt 1884—94), pt Marwood (1875—84)

THROSTON USD (1875—83[53])
pt Throston
TOW LAW USD
pt Cornsay, pt Hedleyhope, pt Wolsingham
WEARDALE RSD
same as PLU less pt Stanhope, pt Wolsingham

WHICKHAM USD
pt Tanfield (1883—94), Whickham (ent 1875—83, pt 1883—94)
WILLINGTON USD (1881[67]—94)
Stockley, Willington

ADMINISTRATIVE COUNTY

For MBs and the associated CB see BOROUGHS

ANNFIELD PLAIN UD (1896[68]—1937[69])
Collierley, Greencroft Within, Kyo
AUCKLAND RD (1894—1937[69])
West Auckland, Auckland St Andrew, Auckland St Helen, North Bedburn, South Bedburn, Binchester, Bolam, Byers Green, Coundon, Coundon Grange, Crook and Billy Row (1894—98), Eldon, Escomb, Evenwood and Barony, Hamsterley, Helmington Row, Hunwick and Helmington, Land Common to Evenwood and Barony and West Auckland, Lynesack and Softley (1894—1937), Merrington, Middlestone, Middridge, Middridge Grange, Newfield, Newton Cap, Old Park, Pollard's Lands; Undivided Moor Common to Lynesack and Softley, Hamsterley and South Bedburn; Westerton, Whitworth Without, Windlestone, Witton le Wear
BISHOP AUCKLAND UD
Bishop Auckland
BARNARD CASTLE RD
West Auckland (1937—39), Cleatlam, Cockfield, Eggleston, Etherley (1939—74), Forest and Frith, Gainford, Headlam, Hilton, Ingleton, Langleydale and Shotton, Langton, Lynesack and Softley (1937—74), Marwood, Middleton in Teesdale, Morton Tinmouth, Newbiggin, Raby with Keverstone, Staindrop, Streatlam and Stainton; Undivided Moor Common to Lynesack and Softley, Hamsterley and South Bedburn (1937—74); Wackerfield, Westwick, Whorlton, Winston, Woodland
BARNARD CASTLE UD
Barnard Castle
BENFIELDSIDE UD (1894—1937[69])
Benfieldside
BILLINGHAM UD (1923[70]—68[59])
Billingham
BLAYDON UD
Blaydon (1936—74), Chopwell (1894—1936), Stella (1894—1936), Winlaton (1894—1936)
BOLDON UD (1936[11]—74)
Boldon
BRANDON AND BYSHOTTLES UD
Brandon and Byshottles
CHESTER LE STREET RD
Barmston (1894—1922), South Biddick, Birtley, Burnmoor, Chester le Street (1894—1909), Cocken (1894—1937), Edmondsley, Harraton, Lambton, Lamesley, Great Lumley, Little Lumley, Ouston, Pelton, Plawsworth, Sacriston (1937—74), Urpeth, Usworth (1894—1922), Waldridge, Washington (1894—1922), Witton Gilbert (1894—1937)

CHESTER LE STREET UD (1909[71]—74)
Chester le Street
CONSETT USD
Consett
CROOK UD (1898[72]—1937[69])
Crook and Billy Row
CROOK AND WILLINGTON UD (1937[69]—74)
Crook and Willington
DARLINGTON RD
Archdeacon Newton, Great Aycliffe, School Aycliffe (1894—1946), Barmpton, Bishopton (1937—74), Blackwell (1894—1967), Brafferton, Great Burdon, Coatham Mundeville, Cockerton (1894—1915), High Coniscliffe, Low Coniscliffe, Denton, Low Dinsdale, Haughton le Skerne (1894—1930), Heighington, Houghton le Side, Hurworth, Killerby, Middleton St George, Morton Palms, Neasham, East and West Newbiggin (1937—74), Piercebridge, Redworth (1894—1937), Sadberge, Sockburn, Great Stainton (1937—74), Little Stainton (1937—74), Summerhouse, Walworth, Whessoe
DURHAM RD
Bearpark, Belmont, Brancepeth, Broom (1894—1937), Cassop cum Quarrington, Coxhoe, Framwellgate Moor, Kelloe (1937—74), Kimblesworth, Moor House (1937—74), Neville's Cross (1894—1935), Pittington, West Rainton (1937—74), St Oswald's (1895—1935), Shadforth, Sherburn, Sherburn House, Shincliffe, Sunderland Bridge, Whitwell House, Witton Gilbert (1937—74)
EASINGTON RD
Burdon, Castle Eden, Cold Hesledon, Dalton le Dale, Easington, Haswell, Hawthorn, Horden (1947—74), Hutton Henry, Kelloe (1894—1937), Monk Hesleden, East Murton, Nesbitt, Peterlee (1956—74), Seaham (1894—1937), Seaton with Slingley, Sheraton with Hulam, Shotton, Thornley, Warden Law (1937—74), Wingate
FELLING UD
Heworth
HARTLEPOOL RD (1894—1936[11])
Brierton, Claxton, Dalton Piercy, Elwick, Elwick Hall, Greatham, Hart, Seaton, Stranton (1894—1932), Thorpe Bulmer, Throston Rural (1894—1932)
HEBBURN UD
Hebburn
HETTON UD (1895[73]—1974)
Hetton (1937—74), Hetton le Hole (1895—1937)
HOUGHTON LE SPRING RD (1894—1937[69])
Great Eppleton, Little Eppleton, East and Middle Herrington, West Herrington, Hetton le Hole (1894—

95), Moor House, Moorsley, Morton Grange, Newbottle, Offerton, Penshaw, East Rainton, West Rainton, Silksworth, Warden Law

HOUGHTON LE SPRING UD
Houghton le Spring

LANCHESTER RD
Collierley (1894—96), Cornsay, Craghead (1894—1937), Ebchester (1894—1937), Esh, Greencroft, Healeyfield, Hedleyhope, Knitsley (1894—1937), Kyo (1894—96), Lanchester, Langley, Medomsley (1894—1937), Muggleswick, Satley, Tanfield (1894—95)

LEADGATE UD (1894—1937[69])
Iveston

RYTON UD
Crawcrook (1894—1914), Ryton, Ryton Woodside (1894—1914)

SEAHAM UD (1937[69]—74)
Seaham

SEAHAM HARBOUR (1894—1937[69])
Dawdon

SEDGEFIELD RD
Bishop Middleham, Bishopton (1894—1937), Bradbury, Butterwick and Oldacres, Chilton, Cornfroth, Elstob, Embleton, Ferryhill, Fishburn, Foxton and Shotton, Garmondsway Moor (1894—1937), Mainsforth, Mordon, East and West Newbiggin (1894—1937), Preston le Skerne, Sedgefield, Great Stainton (1894—1937), Little Stainton (1894—1937), Stillington, Thrislington (1894—1946), Trimdon, Windlestone (1937—74), Woodham

SOUTH SHIELDS RD (1894—1936[11])
Boldon, Boldon Colliery (1895—1936), Harton (1894—1921), Monkton, Whitburn

SHILDON UD (1907[74]—74)
Shildon, East Thickley (1907—37)

SHILDON AND EAST THICKLEY UD (1894—1907[74])
Shildon, East Thickley

SOUTHWICK ON WEAR UD (1894—1928[75])
Southwick

SPENNYMOOR UD
Merrington Lane (1894—1937), Spennymoor (1937—74), Low Spennymoor (1894—1937), Tudhoe (1894—1937), Whitworth (1894—1937)

STANHOPE UD (1894—1937[69])
Stanhope Urban

STANLEY UD
Oxhill (1894—1916), South Moor (1894—1916), Stanley

STOCKTON RD
Aislaby, Cowpen Bewley (1894—1937), Newton Bewley, Billingham (1894—1923), Brierton (1936—74), Carlton, Claxton (1936—74), Dalton Piercy (1936—74), Egglescliffe, Elton, Elwick (1936—74), Elwick Hall (1936—74), Greatham (1936—74), Grindon, Hart (1936—74), East Hartburn (1894—1913), Newsham, Long Newton, Norton (1894—1967), Preston on Tees, Redmarshall, Seaton (1936—67), Whitton, Wolviston (1894—1937), Wolviston (1968—74)

SUNDERLAND RD (1894—1967[24])
Bishopwearmouth Without (1894—1930), Ford, Fulwell (1894—1928), Herrington (1946—67), East and Middle Herrington (1937—46), West Herrington (1937—46), Hylton, Monkwearmouth Without (1894—95), Offerton (1937—67), Ryhope, Silksworth (1937—67), Tunstall

TANFIELD UD (1895[76]—1937[68])
Tanfield

TOW LAW UD
South Cornsay, Tow Law

WASHINGTON UD (1922[77]—74)
Barmston (1922—37), Usworth (1922—37), Washington

WEARDALE RD
Edmondbyers, Hunstanworth, Stanhope, Wolsingham

WHICKHAM UD
Whickham

WILLINGTON UD (1894—1937[69])
Stockley, Willington

NON-METROPOLITAN COUNTY

As constituted 1 Apr 1974, defined in terms of Adm Co units as of 31 Mar.

CHESTER LE STREET DIST
pt Chester le Street RD (South Biddick,[78] Bournmoor, Edmondsley, pt Harraton,[79] Lambton, Great Lumley, Little Lumley, Ouston, Plawsworth, Sacriston, Urpeth, Waldridge), Chester le Street UD

DARLINGTON DIST
CB (assoc with Durham): Darlington CB
from Durham: pt Darlington RD (the pars[80] not in Sedgefield Dist)

DERWENTSIDE DIST
Consett UD, Lanchester RD, Stanley UD

DURHAM DIST
Brandon and Byshottles UD, Durham RD, Durham MB, Land Common to Brancepeth and Brandon and Byshottles

EASINGTON DIST
pt Easington RD (Castle Eden, Cold Hesledon, Dalton le Dale, Easington, Haswell, Hawthorn, Monk Hesleden, Horden, Hutton Henry, East Murton, Nesbitt, Peterlee, Seaton with Slingley, Sheraton with Hulam, Shotton, Thornley, Wingate), Seaham UD

SEDGEFIELD DIST
pt Darlington RD (Great Aycliffe, pt Heighington[80]), Sedgefield RD, Shildon UD, Spennymoor UD

TEESDALE DIST
from Durham: Barnard Castle RD, Barnard Castle UD (incl Lands Common to Lynesack and Softley, Hamsterley and South Bedburn)
from Yorks N Riding: Startforth RD

WEAR VALLEY DIST
Bishop Auckland UD, Crook and Willington UD, Tow Law UD, Weardale RD

GREATER MANCHESTER METROPOLITAN COUNTY

As constituted 1 Apr 1974, defined in terms of Adm Co units as of 31 Mar.

BOLTON METROP DIST
CB (assoc with Lancs): Bolton CB
from Lancs: Blackrod UD, Farnworth MB, Horwich UD, Kearsley UD, Little Lever UD, pt Turton UD (wards of Bradshaw North, Bradshaw South, Bromley Cross, Eagley, pt Egerton ward), Westhoughton UD

BURY METROP DIST
CB (assoc with Lancs): Bury CB
from Lancs: Prestwich MB, Radcliffe MB, pt Ramsbottom UD (wards of Central, East, South, West), Tottington UD, Whitefield UD

MANCHESTER METROP DIST
CB (assoc with Lancs): Manchester CB
from Ches: pt Bucklow RD (Ringway)

OLDHAM METROP DIST
CB (assoc with Lancs): Oldham CB
from Lancs: Chadderton UD, Crompton UD, Failsworth UD, Lees UD, Royton UD
from Yorks W Riding: Saddleworth UD

ROCHDALE METROP DIST
CB (assoc with Lancs): Rochdale CB
from Lancs: Heywood MB, Littleborough UD, Middleton MB, Milnrow UD, Wardle UD

SALFORD METROP DIST
CB (assoc with Lancs): Salford CB
from Lancs: Eccles MB, Irlam UD, Swinton and Pendlebury MB, Worsley UD

STOCKPORT METROP DIST
CB (assoc with Ches): Stockport CB
from Ches: Bredbury and Romiley UD, Cheadle and Gatley UD, Hazel Grove and Bramhall UD, Marple UD

TAMESIDE METROP DIST
from Ches: Dukinfield MB, Hyde MB, Longendale UD, Stalybridge MB
from Lancs: Ashton under Lyne MB, Audenshaw UD, Denton UD, Droylsden UD, Mossley MB

TRAFFORD METROP DIST
from Ches: Altrincham MB, Bowdon UD, pt Bucklow RD (Carrington, Dunham Massey, Partington, Warburton), Hale UD, Sale MB
from Lancs: Stretford MB, Urmston UD

WIGAN METROP DIST
CB (assoc with Lancs): Wigan CB
from Lancs: Abram UD, Aspull UD, pt Ashton in Makerfield UD (all except ward of South), Atherton UD, pt Billinge and Winstanley UD (ward of Billinge Higher End, pt ward of Winstanley), pt Golborne UD (all except wards of Culcheth, Newchurch), Hindley UD, Ince in Makerfield UD, Leigh MB, Orrell UD, Standish with Langtree UD, Tyldesley UD, pt Wigan RD (Haigh, Shevington, Worthington)

HEREFORDSHIRE

ALTERATIONS IN COUNTY BOUNDARIES

As noted by year below, Heref pars gained territory from or lost it to pars in adjoining cos, or were entirely transferred to them. Details of these alterations are noted in Part I of the *Guide* under Herefordshire.

ANCIENT COUNTY (until 1889: Hds, Bors, MBs, PLUs, RSDs, USDs)
1844 Cascob, Cwmyoy, Edvin Loach, Lea, Presteigne, Stottesden, Tenbury, Welsh Bicknor. *1866* Bockleton, Brampton Bryan, Bucknell, Cwmyoy, Leintwardine, Presteigne, Old Radnor. *1883* Lea, Llanrothal, Weston under Penyard. *1884* Edvin Loach, Hope Mansell, Walford.

ADMINISTRATIVE COUNTY (1889—1974: Hds,[1] PLUs, MBs, RDs, UDs)
1889 Richards Castle. *1891* Fwthog. *1893* Edvin Loach. *1894* Brampton Bryan, Bucknell. *1895* Leintwardine North Side, Ludford. *1897* Acton Beauchamp, Cradley, Mathon, Stoke Bliss. *1965* Aston Ingham, Goodrich, Hatfield, Hope Mansell, Lea, Upton Bishop, Weston under Penyard.

(Heref was abol 1974 to help constitute Worcester and Hereford Non-Metrop Co)

HUNDREDS[1]

BROXASH HD
Amberley (1866—87), Avenbury, pt Bockleton (until 1866), Bodenham, Bredenbury, Lower Brockhampton (from 1863), Bromyard, Collington, Little Cowarne, Much Cowarne, Felton, Grendon Bishop, Grendon Warren, Hampton Charles (from 1866), Linton (from 1866), Marden, Norton with Brockhampton (from 1866), Ocle Pychard, Pencombe, Preston Wynne (from 1866), Saltmarshe (from 1858), Upper Sapey, Stanford Bishop, pt Stoke Bliss, Stoke Lacy, Sutton (from joint rating of Sutton St Michael, Sutton St Nicholas), Sutton St Michael (until joint rating), Sutton St Nicholas (until joint rating), Tedstone Delamere, Tedstone Wafer, pt Thornbury, Ullingswick, Wacton, Whitbourne, Winslow (from 1866), Withington, Wolferlow

EWYAS LACY HD
Clodock (until 1866), Craswall (from 1866), Cusop, pt Cwmyoy (until 1866 [reduced pt 1844—66]), Fwthog (from 1866), Llancillo, Llanveynoe (from 1866), Longtown (from 1866), Michaelchurch Escley, Newton (from 1866), Rowlstone, St Margaret's, Walterstone

GREYTREE HD
Aston Ingham, Bartestree (from 1866), Brampton Abbotts, Brockhampton, How Caple, Dormington, Fownhope, pt Foy, Hope Mansell, Lea (pt until 1844, ent 1844—66), Lea (from 1883), Lea Lower[2] (1866—83), Lea Upper (1866—83), Linton, Much Marcle, Mordiford, Putley, Ross, Sollers Hope, Upton Bishop, Walford, Weston under Penyard, Woolhope, Yatton (from 1866)

GRIMSWORTH HD
Bishopstone, Breinton,[3] Bridge Sollers, Brinsop, Brobury, Burghill, Byford, Canon Pyon, Credenhill, Dinmore (from 1858), Hampton Bishop, Holmer (until 1866), Holmer (from 1884), Holmer Within (from 1884), Holmer and Shelwick (1866—84), Huntington[3] (from 1866), Kenchester, Mansell Gamage, Mansell Lacy, Monnington on Wye, Moreton on Lugg, Norton Canon, Pipe and Lyde, Staunton on Wye, Stretton Sugwas, Tupsley[3] (from 1866), Wellington, Wormsley, Yazor

HUNTINGTON HD
Brilley, Clifford, Eardisley, Huntington, Kington, Whitney, Willersley, Winforton

RADLOW HD
Ashperton, Aylton, Bosbury, Coddington, Colwall, Cradley, Donnington, Eastnor, Egleton (from 1866), Evesbatch, Bishop's Frome, Canon Frome, Castle Frome, Ledbury, Lugwardine, Little Marcle, Moreton Jeffreys, Munsley, Parkhold (1866—84), Pixley, Stoke Edith, Stretton Grandison, Tarrington, Westhide (from 1866), Weston Beggard, Yarkhill

STRETFORD HD
Almeley, pt Aymestrey, Birley, Dilwyn, Eardisland, King's Pyon, Kingsland, Kinnersley, pt Letton, Lyonshall, Monkland, Pembridge, Shobdon, pt Staunton on Arrow, Stretford, Weobley[3]

WEBTREE HD
Abbey Dore, Allensmore, Bacton, Blakemere, Bredwardine, Bullingham (until 1866),[3] Lower Bullingham (from 1866), Upper Bullingham[3] (1866—85), Callow, Clehonger, Dinedor, Dorstone, Dulas, Eaton Bishop, Ewyas Harold, Grafton (from 1866), Haywood (from 1858), Hereford All Saints,[3] Hereford St John the Baptist,[3] Hereford St Martin,[3] Hereford St Nicholas,[3] Hereford St Owen,[3] Hereford St Peter,[3] Holme Lacy, Kenderchurch, Kentchurch, Kingstone, Madley, Moccas, Peterchurch, Preston on Wye, St Devereux, Thruxton, Turnastone, Tyberton, Vowchurch, Wormbridge

WIGMORE HD
Adforton (from 1866), Aston, pt Aymestrey, pt Brampton Bryan, pt Bucknell (until 1866), Buckton and Coxall (from 1866), Burrington, Byton, pt Cascob (until 1844), Combe (from 1866), Downton, Elton, Lower Harpton (from 1866), Kinsham (1886—86),

Lower Kinsham (from 1866), Upper Kinsham (until 1886), Knill, Leinthall Starkes, pt Leintwardine (until 1866), pt Leintwardine North Side (from 1866), Lingen, pt Presteigne (until 1866 [reduced pt 1844—66]), pt Old Radnor (until 1866); Rodd, Nash and Little Bampton (from 1866); Stapleton (from 1866), pt Staunton on Arrow, Titley; Walford, Letton and Newton (from 1866); Wigmore, Willey (from 1866)

WOLPHY HD

Brimfield, Croft, Docklow, Edvin Ralph, Eye (until 1866); Eye, Moreton and Ashton (from 1866); Eyton, Ford, New Hampton (from 1858), Hampton Wafer (from 1858), Hatfield, Little Hereford, Hope under Dinmore, Humber, Kimbolton, Laysters, Leominster[3] (until 1866), Leominster Borough[3] (from 1866),

Leominster Out[3] (from 1866), pt Letton, Lucton, pt Ledford, Luston (from 1866), Middleton on the Hill, Newton (from 1866), Orleton, Pudlestone, pt Richards Castle, Sarnesfield, Stoke Prior, pt Tenbury (until 1844), pt Thornbury, Yarpole

WORMELOW HD

Aconbury, Ballingham, Little Birch, Much Birch, Bolstone, Bridstow, King's Caple, Little Dewchurch, Much Dewchurch, Dewsall, pt Foy, Ganarew, Garway, Goodrich, Harewood, Hentland, Kilpeck, Llandinabo, Llangarren, Llanrothal, Llanwarne, Marstow, Orcop, Pencoyd, Peterstow, St Weonards, Sellack, Tretire with Michaelchurch, Treville (from 1858), Welsh Bicknor (from 1844), Welsh Newton, Whitchurch

BOROUGHS

Units with some degree of burghal character[4] are denominated 'Bor'. Those which did not sustain that status until the 19th cent are in italics. MBs were established by the Municipal Corporations Act, 1835,[5] or by later charter.

HEREFORD BOR/MB[6]

pt Breinton (until 1884), pt Upper Bullingham (until 1885), Hereford (1932—74), Hereford All Saints (pt until 1884 [enlarged pt 1866—84], ent 1884—1932), Hereford St John the Baptist (pt until 1884, ent 1884—1932), Hereford St Martin (pt until 1884, ent 1884—1932), Hereford St Nicholas (until 1932), Hereford St Owen (until 1932), Hereford St Peter (until 1932), Hereford The Vineyard (until 1932), pt Holmer (until

1866), pt Holmer and Shelwick (1866—84), Holmer Within (1884—1932), Huntington (until 1932), Tupsley (pt until 1884, ent 1884—1932)

LEOMINSTER BOR/MB

Leominster (pt until 1835, ent 1835—66), Leominster Borough (1866—1974), Leominster Out (1866—1974)

WEOBLEY BOR

Weobley

POOR LAW UNIONS

In Heref Poor Law County:[7]

BROMYARD PLU (Heref, Worcs)

Acton Beauchamp,[8] Avenbury, Bredenbury, Brockhampton (1894—1930), Lower Brockhampton (1863—94), Bromyard, Collington, Little Cowarne, Much Cowarne, Cradley, Edvin Loach,[9] Edvin Ralph, Evesbatch, Felton, Bishop's Frome, Grendon Bishop, Grendon Warren (1836—95), Hampton Charles, Linton, Moreton Jeffreys, Norton (1894—1930), Norton with Brockhampton (1836—94), Ocle Pychard, Pencombe (1836—95), Pencombe with Grendon Warren (1895—1930), Saltmarshe (1858—1930), Upper Sapey, Stanford Bishop, Stoke Lacy, Tedstone Delamere, Tedstone Wafer, Thornbury, Ullingswick, Wacton, Whitbourne, Winslow, Wolferlow

DORE PLU

Abbey Dore, Bacton, Craswall, Dulas, Ewyas Harold, Kenderchurch, Kentchurch, Kilpeck, Kingstone, Llancillo, Llanveynoe, Longtown, Madley, Michaelchurch Escley, Newton, Orcop, Peterchurch, Rowlstone, St Devereux, St Margaret's, Thruxton, Treville, Turnastone, Tyberton, Vowchurch, Walterstone, Wormbridge

HEREFORD PLU

Aconbury, Allensmore (soon after 1836[10]—1930), Amberley (1836—97), Bartestree, Little Birch, Bolstone, Breinton, Lower Bullingham, Upper Bullingham

(1836—85), Burghill, Callow, Clehonger, Credenhill, Little Dewchurch, Much Dewchurch, Dewsall, Dinedor, Dinmore (1858—1930), Dormington, Eaton Bishop (soon after 1836[10]—1930), Fownhope, Grafton, Hampton Bishop, Haywood (1858—1930), Hereford All Saints, Hereford St John the Bishop, Hereford St Martin, Hereford St Nicholas, Hereford St Owen, Hereford St Peter, Hereford The Vineyard (1862—1930), Holme Lacy, Holmer (1884—1930), Holmer and Shelwick (1836—84), Holmer Within (1884—1930), Huntington, Kenchester, Lugwardine, Marden, Mordiford, Moreton on Lugg, Pipe and Lyde, Preston Wynne, Stoke Edith, Stretton Sugwas, Sutton, Tupsley, Wellington, Westhide, Weston Beggard, Withington

KINGTON PLU[10] (Radnor, Heref)

Brilley, Byton (1836—1930), Combe (1836—94), Eardisley, Lower Harpton, Huntington, Kington (1836—94), Kington Rural (1894—1930), Kington Urban (1894—1930), Kinsham (1886—1930), Lower Kinsham (1836—86), Upper Kinsham (1836—86), Knill (1836—1930), Lingen (1836—1930), Lyonshall, Pembridge; Rodd, Nash and Little Brampton (1836—1930); Stapleton (1836—1930), Staunton on Arrow, Titley, Willersley, Willey (1836—1930), Winforton

LEDBURY PLU (Heref, Worcs [1836—97])

Ashperton, Aylton, Bosbury, Coddington, Colwall, Donnington, Eastnor, Egleton, Canon Frome, Castle

Frome, Ledbury (1836—84), Ledbury Rural (1894—1930), Ledbury Urban (1894—1930), Little Marcle, Much Marcle, Mathon (1897—1930), Munsley, Parkhold (1836—84), Pixley, Putley, Stretton Grandison, Tarrington, Wellington Heath (1894—1930), Woolhope, Yarkhill

LEOMINSTER PLU

Aymestry, Bodenham, Croft, Docklow; Eye, Moreton and Ashton; Eyton, Ford, New Hampton (1858—1930), Hampton Wafer (1858—1930), Hatfield, Hope under Dinmore, Humber, Kimbolton, Kingsland, Laysters, Leominster Borough, Leominster Out, Lucton, Luston, Middleton on the Hill, Monkland, Newton, Orleton, Pudlestone, Shobdon, Stoke Prior, Yarpole

ROSS PLU (Heref, Glos)

Aston Ingham (1836—1930), Ballingham, Brampton Abbotts, Bridstow, Brockhampton, How Caple, King's Caple, Foy, Goodrich, Harewood, Hentland, Hope Mansell, Lea (1883—1930), Lea Lower (1836—83), Lea Upper (1836—83), Linton (1836—1930), Llandinabo, Llangarren, Llanwarne, Marstow, Pencoyd, Peterstow, Ross (1836—94), Ross Rural (1894—1930), Ross Urban (1894—1930), St Weonards, Sellack, Sollers Hope, Tretire with Michaelchurch, Upton Bishop, Walford (1836—1930), Weston under Penyard, Yatton

WEOBLEY PLU

Almeley, Birley, Bishopstone, Blakemere (soon after 1836[11]—1930), Bridge Sollers, Brinsop, Brobury, Canon Pyon, Dilwyn, Eardisland, King's Pyon, Kinnersley, Letton (soon after 1836[11]—1930), Mansell Grange, Mansell Lacy, Moccas (soon after 1836[11]—1930), Monington on Wye, Norton Canon (soon after 1836[11]—1930), Preston on Wye (1836—1930), Sarnesfield, Staunton on Wye (1836—1930), Stretford, Weobley, Wormsley, Yazor

In Other Poor Law Counties:

ABERGAVENNY PLU (Monm, Heref [1836—91])

Fwthog[12]

CLEOBURY MORTIMER PLU (Salop, Worcs, Heref [1836—44])

Farley[13]

HAY PLU (Brecon, Heref, Radnor)

Bredwardine, Clifford, Cusop, Dorstone, Whitney

KNIGHTON PLU (Radnor, Salop, Heref)

Adforton, Brampton Bryan, Buckton and Coxall, Letton and Newton, Walford

LUDLOW PLU (Salop, Heref)

Aston, Burrington, Downton, Elton, Leinthall Starkes, Leintwardine[14] (1895—1930), Leintwardine North Side[14] (1836—95), Ludford,[15] Richards Castle[16] (until 1889), Richards Castle[16] (1889—1930), Wigmore

MONMOUTH PLU (Monm, Glos, Heref)

Ganarew, Faraway, Llanrothal, Welsh Bicknor,[17] Welsh Newton, Whitchurch

NEWENT PLU (Glos, Heref [1835—36], Worcs)

Aston Ingham (1835—36), Linton (1835—36), Walford (1835—36)

PRESTEIGNE PLU[10] (Brecon, Heref [1836])

Byton (1836), Combe (1836), Lower Kinsham (1836), Upper Kinsham (1836), Knill (1836), Lingen (1836); Ross, Nash and Little Brampton (1836); Stapleton (1836), Willey (1836)

TENBURY PLU (Worcs, Heref, Salop)

Brimfield, Little Hereford, Stoke Bliss[18]

SANITARY DISTRICTS

ABERGAVENNY RSD
same as PLU for the Heref par

BROMYARD RSD
same as PLU for Heref pars

DORE RSD
same as PLU

HAY RSD
same as PLU for Heref pars

HEREFORD RSD
same as PLU less pt Breinton (1875—84), pt Upper Bullingham (1875—85), Hereford All Saints (pt 1875—84, ent 1884—94), Hereford St John the Baptist (pt 1875—84, ent 1884—94), Hereford St Martin (pt 1875—84, ent 1884—94), Hereford St Nicholas, Hereford St Owen, Hereford the Vineyard, pt Holmer and Shelwick (1875—84), Holmer Within (1884—94), Huntington, Tupsley (pt 1875—84, ent 1884—94)

HEREFORD USD
pt Breinton (1875—84), pt Upper Bullingham (until 1885), Hereford All Saints (pt 1875—84, ent 1884—94), Hereford St John the Baptist (pt 1875—84, ent 1884—94), Hereford St Martin (pt 1875—84, ent 1884—94), Hereford St Nicholas, Hereford St Owen, Hereford St Peter, Hereford The Vineyard, pt Holmer and Shelwick (1875—84), Holmer Within (1884—94), Tupsley (pt 1875—84, ent 1884—94)

KINGTON RSD
same as PLU for Heref pars less pt Kington

KINGTON USD
pt Kington

KNIGHTON RSD
same as PLU for Heref pars

LEDBURY RSD
same as PLU for Heref pars

LEOMINSTER RSD
same as PLU less Leominster Borough, Leominster Out

LEOMINSTER USD
Leominster Borough, Leominster Out

LUDLOW RSD
same as PLU for Heref pars

MONMOUTH RSD
same as PLU for Heref pars

ROSS RSD
same as PLU for Heref pars less pt Bridstow, pt Ross

ROSS USD
pt Bridstow, pt Ross

TENBURY RSD
same as PLU for Heref pars and pt of par

WEOBLEY RSD
same as PLU

ADMINISTRATIVE COUNTY

For MBs see BOROUGHS

BREDWARDINE RD (1894—1934[19])
Bredwardine, Clifford, Cusop, Dorstone, Whitney

BROMYARD RD
Acton Beauchamp (1897—1974), Avenbury, Bredenbury, Brockhampton, Bromyard (1968—74), Collington, Cradley, Little Cowarne, Much Cowarne, Edvin Loach, Edvin Ralph, Evesbatch, Felton, Bishop's Frome, Grendon Bishop, Grendon Warren (1894—95), Hampton Charles, Linton, Moreton Jeffreys, Norton, Ocle Pychard, Pencombe (1894—95), Pencombe with Grendon Warren (1895—1974), Saltmarshe, Upper Sapey, Stanford Bishop, Stoke Lacy, Tedstone Delamere, Tedstone Wafer, Thornbury, Ullingswick, Wacton, Whitbourne, Winslow, Wolferlow

BROMYARD UD (1894[20]—1968[21])
Bromyard

DORE RD (1894—1934[19])
Abbey Dore, Bacton, Craswall, Dulas, Ewyas Harold, Kenderchurch, Kentchurch, Kilpeck, Kingstone, Llancillo, Llanveynoe, Longtown, Madley, Michaelchurch Escley, Newton, Orcop, Peterchurch, Rowlstone, St Devereux, St Margaret's, Thruxton, Treville, Turnastone, Tyberton, Vowchurch, Walterstone, Wormbridge

DORE AND BREDWARDINE RD (1934[19]—74)
Abbey Dore, Bacton, Bredwardine, Clifford, Craswall, Cusop, Dorstone, Dulas, Ewyas Harold, Kenderchurch, Kentchurch, Kilpeck, Kingstone, Llancillo, Llanveynoe, Longtown, Madley, Michaelchurch Escley, Newton, Orcop, Peterchurch, Rowlstone, St Devereux, St Margaret's, Thruxton, Treville, Turnastone, Tyberton, Vowchurch, Walterstone, Wormbridge

HEREFORD RD
Aconbury, Allensmore, Bartestree, Little Birch, Much Birch, Bolstone, Breinton, Lower Bullingham, Burghill, Callow, Clehonger, Credenhill, Little Dewchurch, Much Dewchurch, Dewsall, Dinedor, Dinmore, Dormington, Eaton Bishop, Fownhope, Grafton, Hampton Bishop, Haywood, Holme Lacy, Holmer, Kenchester, Lugwardine, Marden, Mordiford, Moreton on Lugg, Pipe and Lyde, Preston Wynne, Stoke Edith, Stretton Sugwas, Sutton, Wellington, Westhide, Weston Beggard, Withington

KINGTON RD
Brilley, Byton, Combe, Eardisley, Lower Harpton, Huntington, Kington Rural, Kinsham, Knill, Lyonshall, Pembridge; Rodd, Nash and Little Brampton; Stapleton, Staunton on Arrow, Titley, Whitney (1934—74), Willersley, Winforton

KINGTON UD
Kington Urban

LEDBURY RD
Ashperton, Aylton, Bosbury, Coddington, Colwall, Donington, Eastnor, Egleton, Canon Frome, Castle Frome, Ledbury Rural, Ledbury Town (1968—74), Little Marcle, Much Marcle, Mathon (1897—1974), Munsley, Pixley, Putley, Stretton Grandison, Tarrington, Wellington Heath, Woolhope, Yarkhill

LEDBURY UD (1894—1968[21])
Ledbury Urban

LEOMINSTER RD (1894—1930[22])
Aymestry, Bodenham, Brimfield, Croft, Docklow; Eye, Moreton and Ashton; Eyton, Ford, New Hampton, Hampton Wafer, Hatfield, Little Hereford, Hope under Dinmore, Humber, Kimbolton, Kingsland, Laysters, Lucton, Luston, Middleton on the Hill, Monkland, Newton, Orleton, Pudlestone, Shobdon, Stoke Prior, Yarpole

LEOMINSTER AND WIGMORE RD (1930[22]—74)
Adforton, Aston,[23] Aymestry, Bodenham, Brampton Bryan, Brimfield, Buckton and Coxall, Burrington, Croft, Docklow, Downton, Elton; Eye, Moreton and Ashton; Eyton, Ford, New Hampton, Hampton Wafer, Hatfield, Little Hereford, Hope under Dinmore, Humber, Kimbolton, Kingsland, Laysters, Leinthall Starkes, Leintwardine, Lingen, Lucton, Luston, Middleton on the Hill, Monkland, Newton, Orleton, Pudlestone, Richards Castle, Shobdon, Stoke Prior; Walford, Letton and Newton; Wigmore, Willey, Yarpole

ROSS RD (1894—1931[24])
Aston Ingham, Ballingham, Brampton Abbotts, Bridstow, Brockhampton, How Caple, King's Caple, Foy, Goodrich, Harewood, Hentland, Hope Mansell, Lea, Linton, Llandinabo, Llangarren, Llanwarne, Marstow, Pencoyd, Peterstow, Ross Rural, St Weonards, Sellack, Sollers Hope, Tretire with Michaelchurch, Upton Bishop, Walford, Weston under Penyard, Yatton

ROSS UD (1894—1931[25])
Ross Urban

ROSS AND WHITCHURCH RD (1931[24]—74)
Aston Ingham, Ballingham, Brampton Abbotts, Bridstow, Brockhampton, How Caple, King's Caple, Foy, Ganarew, Garway, Goodrich, Harewood, Hentland, Hope Mansell, Lea, Linton, Llandinabo, Llangarren, Llanrothal, Llanwarne, Marstow, Pencoyd, Peterstow, Ross Rural, St Weonards, Sellack, Sollers Hope, Tretire with Michaelchurch, Upton Bishop, Walford, Welsh Bicknor, Welsh Newton, Weston under Penyard, Whitchurch, Yatton

ROSS ON WYE UD (1931[25]—1931)
Ross Urban

WEOBLEY RD
Almeley, Birley, Bishopstone, Blakemere, Bridge Sollers, Brinsop, Brobury, Byford, Canon Pyon, Dilwyn, Eardisland, King's Pyon, Kinnersley, Letton, Mansell Gamage, Mansell Lacy, Moccas, Monnington on Wye, Norton Canon, Preston on Wye, Sarnesfield, Staunton on Wye, Stretford, Weobley, Wormsley, Yazor

WHITCHURCH RD (1894—1931[24])
Garway, Ganarew, Llanrothal, Welsh Bicknor, Welsh Newton, Whitchurch

WIGMORE RD (1894—1930[22])
Adforton, Aston, Buckton and Coxall, Brampton Bryan, Burrington, Downton, Elton, Leinthall Starkes, Leintwardine (1895—1930), pt Leintwardine North Side (1894—95), Lingen, Ludford, Richards Castle; Walford, Letton and Newton; Wigmore, Willey

HEREFORD AND WORCESTER
NON-METROPOLITAN COUNTY

As constituted 1 Apr 1974, defined in terms of Adm Co units as of 31 Mar.

BROMSGROVE DIST
from Worcs: Bromsgrove RD, Bromsgrove UD
HEREFORD DIST
from Heref: Hereford MB
SOUTH HEREFORDSHIRE DIST
from Heref: Dore and Bredwardine RD, Hereford RD, Ross and Whitchurch RD, Ross on Wye UD
LEOMINSTER DIST
from Heref: Kington RD, Kington UD, Leominster MB, Leominster and Wigmore RD, Weobley RD
from Worcs: Tenbury RD
MALVERN HILLS DIST
from Heref: Bromyard RD, Ledbury RD
from Worcs: Malvern UD, Martley UD, Upton upon Severn UD

REDDITCH DIST
from Worcs: Redditch UD
WORCESTER DIST
CB (assoc with Worcs): Worcester CB
from Worcs: pt Droitwich RD (Warndon), pt Pershore RD (St Peter the Great County)
WYCHAVON DIST
from Worcs: Droitwich MB, pt Droitwich RD (the pars not in Worcester Dist), Evesham MB, Evesham RD, pt Pershore RD (the pars not in Worcester Dist)
WYRE FOREST DIST
from Worcs: Bewdley MB, Kidderminster MB, Kidderminster RD, Stourport on Severn UD

HUMBERSIDE NON-METROPOLITAN COUNTY

As constituted 1 Apr 1974, defined in terms of Adm Co units as of 31 Mar.

BEVERLEY DIST
from Yorks E Riding: Beverley MB, Beverley RD, Haltemprice UD

BOOTHFERRY DIST
from Lincs Pts Lind: Isle of Axholm RD
from Yorks E Riding: Howden RD
from Yorks W Riding: Goole MB, Goole RD

CLEETHORPES DIST
from Lincs Pts Lind: Cleethorpes MB, Grimsby RD

GLANFORD DIST
from Lincs Pts Lind: Barton upon Humber UD, Brigg UD, Glanford Brigg RD

GRIMSBY DIST
CB (assoc with Lincs Pts Lind): Grimsby CB

HOLDERNESS DIST
from Yorks E Riding: Bull Sand Fort, Hedon MB, Holderness RD, Hornsea UD, Withernsea UD

KINGSTON UPON HULL DIST
CB (assoc with Yorks E Riding): Kingston upon Hull CB

NORTH WOLDS DIST
from Yorks E Riding: Bridlington MB, pt Bridlington RD (all except Folkton, Hunmanby, Reighton), Driffield RD, Driffield UD, Pocklington RD

SCUNTHORPE DIST
from Lincs Lincs Pts Lind: Scunthorpe MB

LANCASHIRE

ALTERATIONS IN COUNTY BOUNDARIES

As noted by year below, Lancs pars gained territory from or lost it to pars in adjoining cos or county boroughs, or were entirely transferred to them. Details of these alterations are noted in Part I of the *Guide* under Lancashire.

ANCIENT COUNTY (until 1889: Hds, Bors, MBs, PLUs, RSDs, USDs)

1866 Burton in Kendal, Mitton, Rochdale, Thornton in Lonsdale, Whalley. *1884* Warrington. *1885* Woolston with Martinscroft.

ADMINISTRATIVE COUNTY (1889—1974: Hds,[1] PLUs, MBs, RDs, UDs, with assoc CBs of Barrow in Furness, Blackburn, Blackpool [1904—74], Bolton, Bootle, Burnley, Bury, Liverpool, Manchester, Oldham, Preston, Rochdale, St Helen's, Salford, Southport [1905—74], Warrington [1900—74], Wigan)

1889 Ardwick, Ashton under Lyne, Barrow in Furness, Beswick, Birtle cum Bamford, Great Bolton, Little Bolton, Blackburn, Bootle cum Linacre, Briercliffe with Extwistle, Broughton, Burnley, Bury, Butterworth, Castleton, Cheetham, Chorlton upon Medlock, Cliviger, Lower Darwen, West Derby, Droylsden, Eccleston, Elton, Everton, Fishwick, Grimsargh with Brockholes, Habergham Eaves, Halliwell, Little Harwood, Heap, Heaton Norris, Hulme, Ightenhill Park, Kirkdale, Layton with Warbeck; Lea, Ashton, Ingol and Cottam; Livesey, Manchester, Marton, Moss Side, Oldham, Parr, Pendleton, Penwortham, Pilkington, Pilsworth, Preston, Radcliffe; Reedley Hallows, Filly Close and New Laund Booth; Ribbleton, Rumworth, Saddleworth, Salford, Spotland, Stayley, Sutton, Tintwistle, Tonge with Haulgh, Tottington Lower End, Toxteth Park, Walmersley cum Shuttleworth, Wardleworth, Warrington, Wigan, Windle, Withington, Witton, Wuerdle and Wardale. *1890* Blackley, Crumpsall, Gorton, Moston, Newton, Openshaw. *1892* Barton upon Irwell. *1893* Eccleston, Windle. *1895* Dalton. *1896* Latchford. *1897* Blackpool. *1898* Ashton under Lyne, Astley Bridge, Breightmet, Deane, Heaton, Middle Hulton, Over Hulton, Darcy Lever, Great Lever, Lostock, Smithills, Tonge. *1899* Eccleston, *1900* Castleton, Lancashire; Rochdale, Warrington. *1901* Gorton, Heaton Norris, Livesey, Reddish, Witton. *1902* Garston. *1903* Prestwich. *1904* Blackpool, Burnage, Chorlton cum Hardy, Didsbury, Moss Side, Pemberton, Withington. *1905* Fazakerley, Orrell and Ford, Southport. *1909* Gorton, Levenshulme. *1911* Brunshaw, Cliviger, Habergham Eaves, Radcliffe. *1912* Ainsdale, Birkdale. *1913* Allerton, Childwall, Heaton Norris, Little Woolton, Much Woolton. *1918* Bispham with Norbreck, Carleton. *1920* Flixton, Irlam, Rixton with Glazebrook. *1922* Livesey, Ramsgreave. *1926* Habergham Eaves, Ightenhill. *1928* Croxteth Park, West Derby Rural. *1932* Speke. *1933* Birtle cum Bamford, Burtonwood, Chadderton, Cuerdley, Denton, Droylsden, Failsworth, Heywood, Middleton, Norden, Penketh, Radcliffe, Ramsbottom, Rixton with Glazebrook, Great Sankey, Tottington, Unsworth, Walmersley cum Shuttleworth, Winwick with Hulme, Woolston with Martinscroft. *1934* Carleton, Eccleston, Fulwood, Grimsargh with Brockholes, Hardhorn with Newton; Lea, Ashton, Ingol and Cottam; Marton, Ribbleton, Rishton, Windle, Witton. *1935* Broughton West, Dunnerdale with Seathwaite. *1937* Denton, Whitefield. *1940* Ford, Litherland, Netherton, Sefton. *1951* Aintree, Alt, Bardsley, Netherton, Sefton, Woodhouses. *1952* Fulwood, Hale, Halewood, Lea. *1954* Alt, Bardsley, Windle, Winwick, Woodhouses. *1955* Poulton le Fylde. *1956* Kirkby, Lea. *1961* Eccles. *1968* Netherton, Sefton.

NON-METROPOLITAN COUNTY (from 1974: Dists)

1974 Abram, Aintree, Aldingham, Lower Allithwaite, Upper Allithwaite, Altcar, Angerton, Ashton in Makerfield, Ashton under Lyne, Aspull, Atherton, Audenshaw, Billinge and Winstanley, Birkrig Common, Blackrod, Blawith, Bold, Bolton, Broughton East, Broughton West, Burtonwood, Cartmel Fell, Chadderton, Claife, Colton, Coniston, Crompton, Cronton, Great Crosby, Cuerdale, Dalton in Furness, Davyhulme, Denton, Droylsden, Dunnerdale with Seathwaite, Eccles, Eccleston, Egton with Newland, Failsworth, Farnworth, Flixton, Formby, Golborne, Grange, Haigh, Hale, Halewood, Hartshead, Haverthwaite, Hawkshead, Haydock, Heywood, Hindley, Lower Holker, Horwich, Hurst, Huyton with Roby, Ince Blundell, Ince in Makerfield, Irlam, Kearsley, Kirkby, Kirkby Ireleth, Knowsley, Lands Common to Lowick and Subberthwaite, Lees, Leigh, Little Lever, Litherland, Littleborough, Lowick, Lydiate, Maghull, Mansriggs, Melling, Middleton, Milnrow, Mossley, Netherton, Newton le Willows, Orrell, Osmotherley, Penketh, Pennington, Poulton with Fearnhead, Prescot, Prestwich, Radcliffe, Rainford, Rainhill, Ramsbottom, Rixton with Glazebrook, Royton, Great Sankey, Satterthwaite, Seaforth, Sefton, Shevington, Simonswood, Skelwith, Standish with Langtree, Staveley, Stretford, Subberthwaite, Swinton and Pendlebury, Tarbock, Thornton, Torver, Tottington, Turton, Tyldesley with Shakerley, Ulverston, Urmston, Urswick, Wardle, Waterloo, Westhoughton, Whiston, Whitefield, Widnes, Windle, Worsley, Worthington

ASSOCIATED COUNTY BOROUGHS

BARROW IN FURNESS CB
No bdry alt. Transf 1974 to Cumbria.[2]

BLACKBURN CB
Bdry: 1901,[3] 1922,[4] 1934.[5] Transf 1974 to Lancs.[2]

BLACKPOOL CB (1904—74)
Cr 1904 when Blackpool MB constituted a CB.[6] Bdry: 1918,[7] 1934,[5] 1955.[8] Transf 1974 to Lancs.[2]

BOLTON CB
Bdry: 1898.[9] Transf 1974 to Gtr Manch.[2]

BOOTLE CB
Bdry: 1905,[10] 1940,[11] 1951,[12] 1968.[13] Transf 1974 to Merseyside.[2]

BURNLEY CB
Bdry: 1911,[14] 1926.[15] Transf 1974 to Lancs.[2]

BURY CB
Bdry: 1911,[16] 1933,[17] 1933,[18] 1937.[19] Transf 1974 to Gtr Manch.[2]

LIVERPOOL CB
Bdry: 1895,[20] 1902,[21] 1905,[22] 1913,[23] 1928,[24] 1932,[25] 1952,[26] 1956.[27] Transf 1974 to Merseyside.[2]

MANCHESTER CB
Bdry: 1901,[28] 1903,[29] 1904,[30] 1909,[31] 1913,[32] 1931,[33]

1933.[34] Transf 1974 to Gtr Manch.[2]

OLDHAM CB
Bdry: 1951,[35] 1954.[36] Transf 1974 to Gtr Manch.[2]

PRESTON CB
Bdry: 1934,[5] 1952,[37] 1956.[38] Transf 1974 to Lancs.[2]

ROCHDALE CB
Bdry: 1900,[39] 1933.[18] Transf 1974 to Gtr Manch.[2]

ST HELEN'S CB
Bdry: 1894,[40] 1899,[41] 1934,[25] 1954.[42] Transf 1974 to Merseyside.[2]

SALFORD CB
Bdry: 1892,[43] 1961.[44] Transf 1974 to Gtr Manch.[2]

SOUTHPORT CB (1905—74)
Cr 1905 when Southport MB constituted a CB.[45] Bdry: 1912.[46] Transf 1974 to Merseyside.[2]

WARRINGTON CB (1900—74)
Cr 1900 when Warrington MB constituted a CB.[47] Bdry: 1933,[48] 1954.[49] Transf 1974 to Ches.[2]

WIGAN CB
Bdry: 1904.[50] Transf 1974 to Gtr Manch.[2]

HUNDREDS[1]

AMOUNDERNESS HD
Alston (from 1866), Barnacre with Bonds (from 1866), Barton (from 1866), Bilsborrow (from 1866), Bispham (until 1866), Bispham with Norbreck[51] (from 1866), Bleasdale (from 1866), Broughton (from 1866), Bryning with Kellamergh (from 1866), Cabus (from 1866), Carleton (from 1866), Catterall (from 1866), Claughton (from 1866), pt Cleveley (from 1866), Clifton with Salwick (from 1866), Great Eccleston (from 1866), Little Eccleston with Larbreck (from 1866), Elston (from 1866), Elswick (from 1866), Fishwick[51] (from 1866), pt Forton (from 1866), Freckleton (from 1866), Fulwood (from 1866), Garstang, Goosnargh (from 1866), Greenhalgh with Thistleton (from 1866), Grimsargh with Brockholes[51] (from 1866), Haighton (from 1866), Hambleton (from 1866), Hardhorn with Newton (from 1866), pt Holleth (from 1866), Hothersall (from 1866), Inskip with Sowerby (from 1866), Kirkham,[51] Kirkland (from 1866), pt Lancaster[51] (until 1866), Layton with Warbreck[51] (from 1866); Lea, Ashton, Ingol and Cottam[51] (from 1866); Lytham, Marton[51] (from 1866), Medlar with Wesham (from 1866), Myerscough (from 1866), Nateby (from 1866), Newton with Scales (from 1866), pt Pilling (from 1866), Poulton le Fylde, Preesall with Hackinsall (from 1866), Preston,[51] Out Rawcliffe (from 1866), Upper Rawcliffe with Tarnacre (from 1866), Ribbleton[51] (from 1866), Ribby with Wrea (from 1866), pt Ribchester (until 1866), Singleton (from 1866), Stalmine with Staynall (from 1866), St Michael on Wyre (until 1866), Thornton (from 1866); Treales, Roseacre and Wharles (from 1866); Warton (from 1866), Weeton and Preese (from 1866), Westby with Plumpton (from 1866), Whittingham (from 1866),

Winmarleigh (from 1866), Woodplumpton (from 1866), Nether Wyresdale (from 1866)

BLACKBURN HD
Accrington (from 1878), New Accrington (1866—78), Old Accrington (1866—78); Aighton, Bailey and Chaigley (from 1866); Altham (from 1866), Barley with Wheatley Booth (from 1866), Barrowford Booth[51] (from 1866), Billington (from 1866), Blackburn,[51] Higher Booths (from 1866), Lower Booths (from 1866), Little Bowland (from 1866), Briercliffe with Extwistle[51] (from 1866), Burnley[51] (from 1866), pt Bury (until 1866), Chatburn (from 1866), Chipping, Church (from 1866), Clayton le Dale (from 1866), Clayton le Moors (from 1866), Clitheroe[51] (from 1866), Clitheroe Castle (from 1858), Cliviger (from 1866), Colne (from 1866); Cowpe Lench, Newhall Hey and Hall Carr (from 1866); Cuerdale (from 1866), Lower Darwen[51] (from 1866), Over Darwen[51] (from 1866), Dilworth (from 1866), Dinckley (from 1866), Downham (from 1866), Dunnockshaw (from 1866), Dutton (from 1866), Eccleshill[51] (from 1866), Foulridge (from 1866), Goldshaw Booth (from 1866), Habergham Eaves[51] (from 1866), Hapton (from 1866), Great Harwood (from 1866), Little Harwood[51] (from 1866), Haslingden (from 1866), Henheads (from 1866), Heyhouses (from 1858), Higham with West Close Booth (from 1866), Huncoat (from 1866), Ightenhill Park[51] (from 1866), Leagram (from 1866), Livesey[51] (from 1866), Great and Little Marsden[51] (from 1866), Mearley (from 1866), Mellor (from 1866), pt Mitton (until 1866); Little Mitton, Henthorn and Coldcoats (from 1866), Musbury (from 1866), Newchurch (from 1866), Old Laund Booth (from 1866), Osbaldeston (from 1866), Oswaldtwistle (from 1866), Padiham

(from 1866), Pendleton (from 1866), Pleasington (from 1866), Ramsgreave (from 1866), Read (from 1866); Reedley Hallows, Filley Close and New Laund Booth[51] (from 1866); Ribchester, Rishton (from 1866), Roughlee Booth (from 1866), Salesbury (from 1866), Samlesbury (from 1866), Simonstone (from 1866), Thornley with Wheatley (from 1866), Tockholes (from 1866), Trawden (from 1866), Twiston (from 1866), Walton le Dale (from 1866), Whalley[51] (pt until 1866, ent from 1866), Wheatley Carr Booth (from 1866), Wilpshire (from 1866), Wiswell (from 1866), Witton[51] (from 1866), Worsthorne with Hurstwood (from 1866), Worston (from 1866), Yate and Pickup Bank (from 1866)

WEST DERBY HD

Abram (from 1866), Aintree (from 1866), Allerton (from 1866), Altcar, Ashton in Makerfield (from 1845), Astley (from 1866), Atherton (from 1866), Aughton, Bedford (from 1866), Bickerstaffe (from 1866), Billinge Chapel End (from 1866), Billinge Higher End (from 1866), Birkdale (from 1866), Bold (from 1866), Bootle cum Linacre[51] (from 1866), Burscough (from 1866), Burtonwood (from 1866), Childwall, Cronton (from 1866), Great Crosby (from 1866), Little Crosby (from 1866), Croxeth Park (from 1858), Cuerdley (from 1866), Culcheth (from 1866), Dalton (from 1866), West Derby (from 1843), Ditton (from 1866), Downholland (from 1866), Eccleston[51] (from 1866), Everton[51] (from 1866), Fazakerley (from 1866), Formby (from 1866), Garston (from 1866), Golborne (from 1850), Haigh (from 1866), Hale (from 1866), Halewood, Halsall, Haydock (from 1845), Hindley (from 1866); Houghton, Middleton and Arbury (from 1866); Huyton[51] (until 1866), Huyton with Roby[51] (from 1866), Ince Blundell (from 1866), Ince in Makerfield (from 1866), Kenyon (from 1866), Kirkby (from 1866), Kirkdale[51] (from 1866), Knowsley (from 1866), Lathom (from 1866), Leigh (until 1866), West Leigh (from 1866), Litherland (from 1866), Liverpool[51] (from 1699), Lowton (from 1845), Lunt (from 1866), Lydiate (from 1866), Maghull (from 1866), Melling (from 1866), North Meols,[51] Netherton (from 1866), Newchurch Kenyon (1845—66), Newton in Makerfield (from 1841), Ormskirk,[51] Orrell (from 1866), Orrell and Ford (from 1866), Parr[51] (from 1866), Pemberton (from 1866), Penketh (from 1866), Pennington (from 1866), Poulton with Fearnhead (from 1866), Prescot, Rainford (from 1866), Rainhill (from 1866), Rixton with Glazebrook (from 1866), Great Sankey (from 1866), Scarisbrick (from 1866), Sefton, Simonswood (from 1866), Skelmersdale (from 1866), Southworth with Croft (from 1841), Speke (from 1866), Sutton[51] (from 1866), Tarbock (from 1866), Thornton (from 1866), Toxteth Park[51] (from 1858), Tyldesley cum Shakerley (from 1866), Upholland (from 1866), Walton on the Hill,[51] Warrington,[51] Wavertree (from 1866), Whiston (from 1866), Widnes (from 1866), Wigan[51] (pt until 1866, ent from 1866), Windle[51] (from 1866), Winstanley (from 1866), Winwick (until 1866), Winwick with Hulme (from 1866), Woolston with Martinscroft (from 1866), Little Woolton (from 1866), Much Woolton (from 1866)

LEYLAND HD

Adlington (from 1866), Anderton (from 1866), Bispham (from 1866), Bretherton (from 1866), Brindle, Charnock Richard (from 1866), Chorley,[51] Clayton le Woods (from 1866), Coppul (from 1866), Croston,[51] Cuerdon (from 1866), Duxbury (from 1866), Eccleston, Euxton (from 1866), Farington (from 1866), Heapey (from 1866), Heath Charnock (from 1866), Hesketh with Becconsall (from 1821), Heskin (from 1866), Hoghton (from 1866), Hoole (1641—1866), Little Hoole (from 1866), Much Hoole (from 1866), Howick (from 1866), Hutton (from 1866), Leyland, Longton (from 1866), Mawdesley (from 1866), Parbold (from 1866), Penwortham,[51] Rufford (from 1793), Shevington (from 1866), Standish (until 1866), Standish with Langtree (from 1866), Tarleton (from 1821), Ulnes Walton (from 1866), Welsh Whittle (from 1866), Wheelton (from 1866), Whittle le Woods (from 1866), Withnell (from 1866), Worthington (from 1866), Wrightington (from 1866)

LONSDALE HD

Aldcliffe (from 1866), Aldingham, Lower Allithwaite (from 1866), Upper Allithwaite (from 1866), Angerton (from 1858), Arkholme with Cawood (from 1866), Ashton with Stodday (from 1866), Barrow in Furness[51] (from 1866), Blawith (from 1866), Bolton le Sands, Borwick (from 1866), Broughton East (from 1866), Broughton West (from 1866), Bulk (from 1866), Burrow with Burrow (from 1866), pt Burton in Kendal (until 1866), Cantsfield (from 1866), Carnforth (from 1866), Cartmel[51] (until 1866), Cartmel Fell (from 1866), Caton (from 1866), Claife (from 1866), Claughton, pt Cleveley (from 1866), Cockerham, Cockersand Abbey (from 1858), Colton (from 1676), Church Coniston (from 1866), Dalton (from 1866), Dalton in Furness, Dunnerdale with Seathwaite (from 1866), Egton with Newland (from 1866), Ellel (from 1866), Farleton (1866—87), pt Forton (from 1866), Gressingham (from 1866), Halton, Hawkshead (until 1866), Hawkshead and Monk Coniston with Skelwith (from 1866), Heaton with Oxcliffe (from 1866), Heysham, Lower Holker (from 1866), Upper Holker (from 1866), pt Holleth (from 1866), Hornby (1866—87), Hornby with Farleton (from 1887), Ireby (from 1866), Nether Kellet (from 1866), Over Kellet (from 1866), Kirkby Ireleth, Lancaster[51] (pt until 1866, ent from 1866), Leck (from 1866), Lowick (from 1866), Mansriggs (from 1866), Melling[51] (until 1866), Melling with Wrayton (from 1866), Middleton (from 1866), Osmotherley (from 1866), Overton (from 1866), Pennington, pt Pilling (from 1866), Poulton Barre and Torrisholme (from 1866), Priest Hutton (from 1866), Quernmore (from 1866), Roeburndale (from 1866), Satterwaite (from 1866), Scotforth (from 1866), Silverdale (from 1866), Skerton (from 1866), Slyne with Hest (from 1866), Staveley (from 1866), Subberthwaite (from 1866), Tatham, pt Thornton in Lonsdale (until 1866), Thurnham (from 1866), Torver (from 1866), Tunstall, Ulverston,[51] Urswick, Warton[51] (until 1866), Warton with Lindeth (from 1866), Wennington (from 1866), Whittington, Wray with Bolton (from 1866), Over Wyresdale (from 1866), Yealand Convers (from 1866), Yealand Redmayne

(from 1866)

SALFORD HD

Ainsworth (from 1866), Alkrington[51] (from 1866), Anglezarke (from 1866), Ardwick[51] (from 1866), Ashton under Lyne,[51] Ashworth (from 1866), Aspull (from 1866), Barton upon Irwell (from 1866), Beswick[51] (from 1866), Birtle cum Bamford[51] (from 1866), Blackley (from 1866), Blackrod (from 1866), Blatchinworth and Calderbrook (from 1866), Great Bolton[51] (from 1866), Little Bolton[51] (from 1866), Bolton le Moors (until 1866), Bradford[51] (from 1866), Bradshaw (from 1866), Breightmet (from 1866), Broughton[51] (from 1866), Burnage (from 1866), Bury[51] (pt until 1866, ent from 1866), Butterworth (from 1866), Castleton[51] (from 1866), Chadderton (from 1866), Cheetham[51] (from 1866), Chorlton cum Hardy (from 1866), Chorlton on Medlock[51] (from 1866), Clifton (from 1866), Crompton (from 1866), Crumpsall (from 1866), Deane (until 1866), Denton (from 1866), Didsbury (from 1866), Droylsden[51] (from 1866), Eccles (until 1866), Edgeworth (from 1866), Elton (from 1866), Entwistle (from 1866), Failsworth (from 1866), Farnworth (from 1866), Flixton, Gorton (from 1866), Halliwell[51] (from 1866), Harpurhey[51] (from 1866), Harwood (from 1866), Haughton (from 1866), Heap[51] (from 1866), Heaton (from 1866), Great Heaton[51] (from 1866), Little Heaton[51] (from 1866), Heaton Norris[51] (from 1866), Hopwood[51] (from 1866), Horwich (from 1866), Hulme[51] (from 1866), Little Hulton (from 1866), Middle Hulton (from 1866), Over Hulton (from 1866), Kearsley (from 1866), Levenshulme (from 1866), Darcy Lever (from 1866), Great Lever (from 1866), Little Lever (from 1866), Longworth (from 1866), Lostock (from 1866), Manchester,[51] Middleton,[51] Moss Side[51] (from 1866), Moston (from 1866), Newton (from 1866), Oldham[51] (from 1866), Openshaw (from 1866), Pendlebury[51] (from 1866), Pendleton[51] (from 1866), Pilkington[51] (from 1866), Pilsworth[51] (from 1866), Prestwich (from 1866), Quarlton (from 1866), Radcliffe,[51] Reddish (from 1866), Rivington (from 1866), pt Rochdale (until 1866), Royton (from 1866), Rumworth[51] (from 1866), Rusholme[51] (from 1866), Salford[51] (from 1866), Sharples (from 1866), Spotland[51] (from 1866), Stretford (from 1866), Thornham[51] (from 1866), Todmorden and Walsden (from 1866), Tonge[51] (from 1866), Tonge with Haulgh[51] (from 1866), Tottington Higher End (from 1866), Tottington Lower End[51] (from 1866), Turton (from 1866), Urmston (from 1866), Walmersley cum Shuttleworth[51] (from 1866), Wardleworth[51] (from 1866), Westhoughton (from 1866), pt Wigan (until 1866), Withington[51] (from 1866), Worsley (from 1866), Wuerdle and Wardle[51] (from 1866)

BOROUGHS

Units with some degree of burghal character[52] are denominated 'Bor'. Those which did not sustain that status until the 19th cent are in italics. MBs were established by the Municipal Corporations Act, 1835,[53] or by later charter.

ACCRINGTON MB (1878[54]—1974)

Accrington

ASHTON UNDER LYNE MB[55] (1847[56]—1974) [Lancs, Ches (1847—98)]

Ashton under Lyne (pt 1847—94, ent 1894—1974), pt Dukinfield (1847—98), Hartshead (1935—74), Hurst (1927—74)

BACUP MB (1882[57]—1974)

Bacup (1894—1974), pt Newchurch (1882—94), pt Spotland (1882—94)

BARROW IN FURNESS MB[58] (1867[59]—89), CB (1889—1974)

Barrow in Furness (pt 1867—81, ent 1881—1974)

BLACKBURN MB[60] (1851[61]—89), CB (1889—1974)

Blackburn, pt Lower Darwen (1879—93), Little Harwood (pt 1877—79, ent 1879—93), pt Livesey (1877—93), pt Witton (1877—93)

BLACKPOOL MB[62] (1876[63]—1904[6]), CB (1904[6]—74)

pt Bishpam with Norbeck (1879—83), Blackpool (1894—1974), Layton with Warbreck (1876—94), pt Marton (1879—94)

BOLTON LE MOORS BOR, BOLTON MB[64] (1842[65]—89), CB (1889—1974)

Bor: pt Bolton le Moors

MB/CB: Bolton (1895—1974), Great Bolton (1838—95), Little Bolton (pt 1838—85, ent 1885—95), Halliwell (pt 1877—94, ent 1894—95), pt Rumworth (1872—94, ent 1894—95), Tonge with Haulgh (pt 1877—94, ent 1894—95)

BOOTLE CB[66]

Bootle cum Linacre, Orrell (1905—74)

BOOTLE CUM LINACRE MB (1868[67]—89)

Bootle cum Linacre

BURNLEY MB[68] (1861[69]—89), CB (1889—1974)

pt Briercliffe with Extwistle (1889—94), Burnley (pt 1861—94 [enlarged pt 1871—94], ent 1894—1974), pt Habergham Eaves (1871—94 [enlarged pt 1889—94]), pt Ightenhill Park (1889—94); pt Reedley Hallows, Filly Close and New Laund Booth (1889—94)

BURY MB[70] (1876[71]—89), CB (1889—1974)

pt Birtle cum Bamford (1876—94), Bury, pt Elton (1876—94), pt Heap (1876—94), pt Pilkington (1885—94), pt Pilsworth (1876—94), pt Radcliffe (1876—94), pt Tottington Lower End (1876—94), pt Walmersley cum Shuttleworth (1876—94)

CHORLEY BOR, MB (1881[72]—1974)

Bor: pt Croston

MB: Chorley

CLITHEROE BOR/MB[73]

Bor: pt Whalley

MB: Clitheroe

COLNE MB (1895[74]—1974)

Colne

CROSBY MB (1937[75]—74)

Great Crosby, Seaforth, Waterloo

DALTON BOR
pt Dalton
DARWEN MB[76] (1878[77]—1974)
Darwen (1894—1974), Lower Darwen (pt 1879—93, ent 1893—94), Over Darwen (1878—94), pt Eccleshill (1884—94)
WEST DERBY BOR
pt Walton on the Hill
ECCLES MB (1892[78]—1974)
pt Barton upon Irwell (1892—94), Eccles (1894—1974), pt Worsley (1892—94)
FARNWORTH MB (1939[79]—94)
Farnworth
FLEETWOOD MB (1933[80]—74)
Fleetwood
FLOOKBURGH BOR
pt Cartmel
HASLINGDEN MB (1891[81]—1974)
pt Higher Booths (1891—94), pt Lower Booths (1891—94), Haslingden (pt 1891—94, ent 1894—1974), Henheads (1891—94), Musbury (1891—94), pt Tottington Higher End (1891—94), pt Tottington Lower End (1891—94)
HEYWOOD MB (1881[82]—1974)
pt Birtle cum Bamford (1881—94), pt Castleton (1881—94), pt Heap (1881—94), Heywood (1894—1974), pt Hopwood (1881—94), pt Pilsworth (1881—94)
HORNBY MB
pt Melling
KIRKHAM BOR
pt Kirkham
LANCASTER BOR/MB[83]
Lancaster, Lancaster Castle[84] (until 1858)
LEIGH MB (1899[85]—1974)
Leigh
LIVERPOOL BOR/MB/CB
Bor: Liverpool
MB/CB: Allerton (1913—22), Childwall (1913—22), West Derby (pt 1835—95, ent 1895—1922), Everton (1835—1922), Fazakerley (1905—22), Garston (1902—22), Kirkdale (1835—1922), Liverpool, pt Toxteth Park (1835—94), Toxteth Park (1895—1922), Walton on the Hill (1895—1922), Wavertree (1895—1922), Little Woolton (1913—22), Much Woolton (1913—22)
LYTHAM ST ANNE'S MB (1922[86]—74)
Lytham (1922—24), Lytham St Anne's (1924—74), St Anne's on the Sea (1922—24)
MANCHESTER BOR, MB[87] (1838[88]—89), CB (1889—1974) (City from 1853[89])
Bor: pt Manchester
MB/CB: Ardwick (1838—96), Beswick (1838—96), Blackley (1890—96), Bradford (1885—96), Burnage (1904—10), Cheetham (1838—96), Chorlton cum Hardy (1904—10), Chorlton upon Medlock (1838—96), Clayton (1894—96), Crumpsall (1890—96), Didsbury (1904—10), pt Droylsden (1884—94), pt Gorton (1890—94), Gorton (1909—10), West Gorton (1894—96), Harpurhey (1885—96), Hulme (1838—96), Levenshulme (1909—10), Manchester, North Manchester (1896—1916), South Manchester (1896—1916), pt Moss Side (1884—94), Moss Side (1904—

10), Moston (1890—96), Newton (1890—96), Openshaw (1890—96), Rushulme (1885—96), pt Withington (1884—94), Withington (1904—10)
MIDDLETON MB[90] (1886[91]—1974)
Alkrington (1886—94), pt Great Heaton (1891—94), pt Little Heaton (1891—94), pt Hopwood (1886—94), Middleton, pt Thornham (1886—94), Tonge (1886—94)
MORECAMBE MB (1902[92]—28[93])
Morecambe (1924—28), Poulton Barre and Torrisholme (1902—24)
MORECAMBE AND HEYSHAM MB (1928[93]—74)
Morecambe and Heysham
MOSSLEY MB (1885[94]—1974) [*Lancs, Ches, Yorks/ Yorks W Riding (1885—94)*]
pt Ashton under Lyne (1885—94), Mossley (1894—1974), *Saddleworth (the pt in Yorks 1885—89, in Lancs 1889—94), pt Stayley (the pt in Ches, 1885—89, in Lancs 1889—94), pt Tintwistle (the pt in Ches 1885—89, in Lancs 1889—94)*
NELSON MB (1890[95]—1974)
pt Barrowford Booth (1890—94), pt Great and Little Marsden (1890—94), Nelson (1894—1974), pt Wheatley Carr Booth (1890—96)
OLDHAM MB (1849[96]—89), CB (1889—1974)
Oldham
ORMSKIRK BOR
pt Ormskirk
PENWORTHAM BOR
Penwortham
PRESTON BOR/MB[97]/CB
Fishwick (until 1894), pt Grimsargh with Brockholes (1880—94); pt Lea, Ashton, Ingol and Cottam (1880—94 [enlarged pt 1889—94]); pt Penwortham (1889—94), Preston, pt Ribbleton (1880—94)
PRESTWICH MB (1939[98]—74)
Prestwich
RADCLIFFE MB (1935[99]—74)
Radcliffe
RAWTENSTALL MB (1891[100]—1974)
pt Higher Booths (1891—94), pt Lower Booths (1891—94); Cowpe Lench, Newhall Hay and Hall Carr (1891—94); pt Haslingden (1891—94), pt Newchurch (1891—94), Rawtenstall (1894—1974), pt Tottington Higher End (1891—94)
ROBY BOR
pt Huyton with Roby
ROCHDALE BOR,[101] MB[102] (1856[103]—89), CB (1889—1974)
Bor: pt Rochdale
MB/CB: pt Butterworth (1856—94 [enlarged pt 1872—94]), Castleton (pt 1856—72, enlarged pt 1872—94), Rochdale (1894—1974), pt Spotland (1856—94), Wardleworth (pt 1856—72, ent 1872—94), pt Wuerdle and Wardle (1856—94)
ST HELENS MB (1868[104]—89), CB (1889—1974)
pt Eccleston (1868—94), Parr (1868—94), St Helens (1894—1974), Sutton (1868—94), pt Windle (1868—94)
SALFORD BOR, MB[105] (1844[106]—89), CB (1889—1974)
Broughton (pt 1844—53, ent 1853—1919), pt Pendlebury (1853—83), Pendleton (1853—1919), Salford

SOUTHPORT MB[107] (1866[108]—1905[45]), CB (1905[45]—74)

Ainsdale (1912—25), pt North Meols (1866—94), Southport (1894—1974)

STALYBRIDGE MB[109] (1857[110]—1974 [*Ches*, Lancs (1857—89)]

pt Ashton under Lyne (the pt in Lancs 1857—89 [enlarged pt 1881—89], in Ches [the pt as enlarged in 1881] 1889—94), *pt Dukinfield (1857—94), pt Stayley (1857—94 [enlarged pt 1881—94]), Stalybridge (1894—1974)*

STOCKPORT BOR/MB[111]/CB[112] (*Ches*, Lancs (until 1894)]

pt Brinnington (until 1894), pt Cheadle (until 1866), pt Cheadle (1879—94), pt Cheadle Bulkeley (1866—79), pt Cheadle Moseley (1866—79), pt Heaton Norris (1835—94), *Heaton Norris (1913—35), Reddish (1901—74), Stockport*

STRETFORD MB (1933[113]—74)

Stretford

SWINTON AND PENDLEBURY MB (1934[34]—74)

Swinton and Pendlebury

ULVERSTON BOR

pt Ulverston

WARRINGTON BOR, MB[114] (1847[115]—1900[47]), CB (1900[47]—1974) [Lancs, *Ches* (1847—94)]

Bor: pt Warrington

MB: pt Latchford (1847—94), pt Thelwall (1847—84), Warrington (pt 1847—94, ent 1894—1974)

WARTON BOR

pt Warton

WIDNES BOR (1892[116]—1974)

Widnes

WIGAN BOR/MB/CB

Pemberton (1904—20), Wigan

POOR LAW UNIONS

In Lancs Poor Law County:[117]

ASHTON UNDER LYNE PLU (Lancs, Ches)

Alt (1894—1930), Ashton under Lyne, Audenshaw (1894—1930), Bardsley (1894—1930), Crossbank (1894—1914), Denton, Droylesden, Hartshead (1894—1930), Haughton (1837—94), Hurst (1894—1927), Lees (1894—1930), Little Moss (1894—1930), Mossley (1894—1930), Waterloo (1894—1930), Woodhouses (1894—1930)

BARTON UPON IRWELL PLU (1849—1930)

Barton upon Irwell (1849—94), Barton Moss (1894—1930), Clifton, Davyhulme (1894—1930), Eccles (1894—1930), Flixton, Irlam (1894—1930), Stretford, Swinton (1894—1930), Urmston, Worsley

BLACKBURN PLU

Balderstone, Billington, Blackburn, Church, Clayton le Dale, Clayton le Moors, Darwen (1894—1930), Lower Darwen (1837—94), Over Darwen (1837—94), Dinckley, Eccleshill, Great Harwood, Little Harwood (1837—93), Livesey, Mellor, Osbaldeston, Oswaldtwistle, Pleasington, Ramsgreave, Rishton, Salesbury, Tockholes, Wilpshire, Witton (1837—1900), Yate and Pickup Bank

BOLTON PLU

Astley Bridge (1894—98), Belmont (1894—1925), Bolton (1895—1930), Great Bolton (1837—95), Little Bolton (1837—95), Bradshaw (1837—98), Breightmet (1837—98), Deane (1894—98), Edgeworth (1837—1925), Entwistle (1837—98), Farnworth, Halliwell (1837—95), Harwood (1837—98), Heaton (1837—98), Horwich, Little Hulton, Middle Hulton (1837—98), Over Hulton (1837—98), Kearsley, Darcy Lever (1837—98), Great Lever (1837—98), Little Lever, Longworth (1837—98), Lostock (1837—98), Quarlton (1837—98), Rumworth (1837—95), Sharples (1837—94), Smithills (1894—98), Tonge (1894—98), Tonge with Haulgh (1837—95), Turton, Westhoughton

BURNLEY PLU

Altham, Barley with Wheatley Booth, Barrowford (1894—1930), Barrowford Booth (1837—94), Blacko (1894—1930), Briercliffe (1894—1930), Briercliffe with Extwistle (1837—94), Brierfield (1894—1930), Brunshaw (1894—1911), Burnley, Cliviger,[118] Colne, Dunnockshaw, Foulridge, Goldshaw Booth, Habergham Eaves, Hapton, Heyhouses (1837—1904), Higham with West Close Booth, Huncoat (1837—1929), Ightenhill (1894—1930), Ightenhill Park (1837—94), Great and Little Marsden (1837—94), Nelson (1894—1930), Northtown (1894—1930), Old Laund Booth, Padiham, Read, Reedley Hallows (1894—1930); Reedley Hallows, Filley Close and New Laund Booth (soon after 1837[119]—94); Roughlee Booth, Sabden (1904—30), Simonstone, Trawden, Wheatley Carr Booth, Worsthorne with Hurstwood

BURY PLU

Ainsworth, Ashworth (1837—94), Birtle cum Bamford, Bury, Elton (1837—94), Heap (1837—94), Heywood (1894—1930), Hopwood (1837—94), Outwood (1894—1930), Pilkington (1837—94), Pilsworth (1837—94), Radcliffe, Ramsbottom (1894—1930), Tottington (1894—1930), Tottington Lower End (1837—94), Unsworth (1894—1930), Walmersley cum Shuttleworth, Whitefield (1894—1930)

CATON GILBERT UNION (until 1869)

Bolton le Sands, Borwick, Caton, Claughton, Farleton, Gressingham, Halton, Heysham, Hornby, Nether Kellet, Over Kellet, Netherton, Poulton Barre and Torrisholme, Quernmore, Slyne with Hest, Tatham, Wennington, Wray with Botton

CHORLEY PLU

Adlington, Anderton, Anglezarke, Bretherton (soon after 1837[120]—1930), Brindle, Charnock Richard, Chorley, Clayton le Woods, Coppull, Croston, Cuerdon, Duxbury, Eccleston, Euxton, Heapey, Heath Charnock, Heskin, Hoghton, Leyland, Mawdesley, Rivington, Ulnes Walton, Welsh Whittle, Wheelton, Whittle le Woods, Withnell

CHORLTON PLU

Ardwick (1837—96), Burnage (1837—1910), Chorlton on Medlock (1837—96), Chorlton cum Hardy (1837—1910), Didsbury, Gorton (1837—1910), West Gorton (1894—96), Hulme (1837—96), Levenshulme (1837—

1910), South Manchester (1896—1916), Moss Side (1837—1910), Openshaw (1837—1910), Rusholme (1837—96), Stretford (1837—49), Withington (1837—1910)

CLITHEROE PLU (Lancs, Yorks W Riding)
Aighton, Bailey and Chaigley; Little Bowland, Chatburn, Chipping, Clitheroe, Clitheroe Castle (1858—95), Downham, Leagram, Mearley; Little Mitton, Henthorn and Coldcoats; Pendleton, Thornley with Wheatley, Twiston, Whalley, Wiswell, Worston

WEST DERBY PLU
Aintree, Allerton (1837—1922), Bootle cum Linacre, Childwall (1837—1922), Great Crosby, Little Crosby, Croxteth Park (1862—1928), West Derby (1837—1922), West Derby Rural (1895—1928), Everton (1837—1922), Fazakerley (1837—1922), Ford (1905—30), Garston (1837—1922), Ince Blundell, Kirkby, Kirkdale (1837—1922), Litherland, Lunt, Netherton, Orrell (1905—30), Orrell and Ford (1837—1905), Seaforth (1894—1930), Sefton, Thornton, Toxteth Park (1837—57), Walton on the Hill (1837—1922), Waterloo (1894—1930), Wavertree (1837—1922)

FYLDE PLU
Bispham with Norbreck (1837—1918), Blackpool (1894—1930), Bryning with Kellamergh, Carleton, Clifton with Salwick, Little Eccleston with Larbreck, Elswick, Fleetwood (1894—1930), Freckleton, Greenhalgh with Thistleton, Hardhorn with Newton, Kirkham, Layton with Warbreck (1837—94), Lytham (1837—1924), Lytham St Ann's (1924—30), Marton, Medlar with Wesham, Newton with Scales, Poulton le Fylde, Ribby with Wrea, St Anne's on the Sea (1894—1924), Singleton, Thornton; Treales, Roseacre and Wharles; Warton, Weeton and Preese, Westby with Plumptons

GARSTANG PLU
Barnacre with Bonds, Bilsborrow, Bleasdale, Cabus, Catterall, Claughton, Cleveley, Great Eccleston, Forton, Garstang, Hambleton, Holleth, Inskip with Sowerby, Kirkland, Myerscough, Nateby, Pilling, Preesall with Hackinsall, Out Rawcliffe, Upper Rawcliffe with Tarnacre, Stalmine with Staynall, Winmarleigh, Nether Wyresdale

HASLINGDEN PLU
Accrington (1878—1930), New Accrington (1837—78), Old Accrington (1837—78), Bacup (1894—1930), Higher Booths (1837—94), Lower Booths (1837—94); Cowpe Lench, Newhall Hay and Hall Carr (1837—94); Haslingden, Henheads (1837—94), Musbury (1837—94), Newchurch (1837—94), Rawtenstall (1894—1930), Tottington Higher End (1837—94)

LANCASTER PLU
Aldcliffe, Ashton with Stodday, Bolton le Sands (1869—1930), Bulk (1839—1900), Carnforth, Cockerham, Cockersand Abbey (1858—1930), Ellel, Heaton with Oxcliffe, Heysham (1869—1928), Lancaster, Middleton, Morecambe (1924—28), Morecambe and Heysham (1928—30), Overton, Poulton Barre and Torrisholme (1869—1924), Priest Hutton, Scotforth, Silverdale, Skerton (1839—1900), Slyne with Hest (1869—1930), Thurnham, Warton with Lindeth, Over Wyresdale, Yealand Conyers, Yealand Redmayne

LEIGH PLU
Astley, Atherton, Bedford (1837—94), Culceth (1866—1930), Golborne (1850—1930), Kenyon (1866—1930), Leigh (1894—1930), West Leigh (1837—94), Lowton, Newchurch Kenyon (1845—66), Pennington (1837—94), Tyldesley cum Shakerley

LIVERPOOL PAR (1841—1930)
Liverpool

LUNESDALE PLU (1869—1930)
Arkholme with Cawood, Borwick, Burrow with Burrow, Cantsfield, Caton, Claughton, Farleton (1869—87), Gressingham, Halton, Hornby (1866—87), Hornby with Farleton (1887—1930), Ireby, Nether Kellet, Over Kellet, Leck, Melling with Wrayton, Quernmore, Roeburndale, Tatahm, Tunstall, Wennington, Whittington, Wray with Botton

MANCHESTER PLU (1841—50), PAR (1850—1930)
Manchester

OLDHAM PLU
Alkrington (1837—94), Chadderton, Crompton, Middleton, Oldham, Royton, Thornham (1837—94), Tonge (1837—94)

ORMSKIRK PLU
Ainsdale (1894—1925), Altcar, Aughton, Bickerstaffe, Birkdale (1837—1912), Bispham, Burscough, Downholland, Formby, Halsall, Hesketh with Becconsall, Lathom, Lydiate, Maghull, Melling, North Meols, Ormskirk, Rufford, Scarisbrick, Simonswood, Skelmersdale, Southport (1894—1930), Tarleton

PRESCOT PLU
Bold, Cronton, Ditton (1837—1920), Eccleston, Hale, Halewood, Huyton with Roby, Knowsley, Parr (1837—94), Prescot, Rainford, Rainhill, St Helens (1894—1930), Speke, Sutton (1837—94), Tarbock, Whiston, Widnes, Windle, Little Woolton, Much Woolton

PRESTON PLU
Alston, Barton, Bretherton (1837—soon after 1837[119]), Broughton, Cuerdale, Dilworth, Dutton, Elston, Farington, Fishwick (1837—94), Fulwood, Goosnargh, Grimsargh with Brockholes, Haighton, Hothersall, Little Hoole, Much Hoole, Howick, Hutton; Lea, Ashton, Ingol and Cottam; Longton, Penwortham, Preston, Ribbleton, Ribchester, Salmesbury, Walton le Dale, Whittingham (soon after 1837[110]—1930), Woodplumpton

PRESTWICH PLU (1850—1930)
Blackley (1850—96), Beswick (1858—96), Bradford (1850—96), Cheetham (1850—96), Clayton (1894—96), Crumpsall (1850—96), Failsworth, Harpurhey (1850—96), Great Heaton (1850—94), Little Heaton (1850—94), North Manchester (1896—1916), Moston (1850—96), Newton (1850—96), Prestwich

ROCHDALE PLU
Blatchinworth and Calderbrook (1837—94), Butterworth (1837—94), Castleton (1837—94), Castleton by Rochdale (1894—96); Castleton, Lancashire (1894—1900); Littleborough (1894—1930), Milnrow (1894—1930), Norden (1894—1930), Rochdale (1894—1930), Spotland (1837—94), Wardle (1894—1930), Wardleworth (1837—94), Whitworth (1894—1930), Wuerdle and Wardle (1837—94)

SALFORD PLU
Broughton, Pendlebury, Pendleton, Salford

TOXTETH PARK PAR (1857—1922)
Toxteth Park
ULVERSTON PLU
Aldingham, Lower Allithwaite, Upper Allithwaite, Angerton (1858—1930), Barrow in Furness (soon after 1851[119]—1930), Blawith, Broughton East, Broughton West, Cartmel Fell, Claife, Colton, Consiton (1894—1930), Church Coniston (1836—94), Dalton in Furness, Dunnerdale with Seathwaite, Egton with Newland, Grange (1894—1930), Haverthwaite (1927—30), Hawkshead (1894—1930), Hawkshead and Monk Coniston with Skelwith (1836—1930), Lower Holker, Upper Holker, Kirkby Ireleth, Lowick, Mansriggs, Osmotherley, Pennington, Satterwaite, Skelwith (1894—1930), Staveley, Subberthwaite, Torver, Ulverston, Urswick
WARRINGTON PLU
Burtonwood, Cuerdley, Golborne (1837—50), Haydock; Houghton, Middleton and Arbury; Kenyon (1837—45), Newton in Makerfield, Penketh, Poulton with Fearnhead, Rixton with Glazebrook, Great Sankey, Little Sankey (1894—96), Southworth with Croft, Warrington, Winwick with Hulme, Woolston with Martinscroft

WIGAN PLU
Abram, Ashton in Makerfield, Aspull, Billinge and Winstanley (1924—30), Billinge Chapel End (1837—1924), Billinge Higher End (1837—94), Blackrod, Dalton, Haigh, Hindley, Ince in Makerfield, Orrell, Parbold, Pemberton, Shevington, Standish with Langtree, Upholland, Wigan, Winstanley (1837—1924), Worthington, Wrightington

In Other Poor Law Counties:
KENDAL PLU (Westm, Lancs [1836—95])
Dalton
STOCKPORT PLU (Ches, Lancs)
Heaton Norris, Reddish
TODMORDEN PLU (Yorks W Riding, Lancs)
Todmorden and Walsden

SANITARY DISTRICTS

ABRAM USD
Abram
ACCRINGTON USD
Accrington (1878—94), New Accrington (1875—78), Old Accrington (1875—78)
ADLINGTON USD
Adlington
ALLERTON USD
Allerton
ASHTON IN MAKERFIELD USD
Ashton in Makerfield
ASHTON UNDER LYNE RSD
same as PLU for Lancs pars less Ashton under Lyne, Denton, Droylsden (pt 1875—84, ent 1874—94), Haughton
ASHTON UNDER LYNE USD
pt Ashton under Lyne
ASPULL USD
Aspull
ASTLEY BRIDGE USD
pt Little Bolton (1875—85), pt Sharples
ATHERTON USD
Atherton
AUDENSHAW USD
pt Ashton under Lyne
BACUP USD
pt Newchurch, pt Spotland
BARROW IN FURNESS USD
Barrow in Furness (pt 1875—81, ent 1881—94)
BARROWFORD BOOTH USD (1892[121]—94)
pt Barrowford Booth
BARTON, ECCLES, WINTON AND MONTON USD (1875—92[78])
pt Barton upon Irwell
BARTON UPON IRWELL RSD
same as PLU less pt Barton upon Irwell, Stretford, Worsley
BILLINGE USD
Billinge Chapel End, Billinge Higher End, Winstanley

BIRKDALE USD
Birkdale
BLACKBURN RSD
same as PLU less Blackburn, Church, Clayton le Moors, Lower Darwen (pt 1875—79, ent 1879—94), Over Darwen, pt Eccleshill (1884—94), Great Harwood, Little Harwood (pt 1875—79, ent 1879—93), pt Livesey (1875—93), Oswaldtwistle, Rishton (1882—94), pt Witton (1875—93)
BLACKBURN USD[60]
Blackburn, pt Lower Darwen (1879—93), Little Harwood (pt 1877—79, ent 1879—93), pt Livesey (1877—93), pt Witton (1877—93)
BLACKPOOL USD
pt Bispham with Norbreck (1879—83), Layton with Warbreck, pt Marton (1879—94)
BLACKROD USD
Blackrod
BOLTON RSD
same as PLU less Great Bolton, Little Bolton, Farnworth, pt Halliwell (1877—94), Horwich, Little Hulton, Kearsley, Little Lever, pt Rumworth, pt Sharples, pt Tonge with Haulgh (1877—94), Torton, Westhoughton
BOLTON USD[64]
Great Bolton, Little Bolton (pt 1875—85, ent 1885—94), pt Halliwell (1877—94), pt Rumworth, pt Tonge with Haulgh (1877—94)
BOOTLE CUM LINACRE USD
Bootle cum Linacre
BRADFORD USD (1875—85[122])
Bradford
BRIERFIELD USD
pt Great and Little Marsden
BURNLEY RSD
same as PLU less pt Barrowford Booth, Higher Booths, Lower Booths, pt Briercliffe with Extwistle (1889—94), Burnley (pt 1875—89, ent 1889—94), pt Cliviger, Colne, pt Habergham Eaves, pt Hapton, Haslingden,

Henheads (pt 1875—83, ent 1883—94), pt Ightenhill Park (1891—94); Great and Little Marsden, Newchurch, pt Padiham, pt Reedley Hallows, Filly Close and New Laund Booth (1889—94); Trawden, pt Wheatley Carr Booth

BURNLEY USD[68]

pt Briercliffe with Extwistle (1889—94), pt Burnley, pt Habergham Eaves (enlarged pt 1889—94), pt Ightenhill Park (1889—94); pt Reedley Hallows, Filly Close and New Laund Booth (1889—94)

BURY RSD

same as PLU less pt Birtle cum Bamford, Bury, pt Elton (enlarged pt 1883—94), pt Heap, Hopwood, pt Pilkington (reduced pt 1885—94), pt Pilsworth, Radcliffe, Tottington Lower End (pt 1875—83, ent 1883—94), Walmersley cum Shuttleworth (pt 1875—83, ent 1883—94)

BURY USD

pt Birtle cum Bamford, Bury, pt Elton, pt Heap, pt Pilkington, pt Pilsworth, pt Radcliffe, pt Tottington Lower End, pt Walmersley cum Shuttleworth

CASTLETON BY ROCHDALE USD

pt Castleton, pt Hopwood, pt Thornham

CHADDERTON USD

Chadderton

CHILDWALL USD

Childwall

CHORLEY RSD

same as PLU less Adlington, Chorley, Croston, Leyland, Withnell (1893—94)

CHORLEY USD

Chorley

CHORLTON RSD

same as PLU less Ardwick, Burnage, Chorlton cum Hardy, Chorlton on Medlock, Didsbury, Gorton, Hulme, Levenshulme, Moss Side, Openshaw, Rusholme, Withington

CHURCH USD

Church

CLAYTON LE MOORS USD

Clayton le Moors

CLITHEROE RSD

same as PLU for Lancs pars less Clitheroe

CLITHEROE USD

Clitheroe

COLNE USD (Mar[123]—apptd day 1894)

Colne, pt Great and Little Marsden

COLNE AND MARSDEN USD (1875—Mar 1894[123])

Colne, pt Great and Little Marsden

CROMPTON USD

Crompton

GREAT CROSBY USD

pt Great Crosby

LITTLE CROSBY USD

Little Crosby

CROSTON USD

Croston

CRUMPSALL USD (1875—90[124])

Crumpsall

DALTON IN FURNESS USD

Dalton in Furness

DARWEN USD[76] (1878[77]—94)

pt Lower Darwen (pt 1879—93, ent 1893—94), Over

Darwen, pt Eccleshill (1884—94)

OVER DARWEN USD (1875—78[77])

Over Darwen

DENTON USD (1875—84[125])

Denton

DENTON USD (Apr[126]—apptd day 1894)

Denton, Haughton

DENTON AND HAUGHTON USD (1884[125]—94[126])

Denton, Haughton

WEST DERBY RSD

same as PLU less Allerton, Bootle cum Linacre, Childwall, Great Crosby, Little Crosby, pt West Derby, Everton, Garston, Kirkdale, Litherland, Walton on the Hill, Wavertree

WEST DERBY USD

pt West Derby, pt Walton on the Hill

DROYLSDEN USD

pt Droylsden

ECCLES USD (1892[78]—94)

pt Barton upon Irwell, pt Worsley

FAILSWORTH USD

Failsworth

FARNWORTH USD

Farnworth

FLEETWOOD USD[127]

pt Thornton (enlarged pt 1882—94)

FULWOOD USD

Fulwood

FYLDE RSD

same as PLU less pt Bispham with Norbreck (1875—83), Kirkham, Layton with Warbreck, Lytham, pt Marton, pt Thornton (reduced pt 1882—94)

GARSTANG RSD

same as PLU

GARSTON USD

Garston

GORTON USD[128]

pt Gorton (reduced pt 1890—94)

GRANGE USD

pt Lower Allithwaite, pt Upper Allithwaite, pt Broughton East, pt Upper Holker (1875—84)

GREAT HARWOOD USD

Great Harwood

HASLINGDEN USD[129]

pt Higher Booths, pt Lower Booths, pt Haslingden, Henheads (pt 1875—83, ent 1883—94), Musbury (1883—94), pt Tottington Higher End (1891—94), pt Tottington Lower End (1883—94)

HASLINGDEN RSD

same as PLU less Accrington (1878—94), New Accrington (1875—78), Old Accrington (1875—78); Higher Booths (pt 1875—83, ent 1883—94), pt Lower Booths (1875—83); Cowpe Lench, Newhall Hey and Hall Carr (pt 1875—83, ent 1883—94); Haslingden, Henheads (pt 1875—83, ent 1883—94), Musbury (1883—94), Newchurch, Tottington Higher End (pt 1875—83, ent 1883—94), Tottington Lower End (pt 1875—83, ent 1883—94)

HAUGHTON USD (1875—84[125])

Haughton

HAYDOCK USD

Haydock

HEATON NORRIS USD
  pt Heaton Norris
HEYWOOD USD
  pt Birtle cum Bamford, pt Castleton, pt Heap, pt Hopwood, pt Pilsworth
HINDLEY USD
  Hindley
HORWICH USD
  Horwich
LITTLE HULTON USD
  Little Hulton
HURST USD
  pt Ashton under Lyne
HUYTON WITH ROBY USD
  Huyton with Roby
INCE IN MAKERFIELD USD
  Ince in Makerfield
KEARSLEY USD
  Kearsley
KIRKHAM USD
  Kirkham
LANCASTER RSD
  same as PLU less Lancaster, Poulton Barre and Torrisholme
LANCASTER USD
  Lancaster
LATHOM USD (1875—Feb 1894[130])
  Lathom
LATHOM AND BURSCOUGH USD (Feb[130]— appointed day 1894)
  Burscough, Lathom
LEES USD
  pt Ashton under Lyne
LEIGH USD
  Bedford, West Leigh, Pennington
LEIGH RSD
  same as PLU less Atherton, Bedford, West Leigh, Pennington, Tyldesley cum Shakerley
LEVENSHULME USD
  Levenshulme
LITTLE LEVER USD
  Little Lever
LEYLAND USD
  Leyland
LITHERLAND USD
  pt Litherland
LITTLEBOROUGH USD
  Blatchinworth and Calderbrook, pt Butterworth, pt Wuerdle and Wardle
LIVERPOOL USD
  pt West Derby, Everton, Kirkdale, Liverpool, pt Toxteth Park
LONGRIDGE USD (1883[131]—94)
  Alston, Dilworth
LUNESDALE RSD
  same as PLU
LYTHAM USD
  pt Lytham
MANCHESTER USD[87]
  Ardwick, Beswick, Blackley (1890—94), Bradford (1885—94), Cheetham, Chorlton upon Medlock, Crumpsall (1890—94), pt Droylsden (1884—94), pt Gorton (1890—94), Harpurhey (1885—94), Hulme,

Manchester, pt Moss Side (1884—94), Moston (1890—94), Newton (1890—94), Openshaw (1890—94), Rushulme (1885—94), pt Withington (1884—94)
MIDDLETON USD[90] (1886[91]—94)
  Alkrington, pt Great Heaton (1891—94), pt Little Heaton (1891—94), pt Hopwood, Middleton, pt Thornham, Tonge
MIDDLETON AND TONGE USD (1875—86[91])
  Alkrington, pt Hopwood, Middleton, pt Thornham, Tonge
MILNROW USD
  pt Butterworth, pt Castleton
MORECAMBE USD (orig 'Poluton Barre and Torrisholme' USD[132])
  Poulton Barre and Torrisholme
MOSS SIDE USD
  pt Moss Side, pt Withington
MOSSLEY USD[94] (Lancs, Ches 1875—85; Lancs, Ches, Yorks W Riding 1885—94)
  pt Ashton under Lyne, *pt Saddleworth (Yorks W Riding, 1885—94), pt Stayley (Ches 1875—89, Lancs 1889—94), pt Tintwistle (Ches 1875—89, Lancs 1889—94)*
NELSON USD
  pt Barrowford Booth, pt Great and Little Marsden, pt Wheatley Carr Booth
NEWTON HEATH USD (1875—90[124])
  pt Newton
NEWTON IN MAKERFIELD USD
  Newton in Makerfield
NORDEN USD
  pt Spotland
OLDHAM USD
  Oldham
OPENSHAW USD (1875—90[124])
  Openshaw
ORMSKIRK RSD
  same as PLU less Birkdale, Burscough (Feb—apptd day 1894), Lathom, pt North Meols, Ormskirk, Skelmersdale
ORMSKIRK USD
  Ormskirk
ORRELL USD
  Orrell
OSWALDTWISTLE USD
  Oswaldtwistle
PADIHAM AND HAPTON USD
  pt Hapton, pt Padiham
PEMBERTON USD
  Pemberton
POULTON BARRE AND TORRISHOLME USD—see MORECAMBE USD
PRESCOT RSD
  same as PLU less Eccleston, Huyton with Roby, Parr, pt Prescot, Rainford, St Helens (Mar—apptd day 1894), Sutton, Widnes, pt Windle, Little Woolton, Much Woolton
PRESCOT USD
  pt Eccleston, pt Prescot
PRESTON RSD
  same as PLU less Alston (1883—94), Dilworth (1893—94), Fishwick, Fulwood, pt Grimsargh with Brockholes; pt Lea, Ashton, Ingol and Cottam; pt Penwortham (1889—94), pt Ribbleton, Walton le Dale

PRESTON USD[97]
  Fishwick, pt Grimsargh with Brockholes; pt Lea, Ashton, Ingol and Cottam; pt Penwortham (1889—94), Preston, pt Ribbleton

PRESTWICH RSD
  same as PLU less Beswick, Blackley (1890—94), Bradford, Cheetham, Crumpsall, Failsworth, Harpurhey (1885—94), pt Great Heaton (1891—94), pt Little Heaton (1891—94), Moston (1890—94), Newton (pt 1875—90, ent 1890—94), Prestwich

PRESTWICH USD
  Prestwich

RADCLIFFE USD[133]
  pt Radcliffe

RAINFORD USD
  Rainford

RAMSBOTTOM USD[134]
  pt Elton (1883—94), pt Tottington Higher End (1883—94), pt Tottington Lower End, pt Walmersley and Shuttleworth (1883—94)

RAWTENSTALL USD[135]
  pt Higher Booths (1883—94), pt Lower Booths; Cowpe Lench, Newhall Hey and Hall Carr (pt 1875—83, ent 1883—94); pt Haslingden, pt Newchurch, pt Tottington Higher End (1883—94)

REDDISH USD
  Reddish

RISHTON USD (1882[136]—94)
  Rishton

ROCHDALE USD
  pt Butterworth, pt Castleton, pt Spotland, Wardleworth, pt Wuerdle and Wardle

ROYTON USD
  Royton, pt Thornham

RUSHOLME USD (1875—85[122])
  pt Moss Side, Rusholme, pt Withington

ST ANNE'S ON THE SEA USD
  pt Lytham, pt Marton

ST HELENS USD[104]
  pt Eccleston (1875—Mar 1894), Parr (1875—Mar 1894), St Helens (Mar—apptd day 1894), Sutton (1875—Mar 1894), pt Windle (1875—Mar 1894)

SALFORD RSD
  same as PLU less Broughton, Pendlebury (pt 1875—83, ent 1883—94), Pendleton, Salford

SALFORD USD
  Broughton, pt Pendlebury (1875—83), Pendleton (1875—92), Salford

SKELMERSDALE USD
  Skelmersdale

SOUTHPORT USD
  pt North Meols

STALYBRIDGE USD[109] (Ches, Lancs [1875—89])
  pt Ashton under Lyne (enlarged pt 1881—94), pt Dukinfield, pt Stayley (enlarged pt 1881—94)

STANDISH WITH LANGTREE USD
  Standish with Langtree

STOCKPORT RSD
  same as PLU for Lancs pars less Heaton Norris, Reddish

STOCKPORT USD (Ches, Lancs)
  pt Brinnington, pt Cheadle (1879—94), pt Cheadle Bulkeley (1875—79), pt Cheadle Moseley (1875—79), pt Heaton Norris

STRETFORD USD
  Stretford

SWINTON AND PENDLEBURY USD
  Pendlebury (pt 1875—83, ent 1883—94), pt Worsley

TODMORDEN USD (Yorks W Riding, Lancs)
  pt Cliviger[118]

TOXTETH PARK USD
  pt Toxteth Park

TRAWDEN USD
  Trawden

TURTON USD
  Turton

TYLDESLEY WITH SHAKERLEY USD
  Tyldesley cum Shakerley

ULVERSTON RSD
  same as PLU less pt Lower Allithwaite, pt Upper Allithwaite, Barrow in Furness (pt 1875—81, ent 1881—94), pt Broughton East, Dalton in Furness, pt Upper Holker (1875—84), Ulverston

ULVERSTON USD
  Ulverston

UPHOLLAND USD
  Upholland

WALTON LE DALE USD
  Walton le Dale

WALTON ON THE HILL USD
  pt Walton on the Hill

WARRINGTON RSD
  same as PLU for Lancs pars less Haydock, Newton in Makerfield, pt Warrington

WARRINGTON USD[114] (Lancs, Ches)
  pt Chelwall (1875—84), pt Thelwall, pt Warrington

WATERLOO WITH SEAFORTH USD
  pt Great Crosby, pt Litherland

WAVERTREE USD
  Wavertree

WESTHOUGHTON USD
  Westhoughton

WHITEFIELD USD
  pt Pilkington

WHITWORTH USD
  pt Spotland

WIDNES USD
  Widnes

WIGAN RSD
  same as PLU less Abram, Ashton in Makerfield, Aspull, Billinge Chapel End, Billinge Higher End, Hindley, Ince in Makerfield, Orrell, Pemberton, Standish with Langtree, Upholland, Wigan, Winstanley

WIGAN USD
  Wigan

WITHINGTON USD
  Burnage, Chorlton cum Hardy, Didsbury, pt Withington

WITHNELL USD (1893[137]—94)
  Withnell

LITTLE WOOLTON USD
  Little Woolton

MUCH WOOLTON USD
  Much Woolton

WUERDLE AND WARDLE USD
  pt Butterworth, pt Wuerdle and Wardle

ADMINISTRATIVE COUNTY

For MBS and the associated CBs, see BOROUGHS

ABRAM UD
Abram
ADLINGTON UD
Adlington
ALLERTON UD (1894—1913[23])
Allerton
ASHTON IN MAKERFIELD UD
Ashton in Makerfield
ASPULL UD
Aspull
ASTLEY BRIDGE UD (1894—98[138])
Astley Bridge
ATHERTON UD
Atherton
AUDENSHAW UD
Audenshaw
BARROWFORD UD
Barrowford
BARTON UPON IRWELL RD (1894—1933[139])
Barton Moss, Clifton, Davyhulme, Flixton
BILLINGE UD (1894—1924[140])
Billinge Chapel End, Billinge Higher End, Winstanley
BILLINGE AND WINSTANLEY UD (1924[140]—74)
Billinge and Winstanley
BIRKDALE UD[141] (1894—1912[114])
Ainsdale (1905—12), Birkdale
BISPHAM WITH NORBRECK UD (1903[142]—18[7])
Bispham with Norbreck
BLACKBURN RD
Balderstone, Billington, Clayton le Dale, Dinckley, Eccleshill, Livesey, Mellor, Osbaldeston, Pleasington, Ramsgreave, Salesbury, Tockholes, Wilpshire, Witton (1894—1934), Yate and Pickup Bank
BLACKROD UD
Blackrod
BOLTON RD (1894—98[9])
Belmont, Bradshaw, Breightmet, Deane, Edgeworth, Entwistle, Harwood, Heaton, Middle Hulton, Over Hulton, Darcy Lever, Great Lever, Longworth, Lostock, Quarlton, Smithills, Tonge
BRIERFIELD UD
Brierfield
BURNLEY RD
Altham, Barley with Wheatley Booth, Blacko, Briercliffe, Brunshaw (1894—1901), Cliviger, Dunnockshaw, Foulridge, Goldshaw Booth, Habergham Eaves, Hapton, Heyhouses (1894—1904), Higham with West Close Booth, Huncoat (1894—1929), Ightenhill, Northtown, Old Laund Booth, Read, Reedley Hallows, Roughlee Booth, Sabden (1904—74), Simonstone, Wheatley Carr Booth (pt 1894—96, ent 1896—1935), Worsthorne with Hurstwood
BURY RD (1894—1933[18])
Ainsworth, Birtle cum Bamford, Outwood, Tottington (1894—99), Unsworth, Walmersley cum Shuttleworth
CARNFORTH UD (1894[143]—1974)
Carnforth

CASTLETON BY ROCHDALE UD (1894—1900[144])
Castleton by Rochdale (1894—96); Castleton, Lancashire (1896—1900)
CHADDERTON UD
Chadderton
CHILDWALL UD (1894—1913[23])
Childwall
CHORLEY RD
Anderton, Angelzearke, Bretherton, Brindle, Charnock Richard, Clayton le Woods, Coppull, Croston (1934—74), Cuerdon, Duxbury (1894—1934), Eccleston, Euxton, Heapey, Heath Charnock, Heskin, Hoghton, Mawdesley, Rivington, Ulnes Walton, Welsh Whittle (1894—1934), Wheelton, Whittle le Woods
CHURCH UD
Church
CLAYTON LE MOORS UD
Clayton le Moors
CLITHEROE RD
Aighton, Bailey and Chaigley; Little Bowland (1894—1935), Bowland with Leagram (1935—74), Chatburn, Chipping, Downham, Leagram (1894—1935), Mearley, Little Mitton (1935—74); Little Mitton, Henthorn and Coldcoats (1894—1935); Pendleton, Thornley with Wheatley, Twiston, Whalley, Wiswell, Worston
COLNE UD (1894—95[74])
Colne
CROMPTON UD
Crompton
GREAT CROSBY UD (1894—1937[75])
Great Crosby
LITTLE CROSBY UD (1894—1932[145])
Little Crosby
CROSTON UD (1894—1934[5])
Croston
DALTON IN FURNESS UD
Dalton in Furness
DENTON UD
Denton
WEST DERBY UD (1894—95[20])
West Derby
DROYLSDEN UD
Droylsden
FAILSWORTH UD
Failsworth
FARNWORTH UD (1894—1939[79])
Farnworth
FLEETWOOD UD (1894—1933[80])
Fleetwood
FORMBY UD (1905[146]—74)
Formby
FULWOOD UD
Fulwood
FYLDE RD
Bispham with Norbreck (1894—1903), Bryning with Kellamergh (1894—1934), Bryning with Warton (1934—74), Carleton (1894—1934), Clifton with

Salwick (1894—1934), Little Eccleston with Larbreck, Elswick, Freckleton, Greenhalgh with Thistleton, Hardhorn with Newton (1894—1969), Marton (1894—1934), Medlar with Wesham, Newton with Clifton (1934—74), Newton with Scales (1894—1934), Poulton le Fylde (1894—1900), Ribby with Wrea, Singleton, Staining (1969—74), Thornton (1894—1900); Treales, Roseacre and Wharles; Warton (1894—1934), Weeton and Preese, Westby with Plumptons

GARSTANG RD
Barnacre with Bonds, Bilsborrow, Bleasdale, Cabus, Catterall, Claughton, Cleveley (1894—1935), Great Eccleston, Forton, Garstang, Hambleton, Holleth (1894—1935), Inskip with Sowerby, Kirkland, Myerscough, Nateby, Pilling, Preesall with Hackinsall (1894—1900), Out Rawcliffe, Upper Rawcliffe with Tarnacre, Stalmine with Staynall, Winmarleigh, Nether Wyresdale

GARSTON UD (1894—1902[21])
Garston

GOLBORNE UD (1894[147]—1974)
Golborne

GORTON UD (1894—1909[31])
Gorton

GRANGE UD
Grange

GREAT HARWOOD UD
Great Harwood

HAYDOCK UD
Haydock

HEATON NORRIS UD (1894—1913[32])
Heaton Norris

HEYSHAM UD (1899[148]—1928[93])
Heysham

HINDLEY UD
Hindley

HORWICH UD
Horwich

LITTLE HULTON UD (1894—1933[139])
Little Hulton

HURST UD (1894—1927[149])
Hurst

HUYTON WITH ROBY UD
Huyton with Roby

INCE IN MAKERFIELD
Ince in Makerfield

IRLAM UD (1894[150]—1974)
Irlam

KEARSLEY UD
Kearsley

KIRKBY UD (1958[151]—74)
Kirkby

KIRKHAM UD
Kirkham

WEST LANCASHIRE RD
Ainsdale (1894—1905), Aintree (1932—44), Altcar, Aughton, Bickerstaffe, Bispham, Downholland, Ford (1932—54), Formby (1894—1905), Halsall, Hesketh with Becconsall, Ince Blundell (1932—74), Lydiate, Maghull, Melling, North Meols, Netherton (1932—74), Rufford, Scarisbrick, Sefton (1932—74), Simonswood, Tarleton, Thornton (1932—74)

LANCASTER RD
Aldcliffe (1894—1935), Ashton with Stodday, Bolton le Sands, Bulk (1894—1900), Cockerham, Cockersand Abbey (1894—1935), Ellel, Heaton with Oxcliffe, Heysham (1894—99), Middleton, Overton, Priest Hutton, Scotforth, Silverdale, Skerton (1894—1900), Slyne with Hest, Thurnham, Warton (1935—74), Warton with Lindeth (1894—1935), Over Wyresdale, Yealand Conyers, Yealand Redmayne

LATHOM AND BURSCOUGH UD (1894—1931[152])
Burscough, Lathom

LEES UD
Lees

LEIGH RD (1894—1933[18])
Astley, Culcheth, Kenyon, Lowton

LEIGH UD (1894—99[18])
Leigh

LEVENSHULME UD (1894—1909[31])
Levenshulme

LITTLE LEVER UD
Little Lever

LEYLAND UD
Leyland

LIMEHURST RD (1894—1954[153])
Alt, Bardsley, Crossbank (1894—1914), Hartshead (1894—1935), Little Moss, Waterloo, Woodhouses

LITHERLAND UD
Litherland

LITTLEBOROUGH UD
Littleborough

LONGRIDGE UD
Alston, Dilworth

NORTH LONSDALE RD (1960[154]—74)
Aldingham, Lower Allithwaite, Upper Allithwaite, Angerton, Birkrig Common, Blawith, Broughton East, Broughton West, Cartmel Fell, Claife, Colton, Coniston, Dunnerdale with Seathwaite, Egton with Newland, Haverthwaite, Hawkshead, Lower Holker, Kirkby Ireleth, Lands Common to Lowick and Subberthwaite, Lowick, Mansriggs, Osmotherley, Pennington, Satterthwaite, Skelwith, Staveley, Subberthwaite, Torver, Urswick

LUNESDALE RD
Arkholme with Cawood, Borwick, Burrow with Burrow, Cantsfield, Caton, Claughton, Gressingham, Halton, Hornby with Farleton, Ireby, Nether Kellet, Over Kellet, Leck, Melling with Wrayton, Quernmore, Roeburndale, Tatham, Tunstall, Wennington, Whittington, Wray with Botton

LYTHAM UD (1894—1922[86])
Lytham

MILNROW UD
Milnrow

MORECAMBE UD (1894—1902[92])
Poulton Barre and Torrisholme

MOSS SIDE UD (1894—1904[30])
Moss Side

NEWTON IN MAKERFIELD UD (1894—1939[155])
Newton in Makerfield

NEWTON LE WILLOWS UD (1939[155]—74)
Newton in Makerfield (Mar—June 1939), Newton le Willows (June 1939—1974)

NORDEN UD (1894—1933[18])
Norden
ORMSKIRK UD
Burscough (1931—74), Lathom (1931—74), Ormskirk
ORRELL UD
Orrell
OSWALDTWISTLE UD
Oswaldtwistle
PADIHAM UD (1896[156]—1974)
Padiham
PADIHAM AND HAPTON UD (1894—96[156])
Padiham
PEMBERTON UD (1894—1904[50])
Pemberton
POULTON LE FYLDE UD (1900[157]—74)
Poulton le Fylde
PREESALL UD (1910[158]—94)
Preesall with Hackensall
PREESALL WITH HACKENSALL UD (1900[159]—10[158])
Preesall with Hackensall
PRESCOT UD
Prescot
PRESTON RD
Barton, Broughton, Cuerdale, Dutton, Elston (1894—1934), Farington, Goosnargh, Grimsargh (1934—74), Grimsargh with Brockholes (1894—1934), Haighton, Hothersall, Little Hoole, Much Hoole, Howick (1894—1934), Hutton, Lea (1934—74); Lea, Ashton, Ingol and Cottam (1894—1934); Longton, Penwortham, Ribbleton (1894—1934), Ribchester, Samlesbury, Whittingham, Woodplumpton
PRESTWICH UD (1894—1939[98])
Prestwich
RADCLIFFE UD (1894—1935[99])
Radcliffe
RAINFORD UD
Rainford
RAMSBOTTOM UD
Ramsbottom
REDDISH UD (1894—1901[32])
Reddish
RISHTON UD
Rishton
ROYTON UD
Royton
ST ANNE'S ON THE SEA UD (1894—1922[86])
St Anne's on the Sea
SEFTON RD (1894—1932[145])
Aintree, Croxteth Park (1894—1928), West Derby Rural (1894—1928), Fazakerley (1894—1905), Ford (1905—32), Ince Blundell, Kirkby (1894—1922), Lunt, Netherton, Orrell and Ford (1894—1905), Sefton, Thornton
SKELMERSDALE UD (1894—1968[160])
Skelmersdale
SKELMERSDALE AND HOLLAND UD (1968[160]—74)
Skelmersdale, Upholland
STANDISH WITH LANGTREE UD
Standish with Langtree
STRETFORD UD (1894—1933[139])
Stretford
SWINTON AND PENDLEBURY UD (1894—1934[139])
Pendlebury, Swinton

THORNTON UD (1900[161]—1927[162])
Thornton
THORNTON CLEVELEYS UD (1927[162]—74)
Thornton
TOTTINGTON UD (1899[163]—1974)
Tottington
TOXTETH PARK UD (1894—95[20])
Toxteth Park
TRAWDEN UD
Trawden
TURTON UD[9]
Belmont (1898—1925), Edgeworth (1898—1925), Turton
TYLDESLEY UD (1933[18]—74)
Tyldesley cum Shakerley
TYLDESLEY WITH SHAKERLEY UD (1894—1933[18])
Tyldesley cum Shakerley
ULVERSTON RD (1894—1960[154])
Aldingham, Lower Allithwaite, Upper Allithwaite, Angerton, Birkrig Common, Blawith, Broughton East, Broughton West, Cartmel Fell, Claife, Colton, Coniston, Dunnerdale with Seathwaite, Egton with Newland, Haverthwaite (1927—60), Hawkshead, Lower Holker, Upper Holker (1894—1949), Kirkby Ireleth, Lands Common to Lowick and Subberthwaite, Lowick, Mansriggs, Osmotherley, Pennington, Satterthwaite, Skelwith, Staveley, Subberthwaite, Torver, Urswick
ULVERSTON UD
Ulverston
UPHOLLAND UD (1894—1968[160])
Upholland
URMSTON UD (1894[164]—1974)
Davyhulme (1933—74), Flixton (1933—74), Urmston
WALTON LE DALE UD
Walton le Dale
WALTON ON THE HILL UD (1894—95[20])
Walton on the Hill
WARDLE UD (1894[165]—1974)
Wardle
WARRINGTON RD
Burtonwood, Croft (1933—74), Cuerdley; Houghton, Middleton and Arbury (1894—1933); Penketh, Poulton with Fearnhead, Rixton with Glazebrook, Great Sankey, Little Sankey (1894—96), Southworth with Croft (1894—1933), Winwick (1933—74), Winwick with Hulme (1894—1933), Woolston (1933—74), Woolston with Martinscroft (1894—1933)
WATERLOO WITH SEAFORTH UD (1894—1937[75])
Seaforth, Waterloo
WAVERTREE UD (1894—95[20])
Wavertree
WESTHOUGHTON UD
Westhoughton
WHISTON RD
Bold, Cronton, Ditton (1894—1920), Eccleston, Hale, Halewood, Kirkby (1922—58), Knowsley, Rainhill, Speke (1894—1932), Tarbock, Whiston, Windle
WHITEFIELD UD
Whitefield
WHITWORTH UD
Whitworth

WIGAN RD
  Dalton, Haigh, Parbold, Shevington, Worthington, Wrightington
WITHINGTON UD (1894—1904[31])
  Burnage, Chorlton cum Hardy, Didsbury, Withington
WHITHNELL UD
  Withnell

LITTLE WOOLTON UD (1894—1913[23])
  Little Woolton
MUCH WOOLTON UD (1894—1913[23])
  Much Woolton
WORSLEY UD (1894[166]—1974)
  Little Hulton (1935—74), Worsley

NON-METROPOLIAN COUNTY

As constituted 1 Apr 1974, defined in terms of Adm Co units as of 31 Mar. Parts of Adm Co transf to Metrop Cos of Greater Manchester and Merseyside, and to Non-Metrop Cos of Ches and Cumbria, qv.

BLACKBURN DIST
  CB (assoc with Lancs): Blackburn CB
  from Lancs: pt Blackburn RD (Eccleshill, Livesey, Pleasington, Tockholes, Yate and Pickup Bank), Darwen MB, pt Turton UD (all except wards of Bradshaw North, Bradshaw South, Bromley Cross, Eagley, pt ward of Egerton)
BLACKPOOL DIST
  CB (assoc with Lancs): Blackpool CB
BURNLEY DIST
  CB (assoc with Lancs): Burnley CB
  from Lancs: pt Burnley RD (all except pars in Hyndburn, Pendle, Ribble Valley Dists), Padiham UD
CHORLEY DIST
  from Lancs: Adlington UD, Chorley MB, Chorley RD, Withnell UD
FYLDE DIST
  from Lancs: Fylde RD, Kirkham UD, Lytham St Anne's MB
HYNDBURN DIST
  from Lancs: Accrington MB, pt Burnley RD (Altham), Church UD, Clayton le Moors UD, Great Harwood UD, Oswaldtwistle UD, Rishton UD
WEST LANCASHIRE DIST
  from Lancs: pt West Lancashire RD (pt Altcar,[167] Aughton, Bickerstaffe, Bispham, Downholland, Halsall, Hesketh with Becconsall, pt Lydiate,[168] North Meols, Rufford, Scarisbrick, Tarleton), Ormskirk UD, Skelmersdale and Holland UD, pt Wigan RD (Dalton, Parbold, Wrightington)
LANCASTER DIST
  from Lancs: Carnforth UD, Lancaster MB, Lancaster RD, Lunesdale RD, Morecambe and Heysham MB

PENDLE DIST
  from Lancs: Barrowford UD, Brierfield UD, pt Burnley RD (Barley with Wheatley Booth, Blacko, Foulridge, Goldshaw Booth, Higham with West Close Booth; Reedley Hallows, Filly Close and New Laund Booth; Roughlee Booth), Colne MB, Nelson MB, Trawden UD
  from Yorks W Riding: Barnoldswick UD, Earby UD, pt Skipton RD (Bracewell, Brodgen, Salterforth)
PRESTON DIST
  CB (assoc with Lancs): Preston CB
  from Lancs: Fulwood UD, pt Preston RD (all except pars in South Ribble and Ribble Valley Dists)
SOUTH RIBBLE DIST
  from Lancs: Leyland UD, pt Preston RD (Cuerdale, Farington, Little Hoole, Much Hoole, Huttton, Longton, Penwortham, Samlesbury), Walton le Dale UD
RIBBLE VALLEY DIST
  from Lancs: pt Blackburn RD (all except pars in Blackburn Dist), pt Burnley RD (Read, Sabden), Clitheroe MB, Clitheroe RD, Longridge UD, pt Preston RD (Dutton, Hothersall, Ribchester)
  from Yorks W Riding: Bowland RD
ROSSENDALE DIST
  from Lancs: Bacup MB, Haslingden MB, pt Ramsbottom UD (wards of North, Walmersley cum Shuttleworth), Rawtenstall MB, Whitworth UD
WYRE DIST
  from Lancs: Fleetwood MB, Garstang RD, Poulton le Fylde UD, Preesall UD, Thornton Cleveleys UD

LEICESTERSHIRE

ALTERATIONS IN COUNTY BOUNDARIES

As noted by year below, Leics pars gained territory from or lost it to pars in adjoining cos or county boroughs, or were entirely transferred to them. Details of these alterations are noted in Part I of the *Guide* under Leicestershire.

ANCIENT COUNTY (until 1889: Hds, Bors, MBs, PLUs, RSDs, USDs)

1877 Ullesthorpe. *1880* Merevale, Norton juxta Twycross. *1880s* Hinckley, Oakthorpe and Donisthorpe. *1884* Lockington, Packington, Ravenstone, Ravenstone with Snibston. *1885* Merevale, Stoke Dry.

ADMINISTRATIVE COUNTY (1889—1974: Hds,[1] PLUs, MBs, RDs, UDs, with assoc CB of Leicester)

1889 Little Bowden, Leicester All Saints, Leicester Augustine Friars, Leicester Black Friars, Leicester The Castle View, Leicester The Newarke, Leicester St Leonard, Leicester St Margaret, Leicester St Martin, Leicester St Mary, Leicester St Nicholas. *1892* Aylestone, Belgrave, Braunstone, Evington, Freakes Ground, Humberstone, Knighton, Leicester Abbey. *1896* Little Bowden. *1897* Appleby, Ashby Woulds, Blackfordby, Chilcote, Measham, Oakthorpe and Donsithorpe, Nether Seal, Over Seal, Stretton en le Field, Willesley. *1935* Anstey, Beaumont Leys, Birstall, Bittesby, Braunstone, Braunstone Frith, Catthorpe, Claybrooke Parva, Cotesbach, Fenny Drayton, Gilroes, Higham on the Hill, Hinckley, Humberstone, Kirby Muxloe, Leicester Frith, Lubbesthorpe, Lutterworth, New Parks, Sharnford, Shawell, Thurmaston, Thurnby, Ullesthorpe, Wigston Parva. *1936* Evington, Oadby, Wigston Magna. *1939* Wigston Magna. *1965* Appleby Magna, Belvoir, Bottesford, Breedon on the Hill, Broughton and Old Dalby, Buckminster, Burton on the Wolds, Castle Donington, Chilcote, Croxton Kerrial, Hinckley, Market Harborough, Lockington-Hemington, Lubenham, Sproxton, Stretton en le Field, Wymeswold, Wymondham. *1966* Anstey, Birstall, Braunstone, Glen Parva, Glenfields, Kirby Muxloe, Oadby, Scraptoft, Stoughton, Thurcaston, Thurmaston, Thurnby, Wigston Magna. *1969* Wigton Magna.

NON-METROPOLITAN COUNTY (from 1974: Dists)

No bdry alt of Leics pars; gains Rutl Admin Co.

ASSOCIATED COUNTY BOROUGH

LEICESTER CB
Bdry: 1892,[2] 1935,[3] 1936,[4] 1939,[5] 1966,[6] 1969.[7] Transf 1974 to Leics.[8]

HUNDREDS[1]

FRAMLAND HD
Ab Kettleby, Barkestone, Belvoir (from 1858), Bescaby (from 1858), Bottesford, Branston, Nether Broughton, Buckminster, Burton Lazars (from 1866), Long Clawson, Coston, Croxton Kerrial, Little Dalby, Eastwell, Eaton, Edmondthorpe, Feeby (from 1866), Garthorpe, Goadby Marwood, Harby, Harston, Holwell (from 1866), Hose, Kirby Bellars, Knipton, Melton Mowbray, Muston, Cold Overton, Plungar, Redmile, Saltby, Saxby, Scalford, Sewstern (from 1866), Somerby, Sproxton, Stapleford, Stathern, Stonesby, Sysonby (from 1866), Thorpe Arnold, Waltham on the Wolds, Welby (from 1866), Withcote, Wyfordby, Wymondham

GARTREE HD
Billesdon, Blaston, Husbands Bosworth, Great Bowden, Bringhurst, Burrough on the Hill, Burton Overy, Bushby (from 1866), Carlton Curlieu, Cranoe, Drayton (from 1866), Great Easton (from 1866), Evington, Fleckney, Foxton, Frisby (from 1866), Galby, Glen Magna, Glooston, Goadby (from 1866), Gumley, Hallaton, Nevill Holt, Horninghold, Houghton on the Hill, pt Hungerton, Ilston on the Hill (from 1866), Kibworth Beauchamp, Kibworth Harcourt (from 1866), pt Knaptoft (until 1866), Knossington, Church Langton (until 1866), East Langton (from 1866), Thorpe Langton (from 1866), Tur Langton (from 1866), West Langton (from 1866), Laughton, Lubenham, Marefield (from 1866), Market Harborough (from 1866), Newton Harcourt (from 1866), King's Norton, Noseley (from 1858), Owston and Newbold, Pickwell with Leesthorpe, Rolleston (from 1866), Saddington, Scraptoft, Shangton, Slawston, Smeeton Westerby (from 1866), Stockerston, pt Stoke Dry (until 1885), Stonton Wyville, Stoughton (from 1866), Stretton Magna (from 1866), Stretton Parva (from 1866), Theddingworth (pt until 1866, ent from 1866), Thurnby, pt Tilton (until 1866), pt Tugby (until 1866), Welham, Wistow

EAST GOSCOTE HD
Allexton, Asfordby, Ashby Folville, Barkby, Barkby Thorpe (from 1866), Barrow upon Soar (pt until 1866, ent from 1866), Barsby (from 1866), Beeby, Belgrave[9] (pt until 1866, ent from 1866), Cossington, Cotes (from 1866), South Croxton, Great Dalby, Old Dalby, Frisby on the Wreak, Gaddesby, Grimston, Halstead (from

1866), Hoby, Hoton (from 1866), pt Hungerton, Humberstone, Keyham (from 1866), Launde (from 1858), Loddington, Lowesby, East Norton (from 1866), Prestwold, Queniborough, Ragdale, Ratcliffe on the Wreake, Rearsby, Rotherby, pt Rothley (until 1866), Saxelby, Seagrave, Shoby (from 1858), Sileby, Skeffington, Syston, Thorpe Satchville (from 1866), Thrussington, North Thurmaston (from 1866), South Thurmaston (from 1866), Tilton (pt until 1866, ent from 1866), Tugby (pt until 1866, ent from 1866), Twyford, Walton on the Wolds, Wartnaby (from 1866), Whatborough (from 1866), Wycomb and Chadwell (from 1866), Wymeswold

WEST GOSCOTE HD

Anstey (from 1866), Anstey Pastures (from 1858), Ashby de la Zouch, pt Barrow upon Soar (until 1866), Beaumont Leys (from 1858), pt Belgrave (until 1866), Belton, Birstall (from 1866), Blackfordby (from 1866), Bradgate Park (from 1858), Breedon on the Hill, Castle Donington, Charley (from 1858), Coleorton, Cropston (from 1866), Diseworth, Garendon (from 1858), Gilroes (from 1858), Hathern, Hemington (from 1866), Isley Walton (from 1866), Kegworth, Knight Thorpe[9] (from 1866), Langley Priory (from 1858), Leicester Abbey (from 1858), Leicester Frith (from 1858), Leicester St Leonard,[9] Lockington, Loughborough,[9] Maplewell Longdale (from 1866), Mountsorrel (from 1884), Mountsorrel North End (1866—84), Mountsorrel South End (1866—84), Newtown Linford, pt Oakthorpe and Donisthorpe (from 1866), Osgathorpe, Packington (pt until 1866, ent from 1866), Quorndon (from 1866), pt Ravenstone (until 1884), Ravenstone with Snibston (from 1884), Rothley (pt until 1866, ent from 1866), Rothley Temple (from 1858), Seal (until 1866), Over and Nether Seal (from 1866), Shepshed, Staunton Harold (from 1866), Swannington (from 1866), Swepstone, Swithland, Thorpe Acre and Dishley,[9] Thringstone (from 1866), Thurcaston, Ulverscroft (from 1858), Wanlip, Long Whatton, Whitwick, Woodhouse (from 1866), Woodthorpe (from 1866), Worthington (from 1866)

GUTHLAXTON HD

Arnesby, Ashby Magna, Ashby Parva, Aylestone (pt until 1866, ent from 1866), Bittesby (from 1866), Bitteswell, Blaby, Broughton Astley, Bruntingthorpe, Catthorpe, pt Claybrooke (until 1866), Claybrooke Magna (from 1866), Claybrooke Parva (from 1866), Cosby, Cotesbach, Countesthorpe (from 1866), Dunton Bassett, pt Enderby (until 1866), Foston, Freakes Ground (from 1858), Frolesworth, Gilmorton, Glen Parva (from 1866), Kilby, North Kilworth, South Kilworth, Kimcote, Knaptoft (pt until 1866, ent from 1866), Knighton (from 1866), Leicester New Found Pool (from 1858), pt Leicester St Margaret (until 1866), Leire, Lutterworth,[9] Misterton, New Parks (from 1858), Oadby, Peatling Magna, Peatling Parva, Shawell, Shearsby (from 1866), Swinford, Ullesthorpe (from 1866), Walton in Knaptoft (from 1866), Westrill and Starmore (from 1858), Whetstone, Wigston Magna, Wigston Parva (from 1866), Willoughby Waterless

SPARKENHOE HD

pt Appleby, Aston Flamville, Atterton (from 1866), pt Aylestone (until 1866), Bagworth (from 1866), Bardon (from 1858), Barlestone (from 1866), Barton in the Beans (from 1866), Barwell, Bilstone (from 1866), Market Bosworth, Braunstone (from 1866), Braunstone Frith (from 1858), Burbage (from 1866), Cadeby, Carlton (from 1866), Congerstone, Croft, Dadlington (from 1866), Desford, Fenny Drayton, Earl Shilton (from 1866), Elmesthorpe, Enderby (pt until 1866, ent from 1866), Glenfield, Glenfield Frith (from 1858), Gopsall (from 1858), Heather, Higham on the Hill, Hinckley[9] (pt until 1880s, ent from 1880s), Hugglescore and Donington (from 1866), Huncote (from 1866), Ibstock, Kirby Frith (from 1858), Kirby Muxloe (from 1866), Kirkby Mallory, Knoll and Bassett House (from 1858), Leicester Forest East (from 1858), Leicester Forest West (from 1858), Lubbesthorpe (from 1866), Markfield, pt Merevale (until 1880s), Nailstone, Narborough, Newbold Verdon, Normanton le Heath (from 1866), Norton juxta Twycross, Osbaston (from 1866), Odstone (from 1866), Orton on the Hill, Peckleton, Potters Marston (from 1866), Ratby, Ratcliffe Culey, Sapcote, Shackerstone, Sharnford, Sheepy Magna, Sheepy Parva, Shenton (from 1866), Sibson, Snarestone, Stanton under Bardon (from 1866), Stapleton (from 1866), Stoke Golding (from 1866), Stoney Stanton, Sutton Cheney (from 1866), Thornton, Thurlaston, Twycross, Upton (from 1866), Witherley

BOROUGHS

Units with some degree of burghal character[10] are denominated 'Bor'. Those which did not sustain that status until the 19th cent are in italics. MBs were established by the Municipal Corporations Act, 1835,[11] or by later charter.

HINCKLEY BOR
pt Hinckley

LEICESTER BOR[12]/MB/CB[13] (City from 1919[14])
Aylestone (1892—96), Belgrave (1892—96), North Evington (1892—96), West Humberstone (1892—96), Knighton (1892—96), Leicester (1896—1974), Leicester Abbey (1892—96), Leicester All Saints (until 1896), Leicester Augustine Friars (until 1896), Leicester Black Friars (until 1896), Leicester The Castle View (1835—96), Leicester New Found Pool (1892—96), Leicester The Newarke (1835—96), Leicester St Leonard (pt until 1835, ent 1835—96), Leicester St Margaret (pt until 1866 [enlarged pt 1835—66], ent 1866—96), Leicester St Martin (until 1896), Leicester St Mary (pt until 1835, ent 1835—96), Leicester St Nicholas (until 1896)

LOUGHBOROUGH MB[15] (1888[16]—1974)
Knight Thorpe (pt 1888—91, ent 1891—1902), Loughborough (pt 1881—94, ent 1894—1974), pt Thorpe Acre and Dishley (1888—91)

MOUNTSORREL BOR
pt Barrow upon Soar, pt Rothley

POOR LAW UNIONS

In Leics Poor Law County:[17]
ASHBY DE LA ZOUCH PLU (Leics, Derbys)
Appleby[18] (1836—89), Appleby[18] (1889—97), Appleby Magna (1898—1930), Appleby Magna North (1897—98), Appleby Magna South (1897—98), Ashby de la Zouch, Ashby Woulds (1894—1930), Bardon (1862—1930), Blackfordby, Chilcote,[19] Coalville (1894—1930), Coleorton (soon after 1836[20]—1930), Heather, Hugglescote and Donington, Measham,[19] Normanton le Heath, Oakthorpe and Donisthorpe,[21] Osgathorpe (soon after 1836[20]—1930), Packington,[22] Ravenstone[23] (1836—84), Ravenstone with Snibston (1884—1930), Nether Seal[24] (1894—1930), Over Seal[25] (1894—1930), Over and Nether Seal (1836—94), Snarestone, Staunton Harold, Stretton en le Field,[19] Swannington, Swepstone, Thringstone (soon after 1836[20]—1930), Whitwick, Willesley,[19] Worthington (soon after 1836[20]—1930)

BARROW UPON SOAR PLU
Anstey, Anstey Pastures (1858—1930), Barkby, Barkby Thorpe, Barrow upon Soar, Beaumont Leys (1858—1930), Beeby, Belgrave (1837—92), Birstall, Bradgate Park (1858—84), Cossington, Cropston, South Croxton, Gilroes (1858—1930), Leicester Abbey (1858—92), Leicester Frith (1858—1930), Maplewell Longdale (1866—84), Mountsorrel (1884—1930), Mountsorrel North End (1837—84), Mountsorrel South End (1837—84), Newtown Linford, Queniborough, Quorndon, Ratcliffe on the Wreake, Rearsby, Rothley, Rothley Temple (1858—84), Seagrave, Sileby, Swithland, Syston, Thrussington, Thurcaston, Thurmaston (1903—30), North Thurmaston (1837—1903), South Thurmaston (1837—1903), Ulverscroft, Walton on the Wolds, Wanlip, Woodhouse

BILLESDON PLU
Allexton, Billesdon, Burton Overy, Bushby, Carlton Curlieu, Cold Newton, Evington, Frisby, Galby, Glen Magna, Goadby, Halstead, Houghton on the Hill, Humberstone, Hungerton, Ilston on the Hill, Keyham (soon after 1835[20]—1930), Launde (1858—1930), Loddington, Lowesby, Marefield, Newton Harcourt, East Norton, King's Norton, Noseley (1858—1930), Owston and Newbold, Rolleston, Scraptoft, Skeffington, Skelton Magna, Stoughton, Stretton Magna, Stretton Parva, Thurnby (soon after 1835[20]—1930), Tilton, Tugby, Whatborough, Wistow, Withcote

BLABY PLU
Aylestone (1836—92), Blaby, Braunstone, Braunstone Frith (1861—1930), Cosby, Countesthorpe, Croft, Enderby, Foston, Freakes Ground (1861—92), Glenfield, Glenfield Frith (1861—1930), Glen Parva, Huncote, Kilby, Kirby Frith (1861—1930), Kirby Muxloe, Knighton (1836—92), Knoll and Bassett House (1861—1909), Leicester Forest East, Leicester Forest West (1861—1930), Leicester New Found Pool (1861—92), Lubbesthorpe, Narborough, New Parks (1861—1930), Oadby, Potters Marston, Thurlaston,

Whetstone, East Wigston (1894—1930), Wigston Magna

HINCKLEY PLU (Leics, Warws)
Aston Flamville, Barwell, Burbage, Earl Shilton, Elmesthorpe, Higham on the Hill (soon after 1836[20]—1930), Hinckley,[26] Sapcote, Sharnford, Stoke Golding,[27] Stoney Stanton, Wigston Parva (1895—1930)

LEICESTER PLU (1836—96), PAR (1896—1930)
Aylestone (1892—96), Belgrave (1892—96), North Evington (1892—96), West Humberstone (1892—96), Knighton (1892—96), Leicester (1896—1930), Leicester Abbey (1892—96), Leicester All Saints (1836—96), Leicester Augustine Friars (1861—96), Leicester Blackfriars (1861—96), Leicester The Castle View (1836—96), Leicester New Found Pool (1892—96), Leicester The Newarke (1836—96), Leicester St Leonard (1836—96), Leicester St Margaret (1836—96), Leicester St Martin (1836—96), Leicester St Mary (1836—96), Leicester St Nicholas (1836—96)

LOUGHBOROUGH PLU (Leics, Notts)
Belton, Burton on the Wolds, Charley, Cotes, Garendon (1862—1930), Hathern, Holton, Knight Thorpe (1836—1902), Loughborough, Nanpanton (1894—1930), Prestwold, Shepshed, Shepshed Parva (1894—96), Thorpe Acre and Dishley, Long Whatton, Woodthorpe, Wymeswold

LUTTERWORTH PLU (Leics, Warws, Northants [1835—94])
Arnesby, Ashby Magna, Ashby Parva, Bittesby, Bitteswell, Broughton Astley, Bruntingthorpe, Catthorpe, Claybrooke Magna, Claybrooke Parva, Cotesbach, Dunton Bassett, Frolesworth, Gilmorton, North Kilworth, South Kilworth, Kimcote (1835—98), Kimcote and Walton (1898—1930), Knaptoft, Leire, Lutterworth, Misterton, Peatling Magna, Peatling Parva, Shawell, Shearsby, Swinford, Ullesthorpe, Walton in Knaptoft (1835—98), Westrill and Starmore (1895—1930), Wigston Parva (1835—95), Willoughby Waterless

MARKET BOSWORTH PLU
Bagworth, Barlestone, Barton in the Beans, Bilstone, Market Bosworth, Cadeby, Carlton, Congerstone, Dadlington, Desford, Gopsall (1861—1930), Groby (1896—1930), Ibstock, Kirkby Mallory, Markfield, Nailstone, Newbold Verdon, Norton juxta Twycross, Odstone, Orton on the Hill, Osbaston, Peckleton, Ratby, Shackerstone, Shenton, Sibson (soon after 1836[20]—1930), Stanton under Bardon, Stapleton (soon after 1836[20]—1930), Sutton Cheney (soon after 1836[20]—1930), Thornton, Twycross, Upton, Witherley

MARKET HARBOROUGH PLU (Leics, Northants)
Husbands Bosworth, Great Bowden (1835—1927), Little Bowden[28] (1835—1927), Cranoe, Fleckney, Foxton, Glooston, Gumley, Kibworth Beauchamp, Kibworth Harcourt, *Church Langton*,[29] East Langton,[29] Thorpe Langton,[29] Tur Langton,[29] West Langton,[29] Laughton, Lubenham, Market Harborough,

Mowsley, Saddington, Shangton, Smeeton Westerby, Stonton Wyville, Theddingworth,[30] Welham

MELTON MOWBRAY PLU (Leics, Notts)

Ab Kettleby, Asfordby, Ashby Folville, Barsby, Bescaby (1858—1930), Branston, Brooksby, Nether Broughton, Buckminster, Burrough on the Hill, Burton Lazars, Long Clawson, Coston, Great Dalby, Little Dalby, Old Dalby, Dalby on the Wolds, Eastwell, Eaton, Edmondthorpe, Freeby, Frisby on the Wreak, Gaddesby, Garthorpe, Goadby Marwood, Grimston, Harby, Hoby, Holwell, Hose, Kirby Bellars, Melton Mowbray, Pickwell with Leesthorpe, Ragdale, Rotherby, Saltby, Saxby, Saxelby, Scalford, Sewstern, Shoby (1858—1930), Somerby, Sproxton, Stapleford, Stathern, Stonesby, Sysonby, Sysonby with Eye Kettleby[31] (1894—1930), Thorpe Arnold, Thorpe Satchville, Twyford, Waltham on the Wolds, Wartnaby, Welby, Wycomb and Chadwell, Wyfordby, Wymondham

In Other Poor Law Counties:

ATHERSTONE PLU (Warws, Leics)

Atterton (soon after 1836[20]—1930), Fenny Drayton, Merevale,[32] Ratcliffe Culey (soon after 1836[20]—1930), Sheepy Magna, Sheepy Parva, Witherley

BINGHAM PLU (Notts, Leics)

Barkestone, Plungar

GRANTHAM PLU (Lincs Pts Kestev, Leics)

Belvoir (1861—1930), Bottesford, Croxton Kerrial, Harston, Knipton, Muston, Redmile

OAKHAM PLU (Rutl, Leics)

Cold Overton, Knossington

RUGBY PLU (Warws, Leics [1836—95])

Westrill and Starmore (1836—95)

SHARDLOW PLU (Derbys, Leics, Notts)

Breedon on the Hill, Castle Donington, Diseworth, Hemington, Isley Walton, Kegworth, Langley Priory (1861—1930), Lockington

UPPINGHAM PLU (Rutl, Northants, Leics)

Blaston, Bringhurst, Drayton, Great Easton, Hallaton, Nevill Holt, Horninghold, Medbourne, Slawston, Stockerston, Stoke Dry[33]

SANITARY DISTRICTS

ASHBY DE LA ZOUCH RSD

same as PLU for Leics pars less Ashby de la Zouch, Hugglecote and Donington (pt 1892—93, ent 1893—94), pt Ravenstone with Snibston (1889—94 [enlarged pt 1892—94]), pt Swannington (1892—94), Whitwick

ASHBY DE LA ZOUCH UD

pt Ashby de la Zouch, pt Ravenstone with Snibston (1884—94)

ASHBY WOULDS USD

pt Ashby de la Zouch

ATHERSTONE RSD

same as PLU for Leics pars

BARROW UPON SOAR RSD

same as PLU less Belgrave (pt 1875—92, ent 1892—94), Leicester Abbey (1892—94), Quorndon, North Thurmaston, South Thurmaston

BELGRAVE USD (1875—92[13])

pt Belgrave

BILLESDON RSD

same as PLU

BINGHAM RSD

same as PLU for Leics pars

BLABY RSD

same as PLU less Aylestone (1892—94), Knighton (1892—94)

COALVILLE USD (1892[34]—94)

Hugglecote and Donington (pt 1892—93, ent 1893—94), pt Ravenstone with Snibston, pt Swannington, Whitwick

GRANTHAM RSD

same as PLU for Leics pars

HINCKLEY RSD

same as PLU for Leics pars less Hinckley

HINCKLEY USD

Hinckley

LEICESTER USD[35]

Aylestone (1892—94), Belgrave (1892—96), North Evington (1892—94), West Humberstone (1892—94), Knighton (1892—94), Leicester Abbey (1892—94), Leicester All Saints, Leicester Augustine Friars, Leicester Blackfriars, Leicester The Castle View, Leicester New Found Pool (1892—96), Leicester The Newarke, Leicester St Leonard, Leicester St Margaret, Leicester St Martin, Leicester St Mary, Leicester St Nicholas

LOUGHBOROUGH RSD

same as PLU for Leics pars less Knight Thorpe, Loughborough, pt Shepshed (1886—94), Woodthorpe (1875—88)

LOUGHBOROUGH USD

Knight Thorpe, Loughborough, Woodthorpe (1875—88)

LUTTERWORTH RSD

same as PLU for Leics pars

MARKET BOSWORTH RSD

same as PLU

MARKET HARBOROUGH RSD

same as PLU for Leics pars less Great Bowden, Market Harborough

MARKET HARBOROUGH, GREAT AND LITTLE BOWDEN USD (Leics, *Northants*)

Great Bowden, *pt Little Bowden*, Market Harborough

MELTON MOWBRAY RSD

same as PLU for Leics pars less pt Melton Mowbray

MELTON MOWBRAY USD

pt Melton Mowbray

OAKHAM RSD

same as PLU for Leics pars

QUORNDON USD

Quorndon

SHARDLOW RSD
same as PLU for Leics pars
SHEPSHED USD (1886[36]—94)
pt Shepshed
THURMASTON USD
North Thurmaston, South Thurmaston

UPPINGHAM RSD
same as PLU for Leics pars
WHITWICK USD (1875—92[34])
Whitwick

ADMINISTRATIVE COUNTY

For MBs and the associated CB see BOROUGHS

ASHBY DE LA ZOUCH RD
Appleby (1894—97), Appleby Magna (1898—1974), Appleby Magna North (1897—98), Appleby Magna South (1897—98), Bardon, Blackfordby (1894—1936), Chilcote (1897—1974), Coleorton, Heather, Measham (1897—1974), Normanton le Heath, Oakthorpe and Donisthorpe (1897—1974), Osgathorpe, Packington, Ravenstone with Snibston (18 Dec 1894—1974), Nether Seal (1894—97), Over Seal (1894—97), Snarestone, Staunton Harold, Stretton en le Field (1897—1974), Swannington, Swepstone, Thringstone (1894—1936), Willesley (1897—1936), Worthington

ASHBY DE LA ZOUCH UD
Ashby de la Zouch, pt Ravenstone with Snibston (apptd day 1894—18 Dec 1894)

ASHBY WOULDS UD
Ashby Woulds

BARROW UPON SOAR RD
Anstey, Anstey Pastures (1894—1935), Barkby, Barkby Thorpe, Barrow upon Soar, Beaumont Leys (1894—1935), Beeby, Birstall, Burton on the Wolds (1935—74), Cossington, Cotes (1935—74), Cropston (1894—1935), South Croxton, Gilroes (1894—1935), East Goscote (1967—74), Hoton (1935—74), Leicester Frith (1894—1935), Mountsorrel, Newtown Linford, Prestwold (1935—74), Queniborough, Quorndon (1935—74), Ratcliffe on the Wreake, Rearsby, Rothley, Seagrave, Sileby, Swithland, Syston, Thrussington, Thurcaston, Thurmaston (1935—74), Ulverscroft, Walton on the Wolds, Wanlip, Woodhouse, Wymeswold (1935—74)

BELVOIR RD (1894—1935[37])
Barkestone, Belvoir, Bottesford, Croxton Kerrial, Harston, Knipton, Muston, Plungar, Redmile

BILLESDON RD
Allexton, Billesdon, Burton Overy, Bushby (1894—1935), Carlton Curlieu, Cold Newton, Evington (1894—1936), Frisby, Galby (1894—1960), Gaulby (1960—74), Great Glen (1958—74), Glen Magna (1894—1958), Goadby, Halstead (1894—1935), Houghton on the Hill, Humberstone (1894—1935), Hungarton (1947—74), Hungerton (1894—1947), Ilston on the Hill, Keyham, Launde, Loddington, Lowesby, Marefield, Newton Harcourt (1894—1936), East Norton, King's Norton, Noseley, Owston and Newbold, Rolleston, Scraptoft, Skeffington, Stoughton, Stretton Magna, Stretton Parva, Thurnby, Tilton, Tugby, Whatborough, Wistow, Withcote

BLABY RD
Aston Flamville (1936—74), Blaby, Braunstone, Braunstone Frith (1894—1935), Cosby, Countesthorpe, Croft, Elmesthorpe (1936—74), Enderby, Foston (1894—1935), Glenfield (1894—1935), Glenfield Frith (1894—1935), Glenfields (1935—74), Glen Parva, Huncote, Kilby, Kirby Frith (1894—1935), Kirby Muxloe, Knoll and Bassett House (1894—1909), Leicester Forest East (1894—1935), Leicester Forest West, Lubbesthorpe, Narborough, New Parks (1894—1935), Oadby (1894—1913), Potters Marston, Sapcote (1936—74), Sharnford (1936—74), Stoney Stanton (1936—74), Thurlaston, Whetstone, East Wigston (1894—1935), Wigston Parva (1935—74)

CASTLE DONINGTON RD
Belton (1936—74), Breedon on the Hill, Castle Donington, Charley (1936—74), Diseworth (1894—1936), Hemington (1894—1936), Isley cum Langley (1936—74), Isley Walton (1894—1936), Kegworth, Langley Priory (1894—1936), Lockington (1894—1938), Lockington-Hemington (1938—74), Long Whatton (1936—74)

COALVILLE UD
Coalville, Hugglescote and Donington (1894—1936), Whitwick (1894—1936)

HALLATON RD (1894—1935[37])
Blaston, Bringhurst, Drayton, Great Easton, Hallaton, Nevill Holt, Horninghold, Medbourne, Stockerston

HINCKLEY RD (1894—1936[38])
Aston Flamville, Barwell, Burbage, Earl Shilton, Elmesthorpe, Higham on the Hill, Sapcote, Sharnford, Stoke Golding, Stoney Stanton, Wigston Parva (1894—95)

HINCKLEY UD
Hinckley

LOUGHBOROUGH RD (1894—1936[38])
Belton, Burton on the Wolds, Charley, Cotes, Garendon, Hathern, Hoton, Nanpanton, Prestwold, Shepshed Parva (1894—96), Thorpe Acre and Dishley, Long Whatton, Woodthorpe (1894—1935), Wymeswold

LUTTERWORTH RD
Arnesby, Ashby Magna, Ashby Parva, Bittesby, Bitteswell, Broughton Astley, Bruntingthorpe, Catthorpe, Claybrooke Magna, Claybrooke Parva, Cotesbach, Dunton Bassett, Frolesworth, Gilmorton, North Kilworth, South Kilworth, Kimcote (1894—98), Kimcote and Walton (1898—1974), Knaptoft, Leire, Lutterworth, Misterton, Peatling Magna, Peatling Parva, Shawell, Shearsby, Swinford, Ullesthorpe, Walton in Knaptoft (1894—98), Westrill and Starmore, Wigston Parva (1894—95), Willoughby Waterless (1894—1966), Willoughby Waterleys (1966—74)

MARKET BOSWORTH RD

Atterton (1894—1935), Bagworth, Barlestone, Barton in the Beans (1894—1935), Bilstone (1894—1935), Market Bosworth, Cadeby, Carlton, Congerstone (1894—1935), Dadlington (1894—1935), Desford, Fenny Drayton (1894—1935), Gopsall (1894—1935), Groby (1896—1974), Higham on the Hill (1936—74), Ibstock, Kirkby Mallory (1894—1935), Markfield, Nailstone, Newbold Verdon, Norton juxta Twycross (1894—1935), Odstone (1894—1935), Osbaston, Orton on the Hill (1894—1935), Peckleton, Ratby, Ratcliffe Culey (1894—1935), Shackerstone, Sheepy (1935—74), Sheepy Magna (1894—1935), Sheepy Parva (1894—1935), Shenton (1894—1935), Sibson (1894—1935), Stanton under Bardon (1894—1935), Stapleton (1894—1935), Sutton Cheney, Thornton (1894—1935), Twycross, Upton (1894—1935), Witherley

MARKET HARBOROUGH RD

Blaston (1935—74), Husbands Bosworth, Bringhurst (1935—74), Cranoe, Drayton (1935—74), Great Easton (1935—74), Fleckney, Foxton, Glooston, Gumley, Hallaton (1935—74), Nevill Holt (1935—74), Horninghold (1935—74), Kibworth Beauchamp, Kibworth Harcourt, East Langton, Thorpe Langton, Tur Langton, West Langton, Laughton, Lubenham, Medbourne (1935—74), Mowsley, Saddington, Shangton, Slawston, Smeeton Westerby, Stockerston (1935—74), Stonton Wyville, Theddingworth, Welham

MARKET HARBOROUGH UD

Great Bowden (1894—1927), Little Bowden[28] (pt 1894—96, ent 1896—1927), Market Harborough

MELTON AND BELVOIR RD (1935[37]—74)

Ab Kettleby, Asfordby, Ashby Folville (1935—36), Barkestone (1935—36), Barsby (1935—36), Belvoir, Bescaby (1935—36), Bottesford, Branston (1935—36), Bretingby and Wyfordby (1935—36), Brooksby (1935—36), Nether Broughton (1935—36), Broughton and Old Dalby (1936—74), Buckminster, Burrough on the Hill (1935—36), Burton and Dalby (1936—74), Burton Lazars (1935—36), Long Clawson (1935—36), Clawson and Harby (1936—74), Coston (1935—36), Croxton Kerrial, Great Dalby (1935—36), Little Dalby (1935—36), Old Dalby (1935—36), Eastwell (1935—36), Eaton, Edmondthorpe (1935—36), Freeby, Frisby (1936—74), Frisby on the Wreak (1935—36), Gaddesby, Garthorpe, Goadby Marwood (1935—36), Grimston, Harby (1935—36), Harston (1935—36), Hoby (1935—36), Hoby with Rotherby (1936—74), Holwell (1935—36), Hose (1935—36), Kirby Bellars (1935—36), Knipton (1935—36), Knossington, Lands Common to Coston and Garthorpe (1935—36), Muston (1935—36), Cold Overton (1935—36), Pickwell with Leesthorpe (1935—36), Plungar (1935—36), Ragdale (1935—36), Redmile, Rotherby (1935—36), Saltby (1935—36), Saxby (1935—36), Saxelby (1935—36), Scalford, Sewstern (1935—36), Shoby (1935—36), Somerby, Sproxton, Stapleford (1935—36), Stathern, Stonesby (1935—36), Thorpe Arnold (1935—36), Thorpe Satchville (1935—36), Twyford (1935—36), Twyford and Thorpe (1936—74), Waltham (1936—74), Waltham on the Wolds (1935—36), Wartnaby (1935—36), Welby (1935—36), Wycomb and Chadwell (1935—36), Wyfordby (1935—36), Wymondham

MELTON MOWBRAY RD (1894—1935[37])

Ab Kettleby, Asfordby, Ashby Folville, Barsby, Bescaby, Branston, Brooksby, Nether Broughton, Buckminster, Burrough on the Hill, Burton Lazars, Long Clawson, Coston, Great Dalby, Little Dalby, Old Dalby, Eastwell, Eaton, Edmondthorpe, Freeby, Frisby on the Wreak, Gaddesby, Garthorpe, Goadby Marwood, Grimston, Harby, Hoby, Holwell, Hose, Kirby Bellars, Knossington, Lands Common to Coston and Garthorpe (1894—1935), Cold Overton, Pickwell with Leesthorpe, Ragdale, Rotherby, Saltby, Saxby, Saxelby, Scalford, Sewstern, Shoby, Somerby, Sproxton, Stapleford, Stathern, Stonesby, Sysonby (1894—1930), Sysonby and Eye Kettleby[31] (1894—1935), Thorpe Satchville, Thorpe Arnold, Twyford, Waltham on the Wolds, Wartnaby, Welby, Wycomb and Chadwell, Wymondham

MELTON MOWBRAY UD

Melton Mowbray

OADBY UD (1913[39]—74)

Oadby

QUORNDON UD (1894—1935[37])

Quorndon

SHEPSHED UD

Shepshed

THURMASTON UD (1894—1935[37])

Thurmaston (1903—35), North Thurmaston (1894—1903), South Thurmaston (1894—1903)

WIGSTON UD (1930[40]—1974)

Wigston Magna

WIGSTON MAGNA UD (1894[40]—1930[41])

Wigston Magna (pt apptd day—31 Dec 1894, ent 31 Dec 1894—1930)

NON-METROPOLITAN COUNTY

As constituted 1 Apr 1974, defined in terms of Adm Co units as of 31 Mar.

BLABY DIST

Blaby RD

CHARNWOOD DIST

Barrow upon Soar RD, Loughborough MB, Shepshed UD

HARBOROUGH DIST

Billesdon RD, Lutterworth RD, Market Harborough RD, Market Harborough UD

HINCKLEY AND BOSWORTH DIST

Hinckley UD, pt Market Bosworth RD (the pars not in North West Leics Dist)

NORTH WEST LEICESTERSHIRE DIST

Ashby de la Zouch RD, Ashby de la Zouch UD, Ashby Woulds UD, Coalville UD, Castle Donington

RD, pt Market Bosworth RD (Ibstock)
MELTON DIST
  Melton and Belvoir RD, Melton Mowbray UD
OADBY AND WIGSTON DIST
  Oadby UD, Wigston UD

RUTLAND DIST
from Rutl: Rutland Adm Co

LINCOLNSHIRE

ALTERATIONS IN COUNTY BOUNDARIES

As noted by year below, Lincs pars gained territory from or lost it to pars in adjoining cos or county boroughs, or were entirely transferred to them. Details of these alterations are noted in Part I of the *Guide* under Lincolnshire.

ANCIENT COUNTY (until 1889: Hds, Bors, MBs, PLUs, RSDs, USDs)
1840s The parishes in abol Lincoln Liberty and County of Itself (see next entry). *1884* Kettlethorpe. *1886* Misson. *1887* Carlby.

PARTS OF HOLLAND ADMINIS-TRATIVE COUNTY (1889—1974: Waps,[1] PLUs, MBs, RDs, UDs)
1894 Leake. *1897* Central Wingland. *1930* Deeping St Nicholas. *1934* Sutton St Edmund, Tydd St Mary. *1935* Amber Hill, Bicker, Brothertoft, Copping Syke, Fishtoft, Hart's Grounds, Pelham's Lands. *1957* Sutton Bridge.

PARTS OF KESTEVEN ADMINIS-TRATIVE COUNTY (1889—1974: Waps and Soke,[1] PLUs, MBs, RDs, UDs)
1889 Stamford Baron St Martin. *1894* Stamford Baron St Martin. *1920* Boultham, Bracebridge, Bracebridge Heath, North Hykeham, Skellingthorpe. *1930* Deeping St Nicholas. *1935* Dogdyke, Great Hale, South Kyme. *1959* Skellingthorpe. *1965* Colsterworth, Denton, Gunby and Stainby, Sedgebrook, Skillington, Stoke Rochford, South Witham, Woolsthorpe, Wyville cum Hungerton. *1967* Canwick, Skellingthorpe.

PARTS OF LINDSEY ADMINISTRATIVE COUNTY (1889—1974: Waps, Sokes, Hds,[1] PLUs, MBs, RDs, UDs, with assoc CBs of Grimsby, Lincoln)
1889 Bracebridge, Clee with Weelsby, Great Grimsby, Lincoln Bishop's Palace, Lincoln Cold Bath House, Lincoln Holmes Common, Lincoln Monks Liberty, Lincoln St Benedict, Lincoln St Botolph, Lincoln St John in Newport, Lincoln St Margaret in the Close, Lincoln St Mark, Lincoln St Martin, Lincoln St Mary le Wigford with Holmes Common, Lincoln St Mary Magdalen in the Bail, Lincoln St Michael, Lincoln St Nicholas, Lincoln St Paul in the Bail, Lincoln St Peter at Arches, Lincoln St Peter at Gowts, Lincoln St Peter in Eastgate, Lincoln St Swithin, Lincoln South Common. *1895* Lea. *1928* Bradley, Great Coates, Little Coates, Scartho, Weelsby. *1935* Dogdyke, Frithville, Langriville, Wildmore. *1958* Great Coates. *1967* Greetwell, Nettleham, Riseholme. *1968* Great Coates, Waltham, New Waltham, Weelsby.

LINCOLNSHIRE NON-METROPOLITAN COUNTY (from 1974: Dists)
(comprised of Lincoln CB associated with Parts of Lindsey Adm Co, ent Parts of Holland Adm Co, ent Parts of Kesteven Adm Co, and all of Parts of Lindsey Adm Co except the following pars transf to help cr Humberside Non-Metrop Co)
1974 Alkborough, Amcotts, Appleby, Ashby cum Fenby, Aylesby, Barnetby le Wold, Barnoldby le Beck, Barrow upon Humber, Beelsby, Bradley, Belton, Bonby, Bottesford, Glanford Brigg, Brigsley, Broughton, Burringham, Burton upon Stather, East Butterwick, Cadney, Crowle, Croxton, Eastoft, Elsham, Epworth, South Ferriby, Flixborough, Garthorpe, Goxhill, Gunness, Habrough, East Halton, West Halton, Hatcliffe, Haxey, Hawerby cum Beesby, Healing, Hibaldstow, Holme, Horkstow, Humberstone, Immingham, Irby, Keadby with Althorpe, North Killingholme, South Killingholme, Kirmington, Kirton in Lindsey, Laceby, Luddington, Manton, Melton Ross, Messingham, Wold Newton, Owston Ferry, East Ravendale, West Ravendale, Redbourne, Roxby cum Risby, Saxby All Saints, Scawby, Scunthorpe, Stallingborough, Thornton Curtis, Ulceby, Waltham, New Waltham, Weelsby, Whitton, Winteringham, Winterton, Wootton, Worlaby, Wrawby, Wroot

ASSOCIATED COUNTY BOROUGHS

GRIMSBY CB [assoc with Pts Lind]
Bdry: 1928,[2] 1958,[3] 1968.[4] Transf 1974 to Humberside.[5]

LINCOLN LIBERTY (until 1840s) AND COUNTY OF ITSELF (from 1410)[6]
No bdry alt.

LINCOLN CB [assoc with Pts Lind]
Bdry: 1920,[7] 1959,[8] 1967.[9]
Transf 1974 to Lincs.[5]

WAPENTAKES AND HUNDREDS[1]

Parts of Holland
ELLOE WAP
Cowbit, Crowland, *pt Deeping Fen*[10] *(until 1856),* pt Deeping St Nicholas[10] (from 1856), Fleet, Gedney, Gedney Hill (from 1866), Holbeach, Lutton (from 1866), Moulton, Pinchbeck, Spalding,[11] Sutton St Edmund, Sutton St James, Sutton St Mary, Tydd St Mary, Weston, pt Central Wingland[12] (from 1858),

Whaplode
KIRTON WAP

Algar Kirk, Amber Hill (from 1880), Little Beats (from 1858), Bicker, Great Brand End Plot (from 1858), Little Brand End Plot (from 1858), Brothertoft (from 1866), Copping Syke (from 1858), Donington, Drainage Marsh (from 1858), Ferry Corner Plot (from 1858), Fosdyke, Frampton, The Friths (from 1858), Gibbet Hills (from 1858), Gosberton, Hall Hills (from 1858), Hart's Grounds (from 1858), Kirton, Mown Rakes (from 1858), North Forty Foot Bank (from 1858), Pelham's Lands (from 1858), Quadring, Royalty Farm (from 1858), Simon Weir (from 1858), pt Skirbeck (until 1866), Skirbeck Quarter (from 1866), Surfleet, Sutterton, Swineshead, Wigtoft, Wyberton

SKIRBECK WAP

Great Beats (from 1858), Benington, Boston,[11] Butterwick, Fishtoft, Freiston, Leake, Leverton, Pepper Gowt Plot (from 1858), Shuff Fen (from 1858), Skirbeck (pt until 1866, ent from 1866), Wrangle

Parts of Kesteven
ASWARDHURN WAP

Asgarby, Aswarby, Aunsby, Burton Penwardine, Culverthorpe (from 1866), Evedon, Ewerby, Great Hale, Little Hale (from 1866), Heckington, Helpringham, pt Heydour (until 1866), Howell, Ingoldsby, Kelby (from 1866), Kirkby la Thorpe, South Kyme (pt until 1866, ent from 1866), Quarrington, Scredington, Old Sleaford, Swarby, Silk Willoughby

AVELAND WAP

Aslackby, Billingborough, Birthorpe (from 1866), Bourne, Dembleby, Dowsby, Dunsby, Folkingham, Hacconby, Haceby, Horbling, Kirkby Underwood, Laughton, Morton, Newton, Osbournby, Pickworth, Pointon (from 1866), Rippingale, Semperingham, Spanby, Swaton, Threckingham, Walcot (near Folkingham), Scott Willoughby

BELTISLOE WAP

Aunby (from 1866), Bassingthorpe, Bitchfield, Burton Coggles, Castle Bytham, Little Bytham, Careby, pt Colsterworth, Corby, Counthorpe (from 1866), Creeton, Edenham, Gunby, Holywell (from 1866), Irnham,[13] Keisby (from 1866), Lenton, Manthorpe (from 1866), Osgodby (from 1866), Skillington, Stainby, Swayfield, Swinstead, Toft and Lound (from 1866), North Witham, South Witham, Witham on the Hill

BOOTHBY GRAFFOE WAP[14]

Aubourn, Bassingham, Boothby Graffoe, Boultham, Bracebridge (from 1840s), Carlton le Moorland, Coleby, Doddington, Eagle, Eagle Hall (from 1858), Eagle Woodhouse (from 1858), pt Flawford (1858–84), Haddington (from 1866), Harmston, North Hykeham, South Hykeham, Morton (from 1858), Navenby, Norton Disney, North Scarle, Skellingthorpe, Skinnand, Stapleford, Swinderby, Swinethorpe (from 1858), Thorpe on the Hill, Thurlby, Waddington (from 1840s), Welbourn, Wellingore, Whisby (from 1866)

FLAXWELL WAP

Anwick, Ashby de la Launde, Byard's Leap (from 1858), Bloxholm, Brauncewell, Cranwell, Digby, Dorrington, Haverholme Priory (from 1858), Hold-

ingham (from 1866), Leasingham, North Rauceby, South Rauceby, Rowston, Roxholm (from 1866), Ruskington, New Sleaford,[11] pt Temple Bruer with Temple High Grange (from 1858)

GRANTHAM SOKE (until 1830s)

Barkston, Belton, Braceby, pt Colsterworth, Denton, Great Gonerby, pt Grantham,[15] Grantham Grange,[16] Harlaxton, Londonthorpe, Great Ponton, Sapperton, Stoke[17] (from 1776), North Stoke (until 1776), South Stoke (until 1776)

LANGOE WAP[14]

Billinghay, Blankney, Branston (from 1840s), Canwick (from 1840s), Dogdyke (from 1866), Dunston, Potter Hanworth, Heighington (from 1866), Kirkby Green, North Kyme (from 1866), pt South Kyme (until 1866), Martin (from 1866), Mere[14] (from 1858), Metheringham, Nocton, Scopwick, pt Temple Bruer with Temple High Grange (from 1858), Thorpe Tilney (from 1866), Timberland, Walcot (near Billinghay), Washingborough

LOVEDEN WAP

Allington[18] (from 1830s), Ancaster, Barkston (from 1830s), Barrowby (from 1830s), Beckingham, Belton (from 1830s), Long Bennington, Bennington Grange (from 1858), Brant Broughton, Carlton Scroop, Caythorpe, Claypole, Denton (from 1830s), Dry Doddington, Easton[17] (from 1866), Fenton, Foston, Fulbeck, Great Gonersey (from 1830s), Grantham[11] (pt 1830s—66, ent from 1866), Grantham Grange[16] (from 1858), Harlaxton (from 1830s), Harrowby[19] (from 1866), Honington (from 1830s), Hough on the Hill, Hougham, Leadenham, Londonthorpe (from 1830s), Manthorpe cum Little Gonerby[15] (from 1866), Marston, Normanton, Sedgebrook (from 1830s), Stragglethorpe, Stubton, Syston (from 1830s), Westborough, Wyville cum Hungerton (from 1830s)

NESS WAP

Barholm, Baston, Braceborough, Carlby, Market Deeping, West Deeping, *pt Deeping Fen[10] (until 1856),* Deeping St James, pt Deeping St Nicholas[10] (from 1856), Greatford, Langtoft, Stamford All Saints,[20] Stamford St George,[20] Stamford St John,[20] Stamford St Mary,[20] Stamford St Michael,[20] Stowe, Tallington, Thurlby, Uffington, Wilsthorpe (from 1866)

WINNIBRIGGS AND THREO WAP

Allington[18] (until 1830s), Barrowby (until 1830s), Braceby (from 1830s), Boothby Pagnell, pt Colsterworth (from 1830s), pt Grantham[15] (until 1830s), Heydour (pt until 1866, ent from 1866), Honington (until 1830s), Humby (from 1887), Little Humby (1866—87), Great Ponton (from 1830s), Little Ponton, Ropsley, Sapperton (from 1830s), Sedgebrook (until 1830s), Somerby,[11] Spittlegate[15] (from 1866), Stoke (1830s—66), North Stoke[17] (from 1866), South Stoke[17] (from 1866), Stroxton, Syston (until 1830s), Welby, Wilsford, Woolsthorpe, Wyville cum Hungerton (until 1830s)

Parts of Lindsey
ASLACOE WAP

Atterby, Blyborough, Caenby, Cammeringham, Coates, Fillingham, East Firsby, West Firsby (from 1866), Glentham, Glentworth, Hackthorn, Cold

Hanworth, Harpswell, Hemswell, Ingham, Normanby by Spital, Bishop Norton, Owmby, Saxby, Saxilby with Ingleby, Snitterby, Sprindlington, Willoughton

BOLINGBROKE SOKE

Asgarby, Bolingbroke, Carrington[21] (from 1866), Eastville[22] (from 1866), Frithville[21] (from 1866), Hagnaby, Halton Holegate, Hareby, Hundleby, *East Fen*[22], East Keal, West Keal, East Kirkby, Lusby, Mavis Enderby, Midville[22] (from 1866), Miningsby, Raithby, Revesby, Sibsey, Spilsby, Little Steeping, Stickford, Stickney, Thorpe St Peter, Toynton All Saints, Toynton St Peter, *West Fen*[21], West Fen[21] (from 1880), Westville[21] (from 1866)

BRADLEY HAVERSTOE WAP

Ashby cum Fenby, Aylesby, Barnoldby le Beck, Beelsby, Bradley, Brigsley, Cabourne, Clee with Weelsby,[11] Cleethorpes (from 1866), Great Coates, Little Coates, North Coates, Cuxwold, Fulstow, Grainsby, Great Grimsby,[11] Hatcliffe, Hawerby cum Beesby, Healing, Holton le Clay, Humberston, Irby, Laceby, Marsh Chapel, Wold Newton, East Ravendale, West Ravendale (from 1866), Rothwell, Scartho, Swallow, Swinhope, Tetney, North Thoresby, Waithe, Waltham

CALCEWAITH WAP

Aby with Greenfield, Alford, Anderby, Beesby in the Marsh, Belleau, Bilsby, Calceby, Little Cawthorpe, Claxby, Claythorpe (from 1866), Cumberworth, Farlesthorpe, Gayton le Marsh, Hannah cum Hagnaby, Haugh (from 1858), Hogsthorpe, Huttoft, Legbourne, Mablethorpe, Maltby le Marsh, Markby, Mumby, South Reston, Rigsby with Ailby, Saleby with Thoresthorpe, Strubby with Woodthorpe, Sutton in the Marsh, Swaby, Theddlethorpe All Saints, Theddlethorpe St Helen, South Thoresby, Tothill, Trusthorpe, Ulceby with Fordington, Well, Willoughby with Sloothby, Withern with Stain

CANDELSHOE WAP

Addlethorpe, Ashby by Partney, Bratoft, Burgh le Marsh, Candelsby, Croft, Dalby, Driby, Firsby, Friskney, Gunby, Ingoldmells, Irby in the Marsh, Northholme (until 1888), Orby, Partney, Scremby, Skegness, Skendleby, Great Steeping, Sutterby, Wainfleet All Saints,[11] Wainfleet St Mary,[11] Welton le Marsh, Winthorpe

CORRINGHAM WAP

Blyton cum Wharton, pt Burton upon Stather, Cleatham, Corringham, pt East Ferry (from 1866), Gainsborough,[11] Grayingham, Greenhill and Redhill (from 1858), Heapham, Kirton in Lindsey, Laughton (from 1866), Laughton by Gainsborough (until 1866), Lea, pt Manton, Morton (from 1866), Northorpe, Pilham, Scotter, Scotton, Southorpe (from 1858), Springthorpe, East Stockwith (from 1866), Walkerith (from 1866), Wildsworth (from 1866)

GARTREE WAP

Asterby, Baumber, Belchford, Bucknall, Cawkwell, Dalderby, Donington on Bain, Edlington, Gautby, Goulceby, Hemingby, Horsington, Kirkby on Bain, Kirkstead, Langton, Martin, Minting, Ranby, Scamblesby, Scrivelsby, Market Stainton, Stenigot, Stixwould, Great Sturton, Tattershall, Tattershall Thorpe (from 1866), Thornton, Tumby (from 1866),

Waddingworth, Wispington, Woodhall

HILL HD

Ashby Puerorum, Aswardby, Brinkhill, pt Burwell (until 1866), Claxby Pluckacre, Bag Enderby, Fulletby, Greetham, Hagworthingham, Hameringham, Harrington, Ketsby (until 1774), Langton by Spilsby, South Ormsby (until 1774), South Ormsby cum Ketsby (from 1774), Oxcombe, Salmonby, Sausthorpe, Scrafield, Somersby, Tetford, Walmsgate, Winceby, Worlaby (from 1858)

HORNCASTLE SOKE

West Ashby, Coningsby, Wood Enderby, Haltham, Haven Bank (1858—84), Horncastle, Langriville[23] (from 1866), Mareham le Fen, Mareham on the Hill, Moorby, Roughton, Seven Acres (from 1858), Thimbleby, Thornton le Fen[23] (from 1866), High Toynton, Low Toynton, Wildmore[23] (from 1858), *Wildmore Fen*, Wilksby

LAWRES WAP

Aisthorpe, Barlings, Brattleby, Broxholme, Burton, Buslingthorpe, North Carlton, South Carlton, Dunholme, Faldingworth, Fiskerton, Friesthorpe, Grange de Lings (from 1858), Greetwell, Hardwick (from 1866), Nettleham, Reepham, Riseholme, Saxilby with Ingleby, Scampton, Scothern, Snarford, Sudbrooke, Thorpe in the Fallows, pt Torksey,[11] Welton, Cherry Willingham

LOUTH ESK HD

Alvingham, Authorpe, Burwell (pt until 1866, ent from 1866), Calcethorpe, Castle Carlton, Great Carlton, Little Carlton, North Cockerington, South Cockerington, Conisholme, North Elkington, South Elkington, Farforth cum Maidenwell, Gayton le Wold, Grainthorpe, Grimblethorpe (from 1858), Grimoldby, Hallington, Haugham, Keddington, Kelstern, Louth, Louth Park (from 1866), Manby, Muckton, Raithby cum Maltby, North Reston, Ruckland, Saltfleetby All Saints, Saltfleetby St Clement, Saltfleetby St Peter, Skidbrooke with Saltfleet Haven, North Somercotes, South Somercotes, Stewton, Tathwell, Welton le Wold, Withcall, East Wykeham, Yarburgh

LUDBOROUGH WAP

Brackenborough, Covenham St Bartholomew, Covenham St Mary, Fotherby, Little Grimsby, Ludborough, North Ormsby, Utterby, Wytham cum Cadeby

MANLEY WAP

Alkborough, Althorpe, Amcotts (from 1866), Appleby, Ashby (from 1866), Belton, Bottesford, Broughton, Brumby (from 1866), Burringham (from 1866), pt Burton upon Stather, East Butterwick (from 1866), West Butterwick (from 1866), Crosby (from 1866), Crowle, Eastoft (from 1866), Epworth, pt East Ferry (from 1866), Flixborough, Frodingham, Garthorpe (from 1866), Gunness (from 1866), West Halton, Haxey, Hibaldstow, Holme (from 1866), Keadby (from 1866), Luddington, pt Manton, pt Misson (until 1886), Messingham, Newstead (from 1858), Owston, Raventhorpe (from 1866), Redbourne, Risby (until 1717), Roxby (until 1717), Roxby cum Risby (from 1717), Scawby, Scunthorpe (from 1866), Twigmore (from 1866), Waddingham, Whitton, Winteringham, Winterton, Wroot, Yaddlethorpe (1866—87)

WALSHCROFT WAP

Binbrook, pt Caistor (until 1866), Claxby, Croxby, Holton le Moor (from 1866), South Kelsey, Kingerby, Kirkby cum Osgodby, Linwood, Newton by Toft, Normanby le Wold, North Owersby, South Owersby, Market Rasen, Middle Rasen, West Rasen, Stainton le Vale, Tealby, Thoresway, Thorganby, Thornton le Moor, Toft next Newton, Usselby, Walesby, North Willingham

WELL WAP

Brampton (from 1866), Gate Burton, Fenton (from 1866), Kettlethorpe, Kexby (from 1866), Knaith, Marton, Newton on Trent, Stow, Sturton by Stow (from 1866), pt Torksey, Upton, Willingham

WRAGGOE WAP

Apley, Bardney, East Barkwith, West Barkwith, Benniworth, Biscathorpe, Bullington (from 1866), Burgh on Bain, Coldstead (from 1858), Fulnetby (from 1866), Goltho, Hainton, Hatton, Holton cum Beckering, Kirmond le Mire, Langton by Wragby, Legsby, Lissington, Ludford Magna, Ludford Parva, Newball (from 1866), Panton, Rand, Sixhills, Snelland, Sotby, Stainfield, Stainton by Langworth, East Torrington, West Torrington, Tupholme, Wickenby, South Willingham, Wragby

YARBOROUGH WAP

Barnetby le Wold, Barrow upon Humber, Barton upon Humber (from 1866), Barton upon Humber St Mary[11] (until 1888), Barton upon Humber St Peter[11] (until 1888), Bigby, Bonby, Brocklesby, Cadney cum Howsham, Caistor[11] (pt until 1866, ent from 1866), Clixby (from 1866), Croxton, Elsham, South Ferriby, Glanford Brigg (from 1866), Goxhill, Grasby, Habrough, East Halton, Horkstow, Immingham, Keelby, North Kelsey, Killingholme (until 1866), North Killingholme (from 1866), South Killingholme (from 1866), Kirmington, Great Limber, Melton Ross, Nettleton, Riby, Saxby All Saints, Searby cum Ownby, Somerby, Stallingborough, Thornton Curtis, Ulceby, Wootton, Worlaby, Wrawby

BOROUGHS

Units with some degree of burghal character[24] are denominated 'Bor'. Those which did not sustain that status until the 19th cent are in italics. MBs were established by the Municipal Corporations Act, 1835,[25] or by later charter.

BARTON UPON HUMBER BOR [Pts Lind]

Barton upon Humber St Mary, Barton upon Humber St Peter

BOSTON BOR/MB [Pts Holl]

Boston (pt until 1880, ent 1880—94), Hall Hills (1858—1906)

CAISTOR BOR [Pts Lind]

pt Caistor

CLEETHORPES MB (1936[26]—74)

Cleethorpes

GAINSBOROUGH BOR [Pts Lind]

pt Gainsborough

GRANTHAM BOR/MB[27] [Pts Kestev]

Little Gonerby (1894—1909), Grantham (pt [main tp] until 1835, enlarged pt 1835—66, ent 1866—1974), Grantham Grange (1879—1909), pt Harrowby (1879—94), Harrowby Within (1894—1909), pt Manthorpe cum Little Gonerby (1879—94), pt Somerby (1879—94), New Somerby (1894—1909), pt Spittlegate (1879—94), Spittlegate Within (1894—1909)

GREAT GRIMSBY BOR/MB, GRIMSBY CB [Pts Lind]/CB

Clee (1894—1928), pt Clee with Weelsby (1889—94), Grimsby (1928—74), Great Grimsby (until 1928)

LINCOLN LIBERTY (until 1840s) AND COUNTY OF ITSELF (from 1410)[6]

The pars in Lincoln Bor (see following entry) and the following in the Lbty: Bracebridge, Branston, Canwick, Mere, Waddington.

LINCOLN BOR[28]/MB/CB [Pts Lind]

Lincoln (1907—74), Lincoln Bishop's Palace (1835—1907), Lincoln Castle Dykings (1835—88), Lincoln Cold Bath House (1835—1907), Lincoln Holmes Common (1837—88), Lincoln Monks Liberty (1835—1907), Lincoln St Benedict (until 1907), Lincoln St Botolph (until 1907), Lincoln St John in Newport (until 1907), Lincoln St Margaret in the Close (until 1907), Lincoln St Mark (until 1907), Lincoln St Martin (until 1907), Lincoln St Mary le Wigford (until 1888), Lincoln St Mary le Wigford with Holmes Common (1888—1907), Lincoln St Mary Magdalen in the Bail (until 1907), Lincoln St Michael (until 1907), Lincoln St Nicholas (until 1907), Lincoln St Paul in the Bail (until 1907), Lincoln St Peter at Arches (until 1907), Lincoln St Peter at Gowts (until 1907), Lincoln St Peter in Eastgate (until 1907), Lincoln St Swithin (until 1907), Lincoln South Common (until 1907)

LOUTH BOR/MB [Pts Lind]

Louth (pt until 1866, ent 1866—1974)

SCUNTHORPE MB [Pts Lind] (1936[29]—74)

Scunthorpe (1937—74), Scunthorpe and Frodingham (1936—37)

NEW SLEAFORD BOR [Pts Kestev]

New Sleaford

SPALDING BOR [Pts Holl]

Spalding

STAMFORD BOR/MB [Pts Kestev]

Stamford (1930—74), Stamford All Saints (until 1930), Stamford St George (until 1930), Stamford St John (until 1930), Stamford St Mary (until 1930), Stamford St Michael (until 1930), Stamford Baron St Martin[30] (pt 1835—94, ent 1894—1930)

TORKSEY BOR [Pts Lind]

pt Torksey

WAINFLEET BOR [Pts Lind]

Wainfleet All Saints, Wainfleet St Mary

WILLINGTHORPE (alias WESTGATE) BOR [in Lincoln]

uncertain composition

POOR LAW UNIONS

In Lincs Poor Law County:[31]
BOSTON PLU [Pts Holl, Pts Lind]
Algar Kirk, Amber Hill[32] (1862—1930), Great Beats (1862—1906), Little Beats (1862—1906), Benington, Bicker, Boston, Great Brand End Plot (1862—91), Little Brand End Plot (1862—91), Brothertoft, Butterwick, Carrington, Copping Syke (1862—1930), Dogdyke (1836—*ca* 1894), Drainage Marsh (1862—1906), Ferry Corner Plot (1862—1906), Fishtoft, Fosdyke, Frampton, Freiston, The Friths (1866—1906), Frithville, Gibbet Hills (1862—91), Hall Hills (1861—1906), Hart's Grounds (soon after 1836[33]—1930), Kirton, Langriville, Leake (1836—94), Old Leake (1894—1930), Leverton, Mown Rakes (1866—91), North Forty Foot Bank (1862—1906), Pelham's Lands (1862—1930), Pepper Gowt Plot (1862—1906), Royalty Farm (1866—91), Seven Acres (soon after 1836[33]—1906), Shuff Fen (1862—1906), Sibsey, Simon Weir (1862—1906), Skirbeck, Skirbeck Quarter, South of the Witham (1862—1906), Sutterton, Fen, Westville, Wigtoft, Wrangle, Wyberton
BOURNE PLU [Pts Kestev]
Aslackby, Aunby, Baston, Billingborough, Birthorpe, Bourne, Castle Bytham, Little Bytham, Careby, Carlby, Corby, Counthorpe, Creeton (soon after 1836[33]—1930), Market Deeping, Deeping St James, Dowsby, Dunsby, Edenham, Folkingham, Hacconby, Hawthorpe with Bulby[13] (1836—mid cent), Holywell, Horbling, Irnham,[13] Kirkby Underwood, Langtoft, Laughton, Manthorpe, Morton, Pointon, Rippingale, Semperingham, Swayfield, Swinstead, Thurlby, Toft and Lound, Witham on the Hill
CAISTOR PLU [Pts Lind]
Atterby, Bigby, Brocklesby, Buslingthorpe, Cabourne, Caistor, Claxby, Clixby, North Coates, Croxby, Cuxwold, Glentham, Grasby, Holton le Moor, Keelby, North Kelsey, South Kelsey, Kingerby, Kirkby cum Osgodby, Kirmond le Mire, Legsby, Great Limber, Linwood, Lissington, Nettleton, Newton by Toft, Normanby le Wold, Bishop Norton, North Owersby, South Owersby, Market Rasen, Middle Rasen, West Rasen, Riby, Rothwell, Searby cum Ownby, Sixhills, Snitterby, Somerby, Stainton le Vale, Swallow, Swinhope, Tealby, Thoresway, Thorganby, Thornton le Moor, Toft next Newton, East Torrington, Usselby, Waddingham, Walesby, North Willingham
GAINSBOROUGH PLU [Pts Lindsey, Notts]
Blyborough, Blyton cum Wharton, Brampton, Gate Burton, West Butterwick (soon after 1837[33]—1930), Coates, Corringham, Fenton, East Ferry (soon after 1837[33]—1930), Fillingham, Gainsborough, Glentworth, Grayingham, Greenhill and Redhill (1861—1930), Hardwick, Harpswell, Haxey, Heapham, Hemswell, Kettlethorpe, Kexby, Knaith, Laughton, Lea, Marton, Morton, Newton on Trent, Northorpe, Owston (soon after 1837[33]—1912), Owston Ferry (1912—30), Pilham, Scotter, Scotton, Southorpe, Springthorpe, East Stockwith, Stow, Sturton by Stow, Thonock (1895—1930), Torksey, Upton, Walkerith, Wildsworth, Willingham, Willoughton

GLANFORD BRIGG PLU [Pts Lind]
Alkborough, Appleby, Ashby (1837—1919), Barnetby le Wold, Barrow upon Humber, Barton upon Humber St Mary (1837—88), Barton upon Humber St Peter (1837—88), Barton upon Humber (1888—1930), Bonby, Bottesford, Broughton, Brumby (1837—1919), Brumby Rural (1919—30), Burringham, Burton upon Stather, East Butterwick, Cadney cum Howsham, Cleatham, Croxton, Crosby (1837—1919), Elsham, South Ferriby, Flixborough, Frodingham (1837—1919), Glanford Brigg, Goxhill, Gunness (soon after 1837[33]—1930), East Halton, West Halton, Hibaldstow, Holme, Horkstow, North Killingholme, South Killingholme, Kirton in Lindsey, Kirmington, Manton, Melton Ross, Messingham, Newstead (1861—1930), Raventhorpe (soon after 1837[33]—1930), Redbourne, Roxby cum Risby, Saxby All Saints, Scawby, Scunthorpe (1837—1919), Scunthorpe and Frodingham (1919—30), Thornton Curtis, Twigmore, Ulceby, Whitton, Winteringham, Winterton, Wootton, Worlaby, Wrawby, Yaddlethorpe (1837—87)
GRANTHAM PLU [Pts Kestev, Leics]
Ancaster, Barrowby, Bassingthorpe, Belton, Bitchfield, Boothby Pagnell, Braceby, Burton Coggles, Carlton Scroop, Colsterworth, Denton, Easton, Great Gonerby, Little Gonerby (1894—1909), Grantham, Grantham Grange (1866—1909), Gunby, Haceby, Harlaxton, Harrowby (1836—94), Harrowby Within (1894—1909), Harrowby Without (1894—1930), Heydour, Honington, Hough on the Hill, Humby (1887—1930), Little Humby (1836—87), Ingoldsby, Keisby, Lenton, Londonthorpe, Manthorpe (1894—1930), Manthorpe cum Little Gonerby (1836—94), Normanton, Osgodby, Pickworth, Great Ponton, Little Ponton, Ropsley, Sapperton, Skillington, Somerby (1836—94), New Somerby (1894—1909), Old Somerby (1894—1930), Spittlegate (1836—94), Spittlegate Within (1894—1909), Spittlegate Without (1894—1930), Stainby, North Stoke, South Stoke, Stroxton, Welby, North Witham, South Witham, Woolsthorpe, Wyville cum Hungerton
GRIMSBY PLU [Pts Lind]
Ashby cum Fenby, Aylesby, Barnoldby le Beck, Beelsby, Bradley, Brigsley, Clee (1894—1928), Clee with Weelsby (1836—94), Cleethorpes, Great Coates, Little Coates (1836—1928), Grimsby (1928—30), Great Grimsby (1836—1928), Habrough, Hatcliffe, Hawerby cum Beesby, Healing, Humberston, Immingham, Irby, Laceby, Wold Newton, East Ravendale, West Ravendale, Scartho (1836—1928), Stallingborough, Waltham, Weelsby (1894—1930)
HOLBEACH PLU [Pts Holl, Norfolk (until 1897), ent Pts Holl thereafter]
Fleet, Gedney, Gedney Hill, Holbeach, Lutton, Little Sutton (1894—1930), Long Sutton or Sutton St Mary (1894—1930), Sutton Bridge (1894—1930), Sutton St Edmund, Sutton St James, Sutton St Mary (1835—94), Tydd St Mary, Whaplode, Central Wingland[12] (1867—1930)

HORNCASTLE PLU [Pts Lind]

Asgarby, West Ashby, Ashby Puerorum, Asterby, East Barkwith, West Barkwith, Baumber, Belchford, Benniworth, Bucknall, Cawkwell, Claxby Pluckacre, Coningsby, Dalderby, Edlington, Bag Enderby, Wood Enderby, Fulletby, Gautby, Goulceby, Greetham, Hagworthingham, Haltham, Hameringham, Hatton, Haven Bank (1861—84), Hemingby, Horncastle, Horsington, Kirkby on Bain, Kirkstead, Langton, Langton by Wragby, Lusby, Mareham le Fen, Mareham on the Hill, Martin, Miningsby, Minting, Moorby, Panton, Ranby, Revesby, Roughton, Salmonby, Scamblesby, Scrafield, Scrivelsby, Somersby, Sotby, Market Stainton, Stixwould, Great Sturton, Tattershall, Tattershall Thorpe, Tetford, Thimbleby, Thornton, West Torrington, High Toynton, Low Toynton, Tumby, Tupholme, Waddingworth, Wildmore (1880—1930), Wilksby, Winceby, Wispington, Woodhall, Woodhall Spa (1894—1930), Wragby

LINCOLN PLU [Pts Kestev, Pts Lind]

Aisthorpe, Apley, Aubourn, Bardney, Barlings, Boothby Graffoe, Boultham, Bracebridge (1836—1920), Bracebridge Heath (1898—1930), Branston, Brattleby, Broxholme, Bullington, Burton, Caenby, Cammeringham, North Carlton, South Carlton, Canwick, Coldstead (1862—1930), Coleby, Doddington, Dunholme, Dunston, Eagle, Eagle Hall (1862—1930), Eagle Woodhouse (1862—86), Faldingworth, East Firsby, West Firsby, Fiskerton, Friesthorpe, Fulnetby (soon after 1836[33]—1930), Goltho, Grange de Lings (1858—1930), Greetwell, Hackthorn, Haddington, Cold Hanworth, Potter Hanworth, Harmston, Heighington, Holton cum Beckering, North Hykeham, South Hykeham, Ingham, Lincoln (1907—30), Lincoln Bishop's Palace (1861—1907), Lincoln Castle Dykings (1858—88), Lincoln Cold Bath House (1861—1907), Lincoln Holmes Common (1863—88), Lincoln Monks Liberty (1861—1930), Lincoln St Benedict (1836—1907), Lincoln St Botolph (1836—1907), Lincoln St John in Newport, Lincoln St Margaret in the Close (1836—1907), Lincoln St Mark (1836—1907), Lincoln St Martin (1836—1907), Lincoln St Mary Magdalen (1836—1907), Lincoln St Mary le Wigford (1836—88), Lincoln St Mary le Wigford with Holmes Common (1888—1907), Lincoln St Michael (1836—1907), Lincoln St Nicholas (1836—1907), Lincoln St Paul in the Bail (1836—1907), Lincoln St Peter at the Arches (1836—1907), Lincoln St Peter in Eastgate (1836—1907), Lincoln St Peter at Gowts (1836—1907), Lincoln St Swithin (1836—1907), Lincoln South Common, Mere, Metheringham, Morton (1862—1930), Navenby, Nettleham, Newball, Nocton, Normanby by Spital, Owmby, Rand, Reepham, Riseholme, Saxby, Saxilby with Ingleby, Scampton, Scothern, Skellingthorpe, Skinnand, Snarford, Snelland, Sprindlington, Stainfield, Stainton by Langworth, Sudbrooke, Swinethorpe, Thorpe in the Fallows, Thorpe on the Hill, Waddington, Washingborough, Welton, Whisby, Wickenby, Cherry Willingham

LOUTH PLU [Pts Lind]

Aby with Greenfield, Alvingham, Authorpe, Beesby in the Marsh, Belleau, Binbrook,[34] Biscathorpe, Brackenborough, Burwell, Burgh on Bain, Calcethorpe, Castle Carlton, Great Carlton, Little Carlton, Little Cawthorpe, Claythorpe, North Coates, North Cockerington, South Cockerington, Conisholme, Covenham St Bartholomew, Covenham St Mary, Donington on Bain, North Elkington, South Elkington, Farforth cum Maidenwell, Fotherby, Fulstow, Gayton le Marsh, Gayton le Wold, Grainsby, Grainthorpe, Grimblethorpe (1858—1930), Grimoldby, Little Grimsby, Hainton, Hallington, Hannah cum Hagnaby, Haugh (1858—1930), Haugham, Holton le Clay, Keddington, Kelstern, Legbourne, Louth, Louth Park, Ludborough, Ludford Magna, Ludford Parva, Mablethorpe, Walmsgate, Welton le Wold, North Willingham, South Willingham, Withcall, Withern with Stain, Worlaby, Wyham cum Cadeby, East Wykeham (1858—1930), Yarburgh

SLEAFORD PLU [Pts Kestev]

Anwick, Asgarby, Ashby de la Launde, Aswarby, Aunsby, Byard's Leap (1861—1930), Billinghay, Blankney, Bloxholm, Brauncewell, Burton Penwardine, Cranwell, Culverthorpe, Dembleby, Digby, Dogdyke (ca 1894—1930), Dorrington, Evedon, Ewerby, Great Hale, Little Hale, Haverholme Priory (1861—1930), Heckington, Helpringham, Holdingham, Howell, Kelby, Kirkby Green, Kirkby la Thorpe, North Kyme, South Kyme, Leadenham, Leasingham, Martin, Newton, Osbournby, Quarrington, North Rauceby, South Rauceby, Rowston, Roxholm, Ruskington, Scredington, Scopwick, New Sleaford, Old Sleaford, Spanby, Swarby, Swaton, Temple Bruer with Temple High Grange (1861—1930), Thorpe Tilney, Threckingham, Timberland, Walcot (near Billinghay), Walcot (near Folkingham), Welbourn, Wellingore, Scott Willoughby, Silk Willoughby, Wilsford

SPALDING PLU [Pts Holl, Pts Kestev]

Cowbit, Deeping St Nicholas[10] (1862—1930), Donington (soon after 1835[33]—1930), Gosberton, Moulton, Pinchbeck, Quadring, Spalding, Surfleet, Weston

SPILSBY PLU [Pts Lind] Addlethorpe, Alford, Anderby, Ashby by Partney, Aswardby, Bilsby, Bolingbroke, Bratoft, Brinkhill, Burgh le Marsh, Calceby, Candlesby, Chapel St Leonards (1896—1930), Claxby, Croft, Cumberworth, Dalby, Driby, Eastville, Mavis Enderby, Farlesthorpe, Firsby, Friskney, Gunby, Hagnaby, Halton Holegate, Hareby, Harrington, Hogsthorpe, Hundleby, Huttoft, Ingoldmells, Irby in the Marsh, East Keal, West Keal, East Kirkby, Langton by Spilsby, New Leake (1894—1930), Markby, Midville, Mumby, Northholme (1837—88), Orby, South Ormesby cum Ketsby, Partney, Raithby, Rigsby with Ailby, Sausthorpe, Scremby, Skegness, Skendleby, Spilsby, Great Steeping, Little Steeping, Stickford, Stickney, Sutterby, Sutton in the Marsh, Thorpe St Peter, Toynton All Saints, Toynton St Peter, Ulceby with Fordington, Wainfleet All Saints, Wainfleet St Mary, Well, Welton le Marsh, West Fen (1880—1930), Willoughby with Sloothby, Winthorpe (1837—1926)

STAMFORD PLU [Pts Kestev, Northants (1835—89), Soke Peterb (1889—1930), Rutl, Hunts]

Barholm, Braceborough, West Deeping, Greatford, Stamford All Saints, Stamford St George, Stamford St John, Stamford St Mary, Stamford St Michael, Stamford Baron St Martin,[30] Stowe, Tallington, Uffington, Wilsthorpe

In Other Poor Law Counties:

DONCASTER PLU [Yorks W Riding, Notts (1837—95), Pts Lind (1837—86)]
Misson[35]

GOOLE PLU [Yorks W Riding, Pts Lind]
Garthorpe, Luddington

NEWARK PLU [Notts, Pts Lind]
Allington,[18] Barkston, Bassingham, Beckingham, Long Bennington, Bennington Grange (1861—1930), Brant Broughton, Carlton le Moorland, Caythorpe, Claypole,

Dry Doddington, Fenton, Flawford[36] (1866—84), Foston, Fulbeck, Hougham, Marston, Norton Disney, North Scarle, Sedgebrook, Stapleford, Stragglethorpe, Stubton, Swinderby, Syston, Thurlby, Westborough

PETERBOROUGH PLU [Northants, Hunts (1835—89), Pts Holl, Cambs (1835—89), Soke Peterb (1889—1930), Isle of Ely (1889—1930)]
Crowland

THORNE PLU [Yorks W Riding, Pts Lind]
Althorpe, Amcotts, Belton, Crowle,[37] Eastoft, Epworth, Keadby, Wroot

SANITARY DISTRICTS

BARTON UPON HUMBER USD [Pts Lind]
Barton upon Humber (1888—94), Barton upon Humber St Mary (1875—88), Barton upon Humber St Peter (1875—88)

BOSTON RSD
same as PLU less Boston

BOSTON USD [Pts Holl]
Boston

BOURNE RSD
same as PLU

BRIGG USD [Pts Lind]
pt Bigby (1875—92), pt Broughton (1875—92), Glanford Brigg, pt Scawby (1875—92), pt Wraby (1875—92)

BROUGHTON USD [Pts Lind]
Broughton (pt until 1892, ent 1892—94)

BRUMBY AND FRODINGHAM USD [Pts Lind]
Brumby, Frodingham

CAISTOR RSD
same as PLU less pt Bigby (1875—92), Market Rasen

CLEE WITH WEELSBY USD [Pts Lind]
Clee with Weelsby (ent 1875—89, pt 1889—94)

CLEETHORPE WITH THRUNSCOE USD [Pts Lind]
Cleethorpes

CROWLE USD [Pts Lind]
Crowle[37]

GAINSBOROUGH RSD
same as PLU less pt Gainsborough

GAINSBOROUGH USD [Pts Lind]
pt Gainsborough

GLANFORD BRIGG RSD
same as PLU less Barton upon Humber (1888—94), Barton upon Humber St Mary (1875—88), Barton upon Humber St Peter (1875—88), Broughton, Brumby, Frodingham, Roxby cum Risby, pt Scawby (1875—92), Scunthorpe (1890—94), Winterton, pt Wrawby (1875—92)

GRANTHAM RSD
same as PLU for Lincs pars less Grantham, pt Harrowby (1879—94), pt Manthorpe cum Little Gonerby (1879—94), pt Somerby (1879—94), pt Spittlegate (1879—94)

GRANTHAM USD [Pts Kestev]
Grantham, pt Harrowby (1879—94), pt Manthorpe cum Little Gonerby (1879—94), pt Somerby (1879—94), pt Spittlegate (1879—94)

GRIMSBY RSD
same as PLU less Clee with Weelsby, Cleethorpes, Great Grimsby

GREAT GRIMSBY USD (1875—89), GRIMSBY USD (1889—94) [Pts Lind (1875—89), Grimsby CB (1889—94)]
pt Clee with Weelsby (1889—94), Great Grimsby

HOLBEACH RSD
same as PLU for Lincs pars less Holbeach

HOLBEACH USD [Pts Holl]
Holbeach

HORNCASTLE RSD
same as PLU less Horncastle

HORNCASTLE USD [Pts Lind]
Horncastle

LINCOLN RSD
same as PLU less pars and pt of par in Lincoln USD

LINCOLN USD [Pts Lind]
Lincoln Bishop's Palace, Lincoln Castle Dykings, Lincoln Cold Bath House, Lincoln Holmes Common (1875—88), Lincoln Monks Liberty, Lincoln St Benedict, Lincoln St Botolph, Lincoln St John in Newport, Lincoln St Margaret in the Close, Lincoln St Mark, Lincoln St Martin, Lincoln St Mary le Wigford (1875—88), Lincoln St Mary le Wigford with Holmes Common (1888—94), Lincoln St Mary Magdalen in the Bail, Lincoln St Michael, Lincoln St Nicholas, Lincoln St Paul in the Bail, Lincoln St Peter at Arches, Lincoln St Peter at Gowts, Lincoln St Peter in Eastgate, Lincoln St Swithin, Lincoln South Common

LOUTH RSD
same as PLU less Louth

LOUTH USD [Pts Lind]
Louth

NEWARK RSD
same as PLU for Lincs pars

MARKET RASEN USD [Pts Lind]
Market Rasen

ROXBY CUM RISBY USD [Pts Lind]
Roxby cum Risby

RUSKINGTON USD [Pts Kestev]
Ruskington

SCUNTHORPE USD (1890[38]—94) [Pts Lind]
Scunthorpe

SKEGNESS USD (1885[39]—94) [Pts Lind]
Skegness

SLEAFORD RSD
same as PLU less Holdingham, Quarrington, Ruskington, New Sleaford, Old Sleaford
NEW SLEAFORD USD [Pts Kestev]
Holdingham, Quarrington, New Sleaford, Old Sleaford
SPALDING RSD
same as PLU less Spalding (ent 1875—87, pt 1887—88, ent 1888—94)
SPALDING USD [Pts Holl]
Spalding (ent 1875—87, pt 1887—88, ent 1888—94)
SPILSBY RSD
same as PLU less Skegness (1885—94)
STAMFORD RSD
same as PLU less Lincss pars and pt of par in Stamford

USD
STAMFORD USD [Pts Kestev, Northants]
Stamford All Saints, Stamford St George, Stamford St John, Stamford St Mary, Stamford St Michael, pt Stamford Baron St Martin [30]
LONG SUTTON USD [Pts Holl]
pt Sutton St Mary
SUTTON BRIDGE USD [Pts Holl]
pt Sutton St Mary
THORNE RSD
same as PLU for Lincs pars less Crowle[37]
WINTERTON USD [Pts Lind]
Winterton

PARTS OF HOLLAND ADMINISTRATIVE COUNTY

BOSTON RD
Algar Kirk, Amber Hill, Great Beats (1894—1906), Little Beats (1894—1906), Benington, Bicker, Brothertoft, Butterwick, Copping Syke (1894—1935), Drainage Marsh (1894—1906), Ferry Corner Plot (1894—1906), Fishtoft, Fosdyke, Frampton, Freiston, The Friths (1894—1906), Hall Hills (1894—1906), Hart's Grounds, Kirton, Lands Common to Swineshead and Wigtoft (1894—1932), Old Leake, Leverton, North Forty Foot Bank (1894—1906), Pelham's Lands, Pepper Gowt Plot (1894—1906), Shuff Fen (1894—1906), Simon Weir (1894—1906), Skirbeck (1894—1932), Skirbeck Quarter (1894—1932), South of the Witham (1894—1906), Sutterton, Swineshead, Wigtoft, Wrangle, Wyberton
CROWLAND RD (1894—1932[40])
Crowland

EAST ELLOE RD
Fleet, Gedney, Gedney Hill, Holbeach (1932—74), Lutton, Little Sutton, Long Sutton (1932—74), Sutton Bridge (1932—74), Sutton St Edmund, Sutton St James, Tydd St Mary, Whaplode, Central Wingland[12] (pt 1894—97, ent 1897—1954)
HOLBEACH UD (1894—1932[40])
Holbeach
SPALDING RD [Pts Holl, Pts Kestev (1894—1930)]
Cowbit, Crowland (1932—74), Deeping St Nichols[10] (pt 1894—1930, ent 1930—74), Donington, Gosberton, Moulton, Pinchbeck, Quadring, Surfleet, Weston
SPALDING UD
Spalding
LONG SUTTON UD (1894—1932[40])
Long Sutton or Sutton St Mary
SUTTON BRIDGE UD (1894—1932[40])
Sutton Bridge

PARTS OF KESTEVEN ADMINISTRATIVE COUNTY

BOURNE RD (1894—1931[41])
Aslackby, Aunby, Baston, Billingborough, Birthorpe, Bourne (1894—99), Castle Bytham, Little Bytham, Careby, Carlby, Corby, Counthorpe, Creeton, Market Deeping, Deeping St James, Dowsby, Dunsby, Edenham, Folkingham, Hacconby, Holywell, Horbling, Irnham, Kirkby Underwood, Langtoft, Laughton, Manthorpe, Morton, Pointon, Rippingale, Semperingham, Swayfield, Swinstead, Thurlby, Toft and Lound, Witham on the Hill
BOURNE UD (1899[42]—1974)
Bourne
BRACEBRIDGE UD (1898[43]—1920[7])
Bracebridge
BRANSTON RD (1894—1931[41])
Aubourn, Boothby Graffoe, Boultham (1894—1920), Bracebridge (1894—98), Bracebridge Heath (1898—1931), Branston, Canwick, Coleby, Doddington, Dunston, Eagle, Eagle Hall, Haddington, Potter Hanworth, Harmston, Heighington, North Hykeham, South Hykeham, Mere, Metheringham, Morton, Navenby, Nocton, Skellingthorpe, Skinnand, Swinethorpe, Thorpe on the Hill, Waddington, Washingborough,

Whisby
CLAYPOLE RD (1894—1931[41])
Allington, Barkston, Bassingham, Beckingham, Long Bennington, Bennington Grange, Brant Broughton, Carlton le Moorland, Caythorpe, Claypole, Dry Doddington, Fenton, Foston, Fulbeck, Hougham, Marston, Norton Disney, North Scarle, Sedgebrook, Stapleford, Stragglethorpe, Stubton, Swinderby, Syston, Thurlby, Westborough
GRANTHAM RD (1894—1931[41])
Ancaster, Barrowby, Bassingthorpe, Belton, Bitchfield, Boothby Pagnell, Braceby, Burton Coggles, Carlton Scroop, Colsterworth, Denton, Easton, Great Gonerby, Gunby, Haceby, Harlaxton, Harrowby Without, Heydour, Honington, Hough on the Hill, Humby, Ingoldsby, Keisby, Lenton, Londonthorpe, Manthorpe, Normanton, Osgodby, Pickworth, Great Ponton, Little Ponton, Ropsley, Sapperton, Skillington, Old Somerby, Spittlegate Without, Stainby, North Stoke, South Stoke, Stroxton, Welby, North Witham, South Witham, Woolsthorpe, Wyville cum Hungerton
EAST KESTEVEN RD (1931[41]—74)
Anwick, Asgarby and Howell, Ashby de la Launde and

Bloxholm, Aswarby and Swarby, Aunsby and Dembleby, Billinghay, Blankney, Braucewell, Burton Pedwardine, Cranwell and Byard's Leap, Culverthorpe and Kelby, Digby, Dogdyke, Dorrington, Ewerby and Evedon, Great Hale, Little Hale, Heckington, Helpringham, Kirkby la Thorpe, North Kyme, South Kyme, Leasingham, Martin, Newton and Haceby, Osbournby, North Rauceby, South Rauceby, Rowston, Roxholm, Ruskington, Scopwick, Scredington, Swaton, Temple Bruer with Temple High Grange, Threckingham, Timberland, Walcot (near Billinghay), Walcot (near Folkingham), Silk Willoughby, Wilsford

NORTH KESTEVEN RD (1931[41]—74)

Aubourn, Hadington and South Hykeham; Bassingham, Beckingham, Boothby Graffoe, Bracebridge Heath, Branston and Mere, Brant Broughton and Stragglethorpe, Canwick, Carlton le Moorland, Coleby, Doddington and Whisby, Dunston, Eagle and Swinethorpe, Potter Hanworth, Harmston, Heighington, North Hykeham, Leadenham, Metheringham, Navenby, Nocton, Norton Disney, North Scarle, Skellingthorpe, Stapleford, Swinderby, Thorpe on the Hill, Thurlby, Waddington, Washingborough, Welbourn, Wellingore

SOUTH KESTEVEN RD (1931[41]—74)

Aslackby and Laughton, Barholm and Stowe, Baston, Billingborough, Braceborough and Wilsthorpe, Castle Bytham, Little Bytham; Careby, Aunby and Holywell; Carlby, Corby, Counthorpe and Creeton, Market Deeping, West Deeping, Deeping St James, Dowsby, Dunsby, Edenham, Folkingham, Greatford, Hacconby, Horbling, Irnham, Kirkby Underwood, Langtoft, Morton, Pointon and Sempringham, Rippingale, Swayfield, Swinestead, Tallington, Thurlby, Toft with Lound and Manthorpe, Uffington, Witham on the Hill

WEST KESTEVEN RD (1931[41]—74)

Allington, Ancaster, Barkston, Barrowby, Belton and Manthorpe, Long Bennington, Bitchfield and Bassingthorpe, Boothby Pagnell, Braceby and Sapperton, Burton Coggles, Carlton Scroop, Caythorpe, Claypole, Colsterworth, Denton, Easton, Fenton, Foston, Fulbeck, Great Gonerby, Gunby and Stainby, Harlaxton, Heydour, Honington, Hough on the Hill, Hougham, Ingoldsby, Lenton Keisby and Osgodby, Londonthorpe and Harrowby Without, Marston, Normanton, Pickworth, Great Ponton, Little Ponton and Stroxton, Ropsley and Humby, Sedgebrook, Skillington, Old Somerby, Stoke Rochford, Stubton, Syston, Welby, Westborough and Dry Doddington, North Witham, South Witham, Woolsthorpe, Wyville cum Hungerton

RUSKINGTON UD (1894—1931[41])

Ruskington

SLEAFORD RD (1894—1931[41])

Anwick, Asgarby, Ashby de la Launde, Aswarby, Aunsby, Byard's Leap, Billinghay, Blankney, Bloxholm, Braucewell, Burton Penwardine, Cranwell, Culverthorpe, Dembleby, Digby, Dogdyke, Dorrington, Evedon, Ewerby, Great Hale, Little Hale, Haverholme Priory, Heckington, Helpringham, Howell, Kelby, Kirkby Green, Kirkby la Thorpe, North Kyme, South Kyme, Leadenham, Leasingham, Martin, Newton, Osbournby, North Rauceby, South Rauceby, Rowston, Roxholm, Scredington, Scopwick, Spanby, Swarby, Swaton, Temple Bruer with Temple High Grange, Thorpe Tilney, Threckingham, Timberland, Walcot (near Billinghay), Walcot (near Folkingham), Welbourn, Wellingore, Scott Willoughby, Silk Willoughby, Wilsford

SLEAFORD UD

Holdingham, Quarrington, New Sleaford, Old Sleaford

SPALDING RD [Pts Holl, Pts Kestev (1894—1930)]

pt Deeping St Nicholas[10]

UFFINGTON RD (1894—1931[41])

Barholm, Braceborough, West Deeping, Greatford, Stowe, Tallington, Uffington, Wilsthorpe

PARTS OF LINDSEY ADMINISTRATIVE COUNTY

ALFORD UD (1896[44]—1974)

Alford

BARTON UPON HUMBER UD

Barton upon Humber

BRIGG UD

Glanford Brigg

BROUGHTON UD (1894—1923[45])

Broughton

BRUMBY AND FRODINGHAM UD (1894—1919[46])

Brumby, Frodingham

CAISTOR RD

Atterby (1894—1936), Bigby, Brocklesby, Buslingthorpe, Cabourne, Caistor, Claxby, Clixby (1894—1936), Croxby (1894—1936), Cuxwold (1894—1936), Glentham, Grasby, Holton le Moor, Keelby, North Kelsey, South Kelsey, Kingerby (1894—1936), Kirkby cum Osgodby (1894—1936), Kirmond le Mire, Legsby, Great Limber, Linwood, Lissington, Nettleton, Newton by Toft (1894—1936), Normanby le Wold, Bishop Norton, Osgodby (1936—74), Owersby (1936—74), North Owersby (1894—1936), South Owersby (1894—1936), Middle Rasen, West Rasen, Riby, Rothwell, Searby cum Ownby, Sixhills, Snitterby, Somerby, Stainton le Vale, Swallow, Swinhope, Tealby, Thoresway, Thorganby, Thornton le Moor (1894—1936), Toft Newton (1936—74), Toft next Newton (1894—1936), East Torrington (1894—1936), Usselby (1894—1936), Waddingham, Walesby, North Willingham

CLEETHORPE WITH THURNCOE UD (1894—1916[47])

Cleethorpes

CLEETHORPES UD (1916[47]—36[26])

Cleethorpes

CROWLE UD (1894—1936[48])

Crowle

GAINSBOROUGH RD

Blyborough, Blyton (1936—74), Blyton cum Wharton (1894—1936), Brampton, Gate Burton, West Butterwick (1894—1936), Coates (1894—1936), Corringham, Fenton, East Ferry, Fillingham, pt Gainsborough (1894—95), Glentworth, Grayingham, Greenhill and Redhill (1894—1936), Hardwick, Harpswell, Haxey (1894—1936), Heapham, Hemswell, Kettlethorpe, Kexby, Knaith, Lands Common to East Ferry and Scotton (1894—1936), Laughton, Lea, Marton, Morton, Newton on Trent, Northorpe, Owston (1894—1912), Owston Ferry (1912—36), Pilham, Scotter, Scotton, Southorpe (1894—1936), Springthorpe, East Stockwith, Stow, Sturton by Stow, Thonock (1895—1974), Torksey, Upton, Walkerith, Wildsworth, Willingham, Willoughton

GAINSBOROUGH UD

Gainsborough (pt 1894—95, ent 1895—1974)

GLANFORD BRIGG RD

Alkborough, Appleby, Ashby (1894—1919), Barnetby le Wold, Barrow upon Humber, Barton upon Humber, Bonby, Bottesford, Broughton (1923—74), Brumby Rural (1919—36), Burringham, Burton upon Stather, East Butterwick, Cadney (1936—74), Cadney cum Howsham (1894—1936), Cleatham (1894—1936), Croxton, Crosby (1894—1919), Elsham, South Ferriby, Flixborough, Goxhill, Gunness, East Halton, West Halton, Hibaldstow, Holme, Horkstow, North Killingholme, South Killingholme, Kirmington, Kirton in Lindsey, Manton, Melton Ross, Messingham, Newstead (1894—1936), Raventhorpe (1894—1936), Redbourne, Roxby cum Risby (1936—74), Saxby All Saints, Scawby, Thornton Curtis, Twigmore (1894—1936), Ulceby, Whitton, Winteringham, Winterton (1936—74), Wootton, Worlaby, Wrawby

GRIMSBY RD

Ashby cum Fenby, Aylesby, Barnoldby le Beck, Beelsby, Bradley, Brigsley, Great Coates (1894—1968), Little Coates (1894—1928), Habrough, Hatcliffe, Hawerby cum Beesby, Healing, Humberston, Immingham, Irby, Laceby, Wold Newton, East Ravendale, West Ravendale, Scartho (1894—1928), Stallingborough, Waltham, New Waltham (1961—74), Weelsby (1894—1968)

HORNCASTLE RD

Asgarby, West Ashby, Ashby Puerorum (1894—1936), Asterby, East Barkwith, West Barkwith, Baumber, Belchford, Benniworth, Bucknall, Cawkwell, Claxby Pluckacre, Coningsby, Dalderby (1894—1936), Edlington, Bag Enderby (1894—1936), Wood Enderby, Fulletby, Gautby, Goulceby, Greetham, Hagworthingham, Haltham, Hameringham, Hatton, Hemingby, Horsington, Kirkby on Bain, Kirkstead, Langton, Langton by Wragby, Lusby, Mareham le Fen, Mareham on the Hill, Martin (1894—1936), Miningsby, Minting, Moorby, Panton, Ranby, Revesby, Roughton, Salmonby, Scamblesby, Scrafield (1894—1936), Scrivelsby, Somerby, Sotby, Market Stainton, Stixwould, Great Sturton, Tattershall, Tattershall Thorpe, Tetford, Thimbleby, Thornton, West Torrington, High Toynton, Low Toynton, Tumby, Tupholme, Waddingworth, Wildmore, Wilksby (1894—1936), Winceby, Wispington, Woodhall, Woodhall Spa (1894—98), Wragby

HORNCASTLE UD

Horncastle

ISLE OF AXHOLME RD

Althorpe (1894—1958), Amcotts, Belton, West Butterwick (1894—1936), Crowle (1936—74), Eastoft, Epworth, Garthorpe, Haxey (1936—74), Keadby (1894—1958), Keadby with Althorpe (1958—74), Luddington, Owston Ferry (1936—74), Wroot

LOUTH RD

Aby with Greenfield, Alvingham, Authorpe, Beesby in the Marsh, Belleau, Biscathorpe (1894—1936), Brackenborough, Burgh on Bain, Burwell, Calcethorpe, Castle Carlton (1894—1936), Great Carlton, Little Carlton, Little Cawthorpe, Claythorpe, North Coates, North Cockerington, South Cockerington, Conisholme, Covenham St Bartholomew, Covenham St Mary, Donington on Bain, North Elkington, South Elkington, Farforth cum Maidenwell (1894—1936), Fotherby, Fulstow, Gayton le Marsh, Gayton le Wold, Grainsby, Grainthorpe, Grimblethorpe (1894—1936), Grimoldby, Little Grimsby, Hainton, Hallington, Hannah cum Hagnaby, Haugh, Haugh, Haugham, Holton le Clay, Keddington, Kelstern, Legbourne, Louth Park (1894—1936), Ludborough, Ludford (1936—74), Ludford Magna (1894—1936), Ludford Parva (1894—1936), Mablethorpe (1894—96), Maidenwell (1936—74), Maltby le Marsh, Manby, Marsh Chapel, Muckton, North Ormsby, Oxcombe (1894—1936), Raithby cum Maltby, North Reston, South Reston, Ruckland (1894—1936), Saleby with Thoresthorpe, Saltfleetby All Saints, Saltfleetby St Clement, Saltfleetby St Peter, Skidbrooke with Saltfleet Haven, North Somercotes, South Somercotes, Stenigot, Stewton, Strubby with Woodthorpe, Swaby, Tathwell, Theddlethorpe All Saints, Theddlethorpe St Helen, Tetney, North Thoresby, South Thoresby, Tothill, Trusthorpe (1894—1925), Utterby, Waithe, Walmsgate, Welton le Wold, South Willingham, Withcall, Withern with Stain, Worlaby (1894—1936), Wyham cum Cadeby, East Wykeham, Yarburgh

MABLETHORPE UD (1896[49]—1925[50])

Mablethorpe

MABLETHORPE AND SUTTON UD (1925[50]—74)

Mablethorpe, Sutton in the Marsh, Trusthorpe

MARKET RASEN UD

Market Rasen

ROXBY CUM RISBY UD (1894—1936[48])

Roxby cum Risby

SCUNTHORPE UD (1894—1919[46])

Scunthorpe

SCUNTHORPE AND FRODINGHAM UD (1919[46]—36[29])

Scunthorpe and Frodingham

SIBSEY RD (1894—1936[48])

Carrington, Frithville, Langriville, Seven Acres (1894—1906), Sibsey, Thornton le Fen, Westville

SKEGNESS UD

Skegness

SPILSBY RD

Addlethorpe, Alford (1894—96), Anderby, Ashby by Partney, Aswardby, Bilsby, Bolingbroke, Bratoft, Brinkhill, Burgh le Marsh, Calceby, Candlesby, Carrington (1936—74), Chapel St Leonards (1896—1974), Claxby, Croft, Cumberworth, Dalby, Driby, Eastville, Mavis Enderby, Farlesthororpe, Frisby, Friskney, Frithville (1936—74), Gunby, Hagnaby, Halton Holegate, Hareby, Harrington, Hogsthorpe, Hundleby, Huttoft, Ingoldmells, Irby in the Marsh, East Keal,

West Keal, East Kirkby, Langriville (1936—74), Langton by Spilsby, New Leake, Markby, Midville, Mumby, Orby, South Ormsby cum Ketsby, Partney, Raithby, Rigsby with Ailby, Sausthorpe, Scremby, Sibsey (1936—74), Skendleby, Spilsby, Great Steeping, Little Steeping, Stickford, Stickney, Sutterby (1894—1936), Sutton in the Marsh (1894—1925), Thornton le Fen (1936—74), Thorpe St Peter, Toynton All Saints, Toynton St Peter, Ulceby with Fordington, Wainfleet All Saints, Wainfleet St Mary, Welton le Marsh, West Fen, Westville (1936—74), Willoughby with Sloothby, Winthorpe (1894—1926)

WELTON RD

Aisthorpe, Apley, Barlings, Brattleby, Broxholme, Bullington, Burton, Caenby, Cammeringham, North Carlton, South Carlton, Coldstead (1894—1936), Dunholme, Faldingworth, East Firsby (1894—1936), West Firsby, Fiskerton, Friesthorpe, Fulnetby, Goltho, Grange de Lings, Greetwell, Hackthorn, Cold Hanworth, Holton cum Beckering, Ingham, Nettleham, Newball, Normanby by Spital, Owmby, Rand, Reepham, Riseholme, Saxby, Saxilby with Ingleby, Scampton, Scothern, Snarford, Snelland, Sprindlington, Stainfield, Stainton by Langworth, Sudbrooke, Thorpe in the Fallows, Welton, Wickenby, Cherry Willingham

WINTERTON UD (1894—1936[48])

Winterton

WOODHALL SPA UD (1898[51]—1974)

Woodhall Spa

LINCOLNSHIRE NON-METROPOLITAN COUNTY

As constituted 1 Apr 1974, defined in terms of Adm Co units as of 31 Mar.

BOSTON DIST
from Pts Holl: Boston MB, Boston RD

SOUTH HOLLAND DIST
from Pts Holl: East Elloe RD, Spalding UD, Spalding RD

NORTH KESTEVEN DIST
from Pts Kestev: East Kesteven RD, North Kesteven RD, Sleaford UD

SOUTH KESTEVEN DIST
from Pts Kestev: Bourne UD, Grantham MB, South Kesteven RD, West Kesteven RD, Stamford MB

LINCOLN DIST
CB (assoc with Pts Lind): Lincoln CB

EAST LINDSEY DIST
from Pts Lind: Alford UD, Horncastle RD, Horncastle UD, Louth MB, Louth RD, Mablethorpe and Sutton UD, Skegness UD, Spilsby RD, Woodhall Spa UD

WEST LINDSEY DIST
from Pts Lind: Caistor RD, Gainsborough RD, Gainsborough UD, Market Rasen UD, Welton RD

MERSEYSIDE METROPOLITAN COUNTY

As constituted 1 Apr 1974, defined in terms of Adm Co units as of 31 Mar.

BOOTLE METROP DIST
CBs (assoc with Lancs): Bootle CB, Southport CB
from Lancs: Crosby MB, Formby UD, pt West Lancashire RD (Aintree, pt Altcar,[1] Ince Blundell, pt Lydiate,[2] Maghull, Melling, Netherton, Sefton, Thornton), Litherland UD

KNOWSLEY METROP DIST
from Lancs: Huyton with Roby UD, Kirkby UD, pt West Lancashire RD (Simonswood), Prescot UD, pt Whiston RD (all except pars and pts of pars in Ches and in St Helens Metrop Dist of this Metrop Co)

LIVERPOOL METROP DIST
CB (assoc with Lancs): Liverpool CB

ST HELENS METROP DIST
CB (assoc with Lancs): St Helens CB
from Lancs: pt Ashton in Makerfield UD (ward of South), pt Billinge and Winstanley UD (all except ward of Billinge Higher End and pt ward of Winstanley), Haydock UD, Newton le Willows UD, Rainford UD, pt Whiston UD (pt Bold, Eccleston, Rainhill, Windle)

WIRRAL METROP DIST
CBs (assoc with Ches): Birkenhead CB, Wallasey CB
from Ches: Bebington MB, Hoylake UD, Wirral UD

NORTHAMPTONSHIRE

ALTERATIONS IN COUNTY BOUNDARIES

As noted by year below, Northants pars gained territory from or lost it to pars in adjoining cos or county boroughs, or were entirely transferred to them. Details of these alterations are noted in Part I of the *Guide* under Northamptonshire.

ANCIENT COUNTY (until 1889: Hds, Bors, MBs, PLUs, RSDs, USDs)

1844 Farndish, *Luffield Abbey*.[1] *1866* Theddingworth, Warkworth. *1884* Syresham, Warkworth. *1885* Gretton, Thorpe by Water.

ADMINISTRATIVE COUNTY (1889—1974: Hds,[2] PLUs, MBs, RDs, UDs, with assoc CB of Northampton)

1889 Ailsworth, Bainton, Barnack, Borough Fen, Castor, Deeping Gate, Etton, Eye, Glinton, Gunthorpe, Helpston, Marholm, Maxey, Newborough, Northampton All Saints, Northampton Priory of St Andrew, Northampton St Giles, Northampton St Peter, Northampton St Sepulchre, Northborough, Paston, Peakirk, Peterborough [St John the Baptist], Peterborough Minster Close Precincts, Southorpe, Sutton, Thornhaugh, Ufford, Upton, Walton, Wansford, Werrington, Wittering, Wothorpe. *1894* Banbury, Hanslope, Stamford Baron. *1895* Luddington, Lutton, Thurning,

Winwick. *1896* Little Bowden. *1900* Abington, Dallington St James, Duston St James, Far Cotton, Kingsthorpe. *1912* Weston Favell. *1932* Boughton, Dallington, Duston, Far Cotton, Hardingstone, Moulton Park, Weston Favell. *1965* Billing, Boughton, King's Cliffe, Clopton, Duston, Ecton, Fotheringhay, Hardingstone, Great Houghton, Luddington, Lutton, Moulton, Nassington, Thurning, Titmarch, Upton, Warmington, Weston Favell, Wootton, Yarwell. *1969* Billing, Boughton, Moulton, Overstone. *1971* Billing, Brafield on the Green, Cogenhoe, Hardinstone, Harpole, Little Houghton, Overstone, Upton, Wootton.

NON-METROPOLITAN COUNTY (from 1974: Dists)

1974 Brafield on the Green, Collingtree, Courteenhall, Ecton, Great Houghton, Kislingbury, Milton Malsor, Overstone, Rotherscope, Upton, Wootton

ASSOCIATED COUNTY BOROUGH

NORTHAMPTON CB

Bdry: 1900,[3] 1912,[4] 1932,[5] 1965,[6] 1969,[7] 1971.[8]
Transf 1974 to Northants.[9]

HUNDREDS[2]

CLELEY HD

Alderton, Ashton, Cosgrove, Easton Neston, Furtho, Grafton Regis, pt Hanslope, Hartwell, Passenham, Paulerspury, Potterspury, Roade, *Salcey and Hartwell Lodges (1858—1880s[10])*, Shutlanger (from 1866), Stoke Bruerne, Wicken, Yardley Gobion (from 1866)

CORBY HD

Ashley, Beanfield Lawns (from 1858), Blatherwycke, Brampton Ash, Brigstock, Bulwick, East Carlton, Corby, Cottingham, Deene, Deenethorpe (from 1866), Dingley, Fineshade, Geddington, Gretton, Harringworth, Laxton, Middleton (from 1866), Great Oakley, Little Oakley, Newton, Rockingham,[11] Stanion, Stoke Albany, Sutton Bassett, Wakerley, Weekley, Great Weldon, Little Weldon (from 1866), Weston by Welland, Wilbarston

FAWSLEY HD

Ashby St Ledgers, Badby, Barby, Braunston, Catesby,[11] Charwelton, Daventry,[11] Dodford, Everdon, Farthingstone, Fawsley, Hellidon, Kilsby, Litchborough, Newnham, Norton, Preston Capes, Staverton, Stowe Nine Churches, Weedon Beck, Welton

GUILSBOROUGH HD

Cold Ashby, Long Buckby, Claycoton, Coton (from 1866), Cottesbrooke, Great Creaton, Little Creaton (1866—84), Crick, Elkington, Guilsborough, West Haddon, Hollowell (from 1866), Lilbourne, Naseby, pt Ravensthorpe (until 1866), pt Spratton (until 1866), Stanford, Thornby, Watford, Welford, Winwick, Yelvertoft

HAMFORDSHOE HD

Mears Ashby, Earls Barton, Great Doddington, Ecton, Holcot, Sywell, Wellingborough, Wilby

HIGHAM FERRERS HD

Bozeat, Chelveston cum Caldecott, Easton Maudit, pt Farndish (until 1844), Hargrave, Higham Ferrers,[11] Higham Park (from 1858), Irchester, Newton Bromshold, Rounds, Ringstead, Rushden, Stanwick, Strixton, Wollaston

HUXLOE HD

Great Addington, Little Addington, Aldwincle (from 1885), Aldwincle All Saints (until 1885), Aldwincle St Peter (until 1885), Barnwell All Saints, Barton Seagrave, Burton Latimer, Cranford St Andrew, Cranford St John, Denford, Finedon,[11] Grafton Underwood,

710

Irthlingborough, Islip, Kettering, Lilford cum Wigsthorpe, Lowick, Slipton, Sudborough, Twywell, Warkton, Woodford

NASSABOROUGH HD [Soke of Peterb]

Ailsworth (from 1866), Ashton (1866—87), Bainton, Barnack, Borough Fen (from 1858), Castor, Deeping Gate (from 1866), Etton, Eye, Glinton, Gunthorpe (from 1866), Helpston, Marholm, Maxey, Newborough, Northborough, Paston, Peakirk, Pilsgate (1866—87), Southorpe (from 1866), Stamford Baron,[11] Sutton (from 1866), Thornhaugh, Ufford, Upton (from 1866), Walton (from 1866), Wansford, Werrington (from 1866), Wittering, Wothorpe (from 1866)

NAVISFORD HD

Clopton, Pilton, Stoke Doyle, Thrapston, Thorpe Achurch, pt Thurning, Titchmarsh, Wadenhoe

NOBOTTLE GROVE HD

Althorp (from 1858), Chapel Brampton, Church Brampton, Brington, Brockhall, Bugbrooke, Dallington, Duston, Flore, East Haddon, Harlestone, Harpole, Nether Heyford, Upper Heyford, Holdenby, Kislingbury, Ravensthorpe (pt until 1866, ent from 1866), Teeton (from 1866), Upton, Whilton

GREEN'S NORTON HD

Adstone (from 1866), Canons Ashby, Blakesley, Bradden, *pt Luffield Abbey[1] (until 1844)*, Maidford, Moreton Pinkney, Green's Norton, Plumpton, Silverstone, Slapton, Weedon Lois, Whittlebury, Woodend (from 1866)

ORLINGBURY HD

Brixworth, Broughton, Cransley, Faxton (from 1866), Hannington, Hardwick, Great Harrowden, Little Harrowden, Hanging Houghton (from 1866), Isham, Lamport, Mawsley (from 1858), Old, Orlingbury, Pytchley, Scaldwell, Walgrave

POLEBROOK HD

Armston (from 1866), Ashton (from 1866), Barnwell St Andrew, Benefield, Hemington, pt Luddington, Oundle,[11] Polebrook, Warmington, pt Winwick

ROTHWELL HD

Arthingworth (from 1866), Barford (from 1858), Little Bowden, Braybrooke, Clipston, Desborough, Draughton, East Farndon, Glendon, Harrington, Haselbech, Hothorpe (from 1866), Kelmarsh, Loddington, Maidwell, Marston Trussel, Orton (from 1866), Great Oxenden, Rothwell,[11] Rushton, Sibbertoft, Sulby (from 1858), pt Theddingworth (until 1866), Thorpe Lubenham (from 1858), Thorpe Malsor

SPELHOE HD

Abington,[11] Great Billing, Little Billing, Boughton, Kingsthorpe, Moulton, Moulton Park (from 1858), Overstone, Pitsford, Spratton (pt until 1866, ent from 1866), Weston Favell

KING'S SUTTON HD

Astwell and Falcott (from 1858), Aynho, pt Banbury[11] (reduced pt 1866—94), Brackley St James,[11] Brackley St Peter,[11] Chalcombe, Croughton, Culworth, Evenley, Farthinghoe, Helmdon, Hinton in the Hedges, Marston St Lawrence, Middleton Cheney, Newbottle (until 1885), Radstone, Steane, Stuchbury, Kings Sutton (until 1885), Kings Sutton with Newbottle (from 1885), Syresham, Thenford, Thorpe Mandeville, Wappenham, Warkworth, Whitfield

TOWCESTER HD

Abthorpe (from 1737), Gayton, Cold Higham, Pattishall, Tiffield, Towcester[11]

CHIPPING WARDEN HD

Appletree (from 1866), Aston le Walls, Lower Boddington, Upper Boddington, Byfield, Edgcote, Eydon, Greatworth, Stoneton (from 1858), Sulgrave, Chipping Warden, Woodford cum Membris

WILLYBROOK HD

Apethorpe, King's Cliffe, Collyweston, Cotterstock, Duddington, Easton on the Hill, Fotheringhay, Glapthorn, pt Lutton, Nassington, Southwick, Tansor, Woodnewton, Yarwell

WYMERSLEY HD

Castle Ashby, Blisworth, Brafield on the Green, Cogenhoe, Collingtree, Courtenhall, Denton, Grendon, Hackleton (from 1866), Hardingstone, Horton, Great Houghton, Little Houghton, Milton, Piddington, Preston Deanery, Quinton, Rothersthorpe, Whiston, Wootton, Yardley Hastings

BOROUGHS

Units with some degree of burghal character[12] are denominated 'Bor'. Those which did not sustain that status until the 19th cent are in italics. MBs were established by the Municipal Corporations Act, 1835,[13] or by later charter.

BANBURY BOR/MB (Oxon, Northants [until 1894])

Banbury[14] (pt until 1866, ent 1866—1974)

BRACKLEY BOR, MB (1886[15]—1974)

Bor: Brackley St James (when gains sep civ identity), Brackley St Peter
MB: Brackley St Peter

CATESBY BOR

pt Catesby

DAVENTRY BOR/MB

Daventry

FINEDON BOR

Finedon

HIGHAM FERRERS BOR, MB (1886[16]—1974)

Bor: pt Higham Ferrers
MB: Higham Ferrers

KETTERING MB (1938[17]—74)

Kettering

NORTHAMPTON BOR[18]/MB/CB[3]

Abington (1900—13), Dallington St James (1900—13), Duston St James (1900—13), Far Cotton (1900—31), Kingsthorpe (1900—13), Northampton (1900—74), Northampton All Saints (until 1909), Northampton Priory of St Andrew (until 1909), Northampton St Giles (until 1909), Northampton St Peter (until 1909), Northampton St Sepulchre (until 1909)

OUNDLE BOR
pt Oundle
PETERBOROUGH BOR, MB (1874[19]—1974) [Bor in
Northants; MB: Northants, *Hunts (1874—89)*,
Soke Peterb (1889—1965), Hunts & Peterb
(1965—74)]
Bor: pt Peterborough [St John the Baptist]
MB: pt Fletton *(1874—94)*, Fletton Urban (1894—1929),
Peterborough (1929—74), pt Peterborough [St John the
Baptist] (1874—94), Peterborough Minster Close Pre-
cincts (1874—1929), Peterborough Within

(1894—1929), *pt Woodstone (1874—94)*, Woodstone
Urban (1894—1929)
ROCKINGHAM BOR
Rockingham
ROTHWELL BOR
Rothwell
STAMFORD BOR/MB [Lincs Pts Kestev, *pt Northants
(1835—89)*])
pt Stamford Baron St Michael (1835—94)
TOWCESTER BOR
Towcester

POOR LAW UNIONS

In Northants Poor Law County:[20]
BRACKLEY PLU (Northants, Oxon, Bucks)
Astwell and Falcott, Aynho, Brackley St James (1835—
84), Brackley St Peter, Croughton, Culworth, Edgcote
(1835—*ca* 1894), Evenley, Eydon, Farthinghoe, Grea-
tworth, Helmdon, Hinton in the Hedges, Marston St
Lawrence, Moreton Pinkney, Newbottle (1835—85),
Newbottle (1896—1930), Radstone, Steane, Stuchbury,
Sulgrave, Kings Sutton (1835—85), Kings Sutton
(1896—1930), Kings Sutton with Newbottle (1885—
96), Syresham, Thenford, Thorpe Mandeville,
Whitfield
BRIXWORTH PLU
Althorp (1861—1930), Cold Ashby (1836—1930),
Boughton, Chapel Brampton, Church Brampton,
Brington, Brixworth, Coton, Cottesbrooke, Great
Creaton, Little Creaton (1835—84), Draughton,
Faxton, Guilsborough, East Haddon, Hannington,
Harlestone, Haselbech, Holcot, Holdenby, Hollowell,
Hanging Houghton, Lamport, Maidwell, Mawsley
(1862—1930), Moulton, Moulton Park (1861—1930),
Naseby (1836—1930), Old, Overstone (*ca* 1894—
1930), Pitsford, Ravensthorpe, Scaldwell, Spratton,
Teeton, Thornby (1836—1930), Walgrave
DAVENTRY PLU
Canons Ashby, Ashby St Ledgers, Badby, Braunston,
Brockhall, Long Buckby, Byfield, Catesby, Charwell,
Daventry, Dodford, Everdon, Farthingstone, Fawsley,
Flore, West Haddon, Hellidon, Newnham, Norton,
Preston Capes, Staverton, Stowe Nine Churches,
Watford, Weedon Beck, Welton, Winwick, Woodford
cum Membris, Whilton
HARDINGSTONE PLU
Castle Ashby, Brafield on the Green, Cogenhoe,
Collingtree, Courtenhall, Denton, Far Cotton (1895—
1930), Hackleton, Hardingstone, Horton, Great
Houghton, Little Houghton, Milton, Piddington,
Preston Deanry, Quinton, Roade, Rotherstone,
Whiston, Wootton, Yardley Hastings
KETTERING PLU
Barfield (1862—1930), Barton Seagrave, Beanfield
Lawns (1863—1930), Broughton, Burton Latimer, East
Carlton, Corby, Cottingham, Cranford St Andrew,
Cranford St John, Cransley, Desborough, Geddington,
Glendon, Grafton Underwood, Harrington, Kettering,
Loddington, Middleton, Newton, Great Oakley, Little
Oakley, Orton, Pytchley, Rothwell, Rushton, Stanion,
Thorpe Malsor, Warkton, Weekley, Great Weldon

(1894—1930), Little Weldon (1894—1930)
NORTHAMPTON PLU
Abington (1835—1913), Great Billing, Little Billing,
Bugbrooke, Dallington, Dallington St James (1895—
1913), Duston, Duston St James (1895—1913),
Harpole, Nether Heyford, Upper Heyford, Kingsthorpe
(1835—1913), Kislingbury, Northampton (1909—30),
Northampton All Saints (1835—1909), Northampton
Priory of St Andrew (1861—1909), Northampton St
Giles (1835—1909), Northampton St Peter (1835—
1909), Northampton St Sepulchre (1835—1909),
Upton, Weston Favell
OUNDLE PLU (Northants, Hunts)
Apethorpe, Armston, Ashton, Barnwell All Saints,
Barnwell St Andrew, Benefield, Blatherwycke,
Bulwick, King's Cliffe, Cotterstock, Deene, Deeneth-
orpe, Fotheringhay, Glapthorn, Hemington, Lilford
cum Wigsthorpe, Luddington,[21] Lutton,[21] Nassington,
Oundle, Pilton, Polebrook, Southwick, Stoke Doyle,
Tansor, Thorpe Achurch, Thurning,[21] Wadenhoe,
Warmington, Great Weldon (1835—94), Little Weldon
(1835—94), Winwick,[22] Woodnewton, Yarwell
PETERBOROUGH PLU (Northants [1835—89], Soke
Peterb [1889—1930], Cambs [1835—89], Isle of
Ely [1889—1930], Lincs Pts Lind, Hunts)
Ailsworth, Borough Fen (1861—1930), Castor, Deep-
ing Gate, Etton, Eye, Fletton Urban (1894—1929),
Glinton, Gunthorpe (1835—1929), Helpston, Long-
thorpe (1908—29), Marholm, Maxey, Newborough,
Northborough, Paston (1835—1929), Peakirk,
Peterborough (1929—30), Peterborough Minster Close
Precincts (1861—1929), Peterborough [St John the
Baptist] (1835—94), Peterborough Within (1894—
1929), Peterborough Without (1894—1929), Sutton,
Upton (1835—1929), Walton (1835—1929), Werr-
ington (1835—1929), Woodstone Urban (1894—1929)
POTTERSPURY PLU (Northants, Bucks [Sept
1835—1930])
Alderton, Ashton, Cosgrove, Furtho, Grafton Regis,
Hartwell, Passenham, Paulerspury, Potterspury,
Wicken, Yardley Gobion
THRAPSTON PLU (Northants, Hunts)
Great Addington, Little Adington, Aldwincle (1885—
1930), Aldwincle All Saints (1835—85), Aldwincle St
Peter (1835—85), Brigstock, Chelveston cum
Caldecott, Clopton, Denford, Hargrave, Islip, Lowick,
Raunds, Ringstead, Slipton, Stanwick, Sudborough,
Thrapston, Titchmarsh, Twywell, Woodford

TOWCESTER PLU
Abthorpe, Adstone, Blakesley, Blisworth, Bradden, Easton Neston, Gayton, Cold Higham, Litchborough, Maidford, Green's Norton, Pattishall, Plumpton, Shutlanger, Silverstone, Slapton, Stoke Bruerne, Tiffield, Towcester, Wappenham, Weedon Lois, Whittlebury, Woodend

WELLINGBOROUGH PLU (Northants, Beds)
Mears Ashby, Earls Barton, Bozeat, Great Doddington, Easton Maudit, Ecton, Farndish,[23] Finedon, Grendon, Hardwick, Great Harrowden, Little Harrowden, Higham Ferrers, Higham Park (1862—1930), Irchester, Irthlingborough, Isham, Newton Bromshold, Orlingbury, Overstone (1835—ca 1894), Rushden, Strixton, Sywell, Wellingborough, Wilby, Wollaston

In Other Poor Law Counties:
BANBURY PLU (Oxon, Northants, Glos, Warws)
Appletree, Aston le Walls, Banbury,[14] Lower Boddington, Upper Boddington, Chalcombe, Edgcote (ca 1894—1930), Middleton Cheney, Chipping Warden, Warkworth

LUTTERWORTH PLU (Leics, Warws, Northants [1835—94])
Welford

MARKET HARBOROUGH PLU (Leics, Northants)
Arthingworth, Ashley, Little Bowden,[24] Brampton Ash, Braybrooke, Clipston, Dingley, East Frandon, Hothorpe, Kelmarsh, Marston Trussel, Great Oxendon, Sibbertoft, Stoke Albany, Sulby, Sutton Bassett, Thorpe Lubenham (1863—1930), Welford (1894—1930), Weston by Welland, Wilbarston

NEWPORT PAGNELL PLU (Bucks, Northants [1836—94])
Hanslope[25]

RUGBY PLU (Warws, Northants)
Barby, Claycoton, Crick, Elkington, Kilsby, Lilbourne, Stanford, Yelvertoft

SOUTHAM PLU (Warws, Northants [1858—95])
Stoneton[26]

STAMFORD PLU (Lincs Pts Kestev, Northants [1835—89], Soke Peterb [1889—1930], Rutl)
Ashton (1835—77), Bainton, Barnack, Collyweston, Duddington, Easton on the Hill, Pilsgate (1835—87), St Martin Without[27] (1894—1930), Southorpe, Stamford Baron,[28] Thornhaugh, Ufford, Wansford, Wittering, Wothorpe

UPPINGHAM PLU (Rutl, Northants)
Fineshade, Gretton, Harringworth, Laxton, Rockingham, Wakerley

SANITARY DISTRICTS

BANBURY RSD
same as PLU for Northants pars less pt Banbury (the pt in Oxon, in Banbury UD [ent Oxon])

BRACKLEY RSD
same as PLU for Northants pars less Brackley St Peter (1886—94)

BRACKLEY USD (1886[15]—94)
Brackley St Peter

BRIXWORTH RSD
same as PLU

DAVENTRY RSD
same as PLU less Daventry

DAVENTRY USD
Daventry

DESBOROUGH USD (1891[29]—94)
Desborough

HARDINGSTONE RSD
same as PLU less pt Dallington, pt Duston, pt Hardingstone

HARDINGSTONE USD
pt Dallington, pt Duston, pt Hardingstone

HIGHAM FERRERS USD (1886[16]—94)
Higham Ferrers

KETTERING RSD
same as PLU less Desborough (1891—94), Kettering, Rothwell (1891—94)

KETTERING USD
Kettering

KINGSTHORPE USD (1892[30]—94)
Kingsthorpe

LUTTERWORTH RSD
same as PLU for the Northants par

MARKET HARBOROUGH RSD
same as PLU for the Northants pars

NORTHAMPTON RSD
same as PLU less Kingsthorpe (1892—94), Northampton All Saints, Northampton Priory of St Andrew, Northampton St Giles, Northampton St Peter, Northampton St Sepulchre

NORTHAMPTON USD
Northampton All Saints, Northampton Priory of St Andrew, Northampton St Giles, Northampton St Peter, Northampton St Sepulchre

OUNDLE RSD
same as PLU for Northants pars less pt Oundle

OUNDLE USD
pt Oundle

PETERBOROUGH RSD
same as PLU for Northants pars less Peterborough Minster Close Precincts, pt Peterborough [St John the Baptist]

PETERBOROUGH USD (Northants, *Hunts*)
pt Fletton, pt Peterborough [St John the Baptist], Peterborough Minster Close Precincts, *pt Woodstone*

POTTERSPURY RSD
same as PLU for Northants pars

ROTHWELL USD (1891[31]—94)
Rothwell

RUGBY RSD
same as PLU for Northants pars

RUSHDEN USD (1891[32]—94)
Rushden

SOUTHAM RSD
same as PLU for the Northants par

STAMFORD RSD
same as PLU for Northants pars less pt Stamford Baron

STAMFORD USD (Lincs, *Northants*)
pt Stamford Baron

THRAPSTON RSD
  same as PLU for Northants pars
TOWCESTER RSD
  same as PLU
UPPINGHAM RSD
  same as PLU for the Northants pars

WELLINGBOROUGH RSD
  same as PLU for the Northants pars less Higham Ferrers (1886—94), Rushden (1891—94), Wellingborough
WELLINGBOROUGH USD
  Wellingborough

ADMINISTRATIVE COUNTY

For MBs and the associated CB see BOROUGHS.

BRACKLEY RD
  Aston le Walls (1935—74), Astwell and Falcott (1894—1935), Aynho, Boddington (1935—74), Chalcombe (1935—74), Croughton, Culworth, Edgcote (1935—74), Evenley, Eydon, Farthinghoe, Greatworth, Helmdon, Hinton in the Hedges, Marston St Lawrence, Middleton Cheney (1935—74), Moreton Pinkney, Newbottle (1896—1974), Radstone, Steane (1894—1935), Stuchbury (1894—1935), Sulgrave, Kings Sutton (1896—1974), Kings Sutton with Newbottle (1894—96), Syresham, Thenford, Thorpe Mandeville, Chipping Warden (1935—74), Warkworth (1935—74), Whitfield
BRIXWORTH RD
  Althorp, Arthingworth (1935—74), Cold Ashby, Boughton, Chapel Brampton, Church Brampton, Brington, Brixworth, Clipston (1935—74), Coton (1894—1935), Cottesbrooke, Great Creaton, Draughton, East Farndon (1935—74), Faxton (1894—1935), Guilsborough, East Haddon, Hannington, Harlestone, Haselbech, Holcot, Holdenby, Hollowell, Hanging Houghton (1894—1935), Kelmarsh (1935—74), Lamport, Maidwell, Marston Trussel (1935—74), Mawsley (1894—1935), Moulton, Moulton Park (1894—1932), Naseby, Old, Overstone, Great Oxendon (1935—74), Pitsford, Ravensthorpe, Scaldwell, Sibbertoft (1935—74), Spratton, Sulby (1894—1935), Teeton (1894—1935), Thornby, Walgrave, Welford (1935—74)
BURTON LATIMER UD (1923[33]—74)
  Burton Latimer
CORBY UD (1939[34]—74)
  Corby
CRICK RD (1894—1935[35])
  Barby, Claycoton, Crick, Elkington, Kilsby, Lilbourne, Stanford, Yelvertoft
DAVENTRY RD
  Canons Ashby, Ashby St Ledgers, Badby, Barby (1935—74), Braunston, Brockhall, Long Buckby, Byfield, Catesby, Charwelton, Claycoton (1935—74), Crick (1935—74), Dodford, Elkington (1935—74), Everdon, Farthingstone, Fawsley, Flore, West Haddon, Hellidon, Kilsby (1935—74), Lands Common to Badby and Newnham (1894—1935), Lilbourne (1935—74), Newnham, Norton, Preston Capes, Stanford (1935—74), Staverton, Stowe Nine Churches, Watford, Weedon Bec (1935—74), Weedon Beck (1894—1935), Welton, Whilton, Winwick, Woodford cum Membris, Yelvertoft (1935—74)
DESBOROUGH UD
  Desborough

EASTON ON THE HILL RD (1894—1935[35])
  Collyweston, Duddington, Easton on the Hill
FAR COTTON UD (1896[36]—1900[3])
  Far Cotton
FINEDON UD (1894[37]—1935[35])
  Finedon
GRETTON RD (1894—1935[35])
  Fineshade, Gretton, Harringworth, Laxton, Rockingham, Wakerley
HARDINGSTONE RD (1894—1935[35])
  Castle Ashby, Brafield on the Green, Cogenhoe, Collingtree, Courtenhall, Denton, Hackleton, Hardingstone (pt 1894—95, ent 1895—1932), Horton, Great Houghton, Little Houghton, Milton, Piddington, Preston Deanery, Quinton, Roade, Rothersthorpe, Whiston, Wootton, Yardley Hastings
HARDINGSTONE UD (1894—96[36])
  pt Dallington (1894—95), Dallington St James (1895—96), pt Duston (1894—95), Duston St James (1895—96), Far Cotton (1895—96), pt Hardingstone (1894—95)
IRTHLINGBOROUGH UD (1901[38]—74)
  Irthlingborough
KETTERING RD
  Ashley (1935—74), Barford (1894—1935), Bampton Ash (1935—74), Barton Seagrave (1894—1935), Beanfield Lawns (1894—1935), Braybrooke (1894—1935), Broughton, Burton Latimer (1894—1923), East Carlton, Corby (1894—1939), Cottingham, Cranford (1935—74), Cranford St Andrew (1894—1935), Cranford St John (1894—1935), Cransley, Dingley (1935—74), Geddington, Glendon (1894—1935), Grafton Underwood, Gretton (1935—74), Harrington, Loddington, Middleton, Newton, Oakley (1935—67), Great Oakley (1894—1935), Little Oakley (1894—1935), Orton, Pytchley, Rockingham (1935—74), Rushton, Stanion, Stoke Albany (1935—74), Sutton Bassett (1935—74), Thorpe Malsor, Warkton, Weekley, Weldon (1935—74), Great Weldon (1894—1935), Little Weldon (1894—1935), Weston by Welland (1935—74), Wilbarston (1935—74)
KETTERING UD (1894—1938[17])
  Kettering
KINGSTHORPE UD (1894—1900[3])
  Kingsthorpe
MARKET HARBOROUGH UD (Leics, Northants [1894—96])
  pt Little Bowden[39]
MIDDLETON CHENEY RD (1894—1935[35])
  Appletree, Aston le Walls, Lower Boddington, Upper Boddington, Chalcombe, Edgcote, Middleton Cheney,

Chipping Warden, Warkworth

NORTHAMPTON RD

Abington (1894—1900), Castle Ashby (1935—74), Ashton (1935—74), Billing (1935—74), Great Billing (1894—1935), Little Billing (1894—1935), Brafield on the Green (1935—74), Bugbrooke, Cogenhoe (1935—74), Collingtree (1935—74), Courtenhall (1935—74), Dallington (pt 1894—95, ent 1895—1932), Denton (1935—74), Duston (pt 1894—95, ent 1895—1965), Hackleton (1935—74), Hardingstone (1932—74), Harpole, Hartwell (1935—74), Nether Heyford, Upper Heyford, Great Houghton (1935—74), Little Houghton (1935—74), Kislingbury, Milton (1935—60), Milton Malsor (1960—74), Quinton (1935—74), Roade (1935—74), Rothersthorpe (1935—74), Upton, Weston Favell (1894—1965), Wooton (1935—74), Yardley Hastings (1935—74)

OUNDLE RD (1894—1935) (Northants, Hunts)

Apethorpe, Armston, Ashton, Barnwell All Saints, Barnwell St Andrew, Benefield, Blatherwycke, Bulwick, King's Cliffe, Cotterstock, Deene, Deenethorpe, Fotheringhay, Glapthorn, Hemington, Lilford cum Wigsthorpe, Luddington (pt 1894—95, ent 1895—1935), Lutton (pt 1894—95, ent 1895—1935), Nassington, pt Oundle (1894—95), Pilton, Polebrook, Southwick, Stoke Doyle, Tansor, Thorpe Achurch, Thurning (pt 1894—95, ent 1895—1935), Wadenhoe, Warmington, Woodnewton, Yarwell

OUNDLE UD

Oundle (pt 1894—95, ent 1895—1974)

OUNDLE AND THRAPSTON RD (1935[35]—74)

Great Addington, Little Addington, Aldwincle, Apethorpe, Ashton, Barnwell, Benefield, Blatherwycke, Brigstock, Bulwick, Chelveston cum Caldecott, King's Cliffe, Clopton, Collyweston, Cottestock, Deene, Deenethorpe, Denford, Duddington, Easton on the Hill, Fineshade, Fotheringhay, Glapthorn, Hargrave, Harringworth, Hemington, Islip, Laxton, Lilford cum Wigsthorpe, Lowick, Luddington, Lutton, Nassington, Pilton, Polebrook, Ringstead, Southwick, Stoke Doyle, Sudborough, Tansor, Thorpe Achurch, Thrapston, Thurning, Titchmarsh, Twywell, Wadenhoe, Wakerley, Warmington, Woodford, Woodnewton, Yarwell

OXENDON RD (1894—1935[35])

Arthingworth, Ashley, Brampton Ash, Braybrooke, Clipston, Dingley, East Farndon, Hothorpe, Kelmarsh, Marston Trussel, Great Oxendon, Sibbertoft, Stoke Albany, Sulby, Sutton Bassett, Thorpe Lubenham, Welford, Weston by Welland, Wilbarston

POTTERSPURY RD (1894—1935[35])

Alderton, Ashton, Cosgrove, Furtho, Grafton Regis, Hartwell, Lands Common to Potterspury and Yardley Gobion, Passenham, Paulerspury, Potterspury, Wicken, Yardley Gobion

RAUNDS UD (1897[40]—1974)

Raunds

ROTHWELL UD

Rothwell

RUSHDEN UD

Rushden

ST JAMES (NORTHAMPTON) UD (1896[41]—1900[3])

Dallington St James, Duston St James

THRAPSTON RD (1894—1935[35]) (Northants, Hunts)

Great Addington, Little Addington, Aldwincle, Brigstock, Chelveston cum Caldecott, Clopton, Denford, Hargrave, Islip, Lowick, Raunds (1894—97), Ringstead, Slipton, Stanwick, Sudborough, Thrapston, Titchmarsh, Twywell, Woodford

TOWCESTER RD

Abthorpe, Adstone, Blakesley, Blisworth, Bradden, Cosgrove (1935—74), Deanshanger (1948—74), Easton Neston, Furtho (1935—51), Gayton, Grafton Regis (1935—74), Cold Higham, Litchborough, Maidford, Green's Norton, Passenham (1935—48), Pattishall, Paulerspury (1935—74), Plumpton (1894—1935), Potterspury (1935—74), Shutlanger, Silverstone, Slapton, Old Stratford (1951—74), Stoke Bruerne, Tiffield, Towcester, Wappenham, Weedon Lois (1894—1935), Weston and Weedon (1935—74), Whittlebury, Wicken (1935—74), Woodend, Yardley Gobion (1935—74)

WELLINGBOROUGH RD

Mears Ashby, Earls Barton, Bozeat, Great Doddington, Easton Maudit, Ecton, Grendon, Hardwick, Great Harrowden, Little Harrowden, Higham Park (1894—1935), Irchester, Irthlingborough (1894—1901), Isham, Newton Bromshold (1894—1969), Newton Bromswold (1969—74), Orlingbury, Strixton, Sywell, Wilby, Wollaston

WELLINGBOROUGH UD

Wellingborough

NON-METROPOLITAN COUNTY

As consituted 1 Apr 1974, defined in terms of Adm Co units of of 31 Mar.

CORBY DIST

Corby UD, pt Kettering RD (East Carlton, Cottingham, Gretton, Middleton, Rockingham, Stanion, Weldon)

DAVENTRY DIST

pt Brixworth RD (all except the pars in Northampton Dist), Daventry MB, Daventry RD

KETTERING DIST

Burton Latimer UD, Desborough UD, Kettering MB, pt Kettering RD (all except the pars in Corby Dist), Rothwell UD

NORTHAMPTON DIST

CB (assoc with Northants): Northampton CB

from Northants: pt Brixworth RD (pt Overstone[42]), pt Northampton RD (Billing and Hardingstone, pt Brafield on the Green,[42] pt Collingtree,[43] pt Courteenhall,[43] pt Great Houghton,[44] Little Houghton,[44] pt Kislingbury,[45] pt Milton Malsor,[43] pt Rothersthorpe,[46] pt Upton,[45] pt Wootton[46]), pt Wellingborough RD (pt Ecton[42])

EAST NORTHAMPTONSIRE DIST

Higham Ferrers MB, Irthlingborough UD, Oundle UD,

Oundle and Thrapston RD, Raunds UD, Rushden UD, pt Wellingborough RD (Newton Bromswold)

SOUTH NORTHAMPTONSHIRE DIST

Brackley MB, Brackley RD, Northampton RD (all except the pars in Northampton Dist[47]), Towcester RD

WELLINGBOROUGH DIST

pt Wellingborough RD (all except the pars in Northampton Dist), Wellingborough UD

NORTHUMBERLAND

ALTERATIONS IN COUNTY BOUNDARIES

As noted by year below, Northumb pars gained territory from or lost it to pars in adjoining cos or county boroughs, or were entirely transferred to them. Details of these alterations are noted in Part I of the *Guide* under Northumberland.

ANCIENT COUNTY (until 1889: Hds, Bors, MBs, PLUs, RSDs, USDs)

1572 Allendale, Hexham, Lee St John. *1844* Bedlington, Belford,[1] Farne Islands,[2] Holy Island,[3] Monks House,[2] Norham,[4] Tweedmouth. *1887* Hedley Woodside.

ADMINISTRATIVE COUNTY (1889—1974: Wds,[5] PLUs, MBs, RDs, UDs, with assoc CBs of Newcastle upon Tyne, Tynemouth [1904—74])

1889 Byker, Elswick, Heaton, Jesmond, Newcastle upon Tyne All Saints, Newcastle upon Tyne St Andrew, Newcastle upon Tyne St John, Newcastle upon Tyne St Nicholas, Westgate. *1904* Benwell, Chirton, Cullercoats, Fenham, Kenton, Preston, North Shields, Tynemouth, Unnamed, Walker. *1935* West Brunton, East Denton, Earsdon, Fawdon, Kenton, Longbenton, Murton, Seaton Valley, Whitley and Monkseaton.

NON-METROPOLITAN COUNTY (from 1974: Dists)

1974 Brunswick, Dinnington, Gosforth, North Gosforth, Hazlerigg, Longbenton, Moot Hall Precincts, Newburn, Seaton Valley, Wallsend, Whitley and Monkseaton, Woolsington.

ASSOCIATED COUNTY BOROUGHS AND COUNTIES OF THEMSELVES

BERWICK UPON TWEED CO OF ITSELF (from 1835)
no bdry alt

NEWCASTLE UPON TYNE CO OF ITSELF (from 1400), CB
Bdry: 1904,[6] 1935.[7] Transf 1974 to Tyne & Wear.[8]

TYNEMOUTH CB (1904[9]—74)
Bdry: 1935.[7] Transf 1974 to Tyne & Wear.[8]

WARDS[5]

BAMBURGH WD
Adderstone (from 1866), Alnmouth (from 1866), Bamburgh,[10] Bamburgh Castle (from 1866), Beadnell (from 1866), Belford (pt until 1844, ent from 1844), Boulmer and Seaton House (1866—88), Bradford (from 1866), Broxfield (from 1866), Brunton (from 1866), Budle (from 1866), Burton (from 1866), North Charlton (from 1866), South Charlton (from 1866), Chathill (from 1866), Craster (from 1866), Detchant (from 1866), Doxford (from 1866), Dunstan (from 1866), Easington (from 1866), Easington Grange (from 1866), Elford (from 1866), Ellingham, Elwick[11] (from 1866), Embleton, Fallodon (from 1866), Fleetham (from 1866), Glororum (from 1866), Hoppen (1866—87), Howick, Lesbury, Littlehoughton (from 1866), Longhoughton, Lucker (from 1866), Middleton (from 1866), Monks House[12] (from 1858), Mousen (from 1866), Newham (from 1866), Newstead (from 1866), Newton by the Sea (from 1866), Outchester (from 1866), Preston (from 1866), Ratchwood (from 1866), Rennington (from 1866), Rock (from 1866), Ross[13] (from 1866), Shoreston (from 1866), Spindlestone (from 1866), Stamford (from 1866), North Sunderland (from 1866), Swinhoe (from 1866), Tughall (from 1866), Warenford (from 1866), Warenton (from 1866)

BEDLINGTONSHIRE (In Co Durham until 1844, Northumb thereafter)
Bedlington

CASTLE WD
Backworth (from 1866), Bebside (from 1866), Benwell (from 1866), Berwick Hill (from 1866), Brenkley (from 1866), East Brunton (from 1866), West Brunton (from 1866), Burradon (from 1866), Butterlaw (1866—86), Byker[10] (from 1866), Black Callerton (from 1866), High Callerton (from 1866), Little Callerton (from 1866), Chirton[10] (from 1866), Coldcoats (from 1866) Cowpen (from 1866), Coxlodge (from 1866), Cramlington (from 1866), Cullercoats[10] (from 1866), Darras Hall (from 1866), East Denton (from 1866), West Denton (from 1866), Dinnington (from 1818), North Dissington (from 1866), South Dissington (from 1866), pt Eachwick (from 1866), Earsdon, Edington (from 1866), Elswick[10] (from 1866), Fawdon (from 1866), Fenham (from 1866), Gosforth (until 1866), North Gosforth (from 1866), South Gosforth (from 1866), East Hartford (from 1866), West Hartford (from 1866), Hartley (from 1866), Heaton[10] (from 1866), East Heddon (from 1866), Hepscott (from 1866), Higham Dykes (from 1866), Holywell (from 1866), Horton, Horton Grange (from 1866), Jesmond,[10] Kenton (from 1866), Kirkley (from 1866), Longbenton, Mason (from

1866), Meldon, Milbourne (from 1866), Milbourne Grange (from 1866), pt Mitford (until 1866), Molesden (from 1866), Monkseaton (from 1866), pt Morpeth[10] (until 1866), Morpeth Castle (from 1866), Murton (from 1866), Newbiggin (from 1866), Newburn[10] (pt until 1866, ent from 1866), Newburn Hall (from 1866), Newham (from 1866), Newminster Abbey (from 1866), Newsham and South Blyth (from 1866), Ogle (from 1866), Ponteland, Preston (from 1866), Prestwick (from 1866), Riplington (from 1866), Rivergreen (from 1858), Seaton Delaval (from 1866), Seghill (from 1866), North Shields[10] (from 1866), Shilvington (from 1866), Stannington, Sugley (from 1866), Throckley (from 1866), Tranwell and High Church[10] (from 1866), Trewick (from 1866), Twizell (from 1866), Tynemouth,[10] Wallbottle (from 1866), Wallsend (from 1807), Westgate[10] (from 1866), Whalton, Whitley (from 1866), Whorlton (from 1866), Woolsington (from 1866)

COQUETDALE WD

Abberwick (from 1866), Acton and Old Fenton (from 1866), Alnham, Alnwick,[10] Alwinton, Barrow (from 1866), Bassington (from 1866), Beanley (from 1866), New Bewick (from 1866), Old Bewick (from 1866), Bickerton (from 1866), Biddlestone (from 1866), Birling (from 1866), Bolton (from 1866), Brandon (from 1866), Branton (from 1866), pt Brinkburn Chapelry (until 1866), Brinkburn High Ward (from 1866), Brinkburn Low Ward (from 1866), Broome Park (from 1866), Brotherwick (from 1866), Burradon (from 1866), High Buston (from 1866), Low Buston (from 1866), Caistron (from 1866), Callaly and Yetlington (from 1866), Cartington (from 1866), Clennell (from 1866), Crawley (from 1866), Debdon (1866—89), Ditchburn (from 1866), Dueshill (1866—89), Edlingham, Eglingham, Elsdon, Elyhaugh (from 1866), Fairhaugh (from 1866), Fallowlees (from 1866), Farnham (from 1866), Fawdon and Clinch (from 1884); Fawdon, Clinch and Hartside (1866—84); Felton[10] (pt until 1866, ent from 1866), Flotterton (from 1866), Glanton (from 1866), Greens and Glantlees (from 1866), Guyzance (from 1866), Harbottle (from 1866), Harehope (from 1866), Hazon and Hartlaw (from 1866), Hedgeley (from 1866), Hepple (from 1866), Hepple Demesne (1866—89), Hesleyhurst (from 1866), Hollinghill (from 1866), Holystone, Ilderton, Ingram (until 1866); Ingram, Linhope and Greenshawhill (1866—84); Ingram, Linhope, Greenshawhill and Hartside (from 1884); Kidland (from 1858), Learchild (from 1866), Lee Ward (1866—89), Lemmington (from 1866), East Lilburn (from 1866), West Lilburn (from 1866), Linbridge (from 1866), Linsheeles (from 1866), Longframlington (from 1866), Lorbottle (from 1866), North Middleton (from 1866), South Middleton (from 1866), Middleton Hall (from 1866), Monkridge (from 1866), Mount Healey (from 1866), Netherton North Side (from 1866), Netherton South Side (from 1866), Newton on the Moor (from 1866), Newtown (from 1866), Otterburn (from 1866), Pauperhaugh (1866—89), Peels (from 1866), Prendwick (from 1866), Ramshope (1858—86), Raw (from 1866), Reaveley (from 1866), Rochester (1866—86), Rochester Ward (from 1886), Roddam (from

1866), Roseden (from 1866), Rothbury,[10] Great Ryle (from 1866), Little Ryle (from 1866), Scrainwood (from 1866), Sharperton (from 1866), Shawdon (from 1866), Shilbottle, Shipley (from 1866), Snitter (from 1866), Sturton Grange (from 1866), Swarland (from 1866), Thropton (from 1866), Titlington (from 1866), Tosson (from 1889), Great Tosson and Rye Hill (1866—89), Tosson Little (1866—89), High and Low Trewhitt (from 1866), Troughend (from 1866), Unthank (from 1866), Walkmill (from 1866), Warton (from 1866), Whittingham, Whittle (from 1866), Whitton (from 1866), Woodhouse (from 1866), Woodside (from 1866), Woolperton (from 1866), Wreighill (from 1866)

GLENDALE WD

Akeld (from 1866), Branxton, Carham, Chatton, Chillingham, Coldsmouth and Thompson's Walls (from 1866), Coupland (from 1866), Crookhouse (from 1866), Doddington (from 1775), Earle (from 1866), Ewart (from 1866), Ford, Grey's Forest (from 1866), Hethpool (from 1866), Hepburn (from 1866), Howtel (from 1866), Humbleton (from 1866), Kilham (from 1866), Kirknewton, Lanton (from 1866), Lowick, Milfield (from 1866), Nesbit (from 1866), Newtown (from 1866), Paston (from 1866), Selby's Forest (from 1866), Westnewton (from 1866), Wooler, Yeavering (from 1866)

ISLANDSHIRE (In Co Durham until 1844, Northumb thereafter)

Ancroft, Elwick[11] (from 1866), Holy Island, Kyloe, Tweedmouth[10]

MORPETH WD

Acklington (from 1866), Acklington Park (from 1866), Amble (from 1866), High Angerton (from 1866), Low Angerton (from 1866), Ashington and Sheepwash (from 1866), Benridge (from 1866), Bigge's Quarter (from 1866), Bockenfield (from 1866), Bolam (pt until 1866, ent from 1866), Bolam Vicarage (from 1866), Bothal (until 1866), Bothal Demesne (from 1866), pt Brinkburn Chapelry (until 1866), Brinkburn South Side (1866—89), Bullers Green (1866—88), Bullock's Hall (from 1866), Causey Park (from 1866), East Chevington (from 1866), West Chevington (from 1866), Coatyards (from 1866), Cockle Park (from 1866), Corridge (from 1866), Cresswell (from 1866), Earsdon (from 1866), Earsdon Forest (from 1866), Ellington (from 1866), Eshott (from 1866), Ewesley (from 1866), pt Felton (until 1866), Fenrother (from 1866), Freeholders' Quarter (from 1866), Gallowhill (from 1866), Gloster Hill (from 1866), Hadston (from 1866), Hartburn, Hartburn Grange (from 1866), Hauxley (from 1866), Healey and Combhill (from 1866), Hebron (from 1866), Highlaws (from 1866), High and Low Highlaws (from 1866), Hirst (from 1866), Long Horsley (until 1866), Longhirst (from 1866), Longwitton (from 1866), Longshaws (from 1866), Lynmouth (from 1866), North Middleton (from 1866), South Middleton (from 1866), Mitford[10] (pt until 1866, ent from 1866), Morpeth[10] (pt until 1866, ent from 1866), Morwick (from 1866), Netherwitton (from 1866), Newbiggin by the Sea (from 1866), Newton Park (from 1866), Newton Underwood (from 1866), Nunnykirk (from 1866), Nunriding (from 1866), Old

Moor (from 1866), Pegswood (from 1866), Pigdon (from 1866), Riddell's Quarter (from 1866), Ritton Colt Park (from 1866), Ritton White House (from 1866), Rothley (from 1866), North Seaton (from 1866), Spital Hill (from 1866), Stanton (from 1866), East and West Thirston with Shothaugh (from 1866), East Thornton (from 1866), West Thornton (from 1866), Throphill (from 1866), Todburn (from 1866), Todridge (from 1866), Togston (from 1866), Tritlington (from 1866), Ulgham (from 1866), Warkworth[10] (pt until 1866, ent from 1866), Whitridge (from 1866), Widdrington, Wingates (from 1866), Witton Shields (from 1866), Woodhorn,[10] Woodhorn Demesne (from 1866)

NORHAMSHIRE (In Co Durham until 1844, Northumb thereafter)

Cornhill on Tweed (from 1866), Duddo (from 1866), Felkington (from 1866), Grindon (from 1866), Horncliffe (from 1866), Loanend (from 1866), Longridge (from 1866), Norham, Norham Mains (from 1866), Shoreswood (from 1866), Thornton (from 1866), Twizell (from 1866)

TYNEDALE WD

Acomb (from 1866), East Acomb (1866—87), Allendale (from 1572), Anick (1866—87), Anick Grange (1866—87), Apperley (1866—87), Aydon (from 1866), Aydon Castle (from 1866), Great Bavington (from 1866), Little Bavington (from 1866), Bearl (from 1866), Bellingham (from 1866), Bellister (from 1866), Belsay (from 1866), Bingfield (from 1866), Birtley (from 1866), Bitchfield (from 1866), Black Carts and Ryehill (from 1866), Blenkinsopp (from 1866), Bradford (from 1866), Broomhaugh (from 1866), Broomley (from 1866), Bywell (from 1887), Bywell St Andrew (until 1887), Bywell St Peter (until 1887), Cambo (from 1866), Capheaton (from 1866), Carrycoats (from 1866), Catcherside (from 1866), East Charlton (1866—86), West Charlton (1866—86), Cheeseburn Grange (from 1866), Chirdon (from 1866), Chollerton, Clarewood (from 1866), Coanwood (from 1866), Cocklaw (from 1866), Coldwell (from 1866), Corbridge,[10] Corsenside, Crookdean (from 1866), Dalton (from 1866), Deanham (from 1866), Dilston (from 1866), Duke's Hagg (from 1866), pt Eachwick (from 1866), Eltringham (from 1866), Espershields (from 1866), Fairnley (from 1866), Fallowfield (from 1866), Falstone (1811—66), Fawns (from 1866), Featherstone (from 1866), Fenwick (from 1866), High Fotherley (from 1866), Greenleighton (from 1866), Greystead (1811—66), Hallington (from 1866), Halton (from 1866), Halton Shields (1866—87), Haltwhistle,

Little Harle (from 1866), West Harle (from 1866), Harlow Hill (from 1866), Harnham (from 1866), Hartington (from 1866), Hartington Hall (from 1866), Hartleyburn (from 1866), Harwood (from 1866), Haughton (from 1866), Hawick (from 1866), Hawkwell (from 1866), Haydon (from 1866), Healey (from 1866), Black Heddon (from 1866), West Heddon (from 1866), Heddon on the Wall, Hedley (from 1866), Hedley Woodside (from 1866), Henshaw (from 1866), Heugh (from 1866), Hexham[10] (from 1572), Hexhamshire High Quarter (from 1866), Hexhamshire Low Quarter (from 1866), Hexhamshire Middle Quarter (from 1866), Hexhamshire West Quarter (from 1866), Horsley (from 1866), Houghton and Close House (from 1866), Humshaugh (from 1866), Ingoe (from 1866), Kearsley (from 1866), Kirkharle, Kirkhaugh, Kirkheaton (from 1858), Kirkwhelpington, Knarsdale, Lambley, Leemailing (1866—86), Lee St John (1572—1866), Masters Close (from 1858), East Matfen (from 1866), West Matfen (from 1866), Melkridge (from 1866), Mickley (from 1866), Nafferton (from 1866), Nesbitt (from 1866), Newbiggin (1866—87), Newbrough (from 1866), Newlands (from 1866), Newton (from 1866), Newton Hall (from 1866), Nook (from 1866), Ouston (from 1866), Ovingham, Ovington (from 1866), Plashetts and Tynehead (from 1866), Plenmeller (from 1866), Portgate (from 1866), Prudhoe (from 1866), Prudhoe Castle (from 1866), Riding (from 1866), Ridley (from 1866), Rudchester (from 1866), Ryal (from 1866), Sandhoe (from 1866), East Shaftoe (from 1866), West Shaftoe (from 1866), High Shitlington (1866—86), Low Shitlington (1866—86), Shortflatt (from 1866), Shotley (until 1866), Shotley High Quarter (from 1866), Shotley Low Quarter (from 1866), Simonburn, Slaley, Smalesmouth (from 1866), Spital (from 1866), Stamfordham (until 1866), Stelling (from 1866), Stocksfield Hall (1866—87), Styford (from 1866), Sweethope (from 1866), Tarretburn (1866—86), Tarset West (from 1866), Thirlwall (from 1866), Thockrington, Thornbrough (from 1866), Thorneyburn (from 1811), Thorngrafton (from 1866), Wall (from 1866), Wall Town (from 1866), Wallington Demesne (from 1866), Wallridge (from 1866), Warden,[10] Wark (from 1811), Warksburn (1866—86), Wellhaugh (from 1866), Welton (from 1866), West Whelpington (from 1866), Whitchester (from 1866), Whitfield, Great Whittington (from 1866), Little Whittington (from 1866), Whittle (from 1866), Whittonstall (from 1866), Wylam (from 1866)

BOROUGHS

Units with some degree of burghal character[14] are denominated 'Bor'. Those which did not sustain that status until the 19th cent are in italics. MBs were established by the Municipal Corporations Act, 1835,[15] or by later charter.

ALNWICK BOR
Alnwick
BAMBURGH BOR[16]
Bamburgh

BERWICK UPON TWEED BOR/MB[17] (orig co of itself)
Berwick upon Tweed, Tweedmouth (pt 1835—91, ent 1891—1974)
BLYTH MB (1922[18]—74)
Blyth

CORBRIDGE BOR
Corbridge
FELTON BOR
Felton
HARBOTTLE BOR
pt Alnwick
HAYDON BRIDGE BOR
Hexham
HOLY ISLAND BOR
Holy Island
MITFORD BOR
Mitford
MORPETH BOR/MB[19]
Morpeth (pt until 1894, ent 1894—1974), pt Morpeth Castle (1889—94), pt Newminster Abbey (1835—94), pt Tranwell and High Church (1889—94)
NEWBIGGIN ON SEA BOR
pt Woodhorn
NEWBROUGH BOR
pt Warden
NEWBURN BOR
Newburn
NEWCASTLE UPON TYNE CO OF ITSELF (from 1400), BOR/MB/CB
Benwell (1904—14), Byker (1835—1914), Elswick

(1835—1914), Fenham (1904—14), Heaton (1835—1914), Jesmond (1835—1914), Newcastle upon Tyne (1914—74), Newcastle upon Tyne All Saints (until 1914), Newcastle upon Tyne St Andrew (until 1914), Newcastle upon Tyne St John (until 1914), Newcastle upon Tyne St Nicholas (until 1914), Walker (1904—74), Westgate (1835—1914)
NEWTON BOR
pt Warkworth
ROTHBURY BOR
Rothbury
TYNEMOUTH MB (1849[20]—1904), CB (1904—74)
Chirton (1849—1908), Cullercoats (1849—1908), pt Murton (1881—94), Preston (1849—1908), North Shields (1849—1908), Tynemouth, Unnamed (1894—1908)
WALLSEND MB (1901[21]—74)
Wallsend
WARENMOUTH BOR
uncertain composition[22]
WARKWORTH BOR
pt Warkworth
WHITLEY BAY MB (1954[23]—74)
Whitley and Monkseaton

POOR LAW UNIONS

In Northumb Poor Law County:[24]
ALNWICK PLU
Abberwick, Acklington, Acklington Park, Acton and Old Felton, Alnmouth, Alnwick, Amble, Bassington, Beanley, Birling, Bolton, Boulmer and Seaton House (1836—88), Broome Park, Brotherwick, Broxfield, Brunton, High Buston, Low Buston, North Charlton, South Charlton, Craster, Crawley, Denwick (1894—1930), Ditchburn, Doxford, Dunstan, Edlingham, Eglingham, Elyhaugh, Embleton, Fallodon, Felton, Glanton, Gloster Hill, Greens and Glantlees, Guyzance, Harehope, Hauxley, Hazon and Hartlaw, Hedgeley, Howick, Learchild, Lemmington, Lesbury, Littlehoughton, Longhoughton, Morwick, Newton by the Sea, Newton on the Moor, Rennington, Rock, Shawdon, Shilbottle, Shipley, Stamford, Sturton Grange, Swarland, Titlington, Togston, Walkmill, Warkworth, Whittle, Woodhouse
BELFORD PLU
Adderstone, Bamburgh, Bamburgh Castle, Beadnell, Belford,[1] Bradford, Budle, Burton, Chathill, Detchant, Easington, Easington Grange, Elford, Ellingham, Elwick,[1] Farne Islands,[2] Fleetham, Glororum, Hoppen (1836—87), Lucker, Middleton, Monks House[2] (1865—1930), Mousen, Newham, Newstead, Outchester, Preston, Ratchwood, Ross,[1] Shoreston, Spindlestone, North Sunderland, Swinhoe, Tughall, Warenford, Warenton
BELLINGHAM PLU
Great Bavington, Little Bavington, Bellingham, Birtley, Carrycoats, Catcherside, East Charlton (1836—86), West Charlton (1836—86), Chirdon, Coldwell, Corsenside, Crookdean, Fawns, Little Harle, West Harle, Hawick, Kirkharle, Kirkwhelpington,

Leemailing (1836—86), Nook (1836—86), Otterburn, Plashetts and Tynehead, Ramshope (1836—86), Rochester (1836—86), Rochester Ward (1886—1930), High Shitlington (1836—86), Low Shitlington (1836—86), Smalesmouth, Sweethope, Tarretburn (1836—86), Tarset West, Thockrington, Thorneyburn, Troughend, Wark, Warksburn (1836—86), Wellhaugh, West Whelpington
BERWICK PLU (Northumb, Durham [1836—44])
Ancroft,[3] Berwick upon Tweed, Cornhill on Tweed,[4] Duddo,[4] Felkington,[4] Grindon,[4] Holy Island,[3] Horncliffe,[4] Kyloe,[3] Loanend,[4] Longridge,[4] Norham,[4] Norham Mains,[4] Ord (1891—1930), Shoreswood,[4] Thornton,[4] Tweedmouth,[3] Twizell[4]
CASTLE WARD PLU
Belsay, Berwick Hill, Bitchfield, Bolam, Bolam Vicarage, Bradford, Brenkley, East Brunton, West Brunton, Butterlaw (1836—86), Black Callerton, High Callerton, Little Callerton, Capheaton, Cheeseburn Grange, Coldcoats, Coxlodge (1836—1908), Dalton, Darras Hall, East Denton, West Denton, Dinnington, North Dissington, South Dissington, Eachwick, Fawdon, Fenwick, Gallowhill, Gosforth (1908—30), North Gosforth, South Gosforth (1836—1908), Harlow Hill, Harnham, Hawkwell, Black Heddon, East Heddon, West Heddon, Heddon on the Wall, Heugh, Higham Dykes, Horton Grange, Houghton and Close House, Ingoe, Kearsley, Kenton, Kirkheaton, Kirkley, Mason, East Matfen, West Matfen, Milbourne, Milbourne Grange, Nesbitt, Newbiggin, Newburn, Newburn Hall, Newham, Ogle, Ouston, Ponteland, Prestwick, Riplington, Rudchester, Ryal, East Shaftoe, West Shaftoe, Shilvington, Shortflatt, Stannington, Sugley, Throckley, Trewick, Twizell, Wallbottle, Wallridge, Whalton,

Whitchester, Whorlton, Woolsington

GLENDALE PLU

Akeld, New Bewick, Old Bewick, Brandon, Branton, Branxton, Carham, Chatton, Chillingham, Coldsmouth and Thompson's Walls, Coupland, Crookhouse, Doddington, Earle, Ewart, Fawdon and Clinch (1884—1930); Fawdon, Clinch and Hartside (1836—88); Ford, Grey's Forest, Hepburn, Hethpool, Hotwel, Humbleton, Ilderton; Ingham, Linhope and Greenshawhill (1836—84); Ingham, Linhope, Greenshawhill and Hatside (1884—1930); Kilham, Kirknewton, Lanton, East Lilburn, West Lilburn, Lowick, North Middleton, South Middleton, Middleton Hall, Milfield, Nesbit, Newtown, Paston, Plea Piece, Reaveley, Roddam, Roseden, Selby's Forest, Westnewton, Wooler, Wooperton, Yeavering

HALTWHISTLE PLU

Bellister, Blenkinsopp, Coanwood, Featherstone, Haltwhistle, Hartleyburn, Henshaw, Kirkhaugh, Knarsdale, Lambley, Melkridge, Plenmeller, Ridley, Thirlwall, Thorngrafton, Wall Town, Whitfield

HEXHAM PLU

Acomb, East Acomb (1836—87), West Allen (1897—1930), Allendale, Allendale Common, Anick (1836—87), Anick Grange (1836—87), Apperley (1858—87), Aydon, Aydon Castle, Bearl, Bingfield, Black Carts and Ryehill (1858—1930), Broomhaugh, Broomley, Bywell (1887—1930), Bywell St Andrew (1836—87), Bywell St Peter (1836—87), Chollerton, Clarewood, Cocklaw, Corbridge, Dilston, Duke's Hagg, Eltringham, Espershields, Fallowfield, High Fotherley, Hallington, Halton, Halton Shields (1836—87), Haughton, Haydon, Healey, Hedley, Hedley Woodside (1836—87), Hexham, Hexhamshire High Quarter, Hexhamshire Low Quarter, Hexhamshire Middle Quarter, Hexhamshire West Quarter, Horsley, Humshaugh, Masters Close (1858—87), Mickley, Nafferton, Newbiggin (1836—87), Newbrough, Newlands, Newton, Newton Hall, Ovingham, Ovington, Portgate, Prudhoe, Prudhoe Castle, Riding, Sandhoe, Shotley High Quarter, Shotley Low Quarter, Simonburn, Slaley, Spital, Stelling, Stocksfield Hall (1836—87), Styford, Thornborough, Wall, Warden, Welton, Great Whittington, Little Whittington, Whittle, Whittonstall, Wylam

MORPETH PLU (Northumb, Durham [1836—44])

High Angerton, Low Angerton, Ashington (1896—1930), Ashington and Sheepwash (1836—96), Bedlington,[25] Benridge, Bigge's Quarter, Bockenfield, Bothal Demesne, Bullers Green (1836—86), Bullock's Hall, Cambo, Causey Park, East Chevington, West Chevington, Cockle Park, Corridge, Cresswell, Deanham, Earsdon, Earsdon Forest, Edington, Ellington, Eshott, Fenrother, Freeholders' Quarter, Hadston, Hartburn, Hartburn Grange, Hebron, Hepscott, Highlaws, High and Low Highlaws, Hirst, Horlsley Moor, Long Horsley Common, Longhirst, Longshaws, Longwitton, Lynmouth, Meldon, North Middleton,

South Middleton, Mitford, Molesdon, Morpeth, Morpeth Castle, Newbiggin by the Sea, Netherwitton, Newminster (1894—1930), Newminster Abbey (1836—94), Newton Park, Newton Underwood, Nunriding, Old Moor, Pegswood, Pigdon, Riddell's Quarter, Rivergreen, North Seaton, Spital Hill, Stanton, Sheepwash (1896—1930), East and West Thirston with Shothaugh, East Thornton, West Thornton, Throphill, Todridge, Tranwell (1894—1930), Tranwell and High Church (1836—94), Tritlington, Ulgham, Wallington Demesne, Whitridge, Widdrington, Witton Shields, Woodhorn, Woodhorn Demesne

NEWCASTLE UPON TYNE PLU (1836—1914), PAR (1914—30)

Benwell (1836—1914), Byker (1836—1914), Elswick (1836—94), Fenham (1836—1914), Heaton (1836—1914), Jesmond (1836—1914), Newcastle upon Tyne (1914—30), Newcastle upon Tyne All Saints (1836—1914), Newcastle upon Tyne St Andrew (1836—1914), Newcastle upon Tyne St John (1836—1914), Newcastle upon Tyne St Nicholas (1836—1914), Westgate (1836—1914)

ROTHBURY PLU

Alnham, Alwinton, Barrow, Bickerton, Biddlestone, Brinkburn High Ward, Brinkburn Low Ward, Brinkburn South Side (1836—89), Burradon, Caistron, Callaly and Yetlington, Cartington, Clennell, Coatyards, Debdon (1836—89), Debdon (1896—1930), Dueshill (1836—89), Elsdon, Ewesley, Fairhaugh, Fairnley, Fallowlees, Farnham, Flotterton, Greenleighton, Harbottle, Hartington, Hartington Hall, Harwood, Healey and Combhill, Hepple, Hepple Demesne (1836—89), Hesleyhurst, Hollinghill, Holystone, Kidland, Lee Ward (1836—89), Linbridge, Linsheeles, Longframlington, Lorbottle, Monkridge, Mount Healey, Netherton North Side, Netherton South Side, Newtown, Nunnykirk, Pauperhaugh (1836—89), Peels, Prendwick, Raw, Ritton Colt Park, Ritton White House, Rothbury, Rothley, Great Ryle, Little Ryle, Scrainwood, Sharperton, Snitter, Thropton, Todburn, Tosson (1889—1930), Great Tosson and Rye Hill (1836—89), Tosson Little (1836—89), High and Low Trewhitt, Unthank, Warton, Whittingham, Whitton, Wingates, Woodside, Wreighill

TYNEMOUTH PLU

Backworth, Bebside (1836—1920), Blyth (1920—30), Burradon, Camperdown (1899—1912), Chirton (1836—1908), Cowpen (1836—1920), Cramlington, Cullercoats (1836—1908), Earsdon, East Hartford, West Hartford, Hartley (1836—1912), Holywell, Horton, Longbenton, Monkseaton (1836—1913), Murton, Newsham and South Blyth (1836—1920), Preston (1836—1908), Seaton Delaval, Seghill, North Shields (1836—1908), Tynemouth, Unnamed (1894—1908), Walker (1894—1910), Wallsend, Weetslade (1894—1930), Whitley (1836—1913), Whitley and Monkseaton (1913—30), Willington (1894—1910), Willington Quay (1894—1910)

SANITARY DISTRICTS

ALNWICK RSD
same as PLU less pt Alnwick, Amble
ALNWICK AND CANONGATE USD
pt Alnwick
AMBLE USD
Amble
BEDLINGTONSHIRE USD
Bedlington
BELFORD RSD
same as PLU except Farne Islands not in the RSD
BELLINGHAM RSD
same as PLU
BENWELL AND FENHAM USD
Benwell, Fenham
BERWICK RSD
same as PLU less Berwick upon Tweed, Tweedmouth
(pt 1875—91, ent 1891—94)
BERWICK UPON TWEED USD
Berwick upon Tweed, Tweedmouth (pt 1875—91, ent
1891—94)
SOUTH BLYTH USD[26]
Newsham and South Blyth (pt 1875—83, ent 1883—94)
CASTLE WARD RSD
same as PLU less Coxlodge, East Denton, West
Denton, South Gosforth, Newburn, Newburn Hall,
Sugley, Throckley, Wallbottle
COWPEN USD[27]
Cowpen (pt 1875—81, ent 1881—94)
CRAMLINGTON USD
Cramlington
GLENDALE USD
same as PLU
SOUTH GOSFORTH USD
Coxlodge, South Gosforth
HALTWHISLE RSD
same as PLU
HEXHAM RSD
same as PLU less Hexham (ent 1875—83, pt 1883—94)
HEXHAM USD
Hexham (ent 1875—83, pt 1883—94)
HOWDON USD (1875—94[28]**)**
pt Wallsend

MORPETH RSD
same as PLU less Bedlington, Newbiggin by the Sea,
and the pars and pts of pars in Morpeth USD, qv
MORPETH USD[19]
Bullers Green (1875—88), Hepscott (1875—89),
Morpeth (ent 1875—89, pt 1889—94), Morpeth Castle
(ent 1875—89, pt 1889—94), Newminster Abbey (ent
1875—89, pt 1889—94), Tranwell and High Church
(ent 1875—89, pt 1889—94)
NEWBIGGIN BY THE SEA USD
Newbiggin by the Sea
NEWBURN USD (1893[29]**—94)**
East Denton, West Denton, Newburn, Newburn Hall,
Sugley, Throckley, Wallbottle
NEWCASTLE UPON TYNE USD
Byker, Elswick, Heaton, Jesmond, Newcastle upon
Tyne All Saints, Newcastle upon Tyne St Andrew,
Newcastle upon Tyne St John, Newcastle upon St
Nicholas, Westgate
ROTHBURY RSD
same as PLU less Cowpen (pt 1875—81, ent 1881—94)
SEGHILL USD
Seghill
TYNEMOUTH RSD
same as PLU less South Blyth (pt 1875—83, ent 1883—
94), Chirton, Cramlington, Cullercoats, pt
Longbenton, Monkseaton, pt Murton (1881—94),
Preston, Seghill, North Shields, Tynemouth, pt
Wallsend, Whitley
TYNEMOUTH USD
Chirton, Cullercoats, pt Murton (1881—94), Preston,
North Shields, Tynemouth
WALKER USD
pt Longbenton
WALLSEND USD
pt Wallsend
WHITLEY AND MONKSEATON USD
Monkseaton, Whitley
WILLINGTON QUAY USD
pt Willington

ADMINISTRATIVE COUNTY

For MBs and associated CBs, see BOROUGHS.

ALNWICK RD
Abberwick (1894—1955), Acklington, Acklington Park
(1894—1955), Acton and Old Fenton (1894—1955),
Alnmouth, Bassington (1894—1955), Beanley (1894—
1955), Birling (1894—1955), Bolton (1894—1955),
Broome Park (1894—1955), Brotherwick (1894—
1955), Broxfield (1894—1955), Brunton (1894—1955),
High Buston (1894—1955), Low Buston (1894—1955),
North Charlton (1894—1955), South Charlton (1894—
1955), Craster, Crawley (1894—1955), Denwick,
Ditchburn (1894—1955), Doxford (1894—1955), Dunstan (1894—1955), Edlingham, Eglingham, Elyhaugh
(1894—1955), Embleton, Fallodon (1894—1955),
Felton, Glanton, Gloster Hill (1894—1955), Greens
and Glantlees (1894—1955), Guyzance (1894—1955),
Harehope (1894—1955), Hauxley, Hazon and Hartlaw
(1894—1955), Hedgeley, Howick (1894—1955), Learchild (1894—1955), Lemmington (1894—1955),
Lesbury, Littlehoughton (1894—1955), Longhoughton,
Morwick (1894—1955), Newton by the Sea, Newton on
the Moor (1894—1955), Rennington, Rock (1894—
1955), Shawdon (1894—1955), Shilbottle, Shipley
(1894—1955), Stamford (1894—1955), Sturton Grange
(1894—1955), Swarland (1894—1955), Titlington

(1894—1955), Togston, Walkmill (1894—1955), Warkworth, Whittle (1894—1955), Woodhouse (1894—1955)

ALNWICK UD (1896[30]—1974)

Alnwick

ALNWICK AND CANONGATE UD (1894—96[30])

Alnwick

AMBLE UD

Amble

ASHINGTON UD (1896[31]—1974)

Ashington, Hirst (1896—1914)

BEDLINGTONSHIRE UD

Bedlington

BELFORD RD

Adderstone (1894—1955), Adderstone with Lucker (1955—74), Bamburgh, Bamburgh Castle (1894—1955), Beadnell, Belford, Bradford (1894—1955), Budle (1894—1955), Burton (1894—1955), Chathill (1894—1955), Detchant (1894—1955), Easington, Easington Grange (1894—1955), Elford (1894—1955), Ellingham, Elwick (1894—1955), *Farne Islands*[32] (1894—1955), Fleetham (1894—1955), Glororum (1894—1955), Lucker (1894—1955), Middleton, Monks House (1894—1955), Mousen (1894—1955), Newham (1894—1955), Newstead (1894—1955), Outchester (1894—1955), Preston (1894—1955), Ratchwood (1894—1955), Ross (1894—1955), Shoreston (1894—1955), Spindlestone (1894—1955), North Sunderland, Swinhoe (1894—1955), Tughall (1894—1955), Warenford (1894—1955), Warenton (1894—1955)

BELLINGHAM RD

Bavington (1955—74), Great Bavington (1894—1955), Little Bavington (1894—1955), Bellingham, Birtley, Carrycoats (1894—1955), Catcherside (1894—1955), Chirdon (1894—1955), Coldwell (1894—1955), Corsenside, Crookdean (1894—1955), Falstone (1955—74), Fawns (1894—1955), Greystead (1955—74), Little Harle (1894—1955), West Harle (1894—1955), Hawick (1894—1955), Kielder (1955—74), Kirkharle (1894—1955), Kirkwhelpington, Otterburn, Plashetts and Tynehead (1894—1955), Rochester (1955—74), Rochester Ward (1894—1955), Smalesmouth (1894—1955), Sweethope (1894—1955), Tarset (1955—74), Tarset West (1894—1955), Thockrington (1894—1955), Thorneyburn (1894—1955), Troughend (1894—1955), Wark, Wellhaugh (1894—1955), West Whelington (1894—1955)

BENWELL AND FENHAM UD (1894—1904[6])

Benwell, Fenham

BLYTH UD (1894—1922[18])

Bebside (1920—22), Blyth (1920—24), Cowpen (1907—20), Horton (1912—20), Newsham and South Blyth (1894—1920)

CASTLE WARD RD

Belsay, Berwick Hill (1894—1955), Bitchfield (1894—1955), Bolam (1894—1955), Bolam Vicarage (1894—1955), Bradford (1894—1955), Brenkley (1894—1955), Brunswick (1955—74), East Brunton (1894—1955), West Brunton (1894—1955), Black Callerton (1894—1955), High Callerton (1894—1955), Little Callerton (1894—1955), Capheaton, Cheeseburn Grange (1894—1955), Coldcoats (1894—1955), Dalton

(1894—1955), Darras Hall (1894—1955), Dinnington, North Dissington (1894—1955), South Dissington (1894—1955), Eachwick (1894—1955), Fawdon (1894—1955), Fenwick (1894—1955), Gallowhill (1894—1955), North Gosforth, Harlow Hill (1894—1955), Harnham (1894—1955), Hawkwell (1894—1955), Hazelrigg (1955—74), Black Heddon (1894—1955), East Heddon (1894—1955), West Heddon (1894—1955), Heddon on the Wall, Heugh (1894—1955), Higham Dykes (1894—1955), Horton Grange (1894—1955), Houghton and Close House (1894—1955), Ingoe (1894—1955), Kearsley (1894—1955), Kenton (1894—1935), Kirkheaton (1894—1955), Kirkley (1894—1955), Mason (1894—1955), Matfen (1955—74), East Matfen (1894—1955), West Matfen (1894—1955), Milbourne (1894—1955), Milbourne Grange (1894—1955), Nesbitt (1894—1955), Newbiggin (1894—1955), Newham (1894—1955), Ogle (1894—1955), Ouston (1894—1955), Ponteland, Prestwick (1894—1955), Riplington (1894—1955), Rudchester (1894—1955), Ryal (1894—1955), East Shaftoe (1894—1955), West Shaftoe (1894—1955), Shilvington (1894—1955), Shortflatt (1894—1955), Stamfordham (1955—74), Stannington, Trewick (1894—1955), Twizell (1894—1955), Wallridge (1894—1955), Whalton, Whitchester (1894—1955), Whorlton (1894—1955), Woolsington

COWPEN UD (1894—1907[33])

Cowpen

CRAMLINGTON UD[34] (1894—1935[7])

Cramlington, East Hartford (1912—35), West Hartford (1912—35)

EARSDON UD (1894—1935[7])

Backworth, Earsdon, Holywell, Murton

GLENDALE RD

Akeld, Bewick (1955—74), New Bewick (1894—1955), Old Bewick (1894—1955), Bowsden (1955—74), Brandon (1894—1955), Branton (1894—1955), Branxton, Carham, Chatton, Chillingham, Coldsmouth and Thompson's Walls (1894—1955), Coupland (1894—1955), Crookhouse (1894—1955), Doddington, Earle, Ewart, Fawdon and Clinch (1894—1955), Ford, Grey's Forest (1894—1955), Hepburn (1894—1955), Hethpool (1894—1955), Howtel (1894—1955), Humbleton (1894—1955), Ilderton, Ingram (1955—74); Ingram, Linhope, Greenshawhill and Hartside (1894—1955); Kilham, Kirknewton, Lanton (1894—1955), Lilburn (1955—74), East Lilburn (1894—1955), West Lilburn (1894—1955), Lowick, North Middleton (1894—1955), South Middleton (1894—1955), Middleton Hall (1894—1955), Milfield, Nesbit (1894—1955), Newtown (1894—1955), Paston (1894—1955), Plea Piece (1894—1955), Reaveley (1894—1955), Roseden (1894—1955), Roddam, Selby's Forest (1894—1955), Undivided Moor Common to Kirknewton and Lanton (1894—1955), Westnewton (1894—1955), Wooler, Wooperton (1894—1955), Yeavering (1894—1955)

GOSFORTH UD (1895[35]—1974)

Coxlodge (1895—1908), Gosforth (1908—74), South Gosforth (1895—1908)

SOUTH GOSFORTH UD (1894—95[35])

Coxlodge, South Gosforth

HALTWHISTLE RD

Bardon Mill (1955—74), Bellister (1894—1955), Blenkinsopp (1894—1955), Coanwood, Featherstone, Greenhead (1955—74), Haltwhistle, Hartleyburn, Henshaw, Kirkhaugh (1894—1955), Knaresdale (1894—1955), Knaresdale with Kirkhaugh (1967—74), Lambley (1894—1955), Melkridge, Plenmeller (1894—1955), Plenmeller with Whitfield (1955—74), Ridley (1894—1955), Slaggyford (1955—67), Thirlwall, Thorngrafton (1894—1955), Wall Town (1894—1955), Whitfield (1894—1955)

HEXHAM RD

Acomb, West Allen (1897—1974), Allendale, Allendale Common, Aydon (1894—1955), Aydon Castle (1894—1955), Bearl (1894—1955), Bingfield (1894—1955), Black Carts and Ryehill (1894—1955), Blanchland (1955—74), Broomhaugh (1894—1955), Broomhaugh and Riding (1955—74), Broomley (1894—1955), Broomley and Stocksfield (1955—74), Bywell, Chollerton, Clarewood (1894—1955), Cocklaw (1894—1955), Corbridge, Dilston (1894—1955), Duke's Hagg (1894—1955), Eltringham (1894—1910), Espershields (1894—1955), Fallowfield (1894—1955), High Fotherley, Hallington (1894—1955), Halton (1894—1955), Haughton (1894—1955), Haydon, Healey, Hedley, Hexhamshire (1955—74), Hexhamshire High Quarter (1894—1955), Hexhamshire Low Quarter (1894—1955), Hexhamshire Middle Quarter (1894—1955), Hexhamshire West Quarter (1894—1955), Horsley, Humshaugh, Mickley (1894—1910); pt Moorland Common to Hexham and to Hexhamshire High Quarter, Hexhamshire Low Quarter, Hexhamshire Middle Quarter, Hexhamshire West Quarter (1894—1955); Nafferton (1894—1955), Newbrough, Newlands (1894—1955), Newton (1894—1955), Newton Hall (1894—1955), Ovingham, Ovington, Portgate (1894—1955), Prudhoe (1894—1910), Prudhoe Castle (1894—1910), Riding (1894—1955), Sandhoe, Shotley High Quarter (1894—1955), Shotley Low Quarter, Simonburn, Slaley, Spital (1894—1955), Stelling (1894—1955), Styford (1894—1955), Thornborough (1894—1955), Wall, Warden, Welton (1894—1955), Whittington (1955—74), Great Whittington (1894—1955), Little Whittington (1894—1955), Whittle (1894—1955), Whittonstall (1894—1955), Wylam

HEXHAM UD[36]

Hexham, pt Moorland Common to Hexham and to Hexhamshire High Quarter, Hexhamshire Low Quarter, Hexhamshire Middle Quarter, Hexhamshire West Quarter (1894—1955)

LONGBENTON UD (1912[37]—74)

Longbenton

MORPETH RD

High Angerton (1894—1955), Low Angerton (1894—1955), Ashington and Sheepwash (1894—96), Benridge (1894—1955), Bigge's Quarter (1894—1955), Bockenfield (1894—1955), Bothal Demesne (1894—1935), Bullock's Hall (1894—1955), Cambo (1894—1955), Causey Park (1894—1955), East Chevington, West Chevington, Cockle Park (1894—1955), Corridge (1894—1955), Cresswell, Deanham (1894—1955), Earsdon (1894—1955), Earsdon Forest (1894—1955),

Edington (1894—1955), Ellington, Eshott (1894—1955), Fenrother (1894—1955), Freeholders' Quarter (1894—1955), Hadston (1894—1955), Hartburn, Hartburn Grange (1894—1955), Hebron, Hepscott, Highlaws (1894—1955), High and Low Highlaws (1894—1955), Hirst (1894—96), Horsley Moor (1894—1955), Long Horsley Common (1894—1955), Longhirst, Longhorsley (1955—74), Longshaws (1894—1955), Longwitton (1894—1955), Lynmouth, Meldon, North Middleton (1894—1955), South Middleton (1894—1955), Mitford, Molsedon (1894—1935), Morpeth Castle (1894—1935), Netherwitton, Newminster (1894—1935), Newton Park (1894—1955), Newton Underwood (1894—1955), Nunriding (1894—1955), Old Moor (1894—1955), Pegswood, Pigdon (1894—1955), Riddell's Quarter (1894—1955), Rivergreen (1894—1955), North Seaton (1894—1935), Sheepwash (1896—1935), Spital Hill (1894—1955), Stanton (1894—1955), Thirston (1955—74), Thirston (with Shothaugh) (1935—55), East and West Thirston with Shothaugh (1894—1935), East Thornton (1894—1955), West Thornton (1894—1955), Throphill (1894—1955), Todridge (1894—1955), Tranwell (1894—1955), Tritlington, Ulgham, Wallington Demesne, Whitridge (1894—1955), Widdrington, Witton Shields (1894—1955), Woodhorn (1894—1935), Woodhorn Demesne (1894—1913)

NEWBIGGIN BY THE SEA UD

Newbiggin by the Sea, Woodhorn Demesne (1913—74)

NEWBURN UD

East Denton (1894—1935), West Denton (1894—1935), Newburn, Newburn Hall (1894—1935), Sugley (1894—1935), Throckley (1894—1935), Wallbottle (1894—1935)

NEWCASTLE RD (1935[7]—74)

Moot Hall Precinct

NORHAM AND ISLANDSHIRES RD

Ancroft, Cornhill on Tweed, Duddo, Felkington (1894—1955), Grindon (1894—1955), Holy Island, Horncliffe, Kyloe, Loanend (1894—1955), Longridge (1894—1955), Norham, Norham Mains (1894—1955), Ord, Shoreswood, Thornton (1894—1955), Twizell (1894—1955)

PRUDHOE UD (1910[38]—74)

Eltringham, Mickley, Prudhoe, Prudhoe Castle

ROTHBURY RD

Alnham, Alwinton, Barrow (1894—1955), Bickerton (1894—1955), Biddlestone, Brinkburn (1955—74), Brinkburn High Ward (1894—1955), Brinkburn Low Ward (1894—1955), Burradon (1894—1955), Caistron (1894—1935), Callaly (1955—74), Callaly and Yetlington (1894—1955), Cartington, Clennell (1894—1955), Coatyards (1894—1955), Debdon (1896—1955), Elsdon, Ewesley (1894—1955), Fairhaugh (1894—1955), Fairnley (1894—1955), Fallowlees (1894—1955), Farnham (1894—1955), Flotterton (1894—1955), Greenleighton (1894—1955), Harbottle, Hartington (1894—1955), Hartington Hall (1894—1955), Harwood (1894—1955), Healey and Combhill (1894—1955), Hepple, Hesleyhurst, Hollinghill, Holystone (1894—1955), Intermixed Lands Common to Rothbury and Snitter, Kidland (1894—1955), Linbridge (1894—1955), Linsheeles (1894—1955), Longframlington, Lorbottle (1894—1955), Monkridge (1894—1955), Mount Healey (1894—1955), Netherton (1955—74), Netherton North Side (1894—1955), Netherton South Side (1894—1955), Newtown (1894—1955), Nunnykirk, Peels (1894—1955), Prendwick (1894—1955), Raw (1894—1955), Ritton Colt Park (1894—1955), Ritton White House (1894—1955), Rothbury (1894—96), Rothbury (1935—74), Rothley, Great Ryle (1894—1955), Little Ryle (1894—1955), Scrainwood (1894—1955), Sharperton (1894—1955), Snitter, Thropton, Todburn (1894—1955), Tosson, High and Low Trewitt (1894—1955), Unthank (1894—1955), Warton (1894—1955), Whittingham, Whitton (1894—1955), Wingates (1894—1955), Woodside (1894—1955), Wreighill (1894—1955)

ROTHBURY UD (1896[39]—1935[7])
  Rothbury
SEATON DELAVAL UD (1912[37]—35[7])
  Seaton Delaval
SEATON VALLEY UD (1935[7]—74)
  Seaton Valley

SEGHILL UD (1894—1935[7])
  Seghill
TYNEMOUTH RD (1894—1912[37])
  Backworth (1894—97), Bebside, Burradon, Camperdown (1899—1912), Earsdon (1894—97), East Hartford, West Hartford, Hartley, Horton, Holywell (1894—97), Longbenton, Murton (1894—97), Seaton Delaval, Willington (1894—1910)
WALKER UD (1894—1904[6])
  Walker
WALLSEND UD (1894—1901[21])
  Wallsend
WEETSLADE UD (1894[40]—1935[7])
  pt Longbenton (1894), Weetslade (1894—1935)
WHITLEY AND MONKSEATON UD (1894—1944[41])
  Monkseaton (1894—1913), Whitley (1894—1913), Whitley and Monkseaton (1913—44)
WHITLEY BAY UD (1944[41]—54[23])
  Whitley and Monkseaton
WILLINGTON QUAY UD (1894—1910[42])
  Willington Quay

NON-METROPOLITAN COUNTY

As constituted 1 Apr 1974, defined in terms of Adm Co units as of 31 Mar.

ALNWICK DIST
  Alnwick RD, Alnwick UD, Amble UD, Rothbury RD
BERWICK-UPON-TWEED DIST
  Belford RD, Berwick upon Tweed MB, Glendale RD, Norham and Islandshires RD
BLYTH VALLEY DIST
  Blyth MB, pt Seaton Valley UD,[43] pt Whitley Bay MB[44]
CASTLE MORPETH DIST
  pt Castle Ward RD (Belsay, Capheaton, Heddon on the

Wall, Matfen, Ponteland, Stamfordham, Stannington, Whalton), Morpeth MB, Morpeth RD
TYNEDALE DIST
  Bellingham RD, Haltwhistle RD, Hexham RD, Hexham UD, Prudhoe UD
WANSBECK DIST
  Ashington UD, Bedlingtonshire UD, Newbiggin by the Sea UD

NOTTINGHAMSHIRE

ALTERATIONS IN COUNTY BOUNDARIES

As noted by year below, Notts pars gained territory from or lost it to pars in adjoining cos or county boroughs, or were entirely transferred to them. Details of these alterations are noted in Part I of the *Guide* under Nottinghamshire.

ANCIENT COUNTY (until 1889: Waps, Bors, MBs, PLUs, RSDs, USDs)

1866 Blyth, Finningley. *1884* Laneham. *1886* Misson.

ADMINISTRATIVE COUNTY (1889—1974: Waps,[1] PLUs, MBs, RDs, UDs, with assoc CB of Nottingham CB)

1889 Basford, Brewhouse Yard, West Bridgford, Bulwell, Carlton, Lenton, Nottingham St Mary, Nottingham St Nicholas, Nottingham St Peter, Radford, Sneinton, Standard Hill, Wilford. *1895* Auckley, Bole, West Burton, Kirkby in Ashfield, Pinxton, Wallingwells. *1933* Arnold, Beeston, Bestwood Park, Bilborough, Colwick, Wollaton. *1952* West Bridgford, Clifton with Glapton, Ruddington. *1965* Upper Broughton, Willoughby on the Wolds.

NON-METROPOLITAN COUNTY (from 1974: Dists)

1974 Finningley, Harworth.

ASSOCIATED COUNTY BOROUGH AND COUNTY OF ITSELF

NOTTINGHAM CO OF ITSELF (from 1448), CB
Bdry: 1899,[2] 1933,[3] 1952.[4] Transf 1974 to Notts.[5]

WAPENTAKES[1]

BASSETLAW WAP

Askham, pt Auckley (from 1866), Babworth, Barnby Moor (from 1866), Beckingham, Bevercotes, Bilsthorpe, Blyth (pt until 1866, ent from 1866), Bole, Bothamsall, Boughton, Budby (from 1866), West Burton, Carburton (from 1866), Carlton in Lindrick, Clarborough,[6] Clayworth, Clipstone (from 1866), Cottam (from 1866), Cuckney (from 1866), Norton Cuckney (until 1866), Darlton, East Drayton, West Drayton, Dunham, Eakring, Eaton, Edwinstowe, Egmanton, Elkesley, Everton, Finningley (pt until 1866, ent from 1866), Gamston, Gringley on the Hill, Grove, Habblesthorpe (until 1884), Harworth, Haughton, Hayton, Headon cum Upton, Hodsock (from 1866), Holbeck (from 1866), Kirton, pt Kneesall (until 1866), Laneham, Nether Langwith (from 1866), Laxton, North Leverton (until 1884), North Leverton with Habblesthorpe (from 1884), South Leverton, Littleborough, Lound (from 1866), East Markham, Markham Clinton or West Markham, Mattersey, Misson (pt until 1886, ent from 1886), Misterton, Norton (from 1866), Ollerton (from 1866), Ompton (from 1866), Ordsall,[6] Perlethorpe (from 1866), Ragnall, Rampton, Ranskill (from 1866), East Retford,[6] West Retford,[6] Rufford (from 1858), Saundby, Scaftworth (from 1866), Scrooby, Sookholme (from 1866), West Stockwith (from 1866), Stokeham, Sturton le Steeple, Styrrup (from 1866), Sutton (from 1866), Sutton cum Lound (until 1866), Torworth (from 1866), Treswell, Tuxford, Walesby, Walkeringham, pt Wallingwells (from 1858), Welbeck (from 1858), Warsop, Wellow, North Wheatley, South Wheatley, Wiseton (from 1866), Woodhouse Hall (from 1858), Worksop

BINGHAM WAP

Aslockton (from 1866), Bingham, East Bridgford, West Bridgford,[6] Upper Broughton, Clipston (from 1866), Car Colston, Colston Bassett, Cotgrave, Cropwell Bishop, Cropwell Butler (from 1866), Elton, Flintham, Gamston (from 1866), Granby, Hawksworth, Hickling, Holme Pierrepont, Kinoulton, Kneeton, Langar cum Barnstone, Lodge on the Wolds (from 1858), Orston, Owthorpe, Plumtree (pt until 1866, ent from 1866), Radcliffe on Trent, Saxondale (from 1866), Scarrington, Screveton, Shelford, Thoroton, Tithby, Tollerton, Whatton, Wiverton Hall (from 1858)

BROXTOWE WAP

Annesley, Arnold, Attenborough (until 1866), Basford,[6] Beeston, Bestwood Park (from 1877), Bilborough, Blidworth, Bramcote, Brewhouse Yard[6] (from 1858), Bulwell,[6] Chilwell (from 1866), Cossall, Eastwood, Felley (from 1858), Fulwood (from 1858), Greasley, Hucknall Torkard, Hucknall under Huthwaite (from 1866), Kirkby in Ashfield, Lenton,[6] Linby, Mansfield,[6] Mansfield Woodhouse, Newstead (from 1858), Nuthall, Papplewick, Radford,[6] Selston, Skegby, Standard Hill[6] (from 1858), Stapleford, Strelley, Sutton in Ashfield, Teversal, Toton (from 1866), Trowell, Wollaton

NEWARK WAP

Alverton (from 1866), Balderton, Barnby in the Willows, Besthorpe (from 1866), Broadholme (from 1866), North Clifton, South Clifton (from 1866), Coddington, North Collingham, South Collingham, Cotham, Elston, Farndon, Flawborough (from 1866), Girton, Harby (from 1866), Hawton, Kilvington,

726

Langford, Newark upon Trent,[6] South Scarle, Shelton, Sibthorpe, Spalford (from 1866), Staunton, pt East Stoke (until 1866), Syerston, Thorney, Thorpe, Wigsley (from 1866), Winthorpe

RUSHCLIFFE WAP

Barton in Fabis, Bradmore, Bunny, Clifton with Glapton, Costock, Edwalton, Gotham, Keyworth, Kingston on Soar, East Leake, West Leake, Normanton on Soar, Normanton on the Wolds (from 1866), pt Plumtree (until 1866), Ratcliffe on Soar, Rempstone, Ruddington, Stanford on Soar, Stanton on the Wolds, Sutton Bonington,[7] Thorpe in the Glebe, Thrumpton, Widmerpool, Wilford,[6] Willoughby on the Wolds, Wysall

SOUTHWELL AND SCROOBY LBTY (until 1836/37)

(did not affect parochial organisation in Bassetlaw, Thurgarton Hds; tps and other units within pars usually incl [see Part I of the *Guide*]) Askham, Beckingham, Bleasby, Blidworth, Edingley, Everton, Farnsfield, Halam, Halloughton, Hayton, Kirklington, Laneham, Morton, Scrooby, Southwell, Sutton cum Lound, Upton, Woodborough

THURGARTON WAP

Averham, Bathley (from 1866), Bleasby, Bulcote (from 1866), Burton Joyce, Calverton, Carlton (from 1866), Carlton on Trent (from 1866), Caunton, Caythorpe (from 1866), Colwick, Cromwell, Edingley, Elston (from 1866), Epperstone, Farnsfield, Fiskerton (1866—84), Fiskerton cum Morton (from 1884), Fledborough, Gedling, Gonalston, Grassthorpe (from 1866), Gunthorpe (from 1866), Halam, Halloughton, Haywood Oaks (from 1858), Hockerton, Holme, Hoveringham, Kelham, Kersall (from 1866), Kirklington, Kneesall (pt until 1866, ent from 1866), Lambley, Lindhurst (from 1858), Lowdham, Maplebeck, Marnham, Meering (from 1858), Morton (until 1884), North Muskham, South Muskham, Normanton on Trent, Norwell, Norwell Woodhouse (from 1866), Ossington, Oxton, Park Leys (from 1858), Rolleston, Sneinton,[6] Southwell, Staythorpe (from 1866), East Stoke[6] (pt until 1866, ent from 1866), Stoke Bardolph (from 1866), Sutton on Trent, Thurgarton, Upton, Weston, Winkburn, Woodborough

BOROUGHS

Units with some degree of burghal character[8] are denominated 'Bor'. Those which did not sustain that status until the 19th cent are in italics. MBs were established by the Municipal Corporations Act, 1835,[9] or by later charter.

MANSFIELD MB (1891[10]—1974)

Mansfield (pt 1891—94, ent 1894—1974)

NEWARK UPON TRENT BOR/NEWARK MB

Newark upon Trent (ent until 1884, pt 1884—94, ent 1894—1974), pt East Stoke (until 1877)

NOTTINGHAM BOR/MB[11]/CB

Basford (1877—99), Brewhouse Yard (1877—97), pt West Bridgford (1877—94), Bulwell (1877—99), pt Carlton (1877—94), Lenton (pt 1877—94, ent 1894—97), Nottingham St Mary,[12] Nottingham St Nicholas, Nottingham St Peter, Radford (1877—97), pt Wilford (1877—94), North Wilford (1894—97)

[EAST] RETFORD BOR/EAST RETFORD MB[13]

pt Clarborough (1878—94), Ordsall (1878—1921), East Retford, North Retford (1894—1921), West Retford (1878—1921)

WORKSOP MB (1931[14]—74)

Worksop

POOR LAW UNIONS

In Notts Poor Law County:[15]

BASFORD PLU (Notts, Derbys)

Annesley, Arnold, Awsworth (1894—1930), Barton in Fabis, Basford (1836—99), Beeston, Bestwood Park (1877—1930), Bilborough, Bradmore, West Bridgford, Brinsley (1896—1930), Bulwell (1836—99), Bunny, Burton Joyce, Calverton, Carlton, Clifton with Glapton, Colwick, Cossall, Eastwood, Felley, Gamston, Gedling, Gotham, Greasley, Hucknall Torkard, Kimberley (1896—1930), Kirkby in Ashfield, Lambley, Linby, Newstead, Nuthall, Papplewick, Ruddington, Selston, Standard Hill (1862—97), Stoke Bardolph, Strelley, Thrumpton, Trowell, Wilford (1836—94), North Wilford (1894—97), South Wilford (1894—1930), Wollaton, Woodborough

BINGHAM PLU (Notts, Leics)

Aslockton, Barnston cum Langar, Bingham, East Bridgford, Clipston, Car Colston, Colston Bassett, Cotgrave, Cropwell Bishop, Cropwell Butler, Edwalton, Elton, Flawborough, Flintham, Granby, Hawksworth, Hickling, Holme Pierrepont, Keyworth, Kinoulton, Kneeton, Langar cum Barnstone, Lodge on the Wolds (1858—96), Normanton on the Wolds, Orston, Owthorpe, Plumtree, Radcliffe on Trent, Saxondale, Scarrington, Screveton, Shelford, Shelton, Sibthorpe, Stanton on the Wolds, Tithby, Thoroton, Tollerton, Whatton, Widmerpool, Wiverton Hall (1858—1930)

MANSFIELD PLU (Notts, Derbys)

Blidworth, Fulwood (1861—1930), Haywood Oaks (1861—1930), Hucknall under Huthwaite, Lindhurst (1861—1930), Mansfield, Mansfield Woodhouse, Pinxton,[16] Skegby, Sookholme, Sutton in Ashfield, Teversal, Warsop

NEWARK PLU (Notts, Leics)

Alverton, Balderton, Barnby in the Willows, Besthorpe, Broadholme (soon after 1836[17]—1930), North Clifton (soon after 1836[17]—1930), South Clifton, Coddington, North Collingham, South Collingham, Cotham, Farndon, Flawford[18] (1866—84), Girton,

Harby (soon after 1836[17]—1930), Hawton, Kilvington, Langford, Meering (1858—1930), West Newark (1894—1930), Newark upon Trent, South Scarle, Spalford, Staunton, Thorney (soon after 1836[17]—1930), Wigsley (soon after 1836[17]—1930), Winthorpe

NOTTINGHAM PLU (1836—97), PAR (1897—1930)
Nottingham (1897—1930), Nottingham St Mary (1836—97), Nottingham St Nicholas (1836—97), Nottingham St Peter (1836—97)

RADFORD PLU (1836—97)
Brewhouse Yard, Lenton, Radford, Sneinton

EAST RETFORD PLU
Askham, Babworth, Barnby Moor, Bevercotes, Bothamsall, Clarborough, Clayworth, Cottam, Darlton, East Drayton, West Drayton, Dunham, Eaton, Elkesley, Everton, Fledborough, Gamston, Gringley on the Hill, Grove, Habblesthorpe (1836—84), Haughton, Hayton, Headon cum Upton, Laneham, North Leverton (1836—84), North Leverton with Habblesthorpe (1884—1930), South Leverton, Littleborough, Lound, East Markham, Markham Clinton or West Markham, Marnham, Mattersey, Normanton on Trent, Ordall (1836—1921), Ragnall, Rampton, Ranskill, East Retford, North Retford (1894—1921), West Retford (1836—1921), Scaftworth, Scrooby, Stokeham, Sturton le Steeple, Sutton, Torworth, Treswell, Tuxford, North Wheatley, South Wheatley, Wiseton

SOUTHWELL PLU
Averham, Bathley, Bilsthorpe, Bleasby, Boughton, Budby (1836—99), Bulcote, Carlton on Trent, Caunton, Caythorpe, Clipstone, Cromwell, Eakring, Edingley, Edwinstowe, Egmanton, Elston, Epperstone, Farnsfield, Fiskerton (1836—84), Fiskerton cum Morton (1884—1930), Gonalston, Grassthorpe, Gun-

thorpe, Halam, Halloughton, Hockerton, Holme, Hoveringham, Kelham, Kersall, Kirklington, Kirton, Kneesall, Laxton, Lowdham, Maplebeck, Morton (1836—84), North Muskham, South Muskham, Norwell, Norwell Woodhouse, Ollerton, Ompton, Ossington, Oxton, Park Leys (1858—99), Perlethorpe (1836—99), Perlethorpe cum Budby (1899—1930), Rolleston, Rufford, Southwell, Staythorpe, East Stoke, Sutton on Trent, Syerston, Thorpe, Thurgarton, Upton, Walesby, Wellow, Weston, Winkburn

WORKSOP PLU (Notts, Derbys, Yorks W Riding)
Blyth,[19] Carburton, Carlton in Lindrick, Cuckney, Harworth, Hodsock, Holbeck, Nether Langwith, Norton, Styrrup, Wallingwells[20] (1862—1930), Welbeck (1862—1930), Woodhouse Hall (1862—1930), Worksop

In Other Poor Law Counties:

DONCASTER PLU (Yorks W Riding, Notts [1837—95], Lincs Pts Lind [1837—86])
Auckley,[21] Finningley,[22] Misson[23]

GAINSBOROUGH PLU (Lincs Pts Lind, Notts)
Beckingham, Bole, West Burton, Misterton, Saundby, West Stockwith, Walkeringham

LOUGHBOROUGH PLU (Leics, Notts)
Costock, East Leake, West Leake, Normanton on Soar, Rempstone, Stanford on Soar, Sutton Bonington, Thorpe in the Glebe, Willoughby on the Wolds, Wysall

MELTON MOWBRAY PLU (Leics, Notts)
Upper Broughton

SHARDLOW PLU (Derbys, Leics, Notts)
Bramcote, Chilwell, Kingston on Soar, Ratcliffe on Soar, Stapleford, Toton

SANITARY DISTRICTS

ARNOLD USD
Arnold

BASFORD RSD
same as PLU less Arnold, Basford (1877—94), Beeston, pt West Bridgford (1877—94), Bulwell (1877—94), pt Carlton (1877—94), Hucknall Torkard, Standard Hill (1877—94), pt Wilford (1877—94)

BEESTON USD
Beeston

BINGHAM RSD
same as PLU

WEST BRIDGFORD USD (1891[24]—94)
pt West Bridgford

CARLTON USD (1881[25]—94)
pt Carlton

DONCASTER RSD
same as PLU for Notts pars

GAINSBOROUGH RSD
same as PLU for Notts pars

HUCKNALL TORKARD USD
Hucknall Torkard

HUCKNALL UNDER HUTHWAITE USD[26]
pt Fulwood (1883—94), Hucknall under Huthwaite

LOUGHBOROUGH RSD
same as PLU

MANSFIELD RSD
same as PLU less pt Fulwood (1883—94), Hucknall under Huthwaite, Mansfield, Mansfield Woodhouse, Sutton in Ashfield, Warsop

MANSFIELD USD
Mansfield

MANSFIELD WOODHOUSE USD
Mansfield Woodhouse

MELTON MOWBRAY RSD
same as PLU for the Notts par

NEWARK RSD
same as PLU less Newark upon Trent (ent 1875—84, pt 1884—94)

NEWARK UPON TRENT USD
Newark upon Trent (ent 1875—84, pt 1884—94), pt East Stoke (1875—77)

NOTTINGHAM USD
Basford (1877—94), Brewhouse Yard (1877—94), pt West Bridgford (1877—94), Bulwell (1877—94), pt Carlton (1877—94), pt Lenton (1877—94), Nottingham St Mary, Nottingham St Nicholas, Nottingham St Peter, Radford (1877—94), Sneinton (1877—94), Standard Hill (1877—94), pt Wilford (1877—94)

RADFORD RSD
same as PLU less Brewhouse Yard (1877—94), pt Lenton (1877—94), Radford (1877—94), Sneinton (1877—94)

EAST RETFORD RSD
same as PLU less pt Clarborough, Ordsall, East Retford, West Retford

EAST RETFORD USD
pt Clarborough, Ordsall, East Retford, West Retford

SHARDLOW RSD
same as PLU for Notts pars

SOUTHWELL RSD
same as PLU for Notts pars less pt East Stoke (1875—77)

SUTTON IN ASHFIELD USD
Sutton in Ashfield

WARSOP USD
Warsop

WORKSOP RSD
same as PLU less Worksop

WORKSOP USD
Worksop

ADMINISTRATIVE COUNTY

For MBs and the associated CB see BOROUGHS.

ARNOLD UD
Arnold

BASFORD RD
Annesley, Awsworth, Barton in Fabis, Bestwood Park, Bilborough (1894—1933), Bradmore, Brinsley (1896—1974), Bunny, Burton Joyce, Calverton, Clifton with Glapton (1894—1952), Colwick (1894—1935), Cossall, Costock (1935—74), Eastwood (1894—96), Felley, Gamston (1894—1935), Gedling (1894—1935), Gotham, Greasley, Kimberley (1896—1974), Kingston on Soar (1935—74), Kirkby in Ashfield (1894—96), Lambley, East Leake (1935—74), West Leake (1935—74), Linby, Newstead, Normanton on Soar (1935—74), Nuthall, Papplewick, Ratcliffe on Soar (1935—74), Rempstone (1935—74), Ruddington, Selston, Stanford on Soar (1935—74), Stoke Bardolph, Strelley, Sutton Bonington (1935—74), Thorpe in the Glebe (1935—74), Thrumpton, Trowell, South Wilford (1894—1935), Willoughby on the Wolds (1935—74), Wollaton (1894—1933), Woodborough, Wysall (1935—74)

BEESTON UD (1894—1935[27])
Beeston

BEESTON AND STAPLEFORD UD (1935[27]—74)
Beeston and Stapleford

BINGHAM RD
Aslockton, Bingham, East Bridgford, Upper Broughton, Clipston, Car Colston, Colston Bassett, Cotgrave, Cropwell Bishop, Cropwell Butler, Edwalton (1894—1935), Elton, Flawborough, Flintham, Gamston (1935—74), Granby, Hawksworth, Hickling, Holme Pierrepont, Keyworth, Kinoulton, Kneeton, Langar cum Barnstone, Lodge on the Wolds (1894—96), Normanton on the Wolds, Orston, Owthorpe, Plumtree, Radcliffe on Trent, Saxondale, Scarrington, Screveton, Shelford, Shelton, Sibthorpe, Stanton on the Wolds, Thoroton, Tithby, Tollerton, Whatton, Widmerpool, Wiverton Hall

BLYTH AND CUCKNEY RD (1894—1925[28])
Blyth, Carburton, Carlton in Lindrick, Cuckney, Harworth, Hodsock, Holbeck, Nether Langwith, Norton, Styrrup, Wallingwells (pt 1894—95, ent 1895—1925), Welbeck, Woodhouse Hall

WEST BRIDGFORD UD
West Bridgford

EASTWOOD UD (1896[29]—1974)
Eastwood

CARLTON UD
Carlton

EASTWOOD UD (1896[30]—1974)
Eastwood

HUCKNALL UD (1916[31]—74)
Hucknall Torkard

HUCKNALL TORKARD UD (1894—1916[31])
Hucknall Torkard

HUCKNALL UNDER HUTHWAITE UD (1894—1907[32])
pt Fulwood (1894—96), Hucknall under Huthwaite

HUTHWAITE UD (1907[32]—35[27])
Hucknall under Huthwaite

KIRKBY IN ASHFIELD UD (1896[33]—1974)
Kirkby in Ashfield

LEAKE RD[31] (1894—1935[27])
Costock, Kingston on Soar (1927—35), East Leake, West Leake, Normanton on Soar, Ratcliffe on Soar (1927—35), Rempstone, Stanford on Soar, Sutton Bonington, Thorpe in the Glebe, Willoughby on the Wolds, Wysall

MANSFIELD WOODHOUSE UD
Mansfield Woodhouse

MISTERTON RD (1894—1935[27])
Beckingham, Bole, West Burton, Misterton, Saundby, West Stockwith, Walkeringham

NEWARK RD
Alverton, Balderton, Barnby in the Willows, Besthorpe, Broadholme, North Clifton, South Clifton, Coddington, Collingham (1970—*), North Collingham (1894—1970), South Collingham (1894—1970), Cotham, Elston (1935—74), Farndon, Girton, Harby, Hawton, Holme (1935—74), Kilvington, Langford, Meering, West Newark (1894—1935), South Scarle, Spalford, Staunton, East Stoke (1935—74), Syerston (1935—74), Thorney, Thorpe (1935—74), Wigsley, Winthorpe

EAST RETFORD RD
Askham, Babworth, Barnby Moor, Beckingham (1935—74), Bevercotes, Bole (1935—74), Bothamsall, West Burton (1935—74), Clarborough, Clayworth, Cottam, Darlton, East Drayton, West Drayton, Dunham, Eaton, Elkesley, Everton, Finningley, Fledborough, Gamston, Gringley on the Hill, Grove, Haughton, Hayton, Headon cum Upton, Laneham, North Leverton with Habblesthorpe, South Leverton,

Littleborough (1894—1935), Lound, East Markham, Markham Clinton or West Markham, Marnham, Mattersey, Misson, Misterton (1935—74), Normanton on Trent, Ragnall, Rampton, Ranskill, Saundby (1935—74), Scaftworth, Scrooby, West Stockwith (1935—74), Stokeham, Sturton le Steeple, Sutton, Torworth, Treswell, Tuxford, Walkeringham (1935—74), North Wheatley, South Wheatley, Wiseton

SKEGBY RD (1894—1935[27])

Blidworth, Fulwood (pt 1894—96, ent 1896—1935), Haywood Oaks, Lindhurst, Skegby, Sookholme, Teversal

SOUTHWELL RD

Averham, Bathley, Bilsthorpe, Bleasby, Blidworth (1935—74), Boughton, Budby (1894—99), Bulcote, Carlton on Trent, Caunton, Caythorpe, Clipstone, Cromwell, Eakring, Edingley, Edwinstowe, Egmanton, Elston (1894—1935), Epperstone, Farnsfield, Fiskerton cum Morton, Gonalston, Grassthorpe, Gunthorpe, Halam, Halloughton, Haywood Oaks (1935—74), Hockerton, Holme (1894—1935), Hoveringham, Kelham, Kersall, Kirklington, Kirton, Kneesall, Laxton, Lindhurst (1935—74), Lowdham, Maplebeck, North Muskham, South Muskham,

Norwell, Norwell Woodhouse (1894—1935), Ollerton, Ompton, Ossington, Oxton, Park Leys (1894—99), Perlethorpe (1894—99), Perlethorpe cum Budby (1899—1974), Rolleston, Rufford, Southwell, Staythorpe, East Stoke (1894—1935), Sutton on Trent, Sutton on Trent, Syerston (1894—1935), Thorpe (1894—1935), Thurgarton, Upton, Walesby, Wellow, Weston, Winkburn

STAPLEFORD RD (1894—1935[27])

Bramcote, Chilwell, Stapleford, Toton

SUTTON IN ASHFIELD UD

Sutton in Ashfield

UNNAMED RD (1894—1927[34])

Kingston on Soar, Ratcliffe on Soar

WARSOP UD

Warsop

WORKSOP RD (1925[28]—74)

Blyth, Carburton, Carlton in Lindrick, Cuckney, Harworth, Hodsock, Holbeck, Nether Langwith, Norton, Styrrup (1925—51), Styrrup with Oldcotes (1951—74), Wallingwells, Welbeck, Woodhouse Hall (1925—35)

WORKSOP UD (1894—1931[14])

Worksop

NON-METROPOLITAN COUNTY

As consituted 1 Apr 1974, defined in terms of Adm Co units of of 31 Mar.

ASHFIELD DIST

pt Basford RD (Annesley, Felley, Selston), Hucknall UD, Kirkby in Ashfield UD, Sutton in Ashfield UD

BASSETLAW DIST

East Retford MB, East Retford RD (all except Finningley[35]), Worksop MB, Worksop RD (all except pt Harworth[35])

BROXTOWE DIST

pt Basford RD (Awsworth, Brinsley, Cossall, Greasley, Kimberley, Nuthall, Strelley, Trowell), Beeston and Stapleford UD, Eastwood UD

GEDLING DIST

Arnold UD, pt Basford RD (Bestwood Park, Burton Joyce, Calverton, Lambley, Linby, Newstead, Papplewick, Stoke Bardolph, Woodborough), Carlton UD

MANSFIELD DIST

Mansfield MB, Mansfield Woodhouse UD, Warsop UD

NEWARK DIST

Newark MB, Newark RD, Southwell RD

NOTTINGHAM DIST

CB (assoc with Notts): Nottingham CB
from Notts: Nottingham Shire Hall

RUSHCLIFFE DIST

pt Basford RD (the pars neither in Ashfield Dist nor in Broxtowe Dist), Bingham RD, West Bridgford UD

SOKE OF PETERBOROUGH

For MB see BOROUGHS in entries for Northants.

(Soke of Peterborough Adm Co abol 1965 to help cr Hunts and Peterborough Adm Co [see *Guide*, Vol I])

BARNACK RD
Bainton, Barnack, St Martin Without,[1] Southorpe, Thornhaugh, Ufford, Walton (1894—1929), Wansford, Wittering, Wothorpe

PETERBOROUGH RD
Ailsworth, Borough Fen, Castor, Deeping Gate, Etton, Eye, Glinton, Gunthorpe (1894—1929), Helpston, Longthorpe (1908—29), Marholm, Maxey, Newborough, Northborough, Paston (1894—1929), Peakirk, Peterborough Without (1894—1929), Sutton, Upton, Walton (1894—1929), Werrington (1894—1929)

RUTLAND

ALTERATIONS IN COUNTY BOUNDARIES

As noted by year below, Rutl pars gained territory from or lost it to pars in adjoining cos, or were entirely transferred to them. Details of these alterations are noted in Part I of the *Guide* under Rutland.

ANCIENT COUNTY (until 1889: Hds, Soke, Bors, PLUs, RSDs)
1885 Stoke Dry, Thorpe by Water. *1887* Essendine.

ADMINISTRATIVE COUNTY (1889—1974: Hds,[1] PLUs, RDs, UDs)
No bdry alt.

(All Rutl pars transf 1974 to Leics)

HUNDREDS AND SOKE[1]

ALSTOW HD
Ashwell, Barrow (from 1866), Burley, Cottesmore, Exton, Greetham, Horn, Market Overton, Stretton, Teigh, Thistleton, Whissendine, Whitwell

EAST HD
Great Casterton, Little Casterton, Empingham, Essendine, Ketton, Pickworth, Ryhall, Tickencote, Tinwell

MARTINSTLEY HD
Ayston, Beaumont Chase (from 1858), Edith Weston, Hambleton, Lyndon, Manton, Martinsthorpe, Normanton, Preston, Ridlington, pt Uppingham, Wing

OAKHAM SOKE
Belton, Braunston, Brooke, Clipsham, Egleton, Gunthorpe (from 1866), Langham, Leighfield (from 1858), Oakham[2] (until 1866), Oakham Deanshold with Barleythorpe (from 1866), Oakham Lordship (from 1866), Wardley

WRANGDYKE HD
Barrowden, Bisbrooke, Caldecott, Glaston, Liddington, North Luffenham, South Luffenham, Morcott, Pilton, Seaton, Stoke Dry[3] (pt until 1885, ent thereafter), Thorpe by Water[3] (pt 1866—85, ent thereafter), Tixover, pt Uppingham

BOROUGHS

Units with some degree of burghal character[4] are denominated 'Bor'.

OAKHAM BOR
pt Oakham

POOR LAW UNIONS

In Rutl Poor Law County:[5]
OAKHAM PLU (Rutl, Leics)
Ashwell, Barleythorpe (1894—1930), Barrow, Braunston, Brooke, Burley, Cottesmore, Edith Weston, Egleton, Empingham, Exton, Greetham, Gunthorpe, Hambleton, Horn, Langham, Leighfield (1861—1930), Lyndon, Manton, Martinsthorpe, Normanton, Oakham (1894—1930), Oakham (1894—1930), Oakham Deanshold with Barleythorpe (1836—94), Oakham Lordship (1836—94), Market Overton, Stretton, Teigh, Thistleton, Tickencote, Whissendine, Whitwell

UPPINGHAM PLU (Rutl, Leics, Northants)
Ayston, Barrowden, Beaumont Chase (1861—1930), Belton, Bisbrooke, Caldecott, Glaston, Liddington, North Luffenham, South Luffenham, Morcott, Pilton, Preston, Ridlington, Seaton, Stoke Dry,[3] Thorpe by Water,[3] Uppingham, Wardley, Wing

In Other Poor Law Counties:
STAMFORD PLU (Lincs Pts Kestev, Northants, Soke Peterb [1899—1830], Rutl, Hunts)
Great Casterton, Little Casterton, Clipsham, Essendine, Ketton, Pickworth, Ryhall, Tinwell, Tixover

SANITARY DISTRICTS

OAKHAM RSD
same as PLU for Rutl pars
STAMFORD RSD
same as PLU for Rutl pars

UPPINGHAM RSD
same as PLU for Rutl pars

ADMINISTRATIVE COUNTY

KETTON RD

Great Casterton, Little Casterton, Clipsham, Essendine, Ketton, Pickworth, Ryhall, Tinwell, Tixover

OAKHAM RD

Ashwell, Barleythorpe, Barrow, Braunston, Brooke, Burley, Cottesmore, Edith Weston, Egleton, Empingham, Exton, Greetham, Gunthorpe, Hambleton, Horn, Langham, Leighfield, Lyndon, Manton, Martinsthorpe, Normanton, Oakham (1894—1911), Market Overton, Stretton, Teigh, Thistleton, Tickencote, Whissendine, Whitwell

OAKHAM UD (1911[6]—74)

Oakham

UPPINGHAM RD

Ayston, Barrowden, Beaumont Chase, Belton, Bisbrooke, Caldecott, Glaston, Liddington, North Luffenham, South Luffenham, Morcott, Pilton, Preston, Ridlington, Seaton, Stoke Dry, Thorpe by Water, Uppingham, Wardley, Wing

SHROPSHIRE

ALTERATIONS IN COUNTY BOUNDARIES

As noted by year below, Salop pars gained territory from or lost it to pars in adjoining cos, or were entirely transferred to them. Details of these alterations are noted in Part I of the *Guide* under Salop.

ANCIENT COUNTY ([after the redefinitions of borders with the Marches of Wales 1536—1546[1]] until 1889: Hds, Bors, MBs, PLUs, RSDs, USDs)
1844 Halesowen, Llanymynech, Stottesdon. *1866* Alberbury, Bucknell, Clun, Churchstoke, Drayton in Hales, Hyssington, Leintwardine, Llansilin, Llanymnech, Lydham, Mainstone, Mucklestone, Pattingham, Sheriff Hales, Whitchurch, Worthen. *1884* Snead. *1886* Alberbury with Cardeston.

ADMINISTRATIVE COUNTY (1889—1974: Hds,[2] PLUs, MBs, RDs, UDs)
1889 Richard's Castle. *1894* Bucknell. *1895* Bobbington, Dowles, Leintwardine (North Side), Ludford, Sheriff Hales, Tittenley. *1936* Woodcote. *1965* Burford, Chetwynd, Market Drayton, Newport, Sheriff Hales, Sutton upon Turn, Whitchurch Urban.

NON-METROPOLITAN COUNTY (from 1974: Dists)
No bdry alt.

HUNDREDS[2]

After alts of bdry 1536—46 with Marches of Wales.[1]

ALBRIGHTON DIV (from 1836)
Albrighton (from 1866), Astley (from 1866), Battlefield, Broughton, Clive (from 1866), Fitz, Grinshill, Hadnall (from 1866), Haughton Demesne (from 1858), pt Myddle (1836—66), Preston Gubbals, pt Shrewsbury St Alkmund[3] (from 1836), pt Shrewsbury St Chad[3] (from 1836), pt Shrewsbury St Mary[3] (1836—66), Uffington

NORTH BRADFORD HD
Adderley, Cheswardine, Drayton in Hales[3] (pt until 1866, ent from 1866), Child's Ercall, Hinstock, Hodnet, Ightfield, Lee Brockhurst, Moreton Corbet, Moreton Say, pt Mucklestone (until 1866), Norton in Hales, Prees, Shawbury (pt until 1836, ent from 1836), Stanton upon Hine Heath, Stoke upon Tern, pt Wem, Weston under Redcastle (from 1866), Whitchurch (pt until 1866, ent from 1866), Woore (from 1866)

SOUTH BRADFORD HD
Atcham, Bolas Magna, Buildwas, Cherrington (from 1866), Chetwynd, Chetwynd Aston (from 1866), Church Aston (from 1866), Dawley Magna, Eaton Constantine, Edgmond, Ercall Magna, Eyton on the Weald Moors, *Haughton Demesne[5]* (*until 1836*), Kinnersley, Leighton, Lilleshall, Longdon upon Tern, Longford, Newport,[3] Preston upon the Weald Moors, Rodington, pt Sheriff Hales, Stirchley, Tibberton (from 1866), Uffington (until 1836), Uppington, Waters Upton, Upton Magna, Wellington, Withington, Wombridge, Woodcote (from 1866), Wrockwardine, Wrockwardine Wood (from 1884), Wroxeter

BRIDGNORTH LBTY (until 1836)
pt Alveley, Bridgnorth St Leonard,[3] Bridgnorth St Mary Magdalene,[3] pt Quatford,[3] pt Quatt[3]

BRIMSTREE HD
Albrighton,[3] Badger (from 1836), Beckbury (from 1836), pt Bobbington, Boningale, Boscobel (from 1858), Claverley, Deuxhill (1836—by 1841), Don-ington, pt Halesowen (until 1844), Kemberton, Ryton, Shifnal,[3] Stockton, Sutton Maddock, Tong, Worfield

CHIRBURY HD[1]
Brompton and Riston (from 1866), Chirbury, pt Churchstoke (until 1866), pt Hyssington (until 1866), Mucklewick (1866—84), Shelve, Worthen (pt until 1866, ent from 1866)

CONDOVER HD
Acton Burnell,[3] Berrington, Condover, Cound, Cressage (from 1866), Frodesley, Harley, Kenley, Leebotwold, Longnor, Meole Brace[3] (from 1836), Pitchford, Church Preen, Church Pulverbatch, Ruckley and Langley (from 1866), pt Shrewsbury St Chad[3] (from 1836), pt Shrewsbury St Julian[3] (from 1836), Smethcott, Stapleton, Sutton (from 1836), Woolstaston

FORD HD
pt Alberbury (until 1866), Alberbury Lower Quarter (1866—86), Alberbury with Cardeston (from 1886), Bicton (from 1885), Cardeston (until 1886), Ford, Habberley, Great Hanwood (from 1836), Minsterley (from 1866), Pontesbury (pt until 1836, ent from 1836), pt Shrewsbury St Alkmund[3] (from 1836), pt Shrewsbury St Chad[3] (from 1836), pt Shrewsbury St Julian[3] (from 1836), Westbury,[3] Wollaston (from 1866)

MUNSLOW HD
Abdon, Acton Scott, Ashford Bowdler, pt Ashford Carbonell, pt Bitterley, Bromfield, Cardington, Clee St Margaret, Culmington, Diddlebury, Ditton Priors[3] (pt until 1836, ent from 1836), East Hamlet (from 1884), Easthope, Eaton under Haywood (from 1836), Halford (from 1866), Heath (from 1866), Holdgate, Hope Bowdler, Hopton Cangeford, pt Ludford, Ludlow [St Lawrence],[6] Ludlow Castle (from 1858), Munslow, Onibury, pt Richard's Castle,[3] Rushbury, Shipton[3] (from 1836), Stanton Lacy, Stanton Long, Stoke St Milborough (pt 1836—66, ent from 1866), Stokesay, Church Stretton, Tugford, Cold Weston, pt Wistanstow

OSWESTRY HD[1]

West Felton, Kinnerley, Knockin, pt Llansilin (until 1866), Llanyblodwel, Llanymynech (pt until 1866, ent from 1866), Melverley, Oswestry[3] (until 1866), Oswestry Rural (from 1866), Oswestry Town[3] (1866—80s), Oswestry Urban[3] (from 1880s), Ruyton of the Eleven Towns,[3] Selattyn, Sychtyn (from 1866), St Martin's, Whittington

OVERS HD

pt Bitterley, Boraston (from 1866), Burford,[3] Greete, Milson, Nash (from 1866), Neen Sollars, Silvington, Whitton (from 1866)

PIMHILL HD[1]

Baschurch,[3] Ellesmere[3] (pt until 1866, ent from 1866), Fitz (until 1836), Hordley, Loppington, Montford, Myddle (pt until 1866, ent from 1866), Great Ness, Little Ness (from 1866), Petton, pt Shawbury (until 1836), Shrawardine, pt Shrewsbury St Mary (until 1836), Welshampton, pt Wem

PURSLOW HD

Bedstone, Bettws y Crwyn, Bishop's Castle[3] (until 1866), Bishop's Castle[3] (from 1884), Bishop's Castle Borough[3] (1866—84), Bishop's Castle Out (1866—84), Bucknell (pt until 1866, ent from 1866), Clun,[3] Clunbury, Clungunford, Dinmore (1858—84), Edgton, Hill End (1858—84), Hopesay, Hopton Castle, Horderley Hall (1858—84), pt Leintwardine (until 1866), pt Leintwardine (North Side) (from 1866), Llanfair Waterdine, Lydbury North, Lydham[3] (pt until 1866, ent from 1866), Mainstone (pt until 1866, ent from 1866), More, Myndtown, Norbury, Old Church Moor (1858—84), Ratlinghope, Sibdon Carwood, pt Snead (until 1884), Stowe, Wentnor, pt Wistanstow

SHREWSBURY LBTY (until 1836)

Battlefield, Broughton, Grinshill, Great Hanwood, Meole Brace,[3] pt Myddle, pt Pontesbury, Preston Gubbals, pt Shawbury, Shrewsbury Holy Cross with St Giles,[3] Shrewsbury St Alkmund,[3] Shrewsbury St Chad,[3] Shrewsbury St Julian,[3] pt Shrewsbury St Mary,[3] Sutton

STOTTESDEN HD

Acton Round, Alveley[3] (pt until 1836, ent from 1866), pt Ashford Carbonell, Astley Abbots, Aston Botterell, Aston Eyre (from 1866), Billingsley, Burwarton, Caynham, Chelmarsh, Chetton, Cleobury Mortimer,[3] Cleobury North, Coreley, Deuxhill (by 1841), Dowles, Eardington (from 1866), Farlow[7] (from 1866), Glazeley, Highley, Hope Bagot, Hopton Wafers, Kinlet, Loughton (from 1866), Middleton Scriven, Morville, Neen Savage, Neenton, Oldbury, pt Pattingham (until 1866), pt Quatford[3] (until 1866), Quatt[3] (pt until 1835, ent 1835—66), Quatt Jarvis[3] (from 1866), Quatt Malvern (from 1866), Romsley (from 1866), Rudge (from 1866), Sheinton, Sidbury, Stottesdon[3] (pt until 1844, ent from 1844), Tasley, Upton Cressett, Wheathill, Woodhouse (from 1858)

WENLOCK FRANCHISE (until 1836)

Badger, Barrow,[3] Beckbury, Benthall,[3] Broseley,[3] Deuxhill, pt Ditton Priors,[3] Eaton under Haywood, Hughley,[3] Linley,[3] Madeley,[3] Monkhopton,[3] Posenhall,[3] Shipton,[3] pt Stoke St Milborough, Little Wenlock,[3] Much Wenlock,[3] Willey[3]

BOROUGHS[1]

Units with some degree of burghal character[8] are denominated 'Bor'. Those which did not sustain that status until the 19th cent are in italics. MBs were established by the Municipal Corporations Act, 1835,[9] or by later charter.

ACTON BURNELL BOR

Acton Burnell

ALBRIGHTON BOR

Albrighton

BASCHURCH BOR

Baschurch

BISHOP'S CASTLE BOR, MB (1885[10]—1967[11])

pt Bishop's Castle (until 1866), pt Bishop's Castle (1885—94), Bishop's Castle Borough (1866—84), Bishop's Castle Urban (1894—1967)

BRIDGNORTH BOR, MB (1835—1967[11])

pt Alveley (until 1836), Bridgnorth St Leonard, Bridgnorth St Mary Magdalene, Oldbury (1934—67), Quatford (pt 1101[12]—1866, ent 1866—1967), pt Quatt (until 1866), Quatt Jarvis (1866—1934)

BURFORD BOR

Burford

CAUS BOR

pt Westbury

CLEOBURY MORTIMER BOR

Cleobury Mortimer

CLUN BOR

pt Clun

MARKET DRAYTON BOR

pt Drayton in Hales

ELLESMERE BOR

pt Ellesmere

LUDLOW BOR/MB (1835—1967[11])

Ludlow [St Lawrence][6]

LYDHAM BOR

pt Lydham

MADELEY BOR

Madeley

NEWPORT BOR

Newport

OSWESTRY BOR, MB (1835—1967[11])

pt Oswestry (until 1866), Oswestry Town (1866—80s), Oswestry Urban (1880s—1967)

QUATFORD BOR (912—1101[12])

pt Quatford

RICHARD'S CASTLE BOR (Heref, Salop)

Richard's Castle[13]

RUYTON BOR

Ruyton of the Eleven Towns

SHIFNAL BOR

Shifnal

SHREWSBURY BOR[14]/MB
  pt Meole Brace (1835—85), Shrewsbury (1924—74), Shrewsbury Holy Cross with St Giles (1835—1924), pt Shrewsbury St Alkmund (until 1885), Shrewsbury St Chad (pt until 1885, ent 1885—1924), Shrewsbury St Julian (pt until 1885, ent 1885—1924), Shrewsbury St Mary (pt until 1885 [enlarged pt 1835—85], ent 1885—1924)

STOTTESDON BOR
  pt Stottesdon

WENLOCK MB—see following entry
MUCH WENLOCK BOR, WENLOCK MB[15] (1835—1966)
  Barrow, Benthall, Broseley, Ditton Priors (until 1889), Hughley (until 1889), Linley, Madeley (after Madeley Bor loses bor status—1966), Monkhopton (when gains sep civ identity—1889), Posenhall,[5] pt Shipton (until 1889), Little Wenlock, Much Wenlock, Willey

POOR LAW UNIONS

In Salop Poor Law County:[16]
ATCHAM PLU (Salop, Montg)
  Acton Burnell, Alberbury Lower Quarter (1836—86), Alberbury with Cardeston (1886—1930), Albrighton, Astley, Atcham, Battlefield, Berrington, Bicton (1885—1930), Buildwas (1895—1930), Cardeston (1836—86), Condover, Cound, Cressage, Eaton Constantine, Fitz, Ford, Frodesley, Habberley, Great Hanwood, Harley, Haughton Demesne (1858—85), Hughley, Kenley, Leighton, Melverley, Meole Brace (1871—1930), Minsterley, Montford, Pitchford, Pontesbury, Church Preen, Preston Gubbals, Church Pulverbatch, Ruckley and Langley, Sheinton, Shrawardine, Shrewsbury (1924—30), Shrewsbury Holy Cross with St Giles (1871—1924), Shrewsbury St Alkmund (1871—1930), Shrewsbury St Chad (1871—1924), Shrewsbury St Julian (1871—1924), Shrewsbury St Mary (1871—1924), Stapleton, Sutton, Uffington, Unnamed (1894—1901), Unnamed (1894—1901), Uppington, Upton Magna, Westbury, Withington, Woolaston, Wroxeter
BRIDGNORTH PLU
  Acton Round, Alveley, Astley Abbots, Aston Eyre, Billingsley, Bridgnorth St Leonard, Bridgnorth St Mary Magdalen, Burwarton, Chelmarsh, Chetton, Claverley, Cleobury North, Deuxhill, Ditton Priors, Eardington, Glazeley, Middleton Scriven, Monkhopton, Morville, Neenton, Oldbury, Quatford, Quatt (1836—soon after 1836[17]), Quatt Jarvis (soon after 1836[17]—1930), Quatt Malvern (soon after 1836[17]—1930), Romsley, Rudge (1895—1930), Sidbury, Stanton Long, Tasley, Upton Cressett, Worfield
CHURCH STRETTON PLU
  Acton Scott, Cardington, Easthope, Eaton under Haywood, Hope Bowdler, Leebotwold, Longnor, Rushbury, Shipton, Sibdon Carwood, Smethcott, All Stretton (1899—1930), Church Stretton, Little Stretton (1899—1930), Wistanstow, Woolstaston
CLEOBURY MORTIMER PLU (Salop, Worcs, Heref [1836—44])
  Aston Botterell, Cleobury Mortimer, Coreley, Farlow,[7] Highley, Hopton Wafers, Kinlet, Loughton, Milson, Neen Savage, Neen Sollars, Silvington, Stottesdon, Wheathill, Woodhouse (1862—1930)
CLUN PLU (Salop, Montg [1836—84])
  Bishop's Castle (1884—94), Bishop's Castle Borough (1836—84), Bishop's Castle Out (1836—84), Bishop's Castle Rural (1894—1930), Bishop's Castle Urban (1894—1930), Clun, Clunbury, Clungunford, Dinmore (1862—84), Edgton, Hill End (1862—84), Hopesay, Hopton Castle, Horderley Hall (1862—84), Lydbury North, Lydham,[18] Mainstone,[18] More, Mucklewick (soon after 1836[19]—84), Myndtown, Norbury, Old Church Moor (1862—84), Ratlinghope, Shelve, Snead,[20] Wentnor
DRAYTON PLU—see MARKET DRAYTON PLU
ELLESMERE PLU (Salop, Flints)
  Baschurch, Cockshutt (1896—1930), Ellesmere (1836—94), Ellesmere Rural (1894—1930), Ellesmere Urban (1894—1930), Hadnall, Hordley, Myddle, Great Ness, Little Ness, Petton, Welshampton
LUDLOW PLU[21] (Salop, Heref)
  Abdon, Ashford Bowdler, Ashford Carbonnell, Bitterley, Bromfield, Caynham, Clee St Margaret, Culmington, Diddlebury, East Hamlet (1884—1930), Halford, Heath, Holdgate, Hope Bagot, Hopton Cangeford, Leintwardine (North Side),[22] Ludford,[23] Ludlow [St Lawrence],[6] Ludlow Castle (1862—1901), Munslow, Onibury, Richard's Castle[13] (1836—89), Richard's Castle (1889[13]—1930), Stanton Lacy, Stoke St Milborough, Stokesay, Tugford, Cold Weston
MADELEY PLU
  Barrow, Benthall, Broseley, Buildwas (1836—95), Dawley Magna, Linley, Madeley, Posenhall, Stirchley, Little Wenlock, Much Wenlock, Willey
MARKET DRAYTON PLU (orig, 'DRAYTON') (Salop, Staffs)
  Adderley, Cheswardine, Market Drayton (1914—30), Drayton in Hales (1836—1914), Child's Ercall, Hinstock, Hodnet, Moreton Say, Norton in Hales, Stoke upon Tern, Sutton upon Tern (1914—30), Tittenley,[24] Woore
NEWPORT PLU (Salop, Staffs)
  Cherrington, Chetwynd (1836—94), Chetwynd Aston (1836—94), Chetwynd Aston Rural (1894—1930), Chetwynd Aston Urban (1894—96), Chetwynd Rural (1894—1930), Chetwynd Urban (1894—96), Church Aston (1836—94), Church Aston Rural (1894—1930), Church Aston Urban (1894—96), Edgmond, Lilleshall, Longford, Newport, St George's (1898—1930), Tibberton, Woodcote
OSWESTRY PLU (local act 1791)
  West Felton, Kinnerley, Knockin, Llanyblodwel, Llanymench,[25] Oswestry Rural, Oswestry Town (1791—1880s), Oswestry Urban (1880s—1930), Ruyton of the Eleven Towns, St Martin's, Selattyn, Sychtyn, Weston Rhyn (1897—1930), Whittington

SHIFNAL PLU (Salop, Staffs)
> Albrighton, Badger, Beckbury, Bobbington,[26] Boningale, Boscobel (1858—1930), Donington, Kemberton, Priorslee (1898—1930), Ryton, Sheriff Hales, Shifnal, Stockton, Sutton Maddock, Tong

SHREWSBURY INCORP (local act, 1784—1870)/PLU (1870—71)
> Meole Brace, Shrewsbury Holy Cross with St Giles, Shrewsbury St Alkmund, Shrewsbury St Chad, Shrewsbury St Julian, Shrewsbury St Mary

WELLINGTON PLU
> Bolas Magna, Ercall Magna, Eyton on the Weald Moors, Hadley (1898—1930), Kinnersley, Longdon upon Tern, Preston upon the Weald Moors, Rodington, Waters Upton, Wellington (1836—94), Wellington Rural (1894—1930), Wellington Urban (1894—1930), Wombridge, Wrockwardine, Wrockwardine Wood (1884—1930)

WEM PLU
> Broughton, Clive, Grinshill, Ightfield (1836—54), Lee Brockhurst, Loppington, Moreton Corbet, Prees, Shawbury, Stanton upon Hine Heath, Wem (1836—1900), Wem Rural (1900—30), Wem Urban (1900—30), Weston under Redcastle, Whixall (1894—1930)

WHITCHURCH INCORP (1792—1854) (Salop), PLU (1854—1930) (Salop, Ches, Flints)
> Ightfield (1854—1930), Whitchurch (1792—1894), Whitchurch Rural (1894—1930), Whitchurch Urban (1894—1930)

In Other Poor Law Counties:

BROMSGROVE PLU[27] (Worcs, Salop [1836—44], Warws, Staffs)
> Hunnington, Romsley

WEST BROMWICH PLU[27] (Staffs, Salop [1836—44], Worcs)
> Oldbury, Warley Salop

KIDDERMINSTER PLU (Worcs, Staffs [1836—95], Salop [1836—95])
> Dowles[28]

KNIGHTON PLU (Radnor, Heref, Salop)
> Bedstone, Bettws y Crwyn, Bucknell,[29] Llanfair Waterdine, Stowe

MONTGOMERY PLU (Montg, Cardigan, Merioneth, Salop)
> Brompton and Rhiston, Chirbury, Worthen

SEISDON PLU (Staffs, Salop [1836—95])
> Bobbington,[26] Rudge (1836—95)

STOURBRIDGE PLU[27] (Worcs, Salop [1836—44], Staffs)
> Cakemore (1836—1919), Halesowen, Hasbury, Hawne, Hill (1836—1919), Illey, Lapal, Ridgacre

TENBURY PLU (Worcs, Salop, Heref)
> Boraston, Burford, Greete, Nash, Whitton

SANITARY DISTRICTS

ATCHAM RSD
> same as PLU for Salop pars less pt Hughley (1875—89), Meole Brace (1875—94 [reduced pt 1885—94]), Shrewsbury Holy Cross with St Giles, pt Shrewsbury St Alkmund (1875—85), Shrewsbury St Chad (pt 1875—85, ent 1885—94), Shrewsbury St Julian (pt 1875—85, ent 1885—94), Shrewsbury St Mary (pt 1875—85, ent 1885—94)

BISHOP'S CASTLE USD (1885[10]—94)
> pt Bishop's Castle

BRIDGNORTH RSD
> same as PLU less Bridgnorth St Leonard, Bridgnorth St Mary Magdalen, Ditton Priors (1875—89), Quatford, Quatt Jarvis

BRIDGNORTH USD
> Bridgnorth St Leonard, Bridgnorth St Mary Magdalen, Quatford, Quatt Jarvis

BROSELEY USD (1875—89[15])
> Broseley

CHURCH STRETTON RSD
> same as PLU less pt Shipton (1875—89)

CLEOBURY MORTIMER RSD
> same as PLU for Salop pars

CLUN RSD
> same as PLU for Salop pars less pt Bishop's Castle (1885—94)

DAWLEY USD
> Dawley Magna

ELLESMERE RSD
> same as PLU for Salop pars less pt Ellesmere

ELLESMERE USD
> pt Ellesmere

KIDDERMINSTER RSD
> same as PLU for Salop par

KNIGHTON RSD
> same as PLU for Salop pars

LUDLOW RSD
> same as PLU less Ludlow [St Lawrence][6]

LUDLOW USD
> Ludlow [St Lawrence][6]

MADELEY RSD
> Buildwas, Stirchley only

MADELEY USD (1875—89[15])
> Madeley

MARKET DRAYTON RSD
> same as PLU for Salop pars

MONTGOMERY RSD
> same as PLU for Salop pars

NEWPORT RSD
> same as PLU for Salop pars less pt Chetwynd (1893—94), pt Chetwynd Aston (1893—94), pt Church Aston (1893—94), Newport

NEWPORT USD[30]
> pt Chetwynd (1892—94), pt Chetwynd Aston (1892—94), pt Church Aston (1892—94), Newport

OSWESTRY RSD
> same as PLU for Salop pars less Oswestry Town (until 1880s), Oswestry Urban (from 1880s)

OSWESTRY USD
> Oswestry Town (until 1880s), Oswestry Urban (from 1880s)

SEISDON RSD
> same as PLU for Salop pars

SHIFNAL RSD
same as PLU for Salop pars
SHREWSBURY USD
pt Meole Brace (1875—85 [reduced pt 1885—94]), Shrewsbury Holy Cross with St Giles, pt Shrewsbury St Alkmund (1875—85), Shrewsbury St Chad (pt 1875—85, ent 1885—94), Shrewsbury St Julian (pt 1875—85, ent 1885—94), Shrewsbury St Mary (pt 1875—85, ent 1885—94)
TENBURY RSD
same as PLU for Salop pars
WELLINGTON RSD
same as PLU less pt Wellington
WELLINGTON USD
pt Wellington

WEM RSD
same as PLU
WENLOCK USD[15]
Barrow, Benthall, Broseley (1889—94), Ditton Priors (1875—89), Hughley (1875—89), Linley, Madeley (1889—94), Monkhopton (1875—89), Posenhall, pt Shipton (1875—89), Little Wenlock, Much Wenlock (1889—94), Willey
MUCH WENLOCK USD (1875—89[15])
Much Wenlock
WHITCHURCH RSD
same as PLU less pt Whitchurch
WHITCHURCH AND DODDINGTON USD
pt Whitchurch

ADMINISTRATIVE COUNTY

For MBs see BOROUGHS

ATCHAM RD
Acton Burnell, Alberbury with Cardeston, Albrighton (1894—1967), Astley, Atcham, Battlefield (1894—1934), Bayston Hill (1967—74), Berrington, Bicton, Buildwas (1895—1974), Cardington (1934—74), Condover, Cound, Cressage, Eaton Constantine (1894—1934), Fitz (1894—1934), Ford, Frodesley, Habberley (1894—1967), Great Hanwood, Harley, Hughley, Kenley, Leebotwood (1934—74), Leighton, Longnor (1934—74), Melverley (1894—1934), Meole Brace (1894—1934), Minsterley, Montford, Great Ness (1967—74), Little Ness (1967—74), Pimhill (1934—74), Pitchford, Pontesbury, Church Preen, Preston Gubbals (1894—1934), Church Pulverbatch, Ruckley and Langley, Sheinton, Shrawardine (1894—1934), Shrewsbury St Alkmund (1894—1934), Smethcott (1934—74), Stapleton (1894—1967), All Stretton (1934—74), Sutton (1894—1934), Uffington, Uppington, Upton Magna, Westbury, Withington, Wollaston, Woolstaston (1934—74), Wroxeter
BRIDGNORTH RD
Acton Round, Alveley, Astley Abbots, Aston Botterell (1934—74), Aston Eyre, Barrow (1966—74), Billingsley, Bridgnorth (1967—74), Broseley (1966—74), Burwarton, Chelmarsh, Chetton, Claverley, Cleobury North, Deuxhill, Ditton Priors, Eardington, Easthorpe (1934—74), Farlow (1934—74), Glazeley, Highley (1934—74), Kinlet (1934—74), Middleton Scriven, Monkhopton, Morville, Neen Savage (1934—74), Neenton, Oldbury (1894—1934), Quatt Malvern, Romsley, Rudge (1895—1974), Shipton (1934—74), Sidbury, Stanton Long, Stockton (1967—74), Stottesdon (1934—74), Sutton Maddock (1967—74), Tasley, Upton Cressett, Much Wenlock (1966—74), Worfield
BURFORD RD (1894—1934[31])
Boraston, Burford, Greete, Nash, Whitton
CHIRBURY RD (1894—1934[31])
Brompton and Riston, Chirbury, Worthen
CHURCH STRETTON RD (1894—1934[31])
Acton Scott, Cardington, Easthorpe, Eaton under Haywood, Hope Bowdler, Leebotwood, Longnor,

Rushbury, Shipton, Sibdon Carwood, Smethcott, All Stretton (1899—1934), Church Stretton (1894—99), Little Stretton (1899—1934), Wistanstow, Woolstaston
CHURCH STRETTON UD (1899[32]—1966[33])
Church Stretton
CLEOBURY MORTIMER RD (1894—1934[31])
Aston Botterell, Cleobury Mortimer, Coreley, Farlow, Highley, Hopton Wafers, Kinlet, Loughton, Milson, Neen Savage, Neen Sollars, Silvington, Stottesdon, Wheathill, Woodhouse
CLUN RD (1894—1967[33])
Bedstone (1934—67), Bettwys y Crwyn (1934—67), Bishop's Castle Rural (1894—1934), Brompton and Rhiston (1934—67), Bucknell (1934—67), Chirbury (1934—67), Clun, Clunbury, Clungunford, Colebatch (1934—67), Edgton, Hopesay, Hopton Castle, Llanfair Waterdine (1934—67), Lydbury North, Lydham, Mainstone, More, Myndtown, Norbury, Ratlinghope, Shelve, Stowe (1934—67), Wentnor, Worthen (1934—67)
CLUN AND BISHOP'S CASTLE RD (1967[34]—74)
Bedstone, Bettwys y Crwyn, Bishop's Castle, Brompton and Rhiston, Bucknell, Chirbury, Clun, Clunbury, Clungunford, Colebatch, Edgton, Hopesay, Hopton Castle, Llanfair Waterdine, Lydbury North, Lydham, Mainstone, More, Myndtown, Norbury, Ratlinghope, Shelve, Stowe, Wentnor, Worthen
DAWLEY UD
Dawley Magna
DRAYTON RD (1894—1966[35])
Adderley, Cheswardine, Drayton in Hales (1894—1914), Child's Ercall, Hinstock, Hodnet, Ightfield (1934—66), Moreton Say, Norton in Hales, Stoke upon Tern, Sutton upon Tern (1914—66), Tittenley (1895—1934), Woore
ELLESMERE RD (1894—1967[34])
Baschurch, Cockshutt (1896—1967), Ellesmere Rural, Hadnall (1894—1934), Hordley, Myddle, Great Ness, Little Ness, Petton, Welshampton
ELLESMERE UD (1894—1967[34]
Ellesmere Urban

LUDLOW RD

Abdon, Acton Scott (1934—74), Ashford Bowdler, Ashford Carbonell, Bitterley, Boraston (1934—74), Bromfield, Burford (1934—74), Caynham, Clee St Margaret, Cleobury Mortimer (1934—74), Coreley (1934—74), Culmington, Diddlebury, East Hamlet, Eaton under Haywood (1934—74), Greete (1934—74), Halford, Heath, Holdgate (1894—1967), Hope Bagot, Hope Bowdler (1934—74), Hopton Cangeford, Hopton Wafers (1934—74), Loughton (1934—67), Ludford (pt 1894—95, ent 1895—1974), Ludlow (1967—74), Ludlow Castle (1894—1901), Milson (1934—74), Munslow, Nash (1934—74), Neen Sollars (1934—74), Onibury, Richard's Castle, Rushbury (1934—74), Sibdon Carwood (1934—74), Silvington (1934—67), Stanton Lacy, Stoke St Milborough, Stokesay, Church Stretton (1966—74), Little Stretton (1966—74), Tugford, Cold Weston (1894—1967), Wheathill (1934—74), Whitton (1934—74), Wistanstow (1934—74), Woodhouse (1934—67)

MARKET DRAYTON RD (1966[35]—74)

Adderley, Cheswardine, Market Drayton, Child's Ercall, Hinstock, Hodnet, Ightfield, Moreton Say, Norton in Hales, Stoke upon Tern, Sutton upon Tern, Woore

MARKET DRAYTON UD (1914[36]—66[33])

Market Drayton

MADELEY RD (1894—95[37])

Buildwas, Stirchley

NEWPORT RD (1894—1934[31])

Cherrington, Chetwynd Rural, Chetwynd Aston Rural, Church Aston Rural, Edgmond, Lilleshall, Longford, Tibberton, Woodcote

NEWPORT UD

Newport

OAKENGATES UD (1898[38]—1974)

Oakengates (1934—74), Priorslee (1898—1934), St George's (1898—1934), Wombridge (1898—1934), Wrockwardine Wood (1898—1934)

OSWESTRY RD

West Felton, Kinnerley, Knockin, Llanyblodwel,[39] Llanymynech (1894—1967), Llanymynch and Pant (1967—74), Melverley (1934—74), Oswestry (1967—74), Oswestry Rural, Ruyton of the Eleven Towns,[40] St Martin's, Selattyn (1894—1967), Selattyn and Gobowen (1967—74), Sychtyn (1894—1967), Weston Rhyn (1897—1974), Whittington

SHIFNAL RD

Albrighton, Badger, Beckbury, Boningale, Boscobel, Donington, Kemberton, Ryton, Sheriff Hales[41] (pt 1894—95, ent 1895—1974), Shifnal, Stirchley (1895—1966), Stockton (1894—1967), Sutton Maddock (1894—1967), Tong

NORTH SHROPSHIRE RD (1967[34]—74)

Baschurch, Broughton, Clive, Cockshutt, Ellesmere Rural, Ellesmere Urban, Grinshill, Hadnall, Hordley, Lee Brockhurst, Loppington, Moreton Corbet, Myddle, Petton, Prees, Shawbury, Stanton upon Hine Heath, Welshampton, Wem Rural, Wem Urban, Weston under Redcastle, Whitchurch Rural, Whitchurch Urban, Whixall

TEME RD (1894—1934[31])

Bedstone, Bettws y Crwyn, Bucknell, Llanfair Waterdine, Stowe

WELLINGTON RD

Bolas Magna, Cherrington (1934—74), Chetwynd (1934—74), Chetwynd Aston (1934—74), Church Aston (1934—74), Edgmond (1934—74), Ercall Magna, Eyton on the Weald Moors, Hadley (1898—1974), Kinnersley,[42] Lilleshall (1934—74), Longdon upon Tern, Longford (1934—74), Preston upon the Weald Moors, Rodington, Tibberton (1934—74), Waters Upton, Wellington Rural, Little Wenlock (1966—74), Wombridge (1894—98), Woodcote (1934—74), Wrockwardine, Wrockwardine Wood (1894—98)

WELLINGTON UD

Wellington Urban

WEM RD (1894—1967[34])

Broughton, Clive, Grinshill, Hadnall (1934—67), Lee Brockhurst, Loppington, Moreton Corbet, Prees, Shawbury, Stanton upon Hine Heath, Wem (1894—1900), Wem Rural (1900—67), Weston under Redcastle, Whitchurch Rural (1934—67), Whixall

WEM UD (1900[43]—67[34])

Wem Urban

WHITCHURCH RD (1894—1934[31])

Ightfield, Whitchurch Rural

WHITCHURCH UD (1895[44]—1967[34])

Whitchurch Urban

WHITCHURCH AND DODINGTON UD (1894—95[44])

Whitchurch Urban

NON-METROPOLITAN COUNTY

As constituted 1 Apr 1974, defined in terms of Adm Co units as of 31 Mar.

BRIDGNORTH DIST

Bridgnorth RD, pt Shifnal RD (all except the pt in The Wrekin Dist)

OSWESTRY DIST

Oswestry RD

SHREWSBURY DIST

Atcham RD, Shreswbury MB

NORTH SHROPSHIRE DIST

Market Drayton RD, North Shropshire RD

SOUTH SHROPSHIRE DIST

Clun and Bishop's Castle RD, Ludlow RD

THE WREKIN DIST

Dawley UD, Newport UD, Oakengates UD, pt Shifnal RD pt Shifnal RD (pt Shifnal), Wellington RD, Wellington UD

STAFFORDSHIRE

ALTERATIONS IN COUNTY BOUNDARIES

As noted by year below, Staffs pars gained territory from or lost it to pars in adjoining cos or county boroughs, or were entirely transferred to them. Details of these alterations are noted in Part I of the *Guide* under Staffordshire.

ANCIENT COUNTY (until 1889: Hds, Bors, MBs, PLUs, RSDs, USDs)

1844 Broom, Clent, Scropton. *1866* Barthomley, Burton upon Trent, Drayton in Hales, Mucklestone, Oldswinford, Pattingham, Tamworth.

ADMINISTRATIVE COUNTY (1889—1974: Hds,[1] PLUs, MBs, RDs, UDs, with assoc CBs of West Bromwich, Burton upon Trent, Dudley [1966—74], Hanley [1889—1910), Smethwick [1907—66], Stoke on Trent [1910—74], Walsall, Wolverhampton)

1889 Branston, West Bromwich, Burton Extra, Burton upon Trent, Horninglow, Stapenhill, Stoke upon Trent, Walsall Borough, Winshill, Wolverhampton. *1890* Foston and Scropton. *1895* Upper Arley, Bobbington, Croxall, Drayton Bassett, Sheriff Hales. *1903* Rolleston. *1910* Burslem, Fenton, Hanley, Longton, Stoke upon Trent, Tunstall. *1911* Handsworth. *1922* Caverswall, Chell, Milton, Newchapel, Norton in the Moors, Smallthorne, Stoke Rural, Stone Rural, Tren-tham. *1927* Bushbury, Heathtown, Uppen Penn, Wrottesley. *1928* Perry Barr, Warley Woods. *1929* Coseley, Dudley Castle Hill. *1930* Barlaston, Trentham. *1931* Great Barr, Bentley, Rushall, Shenstone, Wednesbury. *1932* Tamworth. *1933* Bushbury, Upper Penn, Wednesfield. *1934* Darlaston, Tipton. *1936* Gnosall. *1954* Brierley Hill, Coseley, Rowley Regis, Sedgley. *1965* Bagnall, Balterley, Barlaston, Betley, Blymhill, Caverswall, Forton, Fulford, Kidsgrove, Newcastle under Lyme, Norton in the Moors, Swynnerton, Tamworth. *1966* Aldridge, Amblecote, Bilston, Brewood, Brierley Hill, Coseley, Darlaston, Essington, Featherstone, Himley, Kinver, Lower Penn, Rowley Regis, Sedgley, Shenstone, Tettenhall, Tipton, Wednesbury, Wednesfield, Weeford, Willenhall, Wombourn, Wrottesley

NON-METROPOLITAN COUNTY (from 1974: Dists)

1974 Aldridge-Brownhills, Burton upon Trent, Stoke on Trent.

ASSOCIATED COUNTY BOROUGHS AND COUNTY OF ITSELF

WEST BROMWICH CB
Bdry: 1897,[2] 1928,[3] 1931,[4] 1931,[5] 1931,[6] 1966 (incl gains pt Smethw. CB, exchanges pts with Walsall CB [both assoc with Staffs], exchanges pts with Birm CB [assoc with Warws]).[7] Transf 1974 to W Midlands.[8]

BURTON UPON TRENT CB
Bdry: 1934.[9] Transf 1974 to Staffs.[8]

DUDLEY CB (1966—74) (assoc with Worcs 1889—1966)
Becomes assoc 1966 with Staffs after bdry alt.[10] Transf 1974 to W Midlands.[8]

HANLEY CB (1889—1910)
Bdry: 1905.[11] Abol 1910 to help cr Stoke on Trent CB.[12]

LICHFIELD CO OF ITSELF (1556—1889)
see listing below under BOROUGHS

SMETHWICK CB (1907—66)
Cr 1907 when Smethw. MB constituted a CB.[13] Bdry: 1928.[14] Abol 1966 pt to W Bromw. CB (assoc with Staffs), pt to help cr Warley CB (assoc with Worcs), pt to Birm CB (assoc with Warws).[7]

STOKE ON TRENT CB (1910—74)
Cr 1910 by union Hanley CB (assoc with Staffs) and Staffs units of Burslem MB, Longton MB, Stoke on Trent MB, Tunstall MB, pt Fenton UD.[12] Bdry: 1922,[15] 1930,[16] 1965.[17] Transf 1974 to Staffs.[8]

WALSALL CB
Bdry: 1890,[18] 1931,[19] 1934,[20] 1966 (incl exchanges pts with W Bromw. CB, gains pt Walsall CB [both assoc with Staffs]).[7] Transf 1974 to W Midlands.[8]

WOLVERHAMPTON CB
Bdry: 1927,[21] 1966 (incl loses pt to Walsall CB [assoc with Staffs]).[7] Transf 1974 to W Midlands.[8]

HUNDREDS[1]

EAST CUTTLESTONE HD
Acton Trussell and Bednall (from 1866), Baswich, Brewood,[22] Brocton (from 1866), pt Bushbury (until 1866), Cannock, Cheslyn Hay (from 1858), Coppenhall (from 1866), Dunston (from 1866), Essington (from 1866), Featherstone (from 1866), Hatherton (from 1866), Hilton (from 1866), Huntington (from 1866), Kinvaston (from 1866), Penkridge[22] (pt until 1866, ent from 1866), Rugeley, Saredon (from 1866), Shareshill, Teddesley Hay (from 1858), pt Wolverhampton[22] (until 1866), Great Wyrley (from 1866)

WEST CUTTLESTONE HD
Blymhill, Bradley, Church Eaton,[22] Forton, Gnosall, Haughton, Lapley, Norbury, pt Penkridge (until 1866),

pt Sheriff Hales, Stretton (from 1866), Weston Jones (from 1866), Weston under Lizard

NORTH OFFLOW HD

Alrewas, Alrewas Hays (1858—85), Anslow (from 1866), Barton under Needwood (from 1866), Branstone[22] (from 1866), King's Bromley, King's Bromley Hays (from 1858), Burton Extra[22] (from 1866), Burton upon Trent[22] (pt until 1866, ent from 1866), Clifton Campville and Haunton, pt Croxall, Curborough and Elmhurst (from 1866), Draycott in the Clay (from 1866), Dunstall (from 1866), Edingale, Fisherwick (from 1866), pt Foston and Scropton[23] (1866—90), Fradley (1866—85), Freeford (from 1858), Fulfen (from 1858), Hanbury, Harlaston (from 1866), Haselour (from 1858), Horninglow (from 1866), Marchington (from 1866), Marchington Woodlands (from 1866), Newborough (from 1866), Orgreave (1866—85), Hamstall Ridware, Mavesyn Ridware, Pipe Ridware, Rolleston, pt Scropton[23] (until 1866), Streethay (from 1866), Stretton (from 1866), Syerscote (from 1866), Tamhorn (from 1858), Tamworth[22] (pt until 1866, ent from 1866), Tatenhill, Thorpe Constantine, Tutbury,[22] Whittington, Wychnor (from 1866), Yoxall

SOUTH OFFLOW HD

Aldridge, Armitage, Great Barr (from 1866), Bentley (from 1866), West Bromwich[22]; Burntwood, Edial and Woodhouses (from 1866); Canwell (from 1858), Darlaston, pt Drayton Bassett, Elford, Farewell and Chorley, Fazeley (from 1866), Hammerwich (from 1866), Handsworth, Harborne, Hints, Hopwas Hays (from 1866), pt Lichfield St Michael (until 1866), Longdon, Norton Canes, Ogley Hay (from 1858), Pelsall (from 1866), Pipehill[22] (from 1866), Rushall, Shenstone, Statfold, Swinfen and Packington (from 1866), pt Tamworth (until 1866), Tipton, Wall (from 1866), Walsall[22] (until 1866), Walsall Borough[22] (from 1866), Walsall Foreign (from 1866), Wednesbury,[22] Wednesfield (from 1866), Weeford, Wiggington (from 1866), Willenhall (from 1866), pt Wolverhampton[22] (until 1866)

NORTH PIREHILL HD

Adbaston, Ashley, Audley,[22] Balterley (from 1866), pt Barthomley (until 1866), Betley, Burslem, Chapel and Hill Chorlton (from 1866), pt Drayton in Hales (until 1866), Eccleshall,[22] Keele, Madeley, Maer, Mucklestone (pt until 1866, ent from 1866), Newcastle under Lyme[22] (from 1834[24]), Norton in the Moors, High Offley, Standon, Stoke upon Trent,[22] Swynnerton, Trentham,[22] Tyrley (from 1866), Whitmore, Wolstanton

SOUTH PIREHILL HD[25]

Barlaston, Blithfield, Abbot's Bromley,[22] Chartley Holme (from 1858), Chebsey, Colton,[22] Cresswell,[26] Ellenhall, Fradswell (from 1866), Gayton, Hopton and Coton[22] (from 1866), Ingestre, Marston (from 1866), Milwich, Newcastle under Lyme (from 1834[24]),[22] Cold Norton (from 1866), Ranton, Ranton Abbey (from 1858), Salt and Enson (from 1866), Sandon, Seighford, pt Stafford St Mary (until 1866), Stone,[22] Stowe, Tillington (from 1858), Tixall, Weston upon Trent, Whitgreave (from 1858), Worston (from 1858), Yarlet (from 1858)

NORTH SEISDON HD

Bilston (from 1866), Bushbury (pt until 1866, ent from 1866), Himley, Kingswinford, Penn (until 1866), Lower Penn (from 1866), Upper Penn (from 1866), Rowley Regis,[22] Sedgley, pt Tettenhall, Wolverhampton[22] (pt until 1866, ent from 1866)

SOUTH SEISDON HD

Amblecote (from 1866), Upper Arley, pt Bobbington, Broom (until 1844), Clent (until 1844), Codsall, Enville, Kinver,[22] pt Oldswinford (until 1866), Patshull, Pattingham (pt until 1866, ent from 1866), pt Tettenhall, Trysull and Seisdon (from 1866), Wombourn, Woodford Grange (from 1858)

NORTH TOTMORE HD

Alstonfield, Blore (from 1866), Blore with Swinscoe (from 1866), Bradnop and Cawdry (from 1866), pt Calton (from 1866), Cauldon, Caverswall, Cheddleton, Consall (from 1866), Dilhorne; Endon, Longsdon and Stanley (from 1866); Fawfieldhead (from 1866), Grindon, Heathylee (from 1866), Heaton (from 1866), Hollinsclough (from 1866), Horton, Ilam, Ipstones, pt Kingsley, pt Leek[22] (until 1866), Leek and Lowe (from 1866), Leekfrith (from 1866), Longnor (from 1866), Okeover, Onecote (from 1866), Quarnford (from 1866), Rushton James (from 1866), Rushton Spencer (from 1866), Tittesworth (from 1866), Warslow and Elkstones (from 1866)

SOUTH TOTMORE HD

Alton,[22] Bradley in the Moors, Bramshall, Butterton (from 1866), pt Calton (from 1866), Calwich (from 1866), Cheadle, Checkley, Cotton (from 1866), Croxden, Denstone (from 1866), Draycott in the Moors, Ellastone, Farley (from 1866), Field (from 1866), Gratwich, pt Kingsley, pt Leek (until 1866), Leigh, Mayfield, Musden Grange (1858—86), Prestwood (from 1866), Ramshorn (from 1866), Rocester, Rudyard (from 1866), Sheen, Stanton (from 1866), Uttoxeter,[22] Waterfall, Wetton, Woodhouses (from 1866), Wootton (from 1866)

BOROUGHS

Units with some degree of burghal character[27] are denominated 'Bor'. Those which did not sustain that status until the 19th cent are in italics. MBs were established by the Municipal Corporations Act, 1835,[28] or by later charter.

ALREWAS BOR
pt Alrewas

ALTON BOR
Alton

BETLEY BOR
pt Audley

BILSTON MB (1933[29]—1966[10])
Bilston

BREWOOD BOR
Brewood
ABBOT'S BROMLEY BOR
Abbot's Bromley
WEST BROMWICH MB (1882[30]—89), CB (1889—1974)
West Bromwich
BURSLEM MB[31] (1878[32]—1910[12])
Burslem (pt 1878—94 [enlarged pt 1891—94], ent 1894—1910)
BURTON UPON TRENT BOR[33], MB (1878[34]—89), CB (1889—1974) (Staffs, *Derbys* 1878—89, ent assoc with Staffs thereafter)
Bor: pt Burton upon Trent
MB/CB: pt Branston (1878—94), Burton upon Trent, Burton Extra (1878—1904), Horninglow (pt 1878—94, ent 1894—1904), *Stapenhill (pt 1878—94, ent 1894—1910), Winshill (pt 1878—94, ent 1894—1910)*
CHURCH EATON BOR
Church Eaton
COLTON BOR
Colton
DUDLEY CB (1966[10]—74)
Dudley
ECCLESHALL BOR
Eccleshall
HANLEY MB (1857[35]—89), CB (1889—1910[12])
Hanley (1894—1910), pt Stoke upon Trent (1857—94 [tp Hanley, pt tp Shelton])
KINVER BOR
Kinver
LEEK BOR
pt Leek
LICHFIELD CO OF ITSELF (1556—1889), BOR/MB (City)
Lichfield The Close, Lichfield The Friary (until 1934), Lichfield St Chad (pt until 1866, ent 1866—1910), Lichfield St Mary, Lichfield St Michael (pt until 1894 [reduced pt 1866—94]), pt Pipehill (1866—94)
LONGTON MB[36] (1865[37]—1910[12])
pt Caverswall (1883—94), Florence (1894—96), Longton (1894—1910), Normancot (1894—96), pt Stoke upon Trent (1865—94 [tp Lane End and Longton]), pt Stone (1884—94), pt Trentham (1884—94), East Vale (1894—96)
NEWBOROUGH BOR[38]
pt Tutbury
NEWBOROUGH (AGARDSLEY) BOR[39]
Constitution not found

NEWCASTLE UNDER LYME BOR/MB
Bor: Newcastle under Lyme (when gains sep civ identity in 16th cent), pt Stoke upon Trent (until Newcastle under Lyme gains sep civ identity 16th cent)
MB: Newcastle under Lyme, pt Stoke upon Trent ([detached pt, tp Penkhull] 1835—78), pt Trentham (1878—94 [the former detached pt of Stoke upon Trent])
PENKRIDGE BOR
pt Penkridge
ROWLEY REGIS MB (1933[29]—66[10])
Rowley Regis
SMETHWICK MB (1899[40]—1907), CB (1907[13]—66[10])
Smethwick, Warley Woods (1928—66)
STAFFORD BOR/MB
pt Castle Church (1835—94), pt Hopton and Coton[41] (1866—86), Stafford (1894—1974), Stafford St Mary and St Chad[42] (pt until 1866, ent 1866—94)
STOKE ON TRENT MB (1874[43]—1910), CB (1910[12]—74) (Made a City 1925[44])
Burslem (1910—22), Fenton (1910—22), Goldenhill (1904—22), Hanley (1910—22), Longton (1910—22), Stoke upon Trent (pt 1874 [pt tp Penkhull, pt tp Shelton]—94, ent 1894—1974), Tunstall (1910—22)
STONE BOR
Stone
TAMWORTH BOR/MB[45] (Staffs, Warws until 1866; ent Staffs 1866—90; pt Staffs, *pt Warws* 1890—94; ent Staffs 1894—1974)
pt Bolehall and Glascote (1890—94), Tamworth[46] (pt until 1866 [enlarged pt 1835—66], ent 1866—1974), *pt Tamworth Castle (1890—94)*
TIPTON MB (1938[47]—66[10])
Tipton
TUTBURY BOR
pt Tutbury
UTTOXETER BOR
Uttoxeter
WALSALL BOR/MB/CB[18]
Bor: pt Walsall
MB/CB: pt Rushall (1890—94), pt Walsall (1835—66), Walsall (1894—1974), Walsall Borough (1866—94), pt Walsall Foreign (1890—94)
WEDNESBURY MB (1886[48]—1974)
Wednesbury
WOLVERHAMPTON BOR, MB (1849[49]—89), CB (1889—1974)
Bor: pt Wolverhampton
MB/CB: Wolverhampton

POOR LAW UNIONS

In Staffs Poor Law County:[50]
ALSTONFIELD GILBERT UNION (until 1869)
Alstonfield, Butterton, Grindon, Wetton
WEST BROMWICH PLU (Staffs, Salop [1836—44], Worcs, Birm CB [1928—30])
West Bromwich, Handsworth (1836—1911), Perry Barr,[51] Warley Woods (1928—30)
BURTON UPON TRENT PLU (Staffs, Derbys)
Anslow, Barton under Needwood, Branston, Burton Extra (1837—1904), Burton upon Trent,[52] Dunstall,

Foston and Scropton,[23] Hanbury, Horninglow (1837—1904), Outwoods (1894—1930), Rolleston,[53] Stapenhill,[33] Stretton, Tatenthill, Tutbury, Winshill,[33] Wychnor
CANNOCK PLU (1870s[54]—1930)
Acton Trussell and Bednall, Brewood, Bushbury, Cannock, Cheslyn Hay, Church Eaton, Coppenhall, Dunston, Essington, Featherstone, Hatherton, Hilton, Huntington, Kinvaston, Lapley, Norton Canes, Penkridge, Saredon, Shareshill, Stretton, Teddesley

Hay, Great Wyrley

CHEADLE PLU

Alton, Bradley in the Moors, Cauldon, Caverswall, Cheadle, Checkley, Cheddleton, Consall, Cotton, Denstone, Dilhorne, Draycott in the Moors, Farley, Forsbrook (1896—1930), Ipstones, Kingsley, Oakamoor (1896—1930)

DUDLEY PLU (Staffs, Worcs)

Coseley (1903—30), Dudley Castle Hill[55] (1867—1929), Rowley Regis, Sedgley, Tipton

LEEK PLU

Bradnop and Cawdry, Butterton, Endon and Stanley (1894—1930); Endon, Longsdon and Stanley (1837—94); Fawfieldhead, Grindon (1869—1930), Heathylee, Heaton, Hollinsclough, Horton, Leek (1894—1930), Leek and Lowe (1837—95), Leekfrith, Longnor, Longsdon (1894—1930), Lowe (1895—1930), Norton in the Moors, Onecote, Quarnford, Rudyard, Rushton James, Rushton Spencer, Sheen, Smallthorne (1894—1922), Tittesworth, Warslow and Elkstones

LICHFIELD PLU

Alrewas, Alrewas Hays (1858—85), Armitage, Brereton (1894—1930), King's Bromley, King's Bromley Hays (1858—1922), Burntwood (1929—30); Burntwood, Edial and Woodhouses (1836—1929); Colton, Curborough and Elmhurst, Elford, Farewell and Chorley, Fisherwick, Fradley (1836—85), Freeford (1858—1930), Fulfen (1858—1930), Hammerwich, Haselour (1858—1930), Longdon, Ogley Hay (soon after 1836[56]—1930), Ogley Hay Rural (1896—1930), Orgreave (1836—85), Pipehill (1894—1930), Hamstall Ridware, Mavesyn Ridware, Pipe Ridware, Rugeley, Shenstone, Shire Oak (1894—1930), Streethay, Swinfen and Packington, Tamhorn (1858—1930), Wall, Weeford, Whittington, Yoxall

NEWCASTLE UNDER LYME PLU

Audley, Balterley, Betley, Chapel and Hill Chorlton, Clayton (1896—1930), Hardings Wood (1894—1930), Keele, Madeley, Maer, Newcastle under Lyme, Whitmore

PENKRIDGE PLU (1836—70s[54])

Acton Trussell and Bednall, Brewood, Bushbury, Cannock, Cheslyn Hay, Church Eaton, Coppenhall, Dunston, Essington, Featherstone, Hatherton, Hilton, Huntington, Kinvaston, Lapley, Norton Canes, Penkridge, Saredon, Shareshill, Stretton, Teddesley Hay, Great Wyrley

SEISDON PLU (Staffs, Salop [1836—95])

Bobbington,[57] Codsall, Enville, Himley, Kinver, Pattingham,[57] Lower Penn, Upper Penn, Swindon (1896—1930), Tettenhall, Trysull and Seisdon, Wombourn, Woodford Grange (1861—1930), Wrottesley (1894—1930)

STAFFORD PLU

Baswich, Bradley, Brocton, Castle Church, Chartley Holme (1858—1930), Colwich, Cresswell (1958—1930), Ellenhall (soon after 1836[56]—1930), Fradswell, Gayton, Haughton, Hopton and Coton, Ingestre, Marston, Ranton, Ranton Abbey (1858—85), Salt and Enson, Seighford, Stafford (1894—1930), Stafford St Mary and St Chad (1836—94), Stowe, Tillington (1858—1917), Tixall, Weston upon Trent, Whitgreave, Worston (1858—1930), Yarlet (1858—1930)

STOKE AND WOLSTANTON PLU (1922—30)

Bagnall, Burslem, Chesterton, Kidsgrove, Newchapel, Silverdale, Stoke upon Trent, Wolstanton

STOKE ON TRENT PLU (1836—1922)

Bagnall (1896—1922), Fenton (1894—1922), Florence (1894—96), Hanley (1894—1922), Longton (1894—1922), Normancot (1894—96), Stoke upon Trent, Stoke Rural (1894—1922), East Vale (1894—96)

STONE PLU

Barlaston, Chebsey, Cold Norton, Eccleshall, Fulford (1897—1930), Hilderstone (1897—1930), Milwich, Sandon, Standon, Stone, Stone Rural (1894—1930), Swynnerton, Trentham

TAMWORTH PLU (Staffs, Warws, Derbys)

Canwell, Clifton Campville and Haunton, Croxall,[58] Drayton Bassett,[59] Edingale, Fazeley, Harlaston, Hints, Hopwas Hays (1865—1930), Statfold, Syerscote, Tamworth,[46] Thorpe Constantine, Wiggington

UTTOXETER PLU (Staffs, Derbys)

Blithfield, Bramshall, Abbot's Bromley, Croxden, Denstone (soon after 1837[56]—1930), Gratwich, Kingston, Leigh, Marchington, Marchington Woodlands, Newborough, Rocester, Uttoxeter, Uttoxeter Rural (1896—1930)

WALSALL PLU

Aldridge, Great Barr, Bentley, Darlaston, Pelsall, Rushall, Walsall (1894—1930), Walsall Borough (1836—94), Walsall Foreign (1836—94), Walsall Wood (1894—1930)

WOLSTANTON AND BURSLEM PLU (1838—1922)

Burslem, Chell (1894—1922), Chesterton (1894—1930), Goldenhill (1894—1922), Kidsgrove (1894—1922), Milton (1894—1922), Newchapel (1894—1922), Silverdale (1894—1922), Tunstall (1894—1922), Wolstanton

WOLVERHAMPTON PLU

Bilston, Heathtown (1894—1922), Short Heath (1894—1930), Wednesfield, Willenhall, Wolverhampton

In Other Poor Law Counties:

ASHBOURNE PLU (Derbys, Staffs)

Alstonfield (1869—1930), Blore with Swinscoe, Calton, Calwich, Ellastone, Ilam, Mayfield, Musden Grange (1858—86), Okeover, Prestwood, Ramshorn, Stanton, Waterfall, Wetton (1869—1930), Woodhouses (1845—1916), Wootton

BROMSGROVE PLU (Worcs, Warws [1836—44], Salop [1836—44])

Clent[60]

CONGLETON PLU (Ches, Staffs)

Biddulph

DRAYTON PLU—see MARKET DRAYTON PLU

KIDDERMINSTER PLU (Worcs, Staffs [1836—95], Salop [1836—95])

Upper Arley,[61] Broom[60]

KING'S NORTON PLU (Worcs, Staffs, Warws [1836—89], Birm CB [1889—1911])

Harborne (1836—1912), Smethwick (1894—1930)

MARKET DRAYTON PLU (cr as 'DRAYTON', soon after 'MARKET DRAYTON') (Salop, Staffs, Ches [1836—95])

Ashley (soon after 1836[56]—1930), Mucklestone,[62]

Tyrley
NEWPORT PLU (Salop, Staffs)
Adbaston, Forton, Gnosall, Norbury, High Offley, Weston Jones

SHIFNAL PLU (Salop, Staffs)
Blymhill, Patshull, Sheriff Hales,[63] Weston under Lizard
STOURBRIDGE PLU (Worcs, Salop [1836—44], Staffs)
Amblecote, Brierley Hill (1894—1930), Kingswinford, Quarry Bank (1894—1930)

SANITARY DISTRICTS

ASHBOURNE RSD
same as PLU for Staffs pars
AUDLEY USD
pt Audley
BIDDULPH USD (1882[64]—94)
Biddulph
BILSTON USD
Bilston
BRIERLEY HILL USD
pt Kingswinford
BROWNHILLS USD
Hammerwich, Norton Canes, pt Ogley Hay, pt Shenstone, pt Walsall Foreign
WEST BROMWICH RSD
same as PLU for Staffs pars less West Bromwich, pt Handsworth, Wednesbury
WEST BROMWICH USD
West Bromwich
BURSLEM USD[31]
pt Burslem (1878—94 [enlarged pt 1891—94])
BURTON UPON TRENT RSD
same as PLU for Staffs pars less pt Branston (1878—94), Burton Extra (1878—94), Burton upon Trent, pt Horninglow (18787—94)
BURTON UPON TRENT USD (Staffs, Derbys)
pt Branston (1878—94), Burton Extra (1878—94), Burton upon Trent
CANNOCK RSD
same as PLU less Cannock, Norton Canes
CANNOCK USD
Cannock
CHEADLE RSD
same as PLU less pt Caverswall
CONGLETON RSD
same as PLU for Staffs par less Biddulph (1882—94)
COSELEY USD
pt Sedgley
DARLASTON USD
Darlaston
DUDLEY RSD
same as PLU for Staffs pars less Dudley Castle Hill (1875—89),[9] Rowley Regis, pt Sedgley, Tipton
DUDLEY USD (Worcs, Staffs)
Dudley Castle Hill (1875—89)
EAST VALE USD (1875—83[36])
pt Caverswall
FENTON USD
pt Stoke upon Trent
HANDSWORTH USD
pt Handsworth
HANLEY USD
pt Stoke upon Trent

HARBORNE USD (1875—91[65])
pt Harborne
HEATH TOWN (or WEDNESFIELD HEATH) USD
pt Wednesfield
KIDDERMINSTER RSD
same as PLU for Staffs pars
KIDSGROVE USD
pt Audley, pt Wolstanton
KING'S NORTON RSD
same as PLU less pt Harborne
LEEK RSD
same as PLU less pt Leek and Lowe, pt Leekfrith, pt Norton in the Moors, pt Tittesworth
LEEK USD
pt Leek and Lowe, pt Leekfrith, pt Tittesworth
LICHFIELD RSD
same as PLU less Lichfield The Close, Lichfield The Friary, Lichfield St Chad, Lichfield St Mary, pt Lichfield St Michael, pt Pipehill
LICHFIELD USD
Lichfield The Close, Lichfield The Friary, Lichfield St Chad, Lichfield St Mary, pt Lichfield St Michael, pt Pipehill
LONGTON USD[36]
pt Caverswall (1883—94), pt Stoke upon Trent, pt Stone (1884—94), pt Trentham (1884—94)
MARKET DRAYTON RSD
same as PLU for Staffs pars
NEWCASTLE UNDER LYME RSD
same as PLU less Audley, Newcastle under Lyme, pt Trentham (1878—94)
NEWCASTLE UNDER LYME USD
Newcastle under Lyme, pt Stoke upon Trent (1875—78), pt Trentham (1878—94)
NEWPORT RSD
same as PLU for Staffs pars
QUARRY BANK USD
pt Kingswinford
ROWLEY REGIS USD
Rowley Regis
RUGELEY USD
pt Rugeley
SEDGLEY USD (1887[66]—94)
pt Sedgley
UPPER SEDGLEY USD (1875—87[66])
pt Sedgley
SEISDON RSD
same as PLU for Staffs pars less pt Tettenhall (1883—94)
SHIFNAL RSD
same as PLU for Staffs pars
SHORT HEATH USD
pt Willenhall

SMALLTHORNE USD
pt Norton in the Moors
SMETHWICK USD
pt Harborne
STAFFORD RSD
same as PLU less pt Castle Church (enlarged pt 1876—94), pt Hopton and Coton (1875—86), Stafford St Mary and St Chad
STAFFORD USD
pt Castle Church (enlarged pt 1876—94), pt Hopton and Coton (1875—86), Stafford St Mary and St Chad
STOKE ON TRENT RSD
same as PLU less pt Stoke upon Trent
STOKE ON TRENT USD
pt Stoke upon Trent
STONE RSD
same as PLU less pt Stone (enlarged pt 1884—94), pt Trentham (ent 1875—78, pt 1878—94 [enlarged pt 1884—94])
STONE USD
pt Stone
STOURBRIDGE RSD
same as PLU for Staffs pars less pt Kingswinford
TAMWORTH RSD
same as PLU for Staffs pars less Tamworth
TAMWORTH USD (ent Staffs 1875—90; pt Staffs, *pt Warws* [1890—94])
pt Bolehall and Glascote (1890—94), Tamworth, *pt Tamworth Castle (1890—94)*

TETTENHALL USD (1883[67]—94)
pt Tettenhall
TIPTON USD
Tipton
TUNSTALL USD
pt Wolstanton
UTTOXETER RSD
same as PLU for Staffs pars
WALSALL RSD
same as PLU less Darlaston, pt Rushall (1890—94), Walsall Borough, Walsall Foreign (pt 1875—90, ent 1890—94)
WALSALL USD
pt Rushall (1890—94), Walsall Borough, pt Walsall Foreign (1890—94)
WEDNESBURY USD
Wednesbury
WEDNESFIELD USD
pt Wednesfield
WILLENHALL USD
pt Willenhall
WOLSTANTON AND BURSLEM RSD
same as PLU less pt Burslem, pt Wolstanton
WOLVERHAMPTON RSD
same as PLU for Staffs pars less Bilston, pt Tettenhall (1883—94), pt Wednesfield, pt Willenhall, Wolverhampton
WOLVERHAMPTON USD
Wolverhampton

ADMINISTRATIVE COUNTY

For MBs and the associated CB see BOROUGHS

ALDRIDGE UD (1934[68]—66[10])
Aldridge, Great Barr, Pelsall, Rushall
ALDRIDGE-BROWNHILLS UD (1966[10]—74)
Aldridge-Brownhills
AMBLECOTE UD (1898[69]—1966[10])
Amblecote
AUDLEY UD (1894—1932[70])
Audley
BIDDULPH UD
Biddulph
BILSTON UD (1894—1933[29])
Bilston
BLORE HEATH RD (1894—1932[71])
Ashley, Mucklestone, Tyrley
BRIERLEY HILL UD (1894—1966[10])
Brierley Hill, Kingswinford, Quarry Bank
BROWNHILLS UD (1894—1966[10])
Hammerwich (1894—96), Norton Canes, Ogley Hay (pt 1894—96, ent 1896—1966), Shire Oak, Walsall Wood
CANNOCK RD
Acton Trussell and Bednall, Blymhill (1934—74), Brewood, Bushbury (1894—1934), Cheslyn Hay, Coppenhall, Dunston, Essington, Featherstone, Hatherton, Hilton, Huntington, Kinvaston (1894—1934), Lapley, Penkridge, Saredon, Shareshill, Stretton, Teddesley Hay, Weston under Lizard (1934—74), Great Wyrley

CANNOCK UD
Cannock
CHEADLE RD
Alton, Blore with Swinscoe (1934—74), Bradley in the Moors (1894—1934), Cauldon (1894—1934), Caverswall, Cheadle, Checkley, Cheddleton, Consall, Cotton, Denstone (1894—1934), Dilhorne, Draycott in the Moors, Farley, Forsbrook (1896—1974), Ipstones, Kingsley, Oakamoor (1896—1974), Waterhouses (1934—74)
COSELEY UD (1894—1966[10])
Coseley
DARLASTON UD (1894—1966[10])
Darlaston
DUDLEY RD (1894—1929[72])
Dudley Castle Hill
FENTON UD (1894—1910[12])
Fenton
GNOSALL RD (1894—1934[68])
Adbaston, Church Eaton, Forton, Gnosall, Norbury, High Offley, Weston Jones
HANDSWORTH UD (1894—1911[73])
Handsworth
HEATHTOWN[74] (or WEDNESFIELD HEATH) UD (1894—1927[21])
Heathtown[74]
KIDSGROVE UD
Hardings Wood, Kidsgrove, Newchapel (1904—74),

Talke (1932—74)

KINGSWINFORD RD (1894—1934[68])
Amblecote (1894—98), Kingswinford

LEEK RD
Alstonfield (1934—74), Bagnall (1922—74), Bradnop and Cawdry, Brown Edge (1965—74), Butterton, Endon and Stanley, Fawfieldhead, Grindon, Heathylee, Heaton, Hollinsclough, Horton, Ilam (1934—74), Leek and Lowe (1894—95), Leekfrith, Longnor, Longsdon, Lowe (1895—1934), Norton in the Moors, Onecote, Quarnford, Rudyard (1894—1934), Rushton (1934—74), Rushton James (1894—1934), Rushton Spencer (1894—1934), Sheen, Tittesworth, Warslow and Elkstones, Wetton (1934—74)

LEEK UD
Leek

LICHFIELD RD
Alrewas, Armitage, Brereton (1894—1934), Brindley Heath (1934—74), King's Bromley, King's Bromley Hays (1894—1922), Burntwood (1929—74); Burntwood, Edial and Woodhouses (1894—1929); Clifton Campville and Haunton (1934—74), Colton, Curborough and Elmhurst, Drayton Bassett (1934—74), Edingale (1894—1934), Elford, Farewell and Chorley, Fazeley (1934—74), Fisherwick, Freeford (1894—1934), Fulfen (1894—1934), Hammerwich, Harlaston (1934—74), Haselour (1894—1934), Hints (1934—74), Longdon, Ogley Hay Rural (1896—1934), Hamstall Ridware, Mavesyn Ridware, Pipe Ridware (1894—1934), Shenstone, Streethay, Swinfen and Packington, Tamhorn (1894—1934), Thorpe Constantine (1934—74), Wall, Weeford, Whittington, Wiggington (1934—74), Yoxall (1894—1934)

MAYFIELD RD (1894—1934[68])
Alstonfield, Blore with Swinscoe, Calton, Calwich, Ellastone, Ilam, Mayfield, Musden Grange, Okeover, Prestwood, Ramshorn, Stanton, Waterfall, Wetton, Woodhouses (1894—1916), Wootton

NEWCASTLE UNDER LYME RD
Ashley (1932—74), Audley Rural (1932—74), Balterley, Betley, Chapel and Hill Chorlton, Clayton (1896—1932), Keele, Madeley, Maer, Mucklestone (1932—74), Tyrley (1932—74), Whitmore

PERRY BARR UD (1894—1928[75])
Perry Barr

QUARRY BANK UD (1894—1934[68])
Quarry Bank

ROWLEY REGIS UD (1894—1933[29])
Rowley Regis

RUGELEY UD
Rugeley

SEDGLEY UD (1894—1966[10])
Sedgley (pt 1894—1903, ent 1903—66)

SEISDON RD
Bobbington (pt 1894—95, ent 1895—1974), Codsall, Enville, Himley, Kinver, Patshull, Pattingham, Lower Penn, Upper Penn (1894—1934), Swindon (1896—1974), Trysull and Seisdon, Wombourn (1894—1966), Wombourne (1966—74), Woodford Grange (1894—1900), Wrottesley

SHORT HEATH UD (1894—1934[68])
Short Heath

SMALLTHORNE UD (1894—1922[15])
Chell (1904—22), Milton (1904—22), Smallthorne

SMETHWICK UD (1894—99[40])
Smethwick

STAFFORD RD
Adbaston (1934—74), Baswich, Bradley, Brocton, Castle Church, Chartley Holme (1894—1934), Church Eaton (1934—74), Colwich, Cresswell, Ellenhall, Forton (1934—74), Fradswell, Gayton, Gnosall (1934—74), Haughton, Hopton and Coton, Ingestre, Marston, Norbury (1934—74), High Offley (1934—74), Ranton, Salt and Enson, Seighford, Stowe, Stretton (1934—74), Tillington (1894—1917), Tixall, Weston under Trent, Whitgreave, Worston (1894—1934), Yarlet (1894—1934)

STOKE UPON TRENT RD (1894—1922[15])
Bagnall (1896—1922), Stoke Rural (1899—1922)

STONE RD
Barlaston, Chebsey, Cold Norton (1894—1932), Eccleshall, Fulford (1897—1974), Hilderstone (1897—1974), Milwich, Sandon, Standon, Stone Rural, Swynnerton, Trentham (1894—1932)

STONE UD
Stone

TAMWORTH RD (Staffs [1894—1932], Warws [1894—1965])
Canwell, Clifton Campville and Haunton, Croxall (pt 1894—95, ent 1895—1934), Drayton Bassett (pt 1894—95, ent 1895—1934), Edingale, Fazeley, Harlaston, Hints, Hopwas Hays, Statfold, Syerscote, Thorpe Constantine, Wiggington

TETTENHALL UD (1894—1966[10])
Tettenhall

TIPTON UD (1894—1938[47])
Tipton

TUNSTALL UD (1894—1910[12])
Tunstall

TUTBURY RD
Anslow, Barton under Needwood, Branston, Dunstall, Hanbury, Outwoods, Rolleston, Stretton, Tatenhill, Tutbury, Wychnor, Yoxall (1934—74)

UNNAMED RD (1894—1934, administered by Shifnal RD Co Council, Salop)
Blymhill, Weston under Lizard

UTTOXETER RD
Blithfield, Bramshall (1894—1934), Abbot's Bromley, Croxden, Denstone (1934—74), Draycott in the Clay, Ellastone (1934—74), Field (1894—1934), Gratwich (1894—1934), Kingston, Leigh, Marchington, Marchington Woodlands (1894—1934), Mayfield (1934—74), Newborough, Okeover (1934—74), Ramshorn (1934—74), Rocester, Stanton (1934—74), Uttoxeter (1894—96), Uttoxeter Rural (1896—1974), Wootton (1934—74)

UTTOXETER UD (1896[76]—1974)
Uttoxeter

WALSALL RD (1894—1934[68])
Aldridge, Great Barr, Bentley, Pelsall, Rushall

WEDNESFIELD UD (1894—1966[10])
Wednesfield

WILLENHALL UD (1894—1966[10])
Short Heath (1934—66), Willenhall

WOLSTANTON RD (1894—1904[77])
Chell, Chesterton, Goldenhill, Milton, Newchapel, Silverdale, Wolstanton

WOLSTANTON UNITED UD (1904[77]—32[79])
Chesterton, Silverdale, Wolstanton

NON-METROPOLITAN COUNTY

As constituted 1 Apr 1974, defined in terms of Adm Co units as of 31 Mar.

CANNOCK CHASE DIST
Cannock UD, pt Lichfield RD (Brindley Heath), Rugeley UD

LICHFIELD DIST
Lichfield MB, pt Lichfield RD (all except Brindley Heath)

NEWCASTLE-UNDER-LYME DIST
Kidsgrove UD, Newcastle under Lyme MB, Newcastle under Lyme RD

STAFFORD DIST
Stafford MB, Stafford RD, Stone RD, Stone UD

EAST STAFFORDSHIRE DIST
CB (assoc with Staffs): Burton upon Trent CB
from Staffs: Tutbury RD, Uttoxeter RD, Uttoxeter RD

SOUTH STAFFORDSHIRE DIST
Cannock RD, Seisdon RD

STAFFORDSHIRE MOORLANDS DIST
Biddulph UD, Cheadle RD, Leek RD, Leek UD

STOKE ON TRENT DIST
CB (assoc with Staffs): Stoke on Trent CB

TAMWORTH DIST
Tamworth MB

TYNE AND WEAR METROPOLITAN COUNTY

As constituted 1 Apr 1974, defined in terms of Adm Co units as of 31 Mar.

GATESHEAD METROP DIST
CB (assoc with Durham): Gateshead CB
from Durham: Blaydon UD, pt Chester le Street RD (Birtley,[1] Lamesley), Felling UD, Ryton UD, Whickham UD

NEWCASTLE UPON TYNE METROP DIST
CB (assoc with Northumb): Newcastle upon Tyne CB, Moot Hall and Precincts
from Northumb: pt Castle Ward RD (Brunswick, Dinnington, North Gosforth, Hazlerigg, Woolsington), Gosforth UD, Newburn UD

SUNDERLAND METROP DIST
CB (assoc with Durham): Sunderland CB

from Durham: pt Chester le Street RD[2] (pts of South Biddick, Birtley, Harraton), pt Easington RD (Burdon, Warden Law), Hetton UD, Houghton le Spring UD, Washington UD

NORTH TYNESIDE METROP DIST
CB (assoc with Northumb): Tynemouth CB
from Northumb: Longbenton UD, pt Seaton Valley UD[3] (wards of Backworth, Earsdon, Shiremoor), Wallsend MB, pt Whitley Bay MB[3]

SOUTH TYNESIDE METROP DIST
CB (assoc with Durham): South Shields CB
from Durham: Boldon UD, Hebburn UD, Jarrow MB

WARWICKSHIRE

ALTERATIONS IN COUNTY BOUNDARIES

As noted by year below, Warws pars gained territory from or lost it to pars in adjoining cos or county boroughs, or were entirely transferred to them. Details of these alterations are noted in Part I of the *Guide* under Warwickshire.

ANCIENT COUNTY (until 1889: Hds, Bors, MBs, PLUs, RSDs, USDs)

1844 Little Compton, Sutton under Brailes, Tardebigge. *1866* Tamworth. *1877* Monks Kirby. *1880* Merevale. *1880s* Hinckley. *1885* Merevale.

COVENTRY CO OF ITSELF (1452—1842[1])

The parishes pt or ent in Coventry Bor (see BOROUGHS below) and the following in the Co: Ansty, Foleshill[2] (1552—1842), Kersley[2] (sep civ identity early—1842), Stivichall[2] (sep civ identity early—1842), Stoke[2] (prob beginning reign Eliz I—1842), pt Walsgrave on Sowe[2] (early 17th cent—1842), Wyken[2] (by 1547—1842)

WARWICKSHIRE ADMINISTRATIVE COUNTY (1889—1974: Hds,[3] PLUs, MBs, RDs, UDs, with assoc CBs of Birmingham, Coventry, Solihull [1964—74])

1889 Aston, Birmingham, Edgbaston, Coventry Holy Trinity, Coventry St Michael, Mollington. *1891* Harborne. *1894* Ilmington, Ipsley, Welford, Weston on Avon. *1895* Drayton Bassett, Mollington, Stoneton. *1896* Batsford, Oldberrow. *1899* Foleshill, Stoke. *1911* Aston Manor, Erdington. *1928* Allesley, Berkswell, Coundon, Coventry Holy Trinity Without, Coventry St Michael Without, Foleshill, Stivichall, Stoke, Stoke Heath, Stoneleigh, Sutton Coldfield, Walsgrave on Sowe. *1931* Alderminster, Bickmarsh, Castle Brom-wich, Clifford Chambers, Dorsington, Ipsley, Long Marston, Minworth, Preston on Stour, Sheldon, Shipston on Stour, Solihull, Sutton Coldfield, Tidmington, Tredington, Welford on Avon, Weston on Avon. *1932* Allesley, Amington and Stonydelph, Baginton, Binley, Bolehall and Glascote, Coundon, Exhall, Foleshill, Keresley, Stivichall, Stoneleigh, Walsgrave on Sowe, Willenhall, Wilnecote and Castle Liberty, Wyken. *1935* Admington, Caldecote, Churchover, Copston Magna, Hartshill, Mancetter, Monks Kirby, Newton and Biggin, Nuneaton, Stretton Baskerville, Wibtoft, Willey. *1956* Allesley, Baginton, Binley, Shilton, Stoneleigh. *1964* Balsall, Bickenhill, Solihull Urban. *1965* Alcester, Allesley, Ansty, Arrow, Baginton, Bedworth, Berkswell, Binley Woods, Brandon and Bretford, Dordon, Glascote, Keresley, Kingsbury, Newton Regis, Polesworth, Ryton on Dunsmore, Sambourne, Shilton, Shuttington, Stoneleigh, Stretton Baskerville, Weethley, Wilnecote and Castle Liberty. *1966* Bickenhill, Castle Bromwich, Kingshurst, Sutton Coldfield. *1969* Studley.

WARWICKSHIRE NON-METROPOLITAN COUNTY (from 1974: Dists)

1974 Allesley, Balsall, Barston, Berkswell, Bickenhill, Castle Bromwich, Chelmsley Wood, Fordbridge, Hampton in Arden, Hockley Heath, Keresley, Kingshurst, Meriden, Sutton Coldfield.

ASSOCIATED COUNTY BOROUGHS AND COUNTY OF ITSELF

BIRMINGHAM CB

Bdry: 1891,[4] 1909,[5] 1911,[6] 1912,[7] 1931,[8] 1964 (incl exchanges pts with Solihull MB as altered area of latter constituted Solihull CB),[9] 1966.[10] Transf 1974 to W Midlands.[11]

COVENTRY CO OF ITSELF (1452—1842[1]), CB

Bdry: 1928,[12] 1932,[13] 1956,[14] 1965.[15] Transf 1974 to W Midlands.[11]

SOLIHULL CB (1964—74)

Cr 1964 when area of Solihull MB altered (incl exchanges pts with Birm CB) and constituted a CB.[9] Transf 1974 to W Midlands.[11]

HUNDREDS[3]

BARLINCHWAY HD[16]

Alcester,[17] Great Alne, Alveston, Arrow, Aston Cantlow, Bearley, Beaudesert, Beausale (from 1866), Bidford on Avon, Billesley, Binton, Budbrooke, Bushwood (from 1866), Claverdon, Coughton, Exhall, Fulbrook, Hampton Lucy, Haseley, Haselor, Hatton, Honiley, pt Ipsley, Kinwarton, Langley (from 1866), Lapworth (from 1833), Loxley, Luddington (from 1664), Morton Bagot, Norton Lindsey, Oversley (from 1866), Packwood (from 1833), Pinley (from 1866), Preston Bagot, Rowington, Salford Priors, Sambourn (from 1866), Sherbourne, Shrewley (from 1866), Snitterfield, Spernall, Old Stratford,[17] Stratford on Avon[17] (from 1866), Studley, Tanworth (from 1833), Temple Grafton, Weethley, pt Welford, pt Weston on Avon, Wixford, Wolverton, Wootton, Wawen,[17] Wroxall

HEMLINGFORD HD

Amington and Stonydelph (from 1866), Ansley, Aston,[17] Atherstone (from 1866), Austrey, Baddesley

Clinton, Baddesley Ensor, Balsall (from 1866), Barston, Baxterley, Bentley (from 1866), Berkswell, Bickenhill, Birmingham,[17] Bolehall and Glascote (from 1866), Caldecote, Chilvers Coton, Coleshill, Corley, Curdworth, Edgbaston,[17] Elmdon, Fillongley, Grendon, Hampton in Arden, Hartshill (from 1866), Kingsbury, Kinwalsey (from 1866), Knowle (from 1866), Mancetter,[17] Lea Marston, Maxstoke, Merevale (pt until 1885, ent from 1885), Meriden, Middleton, Minworth (from 1866), Newton Regis, No Man's Heath (from 1858), Nuneaton,[17] Nuthurst (from 1866), Oldbury (from 1866), Great Packington, Little Packington, Polesworth, Seckington, Sheldon, Shustoke, Shuttington, Solihull,[17] Sutton Coldfield,[17] pt Tamworth[17] (until 1866), Weddington, Nether Whitacre, Over Whitacre, Wilnecote and Castle Liberty (from 1866), Wishaw

KINGTON (sometimes 'KINETON') HD

Atherstone on Stour, Barcheston, Barford, Barton on the Heath, Brailes, Burmington, Chadshunt, Charlecote, Cherington, Chesterton, Combrook (from 1866), Fenny Compton, Little Compton (from 1844), Long Compton, Compton Verney (from 1858), Compton Wynyates, pt Cropredy (until 1866), Avon Dassett, Burton Dassett, Eatington, Farnborough, Gaydon, Halford, Honington, Idlicote, pt Ilmington, Kineton,[17] Lapworth (until 1833), Lighthorne, Butlers Marston, Priors Marston, pt Mollington (from 1866), Moreton Morrell, Newbold Pacey, Oxhill, Packwood (until 1833), Pillerton Hersey, Pillerton Priors, Priors Hardwick, Radway, Ratley and Upton, Shottswell, Lower Shuckburgh, Stourton (from 1866), Stretton on Fosse, Sutton under Brailes (from 1844), pt Bishops Tachbrook, Tanworth (until 1833), Tysoe, Warmington, Wasperton, Wellesbourne (until 1866), Wellesbourne Hastings and Walton (from 1866), Wellesbourne Mountford (from 1866), Whatcote, Whichford, Whitchurch, Great Wolford, Little Wolford (from 1866), Wormleighton

KNIGHTLOW HD

Allesley, Ansty (from 1842), Arley, Ashow, Astley, Baginton, Bedworth, Bilton, Binley, Birdingbury, Bourton on Dunsmore, Brandon and Bretford (from 1866), Brinklow,[17] Brownsover (from 1866), Bubbenhall, Bulkington, Burton Hastings, Chapel Ascote (from 1858), Churchover, pt Claybrooke (until 1866), Clifton upon Dunsmore, Combe Fields (from 1858), Copston Magna (from 1866), Cosford (from 1866), Coundon (from 1866), Coventry Holy Trinity[17] (pt until 1842, ent from 1842), Coventry St Michael[17] (from 1842), Cubbington, Dunchurch, Easenhall (from 1866), Eathorpe (from 1866), Exhall (from 1842), Foleshill (from 1842), Frankton, Grandborough, Guy's Cliffe (from 1858), Harborough Magna, Harbury, Hillmorton, pt Hinckley[17] (until 1880s), Hodnell (from 1858), Hunningham, Bishop's Itchington, Long Itchington, Kenilworth,[17] Keresley (from 1842), Ladbroke, Church Lawford, Little Lawford (from 1866), Long Lawford (from 1866), Leamington Hastings, Leamington Priors,[17] Leek Wootton, Lillington, Marton, Milverton, Monks Kirby, Monks Riding (1858—85), Napton on the Hill, Newbold on Avon, Kings Newnham, Newton and Biggin (from 1866), Offchurch, Pailton (from 1866), Princethorpe (from 1866), Lower Radbourn (from 1858), Upper Radbourn (from 1858), Radford Semele, Rugby,[17] Ryton on Dunsmore, Shilton, Upper Shuckburgh, Southam,[17] Stivichall (from 1842), Stockton, Stoke (from 1842), Stoneleigh, Stretton Baskerville, Stretton on Dunsmore, Stretton under Fosse, pt Bishops Tachbrook, Thurlaston (from 1866), Ufton, Walsgrave on Sowe (pt until 1842, ent from 1842), Wappenbury, Warwick St Mary,[17] Warwick St Nicholas,[17] Watergall (from 1858), Weston under Wetherley, Whitnash, Wibtoft (from 1866), Willenhall[18] (from 1866), Willey, Wills Pastures (from 1858), Willoughby, Withybrook, Wolfhampcote, Wolston, Wolvey, Wyken (from 1858)

BOROUGHS

Units with some degree of burghal character[19] are denominated 'Bor'. Those which did not sustain that status until the 19th cent are in italics. MBs were established by the Municipal Corporations Act, 1835,[20] or by later charter.

ALCESTER BOR
Alcester

ASTON MANOR MB (1903[21]—12[7])
Aston Manor

ATHERSTONE BOR
pt Mancetter

BIRMINGHAM BOR, MB (1838[22]—89), CB[23] (1889—1974)
Aston (pt 1838—94 [enlarged pt (area Saltley USD) 1891—94], ent 1894—1912), Aston Manor (1911—12), Balsall Heath (1894—1912), Birmingham, Edgbaston (1838—1912), Erdington (1911—12), Harborne (pt [area Harborne USD] 1891—94, ent 1894—1912), pt Kings Norton ([area Balsall Heath USD] 1891—94), Quinton (1909—12), Yardley (1911—12)

BRETFORD BOR
pt Wolston

BRINKLOW BOR
Brinklow

COLESHILL BOR
pt Coleshill

COVENTRY BOR/MB/CB[24] [for constitution of the Co of Itself, see entry above]
Coventry (1900—74), pt Coventry Holy Trinity (until 1894), Coventry Holy Trinity Within (1894—1900), pt Coventry St Michael (until 1894), Coventry St Michael Within (1894—1900)

HENLEY IN ARDEN BOR
pt Wootton Wawen

KENILWORTH BOR
Kenilworth

KINETON BOR
  pt Kineton
NUNEATON BOR, MB (1907[25]—74)
  Chilvers Coton (1907—20), Nuneaton
ROYAL LEAMINGTON SPA MB[26] (1875[27]—1974)
  Leamington (1902—74), Leamington Priors (1875—1902), Lillington (pt 1890—94, ent 1894—1902), pt Milverton (1890—94), New Milverton (1894—1902)
RUGBY MB (1932[28]—74)
  Rugby
SOLIHULL BOR, MB (1954[29]—64), CB (1964[9]—74)
  Solihull Urban
SOUTHAM BOR
  Southam

STRATFORD ON AVON BOR/MB[30]
  Alveston (1924—74), pt Old Stratford (until 1894), Old Stratford Within (1894—74), Stratford on Avon
SUTTON COLDFIELD BOR, MB (1885[31]—1974)
  Sutton Coldfield
TAMWORTH BOR/MB[32] (*Staffs*, Warws until 1866; ent *Staffs* 1866—90; pt Staffs, pt Warws 1890—94; ent *Staffs* 1894—1974)
  pt Bolehall and Glascote (1890—94), *Tamworth*[32] (*pt until 1866 [enlarged pt 1835—66;` ent 1866—1974)*), pt Tamworth Castle (1890—94)
WARWICK BOR/MB
  Warwick (1921—74), Warwick St Mary (until 1921), Warwick St Nicholas (until 1921)

POOR LAW UNIONS

In Warws Poor Law County:[33]
ALCESTER PLU (Warws, Worcs)
  Alcester, Great Alne, Arrow, Aston Cantlow, Bidford on Avon, Coughton, Exhall, Haselor, Ipsley,[34] Kinwarton, Morton Bagot, Oldberrow,[35] Oversley, Salford Priors, Sambourn, Spernall, Studley, Weethley, Wixford
ASTON PLU (1836—1911)
  Aston, Aston Manor (1894—1911), Castle Bromwich (1894—1911), Curdworth, Erdington (1894—1911), Minworth, Sutton Coldfield, Water Orton (1894—1911), Wishaw
ATHERSTONE PLU (Warws, Leics)
  Ansley, Atherstone, Baddesley Ensor, Baxterley, Bentley, Grendon, Hartshill, Mancetter, Merevale,[36] Oldbury, Polesworth
BIRMINGHAM INCORP/PLU (1783—1930)
  Aston (1911—12), Aston Manor (1911—12), Balsall Heath (1911—12), Birmingham, Edgbaston (1911—12), Erdington (1911—12), Handsworth (1911—30), Harborne (1911—12), Perry Barr (1928—30), Quinton (1911—12), Yardley (1911—12)
COVENTRY INCORP/PLU
  Coventry (1900—30), Coventry Holy Trinity (until 1894), Coventry Holy Trinity Within (1894—1900), Coventry Holy Trinity Without (1894—1928), Coventry St Michael (until 1894), Coventry St Michael Within (1894—1900), Coventry St Michael Without (1894—1928)
FOLESHILL PLU (Warws, Coventry Co of Itself [1836—42])
  Ansty, Bedworth, Binley, Exhall, Foleshill, Keresley, Shilton, Stoke (1836—1928), Stoke Heath (1920—28), Walsgrave on Sowe, Willenhall, Withybrook, Wyken
MERIDEN PLU
  Allesley, Berkswell, Bickenhill, Castle Bromwich (1911—30), Coleshill, Corley, Coundon, Curdworth (1911—30), Fillongley, Hampton in Arden, Kinwalsey (1836—95), Lea Marston, Maxstoke, Meriden, Minworth (1911—30), Great Packington, Little Packington, Sheldon, Shustoke, Sutton Coldfield (1911—30), Water Orton (1911—30), Nether Whitacre, Over Whitacre, Wishaw (1911—30)
NUNEATON PLU
  Arley, Astley, Bulkington, Burton Hastings (between 1896/1900—1930), Caldecote, Chilvers Coton (1836—1920), Nuneaton, Stretton Baskerville (between 1896/1900—1930), Weddington, Wolvey (between 1896/1900—1930)
RUGBY PLU (Warws, Northants, Leics)
  Bilton, Birdingbury, Bourton on Dunsmore, Brandon and Bretford, Brinklow (soon after 1836[37]—1930), Brownsover, Churchover, Clifton upon Dunsmore, Combe Fields, Cosford, Dunchurch, Easenhall (soon after 1836[37]—1930), Frankton, Grandborough, Harborough Magna, Hillmorton, Church Lawford, Little Lawford, Long Lawford, Leamington Hastings, Marton, Monks Riding (1862—85), Newbold on Avon, Kings Newnham, Newton and Biggin, Princethorpe, Rugby, Ryton on Dunsmore, Stretton on Dunsmore, Thurlaston, Willoughby, Wolfhampcote, Wolston
SOLIHULL PLU (Warws, Worcs [1836—1911])
  Baddesley Clinton, Balsall, Barston, Bushwood, Elmdon, Knowle, Lapworth, Nuthurst, Packwood, Solihull, Tanworth, Yardley[38] (1836—1912)
SOUTHAM PLU
  Chadshunt, Chapel Ascote, Chesterton, Fenny Compton, Burton Dassett, Gaydon, Harbury, Hodnell (1858—1930), Bishop's Itchington, Long Itchington, Ladbroke, Lighthorne, Napton on the Hill, Priors Hardwick, Priors Marston, Lower Radbourn (1858—1930), Upper Radbourn (1858—1930), Lower Shuckburgh, Upper Shuckburgh, Southam, Stockton, Stoneton[39] (1858—1930), Ufton, Watergall (1858—1930), Wills Pastures (1858—1930), Wormleighton
STRATFORD ON AVON PLU (Warws, Glos, Worcs)
  Alveston, Atherstone on Stour, Bearley, Beaudesert, Bickmarsh (1894—1930), Billesley, Binton, Charlecote, Claverdon, Combrook, Compton Verney, Eatington, Fulbrook, Hampton Lucy, Kineton, Langley, Luddington, Loxley, Milcote (1894—1930), Moreton Morrell, Newbold Pacey, Preston Bagot, Snitterfield, Old Stratford (1836—94), Old Stratford and Drayton (1894—1930), Old Stratford Within (1894—1930), Stratford on Avon, Temple Grafton, Welford,[40] Wellesbourne Hastings and Walton, Wellesbourne Mountford, Weston on Avon,[40] Whitchurch, Wolverton, Wootton Wawen
WARWICK PLU
  Ashow, Baginton, Barford, Beausale, Blackdown

(1894—1930), Bubbenhall, Budbrooke, Cubbington, Eathorpe, Guy's Cliffe (1862—1930), Haseley, Hatton, Honiley, Hunningham, Kenilworth, Leamington (1902—30), Leamington Priors (1836—1902), Leek Wootton, Lillington (1836—1902), Milverton (1836—94), New Milverton (1894—1902), Old Milverton, Norton Lindsey, Offchurch, Pinley (1836—86), Radford Semele, Rowington, Sherbourne, Shrewley, Stivichall, Stoneleigh, Bishops Tackbrook, Wappenbury, Warwick (1921—30), Warwick St Mary (1836—1921), Warwick St Nicholas (1836—1921), Wasperton, Weston under Wetherley, Whitnash, Wroxall

In Other Poor Law Counties:
BANBURY PLU (Oxon, Warws)
   Avon Dassett (1836—1930), Farnborough (1836—1930), Mollington[41] (1836—89), Mollington[41] (1889—95), Radway (1836—1930), Ratley and Upton (1836—1930), Shotteswell, Warmington (1836—1930)
CHIPPING NORTON PLU (Oxon, Warws, Glos)
   Barton on the Heath, Little Compton,[42] Long Compton

HINCKLEY PLU (Leics, Warws [1836—80s])
   Burton Hastings (1836—between 1896/1900), Hinckley,[43] Stretton Baskerville (1836—between 1896/1900), Wolvey (between 1896/1900—1930)
KINGS NORTON PLU (Worcs, Warws [1836—1911], Birm CB [1889—1911])
   Balsall Heath[44] (1894—1911), Edgbaston, Harborne[45]
LUTTERWORTH PLU (Leics, Warws, Northants [1835—94])
   Copston Magna, Monks Kirby, Pailton, Stretton under Fosse, Wibtoft, Willey
SHIPSTON ON STOUR PLU (Worcs, Warws, Glos)
   Barcheston, Batsford,[46] Brailes, Burmington, Cherington, Compton Wynyates, Halford, Honington, Idlicote, Ilmington,[47] Butlers Marston, Oxhill, Pillerton Hersey, Pillerton Priors, Stourton, Stretton on Fosse, Sutton under Brailes,[42] Tysoe, Whatcote, Whichford, Great Wolford, Little Wolford
TAMWORTH PLU (Staffs, Warws)
   Amington and Stonydelph, Austrey, Bolehall and Glascote, Drayton Bassett,[48] Kingsbury, Middleton, Newton Regis, No Man's Heath (1861—87), Seckington, Shuttington, Tamworth, Tamworth Castle (1836—94), Wilnecote and Castle Liberty

SANITARY DISTRICTS

ALCESTER RSD
   same as PLU for Warws pars less pt Feckenham, pt Ipsley
ASTON RSD
   same as PLU less pt Aston, Sutton Coldfield
ASTON MANOR USD
   pt Aston
ATHERSTONE RSD
   same as PLU for Warws pars
BANBURY RSD
   same as PLU for Warws pars
BIRMINGHAM USD[23] (Warws, *Worcs*)
   pt Aston (enlarged pt 1891—94), Birmingham, Edgbaston, *pt Harborne (1891—94), pt Kings Norton (1891—94)*
BULKINGTON USD
   Bulkington (ent 1875—83, pt 1883—94)
CHILVERS COTON USD (1875—93[49])
   Chilvers Coton
CHIPPING NORTON RSD
   same as PLU for Warws pars
COVENTRY RSD
   same as PLU less pt Coventry Holy Trinity, pt Coventry St Michael
COVENTRY USD
   pt Coventry Holy Trinity, pt Coventry St Michael
FOLESHILL RSD
   same as PLU
HINCKLEY RSD
   same as PLU for Warws pars
KENILWORTH USD
   Kenilworth
LILLINGTON USD (1875—90[26])
   pt Lillington

LUTTERWORTH RSD
   same as PLU for Warws pars
MERIDEN RSD
   same as PLU
MILVERTON USD (1875—90[26])
   pt Milverton
NUNEATON RSD
   same as PLU less Bulkington (ent 1875—83, pt 1883—94), Chilvers Coton, Nuneaton
NUNEATON USD (1875—93[49])
   Nuneaton
NUNEATON AND CHILVERS COTON USD (1893[49]—94)
   Chilvers Coton, Nuneaton
ROYAL LEAMINGTON SPA USD[26]
   Leamington Priors, pt Lillington (1890—94), pt Milverton (1890—94)
RUGBY RSD
   same as PLU less Rugby
RUGBY USD
   Rugby
SALTLEY USD (1875—91[23])
   pt Aston
SHIPSTON ON STOUR RSD
   same as PLU for Warws pars
SOLIHIULL RSD
   same as PLU for Warws pars
SOUTHAM RSD
   same as PLU for Warws pars
STRATFORD ON AVON RSD
   same as PLU for Warws pars less pt Old Stratford, Stratford on Avon
STRATFORD ON AVON USD
   pt Old Stratford, Stratford on Avon

SUTTON COLDFIELD USD (1885[31]—94)
Sutton Coldfield
TAMWORTH RSD
same as PLU for Warws pars
WARWICK RSD
same as PLU less Kenilworth, Leamington Priors, Lillington (ent 1875—90, pt 1890—94), Milverton (ent 1875—90, pt 1890—94), Warwick St Mary, Warwick St Nicholas
WARWICK USD
Warwick St Mary, Warwick St Nicholas

ADMINISTRATIVE COUNTY

For MBs and the associated CBs see BOROUGHS

ALCESTER RD
Alcester, Great Alne, Arrow, Aston Cantlow, Bidford on Avon, Coughton, Exhall, Haselor, Ipsley (1894—1931), Kinwarton, Morton Bagot, Oldberrow (1896—1974), Oversley (1894—1949), Salford Priors, Sambourn, Spernall, Studley, Weethley, Wixford
ASTON MANOR UD (1894—1903[21])
Aston Manor
ATHERSTONE RD
Ansley, Atherstone, Austrey (1964—74), Baddesley Ensor, Baxterley, Bentley, Caldecote (1932—74), Dordon (1948—74), Grendon, Hartshill, Kingsbury (1964—74), Mancetter, Merevale, Newton Regis (1964—74), Oldbury, Polesworth, Seckington (1964—74), Shuttington (1964—74)
BEDWORTH UD (1928[50]—74)
Bedworth, Bulkington (1938—74)
BRAILES RD (1894—1931[51])
Barcheston, Barton on the Heath, Brailes, Burmington, Cherington, Little Compton, Long Compton, Compton Wynyates, Halford, Honington, Idlicote, Ilmington, Butlers Marston, Oxhill, Pillerton Hersey, Pillerton Priors, Stourton, Stretton on Fosse, Sutton under Brailes, Tysoe, Whatcote, Whichford, Great Wolford, Little Wolford
BULKINGTON UD (1894—1932[52])
Bulkington (pt 1894—95, ent 1895[53]—1932)
CASTLE BROMWICH RD (1894—1911[6])
Castle Bromwich, Curdworth, Minworth, Water Orton, Wishaw
COVENTRY RD (1894—1928[12])
Coventry Holy Trinity Without, Coventry St Michael Without
ERDINGTON UD (1894[54]—1911[6])
Erdington
FARNBOROUGH RD (1894—1932[55])
Avon Dassett, Farnborough, Mollington (1894—95), Radway, Ratley and Upton, Shottswell, Warmington
FOLESHILLL RD (1894—1932[56])
Ansty, Bedworth (1894—1928), Binley, Exhall, Foleshill, Keresley, Shilton, Stoke (1894—1928), Stoke Heath (1920—28), Walsgrave on Sowe, Willenhall, Withybrook, Wyken
KENILWORTH UD
Kenilworth
MERIDEN RD
Allesley, Balsall (1932—74), Barston (1932—74), Berkswell, Bickenhill, Castle Bromwich (1911—74), Chelmsley Wood (1970—74), Coleshill, Corley, Coundon (1894—1931), Curdworth (1912—74), Fillongley, Fordbridge (1970—74), Hampton in Arden, Keresley (1932—74), Kingshurst (1956—74), Kinwalsey (1894—95), Lea Marston, Maxstoke, Meriden, Middleton (1964—74), Minworth (1912—1931), Great Packington, Little Packington, Sheldon (1894—1932), Shustoke, Water Orton (1911—74), Nether Whitacre, Over Whitacre, Wishaw (1912—74)
MONKS KIRBY RD (1894—1932[52])
Copston Magna, Monks Kirby, Pailton, Stretton under Fosse, Wibtoft, Willey
NUNEATON RD (1894—1932[52])
Arley, Astley, Burton Hastings, Caldecote, Stretton Baskerville, Weddington, Wolvey
NUNEATON AND CHILVERS COTON UD (1894—1911[6])
Chilvers Coton, Nuneaton
RUGBY RD
Ansty (1932—74), Arley (1932—74), Astley (1932—74), Bilton (1894—1932), Binley (1932—61), Binley Heath (1961—74), Birdingbury, Bourton on Dunsmore, Brandon and Bretford, Brinklow, Brownsover (1894—1932), Bulkington (1932—38), Churchover, Clifton upon Dunsmore, Combe Fields, Copston Magna (1932—74), Cosford, Dunchurch, Easenhall, Frankton, Grandborough, Harborough Magna, Hillmorton (1894—1932), Church Lawford, Little Lawford, Long Lawford, Leamington Hastings, Marton, Monks Kirby (1932—74), Newbold on Avon (1894—1932), Kings Newnham, Newton and Biggin, Pailton (1932—74), Princethorpe, Ryton on Dunsmore, Shilton (1932—74), Stretton on Dunsmore, Stretton under Fosse (1932—74), Thurlaston, Wibtoft (1932—74), Willey (1932—74), Willoughby, Withybrook (1932—74), Wolfhampcote, Wolston
RUGBY UD (1894—1932[57])
Rugby
SHIPSTON ON STOUR RD (1931[51]—74)
Barcheston, Barton on the Heath, Brailes, Burmington, Cherington, Little Compton, Long Compton, Compton Wynyates, Halford, Honington, Idlicote, Ilmington, Butlers Marston, Oxhill, Pillerton Hersey, Pillerton Priors, Shipston on Stour, Stourton, Stretton on Fosse, Sutton under Brailes, Tidmington, Tredington, Tysoe, Whatcote, Whichford, Great Wolford, Little Wolford
SOLIHULL RD (1894—1932[52])
Baddesley Clinton, Balsall, Barston, Bushwood, Elmdon, Knowle, Lapworth, Nuthurst, Packwood, Solihull, Tanworth
SOLIHULL UD (1932[52]—54[29])
Solihull Urban
SOUTHAM RD
Chadshunt, Chapel Ascote, Chesterton, Fenny Com-

pton, Avon Dassett (1932—74), Burton Dassett, Farnborough (1932—74), Gaydon, Harbury, Hodnell, Bishop's Itchington, Long Itchington, Ladbroke, Lighthorne, Priors Marston, Napton on the Hill, Priors Hardwick, Lower Radbourn, Upper Radbourn, Radway (1932—74), Ratley and Upton (1932—74), Shotteswell (1932—74), Lower Shuckburgh, Upper Shuckburgh, Southam, Stockton, Stoneton (1895—1974), Upton, Warmington (1932—74), Watergall, Wills Pastures, Wormleighton

STRATFORD ON AVON RD

Admington (1935—74), Alderminster (1931—74), Alveston (1894—1924), Atherstone on Stour, Bearley, Beaudesert, Bickmarsh (1894—1931), Billesley, Binton, Charlecote, Claverdon, Clifford Chambers (1931—74), Combrook, Compton Verney, Dorsington (1931—74), Eatington (1894—1948), Ettington (1948—74), Fulbrook, Hampton Lucy, Henley in Arden (1957—74), Hockley Heath (1964—74), Kineton, Langley, Loxley, Luddington, Long Marston (1931—74), Milcote, Moreton Morrell, Newbold Pacey, Preston Bagot, Preston on Stour (1931—74), Quinton (1935—74), Snitterfield, Old Stratford and Drayton, Tanworth (1932—67), Tanworth in Arden (1967—74), Temple Grafton, Ullenhall (1957—74), Welford on Avon (1931—74), Wellesbourne (1952—74), Wellesbourne Hastings and Warton (1894—1952), Wellesbourne Mountford (1894—1952), Weston on Avon (1931—74), Whitchurch, Wolverton, Wootton Wawen

TAMWORTH RD (Staffs, Warws 1894—1932; Warws 1932[58]—65[59])

Amington (1935—64), Amington and Stonydelph (1894—1935), Austrey, Bolehall and Glascote (1894—1957), Glascote (1957—65), Kingsbury, Middleton (1894—1964), Newton Regis, Seckington, Shuttington, Wilnecote and Castle Liberty (1894—1964)

WARWICK RD

Ashow, Baddesley Clinton (1932—74), Baginton, Barford, Beausale, Blackdown, Bubbenhall, Budbrooke, Bushwood (1932—74), Cubbington, Eathorpe, Guy's Cliffe, Haseley, Hatton, Honiley, Hunningham, Lapworth (1932—74), Leek Wootton, Old Milverton, Norton Lindsey, Offchurch, Radford Semele, Rowington, Sherbourne, Shrewley, Stivichall, Stoneleigh, Bishops Tachbrook, Tanworth in Arden (1965—74), Wappenbury, Wasperton, Weston under Wetherley, Whitnash, Wroxall

NON-METROPOLITAN COUNTY

As consituted 1 Apr 1974, defined in terms of Adm Co units of of 31 Mar

NUNEATON DIST

Bedworth UD, Nuneaton MB

RUGBY DIST

Rugby MB, Rugby RD

STRATFORD-ON-AVON DIST

Alcester RD, Shipston on Stour RD, Southam RD, Stratford on Avon MB, pt Stratford on Avon RD (alll except Hockley Heath)

WARWICK DIST

Kenilworth UD, Royal Leamington Spa MB, Warwick MB, Warwick RD

NORTH WARWICKSHIRE DIST

Atherstone RD, pt Meriden RD (Arley, Astley, Coleshill, Corley, Curdworth, Fillongley, Lea Marston, Maxstoke, Middleton, Great Packington, Little Packington, Shustoke, Water Orton, Nether Whitacre, Over Whitacre, Wishaw)

WEST MIDLANDS METROPOLITAN COUNTY

As constituted 1 Apr 1974, defined in terms of Adm Co units as of 31 Mar.

BIRMINGHAM METROP DIST
  CB (assoc with Warws): Birmingham CB
  from Warws: Sutton Coldfield MB
COVENTRY METROP DIST
  CB (assoc with Warws): Coventry CB
  from Warws: pt Meriden RD (Allesley, Keresley)
DUDLEY METROP DIST
  CB (assoc with Staffs): Dudley CB
  from Worcs: Halesowen MB, Stourbridge MB
SANDWELL METROP DIST
  CB (assoc with Staffs): West Bromwich CB
  CB (assoc with Worcs): Warley CB

SOLIHULL METROP DIST
  CB (assoc with Warws): Solihull CB
  from Warws: pt Meriden RD (Balsall, Barston, Berkswell, Bickenhill, Castle Bromwich, Chelmsley Wood, Fordbridge, Hampton in Arden, Kingshurst, Meriden), pt Stratford on Avon RD (Hockley Heath)
WALSALL METROP DIST
  CB (assoc with Staffs): Walsall CB
  from Staffs: Aldridge—Brownhills UD
WOLVERHAMPTON METROP DIST
  CB (assoc with Staffs): Wolverhampton CB

WESTMORLAND

'Westmorland' was orig two sep areas, the Barony of Kendal and the Barony of Westmorland. The Sheriff of the latter received suit from the former in 11 Henry III and from then until 1974 (when the Adm Co was abol to help constitute Cumbria Non-Metrop Co) 'Westmorland' was a sep co. The area of the Barony of Kendal became Kendal Wd and Lonsd. Wd; the Barony of Westmorland, East Wd and West Wd.[1]

ALTERATIONS IN COUNTY BOUNDARIES

As noted by year below, Westm pars gained territory from or lost it to pars in adjoining cos, or gained entire pars. Details of these alterations are noted in Part I of the *Guide* under Westm.

ANCIENT COUNTY (until 1889: Wds, Bors, MBs, PLUs, RSDs, USDs)
No bdry alts.

ADMINISTRATIVE COUNTY (1889—1974: Wds,[2] PLUs, MBs, RDs, UDs)
1895 Dalton. *1911* Hartley, Kaber, Winton.

(Westm was abol 1974 to help constitute Cumbria Non-Metrop Co).

WARDS[2]

EAST WD
Appleby St Laurence,[3] Appleby St Michael or Bongate,[3] Asby, Brough, Crosby Garrett, Dufton, pt Fawcett Forest (from 1866), Hartley (from 1866), Hillbeck (from 1866), Kaber (from 1866), Kirkby Stephen, Kirkby Thore, Mallerstang (from 1866), Long Marton, Milburn (from 1866), Great Musgrave, Little Musgrave (from 1866), Nateby (from 1866), Newbiggin, Ormside, Orton, Ravenstondale, Smardale (from 1866), Soulby (from 1866), Brough Sowerby (from 1866), Temple Sowerby (from 1866), Stainmore (from 1866), Waitby (from 1866), Warcop, Wharton (from 1866), Winton (from 1866)

KENDAL WD
Ambleside (from 1866), Applethwaite (from 1866), Beetham, Burton (pt until 1866, ent from 1866), Crook (from 1866), Crosthwaite and Lyth (from 1866), Docker (from 1866), Farleton (from 1866), pt Fawcett Forest (from 1866), Grasmere, Nether Graveship[3] (from 1866), Grayrigg (from 1866), Haverbrack (from 1866), Helsington (from 1866), Heversham (until 1866), Heversham with Milnthorpe (from 1866), Hincaster (from 1866), Holme (from 1866), Hugill (from 1866), New Hutton (from 1866), Old Hutton and Holmescales (from 1866), Kendal[3] (pt until 1866, ent from 1866), Kentmere (from 1866), Kirkland[3] (from 1866), Lambrigg (from 1866), Langdales (from 1866), Levens (from 1866), Longsleddale (from 1866),

Meathop and Ulpha (from 1866), Natland (from 1866), Patton (from 1866), Preston Patrick (from 1866), Preston Richard (from 1866), Rydal and Loughrigg (from 1866); Scalthwaiterigg, Hay and Hutton in the Hay (from 1866); Sedgwick (from 1866), Skelsmergh (from 1866), Stainton (from 1866), Nether Staveley (from 1866), Over Staveley (from 1866), Strickland Ketel (from 1866), Strickland Roger (from 1866), Troutbeck (from 1866), Underbarrow and Bradleyfield (from 1866), Undermillbeck (from 1866), Whinfell (from 1866), Whitwell and Selside (from 1866), Windermere (until 1866), Witherslack (from 1866)

LONSDALE WD
Barbon (from 1866), Casterton (from 1866), Dillicar (from 1866), Firbank (from 1866), Holme (from 1866), Hutton Roof (from 1866), pt Kendal[3] (until 1866), Killington (from 1866), Kirkby Lonsdale, Lupton (from 1866), Mansergh (from 1866), Middleton (from 1866)

WEST WD
Askham, Bampton, Barton (until 1866), High Barton (from 1866), Bolton (from 1866), Brougham, Cliburn, Clifton, Crosby Ravensworth, Lowther, Martindale (from 1866), King's Meaburn (from 1866), Morland, Newby (from 1866), Patterdale (from 1866), Shap, Sleagill, Sockbridge (from 1866), Great Strickland (from 1866), Little Strickland (from 1866), Thrimby (from 1866), Low Winder (from 1866), Yanwath and Eamont Bridge (from 1866)

BOROUGHS

Units with some degree of burghal character[4] are denominated 'Bor'. Those which did not sustain that status until the 19th cent are in italics. MBs were established by the Municipal Corporations Act, 1835,[5] or by later charter.

APPLEBY BOR, MB (1885[6]—1974)
Bor: pt Appleby St Laurence, pt Appleby St Michael or Bongate
MB: Appleby (1894—1974), pt Appleby St Laurence (1885—94), pt Appleby St Michael or Bongate (1885—94), Bongate (1894—1908)

KENDAL BOR/MB
Nether Graveship (1835—1908), Kendal, Kirkland (1835—1908)
MARKET BROUGH BOR
Brough

POOR LAW UNIONS

In Westm Poor Law County:[7]
EAST WARD PLU
Appleby (1894—1930), Appleby St Laurence (1836—94), Appleby St Michael or Bongate (1836—94), Ashby, Bongate (1894—1908), Brough, Colby (1894—1930), Crackenthorpe (1894—1930), Crosby Garrett, Dufton, Hartley, Hillbeck, Hoff (1894—1930), Kaber, Kirkby Stephen, Kirkby Thore, Mallerstang, Long Marton, Milburn, Murton (1894—1930), Musgrave (1894—1930), Great Musgrave (1836—94), Little Musgrave (1836—94), Nateby, Newbiggin, Ormside, Orton, Ravenstonedale, Smardale (1836—94), Soulby, Brough Sowerby, Temple Sowerby, Stainmore, Tebay (1897—1930), Waitby, Warcop, Wharton, Winton
KENDAL PLU (Westm, Lancs [1836—95])
Ambleside, Arnside (1897—1930), Applethwaite (1836—94), Barbon, Beetham, Bowness on Windermere (1894—1930), Burton, Casterton, Crook, Crosthwaite and Lyth, Dalton,[8] Dillicar, Docker, Farleton, Fawcett Forest, Firbank, Grasmere, Nether Graveship (1836—1908), Grayrigg, Haverbrack, Helsington, Heversham (1896—1930), Heversham with Milnthorpe (1836—96), Hincaster, Holme, Hugill, New Hutton, Old Hutton and Holmescales, Hutton Roof, Kendal, Kentmere, Killington, Kirkby Lonsdale, Kirkland (1836—1908), Lambrigg, Langdales, Levens, Longsleddale, Lupton, Mansergh, Meathop and Ulpha, Middleton, Milnthorpe (1896—1930), Natland, Patton, Preston Patrick, Preston Richard, Rydal and Loughrigg, Scalthwaiterigg (1897—1930); Scalthwaiterigg, Hay and Hutton in the Hay (1836—97); Sedgwick, Skelsmergh, Stainton, Nether Staveley, Over Staveley, Strickland Ketel, Strickland Roger, Troutbeck, Underbarrow and Bradleyfield, Undermillbeck, Whinfell, Whitwell and Selside, Witherslack, Windermere (1894—1930)
WEST WARD PLU
Askham, Bampton, Barton (1894—1930), High Barton (1836—94), Bolton, Brougham, Cliburn, Clifton, Crosby Ravensworth, Lowther, Martindale, King's Meaburn, Morland, Newby, Patterdale, Shap (1896—1905), Shap Rural (1905—30), Shap Urban (1905—30), Sleagill, Sockbridge, Great Strickland, Little Strickland, Thrimby, Low Winder (1836—94), Yanwath and Eamont Bridge

SANITARY DISTRICTS

AMBLESIDE USD
Ambleside, pt Applethwaite
APPLEBY USD (1885[6]—94)
pt Appleby St Laurence, pt Appleby St Michael or Bongate
BOWNESS ON WINDERMERE USD
pt Applethwaite, pt Undermillbeck
EAST WARD RSD
same as PLU less pt Appleby St Laurence (1885—94), pt Appleby St Michael or Bongate (1885—94)
GRASMERE USD[9]
Grasmere (ent 1875—83, pt 1883—91, ent 1891—94), pt Rydal and Loughrigg (1875—83)

KENDAL RSD
same as PLU for Westm pars less pt Applethwaite, Grasmere (ent 1875—83, pt 1883—91, ent 1891—94), Nether Graveship, Kendal, Kirkby Lonsdale, Kirkland, pt Rydal and Loughrigg (1875—83), pt Undermillbeck
KENDAL USD
Nether Graveship, Kendal, Kirkland
KIRKBY LONSDALE USD
Kirkby Lonsdale
WEST WARD RSD
same as PLU
WINDERMERE USD
pt Applethwaite

ADMINISTRATIVE COUNTY

For MBs, see BOROUGHS

AMBLESIDE UD (1894—1935[10])
 Ambleside
BOWNESS ON WINDERMERE UD (1894—1905[11])
 Bowness on Windermere
GRASMERE UD (1894—1935[10])
 Grasmere
KIRKBY LONSDALE UD (1894—1935[10])
 Kirkby Lonsdale
LAKES UD (1935[10]—74)
 Ambleside, Grasmere, Langdales, Patterdale, Rydal and Loughrigg, Troutbeck
SHAP UD (1905[12]—35[10])
 Shap Urban
WEST WARD RD (1894—1935[10])
 Askham, Bampton, Barton, Bolton, Brougham, Cliburn, Clifton, Crosby Ravensworth, Lowther, Martindale, King's Meaburn, Morland, Newby, Patterdale, Shap (1894—1905), Shap Rural (1905—35), Sleagill, Sockbridge, Great Strickland, Little Strickland, Thrimby, Yanworth and Eamont Bridge
EAST WESTMORLAND RD (1894—1935[10])
 Asby, Brough, Colby, Crackenthorpe, Crosby Garrett, Dufton, Hartley, Hillbeck, Hoff, Kaber, Kirkby Stephen, Kirkby Thore, Mallerstang, Long Marton, Milburn, Murton, Musgrave, Nateby, Newbiggin, Ormside, Orton, Ravenstonedale, Soulby, Brough Sowerby, Temple Sowerby, Tebay (1897—1935), Waitby, Warcop, Wharton, Winton
NORTH WESTMORLAND RD (1935[10]—74)
 Asby, Askham, Bampton, Barton, Bolton, Brough, Brougham, Cliburn, Clifton, Colby, Crackenthorpe, Crosby Garrett, Crosby Ravensowrth, Dufton, Hartley, Hillbeck, Hoff, Kaber, Kirkby Stephen, Kirkby Thore, Long Marton, Lowther, Mallerstang, Martindale, King's Meaburn, Milburn, Morland, Murton, Musgrave, Nateby, Newbiggin, Newby, Ormside, Orton, Ravenstonedale, Shap, Shap Rural, Sleagill, Sockbridge, Soulby, Brough Sowerby, Temple Sowerby, Stainmore, Great Strickland, Little Strickland, Tebay, Thrimby, Waitby, Warcop, Wharton, Winton, Yanwath and Eamont Bridge
SOUTH WESTMORLAND RD
 Arnside (1897—1974), Barbon, Beetham, Burton, Casterton, Crook, Crosthwaite and Lyth, Dalton (1895—1974), Dillicar, Docker, Farleton (1894—1935), Fawcett Forest, Firbank, Grayrigg, Haverbrack (1894—1935), Helsington, Heversham (1896—1974), Heversham with Milnthorpe (1894—96), Hincaster, Holme, Hugill, New Hutton, Old Hutton and Holmescales, Hutton Roof, Kentmere, Killington, Kirkby Lonsdale (1935—74), Lambrigg, Langdales (1894—1935), Levens, Longsleddale, Lupton, Mansergh, Meathop and Ulpha, Middleton, Milnthorpe (1896—1974), Natland, Patton, Preston Patrick, Preston Richard, Rydal and Loughrigg (1894—1935), Scalthwaiterigg (1897—1974); Scalthwaiterigg, Hay and Hutton in the Hay (1894—97); Sedgwick, Skelsmergh, Stainton, Nether Staveley, Over Staveley, Strickland Ketel, Strickland Roger, Troutbeck (1894—1935), Underbarrow and Bradleyfield, Undermillbeck (1894—1935), Whinfell, Whitwell and Selside, Witherslack
WINDERMERE UD[12]
 Bowness on Windermere (1905—74), Windermere

WORCESTERSHIRE

ALTERATIONS IN COUNTY BOUNDARIES

As noted by year below, Worcs pars gained territory from or lost it to pars in adjoining cos or county boroughs, or were entirely transferred to them. Details of these alterations are noted in Part I of the *Guide* under Worcestershire.

ANCIENT COUNTY (until 1889: Hds, Bors, MBs, PLUs, RSDs, USDs)
1844 Broom, Clent, Edvin Loach, Halesowen, Icomb, Overbury, Tenbury. *1866* Bockleton, Oldswinford, Stoke Bliss, Tardebigge. *1884* Edvin Loack, Ripple.

ADMINISTRATIVE COUNTY (1889—1974: Hds,[1] PLUs, MBs, RDs, UDs, with assoc CBs of Dudley [1889—1966], Warley [1966—74], Worcester)
1889 Bedwardine St John, Bedwardine St Michael, South Claines, Dudley, South Hallow, Whistones, Worcester All Saints, Worcester Blockhouse, Worcester College Precincts, Worcester St Alban, Worcester St Andrew, Worcester St Clement, Worcester St Helen, Worcester St Martin, Worcester St Nicholas, Worcester St Peter the Great, Worcester St Swithin. *1891* Kings Norton. *1893* Edvin Loach. *1894* Ipsley, Upper Ipsley. *1895* Upper Arley, Dowles. *1896* Batsford, Oldberrow. *1897* Acton Beauchamp, Leigh, West Malvern, Mathon Rural, Stoke Bliss. *1909* Quinton. *1911* Kings Norton, Northfield, Wythall, Yardley. *1914* North Claines,

Worcester St John Bedwardine County. *1928* Oldbury. *1929* Dudley Castle Hill. *1931* Alderminster, Ashton under Hill, Aston Somerville, Beckford, Bickmarsh, Blockley, Chaceley, Childs Wickham, North Claines, Cutsdean, Daylesford, Eldersfield, Evenlode, Hinton on the Green, Cow Honeybourne, Ipsley, Kemerton, Pebworth, Redmarley d'Abitot, Shipston on Stour, Staunton, Teddington, Tidmington, Tredington, Whittington, Worcester St John Bedwardine County, Worcester St Martin County, Worcester St Peter the Great County. *1952* North Claines, Hindlip, Warndon, Whittington, Worcester St Martin County. *1964* Wythall. *1965* Ashton under Hill, Beckford, Bockleton, Bushley, Eldersfield, Inkberrow, Redditch, Tenbury. *1966* Alvechurch, Bredon, Broadway, Cofton Hackett, Frankley, Halesowen, Honeybourne, Oldbury, Pendock, Redditch, Stourbridge, Wythall. *1969* Redditch.

(Worcs was abol 1974 to help constitute Hereford and Worcester Non-Metrop Co)

ASSOCIATED COUNTY BOROUGHS

DUDLEY CB (1889—1966)
Bdry alt: 1929,[2] 1934,[3] 1954.[4] Extended 1966, the reconstituted area then assoc with Staffs 1966—74,[5] qv.

WARLEY CB (1966—74)
Cr 1966 by union pt Birm CB (assoc with Warws), pt West Bromwich CB (assoc with Staffs), pt Dudley CB (assoc with Worcs until 1966), pt Smethwick CB (assoc with Staffs), pt Halesowen MB, pt Oldbury MB (both Worcs), pt Brierley Hill UD, pt Rowley Regis MB, pt Tipton MB (the 3 in Staffs).[5] Transf 1974 to W Midlands.[6]

WORCESTER CB
Bdry alt: 1914,[7] 1931,[8] 1952.[9] Transf 1974 to Heref & Worcs.[6]

HUNDREDS[1]

BLACKENHURST HD
Abbots Morton, Aldington (from 1866), Badsey, Bengeworth,[10] Bretforton, Evesham All Saints,[10] Evesham St Lawrence,[10] Great and Little Hampton, Church Honeybourne, pt Church Lench, North and Middle Littleton, South Littleton, Norton and Lenchwick, Offenham, Oldberrow, Wickhamford

DODDINGTREE HD
Abberley, Acton Beauchamp, Alfrick (from 1866), Areley Kings, Astley, Bayton, Bewdley[10] (from 1866), Bockleton (pt until 1866, ent from 1866), Clifton upon Teme[11] (pt until 1866, ent from 1866), Cotheridge, Doddenham, Eastham, Edvin Loach[12] (from 1844), Hanley Child (from 1866), Hanley William, Hillhampton (from 1866), Kyre Magna, Kyre Parva (from 1866), Lulsley (from 1866), Mamble, Martley, Orleton (from 1866), Ribbesford,[10] Rochford[12] (from

1866), Rock, Lower Sapey, Shelsley Beauchamp, Shelsley Kings (from 1866), Shelsley Walsh, Shrawley, Stanford on Teme, Stockton on Teme, pt Stoke Bliss[13] (until 1866), Suckley, Tenbury[11] (pt until 1844, ent from 1844), Great Witley

HALFSHIRE HD
Belbroughton, Bentley Pauncefoot (from 1866), Bromsgrove, Broom[14] (from 1844), Cakemore[15] (from 1866), Chaddesley Corbett, Churchill, Clent[14] (from 1844), Cofton Hackett, Cradley (from 1866), Cruch (from 1858), Dodderhill,[10] Dodderhill In Liberties[10] (from 1866), Doverdale, Droitwich St Andrew,[10] Droitwich St Nicholas,[10] Droitwich St Peter,[10] Dudley,[10] Dudley Castle (from 1858), Elmbridge (from 1866), Elmley Lovett, Feckenham, Frankley, Grafton Manor (from 1858), Hadzor, Hagley, Halesowen[10] (pt until 1844, ent from 1844), Hampton Lovett, pt Hartlebury (until

759

1866), Hasbury[15] (from 1866), Hawne[15] (from 1866), Hill[15] (from 1866), Hunnington[15] (from 1866), Illey[15] (from 1866), pt Ipsley,[16] Kidderminster[10] (until 1866), Kidderminster Borough[10] (from 1866), Kidderminster Foreign[10] (from 1866), Kington, pt Church Lench, Lapal[15] (from 1866), Lutley (from 1866), Lye (from 1866), Marlborough in the Vines (1858—80), Lower Mitton (from 1866), Upper Mitton (from 1866), Northfield, Kings Norton, Oldbury[15] (from 1866), pt Oldswinford (until 1866), Paper Mills (1858—84), Pedmore, Redditch (from 1866), Ridgacre[15] (from 1866), Romsley[15] (from 1866), Rushock, Salwarpe,[10] Stone, Stourbridge (from 1866), Upper Swinford (from 1866), Tardebigge (pt until 1844, ent 1844—66), Tutnall and Cobley (from 1866), Warley (from 1884), Warley Salop[15] (1866—84), Warley Wigorn (1866—84), Upton Warren, Webheath (from 1866), Westwood Park (from 1858), Wollaston (from 1866), Wollescote (from 1866), pt Wolverley, Yardley[17] (from 1760)

OSWALDSLOW HD[18]

Alvechurch,[10] Bedwardine St John,[10] Bedwardine St Michael,[10] pt Batsford, Berrow, Bishampton, Blockley, Bredicot, Bredon, Bredon's Norton (from 1866), Broadwas, Charlton (from 1866), Churchill, Claines[10] (until 1885), North Claines (from 1885), South Claines[10] (from 1885), Cleeve Prior, Conderton (from 1866), Earls Croome, Hill Croome, Croome d'Abitot, Cropthorne, Crowle, Cutsdean (from 1866), Daylesford, Elmley Castle, Evenlode, Fladbury, Grimley, Hallow (until 1885), North Hallow (from 1885), South Hallow[10] (from 1885), Hanbury, Hartlebury (pt until 1866, ent from 1866), Harvington,

Hill and Moor (from 1866), Himbleton, Hindlip, Holdfast (from 1866), Holt, Huddington, pt Icomb (until 1844), Inkberrow, Kempsey, Kenswick (from 1858), Knighton on Teme (from 1866), Knightwick, Ab Lench (from 1866), Rous Lench, Lindridge, Little Malvern, Netherton (from 1866), Norton juxta Kempsey, Oddingley, Ombersley, Overbury, Pendock, Pensax (from 1866), Redmarley d'Abitot, Ripple (pt until 1866, ent from 1866), Sedgeberrow, Shell (1858—84), Shipston on Stour, Spetchley, Stock and Bradley (from 1866), Stoke Prior, Stoulton, Teddington (from 1866), Throckmorton (from 1866), Tibberton, Tidmington, Tredington, Upton upon Severn[17] (until 1760), Warndon, Welland, White Ladies Aston, Whistones[10] (from 1866), Whittington (from 1866), Wichenford, Little Witley, pt Wolverley, Wyre Piddle

PERSHORE HD[17]

Abberton, Alderminster, Beoley, Besford (from 1866), Birlingham, Birtsmorton, Bransford (from 1866), Bricklehampton (from 1866), Broadway,[10] Broughton Hackett, Bushley, Castlemorton, Chaceley, Great Comberton, Little Comberton, Defford (from 1866), Dormston, Eckington, Eldersfield, Grafton Flyford, Flyford Flavell, Hanley Castle, Leigh, Longdon, Madresfield, Great Malvern, Martin Hussingtree, Mathon, Naunton Beauchamp, Newland (from 1866), Peopleton, Pershore Holy Cross,[10] Pershore St Andrew,[10] North Piddle, Pinvin (from 1866), Pirton, Powick, Queenhill (from 1866), pt Ripple (until 1866), Severn Stoke, Staunton, Strensham, Upton upon Severn (from 1760), Upton Snodbury, Wick (from 1866), Yardley (until 1760)

BOROUGHS

Units with some degree of burghal character[19] are denominated 'Bor'. Those which did not sustain that status until the 19th cent are in italics. MBs were established by the Municipal Corporations Act, 1835,[20] or by later charter.

ALVECHURCH BOR
Alvechurch
BEWDLEY BOR/MB
Bewdley (1866—1974), pt Ribbesford (until 1866)
BROADWAY BOR
Broadway
CLIFTON UPON TEME BOR
pt Clifton upon Teme
DROITWICH BOR/MB
pt Dodderhill (until 1866), Dodderhill In Liberties (1866—84), Droitwich (1920—74), Droitwich St Andrew (until 1920), Droitwich St Nicholas (until 1920), Droitwich St Peter (until 1920), Land Common to Droitwich St Andrew and Droitwich St Peter (The Wrangling Division) (until 1920), Marlborough in the Vines (1835—80), pt Salwarpe (1880—94), Unnamed (1894—1933)
DUDLEY BOR, MB (1865[21]—89), CB (1889—1966[5]) (Worcs, Staffs 1865—89, ent Worcs 1889—1966, the CB assoc with Staffs [qv] 1966—74)
Dudley, Dudley Castle Hill[22] (1865—89)
EVESHAM BOR/MB
Bengeworth (until 1924), Evesham (1924—74),

Evesham All Saints (until 1924), Evesham St Lawrence (until 1924)
HALESOWEN BOR,[23] MB (1936[24]—74) (Worcs, Salop until 1844, MB ent Worcs)
Bor: Halesowen
MB: Cradley, Halesowen, Hasbury, Hawne, Hill and Cakemore, Illey, Lapal, Lutley
KIDDERMINSTER BOR/MB
pt Kidderminster (until 1866), Kidderminster Borough (from 1866), Kidderminster Foreign (1835—94)
OLDBURY MB (1935[25]—66[5])
Oldbury
PERSHORE BOR
Pershore Holy Cross, Pershore St Andrew
STOURBRIDGE MB (1914[26]—74)
Lye (1933—74), Pedmore (1933—74), Stourbridge, Upper Swinford, Wollaston, Wollescote (1933—74)
TENBURY BOR
pt Tenbury
WARLEY CB (1966[5]—74)
Warley
WORCESTER BOR/MB[27]/CB
pt Bedwardine St John (1835—94 [enlarged pt 1885—

94]), Bedwardine St Michael (1835—98), pt Claines (1835—85), South Claines (1885—98), South Hallow (1885—98), Whistones (1835—98), Worcester (1898—1974), Worcester All Saints (until 1898), Worcester Blockhouse (until 1898), Worcester College Precincts (until 1898), Worcester St Alban (until 1898), Worcester St Andrew (until 1898), Worcester St Clement (pt until 1835, ent 1835—98), Worcester St Helen (until 1898), Worcester St John Bedwardine City (1894—98), pt Worcester St Martin (1835—98), Worcester St Martin City (1894—98), Worcester St Nicholas (until 1898), pt Worcester St Peter (1835—94 [enlarged pt 1885—94]), Worcester St Peter the Great City (1894—98), Worcester St Swithin

POOR LAW UNIONS

In Worcs Poor Law County:[28]

BROMSGROVE PLU (Worcs, Warws, Salop, Staffs [1836—44])

Alvechurch, Belbroughton, Bentley Pauncefoot (soon after 1836[29]—1930), Bromsgrove, North Bromsgrove (1894—1930), Beoley (1911—30), Clent,[14] Cofton Hackett, Frankley, Grafton Manor (1863—1930), Hagley, Hunnington,[15] Pedmore, Redditch (soon after 1836[29]—1930), North Redditch (1894—1930), Romsley,[15] Stoke in Bromsgrove (1894—1930), Stoke Prior, Tardebigge (until soon after 1836[30]), Tutnall and Cobley (soon after 1836[29]—1930), Webheath (soon after 1836[29]—1930), Wythall (1911—30)

DROITWICH PLU

Claines (1836—85), North Claines (1885—1930), South Claines (1894—98), Crowle, Crutch (1858—1930), Dodderhill, Dodderhill In Liberties (1836—84), Doverdale, Droitwich (1920—30), Droitwich St Andrew (1836—1920), Droitwich St Nicholas (1836—1920), Droitwich St Peter (1836—1920), Elmbridge, Elmley Lovett, Hadzor, Hampton Lovett, Hanbury, Hartlebury, Himbleton, Hindlip, Huddington, Marlborough in the Vines (1858—80), Martin Hussingtree, Upper Mitton (1894—1928), Oddingley, Ombersley, Paper Mills (1858[31]—84), Salwarpe, Shell (1858—84), Stock and Bradley, Tibberton, Unnamed (1894—1930), Upton Warren, Warndon, Westwood Park (1858—1930)

EVESHAM PLU (Worcs, Glos)

Aldington, Badsey, Bengeworth (1836—1924), Bretforton, Broadway, Cleeve Prior, Evesham (1924—30), Evesham All Saints (1836—1924), Evesham St Lawrence (1836—1924), Great and Little Hampton, Harvington, Church Honeybourne, Ab Lench, Church Lench, Rous Lench, North and Middle Littleton, South Littleton, Norton and Lenchwick, Offenham, Sedgeberrow, Wickhamford

KIDDERMINSTER PLU (Worcs, Staffs, Salop [1836—95])

Upper Arley,[32] Bedwley, Broom,[14] Chaddesley Corbett, Churchill, Dowles,[32] Kidderminster Borough, Kidderminster Foreign, Lower Mitton (1836—1928), Ribbesford, Rushock, Stone, Stourport (1928—30), Wolverley, Wribbenhall (1901—30)

KINGS NORTON PLU (1836—1912) (Worcs, Warws [1836—89], Birm CB [1889—1912], Staffs [1836—94])

Beoley, Kings Norton, Northfield, Unnamed (1894—1911)

MARTLEY PLU

Abberley, Alfrick, Areley Kings, Astley, Bransford, Broadwas, Clifton upon Teme,[11] Cotheridge, Doddenham, Grimley, Hallow (1836—85), North Hallow (1885—1930), South Hallow (1885—98), Hillhmapton, Holt, Kenswick (1861—1930), Knightwick, Leigh, Lulsley, Martley, Pensax, Lower Sapey (*ca* 1894—1930), Shelsley Beauchamp, Shelsley Kings, Shelsley Walsh, Shrawley, Stanford on Teme, Stockton on Teme, Suckley, Wichenford, Great Witley, Little Witley

PERSHORE PLU

Abberton, Besford, Birlingham, Bishampton, Bredicot, Bricklehampton, Broughton Hackett, Charlton, Churchill, Great Comberton, Little Comberton, Cropthorne, Defford, Dormston, Eckington, Elmley Castle, Fladbury, Grafton Flyford, Flyford Flevell, Hill and Moor, Kington, Naunton Beauchamp, Netherton, Norton juxta Kempsey, Peopleton, Pershore Holy Cross, Pershore St Andrew, North Piddle, Pinvin, Pirton, Spetchley, Stoulton, Strensham, Throckmorton, Upton Snodbury, White Ladies Aston, Whittington, Wick, Wyre Piddle

STOURBRIDGE PLU (Worcs, Staffs, Salop [1836—44], Birm CB [1901—11])

Cakemore[15] (1836—1919), Cradley, Halesowen, Hasbury,[15] Hawne,[15] Hill[15] (1836—1911), Hill and Cakemore (1911—30), Illey,[15] Lapal,[15] Lutley, Lye (soon after 1836[29]—1930), Oldswinford (until soon after 1836[30]), Quinton[33] (between 1891/1901—1911), Ridgacre[15] (1836—between 1891/1901), Stourbridge, Upper Swinford (soon after 1836[29]—1930), Wollaston (soon after 1836[29]—1930), Wollaston (soon after 1836[29]—1930), Wollescote

TENBURY PLU (Worcs, Salop, Heref)

Bockleton, Eastham, Hanley Child, Hanley William, Knighton on Teme, Kyre Magna, Kyre Parva, Lindridge, Orleton, Rochford,[12] Stoke Bliss,[13] Tenbury[11]

UPTON UPON SEVERN PLU

Berrow, Birtsmorton, Bushley, Castlemorton, Earls Croome, Hill Croome, Croome d'Abitot, Eldersfield, Guarlford (1894—1930), Hanley Castle, Holdfast, Kempsey, Longdon, Madresfield, Great Malvern, Little Malvern, South Malvern (1894—96), Malvern Link (1894—1930), Malvern Wells (1896—1930), Newland, Powick, Queenhill, Ripple, Severn Stoke, Upton upon Severn, Welland

WORCESTER PLU

Bedwardine St John (1836—94), Bedwardine St Michael (1836—98), Whistones (1836—98), Worcester (1898—1930), Worcester All Saints (1836—98), Worcester Blockhouse (1858—98), Worcester College Precincts (1858—98), Worcester St Alban (1836—98), Worcester St Andrew (1836—98), Worcester St Clement (1836—98), Worcester St Helen (1836—98),

Worcester St John Bedwardine City (1894—98), Worcester St John Bedwardine County (1894—1930), Worcester St Martin (1836—94), Worcester St Martin City (1894—98), Worcester St Martin County (1894—1930), Worcester St Nicholas (1836—98), Worcester St Peter the Great (1836—94), Worcester St Peter the Great City (1894—98), Worcester St Peter the Great County (1894—1930), Worcester St Swithin (1836—98)

In Other Poor Law Counties:
ALCESTER PLU (Warws, Worcs)
Abbots Morton, Feckenham, Feckenham Urban (1894—1930), Inkberrow, Ipsley,[16] Upper Ipsley (1894—1930), Oldberrow[34]
WEST BROMWICH PLU (Staffs, Worcs, Salop [1836—44])
Oldbury,[15] Warley (1844—1908), Warley Salop[15] (1836—44), Warley Wigorn (1836—84)
BROMYARD PLU (Heref, Worcs [1836—*ca* 1894])
Acton Beauchamp,[35] Edvin Loach,[12] Lower Sapey (1836—*ca* 1894)

CLEOBURY MORTIMER PLU (Salop, Worcs)
Bayton, Mamble, Rock
DUDLEY PLU (Staffs, Worcs)
Dudley
LEDBURY PLU (Heref, Worcs)
West Malvern (1897—1930), Mathon (1836—94), Mathon Rural[36] (1894—97), Mathon Urban (1894—97)
NEWENT PLU (Glos, Worcs, Heref)
Redmarley d'Abitot, Staunton
SHIPSTON ON STOUR PLU (Warws, Glos, Worcs)
Batsford,[37] Blockley, Shipston on Stour, Tidmington, Tredington
SOLIHULL PLU (Warws, Worcs [1836—1911])
Yardley (1836—1911)[38]
STOW ON THE WOLD PLU (Glos, Worcs)
Daylesford, Evenlode
STRATFORD ON AVON PLU (Warws, Glos, Worcs)
Alderminster
TEWKESBURY PLU (Glos, Worcs)
Bredon, Bredon's Norton, Chaceley, Conderton, Overbury, Pendock, Teddington
WINCHCOMB PLU (Glos, Worcs)
Cutsdean

SANITARY DISTRICTS

ALCESTER RSD
same as PLU for Worcs pars less pt Feckenham, pt Ipsley
BALSALL HEATH USD (1875—91[39])
pt Kings Norton
BEWDLEY USD
Bewdley
BROMSGROVE RSD
same as PLU less Bromsgrove, pt Grafton Manor, pt Redditch, pt Stoke Prior
BROMSGROVE COUNTRY USD
pt Bromsgrove
BROMSGROVE TOWN USD
pt Bromsgrove, pt Grafton Manor, pt Stoke Prior
WEST BROMWICH RSD
pt Warley only
BROMYARD RSD
same as PLU for Worcs pars
CLEOBURY MORTIMER RSD
same as PLU for Worcs pars
DROITWICH RSD
same as PLU less pt Claines (1875—85), Dodderhill In Liberties (1875—84), Droitwich St Andrew, Droitwich St Nicholas, Droitwich St Peter, Marlborough in the Vines (1875—81), pt Salwarpe (1880—94)
DROITWICH USD
Dodderhill In Liberties (1875—84), Droitwich St Andrew, Droitwich St Nicholas, Droitwich St Peter, Marlborough in the Vines (1875—81), pt Salwarpe (1880—94)
DUDLEY USD (Worcs, Staffs [1875—89])
Dudley
EVESHAM RSD
same as PLU less Bengeworth, Evesham All Saints, Evesham St Lawrence

EVESHAM USD
Bengeworth, Evesham All Saints, Evesham St Lawrence
KIDDERMINSTER RSD
same as PLU less Bewdley, Kidderminster Borough, pt Kidderminster Foreign, Lower Mitton
KIDDERMINSTER USD
Kidderminster Borough, pt Kidderminster Foreign
KINGS NORTON RSD
same as PLU less pt Beoley, pt Kings Norton (1891—94)
LEDBURY RSD
same as PLU for Worcs pars less pt Mathon
GREAT MALVERN USD[40]
pt Hanley Castle (Mar—apptd day 1894), pt Great Malvern (enlarged pt Mar—apptd day 1894)
MALVERN LINK USD[41]
pt Leigh, pt Mathon (1892—94)
MARTLEY RSD
same as PLU less South Hallow (1885—94), pt Leigh
MATHON USD (1875—92[41])
pt Mathon
LOWER MITTON USD (1875—89[42])
Lower Mitton
NEWENT PLU
same as PLU for Worcs pars
OLDBURY USD
Oldbury, pt Warley (1884—94)
PERSHORE RSD
same as PLU
REDDITCH USD[43]
pt Beoley, pt Feckenham, pt Ipsley,[44] Redditch (pt 1875—91, ent 1891—94), pt Webheath
SHIPSTON ON STOUR RSD
same as PLU for Worcs pars

SOLIHULL RSD
    same as PLU for Worcs par
STOURBRIDGE RSD
    same as PLU for Worcs pars less Stourbridge
STOURBRIDGE USD
    Stourbridge
STOURPORT USD (1889[42]—94)
    Lower Mitton
STOW ON THE WOLD RSD
    same as PLU for Worcs pars
STRATFORD ON AVON RSD
    same as PLU for Worcs par
TENBURY RSD
    same as PLU for Worcs pars
TEWKESBURY RSD
    same as PLU for Worcs pars
UPTON ON SEVERN RSD
    same as PLU less pt Hanley Castle (Mar—apptd day

1894), pt Great Malvern (enlarged pt 1892—94)
WINCHCOMB RSD
    same as PLU for Worcs par
WORCESTER RSD
    pt Bedwardine St John (reduced pt 1885—94), pt Worcester St Martin (reduced pt 1885—94), pt Worcester St Peter the Great
WORCESTER USD[27]
    pt Bedwardine St John (enlarged pt 1885—94), Bedwardine St Michael, pt Claines (1875—85), South Claines (1885—94), South Hallow (1885—94), Whistones, Worcester All Saints, Worcester Blockhouse, Worcester College Precincts, Worcester St Alban, Worcester St Andrew, Worcester St Clement, Worcester St Helen, pt Worcester St Martin (enlarged pt 1885—94), Worcester St Nicholas, pt Worcester St Peter the Great, Worcester St Swithin

ADMINISTRATIVE COUNTY

For MBs and the associated CB see BOROUGHS

BROMSGROVE RD
    Alvechurch, Belbroughton, Bentley Pauncefoot, Beoley (1912—74), Clent, Cofton Hackett, Dodford with Grafton (1933—74), Frankley, Grafton Manor (1894—1933), Hagley, Hunnington, Pedmore (1894—1933), North Redditch (1894—1933), Romsley, Stoke Prior, Tutnall and Cobley, Webheath (1894—1933), Wythall (1911—74)
BROMSGROVE UD (1896[45]—1974)
    Bromsgrove, Stoke in Bromsgrove (1896—1933)
NORTH BROMSGROVE UD (1896[46]—1933[47])
    North Bromsgrove
BROMSGROVE COUNTRY UD (1894—96[46])
    North Bromsgrove
BROMSGROVE TOWN UD (1894—96[45])
    Bromsgrove, Stoke in Bromsgrove
DROITWICH RD
    North Claines, Crowle, Crutch (1894—1933), Dodderhill, Doverdale, Elmbridge, Elmley Lovett, Hadzor, Hampton Lovett, Hanbury, Hartlebury, Himbleton, Hindlip, Huddington, Martin Hussingtree, Upper Mitton (1894—97), Oddingley, Ombersley, Salwarpe, Stock and Bradley, Tibberton, Upton Warren, Warndon, Westwood (1937—74), Westwood Park (1894—1937)
EVESHAM RD
    Abbots Morton (1933—74), Aldington, Ashton under Hill (1931—74), Aston Somerville (1931—74), Badsey, Beckford (1933—74), Bickmarsh (1931—74), Bretforton, Broadway, Childs Wickham (1931—74), Cleeve Prior, Conderton (1933—74), Great and Little Hampton (1894—1933), Harvington, Hinton on the Green (1931—74), Honeybourne (1953—74), Church Honeybourne (1894—1953), Cow Honeybourne (1931—53), Inkberrow (1933—74), Kemerton (1933—74), Ab Lench (1894—1933), Church Lench, Rous Lench, North and Middle Littleton, South Littleton, Norton and Lenchwick, Offenham, Overbury (1933—74), Pebworth (1931—74), Sedgeberrow, Wick-

hamford
FECKENHAM RD (1894—1933[47])
    Abbots Morton, Feckenham, Inkberrow
HALESOWEN RD (1894—1925[48])
    Cakemore (1894—1919), Cradley, Halesowen, Hasbury, Hawne, Hill (1894—1919), Hill and Cakemore (1919—25), Illey, Lapal, Lutley, Lye (1894—97), Quinton[49] (1894—1909), Upper Swinford (1894—95), Wollescote (1894—97)
HALESOWEN UD (1925[48]—36[24])
    Cradley, Halesowen, Hasbury, Hawne, Hill and Cakemore, Illey, Lapal, Lutley
KIDDERMINSTER RD
    Upper Arley (1895—1974), Broom (1894—1953), Broome (1935—74), Chaddesley Corbett, Churchill (1894—1933), Churchill and Blakedown (1933—74), Dowles (1895—1933), Kidderminster Foreign, Ribbesford, Rock (1933—74), Rushock, Stone, Wolverley, Wribbenhall (1901—33)
KINGS NORTON RD (1894—98[50])
    Beoley, Kings Norton, Northfield
KINGS NORTON AND NORTHFIELD UD (1898[50]—1912[51])
    Beoley, Kings Norton, Northfield
LYE AND WOLLESCOTE UD (1897[52]—1933[47])
    Lye, Wollescote
MALVERN UD (1898[53]—1974)
    Great Malvern, West Malvern, Malvern Link, Malvern Well
GREAT MALVERN UD (1894—98[53])
    Great Malvern, South Malvern (1894—96), Malvern Wells (1896—98)
MALVERN LINK UD (1894—98[53])
    West Malvern (1897—98), Malvern Link, Mathon Urban (1894—97)
MARTLEY RD
    Abberley, Alfrick, Areley Kings (1894—1933), Astley, Bransford, Broadheath (1952—74), Broadwas, Clifton upon Teme, Cotheridge, Doddenham, Grimley, Hallow

(1952—74), North Hallow (1894—1952), Hillhampton, Holt, Kenswick, Knightwick, Leigh, Lulsley, Martley, Pensax (1894—1933), Lower Sapey, Shelsley Beauchamp, Shelsley Kings, Shelsley Walsh, Shrawley, Stanford on Teme (1894—1933), Stockton on Teme (1894—1933), Suckley, Wichenford, Great Witley, Little Witley, Worcester St John Bedwardine County

OLDBURY UD (1894—1935[25])

Oldbury, pt Warley (1894—95)

PERSHORE RD

Abberton, Besford, Birlingham, Bishampton, Bredicot, Bredon (1933—74), Bredon's Norton (1933—74), Bricklehampton, Broughton Hackett, Charlton, Churchill, Great Comberton, Little Comberton, Cropthorne, Defford, Dormston, Drakes Broughton and Wadborough (1958—74), Eckington, Elmley Castle, Fladbury, Grafton Flyford, Flyford Flavell, Hill and Moor, Kington, Naunton Beauchamp, Netherton, Norton juxta Kempsey, Peopleton, Pershore (1949—74), Pershore Holy Cross (1894—1949), Pershore St Andrew (1894—1949), North Piddle, Pinvin, Pirton, Spetchley, Stoulton, Strensham, Throckmorton, Upton Snodsbury, White Ladies Aston, Whittington, Wick, Worcester St Peter the Great County, Wyre Piddle

REDDITCH UD

Feckenham (1933—74), Feckenham Urban, Ipsley (1931—74), Upper Ipsley, Redditch, Unnamed (1894—1911)

ROCK RD (1894—1933[47])

Bayton, Mamble, Rock

SEPARATE RD (administered by Bromsgrove RD Council) (1911[51]—12[51])

Beoley, Kings Norton, Northfield

SHIPSTON ON STOUR RD (Warws, Glos, Worcs [1894—1931])

Alderminster, Blockley, Shipston on Stour, Tidmington, Tredington

STOURBRIDGE UD (1894—1914[26])

Stourbridge, Upper Swinford (1895—1914), Wollaston

STOURPORT UD[54] (1894—1934[55])

Lower Mitton, Upper Mitton (1897—1928), Stourport (1928—34)

STOURPORT-ON-SEVERN UD (1934[55]—74)

Stourport-on-Severn

STOW ON THE WOLD RD (Glos, Worcs [1894—1931])

Daylesford, Evenlode

TENBURY RD

Bayton (1933—74), Bockleton, Eastham, Hanley (1933—74), Hanley Child (1894—1933), Hanley William (1894—1933), Knighton on Teme, Kyre (1933—74), Kyre Magna (1894—1933), Kyre Parva (1894—1933), Lindridge, Mamble (1933—74), Orleton (1894—1933), Pensax (1933—74), Rochford, Stanford with Orleton (1933—74), Stockton on Teme (1933—74), Stoke Bliss (1897—1974), Tenbury

TEWKESBURY RD (1894—1933[47])

Bredon, Bredon's Norton, Chaceley (1894—1931), Conderton, Kemerton (1931—33), Overbury, Pendock, Teddington (1894—1931)

UNNAMED RD (1894—1931[56])

Redmarley d'Abitot, Staunton

UNNAMED RD (1894—1908[57])

Warley (pt 1894—95, ent 1895—1908)

UPTON UPON SEVERN RD

Berrow, Birtsmorton, Bushley, Castlemorton, Earls Croome, Hill Croome, Croome d'Abitot, Eldersfield, Guarlford, Hanley Castle, Holdfast, Kempsey, Longdon, Madresfield, Little Malvern, Newland, Pendock (1933—74), Powick, Queenhill, Ripple, Severn Stoke, Upton upon Severn, Welland

WINCHCOMB RD (Glos, Worcs [1894—1933])

Beckford (1931—33), Cutsdean

YARDLEY RD (1894—1912[51])

Yardley

YORKSHIRE

ALTERATIONS IN COUNTY BOUNDARIES

As noted by year below, Yorks pars gained territory from or lost it to pars in adjoining cos or county boroughs, or were entirely transferred to them. Details of these alterations are noted in Part I of the *Guide* under Yorkshire.

ANCIENT COUNTY (until 1889: Hds, Bors, MBs, PLUs, RSDs, USDs)
1844 Crayke. *1860s* Crowle. *1866* Blyth, Finningley, Holwick, Mitton, Rochdale. *1884* Thorne. *1887* Thornaby. *1885* Wallingwells.

YORKSHIRE EAST RIDING ADMINIS-TRATIVE COUNTY (1889—1974: Waps,[1] PLUs, MBs, RDs, UDs, with assoc CB of Kingston upon Hull)
1889 Cottingham, Drypool, Garrison Side, Hessle, Kingston upon Hull Holy Trinity and St Mary, Marfleet, Newington, Sculcoates, Southcoates, Sutton and Stoneferry. *1895* Knedlington. *1930* Anlaby, Bilton, Cottingham, Hessle, Sutton on Hull. *1935* Anlaby, Bilton, Cottingham, Kirk Ella, Sutton on Hull, Willerby. *1955* Bilton. *1967* Heslington. *1968* Bilton, Heslington, Wawne

YORKSHIRE NORTH RIDING ADMINIS-TRATIVE COUNTY (1889—1974: Waps,[1] PLUs, MBs, RDs, UDs, with assoc CBs of Middlesbrough [1889—1968] and Teesside [1968—74])
1889 West Acklam, Linthorpe, Marton, Middlesbrough, Normanby, Ormesby. *1894* Sutton Howgrave. *1895* Lower Dunsforth, Upper Dunsforth with Branton Green, Howgrave, Humberton, Linthorpe, Milby, Sutton Howgrave. *1911* Muker. *1913* Linthorpe, Marton, Ormesby. *1929* Marton. *1932* West Acklam, Hemlington, Marton, Ormesby. *1934* Clifton Without, Heworth Without, Huntington, Osbaldwick. *1967* Cleasby. *1968* Clifton Without, Eston, Hemlington, Heworth Without, Huntington, Kirkleatham, Maltby, Marske, Marton, Morton, Newby, Nunthorpe, Ormesby, Osbaldwick, Redcar, Stainton, Thornaby, Wilton.

YORKSHIRE WEST RIDING ADMINIS-TRATIVE COUNTY (1889—1974: Waps,[1] PLUs, MBs, RDs, UDs, with assoc CBs of Barnsley [1913—74], Bradford, Dewsbury [1913—74], Doncaster [1927—74], Halifax, Huddersfield, Leeds, Rotherham [1902—74], Sheffield, Wakefield [1915—74])
1889 Allerton, Chapel Allereton, Almondbury, Armley, Attercliffe cum Darnall, Beeston, Bolton, Bowling, Bradford, Bramley, Brightside Bierlow, Calverley with Farsley, Cliviger, Dalton, Ecclesall Bierlow, Farnley, Halifax, Nether Hallam, Upper Hallam, Heaton, Headingley cum Burley, Heeley, Holbeck, Horton, Huddersfield, Hunslet, Leeds, Lindley cum Quarmby, Lockwood, Manningham, North-

owram, Ovenden, Potter Newton, Pudsey, Seacroft, Sheffield, Skircoat, Southowram, Templenewsham, Wortley. *1890* Longwood. *1894* Nunwick with Howgrave, Saddleworth. *1895* Auckley, Lower Dunsforth, Upper Dunsforth with Branton Green, Humberton, Milby, Newland, Nunwick with Howgrave, Wallingwells. *1897* Todmorden. *1899* North Bierley, Eccleshill, Idle, Thornton, Tong, Wyke. *1900* Northowram, Warley. *1901* Bradfield, Catcliffe, Ecclesfield, Handsworth, Tinsley. *1902* Greetland, Rotherham. *1912* Barwick in Elmet, Roundhay, Seacroft, Shadwell, Southowram, Tinsley. *1913* Barnsley, Dewsbury, Ravensthorpe, Soothill Nether, Stainland with Old Lindley, Thornhill. *1914* Bradfield. *1915* Sandal Magna, Wakefield. *1921* Ardsley, Brinsworth, Ecclesfield, Handsworth, Lupset, Monk Bretton, Worsborough. *1926* Adel cum Eccup. *1927* Doncaster. *1928* Adel cum Eccup, Alwoodley, Austhorpe, Southowram, Sowerby, Templenewsham. *1930* Clayton. *1936* Armthorpe, Barnby Dun with Kirk Sandall, Bentley with Arksey, Brinsworth, Cantley, Dalton, Greasbrough, Loversall, Outwood, Rawmarsh, Stanley, Warmsworth, Wentworth, Whiston. *1937* Acomb, Arthington, Austhorpe, Barwick in Elmet, Bishopthorpe, Bramhope, Brighouse, Dringhouses Without, Esholt, Fixby, Golcar, Horsforth, Knapton, Linthwaite, Middlethorpe Without, Pudsey, Rawdon, Shipley, Stainland with Old Lindley, Swillington, Wigton, Yeadon. *1938* Bradfield, Carlton, South Crosland, Handsworth, Kirkheaton, Lepton, Orgreave, Worsborough. *1951* Cantley, Crigglestone. *1955* Shipley. *1957* Askham Bryan, Austhorpe, Barwick in Elmet. *1967* Aston cum Aughton, Ecclesfield, Wales.

(in 1974, pars in Yorks E Riding were transf pts to Non-Metrop Cos of Humberside (incl assoc CB of Kingston upon Hull), North Yorkshire;
pars in Yorks N Riding were transf pts to the Non-Metrop Cos of Clevland (incl assoc CB of Teesside), Durham, Humberside, North Yorkshire (incl York CB);
pars in Yorks W Riding were transf pts to Metrop Cos of Greater Manchester, South Yorkshire (incl assoc CBs of Barnsley, Doncaster, Rotherham, Sheffield), West Yorkshire (incl assoc CBs of Bradford, Dewsbury, Halifax, Huddersfield, Leeds, Wakefield), pts to Non-Metrop Cos of Cumbria, Humberside, Lancashire, North Yorkshire

ASSOCIATED COUNTY BOROUGHS

BARNSLEY CB (1913—74) [W Riding]
Cr 1913 when Barnsley MB constituted a CB.[2] Bdry: 1921,[3] 1938.[4] Transf 1974 to S Yorks.[5]

BRADFORD CB [W Riding]
Bdry: 1899,[6] 1930,[7] 1937,[8] 1955.[9] Transf 1974 to W Yorks.[5]

DEWSBURY CB (1913—74) [W Riding]
Cr 1913 when Dewsbury MB constituted a CB.[10] Transf 1974 to W Yorks.[5]

DONCASTER CB (1927—74) [W Riding]
Cr 1927 when Doncaster MB constituted a CB.[11] Bdry: 1936,[12] 1951.[13] Transf 1974 to S Yorks.[5]

HALIFAX CB [W Riding]
Bdry: 1892,[14] 1899,[15] 1900,[16] 1902,[17] 1912,[18] 1928.[19] Transf 1974 to W Yorks.[5]

HUDDERSFIELD CB [W Riding]
Bdry: 1890,[20] 1913,[21] 1937,[8] 1938.[4] Transf 1974 to W Yorks.[5]

KINGSTON UPON HULL CO OF ITSELF (from 1440), CB [E Riding]
Bdry: 1897,[22] 1930,[23] 1935,[24] 1955,[25] 1968.[26] Transf 1974 to Humb.[5]

LEEDS CB [W Riding]
Bdry: 1912,[27] 1920,[28] 1926,[29] 1928,[30] 1937,[8] 1957.[31] Transf 1974 to W Riding.[5]

MIDDLESBROUGH CB (1889—1968) [N Riding]
Bdry: 1913,[32] 1929,[33] 1932.[34] Abol 1968 to help cr Teesside CB.[35]

ROTHERHAM CB (1902—74) [W Riding]
Cr 1902 when Rotherham MB constituted a CB.[36] Bdry: 1919,[37] 1921,[38] 1936,[12] 1967.[39] Transf 1974 to S Yorks.[5]

SHEFFIELD CB [W Riding]
Bdry: 1901,[40] 1912,[41] 1914,[42] 1919,[37] 1921,[38] 1929,[43] 1933,[44] 1934,[45] 1938,[46] 1967.[39] Transf 1974 to S Yorks.[5]

TEESSIDE CB (1968—74) [N Riding]
Cr 1968 by union Middlesbrough CB (assoc with N Riding) and areas in Yorks N Riding and Durham.[35] Transf 1974 to Clev.[5]

WAKEFIELD CB (1915—74) [W Riding]
Cr 1915 when Wakefield MB constituted a CB.[47] Bdry: 1921,[48] 1936,[12] 1951.[49] Transf 1974 to W Yorks.[5]

YORK CB [not assoc with any Riding or Adm Co]
Bdry: 1934,[50] 1937,[8] 1957,[51] 1968.[52] Transf 1974 to N Yorks.[5]

WAPENTAKES[1]

East Riding
BUCKROSE WAP
Acklam (until 1866), Acklam with Barthorpe (from 1866), Birdsall, Bughtorpe, Burythorpe, Cowlam, Duggleby (from 1866), Eddlethorpe (from 1866), Fimber (from 1866), Firby (from 1866), Fridaythorpe, North Grimston, Helperthorpe, Heslerton (until 1866), East Heslerton (from 1866), West Heslerton (from 1866), Howsham (from 1866), Kennythorpe (from 1866), Kirby Grindalythe, Kirby Underdale, Kirkham (from 1866), Knapton (from 1866), Langton, Leavening (from 1866), Leppington (from 1866), Luttons Ambo (from 1866), Menethorpe (from 1866), Norton, Raisthorpe and Burdale (from 1866), Rillington, Scagglethorpe (from 1866), Scampston (from 1866), Scrayingham, Settrington, Sherburn, Skirpenbeck, Sledmere, Thirkleby (from 1866), Thixendale (from 1866), Thorpe Bassett, Towthorpe (from 1866), Weaverthorpe, Westow, Wetwang, Wharram le Street, Wharram Percy, Wintringham, Yedingham

DICKERING WAP
Argam, Auburn (from 1866), Bempton, Bessingby, Boynton, Bridlington, Brigham (from 1866), Buckton (from 1866), Burton Agnes, Burton Fleming, Butterwick (from 1866), Carnaby, Cottam (from 1866), Easton (from 1866), Filey (pt until 1866, ent from 1866), Flamborough, Folkton, Fordon (from 1866), Foston on the Wolds, Foxholes (until 1866), Foxholes with Boythorpe (from 1866), Fraisthorpe (from 1866), Ganton, Garton on the Wolds, Gembling (from 1866), Gransmoor (from 1866), Grindale (from 1866), Haisthorpe (from 1866), Harpham (from 1866), Hilder-

thorpe (from 1866), Hunmanby, Great Kelk (from 1866), Little Kelk (from 1858), Kilham, Langtoft, Lowthorpe, Muston, Nafferton, Reighton, Rudston, Ruston Parva, Sewerby cum Marton (from 1866), Speeton (from 1866), Thornholme (from 1866), Thwing, Wansford (from 1866), Willerby, Wilsthorpe (from 1866), Wold Newton

HARTHILL WAP[53]
Aike[54] (from 1866), Allerthorpe, Aughton, Bainton, Barmby on the Moor, Beswick (from 1866), pt Beverley St John[55] (until 1866), Beverley St Martin,[55] Beverley St Mary,[55] Beverley St Nicholas,[55] Bielby (from 1866), Bishop Burton, Bishop Wilton (until 1866), Bishop Wilton with Belthorpe (from 1866), Bolton (from 1866), Bracken (from 1866), pt Brantingham, Breighton and Gunby (from 1866), Broomfleet (from 1866), Bubwith, Catton (until 1866), High Catton (from 1866), Low Catton (from 1866), North Cave (until 1866), North Cave with Everthorpe and Drewton (from 1866), South Cave, Cherry Burton, North Cliffe (from 1866), South Cliffe (from 1866), Cottingham,[56] East Cottingwith (from 1866), North Dalton, South Dalton, Great Driffield, Little Driffield (from 1866), Eastburn (from 1866), Ellerton Priory, Elloughton[56] (until 1866), Elloughton with Brough (from 1866), Emswell with Little Driffield (from 1885), Emswell with Kellythorpe (1866—85), Etton, Everingham, Fangfoss, Faxfleet (from 1866), Foggathorpe (from 1866), Full Sutton, Great Givendale with Grimthorpe, Goodmanham, Gribthorpe (from 1866), Harlthorpe (from 1866), Harswell, Hayton, Holme on the Wolds, Holme upon Spalding Moor, Hotham, Huggate, Hutton

Cranswick, Kilnwick, Kilnwick Percy, Kirkburn (until 1866), Kirkburn and Battleburn (from 1866), Laytham (from 1866), Leconfield (until 1866), Leconfield and Arram (from 1866), Lockington, Lockington in Kilnwick (from 1866), Londesborough (until 1866), Londesborough with Easthorpe (from 1866), Lund, Market Weighton (until 1866), Market Weighton and Arras (from 1866), Melbourne (from 1866), Middleton on the Wolds, Millington with Little Givendale, Molescroft[54] (from 1866), Neswick (from 1866), Newbald (until 1866), North Newbald (from 1866), South Newbald (from 1866), Newton upon Derwent (from 1866), New Village (1858—81), Nunburnholme, Ousethorpe (from 1866), Pocklington,[56] Rotsea (from 1866), Rowley, Sancton (until 1866), Sancton and Houghton (from 1866), Scorborough, Sculcoates,[56] Seaton Ross, Shipton Thorpe (from 1866), Skerne, Skidby, Spaldington (from 1866), East Stamford Bridge (from 1866), Storkhill and Sandholme[54] (from 1866), Storwood (from 1866), Sunderlandwick (from 1866), Sutton upon Derwent, Thearne[54] (from 1866), Thornton, Thorpe le Street (from 1866), Tibthorpe (from 1866), Tickton and Hull Bridge[54] (from 1866), pt Walkington, Waplington (from 1866), Warter, Watton, Wauldby (from 1866), Weel[54] (from 1866), Wilberfoss, Willerby[56] (from 1866), Willitoft (from 1866), Woodmansey and Beverley Parks[54] (from 1866), Wressell, Yapham cum Meltonby (from 1866), Youlthorpe with Gowthorpe (from 1866)

HOLDERNESS WAP

Aldborough, Atwick, Barmston, Beeford, Benningholme and Grange (from 1866), Bewholme and Nunkeeling, pt Beverley St John[56] (until 1866), Bilton (from 1866), Bonwick (from 1866), Brandesburton, Burstwick (until 1866), Burstwick with Skeckling (from 1866), Burton Pidsea, Catfoss (from 1866), Catwick, Coniston (from 1866), Great and Little Cowdens (from 1866), Danthorpe (from 1866); Dringhoe, Upton and Brough (from 1866); Drypool,[56] Dunnington (from 1866), Easington, Ellerby (from 1866), Elstronwick (from 1866), Eske (from 1866), Fitling (from 1866), Flinton (from 1866), North Frodingham, South Frodingham (from 1866), Ganstead (from 1866), Garton (until 1866), Garton with Grimston (from 1866), Goxhill, Halsham, Great Hatfield (from 1866), Little Hatfield (from 1866), Hedon,[56] Hempholme (from 1866), Hilston, Hollym, Holmpton, Hornsea, Humbleton, Keyingham, Kilnsea, Lelley (from 1866), Leven, Lissett (from 1866), Mappleton (until 1866), Mappleton and Rowlston (from 1866), Marfleet,[56] Marton (from 1866), Meaux (from 1866), Moor Town (from 1866), East Newton (from 1866), West Newton with Burton Constable (from 1866), Ottringham, Out Newton (from 1866), Owstwick (from 1866), Owthorne, Partington, Paull, Preston, Rimswell (from 1866), Rise, Long Riston, Roos, Routh, Ryhill and Camerton (from 1866), Seaton and Wassand (from 1866), Sigglesthorne, Skeffling, Skipsea[56]; North Skirlaugh, Rowton and Arnold (from 1866); South Skirlaugh (from 1866), Southcoates[56] (from 1866), Sproatley, Sunk Island, Sutton and Stoneferry,[56] Swine, Thirtleby (from 1866), Thorgumbald (from 1866), Tunstall (from 1866), Ulrome (from 1866),

Waxholme (from 1866), Wawne, Welwick, Winestead, Withernsea (from 1866), Withernwick, Wyton (from 1866)

HOWDENSHIRE WAP

Asselby (from 1866), Balkholme (from 1866), Barmby on the Marsh (from 1866), Belby (from 1866), Bellasize (from 1866), Bishopsoil (from 1880), Blacktoft, pt Brantingham, Cheapsides (from 1866), Cotness (from 1866), Eastrington, Ellerker (from 1866), Gilbderdike (from 1866), Howden,[56] Kilpin (from 1866), Knedlington (from 1866), Laxton (from 1866), Melton (from 1866), Metham (from 1866), Portington and Cavil (from 1866), Saltmarshe (from 1866), Scalby (from 1866), Skelton (from 1866), Thorpe (from 1866), pt Walkington, Wallingfen (from 1881), Welton, Yokefleet (from 1866)

KINGSTON UPON HULL CO (from 1440)

Anlaby (from 1866), Kirk Ella, West Ella (from 1866), North Ferriby, Garrison Side[57] (from 1858), Haltemprice (from 1858), Hessle, Kingston upon Hull Holy Trinity (until jointly rated with St Mary), Kingston upon Hull Holy Trinity and St Mary (from joint rating), Kingston upon Hull St Mary (until jointly rated with Holy Trinity), Newington (from 1877), Swanland (from 1866)

OUSE AND DERWENT WAP

pt Acaster Malbis (until 1866), Barlby (from 1866), Brackenholme with Woodhall (from 1866), Cliffe cum Lund (from 1866), Deighton (from 1866), North Duffield (from 1866), South Duffield (from 1866), Dunnington, Elvington, Escrick, Fulfords Ambo (until 1866), Gate Fulford[56] (from 1866), Water Fulford (from 1866), Grimston (from 1866), Hemingbrough, Heslington (from 1885), Heslington St Lawrence (1866—85), Heslington St Paul (until 1885), Kelfield (from 1866), Kexby (from 1866), Langwith (from 1866), Menthorpe cum Bowthorpe (from 1866), pt Naburn (from 1866), Osgodby (from 1866), Riccall, Skipwith, West Stamford Bridge with Scoreby (from 1866), pt Stillingfleet (until 1866), Stillingfleet with Moreby (from 1866), Thorganby with West Cottingwith, Wheldrake, pt York St Lawrence[36] (until 1866)

North Riding

ALLERTON WAP (or ALLERTONSHIRE)

Birkby, Borrowby (from 1866), Brompton (from 1866), Cotcliffe (from 1858), Crosby (from 1866), Deighton (from 1866), Over Dinsdale (from 1866), Ellerbeck (from 1866), Girsby (from 1866), West Harsley (from 1866), Holme (from 1866), Hornby (from 1866), Hutton Bonville (from 1866), Hutton Conyers (from 1858), Hutton Sessay (from 1866), North Kilvington (from 1866), Kirby Sigston, Knayton with Brawith (from 1866), Landmoth cum Catto (from 1866), Lazenby (from 1858), pt Leake, Northallerton,[56] Norton Conyers (from 1866), Osmotherley, pt North Otterington, pt Pickhill (until 1866), Romanby (from 1866), West Rounton, Sessay, pt Great Smeaton, Little Smeaton (from 1866), pt Sockburn (until 1866), Sowerby under Cotcliffe (from 1866), Thimbleby (from 1866), Thornton le Beans (from 1866), Thornton le Street, pt Wath, Winton (from 1866), High Worsall

(from 1866)

BIRDFORTH WAP

pt Ampleforth (until 1866), pt Ampleforth (from 1887), Ampleforth Birdforth (1866—87), Angram Grange (from 1866), Arden (from 1866), Bagby (from 1866), Balk (from 1866); Bilsdale, West Side (from 1866); Birdforth (from 1866), Boltby (from 1866), Old Byland, Byland Abbey (1866—87), Byland with Wass (from 1887), Carlton Husthwaite (from 1866), Carlton Miniott (from 1866), Catton (from 1866), Cold Kirby, Cowesby, Coxwold, pt Cundall (until 1866), Dale Town (from 1866), Dalton (from 1866), Eldmire with Crakehill (from 1866), Fawdington (from 1866), Felixkirk, Gueldable (1866—88), East Harsley, Hawnby, Hood Grange (from 1866), Husthwaite, Kepwick (from 1866), Kilburn, South Kilvington, Kirby Knowle, pt Kirby Wiske, pt Leake, Murton (from 1858), Newburgh (from 1866), Newsham with Breckenbrough (from 1866), Oldstead (from 1866), pt North Otterington, South Otterington, Oulston (from 1866), Sand Hutton (from 1866), Nether Silton (from 1866), Over Silton, Skipton on Swale (from 1866), Snilesworth (from 1866), Sowerby (from 1866), Sutton under Whitstone Cliffe (from 1866), Thirkleby, Thirlby (from 1866), Thirsk,[56] Thornborough (from 1866), Thornton on the Hill (from 1866), Thornton le Moor (from 1866), Thorpe le Willows (from 1866), pt Topcliffe, Upsall (from 1866), Wass (1866—87), Welbury, Wildon Grange (from 1866), Yearsley (from 1866)

BULMER WAP

Aldwark (from 1866), Alne, pt Barton le Street, Barton le Willows (from 1866), Beningbrough (from 1866), Bossall (until 1866), Bossall with Buttercrambe (from 1866), pt Brafferton, Brandsby cum Stearsby, Bulmer, Claxton (from 1866), Clifton[56] (from 1866), Coneysthorpe (from 1866), Crambe, Crayke (from 1844), Dalby cum Skewsby, Earswick (from 1866), Easingwold, Farlington (from 1866), Flawith (from 1866), Flaxton (from 1866), Foston, Ganthorpe (from 1866), Harton (from 1866), Haxby, Heworth[56] (from 1866), Gate Helmsley, Upper Helmsley, Helperby (from 1866), Henderskelf (from 1866), Holtby, pt Hovingham, Huby (from 1866), Huntington, Huttons Ambo, Lillings Ambo (from 1866), Linton upon Ouse (from 1866), Marton cum Moxby, Murton (from 1866), Myton on Swale, Newton upon Ouse, Osbaldwick, Overton, Raskelf (from 1866), Rawcliffe (from 1866), Sand Hutton (from 1866), Scackleton (from 1866), Sheriff Hutton (until 1866), Sheriff Hutton with Cornbrough (from 1866), Shipton (from 1866), Skelton, Stillington, Stittenham (from 1866), Stockton on the Forest, Strensall, Sutton on the Forest, Terrington (until 1866), Terrington with Wiggenthorpe (from 1866), Tholthorpe (from 1866), Thormanby, Thornton Bridge (from 1866), Thornton le Clay (from 1866), Tollerton (from 1866), Towthorpe (from 1866), Warthill (until 1866), Warthill Copyhold (from 1866), Warthill Freehold (from 1866), Welburn (from 1866), Whenby, Whitwell on the Hill (from 1866), Wiggington, pt York St Cuthbert[56] (until 1866), pt York St Giles[56] (until 1884), pt York St Michael le Belfrey[56] (until 1866); pt York St Olave, Marygate[56] (until 1866);

pt York St Saviour[56] (until 1866), Youlton (from 1866)

EAST GILLING WAP

Ainderby Steeple, pt Barton (from 1866), Bolton upon Swale (from 1866), Brompton on Swale (from 1866), pt Catterick, Cleasby, East Cowton, North Cowton (from 1866), South Cowton (from 1866), Croft, Dalton upon Tees (from 1866), Danby Wiske, pt Easby, Ellerton upon Swale (from 1866), Eryholme (from 1866), pt Gilling (until 1866), Hudswell (from 1866), Kiplin (from 1866), pt Kirby Wiske, Great Langton (from 1866), Little Langton (from 1866), Langton upon Swale (until 1866), pt Manfield, Maunby (from 1866), Middleton Tyas, Morton upon Swale (from 1866), Moulton (from 1866), Newby Wiske (from 1866), Newton Morrell (from 1866), Scorton (from 1866), pt Stanwick St John (from 1866), Stapleton (from 1866), Thrintoft (from 1866), Uckerby (from 1866), Warlaby (from 1866), Whitwell (from 1866), Yafforth (from 1866)

WEST GILLING WAP

Aldbrough (from 1866), Arkengarthdale, Aske (from 1866), Barforth (from 1866), Barningham, pt Barton (from 1866), Boldron (from 1866), Bowes, Brignall, Caldwell (from 1866), Cliffe (from 1866), Cotherstone (from 1866), Dalton (from 1866), pt Easby, Egglestone Abbey (from 1866), Eppleby (from 1866), Forcett with Carkin (from 1866), Gayles (from 1866), Gilling (pt until 1866, ent from 1866), Gilmonby (from 1866), pt Grinton, Holwick (from 1866), Hope (from 1866), Hunderthwaite (from 1866), Hutton Magna (from 1866), Kirby Hill (from 1866), Kirby Ravensworth (until 1866), Lartington (from 1866), East Layton (from 1866), West Layton (from 1866), Lunedale (from 1866), pt Manfield, Marrick, Marske, Melbecks (from 1866), Melsonby, Mickleton (from 1866), Muker (from 1866), New Forest (from 1866), Newsham (from 1866), Ovington (from 1866), Ravensworth (from 1866), Reeth (from 1866), Richmond,[56] Rokeby, Romandkirk, Scargill (from 1866), Skeeby (from 1866), Stanwick (until 1866), pt Stanwick St John (from 1866), Startforth, Washton (from 1866), Wycliffe with Thorpe

HALLIKELD WAP

Ainderby Quernhow (from 1866), pt Aldburgh (until 1866), Asenby (from 1866), Baldersby (from 1866), pt Bedale, pt Brafferton, Burneston, Carthorpe (from 1866), pt Cundall (until 1866), Cundall with Leckby (from 1866), Dishforth (from 1866), pt Lower Dunsforth (from 1866), pt Upper Dunsforth cum Branton Green (from 1866), Ellenthorpe (from 1866); Exelby, Leeming and Newton (from 1866); Gatenby (from 1866), Howe (from 1866), Howgrave (from 1866), pt Humberton (from 1866), Kirby Hill (from 1866), Kirby on the Moor (until 1866), Kirklington (until 1866), Kirklington with Upsland (from 1866), Langthorne (from 1866), Langthorpe (from 1866), Marton le Moor (from 1866), Melmerby (from 1866), Middleton Quernhow (from 1866), pt Milby (from 1866), Norton le Clay (from 1866), pt Nunwick cum Howgrave (from 1866), pt Pickhill (until 1866), Pickhill with Roxby (from 1866), Rainton with Newby (from 1866), Sinderby (from 1866), Sutton Howgrave (from 1866), Swinby with Allerthorpe (from 1866),

East Tanfield (from 1866), West Tanfield (from 1866), Theakston (from 1866), pt Topcliffe

EAST HANG WAP

Ainderby Miers with Holtby (from 1866), Aiskew (from 1866), Appleton (from 1866), Arrathorne (from 1866), pt Bedale, Brough (from 1866), Burrill cum Cowling (from 1866), Burton upon Ure (from 1866), pt Catterick, Clifton upon Ure (from 1866), Colburn (from 1866), Crakenhall (from 1866), Ellenstring (from 1866), Ellingtons (from 1866), Fearby (from 1866), Firby (from 1866), Hackforth (from 1866), Healy with Sutton (from 1866), Hipswell (from 1866), Hornby, pt Hunton (from 1866), Ilton cum Pott (from 1866), Killerby (from 1866), Kirkby Fleetham, Masham, pt Newton le Willows (from 1866), pt Patrick Brompton, Rand Grange (from 1866), Rookwith (from 1866), St Martin (from 1858), Scotton (from 1866), Scruton, Snape (from 1866), Swinton with Watermarske (from 1866), Thirn (from 1866), Thornton Watlass, Tunstall (from 1866), Well

WEST HANG WAP

High Abbotside (from 1866), Low Abbotside (from 1866), Agglethorpe with Coverham (from 1866), Akebar (from 1866), Askrigg (from 1866), Aysgarth, Bainbridge (from 1866), Barden (from 1866), Bellerby (from 1866), Bishopdale (from 1866), Burton cum Walden (from 1866), Caldbergh with East Scrafton (from 1866), Carlton Highdale (from 1866), Carlton Town (from 1866), Carperby cum Thoresby (from 1866), Castle Bolton (from 1866), pt Catterick, Constable Burton (from 1866), Coverham (until 1866), Downholme, pt Easby (until 1866), Ellerton Abbey (from 1866), Finghall, Garriston (from 1866), pt Grinton, Harmby (from 1866), Hauxwell (until 1866), East Hauxwell (from 1866), West Hauxwell (from 1866), Hawes (from 1866), pt Hunton (from 1866), Hutton Hang (from 1866), Leyburn (from 1866), Melmerby (from 1866), Middleham, Newbiggin (from 1866), pt Newton le Willows (from 1866), pt Patrick Brompton, Preston under Soar (from 1866), Redmire (from 1866), West Scrafton (from 1866), Spennithorne, Stainton (from 1866), Thoralby (from 1866), Thornton Rust, Thornton Steward, Walburn (from 1866), Wensley, East Witton (until 1866), East Witton Within (from 1866), East Witton Without (from 1866), West Witton

LANGBAURGH LIBERTY

West Acklam,[56] Aislaby (from 1866), Appleton Wiske (from 1866), Ayton (until 1866), Great Ayton (from 1866), Little Ayton (from 1866), Barnby (from 1866), Borrowby (from 1866), Brotton (from 1866), Broughton (from 1866), Great Busby (from 1866), Little Busby (from 1866), Carlton, Commondale (from 1866), Crathorne, Danby, Easby (from 1866), Easington, Egton (from 1866), Ellerby (from 1866), Eston, Faceby (from 1866), Glaisdale (from 1866), Guisborough, Hemlington (from 1866), Hilton, Hinderwell, Hutton Lowcross (from 1866), Hutton Mulgrave (from 1866), Hutton Rudby (from 1866), Ingleby Arncliffe, Ingleby Barwick (from 1866), Ingleby Greenhow, Kildale, Kilton (from 1866), Kirby in Cleveland, Kirkleatham, Castle Leavington (from 1866), Kirk Leavington,[56] Linthorpe[56] (from 1866), Liverton (from 1866), Loftus, Lythe, Maltby (from 1866), Marske, Marton,[56] Mickleby (from 1866), Middlesbrough,[56] Middleton upon Leven (from 1866), Moorsholm (from 1866), Morton (from 1866), Newby (from 1866), Newton, Newton Mulgrave (from 1866), Normanby[56] (from 1866), Nunthorpe (from 1866), Ormesby,[56] Picton (from 1866), Pinchinthorpe (from 1866), Potto (from 1866), Redcar (from 1866), East Rounton (from 1866), Roxby (from 1866), Rudby in Cleveland, Seamer, Skelton,[56] Skinnigrove (from 1866), Skutterskelfe (from 1866), Stainton, Stanghow (from 1866), Stokesley,[56] Thornaby (from 1866), Tocketts (from 1866), Ugthorpe (from 1866), Upleatham, Upsall (from 1866), Westerdale (from 1866), pt Whitby,[56] Whorlton, Wilton, Low Worsall (from 1866), Yarm[56]

PICKERING LYTHE WAP[58]

Aislaby (from 1866), Allerston, East Ayton (from 1866), West Ayton (from 1866), Barughs Ambo (from 1866), Brompton, Burniston (from 1866), Cawthorne (from 1866), Cayton (from 1886), Cayton with Deepdale and Killerby (1866—86), Cloughton (from 1866), Cropton (from 1866), Ebberston, Ellerburn (until 1866), Falsgrave[56] (from 1866), Farmanby (1866—87), pt Filey (until 1866), Goathland (from 1866), Gristhorpe (from 1866), Great Habton (from 1866), Little Habton (from 1866), Hartoft (from 1866), Hutton Buscel, Irton (from 1866), Kingthorpe (from 1866), Kirby Misperton, Lebberston (from 1866), Levisham, Lockton (from 1866), Marishes (from 1866), Marton (from 1866), Middleton (from 1866), Newby (1866—87), Osgodby (1866—86), Pickering[56]; Rosedale, East Side (from 1866); Ryton (from 1866), Sawdon (1866—86), Scalby, Scarborough,[56] Seamer (from 1866), pt Sinnington, Snainton (from 1866), Staintondale (from 1866), Thornton Dale, Throxenby (from 1866), Troutsdale (from 1866), Wilton (from 1866), Wrelton (from 1866), Wykeham

RYEDALE WAP

Airyholme with Howthorpe and Baxton Howe (from 1866), Amotherby (from 1866), pt Ampleforth (until 1866), pt Ampleforth (from 1887), Ampleforth Oswaldkirk (1866—87), Ampleforth St Peter (1866—87), Appleton le Moors (from 1866), Appleton le Street, pt Barton le Street, Beadlam (from 1866), Bilsdale Midcable (from 1866); Bransdale, West Side (from 1866); Brawby (from 1866), Broughton (from 1866), Butterwick (from 1866), Cawton (from 1866), Coulton (from 1866), Great Edstone, Little Edstone (from 1866), Fadmoor (from 1866); Farndale, East Side (from 1866); Farndale, Low Quarter (from 1866); Farndale, West Side (from 1866); Fryton (from 1866), Gillamoor (from 1866), Gilling East (from 1866), Grimston (from 1866), Harome (from 1866), Helmsley,[56] Hildenley (from 1866), North Holme (from 1866), South Holme (from 1866), pt Hovingham, Hutton le Hole (from 1866), Kirkby Moorside,[56] Kirkdale (from 1866), Laskill Pasture (from 1866), Lastingham, New Malton,[56] Old Malton,[56] Muscoates (from 1866), Nawton (from 1866), Ness (from 1887), East Ness (1866—87), West Ness (1866—87), East Newton and Laysthorpe (from 1866), Normanby, Nunnington, Oswaldkirk, Pockley (from 1866), Rievaulx (from 1866); Rosedale, West Side (from

1866); Salton, Scawton, pt Sinnington, Skiplam (from 1866), Slingsby, Spaunton (from 1866), Sproxton (from 1866), Stonegrave, Swinton (from 1866), Thornton Risebrough (from 1866), Wath (from 1866), Welburn (from 1866), Wombleton (from 1866)

WHITBY STRAND LBTY

Broxa (from 1866), Eskdaleside (1866—85), Eskdaleside cum Ugglebarnby (from 1885), Fylingdales (from 1866), Hackness, Harwood Dale (from 1866), Hawsker with Stainsacre (from 1866), Newholm with Dunsley (from 1866), Ruswarp (from 1866), Silpho (from 1866), Sneaton, Suffield cum Everley (from 1866), Ugglebarnby (1866—85), pt Whitby[56]

West Riding

AGBRIGG WAP

Ackton (from 1866), Almondbury,[56] Altofts (from 1866), Alverthorpe with Thornes[56] (from 1866), Ardsley East, Ardsley West, Austonley (from 1866), Batley[56] (pt until 1866, ent from 1866), pt West Bretton (from 1866), Cartworth (from 1866), Crigglestone (from 1866), Crofton, South Crosland (from 1866), Cumberworth Half (1866—76), Dalton[56] (from 1866), Dewsbury[56] (pt until 1866, ent from 1866), Emley, Farnley Tyas (from 1866), pt Featherstone, Flockton (from 1866), Fulstone (from 1866), Golcar (from 1866), Hepworth (from 1866), Holme (from 1866), Honley (from 1866), Horbury (from 1866), Huddersfield,[56] Kirkburton, Kirkheaton, Lepton (from 1866), Lindley cum Quarmby[56] (from 1866), Lingards (from 1866), Linthwaite (from 1866), Lockwood[56] (from 1866), Lofthouse with Carlton (from 1866), Longwood[56] (from 1866), Marsden in Almondbury (from 1866), Maraden in Huddersfield (from 1866), Meltham (from 1866), Methley, Middleton (from 1866), Mirfield, Morley[56] (from 1866), Netherthong (from 1866), Newland with Woodhouse Moor (from 1858), Normanton, Ossett cum Gawthorpe[56] (from 1866), Oulton with Woodlesford (from 1866), pt Rochdale (until 1866), Rothwell, Saddleworth[56] (from 1866), Sandall Magna, Scammonden (from 1866), Sharlston (from 1866), Shelley (from 1866), Shepley (from 1866), Shitlington (from 1866), Skelmanthorpe (from 1876), Slaithwaite (from 1866), Snydale (from 1866), Soothill (from 1866), Stanley cum Wrenthorpe[56] (from 1866), Thornhill, Thorpe (from 1866), Thurstonland (from 1866), Upperthong (from 1866), Wakefield,[56] Walton (from 1866), Warmfield cum Heath, Whitley Lower (from 1866), Whitley Upper (from 1866), Whitwood (from 1866), Wooldale (from 1866)

AINSTY (WAP in W Riding until 1449, attached to City of York as AINSTY OF YORK 1449—1836, thereafter WAP in W Riding)

Acaster Malbis (pt until 1866, ent from 1866), Acaster Selby (from 1866), Acomb, Angram (from 1866), Appleton Roebuck (from 1866), Askham Bryan, Askham Richard, Bickerton (from 1866), Bilbrough, Bilton, Bishopthorpe, Bolton Percy, Catterton (from 1866), Colton (from 1866), Copmanthorpe (from 1866), Dringhouses[56] (from 1866), Healaugh, Hessay (from 1866), Holgate[56] (from 1866), Hutton Wandesley (from 1866), pt Kirk Hammerton (until 1866), Knapton (from 1866), Long Marston, Middlethorpe[56] (from

1866), Moor Monkton, Newton Kyme cum Toulston, Oxton (from 1866), Nether Poppleton, Upper Poppleton (from 1866), Rufforth, Steeton (from 1866), pt Stillingfleet (until 1866), pt Tadcaster (until 1866), Tadcaster East (from 1866), Thorp Arch, Tockwith (from 1866), Walton, Wighill, Wilstrop (from 1866), pt York Holy Trinity Micklegate[56] (until 1866), pt York St Mary Castlegate[56] (until 1866), pt York St Mary Bishophill Junior[56] (until 1866), pt York St Mary Bishophill Senior[56] (until 1866)

BARKSTONE ASH WAP

Barkston (from 1866), Barlow (from 1866), Biggin (until 1866), Birkin, Bramham (until 1866), Bramham cum Oglethorpe (from 1866), Brayton, Brotherton, Burn (from 1866), Burton Salmon (from 1866), Byram cum Poole (from 1866), Camblesworth (from 1866), Carlton (from 1866), Cawood, Clifford with Boston (from 1866), Drax,[56] Long Drax (from 1866), Fairburn (from 1866), Church Fenton, Little Fenton (from 1866), Monk Fryston, Gateforth (from 1866), Grimston (from 1866), Chapel Haddlesey (from 1866), West Haddlesey (from 1866), Hambleton (from 1866), Hillam (from 1866), Temple Hirst (from 1866), Hirst Courtnay (from 1866), Huddleston cum Lumby (from 1866), Kirkby Wharfe (until 1866), Kirkby Wharfe and North Milford (from 1866), Lead (from 1866), Ledsham, pt Ledston (until 1866), Lotherton cum Aberford (from 1866), Micklefield (from 1866), South Milford (from 1866), Newland (from 1866), Newthorpe (from 1866), Ryther (until 1866), Ryther cum Ossendyke (from 1866), Saxton (until 1866), Saxton with Scarthingwell (from 1866), Selby, Sherburn in Elmet, Snaith (until 1866), Stutton with Hazlewood (from 1866), Sutton (from 1866), pt Tadcaster (until 1866), Tadcaster West (from 1866), Thorpe Willoughby (from 1866), Towton (from 1866), Ulleskelf (from 1866), Wistow

CLARO WAP

pt Addingham, Aldborough[56] (pt until 1866, ent from 1866), Aldfield (from 1866), Allerton Mauleverer (until 1866), Allerton Mauleverer with Hopperton (from 1866), Arkendale (from 1866), Askwith (from 1866), Azerley (from 1866), Beamsley (from 1886), Beamsley in Addingham (1866—86), Beamsley in Skipton (1866—86), Bewerley (from 1866), Bilton with Harrogate[56] (from 1866), Birstwith (from 1866), Blubberhouses (from 1866), Boroughbridge[56] (from 1866), Brearton (from 1866), Burton Leonard, Castley (from 1866), Cattal (from 1866), Clareton (1866—88), Clifton with Norwood (from 1866), Clint (from 1866), Coneythorpe (1866—88), Coneythorpe and Clareton (from 1888), Copgrove, Cowthorpe, Dacre (from 1866), Kirk Deighton, North Deighton (from 1866), Denton (from 1866), Dunkeswick (from 1866), pt Lower Dunsforth (from 1866), pt Upper Dunsforth with Branton Green (from 1866), Farnham, Farnley (from 1866), Felliscliffe (from 1866), Ferrensby (from 1866), Fewston, Flaxby (from 1866), Follifoot (from 1866), Fountains Earth (from 1866), Goldsborough, Grewelthorpe (from 1866), Green Hammerton (from 1866), Kirk Hammerton (pt until 1866, ent from 1866), Hampsthwaite, pt Harewood[56] (until 1866), Hartwith cum Winsley (from 1866), Haverah Park (from 1858), Hazlewood with Storiths (from 1866), pt Humberton (from 1866), Hunsingore, pt Ilkley, Kearby with Netherby (from 1866), Killinghall (from 1866), Kirby Hall, Kirkby Malzeard, Kirkby Overblow, Knaresborough,[56] Laverton (from 1866), Leathley, Lindley (from 1866), Lindrick with Studley Royal and Fountains (from 1858), Linton (from 1866), Marton cum Grafton, Menwith with Darley (from 1866), Middleton (from 1866), pt Milby (from 1866), Minskip (from 1866), Nun Monkton, Nesfield with Langbar (from 1866), Newell with Clifton (from 1866), pt Nidd, pt Otley[56] (until 1866), Great Ouseburn, Little Ouseburn, Pannal,[56] Plompton (from 1866), Great Ribston with Walshford (from 1866), Little Ribston (from 1866), Rigton (from 1866), Ripley, pt Ripon,[56] Roecliffe (from 1866), Scotton (from 1866), Scriven with Tentergate[56] (from 1866), Sicklinghall (from 1866), Skelding (from 1866), pt Skipton[56] (until 1866), Spofforth (until 1866), Spofforth with Stockeld (from 1866), Stainburn (from 1866), South Stainley with Cayton, Staveley, Down Stonebeck (from 1866), Upper Stonebeck (from 1866), Studley Roger (from 1866), Thornville (from 1866), Thornthwaite with Padside (from 1866), Thorpe Underwoods (from 1866), Thruscross (from 1866), Great Timble (from 1866), Little Timble (from 1866), Walkingham Hill with Occaney (from 1866), Weeton (from 1866), Weston, Wetherby (from 1866), Whixley, Widdington (from 1866), Winksley (from 1866)

DONCASTER SOKE

pt Auckley (from 1866), Balby with Hexthorpe (from 1866), Blaxton (from 1866), Doncaster,[56] pt Finningley (until 1866), Loversall (from 1866), Rossington, Long Sandall (1866—86), pt Wallingwells (from 1858), Wheatley (from 1866)

MORLEY WAP

Allerton[56] (from 1866), Barkisland (from 1866), pt Batley[56] (until 1866), North Bierley (from 1866), Birstall (until 1866), Bolton[56] (from 1866), Bowling[56] (from 1866), Bradford,[56] Calverley (until 1866), Calverley with Farsley[56] (from 1866), Churwell (from 1866), Clayton (from 1866), Cleckheaton (from 1866), Clifton (from 1866), pt Dewsbury[56] (until 1866), Drightlington (from 1866), Eccleshill (from 1866), Elland with Greetland (from 1866), Erringden (from 1866), Fixby (from 1866), Gildersome (from 1866), Gomersal (from 1866), Halifax,[56] Hartshead (from 1866), Haworth (from 1866), Heaton (from 1866), Heckmondwike (from 1866), Heltonstall (from 1866), Hipperholme with Brighouse[56] (from 1866), Horton[56] (from 1866), Hunsworth (from 1866), Idle (from 1866), Langfield (from 1866), Liversedge (from 1866), Manningham[56] (from 1866), Midgley (from 1866), Norland (from 1866), Northowram[56] (from 1866), Ovenden[56] (from 1866), Pudsey[56] (from 1866), Rastrick[56] (from 1866), Rishworth (from 1866), Shelf (from 1866), Shipley (from 1866), Skircoat[56] (from 1866), Southowram[56] (from 1866), Sowerby (from 1866), Soyland (from 1866), Stainland with Old Lindley (from 1866), Stansfield (from 1866), Thornton (from 1866), Tong (from 1866), Wadsworth (from 1866), Warley (from 1866), Wilsden (from 1866), Wyke (from 1866)

OSGOLDCROSS WAP

Ackworth, Adlingfleet, Airmyn (from 1866), Askern (from 1866), Badsworth, Balne (from 1866), Beal or Beaghall (from 1866), Burghwallis, Campsall, Carleton (from 1866), Castleford, Cridling Stubbs (from 1866), Darrington, Eastoft (from 1866), Eggborough (from 1866), North Elmsall (from 1866), South Elmsall (from 1866), pt Featherstone, Fenwick (from 1866), Fockerby (from 1866), Ferry Fryston, Glass Houghton (from 1866), Goole (from 1866), Gowdall (from 1866), Haldenby (from 1866), East Hardwick (from 1866), West Hardwick (from 1866), Heck (from 1866), Hensall (from 1866), Hessle (1866—88), Hessle and Hill Top (from 1888), Hill Top (1866—88), Hook (from 1866), Huntwick with Foulby and Nostell (from 1866), Kellington, Kirk Bramwith, South Kirkby, Knottingley (from 1866), Monkhill[56] (from 1866), Moss (from 1866), Norton (from 1866), Ousefleet (from 1866), Owston, Pollington (from 1866), Pontefract,[56] Pontefract Park[56] (from 1858), Purston Jaglin (from 1866), Rawcliffe (from 1866), Reedness (1866—84), Skelbrooke (from 1866), Skellow (from 1866), Kirk Smeaton, Little Smeaton (from 1866), Snaith and Cowick (from 1866), Stapleton (from 1866), Sutton (from 1866), Swinefleet (1866—84), Swinefleet and Reedness (from 1866), Tanshelf[56] (from 1866), Thorpe Audlin (from 1866), Upton (from 1866), Walden Stubbs (from 1866), Whitgift, Whitley (from 1866), Womersley, pt Wragby (until 1866)

RIPON LBTY

Aismunderby with Bondgate[56] (from 1866), High and Low Bishopside (from 1866), Bishopston (from 1866), Bishop Thornton (from 1866), Clotherholme (from 1866), Eavestone (from 1866), Givendale (from 1866), Grantley (from 1866), Bridge Hewick (from 1866), Copt Hewick (from 1866), Ingerthorpe (from 1866), pt Kirklington (until 1866), Markingfield Hall (from 1866), Markington with Wallerthwaite (from 1866), Bishop Monkton (from 1866), Newby with Mulwith (from 1866), pt Nidd, pt Nunwick cum Howgrave (from 1866), pt Ripon,[56] Sawley (from 1866), Sharow (from 1866), Skelton (from 1866), North Stainley with Sleningford (from 1866), Sutton Grange (from 1866), Warsill (from 1866), Westwick (from 1866), Whitcliffe with Thorpe (from 1866)

SKYRACK WAP

Aberford, Adel (until 1866), Adel cum Eccup (from 1866), Chapel Allerton[56] (from 1866), Allerton Bywater (from 1866), Alwoodley (from 1866), Armley[56] (from 1866), Arthington (from 1866), Austhorpe (from 1866), Baildon (from 1866), Bardsey (until 1866), Bardsey cum Rigton (from 1866), Barwick in Elmet, Beeston[56] (from 1866), Bingley,[56] Bramhope (from 1866), Bramley[56] (from 1866), Burley in Wharfedale (from 1866), Carlton (from 1866), Collingham, Esholt (from 1866), Farnley[56] (from 1866), Garforth, Guiseley, Harewood[56] (pt until 1866, ent from 1866), Hawksworth (from 1866), Headingley cum Burley[56] (from 1866), Holbeck[56] (from 1866), Horsforth (from 1866), Hunslet[56] (from 1866), pt Ilkley, East Keswick (from 1866), Kippax, pt Ledston (from 1866), Leeds,[56] Menston (from 1866), Micklethwaite (from 1866), Morton (from 1866), Otley[56] (pt until 1866, ent from

1866), Parlington (from 1866), Pool (from 1866), Potter Newton[56] (from 1866), Great and Little Preston (from 1866), Rawdon (from 1866), Roundhay (from 1866), Scarcroft (from 1866), Seacroft[56] (from 1866), Shadwell (from 1866), Sturton Grange (from 1866), Swillington, Templenewsham[56] (from 1866), Thorner, Thorpe Stapleton (from 1866), Weardley (from 1866), Whitkirk (until 1866), Wigton (from 1866), Wortley[56] (from 1866), Wothersome (from 1866), Wyke (from 1866), Yeadon (from 1866)

STAINCLIFFE AND EWCROSS WAP

pt Addingham, Airton (from 1866), Appletreewick (from 1866), Arncliffe, Austwick (from 1866), Bank Newton (from 1866), Barden (from 1866), Barnoldswick, Bashall Eaves (from 1866), Bentham, Bolton Abbey (from 1866), Bolton by Bowland, Bordley (from 1866), Bowland Forest High (from 1866), Bowland Forest Low (from 1866), Bracewell, West Bradford (from 1866), Bradley's Both (from 1866), Brogden (from 1866), Broughton, Buckden (from 1866), Burnsall, Burton in Lonsdale (from 1866), Calton (from 1866), Carleton, Clapham (until 1866), Clapham cum Newby (from 1866), pt Cliviger (from 1866), Coates (from 1866), Coniston Cold (from 1866), Conistone with Kilnsey (from 1866), Cononley (from 1866), Cowling (from 1866), Cracoe (from 1866), Dent (from 1866), Draughton (from 1866), Easington (from 1866), Elslack (from 1866), Embsay with Eastby (from 1866), Eshton (from 1866), Farnhill (from 1866), Flasby with Winterburn (from 1866), Gargrave, Garsdale (from 1866), Giggleswick, Gisburn, Gisburn Forest (from 1866), Glusburn (from 1866), Grassington (from 1866), Grindleton (from 1866), West Halton (from 1866), Halton East (from 1866), Halton Gill (from 1866), Hanlith, Hartlington, Hawkswick (from 1866), Hebden (from 1866), Hellifield (from 1866), Hetton (from 1866), Horton (from 1866), Horton in Ribblesdale, Ingleton (from 1866), Keighley,[56] Kettlewell with Starbotton, Kildwick, Kirkby in Malham Dale (until 1866), Kirkby Malham (from 1866), Langcliffe (from 1866), Lawkland (from 1866), Linton, Litton (from 1866), Malham (from 1866), Malham Moor (from 1866), Martons Both, Middop (from 1866), pt Mitton (until 1866), Great Mitton (from 1866), Nappa (from 1866), Newsholme (from 1866), Newton (from 1866), Otterburn (from 1866), Paythorne (from 1866), Long Preston, Rathmell (from 1866), Rimington (from 1866), Rylstone (from 1866), Salterforth (from 1866), Sawley (from 1866), Scosthrop (from 1866), Sedbergh, Settle (from 1866), Silsden (from 1866), Skipton[56] (pt until 1866, ent from 1866), Slaidburn, Stainforth (from 1866), Steeton with Eastburn (from 1866), Stirton with Thorlby (from 1866), Sutton (from 1866), Swinden (from 1866), Thornton in Craven, Thornton in Lonsdale (pt until 1866, ent from 1866), Thorpe (from 1866), Thresfield (from 1866), Tosside (from 1858), Waddington (from 1866), pt Whalley (until 1866), Wigglesworth (from 1866)

STAINCROSS WAP

Ardsley (from 1866), Barnsley[56] (from 1866), Barugh (from 1866), pt West Bretton (from 1866), Brierley (from 1866), Carlton (from 1866), Cawthorne, Chevet (from 1866), Clayton West (from 1866), Cudworth (from 1866), Cumberworth (from 1866), pt Darfield, Darton, Denby (from 1866), Dodworth (from 1866), Felkirk (until 1866), Gunthwaite (from 1866), Havercroft with Cold Hiendley (from 1866), Hemsworth, South Hiendley (from 1866), High Hoyland, Hoyland Swaine (from 1866), Hunshelf (from 1866), Ingbirchworth (from 1866), Kexborough (from 1866), Langsett (from 1866), Monk Bretton (from 1866), Notton (from 1866), Oxspring (from 1866), Penistone, Ryhill (from 1866), Shafton (from 1866), Silkstone, Stainbrough (from 1866), Tankersley, Thurgoland (from 1866), Thurlstone (from 1866), Wintersett (from 1866), Woolley (from 1866), Worsbrough (from 1866), Wortley (from 1866), pt Wragby (until 1866)

STRAFFORTH AND TICKHILL WAP

Adwick le Street, Adwick upon Dearne, North and South Anston, Armthorpe, Aston cum Aughton, Austerfield (from 1866), Attercliffe cum Darnall[56] (from 1866), Barnbrough, Barnby upon Don, Bawtry (from 1866), Bentley with Arksey, Brampton Bierlow (from 1866), Brightside Bierlow[56] (from 1866), Ecclesall Bierlow[56] (from 1866), Bilham (from 1866), Billingley (from 1866), pt Blyth[56] (until 1866), Bolton upon Dearne, Bradfield (from 1866), Braithwell, Bramley (from 1866), Brampton en le Morthen (from 1866), Brinsworth[56] (from 1866), Brodsworth, Cadeby (from 1866), Cantley, Carr House and Elm Field (from 1858), Catcliffe (from 1866), Clayton with Frickley, Conisbrough, pt Crowle,[59] Dalton (from 1866), pt Darfield, Denaby (from 1866), Dinnington, Ecclesfield, Edlington, Firbeck, Fishlake, Gildingwells (from 1866), Greasborough[56] (from 1866), Nether Hallam[56] (from 1866), Upper Hallam[56] (from 1866), Hamphall Stubbs (from 1866), Hampole (from 1866), Handsworth[56] (from 1866), Harthill with Woodall, Hatfield, Heeley[56] (from 1880), Hickleton, Hooton Levitt (from 1866), Hooton Pagnell, Hooton Roberts, Great Houghton (from 1866), Little Houghton (from 1866), Hoyland Nether (from 1866), Kimberworth[56] (from 1866), Langthwaite with Tilts (1866—83), Laughton en le Morthen, Letwell (from 1866), Maltby, Marr, High Melton, Mexborough, Orgreave (from 1866), Ravenfield, Rawmarsh, Rotherham,[56] St John's with Throapham (from 1866), Kirk Sandall, Sheffield,[56] Spotbrough, Stainforth (from 1866), Stainton, Stancil with Wellingley and Wilseck (1866—86), Stotfold (from 1858), Swinton (from 1866), Sykehouse (from 1866), Thorne, Thorpe in Balne (from 1866), Thorpe Salvin, Thrybergh, Thurnscoe, Tickhill,[56] Tinsley (from 1866), Todwick, Treeton, Ulley (from 1866), Wadworth, Wales, Warmsworth, Wath upon Dearne, Wentworth[56] (from 1866), Whiston,[56] Wickersley, Wombwell (from 1866), Woodsetts (from 1866)

BOROUGHS

Units with some degree of burghal character[60] are denominated 'Bor'. Those which did not sustain that status until the 19th cent are in italics. MBs were established by the Municipal Corporations Act, 1835,[61] or by later charter.

ALMONDBURY BOR [W Riding]
Almondbury

BARNSLEY MB (1869[62]—1913[2]), CB (1913[2]—74) [W Riding]
Barnsley

BATLEY MB (1868[63]—1974) [W Riding]
Batley

BAWTRY BOR [W Riding]
pt Blyth

BEVERLEY BOR/MB [E Riding]
Beverley (1936—74), pt Beverley St John (until 1866), Beverley St Martin (until 1936), Beverley St Mary (until 1936), Beverley St Mary (until 1936), Beverley St Nicholas (until 1936)

BINGLEY BOR [W Riding]
Bingley

BOOTHAM BOR[64] [City of York]
pt jurisd York St Mary's Abbey

BOROUGHBRIDGE BOR [W Riding]
pt Aldborough

BRADFORD BOR, MB[65] (1847[66]—89), CB (1889—1974) [W Riding] [City from 1897[67]]
Allerton (1882—98), North Bierley (1899—1974), Bolton (1882—98), Bowling (1847—98), Bradford, pt Calverley with Farsley (1882—94), Clayton (1930—74), Eccleshill (1899—1974), Heaton (1882—98), Horton (1847—98), Idle (1899—1974), Manningham (1847—98), pt Pudsey (1882—94), Thornbury (1894—98), Thornton (1899—1974), Tong (1899—1974), Tyersall (1894—98), Wyke (1899—1974)

BRIDLINGTON BOR, MB (1899[68]—1974) [E Riding]
Bridlington, Hilderthorpe (1899—1923)

BRIGHOUSE MB (1893[69]—1974) [W Riding]
Brighouse (1894—1974), pt Hipperholme with Brighouse (1893—94), Rastrick (1893—1915)

BROUGH ON HUMBER BOR[70] [E Riding]
pt Elloughton

CASTLEFORD MB (1955[71]—74) [W Riding]
Castleford

DEWSBURY MB (1862[72]—1913[10]), CB (1913[10]—74) [W Riding]
Dewsbury, Ravensthorpe (1910—25), Soothill Nether (1910—25), Thornhill (1910—25)

DONCASTER BOR/MB (1835—1927[11]), CB (1927[11]—74) [W Riding]
Doncaster

DRAX BOR [W Riding]
Drax

GOOLE MB (1933[73]—74) [W Riding]
Goole

HALIFAX BOR, MB[74] (1848[75]—89), CB (1889—1974) [W Riding]
Halifax, pt Northowram (1848—94), Ovenden (pt 1848—92, ent 1892—94), pt Skircoat (1848—94), pt Southowram (1847—94)

HAREWOOD BOR [W Riding]
Harewood

HARROGATE MB (1884[76]—1974) [W Riding]
pt Bilton with Harrogate (1884—94), Harrogate (1894—1974), pt Knaresborough (1884—88), pt Pannal (1884—94), pt Scriven with Tentergate (1884—88)

HEDON BOR, MB (1861[77]—1974) [E Riding]
Hedon

HELMSLEY BOR [N Riding]
Helmsley

HOWDEN BOR [E Riding]
Howden

HUDDERSFIELD MB[78] (1868[79]—89), CB (1889—1974) [W Riding]
Almondbury (1868—1924), Dalton (1868—1924), Huddersfield, Lindley cum Quarnby (1868—1924), Lockwood (1868—1924), Longwood (1890—1924)

KEIGHLEY MB (1882[80]—1974) [W Riding]
pt Bingley (1882—94), Keighley (pt 1882—94, ent 1894—1974)

KINGSTON UPON HULL BOR[81] (Co of Itself from 1440)/MB/CB [E Riding]
pt Cottingham (1883—94), Cottingham Within (1894—98), Drypool (1835—98), Garrison Side (1835—98), pt Hessle (orig [until Kingston upon Hull Holy Trinity gains sep civ identity], and 1883—94), Hessle Within (1894—98), Kingston upon Hull Holy Trinity (from when gains sep civ identity until jointly rated with St Mary), Kingston upon Hull Holy Trinty and St Mary (joint rating—1974), Kingston upon Hull St Mary (until jointly rated with Holy Trinity), Marfleet (1883—98), Newington (1883—98), Sculcoates, Southcoates (1835—98), pt Sutton and Stoneferry (1835—94), Sutton Within (1894—98)

KIRKBY MOORSIDE BOR [N Riding]
Kirkby Moorside

KNARESBOROUGH BOR [W Riding]
Knaresborough

LEEDS BOR/MB/CB [W Riding] [City from 1893[82]]
Chapel Allerton (until 1904), Armley (until 1904), Armley and Bramley (1904—25), Beeston (until 1904), Bramley (until 1904), Farnley (until 1904), Headingley cum Burley (until 1904), Holbeck (until 1925), Hunslet (until 1925), Leeds, Osmanthorpe (1894—1925), Potter Newton (until 1904), pt Seacroft (1835—94), pt Templenewsham (1835—94), Wortley (until 1904)

NEW MALTON BOR [N Riding]
pt Old Malton (until New Malton gains sep civ identity), New Malton (thereafter)

MIDDLESBROUGH MB[83] (1853[84]—89), CB (1889—1968[35]) [N Riding]
pt West Acklam (1887—94), pt Linthorpe (1866—94), pt Marton (1866—94), Middlesbrough, pt Normanby (1866—94), pt Ormesby (1866—94)

MORLEY MB[85] (1885[86]—1974) [W Riding]
pt Ardsley West (1891—94), Churwell (1891—1937),

Morley

MOSSLEY MB (1884[87]—1974) [Lancs, pt W Riding (1885—94)]

pt Saddleworth

NORTHALLERTON BOR [N Riding]

Northallerton

OSSETT MB (1890[88]—1974) [W Riding]

Ossett

OTLEY BOR [W Riding]

Otley

PICKERING BOR [N Riding]

pt Pickering

POCKLINGTON BOR [E Riding]

Pocklington

PONTEFRACT BOR/MB[89] (sometimes early 'West-cheap') [W Riding]

Monkhill (1875—92), Pontefract, Pontefract Park (1875—1920), Tanshelf (1875—1920))

PUDSEY MB (1900[90]—74) [W Riding]

Pudsey

RAVENSRODD BOR[91] [E Riding]

Ravensrodd

REDCAR MB (1921[92]—68[35]) [N Riding]

Redcar

RICHMOND BOR/MB [N Riding]

Richmond

RIPON BOR/MB [W Riding] [City from 1836]

pt Aismunderby with Bondgate (1835—94), Ripon

ROTHERHAM MB[93] (1871[94]—1902[36]), CB (1902[36]—74) [W Riding]

pt Brinsworth (1879—94), pt Greasborough (1879—94), Kimberworth (ent 1871—83, pt 1883—94), Rotherham, pt Wentworth (1883—94), pt Whiston (1879—94)

ST OLAVE'S BOR[64] [City of York]

Lbty of St Mary's Abbey

SCARBOROUGH BOR[95]/MB [N Riding]

Falsgrave (until 1890), Scarborough

SHEFFIELD BOR, MB (1843[96]—89), CB (1899—1974) [W Riding] [City from 1893[97]]

Attercliffe cum Darnall (1843—1907), Brightside Bierlow (1843—1904), Bradfield Urban (1914—33), Ecclesall (1904—33), Ecclesall Bierlow (1843—1904), Ecclesfield Urban (1921—33), Nether Hallam (1843—1904), Upper Hallam (1843—1904), Handsworth (1921—38), Heeley (1880—1904), Norton Within (1901—04), Sheffield, Tinsley (1912—33)

SKELTON BOR [N Riding]

Skelton

SKIPSEA BOR [E Riding]

Skipsea

SKIPTON BOR [W Riding]

Skipton

SPENBOROUGH MB (1955[71]—74) [W Riding]

Cleckheaton, Gomersal, Liversedge

STOCKTON ON TEES BOR/MB[98] [Durham, pt N Riding (1889—94)]

pt Linthorpe (1889—94)

STOKESLEY BOR [N Riding]

Stokesley

TEESSIDE CB (1967[35]—74) [N Riding]

Teesside

THIRSK BOR [N Riding]

Thirsk

THORNABY ON TEES MB (1892[99]—1974) [N Riding]

Thornaby

TICKHILL BOR [W Riding]

Tickhill

TODMORDEN MB (1896[100]—1974) [W Riding]

Cornholme (1896—97), Langfield (1896—97), Todmorden (1897—1974), Todmorden and Walsden (1896—97)

WAKEFIELD BOR, MB (1848[101]—1915[47]), CB (1915[47]—74) [W Riding] [City from 1888]

pt Alverthorpe with Thornes (1848—94), Lupset (1921—25), Sandal Magna (1909—25), pt Stanley cum Wrenthorpe (1848—94), Wakefield

WHITBY BOR [N Riding]

Whitby

YARM BOR [N Riding]

pt Kirk Leavington (until Yarm gains sep civ identity), Yarm (thereafter)

YORK BOR[102]/MB[103]/CB [not assoc with an Adm Co]

pt Clifton (1884—94), Clifton Within (1894—1900), pt Dringhouses (1884—94), Dringhouses Within (1894—1900), Gate Fulford (pt 1884—94, ent 1894—1900), pt Heworth (1884—94), Heworth Within (1894—1900), Holgate (1884—1900), pt Middlethorpe (1884—94), Middlethorpe Within (1894—1900), York (1900—74), York All Saints North Street (until 1900), York All Saints Pavement (until 1900), *York Castle*,[104] York Davy Hall[105] (until 1900), York Holy Trinity Goodramgate (until 1900); York Holy Trinity, King's Court (until 1900); York Holy Trinity Micklegate (pt until 1866, ent 1866—1900), York Minster Yard with Bedern (1835—1900), York Mint Yard[106] (1835—1900), York St Andrew (until 1900), York St Crux (until 1900); York St Cuthbert, St Helen on the Walls and All Saints, Peaseholme (pt 1586—1866, ent 1866—1900); York St Dennis (until 1900), York St George (until 1900), York St Giles in the Suburbs (pt until 1884, ent 1884—1900); York St Helen, Stonegate (until 1900); York St John, Delpike (until 1900); York St John, Micklegate (until 1900); York St Lawrence (pt until 1866, ent 1866—1900), York St Margaret (until 1900), York St Martin le Grand (until 1900), York St Martin Micklegate with St Gregory (until 1900), York St Mary Bishophill Junior (pt until 1866, ent 1866—1900), York St Mary Bishophill Senior (pt until 1866, ent 1866—1900); York St Mary, Castlegate (until 1900), York St Maurice (until 1900), York St Michael le Belfrey (pt until 1866, ent 1866—1900); York St Michael, Spurriergate (until 1900); York St Nicholas (until 1900); York St Olave, Marygate (pt until 1866, ent 1866—1900); York St Peter the Little (until 1900), York St Peter le Willows (until 1900), York St Sampson (until 1900), York St Saviour (pt until 1866, ent 1866—1900), York St Wilfrid (until 1900)

POOR LAW UNIONS

In Yorks Poor Law County:[107] (Riding/Adm Co as indicated)

AYSGARTH PLU (1869—1930) [N Riding]
High Abbotside, Low Abbotside, Askrigg, Aysgarth, Bainbridge, Bishopdale, Burton cum Walden, Carperby cum Thoresby, Hawes, Newbiggin, Thoralby, Thornton Rust

BAINBRIDGE GILBERT UNION (until 1869) [N Riding]
High Abbotside, Low Abbotside, Askrigg, Aysgarth, Bainbridge, Burton cum Walden, Hawes, Thoralby

BARNSLEY PLU (1850—1930) [W Riding]
Ardsley (1850—1921), Barnsley, Barugh, Billingley, Carlton, Cudworth, Darfield, Darton, Dodworth, Hoyland Nether, Monk Bretton (1850—1921), Notton, Royston, Stainbrough, Wombwell, Woolley, Worsbrough

BARWICK GILBERT UNION (until 1869) [W Riding]
Acaster Selby, Ackton, Alwoodley (until 1861), Appleton Roebuck, Askham Bryan, Barkston, Barwick in Elmet, Bilbrough, Bilton, Bolton Percy, Bramham cum Oglethorpe, Cattal, Catterton, Clifford with Boston, Kirk Deighton, Featherstone, Church Fenton, Ferry Fryston, Hunsingore, Hutton Wandesley, East Keswick (until 1861), Long Marston, Newton Kyme cum Toulston, Normanton, Pontefract Park, Purston Jaglin, Great Ribston with Walshford, Ryther cum Ossendyke, Seacroft, Shadwell, Steeton, Tadcaster East, Thorp Arch, Thornville, Tockwith, Ulleskelf, Walton, Whitwood, Wigton, Wilstrop, Wyke

BEDALE PLU (1839—1920) [N Riding]
Ainderby Miers with Holtby, Aiskew, Bedale, Burneston, Burrill with Cowling, Burton upon Ure, Carthorpe, Clifton upon Ure, Crakehall; Exelby, Leeming and Newton; Firby, Gatenby, Hackforth, Killerby, Kirkby Fleetham, Kirklington cum Upsland, Langthorne, Masham, Rand Grange, Rootwith, Scruton, Snape, Swainby with Allerthorpe, Swinton with Watermarske, Theakston, Thirn, Thornton Walass, Well

BEVERLEY PLU (1836—1930) [E Riding]
Aike, Beverley St Martin, Beverley St Mary, Beverley St Nicholas, Beswick, Brantingham, Bishop Burton, Cherry Burton, South Cave, South Dalton, Ellerker, Elloughton with Brough, Eske, Etton, Holme on the Wolds, Kilnwick, Leconfield and Arram, Leven, Lockington, Lockington in Kilnwick (1836—94), Lund, Meaux, Molescroft, North Newbald, South Newbald, Routh, Rowley, Scorborough, Skidby, Storkhill and Sandholme, Thearne, Tickton and Hull Bridge, Walkington, Wawne, Weel, Woodmansey and Beverley Parks

NORTH BIERLEY PLU (1848—1930) [W Riding]
Allerton (1848—98), North Bierley, Bolton (1848—98), Calverley (1894—1930), Calverley with Farsley (1848—94), Clayton, Cleckheaton, Denholme (1894—1930), Drighlington, Eccleshill (1869—1930), Farsley (1894—1930), Heaton (1848—98), Hunsworth, Idle, Pudsey, Shipley, Thornbury (1894—98), Thornton, Tong, Tyersall (1894—98), Wilsden, Wyke

BRADFORD PLU (1837—98), PAR (1898—1930) [W Riding]
Allerton (1837—48), North Bierley (1837—48), Bolton (1837—48), Bowling (1837—98), Bradford, Calverley with Farsley (1837—48), Clayton (1837—48), Cleckheaton (1837—48), Drighlington (1837—48), Heaton (1837—48), Horton (1837—98), Hunsworth (1837—48), Idle (1837—48), Manningham (1837—98), Pudsey (1837—48), Shipley (1837—48), Thornton (1837—48), Tong (1837—48), Wilsden (1837—48), Wyke (1837—48)

BRAMLEY PLU (1862—1930) [W Riding]
Armley (1869—1904), Armley and Bramley (1904—25), Bramley (1862—1904), Farnley (1869—1904), Gildersome, Wortley (1869—1904)

BRIDLINGTON PLU (1836—1930) [E Riding]
Argam, Auburn (1836—94), Barnston, Bempton, Bessingby, Boynton, Bridlington, Buckton, Burton Agnes, Burton Fleming, Carnaby; Dringhoe, Upton and Brough; Easton, Flamborough, Fordon, Fraisthorpe (1836—96), Fraisthorpe with Auburn and Wilsthorpe (1896—1930), Gransmoor, Grindale, Haisthorpe, Hilderthorpe (1836—1923), Hunmanby, Lissett, Reighton, Rudston, Sewerby cum Marton, Skipsea, Speeton, Thornholme, Thwing, Ulrome, Wilsthorpe (1836—96), Wold Newton

CARLTON GILBERT UNION (until 1869) [W Riding]
Adel cum Eccup, Chapel Allerton, Armley, Arthington, Askwith, Baildon, Beamsley in Addingham, Beamsley in Skipton, Beeston, Bramhope (until 1861), Burley in Wharfedale, Carlton, Churwell, Collingham, Denton, Dunkeswick, Eccleshill, Farnley, Harewood, Hawksworth, Headingley cum Burley, Horsforth (until 1861), Ilkley, Kirkby Overblow (until 1861), Leathley (until 1861), Menston, Middleton, Nesfield with Langbar, Otley, Pool (until 1861), Potter Newton, Rawdon, Rigton (until 1861), Rothwell, Silsden, Templenewsham, Thorner, Weeton, Wortley

DEWSBURY PLU (1837—1930) [W Riding]
Batley, Birkenshaw (1894—1930), Birstall (1894—1930), Dewsbury, Gomersal, Heckmondwike, Liversedge, Mirfield, Morley, Ossett (1890—1930), Ossett cum Gawthorpe (1837—90), Ravensthorpe (1894—1925), Soothill (1837—94), Soothill Nether (1894—1925), Soothill Upper (1894—1910), Thornhill (1837—1925), Whitley Lower (1837—96)

DONCASTER PLU (1837—1930) [W Riding, N Riding (1837—95), Notts (1837—95)]
Adwick le Street, Adwick upon Dearne, Armthorpe, Askern, Auckley,[108] Austerfield, Balby with Hexthorpe (1837—1914), Barnbrough, Barnby Dun with Kirk Sandall (1921—30), Barnby upon Don (1837—1921), Bawtry, Bentley with Arksey, Bilham (1837—1920), Blaxton, Bolton upon Dearne, Braithwell, Brodsworth, Burghwallis, Cadeby, Campsall, Cantley, Carr House and Elm Field (1862—1914), Clayton with Frickley, Conisbrough, Denaby, Doncaster, Edlington, Finningley,[109] Hampole, Hickleton, Hooton Pagnell, Kirk Bramwith, Langthwaite with Tilts (1837—83), Loversall, Marr, High Melton, Mexborough, Moss,

Norton, Owston, Rossington, Kirk Sandall (1837—1921), Long Sandall (1837—86), Skellow (1837—1915), Spotbrough, Stainton, Stainton Urban (1924—30), Stancill with Wellingley and Wilseck (1837—86), Stotfold (1837—1920), Sutton, Thorpe in Balne, Thurnscoe, Tickhill, Tickhill Outer (1894—95), Wadworth, Warmsworth, Whealtey (1837—1914)

DRIFFIELD PLU (1836—1930) [E Riding]

Bainton, Beeford, Bracken, Brigham, Butterwick, Cottam, Cowlam, North Dalton, Great Driffield, Little Driffield (1836—85), Eastburn, Emswell with Little Driffield (1885—1930), Emswell with Kellythorpe (1836—85), Fimber, Foston on the Wolds, Foxholes with Boythorpe, North Frodingham, Garton on the Wolds, Gembling, Harpham, Helperthorpe, Hutton Cranswick, Great Kelk, Little Kelk, Kilham, Kirkburn and Battleburn, Langtoft, Lowthorpe, Luttons Ambo, Middleton on the Wolds, Nafferton, Neswick, Rotsea, Ruston Parva, Skerne, Sledmere, Southburn, Sunderlandwick, Tibthorpe, Towthorpe, Wansford, Watton, Weaverthorpe, Wetwang

EASINGWOLD PLU (1837—1930) [N Riding, Durham (1837—44)]

Aldwark, Alne, Angram Grange, Brafferton, Brandsby cum Stearsby, Carlton Husthwaite, Coxwold, Crayke,[110] Dalby cum Skewsby, Easingwold, Farlington, Flawith, Huby, Husthwaite, Linton upon Ouse, Marton cum Moxby, Myton on Swale, Newburgh, Newton upon Ouse (soon after 1837[111]—1930), Oulston, Raskelf, Stillington, Sutton on the Forest, Tholthorpe, Thormanby, Thornton on the Hill, Whenby, Wildon Grange, Yearsley

ECCLESALL BIERLOW PLU (1837—1930) [W Riding (1837—1904), Derbys]

Ecclesall Bierlow (1837—1904), Nether Hallam (1837—1904), Upper Hallam (1837—1904), Heeley (1880—1904)

GOOLE PLU (1837—1930) [W Riding, Lincs Pts Lind]

Adlingfleet, Airmyn, Eastoft, Fockerby, Goole, Goole Fields (1894—1930), Gowdall, Haldenby, Hook, Ousefleet, Pollington, Rawcliffe, Reedness (1837—48), Reedness (1894—1930), Snaith and Cowick,[112] Swinefleet (1837—84), Swinefleet (1894—1930), Swinefleet and Reedness (1884—94), Whitgift

GUISBOROUGH PLU (1837—1930) [N Riding]

Brotton, Coatham (1899—1921), Commondale, Danby, Easington, Eston (1837—75), Guisborough, Hutton Lowcross, Kilton, Kirkleatham, Liverton, Loftus, Marske, Moorsholm, Morton, Newton, Normanby (1837—75), Ormesby (1837—75), Pinchinthorpe, Redcar, Skelton, Skinnigrove, Stanghow, Tocketts, Upleatham, Upsall, Westerdale, Wilton

HALIFAX PLU (1837—1930) [W Riding]

Barkisland, Brighouse (1894—1930), Clifton,[113] Elland (1894—1930), Elland with Greetland (1837—94), Fixby, Greetland (1894—1930), Upper Greetland (1894—1930), Halifax, Hartshead,[113] Hipperholme (1894—1930), Hipperholme with Brighouse (1837—94), Luddenden Foot (1894—1930), Midgley, Norland, Northowram (1837—1930), Norwood Green and Coley (1894—1930), Ovenden (1837—94), Queensbury (1894—1930), Rastrick (1837—1915), Rishworth, Shelf, Skircoat (1837—99), Southowram, Sowerby,

Sowerby Bridge (1894—1926), Soyland, Stainland with Old Lindley, Warley (1837—1900)

HELMSLEY PLU (orig, 'HELMSLEY BLACKMOOR') (1837—1930) [N Riding]

Ampleforth (1887—1930), Ampleforth Birdforth (1837—87), Ampleforth Oswaldkirk (1837—87), Ampleforth St Peter (1837—87), Arden, Beadlam, Bilsdale Midcable (1837—48); Bilsdale, West Side; Bransdale, West Side (1837—48); Old Byland, Byland Abbey (1837—87), Byland with Wass (1887—1930), Cawton, Cold Kirby, Coulton, Dale Town (soon after 1837[111]—1930), Great Edstone (1837—48), Little Edstone (1837—48), Fadmoor (1837—48); Farndale, East Side (1837—48); Farndale, West Side (1837—48); Farndale, Low Quarter (1837—48); Gillamoor (1837—48), Gilling East, Grimston, Harome, Hawnby, Helmsley, North Holme (1837—48), Hutton le Hole (1837—48), Kirkby Moorside (1837—48), Laskill Pasture, Murton (soon after 1837[111]—1930), Muscoates (1837—48), Nawton (1837—48), East Newton and Laysthorp, Nunnington (1837—48), Oldstead, Oswaldkirk, Pockley, Rievaulx, Scawton, Skiplam (1837—48), Snilesworth (soon after 1837[111]—1930), Sproxton, Stonegrave, Thorpe le Willows, Wass (1837—87), Welburn (1837—48), Wombleton (1837—48)

HEMSWORTH PLU (1850—1930) [W Riding]

Ackworth, Badsworth, Brierley, North Elmsall, South Elmsall, Hamphall Stubbs (soon after 1850[111]—1930), West Hardwick, Havercroft with Cold Hiendley, Hemsworth, Hessle (1850—88), Hessle and Hill Top (1888—1930), South Hiendley, Hill Top (1850—88), Great Houghton, Little Houghton, Huntwick with Foulby and Nostell (soon after 1850[111]—1930), South Kirkby, Ryhill, Shafton, Skelbrooke, Kirk Smeaton, Little Smeaton, Thorpe Audlin, Upton, Walden Stubbs, Wintersett

HOLBECK TP/PAR (1862—69), PLU (1869—1904), PAR (1904—25) [W Riding]

Beeston (1869—1904), Churwell (1869—1904), Holbeck

HOWDEN PLU (1837—1930) [E Riding]

Asselby, Aughton, Barkholme, Barmby on the Marsh, Belby, Bellasize, Bishopsoil (1880—1930), Blacktoft, Brackenholme with Woodhall, Breighton and Gunby, Broomfleet, Bubwith, North Cave with Everthorpe and Drewton, Cheapsides (1858—92), Cotness, Eastrington, Ellerton Priory, Faxfleet, Foggathorpe, Gilberdike, Gribthorpe, Harlthorpe, Hemingbrough, Holme upon Spalding Moor, Hotham, Howden, Kilpin, Knedlington, Laxton, Laytham, Menthorpe cum Bowthorpe, Metham, New Village[114] (1837—81), Portington and Cavil, Saltmarshe, Scalby, Skelton, Spaldington, Thorpe, Wallingfen (1881—1930), Willitoft, Wressell (soon after 1837[111]—1930), Yokefleet

HUDDERSFIELD PLU (1837—1930) [W Riding]

Almondbury (1837—1924), Austonley (1837—1921), Cartworth (1837—1921), South Crosland, Cumberworth, Cumberworth Half (1837—76), Dalton (1837—1924), Farnley Tyas (1837—1925), Fulstone, Golcar, Hepworth, Holme, South Holme (1894—95), Honley, Huddersfield, Kirkburton, Kirkheaton, Lepton, Lindley cum Quarmby (1837—1924), Lingards

(1837—96), Linthwaite, Lockwood (1837—1924), Longwood (1837—1924), Marsden (1898—1930), Marsden in Almondbury (1837—98), Marsden in Huddersfield (1837—98), Meltham, Netherthong (1837—1921), Scammonden, Scholes (1894—1930), Shelley, Shepley, Skelmanthorpe (1876—1930), Slaithwaite, Thurstonland (1837—1925), Thurstonland and Farnley Tyas (1925—30), Upperthong (1837—1921), Whitley Upper, Wooldale (1837—1921)

HULL INCORP [E Riding]

Kingston upon Hull Holy Trinity and St Mary

HUNSLET TP/PAR (1862—69), PLU (1869—1930) [W Riding]

Hunslet (1862—1925), Middleton (1869—1920), Oulton with Woodlesforth (1869—1930), Rothwell (1869—1930), Templenewsham (1869—1927), Thorpe Stapleton (1869—1925)

KEIGHLEY PLU (1837—1930) [W Riding]

Bingley, Bingley Outer (1894—98), Haworth, Keighley, Morton, Oakworth (1894—1930), Oxenhope (1894—1930), Stanbury (1894—1930), Steeton with Eastburn, Sutton

KIRKBY MOORSIDE PLU (1848—1930) [N Riding]

Appleton le Moors (soon after 1848[111]—1930); Bransdale, West Side; Great Edstone, Little Edstone, Fadmoor; Farndale, East Side; Farndale, Low Quarter; Farndale, West Side; Gillamoor, North Holme, Hutton le Hole, Kirkby Moorside, Muscoates, Nawton, Ness (1887—1930), East Ness (soon after 1848[111]—87), West Ness (soon after 1848[111]—87), Normanby (soon after 1848[111]—1930), Nunnington, Salton (soon after 1848[111]—1930), Skiplam, Thornton Riseborough (soon after 1848[111]—1930), Welburn, Wombleton

KNARESBOROUGH PLU (1854—1930) [W Riding]

Bilton (1894—1930), Bilton and Harrogate (1854—94), Brearton, Burton Leonard, Farnham, Fellscliffe, Ferrensby, Flaxby, Follifoot, Goldsborough, Hampsthwaite, Harrogate (1894—1930), Haverah Park, Killinghall, Knaresborough, Knaresborough Outer (1894—1930), Nidd, Pannal, Plompton, Ripley, Scotton, Scriven (1894—1930), Scriven with Tentergate (1854—94), South Stainley with Cayton, Starbeck (1894—1930), Tentergate (1894—95), Walkingham Hill with Occaney

LEEDS GUARDIANS (1844—69), PLU (1869—1912), PAR (1912—30) [W Riding]

Chapel Allerton (1869—1904), Headingley cum Burley (1869—1904), Holbeck (1844—62), Hunslet (1844—62), Leeds, Potter Newton (1869—1904), Roundhay (1869—1912), Seacroft (1869—1912)

LEYBURN PLU (1837—1930) [N Riding]

Agglethorpe with Coverham, Akebar, Arrathorne, Barden, Bellerby, Burrill with Cowling (1837—39), Burton upon Ure (1837—39), Cadbergh with East Scrafton, Carlton Highdale, Carlton Town, Castle Bolton, Clifton upon Ure (1837—39), Colsterdale (1894—1930), Constable Burton, Ellingstring, Ellingtons, Fearby, Finghall, Garriston, Harmby, East Huaxwell, West Huaxwell, Healy with Sutton, Hornby, Hunton, Hutton Hang, Ilton cum Pott (soon after 1837[111]—1930), Leyburn, Melmerby, Middleham, Newton le Willows, Patrick Brompton, Preston, Redmire, Rookwith (1837—39), West Scrafton,

Spennithorne, Thornton Steward, Thirn (1837—39), Wensley, East Witton Within, East Witton Without, West Witton

MALTON PLU (1837—1930) [N Riding, E Riding]

Acklam with Barthorpe, Airyholme with Howthorpe and Baxton Howe, Amotherby, Appleton le Street, Barton le Street, Barton le Willows, Birdsall, Brawby, Broughton, Bulmer, Burythorpe, Butterwick, Coneysthorpe, Crambe, Duggleby, Eddlethorpe, Firby, Foston, Fryton, Ganthorpe, North Grimston, Great Habton, Little Habton, Henderskelf, East Heslerton, West Heslerton, Hildenley, South Holme, Hovingham, Howsham, Huttons Ambo, Kennythorpe, Kirby Grindalythe, Kirkham, Knapton, Langton, Leavening, Leppington, Malton (1896—1930), New Malton (1837—96), Old Malton (1837—96), Menethorpe, Norton, Raisthorpe and Burdale, Rillington, Ryton, Scagglethorpe, Scackleton, Scampston, Settrington, Sheriff Hutton with Cornbrough, Slingsby, Stittenham, Swinton, Terrington with Wigganthorpe, Thirkleby, Thornton le Clay, Thorpe Bassett, Wath, Welburn, Westow, Wharram le Street, Wharram Percy, Whitwell on the Hill, Wintringham, Yedingham

MIDDLESBROUGH PLU (1875—1930) [N Riding]

West Acklam, Eston, Hemlington, Ingleby Barwick, Linthorpe (1875—1913), Maltby, Marton, Middlesbrough, Normanby (1875—1915), Ormesby, Stainton, Thornaby

NORTHALLERTON PLU (1837—1930) [N Riding]

Ainderby Miers with Holtby (1837—39), Ainderby Steeple, Aiskew (1837—39), Appleton Wiske, Bedale (1837—39), Birkby, Borrowby, Brompton, Cotcliffe (1858—1930), East Cowton, South Cowton, Crakenhall (1837—39), Crosby, Danby Wiske, Deighton, Ellerbeck, Firby (1837—39), Gueldable (1837—88), Hackforth (1837—39), East Harlsey, West Harlsey, Hornby, Hutton Bonville, Killerby (1837—39), Kiplin, Kirby Sigston, Kirkby Fleetham (1837—39), Landmoth cum Catto, Langthorne (1837—39), Great Langton, Little Langton, Lazenby (1858—1930), Leake (1858—1930), Morton upon Swale, Northallerton, Osmotherley, North Otterington, Rand Grange (1837—39), Romanby, West Rounton, Scruton (1837—39), Nether Silton, Over Silton, Great Smeaton, Little Smeaton, Sowerby under Cotcliffe, Thimbleby, Thornton le Beans, Thornton Watlass (1837—39), Thrintoft, Warlaby, Welbury, Whitwell, Winton, Yafforth

GREAT OUSEBURN GILBERT UNION (until 1854), PLU (1854—1930) [W Riding, N Riding]

Acomb (1854—1930), Aldborough[115] (1854—1930), Allerton Mauleverer with Hopperton (1854—1930), Arkendale, Baldersby (until 1854), Bickerton (until 1854), Boroughbridge (1854—1930), Burton Leonard (until 1854), Cattal (1869—1930), Clareton[116] (until 1888), Coneythorpe (until 1888), Coneythorpe and Clareton (1888—1930), Copgrove (1854—1930), Dishforth (until 1854), Lower Dunsforth,[117] Upper Dunsforth with Branton Green,[117] Ellenthorpe (1854—1930), Farnham (until 1854), Goldsborough (until 1854), Green Hammerton, Kirk Hammerton, Helperby, Hessay, Humberton[118] (1854—95), Hunsingore (1869—1930), Hutton Conyers (until 1854), Kirby Hall, Kirby Hill, Knapton, Langthorpe, Markington with Wallerthwaite (until 1854), Marton cum Gratton, Milby[118] (1854—95), Minskip, Morton le Moor (until 1854), Bishop Monkton (until 1854), Moor Monkton, Nun Monkton (1854—1930), Norton le Clay, Great Ouseburn, Little Ouseburn, Nether Poppleton (1854—1930), Upper Poppleton (1854—1930), Rainton with Newby (until 1854), Great Ribston with Walshford (1869—1930), Little Ribston (until 1854), Roecliffe (1854—1930), Rufforth, Shipton, Sickinghall (until 1854), Skelton (until 1854), Staveley (1854—1930), Thornton Bridge (1854—1930), Thornville (1869—1930), Thorpe Underwoods (1854—1930), Tollerton, Westwick (1854—1930), Whixley, Widdington, Youlton

PATELEY BRIDGE PLU (1837—1930) [W Riding]
Bewerley, Birstwith (soon after 1837[111]—1930), Bishop Thornton, High and Low Bishopside, Clint, Dacre, Fountains Earth, Hartwith cum Winsley, Menwith with Darley, Down Stonebeck, Upper Stonebeck, Thornthwaite with Padside, Thruscross, Warsill

PATRINGTON PLU (1836—1930) [E Riding]
Burstwick with Skeckling (soon after 1836[111]—1930), Burton Pidsea (soon after 1836[111]—1930), Easington, South Frodingham, Halsham, Hilston, Hollym, Holmpton, Keyingham, Kilnsea, Ottringham, Out Newton, Owstwick, Owthorne, Patrington, Paull, Rimswell, Roos, Ryhill and Camerton, Skeffling, Sunk Island, Thorgumbald, Tunstall, Waxholme, Welwick, Winestead, Withernsea

PENISTONE PLU (1849—1930) [W Riding]
Cawthorne, Clayton West, Denby, Gunthwaite, High Hoyland, Hoyland Swaine, Hunshelf, Ingbirchworth, Kexborough, Langsett, Oxspring, Penistone, Silkstone, Thurgoland, Thurlstone

PICKERING PLU (1837—1930) [N Riding]
Aislaby, Allerston, Appleton le Moors (1837—soon after 1848[111]), Barughs Ambo, Cawthorn, Cropton, Ebberston, Farmanby (1837—87), Hartoft, Kingthorpe, Kirby Misperton, Lastingham, Levisham, Lockton, Marishes, Marton, Middleton, Newton, Normanby (1837—soon after 1848[111]), Pickering; Rosedale, East Side; Rosedale, West Side; Sinnington, Spaunton, Thornton Dale, Thornton Risebrough (1837—soon after 1848[111]), Thurnhill,[119] Wilton, Wrelton

POCKLINGTON PLU (1836—1930) [E Riding]
Alethorpe, Barmby on the Moor, Bielby, Bishop Wilton with Belthorpe, Bolton, Bugthorpe, Burnby, High Catton, Low Catton, North Cliffe, South Cliffe, East Cottingwith, Everingham, Fangfoss, Fridaythorpe, Full Sutton, Great Givendale with Grimthorpe, Goodmanham, Harswell, Hayton, Huggate, Kilnwick Percy, Kirby Underdale, Londesborough with Easthorpe, Market Weighton and Arras, Melbourne, Millington with Little Givendale, Newton upon Derwent, Nunburnholme, Ousethorpe, Pocklington, Sancton and Houghton, Scrayingham, Seaton Ross, Shipton Thorpe, Skirpenbeck, East Stamford Bridge, Storwood, Sutton upon Derwent, Thixendale, Thorpe le Street, Thornton, Waplington, Warter, Wilberfoss, Yapham cum Meltonby, Youlthorpe with Gowthorpe

PONTEFRACT PLU (1862—1930) [W Riding]
Ackton (1869—1930), Balne, Beal or Beaghall (1869—1930), Birkin, Brotherton (1869—1930), Burton Salmon (1869—1930), Byram cum Poole (1862—91), Byram cum Sutton (1891—1930), Carleton (1869—1930), Castleford (1869—1930), Cridling Stubbs, Darrington (1869—1930), Eggborough, Fairburn (1869—1930), Featherstone (1869—1930), Ferry Fryston (1869—1930), Monk Fryston, Glass Houghton (1869—1930), East Hardwick, Heck, Hensall, Hillam, Kellington, Knottingley, Ledston (1869 and only brief time later), Methley (1869—1930), Monkhill (1862—92), Pontefract, Pontefract Park (1869—1920), Purston Jaglin (1869—1930), Snydale, Stapleton, Sutton (1869—91), Tanshelf (1862—1920), Whitley, Whitwood (1869—1930), Womersley

GREAT PRESTON GILBERT UNION (until 1869) [W Riding]
Allerton Bywater, Altofts, Austhorpe (until 1862), Bardsey cum Righton (until 1861), Beal or Beaghall, Birkin (until 1862), Brotherton, Burton Salmon, Byram cum Poole (until 1862), Carleton, Castleford, Crofton, Darrington, Fairburn, Monk Fryston (until 1862), Garforth, Glass Houghton, West Haddlesey, Hambleton, Hillam (until 1862), Kippax, Kirkby Wharfe and North Milford (until 1862), Ledsham, Ledston, Lotherton cum Allerford (until 1862), Methley, Micklefield, Middleton, South Milford, Great and Little Preston, Roundhay, Saxton with Scarthingwell, Sherburn in Elmet, Syndale (until 1862), Stapleton (until 1862), Swillington, Tanshelf (until 1862), Weardley (until 1861), Womersley (until 1862)

REETH PLU (1840—1930) [N Riding]
Arkengarthdale, Ellerton Abbey, Grinton, Marrick, Melbecks, Muker, Reeth

RICHMOND PLU (1837—1930) [N Riding]
Aldbrough, Appleton, Arkengarthdale (1837—40), Aske, Bolton upon Swale, Brompton on Swale, Brough, Calbourn, Caldwell, Catterick, North Cowton, Downholme, Easby, Ellerton Abbey (1837—40), Ellerton upon Swale, Eppleby, Forcett with Carkin, Gayles, Gilling, Grinton (1837—40), Hipswell, Hudswell, Kirby Hill, East Layton, West Layton, Marrick (1837—40), Marske, Melsonby, Middleton Tyas, Moulton, New Forest, Newsham, Ravensworth, Reeth (1837—40), Richmond, St Martin,[120] Scorton, Scotton, Skeeby, Stainton, Stanwick St John, Tunstall, Uckerby, Walburn, Whashton

RIPON PLU (1852—1930) [W Riding, N Riding]
Aismunderby with Bongate (1852—94), Aldfield, Asenby (soon after 1852[111]—1930), Azerley, Baldersby, Bishopton (1852—1900), Clotherholme, Cundall with Leckby (soon after 1852[111]—1930), Dishforth, Eavestone, Givendale, Grantley, Grewelthorpe, Bridge Hewick, Copt Hewick, Howgrave, Hutton Conyers, Ingerthorpe, Kirkby Malzeard, Laverton, Lindrick with Studley Royal Fountains, Littlethorpe (1894—1930), Markingfield Hall (1866—1930), Markington with Wallerthwaite (1854—1930), Marton le Moor, Melmerby, Middleton Quernhow, Bishop Monkton (1854—1930), Newby with Mulwith, Norton Conyers, Nunwick cum Howgrave,[117] Rainton with Newby, Ripon, Sawley, Sharow, Skedling,

Skelton, North Stainley with Sleningford, Studeley Roger, Sutton Grange, Sutton Howgrave, East Tanfield, West Tanfield, Wath, Whitcliffe with Thorpe (1852—94), Winksley

ROTHERHAM PLU (1837—1930) [W Riding, Derbys (1837—94)]

Aston cum Aughton, Bramley, Brampton (1894—97), Brampton Bierlow (1837—94), Brampton Bierlow (1897—1930), Brampton en le Morthen (1837—1923), Brinsworth, Catcliffe, Dalton, Greasbrough, Hooton Levitt, Hooton Roberts, Kimberworth (1837—94), Laughton en le Morthen (1837—1923), Maltby, West Melton (1894—1923), Orgreave, Ravenfield, Rawmarsh, Rotherham, Swinton, Thrybergh, Thurcroft (1923—30), Tinsley, Treeton, Ulley, Wath upon Dearne, Wentworth, Whiston, Wickersley

SADDLEWORTH GILBERT UNION (until 1853), PAR (1853—94), PLU (1894—1930) [W Riding]

Saddleworth, Springhead (1894—1930), Upper Mill (1894—1900)

SCARBOROUGH PLU (1837—1930) [N Riding, E Riding]

East Ayton, West Ayton, Brompton, Broxa, Burniston, Cayton, Cloughton, Falsgrave (1837—90), Filey, Folkton, Ganton, Gristhorpe, Hackness, Harwood Dale, Hutton Buscel, Irton, Lebberston, Muston, Newby (1837—86), Osgodby (1837—86), Sawdon (1837—56), Scalby (1837—1902), Scarborough, Seamer, Sherburn, Silpho, Snainton, Staintondale, Suffield cum Everley, Throxenby (1837—1909), Troutsdale, Willerby, Wykeham

SCULCOATES PLU (1837—1930) [N Riding, E Riding]

Anlaby, Cottingham (1837—94), Cottingham (1898—1930), Cottingham Within (1894—98), Cottingham Without (1894—98), Drypool (1837—98), Kirk Ella, West Ella, North Ferriby, Garrison Side (1858—98), Haltemprice (1862—1930), Hedon, Hessle (1837—94), Hessle (1899—1930), Hessle Within (1894—98), Hessle Without (1894—99), Marfleet (1837—98), Melton, Newington (1877—98), Preston, Sculcoates, Southcoates (1837—98), Sutton and Stoneferry (1837—98), Sutton on Hill (1894—1930), Sutton Within (1894—98), Swanland, Wauldby, Welton, Willerby

SEDBERGH PLU (1840—1930) [W Riding]

Dent, Garsdale, Sedbergh

SELBY PLU (1837—1930) [W Riding, E Riding]

Barlby, Barlow, Biggin (soon after 1837[111]—1930), Brayton, Burn, Camblesforth, Carlton, Cawood, Cliffe cum Lund, Drax, Long Drax, North Duffield, South Duffield, Little Fenton (soon after 1837[111]—1930), Gateforth, Chapel Haddlesey, West Haddlesey (1869—1930), Hambleton (1869—1930), Temple Hirst, Hirst Courtney, Kelfield, Newland, Osgodby, Riccall, Selby, Skipwith, Thorpe Willoughby, Wistow

SETTLE PLU (1837—1930) [W Riding]

Airton, Arncliffe, Austwick, Bentham, Burton in Lonsdale, Clapham cum Newby, Giggleswick, West Halton, Halton Gill, Hanlith, Hawkswick, Hellifield, Horton in Ribblesdale, Ingleton, Kirkby Malham, Langcliffe, Lawkland, Litton, Malham, Malham Moor, Nappa, Otterburn, Long Preston, Rathmell, Scosthrop, Settle, Stainforth, Swinden, Thornton in Lonsdale, Tosside, Wigglesworth

SHEFFIELD PLU (1837—1930) [W Riding]

Attercliffe cum Darnall (1837—1902), Brightside Bierlow (1837—1902), Bradfield Urban (1914—30), Ecclesall (1904—30), Ecclesfield Urban (1921—30), Handsworth (soon after 1837[111]—1930), Sheffield

SKIPTON PLU (1837—1930) [W Riding]

Addingham, Appletreewick, Bank Newton, Barden, Barnoldswick, Beamsley (1886—1930), Beamsley in Addingham (1869—86), Beamsley in Skipton (1869—86), Bolton Abbey, Bordley (soon after 1837[111]—1930), Bracewell, Bradley's Both, Brogden, Broughton, Buckden, Burnsall (soon after 1837[111]—1930), Calton, Carleton, Coates (1837—1923), Coniston Cold, Conistone with Kilnsey, Cononley (soon after 1837[111]—1930), Cowling (soon after 1837[111]—1930), Cracoe, Draughton, Earby (1909—30), Elslack (soon after 1837[111]—1930), Embsay with Eastby, Eshton, Farnhill, Flasby with Winterburn, Gargrave, Glusburn, Grassington, Halton East, Hartlington, Hazlewood with Storiths, Hebden, Hetton, Kettlewell with Starbottom, Kildwick, Linton, Lothersdale (1894—1930), Martons Both, Rylstone, Salterforth, Silsden (1869—1930), Skipton, Stirton with Thorlby, Thornton in Craven, Thorpe, Thresfield

SKIRLAUGH PLU (1837—1930) [E Riding]

Aldborough, Atwick, Benningholme and Grange, Bewholme and Nunkeeling, Bilton, Bonwick, Brandesburton, Catfoss, Catwick, Coniston, Great and Little Cowdens, Danthorpe, Dunnington, Ellerby, Elstronwick, Filing, Flinton, Ganstead, Garton with Grimston, Goxhill, Great Hatfield, Little Hatfield, Hempholme, Hornsea, Humbleton, Lelley, Mappleton and Rowlston, Marton, Moor Town, East Newton, West Newton with Burton Constable, Rise, Long Riston, Seaton and Wassand, Sigglesthorne; North Skirlaugh, Rowton and Arnold; South Skirlaugh, Sproatley, Swine, Thirtleby, Withernwick, Wyton

STOKESLEY PLU (1837—1930) [N Riding]

Great Ayton, Little Ayton, Bilsdale Midcable (1848—1930), Broughton, Great Busby, Little Busby, Carlton, Crathorne, Easby, Faceby, Hemlington (1837—75), Hilton, Hutton Rudby, Ingleby Arncliffe, Ingleby Greenhow, Kildale, Kirby in Cleveland, Castle Leavington (1875—1930), Kirk Leavington (1875—1930), Marton (1837—75), Middleton upon Leven, Newby, Nunthorpe, Picton (1875—1930), Potto, East Rounton, Rudby in Cleveland, Seamer, Sexhow, Skutterskelf, Stokesley, Whorlton, High Worsall (1875—1930), Low Worsall (1875—1930), Yarm (1875—1930)

TADCASTER PLU (1862—1930) [W Riding]

Aberford, Acaster Selby (1869—1930), Allerton Bywater (1869—1930), Appleton Roebuck (1869—1930), Askham Bryan, Austhorpe, Barkston (1869—1930), Barwick in Elmet (1869—1930), Bilbrough (1869—1930), Bolton Percy (1869—1930), Catterton (1869—1930), Colton, Church Fenton (1869—1930), Garforth (1869—1930), Grimston, Healaugh (1864—1930), Huddleston cum Lumby, Kippax (1869—1930), Kirkby Wharfe and North Milford, Lead, Ledsham (1869—1930), Ledston (1869—1930), Lotherton cum Aberford, Micklefield (1869—1930), South Milford (1869—1930), Newthorpe, Newton Kyme cum Toulston (1869—1930),

Oxton, Parlington, Great and Little Preston (1869—1930), Ryther cum Ossendyke (1869—1930), Saxton with Scarthingwell (1869—1930), Sherburn in Elmet (1869—1930), Steeton (1869—1930), Sturton Grange, Stutton with Hazlewood, Swillington (1869—1930), Tadcaster East (1869—1930), Tadcaster West, Towton, Ulleskelf (1869—1930)

THIRSK PLU (1837—1930) [N Riding]
Ainderby Quernhow, Bagby (soon after 1837[111]—1930), Balk, Birdforth (1837[111]—1930), Boltby, Carlton Miniott, Catton, Cowesby, Dalton, Eldmire with Crakenhill, Fawdington (soon after 1837[111]—1930), Felixkirk, Holme, Hood Grange (1858—1930), Howe, Humberton (1895—1930), Hutton Sessay, Kepwick, Kilburn, North Kilvington, South Kilvington, Kirby Knowle, Kirby Wiske, Knayton with Brawith, Maunby, Milby (1895—1930), Newby Wiske, Newsham with Breckenbrough, South Otterington, Pickhill with Roxby, Sand Hutton, Sessay, Sinderby, Skipton on Swale, Sowerby, Sutton under Whitstone Cliffe, Thirkleby, Thirlby, Thirsk, Thornborough, Thornton le Moor, Thornton le Street, Topcliffe, Upsall

THORNE PLU (1837—1930) [W Riding, Lincs Pts Lind]
Crowle,[59] Fishlake, Hatfield, Stainforth, Sykehouse, Thorne

TODMORDEN PLU (1837—1930) [W Riding, Lancs (1837—97]
Blackshaw (1894—1930), Erringden, Hebden Bridge (1894—1930), Heptonstall, Langfield (1837—97), Mytholmroyd (1894—1930), Stansfield (1837—97), Todmorden (1897—1930), Wadsworth

WAKEFIELD PLU (1837—1930) [W Riding]
Altofts (1869—1930), Alverthorpe (1894—1916), Alverthorpe with Thornes (1837—94), Ardsley East, Ardsley West, West Bretton, Chevet (soon after 1837[111]—1930), Crigglestone, Crofton (1869—1930), Emley, Flockton, Horbury, Kirkhamgate (1916—30), Lofthouse with Carleton (soon after 1837[111]—1930), Lupset (1902—25), Newland with Woodhouse Moor (1858—1930), Normanton (1869—1930), Norton Within (1901—04), Oulton with Woodlesford (1837—69), Outwood (1894—1930), Sandal Magna (1837—1925), Sharlston, Stanley (1894—1930), Stanley cum Wrenthorpe (1837—94), Shitlington, Thorpe, Wakefield, Walton, Warmfield cum Heath

WETHERBY PLU (1861—1930) [W Riding]
Angram, Bardsey cum Rigton, Bickerton, Bilton (1869—1930), Boston Spa (1896—1930), Bramham cum Oglethorpe (1869—1930), Clifford (1869—1930), Clifford with Boston (1869—96), Collingham (1869—1930), Cowthorpe, Kirk Deighton (1869—1930), North Deighton, Dunkeswick (1869—1930), Harewood (1869—1930), Healaugh (1861—64), Hutton Wandesley (1869—1930), Kearby with Netherby, East Keswick (1861—1930), Kirkby Overblow (1861—1930), Linton, Long Marston (1869—1930), Micklethwaite, Little Ribston, Rigton (1861—1930), Scarcroft, Shadwell (1869—1912), Sicklinghall, Spofforth with Stockeld, Thorner (1869—1930), Thorp Arch (1869—1930), Tockwith (1869—1930), Walton (1869—1930), Weardley, Weeton (1869—1930), Wetherby, Wighill, Wigton (1869—1930), Wilstrop (1869—1930), Wothersome, Wyke (1869—1930)

WHARFEDALE PLU (1861—1930) [W Riding]
Adel cum Eccup (1869—1928), Alwoodley (1861—1928), Arthington (1869—1930), Askwith, Baildon, Blubberhouses, Bramhope, Burley in Wharfedale, Carlton, Castley, Clifton with Norwood, Denton, Esholt, Farnley, Fewston, Guiseley, Hawksworth, Horsforth, Ilkley, Leathley, Lindley, Menston, Middleton, Nesfield with Langbar, Newall with Clifton, Otley, Pool, Rawdon, Stainburn, Great Timble, Little Timble, Weston (soon after 1861[111]—1930), Yeadon

WHITBY PLU (1837—1930) [N Riding]
Aislaby, Barnby, Borrowby, Egton, Eskdaleside (1837—85), Eskdaleside cum Ugglebarnby (1885—1930), Ellerby, Fylingdales, Glaisdale, Goathland, Hawsker with Stainsacre, Helredale (1894—1925), Hinderwell, Hutton Mulgrave, Lythe, Mickleby, Newholm with Dunsley, Newton Mulgrave, Roxby, Ruswarp (1837—1925), Sneaton, Ugglebarnby (1837—85), Ugthorpe, Whitby

WORTLEY PLU (1838—1930) [W Riding]
Bradfield, Ecclesfield, Hoyland Swaine (1838—49), Hunshelf (1838—49), Ingbirchworth (1838—49), Langsett (1838—49), Oxspring (1838—49), Penistone (1838—49), Stocksbridge (1849—1930), Tankersley, Thurgoland (1838—49), Thurlstone (1838—49), Wortley

YORK PLU (1838—1930) [all 3 Ridings]
Acaster Malbis,[121] Acomb (1837—54), Askham Richard, Beningbrough, Bishopthorpe, Bossall with Buttercrambe, Claxton, Clifton (1837—94), Clifton Within (1894—1900), Clifton Without (1894—1930), Copmanthorpe, Deighton, Dringhouses (1837—94), Dringhouses Within (1894—1900), Dringhouses Without (1894—1930), Dunnington, Earswick, Elvington, Escrick, Flaxton, Gate Fulford (1837—1900), Water Fulford, Grimston, Harton, Haxby, Gate Helmsley, Upper Helmsley, Heslington (1885—1930), Heslington St Lawrence (1837—85), Heslington St Paul (1837—85), Heworth (1837—94), Heworth Within (1894—1900), Heworth Without (1894—1930), Holgate (1837—1900), Holtby, Huntington, Kexby, Langwith, Lillings Ambo, Middlethorpe (1837—94), Middlethorpe Within (1894—1900), Middlethorpe Without (1894—1930), Murton, Naburn, Osbaldwick, Overton, Upper Poppleton (1837—54), Rawcliffe, Sand Hutton, Shipton, Skelton, West Stamford Bridge with Scoreby, Stillingfleet with Moreby, Stockton on the Forest, Strensall, Thorganby with West Cottingham, Towthorpe, Warthill (1925—30), Warthill Copyhold (soon after 1837[111]—1930), Warthill Freehold (soon after 1837[111]—1930), Wheldrake, Wiggington, York (1900—30), York All Saints North Street (1837—1900), York All Saints Pavement (1837—1900), York Castle, York Davy Hill (1861—1900), York Minster Hall with Bedern (1837—1900), York Mint Hall (1837—1900), York Holy Trinity Goodramgate (1837—1900); York Holy Trinity, King's Court (1837—1900); York Holy Trinity Micklegate (1837—1900), York St Andrew (1837—1900), York St Crux (1837—1900), York St Cuthbert (1837—1900), York St Dennis (1837—1900), York St George (1837—1900), York St Giles in the Suburbs (1837—1900); York St Helen, Stonegate (1837—1900); York St John Delpike

(1837—1900); York St John, Micklegate (1837—1900); York St Lawrence (1837—1900), York St Margaret (1837—1900), York St Martin le Grand (1837—1900), York St Martin Micklegate with St Gregory (1837—1900), York St Mary Bishophill Junior (1837—1900), York St Mary Bishophill Senior (1837—1900); York St Mary, Castlegate (1837—1900); York St Maurice (1837—1900), York St Michael le Belfrey (1837—1900), York St Michael, Spurriergate (1837—1900); York St Nicholas (1837—1900); York St Olave, Marygate (1837—1900); York St Peter le Willows (1837—1900), York St Peter the Little (1837—1900), York St Sampson (1837—1900), York St Saviour (1837—1900), York St Wilfrid (1837—1900)

In Other Poor Law Counties:
BURNLEY PLU (1837—1930) [Lancs, W Riding (1837—95)]
Cliviger[122]
CLITHEROE PLU (1837—1930), [Lancs, W Riding]
Bashall Eaves, Bolton by Bowland, Bowland Forest High, Bowland Forest Low, West Bradford, Easington, Gisburn, Gisburn Forest, Grindleton, Horton, Middop, Great Mitton, Newsholme, Newton, Paythorne, Rim-ington, Sawley, Slaidbur, Waddington

DARLINGTON PLU (1837—1930) [Durham, N Riding]
Barton, Cleasby, Cliffe, Croft, Dalton upon Tees, Over Dinsdale, Eryholme, Girsby, Manfield, Newton Morrell, Stapleton

STOCKTON PLU (1837—1930) [Durham, N Riding (1837—75)]
West Acklam, Ingleby Barwick, Castle Leavington, Kirk Leavington, Linthorpe, Maltby, Middlesbrough, Picton (soon after 1837[111]—1930), Stainton, Thornaby, High Worsall, Low Worsall, Yarm

TEESDALE PLU (1837—1930) [Durham, N Riding]
Barforth, Barningham, Boldron, Bowes, Brignall, Cotherstone, Egglestone Abbey, Gilmonby, Holwick, Hope, Hunderthwaite, Hutton Magna, Lartington, Lunedale, Mickleton, Ovington, Rokeby, Romandkirk, Scargill, Startforth, Wycliffe with Thorpe

WORKSOP PLU (1836—1930) [Notts, Derbys, W Riding]
North and South Anston, Dinnington, Firbeck, Gildingwells, Harthill with Woodall, Letwell, St John's with Throapham, Thorpe Salvin, Todwick, Wales, Wallingwells[123] (1862—1930), Woodsetts

SANITARY DISTRICTS

ALLERTON USD (1875—82[65]) [W Riding]
Allerton
ALTOFTS USD [W Riding]
Altofts
ARDSLEY USD (1892[124]—94) [W Riding]
Ardsley
ASKERN USD (1875—81[125]) [W Riding]
Askern
AUSTONLEY USD [W Riding]
Austonley (ent 1875—86, pt 1886—94, pt Cartworth (1886—94), pt Holme (1886—94), pt Upperthong (1886—94)
AYSGARTH RSD [N Riding]
same as PLU
BAILDON USD [W Riding]
Baildon
BARKISLAND USD [W Riding]
Barkisland
BARNOLDSWICK USD (1890[126]—94) [W Riding]
Barnoldswick
BARNSLEY RSD [W Riding]
same as PLU less Ardsley (1892—94), Barnsley, Barugh, Darton, Dodsworth, Hoyland Nether (1890—94), Monk Bretton, Wombwell, Worsborough
BARNSLEY USD [W Riding]
Barnsley
BATLEY USD [W Riding]
Batley
BEDALE RSD [N Riding]
same as PLU less Burton upon Ure, Ilton cum Pott, Kirklington cum Upsland, Masham, Swinton with Warthermarske
BEVERLEY RSD [E Riding]
same as PLU less Beverley St Martin, Beverley St Mary, Beverley St Nicholas

BEVERLEY USD [E Riding]
Beverley St Martin, Beverley St Mary, Beverley St Nicholas
NORTH BIERLEY RSD [W Riding]
pt Clayton (only)
NORTH BIERLEY USD [W Riding]
North Bierley, Wyke
BINGLEY LOCAL GOVERNMENT DIST [W Riding]
pt Bingley
BIRKENSHAW USD [W Riding]
pt Gomersal
BIRSTAL USD [W Riding]
pt Gomersal
BRADFORD USD[65] [W Riding]
Allerton (1882—94), Bolton, Bowling, Bradford, pt Calverley with Farsley (1882—94), Heaton (1882—94), Horton, Manningham, pt Pudsey (1882—94)
BRIDLINGTON RSD [E Riding]
same as PLU less pt Bessingby, Bridlington, pt Hilderthorpe, pt Sewerby cum Marton
BRIDLINGTON USD [E Riding]
pt Bessingby, Bridlington, pt Hilderthorpe, pt Sewerby cum Marton
BRIGHOUSE USD [W Riding]
pt Hipperholme with Brighouse, Rastrick (1893—94)
BROTTON USD (1875—84[127]) [N Riding]
Brotton, Kilton
BURLEY IN WHARFEDALE USD [W Riding]
Burley in Wharfedale
CALVERLEY USD[65] [W Riding]
pt Calverley with Farsley (reduced pt 1882—94)
CARTWORTH USD (1875—84[128]) [W Riding]
pt Cartworth
CASTLEFORD USD [W Riding]
Castleford

SOUTH CAVE AND WALLINGFEN USD [E Riding]
  Broomfleet (ent 1875—80, pt 1880—94), Wallingfen
  (ent 1875—80, pt 1880—94)
CHURWELL USD (1875—91[129]) [W Riding]
  Churwell
CLAYTON USD [W Riding]
  pt Clayton
CLAYTON WEST USD [W Riding]
  Clayton West
CLECKHEATON USD [W Riding]
  Cleckheaton
CLITHEROE RSD [Lancs, W Riding]
  same as PLU for Yorks pars
CLIVIGER USD [Lancs, W Riding]
  Cliviger[122]
COTTINGHAM USD[81] [E Riding]
  Cottingham (ent 1875—83, pt 1883—94)
SOUTH CROSLAND USD [W Riding]
  South Crosland
CUMBERWORTH USD [W Riding]
  Cumberworth (pt 1875—76, ent 1876—94), pt
  Cumberworth Half (1875—76), pt Denby (1885—94)
DARLINGTON RSD [Durham, N Riding]
  same as PLU for Yorks pars
DARTON USD [W Riding]
  Barugh, Darton, Kexborough
DENBY USD [W Riding]
  pt Cumberworth (1885—94), Denby (ent 1875—85, pt
  1885—94)
DENHOLME USD (1887[130]—94) [W Riding]
  pt Thornton
DENHOLME GATE USD (1875—87[130]) [W Riding]
  pt Thornton
DEWSBURY USD [W Riding]
  Dewsbury
DODWORTH USD [W Riding]
  Dodworth
DONCASTER RSD [W Riding, Notts]
  same as PLU for Yorks pars less Askern (1875—81),
  Clayton with Frickley, Doncaster, Mexborough, pt
  Tickhill
DONCASTER USD [W Riding]
  Doncaster
DRIFFIELD RSD [E Riding]
  same as PLU less Great Driffield (ent 1875—83, pt
  1883—85, ent 1885—94)
GREAT DRIFFIELD USD[131] [E Riding]
  Great Driffield (ent 1875—83, pt 1883—85, ent
  1885—94)
DRIGHLINGTON USD [W Riding]
  Drighlington
EASINGWOLD RSD [N Riding]
  same as PLU
ECCLESHILL USD [W Riding]
  Eccleshill
ELLAND USD [W Riding]
  pt Elland with Greetland
EMLEY USD [W Riding]
  Emley
ESTON USD (1884[132]—94) [N Riding]
  Eston
FARNLEY TYAS USD [W Riding]
  Farnley Tyas

FARSLEY USD [W Riding]
  pt Calverley with Farsley
FEATHERSTONE USD [W Riding]
  Ackton, Featherstone, Purton Jaglin, Snydale
FILEY USD [E Riding]
  Filey
FLOCKTON USD [W Riding]
  Flockton
FULSTONE USD [W Riding]
  pt Fulstone, pt Wooldale (1886—94)
GILDERSOME USD [W Riding]
  Gildersome
GOLCAR USD [W Riding]
  Golcar
GOMERSAL USD [W Riding]
  pt Gomersal
GOOLE RSD [W Riding, Lincs Pts Lind]
  same as PLU for Yorks pars less pt Airmyn, pt Goole,
  pt Hook
GOOLE USD [W Riding]
  pt Airmyn, pt Goole, pt Hook
GREASBROUGH USD [W Riding]
  pt Greasbrough
GREETLAND USD [W Riding]
  pt Elland with Greetland
GUISBOROUGH RSD [N Riding]
  same as PLU less Brotton, pt Easington, Guisborough,
  Kilton, Kirkleatham, pt Liverton, pt Loftus, pt Marske,
  Moorsholm, Redcar, Skelton, Skinningrove,
  Stanghow, pt Upleatham
GUISBOROUGH USD [N Riding]
  Guisborough
GUISELEY USD [W Riding]
  Guiseley
GUNTHWAITE AND INGBIRCHWORTH USD [W
  Riding]
  Gunthwaite, Ingbirchworth
HALIFAX RSD [W Riding]
  same as PLU less pt Barkisland, pt Elland with
  Greetland, Halifax, pt Hipperholme with Brighouse, pt
  Midgley, pt Norland, pt Northowram, Ovenden (pt
  1875—92, ent 1892—94), Rishworth, Shelf, pt
  Skircoat, Southowram, Sowerby, Soyland, Stainland
  with Old Lindley, Warley
HALIFAX USD[133] [W Riding]
  Halifax, pt Northowram, Ovenden (pt 1875—92, ent
  1892—94), pt Skircoat, pt Southowram
HANDSWORTH USD [W Riding]
  Handsworth
HARROGATE USD [W Riding]
  pt Bilton with Harrogate (enlarged pt 1884—94), pt
  Knaresborough (1875—88), pt Pannal (enlarged pt
  1888—94), pt Scriven with Tentergate (1875—88)
HAWORTH USD [W Riding]
  pt Haworth
HEATON USD (1875—82[65]) [W Riding]
  Heaton
HEBDEN BRIDGE USD[134] [W Riding]
  pt Erringden (enlarged pt 1891—94), pt Heptonstall, pt
  Stansfield, pt Wadsworth (both reduced[135] and enlarged
  1891)
HECKMONDWIKE USD [W Riding]
  Heckmondwike

HEDON USD [E Riding]
Hedon
HELMSLEY RSD [N Riding]
same as PLU
HEMSWORTH RSD [W Riding]
same as PLU
HEPWORTH USD [W Riding]
pt Fulstone (1886—94), pt Hepworth, pt Wooldale
(1883—94)
HINDERWELL USD [N Riding]
Hinderwell
HIPPERHOLME USD [W Riding]
pt Hipperholme with Brighouse
HOLME USD [W Riding]
Holme (ent 1875—86, pt 1886—94)
HOLMFIRTH USD (1884[128]—94) [W Riding]
pt Austonley (1886—94), pt Cartworth, pt Fulstone, pt
Hepworth, Upperthong (ent 1884—86, pt 1886—94), pt
Wooldale
HONLEY USD [W Riding]
Honley
HORBURY USD [W Riding]
Horbury
HORNSEA USD [E Riding]
Hornsea
HORSFORTH USD [W Riding]
Horsforth
HOWDEN RSD [E Riding]
same as PLU less Broomfleet (ent 1875—80, pt 1880—
94), Wallingfen (ent 1875—80, pt 1880—94)
HOYLAND NETHER USD (1890[136]—94) [W Riding]
Hoyland Nether
HOYLAND SWAINE [W Riding]
Hoyland Swaine
HUDDERSFIELD USD[137] [W Riding]
Almondbury, Dalton, Huddersfield, Lindley cum
Quarmby, Lockwood (1890—94)
HUNSLET RSD [W Riding]
same as PLU less Hunslet, Rothwell, pt
Templenewsham
HUNSWORTH USD [W Riding]
Hunsworth
IDLE USD [W Riding]
pt Idle
ILKLEY USD [W Riding]
Ilkley
KEIGHLEY RSD [W Riding]
same as PLU less pt Bingley, Haworth, pt Keighley
KEIGHLEY USD [W Riding]
pt Bingley, Keighley
KINGSTON UPON HULL USD [E Riding]
Kingston upon Hull Holy Trinity and St Mary
KIRKBY MOORSIDE RSD [N Riding]
same as PLU
KIRKBURTON USD [W Riding]
Kirkburton
KIRKHEATON USD [W Riding]
Kirkheaton
KIRKLEATHAM USD [N Riding]
Kirkleatham
KIRKLINGTON CUM UPSLAND USD [N Riding]
Kirklington cum Upsland

KNARESBOROUGH RSD [W Riding]
same as PLU less pt Bilton with Harrogate, pt
Knaresborough, pt Pannal, pt Scriven with Tentergate
KNARESBOROUGH AND TENTERGATE USD [W
Riding]
pt Knaresborough, pt Scriven with Tentergate
KNOTTINGLEY USD (1892[138]—94) [W Riding]
Knottingley
LEEDS RSD [W Riding]
same as PLU less Chapel Allerton, Headingley cum
Burley, Leeds, Potter Newton, pt Seacroft
LEEDS USD [W Riding]
Chapel Allerton, Armley, Beeston, Bramley, Farnley,
Headingley cum Burley, Holbeck, Hunslet, Leeds,
Potter Newton, pt Seacroft, pt Temsplenewsham,
Wortley
LEPTON USD [W Riding]
Lepton
LEYBURN RSD [N Riding]
same as PLU less Ellingstring, Ellingtons, Fearby,
Healey with Sutton, Ilton cum Pott
LINTHWAITE USD [W Riding]
Linthwaite
LIVERSEDGE USD [W Riding]
Liversedge
LOFTUS USD [N Riding]
pt Easington, pt Liverton, pt Loftus, Skinningrove
LONGWOOD USD (1875—90[137]) [W Riding]
Longwood
LUDDENDEN FOOT USD [W Riding]
pt Midgley, pt Sowerby, pt Warley
MALTON RSD [N Riding, E Riding]
same as PLU less New Malton, Old Malton, Norton
MALTON USD[139] [N Riding, E Riding (1875—90)]
New Malton, Old Malton, Norton (1875—90)
MARSDEN USD (1882[140]—94) [W Riding]
Marsden in Almondbury
MARSDEN IN HUDDERSFIELD USD (1875—82[140])
[W Riding]
Marsden in Huddersfield
MASHAM USD [N Riding]
Burton upon Ure, Ellenstring, Ellingtons, Fearby,
Healey with Sutton, Ilton cum Pott, Masham, Masham
Moor, Swinton with Warthermarske
MELTHAM USD [W Riding]
Meltham
METHLEY USD [W Riding]
Methley
MEXBOROUGH USD [W Riding]
Mexborough
MIDDLESBROUGH RSD [N Riding]
same as PLU less pt West Acklam, Eston (1884—94),
pt Linthorpe, pt Marton, pt Middlesbrough, Normanby
(pt 1875—88, ent 1888—94), pt Ormesby, Thornaby
MIDDLESBROUGH USD [N Riding]
pt West Acklam, pt Linthorpe, pt Marton, pt Middles-
brough, pt Normanby, pt Oresmby
MIDGLEY USD[135] [W Riding]
pt Midgley (reduced pt 1891—94)
MIRFIELD USD [W Riding]
pt Mirfield
MONK BRETTON USD [W Riding]
Monk Bretton

MORLEY USD[129] [W Riding]
  pt Ardsley West (1891—94), Churwell (1891—94), Morley
MOSSLEY USD [Lancs, W Riding]
  pt Saddleworth
MYTHOLMROYD USD (1891[141]—94) [W Riding]
  pt Erringden, pt Midgley, pt Sowerby, pt Wadsworth
NETHERTHONG USD [W Riding]
  Netherthong
NORMANBY USD[142] [N Riding]
  pt Normanby (1888—94)
NORMANTON USD [W Riding]
  Normanton
NORTHALLERTON RSD [N Riding]
  same as PLU less Northallerton
NORTHALLERTON USD [N Riding]
  Northallerton
NORTHOWRAM USD [W Riding]
  pt Northowram
NORTON USD (1890[139]—94) [E Riding]
  Norton
OAKWORTH USD [W Riding]
  pt Haworth, pt Keighley
ORMESBY USD [N Riding]
  pt Ormesby
OSSETT USD (1890[143]—94) [W Riding]
  Ossett
OSSETT CUM GAWTHORPE USD (1875—90[143]) [W Riding]
  Ossett cum Gawthorpe
OTLEY USD [W Riding]
  Otley
GREAT OUSEBURN RSD [W Riding, N Riding]
  same as PLU
OVENDEN USD (1875—92[133]) [W Riding]
  pt Ovenden
OXENHOPE USD [W Riding]
  pt Haworth
PATELEY BRIDGE RSD [W Riding]
  same as PLU
PATRINGTON RSD [E Riding]
  same as PLU
PENISTONE RSD [W Riding]
  same as PLU less Clayton West, Denby, Gunthwaite, Hoyland Swaine, pt Hunshelf, Ingbirchworth, Kexborough, Penistone, Thurlstone
PENISTONE USD [W Riding]
  Penistone
PICKERING RSD [N Riding]
  same as PLU less Pickering
PICKERING USD [N Riding]
  Pickering
POCKLINGTON RSD [E Riding]
  same as PLU less Pocklington (1893—94)
POCKLINGTON USD (1893[144]—94) [E Riding]
  Pocklington
PONTEFRACT RSD [W Riding]
  same as PLU less Acton, Castleford, Featherstone, Knottingley (1892—94), Methley, Monkhill (1875—92), Pontefract, Pontefract Park, Purston Jaglin, Snydale, Tanshelf, Whitwood
PONTEFRACT USD [W Riding]
  Monkhill (1875—92), Pontefract, Pontefract Park,

Tanshelf
PUDSEY USD[65] [W Riding]
  Pudsey (ent 1875—82, pt 1882—94)
QUEENSBURY USD [W Riding]
  pt Clayton, pt Northowram
QUICKMERE MIDDLE DIVISION USD [W Riding]
  pt Saddleworth
RASTRICK USD (1875—93[145]) [W Riding]
  Rastrick
RAVENSTHORPE USD [W Riding]
  pt Mirfield
RAWDON USD [W Riding]
  Rawdon
RAWMARSH USD [W Riding]
  Rawmarsh
REDCAR USD [N Riding]
  pt Marske (1875—86), Redcar, pt Upleatham (1875—86)
REETH RSD [N Riding]
  same as PLU
RICHMOND RSD [N Riding]
  same as PLU less Richmond
RICHMOND USD [N Riding]
  Richmond
RIPON RSD [W Riding, N Riding]
  same as PLU less pt Aismunderby with Bondgate, Ripon
RIPON USD [W Riding]
  pt Aismunderby with Bondgate, Ripon
RISHWORTH USD [W Riding]
  Rishworth
ROTHERHAM RSD [W Riding, Derbys]
  same as PLU for Yorks pars less pt Brampton Bierlow, pt Brimsworth, Greasborough, Kimberworth (ent 1875—83, pt 1883—94), Rawmarsh, Rotherham, Swinton, pt Wath upon Dearne, pt Wentworth (1883—94), pt Whiston
ROTHEHAM USD [W Riding]
  pt Brinsworth, pt Greasborough, Kimberworth (ent 1875—83, pt 1883—94), Rotherham, pt Wentworth (1883—94), pt Whiston
ROTHWELL USD [W Riding]
  Rothwell
SALTBURN BY THE SEA USD [N Riding]
  pt Marske
SANDAL MAGNA USD [W Riding]
  Sandal Magna
SCAMMONDEN USD [W Riding]
  Scammonden
SCARBOROUGH RSD [N Riding, E Riding]
  same as PLU less Falsgrave (1875—90), Filey, Scarborough
SCARBOROUGH USD [N Riding]
  Falsgrave (1875—90), Scarborough
SCHOLES USD[128] [W Riding]
  pt Cartworth (1875—86), pt Fulstone, pt Hepworth (enlarged pt 1886—94), pt Wooldale (enlarged pt 1886—94)
SCULCOATES RSD [E Riding]
  same as PLU less Cottingham, Hedon
SEDBERGH RSD [W Riding]
  same as PLU

SELBY RSD [W Riding]
 same as PLU less Selby
SELBY USD [W Riding]
 Selby
SETTLE RSD [W Riding]
 same as PLU
SHEFFIELD USD [W Riding]
 Attercliffe cum Darnall, Brightside Bierlow, Ecclesall
 Bieriow, Nether Hallam, Upper Hallam, Heeley
 (1880—94), Sheffield
SHELF USD [W Riding]
 Shelf
SHELLEY USD [W Riding]
 Shelley
SHEPLEY USD [W Riding]
 Shepley
SHIPLEY USD[146] [W Riding]
 pt Idle (1891—94), Shipley
SILSDEN USD [W Riding]
 Silsden
SKELMANTHORPE USD [W Riding]
 pt Cumberworth (1875—76), pt Cumberworth Half
 (1875—76), Skelmanthorpe (1876—94)
SKELTON AND BROTTON USD (1884[127]—94) [N
  Riding]
 Brotton, Kilton, Moorsholm, Skelton, Stanghow
SKELTON IN CLEVELAND USD (1875—84[127]) [N
  Riding]
 Moorsholm, Skelton, Stanghow
SKIPTON RSD [W Riding]
 same as PLU less Barnoldswick (1890—94), Silsden,
 Skipton
SKIPTON USD [W Riding]
 Skipton
SKIRLAUGH RSD [E Riding]
 same as PLU less Hornsea
SLAITHWAITE USD [W Riding]
 Lingards, Slaithwaite
SOOTHILL NETHER USD [W Riding]
 pt Soothill
SOOTHILL UPPER USD [W Riding]
 pt Soothill
SOUTH BANK IN NORMANBY (1875—88[142]) [N
  Riding]
 pt Normanby
SOUTHOWRAM USD [W Riding]
 pt Southowram
SOWERBY USD [W Riding]
 pt Sowerby
SOWERBY BRIDGE USD [W Riding]
 pt Norland, pt Skircoat, pt Sowerby, pt Warley
SOYLAND USD [W Riding]
 Soyland
STAINLAND USD [W Riding]
 Stainland with Old Lindley
STOCKSBRIDGE USD [W Riding]
 pt Bradfield, pt Hunshelf
SOUTH STOCKTON USD (1875—92[99]) [N Riding]
 Thornaby
STOKESLEY RSD [N Riding]
 same as PLU
SWINTON USD [W Riding]
 Swinton

TADCASTER RSD [W Riding]
 same as PLU
TEESDALE RSD [Durham, N Riding]
 same as PLU for Yorks pars
THIRSK RSD [N Riding]
 same as PLU
THORNABY ON TEES USD (1892[100]—94) [N Riding]
 Thornaby
THORNE RSD [W Riding, Lincs]
 same as PLU for Yorks pars
THORNHILL USD [W Riding]
 Thornhill, Whitley Lower
THORNTON USD [W Riding]
 pt Thornton
THURLSTONE USD [W Riding]
 Thurlstone
THURSTONLAND USD [W Riding]
 Thurstonland
TICKHILL USD [W Riding]
 pt Tickhill
TODMORDEN RSD [W Riding]
 same as PLU less pt Cliviger, pt Erringden (enlarged pt
 1891—94), pt Heptonstall, Langfield, Stansfield, pt
 Wadsworth (enlarged pt 1891—94)
TODMORDEN USD [W Riding, Lancs (1875—89)]
 pt Cliviger (the pt in Yorks), Langfield, pt Stansfield,
 Todmorden and Walsden[147]
TONG USD [W Riding]
 Tong
UPPER MILL USD [W Riding]
 pt Saddleworth
UPPERTHONG USD (1875—84[128]) [W Riding]
 Upperthong
WAKEFIELD RSD [W Riding]
 same as PLU less Altofts, pt Alverthorpe with Thornes,
 pt Ardsley West (1891—94), Emley, Flockton,
 Horbury, Normanton, Sandal Magna, pt Stanley cum
 Wrenthorpe, Wakefield
WAKEFIELD USD [W Riding]
 pt Alverthorpe with Thornes, pt Stanley cum Wren-
 thorpe, Wakefield
WARLEY USD [W Riding]
 pt Warley
WATH UPON DEARNE USD (1881[148]—94) [W
  Riding]
 pt Brampton Bierlow, pt Wath upon Dearne
WETHERBY RSD [W Riding]
 same as PLU
WHARFEDALE RSD [W Riding]
 same as PLU less Baildon, Burley in Wharfedale,
 Guisley, Horsforth, Ilkley, Otley, Rawdon, Yeadon
WHITBY RSD [N Riding]
 same as PLU less pt Hawsker with Stainsacre,
 Hinderwell, Ruswarp, Whitby
WHITBY USD [N Riding]
 pt Hawsker with Stainsacre, Hinderwell, Ruswarp,
 Whitby
WHITLEY UPPER USD [W Riding]
 Whitley Upper
WHITWOOD USD [W Riding]
 Whitwood
WILSDEN USD [W Riding]
 Wilsden

WINDHILL USD (1875—91[146]) [W Riding]
pt Idle
WOMBWELL USD [W Riding]
Wombwell
WOOLDALE USD (1875—84[128]) [W Riding]
pt Wooldale
WORKSOP RSD [Notts, W Riding, Derbys]
same as PLU for Yorks pars
WORSBOROUGH USD [W Riding]
Worsborough
WORTLEY RSD [W Riding]
same as PLU less pt Bradfield, Clayton West, pt Denby
(1885—94), pt Hunshelf, Kexborough
YEADON USD [W Riding]
Yeadon
YORK RSD [all 3 Ridings]
same as PLU less pars and pts of pars in York USD
YORK USD [all 3 Ridings and City of York]
pt Clifton (1884—94), pt Dringhouses (1884—94), pt
Gate Fulford (1884—94), pt Heworth (1884—94),
Holgate (1884—94), pt Middlethorpe (1884—94), York
All Saints North Street, York All Saints Pavement,
York Castle, York Davy Hall, York Holy Trinity
Goodramgate; York Holy Trinity, King's Court; York
Holy Trinity Micklegate, York Minster Hall with
Beddern, York Mint Yard, York St Andrew, York St
Crux; York St Cuthbert, York St Helen on the Walls
and All Saints Peasholme, York St Dennis, York St
George, York St Giles in the Suburbs (pt 1875—84, ent
1884—94); York St Helen, Stonegate; York St John,
Delpike; York St John, Micklegate; York St Lawrence,
York St Margaret, York St Martin le Grand, York St
Martin Micklegate with St Gregory, York St Mary
Bishopshill Junior, York St Mary Bishopshill Senior;
York St Mary, Castlegate; York St Maurice, York St
Michael le Belfrey; York St Michael, Spurriergate;
York St Nicholas; York St Olave, Marygate; York St
Peter the Little, York St Peter le Willows, York St
Sampson, York St Saviour, York St Wilfrid

YORKSHIRE EAST RIDING ADMINISTRATIVE COUNTY

For MBs and the associated CB see BOROUGHS

BEVERLEY RD
Aike (1894—1935), Beswick, Brantingham, Bishop
Burton, Cherry Burton, South Cave, South Dalton
(1894—1935), Dalton Holme (1935—74), Ellerker,
Elloughton (1935—74), Elloughton with Brough
(1894—1935), Eske (1894—1935), Etton, North
Ferriby (1935—74), Holme on the Wolds (1894—
1935), Kilnwick (1894—1935), Leconfield (1935—74),
Leconfield and Arram (1894—1935), Leven, Lock-
ington, Lund, Meaux (1894—1935), Molescroft,
Newbald (1935—74), North Newbald (1894—1935),
South Newbald (1894—1935), Routh, Rowley,
Scorborough (1894—1935), Skidby, Storkhill and
Sandholme (1894—1935), Swanland (1935—74),
Thearne (1894—1935), Tickton (1935—74), Tickton
and Hull Bridge (1894—1935), Walkington, Wawne,
Weel (1894—1935), Welton (1935—74), Woodmansey
(1935—74), Woodmansey and Beverley Parks
(1894—1935)
BRIDLINGTON RD
Argam (1894—1935), Auburn (1894—96), Barmston,
Bempton, Bessingby (1894—1935), Boynton, Buckton
(1894—1935), Burton Agnes, Burton Fleming,
Carnaby; Dringhoe, Upton and Brough (1894—1935);
Easton (1894—1935), Flamborough, Folkton (1935—
74), Fordon (1894—1935), Fraisthorpe (1894—96),
Fraisthorpe with Auburn and Wilstporpe (1896—1935),
Gransmoor (1894—1935), Grindale, Haisthorpe
(1894—1935), Hunmanby, Lissett (1894—1935),
Muston (1935—74), Reighton, Rudston, Sewerby cum
Marton (1894—1935), Skipsea, Speeton (1894—1935),
Thornholme (1894—1935), Thwing, Ulrome, Wils-
thorpe (1894—96), Wold Newton
BRIDLINGTON UD (1894—99[68])
Bridlington
COTTINGHAM UD (1894—1935[149])
Cottingham

DERWENT RD (1935[149]—74)
Barlby, Cliffe, Deighton, North Duffield, Dunnington,
Elvington, Escrick, Fulford, Hemingbrough, Heslington, Kelfield, Kexby, Naburn, Riccall, Skipwith,
Stillingfleet, Thorganby, Wheldrake
DRIFFIELD RD
Brainton, Beeford, Bracken (1894—1935), Brigham
(1894—1935), Butterwick (1894—1935), Cottam,
Cowlam (1894—1935), North Dalton, Eastburn
(1894—1935), Emswell with Little Driffield (1894—
1935), Fimber, Foston (1935—74), Foston on the
Wolds (1894—1935), Foxholes with Boythorpe
(1894—1935), Fridaythorpe (1935—74), North Frodingham, Garton (1935—74), Garton on the Wolds
(1894—1935), Gembling (1894—1935), Harpham,
Helperthorpe (1894—1935), Hutton Cranswick, Kelk
(1935—74), Great Kelk (1894—1935), Little Kelk
(1894—1935), Kilham, Kirkburn (1935—74), Kirkburn
and Battleburn (1894—1935), Langtoft, Lowthorpe
(1894—1935), Luttons Ambo (1894—1935), Middleton
(1935—74), Middleton on the Wolds (1894—1935),
Nafferton, Neswick (1894—1935), Rotsea (1894—
1935), Ruston Parva (1894—1935), Skerne, Sledmere,
Southburn (1894—1935), Sunderlandwick (1894—
1935), Tibthorpe, Towthorpe (1894—1935), Wansford
(1894—1935), Watton, Weaverthorpe (1894—1935),
Wetwang
DRIFFIELD UD (1935[149]—74)
Driffield
GREAT DRIFFIELD UD (1894—1935[149])
Great Driffield
ESCRICK RD (1894—1935[149])
Deighton, Dunnington, Elvington, Escrick, Water
Fulford, Grimston, Heslington, Kexby, Langwith,
Naburn, West Stamford Bridge with Scoreby, Stilling-
fleet with Moreby, Thorganby with West Cottingwith,
Wheldrake

FILEY UD
  Filey
HALTEMPRICE UD (1935[149]—74)
  Haltemprice
HESSLE UD (1899[150]—1935[149])
  Hessle
HOLDERNESS RD (1935[149]—74)
  Aldborough, Atwick, Bewholme, Bilton, Brandesburton, Bull Fort, Burstwick, Burton Constable, Burton Pidsea, Catwick, Coniston, Easington, Ellerby, Elstronwick, East Garton, Halsham, Hatfield, Hollym, Holmpton, Humbleton, Keyingham, Mappleton, Ottringham, Patrington, Paull, Preston, Rimswell, Rise, Riston, Roos, Seaton, Sigglesthorne, Skeffling, Skirlaugh, Sproatley, Sunk Island, Swine, Thorgumbald, Welwick, Withernwick
HORNSEA UD
  Hornsea
HOWDEN RD
  Asselby, Aughton (1894—1935), Balkholme (1894—1935), Barmby on the Marsh, Belby (1894—1935), Bellasize (1894—1935), Bishopsoil (1894—1935), Blacktoft, Brackenholme with Woodhall (1894—1935), Breighton and Gunby (1894—1935), Broomfleet, Bubwith, North Cave (1935—74), North Cave with Everthorpe and Drewton (1894—1935), Cotness (1894—1935), Eastrington, Ellerton (1935—74), Ellerton Priory (1894—1935), Faxfleet (1894—1935), Foggathorpe, Gilberdike (1894—1935), Gilberdyke (1935—74), Gribthorpe (1894—1935), Harlthorpe (1894—1935), Hemimgbrough (1894—1935), Holme upon Spalding Moor, Hotham, Howden, Kilpin, Knedlington (1894—1935), Laxton, Laytham (1894—1935), Menthorpe cum Bowthorpe (1894—1935), Metham (1894—1935), Newport (1935—74), Portington and Cavil (1894—1935), Saltmarshe (1894—1935), Scalby (1894—1935), Skelton (1894—1935), Spaldington, Thorpe (1894—1935), Wallingfen (1894—1935), Willitoft (1894—1935), Wressell (1894—1935), Wressle (1935—74), Yokefleet (1894—1935)
NORTON RD
  Acklam (1935—74), Acklam with Barthorpe (1894—1935), Birdsall, Burythorpe, Duggleby (1894—1935), Eddlethorpe (1894—1935), Firby, Foxholes (1935—74), Ganton (1935—74), North Grimston (1894—1935), Heslerton (1935—74), East Heslerton (1894—1935), West Heslerton (1894—1935), Howsham, Kennythorpe (1894—1935), Kirby Grindalythe, Kirkham (1894—1935), Knapton (1894—1935), Langton, Leavening, Leppington (1894—1935), Luttons (1935—74), Menethorpe (1894—1935), Raisthorpe and Burdale (1894—1935), Rillington, Scagglethorpe, Scampston, Scrayingham (1935—74), Settrington, Sherburn (1935—74), Thirkleby (1894—1935), Thixendale (1935—74), Thorpe Bassett, Weaverthorpe (1935—74), Westow, Wharram (1935—74), Wharram le Street (1894—1935), Wharram Percy (1894—1935), Willerby (1935—74), Wintringham, Yedingham
NORTON UD
  Norton
PATRINGTON RD (1894—1935[149])
  Burstwick with Skeckling, Burton Pidsea, Easington,

South Frodingham, Halsham, Hilston, Hollym, Holmpton, Keyingham, Kilnsea, Ottringham, Out Newton, Owstwick, Owthorne, Patrington, Paull, Rimswell, Roos, Ryhill and Camerton, Skeffling, Sunk Island, Thorgumbald, Tunstall, Waxholme, Welwick, Winestead, Withernsea (1894—98)
POCKLINGTON RD
  Allerthorpe, Barmby Moor (1935—74), Barmby on the Moor (1894—1935), Bielby, Bishop Wilton (1935—74), Bishop Wilton with Belthorpe (1894—1935), Bolton (1894—1935), Bugthorpe, Burnby (1894—1935), Catton (1935—74), High Catton (1894—1935), Low Catton (1894—1935), North Cliffe (1894—1935), South Cliffe, Cottingwith (1935—74), East Cottingwith (1894—1935), Everingham, Fangfoss, Fridaythorpe (1894—1935), Full Sutton, Great Givendale with Grimthorpe (1894—1935), Goodmanham, Harswell (1894—1935), Hayton, Huggate, Kilnwick Percy (1894—1935), Kirby Underdale, Londesborough (1935—74), Londesborough with Easthorpe (1894—1935), Market Weighton (1935—74), Market Weighton and Arras (1894—1935), Melbourne, Millington (1935—74), Millington with Little Givendale (1894—1935), Newton upon Derwent (1894—1935), Nunburnholme, Ousethorpe (1894—1935), Pocklington (1935—74), Sancton (1935—74), Sancton and Houghton (1894—1935), Scrayingham (1894—1935), Seaton Ross, Shipton Thorpe, Skirpenbeck, Stamford Bridge (1935—74), East Stamford Bridge (1894—1935), Storwood (1894—1935), Sutton upon Derwent, Thixendale (1894—1935), Thorpe le Street (1894—1935), Thornton, Waplington (1894—1935), Warter, Wilberfoss, Yapham (1935—74), Yapham cum Meltonby (1894—1935), Youlthorpe with Gowthorpe (1894—1935)
POCKLINGTON UD (1894—1935[149])
  Pocklington
RICCAL RD (1894—1935[149])
  Barlby, Cliffe cum Lund, North Duffield, South Duffield, Kelfield, Osgodby, Riccall, Skipwith
SCULCOATES RD (1894—1935[149])
  Anlaby, Kirk Ella, West Ella, North Ferriby, Haltemprice, Hessle Without (1894—99), Melton, Preston, Sutton on Hill (1898—1935), Sutton Without (1894—98), Swanland, Wauldby, Welton, Willerby
SHERBURN RD (1894—1935[149])
  Folkton, Ganton, Muston, Sherburn, Willerby
SKIRLAUGH RD (1894—1935[149])
  Aldborough, Atwick, Benningholme and Grange, Bewholme and Nunkeeling, Bilton, Bonwick, Brandesburton, Catfoss, Catwick, Coniston, Great and Little Cowdens, Danthorpe, Dunnington, Ellerby, Elstronwick, Filing, Flinton, Ganstead, Garton with Grimston, Goxhill, Great Hatfield, Little Hatfield, Hempholme, Humbleton, Lelley, Mappleton and Rowlston, Marton, Moor Town, East Newton, West Newton with Burton Constable, Rise. Long Riston, Seaton and Wassand, Sigglesthorne; North Skirlaugh, Rowton and Arnold; South Skirlaugh, Sproatley, Swine, Thirtleby, Withernwick, Wyton
WITHERNSEA UD (1898[151]—1974)
  Withernsea

YORKSHIRE NORTH RIDING ADMINISTRATIVE COUNTY

For MBs and the associated CBs see BOROUGHS

AYSGARTH RD
High Abbotside, Low Abbotside, Abbotside Common (1894—1934), Askrigg, Aysgarth, Bainbridge, Bishopdale, Burton cum Walden, Caperby cum Thoresby, Hawes, Land near Horton Gill Bridge (1894—1934), Mossdale Moor (1894—1934), Newbiggin, Thoralby, Thornton Rust, Wether Fell (1894—1934)

BEDALE RD
Ainderby Miers with Holtby, Aiskew, Bedale, Burneston, Burill with Cowling, Carthorpe, Clifton upon Ure, Crakehall; Exelby, Leeming and Newton; Firby, Gatenby, Hackforth, Howgrave, Killerby, Kirkby Fleetham, Kirklington cum Upsland (1934—74), Langthorne, Rand Grange, Rookwith, Scruton, Snape, Sutton Howgrave, Swainby with Allerthorpe, East Tanfield, West Tanfield, Theakston, Thirn, Thornton Watlass, Well

CROFT RD
Barton, Cleasby, Cliffe, Croft (1894—1971), Croft on Tees (1971—74), Dalton upon Tees, Over Dinsdale, Eryholme, Girsby, Manfield, Newton Morrell, Stapleton

EASINGWOLD RD
Aldwark, Alne, Angram Grange, Beningbrough, Brafferton, Brandsby cum Stearsby, Carlton Husthwaite, Coxwold, Crayke, Dalby cum Skewsby, Easingwold, Farlington, Flawith, Helperby, Huby, Husthwaite, Linton upon Ouse, Marton cum Moxby, Myton on Swale, Newburgh, Newton upon Ouse, Oulston, Overton, Raskelf, Shipton, Stillington, Sutton on the Forest, Tholthorpe, Thormanby, Thornton on the Hill, Tollerton, Whenby, Wildon Grange, Yearsley, Youlton

ESTON UD (1894—1968[35])
Eston

FLAXTON RD
Bossall with Buttercrambe, Claxton, Clifton Without, Earswick, New Earswick (1934—74), Flaxton, Harton, Haxby, Gate Helmsley, Upper Helmsley, Heworth Without, Holtby, Huntington, Lillings Ambo, Murton, Osbaldwick, Rawcliffe, Sand Hutton, Stockton on the Forest, Strensall, Towthorpe, Warthill (1925—74), Warthill Copyhold (1894—1925), Warthill Freehold (1894—1925), Wigginton

GUISBOROUGH RD (1894—1932[152])
Commondale, Danby, Easington, Hutton Lowcross, Kirkleatham (1899—1932), pt Land Common to Danby and Glaisdale (1894—1929), Marske, Morton, Newton, Pinchinthorpe, Tocketts, Upleatham, Upsall, Westerdale, Wilton

GUISBOROUGH UD
Guisborough, Hutton Lowcross (1932—74), Kirkleatham (1932—74), Morton (1932—74), Newton (1932—74), Pinchinthorpe (1932—74), Tocketts (1932—74), Upleatham (1932—74), Upsall (1932—74), Wilton (1932—74)

HELMSLEY RD
Ampleforth, Arden, Beadlam; Bilsdale, West Side; Old Byland, Byland with Wass, Cawton, Cold Kirby, Coulton, Dale Town, Gilling East, Grimston, Harome, Hawnby, Helmsley, Laskill Pasture, Murton, East Newton and Laysthorp, Oldstead, Oswaldkirk, Pockley, Rievaulx, Scawton, Snilesworth, Sproxton, Stonegrave, Thorpe le Willows

HINDERWELL UD (1894—1932[152])
Hinderwell

KIRKBY MOORSIDE RD
Appleton le Moors, Bransdale (1934—74); Bransdale, West Side (1894—1934); Great Edstone, Little Edstone, Fadmoor; Farndale, East Side; Farndale, Low Quarter (1894—1934); Farndale, West Side; Gillamoor, North Holme, Hutton le Hole, Kirkby Moorside, Lastingham (1934—74), Muscoates, Nawton, Ness, Normanby (1894—1934), Nunnington, Salton, Skiplam, Spaunton (1934—74), pt Spaunton Moor (1894—1934), Thornton Risebrough (1894—1934), Welburn, Wombleton

KIRKLEATHAM UD (1894—99[153])
Kirkleatham

KIRKLINGTON CUM UPSLAND (1894—1934[154])
Kirklington cum Upsland

LEYBURN RD
Agglethorpe with Coverham, Akebar, Arrathorne, Barden, Bellerby, Caldbergh with East Scrafton, Carlton Highdale, Carlton Town, Castle Bolton, Constable Burton, Colsterdale (1894—1934), Finghall, Garriston, Harmby, East Hauxwell, West Hauxwell, Hornby, Hunton, Hutton Hang, Leyburn, Melmerby, Middleham, Newton le Willows, Patrick Brompton, Preston, Redmire, West Scrafton, Spennithorne, Thornton Steward, Wensley, East Witton Within, East Witton Without, West Witton

LOFTUS UD
Easington (1932—74), Liverton, Loftus, Skinningrove

MALTON RD
Airyholme with Howthorpe and Baxton Howe, Amotherby, Appleton le Street, Barton le Street, Barton le Willows, Brawby, Broughton, Bulmer, Butterwick, Coneysthorpe, Crambe, Foston, Fryton, Ganthorpe, Great Habton, Little Habton, Henderskelf, Hildenley, South Holme, Hovingham, Huttons Ambo, Ryton, Scackleton, Sheriff Hutton with Cornbrough, Slingsby, Stittenham, Swinton, Terrington with Wigganthorpe, Thornton le Clay, Wath, Welburn, Whitwell on the Hill

MALTON UD
Malton (1896—1974), New Malton (1894—96), Old Malton (1894—96)

MASHAM RD (1934[154]—74)
Burton upon Ure, Colsterdale, Ellenstring, Ellingtons, Fearby, Healey, Ilton cum Pott, Masham, Swinton with Warthermarske

MASHAM UD (1894—1934[154])
Burton upon Ure, Ellenstring, Ellingtons, Fearby, Healey with Sutton, Ilton cum Pott, Masham, pt Masham Moor (1894—1934), Nutwith and Roomer Common (1894—1934), Swinton with Warthermarske

MIDDLESBROUGH RD (1894—1932[152])
West Acklam, Hemlington, Ingleby Barwick, Linthorpe (1894—1913), Maltby, Marton, Ormesby (1913—32), Stainton

NORTHALLERTON RD
Ainderby Steeple, Appleton Wiske, Birkby, Borrowby, Brompton, Cotcliffe, East Cowton, South Cowton, Crosby, Danby Wiske, Deighton, Ellerbeck, East Harsley, West Harsley, Hornby, Hutton Bonville, Kiplin, Kirby Sigston, Landmoth cum Catto, Great Langton, Little Langton, Lazenby, Leake, Morton upon Swale, Osmotherley, North Otterington, Romanby, West Rounton, Nether Silton, Over Silton, Great Smeaton, Little Smeaton, Sowerby under Cotcliffe, Thimbleby, Thornton le Beans, Thrintoft, Warlaby, Welbury, Whitwell, Winton, Yafforth

NORTHALLERTON UD
Northallerton

ORMESBY UD (1894—1913[155])
Ormesby

PICKERING RD
Aislaby, Allerston, Barughs Ambo, Cawthorn, Cropton, Ebberston, Hartoft, Kingthorpe, Kirby Misperton, Lastingham (1894—1934), Levisham, Lockton, Marishes, Marton, Middleton, Newton, Normanby (1934—74); Rosedale, East Side; Rosedale, West Side; Sinnington, Spaunton (1894—1934), pt Spaunton Moor (1894—1934), Thornton Risebrough (1934—74), Thurnhill, Wilton, Wrelton

PICKERING UD
Pickering

REDCAR UD (1894—1922[92])
Coatham (1899—21), Redcar

REETH RD
Arkengarthdale, Ellerton Abbey, Grinton, Marrick, Melbecks, Muker, Reeth

RICHMOND RD
Aldbrough, Appleton, Aske, Bolton upon Swale, Brompton on Swale, Brough, Caldwell, Catterick, Colburn, North Cowton, Dalton, Downholme, Easby, Ellerton upon Swale, Eppleby, Forcett with Carkin, Gayles, Gilling, Hipswell, Hudswell, Kirby Hill, East Layton, West Layton, Marske, Melsonby, Middleton Tyas, Moulton, New Forest, Newsham, Ravensworth, St Martin, Scorton, Scotton, Skeeby, Stainton, Stanwick St John, Tunstall, Uckerby, Walburn, Whaston

SALTBURN AND MARSKE BY THE SEA UD (1932[152]—74)
Marske, Saltburn by the Sea

SALTBURN BY THE SEA UD (1894—1932[152])
Saltburn by the Sea

SCALBY UD (1902[156]—74)
Scalby

SCARBOROUGH RD
East Ayton, West Ayton, Brompton, Broxa, Burniston, Cayton, Cloughton, Gristhorpe, Hackness, Harwood Dale, Hutton Buscel, Irton, Lebberston, Scalby (1894—1902), Seamer, Silpho, Snainton, Staintondale, Suffield cum Everley, Throxenby (1894—1909), Troutsdale, Wykeham

SKELTON AND BROTTON UD
Brotton, Kilton, Moorsholm, Skelton, Stanghow

SOUTH BANK IN NORMANBY UD (1894—1915[157])
Normanby

STARTFORTH RD
Barforth, Barningham, Boldron, Bowes, Brignall, Cotherstone, Egglestone Abbey, Gilmonby, Holwick, Hope, Hunderwaithe, Hutton Magna, Lartington, Lunedale, Mickleton, Ovington, Rokeby, Romaldkirk, Scargill, Startforth, Wycliffe with Thorpe

STOKESLEY RD
Great Ayton, Little Ayton, Bilsdale Midcable, Broughton, Great Busby, Little Busby, Carlton, Crathorne, Easby, Faceby, Hemlington (1932—74), Hilton, Hutton Rudby, Ingleby Arncliffe, Ingleby Barwick (1932—74), Ingleby Greenhow, Kildale, Kirby in Cleveland, Castle Leavington, Kirk Leavington, Maltby (1932—74), Marton (1932—74), Middleton upon Leven, Newby, Nunthorpe, Ormesby (1932—68), Picton, Potto, East Rounton, Rudby in Cleveland, Seamer, Sexhow, Skutterskelfe, Stainton (1932—74), Stokesley, Whorlton, High Worsall (1894—1932), Low Worsall, Yarm

THIRSK RD
Ainderby Quernhow, Bagby, Balk, Birdforth, Boltby, Carlton Miniott, Catton, Cowesby, Dalton, Eldmire with Crakehill, Ellenthorpe, Fawdington, Felixkirk, Holme, Hood Grange, Howe, Humberton (pt 1894—95, ent 1895—1974), Hutton Sessay, Kepwick, Kilburn, North Kilvington, South Kilvington, Kirby Hill, Kirby Knowle, Kirby Whiske, Knayton with Brawith, Langthorpe, Maunby, Milby (pt 1894—95, ent 1895—1974), Newby Whiske, Newsham with Breckenbrough, Norton le Clay, South Otterington, Pickhill with Roxby, Sand Hutton, Sessay, Sinderby, Skipton on Swale, Sowerby, Sutton under Whitstone Cliffe, Thirkleby, Thirlby, Thirsk, Thornborough, Thornton Bridge, Thornton le Moor, Thornton le Street, Topcliffe, Upsall

WATH RD
Asenby, Baldersby, Cundall with Leckby, Dishforth, Hutton Conyers, Marton le Moor, Melmerby, Middleton Quernhow, Norton Conyers, Rainton with Newby, Wath

WHITBY RD
Aislaby, Barnby, Borrowby, Commondale (1932—74), Danby (1932—74), Egton, Ellerby, Eskdaleside cum Ugglebarnby, Fylingdales, Fylingdales Moor (Land Common to Hawsker with Stainsacre and Fylingdales), Glaisdale, Goathland, Hawsker with Stainsacre, Hinderwell (1932—74), Hutton Mulgrave, pt Land Common to Danby and Glaisdale (1894—1929), Lythe, Mickleby, Newholm with Dunsley, Newton Mulgrave, Roxby, Sneaton, Ugthorpe, Westerdale (1932—74)

WHITBY UD
Helredale (1894—1925), Ruswarp (1894—1925), Whitby

YORKSHIRE WEST RIDING ADMINISTRATIVE COUNTY

For MBs and the associated CBs see BOROUGHS

ADWICK LE STREET UD (1915[158]—74)
  Adwick le Street
AIREBOROUGH UD (1937[159]—74)
  Aireborough
ALTOFTS UD (1894—1938[160])
  Altofts
ARDSLEY UD (1894—1921[3])
  Ardsley
ARDSLEY EAST AND WEST UD (1895[161]—1937[159])
  Ardsley East, Ardsley West
BAILDON UD
  Baildon
BALBY WITH HEXTHORPE UD (1895[162]—1914[163])
  Balby with Hexthorpe
BARKISLAND UD (1894—1937[159])
  Barkisland
BARNOLDSWICK UD
  Barnoldswick
BARNSLEY RD (1894—1938[160])
  Billingley, Carlton, Cudworth (1894—1900), Darfield (1894—96), Notton, Royston (1894—96), Stainbrough, Woolley
BENTLEY WITH ARKSEY UD (1911[164]—74)
  Bentley with Arksey
NORTH BIERLEY UD (1894—99[6])
  North Bierley, Wyke
BINGLEY UD[165]
  Bingley, Wilsden (1898—1938)
BINGLEY OUTER UD (1894[166]—98[167])
  Bingley Outer
BIRKENSHAW UD (1894—1937[159])
  Birkenshaw
BIRSTALL UD (1894—1937[159])
  Birstall
BISHOPTHORPE RD (1894—1937[159])
  Acaster Malbis, Askham Richard, Bishopthorpe, Copmanthorpe, Dringhouses Without, Middlethorpe Without
BOLTON UPON DEARNE UD (1899[168]—1937[159])
  Bolton upon Dearne
BOWLAND RD
  Bashall Eaves, Bolton by Bowland, Bowland Forest High, Bowland Forest Low, West Bradford, Easington, Gisburn, Gisburn Forest, Grindleton, Horton, Middop, Great Mitton, Newsholme, Newton, Paythorne, Rimington, Sawley, Slaidburn, Waddington
BURLEY IN WHARFEDALE UD (1894—1937[159])
  Burley in Wharfedale
CALVERLEY UD (1894—1937[159])
  Calverley
CASTLEFORD UD (1894—1955[71])
  Castleford
CLAYTON UD (1894—1930[7])
  Clayton
CLAYTON WEST UD (1894—1938[160])
  Clayton West
CLECKHEATON UD (1894—1915[169])
  Cleckheaton

COLNE VALLEY UD (1937[159]—74)
  Colne Valley
CONISBROUGH UD (1921[170]—74)
  Conisbrough
SOUTH CROSLAND UD (1894—1938[160])
  South Crosland
CUDWORTH UD (1900[171]—74)
  Cudworth
DARFIELD UD (1896[172]—1974)
  Darfield
DARTON UD
  Barugh (1894—1938), Darton, Kexborough (1894—1938)
DEARNE UD (1937[159]—74)
  Dearne
DENBY AND CUMBERWORTH UD (1894—1938[160])
  Cumberworth, Denby
DENBY DALE UD (1938[160]—74)
  Clayton West, Cumberworth, Denby, Emley, Skelmanthorpe
DENHOLME UD
  Denholme
DODWORTH UD
  Dodworth
DONCASTER RD
  Adwick le Street (1894—1915), Adwick upon Dearne, Armthorpe, Askern, Auckley (pt 1894—95, ent 1895—1974), Austerfield, Balby with Hexthorpe (1894—95), Barnbrough (1894—1951), Barnburgh (1951—74), Barnby Dun with Kirk Sandall (1921—74), Barnby upon Don (1894—1921), Bawtry, Bentley with Arksey (1894—1911), Bilham (1894—1920), Blaxton, Bolton upon Dearne (1894—99), Braithwell, Brodsworth, Burghwallis, Cadeby, Campsall (1894—1938), Cantley, Carr House and Elm Field (1894—1914), Clayton with Frickley, Conisbrough (1894—1921), Conisbrough Parks (1921—74), Denaby, Edenthorpe (1956—74), Edlington, Fenwick, Hampole, Hickleton, Hootton Pagnell, Kirk Bramwith, Loversall, Marr, High Melton, Moss, Norton, Owston, Rossington, Kirk Sandall (1894—1921), Skellow (1894—1915), Sprotbrough, Stainton, Stotfold (1894—1920), Sutton (1894—1938), Thorpe in Balne, Thurnscoe (1894—1908), Tickhill Outer (1894—95), Wadworth, Warmsworth, Wheatley (1894—1900)
DRIGHLINGTON UD (1894—1937[159])
  Drighlington
EARBY UD (1909[173]—74)
  Earby
ECCLESHILL UD (1894—99[6])
  Eccleshill
ELLAND UD
  Elland
EMLEY UD (1894—1938[160])
  Emley
FARNLEY TYAS UD (1894—1925[174])
  Farnley Tyas

FARSLEY UD (1894—1937[159])
　Farsley
FEATHERSTONE UD
　Ackton (1894—1938), Ackton and Snydale (1938—74),
　Featherstone, Purston Jaglin (1894—1938), Snydale
　(1894—1938)
FLOCKTON UD (1894—1938[160])
　Flockton
FULSTONE UD (1894—95[175])
　Fulstone
GARFORTH UD (1908[176]—74)
　Garforth
GILDERSOME UD (1894—1937[159])
　Gildersome
GOLCAR UD (1894—1937[159])
　Golcar
GOMERSAL UD (1894—1915[169])
　Gomersal
GOOLE RD
　Adlington, Airmyn, Eastoft, Fockerby, Goole Fields,
　Gowdall, Haldenby, Hook, Ousefleet, Pollington,
　Rawcliffe, Reedness, Snaith and Cowick, Swinefleet,
　Whitgift
GOOLE UD (1894—1933[73])
　Goole
GREASBOROUGH UD (1894—1936[12])
　Greasborough
GREETLAND UD (1894—1937[159])
　Greetland
GUISELEY UD (1894—1937[159])
　Guiseley
GUNTHWAITE AND INGBIRCHWORTH UD
　(1894—1938[160])
　Gunthwaite, Ingbirchworth
HALIFAX RD (1894—1937[159])
　Clifton, Fixby, Upper Greetland, Hartshead, Norland,
　Norwood Green and Coley, Skircoat (1894—99)
HANDSWORTH UD (1894—1921[38])
　Handsworth
HAWORTH UD (1894—1938[160])
　Haworth
HEBDEN BRIDGE UD (1894—1937[159])
　Hebden Bridge
HEBDEN ROYD UD (1937[159]—74)
　Hebden Royd
HECKMONDWIKE UD
　Heckmondwike
HEMSWORTH RD
　Ackworth, Badsworth, Billingley (1894—1938),
　Brierley, North Elmsall, South Elmsall, Hamphall
　Stubbs (1894—1938), West Hardwick, Havercroft with
　Cold Hiendley, Hemsworth (1894—1921), Hessle and
　Hill Top, South Hiendley, Great Houghton, Little
　Houghton, Huntwick with Foulby and Nostell, South
　Kirkby, Ryhill, Shafton, Skelbrooke (1894—1938),
　Kirk Smeaton, Little Smeaton, Thorpe Audlin, Upton,
　Walden Stubbs, Wintersett (1894—1938)
HEMSWORTH UD (1921[177]—74)
　Hemsworth
HEPTON RD (1938[178]—74)
　Blackshaw, Erringden, Heptonstall, Wadsworth
HEPWORTH UD (1894—95[175])
　Hepworth

HIPPERHOLME UD (1894—1937[159])
　Hipperholme
HOLME UD (1894—1938[160])
　Holme, South Holme (1894—95)
HOLMFIRTH UD
　Austonley (1894—1921), Cartworth (1894—1921),
　Holmfirth (1921—74), Netherthong (1912—21),
　Upperthong (1894—1921), Wooldale (1894—1921)
HONLEY UD (1894—1938[160])
　Honely
HORBURY UD
　Horbury
HORSFORTH UD
　Horsforth
HOYLAND NETHER UD
　Hoyland Nether
HOYLAND SWAINE UD (1894—1938[160])
　Hoyland Swaine
HUNSLET RD (1894—1937[159])
　Middleton (1894—1920), Oulton with Woodlesford,
　Templenewsham (1894—1927), Thorpe Stapleton
　(1894—1925)
HUNSWORTH UD (1894—1937[159])
　Hunsworth
IDLE UD (1894—99[6])
　Idle
ILKLEY UD
　Ilkley
KEIGHLEY RD (1894—1938[160])
　Bingley Outer (1894—98), Morton, Steeton with
　Eastburn, Sutton
KIRKBURTON UD
　Flockton (1938—74), Kirkburton
KIRKHEATON UD (1894—1938[160])
　Kirkheaton
KIVETON PARK RD
　North and South Anston, Dinnington (1894—1954),
　Dinnington St John's (1954—74), Firbeck, Gild-
　ingwells, Harthill with Woodall, Letwell, St John's
　with Throapham (1894—1954), Thorpe Salvin,
　Todwick, Wales, Woodsetts
KNARESBOROUGH RD (1894—1938[160])
　Bilton, Brearton, Burton Leonard, Farnham, Fellis-
　cliffe, Ferrensby, Flaxby, Follifoot, Goldsborough,
　Hampsthwaite, Haverah Park, Killinghall, Knaresbor-
　ough Outer, Nidd, Pannal, Plompton, Ripley, Scotton,
　Scriven, Starbeck, South Stainley with Cayton, Walk-
　ingham Hill with Occaney
KNARESBOROUGH UD (1895[179]—1974)
　Knaresborough
KNARESBOROUGH AND TENTERGATE UD
　(1894—95[179])
　Knaresborough, Tentergate
KNOTTINGLEY UD
　Knottingley
LEEDS RD (1894—1912[27])
　Roundhay, Seacroft
LEPTON UD (1894—1938[160])
　Lepton
LINTHWAITE UD (1894—1937[159])
　Linthwaite
LIVERSEDGE UD (1894—1915[169])
　Liversedge

LUDDENDEN FOOT UD (1894—1937[159])
Luddenden Foot
MALTBY UD (1924[180]—74)
Maltby, Stainton Urban
MARSDEN RD (1894—1937[159])
Marsden (1896—1937), Marsden in Almondbury (1894—96), Marsden in Huddersfield (1894—96)
MELTHAM UD
Meltham
METHLEY UD (1894—1937[159])
Methley
MEXBOROUGH UD
Mexborough
MIDGLEY UD (1894—1939[178])
Midgley
MIRFIELD UD
Mirfield
MONK BRETTON UD (1894—1921[3])
Monk Bretton
MYTHOLMROYD UD (1894—1937[159])
Mytholmroyd
NETHERTHONG UD (1894—1912[181])
Netherthong
NEW MILL UD (1895[175]—1938[160])
Fulstone, Hepworth, Scholes
NIDDERDALE RD (1938[160]—74)
Allerton Mauleverer with Hopperton, Arkendale, Boroughbridge, Brearton, Burton Leonard, Cattal, Coneythorpe and Clareton, Copgrove, Dunsforths (1960—74), Lower Dunsforth (1938—60), Upper Dunsforth with Branton Green (1938—60), Farnham, Felliscliffe, Ferrensby, Flaxby, Follifoot, Goldsborough, Green Hammerton, Kirk Hammerton, Hampsthwaite, Haverah Park, Hessay, Hunsingore, Killinghall, Kirby Hall, Knapton, Knaresborough Outer, Marton cum Grafton, Moor Monkton, Nun Monkton, Nidd, Great Ouseburn, Little Ouseburn, Pannal, Plompton, Nether Poppleton, Upper Poppleton, Great Ribston with Washford, Ripley, Roecliffe, Rufforth, Scotton, Scriven, South Stainley with Cayton, Staveley, Thornville, Thorpe Underwoods, Walkingham Hill with Occaney, Westwick, Whixley, Widdington
NORMANTON UD
Normanton
NORTHOWRAM UD (1894—1900[182])
Northowram
OAKWORTH UD (1894—1938[160])
Oakworth, Stanbury
OSGOLDSCROSS RD (1938[160]—74)
Balne, Beal or Beaghall, Birkin, Brotherton, Burton Salmon, Byram cum Sutton, Cridling Stubbs, Darrington, Eggborough, Fairburn, Monk Fryston, East Hardwick, Heck, Hensall, Hillam, Kellington, Stapleton, Whitley, Womersley
OTLEY UD
Otley
GREAT OUSEBURN RD (1894—1938[160])
Acomb (1894—1937), Aldborough, Allerton Mauleverer with Hopperton, Arkendale, Boroughbridge, Cattal, Coneythorpe and Clareton, Copgrove, Lower Dunsforth (pt 1894—95, ent 1895—1938), Upper Dunsforth with Branton Green (pt 1894—95, ent 1895—1938), Green Hammerton, Kirk Hammerton,

Hessay, pt Humberton (1894—95), Hunsingore, Kirby Hall, Knapton, Marton cum Grafton, Minskip, Moor Monkton, Nun Monkton, Great Ouseburn, Little Ouseburn, Nether Poppleton, Upper Poppleton, Great Ribston with Walshford, Roecliffe, Rufforth, Staveley, Thornville, Thorpe Underwoods, Westwick, Whixley, Widdington
OXENHOPE UD (1894—1938[160])
Oxenhope
PATELY BRIDGE RD (1894—1937[159])
Bewerley, Birstwith, High and Low Bishopside, Bishop Thornton, Clint, Dacre, Fountains Earth, Hartwith cum Winsley, Menwith with Darley, Down Stonebeck, Upper Stonebeck, Thornthwaite with Padside, Thruscross, Warsill
PENISTONE RD
Cawthorne, Dunford (1938—74), Gunthwaite and Ingbirchworth (1938—74), High Hoyland, Hunshelf, Langsett, Oxspring, Silkstone, Stainbrough (1938—74), Thurgoland
PENISTONE UD
Penistone
PONTEFRACT RD (1894—1938[160])
Balne, Beal or Beaghall, Birkin, Brotherton, Burton Salmon, Byram cum Sutton, Carleton (1894—1937), Cridling Stubbs, Darrington, Eggborough, Fairburn, Ferry Fryston (1894—1937), Monk Fryston, Glass Houghton (1894—1937), East Hardwick, Heck, Hensall, Hillam, Kellington, Stapleton, Whitley, Womersley
PUDSEY UD (1894—1900[90])
Pudsey
QUEENSBURY UD (1894—1937[159])
Queensbury
QUEENBURY AND SHELF UD (1937[159]—74)
Queenbury and Shelf
QUICKMERE MIDDLE DIVISION UD (1894—95[183])
Springhead
RAVENSTHORPE UD (1894—1910[184])
Ravensthorpe
RAWDON UD (1894—1937[159])
Rawdon
RAWMARSH UD
Rawmarsh
RIPON RD (1894—1938[160])
Aldfield, Azerley, Bishopton (1894—1900), Clotherholme, Eavestone, Givendale, Grantley, Grewelthorpe, Bridge Hewick, Copt Hewick, Ingerthorpe, Kirkby Malzeard, Lands Common to Azerley and Laverton (1894—1937); Lands Common to Grewelthorpe, Kirkby Malzeard and Laverton (1894—1937); Laverton, Lindrick with Studley Royal and Fountains, Littlethorpe, Markingfield Hall, Markington with Wallerthwaite, Bishop Monkton, Newby with Mulwith, Nunwick cum Howgrave (pt 1894—95, ent 1895—1938), Sawly, Sharow, Skedling, Skelton, North Stainley with Sleningford, Studley Roger, Sutton Grange, Winksley
RIPON AND PATELEY BRIDGE RD (1938[160]—74)
Aldfield, Azerley, Bewerly, Birstwith, Bishop Thornton, High and Low Bishopside, Clint, Clotherholme, Dacre, Eavestone, Fountains Earth, Givendale, Grantley, Grewelthorpe, Hartwith cum Winsley,

Bridge Hewick, Copt Hewick, Kirkby Malzeard, Laverton, Lindrick with Studley Royal and Fountains, Littlethorpe, Markingfield Hall, Markington with Wallerthwaite, Menwith with Darley, Newby with Mulwith, Bishop Monkton, Nunwick cum Howgrave, Sawley, Sharow, Skedling, Skelton, North Stainley with Sleningford, Down Stonebeck, Upper Stonebeck, Studley Roger, Sutton Grange, Thornthwaite with Padside, Thruscross, Warsill, Winksley

RIPPONDEN UD (1937[159]—74)
Ripponden

RISHWORTH UD (1894—1937[159])
Rishworth

ROTHERHAM RD
Aston cum Aughton, Bramley, Brampton (1894—97), Brampton Bierlow (1897—1974), Brampton en le Morthen (1894—1923), Brinsworth, Catcliffe, Dalton, Hooton Levitt, Hooton Roberts, Laughton en le Morthen (1894—1923), Maltby (1894—1924), Orgreave, Ravenfield, Thrybergh, Thurcroft (1923—74), Treeton, Ulley, Wentworth, Whiston, Wickersley

ROTHWELL UD
Lofthouse (1937—74), Lofthouse with Carlton (1894—1937), Rothwell, Thorpe (1894—1937)

ROYSTON UD (1896[185]—1974)
Royston

SADDLEWORTH UD (1900[186]—74)
Saddleworth

SANDALL MAGNA UD (1894—1909[187])
Sandall Magna

SCAMMONDEN UD (1894—1937[159])
Scammonden

SCHOLES UD (1894—95[175])
Scholes

SEDBERGH RD
Dent, Garsdale, Sedbergh

SELBY RD
Barlow, Biggin (1894—1938), Brayton, Burn, Camblesforth, Carlton, Cawood, Drax, Long Drax, Little Fenton (1894—1938), Gateforth, Chapel Haddlesey, West Haddlesey, Hambleton, Temple Hirst, Hirst Courtney, Newland, Thorpe Willoughby, Wistow

SELBY UD
Selby

SETTLE RD
Airton, Arncliffe, Austwick, Bentham, Burton in Lonsdale, Clapham cum Newby, Giggleswick, West Halton, Halton Gill, Hanlith, Hawkswick, Hellifield, Horton in Ribbesdale, Ingleton, Kirkby Malham, Langcliffe, Lawkland, Litton, Malham, Malham Moor, Nappa, Otterburn, Long Preston, Rathmell, Scosthrop, Settle, Stainforth, Swinden, Thornton in Lonsdale, Tosside (1894—1938), Wigglesworth

SHELF UD (1894—1937[159])
Shelf

SHELLEY UD (1894—1938[160])
Shelley

SHEPLEY UD (1894—1938[160])
Shepley

SHIPLEY UD
Shipley

SILSDEN UD
Silsden

SKELMANTHORPE UD (1894—1938[160])
Skelmanthorpe

SKIPTON RD
Addingham, Appletreewick, Bank Newton, Barden, Beamsley, Bolton Abbey, Bordley, Bracewell, Bradley's Both, Brogden, Broughton, Buckden, Burnsall, Burnsall and Thorpe Fell (1894—1938), Calton, Carleton, Coates (1894—1923), Coniston Cold, Conistone with Kilnsey, Cononley, Cowling, Cracoe, Draughton, Elslack, Embsay with Eastby, Eshton, Farnhill, Flasby with Winterburn, Gargrave, Glusburn, Grassington, Halton East, Hartlington, Hazlewood with Storiths, Hebden, Hetton, Kettlewell with Starbotton, Kildwick, Linton, Lothersdale, Martons Both, Rylstone, Salterforth, Steeton with Eastburn (1938—74), Stirton with Thorlby, Sutton (1938—74), Thornton in Craven, Thorpe, Thresfield

SKIPTON UD
Skipton

SLAITHWAITE UD (1894—1937[159])
Lingards (1894—96), Slaithwaite

SOOTHILL NETHER UD (1894—1910[184])
Soothill Nether

SOOTHILL UPPER UD (1894—1910[184])
Soothill Upper

SOUTHOWRAM UD (1894—1937[159])
Southowram

SOWERBY UD (1894—1937[159])
Sowerby

SOWERBY BRIDGE UD (1894—1926[188])
Sowerby Bridge

SOWERBY BRIDGE UD (1937[159]—74)
Sowerby Bridge

SOYLAND UD (1894—1937[159])
Soyland

SPENBOROUGH UD (1915[169]—55[71])
Cleckheaton, Gomersal, Liversedge

SPRINGHEAD UD (1895[189]—1937[159])
Springhead

STAINLAND UD (1894—1937[159])
Stainland with Old Lindley

STANLEY UD (1899[190]—1974)
Outwood (1899—1936), Stanley

STOCKSBRIDGE UD
Stocksbridge

SWINTON UD
Swinton

TADCASTER RD
Aberford, Acaster Malbis (1937—74), Acaster Selby, Allerton Bywater (1894—1939), Appleton Roebuck, Askham Bryan, Askham Richard (1937—74), Austhorpe, Barkston, Barwick in Elmet (1894—1970), Barwick in Elmet and Scholes (1970—74), Biggin (1938—74), Bilbrough, Bishopthorpe (1937—74), Bolton Percy, Catterton, Colton, Copmanthorpe (1937—74), Church Fenton, Little Fenton (1937—74), Garforth (1894—1908), Grimston, Healaugh, Huddleston cum Lumby (1894—1937), Huddleston with Newthorpe (1937—74), Kippax (1894—1939), Kirkby Wharfe and North Milford, Lead, Ledsham, Ledston, Lotherton cum Aberford, Micklefield, South Milford, Newthorpe (1894—1937), Newton Kyme cum Toulston, Oxton, Parlington, Great and Little Preston,

Ryther cum Ossendyke, Saxton with Scarthingwell, Sherburn in Elmet, Steeton, Sturton Grange, Stutton with Hazlewood, Swillington, Tadcaster East, Tadcaster West, Towton, Ulleskelf

THORNE RD

Fishlake, Hatfield, Stainforth, Sykehouse, Thorne

THORNHILL UD (1894—1910[184])

Thornhill, Whitley Lower (1894—96)

THORNTON UD (1894—99[6])

Thornton

THURLSTONE UD (1894—1938[191])

Thurlstone

THURNSCOE UD (1908[192]—37[193])

Thurnscoe

THURSTONLAND UD (1894—1925[174])

Thurstonland

THURSTONLAND AND FARNLEY TYAS UD (1925[174]—38[160])

Thurstonland and Farnley Tyas

TICKHILL UD

Tickhill

TODMORDEN RD (1894—1939[178])

Blackshaw, Erringden, Heptonstall, Wadsworth

TODMORDEN UD (1894—96[100])

Cornholme, Langfield, Stansfield, Todmorden and Walsden

TONG UD (1894—99[6])

Tong

UPPER MILL UD (1894—1900[186])

Upper Mill

WAKEFIELD RD

Alverthorpe (1894—1916), West Bretton, Chevet, Crigglestone, Crofton, Kirkhamgate (1916—37), Lupset (1902—21), Newland with Woodhouse Moor, Notton (1938—74), Sharlston, Shitlington 1894—1930s), Sitlington (1930s—74), Walton, Warmfield cum Heath, Wintersett (1938—74), Woolley (1938—74)

WARLEY UD (1894—1900[16])

Warley

WATH UPON DEARNE UD

Wath upon Dearne

WETHERBY RD

Angram, Bardsey cum Rigton, Bickerton (1894—1937), Bilton (1894—1965), Bilton in Ainsty (1965—74), Boston Spa (1896—1974), Bramham cum Oglethorpe, Clifford (1896—1974), Clifford with Boston (1894—96), Collingham, Cowthorpe (1894—1937), Kirk Deighton, North Deighton, Dunkeswick (1894—1937), Harewood, Hutton Wandesley, Kearby with Netherby, East Keswick, Kirkby Overblow, Linton (1894—1937), Long Marston, Micklethwaite (1894—1937), Little Ribston, Rigton (1894—1962), North Rigton (1962—74), Scarcroft, Shadwell (1894—1912), Sicklinghall, Spofforth with Stockeld, Thorner, Thorp Arch, Tockwith, Walton, Weardley (1894—1937), Weeton, Wetherby, Wighill, Wigton (1894—1937), Wilstrop, Wothersome, Wyke (1894—1937)

WHARFEDALE RD

Adel cum Eccup (1894—1928), Alwoodley (1894—1928), Arthington, Askwith, Blubberhouses, Bramhope, Carlton, Castley, Clifton with Norwood (1894—1950), Denton, Esholt (1894—1937), Farnley, Fewston, Hawksworth (1894—1937), Leathley, Lindley, Menston (1894—1937), Middleton, Nesfield with Langbar, Newell with Clifton, Norwood (1950—74), Pool, Stainburn, Great Timble, Little Timble, Weston

WHEATLEY UD (1900[194]—14[195])

Wheatley

WHITLEY UPPER UD (1894—1938[191])

Whitley Upper

WHITWOOD UD (1894—1937[193])

Whitwood

WILSDEN UD (1894—98[167])

Wilsden

WOMBWELL UD

Wombwell

WORSBOROUGH UD (1894—1956[196])

Worsborough

WORSBROUGH UD (1956[196]—74)

Worsborough

WORTLEY RD

Bradfield, Ecclesfield, Tankersley, Wortley

YEADON UD (1894—1937[193])

Yeadon

NORTH YORKSHIRE NON-METROPOLITAN COUNTY

As constituted 1 Apr 1974, defined in terms of Adm Co units as of 31 Mar.

CRAVEN DIST
from Yorks W Riding: Settle RD, pt Skipton RD (all except Addingham, Bracewell, Brogden, Kildwick, Salterforth, Steeton with Eastburn), Skipton UD

HARROGATE DIST
from Yorks N Riding: Masham RD, pt Thirsk RD (Ellenthorpe, Humberton, Kirby Hill, Langthorpe, Miiby, Norton le Clay, Thornton Bridge), Wath RD
from Yorks W Riding: Harrogate MB, Knaresborough UD, Nidderdale RD, Ripon and Pateley Bridge RD, pt Wetherby RD (all except Bardsey cum Rigton, Boston Spa, Bramham cum Oglethorpe, Clifford, Collingham, Harewood, East Keswick, Scarcroft, Thorner, Thorp Arch, Walton, Wetherby, Wothersome), pt Wharfedale RD (all except Arthington, Bramhope, Carlton, Pool)

HAMBLETON DIST
from Yorks N Riding: Bedale RD, pt Croft RD (Over Dinsdale, Girsby), Easingwold RD, Northallerton RD, Northallerton UD, pt Stokesley RD (Great Ayton, Little Ayton, Bilsdale Midcable, Broughton, Great Busby, Little Busby, Carlton, Crathorne, Easby, Faceby, Hutton Rudby, Ingleby Arncliffe, Ingleby Greenhow, Kildale, Kirby in Cleveland, Middleton upon Leven, Newby, Picton, Potto, East Rounton, Rudby in Cleveland, Seamer, Sexhow, Skutterskelfe, Stokesley, Whorlton, High Worsall, Low Worsall), pt Thirsk RD (the pars not in Harrogate Dist)

RICHMONDSHIRE DIST
from Yorks N Riding: Aysgarth RD, pt Croft RD (the pars not in Hambleton Dist), Leyburn RD, Reeth RD, Richmond MB, Richmond RD

RYEDALE DIST
from Yorks E Riding: Norton RD, Norton UD
from Yorks N Riding: Flaxton RD, Helmsley RD, Kirkby Moorside RD, Malton RD, Malton UD, Pickering RD, Pickering UD

SCARBOROUGH DIST
from Yorks E Riding: pt Bridlington RD (Folkton, Hunmanby, Muston, Reighton), Filey UD
from Yorks N Riding: Scalby UD, Scarborough MB, Scarborough RD (incl Fylingdales Moor), Whitby RD, Whitby UD

SELBY DIST
from Yorks E Riding: Derwent RD
from Yorks W Riding: pt Hemsworth RD (Kirk Smeaton, Little Smeaton, Walden Stubbs), pt Osgoldcross RD (all except Darrington, East Hardwick), Selby RD, Selby UD, pt Tadcaster RD (all except Aberford, Austhorpe, Barwick in Elmet and Scholes, Ledsham, Ledston, Lotherton cum Aberford, Micklefield, Parlington, Great and Little Preston, Sturton Grange, Swillington)

YORK DIST
CB (not assoc with any Adm Co): York CB

SOUTH YORKSHIRE METROPOLITAN COUNTY

As constituted 1 Apr 1974, defined in terms of Adm Co units as of 31 Mar.

BARNSLEY METROP DIST
CB (assoc with Yorks W Riding): Barnsley CB
from Yorks W Riding: Cudworth UD, Darfield RD, Darton UD, Dearne UD, Dodworth UD, pt Hemsworth RD (Billingley, Brierley, Great Houghton, Little Houghton, Shafton), Hoyland Nether UD, Penistone RD, Penistone UD, Royston UD, Wombwell UD, Worsbrough UD

DONCASTER METROP DIST
CB (assoc with Yorks W Riding): Doncaster CB
from Notts: pt East Retford RD (Finningley), pt Worksop RD (pt Haworth)

from Yorks W Riding: Adwick le Street UD, Bentley with Arksey UD, Conisbrough UD, Doncaster RD, Mexborough UD, Thorne RD, Tickhill UD

ROTHERHAM METROP DIST
CB (assoc with Yorks W Riding): Rotherham CB
from Yorks W Riding: Kiverton Park RD, Maltby UD, Rawmarsh UD, Rotherham RD, Swinton UD, Wath upon Dearne UD

SHEFFIELD METROP DIST
CB (assoc with Yorks W Riding): Sheffield CB
from Yorks W Riding: Stocksbridge UD, pt Wortley RD (Bradfield, Ecclesfield)

WEST YORKSHIRE METROPOLITAN COUNTY

As constituted 1 Apr 1974, defined in terms of Adm Co units as of 31 Mar.

BRADFORD METROP DIST

CB (assoc with Yorks W Riding): Bradford CB

from Yorks W Riding: Baildon UD, Bingley UD, Denholme UD, Ilkley UD, Keighley MB, pt Queensbury and Shelf UD (all except the wards in Calderdale Metrop Dist), Shipley UD, Silsden UD, pt Skipton RD (Addingham, Kildwick, Steeton with Eastburn)

CALDERDALE METROP DIST

CB (assoc with Yorks W Riding): Halifax CB

from Yorks W Riding: Brighouse MB, Elland UD, Hebden Royd UD, Hepton RD, pt Queensbury and Shelf UD (wards of Shelf East, Shelf West), Ripponden UD, Sowerby Bridge UD, Todmorden MB

KIRKLEES METROP DIST

CBs (assoc with Yorks W Riding): Dewsbury CB, Huddersfield CB

from Yorks W Riding: Batley MB, Colne Valley UD, Denby Dale UD, Heckmondwike UD, Kirkburton UD, Meltham UD, Mirfield UD, Spenborough MB

LEEDS METROP DIST

CB (assoc with Yorks W Riding): Leeds CB

from Yorks W Riding: Aireborough UD, Garforth UD, Horsforth UD, Morley MB, Otley UD, Pudsey MB, Rothwell UD, pt Tadcaster RD (Aberford, Austhorpe, Barwick in Elmet and Scholes, Ledsham, Leston, Lotherton cum Aberford, Micklefield, Parlington, Great and Little Preston, Sturton Grange, Swillington), pt Wetherby RD (Bardsey cum Rigton, Boston Spa, Bramham cum Oglethorpe, Clifford, Collingbam, Harewood, East Keswick, Scarcroft, Thorner, Thorp Arch, Walton, Wetherby, Wothersome), pt Wharfedale RD (Arthington, Bramhope, Carlton, Pool)

WAKEFIELD METROP DIST

CB (assoc with Yorks W Riding): Wakefield CB

from Yorks W Riding: Castleford MB, Featherstone UD, pt Hemsworth RD (the pars transf neither to N Yorks nor to S Yorks), Hemsworth UD, Horbury UD, Knottingley UD, Normanton UD, pt Osgoldcross RD (Darrington, East Hardwick), Ossett MB, Pontefract MB, Stanley UD, Wakefield RD

Part III: Parliamentary Constituencies

CHESHIRE

BOROUGH CONSTITUENCIES[1]

ALTRINCHAM AND SALE PARL BOR/BC (1945—70)

Altrincham MB, Sale MB

ASHTON UNDER LYNE PARL BOR/BC (1832—*) [Lancs, Ches (1867—1918)]

pt Dukinfield (1867—1918)

BEBINGTON BC (1948—70)

Bebington MB, pt Birkenhead CB (wards of Bebington, Devonshire, Egerton, Mersey, Prenton)

BEBINGTON AND ELLESMERE PORT BC (1970—*)

Bebington MB, Ellesmere Port MB

BIRKENHEAD PARL BOR (1859—1918)

pt Higher Bebington, Birkenhead, Claughton with Grange, Oxton, Tranmere

BIRKENHEAD BC (1948—*)

1948—70: pt Birkenhead CB (all except the wards in Bebington BC)

1970—:* pt Birkenhead CB (wards of Argyle, Bebington, Cathcart, Claughton, Cleveland, Clifton, Devonshire, Egerton, Gilbrook, Grange, Holt, Mersey, Oxton, St James)

BIRKENHEAD EAST BC (1918—48)

pt Birkenhead CB (wards of Arglye, Bebington, Clifton, Egerton, Mersey, and the pt of the CB between eastern bdry of Argyle, Bebington, and Mersey wards to the centre of the bed of the River Mersey)

BIRKENHEAD WEST BC (1918—48)

pt Birkenhead CB (wards of Claughton, Cleveland, Grange, Oxton)

CHEADLE BC (1970—*)

Cheadle and Gatley UD, Wilmslow UD

CHESTER PARL BOR (1553—1918) [Ches, Flints (1867—1918)] [1 mbr 1885—1918]

Great Boughton (pt 1832—67, ent 1867—1918), Chester (1885—1918), Chester Abbey Precincts (1553—1885), Chester Holy Trinity (pt 1553—1867, ent 1867—85), Chester St Bridget (1553—1885), Chester St John the Baptist (pt 1553—1867, ent 1867—85), Chester St Martin, Chester St Mary on the Hill (pt 1553—1867, ent 1867—85), Chester St Michael, Chester St Olave, Chester St Oswald (pt 1553—1867, ent 1867—85), Chester St Peter (1553—1885), pt Hoole

(1867—1918), pt Newton by Chester (1867—1918), pt Saltney (1867—1918), Spital Boughton (1553—1885)

HAZEL GROVE BC (1970—*)

Bredbury and Romiley UD, Hazel Grove and Bramhall UD, Marple UD

MACCLESFIELD PARL BOR (1832—1885)

pt Hurdsfield, Macclesfield, pt Sutton, pt Tytherington (1867—85)

STALYBRIDGE PARL BOR (1867—1918) [*Lancs*, Ches]

pt Ashton under Lyne[3] *(enlarged pt 1885—1918)*, pt Dukinfield, *pt Hartshead*, pt Stayley (enlarged pt 1885—1918)

STOCKPORT PARL BOR (1832—1948) (Ches, *Lancs* [1832—1918])

1832—1918: pt Brinnington, pt Cheadle (1885—1918), pt Cheadle Bulkeley (1832—85), pt Cheadle Moseley (1832—85), *pt Heaton Norris*, Stockport

1918—48: Stockport CB

STOCKPORT NORTH BC[2] (1948—*)

pt Stockport CB (wards of Cheadle Heath [1971—*], Edgeley, Heaton Chapel [1971—*], Heaton Lane [1948—71], Heaton Mersey [1971—*], Heaton Moor [1971—*], Heaton Norris [1971—*], Heaton Norris North [1948—71], Heaton Norris South [1948—71], Hollywood [1948—71], Lancashire Hill, Longford [1971—*], Old Road [1948—71], Reddish Green [1971—*], Reddish North [1948—71], Reddish South [1948—71])

STOCKPORT SOUTH BC[4] (1948—*)

pt Stockport CB (wards of Adswood [1971—*], Brinnington [1971—*], Cale Green, Davenport, Heaviley, Hempshaw Lane [1948—71], Little Moor [1971—*], Manor [1971—*], Offerton [1971—*], Portwood [1948—71], St Mary's [1948—71], St Thomas's [1948—71], Shaw Heath [1948—71], Vernon)

WALLASEY PARL BOR/BC (1918—*)

Wallasey CB

WARRINGTON PARL BOR/BC (1832—*) [Lancs, Ches (1832—1918]

Latchford, Thelwall

COUNTY CONSTITUENCIES

1832—1867

NORTHERN DIVISION

Hds of Bucklow, Macclesfield

SOUTHERN DIVISION

Hds of Broxton, Eddisbury, Nantwich, Northwich, Wirral

1867—1885

NORTH DIVISION

Hd of Macclesfield

MID DIVISION

Hds of Bucklow, Northwich

SOUTH DIVISION

Hds of Broxton, Eddisbury, Nantwich, Wirral

1885—1918

ALTRINCHAM DIVISION

Altrincham PSD, pt Stockport PSD, *viz.*, Agden, Altrincham, Ashley, Ashton upon Mersey, Baguley, Bollington, Bowdon, Bramhall, Carrington, pt

Cheadle, Dunham Massey, Northern Etchells, Stockport Etchells, Hale, Handforth, High Legh, Lymm, Millington, Norbury, Northenden, Partington, Rostherne, Sale, Timperley, Warburton

CREWE DIVISION

Crewe MB, pt Nantwich PSD, pt Northwich PSD, *viz.*, Alsager, Alvaston, Arclid, Barthomley, Basford, Betchton, Chorlton, Church Coppenhall, Crewe, Elton, Haslington, Hassall, Hough, Church Lawton, Moreton cum Alcumlow, Nantwich, Odd Rode, Rope, Sandbach, Shavington cum Gresty, Smallwood, Stapeley, Weston, Wheelock, Willaston, Wistaston, Woolstanwood, Wybunbury

EDDISBURY DIVISION

Broxton PSD, pt Chester Castle PSD, pt Eddisbury PSD, pt Nantwich PSD, pt Northwich PSD, *viz.*, Agden, Aldersey, Aldford, Alpraham, Alvanley, Ashton, Aston juxta Mondrum, Audlem, Austerston, Bache, Backford, Baddiley, Baddington, Barrow, Barton, Batherton, Beeston, Bickerton, Bickley, Blacon cum Crabwall, Blakenhall, Bradley, Bradwall, Bridgemere, Brindley, Broomhall, Broxton, Little Budworth, Buerton, Buerton, Bulkeley, Bunbury, Burland, Burton by Tarvin, Burwardsley, Caldecott, Calveley, Capenhurst, Carden, Caughall, Checkley cum Wrinehill, Chester Castle, Chidlow, Cholmondeley, Cholmondeston, Chorley, Chorlton, Chorlton by Backford, Chowley, Christleton, Churton by Aldford, Churton by Farndon, Churton Heath, Claverton, Clotton Hoofield, Clutton, Coddington, Coole Pilate, Monks Coppenhall, Cotton Abbotts, Cotton Edmunds, Crewe, Croughton, Crowton, Cuddington, Cuddington, Darnhall, Delamere, Dodcott cum Wilkesley, Doddington, Dodleston, Duckington, Duddon, Dunham on the Hill, Eaton, Eaton, Eccleston, Eddisbury, Edge, Edgerley, Edleston, Egerton, Elton, Faddiley, Farndon, Frodsham, Frodsham Lordship, Golborne Bellow, Golborne David, Grafton, Hampton, Handley, Hankelow, Hapsford, Harthill, Hatherton, Hatton, Haughton, Helsby, Henhull, Hockenhull, Horton, Horton cum Peele, Hunsterson, Huntington, Hurleston, Huxley, Iddinshall, Ince, Kelsall, Kingsley, Kings Marsh, Kingswood, Lower Kinnerton, Larkton, Lea, Lea by Backford, Lea Newbold, Leighton, Littleton, Macefen, Malpas, Manley, Marbury with Quoisley, Marlston cum Lache, Marton, Marton, Church Minshull, Minshull Vernon, Mollington Banastre, Mollington Tarrant, Moston, Moston, Mouldsworth, Newhall, Newton, pt Newton by Chester, Newton by Frodsham, Newton by Malpas, Newton by Tattenhall, Norbury, Norley, Oakmere, Occlestone, Oldcastle, Onston, Low Oulton, Overton, Peckforton, Picton, Poole, Poulton, Prior's Heys, Pulford, Ridley, Rowton, Rushton, Saighton, Great Saughall, Little Saughall, Church Shocklach, Shocklach Oviatt, Shotwick, Shotwick Park, Sound, Spurstow, Stanlow, Great Stanney, Little Stanney, Bruern Stapleford, Foulk Stapleford, Stockton, Stoke, Stoke, Stretton, Sutton, Guilden Sutton, Tarporley, Tarvin, Tattenhall, Tetton, Thornton le Moors, pt Threapwood, Tilston, Tilstone Fearnall, Tittenley, Tiverton, Bridge Trafford, Mickle Trafford, Wimbolds Trafford, Tushingham cum Grindley, Upton by Chester, Utkinton, Walgherton,

Wardle, Warmingham, Waverton, Weaver, Wervin, Wettenhall, Whitby, Wigland, Willington, Wimboldsley, Wirswall, Woodbank, Woodcott, Worleston, Wrenbury cum Frith, Wychough

HYDE DIVISION

Hyde PSD, pt Stockport PSD, *viz.*, Bredbury, pt Brinnington, Godley, Hattersley, Hollingworth, Hyde, Marple, Matley, Mottram, Newton, Offerton, Romiley, pt Stayley, Tintwistle, Torkington, Werneth

KNUTSFORD DIVISION

Bucklow PSD, pt Daresbury PSD, pt Prestbury PSD, pt Leftwich PSD, pt Northwich PSD, *viz.*, Acton Grange, Adlington, Nether Alderley, Over Alderley, Allostock, Antrobus, Appleton, Aston by Budworth, Bexton, Birches, Blackden, Bollinfee, Bollington, Brereton cum Smethwick, Butley, Byley, Capesthorne, Chelford, Chorley, Cotton, Cranage, Crowley, Daresbury, Davenport, Disley, Fallibroome, Fulshaw, Goostrey cum Barnshaw, Grappenhall, Hatton, pt Hoole, Church Hulme, Keckwick, Kermincham, Kettleshulme, Knutsford Nether, Knutsford Over, Lach Dennis, Leese, Lostock Gralam, Lyme Handley, Macclesfield Forest, Marthall cum Warford, Marton, Mere, Mobberley, Moore, Mooresbarrow cum Parme, Mottram St Andrew, Newhall, Newton, Newton by Daresbury, Ollerton, Nether Peover, Peover Inferior, Peover Superior, Pickmere, Plumbley, Pott Shrigley, Pownall Fee, Poynton with Worth, Prestbury, Preston on the Hill, Rainow, Rudheath, Seven Oaks, Shipbrook, Shurlach, Siddington, Snelson, Somerford, Somerfood Booths, Sproston, Stretton, Stublach, Swettenham, Tabley Inferior, Tabley Superior, Tatton, Taxal, Toft, Twemlow, Tytherington, Upton, Walton Inferior, Walton Superior, Great Warford, Higher Whitley, Lower Whitley, Lower Withington, Old Withington, Woodford, Worth, Yeardsley cum Whalley

MACCLESFIELD DIVISION

Congleton MB, Macclesfield MB, pt Northwich PSD, pt Prestbury PSD, *viz.*, Birtles, Bosley, Buglawton, Congleton, Eaton, Gawsworth, Henbury cum Pexhall, Hulme Walfield, pt Hurdsfield, Macclesfield, Newbold Astbury, Radnor, North Rode, pt Sutton, Wildboarclough, Wincle

NORTHWICH DIVISION

pt Daresbury PSD, pt Eddisbury PSD, pt Leftwich PSD, pt Northwich PSD, Runcorn PSD, *viz.*, Acton, Anderton, Aston by Sutton, Aston Grange, Barnton, Bartington, Bostock, Great Budworth, Clifton, Clive, Cogshall, Comberbach, Croxton, Davenham, Dutton, Eaton, Halton, Hartford, Hulse, Kinderton cum Hulme, Little Leigh, Leftwich, Marbury, Marston, Middlewich, Moulton, Newton, Northwich, Castle Northwich, Norton, Over, Ravenscroft, Runcorn, Stanthorne, Stockham, Sutton, Wallerscoat, Weaverham cum Milton, Weston, Wharton, Whatcroft, Wincham, Winnington, Witton cum Twambrooks

WIRRAL DIVISION

Hd of Wirral PSD, *viz.*, Arrowe, Barnston, pt Higher Bebington, Lower Bebington, Bidston cum Ford, Brimstage, Bromborough, Burton, Caldy, Eastham, Frankby, Gayton, Grange, Greasby, Heswall cum Oldfield, Hoose, Hooton, Irby, West Kirby, Landican,

Ledsham, Leighton, Liscard, Great Meolse, Little Meolse, Moreton, Ness, Great Neston, Little Neston, Netherpool, Newton by Larton, Noctorum, Overpool, Pensby, Poulton cum Spital, Poulton cum Seacombe, Prenton, Puddington, Raby, Saughall Massie, Storeton, Great Sutton, Little Sutton, Thingwall, Childer Thornton, Thornton Hough, Thurstaston, Upton by Birkenhead, Wallasey, Willaston, Woodchurch

1918—1948
ALTRINCHAM DIVISION (1918—45)
Altrincham UD, Ashton upon Mersey UD, Bowdon UD, pt Bucklow RD (the pars not in Knutsford Dv), Cheadle and Gatley UD, Hale UD, Handforth UD, Lymm UD, Sale UD

BUCKLOW DIVISION[5] (1945—48)
Bowdon UD, pt Bucklow RD (the pt in Ches prev in Altrincham Dv and the pt in Lancs in Newton Dv and in Stretford Dv), Cheadle and Gatley UD, Hale UD, Lymm UD, the pt of Manchester CB (assoc with Lancs) in prev Altrincham Dv

CITY OF CHESTER DIVISION
Chester CB, Chester RD, Hoole UD

CREWE DIVISION
Alsager UD, pt Congleton RD (Arclid, Betchton, Hassall, Church Lawton, Moreton cum Alcumlow, Odd Rode, Smallwood, Wheelock), Crewe MB, pt Nantwich RD (Barthomley, Basford, Chorlton, Church Coppenhall, Crewe, Haslington, Hough, Rope, Shavington cum Gresty, Stapeley, Weston, Willaston, Wistaston, Wybunbury), Nantwich UD, Sandbach UD

EDDISBURY DIVISION
Malpas RD, pt Nantwich RD (the pars not in Crewe Dv), pt Northwich RD (Little Budworth, Crowton, Cuddington, Darnhall, Delamere, Eddisbury, Marton, Oakmere, Wimboldsley), pt Runcorn RD (Alvanley, Frodsham, Frodsham Lordship, Helsby, Kingsley, Kingswood, Manley, Newton by Frodsham, Norley), Tarporley UD, Tarvin RD

KNUTSFORD DIVISION[5]
Alderley Edge UD, Bollington UD, pt Bucklow RD (Aston by Budworth, Bexton, Marthall cum Warford, Mere, Mobberley, Ollerton, Peover Inferior, Peover Superior, Pickmere, Plumley, Styal, Tabley Inferior, Tabley Superior, Tatton, Toft), pt Congleton RD (the pars not in Crewe Dv, Macclesfield Dv, Northwich Dv), Hazel Grove and Bramhall UD, Knutsford UD, pt Macclesfield RD (Nether Alderley, Over Alderley, Adlington, Butley, Capesthorne, Chelford, Chorley, Fallibroome, Marton, Mottram St Andrew, Newton, Poynton with Worth, Prestbury, Siddington, Snelson, Tytherington, Upton, Great Warford, Lower Withington, Old Withington, Woodford), pt Northwich RD (Allostock, Byley, Lach Dennis, Lostock Gralam, Nether Peover, Rudheath, Sproston, Whatcroft), pt Runcorn RD (Acton Grange, Antrobus, Appleton, Crowley, Daresbury, Grappenhall, Hatton, Keckwick, Latchford Without, Moore, Newton by Daresbury, Preston on the Hill, Seven Oaks, Stockton Heath, Stretton, Thelwall, Walton Inferior, Walton Superior, Higher Whitley, Lower Whitley), Wilmslow UD

MACCLESFIELD DIVISION
Bredbury and Romiley UD, Buglawton UD, Compstall

UD, Congleton MB, pt Congleton RD (Hulme Walfield, Newbold Astbury), Disley RD, Macclesfield MB, pt Macclesfield RD (the pars not in Knutsford Dv), Marple UD, Yeardsley cum Whaley UD

NORTHWICH DIVISION
pt Congleton RD (Bradwall, Elton, Moston, Tetton), Middlewich UD, pt Northwich RD (the pars neither in Eddisbury Dv or Knutsford Dv), Northwich UD, pt Runcorn RD (the pars neither in Eddisbury Dv or Knutsford Dv), Runcorn UD, Sandbach UD, Winsford UD

STALYBRIDGE AND HYDE DIVISION
Dukinfield MB, Hollingworth UD, Hyde MB, Mottram in Longendale UD, Stalybridge MB, Tintwistle RD

WIRRAL DIVISION
Higher Bebington UD, Lower Bebington UD, Bromborough UD, Ellesmere Port and Whitby UD, Hoylake and West Kirby UD, Neston and Parkgate UD, Wirral RD

1948—1970
CHEADLE COUNTY CONSTITUENCY[6]
Bredbury and Romiley UD, Cheadle and Gatley UD, Hazel Grove and Bramhall UD, Marple UD

CITY OF CHESTER COUNTY CONSTITUENCY
Chester CB, Chester RD, Hoole UD

CREWE COUNTY CONSTITUENCY[7]
Alsager UD (1955—70), Crewe MB, Nantwich RD (ent 1948—55, pt 1955—70 [Barthomley, Crewe, Haslington, Weston]), Nantwich UD (1948—55), Sandbach UD (1955—70)

KNUTSFORD COUNTY CONSTITUENCY[7]
Alderley Edge UD, Alsager UD (1948—55), Bowdon UD, Bucklow RD, Congleton RD, Hale UD, Knutsford UD, Sandbach UD (1948—55), Wilmslow UD

MACCLESFIELD COUNTY CONSTITUENCY
Bollington UD, Congleton MB, Disley RD, Macclesfield MB, Macclesfield RD

NANTWICH COUNTY CONSTITUENCY (1955[7]—70)
Middlewich UD, pt Nantwich RD (all except the pars in Crewe CC), Nantwich UD, pt Northwich RD (Darnhall, Stanthorne, Wimboldsley), pt Tarvin RD (all except the pars in Northwich CC), Winsford UD

NORTHWICH COUNTY CONSTITUENCY[7]
Middlewich UD (1948—55), Northwich RD (ent 1948—55, pt 1955—70 [all except the pars in Nantwich CC]), Northwich UD, Tarvin RD (ent 1948—55, pt 1955—70 [Ashton, Burton by Tarvin, Clotton Hoofield, Cotton Abbotts, Cotton Edmunds, Duddon, Hatton, Hockenhull, Horton cum Peel, Huxley, Iddinshall, Kelsall, Mouldsworth, Prior's Heys, Bruen Stapleford, Foulk Stapleford, Tarvin, Tilstone Fearnall, Tiverton, Waverton, Willington), Winsford UD (1948—55)

RUNCORN COUNTY CONSTITUENCY
Lymm UD, Runcorn RD, Runcorn UD

STALYBRIDGE AND HYDE COUNTY CONSTITUENCY
Dukinfield MB, Hyde MB, Longendale UD, Stalybridge MB, Tintwistle RD

WIRRAL COUNTY CONSTITUENCY
Ellesmere Port UD, Hoylake UD, Neston UD, Wirral RD, Wirral UD

1970—

CITY OF CHESTER COUNTY CONSTITUENCY
Chester CB, Chester RD
CREWE COUNTY CONSTITUENCY
Alsager UD, Crewe MB, pt Nantwich RD (Barthomley, Crewe, Haslington, Weston), Sandbach UD
KNUTSFORD COUNTY CONSTITUENCY
Bowdon UD, Bucklow RD, Congleton RD, Hale UD, Knutsford UD
MACCLESFIELD COUNTY CONSTITUENCY
Alderley Edge UD, Bollington UD, Congleton MB, Disley RD, Macclesfield MB, Macclesfield RD
NANTWICH COUNTY CONSTITUENCY
Middlewich UD, pt Nantwich RD (all except the pars in Crewe CC), Nantwich UD, pt Northwich RD (Darnhall, Stanthorne, Wimboldsley), pt Tarvin RD (Agden, Aldersey, Barton, Beeston, Bickley, Bradley, Broxton, Burwardsley, Caldecott, Carden, Chidlow, Chorlton, Chowley, Churton by Aldford, Churton by Farndon, Clutton, Coddington, Crewe, Cuddington, Duckington, Edge, Edgerley, Farndon, Golborne Bellow, Golborne David, Grafton, Hampton, Handley, Harthill, Horton, Kings Marsh, Larkton, Macefen, Malpas, Newton by Malpas, Newton by Tattenhall, Oldcastle, Overton, Church Shocklach, Shocklach Oviatt, Stockton, Stretton, Tattenhall, Threapwood, Tilston, Tushingham cum Grindley, Wigland, Wychough), Winsford UD
NORTHWICH COUNTY CONSTITUENCY
pt Northwich RD (all except the pars in Nantwich CC), Northwich UD, pt Tarvin RD (Ashton, Burton by Tarvin, Clotton Hoofield, Cotton Abbotts, Cotton Edmunds, Duddon, Hatton, Hockenhull, Horton cum Peel, Huxley, Iddinshall, Kelsall, Mouldsworth, Prior's Heys, Bruen Stapleford, Foulk Stapleford, Tarvin, Tilstone Fearnall, Tiverton, Waverton, Willington)
RUNCORN COUNTY CONSTITUENCY
Lymm UD, Runcorn RD, Runcorn UD
STALYBRIDGE AND HYDE COUNTY CONSTITUENCY
Dukinfield MB, Tintwistle RD, Stalybridge MB
WIRRAL COUNTY CONSTITUENCY
pt Birkenhead CB (the wards of Prenton, Upton), Hoylake UD, Neston UD, Wirral UD

CUMBERLAND

BOROUGH CONSTITUENCIES[1]

CARLISLE PARL BOR/BC[2] (1295—*) [1 mbr, 1885—*]
pt Caldewgate (1835—1918), Carlisle (1918—*), pt Carlisle St Mary (until 1867), pt Carlisle St Cuthbert (until 1867), Eaglesfield Abbey (until 1918), Rickergate (1835—1918), St Mary Within (1867—1918), St Cuthbert Within (1867—1918), pt St Cuthbert Without (1867—1918)

COCKERMOUTH PARL BOR (1295, 1640—1885)
before 1835: pt Brigham [area of Cockermouth]
1835—85: Bridekirk, Brigham, Cockermouth (as tp until 1867, as par 1867—85), pt Dovenby, Eaglesfield, Papcastle
EGREMONT PARL BOR (1295 only)
Egremont
WHITEHAVEN PARL BOR (1835—85)
pt Preston Quarter, Whitehaven

COUNTY CONSTITUENCIES

1832—1885
EASTERN DIVISION
Wards of Cumberland, Eskdale, Leath
WESTERN DIVISION
Wards of Allerdale above Derwent, Allerdale below Derwent

1885—1918
COCKERMOUTH DIVISION
Derwent PSD, Workington PSD, *viz.*, Bewaldeth and Snittlegarth, Blindbothel, Blindcrake Isel and Redmaine, Bothel and Threapland, Brackenthwaite, Brigham, Great Broughton, Little Broughton, Buttermere, Camerton, Great Clifton, Little Clifton, Cloffocks, Cockermouth, Crosscanonby, Dean, Dearham, Dovenby, Eaglesfield, Ellenborough and Ewanrigg, Embleton, Flimby, Gilcrux, Greysouthern, Isel Old Park, Kirkbride, Lorton, Loweswater, Mosser, Oughterside and Allerby, Papcastle, Plumbland, Ribton, Seaton, Setmurthy, Stainburn, Sunderland, Tallentire, Whinfell, Winscales, Workington, Wythop
EGREMONT (or WESTERN) DIVISION
Allerdale Ward above Derwent PSD, Bootle PSD, *viz.*, Arlecdon, Beckermet St Bridget, Beckermet St John, Birker and Austhwaite, Bootle, Cleator, Corney, Distington, Drigg and Carleton, Egremont, Ennerdale and Kinniside, Eskdale and Wasdale, Gosforth, Haile, Harrington, Hensingham, Irton, Lamplugh, Lowside Quarter, Millom, Moresby, Muncaster, Parton, Ponsonby, Preston Quarter, Rottington, St Bees, Salter and Eskett, Sandwith, Ulpha, Waberthwaite, Nether Wasdale, Weddicar, Whicham, Whitbeck, Whitehaven
ESKDALE (or NORTHERN) DIVISION
pt Allerdale Ward below Derwent PSD, Cumberland Ward PSD, Eskdale Ward PSD, Longtown PSD, *viz.*, Aikton, Arthuret, Askerton, Aspatria and Brayton, Beaumont, Bellbank, Bowness, Brampton, Bridekirk, Bromfield, Burgh by Sands, Burtholme, Carlatton, Castle Carrock, Crosby upon Eden, Cummersdale, Cumrew, Cumwhitton, Dalston, Nether Denton, Upper Denton, Farlam, Geltsdale, Grinsdale, Hayton and Mealo, Hethersgill, Holme Abbey, Holme East Waver, Holme Low, Holme St Cuthbert, Irthington, King-

moor, Kingwater, Kirkandrews Middle, Kirkandrews Moat, Kirkandrews Nether, Kirkandrews upon Eden, Kirkbampton, Kirklinton Middle, Langrigg and Mealrigg, Midgeholme, West Newton and Allonby, Nichol Forest, Orton, Oulton, Rockcliffe, pt St Cuthbert Without, Scaleby, Solport, Stanwix, Stapleton, Trough, Walton, Warwick, Waterhead, Westlinton, Wetheral, Wreay
PENRITH (or MID) DIVISION
pt Allerdale Ward below Derwent PSD, Keswick PSD, Leath Ward PSD, *viz.*, Above Derwent, Ainstable, Allhallows, Alston with Garrigill, Bassenthwaite, Berrier and Murrah, Bewcastle, Blencogo, Blennerhassett and Kirkland, Bolton High, Bolton Low, Borrowdale, Bowscale, Briery Cottages, Caldbeck, Castle Sowerby, Castlerigg St John's and Wythburn, Catterlen, Croglin, Culgaith, Dacre, Dundraw, Edenhall, Gamblesby, Glassonby, Greystoke, Hesket in the Forest, Hunsonby and Winskill, Hutton in the Forest, Hutton John, Hutton Roof, Hutton Soil, High Ireby, Low Ireby, Keswick, Kirkland and Blencarn, Kirkoswald, Langwathby, Lazonby, Matterdale, Melmerby, Middlesceugh and Braithwaite, Mosedale, Mungrisdale, Newton Reigny, Ousby, Penrith, Plumpton Wall, Renwick, Great Salkeld, Little Salkeld, Sebergham, Skelton, Skirwith, Skiddaw, Staffield, Threlkeld, Thursby, Torpenhow and Whitrigg, Uldale, Underskiddaw, Watermillock, Waverton, Westward, Wigton, Woodside Quarter

1918—1948
NORTHERN DIVISION
Brampton RD, Carlisle RD, Holme Cultram UD, Longtown RD, pt Wigton RD (the pars not in Workington Dv), Wigton UD
PENRITH AND COCKERMOUTH DIVISION
Alston with Garrigill RD, pt Cockermouth RD (the pars not in Workington Dv), Cockermouth UD, Keswick UD, Penrith RD, Penrith UD
WHITEHAVEN DIVISION
Bootle RD, Cleator Moor UD, Egremont UD, Millom UD, pt Whitehaven RD (the pars not in Workington Dv), Whitehaven MB

WORKINGTON DIVISION
Arlecdon and Frizington UD, Aspatria UD, pt Cockermouth RD (Broughton, Broughton Moor, Camerton, Great Clifton, Little Clifton, Crosscanonby, Dearham, Flimby, Oughterside and Allerby, Ribton, Seaton, Stainburn, Winscales, Workington Rural), Harrington UD, Maryport UD, pt Whitehaven RD (Distington, Moresby, Weddicar), pt Wigton RD (Allonby, Hayton and Mealo, West Newton), Workington MB

1948—1970
PENRITH AND THE BORDER COUNTY CONSTITU-ENCY[2]
Alston with Garrigill RD, Border RD, Penrith RD, Penrith UD, Wigton UD

WHITEHAVEN COUNTY CONSTITUENCY
Ennerdale RD, Millom RD, Whitehaven MB
WORKINGTON COUNTY CONSTITUENCY
Cockermouth RD, Cockermouth UD, Keswick UD, Maryport UD, Workington MB

1970—*
PENRITH AND THE BORDER COUNTY CONSTITU-ENCY
Alston with Garrigill RD, Border RD, Penrith RD, Penrith UD, Wigton UD
WHITEHAVEN COUNTY CONSTITUENCY
Ennerdale RD, Millom RD, Whitehaven MB
WORKINGTON COUNTY CONSTITUENCY
Cockermouth RD, Cockermouth UD, Keswick UD, Maryport UD, Workington MB

DERBYSHIRE

BOROUGH CONSTITUENCIES[1]

CHESTERIELD BC (1948—*)
Chesterfield MB, pt Chesterfield RD (Brimington), Staveley UD

DERBY PARL BOR (1295—1948)
1295—1918: Little Chester (1867—1918), Derby All Saints, pt Derby St Alkmund (enlarged pt 1867—1918), Derby St Michael (pt 1295—1885, ent 1885—1918), Derby St Peter (pt 1295—1885, ent 1885—1918), Derby St Werburgh, Litchurch (1867—1918)
1918—48: Derby CB

DERBY NORTH BC[2] (1948—*)
pt Derby CB (wards of Abbey, Allestree [1970—*], Babington [1948—70], Becket [1948—70], Breadsall [1970—*], Bridge [1948—70], Chaddesden [1970—*], Darley [1970—*], Derwent, Friar Gate, King's Mead [1948—70], Mickleover [1970—*], Rowditch [1948—70], Spondon [1970—*]), pt Shardlow RD (Chaddesden)(1955—70)

DERBY SOUTH BC[2] (1948—*)
pt Derby CB (wards of Alvaston, Arboretum, Babington [1970—*], Castle [1948—70], Chellaston [1970—*], Dale [1948—70], Litchurch, Littleover [1970—*], Normanton, Osmaston, Pear Tree), pt Shardlow RD (Littleover) (1955—70)

COUNTY CONSTITUENCIES

1832—1867

NORTHERN DIVISION
Hds of High Peak, Scarsdale, pt Hd Wirksworth (pt Darley [Wensley and Snitterton], pt Hartington [Hartington Middle Quarter, Hartington Town Quarter, Hartington Upper Quarter], pt Youlgreave [Elton, Middleton and Smerill])

SOUTHERN DIVISION
Hds of Appletree, Morleston and Litchurch, Repton and Gresley, pt Hd Wirksworth (Ashbourne, pt Ashover [Dethick and Lea], Fenny Bentley, Bonsall, pt Bradbourne [main tp, Aldwark, Ballidon, Brassington, Lea Hall], Carsington, pt Crich [Tansley], pt Hartington [Hartington Nether Quarter], Hognaston, Kirk Ireton, Kniveton, Mapleton, Matlock, Parwich, Thorpe, Tissington, pt Wirksworth)

1867—1885

EAST DIVISION
Hd of Scarsdale

NORTH DIVISION
Hds of High Peak, Wirksworth

SOUTH DIVISION
Hds of Appletree, Morleston and Litchurch, Repton and Gresley

1885—1918

CHESTERFIELD DIVISION
pt Alfreton RSD, Chesterfield MB, pt Chesterfield PSD, *viz.*, Ashover, Ault Hucknall, Barlow, Brampton, Brimington, Calow, Chesterfield, Clay Lane, Glapwell, Hasland, Heath, Upper Langwith, Newbold and Dunston, Temple Normanton, Pleasley, Scarcliffe, Stretton, Sutton cum Duckmanton, Tapton, Tupton, Walton, Wingerworth, North Wingfield, Woodthorpe

HIGH PEAK DIVISION
Buxton PSD, Chapel en le Frith PSD, Glossop MB, Glossop PSD, *viz.*, Aston, Bamford; Beard, Thornsett, Ollersett and Whittle; Bradwell, Brough and Shatton, Buxton, Castleton, Chapel en le Frith; Chinley, Bugsworth and Brownside; Derwent, Edale, Fairfield, Fernilee, Glossop, Hartington Upper Quarter, Hayfield, Hope, Hope Woodlands, Ludworth and Chisworth, Mellor, Peak Forest, Thornhill, Wormhill

ILKESTON DIVISION
pt Derby PSD, Smalley PSD, *viz.*, Breaston, Codnor and Loscoe, Codnor Park, Dale Abbey, Denby, Draycott and Church Wilne, Long Eaton, Kirk Hallam, West Hallam, Heanor, Hopwell, Horsley, Horsley Woodhouse, Ilkeston, Mapperley, Morley, Ockbrook, Pentrich, Ripley, Risley, Sandiacre, Sawley and Wilsthorpe, Shipley, Smalley, Stanley, Stanton by Dale

MID DIVISION
pt Alfreton PSD, Belper PSD, *viz.*, Alderwasley, Alfreton, Ashleyhay, Belper, Blackwell, Brackenfield, Crich, Duffield, Hazlewood, Heage, Holbrook, Kilburn, Morton, South Normanton, Pilsley, Pinxton, Shirland and Higham, Shottle and Postern, Tibshelf, Turnditch, Wessington, Windley, South Wingfield

NORTH-EASTERN DIVISION
pt Chesterfield PSD, Eckington PSD, *viz.*, Barlborough, Beauchief, Beighton, Bolsover, Clowne, Coal Aston, Dore, Dronfield, Eckington, Elmton, Holmesfield, Killamarsh, Norton, Staveley, Totley, Unstone, Whittington, Whitwell

SOUTHERN DIVISION
pt Ashbourne PSD, pt Derby PSD, Repton PSD, Swadlincote PSD, *viz.*, Alvaston and Boulton, Allestree, pt Appleby, Ash, Aston upon Trent, Barrow upon Trent, Bearwardcote, The Boundary, Brailsford, Breadsall, Bretby, Burnaston, Caldwell, Calke, Catton, Chaddesden, Chellaston, Chilcote, Coton in the Elms, Croxall, Dalbury Lees, Derby Hills, pt Derby St Alkmund, Drakelow, Little Eaton, Egginton, Elvaston, Etwall, Findern, Foremark, Castle Gresley, Church Gresley, Hartshorne, Ingleby, Kedleston, Kirk Langley, Linton, Littleover, Lullington, Mackworth, Markeaton, Measham, Melbourne, Mercaston, Mickleover, Mugginton, Newton Solney, Normanton, pt Oakthorpe and Donisthorpe, Osmaston, Quarndon,

807

Radbourne, Ravensdale Park, Repton, Rosliston, Shardlow and Great Wilne, Sinfin and Arleston, Sinfin Moor, Smisby, Spondon, Stanton and Newhall, Stanton by Bridge, Stapenhill, Stretton en le Field, Swadlincote, Swarkestone, Ticknall, Trusley, Twyford and Stenson, Walton upon Trent, Weston Underwood, Weston upon Trent, Willesley, Willington, Winshill

WESTERN DIVISION

Appletree PSD, pt Ashbourne PSD, Bakewell PSD, Wirksworth PSD, *viz.*, Abney and Abney Grange, Aldwark, Alkmonton, Ashbourne, Ashford, Atlow, Bakewell, Ballidon, Barton Blount, Baslow and Bubnell, Beeley, Fenny Bentley, Hungry Bentley, Biggin, Birchover, Blackwell, Bonsall, Boyleston, Bradbourne, Bradley, Brassington, Church Broughton, Brushfield, Callow, Calver, Carsington, Chatsworth, Chelmorton, Clifton and Compton, Cromford, Cubley, Curbar, Darley, Dethick and Lea, Doveridge, Eaton and Alsop, Edensor, Edlaston and Wyaston, Elton, Eyam, Eyam Woodlands, Flagg, Foolow, pt Foston and Scropton, Froggatt, Gratton, Grindlow, Nether Haddon, Over Haddon, Hargate Manor, Harthill, Hartington Middle Quarter, Hartington Nether Quarter, Hartington Town Quarter, Hassop, Hathersage, Hatton, Hazlebadge, Highlow, Hilton, Hognaston, Hollington, Hoon, Hopton and Griffe Grange, Great Hucklow, Little Hucklow, Hulland, Hulland Ward, Hulland Ward Intakes, Idridgehay and Alton, Kirk Ireton, Ireton Wood, Ivonbrook Grange, Kniveton, Lea Hall, Litton, Longford, Great Longstone, Little Longstone, Mapleton, Marston Montgomery, Marston on Dove, Matlock, Middleton and Smerrill, Middleton by Wirksworth, Monyash, Newton Grange, Norbury and Roston, Offcote and Underwood, Offerton, Osleston and Thurvaston, Osmaston, Outseats, Nether Padley, Parwich, Pilsley, Rodsley, Rowland, Great Rowsley, Sheldon, Shirley, Snelston, Somersal Herbert, Stanton, Stoke, Stony Middleton, Sturston, Stydd, Sudbury, Sutton on the Hill, Taddington, Tansley, Thorpe, Tideswell, Tissington, Wardlow, Wensley and Snitterton, Wheston, Winster, Wirksworth, Yeaveley, Yeldersley, Youlgreave

1918—1948

BELPER DIVISION

Alfreton UD, Belper RD, Belper UD, Heage UD, pt Repton RD (the pars neither in Southern Dv nor in Western Dv)

CHESTERFIELD DIVISION

Brampton and Walton UD, Chesterfield MB, pt Chesterfield RD (Barlow, Brimington, Calow, Hasland, Temple Normanton, Sutton cum Duckmanton, Tapton, Wingerworth), Whittington and Newbold UD

CLAY CROSS DIVISION

Blackwell RD, pt Chesterfield RD (the pars neither in Chesterfield Dv nor in North Eastern Dv), Clay Cross UD

HIGH PEAK DIVISION

pt Bakewell RD (2 detached pts Outseats), Buxton MB, pt Chapel en le Frith RD (all except 2 detached pts Derwent), Glossop MB, Glossop Dale RD, Hayfield RD, New Mills UD

ILKESTON DIVISION

Heanor UD, Ilkeston MB, Ripley UD, Unnamed RD

NORTH-EASTERN DIVISION

Bolsover UD, pt Chesterfield RD (Beighton, Coal Aston, Dronfield Woodhouse, Eckington, Holmesfield, Killamarsh, Staveley, Unstone), Clowne RD, Dronfield UD, Norton RD

SOUTHERN DIVISION

Alvaston and Boulton UD, Long Eaton UD, Hartshorn and Seals RD, pt Repton RD (Caldwell, Catton, Coton in the Elms, Drakelow, Castle Gresley, Linton, Lullington, Rosliston, Walton upon Trent), Shardlow RD, Swadlincote District UD

WESTERN DIVISION

Ashbourne RD, Ashbourne UD, pt Bakewell RD (all except 2 detached pts of Outseats), Bakewell UD, Baslow and Bubnell UD, Bonsall UD, pt Chapel en le Frith RD (2 detached pts Derwent), North Darley UD, South Darley UD, Matlock UD, Matlock Bath and Scarthin Nick UD, pt Repton RD (Barton Blount, Church Broughton, Foston and Scropton, Hatton, Hilton, Hoon, Marston on Dove, Osleston and Thurvaston, Sutton on the Hill), Sudbury RD, Wirksworth UD

1948—1970

BELPER COUNTY CONSTITUENCY

pt Belper RD (all except Shipley), Belper UD, Repton RD, Swadlincote District UD

BOLSOVER COUNTY CONSTITUENCY

Blackwell RD, Bolsover UD, Clowne RD

NORTH EAST DERBYSHIRE COUNTY CONSTITU-ENCY

pt Chesterfield RD (all except Brimington), Clay Cross UD, Dronfield UD

SOUTH EAST DERBYSHIRE COUNTY CONSTITU-ENCY[2]

Long Eaton UD, Shardlow RD (ent 1948—55, pt 1955—70 [all except Chaddesden, Littleover])

WEST DERBYSHIRE COUNTY CONSTITUENCY

Ashbourne RD, Ashbourne UD, Bakewell RD, Bakewell UD, Matlock UD, Wirksworth UD

HIGH PEAK COUNTY CONSTITUENCY

Buxton MB, Chapel en le Frith RD, Glossop MB, New Mills UD, Whaley Bridge UD

ILKESTON COUNTY CONSTITUENCY

Alfreton UD, pt Belper RD (Shipley), Heanor UD, Ilkeston MB, Ripley UD

1970—*

BELPER COUNTY CONSTITUENCY

pt Belper RD (all except Shipley), Belper UD, Repton RD, Swadlincote UD

BOLSOVER COUNTY CONSTITUENCY

Blackwell RD, Bolsover UD, Clowne RD

NORTH EAST DERBYSHIRE COUNTY CONSTITU-ENCY

pt Chesterfield RD (all except Brimington), Clay Cross UD, Dronfield UD

SOUTH EAST DERBYSHIRE COUNTY CONSTITU-ENCY

South East Derbyshire RD, Long Eaton UD

WEST DERBYSHIRE COUNTY CONSTITUENCY
Ashbourne RD, Ashbourne UD, Bakewell RD, Bakewell UD, Matlock UD, Wirksworth UD

HIGH PEAK COUNTY CONSTITUENCY
Buxton MB, Chapel en le Frith RD, Glossop MB, New Mills UD, Whaley Bridge UD

ILKESTON COUNTY CONSTITUENCY
Alfreton UD, pt Belper RD (Shipley), Heanor UD, Ilkeston MB, Ripley UD

COUNTY DURHAM

BOROUGH CONSTITUENCIES

BLAYDON BC (1970—*)
Blaydon UD, Ryton UD, Whickham UD
DARLINGTON PARL BOR/BC (1867—*) [1 mbr]
1867—1918: pt Cockerton (1885—1918), Darlington (ent 1867—85, pt 1885—1918), pt Haughton le Skerne (1885—1918)
1918—:* Darlington CB
DURHAM PARL BOR (1832—1918) [2 mbrs 1832—85, 1 mbr 1885—1918]
pt Crossgate, Durham Castle and Precincts, Durham College, Durham Magdalen Place, Durham St Mary le Bow [North Bailey], Durham St Mary the Less [South Bailey], Durham St Nicholas, pt Elvet, Framwellgate (pt 1832—67, ent 1867—1918), pt St Giles, pt St Oswald (1832—67)
DURHAM AND FRAMWELLGATE PARL BOR (1661—1832)
Durham St Nicholas, pt St Oswald
GATESHEAD PARL BOR (1832—1948) [1 mbr]
1832—1918: Gateshead, pt Heworth
1918—48: Gateshead CB
GATESHEAD EAST BC[1] (1948—*)
Felling UD (1955—*), pt Gateshead CB (the wards of Claxton [1960—*], East [1948—60], East-Central [1948—55], South-Central [1948—60], Enfield [1960—*], Low Fell [1960—*], North-East [1948—55], South [1948—60], Wrekenton [1960—*])
GATESHEAD WEST BC[1] (1948—*)
pt Gateshead CB (the wards of Askew [1960—*], Bensham [1960—*], Central [1948—60], West-Central [1948—60], Central East [1955—60], Chandless [1960—*], Claremont [1960—*], North [1948—60], North-East [1955—60], North West [1948—60], Riverside [1960—*], Saltwell [1960—*], Shipcote [1960—*], Teams [1960—*], West [1948—60])
HARTLEPOOL BC (1970—*)
Hartlepool CB

THE HARTLEPOOLS PARL BOR/BC[2] (1867—1970) [1 mbr]
1867—1918: Hartlepool, Seaton Carew, Stranton, Throston
1918—70: Hartlepool MB, West Hartlepool CB
JARROW BC[3] (1951—*)
Boldon UD, Felling UD (1951—55), Hebburn UD, Jarrow MB
MORPETH PARL BOR (primarily Northumb, incl from 1832 Bedlington in Durham, that par civ transf 1844 to Northumb, qv)
SOUTH SHIELDS PARL BOR/BC[3] (1832—*) [1 mbr]
South Shields, Westoe (1832—1918)
STOCKTON ON TEES PARL BOR/BC[4] (1867—1970) (Durham, *Yorks N Riding [1867—1948]*)
1867—1918: pt *Linthorpe*, pt Norton, Stockton on Tees, *Thornaby*
1918—70: Stockton on Tees MB, *Thornaby on Tees MB (1918—48)*
SUNDERLAND PARL BOR (1832—1948) [2 mbrs 1832—85, 1 mbr 1885—1918, 2 mbrs 1918—48]
1832—1918: Bishopwearmouth, Bishopwearmouth Panns, Monkwearmouth, Monkwearmouth Shore, pt Ryhope (1867—1918), Southwick, Sunderland
1918—48: Southwick on Wear UD, Sunderland CB
SUNDERLAND NORTH BC[5] (1948—*)
pt Sunderland CB (the wards of Bridge [1948—70], Castletown [1970—*], Central, Colliery, Deptford, Downhill [1970—*)], Ford [1970—*], Fulwell, Hylton Castle [1970—*], Monkwearmouth, Monkwearmouth Shore [1948—70], Pallion [1970—*], Roker, Southwick)
SUNDERLAND SOUTH BC[5] (1948—*)
pt Sunderland CB (the wards of Bishopwearmouth, Hendon, Humbledon, Pallion [1948—70], Park [1948—70], Pennywell [1952—*], Ryhope [1970—*], St Chad's [1970—*], St Michael's, Silksworth [1970—*], Sunderland East [1948—52], Thorney Close [1952—*], Thornhill, West [1948—52])

COUNTY CONSTITUENCIES

Co Durham returned members to Parliament beginning in 1661.

1832—1885[6]
NORTHERN DIVISION
Wds of Chester, Easington
SOUTHERN DIVISION
Wds of Darlington, Stockton

1885—1918
BISHOP AUCKLAND DIVISION
pt Bishop Auckland PSD, *viz.*, Bishop Auckland, Auckland St Andrew, Binchester, Byers Green, Chilton, Coundon, Coundon Grange, Eldon, Escomb,

Helmington Row, Hunwick and Helmington, Merrington, Middlestone, Middridge, Middridge Grange, Newfield, Newton Cap, Old Park, Pollard's Lands, Shildon, East Thickley, Westerton, Whitworth, Windlestone
BARNARD CASTLE DIVISION
pt Bishop Auckland PSD, Barnard Castle and Staindrop PSD, pt Stanhope PSD, Wolsingham PSD, *viz.*, West Auckland, Auckland St Helen, Barnard Castle, North Bedburn, South Bedburn, Bolam, Cleatlam, Cockfield, Crook and Billy Row, Eggleston, Evenwood and

Barony, Forest and Frith, Gainford, Hamsterley, Headlam, Hilton, Ingleton, Langleydale and Shotton, Langton, Lynesack and Softley, Middleton in Teesdale, Morton Tinmouth, Newbiggin, Raby with Keverstone, Staindrop, Stanhope, Streatlam and Stainton, Wackerfield, Westwick, Whorlton, Witton le Wear, Wolsingham, Woodland

CHESTER LE STREET DIVISION

Chester le Street PSD, pt Gateshead PSD, *viz.*, Barmston, Birtley, Chester le Street, Chopwell, Crawcrook, Edmondsley, Harraton, Lamesley, Ouston, Pelton, Plawsworth, Ryton, Ryton Woodside, Stella, Urpeth, Usworth, Waldridge, Washington, Whickham, Winston, Winlaton

HOUGHTON LE SPRING DIVISION

Houghton le Spring PSD, pt Seaham Harbour PSD, Sunderland PSD, *viz.*, South Biddick, Burdon, Burnmoor, Cocken, Dalton le Sale, Great Eppleton, Little Eppleton, Ford, Fulwell, East and Middle Herrington, West Herrington, Hetton le Hole, Houghton le Spring, Hylton, Lambton, Great Lumley, Little Lumley, Moor House, Moorsley, Morton Grange, East Murton, Newbottle, Offerton, Penshaw, East Rainton, West Rainton, pt Ryhope, Seaham, Seaton with Slingley, Silksworth, Tunstall, Warden Law

JARROW DIVISION

pt Gateshead PSD, Jarrow MB, South Shields PSD, *viz.*, Boldon, Harton; Hedworth, Monkton and Jarrow; pt Heworth, Whitburn

MID DIVISION

pt Durham PSD, *viz.*, Bishop Middleham, Brancepeth, Brandon and Byshottles, Broom, Cassop, Cornforth, Coxhoe, pt Crossgate, pt Elvet, Ferryhill, Hett, Kimblesworth, Mainsforth, Pittington, Quarrington, pt St Giles, Shadforth, Sherburn, Sherburn House, Shincliffe, Stockley, Sunderland Bridge, Thrislington, Tudhoe, Whitwell House, Willington, Witton Gilbert

NORTH-WESTERN DIVISION

Lanchester and Consett PSD, pt Stanhope PSD, *viz.*, Benfieldside, Billingside, Collierley, Conside and Knitsley, Cornsay, Ebchester, Edmondbeyers, Esh, Greencroft, Healeyfield, Hedleyhope, Hunstanworth, Iveston, Kyo, Lanchester, Langley, Medomsley, Muggleswick, Satley, Tanfield

SOUTH-EASTERN DIVISION

pt Castle Eden PSD, Darlington PSD, West Hartlepool PSD, pt Seaham Harbour PSD, Stockton on Tees PSD, *viz.*, Aislaby, Archdeacon Newton, Great Aycliffe, School Aycliffe, Barmpton, Cowpen Bewley, Newton Bewley, Billingham, Bishopton, Blackwell, Bradbury, Brafferton, Brierton, Great Burdon, Butterwick and Oldacres, Carlton, Castle Eden, Claxton, Coatham Mundeville, pt Cockerton, Cold Hesledon, High Coniscliffe, Low Coniscliffe, Dalton Piercy, Dawdon, Denton, Low Dinsdale, Easington, Egglescliffe, Elstob, Elton, Elwick, Elwick Hall, Embleton, Fishburn, Foxton and Shotton, Garmondsway Moor, Greatham, Grindon, Hart, East Hartburn, Haswell, Hawthorn, Heighington, Houghton le Side, Hurworth, Hutton Henry, Kelloe, Killerby, Middleton St George, Monk Hesleden, Mordon, Morton Palms, Neasham, Nesbitt, East and West Newbiggin, Newsham, Long

Newton, pt Norton, Piercebridge, Preston le Skerne, Preston on Tees, Redmarshall, Redworth, Sadberge, Sedgefield, Sheraton with Hulam, Shotton, Sockburn, Great Stainton, Little Stainton, Stillington, Summerhouse, Thornley, Thorpe Bulmer, Trimdon, Walworth, Whessoe, Whitton, Wingate, Wolviston, Woodham

1918—1948

BISHOP AUCKLAND DIVISION

pt Auckland RD (the pars neither in Barnard Castle Dv nor in Spennymoor Dv), Bishop Auckland UD, Shildon UD

BARNARD CASTLE DIVISION

pt Auckland RD (South Bedburn, Hamsterley), Barnard Castle RD, Barnard Castle UD, pt Lanchester RD (the pars neither in Consett Dv nor Spennymoor Dv), Stanhope UD, Weardale RD

BLAYDON DIVISION

Blaydon UD, Ryton UD, Tanfield UD, Whickham UD

CHESTER LE STREET DIVISION

Chester le Street RD, Chester le Street UD

CONSETT DIVISION

Annfield Plain UD, Benfieldside UD, Consett UD, Leadgate UD, pt Lanchester RD (Craghead, Ebchester, Healeyfield, Knitsley, Medomsley), Stanley UD

DURHAM DIVISION

Durham MB, pt Durham RD (all except Brancepeth), Hetton UD, pt Houghton le Spring RD (Great Eppleton, Little Eppleton, Moor House, Moorsley, East Rainton, West Rainton)

HOUGHTON LE SPRING DIVISION

pt Houghton le Spring RD (the pars not in Durham Dv), Houghton le Spring UD, South Shields RD, Sunderland RD

JARROW DIVISION

Felling UD, Hebburn UD, Jarrow MB

SEAHAM DIVISION

Easington RD, Seaham Harbour UD

SEDGEFIELD DIVISION

Darlington RD, Hartlepool RD, Sedgefield RD, Stockton RD

SPENNYMOOR DIVISION

pt Auckland RD (North Bedburn, Helmington Row, Hunwick and Helmington), Brandon and Byshottles UD, Crook UD, pt Durham RD (Brancepeth), pt Lanchester RD (Hedleyhope), Spennymoor UD, Tow Law UD, Willington UD

1948—1970

BISHOP AUCKLAND COUNTY CONSTITUENCY[7]

Bishop Auckland UD, Barnard Castle RD, Barnard Castle UD, Shildon UD

BLAYDON COUNTY CONSTITUENCY

Blaydon UD, Ryton UD, Whickham UD

CHESTER LE STREET COUNTY CONSTITUENCY

Chester le Street RD, Chester le Street UD, Washington UD

CONSETT COUNTY CONSTITUENCY

Consett UD, Stanley UD

DURHAM COUNTY CONSTITUENCY

Durham MB, Durham RD, Hetton UD, Spennymoor UD

NORTH WEST DURHAM COUNTY CONSTITU-
ENCY
Brandon and Byshottles UD, Crook and Willington
UD, Lanchester RD, Tow Law UD, Weardale RD
EASINGTON COUNTY CONSTITUENCY
Easington RD
HOUGHTON LE SPRING COUNTY CONSTITU-
ENCY[5]
Houghton le Spring UD, Seaham UD, Sunderland RD
JARROW COUNTY CONSTITUENCY (1948—51[3])
Boldon UD, Felling UD, Hebburn UD, Jarrow MB
SEDGEFIELD COUNTY CONSTITUENCY[8]
Billingham UD, Darlington RD, Sedgefield RD,
Stockton RD

*1970—**
BISHOP AUCKLAND COUNTY CONSTITUENCY
Bishop Auckland UD, Barnard Castle RD, Barnard
Castle UD, Darlington RD, Shildon UD
CHESTER LE STREET COUNTY CONSTITUENCY
Chester le Street RD, Chester le Street UD, Washington
UD

CONSETT COUNTY CONSTITUENCY
Consett UD, Stanley UD
DURHAM COUNTY CONSTITUENCY
Durham MB, pt Durham RD (all except Brancepeth),
Sedgefield RD
NORTH WEST DURHAM COUNTY CONSTITU-
ENCY
Brandon and Byshottles UD, Crook and Willington
UD, pt Durham RD (Brancepeth), Lanchester RD,
Spennymoor UD, Tow Law UD, Weardale RD
EASINGTON COUNTY CONSTITUENCY
pt Easington RD (Castle Eden, Easington, Haswell,
Hawthorn, Horden, Hutton Henry, Monk Hesleden,
Nesbitt, Peterlee, Sheraton with Hulam, Shotton,
Thornley, Wingate), Stockton RD
HOUGHTON LE SPRING COUNTY CONSTITU-
ENCY
pt Easington RD (Burdon, Cold Hesledon, Dalton le
Dale, East Murton, Seaton with Slingley, Warden
Law), Hetton UD, Houghton le Spring UD, Seaham
UD

HEREFORDSHIRE

BOROUGH CONSTITUENCIES[1]

BROMYARD PARL BOR (1305 only)
pt Bromyard

HEREFORD PARL BOR (1295—1918)
pt Breinton (1832—85), pt Upper Bullingham (1832—85), Hereford All Saints (pt 1295—1832, ent 1832—85), Hereford St John the Baptist (pt 1295—1832, ent 1832—85), pt Hereford St Martin, Hereford St Nicholas, Hereford St Owen, Hereford St Peter, Hereford the Vineyard, pt Holmer and Shelwick (1832—85), Huntington (1832—85), pt Tupsley (1832—85)

LEDBURY PARL BOR (1295, 1305 only)
pt Ledbury

LEOMINSTER PARL BOR (1295—1885)
Leominster (pt 1295—1832, ent [incl area Leominster Out] 1832—67), Leominster Borough (1867—85), Leominster Out (1867—85)

LUDLOW PARL BOR (1461—1885 [1 mbr 1867—85])
(*Salop* [1461—1885], Heref [1832—85])
pt Bromfield (1832—85), Ludford[2] (1832—85), *Ludlow [St Lawrence], Ludlow Castle (1832—85), pt Stanton Lacy (1832—85)*

ROSS PARL BOR (1305 only)
pt Ross

WEOBLEY PARL BOR (1295—1306, 1628—1832)
Weobley

COUNTY CONSTITUENCIES

1832—1885
Heref was undivided for parl purposes until 1885.

1885—1918
LEOMINSTER (or NORTHERN) DIVISION
Bredwardine PSD, Bromyard PSD, Kington PSD, Leominster MB, Leominster PSD, Weobley PSD, Wigmore PSD, *viz.*, Adforton, Almeley, Aston, Avenbury, Aymestrey, Birley, Bishopstone, Blakemere, Bodenham, Brampton Bryan, Bredenbury, Bredwardine, Bridge Sollers, Brilley, Brimfield, Brinsop, Brobury, Lower Brockhampton, Bromyard, Buckton and Coxall, Burrington, Byford, Byton, Canon Pyon, Clifford, Collington, Combe, Little Cowarne, Much Cowarne, Cradley, Croft, Cusop, Dilwyn, Docklow, Dorstone, Downton, Eardisland, Eardisley, Edvin Ralph, Elton, Evesbatch; Eye, Moreton and Ashton; Eyton, Felton, Ford, Bishop's Frome, Grendon Bishop, Grendon Warren, New Hampton, Hampton Charles, Hampton Wafer, Lower Harpton, Hatfield, Little Hereford, Hope under Dinmore, Humber, Huntington, Kimbolton, King's Pyon, Kingsland, Kington, Kinnersley, Lower Kinsham, Upper Kinsham, Knill, Laysters, Leinthalll Starkes, pt Leintwardine North Side, Leominster Borough, Leominster Out, Letton, Lingen, Linton, Lucton, pt Ludford, Luston, Lyonshall, Mansell Gamage, Mansell Lacy, Middleton on the Hill, Moccas, Monkland, Monnington on Wye, Moreton Jeffreys, Newton, Norton Canon, Norton with Brockhampton, Ocle Pychard, Orleton, Pembridge, Pencombe, Preston on Wye, Pudlestone, pt Richards Castle; Rodd, Nash and Little Brampton; Saltmarshe, Upper Sapey, Sarnesfield, Shobdon, Stanford Bishop, Stapleton, Staunton on Arrow, Staunton on Wye, pt Stoke Bliss, Stoke Lacy, Stoke Prior, Stretford, Tedstone Delamere, Tedstone Wafer, Thornbury, Titley, Ullingswick, Wacton; Walford, Letton and Newton; Weobley, Whitbourne, Whitney, Wigmore, Willersley, Willey, Winforton, Winslow, Wolferlow, Wormsley, Yarpole, Yazor

ROSS (or SOUTHERN) DIVISION
Dore PSD, Harewood's End PSD, Hereford MB, Hereford PSD, Ledbury PSD, Ross PSD, *viz.*, Abbey Dore, Aconbury, Allensmore, Amberley, Ashperton, Aston Ingham, Aylton, Bacton, Ballingham, Bartestree, Little Birch, Much Birch, Bolstone, Bosbury, Brampton Abbotts, Breinton, Bridstow, Brockhampton, Lower Bullingham, Upper Bullingham, Burghill, Callow, How Caple, King's Caple, Clehonger, Coddington, Colwall, Craswall, Credenhill, Little Dewchurch, Much Dewchurch, Dewsall, Dinedor, Dinmore, Donnington, Dormington, Dulas, Eastnor, Eaton Bishop, Egleton, Ewyas Harold, Fownhope, Foy, Canon Frome, Castle Frome, Fwthog, Ganarew, Garway, Goodrich, Grafton, Hampton Bishop, Harewood, Haywood, Hentland, Hereford All Saints, Hereford St John the Baptist, Hereford St Martin, Hereford St Nicholas, Hereford St Owen, Hereford St Peter, Hereford The Vineyard, Holme Lacy, Holmer, Holmer Within, Hope Mansell, Huntington, Kenchester, Kenderchurch, Kentchurch, Kilpeck, Kingstone, Lea, Ledbury, Linton, Llancillo, Llandinabo, Llangarren, Llanrothal, Llanveynoe, Llanwarne, Longtown, Lugwardine, Madley, Little Marcle, Much Marcle, Marden, Marstow, Michaelchurch Escley, Mordiford, Moreton on Lugg, Munsley, Newton, Orcop, Pencoyd, Peterchurch, Peterstow, Pipe and Lyde, Pixley, Preston Wynne, Putley, Ross, Rowlstone, St Devereux, St Margaret's, St Weonards, Sellack, Sellington, Sollers Hope, Stoke Edith, Stretton Grandison, Stretton Sugwas, Sutton, Tarrington, Thruxton, Tretire with Michaelchurch, Treville, Tupsley, Turnastone, Upton Bishop, Vowchurch, Walford, Walterstone, Welsh Bicknor, Welsh Newton, Westhide, Weston Beggard, Weston under Penyard, Whitchurch, Withington, Woodhope, Wormbridge, Yarkhill, Yatton

1918—1948

HEREFORD DIVISION

Dore RD, Hereford MB, pt Hereford RD (the pars not in Leominster Dv), pt Ledbury RD (the pars not in Leominster Dv), Ledbury UD, Ross RD, Ross UD, Whitchurch RD

LEOMINSTER DIVISION

Bredwardine RD, Bromyard RD, Bromyard UD, pt Hereford RD (Bartestree, Breinton, Burghill, Credenhill, Dinmore, Holmer, Kenchester, Lugwardine, Marden, Moreton on Lugg, Pipe and Lyde, Preston Wynne, Stretton Sugwas, Sutton, Wellington, Westhide, Weston Beggard, Withington), Kington RD, Kington UD, pt Ledbury RD (Ashperton, Bosbury, Coddington, Colwall, Egleton, Canon Frome, Castle Frome, Mathon Rural, Munsley, Pixley, Stretton Grandison, Tarrington, Yarkhill), Leominster MB, Leominster RD, Weobley RD, Wigmore RD

1948—1970

HEREFORD COUNTY CONSTITUENCY

Dore and Bredwardine RD, Hereford MB, pt Hereford RD (Aconbury, Allensmore, Little Birch, Much Birch, Bolstone, Lower Bullingham, Callow, Clehonger, Little Dewchurch, Much Dewchurch, Dewsall, Dinedor, Dormington, Eaton Bishop, Fownhope, Grafton, Hampton Bishop, Haywood, Holme Lacy, Mordisford, Stoke Edith), Ross and Whitchurch RD, Ross on Wye UD

LEOMINSTER COUNTY CONSTITUENCY

Bromyard RD, Bromyard UD, pt Hereford RD (Bartestree, Breinton, Burghill, Credenhill, Dinmore, Holmer, Kenchester, Lugwardine, Marden, Moreton on Lugg, Pipe and Lyde, Preston Wynne, Stretton Sugwas, Sutton, Wellington, Westhide, Weston Beggard, Withington), Kington RD, Kington UD, Ledbury RD, Leominster MB, Leominster and Wigmore RD, Weobley RD

1970—*

HEREFORD COUNTY CONSTITUENCY

Dore and Bredwardine RD, Hereford MB, pt Hereford RD (Aconbury, Allensmore, Little Birch, Much Birch, Bolstone, Lower Bullingham, Callow, Clehonger, Little Dewchurch, Much Dewchurch, Dewsall, Dinedor, Dormington, Eaton Bishop, Fownhope, Grafton, Hampton Bishop, Haywood, Holme Lacy, Mordiford, Stoke Edith), Ross and Whitchurch RD, Ross on Wye UD

LEOMINSTER COUNTY CONSTITUENCY

Bromyard RD, pt Hereford RD (Bartestree, Breinton, Burghill, Credenhill, Dinmore, Holmer, Kenchester, Lugwardine, Marden, Moreton on Lugg, Pipe and Lyde, Preston Wynne, Stretton Sugwas, Sutton, Wellington, Westhide, Weston Beggard, Withington), Kington RD, Kington UD, Ledbury RD, Leominster MB, Leominster and Wigmore RD, Weobley RD

LANCASHIRE

BOROUGH CONSTITUENCIES[1]

ACCRINGTON PARL BOR/BC (1918—*)
Accrington MB, Church UD, Clayton le Moors UD, Oswaldtwistle UD, Rishton UD

ASHTON UNDER LYNE PARL BOR/BC[2] (1832—*) [Lancs, Ches (1867—1918)]
1832—1918: pt Ashton under Lyne (enlarged pt 1867—85, further enlarged pt 1885—1918), *pt Dukinfield (1867—1918)*
1918—:* Ashton under Lyne MB, Droylsden UD (1955—*), Hurst UD, Limehurst RD (1948—55), Mossley MB

BARROW IN FURNESS PARL BOR/BC (1885—*)
Barrow in Furness CB, Dalton in Furness UD (1948—*)

BLACKBURN PARL BOR (1832—1948)
1832—1918: Blackburn, pt Lower Darwen (1885—1918), Little Haywood (pt 1867—85, ent 1885—1918), Livesey (pt 1867—85, ent 1885—1918), Witton (pt 1867—85, ent 1885—1918)
1918—48: Blackburn CB

BLACKBURN BC (1955—*)
pt Blackburn CB (wards of Park, St John's, St Jude's, St Luke's, St Matthew's, St Michael's, St Paul's, St Silas's, St Stephens's, St Thomas's, Trinity)

BLACKBURN EAST BC (1948—55[3])
pt Blackburn CB (wards of St John's, St Mary's, St Matthew's, St Michael's, St Stephen's, St Thomas's, Trinity)

BLACKBURN WEST BC (1948—55[3])
pt Blackburn CB (wards of Park, St Andrew's, St Luke's, St Mark's, St Paul's, St Peter's, St Silas's)

BLACKPOOL PARL BOR[4] (1918—45)
Bispham with Norbreck UD, Blackpool CB, Lytham UD, St Anne's on the Sea UD

BLACKPOOL NORTH PARL BOR/BC[5] (1945—*)
pt Blackpool CB (wards of Alexandra [1945—48], Anchorsholme [1964—*], Bank Hey, Bispham, Brunswick, Claremont, Foxhall [1945—64], Layton, Talbot, Tyldesley [1945—48], Warbreck)

BLACKPOOL SOUTH PARL BOR/BC[6] (1945—*)
pt Blackpool CB (wards of Alexandra [1948—*], Clifton [1964—*], Foxhall [1964—*], Marton, Squires Gate [1964—*], Stanley, Tyldesley [1948—*], Victoria, Waterloo)

BOLTON PARL BOR (1832—1948)
1832—1918: Great Bolton, Little Bolton (pt 1832—67, enlarged pt 1867—85, ent 1885—1918), pt Halliwell (1867—1918), pt Rumworth (1885—1918), pt Sharples (1867—1918), pt Tonge with Haulgh
1918—48: Bolton CB

BOLTON EAST BC (1948—*)
pt Bolton CB (wards of Astley Bridge, Bradford, Church, East, Hulton, Darcy Lever cum Breightmet, Great Lever, North, Tonge)

BOLTON WEST BC (1948—*)
pt Bolton CB (wards of Deane cum Lostock, Derby, Halliwell, Heaton, Rumworth, Smithills, West)

BOOTLE PARL BOR/BC[7] (1918—*)
Bootle CB, Litherland UD (1948—55), Litherland UD (1970—*)

BURNLEY PARL BOR/BC (1867—*)
1867—1918: Burnley, Habergham Eaves
1918—:* Burnley CB

BURY PARL BOR (1832—1948)
1832—1918: pt Birtle cum Bamford (1885—1918), Bury, pt Elton, pt Heap (1885—1918), pt Pilsworth (1885—1918), pt Radcliffe (1885—1918), pt Tottington Lower End (1885—1918), pt Walmersley cum Shuttleworth (1885—1918)
1918—48: Bury CB, Tottington UD

BURY AND RADCLIFFE BC (1948—*)
Bury CB, Radcliffe MB, Tottington UD

CLITHEROE PARL BOR (1558—1885) [1 mbr 1832—85]
1558—1832: pt Whalley [tp Clitheroe]
1832—85: Chatburn, Clitheroe, Clitheroe Castle, Downham, Mearley; Little Mitton, Henthorn and Coldcoats; Pendleton, Twiston, Whalley, Wiswell, Worston

CROSBY BC[8] (1948—*)
Crosby MB, Formby UD (1970—*), pt West Lancashire RD (1948—55: Ford), pt West Lancashire RD (1970—*: Altcar, Ince Blundell, Maghull, pt Sefton, Thornton), Litherland UD (1955—70)

DROYLSDEN BC (1948—55[2])
Audenshaw UD, Denton UD, Droylsden UD, Failsworth UD

ECCLES PARL BOR/BC[9] (1918—*)
Eccles MB, Swinton and Pendlebury MB (1948—*), Swinton and Pendlebury UD (1918—48)

FARNWORTH BC (1970—*)
Farnworth MB, Kearsley UD, Little Lever UD, Worsley UD

INCE BC (1970—*)
Abram UD, Ashton in Makerfield UD, Billinge and Winstanley UD, Ince in Makerfield UD, Orrell UD, Skelmersdale and Holland UD

LANCASTER PARL BOR (irregularly 1295—1359, regularly 1547—1867)
pt Bulk (1832—67), Lancaster

LEIGH PARL BOR/BC (1918—*)
Atherton UD, Leigh MB, Tyldesley UD (1948—*), Tyldesley with Shakerley UD (1918—48)

LIVERPOOL PARL BOR (1295, 1306, 1547—1885)
pt West Derby (1832—85), Everton (1832—85), Kirkdale (1832—85), Liverpool (pt until 1832, ent 1832—85), pt Toxteth Park (1832—85)

LIVERPOOL, ABERCROMBY PARL BOR (1885—1918)
pt Liverpool (wards of Abercromby, Castle Street, Great George, Pitt Street, Rodney Street, St Peter)

LIVERPOOL, WEST DERBY PARL BOR/BC[8] (1885—*)

1885—1918: pt Liverpool (ward of West Derby)

1918—):* pt Liverpool CB (wards of Anfield [1918—48], Breckfield [1918—48], Clubmoor [1955—*], Croxteth [1948—*], West Derby [1918—55], Dovecot [1955—*], Gillmoss [1955—*])

LIVERPOOL, EDGE HILL PARL BOR/BC[10] (1918—*)

pt Liverpool CB (wards of Edge Hill [1918—55], Fairfield [1948—*], Kensington [pt 1918—48, ent 1948—*], Low Hill [1918—55], Low Hill [1970—*], Picton [1955—*], Smithdown [1955—*])

LIVERPOOL, EVERTON PARL BOR (1885—1948)

1885—1918: pt Everton

1918—48: pt Liverpool CB (wards of Everton, Netherfield)

LIVERPOOL, EXCHANGE PARL BOR/BC[10] (1885—1970)

1885—1918: pt Liverpool (wards of Exchange, Lime Street, St Ann, St Paul, Vauxhall)

1918—70: pt Liverpool CB (wards of Abercromby, Brunswick [1948—55], Castle Street [1918—55], Central [1955—70], Exchange [1918—55], Granby [1948—70], Great George [1918—55], Low Hill [1955—70], St Anne's [1918—55], St James [1955—70], St Peter's [1918—55], Vauxhall [pt 1918—48, ent 1948—55])

LIVERPOOL, FAIRFIELD PARL BOR (1918—48)

pt Liverpool CB (wards of Fairfield, pt Kensington, Old Swan)

LIVERPOOL, GARSTON BC[10] (1948—*)

pt Liverpool CB (wards of Aigburth, Allerton, Childwall [1948—55], Garston [1948—55], St Mary's [1955—*], Speke [1955—*], Woolton [1955—*], Little Woolton [1948—55], Much Woolton [1948—55])

LIVERPOOL, KIRKDALE PARL BOR/BC[10] (1885—*)

1885—1918: pt Everton, Kirkdale

1918—:* pt Liverpool CB (wards of Anfield [1948—*], Breckfield [1948—*], Kirkdale [1918—55], Melrose [1955—*], St Domingo [1918—48], St Domingo [1970—*], Tuebrook [1955—*], Westminster [1955—*])

LIVERPOOL, SCOTLAND PARL BOR/BC[10] (1885—1918)

1885—1918: pt Liverpool (ward of Scotland)

1918—70: pt Liverpool CB (wards of Everton [1948—70], Netherfield [1948—70], St Domingo [1948—70], Sandhills, North Scotland [1918—55], South Scotland [1918—55], pt Vauxhall [1918—48], Vauxhall [1955—70])

LIVERPOOL, SCOTLAND EXCHANGE BC (1970—*)

pt Liverpool CB (wards of Abercromby, Central, Everton, Netherfield, St James, Sandhills, Vauxhall)

LIVERPOOL, TOXTETH BC[10] (1948—*)

pt Liverpool CB (wards of Arundel [1955—*], Dingle, Granby [1970—*], Princes Park, St Michael's [1955—*], Sefton Park East [1948—55], Sefton Park West [1948—55])

LIVERPOOL, EAST TOXTETH PARL BOR (1885—1948)

1885—1918: pt Toxteth Park

1918—48: pt Liverpool CB (wards of Aigburth, Granby, Sefton Park East, Sefton Park West)

LIVERPOOL, WEST TOXTETH PARL BOR (1885—1948)

1885—1918: pt Toxteth Park

1918—48: pt Liverpool CB (wards of Brunswick, Dingle, Prince's Park)

LIVERPOOL, WALTON PARL BOR/BC[7] (1885—*)

1885—1918: pt West Derby, pt Everton, pt Walton on the Hill, pt Wavertree

1918—:* pt West Lancashire RD (1948—55: Aintree), pt Liverpool CB (wards of County [1955—*], Fazakerley, Pirrie [1955—*], Walton [1918—55], Warbreck)

LIVERPOOL, WAVERTREE PARL BOR/BC[10] (1918—*)

pt Liverpool CB (wards of Allerton Childwall and Little Woolton [1918—48], Broadgreen [1955—*], Childwall [1955—*], Church [1955—*], Garston [1918—48], Old Swan [1948—*]), Wavertree [1918—55], Wavertree West [1918—55], Much Woolton [1918—48])

MANCHESTER PARL BOR (1832—85) [3 mbrs 1867—85]

Ardwick, Beswick, Bradford, Cheetham, Chorlton upon Medlock, Harpurhey, Hulme, Manchester, Newton

MANCHESTER, ARDWICK PARL BOR/BC[11] (1918—*)

pt Manchester CB (wards of Ardwick, Levenshulme [1970—*], Longsight [1948—*], New Cross [1918—55], New Cross [1970—73], Rusholme [1955—*], St Luke's [1955—73], St Mark's [1918—73])

MANCHESTER, BLACKLEY PARL BOR/BC[12] (1918—*)

pt Manchester CB (wards of Blackley, Charleston [1973—*], Crumpsall, Lightbowne [1973—*], Moston)

MANCHESTER, CENTRAL BC (1970—*)

pt Manchester CB (wards of Beswick, Cheetham, Collegiate Church, Harpurhey, Hugh Oldham, Miles Platting, New Cross, St Peter's)

MANCHESTER, CHEETHAM BC[13] (1948—70)

pt Manchester CB (wards of Cheetham, Collegiate Church, Collyhurst [1948—55], Harpurhey, Hugh Oldham [1955—70], Miles Platting [1955—70], St Michael's [1948—55])

MANCHESTER, CLAYTON PARL BOR/BC (1918—73[12])

pt Manchester CB (wards of Beswick, Bradford, Miles Platting [1948—55], Newton Heath)

MANCHESTER, EAST PARL BOR (1885—1918)

Ardwick, Beswick, Bradford, pt Chorlton upon Medlock

MANCHESTER, EXCHANGE PARL BOR/BC[13] (1918—70)

pt Manchester CB (wards of All Saints' [1948—70], Beswick [1955—70], Cheetham [1918—48], Collegiate Church [1918—48], Exchange [1918—55], Medlock Street [1948—55], New Cross [1955—70], Oxford [1918—55], St Ann's [1918—55], St Clement's [1918—55], St George's [1948—70], St John's [1918—55], St Luke's [1948—55], pt St Michael's [1918—48], St Peter's [1955—70])

MANCHESTER, GORTON PARL BOR/BC[13] (1918—*)

Audenshaw UD (1955—*), Denton UD (1955—*), pt Manchester CB (wards of Gorton North, Gorton South,

Levenshulme [1948—55], Openshaw [1918—55])

MANCHESTER, HULME PARL BOR (1918—48)

pt Manchester CB (wards of Medlock Street, Moss Side West, St George's)

MANCHESTER, MOSS SIDE PARL BOR/BC[12] (1918—*)

pt Manchester CB (wards of Alexandra [1973—*], Alexandra Park [1970—73], All Saints [1918—48], All Saints' [1970—73], Chorlton [1973—*], Chorlton cum Hardy [1948—73], Hulme [1973—*], Lloyd Street [1973—*], Moss Side [1973—*], Moss Side East [1918—73], Moss Side West [1948—73], St George's [1970—73], St Luke's [1918—48])

MANCHESTER, NORTH PARL BOR (1885—1918)

Harpurhey, pt Manchester (ward of St Michael), pt Newton

MANCHESTER, NORTH EAST PARL BOR (1885—1918)

pt Manchester (ward of New Cross, pt ward of Newton)

MANCHESTER, NORTH WEST PARL BOR (1885—1918)

Cheetham, pt Manchester (wards of Collegiate Church, Exchange, Oxford, St Anne's, St Clement's, St James's, St John's)

MANCHESTER, OPENSHAW BC[11] (1955[13]—*)

Failsworth UD, pt Manchester CB (wards of Bradford, Newton Heath, Openshaw [1955—73])

MANCHESTER, PLATTING PARL BOR (1918—48)

pt Manchester CB (wards of Collyhurst, Harpurhey, Miles Platting, pt St Michael's)

MANCHESTER, RUSHOLME PARL BOR (1918—48)

pt Manchester CB (wards of Levenshulme, Longsight, Rusholme)

MANCHESTER, SOUTH PARL BOR (1885—1918)

pt Chorlton upon Medlock, pt Gorton, Moss Side, pt Newton

MANCHESTER, SOUTH WEST PARL BOR (1885—1918)

Hulme

MANCHESTER, WITHINGTON PARL BOR/BC[11] (1918—*)

pt Manchester CB (wards of Barlow Moor [1955—*], Burnage [1955—*], Chorlton cum Hardy [1918—48], Didsbury [1918—48], Didsbury [1970—*], Levenshulme [1955—70], Old Moat [1955—*], Rusholme [1948—55], Withington)

MANCHESTER, WYTHENSHAWE BC[13] (1948—*)

pt Manchester CB (wards of Baguley [1955—*], Benchill [1955—*], Didsbury [1948—70], Levenshulme [1955—70], Northenden [1955—*], Woodhouse Park [1955—*], Wythenshawe [1948—55])

MIDDLETON AND PRESTWICH BC (1970—*)

Middleton MB, Prestwich MB, Whitefield UD

NELSON AND COLNE PARL BOR (1918—48)

Barrowford UD, Brierfield UD, pt Burnley RD (1918—48: pt Foulridge), Colne MB, Nelson MB, Trawden UD

NEWTON PARL BOR (1558—1832)

pt Manchester (tp Newton)

OLDHAM PARL BOR[14] (1832—1948)

1832—1918: pt Ashton under Lyne (1867—1918), Chadderton, Crompton, Oldham, Royton

1918—48: Oldham CB

OLDHAM EAST BC[2] (1948—*)

Lees UD, pt Oldham CB (wards of Bardsley [1955—*], Clarksfield, Mumps, St James, St Mary's, St Paul's, St Peter's, Waterhead)

OLDHAM WEST BC[2] (1948—*)

Chadderton UD, pt Oldham CB (wards of Coldhurst, Hartford, Hollinwood, Werneth, Westwood)

PRESTON PARL BOR[15] (1295—1307, 1326, 1547—1948)

1295—1918: Fishwick (1832—1918), pt Grimsargh with Brockholes (1885—1918); pt Lea, Ashton, Ingol and Cottam (1885—1918); pt Penwortham (1885—1918), Preston (reduced pt from 1867), pt Ribbleton (1885—1918)

1918—48: Fulwood UD, Preston CB

PRESTON NORTH BC[16] (1948—*)

Fulwood UD, pt Preston CB (wards of Deepdale, Fishwick, Moorbrook, Park, Ribbleton)

PRESTON SOUTH BC[16] (1948—*)

pt Preston CB (wards of Ashton, Avenham, Central [1960—*], Christ Church [1948—60], Maudland [1948—60], St John's, St Peter's [1948—60], Savick [1960—*], Trinity [1948—60], Tulketh [1960—*]), Walton le Dale UD

ROCHDALE PARL BOR/BC (1832—*)

1832—1918: pt Butterworth (1867—1918), pt Castleton (enlarged pt 1867—1918), pt Spotland (enlarged pt 1867—1918), Wardleworth (pt 1832—67, ent 1867—1918), pt Wuerdle and Wardle (enlarged pt 1867—1918)

1918—:* Rochdale CB

ROSSENDALE BC (1948—*)

Bacup MB, Haslingden CB, Ramsbsottom UD, Rawtenstall MB

ST HELENS PARL BOR/BC[17] (1885—*)

1885—1918: pt Eccleston, Parr, Sutton, pt Windle

1918—:* St Helens CB

SALFORD PARL BOR (1832—1918) [3 mbrs 1885—1918]

Broughton, pt Pendlebury (1832—85), Pendleton, Salford

SALFORD EAST BC (1948—*)

pt Salford CB (wards of Albert Park, Crescent, Kersal, Mandley Park, Ordsall Park, Regent, St Matthias, Trinity)

SALFORD NORTH PARL BOR (1918—48)

pt Salford CB (wards of Albert Park, Charlestown, Grosvenor, Kersal, St Matthias)

SALFORD SOUTH PARL BOR (1918—48)

pt Salford CB (wards of Crescent, Islington, Ordsall, Regent, Trafford, Trinity, Weaste)

SALFORD WEST PARL BOR[18] (1918—48)

pt Salford CB (wards of Charlestown [1948—*], Claremont [1948—*], Docks [1948—*], Hope [1918—48], Langworthy [1948—*], St Paul's, St Thomas's, Seedley, Weaste [1948—*])

SOUTHPORT PARL BOR/BC (1918—*)

Southport CB

STALYBRIDGE PARL BOR (1867—1918 [Lancs, Ches])

pt Ashton under Lyne (enlarged pt 1885—1918), *pt Dukinfield,* pt Hartshead, *pt Stayley (enlarged pt 1885—1918)*

STOCKPORT PARL BOR (1832—1948) [Ches, Lancs (1832—1918)]
  pt Heaton Norris
STRETFORD BC (1948—*)
  Stretford MB, Urmston UD

WARRINGTON PARL BOR/BC[19] (1832—* [Lancs, Ches [1832—1918]
  1832—1918: *Latchford, Thelwall*, Warrington
  1918—*: Warrington CB
WIGAN PARL BOR/BC (1295, 1306, 1547—*)
  1295—1918: Wigan
  1918—*: Pemberton (1918—48), Wigan CB

COUNTY CONSTITUENCIES

1832—1867
NORTHERN DIVISION
  Hds of Amounderness, Blackburn, Leyland, Lonsdale
SOUTHERN DIVISION
  Hds of West Derby, Salford

1867—1885
NORTH DIVISION
  Hds of Amounderness, Leyland, Lonsdale
NORTH EAST DIVISION
  Hd of Blackburn
SOUTH EAST DIVISION
  Hd of Salford
SOUTH WEST DIVISION
  Hd of West Derby

1885—1918
ACCRINGTON DIVISION
  Accrington MB, Accrington PSD, *viz.*, Accrington, Altham, Church, Clayton le Moors, Hapton, Henheads, Huncoat, Oswaldtwistle
BLACKPOOL DIVISION
  Amounderness PSD, Kirkham PSD, pt Leyland PSD, *viz.*, Alston, Barton, Bispham with Norbreck, Broughton, Bryning with Kellamergh, Carleton, Clifton with Salwick, Little Eccleston with Larbreck, Elston, Elswick, Farington, Freckleton, Goosnargh, Greenhalgh with Thistleton, pt Grimsargh with Brockholes, Haighton, Hardhorn with Newton, Little Hoole, Much Hoole, Hothersall, Howick, Hutton, Kirkham, Layton with Warbreck; pt Lea, Ashton, Ingol and Cottam; Longton, Lytham, Marton, Medlar with Wesham, Newton with Scales, pt Penwortham, Poulton Barre and Torrisholme, Poulton le Fylde, pt Preston, pt Ribbleton, Ribby with Wrea, Singleton, Thornton; Treales, Roseacre and Wharles; Warton, Weeton and Preese, Westby with Plumptons, Whittingham, Woodplumpton
BOOTLE DIVISION
  Bootle MB, pt Childwall PSD, pt Kirkdale PSD, *viz.*, Bootle cum Linacre, Childwall, pt West Derby, Fazakerley, pt Toxteth Park, pt Walton on the Hill, pt Wavertree
CHORLEY DIVISION
  pt Leyland PSD, Leyland Hundred PSD, *viz.*, Adlington, Anderton, Bispham, Bretherton, Brindle, Charnock Richard, Chorley, Clayton le Moors, Coppull, Croston, Cuerdon, Duxbury, Eccleston, Euxton, Heapey, Heath Charnock, Hesketh with Becconsall, Heskin, Hoghton, Leyland, Mawdesley, Parbold, Rufford, Shevington, Standish with Langtree, Tarleton, Ulnes Walton, Welsh Whittle, Wheelston, Whittle le Woods, Withnell, Worthington, Wrightington

CLITHEROE DIVISION
  pt Burnley PSD, Clitheroe MB, pt Clitheroe PSD, Colne PSD, *viz.*, Barley with Wheatley Booth, Barrowford Booth, Chatburn, Clitheroe, Clitheroe Castle, Colne, Downham, Foulridge, Goldshaw Booth, Great and Little Marsden, Mearley; Little Mitton, Henthorn and Coldcoats; Old Laund Booth, Pendleton, Roughlee Booth, Trawden, Twiston, Whalley, Wheatley Carr Booth, Wiswell, Worston
DARWEN DIVISION
  pt Blackburn PSD, pt Clitheroe PSD, Darwen MB, Darwen PSD, Walton le Dale PSD, *viz.*, Aighton, Bailey and Chaigley; Balderstone, Billington, Little Bowland, Briercliffe with Extwistle, Chipping, Clayton le Dale, Cliviger, Cuerdale, pt Lower Darwen, Over Darwen, Dilworth, Dinckley, Dutton, Eccleshill, Great Harwood, Heyhouses, Higham with West Close Booth, Ightenhill Park, Leagram, Mellor, Osbaldeston, Padiham, Pleasington, Ramsgreave, Read; Reedley Hallows, Filly Close and New Laund Booth; Ribchester, Rishton, Salesbury, Samlesbury, Simonstone, Thornley with Wheatley, Tockholes, Walton le Dale, Wilpshire, Worsthorne with Hurstwood, Yate and Pickup Bank
ECCLES DIVISION
  pt Manchester PSD, *viz.*, Barton upon Irwell, Clifton, Flixton, pt Pendlebury, Urmston, Worsley
GORTON DIVISION
  pt Ashton under Lyne PSD, pt Manchester PSD, *viz.*, Denton, pt Gorton, Haughton, Openshaw
HEYWOOD DIVISION
  pt Bury PSD, Heywood MB, pt Middleton PSD, *viz.*, Ainsworth, Ashworth, pt Birtle cum Bamford, pt Elton, pt Heap, Pilkington, pt Pilsworth, pt Radcliffe, pt Spotland, Tottington Higher End, pt Tottington Lower End, pt Walmersley cum Shuttleworth
INCE DIVISION
  pt Wigan PSD, *viz.*, Abram, Haigh, Hindley, Ince in Makerfield, Orrell, Pemberton
LANCASTER DIVISION
  Garstang PSD, Hornby PSD, Lancaster MB, pt South Lonsdale PSD, *viz.*, Aldcliffe, Arkholme with Cawood, Ashton with Stodday, Barnacre with Bonds, Bleasdale, Bulk, Burrow with Burrow, Cabus, Cantsfield, Caton, Catterall, Claughton, Claughton, Cleveley, Cockerham, Cockersand Abbey, Great Eccleston, Ellel, Farleton, Forton, Garstang, Gressingham, Halton, Hambleton, Heaton with Oxcliffe, Heysham, Holleth, Hornby, Inskip with Sowerby, Ireby, Kirkland, Leck, Melling with Wrayton, Middleton, Myerscough, Nateby, Overton, Preesall with Hackinsall, Quernmore, Out Rawcliffe, Upper Rawcliffe with Tarnacre, Roeburndale, Scotforth, Skerton, Slyne with Hest, Stalmine

with Staynall, Tatham, Thurnham, Tunstal, Wennington, Whittington, Winmarleigh, Wray with Botton, Nether Wyresdale, Over Wyresdale

LEIGH DIVISION
Leigh PSD, *viz.*, Astley, Atherton, Bedford, Culceth, Kenyon, West Leigh, Lowton, Pennington, Tyldesley cum Shakerley

NORTH LONSDALE DIVISION
Barrow in Furness PSD, Hawkshead PSD, North Lonsdale PSD, pt South Lonsdale PSD, *viz.*, Aldingham, Lower Allithwaite, Upper Allithwaite, Angerton, Blawith, Bolton le Sands, Borwick, Broughton East, Broughton West, Carnforth, Cartmel Fell, Claife, Church Coniston, Colton, Dalton, Dalton in Furness, Dunnerdale with Seathwaite, Egton cum Newland, Hawkshead and Monk Coniston with Skelwith, Lower Holker, Upper Holker, Nether Kellet, Over Kellet, Kirkby Ireleth, Mansriggs, Osmotherley, Pennington, Priest Hutton, Satterthwaite, Silverdale, Staveley, Subberthwaite, Torver, Ulverston, Urswick, Warton with Lindeth, Yealand Conyers, Yealand Redmayne

MIDDLETON DIVISION
pt Bury PSD, pt Middleton PSD, *viz.*, Alkrington, Blatchinworth and Calderbrook, pt Butterworth, pt Castleton, Hopwood, Middleton, Thornham, Todmorden and Walsden, Tonge, pt Wuerdale and Wardle

NEWTON DIVISION
St Helens PSD, Warrington PSD, pt Wigan PSD, *viz.*, Ashton in Makerfield, Billinge Chapel End, Billinge Higher End, Bold, Burtonwood, Cuerdley, pt Eccleston, Golborne, Haydock, Houghton, Middleton and Arbury, Newton in Makerfield, Penketh, Poulton with Fearnhead, Rainford, Rainhill, Rixton with Glazebrook, Great Sankey, Southworth with Croft, pt Windle, Winstanley, Winwick with Hulme, Woolston with Martinscroft

ORMSKIRK DIVISION
pt Kirkdale PSD, Ormskirk PSD, pt Preston PSD, pt Wigan PSD, *viz.*, Aintree, Aughton, Bickerstaffe, Burscough, Croxteth Park, Dalton, Downholland, Halsall, Kirkby, Knowsley, Lathom, Litherland, Lunt, Lydiate, Maghull, Melling, Netherton, Ormskirk, Orrell and Ford, Prescot, Scarisbrick, Sefton, Simonswood, Skelmersdale, Upholland

PRESTWICH DIVISION
pt Ashton under Lyne PSD, pt Manchester PSD, pt Oldham PSD, *viz.*, pt Ashton under Lyne, Blackley, Crumpsall, Droylsden, Failsworth, Great Heaton, Little Heaton, Moston, Prestwich

RADCLIFFE CUM FARNWORTH DIVISION
pt Bolton PSD, pt Bury PSD, *viz.*, Farnworth, Little Hulton, Kearsley

ROSSENDALE DIVISION
pt Middleton PSD, Rossendale PSD, *viz.*, Higher Booths, Lower Booths; Cowpe Lench, Newhall Hay and Hall Carr; Dunnockshaw, Haslingden, Musbury, Newchurch

SOUTHPORT DIVISION
pt Kirkdale PSD, Southport PSD, *viz.*, Altcar, Birkdale, Great Crosby, Little Crosby, Formby, Ince Blundell, North Meols, Thornton

STRETFORD DIVISION
pt Manchester PSD, *viz.*, Burnage, Chorlton cum Hardy, Didsbury, pt Heaton Norris, Levenshulme, Reddish, Rushulme, Stretford, Withington

WESTHOUGHTON DIVISION
pt Bolton PSD, *viz.*, Anglezarke, Aspull, Blackrod, Bradshaw, Breightmet, Edgeworth, Entwistle, pt Halliwell, Harwood, Heaton, Horwich, Middle Hulton, Over Hulton, Darcy Lever, Great Lever, Little Lever, Longworth, Lostock, Quarlton, Rivington, pt Rumworth, pt Sharples, pt Tonge with Haulgh, Turton, Westhoughton

WIDNES DIVISION
pt Childwall PSD, pt Kirkdale PSD, pt Prescot PSD, *viz.*, Allerton, Cronton, Ditton, Garston, Hale, Halewood, Huyton with Roby, Speke, Tarbock, Whiston, Widnes, Little Woolton, Much Woolton

1918—1948

CHORLEY DIVISION
Adlington UD, Chorley MB, Chorley RD, Croston UD, Leyland UD, pt Wigan RD (Haigh, Parbold, Worthington, Wrightington), Withnell UD

CLITHEROE DIVISION
pt Burnley RD (all except pt Foulridge), Clitheroe MB, Clitheroe RD, Great Harwood UD, Padiham UD

DARWEN DIVISION
Blackburn RD, Darwen MB, Turton UD

FARNWORTH DIVISION
pt Barton upon Irwell RD (Clifton), pt Bury RD (Ainsworth, Outwood), Farnworth UD, Little Hulton UD, Kearsley UD, Little Lever UD, Worsley UD

FYLDE DIVISION[20]
Fleetwood UD, Fyle RD, Kirkham UD, Longridge UD, Poulton le Fylde UD, Preston RD, Thornton UD, Walton le Dale UD

HEYWOOD AND RADCLIFFE DIVISION
pt Bury RD (all except the pars in Farnworth Dv), Heywood MB, Radcliffe UD, Ramsbottom UD, Whitefield UD

INCE DIVISION
Abram UD, Ashton in Makerfield UD, Billinge UD, Ince in Makerfield UD, Orrell UD, Standish with Langtree UD, pt Wigan RD (Shevington)

LANCASTER DIVISION
Garstang RD, Heysham UD, Lancaster MB, pt Lancaster RD (the pars not in Lonsdale Dv), Morecambe MB, Preesall UD

LONSDALE DIVISION
Carnforth UD, Dalton in Furness UD, Grange UD, pt Lancaster RD (Bolton le Sands, Priest Hutton, Silverdale, Slyne with Hest, Warton with Lindeth, Yealand Conyers, Yealand Redmayne), Lunesdale RD, Ulverston RD, Ulverston UD

MIDDLETON AND PRESTWICH DIVISION
Chadderton UD, Middleton MB, Prestwich UD

MOSSLEY DIVISION
Audenshaw UD, Denton UD, Droylsden UD, Failsworth UD, Lees UD, Limehurst RD, Mossley MB

NEWTON DIVISION[21]
Golborne UD, Haydock UD, pt Leigh RD (the pars not in Stretford Dv), Newton in Makerfield UD, Warrington RD

ORMSKIRK DIVISION
Formby UD, West Lancashire RD, Lathom with

Burscough UD, Ormskirk UD, Rainford UD, Sefton RD, Skelmersdale UD, Upholland UD, pt Wigan RD (Dalton)

ROYTON DIVISION

Crompton UD, Littleborough UD, Milnrow UD, Norden UD, Royton UD, Wardle UD, Whitworth UD

STRETFORD DIVISION[22]

pt Barton upon Irwell RD (the pars not in Farnworth Dv), Irlam UD, pt Leigh RD (Astley), Stretford UD, Urmston UD

WATERLOO DIVISION

Great Crosby UD, Little Crosby UD, Litherland UD, Waterloo and Seaforth UD

WESTHOUGHTON DIVISION

Aspull UD, Blackrod UD, Hindley UD, Horwich UD, Westhoughton UD

WIDNES DIVISION

Huyton with Roby UD, Prescot UD, Whiston RD, Widnes MB

1948—1970

CHORLEY COUNTY CONSTITUENCY[3]

Adlington UD, Chorley MB, Chorley RD, Leyland UD, Withnell UD (1955—70)

CLITHEROE COUNTY CONSTITUENCY

Burnley RD, Clitheroe MB, Clitheroe RD, Great Harwood UD, Longridge UD, Padiham UD, pt Preston RD (Dutton, Hothersall, Ribchester)

DARWEN COUNTY CONTITUENCY[3]

pt Blackburn CB (1955—70: wards of St Andrew's, St Francis's, St Mark's), Blackburn RD, Darwen MB, Turton UD, Withnell UD (1948—55)

FARNWORTH COUNTY CONSTITUENCY[23]

Farnworth MB, Kearsley UD, Little Lever UD, Worsley UD

NORTH FYLDE COUNTY CONSTITUENCY[24]

Fleetwood MB, Garstang RD, Poulton le Fylde UD, Preesall UD, Thornton Cleveleys UD

SOUTH FYLDE COUNTY CONSTITUENCY[25]

Fylde RD, Kirkham UD, Lytham St Anne's MB, pt Preston RD (all except the pars in Clitheroe Dv)

HEYWOOD AND ROYTON COUNTY CONSTITUENCY

Crompton UD, Heywood MB, Littleborough UD, Milnrow UD, Royton UD, Wardle UD, Whitworth UD

HUYTON COUNTY CONSTITUENCY[26]

Huyton with Roby UD, Kirkby UD (1960—70), Prescot UD, pt Whiston RD (Eccleston, Kirkby [1948—60], Knowsley, Windle)

INCE COUNTY CONSTITUENCY

Abram UD, Ashton in Makerfield UD, Billinge and Winstanley UD, Ince in Makerfield UD, Orrell UD, Skelmersdale and Upholland UD

LANCASTER COUNTY CONSTITUENCY

Carnforth UD, Lancaster MB, pt Lancaster RD (Ashton with Stodday, Cockerham, Ellel, Heaton with Oxcliffe, Middleton, Overton, Scotforth, Thurnham, Over Wyresdale), Lunesdale RD

MIDDLETON AND PRESTWICH COUNTY CONSTITUENCY

Middleton MB, Prestwich MB, Whitefield UD

MORECAMBE AND LONSDALE COUNTY CONSTITUENCY

Grange UD, pt Lancaster RD (Bolton le Sands, Priest Hutton, Silverdale, Slyne with Hest, Warton, Yealand Conyers, Yealand Redmayne), Morecambe and Heysham MB, Ulverston RD, Ulverston UD

NEWTON COUNTY CONSTITUENCY[19]

Golborne UD, Haydock UD, Irlam UD, Newton le Willows UD, Warrington RD

ORMSKIRK COUNTY CONSTITUENCY[27]

Formby UD, West Lancashire RD (pt 1948—55: all except Aintree, Ford; 1955—70: ent RD), Ormskirk UD, Rainford UD

WESTHOUGHTON COUNTY CONSTITUENCY

Aspull UD, Blackrod UD, Hindley UD, Horwich UD, Standish with Langtree UD, Westhoughton UD, Wigan RD

WIDNES COUNTY CONSTITUENCY[8]

pt Whiston RD (all except Eccleston, Kirkby, Knowsley, Windle), Widnes MB

1970—*

CHORLEY COUNTY CONSTITUENCY

Adlington UD, Chorley MB, Chorley RD, Leyland UD, Withnell UD

CLITHEROE COUNTY CONSTITUENCY

Burnley RD, Clitheroe MB, Clitheroe RD, Great Harwood UD, Longridge UD, Padiham UD, pt Preston RD (Dutton, Hothersall, Ribchester)

DARWEN COUNTY CONSTITUENCY

Blackburn RD, Darwen MB, Turton UD

NORTH FYLDE DIVISION

Fleetwood MB, Garstang RD, Poulton le Fylde UD, Preesall UD, Thornton Cleveleys UD

SOUTH FYLDE DIVISION

Fylde RD, Kirkham UD, Lytham St Anne's MB, pt Preston (all except Dutton, Hothersall, Ribchester)

HEYWOOD AND ROYTON COUNTY CONSTITUENCY

Crompton UD, Heywood MB, Littleborough UD, Milnrow UD, Royton UD, Wardle UD, Whitworth UD

HUYTON COUNTY CONSTITUENCY

Huyton with Roby UD, Prescot UD, pt Whiston RD (Eccleston, Knowsley, Windle)

LANCASTER COUNTY CONSTITUENCY

Carnforth UD, Lancaster MB, pt Lancaster RD (Ashton with Stodday, Cockerham, Ellel, Heaton with Oxcliffe, Middleton, Overton, Scotforth, Thurnham, Over Wyresdale), Lunesdale RD

MORECAMBE AND LONSDALE COUNTY CONSTITUENCY

Grange UD, pt Lancaster RD (Bolton le Sands, Priest Hutton, Silverdale, Slyne with Hest, Warton, Yealand Conyers, Yealand Redmayne), North Lonsdale RD, Morecambe and Heysham MB, Ulverston UD

NEWTON COUNTY CONSTITUENCY

Golborne UD, Haydock UD, Irlam UD, Newton le Willows UD, Warrington RD

ORMSKIRK COUNTY CONSTITUENCY

Formby UD, Kirkby UD, pt West Lancashire RD (Aintree, Aughton, Bickerstaffe, Bispham, Downholland, Halsall, Hesketh with Becconsall, Lydiate, Melling, North Meols, Netherton, Rufford, Scarisbrick, pt Sefton, Simonswood, Tarleton), Ormskirk UD, Rainford UD

WESTHOUGHTON COUNTY CONSTITUENCY

Aspull UD, Blackrod UD, Hindley UD, Horwich UD, Standish with Langtree UD, Westhoughton UD, Wigan RD

WIDNES COUNTY CONSTITUENCY

pt Whiston RD (all except Eccleston, Kirkby, Knowsley, Windle), Widnes MB

LEICESTERSHIRE

BOROUGH CONSTITUENCIES[1]

LEICESTER PARL BOR (1295—1918)
Leicester All Saints, Leicester Augustine Friars, Leicester Black Friars, Leicester The Castle View (1832—1918), Leicester The Newarke (1832—1918), Leicester St Leonard (pt 1295—1832, ent 1832—1918), Leicester St Margaret, Leicester St Martin, Leicester St Mary (pt 1295—1832, ent 1832—1918), Leicester St Nicholas

LEICESTER EAST PARL BOR (1918—48)
pt Leicester CB (wards of Belgrave, West Humberstone, Latimer, Spinney Hill)

LEICESTER EAST BC (1970—*)
pt Leicester CB (wards of Belgrave, Charnwood, Evington, Humberstone, Latimer)

LEICESTER NORTH-EAST BC (1948—70)
pt Leicester CB (wards of Belgrave, Charnwood, Humberstone, Latimer)

LEICESTER NORTH-WEST BC (1948—70)
pt Leicester CB (wards of Abbey, Newton, St Margaret's, Westcotes)

LEICESTER SOUTH PARL BOR (1918—48)
pt Leicester CB (wards of Aylestone, Castle, Charnwood, De Montfort, Knighton, Martin's, Wycliffe)

LEICESTER SOUTH BC[2] (1970—*)
pt Leicester CB (wards of Aylestone, The Castle, De Montfort, Knighton, Spinney Hill, Wycliffe)

LEICESTER SOUTH-EAST BC[3] (1948—70)
pt Leicester CB (wards of Evington, Knighton, Spinney Hill, Wycliffe), Oadby UD (1955—70)

LEICESTER SOUTH-WEST BC (1948—70)
pt Leicester CB (wards of Aylestone, North Braunstone, The Castle, De Montfort)

LEICESTER WEST PARL BOR (1918—48)
pt Leicester CB (wards of Abbey, Newton, St Margaret's, Westcotes, Wyggeston)

LEICESTER WEST BC (1970—*)
pt Leicester CB (wards of The Abbey, North Braunstone, Newton, St Margaret's, Westcotes)

COUNTY CONSTITUENCIES

1832—1885
NORTHERN DIVISION
Hds of Framland, East Goscote, West Goscote, pt Gartree Hd (Burrough on the Hill, Knossington, Marefield (1867—85), Owston with Newbold, Pickwell with Leesthorpe, pt Tilston ([Marefield] 1832—67)
SOUTHERN DIVISION
Hds of Gartree, Guthlaxton, Sparkenhoe, pt Gartree Hd (all except the pars in N'rn Dv)

1885—1918
EASTERN (or MELTON) DIVISION
Belvoir PSD, pt Leicester PSD, pt East Norton PSD, *viz.*, Ab Kettleby, Allexton, Asfordby, Ashby Folville, Barkby, Barkby Thorpe, Barkstone, Barsby, Beeby, Belgrave, Belvoir, Bescaby, Billesdon, Birstall, Bottesford, Branston, Braunstone, Brooksby, Nether Broughton, Buckminster, Burrough on the Hill, Burton Lazars, Bushby, Long Clawson, Cold Newton, Cossington, Coston, South Croxton, Croxton Kerrial, Great Dalby, Little Dalby, Old Dalby, Eastwell, Eaton, Edmondthorpe, Evington, Freeby, Frisby, Frisby on the Wreak, Gaddesby, Galby, Garthorpe, Goadby, Goadby Marwood, Grimston, Halstead, Harby, Harston, Hoby, Holwell, Hose, Houghton on the Hill, Humberstone, Hungerton, Ilston on the Hill, Keyham, Kirby Bellars, Knipton, Knossington, Launde, Loddington, Lowesby, Marefield, Melton Mowbray, Muston, East Norton, King's Norton, Noseley, Cold Overton, Owston and Newbold, Pickwell with Leesthorpe, Plungar, Queniborough, Ragdale, Ratcliffe on the Wreake, Rearsby, Redmile, Rolleston, Rotherby, Saltby, Saxby, Saxelby, Scalford, Scraptoft, Seagrave, Sewstern, Shoby, Sileby, Skeffington, Somerby, Sproxton, Stapleford, Stathern, Stonesby, Stoughton, Stretton Magna, Stretton Parva, Sysonby, Syston, Thorpe Arnold, Thorpe Satchville, Thrussington, North Thurmaston, South Thurmaston, Thurnby, Tilton, Tugby, Twyford, Waltham on the Wolds, Wanlip, Wartnaby, Welby, Whatborough, Withcote, Wycomb and Chadwell, Wyfordby, Wymondham
MID (or LOUGHBOROUGH) DIVISION
pt Ashby de la Zouch PSD, pt Leicester PSD, pt Loughborough PSD, *viz.*, Anstey, Anstey Pastures, Bardon, Barrow upon Soar, Beaumont Leys, Belton, Breedon on the Hill, Burton on the Wolds, Castle Donington, Charley, Cotes, Cropston, Diseworth, Garendon, Gilroes, Hathern, Hemington, Hoton, Isley Walton, Kegworth, Knight Thorpe, Langley Priory, Leicester Abbey, Leicester Frith, Lockington, Loughborough, Markfield, Newtown Linford, Osgathorpe, Prestwold, Quorndon, Ratby, Rothley, Shepshed, Swithland, Thorpe Acre and Dishley, Thringstone, Thurcaston, Ulverscroft, Walton on the Wolds, Long Whatton, Whitwick, Woodhouse, Woodthorpe, Wymeswold
SOUTHERN (or HARBOROUGH) DIVISION
pt Leicester PSD, Lutterworth PSD, Market Harborough PSD, pt East Norton PSD, *viz.*, Arnesby, Ashby Magna, Ashby Parva, Aylestone, Bittesby, Bittesville, Blaby, Blaston, Husbands Bosworth, Great Bowden, Braunstone Frith, Bringhurst, Broughton Astley, Bruntingthorpe, Burton Overy, Carlton Curlieu, Catthorpe, Claybrooke Magna, Claybrooke Parva, Cosby, Cotesbach, Cranoe, Countesthorpe, Croft, Drayton, Dunton Bassett, Great Easton, Enderby, Fleckney, Foston,

Foxton, Freakes Ground, Frolesworth, Gilmorton, Glen Magna, Glen Parva, Glenfield, Glenfield Frith, Glooston, Gumley, Hallaton, Nevill Holt, Horninghold, Huncote, Kibworth Beauchamp, Kibworth Harcourt, Kilby, North Kilworth, South Kilworth, Kimcote, Kirby Frith, Kirby Muxloe, Knaptoft, Knighton, East Langton, Laughton, Thorpe Langton, Tur Langton, West Langton, Leicester Forest East, Leicester New Found Pool, Leire, Lubbesthorpe, Lubenham, Lutterworth, Market Harborough, Medbourne, Misterton, Mowsley, Narborough, New Parks, Newtown Harcourt, Oadby, Peatling Magna, Peatling Parva, Saddington, Shangton, Shawell, Shearsby, Slawston, Smeeton Westerby, Stockerston, pt Stoke Dry, Stonton Wyville, Swinford, Theddingworth, Ullesthorpe, Walton in Knaptoft, Welham, Westrill and Starmore, Whetstone, Wigston Magna, Wigston Parva, Willoughby Waterless, Wistow

WESTERN (or BOSWORTH) DIVISION
pt Ashby de la Zouch PSD, Market Bosworth PSD, *viz.*, pt Appleby, Ashby de la Zouch, Aston Flamville, Atterton, Bagworth, Barlestone, Barton in the Beans, Barwell, Bilstone, Blackfordby, Market Bosworth, Burbage, Cadeby, Carlton, Coleorton, Congerstone, Dadlington, Desford, Fenny Drayton, Earl Shilton, Elmesthorpe, Gopsall, Heather, Higham on the Hill, Hinckley, Hugglescote and Donington, Ibstock, Kirkby Mallory, Knoll and Bassett House, pt Merevale, Nailstone, Newbold Verdon, Normanton le Heath, Norton juxta Twycross, pt Oakthorpe and Donisthorpe, Odstone, Orton on the Hill, Osbaston, Packington, Peckleton, Potters Marston, Ratcliffe Culey, Ravenstone with Snibston, Sapcote, Nether and Over Seal, Shackerstone, Sharnford, Sheepy Magna, Sheepy Parva, Shenton, Sibson, Snarestone, Stanton under Bardon, Stapleton, Staunton Harold, Stoke Golding, Stoney Stanton, Sutton Cheney, Swannington, Swepstone, Thornton, Thurlaston, Twycross, Upton, Witherley, Worthington

1918—1948
BOSWORTH DIVISION
pt Ashby de la Zouch RD (Bardon), Coalville UD, Hinckley RD, Hinckley UD, Market Bosworth RD

HARBOROUGH DIVISION
Blaby RD, Hallaton RD, Lutterworth RD, Market Harborough RD, Market Harborough UD, Oadby UD, Wigston Magna UD
LOUGHBOROUGH DIVISION
pt Ashby de la Zouch RD (all except Bardon), Ashby de la Zouch UD, Ashby Woulds UD, Castle Donington RD, Loughborough MB, Loughborough RD, Shepshed UD
MELTON DIVISION
Barrow upon Soar RD, Belvoir RD, Billesdon RD, Melton Mowbray RD, Melton Mowbray UD, Quorndon UD, Thurmaston UD

1948—1970
BOSWORTH COUNTY CONSTITUENCY[4]
Coalville UD, Hinckley UD, Market Bosworth RD
HARBOROUGH COUNTY CONSTITUENCY[3]
Blaby RD, Lutterworth RD, Market Harborough RD, Market Harborough UD, Oadby UD (1948—55), Wigston UD
LOUGHBOROUGH COUNTY CONSTITUENCY[4]
Ashby de la Zouch RD, Ashby de la Zouch UD, Ashby Woulds UD, Castle Donington RD, Loughborough MB, Shepshed UD
MELTON COUNTY CONSTITUENCY
Barrow upon Soar RD, Billesdon RD, Melton and Belvoir RD, Melton Mowbray UD

*1970—**
BLABY COUNTY CONSTITUENCY
Blaby RD, Lutterworth RD
BOSWORTH COUNTY CONSTITUENCY[5]
Coalville UD, Hinckley UD, Market Bosworth RD
HARBOROUGH COUNTY CONSTITUENCY[2]
Billesdon RD, Market Harborough RD, Market Harborough UD, Oadby UD, Wigston UD
LOUGHBOROUGH COUNTY CONSTITUENCY[5]
Ashby de la Zouch RD, Ashby de la Zouch UD, Ashby Woulds UD, Castle Donington RD, Loughborough MB, Shepshed UD
MELTON COUNTY CONSTITUENCY
Barrow upon Soar RD, Melton and Belvoir RD, Melton Mowbray UD

LINCOLNSHIRE

BOROUGH CONSTITUENCIES[1]

BOSTON PARL BOR (1352—1353, 1547—1918) [1 mbr 1885—1918] [Pts Holl]
  pt Boston (1352—53, 1547—1885, enlarged pt 1832—85, reduced pt 1885—1918), pt Skirbeck (1832—1918)
GRANTHAM PARL BOR (1467—1885) [Pts Kestev]
  Grantham (pt 1467—1867, ent 1867—85), pt Somerby (1832—85)
GRIMSBY PARL BOR/BC[2] (1918—*) [Grimsby CB]
  Cleethorpes UD (1918—48), Grimsby CB
GREAT GRIMSBY PARL BOR (1295—1918) [Pts Lind]
  Bradley (1832—1918), Clee with Weelsby (1832—1918), Cleethorpes (1832—1918), Great Coates (1832—1918), Little Coates (1832—1918), Great Grimsby, Laceby (1832—1918), Scartho (1832—1918), Waltham (1832—1918)
LINCOLN PARL BOR[3] (1295—*) [1 member 1885—*])
  [Linc Co of Itself 1409—1867, Pts Lind 1867—1918, Linc CB 1918—*]
1295—1918: Lincoln Bishop's Palace (1832—1918), Lincoln Castle Dykings (1832—1918), Lincoln Cold Bath House (1837—1918), Lincoln Holmes Common (1832—1918), Lincoln Monks Liberty (1832—1918), Lincoln St Benedict, Lincoln St Botolph, Lincoln St John in Newport, Lincoln St Margaret in the Close, Lincoln St Mark, Lincoln St Martin, Lincoln St Mary le Wigford, Lincoln St Mary Magdalen in the Bail, Lincoln St Michael, Lincoln St Nicholas, Lincoln St Paul in the Bail, Lincoln St Peter at Arches, Lincoln St Peter at Gowts, Lincoln St Peter in Eastgate, Lincoln St Swithin, Lincoln South Common
1918—*: Bracebridge UD (1918—48), Lincoln CB
LOUTH PARL BOR (1306 only) [Pts Lind]
  pt Louth
SPALDING PARL BOR (1328, 1337 only) [Pts Holl]
  Spalding
STAMFORD PARL BOR (1295—1306 irregularly, 1322, 1467—1885) [Pts Kestev, *Northants (1832—85)*]
  Stamford All Saints, Stamford St George, Stamford St John, Stamford St Mary, Stamford St Michael, *Stamford Baron St Martin (1832—85)*
WAINFLEET PARL BOR (1337 only) [Pts Lind]
  Wainfleet All Saints, Wainfleet St Mary

COUNTY CONSTITUENCIES

1832—1867
NORTHERN DIVISION
  Pts Lindsey
SOUTHERN DIVISION
  Pts Holland, Pts Kesteven

1867—1885
NORTH DIVISION
  Pts Lindsey: Waps of Aslacoe, Bradley Haverstoe, Corringham, Ludborough, Manley, Walshcroft, Yarborough, Hd of Louth Esk
MID DIVISION
  Pts Kesteven: Waps of Boothby Graffoe, Langoe
  Pts Lindsey: Waps of Calcewaith, Candleshoe, Gartree, Lawres, Well, Wraggoe; Sokes of Bolingbroke, Horncastle; Hd of Hill
SOUTH DIVISION
  Pts Holland: ent area
  Pts Kesteven: Waps of Aswardhun, Aveland, Beltisloe, Flaxwell, Loveden, Ness, Winnibriggs and Threo

1885—1918
HOLLAND (or SPALDING) DIVISION
  pt Elloe PSD, pt Kirton and Skirbeck PSD, *viz.*, Algar Kirk, Benington, pt Boston, Butterwick, Cowbit, pt Deeping St Nicholas, Fishtoft, Fleet, Fosdyke, Frampton, Freiston, Gedney, Gedney Hill, Gosberton, Holbeach, Kirton, Leake, Leverton, Lutton, Moulton, Pepper Gowt Plot, Pinchbeck, Quadring, Shuff Fen, Simon Weir, pt Skirbeck, Skirbeck Quarter, Spalding, Surfleet, Sutterton, Sutton St Edmund, Sutton St James, Sutton St Mary, Tydd St Mary, Weston, Whaplode, Wigtoft, pt Central Wingland, Wrangle, Wyberton
NORTH KESTEVEN (or SLEAFORD) DIVISION
  pt Kirton and Skirbeck PSD (Pts Holl), pt Lincoln PSD, pt Sleaford PSD (both Pts Kestev), *viz.*, Amber Hill, Ancaster, Anwick, Asgarby, Ashby de la Launde, Aswarby, Aubourn, Aunsby, Bassingham, Great Beats, Little Beats, Bicker, Billinghay, Blankney, Bloxholm, Boothby Graffoe, Boultham, Great Brand End Plot, Little Brand End Plot, Branston, Brauncewell, Brothertoft, Burton Penwardine, Byard's Leap, Canwick, Carlton le Moorland, Caythorpe, Coleby, Copping Syke, Cranwell, Culverthorpe, Dembleby, Digby, Doddington, Dogdyke, Donington, Dorrington, Drainage Marsh, Dunston, Eagle, Eagle Hall, Eagle Woodhouse, Evedon, Ewerby, Ferry Corner Plot, Fulbeck, Gibbet Hills, Haceby, Haddington, Great Hale, Little Hale, Potter Hanworth, Harmston, Hart's Grounds, Haverholme Priory, Heckington, Heighington, Helpringham, Heydour, Holdingham, Howell, North Hykeham, South Hykeham, Kelby, Kirkby Green, Kirkby de la Thorpe, North Kyme, South Kyme, Leadenham, Leasingham, Martin, Metheringham, Morton, Mown Rakes, Navenby, Newton, Nocton, North Forty Foot Bank, Norton Disney, Osbournby, Pelham's Lands, Quarrington, North Rauceby, South Rauceby, Rowston, Roxholm, Royalty Farm, Ruskington, North Scarle, Scopwick, Scredington, Seven Acres, Skellingthorpe, Skinnand, New

Sleaford, Old Sleaford, South of the Witham, Spanby, Stapleford, Swarby, Swaton, Swinderby, Swineshead, Swinethorpe, Temple Bruer with Temple High Grange, Thorpe on the Hill, Thorpe Tilney, Threckingham, Thurlby, Timberland, Waddington, Walcot near Billinghay, Washingborough, Welbourn, Wellingore, Whisby, Scott Willoughby, Silk Willoughby, Wilsford

SOUTH KESTEVEN (or STAMFORD DIVISION)

pt Elloe PSD (Pts Holl), Bourne PSD, Grantham MB, Spittlegate PSD (all Pts Kestev), *viz.*, Allington, Aslackby, Aunby, Barholm, Barkston, Barrowby, Bassingthorpe, Baston, Beckingham, Belton, Long Bennington, Bennington Grange, Billingborough, Birthorpe, Bitchfield, Boothby Pagnell, Bourne, Braceborough, Braceby, Brant Broughton, Burton Coggles, Castle Bytham, Little Bytham, Careby, Carlby, Carlton Scroop, Claypole, Colsterworth, Corby, Counthorpe, Creeton, Crowland, Market Deeping, pt Deeping St Nicholas, Denton, Dry Doddington, Dowsby, Dunsby, Easton, Edenham, Fenton, Folkingham, Foston, Great Gonerby, Grantham, Grantham Grange, Greatford, Gunby, Hacconby, Harlaxton, Harrowby, Holywell, Honington, Horbling, Hough on the Hill, Hougham, Little Humby, Ingoldsby, Irnham, Keisby, Kirkby Underwood, Langtoft, Laughton, Lenton, Londonthorpe, Manthorpe, Manthorpe cum Little Gonerby, Marston, Morton, Normanton, Osgodby, Pickworth, Pointon, Great Ponton, Little Ponton, Rippingale, Ropsley, Sapperton, Sedgebrook, Sempringham, Skillington, Somerby, Spittlegate, Stainby, Stamford All Saints, Stamford St George, Stamford St John, Stamford St Mary, North Stoke, South Stoke, Stowe, Stragglethorpe, Stroxton, Stubton, Swayfield, Swinshead, Syston, Tallington, Thurlby, Toft and Lound, Uffington, Walcot near Folkingham, Welby, Westborough, Wilsthorpe, North Witham, South Witham, Witham on the Hill, Woolsthorpe, Wyville cum Hungerton

EAST LINDSEY (or LOUTH) DIVISION

pt Alford PSD, pt Grimsby PSD, pt Horncastle PSD, Louth MB, Louth PSD, Market Rasen PSD, Wragby PSD, *viz.*, Alvingham, Apley, Ashby by Partney, Asterby, Authorpe, Bardney, East Barkwith, West Barkwith, Baumber, Belchford, Benniworth, Binbrook, Biscathorpe, Brackenborough, Bucknall, Bullington, Burgh on Bain, Burwell, Buslingthorpe, Calcethorpe, Castle Carlton, Great Carlton, Little Carlton, Cawkwell, Little Cawthorpe, Claxby, North Coates, North Cockerington, South Cockerington, Coldstead, Conisholme, Covenham St Bartholomew, Covenham St Mary, Croxby, Donington on Bain, North Elkington, South Elkington, Faldingworth, Farforth cum Maidenwell, Fotherby, Friesthorpe, Fulnetby, Fulstow, Gautby, Gayton le March, Gayton le Wold, Goltho, Goulceby, Grainsby, Grainthorpe, Grimblethorpe, Grimoldby, Little Grimsby, Hainton, Hallington, Hatton, Haugham, Hemingby, Holton cum Beckering, Holton le Clay, Holton le Moor, Horsington, Humberston, Keddington, South Kelsey, Kelstern, Kingerby, Kirkby cum Osgodby, Kirmond le Mire, Langton by Wragby, Legbourne, Legsby, Linwood, Lissington, Ludborough, Ludford Magna, Ludford Parva, Louth, Louth Park, Mablethorpe, Manby, Marsh Chapel,

Minting, Muckton, Newball, Wold Newton, Newton by Toft, Normanby by Spital, North Ormsby, South Ormsby cum Ketsby, North Owersby, South Owersby, Panton, Raithby cum Maltby, Ranby, Rand, Market Rasen, Middle Rasen, West Rasen, North Reston, South Reston, Ruckland, Saltfleetby All Saints, Saltfleetby St Clement, Saltfleetby St Peter, Scamblesby, Sixhills, Skidbrooke with Saltfleet Haven, Snelland, North Somercotes, South Somercotes, Sotby, Stewton, Stainfield, Market Stainton, Stainton by Langworth, Stainton le Vale, Stenigot, Stewton, Stixwould, Great Sturton, Swinhope, Tathwell, Tealby, Tetney, Theddlethorpe All Saints, Theddlethorpe St Helen, North Thoresby, Thoresway, Thorganby, Thornton le Moor, Toft next Newton, East Torrington, West Torrington, Tupholme, Usselby, Utterby, Waddingworth, Walesby, Walmsgate, Welton le Wold, Wickenby, North Willingham, South Willingham, Wispington, Withcall, Wragby, Wyham cum Cadeby, East Wykeham, Yarburgh

NORTH LINDSEY (or BRIGG) DIVISION

Barton upon Humber PSD, Brigg PSD, pt Grimsby PSD, Winterton PSD, *viz.*, Alkborough, Appleby, Ashby, Ashby cum Fenby, Aylesby, Barnetby le Wold, Barnoldby le Beck, Barrow upon Humber, Barton upon Humber St Mary, Barton upon Humber St Peter, Beelsby, Bigby, Bottesford, Brigsley, Brocklesby, Broughton, Brumby, Burringham, Burton upon Stather, East Butterwick, Cabourne, Caistor, Clisby, Crosby, Croxton, Cuxwold, Elsham, South Ferriby, Flixborough, Frodingham, Glanford Brigg, Goxhill, Grasby, Gunness, Habrough, East Halton, West Halton, Hatcliffe, Hawerby cum Beesby, Healing, Hibaldstow, Holme, Horkstow, Immingham, Irby, Keelby, North Kelsey, North Killingholme, South Killingholme, Kirmington, Great Limber, Manton, Melton Ross, Messingham, pt Misson, Nettleton, Newstead, Newton, East Ravendale, West Ravendale, Raventhorpe, Redbourne, Rilby, Rothwell, Roxby cum Risby, Saxby All Saints, Scawby, Scunthorpe, Searby cum Ownby, Snitterby, Somersby, Stallingborough, Swallow, Thornton Curtis, Twigmore, Ulceby, Waddingham, Waithe, Waltham, Whitton, Winteringham, Winterton, Wootton, Worlaby, Wrawby, Yaddlethorpe

SOUTH LINDSEY (or HORNCASTLE) DIVISION

pt Alford PSD, pt Horncastle PSD, Spilsby PSD, *viz.*, Aby with Greenfield, Addlethorpe, Alford, Anderby, Asgarby, West Ashby, Ashby Puerorum, Aswardby, Beesby in the Marsh, Belleau, Bilsby, Bolingbroke, Bratoft, Brinkhill, Burgh le Marsh, Calceby, Candlesby, Carrington, Claxby, Claxby Pluckacre, Claythorpe, Coningsby, Croft, Cumberworth, Dalby, Dalderby, Driby, Eastville, Edlington, Bag Enderby, Mavis Enderby, Wood Enderby, Farlesthorpe, Firsby, Friskney, Frithville, Fulletby, Greetham, Gunby, Hagnaby, Hagworthingham, Haltham, Halton Holegate, Hameringham, Hannah cum Hagnaby, Hareby, Harrington, Haugh, Hogsthorpe, Horncastle, Hundleby, Huttoft, Ingoldmells, Irby in the Marsh, East Keal, West Keal, East Kirkby, Kirkby on Bain, Kirkstead, Langriville, Langton, Langton by Spilsby, Lusby, Maltby le Marsh, Mareham le Fen, Mareham on the Hill, Markby, Martin, Midville, Miningsby, Moorby, Mumby,

Northolme, Orby, South Ormsby cum Ketsby, Oxcombe, Partney, Raithby, Revesby, Rigsby with Ailby, Roughton, Saleby with Thoresthorpe, Salmonby, Sausthorpe, Scrafield, Scremby, Scrivelsby, Sibsey, Skegness, Skendleby, Somerby, Spilsby, Great Steeping, Little Steeping, Stickford, Stickney, Strubby with Woodthorpe, Sutterby, Sutton in the Marsh, Swaby, Tattershall, Tattershall Thorpe, Tetford, Thimbleby, South Thoresby, Thornton, Thornton le Fen, Thorpe St Peter, Tothill, High Toynton, Low Toynton, Toynton All Saints, Toynton St Peter, Trusthorpe, Tumby, Ulceby with Fordington, Wainfleet All Saints, Wainfleet St Mary, Well, Welton le Marsh, Westville, Wildmore, Wilksby, Willoughby with Sloothby, Winceby, Winthorpe, Withern with Stain, Woodhall, Worlaby

WEST LINDSEY (or GAINSBOROUGH) DIVISION
Epworth PSD, Gainsborough PSD, Lincoln PSD, *viz.*, Aisthorpe, Althorpe, Amcotts, Atterby, Barlings, Belton, Blyborough, Blyton cum Wharton, Bracebridge, Brampton, Brattleby, Broxholme, Burton, Gate Burton, East Butterwick, West Butterwick, Caenby, Cammeringham, North Carlton, South Carlton, Cleatham, Coates, Corringham, Crowle, Dunholme, Eastoft, Epworth, Fenton, East Ferry, Fillingham, East Firsby, West Firsby, Fiskerton, Gainsborough, Garthorpe, Glentham, Glentworth, Grayingham, Greenhill and Redhill, Greetwell, Hackthorn, Cold Hanworth, Hardwick, Harpswell, Haxey, Heapham, Hemswell, Ingham, Keadby, Kettlethorpe, Kexby, Kirton in Lindsey, Knaith, Laughton, Lea, Luddington, Marton, pt Misson, Morton, Nettleham, Newton on Trent, Normanby by Spital, Normanby le Wold, Northorpe, Bishop Norton, Owmby, Owston, Pilham, Reepham, Riseholme, Saxby, Saxilby with Ingleby, Scampton, Scotter, Spridlington, Springthorpe, East Stockwith, Stow, Sturton by Stow, Sudbrooke, Thorpe in the Fallows, Torksey, Upton, Walkerith, Welton, Wildsworth, Willingham, Cherry Willingham, Willoughton, Wroot

1918—1948
BRIGG DIVISION [Pts Lind]
Barton upon Humber UD, Brigg UD, Broughton UD, Brumby and Frodingham UD, Glanford Brigg RD, Roxby cum Risby RD, Scunthorpe UD, Winterton UD
GAINSBOROUGH DIVISION [Pts Lind]
Crowle RD, Gainsborough RD, Gainsborough UD, Isle of Axholme RD, Welton RD
GRANTHAM DIVISION [Pts Kestev]
Branston RD, Claypole RD, Grantham MB, pt Grantham RD (Ancaster, Barrowby, Belton, Carlton Scroop, Great Gonerby, Harrowby Without, Heydour, Honington, Hough on the Hill, Londonthorpe, Manthorpe, Normanton, pt Spittlegate Without, Welby), Ruskington UD, Sleaford RD, Sleaford UD
HOLLAND WITH BOSTON DIVISION [Pts Holl]
Adm Co of Pts Holl
HORNCASTLE DIVISION [Pts Lind]
Alford UD, Horncastle RD, Horncastle UD, Sibsey RD, Skegness UD, Spilsby RD, Woodhall Spa UD
LOUTH DIVISION [Pts Lind]
Caistor RD, Grimsby RD, Louth MB, Louth RD,

Mablethorpe UD, Market Rasen UD
RUTLAND AND STAMFORD DIVISION [Pts Kestev, Rutl Adm Co]
Adm Co of Rutl and the following places in Pts Kestev: Bourne RD, Bourne UD, pt Grantham RD (the pars not in Grantham Dv), Stamford MB, Uffington RD

1948—1970
BRIGG COUNTY CONSTITUENCY [Pts Lind]
Barton upon Humber UD, Brigg UD, Glanford Brigg RD, Scunthorpe MB
GAINSBOROUGH COUNTY CONSTITUENCY [Pts Lind]
Caistor RD, Gainsborough RD, Gainsborough UD, Isle of Axholme RD, Market Rasen UD, Welton RD
GRANTHAM COUNTY CONSTITUENCY[3] [Pts Kestev]
Grantham RD, pt East Kesteven RD (the pars not in Rutland and Stamford CC), North Kesteven RD, pt West Kesteven RD (Allington, Ancaster, Barkston, Barrowby, Belton and Manthorpe, Long Bennington, Carlton Scroop, Caythorpe, Claypole, Fenton, Foston, Fulbeck, Great Gonerby, Heydour, Honington, Hough on the Hill, Hougham, Londonthorpe and Harrowby Without, Marston, Normanton, Sedgebrook, Stubton, Syston, Welby, Westborough and Dry Doddington), Sleaford UD
HOLLAND WITH BOSTON COUNTY CONSTITUENCY [Pts Holl]
Adm Co of Pts Holl
HORNCASTLE COUNTY CONSTITUENCY [Pts Lind]
Alford UD, Horncastle RD, Horncastle UD, Mablethorpe and Sutton UD, Skegness UD, Spilsby RD, Woodhall Spa UD
LOUTH COUNTY CONSTITUENCY[2] [Pts Lind]
Cleethorpes MB, Grimsby RD, Louth MB, Louth RD
RUTLAND AND STAMFORD COUNTY CONSTITUENCY [Pts Kestev, Rutl Adm Co]
Adm Co of Rutl and the following places in Pts Kestev: Bourne UD, pt East Kesteven RD (Aswarby and Swarby, Aunsby and Dembleby, Helpringham, Newton and Haceby, Osbournby, Scredington, Swaton, Threckingham, Walcot near Folkingham), South Kesteven RD, pt West Kesteven RD (the pars not in Grantham CC), Stamford MB

1970—*
BRIGG AND SCUNTHORPE COUNTY CONSTITUENCY [Pts Lind]
Barton upon Humber UD, Brigg UD, Glanford Brigg RD, Scunthorpe MB
GAINSBOROUGH COUNTY CONSTITUENCY [Pts Lind]
Caistor RD, Gainsborough RD, Gainsborough UD, Isle of Axholme RD, Market Rasen RD, Welton RD
GRANTHAM COUNTY CONSTITUENCY [Pts Kestev]
Grantham MB, pt East Kesteven RD (the pars not in Rutl and Stamford CC), North Kesteven RD, pt West Kesteven RD (Allington, Ancaster, Barkston, Barrowby, Belton and Manthorpe, Long Bennington, Carlton Scroop, Caythorpe, Claypole, Fenton, Foston, Ful-

beck, Great Gonerby, Haydour, Honington, Hough on the Hill, Hougham, Londonthorpe and Harrowby Without, Marston, Normanton, Sedgebrook, Stubton, Syston, Welby, Westborough and Dry Doddington), Sleaford UD

HOLLAND WITH BOSTON COUNTY CONSTITU-ENCY [Pts Holl]

Adm Co of Pts Holl

HORNCASTLE COUNTY CONSTITUENCY [Pts Lind]

Alford UD, Horncastle RD, Horncastle UD, Mablethorpe and Sutton UD, Skegness UD, Spilsby RD, Woodhall Spa UD

LOUTH COUNTY CONSTITUENCY [Pts Lind]

Cleethorpes MB, Grimsby RD, Louth MB, Louth RD

RUTLAND AND STAMFORD COUNTY CONSTITU-ENCY [Pts Kestev, Rutl Adm Co]

Adm Co of Rutl and the following places in Pts Kestev: Bourne UD, pt East Kesteven RD (Aswarby and Swarby, Aunsby and Dembleby, Helpringham, Newton and Haceby, Osbournby, Scredington, Swaton, Threckingham, Walcot near Folkingham), South Kesteven RD, pt West Kesteven RD (Bitchfield and Bassingthorpe, Boothby Pagnell, Braceby and Sapperton, Burton Coggles, Colsterworth, Denton, Easton, Gunby and Stainby, Harlaxton, Ingoldsby, Lenton Keisby and Osgodby, Great Ponton, Little Ponton and Stroxton, Pickworth, Ropsley and Humby, Skillington, Old Somerby, Stoke Rochford, South Witham, Woolsthorpe, Wyville cum Hungerton

NORTHAMPTONSHIRE

BOROUGH CONSTITUENCIES[1]

BANBURY PARL BOR (1554—1885) (Oxon, Northants [1832—85])
  Banbury (pt [Oxon] 1554—1832, ent [Oxon, Northants] 1832—85)
BRACKLEY PARL BOR (1547—1832)
  Brackley St James (when gains sep civ identity), Brackley St Peter
HIGHAM FERRERS PARL BOR (1558—1832)
  pt Higham Ferrers
NORTHAMPTON PARL BOR/BC (1295—1970)
  1295—1918: pt Dallington (1867—1918), pt Duston (1867—1918), pt Hardingstone (1867—1918), pt Kingsthorpe (1867—1918), Northampton All Saints, Northampton Priory of St Andrew, Northampton St Giles, Northampton St Peter, Northampton St Sepulchre
  1918—1970: Northampton CB

NORTHAMPTON NORTH BC[2] (1970—*)
  pt Northampton CB (wards of Abington, Dallington, Kingsthorpe, Park, St David, St George)
NORTHAMPTON SOUTH BC[2] (1970—*)
  pt Northampton CB (wards of Castle, Delapre, Dunston, St Crispin, South, Weston)
PETERBOROUGH PARL BOR (1547—1918)
  Peterborough [St John the Baptist] (pt 1547—1867, enlarged pt 1832—67, ent 1867—1918), Peterborough Minster Close Precincts
PETERBOROUGH BC (1970—*) [Hunts & Peterb]
  Barnack RD, Peterborough MB, Peterborough RD, Thorney RD[3]
STAMFORD PARL BOR (1295—1306 irregularly, 1322, 1467—1885) (Lincs Pts Kestev, Northants [1832—85])
  pt Stamford Baron St Martin (1832—85)

COUNTY CONSTITUENCIES

1832—1885
NORTHERN DIVISION
  Lbty of Peterborough and Hds of Corby, Hamfordshoe, Higham Ferrers, Huxloe, Navisford, Orlingbury, Polebrook, Rothwell, Willybrook
SOUTHERN DIVISION
  Hds of Cleley, Fawsley, Guilsborough, Nobottle Grove, Green's Norton, Spelhoe, King's Sutton, Towcester, Chipping Warden, Wymersley

1885—1918
EASTERN DIVISION
  pt Kettering PSD, Wellingborough PSD, *viz.,* Little Addington, Mears Ashby, Earls Barton, Bozeat, Broughton, Chelveston cum Caldecott, Cransley, Great Doddington, Easton Maudit, Ecton, Finedon, Grendon, Hardwick, Great Harrowden, Little Harrowden, Higham Ferrers, Higham Park, Irchester, Irthlingborough, Isham, Kettering, Newton Bromshold, Orlingbury, Pytchley, Rushton, Stanwick, Strixton, Sywell, Wellingborough, Wilby, Wollaston
MID DIVISION
  Little Bowden PSD, pt Daventry PSD, pt Kettering PSD, Northampton PSD, *viz.,* Abington, Althorp, Arthingworth, Castle Ashby, Cold Ashby, Ashby St Ledgers, Ashley, Barby, Great Billing, Little Billing, Boughton, Little Bowden, Brafield on the Green, Chapel Brampton, Church Brampton, Brampton Ash, Braybrooke, Brington, Brixworth, Long Buckby, Bugbrooke, Claycoton, Clipston, Cogenhoe, Collingtree, Coton, Cottesbrooke, Courtenhall, Great Creaton, Crick, pt Dallington, Denton, Dingley, Draughton, pt Duston, Elkington, East Farndon, Faxton, Flore, Glendon, Guilsborough, Hackleton, East Haddon, West Haddon, Hannington, pt Hardingstone, Harlestone, Harpole, Harrington, Haselbech, Nether Heyford, Upper Heyford, Holcot, Holdenby, Hollowell, Horton, Hothorpe, Great Houghton, Little Houghton, Kelmarsh, Kilsby, pt Kingsthorpe, Kislingbury, Lamport, Lilbourne, Loddington, Maidwell, Marston Trussel, Mawsley, Milton, Moulton, Moulton Park, Naseby, Old, Orton, Overstone, Great Oxendon, Piddington, Pitsford, Preston Deanery, Quinton, Ravensthorpe, Roade, Rothersthorpe, Rothwell, Rushton, Scaldwell, Sibbertoft, Spratton, Stanford, Stoke Albany, Sulby, Sutton Bassett, Teeton, Thornby, Thorpe Lubenham, Thorpe Malsor, Upton, Walgrave, Watford, Welford, Weston by Welland, Weston Favell, Whiston, Wilbarston, pt Winwick, Wootton, Yardley Hastings, Yelveroft
NORTHERN DIVISION
  pt Kettering PSD, Oundle PSD, Soke of Peterborough, the pt of Stamford MB in Northants, Thrapston PSD, *viz.,* Great Addington, Ailsworth, Aldwincle All Saints, Aldwincle St Peter, Apethorpe, Armston, Ashton, Ashton, Bainton, Barford, Barnack, Barnwell All Saints, Barnwell St Andrew, Barton Seagrave, Beanfield Lawns, Benefield, Blatherwycke, Borough Fen, Brigstock, Bulwick, Burton Latimer, East Carlton, Castor, Clopton, King's Cliffe, Collyweston, Corby, Cotterstock, Cottesbrooke, Cottingham, Cranford St Andrew, Cranford St John, Deene, Deenethorpe, Deeping Gate, Denford, Desborough, Duddington, Easton on the Hill, Etton, Eye, Fineshade, Fotheringhay, Geddington, Glapthorn, Glinton, Grafton Underwood, Gretton, Gunthorpe, Hargrave, Harringworth, Helpston, Hemington, Islip, Laxton, Lilford cum Wigsthorpe, Lowick, pt Luddington, pt Lutton, Marholm, Maxey, Middleton, Nassington, Newborough, Newton, Northborough, Great Oakley, Little

Oakley, Oundle, Paston, Peakirk, Pilsgate, Pilton, Polebrook, Raunds, Ringstead, Rockingham, Rushden, Slipton, Southorpe, Southwick, Stanion, Stoke Doyle, Stuchbury, Sudborough, Kings Sutton, Tansor, Thornhaugh, Thorpe Achurch, pt Thorpe by Water, Thrapston, pt Thurning, Titchmarsh, Twywell, Ufford, Upton, Wadenhoe, Wakerley, Walton, Wansford, Warkton, Warmington, Weekley, Great Weldon, Little Weldon, Werrington, pt Winwick, Wittering, Woodford, Woodnewton, Wothorpe, Yarwell

SOUTHERN DIVISION

Brackley PSD, pt Daventry PSD, Towcester PSD, *viz.*, Abthorpe, Adstone, Alderton, Appletree, Canons Ashby, Ashton, Aston le Walls, Astwell and Falcott, Aynho, Badby, Blakesley, Blisworth, Lower Boddington, Upper Boddington, Brackley St Peter, Bradden, Braunston, Brockhall, Byfield, Catesby, Chalcombe, Charwelton, Cosgrove, Croughton, Culworth, Daventry, Dodford, Easton Neston, Edgcote, Evenley, Everdon, Eydon, Farthinghoe, Farthingstone, Fawsley, Furtho, Gayton, Grafton Regis, Greatworth, pt Hanslope, Hartwell, Hellidon, Helmdon, Cold Higham, Hinton in the Hedges, Litchborough, Maidford, Marston St Lawrence, Middleton Cheney, Moreton Pinkney, Newbottle, Newnham, Norton, Green's Norton, Passenham, Pattishall, Paulerspury, Plumpton, Potterspury, Preston Capes, Radstone, Shutlanger, Silverstone, Slapton, Staverton, Steane, Stoke Bruerne, Stoneton, Stowe Nine Churches, Stuchbury, Sulgrave, Kings Sutton, Syresham, Thenford, Thorpe Mandeville, Tiffield, Towcester, Wappenham, Chipping Warden, Warkworth, Weedon Beck, Weedon Lois, Welton, Whilton, Whitfield, Whittlebury, Wicken, Woodend, Woodford cum Membris, Yardley Gobion

1918—1948
DAVENTRY DIVISION
Brackley MB, Brackley RD, Crick RD, Daventry MB, Daventry RD, Hardingstone RD, Middleton Cheney RD, pt Northampton RD (the pars not in Kettering Dv), Potterspury RD, Towcester RD
KETTERING DIVISION
Brixworth RD, Desborough UD, Kettering RD, Kettering UD, pt Northampton RD (Great Billing, Little Billing, Weston Favell), Oxendon RD, Rothwell UD

PETERBOROUGH DIVISION
Soke of Peterborough Adm Co and the following areas in Northants: Easton on the Hill RD, Gretton RD, the pt of Oundle RD in Northants, Oundle UD, pt of the pt of Thrapston RD in Northants (the Northants pars not in Wellingborough Dv), Wellingborough RD)
WELLINGBOROUGH DIVISION
Finedon UD, Higham Ferrers MB, Irthlingborough UD, Raunds UD, Rushden UD, pt Thrapston RD (Chelveston cum Caldecott, Hargrave, Stanwick), Wellingborough RD, Wellingborough UD

1948—1970
KETTERING COUNTY CONSTITUENCY
Brixworth RD, Burton Latimer UD, Corby UD, Desborough UD, Kettering MB, Kettering RD, Rothwell UD
SOUTH NORTHANTS COUNTY CONSTITUENCY
Brackley MB, Brackley RD, Daventry MB, Daventry RD, Northampton RD, Towcester RD
PETERBOROUGH COUNTY CONSTITUENCY
Soke of Peterb: Barnack RD, Peterborough MB, Peterborough RD
Northants: Oundle UD, pt Oundle and Thrapston RD (the pars not in Wellingborough CC)
WELLINGBOROUGH COUNTY CONSTITUENCY
Higham Ferrers MB, Irthlingborough UD, pt Oundle and Thrapston RD (Chelveston cum Caldecott, Hargrave), Raunds UD, Rushden UD, Wellingborough RD, Wellingborough UD

1970—*
DAVENTRY COUNTY CONSTITUENCY[2]
Brackley MB, Brackley RD, Brixworth RD, Daventry MB, Daventry RD, Northampton RD, Towcester RD
KETTERING COUNTY CONSTITUENCY
Burton Latimer UD, Corby UD, Desborough UD, Kettering MB, Kettering RD, Rothwell UD
WELLINGBOROUGH COUNTY CONSTITUENCY[2]
Higham Ferrers MB, Irthlingborough UD, Oundle UD, Oundle and Thrapston RD, Raunds UD, Rushden UD, Wellingborough RD, Wellingborough UD

NORTHUMBERLAND

BOROUGH CONSTITUENCIES[1]

BAMBURGH PARL BOR (1295 only)
Bamburgh
BERWICK UPON TWEED PARL BOR (1554—1885)
Berwick upon Tweed, Tweedmouth (1835—85)
BLYTH BC[2] (1948—*)
Bedlingtonshire UD, Blyth MB, Seaton Valley UD
CORBRIDGE PARL BOR (1295 only)
Corbridge
MORPETH PARL BOR (1553—1948) [1 mbr 1832—1948]
1553—1832: pt Morpeth
1832—1918: Bedlington,[3] Bullers Green, Cowpen (1867—1918), Hepscott, Morpeth, Morpeth Castle, Newminster Abbey, Newsham and South Blyth (1867—1918), Tranwell and High Church
1918—48: Ashington UD, Bedlingtonshire UD, Blyth UD, Morpeth MB, pt Morpeth RD (Hepscott, Morpeth Castle, Newminster, Tranwell)
NEWCASTLE UPON TYNE PARL BOR/BC (1295—1918)
1295—1832: Newcastle upon Tyne All Saints, Newcastle upon Tyne St Andrew, Newcastle upon Tyne St John, Newcastle upon Tyne St Nicholas
1832—1918: Byker, Elswick, Heaton, Jesmond, Newcastle upon Tyne All Saints, Newcastle upon Tyne St Andrew, Newcastle upon Tyne St John, Newcastle upon Tyne St Nicholas
NEWCASTLE UPON TYNE CENTRAL PARL BOR/BC[4] (1918—*)
pt Newcastle upon Tyne CB (the wards of All Saints [1918—48], Armstrong [1948—*], Benwell [1955—*],
Byker [1948—*], St Anthony's [1948—*], St John's [1918—48], St Nicholas, Stephenson, Westgate [1918—48]), Newcastle upon Tyne RD (1948—*)
NEWCASTLE UPON TYNE EAST PARL BOR/BC (1918—*)
pt Newcastle upon Tyne CB (the wards of Byker [1918—48], Dene [1948—*], Heaton [1948—*], St Anthony's [1918—48], St Lawrence, Walker, Walker Gate [1948—*])
NEWCASTLE UPON TYNE NORTH PARL BOR/BC (1918—*)
pt Newcastle upon Tyne CB (the wards of Arthur's Hill [1948—*], Dene [1918—48], Elswick [1948—*], Heaton [1918—48], Jesmond, St Andrew's [1918—48], St Thomas [1918—48], Sanyford [1948—*], Westgate [1948—*])
NEWCASTLE UPON TYNE WEST PARL BOR/BC[4] (1918—*)
Newburn UD (1948—*), pt Newcastle upon Tyne CB (the wards of Armstrong [1918—48], Arthur's Hill [1918—48], Benwell [1918—55], Elswick [1918—48], Fenham, Kenton [1948—*], Scotswood [1948—*])
TYNEMOUTH PARL BOR/BC (1832—*) [1 mbr]
1832—1918: Chirton, Cullercoats, Preston, North Shields, Tynemouth
1918—:* Tynemouth CB, Whitley Bay UD (1948—70), Whitley Bay MB (1970—*)
WALLSEND PARL BOR/BC (1918—*)
Gosforth UD, Longbenton UD, Wallsend MB, Weetslade UD (1918—48)

COUNTY CONSTITUENCIES

1832—1885
NORTHERN DIVISION
Wards of Bamburgh, Coquetdale, Glendale, Morpeth; Islandshire, Norhamshire
SOUTHERN DIVISION
Wards of Castle, Tynedale

1885—1918
BERWICK UPON TWEED DIVISION
Bamburgh PSD, Berwick upon Tweed MB, pt East Coquetdale PSD, North Coquetdale PSD, Glendale PSD, Norhamshire and Islandshire, *viz.*, Abberwick, Acton and Old Fenton, Adderstone, Akeld, Alnham, Alnmouth, Alnwick, Ancroft, Bamburgh, Bamburgh Castle, Bassington, Beadnell, Beanley, Belford, New Bewick, Old Bewick, Birling, Bolton, Boulmer and Seaton House, Bradford, Brandon, Branton, Branxton, Broome Park, Brotherwick, Broxfield, Brunton, Budle, Burton, High Buston, Low Buston, Callaly and Yetlington, Carham, North Charlton, South Charlton, Chathill, Chatton, Chillingham, Coldsmouth and Thompson's Walls, Cornhill on Tweed, Coupland, Craster, Crawley, Crookhouse, Detchant, Ditchburn, Doddington, Doxford, Duddo, Dunstan, Earle, Easington, Easington Grange, Edlingham, Eglingham, Elford, Ellingham, Elwick, Elyhaugh, Embleton, Ewart, Fallodon, Farne Islands, Fawdon and Clinch, Fellington, Felton, Fleetham, Ford, Glanton, Glororum, Greens and Glantlees, Grey's Forest, Grindon, Guyzance, Harehope, Hazon and Hartlaw, Hedgeley, Hepburn, Hethpool, Holy Island, Hoppen, Horncliffe, Howick, Howtel, Humbleton, Ilderton; Ingram, Linhope, Greenshawhill and Hartside; Kilham, Kirknewton, Kyloe, Lanton, Learchild, Lemmington, Lesbury, East Lilburn, West Lilburn, Littlehoughton, Loanend, Longridge, Longhoughton, Lorbottle, Lowick, Lucker, Midleton, North Middleton, South Middleton, Middleton Hall, Millfield, Monks House, Mousen, Nesbit, Newham, Newstead, Newton by the Sea, Newton on the Moor, Newtown, Norham, Norham Mains, Outchester, Paston, Prendwick, Preston, Ratchwood, Reaveley, Rennington, Rock, Roddam, Roseden, Ross,

Great Ryle, Little Ryle, Scrainwood, Selby's Forest, Shawdon, Shilbottle, Shipley, Shoreston, Shoreswood, Spindlestone, Stamford, Sturton Grange, North Sunderland, Swarland, Swinhoe, Thornton, Titlington, Tughall, Tweedmouth, Twizell, Unthank, Walkmill, Warenford, Warenton, Westnewton, Whittingham, Whittle, Woodhouse, Wooler, Wooperton, Yeavering

HEXHAM DIVISION

Bellingham PSD, West Coquetdale PSD, Haltwhistle PSD, Tynedale PSD, *viz.*, Acomb, East Acomb, Allendale, Alwinton, Anick, Anick Grange, Apperley, Aydon, Aydon Castle, Barrow, Great Bavington, Little Bavington, Bearl, Bellingham, Bellister, Bickerton, Biddlestone, Bingfield, Birtley, Bitchfield, Black Carts and Ryehill, Blenkinsopp, Brinkburn High Ward, Brinkburn Low Ward, Broomhaugh, Broomley, Burradon, Bywell St Andrew, Bywell St Peter, Caistron, Capheaton, Carrycoats, Cartington, Catcherside, East Charlton, West Charlton, Cheeseburn Grange, Chirdon, Chollerton, Clarewood, Clennell, Coanwood, Cocklaw, Coldwell, Corbridge, Corsenside, Crookdean, Debdon, Dilston, Dueshill, Duke's Hagg, Elsdon, Eltringham, Espershields, Fairhaugh, Fairnley, Fallowfield, Fallowlees, Farnham, Fawns, Featherstone, Fenwick, Flotterton, High Fotherley, Greenleighton, Hallington, Halton, Halton Shields, Haltwhistle, Harbottle, Little Harle, West Harle, Harlow Hill, Hartington, Hartington Hall, Hartleyburn, Harwood, Haughton, Hawkwell, Hawick, Haydon, Healey, Black Heddon, West Heddon, Hedley, Hedley Woodside, Henshaw, Hepple, Hepple Demesne, Hesleyhurst, Heugh, Hexham, Hexhamshire High Quarter, Hexhamshire Low Quarter, Hexhamshire Middle Quarter, Hexhamshire West Quarter, Hollinghill, Holystone, Horsley, Humshaugh, Ingoe, Kearsley, Kidland, Kirkharle, Kirkhaugh, Kirkheaton, Kirkwhelpington, Knarsdale, Lambley, Lee Ward, Leemailing, Linbridge, Linsheeles, Longframlington, Masters Close, East Matfen, West Matfen, Melkridge, Mickley, Monkridge, Mount Healey, Nafferton, Nesbitt, Netherton North Side, Netherton South Side, Newbiggin, Newbrough, Newlands, Newton, Newton Hall, Newtown, Nook, Otterburn, Ouston, Ovingham, Ovington, Pauperhaugh, Peels, Plashetts and Tynehead, Plenmeller, Portgate, Prudhoe, Prudhoe Castle, Ramshope, Raw, Riding, Ridley, Rochester, Rothley, Rothley, Ryal, Sandhoe, Sharperton, High Shitlington, Low Shitlington, Shotley High Quarter, Shotley Low Quarter, Simonburn, Slaley, Smalesmouth, Snitter, Spital, Stelling, Stocksfield Hall, Styford, Sweethope, Tarretburn, Tarset West, Thirlwall, Thockrington, Thornborough, Thorneyburn, Thorngrafton, Thropton, Great Tosson and Rye Hill, Tosson Little, High and Low Trewhitt, Troughend, Wall, Wall Town, Wallridge, Warden, Wark, Warksburn, Warton, Wellhaugh, Welton, West Whelpington, Whitfield, Great Whittington, Little Whittington, Whittle, Whitton, Whittonstall, Woodside, Wreighill

TYNESIDE DIVISION

pt Castle East PSD, pt Castle West PSD, *viz.*, Benwell, East Brunton, West Brunton, Butterlaw, Black Callerton, Coxlodge, East Denton, West Denton, Fawdon, Fenham, North Gosforth, South Gosforth, Kenton, Longbenton, Newbiggin, Newburn, Newburn Hall, Sugley, Throckley, Wallbottle, Wallsend, Whorlton, Woolsington

WANSBECK DIVISION

Bedlingtonshire PSD, pt Castle East PSD, pt Castle West PSD, pt East Coquetdale PSD, Morpeth PSD, *viz.*, Acklington, Acklington Park, Amble, High Angerton, Low Angerton, Ashington and Sheepwash, Backworth, Bebside, Belsay, Benridge, Berwick Hall, Bigge's Quarter, Bockenfield, Bolam, Bolam Vicarage, Bothal Demesne, Bradford, Brenkley, Brinkburn South Side, Bullock's Hall, Burradon, High Callerton, Little Callerton, Cambo, Causey Park, East Chevington, West Chevington, Coatyards, Cockle Park, Coldcoats, Corridge, Cramlington, Cresswell, Dalton, Darras Hall, Deanham, Dinnington, North Dissington, South Dissington, Eachwick, Earsdon, Earsdon, Earsdon Forest, Edington, Ellington, Eshott, Ewesley, Fenrother, Freeholders' Quarter, Gallowhill, Gloster Hill, Hadston, Harnham, Hartburn, Hartburn Grange, East Hartford, West Hartford, Hartley, Hauxley, Healey and Combhill, Hebron, East Heddon, West Heddon, Heddon on the Wall, Higham Dykes, Highlaws, High and Low Highlaws, Hirst, Holywell, Horton, Horton Grange, Houghton and Close House, Kirkley, Longhirst, Longshaws, Longwitton, Lynmouth, Mason, Meldon, North Middleton, South Middleton, Milbourne, Milbourne Grange, Mitford, Molesdon, Monkseaton, Morwick, Murton, Netherwitton, Newbiggin by the Sea, Newham, Newton Park, Newton Underwood, Nunnykirk, Nunriding, Ogle, Old Moor, Pegswood, Pigdon, Ponteland, Prestwick, Riddell's Quarter, Riplington, Ritton Colt Park, Ritton White House, Rivergreen, Rudchester, North Seaton, Seaton Delaval, Seghill, East Shaftoe, West Shaftoe, Shilvington, Shortflatt, Spital Hill, Stannington, Stanton, East and West Thirston with Shothaugh, East Thornton, West Thornton, Throphill, Todburn, Todridge, Togston, Trewick, Tritlington, Twizell, Ulgham, Wallington Demesne, Warkworth, Whalton, Whitchester, Whitridge, Whitley, Widdrington, Wingates, Witton Shields, Woodhorn, Woodhorn Demesne, Wylam

1918—1948

BERWICK UPON TWEED DIVISION

Alnwick RD, Alnwick UD, Amble UD, Belford RD, Berwick upon Tweed MB, Farne Islands, Glendale RD, Norham and Islandshires RD, Rothbury RD, Rothbury UD

HEXHAM DIVISION

Bellingham RD, pt Castle Ward RD (Bitchfield, Capheaton, Cheesburn Grange, Fenwick, Harlow Hill, Hawkwell, Black Heddon, Heugh, Ingoe, Kearsley, Kirkheaton, East Matfen, West Matfen, Nesbitt, Ouston, Ryal, Wallridge), Haltwhistle RD, Hexham RD, Hexham UD, Prudhoe UD

WANSBECK DIVISION

pt Castle Ward RD (the pars not in Hexham Dv), Cramlington UD, Earsdon UD, Moot Hall Precincts, pt Morpeth RD (all except Hepscott, Morpeth Castle, Newminster, Tranwell), Newbiggin by the Sea UD, Newburn UD, Seaton Delaval UD, Seghill UD, Whitley and Monkseaton UD

1948—70

BERWICK UPON TWEED COUNTY CONSTITU-ENCY

Alnwick RD, Alnwick UD, Amble UD, Belford RD, Berwick upon Tweed MB, Glendale RD, Norham and Islandshires RD, Rothbury RD

HEXHAM COUNTY CONSTITUENCY

Bellingham RD, Castle Ward RD, Haltwhistle RD, Hexham RD, Hexham UD, Prudhoe UD

MORPETH COUNTY CONSTITUENCY

Ashington UD, Morpeth MB, Morpeth RD, Newbiggin by the Sea UD

*1970—**

BERWICK UPON TWEED COUNTY CONSTITU-ENCY

Alnwick RD, Alnwick UD, Amble UD, Belford RD, Berwick upon Tweed MB, Glendale RD, Norham and Islandshires RD, Rothbury RD

HEXHAM COUNTY CONSTITUENCY[2]

Bellingham RD, Castle Ward RD, Haltwhistle RD, Hexham RD, Hexham UD, Prudhoe UD

MORPETH COUNTY CONSTITUENCY

Ashington UD, Morpeth MB, Morpeth RD, Newbiggin by the Sea UD

NOTTINGHAMSHIRE

BOROUGH CONSTITUENCIES[1]

NEWARK UPON TRENT/NEWARK PARL BOR (1673—1885)
Newark upon Trent, pt East Stoke

NOTTINGHAM PARL BOR (1295—1918)
Basford (1885—1918), Brewhouse Yard (1885—1918), pt West Bridgford (1885—1918), Bulwell (1885—1918), pt Carlton (1885—1918), pt Lenton (1885—1918), Nottingham St Mary, Nottingham St Nicholas, Nottingham St Peter, Radford (1885—1918), Standard Hill (1885—1918), pt Wilford (1885—1918)

NOTTINGHAM CENTRAL PARL BOR/BC[2] (1918—70)
pt Nottingham CB (wards of Forest, Manvers [1956—70], Market, Radford [1956—70], Robin Hood [1918—56], St Ann's [1918—48], St Ann's [1956—70], St Mary's [1948—56], Sherwood [1918—56]), Nottingham RD (1948—70)

NOTTINGHAM EAST PARL BOR/BC (1918—*)
pt Nottingham CB (wards of Bridge [1970—*], Byron [1918—70], Lenton [1970—*], Manvers, Mapperley [1918—70], Market [1970—*], St Ann's [1948—*], St Mary's [1918—48], Trent [1970—*]), Shire Hall (1948—*)

NOTTINGHAM NORTH BC (1956[2]—*)
Hucknall UD (1956—70), pt Nottingham CB (wards of Byron, Forest [1970—*], Mapperley, Portland, Radford [1970—*], St Albans)

NOTTINGHAM NORTH WEST BC (1948—56[2])
pt Nottingham CB (wards of Broxtowe, St Albans, Wollaton)

NOTTINGHAM SOUTH PARL BOR/BC[3] (1918—70)
West Bridgford UD (1956—70), pt Nottingham CB (wards of Bridge, Castle [1918—56], Clifton [1952—70], Lenton [1956—70], Meadows [1918—56], Trent)

NOTTINGHAM WEST PARL BOR (1918—48)
pt Nottingham CB (wards of Broxtowe, St Albans, Wollaton)

NOTTINGHAM WEST BC (1956[2]—*)
pt Nottingham CB (wards of Abbey, Broxtowe, Clifton [1970—*], Robin Hood, University [1970—*], Wollaton)

EAST RETFORD PARL BOR (1316, 1572—1885)
Bassetlaw Wap (1832—85), East Retford

COUNTY CONSTITUENCIES

1832—1885
NORTHERN DIVISION
Broxtowe Wap
SOUTHERN DIVISION
Waps of Bingham, Newark, Rushcliffe, Thurgarton

1885—1918
BASSETLAW DIVISION
pt Mansfield PSD, Retford PSD, East Retford MB, Worksop PSD, *viz.*, Askham, pt Auckley, Babworth, Barnby Moor, Beckingham, Bevercotes, Bilsthorpe, Blyth, Bole, Bothamsall, Boughton, Budby, West Burton, Carburton, Carlton in Lindrick, Clarborough, Clayworth, Clipstone, Cottam, Cuckney, Darlton, East Drayton, West Drayton, Dunham, Eakring, Eaton, Edwinstowe, Egmanton, Elkesley, Everton, Finningley, Gamston, Gringley on the Hill, Grove, Harworth, Haughton, Hayton, Headon cum Upton, Hodsock, Holbeck, Kirton, Laneham, Nether Langwith, Laxton, North Leverton with Habblesthorpe, South Leverton, Littleborough, Lound, East Markham, Markham Clinton or West Markham, Mattersey, pt Misson, Misterton, Norton, Ollerton, Ompton, Ordsall, Perlethorpe, Ragnall, Rampton, Ranskill, East Retford, West Retford, Rufford, Saundby, Scaftworth, Scrooby, Sookholme, West Stockwith, Stokeham, Sturton le Steeple, Styrrup, Sutton, Torworth, Treswell, Tuxford, Walesby, Walkeringham, pt Wallingwells, Welbeck, Warsop, Wellow, North Wheatley, South Wheatley, Wiseton, Woodhouse Hall, Worksop

MANSFIELD DIVISION
pt Mansfield PSD, pt Nottingham PSD, *viz.*, Annesley, Blidworth, Eastwood, Felley, Fulwood, Greasley, Haywood Oaks, Hucknall under Huthwaite, Kirkby in Ashfield, Lindhurst, Mansfield, Mansfield Woodhouse, Selston, Skegby, Sutton in Ashfield, Teversall

NEWARK DIVISION
Bingham PSD, Newark MB, Newark PSD, pt Nottingham PSD, pt Southwell PSD, *viz.*, Alverton, Aslockton, Averham, Balderton, Barnby in the Willows, Bathley, Besthorpe, Bingham, Bleasby, East Bridgford, Broadholme, Upper Broughton, Bulcote, Calverton, Carlton on Trent, Caunton, Caythorpe, North Clifton, South Clifton, Clipston, Coddington, North Collingham, South Collingham, Car Colston, Colston Bassett, Cotgrave, Cotham, Cromwell, Cropwell Bishop, Cropwell Butler, Edingley, Elston, Elton, Epperstone, Farndon, Farnsfield, Fiskerton cum Morton, Flawborough, Fledborough, Flintham, Gamston, Girton, Gonalston, Granby, Grassthorpe, Gunthorpe, Halam, Halloughton, Harby, Hawksworth, Hawton, Hickling, Hockerton, Holme, Holme Pierrepont, Hoveringham, Kelham, Kersall, Kilvington, Kinoulton, Kirklington, Kneesall, Kneeton, Langford, Langar cum Barnstone, Lodge on the Wolds, Lowdham, Maplebeck, Marnham, Meering, North Muskham, South Muskham, Newark upon Trent, Normanton on Trent, Norwell, Norwell Woodhouse, Orston, Ossington, Owthorpe, Oxton, Park Leys, Radcliffe on Trent, Rolleston, Saxondale, South Scarle,

Scarrington, Screveton, Shelford, Shelton, Sibthorpe, Southwell, Spalford, Staunton, Staythorpe, East Stoke, Sutton on Trent, Syerston, Thorney, Thoroton, Thorpe, Tithby, Thurgarton, Tollerton, Upton, Weston, Whatton, Wigsley, Winkburn, Winthorpe, Wiverton Hall

RUSCHCLIFFE DV

pt Nottingham PSD, *viz.*, Arnold, Barton in Fabis, Beeston, Bestwood Park, Bilborough, Bradmore, Bramcote, pt West Bridgford, Bunny, Burton Joyce, pt Carlton, Chilwell, Clifton with Glapton, Colwick, Cossall, Costock, Edwalton, Gedling, Gotham, Hucknall Torkard, Keyworth, Kingston on Soar, Lambley, East Leake, West Leake, pt Lenton, Linby, Newstead, Normanton on the Wolds, Normanton on Soar, Nuthall, Papplewick, Plumtree, Ratcliffe on Soar, Rempstone, Ruddington, Stanford on Soar, Stanton on the Wolds, Stapleford, Stoke Bardolph, Strelley, Sutton Bonington, Thorpe in the Glebe, Thrumpton, Toton, Trowell, Widmerpool, pt Wilford, Willoughby on the Wolds, Wollaton, Woodborough, Wysall

1918—1948

BASSETLAW DIVISION

Blyth and Cuckney RD, Misterton RD, East Retford MB, East Retford RD, pt Skegby RD (Sookholme), Warsop UD

BROXTOWE DIVISION

Arnold UD, pt Basford RD (the pars not in Rushcliffe Dv), Eastwood UD, Hucknall UD, Kirkby in Ashfield UD

MANSFIELD DIVISION

Huthwaite UD, Mansfield MB, Mansfield Woodhouse UD, pt Skegby RD (all except the par in Bassetlaw Dv), Sutton in Ashfield UD

NEWARK DIVISION

Bingham RD, Newark MB, Newark RD, Southwell RD

RUSHCLIFFE DIVISION

pt Basford RD (pars of Awsworth, Barton in Fabis, Bilborough, Bradmore, Bunny, Burton Joyce, Clifton with Glapton, Colwick, Cossall, Gamston, Gedling, Gotham, Nuthall, Ruddington, Stoke Bardolph, Strelley, Thrumpton, Trowell, South Wilford, Wollaton), Beeston UD, West Bridgford UD, Carlton UD, Leake RD, Stapleford RD, Unnamed RD

1948—1970

BASSETLAW COUNTY CONSTITUENCY

East Retford MB, East Retford RD, Warsop UD, Worksop RD, Worksop MB

BROXTOWE COUNTY CONSTITUENCY[2]

pt Basford RD (pars of Annesley, Awsworth, Bestwood Park, Brinsley, Cossall, Felley, Greasley, Kimberley, Linby, Newstead, Nuthall, Papplewick, Selston, Strelley, Trowell), Eastwood UD, Hucknall UD (1948—56), Kirkby in Ashfield UD

CARLTON COUNTY CONSTITUENCY

Arnold UD, pt Basford RD (Burton Joyce, Calverton, Lambley, Stoke Bardolph, Woodborough), Bingham RD, Carlton UD

MANSFIELD COUNTY CONSTITUENCY

Mansfield MB, Sutton in Ashfield UD

NEWARK COUNTY CONSTITUENCY

Mansfield Woodhouse UD, Newark RD, Newark upon Trent MB, Southwell RD

RUSHCLIFFE COUNTY CONSTITUENCY[3]

pt Basford RD (the pars neither in Broxtowe CC nor in Carlton CC), Beeston and Stapleford UD, West Bridgford UD (1948—56)

1970—*

ASHFIELD COUNTY CONSTITUENCY

pt Basford RD (Annesley, Felley, Selston), Hucknall UD, Kirkby in Ashfield UD, Sutton in Ashfield UD

BASSETLAW COUNTY CONSTITUENCY

East Retford MB, East Retford RD, Warsop UD, Worksop MB, Worksop RD

BEESTON COUNTY CONSTITUENCY

pt Basford RD (Awsworth, Brinsley, Cossall, Greasley, Kimberley, Nuthall, Strelley, Trowell), Beeston and Stapleford UD, Eastwood UD

CARLTON COUNTY CONSTITUENCY

Arnold UD, pt Basford RD (Bestwood Park, Burton Joyce, Calverton, Lambley, Linby, Newstead, Papplewick, Stoke Bardolph, Woodborough), Carlton UD

MANSFIELD COUNTY CONSTITUENCY

Mansfield MB

NEWARK COUNTY CONSTITUENCY

Mansfield Woodhouse UD, Newark RD, Newark upon Trent MB, Southwell RD

RUSHCLIFFE COUNTY CONSTITUENCY

Pt Basford RD (Barton in Fabis, Bradmore, Bunny, Costock, Gotham, Kingston on Soar, East Leake, West Leake, Normanton on Soar, Ratcliffe on Soar, Rempstone, Ruddington, Stanford on Soar, Sutton Bonington, Thorpe in the Glebe, Thrumpton, Willoughby on the Wolds, Wysall), Bingham RD, West Bridgford UD

RUTLAND

PARLIAMENTARY CONSTITUENCY

Rutl Parl Co was undivided and existed until 1918. Thereafter it was pt of Northants
Parl Co, in the Rutl and Stamf. Dv/CC.

SHROPSHIRE

BOROUGH CONSTITUENCIES[1]

BISHOP'S CASTLE PARL BOR (1573[2]—1832)
pt Bishop's Castle
BRIDGNORTH PARL BOR (1295—1885)
pt Alveley ([Romsley] 1832—67), Astley Abbots (1832—85), Bridgnorth St Leonard, Bridgnorth St Mary Magdalene, Eardington (1867—85), Oldbury (1832—85), Quatford (pt 1295—1832, ent [incl Eardington] 1832—67), pt Quatt (until 1867), Quatt Jarvis (1867—85), Romsley (1867—85), Tasley (1832—85)
LUDLOW PARL BOR (1461—1885) [1 mbr 1867—85])
(Salop [1461—1832]; Salop, Heref [1832—85])
pt Bromfield (1832—85), Ludford[2] (1832—85), Ludlow [St Lawrence], Ludlow Castle (1832—85), pt Stanton Lacy (1832—85)

SHREWSBURY PARL BOR (1295—1918)
pt Meole Brace (1832—85), Shrewsbury Holy Cross with St Giles (1832—1918), pt Shrewsbury St Alkmund, pt Shrewsbury St Chad, pt Shrewsbury St Julian, pt Shrewsbury St Mary (enlarged pt 1832—1918)
MUCH WENLOCK PARL BOR (1468—1832) [1 mbr 1468—91, 2 mbrs 1491—1832], WENLOCK PARL BOR (1832—85)
Badger, Barrow, Beckbury, Benthall (cr—1885), Broseley, Deuxhill, Ditton Priors, Eaton under Haywood, Hughley, Linley (1867—85), Madeley, Monkhopton (cr—1885), pt Munslow, Posenhall,[4] Shipton (pt 1468—1832, ent 1832—85), Stoke St Milborough, Little Wenlock, Much Wenlock, Willey

COUNTY CONSTITUENCIES

1832—1885
NORTHERN DIVISION
Hds of North Bradford, South Bradford, Oswestry, Pimhill, pt Shrewsbury Lbty (the pt not in Shrewsbury Parl Bor)
SOUTHERN DIVISION
Hds of Brimstree, Chirbury, Condover, Ford, Munslow, Overs, Purslow, Stottesdon Hd, Wenlock Franchise

1885—1918
MID (or WELLINGTON) DIVISION
pt Bradford Newport PSD, pt Bradford Wellington PSD, pt Wenlock MB, *viz.*, Benthall, Broseley, Buildwas, Dawley Magna, Eaton Constantine, Eyton on the Weald Moors, Leighton, Lilleshall, Madeley, Preston upon the Weald Moors, Stirchley, Uppington, Wellington, Little Wenlock, Wombridge, Wrockwardine, Wrockwardine Wood, Wroxeter
NORTHERN (or NEWPORT) DIVISION
pt Albrighton PSD, Bradford Drayton PSD, pt Bradford Newport PSD, pt Bradford Wellington PSD, Bradford Wem PSD, Bradford Whitchurch PSD, Brinstree PSD, pt Pimhill PSD, *viz.*, Adderley, Albrighton, Albrighton, Astley, Atcham, Badger, Battlefield, Beckbury, Bolas Magna, Boningale, Boscobel, Broughton, Cherrington, Cheswardine, Chetwynd, Chetwynd Aston, Church Aston, Clive, Donington, Drayton in Hales, Edgmond, Child's Ercall, Ercall Magna, Grinshill, Hadnall, Haughton Demesne, Hinstock, Hodnet, Ightfield, Kemberton, Kinnersley, Lee Brockhurst, Longdon upon Tern, Longford, Loppington, Moreton Corbet, Moreton Say, Myddle, Newport, Norton in Hales, Prees, Preston Gubbals, Rodington, Ryton, Shawbury, pt Sheriff Hales, Shifnal, pt Shrewsbury St Alkmund, pt Shrewsbury St Chad, pt Shrewsbury St Julian, pt Shrewsbury St Mary, Stanton upon Hine Heath, Stockton, Stoke upon Tern, Sutton Maddock, Tibberton, Tong, Uffington, Waters Upton, Upton Magna, Wem, Weston under Redcastle, Whitchurch, Withington, Woodcote, Woore
SOUTHERN (or LUDLOW) DIVISION
Bishop's Castle PSD, Bridgnorth MB; Brimstree, South and Stottesdon Chelmarsh PSD; Burford PSD, Clun and Parslow PSD, Ludlow MB, Lower Munslow, Upper Munslow and Stottesdon Cleobury PSD, pt Overs and Stottesdon PSD, pt Wenlock MB, *viz.*, Abdon, Acton Round, Acton Scott, Alveley, Ashford Bowdler, Ashford Carbonell, Astley Abbots, Aston Botterell, Aston Eyre, Barrow, Bedstone, Bettws y Crwym, Billingsley, Bishop's Castle, Bitterley, pt Bobbington, Boraston, Bridgnorth St Leonard, Bridgnorth St Mary Magdalen, Bromfield, Bucknell, Burford, Burwarton, Cardington, Caynham, Chelmarsh, Chetton, Claverley, Clee St Margaret, Cleobury Mortimer, Cleobury North, Clun, Clunbury, Clungunford, Coreley, Culmington, Deuxhill, Diddlebury, Ditton Priors, Dowles, Eardington, East Hamlet, Easthorpe, Eaton under Haywood, Edgton, Farlow, Glazeley, Greete, Halford, Heath, Highley, Holdgate, Hope Bagot, Hope Bowdler, Hopesay, Hopton Cangeford, Hopton Castle, Hopton Wafers, Kinlet, pt Leintwardine (North Side), Linley, Llanfair Waterdine, Loughton, pt Ludford, Ludlow Castle, Ludlow [St Lawerence], Lydbury North, Lydham, Mainstone, Middleton Scriven, Milson, More, Morville, Munslow, Myndtown, Nash, Neen Savage, Neen Sollars, Neenton, Norbury, Oldbury, Onibury, Posenhall, Quatford, Quatt Jarvis, Quatt Malvern, Ratlinghope, pt Richard's Castle, Romsley, Rudge, Rushbury, Shipton, Sibdon Carwood, Sidbury, Silvington, Stanton Lacy, Stanton Long, Stoke St Milborough, Stokesay, Stottesdon, Stowe, Church Stretton, Tasley, Tugford, Upton Cressett, Much Wenlock, Wentnor, Cold Weston,

Wheathill, Whitton, Willey, Wistanstow, Woodhouse, Worfield

WESTERN (or OSWESTRY) DIVISION

pt Albrighton PSD, Chirbury PSD, Condover PSD, Ford PSD, Oswestry PSD, pt Pimhill PSD, *viz.*, Acton Burnell, Alberbury Lower Quarter, Baschurch, Berrington, Brompon with Wiston, Cardeston, Chirbury, Condover, Cound, Cressage, Ellesmere, West Felton, Fitz, Ford, Frodesley, Habberley, Great Hanwood, Harley, Hordley, Hughley, Kenley, Kinnerley, Knockin, Leebotwood, pt Llansilin, Llanyblodwel, Llanymynech, Longnor, Melverley, pt Meole Brace, Minsterley, Montford, Great Ness, Little Ness, Oswestry Rural, Oswestry Urban, Petton, Pitchford, Pontesbury, Church Preen, Church Pulverbatch, Ruckley and Langley, Ruyton of the Eleven Towns, St Martin's, Selattyn, Shelve, Sheinton, Shrawardine, Smethcott, Stapleton, Sutton, Sychtyn, Welshampton, Westbury, Whittington, Wollaston, Woolstaston, Worthen

1918—1948

LUDLOW DIVISION

Bishop's Castle MB, Bridgnorth MB, Bridgnorth RD, Burford RD, Church Stretton RD, Church Stretton UD, Cleobury Mortimer RD, Clun RD, Ludlow MB, Ludlow RD, Teme RD

OSWESTRY DIVISION

Drayton RD, Market Drayton UD, Ellesmere RD, Ellesmere UD, Oswestry MB, Oswestry RD, Wem RD, Wem UD, Whitchurch RD, Whitchurch UD

SHREWSBURY DIVISION

Atcham RD, Chirbury RD, Shrewsbury MB

THE WREKIN DIVISION

Dawley UD, Newport RD, Newport UD, Oakengates UD, Shifnal RD, Wellington RD, Wellington UD

1948—1970

LUDLOW COUNTY CONSTITUENCY

Bishop's Castle MB, Bridgnorth MB, Bridgnorth RD, Church Stretton UD, Clun RD, Ludlow MB, Ludlow RD, Wenlock MB

OSWESTRY COUNTY CONSTITUENCY

Drayton RD, Market Drayton UD, Ellesmere RD, Ellesmere UD, Oswestry MB, Oswestry UD, Wem RD, Wem UD, Whitchurch UD

SHREWSBURY COUNTY CONSTITUENCY

Atcham RD, Shrewsbury MB

THE WREKIN COUNTY CONSTITUENCY

Dawley UD, Newport UD, Oakengates UD, Shifnal RD, Wellington RD, Wellington UD

1970—*

LUDLOW COUNTY CONSTITUENCY

Bridgnorth RD, Clun and Bishop's Castle RD, Ludlow RD

OSWESTRY COUNTY CONSTITUENCY

Market Drayton RD, Oswestry RD, North Shropshire RD

SHREWSBURY COUNTY CONSTITUENCY

Atcham RD, Shrewsbury RD

THE WREKIN COUNTY CONSTITUENCY

Dawley UD, Newport UD, Oakengates UD, Shifnal RD, Wellington RD, Wellington UD

STAFFORDSHIRE

BOROUGH CONSTITUENCIES[1]

ALDRIDGE-BROWNHILLS BC (1970—*)
Aldridge-Brownhills UD
BILSTON BC[2] (1948—70)
Bilston MB, Coseley UD, Sedgley UD
WEST BROMWICH PARL BOR/BC (1885—1970)
West Bromwich
WEST BROMWICH EAST BC (1970—*)
pt West Bromwich CB (wards of Great Barr, Charlemont, Friar Park, Hateley Heath, Newton, Sandwell, Tantany)
WEST BROMWICH WEST BC (1970—*)
pt West Bromwich CB (wards of Greets Green, Hill Top, Horseley Heath, Lyng, Market, Tibbington, Tipton Green, Wood Green)
DUDLEY PARL BOR (1295, 1832—*) (Worcs [cr—1970[3]], Staffs [1867—1948, 1970[3]—*])
Dudley Castle Hill (1867—1948), pt Kingswinford (1867—1918: areas of EPs of Brierley Hill, Brockmoor, Pensett, Quarry Bank), pt Rowley Regis (1867—1918: area of Reddal Hill EP)
HANLEY PARL BOR (1885—1918)
Burslem, pt Stoke upon Trent (tp Hanley, pt tp Shelton [neither sep civ, the area of Hanley MB]), pt Wolstanton (ville Rushton Grange, hmlt Sneyd [neither sep civ])
LICHFIELD PARL BOR (1305, 1311—27, 1353, 1553—1885)
Lichfield The Close, Lichfield The Friary, Lichfield St Chad (pt cr—1867, ent 1867—85), Lichfield St Mary, Lichfield St Michael (pt cr—1867, ent 1867—85), pt Pipehill
NEWCASTLE UNDER LYME PARL BOR (1355—*)
until 1918: Newcastle under Lyme (when gains sep civ identity—*), pt Stoke upon Trent (area of Newcastle under Lyme until gains sep civ identity; main pt of tp Penkull, 1832—85), pt Trentham (the former pt of Penkull, 1885—1918), pt Wolstanton (tp Tunstall [not sep civ, the area of Tunstall USD])
1918—*: Audley UD (1918—48), Newcastle under Lyme MB, Newcastle under Lyme RD (1948—*), Wolstanton United UD (1918—48)
ROWLEY REGIS AND TIPTON BC[2] (1948—70)
Rowley Regis MB, Tipton MB
SMETHWICK PARL BOR/BC (1918—70)
Smethwick CB
STAFFORD PARL BOR (1295—1918)
Castle Church (pt 1832—67, ent 1867—1918), pt Hopton and Coton (1866—85), Stafford St Mary and St Chad[4] (pt from sep joint rating—1867, ent 1867—1918)
STOKE ON TRENT PARL BOR (1918—48)
pt Stoke on Trent CB (wards 1—8)
STOKE ON TRENT CENTRAL BC[5] (1948—*)
pt Stoke on Trent CB (wards 10—18 and 28 [1945—55], wards 9—16 [1955—*])
STOKE ON TRENT HANLEY PARL BOR (1918—48)
pt Stoke on Trent CB (wards 9—16)

STOKE ON TRENT NORTH BC[5] (1948—*)
pt Stoke on Trent CB (wards 1—9 and 27 [1948—55], wards 1—8 [1955—*])
STOKE ON TRENT SOUTH BC[5] (1948—*)
pt Stoke on Trent CB (wards 19—26 [1948—55], wards 17—24 [1955—*])
STOKE ON TRENT STOKE PARL BOR (1918—48)
pt Stoke on Trent CB (wards 17—26)
STOKE UPON TRENT PARL BOR (1832—1918)
Burslem (pt 1832—67, ent 1867—85), pt Caverswall (1867—1918), pt Stoke on Trent (1832—85: all except the detached pt of tp Penkull in Newcastle under Lyme Parl Bor; 1885—1918: all except the pt in Hanley Parl Bor, qv above), pt Wolstanton (1832—85: ville Rushton Grange, hmlt Sneyd, tp Tunstall [none sep civ])
TAMWORTH PARL BOR (1563—1885) (Staffs, Warws)
Tamworth (pt 1553—1832, ent 1832—85 [the par Staffs, Warws until 1866, ent Staffs thereafter])
WALSALL PARL BOR/BC (1832—1955[6])
1832—1918: pt Rushall (1867—1918), pt Walsall (1832—67), Walsall Borough (1867—1918)
1918—55: Walsall CB
WALSALL NORTH BC[7] (1955[6]—*)
Brownhills UD (1955—70), pt Walsall CB (wards of Bentley [1970—*], Birchills, Blakenhall, Bloxwich [1955—60], Bloxwich East [1960—*], Bloxwich West [1960—*], Hatherton [1955—70], Leamore, Willenhall North [1970—*], Willenhall South [1970—*])
WALSALL SOUTH BC[7] (1955[6]—*)
Aldridge UD (1955—70), pt Walsall CB (wards of Bridge [1955—70], Caldmore [1955—70], Darlaston North [1970—*], Darlaston South [1970—*], Hatherton [1970—*], Paddock, Palfrey, Pleck, St Matthew's [1970—*])
WEDNESBURY PARL BOR/BC (1867—1970) [1 mbr, 1918—70]
1867—1918: West Bromwich (1867—85), Darlaston, Tipton, Wednesbury
1918—70: Darlaston UD, Tipton UD (1918—48), Wednesbury MB, Wednesfield UD (1948—55), Willenhall UD (1918—48)
WOLVERHAMPTON PARL BOR (1832—1918)
Bilston, Sedgley, Wednesfield, Willenhall, Wolverhampton
WOLVERHAMPTON BILSTON PARL BOR (1918—48)
Bilston UD, Coseley UD, Sedgley UD
WOLVERHAMPTON EAST PARL BOR (1918—48)
Heathtown UD, Short Town UD, Wednesfield UD, Willenhall UD, pt Wolverhampton CB (wards of St James's, St Mary's, St Peter's)
WOLVERHAMPTON NORTH EAST BC[8] (1948—*)
pt Wolverhampton CB (wards of Bushbury, Dunstall [1948—70], Eastfield [1970—*], Heath Town [1948—70], Low Hill, Oxley [1970—*], Park [1948—55], St

James's [1948—70], St Mary's [1948—70], St Peter's [1948—70], Wednesfield Heath [1970—*], Wednesfield North [1970—*], Wednesfield South [1970—*])

WOLVERHAMPTON SOUTH EAST BC (1970—*)
pt Wolverhampton CB (wards of Bilston East, Bilston North, Blakenhall, Ettingshall, Parkfield, Spring Vale)

WOLVERHAMPTON SOUTH WEST BC[8] (1948—*)
pt Wolverhampton CB (wards of Blakenhall and St John's [1948—70], Graisley, Merry Hill [1970—*],

Park [1955—*], Penn, St George's [1948—70], St Mark's and Merridale [1948—70], St Matthew's [1948—70], St Peter's [1970—*], St Philip's [1948—70], Tettenhall Regis [1970—*], Tettenhall Wightwick [1970—*])

WOLVERHAMPTON WEST PARL BOR (1918—48)
pt Wolverhampton CB (wards of Blakenhall, Dunstall, Graisley, Merridale, Park, St George's, St John's, St Mark's, St Matthew's)

COUNTY CONSTITUENCIES

1832—1867
NORTHERN DIVISION
Hds of North Offlow, North Pirehill, South Pirehill, North Totmore, South Totmore
SOUTHERN DIVISION
Hds of East Cuttlestone, West Cuttlestone, South Offlow, North Seisdon, South Seisdon

1867—1885
EAST DIVISION
Hds of North Offlow, South Offlow
NORTH DIVISION
Hds of North Pirehill, North Totmore, South Totmore
WEST DIVISION
Hds of East Cuttlestone, West Cuttlestone, South Pirehill, North Seisdon, South Seisdon

1885—1918
BURTON DIVISION
Burton upon Trent PSD, pt Uttoxeter PSD, *viz.*, Anslow, Barton under Needwood, Blithfield, Bramshall, Branston, Abbot's Bromley, Burton Extra, Burton upon Trent, Draycott in the Clay, Dunstall, Field, pt Foston and Scropton, Gratwich, Hanbury, Horninglow, Kingston, Leigh, Marchington, Marchington Woodlands, Newborough, Rolleston, Stretton, Tatenhill, Tutbury, Uttoxeter, Wychnor
HANDSWORTH DIVISION
West Bromwich PSD, Rushall PSD, Tipton PSD, Wednesbury PSD, *viz.*, Adbaston, Aldridge, Ashley, Great Barr, Bentley, Chebsey, Eccleshall, Ellenhall, Forton, Handsworth, Harborne, Norbury, Cold Norton, High Offley, Pelsall, pt Rushall, Stanton, Swynnerton, Walsall Foreign, Weston Jones
KINGSWINFORD DIVISION
Bilston PSD, Kingswinford PSD, Rowley Regis PSD, Sedgley PSD, Willenhall PSD, Wolverhampton PSD, *viz.*, Amblecote, Upper Arley, pt Bobbington, Bushbury, Codsall, Enville, Himley, pt Kingswinford, Kinver, Patshull, Pattingham, Lower Penn, Upper Penn, Rowley Regis, Tettenhall, Trysull and Seisdon, Wombourn, Woodford Grange
LEEK DIVISION
Cheadle PSD, Leek PSD, pt Uttoxeter PSD, *viz.*, Alstonfield, Alton, Biddulph, Blore with Swinscoe, Bradley in the Moors, Bradnop and Cawdry, Butterton, Calton, Calwich, Cauldon, pt Caverswall, Cheadle, Checkley, Cheddleton, Consall, Cotton, Croxden, Denstone, Dilhorne, Draycott in the Moors; Endon, Longsdon and Stanley; Ellastone, Farley, Fawfield-

head, Grindon, Heathylee, Heaton, Hollingsclough, Horton, Ilam, Ipstones, Kingsley, Leek and Lowe, Leekfrith, Longnor, Mayfield, Musden Grange, Okeover, Onecote, Prestwood, Quarnford, Ramshorn, Rocester, Rudyard, Rushton James, Rushton Spencer, Sheen, Stanton, Tittesworth, Warslow and Elkstones, Waterfall, Wetton, Woodhouses, Wootton
LICHFIELD DIVISION
Elford PSD, pt Penkridge PSD, Rugeley PSD, Shenstone PSD, the pt of Tamworth MB in Staffs, *viz.*, Alrewas, Alrewas Hays, Armitage, King's Bromley, King's Bromley Hays; Burntwood, Edial and Woodhouses; Canwell, Clifton Campville and Haunton, Colton, pt Croxall, Curborough and Elmhurst, Drayton Bassett, Edingale, Elford, Farewell and Chorley, Fazeley, Fisherwick, Fradley, Freeford, Fulfen, Hammerwich, Harlaston, Haselour, Hints, Hopwas Hays, Longdon, Norton Canes, Ogley Hay, Orgreave, Hamstall Ridware, Mavesyn Ridware, Pipe Ridware, Pipehill, Rugeley, Shenstone, Statfold, Streethay, Swinfen and Packington, Syerscote, Tamhorn, Tamworth, Thorpe Constantine, Wall, Weeford, Whittington, Wiggington, Great Wyrley, Yoxall
NORTH-WESTERN DIVISION
pt Eccleshall PSD, Pirehill North PSD, *viz.*, Audley, Balterley, Betley, Burslem, Chapel and Hill Chorlton, Keele, Madeley, Maer, Mucklestone, Norton in the Moors, pt Trentham, Tyrley, Whitmore, pt Wolstanton
WESTERN DIVISION
pt Penkridge PSD, Stafford PSD, Stone PSD, *viz.*, Acton Trussell and Bednall, Barlaston, Baswich, Blymhill, Bradley, Brewood, Brocton, Cannock, Chartley Holme, Cheslyn Hay, Colwich, Church Eaton, Coppenhall, Creswell, Dunston, Essington, Featherstone, Fradswell, Gayton, Gnosall, Hartherton, Haughton, Hilton, Hopton and Coton, Huntington, Ingestre, Kinvaston, Lapley, Marston, Milwich, Penkridge, Ranton, Ranton Abbey, Salt and Enson, Sandon, Saredon, Seighford, Shareshill, pt Sheriff Hales, Stone, Stowe, Stretton, Teddesley Hay, Tillington, Tixall, Weston under Lizard, Weston upon Trent, Whitgreave, Worston, Yarlet

1918—1948
BURTON DIVISION
Burton upon Trent CB, pt Stafford RD (pt Colwich), Tutbury RD, Uttoxeter RD, Uttoxeter UD
CANNOCK DIVISION
Brownhills UD, pt Cannock RD (Bushbury, Cheslyn Hay, Essington, Hilton, Great Wyrley), Cannock UD,

Seisdon RD, Tettenhall UD, pt Walsall RD (Bentley)

KINGSWINFORD DIVISION

Amblecote UD, Brierley Hill UD, Kingswinford RD, Quarry Bank UD, Rowley Regis UD

LEEK DIVISION

Biddulph UD, Kidsgrove UD, Leek RD, Leek UD, Smallthorne UD, Stoke on Trent RD

LICHFIELD DIVISION

Aldridge UD, Lichfield MB, Lichfield RD, Perry Barr UD, Rugeley UD, Tamworth MB, the pt of Tamworth RD in Staffs, pt Walsall RD (all except Bentley)

STAFFORD DIVISION

pt Cannock RD (the pars not in Cannock Dv), Gnosall RD, Stafford MB, pt Stafford RD (all except pt Colwich), Unnamed RD

STONE DIVISION

Blore Heath RD, Cheadle RD, Mayfield RD, Newcastle under Lyme RD, Stone RD, Stone UD

1948—1970

BRIERLEY HILL COUNTY CONSTITUENCY[2]

Amblecote UD, Brierley Hill UD, Seisdon RD, Tettenhall UD

BURTON COUNTY CONSTITUENCY

Burton upon Trent CB, Tutbury RD, Uttoxeter RD, Uttoxeter UD

CANNOCK COUNTY CONSTITUENCY[6]

Brownhills UD (1948—55), Cannock RD, Cannock UD, Wednesfield UD (1955—70)

LEEK COUNTY CONSTITUENCY

Biddulph UD, Cheadle RD, Kidsgrove UD, Leek RD, Leek UD

LICHFIELD AND TAMWORTH COUNTY CONSTITUENCY[6]

Aldridge (1948—55), Lichfield RD, Lichfield MB, Rugeley UD, Tamworth MB

STAFFORD AND STONE COUNTY CONSTITUENCY

Stafford MB, Stafford RD, Stone RD, Stone UD

1970—*

BURTON COUNTY CONSTITUENCY

Burton upon Trent CB, Tutbury RD, Uttoxeter RD, Uttoxeter UD

CANNOCK COUNTY CONSTITUENCY

Cannock UD, pt Lichfield RD (Brindley Heath), Rugeley UD

LEEK COUNTY CONSTITUENCY

Biddulph UD, Cheadle RD, Kidsgrove UD, Leek RD, Leek UD

LICHFIELD AND TAMWORTH COUNTY CONSTITUENCY

Lichfield MB, pt Lichfield RD (all except Brindley Heath), Tamworth MB

STAFFORD AND STONE COUNTY CONSTITUENCY

Stafford MB, Stafford RD, Stone RD, Stone UD

SOUTH WEST STAFFORDSHIRE COUNTY CONSTITUENCY

Cannock RD, Seisdon RD

WARWICKSHIRE

BOROUGH CONSTITUENCIES[1]

ALCESTER PARL BOR (1275 only)
Alcester
ASTON MANOR PARL BOR (1885—1918)
pt Aston (area Aston Manor USD)
BIRMINGHAM PARL BOR (1832—85)
pt Aston, Birmingham, Edgbaston
BIRMINGHAM, ACOCK'S GREEN PARL BOR
(1945—48)
pt Birmingham CB (wards of King's Heath, Moseley,
pt King's Norton ward [prev in Birmingham Moseley
Dv Parl Bor])
BIRMINGHAM, ALL SAINTS BC (1955[2]—70)
pt Birmingham CB (wards of All Saints', Rotton Park,
Soho)
BIRMINGHAM, ASTON PARL BOR/BC[3] (1918—70)
1918—1948: pt Birmingham CB (ward of Aston, pt
wards of All Saints', Lozells, St Mary's)
1918—1970: pt Birmingham CB (wards of Aston,
Gravelly Hill [1955—70], Lozells [1948—55], St
Mary's [1948—49], St Paul's [1948—55], Stockland
Green [1955—70])
BIRMINGHAM, BORDESLEY PARL BOR (1885—
1918)
pt Birmingham MB (wards of Bordeley, St Bartholomew)
BIRMINGHAM, CENTRAL PARL BOR (1885—1918)
pt Birmingham MB (wards of Market Hall, Ladywood,
St Thomas)
BIRMINGHAM, DERITEND PARL BOR (1918—48)
pt Birmingham CB (wards of Deritend, St Bartholomew, St Martin)
BIRMINGHAM, DUDDLESTON PARL BOR (1918—
48)
pt Birmingham CB (wards of Duddleston, Nechells, pt
of wards of Aston, St Mary's)
BIRMINGHAM, EAST PARL BOR (1885—1918)
pt Aston (hmlt Little Bromwich), pt Birmingham MB
(wards of Duddleston, Nechells), Saltley UD
BIRMINGHAM, EDGBASTON PARL BOR/BC[4]
(1918—*)
1885—1918 (Warws, Worcs): Balsall Heath UD
(Warws), pt Birmingham CB (assoc with Warws: ward
of Edgbaston, pt ward of Rotton Park), Harborne UD
(Worcs)
1918—:* pt Birmingham CB (wards of Deritend [1970—
*], Edgbaston, Harborne, Market Hall [1918—70],
Quinton [1970—*])
BIRMINGHAM, ERDINGTON PARL BOR/BC[3]
(1918—55[2])
pt Birmingham CB (wards of Bromford [1948—49],
Erdington [1948—55], Erdington North [1918—48],
Erdington South [1918—48], Gravelly Hill [1948—55],
Stockland Green [1949—55], Washwood Heath
[1918—48], pt ward of Aston [1918—48])
BIRMINGHAM, ERDINGTON BC (1970—*)
pt Birmingham CB (wards of Erdington, Gravelly Hill,

Stockland Green)
BIRMINGHAM, HALL GREEN BC[3] (1948—*)
pt Birmingham CB (wards of Billesley [1970—*],
Brandwood [1955—*], Hall Green, Sparkhill [1948—
55], Springfield [1949—70])
BIRMINGHAM, HANDSWORTH PARL BOR/BC[2]
(1918—*)
pt Birmingham CB (wards of Aston [1970—*],
Handsworth, Lozells [1955—70], Sandwell, Soho
[1918—55])
BIRMINGHAM, KING'S NORTON PARL BOR/BC[3]
(1918—55[2])
1918—48: pt Birmingham CB (wards of Northfield, Selly
Oak, pt King's Norton)
1948—55: pt Birmingham CB (ward of King's Norton)
BIRMINGHAM, LADYWOOD PARL BOR/BC[2]
(1918—*)
pt Birmingham CB (wards of All Saints' [1948—55],
All Saints [1970—*], Duddeston [1948—70], Ladyw-
ood, Rotton Park [1918—55], Rotton Park [1970—*],
St Paul's [1955—70], Soho [1970—*])
BIRMINGHAM, NORTH PARL BOR (1885—1918)
pt Birmingham MB (wards of St George's, St Mary's,
St Stephen's)
BIRMINGHAM, MOSELEY PARL BOR[5] (1918—48)
1918—45: pt Birmingham CB (wards of Acock's Green,
Sparkhill, pt wards of Balsall Heath, Moseley and
King's Heath, King's Norton, Sparkbrook)
1945—48: pt Birmingham CB (wards of Moseley and
King's Heath, Sparkhill, pt ward of King's Norton)
BIRMINGHAM, NORTHFIELD BC[2] (1948—*)
pt Birmingham CB (wards of Longbridge [1970—*],
Northfield, King's Norton [1955—70], Selly Oak
[1948—55], Weoley [1949—*])
BIRMINGHAM, PERRY BARR BC[4] (1948—*)
pt Birmingham CB (wards of Kingstanding [1949—*],
Oscott [1970—*], Perry Barr)
BIRMINGHAM, SELLY OAK BC (1955[2]—*)
pt Birmingham CB (wards of Balsall Heath [1955—70],
Moseley [1970—*], Moseley and King's Heath [1955—
70], King's Norton [1970—*], Selly Oak)
BIRMINGHAM, SMALL HEATH BC[2] (1948—*)
pt Birmingham CB (wards of Deritend [1955—70],
Duddeston [1949—55], Duddeston and Nechells
[1948—49], Newtown [1970—*], St Bartholomew's
[1948—55], Saltley, Small Heath)
BIRMINGHAM, SOUTH PARL BOR (1918—48)
pt Balsall Heath UD, pt Birmingham CB (wards of
Deritend, St Martin's)
BIRMINGHAM, SPARKBROOK PARL BOR/BC[3]
(1918—*)
1918—48: pt Birmingham CB (pt wards of Balsall
Heath, Moseley and King's Heath, Sparkbrook,
Sparkhill
1948—:* pt Birmingham CB (wards of Balsall Heath
[1948—55], Deritend [1949—55], Fox Hollies

[1955—*], St Martin's and Deritend [1948—49], Sparkbrook, Sparkhill [1955—*])

BIRMINGHAM, STECHFORD BC[2] (1948—*)

pt Birmingham CB (wards of Shard End [1970—*], Sheldon [1949—55], Stechford, Washwood Heath)

BIRMINGHAM, WEST PARL BOR (1918—48)

pt Birmingham MB (wards of All Saints', St Paul's, pt ward of Rotton Park)

BIRMINGHAM, WEST BIRMINGHAM PARL BOR (1918—48)

pt Birmingham CB (ward of St Paul's, pt wards of All Saints', Lozells)

BIRMINGHAM, YARDLEY PARL BOR/BC[3] (1918—*)

pt Birmingham CB (wards of Acock's Green [1948—*], Fox Hollies [1949—55], Saltley [1918—48], Sheldon [1955—*], Small Heath [1918—48], Yardley)

COVENTRY PARL BOR (1295—1306, 1315, 1346, 1353, 1472—77, 1529—1945[5]) [1 mbr 1885—1945]

early—1918: Coventry Holy Trinity (pt early—1867, ent 1867—1918), Coventry St Michael (pt early—1867, ent 1867—1918)

1918—45: Coventry CB

COVENTRY EAST PARL BOR/BC[6] (1945[5]—70)

pt Coventry CB (wards of All Saints [1945—48], Charterhouse and Binley [1948—70], Foleshill [1945—48], Harnhall [1945—48], Hill Fields [1945—48], Longford, St Mary's [1945—48], St Paul's [1945—48], Lower Stoke, Upper Stoke, Walsgrave)

COVENTRY NORTH BC[6] (1948—70)

pt Coventry CB (wards of Bablake, Foleshill, Holbrook, Radford, Sherbourne)

COVENTRY NORTH EAST BC (1970—*)

pt Coventry CB (wards of Foleshill, Henley, Longford, Upper Stoke, Wyken)

COVENTRY NORTH WEST BC (1970—*)

pt Coventry CB (wards of Bablake, Holbrook, Radford, Sherbourne)

COVENTRY SOUTH BC[6] (1948—70)

pt Coventry CB (wards of Cheylesmore, Earlsdon, Godiva, St Michael's, Westwood, Whoberley)

COVENTRY SOUTH EAST BC (1970—*)

pt Coventry CB (wards of Binley and Willenhall, Godiva, St Michael's, Lower Stoke)

COVENTRY SOUTH WEST BC (1970—*)

pt Coventry CB (wards of Cheylesmore, Earlsdon, Westwood, Whoberley, Woodlands)

COVENTRY WEST PARL BOR (1945[5]—48)

pt Coventry CB (wards of Bablake, Cheylesmore, Earlsdon, Grey Friars, Radford, Westwood)

NUNEATON BC (1970—*)

Bedworth UD, Nuneaton MB

SOLIHULL BC (1970—*)

Solihull CB

SUTTON COLDFIELD BC (1955[2]—*)

pt Birmingham CB (ward of Erdington [1955—70]), Sutton Coldfield MB

WARWICK PARL BOR (1295—1885)

Warwick St Mary, Warwick St Nicholas

WARWICK AND LEAMINGTON PARL BOR (1885—1918)

Leamington Priors, pt Lillington, pt Milverton, Warwick St Mary, Warwick St Nicholas

COUNTY CONSTITUENCIES

1832—1885

NORTHERN DIVISION

Hemlingford Hd, Coventry Co of Itself, pt Knightlow Hd (pars or pts of pars of Allesley, Arley, Astley, pt Aston, Bedworth, Bilton, Binley, Bourton on Dunsmore, Brandon and Bretford, Brinklow, Brownsover, Bulkington, Burton Hastings, Churchover, Clifton upon Dunsmore, Combe Fields, Copston Magna, Cosford, Coundon, pt Coventry Holy Trinity, pt Coventry St Michael, pt Drayton Bassett, Dunchurch, Easenhall, Frankton, Harborough Magna, Hillmorton, Church Lawford, Little Lawford, Long Lawford, Monks Kirby, Monks Riding, Newbold on Avon, Kings Newnham, Newton and Biggin, Pailton, Princethorpe, Rugby, Ryton on Dunsmore, Shilton, Stretton Baskerville, Stretton on Dunsmore, Stretton under Fosse, Thurlaston, Walsgrave on Sowe, Wibtoft, Willenhall, Willoughby, Willey, Withybrook, Wolston, Wolvey)

SOUTHERN DIVISION

Barlinchway Hd, Kington Hd, pt Knightlow Hd (pars or pts of pars of Ashow, Baginton, Birdingbury, Bubbenhall, Chapel Ascote, Cubbington, Eathorpe, Grandborough, Harbury, pt Hinckley, Hodnell, Hunningham, Bishop's Itchington, Long Itchington, Kenilworth, Ladbroke, Leamington Hastings, Leamington Priors, Leek Wootton, Lillington, Marton, Milverton, Napton on the Hill, Offchurch, Lower Radbourn, Upper Radbourn, Radford Semele, Upper Schuckburgh, Southam, Stockton, Stoneleigh, pt Bishops Tachbrook, Ufton, Wappenbury, Watergall, Weston under Wetherley, Whitnash, Wills Pastures, Wolfhampcote)

1885—1918

NORTHERN (or TAMWORTH) DIVISION

pt Atherstone PSD, Birmingham PSD, pt Coleshill PSD, Solihull PSD, *viz.*, Amington and Stoneydelph, pt Aston, Austrey, Baddesley Clinton, Balsall, Barston, Bickenhill, Bolehall and Glascote, Coleshill, Combrook, Corley, Curdworth, Elmdon, Grendon, Hampton in Arden, Kineton, Kingsbury, Knowle, Lea Marston, Maxstoke, Middleton, Minworth, Newton Regis, No Man's Heath, Polesworth, Seckington, Sheldon, Shustoke, Shuttington, Solihull, Sutton Coldfield, Tamworth Castle, Nether Whitacre, Over Whitacre, Wilnecote and Castle Liberty, Wishaw

NORTH-EASTERN (or NUNEATON) DIVISION

Atherstone PSD, pt Coleshill PSD, Coventry PSD, *viz.*, Allesley, Ansley, Ansty, Arley, Astley, Atherstone, Baddesley Ensor, Baxterley, Bedworth, Bentley, Berkswell, Binley, Brandon and Bretford, Brinklow, Bulkington, Burton Hastings, Caldecote, Chadshunt, Chilvers Coton, Combe Fields, Compton Verney, Copston Magna, Coundon, Easenhall, Exhall, Fillongley, Foleshill, Gaydon, Harborough Magna, Hartshill,

Keresley, Kinwalsey, Lighthorne, Mancetter, Butlers Marston, pt Merevale, Meriden, Monks Kirby, Monks Riding, Nuneaton, Oldbury, Oxhill, Pailton, Great Packington, Little Packington, Pillerton Hersey, Pillerton Priors, Radway, Shilton, Stivichall, Stretton Baskerville, Stretton under Fosse, Tysoe, Walsgrave on Sowe, Weddington, Wibtoft, Willenhall, Willey, Withybrook, Wolvey, Wyken

SOUTH-EASTERN (or RUGBY) DIVISION

Burton Dassett and Kington PSD, pt Kenilworth PSD, Rugby PSD, Southam PSD, viz., Ashow, Baginton, Bilton, Birdingbury, Bourton on Dunsmore, Brownsover, Bubbenhall, Chapel Ascote, Churchover, Clifton upon Dunsmore, Fenny Compton, Cosford, Cubbington, Avon Dassett, Burton Dassett, Dunchurch, Eathorpe, Farnborough, Frankton, Grandborough, Guy's Cliffe, Harbury, Hillmorton, Hodnell, Hunningham, Bishop's Itchington, Long Itchington, Kenilworth, Ladbroke, Church Lawford, Little Lawford, Long Lawford, Leamington Hastings, Leamington Priors, Leek Wootton, Lillington, Priors Marston, Marton, pt Mollington, Napton on the Hill, Newbold on Avon, Kings Newnham, Newton and Biggin, Offchurch, Princethorpe, Priors Hardwick, Lower Radbourn, Upper Radbourn, Radford Semele, Ratley and Upton, Rugby, Ryton on Dunsmore, Shottswell, Lower Shuckburgh, Upper Shuckburgh, Southam, Stockton, Stoneleigh, Stretton on Dunsmore, Thurlaston, Ufton, Wappenbury, Warmington, Watergall, Weston under Wetherley, Whitnash, Willoughby, Wills Pastures, Wolfhampcote, Wolston, Wormleighton

SOUTH-WESTERN (or STRATFORD ON AVON) DIVISION

Alcester PSD, Brailes PSD, Henley PSD, Stratford and Snitterfield PSD, Warwick PSD, Stratford on Avon MB, viz., Alcester, Great Alne, Alveston, Arrow, Aston Cantlow, Atherstone on Stour, Barcheston, Barford, Barton on the Heath, Bearley, Beaudesert, Beausale, Bidford on Avon, Billesley, Binton, Brailes, Budbrooke, Burmington, Bushwood, Charlecote, Cherington, Chesterton, Claverdon, Little Compton, Long Compton, Compton Wynyates, Coughton, Eatington, Exhall, Fulbrook, Halford, Hampton Lucy, Haseley, Haselor, Hatton, Honiley, Honington, Idlicote, pt Ilmington, pt Ipsley, Kinwarton, Langley, Lapworth, Loxley, Luddington, Moreton Morrell, Morton Bagot, Newbold Pacey, Norton Lindsey, Nuthurst, Oversley, Packwood, Pinley, Preston Bagot, Rowington, Salford Priors, Sambourn, Sherbourne, Shrewley, Snitterfield, Spernall, Stourton, Old Stratford, Stratford on Avon, Stretton on Fosse, Studley, Sutton under Brailes, Bishops Tachbrook, Tanworth, Temple Grafton, Wasperton, Weethley, pt Welford, Wellesbourne Hastings and Walton, Wellesbourne Mountford, pt Weston on Avon, Whatcote, Whichford, Whitchurch, Wixford, Great Wolford, Little Wolford, Wolverton, Wootton Wawen, Wroxall

1918—1948

NUNEATON DIVISION[5]

Atherstone RD, Bedworth UD (1945—48), Bulkington UD (1918—45), Coventry RD (1918—45), Foleshill RD (1918—45), Nuneaton MB, Nuneaton RD (1918—45)

RUGBY DIVISION[5]

1918—45: pt Brailes RD (all except pars in Warw. & Leam. Dv), Farnborough RD, Monks Kirby RD, Rugby RD, Rugby UD, Southam RD, pt Stratford on Avon RD (Charlcote, Combrook, Compton Verney, Eatington, Kineton, Loxley, Moreton Morrell, Newbold Pacey, Wellesbourne Hastings, Wellesbourne Mountford)
1945—48: redefined as same area and also the pars in Rugby RD in 1945 heretofore in Nun. Dv

SOLIHULL DIVISION (1945[5]—48)

Solihull UD, the pt of Birm CB in Tamworth Dv as defined in 1918

SUTTON COLDFIELD DIVISION (1945[5]—48)

Meriden RD, Sutton Coldfield MB, Tamworth RD

TAMWORTH DIVISION (1918—45[5])

Meriden RD, Sutton Coldfield MB, the pt of Tamworth RD (Staffs, Warws) in Warws

WARWICK AND LEAMINGTON DIVISION[5]

1918—45: Alcester RD, pt Brailes RD (Ilmington, Stretton on Fosse), Kenilworth UD, Royal Leamington Spa MB, Stratford on Avon MB, pt Stratford on Avon RD (all except the pars in Rugby Dv), Warwick MB, Warwick RD
1945—48: defined as prev existing Dv less the pt of Cov CB since added, but supplemented by the pt of Stratford on Avon RD (prev Tamworth Dv) and Warwick RD (prev Nuneaton Dv and Tamworth Dv)

1948—1970

MERIDEN COUNTY CONSTITUENCY[6] (1955[2]—70)

Atherstone RD, Meriden RD, Tamworth RD

NUNEATON COUNTY CONSTITUENCY[2]

Atherstone RD (1948—55), Bedworth UD, Nuneaton MB

RUGBY COUNTY CONSTITUENCY[6]

Rugby MB, Rugby RD

SOLIHULL COUNTY CONSTITUENCY

Solihull UD

STRATFORD COUNTY CONSTITUENCY

Alcester RD, Shipston on Stour RD, Southam RD, Stratford on Avon MB, Stratford on Avon RD

SUTTON COLDFIELD COUNTY CONSTITUENCY (1945—55[2])

Meriden RD, Sutton Coldfield MB, Tamworth RD

WARWICK AND LEAMINGTON COUNTY CONSTITUENCY[6]

Kenilworth UD, Royal Leamington Spa MB, Warwick RD, Warwick MB

1970—*

MERIDEN COUNTY CONSTITUENCY

Atherstone RD, Meriden RD

NUNEATON COUNTY CONSTITUENCY

Bedworth UD, Nuneaton MB

RUGBY COUNTY CONSTITUENCY

Rugby MB, Rugby RD

STRATFORD ON AVON COUNTY CONSTITUENCY[7]

Alcester RD, Shipston on Stour RD, Southam RD, Stratford on Avon MB, Stratford on Avon RD

WARWICK AND LEAMINGTON COUNTY CONSTITUENCY

Kenilworth UD, Royal Leamington Spa MB, Warwick MB, Warwick RD

WESTMORLAND

BOROUGH CONSTITUENCIES[1]

APPLEBY PARL BOR (1295—1832)
pt Appleby St Laurence, pt Appleby St Michael or Bongate

KENDAL PARL BOR (1832—85) [1 mbr]
Nether Graveship, Kendal, Kirkland

COUNTY CONSTITUENCIES

Westm was undivided for parl purposes before 1885 and after 1918.

1885—1918
APPLEBY OR NORTHERN DIVISION
Ambleside PSD, East Ward PSD, West Ward PSD, *viz.*, Ambleside, Appleby St Laurence, Appleby St Michael or Bongate, Applethwaite, Asby, Askham, Bampton, Barton, Bolton, Brough, Brougham, Cliburn, Clifton, Crosby Garrett, Crosby Ravensworth, Dufton, Grasmere, Hartley, Hillbeck, Kaber, Kirkby Stephen, Kirkby Thore, Langdales, Lowther, Mallerstang, King's Meaburn, Martindale, Long Marton, Milburn, Morland, Great Musgrave, Little Musgrave, Nateby, Newbiggin, Newby, Ormside, Orton, Patterdale, Ravenstonedale, Rydal and Loughrigg, Shap, Sleagill, Smardale, Sockbridge, Soulby, Brough Sowerby, Temple Sowerby, Stainmore, Great Strickland, Little Strickland, Thrimby, Troutbeck, Undermillbeck, Waitby, Warcop, Wharton, Low Winder, Winton, Yanwath and Eamont Bridge

KENDAL OR SOUTHERN DIVISION
Kendal MB, Kendal PSD, Lonsdale PSD, *viz.*, Barbon, Beetham, Burneside, Burton, Casterton, Crook, Crosthwaite and Lyth, Dillicar, Docker, Farleton, Fawcett Forest, Firbank, Nether Graveship, Grayrigg, Haverbrack, Helsington, Heversham with Milnthorpe, Hincaster, Holme, Hugill, Hutton Roof, New Hutton, Old Hutton and Holmescales, Kendal, Kentmere, Killington, Kirkby Lonsdale, Kirkland, Lambrigg, Levens, Longsleddale, Lupton, Mansergh, Meathop and Ulpha, Middleton, Natland, Patton, Preston Patrick, Preston Richard; Scalthwaiterigg, Hay and Hutton in the Hay; Sedgwick, Skelsmergh, Stainton, Nether Staveley, Over Staveley, Strickland Ketel, Strickland Roger, Underbarrow and Bradleyfield, Whinfell, Whitwell and Selside, Witherslack

WORCESTERSHIRE

BOROUGH CONSTITUENCIES[1]

BEWDLEY PARL BOR (1606—1885)
Bewdley (1867—85), pt Kidderminster (1832—67), pt Kidderminster Foreign (1867—85), Lower Mitton (1832—85), Upper Mitton (1867—85), Ribbesford (pt 1606—1832, ent 1832—85)

DROITWICH PARL BOR (1554—1885) [1 mbr 1832—85]
pt Claines (1832—85), Crutch (1832—85), Dodderhill (pt 1554—1832, ent 1832—85), Dodderhill In Liberties (1867—85), Doverdale (1832—85), Droitwich St Andrew, Droitwich St Nicholas, Droitwich St Peter, Elmbridge (1832—85), Hadzor (1832—85), Hampton Lovett (1832—85), pt Hanbury (1832—85 [enlarged pt 1867—85]), Himbleton (1832—85), Hindlip (1832—85), Marlborough in the Vines (1832—85), Martin Hussingtree (1832—85), Oddingley (1832—85), Salwarpe (1832—85), Shell (1832—85), pt Stoke Prior (1867—85), pt Warndon (1832—85), Westwood Park (1832—85)

DUDLEY PARL BOR (1295, 1832—1970[2]) [1 mbr 1832—1970] (Worcs, *Staffs [1867—1948, 1970[2]—*]*)
1832—1918: Dudley, *Dudley Castle Hill (1867—1948), pt Kingswinford (1867—1918: areas of EPs of Brierley Hill, Brockmoor, Pensett, Quarry Bank), pt Rowley Regis (1867—1918: area of Reddal Hill EP)*
1918—70: Dudley CB, Stourbridge MB (1948—70)

EVESHAM PARL BOR (1603—1885) [1 mbr 1867—85]
Bengeworth, Evesham All Saints, Evesham St Lawrence

HALESOWEN AND STOURBRIDGE MB (1970—*)
Halesowen MB, Stourbridge MB

KIDDERMINSTER PARL BOR (1295, 1832—1918) [1 mbr 1832—1918]
pt Kidderminster (until 1867), Kidderminster Borough (1867—1918), pt Kidderminster Foreign (1832—1918 [enlarged pt 1867—1918]), pt Wolverley (1867—1918)

OLDBURY AND HALESOWEN BC (1948—70)
Halesowen MB, Oldbury MB

PERSHORE PARL BOR (1295 only)
Pershore Holy Cross, Pershore St Andrew

WARLEY EAST BC (1970—*)
pt Warley CB (the wards of Abbey, Bearwood, Brandhall, Bristnall, Sandwell, Soho, Uplands, Victorian)

WARLEY WEST BC (1970—*)
pt Warley CB (the wards of Cradley Heath, Langley, Old Hill and Blackheath, Rounds Green, Rowsley, St Paul's, Tividale)

WORCESTER PARL BOR/BC[3] (1295—*)
1295—1918: Bedwardine St John (pt 1832—67, ent 1867—1918), Bedwardine St Michael, pt Claines (1832—1918 [enlarged pt 1867—1918]), pt Hallow (1867—1918), Whistones (1832—1918), Worcester All Saints, Worcester Blockhouse, Worcester College Precincts, Worcester St Alban, Worcester St Andrew, Worcester St Clement (pt 1295—1832, ent 1832—1918), Worcester St Helen, Worcester St Martin (pt 1295—1867, ent 1867—1918), Worcester St Nicholas, Worcester St Peter the Great (pt 1295—1867, 1867—1918), Worcester St Swithin
1918—:* Droitwich MB (1948—*), Droitwich RD (1948—*), Worcester CB

COUNTY CONSTITUENCIES

1832—1885
EASTERN DIVISION
Abberton, Abbots Morton, Alderminster, Aldington, Alvechurch, Badsey, Bentley Pauncefoot, Beoley, Besford, Birlingham, Bishampton, Blockley, Bredon, Bredon's Norton, Bretforton, Bricklehampton, Broadway, Bromsgrove, Broughton Hackett, Cakemore, Charlton, Cleeve Prior, Cofton Hackett, Great Comberton, Little Comberton, Conderton, Cropthorne, Cutsdean, Daylesford, Defford, Dormston, Eckington, Elmley Castle, Evenlode, Feckenham, Fladbury, Grafton Flyford, Flyford Flavell, Grafton Manor, Halesowen, Great and Little Hampton, pt Hanbury, Harvington, Hasbury, Hawne, Hill, Hill and Moor, Church Honeybourne, Hunnington, Illey, Inkberrow, Kings Norton, Kington, Lapal, Ab Lench, Church Lench, Rous Lench, North and Middle Littleton, South Littleton, Naunton Beauchamp, Netherton, Northfield, Norton and Lenchwick, Offenham, Oldberrow, Oldbury, Overbury, Paper Mills, Peopleton, Pershore Holy Cross, Pershore St Andrew, North Piddle, Pinvin, Pirton, Redditch, Ridgacre, Romsley, Sedgeberrow, Shipston on Stour, Stock and Bradley, Stoke Prior (ent 1832—67, pt 1867—85), Strensham, pt Tardebigge (1832—67), Teddington, Throckmorton, Tidmington, Tredington, Tutnall and Cobley, Upton Snodbury, Upton Warren, Warley Salop, Warley Wigorn, pt Warndon, Webheath, Wick, Wickhamford, Wyre Piddle, Yardley

WESTERN DIVISION
Abberley, Acton Beauchamp, Alfrick, Areley Kings, Astley, Bayton, pt Bedwardine St John (1832—67), Belbroughton, Berrow, Bewdley (1832—67), Birtsmorton, pt Bockleton, Bransford, Bredicot, Broadwas, Broom, Bushley, Castlemorton, Chaceley, Chaddesley Corbett, Churchill, Churchill, pt Claines, Clent, Clifton upon Teme, Cotheridge, Cradley, Earls Croome, Hill Croome, Croome d'Abitot, Crowle, Doddenham, Eastham, Edvin Loach, Eldersfield, Elmley Lovett, Frankley, Grimley, Hagley, Hallow (ent 1832—67, pt 1867—85), Hanley Castle, Hanley Child, Hanley William, Hartlebury, Hillhampton,

Holdfast, Holt, Huddington, Kempsey, Kenswick, Kidderminster Foreign (ent 1832—67, pt 1867—85), Knighton on Teme, Knightwick, Kyre Magna, Kyre Parva, Leigh, Lindridge, Longdon, Lulsley, Lutley, Lye, Madresfield, Great Malvern, Little Malvern, Mamble, Martley, Mathon, Upper Mitton (1832—67), Newland, Norton juxta Kempsey, pt Oldswinford (1832—67), Ombersley, Orleton, Pedmore, Pendock, Pensax, Powick, Queenhill, Redmarley d'Abitot, Ripple, Rochford, Rock, Rushock, Lower Sapey, Severn Stoke, Shelsley Beauchamp, Shelsley Kings, Shelsley Walsh, Shrawley, Spetchley, Stanford on Teme, Staunton, Stockton on Teme, pt Stoke Bliss (1832—67), Stone, Stoulton, Stourbridge, Suckley, Upper Swinford, Tenbury, Tibberton, Upton upon Severn, Welland, White Ladies Aston, Whittington, Wichenford, Great Witley, Little Witley, Wollaston, Wollescote, Wolverley (ent 1832—67, pt 1867—85), pt Worcester St Martin (1832—85 [enlarged pt 1867—85]), pt Worcester St Peter the Great (1832—67)

1885—1918
EASTERN DIVISION
pt Bromsgrove PSD, pt Northfield PSD, pt Redditch PSD, *viz.*, Alvechurch, Beoley, pt Bockleton, Bromsgrove, Cofton Hackett, Kings Norton, Oldberrow, Redditch, Tutnall and Cobley, Yardley
MID (or DROITWICH) DIVISION
pt Bromsgrove PSD, Droitwich MB, Droitwich PSD, Kidderminster MB, Kidderminster PSD, pt Redditch PSD, pt Stourbridge PSD, pt Stourport PSD, *viz.*, Belbroughton, Bentley Pauncefoot, Broom, Chaddesley Corbett, Churchill, Clent, Crutch, Dodderhill, Doverdale, Droitwich St Andrew, Droitwich St Nicholas, Droitwich St Peter, Elmbridge, Emley Lovett, Grafton Manor, Hadzor, Hagley, Hampton Lovett, Hanbury, Himbleton, pt Kidderminster Foreign, Lower Mitton, Upper Mitton, Oddingley, Pedmore, Rushock, Salwarpe, Stock and Bradley, Stoke Prior, Stone, Stourbridge, Upper Swinford, Upton Warren, Webheath, Westwood Park, Wollaston, Wollescote, pt Wolverley
NORTHERN DIVISION
Halesowen PSD, pt Northfield PSD, Oldbury PSD, pt Stourbridge PSD, *viz.*, Cakemore, Cradley, Frankley, Halesowen, Hasbury, Hawne, Hill, Hunnington, Illey, Lapal, Lutley, Lye, Northfield, Oldbury, Romsley
SOUTHERN (or EVESHAM) DIVISION
Blockley PSD, Evesham PSD, pt Malvern PSD, Pershore PSD, pt Redditch PSD, Upton upon Severn PSD, *viz.*, Abberton, Abbots Morton, Alderminster, Aldington, Badsey, pt Bedwardine St John, Bengeworth, Berrow, Besford, Birlingham, Birtsmsorton, Bishampton, Blockley, Bredon, Bredon's Norton, Bretforton, Bricklehampton, Broadway, Bushley, Castlemorton, Chaceley, Charlton, Cleeve Prior, Great Comberton, Little Comberton, Conderton, Earls Croome, Hill Croome, Croome d'Abitot, Cropthorne, Cutsdean, Daylesford, Defford, Dormston, Eckington, Eldersfield, Elmley Castle, Evenlode, Evesham All Saints, Evesham St Lawrence, Feckenham, Fladbury, Grafton Flyford, Flyford Flavell, Great and Little Hampton, pt Hanbury, Hanley Castle, Harvington, Hill and Moor, Holdfast, Church Honeybourne, Inkberrow,

Kington, Ab Lench, Church Lench, Rous Lench, North and Middle Littleton, South Littleton, Longdon, Little Malvern, Naunton Beauchamp, Netherton, Norton and Lenchwick, Offenham, Overbury, Pendock, Peopleton, Pershore Holy Cross, Pershore St Andrew, North Piddle, Pinvin, Pirton, Queenhill, Redmarley d'Abitot, Ripple, Sedgeberrow, Severn Stoke, Shipston on Stour, Staunton, Strensham, Teddington, Throckmorton, Tidmington, Tredington, Upton upon Severn, Welland, Wick, Wickhamford, Wyre Piddle
WESTERN (or BEWDLEY) DIVISION
Bewdley MB, Hundred House PSD, pt Malvern PSD, pt Stourport PSD, Tenbury PSD, *viz.*, Abberley, Acton Beauchamp, Alfrick, Areley Kings, Astley, Bayton, pt Bedwardine St John, Bewdley, Bockleton, Bransford, Bredicot, Broadwas, Broughton Hackett, Churchill, pt Claines, Clifton upon Teme, Cotheridge, Crowle, Doddenham, Eastham, Edvin Loach, Grimley, Hallow, Hanley Child, Hanley William, Hartlebury, Hillhampton, Hindlip, Holt, Huddington, Kempsey, Kenswick, Knighton on Teme, Knightwick, Kyre Magna, Kyre Parva, Leigh, Lindridge, Lulsley, Madresfield, Great Malvern, Mamble, Martin Hussingtree, Martley, Mathon, Newland, Norton juxta Kempsey, Ombersley, Orleton, Pensax, Powick, Ribbesford, Rochford, Rock, Lower Sapey, Shelsley Beauchamp, Shelsley Kings, Shelsley Walsh, Shrawley, Spetchley, Stanford on Teme, Stockton on Teme, Stoulton, Suckley, Tenbury, Tibberton, Upton Snodsbury, Warley, Warndon, White Ladies Aston, Whittington, Wichenford, Great Witley, Little Witley, pt Worcester St Martin, pt Worcester St Peter the Great

1918—1948
BEWDLEY DIVISION
Bewdley MB, Malvern UD, Martley RD, Rock RD, Stourport UD, Tenbury RD, pt Tewkesbury RD (Chaceley, Pendock), Unnamed RD, Upton upon Severn RD
EVESHAM DIVISION
Droitwich MB, Droitwich RD, Evesham MB, Evesham RD, Feckenham RD, Pershore RD, Shipston on Stour RD, pt Stow on the Wold RD (the Worcs pars), pt Tewkesbury RD (Bredon, Bredon's Norton, Conderton, Overbury, Teddington), pt Winchcomb RD (the Worcs par)
KIDDERMINSTER DIVISION
Bromsgrove RD, Bromsgrove UD, North Bromsgrove UD, Kidderminster MB, Kidderminster RD, Redditch UD
STOURBRIDGE DIVISION
Halesowen RD, Lye and Wollescote UD, Oldbury UD, Stourbridge MB

1948—1970
BROMSGROVE COUNTY CONSTITUENCY
Bromsgrove RD, Bromsgrove UD, Redditch UD
KIDDERMINSTER COUNTY CONSTITUENCY
Bewdley MB, Kidderminster MB, Kidderminster RD, Martley RD, Stourport on Severn UD, Tenbury RD
SOUTH WORCESTERSHIRE COUNTY CONSTITUENCY[3]
Evesham MB, Evesham RD, Malvern UD, Pershore

RD, Upton upon Severn RD

1970—*

BROMSGROVE AND REDDITCH COUNTY CON-STITUENCY
Bromsgrove RD, Bromsgrove UD, Redditch UD

KIDDERMINSTER COUNTY CONSTITUENCY
Bewdley MB, Kidderminster MB, Kidderminster RD, Martley RD, Stourport on Severn UD, Tenbury RD

SOUTH WORCESTERSHIRE COUNTY CONSTITU-ENCY
Evesham MB, Evesham RD, Malvern UD, Pershore RD, Upton upon Severn RD

YORKSHIRE

BOROUGH CONSTITUENCIES[1]

ALDBOROUGH PARL BOR (1558—1832) [W Riding]
pt Aldborough

BARNSLEY PARL BOR/BC[2] (1918—*) [W Riding]
Ardsley UD (1918—48), Barnsley CB, Darton UD, Monk Bretton UD (1918—48), Worsborough UD (1948—*)

BATLEY AND MORLEY PARL BOR/BC (1918—*) [W Riding]
Batley MB, Morley MB, Ossett MB (1918—48)

BEVERLEY PARL BOR (1295—1306, 1563—1870[3]) [E Riding]
Beverley St Martin, Beverley St Nicholas, Molescroft (1832—70), Storkhill and Sandholme (1832—70), Thearne (1832—70), Tickton and Hull Bridge (1832—70), Weel (1832—70), Woodmansey and Beverley Parks (1832—70)

BOROUGHBRIDGE PARL BOR (1553—1832) [W Riding]
pt Aldborough

BRADFORD PARL BOR (1832—85) [W Riding]
Bowling, Bradford, Horton, Manningham

BRADFORD CENTRAL PARL BOR/BC (1885—1955[4]) [W Riding]
pt Bradford MB/CB (the wards of Bradford Moor [1948—55], East [1918—48], Exchange, Little Horton [1885—1918], Listerhills [1885—1918], Manningham [1918—55], North [1885—1948], North-East [1948—55], South [1918—55], West [1885—1948])

BRADFORD EAST PARL BOR/BC[4] (1885—1970) [W Riding]
pt Bradford MB/CB (the wards of North Bierley East [1948—55], East Bowling, West Bowling [1885—1955], Bradford Moor [1885—1948], East [1885—1918], Exchange [1955—70], Little Horton [1948—70], Listerhills [1955—70], South [1885—1918], South [1955—70], Tong [1918—70])

BRADFORD NORTH PARL BOR/BC[5] (1918—*) [W Riding]
pt Bradford MB/CB (the wards of Allerton [1918—56], Bolton, Bowling [1970—*], Bradford Moor [1955—*], Eccleshill, Heaton [1918—55], Idle, Laisterdyke [1970—*], North East [1955—70], Thornton [1918—48], Undercliffe [1970—*])

BRADFORD SOUTH PARL BOR/BC[4] (1918—*) [W Riding]
pt Bradford CB (the wards of North Brierley East [1918—48], North Brierley East [1955—70], North Brierley West [1918—70], West Bowling [1955—70], Clayton [1948—*], Great Horton [1918—55], Great Horton [1970—*], Little Horton [1918—48], Listerhills [1918—55], Odsal [1970—*], Thornton [1918—55], Tong [1970—*], Wibsey [1970—*], Wyke [1970—*]), Queensbury & Shelf UD (1955—*)

BRADFORD WEST PARL BOR (1885—1918) [W Riding]
pt Bradford MB (the wards of Allerton, Bolton, Heaton, Great Horton, Manningham)

BRADFORD WEST BC (1955[4]—*) [W Riding]
pt Bradford CB (the wards of Allerton, Heaton, Great Horton [1955—70], Little Horton [1970—*], Manningham, Thornton, University [1970—*])

BRIGHOUSE AND SPENBOROUGH BC[4] (1948—*) [W Riding]
Brighouse MB, Heckmondwike UD (1955—*), Queensbury and Shelf UD (1948—55), Spenborough UD

DEWSBURY PARL BOR/BC[4] (1867—*) [W Riding] [1 mbr]
1867—1918: pt Batley, Dewsbury, pt Mirfield, pt Soothill, pt Thornhill
1918—*: Dewsbury CB, Heckmondwike UD (1948—55), Mirfield UD (1948—*), Ossett MB (1948—*)

DONCASTER BC[6] (1948—*) [W Riding]
Doncaster CB

HALIFAX PARL BOR/BC (1832—*) [W Riding]
1832—1918: Halifax, pt Northowram, pt Ovenden (1867—1918), pt Skircoat (1867—1918), pt Southowram
1918—*: Halifax CB

HEDON (1295, 1547—1832) [E Riding]
Hedon

HUDDERSFIELD PARL BOR (1832—1948) [W Riding] [1 mbr]
1832—1918: Almondbury (1867—1918), Huddersfield, Lindley cum Quarmby (1867—1918), pt Linthwaite (1867—1918), Lockwood (1867—1918), pt Longwood (1867—1918)
1918—48: Huddersfield CB

HUDDERSFIELD EAST BC[7] (1948—*) [W Riding]
pt Huddersfield CB (the wards of Almondbury, North Central, South Central, Dalton, Deighton, Farrtown, Newsome [1955—*]), Kirkburton UD (1955—*)

HUDDERSFIELD WEST BC[7] (1948—*) [W Riding]
pt Huddersfield CB (the wards of Birkby, Crosland Moor, Lindley, Longwood, Marsh, Milnsbridge, Newsome [1948—55], Paddock)

KEIGHLEY BC (1948—*) [W Riding]
Denholme UD, Keighley MB, Silsden UD, pt Skipton RD (Steeton with Eastburn, Sutton)

KINGSTON UPON HULL PARL BOR (1304—1885) [E Riding]
Drypool (1832—85), pt Kirk Ella (1867—85), pt North Ferriby (1867—85), Garrison Side (1832—85), Kingston upon Hull Holy Trinity and St Mary (pt from joint rating of Holy Trinity, St Mary, ent 1832—85), Kingston upon Hull St Mary (until joint rating with Holy Trinity), Sculcoates (1832—85), Southcoates (1832—85)

KINGSTON UPON HULL CENTRAL PARL BOR/BC (1885—1955[8]) [E Riding]
pt Kingston upon Hull MB/CB (the wards of Albert [1918—48], Botanic [1948—55], pt Central [1885—

848

1918], East Central [1918—55], West Central [1918—55], Coltman [1918—55], Myton [1918—55], North Newington [1948—55], Paragon, Queen's [1885—1918], Whitefriars [1918—48])

KINGSTON UPON HULL CENTRAL BC (1970—*) [E Riding]

pt Kingston upon Hull CB (the wards of Avenue, Beverley, Botanic, Greenwood, Myton, Newland, University)

KINGSTON UPON HULL EAST PARL BOR/BC[9] (1885—*) [E Riding]

pt Kingston upon Hull MB/CB (the wards of Alexandra [1885—1970], Beverley [1885—1918], Bransholme [1970—*], pt Central [1885—1918], East Central [1955—70], Drypool, Greatfield [1970—*], Holderness [1970—*], Longhill [1970—*], Marfleet [1948—*], Myton [1955—70], Southcoates [1918—70], Stoneferry [1948—*], Sutton [1885—1918], Sutton [1948—*])

KINGSTON UPON HULL HALTEMPRICE BC (1948—55[8]) [E Riding]

Haltemprice UD, pt Kingston upon Hull CB (the wards of Pickering, St Andrews)

KINGSTON UPON HULL NORTH BC[8] (1948—70) [E Riding]

pt Kingston upon Hull CB (the wards of Beverley, Botanic [1955—70], West Central [1955—70], Newland [1955—70], Paragon [1955—70], Park, University)

KINGSTON UPON HULL NORTH WEST PARL BOR (1918—48) [E Riding]

pt Kingston upon Hull CB (the wards of Albert, Botanic, Newland, Park)

KINGSTON UPON HULL SOUTH WEST PARL BOR (1918—48) [E Riding]

pt Kingston upon Hull CB (the wards of Coltman, North Newington, South Newington)

KINGSTON UPON HULL WEST PARL BOR (1885—1918) [E Riding]

pt Kingston upon Hull MB (the wards of Albert, Botanic, Coltman, Newington, Park)

KINGSTON UPON HULL WEST BC (1955[8]—*) [E Riding]

pt Kingston upon Hull CB (the wards of Albert [1955—70], Boothferry [1970—*], Coltman, Derringham [1970—*], Newington [1970—*], North Newington [1955—70], South Newington [1955—70], Pickering, St Andrews)

KNARESBOROUGH PARL BOR (1867—85) [W Riding]

pt Knaresborough, pt Scriven with Tentergate

LEEDS PARL BOR (1832—85) [W Riding]

Chapel Allerton, Armley, Beeston, Bramley, Farnley, Headingley cum Burley, Holbeck, Hunslet, Leeds, Potter Newton, pt Seacroft, pt Templenewsham, Wortley

LEEDS CENTRAL PARL BOR/BC[10] (1885—*) [W Riding]

pt Leeds MB/CB (the wards of Armley and New Wortley [1948—51], Blenheim [1948—51], Blenheim City [1951—*], pt Brunswick [1885—1948], Central [pt 1885—1918, ent 1918—51], pt Headingley [1918—48], Holbeck North [1948—51], Mill Hill [1885—

1948], Mill Hill and South [1948—51], pt North West [1918—48], South [1918—48], Wellington [1951—*], West [1885—1948], Westfield [1948—*])

LEEDS EAST PARL BOR (1918—48) [W Riding]

pt Leeds MB (the ward of East, pt of the wards of Central, North, North East)

LEEDS EAST BC (1955[11]—*) [W Riding]

pt Leeds CB (the wards of Burmantofts, Cross Gates, Halton, Harehills, Osmondthorpe)

LEEDS NORTH PARL BOR/BC[10] (1885—*) [W Riding]

pt Leeds MB/CB (the wards of Allerton [1951—*], pt Brunswick [1885—1948], Headingley [ent 1885—1918, pt 1918—48], Moortown [1951—*], North [pt 1885—1948, ent 1948—51], pt North East [1885—1918], North West [ent 1885—1918, pt 1918—48], Roundhay [1948—*], Woodhouse [1948—*])

LEEDS NORTH EAST PARL BOR/BC[11] (1918—*) [W Riding]

pt Leeds CB (the wards of Allerton [1955—*], Burmantofts [1948—55], Harehills [1948—55], pt North [1918—48], pt North East [1918—48], Potternewton [1948—*], Richmond Hill [1948—55], Rounday [1918—48], Seacroft [1918—48], Shadwell and Crossgates [1918—48], Woodhouse [1955—*])

LEEDS NORTH WEST BC[12] (1948—*) [W Riding]

pt Leeds CB (the wards of Cookridge [1970—*], Headingley [1970—*], Far Headingley [1948—70], Hyde Park [1948—70], Kirkstall, Meanwood [1951—70], Moortown [1955—*], Weetwood [1970—*])

LEEDS SOUTH PARL BOR/BC[10] (1885—*) [W Riding]

pt Leeds MB/CB (the wards of Beeston [1948—*], pt Bramley [1885—1918], Holbeck [1918—48], Holbeck South [1948—51], East Hunslet [1885—1918], West Hunslet [1885—1951], Hunslet Carr and Middleton [1948—70], Middleton and West Hunslet [1970—*], South [1885—1918], pt New Wortley [1918—48])

LEEDS SOUTH EAST PARL BOR/BC[10] (1918—*) [W Riding]

pt Leeds CB (the wards of Blenheim [1955—70], Burley [1970—*], Burmantofts [1970—*], City [1955—*], Cross Gates and Templenewsham [1948—55], East [1918—48], East Hunslet [1918—70], pt North East [1918—48], Osmondthorpe [1948—55], Richmond Hill [1955—*], Westfield [1955—70], Woodhouse [1970—*])

LEEDS WEST PARL BOR/BC[10] (1885—*) [W Riding]

pt Leeds MB/CB (the wards of Armley [1955—*], Armley and Wortley [1885—1948], Bramley [pt 1885—1918, ent 1918—*], Castleton [1970—*], Farnley [1948—55], Holbeck [1885—1918], Stanningley [1955—*], Wellington [1955—70], Wortley [1955—*], New Wortley [ent 1885—1918, pt 1918—48], Wortley and Upper Armley [1948—55])

MALTON PARL BOR (1295, 1298, 1640—1885) [N Riding until 1832, pt N Riding, pt E Riding 1832—85]

until 1832: New Malton

1832—85: New Malton [N Riding], Old Malton [N Riding], Norton [E Riding]

MIDDLESBROUGH PARL BOR (1867—1918) [N Riding]

pt West Acklam (1885—1918), pt Eston, pt Linthorpe,

Middlesbrough, pt Normanby, pt Ormesby

MIDDLESBROUGH EAST PARL BOR/BC[13] (1918—70) [N Riding]

pt Middlesbrough CB (the wards of Berwick Hills [1960—70], Cannon [1948—70], Clairville [1960—70], Cleveland [1948—60], Exchange, Grove Hill, Newport [1948—70], Ormesby [1918—60], North Ormesby [1960—70], St Hilda's, Thorntree [1960—70], Tollesby [1960—70], Vulcan [1918—60])

MIDDLESBROUGH WEST PARL BOR/BC[13] (1918—70) [N Riding]

pt Middlesbrough CB (the wards of Acklam, Ayresome, Cannon [1918—48], Cleveland [1918—48], Crescent [1960—70], Gresham [1960—70], Linthorpe, Newport [1918—48], Park [1960—70], Whinney Banks [1960—70]), Thornaby on Tees MB (1948—70)

NORTHALLERTON PARL BOR (1298, 1640—1885) [N Riding] [1 mbr 1832—85]

Brompton (1867—85), Lazenby (1867—85), Northallerton (pt until 1867, ent 1867—85), Romanby (1867—85)

PICKERING PARL BOR (1295 only) [N Riding]

pt Pickering

PONTEFRACT PARL BOR (1295, 1298, 1620—1918) [W Riding] [1 mbr 1885—1918]

Carleton (1832—1918), Ferry Fryston (1832—1918), Monkhill (1832—1918), Pontefract, Pontefract Park, Tanshelf (1832—1918)

PONTEFRACT BC (1948—70) [W Riding]

Castleford UD, Featherstone UD, Pontefract MB

PONTEFRACT AND CASTLEFORD BC (1970—*) [W Riding]

Castleford MB, Featherstone UD, Pontefract MB

PUDSEY BC (1948—*) [W Riding]

Aireborough UD, Horsforth UD, Pudsey MB

RAVENSRODD PARL BOR (1295, occasionally until 1337) [E Riding]

Ravensrodd

RICHMOND PARL BOR (1585—1885) [N Riding]

pt Catterick (until Hipswell gains sep civ identity), pt Easby, pt Hipswell (when gains sep civ identity), Richmond, St Martin

RIPON PARL BOR (1295, 1307, 1337, 1553—1885) [W Riding]

pt Aismunderby with Bondgate, Ripon

ROTHERHAM PARL BOR/BC (1918—*) [W Riding]

Greasborough UD (1918—48), Rawmarsh UD (1918—48), Rotherham CB

SHEFFIELD PARL BOR (1832—85) [W Riding]

Attercliffe cum Darnall, Brightside Bierlow, Ecclesall Bierlow, Nether Hallam, Upper Hallam, Sheffield

SHEFFIELD, ATTERCLIFFE PARL BOR/BC[14] (1885—*) [W Riding]

Heeley (1885—1918), pt Sheffield MB/CB (the wards of Attercliffe, Birley [1970—*], Darnall [1918—*], Handsworth [1948—*], Park [1885—1918], Mosborough [1970—*], Tinsley [1955—70])

SHEFFIELD, BRIGHTSIDE PARL BOR/BC[14] (1885—*) [W Riding]

pt Sheffield MB/CB (the wards of Brightside, Burngreave [1918—48], Firth Park [1948—*], Nether Shire [1953—*], Southey Green [1955—*], Tinsley [1948—55])

SHEFFIELD, CENTRAL PARL BOR (1885—1948) [W Riding]

pt Sheffield MB/CB (the wards of Broomhall [1918—48], pt St George's [1885—1918], St Peter's, St Philip's)

SHEFFIELD, ECCLESALL PARL BOR (1885—1948) [W Riding]

pt Sheffield MB/CB (the ward of Ecclesall [pt 1885—1918, ent 1918—48], Sharrow [1918—48])

SHEFFIELD, HALAM PARL BOR/BC[14] (1885—*) [W Riding]

pt Sheffield MB/CB (the wards of pt Broomhall [1918—48], Broomhill [1948—*], Crookesmoor [1918—48], Crookesmoor [1955—70], Dore [1970—*], pt Ecclesall [1885—1918], Ecclesall [1948—*], Hallam [1918—*], Nether Hallam [1885—1918], Upper Hallam [1885—1918], Nether Edge [1970—*], pt St George's [1885—1918])

SHEFFIELD, HEELEY BC[14] (1948—*) [W Riding]

pt Sheffield CB (the wards of Beauchief [1970—*], Gleadless [1970—*], Heeley, Intake [1970—*], Nether Edge [1948—70], Norton [1948—70], Sharrow [1955—70], Woodseats [1948—70])

SHEFFIELD, HILLSBOROUGH PARL BOR/BC[14] (1918—*) [W Riding]

pt Sheffield CB (the wards of Cathedral [1955—70], Crookesmoor [1948—55], Hillsborough, Neepsend [1918—48], Owlerton [1948—70], Nether Thorpe [1970—*], Walkley)

SHEFFIELD, NEEPSEND BC[14] (1948—55) [W Riding]

pt Sheffield CB (the wards of Burngreave, Cathedral [1953—55], Neepsend [1948—53], St Peter's [1948—53], St Philip's [1948—53], Southey Green [1953—55])

SHEFFIELD, PARK PARL BOR/BC[14] (1918—*) [W Riding]

pt Sheffield CB (the wards of Burngreave [1955—*], Castle [1970—*], Heeley [1918—48], Manor [1948—*], Moor [1948—70], Park, Sharrow [1948—55], St Philip's [1948—53], Southey Green [1953—55])

STOCKTON ON TEES PARL BOR/BC[15] (1918—70) [N Riding]

Stockton on Tees MB, Thornaby on Tees MB (1918—48)

TEESSIDE, MIDDLESBROUGH BC (1970—*) [N Riding]

pt Teesside CB (the wards of Berwick Hills, Marton, North Ormesby, St Hilda's, Thorntree, Tollesby)

TEESSIDE, REDCAR BC (1970—*) [N Riding]

pt Teesside CB (the wards of Coatham, Eston Grange, Kirkleatham, Ormesby, Redcar, South Bank)

TEESSIDE, STOCKTON BC (1970—*) [N Riding]

pt Teesside CB (the wards of Billingham East, Billingham West, Grangefield, Harthburn, Mile House, North End, Norton, Stockton South)

TEESSIDE, THORNABY (1970—*) [N Riding]

pt Teesside CB (the wards of Acklam, Ayresome, Gresham, Linthorpe, Thornaby East, Thornaby West)

THIRSK PARL BOR (1295, 1553—1885) [N Riding]

Bagby with Islebeck, Carlton Miniott, South Kilvington, Sand Hutton, Sowerby, Thirsk

TICKHILL PARL BOR (1295 only) [W Riding]

pt Tickhill

WAKEFIELD PARL BOR/BC[16] (1832—*) [W Riding] [1 mbr]

1832—1918: pt Alverthorpe with Thornes, pt Sandall Magna (1832—1918), pt Stanley cum Wrenthorpe, Wakefield

1918—:* Horbury UD (1948—*), Royston UD (1955—*), Wakefield CB, pt Wakefield RD (entire RD less Crofton, Newland with Woodhouse Moor [1955—*], Sharlston, Warmfield cum Heath)

WHITBY PARL BOR (1832—85) [N Riding] [1 mbr]
Hawsker with Stainsacre, Ruswarp, Whitby

YARM PARL BOR (1295 only) [N Riding]
Yarm

YORK PARL BOR/BC[17] (1295—*) [not assoc with a Riding]

1295—1918: pt Clifton (1832—1918), pt Dringhouses (1885—1918), pt Gate Fulford (1832—1918), pt Heworth (1832—1918), Holgate (1885—1918), pt Middlethorpe (1832—1918), York All Saints North Street, York All Saints Pavement, York Castle, York Davy Hall, York Holy Trinity Goodramgate; York Holy Trinity, King's Court; York Holy Trinity Micklegate (pt until 1867, ent 1867—1918), York Minster Hall with Bedern (1832—1918), York Mint Yard (1832—1918), York St Andrew, York St Crux; York St Cuthbert, St Helen on the Walls and All Saints Peasholm (pt until 1832, ent 1832—1918); York St Dennis, York St George, York St Giles in the Suburbs (pt until 1885, ent 1885—1918); York St Helen, Stonegate; York St John, Delpike; York St John, Micklegate; York St Lawrence (pt until 1867, ent 1867—1918), York St Margaret, York St Martin le Grand, York St Martin Micklegate with St Gregory, York St Mary Bishophill Junior (pt until 1867, ent 1867—1918), York St Mary Bishophill Senior (pt until 1867, ent 1867—1918); York St Mary, Castlegate; York St Maurice, York St Michael le Belfrey (pt until 1867, ent 1867—1918), York St Michael Spurriergate (pt until 1832, ent 1832—1918), York St Nicholas; York St Olave, Marygate (pt until 1832, ent 1832—1918); York St Peter the Little, York St Peter le Willows, York St Sampson, York St Saviour (pt until 1867, ent 1867—1918)

1918—:* York CB

COUNTY CONSTITUENCIES

East Riding
1832—1885
EAST RIDING DIVISION
East Riding of Yorkshire

1885—1918
BUCKROSE DIVISION
Bainton Beacon PSD, Buckrose PSD, Dockering PSD, *viz.,* Acklam with Barthorpe, Agram, Auburn, Bainton, Barmston, Beeford, Bempton, Bessingby, Birdsall, Boynton, Bracken, Bridlington, Brigham, Buckton, Burton Agnes, Burton Fleming, Burythorpe, Butterwick, Carnaby, Cottam, Cowlam, North Dalton, Great Driffield, Little Driffield, Duggleby, Eastburn, Easton, Eddlethorpe, Emswell with Kellythorpe, Filey, Fimber, Firby, Flamborough, Folkton, Fordon, Foston on the Wolds, Foxholes with Boythorpe, Fraisthorpe, Fridaythorpe, North Frodingham, Ganton, Garton on the Wolds, Gembling, Gransmoor, North Grimton, Grindale, Haisthorpe, Harpham, Helperthorpe, East Heslerton, West Heslerton, Hilderthorpe, Howsham, Hunmanby, Hutton Cranswick, Great Kelk, Little Kelk, Kennythorpe, Kilham, Kilnwick, Kirby Grindalyth, Kirkburn and Battleburn, Kirkham, Knapton, Langtoft, Langton, Leavening, Leppington, Lissett, Lowthorpe, Lund, Luttons Ambo, Menethorpe, Middleton on the Wolds, Muston, Nafferton, Neswick, Norton, Raisthorpe and Burdale, Reighton, Rillington, Rotsea, Rudston, Ruston Parva, Scagglethorpe, Scampston, Scrayingham, Settrington, Sewerby cum Marton, Sherburn, Skerne, Sledmere, Southburn, Speeton, Sunderlandwick, Thirkleby, Thornholme, Thorpe Bassett, Thwing, Tibthorpe, Towthorpe, Ulrome, Wansford, Watton, Weaverthorpe, Westow, Wetwang, Wharram le Street, Wharram Percy, Willerby, Wilsthorpe, Wintringham, Wold Newton, Yedingham

HOLDERNESS DIVISION
Beverley MB, Middle Holderness PSD, North Holderness PSD, South Holderness PSD, North Hunsley Beacon PSD, *viz.,* Aike, Aldborough, Atwick, Benningholme and Grange, Beswick, Beverley St Martin, Beverley St Mary, Beverley St Nicholas, Bewholme and Nunkeeling, Bilton, Bishop Burton, Bonwick, Brandesburton, Burstwick with Skeckling, Burton Pidsea, Catfoss, Catwick, Cherry Burton, Coniston, Great and Little Cowdens, South Dalton, Danthorpe; Dringhoe, Upton and Brough; Dunnington, Easington, pt Kirk Ella, Ellerby, Elstronwick, Eske, Etton, Fitling, Flinton, South Frodingham, Ganstead, Garton with Grimston, Goxhill, Halsham, Great Hatfield, Little Hatfield, Hedon, Hempholme, Hilston, Hollym, Holme on the Wolds, Holmpton, Hornsea, Humbleton, Keyingham, Kilnsea, Leconfield and Arram, Lelley, Leven, Lockington, Lockington in Kilnwick, Mappleton and Rowlston, Marton, Meaux, Molescroft, Moor Town, North Newbald, East Newton, Out Newton, West Newton with Burton Constable, Ottringham, Oswtwick, Owthorne, Patrington, Paull, Preston, Rimswell, Rise, Long Riston, Roos, Routh, Ryhill and Camerton, Scorborough, Seaton and Wassand, Sigglesthorne, Skeffling, Skipsea; North Skirlaugh, Rowton and Arnold; South Skirlaugh, Sproatley, Storkhill and Sandholme, Sunk Island, pt Sutton and Stoneferry, Swine, Thearne, Thirtleby, Thorgumbald, Tickton and Hill Bridge, Tunstall, Walkington, Wawne, Waxholme, Weel, Welwick, Winestead, Withernsea, Withernwick, Woodmansey and Beverley Parks, Wyton

HOWDENSHIRE DIVISION
Holme Beacon PSD, Howdenshire PSD, South Hunsley Beacon PSD, pt Ouse and Derwent PSD, Wilton Beacon PSD, *viz.,* Allerthorpe, Anlaby, Asselby, Aughton, Balkholme, Barlby, Barmby on the Marsh,

Barmby on the Moor, Belby, Bellasize, Bielby, Bishop Wilton with Belthorpe, Bishopsoil, Blacktoft, Bolton, Brackenholme with Woodhall, Brantingham, Breighton and Gunby, Broomfleet, Bubwith, Bugthorpe, Burnby, High Catton, Low Catton, North Cave with Everthorpe and Drewton, South Cave, Cheapsides, North Cliffe, South Cliffe, Cliffe cum Lund, Cotness, pt Cottingham, East Cottingwith, Deighton, North Duffield, South Duffield, Dunnington, Eastrington, Kirk Ella, West Ella, Ellerker, Ellerton Priory, Elloughton with Brough, Elvington, Escrick, Everingham, Fangfoss, Faxfleet, pt North Ferriby, Foggathorpe, pt Gate Fulford, Water Fulford, Full Sutton, Gilberdike, Great Givendale with Grimthorpe, Goodmanham, Gribthorpe, Grimston, Haltemprice, Harlthorpe, Harswell, Hayton, Hemingbrough, Heslington St Lawrence, Heslington St Paul, Hessle, Holme upon Spalding Moor, Hotham, Howden, Huggate, Kelfield, Kexby, Kilnwick Percy, Kilpin, Kirby Underdale, Knedlington, Langwith, Laxton, Laytham, Londesborough with Easthorpe, Market Weighton and Arras, Melbourne, Melton, Menthorpe cum Bowthorpe, Metham, Millington with Little Givendale, Naburn, South Newbald, Newton upon Derwent, Nunburnholme, Osgodby, Ousethorpe, Pocklington, Portington and Cavil, Ricall, Rowley, Saltmarshe, Sancton and Houghton, Scalby, Seaton Ross, Shipton Thorpe, Skelton, Skidby, Skipwith, Skirpenbeck, Spadlington, East Stamford Bridge, West Stamford Bridge with Scoreby, Stillingfleet with Moreby, Storwood, Sutton upon Derwent, Swanland, Thixendale, Thorganby with West Cottingwith, Thornton, Thorpe, Thorpe le Street, Wallingfen, Waplington, Warter, Wauldby, Welton, Wheldrake, Wilberfoss, Willerby, Willitoft, Wressell, Yapham cum Meltonby, Yokefleet, Youlthorpe with Gowthorpe

1918—1948
BUCKROSE DIVISION
Bridlington MB, Bridlington RD, Driffield RD, Great Driffield UD, Filey UD, Norton RD, Norton UD, Sherburn RD
HOLDERNESS DIVISION
Beverley MB, pt Beverley RD (the pars not in Howdenshire Dv), Cottingham UD, Hedon MB, Hornsea UD, Patrington RD, pt Sculcoates RD (Preston, Sutton), Skirlaugh RD, Withernsea UD
HOWDENSHIRE DIVISION
pt Beverley RD (Brantingham, South Cave, Ellerker, Elloughton with Brough), Escrick RD, Hessle UD, Howden RD, Pocklington RD, Pocklington UD, Riccall RD, pt Sculcoates RD (the pars not in Holderness Dv)

1948—1970
BEVERLEY COUNTY CONSTITUENCY (1948—55[8])
Beverley MB, Beverley RD, Derwent RD, Howden RD, Norton RD, Norton UD, Pocklington RD
BRIDLINGTON COUNTY CONSTITUENCY[9]
Bridlington MB, Bridlington RD, Driffield RD (1948—55), Driffield UD (1948—55), Filey UD, Hedon MB, Holderness RD, Hornsea UD, Withernsea UD

HALTEMPRICE COUNTY CONSTITUENCY (1955[8]—70)
Beverley MB, Beverley RD, Haltemprice UD
HOWDEN COUNTY CONSTITUENCY (1955[8]—70)
Derwent RD, Driffield RD, Driffield UD, Howden RD, Norton RD, Norton UD, Pocklington RD

1970—*
BRIDLINGTON COUNTY CONSTITUENCY
Bridlington MB, Bridlington RD, Filey UD, Hedon MB, Holderness RD, Hornsea UD, Withernsea UD
HALTEMPRICE COUNTY CONSTITUENCY
Beverley MB, Beverley RD, Haltemprice UD
HOWDEN COUNTY CONSTITUENCY
Derwent RD, Driffield RD, Driffield UD, Howden RD, Norton RD, Norton UD, Pocklington RD

North Riding
1832—1885
NORTH RIDING DIVISION
North Riding of Yorkshire and Ainsty Wap in West Riding

1885—1918
CLEVELAND DIVISION
pt East Langbarugh PSD, North Langbarugh PSD, West Langbarugh PSD, Yarm PSD, *viz.*, pt West Acklam, Appleton Wiske, Great Ayton, Little Ayton, Brotton, Broughton, Great Busby, Little Busby, Carlton, Commondale, Crathorne, Over Dinsdale, Easby, pt Eston, Faceby, Girsby, Guisborough, Hemlington, Hilton, Hornby, Hutton Lowcross, Hutton Rudby, Ingleby Arncliffe, Ingleby Barwick, Ingleby Greenhow, Kildale, Kilton, Kirby in Cleveland, Kirkleatham, Castle Leavington, Kirk Leavington, pt Linthorpe, Liverton, Loftus, Maltby, Marske, Marton, Middleton upon Leven, Mooresholm, Morton, Newby, Newton, pt Normanby, Nunthorpe, pt Ormesby, Picton, Pinchinthorpe, Potto, Redcar, East Rounton, Rudby in Cleveland, Seamer, Sexhow, Skelton, Skinningrove, Skutterskelfe, Great Smeaton, Stainton, Stanghow, Stokesley, Thornaby, Tocketts, Upleatham, Upsall, Westerdale, Whorlton, Wilton, High Worsall, Low Worsall, Yarm
RICHMOND DIVISION
Allertonshire PSD, East Gilling PSD, West Gilling PSD, Greta Bridge PSD, East Hang PSD, West Hang PSD, Richmond MB, *viz.*, High Abbotside, Low Abbotside, Agglethorpe with Coverham, Ainderby Miers with Holtby, Ainderby Steeple, Aiskew, Akebar, Aldbrough, Appleton, Arkengarthdale, Arrathorne, Aske, Askrigg, Aysgarth, Bainbridge, Barden, Barforth, Barningham, Barton, Bedale, Bellerby, Birklby, Bishopdale, Boldron, Bolton upon Swale, Borrowby, Bowes, Brignall, Brompton, Brompton on Swale, Brough, Burrill with Cowling, Burton cum Walden, Burton upon Ure, Caldbergh with East Scrafton, Caldwell, Carkin, Carlton Highdale, Carlton Town, Carperby cum Thoresby, Castle Bolton, Catterick, Cleasby, Clifton upon Ure, Colburn, Constable Burton, Cotherstone, Cotcliffe, East Cowton, North Cowton, South Cowton, Crakenhall, Croft, Crosby, Dalton, Dalton upon Tees, Danby Wiske, Deighton, Down-

holme, Easby, Egglestone Abbey, Ellerbeck, Ellerton Abbey, Ellerton upon Swale, Ellingstring, Ellingston, Eppleby, Eryholme; Exelby, Leeming and Newton; Fearby, Finghall, Firby, Forcett with Carkin, Garriston, Gayles, Gilling, Gilmonby, Grinton, Hackfroth, Harmby, East Harsley, West Harsley, East Hauxwell, West Hauxwell, Hawes, Healy with Sutton, Hipswell, Holwick, Hope, Hornby, Hudswell, Hunderthwaite, Hunton, Hutton Bonville, Hutton Hang, Hutton Magna, Ilton cum Pott, Killerby, Kiplin, Kirby Sigston, Kirkby Fleetham, Kirkby Ravensworth, Knayton with Brawith, Landmoth cum Catto, Langthorne, Great Langton, Little Langton, Lartington, East Layton, West Layton, Lazenby, Leake, Leyburn, Lunedale, Manfield, Marrick, Marske, Masham, Melbecks, Melmerby, Melsonby, Mickleton, Middleham, Middleton Tyas, Morton upon Swale, Moulton, Muker, New Forest, Newbiggin, Newby Wiske, Newsham, Newton Morrell, Northallerton, Osmotherley, North Otterington, Ovington, Patrick Brompton, Preston under Soar, Rand Grange, Ravensworth, Redmire, Reeth, Richmond, Rokesby, Romaldkirk, Romanby, Rookwith, West Rounton, St Martin, Scargill, Scorton, Scotton, West Scrafton, Scrunton, Skeeby, Little Smeaton, Snape, Sowerby under Cotcliffe, Spennithorne, Stainton, Stanwick St John, Stapleton, Startforth, Swinton with Warthermarske, Thimbleby, Thirn, Thorlaby, Thornton le Beans, Thornton Rust, Thornton Steward, Thornton Watlass, Thrintoft, Tunstall, Uckerby, Walburn, Warlaby, Welbury, Well, Wensley, Whaston, Whitwell, Winton, East Witton Within, East Witton Without, West Witton, Wycliffe with Thorpe, Yafforth

THIRSK AND MALTON DIVISION

Ainsty Wap, Birdforth PSD, pt East Bulmer PSD, West Bulmer PSD, Hallikeld PSD, Malton PSD, viz., Acaster Malbis, Acaster Selby, Acomb, Ainderby Quernhow, Airyholme with Howthorpe and Baxton Howe, Aldwark, Alne, Amotherby, Angram, Angram Grange, Appleton le Street, Appleton Roebuck, Arden, Asenby, Askham Bryan, Askham Richard, Bagby, Baldersby, Balk, Barton le Street, Barton le Willows, Benningbrough, Bickerton, Bilbrough; Bilsdale, West Side; Bilton, Birdforth, Bishopthorpe, Boltby, Bolton Percy, Bossall with Buttercrambe, Brafferton, Brandsby cum Stearsby, Broughton, Bulmer, Burneston, Butterwick, Old Byland, Byland Abbey, Carlton Husthwaite, Carlton Miniott, Carthorpe, Catterton, Catton, Claxton, pt Clifton, Cold Kirby, Colton, Coneysthorpe, Copmanthorpe, Cowesby, Coxwold, Crambe, Crayke, Cundall with Leckby, Dalby cum Skewsby, Dale Town, Dalton, Dishforth, pt Dringhouses, Earswick, Easingwold, Eldmire with Crakenhill, Farlington, Fawdington, Felixkirk, Flawith, Flaxton, Foston, Fryton, Ganthorpe, Gatenby, Gueldable, Harton, Hawnby, Haxby, Healaugh, Gate Helmsley, Upper Helmsley, Helperby, Hendershelf, Hessay, pt Heworth, Hildenley, Holme, South Holme, Holtby, Hood Grange, Hovingham, Howe, Howgrave, Huby, Humberton, Huntington, Husthwaite, Hutton Conyers, Hutton Sessay, Hutton Wandesley, Huttons Ambo, Kepwick, Kilburn, North Kilvington, South Kilvington, Kirby Hill, Kirby Knowle, Kirby Wiske,

Kirklington cum Upsland, Knapton, Langthorpe, Lillings Ambo, Linton upon Ouse, New Malton, Old Malton, Long Marston, Marton cum Moxby, Marton le Moor, Maunby, Melmerby, Middlethorpe, Middleton Quernhow, Moor Monkton, Murton, Myton on Swale, Newburgh, Newsham with Breckenbrough, Newton Kyme cum Toulston, Newton upon Ouse, Norton Conyers, Norton le Clay, Oldstead, Osbaldwick, South Otterington, Oulston, Overton, Oxton, Pickhill with Roxby, Nether Poppleton, Upper Poppleton, Rainton with Newby, Raskelf, Rawcliffe, Rufforth, Sand Hutton, Scackleton, Sessay, Sheriff Hutton with Cornbrough, Shipton, Sinderby, Nether Silton, Over Silton, Skelton, Skipton on Swale, Slingsby, Snilesworth, Sowerby, Steeton, Stittenham, Stillington, Stockton on the Forest, Strensall, Sutton Howgrave, Sutton on the Forest, Sutton under Whitstone Cliff, Swainby with Allerthorpe, Swinton, Tadcaster East, East Tanfield, West Tanfield, Terrington with Wigganthorpe, Theakston, Thirkleby, Thirlby, Thirsk, Tholthorpe, Thormanby, Thornborough, Thornton Bridge, Thornton on the Hill, Thornton le Clay, Thornton le Moor, Thornton le Street, Thorp Arch, Thorpe le Willows, Tockwith, Tollerton, Topcliffe, Towthorpe, Upsall, Walton, Warthill Copyhold, Warthill Freehold, Wass, Wath, Welburn, Whenby, Whitwell on the Hill, Wighill, Wigginton, Wildon Grange, Wilstrop, Yearsley

WHITBY DIVISION

pt East Langbaurgh PSD, East Pickering Lythe PSD, West Pickering Lythe PSD, Ryedale PSD, Whitby Strand PSD, Scarbrough MB, viz., Aislaby, Aislaby, Allerston, Ampleforth Birdforth, Ampleforth Oswaldkirk, Ampleforth St Peter, Appleton le Moors, East Ayton, West Ayton, Barnby, Barughs Ambo, Beadlam, Bilsdale Midcable, Borrowby; Bransdale, West Side; Brawby, Brompton, Broxa, Burniston, Cawthorn, Cawton, Cayton, Cloughton, Coulton, Cropton, Danby, Easington, Ebberston, Great Edstone, Little Edstone, Egton, Ellerby, Eskdaleside, Fadmore, Farmanby; Farndale, East Side; Farndale, Low Quarter; Farndale, West Side; Fylingdales, Gillamoor, Gilling East, Glaisdale, Goathland, Grimston, Gristhorpe, Great Habton, Little Habton, Hackness, Harome, Hartoft, Harwood Dale, Hawsker with Stainsacre, Helmsley, Hinderwell, North Holme, Hutton Buscel, Hutton le Hole, Hutton Mulgrave, Irton, Kingthorpe, Kirby Misperton, Kirkby Moorside, Laskill Pasture, Lastingham, Lebberston, Levisham, Lockton, Lythe, Marishes, Marton, Mickleby, Middleton, Muscoates, Nawton, East Ness, West Ness, Newholm with Dunsley, Newton, East Newton and Laysthorp, Newton Mulgrave, Normanby, Nunington, Osgodby, Oswaldkirk, Pickering, Pockley, Rievaulx; Rosedale, East Side; Rosedale, West Side; Roxby, Ruswarp, Ryton, Salton, Sawdon, Scalby, Scarborough, Scawton, Seamer, Silpho, Sinnington, Skiplam, Snainton, Sneaton, Spaunton, Sproxton, Staintondale, Stonegrave, Suffield cum Everley, Thornton le Dale, Thornton Risebrough, Throxenby, Troutsdale, Ugglebarnby, Ugthorpe, Welburn, Whitby, Wilton, Wombleton, Wrelton, Wykeham

1918—1948

CLEVELAND DIVISION

Eston UD, pt Guisborough RD (the pars not in Scarborough & Whitby Dv), Guisborough UD, Hinderwell UD, Loftus UD, Middlesbrough RD, Redcar UD, Saltburn by the Sea UD, Skelton and Brotton UD

RICHMOND DIVISION

Aysgarth RD, Bedale RD, Croft RD, Kirlington cum Upsland UD, Leyburn RD, Masham UD, Northallerton RD, Northallerton UD, Reeth RD, Richmond MB, Richmond RD, Startforth RD, Stokesley RD

SCARBOROUGH AND WHITBY DIVISION

pt Guisborough RD (Commondale, Danby, Westerdale), pt Pickering RD (Allerston, Ebberston, Kingthorpe, Levisham, Lockton, Marishes, Newton, Thornton Dale, Wilton), Pickering UD, Scalby UD, Scarborough MB, Scarborough RD, Whitby RD, Whitby UD

THIRSK AND MALTON DIVISION

Easingwold RD, Flaxton RD, Helmsley RD, Kirkby Moorside RD, Malton RD, Malton UD, pt Pickering RD (all except the pars in Scarborough & Whitby Dv), Thirsk RD, Wath RD

1948—1970

CLEVELAND COUNTY CONSTITUENCY

Eston UD, Guisborough UD, Loftus UD, Redcar MB, Saltburn and Marske by the Sea UD, Skelton and Brotton UD

RICHMOND COUNTY CONSTITUENCY

Aysgarth RD, Croft RD, Leyburn RD, Masham RD, Northallerton RD, Northallerton UD, Reeth RD, Richmond MB, Richmond RD, Startforth RD, Stokesley RD

SCARBOROUGH AND WHITBY COUNTY CONSTITUENCY

pt Pickering RD (Allerston, Ebberston, Kingthorpe, Levisham, Lockton, Newton, Marishes, Thornton Dale, Wilton), Pickering UD, Scalby UD, Scarborough MB, Scarborough RD, Whitby RD, Whitby UD

THIRSK AND MALTON COUNTY CONSTITUENCY

Bedale RD, Easingwold RD, Flaxton RD, Helmsley RD, Kirkby Moorside RD, Malton RD, Malton UD, pt Pickering RD (all except the pars in Scarborough & Whitby CC), Thirsk RD, Wath RD

1970—*

CLEVELAND AND WHITBY COUNTY CONSTITUENCY

Guisborough UD, Loftus UD, Saltburn and Marske by the Sea UD, Skelton and Brotton UD, Whitby RD, Whitby UD

RICHMOND COUNTY CONSTITUENCY

Aysgarth RD, Croft RD, Leyburn RD, Masham RD, Northallerton RD, Northallerton UD, Reeth RD, Richmond MB, Richmond RD, Startforth RD, Stokesley RD

SCARBOROUGH COUNTY CONSTITUENCY

Pickering RD, Pickering UD, Scalby UD, Scarborough MB, Scarborough RD

THIRSK AND MALTON COUNTY CONSTITUENCY

Bedale RD, Easingwold RD, Flaxton RD, Helmsley RD, Kirkby Moorside RD, Malton RD, Malton UD,

Thirsk RD, Wath RD

West Riding

1832—1867

WEST RIDING DIVISION

West Riding of Yorkshire

1867—1885[18]

EASTERN DIVISION OF THE WEST RIDING

Morley Wap, Ripon Lbty

NORTHERN DIVISION OF THE WEST RIDING

Waps of Barkstone Ash, Claro, Osgoldcross, Skyrack, Staincliffe and Ewecross

SOUTHERN DIVISION OF THE WEST RIDING

Doncaster Soke, Waps of Agbrigg, Staincross, Strafforth and Tickhill

1885—1918

BARKSTON ASH DIVISION

Lower Barkston Ash PSD, pt Upper Barkston Ash PSD, pt Skyrack PSD, pt Wetherby PSD, other specified pars, *viz.*, Aberford, Adel cum Eccup, Alwoodley, Austhorpe, Bardsey cum Rigton, Barkston, Barlow, Barwick in Elmet, Biggin, Birkin, Bramham cum Oglethorpe, Brayton, Burn, Burton Salmon, Byram cum Pool, Camblesforth, Carlton, Cawood, Clifford with Boston, Collingham, Cowthorpe, Kirk Deighton, North Deighton, Drax, Long Drax, Dunkeswick, Church Fenton, Little Fenton, Monk Fryston, Garforth, Gateforth, Grimston, Chapel Hadlesey, West Haddlesey, Hambleton, Harewood, Hillam, Temple Hirst, Hirst Courtney, Huddleston cum Lumby, Kearby with Netherby, East Keswick, Kirkby Wharfe and North Milford, Lead, Linton, Lotherton cum Aberford, Micklefield, Micklethwaite, South Milford, Newland, Newthorpe, Newton Kyme cum Toulston, Parlington, Great and Little Preston, Little Ribston, Roundhay, Ryther cum Ossendyke, Saxton with Scarthingwell, Scarcroft, pt Seacroft, Selby, Shadwell, Sherburn, Sicklinghall, Spofforth with Stockeld, Sturton Grange, Sutton, Sutton with Hazlewood, Swillington, Tadcaster West, pt Templenewsham, Thorner, Thorpe Stapleton, Thorpe Willoughby, Towton, Ulleskelf, Weardley, Wetherby, Wiston, Wistow, Wotherseome, Wyke

BARNSLEY DIVISION

pt Staincross PSD, other specified pars, *viz.*, Ardsley, Barnsley, Barugh, Billingley, Brierley, Carlton, Cudworth, Darfield, Darton, Havercroft with Cold Hiendley, Hemsworth, South Hiendley, Great Houghton, Little Houghton, Kexborough, Monk Bretton, Notton, Royston, Ryhill, Shafton, Wintersett, Wombwell, Woolley

COLNE VALLEY DIVISION

pt Upper Agbrigg PSD, *viz.*, South Crosland, Golcar, Honley, Lingards, pt Linthwaite, pt Longwood, Marsden in Almondbury, Marsden in Huddersfield, Meltham, Saddleworth, Scammonden, Slaithwaite

DONCASTER DIVISION

Doncaster MB, pt Lower Strafforth and Tickhill PSD, *viz.*, Adwick le Street, Adwick upon Dearne, North and South Anston, Armthorpe, pt Auckley, Austerfield, Balby with Hexthorpe, Barnborough, Barnby upon Don, Bawtry, Bentley with Arksey, Bilham, Blaxton,

Bolton upon Dearne, Braithwell, Brodsworth, Cadeby, Cantley, Carr House and Elm Field, Clayton with Frickley, Conisbrough, Crowle, Dinnington, Doncaster, Edlington, Firbeck, Fishlake, Gildingwells, Hamphall Stubbs, Hampole, Harthill with Woodall, Hatfield, Hickleton, Hootton Levitt, Hootton Pagnell, Laughton en le Morthen, Letwell, Loversall, Maltby, Marr, High Melton, Mexborough, Rossington, St John's with Throapham, Kirk Sandall, Long Sandall, Spotbrough, Stancill with Wellingley and Wilseck, Stainforth, Stotfold, Sykehouse, Thorne, Thorpe in Balne, Thorpe Salvin, Thurnscoe, Tickhill, Todwick, Wadsworth, Wales, Warmsworth, Wheatley, Woodsetts

ELLAND DIVISION

specified pars, *viz.*, Elland with Greetland, Fixby, Hipperholme with Brighouse, pt Northowram, pt Ovenden, Rastrick, Shelf, pt Southowram, Stainland with Old Lindley

HALLAMSHIRE DIVISION

pt Staincross PSD, pt Upper Strafforth and Tickhill PSD, *viz.*, Brampton Bierlow, Bradfield, Ecclesfield, Handsworth, Hoyland Nether, Tankersley, Wath upon Dearne, Wentworth, Wortley

HOLMFIRTH DIVISION

pt Upper Agbrigg PSD, pt Staincross PSD, *viz.*, Austonley, Cartworth, Cawthorne, Clayton West, Cumberworth, Denby, Dodworth, Farnley Tyas, Fulstone, Gunthwaite, Hepworth, Holme, Hoyland, Hoyland Swaine, Hunshelf, Ingbirchworth, Kirkburton, Langsett, Lepton, Netherthong, Oxspring, Penistone, Shelley, Shepley, Silkstone, Skelmanthorpe, Stainbrough, Thurgoland, Thurstonland, Upperthong, Whitley Upper, Wooldale, Worsbrough

KEIGHLEY DIVISION

pt Staincliffe and Ewecross PSD, other specified pars, *viz.*, Cowling, Glusburn, Haworth, Keighley, Steeton with Eastburn, Sutton, Thornton, Wilsden

MORLEY DIVISION

pt Lower Agbrigg PSD, Batley MB, Dewsbury MB, pt Dewsbury PSD, *viz.*, Ardsley East, Ardsley West, pt Batley, Lofthouse with Carlton, Middleton, pt Mirfield, Morley, Ossett cum Gawthorpe, pt Soothill, pt Thornhill, Thorpe, Whitley Lower

NORMANTON DIVISION

pt Lower Agbrigg PSD, *viz.*, Ackston, Altofts, pt Alverthorpe with Thornes, West Bretton, Chevet, Crigglestone, Crofton, Emley, Flockton, Horbury, Methley, Newland with Woodhouse Moor, Normanton, Oulton with Woodlesford, Rothwell, Sandal Magna, Sharlston, Shitlington, Snydale, pt Stanley cum Wrenthorpe, Walton, Warmfield cum Heath, Whitwood

OSGOLDCROSS DIVISION

pt Upper Barkston Ash PSD, Osgoldcross Wap, Pontefract MB, pt Skyrack PSD, *viz.*, Ackworth, Adlingfleet, Airmyn, Allerton Bywater, Askern, Badsworth, Balne, Beal or Beaghall, Brotherton, Burghwallis, Campsall, Castleford, Cridling Stubbs, Darrington, Eastoft, Eggborough, North Elmsall, Fairburn, Featherstone, Fenwick, Fockerby, Glass Houghton, Goole, Gowdall, Haldenby, East Hardwick, West Hardwick, Heck, Hensall, Hessle, Hill Top,

Hook, Huntwick with Foulby and Nostell, Kellington, Kippax, Kirk Bramwith, South Kirkby, Knottingley, Ledsham, Ledstone, Moss, Ousefleet, Owston, Pollington, Purston Jaglin, Rawcliffe, Skelbrooke, Skellow, Kirk Smeaton, Little Smeaton, Snaith and Cowick, Stapleton, Sutton, Swinefleet and Reedness, Thorpe Audlin, Upton, Walden Stubbs, Whitgift, Whitley, Womersley

OTLEY DIVISION

Otley PSD, other specified pars, *viz.*, Arthington, Askwith, Balidon, Beamsley in Addingham, Beamsley in Skipton, Bingley, Blubberhouses, Bramhope, Burley in Wharfedale, Carlton, Castley, Clifton with Norwood, Denton, Esholt, Farnley, Fewston, Guiseley, Hawksworth, Hazlewood with Storiths, Ilkley, Leathley, Lindley, Menston, Middleton, Morton, Newfield with Langbar, Newell with Clifton, Otley, Pool, Stainburn, Thruscross, Great Timble, Little Timble, Weston, Yeadon

PUDSEY DIVISION

pt Skyrack PSD, other specified pars, *viz.*, pt Calverley with Farsley, Churwell, Drighlington, Gildersome, Horsforth, Hunsworth, pt Pudsey, Rawdon, Tong

RIPON DIVISION

Claro PSD, Kirkby Malzeard PSD, Ripon Lbty, Ripon MB, *viz.*, Aismunderby with Bondgate, Aldborough, Aldfield, Allerton Mauleverer with Hopperton, Arkendale, Azerley, Bewerley, Bilton with Harrogate, Birstwith, Bishop Thornton, High and Low Bishopside, Bishopton, Boroughbridge, Brearton, Burton Leonard, Cattal, Clareton, Clint, Clotherholme, Coneythorpe, Copgrove, Dacre, pt Lower Dunsforth, pt Upper Dunsforth with Branton Green, Eavestone, Farnham, Felliscliffe, Ferrensby, Flaxby, Follifoot, Fountains Earth, Givendale, Goldsborough, Grantley, Green Hammerton, Kirk Hammerton, Grewelthorpe, Hampsthwaite, Hartwith cum Winsley, Haverah Park, Bridge Hewick, Copt Hewick, pt Humberton, Hunsingore, Ingerthorpe, Kirby Hall, Kirkby Malzeard, Kirkby Overblow, Killinghall, Knaresborough, Laverton, Lindrick with Studley Royal and Fountains, Markingfield Hall, Markington with Wallerthwaite, Marton cum Grafton, Menwith with Darley, pt Milby, Minskip, Bishop Monkton, Nun Monkton, Newby with Mulwith, Nidd, pt Nunwick cum Howgrave, Great Ouseburn, Little Ouseburn, Pannal, Plompton, Great Ribston with Walshford, Rigton, Ripley, Ripon, Roecliffe, Sawley, Scotton, Scriven with Tentergate, Sharrow, Skelton, North Stainley with Sleningford, South Stainley with Cayton, Staveley, Down Stonebeck, Up Stonebeck, Studley Roger, Sutton Grange, Thornthwaite with Padside, Thornville, Thorpe Underwood, Walkingham Hill with Occaney, Warsill, Weeton, Westwick, Whitcliffe with Thorpe, Whixley, Widdington, Winksley

ROTHERHAM DIVISION

Rotherham MB, pt Upper Strafforth and Tickhill PSD, *viz.*, Aston cum Aughton, Bramley, Brampton en le Morthen, Brinsworth, Catcliffe, Dalton, Denaby, Greasbrough, Hooton Roberts, Kimberworth, Orgreave, Ravenfield, Rawmarsh, Rotherham, Swinton, Thrybergh, Tinsley, Treeton, Ulley, Wallingwells, Whiston, Wickersley

SHIPLEY DIVISION
pt East Morley PSD, *viz.*, North Bierley, Clayton, Eccleshill, Idle, Shipley

SKIPTON DIVISION
pt Staincliffe and Ewecross PSD, *viz.*, Addingham, Airton, Appletreewick, Arncliffe, Austwick, Bank Newton, Barden, Barnoldswick, Bashall Eaves, Bentham, Bolton Abbey, Bolton by Bowland, Bowland Forest High, Bowland Forest Low, Bordley, Bracewell, West Bradford, Bradley's Both, Brogden, Broughton, Buckden, Burnsall, Burton in Lonsdale, Calton, Carleton, Clapham cum Newby, Coates, Coniston Cold, Conistone with Kilnsey, Cononley, Cracoe, Dent, Draughton, Easington, Elslack, Embsay with Eastby, Eshton, Farnhill, Flasby with Winterburn, Gargrave, Garsdale, Giggleswick, Gisburn, Gisburn Forest, Grassington, Grindleton, West Halton, Halton East, Halton Gill, Hanlith, Hartlington, Hawkswick, Hebden, Hellifield, Hetton, Horton, Horton in Ribblesdale, Ingleton, Kettlewell with Starbotton, Kildwick, Kirkby Malham, Langcliffe, Lawkland, Linton, Litton, Malham, Malham Moor, Martons Both, Middop, Great Mitton, Nappa, Newsholme, Newton, Otterburn, Paythorne, Long Preston, Rathmell, Rimington, Rylstone, Salterforth, Sawley, Scosthrop, Sedgbergh, Silsden, Slaidburn, Stainforth, Stirton with Thorlby, Swinden, Thornton in Craven, Thornton in Lonsdale, Thorpe, Thresfield, Tosside, Waddington, Wigglesworth

SOWERBY DIVISION
specified pars, *viz.*, Barkisland, Erringden, Heptonstall, Langfield, Midgley, Norland, Rishworth, pt Skircoat, Sowerby, Soyland, Stansfield, Wadworth, Warley

SPEN VALLEY DIVISION
pt Dewsbury PSD, other specified pars, *viz.*, Cleckheaton, Clifton, Gomersal, Hartshead, Heckmondwike, Liversedge, Wyke

1918—1948

BARKSTON ASH DIVISION
Bishopthorpe RD, Garforth UD, pt Great Ouseburn RD (Acomb, Hessay, Knapton, Moor Monkton, Nether Poppleton, Upper Poppleton, Rufforth), Selby RD, Selby UD, Tadcaster RD, Wetherley RD

COLNE VALLEY DIVISION
South Crosland UD, Farnley Tyas UD, Golcar UD, Holme UD, Holmfirth UD, Honley UD, Linthwaite UD, Marsden UD, Meltham UD, New Mill UD, Saddleworth UD, Scammonden UD, Slaithwaite UD, Springhead UD, Thurstonland UD

DON VALLEY DIVISION
Doncaster RD, Mexborough UD, Thorne RD, Tickhill UD

DONCASTER DIVISION
Adwick le Street UD, Bentley with Arksey UD, Doncaster MB

ELLAND DIVISION
Brighouse MB, Clayton UD, Elland UD, Greetland UD, pt Halifax RD (all except the pars in Sowerby Dv), Hipperholme UD, Queensbury UD, Shelf UD, Southowram UD, Stainland UD

HEMSWORTH DIVISION
pt Barnsley RD (the pars not in Wentworth Dv), Cudworth UD, Hemsworth RD, Royston UD

KEIGHLEY DIVISION
Denholme UD, Haworth UD, Keighley MB, Keighley RD, Oakworth UD, Oxenhope UD, Silsden UD

NORMANTON DIVISION
Altofts UD, Castleford UD, Featherstone UD, Methley UD, Normanton UD, Whitwood UD

PENISTONE DIVISION
Clayton West UD, Denby and Cumberworth UD, Gunthwaite and Ingbirchworth UD, Hoyland Swaine UD, Kirkburton UD, Penistone RD, Penistone UD, Shelley UD, Shepley UD, Skelmanthorpe UD, Stocksbridge UD, Thurlstone UD, Wortley RD

PONTEFRACT DIVISION
Goole RD, Goole UD, Knottingley UD, Pontefract MB, Pontefract RD

PUDSEY AND OTLEY DIVISION
Burley in Wharfedale UD, Calverley UD, Farsley UD, Horsforth UD, Ilkley UD, Otley UD, Pudsey MB, Rawdon UD, pt Wharfedale RD (the pars not in Shipley Dv)

RIPON DIVISION
Harrogate MB, Knaresborough RD, Knaresborough UD, pt Great Ouseburn RD (the pars not in Barkston Ash Dv), Pateley Bridge RD, Ripon MB, Ripon RD

ROTHER VALLEY DIVISION
Handsworth UD, Kniveton Park RD, pt Rotherham RD (the pars not in Wentworth Dv), Swinton UD

ROTHWELL DIVISION
Ardsley East and West UD, Emley UD, Flockton UD, Horbury UD, Hunslet RD, Rothwell UD, Stanley UD, Wakefield RD

SHIPLEY DIVISION
Baildon UD, Bingley UD, Guiseley UD, Shipley UD, pt Wharfedale RD (Esholt, Hawksworth, Menston), Yeadon UD

SKIPTON DIVISION
Barnoldswick UD, Bowland RD, Earby UD, Sedbergh RD, Settle RD, Skipton RD, Skipton UD

SOWERBY DIVISION
Barkisland UD, pt Halifax RD (Norland), Hebden Bridge UD, Luddenden Foot UD, Midgley UD, Mytholmroyd UD, Rishworth UD, Sowerby UD, Sowerby Bridge UD, Soyland UD, Todmorden MB, Todmorden RD

SPEN VALLEY DIVISION
Birkenshaw UD, Birstall UD, Drighlington UD, Gildersome UD, Heckmondwike UD, Hunsworth UD, Kirkheaton UD, Lepton UD, Mirfield UD, Spenborough UD, Whitley UD

WENTWORTH DIVISION
pt Barnsley RD (Billingley, Stainborough), Bolton upon Dearne UD, Darfield UD, Dodworth UD, Hoyland Nether UD, pt Rotherham RD (Brampton Bierlow, Wentworth), Thurnscoe UD, Wath upon Dearne UD, Wombwell UD, Worsborough UD

1948—1970

BARKSTON ASH COUNTY CONSTITUENCY[19]
Garforth UD, pt Nidderdale RD (Hessay, Knapton, Moor Monkton, Nether Poppleton, Upper Poppleton,

Rufforth), Selby RD, Selby UD, pt Tadcaster RD (the pars not in Normanton CC)
COLNE VALLEY COUNTY CONSTITUENCY[7]
Colne Valley UD, Denby Dale UD (1955—70), Holmfirth UD, Kirkburton UD (1948—55), Meltham UD, Saddleworth UD
DEARNE VALLEY COUNTY CONSTITUENCY
Conisbrough UD, Darfield UD, Mexborough UD, Swinton UD, Wath upon Dearne UD, Wombwell UD
DON VALLEY COUNTY CONSTITUENCY[6]
Adwick le Street UD, Bentley with Arksey UD, Doncaster RD, Pickhill UD
GOOLE COUNTY CONSTITUENCY
Goole MB, Goole RD, Knottingley UD, Osgoldcross RD, Thorne RD
HARROGATE COUNTY CONSTITUENCY
Harrogate MB, Knaresborough UD, pt Nidderdale RD (the pars not in Barkston Ash CC)
HEMSWORTH COUNTY CONSTITUENCY[16]
Curdworth UD, Dearne UD, Hemsworth RD, Hemsworth UD, Royston UD (1948—55)
NORMANTON COUNTY CONSTITUENCY[16]
Normanton UD, Rothwell UD, Stanley UD, pt Tadcaster RD (Great and Little Preston, Swillington), pt Wakefield RD (Crofton, Newland with Woodhouse Moor [1949—70], Sharlston, Warmfield cum Heath)
PENISTONE COUNTY CONSTITUENCY[7]
Denby Dale (1948—55), Dodworth UD, Hoyland Nether UD, Penistone RD, Penistone UD, Stocksbridge UD, Wortley RD
RIPON COUNTY CONSTITUENCY
Ilkley UD, Otley UD, Ripon MB, Ripon and Pateley Bridge RD, Wharfedale RD
ROTHER VALLEY COUNTY CONSTITUENCY
Kiveton Park RD, Maltby UD, Rawmarsh UD, Rotherham RD
SHIPLEY COUNTY CONSTITUENCY[5]
Baildon UD, Bingley UD, Shipley UD
SKIPTON COUNTY CONSTITUENCY
Barnoldswick UD, Bowland RD, Earby UD, Sedbergh RD, Settle RD, pt Skipton RD (the pars not in Keighley BC), Skipton UD
SOWERBY COUNTY CONSTITUENCY
Elland UD, Hebden Royd UD, Hepton RD, Ripponden UD, Sowerby Bridge UD, Todmorden MB

1970—
BARKSTON ASH COUNTY CONSTITUENCY
Garforth UD, pt Nidderdale RD (Hessay, Knapton, Moor Monkton, Nether Poppleton, Upper Poppleton, Rufforth), Selby RD, Selby UD, pt Tadcaster RD (the pars not in Normanton CC)
COLNE VALLEY COUNTY CONSTITUENCY[7]
Colne Valley UD, Denby Dale UD, Holmfirth UD, Meltham UD, Saddleworth UD
DEARNE VALLEY COUNTY CONSTITUENCY
Conisbrough UD, Darfield UD, Mexborough UD, Swinton UD, Wath upon Dearne UD, Wombwell UD
DON VALLEY COUNTY CONSTITUENCY
Adwick le Street UD, Bentley with Arksey UD, Doncaster RD, Pickhill UD
GOOLE COUNTY CONSTITUENCY
Goole MB, Goole RD, Knottingley UD, Osgoldcross RD, Thorne RD
HARROGATE COUNTY CONSTITUENCY
Harrogate MB, Knaresborough UD, pt Nidderdale RD (the pars not in Barkston Ash CC)
HEMSWORTH COUNTY CONSTITUENCY
Curdworth UD, Dearne UD, Hemsworth RD, Hemsworth UD
NORMANTON COUNTY CONSTITUENCY
Normanton UD, Rothwell UD, Stanley UD, pt Tadcaster RD (Great and Little Preston, Swillington), pt Wakefield RD (Crofton, Newland with Woodhouse Moor, Sharlston, Warmfield cum Heath)
PENISTONE COUNTY CONSTITUENCY
Dodworth UD, Hoyland Nether UD, Penistone RD, Penistone UD, Stocksbridge UD, Wortley RD
RIPON COUNTY CONSTITUENCY
Ilkley UD, Otley UD, Ripon MB, Ripon and Pateley Bridge RD, Wharfedale RD
ROTHER VALLEY COUNTY CONSTITUENCY
Kiveton Park RD, Maltby UD, Rawmarsh UD, Rotherham RD
SHIPLEY COUNTY CONSTITUENCY
Baildon UD, Bingley UD, Shipley UD
SKIPTON COUNTY CONSTITUENCY
Barnoldswick UD, Bowland RD, Earby UD, Sedbergh RD, Settle RD, pt Skipton RD (the pars not in Keighley BC), Skipton UD
SOWERBY COUNTY CONSTITUENCY
Elland UD, Hebden Royd UD, Hepton RD, Ripponden UD, Sowerby Bridge UD, Todmorden MB

Part IV: The Dioceses of England

BIRMINGHAM

Cr 1905 from Worcester dioc.[1] Primarily Warws, incl pars in Staffs and in Worcs.

ORGANISATION IN ARCHDEACONRIES
AND RURAL DEANERIES

ASTON AD (1906—*)
Aston,[2] East Birmingham (1906—57), Bordesley, Coleshill (1957—*), Polesworth, Solihull, Sutton Coldfield, Yardley (1957—*)

BIRMINGHAM AD
Aston (1905—06), Birmingham (1905), East Birmingham (1905—06), Birmingham Central (1905—57), Birmingham City (1957—*), Bordesley (1905—06), Coleshill (1905), Edgbaston, Handsworth, Harborne (1905—29), King's Norton, Moseley (1957—*), Northfield (1905), Polesworth (1905—06), Smethwick (1929—66), Solihull (1905—06), Sutton Coldfield (1905—06), Warley (1966—*)

ALTERATIONS IN ARCHDEACONRIES
AND RURAL DEANERIES

In 1905,[3] 1905,[4] 1906,[5] 1919,[6] 1929,[7] 1957,[8] 1966.[9]

BLACKBURN

Cr 1926 from Manchester dioc.[1] Lancs pars.

ORGANISATION IN ARCHDEACONRIES
AND RURAL DEANERIES

BLACKBURN AD
Accrington, Blackburn, Burnley, Chorley (1964—*), Darwen (1964—*), Leyland, Pendle (1970—*), Whalley

LANCASTER AD
Blackpool (1963—*), The Fylde, Garstang, Lancaster, Preston, Tunstall

ALTERATIONS IN ARCHDEACONRIES
AND RURAL DEANERIES

In 1927,[2] 1928,[3] 1963,[4] 1964,[5] 1970.[6]

BRADFORD

Cr 1919 from Ripon dioc, Wakefield dioc.[1] Primarily Yorks; incl pars in Lancs.

ORGANISATION IN ARCHDEACONRIES
AND RURAL DEANERIES

BRADFORD AD (1921—*)
Airedale (1971—*), Bowling (1921—71), Bowling and Horton (1971—*), Bradford (1921—71), Calverley, Horton (1921—71), Otley

CRAVEN AD
Bolland (1921—*), Bradford (1919—21), Clapham (1919—21), South Craven (1921—*); Craven, Eastern Dv (1919—21); Craven, Northern Dv (1919—21); Craven, Southern Dv (1919—21); Craven, Western Dv (1919—21); Ewecross (1921—*), Otley (1919—21), Sedbergh (1926—71), Settle (1926—71), Skipton (1921—*)

ALTERATIONS IN ARCHDEACONRIES AND RURAL DEANERIES

In 1921,[2] 1926,[3] 1935,[4] 1959,[5] 1971.[6]

CARLISLE

Primarily Cumb and Westm pars; incl pars in Lancs.

ORGANISATION IN ARCHDEACONRIES AND RURAL DEANERIES

CARLISLE AD
Allerdale (until 1859), Appleby (1859—82), Appleby (1970—*), Appleby and Kirkby Stephen (1882—1970), Brampton (1859—*), Carlisle (until 1871), Carlisle (1926—*), Carlisle North (1871—1926), Carlisle South (1871—1926), Cumberland (1857—59), Greystoke (1859—82), Keswick (1859—84), Kirkby Stephen (1859—82), Kirkoswald (1926—70), Lowther (1859—1970), Maryport (1871—1959), Penrith (1859—82), Penrith (1926—*), Penrith East (1882—1926), Penrith West (1882—1926), Westmorland (until 1856), Wigton (1859—1970)

WEST CUMBERLAND AD (1959—*)
Calder (1970—*), Cockermouth and Workington (1959—70), Derwent (1970—*), Gosforth (1959—70), Keswick (1959—70), Maryport (1959—70), Solway (1970—*), Whitehaven (1959—70)

FURNESS AD (1884—1959)
Cartmel, Dalton, Gosforth, Ulverston

WESTMORLAND AD (1856—1959)
Aldingham (1859—82), Ambleside (1859—1959), Cartmel (1859—1959), Cockermouth (1859—82), Cockermouth and Workington (1882—1959), Copeland [sometimes 'Coupland'] (1856—59), Dalton (1884—1959), Furness (1970—*), Furness and Cartmel (1856—59), Gosforth (1859—84), Kendal, Keswick (1884—1959), Kirkby Lonsdale, Ulverston (1859—84), Westmorland (1856—59), Whitehaven (1859—1959)

WESTMORLAND AND FURNESS AD (1959—*)
Ambleside (1959—70), Cartmel (1959—70), Dalton (1959—70), Furness (1970—*), Kendal, Kirkby Lonsdale (1959—70), Ulverston (1959—70), Windermere (1970—*)

ALTERATIONS IN ARCHDEACONRIES AND RURAL DEANERIES

In 1856,[1] 1859,[2] 1871,[2] 1882,[3] 1884,[4] 1919,[5] 1926,[6] 1954,[7] 1959,[8] 1973.[9]

CHESTER

Cr 1541 from York dioc, Lichfield and Coventry dioc.[1] Orig Ches and Lancs, primarily Ches after 1880.

ORGANISATION IN ARCHDEACONRIES AND RURAL DEANERIES

CHESTER AD [from Lichfield and Coventry dioc]
Bangor (1541—1847), Birkenhead (1888—*), Blackburn[2] (1541—1844), Great Budworth (1935—*), Chester, Frodsham (1541—1869), Frodsham (1880—*), Frodsham East (1869—80), Frodsham West (1869—80), Leyland[2] (1541—1844), Macclesfield (1541—1873), Macclesfield North (1873—80), Macclesfield South (1873—80), Malpas, Manchester (1541—1844), Middlewich, Nantwich (1541—1966), Wallasey (1907—*), Warrington (1541—1844), Wirral (1541—1847), Wirral (1880—1935), Wirral North (1935—*), Wirral South (1935—*)

LIVERPOOL AD (1847—80 [help cr Liverpool dioc])
North Meols and Ormskirk (1848—80), Prescot, Warrington[2] (1847—80), Wigan (1848—80), Winwick (1848—80), Wirral

MACCLESFIELD AD (1880—*)
Bowdon, Congleton, Fernilee (1966—*), Knutsford

(1935—*), Macclesfield, Mottram (1888—*), Nantwich (1966—*), Stockport

MANCHESTER AD (1844—47 [help cr Manchester dioc])
Amounderness, Blackburn,[2] Leyland,[2] Manchester,[2] Warrington[2]

RICHMOND AD (1541 [from York dioc]—1836 [help cr Ripon dioc])
Amounderness (1541—1836), Boroughbridge (1541—1836), Catterick (1541—1836), Copeland [sometimes 'Coupland'], Furness and Cartmel, Kendal (1541—1836), Kirkby Lonsdale (1541—1836), Richmond (1541—1836)

ALTERATIONS IN ARCHDEACONRIES
AND RURAL DEANERIES

In 1836[3] 1844,[4] 1845,[5] 1849,[6] 1856,[7] 1869,[8] 1873,[8] 1880,[9] 1880,[10] 1888,[11] 1907,[12] 1934,[13] 1935,[14] 1954,[15] 1966,[16] 1970.[17]

COVENTRY

Cr 1918 from Worcester dioc.[1] Warws pars.

ORGANISATION IN ARCHDEACONRIES
AND RURAL DEANERIES

COVENTRY AD
Atherstone (1918—63), Baginton (1918—21), Bedworth (1963—*), Coventry (1918—63), Coventry East (1963—*), Coventry North (1963—*), Coventry South (1963—*), Dassett Magna (1918—21), Dewchurch (1921—*), Kenilworth (1918—21), Leamington (1918—21), Monks Kirby (1918—63), Nuneaton (1963—*), Rugby (1921—*), Rugby and Dewchurch (1918—21), Southam (1918—21)

WARWICK AD
Alcester, Dassett Magna (1921—*), Kineton (1921—63), North Kineton (1918—21), South Kineton (1918—21), Leamington (1921—*), Shipston (1921—*), Southam (1921—*), Stratford on Avon (1963—*), Warwick

ALTERATIONS IN ARCHDEACONRIES
AND RURAL DEANERIES

In 1919,[2] 1921,[3] 1963,[4] 1963,[5] 1970.[6]

DERBY

Cr 1927 from Southwell dioc.[1] Derbys pars.

ORGANISATION IN ARCHDEACONRIES
AND RURAL DEANERIES

CHESTERFIELD AD
Alfreton, Bakewell (1971—*), Bolsover, Buxton (1971—*), Chesterfield, Eyam, Glossop, Heanor, Staveley

DERBY AD
Ashbourne, Bakewell (1927—71), Buxton (1927—71), Derby, Duffield, Ilkeston, Longford, Melbourne, Repton, Wirksworth

ALTERATIONS IN ARCHDEACONRIES
AND RURAL DEANERIES

In 1955,[2] 1971.[3]

DURHAM

Durham pars; incl Northumb pars until 1882.

ORGANISATION IN ARCHDEACONRIES
AND RURAL DEANERIES

AUCKLAND AD (1882—*)
Auckland, Barnard Castle (1924—*), Darlington, Hartlepool (1888—*), Stanhope, Stockton

DURHAM AD
Auckland (until early 19th cent), Auckland (1880—82), Chester (Eastern Dv) (1874—80), Chester (Western Dv) (1874—80), Chester le Street (before 1535—early 19th cent), Chester le Street (1842—74), Chester le Street (1880—*), Darlington (before 1291—early 19th cent), Darlington (1842—74), Darlington (1880—82), Darlington (Northern Dv) (1874—80), Darlington (Southern Dv) (1874—80), Durham (until 1842), Durham (1880—*), Easington (1842—74), Easington (1880—*), Easington (Northern Dv) (1874—80), Easington (Southern Dv) (1874—80), Gateshead (1891—*), Houghton le Spring (1880—*), Jarrow (1880—*), Lanchester (until early 19th cent), Lanchester (1891—

), Ryton (1880—91), Stanhope (1880—82), Stockton (1842—82), Wearmouth (1880—)

LINDISFARNE AD (1845—82 [help cr Newcastle dioc])
Alnwick, Bamburgh (1845—84), Morpeth, Norham, Rothbury

NORTHUMBERLAND AD (until 1882 [help cr Newcastle dioc])
Alnwick (until 1845), Bamburgh (until 1845), Bellingham (1845—82), Corbridge, Hexham (1845—82), Morpeth (until 1845), Newcastle upon Tyne (until 1877), Newcastle upon Tyne (Eastern Division) (1877—82), Newcastle upon Tyne (Northern Division) (1874—77), Newcastle upon Tyne (Southern Division) (1874—77), Newcastle upon Tyne (Western Division) (1877—82)

ALTERATIONS IN ARCHDEACONRIES
AND RURAL DEANERIES

In 1842,[1] 1845,[2] 1874,[2] 1877,[2] 1880,[2] 1882,[3] 1882,[4] 1888,[5] 1891,[6] 1924,[7] 1965.[8]

HEREFORD

Heref and Salop pars; incl pars in Worcs.

ORGANISATION IN ARCHDEACONRIES
AND RURAL DEANERIES

HEREFORD AD
Abbey Dore (1898—1972), Abbeydore (1972—*), Archenfield (until 1923), Bromyard (1898—*), Frome (until 1878), North Frome (1878—98), South Frome (1878—98), Hereford (until 1923), Hereford (City) (1923—72), Hereford City (1972—*), Hereford Rural (1972—*), Hereford (South) (1923—72), Kingsland (1898—1923), Kington (1898—1972), Kington and Weobley (1972—*), Ledbury (1898—*), Leominster (until 1878), Leominster (1898—*), Leominster 1 (1878—98), Leominster 2 (1878—98), Ross (until 1923), Ross and Archenfield (1923—*), Weobley (until 1878), Weobley (1898—1972), Weobley 1 (1878—98), Weobley 2 (1878—98), Weobley 3 (1878—98), Weston (until 1972), Wigmore (1923—58)

LUDLOW AD (1876—*)
Bewdley (1898—1919), Bishop's Castle (1898—1923),

Bridgnorth, Burford (1876—78), Burford (1898—1972), Burford (East) (1878—98), Burford (West) (1878—98), Church Stretton (1898—1923), Clun (1876—1972), Clun Forest (1972—-*), Condover (1905—*), Ludlow, Montgomery (1898—1923), Pontesbury (1876—78), Pontesbury (1898—*), Pontesbury (1) (1878—98), Pontesbury (2) (1878—98), Stokesay (1923—72), Stottesdon (1876—1955), Telford Severn Gorge (1972—*), Wenlock (1876—78), Wenlock (1898—1972), Wenlock (1) (1878—98), Wenlock (2) (1878—98)

SALOP AD (until 1876)
Bridgnorth (1846—76), Burford, Clun (1842—76), Clun and Wenlock (until 1842), Ludlow, Pontesbury, Stottesdon, Wenlock (1842—76)

ALTERATIONS IN ARCHDEACONRIES
AND RURAL DEANERIES

In 1842,[1] 1847,[2] 1876,[3] 1878,[4] 1898,[5] 1905,[6] 1919,[7] 1923,[8] 1946,[9] 1955,[10] 1958,[11] 1972.[12]

LEICESTER

Cr 1926 from Peterborough dioc.[1] Leics pars.

ORGANISATION IN ARCHDEACONRIES
AND RURAL DEANERIES

LEICESTER AD
Christianity, Framland I, Framland II, Framland III (1926—61), Gartree I, Gartree II, Gartree III, Goscote I, Goscote II

LOUGHBOROUGH AD
East Akeley, South Akeley, West Akeley, Guthlaxton I, Guthlaxton II, Guthlaxton III, Sparkenhoe I, Sparkenhoe II, Sparkenhoe III

ALTERATIONS IN ARCHDEACONRIES
AND RURAL DEANERIES

In 1928,[2] 1961,[3] 1966.[4]

LICHFIELD

Cr 1837 from Lichfield and Coventry dioc.[1] Salop and Staffs pars; incl Derbys pars 1837—84.

ORGANISATION IN ARCHDEACONRIES
AND RURAL DEANERIES[2]

DERBY AD (1837—84 [help cr Southwell dioc])
Alfreton (1846—84), Ashbourne, Ashover (1846—84), Bakewell (1847—84), Bolsover (1875—84), Brampton (1846—84), Buxton (1847—84), Castilar (1837—46), Castleton (1846—84), Chesterfield, Cubley (1846—84), Derby, Duffield (1846—84), Eyam (1846—84), Hartshorn (1846—84), High Peak [sometimes 'Alto Pecco'] (1837—46), Lullington (1855—84), Ockbrook (1846—84), Radbourne (1846—84), Repton (1837—46), Stanton by Bridge (1846—84), Staveley (1846—84), Willington (1846—47), Wirksworth (1846—84), Youlgreave (1846—47)

SALOP AD
Condover (1837—1905), Edgmond (1859—*), Ellesmere (1837—*), Hodnet (1859—*), Market Drayton (1837—59), Newport (1837—59), Oswestry (1920—*), Salop (1837), Shifnal (1837—*), Shrewsbury (1837—*), Wellington (1837—59), Wem (1837—1962), Wem and Whitchurch (1962—*), Whitchurch (1863—1962), Wrockwardine (1859—*)

STAFFORD AD
Alstonfield (1851—77), Brewood (1851—94), Eccleshall (1851—1923), Cheadle (1851—77), Eccleshall (1851—77), Handsworth (1851—1906), Himley (1851—*), Lapley and Trysull (1837—51), Leek (1835—77), Leek and Alton (1837—51), Lichfield (1851—*), Newcastle and Stone (1837—51), Newcastle under Lyme (1851—77), Penkridge (1851—*), Rugeley (1851—*), Stafford (1851—*), Stoke upon Trent (1837—51), Tamworth (1851—*), Tamworth and Tutbury (1837—51), Trentham (1851—77), Trysull (1851—*), Tutbury (1851—*), Uttoxeter (1851—77), Walsall (1851—*), Wednesbury (1894—*), West Bromwich (1894—*), Wolverhampton (1851—*)

STOKE ON TRENT AD (1877—*)
Alstonfield, Cheadle, Eccleshall, Hamley (1894—1920), Leek, Newcastle under Lyme, Stoke (North) (1962—*), Trentham, Uttoxeter

ALTERATIONS IN ARCHDEACONRIES
AND RURAL DEANERIES

In 1846,[3] 1847,[3] 1851,[3] 1855,[3] 1859,[3] 1863,[3] 1875,[3] 1877,[4] 1884,[5] 1886,[6] 1894,[7] 1905,[8] 1906,[9] 1920,[10] 1924,[11] 1962.[12]

LICHFIELD AND COVENTRY

Styled LICHFIELD 1053—1075, CHESTER 1075—1102, COVENTRY 1102—1128, COVENTRY AND LICHFIELD 1228—Reformation, LICHFIELD AND COVENTRY Reformation—1837 at which time abolished.[1]

Warws, Derbys, Salop, Staffs pars; incl Ches pars until 1541.

CHESTER AD (until 1541 [help cr Chester dioc][2])
Blackburn (before 1535—1541), Broxton (until after 1382), Chester, Frodsham, Leyland, Macclesfield, Malpas (after 1382—1541), Manchester (before 1541—1541), Manchester and Blackburn (before 1291—before 1535), Middlewich, Nantwich, Warrington, Wirral

COVENTRY AD [transf to Worcester dioc]
Arden, Coventry, Marton, Stonleigh

DERBY AD [help cr Lichfield dioc]
Ashbourne, Castilar, Chestfield, Derby, High Peak, Repton

SALOP AD [help cr Lichfield dioc]
Newport, Salop

STAFFORD AD [help cr Lichfield dioc]
Lapley and Trysull, Leek and Alton, Newcastle (until early 14th cent), Newcastle and Stone (early 14th cent—1837), Stafford (until early 14th cent), Tamworth and Tutbury

ALTERATIONS IN ARCHDEACONRIES
AND RURAL DEANERIES

None made after medieval period.

LINCOLN

Primarily Lincs; incl Oxon pars until 1542; Hunts pars until 1837; Beds, Bucks, pt of Herts pars until 1845 (see Volume I of the *Guide* for those 5 cos); incl Rutl and Northants pars until 1541, Leics until 1837; incl Notts pars 1839—1884.

ORGANISATION IN ARCHDEACONRIES
AND RURAL DEANERIES

BEDFORD AD (until 1837 [transf to Ely dioc])
Bedford, Clapham, Dunstable, Eaton, Fleete, Shefford

BUCKINGHAM AD (until 1837 [transf to Oxford dioc])
Buckingham, Burnham, Mursley, Newport, Waddesdon, Wendover, Wycombe

HUNTINGDON AD (until 1845 [transf to Ely dioc])
Baldock, Berkhampstead, Hertford, Hitchin, Huntingdon (until 1837), Leightonstone (until 1837), St Ives (until 1837), St Neots (until 1837), Yaxley (until 1837)

LEICESTER AD (until 1837 [transf to Peterb dioc])
Akeley, Christianity, Framland, Gartree, Goscote, Guthlaxton, Sparkenhoe

LINCOLN AD
Aswardhurn with Lafford (until 1866), Aswardhurn with Lafford 1 (1866—84), Aswardhurn with Lafford 2 (1866—84), Aveland (until 1866), Aveland (1910—68), Aveland 1 (1866—1910), Aveland 2 (1866—1910), Aveland and Ness with Stamford (1968—*), Beltisloe (until 1866), Beltisloe (1873—*), Beltisloe 1 (1866—73), Beltisloe 2 (1866—73), Bolingbroke (until 1933), Calcewaith (until 1866), Calcewaith 1 (1866—1910), Calcewaith 2 (1866—1910), Calcewaith (North) (1910—33), Calcewaith (South) (1910—68), Candleshoe (until 1866), Candleshoe (1910—33), Candleshoe 1 (1866—1910), Candleshoe 2 (1866—1910), Christianity, East Elloe (1877—1910), West Elloe (1877—1910), Elloe (East) (1910—*), Elloe (West) (1910—*), Gartree (until 1877), Graffoe, Grantham

(until 1866), Grantham (1968—*), Grantham 1 (1866—1910), Grantham 2 (1866—1910), North Grantham (1910—68), South Grantham (1910—68), Grimsby (until 1866), Grimsby 1 (1866—1910), Grimsby 2 (1866—1910), Hill (until 1866), Hill 1 (1866—1910), Hill 2 (1866—1910), Holland (until 1866), Holland (East) (1910—*), Holland (West) (1910—*), North Holland 1 (1866—1910), North Holland 2 (1866—1910), South Holland 1 (1866—77), South Holland 2 (1866—77), Horncastle (until 1876), Lafford (1968—*), Lafford 1 (1884—1910), Lafford 2 (1884—1910), Lafford (North) (1910—68), Lafford (South) (1884—1910), Longoboby (until 1968), Louthesk and Ludborough (until 1863), Louthesk and Ludborough 1 (1863—76), Louthesk and Ludborough 2 (1863—76), Louthesk and Ludborough 3 (1863—76), Loveden, Ness (until 1968), Stamford (until 1968), Walshcroft (until 1866), Walshcroft (1873—76), Walshcroft 1 (1866—73), Walshcroft 2 (1866—73), Wraggoe (until 1876), Yarborough (until 1863), Yarborough 1 (1863—76), Yarborough 2 (1863—76)

LINDSEY AD (1933—*)

Bolingbroke, Caistor, Calcewaith (North) (1933—68), Calcewaith and Candleshoe (1968—*), Candleshoe (1933—68), Gartree (1933—68), Grimsby (North) (1933—68), Grimsby (South) (1933—68), Grimsby and Cleethorpes, Haverstoe (1968—*), Hill (North) (1933—68), Hill (South) (1933—68), Horncastle, Louthesk (1968—*), Louthesk (East) (1933—68), Louthesk (West) (1933—68), Ludborough (1933—68)

NORTHAMPTON AD (until 1541 [cr Peterborough dioc])

Alstow Hundred, Brackley, Daventry, East Hundred, Haddon, Higham Ferrers, Northampton, Oakham Soke, Oundle, Peterborough, Preston, Rothwell, Rutland (or Martinsley), Weldon, Wrangdyke

NOTTINGHAM AD (1839 [transf from York dioc]—84 [help cr Southwell dioc])

Bingham (1839—57), Bingham (1877—84), South Bingham (1877—84), West Bingham (1877—84), Bingham 1 (1857—77), Bingham 2 (1857—77), Bingham 3 (1857—77), Collingham (1877—84), Mansfield (1877—84), Newark (1839—57), Newark (1877—84), Newark 1 (1857—77), Newark 2 (1857—77), Nottingham (1839—57), Nottingham (1877—84), Nottingham 1 (1857—77), Nottingham 2 (1857—77), Nottingham 3 (1857—77), Retford (1839—57), Retford (1877—84), Retford 1 (1857—77), Retford 2 (1857—77), Retford 3 (1857—77), Southwell (1841—84), Tuxford (1877—84), Worksop (1877—84)

OXFORD AD (until 1542 [cr Oxford dioc])

Aston, Bicester, Cuddesdon, Deddington, Henley, Chipping Norton, Oxford, Witney, Woodstock

STOW AD

Aslacoe (until 1968), Caistor (1910—33), Corringham, Gartree (1877—1933), Grimsby 1 (1876—1910), Grimsby 2 (1876—1910), Grimsby (North) (1910—33), Grimsby (South) (1910—33), Grimsby and Cleethorpes (1910—33), Hill 1 (1877—1910), Hill (North) (1910—68), Hill (South) (1910—68), Horncastle (1876—1933), Isle of Axholme (1857—*), Lawres (until 1866), Lawres (1968—*), Lawres 1 (1866—1910), Lawres 2 (1866—1910), Lawres (East) (1910—68), Lawres (West) (1910—68), Louthesk (East) (1910—33), Louthesk (West) (1910—33), Louthesk and Ludborough 1 (1876—1910), Louthesk and Ludborough 2 (1876—1910), Louthesk and Ludborough 3 (1876—1910), Ludborough (1910—33), Manlake, Walshcroft (1876—1910), Walshcroft (East) (1910—68), Walshcroft (West) (1910—68), West Wold (1968—*), Wraggoe (1876—1968), Yarborough (1968—*), Yarborough 1 (1876—1910), Yarborough 2 (1876—1910), Yarborough (North) (1910—68), Yarborough (South) (1910—68)

ALTERATIONS IN ARCHDEACONRIES AND RURAL DEANERIES

In 1541,[1] 1542,[2] 1837,[3] 1837,[4] 1839,[5] 1839,[6] 1841,[7] 1845,[8] 1857,[9] 1860,[9] 1863,[9] 1866,[9] 1873,[9] 1876,[10] 1877,[11] 1884,[12] 1910,[13] 1933,[14] 1968.[15]

LIVERPOOL

Cr 1880 from Chester dioc.[1] Lancs pars.

ORGANISATION IN ARCHDEACONRIES AND RURAL DEANERIES

LIVERPOOL AD

Bootle (1895—*), Childwall (1949—*), West Derby (1949—*), Liverpool (1949—*), Liverpool North (1880—1949), Liverpool South (1880), North Meols (1887—1949), North Meols and Ormskirk (1880—87), Ormskirk (1887—1949), Prescot (1880), Toxteth (1949—*), Walton (1882—*), Wigan (1880—1949), Winwick (1880)

WARRINGTON AD (1880—*)
Childwall (1882—1949), West Derby (1902—49), Farnworth (1949—*), Liverpool South (1880—1949), North Meols (1949—*), Ormskirk (1949—*), Prescot, Toxteth (1882—1949), Warrington (1949—*), Wigan (1949—*), Winwick (1880—1949)

ALTERATIONS IN ARCHDEACONRIES AND RURAL DEANERIES

In 1880,[2] 1882,[3] 1887,[4] 1895,[5] 1902,[6] 1906,[7] 1920,[8] 1949,[9] 1971.[10]

MANCHESTER

Cr 1847 from Chester dioc.[1] Lancs pars; incl small number of pars in Yorks W Riding.

ORGANISATION IN ARCHDEACONRIES AND RURAL DEANERIES

BLACKBURN AD (1877—1926 [help cr Blackburn dioc])
Accrington (1912—26), Blackburn, Burnley, Leyland, Rossendale (1912—26), Whalley

LANCASTER AD (1847—1926 [help cr Blackburn dioc])
Amounderness (1847—52), The Fylde (1852—1926), Garstang (1852—1926), Lancaster (1852—1926), Preston (1852—1926), Tunstall (1848—1926)

MANCHESTER AD
Accrington (1866—72), Ardwick (1872—*), Ashton under Lyne (1847—1929), Blackburn (1847—77), Bolton le Moors (1847—93), Bolton North (1893—1901), Bolton South (1893—1901), Burnley (1872—77), Bury (1850—1910), Cathedral (1872—*), Cheetham (1872—*), Chorlton (1855—66), Chorlton and Hulme (1866—69), Eccles (1850—66), Eccles and Salford (1866—72), Heaton (1912—*), Hulme (1869—*), Leigh (1933—*), Leyland (1847—77), Manchester (1847—72), North Meols (1847—48), Oldham (1872—1910), Oldham (1929—*), Prestwich (1851—72), Prestwich and Middleton (1872—1910), Rochdale (1847—1910), Salford (1872—*), Stretford (1933—*), Whalley (1847—77), Withington (1965—*)

ROCHDALE AD (1910—*)
Ashton under Lyne (1910—29), Bolton le Moors, Bury, Deane (1968—*), Farnworth (1968—*), Middleton (1912—*), Oldham, Prestwich and Middleton (1919—12), Radcliffe and Prestwich (1912—*), Rochdale, Rossendale (1927—*), Walmsley (1968—*)

ALTERATIONS IN ARCHDEACONRIES AND RURAL DEANERIES

In 1850,[2] 1851,[2] 1852,[2] 1855,[2] 1866,[2] 1869,[2] 1872,[2] 1873,[3] 1877,[3] 1893,[4] 1901,[5] 1903,[6] 1910,[7] 1912,[8] 1923,[9] 1926,[10] 1927,[11] 1929,[12] 1933,[13] 1934,[14] 1956,[15] 1961,[16] 1964,[17] 1965,[18] 1967,[19] 1968.[20]

NEWCASTLE

Cr 1882 from Durham dioc.[1] Northumb pars.

ORGANISATION IN ARCHDEACONRIES AND RURAL DEANERIES

LINDISFARNE AD
Alnwick, Bamburgh (1882—1969), Bamburgh and Glendale (1969—*), Glendale (1899—1969), Morpeth, Norham, Rothbury

NORTHUMBERLAND AD
Bedlington (1884—*), Bellingham, Corbridge, Hexham, Newcastle (1884—1967), Newcastle Central (1967—*), Newcastle East (1967—*), Newcastle West (1967—*), Newcastle upon Tyne (Eastern Dv) (1882—84), Newcastle upon Tyne (Western Dv) (1882—84), Tynemouth (1884—*)

ALTERATIONS IN ARCHDEACONRIES
AND RURAL DEANERIES

In 1884,[2] 1899,[3] 1954,[4] 1967,[5] 1969.[6]

PETERBOROUGH

Cr 1541 from Lincoln dioc.[1] Northants and Rutl pars. Incl Leics pars 1837—1926.

ORGANISATION IN ARCHDEACONRIES
AND RURAL DEANERIES

LEICESTER AD (1837 [transf from Linc dioc]—1926 [help cr Leicester dioc])
Akeley (1837—66), East Akeley (1875—1926), South Akeley (1893—26), West Akeley (1875—1926), Akeley I (1866—75), Akeley II (1866—75), Christianity, Framland (1837—66), Framland I (1866—1926), Framland II (1866—1926), Framland III (1866—1926), Framland IV (1866—73), Gartree (1837—66), Gartree I (1866—1926), Gartree II (1866—1926), Gartree III (1873—1926), Goscote (1837—66), Goscote I (1866—1921), Goscote II (1866—1926), Guthlaxton (1837—66), Guthlaxton I (1866—1926), Guthlaxton II (1866—1921), Guthlaxton III (1866—1921), Sparkenhoe (1837—66), Sparkenhoe I (1866—1921), Sparkenhoe II (1866—1921)

LOUGHBOROUGH AD (1921—26 [help cr Leicester dioc])
Guthlaxton I, Guthlaxton II, Guthlaxton III, Sparkenhoe I, Sparkenhoe II

NORTHAMPTON AD
Alstow Hundred (1541—1842), Brackley (1541—1867), Brackley (1954—*), Brackley I (1867—1954), Brackley II (1867—1954), Brackley III (1867—1954), Brackley IV (1867—75), Brampton (1954—55), Brixworth (1954—*), Culworth (1954—70), Daventry, East Hundred (1541—1842), Haddon (1541—1867), Haddon (1954—70), Haddon I (1867—1954), Haddon II (1867—1954), Higham (1954—*), Higham Ferrers (1541—1867), Higham Ferrers I (1867—1954), Higham Ferrers II (1867—75), Higham Ferrers III (1867—75), Northampton, Oakham (1541—1842), Oundle (1541—1867), Oundle I (1867—75), Oundle II[2] (1867—75), Oundle III[3] (1867—75), Oundle IV (1867—73), Peterborough (1541—1867), Peterborough I (1867—75), Peterborough II (1867—75), Preston (1541—1867), Preston (1954—70), Preston I (1867—1954), Preston II (1867—1954), Preston III (1867—73), Rothwell (1541—1867), Rothwell (1954—70), Rothwell I (1867—1954), Rothwell II (1867—1954), Rothwell III (1867—1954), Rutland (1842—67), Rutland I (1867—75), Rutland II (1867—75), Rutland III (1867—75), Rutland IV (1867—73), Rutland (or Martinsley) (1541—1842), Towcester (1954—*), Weedon (1873—1970), Weldon (1541—1867), Weldon I (1867—75), Weldon II (1867—75), Wellingborough (1954—*), Wootton (1954—*), Wrangdyke (1541—1842)

OAKHAM AD (1875—*)
Barnack (1954—*), Corby (1970—*), Higham (1954—*), Higham Ferrers I (1875—1954), Higham Ferrers II (1875—1954), Higham Ferrers III (1875—81), Kettering (1954—*), Ketton (1954—63), King's Cliffe (1954—60), Oakham (1954—70), Oundle (1954—*), Oundle I (1875—1954), Oundle II[2] (1875—1954), Oundle III[3] (1875—77), Peterborough (1954—*), Peterborough I (1875—1954), Peterborough II (1875—1954), Rutland (1970—*), Rutland I (1875—1954), Rutland II (1875—1954), Rutland III (1875—1954), Thrapston (1954—70), Uppingham (1954—70), Weldon (1954—70), Weldon I (1875—1954), Weldon II (1875—1954)

ALTERATIONS IN ARCHDEACONRIES
AND RURAL DEANERIES

In 1837,[4] 1842,[5] 1851,[6] 1866,[5] 1867,[5] 1873,[5] 1875,[7] 1876,[8] 1877,[5] 1881,[9] 1893,[10] 1926,[11] 1954,[12] 1955,[13] 1960,[14] 1963,[15] 1969,[16] 1970.[17]

RIPON

Cr 1836 from York dioc.[1] Yorks pars; incl some pars in Lancs.

ORGANISATION IN ARCHDEACONRIES
AND RURAL DEANERIES

CRAVEN AD (1836—1919 [cr Bradford dioc] [pt transf 1888 to cr Wakefield dioc])
Birstall (1866—88), Bradford (1857—1919), Craven (1836—57); Craven, Eastern Dv (1905—19); Craven, Northern Dv (1857—1919); Craven, Southern Dv (1857—1919); Craven, Western Dv (1857—1919); Dewsbury (1857—88), Halifax (1857—88), Huddersfield (1857—88), Leeds (1857—94), Otley (1857—94), Pontefract (1836—57), Silkstone (1857—88), Wakefield (1857—88), Wetherby (1857—94), Whitkirk (1861—94)

LEEDS AD (1921—*)
Allerton (1971—*), Armley (1971—*), Boroughbridge, Harrogate (1971—*), Headingley (1971—*), Knaresborough, Leeds, Wetherby, Whitkirk

RICHMOND AD
Amounderness (1836—44), Bedale (1928—*), Boroughbridge (1836—94), Catterick (1836—57), Catterick East[2] (1857—1928), Catterick West[2] (1857—1928), Clapham (1848—94), Kirkby Lonsdale (1836—49), Knaresborough (1870—94), Masham (1877—1905), Nidderdale (1905—21), Richmond (1836—57), Richmond East[2] (1857—*), Richmond North (1863—*), Richmond West[2] (1857—*), Ripon (1849—94), Ripon (1921—*), Wensleydale (1928—*)

RIPON AD (1894—1921)
Boroughbridge, Clapham (1894—1919), Knaresborough, Leeds, Otley,[3] Ripon, Wetherby, Whitkirk

ALTERATIONS IN ARCHDEACONRIES
AND RURAL DEANERIES

In 1849,[4] 1857,[4] 1861,[4] 1863,[4] 1866,[4] 1870,[4] 1877,[5] 1883,[4] 1888,[6] 1894,[7] 1905,[8] 1919,[9] 1921,[10] 1928,[11] 1971.[12]

SHEFFIELD

Cr 1914 from York dioc, Southwell dioc.[1] Yorks pars; incl some pars in Derbys.

ORGANISATION IN ARCHDEACONRIES
AND RURAL DEANERIES

DONCASTER AD
Doncaster, Snaith, Wath

SHEFFIELD AD
Attercliffe (1942—*), Eccleshall (1942—*), Ecclesield, Hallam (1942—*), Handsworth (1927—42), Laughton (1942—*), Rotherham, Sheffield (1914—42), Tankersley (1942—*)

ALTERATIONS IN ARCHDEACONRIES
AND RURAL DEANERIES

In 1914,[2] 1927,[3] 1942.[4]

SOUTHWELL

Cr 1884 from Lichfield dioc, Lincoln dioc.[1] Notts pars; incl Derbys pars
1884—1927.

ORGANISATION IN ARCHDEACONRIES AND RURAL DEANERIES

CHESTERFIELD AD (1910—27 [help cr Derby dioc])
Alfreton, Bolsover (1920—27), Chesterfield, Eyam, Glossop, Heanor (1920—27), Staveley

DERBY AD (1884 [from Lichfield dioc]—1927 [help cr Derby dioc])
Alfreton (1884—1910), Ashbourne, Ashover (1884—87), Bakewell, Bolsover (1884—87), Brampton (1884—87), Buxton, Castleton (1884—87), Chesterfield (1884—1910), Cubley (1884—87), Derby, Dronfield (1887—1910), Duffield, Eyam (1884—1910), Glossop (1887—1910), Hartshorne (1884—87), Ilkeston (1887—1927), Longford (1887—1927), Lullington (1884—87), Melbourne (1887—1927), Repton (1887—1927), Ockbrook (1884—87), Radbourne (1884—87), Stanton by Bridge (1884—87), Staveley (1887—1910), Wirksworth

NEWARK AD (1912—*)
Bawtry, Mansfield, Newark, Retford, Tuxford, Worksop

NOTTINGHAM AD [from Lincoln dioc]
Bawtry (1887—1912), Beeston (1910—*), Bingham, South Bingham, West Bingham, Bulwell (1887—*), Collingham (1884—87), Gedling (1887—*), Mansfield (1884—1912), Newark (1884—1912), Newark East (1887—1910), Norwell (1887—1912), Nottingham, Retford (1884—1912), Southwell, Tuxford (1884—1912), Worksop (1884—1912)

ALTERATIONS IN ARCHDEACONRIES AND RURAL DEANERIES

In 1887,[2] 1910,[3] 1912,[4] 1914,[5] 1920,[6] 1927,[7] 1957.[8]

WAKEFIELD

Cr 1888 from Ripon dioc.[1] Yorks pars; incl some pars in Lancs.

ORGANISATION IN ARCHDEACONRIES AND RURAL DEANERIES

HALIFAX AD
Almondbury (1968—*), Birstall (1888—1927), Blackmoorfoot (1968—*), Brighouse and Elland (1967—*), Calder Valley (1967—*), Dewsbury (1888—1927), Halifax, Huddersfield (1927—*), Kirkburton (1968—*)

HUDDERSFIELD AD (1888—1927)
Hemsworth (1919—27), Huddersfield, Pontefract (1919—27), Silkstone, Wakefield

PONTEFRACT AD (1927—*)
Barnsley, Birstall, Chevet (1973—*), Dewsbury, Pontefract, Wakefield

ALTERATIONS IN ARCHDEACONRIES AND RURAL DEANERIES

In 1888,[2] 1889,[3] 1913,[4] 1920,[5] 1927,[6] 1954,[7] 1967,[8] 1968,[9] 1973.[10]

WORCESTER

Worcs pars; incl Warws until pt severed 1905 to help cr Birmingham dioc, pt severed 1918 to help cr Coventry dioc.

ORGANISATION IN ARCHDEACONRIES AND RURAL DEANERIES

BIRMINGHAM AD (1892—1905 [help cr Birmingham dioc])
Aston,[1] Birmingham, Coleshill, Northfield, Polesworth, Sutton Coldfield, Solihull

COVENTRY AD (1837 [transf from Lichfield and Coventry dioc]—1918 [help cr Coventry dioc])
Arden (1837—54), Atherstone (1854—1918), Baginton (1854—1918), Birmingham (1854—92), Coleshill (1854—92), Coventry, Dassett Magna (1854—1918), Dunchurch (1854—1907), Kenilworth (1907—18), Leamington (1854—1918), Marton (1837—54), Monk's Kirby (1854—1918), Polesworth (1854—92), Rugby (1854—1907), Rugby and Dunchurch (1907—18), Solihull (1854—92), Southam (1854—1918), Stoneleigh or Stonley (1837—54), Sutton Coldfield (1860—92)

DUDLEY AD (1921—*)
Bewdley (1921—26), Bromsgrove, Droitwich, Dudley, Kidderminster, Lindridge (1926—73), Mitton (1921—73), Stourbridge (1974—*), Stourport (1974—*), Swinford (1921—73)

WARWICK AD (1910—18 [help cr Coventry dioc])
Alcester, Blockley, Dudley, Evesham, Feckenham, North Kineton, South Kineton, Pershore, Warwick

WORCESTER AD
Alcester (1861—1910), Bewdley (1919—21), Blockley (until 1918), Bredon (1861—1973), Bromsgrove (1892—1921), Droitwich (until 1921), Dudley (1880—1921), Evesham, Feckenham (1861—1910), Feckenham (1919—73), Kidderminster (until 1921), Kineton (until 1861), North Kineton (1861—1910), South Kineton (1861—1910), Malvern (1974—*), Martley (1921—73), Martley and Worcester West (1974—*), Mitton (1921—73), Northfield (1880—92), Pershore (until 1910), Pershore (1919—*), Powyke (until 1973), Stourport (1974—*), Swinford (1907—73), Upton (1861—*), Warwick (until 1910), Worcester (until 1861), Worcester (1926—73), Inner Worcester (1921—26), Outer Worcester (1921—26), Worcester East (1861—1921), Worcester East (1974—*), Worcester West (1861—1921)

ALTERATIONS IN ARCHDEACONRIES AND RURAL DEANERIES

In 1836,[2] 1837,[3] 1854,[4] 1860,[4] 1861,[4] 1862,[4] 1880,[4] 1880s,[5] 1892,[6] 1905,[7] 1905,[8] 1907,[9] 1910,[10] 1918,[11] 1919,[12] 1921,[13] 1926,[14] 1971,[15] 1974.[16]

YORK

Yorks pars; incl Lancs pars until 1541, Notts pars until 1837; incl some Lancs pars.

ORGANISATION IN ARCHDEACONRIES AND RURAL DEANERIES

CLEVELAND AD
Bulmer (until 1913), Cleveland (until 1862), Easingwold (1862—1913), Guisborough (1862—78), Guisborough (1924—*), Helmsley (1862—*), Malton (1862—*), Middlesbrough (1878—*), Northallerton (1862—*), Pickering (1928—*), Riddal (until 1862), Ripon (until 1836), Stokesley (1862—*), Thirsk (1862—*), Whitby (1878—*)

DONCASTER AD (1913—14 [help cr Sheffield dioc])
Doncaster, Snaith, Wath

EAST RIDING AD
Beverley (1866—*), Bridlington (1866—*), Buckrose (until 1857), Buckrose (1866—1936), East Buckrose (1857—66), West Buckrose (1857—66), Dickering (until 1862), North Dickering (1862—66), South Dickering (1862—66), Escrick (1896—1913), Harthill (1866—*) , North Harthill (1857—66), South Harthill (1857—66), West Harthill (1857—66), Harthill and Hull (until 1857), Hedon (1866—1916), Holderness (until 1849), North Holderness (1849—66), North Holderness (1916—*), South Holderness (1849—66), South Holderness (1916—*), Hornsea (1866—1916), Howden (1866—*), Kingston upon Hull (1869—*),

Pocklington (1866—1936), Scarborough (1866—*), Settrington (1887—1922), Weighton (1866—1936)

NOTTINGHAM AD (until 1839 [transf to Peterb dioc])
Bingham, Newark, Nottingham, Retford

RICHMOND AD (until 1541 [help cr Chester dioc])
Amounderness (before 1291—1541), Boroughbridge, Catterick, Copeland [sometimes 'Coupland'] (before 1291—before 1535), Furness and Cartmel (before 1535—1541), Kendal (before 1535—1541), Kirkby Lonsdale (before 1535—1541), Kirkby Lonsdale and Kendal (before 1291—before 1535), Lancaster (until before 1291), Richmond

SHEFFIELD AD (1884—1914 [help cr Sheffield dioc])
Ecclesfield, Rotherham, Sheffield, Wath (1884—1913)

YORK AD (1928—*)
Ainsty, Buckrose (1936—*), Bulmer, Easingwold, Escrick, Pocklington (1936—*), Selby, Tadcaster, Weighton (1936—*), City of York

YORK AND WEST RIDING AD (until 1928)
Ainsty (until 1820), Ainsty (1862—1928), New Ainsty (1820—62), Old Ainsty (1820—62), Bishopthorpe (1871—96), Bulmer (1913—28), Craven (until 1836), Doncaster (until 1913), Easingwold (1913—28), Ecclesfield (1862—84), Escrick (1913—28), Hemsworth (1916—19), Pontefract (until 1836), Pontefract (1857—1919), Rotherham (1857—84), Selby (1862—1928), Sheffield (1862—84), Snaith (1871—1913), Tadcaster (1862—71), Tadcaster (1922—28), Wath (1871—84), City of York (until 1836), City of York (1862—1928), City of York and Ainsty (1836—62)

ALTERATIONS IN ARCHDEACONRIES
AND RURAL DEANERIES

In 1820,[1] 1836,[2] 1849,[3] 1857,[3] 1862,[3] 1866,[3] 1869,[3] 1871,[3] 1877,[4] 1878,[5] 1884,[6] 1887,[7] 1894,[8] 1896,[9] 1913,[10] 1916,[11] 1916,[12] 1919,[13] 1922,[14] 1924,[15] 1928,[16] 1936,[17] 1958,[18] 1969.[19]

Notes for Entries

PART I: THE PARISHES OF ENGLAND

CHESHIRE

[1]George Ormerod, *The History of the County Palatine and City of Chester* . . . (2nd ed, ed Thomas Helsby, 1882), III, 341. Hereafter, 'Ormerod'. [2]Ormerod III, 443—44. [3]PC augmented by Commissioners of QAB. [4]29 & 30 Vict, *c* 113. [5]17 Jan, *Lond Gaz.* [6]24 Mar, LGBO 22407. [7]1 Apr, MHealthO 84735. [8]1 Apr, *Lond Gaz.* [9]23 Feb, MHousLG Decl. [10]1 Jan, 20 Vict, *c* 19. [11]5 Dec, *Lond Gaz.* [12]27 Feb, *Lond Gaz.* [13]1 Apr, 23 & 34 Geo V, *c* vii. [14]10 Aug, *Lond Gaz.* [15]3 Aug, *Lond Gaz.* [16]19 Aug, *Lond Gaz.* [17]1 Oct, LGBO 55100. [18]5 Sept, LGBO 31737. [19]Apptd day, 56 & 57 Vict, *c* 73 and Co Council Naming O. [20]30 Sept, LGBO 33124. [21]1 Apr, MHousLGO 198. [22]Authority not found, cited *Kelly's Directory* (1914), 658 and Ormerod II, 278. [23]19 July, *Lond Gaz.* [24]9 Aug, *Lond Gaz.* [25]24 Oct, *Lond Gaz.* [26]28 Aug, *Lond Gaz.* [27]1 Oct, LGBO 66417. [28]1 Apr, 20 & 21 Eliz II, *c* 70. [29]24 Jan, *Lond Gaz.* [30]5 Nov, *Lond Gaz.* [31]31 July, *Lond Gaz.* [32]19 Apr, *Lond Gaz.* [33]27 May, *Lond Gaz.* [34]29 Sept, LGBO 39600. [35]20 Dec, LGBO 15116. [36]20 Dec, LGBO 15115. [37]9 Nov, LGBProvO 1167. [38]1 Oct, LGBO 36382. [39]27 Sept, *Lond Gaz.* [40]1 Apr, MHealthO 77044. [41]4 Mar, *Lond Gaz.* [42]1 Apr, MHealthO 93474. [43]30 Sept, Instr Bp Chester, Part Dist. [44]30 Sept, LGBO 51067. [45]OC 26 Aug, reported *Parl Papers* 1897, LXVII, Pt VI, 174. [46]Authority not found, reported in *Kelly's Directory* (1914), 49. [47]Authority not found, reported in *Kelly's Directory* (1914), 204. [48]21 May, *Lond Gaz.* [49]OC 19 May, reported *Parl Papers* 1890—91, LXI, 56. [50]2 Aug, *Lond Gaz.* [51]30 Oct, *Lond Gaz.* [52]1 Apr, MHousLGO 27990. [53]3 May, *Lond Gaz.* [54]30 Nov, *Lond Gaz.* [55]16 Feb, *Lond Gaz.* [56]25 Mar, 45 & 46 Vict., *c* 58. [57]18 June, Instr Bp Chester, Part Dist. [58]1 Apr, 20 & 21 Vict, *c* clxxiii. [59]20 Aug, *Lond Gaz.* [60]8 Jan, *Lond Gaz* (OC 18 Dec 1936). [61]28 Oct, *Lond Gaz.* [62]29 Nov, *Lond Gaz.* [63]24 Feb, *Lond Gaz.* [64]Authority not found, reported in *Kelly's Directory* (1914), 60. [65]Not orig rated in the PLU, incl in it soon after. [66]1 Apr, MHousLGO 9439. [67]8 Sept, *Lond Gaz.* [68]16 May, *Lond Gaz.* [69]1 Apr, LGBO 37379. [70]4 June, Instr Bp Chester, Part Dist. [71]10 May, *Lond Gaz.* [72]1 Apr, MHealthO 67350. [73]4 May, *Lond Gaz.* [74]31 Mar, 60 & 61 Vict, *c* xcix. [75]1 Apr, LGBO 56268. [76]21 Dec, *Lond Gaz.* [77]5 June, *Lond Gaz.* [78]25 Oct, *Lond Gaz.* [79]21 Nov, lic min (*Lond Gaz*, 25 Oct 1963). [80]24 Nov, *Lond Gaz.* [81]1 July (*Lond Gaz*, 29 June). [82]Act of Parliament noted in Ormerod, 488. [83]Presumed in this EP by process of elimination because these tps neither in orders cr Malpas St Chad nor refounding Malpas. [84]Instr Bp Chester, Part Dist. [85]3 Feb, *Lond Gaz.* [86]31 Oct, *Lond Gaz.* [87]12 May, *Lond Gaz.* [88]Yr eff (*Lond Gaz*, 29 Nov 1957). [89]8 Jan, *Lond Gaz.* [90]1 Apr, 17 & 18 Geo V, *c* cxxii. [91]1 Apr, 17 & 18 Geo V, *c* cv. [92]25 Mar, LGBO 28045, confirming Ches Co Council O eff 14 Mar. [93]Authority not found; date noted in census records. [94]9 June, Instr Bp Chester, Part Dist. [95]14 Jan, Instr Bp Chester, Part Dist. [96]Authority not found; date noted in census records. [97]22 July, *Lond Gaz.* [98]6 Aug, *Lond Gaz.* [99]16 Dec, Instr Bp Chester, Part Dist. [100]4 Aug, *Lond Gaz.* [101]21 July, *Lond Gaz.* [102]1 Aug (*Lond Gaz.*, 28 July). [103]14 Feb, *Lond Gaz.* [104]1 May (*Lond Gaz.*, 29 Apr). [105]Ormerod III, 711. [106]18 Dec, *Lond Gaz.* [107]8 Dec, *Lond Gaz.* [108]9 Nov, LGB ProvO 1440, conf by 61 & 62 Vict, *c* lxxxiii. [109]1 Apr, SI 1965/223. [110]24 Mar, LGBO 22377. [111]30 Sept, LGBO 31606. [112]30 Sept, LGBO 31659. [113]1 July (*Lond Gaz.*, 22 June). [114]11 Mar, *Lond Gaz.* [115]30 Sept, LGBO 41128. [116]28 Nov, *Lond Gaz.* [117]17 Dec, LGBO 7885. [118]23 Aug, *Lond Gaz.* [119]30 Sept, LGBO 41375. [120]10 Mar, *Lond Gaz.* [121]11 Apr, Instr Bp Chester, Part Dist. [122]Authority not found, reported in *Kelly's Directory* (1914), 659 and Ormerod I, 548. [123]Apptd day, 56 & 57 Vict, *c* 73. [124]15 Sept, *Lond Gaz.* [125]2 Apr 1839, *Lond Gaz* (OC 6 Oct 1838). [126]9 Nov, 1 Edw VII, *c* clxix. [127]30 Sept, LGBO 43459. [128]Yr eff (*Lond Gaz.*, 16 Apr 1963). [129]1 Apr, SI 1952/588. [130]7 May, SI 1953/742. [131]1 July (*Lond Gaz.*, 25 June). [132]26 Mar, *Lond Gaz.* [133]18 May, *Lond Gaz.* [134]15 Oct, *Lond Gaz.* [135]16 July, *Lond Gaz.* [136]15 Jan, *Lond Gaz.* [137]3 June, *Lond Gaz.* [138]Apptd day, LGBO 31812. [139]1 July (*Lond Gaz.*, 29 June). [140]Ormerod II, 406. [141]30 Sept, LGBO 33125. [142]11 June, *Lond Gaz.* [143]Authority not found; reported in *Kelly's Directory* (1914), 276. [144]15 July, *Lond Gaz* (OC 16 Oct 1853). [145]15 July 1834, *Lond Gaz* (OC 16 Oct 1833). [146]19 Mar, *Lond Gaz.* [147]10 Mar, *Lond Gaz.* [148]29 Dec, *Lond Gaz.* [149]Authority not found; reported in *Kelly's Directory* (1914), 400. [150]Authority not found, reported in *Kelly's Directory* (1914), 641. [151]Ormerod II, 223—24. [152]1 Nov (*Lond Gaz.*, 28 Oct). [153]25 Apr, *Lond Gaz.* [154]30 Sept, LGBO 31605. [155]22 Oct, *Lond Gaz.* [156]14 Apr, *Lond Gaz.* [157]24 Mar, LGBO 22404. [158]Aug 1859, Instr Bp Chester, Part Dist. [159]OC 6 Apr, reported in *Parl Papers* 1872, XLVI, 13. [160]1 Apr, 9 & 10 Geo V, *c* lxxviii. [161]2 Oct, SI 1945/701. [162]24 Mar, *Lond Gaz.* [163]15 May, *Lond Gaz.* [164]27 Oct, *Lond Gaz.* [165]2 Apr, *Lond Gaz.* [166]24 Dec, *Lond Gaz.* [167]Yr lic min (*Lond Gaz.*, 15 May). [168]3 May, LGBProvO 8065 confirmed by 42 & 43 Vict, *c* cxi. [169]31 Mar, MHealthO 73725. [170]25 Feb, *Lond Gaz.* [171]9 Apr, *Lond Gaz.* [172]30 Nov, *Lond Gaz.* [173]47 & 48 Vict, *c* ccxxxix. [174]1 Apr, SI 1954/317. [175]Jan 1973 (*Lond Gaz.*, 30 June 1972). [176]Authority not found; Part Dist, date of cr noted in census reports. [177]13 Aug, *Lond Gaz.* [178]OC 6 Feb, reported *Parl Papers* 1890—91, LXI, 56. [179]OC 15 Sept, reported *Parl Papers* 1890—91, LXI, 57. [180]23 Dec, *Lond Gaz.* [181]1 Dec (*Lond Gaz.*, 28 Nov). [182]OC 27 Apr, reported *Parl Papers* 1872, XLVI, 12. [183]Ormerod I, 315. [184]10 July, *Lond Gaz.* [185]22 Aug, *Lond Gaz.* [186]16 Oct, *Lond Gaz.* [187]12 Oct, *Lond Gaz.* [188]OC 11 July, reported *Parl Papers* 1872, XLVI, 12. [189]17 Aug, *Lond Gaz.* [190]20 Feb, *Lond Gaz.* [191]1 Aug, *Lond Gaz.* [192]5 Aug, *Lond Gaz.* [193]17 May, *Lond Gaz.* [194]30 Sept, LGBO 36967. [195]10 July, *Lond Gaz.* [196]13 Feb, *Lond Gaz.* [197]14 Dec, *Lond Gaz.* [198]3 July, *Lond Gaz.* [199]24 Mar, LGBO 30136. [200]5 Jan, *Lond Gaz.* [201]7 Apr, *Lond Gaz.* [202]24 Mar, LGBO 22406. [203]24 Mar, LGBO 22880. [204]23 Apr, *Lond Gaz.* [205]20 Dec, LGBO 15118. [206]2 Dec, *Lond Gaz.* [207]OC 17 May, reported *Parl Papers* 1890—91, LXI, 55. [208]1 Apr, MHousLGO 4238. [209]52 Geo III, *c* 136. [210]14 Aug, *Lond Gaz.* [211]Apptd day, LGBO 32236. [212]14 Oct, *Lond Gaz.* [213]1 Apr, 26 Geo V & 1 Edw VIII, *c* x. [214]1 June, *Lond Gaz.* [215]9 Nov, LGBProvO 1416. [216]15 Aug, LGBO

63696. [217]11 Dec, *Lond Gaz.* [218]10 Jan, *Lond Gaz* (OC 24 Sept 1842). [219]10 Feb, *Lond Gaz.* [220]10 June, *Lond Gaz.* [221]28 Mar, *Lond Gaz.* [222]5 Mar, *Lond Gaz.* [223]Yr vac (*Lond Gaz.*, 13 Mar 1973). [224]16 Sept, *Lond Gaz.* [225]28 Apr, *Lond Gaz.* [226]1 July (*Lond Gaz.*, 8 June). [227]29 Sept, *Lond Gaz.* [228]31 Mar, *Lond Gaz.* [229]1 Dec (*Lond Gaz.*, 1 Nov). [230]1 Apr, LGBO 56293. [231]1 Apr, MHealthO 109856. [232]1 Apr, MHousLGO 9439. [233]1 Apr, MHousLGO 28164. [234]1 Apr, MHousLGO 45725. [235]9 Mar, *Lond Gaz.* [236]30 June, *Lond Gaz.* [237]28 June, *Lond Gaz.* [238]26 Oct, *Lond Gaz.* [239]17 Aug, *Lond Gaz.* [240]8 Oct, *Lond Gaz.* [241]Authority not found; date noted in census records. [242]7 Dec, *Lond Gaz.* [243]24 Nov, *Lond Gaz.* [244]8 Mar, SI 1955/377. [245]26 Jan, *Lond Gaz.* [246]7 May, *Lond Gaz.* [247]1 Oct, MHealthO 68687. [248]28 Oct, lic min (*Lond Gaz.*, 16 June). [249]24 Mar, LGBO 23295. [250]Apptd day, LGBO 31615. [251]1 Apr, LGBO 63198. [252]27 July, *Lond Gaz.* [253]13 Mar, *Lond Gaz.* [254]1 Apr, 22 & 23 Geo V, *c* lxxxviii. [255]1 Apr, MHousLGO 3463. [256]1 Apr, LGBO 40700. [257]24 Mar, LGBO 15915. [258]1 Apr, MHousLGO 4918. [259]20 May, *Lond Gaz.* [260]Yr lic min (*Lond Gaz.*, 31 May). [261]Yr eff (*Lond Gaz.*, 26 Oct 1972). [262]29 Sept, LGBO 31609. [263]9 Dec, *Lond Gaz.* [264]1 Apr, 24 & 25 Geo V, *c* lvi. [265]1 Apr, MHealthO 100212. [266]6 July, *Lond Gaz.* [267]3 Mar, *Lond Gaz.* [268]23 Jan, *Lond Gaz.* [269]26 July, Instr Bp Chester, Part Dist. [270]9 July, *Lond Gaz.* [271]24 Mar, LGBO 22879. [272]3 Jan, Instr Bp Chester, Part Dist. [273]30 Sept, LGBO 31603. [274]22 Jan, *Lond Gaz.* [275]9 Dec, *Lond Gaz.* [276]2 Oct, *Lond Gaz.* [277]2 Oct, *Lond Gaz.* [278]30 Sept, LGBO 31604. [279]20 Dec, LGBO 15117. [280]OC 20 Oct, reported *Parl Papers* 1890—91, LXI, 55. [281]26 July, Instr Bp Chester. [282]Authority not found; date and mother pars reported in census reports. [283]1 Apr, LGBO 32560. [284]22 Apr, *Lond Gaz.* [285]24 Mar, LGBO 14976. [286]24 Mar, LGBO 14973. [287]Apptd day, LGBO 31665. [288]1 July (*Lond Gaz.*, 22 June). [289]30 Sept, LGBO 31631. [290]5 July, *Lond Gaz.* [291]1 Apr, LGBO 58295. [292]OC 11 Dec; see Ormerod I, 576. [293]Proposed OC published in *Lond Gaz* 30 Jan 1874, confirmed by OC published in *Lond Gaz* 23 Dec 1881. [294]23 Nov, *Lond Gaz.* [295]8 May, *Lond Gaz.* [296]16 Apr, *Lond Gaz.* [297]6 Mar, *Lond Gaz.* [298]1 Nov (*Lond Gaz.*, 30 Oct). [299]25 May, *Lond Gaz.* [300]OC 5 Feb, reported *Parl Papers* 1872, XLVI, 22. [301]22 Dec, date instr and deed. [302]1 Apr, MLocal Govt PlanningO 537. [303]1 Oct, MHealthO 72033. [304]25 Mar, LGBO 41687. [305]Authority not found; date reported in census reports. [306]24 Mar, LGBO 23293. [307]Statute 33 Henry VIII, reported in Ormerod II, 145. [308]13 Jan, *Lond Gaz.* [309]24 Mar, LGBO 23294. [310]Authority not found, reported in *Kelly's Directory* (1914), 74 and Ormerod II, 528. [311]7 Mar, *Lond Gaz.* [312]9 Jan, *Lond Gaz.* [313]14 May, *Lond Gaz.* [314]19 Feb, *Lond Gaz.* [315]21 Dec, LGBO 11688 with supplementary order 2 Apr 1881, LGBO 12357. [316]28 July, *Lond Gaz.* [317]Authority not found, reported in *Kelly's Directory* (1914), 527. [318]1 Oct, LGBO 33391. [319]Yr vac (*Lond Gaz*, 1 July 1921). [320]27 Mar, *Lond Gaz.* [321]6 Nov, *Lond Gaz.* [322]8 Feb, *Lond Gaz.* [323]Authority not found, reported in *Kelly's Directory* (1914), 534. [324]Authority not found, reported in *Kelly's Directory* (1914), 678. [325]29 May, *Lond Gaz.* [326]31 Dec, *Lond Gaz.* [327]Authority not found, reported in *Kelly's Directory* (1914), 680. [328]22 Nov, *Lond Gaz.* [329]1 Apr, MHealthO 107413. [330]16 Aug, *Lond Gaz.* [331]24 Mar, LGBO 22405. [332]Authority not found, reported in *Kelly's Directory* (1914), 557 and Ormerod II, 480. [333]24 May, Instr Bp Chester, Part Dist. [334]9 Nov, 3 & 4 Geo V, *c* cxxxvii. [335]1 Apr, MHealthO 89198. [336]17 Dec, *Lond Gaz.* [337]9 Nov, *Lond Gaz.* [338]5 May, *Lond Gaz.* [339]7 June, *Lond Gaz.* [340]25 Mar, LGBO 14975. [341]30 May, *Lond Gaz.* [342]30 Sept, 59 & 60 Vict, *c* ccxxxvi. [343]29 Aug, *Lond Gaz.* [344]30 Sept, 58 & 59 Vict, *c* lxxxvi. [345]27 Apr, *Lond Gaz.* [346]6 Mar, *Lond Gaz.* [347]1 June (*Lond Gaz*, 7 May). [348]24 Mar, LGBO 22378.

CUMBERLAND

[1]29 & 39 Vict, *c* 113. [2]Not orig rated in the PLU (1838), incl soon thereafter. [3]23 Aug, MHealth Decl. [4]1 Apr, MHealthO 78137. [5]20 July, *Lond Gaz.* [6]PC augmented by Commissioners of QAB. [7]20 Feb, *Lond Gaz.* [8]Apptd day, LGBO 32309. [9]2 Jan, *Lond Gaz* (OC 23 Dec 1845). [10]11 Jan, *Lond Gaz.* [11]25 Mar, 45 & 46 Vict, *c* 58. [12]4 Nov, *Lond Gaz.* [13]24 Mar, LGBO 19603. [14]1 Apr, 14 Geo VI, *c* xix. [15]1 Apr, SI 1951/322. [16]Joseph Nicholson and Richard Burn, *The History and Antiquities of the Counties of Westmorland and Cumberland* (1777), II, 226. Hereafter 'Nicholson and Burn'. [17]17 Dec, LGBO 13097. [18]1 Apr, MHealth O 80628. [19]1 Nov, *Lond Gaz.* [20]31 May, *Lond Gaz.* [21]Apptd day, LGBO 31782. [22]Apptd day, 57 & 58 Vict, *c* 58 and Co Council Naming O. [23]9 Nov, 2 & 3 Geo V, *c* cxxxvii. [24]26 Mar, *Lond Gaz.* [25]31 Mar, *Lond Gaz.* [26]24 Mar, LGBO 20183. [27]12 Apr, Instr Bp Carlisle & CBC, Part Dist, reported in *Parl Papers* 1870, LXIV, 139—43. [28]19 May, *Lond Gaz.* [29]23 June, *Lond Gaz.* [30]15 Aug, 4 Edw VII, *c* ccxlv. [31]Not orig rated in the PLU (1837), incl soon thereafter. [32]11 Sept, *Lond Gaz.* [33]15 Aug, *Lond Gaz.* [34]6 Apr, *Lond Gaz.* [35]24 Mar, LGBO 20630. [36]25 Mar, LGBO 14681. [37]15 Sept, *Lond Gaz.* [38]1 Jan, 20 Vict, *c* 19. [39]11 Dec, Instr Bp Carl. [40]12 Nov, LGBO 32125. [41]28 Aug, *Lond Gaz.* [42]23 Nov, *Lond Gaz.* [43]12 Aug, *Lond Gaz.* [44]1 Oct, LGBO 38315. [45]25 Mar, LGBO 14681, 14682, 14683. [46]12 June, MHealth Decl. [47]1 Apr, Dept EnvironO 3709. [48]12 Sept, *Lond Gaz.* [49]19 Aug, *Lond Gaz.* [50]Apptd day, LGBO 31664. [51]Nicholson and Burn, II, 108. [52]29 Aug, *Lond Gaz.* [53]Nicholson and Burn, II, 514. [54]29 Oct, *Lond Gaz.* [55]8 Aug, *Lond Gaz.* [56]5 Nov, *Lond Gaz.* [57]10 June, *Lond Gaz.* [58]1 Feb, *Lond Gaz.* [59]14 Jan, *Lond Gaz.* [60]8 June, *Lond Gaz.* [61]Year lic min (*Lond Gaz*, 27 Nov 1959). [62]30 May, *Lond Gaz.* [63]26 Jan, *Lond Gaz.* [64]24 Dec, *Lond Gaz.* [65]22 July, *Lond Gaz.* [66]15 Oct, *Lond Gaz.* [67]27 Apr, *Lond Gaz.* [68]25 Mar, LGBO 19602. [69]19 Mar, *Lond Gaz.* [70]25 Mar, LGBO 19633. [71]7 Dec, *Lond Gaz.* [72]15 May, *Lond Gaz.* [73]31 Jan, *Lond Gaz.* [74]28 July, *Lond Gaz.* [75]23 Aug, *Lond Gaz.* [76]31 Oct, *Lond Gaz.* [77]Nicholson and Burn, II, 494. [78]6 Dec, *Lond Gaz.* [79]4 Apr, *Lond Gaz.* [80]25 Mar, LGBO 14683. [81]22 Dec, *Lond Gaz.* [82]1 Jan, *Lond Gaz.* [83]15 Nov, *Lond Gaz.* [84]1 Oct, LGBO 43157. [85]10 Aug, MHealth Decl. [86]Nicholson and Burn, II, 475. [87]Nicholson and Burn, II, 448. [88]17 Dec, LGBO 13093. [89]1 Apr, MHealthO 73050. [90]24 Mar, LGBO 20709. [91]27 May, *Lond Gaz.* [92]25 Mar, LGBO 14682. [93]25 Mar, LGBO 19520. [94]26 Sept, Instr Bp Carlisle. [95]24 Apr, Instr Bp Carlisle & CBC, Part Dist. [96]1 Apr, LGBO 35440. [97]18 Oct, Instr Bp Carlisle, Part Dist, reported in *Parl Papers* 1870, LXIV, 139—43. [98]17 Dec, LGBO 13093, 13095, 13098. [99]27 July, *Lond Gaz.*

[100]27 June, *Lond Gaz*. [101]Nicholson and Burn II, 338—39. [102]15 Jan, *Lond Gaz*. [103]4 Mar, *Lond Gaz*. [104]Nicholson and Burn, II, 177—78. [105]6 Dec, Instr Bp Carlisle, Part Dist, reported in *Parl Papers* 1870, LXIV, 139—43. [106]24 Mar, LGBO 20185. [107]30 June, Instr Bp Carlisle. [108]Date of cr and of incl in the PLU from Whitehaven PLU records; information kindly supplied by Cumbria RO. [109]17 Dec, LGBO 13098. [110]9 Nov, *Lond Gaz*. [111]3 May, *Lond Gaz*. [112]Nicholson and Burn, II, 506—07. [113]1 Mar, *Lond Gaz*. [114]25 Mar, LGBO 19519. [115]14 Apr, *Lond Gaz*. [116]27 Nov, *Lond Gaz*. [117]1 Apr, 23 & 24 Geo V, *c* vii. [118]31 Mar, 62 & 63 Vict, *c* ccc. [119]OC 1 Jan (*Lond Gaz*, 20 Dec 1934). [120]Nicholson and Burn, II, 394—95. [121]8 Mar, *Lond Gaz*. [122]17 Dec, LGBO 13093, 13094. [123]26 Mar, LGBO 34096. [124]1 Apr, LGBO 33602. [125]11 Aug, *Lond Gaz*. [126]17 Dec, LGBO 13095, 13096. [127]OC 21 Dec, reported in *Parl Papers* 1870, LXIV, 139—43. [128]9 Nov, 62 & 63 Vict, *c* cclx. [129]1 Jan, MHousLG Decl. [130]1 Apr, 25 & 26 Geo V, *c* v. [131]Nicholson and Burn, II, 326—29. Cumbria RO states that the par sep eccl from 1338. [132]24 Mar, LGBO 20184. [133]9 Oct, *Lond Gaz*. [134]6 Jan, *Lond Gaz*. [135]9 Oct, *Lond Gaz*.

DERBYSHIRE

[1]25 Jan, *Lond Gaz*. [2]17 Oct, *Lond Gaz*. [3]29 & 30 Vict, *c* 113. [4]10 Aug, *Lond Gaz*. [5]25 Mar, LGBO 19657. [6]Not orig rated in the PLU, included in it soon thereafter. [7]1 Apr, MHealthO 77674. [8]16 June, *Lond Gaz*. [9]PC augmented by Commissioners of QAB. [10]25 Oct, *Lond Gaz*. [11]25 Nov, *Lond Gaz*. [12]16 Jan, *Lond Gaz*. [13]25 Mar, LGBO 19531. [14]30 Apr, *Lond Gaz*. [15]28 June, *Lond Gaz*. [16]OC 15 Jan, reported in *Parl Papers* 1872, XLVI, 19. [17]1 Apr, SI 1968/44. [18]24 Oct, *Lond Gaz*. [19]2 Feb, *Lond Gaz*. [20]24 Mar, LGBO 15290, LGBO 15291. [21]25 May, *Lond Gaz*. [22]9 Nov, 1 Edw VII, *c* cclxvii. [23]1 Apr, 17 & 18 Geo V, *c* xcii. [24]3 Feb, *Lond Gaz*. [25]2 July, *Lond Gaz*. [26]51 & 52 Vict, *c* 41. [27]30 Sept, 60 & 61 Vict, *c* cxxxix. [28]J. Charles Cox, *Notes on the Churches of Derbyshire* (1875—79, 4 vols) I, 489—92. Hereafter, 'Cox'. [29]Cox I, 505—06. [30]17 May, *Lond Gaz*. [31]Apptd day, LGBO 32243. [32]1 Apr, MHealthO 69041. [33]After *Valor* (1535) but before *Liber Regis* (1786). [34]OC 5 Feb, reported in *Parl Papers* 1872, XLVI, 22. [35]OC 25 June, reported in *Parl Papers* 1890—91, LXI,51. [36]31 Mar, MHousLG Decl. [37]11 Aug, *Lond Gaz*. [38]9 Nov, *Lond Gaz*. [39]13 July, *Lond Gaz*. [40]21 Nov, *Lond Gaz*. [41]30 Sept, LGBO 31701. [42]1 Oct, LGBO 45287. [43]30 Oct, *Lond Gaz*. [44]16 Apr, *Lond Gaz*. [45]26 Mar, *Lond Gaz*. [46]1 Apr, MHealthO 79528. [47]2 May, LGB ProvO 4374. [48]14 Aug, *Lond Gaz*. [49]1 May (*Lond Gaz*, 17 Apr). [50]25 Mar, LGBO 17808. [51]25 July, *Lond Gaz*. [52]2 & 3 Wm IV, *c* 64 and 7 & 8 Vict, *c* 61. [53]6 Feb, *Lond Gaz*. [54]25 Mar, LGBO 18462. [55]25 Mar, LGBO 17808. [56]20 Vict, *c* 19. [57]15 Oct, *Lond Gaz*. [58]1 Jan (*Lond Gaz*, 18 Dec 1973). [59]31 Oct, 63 & 64 Vict, *c* ccxxii. [60]1 Apr, 23 & 24 Geo V, *c* lxx. [61]1 Apr, MHousLGO 25331. [62]15 Jan, lic min (*Lond Gaz*, 4 Dec 1956). [63]3 Sept, *Lond Gaz*. [64]10 Feb, *Lond Gaz*. [65]17 Aug, *Lond Gaz*. [66]28 Mar, *Lond Gaz*. [67]25 Mar, 45 & 46 Vict, *c* 58. [68]25 Mar, LGBO 18121. [69]14 Sept, *Lond Gaz*. [70]OC 1 Mar, reported in *Parl Papers* 1872, XLVI, 19. [71]26 Mar, LGBO 30633. [72]9 Nov, 10 Edw VII & 1 Geo V, *c* lxxxiii. [73]9 Nov, 10 & 11 Geo V, *c* cxxvi. [74]23 Sept

1834, *Lond Gaz* (OC 1 Aug 1832). [75]16 Nov, lic min (*Lond Gaz*, 24 Aug). [76]8 Feb, *Lond Gaz*. [77]8 May, *Lond Gaz*. [78]18 Nov, lic min (*Lond Gaz*, 22 Oct 1954). [79]1 Apr, SI 1965/24. [80]25 Mar, LGBO 17809. [81]Apptd day, LGBO 31969. [82]OC 3 Sept, reported in *Parl Papers* 1872, XLVI, 18. [83]25 Mar, LGBO 14576. [84]25 Mar, LGBO 17807. [85]19 Mar, *Lond Gaz*. [86]Apptd day, LGBO 32024. [87]After *Valor* (1535) but before *Liber Regis* (1786). [88]1 Mar, *Lond Gaz* (OC 10 Dec 1841). [89]21 May, *Lond Gaz*. [90]Apptd day, LGBO 31843. [91]Apptd day, LGBO 32058. [92]Authority not found; so listed in Lewis, *Topographical Dictionary*, sub 'Calke'. [93]13 Jan, *Lond Gaz*. [94]OC 3 Feb, reported in *Parl Papers* 1872, XLVI, 19. [95]1 Apr, 26 Geo V & 1 Edw VIII, *c* x. [96]2 Dec, *Lond Gaz*. [97]29 June, *Lond Gaz*. [98]15 July, *Lond Gaz*. [99]56 & 57 Vict, *c* 73 and Co Council Naming O. [100]Cox I, 184. [101]26 Mar, LGBO 37890. [102]7 Feb, *Lond Gaz*. [103]4 Nov, Instr Bp Lichf, Part Dist. [104]7 Apr, *Lond Gaz*. [105]30 Sept, 60 & 61 Vict, *c* cxxxix. [106]24 Aug, *Lond Gaz*. [107]1 Apr, LGBO 34064. [108]6 Feb, *Lond Gaz*. [109]17 July, *Lond Gaz*. [110]22 Mar, *Lond Gaz*. [111]1 Oct, *Lond Gaz*. [112]21 June, *Lond Gaz*. [113]16 Dec, *Lond Gaz*. [114]25 Jan, *Lond Gaz*. [115]10 Mar, *Lond Gaz*. [116]8 Mar, *Lond Gaz*. [117]1 Oct, LGBO 36015. [118]30 Sept, 58 & 59 Vict., *c* lxxxvi. [119]Sometimes but not always sep listed in *Clergy List*. [120]25 Mar, LGBO 15290. [121]Aug, *Lond Gaz*. [122]15 Jan 1847, *Lond Gaz* (OC 19 Dec 1846). [123]9 Mar, *Lond Gaz*. [124]26 Feb, *Lond Gaz*. [125]6 June, *Lond Gaz*. [126]1 Dec, *Lond Gaz*. [127]5 Sept, *Lond Gaz*. [128]4 Oct, *Lond Gaz*. [129]6 May, *Lond Gaz*. [130]1 Jan, *Lond Gaz*. [131]1 Nov (*Lond Gaz*, 3 Oct). [132]1 Apr (*Lond Gaz*, 28 Mar). [133]4 Aug, *Lond Gaz*. [134]6 Apr, *Lond Gaz*. [135]28 Nov,*Lond Gaz*. [136]15 May, *Lond Gaz*. [137]Authority not found; year cited in census reports. [138]20 Feb, *Lond Gaz*. [139]14 May, *Lond Gaz*. [140]OC 13 Aug, reported in *Parl Papers* 1890—91, LXI, 54. [141]53 & 54 Vict, *c* liv. [142]16 May, *Lond Gaz*. [143]1 Apr, 18 & 19 Geo V, *c* lxxxvii. [144]14 Feb, *Lond Gaz*. [145]Apptd day, LGBO 32161. [146]8 Oct, *Lond Gaz*. [147]OC 24 Mar, reported in *Parl Papers* 1872, XLVI, 22. [148]1 Jan 1974 (*Lond Gaz*, 18 Dec 1973). [149]OC 6 May, reported in *Parl Papers* 1872, XLVI, 20. [150]OC 2 May, reported in *Parl Papers* 1872, XLVI, 20. [151]Apptd day, LGBO 31810. [152]28 July, *Lond Gaz*. [153]24 Nov, *Lond Gaz*. [154]1 Oct, LGBO 36016. [155]11 Apr, *Lond Gaz*. [156]30 June, *Lond Gaz*. [157]OC 1 Mar, reported in *Parl Papers* 1872, XLVI, 18. [158]1 Oct, MHealthO 67306. [159]OC 10 June, reported in *Parl Papers* 1872, XLVI, 18. [160]4 Jan 1842, *Lond Gaz* (OC 21 Oct 1841). [161]OC 10 June, reported in *Parl Papers* 1872, XLVI, 18. [162]1 Feb, *Lond Gaz*. [163]9 Aug, *Lond Gaz*. [164]30 Sept, LGBO 38251. [165]57 & 58 Vict, *c* 58. [166]4 Mar, LGBO 36072. [167]14 July, *Lond Gaz*. [168]Charter of incorp and 6 & 7 Geo V, *c* l (fifty). [169]24 June, *Lond Gaz*. [170]28 Dec, OC reported in *Parl Papers* 1872, XLVI, 22. [171]22 May, O Derbys and Staffs Co Councils, conf by LGBO 26017. [172]1 Dec (*Lond Gaz*, 30 Nov). [173]Year lic min (*Lond Gaz*, 18 Aug). [174]7 Aug, *Lond Gaz*. [175]*Eleventh Report . . . Poor Law Commissioners* IX, 741. [176]22 July, *Lond Gaz*. [177]25 Mar, LGBO 17810. [178]6 July, *Lond Gaz*. [179]18 Feb, *Lond Gaz*. [180]22 Oct, *Lond Gaz*. [181]OC 2 Feb, reported in *Parl Papers* 1890—91, LXI, 54. [182]27 Sept, *Lond Gaz*. [183]25 Mar, LGBO 19659. [184]25 Mar, LGBO 19658. [185]22 Jan, *Lond Gaz*. [186]24 Mar, LGBO 22100. [187]19 Jan, *Lond*

Gaz. [188]7 May, *Lond Gaz.* [189]24 Mar, LGBO 14664. [190]OC 28 Dec, reported in *Parl Papers* 1872, XLVI, 22. [191]Year lic min (*Lond Gaz*, 22 Oct 1954). [192]1 Oct, LGBO 45968. [193]1 Jan (*Lond Gaz*, 31 Dec 1973). [194]19 May, *Lond Gaz.* [195]20 Apr, *Lond Gaz.* [196]24 Mar, LGBO 15272. [197]27 Oct, LGBO 61219. [198]24 Mar, LGBO 20648. [199]24 Mar, LGBO 15271. [200]24 Mar, LGBO 15277. [201]1 Apr, MHousLGO 4143. [202]4 Sept, *Lond Gaz.* [203]1 Apr, LGBO 43684. [204]24 Mar, LGBO 15277. [205]11 Jan, *Lond Gaz.* [206]6 Nov, *Lond Gaz.* [207]30 Jan, *Lond Gaz.* [208]1 June (*Lond Gaz*, 31 May). [209]30 Sept, 58 & 59 Vict, *c* xci. [210]4 May, *Lond Gaz.* [211]1 Apr, LGBO 46368. [212]1 Mar, LGBO 10465. [213]1 Mar, LGBO 10464. [214]Apptd day, LGBO 31596. [215]OC 22 Oct, reported in *Parl Papers* 1872, XLVI, 20. [216]24 Mar, LGBO 15292. [217]31 Dec, *Lond Gaz* (and supplemental order 2 Jan, *Lond Gaz*). [218]16 Aug, *Lond Gaz.* [219]3 June, *Lond Gaz.* [220]18 Nov, *Lond Gaz.* [221]25 Mar, LGBO 19533. [222]24 Mar, LGBO 14273. [223]24 Mar, LGBO 15273. [224]31 Mar, LGBO 46186. [225]1 Apr, 20 & 21 Eliz II, *c* 70. [226]27 May, *Lond Gaz.*

COUNTY DURHAM

[1]29 & 30 Vict, *c* 113. [2]20 & 21 Eliz II, *c* 70. [3]PC augmented by Commissioners of QAB. [4]2 & 3 Wm IV, *c* 64 and 7 & 8 Vict, *c* 61. [5]13 Mar, *Lond Gaz.* [6]24 May, *Lond Gaz.* [7]14 May, *Lond Gaz.* [8]1 Aug, *Lond Gaz.* [9]1 Apr, 5 & 6 Geo V, *c* ii. [10]1 Oct, 20 & 21 Geo V, *c* cxxi. [11]29 Aug, *Lond Gaz.* [12]45 & 46 Vict, *c* 58. [13]25 Mar, LGBO 17588. [14]Apptd day, LGBO 31709. [15]1 Apr, MHealthO 86335. [16]17 July, MHealth Decl. [17]William Fordyce, *The History and Antiquities of the County Palatine of Durham* (1853), I, 608–09. Hereafter 'Fordyce'. [18]15 Sept, *Lond Gaz.* [19]20 Aug, *Lond Gaz.* [20]3 May, *Lond Gaz.* [21]30 Apr, *Lond Gaz.* [22]21 June, *Lond Gaz.* [23]4 Mar, *Lond Gaz.* [24]2 Nov, *Lond Gaz.* [25]13 July, *Lond Gaz.* [26]6 Apr, *Lond Gaz.* [27]27 July, *Lond Gaz.* [28]Year lic min (*Lond Gaz* 24 Sept 1957). [29]13 Oct, *Lond Gaz.* [30]24 Mar, LGBO 16363. [31]1 Apr, MHousLGO 1481. [32]1 Apr, MHousLGO 41588. [33]25 Mar, LGBO 17495. [34]1 Apr, MHealthO 104825. [35]27 Aug, *Lond Gaz.* [36]21 Apr, *Lond Gaz.* [37]OC 19 June, reported in *Parl Papers* 1872, XLVI, 19. [38]24 Mar, LGBO 16614. [39]57 & 58 Vict, *c* 58 and Co Council Naming O. [40]2 Sept, *Lond Gaz.* [41]25 May, *Lond Gaz.* [42]17 May, *Lond Gaz.* [43]17 Dec, *Lond Gaz.* [44]14 May, *Lond Gaz.* [45]22 Aug, *Lond Gaz.* [46]18 Aug, *Lond Gaz.* [47]57 & 58 Vict, *c* 58 and Co Council Naming O. [48]5 Oct, LGBO 32982. [49]1 Apr, MHealthO 81424. [50]1 Apr, MHealthO 104821. [51]4 Nov, *Lond Gaz.* [52]10 Feb, *Lond Gaz.* [53]1 Oct, LGBO 34879. [54]1 Apr, MHousLGO 7056. [55]26 Mar, *Lond Gaz.* [56]19 Apr, *Lond Gaz.* [57]12 July, *Lond Gaz.* [58]3 Sept, *Lond Gaz.* [59]24 Mar, LGBO 20915. [60]24 Mar, LGBO 20955. [61]30 Sept, LGBO 31655. [62]7 Mar, *Lond Gaz.* [63]17 June, *Lond Gaz.* [64]1 Apr, SI 1967/396. [65]2 Jan, *Lond Gaz.* [66]6 Aug, *Lond Gaz.* [67]18 Feb, *Lond Gaz.* [68]16 Jan 1959, lic min (*Lond Gaz* 25 Nov 1958). [69]30 May, *Lond Gaz.* [70]17 Jan 1843, *Lond Gaz* (OC 24 Sept 1842). [71]25 Mar, LGBO 17589. [72]11 Jan, *Lond Gaz.* [73]10 Aug, *Lond Gaz.* [74]29 Oct, *Lond Gaz.* [75]29 Jan, *Lond Gaz.* [76]4 Apr, *Lond Gaz.* [77]3 Mar, *Lond Gaz.* [78]5 Geo I, *c* xix. [79]31 Mar, *Lond Gaz.* [80]9 Nov, LGBProvO 1074. [81]25 Mar, LGBO

35995. [82]21 Nov, *Lond Gaz.* [83]3 Mar, *Lond Gaz.* [84]7 Dec, *Lond Gaz.* [85]28 Aug, *Lond Gaz.* [86]13 Dec, *Lond Gaz.* [87]26 July, *Lond Gaz.* [88]31 Dec, *Lond Gaz.* [89]1 May (*Lond Gaz*, 30 Apr). [90]18 Apr, *Lond Gaz.* [91]1 Mar (*Lond Gaz* 6 Feb). [92]4 Dec lic min (*Lond Gaz* 6 Nov). [93]1 Apr, 17 & 18 Geo V, *c* xcvii. [94]28 July, *Lond Gaz.* [95]4 July, *Lond Gaz.* [96]1 Apr, SI 1967/67. [97]1 Apr, MHealthO 83526. [98]26 Mar, LGBO 34420. [99]23 Aug, *Lond Gaz.* [100]23 Nov, *Lond Gaz.* [101]1 Apr, LGBO 32574. [102]9 Nov, 1 Edw VII, *c* clxix. [103]1 Nov, 11 & 12 Geo V, *c* cxviii. [104]1 Apr, 14 Geo VI, *c* lix. [105]1 Apr, MHousLGO 27989. [106]9 Apr, *Lond Gaz.* [107]19 Dec, *Lond Gaz.* [108]4 Aug, *Lond Gaz.* [109]21 Jan, *Lond Gaz.* [110]18 Dec, *Lond Gaz.* [111]15 Aug, *Lond Gaz.* [112]21 Dec, LGBO 13173, 13176, 13177. [113]OC 31 Mar, reported in *Parl Papers* 1872, LXVI, 21. [114]15 Aug, *Lond Gaz.* [115]25 Apr, *Lond Gaz.* [116]21 Dec, LGBO 13172. [117]1 Apr, SI 1967/174. [118]1 Apr, SI 1967/66. [119]21 May, *Lond Gaz.* [120]22 Dec, *Lond Gaz.* [121]13 Feb, *Lond Gaz.* [122]1 Apr, LGBO 57677. [123]9 Aug, *Lond Gaz.* [124]24 Mar, LGBO 19069. [125]18 Mar, *Lond Gaz.* [126]10 June, *Lond Gaz.* [127]1 Apr, MHousLGO 3321. [128]1 Apr, MHealthO 104811. [129]1 Apr, MHousLGO 5882. [130]24 July, *Lond Gaz.* [131]25 Oct, *Lond Gaz.* [132]2 Aug, *Lond Gaz.* [133]13 June, *Lond Gaz.* [134]7 Feb, *Lond Gaz.* [135]21 Dec, LGBO 13174. [136]25 Mar, LGBO 17125, 17127. [137]25 July, SI 1952/1348. [138]1 Oct, MHealthO 67139. [139]3 Dec, *Lond Gaz.* [140]30 June, *Lond Gaz.* [141]27 Oct, *Lond Gaz.* [142]16 Feb, *Lond Gaz.* [143]10 Oct, *Lond Gaz.* [144]1 Apr, MHealthO 104793. [145]18 Oct, *Lond Gaz.* [146]6 Nov, reported in *Parl Papers* 1870, LXIV. [147]29 Feb, *Lond Gaz.* [148]1 Oct, LGBO 42894. [149]*VCH Durham* III, 264. [150]14 Nov, *Lond Gaz.* [151]11 Dec, *Lond Gaz.* [152]18 Jan 1952, lic min (*Lond Gaz* 11 Dec 1951). [153]27 June, *Lond Gaz.* [154]28 Apr, *Lond Gaz.* [155]17 Nov, *Lond Gaz.* [156]24 Mar, LGBO 16365. [157]26 May, *Lond Gaz.* [158]Apptd day, LGBO 31653. [159]24 Mar, LGBO 16613. [160]1 July, *Lond Gaz.* [161]1 Apr, MHousLGO 3916. [162]25 Mar, LGBO 17128. [163]21 Dec, *Lond Gaz.* [164]1 Oct, LGBO 66418. [165]1 Apr, MHealthO 104819. [166]1 Apr, MHousLGO 5813. [167]30 Sept, LGBO 34883. [168]28 June, *Lond Gaz.* [169]1 Apr, LGBO 61646. [170]22 Mar, *Lond Gaz.* [171]5 Feb, *Lond Gaz.* [172]9 Nov, 5 Edw VII, *c* cvii. [173]1 Apr, LGBO 63385. [174]5 Sept, *Lond Gaz.* [175]7 Nov, *Lond Gaz.* [176]26 Jan, *Lond Gaz.* [177]1 Apr, 21 & 22 Geo V, *c* ciii. [178]1 Apr, 15 & 16 Geo VI & 1 Eliz II, *c* xlix. [179]7 May, SI 1953/741. [180]24 Apr, *Lond Gaz.* [181]12 Apr, *Lond Gaz.* [182]1 Nov (*Lond Gaz* 30 Oct). [183]2 Apr, *Lond Gaz.* [184]10 July, *Lond Gaz.* [185]15 May, *Lond Gaz.* [186]9 July, *Lond Gaz.* [187]Year Bolam with Heighington united benefice effective (date kindly supplied by Durham RO). [188]6 May, *Lond Gaz.* [189]Year new incumbent Middleton St George (information kindly supplied by Durham RO). [190]OC 4 Feb, reported in *Parl Papers* 1872, XLVI, 21. [191]28 May, *Lond Gaz.* [192]17 Oct, lic min (*Lond Gaz*, 29 July). [193]1 Apr, SI 1955/413. [194]1 Jan, 20 Vict, *c* 19. [195]*VCH Durham* III, 189. [196]10 Sept, *Lond Gaz.* [197]Robert Surtees, *The History and Antiquities of the County Palatine of Durham* (1840), IV, 81–82. [198]31 July, *Lond Gaz.* [199]No institutions to Durham St Mary the Less after 1578. [200]31 Jan, *Lond Gaz.* [201]Fordyce I, 415. [202]Fordyce I, 417. [203]13 Jan, *Lond Gaz.* [204]20 May, *Lond Gaz.* [205]1 Apr, LGBO 63059. [206]1 Apr, MHousLGO 5934. [207]9 May, *Lond*

Gaz. [208]18 Feb 1957, lic min (*Lond Gaz* 21 Dec 1956). [209]22 Sept, *Lond Gaz.* [210]19 June, *Lond Gaz.* [211]25 Mar, LGBO 17127. [212]1 Oct, LGBO 34610. [213]1 Apr, MHealthO 104812. [214]11 Nov, *Lond Gaz.* [215]5 Aug, *Lond Gaz.* [216]12 June, *Lond Gaz.* [217]4 Jan, *Lond Gaz.* [218]3 Apr, *Lond Gaz.* [219]*VCH Durham* III, 235. [220]9 Nov, 3 & 4 Geo V, *c* cxliii. [221]1 Oct, SI 1951/1184. [222]25 Mar, LGBO 19070. [223]3 Oct, *Lond Gaz.* [224]1 Apr, MHealthO 104817. [225]18 Sept, *Lond Gaz.* [226]25 Mar, LGBO 19071. [227]Apptd day, LGBO 31654. [228]Apptd day, LGBO 32175. [229]OC 31 Mar, reported in *Parl Papers* 1872, LXVI, 21. [230]1 Apr, 25 & 26 Geo V, *c* cxxxv. [231]1 Apr, SI 1967/66. [232]17 Mar, SI 1952/453. [233]29 June, *Lond Gaz.* [234]26 June, reported in *Parl Papers* 1890—91, LXI, 57. [235]11 May, *Lond Gaz.* [236]24 Mar, LGBO 20308. [237]*VCH Durham* III, 204. [238]1 Apr, LGBO 50062. [239]1 Apr, 22 & 23 Geo V, *c* lxxviii. [240]1 Apr, 1 & 2 Eliz II, *c* xxvii. [241]Fordyce II, 788. [242]30 Aug, *Lond Gaz.* [243]31 May, *Lond Gaz.* [244]19 May, *Lond Gaz.* [245]15 Dec, *Lond Gaz.* [246]4 Feb, *Lond Gaz.* [247]Date not found; 1973 is date of team ministry in which incl (informed kindly supplied by Durham RO); the order in *Lond Gaz* 27 Oct 1972. [248]12 Aug, *Lond Gaz.* [249]14 Aug, *Lond Gaz.* [250]10 Mar, *Lond Gaz.* [251]1 Apr, MHealthO 104818. [252]1 Oct, LGBO 35002. [253]20 Dec, LGBO 13145. [254]1 Oct, LGBO 47853. [255]9 Nov, LGBProvO 1361. [256]8 Feb, *Lond Gaz.* [257]9 Nov, *Lond Gaz.* [258]22 Oct, *Lond Gaz.* [259]1 Jan, *Lond Gaz.* [260]Statute 12 Anne, cited in *VCH Durham* III, 364. [261]26 Apr, *Lond Gaz.* [262]7 Jan, *Lond Gaz.* [263]9 Nov, LGBProvO 1354. [264]1 Apr, LGBO 66963. [265]18 Jan, *Lond Gaz.* [266]13 Aug, *Lond Gaz.* [267]29 Mar, *Lond Gaz.* [268]24 Mar, *Lond Gaz.* [269]2 July, *Lond Gaz.* [270]OC 30 June, reported in *Parl Papers* 1872, XLVI, 18. [271]17 Aug, *Lond Gaz.* [272]OC 27 Aug, reported in *Parl Papers* 1872, XLVI, 21. [273]20 Feb, *Lond Gaz.* [274]1 Dec, *Lond Gaz.* [275]8 Apr, *Lond Gaz.* [276]1 Apr, LGBO 61380. [277]1 Oct, MHealthO 67119. [278]28 Oct, *Lond Gaz.* [279]30 Jan, *Lond Gaz.* [280]24 Mar, LGBO 16364. [281]21 Dec, LGBO 13195. [282]25 Nov, *Lond Gaz.* [283]30 Mar, *Lond Gaz.* [284]1 Apr, MHealthO 104864. [285]1 Apr, 14 Geo V, *c* liv. [286]25 Mar, LGBO 18972. [287]4 Dec, *Lond Gaz.* [288]15 Feb, *Lond Gaz.* [289]23 May, *Lond Gaz.* [290]1 Apr, MHealthO 106135. [291]10 Jan, *Lond Gaz.* [292]OC 27 Feb, reported in *Parl Papers* 1872, XLVI, 19. [293]25 Feb, *Lond Gaz.* [294]6 Nov, *Lond Gaz.* [295]OC 27 Aug, reported in *Parl Papers* 1872, XLVI, 21. [296]23 June, *Lond Gaz.* [297]12 Jan, *Lond Gaz.* [298]1 Nov (*Lond Gaz* 3 Oct). [299]OC 27 Aug, reported in *Parl Papers* 1872, XLVI, 21. [300]14 Oct, *Lond Gaz.* [301]OC 1 Aug, reported in *Parl Papers* 1897, LXVII, Pt VI, 174. [302]15 June, LGBO 32272. [303]31 Mar, LGBO 39484. [304]11 Aug, *Lond Gaz.* [305]1 Apr, LGBO 56678. [306]Apptd day, LGBO 13172, 13176. [307]24 Dec, *Lond Gaz.* [308]5 Dec, *Lond Gaz.* [309]9 Nov, LGBProvO 1074. [311]16 May, *Lond Gaz.* [312]26 Nov, *Lond Gaz.* [313]19 Aug, *Lond Gaz.* [314]28 Feb, *Lond Gaz.* [315]1 June, *Lond Gaz.* [316]15 June, LGBO 32272. [317]1 Oct, LGBO 64332. [318]1 Apr, MHealthO 104826. [319]24 Mar, LGBO 16615. [320]24 Mar, LGBO 20697. [321]24 Mar, LGBO 20698. [322]8 Jan, *Lond Gaz.* [323]17 July, *Lond Gaz.* [324]Year lic min (*Lond Gaz* 31 July). [325]25 Mar, LGBO 17125. [326]OC 10 Nov, reported in *Parl Papers* 1872, XLVI, 22. [327]21 Dec, LGBO 13175. [328]25 Mar, LGBO 17126. [329]25 Mar, LGBO 17125, 17126. [330]8 Aug, *Lond*

Gaz. [331]28 Oct, *Lond Gaz.* [332]19 July, *Lond Gaz.* [333]4 Jan, 1843, *Lond Gaz.* [334]30 Mar, LGBO 36023. [335]1 Apr, SI 1951/326. [336]17 Aug, *Lond Gaz.* [337]16 Apr, *Lond Gaz.* [338]11 Feb, *Lond Gaz.* [339]4 Sept, *Lond Gaz.* [340]12 Mar, *Lond Gaz.* [341]28 Mar, *Lond Gaz.* [342]20 Oct, *Lond Gaz.* [343]21 Dec, LGBO 13173, 13176, 13177. [344]24 Mar, LGBO 20699. [345]30 Sept, LGBProvO 1088. [346]29 Dec, *Lond Gaz.* [347]OC 4 Feb, reported in *Parl Papers* 1890—91, LXI, 53. [348]57 & 58 Vict, *c* 58. [349]22 Feb, *Lond Gaz.* [350]5 Nov, *Lond Gaz.* [351]21 Dec, LGBO 13176, 13177. [353]1 Apr, MHealthO 104820.

HEREFORDSHIRE

[1]29 Mar, *Lond Gaz.* [2]30 Sept, 60 & 61 Vict, *c* lxxv. [3]29 & 30 Vict, *c* 113. [4]Not orig rated in schedule of pars in the PLU, incl soon thereafter. [5]25 Mar, 45 & 46 Vict, *c* 58. [6]24 Mar, LGBO 20078. [7]OC 18 Mar, reported in *Parl Papers* 1890—91, LXI, 54. [8]24 Mar, LGBO 16128. [9]25 Mar, LGBO 16127. [10]25 Mar, LGBO 16129. [11]1 Apr, SI 1965/223. [12]24 Mar, LGBO 16001. [13]24 Mar, LGBO 16006. [14]OC 29 June, reported in *Parl Papers* 1890—91, LXI, 56. [15]2 Nov, *Lond Gaz.* [16]14 July, *Lond Gaz.* [17]John Duncomb, *Collections towards the History and Antiquities of the County of Hereford* (7 vols, completed by others, 1804), IV, 16 (hereafter, 'Duncomb'). [18]PC augmented by Commissioners of QAB. [19]24 Dec, *Lond Gaz.* [20]Duncomb V, 60. [21]24 Mar, LGBO 16140. [22]Year vac (*Lond Gaz*, 2 Nov 1928). [23]Duncomb V, 73. [24]24 Mar, LGBO 15956. [25]14 Feb, *Lond Gaz.* [26]29 Aug, Part Dist, reported in *Parl Papers* 1870, LXIV, 162. [27]24 Mar, LGBO 16008. [28]Per statutory authority, cited in Duncomb II, 332. [29]24 Mar, LGBO 16111. [30]28 Oct, *Lond Gaz.* [31]30 Sept, LGBO 31670. [32]OC 5 Aug 1875. [33]Year vac (*Lond Gaz*, 8 Nov 1930). [34]22 Oct, *Lond Gaz.* [35]24 Mar, LGBO 16145. [36]24 Mar, LGBO 16561. [37]24 Mar, LGBO 16109. [38]Apptd day, LGBO 31669. [39]1 Apr, MHealthO 75349. [40]Duncomb IV, 6. [41]1 Mar (*Lond Gaz*, 11 Feb). [42]24 Mar, LGBO 16112. [43]29 Sept, LGBO 31685. [44]OC 30 July, reported in *Parl Papers* 1897, LXVII, Pt VI, 174. [45]24 Mar, LGBO 16002. [46]24 Mar, LGBO 16119. [47]24 Mar, LGBO 16004. [48]24 Mar, LGBO 16003. [49]Apptd day, LGBO 32084. [50]25 Mar, LGBO 16142. [51]24 Mar, LGBO 16141. [52]25 Mar, LGBO 17900. [53]29 Oct, *Lond Gaz.* [54]*Liber Regis* (1786), 336. [55]2 & 3 Wm IV, *c* 64 and 7 & 8 Vict, *c* 61. [56]24 Mar, LGBO 16144. [57]23 Dec, *Lond Gaz.* [58]23 Jan, Part Dist, reported in *Parl Papers* 1870, LXIV, 162. [59]5 July, *Lond Gaz.* [60]Authority and date not found, after 1898 and before 1923 (union appears in a sched of par changes in RDns at this time). [61]3 Nov, *Lond Gaz.* [62]Duncomb II, 108. [63]31 Mar, 59 & 60 Vict, *c* lxxii. [64]30 Sept, LGBProvO 1380, confirmed by 60 & 61 Vict, *c* lxxv. [65]1 Dec (*Lond Gaz*, 17 Nov). [66]1 Feb (*Lond Gaz*, 23 Jan). [67]OC 1 May, reported in *Parl Papers* 1872, XLVI, 19. [68]OC 30 Aug, reported in *Parl Papers* 1872, XLVI, 21. [69]1 Jan, 20 Vict, *c* 19. [70]24 Mar, LGBO 20077. [71]24 Mar, LGBO 16110. [72]8 Jan, *Lond Gaz.* [73]Authority not found. [74]24 Mar, LGBO 16590. [75]28 July, *Lond Gaz.* [76]*VCH Worcs* IV, 275. [77]3 Mar, *Lond Gaz.* [78]24 Mar, LGBO 16007. [79]56 & 57 Vict, *c* cxxxii. [80]Year vac (*Lond Gaz*, 12 Oct 1956). [81]OC 29 Nov, reported in *Parl Papers* 1890—91, LXI, 56. [82]Union

effective 1923; date of Gazetting not found. [83]14 Mar, *Lond Gaz.* [84]Year vac (*Lond Gaz*, 14 June 1940). [85]24 Mar, LGBO 16009. [86]11 May, *Lond Gaz.* [87]28 Feb, *Lond Gaz.* [88]24 Mar, LGBO 16005. [89]30 Oct, *Lond Gaz.* [90]OC 11 Dec 1845. [91]24 Mar, LGBO 20075. [92]56 & 57 Vict, *c* cxxxii. [93]30 Sept, LGBO 33557. [94]13 Mar, *Lond Gaz.* [95]24 Mar, LGBO 16147. [96]1 Oct, MHealthO 76635. [97]OC 13 July, reported in *Parl Papers* 1872, XLVI, 19. [98]24 Mar, LGBO 16146. [99]14 Jan, *Lond Gaz.* [100]16 Mar, Part Dist, reported in *Parl Papers* 1870, LXIV, 162. [101]Authority for union not found. [102]24 Mar, LGBO 14591. [103]24 Mar, LGBO 21627. [104]1 Jan, Part Dist, reported in *Parl Papers* 1870, LXIV, 162. [105]24 Mar, LGBO 16149. [106]57 & 58 Vict, *c* 58 and Co Council Naming O. [107]25 Mar, LGBO 18747. [108]Authority not found. [109]25 Mar, LGBO 14593. [110]25 Mar, LGBO 14594. [111]Apptd day, LGBO 31650. [112]Apptd day, LGBO 31450. [113]25 Mar, Part Dist, reported in *Parl Papers* 1870, LXIV, 162. [114]1 Apr, SI 1967/1940. [115]9 Nov, *Lond Gaz.* [116]26 Mar, Part Dist, Instr. [117]OC 17 May, reported in *Parl Papers* 1890—91, LXI, 154. [118]25 Mar, LGBO 14632. [119]1 Aug, *Lond Gaz.* [120]24 Mar, LGBO 20079. [121]24 Mar, LGBO 16131. [122]24 Mar, LGBO 20076. [123]Duncomb V, 105. [124]24 Mar, LGBO 16130. [125]11 Dec, vac (*Lond Gaz*, 6 Nov). [126]OC 27 Aug, reported in *Parl Papers* 1872, XLVI, 20. [127]51 & 52 Vict, *c* 41. [128]1 Oct, LGBO 48235. [129]OC 3 Apr, reported in *Parl Papers* 1872, XLVI, 18. [130]OC 11 Aug, reported in *Parl Papers* 1872, XLVI, 7. [131]24 Mar, LGBO 14523. [132]24 Mar, LGBO 15515. [133]1 May (*Lond Gaz*, 16 Apr). [134]25 Mar, LGBO 14592.

LANCASHIRE

[1]3 Feb, *Lond Gaz.* [2]13 June, *Lond Gaz.* [3]26 Apr, *Lond Gaz.* [4]29 & 30 Vict, *c* 113. [5]1 Aug, *Lond Gaz.* [6]14 June, *Lond Gaz.* [7]27 Aug, MHousLG Decl. [8]2 July, *Lond Gaz.* [9]18 July, *Lond Gaz.* [10]15 Dec, *Lond Gaz.* [11]14 Jan, *Lond Gaz.* [12]PC augmented by Commissioners of QAB. [13]20 May, *Lond Gaz.* [14]6 May, LGBProvO 7930, confirmed by 41 & 42 Vict, *c* civ. [15]1 Apr, 18 & 19 Geo V, *c* xcv. [16]28 Mar, *Lond Gaz.* [17]14 Feb, *Lond Gaz.* [18]8 Oct, *Lond Gaz.* [19]8 May, *Lond Gaz.* [20]22 Jan, *Lond Gaz.* [21]27 June, *Lond Gaz.* [22]19 July, *Lond Gaz.* [23]16 Aug, *Lond Gaz.* [24]15 May, *Lond Gaz.* [25]22 Sept, lic min (*Lond Gaz* 15 May). [26]27 Aug, *Lond Gaz.* [27]6 Mar, *Lond Gaz.* [28]1 July 1875, Instr Eccl Commissioners and Bp Chester, Part Dist. [29]24 Jan, *Lond Gaz.* [30]25 Feb, *Lond Gaz.* [31]25 Mar, 45 & 46 Vict, *c* 58. [32]Apptd day, LGBO 31626. [33]6 July, *Lond Gaz.* [34]1 Apr, MHealthO 69796. [35]21 May, *Lond Gaz.* [36]30 Sept, 61 & 62 Vict, *c* ccxlii. [37]1 Oct, MHealthO 77457. [39]1 Apr, 14 Geo VI, *c* lxiii. [40]1 Apr, 20 & 21 Eliz II, *c* 70. [41]26 Feb, *Lond Gaz.* [42]14 Sept, *Lond Gaz.* [43]1 Apr, MHealthO 80451. [44]13 May, *Lond Gaz.* [45]Apptd day, LGBO 31625. [46]9 Nov 1876, Instr Bp, Part Dist. [47]1 Apr, 11 & 12 Geo V, *c* lxxiv. [48]31 July, *Lond Gaz.* [49]28 July, *Lond Gaz.* [50]13 Mar, *Lond Gaz.* [51]24 Mar, LGBO 16388. [52]24 Mar, LGBO 16390. [53]24 Mar, LGBO 16391. [54]24 Mar, LGBO 16392. [55]24 Mar, LGBO 16394. [56]24 Mar, LGBO 16395. [57]24 Mar, LGBO 16393. [58]Apptd day, LGBO 31644. [59]1 Apr, LGBO 61474. [60]1 Apr, MHealthO 71713. [61]20 May, MHealthO 109121. [62]8 Feb, *Lond Gaz.* [63]Apptd day, LGBO 32237.

[64]1 Apr, 14 Geo VI, *c* lv. [65]1 Apr, SI 1955/16. [66]18 July, SI 1951/1236. [67]*VCH Lancs* III, 225—26. [68]31 Oct, reported in *Parl Papers* 1870, LXIV, 159. [69]31 Aug, *Lond Gaz.* [70]13 Aug, *Lond Gaz.* [71]7 Feb, *Lond Gaz.* [72]5 Aug, *Lond Gaz.* [73]24 June, *Lond Gaz.* [74]29 Mar 1839, *Lond Gaz* (OC 14 Sept 1838). [75]4 July, *Lond Gaz.* [76]Year vac (*Lond Gaz* 11 May 1928). [77]Year vac (*Lond Gaz* 9 Feb 1937). [78]22 Aug, *Lond Gaz.* [79]7 Aug, *Lond Gaz.* [80]1 Jan, 20 Vict, *c* 19. [81]*VCH Lancs* IV, 280. [82]26 May, LGBO 33847. [83]1 July, *Lond Gaz.* [84]27 July, *Lond Gaz.* [85]14 May, *Lond Gaz.* [86]6 Dec, *Lond Gaz.* [87]9 July, *Lond Gaz.* [88]17 Dec, *Lond Gaz.* [89]12 Oct, *Lond Gaz.* [90]25 July, *Lond Gaz.* [91]15 Sept, *Lond Gaz.* [92]8 & 9 Vict, *c* ix. [93]*VCH Lancs* IV, 147. [94]30 Aug, *Lond Gaz.* [95]25 Aug, *Lond Gaz.* [96]2 Apr, *Lond Gaz.* [97]Apptd day, LGBO 32236. [98]Apptd day, LGBO 32242. [99]9 Nov, LGBProvO 1416. [100]1 Apr, 16 & 17 Geo V, *c* lxi. [101]19 Jan, SI 1955/16. [102]30 Oct, *Lond Gaz.* [103]12 Apr, *Lond Gaz.* [104]19 May, *Lond Gaz.* [105]17 Apr, *Lond Gaz.* [106]Reported in *Parl Papers* 1870, LXIV, 159. [107]14 July, *Lond Gaz.* [108]30 July, *Lond Gaz.* [109]12 June, *Lond Gaz.* [110]21 Mar, *Lond Gaz.* [111]3 June, *Lond Gaz.* [112]14 Oct, *Lond Gaz.* [113]4 Aug, *Lond Gaz.* [114]1 Apr (*Lond Gaz* 3 Mar). [115]Apptd day, LGBO 31671. [116]3 Apr, *Lond Gaz.* [117]24 Apr, *Lond Gaz.* [118]5 June, *Lond Gaz.* [119]10 Jan, *Lond Gaz.* [120]Apptd day, LGBO 31690. [121]23 Jan, *Lond Gaz.* [122]29 Sept, LGBO 31736. [123]11 July, *Lond Gaz.* [124]3 Sept, *Lond Gaz.* [125]30 Nov, *Lond Gaz.* [126]1 Apr, MHealthO 75239. [127]10 Aug, MHousLG Decl. [128]5 Mar, *Lond Gaz.* [129]Apptd day, LGBO 32291. [130]Registers from 1564, Baines, *History of Lancashire* II, 46; hereafter, 'Baines'. [131]17 June, *Lond Gaz.* [132]6 Feb, *Lond Gaz.* [133]20 Sept, *Lond Gaz.* [134]2 Oct, *Lond Gaz.* [135]23 Dec, *Lond Gaz.* [136]12 Mar, lic min (*Lond Gaz* 28 Feb). [137]19 Jan, *Lond Gaz.* [138]Year lic min (*Lond Gaz* 29 Jan). [139]10 Aug, *Lond Gaz.* [140]8 Mar, *Lond Gaz.* [141]18 Apr, *Lond Gaz.* [142]3 Aug, Instr, Part Dist. [143]2 Mar, *Lond Gaz.* [144]3 Dec, *Lond Gaz.* [145]21 Jan, lic min (*Lond Gaz* 25 Dec 1964). [146]26 May, *Lond Gaz.* [147]10 Feb, *Lond Gaz.* [148]Year lic min (*Lond Gaz* 24 Sept 1955). [149]16 May, *Lond Gaz.* [150]29 Oct, *Lond Gaz.* [151]3 Mar, *Lond Gaz.* [152]1 Feb, *Lond Gaz.* [153]19 Dec, *Lond Gaz.* [154]4 Mar, *Lond Gaz.* [155]24 Mar, LGBO 20097. [156]Not sep rated in PLU as late as 1851 (rated with Dalton in Furness); incl in PLU soon thereafter as sep rated. [157]15 Oct, *Lond Gaz.* [158]1 May, LGBO 7880. [159]23 Aug, *Lond Gaz.* [160]21 Dec, *Lond Gaz.* [161]2 Feb, *Lond Gaz.* [162]9 Feb, *Lond Gaz.* [163]1 Apr, lic min (*Lond Gaz* 31 Mar). [164]Apptd day, LGBO 31617. [165]*VCH Lancs* VII, 123. [166]OC 10 Oct, reported in *Parl Papers* 1870, LXIV, 159. [167]Apptd day, LGBO 32199. [168]26 June, *Lond Gaz.* [169]Apptd day, LGBO 31687. [170]30 Sept, LGBO 34989. [171]1 Apr, MHealthO 77201. [172]1 Mar, *Lond Gaz.* [173]1 June, 54 & 55 Vict, *c* ccxxi. [174]Apptd day, LGBO 31667. [175]Apptd day, LGBO 31688. [176]9 Nov, LGBProvO 1639, confirmed by 63 & 64 Vict, *c* cclxxviii. [177]30 Jan, *Lond Gaz.* [178]29 Sept, *Lond Gaz.* [179]1 July (*Lond Gaz* 29 June). [180]1 & 2 Geo IV, *c* 103. [181]22 Nov, *Lond Gaz.* [182]5 May, *Lond Gaz.* [183]6 Aug, *Lond Gaz.* [184]1 Apr, MHealthO 69462. [185]5 Sept, *Lond Gaz.* [186]12 Dec, *Lond Gaz.* [187]Liverpool and Wigan Churches Act, 1904 (local act, citation by regnal year and chapter not found). [188]Year vac (*Lond Gaz* 1 Feb 1929). [189]*VCH Lancs* VII, 218. [190]8

[191]Dec, *Lond Gaz.* [191]1 Apr, MHealthO 68872. [192] *VCH Lancs* IV, 96. [193]14 Nov, *Lond Gaz.* [194]11 Feb, *Lond Gaz.* [195]12 May, *Lond Gaz.* [196]16 Oct, *Lond Gaz.* [197]20 Oct, lic min (*Lond Gaz* 16 Oct). [198]*VCH Lancs* IV, 308. [199]16 June, *Lond Gaz.* [200]28 June, *Lond Gaz.* [201]20 Aug, *Lond Gaz.* [202]14 Aug, *Lond Gaz.* [203]9 May, *Lond Gaz.* [204]8 Nov, *Lond Gaz.* [205]11 Oct, *Lond Gaz.* [206]28 Apr, *Lond Gaz.* [207]1 Apr, 1 & 2 Geo V, *c* clxxxv. [208]13 Dec, *Lond Gaz.* [209]15 Apr, *Lond Gaz.* [210]*VCH Lancs* VII, 244. [211]Reported in *Parl Papers* 1870, LXIV, 159. [212]22 Dec, *Lond Gaz.* [213]4 Apr, *Lond Gaz.* [214]4 Apr, *Lond Gaz.* [215]24 Nov, LGBO 6910. [216]25 Mar, LGBO 14712. [217]Apptd day, LGBO 31813. [218]1 Apr, 7 & 8 Geo V, *c* lii. [219]Reported in *Parl Papers* 1870, LXIV, 159. [220]Baines, II, 92. [221]18 Dec, *Lond Gaz.* [222]8 July, *Lond Gaz.* [223]25 Mar, 55 & 56 Vict, *c* cxviii. [224]9 Nov, 1 Edw VII, *c* ccxxiii. [225]1 Oct, 12 & 13 Geo V, *c* xx. [226]1 Apr, MHealthO 78129. [227]3 July, *Lond Gaz.* [228]18 Oct, *Lond Gaz.* [229]Year vac (*Lond Gaz* 15 Apr 1955). [230]7 Mar, *Lond Gaz.* [231]28 Nov, *Lond Gaz.* [232]11 Aug, *Lond Gaz.* [233]16 Feb, *Lond Gaz.* [234]22 Apr, *Lond Gaz.* [235]11 Mar, *Lond Gaz.* [236]19 Feb, *Lond Gaz.* [237]13 July, *Lond Gaz.* [238]4 Dec, *Lond Gaz.* [239]7 May, *Lond Gaz.* [240]1 Dec (*Lond Gaz* 17 Nov). [241]29 Mar, *Lond Gaz.* [242]7 Nov, *Lond Gaz.* [243]29 July, *Lond Gaz.* [244]29 June, *Lond Gaz.* [245]25 Mar, *Lond Gaz.* [246]27 Apr, LGBO 36320. [247]1 Apr, SI 1955/415. [248]15 June, SI 1956/818. [249]15 Nov, *Lond Gaz.* [250]9 Mar, *Lond Gaz.* [251]23 Mar, *Lond Gaz.* [252]Year lic min (*Lond Gaz* 24 Sept). [253]26 Nov, lic min (*Lond Gaz* 12 Oct). [254]10 Mar, *Lond Gaz.* [255]26 Nov, lic min (*Lond Gaz* 12 Oct). [256]2 Aug, *Lond Gaz.* [257]Apptd day, LGBO 31646. [258]6 June, *Lond Gaz.* [259]16 Apr, *Lond Gaz.* [260]1 Jan (*Lond Gaz.* 22 Dec 1970). [261]*VCH Lancs* III, 389–92. [262]12 July, *Lond Gaz.* [263]30 Sept, LGBO 33407. [264]28 May, *Lond Gaz.* [265]28 Feb, *Lond Gaz.* [266]12 Nov, *Lond Gaz.* [267]25 Mar, LGBO 17905. [268]10 Apr, *Lond Gaz.* [269]20 Dec, *Lond Gaz.* [270]17 Nov, *Lond Gaz.* [271]Baines, I, 554. [272]11 May, *Lond Gaz.* [273]31 Mar, *Lond Gaz.* [274]13 Apr, *Lond Gaz.* [275]1 Feb (*Lond Gaz* 23 Jan). [276]25 Oct, *Lond Gaz.* [277]1 Mar (*Lond Gaz* 10 Feb). [278]1 Nov (*Lond Gaz* 29 Oct). [279]23 Apr, *Lond Gaz.* [280]31 Oct, *Lond Gaz.* [281]22 Feb, *Lond Gaz.* [282]24 Mar, LGBO 19997. [283]17 Mar, *Lond Gaz.* [284]OC 6 Oct, reported in *Parl Papers* 1872, XLVI, 19. [285]Year vac (LG 24 May 1957). [286]16 Jan, *Lond Gaz.* [287]20 Feb, *Lond Gaz.* [288]18 Jan 1840, Instr Bp Chester, Part Dist, and OC reported in *Lond Gaz* 5 Sept 1862. [289]1 June (*Lond Gaz* 30 May). [290]21 Sept, Instr, Part Dist. [291]Orig rated in Preston PLU, incl in Chorley PLU before 1851; exact date of transfer not found. [292]20 Aug, Instr, Part Dist. [293]3 Jan, *Lond Gaz.* [294]6 Oct, *Lond Gaz.* [295]Apptd day, LGBO 31666. [296]15 July, *Lond Gaz.* [297]6 May, *Lond Gaz.* [298]9 Nov, LGBProvO 1365, confirmed by 60 & 61 Vict, *c* cxlii. [299]1 Nov (*Lond Gaz* 28 Oct). [300]1 Apr, *Lond Gaz.* [301]7 June, *Lond Gaz.* [302]5 Apr, *Lond Gaz.* [303]*VCH Lancs* VII, 280. [304]5 Feb, *Lond Gaz.* [305]31 Jan, *Lond Gaz.* [306]Authority not found; date cited in census reports. [307]1 Apr, 25 & 26 Geo V, *c* v. [308]9 Nov, 1 & 2 Geo V, *c* cxliv. [309]9 Nov, LGBProvO 1586. [310]1 Oct, LGBO 55101. [311]1 Apr, 15 & 16 Geo V, *c* xcii. [312]16 Jan 1846, *Lond Gaz* (OC 23 Dec 1845). [313]9 Dec, *Lond Gaz.* [314]19 Aug, *Lond Gaz.* [315]27 Feb, *Lond Gaz.* [316]12 Mar, *Lond Gaz.* [317]28 Aug, *Lond Gaz.* [318]Year vac (*Lond Gaz* 29 Sept 1969).

[319]7 July, *Lond Gaz.* [320]30 May, lic min (*Lond Gaz* 22 May). [321]22 July, *Lond Gaz.* [322]3 Aug, *Lond Gaz.* [323]12 Aug, *Lond Gaz.* [324]1 Apr, 22 & 23 Geo V, *c* lxxxviii. [325]8 Jan, *Lond Gaz* (OC 18 Dec 1936). [326]23 Feb 1844, *Lond Gaz* (OC 13 Dec 1843). [327]20 Nov, *Lond Gaz.* [328]26 Aug, *Lond Gaz.* [329]9 Nov, 1 & 2 Geo V, *c* cxliv. [330]1 Apr, 22 & 23 Geo V, *c* lxix. [331]1 Apr, MHealthO 87428. [332]25 Jan, *Lond Gaz.* [333]14 Mar, reported in *Parl Papers* 1870, LXIV, 159. [334]30 June, *Lond Gaz.* [335]31 Dec, *Lond Gaz.* [336]26 Mar, *Lond Gaz.* [337]27 Sept, *Lond Gaz.* [338]1 Apr, *Lond Gaz.* [339]15 Mar, SI 1945/701. [340]5 Dec, *Lond Gaz.* [341]24 Mar, LGBO 16389. [342]13 Jan, *Lond Gaz.* [343]Apptd day, LGBO 32287. [344]25 Nov, *Lond Gaz.* [345]5 Nov, O Lancs Co Council. [346]22 Mar, *Lond Gaz.* [347]4 Feb, *Lond Gaz.* [348]22 Oct, *Lond Gaz.* [349]31 May, *Lond Gaz.* [350]20 Mar, *Lond Gaz.* [351]1 Apr (*Lond Gaz* 28 Mar). [352]1 Aug (*Lond Gaz* 20 July). [353]*VCH Lancs* IV, 262. [354]19 June, *Lond Gaz.* [355]2 Sept, *Lond Gaz.* [356]19 Oct, *Lond Gaz.* [357]20 Oct, *Lond Gaz.* [358]27 May, *Lond Gaz.* [359]*VCH Lancs* II, 127-28. [360]29 Aug, *Lond Gaz.* [361]*VCH Lancs* VII, 23. [362]33 Geo III, *c* 24. [363]1 Apr, MHealthO 76291. [364]18 May, *Lond Gaz.* [365]2 Dec, *Lond Gaz.* [366]12 Sept, *Lond Gaz.* [367]29 Mar, *Lond Gaz.* [368]22 May, *Lond Gaz.* [369]26 Jan, *Lond Gaz.* [370]1 July (*Lond Gaz* 25 June). [371]21 July, *Lond Gaz.* [372]23 Sept, *Lond Gaz.* [373]Apptd day, LGBO 32236. [374]1 Mar (*Lond Gaz* 6 Feb). [375]24 Mar, LGBO 20100. [376]1 Mar (*Lond Gaz* 12 Feb). [377]Part Dist, cited *VCH Lancs* VII, 165. [378]9 Nov, LGBProvO 1079. [379]17 Jan, *Lond Gaz.* [380]Baines, II, 19. [381]13 Feb, *Lond Gaz.* [382]Apptd day, LGBO 31992. [383]1 Apr, LGBO 61428. [384]4 May, *Lond Gaz.* [385]24 Mar, LGBO 20099. [386]17 Oct, *Lond Gaz.* [387]1 Dec, *Lond Gaz.* [388]9 Sept, vac (*Lond Gaz* 28 July). [389]26 Mar, LGBO 30592. [390]28 Mar, LGBO 30724. [391]8 Aug, *Lond Gaz.* [392]*VCH Lancs* VII, 370–74. [393]*VCH Lancs* VIII, 383–86. [394]1 Apr, MHealthO 71518. [395]23 July, *Lond Gaz.* [396]Apptd day, LGBO 32059. [397]23 Jan, *Lond Gaz.* [398]OC 15 Jan, reported in *Parl Papers* 1872, XLVI, 19. [399]3 Dec, *Lond Gaz*, on authority of 4 & 5 Vict, *c* 9. [400]4 Vict, *c* 9. [401]17 Dec, LGBO 7401. [402]Apptd day, LGBO 31614. [403]1 Apr, MHealthO 76293. [404]1 Apr, 4 & 5 Eliz II, *c* xxxii. [405]30 Mar, SI 1960/463. [406]26 Oct, *Lond Gaz.* [407]1 Apr, LGBO 55543. [408]1 Apr, LGBO 61822. [409]16 Chas I, *c* 6 (private act). [410]1 Apr, 17 & 18 Geo V, *c* lxxxviii. [411]1 Apr, MHealthO 89198. [412]1 Apr, 23 & 24 Geo V, *c* vii. [413]30 Sept, 58 & 59 Vict, *c* lxxxix. [414]1 Apr, MHousLGO 34441. [415]Apptd day, LGBO 31674; see also 30 Sept 1895, LGBO 33324. [416]27 Jan, *Lond Gaz.* [417]20 Sept, lic min (*Lond Gaz* 3 Aug). [418]23 Jan, lic min (*Lond Gaz* 21 Dec 1967). [419]*VCH Lancs* V, 3. [420]10 Jan 1854, *Lond Gaz* (OC 29 Dec 1853). [421]13 Jan 1829, *Lond Gaz* (OC 23 July 1828). [422]*VCH Lancs* IV, 319. [423]Apptd day, LGBO 31624. [424]6 & 7 Vict, *c* 16. [425]9 Nov, LGBProvO 1147. [426]24 Mar, *Lond Gaz.* [427]10 Dec 1863, Instr Eccl Commissioners and Bp Chester, Part Dist. [428]3 Aug, reported in *Parl Papers* 1870, LXIV, 159. [429]27 Oct, *Lond Gaz.* [430]*VCH Lancs* IV, 19. [431]23 Nov, *Lond Gaz.* [432]*VCH Lancs* IV, 18. [433]4 Nov, *Lond Gaz.* [434]Year lic min (*Lond Gaz* 12 Oct 1951). [435]1 Apr (*Lond Gaz* 30 Mar). [436]24 Nov, *Lond Gaz.* [437]19 Mar, *Lond Gaz.* [438]17 Dec, LGBO 7402. [439]7 Jan, *Lond Gaz.* [440]24 Mar, LGBO 22623. [441]Apptd day, LGBO 32056. [442]23 May, *Lond Gaz.* [443]25 Mar, reported in *Parl*

Papers 1870, LXIV, 159. [444]Baines, I, 598. [445]25 May, *Lond Gaz*. [446]1 Jan, *Lond Gaz*. [447]1 Apr, SI 1960/2204. [448]11 Mar, SI 1964/275. [449]17 July, *Lond Gaz*. [450]Apptd day, LGBO 32172. [451]25 Mar, 56 & 57 Vict, *c* ccxv. [452]31 Mar, 61 & 62 Vict, *c* cclviii. [453]1 Apr, MHealthO 76292. [454]29 May, *Lond Gaz*. [455]Year consecr church (*Lond Gaz*, 7 Dec 1951). [456]12 July, lic min (*Lond Gaz*, 2 Dec 1960). [457]31 Mar, reported in *Parl Papers* 1870, LXIV, 159. [458]1 Mar (*Lond Gaz*, 12 Feb). [459]1 Apr, MHousLGO 9406. [460]25 June, LGBO 30905. [461]15 Aug, *Lond Gaz*. [462]17 Aug, *Lond Gaz*. [463]6 Sept, *Lond Gaz*. [464]*VCH Lancs* III, 21. [465]26 July, *Lond Gaz*. [466]13 Apr, reported in *Parl Papers* 1870, LXIV, 159. [467]7 Dec 1849, Instr Bp Chester, Part Dist. [468]Union 1948 presumed since one incumbent assumes the cure that year. [469]Year of union; information kindly supplied by Legal Officer, Liverp Dioc Registry. [470]6 Apr, *Lond Gaz*. [471]1 Dec (*Lond Gaz*. 13 Nov). [472]Privately erected 1849; authority not found. [473]25 Apr (information kindly supplied by Records Officer of the Church Commissioners). [474]5 Nov, *Lond Gaz*. [475]25 Dec, *Lond Gaz*. [476]8 Sept, *Lond Gaz*. [477]1 Apr (*Lond Gaz* 3 Mar). [478]29 Apr, *Lond Gaz*. [479]24 Mar, LGBO 20271. [480]3 Feb 1957 (*Lond Gaz*, 7 Dec 1956). [481]7 Dec, Instr Bp Manch, reported *Lond Gaz* 22 Dec. [482]Apptd day, LGBO 31607. [483]16 Oct, reported in *Parl Papers* 1870, LXIV, 159. [484]1 Apr, 9 & 10 Geo V, *c* lxxix. [485]9 Nov, 5 Edw VII, *c* cliv. [486]1 Apr, 2 & 3 Geo VI, *c* lxxxv. [487]1 Apr, MHousLGO 3969. [488]19 Jan, SI 1955/15. [489]26 Jan, reported in *Parl Papers* 1890—91, LXI, 53. [490]1 Apr, SI 1952/589. [491]17 Sept, *Lond Gaz*. [492]30 May, *Lond Gaz*. [493]13 Oct, *Lond Gaz*. [494]31 Oct, reported in *Parl Papers* 1870, LXIV, 159. [495]1 Apr, MHousLGO 40664. [496]31 Mar, LGBO 37367. [497]1 Apr, LGBO 45918. [498]OC 21 Jan, reported in *Parl Papers* 1872, XLVI, 18. [499]OC 21 Jan, reported in *Parl Papers* 1872, XLVI, 18. [500]9 Nov, LGBProvO 712 conf by 53 & 54 Vict, *c* ccxxviii. [501]Apptd day, LGBO 31635. [502]9 Nov, 1 Edw VII, *c* cxciii. [503]*VCH Lancs* VII, 113. [504]1 Apr, 14 & 15 Geo VI, *c* xlvi. [505]22 June, *Lond Gaz*. [506]12 Oct, lic min (*Lond Gaz* 4 Dec). [507]10 May, *Lond Gaz*. [508]OC 21 Jan, reported in *Parl Papers* 1872, XLVI, 18. [509]1 Apr, MHousLG Decl. [510]1 July (*Lond Gaz*, 30 June). [511]Apr 1864, Instr, Part Dist. [512]18 Sept, *Lond Gaz*. [513]13 Sept, *Lond Gaz*. [514]Apptd day, LGBO 32103. [515]*VCH Lancs* IV, 325. [516]Apptd day, LGBO 31812. [517]9 Nov, 3 & 4 Geo V, *c* cxxxi. [518]9 Nov, 3 & 4 Geo V, *c* xcii. [519]24 & 25 Geo V, *c* lvi. [520]20 Jan, lic min (*Lond Gaz* 24 Dec 1965). [521]Baines, II, 191. [522]17 Feb, *Lond Gaz*. [523]12 Jan, *Lond Gaz*. [524]3 May, *Lond Gaz*. [525]22 Oct, LGBO 7119. [526]21 Nov, *Lond Gaz*. [527]21 June 1836, *Lond Gaz* (OC 23 Mar 1831). [528]22 Sept, *Lond Gaz*. [529]27 Dec, Instr, Part Dist. [530]4 June, *Lond Gaz*. [531]5 Jan, *Lond Gaz*. [532]*VCH Lancs* II, 168. [533]9 Aug, *Lond Gaz*. [534]Year lic min (*Lond Gaz* 1 June 1951). [535]17 Dec, LGBO 7403. [536]30 Mar, SI 1960/463. [537]Orig rated in Warrington PLU, incl in Leigh PLU before 1851; exact date of transfer not found, perhaps at date par cr in 1845. [538]1 Apr, MHousLG Decl. [539]1 Apr, MHousLGO 7185. [540]1 Apr, MHousLGO 40409. [541]11 Jan, *Lond Gaz*. [542]1 Aug, *Lond Gaz*. [543]OC 21 Jan, reported in *Parl Papers* 1872, XLVI, 18. [544]OC 23 Oct, reported in *Parl Papers* 1872, XLVI, 19. [545]OC 21 Jan, reported in *Parl Papers* 1872, XLVI, 18. [546]OC 21 Jan, reported in *Parl Papers* 1872, XLVI, 18. [547]OC 6 Apr, reported in *Parl Papers* 1872, XLVI, 20. [548]10 July, reported in *Parl Papers* 1870, LXIV, 159. [549]Authority not found. [550]*VCH Lancs* VII, 255. [551]13 Feb, Instr Bp Chester, Part Dist. [552]2 Aug, *Lond Gaz*. [553]24 Oct, *Lond Gaz*. [554]13 Mar, *Lond Gaz*. [555]24 Mar, LGBO 14973. [556]Apptd day, LGBO 31665. [557]9 Nov, LGBProvO 1167. [558]30 Sept, LGBO 38100. [559]1 Apr, LGBO 61801. [560]1 Apr, SI 1956/370. [561]7 May, SI 1953/743. [562]30 Mar, SI 1960/461. [563]46 & 47 Vict, *c* cxv. [564]12 Feb, *Lond Gaz*. [565]28 Nov, Instr, Part Dist. [566]15 Jan, *Lond Gaz*. [567]28 Oct, *Lond Gaz*. [568]OC 29 Sept, reported in *Parl Papers* 1870, LXIV, 159. [569]26 June, Instr, Part Dist. [570]17 July, lic min (*Lond Gaz* 28 Oct 1960). [571]1 May 1916 (LG 3 May). [572]10 & 11 Wm III, *c* xxxvi. [573]25 June, *Lond Gaz*. [574]9 Jan, *Lond Gaz*. [575]7 Dec, *Lond Gaz*. [576]7 Dec, *Lond Gaz*. [577]18 Mar, Reorganisation Areas Measure (*ca* 1947, before the union when Liverpool St Alban Bevington abol). [578]1 Nov (*Lond Gaz* 2 Oct). [579]Church closed 6 May, information kindly supplied by Legal Officer, Liverp Dioc Registry. [580]Year vac (*Lond Gaz* 1 Feb 1929). [581]Information kindly supplied by Legal Officer, Liverp Dioc Registry. [582]1 Nov, vac (*Lond Gaz* 29 Oct). [583]Year vac (*Lond Gaz*, 14 June 1929). [584]Year vac (*Lond Gaz*, 10 May 1929). [585]26 Sept, *Lond Gaz*. [586]1 Apr, SI 1954/414. [587]12 Aug, LGBO 58265. [588]1 Apr, 13 & 14 Geo V, *c* lxxxvi. [589]16 Apr, Instr, Part Dist. [590]*VCH Lancs* IV, 215—16. [591]1 Apr, LGBO 63892. [592]1 Apr, 20 & 21 Geo V, *c* clxxiii. [593]7 Anne, *c* 6, cited in *VCH Lancs* IV, 246—47. [594]26 Geo II, *c* 45 cited in *VCH Lancs* IV, 248. [595]*VCH Lancs* IV, 248. [596]*VCH Lancs* IV, 248. [597]13 Aug, *Lond Gaz*. [598]6 Dec 1842, Part Dist. [599]9 Nov, 3 Edw VII, *c* ccxiii. [600]10 July, *Lond Gaz*. [601]Year vac (*Lond Gaz*, 26 Oct). [602]18 Mar, *Lond Gaz*. [603]Year vac (*Lond Gaz*, 10 May 1929). [604]16 Sept, *Lond Gaz*. [605]Year lic min (*Lond Gaz*, 19 Apr). [606]8 Feb 1842. [607]8 Feb, reported in *Parl Papers* 1870, LXIV, 159. [608]17 Dec, LGBO 7218. [609]18 Aug, *Lond Gaz*. [610]Apptd day, LGBO 31645. [611]9 Nov, 63 & 64 Vict, *c* lxvi. [612]27 Nov, MHealth Decl. [613]11 Dec, *Lond Gaz*. [614]9 Apr, *Lond Gaz*. [615]1 Aug, 14 & 15 Geo V, *c* lv. [616]1 Oct, 18 & 19 Geo V, *c* cxix. [617]1 Apr, MHousLGO 18596. [618]21 June, *Lond Gaz*. [619]Apptd day, LGBO 31874. [620]29 Dec, *Lond Gaz*. [621]8 Sept, LGBO 35027. [622]Year lic min (*Lond Gaz* 22 Feb). [623]1 Apr, SI 1968/527. [624]1 June (*Lond Gaz* 31 May). [625]11 Sept, *Lond Gaz*. [626]1 June (*Lond Gaz* 31 May). [627]1 June, MHealth Decl. [628]10 June, *Lond Gaz*. [629]Baines, I, 465. [630]16 Dec, *Lond Gaz*. [631]6 Jan, lic min (*Lond Gaz* 29 Nov 1963). [632]14 Dec, *Lond Gaz*. [633]30 Mar, *Lond Gaz*. [634]21 Sept, *Lond Gaz*. [635]4 Dec 1838, Instr Bp Chester, Part Dist. [636]1 Dec (*Lond Gaz* 6 Nov). [637]30 Sept, LGBO 35308. [638]13 Nov, *Lond Gaz*. [639]1 Apr, LGBO 65884. [640]1 May, *Lond Gaz*. [641]25 Mar, LGBO 14672. [642]Apptd day, LGBO 31961. [643]18 Nov, reported in *Parl Papers* 1870, LXIV, 159. [644]28 Dec, reported in *Parl Papers* 1872, XLVI, 19. [645]1 Oct, LGBO 61970. [646]31 & 32 Vict, *c* 46. [647]Authority not found; date cited in census records. [648]13 Dec 1838, Instr Bp Chester, Part Dist. [649]30 Nov, reported in *Parl Papers* 1870, LXIV, 159. [650]2 Jan, *Lond Gaz*. [651]1 May (*Lond Gaz*, 30 Apr). [652]25 Apr, *Lond Gaz*. [653]6 Jan, LGBO 33855. [654]5 July, *Lond Gaz*. [655]24 May, *Lond Gaz*. [656]15 Feb, *Lond Gaz*. [657]Not exempt from poor law rates but not orig rated sep in the PLU; exact date of sep rating not found, but before 1858 when ex-par places explicitly assigned to PLUs. [658]1 Apr, SI 1954/202. [659]Instr cited in *Eccl Commissioners Reports* XI, 500, also noting instr in 1842, 1846. [660]Part Dist, cited in *Eccl Commissioners Reports* 1870, XI, 501. [661]13 Dec (*Lond Gaz*, 4 May). [662]Apptd day, LGBO 31665. [663]24 Apr, lic min (*Lond Gaz* 3 Apr). [664]1 Sept (*Lond Gaz*, 7 Aug). [665]16 Mar, *Lond Gaz.* [666]1 Apr, LGBO 49299. [667]15 June, SI 1956/821. [668]1 Apr, *Lond Gaz.* [669]Year lic min (*Lond Gaz*, 26 Oct 1960). [670]11 Nov, Instr Bp Manch, reported *Lond Gaz*, 10 Dec. [671]Year vac (*Lond Gaz*, 9 Feb 1940). [672]*VCH Lancs* III, 43. [673]Year vac (*Lond Gaz*, 5 May 1929). [674]22 Feb, Instr, Part Dist. [675]1 June, reported in *Parl Papers* 1870, LXIV, 159. [676]1 May (*Lond Gaz*, 3 Apr). [677]24 Mar, LGBO 14976. [678]30 Sept, LGBO 38100. [679]1 Apr, SI 1954/319. [680]19 Jan, SI 1955/17. [681]1 Apr, LGBO 39579. [682]24 Feb, *Lond Gaz.* [683]1 Nov (*Lond Gaz*, 22 Oct). [685]25 Mar, LGBO 14975.

LEICESTERSHIRE

[1]29 & 30 Vict, *c* 113. [2]24 Mar, LGBO 16432. [3]1 Apr, MHealthO 84988. [4]Yr vac (*Lond Gaz*, 4 Aug 1931). [5]28 Mar, *Lond Gaz.* [6]Yr vac (*Lond Gaz*, 26 Apr 1927). [7]13 Apr, *Lond Gaz.* [8]24 Mar, LGBO 16574. [9]1 Apr, MHealthO 81175. [10]1 Apr, MHealthO 85391. [11]1 Apr, MHousLGO 3241. [12]1 Apr, SI 1966/78. [13]31 Jan, *Lond Gaz.* [14]1 Jan, 20 Vict, *c* 19. [15]51 & 52 Vict, *c* 41. [16]O Leics Co Council. [17]30 Sept, LGBO 38295. [18]1 Apr, SI 1965/24. [19]Yr vac (*Lond Gaz*, 7 Dec 1926). [20]15 Feb, *Lond Gaz.* [21]24 Mar, LGBO 15277. [22]57 & 58 Vict, *c* 58 and Co Council Naming O. [23]1 Apr, MHealthO 84292. [24]1 Apr, MHousLGO 5830. [25]PC augmented by Commissioners of QAB. [26]10 Mar, *Lond Gaz.* [27]6 July, *Lond Gaz.* [28]45 & 46 Vict, *c* 58. [29]26 Nov, LGBO 6887. [30]26 Nov, LGBO 6928. [31]26 Nov, LGBO 6929. [32]60 & 61 Vict, *c* cxxxix. [33]Not orig rated in the PLU, incl soon thereafter. [34]25 Mar, LGBO 18173. [35]30 June, *Lond Gaz.* [36]OC 11 Aug, reported in *Parl Papers* 1902, L, 595—96. [37]25 Mar, LGBO 17594. [38]1 Jan, 54 & 55 Vict, *c* c. [39]26 Mar, LGBO 32954. [40]OC 26 Aug, reported in *Parl Papers* 1890—91, LXI, 54. [41]Yr lic min (*Lond Gaz*, 7 Dec). [42]10 Apr, lic min (*Lond Gaz*, 16 Mar). [43]25 Mar, LGBO 18578. [44]16 May, *Lond Gaz.* [45]31 Dec, LGBO 31786. [46]1 Apr, MHousLGO 3843. [47]1 Apr, MHousLGO 41025. [48]19 Jan, SI 1955/18. [49]5 Jan, SI 1971/2108. [50]8 Mar, *Lond Gaz.* [51]26 Jan, *Lond Gaz.* [52]1 Mar, lic min (*Lond Gaz*, 26 Jan). [53]4 Feb, *Lond Gaz.* [54]1 Apr, LGBO 35403. [55]1 Oct, LGBO 61965. [56]Authority not found; year of cr noted in *Crockford's* (1947), 1565. [57]4 Aug, *Lond Gaz.* [58]24 Mar, LGBO 16572. [59]1 Oct, LGBO 34242. [60]14 Sept, *Lond Gaz.* [61]24 Mar, LGBO 16573. [62]1 Oct, LGBO 66441. [63]1 Apr, MHealthO 84311. [64]30 Mar, *Lond Gaz.* [65]15 July, *Lond Gaz.* [66]14 Aug, *Lond Gaz.* [67]17 Oct, lic min (*Lond Gaz*, 12 Sept). [68]23 Aug, *Lond Gaz.* [69]23 Oct, *Lond Gaz.* [70]7 Dec, *Lond Gaz.* [71]1 Apr, SI 1966/78. [72]1 Apr, 25 & 26 Geo V, *c* iv. [73]OC 16 May, reported in *Parl Papers* 1890—91, LXI, 54. [74]16 Mar, *Lond Gaz.* [75]24 Mar, LGBO 15270. [76]So noted in secondary sources; citation not found. [77]29 July, *Lond Gaz.* [78]15 May, *Lond Gaz.* [79]OC 23 Jan, reported in

Parl Papers 1872, XLVI, 21. [80]24 Mar, LGBO 16547. [81]20 May, *Lond Gaz.* [82]1 Apr, MHealthO 68901. [83]1 Oct, MHealthO 71978. [84]OC 9 Mar, reported in *Parl Papers* 1902, L, 595—96. [85]51 & 52 Vict, *c* 41. [86]1 Oct, LGBO 34695. [87]OC 28 Oct, reported in *Parl Papers* 1897, LXVII, Pt VI, 174. [88]20 Aug, *Lond Gaz.* [89]6 Aug, *Lond Gaz.* [90]1 Apr, MHealthO 85005. [91]3 June, *Lond Gaz.* [92]26 Nov, *Lond Gaz.* [93]25 Mar, LGBO 17595. [94]24 Mar, LGBO 16423. [95]1 Apr, MHealthO 72314. [96]24 Mar, LGBO 16575. [97]3 Mar, *Lond Gaz.* [98]25 Mar, LGBO 16579. [99]25 Mar, LGBO 16578. [100]29 June, *Lond Gaz.* [101]1 Apr, SI 1965/223. [102]25 Mar, LGBO 17908. [103]Augmented 1840 and also Part Dist, Instr 29 June and 26 July, reported in *Parl Papers* 1870, LXIV, 173. [104]29 Sept, LGBO 31758. [105]1 Apr, LGBO 56736. [106]1 Aug, *Lond Gaz.* [107]24 Mar, LGBO 15275. [108]*VCH Leics* V, 83. [109]OC 18 May, reported in *Parl Papers* 1872, XLVI, 21. [110]John Nichols, *The History and Antiquities of the County of Leicester* (4 vols., 1795—1811), III, 768; hereafter, 'Nichols'. [111]25 Mar, Part Dist, reported in *Parl Papers* 1870, LXIV, 173. [112]16 Aug, *Lond Gaz.* [113]8 Oct, *Lond Gaz.* [114]Authority not found; year of cr noted in *Kelley's Directory* (1932), 79. [115]25 Mar, LGBO 18143. [116]1 June, *Lond Gaz.* [117]OC 3 Aug, reported in *Parl Papers* 1872, XLVI, 22. [118]12 Aug, *Lond Gaz.* [119]30 Sept, lic min (*Lond Gaz*, 30 May). [120]*VCH Leics* V, 88. [121]2 Feb, *Lond Gaz.* [122]OC 7 July, reported in *Parl Papers* 1890—91, LXI, 53. [123]11 Feb, MHousLG Decl. [124]25 Mar, LGBO 26416. [125]26 Nov, LGBO 6926. [126]8 Dec, MHousLG Decl. [127]1 Oct, MHealthO 72492. [128]OC 7 Feb, reported in *Parl Papers* 1890—91, LXI, 55. [129]11 Jan, consecr church (*Lond Gaz*, 30 May 1952). [130]*VCH Leics* V, 114. [131]11 Sept, *Lond Gaz.* [132]1 Apr, MHousLGO 26189. [133]OC 9 Aug, reported in *Parl Papers* 1890—91, LXI, 55. [134]1 Apr, LGBO 34063. [135]1 Apr, MHealthO 84987. [136]*VCH Warws* VI, 120. [137]OC 9 May, Part Dist, reported in *Parl Papers* LXIV, 173. [138]16 Apr, *Lond Gaz.* [139]OC 9 Sept, reported in *Parl Papers* 1872, XLVI, 21. [140]7 June, lic min (*Lond Gaz*, 28 Mar). [141]13 Oct, *Lond Gaz.* [142]1 Nov (*Lond Gaz*, 28 Oct). [143]11 May, *Lond Gaz.* [144]Orig a chap, long since demolished and in Narborough by *temp* Lewis, *Topographical Dictionary* (1835), sub 'Narborough'. [145]15 Nov, *Lond Gaz.* [146]*Liber Regis*, 555. [147]26 Feb, *Lond Gaz.* [148]29 July, Hungarton Civil Parish (Alteration of Name) O, 1947 (citation by order number not found). [149]OC 5 Mar, reported in *Parl Papers* 1872, XLVI, 19. [150]*VCH Leics* V, 339. [151]26 Nov, LGBO 6927. [152]31 Mar, LGBO 36969. [153]1 Oct, LGBO 46276. [154]Authority not found; year of cr noted in *Crockford's* (1947), 1634, and in *Kelley's Directory* (1932), 132. [155]1 Oct, LGBO 44516. [156]25 Mar, LGBO 17496. [157]17 July, *Lond Gaz.* [158]25 June, *Lond Gaz.* [159]19 Dec, *Lond Gaz.* [160]29 May, *Lond Gaz.* [161]1 Oct, LGBO 53488. [162]25 Mar, LGBO 17906. [163]1 Apr, MHealthO 71746. [164]1 Apr, MHealthO 98241. [165]1 Apr, SI 1969/340. [166]5 Jan, SI 1971/2111. [167]Authority not found; noted in *Kelley's Directory* for Leics (1904), 116. [168]OC 31 July, reported in *Parl Papers* 1890—91, LXI, 56. [169]OC 10 Apr, Part Dist, reported in *Parl Papers* 1870, LXIV, 113. [170]13 Aug, *Lond Gaz.* [171]6 June, *Lond Gaz.* [172]13 Jan, *Lond Gaz.* [173]23 Jan, Part Dist, reported in *Parl Papers* 1870, 173. [174]2 July, *Lond Gaz.* [175]6 May, *Lond Gaz.* [176]4 Nov, *Lond Gaz.*

[177]VCH Leics IV, 347. [178]9 Dec, Lond Gaz. [179]8 Aug, Lond Gaz. [180]Nichols I, 328. [181]9 Jan 1829, Lond Gaz (OC, 28 June 1828). [182]11 Dec, Part Dist, reported in Parl Papers 1870, LXIV, 173. [183]13 Nov, Lond Gaz. [184]11 Aug, Lond Gaz. [185]8 June, Lond Gaz. [186]Area of Frog Island within Bor in Middle Ages, considered ent outside Bor by temp Eliz I, brought within Bor by charter of 1599 but disputed, sometimes concurrent jurisd until within MB 1835. [187]OC 30 June, reported in Parl Papers 1890—91, LXI, 57. [188]See VCH Leics VIII, 375 for dispute over area outside orig Bor bdry, incl bringing ent par within Bor in charter of 1599 (not sustained) and subsequent disputes until the par finally ent in MB in 1835. [189]23 Apr, Lond Gaz. [190]5 Apr, Lond Gaz. [191]Nichols I, 327. [192]Nichols I, 327-28. [193]14 May, MHealth Decl. [194]25 May, Lond Gaz. [195]22 Aug, Lond Gaz. [196]18 May, Lond Gaz. [197]24 Mar, Lond Gaz. [198]19 Nov, lic min (Lond Gaz, 30 May). [199]24 Mar, LGBO 16576. [200]25 October (on cr of the United Benefice of Lyndon and Thornton); information kindly supplies by Leics Co Record Office. [201]1 Oct, MHealthO 74868. [202]1 July (Lond Gaz, 8 June). [203]11 Dec, LGBO 11584. [204]11 Dec, LGBO 11585. [205]25 Mar, LGBO 18174. [206]25 Feb, Lond Gaz. [207]12 May and 24 Oct, Part Dist, reported in Parl Papers 1870, LXIV, 173. [208]Authority not found; year of cr noted in Kelley's Directory (1932), 740, and in civ census records. [209]24 Mar, LGBO 20648. [210]16 Dec, Lond Gaz. [211]VCH Leics V, 264. [212]VCH Leics III, 195. [213]VCH Leics V, 273-74. [214]11 Jan, Lond Gaz. [215]Liber Regis, 549. [216]VCH Leics V, 279. [217]1 Apr, MHealthO 84986. [218]18 Dec, LGBO 32244. [219]1 Oct, LGBO 59082. [220]29 Sept, LGBO 31759. [221]24 Mar, LGBO 15271. [222]5 July, Lond Gaz. [223]1 Oct, LGBO 35248. [224]VCH Leics I, 400. [225]25 Mar, LGBO 17137. [226]1 Apr, MHousLGO 34130. [227]30 Sept, LGBO 45605. [228]17 Dec, LGBO 7426. [229]29 Oct, Lond Gaz. [230]26 Sept, MHousLG Decl.

LINCOLNSHIRE

[1]Liber Regis, 414. [2]24 Mar, LGBO 22180. [3]1 Apr, MHealthO 70504. [4]1 Apr, MHousLGO 8423. [5]After Valor (1535) but before Liber Regis (1786). [6]PC augmented by commissioners of QAB. [7]7 Nov, Lond Gaz. [8]19 July, Lond Gaz. [9]24 Dec, LGBO 11660. [10]20 & 21 Eliz II, c 70. [11]OC 15 Oct, reported in Parl Papers 1890—91, LXI, 55. [12]Dorothy M. Owen, 'Medieval Chapels in Lincolnshire', Lincolnshire History and Archaeology, X (1975), 15; hereafter, 'Owen'. [13]29 & 30 Vict, c 30. [14]OC 19 June, reported in Parl Papers 1872, XLVI, 19. [15]1 Apr, MHousLGO 4867. [16]1 Apr, 25 & 26 Geo V, c vii. [17]25 Mar, LGBO 18159. [18]1 Apr, MHousLGO 34616. [19]1 Apr, MHealthO 74993. [20]25 Mar, LGBO 17800. [21]The Co of the Pts of Lind (Scunthorpe and Frodingham) Conf O, 1919 (citation by order number not found). [22]Liber Regis, 402. [23]24 Dec, LGBO 11668. [24]7 Sept, Lond Gaz. [25]OC 30 Nov, reported in Parl Papers 1872, XLVI, 14. [26]24 Dec, LGBO 11663. [27]30 Aug, Lond Gaz. [28]1 Apr, MHealthO 84619. [29]OC 13 Nov, reported in Parl Papers 1872, XLVI, 13. [30]22 July, Lond Gaz. [31]45 & 46 Vict, c 58. [32]Liber Regis, 457. [33]1 Apr, MHousLGO 1307. [34]1 Oct, MHealthO 74837. [35]1 Oct, MHealthO 75973. [36]7 June, Lond Gaz. [37]24 Mar, LGBO 19999. [38]1 Jan, 20 Vict, c 19. [39]1 Apr, LGBO 48329. [40]Owen, 16. [41]Year vac (Lond Gaz, 18 Dec 1931). [42]11 Nov, Lond Gaz. [43]25 July, Lond Gaz. [44]24 Mar, LGBO 20992. [45]24 Mar, LGBO 16598. [46]1 July (Lond Gaz, 4 June). [47]24 Dec, LGBO 11667. [48]10 Mar, Lond Gaz. [49]13 Aug, Lond Gaz. [50]26 Mar, LGBO 26921. [51]30 Apr, Lond Gaz. [52]OC 6 Apr, reported in Parl Papers 1872, XLVI, 13. [53]Year consecr church (Lond Gaz, 23 Apr 1969). [54]25 Mar, LGBO 19494. [55]24 Dec, LGBO 11673. [56]Liber Regis, 409. [57]4 Aug, Lond Gaz. [58]24 Dec, LGBO 11672. [59]1 Apr, LGBO 40052. [60]1 Apr, MHealthO 76263. [61]2 July, Lond Gaz. [62]OC 6 Apr, reported in Parl Papers 1890—91, LXI, 57. [63]24 Mar, LGBO 19996. [64]15 Oct, Lond Gaz. [65]6 July, lic min (Lond Gaz, 18 Mar). [66]1 May (Lond Gaz, 26 Apr). [67]10 & 11 Geo V, c cxvii. [68]30 June, Lond Gaz. [69]1 Apr, LGBO 37114. [70]1 Nov (Lond Gaz, 29 Oct). [71]William White, History, Gazetteer and Directory of Lincolnshire, 268; hereafter, 'White'. [72]1 Apr, 17 & 18 Geo V, c lxxvii. [73]26 Mar, LGBO 26737. [74]Liber Regis, 404; Owen, 16 says Dunsby never sep but rated in Valor as a rectory. [75]24 Mar, LGBO 20263. [76]24 Dec, LGBO 11661. [77]1 Apr, MHealthO 76077. [78]1 Apr, 25 & 26 Geo V, c viii. [79]17 Nov, Lond Gaz. [80]13 Nov, Lond Gaz. [81]24 Mar, LGBO 19648. [82]24 Mar, LGBO 20262. [83]9 May, Lond Gaz. [84]Not orig rated in the PLU, but soon after incl in it. [85]25 Mar, LGBO 19493. [86]1 Apr, MHousLGO 26933. [87]Liber Regis, 415. [88]26 June, Lond Gaz. [89]1 Apr, SI 1967/88. [90]24 Mar, LGBO 20219. [91]12 Feb, Lond Gaz. [92]52 Geo III, c 3. [93]White, 774. [94]27 Jan, Lond Gaz. [95]1 Apr, LGBO 33922. [96]8 Feb, Lond Gaz. [97]Liber Regis, 461. [98]12 Dec, Lond Gaz. [99]23 Oct, Lond Gaz. [100]10 Feb, Lond Gaz. [101]14 May, Lond Gaz. [102]57 & 58 Vict, c 58 and Co Council Namimg O. [103]21 Feb, Lond Gaz. [104]1 Oct, MHealthO 67605. [105]1 Apr, MHealthO 71641. [106]1 Apr, SI 1958/463. [107]1 Apr, SI 1967/1820. [108]30 Mar, SI 1960/453. [109]21 Dec, Lond Gaz. [110]21 Mar, Lond Gaz. [111]8 Nov, Lond Gaz. [112]29 May, Lond Gaz. [113]1 Apr, SI 1965/24. [114]24 Dec, LGBO 11665. [115]24 Dec, LGBO 11664. [116]24 Mar, LGBO 16562. [117]24 Mar, LGBO 16564. [118]24 Mar, LGBO 16565. [119]1 Apr, LGBO 46339. [120]24 Mar, LGBO 20994. [121]White, 821. [122]24 Mar, LGBO 20163. [123]1 Apr, MHealthO 75838. [124]22 Mar, Lond Gaz. [125]23 Aug, Lond Gaz. [126]14 Oct, Lond Gaz. [127]30 Sept, lic min (Lond Gaz, 23 May). [128]No explicit order amending co boundaries found. [129]25 Sept, Lond Gaz. [130]24 Mar, LGBO 20166. [131]Liber Regis, 423. [132]White, 825. [133]31 Mar, MHealthO 74205. [134]16 Oct, Lond Gaz. [135]27 June, Lond Gaz. [136]25 Mar, LGBO 19650. [137]24 Mar, LGBO 16600. [138]OC 12 Dec, reported in Parl Papers 1872, XLVI, 13. [139]24 Dec, LGBO 11669. [140]24 Mar, LGBO 16566. [141]24 Mar, LGBO 18158. [142]24 Mar, LGBO 20655. [143]White, 228. [144]Liber Regis, 451. [145]4 June, Lond Gaz. [146]25 Mar, LGBO 17146. [147]Authority not found; after Liber Regis (1786) but not in report of unions by Orders in Council (beginning 1838). [148]23 Sept, Lond Gaz. [149]Owen, 18. [150]24 Mar, LGBO 15303. [151]28 June, Lond Gaz. [152]Liber Regis, 399 and White, 716. [153]White, 777. [154]24 Dec, LGBO 11671. [155]29 Dec, Lond Gaz. [156]30 Sept, LGBProvO 1112. [157]10 July, Lond Gaz. [158]24 Jan, Lond Gaz. [159]25 May, Lond Gaz. [160]24 Mar, LGBO 16595. [161]Apptd day, LGBO 32114. [162]1 Apr, LGBO

52466. [163]1 Oct, MHealthO 70214. [164]17 Dec, *Lond Gaz.* [165]6 Feb, *Lond Gaz.* [166]4 Mar, OC reported in *Parl Papers* 1872, XLVI, 18. [167]21 Jan, *Lond Gaz.* [168]11 Apr, *Lond Gaz.* [169]White, 580. [170]28 Mar, *Lond Gaz.* [171]5 Nov, *Lond Gaz.* [172]26 Sept, *Lond Gaz.* [173]24 Mar, LGBO 21000. [174]*Liber Regis*, 406. [175]4 Feb, OC reported in *Parl Papers* 1872, XLVI, 14. [176]Authority not found; first registers from 1680. [177]*Liber Regis*, 400. [178]30 Oct, *Lond Gaz.* [179]24 Dec, LGBO 11666. [180]*Liber Regis*, 449 (without date, found elsewhere). [181]Joint patron, then united par, *Liber Regis*, 433—34. [182]24 Mar, LGBO 20995. [183]Authority and date of union not found, after *Liber Regis* (1786). [184]31 Dec, *Lond Gaz.* [185]24 Mar, LGBO 20656. [186]17 July, *Lond Gaz.* [187]24 Mar, LGBO 22181. [188]16 Apr, *Lond Gaz.* [189]1 Apr, *Lond Gaz.* [190]29 Sept, *Lond Gaz.* [191]24 Mar, LGBO 21368. [192]24 Mar, LGBO 21001. [193]24 Mar, LGBO 20264. [194]24 Dec, LGBO 11670. [195]30 Sept, LGBO 34548. [196]OC 4 Dec, reported in *Parl Papers* 1890—91, LXI, 56. [197]24 Mar, LGBO 20261. [198]Ruins of St Nicholas used 1795 in rebuilding of St Mary's, White, 476. [199]27 Aug, *Lond Gaz.* [200]24 Mar, LGBO 16620. [201]16 Feb, *Lond Gaz.* [202]24 Mar, LGBO 16534. [203]1 Oct, LGBO 34813. [204]21 June, *Lond Gaz.* [205]Apptd day, LGBO 31809. [206]*Liber Regis*, 403. [207]Thomas Allen, *History of the County of Lincoln* (1834) I, 52 ff; hereafter, 'Allen'. [208]1 Apr, LGBO 49039. [209]SI 1958/1175. [210]30 Mar, SI 1960/456. [211]22 Apr, *Lond Gaz.* [212]24 Mar, LGBO 22095. [213]24 Mar, LGBO 22094. [214]24 Mar, LGBO 22097. [215]10 Dec (*Lond Gaz*, 28 Nov). [216]31 July, *Lond Gaz.* [217]OC 4 June, reported in *Parl Papers* 1872, XLVI, 12. [218]29 Nov, lic min (*Lond Gaz*, 26 Oct). [219]24 Mar, LGBO 22096. [220]1 Aug (*Lond Gaz*, 30 July). [221]11 Aug, *Lond Gaz.* [222]1 Feb, *Lond Gaz.* [223]OC 7 July, reported in *Parl Papers* 1890—91, XLI, 55. [224]1 Jan, *Lond Gaz.* [225]28 July, *Lond Gaz.* [226]OC 30 June, reported in *Parl Papers* 1872, XLVI, 13. [227]OC 30 Nov, reported in *Parl Papers* 1890—91, LXI, 54. [228]*Liber Regis*, 414—15. [229]White, 505. [230]29 Sept, LGBO 31760. [231]OC 25 July, reported in *Parl Papers* 1890—91, LXI, 54. [232]*Liber Regis*, 412. [233]20 May, LGBO (number not cited in reference to census of 1891). [234]20 May, *Lond Gaz.* [235]Authority not found; date of cr noted in *Crockford's* (1947), 1782. [236]24 Mar, LGBO 22182. [237]*Poor Law Commissioners Report* 1859, IX, sub Lincs. [238]2 Nov, O Pts Lind Co Council. [239]OC 23 Jan, reported in *Parl Papers* 1872, XLVI, 14. [240]24 Dec, LGBO 11662. [241]11 Mar, *Lond Gaz.* [242]1 Dec, *Lond Gaz.* [243]24 Mar, LGBO 21369. [244]23 Mar, *Lond Gaz.* [245]White, 452. [246]3 Dec, *Lond Gaz.* [247]White, 561. [248]24 Mar, LGBO 16563. [249]OC 26 Jan, reported in *Parl Papers* 1890—91, XLI, 55. [250]12 May, *Lond Gaz.* [251]*Liber Regis*, 455. [252]23 Dec, *Lond Gaz.* [253]1 Dec (*Lond Gaz*, 16 Nov). [254]24 Mar, LGBO 20993. [255]3 Aug, *Lond Gaz.* [256]25 Mar, LGBO 17145. [257]1 Apr, MHealth Decl. [258]30 May, *Lond Gaz.* [259]Owen, 20. [260]*Liber Regis*, 407. [261]18 Oct, *Lond Gaz.* [262]15 May, *Lond Gaz.* [263]1 Oct, LGBO 52063. [264]Owen, 21. [265]Authority for cr not found; date from *Crockford's* (1947), 1754. [266]Authority and date not found; date of registers from *Original Parish Registers in Record Offices and Libraries* (Cambridge Group for the History of Population and Social Structure, 1974), 60. [267]Allen, VIII, 318—40. [268]1 Nov (*Lond Gaz*, 28 Oct). [269]27 July,

Instr, Part Dist. [270]1 Apr, MHousLGO 3724. [271]1 Apr, SI 1957/414. [272]1 Apr, 23 & 24 Geo V, *c* lxv. [273]OC 22 Feb, reported in *Parl Papers* 1890—91, LXI, 54. [274]OC 27 Apr, reported in *Parl Papers* 1872, XLVI, 12. [275]9 Nov, LGBProvO 1326. [276]1 Nov (*Lond Gaz*, 22 Oct). [277]28 Aug, *Lond Gaz.* [278]1 Apr, MHousLGO 8987. [279]15 Aug, *Lond Gaz.* [280]*Liber Regis*, 453, and White, 239.

NORTHAMPTONSHIRE

[1]9 Nov, 63 & 64 Vict, *c* clxxxiii. [2]1 Apr, LGBO 43787. [3]1 Nov, 1 & 2 Geo V, *c* lxiv. [4]1 Apr, LGBO 59994. [5]1 Jan, *Lond Gaz.* [6]7 Dec, *Lond Gaz.* [7]16 Apr, *Lond Gaz.* [8]Act of Parl (not found), noted by year only in Lewis, *Topographical Dictionary* (1835), I, sub 'Abthorpe'. [9]28 Dec, MHousLG Decl. [10]29 & 30 Vict, *c* 113. [11]PC augmented by Commissioners of QAB. [12]1 Apr, SI 1965/2175. [13]25 Mar, LGBO 14671. [14]1 Apr, MHealthO 80296. [15]25 Mar, LGBO 17778. [16]5 Dec, *Lond Gaz.* [17]1 Jan, 20 Vict, *c* 19. [18]31 & 32 Vict, *c* cxvii. [19]John Bridges, *The History and Antiquities of Northamptonshire* (ed. Peter Whalley, 1791), I, 283—84; hereafter, 'Bridges'. [20]25 Mar, LGBO 17763. [21]25 Mar, 45 & 46 Vict, *c* 58. [22]24 Mar, LGBO 20217. [23]24 Mar, LGBO 15248. [24]25 Mar, LGBO 15983. [25]57 & 58 Vict, *c* 58 and Co Council Naming O. [26]20 Jan 1846 (*Lond Gaz*, 23 Dec 1845). [27]11 Feb, LGBO. [28]Bridges II, 23. [29]1 Apr, MHealthO 80296. [30]24 Mar, LGBO 20216. [31]*VCH Northants* III, 71. [32]3 Mar, *Lond Gaz.* [33]20 Jan, *Lond Gaz.* [34]1 Feb, lic min (*Lond Gaz*, 20 Jan). [35]1 Oct, LGBO 33586. [36]1 Apr, SI 1965/250. [37]1 Apr, SI 1969/494. [38]1 Apr, SI 1971/575. [39]12 Apr, SI 1973/604. [40]25 Mar, LGBO 14659. [41]Bridges I, 278. [42]Bridges II, 321. [43]25 Mar, LGBO 17762. [44]Year vac (*Lond Gaz*, 16 May 1930). [45]Bridges I, 103—05. [46]1 Sept, *Lond Gaz.* [47]2 Oct, *Lond Gaz.* [48]26 May, *Lond Gaz.* [49]30 May, *Lond Gaz.* [50]1 Apr, 21 & 22 Geo V, *c* xxix. [51]3 Dec, *Lond Gaz.* [52]1 Apr, LGBO 53409. [53]OC 28 Oct, reported in *Parl Papers* 1897, LXVII, Pt VI, 174. [54]20 Aug, *Lond Gaz.* [55]24 Mar, LGBO 15984. [56]24 Mar, LGBO 15985. [57]24 Mar, LGBO 15986. [58]15 Feb, MHousLG Decl. [59]25 Mar, LGBO 14660. [60]1 Apr, 20 & 21 Eliz II, *c* 70. [61]Bridges I, 492. [62]24 Mar, LGBO 16459. [63]24 Mar, LGBO 15251. [64]Bridges II, 293. [65]25 Mar, LGBO 17914. [66]OC 25 June, reported in *Parl Papers* 1872, XLVI, 19. [67]28 Sept, MHousLG Decl. [68]Bridges I, 72—73. [69]21 Dec, *Lond Gaz.* [70]26 July, *Lond Gaz.* [71]1 Apr, MHousLGO 34561. [72]3 Jan, *Lond Gaz.* [73]1 Apr, MHealthO 100378. [74]1 Apr, MHousLGO 1445. [75]1 Apr, MHousLGO 4876. [76]1 Apr, MHousLGO 27639. [77]1 Apr, Dept Environm O 3576. [78]8 Mar, *Lond Gaz.* [79]4 Dec, *Lond Gaz.* [80]2 July, *Lond Gaz.* [81]1 Apr, LGBO 63823. [82]1 Apr, MHousLGO 548. [83]11 Aug, *Lond Gaz.* [84]7 May, *Lond Gaz.* [85]25 Mar, LGBO 17915. [86]24 Mar, LGBO 16273. [87]1 Apr, LGBO 32548. [88]13 Aug, *Lond Gaz.* [89]5 Oct, lic min (*Lond Gaz*, 28 June). [90]15 Sept, *Lond Gaz.* [91]1 Feb (*Lond Gaz*, 23 Jan). [92]11 Nov, O Northants Co Council. [93]25 Mar, LGBO 17761. [94]OC 18 Aug, reported in *Parl Papers* 1897, LXVII, Pt VI, 173. [95]Date and authority not found; date of 1st registers from *Original Parish Registers in Record Offices and Libraries* (1974), 73. [96]29 June, *Lond Gaz.* [97]Bridges I, 565—66. [98]29 Oct, *Lond Gaz.* [99]3 May, *Lond Gaz.* [100]28 Oct, *Lond*

Gaz. [101]2 & 3 Wm IV, *c* 64 and 7 & 8 Vict, *c* 61. [102]1 Apr, SI 1965/24. [103]1 Apr, MHealthO 81163. [104]Apptd day, 57 & 58 Vict, *c* 58. [105]1 Apr, 18 & 19 Geo V, *c* xix. [106]29 July, *Lond Gaz.* [107]Bridges II, 323—24. [108]1 July (*Lond Gaz,* 22 June). [109]12 Oct, *Lond Gaz.* [110]OC 7 Jan, reported in *Parl Papers* 1872, XLVI, 21. [111]25 Mar, LGBO 19413. [112]19 Jan, *Lond Gaz.* [113]25 Mar, LGBO 17137. [114]21 June, *Lond Gaz.* [115]2 May, *Lond Gaz.* [116]28 July, *Lond Gaz.* [117]Apptd day, LGBO 31794. [118]Bridges I, 304. [119]Salcey and Hartwell Lodges an ex-par place, neither made a sep CP 1858 nor incl in another par; noted in census of 1871 as still ex-par, but disappears from list of civil parishes before census of 1891; no explicit order for its inclusion in Hartwell AP found. [120]Bridges I, 202—03. [121]4 Sept, *Lond Gaz.* [122]OC 6 Nov, reported in *Parl Papers* 1872, XLVI, 13. [123]Bridges II, 36—37. [124]Bridges II, 41. [125]15 Feb, *Lond Gaz.* [126]31 Mar, *Lond Gaz.* [127]OC 9 Mar, reported in *Parl Papers* 1872, XLVI, 19. [128]29 Aug, *Lond Gaz.* [129]7 June, *Lond Gaz.* [130]1 Apr, lic min (*Lond Gaz,* 31 Mar). [131]18 Geo III, *c* 9, noted in *VCH Northants* III, 230. [132]OC 19 June, reported in *Parl Papers* 1872, XLVI, 19. [133]1 Nov, LGBO 52611. [134]17 Dec (*Lond Gaz,* 7 Aug). [135]30 Sept, 58 & 59 Vict, *c* lxxxix. [136]Bridges II, 463. [137]Bridges II, 47—50. [138]25 Mar, LGBO 15989. [139]24 Mar, LGBO 15249. [140]11 May, MHousLG Decl. [141]25 Mar, LGBO 15988. [142]1 Apr, LGBO 33900. [143]15 May, MHousLG Decl. [144]1 Apr, LGBO 53409. [145]Bridges I, 450. [146]Bridges I, 451. [147]25 Mar, Part Dist, reported in *Parl Papers* 1870, LXIV, 173. [148]30 Sept, *Lond Gaz.* [149]Bridges I, 448—49. [150]21 Nov, Part Dist, reported in *Parl Papers* 1870, LXIV, 173. [151]24 July, *Lond Gaz.* [152]23 May, *Lond Gaz.* [153]24 Dec, *Lond Gaz.* [154]25 Mar, LGBO 18191. [155]Bridges I, 304. [156]23 June, *Lond Gaz.* [157]20 July, *Lond Gaz.* [158]8 Jan, *Lond Gaz.* [159]28 Dec, reported in *Parl Papers* 1872, XLVI, 19. [160]1 Apr (*Lond Gaz,* 28 Mar). [161]OC 11 Mar, reported in *Parl Papers* 1872, XLVI, 20. [162]OC 3 Mar, reported in *Parl Papers* 1890—91, LXI, 57. [163]10 Apr, *Lond Gaz.* [164]30 Aug, *Lond Gaz.* [165]10 Aug, *Lond Gaz.* [166]4 May, *Lond Gaz.* [167]31 May, *Lond Gaz.* [168]17 Mar, *Lond Gaz.* [169]14 Aug, *Lond Gaz.* [170]30 Oct, *Lond Gaz.* [171]26 Mar, *Lond Gaz.* [172]14 Oct, *Lond Gaz.* [173]Date of union not found; held by same incumbent in 1786 (*Liber Regis,* 838). [174]25 Mar, LGBO 14658. [175]Bridges II, 592—93. [176]30 Sept, 58 & 59 Vict, *c* lxxxvi. [177]24 Mar, LGBO 16460. [178]24 Mar, LGBO 16416. [179]23 Aug, *Lond Gaz.* [180]Bridges I, 597—99. [181]29 Jan, *Lond Gaz.* [182]24 Mar, LGBO 20218. [183]24 Mar, LGBO 15250. [184]16 May, O Northants Co Council. [185]18 Oct, *Lond Gaz.* [186]29 Apr, *Lond Gaz.* [187]1 Apr, lic min (*Lond Gaz,* 28 Feb). [188]16 Dec, *Lond Gaz.* [189]19 Oct, lic min (*Lond Gaz,* 30 May). [190]Bridges I, 329—33.

NORTHUMBERLAND

[1]29 & 30 Vict, *c* 113. [2]1 Apr, MHousLGO 4894. [3]30 Sept, *Lond Gaz.* [4]25 Mar, 45 & 46 Vict, *c* 58. [5]24 Mar, LGBO 20952. [6]24 Mar, LGBO 22141. [7]1 July, *Lond Gaz.* [8]1 Apr, MHousLGO 4837. [9]1 Apr, MHousLGO 4862. [10]Priv statute, 14 Eliz I. [11]Augmented as PC Commissioners of QAB. [12]1 Apr, LGBO 34574. [13]22 May, *Lond Gaz.* [14]13 Feb, *Lond Gaz.* [15]24 Mar, LGBO 22897. [16]1 Apr, MHousLGO 4843. [17]20 Feb, *Lond Gaz.*

[18]30 Sept, LGBO 31327. [19]30 Oct, *Lond Gaz.* [20]Edward Bateson, *A History of Northumberland* (15 vols; 1893—1940), XV, 406—08. Henceforth, 'Bateson'. [21]25 Mar, LGBO 14548. [22]25 Mar, LGBO 15549. [23]5 Feb, *Lond Gaz.* [24]OC 5 July, reported in *Parl Papers* 1890—91, LXI, 57. [25]2 & 3 Wm IV, *c* 64, and 7 & 8 Vict, *c* 61. [26]24 Mar, LGBO 20487. [27]14 Sept, *Lond Gaz.* [28]1 Apr, MHousLGO 4893. [29]24 Mar, LGBO 20948. [30]24 Mar, LGBO 20950. [31]31 Mar, LGBO 33456. [32]17 Dec, reported in *Parl Papers* 1890—91, LXI, 54. [33]1 Apr, LGBO 61771. [34]1 Apr, MHealthO 81246. [35]3 Aug, *Lond Gaz.* [36]24 Mar, LGBO 20946. [37]1 Apr, MHousLGO 4871. [38]20 Dec, LGBO 13081, 13083. [39]4 Apr, *Lond Gaz.* [40]30 May, *Lond Gaz.* [41]20 July, *Lond Gaz.* [42]9 June, *Lond Gaz.* [43]Authority not found; dated noted in census reports. [44]24 Mar, LGBO 19985. [45]1 Apr, MHousLGO 4872. [46]25 Mar, LGBO 15551. [47]1 Apr, MHousLGO 6785. [48]1 Apr, LGBO 65934. [49]1 Apr, LGBO 35514. [50]15 Sept, *Lond Gaz.* [51]23 Feb, *Lond Gaz.* [52]51 Geo III, *c* cxciv. [53]25 Mar, LGBO 17750. [54]1 Apr, MHousLGO 4870. [55]20 May, *Lond Gaz.* [56]10 Apr, *Lond Gaz.* [57]19 May, *Lond Gaz.* [58]24 Oct, *Lond Gaz.* [59]29 Mar, lic min (*Lond Gaz,* 2 July 1954). [60]4 Jan, *Lond Gaz.* [61]17 Jan, *Lond Gaz* (OC, 2 Nov 1842). [62]1 Apr, LGBO 60720. [63]15 May, *Lond Gaz.* [64]12 Aug, *Lond Gaz.* [65]8 Jan, *Lond Gaz.* [66]5 Nov, *Lond Gaz.* [67]See comments above on border status. [68]John Scott, *Berwick upon Tweed* (1888), 337. [69]12 July, *Lond Gaz.* [70]31 Oct, *Lond Gaz.* [71]3 Jan, *Lond Gaz* (OC, 29 Dec 1887). [72]24 Mar, LGBO 20954. [73]OC 25 Mar, reported in *Parl Papers* 1890—91, LXI, 57. [74]10 July, *Lond Gaz.* [75]18 May, *Lond Gaz.* [76]25 Mar, LGBO 19409. [77]9 Nov, *Lond Gaz.* [78]12 Jan, *Lond Gaz.* [79]24 Mar, LGBO 22139. [80]15 Dec, *Lond Gaz.* [81]24 Mar, LGBO 22142. [82]25 June, *Lond Gaz.* [83]Bateson VIII, 487-88. [84]24 Mar, LGBO 22901. [85]27 Oct, *Lond Gaz.* [86]24 Mar, LGBO 20946, 20950. [87]4 Aug, MHousLG Decl. [88]30 June, *Lond Gaz.* [89]1 Apr, 20 & 21 Eliz. II, *c* 70. [90]31 Jan, *Lond Gaz.* [91]24 Mar, LGBO 22137. [92]12 June, *Lond Gaz.* [93]12 May, *Lond Gaz.* [94]1 Apr, LGBO 56450. [95]24 Mar, LGBO 19486. [96]23 June, *Lond Gaz.* [97]23 June, *Lond Gaz.* [98]1 Apr, *Lond Gaz.* [99]5 Jan, *Lond Gaz.* [100]14 July, *Lond Gaz.* [101]6 Oct, *Lond Gaz.* [102]24 Aug, *Lond Gaz.* [103]27 Feb, *Lond Gaz.* [104]1 May, *Lond Gaz.* [105]26 May, *Lond Gaz.* [106]10 Dec, *Lond Gaz.* [107]23 Feb, *Lond Gaz.* [108]1 Apr, LGBO 38305. [109]Bateson, XI, 12. [110]31 Aug, *Lond Gaz.* [111]Bateson, XIV, 175. [112]OC 19 May, reported in *Parl Papers* 1903, L, 596. [113]6 Feb, *Lond Gaz.* [114]16 Apr, *Lond Gaz.* [115]20 Dec, LGBO 13083. [116]24 Mar, LGBO 22860. [117]1 Apr, LGBO 49420. [118]Bateson, IV, 384—86. [119]1 Jan, 20 Vict, *c* 19. [120]24 Mar, LGBO 20951. [121]Lewis, *Typographical Dictionary* (1835), I, sub 'Corbridge'. [122]John Hodgson, *A History of Northumberland* (1832), Pt II, I, 170—71. Hereafter, 'Hodgson'. [123]29 Nov, *Lond Gaz.* [124]1 Apr, LGBO 51728. [125]14 July, lic min (*Lond Gaz,* 30 May). [126]*Kelley's Directory* (1904), 112. [127]26 Jan, *Lond Gaz.* [128]28 Oct, *Lond Gaz.* [129]23 Apr, *Lond Gaz.* [130]12 Aug, *Lond Gaz.* [131]13 Nov, *Lond Gaz.* [132]24 Mar, LGBO 22902. [133]1 Apr, LGBO 34328. [134]1 Dec, *Lond Gaz.* [135]26 Mar, *Lond Gaz.* [136]OC 27 Feb, reported in *Parl Papers* 1890—91, LXI, 56. [137]4 Feb, reported in *Parl Papers* 1872, XLVI, 21. [138]16 Mar, LGBO 8452. [139]1 Apr, MHousLGO 4841. [140]10 Mar, *Lond Gaz.* [141]24

Mar, LGBO 22903. [142]20 Dec, LGBO 13082, 13083. [143]24 Mar, LGBO 22138. [144]14 Oct, *Lond Gaz*. [145]18 Dec, *Lond Gaz*. [146]21 Apr, *Lond Gaz*. [147]12 Sept, *Lond Gaz*. [148]11 Dec, *Lond Gaz*. [149]10 July, *Lond Gaz*. [150]22 Mar, 51 & 52 Vict, *c cvii*. [151]4 Aug, *Lond Gaz*. [152]Bateson, XV, 173. [153]24 Mar, LGBO 19485. [154]1 Apr, MHealthO 81246. [155]24 Mar, LGBO 14765. [156]24 Mar, LGBO 19934. [157]OC 23 Feb, reported in *Parl Papers* 1897, LXVII, Pt VI, 173. [158]24 Mar, LGBO 22140, 22141. [159]13 July, *Lond Gaz*. [160]Bateson, XI, 289. [161]*Kelley's Directory* (1910), 132—33. [162]1 Apr, MHousLGO 7714. [163]13 Oct, *Lond Gaz*. [164]24 Mar, LGBO 20955. [165]24 Mar, LGBO 22898. [166]1 Apr, MHousLGO 19566. [167]24 Mar, LGBO 22899. [168]Bateson, III, 200—03. [169]10 Aug, *Lond Gaz*. [170]Bateson, III, 200. [171]1 Apr, LGBO 39885. [172]1 Apr, LGBO 52286. [173]12 Nov, LGBO 11459. [174]24 Mar, LGBO 19986. [175]13 June, *Lond Gaz*. [176]14 Dec, consecr church (*Lond Gaz* 6 Oct 1953). This par may have come into existence earlier, between the gazetting in 1953 (when there was already a curate) and the consecr in 1957, but no notice thus found. [177]23 Sept, *Lond Gaz*. [178]Bateson, XIV, 201. [179]24 Mar, LGBO 14766. [180]19 Mar, *Lond Gaz*. [181]9 Nov, 4 Edw VII, *c ccxx*. [182]18 May, *Lond Gaz*. [183]3 Aug, Decl MHousLG. [184]Hodgson, pt II, VIII, 91—96. [185]Bateson, II, 390. [186]30 Sept, LGBO 31332. [187]9 Nov, 10 Edw VII & 1 Geo V, *c lxxxix*. [188]Year effective (*Lond Gaz* 12 Sept 1960). [189]12 June, *Lond Gaz*. [190]24 Mar, LGBO 20949. [191]20 Dec, LGBO 13081, 13082, 13083. [192]1 Apr, LGBO 59801. [193]26 Oct, *Lond Gaz*. [194]57 & 58 Vict, *c 58*. [195]26 Oct, reported in *Parl Papers* 1890—91, LXI, 53. [196]30 Sept, LGBO 31326. [197]24 Mar, LGBO 14767. [198]24 Mar, LGBO 20947. [199]1 Apr, LGBO 54217. [200]1 Apr, LGBO 66913. [201]1 Apr, *Lond Gaz*. [202]28 Sept, *Lond Gaz*. [203]17 Apr, *Lond Gaz*. [204]OC 28 June, reported in *Parl Papers* 1897, LXVII, Pt VI, 174. [205]14 Feb, *Lond Gaz* (OC, 10 Dec 1842). [206]5 Feb, Part Dist, reported in *Parl Papers* 1870. [207]4 Nov, *Lond Gaz*. [208]14 Feb, *Lond Gaz*. [209]14 May, *Lond Gaz*. [210]16 Feb, *Lond Gaz*. [211]26 Mar, LGBO 26635. [212]24 Mar, LGBO 22900. [213]1 Apr, LGBO 66002. [214]1 Apr, MHousLGO 41582. [215]5 Jan, SI 1971/2107. [216]3 Nov, MHousLG Decl. [217]15 Aug, *Lond Gaz*. [218]24 Mar, LGBO 22140. [219]13 Mar, *Lond Gaz*. [220]3 July, *Lond Gaz*. [221]24 Mar, *Lond Gaz*. [222]15 Dec, lic min (*Lond Gaz*, 17 Nov). [223]Bateson, XIII, 444—52. [224]30 Sept, LGBO 31487. [225]15 July, *Lond Gaz*. [226]1 Apr, LGBO 59347.

NOTTINGHAMSHIRE

[1]*Liber Regis*, 1167. [2]29 & 30 Vict, *c 113*. [3]1 Apr, MHealthO 78578. [4]Authority not found and not known by Notts RO. [5]1 Apr, 22 & 23 Geo V, *c lxxx*. [6]19 May, *Lond Gaz*. [7]OC 10 Nov, reported in *Parl Papers* 1872, XLVI, 22. [8]OC 24 Feb, reported in *Parl Papers* 1872, XLVI, 22. [9]22 Dec, *Lond Gaz*. [10]28 Aug, *Lond Gaz*. [11]26 May, *Lond Gaz*. [12]30 Sept, 58 & 59 Vict, *c xci*. [13]After *Valor* (1535) but before *Liber Regis* (1786). [14]6 Aug, *Lond Gaz*. [15]PC augmented by commissioners of QAB. [16]Apptd day, LGBO 31838. [17]7 Aug, *Lond Gaz*. [18]4 Nov, *Lond Gaz*. [19]7 Dec, *Lond Gaz*. [20]24 Mar, LGBO 15303. [21]1 Apr, 14 & 15 Geo VI, *c xxxi*. [22]1 Apr, LGBO 39566.

[23]24 June, Instr, Part Dist. [24]30 Mar, *Lond Gaz*. [25]21 May, *Lond Gaz*. [26]14 Oct, *Lond Gaz*. [27]30 Aug, *Lond Gaz*. [28]28 Mar, *Lond Gaz*. [29]OC 31 July, reported in *Parl Papers* 1872, XLVI, 20. [30]27 June, *Lond Gaz*. [31]15 May, *Lond Gaz*. [32]9 Oct, LGBO 6909. [33]25 Mar, LGBO 14566. [34]Robert Thoroton, *The Antiquities of Nottinghamshire* (enlarged ed [by John Throsby], 3 vols, 1790—96), III, 357; hereafter, 'Thoroton'. [35]Year vac (*Lond Gaz*, 22 Feb 1965). [36]OC 5 Nov, reported in *Parl Papers* 1872, XLVI, 12. [37]27 Feb, *Lond Gaz*. [38]22 Feb, *Lond Gaz*. [39]1 Nov (*Lond Gaz*, 28 Oct). [40]Thoroton III, 256. [41]25 Mar, 45 & 46 Vict, *c 58*. [42]30 Mar, lic min (*Lond Gaz*, 13 Feb). [43]3 Mar, *Lond Gaz*. [44]28 Feb, *Lond Gaz*. [45]Authority not found; appears as sep PC by *Clergy List* of 1841. [46]William White, *History, Gazetteer, and Directory of Nottinghamshire* (1832), 433. [47]24 Mar, LGBO 16618. [48]18 Dec, *Lond Gaz*. [49]1 Jan, 20 Vict, *c 19*. [50]5 Mar, *Lond Gaz*. [51]26 Mar, LGBO 35199. [52]24 Mar, LGBO 23857. [53]Apptd day, LGBO 31837. [54]25 July, SI 1952/1347. [55]OC 9 Oct; information kindly supplied by Notts RO. [56]28 June, *Lond Gaz*. [57]1 Apr, LGBO 33702. [58]10 May, *Lond Gaz*. [59]Not orig rated in the PLU but incl soon thereafter. [60]1 Apr, SI 1965/24. [61]1 Oct, LGBO 40035. [62]8 May, *Lond Gaz*. [63]25 Mar, LGBO 19495. [64]13 May, *Lond Gaz*. [65]11 Sept, *Lond Gaz*. [66]21 Aug, *Lond Gaz*. [67]25 Mar, LGBO 18120. [68]7 June, *Lond Gaz*. [69]19 July, *Lond Gaz*. [70]OC 12 May, reported in *Parl Papers* 1890—91, LXI, 53. [71]26 Oct, *Lond Gaz*. [72]13 Nov, *Lond Gaz*. [73]9 Oct, LGBO 6979. [74]Apptd day, LGBO 31857. [75]10 Feb, *Lond Gaz*. [76]1 Dec (*Lond Gaz*, 16 Nov). [77]OC 17 Mar, reported in *Parl Papers* 1890—91, LXI, 53. [78]OC 4 Feb, reported in *Parl Papers* 1890—91, LXI, 55. [79]24 Mar, LGBO 16621. [80]29 Jan, *Lond Gaz*. [81]2 Aug, *Lond Gaz*. [82]8 July, *Lond Gaz*. [83]Authority for cr not found; date of 1st registers from *Original Parish Registers in Record Offices and Libraries* (Cambridge Group for the History of Population and Social Structure), third supplement (1980), 47. [84]1 Apr, MHousLGO 45760. [85]1 Oct, LGBO 34663. [86]OC 24 May, information kindly supplied by Notts RO. [87]19 Jan, *Lond Gaz*. [88]Authority for cr not found; date of first registers from *Original Parish Registers* (1974), 77. [89]1 Apr, MHealthO 111030. [90]24 Mar, LGBO 15305. [91]Act of Parl for noble patron, noted in *Kelley's Directory* (1899), 359, but a later *Crockford's* (1947), 1723, states 1876 as date of sep from Edwinstowe. [92]OC 29 June, reported in *Parl Papers* 1890—91, LXI, 54. [93]1 Apr, MHousLGO 6573. [94]OC 24 Mar, reported in *Parl Papers* 1890—91, LXI, 55. [95]24 Mar, LGBO 15306. [96]Date of 1876 noted in Directories, according to information kindly supplied by Notts RO. [97]24 Mar, LGBO 15304. [98]9 Oct, LGBO 6991. [99]1 Apr, 20 & 21 Eliz II, *c 70*. [100]24 Mar, LGBO 15307. [101]6 Nov, *Lond Gaz*. [102]24 Mar, LGBO 14664. [103]23 Jan, LGBO 33596. [104]29 July, LGBO 36643. [105]17 Aug, *Lond Gaz*. [106]9 Oct, LGBO 6989. [107]9 Oct, LGBO 6990. [108]12 Sept, LGBO 40034. [109]24 Mar, LGBO 16619. [110]24 Mar, LGBO 22953. [111]Date of union noted in Directories; information kindly supplied by Notts RO. [112]24 Mar, LGBO 15302. [113]OC 27 June, reported in *Parl Papers* 1872, XLVI, 13. [114]6 Mar, *Lond Gaz*. [115]5 May, *Lond Gaz*. [116]14 Sept, *Lond Gaz*. [117]21 June, *Lond Gaz*. [118]1 Apr, LGBO 39087. [119]14 Nov, *Lond Gaz*. [120]30 May, *Lond Gaz*. [121]13 Dec,

Lond Gaz. [122]30 Oct, *Lond Gaz.* [123]24 Mar, LGBO 16620. [124]11 Dec, LGBO 11564. [125]11 Dec, LGBO 11565. [126]OC 20 Nov, reported in *Parl Papers* 1897, LXVII, Pt VI, 174. [127]25 Mar, LGBO 17780. [128]Apptd day, LGBO 31839. [129]17 Mar, *Lond Gaz.* [130]6 Jan 1857, *Lond Gaz* (OC, 29 Dec 1856). [131]4 June, *Lond Gaz.* [132]1 May, *Lond Gaz.* [133]20 May, LGBO (number not found), cited in Census of 1891. [134]6 Sept, *Lond Gaz.* [135]Authority not found; date kindly supplied by Notts RO. [136]Apptd day, LGBO 31856. [137]Authority not found; date of cr noted in *Crockford's* (1947), 1708. [138]4 Mar, *Lond Gaz.* [139]9 Oct, LGBO 4342. [140]10 Mar, *Lond Gaz.* [141]Year vac (*Lond Gaz*, 25 Nov 1958). [142]12 Mar, *Lond Gaz.* [143]1 Nov (*Lond Gaz*, 27 Oct). [144]30 Apr, *Lond Gaz.* [145]21 Jan, *Lond Gaz.* [146]10 Aug, *Lond Gaz.* [147]6 May, *Lond Gaz.* [148]12 May, *Lond Gaz.* [149]9 Nov, *Lond Gaz.* [150]21 Dec, *Lond Gaz.* [151]16 Apr, *Lond Gaz.* [152]13 Feb, *Lond Gaz.* [153]Noted in *Kelley's Directory* (1940). [154]18 Sept, *Lond Gaz.* [155]1 Aug, *Lond Gaz.* [156]28 July, *Lond Gaz.* [157]28 Mar, *Lond Gaz.* [158]3 Mar, Instr, Part Dist. [159]5 Feb 1839, *Lond Gaz* (OC, 29 Nov 1838). [160]27 Nov, Instr, Part Dist. [161]1 Dec, *Lond Gaz.* [162]Year vac (*Lond Gaz*, 26 Feb 1926). [163]14 Aug, LGBO 6573. [164]1 Apr, LGBO 66674. [165]1 Oct, *Lond Gaz.* [166]29 Apr, *Lond Gaz.* [167]OC 29 June, reported in *Parl Papers* 1897, LXVII, Pt VI, 173. [168]Authority for cr not found; date of 1st registers from *Original Parish Registers* (1974), 79. [169]2 Dec, *Lond Gaz.* [170]12 Sept, *Lond Gaz.* [171]15 Jan, *Lond Gaz.* [172]4 Aug, *Lond Gaz.* [173]10 June, order not found but so noted in census records. [174]Information kindly supplied by Notts RO. [175]31 July, MHousLG Decl. [176]Thoroton I, 14—19. [177]18 Oct, *Lond Gaz.* [178]OC 8 May, reported in *Parl Papers* 1872, XLVI, 17. [179]Information kindly supplied by Notts RO. [180]5 Nov, *Lond Gaz.* [181]17 June, *Lond Gaz.*

RUTLAND

[1]Apptd, day, LGBO 31977. [2]29 & 30 Vict, *c* 113. [3]3 Mar, *Lond Gaz.* [4]1 Jan, 20 Vict, *c* 19. [5]25 Mar, LGBO 17766. [6]25 Mar, LGBO 17137. [7]OC 29 Nov, reported in *Parl Papers* 1890—91, LXI, 54. [8]30 Oct, *Lond Gaz.* [9]17 Aug, *Lond Gaz.* [10]Yr vac (*Lond Gaz*, 7 Feb 1928). [11]24 Mar, LGBO 20219. [12]*VCH Rutl* II, 158. [13]1 Aug (*Lond Gaz*, 28 July). [14]13 Sept, *Lond Gaz.* [15]Exact date not found; range of years in *VCH Rutl* II, 52. [16]Authority not found; date of union noted in *VCH Rutl*, II, 158.

SHROPSHIRE

[1]24 Mar, LGBO 15926. [2]1 Apr, SI 1966/1529. [3]29 & 30 Vict, *c* 113. [4]PC augmented by Commissioners of QAB. [5]25 Mar, LGBO 14440. [6]1 Apr, MHealthO 77933. [7]14 June, *Lond Gaz.* [8]25 Mar, LGBO 17486. [9]31 May, *Lond Gaz.* [10]30 Oct, *Lond Gaz.* [11]29 Nov, *Lond Gaz.* [12]29 Nov, *Lond Gaz.* [13]15 Oct, *Lond Gaz.* [14]22 June, *Lond Gaz.* [15]OC 18 Mar, reported in *Parl Papers* 1890—91, LXI, 54. [16]28 Aug, *Lond Gaz.* [17]*Original Parish Registers in Record Offices and Libraries*, 3rd Supplement (1980), 51. Hereafter, *Original Parish Registers.* [18]1 Apr, SI 1966/8. [19]25 Mar, LGBO 17485. [20]25 Mar, LGBO 17487. [21]*Original Parish Registers*, 2nd Supplement (1978), 37. [22]26 May, *Lond Gaz.* [23]24 July, *Lond*

Gaz. [24]OC 17 May, reported in *Parl Papers* 1890—91, LXI, 55. [25]14 Sept, *Lond Gaz.* [26]24 Mar, LGBO 16544. [27]8 July, *Lond Gaz.* [28]28 May, *Lond Gaz.* [29]25 Oct, *Lond Gaz.* [30]12 June, *Lond Gaz.* [31]24 June, LGBO 43130. [32]1 Oct, LGBO 43130. [33]24 Mar, LGBO 16350. [34]Apptd day, LGBO 32010. [35]24 Mar, LGBO 15929. [36]23 Feb, *Lond Gaz.* [37]23 May, *Lond Gaz.* [38]30 Sept, 58 & 59 Vict, *c* viii. [39]OC 2 Feb, reported in *Parl Papers* 1872, XLVI, 20. [40]24 Mar, LGBO 15167. [41]1 Jan, 20 Vict, *c* 19. [42]13 Aug, *Lond Gaz.* [43]45 & 46 Vict, *c* 58. [44]Authority not found; date of 1st registers cited in *Kelley's Directory* (1900), 120. [45]7 Feb. *Lond Gaz.* [46]30 Sept, LGBO 31670. [47]1 Apr, SI 1965/2139. [48]Samuel Bagshaw, *History, Gazeteer, and Directory of the County Palatine of Chester* (Sheffield, 1850), 666. [49]10 May, *Lond Gaz.* [50]30 Nov, *Lond Gaz.* [51]7 May, *Lond Gaz.* [52]OC 30 July, reported in *Parl Papers* 1897, LXVII, Pt VI, 174. [53]2 Nov, *Lond Gaz.* [54]14 Feb, *Lond Gaz.* [55]5 Feb, *Lond Gaz.* [56]25 Mar, LGBO 14439. [57]13 Jan, *Lond Gaz* (OC 29 Dec 1856). [58]OC 21 Nov, reported in *Parl Papers* 1897, LXVII, Pt VI, 174. [59]27 Sept, LGBO 11203. [60]27 Sept, LGBO 11204. [61]Apptd day, 57 & 58 Vict, *c* 58 and Co Council Naming O. [62]26 Mar, LGBO 33957. [63]30 Dec, *Lond Gaz.* [64]9 July, *Lond Gaz.* [65]12 July, *Lond Gaz.* [66]18 Dec, *Lond Gaz.* [67]23 Mar, *Lond Gaz.* [68]9 Oct, LGBO 6939. [69]1 Apr, MHealthO 95859. [70]8 Apr, Instr, Part Dist. [71]*Original Parish Registers*, 3rd Supplement (1980), 57. [72]*Shropshire Parish Documents* (1894), 315. [73]*Original Parish Registers*, 1st Supplement (1976), 36. [74]27 Feb, *Lond Gaz.* [75]24 Mar, LGBO 13631. [76]25 July, *Lond Gaz.* [77]1 Apr, LGBO 33899. [78]*VCH Salop* VIII, 113—14. [79]*VCH Salop* VIII, 53. [80]22 Mar, *Lond Gaz.* [81]28 July, *Lond Gaz.* [82]4 Oct, *Lond Gaz.* [83]8 June, *Lond Gaz.* [84]24 Mar, LGBO 16351. [85]15 Oct, *Lond Gaz.* [86]13 Aug, Instr, Part Dist. [87]30 Sept, 58 & 59 Vict, *c* lxxxvi. [88]19 Jan, *Lond Gaz.* [89]8 Sept, *Lond Gaz.* [90]6 Jan, *Lond Gaz* (OC 29 Dec 1856). [91]1 Apr, LGBO 61468. [92]OC 28 June, reported in *Parl Papers* 1890—91, LXI, 56. [93]1 Edw VII, *c* clxvii. [94]25 Mar, LGBO 13693. [95]24 Mar, LGBO 16352. [96]OC 22 Mar, reported in *Parl Papers* 1872, XLVI, 17. [97]26 Sept, *Lond Gaz.* [98]Authority not found; cr noted in *Crockford's* (1947), 1840. [99]5 Sept, LGBO 9732. [100]5 Sept, LGBO 9730. [101]Apptd day, LGBO 32128. [102]7 July, *Lond Gaz.* [103]19 Mar, *Lond Gaz.* [104]24 Mar, LGBO 16636. [105]Endowed by Duke of Cleves and augmented QAB, noted in *Kelley's Directory* (1900), 188. [106]Authority not found. [107]1 Oct, LGBO 48032. [108]11 July, *Lond Gaz.* [109]2 & 3 Wm IV, *c* 64 and 7 & 8 Vict, *c* 61. [110]15 Aug, *Lond Gaz.* [111]9 Oct, LGBO 6897. [112]28 Oct, *Lond Gaz.* [113]7 Nov, *Lond Gaz.* [114]31 Mar, *Lond Gaz.* [115]4 Feb, *Lond Gaz.* [116]1 Oct, LGBO 37838. [117]1 Apr, LGBO 44632. [118]OC 22 Oct, reported in *Parl Papers* 1872, XLVI, 20. [119]OC 11 Aug, reported in *Parl Papers* 1872, XLVI, 17. [120]8 Aug, Instr Bp, Part Dist, reported in *Parl Papers* 1870, LXVI, 182. [121]Year union noted in *Crockford's* (1887). [122]1 Apr, MHealthO 107144. [123]25 Mar, LGBO 177484. [124]31 Jan, *Lond Gaz.* [125]4 Aug, *Lond Gaz.* [126]Date of 1st registers noted in *Kelley's Directory* (1900), 152. [127]24 Mar, LGBO 15928. [128]OC 29 Nov, reported in *Parl Papers* 1872, XLVI, 20. [129]24 Mar, LGBO 15927. [130]20 Aug, *Lond Gaz.* [131]30 Apr, *Lond Gaz.* [132]25 Mar, LGBO 14701. [133]1 Apr, MHealthO 70489. [134]19 Aug, *Lond Gaz.* [135]25

Mar, LGBO 17900. [136]1 Apr, LGBO 37030. [137]Authority not found. [138]OC 13 Aug, reported in *Parl Papers* 1890—91, LXI, 56. [139]OC 22 Mar, reported in *Parl Papers* 1890—91, LXI, 56. [140]Note not used. [141]13 Aug, *Lond Gaz*. [142]27 Sept, LGBO 11205. [143]OC 27 June, reported in *Parl Papers* 1897, LXVII, Pt VI, 174. [144]24 Mar, LGBO 16350. [145]22 July, *Lond Gaz*. [146]2 Oct, *Lond Gaz*. [147]25 Mar, LGBO 13694. [148]Not orig rated in the PLU, incl soon thereafter. [149]21 Jan, *Lond Gaz* (OC 21 Oct 1841). [150]25 Mar, LGBO 13632. [151]Year vac (*Lond Gaz*, 26 Oct 1973). [152]*Liber Regis* (1786), 188. [153]OC 20 Nov, reported in *Parl Papers* 1872, XLVI, 20. [154]31 July, *Lond Gaz*. [155]29 Apr, *Lond Gaz*. [156]14 Aug, LGBO 9179. [157]2 Dec, *Lond Gaz*. [158]24 Mar, LGBO 16275. [159]1 Apr, MHealthO 107144. [160]*VCH Salop* VIII, 127. [161]Apptd day, LGBO 31866. [162]8 Mar, *Lond Gaz*. [163]24 Mar, LGBO 16637. [164]1 May, *Lond Gaz*. [165]1 Apr, LGBO 37030. [166]Not mentioned in the act; see *VCH Salop* III, 41. [167]1 Oct, LGBO 36552. [168]8 May, *Lond Gaz*. [169]15 Mar, *Lond Gaz*. [170]1 Apr, MHealthO 68776. [171]Date not found; before *Liber Regis* (1786). [172]13 Jan, *Lond Gaz* (OC 29 Dec 1856). [173]11 Aug, *Lond Gaz*. [174]19 May, *Lond Gaz*. [175]1 Oct, LGBO 39881. [176]OC 13 June, reported in *Parl Papers* 1872, XLVI, 20. [177]OC 6 Aug, reported in *Parl Papers* 1890—91, LXI, 55. [178]2 Aug, *Lond Gaz*. [179]OC 27 May, reported in *Parl Papers* 1890—91, LXI, 55. [180]1 Apr, LGBO 41000. [181]Apptd day, LGBO 31763. [182]21 Aug, MHealth Decl. [183]19 Dec, *Lond Gaz*.

STAFFORDSHIRE

[1]*VCH Staffs* V, 51. [2]29 & 30 Vict, *c* 113. [3]PC augmented by Commissioners of QAB. [4]1 Apr, MHealthO 77777. [5]OC 11 May, reported in *Parl Papers* 1872, XLVI, 19. [6]1 Apr, SI 1965/223. [7]1 Apr, 20 & 21 Eliz II, *c* 70. [8]45 & 46 Vict, *c* 58. [9]25 Mar, LGBO 16635. [10]1 Jan, 20 Vict, *c* 19. [11]21 June, *Lond Gaz*. [12]15 Aug, *Lond Gaz*. [13]22 July, *Lond Gaz*. [14]28 Aug, *Lond Gaz*. [15]1 Oct, LGBO 35059. [16]Instr Bp Worc & CBC, Part Dist, reported in *Parl Papers* 1870, LXIV, 181. [17]3 Oct, Instr Bp Worc, Part Dist. [18]1 Apr, LGBO 84985. [19]25 Jan, *Lond Gaz*. [20]Date sep identity lost not found, but by 1874. [21]15 Oct, *Lond Gaz*. [22]31 Dec 1884 and 2 Jan 1885, *Lond Gaz*. [23]30 May, *Lond Gaz*. [24]29 Oct, *Lond Gaz*. [25]30 Sept, 58 & 59 Vict, *c* lxxxvi. [26]Not orig rated in the PLU, incl soon thereafter. [27]1 Apr, MHealthO 76042. [28]27 Oct, *Lond Gaz*. [29]9 Aug, *Lond Gaz*. [30]17 Jan, *Lond Gaz*. [31]27 Sept, *Lond Gaz*. [32]Apptd day, LGBO 31886. [33]21 July, *Lond Gaz*. [34]1 Apr, LGBO 34059. [35]1 Apr, SI 1964/113. [36]1 Apr, 20 & 21 Geo V, *c* xxvii. [37]12 Mar, *Lond Gaz*. [38]1 Apr, 20 & 21 Geo V, *c* clxx. [39]1 Apr, 20 & 21 Geo V, *c* cxx. [40]1 Apr, 20 & 21 Geo V, *c* lxxxv. [41]25 Mar, LGBO 17808. [42]16 Aug, LGBO 29724. [43]24 Aug, *Lond Gaz*. [44]18 May, *Lond Gaz*. [45]25 Mar, LGBO 17888. [46]28 June, *Lond Gaz*. [47]13 May, *Lond Gaz*. [48]34 & 35 Henry VIII, *c* 26. [49]16 Jan, *Lond Gaz*. [50]5 Feb, *Lond Gaz*. [51]29 Nov, *Lond Gaz*. [52]26 July, Instr Bp Lichf, Part Dist. [53]8 July, *Lond Gaz*. [54]3 Sept, *Lond Gaz*. [55]23 Jan, *Lond Gaz*. [56]30 June, *Lond Gaz*. [57]21 Apr, *Lond Gaz*. [58]10 Mar, *Lond Gaz*. [59]10 Sept, *Lond Gaz*. [60]26 July, lic min (*Lond Gaz*, 18 May). [61]19 Mar, *Lond Gaz*. [62]9 Jan 1852, *Lond Gaz* (OC, 26 Dec 1851). [63]13 July, *Lond Gaz*. [64]25 Feb, *Lond Gaz*. [65]6 May, *Lond Gaz*. [66]13 June, *Lond Gaz*. [67]22 Feb, *Lond Gaz*. [68]19 Aug, *Lond Gaz*. [69]17 Jan 1832, *Lond Gaz* (OC, 10 Aug 1831). [70]4 May, *Lond Gaz*. [71]5 Nov, *Lond Gaz*. [72]1 Jan, *Lond Gaz*. [73]30 Sept, 58 & 59 Vict, session 2, *c* viii. [74]25 Mar, LGBO 17892. [75]16 Sept, *Lond Gaz*. [76]Apptd day, LGBO 31969. [77]4 Feb, *Lond Gaz*. [78]15 Feb, *Lond Gaz*. [79]8 Sept, *Lond Gaz*. [80]26 Mar, *Lond Gaz*. [81]20 May, *Lond Gaz*. [82]Apptd day, LGBO 31887. [83]2 July, *Lond Gaz*. [84]14 Dec, *Lond Gaz*. [85]18 Sept, *Lond Gaz*. [86]29 July, *Lond Gaz*. [87]Apptd day, LGBO 32117. [88]1 Apr, 1 & 2 Eliz II, *c* xxxv. [89]15 Feb, SI 1955/71. [90]20 Oct, *Lond Gaz*. [91]Walter Noble Landor, *Staffordshire Incumbents and Parochial Records (1530—1680)* (*Historical Collections of Staffordshire* [for 1915]), 134; hereafter, 'Landor'. [92]1 Apr, MHealthO 67258. [93]*VCH Staffs* XVII, 50. [94]9 Nov, LGBProvO 1342, confirmed by 60 & 61 Vict, *c* liii. [95]1 Apr, 17 & 18 Geo V, *c* lxxxvi. [96]1 Apr, 17 & 18 Geo V, *c* cii. [97]1 Apr, 20 & 21 Geo V, *c* cxxv. [98]24 Feb 1837, *Lond Gaz* (OC, 22 Dec 1836). [99]14 Sept, *Lond Gaz*. [100]11 Mar, *Lond Gaz*. [101]11 June, *Lond Gaz*. [102]7 Aug, *Lond Gaz*. [103]3 May, *Lond Gaz*. [104]4 Mar, *Lond Gaz*. [105]10 July, *Lond Gaz*. [106]14 Oct, *Lond Gaz*. [107]2 & 3 Wm IV, *c* 64 and 7 & 8 Vict, *c* 61. [108]6 Jan 1857, *Lond Gaz* (OC, 29 Dec). [109]23 Dec, *Lond Gaz*. [110]Effective 1849 on vacancy of rectory of Stoke upon Trent, per statutory authority 47 Geo III, session 2, *c* cxiv. [111]OC 16 Dec, reported in *Parl Papers* L, 1902, 595—96. [112]30 Oct, lic min (*Lond Gaz*, 30 June). [113]1 Apr, MHealthO 73138. [114]5 Feb, *Lond Gaz*. [115]18 Dec, LGBO 10283. [116]Apptd day, LGBO 31833. [117]1 Apr, 11 & 12 Geo V, *c* ciii. [118]24 Jan, *Lond Gaz*. [119]3 June, *Lond Gaz*. [120]31 Dec, *Lond Gaz*. [121]23 Dec, *Lond Gaz*. [122]15 Sept, *Lond Gaz*. [123]24 Oct, *Lond Gaz*. [124]31 Mar, LGBO 46186. [125]1 Mar 1842, *Lond Gaz* (OC, 10 Dec 1841). [126]21 May, *Lond Gaz*. [127]25 Nov, *Lond Gaz*. [128]1 Apr, MHealthO 77674. [129]2 Sept, *Lond Gaz*. [130]18 Nov, *Lond Gaz*. [131]30 June, *Lond Gaz*. [132]5 Jan 1934, *Lond Gaz* (OC, 21 Dec 1933). [133]1 Apr, 16 & 17 Geo V, *c* cvi. [134]1 Apr, 22 & 23 Geo V, *c* xc. [135]Year lic min (*Lond Gaz*, 12 Oct 1951). [136]20 May, lic min (*Lond Gaz*, 21 Jan). [137]27 Feb, *Lond Gaz*. [138]22 Mar, *Lond Gaz*. [139]1 Dec, *Lond Gaz*. [140]25 Mar, LGBO 19535. [141]13 Mar, *Lond Gaz*. [142]*VCH Staffs* V, 63. [143]3 Nov, *Lond Gaz*. [144]4 Sept, *Lond Gaz*. [145]11 Aug, *Lond Gaz*. [146]Date of cr shown in *Crockford's* as 1920, but may only have been a Conventual Dist then and sep later. [147]1 Oct, LGBO 35202. [148]*VCH Staffs* V, 82-83. [149]Apptd day, LGBO 31885. [150]1 Apr, 6 & 7 Geo V, *c* xxxiv. [151]23 July, *Lond Gaz*. [152]31 July, *Lond Gaz*. [153]14 July, *Lond Gaz*. [154]Apptd day, 57 & 58 Vict, *c* 58 and Co Council Naming O. [155]3 Feb, *Lond Gaz*. [156]29 June, *Lond Gaz*. [157]24 Nov, *Lond Gaz*. [158]1 Oct, LGBO 34525. [159]2 Dec, *Lond Gaz*. [160]5 Mar, *Lond Gaz*. [161]30 Sept, LGBO 29724. [162]20 Aug, *Lond Gaz*. [163]3 Dec, *Lond Gaz*. [164]Landor, 60. [165]1 Oct, LGBO 39185. [166]1 Apr, LGBO 43817. [167]13 Oct, *Lond Gaz*. [168]12 Apr, *Lond Gaz*. [169]1 Apr, MHealthO 75877. [170]1 Apr, LGBO 33910. [171]1 Apr, LGBO 34243. [172]9 Nov, 11 & 12 Geo V, *c* lxviii. [173]1 Oct, 17 & 18 Geo V, *c* xlvii. [174]*VCH Staffs* III, 50. [175]OC 11 Aug, reported in *Parl Papers* 1872, XLVI, 19. [176]10 Feb, *Lond Gaz*. [177]Stebbing Shaw, *The History and Antiquities of Staffordshire* (1798—1801), II, 410, and Lewis, *Topographical Dic-*

tionary, sub 'Statfold'. [178]31 Aug, *Lond Gaz*. [179]Landor, 71—72. [180]24 Apr, *Lond Gaz*. [181]25 Mar, LGBO 17891. [182]OC 3 Feb, reported in *Parl Papers 1872*, XLVI, 19. [183]25 Mar, LGBO 17937. [184]1 Sept, *Lond Gaz*. [185]OC 11 Aug, reported in *Parl Papers 1872*, XLVI, 20. [186]9 May, *Lond Gaz*. [187]Year lic min (*Lond Gaz*, 24 Oct 1952). [188]30 Sept, LGBO 45673. [189]1 Apr, 18 & 19 Geo V, *c* cv. [190]16 Dec, *Lond Gaz*. [191]25 Apr, *Lond Gaz*. [192]27 Apr, *Lond Gaz*. [193]17 Dec, *Lond Gaz*. [194]Year vac (*Lond Gaz*, 5 Feb 1929). [195]Year lic min (*Lond Gaz*, 11 Dec 1951). [196]OC 8 Aug, reported in *Parl Papers 1903*, L, 595—96. [197]Landor, 79—80. [198]6 Jan 1857, *Lond Gaz* (OC, 29 Dec 1856). [199]1 Apr, MHealthO 78462. [200]1 Apr, MHealthO 88496. [201]4 Oct, *Lond Gaz*. [202]18 Oct, *Lond Gaz*. [203]1 Nov (*Lond Gaz*, 30 Oct). [204]Landor, 227. [205]1 Apr, LGBO 34223. [206]*VCH Worcs* III, 103. [207]14 Mar, *Lond Gaz*. [208]1 Apr, LGBO 33052. [209]9 Oct, *Lond Gaz*. [210]25 Mar, LGBO 17890. [211]Apptd day, LGBO 31834. [212]25 Dec, *Lond Gaz*. [213]10 Aug, *Lond Gaz*. [214]1 Apr, 21 & 22 Geo V, *c* xlv. [215]11 Oct, *Lond Gaz*. [216]*VCH Staffs* VIII, 214. [217]31 Mar, 8 Edw VII, *c* lxiv. [218]20 Aug, *Lond Gaz*. [219]17 June, *Lond Gaz*. [220]1 Apr, LGBO 33910. [221]15 June, *Lond Gaz*. [222]25 Mar, LGBO 17807. [223]30 Sept, LGBO 26017. [224]1 Apr, LGBO 35994. [225]Landor, 105. [226]21 Aug, MHealth Decl. [227]11 Feb 1853, *Lond Gaz* (OC 28 Dec 1852). [228]16 Apr, *Lond Gaz*. [229]13 Nov, *Lond Gaz*. [230]23 Oct, *Lond Gaz*. [231]30 Jan 1964, lic min (*Lond Gaz*, 25 Oct 1963). [232]10 June, *Lond Gaz*. [233]Authority not found. [234]26 Mar, LGBO 29564. [235]1 Oct, MHealthO 74847. [236]10 Dec, *Lond Gaz*. [237]Inst Aug 1862, Part Dist. [238]16 Jan, *Lond Gaz*. [239]9 Nov, 5 Edw VII, *c* cvii. [240]15 Apr, *Lond Gaz*. [241]20 June, *Lond Gaz*. [242]17 May, *Lond Gaz*. [243]*VCH Warws* VII, 362. [244]1 Apr, 1 & 2 Geo V, *c* xxxvi. [245]28 Oct, *Lond Gaz*. [246]8 Feb, *Lond Gaz*. [247]17 Mar, *Lond Gaz*. [248]17 Feb, *Lond Gaz*. [249]19 May, *Lond Gaz*. [250]31 Mar, LGBO 35993. [251]Church built by lord of manor, noted in *VCH Staffs* III, 88. [252]3 Apr, *Lond Gaz*. [253]25 Mar, LGBO 17889. [254]28 July, MHealth Decl. [255]Landor, xxxii. [256]Landor, 230—31. [257]27 Mar, LGBO 19532. [258]Landor, 133. [259]Apptd day, LGBO 32249. [260]25 Nov, *Lond Gaz*. [261]22 Jan, lic min (*Lond Gaz*, 25 Nov 1966). [262]2 Oct, *Lond Gaz*. [263]6 Feb, *Lond Gaz*. [264]15 May, *Lond Gaz*. [265]Apptd day, LGBO 31940. [266]15 May, prob by Co Council Naming O. [267]18 Feb, *Lond Gaz*. [268]1 Oct, LGBO 35040. [269]*VCH Staffs* VIII, 273. [270]Authority not found, noted on map in *VCH Staffs* VIII, 259. [271]13 Dec, *Lond Gaz*. [272]OC 12 Dec, reported in *Parl Papers 1872*, XLVI, 13. [273]1 Jan (*Lond Gaz*, 31 Dec 1973). [274]1 Apr, LGBO 33050. [275]21 Jan 1842, *Lond Gaz* (OC 21 Oct 1841). [276]1 Oct, LGBProvO 3167. [277]8 Aug, *Lond Gaz*. [278]28 Mar, *Lond Gaz*. [279]24 June, *Lond Gaz*. [280]29 Mar, *Lond Gaz*. [281]1 Apr, LGBO 33832. [282]21 Jan, *Lond Gaz*. [283]1 Apr, LGBO 63911. [284]25 Aug, *Lond Gaz*. [285]31 Oct, *Lond Gaz*. [286]*VCH Staffs* V, 179. [287]*VCH Staffs* IV, 167. [288]6 Aug, *Lond Gaz*. [289]1 Apr, 17 & 18 Geo V, *c* xcii. [290]Year consecr church (*Lond Gaz*, 1 July 1949). [291]30 Oct, *Lond Gaz*. [292]6 Sept, *Lond Gaz*. [293]14 Feb, *Lond Gaz*. [294]Landor, 304. [295]1 Oct, LGBO 45968. [296]23 May, *Lond Gaz*. [297]28 Nov, *Lond Gaz*. [298]Apptd day, LGBO 31892. [299]29 Dec, *Lond Gaz*. [300]Landor, 224. [301]10 Jan, *Lond Gaz*. [302]6 Aug, *Lond Gaz*. [303]1 Apr, LGBO 55811. [304]1 Apr, MHousLGO 6558. [305]1 Oct, LGBO 33282. [306]25 July, *Lond Gaz*. [307]1 July, *Lond Gaz*. [308]14 Jan, *Lond Gaz*. [309]2 Oct, *Lond Gaz*. [310]*VCH Staffs* VIII, 252 ff. [311]Apptd day, LGBO 32249. [312]1 Apr, MHousLGO 5904. [313]1 Apr, LGBO 33251. [314]21 Mar, *Lond Gaz*. [315]Apptd day, LGBO 31651. [316]1 Apr, SI 1964/1161. [317]Apptd day, LGBO 31893. [318]23 June, *Lond Gaz*. [319]9 Aug, *Lond Gaz*. [320]22 June, *Lond Gaz*. [321]11 Feb, *Lond Gaz*. [322]1 Apr, *Lond Gaz*. [323]OC 3 May, reported in *Parl Papers 1890—91*, LXI, 54. [324]1 Apr, LGBO 40311. [325]Beresford & Finberg, 163. [326]1 Oct, LGBO 26017. [327]1 Apr, LGBO 33990. [328]1 Apr, MHousLGO 27858. [329]12 Aug, *Lond Gaz*. [330]14 May, *Lond Gaz*. [331]26 Feb, *Lond Gaz*. [332]26 May, *Lond Gaz*. [333]1 May (*Lond Gaz*, 3 Apr). [334]1 Apr, 17 & 18 Geo V, *c* lxv. [335]2 Nov, *Lond Gaz*. [336]9 Sept, *Lond Gaz*. [337]13 Oct, Instr Bp Lichf, Part Dist. [338]Authority not found; dated cited in census reports. [339]Authority for cr not found; date of 29 June 1844 given in census for 1851; date of 1835 cited in *Kelly's Directory* (1908), 539. [340]24 Mar, *Lond Gaz*. [341]9 Feb, *Lond Gaz*. [342]11 July, *Lond Gaz*. [343]Authority not found. [344]26 July, *Lond Gaz*. [345]1 Mar (*Lond Gaz*, 20 Feb).

WARWICKSHIRE

[1]25 & 26 Geo V, *c* vi. [2]*VCH Warws* III, 17. [3]1 Apr, MHealthO 108580. [4]1 Apr, SI 1965/223. [5]OC 9 Dec, reported in *Parl Papers 1890—91*, LXI, 55. [6]1 Apr, 21 & 22 Geo V, *c* ix. [7]*VCH Warws* VII, 7. [8]1 Apr, 17 & 18 Geo V, *c* xci. [9]1 Apr, 21 & 22 Geo V, *c* lvi. [10]1 Apr, SI 1956/446. [11]1 Apr, SI 1965/222. [12]1 Apr, 20 & 21 Eliz II, *c* 70. [13]30 Mar, SI 1960/450. [14]9 May, *Lond Gaz*. [15]12 Mar, *Lond Gaz*. [16]Year lic min (*Lond Gaz*, 23 Oct 1959). [17]*Crockford's* (1947), 1557. [18]1 Apr, MHealthO 80866. [19]1 Apr, MHousLGO 5447. [20]1 Apr, MHousLGO 7197. [21]1 Apr, SI 1964/1161. [22]29 & 30 Vict, *c* 113. [23]1 Apr, 21 & 22 Geo V, *c* xlv. [24]*VCH Warws* IV, 215. [25]PC augmented by Commissioners of QAB. [26]1 Apr, MHealthO 76114. [27]*VCH Warws* VI, 14. [28]9 Aug, *Lond Gaz*. [29]22 Feb, *Lond Gaz*. [30]1 July (*Lond Gaz*, 4 June). [31]26 Mar, *Lond Gaz*. [32]*Liber Regis* (1786), 211. [33]27 Sept, *Lond Gaz*. [34]22 Aug, *Lond Gaz*. [35]Apptd day, LGBO 31859. [36]1 Apr 1912, 1 & 2 Geo V, *c* xxxvi. [37]Instr Bp Worc, Part Dist. [38]22 Sept, *Lond Gaz*. [39]1 Dec (*Lond Gaz*, 16 Nov). [40]24 Mar, *Lond Gaz*. [41]*VCH Warws* III, 365. [42]25 Feb, *Lond Gaz*. [43]Instr Bp Worc, Part Dist, reported *Parl Papers 1870*, LXIV, 181. [44]28 Aug, *Lond Gaz*. [45]17 Aug, *Lond Gaz*. [46]*VCH Warws* VI, 382. [47]28 Dec, Instr Bp Worc, Part Dist. [48]7 May, *Lond Gaz*. [49]Instr Bp Worc, Part Dist, reported *Parl Papers 1870*, XLIV, 181. [50]1 Jan 1886, *Lond Gaz* (OC, 29 Dec 1885). [51]19 Aug, *Lond Gaz*. [52]11 Dec, *Lond Gaz*. [53]8 Mar, *Lond Gaz*. [54]1 Aug, *Lond Gaz*. [55]13 Oct, *Lond Gaz*. [56]3 Mar, *Lond Gaz*. [57]*VCH Warws* IV, 19. [58]*VCH Warws* V, 21. [59]*VCH Warws* VI, 25. [60]15 Sept, *Lond Gaz*. [61]1 Apr, MHealthO 75688. [62]1 Apr, SI 1964/170. [63]Year lic min (*Lond Gaz*, 19 June). [64]Apptd day, 57 & 58 Vict, *c* 58 and Co Council Naming O. [65]24 Mar, LGBO 16634. [66]1 Jan, MHousLGO 3877. [67]22 Mar, *Lond Gaz*. [68]OC 23 Nov, reported in *Parl Papers 1897*, LXXVII, Pt VI, 173. [69]*VCH Warws* III, 44. [70]1 Apr, MHealthO 67629. [71]1 Apr, MHousLGO 6498. [72]*VCH Warws* III, 211. [73]30 Jan, *Lond Gaz*. [74]1 Apr, MHealthO 75388. [75]2 Mar, *Lond*

Gaz. [76]17 Aug, LGBO 6465. [77]1 Apr, MHousLGO 7180. [78]1 Apr, MHousLGO 45717. [79]3 Jan, *Lond Gaz.* [80]Apptd day, LGBO 32074. [81]24 Dec, *Lond Gaz.* [82]14 Mar, *Lond Gaz.* [83]*VCH Warws* VII, 37. [84]14 June, MHousLG Decl. [85]54 & 55 Vict, *c* clxi. [86]9 Edw VII, *c* cxxii. [87]9 Nov 1911, 1 & 2 Geo V, *c* xxxvi. [88]1 Oct, MHealthO 74847. [89]1 Apr, MHealthO 75387. [90]*VCH Warws* VII, 377, per authority 7 Anne, *c* xiii. [91]*VCH Warws* VII, 371. [92]Instr Bp Worc, Part Dist, reported *Parl Papers* 1870, LXIV, 181. [93]19 July, *Lond Gaz.* [94]14 May, *Lond Gaz.* [95]Instr Bp Worc, Part Dist, reported *Parl Papers* 1870, LXIV, 181. [96]Instr Bp Worc, Part Dist, reported *Parl Papers* 1870, LXIV, 181. [97]Instr Bp Worc, Part Dist, reported *Parl Papers* 1870, LXIV, 181. [98]19 Dec, *Lond Gaz.* [99]1 June, *Lond Gaz,* also noted *VCH Warws* VII, 361. [100]20 June, *Lond Gaz.* [101]28 June, *Lond Gaz.* [102]30 June, *Lond Gaz.* [103]10 Aug, *Lond Gaz.* [104]9 Dec, *Lond Gaz.* [105]1 Mar (*Lond Gaz,* 12 Feb). [106]18 Oct, *Lond Gaz.* [107]20 May, *Lond Gaz.* [108]1 May (*Lond Gaz,* 3 Apr). [109]16 May, *Lond Gaz.* [110]24 Jan, *Lond Gaz.* [111]6 July, *Lond Gaz.* [112]60 & 61 Vict, *c* ccxi. [113]31 July, *Lond Gaz.* [114]12 Sept, *Lond Gaz.* [115]22 June, *Lond Gaz.* [116]21 June, *Lond Gaz.* [117]27 Nov, *Lond Gaz.* [118]2 Jan 1866, *Lond Gaz* (OC, 28 Dec 1865). [119]3 Feb, *Lond Gaz.* [120]16 July, *Lond Gaz.* [121]5 Aug, *Lond Gaz.* [122]22 July, *Lond Gaz.* [123]OC 19 May, reported in *Parl Papers* 1890—91, LXI, 57. [124]1 Oct (*Lond Gaz,* 5 Sept). [125]1 Dec (*Lond Gaz,* 17 Nov). [126]29 Feb, *Lond Gaz.* [127]11 Apr, *Lond Gaz.* [128]1 Dec, *Lond Gaz.* [129]1 July, *Lond Gaz.* [130]2 July, *Lond Gaz.* [131]*VCH Warws* VII, 394. [132]4 Apr, *Lond Gaz.* [133]1 Oct, *Lond Gaz.* [134]4 May, *Lond Gaz.* [135]14 Sept, *Lond Gaz.* [136]Year lic min (*Lond Gaz,* 20 July). [137]Apptd day, LGBO 31651. [138]13 Nov, MHousLG Decl. [139]14 Feb, *Lond Gaz.* [140]14 Apr, *Lond Gaz.* [141]9 Mar, *Lond Gaz.* [142]1 Feb (*Lond Gaz,* 23 Jan). [143]23 Aug, *Lond Gaz.* [144]21 June, *Lond Gaz.* [145]14 Oct, *Lond Gaz.* [146]9 Nov, *Lond Gaz.* [147]*VCH Warws* V, 174. [148]*VCH Warws* VI, 72. [149]*VCH Warws* VI, 45. [150]Not orig rated in schedule of pars in PLU, incl soon thereafter. [151]25 Mar, LGBO 17792. [152]*VCH Warws* VI, 212. [153]25 Mar, 45 & 46 Vict, *c* 58. [154]1 Apr, MHealthO 95455. [155]1 Apr, 1 & 2 Geo VI, *c* ix. [156]*VCH Warws* V, 27. [157]19 May, *Lond Gaz.* [158]25 Mar, LGBO 18144. [159]1 Apr, MHealthO 75389. [160]25 & 26 Geo V, *c* iv. [161]27 May, lic min (*Lond Gaz,* 28 Feb). [162]Year lic min (*Lond Gaz,* 21 Dec 1967). [163]7 Apr, lic min (*Lond Gaz,* 1 Feb). [164]OC 22 Feb, reported in *Parl Papers* 1890—91, LXI, 54. [165]*VCH Warws* VI, 114. [166]1 Jan, 20 Vict, *c* 19. [167]*VCH Warws* V, 38. [168]25 Mar, LGBO 19666. [169]Year lic min (*Lond Gaz,* 1 July 1969). [170]*VCH Warws* V, 27. [171]Year lic min (*Lond Gaz,* 19 Apr). [172]25 Mar, LGBO 18145. [173]1 Oct, LGBO 66289. [174]6 Nov, *Lond Gaz.* [175]OC 14 Nov, reported in *Parl Papers* 1872, XLVI, 19. [176]OC 9 Jan, reported in *Parl Papers* 1872, XLVI, 20. [177]*VCH Warws* VI, 207. [178]*VCH Warws* IV, 116. [179]*VCH Warws* IV, 56, 255, 258. [180]1 Apr, MHousLGO 5265. [181]27 June, *Lond Gaz.* [182]Year lic min (*Lond Gaz,* 22 Feb). [183]*VCH Warws* V, 107. [184]*VCH Warws* V, 59—60. [185]2 & 3 Wm IV, *c* 64 and 7 & 8 Vict, *c* 61. [186]18 Feb, *Lond Gaz.* [187]26 Mar, LGBO 40918. [188]4 Nov, *Lond Gaz.* [189]1 May (*Lond Gaz,* 3 Apr). [190]1 June (*Lond Gaz,* 31 May). [191]24 Mar, LGBO 16425. [192]15 Nov, *Lond Gaz.* [193]26 July, *Lond Gaz.* [194]29 Oct, *Lond Gaz.* [195]31 Jan, *Lond Gaz.* [196]9 Nov, 62

& 63 Vict, *c* cxlix. [197]Sep par 1939 (built 1929), *VCH Warws* VIII, 320. [198]24 Feb, *Lond Gaz.* [199]Year lic min (*Lond Gaz,* 24 Oct). [200]1 Jan, *Lond Gaz.* [201]18 Sept, *Lond Gaz.* [202]29 June, *Lond Gaz.* [203]*VCH Warws* VI, 91. [204]*VCH Warws* VII, 340. [205]William Dugdale, *The Antiquities of Warwickshire* (1730), I, 203—04; *VCH Warws* VII, 336. [206]*VCH Warws* VIII, 336, 358—59. [207]*VCH Warws* VIII, 342. [208]*VCH Warws* VIII, 344. [209]11 Aug, *Lond Gaz.* [210]OC 14 Nov, reported in *Parl Papers* 1872, XLVI, 19. [211]OC 9 Jan, reported in *Parl Papers* 1872, XLVI, 20. [212]*VCH Warws* VI, 78. [213]25 Mar, LGBO 21023. [214]14 Feb, *Lond Gaz.* [215]Year union effective; information kindly supplied by Records Office, Church Commissioners. [216]1 Apr, MHealthO 107487. [217]22 Dec, *Lond Gaz.* [218]24 May, lic min (*Lond Gaz,* 2 Aug 1966). [219]25 Sept, *Lond Gaz.* [220]30 Sept, 58 & 59 Vict, *c* lxxxvi. [221]14 Dec, *Lond Gaz.* [222]10 Nov, Parish of Ettington (Change of Name) O, 1948; citation by number of order not found. [223]*VCH Warws* VII, 362. [224]22 May, Instr Bp Worc, Part Dist. [225]Instr Bp Worc, Part Dist, reported *Parl Papers* 1870, LXIV, 181. [226]31 Aug, Instr Bp Worc, Part Dist. [227]Instr Bp Worc, Part Dist, reported *Parl Papers* 1870, LXIV, 181. [228]6 Dec, *Lond Gaz.* [229]17 Feb, *Lond Gaz.* [230]9 Oct, *Lond Gaz.* [231]30 Apr, *Lond Gaz.* [232]31 Oct, *Lond Gaz.* [233]20 Mar, lic min (*Lond Gaz,* 25 May). [234]Year lic min (*Lond Gaz,* 27 Aug). [235]25 Mar, LGBO 18161. [236]27 Oct, *Lond Gaz.* [237]13 May, *Lond Gaz.* [238]*VCH Warws* III, 193. [239]30 Sept, LGBO 33558. [240]Authority not found; date of cr cited in *Crockford's* (1947), 1635. [241]26 May, *Lond Gaz.* [242]28 Jan, lic min (*Lond Gaz,* 29 Nov 1963). [243]4 Oct, *Lond Gaz.* [244]23 Dec, *Lond Gaz.* [245]4 June, lic min (*Lond Gaz,* 2 Nov 1956). [246]*VCH Warws* III, 94. [247]5 Sept, *Lond Gaz.* [248]15 May, lic min (*Lond Gaz,* 16 Feb). [249]30 Oct, lic min (*Lond Gaz,* 12 July). [250]6 Jan, *Lond Gaz.* [251]5 Jan 1934 (*Lond Gaz,* 21 Dec 1933). [252]*VCH Warws* VIII, 534—35. [253]18 Jan, *Lond Gaz.* [254]*VCH Warws* V, 189. [255]*VCH Warws* V, 132, 189. [256]7 July, *Lond Gaz.* [257]11 Jan, *Lond Gaz.* [258]10 Oct, *Lond Gaz.* [259]Authority not found by compiler or by editors of *VCH Warws* VI, 120. [260]9 July, lic min (*Lond Gaz,* 19 Mar). [261]7 Nov, *Lond Gaz.* [262]*VCH Warws* VI, 120. [263]Apptd day, LGBO 32068. [264]10 Feb, *Lond Gaz.* [265]*VCH Warws* VI, 142. [266]5 Apr, Instr Bp Worc, Part Dist. [267]25 May, *Lond Gaz.* [268]1 Apr, MHousLGO 4068. [269]17 Dec, *Lond Gaz.* [270]14 Feb, *Lond Gaz.* [271]2 Aug, *Lond Gaz.* [272]23 Jan, lic min (*Lond Gaz,* 1 Mar 1966). [273]1 Apr, LGBO 42358. [274]1 Apr, 15 & 16 Geo VI & 1 Eliz II, *c* xvi. [275]25 June, *Lond Gaz.* [276]*VCH Warws* VI, 160. [277]Instr Bp Worc, Part Dist, reported *Parl Papers* 1870, LXIV, 181. [278]9 Feb, *Lond Gaz.* [279]*VCH Warws* VI, 163. [280]*VCH Warws* VI, 167. [281]5 Apr, *Lond Gaz.* [282]*VCH Warws* III, 221. [283]19 Feb, *Lond Gaz.* [284]11 Dec, LGBO 11584. [285]OC 1 Aug, reported in *Parl Papers* 1872, XLVI, 21. [286]29 June, lic min (*Lond Gaz,* 30 Mar). [287]1 Mar, *Lond Gaz.* [288]*VCH Warws* IV, 147. [289]11 Dec, LGBO 11585. [290]25 Mar, LGBO 18174. [291]25 Feb, *Lond Gaz.* [292]51 & 52 Vict, *c* 41. [293]30 Sept, 58 & 59 Vict, sess 2, *c* viii. [294]*VCH Warws* VI, 268. [295]17 Dec, LGBO 7426. [296]1 Nov (*Lond Gaz,* 27 Oct). [297]28 Mar, *Lond Gaz.* [298]24 Mar, LGBO 20648. [299]16 Dec, *Lond Gaz.* [300]30 Sept, 59 & 60 Vict, *c* lxxv. [301]6 Aug, *Lond Gaz.* [302]25 Mar, LGBO 17278. [303]1 Apr, 17 & 18 Geo V, *c* cii. [304]1 Apr,

17 & 18 Geo V, *c* cxii. [305]*VCH Warws* V, 136—37. [306]25 Mar, LGBO 19668. [307]3 July, *Lond Gaz.* [308]21 Mar, *Lond Gaz.* [309]16 Oct, *Lond Gaz.* [310]*VCH Warws* VI, 244. [311]25 Mar, LGBO 19667. [312]2 Apr, *Lond Gaz.* [313]8 Nov, *Lond Gaz.* [314]1 Apr, MHousLGO 10514. [315]26 Jan, *Lond Gaz.* [316]Still sep in 1907, sep identity lost soon after, authority not found; see *VCH Warws* VI, 219. [317]10 May, *Lond Gaz.* [318]10 June, *Lond Gaz.* [319]26 Aug, *Lond Gaz.* [320]12 Aug, *Lond Gaz.* [321]12 June, *Lond Gaz.* [322]1 Oct, LGBO 66290. [323]11 Sept, *Lond Gaz.* [324]58 & 59 Vict, *c* lxxxvi. [325]*VCH Warws* V, 156; *VCH Worcs* III, 276. [326]1 Apr, SI 1969/361. [327]5 Jan, SI 1971/2109. [328]1 Apr, 20 & 21 Geo V, *c* lxxxv. [329]6 Aug, Instr Bp Worc, Part Dist. [330]Instr Bp Worc, Part Dist, reported *Parl Papers* 1870, LXIV, 181. [331]Exact date in year not found (*Lond Gaz*, 24 Feb). [332]30 Sept, LGBO 33305. [333]29 Nov, MHousLG Decl. [334]23 May, *Lond Gaz.* [335]*VCH Worcs* III, 223. [336]OC 25 July, reported in *Parl Papers* 1872, XLVI, 21. [337]*VCH Warws* V, 198. [338]1 Oct, MHealthO 67205. [339]15 Oct, *Lond Gaz.* [340]31 Dec, 4 Edw VII, *c* xxvii. [341]1 Apr, MHousLG Planning O 571. [342]27 Apr, lic min (*Lond Gaz*, 2 Feb). [343]25 Mar, LGBO 17279.

WESTMORLAND

[1]Joseph Nicholson and Richard Burn, *The History and Antiquities of the Counties of Westmorland and Cumberland* (1777) I, 148 and I, 176—77, respectively. Hereafter, 'Nicholson and Brun'. [2]29 & 30 Vict, *c* 113. [3]PC augmented Commissioners of QAB. [4]15 Sept, *Lond Gaz.* [5]25 Mar, LGBO 19477. [6]Apptd day, LGBO 31578. [7]31 Aug, *Lond Gaz.* [8]1 Apr, LGBO 51820. [9]10 Feb, *Lond Gaz.* [10]13 Jan, *Lond Gaz.* [11]Nicholson and Burn I, 187. [12]8 Aug, Instr CBC, Part Dist, reported in *Parl Papers* 1870, LXIV, 139—43. [13]5 Dec, *Lond Gaz.* [14]14 Aug, *Lond Gaz.* [15]5 Aug, *Lond Gaz.* [16]8 Feb, *Lond Gaz.* [17]1 Apr, LGBO 35557. [18]1 Apr, MHealthO 78796. [19]25 Mar, 45 & 46 Vict, *c* 58. [20]25 May, *Lond Gaz.* [21]11 July, *Lond Gaz.* [22]29 Nov, *Lond Gaz.* [23]24 Mar, LGBO 21490. [24]24 Mar, *Lond Gaz.* [25]8 Oct, MHealthO 83424. [26]Nicholson and Brun I, 568. [27]18 Dec, *Lond Gaz.* [28]30 Aug, *Lond Gaz.* [29]1 Dec, *Lond Gaz.* [30]17 Aug, Instr Bp Carlisle, Part Dist, reported in *Parl Papers* 1870, LXIV, 139—43. [31]Nicholson and Burn, I, 141. [32]1 Apr, MHousLG PlanningO 549. [33]24 July, *Lond Gaz.* [34]15 Jan, *Lond Gaz.* [35]25 Mar, LGBO 19478. [36]30 Sept, 58 & 59 Vict, *c* lxxxix. [37]Nicholson and Burn, I, 264. [38]6 Aug, *Lond Gaz.* [39]14 June, *Lond Gaz.* [40]11 Dec, LGBO 11567. [41]11 Dec, LGBO 11568. [42]1 Apr, 7 Edw VII, *c* lxxxii. [43]Nicholson and Burn, I, 114. [44]1 & 2 Geo V, *c* clxxx. [45]Nicholson and Burn, I, 103. [46]1 Apr, MHousLGO 45726. [47]15 Apr, Instr Bp Carlisle, Part Dist. [48]Nicholson and Burn, I, 210. [49]OC 3 Mar, reported in *Parl Papers* 1890, LXI, 55. [50]1 Oct, LGBO 34951. [51]Nicholson and Burn, I, 108. [52]1 Apr, LGBO 35196. [53]7 Dec, *Lond Gaz.* [54]Nicholson and Burn, I, 176—77. [55]Nicholson and Burn, I, 105. [56]*Kelley's Directory* (1906), 123. [57]Nicholson and Burn, I, 146. [58]9 Nov, LGBO 65068. [59]28 Apr, *Lond Gaz.* [60]13 Aug, *Lond Gaz.* [61]13 Sept, *Lond Gaz.* [62]Nicholson and Burn, I, 252; chap augmented in year when built. [63]13 Mar, *Lond Gaz.* [64]Nicholson and Burn, I, 260. [65]Nicholson and Burn, I, 553. [66]15 May, *Lond Gaz.* [67]29 Oct, *Lond Gaz.* [68]22 Mar, *Lond Gaz.*

[69]Nicholson and Burn, I, 450—55. [70]OC 9 Aug, reported in *Parl Papers* 1872, XLVI, 22. [71]29 Aug, *Lond Gaz.* [72]1 and 4 Jan, *Lond Gaz* (OC, 31 Dec 1883). [73]9 July, *Lond Gaz.* [74]1 Apr, LGBO 45299.

WORCESTERSHIRE

[1]17 Dec, LGBO 13062. [2]25 Mar, LGBO 16082. [3]Year vac (*Lond Gaz*, 15 Sept 1939). [4]1 Mar, *Lond Gaz.* [5]Authority not found, cited in *VCH Warws* VII, 378. [6]14 Feb, *Lond Gaz.* [7]13 Nov, *Lond Gaz.* [8]12 July, *Lond Gaz.* [9]6 Jan, *Lond Gaz.* [10]30 Sept, 60 & 61 Vict, *c* lxxv. [11]1 Apr, 21 & 22 Geo V, *c* ix. [12]29 & 30 Vict, *c* 113. [13]1 Oct, MHealthO 67265. [14]1 Apr, MHealthO 76790. [15]Authority not found; date of union cited in *VCH Worcs* IV, 360. [16]24 Mar, LGBO 16079. [17]Apptd day, LGBO 32061. [18]5 Aug, *Lond Gaz.* [19]6 Aug, *Lond Gaz.* [20]31 Mar, MHealthO 73905. [21]1 Apr, SI 1965/2139. [22]26 Aug, *Lond Gaz.* [23]14 Oct, *Lond Gaz.* [24]Instr Bp Worc & CBC, Part Dist, reported in *Parl Papers* 1870, LXIV, 181. [25]3 Oct, Instr Bp Lichf, Part Dist. [26]25 Jan, *Lond Gaz.* [27]*VCH Worcs* IV, 230. [28]1 Oct, LGBO 66666. [29]30 Sept, 58 & 59 Vict, *c* lxxxvi. [30]1 Apr, MHousLGO 3462. [31]PC augmented by Commissioners of QAB. [32]10 Oct, *Lond Gaz.* [33]*VCH Worcs* II, 358. [34]1 Apr, MHealthO 108860. [35]31 Jan, *Lond Gaz.* [36]7 Mar, *Lond Gaz.* [37]9 Mar, *Lond Gaz.* [38]11 July, *Lond Gaz.* [39]1 Feb (*Lond Gaz*, 23 Jan). [40]Cr by deed Nov 1862. [41]Instr Eccl Commissioners, Part Dist, reported in *Parl Papers* 1870, LXVI, 181. [42]23 Mar, *Lond Gaz.* [43]5 Dec, lic min (*Lond Gaz*, 11 Sept). [44]30 Sept, 59 & 60 Vict, *c* lxxiv. [45]9 Oct, LGBO 6940. [46]*VCH Worcs* IV, 240. [47]*VCH Worcs* II, 509—10. [48]Apptd day, LGBO 32069. [49]*VCH Worcs* III, 411. [50]1 Apr, LGBO 36842. [51]1 Apr, MHealthO 68956. [52]Not orig rated in the PLU, incl in it soon thereafter. [53]57 & 58 Vict, *c* 58 and Co Council Naming O. [54]1 Apr, MHousLGO 23544. [55]*VCH Worcs* III, 260. [56]25 Mar, 45 & 46 Vict, *c* 58. [57]28 June, *Lond Gaz.* [58]11 Aug, *Lond Gaz.* [59]30 June, *Lond Gaz.* [60]34 & 35 Henry VIII, *c* 26. [61]*VCH Worcs* IV, 314. [62]9 Aug, *Lond Gaz.* [63]19 Jan, *Lond Gaz.* [64]26 Oct, *Lond Gaz.* [65]18 Apr, *Lond Gaz.* [66]18 Jan, *Lond Gaz.* [67]*VCH Worcs* IV, 28. [68]13 July, *Lond Gaz.* [69]28 Nov, *Lond Gaz.* [70]*VCH Worcs* III, 276 and *VCH Warws* V, 156. [71]19 Mar, *Lond Gaz.* [72]28 July, *Lond Gaz.* [73]OC 19 July, reported in *Parl Papers* 1872, XLVI, 21. [74]July 1973 (*Lond Gaz*, 23 Jan). [75]*VCH Worcs* IV, 110. [76]Year vac (*Lond Gaz*, 24 July 1924). [77]*VCH Worcs* III, 556—57. [78]*VCH Worcs* III, 279. [79]25 Dec, *Lond Gaz.* [80]13 Oct, *Lond Gaz.* [81]13 June, *Lond Gaz.* [82]1 Apr, MHousLGO 1451. [83]24 Mar, LGBO 16080. [84]Year lic min (*Lond Gaz*, 3 July 1952). [85]*VCH Worcs* III, 123. [86]1 Jan, 20 Vict, *c* 19. [87]12 June, *Lond Gaz.* [88]OC 6 July, reported in *Parl Papers* 1872, XLVI, 18. [89]22 Dec, LGBO 11586. [90]Apptd day, LGBO 31982. [91]18 Mar, *Lond Gaz.* [92]23 Jan, *Lond Gaz.* [93]13 Aug, *Lond Gaz.* [94]14 May, *Lond Gaz.* [95]2 & 3 Wm IV, *c* 64 and 7 & 8 Vict, *c* 61. [96]1 Apr, LGBO 64543. [97]OC 6 Sept, reported in *Parl Papers* 1890—91, 54. [98]*VCH Worcs* III, 205. [99]*VCH Worcs* III, 212. [100]22 Aug, *Lond Gaz.* [101]1 Apr, MHealthO 108861. [102]OC 29 June, reported in *Parl Papers* 1890—91, LXI, 57. [103]*VCH Worcs* III, 299. [104]Year vac (*Lond Gaz*, 25 July 1924). [105]*VCH Worcs* III, 306. [106]48 & 49 Vict, *c* clxiv. [107]2 May, *Lond Gaz.* [108]18

Sept, *Lond Gaz.* [109]24 Aug, *Lond Gaz.* [110]OC 8 Mar, reported in *Parl Papers* 1897, pt VI, 174. [111]14 June, *Lond Gaz.* [112]9 Nov, 4 & 5 Geo V, *c* cxxxiv. [113]1 Oct, 21 & 22 Geo V, *c* xxxiv. [114]1 Apr, 14 & 15 Geo VI, *c* xliv. [115]25 July, SI 1952/1350. [116]*VCH Worcs* III, 50. [117]OC 11 Aug, reported in *Parl Papers* 1872, XLVI, 19. [118]*VCH Worcs* II, 90 says that Clent was transf to dioc Heref before 1535, but it was noted as still in Kidderm. RDn in *Liber Regis* (1786). [119]*VCH Worcs* IV, 331. [120]1 Apr, (*Lond Gaz*, 3 Mar). [121]OC 26 July, reported in *Parl Papers* 1872, XLVI, 22. [122]OC 8 Feb, reported in *Parl Papers* 1872, XLVI, 22. [123]9 Nov, 1 & 2 Geo V, *c* xxxvi. [124]5 Aug, lic min (*Lond Gaz*, 3 Sept). [125]4 May, *Lond Gaz.* [126]Instr Bp, Part Dist, reported in *Parl Papers* 1870, XLVI, 181. [127]24 Mar, LGBO 16081. [128]12 Aug, *Lond Gaz.* [129]29 May, *Lond Gaz.* [130]31 July, lic min (*Lond Gaz*, 26 May). [131]15 Feb, *Lond Gaz.* [132]29 Feb, *Lond Gaz.* [133]8 Aug, Instr Bp, Part Dist, reported in *Parl Papers* 1870, LXVI, 182. [134]1 Apr, 20 & 21 Eliz II, *c* 70. [135]24 Mar, LGBO 16057. [136]*VCH Worcs* IV, 184. [137]1 Nov (*Lond Gaz*, 30 Oct). [138]*VCH Worcs* III, 412. [139]*VCH Worcs* III, 441. [140]OC 7 Feb, reported in *Parl Papers* 1890—91, XLI, 54. [141]*VCH Worcs* III, 234. [142]*VCH Worcs* III, 237. [143]24 Mar, LGBO 16029. [144]14 Aug, *Lond Gaz.* [145]24 Mar, LGBO 16026. [146]*VCH Worcs* IV, 68. [147]1 Apr, MHousLGO 7176. [148]1 Apr, LGBO 65925. [149]1 Apr, SI 1967/1787. [150]1 Apr (*Lond Gaz*, 28 Mar). [151]*VCH Worcs* III, 88. [152]24 Mar, LGBO 16027. [153]22 Dec, LGBO 11588. [154]*VCH Worcs* III, 103. [155]1 Apr, 18 & 19 Geo V, *c* cv. [156]1 Apr, MHealthO 77777. [157]1 Apr, 1 & 2 Eliz II, *c* xxxv. [158]15 Oct, *Lond Gaz.* [159]20 Feb, *Lond Gaz.* [160]5 Dec, *Lond Gaz.* [161]16 Sept, *Lond Gaz.* [162]1 July, *Lond Gaz.* [163]29 July, *Lond Gaz.* [164]20 Aug, lic min (*Lond Gaz*, 30 May). [165]4 Apr, *Lond Gaz.* [166]*VCH Worcs* IV, 272. [167]30 Nov, *Lond Gaz.* [168]24 Mar, LGBO 15167. [169]24 Mar, LGBO 16007. [170]56 & 57 Vict, *c* cxxxii. [171]*VCH Worcs* IV, 82. [172]*VCH Worcs* II, 386. [173]Apptd day, 56 & 57 Vict, *c* 73 and Co Council Naming O. [174]11 Jan, *Lond Gaz.* [175]1 Dec, *Lond Gaz.* [176]6 Nov, *Lond Gaz.* [177]15 May, lic min (*Lond Gaz*, 16 Feb). [178]30 Oct, lic min (*Lond Gaz*, 12 July). [179]OC 23 Oct, reported in *Parl Papers* 1890—91, LXI, 55. [180]Apptd day, LGBO 31982. [181]22 Feb, *Lond Gaz.* [182]Apptd day, LGBO 32060. [183]1 Oct, MHealthO 67606. [184]18 Jan, *Lond Gaz.* [185]*VCH Worcs* III, 378. [186]28 July, MHousLG Decl. [187]*VCH Worcs* III, 408. [188]1 Oct, LGBO 34716. [189]1 Apr, LGBO 37597. [190]Authority not found; cited in *VCH Worcs* IV, 100. [191]1 Dec (*Lond Gaz*, 16 Nov). [192]OC 13 Aug, reported in *Parl Papers* 1890—91, LXI, 55. [193]15 July, *Lond Gaz.* [194]16 Feb, *Lond Gaz.* [195]2 Aug, *Lond Gaz.* [196]24 Mar, LGBO 16028. [197]*VCH Worcs* III, 401. [198]6 Dec, lic min (*Lond Gaz*, 17 Nov). [199]17 Nov, Instr Bp, Part Dist, reported in *Parl Papers* 1870, LXVI, 182. [200]*VCH Worcs* III, 407. [201]1 Apr, MHousLGO 7143. [202]24 June, reported in *Parl Papers* 1890—91, LXI, 57. [203]Year vac (*Lond Gaz*, 10 Feb 1933). [204]1 Apr, *Lond Gaz.* [205]26 May, *Lond Gaz.* [206]23 Aug, *Lond Gaz.* [207]Apptd day, LGBO 32137. [208]2 & 3 Geo V, *c* cxxxi. [209]1 Apr, LGBO 42285. [210]OC 12 Aug, reported in *Parl Papers* 1890—91, LXI, 57. [211]13 Jan, *Lond Gaz.* [212]Apptd day, 56 & 57 Vict, *c* 73 and Co Council Naming O. [213]1 Apr, 21 & 22 Geo V, *c* xxxiv. [214]1 Mar, Instr Bp, Part Dist. [215]17 Dec, *Lond Gaz.* [216]OC 2 Oct, reported in *Parl Papers* 1872, XLVI, 18. [217]*VCH Worcs* IV, 284—85. [218]*VCH Worcs* IV, 353. [219]12 May, *Lond Gaz.* [220]19 Sept, lic Min (*Lond Gaz*, 30 May). [221]23 Jan, lic min (*Lond Gaz*, 1 Mar 1966). [222]13 Dec, Instr, Part Dist. [223]Instr CBC, Part Dist, reported in *Parl Papers* 1870, LXVI, 181. [224]28 July, *Lond Gaz.* [225]OC 14 Aug, reported in *Parl Papers* 1890—91, LXI, 56. [226]25 Mar, LGBO 17916. [227]5 Mar, *Lond Gaz.* [228]11 June, Instr Bp Worc, Part Dist. [229]Instr CBC, Part Dist, reported in *Parl Papers* 1870, LXVI, 181. [230]17 Jan, *Lond Gaz.* [231]3 Oct, *Lond Gaz.* [232]4 Nov, *Lond Gaz.* [233]29 Sept, lic min (*Lond Gaz*, 6 Aug). [234]24 Mar, LGBO 16056. [235]15 Jan, *Lond Gaz.* [236]22 Mar, *Lond Gaz.* [237]OC 13 Aug, reported in *Parl Papers* 1879, pt VI, 174. [238]9 Nov, *Lond Gaz.* [239]*VCH Worcs* III, 453. [240]1 Apr, LGBO 40254. [241]59 & 60 Vict, *c* lxxii. [242]1 Oct, LGBO 38126. [243]9 Oct, LGBO 6940. [244]Apptd day, LGBO 32006. [245]1 Apr, MHealthO 72393. [246]5 Feb, *Lond Gaz.* [247]OC 17 May, reported in *Parl Papers* 1890—91, LXI, 56. [248]10 June, *Lond Gaz.* [249]29 Nov, lic min (*Lond Gaz*, 6 Aug). [250]28 Sept, lic min (*Lond Gaz*, 7 Aug). [251]25 Mar, LGBO 16030. [252]4 Aug, *Lond Gaz.* [253]*VCH Worcs* II, 423. [254]10 Sept, Instr Bp, Part Dist. [255]30 Sept, 59 & 60 Vict, *c* lxxv. [256]24 Mar, LGBO 16429. [257]1 Oct, LGBO 33031. [258]30 Sept, LGBO 52440. [259]1 Apr, 17 & 18 Geo V, *c* lxv. [260]5 Sept, *Lond Gaz.* [261]Presumed rated in PLU when a sep CP; not incl in list of additions in reports of Poor Law Commissioners. [262]1 Apr, MHealthO 73156. [263]1 Apr, MHealthO 108298. [264]1 Apr, MHousLGO 4925. [265]*VCH Worcs* IV, 207, 211. [266]*VCH Worcs* IV, 162. [267]1 Apr, MHousLGO 4921. [268]Explicit order not found; 'Ridgacre' in 1891 census and 'Quinton' in 1901 census. [269]28 Feb, *Lond Gaz.* [270]4 Sept, *Lond Gaz.* [271]Year lic min (*Lond Gaz*, 6 Oct 1953). [272]14 Apr, *Lond Gaz.* [273]Orig rated in Tardebigge, sep rated soon after. [274]1 Apr, LGBO 46309. [275]1 Apr, SI 1969/340. [276]15 Aug, *Lond Gaz.* [277]Presumed licensed same year as order (*Lond Gaz*, 29 Mar 1957). [278]24 Mar, LGBO 16058. [279]OC 3 Apr, reported in *Parl Papers* 1872, XLVI, 18. [280]12 Feb, *Lond Gaz.* [281]10 Feb, *Lond Gaz.* [282]6 Geo I, *c* ix. [283]8 May, *Lond Gaz.* [284]*VCH Worcs* III, 527. [285]27 July, *Lond Gaz.* [286]9 Aug, MHealth Decl. [287]*VCH Worcs* III, 223. [288]*VCH Worcs* III, 553. [289]8 Nov, MHealth Decl. [290]*VCH Worcs* III, 517—18. [291]24 Mar, LGBO 6060. [292]*VCH Worcs* III, 566. [293]*VCH Worcs* II, 429. [294]14 Apr, *Lond Gaz.* [295]*VCH Worcs* IV, 411. [296]*VCH Worcs* IV, 410. [297]4 Oct, lic min (*Lond Gaz*, 13 May). [298]1 Apr, SI 1964/170.

YORKSHIRE

[1]20 Aug, *Lond Gaz.* [2]29 & 30 Vict, *c* 113. [3]1 Apr, MHealthO 77607. [4]25 Mar, LGBO 19642. [5]1 Apr, 20 & 21 Eliz II, *c* 70. [6]OC 17 Dec (York dioc OC file, 464). [7]OC 27 Aug, reported in *Parl Papers* 1872, XLVI, 18. [8]*VCH Yorks E Riding* III, 74. [9]PC augmented by Commissioners of QAB. [10]15 Nov, *Lond Gaz.* [11]29 Oct, *Lond Gaz.* [12]25 Mar, *Lond Gaz.* [13]1 Apr, MHealthO 80872. [14]1 Nov (*Lond Gaz*, 3 Oct). [15]*VCH Yorks N Riding* II, 223. [16]45 & 46 Vict, *c* 58. [17]24 Mar, LGBO 20196. [18]Apptd day, LGBO 31986. [19]9 Nov, 3 & 4 Geo V, *c* cxlii. [20]1 Apr, MHealthO 76121. [21]17 Jan, *Lond Gaz.* [22]23 May, *Lond Gaz.* [23]10 Aug, *Lond Gaz.* [24]6 Nov, *Lond Gaz.* [25]OC 9 Mar (York dioc OC file). [26]2 June, lic

min (*Lond Gaz*, 4 Apr). [27]30 May, *Lond Gaz.* [28]1 Apr, MHealthO 93469. [29]27 Oct, *Lond Gaz.* [30]25 Oct, *Lond Gaz.* [31]1 Apr, MHealthO 87427. [32]OC 20 Dec (York dioc OC file). [33]5 July, lic min (*Lond Gaz*, 14 May). [34]7 Feb, *Lond Gaz.* [35]11 Aug, *Lond Gaz.* [36]24 Jan, *Lond Gaz.* [37]31 Aug, *Lond Gaz.* [38]1 Apr, 15 & 16 Geo V, *c* lx. [39]1 Apr, 17 & 18 Geo V, *c* ci. [40]25 Sept, *Lond Gaz.* [41]1 Aug, *Lond Gaz.* [42]25 Mar, LGBO 13181. [43]1 Apr, MHealthO 62619. [44]28 Nov, *Lond Gaz.* [45]27 May, *Lond Gaz.* [46]27 Feb, *Lond Gaz.* [47]Apptd day, LGBO 31724. [48]21 Nov, *Lond Gaz.* [49]24 Mar, LGBO 20784. [50]OC 7 Jan, reported in *Parl Papers* 1872, XLVI, 21. [51]1 Apr, MHealthO 76122. [52]45 & 46 Vict, *c* 58. [53]Apptd day, LGBO 31730. [54]18 Sept, *Lond Gaz.* [55]12 Nov, *Lond Gaz.* [56]6 Aug, *Lond Gaz.* [57]1 Feb (*Lond Gaz*, 23 Jan). [58]George Lawton, ed., *Collectio Rerum Ecclesiasticarum de Diocesi Eboracensi* (new ed., 1842), 374; hereafter 'Lawton'. [59]25 Mar, LGBO 16993. [60]15 June, *Lond Gaz.* [61]*VCH Yorks N Riding* II, 424. [62]Lawton, 316. [63]2 Dec, *Lond Gaz.* [64]11 Feb, *Lond Gaz.* [65]25 Mar, 60 & 61 Vict, *c* cclx. [66]21 Mar, *Lond Gaz.* [67]28 June, *Lond Gaz.* [68]3 Aug, *Lond Gaz.* [69]26 Mar, LGBO 45137. [70]27 Aug, *Lond Gaz.* [71]8 Oct, *Lond Gaz.* [72]11 Aug, *Lond Gaz.* [73]18 Oct, *Lond Gaz.* [74]1 Jan, *Lond Gaz.* [75]24 Mar, LGBO 16611. [76]1 Apr, MHealthO 100248. [77]22 Feb, *Lond Gaz.* [78]1 Dec (*Lond Gaz*, 16 Nov). [79]7 Mar, *Lond Gaz* (OC, 10 Dec 1842). [80]10 Nov, *Lond Gaz.* [81]17 July, *Lond Gaz.* [82]30 Jan, *Lond Gaz.* [83]1 Apr, MHealthO 68890. [84]11 Nov 1845, Part Dist, reported in *Parl Papers* 1870, LXIV, 175. [85]27 Mar, *Lond Gaz.* [86]17 Aug, *Lond Gaz.* [87]8 Sept, *Lond Gaz.* [88]31 Dec, *Lond Gaz.* [89]15 Aug, *Lond Gaz.* [90]14 May, *Lond Gaz.* [91]3 Sept, *Lond Gaz.* [92]7 Jan, *Lond Gaz.* [93]7 Mar, *Lond Gaz.* [94]5 Jan, *Lond Gaz.* [95]57 & 58 Vict, *c* 58 and Co Council Naming O. [96]9 Nov, 58 & 59 Vict, *c* xiii. [97]1 Oct, LGBO 40224. [98]9 Nov, 63 & 64 Vict, *c* clxxxi. [99]9 Nov, 1 Edw VII, *c* cxlviii. [100]1 Apr, LGBO 43618. [101]1 Apr, LGBO 64168. [102]24 Mar, LGBO 16014. [103]24 Mar, LGBO 19087. [104]OC 24 Mar. [105]1 Apr, LGBO 62276. [106]Year vicarage (*Lond Gaz*, 1 June 1951). [107]7 Aug, *Lond Gaz.* [108]Lawton, 170; Thomas Langdale, ed., *A Topographical Dictionary of Yorkshire* (1809), 218. [109]14 Dec, *Lond Gaz.* [110]12 Sept, *Lond Gaz.* [111]15 Sept, *Lond Gaz.* [112]Not orig rated in schedule for PLU, incl soon after. [113]16 Feb, *Lond Gaz.* [114]35 & 36 Vict, *c* xiv. [115]17 May, *Lond Gaz.* [116]1 Apr, 9 & 10 Geo V, *c* liii. [117]6 Dec, *Lond Gaz.* [118]Apptd day, LGBO 31729. [119]12 Aug, *Lond Gaz.* [120]*VCH Yorks E Riding* II, 7. [121]4 Feb, *Lond Gaz.* [122]15 Apr, *Lond Gaz.* [123]15 Jan 1958, lic min (*Lond Gaz*, 15 Apr 1958). [124]26 Mar, LGBO 45137. [125]5 Nov, *Lond Gaz.* [126]15 July, *Lond Gaz.* [127]31 Aug, *Lond Gaz.* [128]1 June (*Lond Gaz*, 3 Mar). [129]1 Apr, 14 & 15 Geo V, *c* lxxxix. [130]8 Dec, *Lond Gaz.* [131]29 May, *Lond Gaz.* [132]1 Apr, MHealthO 84517. [133]23 July, *Lond Gaz.* [134]4 July, lic min (*Lond Gaz*, 22 July). [135]24 Mar, LGBO 16602. [136]5 Sept, *Lond Gaz.* [137]4 Mar, *Lond Gaz.* [138]10 June, *Lond Gaz.* [139]1 Apr, MHousLGO 6543. [140]30 Mar, SI 1960/455. [141]21 Dec, *Lond Gaz.* [142]21 Dec, LGBO 11613. [143]9 Mar, *Lond Gaz.* [144]1 Apr, SI 1967/104. [145]1 Nov (*Lond Gaz*, 30 Oct). [146]4 May, *Lond Gaz.* [147]21 Oct, *Lond Gaz.* [148]20 Oct, *Lond Gaz.* [149]15 Dec, *Lond Gaz.* [150]Year when united benefice of Attercliffe with Carbrook became effective. [151]1 Apr, 63 & 64 Vict, *c* ccxxii. [152]Lawton, 294. [153]26 Mar, LGBO 26767. [154]30 Sept, 58 & 59 Vict, *c* xci. [155]OC 28 June, reported in *Parl Papers* 1872, XLVI, 20. [156]1 Apr, 4 & 5 Eliz II, *c* lxxv. [157]25 Mar, LGBO 18582. [158]Apptd day, LGBO 31925. [159]1 Apr, LGBO 66604. [160]24 Mar, *Lond Gaz.* [161]OC 31 July, reported in *Parl Papers* 1890—91, LXI, 56. [162]24 Mar, LGBO 19552. [163]12 June, *Lond Gaz.* [164]OC 31 July, reported in *Parl Papers* 1890—91, LXI, 56. [165]24 Mar, LGBO 20188. [166]11 Sept, *Lond Gaz.* [167]9 Nov, 4 & 5 Geo V, *c* clxxx. [168]18 Dec, *Lond Gaz.* [169]OC 18 Dec (York dioc OC file, 616). [170]By deed Jan 1859. [171]21 Dec, *Lond Gaz.* [172]21 Dec, LGBO 11617. [173]6 Apr, *Lond Gaz.* [174]25 Oct, *Lond Gaz.* [175]5 Feb, *Lond Gaz.* [176]25 Mar, LGBO 19553. [177]30 Aug, *Lond Gaz.* [178]Lawton, 129—30. [179]25 Mar, LGBO 17029. [180]25 Feb, *Lond Gaz.* [181]25 Mar, LGBO 14705. [182]OC 9 July, reported in *Parl Papers* 1872, XLVI, 21. [183]*VCH Yorks E Riding* III, 144. [184]1 Oct, LGBO 42567. [185]Date and authority not found; appears as separate in *Clergy List* (1835). [186]OC 7 May (York dioc OC file, 593). [187]1 Nov, MHousLG Decl. [188]10 July, *Lond Gaz.* [189]24 Mar, 416616. [190]1 Oct, MHealthO 67318. [191]OC 30 Dec, reported in *Parl Papers* 1890—91, XLI, 54. [192]1 Apr, MHealthO 68662. [193]26 July, *Lond Gaz.* [194]26 May, *Lond Gaz.* [195]17 Feb, *Lond Gaz.* [196]9 Aug, *Lond Gaz.* [197]3 June, *Lond Gaz.* [198]2 July, *Lond Gaz.* [199]1 July (*Lond Gaz*, 30 June). [200]*VCH Yorks N Riding* I, 154. [201]16 May, *Lond Gaz.* [202]9 Nov, 2 & 3 Geo V, *c* cxxxviii. [203]1 Nov, declaration of MHousLG. [204]1 Aug, *Lond Gaz.* [205]1 June (*Lond Gaz*, 2 May). [206]Lawton, 145. [207]31 Mar, 9 Edw VII, *c* clxii. [208]6 Mar, *Lond Gaz.* [209]19 Mar, *Lond Gaz.* [210]7 Nov, *Lond Gaz.* [211]23 Aug, *Lond Gaz.* [212]Year lic min (*Lond Gaz*, 10 Oct). [213]29 Nov, *Lond Gaz.* [214]14 Nov, *Lond Gaz.* [215]Year lic min (*Lond Gaz*, 4 Nov). [216]13 Dec, *Lond Gaz.* [217]19 Nov, *Lond Gaz.* [218]23 Dec, *Lond Gaz.* [219]26 May, *Lond Gaz.* [220]17 Sept, *Lond Gaz.* [221]5 July, *Lond Gaz.* [222]22 Mar, *Lond Gaz.* [223]OC 30 Nov, reported in *Parl Papers* 1890—91, LXI, 56. [224]25 Mar, LGBO 22920. [225]20 May, *Lond Gaz.* [226]3 Dec, *Lond Gaz.* [227]1 Apr, MHousLGO 3357. [228]10 June, date vac (*Lond Gaz*, 25 Mar). [229]28 Aug, *Lond Gaz.* [230]21 Dec, LGBO 11621. [231]2 May, *Lond Gaz.* [232]Lawton, 287. [233]*VCH Yorks E Riding* II, 14. [234]25 June, *Lond Gaz.* [235]OC 26 Feb, reported in *Parl Papers* 1872, XLVI, 22. [236]17 May, date vac (*Lond Gaz*, 23 Mar). [237]19 Apr, *Lond Gaz.* [238]9 Nov, 63 & 64 Vict, *c* clxxix. [239]Apptd day, LGBO 32083. [240]1 Oct, 13 & 14 Geo V, *c* xliv. [241]1 Apr, MHealthO 85377. [242]Lawton, 319. [243]45 & 46 Vict, *c* 58. [244]Lawton, 326. [245]27 Dec, *Lond Gaz.* [246]8 Jan, *Lond Gaz.* [247]2 Mar, *Lond Gaz.* [248]1 Apr, MHealthO 65899. [249]1 June, MHousLG Decl. [250]1 Mar, *Lond Gaz.* [251]1 Apr, 19 & 20 Geo V, *c* lxxxviii. [252]1 Apr, SI 1955/359. [253]1 Apr, SI 1968/128. [254]15 June, SI 1956/822. [255]6 May, *Lond Gaz.* [256]5 Aug, *Lond Gaz.* [257]Apptd day, 57 & 58 Vict, *c* 58, and Co Council Naming O. [258]15 Apr, LGBO 32893. [259]10 Feb, *Lond Gaz.* [260]13 Jan, *Lond Gaz* (OC, 28 June 1828). [261]24 Mar, LGBO 21401. [262]Apptd day, LGBO 31733. [263]8 Aug, *Lond Gaz.* [264]12 Sept, *Lond Gaz.* [265]Apptd day, LGBO 31732. [266]26 Mar, LGBO 37539. [267]24 Aug, *Lond Gaz.* [268]14 Apr, *Lond Gaz.* [269]17 Nov, *Lond Gaz.* [270]17 June, *Lond Gaz.* [271]9 Nov, 58 & 59 Vict, *c* xiv. [272]26 Mar, LGBO 34241. [273]12 July, *Lond Gaz.* [274]OC 21 July, reported in *Parl Papers* 1872, XLVI, 20. [275]27 July,

Lond Gaz. [276]24 Mar, LGBO 14821. [277]24 Nov, *Lond Gaz.* [278]12 Dec, *Lond Gaz.* [279]OC 5 Mar, reported in *Parl Papers* 1890—91, LXI, 55. [280]9 Nov, 63 & 64 Vict, c lxxix. [281]9 Nov, charter incorp Todmorden MB. [282]21 Dec, LGBO 11619. [283]21 Dec, LGBO 11618. [284]8 Feb, *Lond Gaz.* [285]Robert Thoroton, *The Antiquities of Nottinghamshire* (enlarged ed [by John Thorsby], 3 vols, 1790—96), III, 357. [286]24 Mar, LGBO 20187. [287]24 Dec, *Lond Gaz.* [288]2 Aug, *Lond Gaz.* [289]14 Apr 1966, vac (*Lond Gaz*, 1 Nov 1965). [290]23 June, *Lond Gaz.* [291]24 Mar, LGBO 22257. [292]OC 26 June, reported in *Parl Papers* 1872, XLVI, 21. [293]28 May, *Lond Gaz.* [294]OC 7 Feb, reported in *Parl Papers* 1872, XLVI, 20. [295]1 Apr, LGBO 33556. [296]*VCH Yorks N Riding* I, 48. [297]16 Jan, *Lond Gaz.* [298]19 May, *Lond Gaz.* [299]3 May, *Lond Gaz.* [300]8 Mar, *Lond Gaz.* [301]30 Oct, *Lond Gaz.* [302]31 Mar, *Lond Gaz.* [303]Apptd day, LGBO 31735. [304]31 Oct, 63 & 64 Vict, c ccxxii. [305]31 Mar, MHealthO 74102. [306]1 Apr, MHealthO 90885. [307]Apptd day, LGBO 32129. [308]30 Aug, *Lond Gaz.* [309]6 Feb, *Lond Gaz.* [310]10 Jan, *Lond Gaz.* [311]15 June, SI 1956/819. [312]2 Sept, *Lond Gaz.* [313]23 Oct 1841, Part Dist, reported in *Parl Papers* 1870, LXIV, 175. [314]2 Aug 1842, Part Dist, reported in *Parl Papers* 1870, LXIV, 175. [315]17 Oct 1842, Part Dist, reported in *Parl Papers* 1870, LXIV, 175. [316]7 Sept, *Lond Gaz.* [317]31 Jan, *Lond Gaz.* [318]21 May, *Lond Gaz.* [319]22 Sept, *Lond Gaz.* [320]Year vac (*Lond Gaz* 19 Dec 1922). [321]24 Oct, *Lond Gaz.* [322]3 July, *Lond Gaz.* [323]3 May 1966, vac (*Lond Gaz*, 1 Mar). [324]2 Nov, *Lond Gaz.* [325]22 Aug, *Lond Gaz.* [326]13 Oct, *Lond Gaz.* [327]29 Aug, *Lond Gaz.* [328]11 July, O Yorks W Riding Co Council. [329]19 July, O Yorks W Riding Co Council. [330]25 July, *Lond Gaz.* [331]21 Dec, LGBO 13201. [332]21 Dec, LGBO 13200. [333]31 Oct, *Lond Gaz.* [334]25 Mar, LGBO 16994. [335]1 Apr, LGBO 32495. [336]5 Apr, *Lond Gaz.* [337]1 Jan 1973 (*Lond Gaz*, 29 Dec 1972). [338]11 June, *Lond Gaz.* [339]22 Dec, *Lond Gaz.* [340]25 Mar, LGBO 14708. [341]Apptd day, LGBO 32120. [342]Year vac (*Lond Gaz*, 22 July 1932). [343]18 Feb, *Lond Gaz.* [344]1 Edw VII, c cxc. [345]3 Mar, O Archbp York under Private Patronage Act, reported in *Parl Papers* 1870, LXIV, 184. [346]18 Aug, *Lond Gaz.* [347]24 Mar, LGBO 22105. [348]1 Apr, LGBO 62158. [349]24 Mar, LGBO 16604. [350]14 Mar, *Lond Gaz.* [351]1 Apr, LGBO 63268. [352]27 May, Part Dist, reported in *Parl Papers* 1870, LXIV, 184. [353]14 Jan, *Lond Gaz.* [354]16 Apr, *Lond Gaz.* [355]May, Part Dist, by deed. [356]Year vac (*Lond Gaz*, 31 Jan 1922). [357]22 Nov, LGBO 6861. [358]Apptd day, LGBO 31844. [359]1 Apr, 1 & 2 Geo V, c lxxxiv. [360]9 Nov, 11 & 12 Geo V, c lxix. [361]OC 2 Oct, reported in *Parl Papers* 1872, XLVI, 18. [362]1 Oct, MHealthO 79190. [363]13 June, *Lond Gaz.* [364]9 May, *Lond Gaz.* [365]1 Oct, *Lond Gaz.* [366]10 Oct, *Lond Gaz.* [367]4 Aug, *Lond Gaz.* [368]1 May, *Lond Gaz.* [369]19 Aug, *Lond Gaz.* [370]Year sep EP, erected on authority 1 Edw VII, c cxc. [371]First appearance in clergy; authority and exact date not found. [372]OC 24 Dec (York dioc OC file, 727). [373]1 Apr, MHousLGO 14991. [374]*VCH Yorks E Riding* II, 196. [375]*VCH Yorks E Riding* II, 226. [376]24 Mar, LGBO 16430. [377]1 Apr, MHousLGO 1444. [378]*VCH Yorks E Riding* II, 123. [379]1 Nov, O E Riding Co Council. [380]OC 3 Feb (York dioc OC file, 157). [381]25 Mar, LGBO 19662. [382]30 Apr, *Lond Gaz.* [383]13 Sept, *Lond Gaz.* [384]24 Mar, LGBO 19086. [385]26 Mar, LGBO 25974. [386]1 Apr, MHealthO 66454. [387]25 Mar, LGBO 14706. [388]1 Apr, 14 Geo VI, c xl. [389]1 Apr, SI 1951/323. [390]*VCH Yorks N Riding* II, 233. [391]*VCH Yorks E Riding* II, 129. [392]1 Jan, 20 Vict, c 19. [393]23 Oct, Part Dist, reported in *Parl Papers* 1870, LXIV, 175. [394]1 Dec, *Lond Gaz.* [395]27 June, *Lond Gaz.* [396]1 Feb (*Lond Gaz*, 29 Jan). [397]OC 28 June, reported in *Parl Papers* 1890—91, LXI, 55. [398]OC 25 Mar, reported in *Parl Papers* 1890—91, LXI, 57. [399]29 Mar, *Lond Gaz.* [400]23 Feb, *Lond Gaz.* [401]25 Mar, LGBO 19554. [402]26 July, LGBO 20475. [403]1 Apr, SI 1953/469. [404]12 Apr, *Lond Gaz.* [405]3 Nov, *Lond Gaz.* [406]31 July, *Lond Gaz.* [407]26 Mar, LGBO 27653. [408]24 Mar, LGBO 22397. [409]Apptd day, LGBO 32122. [410]Lawton, 195. [411]1 Apr, SI 1967/67. [412]6 June, *Lond Gaz.* [413]7 May, *Lond Gaz.* [414]Sept, *Lond Gaz.* [415]8 Nov, *Lond Gaz.* [416]24 Mar, LGBO 16263. [417]Apptd day, LGBO 31643. [418]21 Jan, *Lond Gaz.* [419]6 July, *Lond Gaz.* [420]5 Dec, *Lond Gaz.* [421]1 Nov, MHealth Decl. [422]26 Mar, LGBO 39884. [423]1 Apr, SI 1967/1868. [424]Apptd day, LGBO 31992. [425]1 Apr, LGBO 38692. [426]1 Oct, LGBO 66324. [427]1 Apr, LGBO 66763. [428]17 Dec, *Lond Gaz.* [429]23 Dec, LGBO 11659. [430]Apptd day, 57 & 58 Vict, c 58, and Co Council Naming O. [431]22 Dec, LGBO 13182. [432]20 Nov, *Lond Gaz.* [433]Oct 1954, lic min (*Lond Gaz*, 20 Nov 1953). [434]8 June, *Lond Gaz.* [435]13 Mar, *Lond Gaz.* [436]OC 31 Jan, reported in *Parl Papers* 1872, XLVI, 18. [437]OC 28 Dec (York dioc OC file, 259). [438]30 Sept, LGBO 36649. [439]10 Apr, *Lond Gaz.* [440]*VCH Yorks E Riding* IV, 169. [441]OC 12 Apr, reported in *Parl Papers* 1872, XLVI, 20. [442]5 Dec, LGBO 9873. [443]Apptd day, 57 & 58 Vict, c 58 & Co Council Naming O. [444]30 Sept, 60 & 61 Vict, c ccxliv. [445]25 Mar, LGBO 37837. [446]32 & 33 Vict, c xxx. [447]*VCH Yorks N Riding* II, 39. [448]2 & 3 Wm IV, c 64 and 7 & 8 Vict, c 61. [449]Apptd day, LGBO 31738. [450]16 Apr, LGBO 8986. [451]17 Feb, MHousLG Decl. [452]OC 26 Jan. [453]27 June, reported in *Parl Papers* 1870, LXIV, 184. [454]30 Mar, *Lond Gaz.* [455]1 Mar (*Lond Gaz*, 20 Feb). [456]7 Nov, *Lond Gaz.* [457] No explicit order amending co boundaries found. [458]Lawton, 228. [459]23 Feb, LGBProvO 3479, confirmed by 42 & 43 Vict, c cvi. [460]25 Mar, LGBO 16947. [461]12 Jan, *Lond Gaz.* [462]Year abol, vac (*Lond Gaz*, 27 Feb 1934). [463]24 July, *Lond Gaz.* [464]17 Dec, LGBO 12859. [465]18 Apr, *Lond Gaz.* [466]OC 6 Jan (York dioc OC file, 189). [467]15 Nov, MHealthO 73815. [468]18 May, *Lond Gaz.* [469]Augmented 1722 as PC (Lawton, 183). [470]29 June, *Lond Gaz.* [471]1 Apr, MHousLGO 7713. [472]30 Mar, SI 1960/449. [473]11 Dec, *Lond Gaz.* [474]1 Mar (*Lond Gaz*, 14 Feb). [475]19 July, *Lond Gaz.* [476]1 Apr, MHealthO 69700. [477]29 Apr, *Lond Gaz.* [478]13 Aug, *Lond Gaz.* [479]1 Apr, MHousLGO 4119. [480]30 Nov, *Lond Gaz.* [481]29 Feb, *Lond Gaz.* [482]7 June, *Lond Gaz.* [483]25 Mar, LGBO 16605. [484]24 Mar, LGBO 22061. [485]20 July, *Lond Gaz.* [486]20 Dec, *Lond Gaz.* [487]9 Mar, *Lond Gaz.* [488]22 Oct, *Lond Gaz.* [489]28 Apr, *Lond Gaz.* [490]30 Sept, 58 & 59 Vict, c vii. [491]1 Apr, MHousLGO 8386. [492]28 July, *Lond Gaz.* [493]1 July, *Lond Gaz.* [494]16 Sept, *Lond Gaz.* [495]1 Oct, LGBO 53399. [496]12 Oct, *Lond Gaz.* [497]Year of cr, effective before 19 Dec (information kindly supplied by Records Officer, Church Commissioners (file NB 43/98B [*Lond Gaz* 30 Jan 1923]). [498]1 & 2 Geo V, c clxxx. [499]24 Mar, LGBO 16600. [500]25 Mar, LGBO 19556. [501]1 Apr, 3 Edw VII, c cclv. [503]Apptd day, LGBO 31668. [504]1 Apr, 22 & 23 Geo V, c xv. [505]22 Oct, LGBO 7252. [506]9 Oct, LGBO 6994. [507]18 July, *Lond Gaz.* [508]24 Feb, *Lond Gaz.* [509]1 Apr, MHousLGO 6511. [510]13 June, Instr, Part Dist. [511]8 Nov, *Lond Gaz.* [512]25 Mar, consecr church (*Lond Gaz*, 29 Nov 1938). [513]11 Jan 1941, consecr church (*Lond Gaz*, 8 Nov 1938). [514]29 Dec, *Lond Gaz.* [515]1 Apr, *Lond Gaz.* [516]5 June, *Lond Gaz.* [517]1 Apr, MHousLGO 5828. [518]Year abol, effective vac (*Lond Gaz*, 26 Oct 1937). [519]16 Dec, LGBO 8296. [520]28 Mar, *Lond Gaz.* [521]15 Jan, *Lond Gaz.* [522]22 July, *Lond Gaz.* [523]3 Mar, *Lond Gaz.* [524]Year vac (*Lond Gaz*, 7 Nov 1930). [525]25 Mar, LGBO 19660. [526]25 Mar, LGBO 19661. [527]1 Oct, LGBO 33854. [528]*VCH Yorks E Riding* IV, 95. [529]*VCH Yorks E Riding* IV, 101. [530]2 July, Instr, Part Dist, reported in *Parl Papers* 1870, LXIV, 183. [531]*VCH Yorks E Riding* II, 89. [532]14 Sept, *Lond Gaz.* [533]Apptd day, LGBO 31740. [534]10 May, Instr Bp Ripon, Part Dist. [535]*VCH Yorks N Riding* II, 525. [536]1 Apr, LGBO 66566. [537]1 Apr, SI 1967/396. [538]24 Mar, LGBO 20788. [539]Lawton, 68. [540]11 Apr, Part Dist, reported in *Parl Papers* 1870, LXIV, 175. [541]*VCH Yorks N Riding* II, 538. [542]21 July, *Lond Gaz.* [543]2 Feb, *Lond Gaz.* [544]Year lic min (*Lond Gaz*, 12 Oct 1951). [545]1 May (*Lond Gaz*, 26 Apr). [546]*VCH Yorks N Riding* II, 186—87. [547]24 Mar, LGBO 19604. [548]24 Mar, LGBO 20786. [549]1 Nov (*Lond Gaz*, 26 Oct). [550]1 Apr, MHealthO 71638. [551]9 Nov, *Lond Gaz.* [552]1 Apr, MHealthO 69748. [553]10 Mar, *Lond Gaz.* [554]*VCH Yorks E Riding* I, 294. [555]OC 16 Apr (York dioc OC file, 550). [556]24 Mar, LGBO 16597. [557]24 Mar, LGBO 16599. [558]24 Mar, LGBO 16598. [559]OC 13 May, reported in *Parl Papers* 1890—91, LXI, 57. [560]26 Oct 1838, Part Dist, reported in *Parl Papers* 1870, LXIV, 175. [561]16 July, MHousLG Decl. [562]*VCH Yorks N Riding* I, 71. [563]1 Feb (*Lond Gaz*, 23 Jan 1973). [564]10 Sept, *Lond Gaz.* [565]1 Nov, *Lond Gaz.* [566]24 Mar, LGBO 21718. [567]*VCH Yorks E Riding* II, 244. [568]28 Feb, *Lond Gaz.* [569]*VCH City of York*, 399; *VCH Yorks E Riding* III, 34. [570]1 Oct, LGBO 33042. [571]1 Apr, LGBO 57578. [572]OC 8 May, reported in *Parl Papers* 1872, XLVI, 17. [573]Authority not found; date noted in secondary sources. [574]Year effective and so noted in census records; authority not found. [575]24 June, *Lond Gaz.* [576]14 Feb, *Lond Gaz.* [577]1 Jan 1974 (*Lond Gaz*, 18 Dec 1973). [578]4 Apr, *Lond Gaz.* [579]16 Sept, lic min (*Lond Gaz*, 1 July). [580]1 Aug (*Lond Gaz*, 20 July). [581]9 Nov, 2 Edw VII, c cxxiv. [582]18 June, *Lond Gaz.* [583]31 Aug, *Lond Gaz.* [584]1 May 1841, Part Dist, reported in *Parl Papers* 1870, LXIV, 175. [585]28 Jan, *Lond Gaz.* [586]14 Sept, *Lond Gaz.* [587]26 Feb, *Lond Gaz.* [588]Apptd day, LGBO 32142. [589]9 Nov, 62 & 63 Vict, c cxi. [590]9 Nov, 63 & 64 Vict, c ccxxxiv. [591]9 Nov, 2 & 3 Geo V, c cxxxiii. [592]1 Oct, 18 & 19 Geo V, c lxiii. [593]13 Feb, *Lond Gaz.* [594]2 Apr, *Lond Gaz.* [595]15 Feb, *Lond Gaz.* [596]23 Jan, *Lond Gaz.* [597]9 Oct, LGBO 6995. [598]20 Feb, *Lond Gaz.* [599]14 Feb, *Lond Gaz.* [600]1 July (*Lond Gaz*, 30 June). [601]*VCH Yorks N Riding* II, 30. [602]31 Aug, *Lond Gaz.* [603]25 Mar, LGBO 18120. [604]Lawton, 232. [605]15 May, *Lond Gaz.* [606]10 Oct, consecr church (*Lond Gaz*, 15 Sept 1959). [607]24 Mar, LGBO 42280. [608]Lawton, 383. [609]11 Nov, *Lond Gaz.* [610]30 Jan, Instr, Part Dist, reported in *Parl Papers* 1870, LXIV, 187. [611]OC 20 Oct, reported in *Parl Papers* 1890—91, LXI, 53. [612]1 Apr, MHealthO 69365. [613]24 Mar, LGBO 22800. [614]20 Mar,

Lond Gaz. [615]OC 14 Aug, reported in *Parl Papers* 1890—91, XLI, 54. [616]24 Mar, LGBO 14789. [617]*VCH Yorks E Riding* III, 73. [618]*VCH Yorks E Riding* I, 287; Lawton, 388; 13 Chas II, c ii (private). [619]7 Dec, *Lond Gaz.* [620]*Valor.* [621]6 Oct, *Lond Gaz.* [622]*VCH Yorks N Riding* II, 239. [623]9 Nov, LGBProvO 1504. [624]24 Mar, LGBO 21382. [625]11 May, *Lond Gaz.* [626]11 Oct, *Lond Gaz.* [627]Year vac (*Lond Gaz*, 16 Apr 1937). [628]26 Mar, LGBO 39006. [629]LGBO 58473. [630]28 Mar, *Lond Gaz.* [631]1 June (*Lond Gaz*, 30 May). [632]OC 20 Mar (York dioc OC file, 620). [633]21 Dec, LGBO 11620. [634]30 Sept, LGBProvO 1126, confirmed by 58 & 59 Vict, session 2, c viii. [635]Lawton, 240. [636]3 Oct, *Lond Gaz.* [637]15 Oct, *Lond Gaz.* [638]Incumbent from 1859, Church Commissioners NB 40/106. [639]28 Feb 1926, vac (*Lond Gaz*, 26 Mar 1922). [640]5 Mar, *Lond Gaz* (Reorganisation Areas Measure). [641]Year vac (*Lond Gaz*, 5 Mar 1957). [642]Year vicarage (*Lond Gaz*, 4 Apr 1950). [643]*VCH Yorks E Riding* II, 281, 301. [644]*VCH Yorks E Riding* II, 308. [645]30 Sept, LGBO 35101. [646]1 Apr, 9 & 10 Geo V, c liii. [647]11 Mar, *Lond Gaz.* [648]1 Nov (*Lond Gaz*, 29 Oct). [649]24 Mar, LGBO 22106. [650]1 Apr, SI 1955/387. [651]13 Nov, Part Dist, by deed. [652]22 May, *Lond Gaz.* [653]1 Nov (*Lond Gaz*, 30 Oct). [654]18 Mar, *Lond Gaz.* [655]27 Jan, *Lond Gaz.* [656]25 Mar, LGBO 19517. [657]19 Dec, *Lond Gaz.* [658]25 July, *Lond Gaz.* [659]30 June, *Lond Gaz.* [660]5 Mar, *Lond Gaz.* [661]19 Jan, *Lond Gaz.* [662]1 July (*Lond Gaz*, 14 June). [663]30 Sept, LGBO 33134. [664]1 Oct, LGBO 46506. [665]30 Sept, 58 & 59 Vict, c lxxxix. [666]30 Sept, LGBO 36649. [667]24 Mar, LGBO 22556. [668]OC 23 Oct, reported in *Parl Papers* 1890—91, LXI, 55. [669]12 Mar, *Lond Gaz.* [670]OC 11 Oct (York dioc OC file, 491). [671]Year vac (*Lond Gaz*, 9 Oct 1933). [672]Lawton, 91; act of Parl 22 Geo III. [673]Lawton, 92. [674]7 Nov, Part Dist, reported in *Parl Papers* 1870, LXIV, 175. [675]19 Sept, *Lond Gaz.* [676]16 Dec, *Lond Gaz.* [677]Year abol (incumbent no longer in benefice). [678]Yr effective; authority not found. [679]16 Apr, *Lond Gaz.* [680]3 Apr, *Lond Gaz.* [681]Year vac, on statutory authority of 1 Edw VII, c cxc. [682]28 July 1939, Church Commissioners NB30/121. [683]OC 28 July (York dioc OC file, 513). [684]30 Sept, LGBO 34688. [685]25 Mar, *Lond Gaz.* [686]30 Sept, LGBProvO 1088, confirmed by 58 & 59 Vict, c lxxxix. [687]Apptd day, LGBO 31761. [688]1 Apr, LGBO 66301. [689]9 Nov, 3 & 4 Geo V, c xcv. [690]*VCH Yorks E Riding* II, 323. [691]Apptd day, LGBO 31741. [692]Year lic min (*Lond Gaz*, 29 Jan). [693]9 Nov, 11 & 12 Geo V, c xcvi. [694]1 Apr, 14 & 15 Geo V, c lxxi. [695]30 Oct, *Lond Gaz.* [696]8 Oct, *Lond Gaz.* [697]13 Nov, *Lond Gaz.* [698]8 May, *Lond Gaz.* [699]Lawton, 452. [700]24 Mar, LGBO 20785. [701]OC 27 June, reported in *Parl Papers* 1890—91, XLI, 54. [702]26 Mar, LGBO 37629. [703]25 Mar, LGBO 19518. [704]1 Oct, 19 & 20 Geo V, c xxiii. [705]1 Apr, MHousLGO 8386. [706]15 Mar, *Lond Gaz.* [707]24 Mar, LGBO 21638. [708]1 Apr, MHealthO 68250. [709]2 Dec, LGBO 11616. [710]Lawton, 211. [711]25 Mar, LGBO 13183. [712]6 Dec, lic min (*Lond Gaz*, 17 Nov). [713]Supplemental O (*Lond Gaz*, 30 June 1967). [714]26 Nov, lic min (*Lond Gaz*, 12 Oct). [715]24 Mar, LGBO 20787. [716]1 Oct, 432885. [717]25 Mar, LGBO 27584. [718]24 Mar, LGBO 22396. [719]1 June, lic min (*Lond Gaz*, 1 May). [720]Year vac (*Lond Gaz*, 11 June 1937). [721]*VCH Yorks N Riding* I, 197. [722]1 & 2 Geo V, c clxxx. [723]27 Jan, deed of Mayor on statutory authority of 1 Edw VI, c 9; see *VCH*

City of York, 367—68. [724]OC 12 Aug (York dioc OC file, 459). [725]26 Feb, *Lond Gaz*. [726]24 Mar, LGBO 20789. [727]Year vac (*Lond Gaz*, 26 Nov 1937). [728]17 July, LGBProvO 11613, conf by 44 Vict, *c* xvii. [729]Year vac (*Lond Gaz*, 31 May). [730]25 Mar, LGBO 1955. [731]1 Oct, LGBO 36632. [732]30 Sept, LGBO 45657. [733]14 Dec, LGBO 6846. [734]Apptd day, LGBO 31739. [735]Year vac (*Lond Gaz*, 30 Jan 1923). [736]1 Apr, LGBO 46064. [737]Apptd day, LGBO 32122. [738]Apptd day, LGBO 32268. [739]Lawton, 413. [740]Charter incorp of Ossett MB. [741]27 Nov, *Lond Gaz*. [742]29 Sept, *Lond Gaz*. [743]7 Oct, *Lond Gaz*. [744]OC 15 Jan, reported in *Parl Papers* 1890—91, LXI, 56. [745]1 Oct, LGBO 34760. [746]1 Oct, LGBO 56590. [747]2 Jan, *Lond Gaz*. [748]24 Mar, LGBO 22801. [749]9 June, *Lond Gaz*. [750]Lawton, 211. [751] 25 Mar, LGBO 19656. [752]24 Mar, LGBO 16601. [753]Apptd day, LGBO 31724. [754]25 Mar, LGBO 14707. [755]1 Feb, MHousLG Decl. [756]9 July, Instr, Part Dist, reported in *Parl Papers* 1870, LXIV, 187. [757]4 Dec, *Lond Gaz*. [758]6 Sept, *Lond Gaz*. [759]1 Apr, MHousLGO 1443. [760]Year lic min (*Lond Gaz*, 6 Dec 1955). [761]1 Apr, LGBO 39497. [762]9 July, *Lond Gaz*. [763]25 Mar, LGBO 18164. [764]OC 10 Aug, reported in *Parl Papers* 1890—91, LXI, 57. [765]1 Apr, LGBO 53387. [766]1 Apr, 3 & 4 Geo V, *c* cxxxiv. [767]24 Mar, LGBO 20788. [768]Cr by deed 1863. [769]25 Mar, LGBO 17030. [770]1 Apr, 18 & 19 Geo V, *c* lxxxvii. [771]Year vac (*Lond Gaz*, 11 June 1937). [772]1 Jan (*Lond Gaz*, 18 Dec 1973). [773]OC 14 Aug, reported in *Parl Papers* 1890—91, LXI, 56. [774]Year vac (*Lond Gaz*, 19 Feb 1937). [775]1 Apr, LGBO 33526. [776]14 Aug, *Lond Gaz*. [777]1 Apr, LGBO 46257. [778]1 Nov (*Lond Gaz*, 24 Oct). [779]1 Apr, MHealthO 70508. [780]1 June (*Lond Gaz*, 2 May). [781]1 Apr, MHousLGO 4152. [782]Apptd day, LGBO 32236. [783]OC 19 June, reported in *Parl Papers* 1872, XLVI, 18. [784]25 Mar, LGBO 18166. [785]25 Mar, LGBO 18165. [786]1 Oct, MHealthO 69013. [787]1 June (*Lond Gaz*, 31 May 1973). [788]OC 3 Feb, reported in *Parl Papers* 1872, XLVI, 20. [789]Lawton, 197; *Kelley's Directory* (1889), 653. [790]1 Oct, MHealthO 70163. [791]24 Mar, LGBO 20699. [792]1 Mar (*Lond Gaz*, 10 Feb). [793]29 Jan, *Lond Gaz*. [794]30 Sept, Part Dist, reported in *Parl Papers* 1870, LXIV, 175. [795]26 Mar, LGBO 33789. [796]24 Mar, LGBO 22555. [797]31 Mar, LGBO 33786. [798]4 July, *Lond Gaz*. [799]Date and authority for loss of sep eccl status not found. The par appears in the schedule of alterations in RDns in 1927. [800]Apptd day, LGBO 31728. [801]1 Apr, 14 Geo VI, *c* xiii. [802]6 Mar 1844, Part Dist, reported in *Parl Papers* 1870, LXIV, 175. [803]4 Oct, *Lond Gaz*. [804]23 Mar, *Lond Gaz*. [805]1 Apr, MHealthO 69356. [806]12 Feb, *Lond Gaz*. [807]OC 21 July, reported in *Parl Papers* 1890—91, LXI, 55. [808]17 Dec, LGBO 8890. [809]15 Oct, *Lond Gaz*. [810]25 Sept, *Lond Gaz*. [811]*VCH City of York*, passim. [812]Action of York officials in 1586 on authority of earlier statute (1547), 1 Edw VI, *c* 9. [813]9 Oct, *Lond Gaz*. [814]5 Mar, *Lond Gaz*. [815]24 Mar, LGBO 22060. [816]24 Mar, LGBO 22059. [817]OC 26 Mar, reported in *Parl Papers* 1890—91, LXI, 56. [818]OC 12 Aug, reported in *Parl Papers* 1890—91, LXI, 57. [819]21 Dec, date of vac (*Lond Gaz*, 11 Oct). [820]26 Nov, lic min (*Lond Gaz*, 12 Oct).

PART II: LOCAL GOVERNMENT UNITS

CHESHIRE

[1]Pars within hundreds from late 16th cent only and not shown after cr of Adm Co in 1889. [2]1 Apr, 17 & 18 Geo V, *c* cv. [3]1 Apr, MHealthO 77044. [4]1 Apr, 20 & 21 Eliz II, *c* 70. [5]9 Nov, 9 Nov, LGB ProvO 1440, conf by 61 & 62 Vict, *c* lxxxiii. [6]1 Apr, MHealthO 84735. [7]1 Apr, SI 1954/317. [8]9 Nov, 1 Edw VII, *c* clxix. [9]9 Nov, 3 & 4 Geo V, *c* cxxxvii. [10]1 Apr, 24 & 25 Geo V, *c* lvi. [11]1 Apr, MHealthO 89198. [12]1 Apr, SI 1952/588. [13]1 Apr, LGBO 58295, conf by 2 & 3 Geo V, *c* cxxvii. [14]1 Apr, 17 & 18 Geo V, *c* ccxxii. [15]At some time pt or ent in a Borough; see BOROUGHS. [16]Based on Beresford & Finberg *Hand-List* and secondary sources with no addtl research. [17]5 & 6 Wm IV, *c* 76. [18]9 Nov, charter incorp, Altrincham UD, Bebington UD constituted respective MBs. [19]Year charter incorp. [20]13 Aug, charter incorp. Extension 1891 to incl the middle of the bed of River Mersey, 54 & 55 Vict, *c* lxxxvii. [21]Extension 1892, 9 Nov, 55 & 56 Vict, *c* cci. [22]27 Apr, charter incorp. [23]OC 14 July, Dukinfield UD constitued Dukinfield MB. [24]23 May, charter incorp. [25]Year charter incorp. [26]Year charter incorp. [27]Ches par, the pt in Mossley MB in Lancs 1889—94. [28]1 Apr, Sale UD constituted a MB, MHealthO 84735. [29]Extension 1881, 11 Aug, 44 & 45 Vict, *c* cxci. [30]Year charter incorp. [31]9 Nov, chater incorp. [32]Not co-terminous with Anc or Adm Co. [33]Altrincham PLU, RD renamed 1895 Bucklow PLU, RD. [34]Not orig rated in the PLU, incl soon thereafter. [35]Great Barrow, Little Barrow each orig sep rated in Gt Budw. PLU, rated soon thereafter jointly as 'Barrow'. [36]Ches, Flints until 1866, ent Ches thereafter. [37]2 Geo III, *c* xlv. [38]Ches par, the pt in New Mills USD in Derbys 1889—94. [39]Ches par transf 1895 to Salop. [40]Ches, Lancs until 1889, the latter in Warr. CB ([assoc with Lancs] pt 1889—94, ent 1894—1974). [41]Ches, Salop until 1866, ent Ches thereafter. [42]Ches, Flints until 1896, ent Ches thereafter. [43]5 Sept, LGBO 31737. [44]24 Jan, LGBO 30586. [45]2 Aug, LGBO 20464. [46]O Ches Co Council, 15 Jan, conf by LGBO 26531. [47]Extension 1893, 15 Apr, LGBO 29250. [48]14 May, LGBO 32764. [49]1 Oct, MHealthO 74933. [50]1 Apr, MHealthO 67350. [51]1 Apr, MHealthO 84735. [52]1 Apr, LGBO 42748. [53]1 Apr, LGBO 42750. [54]1 Apr, LGBO 40700. [55]30 Sept, LGBO 46565. [56]30 Sept, LGBO 41375. [57]60 & 61 Vict, *c* ci. [58]1 Apr, LGBO 32560. [59]1 Apr, 26 Geo V & 1 Edw VIII, *c* x. [60]The pt transf to Merseyside to be 'Bold' par there, the pt transf to Ches (the pt in Warrington New Town) added to Great Sankey CP.

CUMBERLAND

[1]Pars within wards from late 16th cent only and not shown after cr of Adm Co in 1889. [2]1 Apr, 3 & 4 Geo V, *c* cxxxiv. [3]1 Apr, 14 Geo. VI, c. xix. [4]At some time pt or ent in a Borough; see BOROUGHS. [5]Based on Beresford & Finberg *Hand-List* and secondary sources with no addtl research. [6]5 & 6 Wm IV, *c* 76. [7]Extension 1887, 50 & 51

Vict, *c* xix. [8]Beresford & Finsberg, 84. [9]OC 27 June, Whitehaven UD constituted Whitehaven MB. [10]10 Aug, charter incorp; Workington USD existed before incorp of MB in 1883 (and had been enlarged 29 Nov 1882 by 45 & 46 Vict., c. xcviii); the area of the MB was not as large as that of the USD. [11]Not co-terminous with anc or adm co. [12]Not orig rated in the PLU, incl soon thereafter. [13]24 Apr, LGBO 13590. [13]Authority not found. [15]Extension 1890, 14 Aug, O Cumb Co Council. [16]O Cumb Co Council, conf by LGBO 26559, 31 Jan 1891. [17]28 Sept 1894, the UD enlarged so that the formerly rural pt of Arlecdon brought into the UD, LGBO 31577. [18]1 Apr, MHealthO 80628. [19]1 Apr, MHealthO 78137. [20]1 Oct, pt of Keswick UD transf to Cockermouth RD, LGBO 39949. [21]Area of UD enlarged 1894, (incl Ellenborough and Ewanrigg made ent in the UD), apptd day, LGBO 31884.

DERBYSHIRE

[1]Pars within hundreds from late 16th cent only and not shown after cr of Adm Co in 1889. [2]53 & 54 Vict, *c* liv. [3]31 Oct, 63 & 64 Vict, *c* ccxxii. [4]1 Apr, 17 & 18 Geo V, *c* xcii. [5]1 Apr, MHealthO 77674. [6]1 Apr, SI 1968/44. [7]Tp Scropton and Foston in Scropton AP pt Derbys, pt Staffs, pt of the pt in Derbys transf 1844 to Staffs; the tp became a sep CP 1866 pt in Derbys, pt in Staffs; the pt in Staffs lost 1890 and the par ent Derbys thereafter. [8]At some time pt or ent in a Borough; see BOROUGHS. [9]Pinxton considered most of 19th cent and earlier to be ent Derbys; by 1891 census pt deemed to be in Notts, by bdry alt 1895 the par made ent Derbys. [10]Based on Beresford & Finberg *Hand-List* and secondary sources with no addtl research. [11]5 & 6 Wm IV, *c* 76. [12]Charter incorp. [13]Derbys pars of Stapenhill, Winshill each incl in Burton upon Trent MB at its incorp; each pt Derbys, pt CB 1889—94; by bdry alts 1894 each made ent in the CB (assoc with Staffs). [14]1 Jan, charter incorp, and 6 & 7 Geo V, *c* l (fifty), Buxton UD constituted a MB. [15]Extension 1892, 9 Nov, LGB ProvO 882 confirmed by 55 & 56 Vict, *c* ccxxiv; the pts added in 1892 to the MB and USD transf 26 Mar 1894 to Chesterfield AP so that the enlarged latter alone constituted the MB and USD from 26 Mar 1894. [16]Extension 1877, 40 & 41 Vict, *c* cxviii; extension 1890, 53 & 54 Vict, *c* liv; extension 1891, 54 & 55 Vict, *c* lxxi. [17]Charter incorp. [18]14 Jan, charter incorp. [19]Not co-terminous with Anc or Adm Co. [20]Not orig rated in the PLU, included in it soon thereafter. [21]Disley ent Ches until 1889; pt Ches, pt Derbys 1889—94; ent Ches from 1894. [22]King's Norton in Melbourne orig rated at cr of Shardlow PLU, sep civ status not sustained. [23]Appleby mostly Leics, pt Derbys until 1889; from 1889, 2 CPs, one in each co, each 'Appleby'. [24]Cr 1894 in Leics as 'Nether Seal', transf 1897 to Derbys where called 'Netherseal'. [25]Oakthorpe (ent Derbys) and Donisthorpe (pt Derbys, in Stretton en le Field, Church Gresley, Measham; pt Leics) a sep CP 1866 with pt in each co, made 1897 ent Leics. [26]Cr 1894 in Leics as 'Over Seal', transf 1897 to Derbys where called 'Overseal'. [27]Packington, Ravenstone each mostly Leics, pt Derbys; in 1884, 'Ravenstone with Snibston' cr to be ent Leics incl the pts in Derbys of Packington. [28]Derbys until 1897, Leics thereafter. [29]Chilcote the only

Derbys pt of Burton upon Trent (o'wise Staffs); Chilcote transf 1897 to Leics. [30]Croxall pt Derbys, pt Staffs until 1895, ent Staffs thereafter. [31]Alfreton made ent in the USD 17 Apr 1888, LGB ProvO 531. [32]14 Aug, LGBO 30052. [33]By mid 20th cent called 'Rowsley'. [33]28 Jan, LGBO 29350. [34]1 Jan, MHousLG Decl. [35]Extension 1899, 1 Apr, LGBO 39199. [36]1 Oct, MHealthO 69162. [37]1 Apr, LGBO 56460. [38]31 Mar, MHealth Decl. [39]26 Geo V and 1 Edw VIII, *c* x. [40]9 Nov, 10 & 11 Geo V, *c* cxxvi.

COUNTY DURHAM

[1]Incl area of orig co Sadberge which was in Northumb until 1189, in Durham thereafter until mid 15th cent when constituent pars were transf to other Wds: to Darlington Wd: Coniscliffe, Gainford; to Stockton Wd: Low Dinsdale, Elton, Elwick Hall, Egglescliffe, pt Haughton le Skerne (areas of Coatham Mundeville, Sadberge), pt Greatham (all except area Claxton), Hurworth, Middleton St George, Long Newton, Great Stainton, Stranton; pt to Easington Wd, pt to Stockton Wd: Hart. [2]Mostly Northumb, pt Durham, the latter transf 1844 to Northumb. [3]Mostly Durham, pt Northumb, the former transf 1844 to Northumb. [4]Main tp and other tps, all constituting Norhamshire, transf 1844 to Northumb. [5]Pars within wards from late 16th cent only and not shown after cr of Adm Co in 1889. [6]1 Apr, 5 & 6 Geo V, *c* ii. [7]1 Apr, MHealthO 83526. [8]1 Apr, SI 1967/67. [9]1 Apr, 20 & 21 Eliz II, *c* 70. [10]1 Apr, 22 & 23 Geo V, *c* lxxviii. [11]1 Apr, MHealthO 83526. [12]1 Apr, 1 & 2 Eliz II, *c* xxvii. [13]1 Apr, SI 1967/174. [14]1 Oct, 2 Edw VII, *c* ccx. [15]1 Apr, 21 & 22 Geo V, *c* ciii. [16]1 Apr, 15 & 16 Geo VI & 1 Eliz II, *c* xlix. [17]9 Nov, 5 Edw VII, *c* cvii. [18]1 Nov, 11 & 12 Geo V, *c* cxviii. [19]1 Apr, 14 Geo VI, *c* lix. [20]9 Nov, LGBProvO 1074. [21]1 Apr, 17 & 18 Geo V, *c* xcvii. [22]1 Apr, 25 & 26 Geo V, *c* cxxv. [23]1 Apr, 14 Geo VI, *c* liv. [24]1 Apr, SI 1967/66. [25]Orig sep co, early incl in Durham. [26]Pt Eas. Wd until 1866: tps Lambton, Great Lumley, Little Lumley; pt Durham Wd 1829—66: tp Plawsworth; Chester Wd, pt until 1829: remainder, incl tp Chester le Street and tp Plawsworth; 1829-66: same area less Plawsworth; ent from 1866. [27]At some time pt or ent in a Borough; see BOROUGHS. [28]Orig AP, later deemed ex-par, sep CP 1858. [29]Chap Esh in Lanchester AP transf 1829 from Chester Wd to Durham Wd. [30]Ent par with its tps transf 1829 from Chester Wd to Easington Wd. [31]Tps Broomgate, Crossgate, Elvet, Framwellgate, all in St Oswald, transf 1829 from Chester Wd to Durham Wd. [32]Ent par with its tps and chaps transf 1829 from Chester Wd to Durham Wd. [33]Tp in Haughton le Skerne AP, transf 1829 from Stockton Wd to Darlington Wd. [34]Main tp and tp Neasham transf 1829 from Stockton Wd to Darlington Wd. [35]Tps Ferryhill, Hett in Merrington AP transf 1829 to Darlington Wd. [36]Tp Sunderland Bridge in St Oswald transf 1829 from Chester Wd to Durham Wd; tp Shincliffe in same par transf 1829 from Easington Wd to Durham Wd. [37]Pt Yorks (N Riding), pt Durham (Stockton Wd) until 1829, the latter pt transf 1829 to Darlington Wd. [38]13 July, 6 Geo IV, *c* 43. [39]Tps Cornforth, Garmondsway Moor, Mainforth, Thrislington in Bishop Middleham AP transf 1829 from Stockton Wd to Durham Wd. [40]Tps Cassop, Coxhoe, Quarrington in

Kelloe AP transf 1829 from Easington Wd to Durham Wd. [41]Ex-par area in Easington Wd, transf 1829 to Durham Wd, sep CP 1858, in Durham MB from 1835. [42]Tps Moor House, Moorsley in Houghton le Spring AP transf 1829 from Easington Wd to Durham Wd. [43]Tps Shadforth, Sherburn in Pittington AP transf 1829 from Easington Wd to Durham Wd. [44]Based on Beresford & Finberg *Hand-List* and secondary sources with no addtl research. [45]5 & 6 Wm IV, *c* 76. [46]Extension 1872, 35 & 36 Vict, *c* cxii. [47]13 Sept, charter incorp. [48]Charter of Bp Pilkington. [49]For distinction between Old Borough and Bishop's Borough, incl boundaries, see *VCH Durham* III, 54—61. [50]For distinction in areas as between the Barony and Borough, see *VCH Durham* III, 61—62. [51]For doubt about the pre-1835 Bor status of Gateshead, see *Parl Papers* 1835, XXV, 1525. [52]5 Dec, charter incorp. [53]Extension 1883, 25 Aug, LGBProvO 84, conf by 46 & 47 Vict, *c* cxxiv. [54]12 July, charter incorp. [55]Extension 1884, 47 & 48 Vict, *c* cxxxiv. [56]13 May, charter incorp. [57]3 Sept, charter incorp. [58]Extension 1852 to gain a larger pt of Stockton on Tees CP, 15 & 16 Vict, *c* xviii; extension 1889 to incl the area in Linthorpe in Yorks N Riding, 52 & 53 Vict, *c* xcii. [59]1 Apr, SI 1967/396. Pt of areas in Durham, incl this assoc CB, severed to help cr Teesside CB (assoc with Yorks N Riding), qv in entries for Yorks. [60]Borough enlarged 1867, Sunderland Improvement and Extension Act, 1878; for early doubts about the status of this MB, see William Fordyce, *The History and Antiquities of the County Palatine of Durham* (1853), II, 481—55. [61]Not co-terminous with Anc or Adm Co. [62]Tp Ross, pt tp Elwick each in Durham until 1844, ent Northumb thereafter (see entry under 'Belford' in Part I of the *Guide* for details). [63]29 Mar, LGBProvO 640, the pt of Startforth (Yorks N Riding) transf to Teesdale RSD. [64]Extension 1884, 9 Apr, LGBProvO 560. [65]Extension 1887, 7 May, LGBProvO 496. [66]31 Mar, LGBO 28086. [67]29 Sept, LGBO 11996, confirmed by 44 & 45 Vict, *c* lxi. [68]1 Oct, LGBO 35002. [69]1 Apr, MHealthO 86335. [70]1 Apr, MHealthO 68229. [71]1 Apr, LGBO 52989. [72]1 Apr, LGBO 37374. [73]1 May, LGBO 32271. [74]31 July, O Durham Co Council. [75]1 Apr, 17 & 18 Geo V, *c* xcvii. [76]15 June, LGBO 32273. [77]1 Apr, MHealthO 67552. [78]The pt remaining in Durham to be 'South Biddick' par; the pt of the par transf to Tyne & Wear not to be in a par. [79]The pt of Harraton remaining in Durham to be 'North Lodge' the pt transf to Tyne & Wear not to be in a par so that after 31 Mar 1974, 'Harraton' has no sep civ identity. [80]The pt of Heighington remains as 'Heighington' par in Darlington Dist; the pt in Sedgefield Dist transf to Great Aycliffe.

HEREFORDSHIRE

[1]Pars within hundreds from late 16th cent only and not shown after cr of Adm Co in 1889. [2]Tp in Lea AP, transf 1844 from Glos to Heref, sep CP 1866 in Heref. [3]At some time pt or ent in a Borough; see BOROUGHS. [4]Based on Beresford & Finberg *Hand-List* and secondary sources with no addtl research. [5]5 & 6 Wm IV, *c* 76. [6]Extension 1884, 24 Mar, LGBO 16147. [7]Not co-terminous with Anc or Adm Co. [8]Worcs until 1897, Heref thereafter. [9]Heref until 1844, Worcs thereafter. [10]Tp Litton and Cascob (pt Heref, pt Radnor) sep rated

1836 in Presteigne PLU, transf 1836 to Kington PLU, the tp made 1844 ent Radnor. [11]Not orig rated in the PLU, incl in it soon thereafter. [12]Heref until 1891, Monm thereafter. [13]Heref until 1844, Salop thereafter. [14]Leintwardine North Side pt Heref, pt Salop, made 1895 ent Heref where then called 'Leintwardine'. [15]Salop, Heref until 1895, ent Salop thereafter. [16]Richards Castle pt Salop, pt Heref, divided 1889 into 2 pars of same name, one in each co. [17]Monm until 1844, Heref thereafter. [18]Worcs, Heref until 1897, ent Worcs thereafter. [19]1 Apr, MHealthO 77659. [20]Apptd day, LGBO 32084. [21]1 Apr, MHousLGO 33155. [22]31 Mar, MHealthO 73959. [23]By late 20th cent called 'Pipe Aston'. [24]1 Apr, MHealthO 75349. [25]16 May, O Heref Co Council.

LANCASHIRE

[1]Pars within hundreds from late 16th cent only and not shown after cr of Adm Co in 1889. [2]1 Apr, 20 & 21 Eliz II, *c* 70. [3]9 Nov, 1 Edw VII, *c* ccxxiii. [4]1 Oct, 12 & 13 Geo V, *c* xx. [5]1 Apr, MHealthO 78129. [6]1 Oct, 4 Edw VII, *c* clxiii. [7]1 Apr, 7 & 8 Geo V, *c* lii. [8]1 Apr, SI 1955/415. [9]30 Sept, 61 & 62 Vict, *c* ccxlii; incl extension of Turton UD. [10]9 Nov, 5 Edw VII, *c* cliv. [11]1 Apr, 2 & 3 Geo VI, *c* lxxxv. [12]1 Apr, 14 Geo VI, *c* lxiii. [13]1 Apr, SI 1968/527. [14]9 Nov, 1 & 2 Geo V, *c* cxliv. [15]1 Apr, 15 & 16 Geo V, *c* xcii. [16]9 Nov, 1 & 2 Geo V, *c* cxliv. [17]1 Apr, 22 & 23 Geo V, *c* lxix. [18]1 Oct, MHealthO 77457. [19]1 Apr, MHealthO 87428. [20]9 Nov, LGBProv O 1147, confirmed by 58 & 59 Vict, session 2, *c* vii. [21]9 Nov, 2 Edw VII, *c* ccxl. [22]9 Nov, 5 Edw VII, *c* lxxvii. [23]9 Nov, 3 & 4 Geo V, *c* lxxxi. [24]1 Apr, 17 & 18 Geo V, *c* lxxxviii. [25]1 Apr, 23 & 24 Geo V, *c* lxxv. [26]1 Apr, 14 & 15 Geo VI, *c* xlvi. [27]1 Apr, MHousLGO Decl. [28]9 Nov, 1 Edw VII, *c* xciii. [29]9 Nov, 3 Edw VII, *c* ccxiii. [30]9 Nov, 4 Edw VII, *c* ccxxxv. [31]9 Nov, 9 Edw VII, *c* lvii. [32]9 Nov, 3 & 4 Geo V, *c* cxxxi. [33]1 Apr, 20 & 21 Geo V, *c* clxxiii. [34]1 Apr, MHealthO 77201. [35]1 Apr, 14 Geo VI, *c* 55. [36]1 Apr, SI 1955/16. [37]1 Apr, SI 1952/589. [38]1 Apr, SI 1956/370. [39]9 Nov, 63 & 64 Vict, *c* cclxxxviii. [40]25 Mar, 56 & 57 Vict, *c* ccxv. [41]31 Mar, 61 & 62 Vict, *c* cclviii. [42]1 Apr, SI 1954/202. [43]1 June, 54 & 55 Vict, *c* ccxxi. [44]1 Apr, SI 1960/2204. [45]1 Oct, 5 Edw VII, *c* ii. [46]1 Apr, 1 & 2 Geo V, *c* lxxxv. [47]1 Oct, LBPProvO 1629, confirmed by 63 & 64 Vict, *c* clxxxviii. [48]1 Apr, 22 & 23 Geo V, *c* lxxxviii. [49]1 Apr, SI 1954/319. [50]1 Apr, MHealthO 65884. [51]At some time pt or ent in a Bor; see BOROUGHS listing. [52]Based on Beresford & Finberg *Hand-List* and on other secondary sources with no addtl research. [53]5 & 6 Wm IV, *c* 76. [54]Feb 1878, charter incorp. [55]Gains 1895 the pt of Dukinfield CP (Ches) in the MB, 61 & 62 Vict, *c* lxxxiii; gains 1927 Hurst UD & CP, 1 Apr, 16 & 17 Geo V, *c* lxi; gains 1935 Hartshead CP from Limehurst RD, 1 Apr, MHealthO 80451. [56]29 Sept, charter incorp. [57]25 July, charter incorp. [58]Extensions in 1872 and 1875, noted *VCH Lancs* VIII, 314; extension 1881, 44 & 45 Vict, *c* cxxi. [59]13 June, charter incorp. [60]Extension 1877, 40 & 41 Vict, *c* cxv; extension 1879, 42 & 43 Vict, *c* cxvi. [61]28 Aug, charter incorp. [62]Extendsion 1879, 42 & 43 Vict, *c* cxcix; gains 1897 foreshore, 27 Apr, LGBO 36320. [63]21 Jan, charter incorp. [64]Extension 1872, 35 & 36 Vict, *c* lxxviii; extended 1877, 40 & 41 Vict, *c* clxxxviii and also 42 &

43 Vict, *c* ciii; gains 1898 area Astley Bridge UD & CP, 30 Sept, 61 & 62 Vict, *c* ccxlii. [65]11 Oct, charter incorp. [66]Gains 1905 pt of Orrell and Ford CP (constituted 'Orrell' CP) from Sefton RD, 9 Nov, 5 Edw VII, *c* cliv. [67]30 Dec, charter incorp. [68]Extension 1871, 34 & 35 Vict, *c* cliv; extension 1889, 52 & 53 Vict, *c* lv. [69]24 Oct, charter incorp. [70]Extension 1885, 48 & 49 Vict, *c* cxlvi. [71]9 Sept, charter incorp. [72]17 June, charter incorp. [73]Extension 1895, gaining area Clitheroe Castle CP (not prev in the MB), 58 & 59 Vict, *c* lxxxv. [74]29 June, OC, Colne UD incorp as a MB. [75]9 Nov, charter incorp, Great Crosby UD and Waterloo with Seaforth UD united to constitute Crosby MB. [76]Extension 1879, 42 & 43 Vict, *c* ccii; extended 1884, 47 & 48 Vict, *c* ccx. [77]Year charter incorp; this incorp changes the name of the USD from 'Over Darwen' to 'Darwen'. [78]9 May, OC, the UD of Barton, Eccles, Winton, and Monton incorp as 'Eccles' MB. [79]9 Nov, charter incorp, Farnworth UD constituted a MB. [80]9 Nov, charter incorp, Fleetwood UD constituted a MB. [81]Year charter incorp. [82]18 Feb, charter incorp. [83]Extension 1888, 51 & 52 Vict, *c* clv; extended 1900, 9 Nov, LGBProvO 1586, confirmed by 63 & 64 Vict, *c* ccxxxvi, both changes affecting pts of pars transf to Lancaster CP and not ent pars. [84]Lancaster Castle, an ex-par place, was within the Bor/MB, and was listed sep; it was not sep rated for poor rates and thus became pt 1858 of Lancaster AP. [85]14 July, charter incorp, Leigh UD constituted a MB. [86]9 Nov, charter incorp, Lytham UD and St Anne's on the Sea UD united to constitute Lytham St Anne's MB. [87]Extension 1884, 47 & 48 Vict, *c* ccxv; extension 1885, 48 & 49 Vict, *c* cxxvi; other extensions after constitued a CB. [88]23 Oct, charter incorp. [89]By letters patent 29 Mar 1853. [90]Extension 1891, 9 Nov, LGBProvO 807, confirmed by 54 & 55 Vict, *c* ccxxxiii. [91]21 July, charter incorp. [92]By OC 11 June, Morecambe UD constituted a MB. [93]Union of Heysham UD, Morecambe MB to cr Morecambe and Heysham MB, 18 & 19 Geo V, *c* cxix. [94]Chartered by provisions of 48 & 49 Vict, *c* clxxx, incl gains at that time pt Saddleworth (Yorks W Riding), pt Tintwistle (Ches). [95]Year charter incorp. [96]13 June, charter incorp. [97]Extension 1880, 43 & 44 Vict, *c* cxviii; extended 1889, 1 June, 51 & 52 Vict, *c* clxxiii. [98]9 Nov, charter incorp, Prestwich UD made a MB. [99]9 Nov, charter incorp, Radcliffe UD made a MB. [100]Year charter incorp. [101]The bor ent Lancs, but pt of Rochdale AP in Yorks; see Part I of the *Guide*. [102]Extension 1872, 35 & 36 Vict, *c* xlix. [103]9 Sept, charter incorp. [104]Year charter incorp. [105]Extension 1853, 16 & 17 Vict, *c* xxxii. [106]16 Apr, charter incorp, confirmed by 11 & 12 Vict, *c* xciii. [107]Three small extensions adding further pts of North Meols to the MB, in 1871, 1875, 1885, noted in *VCH Lancs* III, 235. [108]Year charter incorp. [109]Extension 1881, 11 Aug, 44 & 45 Vict, *c* cxiii. [110]Year charter incorp. [111]Pt Heaton Norris (Lancs) in this MB, that pt becomming therefore 1889 assoc with Ches. [112]Extension 1901 (gains ent Reddish UD & CP [which CP became a constituent par in the CB], pt Heaton Norris UD & CP, both Lancs), 1 Edw VII, *c* clxix; extension 1913 (gains Heaton Norris UD & CP [which CP became a constituent par in the CB] from Lancs), 9 Nov, 3 & 4 Geo V, *c* xciii. [113]9 Nov, charter incorp, Stretford UD constituted a MB. [114]Extension (pts of pars only) in 1890, 53 & 54 Vict, *c*

ccxxxvi; in 1895, 58 & 59 Vict, *c* xli; in 1896, 59 & 60 Vict, *c* cxiii (incl gains areas in Ches, qv in Part I of the *Guide*). [115]Chartered on statutory authority of 11 & 12 Vict, *c* xciii. [116]9 June, OC, Widnes USD constituted a MB. [117]Not co-terminous with Anc or Adm Co. [118]Lancs par, pt in Yorks W Riding (the pt in Todmorden USD) 1889—94, thereafter ent Lancs. [119]Not orig rated in the PLU, incl soon thereafter. [120]Not orig rated in the PLU, incl soon after date shown, transf from Preston PLU to Chorley PLU. [121]24 June, O Co Palatine Lancs, confirmed LGBO 28213. [122]Transf 1885 to Manch MB & USD, 48 & 49 Vict, *c* ccxxviii. [123]28 Mar, LGBO 30724. [124]Transf 1890 to Manch MB & USD, 53 & 54 Vict, *c* ccxxviii. [125]5 June, LGBProvO 284. [126]19 Apr, LGBO 31060. [127]Enlarged 1882, 22 May, LGBProvO 63. [128]Reduced 1890 when pt of Gorton CP transf to Manch CB & USD, 53 & 54 Vict, *c* ccxxviii. [129]Extension 1883, 46 & 47 Vict, *c* ccxxv; extension 1891 when Haslingden incorp as a MB, qv in BOROUGHS listing. [130]1 Feb, LGBO 30737. [131]16 Feb, LGBO 14845. [132]Orig 'Poulton Barre and Torrisholme' USD, later called 'Morecambe' USD; date and authority not found. [133]Extension 25 June 1894 when Radcliffe CP gains pt Whitefield UD & Pilkington CP, pt Elton CP, LGBO 30905. [134]Extension 25 Mar 1883, LGBProvO 139. [135]Extension 25 Mar 1883, LGBProvO 139; Lower Booths, Newchurch also affected by civ bdry alts 1883 (see Part I). [136]23 June, LGBO 13785. [137]13 Feb, LGBO 29232. [138]30 Sept, 61 & 62 Vict, *c* ccxlii. [139]1 Apr, LGBO 77201. [140]5 May, O Lancs Co Council. [141]Extension 1905, 1 Apr, LGBO 47745. [142]1 Apr, LGBO 44836. [143]Apptd day, LGBO 31573. [144]9 Nov, LGBProvO 1639, confirmed by 63 & 64 Vict, *c* clxxviii. [145]1 Apr, MHealthO 76293. [146]4 Aug, O Formby UD Council, 1905. [147]Apptd day, LGBO 31458. [148]1 Apr, LGBO 39511. [149]1 Apr, 16 & 17 Geo V, *c* lxi. [150]Apptd day, LGBO 31579. [151]1 Apr, MHousLGO 7185. [152]1 Apr, MHealthO 75239. [153]1 Apr, SI 1954/16. [154]1 Apr, MHousLG Decl. [155]1 Mar, renamed by Lancs Co Council O. [156]9 Sept, O Lancs Co Council. [157]1 Apr, LGBO 40342. [158]4 Aug, renaming by Lancs Co Council O. [159]1 Apr, LGBO 40650. [160]1 Apr, MHousLGO 34441. [161]1 Apr, LGBO 40339. [162]5 May, O Lancs Co Council. [163]1 Apr, LGBO 39522. [164]Apptd day, LGBO 31746. [165]Apptd day, LGBO 31828. [166]Apptd day, LGBO 31804. [167]The pt of Altcar remaining in Lancs to be 'Great Altcar' while the pt transf to Merseyside to be 'Altcar' par. [168]The pt transf to Merseyside to be 'Lydiate' par there; the pt remaining in Lancs transf to Downholland CP.

LEICESTERSHIRE

[1]Pars within hundreds from late 16th cent only and not shown after cr of Adm Co in 1889. [2]1 Jan, 54 & 55 Vict, *c* c. [3]1 Apr, MHealthO 81175. [4]1 Apr, MHealthO 84292. [5]1 Apr, MHealthO 98241. [6]1 Apr, SI 1966/78. [7]1 Apr, SI 1966/340. [8]1 Apr, 20 & 21 Eliz II, *c* 70. [9]At some time pt or ent in a Borough; see BOROUGHS. [10]Based on Beresford & Finberg *Hand-List* and secondary sources with no addtl research. [11]5 & 6 Wm IV, *c* 76. [12]See notes in Part I for disputes over inclusion in Bor or not before 1835 of Leicester The Newarke, Leicester St Leonard, Leicester St Mary (for details see *VCH Leics* VIII, 338

ff). [13]Extension 1892, 1 Jan, 54 & 55 Vict, *c* c. [14]4 Sept, royal charter. [15]Extension 1891, 25 Mar, O Leics Co Council, confirmed by LGBO 26416. [16]10 Aug, charter incorp. [17]Not co-terminous with Anc or Adm Co. [18]Pt Leics, pt Derbys, divided 1889 into 2 pars of same name, one in each co. [19]Derbys until 1897, Leics thereafter. [20]Not orig rated in the PLU, incl in it soon thereafter. [21]Pt Derbys, pt Leics until 1880s, ent Derbys 1880s—97, ent Leics from 1897. [22]Pt Derbys, pt Leics until 1884, ent Leics thereafter. [23]Pt Leics, pt Derbys. [24]Leics 1894—97, Derbys thereafter as 'Netherseal'. [25]Leics 1894—97, Derbys thereafter as 'Overseal'. [26]Pt Leics, pt Warws until 1880s, ent Leics thereafter. [27]Orig rated as pt of Hinckly, sep rated soon thereafter. [28]Northants until 1889; pt Northants, pt Leics 1889—96; ent Leics 1896—1927. [29]Church Langton orig rated in the PLU, its 4 constituent tps (East Langton, Thorpe Langton, Tur Langton, West Langton) sep rated soon thereafter and Church Langton then has no sep civ identity. [30]Incl in Northants hmlt Hothorpe (sep rated, sep CP 1866 in that co). [31]Sysonby with Eye Kettleby (cr 1894) called 'Eye Kettleby' by time of civ abol 1935. [32]Pt Warws, pt Leics until 1885, ent Warws thereafter. [33]Rutl, Leics until 1885, ent Rutl thereafter. [34]31 May, O Leics Co Council confirmed by LGBO 28085. [35]For extensions 1892, see note 2 above. [36]18 Dec, LGBO 20905. [37]1 Apr, MHealthO 81175. [38]1 Apr, MHealthO 84988. [39]1 Oct, LGBO 60780. [40]Authority not found; year of renaming from 'Wigston Magna' UD to 'Wigston' UD noted in *VCH Leics* III, 202. [41]Apptd day, LGBO 31777.

LINCOLNSHIRE

[1]Lbty abol and pars transf to Waps in early 1840s (date not found). [2]Pars within hundreds from late 16th cent only and not shown after cr of Adm Co in 1889. [3]1 Apr, 17 & 18 Geo V, *c* lxxvii. [4]1 Apr, SI 1958/463. [5]1 Apr, SI 1967/1820. [6]1 Apr, 20 & 21 Eliz II, *c* 70. [7]9 Nov, 10 & 11 Geo V, *c* cxvii. [8]1 Apr, SI 1958/1175. [9]24 Mar, LGBO 11660. [10]Deeping Fen reclaimed by drainage beginning in 1595, pt Pts Holl (Elloe Wap), pt Pts Kestev (Ness Wap), made a sep par 1856 as 'Deeping St Nicholas' with pt in each of the Pts (remains pt in Pts Kestev until 1930, ent Pts Holl Adm Co thereafter. [11]At some time pt or ent in a Bor; see BOROUGHS). [12]Pt Lincs Pts Holl, pt Norfolk until 1897, ent Lincs Pts Holl thereafter. [13]Irnham incl tp Hawthorpe with Bulby (sep rated in Bourne PLU at time of cr of that PLU in 1836), sep civ identity not sustained and the tp incl again in Irnham AP by mid cent. [14]On abol of Lincoln Liberty and County of Itself, all pars transf to Pts Kestev: Bracebridge and Waddington to Boothby Graffoe Wap; Branston, Canwick, Mere (ex-par place, sep CP 1858), to Langoe Wap. [15]Pt Grantham par in Grantham Soke & Bor (3 tps of Harrowby, Manthorpe cum Little Gonerby, Spittlegate [each a sep CP 1866, the 1st two in Loveden Wap, the last in Winnibrigs & Threo Wap and in Grantham MB]). [16]Grantham Grange ex-par place (sep CP 1858) in Grantham Soke & Bor. [17]When Stoke CP cr 1776 by union North Stoke AP, South Stoke AP, remains in Grantham Soke (consists from 1776 of 3 tps of Easton, North Stoke, South Stoke) until 1830s, thereafter Easton in Loveden Wap, the other tps in Winnibriggs & Threo

Wap (each a sep CP 1866); Manthorpe cum Little Gonerby pt in Grantham MB. [18]'Allington' a rating as a single tp for poor law purposes consisting of East Allington CP (sep civ identity early from Sedgebrook AP), West Allington AP. [19]Harrowby pt in a Bor; see BOROUGHS. For orig organisation in Grantham Soke, see note 15. [20]In Stamford Bor and Soke. [21]West Fen an ex-par place reclaimed by draining, the tps of Carrington, Frithville, Westville each cr from it in 1812, each a sep CP 1866; see Part I of the *Guide* for the composition of West Fen CP cr in 1880. [22]East Fen an ex-par place reclaimed by draining, the tps of Eastville, Midville each cr from it in 1812, each a sep CP 1866. [23]Wildmore Fen an ex-par place reclaimed by draining, Langriville, Thornton le Fen each cr a parochial chap from it 1812, each a sep CP 1866; Wildmore also cr a parochial chap from it in 1812, but see Part I of the *Guide* for composition of Wildmore CP cr in 1880. [24]Based on Beresford & Finberg's *Hand-List* and secondary sources with no addtl research. [25]5 & 6 Wm IV, *c* 76. [26]9 Nov, charter incorp, Cleethorpes UD constituted a MB. [27]Extension 1879, 14 & 15 Geo VI, *c* lxxiii. [28]Pars from late 16th cent only; for earlier pars abol before that time, see Part I of the *Guide*. [29]9 Nov, charter incorp, Scunthorpe and Frodingham UD constituted 'Scunthorpe' MB. [30]Stamford Baron St Martin ent Northants until 1889 but pt in Stamford MB from 1835 (the MB o'wise ent Lincs Pts Kestev; from 1889—94 the pt in the MB in Lincs Pts Kestev, the remainder in Soke Peterb; after bdry alt 1894, the par ent Lincs Pts Kestev thereafter until civ abol 1930. [31]Not co-terminous with Anc or Adm Co. [32]Amber Hill rated in Boston PLU from 1862, although only cr a CP in 1880. [33]Not orig rated in the PLU, incl soon thereafter. [34]Binbrook St Mary, Binbrook St Gabriel each orig sep rated 1837 at cr of Louth PLU, rated prob from 1840s together as 'Binbrook'. [35]Pts Lind, Notts until 1886, ent Notts thereafter. [36]Flawford an ex-par place, pt in Notts, pt in Pts Lind, sep CP 1858. [37]Crowle pt Yorks W Riding (moorland, uninhabited until late 19th cent), remainder in Pts Lind, the par considered ent Lincs by census of 1871. [38]10 June, O Pts Lind Co Council, conf by LGBO 26299 (dated 17 Oct). [39]22 July, LGBO 18981. [40]1 Apr, MHealthO 75838. [41]1 Apr, MHealthO 74993. [42]1 Apr, LGBO 38377. [43]1 Apr, LGBO 37114. [44]15 Apr, LGBO 34380. [45]1 Oct, MHealthO 68714. [46]1 Oct, The Co of the Pts of Lind (Scunthorpe and Frodingham) Confirmation O, 1919 [so listed in census report of 1921; citation by statutory citation or order number not found]. [47]28 Jan, Pts Lind Co Coucil O. [48]1 Apr, MHealthO 84619. [49]1 Oct, LGBO 34984. [50]1 Apr, MHealthO 69577. [51]1 Apr, LGBO 37321.

MERSEYSIDE

[1]The pt of Altcar remaining in Lancs to be 'Great Altcar' while the pt transf to Merseyside to be 'Altcar' par. [2]The pt transf to Merseyside to be 'Lydiate' par there; the pt remaining in Lancs transf to Downholland CP.

NORTHAMPTONSHIRE

[1]Ex-par place, Northants, Bucks, made 1844 ent Bucks, not a CP in the latter co until 1858. [2]Pars within hundreds from late 16th cent only and not shown after cr of Adm Co in 1889. [3]Extension 1900 of Northampton CB when gains Far Cotton UD, Kingsthorpe UD, St James (Northampton) UD, Abington AP from N'htn. RD, 9 Nov, LGBProvO 1623, conf by 63 & 64 Vict, c lxxxiii. [4]1 Apr, LGBO 59994. [5]1 Apr, 1 Apr, 21 & 22 Geo V, c xxix. [6]1 Apr, SI 1965/250. [7]1 Apr, SI 1969/494. [8]1 Apr, SI 1971/575. [9]1 Apr, 20 & 21 Eliz II, c 70. [10]Salcey and Hartwell Lodges an ex-par place; noted in census of 1871 as still ex-par, but disappears from list of civil parishes before census of 1891; no explicit order found for its inclusion in Hartwell AP. [11]At some time pt or ent in a Bor or MB; see BOROUGHS. [12]Based on Beresford & Finberg's *Hand-List* and secondary sources with no addtl research. [13]5 & 6 Wm IV, c 76. [14]See Part I of the *Guide* for the pts of Banbury in Oxon and in Northants. [15]24 Sept, charter incorp. [16]26 June, charter incorp. [17]Charter incorp. [18]Pars abol before 17th cent not included in list; see Part I of the *Guide* for those pars. [19]Charter incorp. [20]Not co-terminous with Anc or Adm Co. [21]Northants, Hunts until 1895, ent Northants thereafter. [22]Hunts, Northants until 1895, ent Hunts thereafter. [23]Beds, Northants until 1844, ent Beds thereafter. [24]Northants until 1889; pt Northants, pt Leics 1889—96; ent Leics thereafter. [25]Bucks, Northants until 1894, ent Bucks thereafter. [26]Northants until 1895, Warws thereafter. [27]Cr 1894 as 'St Martin Without', later called 'Stamford Baron St Martin's Without'. [28]Northants par, the pt in Stamford MB in Lincs Pts Kestev 1889—94, the remainder ent Northants thereafter. [29]O Northants Co Council, conf 3 Sept by LGBO 27418. [30]O Northants Co Council, conf 9 Dec by LGBO 29121. [31]O Northants Co Council, conf 30 Sept by LGBO 27530. [32]O Northants Co Council, conf 25 Mar by LGBO 26690. [33]1 Oct, MHealthO 68406. [34]1 Apr, MHealthO 100378. [35]1 Apr, MHealthO 80296. [36]1 Apr, LGBO 34373. [37]Apptd day, LGBO 31860. [38]1 Oct, LGBO 43004. [39]Little Bowden made 1896 ent Leics. [40]1 Oct, LGBO 37051. [41]1 Apr, LGBO 34373. [42]The pts of Overstone, Brafield on the Green, Ecton, all in Northampton Dist, cease to be in a par; Overstone as reduced continues to exist in Daventry Dist, and the other 2 as reduced continues to exist in South Northamptonshire Dist. [43]The pts of Collingtree, Courteenhall in Northampton Dist united as 'Collingtree'; the pts of Collingtree, Milton Malsor in South Northamptonshire Dist united as 'Milton Malsor'; the pt of Courteenhall in South Northamptonshire Dist as reduced to be 'Courteenhall' in that Dist. [44]The pts of Great Houghton, Little Houghton in Northampton Dist united as 'Great Houghton'; the pt of each in South Northamptonshire Dist united as 'Little Houghton'. [45]The pts of Kislingbury, Upton in Northampton Dist united as 'Upton'; the area of Kislingbury as reduced to be 'Kislingbury' in South Northamptonshire Dist; the pt of Upton in South Northamptonsire Dist transf to Harpole. [46]The pt of Rothersthorpe in Northampton Dist united with the pts of Milton Malsor, Wootton in that Dist as 'Wootton'; the area of Rothersthorpe as reduced to be 'Rothersthorpe' in South Northamptonshire Dist. [47]See preeceeding specifics on altered areas of pars affecting this Dist.

NORTHUMBERLAND

[1]Belford pt in Durham, pt Northumb until 1844, ent Northumb thereafter; incl tp Elwick (pt Durham, pt Northumb until 1844, ent Northumb thereafter), tp Ross (Durham, transf 1844 to Northumb), all 3 sep rated for poor law purposes. [2]Ex-par place, transf 1844 from Durham to Northumb. [3]Holy Island (Northumb) incl in Durham Ancroft, Kyloe, Tweedmouth, those 3 tps transf 1844 to Northumb. [4]Norham incl Cornhill on Tweed, Duddo, Felkington, Grindon, Horncliffe, Loanend, Longridge, Norham Mains, Shoreswood, Thornton, Twizell, all areas transf 1844 from Durham to Northumb. [5]Pars within wards from late 16th cent only and not shown after cr of Adm Co in 1889. [6]9 Nov, 4 Edw VII, c ccxx. [7]1 Apr, MHealthO 81246. [8]1 Apr, 20 & 21 Eliz II, c 70. [9]Edw VII, c cvii. [10]At some time pt or ent in a Borough; see BOROUGHS. [11]Durham, Northumb until 1844 while tp, ent Northumb from 1844, sep par 1866. [12]In Durham until 1844 while ex-par, in Northumb from 1844, sep par 1858. [13]In Durham until 1844 while tp, in Northumb from 1844, sep par 1866. [14]Based on Bereford & Finberg's *Hand-List* and secondary sources with no addtl research. [15]5 & 6 Wm IV, c 76. [16]Orig area of 'Bamburgshire', early a sep franchise. [17]Extension 1891, 24 Feb, O Northumb Co Council, conf by LGBO 26635. [18]9 Nov, Blyth UD constituted Blyth MB. [19]Area altered in 1889, the MB enlarged and the UD reduced in area to become coterminous, LGBProvO 624, conf by 52 & 53 Vict, c cxii. [20]Year charter incorp. [21]9 Nov, charter incorp (dated 9 Feb). [22]Beresford & Finburg, 146. [23]24 May, charter incorp, Whitley Bay UD constituted Whitley Bay MB. [24]Not co-terminous with Anc or Adm Co. [25]Durham par (the only one in this PLU) transf to Northumb 1844 for civ purposes. [26]Extension 1883, 25 Mar, 45 & 46 Vict, c lxi. [27]Extension 1881, 29 Sept, 45 & 46 Vict, c cii. [28]USD abol 30 Sept, LGBO 31487. [29]2 Mar, LGBO 29233. [30]5 Nov, renaming by O Northumb Co Council. [31]31 Mar, LGBO 33456. [32]Farne Islands ex-par place, not pt of Belford RD but returned with that RD in census reports for convenience's sake. [33]1 Apr, LGBO 49315. [34]Extension 1912, 1 Apr, LGBO 56450. [35]14 Mar, renaming by O Northumb Co Council. [36]Hexham par made ent in UD on apptd day 1894, LGBO 31489. [37]1 Apr, LGBO 56450. [38]1 Apr, LGBO 54447. [39]1 Apr, LGBO 34328. [40]Apptd day, LGBO 31533. [41]1 Jan, renaming O Northumb Co Council. [42]9 Nov, 10 Edw VII & 1 Geo V, c lxxxix. [43]Entire UD except wds of Beckworth, Earsdon, Shiremoor. [44]As defined in the act, per authority cited in note 8.

NOTTINGHAMSHIRE

[1]Pars within hundreds from late 16th cent only and not shown after cr of Adm Co in 1889. [2]1 Apr, LGBO 39566. [3]1 Apr, 22 & 23 Geo V, c lxxx. [4]1 Apr, 14 & 15 Geo VI, c xxxi. [5]1 Apr, 20 & 21 Eliz II, c 70. [6]At some time pt or ent in a Bor; see BOROUGHS. [7]'Sutton Bonington' is the joint rating for poor law purposes of 2 APs of Sutton

Bonington St Anne, Sutton Bonington St Michael. [8]Based on Beresford & Finberg *Hand-List* and secondary sources with no addtl research. [9]5 & 6 Wm IV, *c* 76. [10]9 May, charter incorp. [11]40 & 41 Vict, *c* xxxi. [12]The par of Nottingham St Mary pt in Nott. Bor; when Sneinton gains sep civ identity, Nottingham St Mary ent in Bor thereafter. [13]Extension 1878, 41 & 42 Vict, *c* clxxix. [14]9 Nov, Worksop UD cconstituted a MB. [15]Not co-terminous with Anc or Adm Co. [16]Pinxton considered ent Derbys in 19th cent, deemed by census of 1891 to be pt Notts; after bdry alts 1895, ent Derbys thereafter. [17]Not orig rated in the PLU but incl soon thereafter. [18]Pt Notts, pt Lincs, abol 1884. [19]Blyth AP pt Notts, pt Yorks W Riding until 1866; main tp listed above. [20]Wallingwells pt Nott, pt Yorks W Riding until 1895, ent Notts thereafter. [21]Pt Notts, pt Yorks W Riding until 1895, ent Yorks W Riding thereafter. [22]Pt Notts, pt Yorks W Riding until 1866, ent Notts thereafter. [23]Pt Notts, pt Yorks W Riding until 1886, ent Notts thereafter. [24]O Notts Co Council, conf by LGBO 26979 dated 16 July. [25]13 Dec, LGBO 13038. [26]Extension 1883, 19 May, LGBProvO 99. [27]1 Apr, MHealth0 78578. [28]5 May, O Notts Co Council, Blyth and Cuckney RD renamed Worksop RD. [29]1 Oct, LGBO 34809. [30]1 Oct, LGBO 34809. [31]25 Jan, O Notts Co Council, Hucknall Torkard UD renamed Hucknall UD. [32]30 Apr, O Notts Co Council, Hucknall under Huthwaite UD renamed Huthwaite UD. [33]1 Apr, LGBO 33898. [34]1 Apr, MHealthO 71463, Unnamed RD abol and its pars transf to Leake RD. [35]Finningley, pt Harworth transf to S Yorks; the remainder of the latter to be 'Harworth' in Notts.

RUTLAND

[1]Pars within hundreds from late 16th cent only and not shown after cr of Adm Co in 1889. [2]At some time pt or ent in a Borough; see BOROUGHS. [3]Stoke Dry, Thorpe by Water each pt Leics, pt Rutl until 1885, each ent Rutl from 1885. [4]Based on Beresford & Finberg *Hand-List* and secondary sources with no addtl research. [5]Not co-terminous with Anc or Adm Co. [6]1 Nov, LGBO 56440.

SHROPSHIRE

[1]In 1536 (27 Henry VIII, *c* 26) Oswestry Hd cr in Salop comprised of marcher lordships of Oswestry, Knockin, Maesbrook, prev in Marches; a par in Marches incl thereafter in Salop (Ellesmere in Pimhill Hd), area of Down (not sep later civ) transf to Chirbury Hd; Salop par transf to Marches (Clun); in 1543 (34 & 35 Henry VIII, *c* 26) pt Llanyblodwel (Aber Tanat) transf from Montg to Salop; in 1546 (37 Henry VIII, *c* xxxii) Clun transf back from Montg to Salop; for these changes and for uncertain inclusion and changes, see *VCH Salop* III, 41—42. For other areas exempt from co jurisd, see *VCH Salop* III, 45 ff. [2]Pars within hundreds from late 16th cent only and not shown after cr of Adm Co in 1889. [3]At some time pt or ent in a Borough; see BOROUGHS. [4]Posenhall in Much Wenlock Bor/MB, but ex-par and not a sep CP until 1858. [5]Haughton Demesne ex-par place in South Bradford Hd, sep CP 1858 (after transf 1836 to Albrighton Dv). [6]'Ludlow' called 'Ludlow St Lawrence'

in 19th cent; in Ludlow Bor/MB. [7]Chap Farlow (Heref) in Stottesdon AP, the chap transf 1844 to Salop, sep CP 1866. [8]Based on Beresford & Finberg *Hand-List* and secondary sources with no addtl research. [9]5 & 6 Wm IV, *c* 76. [10]24 June, charter incorp. [11]1 Apr, SI 1966/1529. [12]Abol of Quatford Bor and its transf to Bridgnorth Bor noted in Beresford & Finberg, 153. [13]Heref, Salop until 1889, divided 1889 into 2 sep pars, each 'Richard's Castle', one in each co, the one in Salop sometimes early called 'Richard's Castle (Salop)'. [14]On extra-municipal liberties 1495, 1542, see *VCH Salop* III, 47. [15]Area of Wenlock MB reduced in 1889 regard to some constituent pars, and USDs of Broseley, Madeley (each constituted of pars already in Wenlock MB) abol and merged into Wenlock USD, LGB ProvO 636, conf by 52 & 53 Vict, *c* xxii. [16]Not co-terminous with Anc or Adm Co. [17]Quatt orig rated in Bridgnorth PLU, but its constituent areas of Quatt Jarvis, Quatt Malvern sep rated soon after and Quatt does not retain sep civ identity. [18]Salop, Montg until 1866, ent Salop thereafter. [19]Mucklewick orig rated in Hyssington, sep rated soon thereafter. [20]Montg, Salop until 1884, ent Montg thereafter. [21]Ex-par place of Skirmage sep rated 1865, sep status not sustained and incl soon thereafter in Diddlesbury. [22]Heref, Salop until 1895, ent Heref thereafter where called 'Leintwardine'. [23]Heref, Salop until 1895, ent Salop thereafter. [24]Ches par transf 1895 to Salop. [25]Salop, Denb until 1844; Salop, Montg 1844—66; ent Salop thereafter. [26]Staffs, Salop until 1895, ent Staffs thereafter. [27]Salop pars sep rated in this PLU were orig pt of Halesowen AP, and were transf 1844 to Worcs. [28]Salop par transf 1895 to Worcs. [29]Salop, Heref until 1894, ent Salop thereafter. [30]Extension 1893, 25 Mar, LGBO 28404. [31]1 Apr, MHealthO 77933. [32]1 Oct, LGBO 39881. [33]1 Apr, SI 1966/8. [34]1 Apr, SI 1966/1529. [35]1 Apr, SI 1965/2139. [36]1 Apr, LGBO 61468. [37]Authority not found, abol noted *VCH Salop* II, 215. [38]1 Apr, LGBO 37030. [39]By 1971 census called 'Llanyblodwell'. [40]By 1971 census called 'Ruyton XI Towns'. [41]By 1971 census called 'Sheriffhales'. [42]By 1971 census called 'Kynnersley'. [43]1 Apr, LGBO 41000. [44]26 Jan, O Salop Co Council, 'Whitchurch and Dodington' UD renamed 'Whitchurch'.

STAFFORDSHIRE

[1]Pars within hundreds from late 16th cent only and not shown after cr of Adm Co in 1889. [2]9 Nov, LGBProvO 1342, conf by 60 & 61 Vict, *c* lxxii. [3]17 & 18 Geo V, *c* lxxxvi. [4]1 Apr, 20 & 21 Geo V, *c* clxx. [5]1 Apr, 20 & 21 Geo V, *c* cxx. [6]1 Apr, 20 & 21 Geo V, *c* cxxv. [7]1 Apr, SI 1965/223. [8]1 Apr, 20 & 21 Eliz II, *c* 70. [9]1 Apr, MHealthO 77674. [10]1 Apr, SI 1965/223. [11]9 Nov, 5 Edw VII, *c* cvii. [12]31 Mar, 8 Edw VII, *c* lxiv. [13]6 Edw VII, *c* cv. [14]1 Apr, 17 & 18 Geo V, *c* lxv. [15]1 Apr, 11 & 12 Geo V, *c* ciii. [16]1 Apr, 20 & 21 Geo V, *c* xxvii. [17]1 Apr, SI 1964/113. [18]Extension 1890, 53 & 54 Vict, *c* cxxx. [19]1 Apr, 20 & 21 Geo V, *c* clxx. [20]1 Apr, MHealthO 78462. [21]1 Apr, 16 & 17 Geo V, *c* cvi. [22]At some time pt or ent in a Borough; see BOROUGHS. [23]Scropton consisted of sole tp Foston and Scropton (sep CP 1866), pt Derbys, pt Staffs, pt but not all of the area in Derbys transf 1844 to Staffs, the par ent Derbys from 1890. [24]Transf Newcastle under Lyme from South Pirehill Hd to North Pirehill Hd,

O Staffs Quarter Sessions, cited in *VCH Staffs* VIII, 1. [25]Incl Stafford Bor/MB. [26]Cresswell orig a sep AP, by 1549 free chap, civ ex-par after 1633, sep CP 1858. [27]Based on Beresford & Finberg *Hand-List* and secondary sources with no addtl research. [28]5 & 6 Wm IV, *c* 76. [29]9 Nov, by charters incorp with same date, Bilston UD and Rowley Regis UD each constituted a MB. [30]18 Aug, charter incorp. [31]Extension 1891, 9 Nov, LGBProvO 813, conf by 54 & 55 Vict, *c* ccxxiii. [32]39 & 40 Vict, *c* xcvii. [33]Stapenhill, Winshill each a Derbys par, the pts of each in the MB become 1889 pt in Burton upon Trent CB (assoc with Staffs). [34]39 & 40 Vict, *c* xcvii. [35]22 Aug, charter incorp, corrected by 20 & 21 Vict, *c* xxv. [36]Extension 1883 (East Vale USD [pt Caverswall] abol, ent to Longton MB), 46 & 47 Vict, *c* lxii; extension 1884, 47 & 48 Vict, *c* xxvii. [37]29 & 30 Vict, *c* xxiv. [38]Not certain that this Bor was in Tutbury; see Beresford & Finberg, 163. [39]See Beresford & Finberg, 162. [40]19 May, chartered by OC. [41]Hopton and Coton a tp in Stafford St Mary AP/Stafford St Mary and St Chad CP, pt in Staff Bor/MB before becomes sep CP 1866. [42]Ent Stafford St Chad, pt Stafford St Mary (see prev note concerning Hopton and Coton), so that this par ent MB after Hopton and Coton gains 1866 sep civ identity in Bor/MB; the two sep existed early, then jointly rated for poor law purposes as 'Stafford St Mary and St Chad' as listed in entry for BOROUGHS. [43]36 & 37 Vict, *c* ccxvi. [44]5 July, announced by Geo V and conf in *Lond Gaz.* [45]Extension 1890, 9 Nov, LGBProvO 693, conf by 53 & 54 Vict, *c* ccxxxvii. [46]Main tp of Tamworth in Staffs, Warws (see Part I of the *Guide*); pt before and after enlargement of area on constitution 1835 of the MB in both cos; Tamworth ent Staffs from 1866 when areas in Warws gain sep civ identity in that co. [47]9 Nov, by charter incorp, Tipton UD constitued a MB. [48]Year charter incorp. [49]Year charter incorp. [50]Not co-terminous with Anc or Adm Co. [51]Staffs until 1928, in Birm CB (assoc with Warws) 1928—30. [52]Staffs, Derbys until 1866, ent Staffs thereafter. [53]Considered in 19th cent and earlier to be ent Staffs, a small pt without population deemed later to be in Derbys, the latter transf 1903 to a Derbys par and Rolleston ent Staffs thereafter. [54]Workhouse in Penkridge PLU transf 1872 to Cannock, and by 1880 the PLU renamed 'Cannock' (*VCH Staffs* V, 19, 52 [the later reference citing directory of 1880]). [55]In Dudley MB (1865—89) but excluded from Dudley CB and thereafter (1889—1929) in Staffs. [56]Not orig rated in the PLU, incl in it soon thereafter. [57]Staffs, Salop until 1895, ent Staffs thereafter. [58]Derbys, Staffs until 1895, ent Staffs thereafter. [59]Staffs, Warws until 1895, ent Staffs thereafter. [60]Staffs until 1844, Worcs thereafter. [61]Staffs until 1895, Worcs thereafter. [62]Staffs, Salop until 1866, ent Staffs thereafter. [63]Salop, Staffs until 1895, ent Salop thereafter as 'Sheriffhales'. [64]25 Mar, LGBO 13328. [65]9 Nov, 54 & 55 Vict, *c* clxi. [66]18 Apr, Upper Sedgley USD renamed Sedgley USD, LGBO 21378. [67]12 July, LGBO 15446. [68]1 Apr, MHealthO 77777. [69]1 Apr, LGBO 36640. [70]1 Apr, MHealthO 75877. [71]1 Apr, MHealthO 76042. [72]1 Apr, 18 & 19 Geo V, *c* cv. [73]9 Nov, 1 & 2 Geo V, *c* xxxvi. [74]Cr as 'Heath Town', later 'Heathtown'. [75]1 Apr, 17 & 18 Geo V, *c* cii. [76]1 Apr, LGBO 33990. [77]1 Apr, LGBO 43817.

WARWICKSHIRE

[1]Charter Henry VI annuled 1842; information kindly supplied by Warws RO. [2]Orig pt Coventry St Michael. Walsgrave on Sowe orig called 'Sowe'. [3]Pars within hundreds from late 16th cent only and not shown after cr of Adm Co in 1889. [4]54 & 55 Vict, *c* clxi. [5]9 Edw VII, *c* cxxii. [6]9 Nov 1911, 1 & 2 Geo V, *c* xxxvi. [7]1 Apr 1912, 1 & 2 Geo V, *c* xxxvi. [8]1 Apr, MHealthO 75387. [9]1 Apr, SI 1964/170. [10]1 Apr, SI 1965/223. [11]1 Apr, 20 & 21 Eliz II, *c* 70. [12]1 Apr, 17 & 18 Geo V, *c* xci. [13]1 Apr, 21 & 22 Geo V, *c* lvi. [14]1 Apr, SI 1956/446. [15]1 Apr, SI 1965/222. [16]Barlinchway Hd incl Pathlow Lbty (until middle of 17th cent). Entries not made in Part I; for constituent pars, see *VCH Warws* III, 6. [17]At some time pt or ent in a Borough; see BOROUGHS. [18]In Cov Co until 1842, sep CP 1866. [19]Based on Beresford & Finberg *Hand-List* and secondary sources with no addtl research. [20]5 & 6 Wm IV, *c* 76. [21]Exact date of charter incorp not found; its reception celebrated 2 Sept 1903 (information kindly supplied by Editor of *VCH* from *Catalogue of the Birmingham Collection* (1918), 70). [22]Year charter incorp. [23]Extension 1891, LGBProv O 786, conf by 1 Edw VII, *c* ccxxxi. [24]Extension (not found which pars affected, prob pt only of one or other added), 9 Nov, LGBProvO 733, conf by 53 & 54 Vict, *c* ccii. [25]Chartered by OC 6 July. [26]Extension 1890, 9 Nov, areas of Lillington USD, Milverton USD added to Royal Leamington Spa MB. [27]Year charter incorp. [28]9 Nov, charter incorp. [29]24 May, charter incorp. [30]Alteration 1879 (not seen), 42 & 43 Vict, *c* cix. [31]12 Dec, charter incorp, Sutton Coldfield UD constitued a MB. [32]Staffs, Warws until 1866, ent Staffs thereafter. [33]Not co-terminous with Anc or Adm Co. [34]Warws, Worcs until 1894, ent Worcs thereafter. [35]Worcs until 1896, Warws thereafter. [36]Warws, Leics until 1885, ent Warws thereafter. [37]Not orig rated in the PLU, incl in it soon thereafter. [38]Staffs until 1911, Birm CB (1911—12). [39]Northants (1858—1895), Warws thereafter. [40]Glos, Warws until 1894, ent Glos thereafter. [41]Oxon, Warws until 1889, becomes 1889 two sep CPs, each 'Mollington', one in Oxon, one in Warws, the former abol 1895 ent to the latter. [42]Glos until 1844, Warws thereafter. [43]Leics, Warws until considered 1880s ent Leics. [44]Cr 1894 from the pt of Kings Norton (Worcs) in Birm CB. [45]Staffs par, pt Birm CB (1891—94), ent Birm CB (1894—1911). [46]Glos, Warws until 1896, ent Glos thereafter. [47]Glos, Warws until 1894, ent Warws thereafter. [48]Staffs, Warws until 1895, ent Staffs thereafter. [49]25 Mar, O Warws Co Council, conf by LGBO 29203. [50]1 Oct, LGBO 72867. [51]1 Apr, 21 & 22 Geo V, *c* ix. [52]1 Apr, MHealthO 76114. [53]20 Dec, LGBO 33596, the par of Bulkington made ent in the UD. [54]Apptd day, LGBO 31873. [55]1 Apr, MHealthO 75379. [56]1 Apr, 21 & 22 Geo V, *c* lvi. [57]1 Apr, MHealthO 75688. [58]1 Apr, 21 & 22 Geo V, *c* xlv. [59]1 Apr, SI 1969/361.

WESTMORLAND

[1]Joseph Nicholson and Richard Burn, *The History and Antiquities of the Counties of Westmorland and Cumberland* (1777) I, 34; pt of the tp of Fawcett Forest

was later reckoned in East Wd and thus in the orig area of the Barony of Westmorland, but the major pt was in the orig area of the Barony of Kendal. [2]Pars within wards from late 16th cent only and not shown after cr of Adm Co in 1889. [3]At some time pt or ent in a Borough; see BOROUGHS. [4]Based on Beresford & Finberg *Hand-List* and secondary sources with no addtl research. [5]5 & 6 Wm IV, *c* 76. [6]24 June, charter incorp. [7]Not co-terminous with Anc or Adm Co. [8]Lancs par transf 1895 to Westm. [9]Extension 1891, O Westm Co Council, conf by LGBO 26832, dated 31 Mar. [10]1 Apr, MHealthO 78796. [11]1 Apr, LGBO 47425. [12]Changes in 1905, 1 Apr, LGBO 45299.

WORCESTERSHIRE

[1]Pars within hundreds from late 16th cent only and not shown after cr of Adm Co in 1889. [2]1 Apr, 18 & 19 Geo V, *c* cv. [3]1 Apr, MHealthO 77777. [4]1 Apr, 1 & 2 Eliz II, *c* xxxv. [5]1 Apr, SI 1965/2139. [6]1 Apr, 20 & 21 Eliz II, *c* 70. [7]9 Nov, 4 & 5 Geo V, *c* cxxxiv. [8]1 Oct, 21 & 22 Geo V, *c* xxxiv. [9]1 Apr, 14 & 15 Geo V, *c* xliv. [10]At some time pt or ent in a Borough; see BOROUGHS. [11]Worcs, Heref until 1844, ent Worcs thereafter; pt in Bor. [12]Heref until 1844, Worcs thereafter. [13]Heref, Worcs until 1866, ent Heref 1866—97, transf 1897 to Worcs. [14]Staffs until 1844, Worcs thereafter. [15]A pt of Halesowen AP, transf 1844 from Salop to Worcs. [16]Warws, Worcs until 1894, ent Warws thereafter. [17]Transfers 1760 among Hds, 1 Geo III, *c* 2. [18]Incl area of Worcester Bor; parishes whose names begin with 'Worcester' not incl in the list for this Hd; see Worcester Bor/MB. [19]Based on Beresford & Finberg *Hand-List* and secondary sources with no addtl research. [20]5 & 6 Wm IV, *c* 76. [21]13 Apr, charter incorp. [22]Dudley Castle Hill in Staffs, incl in MB 1865—89 but not incl in CB 1889, the area abol 1929 and incl in Dudley AP and thus in the CB. [23]Worcs, Salop until 1844, ent Worcs thereafter. [24]9 Nov, charter incorp. [25]9 Nov, charter incorp. [26]9 Nov, charter incorp. [27]Extension 1891, 48 & 49 Vict, *c* clxiv. [28]Not co-terminous with Anc or Adm Co. [29]Not orig rated in the PLU, incl in it soon thereafter. [30]Mother par orig rated in the PLU; all subordinate subunits soon sep rated thereafter and this par no longer rated for poor law purposes. [31]Presumed rated in PLU when became a sep CP; not mentioned in any schedule of additions to PLUs as were other ex-par places. [32]Salop until 1895, Worcs thereafter. [33]Worcs until 1909, Birm CB (assoc with Warws) 1909—11. [34]Worcs until 1896, Warws thereafter. [35]Worcs until 1897, Heref thereafter. [36]Worcs 1894—97, Heref thereafter as 'Mathon'. [37]Glos, Worcs until 1896, ent Glos thereafter. [38]Worcs until 1911, Birm PLU & CB (assoc with Warws) (1911—12). [39]9 Nov, LGB ProvO 786, conf by 54 & 55 Vict, *c* clxi. [40]Extension 1894, 1 Mar, LGBO 30634. [41]Extension 1892, 7 Feb, LGBO 27699. [42]4 Mar, LGBO 24094. [43]Extension 1891, 4 Oct, LGBO 31228. [44]The pt in Worcs. [45]8 June, O Worcs Co Council. [46]26 June, O Worcs Co Council. [47]1 Apr, MHealthO 76790. [48]1 Apr, MHealthO 69527. [49]The name of par 'Ridgacre' changed to 'Quinton' between 1891 and 1901 (the former appearing in the census of 1891 and the latter in the census of 1901). The entry for the RD presumes the change was made by 1894 and would need to be revised if

the change came later. [50]1 Oct, LGBO 38127. [51]9 Nov, 1 & 2 Geo V, *c* xxxvi. Some changes effective 9 Nov 1911 and others 1 Apr 1912. [52]1 Oct, LGBO 36508. [53]1 Apr, LGBO 37597. [54]Extension 1897, 1 Apr, LGBO 34678. [55]9 Aug, MHealth Decl, 'Stourport' UD renamed 'Stourport-on-Severn' UD. [56]1 Apr, 21 & 22 Geo V, *c* ix. [57]RD consisted of the pt of Warley not in Oldbury UD, then (after 1895) of the ent par until its abol 1908, 30 Sept, LGBO 52440.

YORKSHIRE

[1]Pars within wapentakes from late 16th cent only and not shown after cr of Adm Co in 1889. [2]1 Apr, 2 & 3 Geo V, *c* cxxxviii. [3]9 Nov, 11 & 12 Geo V, *c* cii. [4]1 Apr, MHealthO 93469. [5]1 Apr, 20 & 21 Eliz II, *c* 70. [6]9 Nov, 62 & 63 Vict, *c* cxlix. [7]1 Apr, 20 & 21 Geo V, *c* xliii. [8]1 Apr, MHealth O 87427. [9]1 Apr, SI 1955/387. [10]1 Apr, 2 & 3 Geo V, *c* cxxxviii. [11]1 Apr, 16 & 17 Geo V, *c* xxvii. [12]1 Apr, MHealthO 84517. [13]1 Apr, 14 Geo VI, *c* xl. [14]9 Nov, 55 & 56 Vict, *c* cccxii. [15]9 Nov, 63 & 63 Vict, *c* cxi. [16]9 Nov, 63 & 64 Vict, *c* ccxxxvi. [17]9 Nov, 2 Edw VII, *c* cxxiv. [18]9 Nov, 2 & 3 Geo V, *c* cxxxiii. [19]1 Oct, 18 & 19 Geo V, *c* lxiii. [20]9 Nov, LGBProvO 720. [21]9 Nov, 3 & 4 Geo V, *c* xcv. [22]30 Sept, 60 & 61 Vict, *c* ccxliv. [23]1 Apr, 19 & 20 Geo V, *c* lxxxviii. [24]1 Apr, MHealthO 80872. [25]1 Apr, SI 1955/359. [26]1 Apr, MHousLGO 32862. [27]9 Nov, 2 & 3 Geo V, *c* cxxxviii. [28]1 Apr, 9 & 10 Geo V, *c* liii. [29]1 Apr, 15 & 16 Geo V, *c* lx. [30]1 Apr, 17 & 18 Geo V, *c* ci. [31]1 Apr, 4 & 5 Eliz II, *c* lxxxv. [32]9 Nov, 3 & 4 Geo V, *c* cxlii. [33]1 Oct, 19 & 20 Geo V, *c* xxiii. [34]1 Apr, MHealthO 76121. [35]1 Apr, MHousLGO 27305. [36]1 Oct, 2 Edw VII, *c* ccx. [37]31 Mar, 8 & 9 Geo V, *c* lxi. [38]9 Nov, 11 & 12 Geo V, *c* lxix. [39]1 Apr, MHousLGO 25331. [40]31 Oct, 63 & 64 Vict, *c* ccxxii. [41]1 Apr, 1 & 2 Geo V, *c* clxxxiv. [42]1 Oct, 4 & 5 Geo V, *c* lxxxix. [43]1 Apr, 18 & 19 Geo V, *c* lxxxvii. [44]1 Apr, 22 & 23 Geo V, *c* xv. [45]1 Apr, 22 & 23 Geo V, *c* lxx. [46]1 Apr, MHealthO 90885. [47]1 Apr, 4 & 5 Geo V, *c* clxxxii. [48]9 Nov, 11 & 12 Geo V, *c* xcvi. [49]1 Apr, 14 Geo VI, *c* xiii. [50]1 Apr, MHealthO 77607. [51]1 Apr, MHousLGO 6543. [52]1 Apr, MHousLGO 32437. [53]Incl Beverley Liberty and Bor. [54]In Beverley Lbty. [55]In Beverley Lbty and Bor. [56]At some time pt or ent in a Bor or MB; see BOROUGHS. [57]Incl 1802 in Kingston upon Hull Co , 42 Geo III, *c* xci. [58]Ex-par Turnhill sometimes deemed sep CP in this Wap, sep status not sustained. [59]Several areas of Crowle (mainly Lincs Pts Lindsey) deemed in Yorks W Riding in this Wap, considered ent Lincs by time of census of 1871. [60]Based on Beresford & Finberg *Hand-List* and secondary sources with no addtl research. [61]5 & 6 Wm IV, *c* 76. [62]5 July, charter incorp. [63]8 Dec, charter incorp. [64]For Lbty St Mary's Abbey in York, incl Bootham Bor and St Olave's Bor, see *VCH City of York, passim*. [65]Extension 1882, 1 May, 44 & 45 Vict, *c* cxxii, incl abol of Allerton USD. [66]Charter incorp. [67]10 July, letters patent. [68]Charter incorp, Bridlington UD constituted a MB. [69]10 Aug, charter incorp. [70]Effort to sustained bor, erected *ca* 1239, seemingly not successful, *VCH Yorks E Riding* IV, 95. [71]13 May, charter incorp. [72]11 Apr, charter incorp. [73]9 Nov, charter incorp. [74]Extension 1882, 9 Nov, 55 & 56 Vict, *c* ccxxii. [75]Charter incorp. [76]1 Feb, charter incorp. [77]Charter

incorp. [78]Extension 1890, 9 Nov, LGBProvO 720. [79]7 July, charter incorp. [80]28 July, charter incorp. [81]Extension 1883, 1 Apr, 45 & 46 Vict, c cxv. [82]Letters patent. [83]Extension 1866, 29 & 30 Vict, c cxliii. [84]Charter incorp. [85]Extension 1891, 53 & 54 Vict, c cciv. [86]12 Dec, charter incorp. [87]Charter incorp. [88]16 July, charter incorp. [89]Extension 1875, 38 & 39 Vict, c xxxii. [90]Nov, charter incorp. [91]Area lost into sea at an early date. [92]9 Nov, charter incorp. [93]Extension 1879, 42 & 43 Vict, c cxxi. [94]Aug, charter incorp. [95]Temporarily a co of itself temp Rchd III; see VCH Yorks N Riding. [96]Charter incorp. [97]Letters patent. [98]Extension incl pt Linthorpe in N Riding, 52 & 53 Vict, c xcii; for remainder see entry in Durham. [99]5 Aug, charter incorp (to incl ent par Thornaby, hence South Stockton USD (pt Thornaby) abol at same time. [100]2 June, charter incorp. [101]15 Mar, charter incorp. [102]Pars which were abol 1586 or earlier, or which disappeared earlier, not listed; for these see Part I of the Guide. For early boundaries of the Bor, see VCH City of York, 311—21. [103]Extension 1884, 47 & 48 Vict, c ccxxxii. [104]Within area but not within jurisd of City (although noted as within area in Municipal Corporations Act, 1835). [105]Ex-par lbty, acquired by city shortly after 1719, VCH City of York, 496. [106]Orig Hospital of St Leonards. [107]Not co-terminous with Anc or Adm Co. [108]Yorks W Riding, Notts until 1895, ent Yorks W Riding thereafter. [109]Tp in Notts, pt of Finningley par (Notts, Yorks W Riding until 1866), ent Notts thereafter. [110]Durham until 1844, Yorks N Riding thereafter. [111]Not orig rated in the PLU, incl in it soon thereafter. [112]'East and West Cowick' orig sep rated, thereafter in Snaith as 'Snaith and Cowick'. [113]Hartshead orig rated with Clifton, sep rated later. [114]Orig rated under name 'Wallingfen'. [115]Yorks W Riding, Yorks E Riding until 1866, ent Yorks W Riding thereafter. [116]Clareton orig rated with Coneythorpe, sep rated thereafter. [117]Yorks W Riding, Yorks N Riding until 1895, ent Yorks W Riding thereafter. [118]Yorks N Riding, Yorks W Riding until 1895, ent Yorks N Riding thereafter (at which time transf to Thirsk PLU). [119]Thurnhill sep rated and sep CP 1858 in Pickering PLU, sep identity not sustained and incl thereafter in Middleton. [120]St Martin orig rated in Richmond PLU, but noted as incl in that PLU only from 1858 in a subsequent report of the Poor Law Commissioners. [121]Yorks E Riding, Yorks W Riding (Ainsty) until 1866, ent Yorks W Riding thereafter. [122]Mostly Lancs, pt Yorks W Riding until 1895, ent Lancs thereafter. [123]Notts, Yorks W Riding until 1895, ent Notts thereafter. [124]5 Sept, O W Riding Co Council, conf by LGBO 28723. [125]29 Sept, LGBProvO 11724, conf by 44 & 45 Vict, c xcviii. [126]7 Oct, O W Riding Co Council, conf by LGBO 26223. [127]7 June, Skelton and Brotton USD cr by union of Brotton USD, Skelton and Cleveland USD, LGBProvO 271. [128]16 May, LGBProvO 236; Hepworth, Wooldale each gain 1884 pt in Cartworth

USD. [129]6 June, LGBProvO 808, conf by 54 & 55 Vict, c ccxxiii. [130]14 Jan, LGBO 21040, Denholme Gate USD renamed Denholme USD. [131]26 Mar, LGBProvO 325. [132]24 Mar, LGBO 17004. [133]Extension 1892 (gains Ovenden USD), 9 Nov, LGBProvO 848. [134]Extension 1891, 30 July, LGBO 26677. [135]Reduction 1891, 30 July, LGBO 26676. [136]5 Nov, O W Riding Co Council, conf by LGBO 26316. [137]Extension 1890 (gains abol Longwood USD), 9 Nov, LGBO 26316. [138]18 Jan, O W Riding Co Council, conf by LGBO 27640. [139]6 Dec, O E Riding Co Council, conf by LGBO 25691, Norton severed from Malton USD to cr Norton USD. [140]29 Sept, LGBProvO 8, conf by 45 & 46 Vict, c clxx. [141]30 July, O W Riding Co Council, conf by LGBO 26676. [142]17 May, LGBProvO 589, all of Normanby not in Middlesb. MB made pt of USD, prev 'South Bank in Normanby' USD, thereafter 'Normanby' USD. [143]'Ossett cum Gawthorpe' USD and par until constitution of Ossett MB (see note 88), 'Ossett' MB, USD, par thereafter. [144]18 July, LGBO 29872. [145]Rastrick USD incl in Brighouse MB when latter chartered 1893. [146]28 Oct, Windhill USD abol by O W Riding Co Council, conf by LGBO 27431, and constituent area (pt Idle) transf to Shipley USD. [147]Lancs until 1889, Yorks W Riding 1897—97. [148]44 & 45 Vict, c clxii. [149]1 Apr, MHealthO 80872. [150]1 Apr, LGBO 38739. [151]1 Oct, LGBO 38262. [152]1 Apr, MHealthO 76122. [153]1 Apr, LGBO 38692. [154]1 Apr, MHealthO 77607. [155]9 Nov, 3 & 4 Geo V, c xcv. [156]1 Apr, LGBO 42863. [157]1 Apr, MHealthO 62276. [158]1 Apr, MHealthO 62619. [159]1 Apr, MHealthO 87427. [160]1 Apr, MHealthO 93469. [161]1 Oct, LGBO 33163. [162]1 Apr, LGBO 34339. [163]9 Nov, 4 & 5 Geo V, c clxxx. [164]1 Apr, LGBO 56419. [165]15 Apr, LGBO 37539. [166]57 & 58 Vict, c 58. [167]26 Mar, LGBO 37539. [168]1 Oct, LGBO 39883. [169]1 Apr, LGBO 62769. [170]1 Apr, MHealthO 66454. [171]1 Apr, LGBO 41103. [172]1 Apr, LGBO 33454. [173]1 Oct, LGBO 53399. [174]1 Apr, MHealthO 69748. [175]1 Oct, LGBO 33042. [176]1 Apr, LGBO 51386. [177]1 Apr, MHealthO 66924. [178]1 Apr, MHealthO 100248. [179]30 Sept, LGBO 33134. [180]1 Oct, MHealthO 69013. [181]1 Apr, LGBO 58473. [182]9 Nov, 63 & 64 Vict, c ccxxxiv. [183]3 Jan, LGBO 32136. [184]31 Mar, 9 Edw VII, c clxii. [185]31 Mar, LGBO 33621. [186]1 Apr, LGBO 39497. [187]9 Nov, 9 Edw VII, c cxxii. [188]1 Apr, MHealthO 70508. [189]3 Jan, LGBO 32136. [190]1 Apr, LGBO 39517. [191]1 Apr, MHealthO 93469. [192]1 Oct, LGBO 51879. [193]1 Apr, MHealthO 87427. [194]1 Apr, LGBO 41097. [195]9 Nov, 4 & 5 Geo V, c clxxx. [196]1 Feb, MHousLG Decl.

SOUTH YORKSHIRE

[1]The pt of Haworth to be in S Yorks transf to Bawtry CP, the pt remaining in Notts to be 'Harworth Bircotes' CP.

PART III: PARLIAMENTARY CONSTITUENCIES

CHESHIRE

[1]Dates of medieval representation taken from list of MPs in Parl Papers with no addtl research. [2]Changes in constituent wards, 5 Jan, SI 1971/2115. [3]Primarily Lancs; see Part I of the Guide. [4]Bdry alt 1953, 7 May, affecting Southport South BC (Stockport) and Cheadle CC (Bredbury and Romiley), SI 1953/742; changes in

constituent wards 1971 as in note 2 above, SI 1971/2115. [5]In addition to transfers of ent pars involved in the abol 1945 of Altrincham Dv and cr of Bucklow Dv (noted in place in the entries), there were changes in parl boundaries affecting the following places: (a) Baguley, Northern Etchells, Northenden (prev Ches, Altrincham Dv) had been abol 1931 ent to Manchester CB, but their areas remained in Ches Parl Co and became constituent areas in Bucklow Dv; (b) pts of Carrington, Partington (all prev Ches, Altrincham Dv) lost civ 1920 to Lancs (Irlam UD) transf to Lancs Parl Co, Stretford Dv, as was the pt of Carrington transf 1920 to Flixton, Lancs, and subsequently 1933 to Urmston UD; but the pts which Carrington, Partington each gained civ from Lancs in 1920 remained in Ches Parl Co; (c) the pts of Warrington, Partington (all prev Ches, Altrincham Dv) lost civ 1920 to Lancs (Warrington RD) transf to Lancs Parl Co, Newton Dv; (d) the pt of Grappenhall (prev Ches, Knutsford Dv) transf civ 1936 to Lymm UD to help constitute Bucklow Dv; (e) the parts of Handforth (abol civ 1936), Cheadle and Gateley (cr 1930) (both Ches, Altrincham Dv) lost civ 1936 to Wilmslow UD transf to Knutsford Dv. [6]Bdry alt 1953, as in note 4 above, SI 1953/742. [7]Changes in constituent areas 1955, incl cr of Nantwich CC, 19 Jan, SI 1955/4.

CUMBERLAND

[1]Dates of medieval representation taken from list of MPs in *Parl Papers* with no addtl research. [2]Bdry alt 1951, 1 Jan, affecting Carlisle BC (Carlisle) and Penrith and the Border CC (Beaumont, Cummersdale, Kingmoor, St Cuthbert Without, Stanwix, Wetheral), SI 1951/322.

DERBYSHIRE

[1]Dates of medieval representation taken from list of MPs in *Parl Papers* with no addtl research. [2]Changes in constituent areas, 19 Jan, SI 1955/5.

COUNTY DURHAM

[1]Changes 1955 in constituent areas and wards, 19 Jan, SI 1955/7; changes 1960 in constituent areas, 30 Mar, SI 1960/451. [2]Bdry alt 1953, 7 May, affecting Sedgefield CC (Dalton Piercy, Greatham, Seaton) and The Hartlepools BC (West Hartlepool), SI 1953/741. [3]Bdry alt 1951, 1 Apr, affecting South Shields BC, Jarrow BC (the pt of South Shields CB gained civ 1951 from Boldon transf parl 1951 to South Shields BC and not to help cr Jarrow BC), SI 1951/326. [4]Bdry alt 1952, 25 July, affecting Stockton on Tees BC (Stockton on Tees) and Sedgefield CC (Elton, Norton, Preston on Tees), SI 1952/1348. [5]Bdry alt 1952, 17 Mar, affecting Sunderland North BC, Sunderland South BC (Sunderland), Houghton le Spring CC (Ford, Herrington, Hylton, Silksworth), SI 1952/453. [6]The schedule of the act of 1832 cites Wards as they existed before the changes of 1829. [7]Bdry alt 1953, 7 May, affecting Bishop Auckland CC (Shildon) and Sedgefield CC (Great Aycliffe), SI 1953/741. [8]Bdry alt 1952 as in note 4; bdry alt 1953 as in notes 2 and 7.

HEREFORDSHIRE

[1]Dates of medieval representation taken from list of MPs in *Parl Papers* with no addtl research. [2]Pt Salop, pt Heref (1832—85).

LANCASHIRE

[1]Dates of medieval representation taken from list of MPs in *Parl Papers* with no addtl research. [2]Bdry alt 1951, 18 July, affecting Ashton under Lyne BC (Alt, Bardsley, Woodhouses), Oldham West BC (Oldham), SI 1951/1236; changes 1955 in constituencies, affecting Oldham East BC, and also bdry alt 1955, 19 Jan, affecting Oldham East BC, Oldham West BC (Oldham), Ashton under Lyne BC (Alt, Bardsley, Little Moss, Mossley, Woodhouses), SI 1955/16. [3]Changes 1955 in constituent areas, 19 Jan, SI 1955/14. [4]The pt of Carleton to become a pt of Blackpool CB 1 Apr 1918 incl for parl purposes in Blackpool Parl Bor and not in Fylde Dv. [5]Bdry alt 1956, 15 June, affecting Blackpool North BC (Blackpool) and North Fylde CC (Poulton le Fylde), SI 1956/818; changes 1964 in constituent wards, 11 Mar, SI 1964/273. [6]Changes 1964 in constituent wards, 11 Mar, SI 1964/273. [7]Bdry alt 1955, 15 Jan, affecting Bootle BC (Bootle) and Liverpool, Walton BC (Aintree), SI 1955/15. [8]Bdry alt and change of constituencies 1955, 15 Jan, affecting Crosby BC (Ford, Litherland), Huyton CC (Windle), Liverpool, West Derby BC (Liverpool), Ormskirk CC (Sefton), St Helens BC (St Helens), Widnes CC (Hale, Halewood), SI 1955/15; bdry alt 1960, 30 Mar, affecting Crosby BC (Great Crosby), Huyton CC (Kirkby, Knowsley), Liverpool, West Derby BC (Liverpool), Ormskirk CC (Ince Blundell, Seftin, Simonswood, Thornton), SI 1960/463. [9]Bdry alt 1956, 15 June, affecting Eccles BC (Swinton and Pendlebury) and Farnworth CC (Worsley), SI 1956/821; bdry alt 1964, 11 Mar, affecting Salford West BC (Salford) and Eccles BC (Eccles), SI 1964/275. [10]Changes 1955 in constituent areas and wards, 19 Jan, SI 1955/15. [11]Changes 1955 in constituent wards, 19 Jan, SI 1955/16; changes 1973 in constituent wards, 12 Apr, SI 1973/60. [12]Changes 1973 in constituent wards, abol of several Manchester BCs, 12 Apr, SI 1973/606. [13]Changes 1955 in constituent areas and wards, 19 Jan, SI 1955/16. [14]Statute of 1885 stated that so much of Oldham MB as not incl in Oldham Parl Bor (1867—85) to be added to the Parl Bor; any pt not prev in that Parl Bor or added by civ bdry alt not found. [15]Statute of 1867 excluded so much of the MB as lay on the south side of the River Ribble, affecting Preston par. [16]Bdry alt 1953, 7 May, affecting Preston North BC (Fulwood), Preston South BC (Preton), South Fylde CC (Lea), SI 1953/743; changes 1960 in constituent wards in Preston South BC, and bdry alt at same time, 30 Mar, affecting Preston South BC (Preston) and South Fylde CC (Lea), SI 1960/461. [17]Bdry alt 1955, 19 Jan, affecting pars as in note 8 above, SI 1955/17. [18]Bdry alt 1964, 15 June, affecting pars as in note 9 above, SI 1964/275. [19]Bdry alt 1955, 19 Jan, affecting Newton CC (Winwick), Warrington BC (Warrington), SI 1955/17. [20]See note 4 for changes affected by act of 1918; bdry alt 1945, 15 May, affecting Carleton,

Hardhorn with Newton, Marton, SI 1945/701. [21]Bdry alt 1945, 15 May, affecting Culceth, Rixton with Glazebrook, Woolston with Martinscroft, SI 1945/701. [22]Bdry alt 1945, 15 Mar, affecting Davyhulme, Flixton, Irlam, SI 1945/701. [23]Bdry alt 1956, 15 June, affecting pars as in note 9, SI 1956/881. [24]Bdry alt 1955, 15 June, affecting pars as in note 5, SI 1955/818. [25]Bdry alt 1953, 7 May, affecting pars as in note 16, SI 1953/743. [26]Bdry alt 1955, 19 Jan, affecting pars as in note 8, SI 1955/15; changes 1960 in constituent areas, 30 Mar, SI 1960/461. [27]Changes 1955 in constituent areas, 19 Jan, SI 1955/15; bdry alt 1960, 30 Mar, affecting pars as in note 8, SI 1960/461.

LEICESTERSHIRE

[1]Dates of medieval representation taken from list of MPs in *Parl Papers* with no addtl research. [2]Bdry alt 1972, 5 Jan, affecting Leicester South BC (Leicester), Harborough CC (Wigston), SI 1971/2111. [3]Changes in constituent areas, 19 Jan, SI 1955/19. [4]Bdry alt 1955, 19 Jan, affecting Bosworth CC (Coalville), Loughborough CC (Bardon), SI 1955/18. [5]Bdry alt 1972, 5 Jan, affecting Bosworth CC (Coalville), Loughborough CC (Bardon, Belton, Osgathorpe), SI 1971/2108.

LINCOLNSHIRE

[1]Dates of medieval representation taken from list of MPs in *Parl Papers* with no addtl research. [2]Bdry alt 1960, 30 Mar, affecting Grimsby BC (Grimsby), Louth CC (Great Coates), SI 1960/453. [3]Bdry alt 1960, 30 Mar, affecting Lincoln BC (Lincoln), Grantham CC (Skellingthorpe), SI 1960/456.

NORTHAMPTONSHIRE

[1]Dates of medieval representation taken from list of MPs in *Parl Papers* with no addtl research. [2]Bdry alt 1973, 12 Apr, affecting Daventry CC (Billing, Boughton, Brafield on the Green, Cogenhoe, Hardingstone, Harpole, Little Houghton, Moulton, Overstone, Upton, Wootton), Wellingborough CC (Ecton), Northampton North BC (Northampton), Northampton South BC (Northampton), SI 1973/604. [3]Thorney RD consists of Hunts pars transf 1965 to help cr Hunts & Peterb; see Vol. I of the *Guide*.

NORTHUMBERLAND

[1]Dates of medieval representation taken from list of MPs in *Parl Papers* with no addtl research. [2]Bdry alt 1972, 5 Jan, affecting Blyth BC (Seaton Valley CP) and Hexham CC (Stannington AP), SI 1971/2107. [3]Durham par, transf to Northumb 1832 for parl purposes, 1844 for civ purposes. [4]Changes 1955 in constituent wards, 15 Feb, SI 1955/168.

NOTTINGHAMSHIRE

[1]Dates of medieval representation taken from list of MPs in *Parl Papers* with no addtl research. [2]Changes 1956 in constituent areas and wards, 15 June, SI 1956/823. [3]Changes 1952 in constituent wards of Nottingham South BC and bdry alt at the same time, 25 July, affecting Nottingham South BC (Nottingham) and Rushcliffe CC (West Bridgford, Clifton with Glapton, Ruddington), SI 1952/1347; changes 1956 in constituent wards of Nottingham South BC, 15 June, SI 1956/823.

SHROPSHIRE

[1]Dates of medieval representation taken from list of MPs in *Parl Papers* with no addtl research. [2]Elections from 1584. [3]Pt Salop, pt Heref. [4]Ex-par place, sep CP 1858.

STAFFORDSHIRE

[1]Dates of medieval representation taken from list of MPs in *Parl Papers* with no addtl research. [2]Bdry alt 1955, 15 Feb, affecting Bilston BC (Coseley, Sedgley), Rowley Regis and Tipton BC (Rowley Regis), Brierley Hill CC (Brierley Hill UD), SI 1955/171. [3]Dudley in Worcs, Dudley CB assoc with CB (1889—1966), assoc with Staffs (1966—*) so that the BC assoc with Staffs (1970—*). [4]Stafford St Mary and St Chad and joint rating of Stafford St Mary (ent in the Parl Bor), Stafford St Chad (pt in the Parl Bor). [5]Changes in constituent wards, 15 Feb, SI 1955/172. [6]Abol of Walsall BC, cr of Walsall North BC, Walsall South BC, changes in constituent areas in Cannock CC, Lichfield and Tamworth CC, 15 Feb, SI 1955/170. [7]Changes 1960 in constituent wards, 30 Mar, SI 1960/464. [8]Changes 1955 in constituent wards, 15 Feb, SI 1955/173.

WARWICKSHIRE

[1]Dates of medieval representation taken from list of MPs in *Parl Papers* with no addtl research. [2]Cr and abol of BCs, CCs, changes in constituent wards and areas of others, 19 Jan, SI 1955/177. [3]Changes 1949 in constituent wards, OC, 28 July, confirmed by SI 1949/2196; changes 1955 in constituent wards, as in note 2 above, SI 1955/177. [4]Changes 1949 in constituent wards, as in note 3 above, SI 1949/2196. [5]Cr and abol of constituencies, changes in constituent areas, 11 June 1945, SI 1945/701. [6]Bdry alt 1960, 30 Mar, affecting Coventry BCs (Coventry), Meriden CC (Allesley), Rugby CC (Binley), Warwick and Leamington CC (Baginton, Stoneleigh), SI 1960/450. [7]Bdry alt 1972, 5 Jan, affecting Stratford on Avon CC (Studley) and Worcs constituency of Bromsgrove and Redditch CC (Redditch), SI 1971/2109.

WESTMORLAND

[1]Dates of medieval representation taken from list of MPs in *Parl Papers* with no addtl research.

WORCESTERSHIRE

[1]Dates of medieval representation taken from list of MPs in *Parl Papers* with no addtl research. [2]Dudley CB became assoc 1966 with Staffs; see entries in Staffs for Dudley BCs (1970—*). [3]Bdry alt 1952, 25 July, affecting Worcester BC (Worcester [also affects boundaries of

North Claines, Hindlip, Warndon, but all remain in same BC]), South Worcestershire CC (Whittington), SI 1952/1350.

YORKSHIRE

[1]Dates of medieval representation taken from list of MPs in *Parl Papers* with no addtl research. [2]Bdry alt 1960, 30 Mar, affecting Barnsley BC (Darton) and Wakefield CC (Woolley), SI 1960/449. [3]Disfranchised 1870, 33 & 34 Vict, *c* 21. [4]Cr and abol of BCs in 1955, changes in constituent wards and areas of others, 15 Feb, SI 1955/180. [5]Changes 1955 in constituent wards, as in note 4 above, SI 1955/180; change 1956 in constituent ward and bdry alt, 15 June, affecting Bradford North BC (Bradford) and Shipley CC (Shipley), SI 1956/819. [6]Bdry alt 1951, 1 Apr, affecting Doncaster BC (Doncaster) and Don Valley CC (Cantley), SI 1951/323. [7]Changes 1955 in constituent areas and wards, 15 Feb, SI 1955/179. [8]Cr and abol of BCs and CCs in 1955, changes in constituent areas and wards of others, 15 Feb, SI 1955/178. [9]Changes 1955 in constituent areas and wards as in note 8 above, SI 1955/178; bdry alt 1956, 15 June, affecting Kingston upon Hull East BC (Sculcoates) and Bridlington CC (Bilton), SI 1956/822. [10]Changes 1951 in constituent wards, 1 Apr, SI 1951/320. [11]Cr of BC 1955 and changes in constituent wards of others, 15 Feb, SI 1955/182; bdry alt 1960, 30 Mar, affecting Leeds East BC and Leeds North East BC (Leeds), Barkston Ash CC (Austhorpe, Barwick in Elmet), SI 1960/455. [12]Changes 1951 in constituent wards, as in note 10 above, SI 1955/178; changes 1955 in constituent wards, as in note 11 above, SI 1955/182. [13]Changes 1960 in constituent wards, 30 Mar, SI 1960/457. [14]Redefinition 1953 of wards in constituencies (after civ redefinition 30 Jan 1952), 7 May, SI 1953/746; changes 1955 in constituent wards, 15 Feb, SI 1955/183. [15]Bdry alt 1952, SI 1952/1348. [16]Changes 1949 in constituent areas, 10 Aug, SI 1949/1439; changes in constituent areas and wards 1955, 15 Feb, SI 1955/181. [17]Bdry alt in 1960, 30 Mar, affecting York BC (York), Barkston Ash CC (Askham Bryan), SI 1960/455. [18]Orig definition of constituencies (1867: 30 & 31 Vict, *c* 102) replaced by redefinition (1868: 31 & 32 Vict, *c* 46). [19]Bdry alts 1960, as in notes 11 and 17 above, SI 1960/455.

PART IV: THE DIOCESES OF ENGLAND

BIRMINGHAM

[1]13 Jan, *Lond Gaz*. [2]Orig called 'Aston juxta Birmingham'. [3]11 July, *Lond Gaz*. [4]11 Aug, *Lond Gaz*. [5]23 Oct, *Lond Gaz*. [6]31 Oct, *Lond Gaz*. [7]30 Aug, *Lond Gaz*. [8]17 Oct, *Lond Gaz*. [9]19 May, *Lond Gaz*.

BLACKBURN

[1]12 Nov, *Lond Gaz*. [2]4 Nov, *Lond Gaz*. [3]3 Apr, *Lond Gaz*. [4]1 Mar, *Lond Gaz*. [5]3 Apr, *Lond Gaz*. [6]Yr Instr Bp Blackb (*Lond Gaz*, 17 Apr 1970).

BRADFORD

[1]25 Nov, *Lond Gaz*. [2]25 Feb, *Lond Gaz*. [3]2 Mar, *Lond Gaz*. [4]16 Aug, *Lond Gaz*. [5]15 May, *Lond Gaz*. [6]29 July, *Lond Gaz* (2 orders).

CARLISLE

[1]5 Feb, avoidance of see (*Lond Gaz*, 31 Aug 1847). [2]First appearance in *Clergy List*. [3]21 Mar, *Lond Gaz*. [4]27 May, *Lond Gaz*. [5]30 May, *Lond Gaz*. [6]13 Aug, *Lond Gaz*. [7]1 Jan, *Lond Gaz*. [8]7 Aug, *Lond Gaz*. [9]13 Mar, *Lond Gaz*.

CHESTER

[1]4 Aug, Rymer, *Foedera*, XIV, 717. [2]A number of Rural Deaneries were subdivided as appears in the *Clergy List* for 1847 and slightly later, which however did not persist and which are therefore not shown in the list in the text: Blackburn into the 2 pts of Blackburn, Whalley (1847 only); Leyland into the 2 pts of North Meols, Wigan (1847 only); Manchester into the 4 pts of Aston, Bolton, Manchester, Rochdale (1847 only); Warrington into the 4 pts of Liverpool North, Liverpool South, Prescot, Winwick (1847—80). [3]7 Oct, *Lond Gaz*. [4]Year effective (exact day not found). [5]31 Aug, *Lond Gaz*. [6]17 Aug, *Lond Gaz*. [7]5 Feb, avoidance of see of Carlisle (*Lond Gaz*, 31 Aug 1847). [8]First appearance in *Clergy List*. [9]3 Aug, *Lond Gaz*. [10]21 Sept, *Lond Gaz*. [11]21 Dec, *Lond Gaz*. [12]19 Feb, *Lond Gaz*. [13]1 Nov, *Lond Gaz*. [14]14 Mar, *Lond Gaz*. [15]22 Oct, *Lond Gaz*. [16]12 Apr, *Lond Gaz*. [17]Yr Instr Bp Chester (*Lond Gaz*, 2 Oct 1970).

COVENTRY

[1]6 Sept, *Lond Gaz*. [2]31 Oct, *Lond Gaz*. [3]15 Feb, *Lond Gaz*. [4]28 June, *Lond Gaz*. [5]2 Aug, *Lond Gaz*. [6]14 Dec, *Lond Gaz*.

DERBY

[1]1 July, *Lond Gaz*. [2]5 Aug, *Lond Gaz*. [3]24 May, *Lond Gaz*.

DURHAM

[1]First appearance in *Clergy List*. [2]9 July, *Lond Gaz*. [3]23 May, *Lond Gaz*. [4]29 Aug, *Lond Gaz*. [5]3 Jan, *Lond Gaz*. [6]30 June, *Lond Gaz*. [7]18 Jan, *Lond Gaz*. [8]25 June, *Lond Gaz*.

HEREFORD

[1]First appearance in *Clergy List*. [2]1 Jan (*Lond Gaz*, 15 Dec 1848). [3]4 Apr, *Lond Gaz*. [4]2 Dec, *Lond Gaz*. [5]11 July, *Lond Gaz*. [6]31 Oct, *Lond Gaz*. [7]12 Oct, *Lond Gaz*. [8]9 Aug, *Lond Gaz*. [9]15 Apr, *Lond Gaz*. [10]23 Dec, *Lond Gaz*. [11]2 June, *Lond Gaz*. [12]Exact date for changes in 1972 not found.

LEICESTER

[1]12 Nov, *Lond Gaz.* [2]13 Nov, *Lond Gaz.* [3]20 Jan, *Lond Gaz.* [4]12 Apr, *Lond Gaz.*

LICHFIELD

[1]6 & 7 Wm IV, *c* 77 and 24 Jan, *Lond Gaz.* [2]Note that dates for cr and abol of Rural Deaneries differs in *Clergy List* and *VCH* drawing on county reports; dates drawn from latter. [3]First appearance in *Clergy List.* [4]11 July, *Lond Gaz.* [5]8 July, *Lond Gaz.* [6]28 Sept, *Lond Gaz.* [7]30 Nov, *Lond Gaz.* [8]11 July, *Lond Gaz.* [9]23 Oct, *Lond Gaz.* [10]21 May, *Lond Gaz.* [11]18 Jan, *Lond Gaz,* [12]26 Oct, *Lond Gaz.*

LICHFIELD AND COVENTRY

[1]6 & 7 Wm IV, *c* 77 and 24 Jan, *Lond Gaz.* [2]4 Aug, Rymer, *Foedera,* XIV, 717.

LINCOLN

[1]4 Sept, Letters Patent for erection of dioc Peterborough printed in Rymer, *Foedera* XIV, 731. [2]1 Sept, Letters Patent for erection of dioc Osney printed in Rymer XIV, 754; name changed to 'Oxford' when see transfered there. [3]30 May, *Lond Gaz.* [4]18 Aug, *Lond Gaz.* [5] 1 May, vac of dioc Peterb (*Lond Gaz,* 5 Sept 1837). [6]23 Apr, *Lond Gaz.* [7]8 June, *Lond Gaz.* [8]20 Aug, *Lond Gaz.* [9]First appearance in *Clergy List.* [10]4 Apr, *Lond Gaz.* [11]30 Oct, *Lond Gaz.* [12]8 July, *Lond Gaz.* [13]9 Aug, *Lond Gaz.* [14]22 Dec, *Lond Gaz.* [15]31 Dec, *Lond Gaz* (2 orders).

LIVERPOOL

[1]2 July, *Lond Gaz.* [2]OC 24 Mar, effective 9 Apr. [3]14 July, *Lond Gaz.* [4]9 Dec, *Lond Gaz.* [5]17 May, *Lond Gaz.* [6]25 Mar, *Lond Gaz.* [7]10 Apr, *Lond Gaz.* [8]10 Dec, *Lond Gaz.* [9]20 Dec, *Lond Gaz.* [10]27 May, *Lond Gaz.*

MANCHESTER

[1]31 Aug, *Lond Gaz.* [2]First appearance in *Clergy List.* [3]17 Aug, *Lond Gaz.* [4]4 July, *Lond Gaz.* [5]19 Mar, *Lond Gaz.* [6]17 July, *Lond Gaz.* [7]3 June, *Lond Gaz.* [8]11 Oct, *Lond Gaz.* [9]16 Feb, *Lond Gaz.* [10]12 Nov, *Lond Gaz.* [11]4 Nov, *Lond Gaz.* [12]1 Feb, *Lond Gaz.* [13]25 Apr, *Lond Gaz.* [14]14 Mar, *Lond Gaz.* [15]24 June, *Lond Gaz.* [16]4 Aug, *Lond Gaz.* [17]15 May, *Lond Gaz.* [18]24 June, *Lond Gaz.* [19]26 May, *Lond Gaz.* [20]4 Apr, *Lond Gaz.*

NEWCASTLE

[1]23 May, *Lond Gaz.* [2]1 July, *Lond Gaz.* [3]3 Feb, *Lond Gaz.* [4]22 Oct, *Lond Gaz.* [5]17 Nov, *Lond Gaz.* [6]25 Mar, *Lond Gaz.*

PETERBOROUGH

[1]Rymer, *Foedera.* [2]Sometimes 'Oundle South'. [3]Sometimes 'Oundle North'. [4]5 Sept, *Lond Gaz.* [5]First appearance in *Clergy List.* [6]1 Aug, *Lond Gaz.* [7]29 June, *Lond Gaz.* [8]27 Oct, *Lond Gaz.* [9]13 May, *Lond Gaz.* [10]19 May, *Lond Gaz.* [11]12 Nov, *Lond Gaz.* [12]23 Feb, *Lond Gaz.* [13]6 Dec, *Lond Gaz.* [14]9 Feb, *Lond Gaz.* [15] 28 June (2 orders). [16]9 Dec, *Lond Gaz.* [17]Yr Instr Bp Peterb (*Lond Gaz,* 24 Feb 1970).

RIPON

[1]7 Oct, *Lond Gaz.* [2]Sometimes early called 'Eastern' instead of 'East', 'Western' instead of 'West'. [3]Most of Otley transf 1919 to help cr Bradford dioc; a small remnant remained as Otley RDn in Ripon dioc 1919—21. [4]First appearance in *Clergy List.* [5]21 Dec, *Lond Gaz.* [6]20 Nov, *Clergy List.* [7]31 Aug, *Lond Gaz.* [8]11 July, *Lond Gaz.* [9]25 Nov, *Lond Gaz.* [10]15 Mar, *Lond Gaz.* [11]14 Aug, *Lond Gaz.* [12]13 July, *Lond Gaz.*

SHEFFIELD

[1]23 Jan, *Lond Gaz.* [2]4 Sept, *Lond Gaz.* [3]15 July, *Lond Gaz.* [4]16 Oct, *Lond Gaz.*

SOUTHWELL

[1]8 July, *Lond Gaz.* [2]27 Sept, *Lond Gaz.* [3]18 Oct, *Lond Gaz.* [4]11 June, *Lond Gaz.* [5]4 Sept, *Lond Gaz.* [6]19 Oct, *Lond Gaz.* [7]1 July, *Lond Gaz.* [8]2 Aug, *Lond Gaz.*

WAKEFIELD

[1]17 May, *Lond Gaz.* [2]20 Nov, *Lond Gaz.* [3]5 Feb, *Lond Gaz.* [4]21 Feb, *Lond Gaz.* [5]30 Apr, *Lond Gaz.* [6]15 Feb, *Lond Gaz.* [7]22 Oct, *Lond Gaz.* [8]21 Dec, *Lond Gaz.* [9]11 June, *Lond Gaz.* [10]9 Mar, *Lond Gaz.*

WORCESTER

[1]Orig called 'Aston juxta Birmingham'. [2]24 Jan, *Lond Gaz.* [3]18 Aug, *Lond Gaz.* [4]First appearance in *Clergy List.* [5]Transf Oldbury from Hereford dioc to Worcester dioc. [6]Less than ten changes, effective date not found for transf of these pars; see Part I of the *Guide.* [7]12 Aug, *Lond Gaz.* [8]13 Jan, *Lond Gaz.* [9]11 July, *Lond Gaz.* [10]23 Aug, *Lond Gaz.* [11]21 Jan, *Lond Gaz.* [12]6 Sept, *Lond Gaz.* [13]31 Oct, *Lond Gaz.* [14]15 Feb, *Lond Gaz.* [15]14 Oct, *Lond Gaz.* [16]16 Nov 1973, *Lond Gaz.*

YORK

[1]Exact date of rearrangement of Ainsty RDns not found. [2]7 Oct, *Lond Gaz.* [3]First appearance in *Clergy List.* [4]21 Dec, *Lond Gaz.* [5]5 Apr, *Lond Gaz.* [6]18 Apr, *Lond Gaz.* [7]27 Sept, *Lond Gaz.* [8]31 Aug, *Lond Gaz.* [9]10 Mar, *Lond Gaz.* [10]18 Feb, *Lond Gaz.* [11]14 Jan, *Lond Gaz.* [12]19 Dec, *Lond Gaz.* [13]23 Dec, *Lond Gaz.* [14]7 Apr, *Lond Gaz.* [15]15 Aug, *Lond Gaz.* [16]30 Mar, *Lond Gaz.* [17]6 Nov, *Lond Gaz.* [18]31 Jan, *Lond Gaz.* [19]14 Feb, *Lond Gaz.*

CORRIGENDA FOR VOLUME I

Entries as in the reprint of Volume I and additional changes. Page of entry, name of entry, corrected and/or added information. Most elaborated entries (e.g., the three for page 9 below) show name(s) of entire parish(es) gained to be consistent with other entries, whereas for the former, in the first printing, the date and authority only were cited.

7 HYDE: [Civ bdry:] 1907 (exchanges pts with Flamstead AP, Harpenden Rural CP, both Herts),[26]

8 MELCHBOURNE: Incl chap Knotting (sep par 1176[76]).

9 PODINGTON: [Civ bdry:] 1884 (gains Farndish AP),[59]

9 SHARNBROOK: [Civ bdry:] 1895 (gains Colworth Farm CP),[51]

9 SHEFFORD: [Civ bdry:] 1933 (gains Shefford Hardwick CP).[4]

15 AVINGTON: Abol civ 1934 [corrected date]

19 HAMPSTEAD NORREYS: [corrected spelling par name]

20 INGLESHAM: [pt in Berks] transf to Wilts 1832 for parl purposes, 1844 for civ purposes.[27]

20 KINGSTON BAGPUIZE WITH SOUTHMOOR: Cr 1971 by union . . . Draycot Moor CP.[93] [corrected spelling]

20 KINTBURY: [Civ bdry:] 1934 (gains Avington AP).[3]

22 RADLEY: [Civ bdry:] 1900 [in lieu of 1894] (gains Bagley Wood CP, Chandlings Farm CP),[26]

24 SULHAMSTEAD ABBOTS: [LG] [add:] Abol civ 1934 to help cr Sulhamstead CP.[3]

25 TWYFORD: Eccl Sonn. RDn (1874—1973).

27 WYTHAM: [Civ bdry:] 1900 (gains Seacourt CP).[164]

29 Local Government Sequences: SEQ 11 Cott. Hd,

31 AYLESBURY: [chaps] as 'Bierton with Broughton',[17] qv for later eccl separation),

31 BLETCHLEY: [Civ bdry:] 1934 (gains Fenny Stratford CP, Simpson AP, Water Eaton CP),[3]

34 ETON: [Civ bdry:] 1934 (gains Eton Wick CP).[3]

39 QUAINTON: [Civ bdry:] 1886 [in lieu of 1885] (gains Shipton Lee CP),[155]

39 SHENLEY: [LG] each sep rated for poor law purposes and each sep CP 1866,[2]

42 WEXHAM: [Civ bdry:] 1901 (gains Upton cum Chalvey AP),[178]

43 WOTTON UNDERWOOD: [Eccl] Wadd. RDn (1874—1921).

44 WEST WYCOMBE RURAL: Abol civ 1934 . . . pt to Hughendon AP.[3] [corrected spelling]

48 CP1—CAMBRIDGE: [Bdry:] 1923 (gains Chesterton AP),[25] 1934 (gains Cherry Hinton AP).[26]

49 CLAPTON: Shingay RDn,

50 FORDHAM: [Civ bdry:] 1953 (gains Landwade CP).[85]

54 UPWELL: [CP] Cr 1889 from the IoE pt of Upwell AP.[111]

54 WELNEY: [CP] Cr 1889 from the IoE pt of Welney CP.[111]

55 WILBURTON: [Civ bdry:] 1933 (gains Grunty Fen CP).[72]

55 WISBECH ST PETER: Usual civ spelling; for eccl see following entry.

58 BLISLAND: [Civ bdry:] 1934 (gains Temple AP).[6]

60 CORNELLY: Abol civ 1934 ent to Tregony CP.[6] [corrected spelling]

61 GERRANS: [Civ bdry:] 1934 (gains St Anthony in Rushland CP).[6]

61 HAYLE: [Civ bdry:] 1935 (gains East Phillack CP),[56] 1938 (gains West Phillack CP).[53]

62 KENWYN: [LG] pt Truro Bor/MB (enlarged pt 1835—94),

64 LOSTWITHIEL: [Civ bdry:] 1896 (gains Lanlivery Urban CP),[70]

64 MARAZION: [Parl] West Dv (1832—85),

65 MYLOR: [add] Eccl Seq 6.

65 PADSTOW URBAN: [Bdry:] [add] 1934 (gains Padstow Rural CP).[6]

65 PENZANCE: [Civ bdry:] 1894 ([add] gains Madron in Penzance CP, gains Penzance in Madron CP),[17]

70 SALTASH: [Civ bdry:] 1934 (gains St Stephens AP).[6]

76 AXMINSTER: Abol civ 1915 . . . pt to cr Axmin. UD . . . CP.[30] [corrected abbreviation]

81 COLATON RALEIGH: [Civ bdry:] 1894 (gains Dotton CP).[147]

82 DALWOOD: sep CP 1866[81] but not sep eccl [in lieu of civ] identity.

86 HARPFORD: [Civ bdry:] 1935 (gains Newton Poppleford CP, Venn Ottery CP).[1]

89 LOXBEARE: [Civ bdry:] 1885 (gains Calverleigh AP).[124]

91 NEWTON ST CYRES: [Civ bdry:] 1894 [in lieu of 1884] (gains Highley St Mary CP, Sherwood Villa CP).[245]

92 OLDRIDGE: [add:] Eccl Kenn RDn.

93 CP1—PLYMOUTH: [Bdry:] 1939 (gains Compton Gifford CP),[55] 1951 (gains St Budeaux CP),[57]

93 PLYMPTON ST MARY: [Civ bdry:] 1894 (gains Chelson Meadow CP).[130]

94 REVELSTOKE: Abol civ 1935 to help cr Newton and Noss CP.[1]

96 SALCOMBE: sep CP 1894 (the pt in Salcombe USD).[47] LG Kingsbr. PLU, Salcombe UD. [corrected spellings]

96 SAMPFORD COURTENAY: [Civ bdry:] 1894 (gains Honeychurch AP).[245]

96 SIDMOUTH: [Civ bdry:] 1931 (gains Salcombe Regis AP, Sidbury AP),[346]

98 NORTH TAWTON: [Civ bdry:] [add] between 1820—50 (gains Broad Nymet AP).[84]

99 THORNCOMBE: Transf to Devon 1832 for parl

purposes, 1844 for civ purposes.[27] [omit transf to Dorset 1896]

99 TORBRYAN: [Civ bdry:] 1885 (gains Denbury AP).[363]

101 WOLBOROUGH: [corrected spelling par name]

102 EAST WORLINGTON: [Civ bdry:] 1885 (gains West Worlington AP).[375]

106 ALMER: Abol civ 1933 [in lieu of 1935]

106 ANDERSON: for eccl see 'Winterbourne Anderson'. [corrected spelling]; [Civ bdry:] 1933 (gains Winterborne Tomson AP).[2]

108 BUCKLAND RIPERS: Abol civ 1894 to help reconstitute Radipole AP.[70] [corrected information]

111 GUSSAGE ALL SAINTS: [corrected spelling par name]

112 HOLNEST: eccl severed 1929 to help cr Wotton Glanville with Holnest EP,

113 LYDLINCH: [Civ bdry:] 1884 (gains Stock Gaylard AP).[163]

114 MAPPOWDER: [Eccl] Cerne RDn (1872—1937).

115 MINTERNE MAGNA: [Civ bdry:] 1933 (gains Gorewood CP).[2]

116 WEST PARLEY: West Moors CP cr 1956 from [corrected spelling] West Parley AP . . .

116 PENTRIDGE: [Civ bdry:] 1933 (. . . West Woodyates CP).[2] [corrected description of par status]

117 RADIPOLE: [Civ bdry:] 1894 (. . . the residue combined with Buckland Ripers AP as reconstituted Radipole par),[15]

118 CP1—SHAFTESBURY: [Civ bdry:] 1921 (gains Alcester CP),[6]

121 UPWEY: Abol civ 1933 . . . Chickerell [corrected spelling] AP.[2]

123 WINTERBORNE PHILLIPSTON: [corrected spelling par name]

129 ASHINGDON: [Civ bdry:] 1949 [corrected date] (gains South Frambridge AP).[9]

131 BIRCH: [Civ bdry:] 1949 (gains Messing AP).[9]

132 BRENTWOOD: [Civ bdry:] 1934 (gains Ingrave AP).[17]

133 CANEWDON: [Civ bdry:] 1946 (gains Eastwood AP).[20]

139 WEST HAM: [LG] MB (1886—89), CB (1889—1965).

140 Pages in incorrect alphabetical order in first printing: correct sequence of placement using page numbers in first printing is 140, 144, 143, 142, 141

146 NETTESWELL: [Civ bdry:] [add] 1935 (loses pt to Gilston AP, Herts), (authority for change: 1 Apr, MHealthO 80108).

147 GREAT PARNDON: [Civ bdry:] [add] 1935 (loses pt to Eastwick AP, Herts), (authority for change: as for NETTESWELL, above).

148 QUENDON AND RICKLING: Cr 1949 . . . Rickling [corrected spelling] AP.[14]

149 ROYDON: [Civ bdry:] [add] 1935 (loses pt to Eastwick AP, Herts), (authority for change: as for NETTESWELL, above).

150 SOUTHEND ON SEA: [Civ bdry:] 1933 (gains South Shoebury AP).[111]

151 STANSTEAD MOUNTFITCHET: [add] Later called 'Stansted Mountfitchet'.

152 MARKS TEY: [Civ bdry:] 1949 (gains Little Tey AP).[9]

157 WITHAM: [Civ bdry:] 1933 (gains Rivenhall AP).[184]

163 AUST: [Civ bdry:] 1935 (gains Elberton AP).[2]

164 BATSFORD: [LG] pt Worcs (Kington Hd),; [Civ bdry:] 1935 (gains Lower Lemington CP).[2]

165 BLAISDON: [Civ bdry:] 1935 (gains Flaxley AP).[2]

165 CP1—BRISTOL: 1904 (gains Horfield AP, Shirehampton CP, Westbury-on-Trym AP),[287]; 1933 (gains Brislington CP, Somerset),[87]

168 CHARLTON KINGS: [corrected spelling par name]

169 CHURCHAM: [Civ bdry:] 1935 (gains Bulley CP).[2]

170 COLEFORD: Chap in Newland AP, sep EP 1772,[13]

170 COLN ST DENNIS: [Civ bdry:] 1935 (gains Coln Rogers AP).[2]

171 CONDICOTE: [corrected spelling par name]

171 EAST DEAN: [Civ bdry:] 1884 (gains Hinders Lane and Dockham CP),[209]

171 DIDMARTON: [Civ bdry:] [add] 1883 (gains Oldbury on the Hill AP),[222]

171 DODINGTON: [Civ bdry:] 1935 (gains Wapley and Codrington AP).[2]

172 DRIFFIELD: [Civ bdry:] 1935 (gains Harnhill AP).[2]

172 DUMBLETON: [Civ bdry:] 1935 (gains Great Washbourne AP, Little Washbourne CP, Wormington AP),[2] 1965 (loses pt to Beckford AP, pt to Ashton under Hill CP, both Worcs).[29]

172 DYMOCK: [Civ bdry:] 1935 (gains Preston AP).[2]

172 EBRINGTON: [Civ bdry:] 1935 (gains Hidcote Bartrim CP).[2]

173 FORTHAMPTON: [Civ bdry:] 1965 (loses pt to Eldersfield AP, pt to Bushley CP, both Worcs).[29]

174 CP1—GLOUCESTER: [Bdry:] 1951 (gains Wotton Vill CP),[46]

175 TEMPLE GUITING: [Eccl bdry:] Gains 1912 chap Cutsdean from Bredon with Bredon's Norton AP, Worcs, to cr Temple Guiting with Cutsdean EP. (authority for change: VCH Worcs III, 279).

175 TEMPLE GUITING WITH CUTSDEAN: EP Cr 1912 by union Temple Guting AP, chap Cutsdean from Bredon with Bredon's Norton AP, Worcs. (authority for change as in prev entry).

176 HAWLING: [Civ bdry:] 1935 (gains Roel CP).[2]

177 HENBURY: [Civ bdry:] [add] 1896 (gains Compton Greenfield AP),[205]

178 ICOMB: [Civ bdry:] 1935 (gains Church Icomb CP).[2]

178 KINGSCOTE: [Civ bdry:] 1935 (gains Newington Bagpath AP).[2]

179 LEA: pt Hereford [corrected spelling]

180 LONGFORD: Cr 1885 from . . . Twigworth CP, . . . [corrected description of par status]

181 MITCHELDEAN: [Civ bdry:] 1935 (gains Abenhall AP),[2]

181 MOCKING HAZEL WOOD: [corrected spelling par name]

182 OXENTON: [Civ bdry:] 1935 (gains Woolstone AP).[2]

182 PAINSWICK: *LG* Painswick Bor (status not sustained), Bisley Hd, Stroud PLU, pt Stroud USD, pt Stroud RSD, Stroud RD.

183 POULTON: Fairford RDn (1887—*). [corrected spelling]

183 PRESTBURY: [*Eccl*] 1953 (help cr Lynworth EP).[318]

183 PRESTON ON STOUR: [*Eccl*] Camp. RDn (until 1919), Cov & Lichf dioc thereafter (see entry in Warws).

184 RUDFORD: [Civ bdry:] 1935 (gains Highleadon CP).[2]

185 UPPER SLAUGHTER: [Civ bdry:] 1935 (gains Eyford AP).[2]

187 STONEHOUSE: [Civ bdry:] 1884 (gains Haywards Field CP),[285]

187 STROUD: [Civ bdry:] 1936 (gains Uplands CP).[69]

187 TEDDINGTON: [Civ bdry:] 1935 (gains Alstone CP),[2]

188 TEWKSBURY HOLY TRINITY: [add] [Bdry:] 1966 (gains pt Bredon with Bredon's Norton AP, Worcs). (authority for change, 25 Dec, *Lond Gaz*).

188 TORMARTON: [Civ bdry:] 1935 (gains West Littleton CP).[2]

189 UPTON ST LEONARDS: [Civ bdry:] 1935 (incl . . . and gains Prinknash Park CP),[2]

192 YANWORTH: [Civ bdry:] 1935 (gains Stowell AP).[2]

193 [in list of ABBREVIATIONS:] Hartley Wintney [corrected spelling]

197 ASHEY: [corrected spelling par name for 2nd par listed as 'ASHLEY', and change alphabetical order of pars]

199 CP1—BOURNEMOUTH: [Bdry:] [add] 1895 (gains pt Holdenhurst CP),[324]; 1901 (gains pt Southbourne CP),[115]; 1902 ([omit reference to Southbourne CP]),[116]; 1914 (gains pt Holdenhurst CP),[117]

201 BURTON: Cr 1877 from Christchurch AP.[167] [corrected spelling]

201 CALBOURNE: [incl pt from Shalfleet AP][168] [in lieu of Shinfleet]

202 CHRISTCHURCH: Incl area Highcliffe (. . . sep CP 1897 . . .) [corrected date]; [Addtl civ bdry alt:] [add:] 1933 (gains Highcliffe AP),[119]

206 KNIGHTS ENHAM: [Eccl bdry:] 1973 (exchanges pts with Smannell EP which is then renamed 'Smannell with Enham Alamein').[263] [corrected spelling]

207 FAREHAM: [Eccl bdry:] 1957 (cr Fareham St John the Evangelist EP).[269]

207 FARINGDON: [Eccl bdry:] 1973 [corrected date]

210 HIGHCLIFFE: [Civ bdry:] 1901, [correct authority is 1 Edw VII, *c* clxviii]; Abol civ 1932 [corrected date]

211 HOUND: [Civ bdry:] 1894 (cr Sholing CP),[114] [corrected footnote number]

212 KINGSTON: Abol civ 1933 ent to Shorwell CP.[42] [corrected spelling]

216 NURSLING AND ROWNHAMS: [corrected spelling par name]

218 POKESDOWN: [top of right column] CP Cr 1894 from Christchurch AP.[189] *LG* Bournem. & Christch. PLU (1894—1900), Christch. PLU (1900—02), RD (1894—95), Pokesdown UD (1895—1901), Bournem. CB (1901—02).

218 PORTSMOUTH: [Eccl bdry:] 1955 (incl gains Portsea St John EP, Portsea St George EP).[336]

220 SANDOWN-SHANKLIN: CP [in lieu of EP]

220 EAST SHANKLIN: CP Cr 1894 from the pt of Brading AP in Shanklin UD.[3] [corrected description of status]

221 SHERFIELD-ON-LODDON: [*LG*] Odiham Hd (until 1834), Basingst. Hd (from 1834),

221 SMANNELL WITH ENHAM ALAMEIN: . . . after exchanges pts with Knights Enham AP.[263] [corrected spelling]

222 SOUTHBOURNE: [delete bdry alt 1901]; Abol civ 1901 pt to Bournem. CB and CP, pt to Highcliffe CP. (authority as for HIGHCLIFFE [p. 210], above).

229 WINTON: [to *LG* add:] Christch. RD (1894—98),

229 WOODMANCOTT: [*LG*] Mainsbr. Hd (until 1834), Holdshot Hd (from 1834),

230 YATELEY: [*LG*:] Crondall Hd, [corrected spelling]

235 COTTERED: [Civ bdry:] 1955 (gains Throcking AP).[87]

237 HERTINGFORDBY: [Civ bdry:] 1924 (gains St Andrew Rural CP),[16]

238 HITCHIN URBAN: [Bdry:] 1921 (gains Walworth CP),[169]

239 LEAVESDEN: [corrected spelling par name]

239 LETCHWORTH: [Civ bdry:] 1908 (gains Norton AP),[191] 1935 (gains Willian AP),[4]

242 ST ANDREW RURAL: Abol 1924 ent to Hertingfordbury AP.[161] [corrected footnote]

243 TRING RURAL: [Bdry: (in lieu of Civ bdry:)] 1964 (gains Puttenham AP).[208]

251 LUDDINGTON IN THE BROOK: pt Northants (Polebrook Hd, usually civ 'Luddington'); [*Eccl*] Oundle RDn. Abol eccl 1849 to help cr Luddington with Helmington EP, qv in entries for Northants. (authority for change, OC 6 Nov, reported in *Parl Papers* 1872, XLVI, 13).

260 BELVEDERE ALL SAINTS: [Bdry:] 1955 (help cr Bexleyheath St Peter EP),[67]

261 BRABOURNE: [Civ bdry:] 1934 (gains Bircholt AP).[19]

263 BURMARSH: [Civ bdry:] [add to 1934:] (. . . and gains Easebridge AP).[19]

264 CAPEL: [Bdry:] 1885 (gains Tudeley AP),[164]

266 CHILLENDEN: Abol civ . . . to Goodnestone AP.[6] [corrected spelling]

266 CHILLENDEN WITH KNOWLTON [corrected spelling par name]; Cr 1940 by union Chillenden AP, . . . [corrected spelling]

267 COOLING: [*Eccl*] Cliffe at Hoo RDn (1909—58). Abol eccl 1958 to help cr Cliffe at Hoo with Cooling EP.[218]

269 CP1—DOVER: [add to list of pars united to cr this par:] East Cliffe CP

270 EYNESFORD: [Civ bdry:] [add to entry for 1955:]

1955 . . ., gains Lullingstone AP).[29]

270 EYTHORNE: [Civ bdry:] 1935 (gains Barfreston AP).[6]

271 FAVERSHAM: [Eccl bdry:] 1947.[117]

272 GILLINGHAM: [LG] pt Chatham MB & USD (1890—94),

272 AP1—GILLINGHAM [ST MARY THE VIRGIN]: [Civ bdry:] 1913 (gains Lidsing CP),[314]

272 GOODNESTONE [1st of 2]: [Civ bdry:] 1935 (gains Chillenden AP, Knowlton AP).[6]

272 GOODNESTONE [2nd of 2]: [Eccl bdry:] 1947.[117]

273 AP1—GRAVESEND: [Civ bdry:] 1935 (gains Chalk AP, Denton AP).[6]

274 HARBLEDOWN: [Civ bdry:] [add to entry for 1934:] 1934 (. . ., gains St Nicholas Hospital CP).[150]

274 LOWER HARDRES: [Civ bdry:] 1934 (gains Nackington AP).[19]

275 HERNE BAY: [Bdry:] 1934 (gains Herne AP, Reculver AP).[19]

279 AP1—MAIDSTONE: [Civ bdry:] 1934 (gains Allington AP).[19]

282 NORTHBOURNE: [Addtl civ bdry alt:] 1935 (gains Betteshanger AP, Ham AP).[6]

282 OARE: [Eccl bdry:] 1947.[117]

283 ORPINGTON: [Addtl civ bdry alt:] [add to entry for 1934:] 1934 (. . . and gains Chelsfield AP, Cudham AP, Downe CP, Knockholt CP).[19]

284 POULTON WITHIN: [corrected spelling par name]; Cr 1894 from the pt of Poulton AP . . . [corrected description of status]

286 OLD ROMNEY: [Civ bdry:] 1934 (gains Midley AP).[19]

287 ST LAWRENCE: [LG] pt Ramsgate MB (1884—94),

290 SPELDHURST: [Civ bdry:] 1934 (gains Ashurst AP).[19]

291 STELLING MINNIS: [Bdry:] 1968 (gains Stelling CP).[452]

291 SUTTON: [Civ bdry:] 1935 (gains Little Mongeham AP).[19]

292 THANNINGON WITHOUT: [Bdry:] 1934 (gains Milton AP).[19]

294 WHITSTABLE: Abol civ 1934 the pt constituted [corrected spelling]

295 WINGHAM: Incl . . . areas . . . Womenswold [corrected spelling]

295 EP1—WOOLWICH HOLY TRINITY: [corrected spelling par name]

298 AP16—ST ANDREW UNDERSHAFT: United 1562 to help cr united par

309 BROMLEY LB: Bdry alt: 1969 (cr Knockholt CP to be in Kent). (authority for change: 1 Apr, SI 1968/2020)

310 CROYDON LB: Bdry alt: 1969 (gains pt Banstead AP, Surrey). (authority for change: as for Bromley LB in prev entry)

317 BRONDESBURY CHRIST CHURCH: Brent RDn (1967—71).

330 HOXTON: [Eccl] St Sepulchre RDn (1861—70), Shored. RDn (1870—1967), Hack. RDn (1967—*).

340 ST GEORGE HANOVER SQUARE: [LG] St Geo. Hanov. Sq. Vestry

344 SPITALFIELDS: [Eccl] Step. RDn (1901—11).

358 BOWTHORPE: Abol civ 1935 ent to Costessey AP.[1] [corrected spelling]

361 COSTESSEY: [corrected spelling par name]

362 EATON: [corrected spelling of par name in lieu of EASTON (2nd of that name)]

365 EAST HARLING: LG Guiltc. Hd, [corrected abbreviation]

367 HORSTEAD WITH STANNINGHALL: Civ union 16th cent of Horstead AP [corrected spelling] . . .

369 KNAPTON: Abol civ 1935 ent to Paston AP.[134] [corrected footnote number]

369 LETHERINGSETT WITH GLANDFORD: [corrected spelling par name]

375 POSTWICK: [Civ bdry:] 1935 (incl gains Witton AP).[1]

381 TERRINGTON ST CLEMENT: [Civ bdry:] 1897, (authority for change as for CENTRAL WINGLAND below).

383 WALPOLE ST ANDREW: [Civ bdry:] 1897, (authority for change as for CENTRAL WINGLAND below).

383 WALPOLE ST PETER: [Civ bdry:] 1897, (authority for change as for CENTRAL WINGLAND below).

384 WALSOKEN: [Civ bdry:] [to entry for 1934, add:] loses pt to Wisbech St Peter AP, Cambs)

386 CENTRAL WINGLAND: [add entire entry:] Pt Lincs Pts Holl (Elloe Wap), pt Norfolk (Freebridge Marshland Hd). Ex-par place, sep CP 1858.[4] LG Holbeach PLU (1867—1930), RSD, pt sep RD in Norfolk (1894—97), East Elloe RD (pt 1894—97, ent 1897—1954). Bdry: 1897 (exchanges pts with Terrington St Clement AP, gains pts Walpole St Andrew AP, Walpole St Peter AP, all Norfolk, and gains pt Tydd St Giles AP, Lincs Pts Holl, and the reconstituted par ent Lincs Pts Holl thereafter. See entry in Lincs for civ abol and other organisation). (authority for change 1897: 9 Nov, LGBProvO 1326).

393 BODICOTE: [Civ bdry:] 1884 (gains pt Warkworth AP, Northants),[50]

394 CHINNOR: [Civ bdry:] 1932 (gains Emmington AP),[8]

395 CLIFTON HAMPDEN: [Civ bdry:] 1932 (gains Burcott CP).[8]

396 DENTON: [Bdry:] 1932 (gains Chippinghurst AP).[8]

402 MOLLINGTON: In 1889 becomes 2 sep pars, each 'Mollington',

404 OXFORD UNIVERSITY COLLEGES AND HALLS: [add] Parl Univ was sep Parl Bor (1604—1948).

405 STADHAMPTON: [Civ bdry:] 1932 ([add:], gains Ascott CP).[8]

406 SWERFORD: [Eccl] Sometimes as 'Swerford with Showell', Seq 8.

408 LITTLE WITTENHAM: [corrected spelling par name]

414 BADGWORTH: [Civ bdry:] 1933 (gains Biddenham AP).[3]

415 CP1—BATH: Bdry: [in lieu of Civ bdry:]; 1911

(gains Twerton or Twiverton CP),[42]

417 WEST BRADLEY: [Civ bdry:] 1933 (gains Hornblotton AP).[3]

419 BROMPTON REGIS: [Civ bdry:] 1933 (gains Withiel Florey AP).[3]

419 BRUTON WITH WYKE CHAMPFLOWER AND REDLYNCH: Cr 1971 by union Bruton and Redlynch EP, Wyke Champflower EP,[142]

419 BRYMPTON: [Civ bdry:] 1933 (gains Lufton AP, Thorne AP).[3]

419 SOUTH CADBURY: [Civ bdry:] 1933 (gains Sutton Montis AP).[3]

420 CHARLCOMBE: [Civ bdry:] 1933 (gains Langridge AP, Woolley AP),[3]

420 CHARLTON HORETHORNE: [Civ bdry:] 1933 (gains Stowell AP).[3]

420 CHEDDAR: [Civ bdry:] 1933 (gains Nyland cum Batcombe AP),[3]

421 CHILTON CANTELO: [Civ bdry:] 1933 (gains Ashington AP).[3]

421 CHIPSTABLE: [Civ bdry:] 1933 (gains Raddington AP).[3]

422 CLOSWORTH: [Civ bdry:] 1933 (gains Pendomer AP, Sutton Bingham AP).[3]

423 COMPTON DANDO: [Civ bdry:] 1933 (gains Burnett AP, Queen Charlton CP),[3]

423 COMPTON PAUNCEFOOT: [Civ bdry:] 1933 (gains Blackford CP).[3]

424 CURRY RIVEL: [Civ bdry:] 1933 (gains Earnshill AP).[3]

426 FIVEHEAD: [Civ bdry:] 1933 (gains Swell AP).[3]

427 WEST HARPTREE: [Civ bdry:] 1933 (gains North Widcombe CP).[3]

427 HEMINGTON: [Civ bdry:] 1933 (gains Foxcote AP, Hardington AP).[3]

428 HOLFORD: [Civ bdry:] 1933 (gains Dodington AP).[3]

429 ILCHESTER: [Civ bdry:] 1933 (gains Northover AP),[3]

429 KEYNSHAM: [Addtl civ bdry alt:] 1938 ([add:] gains Saltford AP . . ., 'Unannexed Area' [corrected spelling]),[229]

430 KNOWLE ST GILES: [Civ bdry:] 1933 (gains Cricket Malherbie AP).[3]

430 LANGFORD BUDVILLE: [Civ bdry:] 1933 (gains Runnington AP).[3]

431 LOVINGTON: [Civ bdry:] 1933 (gains Wheathill AP).[3]

431 LOXTON: [Civ bdry:] 1933 (gains Christon AP).[3]

431 LUCCOMBE: [Civ bdry:] 1933 (gains Stoke Perro AP).[3]

431 LULLINGTON: [Civ bdry:] 1933 (gains Laverton AP, Orchardleigh AP).[3]

431 MARKSBURY: [Civ bdry:] 1933 (gains Stanton Prior AP).[3]

433 NORTON FITZWARREN: [Civ bdry:] 1933 (gains Heathfield AP).[3]

433 NORTON ST PHILIP: [Civ bdry:] 1933 (gains Farleigh Hungerford AP),[3]

433 NUNNEY: [Civ bdry:] 1933 (gains Marston Bigot AP),[3]

433 OARE: [Civ bdry:] 1933 (gains Culbone AP).[3]

433 ORCHARD PORTMAN: [Civ bdry:] 1933 (gains

Thurlbear CP).[3]

434 NORTH PETHERTON: [Civ bdry:] 1933 (gains St Michaelchurch CP),[3]

434 PITMINSTER: [Civ bdry:] 1933 (gains Angersleigh AP).[3]

436 SELWOOD: [Civ bdry:] 1933 (gains Rodden CP).[3]

436 SHIPHAM: [Civ bdry:] 1933 (gains Rowberrow AP).[3]

436 SPARKFORD: [Civ bdry:] 1933 (gains Weston Bampfylde AP).[3]

436 SPAXTON: [Civ bdry:] 1933 (gains Aisholt AP).[3]

437 STAWLEY: [Civ bdry:] 1933 (gains Kittisford AP).[3]

439 CP3—TAUNTON ST JAMES WITHOUT: Abol 1932 . . . [corrected date]

439 TELLISFORD: [Civ bdry:] 1933 (gains Woolverton AP).[3]

440 WANSTROW: [Civ bdry:] 1933 (gains Cloford AP).[3]

442 AP1—WESTON-SUPER-MARE: [Civ bdry:] 1933 (gains Uphill AP).[3]

443 WITHYPOOL: [Civ bdry:] 1933 (gains Hawkridge AP).[3]

444 YEOVILTON: [Civ bdry:] 1933 (gains Podimore AP).[3]

460 LOWESTOFT: [Civ bdry:] 1934.[7] [corrected footnote number]

460 MENDHAM: Incl chap Metfield (Donative since 1570,[155] later considered distinctive civ and eccl).

462 REDLINGFIELD: Former priory [corrected spelling] church

466 WESTERFIELD: [Civ bdry:] 1894 (. . . Westerfield in Ipswich CP),[26] [corrected description of status]

467 LITTLE WHELNETHAM: [corrected spelling par name]

478 CROYDON: [LG] Croy. MB (1883—89), CB (1889—1965).

483 KINGSTON UPON THAMES: Incl . . . chap East Molesey [corrected spelling]

487 PENGE: [Eccl] Streath. RDn (1871—73), Cambw. RDn (1873—79),

488 REIGATE BOROUGH: CP2—REIGATE BOROUGH

493 TONGHAM: Farn. RDn (1873—between 1939/57), Aldershot RDn (between 1939/57—*).

507 CUCKFIELD: [Civ bdry:] 1894 (the pt in Hayward's Heath USD [corrected description unit status]

526 CP1—WORTHING: [Bdry:] 1902 (gains Heene CP),[103]

530 BARFORD ST MARTIN: [Civ bdry:] 1934 (gains Groveley Wood CP).[1]

531 BISHOPSTONE: [Civ bdry:] 1934 (gains Little Hinton AP).[1]

532 BRITFORD: [Civ bdry:] 1934 (gains Nuneaton and Bodenham CP),[1]

533 BROMHAM: [Civ bdry:] 1934 (gains Chittoe CP).[1]

533 ALL CANNINGS: [Addtl civ bdry alt:] 1934 (gains Allington CP).[1]

534 CHERHILL: [Civ bdry:] 1934 (gains Yatesbury AP).[1]

534 CHIPPENHAM WITHIN: [Bdry:] 1934 (gains

Langley Burrell Within CP),[1]

534 CHISELDON: [Civ bdry:] 1894 (gains Draycot Foliat AP),[120]

535 COOMBE BISSETT: [Addtl civ bdry alt:] 1934 (gains Homington AP).[1]

536 LONGBRIDGE DEVERILL: [Addtl civ bdry alt:] 1934 (incl gains Hill Deverill [in lieu of Kingston Deverill] AP).[1]

537 DINTON: [Addtl civ bdry alt:] 1934 (gains Baverstock AP).[1]

537 DOWNTON: [Addtl civ bdry alt:] 1894 (gains Langley Wood CP),[120]

538 EBBESBOURNE WAKE: [Civ bdry:] 1894 (gains Fifield Bavant AP).[120]

539 GARSDON: Abol civ 1934 ent to Lea and Cleverton AP.[1] [corrected spelling]

539 GRITTLETON: [Civ bdry:] 1934 (gains Leigh Delamere AP, Littleton Drew AP).[1]

540 HILMARTON: [Civ bdry:] 1890 (gains Highway CP).[43]

542 SOMERFORD KEYNES: [add:] Civ bdry: 1894 (gains Shorncott AP).[257]

542 LANDFORD: [Civ bdry:] 1896 (gains Earldoms CP).[165]

542 STEEPLE LANGFORD: [Civ bdry:] 1934 (gains Little Langford AP).[1]

542 LANGLEY BURRELL WITHOUT: [Bdry:] 1934 (gains Hardenhuish AP, Kellaways CP),[1]

542 LATTON: [Civ bdry:] 1896 (gains Eisey AP).[118]

543 LEA AND CLEVERTON: [Civ bdry:] 1934 (gains Garsdon AP).[1]

543 LUCKINGTON: [Civ bdry:] 1934 (gains Alderton AP).[1]

544 MALMESBURY ST PAUL WITHOUT: [Bdry:] 1896 (gains Westport St Mary Without CP),[118]

545 NETHERHAMPTON: [Civ bdry:] 1934 (gains West Harnham CP),[1]

545 NETTLETON: [Civ bdry:] 1934 (gains West Kington AP),[1]

545 NORTON: [Civ bdry:] 1934 (gains Foxley AP).[1]

547 REDLYNCH: [Civ bdry:] 1934 (gains Morgan's Vale and Woodfalls CP).[1]

548 SEMINGTON: [Bdry:] 1894 (gains Whaddon AP).[120]

549 STERT: [Bdry:] 1894 (gains Fullaway CP).[120]

549 STRATFORD SUB CASTLE: [Civ bdry:] 1894 (gains Old Sarum CP),[120]

549 SUTTON BENGER: [Civ bdry:] 1934 ([add:] gains Draycot Cerne AP),[1]

551 WESTPORT ST MARY WITHIN: [Bdry:] 1897 (gains Brokenborough Within CP).[87]

560 LUTTON RD: Billington [corrected spelling] (1933—74),

563 KINTBURY EAGLE HD: Chaddleworth, [corrected spelling],

563 SHRIVENHAM HD: Fernham (from 1866),

564 *WOKINGHAM BOR*, MB (1835—1974)

565 [add section on SANITARY DISTRICTS as follows:]

ABINGDON USD
pt Abingdon St Helen (enlarged pt 1890—94), Abingdon St Nicholas (ent 1875—83, pt 1883—94), pt Culham (1890—94), pt Sutton Wick (1890—94)

MAIDENHEAD USD
pt Bray, pt Cookham

NEWBURY USD
pt Greenham (1878—94), Newbury, pt Speen (1878—94)

OXFORD USD (Oxon, Berks)
pt North Hinksey, pt South Hinksey (1889—94), pt Seacourt

READING USD
pt Burghfield (1887—89), pt Earley (1887—89), pt Reading St Giles (enlarged pt 1887—94), Reading St Lawrence, Reading St Mary (pt 1875—1887, ent 1887—94), pt Shinfield (1887—89), pt Sonning (1887—89), pt Tilehurst (1887—89)

WALLINGFORD USD
pt Wallingford All Hallows, pt Wallingford Castle Precincts, Wallingford St Leonard, Wallingford St Mary le More, Wallingford St Peter

WANTAGE USD
Wantage

NEW WINDSOR USD
pt Clewer, New Windsor, pt Windsor Castle (1886—94)

WOKINGHAM USD
pt Wokingham

565 EASTHAMPTON RD: Crowthorne, [corrected spelling]

570 WYCOMBE RD: Fingest and Lane End (1937—74), [corrected date]

572 FLENDISH HD: Horningsea, [corrected spelling]

583 SOUTH MOLTON HD: West Anstey, [corrected spelling]

586 NEWTON ABBOT PLU: Denbury (1836—85), [corrected dates]

592 SHERBORNE HD: Beer Hackett, [corrected spelling]

593 BEAMINSTER PLU: Broadwindsor, [corrected spelling]

594 SHERBORNE PLU: [added title]; Beer Hackett, [corrected spelling]

595 POOLE RD: [delete:] Branksome (1894—1905)

596 SHERBORNE RD: Beer Hackett, [corrected spelling]

596 WIMBORNE AND CRANBORNE RD: [add:] West Moors,

596 WEST DORSET DIST: Bridport [corrected spelling]

597 CLAVERING HD: Stanstead Mountfitchet [corrected spelling]

599 WEST HAM: MB (1886—89), CB (1889—1965).

599 BILLERICAY PLU: Thundersley (1835—47),

600 SAFFRON WALDEN PLU: Rickling, [corrected spelling]

601 SOUTHEND ON SEA USD: Prittlewell, [corrected spelling]

603 SAFFRON WALDEN RD: Rickling (1894—1946), [corrected dates]

605 ADMINISTRATIVE COUNTY: . . . with associated CBs of Bristol, . . . [corrected spelling]

607 BRISTOL BOR/MB/CB: pt Westbury-on-Trym (1880s—94)

608 NORTHLEACH PLU: Shipton (1871—1930), [added dates]; [add:] Shipton Oliffe (1836—71), Shipton Spllars (1836—71),

609 TETBURY PLU: Westonbirt [corrected spelling]

609 KEYNSHAM PLU: Bitton, [corrected spelling]

612 TETBURY RD: Westonbirt [corrected spelling]

613 HAMPSHIRE ADMINISTRATIVE COUNTY: *1901* [add:] Southbourne; *1902* [delete:] Southbourne.

614 CRONDALL HD: Hawley with Minley, [corrected spelling]

616 BOURNEMOUTH AND CHRISTCHURCH PLU: Bournemouth (1894—1900), [added dates]; Highcliffe (1897—1900), [corrected date]

617 CHRISTCHURCH PLU: Southbourne (1900—01), [corrected date]

618 ISLE OF WIGHT INCORP: Bembridge (1896—1930), [corrected spelling]

619 ANDOVER RD: Appleshaw, [corrected spelling]

620 CHRISTCHURCH RD: Southbourne (1894—1901), Winton (1894—98) [corrected dates]

621 ISLE OF WIGHT RD: [add:] Bembridge, . . . Totland,

622 SOUTH WIGHT DIST: [corrected name]

636 MALLING PLU: Stansted, [corrected spelling]

637 DOVER RSD: pt Poulton [pt for ent period 1875—94]

639 THANET RSD: Ramsgate (1884—94)

646 ALTERATIONS IN BOUNDARIES: [corrected text:] The boundaries of Greater London were altered in 1969 (see Part I of the *Guide* under Bromley LB, Croydon LB) and in 1970 (see Part I under Richmond upon Thames LB)

649 ST MARGARET AND ST JOHN PARS: Evangelist [corrected spelling]

652 ADMINISTRATIVE COUNTY: *1968* Costessey, [corrected spelling]

652 NON-METROPOLITAN COUNTY: [corrected spelling in heading]

653 FREEBRIDGE MARSHLAND HD: [add] pt Central Wingland,

654 LAUNDITCH HD: Weasenham St Peter,

654 NORWICH BOR/MB/CB: Eaton [in lieu of Easton]; Trowse with Newton [in lieu of Troswe with Newton]

656 HENSTEAD PLU: [corrected spelling of heading]

657 BLOFIELD RSD: [corrected spelling of heading]

657 HOLBEACH PLU: [add entire entry:] (Lincs Pts Holl, Norfolk [1867—97]) Central Wingland (1867—1930)

659 HENSTEAD RD: Stoke Holy Cross, [corrected spelling]

664 BICESTER PLU: Charlton-on-Otmoor, [corrected spelling]

669 HORETHORNE HD: Charlton Horethorne (until 1887), [corrected spelling]

671 BATH PLU: Woolley [corrected spelling]

675 WELLINGTON RD: Bathealton, [corrected spelling]

678 HARTISMERE HD: Rickinghall Superior, [corrected spelling]

678 SAMFORD HD: Shelley, [corrected spelling]

680 SAMFORD PLU: Shelley, [corrected spelling]

683 SAMFORD RD: Shelley, [corrected spelling]; Great Wenham [corrected spelling]

683 WAINFORD RD: Barsham, [corrected spelling]

686 REIGATE HD: Merstham, [corrected spelling]

687 REIGATE PLU: Merstham, [corrected spelling]

687 EPSOM USD: [corrected spelling of heading]

688 CROYDON RD: [add:] Penge,

689 REIGATE RD: Merstham, [corrected spelling]

707 NORTH WILTSHIRE DIST: Wootton Bassett [corrected spelling]

716 WESTERN OR CHESTERTON DIST: Trumpington, [corrected spelling]

751 NORWICH: Eaton, [corrected spelling]

761 NORTHERN OR LOWESTOFT DIVISION: South Elmham St Margaret, [corrected spelling]

822 HERTFORDSHIRE: [note 1] cr of Adm Co in 1889.

823 HUNTS: [note 1] cr of Adm Co in 1889.

827 NORFOLK: [4] (both Central Norfolk CC) [corrected spelling]

828 SURREY: [7] (Chaldon, Merstham) [corrected spelling]